America's Top-Rated Smaller Cities: A Statistical Handbook

Volume 1: Alabama – New Jersey

2016/17

Eleventh Edition

America's Top-Rated Smaller Cities: A Statistical Handbook

Volume 1: Alabama – New Jersey

A UNIVERSAL REFERENCE BOOK

Grey House Publishing

PUBLISHER: Leslie Mackenzie
EDITORIAL DIRECTOR: Laura Mars
SENIOR EDITOR: David Garoogian

CONTRIBUTING WRITERS: Kelsey Draper; Michael Moglia
MARKETING DIRECTOR: Jessica Moody

A Universal Reference Book
Grey House Publishing, Inc.
4919 Route 22
Amenia, NY 12501
518.789.8700
Fax 845.373.6390
www.greyhouse.com
e-mail: books @greyhouse.com

Eleventh Edition
Printed in Canada

America's top-rated smaller cities : a statistical handbook. — 1st ed. (1994–1995)-

2 v.; 27.5 cm.
Biennial
Title varies.
ISSN: 1094-4893

1. Cities and towns—Ratings—United States—Statistics. 2. Cities and towns—United States—Statistics.
3. Social indicators—United States. 4. Quality of life—United States—Statistics.
HT123.A6692
307.76/0973/05

ISBN: 978-1-61925-925-6

Table of Contents

Bella Vista, Arkansas

Aliso Viejo, California

Cupertino, California

Danville, California

Folsom, California

Foster City, California

Los Altos, California

Rancho Palos Verdes, California

San Ramon, California

Saratoga, California

Yorba Linda, California

Broomfield, Colorado

Lafayette, Colorado

Parker, Colorado

Cheshire, Connecticut

Glastonbury, Connecticut

Newtown, Connecticut

Ridgefield, Connecticut

South Windsor, Connecticut

Westport, Connecticut

Oviedo, Florida

Parkland, Florida

Weston, Florida

Alpharetta, Georgia

Johns Creek, Georgia

Peachtree City, Georgia

Meridian, Idaho

Northbrook, Illinois

O'Fallon, Illinois

Plainfield, Illinois

Wilmette, Illinois

Carmel, Indiana

Fishers, Indiana

Ankeny, Iowa

Marion, Iowa

Leawood, Kansas

Lenexa, Kansas

Independence, Kentucky

Bowie, Maryland

Lexington, Massachusetts

Needham, Massachusetts

Shrewsbury, Massachusetts

Wellesley, Massachusetts

Bloomfield, Michigan

Grand Blanc, Michigan

Northville, Michigan

Novi, Michigan

Eden Prairie, Minnesota

Lee's Summit, Missouri

O'Fallon, Missouri

Bozeman, Montana

Merrimack, New Hampshire

Bernards, New Jersey

Evesham, New Jersey

Marlboro, New Jersey

Princeton, New Jersey

Ridgewood, New Jersey

South Brunswick, New Jersey

West Windsor, New Jersey

Places profiled in this edition of *America's Top-Rated Smaller Cities*

By City

Aliso Viejo (city), CA
Allen (city), TX
Alpharetta (city), GA
Ankeny (city), IA
Apex (town), NC
Ballwin (city), MO
Beavercreek (city), OH
Bella Vista (town), AR
Bernards (township), NJ
Bethlehem (town), NY
Bloomfield (township), MI
Bowie (city), MD
Bozeman (city), MT
Brentwood (city), TN
Broomfield (city), CO
Carmel (city), IN
Cedar Park (city), TX
Cheshire (town), CT
Chesterfield (city), MO
Collierville (town), TN
Coppell (city), TX
Cornelius (town), NC
Cranberry (township), PA
Cupertino (city), CA
Danville (town), CA
Draper (city), UT
Dublin (city), OH
Eastchester (town), NY
Eden Prairie (city), MN
Edmond (city), OK
Evesham (township), NJ
Fishers (town), IN
Flower Mound (town), TX
Folsom (city), CA
Foster City (city), CA
Franklin (city), TN
Friendswood (city), TX
Germantown (city), TN
Glastonbury (town), CT
Grand Blanc (township), MI
Guilderland (town), NY
Hampden (township), PA
Holly Springs (town), NC
Huntersville (town), NC
Independence (city), KY
Johns Creek (city), GA
Keller (city), TX
Kirkland (city), WA
Lafayette (city), CO
Lake Oswego (city), OR
League City (city), TX
Leawood (city), KS
Lee's Summit (city), MO
Leesburg (town), VA
Lehi (city), UT
Lenexa (city), KS
Lexington (town), MA
Los Altos (city), CA
Lower Makefield (township), PA
Madison (city), AL
Mamaroneck (town), NY
Manheim (township), PA
Manlius (town), NY
Maple Grove (city), MN
Marion (city), IA
Marlboro (township), NJ
Mason (city), OH
McCandless (township), PA
Menomonee Falls (village), WI
Meridian (city), ID
Merrimack (town), NH
Mount Lebanon (township), PA
Mount Pleasant (town), SC
Needham (town), MA
Newtown (town), CT
Northbrook (village), IL
Northville (township), MI
Novi (city), MI
O'Fallon (city), IL
O'Fallon (city), MO
Orchard Park (town), NY
Oviedo (city), FL
Parker (town), CO
Parkland (city), FL
Peachtree City (city), GA
Pflugerville (city), TX
Plainfield (village), IL
Princeton (borough), NJ
Queen Creek (town), AZ
Rancho Palos Verdes (city), CA
Redmond (city), WA
Richland (city), WA
Ridgefield (town), CT
Ridgewood (village), NJ
Rio Rancho (city), NM
Sahuarita (town), AZ
Sammamish (city), WA
San Ramon (city), CA
Saratoga (city), CA
Schertz (city), TX
Shrewsbury (town), MA
South Brunswick (township), NJ
South Jordan (city), UT
South Kingstown (town), RI
South Windsor (town), CT
Southlake (city), TX
Spring Hill (city), TN
Stow (city), OH
Sugar Land (city), TX
Sun Prairie (city), WI
Syracuse (city), UT
Tredyffrin (township), PA
Upper Arlington (city), OH
Upper Dublin (township), PA
Vestavia Hills (city), AL
Webster (town), NY
Wellesley (town), MA
West Fargo (city), ND
West Linn (city), OR
West Windsor (township), NJ
Westlake (city), OH
Weston (city), FL
Westport (town), CT
Wilmette (village), IL
Woodbury (city), MN
Yorba Linda (city), CA

By State

Madison (city), AL
Vestavia Hills (city), AL
Queen Creek (town), AZ
Sahuarita (town), AZ
Bella Vista (town), AR
Aliso Viejo (city), CA
Cupertino (city), CA
Danville (town), CA
Folsom (city), CA
Foster City (city), CA
Los Altos (city), CA
Rancho Palos Verdes (city), CA
San Ramon (city), CA
Saratoga (city), CA
Yorba Linda (city), CA
Broomfield (city), CO
Lafayette (city), CO
Parker (town), CO
Cheshire (town), CT
Glastonbury (town), CT
Newtown (town), CT
Ridgefield (town), CT
South Windsor (town), CT
Westport (town), CT
Oviedo (city), FL
Parkland (city), FL
Weston (city), FL
Alpharetta (city), GA
Johns Creek (city), GA
Peachtree City (city), GA
Meridian (city), ID
Northbrook (village), IL
O'Fallon (city), IL
Plainfield (village), IL
Wilmette (village), IL
Carmel (city), IN
Fishers (town), IN
Ankeny (city), IA
Marion (city), IA
Leawood (city), KS
Lenexa (city), KS
Independence (city), KY
Bowie (city), MD
Lexington (town), MA
Needham (town), MA
Shrewsbury (town), MA
Wellesley (town), MA
Bloomfield (township), MI
Grand Blanc (township), MI
Northville (township), MI
Novi (city), MI
Eden Prairie (city), MN
Maple Grove (city), MN
Woodbury (city), MN
Ballwin (city), MO
Chesterfield (city), MO
Lee's Summit (city), MO
O'Fallon (city), MO
Bozeman (city), MT
Merrimack (town), NH
Bernards (township), NJ
Evesham (township), NJ
Marlboro (township), NJ
Princeton (borough), NJ
Ridgewood (village), NJ
South Brunswick (township), NJ
West Windsor (township), NJ
Rio Rancho (city), NM
Bethlehem (town), NY
Eastchester (town), NY
Guilderland (town), NY
Mamaroneck (town), NY
Manlius (town), NY
Orchard Park (town), NY
Webster (town), NY
Apex (town), NC
Cornelius (town), NC
Holly Springs (town), NC
Huntersville (town), NC
West Fargo (city), ND
Beavercreek (city), OH
Dublin (city), OH
Mason (city), OH
Stow (city), OH
Upper Arlington (city), OH
Westlake (city), OH
Edmond (city), OK
Lake Oswego (city), OR
West Linn (city), OR
Cranberry (township), PA
Hampden (township), PA
Lower Makefield (township), PA
Manheim (township), PA
McCandless (township), PA
Mount Lebanon (township), PA
Tredyffrin (township), PA
Upper Dublin (township), PA
South Kingstown (town), RI
Mount Pleasant (town), SC
Brentwood (city), TN
Collierville (town), TN
Franklin (city), TN
Germantown (city), TN
Spring Hill (city), TN
Allen (city), TX
Cedar Park (city), TX
Coppell (city), TX
Flower Mound (town), TX
Friendswood (city), TX
Keller (city), TX
League City (city), TX
Pflugerville (city), TX
Schertz (city), TX
Southlake (city), TX
Sugar Land (city), TX
Draper (city), UT
Lehi (city), UT
South Jordan (city), UT
Syracuse (city), UT
Leesburg (town), VA
Kirkland (city), WA
Redmond (city), WA
Richland (city), WA
Sammamish (city), WA
Menomonee Falls (village), WI
Sun Prairie (city), WI

Introduction

This is the eleventh edition of *America's Top-Rated Smaller Cities*—current, concise statistical profiles of top U.S. cities with populations between 25,000 and 100,000. The 2016/17 edition features 126 cities, 32 which are new to this edition, including 26 never before profiled. There are many ways to research new places to live. The Internet can provide important details, like the cost of various lifestyles in various cities, and which schools are top rated, but only *America's Top-Rated Smaller Cities* gives you a complete picture. We've done the extensive research necessary to compile comprehensive profiles and comparative statistics that will educate and prepare you—and your business—for relocation.

Praise for previous editions:

> "Patrons…will value this compilation of statistics on the 124 most desirable (statistically speaking)…cities…An exhaustive [resource] essential for libraries."
>
> —*Library Journal*

> "…These volumes provide excellent, comprehensive information on smaller urban communities…a valuable resource for graduating college students. Career professionals…will find these volumes useful…"
>
> —*Choice*

> "A quick and handy reference tool, this work will have a wide and grateful audience…recommended for public and academic libraries."
>
> —*ARBA*

To expand our available city choices, selection is not limited to incorporated cities, but includes towns and townships. This availed us many top-rated communities not designated as cities. Final selection was based on our unique rating system, using six key criteria: population growth, income, housing affordability, crime rate, educational attainment, and unemployment.

FEATURES

The city rankings for each of the 126 city chapters now comprise information from hundreds of books, magazines, newspapers and research reports. Interesting "top-city" rankings include...**Best Cities for Jobs, Best Cities for Singles, Best Cities for Moviemakers,** and **Most Inventive Cities.** You'll also learn which cities are the most...**Allergy Prone, Literate, Frugal,** and **Debt-Ridden.**

New topics include *Disability Status* and *Freeway Commuter Stress Index.* Expanded topics: *Bankruptcy Filings* now include business filings; *Air Quality Trends: Ozone* now includes data from 1990 through 2014.

ARRANGEMENT

America's Top-Rated Smaller Cities is arranged in two volumes—Volume 1 has 67 city chapters, Alabama to New Jersey, and Volume 2 has 59 city chapters, New Mexico to Wisconsin. Each city chapter is divided into three sections: **Background & Rankings; Business Environment;** and **Living Environment**. Both volumes include **100 Honorable Mention Cities,** five **Maps** that indicate the location of each of the 126 cities, and five **Appendices,** with comparative rankings and resource information on all cities. Here is a detailed look:

City Background

Each of the 126 city chapters begins with an informative background. These page-long narratives combine history with current events, and touch on the city's environment, politics, employment, and cultural offerings, along with some interesting trivia.

Rankings

This section has 18 ranking categories, including *Business/Finance, Health, Women/Minorities, Retirement, Family, Safety, Recreation,* and *Dating/Romance.* It contains data from 312 books, articles, and research reports, and is presented in an easy-to-read, bulleted format. You'll find rankings—and several scores and figures—on a wide variety of topics, such as **Best Cities for Seniors, Best Cities for College Graduates, Best Cities for Families,**

Best Cities for Hispanics, Best Places for Newlyweds, Best Cities to Flip a House, Best Cities for Dogs, Best Cities for Wheelchair Users, Best Places for Business and Career, and hundreds more.

Sources for these Rankings include both well-known magazines and other media, including *Forbes, Fortune, Inc. Magazine, Working Mother, BusinessWeek, Kiplinger's Personal Finance, Men's Journal,* and *Travel + Leisure,* as well as resources not as well known, such as the *Asthma & Allergy Foundation of America, The Advocate, Black Enterprise, National Civic League, The National Coalition for the Homeless, MovieMaker Magazine, Center for Digital Government, U.S. Conference of Mayors,* and the *Milken Institute.*

Business Environment—Statistical Tables
Each city chapter in *America's Top-Rated Smaller Cities* includes 39 tables with business related data for seven topics. Over 95% of statistical data has been updated. Here is where you will find hard facts and figures on city finances, population demographics, income, bankruptcy rates, employment, and taxes. Again, our editors have used sources that are obvious, such as the *U.S. Census Bureau* and the *Bureau of Labor Statistics,* and more obscure ones, like *The Council for Community and Economic Research, Texas Transportation Institute,* and *Federation of Tax Administrators.*

Living Environment—Statistical Tables
The business tables are followed by 42 tables with data related to nine living environment topics. These include information on housing, healthcare, cost-of-living, education, air quality, and climate. Sources include the *U.S. Environmental Protection Agency, Federal Bureau of Investigation, Centers for Disease Control and Prevention,* and *National Center for Education Statistics,* as well as *The Grey House Performing Arts Directory.*

The availability of statistics is related to both a city's size and how data is gathered. Some statistics represent the Metropolitan Statistical Area the city is part of, and some are not available at all, indicated by n/a.

Five Appendices

- **A—Comparative Statistics:** A city-by city comparison of hundreds of variables spread out over 74 tables that offers both an overview of the city, and a broad geographical profile.
- **B—Metropolitan Area Definitions:** In straight alpha-by-city order, this includes the counties/cities that combine to form each city's Metropolitan Statistical Area, Micropolitan Statistical Area, Metropolitan Division, New England City and Town Area, and New England City and Town Area Division.
- **C—Government Type and County:** This appendix includes the government structure of each place included in this book. It also includes the county or county equivalent in which each place is located.
- **D—Chambers of Commerce:** Alpha-by-city, includes address, phone and fax numbers, and websites of additional city resources.
- **E—State Departments of Labor and Employment:** Another source for additional economic and employment data for each city, with address and phone number for easy access.

The material provided by public and private agencies and organizations was supplemented by library sources and Internet sites. This edition is designed for individuals considering relocating a residence or business; professionals considering expanding a business or changing careers; corporations considering relocation or additional offices; government agencies; general and market researchers; real estate consultants; human resource personnel; urban planners; investors; and urban government students. With more content and more coverage, this edition is our strongest and most informative to date.

Honorable Mentions

These places did not make our editor's final cut, however, they were on our preliminary list.

By City

Algonquin (village), IL
Andover (town), MA
Apple Valley (city), MN
Arlington (town), MA
Arlington Heights (village), IL
Bartlett (village), IL
Belmont (city), CA
Belmont (town), MA
Bethel Park (municipality), PA
Bettendorf (city), IA
Bridgewater (township), NJ
Brookfield (city), WI
Buffalo Grove (village), IL
Canton (charter township), MI
Carmel (town), NY
Castle Rock (town), CO
Chelmsford (town), MA
Cottage Grove (city), MN
Cottonwood Heights (city), UT
Downers Grove (village), IL
Dublin (city), CA
Eagan (city), MN
Edina (city), MN
Elmhurst (city), IL
Fairfield (town), CT
Farmington (town), CT
Franklin (township), NJ
Franklin Town (city), MA
Glen Ellyn (village), IL
Glenview (village), IL
Greenwich (town), CT
Haverford (township), PA
Highland Park (city), IL
Hillsborough (township), NJ
Hoover (city), AL
Horsham (township), PA
Huntley (village), IL
Issaquah (city), WA
Kaysville (city), UT
Kirkwood (city), MO
Lakeville (city), MN
Lancaster (town), NY
Livingston (township), NJ
Lockport (city), IL
Los Gatos (town), CA
Lower Merion (township), PA
Lower Providence (township), PA
Mahwah (township), NJ
Manalapan (township), NJ
Manhattan Beach (city), CA
Mansfield (city), TX
Melrose (city), MA
Middletown (township), NJ
Milton (city), GA
Milton (town), MA
Minnetonka (city), MN
Monroe (township), NJ
Montgomery (township), PA
Mount Olive (township), NJ
Natick (town), MA
Newport Beach (city), CA
Newton (city), MA
North Andover (town), MA
North Ridgeville (city), OH
Northampton (township), PA
Orland Park (village), IL
Oswego (village), IL
Palo Alto (city), CA
Park Ridge (city), IL
Parsippany-Troy Hills (township), NJ
Pearland (city), TX
Pittsford (town), NY
Pleasant Grove (city), UT
Pleasanton (city), CA
Plymouth (charter township), MI
Plymouth (city), MN
Radnor (township), PA
Rancho Santa Margarita (city), CA
Randolph (township), NJ
Rockwall (city), TX
Roswell (city), GA
Royal Oak (city), MI
Saint Charles (city), IL
Savage (city), MN
Shakopee (city), MN
Shawnee (city), KS
Shoreview (city), MN
Troy (city), MI
Urbandale (city), IA
Vernon Hills (village), IL
Wake Forest (town), NC
Wall (township), NJ
West Bloomfield (charter twp), MI
West Des Moines (city), IA
Westerville (city), OH
Westfield (city), IN
Westfield (town), NJ
Wheaton (city), IL
Wildwood (city), MO
Wylie (city), TX

By State

Hoover (city), AL
Belmont (city), CA
Dublin (city), CA
Los Gatos (town), CA
Manhattan Beach (city), CA
Newport Beach (city), CA
Palo Alto (city), CA
Pleasanton (city), CA
Rancho Santa Margarita (city), CA
Castle Rock (town), CO
Fairfield (town), CT
Farmington (town), CT
Greenwich (town), CT
Milton (city), GA
Roswell (city), GA
Algonquin (village), IL
Arlington Heights (village), IL
Bartlett (village), IL
Buffalo Grove (village), IL
Downers Grove (village), IL
Elmhurst (city), IL
Glen Ellyn (village), IL
Glenview (village), IL
Highland Park (city), IL
Huntley (village), IL
Lockport (city), IL
Orland Park (village), IL
Oswego (village), IL
Park Ridge (city), IL
Saint Charles (city), IL
Vernon Hills (village), IL
Wheaton (city), IL
Westfield (city), IN
Bettendorf (city), IA
Urbandale (city), IA
West Des Moines (city), IA
Shawnee (city), KS
Andover (town), MA
Arlington (town), MA
Belmont (town), MA
Chelmsford (town), MA
Franklin Town (city), MA
Melrose (city), MA
Milton (town), MA
Natick (town), MA
Newton (city), MA
North Andover (town), MA
Canton (charter township), MI
Plymouth (charter township), MI
Royal Oak (city), MI
Troy (city), MI
West Bloomfield (charter twp), MI
Apple Valley (city), MN
Cottage Grove (city), MN
Eagan (city), MN
Edina (city), MN
Lakeville (city), MN
Minnetonka (city), MN
Plymouth (city), MN
Savage (city), MN
Shakopee (city), MN
Shoreview (city), MN
Kirkwood (city), MO
Wildwood (city), MO
Bridgewater (township), NJ
Franklin (township), NJ
Hillsborough (township), NJ
Livingston (township), NJ
Mahwah (township), NJ
Manalapan (township), NJ
Middletown (township), NJ
Monroe (township), NJ
Mount Olive (township), NJ
Parsippany-Troy Hills (township), NJ
Randolph (township), NJ
Wall (township), NJ
Westfield (town), NJ
Carmel (town), NY
Lancaster (town), NY
Pittsford (town), NY
Wake Forest (town), NC
North Ridgeville (city), OH
Westerville (city), OH
Bethel Park (municipality), PA
Haverford (township), PA
Horsham (township), PA
Lower Merion (township), PA
Lower Providence (township), PA
Montgomery (township), PA
Northampton (township), PA
Radnor (township), PA
Mansfield (city), TX
Pearland (city), TX
Rockwall (city), TX
Wylie (city), TX
Cottonwood Heights (city), UT
Kaysville (city), UT
Pleasant Grove (city), UT
Issaquah (city), WA
Brookfield (city), WI

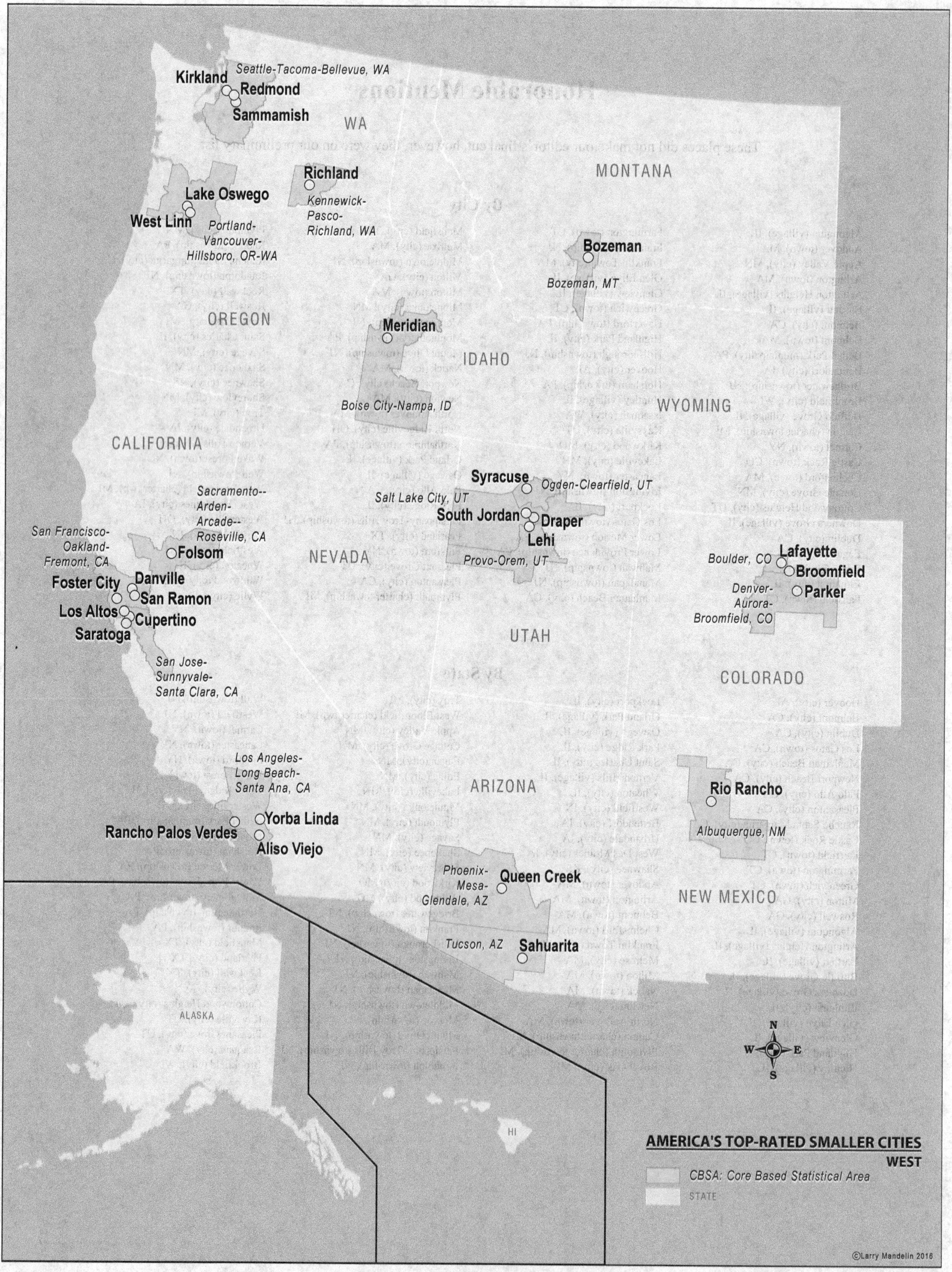

Seattle-Tacoma-Bellevue, WA
Kirkland
Redmond
Sammamish
WA
Richland
Kennewick-Pasco-Richland, WA
Lake Oswego
West Linn
Portland-Vancouver-Hillsboro, OR-WA
MONTANA
Bozeman
Bozeman, MT
OREGON
Meridian
IDAHO
Boise City-Nampa, ID
WYOMING
CALIFORNIA
Syracuse
Ogden-Clearfield, UT
Salt Lake City, UT
South Jordan
Draper
Lehi
Provo-Orem, UT
Sacramento--Arden-Arcade--Roseville, CA
Folsom
San Francisco-Oakland-Fremont, CA
NEVADA
Foster City
Danville
San Ramon
Los Altos
Cupertino
Saratoga
San Jose-Sunnyvale-Santa Clara, CA
Boulder, CO
Lafayette
Broomfield
Parker
Denver-Aurora-Broomfield, CO
UTAH
COLORADO
Los Angeles-Long Beach-Santa Ana, CA
Yorba Linda
Rancho Palos Verdes
Aliso Viejo
ARIZONA
Rio Rancho
Albuquerque, NM
Phoenix-Mesa-Glendale, AZ
Queen Creek
NEW MEXICO
Tucson, AZ
Sahuarita
ALASKA
HI
N
W
E
S
AMERICA'S TOP-RATED SMALLER CITIES
WEST
CBSA: Core Based Statistical Area
STATE
©Larry Mandelin 2016

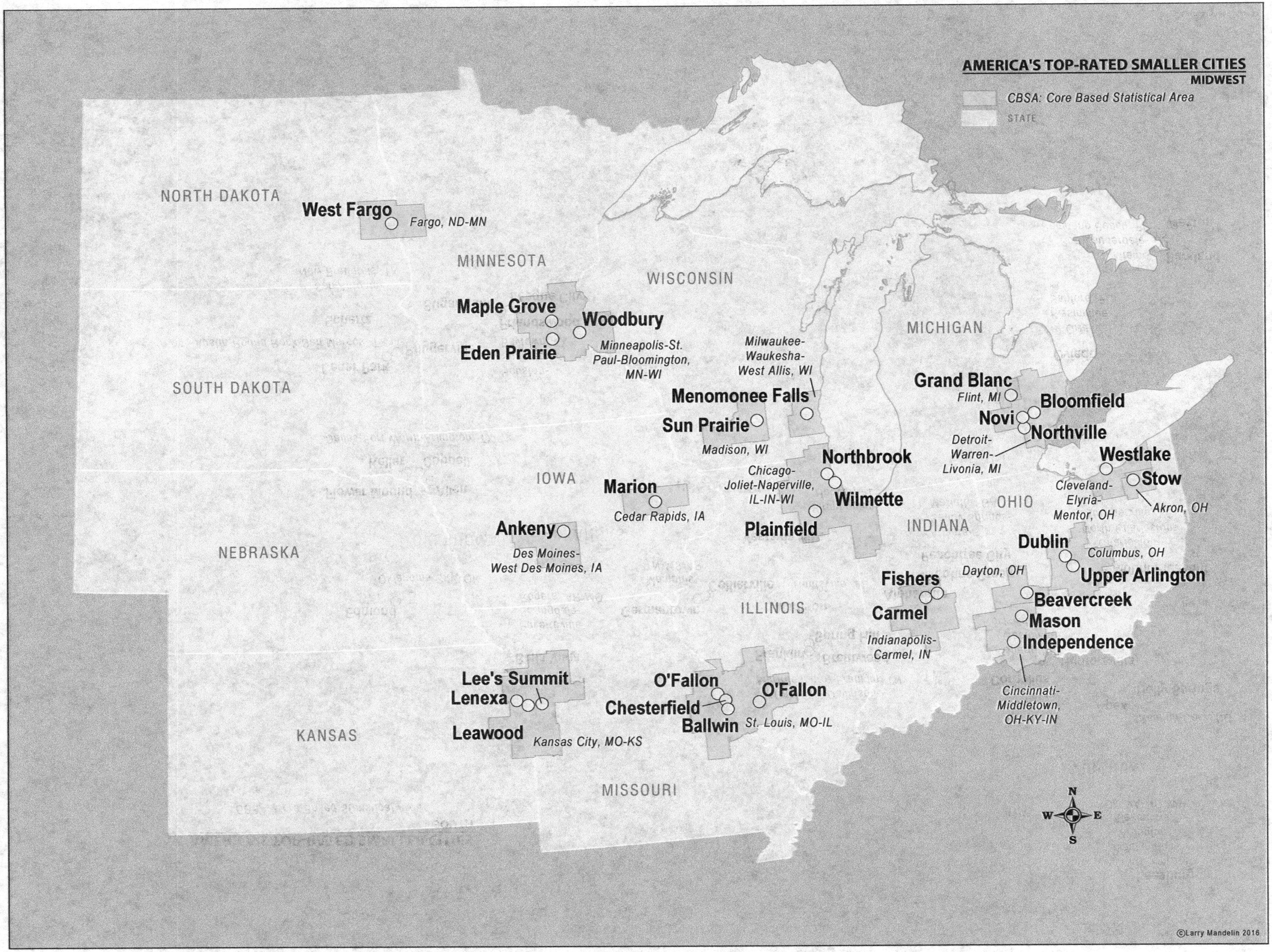
AMERICA'S TOP-RATED SMALLER CITIES
MIDWEST
CBSA: Core Based Statistical Area
STATE
NORTH DAKOTA
West Fargo
Fargo, ND-MN
MINNESOTA
WISCONSIN
Maple Grove
Woodbury
Eden Prairie
Minneapolis-St. Paul-Bloomington, MN-WI
SOUTH DAKOTA
MICHIGAN
Milwaukee-Waukesha-West Allis, WI
Menomonee Falls
Sun Prairie
Madison, WI
Grand Blanc
Flint, MI
Bloomfield
Novi
Northville
Detroit-Warren-Livonia, MI
Northbrook
Chicago-Joliet-Naperville, IL-IN-WI
Wilmette
Plainfield
Westlake
Stow
Cleveland-Elyria-Mentor, OH
Akron, OH
IOWA
Marion
Cedar Rapids, IA
OHIO
INDIANA
Ankeny
Des Moines-West Des Moines, IA
NEBRASKA
Dublin
Columbus, OH
Upper Arlington
Dayton, OH
Fishers
Carmel
Indianapolis-Carmel, IN
ILLINOIS
Beavercreek
Mason
Independence
Cincinnati-Middletown, OH-KY-IN
Lee's Summit
Lenexa
Leawood
Kansas City, MO-KS
O'Fallon
Chesterfield
Ballwin
O'Fallon
St. Louis, MO-IL
KANSAS
MISSOURI
N
W
E
S
©Larry Mandelin 2016

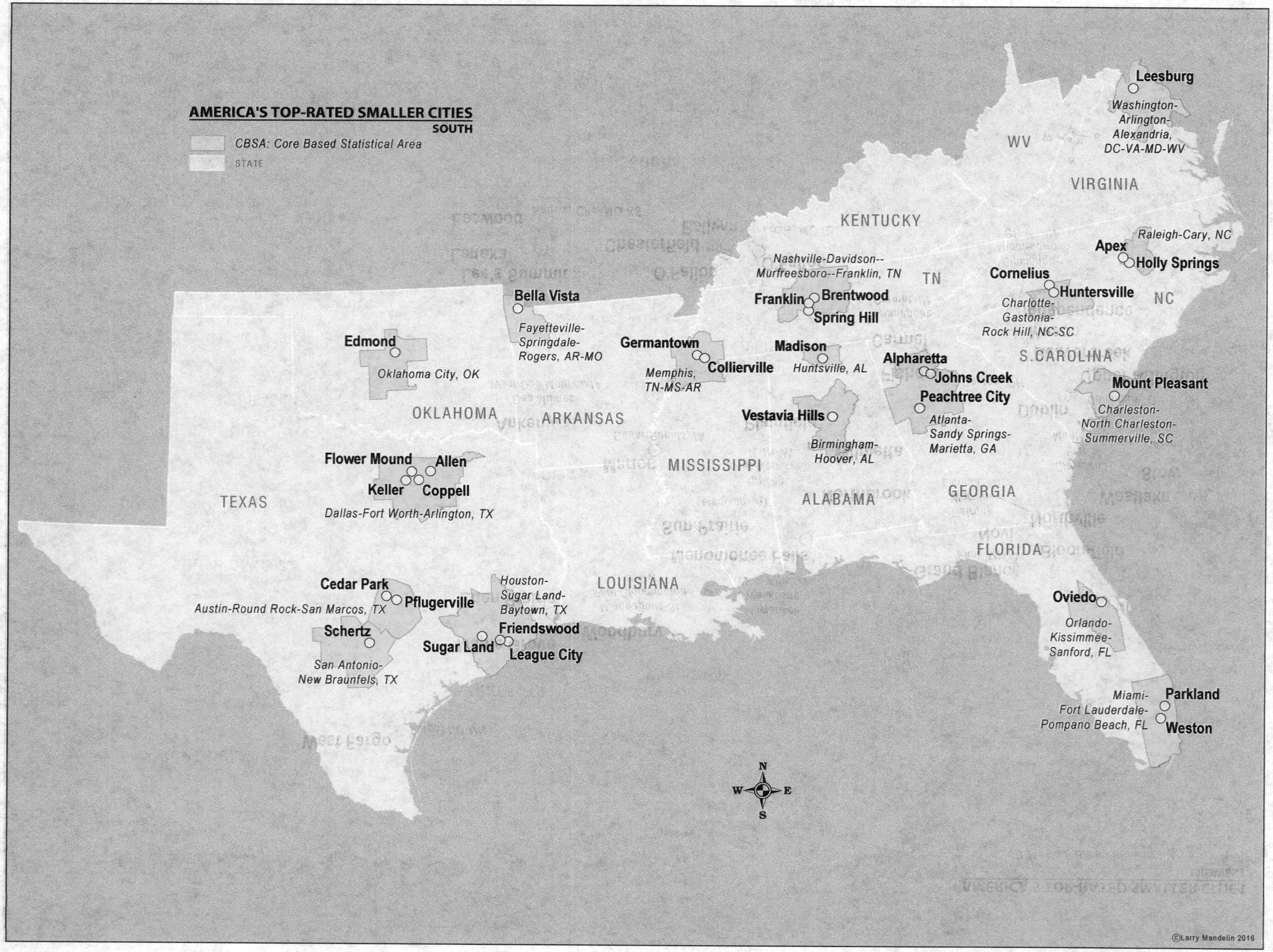
AMERICA'S TOP-RATED SMALLER CITIES
SOUTH
CBSA: Core Based Statistical Area
STATE
Leesburg
Washington-Arlington-Alexandria, DC-VA-MD-WV
WV
VIRGINIA
KENTUCKY
Raleigh-Cary, NC
Apex
Holly Springs
Nashville-Davidson--Murfreesboro--Franklin, TN
TN
Cornelius
Huntersville
NC
Franklin
Brentwood
Spring Hill
Charlotte-Gastonia-Rock Hill, NC-SC
Bella Vista
Fayetteville-Springdale-Rogers, AR-MO
Edmond
Oklahoma City, OK
Germantown
Collierville
Memphis, TN-MS-AR
Madison
Huntsville, AL
Alpharetta
Johns Creek
Peachtree City
Atlanta-Sandy Springs-Marietta, GA
S.CAROLINA
Mount Pleasant
Charleston-North Charleston-Summerville, SC
OKLAHOMA
ARKANSAS
Vestavia Hills
Birmingham-Hoover, AL
Flower Mound
Allen
Keller
Coppell
Dallas-Fort Worth-Arlington, TX
TEXAS
MISSISSIPPI
ALABAMA
GEORGIA
FLORIDA
Cedar Park
Pflugerville
Austin-Round Rock-San Marcos, TX
Houston-Sugar Land-Baytown, TX
LOUISIANA
Friendswood
Sugar Land
League City
Schertz
San Antonio-New Braunfels, TX
Oviedo
Orlando-Kissimmee-Sanford, FL
Miami-Fort Lauderdale-Pompano Beach, FL
Parkland
Weston
N
W
E
S
©Larry Mandelin 2016

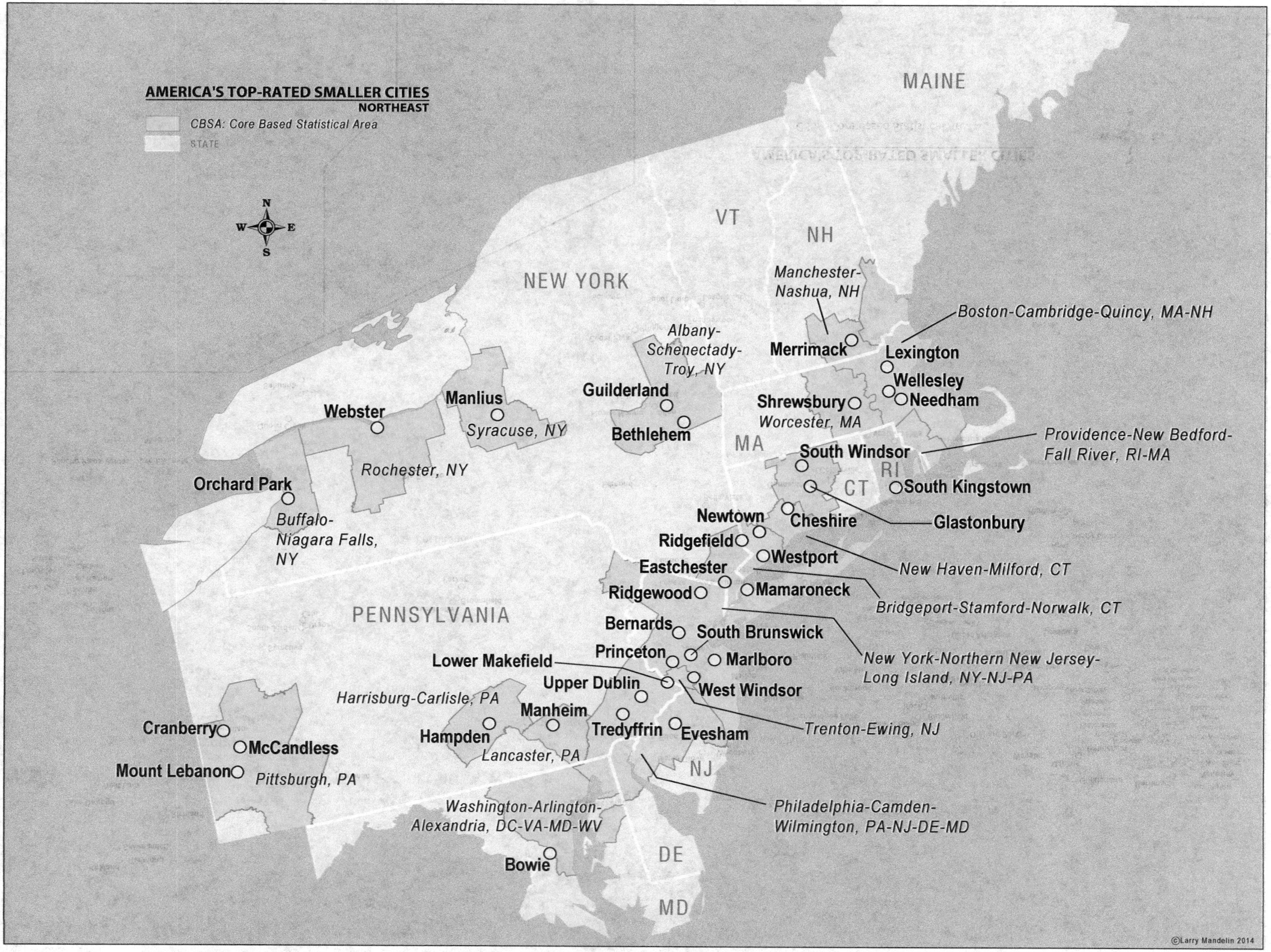
AMERICA'S TOP-RATED SMALLER CITIES
NORTHEAST
CBSA: Core Based Statistical Area
STATE
N
W
E
S
MAINE
VT
NH
NEW YORK
MA
RI
CT
PENNSYLVANIA
NJ
DE
MD
Manchester-Nashua, NH
Merrimack
Boston-Cambridge-Quincy, MA-NH
Lexington
Wellesley
Needham
Shrewsbury
Worcester, MA
Providence-New Bedford-Fall River, RI-MA
South Windsor
South Kingstown
Glastonbury
Cheshire
Newtown
Ridgefield
Westport
New Haven-Milford, CT
Eastchester
Mamaroneck
Ridgewood
Bridgeport-Stamford-Norwalk, CT
Bernards
South Brunswick
Princeton
Marlboro
Lower Makefield
Upper Dublin
West Windsor
New York-Northern New Jersey-Long Island, NY-NJ-PA
Trenton-Ewing, NJ
Tredyffrin
Evesham
Philadelphia-Camden-Wilmington, PA-NJ-DE-MD
Albany-Schenectady-Troy, NY
Guilderland
Bethlehem
Manlius
Syracuse, NY
Webster
Rochester, NY
Orchard Park
Buffalo-Niagara Falls, NY
Harrisburg-Carlisle, PA
Manheim
Hampden
Lancaster, PA
Cranberry
McCandless
Mount Lebanon
Pittsburgh, PA
Washington-Arlington-Alexandria, DC-VA-MD-WV
Bowie
©Larry Mandelin 2014

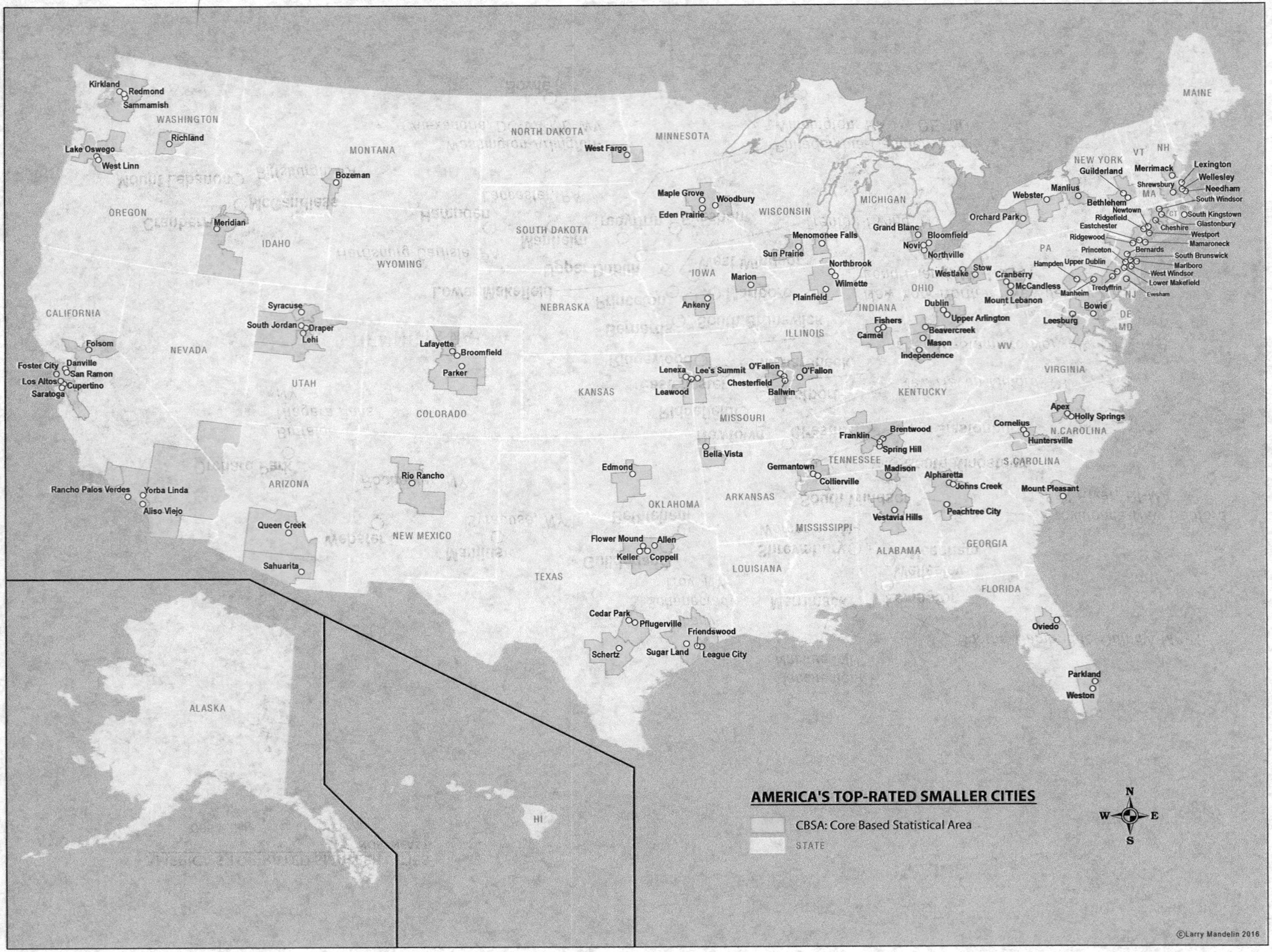
AMERICA'S TOP-RATED SMALLER CITIES
CBSA: Core Based Statistical Area
STATE
N
W
E
S
WASHINGTON
OREGON
CALIFORNIA
NEVADA
IDAHO
MONTANA
WYOMING
UTAH
ARIZONA
COLORADO
NEW MEXICO
NORTH DAKOTA
SOUTH DAKOTA
NEBRASKA
KANSAS
OKLAHOMA
TEXAS
MINNESOTA
IOWA
MISSOURI
ARKANSAS
LOUISIANA
WISCONSIN
ILLINOIS
MICHIGAN
INDIANA
OHIO
KENTUCKY
TENNESSEE
MISSISSIPPI
ALABAMA
GEORGIA
FLORIDA
S.CAROLINA
N.CAROLINA
VIRGINIA
WV
PA
NEW YORK
VT
NH
MAINE
MA
CT
RI
NJ
DE
MD
ALASKA
HI
Kirkland
Redmond
Sammamish
Richland
Lake Oswego
West Linn
Bozeman
Meridian
Folsom
Foster City
Danville
San Ramon
Los Altos
Cupertino
Saratoga
Rancho Palos Verdes
Yorba Linda
Aliso Viejo
Syracuse
South Jordan
Draper
Lehi
Queen Creek
Sahuarita
Lafayette
Broomfield
Parker
Rio Rancho
West Fargo
Maple Grove
Woodbury
Eden Prairie
Ankeny
Marion
Sun Prairie
Menomonee Falls
Northbrook
Wilmette
Plainfield
Lenexa
Lee's Summit
Leawood
O'Fallon
Chesterfield
Ballwin
O'Fallon
Bella Vista
Edmond
Flower Mound
Allen
Keller
Coppell
Cedar Park
Pflugerville
Schertz
Sugar Land
Friendswood
League City
Germantown
Collierville
Franklin
Brentwood
Spring Hill
Madison
Vestavia Hills
Alpharetta
Johns Creek
Peachtree City
Fishers
Carmel
Grand Blanc
Bloomfield
Novi
Northville
Dublin
Upper Arlington
Beavercreek
Mason
Independence
Westlake
Stow
Cranberry
McCandless
Mount Lebanon
Orchard Park
Webster
Manlius
Guilderland
Bethlehem
Merrimack
Lexington
Wellesley
Needham
Shrewsbury
South Windsor
South Kingstown
Glastonbury
Newtown
Ridgefield
Cheshire
Eastchester
Westport
Ridgewood
Mamaroneck
Princeton
Bernards
South Brunswick
Hampden
Upper Dublin
Marlboro
West Windsor
Manheim
Tredyffrin
Lower Makefield
Evesham
Bowie
Leesburg
Apex
Holly Springs
Cornelius
Huntersville
Mount Pleasant
Oviedo
Parkland
Weston
©Larry Mandelin 2016

Madison, Alabama

Background

Madison is located just south of the Tennessee border, and adjacent to and just west of the Huntsville metropolitan area, convenient to the region's many business, education, and cultural resources.

Madison is one of the fastest-growing cities in Alabama. It is a prosperous community, boasting Alabama's most highly educated workforce. The town has labored to preserve its small-town atmosphere, with a responsive and proactive city government, a low crime rate, and excellent schools. Huntsville International Airport, which was an Intermodal Center and is now designated a Port of Entry for international travelers, is just next door.

The first known settler in what was to become the city of Madison was John Cartwright, in 1818, who arrived when the site was still largely wild and part of the newly acquired Mississippi Territory. He received a land grant from the federal government for a plot first known as Madison Station. After Cartwright sold his property to the Palmer family, the little settlement was referred to for some time simply as the "the Palmer place." The arrival of rail travel was important in Madison's history, and the Norfolk Southern Railway still runs through town.

The community began to take its modern shape in 1856, as a stop on the Memphis and Charleston Railroad line, and in 1858, one of the residents, Judge Clemons, planned out a town in lots along the rail line measuring 66 feet by 198 feet. On one of these lots a house was built for T. J. Clay, the town's first station manager, and soon new residents were moving in to take advantage of the fertile surrounding farmland and the convenience of nearby transport. This rail-centered row of houses developed into the town's first commercial district and became Main Street. Mill operator J. J. Akers, blacksmith S. D. Doolittle, and the merchants Walter and Thomas Hopkins and James Bibb were among "Madison Station's" more prominent businessmen.

During the Civil War, of course, further development was curtailed. Many local men fought during the conflict, and a significant battle, "the Affair at Madison Station," was fought at Madison on May 17, 1864. Federal troops fought successfully to control the rail line, which was strategically important in transporting men and supplies to Georgia. Causalities on the Confederate side were 18 killed and 55 wounded, while the Union suffered one death and three wounded. Sixty-six prisoners were taken by the Union Army. With the close of hostilities, development began anew, and in 1869 the merchant James Bibb and others moved to incorporate the town, to be known henceforth as Madison, in honor of the nation's fourth president.

The city, which came close to doubling in population between 1990 and 2000, has in the recent past constructed a new library, fire station, recreation center, and invested in necessary road and drainage projects. One new high school and two elementary schools have also been established.

Nearby institutions of higher learning include Alabama A&M University, Oakwood College, and the University of Alabama at Huntsville.

Madison has a temperate climate. Summers are characterized by warm and humid weather, with rather frequent thunderstorms. Winters are usually cool, but vary considerably from year to year. Cold air masses from the northwest dominate during the winter, but at times air flowing north from the Gulf of Mexico brings warmer temperatures. Spring comes early and brings changeable weather, with rainstorms. Fall is usually clear, dry, and pleasant.

Rankings

Business/Finance Rankings

- The personal finance site NerdWallet analyzed 183 American metropolitan areas with populations over 250,000 and more than 15,000 businesses to rank where entrepreneurs find the most success. Criteria included area economy, annual income, housing cost, unemployment rate, and the success rate of area businesses. Huntsville* ranked #83. *www.nerdwallet.com, "Best Places to Start a Business," April 27, 2015*
- The Huntsville* metro area appeared on the Milken Institute "2015 Best Performing Cities" list. Rank: #140 out of 200 large metro areas. Criteria: job growth; wage and salary growth; high-tech output growth. *Milken Institute, "Best-Performing Cities 2015," December 2015*
- *Forbes* ranked the 200 most populous metro areas to determine the nation's "Best Places for Business and Careers." The Huntsville* metro area was ranked #96. Criteria: costs (business and living); job growth (past and projected); income growth; educational attainment (college and high school); projected economic growth; cultural and recreational opportunities; net migration patterns; number of highly ranked colleges. *Forbes, "The Best Places for Business and Careers 2015," July 29, 2015*

Education Rankings

- Personal finance website *WalletHub* analyzed the 150 largest U.S. metropolitan statistical areas to determine where the most educated Americans are choosing to settle. Criteria: education quality and attainment gap; education levels; percentage of workers with degrees; public school rankings; quality and size of each metro area's universities. Huntsville* was ranked #25 (#1 = most educated city). *www.WalletHub.com, "2015's Most and Least Educated Cities*

Environmental Rankings

- The Huntsville* metro area came in at #258 for the relative comfort of its climate on Sperling's list of "chill cities," as measured by the Sperling Heat Index. All 361 metro areas are included. Criteria included daytime high temperatures, nighttime low temperatures, dew point, and relative humidity at the high temperatures. *www.bertsperling.com, "Sperling's Chill Cities," July 18, 2013*
- Sperling's BestPlaces assessed 379 metropolitan areas of the United States for the likelihood of dangerously extreme weather events or earthquakes. In general the Southeast and South-Central regions have the highest risk of weather extremes and earthquakes, while the Pacific Northwest enjoys the lowest risk. Of the least risky metropolitan areas, the Huntsville* metro area was ranked #351. *www.bestplaces.net, "Safest Places from Natural Disasters," April 2011*
- Huntsville* was highlighted as one of the top 25 cleanest metro areas for short-term particle pollution (24-hour PM 2.5) in the U.S. during 2011 through 2013. Monitors in these cities reported no days with unhealthful PM 2.5 levels. *American Lung Association, State of the Air 2015*

Health/Fitness Rankings

- The Huntsville* metro area ranked #52 out of 190 in The Gallup-Healthways Well-Being Index. Criteria: purpose; social well being; financial health; community and physical health. Results are based on telephone interviews with adults, aged 18 and older, living in metropolitan areas in the 50 U.S. states and the District of Columbia. *Gallup-Healthways, "State of American Well-Being," February 23, 2016*

Safety Rankings

- The National Insurance Crime Bureau ranked 380 metro areas in the U.S. in terms of per capita rates of vehicle theft. The Huntsville* metro area ranked #159 (#1 = highest rate). Criteria: number of vehicle theft offenses per 100,000 inhabitants in 2014. *National Insurance Crime Bureau, "Hot Spots 2014," June 24, 2015*

Seniors/Retirement Rankings

- From its Best Cities for Successful Aging indexes, the Milken Institute generated rankings for metropolitan areas, weighing data in eight categories—health care, wellness, living arrangements, transportation, financial characteristics, education and employment opportunities, community engagement, and overall livability. The Huntsville* metro area was ranked #124 overall in the small metro area category. *Milken Institute, "Best Cities for Successful Aging, 2014"*

***Madison is located within the Huntsville, AL Metropolitan Statistical Area.**

Business Environment

CITY FINANCES

City Government Finances

Component	2012 ($000)	2012 ($ per capita)
Total Revenues	58,416	1,360
Total Expenditures	56,321	1,311
Debt Outstanding	75,125	1,749
Cash and Securities[1]	15,092	351

Note: (1) Cash and security holdings of a government at the close of its fiscal year, including those of its dependent agencies, utilities, and liquor stores.
Source: U.S Census Bureau, State & Local Government Finances 2012

City Government Revenue by Source

Source	2012 ($000)	2012 ($ per capita)
General Revenue		
From Federal Government	1,216	28
From State Government	4,648	108
From Local Governments	0	0
Taxes		
Property	13,058	304
Sales and Gross Receipts	15,206	354
Personal Income	0	0
Corporate Income	0	0
Motor Vehicle License	0	0
Other Taxes	6,629	154
Current Charges	8,277	192
Liquor Store	0	0
Utility	7,049	164
Employee Retirement	0	0

Source: U.S Census Bureau, State & Local Government Finances 2012

City Government Expenditures by Function

Function	2012 ($000)	2012 ($ per capita)	2012 (%)
General Direct Expenditures			
Air Transportation	0	0	0.0
Corrections	0	0	0.0
Education	0	0	0.0
Employment Security Administration	0	0	0.0
Financial Administration	1,404	32	2.4
Fire Protection	5,489	127	9.7
General Public Buildings	0	0	0.0
Governmental Administration, Other	14,408	335	25.5
Health	0	0	0.0
Highways	7,277	169	12.9
Hospitals	0	0	0.0
Housing and Community Development	0	0	0.0
Interest on General Debt	3,083	71	5.4
Judicial and Legal	1,192	27	2.1
Libraries	550	12	0.9
Parking	0	0	0.0
Parks and Recreation	3,520	81	6.2
Police Protection	7,047	164	12.5
Public Welfare	0	0	0.0
Sewerage	6,140	142	10.9
Solid Waste Management	0	0	0.0
Veterans' Services	0	0	0.0
Liquor Store	0	0	0.0
Utility	6,140	142	10.9
Employee Retirement	0	0	0.0

Source: U.S Census Bureau, State & Local Government Finances 2012

DEMOGRAPHICS

Population Growth

Area	1990 Census	2000 Census	2010 Census	2014* Estimate	Population Growth (%) 1990-2014	2010-2014
City	16,813	29,329	42,938	44,866	166.9	4.5
MSA[1]	293,047	342,376	417,593	430,396	46.9	3.1
U.S.	248,709,873	281,421,906	308,745,538	314,107,084	26.3	1.7

Note: (1) Figures cover the Huntsville, AL Metropolitan Statistical Area—see Appendix B for areas included; (*) 2010-2014 5-year estimated population
Source: U.S. Census Bureau, 1990 Census, Census 2000, Census 2010, 2010-2014 American Community Survey 5-Year Estimates

Household Size

Area	Persons in Household (%) One	Two	Three	Four	Five	Six	Seven or More	Average Household Size
City	23.4	33.2	17.9	16.8	6.0	1.9	0.4	2.75
MSA[1]	29.5	34.3	16.1	12.8	4.8	1.4	0.7	2.50
U.S.	27.5	33.5	15.8	13.1	6.0	2.3	1.4	2.64

Note: (1) Figures cover the Huntsville, AL Metropolitan Statistical Area—see Appendix B for areas included
Source: U.S. Census Bureau, 2010-2014 American Community Survey 5-Year Estimates

Race

Area	White Alone[2] (%)	Black Alone[2] (%)	Asian Alone[2] (%)	AIAN[3] Alone[2] (%)	NHOPI[4] Alone[2] (%)	Other Race Alone[2] (%)	Two or More Races (%)
City	75.1	14.7	5.6	0.8	0.2	0.7	2.8
MSA[1]	71.5	21.7	2.2	0.6	0.1	1.1	2.7
U.S.	73.8	12.6	5.0	0.8	0.2	4.7	2.9

Note: (1) Figures cover the Huntsville, AL Metropolitan Statistical Area—see Appendix B for areas included; (2) Alone is defined as not being in combination with one or more other races; (3) American Indian and Alaska Native; (4) Native Hawaiian and Other Pacific Islander
Source: U.S. Census Bureau, 2010-2014 American Community Survey 5-Year Estimates

Hispanic or Latino Origin

Area	Total (%)	Mexican (%)	Puerto Rican (%)	Cuban (%)	Other (%)
City	4.5	2.2	1.4	0.1	0.9
MSA[1]	4.9	3.3	0.6	0.1	0.8
U.S.	16.9	10.8	1.6	0.6	3.8

Note: Persons of Hispanic or Latino origin can be of any race; (1) Figures cover the Huntsville, AL Metropolitan Statistical Area—see Appendix B for areas included
Source: U.S. Census Bureau, 2010-2014 American Community Survey 5-Year Estimates

Ancestry

Area	German	Irish	English	American	Italian	Polish	French[2]	Scottish	Dutch
City	13.2	9.8	11.9	11.6	2.7	1.8	1.8	2.2	1.2
MSA[1]	9.9	9.2	9.9	13.9	2.2	1.0	1.8	2.0	0.9
U.S.	14.9	10.8	8.0	7.1	5.5	3.0	2.7	1.7	1.4

Note: Figures are the percentage of the total population reporting a particular ancestry. The nine most commonly reported ancestries in the U.S. are shown. Figures include multiple ancestries (e.g. if a person reported being Irish and Italian, they were included in both columns); (1) Figures cover the Huntsville, AL Metropolitan Statistical Area—see Appendix B for areas included; (2) Excludes Basque
Source: U.S. Census Bureau, 2010-2014 American Community Survey 5-Year Estimates

Foreign-Born Population

Area	Percent of Population Born in								
	Any Foreign Country	Asia	Mexico	Europe	Carribean	Central America[2]	South America	Africa	Canada
City	7.8	4.4	0.5	1.6	0.0	0.1	0.4	0.4	0.3
MSA[1]	5.2	1.8	1.4	0.8	0.3	0.3	0.2	0.4	0.1
U.S.	13.1	3.8	3.7	1.5	1.2	1.0	0.9	0.6	0.3

Note: (1) Figures cover the Huntsville, AL Metropolitan Statistical Area—see Appendix B for areas included; (2) Excludes Mexico.
Source: U.S. Census Bureau, 2010-2014 American Community Survey 5-Year Estimates

Marital Status

Area	Never Married	Now Married[2]	Separated	Widowed	Divorced
City	27.6	58.3	1.0	4.0	9.1
MSA[1]	29.2	51.1	1.8	5.8	12.0
U.S.	32.5	48.4	2.2	5.9	10.9

Note: Figures are percentages and cover the population 15 years of age and older; (1) Figures cover the Huntsville, AL Metropolitan Statistical Area—see Appendix B for areas included; (2) Excludes separated
Source: U.S. Census Bureau, 2010-2014 American Community Survey 5-Year Estimates

Disability Status

Area	All Ages	Under 18 Years Old	18 to 64 Years Old	65 Years and Over
City	7.9	1.8	6.7	36.0
MSA[1]	12.6	3.8	10.6	38.5
U.S.	12.3	4.1	10.2	36.3

Note: Figures show percent of the civilian noninstitutionalized population that reported having a disability. Disability status is determined from from six types of difficulty: vision, hearing, cognitive, ambulatory, self-care, and independent living. For children under 5 years old, hearing and vision difficulty are used to determine disability status. For children between the ages of 5 and 14, disability status is determined from hearing, vision, cognitive, ambulatory, and self-care difficulties. For people aged 15 years and older, they are considered to have a disability if they have difficulty with any one of the six difficulty types; (1) Figures cover the Huntsville, AL Metropolitan Statistical Area—see Appendix B for areas included.
Source: U.S. Census Bureau, 2010-2014 American Community Survey 5-Year Estimates

Age

Area	Percent of Population									Median Age
	Under Age 5	Age 5–19	Age 20–34	Age 35–44	Age 45–54	Age 55–64	Age 65–74	Age 75–84	Age 85+	
City	5.8	23.2	18.6	13.5	18.4	11.4	6.2	1.9	1.1	37.1
MSA[1]	6.1	19.9	20.4	13.0	15.7	12.1	7.4	4.0	1.5	37.9
U.S.	6.4	19.9	20.6	13.0	14.1	12.3	7.6	4.3	1.9	37.4

Note: (1) Figures cover the Huntsville, AL Metropolitan Statistical Area—see Appendix B for areas included
Source: U.S. Census Bureau, 2010-2014 American Community Survey 5-Year Estimates

Gender

Area	Males	Females	Males per 100 Females
City	22,341	22,525	99.2
MSA[1]	212,007	218,389	97.1
U.S.	154,515,159	159,591,925	96.8

Note: (1) Figures cover the Huntsville, AL Metropolitan Statistical Area—see Appendix B for areas included
Source: U.S. Census Bureau, 2010-2014 American Community Survey 5-Year Estimates

Religious Groups by Family

Area	Catholic	Baptist	Non-Den.	Methodist[2]	Lutheran	LDS[3]	Pentecostal	Presbyterian[4]	Muslim[5]	Judaism
MSA[1]	3.9	27.6	3.1	7.5	0.7	1.1	1.2	1.7	0.2	0.1
U.S.	19.1	9.3	4.0	4.0	2.3	2.0	1.9	1.6	0.8	0.7

Note: Figures are the number of adherents as a percentage of the total population; (1) Figures cover the Huntsville, AL Metropolitan Statistical Area—see Appendix B for areas included; (2) Methodist/Pietist; (3) Latter Day Saints; (4) Reformed; (5) Figures are estimates
Source: Association of Statisticians of American Religious Bodies, 2010 U.S. Religion Census: Religious Congregations & Membership Study

Religious Groups by Tradition

Area	Catholic	Evangelical Protestant	Mainline Protestant	Other Tradition	Black Protestant	Orthodox
MSA[1]	3.9	33.3	9.6	1.8	1.8	<0.1
U.S.	19.1	16.2	7.3	4.3	1.6	0.3

Note: Figures are the number of adherents as a percentage of the total population; (1) Figures cover the Huntsville, AL Metropolitan Statistical Area—see Appendix B for areas included
Source: Association of Statisticians of American Religious Bodies, 2010 U.S. Religion Census: Religious Congregations & Membership Study

ECONOMY

Gross Metropolitan Product

Area	2013	2014	2015	2016	Rank[2]
MSA[1]	22.9	23.6	24.5	25.7	102

Note: Figures are in billions of dollars; (1) Figures cover the Huntsville, AL Metropolitan Statistical Area—see Appendix B for areas included; (2) Rank is based on 2016 data and ranges from 1 to 381
Source: The U.S. Conference of Mayors, U.S. Metro Economies: GMP and Employment 2014-2016, June 2015

Economic Growth

Area	2011-13 (%)	2014 (%)	2015 (%)	2016 (%)	Rank[2]
MSA[1]	0.7	1.3	2.2	3.0	83
U.S.	2.2	2.4	2.3	2.9	–

Note: Figures are real gross metropolitan product (GMP) growth rates and represent annual average percent change; (1) Figures cover the Huntsville, AL Metropolitan Statistical Area—see Appendix B for areas included; (2) Rank is based on 2016 data and ranges from 1 to 381
Source: The U.S. Conference of Mayors, U.S. Metro Economies: GMP and Employment 2014-2016, June 2015

Metropolitan Area Exports

Area	2009	2010	2011	2012	2013	2014	Rank[2]
MSA[1]	1,136.5	986.8	1,293.3	1,491.5	1,518.6	1,440.4	127

Note: Figures are in millions of dollars; (1) Figures cover the Huntsville, AL Metropolitan Statistical Area—see Appendix B for areas included; (2) Rank is based on 2014 data and ranges from 1 to 385
Source: U.S. Department of Commerce, International Trade Administration, Office of Trade & Industry Information, Manufacturing & Services, data extracted March 10, 2016

Building Permits

Area	Single-Family			Multi-Family			Total		
	2014	2015p	Pct. Chg.	2014	2015p	Pct. Chg.	2014	2015p	Pct. Chg.
City	338	466	37.9	0	0	-	338	466	37.9
MSA[1]	1,784	2,116	18.6	1,033	486	-53.0	2,817	2,602	-7.6
U.S.	640,300	690,800	7.9	411,800	487,600	18.4	1,052,100	1,178,400	12.0

Note: (1) Figures cover the Huntsville, AL Metropolitan Statistical Area—see Appendix B for areas included; Figures represent new, privately-owned housing units authorized (unadjusted data); All permit data are based on estimates with imputation; (p) preliminary data.
Source: U.S. Census Bureau, Manufacturing, Mining, and Construction Statistics, Building Permits, 2014, 2015

Bankruptcy Filings

Area	Business Filings			Nonbusiness Filings		
	2014	2015	% Chg.	2014	2015	% Chg.
Madison County	35	25	-28.6	1,334	1,316	-1.3
U.S.	26,983	24,735	-8.3	909,812	819,760	-9.9

Note: Business filings include Chapter 7, Chapter 11, Chapter 12, and Chapter 13; Nonbusiness filings include Chapter 7, Chapter 11, and Chapter 13
Source: Administrative Office of the U.S. Courts, Business and Nonbusiness Bankruptcy, County Cases Commenced by Chapter of the Bankruptcy Code, During the 12- Month Period Ending December 31, 2014 and Business and Nonbusiness Bankruptcy, County Cases Commenced by Chapter of the Bankruptcy Code, During the 12- Month Period Ending December 31, 2015

Housing Vacancy Rates

Area	Gross Vacancy Rate[2] (%)			Year-Round Vacancy Rate[3] (%)			Rental Vacancy Rate[4] (%)			Homeowner Vacancy Rate[5] (%)		
	2013	2014	2015	2013	2014	2015	2013	2014	2015	2013	2014	2015
MSA[1]	n/a	n/a	n/a	n/a	n/a	n/a	n/a	n/a	n/a	n/a	n/a	n/a
U.S.	13.6	13.4	12.9	10.7	10.4	10.0	8.3	7.6	7.1	2.0	1.9	1.8

Note: (1) Figures cover the Huntsville, AL Metropolitan Statistical Area—see Appendix B for areas included; (2) The percentage of the total housing inventory that is vacant; (3) The percentage of the housing inventory (excluding seasonal units) that is year-round vacant; (4) The percentage of rental inventory that is vacant for rent; (5) The percentage of homeowner inventory that is vacant for sale; n/a not available
Source: U.S. Census Bureau, Housing Vacancies and Homeownership Annual Statistics: 2015

INCOME

Income

Area	Per Capita ($)	Median Household ($)	Average Household ($)
City	42,284	92,965	112,609
MSA[1]	30,960	55,881	77,454
U.S.	28,555	53,482	74,596

Note: (1) Figures cover the Huntsville, AL Metropolitan Statistical Area—see Appendix B for areas included
Source: U.S. Census Bureau, 2010-2014 American Community Survey 5-Year Estimates

Household Income Distribution

Area	Percent of Households Earning							
	Under $15,000	$15,000 -24,999	$25,000 -34,999	$35,000 -49,999	$50,000 -74,999	$75,000 -99,000	$100,000 -149,999	$150,000 and up
City	3.7	5.6	7.6	10.5	16.1	10.0	23.0	23.5
MSA[1]	12.2	9.6	10.2	13.2	16.5	11.8	15.3	11.1
U.S.	12.5	10.7	10.2	13.5	17.8	12.2	13.0	10.0

Note: (1) Figures cover the Huntsville, AL Metropolitan Statistical Area—see Appendix B for areas included
Source: U.S. Census Bureau, 2010-2014 American Community Survey 5-Year Estimates

Poverty Rate

Area	All Ages	Under 18 Years Old	18 to 64 Years Old	65 Years and Over
City	6.6	9.1	5.9	4.3
MSA[1]	13.5	18.9	12.6	8.2
U.S.	15.6	21.9	14.6	9.4

Note: Figures are percentage of people whose income during the past 12 months was below the poverty level; (1) Figures cover the Huntsville, AL Metropolitan Statistical Area—see Appendix B for areas included
Source: U.S. Census Bureau, 2010-2014 American Community Survey 5-Year Estimates

EMPLOYMENT

Labor Force and Employment

Area	Civilian Labor Force			Workers Employed		
	Dec. 2014	Dec. 2015	% Chg.	Dec. 2014	Dec. 2015	% Chg.
City	22,885	23,243	1.5	22,019	22,180	0.7
MSA[1]	206,534	208,299	0.8	196,222	197,695	0.7
U.S.	155,521,000	157,245,000	1.1	147,190,000	149,703,000	1.7

Note: Data is not seasonally adjusted and covers workers 16 years of age and older; (1) Figures cover the Huntsville, AL Metropolitan Statistical Area—see Appendix B for areas included
Source: Bureau of Labor Statistics, Local Area Unemployment Statistics

Unemployment Rate

Area	2015											
	Jan.	Feb.	Mar.	Apr.	May	Jun.	Jul.	Aug.	Sep.	Oct.	Nov.	Dec.
City	4.8	4.4	4.5	4.1	4.7	5.2	5.1	5.1	4.5	4.4	4.4	4.6
MSA[1]	5.6	5.2	5.3	4.8	5.5	6.1	6.1	5.9	5.3	5.0	5.0	5.1
U.S.	6.1	5.8	5.6	5.1	5.3	5.5	5.6	5.2	4.9	4.8	4.8	4.8

Note: Data is not seasonally adjusted and covers workers 16 years of age and older; (1) Figures cover the Huntsville, AL Metropolitan Statistical Area—see Appendix B for areas included
Source: Bureau of Labor Statistics, Local Area Unemployment Statistics

Employment by Occupation

Occupation Classification	City (%)	MSA[1] (%)	U.S. (%)
Management, Business, Science, and Arts	57.7	42.7	36.4
Natural Resources, Construction, and Maintenance	4.3	7.5	9.0
Production, Transportation, and Material Moving	6.9	11.5	12.1
Sales and Office	19.3	23.1	24.4
Service	11.8	15.2	18.2

Note: Figures cover employed civilians 16 years of age and older; (1) Figures cover the Huntsville, AL Metropolitan Statistical Area—see Appendix B for areas included
Source: U.S. Census Bureau, 2010-2014 American Community Survey 5-Year Estimates

Employment by Industry

Sector	MSA[1]		U.S.
	Number of Employees	Percent of Total	Percent of Total
Construction, Mining, and Logging	8,300	3.7	5.0
Education and Health Services	20,100	9.0	15.7
Financial Activities	6,300	2.8	5.7
Government	48,700	21.8	15.5
Information	2,600	1.1	1.9
Leisure and Hospitality	19,500	8.7	10.4
Manufacturing	23,600	10.5	8.6
Other Services	7,000	3.1	3.9
Professional and Business Services	52,700	23.6	13.9
Retail Trade	25,400	11.3	11.3
Transportation, Warehousing, and Utilities	3,100	1.3	3.9
Wholesale Trade	5,900	2.6	4.1

Note: Figures are non-farm employment as of December 2015. Figures are not seasonally adjusted and include workers 16 years of age and older; (1) Figures cover the Huntsville, AL Metropolitan Statistical Area—see Appendix B for areas included; n/a not available
Source: Bureau of Labor Statistics, Current Employment Statistics, Employment, Hours, and Earnings

Occupations with Greatest Projected Employment Growth: 2012 – 2022

Occupation[1]	2012 Employment	2022 Projected Employment	Numeric Employment Change	Percent Employment Change
Registered Nurses	46,040	54,670	8,630	18.7
Team Assemblers	29,770	36,190	6,420	21.6
Retail Salespersons	59,400	65,790	6,390	10.8
Secretaries and Administrative Assistants, Except Legal, Medical, and Executive	42,330	48,520	6,190	14.6
Combined Food Preparation and Serving Workers, Including Fast Food	40,870	46,690	5,820	14.2
Personal Care Aides	10,730	15,650	4,920	45.9
Laborers and Freight, Stock, and Material Movers, Hand	34,790	38,910	4,120	11.8
Customer Service Representatives	30,640	34,660	4,020	13.1
Heavy and Tractor-Trailer Truck Drivers	31,860	35,690	3,830	12.0
Janitors and Cleaners, Except Maids and Housekeeping Cleaners	27,930	31,490	3,560	12.7

Note: Projections cover Alabama; (1) Sorted by numeric employment change
Source: www.projectionscentral.com, State Occupational Projections, 2012–2022 Long-Term Projections

Fastest Growing Occupations: 2012 – 2022

Occupation[1]	2012 Employment	2022 Projected Employment	Numeric Employment Change	Percent Employment Change
Engine and Other Machine Assemblers	2,150	3,430	1,280	59.7
Occupational Therapy Assistants	360	530	170	49.6
Personal Care Aides	10,730	15,650	4,920	45.9
Diagnostic Medical Sonographers	1,130	1,630	500	44.5
Physical Therapist Assistants	1,870	2,680	810	43.4
Computer Numerically Controlled Machine Tool Programmers, Metal and Plastic	290	410	120	42.3
Helpers—Brickmasons, Blockmasons, Stonemasons, and Tile and Marble Setters	340	490	150	42.0
Biological Science Teachers, Postsecondary	1,730	2,460	730	41.9
Insulation Workers, Mechanical	550	770	220	40.6
Home Health Aides	8,340	11,710	3,370	40.4

Note: Projections cover Alabama; (1) Sorted by percent employment change and excludes occupations with numeric employment change less than 100
Source: www.projectionscentral.com, State Occupational Projections, 2012–2022 Long-Term Projections

Average Wages

Occupation	$/Hr.	Occupation	$/Hr.
Accountants and Auditors	36.90	Maids and Housekeeping Cleaners	8.46
Automotive Mechanics	17.29	Maintenance and Repair Workers	19.72
Bookkeepers	17.75	Marketing Managers	65.00
Carpenters	16.16	Nuclear Medicine Technologists	n/a
Cashiers	9.31	Nurses, Licensed Practical	17.52
Clerks, General Office	12.28	Nurses, Registered	27.61
Clerks, Receptionists/Information	12.10	Nursing Assistants	11.63
Clerks, Shipping/Receiving	14.44	Packers and Packagers, Hand	11.61
Computer Programmers	47.04	Physical Therapists	46.15
Computer Systems Analysts	40.71	Postal Service Mail Carriers	24.72
Computer User Support Specialists	24.24	Real Estate Brokers	34.44
Cooks, Restaurant	10.52	Retail Salespersons	11.85
Dentists	87.51	Sales Reps., Exc. Tech./Scientific	28.38
Electrical Engineers	47.71	Sales Reps., Tech./Scientific	43.33
Electricians	18.98	Secretaries, Exc. Legal/Med./Exec.	17.35
Financial Managers	63.42	Security Guards	12.52
First-Line Supervisors/Managers, Sales	19.82	Surgeons	n/a
Food Preparation Workers	8.94	Teacher Assistants*	9.22
General and Operations Managers	64.69	Teachers, Elementary School*	24.73
Hairdressers/Cosmetologists	14.75	Teachers, Secondary School*	24.42
Internists	n/a	Telemarketers	n/a
Janitors and Cleaners	10.55	Truck Drivers, Heavy/Tractor-Trailer	18.61
Landscaping/Groundskeeping Workers	10.16	Truck Drivers, Light/Delivery Svcs.	14.34
Lawyers	66.06	Waiters and Waitresses	10.14

Note: Wage data covers the Huntsville, AL Metropolitan Statistical Area—see Appendix B for areas included; (*) Hourly wages for elementary/secondary school teachers and teacher assistants were calculated by the editors from annual wage data based on a 40 hour work week; n/a not available.
Source: Bureau of Labor Statistics, Metro Area Occupational Employment and Wage Estimates, May 2015

TAXES

State Corporate Income Tax Rates

State	Tax Rate (%)	Income Brackets ($)	Num. of Brackets	Financial Institution Tax Rate (%)[a]	Federal Income Tax Ded.
Alabama	6.5	Flat rate	1	6.5	Yes

Note: Tax rates as of January 1, 2016; (a) Rates listed are the corporate income tax rate applied to financial institutions or excise taxes based on income. Some states have other taxes based upon the value of deposits or shares.
Source: Federation of Tax Administrators, "State Corporate Income Tax Rates, 2016"

State Individual Income Tax Rates

State	Tax Rate (%)	Income Brackets ($)	Num. of Brackets	Personal Exempt. ($)[1] Single	Personal Exempt. ($)[1] Dependents	Fed. Inc. Tax Ded.
Alabama	2.0 - 5.0	500 - 3,001 (b)	3	1,500	500 (e)	Yes

Note: Tax rates as of January 1, 2016; Local- and county-level taxes are not included; n/a not applicable; (1) Married joint filers generally receive double the single exemption; (b) For joint returns, taxes are twice the tax on half the couple's income; (e) In Alabama, the per-dependent exemption is $1,000 for taxpayers with state AGI of $20,000 or less, $500 with AGI from $20,001 to $100,000, and $300 with AGI over $100,000.
Source: Federation of Tax Administrators, "State Individual Income Tax Rates, 2016"

Various State and Local Tax Rates

State	State and Local Sales and Use (%)	State Sales and Use (%)	Gasoline[1] (¢/gal.)	Cigarette[2] ($/pack)	Spirits[3] ($/gal.)	Wine[4] ($/gal.)	Beer[5] ($/gal.)
Alabama	9.50	4.0	20.87	0.675	18.25 (g)	1.70 (l)	1.07 (r)

Note: All tax rates as of January 1, 2016; (1) The American Petroleum Institute has developed a methodology for determining the average tax rate on a gallon of fuel. Rates may include any of the following: excise taxes, environmental fees, storage tank fees, other fees or taxes, general sales tax, and local taxes. In states where gasoline is subject to the general sales tax, or where the fuel tax is based on the average sale price, the average rate determined by API is sensitive to changes in the price of gasoline. States that fully or partially apply general sales taxes to gasoline: CA, CO, GA, IL, IN, MI, NY; (2) The federal excise tax of $1.0066 per pack and local taxes are not included; (3) Rates are those applicable to off-premise sales of 40% alcohol by volume (a.b.v.) distilled spirits in 750ml containers. Local excise taxes are excluded; (4) Rates are those applicable to off-premise sales of 11% a.b.v. non-carbonated wine in 750ml containers; (5) Rates are those applicable to off-premise sales of 4.7% a.b.v. beer in 12 ounce containers; (g) Control states, where the government controls all sales. Products can be subject to ad valorem mark-up as well as excise taxes; (l) Different rates also applicable according to alcohol content, place of production, size of container, place purchased (on- or off-premise or on board airlines) or type of wine (carbonated, vermouth, etc.); (r) Includes the statewide local rate in Alabama ($0.52) and Georgia ($0.53).
Source: Tax Foundation, 2016 Facts & Figures: How Does Your State Compare?

State Business Tax Climate Index Rankings

State	Overall Rank	Corporate Tax Rank	Individual Income Tax Rank	Sales Tax Rank	Unemployment Insurance Tax Rank	Property Tax Rank
Alabama	29	25	22	41	26	17

Note: The index is a measure of how each state's tax laws affect economic performance. The lower the rank, the more favorable a state's tax system is for business. States without a given tax are given a ranking of 1. The scores/rankings for the District of Columbia do not affect other states. The 2016 index represents the tax climate as of July 1, 2015 (the beginning of Fiscal Year 2016).
Source: Tax Foundation, State Business Tax Climate Index 2016

TRANSPORTATION

Means of Transportation to Work

Area	Car/Truck/Van: Drove Alone	Car/Truck/Van: Car-pooled	Public Transportation: Bus	Public Transportation: Subway	Public Transportation: Railroad	Bicycle	Walked	Other Means	Worked at Home
City	90.7	6.1	0.1	0.0	0.0	0.3	0.1	0.7	2.0
MSA[1]	86.7	7.6	0.3	0.0	0.0	0.1	1.0	1.2	2.9
U.S.	76.4	9.6	2.6	1.8	0.6	0.6	2.8	1.3	4.4

Note: Figures are percentages and cover workers 16 years of age and older; (1) Figures cover the Huntsville, AL Metropolitan Statistical Area—see Appendix B for areas included
Source: U.S. Census Bureau, 2010-2014 American Community Survey 5-Year Estimates

Travel Time to Work

Area	Less Than 10 Minutes	10 to 19 Minutes	20 to 29 Minutes	30 to 44 Minutes	45 to 59 Minutes	60 to 89 Minutes	90 Minutes or More
City	10.5	42.0	31.6	13.2	1.2	1.0	0.4
MSA[1]	11.1	34.0	28.2	19.4	4.4	1.7	1.1
U.S.	13.3	29.6	21.0	20.2	7.7	5.7	2.6

Note: Figures are percentages and include workers 16 years old and over; (1) Figures cover the Huntsville, AL Metropolitan Statistical Area—see Appendix B for areas included
Source: U.S. Census Bureau, 2010-2014 American Community Survey 5-Year Estimates

Freeway Travel Time Index

Area	1985	1990	1995	2000	2005	2010	2014
Urban Area Rank[1,2]	n/a	n/a	n/a	n/a	n/a	n/a	n/a
Urban Area Index[1]	n/a	n/a	n/a	n/a	n/a	n/a	n/a
Average Index[3]	1.09	1.11	1.14	1.17	1.20	1.19	1.20

Note: Freeway Travel Time Index—the ratio of travel time in the peak period to the travel time at free-flow conditions. For example, a value of 1.30 indicates a 20-minute free-flow trip takes 26 minutes in the peak (20 minutes x 1.30 = 26 minutes); (1) Data for the Huntsville, AL urban area was not available; (2) Rank is based on 101 urban areas (#1 = highest travel time index); (3) Average of 101 urban areas
Source: Texas Transportation Institute, 2015 Urban Mobility Scorecard, August 2015

Freeway Commuter Stress Index

Area	1985	1990	1995	2000	2005	2010	2014
Urban Area Rank[1,2]	n/a	n/a	n/a	n/a	n/a	n/a	n/a
Urban Area Index[1]	n/a	n/a	n/a	n/a	n/a	n/a	n/a
Average Index[3]	1.13	1.16	1.19	1.22	1.25	1.24	1.25

Note: The Freeway Commuter Stress Index is the same as the Freeway Travel Time Index (see table above) except that it includes only the travel in the peak directions during the peak periods; the TTI includes travel in all directions during the peak period. Thus, the CSI is more indicative of the work trip experienced by each commuter on a daily basis. (1) Data for the Huntsville, AL urban area was not available; (2) Rank is based on 101 urban areas (#1 = highest stress index); (3) Average of 101 urban areas
Source: Texas Transportation Institute, 2015 Urban Mobility Scorecard, August 2015

Living Environment

COST OF LIVING

Cost of Living Index

Composite Index	Groceries	Housing	Utilities	Transportation	Health Care	Misc. Goods/ Services
91.3	93.6	73.3	101.2	95.4	94.9	100.8

Note: The Cost of Living Index measures regional differences in the cost of consumer goods and services, excluding taxes and non-consumer expenditures, for professional and managerial households in the top income quintile. It is based on more than 50,000 prices covering almost 60 different items for which prices are collected three times a year by chambers of commerce, economic development organizations or university applied economic centers in each participating urban area. The numbers shown should be read as a percentage above or below the national average of 100. For example, a value of 115.4 in the groceries column indicates that grocery prices are 15.4% higher than the national average. Small differences in the index numbers should not be interpreted as significant; Figures cover the Huntsville AL urban area.
Source: The Council for Community and Economic Research, ACCRA Cost of Living Index, 2015

Grocery Prices

Area[1]	T-Bone Steak ($/pound)	Frying Chicken ($/pound)	Whole Milk ($/half gal.)	Eggs ($/dozen)	Orange Juice ($/64 oz.)	Coffee ($/11.5 oz.)
City[2]	11.50	1.21	2.07	2.10	3.30	4.19
Avg.	10.99	1.43	2.25	2.26	3.58	4.48
Min.	7.16	0.98	1.30	1.35	2.88	2.98
Max.	14.13	2.43	3.85	4.81	6.39	7.56

Note: (1) Values for the local area are compared with the average, minimum and maximum values for all 292 areas in the Cost of Living Index; (2) Figures cover the Huntsville AL urban area; **T-Bone Steak** *(price per pound);* **Frying Chicken** *(price per pound, whole fryer);* **Whole Milk** *(half gallon carton);* **Eggs** *(price per dozen, Grade A, large);* **Orange Juice** *(64 oz. Tropicana or Florida Natural);* **Coffee** *(11.5 oz. can, vacuum-packed, Maxwell House, Hills Bros, or Folgers).*
Source: The Council for Community and Economic Research, ACCRA Cost of Living Index, 2015

Housing and Utility Costs

Area[1]	New Home Price ($)	Apartment Rent ($/month)	All Electric ($/month)	Part Electric ($/month)	Other Energy ($/month)	Telephone ($/month)
City[2]	219,464	778	153.20	-	-	32.84
Avg.	312,874	945	179.30	95.07	72.96	28.11
Min.	178,682	479	116.28	43.14	26.46	10.01
Max.	1,472,476	3,984	504.25	189.44	421.11	43.06

Note: (1) Values for the local area are compared with the average, minimum and maximum values for all 292 areas in the Cost of Living Index; (2) Figures cover the Huntsville AL urban area; **New Home Price** *(2,400 sf living area, 8,000 sf lot, in urban area with full utilities);* **Apartment Rent** *(950 sf 2 bedroom/1.5 or 2 bath, unfurnished, excluding all utilities except water);* **All Electric** *(average monthly cost for an all-electric home);* **Part Electric** *(average monthly cost for a part-electric home);* **Other Energy** *(average monthly cost for natural gas, fuel oil, coal, wood, and any other forms of energy except electricity);* **Telephone** *(price includes basic monthly rate for a private residential line plus additional local usage charges incurred by a family of four).*
Source: The Council for Community and Economic Research, ACCRA Cost of Living Index, 2015

Health Care, Transportation, and Other Costs

Area[1]	Doctor ($/visit)	Dentist ($/visit)	Optometrist ($/visit)	Gasoline ($/gallon)	Beauty Salon ($/visit)	Men's Shirt ($)
City[2]	78.61	91.92	111.44	2.21	33.47	31.00
Avg.	105.15	89.02	99.78	2.38	35.30	28.10
Min.	66.87	56.09	48.53	1.95	18.91	13.38
Max.	182.34	150.36	228.33	4.09	67.91	63.80

Note: (1) Values for the local area are compared with the average, minimum and maximum values for all 292 areas in the Cost of Living Index; (2) Figures cover the Huntsville AL urban area; **Doctor** *(general practitioners routine exam of an established patient);* **Dentist** *(adult teeth cleaning and periodic oral examination);* **Optometrist** *(full vision eye exam for established adult patient);* **Gasoline** *(one gallon regular unleaded, national brand, including all taxes, cash price at self-service pump if available);* **Beauty Salon** *(woman's shampoo, trim, and blow-dry);* **Men's Shirt** *(cotton/polyester dress shirt, pinpoint weave, long sleeves).*
Source: The Council for Community and Economic Research, ACCRA Cost of Living Index, 2015

HOUSING

House Price Index (HPI)

Area	National Ranking[2]	Quarterly Change (%)	One-Year Change (%)	Five-Year Change (%)
MSA[1]	209	0.80	2.40	-0.00
U.S.[3]	–	1.45	5.76	22.85

Note: The HPI is a weighted repeat sales index. It measures average price changes in repeat sales or refinancings on the same properties. This information is obtained by reviewing repeat mortgage transactions on single-family properties whose mortgages have been purchased or securitized by Fannie Mae or Freddie Mac in January 1975; (1) Huntsville Metropolitan Statistical Area—see Appendix B for areas included; (2) Rankings are based on annual percentage change for all metro areas containing at least 15,000 transactions over the last 10 years and ranges from 1 to 266; (3) figures based on a weighted average of Census Division estimates using a seasonally adjusted, purchase-only index; all figures are for the period ending December 31, 2015
Source: Federal Housing Finance Agency, House Price Index, February 25, 2016

Median Single-Family Home Prices

Area	2013	2014	2015p	Percent Change 2014 to 2015
MSA[1]	171.6	171.1	173.7	1.5
U.S. Average	197.4	208.9	223.9	7.2

Note: Figures are median sales prices of existing single-family homes in thousands of dollars; (p) preliminary; n/a not available; (1) Huntsville, AL Metropolitan Statistical Area—see Appendix B for areas included
Source: National Association of Realtors, Median Sales Price of Existing Single-Family Homes for Metropolitan Areas, 4th Quarter 2015

Qualifying Income Based on Median Sales Price of Existing Single-Family Homes

Area	With 5% Down ($)	With 10% Down ($)	With 20% Down ($)
MSA[1]	39,259	37,193	33,060
U.S. Average	49,535	46,928	41,714

Note: Figures are preliminary; Qualifying income is based on a mortgage rate of 4.1%. Monthly principal and interest payment is limited to 25% of income; n/a not available; (1) Huntsville, AL Metropolitan Statistical Area—see Appendix B for areas included
Source: National Association of Realtors, Qualifying Income Based on Median Sales Price of Existing Single-Family Homes for Metropolitan Areas, 4th Quarter 2015

Median Apartment Condo-Coop Home Prices

Area	2013	2014	2015p	Percent Change 2014 to 2015
MSA[1]	n/a	n/a	n/a	n/a
U.S. Average	194.9	204.3	210.7	3.1

Note: Figures are median sales prices of existing apartment condo-coop homes in thousands of dollars; (p) preliminary; n/a not available; (1) Huntsville, AL Metropolitan Statistical Area—see Appendix B for areas included
Source: National Association of Realtors, Median Sales Price of Existing Apartment Condo-Coop Homes for Metropolitan Areas, 4th Quarter 2015

Gross Monthly Rent

Area	Under $200	$200 -299	$300 -499	$500 -749	$750 -999	$1,000 -1,499	$1,500 and up	Median ($)
City	0.4	1.2	4.2	24.6	34.9	24.7	10.1	857
MSA[1]	1.1	4.3	10.3	36.8	25.2	17.5	4.7	733
U.S.	1.5	3.2	7.4	21.0	24.1	26.9	15.9	920

Note: Figures are percentages except for Median; Gross rent is the contract rent plus the estimated average monthly cost of utilities (electricity, gas, and water and sewer) and fuels (oil, coal, kerosene, wood, etc.) if these are paid by the renter (or paid for the renter by someone else); (1) Figures cover the Huntsville, AL Metropolitan Statistical Area—see Appendix B for areas included
Source: U.S. Census Bureau, 2010-2014 American Community Survey 5-Year Estimates

Homeownership Rate

Area	2008 (%)	2009 (%)	2010 (%)	2011 (%)	2012 (%)	2013 (%)	2014 (%)	2015 (%)
MSA[1]	n/a	n/a	n/a	n/a	n/a	n/a	n/a	n/a
U.S.	67.8	67.4	66.9	66.1	65.4	65.1	64.5	63.7

Note: (1) Figures cover the Huntsville, AL Metropolitan Statistical Area—see Appendix B for areas included; n/a not available
Source: U.S. Census Bureau, Housing Vacancies and Homeownership Annual Statistics: 2015

Year Housing Structure Built

Area	2010 or Later	2000 -2009	1990 -1999	1980 -1989	1970 -1979	1960 -1969	1950 -1959	1940 -1949	Before 1940	Median Year
City	3.1	32.4	29.9	22.3	6.2	4.2	0.9	0.4	0.6	1995
MSA[1]	2.4	21.9	19.7	16.2	12.6	14.3	7.4	2.3	3.2	1986
U.S.	1.0	14.9	13.9	13.8	15.8	11.0	10.8	5.4	13.3	1976

Note: Figures are percentages except for Median Year; (1) Figures cover the Huntsville, AL Metropolitan Statistical Area—see Appendix B for areas included
Source: U.S. Census Bureau, 2010-2014 American Community Survey 5-Year Estimates

HEALTH

Health Risk Data

Category	MSA[1] (%)	U.S. (%)
Adults aged 18–64 who have any kind of health care coverage	81.3	79.6
Adults who reported being in good or excellent health	78.8	83.1
Adults who are current smokers	22.0	19.6
Adults who are heavy drinkers[2]	4.1	6.1
Adults who are binge drinkers[3]	11.4	16.9
Adults who are overweight (BMI 25.0 - 29.9)	36.8	35.8
Adults who are obese (BMI 30.0 - 99.8)	29.4	27.6
Adults who participated in any physical activities in the past month	73.8	77.1
Adults 50+ who have ever had a sigmoidoscopy or colonoscopy	68.0	67.3
Women aged 40+ who have had a mammogram within the past two years	81.8	74.0
Men aged 40+ who have had a PSA test within the past two years	44.7	45.2
Adults aged 65+ who have had flu shot within the past year	54.8	60.1
Adults who always wear a seatbelt	94.8	93.8

Note: Data as of 2012 unless otherwise noted; (1) Figures cover the Huntsville, AL Metropolitan Statistical Area—see Appendix B for areas included; (2) Heavy drinkers are classified as males having more than two drinks per day or females having more than one drink per day; (3) Binge drinkers are classified as males having five or more drinks on one occasion or females having four or more drinks on one occasion
Source: Centers for Disease Control and Prevention, Behaviorial Risk Factor Surveillance System, SMART: Selected Metropolitan/Micropolitan Area Risk Trends, 2012 (Note: the CDC has discontinued this dataset but will be releasing a replacement in mid-2016)

Chronic Health Indicators

Category	MSA[1] (%)	U.S. (%)
Adults who have ever been told they had a heart attack	3.9	4.5
Adults who have ever been told they had a stroke	n/a	2.9
Adults who have been told they currently have asthma	8.6	8.9
Adults who have ever been told they have arthritis	29.9	25.7
Adults who have ever been told they have diabetes[2]	8.8	9.7
Adults who have ever been told they had skin cancer	8.1	5.7
Adults who have ever been told they had any other types of cancer	6.4	6.5
Adults who have ever been told they have COPD	6.8	6.2
Adults who have ever been told they have kidney disease	1.8	2.5
Adults who have ever been told they have a form of depression	20.8	18.0

Note: Data as of 2012 unless otherwise noted; n/a not available; (1) Figures cover the Huntsville, AL Metropolitan Statistical Area—see Appendix B for areas included; (2) Figures do not include pregnancy-related, borderline, or pre-diabetes
Source: Centers for Disease Control and Prevention, Behaviorial Risk Factor Surveillance System, SMART: Selected Metropolitan/Micropolitan Area Risk Trends, 2012 (Note: the CDC has discontinued this dataset but will be releasing a replacement in mid-2016)

Mortality Rates for the Top 10 Causes of Death in the U.S.

ICD-10[a] Sub-Chapter	ICD-10[a] Code	Age-Adjusted Mortality Rate[1] per 100,000 population	
		County[2]	U.S.
Malignant neoplasms	C00-C97	155.9	163.6
Ischaemic heart diseases	I20-I25	54.0	102.2
Other forms of heart disease	I30-I51	136.0	50.1
Chronic lower respiratory diseases	J40-J47	41.6	41.4
Organic, including symptomatic, mental disorders	F01-F09	47.9	38.5
Cerebrovascular diseases	I60-I69	39.7	36.5
Other external causes of accidental injury	W00-X59	18.8	27.5
Other degenerative diseases of the nervous system	G30-G31	29.4	26.3
Diabetes mellitus	E10-E14	14.1	21.1
Hypertensive diseases	I10-I15	10.1	19.7

Note: (a) ICD-10 = International Classification of Diseases 10th Revision; (1) Mortality rates are a three year average covering 2012-2014; (2) Figures cover COUNTY NOT FOUND!!!!!!.
Source: Centers for Disease Control and Prevention, National Center for Health Statistics. Underlying Cause of Death 1999-2014 on CDC WONDER Online Database, released 2015.

Mortality Rates for Selected Causes of Death

ICD-10[a] Sub-Chapter	ICD-10[a] Code	Age-Adjusted Mortality Rate[1] per 100,000 population	
		County[2]	U.S.
Assault	X85-Y09	6.8	5.1
Diseases of the liver	K70-K76	12.4	13.5
Human immunodeficiency virus (HIV) disease	B20-B24	2.0	2.1
Influenza and pneumonia	J09-J18	12.8	15.2
Intentional self-harm	X60-X84	13.3	12.7
Malnutrition	E40-E46	Unreliable	0.9
Obesity and other hyperalimentation	E65-E68	Unreliable	1.9
Renal failure	N17-N19	18.0	13.0
Transport accidents	V01-V99	13.9	11.6
Viral hepatitis	B15-B19	1.6	2.1

Note: (a) ICD-10 = International Classification of Diseases 10th Revision; (1) Mortality rates are a three year average covering 2012-2014; (2) Figures cover COUNTY NOT FOUND!!!!!!; Data are Suppressed when the data meet the criteria for confidentiality constraints; Mortality rates are flagged as Unreliable when the rate would be calculated with a numerator of 20 or less.
Source: Centers for Disease Control and Prevention, National Center for Health Statistics. Underlying Cause of Death 1999-2014 on CDC WONDER Online Database, released 2015.

Health Insurance Coverage

Area	With Health Insurance	With Private Health Insurance	With Public Health Insurance	Without Health Insurance	Population Under Age 18 Without Health Insurance
City	92.7	85.9	17.7	7.3	3.3
MSA[1]	87.6	73.8	26.7	12.4	3.6
U.S.	85.8	65.8	31.1	14.2	7.1

Note: Figures are percentages that cover the civilian noninstitutionalized population; (1) Figures cover the Huntsville, AL Metropolitan Statistical Area—see Appendix B for areas included
Source: U.S. Census Bureau, 2010-2014 American Community Survey 5-Year Estimates

Number of Medical Professionals

Area	MDs[3]	DOs[3,4]	Dentists	Podiatrists	Chiropractors	Optometrists
County[1] (number)	940	38	194	13	78	64
County[1] (rate[2])	270.8	10.9	55.4	3.7	22.3	18.3
U.S. (rate[2])	272.5	20.9	64.7	5.8	25.9	15.2

Note: Data as of 2014 unless noted; (1) Data covers Madison County; (2) Rate per 100,000 population; (3) Data as of 2013 and includes all active, non-federal physicians; (4) Doctor of Osteopathic Medicine
Source: U.S. Department of Health and Human Services, Health Resources and Services Administration, Bureau of Health Professions, Area Resource File (ARF) 2014-2015

EDUCATION

Public School District Statistics

District Name	Schls	Pupils	Pupil/ Teacher Ratio	Minority Pupils[1] (%)	Free Lunch Eligible[2] (%)	IEP[3] (%)
Madison City	11	9,554	18.1	35.4	18.5	10.1
Madison County	29	19,741	16.9	31.8	30.2	10.4

Note: Table includes school districts with 100 or more students; (1) Percentage of students that are not non-Hispanic white; (2) Percentage of students that are eligible for the free lunch program; (3) Percentage of students that have an Individualized Education Program.
Source: U.S. Department of Education, National Center for Education Statistics, Common Core of Data, Local Education Agency (School District) Universe Survey: School Year 2013-2014; U.S. Department of Education, National Center for Education Statistics, Common Core of Data, Public Elementary/Secondary School Universe Survey: School Year 2013-2014

Highest Level of Education

Area	Less than H.S.	H.S. Diploma	Some College, No Deg.	Associate Degree	Bachelor's Degree	Master's Degree	Prof. School Degree	Doctorate Degree
City	4.3	13.3	20.4	6.8	33.1	17.5	2.0	2.5
MSA[1]	11.5	23.3	22.0	7.8	22.3	10.3	1.5	1.4
U.S.	13.7	28.0	21.2	7.9	18.3	7.8	2.0	1.3

Note: Figures cover persons age 25 and over; (1) Figures cover the Huntsville, AL Metropolitan Statistical Area—see Appendix B for areas included
Source: U.S. Census Bureau, 2010-2014 American Community Survey 5-Year Estimates

Educational Attainment by Race

Area	High School Graduate or Higher (%)					Bachelor's Degree or Higher (%)				
	Total	White	Black	Asian	Hisp.[2]	Total	White	Black	Asian	Hisp.[2]
City	95.7	96.9	96.6	85.1	83.8	55.2	58.3	40.9	60.1	51.5
MSA[1]	88.5	89.5	86.2	86.8	62.5	35.4	37.6	26.2	53.1	23.2
U.S.	86.3	88.4	83.2	85.8	64.1	29.3	30.6	19.0	50.9	13.9

Note: Figures shown cover persons 25 years old and over; (1) Figures cover the Huntsville, AL Metropolitan Statistical Area—see Appendix B for areas included; (2) People of Hispanic origin can be of any race
Source: U.S. Census Bureau, 2010-2014 American Community Survey 5-Year Estimates

School Enrollment by Grade and Control

Area	Preschool (%)		Kindergarten (%)		Grades 1 - 4 (%)		Grades 5 - 8 (%)		Grades 9 - 12 (%)	
	Public	Private	Public	Private	Public	Private	Public	Private	Public	Private
City	62.7	37.3	72.4	27.6	91.0	9.0	91.7	8.3	89.9	10.1
MSA[1]	45.3	54.7	83.7	16.3	86.6	13.4	87.3	12.7	87.3	12.7
U.S.	57.4	42.6	87.8	12.2	89.8	10.2	89.9	10.1	90.6	9.4

Note: Figures shown cover persons 3 years old and over; (1) Figures cover the Huntsville, AL Metropolitan Statistical Area—see Appendix B for areas included
Source: U.S. Census Bureau, 2010-2014 American Community Survey 5-Year Estimates

Average Salaries of Public School Classroom Teachers

Area	2013-14		2014-15		Percent Change 2013-14 to 2014-15	Percent Change 2004-05 to 2014-15
	Dollars	Rank[1]	Dollars	Rank[1]		
Alabama	48,720	35	49,497	35	1.59	29.6
U.S. Average	56,610	–	57,379	–	1.36	20.8

Note: (1) State rank ranges from 1 to 51 where 1 indicates highest salary.
Source: National Education Association, Rankings & Estimates: Rankings of the States 2014 and Estimates of School Statistics 2015, March 2015

Higher Education

Four-Year Colleges			Two-Year Colleges			Medical Schools[1]	Law Schools[2]	Voc/ Tech[3]
Public	Private Non-profit	Private For-profit	Public	Private Non-profit	Private For-profit			
0	0	1	0	0	0	0	0	1

Note: Figures cover institutions located within the city limits and include main campuses only; (1) includes schools accredited by the Liaison Committee on Medical Education and the American Osteopathic Association's Commission on Osteopathic College Accreditation; (2) includes ABA-accredited schools, schools with provisional ABA accreditation, and state accredited schools; (3) includes all schools with programs that are less than 2 years.

Source: National Center for Education Statistics, Integrated Postsecondary Education System (IPEDS), 2014-15; Association of American Medical Colleges, Member List, March 21, 2016; American Osteopathic Association, Member List, March 21, 2016; Law School Admission Council, Official Guide to ABA-Approved Law Schools Online, March 21, 2016; Wikipedia, List of Medical Schools in the United States, March 21, 2016; Wikipedia, List of Law Schools in the United States, March 21, 2016

According to *U.S. News & World Report,* the Huntsville, AL metro area is home to one of the best national universities in the U.S.: **University of Alabama–Huntsville** (#187 tie). The indicators used to capture academic quality fall into a number of categories: assessment by administrators at peer institutions; retention of students; faculty resources; student selectivity; financial resources; alumni giving; high school counselor ratings of colleges; and graduation rate. *U.S. News & World Report, "America's Best Colleges 2016"*

PRESIDENTIAL ELECTION

2012 Presidential Election Results

Area	Obama (%)	Romney (%)	Other (%)
Madison County	40.0	58.6	1.4
U.S.	51.0	47.2	1.8

Note: Results may not add to 100% due to rounding

Source: Dave Leip's Atlas of U.S. Presidential Elections

EMPLOYERS

Major Employers

Company Name	Industry
Avocent Corporation	Computer peripheral equip
City of Huntsville	Mayor's office
City of Huntsville	Town council
COLSA Corporation	Commercial research laboratory
County of Madison	Executive offices
Dynetics	Engineering laboratory/except testing
General Dynamics C4 Systems	Defense systems equipment
Healthcare Auth - City of Huntsville	General government
Intergraph Process & Bldg Solutions	Systems software development
Qualitest Products	Drugs & drug proprietaries
Science Applications Int'l Corporation	Computer processing services/commercial research lab
Teledyne brown Engineering	Energy research
The Army, United States Department of	Army
The Boeing Company	Aircraft/guided missiles/space vehicles
United States Department of the Army	Army

Note: Companies shown are located within the Huntsville, AL Metropolitan Statistical Area.

Source: Hoovers.com; Wikipedia

PUBLIC SAFETY

Crime Rate

Area	All Crimes	Violent Crimes: Murder	Violent Crimes: Rape[3]	Violent Crimes: Robbery	Violent Crimes: Aggrav. Assault	Property Crimes: Burglary	Property Crimes: Larceny -Theft	Property Crimes: Motor Vehicle Theft
City	2,353.5	4.3	23.7	43.1	251.9	325.1	1,612.8	92.6
Metro[1]	3,651.8	5.2	41.8	107.9	322.8	693.8	2,254.2	226.0
U.S.	2,971.8	4.5	36.6	102.2	232.5	542.5	1,837.3	216.2

Note: Figures are crimes per 100,000 population; (1) Figures cover the Huntsville, AL Metropolitan Statistical Area—see Appendix B for areas included; (3) The city and U.S. figures shown were reported using the revised Uniform Crime Reporting (UCR) definition of rape. The suburban and metro area figures shown are an aggregate total of the data submitted using both the revised and legacy UCR definitions.
Source: FBI Uniform Crime Reports, 2014

Hate Crimes

Area	Number of Quarters Reported	Race	Religion	Sexual Orientation	Ethnicity	Disability	Gender	Gender Identity
		Number of Incidents per Bias Motivation						
City	n/a	n/a	n/a	n/a	n/a	n/a	n/a	n/a
U.S.	4	2,568	1,014	1,017	648	84	33	98

Note: n/a not available.
Source: Federal Bureau of Investigation, Hate Crime Statistics 2014

Identity Theft Consumer Complaints

Area	Complaints	Complaints per 100,000 Population	Rank[2]
MSA[1]	519	117.7	132
U.S.	490,220	152.4	-

Note: (1) Figures cover the Huntsville, AL Metropolitan Statistical Area—see Appendix B for areas included; (2) Rank ranges from 1 to 379 where 1 indicates greatest number of identity theft complaints per 100,000 population
Source: Federal Trade Commission, Consumer Sentinel Network Data Book for January–December 2015

Fraud and Other Consumer Complaints

Area	Complaints	Complaints per 100,000 Population	Rank[2]
MSA[1]	1,710	387.7	130
U.S.	2,593,159	806.0	-

Note: (1) Figures cover the Huntsville, AL Metropolitan Statistical Area—see Appendix B for areas included; (2) Rank ranges from 1 to 379 where 1 indicates greatest number of identity theft complaints per 100,000 population
Source: Federal Trade Commission, Consumer Sentinel Network Data Book for January–December 2015

RECREATION

Culture

Dance[1]	Theatre[1]	Instrumental Music[1]	Vocal Music[1]	Series and Festivals	Museums and Art Galleries[2]	Zoos and Aquariums[3]
0	0	0	0	0	0	0

Note: (1) Professional perfoming groups; (2) Based on organizations with SIC code 8412; (3) AZA-accredited
Source: The Grey House Performing Arts Directory, 2015-16; Association of Zoos & Aquariums, AZA Member Zoos & Aquariums, March 25, 2016; www.AccuLeads.com, March 29, 2016

Professional Sports Teams

Team Name	League	Year Established
No teams are located in the metro area		

Source: Wikipedia, Major Professional Sports Teams of the United States and Canada, March 24, 2016

CLIMATE

Average and Extreme Temperatures

Temperature	Jan	Feb	Mar	Apr	May	Jun	Jul	Aug	Sep	Oct	Nov	Dec	Yr.
Extreme High (°F)	76	82	88	92	96	101	104	103	101	91	84	77	104
Average High (°F)	49	54	63	73	80	87	90	89	83	73	62	52	71
Average Temp. (°F)	39	44	52	61	69	76	80	79	73	62	51	43	61
Average Low (°F)	30	33	41	49	58	65	69	68	62	50	40	33	50
Extreme Low (°F)	-11	5	6	26	36	45	53	52	37	28	15	-3	-11

Note: Figures cover the years 1958-1995
Source: National Climatic Data Center, International Station Meteorological Climate Summary, 9/96

Average Precipitation/Snowfall/Humidity

Precip./Humidity	Jan	Feb	Mar	Apr	May	Jun	Jul	Aug	Sep	Oct	Nov	Dec	Yr.
Avg. Precip. (in.)	5.0	5.0	6.6	4.8	5.1	4.3	4.6	3.5	4.1	3.3	4.7	5.7	56.8
Avg. Snowfall (in.)	2	1	1	Tr	0	0	0	0	0	Tr	Tr	1	4
Avg. Rel. Hum. 7am (%)	82	81	79	78	79	81	84	86	85	86	84	81	82
Avg. Rel. Hum. 4pm (%)	60	56	51	46	51	53	56	55	54	51	55	60	54

Note: Figures cover the years 1958-1995; Tr = Trace amounts (<0.05 in. of rain; <0.5 in. of snow)
Source: National Climatic Data Center, International Station Meteorological Climate Summary, 9/96

Weather Conditions

Temperature			Daytime Sky			Precipitation		
10°F & below	32°F & below	90°F & above	Clear	Partly cloudy	Cloudy	0.01 inch or more precip.	0.1 inch or more snow/ice	Thunder-storms
2	66	49	70	118	177	116	2	54

Note: Figures are average number of days per year and cover the years 1958-1995
Source: National Climatic Data Center, International Station Meteorological Climate Summary, 9/96

HAZARDOUS WASTE

Superfund Sites

Madison has no sites on the EPA's Superfund Final National Priorities List. There are a total of 1,323 Superfund sites on the list in the U.S. *U.S. Environmental Protection Agency, Final National Priorities List, March 18, 2016*

AIR & WATER QUALITY

Air Quality Trends: Ozone

	1990	1995	2000	2005	2010	2011	2012	2013	2014
MSA[1]	0.079	0.080	0.088	0.075	0.071	0.072	0.076	0.064	0.064

Note: (1) Data covers the Huntsville, AL Metropolitan Statistical Area—see Appendix B for areas included. The values shown are the composite ozone concentration averages among trend sites based on the highest fourth daily maximum 8-hour concentration in parts per million. These trends are based on sites having an adequate record of monitoring data during the trend period. Data from exceptional events are included.
Source: U.S. Environmental Protection Agency, Air Quality Monitoring Information, "Air Quality Trends by City, 1990-2014"

Air Quality Index

Area	Percent of Days when Air Quality was...[2]					AQI Statistics[2]	
	Good	Moderate	Unhealthy for Sensitive Groups	Unhealthy	Very Unhealthy	Maximum	Median
MSA[1]	90.4	9.6	0.0	0.0	0.0	71	34.5

Note: (1) Data covers the Huntsville, AL Metropolitan Statistical Area—see Appendix B for areas included; (2) Based on 334 days with AQI data in 2015. Air Quality Index (AQI) is an index for reporting daily air quality. EPA calculates the AQI for five major air pollutants regulated by the Clean Air Act: ground-level ozone, particle pollution (aka particulate matter), carbon monoxide, sulfur dioxide, and nitrogen dioxide. The AQI runs from 0 to 500. The higher the AQI value, the greater the level of air pollution and the greater the health concern. There are six AQI categories: "Good" AQI is between 0 and 50. Air quality is considered satisfactory; "Moderate" AQI is between 51 and 100. Air quality is acceptable; "Unhealthy for Sensitive Groups" When AQI values are between 101 and 150, members of sensitive groups may experience health effects; "Unhealthy" When AQI values are between 151 and 200 everyone may begin to experience health effects; "Very Unhealthy" AQI values between 201 and 300 trigger a health alert; "Hazardous" AQI values over 300 trigger warnings of emergency conditions (not shown).
Source: U.S. Environmental Protection Agency, Air Quality Index Report, 2015

Air Quality Index Pollutants

Area	Percent of Days when AQI Pollutant was...[2]					
	Carbon Monoxide	Nitrogen Dioxide	Ozone	Sulfur Dioxide	Particulate Matter 2.5	Particulate Matter 10
MSA[1]	0.0	0.0	61.4	0.0	22.2	16.5

Note: (1) Data covers the Huntsville, AL Metropolitan Statistical Area—see Appendix B for areas included; (2) Based on 334 days with AQI data in 2015. The Air Quality Index (AQI) is an index for reporting daily air quality. EPA calculates the AQI for five major air pollutants regulated by the Clean Air Act: ground-level ozone, particle pollution (also known as particulate matter), carbon monoxide, sulfur dioxide, and nitrogen dioxide. The AQI runs from 0 to 500. The higher the AQI value, the greater the level of air pollution and the greater the health concern.
Source: U.S. Environmental Protection Agency, Air Quality Index Report, 2015

Maximum Air Pollutant Concentrations: Particulate Matter, Ozone, CO and Lead

	Particulate Matter 10 (ug/m^3)	Particulate Matter 2.5 Wtd AM (ug/m^3)	Particulate Matter 2.5 24-Hr (ug/m^3)	Ozone (ppm)	Carbon Monoxide (ppm)	Lead (ug/m^3)
MSA[1] Level	62	9	21	0.064	n/a	n/a
NAAQS[2]	150	15	35	0.075	9	0.15
Met NAAQS[2]	Yes	Yes	Yes	Yes	n/a	n/a

Note: (1) Data covers the Huntsville, AL Metropolitan Statistical Area—see Appendix B for areas included; Data from exceptional events are included; (2) National Ambient Air Quality Standards; ppm = parts per million; ug/m^3 = micrograms per cubic meter; n/a not available.
Concentrations: Particulate Matter 10 (coarse particulate)—highest second maximum 24-hour concentration; Particulate Matter 2.5 Wtd AM (fine particulate)—highest weighted annual mean concentration; Particulate Matter 2.5 24-Hour (fine particulate)—highest 98th percentile 24-hour concentration; Ozone—highest fourth daily maximum 8-hour concentration; Carbon Monoxide—highest second maximum non-overlapping 8-hour concentration; Lead—maximum running 3-month average
Source: U.S. Environmental Protection Agency, Air Quality Monitoring Information, "Air Quality Statistics by City, 2014"

Maximum Air Pollutant Concentrations: Nitrogen Dioxide and Sulfur Dioxide

	Nitrogen Dioxide AM (ppb)	Nitrogen Dioxide 1-Hr (ppb)	Sulfur Dioxide AM (ppb)	Sulfur Dioxide 1-Hr (ppb)	Sulfur Dioxide 24-Hr (ppb)
MSA[1] Level	n/a	n/a	n/a	n/a	n/a
NAAQS[2]	53	100	30	75	140
Met NAAQS[2]	n/a	n/a	n/a	n/a	n/a

Note: (1) Data covers the Huntsville, AL Metropolitan Statistical Area—see Appendix B for areas included; Data from exceptional events are included; (2) National Ambient Air Quality Standards; ppm = parts per million; ug/m^3 = micrograms per cubic meter; n/a not available.
Concentrations: Nitrogen Dioxide AM—highest arithmetic mean concentration; Nitrogen Dioxide 1-Hr—highest 98th percentile 1-hour daily maximum concentration; Sulfur Dioxide AM—highest annual mean concentration; Sulfur Dioxide 1-Hr—highest 99th percentile 1-hour daily maximum concentration; Sulfur Dioxide 24-Hr—highest second maximum 24-hour concentration
Source: U.S. Environmental Protection Agency, Air Quality Monitoring Information, "Air Quality Statistics by City, 2014"

Drinking Water

Water System Name	Pop. Served	Primary Water Source Type	Violations[1]	
			Health Based	Monitoring/ Reporting
Madison Water Works & Sewer	39,051	Purchased Surface	0	0

Note: (1) Based on violation data from January 1, 2015 to December 31, 2015 (includes unresolved violations from earlier years)
Source: U.S. Environmental Protection Agency, Office of Ground Water and Drinking Water, Safe Drinking Water Information System (based on data extracted April 29, 2016)

Vestavia Hills, Alabama

Background

Located merely six miles south of Birmingham, in Jefferson County, hilltop Vestavia Hills is a comfortable bedroom community offering good schools, a wealthy average household income and a low crime rate. Its proximity to Birmingham affords its resident easy access to jobs in the city.

The city's comfortable lifestyle is reflected in its roots. Former Birmingham mayor George Ward decided to build an elaborate home on 20 acres atop Shades Mountain. He styled his home after the Temple of Vesta, located near the Tiber River and named for the Roman goddess of the earth. The classically inclined Ward's home was completed in 1925, but later was destroyed. However, his Temple of Sibyl at Tivoli replica, which served as his gazebo, now stands at the northern entry to the city, a symbol of Vestavia Hills.

A subdivision was planned for the mountaintop in 1946. The city was incorporated in 1950, and has experienced continued healthy growth, doubling in size from 1960 to 1970, and again by 1980.

Among its recreational facilities is Wald Park, with five baseball fields, a swimming pool, a walking track, picnic areas, the civic center, a senior's lodge, a skate park, and a community playground. Also in town is Byrd Park, also with picnic areas, playground, and walking track. Vestavia Hills's Liberty Park Sports Complex has four softball fields for youth, five for adults, four soccer fields, and one football field.

The Vestavia Hills City School System consistently rate in Alabama's top three on standardized tests, and the city's high school boasts a significant number of National Merit Finalists each year.

Easy access to I-495, I-65, and other major highways not only simplifies life for commuters, but Vestavia Hills residents can take advantage of the considerable arts and other attractions in Birmingham. These include the Alabama Theater, the Alabama Symphony Orchestra, Birmingham Children's Theatre, and the Alys Robinson Stephens Performing Arts Center, which draws noted national performers from the fields of classical music, pop, jazz, dance, and more. The Birmingham-Shuttlesworth International Airport offers commercial flights to and from the area.

The climate in Vestavia Hills is temperate. Prevailing winds from the northwest are frequently broken up by warm air flowing up from the Gulf of Mexico. Winters are cooler than in the semi-tropical southern part of the state, but seldom does the temperature remain below freezing, even in cold spells. Summers are long, hot, and humid, but exceedingly hot temperatures—over 100 degrees—are rare. Fall is dry and pleasant.

Rankings

Business/Finance Rankings

- The personal finance site NerdWallet analyzed 183 American metropolitan areas with populations over 250,000 and more than 15,000 businesses to rank where entrepreneurs find the most success. Criteria included area economy, annual income, housing cost, unemployment rate, and the success rate of area businesses. Birmingham* ranked #58. *www.nerdwallet.com, "Best Places to Start a Business," April 27, 2015*

- Based on the U.S. Department of Labor's Occupational Information Network Data Collection Program, the Brookings Institution defined job opportunities for STEM workers at various levels of educational attainment. The Birmingham* metro area was one of the ten metro areas where workers in low-education-level STEM jobs earn the highest relative wages. *www.brookings.edu, "The Hidden Stem Economy," June 10, 2013*

- Based on metro area social media reviews, the employment opinion group Glassdoor surveyed 50 of the largest U.S. metro areas and equally weighed cost of living, hiring opportunity, and job satisfaction to compose a list of "25 Best Cities for Jobs." The Birmingham* metro area was ranked #40 in overall job satisfaction. *www.glassdoor.com, "Best Cities for Jobs," May 19, 2015*

- In a survey of economic confidence in the nation's 50 largest metropolitan areas conducted January–December 2014, the Birmingham* metro area placed #50, according to Gallup's 2014 Economic Confidence Index. *Gallup, "San Jose and San Francisco Lead in Economic Confidence," March 19, 2015*

- The Brookings Institution ranked the 100 largest metro areas in the U.S. based on income inequality. Birmingham* was ranked #23 (#1 = greatest ineqality). Criteria: the "95/20 ratio," a figure representing the income at which a household earns more than 95 percent of all other households, divided by the income at which a household earns more than only 20 percent of all other households. *Brookings Institution, "Income Inequality, 100 Largest U.S. Metro Areas, 2007-2014," January 14, 2016*

- The Birmingham* metro area was identified as one of the most affordable metropolitan areas in America by *Forbes*. The area ranked #1 out of 20 based on the National Association of Home Builders/Wells Fargo Housing Affordability Index and Sperling's Best Places' cost-of-living index. *Forbes.com, "America's Most Affordable Cities in 2015," March 12, 2015*

- The Birmingham* metro area appeared on the Milken Institute "2015 Best Performing Cities" list. Rank: #181 out of 200 large metro areas. Criteria: job growth; wage and salary growth; high-tech output growth. *Milken Institute, "Best-Performing Cities 2015," December 2015*

- *Forbes* ranked the 200 most populous metro areas to determine the nation's "Best Places for Business and Careers." The Birmingham* metro area was ranked #150. Criteria: costs (business and living); job growth (past and projected); income growth; educational attainment (college and high school); projected economic growth; cultural and recreational opportunities; net migration patterns; number of highly ranked colleges. *Forbes, "The Best Places for Business and Careers 2015," July 29, 2015*

Education Rankings

- Personal finance website *WalletHub* analyzed the 150 largest U.S. metropolitan statistical areas to determine where the most educated Americans are choosing to settle. Criteria: education quality and attainment gap; education levels; percentage of workers with degrees; public school rankings; quality and size of each metro area's universities. Birmingham* was ranked #90 (#1 = most educated city). *www.WalletHub.com, "2015's Most and Least Educated Cities*

Environmental Rankings

- The Birmingham* metro area came in at #268 for the relative comfort of its climate on Sperling's list of "chill cities," as measured by the Sperling Heat Index. All 361 metro areas are included. Criteria included daytime high temperatures, nighttime low temperatures, dew point, and relative humidity at the high temperatures. *www.bertsperling.com, "Sperling's Chill Cities," July 18, 2013*

- Sperling's BestPlaces assessed 379 metropolitan areas of the United States for the likelihood of dangerously extreme weather events or earthquakes. In general the Southeast and South-Central regions have the highest risk of weather extremes and earthquakes, while the Pacific Northwest enjoys the lowest risk. Of the least risky metropolitan areas, the Birmingham* metro area was ranked #372. *www.bestplaces.net, "Safest Places from Natural Disasters," April 2011*

- Birmingham* was highlighted as one of the 25 metro areas most polluted by year-round particle pollution (Annual PM 2.5) in the U.S. during 2011 through 2013. The area ranked #17. *American Lung Association, State of the Air 2015*

Health/Fitness Rankings

- For each of the 50 most populous metro areas in the United States, the American College of Sports Medicine's American Fitness Index evaluated infrastructure, community assets, and policies that encourage healthy and fit lifestyles, including preventive health behaviors, levels of chronic disease conditions, health care access, and community resources and policies that support physical activity. The Birmingham* metro area ranked #44 for "community fitness." *www.americanfitnessindex.org, "ACSM American Fitness Index Health and Community Fitness Status of the 50 Largest Metropolitan Areas," May 2015*

- Birmingham* was identified as a "2016 Spring Allergy Capital." The area ranked #41 out of 100. Three groups of factors were used to identify the most severe cities for people with allergies during the spring season: annual pollen levels; medicine utilization; access to board-certified allergists. *Asthma and Allergy Foundation of America, "Spring Allergy Capitals 2016"*

- Birmingham* was identified as a "2015 Asthma Capital." The area ranked #44 out of the nation's 100 largest metropolitan areas. Criteria: estimated prevalence; self-reported prevalence; crude death rate for asthma; annual pollen score; annual air quality; public smoking laws; number of board-certified asthma specialists; school inhaler access laws; rescue medication use; controller medication use; ER visits for asthma; uninsured rate; poverty rate. *Asthma and Allergy Foundation of America, "Asthma Capitals 2015"*

- The Birmingham* metro area ranked #109 out of 190 in The Gallup-Healthways Well-Being Index. Criteria: purpose; social well being; financial health; community and physical health. Results are based on telephone interviews with adults, aged 18 and older, living in metropolitan areas in the 50 U.S. states and the District of Columbia. *Gallup-Healthways, "State of American Well-Being," February 23, 2016*

Real Estate Rankings

- Birmingham* was ranked #96 out of 225 metro areas in terms of housing affordability in 2015 by the National Association of Home Builders (#1 = most affordable). Criteria: the share of homes sold in that area affordable to a family earning the local median income, based on standard mortgage underwriting criteria. *National Association of Home Builders®, NAHB-Wells Fargo Housing Opportunity Index, 4th Quarter 2015*

Safety Rankings

- Birmingham* was identified as one of the least disaster-proof places in the U.S. in terms of its vulnerability to natural and non-natural disasters. The city ranked #3 out of 5. Rankings are based on the U.S. Center for Disease Control's Cities Readiness Initiative (CRI), which assesses local emergency-management plans, protocols and capabilities for 72 Metropolitan Statistical Areas and four non-MSA large cities. *Forbes, "America's Most and Least Disaster-Proof Cities," December 12, 2011*

- The National Insurance Crime Bureau ranked 380 metro areas in the U.S. in terms of per capita rates of vehicle theft. The Birmingham* metro area ranked #67 (#1 = highest rate). Criteria: number of vehicle theft offenses per 100,000 inhabitants in 2014. *National Insurance Crime Bureau, "Hot Spots 2014," June 24, 2015*

Seniors/Retirement Rankings

- From its Best Cities for Successful Aging indexes, the Milken Institute generated rankings for metropolitan areas, weighing data in eight categories—health care, wellness, living arrangements, transportation, financial characteristics, education and employment opportunities, community engagement, and overall livability. The Birmingham* metro area was ranked #45 overall in the large metro area category. *Milken Institute, "Best Cities for Successful Aging, 2014"*

Miscellaneous Rankings

- Mars Chocolate North America, the makers of COMBOS®, in partnership with Sperling's BestPlaces, ranked 50 major metro areas in terms of their "manliness." The Birmingham* metro area ranked #5. Criteria: number of professional sports teams; number of nearby NASCAR tracks and racing events; manly lifestyle; concentration of manly retail stores; manly occupations per capita; salty snack sales; "Board of Manliness" rankings. *Mars Chocolate North America, "America's Manliest Cities 2012"*
- The National Alliance to End Homelessness ranked the 100 most populous metro areas with the highest rate of homelessness. The Birmingham* metro area ranked #40. Criteria: number of homeless people per 10,000 population in 2011. *National Alliance to End Homelessness, The State of Homelessness in America 2012*

Vestavia Hills is located within the Birmingham-Hoover, AL Metropolitan Statistical Area.

Business Environment

CITY FINANCES

City Government Finances

Component	2012 ($000)	2012 ($ per capita)
Total Revenues	34,238	1,006
Total Expenditures	34,630	1,017
Debt Outstanding	41,605	1,222
Cash and Securities[1]	15,121	444

Note: (1) Cash and security holdings of a government at the close of its fiscal year, including those of its dependent agencies, utilities, and liquor stores.
Source: U.S Census Bureau, State & Local Government Finances 2012

City Government Revenue by Source

Source	2012 ($000)	2012 ($ per capita)
General Revenue		
From Federal Government	569	16
From State Government	598	17
From Local Governments	640	18
Taxes		
Property	13,139	386
Sales and Gross Receipts	10,276	301
Personal Income	0	0
Corporate Income	0	0
Motor Vehicle License	87	2
Other Taxes	5,616	165
Current Charges	1,741	51
Liquor Store	0	0
Utility	0	0
Employee Retirement	0	0

Source: U.S Census Bureau, State & Local Government Finances 2012

City Government Expenditures by Function

Function	2012 ($000)	2012 ($ per capita)	2012 (%)
General Direct Expenditures			
Air Transportation	0	0	0.0
Corrections	2	< 1	< 0.1
Education	0	0	0.0
Employment Security Administration	0	0	0.0
Financial Administration	464	13	1.3
Fire Protection	6,690	196	19.3
General Public Buildings	229	6	0.6
Governmental Administration, Other	1,945	57	5.6
Health	7	< 1	< 0.1
Highways	1,673	49	4.8
Hospitals	0	0	0.0
Housing and Community Development	0	0	0.0
Interest on General Debt	1,901	55	5.4
Judicial and Legal	149	4	0.4
Libraries	2,079	61	6.0
Parking	0	0	0.0
Parks and Recreation	5,665	166	16.3
Police Protection	4,430	130	12.7
Public Welfare	0	0	0.0
Sewerage	1	< 1	< 0.1
Solid Waste Management	2,571	75	7.4
Veterans' Services	0	0	0.0
Liquor Store	0	0	0.0
Utility	61	1	0.1
Employee Retirement	0	0	0.0

Source: U.S Census Bureau, State & Local Government Finances 2012

DEMOGRAPHICS

Population Growth

Area	1990 Census	2000 Census	2010 Census	2014* Estimate	Population Growth (%) 1990-2014	Population Growth (%) 2010-2014
City	22,183	24,476	34,033	34,061	53.5	0.1
MSA[1]	956,894	1,052,238	1,128,047	1,135,534	18.7	0.7
U.S.	248,709,873	281,421,906	308,745,538	314,107,084	26.3	1.7

Note: (1) Figures cover the Birmingham-Hoover, AL Metropolitan Statistical Area—see Appendix B for areas included; (*) 2010-2014 5-year estimated population
Source: U.S. Census Bureau, 1990 Census, Census 2000, Census 2010, 2010-2014 American Community Survey 5-Year Estimates

Household Size

Area	Persons in Household (%) One	Two	Three	Four	Five	Six	Seven or More	Average Household Size
City	29.7	32.8	14.4	15.1	6.4	1.0	0.3	2.45
MSA[1]	28.3	34.4	16.8	12.8	5.0	1.6	0.8	2.55
U.S.	27.5	33.5	15.8	13.1	6.0	2.3	1.4	2.64

Note: (1) Figures cover the Birmingham-Hoover, AL Metropolitan Statistical Area—see Appendix B for areas included
Source: U.S. Census Bureau, 2010-2014 American Community Survey 5-Year Estimates

Race

Area	White Alone[2] (%)	Black Alone[2] (%)	Asian Alone[2] (%)	AIAN[3] Alone[2] (%)	NHOPI[4] Alone[2] (%)	Other Race Alone[2] (%)	Two or More Races (%)
City	90.0	3.3	5.2	0.2	0.0	0.7	0.6
MSA[1]	66.8	28.5	1.3	0.3	0.0	2.0	1.1
U.S.	73.8	12.6	5.0	0.8	0.2	4.7	2.9

Note: (1) Figures cover the Birmingham-Hoover, AL Metropolitan Statistical Area—see Appendix B for areas included; (2) Alone is defined as not being in combination with one or more other races; (3) American Indian and Alaska Native; (4) Native Hawaiian and Other Pacific Islander
Source: U.S. Census Bureau, 2010-2014 American Community Survey 5-Year Estimates

Hispanic or Latino Origin

Area	Total (%)	Mexican (%)	Puerto Rican (%)	Cuban (%)	Other (%)
City	1.4	0.6	0.1	0.0	0.7
MSA[1]	4.3	3.3	0.2	0.1	0.7
U.S.	16.9	10.8	1.6	0.6	3.8

Note: Persons of Hispanic or Latino origin can be of any race; (1) Figures cover the Birmingham-Hoover, AL Metropolitan Statistical Area—see Appendix B for areas included
Source: U.S. Census Bureau, 2010-2014 American Community Survey 5-Year Estimates

Ancestry

Area	German	Irish	English	American	Italian	Polish	French[2]	Scottish	Dutch
City	9.7	11.6	17.9	14.6	5.2	1.1	3.8	4.7	1.0
MSA[1]	6.9	9.3	9.3	15.3	2.3	0.7	1.6	2.2	0.9
U.S.	14.9	10.8	8.0	7.1	5.5	3.0	2.7	1.7	1.4

Note: Figures are the percentage of the total population reporting a particular ancestry. The nine most commonly reported ancestries in the U.S. are shown. Figures include multiple ancestries (e.g. if a person reported being Irish and Italian, they were included in both columns); (1) Figures cover the Birmingham-Hoover, AL Metropolitan Statistical Area—see Appendix B for areas included; (2) Excludes Basque
Source: U.S. Census Bureau, 2010-2014 American Community Survey 5-Year Estimates

Foreign-Born Population

Area	Percent of Population Born in								
	Any Foreign Country	Asia	Mexico	Europe	Carribean	Central America[2]	South America	Africa	Canada
City	6.4	4.0	0.5	1.2	0.0	0.1	0.0	0.3	0.2
MSA[1]	3.9	1.1	1.8	0.3	0.1	0.3	0.1	0.2	0.1
U.S.	13.1	3.8	3.7	1.5	1.2	1.0	0.9	0.6	0.3

Note: (1) Figures cover the Birmingham-Hoover, AL Metropolitan Statistical Area—see Appendix B for areas included; (2) Excludes Mexico.
Source: U.S. Census Bureau, 2010-2014 American Community Survey 5-Year Estimates

Marital Status

Area	Never Married	Now Married[2]	Separated	Widowed	Divorced
City	20.9	61.3	0.7	6.8	10.3
MSA[1]	29.3	48.7	2.4	6.9	12.7
U.S.	32.5	48.4	2.2	5.9	10.9

Note: Figures are percentages and cover the population 15 years of age and older; (1) Figures cover the Birmingham-Hoover, AL Metropolitan Statistical Area—see Appendix B for areas included; (2) Excludes separated
Source: U.S. Census Bureau, 2010-2014 American Community Survey 5-Year Estimates

Disability Status

Area	All Ages	Under 18 Years Old	18 to 64 Years Old	65 Years and Over
City	8.2	1.9	4.5	32.6
MSA[1]	15.0	4.4	13.6	40.3
U.S.	12.3	4.1	10.2	36.3

Note: Figures show percent of the civilian noninstitutionalized population that reported having a disability. Disability status is determined from from six types of difficulty: vision, hearing, cognitive, ambulatory, self-care, and independent living. For children under 5 years old, hearing and vision difficulty are used to determine disability status. For children between the ages of 5 and 14, disability status is determined from hearing, vision, cognitive, ambulatory, and self-care difficulties. For people aged 15 years and older, they are considered to have a disability if they have difficulty with any one of the six difficulty types; (1) Figures cover the Birmingham-Hoover, AL Metropolitan Statistical Area—see Appendix B for areas included.
Source: U.S. Census Bureau, 2010-2014 American Community Survey 5-Year Estimates

Age

Area	Percent of Population									Median Age
	Under Age 5	Age 5–19	Age 20–34	Age 35–44	Age 45–54	Age 55–64	Age 65–74	Age 75–84	Age 85+	
City	5.6	21.2	15.7	13.8	14.8	13.0	7.2	5.3	3.4	41.0
MSA[1]	6.5	19.6	20.1	13.2	14.1	12.8	7.8	4.3	1.6	38.1
U.S.	6.4	19.9	20.6	13.0	14.1	12.3	7.6	4.3	1.9	37.4

Note: (1) Figures cover the Birmingham-Hoover, AL Metropolitan Statistical Area—see Appendix B for areas included
Source: U.S. Census Bureau, 2010-2014 American Community Survey 5-Year Estimates

Gender

Area	Males	Females	Males per 100 Females
City	16,440	17,621	93.3
MSA[1]	546,799	588,735	92.9
U.S.	154,515,159	159,591,925	96.8

Note: (1) Figures cover the Birmingham-Hoover, AL Metropolitan Statistical Area—see Appendix B for areas included
Source: U.S. Census Bureau, 2010-2014 American Community Survey 5-Year Estimates

Religious Groups by Family

Area	Catholic	Baptist	Non-Den.	Methodist[2]	Lutheran	LDS[3]	Pente-costal	Presby-terian[4]	Muslim[5]	Judaism
MSA[1]	5.7	39.0	7.0	7.8	0.3	0.6	4.8	2.1	0.3	0.3
U.S.	19.1	9.3	4.0	4.0	2.3	2.0	1.9	1.6	0.8	0.7

Note: Figures are the number of adherents as a percentage of the total population; (1) Figures cover the Birmingham-Hoover, AL Metropolitan Statistical Area—see Appendix B for areas included; (2) Methodist/Pietist; (3) Latter Day Saints; (4) Reformed; (5) Figures are estimates
Source: Association of Statisticians of American Religious Bodies, 2010 U.S. Religion Census: Religious Congregations & Membership Study

Religious Groups by Tradition

Area	Catholic	Evangelical Protestant	Mainline Protestant	Other Tradition	Black Protestant	Orthodox
MSA[1]	5.7	45.2	8.3	1.4	10.1	0.1
U.S.	19.1	16.2	7.3	4.3	1.6	0.3

Note: Figures are the number of adherents as a percentage of the total population; (1) Figures cover the Birmingham-Hoover, AL Metropolitan Statistical Area—see Appendix B for areas included
Source: Association of Statisticians of American Religious Bodies, 2010 U.S. Religion Census: Religious Congregations & Membership Study

ECONOMY

Gross Metropolitan Product

Area	2013	2014	2015	2016	Rank[2]
MSA[1]	59.7	61.3	63.7	66.3	50

Note: Figures are in billions of dollars; (1) Figures cover the Birmingham-Hoover, AL Metropolitan Statistical Area—see Appendix B for areas included; (2) Rank is based on 2016 data and ranges from 1 to 381
Source: The U.S. Conference of Mayors, U.S. Metro Economies: GMP and Employment 2014-2016, June 2015

Economic Growth

Area	2011-13 (%)	2014 (%)	2015 (%)	2016 (%)	Rank[2]
MSA[1]	1.9	1.0	2.3	2.2	236
U.S.	2.2	2.4	2.3	2.9	–

Note: Figures are real gross metropolitan product (GMP) growth rates and represent annual average percent change; (1) Figures cover the Birmingham-Hoover, AL Metropolitan Statistical Area—see Appendix B for areas included; (2) Rank is based on 2016 data and ranges from 1 to 381
Source: The U.S. Conference of Mayors, U.S. Metro Economies: GMP and Employment 2014-2016, June 2015

Metropolitan Area Exports

Area	2009	2010	2011	2012	2013	2014	Rank[2]
MSA[1]	1,449.8	1,687.7	2,383.2	1,939.2	1,865.2	1,803.4	111

Note: Figures are in millions of dollars; (1) Figures cover the Birmingham-Hoover, AL Metropolitan Statistical Area—see Appendix B for areas included; (2) Rank is based on 2014 data and ranges from 1 to 385
Source: U.S. Department of Commerce, International Trade Administration, Office of Trade & Industry Information, Manufacturing & Services, data extracted March 10, 2016

Building Permits

Area	Single-Family			Multi-Family			Total		
	2014	2015p	Pct. Chg.	2014	2015p	Pct. Chg.	2014	2015p	Pct. Chg.
City	109	88	-19.3	0	272	-	109	360	230.3
MSA[1]	2,318	2,468	6.5	1,046	1,190	13.8	3,364	3,658	8.7
U.S.	640,300	690,800	7.9	411,800	487,600	18.4	1,052,100	1,178,400	12.0

Note: (1) Figures cover the Birmingham-Hoover, AL Metropolitan Statistical Area—see Appendix B for areas included; Figures represent new, privately-owned housing units authorized (unadjusted data); All permit data are based on estimates with imputation; (p) preliminary data.
Source: U.S. Census Bureau, Manufacturing, Mining, and Construction Statistics, Building Permits, 2014, 2015

Bankruptcy Filings

Area	Business Filings 2014	Business Filings 2015	Business Filings % Chg.	Nonbusiness Filings 2014	Nonbusiness Filings 2015	Nonbusiness Filings % Chg.
Jefferson County	55	54	-1.8	4,020	4,336	7.9
U.S.	26,983	24,735	-8.3	909,812	819,760	-9.9

Note: Business filings include Chapter 7, Chapter 11, Chapter 12, and Chapter 13; Nonbusiness filings include Chapter 7, Chapter 11, and Chapter 13

Source: Administrative Office of the U.S. Courts, Business and Nonbusiness Bankruptcy, County Cases Commenced by Chapter of the Bankruptcy Code, During the 12- Month Period Ending December 31, 2014 and Business and Nonbusiness Bankruptcy, County Cases Commenced by Chapter of the Bankruptcy Code, During the 12- Month Period Ending December 31, 2015

Housing Vacancy Rates

Area	Gross Vacancy Rate[2] (%)			Year-Round Vacancy Rate[3] (%)			Rental Vacancy Rate[4] (%)			Homeowner Vacancy Rate[5] (%)		
	2013	2014	2015	2013	2014	2015	2013	2014	2015	2013	2014	2015
MSA[1]	14.2	14.3	16.0	13.2	13.8	15.6	9.9	13.0	17.7	1.8	2.7	2.2
U.S.	13.6	13.4	12.9	10.7	10.4	10.0	8.3	7.6	7.1	2.0	1.9	1.8

Note: (1) Figures cover the Birmingham-Hoover, AL Metropolitan Statistical Area—see Appendix B for areas included; (2) The percentage of the total housing inventory that is vacant; (3) The percentage of the housing inventory (excluding seasonal units) that is year-round vacant; (4) The percentage of rental inventory that is vacant for rent; (5) The percentage of homeowner inventory that is vacant for sale

Source: U.S. Census Bureau, Housing Vacancies and Homeownership Annual Statistics: 2015

INCOME

Income

Area	Per Capita ($)	Median Household ($)	Average Household ($)
City	51,102	81,352	126,102
MSA[1]	26,706	48,438	67,422
U.S.	28,555	53,482	74,596

Note: (1) Figures cover the Birmingham-Hoover, AL Metropolitan Statistical Area—see Appendix B for areas included

Source: U.S. Census Bureau, 2010-2014 American Community Survey 5-Year Estimates

Household Income Distribution

Area	Percent of Households Earning: Under $15,000	$15,000 -24,999	$25,000 -34,999	$35,000 -49,999	$50,000 -74,999	$75,000 -99,000	$100,000 -149,999	$150,000 and up
City	5.6	7.5	8.8	10.5	14.6	10.0	17.3	25.7
MSA[1]	14.4	11.8	11.1	13.9	17.6	11.6	11.7	7.9
U.S.	12.5	10.7	10.2	13.5	17.8	12.2	13.0	10.0

Note: (1) Figures cover the Birmingham-Hoover, AL Metropolitan Statistical Area—see Appendix B for areas included

Source: U.S. Census Bureau, 2010-2014 American Community Survey 5-Year Estimates

Poverty Rate

Area	All Ages	Under 18 Years Old	18 to 64 Years Old	65 Years and Over
City	4.6	3.8	5.6	2.3
MSA[1]	16.9	24.9	15.4	9.6
U.S.	15.6	21.9	14.6	9.4

Note: Figures are percentage of people whose income during the past 12 months was below the poverty level; (1) Figures cover the Birmingham-Hoover, AL Metropolitan Statistical Area—see Appendix B for areas included

Source: U.S. Census Bureau, 2010-2014 American Community Survey 5-Year Estimates

EMPLOYMENT

Labor Force and Employment

Area	Civilian Labor Force			Workers Employed		
	Dec. 2014	Dec. 2015	% Chg.	Dec. 2014	Dec. 2015	% Chg.
City	17,197	17,330	0.7	16,702	16,758	0.3
MSA[1]	530,623	535,298	0.8	504,964	506,858	0.3
U.S.	155,521,000	157,245,000	1.1	147,190,000	149,703,000	1.7

Note: Data is not seasonally adjusted and covers workers 16 years of age and older; (1) Figures cover the Birmingham-Hoover, AL Metropolitan Statistical Area—see Appendix B for areas included
Source: Bureau of Labor Statistics, Local Area Unemployment Statistics

Unemployment Rate

Area	2015											
	Jan.	Feb.	Mar.	Apr.	May	Jun.	Jul.	Aug.	Sep.	Oct.	Nov.	Dec.
City	3.9	3.7	3.6	3.4	4.0	4.0	4.2	4.2	3.6	3.5	3.2	3.3
MSA[1]	5.5	5.1	5.1	4.8	5.5	5.9	6.0	5.9	5.4	5.1	5.2	5.3
U.S.	6.1	5.8	5.6	5.1	5.3	5.5	5.6	5.2	4.9	4.8	4.8	4.8

Note: Data is not seasonally adjusted and covers workers 16 years of age and older; (1) Figures cover the Birmingham-Hoover, AL Metropolitan Statistical Area—see Appendix B for areas included
Source: Bureau of Labor Statistics, Local Area Unemployment Statistics

Employment by Occupation

Occupation Classification	City (%)	MSA[1] (%)	U.S. (%)
Management, Business, Science, and Arts	62.7	36.7	36.4
Natural Resources, Construction, and Maintenance	2.7	9.0	9.0
Production, Transportation, and Material Moving	3.5	12.3	12.1
Sales and Office	22.7	26.0	24.4
Service	8.4	16.1	18.2

Note: Figures cover employed civilians 16 years of age and older; (1) Figures cover the Birmingham-Hoover, AL Metropolitan Statistical Area—see Appendix B for areas included
Source: U.S. Census Bureau, 2010-2014 American Community Survey 5-Year Estimates

Employment by Industry

Sector	MSA[1]		U.S.
	Number of Employees	Percent of Total	Percent of Total
Construction	26,100	5.0	4.5
Education and Health Services	70,900	13.6	15.7
Financial Activities	42,200	8.1	5.7
Government	82,400	15.8	15.5
Information	8,200	1.5	1.9
Leisure and Hospitality	48,200	9.2	10.4
Manufacturing	37,300	7.1	8.6
Mining and Logging	2,900	0.5	0.5
Other Services	23,800	4.5	3.9
Professional and Business Services	65,000	12.4	13.9
Retail Trade	61,700	11.8	11.3
Transportation, Warehousing, and Utilities	23,000	4.4	3.9
Wholesale Trade	28,900	5.5	4.1

Note: Figures are non-farm employment as of December 2015. Figures are not seasonally adjusted and include workers 16 years of age and older; (1) Figures cover the Birmingham-Hoover, AL Metropolitan Statistical Area—see Appendix B for areas included
Source: Bureau of Labor Statistics, Current Employment Statistics, Employment, Hours, and Earnings

Occupations with Greatest Projected Employment Growth: 2012 – 2022

Occupation[1]	2012 Employment	2022 Projected Employment	Numeric Employment Change	Percent Employment Change
Registered Nurses	46,040	54,670	8,630	18.7
Team Assemblers	29,770	36,190	6,420	21.6
Retail Salespersons	59,400	65,790	6,390	10.8
Secretaries and Administrative Assistants, Except Legal, Medical, and Executive	42,330	48,520	6,190	14.6
Combined Food Preparation and Serving Workers, Including Fast Food	40,870	46,690	5,820	14.2
Personal Care Aides	10,730	15,650	4,920	45.9
Laborers and Freight, Stock, and Material Movers, Hand	34,790	38,910	4,120	11.8
Customer Service Representatives	30,640	34,660	4,020	13.1
Heavy and Tractor-Trailer Truck Drivers	31,860	35,690	3,830	12.0
Janitors and Cleaners, Except Maids and Housekeeping Cleaners	27,930	31,490	3,560	12.7

Note: Projections cover Alabama; (1) Sorted by numeric employment change
Source: www.projectionscentral.com, State Occupational Projections, 2012–2022 Long-Term Projections

Fastest Growing Occupations: 2012 – 2022

Occupation[1]	2012 Employment	2022 Projected Employment	Numeric Employment Change	Percent Employment Change
Engine and Other Machine Assemblers	2,150	3,430	1,280	59.7
Occupational Therapy Assistants	360	530	170	49.6
Personal Care Aides	10,730	15,650	4,920	45.9
Diagnostic Medical Sonographers	1,130	1,630	500	44.5
Physical Therapist Assistants	1,870	2,680	810	43.4
Computer Numerically Controlled Machine Tool Programmers, Metal and Plastic	290	410	120	42.3
Helpers—Brickmasons, Blockmasons, Stonemasons, and Tile and Marble Setters	340	490	150	42.0
Biological Science Teachers, Postsecondary	1,730	2,460	730	41.9
Insulation Workers, Mechanical	550	770	220	40.6
Home Health Aides	8,340	11,710	3,370	40.4

Note: Projections cover Alabama; (1) Sorted by percent employment change and excludes occupations with numeric employment change less than 100
Source: www.projectionscentral.com, State Occupational Projections, 2012–2022 Long-Term Projections

Average Wages

Occupation	$/Hr.	Occupation	$/Hr.
Accountants and Auditors	33.02	Maids and Housekeeping Cleaners	8.79
Automotive Mechanics	21.05	Maintenance and Repair Workers	18.76
Bookkeepers	18.89	Marketing Managers	71.08
Carpenters	17.70	Nuclear Medicine Technologists	31.26
Cashiers	8.93	Nurses, Licensed Practical	18.41
Clerks, General Office	12.18	Nurses, Registered	28.38
Clerks, Receptionists/Information	12.82	Nursing Assistants	10.74
Clerks, Shipping/Receiving	14.60	Packers and Packagers, Hand	10.02
Computer Programmers	37.71	Physical Therapists	40.96
Computer Systems Analysts	35.89	Postal Service Mail Carriers	24.56
Computer User Support Specialists	23.32	Real Estate Brokers	n/a
Cooks, Restaurant	10.50	Retail Salespersons	12.92
Dentists	68.83	Sales Reps., Exc. Tech./Scientific	33.37
Electrical Engineers	45.00	Sales Reps., Tech./Scientific	42.34
Electricians	22.93	Secretaries, Exc. Legal/Med./Exec.	17.26
Financial Managers	65.09	Security Guards	10.69
First-Line Supervisors/Managers, Sales	21.83	Surgeons	98.93
Food Preparation Workers	9.46	Teacher Assistants*	10.53
General and Operations Managers	63.70	Teachers, Elementary School*	24.73
Hairdressers/Cosmetologists	11.48	Teachers, Secondary School*	24.58
Internists	120.46	Telemarketers	13.15
Janitors and Cleaners	10.41	Truck Drivers, Heavy/Tractor-Trailer	21.98
Landscaping/Groundskeeping Workers	12.59	Truck Drivers, Light/Delivery Svcs.	14.63
Lawyers	58.47	Waiters and Waitresses	9.61

Note: Wage data covers the Birmingham-Hoover, AL Metropolitan Statistical Area—see Appendix B for areas included; (*) Hourly wages for elementary/secondary school teachers and teacher assistants were calculated by the editors from annual wage data based on a 40 hour work week; n/a not available.
Source: Bureau of Labor Statistics, Metro Area Occupational Employment and Wage Estimates, May 2015

TAXES

State Corporate Income Tax Rates

State	Tax Rate (%)	Income Brackets ($)	Num. of Brackets	Financial Institution Tax Rate (%)[a]	Federal Income Tax Ded.
Alabama	6.5	Flat rate	1	6.5	Yes

Note: Tax rates as of January 1, 2016; (a) Rates listed are the corporate income tax rate applied to financial institutions or excise taxes based on income. Some states have other taxes based upon the value of deposits or shares.
Source: Federation of Tax Administrators, "State Corporate Income Tax Rates, 2016"

State Individual Income Tax Rates

State	Tax Rate (%)	Income Brackets ($)	Num. of Brackets	Personal Exempt. ($)[1]		Fed. Inc. Tax Ded.
				Single	Dependents	
Alabama	2.0 - 5.0	500 - 3,001 (b)	3	1,500	500 (e)	Yes

Note: Tax rates as of January 1, 2016; Local- and county-level taxes are not included; n/a not applicable; (1) Married joint filers generally receive double the single exemption; (b) For joint returns, taxes are twice the tax on half the couple's income; (e) In Alabama, the per-dependent exemption is $1,000 for taxpayers with state AGI of $20,000 or less, $500 with AGI from $20,001 to $100,000, and $300 with AGI over $100,000.
Source: Federation of Tax Administrators, "State Individual Income Tax Rates, 2016"

Various State and Local Tax Rates

State	State and Local Sales and Use (%)	State Sales and Use (%)	Gasoline[1] (¢/gal.)	Cigarette[2] ($/pack)	Spirits[3] ($/gal.)	Wine[4] ($/gal.)	Beer[5] ($/gal.)
Alabama	9.00	4.0	20.87	0.675	18.25 (g)	1.70 (l)	1.07 (r)

Note: All tax rates as of January 1, 2016; (1) The American Petroleum Institute has developed a methodology for determining the average tax rate on a gallon of fuel. Rates may include any of the following: excise taxes, environmental fees, storage tank fees, other fees or taxes, general sales tax, and local taxes. In states where gasoline is subject to the general sales tax, or where the fuel tax is based on the average sale price, the average rate determined by API is sensitive to changes in the price of gasoline. States that fully or partially apply general sales taxes to gasoline: CA, CO, GA, IL, IN, MI, NY; (2) The federal excise tax of $1.0066 per pack and local taxes are not included; (3) Rates are those applicable to off-premise sales of 40% alcohol by volume (a.b.v.) distilled spirits in 750ml containers. Local excise taxes are excluded; (4) Rates are those applicable to off-premise sales of 11% a.b.v. non-carbonated wine in 750ml containers; (5) Rates are those applicable to off-premise sales of 4.7% a.b.v. beer in 12 ounce containers; (g) Control states, where the government controls all sales. Products can be subject to ad valorem mark-up as well as excise taxes; (l) Different rates also applicable according to alcohol content, place of production, size of container, place purchased (on- or off-premise or on board airlines) or type of wine (carbonated, vermouth, etc.); (r) Includes the statewide local rate in Alabama ($0.52) and Georgia ($0.53).
Source: Tax Foundation, 2016 Facts & Figures: How Does Your State Compare?

State Business Tax Climate Index Rankings

State	Overall Rank	Corporate Tax Rank	Individual Income Tax Rank	Sales Tax Rank	Unemployment Insurance Tax Rank	Property Tax Rank
Alabama	29	25	22	41	26	17

Note: The index is a measure of how each state's tax laws affect economic performance. The lower the rank, the more favorable a state's tax system is for business. States without a given tax are given a ranking of 1. The scores/rankings for the District of Columbia do not affect other states. The 2016 index represents the tax climate as of July 1, 2015 (the beginning of Fiscal Year 2016).
Source: Tax Foundation, State Business Tax Climate Index 2016

TRANSPORTATION

Means of Transportation to Work

Area	Car/Truck/Van		Public Transportation			Bicycle	Walked	Other Means	Worked at Home
	Drove Alone	Car-pooled	Bus	Subway	Railroad				
City	88.5	4.9	0.1	0.0	0.0	0.2	1.7	0.5	4.0
MSA[1]	85.2	9.3	0.6	0.0	0.0	0.1	1.0	0.7	2.9
U.S.	76.4	9.6	2.6	1.8	0.6	0.6	2.8	1.3	4.4

Note: Figures are percentages and cover workers 16 years of age and older; (1) Figures cover the Birmingham-Hoover, AL Metropolitan Statistical Area—see Appendix B for areas included
Source: U.S. Census Bureau, 2010-2014 American Community Survey 5-Year Estimates

Travel Time to Work

Area	Less Than 10 Minutes	10 to 19 Minutes	20 to 29 Minutes	30 to 44 Minutes	45 to 59 Minutes	60 to 89 Minutes	90 Minutes or More
City	9.6	41.9	30.4	13.7	2.0	1.5	1.0
MSA[1]	9.6	27.6	23.3	24.0	8.9	4.7	1.7
U.S.	13.3	29.6	21.0	20.2	7.7	5.7	2.6

Note: Figures are percentages and include workers 16 years old and over; (1) Figures cover the Birmingham-Hoover, AL Metropolitan Statistical Area—see Appendix B for areas included
Source: U.S. Census Bureau, 2010-2014 American Community Survey 5-Year Estimates

Freeway Travel Time Index

Area	1985	1990	1995	2000	2005	2010	2014
Urban Area Rank[1,2]	81	90	77	72	82	82	81
Urban Area Index[1]	1.04	1.05	1.09	1.13	1.13	1.13	1.14
Average Index[3]	1.09	1.11	1.14	1.17	1.20	1.19	1.20

Note: Freeway Travel Time Index—the ratio of travel time in the peak period to the travel time at free-flow conditions. For example, a value of 1.30 indicates a 20-minute free-flow trip takes 26 minutes in the peak (20 minutes x 1.30 = 26 minutes); (1) Covers the Birmingham AL urban area; (2) Rank is based on 101 urban areas (#1 = highest travel time index); (3) Average of 101 urban areas
Source: Texas Transportation Institute, 2015 Urban Mobility Scorecard, August 2015

Freeway Commuter Stress Index

Area	1985	1990	1995	2000	2005	2010	2014
Urban Area Rank[1,2]	66	84	76	70	81	82	79
Urban Area Index[1]	1.07	1.08	1.12	1.16	1.16	1.16	1.17
Average Index[3]	1.13	1.16	1.19	1.22	1.25	1.24	1.25

Note: The Freeway Commuter Stress Index is the same as the Freeway Travel Time Index (see table above) except that it includes only the travel in the peak directions during the peak periods; the TTI includes travel in all directions during the peak period. Thus, the CSI is more indicative of the work trip experienced by each commuter on a daily basis. (1) Covers the Birmingham AL urban area; (2) Rank is based on 101 urban areas (#1 = highest stress index); (3) Average of 101 urban areas

Source: Texas Transportation Institute, 2015 Urban Mobility Scorecard, August 2015

Living Environment

COST OF LIVING

Cost of Living Index

Composite Index	Groceries	Housing	Utilities	Trans-portation	Health Care	Misc. Goods/ Services
91.7	101.4	80.6	97.5	90.5	84.2	96.9

Note: The Cost of Living Index measures regional differences in the cost of consumer goods and services, excluding taxes and non-consumer expenditures, for professional and managerial households in the top income quintile. It is based on more than 50,000 prices covering almost 60 different items for which prices are collected three times a year by chambers of commerce, economic development organizations or university applied economic centers in each participating urban area. The numbers shown should be read as a percentage above or below the national average of 100. For example, a value of 115.4 in the groceries column indicates that grocery prices are 15.4% higher than the national average. Small differences in the index numbers should not be interpreted as significant; Figures cover the Birmingham AL urban area.
Source: The Council for Community and Economic Research, ACCRA Cost of Living Index, 2015

Grocery Prices

Area[1]	T-Bone Steak ($/pound)	Frying Chicken ($/pound)	Whole Milk ($/half gal.)	Eggs ($/dozen)	Orange Juice ($/64 oz.)	Coffee ($/11.5 oz.)
City[2]	10.25	1.32	2.45	2.44	4.14	4.19
Avg.	10.99	1.43	2.25	2.26	3.58	4.48
Min.	7.16	0.98	1.30	1.35	2.88	2.98
Max.	14.13	2.43	3.85	4.81	6.39	7.56

Note: (1) Values for the local area are compared with the average, minimum and maximum values for all 292 areas in the Cost of Living Index; (2) Figures cover the Birmingham AL urban area; **T-Bone Steak** *(price per pound);* **Frying Chicken** *(price per pound, whole fryer);* **Whole Milk** *(half gallon carton);* **Eggs** *(price per dozen, Grade A, large);* **Orange Juice** *(64 oz. Tropicana or Florida Natural);* **Coffee** *(11.5 oz. can, vacuum-packed, Maxwell House, Hills Bros, or Folgers).*
Source: The Council for Community and Economic Research, ACCRA Cost of Living Index, 2015

Housing and Utility Costs

Area[1]	New Home Price ($)	Apartment Rent ($/month)	All Electric ($/month)	Part Electric ($/month)	Other Energy ($/month)	Telephone ($/month)
City[2]	243,880	833	-	103.98	74.91	24.33
Avg.	312,874	945	179.30	95.07	72.96	28.11
Min.	178,682	479	116.28	43.14	26.46	10.01
Max.	1,472,476	3,984	504.25	189.44	421.11	43.06

Note: (1) Values for the local area are compared with the average, minimum and maximum values for all 292 areas in the Cost of Living Index; (2) Figures cover the Birmingham AL urban area; **New Home Price** *(2,400 sf living area, 8,000 sf lot, in urban area with full utilities);* **Apartment Rent** *(950 sf 2 bedroom/1.5 or 2 bath, unfurnished, excluding all utilities except water);* **All Electric** *(average monthly cost for an all-electric home);* **Part Electric** *(average monthly cost for a part-electric home);* **Other Energy** *(average monthly cost for natural gas, fuel oil, coal, wood, and any other forms of energy except electricity);* **Telephone** *(price includes basic monthly rate for a private residential line plus additional local usage charges incurred by a family of four).*
Source: The Council for Community and Economic Research, ACCRA Cost of Living Index, 2015

Health Care, Transportation, and Other Costs

Area[1]	Doctor ($/visit)	Dentist ($/visit)	Optometrist ($/visit)	Gasoline ($/gallon)	Beauty Salon ($/visit)	Men's Shirt ($)
City[2]	90.61	66.78	109.22	2.18	30.89	36.41
Avg.	105.15	89.02	99.78	2.38	35.30	28.10
Min.	66.87	56.09	48.53	1.95	18.91	13.38
Max.	182.34	150.36	228.33	4.09	67.91	63.80

Note: (1) Values for the local area are compared with the average, minimum and maximum values for all 292 areas in the Cost of Living Index; (2) Figures cover the Birmingham AL urban area; **Doctor** *(general practitioners routine exam of an established patient);* **Dentist** *(adult teeth cleaning and periodic oral examination);* **Optometrist** *(full vision eye exam for established adult patient);* **Gasoline** *(one gallon regular unleaded, national brand, including all taxes, cash price at self-service pump if available);* **Beauty Salon** *(woman's shampoo, trim, and blow-dry);* **Men's Shirt** *(cotton/polyester dress shirt, pinpoint weave, long sleeves).*
Source: The Council for Community and Economic Research, ACCRA Cost of Living Index, 2015

HOUSING

House Price Index (HPI)

Area	National Ranking[2]	Quarterly Change (%)	One-Year Change (%)	Five-Year Change (%)
MSA[1]	176	-0.10	3.40	5.50
U.S.[3]	–	1.45	5.76	22.85

Note: The HPI is a weighted repeat sales index. It measures average price changes in repeat sales or refinancings on the same properties. This information is obtained by reviewing repeat mortgage transactions on single-family properties whose mortgages have been purchased or securitized by Fannie Mae or Freddie Mac in January 1975; (1) Birmingham-Hoover Metropolitan Statistical Area—see Appendix B for areas included; (2) Rankings are based on annual percentage change for all metro areas containing at least 15,000 transactions over the last 10 years and ranges from 1 to 266; (3) figures based on a weighted average of Census Division estimates using a seasonally adjusted, purchase-only index; all figures are for the period ending December 31, 2015

Source: Federal Housing Finance Agency, House Price Index, February 25, 2016

Median Single-Family Home Prices

Area	2013	2014	2015p	Percent Change 2014 to 2015
MSA[1]	165.1	167.9	178.5	6.3
U.S. Average	197.4	208.9	223.9	7.2

Note: Figures are median sales prices of existing single-family homes in thousands of dollars; (p) preliminary; n/a not available; (1) Birmingham-Hoover, AL Metropolitan Statistical Area—see Appendix B for areas included

Source: National Association of Realtors, Median Sales Price of Existing Single-Family Homes for Metropolitan Areas, 4th Quarter 2015

Qualifying Income Based on Median Sales Price of Existing Single-Family Homes

Area	With 5% Down ($)	With 10% Down ($)	With 20% Down ($)
MSA[1]	38,347	36,329	32,292
U.S. Average	49,535	46,928	41,714

Note: Figures are preliminary; Qualifying income is based on a mortgage rate of 4.1%. Monthly principal and interest payment is limited to 25% of income; n/a not available; (1) Birmingham-Hoover, AL Metropolitan Statistical Area—see Appendix B for areas included

Source: National Association of Realtors, Qualifying Income Based on Median Sales Price of Existing Single-Family Homes for Metropolitan Areas, 4th Quarter 2015

Median Apartment Condo-Coop Home Prices

Area	2013	2014	2015p	Percent Change 2014 to 2015
MSA[1]	n/a	n/a	n/a	n/a
U.S. Average	194.9	204.3	210.7	3.1

Note: Figures are median sales prices of existing apartment condo-coop homes in thousands of dollars; (p) preliminary; n/a not available; (1) Birmingham-Hoover, AL Metropolitan Statistical Area—see Appendix B for areas included

Source: National Association of Realtors, Median Sales Price of Existing Apartment Condo-Coop Homes for Metropolitan Areas, 4th Quarter 2015

Gross Monthly Rent

Area	Under $200	$200 -299	$300 -499	$500 -749	$750 -999	$1,000 -1,499	$1,500 and up	Median ($)
City	0.0	0.0	0.4	9.2	33.1	32.6	24.7	1,093
MSA[1]	1.4	3.9	10.2	28.3	29.2	21.3	5.8	797
U.S.	1.5	3.2	7.4	21.0	24.1	26.9	15.9	920

Note: Figures are percentages except for Median; Gross rent is the contract rent plus the estimated average monthly cost of utilities (electricity, gas, and water and sewer) and fuels (oil, coal, kerosene, wood, etc.) if these are paid by the renter (or paid for the renter by someone else); (1) Figures cover the Birmingham-Hoover, AL Metropolitan Statistical Area—see Appendix B for areas included

Source: U.S. Census Bureau, 2010-2014 American Community Survey 5-Year Estimates

Homeownership Rate

Area	2008 (%)	2009 (%)	2010 (%)	2011 (%)	2012 (%)	2013 (%)	2014 (%)	2015 (%)
MSA[1]	73.3	75.1	76.2	76.1	73.2	72.1	71.9	71.3
U.S.	67.8	67.4	66.9	66.1	65.4	65.1	64.5	63.7

Note: (1) Figures cover the Birmingham-Hoover, AL Metropolitan Statistical Area—see Appendix B for areas included
Source: U.S. Census Bureau, Housing Vacancies and Homeownership Annual Statistics: 2015

Year Housing Structure Built

Area	2010 or Later	2000 -2009	1990 -1999	1980 -1989	1970 -1979	1960 -1969	1950 -1959	1940 -1949	Before 1940	Median Year
City	0.2	14.7	15.1	15.5	20.3	20.1	11.3	2.3	0.4	1978
MSA[1]	1.1	16.6	17.1	13.7	16.6	11.6	10.9	5.3	7.0	1979
U.S.	1.0	14.9	13.9	13.8	15.8	11.0	10.8	5.4	13.3	1976

Note: Figures are percentages except for Median Year; (1) Figures cover the Birmingham-Hoover, AL Metropolitan Statistical Area—see Appendix B for areas included
Source: U.S. Census Bureau, 2010-2014 American Community Survey 5-Year Estimates

HEALTH

Health Risk Data

Category	MSA[1] (%)	U.S. (%)
Adults aged 18–64 who have any kind of health care coverage	77.4	79.6
Adults who reported being in good or excellent health	78.3	83.1
Adults who are current smokers	21.5	19.6
Adults who are heavy drinkers[2]	4.4	6.1
Adults who are binge drinkers[3]	11.7	16.9
Adults who are overweight (BMI 25.0 - 29.9)	33.4	35.8
Adults who are obese (BMI 30.0 - 99.8)	34.3	27.6
Adults who participated in any physical activities in the past month	75.4	77.1
Adults 50+ who have ever had a sigmoidoscopy or colonoscopy	71.9	67.3
Women aged 40+ who have had a mammogram within the past two years	78.5	74.0
Men aged 40+ who have had a PSA test within the past two years	50.8	45.2
Adults aged 65+ who have had flu shot within the past year	63.7	60.1
Adults who always wear a seatbelt	93.7	93.8

Note: Data as of 2012 unless otherwise noted; (1) Figures cover the Birmingham-Hoover, AL Metropolitan Statistical Area—see Appendix B for areas included; (2) Heavy drinkers are classified as males having more than two drinks per day or females having more than one drink per day; (3) Binge drinkers are classified as males having five or more drinks on one occasion or females having four or more drinks on one occasion
Source: Centers for Disease Control and Prevention, Behaviorial Risk Factor Surveillance System, SMART: Selected Metropolitan/Micropolitan Area Risk Trends, 2012 (Note: the CDC has discontinued this dataset but will be releasing a replacement in mid-2016)

Chronic Health Indicators

Category	MSA[1] (%)	U.S. (%)
Adults who have ever been told they had a heart attack	4.8	4.5
Adults who have ever been told they had a stroke	4.4	2.9
Adults who have been told they currently have asthma	7.8	8.9
Adults who have ever been told they have arthritis	31.1	25.7
Adults who have ever been told they have diabetes[2]	11.3	9.7
Adults who have ever been told they had skin cancer	7.0	5.7
Adults who have ever been told they had any other types of cancer	5.3	6.5
Adults who have ever been told they have COPD	8.8	6.2
Adults who have ever been told they have kidney disease	1.9	2.5
Adults who have ever been told they have a form of depression	20.4	18.0

Note: Data as of 2012 unless otherwise noted; (1) Figures cover the Birmingham-Hoover, AL Metropolitan Statistical Area—see Appendix B for areas included; (2) Figures do not include pregnancy-related, borderline, or pre-diabetes
Source: Centers for Disease Control and Prevention, Behaviorial Risk Factor Surveillance System, SMART: Selected Metropolitan/Micropolitan Area Risk Trends, 2012 (Note: the CDC has discontinued this dataset but will be releasing a replacement in mid-2016)

Mortality Rates for the Top 10 Causes of Death in the U.S.

ICD-10[a] Sub-Chapter	ICD-10[a] Code	Age-Adjusted Mortality Rate[1] per 100,000 population	
		County[2]	U.S.
Malignant neoplasms	C00-C97	180.9	163.6
Ischaemic heart diseases	I20-I25	83.6	102.2
Other forms of heart disease	I30-I51	101.4	50.1
Chronic lower respiratory diseases	J40-J47	39.3	41.4
Organic, including symptomatic, mental disorders	F01-F09	54.5	38.5
Cerebrovascular diseases	I60-I69	54.7	36.5
Other external causes of accidental injury	W00-X59	33.3	27.5
Other degenerative diseases of the nervous system	G30-G31	25.4	26.3
Diabetes mellitus	E10-E14	24.5	21.1
Hypertensive diseases	I10-I15	18.1	19.7

Note: (a) ICD-10 = International Classification of Diseases 10th Revision; (1) Mortality rates are a three year average covering 2012-2014; (2) Figures cover COUNTY NOT FOUND!!!!!!.
Source: Centers for Disease Control and Prevention, National Center for Health Statistics. Underlying Cause of Death 1999-2014 on CDC WONDER Online Database, released 2015.

Mortality Rates for Selected Causes of Death

ICD-10[a] Sub-Chapter	ICD-10[a] Code	Age-Adjusted Mortality Rate[1] per 100,000 population	
		County[2]	U.S.
Assault	X85-Y09	14.2	5.1
Diseases of the liver	K70-K76	14.8	13.5
Human immunodeficiency virus (HIV) disease	B20-B24	4.0	2.1
Influenza and pneumonia	J09-J18	17.1	15.2
Intentional self-harm	X60-X84	12.2	12.7
Malnutrition	E40-E46	1.7	0.9
Obesity and other hyperalimentation	E65-E68	1.6	1.9
Renal failure	N17-N19	19.9	13.0
Transport accidents	V01-V99	16.2	11.6
Viral hepatitis	B15-B19	2.0	2.1

Note: (a) ICD-10 = International Classification of Diseases 10th Revision; (1) Mortality rates are a three year average covering 2012-2014; (2) Figures cover COUNTY NOT FOUND!!!!!!; Data are Suppressed when the data meet the criteria for confidentiality constraints; Mortality rates are flagged as Unreliable when the rate would be calculated with a numerator of 20 or less.
Source: Centers for Disease Control and Prevention, National Center for Health Statistics. Underlying Cause of Death 1999-2014 on CDC WONDER Online Database, released 2015.

Health Insurance Coverage

Area	With Health Insurance	With Private Health Insurance	With Public Health Insurance	Without Health Insurance	Population Under Age 18 Without Health Insurance
City	97.0	90.4	19.5	3.0	1.0
MSA[1]	87.9	68.4	31.3	12.1	4.5
U.S.	85.8	65.8	31.1	14.2	7.1

Note: Figures are percentages that cover the civilian noninstitutionalized population; (1) Figures cover the Birmingham-Hoover, AL Metropolitan Statistical Area—see Appendix B for areas included
Source: U.S. Census Bureau, 2010-2014 American Community Survey 5-Year Estimates

Number of Medical Professionals

Area	MDs[3]	DOs[3,4]	Dentists	Podiatrists	Chiropractors	Optometrists
County[1] (number)	3,796	87	540	30	94	191
County[1] (rate[2])	575.9	13.2	81.7	4.5	14.2	28.9
U.S. (rate[2])	272.5	20.9	64.7	5.8	25.9	15.2

Note: Data as of 2014 unless noted; (1) Data covers Jefferson County; (2) Rate per 100,000 population; (3) Data as of 2013 and includes all active, non-federal physicians; (4) Doctor of Osteopathic Medicine
Source: U.S. Department of Health and Human Services, Health Resources and Services Administration, Bureau of Health Professions, Area Resource File (ARF) 2014-2015

Best Hospitals

According to *U.S. News,* the Birmingham-Hoover, AL metro area is home to one of the best hospitals in the U.S.: **University of Alabama Hospital at Birmingham** (6 specialties). The hospital listed was nationally ranked in at least one adult specialty. Only 137 hospitals nationwide were nationally ranked in one or more specialties. Fifteen hospitals in the U.S. made the Honor Roll with high scores in at least six specialties. *U.S. News Online, "America's Best Children's Hospitals 2015-16"*

According to *U.S. News,* the Birmingham-Hoover, AL metro area is home to one of the best children's hospitals in the U.S.: **Children's Hospital of Alabama at UAB** (7 specialties). The hospital listed was highly ranked in at least one pediatric specialty. Eighty-three children's hospitals in the U.S. were nationally ranked in at least one specialty. Twelve children's hospitals in the U.S. made the Honor Roll with high scores in at least three specialties. *U.S. News Online, "America's Best Children's Hospitals 2015-16"*

EDUCATION

Public School District Statistics

District Name	Schls	Pupils	Pupil/ Teacher Ratio	Minority Pupils[1] (%)	Free Lunch Eligible[2] (%)	IEP[3] (%)
Vestavia Hills City	8	6,762	16.0	16.5	7.1	6.8

Note: Table includes school districts with 100 or more students; (1) Percentage of students that are not non-Hispanic white; (2) Percentage of students that are eligible for the free lunch program; (3) Percentage of students that have an Individualized Education Program.

Source: U.S. Department of Education, National Center for Education Statistics, Common Core of Data, Local Education Agency (School District) Universe Survey: School Year 2013-2014; U.S. Department of Education, National Center for Education Statistics, Common Core of Data, Public Elementary/Secondary School Universe Survey: School Year 2013-2014

Highest Level of Education

Area	Less than H.S.	H.S. Diploma	Some College, No Deg.	Associate Degree	Bachelor's Degree	Master's Degree	Prof. School Degree	Doctorate Degree
City	2.2	10.0	16.3	4.4	37.3	17.4	8.1	4.4
MSA[1]	13.8	28.1	22.8	7.6	17.4	6.9	2.3	1.2
U.S.	13.7	28.0	21.2	7.9	18.3	7.8	2.0	1.3

Note: Figures cover persons age 25 and over; (1) Figures cover the Birmingham-Hoover, AL Metropolitan Statistical Area—see Appendix B for areas included

Source: U.S. Census Bureau, 2010-2014 American Community Survey 5-Year Estimates

Educational Attainment by Race

Area	High School Graduate or Higher (%)					Bachelor's Degree or Higher (%)				
	Total	White	Black	Asian	Hisp.[2]	Total	White	Black	Asian	Hisp.[2]
City	97.8	98.1	89.0	99.3	90.9	67.1	67.5	40.1	85.9	40.8
MSA[1]	86.2	87.8	84.2	91.1	56.7	27.8	31.1	18.6	59.8	12.6
U.S.	86.3	88.4	83.2	85.8	64.1	29.3	30.6	19.0	50.9	13.9

Note: Figures shown cover persons 25 years old and over; (1) Figures cover the Birmingham-Hoover, AL Metropolitan Statistical Area—see Appendix B for areas included; (2) People of Hispanic origin can be of any race

Source: U.S. Census Bureau, 2010-2014 American Community Survey 5-Year Estimates

School Enrollment by Grade and Control

Area	Preschool (%)		Kindergarten (%)		Grades 1 - 4 (%)		Grades 5 - 8 (%)		Grades 9 - 12 (%)	
	Public	Private	Public	Private	Public	Private	Public	Private	Public	Private
City	25.8	74.2	80.5	19.5	89.0	11.0	91.2	8.8	94.2	5.8
MSA[1]	40.7	59.3	81.7	18.3	90.5	9.5	90.4	9.6	89.9	10.1
U.S.	57.4	42.6	87.8	12.2	89.8	10.2	89.9	10.1	90.6	9.4

Note: Figures shown cover persons 3 years old and over; (1) Figures cover the Birmingham-Hoover, AL Metropolitan Statistical Area—see Appendix B for areas included

Source: U.S. Census Bureau, 2010-2014 American Community Survey 5-Year Estimates

Average Salaries of Public School Classroom Teachers

Area	2013-14 Dollars	2013-14 Rank[1]	2014-15 Dollars	2014-15 Rank[1]	Percent Change 2013-14 to 2014-15	Percent Change 2004-05 to 2014-15
Alabama	48,720	35	49,497	35	1.59	29.6
U.S. Average	56,610	–	57,379	–	1.36	20.8

Note: (1) State rank ranges from 1 to 51 where 1 indicates highest salary.
Source: National Education Association, Rankings & Estimates: Rankings of the States 2014 and Estimates of School Statistics 2015, March 2015

Higher Education

Four-Year Colleges			Two-Year Colleges			Medical Schools[1]	Law Schools[2]	Voc/ Tech[3]
Public	Private Non-profit	Private For-profit	Public	Private Non-profit	Private For-profit			
0	0	0	0	0	0	0	0	0

Note: Figures cover institutions located within the city limits and include main campuses only; (1) includes schools accredited by the Liaison Committee on Medical Education and the American Osteopathic Association's Commission on Osteopathic College Accreditation; (2) includes ABA-accredited schools, schools with provisional ABA accreditation, and state accredited schools; (3) includes all schools with programs that are less than 2 years.
Source: National Center for Education Statistics, Integrated Postsecondary Education System (IPEDS), 2014-15; Association of American Medical Colleges, Member List, March 21, 2016; American Osteopathic Association, Member List, March 21, 2016; Law School Admission Council, Official Guide to ABA-Approved Law Schools Online, March 21, 2016; Wikipedia, List of Medical Schools in the United States, March 21, 2016; Wikipedia, List of Law Schools in the United States, March 21, 2016

According to *U.S. News & World Report,* the Birmingham-Hoover, AL metro area is home to one of the best national universities in the U.S.: **University of Alabama–Birmingham** (#149 tie). The indicators used to capture academic quality fall into a number of categories: assessment by administrators at peer institutions; retention of students; faculty resources; student selectivity; financial resources; alumni giving; high school counselor ratings of colleges; and graduation rate. *U.S. News & World Report, "America's Best Colleges 2016"*

According to *U.S. News & World Report,* the Birmingham-Hoover, AL metro area is home to one of the best liberal arts colleges in the U.S.: **Birmingham–Southern College** (#120 tie). The indicators used to capture academic quality fall into a number of categories: assessment by administrators at peer institutions; retention of students; faculty resources; student selectivity; financial resources; alumni giving; high school counselor ratings of colleges; and graduation rate. *U.S. News & World Report, "America's Best Colleges 2016"*

According to *U.S. News & World Report,* the Birmingham-Hoover, AL metro area is home to one of the top 75 medical schools for research in the U.S.: **University of Alabama–Birmingham, School of Medicine** (#35 tie). The rankings are based on a weighted average of 11 measures of quality: quality assessment; peer assessment score; assessment score by residency directors; research activity; total research activity; average research activity per faculty member; student selectivity; median MCAT total score; median undergraduate GPA; acceptance rate; and faculty resources. *U.S. News & World Report, "America's Best Graduate Schools, Medical, 2017"*

PRESIDENTIAL ELECTION

2012 Presidential Election Results

Area	Obama (%)	Romney (%)	Other (%)
Jefferson County	52.6	46.6	0.8
U.S.	51.0	47.2	1.8

Note: Results may not add to 100% due to rounding
Source: Dave Leip's Atlas of U.S. Presidential Elections

EMPLOYERS

Major Employers

Company Name	Industry
9 Mercedes-Benz U.S. International	Inc.
Alabama Power Company	Utilties
American Cast Iron Pipe Company	Metal fabrication
AT&T	Information
Baptist Health System	Inc.
BBVA Compass	Financial services
Birmingham Veterans Affairs Medical Center	Healthcare
Blue Cross-Blue Shield of Alabama	Financial services
Brookwood Medical Center	Healthcare
Children's Health System	Healthcare
Drummond Company	Inc.
EBSCO Industries	Inc.
Honda Manufacturing of Alabama	LLC
Marshall Durbin Food Corporation	Food processing
McDonald's/CLP Corp	Food and beverage
Medical West	Education and healthcare
Regions Financial Corporation	Financial services
Southern Company Services	Utilties
Southern Progress Corporation	Publishing
St Vincent's Health System	Education and healthcare
Trinity Medical Center	Healthcare
U.S. Social Security Administration	Government
U.S. Steel-Fairfield Works	Metal fabrication
University of Alabama at Birmingham	Education and healthcare
Wells Fargo	Financial services

Note: Companies shown are located within the Birmingham-Hoover, AL Metropolitan Statistical Area.
Source: Hoovers.com; Wikipedia

PUBLIC SAFETY

Crime Rate

Area	All Crimes	Violent Crimes				Property Crimes		
		Murder	Rape[3]	Robbery	Aggrav. Assault	Burglary	Larceny -Theft	Motor Vehicle Theft
City	1,405.5	0.0	0.0	17.6	47.0	217.6	1,061.5	61.7
Metro[1]	n/a	7.8	43.4	161.1	364.1	923.0	n/a	255.6
U.S.	2,971.8	4.5	36.6	102.2	232.5	542.5	1,837.3	216.2

Note: Figures are crimes per 100,000 population; (1) Figures cover the Birmingham-Hoover, AL Metropolitan Statistical Area—see Appendix B for areas included; (3) The city and U.S. figures shown were reported using the revised Uniform Crime Reporting (UCR) definition of rape. The suburban and metro area figures shown are an aggregate total of the data submitted using both the revised and legacy UCR definitions.
Source: FBI Uniform Crime Reports, 2014

Hate Crimes

Area	Number of Quarters Reported	Number of Incidents per Bias Motivation						
		Race	Religion	Sexual Orientation	Ethnicity	Disability	Gender	Gender Identity
City	n/a	n/a	n/a	n/a	n/a	n/a	n/a	n/a
U.S.	4	2,568	1,014	1,017	648	84	33	98

Note: n/a not available.
Source: Federal Bureau of Investigation, Hate Crime Statistics 2014

Identity Theft Consumer Complaints

Area	Complaints	Complaints per 100,000 Population	Rank[2]
MSA[1]	1,207	105.5	180
U.S.	490,220	152.4	-

Note: (1) Figures cover the Birmingham-Hoover, AL Metropolitan Statistical Area—see Appendix B for areas included; (2) Rank ranges from 1 to 379 where 1 indicates greatest number of identity theft complaints per 100,000 population
Source: Federal Trade Commission, Consumer Sentinel Network Data Book for January–December 2015

Fraud and Other Consumer Complaints

Area	Complaints	Complaints per 100,000 Population	Rank[2]
MSA[1]	5,228	457.1	42
U.S.	2,593,159	806.0	-

Note: (1) Figures cover the Birmingham-Hoover, AL Metropolitan Statistical Area—see Appendix B for areas included; (2) Rank ranges from 1 to 379 where 1 indicates greatest number of identity theft complaints per 100,000 population
Source: Federal Trade Commission, Consumer Sentinel Network Data Book for January–December 2015

RECREATION

Culture

Dance[1]	Theatre[1]	Instrumental Music[1]	Vocal Music[1]	Series and Festivals	Museums and Art Galleries[2]	Zoos and Aquariums[3]
0	0	0	0	0	0	0

Note: (1) Professional perfoming groups; (2) Based on organizations with SIC code 8412; (3) AZA-accredited
Source: The Grey House Performing Arts Directory, 2015-16; Association of Zoos & Aquariums, AZA Member Zoos & Aquariums, March 25, 2016; www.AccuLeads.com, March 29, 2016

Professional Sports Teams

Team Name	League	Year Established
No teams are located in the metro area		

Source: Wikipedia, Major Professional Sports Teams of the United States and Canada, March 24, 2016

CLIMATE

Average and Extreme Temperatures

Temperature	Jan	Feb	Mar	Apr	May	Jun	Jul	Aug	Sep	Oct	Nov	Dec	Yr.
Extreme High (°F)	81	83	89	92	99	102	106	103	100	94	84	80	106
Average High (°F)	53	58	66	75	82	88	90	90	84	75	64	56	74
Average Temp. (°F)	43	47	54	63	70	77	80	80	74	63	53	46	63
Average Low (°F)	33	36	42	50	58	66	70	69	63	51	41	35	51
Extreme Low (°F)	-6	3	2	26	36	42	51	52	37	27	5	1	-6

Note: Figures cover the years 1948-1995
Source: National Climatic Data Center, International Station Meteorological Climate Summary, 9/96

Average Precipitation/Snowfall/Humidity

Precip./Humidity	Jan	Feb	Mar	Apr	May	Jun	Jul	Aug	Sep	Oct	Nov	Dec	Yr.
Avg. Precip. (in.)	5.0	4.8	5.9	4.6	4.4	3.8	5.1	3.8	4.1	2.9	4.3	4.8	53.5
Avg. Snowfall (in.)	1	Tr	Tr	Tr	0	0	0	0	0	Tr	Tr	Tr	2
Avg. Rel. Hum. 7am (%)	82	81	78	76	76	78	81	82	81	82	82	82	80
Avg. Rel. Hum. 4pm (%)	57	53	48	46	51	54	58	55	54	50	52	58	53

Note: Figures cover the years 1948-1995; Tr = Trace amounts (<0.05 in. of rain; <0.5 in. of snow)
Source: National Climatic Data Center, International Station Meteorological Climate Summary, 9/96

Weather Conditions

Temperature			Daytime Sky			Precipitation		
10°F & below	32°F & below	90°F & above	Clear	Partly cloudy	Cloudy	0.01 inch or more precip.	0.1 inch or more snow/ice	Thunder-storms
1	57	59	91	161	113	119	1	57

Note: Figures are average number of days per year and cover the years 1948-1995
Source: National Climatic Data Center, International Station Meteorological Climate Summary, 9/96

HAZARDOUS WASTE

Superfund Sites

Vestavia Hills has no sites on the EPA's Superfund Final National Priorities List. There are a total of 1,323 Superfund sites on the list in the U.S. *U.S. Environmental Protection Agency, Final National Priorities List, March 18, 2016*

AIR & WATER QUALITY

Air Quality Trends: Ozone

	1990	1995	2000	2005	2010	2011	2012	2013	2014
MSA[1]	0.093	0.096	0.091	0.082	0.075	0.078	0.077	0.066	0.066

Note: (1) Data covers the Birmingham-Hoover, AL Metropolitan Statistical Area—see Appendix B for areas included. The values shown are the composite ozone concentration averages among trend sites based on the highest fourth daily maximum 8-hour concentration in parts per million. These trends are based on sites having an adequate record of monitoring data during the trend period. Data from exceptional events are included.
Source: U.S. Environmental Protection Agency, Air Quality Monitoring Information, "Air Quality Trends by City, 1990-2014"

Air Quality Index

Area	Percent of Days when Air Quality was...[2]					AQI Statistics[2]	
	Good	Moderate	Unhealthy for Sensitive Groups	Unhealthy	Very Unhealthy	Maximum	Median
MSA[1]	57.3	41.6	0.8	0.0	0.3	356	48

Note: (1) Data covers the Birmingham-Hoover, AL Metropolitan Statistical Area—see Appendix B for areas included; (2) Based on 365 days with AQI data in 2015. Air Quality Index (AQI) is an index for reporting daily air quality. EPA calculates the AQI for five major air pollutants regulated by the Clean Air Act: ground-level ozone, particle pollution (aka particulate matter), carbon monoxide, sulfur dioxide, and nitrogen dioxide. The AQI runs from 0 to 500. The higher the AQI value, the greater the level of air pollution and the greater the health concern. There are six AQI categories: "Good" AQI is between 0 and 50. Air quality is considered satisfactory; "Moderate" AQI is between 51 and 100. Air quality is acceptable; "Unhealthy for Sensitive Groups" When AQI values are between 101 and 150, members of sensitive groups may experience health effects; "Unhealthy" When AQI values are between 151 and 200 everyone may begin to experience health effects; "Very Unhealthy" AQI values between 201 and 300 trigger a health alert; "Hazardous" AQI values over 300 trigger warnings of emergency conditions (not shown).
Source: U.S. Environmental Protection Agency, Air Quality Index Report, 2015

Air Quality Index Pollutants

Area	Percent of Days when AQI Pollutant was...[2]					
	Carbon Monoxide	Nitrogen Dioxide	Ozone	Sulfur Dioxide	Particulate Matter 2.5	Particulate Matter 10
MSA[1]	0.0	2.7	16.7	1.6	77.8	1.1

Note: (1) Data covers the Birmingham-Hoover, AL Metropolitan Statistical Area—see Appendix B for areas included; (2) Based on 365 days with AQI data in 2015. The Air Quality Index (AQI) is an index for reporting daily air quality. EPA calculates the AQI for five major air pollutants regulated by the Clean Air Act: ground-level ozone, particle pollution (also known as particulate matter), carbon monoxide, sulfur dioxide, and nitrogen dioxide. The AQI runs from 0 to 500. The higher the AQI value, the greater the level of air pollution and the greater the health concern.
Source: U.S. Environmental Protection Agency, Air Quality Index Report, 2015

Maximum Air Pollutant Concentrations: Particulate Matter, Ozone, CO and Lead

	Particulate Matter 10 (ug/m^3)	Particulate Matter 2.5 Wtd AM (ug/m^3)	Particulate Matter 2.5 24-Hr (ug/m^3)	Ozone (ppm)	Carbon Monoxide (ppm)	Lead (ug/m^3)
MSA[1] Level	98	11.8	26	0.065	2	n/a
NAAQS[2]	150	15	35	0.075	9	0.15
Met NAAQS[2]	Yes	Yes	Yes	Yes	Yes	n/a

Note: (1) Data covers the Birmingham-Hoover, AL Metropolitan Statistical Area—see Appendix B for areas included; Data from exceptional events are included; (2) National Ambient Air Quality Standards; ppm = parts per million; ug/m^3 = micrograms per cubic meter; n/a not available.
Concentrations: Particulate Matter 10 (coarse particulate)—highest second maximum 24-hour concentration; Particulate Matter 2.5 Wtd AM (fine particulate)—highest weighted annual mean concentration; Particulate Matter 2.5 24-Hour (fine particulate)—highest 98th percentile 24-hour concentration; Ozone—highest fourth daily maximum 8-hour concentration; Carbon Monoxide—highest second maximum non-overlapping 8-hour concentration; Lead—maximum running 3-month average
Source: U.S. Environmental Protection Agency, Air Quality Monitoring Information, "Air Quality Statistics by City, 2014"

Maximum Air Pollutant Concentrations: Nitrogen Dioxide and Sulfur Dioxide

	Nitrogen Dioxide AM (ppb)	Nitrogen Dioxide 1-Hr (ppb)	Sulfur Dioxide AM (ppb)	Sulfur Dioxide 1-Hr (ppb)	Sulfur Dioxide 24-Hr (ppb)
MSA[1] Level	14	51	n/a	41	n/a
NAAQS[2]	53	100	30	75	140
Met NAAQS[2]	Yes	Yes	n/a	Yes	n/a

Note: (1) Data covers the Birmingham-Hoover, AL Metropolitan Statistical Area—see Appendix B for areas included; Data from exceptional events are included; (2) National Ambient Air Quality Standards; ppm = parts per million; ug/m^3 = micrograms per cubic meter; n/a not available.

Concentrations: Nitrogen Dioxide AM—highest arithmetic mean concentration; Nitrogen Dioxide 1-Hr—highest 98th percentile 1-hour daily maximum concentration; Sulfur Dioxide AM—highest annual mean concentration; Sulfur Dioxide 1-Hr—highest 99th percentile 1-hour daily maximum concentration; Sulfur Dioxide 24-Hr—highest second maximum 24-hour concentration

Source: U.S. Environmental Protection Agency, Air Quality Monitoring Information, "Air Quality Statistics by City, 2014"

Drinking Water

Water System Name	Pop. Served	Primary Water Source Type	Violations[1] Health Based	Violations[1] Monitoring/ Reporting
Birmingham Water Works Board	591,243	Surface	0	0

Note: (1) Based on violation data from January 1, 2015 to December 31, 2015 (includes unresolved violations from earlier years)

Source: U.S. Environmental Protection Agency, Office of Ground Water and Drinking Water, Safe Drinking Water Information System (based on data extracted April 29, 2016)

Queen Creek, Arizona

Background

Queen Creek is one of Arizona's best kept secrets. In southeast Maricopa and Pinal counties and covering 25.8 square miles, it is an oasis in the eastern valley of the Phoenix metropolitan area and one of the fastest growing towns in Arizona.

Queen Creek was incorporated in 1989 and has grown from its rich rural roots into one of the most innovative and family-oriented home towns in Arizona. When Arizona became a state in 1912, the community that formed at Queen Creek was steeped in the neighborliness and rural tradition that is still present today. In the 1920s, an influx of immigrants from Mexico came to work in the mines in southern Arizona. They also picked cotton alongside German prisoners of war during the 1940s. Immigrants from the Philippines also contributed to the agricultural labor force.

Agriculture still plays a major role in Queen Creek's economy, and has been thoughtfully considered as the city continues to grow. The fertile land in the valley below the San Tan Mountains offered a safe haven for the early Native American communities and homesteaders who came to farm and ranch along the Queen Creek Wash. This area is a key element in the town's planning for future recreational trails and open space. Citrus, cotton, pecans, vegetables, and other crops still provide for local families and farms in the area.

Today, Queen Creek faces rapid expansion and inevitable growth as the area draws new residents. The townspeople strive to preserve its cultural diversity and the benefits of rural life and small town living while providing economic and recreational opportunities. The town is served by six public school districts, charter schools, and a private school. Local theater, charming boutiques, and quaint restaurants speak to the kinds of experiences that are exemplified in the community's slogan, "comforts of the country, convenience of a city." Queen Creek prides itself as a 'first-name' community where people know each other by name and take time and effort to know their neighbors.

Queen Creek's San Tan Mountains and valley provide an exquisite backdrop for one of America's best small towns. The scenic views of Queen Creek are unparalleled, with the San Tan Mountains to the south and the Superstition Mountains to the northeast. San Tan Mountain Regional Park offers residents and visitors beauty, outdoor recreation, and more than 10,000 acres of the Sonoran Desert. A family town, Queen Creek offers an active equestrian scene and the Horseshoe Park and Equestrian Centre provides opportunities for both English and Western style events such as jumping competitions, roping, team penning, and barrel racing. Other outdoor activities include golfing, biking, and walking.

Each year, the town of Queen Creek attracts thousands of visitors, who participate in many seasonal and cultural events, including picking fruit and vegetable crops and visiting the olive mill. Since 2003, the American Heritage Festival has been the largest annual educational living history event not only in Arizona but in the entire southwest. Historical sites include the Old Main school building and the ruins of a Butterfield Stage coach stop. Plans for expanding the foundation of parks and trails are in the works as population inreases.

Queen Creek residents enjoy the benefits of small town living close to a bustling metropolitan area. The city boasts low crime rates, easy commuting to and from metro Phoenix, excellent air quality, and access to numerous recreational activities. It is a world apart from city life despite its close proximity to the metropolitan area.

Queen Creek enjoys 330 days of sunshine a year making it one of the sunniest places to live in Arizona. The town gets approximately 9 inches of rain per year and no snow. The highs during summer are around 100 and can drop into the upper 30s during winter.

Rankings

General Rankings

- The Phoenix* metro area was identified as one of America's fastest-growing areas in terms of population and economy by *Forbes*. The area ranked #11 out of 20. The 100 most populous metro areas in the U.S. were evaluated on the following criteria: estimated population growth; job growth; gross metropolitan product growth; unemployment; median salaries for college-educated workers. *Forbes, "America's Fastest-Growing Cities 2015," January 27, 2015*

- Phoenix* was identified as one of America's fastest-growing major metropolitan areas in terms of population growth by CNNMoney.com. The area ranked #6 out of 10. Criteria: population growth between July 2013 and July 2014. *CNNMoney, "10 Fastest-Growing Cities," May 27, 2015*

Business/Finance Rankings

- The personal finance site NerdWallet analyzed 183 American metropolitan areas with populations over 250,000 and more than 15,000 businesses to rank where entrepreneurs find the most success. Criteria included area economy, annual income, housing cost, unemployment rate, and the success rate of area businesses. Phoenix* ranked #137. *www.nerdwallet.com, "Best Places to Start a Business," April 27, 2015*

- The finance website Wall St. Cheat Sheet ranked the nation's largest metro areas on prospects for high-wage job creation in over the next five years. Based on analysis by CareerBuilder and Economic Modeling Specialists International (EMSI), The Phoenix* metro area ranked #3. *wallstcheatsheet.com, "Top 10 Cities for High-Wage Job Growth," December 8, 2013*

- Based on metro area social media reviews, the employment opinion group Glassdoor surveyed 50 of the largest U.S. metro areas and equally weighed cost of living, hiring opportunity, and job satisfaction to compose a list of "25 Best Cities for Jobs." The Phoenix* metro area was ranked #46 in overall job satisfaction. *www.glassdoor.com, "Best Cities for Jobs," May 19, 2015*

- In a survey of economic confidence in the nation's 50 largest metropolitan areas conducted January–December 2014, the Phoenix* metro area placed #26, according to Gallup's 2014 Economic Confidence Index. *Gallup, "San Jose and San Francisco Lead in Economic Confidence," March 19, 2015*

- The Brookings Institution ranked the 100 largest metro areas in the U.S. based on income inequality. Phoenix* was ranked #46 (#1 = greatest ineqality). Criteria: the "95/20 ratio," a figure representing the income at which a household earns more than 95 percent of all other households, divided by the income at which a household earns more than only 20 percent of all other households. *Brookings Institution, "Income Inequality, 100 Largest U.S. Metro Areas, 2007-2014," January 14, 2016*

- Payscale.com ranked the 20 largest metro areas in terms of wage growth. The Phoenix* metro area ranked #19. Criteria: private-sector wage growth between the 1st quarter of 2015 and the 1st quarter of 2016. *PayScale, "Wage Trends by Metro Area," 1st Quarter, 2016*

- The Phoenix* metro area was identified as one of the most debt-ridden places in America by the finance site Credit.com. The metro area was ranked #6. Criteria: residents' average personal debt load and average credit scores. *Credit.com, "The Most Debt-Ridden Cities," May 1, 2014*

- Phoenix* was identified as one of America's most frugal metro areas by *Coupons.com*. The city ranked #18 out of 25. Criteria: online coupon usage. *Coupons.com, "Top 25 Most Frugal Cities of 2014," May 11, 2015*

- Phoenix* was identified as one of America's most frugal metro areas by *Coupons.com*. The city ranked #19 out of 25. Criteria: Grocery IQ and coupons.com mobile app usage. *Coupons.com, "Top 25 Most On-the-Go Frugal Cities of 2013," April 10, 2014*

- The Phoenix* metro area appeared on the Milken Institute "2015 Best Performing Cities" list. Rank: #62 out of 200 large metro areas. Criteria: job growth; wage and salary growth; high-tech output growth. *Milken Institute, "Best-Performing Cities 2015," December 2015*

- *Forbes* ranked the 200 most populous metro areas to determine the nation's "Best Places for Business and Careers." The Phoenix* metro area was ranked #44. Criteria: costs (business and living); job growth (past and projected); income growth; educational attainment (college and high school); projected economic growth; cultural and recreational opportunities; net migration patterns; number of highly ranked colleges. *Forbes, "The Best Places for Business and Careers 2015," July 29, 2015*

Education Rankings

- Personal finance website *WalletHub* analyzed the 150 largest U.S. metropolitan statistical areas to determine where the most educated Americans are choosing to settle. Criteria: education quality and attainment gap; education levels; percentage of workers with degrees; public school rankings; quality and size of each metro area's universities. Phoenix* was ranked #76 (#1 = most educated city). *www.WalletHub.com, "2015's Most and Least Educated Cities*

Environmental Rankings

- The Phoenix* metro area came in at #359 for the relative comfort of its climate on Sperling's list of "chill cities," as measured by the Sperling Heat Index. All 361 metro areas are included. Criteria included daytime high temperatures, nighttime low temperatures, dew point, and relative humidity at the high temperatures. *www.bertsperling.com, "Sperling's Chill Cities," July 18, 2013*
- Sperling's BestPlaces assessed 379 metropolitan areas of the United States for the likelihood of dangerously extreme weather events or earthquakes. In general the Southeast and South-Central regions have the highest risk of weather extremes and earthquakes, while the Pacific Northwest enjoys the lowest risk. Of the least risky metropolitan areas, the Phoenix* metro area was ranked #120. *www.bestplaces.net, "Safest Places from Natural Disasters," April 2011*
- The U.S. Environmental Protection Agency (EPA) released a list of U.S. metropolitan areas with the most ENERGY STAR certified buildings in 2015. The Phoenix* metro area was ranked #10 out of 25. *U.S. Environmental Protection Agency, "Top Cities With the Most ENERGY STAR Certified Buildings in 2016," March 30, 2016*
- Phoenix* was highlighted as one of the 25 most ozone-polluted metro areas in the U.S. during 2011 through 2013. The area ranked #10. *American Lung Association, State of the Air 2015*
- Phoenix* was highlighted as one of the 25 metro areas most polluted by short-term particle pollution (24-hour PM 2.5) in the U.S. during 2011 through 2013. The area ranked #12. *American Lung Association, State of the Air 2015*

Health/Fitness Rankings

- For each of the 50 most populous metro areas in the United States, the American College of Sports Medicine's American Fitness Index evaluated infrastructure, community assets, and policies that encourage healthy and fit lifestyles, including preventive health behaviors, levels of chronic disease conditions, health care access, and community resources and policies that support physical activity. The Phoenix* metro area ranked #37 for "community fitness." *www.americanfitnessindex.org, "ACSM American Fitness Index Health and Community Fitness Status of the 50 Largest Metropolitan Areas," May 2015*
- The Phoenix* metro area was identified as one of the worst cities for bed bugs in America by pest control company Orkin. The area ranked #23 out of 50 based on the number of bed bug treatments Orkin performed from January to December 2015. *Orkin, "Chicago Tops Bed Bug Cities List for Fourth Year in a Row," January 13, 2016*
- Phoenix* was identified as a "2016 Spring Allergy Capital." The area ranked #62 out of 100. Three groups of factors were used to identify the most severe cities for people with allergies during the spring season: annual pollen levels; medicine utilization; access to board-certified allergists. *Asthma and Allergy Foundation of America, "Spring Allergy Capitals 2016"*

- Phoenix* was identified as a "2015 Asthma Capital." The area ranked #46 out of the nation's 100 largest metropolitan areas. Criteria: estimated prevalence; self-reported prevalence; crude death rate for asthma; annual pollen score; annual air quality; public smoking laws; number of board-certified asthma specialists; school inhaler access laws; rescue medication use; controller medication use; ER visits for asthma; uninsured rate; poverty rate. *Asthma and Allergy Foundation of America, "Asthma Capitals 2015"*

- The Phoenix* metro area ranked #58 out of 190 in The Gallup-Healthways Well-Being Index. Criteria: purpose; social well being; financial health; community and physical health. Results are based on telephone interviews with adults, aged 18 and older, living in metropolitan areas in the 50 U.S. states and the District of Columbia. *Gallup-Healthways, "State of American Well-Being," February 23, 2016*

Real Estate Rankings

- According to Penske Truck Rental, the Phoenix* metro area was named the #2 moving destination in 2015, based on one-way consumer truck rental reservations made through Penske's website and reservations call center. *blog.gopenske.com, "Penske Truck Rental's 2015 Top Moving Destinations List," February 3, 2016*

- The Phoenix* metro area was identified as one of the 15 worst housing markets for the next five years." Criteria: projected annualized change in home prices between the fourth quarter 2012 and the fourth quarter 2017. *The Business Insider, "The 15 Worst Housing Markets for the Next Five Years," May 22, 2013*

- Phoenix* was ranked #145 out of 225 metro areas in terms of housing affordability in 2015 by the National Association of Home Builders (#1 = most affordable). Criteria: the share of homes sold in that area affordable to a family earning the local median income, based on standard mortgage underwriting criteria. *National Association of Home Builders®, NAHB-Wells Fargo Housing Opportunity Index, 4th Quarter 2015*

Safety Rankings

- The National Insurance Crime Bureau ranked 380 metro areas in the U.S. in terms of per capita rates of vehicle theft. The Phoenix* metro area ranked #75 (#1 = highest rate). Criteria: number of vehicle theft offenses per 100,000 inhabitants in 2014. *National Insurance Crime Bureau, "Hot Spots 2014," June 24, 2015*

Seniors/Retirement Rankings

- From its Best Cities for Successful Aging indexes, the Milken Institute generated rankings for metropolitan areas, weighing data in eight categories—health care, wellness, living arrangements, transportation, financial characteristics, education and employment opportunities, community engagement, and overall livability. The Phoenix* metro area was ranked #90 overall in the large metro area category. *Milken Institute, "Best Cities for Successful Aging, 2014"*

Sports/Recreation Rankings

- According to the personal finance website NerdWallet, the Phoenix* metro area, at #7, is one of the nation's top dozen metro areas for sports fans. Criteria included the presence of all four major sports—MLB, NFL, NHL, and NBA, fan enthusiasm (as measured by game attendance), ticket affordability, and "sports culture," that is, number of sports bars. *www.nerdwallet.com, "Best Cities for Sports Fans," May 5, 2013*

Miscellaneous Rankings

- The watchdog site Charity Navigator conducts an annual study of charities in the nation's major markets both to analyze statistical differences in their financial, accountability, and transparency practices and to track year-to-year variations in individual communities. The Phoenix* metro area was ranked #11 among the 30 metro markets in the rating dimension of Overall Score. *www.charitynavigator.org, "Metro Market Study 2015," June 5, 2015*

- Mars Chocolate North America, the makers of COMBOS®, in partnership with Sperling's BestPlaces, ranked 50 major metro areas in terms of their "manliness." The Phoenix* metro area ranked #25. Criteria: number of professional sports teams; number of nearby NASCAR tracks and racing events; manly lifestyle; concentration of manly retail stores; manly occupations per capita; salty snack sales; "Board of Manliness" rankings. *Mars Chocolate North America, "America's Manliest Cities 2012"*
- The National Alliance to End Homelessness ranked the 100 most populous metro areas with the highest rate of homelessness. The Phoenix* metro area ranked #60. Criteria: number of homeless people per 10,000 population in 2011. *National Alliance to End Homelessness, The State of Homelessness in America 2012*

Queen Creek is located within the Phoenix-Mesa-Scottsdale, AZ Metropolitan Statistical Area.

Business Environment

CITY FINANCES

City Government Finances

Component	2012 ($000)	2012 ($ per capita)
Total Revenues	59,909	2,272
Total Expenditures	59,711	2,265
Debt Outstanding	165,601	6,282
Cash and Securities[1]	33,704	1,278

Note: (1) Cash and security holdings of a government at the close of its fiscal year, including those of its dependent agencies, utilities, and liquor stores.
Source: U.S Census Bureau, State & Local Government Finances 2012

City Government Revenue by Source

Source	2012 ($000)	2012 ($ per capita)
General Revenue		
From Federal Government	0	0
From State Government	7,952	301
From Local Governments	15	0
Taxes		
Property	6,218	235
Sales and Gross Receipts	12,220	463
Personal Income	0	0
Corporate Income	0	0
Motor Vehicle License	0	0
Other Taxes	2,198	83
Current Charges	19,119	725
Liquor Store	0	0
Utility	9,357	354
Employee Retirement	0	0

Source: U.S Census Bureau, State & Local Government Finances 2012

City Government Expenditures by Function

Function	2012 ($000)	2012 ($ per capita)	2012 (%)
General Direct Expenditures			
Air Transportation	0	0	0.0
Corrections	1	< 1	< 0.1
Education	0	0	0.0
Employment Security Administration	0	0	0.0
Financial Administration	631	23	1.0
Fire Protection	5,347	202	8.9
General Public Buildings	1,159	43	1.9
Governmental Administration, Other	7,846	297	13.1
Health	11	< 1	< 0.1
Highways	3,104	117	5.1
Hospitals	0	0	0.0
Housing and Community Development	696	26	1.1
Interest on General Debt	4,624	175	7.7
Judicial and Legal	326	12	0.5
Libraries	15	< 1	< 0.1
Parking	0	0	0.0
Parks and Recreation	6,614	250	11.0
Police Protection	0	0	0.0
Public Welfare	0	0	0.0
Sewerage	2,935	111	4.9
Solid Waste Management	1,234	46	2.0
Veterans' Services	0	0	0.0
Liquor Store	0	0	0.0
Utility	7,726	293	12.9
Employee Retirement	0	0	0.0

Source: U.S Census Bureau, State & Local Government Finances 2012

DEMOGRAPHICS

Population Growth

Area	1990 Census	2000 Census	2010 Census	2014* Estimate	Population Growth (%) 1990-2014	2010-2014
City	2,860	4,316	26,361	28,529	897.5	8.2
MSA[1]	2,238,480	3,251,876	4,192,887	4,337,542	93.8	3.5
U.S.	248,709,873	281,421,906	308,745,538	314,107,084	26.3	1.7

Note: (1) Figures cover the Phoenix-Mesa-Scottsdale, AZ Metropolitan Statistical Area—see Appendix B for areas included; (*) 2010-2014 5-year estimated population
Source: U.S. Census Bureau, 1990 Census, Census 2000, Census 2010, 2010-2014 American Community Survey 5-Year Estimates

Household Size

Area	Persons in Household (%) One	Two	Three	Four	Five	Six	Seven or More	Average Household Size
City	13.6	26.6	16.7	20.8	11.2	7.7	3.1	3.36
MSA[1]	26.6	34.5	14.4	12.7	6.5	3.0	2.0	2.75
U.S.	27.5	33.5	15.8	13.1	6.0	2.3	1.4	2.64

Note: (1) Figures cover the Phoenix-Mesa-Scottsdale, AZ Metropolitan Statistical Area—see Appendix B for areas included
Source: U.S. Census Bureau, 2010-2014 American Community Survey 5-Year Estimates

Race

Area	White Alone[2] (%)	Black Alone[2] (%)	Asian Alone[2] (%)	AIAN[3] Alone[2] (%)	NHOPI[4] Alone[2] (%)	Other Race Alone[2] (%)	Two or More Races (%)
City	86.9	2.8	1.2	1.5	0.1	6.2	1.3
MSA[1]	80.0	5.1	3.5	2.2	0.2	5.9	3.0
U.S.	73.8	12.6	5.0	0.8	0.2	4.7	2.9

Note: (1) Figures cover the Phoenix-Mesa-Scottsdale, AZ Metropolitan Statistical Area—see Appendix B for areas included; (2) Alone is defined as not being in combination with one or more other races; (3) American Indian and Alaska Native; (4) Native Hawaiian and Other Pacific Islander
Source: U.S. Census Bureau, 2010-2014 American Community Survey 5-Year Estimates

Hispanic or Latino Origin

Area	Total (%)	Mexican (%)	Puerto Rican (%)	Cuban (%)	Other (%)
City	17.7	11.0	1.4	0.2	5.1
MSA[1]	29.8	26.8	0.6	0.2	2.3
U.S.	16.9	10.8	1.6	0.6	3.8

Note: Persons of Hispanic or Latino origin can be of any race; (1) Figures cover the Phoenix-Mesa-Scottsdale, AZ Metropolitan Statistical Area—see Appendix B for areas included
Source: U.S. Census Bureau, 2010-2014 American Community Survey 5-Year Estimates

Ancestry

Area	German	Irish	English	American	Italian	Polish	French[2]	Scottish	Dutch
City	17.9	11.8	11.9	4.8	5.0	1.9	4.1	3.5	2.8
MSA[1]	14.5	9.3	8.3	5.8	4.6	2.6	2.4	1.7	1.4
U.S.	14.9	10.8	8.0	7.1	5.5	3.0	2.7	1.7	1.4

Note: Figures are the percentage of the total population reporting a particular ancestry. The nine most commonly reported ancestries in the U.S. are shown. Figures include multiple ancestries (e.g. if a person reported being Irish and Italian, they were included in both columns); (1) Figures cover the Phoenix-Mesa-Scottsdale, AZ Metropolitan Statistical Area—see Appendix B for areas included; (2) Excludes Basque
Source: U.S. Census Bureau, 2010-2014 American Community Survey 5-Year Estimates

Foreign-Born Population

Area	Any Foreign Country	Asia	Mexico	Europe	Carribean	Central America[2]	South America	Africa	Canada
	Percent of Population Born in								
City	4.0	0.9	1.4	0.8	0.1	0.0	0.1	0.1	0.5
MSA[1]	14.4	2.9	7.9	1.4	0.2	0.5	0.3	0.4	0.7
U.S.	13.1	3.8	3.7	1.5	1.2	1.0	0.9	0.6	0.3

Note: (1) Figures cover the Phoenix-Mesa-Scottsdale, AZ Metropolitan Statistical Area—see Appendix B for areas included; (2) Excludes Mexico.
Source: U.S. Census Bureau, 2010-2014 American Community Survey 5-Year Estimates

Marital Status

Area	Never Married	Now Married[2]	Separated	Widowed	Divorced
City	21.4	65.5	1.1	2.8	9.3
MSA[1]	33.1	47.9	1.8	5.1	12.2
U.S.	32.5	48.4	2.2	5.9	10.9

Note: Figures are percentages and cover the population 15 years of age and older; (1) Figures cover the Phoenix-Mesa-Scottsdale, AZ Metropolitan Statistical Area—see Appendix B for areas included; (2) Excludes separated
Source: U.S. Census Bureau, 2010-2014 American Community Survey 5-Year Estimates

Disability Status

Area	All Ages	Under 18 Years Old	18 to 64 Years Old	65 Years and Over
City	6.3	2.1	6.8	27.5
MSA[1]	10.4	3.3	8.6	32.6
U.S.	12.3	4.1	10.2	36.3

Note: Figures show percent of the civilian noninstitutionalized population that reported having a disability. Disability status is determined from from six types of difficulty: vision, hearing, cognitive, ambulatory, self-care, and independent living. For children under 5 years old, hearing and vision difficulty are used to determine disability status. For children between the ages of 5 and 14, disability status is determined from hearing, vision, cognitive, ambulatory, and self-care difficulties. For people aged 15 years and older, they are considered to have a disability if they have difficulty with any one of the six difficulty types; (1) Figures cover the Phoenix-Mesa-Scottsdale, AZ Metropolitan Statistical Area—see Appendix B for areas included.
Source: U.S. Census Bureau, 2010-2014 American Community Survey 5-Year Estimates

Age

Area	Under Age 5	Age 5–19	Age 20–34	Age 35–44	Age 45–54	Age 55–64	Age 65–74	Age 75–84	Age 85+	Median Age
	Percent of Population									
City	10.4	30.7	15.4	17.6	11.6	7.7	4.6	1.6	0.3	30.3
MSA[1]	7.0	21.4	21.1	13.5	12.9	10.9	7.6	4.1	1.6	35.4
U.S.	6.4	19.9	20.6	13.0	14.1	12.3	7.6	4.3	1.9	37.4

Note: (1) Figures cover the Phoenix-Mesa-Scottsdale, AZ Metropolitan Statistical Area—see Appendix B for areas included
Source: U.S. Census Bureau, 2010-2014 American Community Survey 5-Year Estimates

Gender

Area	Males	Females	Males per 100 Females
City	14,090	14,439	97.6
MSA[1]	2,153,952	2,183,590	98.6
U.S.	154,515,159	159,591,925	96.8

Note: (1) Figures cover the Phoenix-Mesa-Scottsdale, AZ Metropolitan Statistical Area—see Appendix B for areas included
Source: U.S. Census Bureau, 2010-2014 American Community Survey 5-Year Estimates

Religious Groups by Family

Area	Catholic	Baptist	Non-Den.	Methodist[2]	Lutheran	LDS[3]	Pente-costal	Presby-terian[4]	Muslim[5]	Judaism
MSA[1]	13.3	3.4	5.1	1.0	1.6	6.1	2.9	0.6	0.1	0.3
U.S.	19.1	9.3	4.0	4.0	2.3	2.0	1.9	1.6	0.8	0.7

Note: Figures are the number of adherents as a percentage of the total population; (1) Figures cover the Phoenix-Mesa-Glendale, AZ Metropolitan Statistical Area—see Appendix B for areas included; (2) Methodist/Pietist; (3) Latter Day Saints; (4) Reformed; (5) Figures are estimates
Source: Association of Statisticians of American Religious Bodies, 2010 U.S. Religion Census: Religious Congregations & Membership Study

Religious Groups by Tradition

Area	Catholic	Evangelical Protestant	Mainline Protestant	Other Tradition	Black Protestant	Orthodox
MSA[1]	13.3	13.2	2.6	7.8	0.1	0.3
U.S.	19.1	16.2	7.3	4.3	1.6	0.3

Note: Figures are the number of adherents as a percentage of the total population; (1) Figures cover the Phoenix-Mesa-Glendale, AZ Metropolitan Statistical Area—see Appendix B for areas included
Source: Association of Statisticians of American Religious Bodies, 2010 U.S. Religion Census: Religious Congregations & Membership Study

ECONOMY

Gross Metropolitan Product

Area	2013	2014	2015	2016	Rank[2]
MSA[1]	209.5	219.0	228.4	241.4	15

Note: Figures are in billions of dollars; (1) Figures cover the Phoenix-Mesa-Scottsdale, AZ Metropolitan Statistical Area—see Appendix B for areas included; (2) Rank is based on 2016 data and ranges from 1 to 381
Source: The U.S. Conference of Mayors, U.S. Metro Economies: GMP and Employment 2014-2016, June 2015

Economic Growth

Area	2011-13 (%)	2014 (%)	2015 (%)	2016 (%)	Rank[2]
MSA[1]	2.4	2.8	2.8	3.7	27
U.S.	2.2	2.4	2.3	2.9	–

Note: Figures are real gross metropolitan product (GMP) growth rates and represent annual average percent change; (1) Figures cover the Phoenix-Mesa-Scottsdale, AZ Metropolitan Statistical Area—see Appendix B for areas included; (2) Rank is based on 2016 data and ranges from 1 to 381
Source: The U.S. Conference of Mayors, U.S. Metro Economies: GMP and Employment 2014-2016, June 2015

Metropolitan Area Exports

Area	2009	2010	2011	2012	2013	2014	Rank[2]
MSA[1]	7,947.5	9,342.7	10,914.4	10,834.2	11,473.5	12,764.4	25

Note: Figures are in millions of dollars; (1) Figures cover the Phoenix-Mesa-Scottsdale, AZ Metropolitan Statistical Area—see Appendix B for areas included; (2) Rank is based on 2014 data and ranges from 1 to 385
Source: U.S. Department of Commerce, International Trade Administration, Office of Trade & Industry Information, Manufacturing & Services, data extracted March 10, 2016

Building Permits

Area	Single-Family			Multi-Family			Total		
	2014	2015p	Pct. Chg.	2014	2015p	Pct. Chg.	2014	2015p	Pct. Chg.
City	693	987	42.4	0	0	-	693	987	42.4
MSA[1]	11,557	16,940	46.6	8,784	6,006	-31.6	20,341	22,946	12.8
U.S.	640,300	690,800	7.9	411,800	487,600	18.4	1,052,100	1,178,400	12.0

Note: (1) Figures cover the Phoenix-Mesa-Scottsdale, AZ Metropolitan Statistical Area—see Appendix B for areas included; Figures represent new, privately-owned housing units authorized (unadjusted data); All permit data are based on estimates with imputation; (p) preliminary data.
Source: U.S. Census Bureau, Manufacturing, Mining, and Construction Statistics, Building Permits, 2014, 2015

Bankruptcy Filings

Area	Business Filings 2014	Business Filings 2015	Business Filings % Chg.	Nonbusiness Filings 2014	Nonbusiness Filings 2015	Nonbusiness Filings % Chg.
Maricopa County	545	496	-9.0	13,283	11,293	-15.0
U.S.	26,983	24,735	-8.3	909,812	819,760	-9.9

Note: Business filings include Chapter 7, Chapter 11, Chapter 12, and Chapter 13; Nonbusiness filings include Chapter 7, Chapter 11, and Chapter 13

Source: Administrative Office of the U.S. Courts, Business and Nonbusiness Bankruptcy, County Cases Commenced by Chapter of the Bankruptcy Code, During the 12- Month Period Ending December 31, 2014 and Business and Nonbusiness Bankruptcy, County Cases Commenced by Chapter of the Bankruptcy Code, During the 12- Month Period Ending December 31, 2015

Housing Vacancy Rates

Area	Gross Vacancy Rate[2] (%)			Year-Round Vacancy Rate[3] (%)			Rental Vacancy Rate[4] (%)			Homeowner Vacancy Rate[5] (%)		
	2013	2014	2015	2013	2014	2015	2013	2014	2015	2013	2014	2015
MSA[1]	18.4	17.5	15.3	11.5	11.3	9.5	9.7	9.7	6.3	2.4	2.9	2.0
U.S.	13.6	13.4	12.9	10.7	10.4	10.0	8.3	7.6	7.1	2.0	1.9	1.8

Note: (1) Figures cover the Phoenix-Mesa-Scottsdale, AZ Metropolitan Statistical Area—see Appendix B for areas included; (2) The percentage of the total housing inventory that is vacant; (3) The percentage of the housing inventory (excluding seasonal units) that is year-round vacant; (4) The percentage of rental inventory that is vacant for rent; (5) The percentage of homeowner inventory that is vacant for sale

Source: U.S. Census Bureau, Housing Vacancies and Homeownership Annual Statistics: 2015

INCOME

Income

Area	Per Capita ($)	Median Household ($)	Average Household ($)
City	30,547	83,809	102,621
MSA[1]	26,893	53,310	72,307
U.S.	28,555	53,482	74,596

Note: (1) Figures cover the Phoenix-Mesa-Scottsdale, AZ Metropolitan Statistical Area—see Appendix B for areas included

Source: U.S. Census Bureau, 2010-2014 American Community Survey 5-Year Estimates

Household Income Distribution

Area	Percent of Households Earning: Under $15,000	$15,000 -24,999	$25,000 -34,999	$35,000 -49,999	$50,000 -74,999	$75,000 -99,000	$100,000 -149,999	$150,000 and up
City	4.9	3.9	7.6	9.8	16.3	15.9	23.9	17.7
MSA[1]	11.4	10.3	10.6	14.6	18.7	12.4	13.2	8.9
U.S.	12.5	10.7	10.2	13.5	17.8	12.2	13.0	10.0

Note: (1) Figures cover the Phoenix-Mesa-Scottsdale, AZ Metropolitan Statistical Area—see Appendix B for areas included

Source: U.S. Census Bureau, 2010-2014 American Community Survey 5-Year Estimates

Poverty Rate

Area	All Ages	Under 18 Years Old	18 to 64 Years Old	65 Years and Over
City	8.6	11.6	6.7	5.8
MSA[1]	17.1	24.5	16.0	8.0
U.S.	15.6	21.9	14.6	9.4

Note: Figures are percentage of people whose income during the past 12 months was below the poverty level; (1) Figures cover the Phoenix-Mesa-Scottsdale, AZ Metropolitan Statistical Area—see Appendix B for areas included

Source: U.S. Census Bureau, 2010-2014 American Community Survey 5-Year Estimates

EMPLOYMENT

Labor Force and Employment

Area	Civilian Labor Force			Workers Employed		
	Dec. 2014	Dec. 2015	% Chg.	Dec. 2014	Dec. 2015	% Chg.
City	14,540	14,806	1.8	13,918	14,253	2.4
MSA[1]	2,140,674	2,175,140	1.6	2,023,418	2,072,215	2.4
U.S.	155,521,000	157,245,000	1.1	147,190,000	149,703,000	1.7

Note: Data is not seasonally adjusted and covers workers 16 years of age and older; (1) Figures cover the Phoenix-Mesa-Scottsdale, AZ Metropolitan Statistical Area—see Appendix B for areas included
Source: Bureau of Labor Statistics, Local Area Unemployment Statistics

Unemployment Rate

Area	2015											
	Jan.	Feb.	Mar.	Apr.	May	Jun.	Jul.	Aug.	Sep.	Oct.	Nov.	Dec.
City	4.4	3.9	3.8	3.7	3.6	4.4	4.5	4.6	4.6	4.2	3.9	3.7
MSA[1]	5.8	5.4	4.8	4.8	4.6	5.4	5.7	5.8	5.5	5.2	5.0	4.7
U.S.	6.1	5.8	5.6	5.1	5.3	5.5	5.6	5.2	4.9	4.8	4.8	4.8

Note: Data is not seasonally adjusted and covers workers 16 years of age and older; (1) Figures cover the Phoenix-Mesa-Scottsdale, AZ Metropolitan Statistical Area—see Appendix B for areas included
Source: Bureau of Labor Statistics, Local Area Unemployment Statistics

Employment by Occupation

Occupation Classification	City (%)	MSA[1] (%)	U.S. (%)
Management, Business, Science, and Arts	44.3	36.2	36.4
Natural Resources, Construction, and Maintenance	5.7	8.5	9.0
Production, Transportation, and Material Moving	8.0	9.6	12.1
Sales and Office	29.3	27.1	24.4
Service	12.7	18.6	18.2

Note: Figures cover employed civilians 16 years of age and older; (1) Figures cover the Phoenix-Mesa-Scottsdale, AZ Metropolitan Statistical Area—see Appendix B for areas included
Source: U.S. Census Bureau, 2010-2014 American Community Survey 5-Year Estimates

Employment by Industry

Sector	MSA[1]		U.S.
	Number of Employees	Percent of Total	Percent of Total
Construction	101,200	5.0	4.5
Education and Health Services	291,900	14.7	15.7
Financial Activities	171,800	8.6	5.7
Government	239,500	12.0	15.5
Information	38,300	1.9	1.9
Leisure and Hospitality	210,900	10.6	10.4
Manufacturing	121,200	6.1	8.6
Mining and Logging	3,300	0.1	0.5
Other Services	65,700	3.3	3.9
Professional and Business Services	342,200	17.2	13.9
Retail Trade	246,700	12.4	11.3
Transportation, Warehousing, and Utilities	72,900	3.6	3.9
Wholesale Trade	79,100	3.9	4.1

Note: Figures are non-farm employment as of December 2015. Figures are not seasonally adjusted and include workers 16 years of age and older; (1) Figures cover the Phoenix-Mesa-Scottsdale, AZ Metropolitan Statistical Area—see Appendix B for areas included
Source: Bureau of Labor Statistics, Current Employment Statistics, Employment, Hours, and Earnings

Occupations with Greatest Projected Employment Growth: 2012 – 2022

Occupation[1]	2012 Employment	2022 Projected Employment	Numeric Employment Change	Percent Employment Change
Combined Food Preparation and Serving Workers, Including Fast Food	50,540	68,080	17,540	34.7
Customer Service Representatives	64,570	81,660	17,090	26.5
Retail Salespersons	88,270	102,400	14,130	16.0
Construction Laborers	28,290	42,000	13,710	48.5
Registered Nurses	48,660	61,130	12,470	25.6
Waiters and Waitresses	48,150	59,900	11,750	24.4
General and Operations Managers	46,340	57,660	11,320	24.4
Secretaries and Administrative Assistants, Except Legal, Medical, and Executive	45,880	56,340	10,460	22.8
Personal Care Aides	22,040	30,960	8,920	40.5
Office Clerks, General	49,260	58,180	8,920	18.1

Note: Projections cover Arizona; (1) Sorted by numeric employment change
Source: www.projectionscentral.com, State Occupational Projections, 2012–2022 Long-Term Projections

Fastest Growing Occupations: 2012 – 2022

Occupation[1]	2012 Employment	2022 Projected Employment	Numeric Employment Change	Percent Employment Change
Helpers—Brickmasons, Blockmasons, Stonemasons, and Tile and Marble Setters	370	610	240	65.9
Brickmasons and Blockmasons	840	1,370	530	63.5
Helpers—Electricians	790	1,280	490	61.6
Cement Masons and Concrete Finishers	4,000	6,210	2,210	55.2
Diagnostic Medical Sonographers	1,240	1,920	680	54.9
Tile and Marble Setters	1,370	2,130	760	54.9
Millwrights	400	610	210	54.7
Fence Erectors	370	570	200	54.5
Computer Numerically Controlled Machine Tool Programmers, Metal and Plastic	360	550	190	53.2
Solar Photovoltaic Installers	220	340	120	52.5

Note: Projections cover Arizona; (1) Sorted by percent employment change and excludes occupations with numeric employment change less than 100
Source: www.projectionscentral.com, State Occupational Projections, 2012–2022 Long-Term Projections

Average Wages

Occupation	$/Hr.	Occupation	$/Hr.
Accountants and Auditors	33.16	Maids and Housekeeping Cleaners	10.33
Automotive Mechanics	19.59	Maintenance and Repair Workers	17.82
Bookkeepers	18.26	Marketing Managers	57.96
Carpenters	19.55	Nuclear Medicine Technologists	37.87
Cashiers	10.31	Nurses, Licensed Practical	24.62
Clerks, General Office	16.85	Nurses, Registered	35.34
Clerks, Receptionists/Information	13.39	Nursing Assistants	14.21
Clerks, Shipping/Receiving	15.95	Packers and Packagers, Hand	11.28
Computer Programmers	39.92	Physical Therapists	40.14
Computer Systems Analysts	43.97	Postal Service Mail Carriers	24.88
Computer User Support Specialists	24.43	Real Estate Brokers	32.71
Cooks, Restaurant	11.50	Retail Salespersons	12.07
Dentists	75.56	Sales Reps., Exc. Tech./Scientific	29.63
Electrical Engineers	50.79	Sales Reps., Tech./Scientific	41.79
Electricians	23.49	Secretaries, Exc. Legal/Med./Exec.	17.04
Financial Managers	59.68	Security Guards	13.85
First-Line Supervisors/Managers, Sales	20.03	Surgeons	127.07
Food Preparation Workers	10.42	Teacher Assistants*	12.06
General and Operations Managers	51.00	Teachers, Elementary School*	20.48
Hairdressers/Cosmetologists	12.18	Teachers, Secondary School*	23.77
Internists	84.97	Telemarketers	13.83
Janitors and Cleaners	11.49	Truck Drivers, Heavy/Tractor-Trailer	20.26
Landscaping/Groundskeeping Workers	11.74	Truck Drivers, Light/Delivery Svcs.	16.21
Lawyers	63.45	Waiters and Waitresses	10.61

Note: Wage data covers the Phoenix-Mesa-Glendale, AZ Metropolitan Statistical Area—see Appendix B for areas included; (*) Hourly wages for elementary/secondary school teachers and teacher assistants were calculated by the editors from annual wage data based on a 40 hour work week; n/a not available.
Source: Bureau of Labor Statistics, Metro Area Occupational Employment and Wage Estimates, May 2015

TAXES

State Corporate Income Tax Rates

State	Tax Rate (%)	Income Brackets ($)	Num. of Brackets	Financial Institution Tax Rate (%)[a]	Federal Income Tax Ded.
Arizona	5.5 (b)	Flat rate	1	5.5 (b)	No

Note: Tax rates as of January 1, 2016; (a) Rates listed are the corporate income tax rate applied to financial institutions or excise taxes based on income. Some states have other taxes based upon the value of deposits or shares; (b) Arizona minimum tax is $100. Tax rate is scheduled to decrease to 4.9% in tax years 2017.
Source: Federation of Tax Administrators, "State Corporate Income Tax Rates, 2016"

State Individual Income Tax Rates

State	Tax Rate (%)	Income Brackets ($)	Num. of Brackets	Personal Exempt. ($)[1] Single	Personal Exempt. ($)[1] Dependents	Fed. Inc. Tax Ded.
Arizona (a)	2.59 - 4.54	10,163 - 152,434 (b)	5	2,100	2,300	No

Note: Tax rates as of January 1, 2016; Local- and county-level taxes are not included; n/a not applicable; (1) Married joint filers generally receive double the single exemption; (a) 18 states have statutory provision for automatically adjusting to the rate of inflation the dollar values of the income tax brackets, standard deductions, and/or personal exemptions. Massachusetts, Michigan, and Nebraska index the personal exemptiononly. Oregon does not index the income brackets for $125,000 and over. Maine has suspended indexing for 2014 and 2015; (b) For joint returns, taxes are twice the tax on half the couple's income.
Source: Federation of Tax Administrators, "State Individual Income Tax Rates, 2016"

Various State and Local Tax Rates

State	State and Local Sales and Use (%)	State Sales and Use (%)	Gasoline[1] (¢/gal.)	Cigarette[2] ($/pack)	Spirits[3] ($/gal.)	Wine[4] ($/gal.)	Beer[5] ($/gal.)
Arizona	8.55	5.6	19	2.00	3.00	0.84 (l)	0.35

Note: All tax rates as of January 1, 2016; (1) The American Petroleum Institute has developed a methodology for determining the average tax rate on a gallon of fuel. Rates may include any of the following: excise taxes, environmental fees, storage tank fees, other fees or taxes, general sales tax, and local taxes. In states where gasoline is subject to the general sales tax, or where the fuel tax is based on the average sale price, the average rate determined by API is sensitive to changes in the price of gasoline. States that fully or partially apply general sales taxes to gasoline: CA, CO, GA, IL, IN, MI, NY; (2) The federal excise tax of $1.0066 per pack and local taxes are not included; (3) Rates are those applicable to off-premise sales of 40% alcohol by volume (a.b.v.) distilled spirits in 750ml containers. Local excise taxes are excluded; (4) Rates are those applicable to off-premise sales of 11% a.b.v. non-carbonated wine in 750ml containers; (5) Rates are those applicable to off-premise sales of 4.7% a.b.v. beer in 12 ounce containers; (l) Different rates also applicable according to alcohol content, place of production, size of container, place purchased (on- or off-premise or on board airlines) or type of wine (carbonated, vermouth, etc.).
Source: Tax Foundation, 2016 Facts & Figures: How Does Your State Compare?

State Business Tax Climate Index Rankings

State	Overall Rank	Corporate Tax Rank	Individual Income Tax Rank	Sales Tax Rank	Unemployment Insurance Tax Rank	Property Tax Rank
Arizona	24	22	19	49	9	6

Note: The index is a measure of how each state's tax laws affect economic performance. The lower the rank, the more favorable a state's tax system is for business. States without a given tax are given a ranking of 1. The scores/rankings for the District of Columbia do not affect other states. The 2016 index represents the tax climate as of July 1, 2015 (the beginning of Fiscal Year 2016).
Source: Tax Foundation, State Business Tax Climate Index 2016

TRANSPORTATION

Means of Transportation to Work

Area	Car/Truck/Van		Public Transportation			Bicycle	Walked	Other Means	Worked at Home
	Drove Alone	Car-pooled	Bus	Subway	Railroad				
City	79.1	7.6	0.1	0.1	0.0	0.1	0.7	2.4	10.0
MSA[1]	76.6	11.3	2.0	0.0	0.0	0.8	1.5	1.8	5.9
U.S.	76.4	9.6	2.6	1.8	0.6	0.6	2.8	1.3	4.4

Note: Figures are percentages and cover workers 16 years of age and older; (1) Figures cover the Phoenix-Mesa-Scottsdale, AZ Metropolitan Statistical Area—see Appendix B for areas included
Source: U.S. Census Bureau, 2010-2014 American Community Survey 5-Year Estimates

Travel Time to Work

Area	Less Than 10 Minutes	10 to 19 Minutes	20 to 29 Minutes	30 to 44 Minutes	45 to 59 Minutes	60 to 89 Minutes	90 Minutes or More
City	9.0	12.7	23.5	28.7	16.3	7.7	2.1
MSA[1]	10.0	27.2	23.4	24.8	8.6	4.5	1.5
U.S.	13.3	29.6	21.0	20.2	7.7	5.7	2.6

Note: Figures are percentages and include workers 16 years old and over; (1) Figures cover the Phoenix-Mesa-Scottsdale, AZ Metropolitan Statistical Area—see Appendix B for areas included
Source: U.S. Census Bureau, 2010-2014 American Community Survey 5-Year Estimates

Freeway Travel Time Index

Area	1985	1990	1995	2000	2005	2010	2014
Urban Area Rank[1,2]	5	7	13	17	17	20	19
Urban Area Index[1]	1.20	1.21	1.22	1.25	1.28	1.26	1.27
Average Index[3]	1.09	1.11	1.14	1.17	1.20	1.19	1.20

Note: Freeway Travel Time Index—the ratio of travel time in the peak period to the travel time at free-flow conditions. For example, a value of 1.30 indicates a 20-minute free-flow trip takes 26 minutes in the peak (20 minutes x 1.30 = 26 minutes); (1) Covers the Phoenix-Mesa AZ urban area; (2) Rank is based on 101 urban areas (#1 = highest travel time index); (3) Average of 101 urban areas
Source: Texas Transportation Institute, 2015 Urban Mobility Scorecard, August 2015

Freeway Commuter Stress Index

Area	1985	1990	1995	2000	2005	2010	2014
Urban Area Rank[1,2]	14	17	19	20	18	25	27
Urban Area Index[1]	1.24	1.25	1.27	1.30	1.33	1.30	1.31
Average Index[3]	1.13	1.16	1.19	1.22	1.25	1.24	1.25

Note: The Freeway Commuter Stress Index is the same as the Freeway Travel Time Index (see table above) except that it includes only the travel in the peak directions during the peak periods; the TTI includes travel in all directions during the peak period. Thus, the CSI is more indicative of the work trip experienced by each commuter on a daily basis. (1) Covers the Phoenix-Mesa AZ urban area; (2) Rank is based on 101 urban areas (#1 = highest stress index); (3) Average of 101 urban areas

Source: Texas Transportation Institute, 2015 Urban Mobility Scorecard, August 2015

Living Environment

COST OF LIVING

Cost of Living Index

Composite Index	Groceries	Housing	Utilities	Transportation	Health Care	Misc. Goods/ Services
95.9	98.5	95.1	96.7	99.8	97.2	93.9

Note: The Cost of Living Index measures regional differences in the cost of consumer goods and services, excluding taxes and non-consumer expenditures, for professional and managerial households in the top income quintile. It is based on more than 50,000 prices covering almost 60 different items for which prices are collected three times a year by chambers of commerce, economic development organizations or university applied economic centers in each participating urban area. The numbers shown should be read as a percentage above or below the national average of 100. For example, a value of 115.4 in the groceries column indicates that grocery prices are 15.4% higher than the national average. Small differences in the index numbers should not be interpreted as significant; Figures cover the Phoenix AZ urban area.
Source: The Council for Community and Economic Research, ACCRA Cost of Living Index, 2015

Grocery Prices

Area[1]	T-Bone Steak ($/pound)	Frying Chicken ($/pound)	Whole Milk ($/half gal.)	Eggs ($/dozen)	Orange Juice ($/64 oz.)	Coffee ($/11.5 oz.)
City[2]	11.14	1.83	1.73	2.12	3.69	4.68
Avg.	10.99	1.43	2.25	2.26	3.58	4.48
Min.	7.16	0.98	1.30	1.35	2.88	2.98
Max.	14.13	2.43	3.85	4.81	6.39	7.56

Note: (1) Values for the local area are compared with the average, minimum and maximum values for all 292 areas in the Cost of Living Index; (2) Figures cover the Phoenix AZ urban area; **T-Bone Steak** *(price per pound);* **Frying Chicken** *(price per pound, whole fryer);* **Whole Milk** *(half gallon carton);* **Eggs** *(price per dozen, Grade A, large);* **Orange Juice** *(64 oz. Tropicana or Florida Natural);* **Coffee** *(11.5 oz. can, vacuum-packed, Maxwell House, Hills Bros, or Folgers).*
Source: The Council for Community and Economic Research, ACCRA Cost of Living Index, 2015

Housing and Utility Costs

Area[1]	New Home Price ($)	Apartment Rent ($/month)	All Electric ($/month)	Part Electric ($/month)	Other Energy ($/month)	Telephone ($/month)
City[2]	292,558	880	194.92	-	-	19.99
Avg.	312,874	945	179.30	95.07	72.96	28.11
Min.	178,682	479	116.28	43.14	26.46	10.01
Max.	1,472,476	3,984	504.25	189.44	421.11	43.06

Note: (1) Values for the local area are compared with the average, minimum and maximum values for all 292 areas in the Cost of Living Index; (2) Figures cover the Phoenix AZ urban area; **New Home Price** *(2,400 sf living area, 8,000 sf lot, in urban area with full utilities);* **Apartment Rent** *(950 sf 2 bedroom/1.5 or 2 bath, unfurnished, excluding all utilities except water);* **All Electric** *(average monthly cost for an all-electric home);* **Part Electric** *(average monthly cost for a part-electric home);* **Other Energy** *(average monthly cost for natural gas, fuel oil, coal, wood, and any other forms of energy except electricity);* **Telephone** *(price includes basic monthly rate for a private residential line plus additional local usage charges incurred by a family of four).*
Source: The Council for Community and Economic Research, ACCRA Cost of Living Index, 2015

Health Care, Transportation, and Other Costs

Area[1]	Doctor ($/visit)	Dentist ($/visit)	Optometrist ($/visit)	Gasoline ($/gallon)	Beauty Salon ($/visit)	Men's Shirt ($)
City[2]	97.83	98.67	84.67	2.49	28.33	23.10
Avg.	105.15	89.02	99.78	2.38	35.30	28.10
Min.	66.87	56.09	48.53	1.95	18.91	13.38
Max.	182.34	150.36	228.33	4.09	67.91	63.80

Note: (1) Values for the local area are compared with the average, minimum and maximum values for all 292 areas in the Cost of Living Index; (2) Figures cover the Phoenix AZ urban area; **Doctor** *(general practitioners routine exam of an established patient);* **Dentist** *(adult teeth cleaning and periodic oral examination);* **Optometrist** *(full vision eye exam for established adult patient);* **Gasoline** *(one gallon regular unleaded, national brand, including all taxes, cash price at self-service pump if available);* **Beauty Salon** *(woman's shampoo, trim, and blow-dry);* **Men's Shirt** *(cotton/polyester dress shirt, pinpoint weave, long sleeves).*
Source: The Council for Community and Economic Research, ACCRA Cost of Living Index, 2015

HOUSING

House Price Index (HPI)

Area	National Ranking[2]	Quarterly Change (%)	One-Year Change (%)	Five-Year Change (%)
MSA[1]	55	0.80	7.70	43.60
U.S.[3]	–	1.45	5.76	22.85

Note: The HPI is a weighted repeat sales index. It measures average price changes in repeat sales or refinancings on the same properties. This information is obtained by reviewing repeat mortgage transactions on single-family properties whose mortgages have been purchased or securitized by Fannie Mae or Freddie Mac in January 1975; (1) Phoenix-Mesa-Scottsdale Metropolitan Statistical Area—see Appendix B for areas included; (2) Rankings are based on annual percentage change for all metro areas containing at least 15,000 transactions over the last 10 years and ranges from 1 to 266; (3) figures based on a weighted average of Census Division estimates using a seasonally adjusted, purchase-only index; all figures are for the period ending December 31, 2015

Source: Federal Housing Finance Agency, House Price Index, February 25, 2016

Median Single-Family Home Prices

Area	2013	2014	2015[p]	Percent Change 2014 to 2015
MSA[1]	183.6	198.5	216.4	9.0
U.S. Average	197.4	208.9	223.9	7.2

Note: Figures are median sales prices of existing single-family homes in thousands of dollars; (p) preliminary; n/a not available; (1) Phoenix-Mesa-Scottsdale, AZ Metropolitan Statistical Area—see Appendix B for areas included

Source: National Association of Realtors, Median Sales Price of Existing Single-Family Homes for Metropolitan Areas, 4th Quarter 2015

Qualifying Income Based on Median Sales Price of Existing Single-Family Homes

Area	With 5% Down ($)	With 10% Down ($)	With 20% Down ($)
MSA[1]	49,157	46,570	41,395
U.S. Average	49,535	46,928	41,714

Note: Figures are preliminary; Qualifying income is based on a mortgage rate of 4.1%. Monthly principal and interest payment is limited to 25% of income; n/a not available; (1) Phoenix-Mesa-Scottsdale, AZ Metropolitan Statistical Area—see Appendix B for areas included

Source: National Association of Realtors, Qualifying Income Based on Median Sales Price of Existing Single-Family Homes for Metropolitan Areas, 4th Quarter 2015

Median Apartment Condo-Coop Home Prices

Area	2013	2014	2015[p]	Percent Change 2014 to 2015
MSA[1]	105.0	109.1	121.2	11.1
U.S. Average	194.9	204.3	210.7	3.1

Note: Figures are median sales prices of existing apartment condo-coop homes in thousands of dollars; (p) preliminary; n/a not available; (1) Phoenix-Mesa-Scottsdale, AZ Metropolitan Statistical Area—see Appendix B for areas included

Source: National Association of Realtors, Median Sales Price of Existing Apartment Condo-Coop Homes for Metropolitan Areas, 4th Quarter 2015

Gross Monthly Rent

Area	Under $200	$200 -299	$300 -499	$500 -749	$750 -999	$1,000 -1,499	$1,500 and up	Median ($)
City	0.0	0.0	1.5	1.9	16.3	41.5	38.8	1,305
MSA[1]	0.6	1.1	4.1	21.0	27.9	32.6	12.7	953
U.S.	1.5	3.2	7.4	21.0	24.1	26.9	15.9	920

Note: Figures are percentages except for Median; Gross rent is the contract rent plus the estimated average monthly cost of utilities (electricity, gas, and water and sewer) and fuels (oil, coal, kerosene, wood, etc.) if these are paid by the renter (or paid for the renter by someone else); (1) Figures cover the Phoenix-Mesa-Scottsdale, AZ Metropolitan Statistical Area—see Appendix B for areas included

Source: U.S. Census Bureau, 2010-2014 American Community Survey 5-Year Estimates

Homeownership Rate

Area	2008 (%)	2009 (%)	2010 (%)	2011 (%)	2012 (%)	2013 (%)	2014 (%)	2015 (%)
MSA[1]	70.2	69.8	66.5	63.3	63.1	62.2	61.9	61.0
U.S.	67.8	67.4	66.9	66.1	65.4	65.1	64.5	63.7

Note: (1) Figures cover the Phoenix-Mesa-Scottsdale, AZ Metropolitan Statistical Area—see Appendix B for areas included
Source: U.S. Census Bureau, Housing Vacancies and Homeownership Annual Statistics: 2015

Year Housing Structure Built

Area	2010 or Later	2000 -2009	1990 -1999	1980 -1989	1970 -1979	1960 -1969	1950 -1959	1940 -1949	Before 1940	Median Year
City	3.5	82.9	6.4	3.7	1.6	0.5	0.9	0.4	0.2	2004
MSA[1]	1.0	28.0	20.9	18.3	16.8	7.0	5.5	1.4	1.0	1990
U.S.	1.0	14.9	13.9	13.8	15.8	11.0	10.8	5.4	13.3	1976

Note: Figures are percentages except for Median Year; (1) Figures cover the Phoenix-Mesa-Scottsdale, AZ Metropolitan Statistical Area—see Appendix B for areas included
Source: U.S. Census Bureau, 2010-2014 American Community Survey 5-Year Estimates

HEALTH

Health Risk Data

Category	MSA[1] (%)	U.S. (%)
Adults aged 18–64 who have any kind of health care coverage	75.3	79.6
Adults who reported being in good or excellent health	83.2	83.1
Adults who are current smokers	16.9	19.6
Adults who are heavy drinkers[2]	5.0	6.1
Adults who are binge drinkers[3]	15.5	16.9
Adults who are overweight (BMI 25.0 - 29.9)	35.8	35.8
Adults who are obese (BMI 30.0 - 99.8)	25.3	27.6
Adults who participated in any physical activities in the past month	77.3	77.1
Adults 50+ who have ever had a sigmoidoscopy or colonoscopy	63.0	67.3
Women aged 40+ who have had a mammogram within the past two years	68.5	74.0
Men aged 40+ who have had a PSA test within the past two years	44.4	45.2
Adults aged 65+ who have had flu shot within the past year	54.1	60.1
Adults who always wear a seatbelt	94.3	93.8

Note: Data as of 2012 unless otherwise noted; (1) Figures cover the Phoenix-Mesa-Scottsdale, AZ Metropolitan Statistical Area—see Appendix B for areas included; (2) Heavy drinkers are classified as males having more than two drinks per day or females having more than one drink per day; (3) Binge drinkers are classified as males having five or more drinks on one occasion or females having four or more drinks on one occasion
Source: Centers for Disease Control and Prevention, Behaviorial Risk Factor Surveillance System, SMART: Selected Metropolitan/Micropolitan Area Risk Trends, 2012 (Note: the CDC has discontinued this dataset but will be releasing a replacement in mid-2016)

Chronic Health Indicators

Category	MSA[1] (%)	U.S. (%)
Adults who have ever been told they had a heart attack	4.7	4.5
Adults who have ever been told they had a stroke	2.6	2.9
Adults who have been told they currently have asthma	8.6	8.9
Adults who have ever been told they have arthritis	23.8	25.7
Adults who have ever been told they have diabetes[2]	9.8	9.7
Adults who have ever been told they had skin cancer	6.5	5.7
Adults who have ever been told they had any other types of cancer	6.2	6.5
Adults who have ever been told they have COPD	5.5	6.2
Adults who have ever been told they have kidney disease	3.5	2.5
Adults who have ever been told they have a form of depression	18.2	18.0

Note: Data as of 2012 unless otherwise noted; (1) Figures cover the Phoenix-Mesa-Scottsdale, AZ Metropolitan Statistical Area—see Appendix B for areas included; (2) Figures do not include pregnancy-related, borderline, or pre-diabetes
Source: Centers for Disease Control and Prevention, Behaviorial Risk Factor Surveillance System, SMART: Selected Metropolitan/Micropolitan Area Risk Trends, 2012 (Note: the CDC has discontinued this dataset but will be releasing a replacement in mid-2016)

Mortality Rates for the Top 10 Causes of Death in the U.S.

ICD-10[a] Sub-Chapter	ICD-10[a] Code	Age-Adjusted Mortality Rate[1] per 100,000 population	
		County[2]	U.S.
Malignant neoplasms	C00-C97	144.1	163.6
Ischaemic heart diseases	I20-I25	92.9	102.2
Other forms of heart disease	I30-I51	23.0	50.1
Chronic lower respiratory diseases	J40-J47	42.1	41.4
Organic, including symptomatic, mental disorders	F01-F09	24.3	38.5
Cerebrovascular diseases	I60-I69	28.3	36.5
Other external causes of accidental injury	W00-X59	31.0	27.5
Other degenerative diseases of the nervous system	G30-G31	39.0	26.3
Diabetes mellitus	E10-E14	23.1	21.1
Hypertensive diseases	I10-I15	25.8	19.7

Note: (a) ICD-10 = International Classification of Diseases 10th Revision; (1) Mortality rates are a three year average covering 2012-2014; (2) Figures cover COUNTY NOT FOUND!!!!!!.
Source: Centers for Disease Control and Prevention, National Center for Health Statistics. Underlying Cause of Death 1999-2014 on CDC WONDER Online Database, released 2015.

Mortality Rates for Selected Causes of Death

ICD-10[a] Sub-Chapter	ICD-10[a] Code	Age-Adjusted Mortality Rate[1] per 100,000 population	
		County[2]	U.S.
Assault	X85-Y09	5.3	5.1
Diseases of the liver	K70-K76	13.5	13.5
Human immunodeficiency virus (HIV) disease	B20-B24	1.7	2.1
Influenza and pneumonia	J09-J18	7.5	15.2
Intentional self-harm	X60-X84	15.5	12.7
Malnutrition	E40-E46	0.5	0.9
Obesity and other hyperalimentation	E65-E68	2.4	1.9
Renal failure	N17-N19	2.5	13.0
Transport accidents	V01-V99	10.5	11.6
Viral hepatitis	B15-B19	3.9	2.1

Note: (a) ICD-10 = International Classification of Diseases 10th Revision; (1) Mortality rates are a three year average covering 2012-2014; (2) Figures cover COUNTY NOT FOUND!!!!!!; Data are Suppressed when the data meet the criteria for confidentiality constraints; Mortality rates are flagged as Unreliable when the rate would be calculated with a numerator of 20 or less.
Source: Centers for Disease Control and Prevention, National Center for Health Statistics. Underlying Cause of Death 1999-2014 on CDC WONDER Online Database, released 2015.

Health Insurance Coverage

Area	With Health Insurance	With Private Health Insurance	With Public Health Insurance	Without Health Insurance	Population Under Age 18 Without Health Insurance
City	95.4	86.0	16.0	4.6	3.5
MSA[1]	83.7	62.3	31.4	16.3	11.4
U.S.	85.8	65.8	31.1	14.2	7.1

Note: Figures are percentages that cover the civilian noninstitutionalized population; (1) Figures cover the Phoenix-Mesa-Scottsdale, AZ Metropolitan Statistical Area—see Appendix B for areas included
Source: U.S. Census Bureau, 2010-2014 American Community Survey 5-Year Estimates

Number of Medical Professionals

Area	MDs[3]	DOs[3,4]	Dentists	Podiatrists	Chiropractors	Optometrists
County[1] (number)	9,486	1,299	2,602	243	1,381	563
County[1] (rate[2])	236.4	32.4	63.7	5.9	33.8	13.8
U.S. (rate[2])	272.5	20.9	64.7	5.8	25.9	15.2

Note: Data as of 2014 unless noted; (1) Data covers Maricopa County; (2) Rate per 100,000 population; (3) Data as of 2013 and includes all active, non-federal physicians; (4) Doctor of Osteopathic Medicine
Source: U.S. Department of Health and Human Services, Health Resources and Services Administration, Bureau of Health Professions, Area Resource File (ARF) 2014-2015

Best Hospitals

According to *U.S. News,* the Phoenix-Mesa-Scottsdale, AZ metro area is home to four of the best hospitals in the U.S.: **Banner Estrella Medical Center** (1 specialty); **Banner Good Samaritan Medical Center** (4 specialties); **Mayo Clinic** (12 specialties); **St. Joseph's Hospital and Medical Center** (1 specialty). The hospitals listed were nationally ranked in at least one adult specialty. Only 137 hospitals nationwide were nationally ranked in one or more specialties. Fifteen hospitals in the U.S. made the Honor Roll with high scores in at least six specialties. *U.S. News Online, "America's Best Children's Hospitals 2015-16"*

According to *U.S. News,* the Phoenix-Mesa-Scottsdale, AZ metro area is home to one of the best children's hospitals in the U.S.: **Phoenix Children's Hospital** (9 specialties). The hospital listed was highly ranked in at least one pediatric specialty. Eighty-three children's hospitals in the U.S. were nationally ranked in at least one specialty. Twelve children's hospitals in the U.S. made the Honor Roll with high scores in at least three specialties. *U.S. News Online, "America's Best Children's Hospitals 2015-16"*

EDUCATION

Public School District Statistics

District Name	Schls	Pupils	Pupil/ Teacher Ratio	Minority Pupils[1] (%)	Free Lunch Eligible[2] (%)	IEP[3] (%)
American Leadership Academy	5	3,111	n/a	24.3	9.5	7.7
Benjamin Franklin Charter School	5	2,549	n/a	20.1	n/a	6.9
Cambridge Academy East Inc	2	568	n/a	29.8	n/a	10.4
Chandler Unified District #80	42	41,257	19.5	44.1	25.2	11.8
Coolidge Unified District	7	3,693	21.4	67.7	64.4	12.9
East Valley Institute of Tech	48	126	1.8	45.2	n/a	n/a
Eduprize Schools LLC	3	3,748	n/a	26.1	3.8	8.6
Heritage Academy Inc.	2	699	n/a	19.5	n/a	4.6
Higley Unified School District	13	11,251	21.4	32.8	15.3	11.3
J O Combs USD	7	4,510	24.1	39.0	35.0	15.3
Lead Charter Schools	4	495	n/a	28.1	17.0	16.0
Leading Edge Academy	2	336	n/a	41.4	15.2	11.6
Legacy Traditional Charter	3	2,108	n/a	28.9	n/a	4.6
Patriot Academy Inc.	1	106	n/a	31.1	n/a	1.9
Queen Creek Unified District	7	5,051	20.0	31.1	25.9	12.9

Note: Table includes school districts with 100 or more students; (1) Percentage of students that are not non-Hispanic white; (2) Percentage of students that are eligible for the free lunch program; (3) Percentage of students that have an Individualized Education Program.
Source: U.S. Department of Education, National Center for Education Statistics, Common Core of Data, Local Education Agency (School District) Universe Survey: School Year 2013-2014; U.S. Department of Education, National Center for Education Statistics, Common Core of Data, Public Elementary/Secondary School Universe Survey: School Year 2013-2014

Highest Level of Education

Area	Less than H.S.	H.S. Diploma	Some College, No Deg.	Associate Degree	Bachelor's Degree	Master's Degree	Prof. School Degree	Doctorate Degree
City	4.0	16.2	29.4	12.7	25.7	8.6	2.0	1.4
MSA[1]	13.6	23.9	25.3	8.5	18.6	7.5	1.8	1.1
U.S.	13.7	28.0	21.2	7.9	18.3	7.8	2.0	1.3

Note: Figures cover persons age 25 and over; (1) Figures cover the Phoenix-Mesa-Scottsdale, AZ Metropolitan Statistical Area—see Appendix B for areas included
Source: U.S. Census Bureau, 2010-2014 American Community Survey 5-Year Estimates

Educational Attainment by Race

Area	High School Graduate or Higher (%)					Bachelor's Degree or Higher (%)				
	Total	White	Black	Asian	Hisp.[2]	Total	White	Black	Asian	Hisp.[2]
City	96.0	97.0	90.2	96.1	90.1	37.7	38.5	38.8	66.1	24.3
MSA[1]	86.4	87.9	88.8	87.5	63.4	28.8	29.7	22.7	53.0	10.6
U.S.	86.3	88.4	83.2	85.8	64.1	29.3	30.6	19.0	50.9	13.9

Note: Figures shown cover persons 25 years old and over; (1) Figures cover the Phoenix-Mesa-Scottsdale, AZ Metropolitan Statistical Area—see Appendix B for areas included; (2) People of Hispanic origin can be of any race
Source: U.S. Census Bureau, 2010-2014 American Community Survey 5-Year Estimates

School Enrollment by Grade and Control

Area	Preschool (%)		Kindergarten (%)		Grades 1 - 4 (%)		Grades 5 - 8 (%)		Grades 9 - 12 (%)	
	Public	Private	Public	Private	Public	Private	Public	Private	Public	Private
City	38.0	62.0	97.4	2.6	90.8	9.2	89.9	10.1	82.8	17.2
MSA[1]	58.0	42.0	92.0	8.0	92.8	7.2	94.4	5.6	94.0	6.0
U.S.	57.4	42.6	87.8	12.2	89.8	10.2	89.9	10.1	90.6	9.4

Note: Figures shown cover persons 3 years old and over; (1) Figures cover the Phoenix-Mesa-Scottsdale, AZ Metropolitan Statistical Area—see Appendix B for areas included
Source: U.S. Census Bureau, 2010-2014 American Community Survey 5-Year Estimates

Average Salaries of Public School Classroom Teachers

Area	2013-14		2014-15		Percent Change 2013-14 to 2014-15	Percent Change 2004-05 to 2014-15
	Dollars	Rank[1]	Dollars	Rank[1]		
Arizona	45,335	45	45,406	47	0.16	13.4
U.S. Average	56,610	–	57,379	–	1.36	20.8

Note: (1) State rank ranges from 1 to 51 where 1 indicates highest salary.
Source: National Education Association, Rankings & Estimates: Rankings of the States 2014 and Estimates of School Statistics 2015, March 2015

Higher Education

Four-Year Colleges			Two-Year Colleges			Medical Schools[1]	Law Schools[2]	Voc/ Tech[3]
Public	Private Non-profit	Private For-profit	Public	Private Non-profit	Private For-profit			
0	0	0	0	0	0	0	0	0

Note: Figures cover institutions located within the city limits and include main campuses only; (1) includes schools accredited by the Liaison Committee on Medical Education and the American Osteopathic Association's Commission on Osteopathic College Accreditation; (2) includes ABA-accredited schools, schools with provisional ABA accreditation, and state accredited schools; (3) includes all schools with programs that are less than 2 years.
Source: National Center for Education Statistics, Integrated Postsecondary Education System (IPEDS), 2014-15; Association of American Medical Colleges, Member List, March 21, 2016; American Osteopathic Association, Member List, March 21, 2016; Law School Admission Council, Official Guide to ABA-Approved Law Schools Online, March 21, 2016; Wikipedia, List of Medical Schools in the United States, March 21, 2016; Wikipedia, List of Law Schools in the United States, March 21, 2016

According to *U.S. News & World Report,* the Phoenix-Mesa-Scottsdale, AZ metro area is home to one of the best national universities in the U.S.: **Arizona State University–Tempe** (#129 tie). The indicators used to capture academic quality fall into a number of categories: assessment by administrators at peer institutions; retention of students; faculty resources; student selectivity; financial resources; alumni giving; high school counselor ratings of colleges; and graduation rate. *U.S. News & World Report, "America's Best Colleges 2016"*

According to *U.S. News & World Report,* the Phoenix-Mesa-Scottsdale, AZ metro area is home to one of the top 100 law schools in the U.S.: **Arizona State University, Sandra Day O'Connor College of Law** (#25 tie). The rankings are based on a weighted average of 12 measures of quality: peer assessment score; assessment score by lawyers/judges; median LSAT scores; median undergrad GPA; acceptance rate; employment rates for graduates; placement success; bar passage rate; faculty resources; expenditures per student; student/faculty ratio; and library resources. *U.S. News & World Report, "America's Best Graduate Schools, Law, 2017"*

According to *U.S. News & World Report,* the Phoenix-Mesa-Scottsdale, AZ metro area is home to one of the top 75 business schools in the U.S.: **Arizona State University, W. P. Carey School of Business** (#35 tie). The rankings are based on a weighted average of the following nine measures: quality assessment; peer assessment; recruiter assessment; placement success; mean starting salary and bonus; student selectivity; mean GMAT and GRE scores; mean undergraduate GPA; and acceptance rate. *U.S. News & World Report, "America's Best Graduate Schools, Business, 2017"*

PRESIDENTIAL ELECTION

2012 Presidential Election Results

Area	Obama (%)	Romney (%)	Other (%)
Maricopa County	43.1	54.9	2.0
U.S.	51.0	47.2	1.8

Note: Results may not add to 100% due to rounding
Source: Dave Leip's Atlas of U.S. Presidential Elections

EMPLOYERS

Major Employers

Company Name	Industry
Arizona Dept of Transportation	Regulation, administration of transportation
Arizona State University	University
Avnet	Electronic parts & equipment, nec
Carter & Burgess	Engineering services
Chase Bankcard Services	State commercial banks
City of Mesa	Executive offices
City of Phoenix	Administration of social & human resources
General Dynamics C4 Systems	Communications equipment, nec
Grand Canyon Education	Colleges & universities
Honeywell International	Aircraft engines & engine parts
Lockheed Martin Corporation	Search & navigation equipment
Paramount Building Solutions	Janitorial service, contract basis
Salt River Pima-Maricopa Indian Community	Gambling establishment
Scottsdale Healthcare Corp.	Hospital management
Scottsdale Healthcare Osborn Med Ctr	General medical & surgical hospitals
Swift Transportation Company	Trucking, except local
The Boeing Company	Helicopters
Veterans Health Administration	General medical & surgical hospitals

Note: Companies shown are located within the Phoenix-Mesa-Scottsdale, AZ Metropolitan Statistical Area.
Source: Hoovers.com; Wikipedia

PUBLIC SAFETY

Crime Rate

Area	All Crimes	Violent Crimes				Property Crimes		
		Murder	Rape[3]	Robbery	Aggrav. Assault	Burglary	Larceny -Theft	Motor Vehicle Theft
City	n/a	n/a	n/a	n/a	n/a	n/a	n/a	n/a
Metro[1]	n/a	4.8	29.5	115.3	242.8	731.0	2,219.4	n/a
U.S.	3,108.6	4.5	35.9	109.0	229.6	610.5	1,901.9	221.3

Note: Figures are crimes per 100,000 population; (1) Figures cover the Phoenix-Mesa-Scottsdale, AZ Metropolitan Statistical Area—see Appendix B for areas included; n/a not available; (3) The city and U.S. figures shown were reported using the revised Uniform Crime Reporting (UCR) definition of rape. The suburban and metro area figures shown are an aggregate total of the data submitted using both the revised and legacy UCR definitions.
Source: FBI Uniform Crime Reports, 2013 (data for 2014 was not available)

Hate Crimes

Area	Number of Quarters Reported	Number of Incidents per Bias Motivation						
		Race	Religion	Sexual Orientation	Ethnicity	Disability	Gender	Gender Identity
City	n/a	n/a	n/a	n/a	n/a	n/a	n/a	n/a
U.S.	4	2,568	1,014	1,017	648	84	33	98

Note: n/a not available.
Source: Federal Bureau of Investigation, Hate Crime Statistics 2014

Identity Theft Consumer Complaints

Area	Complaints	Complaints per 100,000 Population	Rank[2]
MSA[1]	6,534	145.6	62
U.S.	490,220	152.4	-

Note: (1) Figures cover the Phoenix-Mesa-Scottsdale, AZ Metropolitan Statistical Area—see Appendix B for areas included; (2) Rank ranges from 1 to 379 where 1 indicates greatest number of identity theft complaints per 100,000 population
Source: Federal Trade Commission, Consumer Sentinel Network Data Book for January–December 2015

Fraud and Other Consumer Complaints

Area	Complaints	Complaints per 100,000 Population	Rank[2]
MSA[1]	20,978	467.3	34
U.S.	2,593,159	806.0	-

Note: (1) Figures cover the Phoenix-Mesa-Scottsdale, AZ Metropolitan Statistical Area—see Appendix B for areas included; (2) Rank ranges from 1 to 379 where 1 indicates greatest number of identity theft complaints per 100,000 population
Source: Federal Trade Commission, Consumer Sentinel Network Data Book for January–December 2015

RECREATION

Culture

Dance[1]	Theatre[1]	Instrumental Music[1]	Vocal Music[1]	Series and Festivals	Museums and Art Galleries[2]	Zoos and Aquariums[3]
0	0	0	0	0	0	0

Note: (1) Professional perfoming groups; (2) Based on organizations with SIC code 8412; (3) AZA-accredited
Source: The Grey House Performing Arts Directory, 2015-16; Association of Zoos & Aquariums, AZA Member Zoos & Aquariums, March 25, 2016; www.AccuLeads.com, March 29, 2016

Professional Sports Teams

Team Name	League	Year Established
Arizona Cardinals	National Football League (NFL)	1988
Arizona Diamondbacks	Major League Baseball (MLB)	1998
Phoenix Coyotes	National Hockey League (NHL)	1996
Phoenix Suns	National Basketball Association (NBA)	1968

Note: Includes teams located in the Phoenix-Mesa-Scottsdale, AZ Metropolitan Statistical Area.
Source: Wikipedia, Major Professional Sports Teams of the United States and Canada, March 24, 2016

CLIMATE

Average and Extreme Temperatures

Temperature	Jan	Feb	Mar	Apr	May	Jun	Jul	Aug	Sep	Oct	Nov	Dec	Yr.
Extreme High (°F)	88	92	100	105	113	122	118	116	118	107	93	88	122
Average High (°F)	66	70	75	84	93	103	105	103	99	88	75	67	86
Average Temp. (°F)	53	57	62	70	78	88	93	91	85	74	62	54	72
Average Low (°F)	40	44	48	55	63	72	80	78	72	60	48	41	59
Extreme Low (°F)	17	22	25	37	40	51	66	61	47	34	27	22	17

Note: Figures cover the years 1948-1990
Source: National Climatic Data Center, International Station Meteorological Climate Summary, 9/96

Average Precipitation/Snowfall/Humidity

Precip./Humidity	Jan	Feb	Mar	Apr	May	Jun	Jul	Aug	Sep	Oct	Nov	Dec	Yr.
Avg. Precip. (in.)	0.7	0.6	0.8	0.3	0.1	0.1	0.8	1.0	0.7	0.6	0.6	0.9	7.3
Avg. Snowfall (in.)	Tr	Tr	0	0	0	0	0	0	0	0	0	Tr	Tr
Avg. Rel. Hum. 5am (%)	68	63	56	45	37	33	47	53	50	53	59	66	53
Avg. Rel. Hum. 5pm (%)	34	28	24	17	14	12	21	24	23	24	28	34	24

Note: Figures cover the years 1948-1990; Tr = Trace amounts (<0.05 in. of rain; <0.5 in. of snow)
Source: National Climatic Data Center, International Station Meteorological Climate Summary, 9/96

Weather Conditions

Temperature			Daytime Sky			Precipitation		
10°F & below	32°F & below	90°F & above	Clear	Partly cloudy	Cloudy	0.01 inch or more precip.	0.1 inch or more snow/ice	Thunder-storms
0	10	167	186	125	54	37	< 1	23

Note: Figures are average number of days per year and cover the years 1948-1990
Source: National Climatic Data Center, International Station Meteorological Climate Summary, 9/96

HAZARDOUS WASTE

Superfund Sites

Queen Creek has no sites on the EPA's Superfund Final National Priorities List. There are a total of 1,323 Superfund sites on the list in the U.S. *U.S. Environmental Protection Agency, Final National Priorities List, March 18, 2016*

AIR & WATER QUALITY

Air Quality Trends: Ozone

	1990	1995	2000	2005	2010	2011	2012	2013	2014
MSA[1]	0.080	0.087	0.082	0.077	0.076	0.077	0.080	0.076	0.075

Note: (1) Data covers the Phoenix-Mesa-Scottsdale, AZ Metropolitan Statistical Area—see Appendix B for areas included. The values shown are the composite ozone concentration averages among trend sites based on the highest fourth daily maximum 8-hour concentration in parts per million. These trends are based on sites having an adequate record of monitoring data during the trend period. Data from exceptional events are included.
Source: U.S. Environmental Protection Agency, Air Quality Monitoring Information, "Air Quality Trends by City, 1990-2014"

Air Quality Index

Area	Percent of Days when Air Quality was...[2]					AQI Statistics[2]	
	Good	Moderate	Unhealthy for Sensitive Groups	Unhealthy	Very Unhealthy	Maximum	Median
MSA[1]	18.6	71.2	6.6	0.8	2.7	881	66

Note: (1) Data covers the Phoenix-Mesa-Scottsdale, AZ Metropolitan Statistical Area—see Appendix B for areas included; (2) Based on 365 days with AQI data in 2015. Air Quality Index (AQI) is an index for reporting daily air quality. EPA calculates the AQI for five major air pollutants regulated by the Clean Air Act: ground-level ozone, particle pollution (aka particulate matter), carbon monoxide, sulfur dioxide, and nitrogen dioxide. The AQI runs from 0 to 500. The higher the AQI value, the greater the level of air pollution and the greater the health concern. There are six AQI categories: "Good" AQI is between 0 and 50. Air quality is considered satisfactory; "Moderate" AQI is between 51 and 100. Air quality is acceptable; "Unhealthy for Sensitive Groups" When AQI values are between 101 and 150, members of sensitive groups may experience health effects; "Unhealthy" When AQI values are between 151 and 200 everyone may begin to experience health effects; "Very Unhealthy" AQI values between 201 and 300 trigger a health alert; "Hazardous" AQI values over 300 trigger warnings of emergency conditions (not shown).
Source: U.S. Environmental Protection Agency, Air Quality Index Report, 2015

Air Quality Index Pollutants

Area	Percent of Days when AQI Pollutant was...[2]					
	Carbon Monoxide	Nitrogen Dioxide	Ozone	Sulfur Dioxide	Particulate Matter 2.5	Particulate Matter 10
MSA[1]	0.0	3.8	31.0	0.0	24.7	40.5

Note: (1) Data covers the Phoenix-Mesa-Scottsdale, AZ Metropolitan Statistical Area—see Appendix B for areas included; (2) Based on 365 days with AQI data in 2015. The Air Quality Index (AQI) is an index for reporting daily air quality. EPA calculates the AQI for five major air pollutants regulated by the Clean Air Act: ground-level ozone, particle pollution (also known as particulate matter), carbon monoxide, sulfur dioxide, and nitrogen dioxide. The AQI runs from 0 to 500. The higher the AQI value, the greater the level of air pollution and the greater the health concern.
Source: U.S. Environmental Protection Agency, Air Quality Index Report, 2015

Maximum Air Pollutant Concentrations: Particulate Matter, Ozone, CO and Lead

	Particulate Matter 10 (ug/m³)	Particulate Matter 2.5 Wtd AM (ug/m³)	Particulate Matter 2.5 24-Hr (ug/m³)	Ozone (ppm)	Carbon Monoxide (ppm)	Lead (ug/m³)
MSA[1] Level	985	10.9	37	0.08	3	0.05
NAAQS[2]	150	15	35	0.075	9	0.15
Met NAAQS[2]	No	Yes	No	No	Yes	Yes

Note: (1) Data covers the Phoenix-Mesa-Scottsdale, AZ Metropolitan Statistical Area—see Appendix B for areas included; Data from exceptional events are included; (2) National Ambient Air Quality Standards; ppm = parts per million; ug/m³ = micrograms per cubic meter; n/a not available.
Concentrations: Particulate Matter 10 (coarse particulate)—highest second maximum 24-hour concentration; Particulate Matter 2.5 Wtd AM (fine particulate)—highest weighted annual mean concentration; Particulate Matter 2.5 24-Hour (fine particulate)—highest 98th percentile 24-hour concentration; Ozone—highest fourth daily maximum 8-hour concentration; Carbon Monoxide—highest second maximum non-overlapping 8-hour concentration; Lead—maximum running 3-month average
Source: U.S. Environmental Protection Agency, Air Quality Monitoring Information, "Air Quality Statistics by City, 2014"

Maximum Air Pollutant Concentrations: Nitrogen Dioxide and Sulfur Dioxide

	Nitrogen Dioxide AM (ppb)	Nitrogen Dioxide 1-Hr (ppb)	Sulfur Dioxide AM (ppb)	Sulfur Dioxide 1-Hr (ppb)	Sulfur Dioxide 24-Hr (ppb)
MSA[1] Level	25	64	n/a	8	n/a
NAAQS[2]	53	100	30	75	140
Met NAAQS[2]	Yes	Yes	n/a	Yes	n/a

Note: (1) Data covers the Phoenix-Mesa-Scottsdale, AZ Metropolitan Statistical Area—see Appendix B for areas included; Data from exceptional events are included; (2) National Ambient Air Quality Standards; ppm = parts per million; ug/m³ = micrograms per cubic meter; n/a not available.
Concentrations: Nitrogen Dioxide AM—highest arithmetic mean concentration; Nitrogen Dioxide 1-Hr—highest 98th percentile 1-hour daily maximum concentration; Sulfur Dioxide AM—highest annual mean concentration; Sulfur Dioxide 1-Hr—highest 99th percentile 1-hour daily maximum concentration; Sulfur Dioxide 24-Hr—highest second maximum 24-hour concentration
Source: U.S. Environmental Protection Agency, Air Quality Monitoring Information, "Air Quality Statistics by City, 2014"

Drinking Water

Water System Name	Pop. Served	Primary Water Source Type	Violations[1]	
			Health Based	Monitoring/ Reporting
Town of Queen Creek	67,964	Ground	0	0

Note: (1) Based on violation data from January 1, 2015 to December 31, 2015 (includes unresolved violations from earlier years)
Source: U.S. Environmental Protection Agency, Office of Ground Water and Drinking Water, Safe Drinking Water Information System (based on data extracted April 29, 2016)

Sahuarita, Arizona

Background

Sahuarita, in Pima County, Arizona, is located south of the Tohono O'odham Nation and approximately 15 miles south of Tucson just 40 minutes north of the Mexico border. Uniquely positioned to capture 24 million annual visitors from Mexico, Sahuarita is overflowing with retail opportunities, executive living and a viable center for companies and employers to conduct business with Mexico.

The first known inhabitants of the Sahuarita region were the Hohokam people, who are considered to be ancestors of the modern day Tohono O'odham Nation. The Hohokam are known for their innovations in and extensive use of irrigation practices in this dry, desert climate. They established extensive trade routes throughout the region, and many cultural influences are evident in the area.

Sahuarita was incorporated in 1994 and has a total area of 15.2 square miles. The Santa Cruz River runs through the desert town and flows north towards Tucson. Madera Canyon lies just southeast of the town and is an important landmark. Madera Canyon is a spectacular day trip site and ideal birdwatching point.

The town of Sahuarita operates under a seven-member town council, including a mayor and vice mayor. The town council oversees all issues related to Sahuarita including residential and commercial development and natural preservation of land.

Sahuarita is one of Arizona's fastest growing communities and is comprised of three planned communities and eleven small neighborhoods. The town has 92 acres of public land and private parks and recreation facilities, with approximately 125 additional acres of proposed parkland. Sahuarita is known for its high quality of life, affordable housing options, safe and quiet streets, modern schools, and scenic beauty. There are many shopping options, from small shops to major shopping centers. The newest commercial development is Rancho Sahuarita Marketplace, 450 acres of retail, commercial, and dining establishments. It is the town's primary retail center, and includes the convenience of grocery, banking, restaurants, retail shops, and medical services, and located close to the old-fashioned main street of Sahuarita.

Sahuarita's workforce is highly educated, with many residents working in high tech and computer industries. Other major employment sectors include management, business and financial services, architecture and engineering, healthcare, and protective services. Sahuarita is a uniquely business friendly municipality—the town doesn't charge impact fees, business license fees or property tax. These measures are designed to encourage and facilitate business growth in the area which in turn will encourage residential growth. New recreation and retail developments are in the works, and family-friendly facilities presently include a club house, water park, lake, and miles of landscaped trails and walking paths.

The climate in Sahuarita is hot during the summer months when the temperatures tend to hover in the 80s and 90s. During the winter, temperatures fall into the 50s, with an occasional dip into lower temperatures. The warmest month is June and the coldest month in January, and rainfall is fairly evenly distributed throughout the year with an average of 15.5 annual precipitation. There are about 287 days of sunshine per year and the temperature variations between night and day tend to be moderate during both the summer and winter months.

Rankings

Business/Finance Rankings

- The personal finance site NerdWallet analyzed 183 American metropolitan areas with populations over 250,000 and more than 15,000 businesses to rank where entrepreneurs find the most success. Criteria included area economy, annual income, housing cost, unemployment rate, and the success rate of area businesses. Tucson* ranked #148. *www.nerdwallet.com, "Best Places to Start a Business," April 27, 2015*
- The Brookings Institution ranked the 100 largest metro areas in the U.S. based on income inequality. Tucson* was ranked #39 (#1 = greatest ineqality). Criteria: the "95/20 ratio," a figure representing the income at which a household earns more than 95 percent of all other households, divided by the income at which a household earns more than only 20 percent of all other households. *Brookings Institution, "Income Inequality, 100 Largest U.S. Metro Areas, 2007-2014," January 14, 2016*
- The finance site *24/7 Wall St.* identified the metropolitan areas that have the smallest and largest pay disparities between men and women, comparing the median earnings for the past 12 months of both men and women working full-time in the country's 100 largest metropolitan statistical areas. Of the ten best-paying metros for women, the Tucson* metro area ranked #5. *24/7 Wall St., "The Best (and Worst) Paying Cities for Women," March 6, 2015*
- The Tucson* metro area appeared on the Milken Institute "2015 Best Performing Cities" list. Rank: #175 out of 200 large metro areas. Criteria: job growth; wage and salary growth; high-tech output growth. *Milken Institute, "Best-Performing Cities 2015," December 2015*
- *Forbes* ranked the 200 most populous metro areas to determine the nation's "Best Places for Business and Careers." The Tucson* metro area was ranked #103. Criteria: costs (business and living); job growth (past and projected); income growth; educational attainment (college and high school); projected economic growth; cultural and recreational opportunities; net migration patterns; number of highly ranked colleges. *Forbes, "The Best Places for Business and Careers 2015," July 29, 2015*

Education Rankings

- Personal finance website *WalletHub* analyzed the 150 largest U.S. metropolitan statistical areas to determine where the most educated Americans are choosing to settle. Criteria: education quality and attainment gap; education levels; percentage of workers with degrees; public school rankings; quality and size of each metro area's universities. Tucson* was ranked #51 (#1 = most educated city). *www.WalletHub.com, "2015's Most and Least Educated Cities*

Environmental Rankings

- The Tucson* metro area came in at #344 for the relative comfort of its climate on Sperling's list of "chill cities," as measured by the Sperling Heat Index. All 361 metro areas are included. Criteria included daytime high temperatures, nighttime low temperatures, dew point, and relative humidity at the high temperatures. *www.bertsperling.com, "Sperling's Chill Cities," July 18, 2013*
- Sperling's BestPlaces assessed 379 metropolitan areas of the United States for the likelihood of dangerously extreme weather events or earthquakes. In general the Southeast and South-Central regions have the highest risk of weather extremes and earthquakes, while the Pacific Northwest enjoys the lowest risk. Of the least risky metropolitan areas, the Tucson* metro area was ranked #100. *www.bestplaces.net, "Safest Places from Natural Disasters," April 2011*

Health/Fitness Rankings

- Tucson* was identified as a "2016 Spring Allergy Capital." The area ranked #24 out of 100. Three groups of factors were used to identify the most severe cities for people with allergies during the spring season: annual pollen levels; medicine utilization; access to board-certified allergists. *Asthma and Allergy Foundation of America, "Spring Allergy Capitals 2016"*

- Tucson* was identified as a "2015 Asthma Capital." The area ranked #75 out of the nation's 100 largest metropolitan areas. Criteria: estimated prevalence; self-reported prevalence; crude death rate for asthma; annual pollen score; annual air quality; public smoking laws; number of board-certified asthma specialists; school inhaler access laws; rescue medication use; controller medication use; ER visits for asthma; uninsured rate; poverty rate. *Asthma and Allergy Foundation of America, "Asthma Capitals 2015"*
- The Tucson* metro area ranked #91 out of 190 in The Gallup-Healthways Well-Being Index. Criteria: purpose; social well being; financial health; community and physical health. Results are based on telephone interviews with adults, aged 18 and older, living in metropolitan areas in the 50 U.S. states and the District of Columbia. *Gallup-Healthways, "State of American Well-Being," February 23, 2016*

Real Estate Rankings

- The Tucson* metro area was identified as one of 14 best housing markets for the next five years. Criteria: projected annualized change in home prices between the fourth quarter 2012 and the fourth quarter 2017. *The Business Insider, "The 14 Best Housing Markets for the Next Five Years," May 20, 2013*
- Tucson* was ranked #100 out of 225 metro areas in terms of housing affordability in 2015 by the National Association of Home Builders (#1 = most affordable). Criteria: the share of homes sold in that area affordable to a family earning the local median income, based on standard mortgage underwriting criteria. *National Association of Home Builders®, NAHB-Wells Fargo Housing Opportunity Index, 4th Quarter 2015*

Safety Rankings

- The National Insurance Crime Bureau ranked 380 metro areas in the U.S. in terms of per capita rates of vehicle theft. The Tucson* metro area ranked #87 (#1 = highest rate). Criteria: number of vehicle theft offenses per 100,000 inhabitants in 2014. *National Insurance Crime Bureau, "Hot Spots 2014," June 24, 2015*

Seniors/Retirement Rankings

- From its Best Cities for Successful Aging indexes, the Milken Institute generated rankings for metropolitan areas, weighing data in eight categories—health care, wellness, living arrangements, transportation, financial characteristics, education and employment opportunities, community engagement, and overall livability. The Tucson* metro area was ranked #47 overall in the large metro area category. *Milken Institute, "Best Cities for Successful Aging, 2014"*

Women/Minorities Rankings

- *24/7 Wall St.* compared median earnings over a 12-month period for men and women who worked full-time, year-round, and employment composition by sector to identify the best-paying cities for women. Of the largest 100 U.S. metropolitan areas, Tucson* was ranked #5 in pay disparity. *24/7 Wall St., "The Best (and Worst) Paying Cities for Women," March 6, 2015*

Miscellaneous Rankings

- Of the American metro areas that allow medical or recreational use of marijuana, the Tucson* metro area was identified by CNBC editors as one of the most livable for marijuana lovers. Criteria included the Sperling's BestPlaces assessment of marijuana-friendly cities in terms of sound economy, cultural diversity, and a healthy population, plus cost-of-living index and high-quality schools. *www.cnbc.com, "The Best Cities to Live for Marijuana Lovers," February 5, 2014*
- The National Alliance to End Homelessness ranked the 100 most populous metro areas with the highest rate of homelessness. The Tucson* metro area ranked #19. Criteria: number of homeless people per 10,000 population in 2011. *National Alliance to End Homelessness, The State of Homelessness in America 2012*

Sahuarita is located within the Tucson, AZ Metropolitan Statistical Area.

Business Environment

CITY FINANCES

City Government Finances

Component	2012 ($000)	2012 ($ per capita)
Total Revenues	26,622	1,053
Total Expenditures	22,430	888
Debt Outstanding	56,876	2,251
Cash and Securities[1]	22,717	899

Note: (1) Cash and security holdings of a government at the close of its fiscal year, including those of its dependent agencies, utilities, and liquor stores.
Source: U.S Census Bureau, State & Local Government Finances 2012

City Government Revenue by Source

Source	2012 ($000)	2012 ($ per capita)
General Revenue		
From Federal Government	243	9
From State Government	8,010	317
From Local Governments	4,383	173
Taxes		
Property	290	11
Sales and Gross Receipts	6,594	261
Personal Income	0	0
Corporate Income	0	0
Motor Vehicle License	0	0
Other Taxes	3,093	122
Current Charges	2,545	100
Liquor Store	0	0
Utility	0	0
Employee Retirement	0	0

Source: U.S Census Bureau, State & Local Government Finances 2012

City Government Expenditures by Function

Function	2012 ($000)	2012 ($ per capita)	2012 (%)
General Direct Expenditures			
Air Transportation	0	0	0.0
Corrections	0	0	0.0
Education	0	0	0.0
Employment Security Administration	0	0	0.0
Financial Administration	900	35	4.0
Fire Protection	0	0	0.0
General Public Buildings	445	17	1.9
Governmental Administration, Other	2,059	81	9.1
Health	0	0	0.0
Highways	6,266	248	27.9
Hospitals	0	0	0.0
Housing and Community Development	0	0	0.0
Interest on General Debt	2,589	102	11.5
Judicial and Legal	951	37	4.2
Libraries	0	0	0.0
Parking	0	0	0.0
Parks and Recreation	1,305	51	5.8
Police Protection	5,136	203	22.8
Public Welfare	0	0	0.0
Sewerage	1,746	69	7.7
Solid Waste Management	0	0	0.0
Veterans' Services	0	0	0.0
Liquor Store	0	0	0.0
Utility	0	0	0.0
Employee Retirement	0	0	0.0

Source: U.S Census Bureau, State & Local Government Finances 2012

DEMOGRAPHICS

Population Growth

Area	1990 Census	2000 Census	2010 Census	2014* Estimate	Population Growth (%) 1990-2014	Population Growth (%) 2010-2014
City	1,752	3,242	25,259	26,441	1,409.2	4.7
MSA[1]	666,880	843,746	980,263	993,144	48.9	1.3
U.S.	248,709,873	281,421,906	308,745,538	314,107,084	26.3	1.7

Note: (1) Figures cover the Tucson, AZ Metropolitan Statistical Area—see Appendix B for areas included; (*) 2010-2014 5-year estimated population
Source: U.S. Census Bureau, 1990 Census, Census 2000, Census 2010, 2010-2014 American Community Survey 5-Year Estimates

Household Size

Area	Persons in Household (%) One	Two	Three	Four	Five	Six	Seven or More	Average Household Size
City	16.9	37.0	15.6	17.0	8.5	3.0	1.6	2.88
MSA[1]	30.8	35.2	14.0	10.4	5.6	2.4	1.3	2.50
U.S.	27.5	33.5	15.8	13.1	6.0	2.3	1.4	2.64

Note: (1) Figures cover the Tucson, AZ Metropolitan Statistical Area—see Appendix B for areas included
Source: U.S. Census Bureau, 2010-2014 American Community Survey 5-Year Estimates

Race

Area	White Alone[2] (%)	Black Alone[2] (%)	Asian Alone[2] (%)	AIAN[3] Alone[2] (%)	NHOPI[4] Alone[2] (%)	Other Race Alone[2] (%)	Two or More Races (%)
City	84.9	3.7	4.2	0.5	0.1	2.9	3.7
MSA[1]	78.8	3.6	2.7	3.2	0.1	8.2	3.5
U.S.	73.8	12.6	5.0	0.8	0.2	4.7	2.9

Note: (1) Figures cover the Tucson, AZ Metropolitan Statistical Area—see Appendix B for areas included; (2) Alone is defined as not being in combination with one or more other races; (3) American Indian and Alaska Native; (4) Native Hawaiian and Other Pacific Islander
Source: U.S. Census Bureau, 2010-2014 American Community Survey 5-Year Estimates

Hispanic or Latino Origin

Area	Total (%)	Mexican (%)	Puerto Rican (%)	Cuban (%)	Other (%)
City	30.2	26.3	0.7	0.1	3.1
MSA[1]	35.4	32.1	0.6	0.2	2.5
U.S.	16.9	10.8	1.6	0.6	3.8

Note: Persons of Hispanic or Latino origin can be of any race; (1) Figures cover the Tucson, AZ Metropolitan Statistical Area—see Appendix B for areas included
Source: U.S. Census Bureau, 2010-2014 American Community Survey 5-Year Estimates

Ancestry

Area	German	Irish	English	American	Italian	Polish	French[2]	Scottish	Dutch
City	12.3	13.7	9.9	2.9	5.4	3.4	1.8	1.3	1.8
MSA[1]	14.5	10.2	8.8	3.5	4.6	2.4	2.8	1.9	1.5
U.S.	14.9	10.8	8.0	7.1	5.5	3.0	2.7	1.7	1.4

Note: Figures are the percentage of the total population reporting a particular ancestry. The nine most commonly reported ancestries in the U.S. are shown. Figures include multiple ancestries (e.g. if a person reported being Irish and Italian, they were included in both columns); (1) Figures cover the Tucson, AZ Metropolitan Statistical Area—see Appendix B for areas included; (2) Excludes Basque
Source: U.S. Census Bureau, 2010-2014 American Community Survey 5-Year Estimates

Foreign-Born Population

Area	Percent of Population Born in								
	Any Foreign Country	Asia	Mexico	Europe	Carribean	Central America[2]	South America	Africa	Canada
City	10.0	1.9	4.7	1.1	0.2	0.2	1.1	0.1	0.6
MSA[1]	12.8	2.2	7.7	1.2	0.1	0.3	0.3	0.4	0.4
U.S.	13.1	3.8	3.7	1.5	1.2	1.0	0.9	0.6	0.3

Note: (1) Figures cover the Tucson, AZ Metropolitan Statistical Area—see Appendix B for areas included; (2) Excludes Mexico.
Source: U.S. Census Bureau, 2010-2014 American Community Survey 5-Year Estimates

Marital Status

Area	Never Married	Now Married[2]	Separated	Widowed	Divorced
City	18.8	64.7	1.6	4.3	10.7
MSA[1]	33.4	45.4	2.1	6.1	13.1
U.S.	32.5	48.4	2.2	5.9	10.9

Note: Figures are percentages and cover the population 15 years of age and older; (1) Figures cover the Tucson, AZ Metropolitan Statistical Area—see Appendix B for areas included; (2) Excludes separated
Source: U.S. Census Bureau, 2010-2014 American Community Survey 5-Year Estimates

Disability Status

Area	All Ages	Under 18 Years Old	18 to 64 Years Old	65 Years and Over
City	7.9	4.3	6.7	18.6
MSA[1]	13.7	4.2	11.6	34.5
U.S.	12.3	4.1	10.2	36.3

Note: Figures show percent of the civilian noninstitutionalized population that reported having a disability. Disability status is determined from from six types of difficulty: vision, hearing, cognitive, ambulatory, self-care, and independent living. For children under 5 years old, hearing and vision difficulty are used to determine disability status. For children between the ages of 5 and 14, disability status is determined from hearing, vision, cognitive, ambulatory, and self-care difficulties. For people aged 15 years and older, they are considered to have a disability if they have difficulty with any one of the six difficulty types; (1) Figures cover the Tucson, AZ Metropolitan Statistical Area—see Appendix B for areas included.
Source: U.S. Census Bureau, 2010-2014 American Community Survey 5-Year Estimates

Age

Area	Percent of Population									Median Age
	Under Age 5	Age 5–19	Age 20–34	Age 35–44	Age 45–54	Age 55–64	Age 65–74	Age 75–84	Age 85+	
City	9.6	22.8	17.5	14.1	9.6	9.6	10.2	5.5	1.2	35.1
MSA[1]	6.1	19.5	21.0	11.6	12.6	12.7	9.2	5.3	2.1	37.9
U.S.	6.4	19.9	20.6	13.0	14.1	12.3	7.6	4.3	1.9	37.4

Note: (1) Figures cover the Tucson, AZ Metropolitan Statistical Area—see Appendix B for areas included
Source: U.S. Census Bureau, 2010-2014 American Community Survey 5-Year Estimates

Gender

Area	Males	Females	Males per 100 Females
City	13,086	13,355	98.0
MSA[1]	488,310	504,834	96.7
U.S.	154,515,159	159,591,925	96.8

Note: (1) Figures cover the Tucson, AZ Metropolitan Statistical Area—see Appendix B for areas included
Source: U.S. Census Bureau, 2010-2014 American Community Survey 5-Year Estimates

Religious Groups by Family

Area	Catholic	Baptist	Non-Den.	Methodist[2]	Lutheran	LDS[3]	Pentecostal	Presbyterian[4]	Muslim[5]	Judaism
MSA[1]	20.7	3.3	3.7	1.3	1.5	2.9	1.5	1.0	<0.1	0.5
U.S.	19.1	9.3	4.0	4.0	2.3	2.0	1.9	1.6	0.8	0.7

Note: Figures are the number of adherents as a percentage of the total population; (1) Figures cover the Tucson, AZ Metropolitan Statistical Area—see Appendix B for areas included; (2) Methodist/Pietist; (3) Latter Day Saints; (4) Reformed; (5) Figures are estimates
Source: Association of Statisticians of American Religious Bodies, 2010 U.S. Religion Census: Religious Congregations & Membership Study

Religious Groups by Tradition

Area	Catholic	Evangelical Protestant	Mainline Protestant	Other Tradition	Black Protestant	Orthodox
MSA[1]	20.7	10.0	3.7	4.5	0.4	0.2
U.S.	19.1	16.2	7.3	4.3	1.6	0.3

Note: Figures are the number of adherents as a percentage of the total population; (1) Figures cover the Tucson, AZ Metropolitan Statistical Area—see Appendix B for areas included
Source: Association of Statisticians of American Religious Bodies, 2010 U.S. Religion Census: Religious Congregations & Membership Study

ECONOMY

Gross Metropolitan Product

Area	2013	2014	2015	2016	Rank[2]
MSA[1]	35.4	36.3	37.5	39.4	74

Note: Figures are in billions of dollars; (1) Figures cover the Tucson, AZ Metropolitan Statistical Area—see Appendix B for areas included; (2) Rank is based on 2016 data and ranges from 1 to 381
Source: The U.S. Conference of Mayors, U.S. Metro Economies: GMP and Employment 2014-2016, June 2015

Economic Growth

Area	2011-13 (%)	2014 (%)	2015 (%)	2016 (%)	Rank[2]
MSA[1]	1.4	0.9	1.7	2.8	116
U.S.	2.2	2.4	2.3	2.9	–

Note: Figures are real gross metropolitan product (GMP) growth rates and represent annual average percent change; (1) Figures cover the Tucson, AZ Metropolitan Statistical Area—see Appendix B for areas included; (2) Rank is based on 2016 data and ranges from 1 to 381
Source: The U.S. Conference of Mayors, U.S. Metro Economies: GMP and Employment 2014-2016, June 2015

Metropolitan Area Exports

Area	2009	2010	2011	2012	2013	2014	Rank[2]
MSA[1]	1,978.0	2,099.3	2,309.9	2,508.2	2,589.8	2,277.3	95

Note: Figures are in millions of dollars; (1) Figures cover the Tucson, AZ Metropolitan Statistical Area—see Appendix B for areas included; (2) Rank is based on 2014 data and ranges from 1 to 385
Source: U.S. Department of Commerce, International Trade Administration, Office of Trade & Industry Information, Manufacturing & Services, data extracted March 10, 2016

Building Permits

Area	Single-Family			Multi-Family			Total		
	2014	2015p	Pct. Chg.	2014	2015p	Pct. Chg.	2014	2015p	Pct. Chg.
City	183	271	48.1	0	0	-	183	271	48.1
MSA[1]	2,296	2,477	7.9	954	1,055	10.6	3,250	3,532	8.7
U.S.	640,300	690,800	7.9	411,800	487,600	18.4	1,052,100	1,178,400	12.0

Note: (1) Figures cover the Tucson, AZ Metropolitan Statistical Area—see Appendix B for areas included; Figures represent new, privately-owned housing units authorized (unadjusted data); All permit data are based on estimates with imputation; (p) preliminary data.
Source: U.S. Census Bureau, Manufacturing, Mining, and Construction Statistics, Building Permits, 2014, 2015

Bankruptcy Filings

Area	Business Filings			Nonbusiness Filings		
	2014	2015	% Chg.	2014	2015	% Chg.
Pima County	75	71	-5.3	2,460	2,214	-10.0
U.S.	26,983	24,735	-8.3	909,812	819,760	-9.9

Note: Business filings include Chapter 7, Chapter 11, Chapter 12, and Chapter 13; Nonbusiness filings include Chapter 7, Chapter 11, and Chapter 13
Source: Administrative Office of the U.S. Courts, Business and Nonbusiness Bankruptcy, County Cases Commenced by Chapter of the Bankruptcy Code, During the 12- Month Period Ending December 31, 2014 and Business and Nonbusiness Bankruptcy, County Cases Commenced by Chapter of the Bankruptcy Code, During the 12- Month Period Ending December 31, 2015

Housing Vacancy Rates

Area	Gross Vacancy Rate[2] (%)			Year-Round Vacancy Rate[3] (%)			Rental Vacancy Rate[4] (%)			Homeowner Vacancy Rate[5] (%)		
	2013	2014	2015	2013	2014	2015	2013	2014	2015	2013	2014	2015
MSA[1]	14.5	10.0	11.8	12.5	8.4	9.8	13.9	9.0	10.1	1.9	2.1	1.7
U.S.	13.6	13.4	12.9	10.7	10.4	10.0	8.3	7.6	7.1	2.0	1.9	1.8

Note: (1) Figures cover the Tucson, AZ Metropolitan Statistical Area—see Appendix B for areas included; (2) The percentage of the total housing inventory that is vacant; (3) The percentage of the housing inventory (excluding seasonal units) that is year-round vacant; (4) The percentage of rental inventory that is vacant for rent; (5) The percentage of homeowner inventory that is vacant for sale
Source: U.S. Census Bureau, Housing Vacancies and Homeownership Annual Statistics: 2015

INCOME

Income

Area	Per Capita ($)	Median Household ($)	Average Household ($)
City	26,856	65,183	76,183
MSA[1]	25,524	46,233	63,627
U.S.	28,555	53,482	74,596

Note: (1) Figures cover the Tucson, AZ Metropolitan Statistical Area—see Appendix B for areas included
Source: U.S. Census Bureau, 2010-2014 American Community Survey 5-Year Estimates

Household Income Distribution

Area	Percent of Households Earning							
	Under $15,000	$15,000 -24,999	$25,000 -34,999	$35,000 -49,999	$50,000 -74,999	$75,000 -99,000	$100,000 -149,999	$150,000 and up
City	3.2	6.2	5.2	14.4	30.1	18.8	14.8	7.3
MSA[1]	14.8	12.1	11.7	14.8	17.7	11.3	11.0	6.6
U.S.	12.5	10.7	10.2	13.5	17.8	12.2	13.0	10.0

Note: (1) Figures cover the Tucson, AZ Metropolitan Statistical Area—see Appendix B for areas included
Source: U.S. Census Bureau, 2010-2014 American Community Survey 5-Year Estimates

Poverty Rate

Area	All Ages	Under 18 Years Old	18 to 64 Years Old	65 Years and Over
City	6.3	10.3	5.0	2.7
MSA[1]	19.0	26.7	19.2	8.3
U.S.	15.6	21.9	14.6	9.4

Note: Figures are percentage of people whose income during the past 12 months was below the poverty level; (1) Figures cover the Tucson, AZ Metropolitan Statistical Area—see Appendix B for areas included
Source: U.S. Census Bureau, 2010-2014 American Community Survey 5-Year Estimates

EMPLOYMENT

Labor Force and Employment

Area	Civilian Labor Force			Workers Employed		
	Dec. 2014	Dec. 2015	% Chg.	Dec. 2014	Dec. 2015	% Chg.
City	11,359	11,522	1.4	10,817	11,018	1.8
MSA[1]	465,594	470,703	1.0	438,925	447,052	1.8
U.S.	155,521,000	157,245,000	1.1	147,190,000	149,703,000	1.7

Note: Data is not seasonally adjusted and covers workers 16 years of age and older; (1) Figures cover the Tucson, AZ Metropolitan Statistical Area—see Appendix B for areas included
Source: Bureau of Labor Statistics, Local Area Unemployment Statistics

Unemployment Rate

Area	2015											
	Jan.	Feb.	Mar.	Apr.	May	Jun.	Jul.	Aug.	Sep.	Oct.	Nov.	Dec.
City	5.4	5.3	4.5	4.5	4.3	5.4	5.7	5.8	5.2	4.7	4.5	4.4
MSA[1]	5.9	5.6	4.9	5.1	4.9	5.9	6.2	6.1	5.7	5.5	5.3	5.0
U.S.	6.1	5.8	5.6	5.1	5.3	5.5	5.6	5.2	4.9	4.8	4.8	4.8

Note: Data is not seasonally adjusted and covers workers 16 years of age and older; (1) Figures cover the Tucson, AZ Metropolitan Statistical Area—see Appendix B for areas included
Source: Bureau of Labor Statistics, Local Area Unemployment Statistics

Employment by Occupation

Occupation Classification	City (%)	MSA[1] (%)	U.S. (%)
Management, Business, Science, and Arts	39.3	36.3	36.4
Natural Resources, Construction, and Maintenance	8.0	8.8	9.0
Production, Transportation, and Material Moving	6.3	8.3	12.1
Sales and Office	26.9	25.2	24.4
Service	19.6	21.5	18.2

Note: Figures cover employed civilians 16 years of age and older; (1) Figures cover the Tucson, AZ Metropolitan Statistical Area—see Appendix B for areas included
Source: U.S. Census Bureau, 2010-2014 American Community Survey 5-Year Estimates

Employment by Industry

Sector	MSA[1]		U.S.
	Number of Employees	Percent of Total	Percent of Total
Construction	14,300	3.7	4.5
Education and Health Services	65,300	17.1	15.7
Financial Activities	18,700	4.9	5.7
Government	80,500	21.1	15.5
Information	4,700	1.2	1.9
Leisure and Hospitality	43,700	11.4	10.4
Manufacturing	23,200	6.0	8.6
Mining and Logging	2,200	0.5	0.5
Other Services	12,700	3.3	3.9
Professional and Business Services	52,300	13.7	13.9
Retail Trade	44,700	11.7	11.3
Transportation, Warehousing, and Utilities	10,700	2.8	3.9
Wholesale Trade	7,900	2.0	4.1

Note: Figures are non-farm employment as of December 2015. Figures are not seasonally adjusted and include workers 16 years of age and older; (1) Figures cover the Tucson, AZ Metropolitan Statistical Area—see Appendix B for areas included
Source: Bureau of Labor Statistics, Current Employment Statistics, Employment, Hours, and Earnings

Occupations with Greatest Projected Employment Growth: 2012 – 2022

Occupation[1]	2012 Employment	2022 Projected Employment	Numeric Employment Change	Percent Employment Change
Combined Food Preparation and Serving Workers, Including Fast Food	50,540	68,080	17,540	34.7
Customer Service Representatives	64,570	81,660	17,090	26.5
Retail Salespersons	88,270	102,400	14,130	16.0
Construction Laborers	28,290	42,000	13,710	48.5
Registered Nurses	48,660	61,130	12,470	25.6
Waiters and Waitresses	48,150	59,900	11,750	24.4
General and Operations Managers	46,340	57,660	11,320	24.4
Secretaries and Administrative Assistants, Except Legal, Medical, and Executive	45,880	56,340	10,460	22.8
Personal Care Aides	22,040	30,960	8,920	40.5
Office Clerks, General	49,260	58,180	8,920	18.1

Note: Projections cover Arizona; (1) Sorted by numeric employment change
Source: www.projectionscentral.com, State Occupational Projections, 2012–2022 Long-Term Projections

Fastest Growing Occupations: 2012 – 2022

Occupation[1]	2012 Employment	2022 Projected Employment	Numeric Employment Change	Percent Employment Change
Helpers—Brickmasons, Blockmasons, Stonemasons, and Tile and Marble Setters	370	610	240	65.9
Brickmasons and Blockmasons	840	1,370	530	63.5
Helpers—Electricians	790	1,280	490	61.6
Cement Masons and Concrete Finishers	4,000	6,210	2,210	55.2
Diagnostic Medical Sonographers	1,240	1,920	680	54.9
Tile and Marble Setters	1,370	2,130	760	54.9
Millwrights	400	610	210	54.7
Fence Erectors	370	570	200	54.5
Computer Numerically Controlled Machine Tool Programmers, Metal and Plastic	360	550	190	53.2
Solar Photovoltaic Installers	220	340	120	52.5

Note: Projections cover Arizona; (1) Sorted by percent employment change and excludes occupations with numeric employment change less than 100
Source: www.projectionscentral.com, State Occupational Projections, 2012–2022 Long-Term Projections

Average Wages

Occupation	$/Hr.	Occupation	$/Hr.
Accountants and Auditors	27.57	Maids and Housekeeping Cleaners	9.62
Automotive Mechanics	19.17	Maintenance and Repair Workers	16.65
Bookkeepers	17.28	Marketing Managers	52.73
Carpenters	17.47	Nuclear Medicine Technologists	n/a
Cashiers	10.76	Nurses, Licensed Practical	23.18
Clerks, General Office	16.20	Nurses, Registered	32.28
Clerks, Receptionists/Information	12.69	Nursing Assistants	13.11
Clerks, Shipping/Receiving	14.82	Packers and Packagers, Hand	10.47
Computer Programmers	36.77	Physical Therapists	42.61
Computer Systems Analysts	37.61	Postal Service Mail Carriers	25.44
Computer User Support Specialists	23.31	Real Estate Brokers	35.70
Cooks, Restaurant	10.91	Retail Salespersons	11.93
Dentists	70.15	Sales Reps., Exc. Tech./Scientific	23.79
Electrical Engineers	37.40	Sales Reps., Tech./Scientific	37.14
Electricians	22.24	Secretaries, Exc. Legal/Med./Exec.	15.75
Financial Managers	45.92	Security Guards	11.50
First-Line Supervisors/Managers, Sales	19.70	Surgeons	126.79
Food Preparation Workers	10.62	Teacher Assistants*	11.74
General and Operations Managers	38.38	Teachers, Elementary School*	18.46
Hairdressers/Cosmetologists	11.55	Teachers, Secondary School*	18.98
Internists	n/a	Telemarketers	9.95
Janitors and Cleaners	11.20	Truck Drivers, Heavy/Tractor-Trailer	18.53
Landscaping/Groundskeeping Workers	12.00	Truck Drivers, Light/Delivery Svcs.	16.26
Lawyers	51.38	Waiters and Waitresses	10.54

Note: Wage data covers the Tucson, AZ Metropolitan Statistical Area—see Appendix B for areas included; (*) Hourly wages for elementary/secondary school teachers and teacher assistants were calculated by the editors from annual wage data based on a 40 hour work week; n/a not available.
Source: Bureau of Labor Statistics, Metro Area Occupational Employment and Wage Estimates, May 2015

TAXES

State Corporate Income Tax Rates

State	Tax Rate (%)	Income Brackets ($)	Num. of Brackets	Financial Institution Tax Rate (%)[a]	Federal Income Tax Ded.
Arizona	5.5 (b)	Flat rate	1	5.5 (b)	No

Note: Tax rates as of January 1, 2016; (a) Rates listed are the corporate income tax rate applied to financial institutions or excise taxes based on income. Some states have other taxes based upon the value of deposits or shares; (b) Arizona minimum tax is $100. Tax rate is scheduled to decrease to 4.9% in tax years 2017.
Source: Federation of Tax Administrators, "State Corporate Income Tax Rates, 2016"

State Individual Income Tax Rates

State	Tax Rate (%)	Income Brackets ($)	Num. of Brackets	Personal Exempt. ($)[1] Single	Personal Exempt. ($)[1] Dependents	Fed. Inc. Tax Ded.
Arizona (a)	2.59 - 4.54	10,163 - 152,434 (b)	5	2,100	2,300	No

Note: Tax rates as of January 1, 2016; Local- and county-level taxes are not included; n/a not applicable; (1) Married joint filers generally receive double the single exemption; (a) 18 states have statutory provision for automatically adjusting to the rate of inflation the dollar values of the income tax brackets, standard deductions, and/or personal exemptions. Massachusetts, Michigan, and Nebraska index the personal exemptiononly. Oregon does not index the income brackets for $125,000 and over. Maine has suspended indexing for 2014 and 2015; (b) For joint returns, taxes are twice the tax on half the couple's income.
Source: Federation of Tax Administrators, "State Individual Income Tax Rates, 2016"

Various State and Local Tax Rates

State	State and Local Sales and Use (%)	State Sales and Use (%)	Gasoline[1] (¢/gal.)	Cigarette[2] ($/pack)	Spirits[3] ($/gal.)	Wine[4] ($/gal.)	Beer[5] ($/gal.)
Arizona	8.10	5.6	19	2.00	3.00	0.84 (l)	0.35

Note: All tax rates as of January 1, 2016; (1) The American Petroleum Institute has developed a methodology for determining the average tax rate on a gallon of fuel. Rates may include any of the following: excise taxes, environmental fees, storage tank fees, other fees or taxes, general sales tax, and local taxes. In states where gasoline is subject to the general sales tax, or where the fuel tax is based on the average sale price, the average rate determined by API is sensitive to changes in the price of gasoline. States that fully or partially apply general sales taxes to gasoline: CA, CO, GA, IL, IN, MI, NY; (2) The federal excise tax of $1.0066 per pack and local taxes are not included; (3) Rates are those applicable to off-premise sales of 40% alcohol by volume (a.b.v.) distilled spirits in 750ml containers. Local excise taxes are excluded; (4) Rates are those applicable to off-premise sales of 11% a.b.v. non-carbonated wine in 750ml containers; (5) Rates are those applicable to off-premise sales of 4.7% a.b.v. beer in 12 ounce containers; (l) Different rates also applicable according to alcohol content, place of production, size of container, place purchased (on- or off-premise or on board airlines) or type of wine (carbonated, vermouth, etc.).
Source: Tax Foundation, 2016 Facts & Figures: How Does Your State Compare?

State Business Tax Climate Index Rankings

State	Overall Rank	Corporate Tax Rank	Individual Income Tax Rank	Sales Tax Rank	Unemployment Insurance Tax Rank	Property Tax Rank
Arizona	24	22	19	49	9	6

Note: The index is a measure of how each state's tax laws affect economic performance. The lower the rank, the more favorable a state's tax system is for business. States without a given tax are given a ranking of 1. The scores/rankings for the District of Columbia do not affect other states. The 2016 index represents the tax climate as of July 1, 2015 (the beginning of Fiscal Year 2016).
Source: Tax Foundation, State Business Tax Climate Index 2016

TRANSPORTATION

Means of Transportation to Work

Area	Car/Truck/Van		Public Transportation			Bicycle	Walked	Other Means	Worked at Home
	Drove Alone	Car-pooled	Bus	Subway	Railroad				
City	79.0	12.9	0.0	0.0	0.0	0.1	0.8	2.8	4.3
MSA[1]	76.5	9.9	2.6	0.0	0.0	1.8	2.4	2.1	4.7
U.S.	76.4	9.6	2.6	1.8	0.6	0.6	2.8	1.3	4.4

Note: Figures are percentages and cover workers 16 years of age and older; (1) Figures cover the Tucson, AZ Metropolitan Statistical Area—see Appendix B for areas included
Source: U.S. Census Bureau, 2010-2014 American Community Survey 5-Year Estimates

Travel Time to Work

Area	Less Than 10 Minutes	10 to 19 Minutes	20 to 29 Minutes	30 to 44 Minutes	45 to 59 Minutes	60 to 89 Minutes	90 Minutes or More
City	9.7	20.6	22.0	30.9	12.2	3.1	1.5
MSA[1]	10.9	30.0	24.6	23.1	6.9	2.9	1.7
U.S.	13.3	29.6	21.0	20.2	7.7	5.7	2.6

Note: Figures are percentages and include workers 16 years old and over; (1) Figures cover the Tucson, AZ Metropolitan Statistical Area—see Appendix B for areas included
Source: U.S. Census Bureau, 2010-2014 American Community Survey 5-Year Estimates

Freeway Travel Time Index

Area	1985	1990	1995	2000	2005	2010	2014
Urban Area Rank[1,2]	26	25	32	28	35	29	32
Urban Area Index[1]	1.10	1.14	1.16	1.20	1.21	1.22	1.22
Average Index[3]	1.09	1.11	1.14	1.17	1.20	1.19	1.20

Note: Freeway Travel Time Index—the ratio of travel time in the peak period to the travel time at free-flow conditions. For example, a value of 1.30 indicates a 20-minute free-flow trip takes 26 minutes in the peak (20 minutes x 1.30 = 26 minutes); (1) Covers the Tucson AZ urban area; (2) Rank is based on 101 urban areas (#1 = highest travel time index); (3) Average of 101 urban areas
Source: Texas Transportation Institute, 2015 Urban Mobility Scorecard, August 2015

Freeway Commuter Stress Index

Area	1985	1990	1995	2000	2005	2010	2014
Urban Area Rank[1,2]	42	42	46	40	41	40	40
Urban Area Index[1]	1.11	1.15	1.17	1.21	1.23	1.23	1.24
Average Index[3]	1.13	1.16	1.19	1.22	1.25	1.24	1.25

Note: The Freeway Commuter Stress Index is the same as the Freeway Travel Time Index (see table above) except that it includes only the travel in the peak directions during the peak periods; the TTI includes travel in all directions during the peak period. Thus, the CSI is more indicative of the work trip experienced by each commuter on a daily basis. (1) Covers the Tucson AZ urban area; (2) Rank is based on 101 urban areas (#1 = highest stress index); (3) Average of 101 urban areas
Source: Texas Transportation Institute, 2015 Urban Mobility Scorecard, August 2015

Living Environment

COST OF LIVING

Cost of Living Index

Composite Index	Groceries	Housing	Utilities	Transportation	Health Care	Misc. Goods/ Services
92.9	96.7	83.5	91.5	96.7	103.6	97.0

Note: The Cost of Living Index measures regional differences in the cost of consumer goods and services, excluding taxes and non-consumer expenditures, for professional and managerial households in the top income quintile. It is based on more than 50,000 prices covering almost 60 different items for which prices are collected three times a year by chambers of commerce, economic development organizations or university applied economic centers in each participating urban area. The numbers shown should be read as a percentage above or below the national average of 100. For example, a value of 115.4 in the groceries column indicates that grocery prices are 15.4% higher than the national average. Small differences in the index numbers should not be interpreted as significant; Figures cover the Tucson AZ urban area.
Source: The Council for Community and Economic Research, ACCRA Cost of Living Index, 2015

Grocery Prices

Area[1]	T-Bone Steak ($/pound)	Frying Chicken ($/pound)	Whole Milk ($/half gal.)	Eggs ($/dozen)	Orange Juice ($/64 oz.)	Coffee ($/11.5 oz.)
City[2]	11.20	1.31	1.68	2.12	3.28	4.88
Avg.	10.99	1.43	2.25	2.26	3.58	4.48
Min.	7.16	0.98	1.30	1.35	2.88	2.98
Max.	14.13	2.43	3.85	4.81	6.39	7.56

Note: (1) Values for the local area are compared with the average, minimum and maximum values for all 292 areas in the Cost of Living Index; (2) Figures cover the Tucson AZ urban area; **T-Bone Steak** *(price per pound);* **Frying Chicken** *(price per pound, whole fryer);* **Whole Milk** *(half gallon carton);* **Eggs** *(price per dozen, Grade A, large);* **Orange Juice** *(64 oz. Tropicana or Florida Natural);* **Coffee** *(11.5 oz. can, vacuum-packed, Maxwell House, Hills Bros, or Folgers).*
Source: The Council for Community and Economic Research, ACCRA Cost of Living Index, 2015

Housing and Utility Costs

Area[1]	New Home Price ($)	Apartment Rent ($/month)	All Electric ($/month)	Part Electric ($/month)	Other Energy ($/month)	Telephone ($/month)
City[2]	253,513	839	-	103.26	63.52	23.09
Avg.	312,874	945	179.30	95.07	72.96	28.11
Min.	178,682	479	116.28	43.14	26.46	10.01
Max.	1,472,476	3,984	504.25	189.44	421.11	43.06

Note: (1) Values for the local area are compared with the average, minimum and maximum values for all 292 areas in the Cost of Living Index; (2) Figures cover the Tucson AZ urban area; **New Home Price** *(2,400 sf living area, 8,000 sf lot, in urban area with full utilities);* **Apartment Rent** *(950 sf 2 bedroom/1.5 or 2 bath, unfurnished, excluding all utilities except water);* **All Electric** *(average monthly cost for an all-electric home);* **Part Electric** *(average monthly cost for a part-electric home);* **Other Energy** *(average monthly cost for natural gas, fuel oil, coal, wood, and any other forms of energy except electricity);* **Telephone** *(price includes basic monthly rate for a private residential line plus additional local usage charges incurred by a family of four).*
Source: The Council for Community and Economic Research, ACCRA Cost of Living Index, 2015

Health Care, Transportation, and Other Costs

Area[1]	Doctor ($/visit)	Dentist ($/visit)	Optometrist ($/visit)	Gasoline ($/gallon)	Beauty Salon ($/visit)	Men's Shirt ($)
City[2]	121.93	89.60	91.60	2.23	43.60	34.05
Avg.	105.15	89.02	99.78	2.38	35.30	28.10
Min.	66.87	56.09	48.53	1.95	18.91	13.38
Max.	182.34	150.36	228.33	4.09	67.91	63.80

Note: (1) Values for the local area are compared with the average, minimum and maximum values for all 292 areas in the Cost of Living Index; (2) Figures cover the Tucson AZ urban area; **Doctor** *(general practitioners routine exam of an established patient);* **Dentist** *(adult teeth cleaning and periodic oral examination);* **Optometrist** *(full vision eye exam for established adult patient);* **Gasoline** *(one gallon regular unleaded, national brand, including all taxes, cash price at self-service pump if available);* **Beauty Salon** *(woman's shampoo, trim, and blow-dry);* **Men's Shirt** *(cotton/polyester dress shirt, pinpoint weave, long sleeves).*
Source: The Council for Community and Economic Research, ACCRA Cost of Living Index, 2015

HOUSING

House Price Index (HPI)

Area	National Ranking[2]	Quarterly Change (%)	One-Year Change (%)	Five-Year Change (%)
MSA[1]	156	2.40	4.00	6.70
U.S.[3]	–	1.45	5.76	22.85

Note: The HPI is a weighted repeat sales index. It measures average price changes in repeat sales or refinancings on the same properties. This information is obtained by reviewing repeat mortgage transactions on single-family properties whose mortgages have been purchased or securitized by Fannie Mae or Freddie Mac in January 1975; (1) Tucson Metropolitan Statistical Area—see Appendix B for areas included; (2) Rankings are based on annual percentage change for all metro areas containing at least 15,000 transactions over the last 10 years and ranges from 1 to 266; (3) figures based on a weighted average of Census Division estimates using a seasonally adjusted, purchase-only index; all figures are for the period ending December 31, 2015
Source: Federal Housing Finance Agency, House Price Index, February 25, 2016

Median Single-Family Home Prices

Area	2013	2014	2015[p]	Percent Change 2014 to 2015
MSA[1]	169.6	175.8	182.9	4.0
U.S. Average	197.4	208.9	223.9	7.2

Note: Figures are median sales prices of existing single-family homes in thousands of dollars; (p) preliminary; n/a not available; (1) Tucson, AZ Metropolitan Statistical Area—see Appendix B for areas included
Source: National Association of Realtors, Median Sales Price of Existing Single-Family Homes for Metropolitan Areas, 4th Quarter 2015

Qualifying Income Based on Median Sales Price of Existing Single-Family Homes

Area	With 5% Down ($)	With 10% Down ($)	With 20% Down ($)
MSA[1]	41,328	39,152	34,802
U.S. Average	49,535	46,928	41,714

Note: Figures are preliminary; Qualifying income is based on a mortgage rate of 4.1%. Monthly principal and interest payment is limited to 25% of income; n/a not available; (1) Tucson, AZ Metropolitan Statistical Area—see Appendix B for areas included
Source: National Association of Realtors, Qualifying Income Based on Median Sales Price of Existing Single-Family Homes for Metropolitan Areas, 4th Quarter 2015

Median Apartment Condo-Coop Home Prices

Area	2013	2014	2015[p]	Percent Change 2014 to 2015
MSA[1]	107.7	112.3	119.7	6.6
U.S. Average	194.9	204.3	210.7	3.1

Note: Figures are median sales prices of existing apartment condo-coop homes in thousands of dollars; (p) preliminary; n/a not available; (1) Tucson, AZ Metropolitan Statistical Area—see Appendix B for areas included
Source: National Association of Realtors, Median Sales Price of Existing Apartment Condo-Coop Homes for Metropolitan Areas, 4th Quarter 2015

Gross Monthly Rent

Area	Under $200	$200 -299	$300 -499	$500 -749	$750 -999	$1,000 -1,499	$1,500 and up	Median ($)
City	0.0	0.0	0.0	4.8	11.4	53.4	30.4	1,260
MSA[1]	1.0	1.6	8.9	31.7	24.6	24.5	7.7	813
U.S.	1.5	3.2	7.4	21.0	24.1	26.9	15.9	920

Note: Figures are percentages except for Median; Gross rent is the contract rent plus the estimated average monthly cost of utilities (electricity, gas, and water and sewer) and fuels (oil, coal, kerosene, wood, etc.) if these are paid by the renter (or paid for the renter by someone else); (1) Figures cover the Tucson, AZ Metropolitan Statistical Area—see Appendix B for areas included
Source: U.S. Census Bureau, 2010-2014 American Community Survey 5-Year Estimates

Homeownership Rate

Area	2008 (%)	2009 (%)	2010 (%)	2011 (%)	2012 (%)	2013 (%)	2014 (%)	2015 (%)
MSA[1]	63.5	65.5	64.3	67.2	64.9	66.1	66.7	61.4
U.S.	67.8	67.4	66.9	66.1	65.4	65.1	64.5	63.7

Note: (1) Figures cover the Tucson, AZ Metropolitan Statistical Area—see Appendix B for areas included
Source: U.S. Census Bureau, Housing Vacancies and Homeownership Annual Statistics: 2015

Year Housing Structure Built

Area	2010 or Later	2000 -2009	1990 -1999	1980 -1989	1970 -1979	1960 -1969	1950 -1959	1940 -1949	Before 1940	Median Year
City	4.4	75.9	10.9	1.9	3.1	2.2	0.6	0.7	0.4	2004
MSA[1]	0.9	19.7	17.9	17.5	20.7	9.2	8.6	3.1	2.4	1983
U.S.	1.0	14.9	13.9	13.8	15.8	11.0	10.8	5.4	13.3	1976

Note: Figures are percentages except for Median Year; (1) Figures cover the Tucson, AZ Metropolitan Statistical Area—see Appendix B for areas included
Source: U.S. Census Bureau, 2010-2014 American Community Survey 5-Year Estimates

HEALTH

Health Risk Data

Category	MSA[1] (%)	U.S. (%)
Adults aged 18–64 who have any kind of health care coverage	79.7	79.6
Adults who reported being in good or excellent health	81.2	83.1
Adults who are current smokers	16.4	19.6
Adults who are heavy drinkers[2]	5.6	6.1
Adults who are binge drinkers[3]	17.5	16.9
Adults who are overweight (BMI 25.0 - 29.9)	36.6	35.8
Adults who are obese (BMI 30.0 - 99.8)	22.9	27.6
Adults who participated in any physical activities in the past month	79.0	77.1
Adults 50+ who have ever had a sigmoidoscopy or colonoscopy	69.4	67.3
Women aged 40+ who have had a mammogram within the past two years	75.5	74.0
Men aged 40+ who have had a PSA test within the past two years	47.2	45.2
Adults aged 65+ who have had flu shot within the past year	50.6	60.1
Adults who always wear a seatbelt	96.5	93.8

Note: Data as of 2012 unless otherwise noted; (1) Figures cover the Tucson, AZ Metropolitan Statistical Area—see Appendix B for areas included; (2) Heavy drinkers are classified as males having more than two drinks per day or females having more than one drink per day; (3) Binge drinkers are classified as males having five or more drinks on one occasion or females having four or more drinks on one occasion
Source: Centers for Disease Control and Prevention, Behaviorial Risk Factor Surveillance System, SMART: Selected Metropolitan/Micropolitan Area Risk Trends, 2012 (Note: the CDC has discontinued this dataset but will be releasing a replacement in mid-2016)

Chronic Health Indicators

Category	MSA[1] (%)	U.S. (%)
Adults who have ever been told they had a heart attack	3.3	4.5
Adults who have ever been told they had a stroke	2.9	2.9
Adults who have been told they currently have asthma	8.7	8.9
Adults who have ever been told they have arthritis	25.7	25.7
Adults who have ever been told they have diabetes[2]	11.8	9.7
Adults who have ever been told they had skin cancer	8.1	5.7
Adults who have ever been told they had any other types of cancer	7.8	6.5
Adults who have ever been told they have COPD	6.2	6.2
Adults who have ever been told they have kidney disease	4.3	2.5
Adults who have ever been told they have a form of depression	20.9	18.0

Note: Data as of 2012 unless otherwise noted; (1) Figures cover the Tucson, AZ Metropolitan Statistical Area—see Appendix B for areas included; (2) Figures do not include pregnancy-related, borderline, or pre-diabetes
Source: Centers for Disease Control and Prevention, Behaviorial Risk Factor Surveillance System, SMART: Selected Metropolitan/Micropolitan Area Risk Trends, 2012 (Note: the CDC has discontinued this dataset but will be releasing a replacement in mid-2016)

Mortality Rates for the Top 10 Causes of Death in the U.S.

ICD-10[a] Sub-Chapter	ICD-10[a] Code	Age-Adjusted Mortality Rate[1] per 100,000 population	
		County[2]	U.S.
Malignant neoplasms	C00-C97	148.8	163.6
Ischaemic heart diseases	I20-I25	93.9	102.2
Other forms of heart disease	I30-I51	30.6	50.1
Chronic lower respiratory diseases	J40-J47	41.4	41.4
Organic, including symptomatic, mental disorders	F01-F09	28.8	38.5
Cerebrovascular diseases	I60-I69	31.0	36.5
Other external causes of accidental injury	W00-X59	35.9	27.5
Other degenerative diseases of the nervous system	G30-G31	33.3	26.3
Diabetes mellitus	E10-E14	24.6	21.1
Hypertensive diseases	I10-I15	24.9	19.7

Note: (a) ICD-10 = International Classification of Diseases 10th Revision; (1) Mortality rates are a three year average covering 2012-2014; (2) Figures cover COUNTY NOT FOUND!!!!!!.
Source: Centers for Disease Control and Prevention, National Center for Health Statistics. Underlying Cause of Death 1999-2014 on CDC WONDER Online Database, released 2015.

Mortality Rates for Selected Causes of Death

ICD-10[a] Sub-Chapter	ICD-10[a] Code	Age-Adjusted Mortality Rate[1] per 100,000 population	
		County[2]	U.S.
Assault	X85-Y09	6.0	5.1
Diseases of the liver	K70-K76	17.9	13.5
Human immunodeficiency virus (HIV) disease	B20-B24	1.6	2.1
Influenza and pneumonia	J09-J18	10.9	15.2
Intentional self-harm	X60-X84	18.3	12.7
Malnutrition	E40-E46	0.9	0.9
Obesity and other hyperalimentation	E65-E68	2.8	1.9
Renal failure	N17-N19	4.6	13.0
Transport accidents	V01-V99	11.7	11.6
Viral hepatitis	B15-B19	3.8	2.1

Note: (a) ICD-10 = International Classification of Diseases 10th Revision; (1) Mortality rates are a three year average covering 2012-2014; (2) Figures cover COUNTY NOT FOUND!!!!!!; Data are Suppressed when the data meet the criteria for confidentiality constraints; Mortality rates are flagged as Unreliable when the rate would be calculated with a numerator of 20 or less.
Source: Centers for Disease Control and Prevention, National Center for Health Statistics. Underlying Cause of Death 1999-2014 on CDC WONDER Online Database, released 2015.

Health Insurance Coverage

Area	With Health Insurance	With Private Health Insurance	With Public Health Insurance	Without Health Insurance	Population Under Age 18 Without Health Insurance
City	93.3	78.3	29.2	6.7	5.2
MSA[1]	85.5	60.8	37.4	14.5	10.7
U.S.	85.8	65.8	31.1	14.2	7.1

Note: Figures are percentages that cover the civilian noninstitutionalized population; (1) Figures cover the Tucson, AZ Metropolitan Statistical Area—see Appendix B for areas included
Source: U.S. Census Bureau, 2010-2014 American Community Survey 5-Year Estimates

Number of Medical Professionals

Area	MDs[3]	DOs[3,4]	Dentists	Podiatrists	Chiropractors	Optometrists
County[1] (number)	3,507	230	579	51	191	145
County[1] (rate[2])	351.4	23.0	57.6	5.1	19.0	14.4
U.S. (rate[2])	272.5	20.9	64.7	5.8	25.9	15.2

Note: Data as of 2014 unless noted; (1) Data covers Pima County; (2) Rate per 100,000 population; (3) Data as of 2013 and includes all active, non-federal physicians; (4) Doctor of Osteopathic Medicine
Source: U.S. Department of Health and Human Services, Health Resources and Services Administration, Bureau of Health Professions, Area Resource File (ARF) 2014-2015

Best Hospitals

According to *U.S. News,* the Tucson, AZ metro area is home to two of the best hospitals in the U.S.: **Banner-University Medical Center Tucson** (3 specialties); **University of Arizona Medical Center** (1 specialty). The hospitals listed were nationally ranked in at least one adult specialty. Only 137 hospitals nationwide were nationally ranked in one or more specialties. Fifteen hospitals in the U.S. made the Honor Roll with high scores in at least six specialties. *U.S. News Online, "America's Best Children's Hospitals 2015-16"*

EDUCATION

Public School District Statistics

District Name	Schls	Pupils	Pupil/ Teacher Ratio	Minority Pupils[1] (%)	Free Lunch Eligible[2] (%)	IEP[3] (%)
Great Expectations Academy	1	328	n/a	36.9	13.1	9.8
Sahuarita Unified District	8	5,538	18.3	58.5	24.3	10.0

Note: Table includes school districts with 100 or more students; (1) Percentage of students that are not non-Hispanic white; (2) Percentage of students that are eligible for the free lunch program; (3) Percentage of students that have an Individualized Education Program.
Source: U.S. Department of Education, National Center for Education Statistics, Common Core of Data, Local Education Agency (School District) Universe Survey: School Year 2013-2014; U.S. Department of Education, National Center for Education Statistics, Common Core of Data, Public Elementary/Secondary School Universe Survey: School Year 2013-2014

Highest Level of Education

Area	Less than H.S.	H.S. Diploma	Some College, No Deg.	Associate Degree	Bachelor's Degree	Master's Degree	Prof. School Degree	Doctorate Degree
City	4.9	20.0	29.7	10.2	23.4	9.6	0.9	1.2
MSA[1]	12.5	22.8	26.2	8.4	17.6	8.5	2.0	1.9
U.S.	13.7	28.0	21.2	7.9	18.3	7.8	2.0	1.3

Note: Figures cover persons age 25 and over; (1) Figures cover the Tucson, AZ Metropolitan Statistical Area—see Appendix B for areas included
Source: U.S. Census Bureau, 2010-2014 American Community Survey 5-Year Estimates

Educational Attainment by Race

Area	High School Graduate or Higher (%)					Bachelor's Degree or Higher (%)				
	Total	White	Black	Asian	Hisp.[2]	Total	White	Black	Asian	Hisp.[2]
City	95.1	95.4	97.8	96.7	90.8	35.2	36.6	43.8	15.1	23.1
MSA[1]	87.5	89.5	88.8	86.9	72.5	30.1	32.1	22.5	46.5	13.6
U.S.	86.3	88.4	83.2	85.8	64.1	29.3	30.6	19.0	50.9	13.9

Note: Figures shown cover persons 25 years old and over; (1) Figures cover the Tucson, AZ Metropolitan Statistical Area—see Appendix B for areas included; (2) People of Hispanic origin can be of any race
Source: U.S. Census Bureau, 2010-2014 American Community Survey 5-Year Estimates

School Enrollment by Grade and Control

Area	Preschool (%)		Kindergarten (%)		Grades 1 - 4 (%)		Grades 5 - 8 (%)		Grades 9 - 12 (%)	
	Public	Private	Public	Private	Public	Private	Public	Private	Public	Private
City	77.8	22.2	90.1	9.9	97.9	2.1	95.7	4.3	90.3	9.7
MSA[1]	57.6	42.4	87.1	12.9	91.7	8.3	92.5	7.5	92.5	7.5
U.S.	57.4	42.6	87.8	12.2	89.8	10.2	89.9	10.1	90.6	9.4

Note: Figures shown cover persons 3 years old and over; (1) Figures cover the Tucson, AZ Metropolitan Statistical Area—see Appendix B for areas included
Source: U.S. Census Bureau, 2010-2014 American Community Survey 5-Year Estimates

Average Salaries of Public School Classroom Teachers

Area	2013-14		2014-15		Percent Change 2013-14 to 2014-15	Percent Change 2004-05 to 2014-15
	Dollars	Rank[1]	Dollars	Rank[1]		
Arizona	45,335	45	45,406	47	0.16	13.4
U.S. Average	56,610	–	57,379	–	1.36	20.8

Note: (1) State rank ranges from 1 to 51 where 1 indicates highest salary.
Source: National Education Association, Rankings & Estimates: Rankings of the States 2014 and Estimates of School Statistics 2015, March 2015

Higher Education

Four-Year Colleges			Two-Year Colleges			Medical Schools[1]	Law Schools[2]	Voc/ Tech[3]
Public	Private Non-profit	Private For-profit	Public	Private Non-profit	Private For-profit			
0	0	0	0	0	0	0	0	0

Note: Figures cover institutions located within the city limits and include main campuses only; (1) includes schools accredited by the Liaison Committee on Medical Education and the American Osteopathic Association's Commission on Osteopathic College Accreditation; (2) includes ABA-accredited schools, schools with provisional ABA accreditation, and state accredited schools; (3) includes all schools with programs that are less than 2 years.

Source: National Center for Education Statistics, Integrated Postsecondary Education System (IPEDS), 2014-15; Association of American Medical Colleges, Member List, March 21, 2016; American Osteopathic Association, Member List, March 21, 2016; Law School Admission Council, Official Guide to ABA-Approved Law Schools Online, March 21, 2016; Wikipedia, List of Medical Schools in the United States, March 21, 2016; Wikipedia, List of Law Schools in the United States, March 21, 2016

According to *U.S. News & World Report,* the Tucson, AZ metro area is home to one of the best national universities in the U.S.: **University of Arizona** (#121 tie). The indicators used to capture academic quality fall into a number of categories: assessment by administrators at peer institutions; retention of students; faculty resources; student selectivity; financial resources; alumni giving; high school counselor ratings of colleges; and graduation rate. *U.S. News & World Report, "America's Best Colleges 2016"*

According to *U.S. News & World Report,* the Tucson, AZ metro area is home to one of the top 100 law schools in the U.S.: **University of Arizona, James E. Rogers College of Law** (#40 tie). The rankings are based on a weighted average of 12 measures of quality: peer assessment score; assessment score by lawyers/judges; median LSAT scores; median undergrad GPA; acceptance rate; employment rates for graduates; placement success; bar passage rate; faculty resources; expenditures per student; student/faculty ratio; and library resources. *U.S. News & World Report, "America's Best Graduate Schools, Law, 2017"*

According to *U.S. News & World Report,* the Tucson, AZ metro area is home to one of the top 75 medical schools for research in the U.S.: **University of Arizona, College of Medicine** (#63 tie). The rankings are based on a weighted average of 11 measures of quality: quality assessment; peer assessment score; assessment score by residency directors; research activity; total research activity; average research activity per faculty member; student selectivity; median MCAT total score; median undergraduate GPA; acceptance rate; and faculty resources. *U.S. News & World Report, "America's Best Graduate Schools, Medical, 2017"*

According to *U.S. News & World Report,* the Tucson, AZ metro area is home to one of the top 75 business schools in the U.S.: **University of Arizona, Eller College of Management** (#60 tie). The rankings are based on a weighted average of the following nine measures: quality assessment; peer assessment; recruiter assessment; placement success; mean starting salary and bonus; student selectivity; mean GMAT and GRE scores; mean undergraduate GPA; and acceptance rate. *U.S. News & World Report, "America's Best Graduate Schools, Business, 2017"*

PRESIDENTIAL ELECTION

2012 Presidential Election Results

Area	Obama (%)	Romney (%)	Other (%)
Pima County	52.1	46.1	1.8
U.S.	51.0	47.2	1.8

Note: Results may not add to 100% due to rounding

Source: Dave Leip's Atlas of U.S. Presidential Elections

EMPLOYERS

Major Employers

Company Name	Industry
Afni Inc	Customer contact
APAC Customer Service	Customer care outsourcing
Asarco LLC	Mining, smelting and refining
Bashas' Inc	Grocery
Carondelet Health Network	Healthcare
Circle K Stores	Convenience stores
Citi	Banking
Corrections Corp. of America	Prison and detention center management
Freeport-McMoRan Copper & Gold	Copper and gold producer
Fry's Food Stores	Grocery
GEICO	Insurance
IBM	Data management, cloud computing, manufacturing
Northwest Medical Center	Healthcare
Raytheon Missile Systems	Defense contractor
Safeway Inc.	Grocery
Sol Casinos	Gaming
Southern Arizona VA Health Care	Healthcare
Target	Retail
TEP/UniSource Energy	Energy corp
TMC HealthCare	Healthcare
UA Healthcare	Healthcare
Union Pacific Railroad	Freight railroad
University of Arizona	Education
Ventana Medical Systems, Inc.	Healthcare
Wal-Mart Stores	Retail
Walgreens	Retail

Note: Companies shown are located within the Tucson, AZ Metropolitan Statistical Area.
Source: Hoovers.com; Wikipedia

PUBLIC SAFETY

Crime Rate

Area	All Crimes	Violent Crimes: Murder	Violent Crimes: Rape[3]	Violent Crimes: Robbery	Violent Crimes: Aggrav. Assault	Property Crimes: Burglary	Property Crimes: Larceny -Theft	Property Crimes: Motor Vehicle Theft
City	1,477.6	0.0	7.4	11.0	14.7	187.5	1,198.2	58.8
Metro[1]	n/a	n/a	n/a	n/a	n/a	n/a	n/a	n/a
U.S.	2,971.8	4.5	36.6	102.2	232.5	542.5	1,837.3	216.2

Note: Figures are crimes per 100,000 population; (1) Figures cover the Tucson, AZ Metropolitan Statistical Area—see Appendix B for areas included; n/a not available; (3) The city and U.S. figures shown were reported using the revised Uniform Crime Reporting (UCR) definition of rape. The suburban and metro area figures shown are an aggregate total of the data submitted using both the revised and legacy UCR definitions.
Source: FBI Uniform Crime Reports, 2014

Hate Crimes

Area	Number of Quarters Reported	Number of Incidents per Bias Motivation: Race	Religion	Sexual Orientation	Ethnicity	Disability	Gender	Gender Identity
City	4	0	0	0	0	0	0	0
U.S.	4	2,568	1,014	1,017	648	84	33	98

Source: Federal Bureau of Investigation, Hate Crime Statistics 2014

Identity Theft Consumer Complaints

Area	Complaints	Complaints per 100,000 Population	Rank[2]
MSA[1]	1,399	139.3	73
U.S.	490,220	152.4	-

Note: (1) Figures cover the Tucson, AZ Metropolitan Statistical Area—see Appendix B for areas included; (2) Rank ranges from 1 to 379 where 1 indicates greatest number of identity theft complaints per 100,000 population
Source: Federal Trade Commission, Consumer Sentinel Network Data Book for January–December 2015

Fraud and Other Consumer Complaints

Area	Complaints	Complaints per 100,000 Population	Rank[2]
MSA[1]	4,311	429.2	65
U.S.	2,593,159	806.0	-

Note: (1) Figures cover the Tucson, AZ Metropolitan Statistical Area—see Appendix B for areas included; (2) Rank ranges from 1 to 379 where 1 indicates greatest number of identity theft complaints per 100,000 population
Source: Federal Trade Commission, Consumer Sentinel Network Data Book for January–December 2015

RECREATION

Culture

Dance[1]	Theatre[1]	Instrumental Music[1]	Vocal Music[1]	Series and Festivals	Museums and Art Galleries[2]	Zoos and Aquariums[3]
0	0	0	0	0	0	0

Note: (1) Professional perfoming groups; (2) Based on organizations with SIC code 8412; (3) AZA-accredited
Source: The Grey House Performing Arts Directory, 2015-16; Association of Zoos & Aquariums, AZA Member Zoos & Aquariums, March 25, 2016; www.AccuLeads.com, March 29, 2016

Professional Sports Teams

Team Name	League	Year Established
No teams are located in the metro area		

Source: Wikipedia, Major Professional Sports Teams of the United States and Canada, March 24, 2016

CLIMATE

Average and Extreme Temperatures

Temperature	Jan	Feb	Mar	Apr	May	Jun	Jul	Aug	Sep	Oct	Nov	Dec	Yr.
Extreme High (°F)	87	92	99	104	107	117	114	108	107	101	90	84	117
Average High (°F)	64	68	73	81	89	99	99	96	94	84	73	65	82
Average Temp. (°F)	51	54	59	66	74	84	86	84	81	71	59	52	69
Average Low (°F)	38	40	44	51	58	68	74	72	67	57	45	39	55
Extreme Low (°F)	16	20	20	33	38	47	62	61	44	26	24	16	16

Note: Figures cover the years 1946-1990
Source: National Climatic Data Center, International Station Meteorological Climate Summary, 9/96

Average Precipitation/Snowfall/Humidity

Precip./Humidity	Jan	Feb	Mar	Apr	May	Jun	Jul	Aug	Sep	Oct	Nov	Dec	Yr.
Avg. Precip. (in.)	0.9	0.7	0.7	0.3	0.1	0.2	2.5	2.2	1.4	0.9	0.6	0.9	11.6
Avg. Snowfall (in.)	Tr	Tr	Tr	Tr	0	0	0	0	0	0	Tr	Tr	2
Avg. Rel. Hum. 5am (%)	62	58	52	41	34	32	58	65	55	52	54	61	52
Avg. Rel. Hum. 5pm (%)	31	26	22	16	13	13	29	32	26	24	27	33	24

Note: Figures cover the years 1946-1990; Tr = Trace amounts (<0.05 in. of rain; <0.5 in. of snow)
Source: National Climatic Data Center, International Station Meteorological Climate Summary, 9/96

Weather Conditions

Temperature			Daytime Sky			Precipitation		
10°F & below	32°F & below	90°F & above	Clear	Partly cloudy	Cloudy	0.01 inch or more precip.	0.1 inch or more snow/ice	Thunder-storms
0	18	140	177	119	69	54	2	42

Note: Figures are average number of days per year and cover the years 1946-1990
Source: National Climatic Data Center, International Station Meteorological Climate Summary, 9/96

HAZARDOUS WASTE

Superfund Sites

Sahuarita has no sites on the EPA's Superfund Final National Priorities List. There are a total of 1,323 Superfund sites on the list in the U.S. *U.S. Environmental Protection Agency, Final National Priorities List, March 18, 2016*

AIR & WATER QUALITY

Air Quality Trends: Ozone

	1990	1995	2000	2005	2010	2011	2012	2013	2014
MSA[1]	0.073	0.078	0.074	0.075	0.068	0.072	0.069	0.069	0.065

Note: (1) Data covers the Tucson, AZ Metropolitan Statistical Area—see Appendix B for areas included. The values shown are the composite ozone concentration averages among trend sites based on the highest fourth daily maximum 8-hour concentration in parts per million. These trends are based on sites having an adequate record of monitoring data during the trend period. Data from exceptional events are included.
Source: U.S. Environmental Protection Agency, Air Quality Monitoring Information, "Air Quality Trends by City, 1990-2014"

Air Quality Index

Area	Percent of Days when Air Quality was...[2]					AQI Statistics[2]	
	Good	Moderate	Unhealthy for Sensitive Groups	Unhealthy	Very Unhealthy	Maximum	Median
MSA[1]	78.6	21.4	0.0	0.0	0.0	95	43

Note: (1) Data covers the Tucson, AZ Metropolitan Statistical Area—see Appendix B for areas included; (2) Based on 365 days with AQI data in 2015. Air Quality Index (AQI) is an index for reporting daily air quality. EPA calculates the AQI for five major air pollutants regulated by the Clean Air Act: ground-level ozone, particle pollution (aka particulate matter), carbon monoxide, sulfur dioxide, and nitrogen dioxide. The AQI runs from 0 to 500. The higher the AQI value, the greater the level of air pollution and the greater the health concern. There are six AQI categories: "Good" AQI is between 0 and 50. Air quality is considered satisfactory; "Moderate" AQI is between 51 and 100. Air quality is acceptable; "Unhealthy for Sensitive Groups" When AQI values are between 101 and 150, members of sensitive groups may experience health effects; "Unhealthy" When AQI values are between 151 and 200 everyone may begin to experience health effects; "Very Unhealthy" AQI values between 201 and 300 trigger a health alert; "Hazardous" AQI values over 300 trigger warnings of emergency conditions (not shown).
Source: U.S. Environmental Protection Agency, Air Quality Index Report, 2015

Air Quality Index Pollutants

Area	Percent of Days when AQI Pollutant was...[2]					
	Carbon Monoxide	Nitrogen Dioxide	Ozone	Sulfur Dioxide	Particulate Matter 2.5	Particulate Matter 10
MSA[1]	0.0	2.5	65.8	0.0	5.5	26.3

Note: (1) Data covers the Tucson, AZ Metropolitan Statistical Area—see Appendix B for areas included; (2) Based on 365 days with AQI data in 2015. The Air Quality Index (AQI) is an index for reporting daily air quality. EPA calculates the AQI for five major air pollutants regulated by the Clean Air Act: ground-level ozone, particle pollution (also known as particulate matter), carbon monoxide, sulfur dioxide, and nitrogen dioxide. The AQI runs from 0 to 500. The higher the AQI value, the greater the level of air pollution and the greater the health concern.
Source: U.S. Environmental Protection Agency, Air Quality Index Report, 2015

Maximum Air Pollutant Concentrations: Particulate Matter, Ozone, CO and Lead

	Particulate Matter 10 (ug/m^3)	Particulate Matter 2.5 Wtd AM (ug/m^3)	Particulate Matter 2.5 24-Hr (ug/m^3)	Ozone (ppm)	Carbon Monoxide (ppm)	Lead (ug/m^3)
MSA[1] Level	143	6.3	17	0.069	1	0
NAAQS[2]	150	15	35	0.075	9	0.15
Met NAAQS[2]	Yes	Yes	Yes	Yes	Yes	Yes

Note: (1) Data covers the Tucson, AZ Metropolitan Statistical Area—see Appendix B for areas included; Data from exceptional events are included; (2) National Ambient Air Quality Standards; ppm = parts per million; ug/m^3 = micrograms per cubic meter; n/a not available.
Concentrations: Particulate Matter 10 (coarse particulate)—highest second maximum 24-hour concentration; Particulate Matter 2.5 Wtd AM (fine particulate)—highest weighted annual mean concentration; Particulate Matter 2.5 24-Hour (fine particulate)—highest 98th percentile 24-hour concentration; Ozone—highest fourth daily maximum 8-hour concentration; Carbon Monoxide—highest second maximum non-overlapping 8-hour concentration; Lead—maximum running 3-month average
Source: U.S. Environmental Protection Agency, Air Quality Monitoring Information, "Air Quality Statistics by City, 2014"

Maximum Air Pollutant Concentrations: Nitrogen Dioxide and Sulfur Dioxide

	Nitrogen Dioxide AM (ppb)	Nitrogen Dioxide 1-Hr (ppb)	Sulfur Dioxide AM (ppb)	Sulfur Dioxide 1-Hr (ppb)	Sulfur Dioxide 24-Hr (ppb)
MSA[1] Level	11	43	n/a	6	n/a
NAAQS[2]	53	100	30	75	140
Met NAAQS[2]	Yes	Yes	n/a	Yes	n/a

Note: (1) Data covers the Tucson, AZ Metropolitan Statistical Area—see Appendix B for areas included; Data from exceptional events are included; (2) National Ambient Air Quality Standards; ppm = parts per million; ug/m^3 = micrograms per cubic meter; n/a not available.

Concentrations: Nitrogen Dioxide AM—highest arithmetic mean concentration; Nitrogen Dioxide 1-Hr—highest 98th percentile 1-hour daily maximum concentration; Sulfur Dioxide AM—highest annual mean concentration; Sulfur Dioxide 1-Hr—highest 99th percentile 1-hour daily maximum concentration; Sulfur Dioxide 24-Hr—highest second maximum 24-hour concentration

Source: U.S. Environmental Protection Agency, Air Quality Monitoring Information, "Air Quality Statistics by City, 2014"

Drinking Water

Water System Name	Pop. Served	Primary Water Source Type	Violations[1] Health Based	Violations[1] Monitoring/ Reporting
Sahuarita Water Company	16,200	Ground	0	0

Note: (1) Based on violation data from January 1, 2015 to December 31, 2015 (includes unresolved violations from earlier years)

Source: U.S. Environmental Protection Agency, Office of Ground Water and Drinking Water, Safe Drinking Water Information System (based on data extracted April 29, 2016)

Bella Vista, Arkansas

Background

Bella Vista is an Ozark Mountain city located on the Arkansas-Missouri border in the northwest corner of Arkansas about 25 miles east of the Oklahoma line. The city is situated along I-540 north of I-40, a major interstate that crosses the country east to west.

Incorporated in 2007, Bella Vista grew from a planned recreational community built in 1965. Seven "village lakes" ranging in size from about 35 to 477 acres lie in and around the community and provide abundant recreational opportunities. The largest, at 477 acres, is Lake Lomand, with a depth of 80 feet. Lake Lomand is large enough to accommodate water skiers as well as fishers, who find bass, bluegill, crappie and catfish in its coves. Further enhancing Bella Vista's recreational opportunities are two fitness centers, two swimming pools, a variety of tennis courts, parks, and even two mini-golf courses (as well as eight golf courses).

The city's proximity to Bentonville, both within Benton County, tie the two together economically, shares a Chamber of Commerce. Bentonville's largest employers include Wal-Mart, Mercy Health System of Northwest Arkansas and the Bentonville School District. Three other major employers are Northwest Health System, the city of Bentonville and Northwest Arkansas Community College. ConAgra Foods also operates in Bentonville.

Bella Vista's children attend one of two school districts, either the Bentonville Public Schools or the Gravette Public Schools. Cooper Elementary School is located in Bella Vista and there's a Montessori school in town. Higher educational offerings in the region include the University of Arkansas, the state's land-grant school with 200 academic programs that is a 40-minute drive from Bella Vista in Fayetteville. Northwest Arkansas Community College is in Bentonville.

Bella Vista also taps into Bentonville's cultural scene, which include the new Crystal Bridges Museum of American Art with works by major artists such as Thomas Hart Benton, Claes Oldenburg, and Andy Warhol.

Bella Vista's climate is summer highs of 90, winter lows of about 23 degrees, and average rainfall just over 45 inches per year.

Rankings

Business/Finance Rankings

- The personal finance site NerdWallet analyzed 183 American metropolitan areas with populations over 250,000 and more than 15,000 businesses to rank where entrepreneurs find the most success. Criteria included area economy, annual income, housing cost, unemployment rate, and the success rate of area businesses. Fayetteville* ranked #74. *www.nerdwallet.com, "Best Places to Start a Business," April 27, 2015*
- The Fayetteville* metro area appeared on the Milken Institute "2015 Best Performing Cities" list. Rank: #24 out of 200 large metro areas. Criteria: job growth; wage and salary growth; high-tech output growth. *Milken Institute, "Best-Performing Cities 2015," December 2015*
- *Forbes* ranked the 200 most populous metro areas to determine the nation's "Best Places for Business and Careers." The Fayetteville* metro area was ranked #23. Criteria: costs (business and living); job growth (past and projected); income growth; educational attainment (college and high school); projected economic growth; cultural and recreational opportunities; net migration patterns; number of highly ranked colleges. *Forbes, "The Best Places for Business and Careers 2015," July 29, 2015*

Education Rankings

- Personal finance website *WalletHub* analyzed the 150 largest U.S. metropolitan statistical areas to determine where the most educated Americans are choosing to settle. Criteria: education quality and attainment gap; education levels; percentage of workers with degrees; public school rankings; quality and size of each metro area's universities. Fayetteville* was ranked #105 (#1 = most educated city). *www.WalletHub.com, "2015's Most and Least Educated Cities*

Environmental Rankings

- The Fayetteville* metro area came in at #237 for the relative comfort of its climate on Sperling's list of "chill cities," as measured by the Sperling Heat Index. All 361 metro areas are included. Criteria included daytime high temperatures, nighttime low temperatures, dew point, and relative humidity at the high temperatures. *www.bertsperling.com, "Sperling's Chill Cities," July 18, 2013*
- Sperling's BestPlaces assessed 379 metropolitan areas of the United States for the likelihood of dangerously extreme weather events or earthquakes. In general the Southeast and South-Central regions have the highest risk of weather extremes and earthquakes, while the Pacific Northwest enjoys the lowest risk. Of the least risky metropolitan areas, the Fayetteville* metro area was ranked #282. *www.bestplaces.net, "Safest Places from Natural Disasters," April 2011*
- Fayetteville* was highlighted as one of the top 25 cleanest metro areas for short-term particle pollution (24-hour PM 2.5) in the U.S. during 2011 through 2013. Monitors in these cities reported no days with unhealthful PM 2.5 levels. *American Lung Association, State of the Air 2015*

Health/Fitness Rankings

- The Gallup-Healthways Well-Being Index tracks Americans' optimism about their communities and satisfaction with the metro areas in which they live. At least 300 adult residents in each of 189 U.S. metropolitan areas were asked whether their metro was improving and the Fayetteville* metro area placed among the top ten in the percentage of residents who were optimistic about their metro area. *www.gallup.com, "City Satisfaction Highest in Fort Collins-Loveland, Colo.," April 11, 2014*
- The Fayetteville* metro area ranked #68 out of 190 in The Gallup-Healthways Well-Being Index. Criteria: purpose; social well being; financial health; community and physical health. Results are based on telephone interviews with adults, aged 18 and older, living in metropolitan areas in the 50 U.S. states and the District of Columbia. *Gallup-Healthways, "State of American Well-Being," February 23, 2016*

Real Estate Rankings

- With data from RealtyTrac, Yahoo! Finance researchers listed the housing markets in which housing affordability is improving most, factoring in interest rates as well as median home prices. The Fayetteville* metro area was among the most affordable housing markets. *news.yahoo.com, "10 Cities Where Ordinary People Can No Longer Afford Homes," March 5, 2014*

Safety Rankings

- Farmers Insurance, in partnership with Sperling's BestPlaces, ranked metro areas in the U.S. as the "Most Secure Places to Live." The Fayetteville* metro area ranked #17 out of the top 20 in the mid-size city category (150,000 to 500,000 residents). Criteria: economic stability; crime statistics; extreme weather; risk of natural disasters; housing depreciation; foreclosures; air quality; environmental hazards; life expectancy; motor vehicle fatalities; and employment numbers. *Farmers Insurance Group of Companies, "Most Secure U.S. Places to Live in the U.S.," June 25, 2013*
- Bella Vista was identified as one of the safest cities in America by NeighborhoodScout. The city ranked #22 out of 100. Criteria: number of violent and property crimes per 1,000 residents. The editors only considered cities with 25,000 or more residents. *NeighborhoodScout, "Safest Cities in America 2016"*
- The National Insurance Crime Bureau ranked 380 metro areas in the U.S. in terms of per capita rates of vehicle theft. The Fayetteville* metro area ranked #215 (#1 = highest rate). Criteria: number of vehicle theft offenses per 100,000 inhabitants in 2014. *National Insurance Crime Bureau, "Hot Spots 2014," June 24, 2015*

Seniors/Retirement Rankings

- From its Best Cities for Successful Aging indexes, the Milken Institute generated rankings for metropolitan areas, weighing data in eight categories—health care, wellness, living arrangements, transportation, financial characteristics, education and employment opportunities, community engagement, and overall livability. The Fayetteville* metro area was ranked #116 overall in the small metro area category. *Milken Institute, "Best Cities for Successful Aging, 2014"*

Bella Vista is located within the Fayetteville-Springdale-Rogers, AR-MO Metropolitan Statistical Area.

Business Environment

CITY FINANCES

City Government Finances

Component	2012 ($000)	2012 ($ per capita)
Total Revenues	12,196	460
Total Expenditures	12,060	455
Debt Outstanding	0	0
Cash and Securities[1]	5,233	197

Note: (1) Cash and security holdings of a government at the close of its fiscal year, including those of its dependent agencies, utilities, and liquor stores.
Source: U.S Census Bureau, State & Local Government Finances 2012

City Government Revenue by Source

Source	2012 ($000)	2012 ($ per capita)
General Revenue		
From Federal Government	256	9
From State Government	1,728	65
From Local Governments	3,986	150
Taxes		
Property	772	29
Sales and Gross Receipts	2,437	92
Personal Income	0	0
Corporate Income	0	0
Motor Vehicle License	0	0
Other Taxes	127	4
Current Charges	2,587	97
Liquor Store	0	0
Utility	0	0
Employee Retirement	0	0

Source: U.S Census Bureau, State & Local Government Finances 2012

City Government Expenditures by Function

Function	2012 ($000)	2012 ($ per capita)	2012 (%)
General Direct Expenditures			
Air Transportation	0	0	0.0
Corrections	0	0	0.0
Education	0	0	0.0
Employment Security Administration	0	0	0.0
Financial Administration	277	10	2.2
Fire Protection	3,289	124	27.2
General Public Buildings	41	1	0.3
Governmental Administration, Other	553	20	4.5
Health	0	0	0.0
Highways	3,139	118	26.0
Hospitals	0	0	0.0
Housing and Community Development	0	0	0.0
Interest on General Debt	0	0	0.0
Judicial and Legal	0	0	0.0
Libraries	75	2	0.6
Parking	0	0	0.0
Parks and Recreation	0	0	0.0
Police Protection	2,401	90	19.9
Public Welfare	0	0	0.0
Sewerage	0	0	0.0
Solid Waste Management	1,665	62	13.8
Veterans' Services	0	0	0.0
Liquor Store	0	0	0.0
Utility	0	0	0.0
Employee Retirement	0	0	0.0

Source: U.S Census Bureau, State & Local Government Finances 2012

DEMOGRAPHICS

Population Growth

Area	1990 Census	2000 Census	2010 Census	2014* Estimate	Population Growth (%) 1990-2014	2010-2014
City	9,091	16,582	26,461	27,273	200.0	3.1
MSA[1]	239,474	347,045	463,204	483,396	101.9	4.4
U.S.	248,709,873	281,421,906	308,745,538	314,107,084	26.3	1.7

Note: (1) Figures cover the Fayetteville-Springdale-Rogers, AR-MO Metropolitan Statistical Area—see Appendix B for areas included; (*) 2010-2014 5-year estimated population
Source: U.S. Census Bureau, 1990 Census, Census 2000, Census 2010, 2010-2014 American Community Survey 5-Year Estimates

Household Size

Area	Persons in Household (%) One	Two	Three	Four	Five	Six	Seven or More	Average Household Size
City	19.5	55.1	8.9	9.3	3.6	1.9	1.3	2.33
MSA[1]	24.4	34.4	15.7	14.0	6.8	2.7	1.8	2.66
U.S.	27.5	33.5	15.8	13.1	6.0	2.3	1.4	2.64

Note: (1) Figures cover the Fayetteville-Springdale-Rogers, AR-MO Metropolitan Statistical Area—see Appendix B for areas included
Source: U.S. Census Bureau, 2010-2014 American Community Survey 5-Year Estimates

Race

Area	White Alone[2] (%)	Black Alone[2] (%)	Asian Alone[2] (%)	AIAN[3] Alone[2] (%)	NHOPI[4] Alone[2] (%)	Other Race Alone[2] (%)	Two or More Races (%)
City	95.9	0.7	1.1	0.7	0.2	0.1	1.4
MSA[1]	84.1	2.2	2.7	1.3	1.1	5.8	2.7
U.S.	73.8	12.6	5.0	0.8	0.2	4.7	2.9

Note: (1) Figures cover the Fayetteville-Springdale-Rogers, AR-MO Metropolitan Statistical Area—see Appendix B for areas included; (2) Alone is defined as not being in combination with one or more other races; (3) American Indian and Alaska Native; (4) Native Hawaiian and Other Pacific Islander
Source: U.S. Census Bureau, 2010-2014 American Community Survey 5-Year Estimates

Hispanic or Latino Origin

Area	Total (%)	Mexican (%)	Puerto Rican (%)	Cuban (%)	Other (%)
City	3.9	3.3	0.1	0.0	0.5
MSA[1]	15.3	11.5	0.3	0.1	3.4
U.S.	16.9	10.8	1.6	0.6	3.8

Note: Persons of Hispanic or Latino origin can be of any race; (1) Figures cover the Fayetteville-Springdale-Rogers, AR-MO Metropolitan Statistical Area—see Appendix B for areas included
Source: U.S. Census Bureau, 2010-2014 American Community Survey 5-Year Estimates

Ancestry

Area	German	Irish	English	American	Italian	Polish	French[2]	Scottish	Dutch
City	18.8	10.3	13.1	9.2	3.3	1.3	2.6	3.4	1.8
MSA[1]	13.0	10.3	9.0	8.5	2.0	1.1	2.2	2.0	1.4
U.S.	14.9	10.8	8.0	7.1	5.5	3.0	2.7	1.7	1.4

Note: Figures are the percentage of the total population reporting a particular ancestry. The nine most commonly reported ancestries in the U.S. are shown. Figures include multiple ancestries (e.g. if a person reported being Irish and Italian, they were included in both columns); (1) Figures cover the Fayetteville-Springdale-Rogers, AR-MO Metropolitan Statistical Area—see Appendix B for areas included; (2) Excludes Basque
Source: U.S. Census Bureau, 2010-2014 American Community Survey 5-Year Estimates

Foreign-Born Population

Area	Percent of Population Born in								
	Any Foreign Country	Asia	Mexico	Europe	Carribean	Central America[2]	South America	Africa	Canada
City	3.6	0.8	0.6	1.7	0.1	0.1	0.0	0.2	0.2
MSA[1]	10.9	1.9	5.4	0.5	0.1	1.7	0.3	0.1	0.1
U.S.	13.1	3.8	3.7	1.5	1.2	1.0	0.9	0.6	0.3

Note: (1) Figures cover the Fayetteville-Springdale-Rogers, AR-MO Metropolitan Statistical Area—see Appendix B for areas included; (2) Excludes Mexico.
Source: U.S. Census Bureau, 2010-2014 American Community Survey 5-Year Estimates

Marital Status

Area	Never Married	Now Married[2]	Separated	Widowed	Divorced
City	13.5	72.0	0.3	6.4	7.7
MSA[1]	27.7	54.8	1.5	5.1	10.9
U.S.	32.5	48.4	2.2	5.9	10.9

Note: Figures are percentages and cover the population 15 years of age and older; (1) Figures cover the Fayetteville-Springdale-Rogers, AR-MO Metropolitan Statistical Area—see Appendix B for areas included; (2) Excludes separated
Source: U.S. Census Bureau, 2010-2014 American Community Survey 5-Year Estimates

Disability Status

Area	All Ages	Under 18 Years Old	18 to 64 Years Old	65 Years and Over
City	13.6	1.4	7.3	29.1
MSA[1]	10.8	3.5	9.2	36.5
U.S.	12.3	4.1	10.2	36.3

Note: Figures show percent of the civilian noninstitutionalized population that reported having a disability. Disability status is determined from from six types of difficulty: vision, hearing, cognitive, ambulatory, self-care, and independent living. For children under 5 years old, hearing and vision difficulty are used to determine disability status. For children between the ages of 5 and 14, disability status is determined from hearing, vision, cognitive, ambulatory, and self-care difficulties. For people aged 15 years and older, they are considered to have a disability if they have difficulty with any one of the six difficulty types; (1) Figures cover the Fayetteville-Springdale-Rogers, AR-MO Metropolitan Statistical Area—see Appendix B for areas included.
Source: U.S. Census Bureau, 2010-2014 American Community Survey 5-Year Estimates

Age

Area	Percent of Population									Median Age
	Under Age 5	Age 5–19	Age 20–34	Age 35–44	Age 45–54	Age 55–64	Age 65–74	Age 75–84	Age 85+	
City	5.9	13.7	12.1	11.7	11.8	11.8	17.7	10.2	5.0	50.2
MSA[1]	7.4	22.2	22.6	13.4	12.5	10.2	6.7	3.5	1.5	33.5
U.S.	6.4	19.9	20.6	13.0	14.1	12.3	7.6	4.3	1.9	37.4

Note: (1) Figures cover the Fayetteville-Springdale-Rogers, AR-MO Metropolitan Statistical Area—see Appendix B for areas included
Source: U.S. Census Bureau, 2010-2014 American Community Survey 5-Year Estimates

Gender

Area	Males	Females	Males per 100 Females
City	13,147	14,126	93.1
MSA[1]	240,613	242,783	99.1
U.S.	154,515,159	159,591,925	96.8

Note: (1) Figures cover the Fayetteville-Springdale-Rogers, AR-MO Metropolitan Statistical Area—see Appendix B for areas included
Source: U.S. Census Bureau, 2010-2014 American Community Survey 5-Year Estimates

Religious Groups by Family

Area	Catholic	Baptist	Non-Den.	Methodist[2]	Lutheran	LDS[3]	Pentecostal	Presbyterian[4]	Muslim[5]	Judaism
MSA[1]	9.1	22.9	5.7	4.8	0.8	1.7	2.2	0.9	0.1	<0.1
U.S.	19.1	9.3	4.0	4.0	2.3	2.0	1.9	1.6	0.8	0.7

Note: Figures are the number of adherents as a percentage of the total population; (1) Figures cover the Fayetteville-Springdale-Rogers, AR-MO Metropolitan Statistical Area—see Appendix B for areas included; (2) Methodist/Pietist; (3) Latter Day Saints; (4) Reformed; (5) Figures are estimates
Source: Association of Statisticians of American Religious Bodies, 2010 U.S. Religion Census: Religious Congregations & Membership Study

Religious Groups by Tradition

Area	Catholic	Evangelical Protestant	Mainline Protestant	Other Tradition	Black Protestant	Orthodox
MSA[1]	9.1	32.6	7.0	2.1	0.1	<0.1
U.S.	19.1	16.2	7.3	4.3	1.6	0.3

Note: Figures are the number of adherents as a percentage of the total population; (1) Figures cover the Fayetteville-Springdale-Rogers, AR-MO Metropolitan Statistical Area—see Appendix B for areas included
Source: Association of Statisticians of American Religious Bodies, 2010 U.S. Religion Census: Religious Congregations & Membership Study

ECONOMY

Gross Metropolitan Product

Area	2013	2014	2015	2016	Rank[2]
MSA[1]	23.8	25.3	26.3	27.9	93

Note: Figures are in billions of dollars; (1) Figures cover the Fayetteville-Springdale-Rogers, AR-MO Metropolitan Statistical Area—see Appendix B for areas included; (2) Rank is based on 2016 data and ranges from 1 to 381
Source: The U.S. Conference of Mayors, U.S. Metro Economies: GMP and Employment 2014-2016, June 2015

Economic Growth

Area	2011-13 (%)	2014 (%)	2015 (%)	2016 (%)	Rank[2]
MSA[1]	3.7	4.8	3.2	4.2	7
U.S.	2.2	2.4	2.3	2.9	–

Note: Figures are real gross metropolitan product (GMP) growth rates and represent annual average percent change; (1) Figures cover the Fayetteville-Springdale-Rogers, AR-MO Metropolitan Statistical Area—see Appendix B for areas included; (2) Rank is based on 2016 data and ranges from 1 to 381
Source: The U.S. Conference of Mayors, U.S. Metro Economies: GMP and Employment 2014-2016, June 2015

Metropolitan Area Exports

Area	2009	2010	2011	2012	2013	2014	Rank[2]
MSA[1]	811.4	678.0	568.1	667.6	699.0	786.9	181

Note: Figures are in millions of dollars; (1) Figures cover the Fayetteville-Springdale-Rogers, AR-MO Metropolitan Statistical Area—see Appendix B for areas included; (2) Rank is based on 2014 data and ranges from 1 to 385
Source: U.S. Department of Commerce, International Trade Administration, Office of Trade & Industry Information, Manufacturing & Services, data extracted March 10, 2016

Building Permits

Area	Single-Family			Multi-Family			Total		
	2014	2015p	Pct. Chg.	2014	2015p	Pct. Chg.	2014	2015p	Pct. Chg.
City	51	68	33.3	0	0	-	51	68	33.3
MSA[1]	2,388	2,816	17.9	965	976	1.1	3,353	3,792	13.1
U.S.	640,300	690,800	7.9	411,800	487,600	18.4	1,052,100	1,178,400	12.0

Note: (1) Figures cover the Fayetteville-Springdale-Rogers, AR-MO Metropolitan Statistical Area—see Appendix B for areas included; Figures represent new, privately-owned housing units authorized (unadjusted data); All permit data are based on estimates with imputation; (p) preliminary data.
Source: U.S. Census Bureau, Manufacturing, Mining, and Construction Statistics, Building Permits, 2014, 2015

Bankruptcy Filings

Area	Business Filings			Nonbusiness Filings		
	2014	2015	% Chg.	2014	2015	% Chg.
Benton County	29	33	13.8	656	576	-12.2
U.S.	26,983	24,735	-8.3	909,812	819,760	-9.9

Note: Business filings include Chapter 7, Chapter 11, Chapter 12, and Chapter 13; Nonbusiness filings include Chapter 7, Chapter 11, and Chapter 13

Source: Administrative Office of the U.S. Courts, Business and Nonbusiness Bankruptcy, County Cases Commenced by Chapter of the Bankruptcy Code, During the 12- Month Period Ending December 31, 2014 and Business and Nonbusiness Bankruptcy, County Cases Commenced by Chapter of the Bankruptcy Code, During the 12- Month Period Ending December 31, 2015

Housing Vacancy Rates

Area	Gross Vacancy Rate² (%)			Year-Round Vacancy Rate³ (%)			Rental Vacancy Rate⁴ (%)			Homeowner Vacancy Rate⁵ (%)		
	2013	2014	2015	2013	2014	2015	2013	2014	2015	2013	2014	2015
MSA[1]	n/a	n/a	n/a	n/a	n/a	n/a	n/a	n/a	n/a	n/a	n/a	n/a
U.S.	13.6	13.4	12.9	10.7	10.4	10.0	8.3	7.6	7.1	2.0	1.9	1.8

Note: (1) Figures cover the Fayetteville-Springdale-Rogers, AR-MO Metropolitan Statistical Area—see Appendix B for areas included; (2) The percentage of the total housing inventory that is vacant; (3) The percentage of the housing inventory (excluding seasonal units) that is year-round vacant; (4) The percentage of rental inventory that is vacant for rent; (5) The percentage of homeowner inventory that is vacant for sale; n/a not available

Source: U.S. Census Bureau, Housing Vacancies and Homeownership Annual Statistics: 2015

INCOME

Income

Area	Per Capita ($)	Median Household ($)	Average Household ($)
City	31,734	62,500	74,892
MSA[1]	25,291	48,627	67,424
U.S.	28,555	53,482	74,596

Note: (1) Figures cover the Fayetteville-Springdale-Rogers, AR-MO Metropolitan Statistical Area—see Appendix B for areas included

Source: U.S. Census Bureau, 2010-2014 American Community Survey 5-Year Estimates

Household Income Distribution

Area	Percent of Households Earning							
	Under $15,000	$15,000 -24,999	$25,000 -34,999	$35,000 -49,999	$50,000 -74,999	$75,000 -99,000	$100,000 -149,999	$150,000 and up
City	5.2	7.7	9.4	15.4	23.0	15.1	16.3	8.0
MSA[1]	13.0	11.2	11.5	15.4	18.4	10.6	11.8	8.0
U.S.	12.5	10.7	10.2	13.5	17.8	12.2	13.0	10.0

Note: (1) Figures cover the Fayetteville-Springdale-Rogers, AR-MO Metropolitan Statistical Area—see Appendix B for areas included

Source: U.S. Census Bureau, 2010-2014 American Community Survey 5-Year Estimates

Poverty Rate

Area	All Ages	Under 18 Years Old	18 to 64 Years Old	65 Years and Over
City	4.3	2.5	5.9	2.9
MSA[1]	16.4	21.6	15.7	8.2
U.S.	15.6	21.9	14.6	9.4

Note: Figures are percentage of people whose income during the past 12 months was below the poverty level; (1) Figures cover the Fayetteville-Springdale-Rogers, AR-MO Metropolitan Statistical Area—see Appendix B for areas included

Source: U.S. Census Bureau, 2010-2014 American Community Survey 5-Year Estimates

EMPLOYMENT

Labor Force and Employment

Area	Civilian Labor Force			Workers Employed		
	Dec. 2014	Dec. 2015	% Chg.	Dec. 2014	Dec. 2015	% Chg.
City	11,292	11,713	3.7	10,759	11,255	4.6
MSA[1]	241,432	250,333	3.6	231,793	242,314	4.5
U.S.	155,521,000	157,245,000	1.1	147,190,000	149,703,000	1.7

Note: Data is not seasonally adjusted and covers workers 16 years of age and older; (1) Figures cover the Fayetteville-Springdale-Rogers, AR-MO Metropolitan Statistical Area—see Appendix B for areas included
Source: Bureau of Labor Statistics, Local Area Unemployment Statistics

Unemployment Rate

Area	2015											
	Jan.	Feb.	Mar.	Apr.	May	Jun.	Jul.	Aug.	Sep.	Oct.	Nov.	Dec.
City	5.4	5.0	4.7	4.6	4.6	4.6	5.2	4.2	4.2	4.0	3.8	3.9
MSA[1]	4.7	4.4	4.2	4.0	4.3	4.2	4.3	3.6	3.5	3.4	3.1	3.2
U.S.	6.1	5.8	5.6	5.1	5.3	5.5	5.6	5.2	4.9	4.8	4.8	4.8

Note: Data is not seasonally adjusted and covers workers 16 years of age and older; (1) Figures cover the Fayetteville-Springdale-Rogers, AR-MO Metropolitan Statistical Area—see Appendix B for areas included
Source: Bureau of Labor Statistics, Local Area Unemployment Statistics

Employment by Occupation

Occupation Classification	City (%)	MSA[1] (%)	U.S. (%)
Management, Business, Science, and Arts	41.2	34.3	36.4
Natural Resources, Construction, and Maintenance	6.9	9.4	9.0
Production, Transportation, and Material Moving	8.7	15.6	12.1
Sales and Office	29.4	25.1	24.4
Service	13.8	15.6	18.2

Note: Figures cover employed civilians 16 years of age and older; (1) Figures cover the Fayetteville-Springdale-Rogers, AR-MO Metropolitan Statistical Area—see Appendix B for areas included
Source: U.S. Census Bureau, 2010-2014 American Community Survey 5-Year Estimates

Employment by Industry

Sector	MSA[1]		U.S.
	Number of Employees	Percent of Total	Percent of Total
Construction, Mining, and Logging	10,000	4.1	5.0
Education and Health Services	26,400	10.8	15.7
Financial Activities	6,900	2.8	5.7
Government	34,300	14.1	15.5
Information	2,000	0.8	1.9
Leisure and Hospitality	24,500	10.0	10.4
Manufacturing	26,700	10.9	8.6
Other Services	7,200	2.9	3.9
Professional and Business Services	48,600	20.0	13.9
Retail Trade	27,600	11.3	11.3
Transportation, Warehousing, and Utilities	16,800	6.9	3.9
Wholesale Trade	12,000	4.9	4.1

Note: Figures are non-farm employment as of December 2015. Figures are not seasonally adjusted and include workers 16 years of age and older; (1) Figures cover the Fayetteville-Springdale-Rogers, AR-MO Metropolitan Statistical Area—see Appendix B for areas included; n/a not available
Source: Bureau of Labor Statistics, Current Employment Statistics, Employment, Hours, and Earnings

Occupations with Greatest Projected Employment Growth: 2012 – 2022

Occupation[1]	2012 Employment	2022 Projected Employment	Numeric Employment Change	Percent Employment Change
Personal Care Aides	14,440	21,490	7,050	48.9
Combined Food Preparation and Serving Workers, Including Fast Food	22,610	29,320	6,710	29.7
Retail Salespersons	38,060	41,570	3,510	9.2
Heavy and Tractor-Trailer Truck Drivers	35,670	39,160	3,490	9.8
Waiters and Waitresses	18,660	22,120	3,460	18.6
Registered Nurses	23,090	26,530	3,440	14.9
Nursing Assistants	19,380	22,290	2,910	15.0
Home Health Aides	8,510	11,390	2,880	33.9
Secretaries and Administrative Assistants, Except Legal, Medical, and Executive	23,770	26,450	2,680	11.3
Customer Service Representatives	18,190	20,740	2,550	14.0

Note: Projections cover Arkansas; (1) Sorted by numeric employment change
Source: www.projectionscentral.com, State Occupational Projections, 2012–2022 Long-Term Projections

Fastest Growing Occupations: 2012 – 2022

Occupation[1]	2012 Employment	2022 Projected Employment	Numeric Employment Change	Percent Employment Change
Personal Care Aides	14,440	21,490	7,050	48.9
Health Specialties Teachers, Postsecondary	470	690	220	48.6
Nursing Instructors and Teachers, Postsecondary	640	930	290	45.3
Diagnostic Medical Sonographers	380	540	160	41.1
Food Scientists and Technologists	340	470	130	38.6
Home Health Aides	8,510	11,390	2,880	33.9
Nurse Practitioners	790	1,040	250	30.9
Meeting, Convention, and Event Planners	340	450	110	30.8
Psychiatric Technicians	590	760	170	30.3
Cooks, Restaurant	8,230	10,700	2,470	29.9

Note: Projections cover Arkansas; (1) Sorted by percent employment change and excludes occupations with numeric employment change less than 100
Source: www.projectionscentral.com, State Occupational Projections, 2012–2022 Long-Term Projections

Average Wages

Occupation	$/Hr.	Occupation	$/Hr.
Accountants and Auditors	29.64	Maids and Housekeeping Cleaners	8.92
Automotive Mechanics	17.26	Maintenance and Repair Workers	16.10
Bookkeepers	16.88	Marketing Managers	70.65
Carpenters	16.73	Nuclear Medicine Technologists	n/a
Cashiers	9.04	Nurses, Licensed Practical	19.66
Clerks, General Office	12.24	Nurses, Registered	27.00
Clerks, Receptionists/Information	11.98	Nursing Assistants	10.53
Clerks, Shipping/Receiving	14.41	Packers and Packagers, Hand	11.62
Computer Programmers	n/a	Physical Therapists	35.20
Computer Systems Analysts	32.59	Postal Service Mail Carriers	24.41
Computer User Support Specialists	18.99	Real Estate Brokers	n/a
Cooks, Restaurant	11.43	Retail Salespersons	11.36
Dentists	99.55	Sales Reps., Exc. Tech./Scientific	36.32
Electrical Engineers	38.34	Sales Reps., Tech./Scientific	44.72
Electricians	18.47	Secretaries, Exc. Legal/Med./Exec.	15.83
Financial Managers	68.74	Security Guards	13.34
First-Line Supervisors/Managers, Sales	16.62	Surgeons	n/a
Food Preparation Workers	9.03	Teacher Assistants*	9.51
General and Operations Managers	47.63	Teachers, Elementary School*	23.95
Hairdressers/Cosmetologists	11.88	Teachers, Secondary School*	27.23
Internists	n/a	Telemarketers	11.11
Janitors and Cleaners	10.93	Truck Drivers, Heavy/Tractor-Trailer	21.07
Landscaping/Groundskeeping Workers	11.85	Truck Drivers, Light/Delivery Svcs.	14.34
Lawyers	63.97	Waiters and Waitresses	9.07

Note: Wage data covers the Fayetteville-Springdale-Rogers, AR-MO Metropolitan Statistical Area—see Appendix B for areas included; (*) Hourly wages for elementary/secondary school teachers and teacher assistants were calculated by the editors from annual wage data based on a 40 hour work week; n/a not available.
Source: Bureau of Labor Statistics, Metro Area Occupational Employment and Wage Estimates, May 2015

TAXES

State Corporate Income Tax Rates

State	Tax Rate (%)	Income Brackets ($)	Num. of Brackets	Financial Institution Tax Rate (%)[a]	Federal Income Tax Ded.
Arkansas	1.0 - 6.5	3,000 - 100,001	6	1.0 - 6.5	No

Note: Tax rates as of January 1, 2016; (a) Rates listed are the corporate income tax rate applied to financial institutions or excise taxes based on income. Some states have other taxes based upon the value of deposits or shares.
Source: Federation of Tax Administrators, "State Corporate Income Tax Rates, 2016"

State Individual Income Tax Rates

State	Tax Rate (%)	Income Brackets ($)	Num. of Brackets	Personal Exempt. ($)[1] Single	Personal Exempt. ($)[1] Dependents	Fed. Inc. Tax Ded.
Arkansas (a)	0.9 - 6.9	4,299 - 35,100	6	26 (c)	26 (c)	No

Note: Tax rates as of January 1, 2016; Local- and county-level taxes are not included; n/a not applicable; (1) Married joint filers generally receive double the single exemption; (a) 18 states have statutory provision for automatically adjusting to the rate of inflation the dollar values of the income tax brackets, standard deductions, and/or personal exemptions. Massachusetts, Michigan, and Nebraska index the personal exemptiononly. Oregon does not index the income brackets for $125,000 and over. Maine has suspended indexing for 2014 and 2015; (c) The personal exemption takes the form of a tax credit instead of a deduction
Source: Federation of Tax Administrators, "State Individual Income Tax Rates, 2016"

Various State and Local Tax Rates

State	State and Local Sales and Use (%)	State Sales and Use (%)	Gasoline[1] (¢/gal.)	Cigarette[2] ($/pack)	Spirits[3] ($/gal.)	Wine[4] ($/gal.)	Beer[5] ($/gal.)
Arkansas	8.50	6.5	21.80	1.15	6.88 (i)(j)	1.35 (o)(p)	0.20 (s)(t)

Note: All tax rates as of January 1, 2016; (1) The American Petroleum Institute has developed a methodology for determining the average tax rate on a gallon of fuel. Rates may include any of the following: excise taxes, environmental fees, storage tank fees, other fees or taxes, general sales tax, and local taxes. In states where gasoline is subject to the general sales tax, or where the fuel tax is based on the average sale price, the average rate determined by API is sensitive to changes in the price of gasoline. States that fully or partially apply general sales taxes to gasoline: CA, CO, GA, IL, IN, MI, NY; (2) The federal excise tax of $1.0066 per pack and local taxes are not included; (3) Rates are those applicable to off-premise sales of 40% alcohol by volume (a.b.v.) distilled spirits in 750ml containers. Local excise taxes are excluded; (4) Rates are those applicable to off-premise sales of 11% a.b.v. non-carbonated wine in 750ml containers; (5) Rates are those applicable to off-premise sales of 4.7% a.b.v. beer in 12 ounce containers; (i) Includes case fees and/or bottle fees which may vary with size of container; (j) Includes sales taxes specific to alcoholic beverages; (o) Includes case fees and/or bottle fees which may vary with size of container; (p) Includes sales taxes specific to alcoholic beverages; (s) Includes sales taxes specific to alcoholic beverages; (t) Includes case fees and/or bottle fees which may vary with the size of container.
Source: Tax Foundation, 2016 Facts & Figures: How Does Your State Compare?

State Business Tax Climate Index Rankings

State	Overall Rank	Corporate Tax Rank	Individual Income Tax Rank	Sales Tax Rank	Unemployment Insurance Tax Rank	Property Tax Rank
Arkansas	38	42	29	43	43	27

Note: The index is a measure of how each state's tax laws affect economic performance. The lower the rank, the more favorable a state's tax system is for business. States without a given tax are given a ranking of 1. The scores/rankings for the District of Columbia do not affect other states. The 2016 index represents the tax climate as of July 1, 2015 (the beginning of Fiscal Year 2016).
Source: Tax Foundation, State Business Tax Climate Index 2016

TRANSPORTATION

Means of Transportation to Work

Area	Car/Truck/Van		Public Transportation			Bicycle	Walked	Other Means	Worked at Home
	Drove Alone	Car-pooled	Bus	Subway	Railroad				
City	83.6	9.1	0.4	0.0	0.0	0.0	1.0	0.5	5.5
MSA[1]	80.2	11.4	0.5	0.0	0.0	0.3	2.2	1.0	4.4
U.S.	76.4	9.6	2.6	1.8	0.6	0.6	2.8	1.3	4.4

Note: Figures are percentages and cover workers 16 years of age and older; (1) Figures cover the Fayetteville-Springdale-Rogers, AR-MO Metropolitan Statistical Area—see Appendix B for areas included
Source: U.S. Census Bureau, 2010-2014 American Community Survey 5-Year Estimates

Travel Time to Work

Area	Less Than 10 Minutes	10 to 19 Minutes	20 to 29 Minutes	30 to 44 Minutes	45 to 59 Minutes	60 to 89 Minutes	90 Minutes or More
City	8.3	19.5	33.4	27.2	7.8	2.2	1.7
MSA[1]	16.3	35.8	23.0	16.4	5.1	1.9	1.3
U.S.	13.3	29.6	21.0	20.2	7.7	5.7	2.6

Note: Figures are percentages and include workers 16 years old and over; (1) Figures cover the Fayetteville-Springdale-Rogers, AR-MO Metropolitan Statistical Area—see Appendix B for areas included
Source: U.S. Census Bureau, 2010-2014 American Community Survey 5-Year Estimates

Freeway Travel Time Index

Area	1985	1990	1995	2000	2005	2010	2014
Urban Area Rank[1,2]	n/a	n/a	n/a	n/a	n/a	n/a	n/a
Urban Area Index[1]	n/a	n/a	n/a	n/a	n/a	n/a	n/a
Average Index[3]	1.09	1.11	1.14	1.17	1.20	1.19	1.20

Note: Freeway Travel Time Index—the ratio of travel time in the peak period to the travel time at free-flow conditions. For example, a value of 1.30 indicates a 20-minute free-flow trip takes 26 minutes in the peak (20 minutes x 1.30 = 26 minutes); (1) Data for the Fayetteville-Springdale-Rogers, AR-MO urban area was not available; (2) Rank is based on 101 urban areas (#1 = highest travel time index); (3) Average of 101 urban areas
Source: Texas Transportation Institute, 2015 Urban Mobility Scorecard, August 2015

Freeway Commuter Stress Index

Area	1985	1990	1995	2000	2005	2010	2014
Urban Area Rank[1,2]	n/a	n/a	n/a	n/a	n/a	n/a	n/a
Urban Area Index[1]	n/a	n/a	n/a	n/a	n/a	n/a	n/a
Average Index[3]	1.13	1.16	1.19	1.22	1.25	1.24	1.25

Note: The Freeway Commuter Stress Index is the same as the Freeway Travel Time Index (see table above) except that it includes only the travel in the peak directions during the peak periods; the TTI includes travel in all directions during the peak period. Thus, the CSI is more indicative of the work trip experienced by each commuter on a daily basis. (1) Data for the Fayetteville-Springdale-Rogers, AR-MO urban area was not available; (2) Rank is based on 101 urban areas (#1 = highest stress index); (3) Average of 101 urban areas
Source: Texas Transportation Institute, 2015 Urban Mobility Scorecard, August 2015

Living Environment

COST OF LIVING

Cost of Living Index

Composite Index	Groceries	Housing	Utilities	Trans-portation	Health Care	Misc. Goods/ Services
88.3	91.5	76.1	103.6	93.8	90.9	90.3

Note: The Cost of Living Index measures regional differences in the cost of consumer goods and services, excluding taxes and non-consumer expenditures, for professional and managerial households in the top income quintile. It is based on more than 50,000 prices covering almost 60 different items for which prices are collected three times a year by chambers of commerce, economic development organizations or university applied economic centers in each participating urban area. The numbers shown should be read as a percentage above or below the national average of 100. For example, a value of 115.4 in the groceries column indicates that grocery prices are 15.4% higher than the national average. Small differences in the index numbers should not be interpreted as significant; Figures cover the Fayetteville AR urban area.
Source: The Council for Community and Economic Research, ACCRA Cost of Living Index, 2015

Grocery Prices

Area[1]	T-Bone Steak ($/pound)	Frying Chicken ($/pound)	Whole Milk ($/half gal.)	Eggs ($/dozen)	Orange Juice ($/64 oz.)	Coffee ($/11.5 oz.)
City[2]	10.76	1.03	2.22	2.17	3.51	3.98
Avg.	10.99	1.43	2.25	2.26	3.58	4.48
Min.	7.16	0.98	1.30	1.35	2.88	2.98
Max.	14.13	2.43	3.85	4.81	6.39	7.56

Note: (1) Values for the local area are compared with the average, minimum and maximum values for all 292 areas in the Cost of Living Index; (2) Figures cover the Fayetteville AR urban area; **T-Bone Steak** *(price per pound);* **Frying Chicken** *(price per pound, whole fryer);* **Whole Milk** *(half gallon carton);* **Eggs** *(price per dozen, Grade A, large);* **Orange Juice** *(64 oz. Tropicana or Florida Natural);* **Coffee** *(11.5 oz. can, vacuum-packed, Maxwell House, Hills Bros, or Folgers).*
Source: The Council for Community and Economic Research, ACCRA Cost of Living Index, 2015

Housing and Utility Costs

Area[1]	New Home Price ($)	Apartment Rent ($/month)	All Electric ($/month)	Part Electric ($/month)	Other Energy ($/month)	Telephone ($/month)
City[2]	250,223	642	-	79.71	78.12	33.40
Avg.	312,874	945	179.30	95.07	72.96	28.11
Min.	178,682	479	116.28	43.14	26.46	10.01
Max.	1,472,476	3,984	504.25	189.44	421.11	43.06

Note: (1) Values for the local area are compared with the average, minimum and maximum values for all 292 areas in the Cost of Living Index; (2) Figures cover the Fayetteville AR urban area; **New Home Price** *(2,400 sf living area, 8,000 sf lot, in urban area with full utilities);* **Apartment Rent** *(950 sf 2 bedroom/1.5 or 2 bath, unfurnished, excluding all utilities except water);* **All Electric** *(average monthly cost for an all-electric home);* **Part Electric** *(average monthly cost for a part-electric home);* **Other Energy** *(average monthly cost for natural gas, fuel oil, coal, wood, and any other forms of energy except electricity);* **Telephone** *(price includes basic monthly rate for a private residential line plus additional local usage charges incurred by a family of four).*
Source: The Council for Community and Economic Research, ACCRA Cost of Living Index, 2015

Health Care, Transportation, and Other Costs

Area[1]	Doctor ($/visit)	Dentist ($/visit)	Optometrist ($/visit)	Gasoline ($/gallon)	Beauty Salon ($/visit)	Men's Shirt ($)
City[2]	91.43	78.47	93.33	2.14	32.26	16.03
Avg.	105.15	89.02	99.78	2.38	35.30	28.10
Min.	66.87	56.09	48.53	1.95	18.91	13.38
Max.	182.34	150.36	228.33	4.09	67.91	63.80

Note: (1) Values for the local area are compared with the average, minimum and maximum values for all 292 areas in the Cost of Living Index; (2) Figures cover the Fayetteville AR urban area; **Doctor** *(general practitioners routine exam of an established patient);* **Dentist** *(adult teeth cleaning and periodic oral examination);* **Optometrist** *(full vision eye exam for established adult patient);* **Gasoline** *(one gallon regular unleaded, national brand, including all taxes, cash price at self-service pump if available);* **Beauty Salon** *(woman's shampoo, trim, and blow-dry);* **Men's Shirt** *(cotton/polyester dress shirt, pinpoint weave, long sleeves).*
Source: The Council for Community and Economic Research, ACCRA Cost of Living Index, 2015

HOUSING

House Price Index (HPI)

Area	National Ranking[2]	Quarterly Change (%)	One-Year Change (%)	Five-Year Change (%)
MSA[1]	145	1.60	4.30	13.10
U.S.[3]	–	1.45	5.76	22.85

Note: The HPI is a weighted repeat sales index. It measures average price changes in repeat sales or refinancings on the same properties. This information is obtained by reviewing repeat mortgage transactions on single-family properties whose mortgages have been purchased or securitized by Fannie Mae or Freddie Mac in January 1975; (1) Fayetteville-Springdale-Rogers Metropolitan Statistical Area—see Appendix B for areas included; (2) Rankings are based on annual percentage change for all metro areas containing at least 15,000 transactions over the last 10 years and ranges from 1 to 266; (3) figures based on a weighted average of Census Division estimates using a seasonally adjusted, purchase-only index; all figures are for the period ending December 31, 2015

Source: Federal Housing Finance Agency, House Price Index, February 25, 2016

Median Single-Family Home Prices

Area	2013	2014	2015[p]	Percent Change 2014 to 2015
MSA[1]	n/a	n/a	n/a	n/a
U.S. Average	197.4	208.9	223.9	7.2

Note: Figures are median sales prices of existing single-family homes in thousands of dollars; (p) preliminary; n/a not available; (1) Fayetteville-Springdale-Rogers, AR-MO Metropolitan Statistical Area—see Appendix B for areas included

Source: National Association of Realtors, Median Sales Price of Existing Single-Family Homes for Metropolitan Areas, 4th Quarter 2015

Qualifying Income Based on Median Sales Price of Existing Single-Family Homes

Area	With 5% Down ($)	With 10% Down ($)	With 20% Down ($)
MSA[1]	n/a	n/a	n/a
U.S. Average	49,535	46,928	41,714

Note: Figures are preliminary; Qualifying income is based on a mortgage rate of 4.1%. Monthly principal and interest payment is limited to 25% of income; n/a not available; (1) Fayetteville-Springdale-Rogers, AR-MO Metropolitan Statistical Area—see Appendix B for areas included

Source: National Association of Realtors, Qualifying Income Based on Median Sales Price of Existing Single-Family Homes for Metropolitan Areas, 4th Quarter 2015

Median Apartment Condo-Coop Home Prices

Area	2013	2014	2015[p]	Percent Change 2014 to 2015
MSA[1]	n/a	n/a	n/a	n/a
U.S. Average	194.9	204.3	210.7	3.1

Note: Figures are median sales prices of existing apartment condo-coop homes in thousands of dollars; (p) preliminary; n/a not available; (1) Fayetteville-Springdale-Rogers, AR-MO Metropolitan Statistical Area—see Appendix B for areas included

Source: National Association of Realtors, Median Sales Price of Existing Apartment Condo-Coop Homes for Metropolitan Areas, 4th Quarter 2015

Gross Monthly Rent

Area	Under $200	$200 -299	$300 -499	$500 -749	$750 -999	$1,000 -1,499	$1,500 and up	Median ($)
City	0.0	0.8	3.2	15.0	39.0	28.2	13.8	964
MSA[1]	0.8	1.8	12.1	38.0	28.4	15.2	3.7	732
U.S.	1.5	3.2	7.4	21.0	24.1	26.9	15.9	920

Note: Figures are percentages except for Median; Gross rent is the contract rent plus the estimated average monthly cost of utilities (electricity, gas, and water and sewer) and fuels (oil, coal, kerosene, wood, etc.) if these are paid by the renter (or paid for the renter by someone else); (1) Figures cover the Fayetteville-Springdale-Rogers, AR-MO Metropolitan Statistical Area—see Appendix B for areas included

Source: U.S. Census Bureau, 2010-2014 American Community Survey 5-Year Estimates

Homeownership Rate

Area	2008 (%)	2009 (%)	2010 (%)	2011 (%)	2012 (%)	2013 (%)	2014 (%)	2015 (%)
MSA[1]	n/a	n/a	n/a	n/a	n/a	n/a	n/a	n/a
U.S.	67.8	67.4	66.9	66.1	65.4	65.1	64.5	63.7

Note: (1) Figures cover the Fayetteville-Springdale-Rogers, AR-MO Metropolitan Statistical Area—see Appendix B for areas included; n/a not available
Source: U.S. Census Bureau, Housing Vacancies and Homeownership Annual Statistics: 2015

Year Housing Structure Built

Area	2010 or Later	2000 -2009	1990 -1999	1980 -1989	1970 -1979	1960 -1969	1950 -1959	1940 -1949	Before 1940	Median Year
City	0.3	27.9	25.9	25.4	15.5	3.2	0.5	0.6	0.8	1992
MSA[1]	1.5	26.5	24.8	16.3	13.5	6.9	4.0	2.4	4.0	1991
U.S.	1.0	14.9	13.9	13.8	15.8	11.0	10.8	5.4	13.3	1976

Note: Figures are percentages except for Median Year; (1) Figures cover the Fayetteville-Springdale-Rogers, AR-MO Metropolitan Statistical Area—see Appendix B for areas included
Source: U.S. Census Bureau, 2010-2014 American Community Survey 5-Year Estimates

HEALTH

Health Risk Data

Category	MSA[1] (%)	U.S. (%)
Adults aged 18–64 who have any kind of health care coverage	67.0	79.6
Adults who reported being in good or excellent health	79.7	83.1
Adults who are current smokers	20.1	19.6
Adults who are heavy drinkers[2]	4.0	6.1
Adults who are binge drinkers[3]	12.6	16.9
Adults who are overweight (BMI 25.0 - 29.9)	34.6	35.8
Adults who are obese (BMI 30.0 - 99.8)	29.1	27.6
Adults who participated in any physical activities in the past month	74.8	77.1
Adults 50+ who have ever had a sigmoidoscopy or colonoscopy	56.7	67.3
Women aged 40+ who have had a mammogram within the past two years	62.9	74.0
Men aged 40+ who have had a PSA test within the past two years	40.8	45.2
Adults aged 65+ who have had flu shot within the past year	56.6	60.1
Adults who always wear a seatbelt	93.8	93.8

Note: Data as of 2012 unless otherwise noted; (1) Figures cover the Fayetteville-Springdale-Rogers, AR-MO Metropolitan Statistical Area—see Appendix B for areas included; (2) Heavy drinkers are classified as males having more than two drinks per day or females having more than one drink per day; (3) Binge drinkers are classified as males having five or more drinks on one occasion or females having four or more drinks on one occasion
Source: Centers for Disease Control and Prevention, Behaviorial Risk Factor Surveillance System, SMART: Selected Metropolitan/Micropolitan Area Risk Trends, 2012 (Note: the CDC has discontinued this dataset but will be releasing a replacement in mid-2016)

Chronic Health Indicators

Category	MSA[1] (%)	U.S. (%)
Adults who have ever been told they had a heart attack	6.0	4.5
Adults who have ever been told they had a stroke	3.0	2.9
Adults who have been told they currently have asthma	7.7	8.9
Adults who have ever been told they have arthritis	20.6	25.7
Adults who have ever been told they have diabetes[2]	9.4	9.7
Adults who have ever been told they had skin cancer	5.7	5.7
Adults who have ever been told they had any other types of cancer	6.1	6.5
Adults who have ever been told they have COPD	6.8	6.2
Adults who have ever been told they have kidney disease	2.5	2.5
Adults who have ever been told they have a form of depression	20.0	18.0

Note: Data as of 2012 unless otherwise noted; (1) Figures cover the Fayetteville-Springdale-Rogers, AR-MO Metropolitan Statistical Area—see Appendix B for areas included; (2) Figures do not include pregnancy-related, borderline, or pre-diabetes
Source: Centers for Disease Control and Prevention, Behaviorial Risk Factor Surveillance System, SMART: Selected Metropolitan/Micropolitan Area Risk Trends, 2012 (Note: the CDC has discontinued this dataset but will be releasing a replacement in mid-2016)

Mortality Rates for the Top 10 Causes of Death in the U.S.

ICD-10[a] Sub-Chapter	ICD-10[a] Code	Age-Adjusted Mortality Rate[1] per 100,000 population County[2]	U.S.
Malignant neoplasms	C00-C97	164.8	163.6
Ischaemic heart diseases	I20-I25	109.9	102.2
Other forms of heart disease	I30-I51	36.7	50.1
Chronic lower respiratory diseases	J40-J47	49.4	41.4
Organic, including symptomatic, mental disorders	F01-F09	54.7	38.5
Cerebrovascular diseases	I60-I69	45.5	36.5
Other external causes of accidental injury	W00-X59	28.4	27.5
Other degenerative diseases of the nervous system	G30-G31	20.2	26.3
Diabetes mellitus	E10-E14	21.6	21.1
Hypertensive diseases	I10-I15	10.1	19.7

Note: (a) ICD-10 = International Classification of Diseases 10th Revision; (1) Mortality rates are a three year average covering 2012-2014; (2) Figures cover COUNTY NOT FOUND!!!!!!.
Source: Centers for Disease Control and Prevention, National Center for Health Statistics. Underlying Cause of Death 1999-2014 on CDC WONDER Online Database, released 2015.

Mortality Rates for Selected Causes of Death

ICD-10[a] Sub-Chapter	ICD-10[a] Code	Age-Adjusted Mortality Rate[1] per 100,000 population County[2]	U.S.
Assault	X85-Y09	Suppressed	5.1
Diseases of the liver	K70-K76	11.4	13.5
Human immunodeficiency virus (HIV) disease	B20-B24	Suppressed	2.1
Influenza and pneumonia	J09-J18	9.8	15.2
Intentional self-harm	X60-X84	14.2	12.7
Malnutrition	E40-E46	Suppressed	0.9
Obesity and other hyperalimentation	E65-E68	Unreliable	1.9
Renal failure	N17-N19	11.3	13.0
Transport accidents	V01-V99	9.7	11.6
Viral hepatitis	B15-B19	Unreliable	2.1

Note: (a) ICD-10 = International Classification of Diseases 10th Revision; (1) Mortality rates are a three year average covering 2012-2014; (2) Figures cover COUNTY NOT FOUND!!!!!!; Data are Suppressed when the data meet the criteria for confidentiality constraints; Mortality rates are flagged as Unreliable when the rate would be calculated with a numerator of 20 or less.
Source: Centers for Disease Control and Prevention, National Center for Health Statistics. Underlying Cause of Death 1999-2014 on CDC WONDER Online Database, released 2015.

Health Insurance Coverage

Area	With Health Insurance	With Private Health Insurance	With Public Health Insurance	Without Health Insurance	Population Under Age 18 Without Health Insurance
City	93.9	81.5	37.5	6.1	2.7
MSA[1]	83.9	64.9	28.3	16.1	7.3
U.S.	85.8	65.8	31.1	14.2	7.1

Note: Figures are percentages that cover the civilian noninstitutionalized population; (1) Figures cover the Fayetteville-Springdale-Rogers, AR-MO Metropolitan Statistical Area—see Appendix B for areas included
Source: U.S. Census Bureau, 2010-2014 American Community Survey 5-Year Estimates

Number of Medical Professionals

Area	MDs[3]	DOs[3,4]	Dentists	Podiatrists	Chiropractors	Optometrists
County[1] (number)	304	32	107	7	76	32
County[1] (rate[2])	128.1	13.5	44.2	2.9	31.4	13.2
U.S. (rate[2])	272.5	20.9	64.7	5.8	25.9	15.2

Note: Data as of 2014 unless noted; (1) Data covers Benton County; (2) Rate per 100,000 population; (3) Data as of 2013 and includes all active, non-federal physicians; (4) Doctor of Osteopathic Medicine
Source: U.S. Department of Health and Human Services, Health Resources and Services Administration, Bureau of Health Professions, Area Resource File (ARF) 2014-2015

EDUCATION

Public School District Statistics

District Name	Schls	Pupils	Pupil/ Teacher Ratio	Minority Pupils[1] (%)	Free Lunch Eligible[2] (%)	IEP[3] (%)
Bentonville School District	18	15,081	14.6	24.4	20.1	10.6

Note: Table includes school districts with 100 or more students; (1) Percentage of students that are not non-Hispanic white; (2) Percentage of students that are eligible for the free lunch program; (3) Percentage of students that have an Individualized Education Program.
Source: U.S. Department of Education, National Center for Education Statistics, Common Core of Data, Local Education Agency (School District) Universe Survey: School Year 2013-2014; U.S. Department of Education, National Center for Education Statistics, Common Core of Data, Public Elementary/Secondary School Universe Survey: School Year 2013-2014

Highest Level of Education

Area	Less than H.S.	H.S. Diploma	Some College, No Deg.	Associate Degree	Bachelor's Degree	Master's Degree	Prof. School Degree	Doctorate Degree
City	5.5	26.3	24.2	9.5	22.1	10.2	1.3	1.0
MSA[1]	15.8	30.3	20.8	5.2	17.7	7.2	1.7	1.3
U.S.	13.7	28.0	21.2	7.9	18.3	7.8	2.0	1.3

Note: Figures cover persons age 25 and over; (1) Figures cover the Fayetteville-Springdale-Rogers, AR-MO Metropolitan Statistical Area—see Appendix B for areas included
Source: U.S. Census Bureau, 2010-2014 American Community Survey 5-Year Estimates

Educational Attainment by Race

Area	High School Graduate or Higher (%)					Bachelor's Degree or Higher (%)				
	Total	White	Black	Asian	Hisp.[2]	Total	White	Black	Asian	Hisp.[2]
City	94.5	94.7	65.8	91.9	55.8	34.5	34.7	16.8	45.5	15.1
MSA[1]	84.2	86.4	88.0	89.0	42.4	27.9	28.3	28.3	60.6	9.4
U.S.	86.3	88.4	83.2	85.8	64.1	29.3	30.6	19.0	50.9	13.9

Note: Figures shown cover persons 25 years old and over; (1) Figures cover the Fayetteville-Springdale-Rogers, AR-MO Metropolitan Statistical Area—see Appendix B for areas included; (2) People of Hispanic origin can be of any race
Source: U.S. Census Bureau, 2010-2014 American Community Survey 5-Year Estimates

School Enrollment by Grade and Control

Area	Preschool (%)		Kindergarten (%)		Grades 1 - 4 (%)		Grades 5 - 8 (%)		Grades 9 - 12 (%)	
	Public	Private	Public	Private	Public	Private	Public	Private	Public	Private
City	20.7	79.3	92.5	7.5	78.4	21.6	83.1	16.9	90.9	9.1
MSA[1]	63.0	37.0	91.4	8.6	92.3	7.7	92.3	7.7	93.3	6.7
U.S.	57.4	42.6	87.8	12.2	89.8	10.2	89.9	10.1	90.6	9.4

Note: Figures shown cover persons 3 years old and over; (1) Figures cover the Fayetteville-Springdale-Rogers, AR-MO Metropolitan Statistical Area—see Appendix B for areas included
Source: U.S. Census Bureau, 2010-2014 American Community Survey 5-Year Estimates

Average Salaries of Public School Classroom Teachers

Area	2013-14		2014-15		Percent Change 2013-14 to 2014-15	Percent Change 2004-05 to 2014-15
	Dollars	Rank[1]	Dollars	Rank[1]		
Arkansas	47,319	41	48,017	40	1.48	18.6
U.S. Average	56,610	–	57,379	–	1.36	20.8

Note: (1) State rank ranges from 1 to 51 where 1 indicates highest salary.
Source: National Education Association, Rankings & Estimates: Rankings of the States 2014 and Estimates of School Statistics 2015, March 2015

Higher Education

Four-Year Colleges			Two-Year Colleges			Medical Schools[1]	Law Schools[2]	Voc/ Tech[3]
Public	Private Non-profit	Private For-profit	Public	Private Non-profit	Private For-profit			
0	0	0	0	0	0	0	0	0

Note: Figures cover institutions located within the city limits and include main campuses only; (1) includes schools accredited by the Liaison Committee on Medical Education and the American Osteopathic Association's Commission on Osteopathic College Accreditation; (2) includes ABA-accredited schools, schools with provisional ABA accreditation, and state accredited schools; (3) includes all schools with programs that are less than 2 years.

Source: National Center for Education Statistics, Integrated Postsecondary Education System (IPEDS), 2014-15; Association of American Medical Colleges, Member List, March 21, 2016; American Osteopathic Association, Member List, March 21, 2016; Law School Admission Council, Official Guide to ABA-Approved Law Schools Online, March 21, 2016; Wikipedia, List of Medical Schools in the United States, March 21, 2016; Wikipedia, List of Law Schools in the United States, March 21, 2016

According to *U.S. News & World Report,* the Fayetteville-Springdale-Rogers, AR-MO metro area is home to one of the best national universities in the U.S.: **University of Arkansas** (#129 tie). The indicators used to capture academic quality fall into a number of categories: assessment by administrators at peer institutions; retention of students; faculty resources; student selectivity; financial resources; alumni giving; high school counselor ratings of colleges; and graduation rate. *U.S. News & World Report, "America's Best Colleges 2016"*

According to *U.S. News & World Report,* the Fayetteville-Springdale-Rogers, AR-MO metro area is home to one of the top 100 law schools in the U.S.: **University of Arkansas–Fayetteville, School of Law** (#86 tie). The rankings are based on a weighted average of 12 measures of quality: peer assessment score; assessment score by lawyers/judges; median LSAT scores; median undergrad GPA; acceptance rate; employment rates for graduates; placement success; bar passage rate; faculty resources; expenditures per student; student/faculty ratio; and library resources. *U.S. News & World Report, "America's Best Graduate Schools, Law, 2017"*

According to *U.S. News & World Report,* the Fayetteville-Springdale-Rogers, AR-MO metro area is home to one of the top 75 business schools in the U.S.: **University of Arkansas–Fayetteville, Sam M. Walton College of Business** (#63 tie). The rankings are based on a weighted average of the following nine measures: quality assessment; peer assessment; recruiter assessment; placement success; mean starting salary and bonus; student selectivity; mean GMAT and GRE scores; mean undergraduate GPA; and acceptance rate. *U.S. News & World Report, "America's Best Graduate Schools, Business, 2017"*

PRESIDENTIAL ELECTION

2012 Presidential Election Results

Area	Obama (%)	Romney (%)	Other (%)
Benton County	28.6	68.9	2.5
U.S.	51.0	47.2	1.8

Note: Results may not add to 100% due to rounding
Source: Dave Leip's Atlas of U.S. Presidential Elections

EMPLOYERS

Major Employers

Company Name	Industry
Allens, Inc.	Manufacturing
Arkansas Western Gas	Utilities
Arvest Bank	Financial
Ayrshire Electronics	Manufacturing
City of Fayetteville	Government
Fayetteville School District	Education
J.B. Hunt Transport, Inc.	Transportation & utilities
Mercy Northwest Arkansas	Education & health services
Northwest Health System	Education & health services
Simmons Foods, Inc.	Manufacturing
Superior Industries	Manufacturing
Tyson Foods	Food manufacturing
University of Arkansas	Education
Veterans Administration Medical	Medical
Wal-Mart Stores	Retail
Washington Regional	Education & health services

Note: Companies shown are located within the Fayetteville-Springdale-Rogers, AR-MO Metropolitan Statistical Area.
Source: Hoovers.com; Wikipedia

PUBLIC SAFETY

Crime Rate

Area	All Crimes	Violent Crimes				Property Crimes		
		Murder	Rape[3]	Robbery	Aggrav. Assault	Burglary	Larceny -Theft	Motor Vehicle Theft
City	738.0	0.0	43.0	0.0	96.7	111.1	480.1	7.2
Metro[1]	n/a	n/a	n/a	n/a	n/a	n/a	n/a	n/a
U.S.	2,971.8	4.5	36.6	102.2	232.5	542.5	1,837.3	216.2

Note: Figures are crimes per 100,000 population; (1) Figures cover the Fayetteville-Springdale-Rogers, AR-MO Metropolitan Statistical Area—see Appendix B for areas included; n/a not available; (3) The city and U.S. figures shown were reported using the revised Uniform Crime Reporting (UCR) definition of rape. The suburban and metro area figures shown are an aggregate total of the data submitted using both the revised and legacy UCR definitions.
Source: FBI Uniform Crime Reports, 2014

Hate Crimes

Area	Number of Quarters Reported	Number of Incidents per Bias Motivation						
		Race	Religion	Sexual Orientation	Ethnicity	Disability	Gender	Gender Identity
City	4	0	0	0	0	0	0	0
U.S.	4	2,568	1,014	1,017	648	84	33	98

Source: Federal Bureau of Investigation, Hate Crime Statistics 2014

Identity Theft Consumer Complaints

Area	Complaints	Complaints per 100,000 Population	Rank[2]
MSA[1]	376	75.0	339
U.S.	490,220	152.4	-

Note: (1) Figures cover the Fayetteville-Springdale-Rogers, AR-MO Metropolitan Statistical Area—see Appendix B for areas included; (2) Rank ranges from 1 to 379 where 1 indicates greatest number of identity theft complaints per 100,000 population
Source: Federal Trade Commission, Consumer Sentinel Network Data Book for January–December 2015

Fraud and Other Consumer Complaints

Area	Complaints	Complaints per 100,000 Population	Rank[2]
MSA[1]	1,648	328.5	252
U.S.	2,593,159	806.0	-

Note: (1) Figures cover the Fayetteville-Springdale-Rogers, AR-MO Metropolitan Statistical Area—see Appendix B for areas included; (2) Rank ranges from 1 to 379 where 1 indicates greatest number of identity theft complaints per 100,000 population
Source: Federal Trade Commission, Consumer Sentinel Network Data Book for January–December 2015

RECREATION

Culture

Dance[1]	Theatre[1]	Instrumental Music[1]	Vocal Music[1]	Series and Festivals	Museums and Art Galleries[2]	Zoos and Aquariums[3]
0	0	0	0	0	0	0

Note: (1) Professional perfoming groups; (2) Based on organizations with SIC code 8412; (3) AZA-accredited
Source: The Grey House Performing Arts Directory, 2015-16; Association of Zoos & Aquariums, AZA Member Zoos & Aquariums, March 25, 2016; www.AccuLeads.com, March 29, 2016

Professional Sports Teams

Team Name	League	Year Established
No teams are located in the metro area		

Source: Wikipedia, Major Professional Sports Teams of the United States and Canada, March 24, 2016

CLIMATE

Average and Extreme Temperatures

Temperature	Jan	Feb	Mar	Apr	May	Jun	Jul	Aug	Sep	Oct	Nov	Dec	Yr.
Extreme High (°F)	81	86	94	95	98	105	111	110	105	96	86	82	111
Average High (°F)	48	54	63	74	81	89	93	93	85	76	62	52	73
Average Temp. (°F)	38	43	51	62	70	78	82	81	74	63	50	41	61
Average Low (°F)	27	31	39	49	58	67	71	69	62	49	38	30	49
Extreme Low (°F)	-10	-9	7	22	35	47	50	51	33	22	8	-5	-10

Note: Figures cover the years 1948-1995
Source: National Climatic Data Center, International Station Meteorological Climate Summary, 9/96

Average Precipitation/Snowfall/Humidity

Precip./Humidity	Jan	Feb	Mar	Apr	May	Jun	Jul	Aug	Sep	Oct	Nov	Dec	Yr.
Avg. Precip. (in.)	2.3	2.8	3.7	4.2	5.3	3.6	3.4	2.8	3.3	3.5	3.9	3.0	41.8
Avg. Snowfall (in.)	3	2	1	Tr	0	0	0	0	0	Tr	1	1	6
Avg. Rel. Hum. 6am (%)	81	81	79	82	88	89	89	89	89	87	83	82	85
Avg. Rel. Hum. 3pm (%)	55	50	46	46	52	52	49	47	48	45	48	53	49

Note: Figures cover the years 1948-1995; Tr = Trace amounts (<0.05 in. of rain; <0.5 in. of snow)
Source: National Climatic Data Center, International Station Meteorological Climate Summary, 9/96

Weather Conditions

Temperature			Daytime Sky			Precipitation		
10°F & below	32°F & below	90°F & above	Clear	Partly cloudy	Cloudy	0.01 inch or more precip.	0.1 inch or more snow/ice	Thunder-storms
3	76	76	117	121	127	98	5	59

Note: Figures are average number of days per year and cover the years 1948-1995
Source: National Climatic Data Center, International Station Meteorological Climate Summary, 9/96

HAZARDOUS WASTE

Superfund Sites

Bella Vista has no sites on the EPA's Superfund Final National Priorities List. There are a total of 1,323 Superfund sites on the list in the U.S. *U.S. Environmental Protection Agency, Final National Priorities List, March 18, 2016*

AIR & WATER QUALITY

Air Quality Trends: Ozone

	1990	1995	2000	2005	2010	2011	2012	2013	2014
MSA[1]	n/a	n/a	n/a	n/a	n/a	n/a	n/a	n/a	n/a

Note: (1) Data covers the Fayetteville-Springdale-Rogers, AR-MO Metropolitan Statistical Area—see Appendix B for areas included; n/a not available. The values shown are the composite ozone concentration averages among trend sites based on the highest fourth daily maximum 8-hour concentration in parts per million. These trends are based on sites having an adequate record of monitoring data during the trend period. Data from exceptional events are included.

Source: U.S. Environmental Protection Agency, Air Quality Monitoring Information, "Air Quality Trends by City, 1990-2014"

Air Quality Index

Area	Percent of Days when Air Quality was...[2]					AQI Statistics[2]	
	Good	Moderate	Unhealthy for Sensitive Groups	Unhealthy	Very Unhealthy	Maximum	Median
MSA[1]	93.2	6.8	0.0	0.0	0.0	74	34

Note: (1) Data covers the Fayetteville-Springdale-Rogers, AR-MO Metropolitan Statistical Area—see Appendix B for areas included; (2) Based on 365 days with AQI data in 2015. Air Quality Index (AQI) is an index for reporting daily air quality. EPA calculates the AQI for five major air pollutants regulated by the Clean Air Act: ground-level ozone, particle pollution (aka particulate matter), carbon monoxide, sulfur dioxide, and nitrogen dioxide. The AQI runs from 0 to 500. The higher the AQI value, the greater the level of air pollution and the greater the health concern. There are six AQI categories: "Good" AQI is between 0 and 50. Air quality is considered satisfactory; "Moderate" AQI is between 51 and 100. Air quality is acceptable; "Unhealthy for Sensitive Groups" When AQI values are between 101 and 150, members of sensitive groups may experience health effects; "Unhealthy" When AQI values are between 151 and 200 everyone may begin to experience health effects; "Very Unhealthy" AQI values between 201 and 300 trigger a health alert; "Hazardous" AQI values over 300 trigger warnings of emergency conditions (not shown).

Source: U.S. Environmental Protection Agency, Air Quality Index Report, 2015

Air Quality Index Pollutants

Area	Percent of Days when AQI Pollutant was...[2]					
	Carbon Monoxide	Nitrogen Dioxide	Ozone	Sulfur Dioxide	Particulate Matter 2.5	Particulate Matter 10
MSA[1]	0.0	0.0	86.0	0.0	14.0	0.0

Note: (1) Data covers the Fayetteville-Springdale-Rogers, AR-MO Metropolitan Statistical Area—see Appendix B for areas included; (2) Based on 365 days with AQI data in 2015. The Air Quality Index (AQI) is an index for reporting daily air quality. EPA calculates the AQI for five major air pollutants regulated by the Clean Air Act: ground-level ozone, particle pollution (also known as particulate matter), carbon monoxide, sulfur dioxide, and nitrogen dioxide. The AQI runs from 0 to 500. The higher the AQI value, the greater the level of air pollution and the greater the health concern.

Source: U.S. Environmental Protection Agency, Air Quality Index Report, 2015

Maximum Air Pollutant Concentrations: Particulate Matter, Ozone, CO and Lead

	Particulate Matter 10 (ug/m^3)	Particulate Matter 2.5 Wtd AM (ug/m^3)	Particulate Matter 2.5 24-Hr (ug/m^3)	Ozone (ppm)	Carbon Monoxide (ppm)	Lead (ug/m^3)
MSA[1] Level	n/a	8.7	21	0.064	n/a	n/a
NAAQS[2]	150	15	35	0.075	9	0.15
Met NAAQS[2]	n/a	Yes	Yes	Yes	n/a	n/a

Note: (1) Data covers the Fayetteville-Springdale-Rogers, AR-MO Metropolitan Statistical Area—see Appendix B for areas included; Data from exceptional events are included; (2) National Ambient Air Quality Standards; ppm = parts per million; ug/m^3 = micrograms per cubic meter; n/a not available.

Concentrations: Particulate Matter 10 (coarse particulate)—highest second maximum 24-hour concentration; Particulate Matter 2.5 Wtd AM (fine particulate)—highest weighted annual mean concentration; Particulate Matter 2.5 24-Hour (fine particulate)—highest 98th percentile 24-hour concentration; Ozone—highest fourth daily maximum 8-hour concentration; Carbon Monoxide—highest second maximum non-overlapping 8-hour concentration; Lead—maximum running 3-month average

Source: U.S. Environmental Protection Agency, Air Quality Monitoring Information, "Air Quality Statistics by City, 2014"

Maximum Air Pollutant Concentrations: Nitrogen Dioxide and Sulfur Dioxide

	Nitrogen Dioxide AM (ppb)	Nitrogen Dioxide 1-Hr (ppb)	Sulfur Dioxide AM (ppb)	Sulfur Dioxide 1-Hr (ppb)	Sulfur Dioxide 24-Hr (ppb)
MSA[1] Level	n/a	n/a	n/a	n/a	n/a
NAAQS[2]	53	100	30	75	140
Met NAAQS[2]	n/a	n/a	n/a	n/a	n/a

Note: (1) Data covers the Fayetteville-Springdale-Rogers, AR-MO Metropolitan Statistical Area—see Appendix B for areas included; Data from exceptional events are included; (2) National Ambient Air Quality Standards; ppm = parts per million; ug/m^3 *= micrograms per cubic meter; n/a not available.*
Concentrations: Nitrogen Dioxide AM—highest arithmetic mean concentration; Nitrogen Dioxide 1-Hr—highest 98th percentile 1-hour daily maximum concentration; Sulfur Dioxide AM—highest annual mean concentration; Sulfur Dioxide 1-Hr—highest 99th percentile 1-hour daily maximum concentration; Sulfur Dioxide 24-Hr—highest second maximum 24-hour concentration
Source: U.S. Environmental Protection Agency, Air Quality Monitoring Information, "Air Quality Statistics by City, 2014"

Drinking Water

Water System Name	Pop. Served	Primary Water Source Type	Violations[1]	
			Health Based	Monitoring/ Reporting
Bella Vista POA	26,461	Purchased Surface	0	0

Note: (1) Based on violation data from January 1, 2015 to December 31, 2015 (includes unresolved violations from earlier years)
Source: U.S. Environmental Protection Agency, Office of Ground Water and Drinking Water, Safe Drinking Water Information System (based on data extracted April 29, 2016)

Aliso Viejo, California

Background

Aliso Viejo, Orange County's first planned community, carved its 6,600 acres (6.9 square miles) out of the former 22,000-acre Moulton ranch, granted to the Moulton family by the Mexican government in 1842. Since its inception in 1982, the town has targeted its housing stock to middle- and upper-middle income homebuyers with such success that lotteries were held to control the massive influx of settlers, which by 2000 had earned the suburb the top population growth slot in the county. Aliso Viejo is also Orange County's newest city, incorporated in July 1, 2001, and its slogan is "Since 2001."

The City of Aliso Viejo lies 57 miles south of Los Angeles, approximately 10 miles from the John Wayne Airport, 20 miles south of Santa Ana (the County Seat), and 3 miles inland of the Pacific Ocean. The 3,400-acre Aliso and Wood Canyons Regional Park abuts three sides of the community. Scenic canyons, rock formations, oak and sycamore groves, a fresh water marsh and miles of hiking and biking trails with more than 90 species of birds may be observed at the two parks.

Taking advantage of the mild southern California climate, the town boasts a wide program of recreational programs and services for children and adults including dance classes, CPR training, Summer Youth Drop-In park programs, youth sport camps, tennis lessons, T'ai Chi, dog obedience, golf lessons, and yoga. The community association maintains and operates parks, slopes, medians and landscaped areas throughout the city. The town also sponsors an annual golf tournament benefiting the community's families and children through the establishment of after-school homework tutoring programs at the Jack Nicklaus-designed 18-hole course at the Aliso Viejo Golf Club.

The Don Juan Avila and Oak Grove elementary schools rank well above average on the Academic Performance Index and were among 35 elementary schools in Orange County named California Distinguished Schools. Located minutes from the community, California State Fullerton and University of California Irvine offer opportunities for higher education.

Aliso Viego's top employers include UPS, Pacific Life, Pepsi, 3tera (cloud computing), Buy.com, Ketel One, Marie Callender's, Qlogic and Smith Micro Software. Aliso Viejo offers residential, business, and retail centers to meet most all citizens' needs.

Rankings

General Rankings

- Los Angeles* was identified as one of America's fastest-growing major metropolitan areas in terms of population growth by CNNMoney.com. The area ranked #3 out of 10. Criteria: population growth between July 2013 and July 2014. *CNNMoney, "10 Fastest-Growing Cities," May 27, 2015*

Business/Finance Rankings

- The personal finance site NerdWallet analyzed 183 American metropolitan areas with populations over 250,000 and more than 15,000 businesses to rank where entrepreneurs find the most success. Criteria included area economy, annual income, housing cost, unemployment rate, and the success rate of area businesses. Los Angeles* ranked #109. *www.nerdwallet.com, "Best Places to Start a Business," April 27, 2015*
- Based on the U.S. Department of Labor's Occupational Information Network Data Collection Program, the Brookings Institution defined job opportunities for STEM workers at various levels of educational attainment. The Anaheim* metro area was one of the ten metro areas where workers in low-education-level STEM jobs earn the lowest relative wages. *www.brookings.edu, "The Hidden Stem Economy," June 10, 2013*
- Based on metro area social media reviews, the employment opinion group Glassdoor surveyed 50 of the largest U.S. metro areas and equally weighed cost of living, hiring opportunity, and job satisfaction to compose a list of "25 Best Cities for Jobs." The Los Angeles* metro area was ranked #16 in overall job satisfaction. *www.glassdoor.com, "Best Cities for Jobs," May 19, 2015*
- In a survey of economic confidence in the nation's 50 largest metropolitan areas conducted January–December 2014, the Los Angeles* metro area placed #11, according to Gallup's 2014 Economic Confidence Index. *Gallup, "San Jose and San Francisco Lead in Economic Confidence," March 19, 2015*
- The Brookings Institution ranked the 100 largest metro areas in the U.S. based on income inequality. Los Angeles* was ranked #7 (#1 = greatest ineqality). Criteria: the "95/20 ratio," a figure representing the income at which a household earns more than 95 percent of all other households, divided by the income at which a household earns more than only 20 percent of all other households. *Brookings Institution, "Income Inequality, 100 Largest U.S. Metro Areas, 2007-2014," January 14, 2016*
- The finance site *24/7 Wall St.* identified the metropolitan areas that have the smallest and largest pay disparities between men and women, comparing the median earnings for the past 12 months of both men and women working full-time in the country's 100 largest metropolitan statistical areas. Of the ten best-paying metros for women, the Los Angeles* metro area ranked #2. *24/7 Wall St., "The Best (and Worst) Paying Cities for Women," March 6, 2015*
- Payscale.com ranked the 20 largest metro areas in terms of wage growth. The Los Angeles* metro area ranked #16. Criteria: private-sector wage growth between the 1st quarter of 2015 and the 1st quarter of 2016. *PayScale, "Wage Trends by Metro Area," 1st Quarter, 2016*
- The Anaheim* metro area appeared on the Milken Institute "2015 Best Performing Cities" list. Rank: #46 out of 200 large metro areas. Criteria: job growth; wage and salary growth; high-tech output growth. *Milken Institute, "Best-Performing Cities 2015," December 2015*
- *Forbes* ranked the 200 most populous metro areas to determine the nation's "Best Places for Business and Careers." The Anaheim* metro area was ranked #62. Criteria: costs (business and living); job growth (past and projected); income growth; educational attainment (college and high school); projected economic growth; cultural and recreational opportunities; net migration patterns; number of highly ranked colleges. *Forbes, "The Best Places for Business and Careers 2015," July 29, 2015*

Education Rankings

- Personal finance website *WalletHub* analyzed the 150 largest U.S. metropolitan statistical areas to determine where the most educated Americans are choosing to settle. Criteria: education quality and attainment gap; education levels; percentage of workers with degrees; public school rankings; quality and size of each metro area's universities. Los Angeles* was ranked #87 (#1 = most educated city). *www.WalletHub.com, "2015's Most and Least Educated Cities*

Environmental Rankings

- The Los Angeles* metro area came in at #148 for the relative comfort of its climate on Sperling's list of "chill cities," as measured by the Sperling Heat Index. All 361 metro areas are included. Criteria included daytime high temperatures, nighttime low temperatures, dew point, and relative humidity at the high temperatures. *www.bertsperling.com, "Sperling's Chill Cities," July 18, 2013*
- Sperling's BestPlaces assessed 379 metropolitan areas of the United States for the likelihood of dangerously extreme weather events or earthquakes. In general the Southeast and South-Central regions have the highest risk of weather extremes and earthquakes, while the Pacific Northwest enjoys the lowest risk. Of the least risky metropolitan areas, the Anaheim* metro area was ranked #198. *www.bestplaces.net, "Safest Places from Natural Disasters," April 2011*
- Los Angeles* was identified as one of America's dirtiest metro areas by *Forbes.* The area ranked #17 out of 20. Criteria: air quality; water quality; toxic releases; superfund sites. *Forbes, "America's 20 Dirtiest Cities," December 10, 2012*
- The U.S. Environmental Protection Agency (EPA) released a list of U.S. metropolitan areas with the most ENERGY STAR certified buildings in 2015. The Los Angeles* metro area was ranked #2 out of 25. *U.S. Environmental Protection Agency, "Top Cities With the Most ENERGY STAR Certified Buildings in 2016," March 30, 2016*
- Los Angeles* was highlighted as one of the 25 most ozone-polluted metro areas in the U.S. during 2011 through 2013. The area ranked #1. *American Lung Association, State of the Air 2015*
- Los Angeles* was highlighted as one of the 25 metro areas most polluted by year-round particle pollution (Annual PM 2.5) in the U.S. during 2011 through 2013. The area ranked #5. *American Lung Association, State of the Air 2015*
- Los Angeles* was highlighted as one of the 25 metro areas most polluted by short-term particle pollution (24-hour PM 2.5) in the U.S. during 2011 through 2013. The area ranked #5. *American Lung Association, State of the Air 2015*

Health/Fitness Rankings

- Analysts who tracked obesity rates in the nation's largest metro areas (populations above one million) found that the Anaheim* metro area was one of the ten major metros where residents were least likely to be obese, defined as a BMI score of 30 or above. *www.gallup.com, "Boulder, Colo., Residents Still Least Likely to Be Obese," April 4, 2014*
- For each of the 50 most populous metro areas in the United States, the American College of Sports Medicine's American Fitness Index evaluated infrastructure, community assets, and policies that encourage healthy and fit lifestyles, including preventive health behaviors, levels of chronic disease conditions, health care access, and community resources and policies that support physical activity. The Los Angeles* metro area ranked #23 for "community fitness." *www.americanfitnessindex.org, "ACSM American Fitness Index Health and Community Fitness Status of the 50 Largest Metropolitan Areas," May 2015*
- The Los Angeles* metro area was identified as one of the worst cities for bed bugs in America by pest control company Orkin. The area ranked #2 out of 50 based on the number of bed bug treatments Orkin performed from January to December 2015. *Orkin, "Chicago Tops Bed Bug Cities List for Fourth Year in a Row," January 13, 2016*

- Los Angeles* was identified as a "2016 Spring Allergy Capital." The area ranked #67 out of 100. Three groups of factors were used to identify the most severe cities for people with allergies during the spring season: annual pollen levels; medicine utilization; access to board-certified allergists. *Asthma and Allergy Foundation of America, "Spring Allergy Capitals 2016"*
- Los Angeles* was identified as a "2015 Asthma Capital." The area ranked #52 out of the nation's 100 largest metropolitan areas. Criteria: estimated prevalence; self-reported prevalence; crude death rate for asthma; annual pollen score; annual air quality; public smoking laws; number of board-certified asthma specialists; school inhaler access laws; rescue medication use; controller medication use; ER visits for asthma; uninsured rate; poverty rate. *Asthma and Allergy Foundation of America, "Asthma Capitals 2015"*
- The Los Angeles* metro area ranked #40 out of 190 in The Gallup-Healthways Well-Being Index. Criteria: purpose; social well being; financial health; community and physical health. Results are based on telephone interviews with adults, aged 18 and older, living in metropolitan areas in the 50 U.S. states and the District of Columbia. *Gallup-Healthways, "State of American Well-Being," February 23, 2016*

Real Estate Rankings

- With data from RealtyTrac, Yahoo! Finance researchers listed the housing markets in which housing affordability is improving most, factoring in interest rates as well as median home prices. The Los Angeles* metro area was among the least affordable housing markets. *news.yahoo.com, "10 Cities Where Ordinary People Can No Longer Afford Homes," March 5, 2014*
- The Los Angeles* metro area was identified as one of the nations's 20 hottest housing markets in 2016. Criteria: listing views as an indicator of demand and median days on the market as an indicator of supply. The area ranked #12. *Realtor.com, "The 20 Hottest U.S. Real Estate Markets in February 2016," February 25, 2016*
- The Anaheim* metro area was identified as one of the 20 least affordable housing markets in the U.S. in 2015. The area ranked #3 out of 179 markets. Criteria: qualification for a mortgage loan on a typical home. *National Association of Realtors®, Affordability Index of Existing Single-Family Homes for Metropolitan Areas, 2015*
- Los Angeles* was ranked #224 out of 225 metro areas in terms of housing affordability in 2015 by the National Association of Home Builders (#1 = most affordable). Criteria: the share of homes sold in that area affordable to a family earning the local median income, based on standard mortgage underwriting criteria. *National Association of Home Builders®, NAHB-Wells Fargo Housing Opportunity Index, 4th Quarter 2015*

Safety Rankings

- Farmers Insurance, in partnership with Sperling's BestPlaces, ranked metro areas in the U.S. as the "Most Secure Places to Live." The Anaheim* metro area ranked #19 out of the top 20 in the large metro area category (500,000 or more residents). Criteria: economic stability; crime statistics; extreme weather; risk of natural disasters; housing depreciation; foreclosures; air quality; environmental hazards; life expectancy; motor vehicle fatalities; and employment numbers. *Farmers Insurance Group of Companies, "Most Secure U.S. Places to Live in the U.S.," June 25, 2013*
- The National Insurance Crime Bureau ranked 380 metro areas in the U.S. in terms of per capita rates of vehicle theft. The Los Angeles* metro area ranked #39 (#1 = highest rate). Criteria: number of vehicle theft offenses per 100,000 inhabitants in 2014. *National Insurance Crime Bureau, "Hot Spots 2014," June 24, 2015*

Seniors/Retirement Rankings

- From its Best Cities for Successful Aging indexes, the Milken Institute generated rankings for metropolitan areas, weighing data in eight categories—health care, wellness, living arrangements, transportation, financial characteristics, education and employment opportunities, community engagement, and overall livability. The Los Angeles* metro area was ranked #66 overall in the large metro area category. *Milken Institute, "Best Cities for Successful Aging, 2014"*

Sports/Recreation Rankings

- *Card Player* magazine scoured North America to identify the top five metropolitan areas where a player can access the types of games that make launching a poker career possible. The Los Angeles* metro area ranked #1. *Card Player, "The Top Five Cities to Launch Your Poker Career," April 2, 2014*

Transportation Rankings

- Los Angeles* was identified as one of the most congested metro areas in the U.S. The area ranked #2 out of 10. Criteria: yearly delay per auto commuter in hours. *Texas A&M Transportation Institute, "2015 Urban Mobility Scorecard," August 2015*
- The Los Angeles* metro area appeared on *Forbes* list of places with the most extreme commutes. The metro area ranked #5 out of 10. Criteria: average travel time; percentage of mega commuters. Mega-commuters travel more than 90 minutes and 50 miles each way to work. *Forbes.com, "The Cities with the Most Extreme Commutes," March 5, 2013*

Women/Minorities Rankings

- *24/7 Wall St.* compared median earnings over a 12-month period for men and women who worked full-time, year-round, and employment composition by sector to identify the best-paying cities for women. Of the largest 100 U.S. metropolitan areas, Los Angeles* was ranked #2 in pay disparity. *24/7 Wall St., "The Best (and Worst) Paying Cities for Women," March 6, 2015*

Miscellaneous Rankings

- The watchdog site Charity Navigator conducts an annual study of charities in the nation's major markets both to analyze statistical differences in their financial, accountability, and transparency practices and to track year-to-year variations in individual communities. The Los Angeles* metro area was ranked #4 among the 30 metro markets in the rating dimension of Overall Score. *www.charitynavigator.org, "Metro Market Study 2015," June 5, 2015*
- The Harris Poll's Happiness Index survey revealed that of the top ten U.S. markets, the Los Angeles* metro area residents ranked #5 in happiness. Criteria included strong assent to positive statements and strong disagreement with negative ones, and degree of agreement with a series of statements about respondents' personal relationships and general outlook. *www.harrisinteractive.com, "Dallas/Fort Worth Is "Happiest" City among America's Top Ten Markets," September 4, 2013*
- Energizer Personal Care, the makers of Edge® shave gel, in partnership with Sperling's BestPlaces, ranked 50 major metro areas in terms of everyday irritations. The Los Angeles* metro area ranked #6 the 50 metro area most iritating to guys. Criteria: high male-to-female ratio; poor sports team performance and high ticket prices; slow traffic; lack of job availability; unaffordable housing; extreme weather; lack of nightlife and fitness options. *Energizer Personal Care, "Most Irritatng Cities for Guys," August 26, 2013*
- Mars Chocolate North America, the makers of COMBOS®, in partnership with Sperling's BestPlaces, ranked 50 major metro areas in terms of their "manliness." The Los Angeles* metro area ranked #46. Criteria: number of professional sports teams; number of nearby NASCAR tracks and racing events; manly lifestyle; concentration of manly retail stores; manly occupations per capita; salty snack sales; "Board of Manliness" rankings. *Mars Chocolate North America, "America's Manliest Cities 2012"*
- The National Alliance to End Homelessness ranked the 100 most populous metro areas with the highest rate of homelessness. The Los Angeles* metro area ranked #6. Criteria: number of homeless people per 10,000 population in 2011. *National Alliance to End Homelessness, The State of Homelessness in America 2012*

Aliso Viejo is located within the Los Angeles-Long Beach-Anaheim, CA Metropolitan Statistical Area and the Anaheim-Santa Ana-Irvine, CA Metropolitan Division.

Business Environment

CITY FINANCES

City Government Finances

Component	2012 ($000)	2012 ($ per capita)
Total Revenues	18,953	396
Total Expenditures	22,221	464
Debt Outstanding	34,030	711
Cash and Securities[1]	37,778	789

Note: (1) Cash and security holdings of a government at the close of its fiscal year, including those of its dependent agencies, utilities, and liquor stores.
Source: U.S Census Bureau, State & Local Government Finances 2012

City Government Revenue by Source

Source	2012 ($000)	2012 ($ per capita)
General Revenue		
From Federal Government	0	0
From State Government	1,375	28
From Local Governments	0	0
Taxes		
Property	6,627	138
Sales and Gross Receipts	5,443	113
Personal Income	0	0
Corporate Income	0	0
Motor Vehicle License	0	0
Other Taxes	1,968	41
Current Charges	2,644	55
Liquor Store	0	0
Utility	0	0
Employee Retirement	0	0

Source: U.S Census Bureau, State & Local Government Finances 2012

City Government Expenditures by Function

Function	2012 ($000)	2012 ($ per capita)	2012 (%)
General Direct Expenditures			
Air Transportation	0	0	0.0
Corrections	0	0	0.0
Education	0	0	0.0
Employment Security Administration	0	0	0.0
Financial Administration	302	6	1.3
Fire Protection	0	0	0.0
General Public Buildings	518	10	2.3
Governmental Administration, Other	3,782	79	17.0
Health	220	4	0.9
Highways	3,397	71	15.2
Hospitals	0	0	0.0
Housing and Community Development	108	2	0.4
Interest on General Debt	2,010	42	9.0
Judicial and Legal	0	0	0.0
Libraries	0	0	0.0
Parking	0	0	0.0
Parks and Recreation	1,750	36	7.8
Police Protection	6,266	131	28.1
Public Welfare	0	0	0.0
Sewerage	0	0	0.0
Solid Waste Management	0	0	0.0
Veterans' Services	0	0	0.0
Liquor Store	0	0	0.0
Utility	0	0	0.0
Employee Retirement	0	0	0.0

Source: U.S Census Bureau, State & Local Government Finances 2012

DEMOGRAPHICS

Population Growth

Area	1990 Census	2000 Census	2010 Census	2014* Estimate	Population Growth (%) 1990-2014	Population Growth (%) 2010-2014
City	8,963	40,166	47,823	49,437	451.6	3.4
MSA[1]	11,273,720	12,365,627	12,828,837	13,060,534	15.8	1.8
U.S.	248,709,873	281,421,906	308,745,538	314,107,084	26.3	1.7

Note: (1) Figures cover the Los Angeles-Long Beach-Anaheim, CA Metropolitan Statistical Area—see Appendix B for areas included; (*) 2010-2014 5-year estimated population
Source: U.S. Census Bureau, 1990 Census, Census 2000, Census 2010, 2010-2014 American Community Survey 5-Year Estimates

Household Size

Area	Persons in Household (%) One	Two	Three	Four	Five	Six	Seven or More	Average Household Size
City	24.8	30.4	19.6	17.4	4.7	1.8	1.0	2.60
MSA[1]	24.5	28.0	16.6	15.4	8.3	3.8	3.1	3.03
U.S.	27.5	33.5	15.8	13.1	6.0	2.3	1.4	2.64

Note: (1) Figures cover the Los Angeles-Long Beach-Anaheim, CA Metropolitan Statistical Area—see Appendix B for areas included
Source: U.S. Census Bureau, 2010-2014 American Community Survey 5-Year Estimates

Race

Area	White Alone[2] (%)	Black Alone[2] (%)	Asian Alone[2] (%)	AIAN[3] Alone[2] (%)	NHOPI[4] Alone[2] (%)	Other Race Alone[2] (%)	Two or More Races (%)
City	70.0	2.7	15.5	0.3	0.0	5.5	6.0
MSA[1]	55.7	6.8	15.1	0.5	0.3	17.9	3.8
U.S.	73.8	12.6	5.0	0.8	0.2	4.7	2.9

Note: (1) Figures cover the Los Angeles-Long Beach-Anaheim, CA Metropolitan Statistical Area—see Appendix B for areas included; (2) Alone is defined as not being in combination with one or more other races; (3) American Indian and Alaska Native; (4) Native Hawaiian and Other Pacific Islander
Source: U.S. Census Bureau, 2010-2014 American Community Survey 5-Year Estimates

Hispanic or Latino Origin

Area	Total (%)	Mexican (%)	Puerto Rican (%)	Cuban (%)	Other (%)
City	16.5	11.7	0.3	0.1	4.3
MSA[1]	44.8	35.0	0.5	0.4	8.9
U.S.	16.9	10.8	1.6	0.6	3.8

Note: Persons of Hispanic or Latino origin can be of any race; (1) Figures cover the Los Angeles-Long Beach-Anaheim, CA Metropolitan Statistical Area—see Appendix B for areas included
Source: U.S. Census Bureau, 2010-2014 American Community Survey 5-Year Estimates

Ancestry

Area	German	Irish	English	American	Italian	Polish	French[2]	Scottish	Dutch
City	12.9	11.7	9.5	3.5	6.8	2.4	3.3	1.8	1.2
MSA[1]	6.0	4.8	4.4	3.2	3.0	1.3	1.4	1.0	0.7
U.S.	14.9	10.8	8.0	7.1	5.5	3.0	2.7	1.7	1.4

Note: Figures are the percentage of the total population reporting a particular ancestry. The nine most commonly reported ancestries in the U.S. are shown. Figures include multiple ancestries (e.g. if a person reported being Irish and Italian, they were included in both columns); (1) Figures cover the Los Angeles-Long Beach-Anaheim, CA Metropolitan Statistical Area—see Appendix B for areas included; (2) Excludes Basque
Source: U.S. Census Bureau, 2010-2014 American Community Survey 5-Year Estimates

Foreign-Born Population

Area	Percent of Population Born in								
	Any Foreign Country	Asia	Mexico	Europe	Carribean	Central America[2]	South America	Africa	Canada
City	22.5	14.3	3.0	1.8	0.3	0.4	1.5	0.7	0.5
MSA[1]	33.8	12.3	13.3	1.7	0.3	4.3	0.9	0.5	0.3
U.S.	13.1	3.8	3.7	1.5	1.2	1.0	0.9	0.6	0.3

Note: (1) Figures cover the Los Angeles-Long Beach-Anaheim, CA Metropolitan Statistical Area—see Appendix B for areas included; (2) Excludes Mexico.
Source: U.S. Census Bureau, 2010-2014 American Community Survey 5-Year Estimates

Marital Status

Area	Never Married	Now Married[2]	Separated	Widowed	Divorced
City	29.7	55.9	1.2	3.0	10.2
MSA[1]	39.6	44.3	2.5	5.0	8.6
U.S.	32.5	48.4	2.2	5.9	10.9

Note: Figures are percentages and cover the population 15 years of age and older; (1) Figures cover the Los Angeles-Long Beach-Anaheim, CA Metropolitan Statistical Area—see Appendix B for areas included; (2) Excludes separated
Source: U.S. Census Bureau, 2010-2014 American Community Survey 5-Year Estimates

Disability Status

Area	All Ages	Under 18 Years Old	18 to 64 Years Old	65 Years and Over
City	5.1	2.6	3.6	29.7
MSA[1]	9.2	2.8	6.8	36.1
U.S.	12.3	4.1	10.2	36.3

Note: Figures show percent of the civilian noninstitutionalized population that reported having a disability. Disability status is determined from from six types of difficulty: vision, hearing, cognitive, ambulatory, self-care, and independent living. For children under 5 years old, hearing and vision difficulty are used to determine disability status. For children between the ages of 5 and 14, disability status is determined from hearing, vision, cognitive, ambulatory, and self-care difficulties. For people aged 15 years and older, they are considered to have a disability if they have difficulty with any one of the six difficulty types; (1) Figures cover the Los Angeles-Long Beach-Anaheim, CA Metropolitan Statistical Area—see Appendix B for areas included.
Source: U.S. Census Bureau, 2010-2014 American Community Survey 5-Year Estimates

Age

Area	Percent of Population									Median Age
	Under Age 5	Age 5–19	Age 20–34	Age 35–44	Age 45–54	Age 55–64	Age 65–74	Age 75–84	Age 85+	
City	8.5	19.8	19.8	18.4	17.7	8.7	5.1	1.0	1.0	36.1
MSA[1]	6.4	20.0	22.6	14.2	14.0	11.0	6.4	3.6	1.7	35.6
U.S.	6.4	19.9	20.6	13.0	14.1	12.3	7.6	4.3	1.9	37.4

Note: (1) Figures cover the Los Angeles-Long Beach-Anaheim, CA Metropolitan Statistical Area—see Appendix B for areas included
Source: U.S. Census Bureau, 2010-2014 American Community Survey 5-Year Estimates

Gender

Area	Males	Females	Males per 100 Females
City	23,511	25,926	90.7
MSA[1]	6,438,759	6,621,775	97.2
U.S.	154,515,159	159,591,925	96.8

Note: (1) Figures cover the Los Angeles-Long Beach-Anaheim, CA Metropolitan Statistical Area—see Appendix B for areas included
Source: U.S. Census Bureau, 2010-2014 American Community Survey 5-Year Estimates

Religious Groups by Family

Area	Catholic	Baptist	Non-Den.	Methodist[2]	Lutheran	LDS[3]	Pentecostal	Presbyterian[4]	Muslim[5]	Judaism
MSA[1]	33.8	2.7	3.6	1.0	0.6	1.7	1.7	0.9	0.7	0.9
U.S.	19.1	9.3	4.0	4.0	2.3	2.0	1.9	1.6	0.8	0.7

Note: Figures are the number of adherents as a percentage of the total population; (1) Figures cover the Los Angeles-Long Beach-Santa Ana, CA Metropolitan Statistical Area—see Appendix B for areas included; (2) Methodist/Pietist; (3) Latter Day Saints; (4) Reformed; (5) Figures are estimates

Source: Association of Statisticians of American Religious Bodies, 2010 U.S. Religion Census: Religious Congregations & Membership Study

Religious Groups by Tradition

Area	Catholic	Evangelical Protestant	Mainline Protestant	Other Tradition	Black Protestant	Orthodox
MSA[1]	33.8	9.0	2.3	4.6	0.8	0.6
U.S.	19.1	16.2	7.3	4.3	1.6	0.3

Note: Figures are the number of adherents as a percentage of the total population; (1) Figures cover the Los Angeles-Long Beach-Santa Ana, CA Metropolitan Statistical Area—see Appendix B for areas included

Source: Association of Statisticians of American Religious Bodies, 2010 U.S. Religion Census: Religious Congregations & Membership Study

ECONOMY

Gross Metropolitan Product

Area	2013	2014	2015	2016	Rank[2]
MSA[1]	826.8	859.7	887.9	930.8	2

Note: Figures are in billions of dollars; (1) Figures cover the Los Angeles-Long Beach-Anaheim, CA Metropolitan Statistical Area—see Appendix B for areas included; (2) Rank is based on 2016 data and ranges from 1 to 381

Source: The U.S. Conference of Mayors, U.S. Metro Economies: GMP and Employment 2014-2016, June 2015

Economic Growth

Area	2011-13 (%)	2014 (%)	2015 (%)	2016 (%)	Rank[2]
MSA[1]	1.5	2.6	2.0	3.0	83
U.S.	2.2	2.4	2.3	2.9	–

Note: Figures are real gross metropolitan product (GMP) growth rates and represent annual average percent change; (1) Figures cover the Los Angeles-Long Beach-Anaheim, CA Metropolitan Statistical Area—see Appendix B for areas included; (2) Rank is based on 2016 data and ranges from 1 to 381

Source: The U.S. Conference of Mayors, U.S. Metro Economies: GMP and Employment 2014-2016, June 2015

Metropolitan Area Exports

Area	2009	2010	2011	2012	2013	2014	Rank[2]
MSA[1]	51,528.3	62,167.6	72,688.9	75,007.5	76,305.7	75,471.2	3

Note: Figures are in millions of dollars; (1) Figures cover the Los Angeles-Long Beach-Anaheim, CA Metropolitan Statistical Area—see Appendix B for areas included; (2) Rank is based on 2014 data and ranges from 1 to 385

Source: U.S. Department of Commerce, International Trade Administration, Office of Trade & Industry Information, Manufacturing & Services, data extracted March 10, 2016

Building Permits

Area	Single-Family			Multi-Family			Total		
	2014	2015p	Pct. Chg.	2014	2015p	Pct. Chg.	2014	2015p	Pct. Chg.
City	0	0	-	0	637	-	0	637	-
MSA[1]	8,300	8,458	1.9	18,650	25,211	35.2	26,950	33,669	24.9
U.S.	640,300	690,800	7.9	411,800	487,600	18.4	1,052,100	1,178,400	12.0

Note: (1) Figures cover the Los Angeles-Long Beach-Anaheim, CA Metropolitan Statistical Area—see Appendix B for areas included; Figures represent new, privately-owned housing units authorized (unadjusted data); All permit data are based on estimates with imputation; (p) preliminary data.

Source: U.S. Census Bureau, Manufacturing, Mining, and Construction Statistics, Building Permits, 2014, 2015

Bankruptcy Filings

Area	Business Filings			Nonbusiness Filings		
	2014	2015	% Chg.	2014	2015	% Chg.
Orange County	397	424	6.8	7,279	5,898	-19.0
U.S.	26,983	24,735	-8.3	909,812	819,760	-9.9

Note: Business filings include Chapter 7, Chapter 11, Chapter 12, and Chapter 13; Nonbusiness filings include Chapter 7, Chapter 11, and Chapter 13
Source: Administrative Office of the U.S. Courts, Business and Nonbusiness Bankruptcy, County Cases Commenced by Chapter of the Bankruptcy Code, During the 12- Month Period Ending December 31, 2014 and Business and Nonbusiness Bankruptcy, County Cases Commenced by Chapter of the Bankruptcy Code, During the 12- Month Period Ending December 31, 2015

Housing Vacancy Rates

Area	Gross Vacancy Rate[2] (%)			Year-Round Vacancy Rate[3] (%)			Rental Vacancy Rate[4] (%)			Homeowner Vacancy Rate[5] (%)		
	2013	2014	2015	2013	2014	2015	2013	2014	2015	2013	2014	2015
MSA[1]	6.2	5.8	5.4	5.7	5.5	5.0	4.2	4.6	3.3	1.2	0.8	0.8
U.S.	13.6	13.4	12.9	10.7	10.4	10.0	8.3	7.6	7.1	2.0	1.9	1.8

Note: (1) Figures cover the Los Angeles-Long Beach-Anaheim, CA Metropolitan Statistical Area—see Appendix B for areas included; (2) The percentage of the total housing inventory that is vacant; (3) The percentage of the housing inventory (excluding seasonal units) that is year-round vacant; (4) The percentage of rental inventory that is vacant for rent; (5) The percentage of homeowner inventory that is vacant for sale
Source: U.S. Census Bureau, Housing Vacancies and Homeownership Annual Statistics: 2015

INCOME

Income

Area	Per Capita ($)	Median Household ($)	Average Household ($)
City	44,986	102,325	119,475
MSA[1]	29,506	60,337	86,928
U.S.	28,555	53,482	74,596

Note: (1) Figures cover the Los Angeles-Long Beach-Anaheim, CA Metropolitan Statistical Area—see Appendix B for areas included
Source: U.S. Census Bureau, 2010-2014 American Community Survey 5-Year Estimates

Household Income Distribution

Area	Percent of Households Earning							
	Under $15,000	$15,000 -24,999	$25,000 -34,999	$35,000 -49,999	$50,000 -74,999	$75,000 -99,000	$100,000 -149,999	$150,000 and up
City	4.2	3.2	3.6	7.3	14.2	16.1	23.5	27.9
MSA[1]	11.3	9.8	9.1	12.2	16.6	12.1	14.5	14.4
U.S.	12.5	10.7	10.2	13.5	17.8	12.2	13.0	10.0

Note: (1) Figures cover the Los Angeles-Long Beach-Anaheim, CA Metropolitan Statistical Area—see Appendix B for areas included
Source: U.S. Census Bureau, 2010-2014 American Community Survey 5-Year Estimates

Poverty Rate

Area	All Ages	Under 18 Years Old	18 to 64 Years Old	65 Years and Over
City	5.2	5.6	4.7	8.8
MSA[1]	17.1	24.0	15.4	12.2
U.S.	15.6	21.9	14.6	9.4

Note: Figures are percentage of people whose income during the past 12 months was below the poverty level; (1) Figures cover the Los Angeles-Long Beach-Anaheim, CA Metropolitan Statistical Area—see Appendix B for areas included
Source: U.S. Census Bureau, 2010-2014 American Community Survey 5-Year Estimates

EMPLOYMENT

Labor Force and Employment

Area	Civilian Labor Force			Workers Employed		
	Dec. 2014	Dec. 2015	% Chg.	Dec. 2014	Dec. 2015	% Chg.
City	29,342	29,700	1.2	28,271	28,758	1.7
MD[1]	1,584,967	1,602,110	1.0	1,511,008	1,537,037	1.7
U.S.	155,521,000	157,245,000	1.1	147,190,000	149,703,000	1.7

Note: Data is not seasonally adjusted and covers workers 16 years of age and older; (1) Figures cover the Anaheim-Santa Ana-Irvine, CA Metropolitan Division—see Appendix B for areas included
Source: Bureau of Labor Statistics, Local Area Unemployment Statistics

Unemployment Rate

Area	2015											
	Jan.	Feb.	Mar.	Apr.	May	Jun.	Jul.	Aug.	Sep.	Oct.	Nov.	Dec.
City	3.9	3.6	3.4	3.2	3.3	3.4	3.7	3.5	3.1	3.4	3.3	3.2
MD[1]	5.0	4.6	4.4	4.1	4.2	4.3	4.7	4.5	4.0	4.3	4.2	4.1
U.S.	6.1	5.8	5.6	5.1	5.3	5.5	5.6	5.2	4.9	4.8	4.8	4.8

Note: Data is not seasonally adjusted and covers workers 16 years of age and older; (1) Figures cover the Anaheim-Santa Ana-Irvine, CA Metropolitan Division—see Appendix B for areas included
Source: Bureau of Labor Statistics, Local Area Unemployment Statistics

Employment by Occupation

Occupation Classification	City (%)	MSA[1] (%)	U.S. (%)
Management, Business, Science, and Arts	56.5	36.5	36.4
Natural Resources, Construction, and Maintenance	2.6	7.5	9.0
Production, Transportation, and Material Moving	4.4	12.1	12.1
Sales and Office	25.6	25.2	24.4
Service	10.9	18.6	18.2

Note: Figures cover employed civilians 16 years of age and older; (1) Figures cover the Los Angeles-Long Beach-Anaheim, CA Metropolitan Statistical Area—see Appendix B for areas included
Source: U.S. Census Bureau, 2010-2014 American Community Survey 5-Year Estimates

Employment by Industry

Sector	MD[1]		U.S.
	Number of Employees	Percent of Total	Percent of Total
Construction	96,100	6.0	4.5
Education and Health Services	203,200	12.8	15.7
Financial Activities	118,700	7.5	5.7
Government	161,200	10.2	15.5
Information	25,800	1.6	1.9
Leisure and Hospitality	209,100	13.2	10.4
Manufacturing	157,100	9.9	8.6
Mining and Logging	600	<0.1	0.5
Other Services	48,100	3.0	3.9
Professional and Business Services	290,700	18.4	13.9
Retail Trade	159,100	10.0	11.3
Transportation, Warehousing, and Utilities	28,100	1.7	3.9
Wholesale Trade	81,900	5.1	4.1

Note: Figures are non-farm employment as of December 2015. Figures are not seasonally adjusted and include workers 16 years of age and older; (1) Figures cover the Anaheim-Santa Ana-Irvine, CA Metropolitan Division—see Appendix B for areas included
Source: Bureau of Labor Statistics, Current Employment Statistics, Employment, Hours, and Earnings

Occupations with Greatest Projected Employment Growth: 2012 – 2022

Occupation[1]	2012 Employment	2022 Projected Employment	Numeric Employment Change	Percent Employment Change
Personal Care Aides	386,900	587,200	200,300	51.8
Combined Food Preparation and Serving Workers, Including Fast Food	286,000	362,400	76,400	26.7
Retail Salespersons	468,400	528,100	59,700	12.7
Laborers and Freight, Stock, and Material Movers, Hand	270,500	322,300	51,800	19.1
Waiters and Waitresses	246,100	290,300	44,200	18.0
Registered Nurses	254,500	297,400	42,900	16.9
General and Operations Managers	253,800	295,700	41,900	16.5
Secretaries and Administrative Assistants, Except Legal, Medical, and Executive	212,800	250,100	37,300	17.5
Cashiers	357,800	392,600	34,800	9.7
Cooks, Restaurant	116,900	150,600	33,700	28.8

Note: Projections cover California; (1) Sorted by numeric employment change
Source: www.projectionscentral.com, State Occupational Projections, 2012–2022 Long-Term Projections

Fastest Growing Occupations: 2012 – 2022

Occupation[1]	2012 Employment	2022 Projected Employment	Numeric Employment Change	Percent Employment Change
Economists	3,100	5,100	2,000	64.5
Helpers—Brickmasons, Blockmasons, Stonemasons, and Tile and Marble Setters	2,900	4,600	1,700	58.6
Brickmasons and Blockmasons	5,100	8,000	2,900	56.9
Insulation Workers, Floor, Ceiling, and Wall	1,600	2,500	900	56.3
Stonemasons	1,100	1,700	600	54.5
Insulation Workers, Mechanical	1,100	1,700	600	54.5
Personal Care Aides	386,900	587,200	200,300	51.8
Foresters	1,200	1,800	600	50.0
Terrazzo Workers and Finishers	1,100	1,600	500	45.5
Mechanical Door Repairers	1,100	1,600	500	45.5

Note: Projections cover California; (1) Sorted by percent employment change and excludes occupations with numeric employment change less than 100
Source: www.projectionscentral.com, State Occupational Projections, 2012–2022 Long-Term Projections

Average Wages

Occupation	$/Hr.	Occupation	$/Hr.
Accountants and Auditors	37.26	Maids and Housekeeping Cleaners	11.34
Automotive Mechanics	25.15	Maintenance and Repair Workers	19.96
Bookkeepers	21.75	Marketing Managers	65.03
Carpenters	24.95	Nuclear Medicine Technologists	52.24
Cashiers	11.29	Nurses, Licensed Practical	24.65
Clerks, General Office	16.51	Nurses, Registered	42.74
Clerks, Receptionists/Information	14.99	Nursing Assistants	13.85
Clerks, Shipping/Receiving	15.87	Packers and Packagers, Hand	11.64
Computer Programmers	39.49	Physical Therapists	45.41
Computer Systems Analysts	45.84	Postal Service Mail Carriers	25.84
Computer User Support Specialists	28.56	Real Estate Brokers	n/a
Cooks, Restaurant	12.43	Retail Salespersons	13.50
Dentists	84.50	Sales Reps., Exc. Tech./Scientific	30.76
Electrical Engineers	53.89	Sales Reps., Tech./Scientific	41.69
Electricians	25.64	Secretaries, Exc. Legal/Med./Exec.	18.85
Financial Managers	68.25	Security Guards	12.56
First-Line Supervisors/Managers, Sales	21.08	Surgeons	87.38
Food Preparation Workers	11.02	Teacher Assistants*	16.42
General and Operations Managers	66.05	Teachers, Elementary School*	36.66
Hairdressers/Cosmetologists	14.23	Teachers, Secondary School*	38.38
Internists	129.18	Telemarketers	13.81
Janitors and Cleaners	12.80	Truck Drivers, Heavy/Tractor-Trailer	20.45
Landscaping/Groundskeeping Workers	12.75	Truck Drivers, Light/Delivery Svcs.	18.28
Lawyers	76.75	Waiters and Waitresses	13.53

Note: Wage data covers the Santa Ana-Anaheim-Irvine, CA Metropolitan Division—see Appendix B for areas included; (*) Hourly wages for elementary/secondary school teachers and teacher assistants were calculated by the editors from annual wage data based on a 40 hour work week; n/a not available.
Source: Bureau of Labor Statistics, Metro Area Occupational Employment and Wage Estimates, May 2015

TAXES

State Corporate Income Tax Rates

State	Tax Rate (%)	Income Brackets ($)	Num. of Brackets	Financial Institution Tax Rate (%)[a]	Federal Income Tax Ded.
California	8.84 (c)	Flat rate	1	10.84 (c)	No

Note: Tax rates as of January 1, 2016; (a) Rates listed are the corporate income tax rate applied to financial institutions or excise taxes based on income. Some states have other taxes based upon the value of deposits or shares; (c) Minimum tax is $800 in California, $100 in District of Columbia, $50 in North Dakota (banks), $500 in Rhode Island, $200 per location in South Dakota (banks), $100 in Utah, $250 in Vermont.
Source: Federation of Tax Administrators, "State Corporate Income Tax Rates, 2016"

State Individual Income Tax Rates

State	Tax Rate (%)	Income Brackets ($)	Num. of Brackets	Personal Exempt. ($)[1] Single	Personal Exempt. ($)[1] Dependents	Fed. Inc. Tax Ded.
California (a)	1.0 - 12.3 (f)	7,850- 526,443 (b)	9	109 (c)	337 (c)	No

Note: Tax rates as of January 1, 2016; Local- and county-level taxes are not included; n/a not applicable; (1) Married joint filers generally receive double the single exemption; (a) 18 states have statutory provision for automatically adjusting to the rate of inflation the dollar values of the income tax brackets, standard deductions, and/or personal exemptions. Massachusetts, Michigan, and Nebraska index the personal exemptiononly. Oregon does not index the income brackets for $125,000 and over. Maine has suspended indexing for 2014 and 2015; (b) For joint returns, taxes are twice the tax on half the couple's income; (c) The personal exemption takes the form of a tax credit instead of a deduction; (f) California imposes an additional 1% tax on taxable income over $1 million, making the maximum rate 13.3% over $1 million.
Source: Federation of Tax Administrators, "State Individual Income Tax Rates, 2016"

Various State and Local Tax Rates

State	State and Local Sales and Use (%)	State Sales and Use (%)	Gasoline[1] (¢/gal.)	Cigarette[2] ($/pack)	Spirits[3] ($/gal.)	Wine[4] ($/gal.)	Beer[5] ($/gal.)
California	8.00	7.50 (b)	40.62	0.87	3.30 (f)	0.20 (l)	0.08

Note: All tax rates as of January 1, 2016; (1) The American Petroleum Institute has developed a methodology for determining the average tax rate on a gallon of fuel. Rates may include any of the following: excise taxes, environmental fees, storage tank fees, other fees or taxes, general sales tax, and local taxes. In states where gasoline is subject to the general sales tax, or where the fuel tax is based on the average sale price, the average rate determined by API is sensitive to changes in the price of gasoline. States that fully or partially apply general sales taxes to gasoline: CA, CO, GA, IL, IN, MI, NY; (2) The federal excise tax of $1.0066 per pack and local taxes are not included; (3) Rates are those applicable to off-premise sales of 40% alcohol by volume (a.b.v.) distilled spirits in 750ml containers. Local excise taxes are excluded; (4) Rates are those applicable to off-premise sales of 11% a.b.v. non-carbonated wine in 750ml containers; (5) Rates are those applicable to off-premise sales of 4.7% a.b.v. beer in 12 ounce containers; (b) Three states levy mandatory, statewide local add-on sales taxes at the state level: California (1%), Utah (1.25%), and Virginia (1%). We include these in their state sales tax rates; (f) Different rates are also applicable according to alcohol content, place of production, size of container, or place purchased (on- or off-premise or onboard airlines); (l) Different rates also applicable according to alcohol content, place of production, size of container, place purchased (on- or off-premise or on board airlines) or type of wine (carbonated, vermouth, etc.).
Source: Tax Foundation, 2016 Facts & Figures: How Does Your State Compare?

State Business Tax Climate Index Rankings

State	Overall Rank	Corporate Tax Rank	Individual Income Tax Rank	Sales Tax Rank	Unemployment Insurance Tax Rank	Property Tax Rank
California	48	35	50	40	13	13

Note: The index is a measure of how each state's tax laws affect economic performance. The lower the rank, the more favorable a state's tax system is for business. States without a given tax are given a ranking of 1. The scores/rankings for the District of Columbia do not affect other states. The 2016 index represents the tax climate as of July 1, 2015 (the beginning of Fiscal Year 2016).
Source: Tax Foundation, State Business Tax Climate Index 2016

TRANSPORTATION

Means of Transportation to Work

Area	Car/Truck/Van		Public Transportation			Bicycle	Walked	Other Means	Worked at Home
	Drove Alone	Car-pooled	Bus	Subway	Railroad				
City	78.8	9.3	0.8	0.0	0.1	0.2	1.6	0.5	8.6
MSA[1]	73.9	10.3	5.3	0.4	0.2	0.9	2.6	1.3	5.1
U.S.	76.4	9.6	2.6	1.8	0.6	0.6	2.8	1.3	4.4

Note: Figures are percentages and cover workers 16 years of age and older; (1) Figures cover the Los Angeles-Long Beach-Anaheim, CA Metropolitan Statistical Area—see Appendix B for areas included
Source: U.S. Census Bureau, 2010-2014 American Community Survey 5-Year Estimates

Travel Time to Work

Area	Less Than 10 Minutes	10 to 19 Minutes	20 to 29 Minutes	30 to 44 Minutes	45 to 59 Minutes	60 to 89 Minutes	90 Minutes or More
City	11.2	25.5	24.9	25.2	5.5	5.3	2.5
MSA[1]	8.1	26.1	20.5	24.9	9.2	8.2	3.0
U.S.	13.3	29.6	21.0	20.2	7.7	5.7	2.6

Note: Figures are percentages and include workers 16 years old and over; (1) Figures cover the Los Angeles-Long Beach-Anaheim, CA Metropolitan Statistical Area—see Appendix B for areas included
Source: U.S. Census Bureau, 2010-2014 American Community Survey 5-Year Estimates

Freeway Travel Time Index

Area	1985	1990	1995	2000	2005	2010	2014
Urban Area Rank[1,2]	1	1	1	1	1	1	1
Urban Area Index[1]	1.31	1.34	1.38	1.41	1.44	1.42	1.43
Average Index[3]	1.09	1.11	1.14	1.17	1.20	1.19	1.20

Note: Freeway Travel Time Index—the ratio of travel time in the peak period to the travel time at free-flow conditions. For example, a value of 1.30 indicates a 20-minute free-flow trip takes 26 minutes in the peak (20 minutes x 1.30 = 26 minutes); (1) Covers the Los Angeles-Long Beach-Anaheim CA urban area; (2) Rank is based on 101 urban areas (#1 = highest travel time index); (3) Average of 101 urban areas
Source: Texas Transportation Institute, 2015 Urban Mobility Scorecard, August 2015

Freeway Commuter Stress Index

Area	1985	1990	1995	2000	2005	2010	2014
Urban Area Rank[1,2]	1	1	1	1	1	1	1
Urban Area Index[1]	1.49	1.52	1.56	1.59	1.63	1.61	1.62
Average Index[3]	1.13	1.16	1.19	1.22	1.25	1.24	1.25

Note: The Freeway Commuter Stress Index is the same as the Freeway Travel Time Index (see table above) except that it includes only the travel in the peak directions during the peak periods; the TTI includes travel in all directions during the peak period. Thus, the CSI is more indicative of the work trip experienced by each commuter on a daily basis. (1) Covers the Los Angeles-Long Beach-Anaheim CA urban area; (2) Rank is based on 101 urban areas (#1 = highest stress index); (3) Average of 101 urban areas

Source: Texas Transportation Institute, 2015 Urban Mobility Scorecard, August 2015

Living Environment

COST OF LIVING

Cost of Living Index

Composite Index	Groceries	Housing	Utilities	Trans-portation	Health Care	Misc. Goods/ Services
148.8	107.6	244.7	113.9	135.0	107.6	104.8

Note: The Cost of Living Index measures regional differences in the cost of consumer goods and services, excluding taxes and non-consumer expenditures, for professional and managerial households in the top income quintile. It is based on more than 50,000 prices covering almost 60 different items for which prices are collected three times a year by chambers of commerce, economic development organizations or university applied economic centers in each participating urban area. The numbers shown should be read as a percentage above or below the national average of 100. For example, a value of 115.4 in the groceries column indicates that grocery prices are 15.4% higher than the national average. Small differences in the index numbers should not be interpreted as significant; Figures cover the Orange County CA urban area.
Source: The Council for Community and Economic Research, ACCRA Cost of Living Index, 2015

Grocery Prices

Area[1]	T-Bone Steak ($/pound)	Frying Chicken ($/pound)	Whole Milk ($/half gal.)	Eggs ($/dozen)	Orange Juice ($/64 oz.)	Coffee ($/11.5 oz.)
City[2]	11.16	1.48	2.43	3.59	3.52	5.35
Avg.	10.99	1.43	2.25	2.26	3.58	4.48
Min.	7.16	0.98	1.30	1.35	2.88	2.98
Max.	14.13	2.43	3.85	4.81	6.39	7.56

Note: (1) Values for the local area are compared with the average, minimum and maximum values for all 292 areas in the Cost of Living Index; (2) Figures cover the Orange County CA urban area; **T-Bone Steak** *(price per pound);* **Frying Chicken** *(price per pound, whole fryer);* **Whole Milk** *(half gallon carton);* **Eggs** *(price per dozen, Grade A, large);* **Orange Juice** *(64 oz. Tropicana or Florida Natural);* **Coffee** *(11.5 oz. can, vacuum-packed, Maxwell House, Hills Bros, or Folgers).*
Source: The Council for Community and Economic Research, ACCRA Cost of Living Index, 2015

Housing and Utility Costs

Area[1]	New Home Price ($)	Apartment Rent ($/month)	All Electric ($/month)	Part Electric ($/month)	Other Energy ($/month)	Telephone ($/month)
City[2]	809,108	1,998	-	129.72	57.14	33.57
Avg.	312,874	945	179.30	95.07	72.96	28.11
Min.	178,682	479	116.28	43.14	26.46	10.01
Max.	1,472,476	3,984	504.25	189.44	421.11	43.06

Note: (1) Values for the local area are compared with the average, minimum and maximum values for all 292 areas in the Cost of Living Index; (2) Figures cover the Orange County CA urban area; **New Home Price** *(2,400 sf living area, 8,000 sf lot, in urban area with full utilities);* **Apartment Rent** *(950 sf 2 bedroom/1.5 or 2 bath, unfurnished, excluding all utilities except water);* **All Electric** *(average monthly cost for an all-electric home);* **Part Electric** *(average monthly cost for a part-electric home);* **Other Energy** *(average monthly cost for natural gas, fuel oil, coal, wood, and any other forms of energy except electricity);* **Telephone** *(price includes basic monthly rate for a private residential line plus additional local usage charges incurred by a family of four).*
Source: The Council for Community and Economic Research, ACCRA Cost of Living Index, 2015

Health Care, Transportation, and Other Costs

Area[1]	Doctor ($/visit)	Dentist ($/visit)	Optometrist ($/visit)	Gasoline ($/gallon)	Beauty Salon ($/visit)	Men's Shirt ($)
City[2]	96.52	104.00	101.81	3.38	59.39	26.79
Avg.	105.15	89.02	99.78	2.38	35.30	28.10
Min.	66.87	56.09	48.53	1.95	18.91	13.38
Max.	182.34	150.36	228.33	4.09	67.91	63.80

Note: (1) Values for the local area are compared with the average, minimum and maximum values for all 292 areas in the Cost of Living Index; (2) Figures cover the Orange County CA urban area; **Doctor** *(general practitioners routine exam of an established patient);* **Dentist** *(adult teeth cleaning and periodic oral examination);* **Optometrist** *(full vision eye exam for established adult patient);* **Gasoline** *(one gallon regular unleaded, national brand, including all taxes, cash price at self-service pump if available);* **Beauty Salon** *(woman's shampoo, trim, and blow-dry);* **Men's Shirt** *(cotton/polyester dress shirt, pinpoint weave, long sleeves).*
Source: The Council for Community and Economic Research, ACCRA Cost of Living Index, 2015

HOUSING

House Price Index (HPI)

Area	National Ranking[2]	Quarterly Change (%)	One-Year Change (%)	Five-Year Change (%)
MD[1]	88	1.00	6.10	29.10
U.S.[3]	–	1.45	5.76	22.85

Note: The HPI is a weighted repeat sales index. It measures average price changes in repeat sales or refinancings on the same properties. This information is obtained by reviewing repeat mortgage transactions on single-family properties whose mortgages have been purchased or securitized by Fannie Mae or Freddie Mac in January 1975; (1) Anaheim-Santa Ana-Irvine Metropolitan Division—see Appendix B for areas included; (2) Rankings are based on annual percentage change for all metro areas containing at least 15,000 transactions over the last 10 years and ranges from 1 to 266; (3) figures based on a weighted average of Census Division estimates using a seasonally adjusted, purchase-only index; all figures are for the period ending December 31, 2015

Source: Federal Housing Finance Agency, House Price Index, February 25, 2016

Median Single-Family Home Prices

Area	2013	2014	2015[p]	Percent Change 2014 to 2015
MD[1]	651.7	687.9	707.5	2.8
U.S. Average	197.4	208.9	223.9	7.2

Note: Figures are median sales prices of existing single-family homes in thousands of dollars; (p) preliminary; n/a not available; (1) Anaheim-Santa Ana-Irvine, CA Metropolitan Division—see Appendix B for areas included

Source: National Association of Realtors, Median Sales Price of Existing Single-Family Homes for Metropolitan Areas, 4th Quarter 2015

Qualifying Income Based on Median Sales Price of Existing Single-Family Homes

Area	With 5% Down ($)	With 10% Down ($)	With 20% Down ($)
MD[1]	157,636	149,340	132,746
U.S. Average	49,535	46,928	41,714

Note: Figures are preliminary; Qualifying income is based on a mortgage rate of 4.1%. Monthly principal and interest payment is limited to 25% of income; n/a not available; (1) Anaheim-Santa Ana-Irvine, CA Metropolitan Division—see Appendix B for areas included

Source: National Association of Realtors, Qualifying Income Based on Median Sales Price of Existing Single-Family Homes for Metropolitan Areas, 4th Quarter 2015

Median Apartment Condo-Coop Home Prices

Area	2013	2014	2015[p]	Percent Change 2014 to 2015
MD[1]	n/a	n/a	n/a	n/a
U.S. Average	194.9	204.3	210.7	3.1

Note: Figures are median sales prices of existing apartment condo-coop homes in thousands of dollars; (p) preliminary; n/a not available; (1) Anaheim-Santa Ana-Irvine, CA Metropolitan Division—see Appendix B for areas included

Source: National Association of Realtors, Median Sales Price of Existing Apartment Condo-Coop Homes for Metropolitan Areas, 4th Quarter 2015

Gross Monthly Rent

Area	Under $200	$200 -299	$300 -499	$500 -749	$750 -999	$1,000 -1,499	$1,500 and up	Median ($)
City	0.0	0.1	1.3	2.1	2.7	14.5	79.3	1,862
MSA[1]	0.5	1.9	2.5	6.4	16.4	37.2	35.0	1,284
U.S.	1.5	3.2	7.4	21.0	24.1	26.9	15.9	920

Note: Figures are percentages except for Median; Gross rent is the contract rent plus the estimated average monthly cost of utilities (electricity, gas, and water and sewer) and fuels (oil, coal, kerosene, wood, etc.) if these are paid by the renter (or paid for the renter by someone else); (1) Figures cover the Los Angeles-Long Beach-Anaheim, CA Metropolitan Statistical Area—see Appendix B for areas included

Source: U.S. Census Bureau, 2010-2014 American Community Survey 5-Year Estimates

Homeownership Rate

Area	2008 (%)	2009 (%)	2010 (%)	2011 (%)	2012 (%)	2013 (%)	2014 (%)	2015 (%)
MSA[1]	52.1	50.4	49.7	50.1	49.9	48.7	49.0	49.1
U.S.	67.8	67.4	66.9	66.1	65.4	65.1	64.5	63.7

Note: (1) Figures cover the Los Angeles-Long Beach-Anaheim, CA Metropolitan Statistical Area—see Appendix B for areas included
Source: U.S. Census Bureau, Housing Vacancies and Homeownership Annual Statistics: 2015

Year Housing Structure Built

Area	2010 or Later	2000 -2009	1990 -1999	1980 -1989	1970 -1979	1960 -1969	1950 -1959	1940 -1949	Before 1940	Median Year
City	1.8	13.3	56.1	22.1	4.7	0.7	0.3	0.3	0.6	1994
MSA[1]	0.5	6.8	7.5	12.6	16.5	16.0	19.0	8.9	12.2	1966
U.S.	1.0	14.9	13.9	13.8	15.8	11.0	10.8	5.4	13.3	1976

Note: Figures are percentages except for Median Year; (1) Figures cover the Los Angeles-Long Beach-Anaheim, CA Metropolitan Statistical Area—see Appendix B for areas included
Source: U.S. Census Bureau, 2010-2014 American Community Survey 5-Year Estimates

HEALTH

Health Risk Data

Category	MD[1] (%)	U.S. (%)
Adults aged 18–64 who have any kind of health care coverage	82.4	79.6
Adults who reported being in good or excellent health	87.0	83.1
Adults who are current smokers	10.0	19.6
Adults who are heavy drinkers[2]	5.3	6.1
Adults who are binge drinkers[3]	19.5	16.9
Adults who are overweight (BMI 25.0 - 29.9)	38.2	35.8
Adults who are obese (BMI 30.0 - 99.8)	21.5	27.6
Adults who participated in any physical activities in the past month	84.4	77.1
Adults 50+ who have ever had a sigmoidoscopy or colonoscopy	69.5	67.3
Women aged 40+ who have had a mammogram within the past two years	77.4	74.0
Men aged 40+ who have had a PSA test within the past two years	45.6	45.2
Adults aged 65+ who have had flu shot within the past year	65.0	60.1
Adults who always wear a seatbelt	n/a	93.8

Note: Data as of 2012 unless otherwise noted; n/a not available; (1) Figures cover the Anaheim-Santa Ana-Irvine, CA Metropolitan Division—see Appendix B for areas included; (2) Heavy drinkers are classified as males having more than two drinks per day or females having more than one drink per day; (3) Binge drinkers are classified as males having five or more drinks on one occasion or females having four or more drinks on one occasion
Source: Centers for Disease Control and Prevention, Behaviorial Risk Factor Surveillance System, SMART: Selected Metropolitan/Micropolitan Area Risk Trends, 2012 (Note: the CDC has discontinued this dataset but will be releasing a replacement in mid-2016)

Chronic Health Indicators

Category	MD[1] (%)	U.S. (%)
Adults who have ever been told they had a heart attack	2.2	4.5
Adults who have ever been told they had a stroke	n/a	2.9
Adults who have been told they currently have asthma	5.7	8.9
Adults who have ever been told they have arthritis	18.1	25.7
Adults who have ever been told they have diabetes[2]	9.4	9.7
Adults who have ever been told they had skin cancer	7.5	5.7
Adults who have ever been told they had any other types of cancer	8.4	6.5
Adults who have ever been told they have COPD	4.3	6.2
Adults who have ever been told they have kidney disease	1.9	2.5
Adults who have ever been told they have a form of depression	9.2	18.0

Note: Data as of 2012 unless otherwise noted; n/a not available; (1) Figures cover the Anaheim-Santa Ana-Irvine, CA Metropolitan Division—see Appendix B for areas included; (2) Figures do not include pregnancy-related, borderline, or pre-diabetes
Source: Centers for Disease Control and Prevention, Behaviorial Risk Factor Surveillance System, SMART: Selected Metropolitan/Micropolitan Area Risk Trends, 2012 (Note: the CDC has discontinued this dataset but will be releasing a replacement in mid-2016)

Mortality Rates for the Top 10 Causes of Death in the U.S.

ICD-10[a] Sub-Chapter	ICD-10[a] Code	Age-Adjusted Mortality Rate[1] per 100,000 population	
		County[2]	U.S.
Malignant neoplasms	C00-C97	139.1	163.6
Ischaemic heart diseases	I20-I25	92.9	102.2
Other forms of heart disease	I30-I51	38.3	50.1
Chronic lower respiratory diseases	J40-J47	28.8	41.4
Organic, including symptomatic, mental disorders	F01-F09	22.3	38.5
Cerebrovascular diseases	I60-I69	34.3	36.5
Other external causes of accidental injury	W00-X59	16.2	27.5
Other degenerative diseases of the nervous system	G30-G31	36.8	26.3
Diabetes mellitus	E10-E14	14.4	21.1
Hypertensive diseases	I10-I15	16.0	19.7

Note: (a) ICD-10 = International Classification of Diseases 10th Revision; (1) Mortality rates are a three year average covering 2012-2014; (2) Figures cover COUNTY NOT FOUND!!!!!!.
Source: Centers for Disease Control and Prevention, National Center for Health Statistics. Underlying Cause of Death 1999-2014 on CDC WONDER Online Database, released 2015.

Mortality Rates for Selected Causes of Death

ICD-10[a] Sub-Chapter	ICD-10[a] Code	Age-Adjusted Mortality Rate[1] per 100,000 population	
		County[2]	U.S.
Assault	X85-Y09	1.8	5.1
Diseases of the liver	K70-K76	11.9	13.5
Human immunodeficiency virus (HIV) disease	B20-B24	1.0	2.1
Influenza and pneumonia	J09-J18	16.4	15.2
Intentional self-harm	X60-X84	10.0	12.7
Malnutrition	E40-E46	0.2	0.9
Obesity and other hyperalimentation	E65-E68	0.7	1.9
Renal failure	N17-N19	8.0	13.0
Transport accidents	V01-V99	6.5	11.6
Viral hepatitis	B15-B19	2.1	2.1

Note: (a) ICD-10 = International Classification of Diseases 10th Revision; (1) Mortality rates are a three year average covering 2012-2014; (2) Figures cover COUNTY NOT FOUND!!!!!!; Data are Suppressed when the data meet the criteria for confidentiality constraints; Mortality rates are flagged as Unreliable when the rate would be calculated with a numerator of 20 or less.
Source: Centers for Disease Control and Prevention, National Center for Health Statistics. Underlying Cause of Death 1999-2014 on CDC WONDER Online Database, released 2015.

Health Insurance Coverage

Area	With Health Insurance	With Private Health Insurance	With Public Health Insurance	Without Health Insurance	Population Under Age 18 Without Health Insurance
City	90.8	84.1	11.4	9.2	3.8
MSA[1]	80.3	56.7	29.9	19.7	8.2
U.S.	85.8	65.8	31.1	14.2	7.1

Note: Figures are percentages that cover the civilian noninstitutionalized population; (1) Figures cover the Los Angeles-Long Beach-Anaheim, CA Metropolitan Statistical Area—see Appendix B for areas included
Source: U.S. Census Bureau, 2010-2014 American Community Survey 5-Year Estimates

Number of Medical Professionals

Area	MDs[3]	DOs[3,4]	Dentists	Podiatrists	Chiropractors	Optometrists
County[1] (number)	9,654	595	3,265	180	1,402	753
County[1] (rate[2])	309.2	19.1	103.8	5.7	44.6	23.9
U.S. (rate[2])	272.5	20.9	64.7	5.8	25.9	15.2

Note: Data as of 2014 unless noted; (1) Data covers Orange County; (2) Rate per 100,000 population; (3) Data as of 2013 and includes all active, non-federal physicians; (4) Doctor of Osteopathic Medicine
Source: U.S. Department of Health and Human Services, Health Resources and Services Administration, Bureau of Health Professions, Area Resource File (ARF) 2014-2015

Best Hospitals

According to *U.S. News,* the Anaheim-Santa Ana-Irvine, CA metro area is home to one of the best hospitals in the U.S.: **University of California, Irvine Medical Center** (2 specialties). The hospital listed was nationally ranked in at least one adult specialty. Only 137 hospitals nationwide were nationally ranked in one or more specialties. Fifteen hospitals in the U.S. made the Honor Roll with high scores in at least six specialties. *U.S. News Online, "America's Best Children's Hospitals 2015-16"*

According to *U.S. News,* the Anaheim-Santa Ana-Irvine, CA metro area is home to one of the best children's hospitals in the U.S.: **Children's Hospital of Orange County** (8 specialties). The hospital listed was highly ranked in at least one pediatric specialty. Eighty-three children's hospitals in the U.S. were nationally ranked in at least one specialty. Twelve children's hospitals in the U.S. made the Honor Roll with high scores in at least three specialties. *U.S. News Online, "America's Best Children's Hospitals 2015-16"*

EDUCATION

Public School District Statistics

District Name	Schls	Pupils	Pupil/ Teacher Ratio	Minority Pupils[1] (%)	Free Lunch Eligible[2] (%)	IEP[3] (%)
Capistrano Unified	63	53,833	28.8	40.8	17.4	9.0

Note: Table includes school districts with 100 or more students; (1) Percentage of students that are not non-Hispanic white; (2) Percentage of students that are eligible for the free lunch program; (3) Percentage of students that have an Individualized Education Program.
Source: U.S. Department of Education, National Center for Education Statistics, Common Core of Data, Local Education Agency (School District) Universe Survey: School Year 2013-2014; U.S. Department of Education, National Center for Education Statistics, Common Core of Data, Public Elementary/Secondary School Universe Survey: School Year 2013-2014

Highest Level of Education

Area	Less than H.S.	H.S. Diploma	Some College, No Deg.	Associate Degree	Bachelor's Degree	Master's Degree	Prof. School Degree	Doctorate Degree
City	4.6	11.3	18.0	9.2	38.8	13.2	2.9	1.9
MSA[1]	21.5	19.9	19.9	7.1	20.7	7.2	2.4	1.3
U.S.	13.7	28.0	21.2	7.9	18.3	7.8	2.0	1.3

Note: Figures cover persons age 25 and over; (1) Figures cover the Los Angeles-Long Beach-Anaheim, CA Metropolitan Statistical Area—see Appendix B for areas included
Source: U.S. Census Bureau, 2010-2014 American Community Survey 5-Year Estimates

Educational Attainment by Race

Area	High School Graduate or Higher (%)					Bachelor's Degree or Higher (%)				
	Total	White	Black	Asian	Hisp.[2]	Total	White	Black	Asian	Hisp.[2]
City	95.4	97.0	96.8	96.7	80.6	56.9	57.0	64.4	67.7	28.8
MSA[1]	78.5	81.1	88.5	87.2	57.4	31.7	33.6	23.9	50.0	11.1
U.S.	86.3	88.4	83.2	85.8	64.1	29.3	30.6	19.0	50.9	13.9

Note: Figures shown cover persons 25 years old and over; (1) Figures cover the Los Angeles-Long Beach-Anaheim, CA Metropolitan Statistical Area—see Appendix B for areas included; (2) People of Hispanic origin can be of any race
Source: U.S. Census Bureau, 2010-2014 American Community Survey 5-Year Estimates

School Enrollment by Grade and Control

Area	Preschool (%)		Kindergarten (%)		Grades 1 - 4 (%)		Grades 5 - 8 (%)		Grades 9 - 12 (%)	
	Public	Private	Public	Private	Public	Private	Public	Private	Public	Private
City	30.3	69.7	75.2	24.8	84.2	15.8	86.2	13.8	90.4	9.6
MSA[1]	58.3	41.7	88.2	11.8	90.3	9.7	90.6	9.4	91.8	8.2
U.S.	57.4	42.6	87.8	12.2	89.8	10.2	89.9	10.1	90.6	9.4

Note: Figures shown cover persons 3 years old and over; (1) Figures cover the Los Angeles-Long Beach-Anaheim, CA Metropolitan Statistical Area—see Appendix B for areas included
Source: U.S. Census Bureau, 2010-2014 American Community Survey 5-Year Estimates

Average Salaries of Public School Classroom Teachers

Area	2013-14		2014-15		Percent Change	Percent Change
	Dollars	Rank[1]	Dollars	Rank[1]	2013-14 to 2014-15	2004-05 to 2014-15
California	71,396	4	72,535	4	1.59	25.9
U.S. Average	56,610	–	57,379	–	1.36	20.8

Note: (1) State rank ranges from 1 to 51 where 1 indicates highest salary.
Source: National Education Association, Rankings & Estimates: Rankings of the States 2014 and Estimates of School Statistics 2015, March 2015

Higher Education

Four-Year Colleges			Two-Year Colleges			Medical Schools[1]	Law Schools[2]	Voc/ Tech[3]
Public	Private Non-profit	Private For-profit	Public	Private Non-profit	Private For-profit			
0	1	0	0	0	0	0	0	0

Note: Figures cover institutions located within the city limits and include main campuses only; (1) includes schools accredited by the Liaison Committee on Medical Education and the American Osteopathic Association's Commission on Osteopathic College Accreditation; (2) includes ABA-accredited schools, schools with provisional ABA accreditation, and state accredited schools; (3) includes all schools with programs that are less than 2 years.
Source: National Center for Education Statistics, Integrated Postsecondary Education System (IPEDS), 2014-15; Association of American Medical Colleges, Member List, March 21, 2016; American Osteopathic Association, Member List, March 21, 2016; Law School Admission Council, Official Guide to ABA-Approved Law Schools Online, March 21, 2016; Wikipedia, List of Medical Schools in the United States, March 21, 2016; Wikipedia, List of Law Schools in the United States, March 21, 2016

According to *U.S. News & World Report,* the Anaheim-Santa Ana-Irvine, CA metro division is home to one of the best national universities in the U.S.: **University of California–Irvine** (#39 tie). The indicators used to capture academic quality fall into a number of categories: assessment by administrators at peer institutions; retention of students; faculty resources; student selectivity; financial resources; alumni giving; high school counselor ratings of colleges; and graduation rate. *U.S. News & World Report, "America's Best Colleges 2016"*

According to *U.S. News & World Report,* the Anaheim-Santa Ana-Irvine, CA metro division is home to one of the best liberal arts colleges in the U.S.: **Soka University of America** (#45 tie). The indicators used to capture academic quality fall into a number of categories: assessment by administrators at peer institutions; retention of students; faculty resources; student selectivity; financial resources; alumni giving; high school counselor ratings of colleges; and graduation rate. *U.S. News & World Report, "America's Best Colleges 2016"*

According to *U.S. News & World Report,* the Anaheim-Santa Ana-Irvine, CA metro division is home to one of the top 100 law schools in the U.S.: **University of California–Irvine, School of Law** (#28 tie). The rankings are based on a weighted average of 12 measures of quality: peer assessment score; assessment score by lawyers/judges; median LSAT scores; median undergrad GPA; acceptance rate; employment rates for graduates; placement success; bar passage rate; faculty resources; expenditures per student; student/faculty ratio; and library resources. *U.S. News & World Report, "America's Best Graduate Schools, Law, 2017"*

According to *U.S. News & World Report,* the Anaheim-Santa Ana-Irvine, CA metro division is home to one of the top 75 medical schools for research in the U.S.: **University of California–Irvine, School of Medicine** (#44 tie). The rankings are based on a weighted average of 11 measures of quality: quality assessment; peer assessment score; assessment score by residency directors; research activity; total research activity; average research activity per faculty member; student selectivity; median MCAT total score; median undergraduate GPA; acceptance rate; and faculty resources. *U.S. News & World Report, "America's Best Graduate Schools, Medical, 2017"*

According to *U.S. News & World Report,* the Anaheim-Santa Ana-Irvine, CA metro division is home to one of the top 75 business schools in the U.S.: **University of California–Irvine, Paul Merage School of Business** (#48 tie). The rankings are based on a weighted average of the following nine measures: quality assessment; peer assessment; recruiter assessment; placement success; mean starting salary and bonus; student selectivity; mean GMAT and GRE scores; mean undergraduate GPA; and acceptance rate. *U.S. News & World Report, "America's Best Graduate Schools, Business, 2017"*

PRESIDENTIAL ELECTION

2012 Presidential Election Results

Area	Obama (%)	Romney (%)	Other (%)
Orange County	45.4	52.4	2.2
U.S.	51.0	47.2	1.8

Note: Results may not add to 100% due to rounding
Source: Dave Leip's Atlas of U.S. Presidential Elections

EMPLOYERS

Major Employers

Company Name	Industry
City of Los Angeles	General government
County of Los Angeles	General government
Decton	Employment agencies
Disney Enterprises	Motion picture production & distribution
Disney Worldwide Services	Telecommunication equipment repair (except telephones)
Electronic Arts	Home entertainment computer software
King Holding Corporation	Bolts, nuts, rivets, & washers
Securitas Security Services USA	Security guard service
Team-One Employment Specialists	Employment agencies
The Boeing Company	Aircraft
The Boeing Company	Aircraft engines & engine parts
The Walt Disney Company	Television broadcasting stations
UCLA Health System	Home health care services
UCLA Medical Group	Medical centers
University of California, Irvine	University
University of Southern California	Colleges & universities
Veterans Health Administration	Administration of veterans' affairs
Warner Bros. Entertainment	Motion picture & video production

Note: Companies shown are located within the Los Angeles-Long Beach-Anaheim, CA Metropolitan Statistical Area.
Source: Hoovers.com; Wikipedia

PUBLIC SAFETY

Crime Rate

Area	All Crimes	Violent Crimes: Murder	Violent Crimes: Rape[3]	Violent Crimes: Robbery	Violent Crimes: Aggrav. Assault	Property Crimes: Burglary	Property Crimes: Larceny -Theft	Property Crimes: Motor Vehicle Theft
City	607.8	2.0	9.9	9.9	47.4	88.8	416.4	33.5
Metro[1]	1,932.9	1.9	20.6	61.7	114.0	293.2	1,241.9	199.5
U.S.	2,971.8	4.5	36.6	102.2	232.5	542.5	1,837.3	216.2

Note: Figures are crimes per 100,000 population; (1) Figures cover the Anaheim-Santa Ana-Irvine, CA Metropolitan Division—see Appendix B for areas included; (3) The city and U.S. figures shown were reported using the revised Uniform Crime Reporting (UCR) definition of rape. The suburban and metro area figures shown are an aggregate total of the data submitted using both the revised and legacy UCR definitions.
Source: FBI Uniform Crime Reports, 2014

Hate Crimes

Area	Number of Quarters Reported	Race	Religion	Sexual Orientation	Ethnicity	Disability	Gender	Gender Identity
City	4	0	0	0	0	0	0	0
U.S.	4	2,568	1,014	1,017	648	84	33	98

Number of Incidents per Bias Motivation (columns Race through Gender Identity)

Source: Federal Bureau of Investigation, Hate Crime Statistics 2014

Identity Theft Consumer Complaints

Area	Complaints	Complaints per 100,000 Population	Rank[2]
MSA[1]	19,791	149.2	55
U.S.	490,220	152.4	-

Note: (1) Figures cover the Los Angeles-Long Beach-Anaheim, CA Metropolitan Statistical Area—see Appendix B for areas included; (2) Rank ranges from 1 to 379 where 1 indicates greatest number of identity theft complaints per 100,000 population
Source: Federal Trade Commission, Consumer Sentinel Network Data Book for January–December 2015

Fraud and Other Consumer Complaints

Area	Complaints	Complaints per 100,000 Population	Rank[2]
MSA[1]	48,981	369.3	172
U.S.	2,593,159	806.0	-

Note: (1) Figures cover the Los Angeles-Long Beach-Anaheim, CA Metropolitan Statistical Area—see Appendix B for areas included; (2) Rank ranges from 1 to 379 where 1 indicates greatest number of identity theft complaints per 100,000 population
Source: Federal Trade Commission, Consumer Sentinel Network Data Book for January–December 2015

RECREATION

Culture

Dance[1]	Theatre[1]	Instrumental Music[1]	Vocal Music[1]	Series and Festivals	Museums and Art Galleries[2]	Zoos and Aquariums[3]
0	0	0	0	0	0	0

Note: (1) Professional perfoming groups; (2) Based on organizations with SIC code 8412; (3) AZA-accredited
Source: The Grey House Performing Arts Directory, 2015-16; Association of Zoos & Aquariums, AZA Member Zoos & Aquariums, March 25, 2016; www.AccuLeads.com, March 29, 2016

Professional Sports Teams

Team Name	League	Year Established
Anaheim Ducks	National Hockey League (NHL)	1993
C.D. Chivas USA	Major League Soccer (MLS)	2004
Los Angeles Angels of Anaheim	Major League Baseball (MLB)	1961
Los Angeles Clippers	National Basketball Association (NBA)	1984
Los Angeles Dodgers	Major League Baseball (MLB)	1958
Los Angeles FC	Major League Soccer (MLS)	2018
Los Angeles Galaxy	Major League Soccer (MLS)	1996
Los Angeles Kings	National Hockey League (NHL)	1967
Los Angeles Lakers	National Basketball Association (NBA)	1960
Los Angeles Rams	National Hockey League (NHL)	2016

Note: Includes teams located in the Los Angeles-Long Beach-Anaheim, CA Metropolitan Statistical Area.
Source: Wikipedia, Major Professional Sports Teams of the United States and Canada, March 24, 2016

CLIMATE

Average and Extreme Temperatures

Temperature	Jan	Feb	Mar	Apr	May	Jun	Jul	Aug	Sep	Oct	Nov	Dec	Yr.
Extreme High (°F)	89	91	97	108	102	107	112	104	112	105	95	93	112
Average High (°F)	68	69	69	72	73	77	82	83	83	79	73	68	75
Average Temp. (°F)	56	58	58	61	64	68	72	74	72	67	61	56	64
Average Low (°F)	44	46	48	50	55	59	62	64	61	56	48	43	53
Extreme Low (°F)	28	29	31	34	38	42	45	48	44	30	32	25	25

Note: Figures cover the years 1945-1995
Source: National Climatic Data Center, International Station Meteorological Climate Summary, 9/96

Average Precipitation/Snowfall/Humidity

Precip./Humidity	Jan	Feb	Mar	Apr	May	Jun	Jul	Aug	Sep	Oct	Nov	Dec	Yr.
Avg. Precip. (in.)	2.7	2.4	2.2	0.8	0.2	0.1	Tr	0.1	0.4	0.3	1.3	1.5	11.9
Avg. Snowfall (in.)	0	0	0	0	0	0	0	0	0	0	0	Tr	Tr
Avg. Rel. Hum. 7am (%)	78	81	82	79	77	79	80	81	81	80	79	79	80
Avg. Rel. Hum. 4pm (%)	56	57	57	55	58	59	57	57	56	57	56	57	57

Note: Figures cover the years 1945-1995; Tr = Trace amounts (<0.05 in. of rain; <0.5 in. of snow)
Source: National Climatic Data Center, International Station Meteorological Climate Summary, 9/96

Weather Conditions

Temperature			Daytime Sky			Precipitation		
10°F & below	32°F & below	90°F & above	Clear	Partly cloudy	Cloudy	0.01 inch or more precip.	0.1 inch or more snow/ice	Thunder-storms
0	2	18	95	192	78	41	0	4

Note: Figures are average number of days per year and cover the years 1945-1995
Source: National Climatic Data Center, International Station Meteorological Climate Summary, 9/96

HAZARDOUS WASTE

Superfund Sites

Aliso Viejo has no sites on the EPA's Superfund Final National Priorities List. There are a total of 1,323 Superfund sites on the list in the U.S. *U.S. Environmental Protection Agency, Final National Priorities List, March 18, 2016*

AIR & WATER QUALITY

Air Quality Trends: Ozone

	1990	1995	2000	2005	2010	2011	2012	2013	2014
MSA[1]	0.123	0.106	0.087	0.080	0.073	0.075	0.076	0.072	0.080

Note: (1) Data covers the Los Angeles-Long Beach-Anaheim, CA Metropolitan Statistical Area—see Appendix B for areas included. The values shown are the composite ozone concentration averages among trend sites based on the highest fourth daily maximum 8-hour concentration in parts per million. These trends are based on sites having an adequate record of monitoring data during the trend period. Data from exceptional events are included.
Source: U.S. Environmental Protection Agency, Air Quality Monitoring Information, "Air Quality Trends by City, 1990-2014"

Air Quality Index

Area	Percent of Days when Air Quality was...[2]					AQI Statistics[2]	
	Good	Moderate	Unhealthy for Sensitive Groups	Unhealthy	Very Unhealthy	Maximum	Median
MSA[1]	19.7	57.8	19.5	3.0	0.0	182	67

Note: (1) Data covers the Los Angeles-Long Beach-Anaheim, CA Metropolitan Statistical Area—see Appendix B for areas included; (2) Based on 365 days with AQI data in 2015. Air Quality Index (AQI) is an index for reporting daily air quality. EPA calculates the AQI for five major air pollutants regulated by the Clean Air Act: ground-level ozone, particle pollution (aka particulate matter), carbon monoxide, sulfur dioxide, and nitrogen dioxide. The AQI runs from 0 to 500. The higher the AQI value, the greater the level of air pollution and the greater the health concern. There are six AQI categories: "Good" AQI is between 0 and 50. Air quality is considered satisfactory; "Moderate" AQI is between 51 and 100. Air quality is acceptable; "Unhealthy for Sensitive Groups" When AQI values are between 101 and 150, members of sensitive groups may experience health effects; "Unhealthy" When AQI values are between 151 and 200 everyone may begin to experience health effects; "Very Unhealthy" AQI values between 201 and 300 trigger a health alert; "Hazardous" AQI values over 300 trigger warnings of emergency conditions (not shown).
Source: U.S. Environmental Protection Agency, Air Quality Index Report, 2015

Air Quality Index Pollutants

Area	Percent of Days when AQI Pollutant was...[2]					
	Carbon Monoxide	Nitrogen Dioxide	Ozone	Sulfur Dioxide	Particulate Matter 2.5	Particulate Matter 10
MSA[1]	0.0	1.9	49.0	0.0	48.5	0.5

Note: (1) Data covers the Los Angeles-Long Beach-Anaheim, CA Metropolitan Statistical Area—see Appendix B for areas included; (2) Based on 365 days with AQI data in 2015. The Air Quality Index (AQI) is an index for reporting daily air quality. EPA calculates the AQI for five major air pollutants regulated by the Clean Air Act: ground-level ozone, particle pollution (also known as particulate matter), carbon monoxide, sulfur dioxide, and nitrogen dioxide. The AQI runs from 0 to 500. The higher the AQI value, the greater the level of air pollution and the greater the health concern.
Source: U.S. Environmental Protection Agency, Air Quality Index Report, 2015

Maximum Air Pollutant Concentrations: Particulate Matter, Ozone, CO and Lead

	Particulate Matter 10 (ug/m³)	Particulate Matter 2.5 Wtd AM (ug/m³)	Particulate Matter 2.5 24-Hr (ug/m³)	Ozone (ppm)	Carbon Monoxide (ppm)	Lead (ug/m³)
MSA[1] Level	95	12.6	35	0.097	4	0.07
NAAQS[2]	150	15	35	0.075	9	0.15
Met NAAQS[2]	Yes	Yes	Yes	No	Yes	Yes

Note: (1) Data covers the Los Angeles-Long Beach-Anaheim, CA Metropolitan Statistical Area—see Appendix B for areas included; Data from exceptional events are included; (2) National Ambient Air Quality Standards; ppm = parts per million; ug/m³ = micrograms per cubic meter; n/a not available.
Concentrations: Particulate Matter 10 (coarse particulate)—highest second maximum 24-hour concentration; Particulate Matter 2.5 Wtd AM (fine particulate)—highest weighted annual mean concentration; Particulate Matter 2.5 24-Hour (fine particulate)—highest 98th percentile 24-hour concentration; Ozone—highest fourth daily maximum 8-hour concentration; Carbon Monoxide—highest second maximum non-overlapping 8-hour concentration; Lead—maximum running 3-month average
Source: U.S. Environmental Protection Agency, Air Quality Monitoring Information, "Air Quality Statistics by City, 2014"

Maximum Air Pollutant Concentrations: Nitrogen Dioxide and Sulfur Dioxide

	Nitrogen Dioxide AM (ppb)	Nitrogen Dioxide 1-Hr (ppb)	Sulfur Dioxide AM (ppb)	Sulfur Dioxide 1-Hr (ppb)	Sulfur Dioxide 24-Hr (ppb)
MSA[1] Level	27	69	n/a	9	n/a
NAAQS[2]	53	100	30	75	140
Met NAAQS[2]	Yes	Yes	n/a	Yes	n/a

Note: (1) Data covers the Los Angeles-Long Beach-Anaheim, CA Metropolitan Statistical Area—see Appendix B for areas included; Data from exceptional events are included; (2) National Ambient Air Quality Standards; ppm = parts per million; ug/m³ = micrograms per cubic meter; n/a not available.
Concentrations: Nitrogen Dioxide AM—highest arithmetic mean concentration; Nitrogen Dioxide 1-Hr—highest 98th percentile 1-hour daily maximum concentration; Sulfur Dioxide AM—highest annual mean concentration; Sulfur Dioxide 1-Hr—highest 99th percentile 1-hour daily maximum concentration; Sulfur Dioxide 24-Hr—highest second maximum 24-hour concentration
Source: U.S. Environmental Protection Agency, Air Quality Monitoring Information, "Air Quality Statistics by City, 2014"

Drinking Water

Water System Name	Pop. Served	Primary Water Source Type	Violations[1] Health Based	Violations[1] Monitoring/ Reporting
El Toro Water District	48,628	Purchased Surface	0	0

Note: (1) Based on violation data from January 1, 2015 to December 31, 2015 (includes unresolved violations from earlier years)
Source: U.S. Environmental Protection Agency, Office of Ground Water and Drinking Water, Safe Drinking Water Information System (based on data extracted April 29, 2016)

Cupertino, California

Background

The city of Cupertino is a vibrant presence in the San Francisco Bay Area, a major source of information-age innovation, and a comfortable California residential community. It offers a unique blend of high technology employment and open space. Cupertino appears in European history after 1776, when the Spanish explorer, Captain Juan Bautista de Anza led a group into the area from his landing place at Monterey. De Anza's scribe, the Franciscan priest, Pedro Font, named a nearby creek for St. Joseph Cupertino and while the waterway later became Stephen's Creek, the Italian saint's name was later given to a local winery, then the post office, and subsequently to the town.

By the late 1800s, vineyards were the primary agriculture in the area, but were devastated by the infamous phylloxera infestation that raged through Europe and the New World. In the wake of this devastation, many farmers switched from grapes to fruit or almond trees, resulting in a richer variety of agriculture. Tourist trade increased, to enjoy what was called "Valley of Heart's Delight."

This mix of agriculture and tourism lasted until the late 1940s, when the Bay Area experienced postwar suburban expansion. As a result, Cupertino became incorporated in 1955 as one of Santa Clara County's 13 cities.

In the mid-1960s, many electronics firms moved into the area, De Anza College was established, and Cupertino moved into its present status as a hub of the information technology universe.

Most famously, Apple Computer came to Cupertino in the late 1970s and the city is still known for its private sector specialization of cutting-edge electronics and information technology. In addition to Apple Computer, Durect Corporation, Portal Software, and Symantec Corporation have headquarters here.

The city is regularly recognized for its services and programs, and most recently received the Helen Putnam Award for service and the American Planning Association Award.

The city is convenient to major hospitals, including Kaiser Foundation Hospital. El Camino Hospital, and Community Hospital Los Gatos.

The Cupertino Union School District is recognized in the state, and nationally, as one of the premier public school districts in the nation, and its diverse student population are testimony to the international drawing power of the city's knowledge-based industries: the schools test high. Colleges and universities in the area include the town's own De Anza College, and within fifteen miles of the city are West Valley College, Foothill College, San Jose City College, Mission College, and Stanford University.XXX

The city is served by three major airports, San Jose International (11 miles), San Francisco International (32 miles), and Oakland International (42 miles).

Rankings

General Rankings

- The San Jose* metro area was identified as one of America's fastest-growing areas in terms of population and economy by *Forbes*. The area ranked #17 out of 20. The 100 most populous metro areas in the U.S. were evaluated on the following criteria: estimated population growth; job growth; gross metropolitan product growth; unemployment; median salaries for college-educated workers. *Forbes, "America's Fastest-Growing Cities 2015," January 27, 2015*

Business/Finance Rankings

- The personal finance site NerdWallet analyzed 183 American metropolitan areas with populations over 250,000 and more than 15,000 businesses to rank where entrepreneurs find the most success. Criteria included area economy, annual income, housing cost, unemployment rate, and the success rate of area businesses. San Jose* ranked #42. *www.nerdwallet.com, "Best Places to Start a Business," April 27, 2015*

- TransUnion ranked the nation's metro areas by average credit score, calculated on the VantageScore system, developed by the three major credit-reporting bureaus—TransUnion, Experian, and Equifax. The San Jose* metro area was among the ten cities with the highest collective credit score, meaning that its residents posed the lowest average consumer credit risk. *www.usatoday.com, "Metro Areas' Average Credit Rating Revealed," February 7, 2013*

- Based on the U.S. Department of Labor's Occupational Information Network Data Collection Program, the Brookings Institution defined job opportunities for STEM workers at various levels of educational attainment. The San Jose* metro area was placed among the ten large metro areas with the highest demand for high-level STEM knowledge. *www.brookings.edu, "The Hidden Stem Economy," June 10, 2013*

- According to data by the Bureau of Economic Analysis (BEA) and the Bureau of Labor Statistics (BLS), the San Jose* metro area has the fastest-growing GDP (gross domestic product) and positive employment trends, at #9. *247wallst.com, "Cities With the Fastest Growing (and Shrinking) Economies," September 29, 2015*

- 24/7 Wall Street used Brookings Institution research on 50 advanced industries to identify the proportion of workers in the nation's largest metropolitan areas that were employed in jobs requiring knowledge in the science, technology, engineering, or math (STEM) fields. The San Jose* metro area was #1. *247wallst.com, "15 Cities with the Most High-Tech Jobs," March 13, 2015*

- Based on metro area social media reviews, the employment opinion group Glassdoor surveyed 50 of the largest U.S. metro areas and equally weighed cost of living, hiring opportunity, and job satisfaction to compose a list of "25 Best Cities for Jobs," The San Jose* metro area was ranked #2 in overall job satisfaction. *www.glassdoor.com, "Best Cities for Jobs," May 19, 2015*

- In a survey of economic confidence in the nation's 50 largest metropolitan areas conducted January–December 2014, the San Jose* metro area placed #1, according to Gallup's 2014 Economic Confidence Index. *Gallup, "San Jose and San Francisco Lead in Economic Confidence," March 19, 2015*

- The Brookings Institution ranked the 100 largest metro areas in the U.S. based on income inequality. San Jose* was ranked #17 (#1 = greatest ineqality). Criteria: the "95/20 ratio," a figure representing the income at which a household earns more than 95 percent of all other households, divided by the income at which a household earns more than only 20 percent of all other households. *Brookings Institution, "Income Inequality, 100 Largest U.S. Metro Areas, 2007-2014," January 14, 2016*

- *Forbes* ranked the largest metro areas in the U.S. in terms of the "Best Cities for Young Professionals." The San Jose* metro area ranked #11 out of 15. Criteria: job growth; unemployment rate; median salary of college graduates age 24 to 34; cost of living; number of small businesses per capita; number of large companies; percentage of population 25 years of age and older with college degrees. *Forbes.com, "America's 15 Best Cities for Young Professionals," August 18, 2014*

- The San Jose* metro area appeared on the Milken Institute "2015 Best Performing Cities" list. Rank: #1 out of 200 large metro areas. Criteria: job growth; wage and salary growth; high-tech output growth. *Milken Institute, "Best-Performing Cities 2015," December 2015*

- *Forbes* ranked the 200 most populous metro areas to determine the nation's "Best Places for Business and Careers." The San Jose* metro area was ranked #42. Criteria: costs (business and living); job growth (past and projected); income growth; educational attainment (college and high school); projected economic growth; cultural and recreational opportunities; net migration patterns; number of highly ranked colleges. *Forbes, "The Best Places for Business and Careers 2015," July 29, 2015*

Dating/Romance Rankings

- *Forbes* reports that the San Jose* metro area made Rent.com's Best Cities for Newlyweds list for 2013, based on Bureau of Labor Statistics and Census Bureau data on number of married couples, percentage of families with children under age six, average annual income, cost of living, and availability of rentals. *www.forbes.com, "The 10 Best Cities for Newlyweds to Live and Work In," May 30, 2013*

- CreditDonkey, a financial education website, sought out the ten best U.S. cities for newlyweds, considering the number of married couples, divorce rate, average credit score, and average number of hours worked per week in metro areas with a million or more residents. The San Jose* metro area placed #2. *www.creditdonkey.com, "Study: Best Cities for Newlyweds," November 30, 2013*

Education Rankings

- Based on a Brookings Institution study, *24/7 Wall St.* identified the ten U.S. metropolitan areas with the most average patent filings per million residents between 2007 and 2011. San Jose* ranked #1. *24/7 Wall St., "America's Most Innovative Cities," February 1, 2013*

- The San Jose* metro area was selected as one of America's most innovative cities" by *The Business Insider*. The metro area was ranked #1 out of 20. Criteria: patents per capita. *The Business Insider, "The 20 Most Innovative Cities in the U.S.," February 1, 2013*

- San Jose* was identified as one of America's "smartest" metropolitan areas by *The Business Journals*. The area ranked #5 out of 10. Criteria: percentage of adults (25 and older) with high school diplomas, bachelor's degrees and graduate degrees. *The Business Journals, "Where the Brainpower Is: Exclusive U.S. Rankings, Insights," February 27, 2014*

- Personal finance website *WalletHub* analyzed the 150 largest U.S. metropolitan statistical areas to determine where the most educated Americans are choosing to settle. Criteria: education quality and attainment gap; education levels; percentage of workers with degrees; public school rankings; quality and size of each metro area's universities. San Jose* was ranked #14 (#1 = most educated city). *www.WalletHub.com, "2015's Most and Least Educated Cities*

Environmental Rankings

- The San Jose* metro area came in at #48 for the relative comfort of its climate on Sperling's list of "chill cities," as measured by the Sperling Heat Index. All 361 metro areas are included. Criteria included daytime high temperatures, nighttime low temperatures, dew point, and relative humidity at the high temperatures. *www.bertsperling.com, "Sperling's Chill Cities," July 18, 2013*

- Sperling's BestPlaces assessed 379 metropolitan areas of the United States for the likelihood of dangerously extreme weather events or earthquakes. In general the Southeast and South-Central regions have the highest risk of weather extremes and earthquakes, while the Pacific Northwest enjoys the lowest risk. Of the least risky metropolitan areas, the San Jose* metro area was ranked #69. *www.bestplaces.net, "Safest Places from Natural Disasters," April 2011*

- San Jose* was identified as one of America's dirtiest metro areas by *Forbes*. The area ranked #8 out of 20. Criteria: air quality; water quality; toxic releases; superfund sites. *Forbes, "America's 20 Dirtiest Cities," December 10, 2012*

- The U.S. Environmental Protection Agency (EPA) released a list of U.S. metropolitan areas with the most ENERGY STAR certified buildings in 2015. The San Jose* metro area was ranked #17 out of 25. *U.S. Environmental Protection Agency, "Top Cities With the Most ENERGY STAR Certified Buildings in 2016," March 30, 2016*

- The U.S. Environmental Protection Agency (EPA) released a list of mid-size U.S. metropolitan areas with the most ENERGY STAR certified buildings in 2015. The San Jose* metro area was ranked #1 out of 10. *U.S. Environmental Protection Agency, "Top Cities With the Most ENERGY STAR Certified Buildings in 2016," March 30, 2016*

- San Jose* was highlighted as one of the 25 metro areas most polluted by year-round particle pollution (Annual PM 2.5) in the U.S. during 2011 through 2013. The area ranked #7. *American Lung Association, State of the Air 2015*

- San Jose* was highlighted as one of the 25 metro areas most polluted by short-term particle pollution (24-hour PM 2.5) in the U.S. during 2011 through 2013. The area ranked #6. *American Lung Association, State of the Air 2015*

Health/Fitness Rankings

- Analysts who tracked obesity rates in the nation's largest metro areas (populations above one million) found that the San Jose* metro area was one of the ten major metros where residents were least likely to be obese, defined as a BMI score of 30 or above. *www.gallup.com, "Boulder, Colo., Residents Still Least Likely to Be Obese," April 4, 2014*

- Analysts who tracked obesity rates in 100 of the nation's most populous areas found that the San Jose* metro area was one of the ten communities where residents were least likely to be obese, defined as a BMI score of 30 or above. *www.gallup.com, "Colorado Springs Residents Least Likely to Be Obese," May 28, 2015*

- For each of the 50 most populous metro areas in the United States, the American College of Sports Medicine's American Fitness Index evaluated infrastructure, community assets, and policies that encourage healthy and fit lifestyles, including preventive health behaviors, levels of chronic disease conditions, health care access, and community resources and policies that support physical activity. The San Jose* metro area ranked #10 for "community fitness." *www.americanfitnessindex.org, "ACSM American Fitness Index Health and Community Fitness Status of the 50 Largest Metropolitan Areas," May 2015*

- San Jose* was identified as a "2016 Spring Allergy Capital." The area ranked #86 out of 100. Three groups of factors were used to identify the most severe cities for people with allergies during the spring season: annual pollen levels; medicine utilization; access to board-certified allergists. *Asthma and Allergy Foundation of America, "Spring Allergy Capitals 2016"*

- San Jose* was identified as a "2015 Asthma Capital." The area ranked #97 out of the nation's 100 largest metropolitan areas. Criteria: estimated prevalence; self-reported prevalence; crude death rate for asthma; annual pollen score; annual air quality; public smoking laws; number of board-certified asthma specialists; school inhaler access laws; rescue medication use; controller medication use; ER visits for asthma; uninsured rate; poverty rate. *Asthma and Allergy Foundation of America, "Asthma Capitals 2015"*

- The San Jose* metro area ranked #15 out of 190 in The Gallup-Healthways Well-Being Index. Criteria: purpose; social well being; financial health; community and physical health. Results are based on telephone interviews with adults, aged 18 and older, living in metropolitan areas in the 50 U.S. states and the District of Columbia. *Gallup-Healthways, "State of American Well-Being," February 23, 2016*

Real Estate Rankings

- With data from RealtyTrac, Yahoo! Finance researchers listed the housing markets in which housing affordability is improving most, factoring in interest rates as well as median home prices. The San Jose* metro area was among the least affordable housing markets. *news.yahoo.com, "10 Cities Where Ordinary People Can No Longer Afford Homes," March 5, 2014*

- The San Jose* metro area was identified as one of the nations's 20 hottest housing markets in 2016. Criteria: listing views as an indicator of demand and median days on the market as an indicator of supply. The area ranked #2. *Realtor.com, "The 20 Hottest U.S. Real Estate Markets in February 2016," February 25, 2016*
- San Jose* was ranked #15 in the top 20 out of 266 metro areas in terms of house price appreciation in 2015 (#1 = highest rate). *Federal Housing Finance Agency, House Price Index, 4th Quarter 2015*
- The San Jose* metro area was identified as one of the 20 least affordable housing markets in the U.S. in 2015. The area ranked #1 out of 179 markets. Criteria: qualification for a mortgage loan on a typical home. *National Association of Realtors®, Affordability Index of Existing Single-Family Homes for Metropolitan Areas, 2015*
- San Jose* was ranked #220 out of 225 metro areas in terms of housing affordability in 2015 by the National Association of Home Builders (#1 = most affordable). Criteria: the share of homes sold in that area affordable to a family earning the local median income, based on standard mortgage underwriting criteria. *National Association of Home Builders®, NAHB-Wells Fargo Housing Opportunity Index, 4th Quarter 2015*

Safety Rankings

- Farmers Insurance, in partnership with Sperling's BestPlaces, ranked metro areas in the U.S. as the "Most Secure Places to Live." The San Jose* metro area ranked #7 out of the top 20 in the large metro area category (500,000 or more residents). Criteria: economic stability; crime statistics; extreme weather; risk of natural disasters; housing depreciation; foreclosures; air quality; environmental hazards; life expectancy; motor vehicle fatalities; and employment numbers. *Farmers Insurance Group of Companies, "Most Secure U.S. Places to Live in the U.S.," June 25, 2013*
- The National Insurance Crime Bureau ranked 380 metro areas in the U.S. in terms of per capita rates of vehicle theft. The San Jose* metro area ranked #10 (#1 = highest rate). Criteria: number of vehicle theft offenses per 100,000 inhabitants in 2014. *National Insurance Crime Bureau, "Hot Spots 2014," June 24, 2015*

Seniors/Retirement Rankings

- From its Best Cities for Successful Aging indexes, the Milken Institute generated rankings for metropolitan areas, weighing data in eight categories—health care, wellness, living arrangements, transportation, financial characteristics, education and employment opportunities, community engagement, and overall livability. The San Jose* metro area was ranked #65 overall in the large metro area category. *Milken Institute, "Best Cities for Successful Aging, 2014"*

Transportation Rankings

- San Jose* was identified as one of the most congested metro areas in the U.S. The area ranked #5 out of 10. Criteria: yearly delay per auto commuter in hours. *Texas A&M Transportation Institute, "2015 Urban Mobility Scorecard," August 2015*

Miscellaneous Rankings

- The National Alliance to End Homelessness ranked the 100 most populous metro areas with the highest rate of homelessness. The San Jose* metro area ranked #7. Criteria: number of homeless people per 10,000 population in 2011. *National Alliance to End Homelessness, The State of Homelessness in America 2012*

Cupertino is located within the San Jose-Sunnyvale-Santa Clara, CA Metropolitan Statistical Area.

Business Environment

CITY FINANCES

City Government Finances

Component	2012 ($000)	2012 ($ per capita)
Total Revenues	60,366	1,035
Total Expenditures	59,233	1,015
Debt Outstanding	43,940	753
Cash and Securities[1]	51,344	880

Note: (1) Cash and security holdings of a government at the close of its fiscal year, including those of its dependent agencies, utilities, and liquor stores.
Source: U.S Census Bureau, State & Local Government Finances 2012

City Government Revenue by Source

Source	2012 ($000)	2012 ($ per capita)
General Revenue		
From Federal Government	211	3
From State Government	1,788	30
From Local Governments	0	0
Taxes		
Property	18,339	314
Sales and Gross Receipts	20,275	347
Personal Income	0	0
Corporate Income	0	0
Motor Vehicle License	0	0
Other Taxes	4,238	72
Current Charges	12,016	206
Liquor Store	0	0
Utility	0	0
Employee Retirement	0	0

Source: U.S Census Bureau, State & Local Government Finances 2012

City Government Expenditures by Function

Function	2012 ($000)	2012 ($ per capita)	2012 (%)
General Direct Expenditures			
Air Transportation	0	0	0.0
Corrections	0	0	0.0
Education	0	0	0.0
Employment Security Administration	0	0	0.0
Financial Administration	742	12	1.2
Fire Protection	0	0	0.0
General Public Buildings	0	0	0.0
Governmental Administration, Other	8,954	153	15.1
Health	0	0	0.0
Highways	7,054	120	11.9
Hospitals	0	0	0.0
Housing and Community Development	1,073	18	1.8
Interest on General Debt	1,883	32	3.1
Judicial and Legal	619	10	1.0
Libraries	0	0	0.0
Parking	0	0	0.0
Parks and Recreation	15,148	259	25.5
Police Protection	8,446	144	14.2
Public Welfare	0	0	0.0
Sewerage	0	0	0.0
Solid Waste Management	1,563	26	2.6
Veterans' Services	0	0	0.0
Liquor Store	0	0	0.0
Utility	0	0	0.0
Employee Retirement	0	0	0.0

Source: U.S Census Bureau, State & Local Government Finances 2012

DEMOGRAPHICS

Population Growth

Area	1990 Census	2000 Census	2010 Census	2014* Estimate	Population Growth (%) 1990-2014	Population Growth (%) 2010-2014
City	44,842	50,546	58,302	59,787	33.3	2.5
MSA[1]	1,534,280	1,735,819	1,836,911	1,898,457	23.7	3.4
U.S.	248,709,873	281,421,906	308,745,538	314,107,084	26.3	1.7

Note: (1) Figures cover the San Jose-Sunnyvale-Santa Clara, CA Metropolitan Statistical Area—see Appendix B for areas included; (*) 2010-2014 5-year estimated population
Source: U.S. Census Bureau, 1990 Census, Census 2000, Census 2010, 2010-2014 American Community Survey 5-Year Estimates

Household Size

Area	Persons in Household (%) One	Two	Three	Four	Five	Six	Seven or More	Average Household Size
City	19.6	24.2	22.2	25.5	6.2	1.2	0.8	2.90
MSA[1]	21.3	29.2	18.6	17.6	7.6	2.8	2.5	2.95
U.S.	27.5	33.5	15.8	13.1	6.0	2.3	1.4	2.64

Note: (1) Figures cover the San Jose-Sunnyvale-Santa Clara, CA Metropolitan Statistical Area—see Appendix B for areas included
Source: U.S. Census Bureau, 2010-2014 American Community Survey 5-Year Estimates

Race

Area	White Alone[2] (%)	Black Alone[2] (%)	Asian Alone[2] (%)	AIAN[3] Alone[2] (%)	NHOPI[4] Alone[2] (%)	Other Race Alone[2] (%)	Two or More Races (%)
City	30.8	0.6	65.0	0.2	0.3	0.6	2.5
MSA[1]	50.3	2.6	32.2	0.5	0.4	9.4	4.5
U.S.	73.8	12.6	5.0	0.8	0.2	4.7	2.9

Note: (1) Figures cover the San Jose-Sunnyvale-Santa Clara, CA Metropolitan Statistical Area—see Appendix B for areas included; (2) Alone is defined as not being in combination with one or more other races; (3) American Indian and Alaska Native; (4) Native Hawaiian and Other Pacific Islander
Source: U.S. Census Bureau, 2010-2014 American Community Survey 5-Year Estimates

Hispanic or Latino Origin

Area	Total (%)	Mexican (%)	Puerto Rican (%)	Cuban (%)	Other (%)
City	4.7	3.0	0.3	0.0	1.4
MSA[1]	27.7	23.5	0.4	0.1	3.6
U.S.	16.9	10.8	1.6	0.6	3.8

Note: Persons of Hispanic or Latino origin can be of any race; (1) Figures cover the San Jose-Sunnyvale-Santa Clara, CA Metropolitan Statistical Area—see Appendix B for areas included
Source: U.S. Census Bureau, 2010-2014 American Community Survey 5-Year Estimates

Ancestry

Area	German	Irish	English	American	Italian	Polish	French[2]	Scottish	Dutch
City	5.4	3.7	4.0	2.2	2.8	0.7	1.2	1.2	0.5
MSA[1]	7.2	5.5	5.2	2.0	4.5	1.2	1.6	1.2	0.8
U.S.	14.9	10.8	8.0	7.1	5.5	3.0	2.7	1.7	1.4

Note: Figures are the percentage of the total population reporting a particular ancestry. The nine most commonly reported ancestries in the U.S. are shown. Figures include multiple ancestries (e.g. if a person reported being Irish and Italian, they were included in both columns); (1) Figures cover the San Jose-Sunnyvale-Santa Clara, CA Metropolitan Statistical Area—see Appendix B for areas included; (2) Excludes Basque
Source: U.S. Census Bureau, 2010-2014 American Community Survey 5-Year Estimates

Foreign-Born Population

Area	Percent of Population Born in								
	Any Foreign Country	Asia	Mexico	Europe	Carribean	Central America[2]	South America	Africa	Canada
City	50.3	43.6	0.6	3.8	0.1	0.1	0.5	0.6	0.8
MSA[1]	36.9	22.9	8.1	2.9	0.1	1.0	0.7	0.5	0.5
U.S.	13.1	3.8	3.7	1.5	1.2	1.0	0.9	0.6	0.3

Note: (1) Figures cover the San Jose-Sunnyvale-Santa Clara, CA Metropolitan Statistical Area—see Appendix B for areas included; (2) Excludes Mexico.
Source: U.S. Census Bureau, 2010-2014 American Community Survey 5-Year Estimates

Marital Status

Area	Never Married	Now Married[2]	Separated	Widowed	Divorced
City	22.7	65.4	0.7	5.9	5.4
MSA[1]	32.5	53.2	1.7	4.5	8.2
U.S.	32.5	48.4	2.2	5.9	10.9

Note: Figures are percentages and cover the population 15 years of age and older; (1) Figures cover the San Jose-Sunnyvale-Santa Clara, CA Metropolitan Statistical Area—see Appendix B for areas included; (2) Excludes separated
Source: U.S. Census Bureau, 2010-2014 American Community Survey 5-Year Estimates

Disability Status

Area	All Ages	Under 18 Years Old	18 to 64 Years Old	65 Years and Over
City	6.1	1.2	3.6	29.6
MSA[1]	7.7	2.2	5.2	33.5
U.S.	12.3	4.1	10.2	36.3

Note: Figures show percent of the civilian noninstitutionalized population that reported having a disability. Disability status is determined from from six types of difficulty: vision, hearing, cognitive, ambulatory, self-care, and independent living. For children under 5 years old, hearing and vision difficulty are used to determine disability status. For children between the ages of 5 and 14, disability status is determined from hearing, vision, cognitive, ambulatory, and self-care difficulties. For people aged 15 years and older, they are considered to have a disability if they have difficulty with any one of the six difficulty types; (1) Figures cover the San Jose-Sunnyvale-Santa Clara, CA Metropolitan Statistical Area—see Appendix B for areas included.
Source: U.S. Census Bureau, 2010-2014 American Community Survey 5-Year Estimates

Age

Area	Percent of Population									Median Age
	Under Age 5	Age 5–19	Age 20–34	Age 35–44	Age 45–54	Age 55–64	Age 65–74	Age 75–84	Age 85+	
City	5.9	22.9	12.1	17.9	17.7	10.4	6.7	4.1	2.3	40.2
MSA[1]	6.7	19.4	21.4	15.2	14.6	10.9	6.4	3.6	1.6	36.6
U.S.	6.4	19.9	20.6	13.0	14.1	12.3	7.6	4.3	1.9	37.4

Note: (1) Figures cover the San Jose-Sunnyvale-Santa Clara, CA Metropolitan Statistical Area—see Appendix B for areas included
Source: U.S. Census Bureau, 2010-2014 American Community Survey 5-Year Estimates

Gender

Area	Males	Females	Males per 100 Females
City	29,342	30,445	96.4
MSA[1]	953,276	945,181	100.9
U.S.	154,515,159	159,591,925	96.8

Note: (1) Figures cover the San Jose-Sunnyvale-Santa Clara, CA Metropolitan Statistical Area—see Appendix B for areas included
Source: U.S. Census Bureau, 2010-2014 American Community Survey 5-Year Estimates

Religious Groups by Family

Area	Catholic	Baptist	Non-Den.	Methodist[2]	Lutheran	LDS[3]	Pente-costal	Presby-terian[4]	Muslim[5]	Judaism
MSA[1]	26.0	1.3	4.2	1.0	0.5	1.4	1.1	0.7	1.0	0.6
U.S.	19.1	9.3	4.0	4.0	2.3	2.0	1.9	1.6	0.8	0.7

Note: Figures are the number of adherents as a percentage of the total population; (1) Figures cover the San Jose-Sunnyvale-Santa Clara, CA Metropolitan Statistical Area—see Appendix B for areas included; (2) Methodist/Pietist; (3) Latter Day Saints; (4) Reformed; (5) Figures are estimates
Source: Association of Statisticians of American Religious Bodies, 2010 U.S. Religion Census: Religious Congregations & Membership Study

Religious Groups by Tradition

Area	Catholic	Evangelical Protestant	Mainline Protestant	Other Tradition	Black Protestant	Orthodox
MSA[1]	26.0	8.2	2.4	6.8	0.1	0.4
U.S.	19.1	16.2	7.3	4.3	1.6	0.3

Note: Figures are the number of adherents as a percentage of the total population; (1) Figures cover the San Jose-Sunnyvale-Santa Clara, CA Metropolitan Statistical Area—see Appendix B for areas included
Source: Association of Statisticians of American Religious Bodies, 2010 U.S. Religion Census: Religious Congregations & Membership Study

ECONOMY

Gross Metropolitan Product

Area	2013	2014	2015	2016	Rank[2]
MSA[1]	196.8	210.1	220.3	233.3	16

Note: Figures are in billions of dollars; (1) Figures cover the San Jose-Sunnyvale-Santa Clara, CA Metropolitan Statistical Area—see Appendix B for areas included; (2) Rank is based on 2016 data and ranges from 1 to 381
Source: The U.S. Conference of Mayors, U.S. Metro Economies: GMP and Employment 2014-2016, June 2015

Economic Growth

Area	2011-13 (%)	2014 (%)	2015 (%)	2016 (%)	Rank[2]
MSA[1]	3.8	3.4	3.7	4.1	9
U.S.	2.2	2.4	2.3	2.9	–

Note: Figures are real gross metropolitan product (GMP) growth rates and represent annual average percent change; (1) Figures cover the San Jose-Sunnyvale-Santa Clara, CA Metropolitan Statistical Area—see Appendix B for areas included; (2) Rank is based on 2016 data and ranges from 1 to 381
Source: The U.S. Conference of Mayors, U.S. Metro Economies: GMP and Employment 2014-2016, June 2015

Metropolitan Area Exports

Area	2009	2010	2011	2012	2013	2014	Rank[2]
MSA[1]	21,405.7	26,333.0	26,712.1	26,687.6	23,413.1	21,128.7	16

Note: Figures are in millions of dollars; (1) Figures cover the San Jose-Sunnyvale-Santa Clara, CA Metropolitan Statistical Area—see Appendix B for areas included; (2) Rank is based on 2014 data and ranges from 1 to 385
Source: U.S. Department of Commerce, International Trade Administration, Office of Trade & Industry Information, Manufacturing & Services, data extracted March 10, 2016

Building Permits

Area	Single-Family			Multi-Family			Total		
	2014	2015p	Pct. Chg.	2014	2015p	Pct. Chg.	2014	2015p	Pct. Chg.
City	41	52	26.8	2	127	6,250.0	43	179	316.3
MSA[1]	1,861	1,954	5.0	8,176	4,364	-46.6	10,037	6,318	-37.1
U.S.	640,300	690,800	7.9	411,800	487,600	18.4	1,052,100	1,178,400	12.0

Note: (1) Figures cover the San Jose-Sunnyvale-Santa Clara, CA Metropolitan Statistical Area—see Appendix B for areas included; Figures represent new, privately-owned housing units authorized (unadjusted data); All permit data are based on estimates with imputation; (p) preliminary data.
Source: U.S. Census Bureau, Manufacturing, Mining, and Construction Statistics, Building Permits, 2014, 2015

Bankruptcy Filings

Area	Business Filings 2014	Business Filings 2015	Business Filings % Chg.	Nonbusiness Filings 2014	Nonbusiness Filings 2015	Nonbusiness Filings % Chg.
Santa Clara County	147	124	-15.6	3,173	2,413	-24.0
U.S.	26,983	24,735	-8.3	909,812	819,760	-9.9

Note: Business filings include Chapter 7, Chapter 11, Chapter 12, and Chapter 13; Nonbusiness filings include Chapter 7, Chapter 11, and Chapter 13
Source: Administrative Office of the U.S. Courts, Business and Nonbusiness Bankruptcy, County Cases Commenced by Chapter of the Bankruptcy Code, During the 12- Month Period Ending December 31, 2014 and Business and Nonbusiness Bankruptcy, County Cases Commenced by Chapter of the Bankruptcy Code, During the 12- Month Period Ending December 31, 2015

Housing Vacancy Rates

Area	Gross Vacancy Rate[2] (%) 2013	2014	2015	Year-Round Vacancy Rate[3] (%) 2013	2014	2015	Rental Vacancy Rate[4] (%) 2013	2014	2015	Homeowner Vacancy Rate[5] (%) 2013	2014	2015
MSA[1]	5.0	4.7	5.7	4.9	4.5	5.6	3.0	2.9	3.5	0.6	0.6	0.9
U.S.	13.6	13.4	12.9	10.7	10.4	10.0	8.3	7.6	7.1	2.0	1.9	1.8

Note: (1) Figures cover the San Jose-Sunnyvale-Santa Clara, CA Metropolitan Statistical Area—see Appendix B for areas included; (2) The percentage of the total housing inventory that is vacant; (3) The percentage of the housing inventory (excluding seasonal units) that is year-round vacant; (4) The percentage of rental inventory that is vacant for rent; (5) The percentage of homeowner inventory that is vacant for sale
Source: U.S. Census Bureau, Housing Vacancies and Homeownership Annual Statistics: 2015

INCOME

Income

Area	Per Capita ($)	Median Household ($)	Average Household ($)
City	55,867	134,872	159,497
MSA[1]	42,176	92,960	123,393
U.S.	28,555	53,482	74,596

Note: (1) Figures cover the San Jose-Sunnyvale-Santa Clara, CA Metropolitan Statistical Area—see Appendix B for areas included
Source: U.S. Census Bureau, 2010-2014 American Community Survey 5-Year Estimates

Household Income Distribution

Area	Percent of Households Earning: Under $15,000	$15,000 -24,999	$25,000 -34,999	$35,000 -49,999	$50,000 -74,999	$75,000 -99,000	$100,000 -149,999	$150,000 and up
City	5.1	4.5	2.8	5.5	9.3	8.2	18.8	45.7
MSA[1]	6.9	6.1	6.1	8.8	13.4	11.8	18.6	28.2
U.S.	12.5	10.7	10.2	13.5	17.8	12.2	13.0	10.0

Note: (1) Figures cover the San Jose-Sunnyvale-Santa Clara, CA Metropolitan Statistical Area—see Appendix B for areas included
Source: U.S. Census Bureau, 2010-2014 American Community Survey 5-Year Estimates

Poverty Rate

Area	All Ages	Under 18 Years Old	18 to 64 Years Old	65 Years and Over
City	4.1	2.2	4.2	7.2
MSA[1]	10.0	11.9	9.5	8.7
U.S.	15.6	21.9	14.6	9.4

Note: Figures are percentage of people whose income during the past 12 months was below the poverty level; (1) Figures cover the San Jose-Sunnyvale-Santa Clara, CA Metropolitan Statistical Area—see Appendix B for areas included
Source: U.S. Census Bureau, 2010-2014 American Community Survey 5-Year Estimates

EMPLOYMENT

Labor Force and Employment

Area	Civilian Labor Force			Workers Employed		
	Dec. 2014	Dec. 2015	% Chg.	Dec. 2014	Dec. 2015	% Chg.
City	29,487	30,359	2.9	28,453	29,448	3.4
MSA[1]	1,039,234	1,068,398	2.8	992,810	1,027,507	3.4
U.S.	155,521,000	157,245,000	1.1	147,190,000	149,703,000	1.7

Note: Data is not seasonally adjusted and covers workers 16 years of age and older; (1) Figures cover the San Jose-Sunnyvale-Santa Clara, CA Metropolitan Statistical Area—see Appendix B for areas included
Source: Bureau of Labor Statistics, Local Area Unemployment Statistics

Unemployment Rate

Area	2015											
	Jan.	Feb.	Mar.	Apr.	May	Jun.	Jul.	Aug.	Sep.	Oct.	Nov.	Dec.
City	3.8	3.5	3.3	3.1	3.2	3.2	3.4	3.2	2.9	3.1	3.1	3.0
MSA[1]	4.8	4.4	4.2	3.9	4.0	4.0	4.3	4.1	3.7	4.0	3.9	3.8
U.S.	6.1	5.8	5.6	5.1	5.3	5.5	5.6	5.2	4.9	4.8	4.8	4.8

Note: Data is not seasonally adjusted and covers workers 16 years of age and older; (1) Figures cover the San Jose-Sunnyvale-Santa Clara, CA Metropolitan Statistical Area—see Appendix B for areas included
Source: Bureau of Labor Statistics, Local Area Unemployment Statistics

Employment by Occupation

Occupation Classification	City (%)	MSA[1] (%)	U.S. (%)
Management, Business, Science, and Arts	77.4	49.7	36.4
Natural Resources, Construction, and Maintenance	1.4	6.9	9.0
Production, Transportation, and Material Moving	2.6	8.3	12.1
Sales and Office	13.4	20.1	24.4
Service	5.3	15.1	18.2

Note: Figures cover employed civilians 16 years of age and older; (1) Figures cover the San Jose-Sunnyvale-Santa Clara, CA Metropolitan Statistical Area—see Appendix B for areas included
Source: U.S. Census Bureau, 2010-2014 American Community Survey 5-Year Estimates

Employment by Industry

Sector	MSA[1]		U.S.
	Number of Employees	Percent of Total	Percent of Total
Construction	44,500	4.1	4.5
Education and Health Services	161,400	15.1	15.7
Financial Activities	35,600	3.3	5.7
Government	94,000	8.7	15.5
Information	77,200	7.2	1.9
Leisure and Hospitality	96,900	9.0	10.4
Manufacturing	161,800	15.1	8.6
Mining and Logging	200	<0.1	0.5
Other Services	27,800	2.6	3.9
Professional and Business Services	223,400	20.9	13.9
Retail Trade	92,200	8.6	11.3
Transportation, Warehousing, and Utilities	17,100	1.6	3.9
Wholesale Trade	36,600	3.4	4.1

Note: Figures are non-farm employment as of December 2015. Figures are not seasonally adjusted and include workers 16 years of age and older; (1) Figures cover the San Jose-Sunnyvale-Santa Clara, CA Metropolitan Statistical Area—see Appendix B for areas included
Source: Bureau of Labor Statistics, Current Employment Statistics, Employment, Hours, and Earnings

Occupations with Greatest Projected Employment Growth: 2012 – 2022

Occupation[1]	2012 Employment	2022 Projected Employment	Numeric Employment Change	Percent Employment Change
Personal Care Aides	386,900	587,200	200,300	51.8
Combined Food Preparation and Serving Workers, Including Fast Food	286,000	362,400	76,400	26.7
Retail Salespersons	468,400	528,100	59,700	12.7
Laborers and Freight, Stock, and Material Movers, Hand	270,500	322,300	51,800	19.1
Waiters and Waitresses	246,100	290,300	44,200	18.0
Registered Nurses	254,500	297,400	42,900	16.9
General and Operations Managers	253,800	295,700	41,900	16.5
Secretaries and Administrative Assistants, Except Legal, Medical, and Executive	212,800	250,100	37,300	17.5
Cashiers	357,800	392,600	34,800	9.7
Cooks, Restaurant	116,900	150,600	33,700	28.8

Note: Projections cover California; (1) Sorted by numeric employment change
Source: www.projectionscentral.com, State Occupational Projections, 2012–2022 Long-Term Projections

Fastest Growing Occupations: 2012 – 2022

Occupation[1]	2012 Employment	2022 Projected Employment	Numeric Employment Change	Percent Employment Change
Economists	3,100	5,100	2,000	64.5
Helpers—Brickmasons, Blockmasons, Stonemasons, and Tile and Marble Setters	2,900	4,600	1,700	58.6
Brickmasons and Blockmasons	5,100	8,000	2,900	56.9
Insulation Workers, Floor, Ceiling, and Wall	1,600	2,500	900	56.3
Stonemasons	1,100	1,700	600	54.5
Insulation Workers, Mechanical	1,100	1,700	600	54.5
Personal Care Aides	386,900	587,200	200,300	51.8
Foresters	1,200	1,800	600	50.0
Terrazzo Workers and Finishers	1,100	1,600	500	45.5
Mechanical Door Repairers	1,100	1,600	500	45.5

Note: Projections cover California; (1) Sorted by percent employment change and excludes occupations with numeric employment change less than 100
Source: www.projectionscentral.com, State Occupational Projections, 2012–2022 Long-Term Projections

Average Wages

Occupation	$/Hr.	Occupation	$/Hr.
Accountants and Auditors	48.36	Maids and Housekeeping Cleaners	15.18
Automotive Mechanics	25.59	Maintenance and Repair Workers	23.36
Bookkeepers	23.98	Marketing Managers	94.90
Carpenters	29.24	Nuclear Medicine Technologists	57.52
Cashiers	12.25	Nurses, Licensed Practical	28.36
Clerks, General Office	19.84	Nurses, Registered	58.47
Clerks, Receptionists/Information	17.28	Nursing Assistants	15.92
Clerks, Shipping/Receiving	17.59	Packers and Packagers, Hand	12.48
Computer Programmers	45.16	Physical Therapists	47.60
Computer Systems Analysts	55.19	Postal Service Mail Carriers	26.04
Computer User Support Specialists	37.61	Real Estate Brokers	n/a
Cooks, Restaurant	13.19	Retail Salespersons	14.30
Dentists	91.18	Sales Reps., Exc. Tech./Scientific	35.36
Electrical Engineers	64.71	Sales Reps., Tech./Scientific	56.30
Electricians	36.59	Secretaries, Exc. Legal/Med./Exec.	22.03
Financial Managers	82.91	Security Guards	15.74
First-Line Supervisors/Managers, Sales	24.43	Surgeons	125.24
Food Preparation Workers	11.88	Teacher Assistants*	15.16
General and Operations Managers	76.18	Teachers, Elementary School*	36.39
Hairdressers/Cosmetologists	12.87	Teachers, Secondary School*	36.28
Internists	112.31	Telemarketers	17.42
Janitors and Cleaners	13.50	Truck Drivers, Heavy/Tractor-Trailer	20.79
Landscaping/Groundskeeping Workers	15.50	Truck Drivers, Light/Delivery Svcs.	18.60
Lawyers	98.08	Waiters and Waitresses	13.01

Note: Wage data covers the San Jose-Sunnyvale-Santa Clara, CA Metropolitan Statistical Area—see Appendix B for areas included; (*) Hourly wages for elementary/secondary school teachers and teacher assistants were calculated by the editors from annual wage data based on a 40 hour work week; n/a not available.
Source: Bureau of Labor Statistics, Metro Area Occupational Employment and Wage Estimates, May 2015

TAXES

State Corporate Income Tax Rates

State	Tax Rate (%)	Income Brackets ($)	Num. of Brackets	Financial Institution Tax Rate (%)[a]	Federal Income Tax Ded.
California	8.84 (c)	Flat rate	1	10.84 (c)	No

Note: Tax rates as of January 1, 2016; (a) Rates listed are the corporate income tax rate applied to financial institutions or excise taxes based on income. Some states have other taxes based upon the value of deposits or shares; (c) Minimum tax is $800 in California, $100 in District of Columbia, $50 in North Dakota (banks), $500 in Rhode Island, $200 per location in South Dakota (banks), $100 in Utah, $250 in Vermont.
Source: Federation of Tax Administrators, "State Corporate Income Tax Rates, 2016"

State Individual Income Tax Rates

State	Tax Rate (%)	Income Brackets ($)	Num. of Brackets	Personal Exempt. ($)[1]		Fed. Inc. Tax Ded.
				Single	Dependents	
California (a)	1.0 - 12.3 (f)	7,850- 526,443 (b)	9	109 (c)	337 (c)	No

Note: Tax rates as of January 1, 2016; Local- and county-level taxes are not included; n/a not applicable; (1) Married joint filers generally receive double the single exemption; (a) 18 states have statutory provision for automatically adjusting to the rate of inflation the dollar values of the income tax brackets, standard deductions, and/or personal exemptions. Massachusetts, Michigan, and Nebraska index the personal exemptiononly. Oregon does not index the income brackets for $125,000 and over. Maine has suspended indexing for 2014 and 2015; (b) For joint returns, taxes are twice the tax on half the couple's income; (c) The personal exemption takes the form of a tax credit instead of a deduction; (f) California imposes an additional 1% tax on taxable income over $1 million, making the maximum rate 13.3% over $1 million.
Source: Federation of Tax Administrators, "State Individual Income Tax Rates, 2016"

Various State and Local Tax Rates

State	State and Local Sales and Use (%)	State Sales and Use (%)	Gasoline[1] (¢/gal.)	Cigarette[2] ($/pack)	Spirits[3] ($/gal.)	Wine[4] ($/gal.)	Beer[5] ($/gal.)
California	8.75	7.50 (b)	40.62	0.87	3.30 (f)	0.20 (l)	0.08

Note: All tax rates as of January 1, 2016; (1) The American Petroleum Institute has developed a methodology for determining the average tax rate on a gallon of fuel. Rates may include any of the following: excise taxes, environmental fees, storage tank fees, other fees or taxes, general sales tax, and local taxes. In states where gasoline is subject to the general sales tax, or where the fuel tax is based on the average sale price, the average rate determined by API is sensitive to changes in the price of gasoline. States that fully or partially apply general sales taxes to gasoline: CA, CO, GA, IL, IN, MI, NY; (2) The federal excise tax of $1.0066 per pack and local taxes are not included; (3) Rates are those applicable to off-premise sales of 40% alcohol by volume (a.b.v.) distilled spirits in 750ml containers. Local excise taxes are excluded; (4) Rates are those applicable to off-premise sales of 11% a.b.v. non-carbonated wine in 750ml containers; (5) Rates are those applicable to off-premise sales of 4.7% a.b.v. beer in 12 ounce containers; (b) Three states levy mandatory, statewide local add-on sales taxes at the state level: California (1%), Utah (1.25%), and Virginia (1%). We include these in their state sales tax rates; (f) Different rates are also applicable according to alcohol content, place of production, size of container, or place purchased (on- or off-premise or onboard airlines); (l) Different rates also applicable according to alcohol content, place of production, size of container, place purchased (on- or off-premise or on board airlines) or type of wine (carbonated, vermouth, etc.).
Source: Tax Foundation, 2016 Facts & Figures: How Does Your State Compare?

State Business Tax Climate Index Rankings

State	Overall Rank	Corporate Tax Rank	Individual Income Tax Rank	Sales Tax Rank	Unemployment Insurance Tax Rank	Property Tax Rank
California	48	35	50	40	13	13

Note: The index is a measure of how each state's tax laws affect economic performance. The lower the rank, the more favorable a state's tax system is for business. States without a given tax are given a ranking of 1. The scores/rankings for the District of Columbia do not affect other states. The 2016 index represents the tax climate as of July 1, 2015 (the beginning of Fiscal Year 2016).
Source: Tax Foundation, State Business Tax Climate Index 2016

TRANSPORTATION

Means of Transportation to Work

Area	Car/Truck/Van: Drove Alone	Car/Truck/Van: Car-pooled	Public Transportation: Bus	Public Transportation: Subway	Public Transportation: Railroad	Bicycle	Walked	Other Means	Worked at Home
City	79.6	9.5	1.3	0.2	0.5	0.7	1.4	1.0	5.7
MSA[1]	76.5	10.5	2.2	0.2	1.1	1.8	1.9	1.4	4.6
U.S.	76.4	9.6	2.6	1.8	0.6	0.6	2.8	1.3	4.4

Note: Figures are percentages and cover workers 16 years of age and older; (1) Figures cover the San Jose-Sunnyvale-Santa Clara, CA Metropolitan Statistical Area—see Appendix B for areas included
Source: U.S. Census Bureau, 2010-2014 American Community Survey 5-Year Estimates

Travel Time to Work

Area	Less Than 10 Minutes	10 to 19 Minutes	20 to 29 Minutes	30 to 44 Minutes	45 to 59 Minutes	60 to 89 Minutes	90 Minutes or More
City	7.6	21.4	32.0	28.1	6.4	3.6	0.9
MSA[1]	8.4	29.2	25.7	22.3	7.4	5.3	1.9
U.S.	13.3	29.6	21.0	20.2	7.7	5.7	2.6

Note: Figures are percentages and include workers 16 years old and over; (1) Figures cover the San Jose-Sunnyvale-Santa Clara, CA Metropolitan Statistical Area—see Appendix B for areas included
Source: U.S. Census Bureau, 2010-2014 American Community Survey 5-Year Estimates

Freeway Travel Time Index

Area	1985	1990	1995	2000	2005	2010	2014
Urban Area Rank[1,2]	16	7	10	9	8	6	3
Urban Area Index[1]	1.15	1.21	1.23	1.28	1.32	1.34	1.38
Average Index[3]	1.09	1.11	1.14	1.17	1.20	1.19	1.20

Note: Freeway Travel Time Index—the ratio of travel time in the peak period to the travel time at free-flow conditions. For example, a value of 1.30 indicates a 20-minute free-flow trip takes 26 minutes in the peak (20 minutes x 1.30 = 26 minutes); (1) Covers the San Jose CA urban area; (2) Rank is based on 101 urban areas (#1 = highest travel time index); (3) Average of 101 urban areas
Source: Texas Transportation Institute, 2015 Urban Mobility Scorecard, August 2015

Freeway Commuter Stress Index

Area	1985	1990	1995	2000	2005	2010	2014
Urban Area Rank[1,2]	14	7	8	7	7	5	5
Urban Area Index[1]	1.24	1.31	1.33	1.39	1.43	1.45	1.50
Average Index[3]	1.13	1.16	1.19	1.22	1.25	1.24	1.25

Note: The Freeway Commuter Stress Index is the same as the Freeway Travel Time Index (see table above) except that it includes only the travel in the peak directions during the peak periods; the TTI includes travel in all directions during the peak period. Thus, the CSI is more indicative of the work trip experienced by each commuter on a daily basis. (1) Covers the San Jose CA urban area; (2) Rank is based on 101 urban areas (#1 = highest stress index); (3) Average of 101 urban areas

Source: Texas Transportation Institute, 2015 Urban Mobility Scorecard, August 2015

Living Environment

COST OF LIVING

Cost of Living Index

Composite Index	Groceries	Housing	Utilities	Trans- portation	Health Care	Misc. Goods/ Services
n/a	n/a	n/a	n/a	n/a	n/a	n/a

Note: The Cost of Living Index measures regional differences in the cost of consumer goods and services, excluding taxes and non-consumer expenditures, for professional and managerial households in the top income quintile. It is based on more than 50,000 prices covering almost 60 different items for which prices are collected three times a year by chambers of commerce, economic development organizations or university applied economic centers in each participating urban area. The numbers shown should be read as a percentage above or below the national average of 100. For example, a value of 115.4 in the groceries column indicates that grocery prices are 15.4% higher than the national average. Small differences in the index numbers should not be interpreted as significant; n/a not available.
Source: The Council for Community and Economic Research, ACCRA Cost of Living Index, 2015

Grocery Prices

Area[1]	T-Bone Steak ($/pound)	Frying Chicken ($/pound)	Whole Milk ($/half gal.)	Eggs ($/dozen)	Orange Juice ($/64 oz.)	Coffee ($/11.5 oz.)
City[2]	n/a	n/a	n/a	n/a	n/a	n/a
Avg.	10.99	1.43	2.25	2.26	3.58	4.48
Min.	7.16	0.98	1.30	1.35	2.88	2.98
Max.	14.13	2.43	3.85	4.81	6.39	7.56

Note: (1) Values for the local area are compared with the average, minimum and maximum values for all 292 areas in the Cost of Living Index; (2) Figures cover the Cupertino CA urban area; n/a not available; **T-Bone Steak** *(price per pound);* **Frying Chicken** *(price per pound, whole fryer);* **Whole Milk** *(half gallon carton);* **Eggs** *(price per dozen, Grade A, large);* **Orange Juice** *(64 oz. Tropicana or Florida Natural);* **Coffee** *(11.5 oz. can, vacuum-packed, Maxwell House, Hills Bros, or Folgers).*
Source: The Council for Community and Economic Research, ACCRA Cost of Living Index, 2015

Housing and Utility Costs

Area[1]	New Home Price ($)	Apartment Rent ($/month)	All Electric ($/month)	Part Electric ($/month)	Other Energy ($/month)	Telephone ($/month)
City[2]	n/a	n/a	n/a	n/a	n/a	n/a
Avg.	312,874	945	179.30	95.07	72.96	28.11
Min.	178,682	479	116.28	43.14	26.46	10.01
Max.	1,472,476	3,984	504.25	189.44	421.11	43.06

Note: (1) Values for the local area are compared with the average, minimum and maximum values for all 292 areas in the Cost of Living Index; (2) Figures cover the Cupertino CA urban area; n/a not available; **New Home Price** *(2,400 sf living area, 8,000 sf lot, in urban area with full utilities);* **Apartment Rent** *(950 sf 2 bedroom/1.5 or 2 bath, unfurnished, excluding all utilities except water);* **All Electric** *(average monthly cost for an all-electric home);* **Part Electric** *(average monthly cost for a part-electric home);* **Other Energy** *(average monthly cost for natural gas, fuel oil, coal, wood, and any other forms of energy except electricity);* **Telephone** *(price includes basic monthly rate for a private residential line plus additional local usage charges incurred by a family of four).*
Source: The Council for Community and Economic Research, ACCRA Cost of Living Index, 2015

Health Care, Transportation, and Other Costs

Area[1]	Doctor ($/visit)	Dentist ($/visit)	Optometrist ($/visit)	Gasoline ($/gallon)	Beauty Salon ($/visit)	Men's Shirt ($)
City[2]	n/a	n/a	n/a	n/a	n/a	n/a
Avg.	105.15	89.02	99.78	2.38	35.30	28.10
Min.	66.87	56.09	48.53	1.95	18.91	13.38
Max.	182.34	150.36	228.33	4.09	67.91	63.80

Note: (1) Values for the local area are compared with the average, minimum and maximum values for all 292 areas in the Cost of Living Index; (2) Figures cover the Cupertino CA urban area; n/a not available; **Doctor** *(general practitioners routine exam of an established patient);* **Dentist** *(adult teeth cleaning and periodic oral examination);* **Optometrist** *(full vision eye exam for established adult patient);* **Gasoline** *(one gallon regular unleaded, national brand, including all taxes, cash price at self-service pump if available);* **Beauty Salon** *(woman's shampoo, trim, and blow-dry);* **Men's Shirt** *(cotton/polyester dress shirt, pinpoint weave, long sleeves).*
Source: The Council for Community and Economic Research, ACCRA Cost of Living Index, 2015

HOUSING

House Price Index (HPI)

Area	National Ranking[2]	Quarterly Change (%)	One-Year Change (%)	Five-Year Change (%)
MSA[1]	15	1.20	11.30	51.20
U.S.[3]	–	1.45	5.76	22.85

Note: The HPI is a weighted repeat sales index. It measures average price changes in repeat sales or refinancings on the same properties. This information is obtained by reviewing repeat mortgage transactions on single-family properties whose mortgages have been purchased or securitized by Fannie Mae or Freddie Mac in January 1975; (1) San Jose-Sunnyvale-Santa Clara Metropolitan Statistical Area—see Appendix B for areas included; (2) Rankings are based on annual percentage change for all metro areas containing at least 15,000 transactions over the last 10 years and ranges from 1 to 266; (3) figures based on a weighted average of Census Division estimates using a seasonally adjusted, purchase-only index; all figures are for the period ending December 31, 2015

Source: Federal Housing Finance Agency, House Price Index, February 25, 2016

Median Single-Family Home Prices

Area	2013	2014	2015p	Percent Change 2014 to 2015
MSA[1]	780.0	860.0	950.4	10.5
U.S. Average	197.4	208.9	223.9	7.2

Note: Figures are median sales prices of existing single-family homes in thousands of dollars; (p) preliminary; n/a not available; (1) San Jose-Sunnyvale-Santa Clara, CA Metropolitan Statistical Area—see Appendix B for areas included

Source: National Association of Realtors, Median Sales Price of Existing Single-Family Homes for Metropolitan Areas, 4th Quarter 2015

Qualifying Income Based on Median Sales Price of Existing Single-Family Homes

Area	With 5% Down ($)	With 10% Down ($)	With 20% Down ($)
MSA[1]	209,085	198,080	176,071
U.S. Average	49,535	46,928	41,714

Note: Figures are preliminary; Qualifying income is based on a mortgage rate of 4.1%. Monthly principal and interest payment is limited to 25% of income; n/a not available; (1) San Jose-Sunnyvale-Santa Clara, CA Metropolitan Statistical Area—see Appendix B for areas included

Source: National Association of Realtors, Qualifying Income Based on Median Sales Price of Existing Single-Family Homes for Metropolitan Areas, 4th Quarter 2015

Median Apartment Condo-Coop Home Prices

Area	2013	2014	2015p	Percent Change 2014 to 2015
MSA[1]	n/a	n/a	n/a	n/a
U.S. Average	194.9	204.3	210.7	3.1

Note: Figures are median sales prices of existing apartment condo-coop homes in thousands of dollars; (p) preliminary; n/a not available; (1) San Jose-Sunnyvale-Santa Clara, CA Metropolitan Statistical Area—see Appendix B for areas included

Source: National Association of Realtors, Median Sales Price of Existing Apartment Condo-Coop Homes for Metropolitan Areas, 4th Quarter 2015

Gross Monthly Rent

Area	Under $200	$200 -299	$300 -499	$500 -749	$750 -999	$1,000 -1,499	$1,500 and up	Median ($)
City	0.2	0.0	2.7	0.3	1.7	6.6	88.5	2,000+
MSA[1]	0.5	1.5	2.6	3.7	6.5	28.1	57.1	1,629
U.S.	1.5	3.2	7.4	21.0	24.1	26.9	15.9	920

Note: Figures are percentages except for Median; Gross rent is the contract rent plus the estimated average monthly cost of utilities (electricity, gas, and water and sewer) and fuels (oil, coal, kerosene, wood, etc.) if these are paid by the renter (or paid for the renter by someone else); (1) Figures cover the San Jose-Sunnyvale-Santa Clara, CA Metropolitan Statistical Area—see Appendix B for areas included

Source: U.S. Census Bureau, 2010-2014 American Community Survey 5-Year Estimates

Homeownership Rate

Area	2008 (%)	2009 (%)	2010 (%)	2011 (%)	2012 (%)	2013 (%)	2014 (%)	2015 (%)
MSA[1]	54.6	57.2	58.9	60.4	58.6	56.4	56.4	50.7
U.S.	67.8	67.4	66.9	66.1	65.4	65.1	64.5	63.7

Note: (1) Figures cover the San Jose-Sunnyvale-Santa Clara, CA Metropolitan Statistical Area—see Appendix B for areas included
Source: U.S. Census Bureau, Housing Vacancies and Homeownership Annual Statistics: 2015

Year Housing Structure Built

Area	2010 or Later	2000 -2009	1990 -1999	1980 -1989	1970 -1979	1960 -1969	1950 -1959	1940 -1949	Before 1940	Median Year
City	0.5	7.7	12.2	11.2	22.0	27.5	15.4	2.7	0.8	1972
MSA[1]	0.7	9.8	10.6	12.7	22.6	18.9	15.4	4.2	5.2	1973
U.S.	1.0	14.9	13.9	13.8	15.8	11.0	10.8	5.4	13.3	1976

Note: Figures are percentages except for Median Year; (1) Figures cover the San Jose-Sunnyvale-Santa Clara, CA Metropolitan Statistical Area—see Appendix B for areas included
Source: U.S. Census Bureau, 2010-2014 American Community Survey 5-Year Estimates

HEALTH

Health Risk Data

Category	MSA[1] (%)	U.S. (%)
Adults aged 18–64 who have any kind of health care coverage	82.5	79.6
Adults who reported being in good or excellent health	88.2	83.1
Adults who are current smokers	9.6	19.6
Adults who are heavy drinkers[2]	4.3	6.1
Adults who are binge drinkers[3]	16.4	16.9
Adults who are overweight (BMI 25.0 - 29.9)	33.0	35.8
Adults who are obese (BMI 30.0 - 99.8)	15.9	27.6
Adults who participated in any physical activities in the past month	83.6	77.1
Adults 50+ who have ever had a sigmoidoscopy or colonoscopy	72.3	67.3
Women aged 40+ who have had a mammogram within the past two years	82.7	74.0
Men aged 40+ who have had a PSA test within the past two years	31.4	45.2
Adults aged 65+ who have had flu shot within the past year	54.1	60.1
Adults who always wear a seatbelt	n/a	93.8

Note: Data as of 2012 unless otherwise noted; n/a not available; (1) Figures cover the San Jose-Sunnyvale-Santa Clara, CA Metropolitan Statistical Area—see Appendix B for areas included; (2) Heavy drinkers are classified as males having more than two drinks per day or females having more than one drink per day; (3) Binge drinkers are classified as males having five or more drinks on one occasion or females having four or more drinks on one occasion
Source: Centers for Disease Control and Prevention, Behaviorial Risk Factor Surveillance System, SMART: Selected Metropolitan/Micropolitan Area Risk Trends, 2012 (Note: the CDC has discontinued this dataset but will be releasing a replacement in mid-2016)

Chronic Health Indicators

Category	MSA[1] (%)	U.S. (%)
Adults who have ever been told they had a heart attack	3.8	4.5
Adults who have ever been told they had a stroke	n/a	2.9
Adults who have been told they currently have asthma	8.4	8.9
Adults who have ever been told they have arthritis	17.2	25.7
Adults who have ever been told they have diabetes[2]	7.4	9.7
Adults who have ever been told they had skin cancer	4.1	5.7
Adults who have ever been told they had any other types of cancer	3.9	6.5
Adults who have ever been told they have COPD	2.7	6.2
Adults who have ever been told they have kidney disease	2.9	2.5
Adults who have ever been told they have a form of depression	11.3	18.0

Note: Data as of 2012 unless otherwise noted; n/a not available; (1) Figures cover the San Jose-Sunnyvale-Santa Clara, CA Metropolitan Statistical Area—see Appendix B for areas included; (2) Figures do not include pregnancy-related, borderline, or pre-diabetes
Source: Centers for Disease Control and Prevention, Behaviorial Risk Factor Surveillance System, SMART: Selected Metropolitan/Micropolitan Area Risk Trends, 2012 (Note: the CDC has discontinued this dataset but will be releasing a replacement in mid-2016)

Mortality Rates for the Top 10 Causes of Death in the U.S.

ICD-10[a] Sub-Chapter	ICD-10[a] Code	Age-Adjusted Mortality Rate[1] per 100,000 population	
		County[2]	U.S.
Malignant neoplasms	C00-C97	129.7	163.6
Ischaemic heart diseases	I20-I25	68.0	102.2
Other forms of heart disease	I30-I51	21.9	50.1
Chronic lower respiratory diseases	J40-J47	22.8	41.4
Organic, including symptomatic, mental disorders	F01-F09	6.6	38.5
Cerebrovascular diseases	I60-I69	26.5	36.5
Other external causes of accidental injury	W00-X59	16.7	27.5
Other degenerative diseases of the nervous system	G30-G31	48.0	26.3
Diabetes mellitus	E10-E14	22.4	21.1
Hypertensive diseases	I10-I15	29.7	19.7

Note: (a) ICD-10 = International Classification of Diseases 10th Revision; (1) Mortality rates are a three year average covering 2012-2014; (2) Figures cover COUNTY NOT FOUND!!!!!!.
Source: Centers for Disease Control and Prevention, National Center for Health Statistics. Underlying Cause of Death 1999-2014 on CDC WONDER Online Database, released 2015.

Mortality Rates for Selected Causes of Death

ICD-10[a] Sub-Chapter	ICD-10[a] Code	Age-Adjusted Mortality Rate[1] per 100,000 population	
		County[2]	U.S.
Assault	X85-Y09	2.8	5.1
Diseases of the liver	K70-K76	9.6	13.5
Human immunodeficiency virus (HIV) disease	B20-B24	0.7	2.1
Influenza and pneumonia	J09-J18	12.4	15.2
Intentional self-harm	X60-X84	7.9	12.7
Malnutrition	E40-E46	Unreliable	0.9
Obesity and other hyperalimentation	E65-E68	1.0	1.9
Renal failure	N17-N19	2.5	13.0
Transport accidents	V01-V99	6.3	11.6
Viral hepatitis	B15-B19	2.3	2.1

Note: (a) ICD-10 = International Classification of Diseases 10th Revision; (1) Mortality rates are a three year average covering 2012-2014; (2) Figures cover COUNTY NOT FOUND!!!!!!; Data are Suppressed when the data meet the criteria for confidentiality constraints; Mortality rates are flagged as Unreliable when the rate would be calculated with a numerator of 20 or less.
Source: Centers for Disease Control and Prevention, National Center for Health Statistics. Underlying Cause of Death 1999-2014 on CDC WONDER Online Database, released 2015.

Health Insurance Coverage

Area	With Health Insurance	With Private Health Insurance	With Public Health Insurance	Without Health Insurance	Population Under Age 18 Without Health Insurance
City	96.6	88.4	16.1	3.4	0.9
MSA[1]	89.3	73.0	24.2	10.7	3.9
U.S.	85.8	65.8	31.1	14.2	7.1

Note: Figures are percentages that cover the civilian noninstitutionalized population; (1) Figures cover the San Jose-Sunnyvale-Santa Clara, CA Metropolitan Statistical Area—see Appendix B for areas included
Source: U.S. Census Bureau, 2010-2014 American Community Survey 5-Year Estimates

Number of Medical Professionals

Area	MDs[3]	DOs[3,4]	Dentists	Podiatrists	Chiropractors	Optometrists
County[1] (number)	7,351	153	2,028	112	738	460
County[1] (rate[2])	392.9	8.2	107.0	5.9	39.0	24.3
U.S. (rate[2])	272.5	20.9	64.7	5.8	25.9	15.2

Note: Data as of 2014 unless noted; (1) Data covers Santa Clara County; (2) Rate per 100,000 population; (3) Data as of 2013 and includes all active, non-federal physicians; (4) Doctor of Osteopathic Medicine
Source: U.S. Department of Health and Human Services, Health Resources and Services Administration, Bureau of Health Professions, Area Resource File (ARF) 2014-2015

Best Hospitals

According to *U.S. News,* the San Jose-Sunnyvale-Santa Clara, CA metro area is home to one of the best hospitals in the U.S.: **Stanford Hospital and Clinics** (Honor Roll/13 specialties). The hospital listed was nationally ranked in at least one adult specialty. Only 137 hospitals nationwide were nationally ranked in one or more specialties. Fifteen hospitals in the U.S. made the Honor Roll with high scores in at least six specialties. *U.S. News Online, "America's Best Children's Hospitals 2015-16"*

According to *U.S. News,* the San Jose-Sunnyvale-Santa Clara, CA metro area is home to one of the best children's hospitals in the U.S.: **Lucile Packard Children's Hospital at Stanford** (9 specialties). The hospital listed was highly ranked in at least one pediatric specialty. Eighty-three children's hospitals in the U.S. were nationally ranked in at least one specialty. Twelve children's hospitals in the U.S. made the Honor Roll with high scores in at least three specialties. *U.S. News Online, "America's Best Children's Hospitals 2015-16"*

EDUCATION

Public School District Statistics

District Name	Schls	Pupils	Pupil/ Teacher Ratio	Minority Pupils[1] (%)	Free Lunch Eligible[2] (%)	IEP[3] (%)
Cupertino Union	25	19,194	24.4	82.5	4.2	6.9
Fremont Union High	6	10,710	24.8	79.2	11.9	8.9

Note: Table includes school districts with 100 or more students; (1) Percentage of students that are not non-Hispanic white; (2) Percentage of students that are eligible for the free lunch program; (3) Percentage of students that have an Individualized Education Program.
Source: U.S. Department of Education, National Center for Education Statistics, Common Core of Data, Local Education Agency (School District) Universe Survey: School Year 2013-2014; U.S. Department of Education, National Center for Education Statistics, Common Core of Data, Public Elementary/Secondary School Universe Survey: School Year 2013-2014

Best High Schools

According to *U.S. News,* Cupertino is home to two of the best high schools in the U.S.: **Monta Vista High School** (#103); **Homestead High** (#454); Nearly 20,000 schools were ranked based on their performance on state assessments and how well they prepare students for college. Schools with the highest unrounded College Readiness Index values were numerically ranked from No. 1 to No. 500 and were the gold medal winners. *U.S. News & World Report, "Best High Schools 2015"*

Highest Level of Education

Area	Less than H.S.	H.S. Diploma	Some College, No Deg.	Associate Degree	Bachelor's Degree	Master's Degree	Prof. School Degree	Doctorate Degree
City	3.5	6.2	10.2	4.5	33.1	31.2	4.1	7.3
MSA[1]	13.5	15.7	17.2	7.1	25.7	14.9	2.7	3.3
U.S.	13.7	28.0	21.2	7.9	18.3	7.8	2.0	1.3

Note: Figures cover persons age 25 and over; (1) Figures cover the San Jose-Sunnyvale-Santa Clara, CA Metropolitan Statistical Area—see Appendix B for areas included
Source: U.S. Census Bureau, 2010-2014 American Community Survey 5-Year Estimates

Educational Attainment by Race

Area	High School Graduate or Higher (%)					Bachelor's Degree or Higher (%)				
	Total	White	Black	Asian	Hisp.[2]	Total	White	Black	Asian	Hisp.[2]
City	96.5	95.9	97.9	97.3	85.7	75.6	60.2	30.9	85.5	41.0
MSA[1]	86.5	88.4	91.8	89.2	65.6	46.5	44.1	31.5	61.2	14.3
U.S.	86.3	88.4	83.2	85.8	64.1	29.3	30.6	19.0	50.9	13.9

Note: Figures shown cover persons 25 years old and over; (1) Figures cover the San Jose-Sunnyvale-Santa Clara, CA Metropolitan Statistical Area—see Appendix B for areas included; (2) People of Hispanic origin can be of any race
Source: U.S. Census Bureau, 2010-2014 American Community Survey 5-Year Estimates

School Enrollment by Grade and Control

Area	Preschool (%)		Kindergarten (%)		Grades 1 - 4 (%)		Grades 5 - 8 (%)		Grades 9 - 12 (%)	
	Public	Private	Public	Private	Public	Private	Public	Private	Public	Private
City	16.8	83.2	83.0	17.0	93.2	6.8	92.4	7.6	91.3	8.7
MSA[1]	34.4	65.6	81.9	18.1	87.1	12.9	87.7	12.3	89.1	10.9
U.S.	57.4	42.6	87.8	12.2	89.8	10.2	89.9	10.1	90.6	9.4

Note: Figures shown cover persons 3 years old and over; (1) Figures cover the San Jose-Sunnyvale-Santa Clara, CA Metropolitan Statistical Area—see Appendix B for areas included
Source: U.S. Census Bureau, 2010-2014 American Community Survey 5-Year Estimates

Average Salaries of Public School Classroom Teachers

Area	2013-14		2014-15		Percent Change 2013-14 to 2014-15	Percent Change 2004-05 to 2014-15
	Dollars	Rank[1]	Dollars	Rank[1]		
California	71,396	4	72,535	4	1.59	25.9
U.S. Average	56,610	–	57,379	–	1.36	20.8

Note: (1) State rank ranges from 1 to 51 where 1 indicates highest salary.
Source: National Education Association, Rankings & Estimates: Rankings of the States 2014 and Estimates of School Statistics 2015, March 2015

Higher Education

Four-Year Colleges			Two-Year Colleges			Medical Schools[1]	Law Schools[2]	Voc/ Tech[3]
Public	Private Non-profit	Private For-profit	Public	Private Non-profit	Private For-profit			
0	0	0	1	0	0	0	0	0

Note: Figures cover institutions located within the city limits and include main campuses only; (1) includes schools accredited by the Liaison Committee on Medical Education and the American Osteopathic Association's Commission on Osteopathic College Accreditation; (2) includes ABA-accredited schools, schools with provisional ABA accreditation, and state accredited schools; (3) includes all schools with programs that are less than 2 years.
Source: National Center for Education Statistics, Integrated Postsecondary Education System (IPEDS), 2014-15; Association of American Medical Colleges, Member List, March 21, 2016; American Osteopathic Association, Member List, March 21, 2016; Law School Admission Council, Official Guide to ABA-Approved Law Schools Online, March 21, 2016; Wikipedia, List of Medical Schools in the United States, March 21, 2016; Wikipedia, List of Law Schools in the United States, March 21, 2016

According to *U.S. News & World Report,* the San Jose-Sunnyvale-Santa Clara, CA metro area is home to one of the best national universities in the U.S.: **Stanford University** (#4 tie). The indicators used to capture academic quality fall into a number of categories: assessment by administrators at peer institutions; retention of students; faculty resources; student selectivity; financial resources; alumni giving; high school counselor ratings of colleges; and graduation rate. *U.S. News & World Report, "America's Best Colleges 2016"*

According to *U.S. News & World Report,* the San Jose-Sunnyvale-Santa Clara, CA metro area is home to one of the top 100 law schools in the U.S.: **Stanford University, Law School** (#2 tie). The rankings are based on a weighted average of 12 measures of quality: peer assessment score; assessment score by lawyers/judges; median LSAT scores; median undergrad GPA; acceptance rate; employment rates for graduates; placement success; bar passage rate; faculty resources; expenditures per student; student/faculty ratio; and library resources. *U.S. News & World Report, "America's Best Graduate Schools, Law, 2017"*

According to *U.S. News & World Report,* the San Jose-Sunnyvale-Santa Clara, CA metro area is home to one of the top 75 medical schools for research in the U.S.: **Stanford University, School of Medicine** (#2). The rankings are based on a weighted average of 11 measures of quality: quality assessment; peer assessment score; assessment score by residency directors; research activity; total research activity; average research activity per faculty member; student selectivity; median MCAT total score; median undergraduate GPA; acceptance rate; and faculty resources. *U.S. News & World Report, "America's Best Graduate Schools, Medical, 2017"*

According to *U.S. News & World Report,* the San Jose-Sunnyvale-Santa Clara, CA metro area is home to one of the top 75 business schools in the U.S.: **Stanford University, Graduate School of Business** (#2 tie). The rankings are based on a weighted average of the following nine measures: quality assessment; peer assessment; recruiter assessment; placement success; mean starting salary and bonus; student selectivity; mean GMAT and GRE scores; mean

undergraduate GPA; and acceptance rate. *U.S. News & World Report, "America's Best Graduate Schools, Business, 2017"*

PRESIDENTIAL ELECTION

2012 Presidential Election Results

Area	Obama (%)	Romney (%)	Other (%)
Santa Clara County	69.9	27.6	2.5
U.S.	51.0	47.2	1.8

Note: Results may not add to 100% due to rounding
Source: Dave Leip's Atlas of U.S. Presidential Elections

EMPLOYERS

Major Employers

Company Name	Industry
Adobe Systems Inc	Publishers-computer software (mfrs)
Advanced Micro Devices Inc	Semiconductor devices (mfrs)
Apple Inc	Computers-electronic-manufacturers
Applied Materials Inc	Semiconductor manufacturing equip (mfrs)
Bon Appetit-Cafe Adobe	Restaurant management
California's Great America	Amusement & theme parks
Christopher Ranch	Garlic manufacturers
Cisco Systems Inc	Computer peripherals
E Bay Inc	E-commerce
Flextronics	Solar energy equipment-manufacturers
General Motors Advanced Tech	Automobile-manufacturers
Hewlett-Packard	Computers-electronic-manufacturers
Intel Corp	Semiconductor devices (mfrs)
Kaiser Permanente Med Center	Hospitals
Kaiser Permanente Medical Ctr	Hospitals
Lockheed Martin Space Systems	Satellite equipment & systems-mfrs
Microsoft Corp	Computer software-manufacturers
NASA	Government offices-us
Net App Inc	Computer storage devices

Note: Companies shown are located within the San Jose-Sunnyvale-Santa Clara, CA Metropolitan Statistical Area.
Source: Hoovers.com; Wikipedia

PUBLIC SAFETY

Crime Rate

Area	All Crimes	Violent Crimes				Property Crimes		
		Murder	Rape[3]	Robbery	Aggrav. Assault	Burglary	Larceny -Theft	Motor Vehicle Theft
City	1,760.1	0.0	6.6	31.4	28.1	434.3	1,182.2	77.6
Metro[1]	2,496.5	2.3	25.2	80.4	142.0	469.8	1,272.0	504.9
U.S.	2,971.8	4.5	36.6	102.2	232.5	542.5	1,837.3	216.2

Note: Figures are crimes per 100,000 population; (1) Figures cover the San Jose-Sunnyvale-Santa Clara, CA Metropolitan Statistical Area—see Appendix B for areas included; (3) The city and U.S. figures shown were reported using the revised Uniform Crime Reporting (UCR) definition of rape. The suburban and metro area figures shown are an aggregate total of the data submitted using both the revised and legacy UCR definitions.
Source: FBI Uniform Crime Reports, 2014

Hate Crimes

Area	Number of Quarters Reported	Number of Incidents per Bias Motivation						
		Race	Religion	Sexual Orientation	Ethnicity	Disability	Gender	Gender Identity
City	4	0	1	0	0	0	0	0
U.S.	4	2,568	1,014	1,017	648	84	33	98

Source: Federal Bureau of Investigation, Hate Crime Statistics 2014

Identity Theft Consumer Complaints

Area	Complaints	Complaints per 100,000 Population	Rank[2]
MSA[1]	2,693	137.9	74
U.S.	490,220	152.4	-

Note: (1) Figures cover the San Jose-Sunnyvale-Santa Clara, CA Metropolitan Statistical Area—see Appendix B for areas included; (2) Rank ranges from 1 to 379 where 1 indicates greatest number of identity theft complaints per 100,000 population
Source: Federal Trade Commission, Consumer Sentinel Network Data Book for January–December 2015

Fraud and Other Consumer Complaints

Area	Complaints	Complaints per 100,000 Population	Rank[2]
MSA[1]	6,862	351.4	213
U.S.	2,593,159	806.0	-

Note: (1) Figures cover the San Jose-Sunnyvale-Santa Clara, CA Metropolitan Statistical Area—see Appendix B for areas included; (2) Rank ranges from 1 to 379 where 1 indicates greatest number of identity theft complaints per 100,000 population
Source: Federal Trade Commission, Consumer Sentinel Network Data Book for January–December 2015

RECREATION

Culture

Dance[1]	Theatre[1]	Instrumental Music[1]	Vocal Music[1]	Series and Festivals	Museums and Art Galleries[2]	Zoos and Aquariums[3]
0	0	0	0	0	0	0

Note: (1) Professional perfoming groups; (2) Based on organizations with SIC code 8412; (3) AZA-accredited
Source: The Grey House Performing Arts Directory, 2015-16; Association of Zoos & Aquariums, AZA Member Zoos & Aquariums, March 25, 2016; www.AccuLeads.com, March 29, 2016

Professional Sports Teams

Team Name	League	Year Established
San Jose Earthquakes	Major League Soccer (MLS)	1996
San Jose Sharks	National Hockey League (NHL)	1991

Note: Includes teams located in the San Jose-Sunnyvale-Santa Clara, CA Metropolitan Statistical Area.
Source: Wikipedia, Major Professional Sports Teams of the United States and Canada, March 24, 2016

CLIMATE

Average and Extreme Temperatures

Temperature	Jan	Feb	Mar	Apr	May	Jun	Jul	Aug	Sep	Oct	Nov	Dec	Yr.
Extreme High (°F)	76	82	83	95	103	104	105	101	105	100	87	76	105
Average High (°F)	57	61	63	67	70	74	75	75	76	72	65	58	68
Average Temp. (°F)	50	53	55	58	61	65	66	67	66	63	56	50	59
Average Low (°F)	42	45	46	48	51	55	57	58	57	53	47	42	50
Extreme Low (°F)	21	26	30	32	38	43	45	47	41	33	29	23	21

Note: Figures cover the years 1945-1993
Source: National Climatic Data Center, International Station Meteorological Climate Summary, 9/96

Average Precipitation/Snowfall/Humidity

Precip./Humidity	Jan	Feb	Mar	Apr	May	Jun	Jul	Aug	Sep	Oct	Nov	Dec	Yr.
Avg. Precip. (in.)	2.7	2.3	2.2	0.9	0.3	0.1	Tr	Tr	0.2	0.7	1.7	2.3	13.5
Avg. Snowfall (in.)	Tr	Tr	Tr	0	0	0	0	0	0	0	0	Tr	Tr
Avg. Rel. Hum. 7am (%)	82	82	80	76	74	73	77	79	79	79	81	82	79
Avg. Rel. Hum. 4pm (%)	62	59	56	52	53	54	58	58	55	54	59	63	57

Note: Figures cover the years 1945-1993; Tr = Trace amounts (<0.05 in. of rain; <0.5 in. of snow)
Source: National Climatic Data Center, International Station Meteorological Climate Summary, 9/96

Weather Conditions

Temperature			Daytime Sky			Precipitation		
10°F & below	32°F & below	90°F & above	Clear	Partly cloudy	Cloudy	0.01 inch or more precip.	0.1 inch or more snow/ice	Thunder-storms
0	5	5	106	180	79	57	< 1	6

Note: Figures are average number of days per year and cover the years 1945-1993
Source: National Climatic Data Center, International Station Meteorological Climate Summary, 9/96

HAZARDOUS WASTE

Superfund Sites

Cupertino has one hazardous waste site on the EPA's Superfund Final National Priorities List: **Intersil Inc./Siemens Components**. There are a total of 1,323 Superfund sites on the list in the U.S. *U.S. Environmental Protection Agency, Final National Priorities List, March 18, 2016*

AIR & WATER QUALITY

Air Quality Trends: Ozone

	1990	1995	2000	2005	2010	2011	2012	2013	2014
MSA[1]	0.079	0.085	0.070	0.065	0.073	0.065	0.064	0.064	0.069

Note: (1) Data covers the San Jose-Sunnyvale-Santa Clara, CA Metropolitan Statistical Area—see Appendix B for areas included. The values shown are the composite ozone concentration averages among trend sites based on the highest fourth daily maximum 8-hour concentration in parts per million. These trends are based on sites having an adequate record of monitoring data during the trend period. Data from exceptional events are included.
Source: U.S. Environmental Protection Agency, Air Quality Monitoring Information, "Air Quality Trends by City, 1990-2014"

Air Quality Index

Area	Percent of Days when Air Quality was...[2]					AQI Statistics[2]	
	Good	Moderate	Unhealthy for Sensitive Groups	Unhealthy	Very Unhealthy	Maximum	Median
MSA[1]	67.1	31.0	1.9	0.0	0.0	135	44

Note: (1) Data covers the San Jose-Sunnyvale-Santa Clara, CA Metropolitan Statistical Area—see Appendix B for areas included; (2) Based on 365 days with AQI data in 2015. Air Quality Index (AQI) is an index for reporting daily air quality. EPA calculates the AQI for five major air pollutants regulated by the Clean Air Act: ground-level ozone, particle pollution (aka particulate matter), carbon monoxide, sulfur dioxide, and nitrogen dioxide. The AQI runs from 0 to 500. The higher the AQI value, the greater the level of air pollution and the greater the health concern. There are six AQI categories: "Good" AQI is between 0 and 50. Air quality is considered satisfactory; "Moderate" AQI is between 51 and 100. Air quality is acceptable; "Unhealthy for Sensitive Groups" When AQI values are between 101 and 150, members of sensitive groups may experience health effects; "Unhealthy" When AQI values are between 151 and 200 everyone may begin to experience health effects; "Very Unhealthy" AQI values between 201 and 300 trigger a health alert; "Hazardous" AQI values over 300 trigger warnings of emergency conditions (not shown).
Source: U.S. Environmental Protection Agency, Air Quality Index Report, 2015

Air Quality Index Pollutants

Area	Percent of Days when AQI Pollutant was...[2]					
	Carbon Monoxide	Nitrogen Dioxide	Ozone	Sulfur Dioxide	Particulate Matter 2.5	Particulate Matter 10
MSA[1]	0.0	2.5	51.0	0.0	46.3	0.3

Note: (1) Data covers the San Jose-Sunnyvale-Santa Clara, CA Metropolitan Statistical Area—see Appendix B for areas included; (2) Based on 365 days with AQI data in 2015. The Air Quality Index (AQI) is an index for reporting daily air quality. EPA calculates the AQI for five major air pollutants regulated by the Clean Air Act: ground-level ozone, particle pollution (also known as particulate matter), carbon monoxide, sulfur dioxide, and nitrogen dioxide. The AQI runs from 0 to 500. The higher the AQI value, the greater the level of air pollution and the greater the health concern.
Source: U.S. Environmental Protection Agency, Air Quality Index Report, 2015

Maximum Air Pollutant Concentrations: Particulate Matter, Ozone, CO and Lead

	Particulate Matter 10 (ug/m^3)	Particulate Matter 2.5 Wtd AM (ug/m^3)	Particulate Matter 2.5 24-Hr (ug/m^3)	Ozone (ppm)	Carbon Monoxide (ppm)	Lead (ug/m^3)
MSA[1] Level	52	8.4	27	0.073	2	0.13
NAAQS[2]	150	15	35	0.075	9	0.15
Met NAAQS[2]	Yes	Yes	Yes	Yes	Yes	Yes

Note: (1) Data covers the San Jose-Sunnyvale-Santa Clara, CA Metropolitan Statistical Area—see Appendix B for areas included; Data from exceptional events are included; (2) National Ambient Air Quality Standards; ppm = parts per million; ug/m^3 = micrograms per cubic meter; n/a not available.

Concentrations: Particulate Matter 10 (coarse particulate)—highest second maximum 24-hour concentration; Particulate Matter 2.5 Wtd AM (fine particulate)—highest weighted annual mean concentration; Particulate Matter 2.5 24-Hour (fine particulate)—highest 98th percentile 24-hour concentration; Ozone—highest fourth daily maximum 8-hour concentration; Carbon Monoxide—highest second maximum non-overlapping 8-hour concentration; Lead—maximum running 3-month average

Source: U.S. Environmental Protection Agency, Air Quality Monitoring Information, "Air Quality Statistics by City, 2014"

Maximum Air Pollutant Concentrations: Nitrogen Dioxide and Sulfur Dioxide

	Nitrogen Dioxide AM (ppb)	Nitrogen Dioxide 1-Hr (ppb)	Sulfur Dioxide AM (ppb)	Sulfur Dioxide 1-Hr (ppb)	Sulfur Dioxide 24-Hr (ppb)
MSA[1] Level	13	55	n/a	2	n/a
NAAQS[2]	53	100	30	75	140
Met NAAQS[2]	Yes	Yes	n/a	Yes	n/a

Note: (1) Data covers the San Jose-Sunnyvale-Santa Clara, CA Metropolitan Statistical Area—see Appendix B for areas included; Data from exceptional events are included; (2) National Ambient Air Quality Standards; ppm = parts per million; ug/m^3 = micrograms per cubic meter; n/a not available.

Concentrations: Nitrogen Dioxide AM—highest arithmetic mean concentration; Nitrogen Dioxide 1-Hr—highest 98th percentile 1-hour daily maximum concentration; Sulfur Dioxide AM—highest annual mean concentration; Sulfur Dioxide 1-Hr—highest 99th percentile 1-hour daily maximum concentration; Sulfur Dioxide 24-Hr—highest second maximum 24-hour concentration

Source: U.S. Environmental Protection Agency, Air Quality Monitoring Information, "Air Quality Statistics by City, 2014"

Drinking Water

Water System Name	Pop. Served	Primary Water Source Type	Violations[1]	
			Health Based	Monitoring/ Reporting
City of Cupertino	14,207	Purchased Surface	0	0

Note: (1) Based on violation data from January 1, 2015 to December 31, 2015 (includes unresolved violations from earlier years)

Source: U.S. Environmental Protection Agency, Office of Ground Water and Drinking Water, Safe Drinking Water Information System (based on data extracted April 29, 2016)

Danville, California

Background

Danville is highly regarded for its small-town atmosphere and outstanding quality of life. Often referred to as the "Heart of the San Ramon Valley," Danville was incorporated as a city in 1982 and is governed by a mayor-council form of government with day-to-day operations performed by a Town Manager.

The Danville area's original Indian inhabitants were semi-nomadic peoples who lived most of the year by the banks of neighboring creeks, and in summer camped on the slopes of the spectacular Mount Diablo. During the Spanish period, it became part of the grazing land for Mission San Jose, under a Mexican land grant—Rancho San Ramon. Later, as Americans were drawn to the area during the California Gold Rush, the modern growth of the town began in earnest. In 1854, Daniel and Andrew Inman bought 400 acres of Old Town Danville with their mining earnings, and by 1858, the community boasted a hotel, a blacksmith, and a general store. The town's connection to its Old West history is preserved in the downtown cluster of narrow roads and the great number of early buildings that still remain. The painstakingly restored Southern Pacific Railroad Depot, now the site of the Museum of the San Ramon Valley, is on the National Register of Historic Places.

A remarkable variety of famous figures have lived in or visited Danville. A Queen Anne cottage, on Railroad Avenue, was built by a direct descendent of Daniel Boone. Tao House, on the western hills of Danville, was the home of Eugene and Carlotta O'Neill from 1937 to 1944 and is now a National Historic Site. O'Neill wrote his last and most famous plays here—*The Iceman Cometh, Long Day's Journey Into Night,* and *A Moon for the Misbegotten.* The former heavyweight champion of the world, Jack Dempsey, sold war bonds here during World War II. The San Ramon Valley Little League All-Stars, coached by Bill Ross, were the U.S. champions in 1978.

Danville operates and maintains an extensive system of parks and recreational resources—ball fields, tennis courts, picnic facilities, playground equipment, and walking trails. The Iron Horse Trail provides miles of paths for biking and walking. Diablo Vista Park, just one of Danville's parks, is known for the mosaic "water-snake" that winds down a hillside, while 43-acre Oak Hill Park offers a quiet country setting with a spectacular view of Mt. Diablo. Oak Hill is also the site of many special events that are sponsored by Danville, including a youth day camp and the summer music programs.

The Fourth of July Parade, the Lighting of Old Town Danville, Danville Summerfest, Thursday Night Street Festival, and a weekly farmer's market are just a few of Danville's community events. The Village Theatre offers live theater productions, and also houses an art gallery. "Music in the Park" is a summer concert series, featuring local groups. World-class restaurants draw people from as far away as San Francisco, and one of these restaurants, Bridges, was made famous when scenes for the movie *Mrs. Doubtfire* were filmed there.

Major employers in Danville include Costco and the Crow Canyon Country Club.

Danville is a uniquely scenic town, and from its Mount Diablo one can see a vista more extensive than from most any mountain in the world, and see it with sunshine more than 300 days of the year.

Rankings

General Rankings

- The San Francisco* metro area was identified as one of America's fastest-growing areas in terms of population and economy by *Forbes*. The area ranked #7 out of 20. The 100 most populous metro areas in the U.S. were evaluated on the following criteria: estimated population growth; job growth; gross metropolitan product growth; unemployment; median salaries for college-educated workers. *Forbes, "America's Fastest-Growing Cities 2015," January 27, 2015*

Business/Finance Rankings

- The personal finance site NerdWallet analyzed 183 American metropolitan areas with populations over 250,000 and more than 15,000 businesses to rank where entrepreneurs find the most success. Criteria included area economy, annual income, housing cost, unemployment rate, and the success rate of area businesses. Oakland* ranked #19. *www.nerdwallet.com, "Best Places to Start a Business," April 27, 2015*

- TransUnion ranked the nation's metro areas by average credit score, calculated on the VantageScore system, developed by the three major credit-reporting bureaus—TransUnion, Experian, and Equifax. The Oakland* metro area was among the ten cities with the highest collective credit score, meaning that its residents posed the lowest average consumer credit risk. *www.usatoday.com, "Metro Areas' Average Credit Rating Revealed," February 7, 2013*

- Based on the U.S. Department of Labor's Occupational Information Network Data Collection Program, the Brookings Institution defined job opportunities for STEM workers at various levels of educational attainment. The Oakland* metro area was one of the ten metro areas where workers in low-education-level STEM jobs earn the lowest relative wages. *www.brookings.edu, "The Hidden Stem Economy," June 10, 2013*

- 24/7 Wall Street used Brookings Institution research on 50 advanced industries to identify the proportion of workers in the nation's largest metropolitan areas that were employed in jobs requiring knowledge in the science, technology, engineering, or math (STEM) fields. The San Francisco* metro area was #5. *247wallst.com, "15 Cities with the Most High-Tech Jobs," March 13, 2015*

- Based on metro area social media reviews, the employment opinion group Glassdoor surveyed 50 of the largest U.S. metro areas and equally weighed cost of living, hiring opportunity, and job satisfaction to compose a list of "25 Best Cities for Jobs." The San Francisco* metro area was ranked #1 in overall job satisfaction. *www.glassdoor.com, "Best Cities for Jobs," May 19, 2015*

- In a survey of economic confidence in the nation's 50 largest metropolitan areas conducted January–December 2014, the San Francisco* metro area placed #2, according to Gallup's 2014 Economic Confidence Index. *Gallup, "San Jose and San Francisco Lead in Economic Confidence," March 19, 2015*

- The Brookings Institution ranked the 100 largest metro areas in the U.S. based on income inequality. San Francisco* was ranked #3 (#1 = greatest ineqality). Criteria: the "95/20 ratio," a figure representing the income at which a household earns more than 95 percent of all other households, divided by the income at which a household earns more than only 20 percent of all other households. *Brookings Institution, "Income Inequality, 100 Largest U.S. Metro Areas, 2007-2014," January 14, 2016*

- *Forbes* ranked the largest metro areas in the U.S. in terms of the "Best Cities for Young Professionals." The San Francisco* metro area ranked #15 out of 15. Criteria: job growth; unemployment rate; median salary of college graduates age 24 to 34; cost of living; number of small businesses per capita; number of large companies; percentage of population 25 years of age and older with college degrees. *Forbes.com, "America's 15 Best Cities for Young Professionals," August 18, 2014*

- Payscale.com ranked the 20 largest metro areas in terms of wage growth. The San Francisco* metro area ranked #3. Criteria: private-sector wage growth between the 1st quarter of 2015 and the 1st quarter of 2016. *PayScale, "Wage Trends by Metro Area," 1st Quarter, 2016*

- San Francisco* was identified as one of America's most frugal metro areas by *Coupons.com*. The city ranked #1 out of 25. Criteria: online coupon usage. *Coupons.com, "Top 25 Most Frugal Cities of 2014," May 11, 2015*

- The Oakland* metro area appeared on the Milken Institute "2015 Best Performing Cities" list. Rank: #39 out of 200 large metro areas. Criteria: job growth; wage and salary growth; high-tech output growth. *Milken Institute, "Best-Performing Cities 2015," December 2015*

- *Forbes* ranked the 200 most populous metro areas to determine the nation's "Best Places for Business and Careers." The Oakland* metro area was ranked #25. Criteria: costs (business and living); job growth (past and projected); income growth; educational attainment (college and high school); projected economic growth; cultural and recreational opportunities; net migration patterns; number of highly ranked colleges. *Forbes, "The Best Places for Business and Careers 2015," July 29, 2015*

Dating/Romance Rankings

- CreditDonkey, a financial education website, sought out the ten best U.S. cities for newlyweds, considering the number of married couples, divorce rate, average credit score, and average number of hours worked per week in metro areas with a million or more residents. The San Francisco* metro area placed #9. *www.creditdonkey.com, "Study: Best Cities for Newlyweds," November 30, 2013*

Education Rankings

- The San Francisco* metro area was selected as one of the world's most inventive cities by *Forbes*. The area was ranked #3 out of 15. Criteria: patent applications per capita. *Forbes, "World's 15 Most Inventive Cities," July 9, 2013*

- Based on a Brookings Institution study, *24/7 Wall St.* identified the ten U.S. metropolitan areas with the most average patent filings per million residents between 2007 and 2011. Oakland* ranked #8. *24/7 Wall St., "America's Most Innovative Cities," February 1, 2013*

- The Oakland* metro area was selected as one of America's most innovative cities" by *The Business Insider*. The metro area was ranked #8 out of 20. Criteria: patents per capita. *The Business Insider, "The 20 Most Innovative Cities in the U.S.," February 1, 2013*

- Oakland* was identified as one of America's "smartest" metropolitan areas by *The Business Journals*. The area ranked #7 out of 10. Criteria: percentage of adults (25 and older) with high school diplomas, bachelor's degrees and graduate degrees. *The Business Journals, "Where the Brainpower Is: Exclusive U.S. Rankings, Insights," February 27, 2014*

- Personal finance website *WalletHub* analyzed the 150 largest U.S. metropolitan statistical areas to determine where the most educated Americans are choosing to settle. Criteria: education quality and attainment gap; education levels; percentage of workers with degrees; public school rankings; quality and size of each metro area's universities. San Francisco* was ranked #20 (#1 = most educated city). *www.WalletHub.com, "2015's Most and Least Educated Cities*

Environmental Rankings

- The San Francisco* metro area came in at #28 for the relative comfort of its climate on Sperling's list of "chill cities," as measured by the Sperling Heat Index. All 361 metro areas are included. Criteria included daytime high temperatures, nighttime low temperatures, dew point, and relative humidity at the high temperatures. *www.bertsperling.com, "Sperling's Chill Cities," July 18, 2013*

- Sperling's BestPlaces assessed 379 metropolitan areas of the United States for the likelihood of dangerously extreme weather events or earthquakes. In general the Southeast and South-Central regions have the highest risk of weather extremes and earthquakes, while the Pacific Northwest enjoys the lowest risk. Of the least risky metropolitan areas, the Oakland* metro area was ranked #76. *www.bestplaces.net, "Safest Places from Natural Disasters," April 2011*

- The U.S. Environmental Protection Agency (EPA) released a list of U.S. metropolitan areas with the most ENERGY STAR certified buildings in 2015. The San Francisco* metro area was ranked #3 out of 25. *U.S. Environmental Protection Agency, "Top Cities With the Most ENERGY STAR Certified Buildings in 2016," March 30, 2016*

Health/Fitness Rankings

- Analysts who tracked obesity rates in the nation's largest metro areas (populations above one million) found that the Oakland* metro area was one of the ten major metros where residents were least likely to be obese, defined as a BMI score of 30 or above. *www.gallup.com, "Boulder, Colo., Residents Still Least Likely to Be Obese," April 4, 2014*
- Analysts who tracked obesity rates in 100 of the nation's most populous areas found that the San Francisco* metro area was one of the ten communities where residents were least likely to be obese, defined as a BMI score of 30 or above. *www.gallup.com, "Colorado Springs Residents Least Likely to Be Obese," May 28, 2015*
- For each of the 50 most populous metro areas in the United States, the American College of Sports Medicine's American Fitness Index evaluated infrastructure, community assets, and policies that encourage healthy and fit lifestyles, including preventive health behaviors, levels of chronic disease conditions, health care access, and community resources and policies that support physical activity. The San Francisco* metro area ranked #4 for "community fitness." *www.americanfitnessindex.org, "ACSM American Fitness Index Health and Community Fitness Status of the 50 Largest Metropolitan Areas," May 2015*
- *Business Insider* reported Trulia's analysis of the 100 largest U.S. metro areas to identify the nation's best cities for weight loss, based on healthful food options, access to outdoor activities, weight-loss centers, gyms, and opportunities to bike or walk to work. San Francisco* ranked #1. *Businessinsider.com, "These Are the Best US Cities for Weight loss," January 17, 2013*
- The San Francisco* metro area was identified as one of the worst cities for bed bugs in America by pest control company Orkin. The area ranked #14 out of 50 based on the number of bed bug treatments Orkin performed from January to December 2015. *Orkin, "Chicago Tops Bed Bug Cities List for Fourth Year in a Row," January 13, 2016*
- San Francisco* was identified as a "2016 Spring Allergy Capital." The area ranked #80 out of 100. Three groups of factors were used to identify the most severe cities for people with allergies during the spring season: annual pollen levels; medicine utilization; access to board-certified allergists. *Asthma and Allergy Foundation of America, "Spring Allergy Capitals 2016"*
- San Francisco* was identified as a "2015 Asthma Capital." The area ranked #100 out of the nation's 100 largest metropolitan areas. Criteria: estimated prevalence; self-reported prevalence; crude death rate for asthma; annual pollen score; annual air quality; public smoking laws; number of board-certified asthma specialists; school inhaler access laws; rescue medication use; controller medication use; ER visits for asthma; uninsured rate; poverty rate. *Asthma and Allergy Foundation of America, "Asthma Capitals 2015"*
- The San Francisco* metro area ranked #30 out of 190 in The Gallup-Healthways Well-Being Index. Criteria: purpose; social well being; financial health; community and physical health. Results are based on telephone interviews with adults, aged 18 and older, living in metropolitan areas in the 50 U.S. states and the District of Columbia. *Gallup-Healthways, "State of American Well-Being," February 23, 2016*

Real Estate Rankings

- With data from RealtyTrac, Yahoo! Finance researchers listed the housing markets in which housing affordability is improving most, factoring in interest rates as well as median home prices. The San Francisco* metro area was among the least affordable housing markets. *news.yahoo.com, "10 Cities Where Ordinary People Can No Longer Afford Homes," March 5, 2014*

- The San Francisco* metro area was identified as one of the nations's 20 hottest housing markets in 2016. Criteria: listing views as an indicator of demand and median days on the market as an indicator of supply. The area ranked #1. *Realtor.com, "The 20 Hottest U.S. Real Estate Markets in February 2016," February 25, 2016*

- Oakland* was ranked #13 in the top 20 out of 266 metro areas in terms of house price appreciation in 2015 (#1 = highest rate). *Federal Housing Finance Agency, House Price Index, 4th Quarter 2015*

- The San Francisco* metro area was identified as one of the 10 best condo markets in the U.S. in 2015. The area ranked #6 out of 61 markets. Criteria: year-over-year change of median sales price of existing apartment condo-coop homes between the 4th quarter of 2014 and the 4th quarter of 2015. *National Association of Realtors®, Median Sales Price of Existing Apartment Condo-Coop Homes for Metropolitan Areas, 4th Quarter 2015*

- The San Francisco* metro area was identified as one of the 20 least affordable housing markets in the U.S. in 2015. The area ranked #4 out of 179 markets. Criteria: qualification for a mortgage loan on a typical home. *National Association of Realtors®, Affordability Index of Existing Single-Family Homes for Metropolitan Areas, 2015*

- Oakland* was ranked #213 out of 225 metro areas in terms of housing affordability in 2015 by the National Association of Home Builders (#1 = most affordable). Criteria: the share of homes sold in that area affordable to a family earning the local median income, based on standard mortgage underwriting criteria. *National Association of Home Builders®, NAHB-Wells Fargo Housing Opportunity Index, 4th Quarter 2015*

Safety Rankings

- Farmers Insurance, in partnership with Sperling's BestPlaces, ranked metro areas in the U.S. as the "Most Secure Places to Live." The San Francisco* metro area ranked #8 out of the top 20 in the large metro area category (500,000 or more residents). Criteria: economic stability; crime statistics; extreme weather; risk of natural disasters; housing depreciation; foreclosures; air quality; environmental hazards; life expectancy; motor vehicle fatalities; and employment numbers. *Farmers Insurance Group of Companies, "Most Secure U.S. Places to Live in the U.S.," June 25, 2013*

- The National Insurance Crime Bureau ranked 380 metro areas in the U.S. in terms of per capita rates of vehicle theft. The San Francisco* metro area ranked #1 (#1 = highest rate). Criteria: number of vehicle theft offenses per 100,000 inhabitants in 2014. *National Insurance Crime Bureau, "Hot Spots 2014," June 24, 2015*

Seniors/Retirement Rankings

- From its Best Cities for Successful Aging indexes, the Milken Institute generated rankings for metropolitan areas, weighing data in eight categories—health care, wellness, living arrangements, transportation, financial characteristics, education and employment opportunities, community engagement, and overall livability. The Oakland* metro area was ranked #17 overall in the large metro area category. *Milken Institute, "Best Cities for Successful Aging, 2014"*

Sports/Recreation Rankings

- According to the personal finance website NerdWallet, the San Francisco* metro area, at #5, is one of the nation's top dozen metro areas for sports fans. Criteria included the presence of all four major sports—MLB, NFL, NHL, and NBA, fan enthusiasm (as measured by game attendance), ticket affordability, and "sports culture," that is, number of sports bars. *www.nerdwallet.com, "Best Cities for Sports Fans," May 5, 2013*

Transportation Rankings

- San Francisco* was identified as one of the most congested metro areas in the U.S. The area ranked #3 out of 10. Criteria: yearly delay per auto commuter in hours. *Texas A&M Transportation Institute, "2015 Urban Mobility Scorecard," August 2015*

- The San Francisco* metro area appeared on *Forbes* list of places with the most extreme commutes. The metro area ranked #1 out of 10. Criteria: average travel time; percentage of mega commuters. Mega-commuters travel more than 90 minutes and 50 miles each way to work. *Forbes.com, "The Cities with the Most Extreme Commutes," March 5, 2013*

Miscellaneous Rankings

- The watchdog site Charity Navigator conducts an annual study of charities in the nation's major markets both to analyze statistical differences in their financial, accountability, and transparency practices and to track year-to-year variations in individual communities. The San Francisco* metro area was ranked #9 among the 30 metro markets in the rating dimension of Overall Score. *www.charitynavigator.org, "Metro Market Study 2015," June 5, 2015*

- The Harris Poll's Happiness Index survey revealed that of the top ten U.S. markets, the San Francisco* metro area residents ranked #10 in happiness. Criteria included strong assent to positive statements and strong disagreement with negative ones, and degree of agreement with a series of statements about respondents' personal relationships and general outlook. *www.harrisinteractive.com, "Dallas/Fort Worth Is "Happiest" City among America's Top Ten Markets," September 4, 2013*

- Mars Chocolate North America, the makers of COMBOS®, in partnership with Sperling's BestPlaces, ranked 50 major metro areas in terms of their "manliness." The Oakland* metro area ranked #48. Criteria: number of professional sports teams; number of nearby NASCAR tracks and racing events; manly lifestyle; concentration of manly retail stores; manly occupations per capita; salty snack sales; "Board of Manliness" rankings. *Mars Chocolate North America, "America's Manliest Cities 2012"*

- The National Alliance to End Homelessness ranked the 100 most populous metro areas with the highest rate of homelessness. The San Francisco* metro area ranked #12. Criteria: number of homeless people per 10,000 population in 2011. *National Alliance to End Homelessness, The State of Homelessness in America 2012*

Danville is located within the San Francisco-Oakland-Hayward, CA Metropolitan Statistical Area and the Oakland-Hayward-Berkeley, CA Metropolitan Division.

Business Environment

CITY FINANCES

City Government Finances

Component	2012 ($000)	2012 ($ per capita)
Total Revenues	35,042	833
Total Expenditures	34,679	824
Debt Outstanding	12,865	306
Cash and Securities[1]	91,746	2,182

Note: (1) Cash and security holdings of a government at the close of its fiscal year, including those of its dependent agencies, utilities, and liquor stores.
Source: U.S Census Bureau, State & Local Government Finances 2012

City Government Revenue by Source

Source	2012 ($000)	2012 ($ per capita)
General Revenue		
From Federal Government	0	0
From State Government	6,430	152
From Local Governments	0	0
Taxes		
Property	13,117	312
Sales and Gross Receipts	6,323	150
Personal Income	0	0
Corporate Income	0	0
Motor Vehicle License	0	0
Other Taxes	2,333	55
Current Charges	3,655	86
Liquor Store	0	0
Utility	0	0
Employee Retirement	0	0

Source: U.S Census Bureau, State & Local Government Finances 2012

City Government Expenditures by Function

Function	2012 ($000)	2012 ($ per capita)	2012 (%)
General Direct Expenditures			
Air Transportation	0	0	0.0
Corrections	0	0	0.0
Education	0	0	0.0
Employment Security Administration	0	0	0.0
Financial Administration	728	17	2.0
Fire Protection	0	0	0.0
General Public Buildings	0	0	0.0
Governmental Administration, Other	9,706	230	27.9
Health	364	8	1.0
Highways	7,566	179	21.8
Hospitals	0	0	0.0
Housing and Community Development	141	3	0.4
Interest on General Debt	503	11	1.4
Judicial and Legal	639	15	1.8
Libraries	1	< 1	< 0.1
Parking	0	0	0.0
Parks and Recreation	7,418	176	21.3
Police Protection	7,276	173	20.9
Public Welfare	0	0	0.0
Sewerage	0	0	0.0
Solid Waste Management	0	0	0.0
Veterans' Services	0	0	0.0
Liquor Store	0	0	0.0
Utility	0	0	0.0
Employee Retirement	0	0	0.0

Source: U.S Census Bureau, State & Local Government Finances 2012

DEMOGRAPHICS

Population Growth

Area	1990 Census	2000 Census	2010 Census	2014* Estimate	Population Growth (%) 1990-2014	Population Growth (%) 2010-2014
City	32,328	41,715	42,039	42,891	32.7	2.0
MSA[1]	3,686,592	4,123,740	4,335,391	4,466,251	21.1	3.0
U.S.	248,709,873	281,421,906	308,745,538	314,107,084	26.3	1.7

Note: (1) Figures cover the San Francisco-Oakland-Hayward, CA Metropolitan Statistical Area—see Appendix B for areas included; (*) 2010-2014 5-year estimated population
Source: U.S. Census Bureau, 1990 Census, Census 2000, Census 2010, 2010-2014 American Community Survey 5-Year Estimates

Household Size

Area	Persons in Household (%) One	Two	Three	Four	Five	Six	Seven or More	Average Household Size
City	20.7	34.1	14.7	20.8	7.0	1.9	0.5	2.74
MSA[1]	28.1	31.4	16.2	14.0	5.8	2.3	1.7	2.67
U.S.	27.5	33.5	15.8	13.1	6.0	2.3	1.4	2.64

Note: (1) Figures cover the San Francisco-Oakland-Hayward, CA Metropolitan Statistical Area—see Appendix B for areas included
Source: U.S. Census Bureau, 2010-2014 American Community Survey 5-Year Estimates

Race

Area	White Alone[2] (%)	Black Alone[2] (%)	Asian Alone[2] (%)	AIAN[3] Alone[2] (%)	NHOPI[4] Alone[2] (%)	Other Race Alone[2] (%)	Two or More Races (%)
City	83.4	1.1	11.5	0.2	0.1	0.4	3.4
MSA[1]	54.0	8.0	24.0	0.5	0.7	7.5	5.4
U.S.	73.8	12.6	5.0	0.8	0.2	4.7	2.9

Note: (1) Figures cover the San Francisco-Oakland-Hayward, CA Metropolitan Statistical Area—see Appendix B for areas included; (2) Alone is defined as not being in combination with one or more other races; (3) American Indian and Alaska Native; (4) Native Hawaiian and Other Pacific Islander
Source: U.S. Census Bureau, 2010-2014 American Community Survey 5-Year Estimates

Hispanic or Latino Origin

Area	Total (%)	Mexican (%)	Puerto Rican (%)	Cuban (%)	Other (%)
City	5.8	3.5	0.1	0.1	2.0
MSA[1]	21.8	14.8	0.6	0.2	6.2
U.S.	16.9	10.8	1.6	0.6	3.8

Note: Persons of Hispanic or Latino origin can be of any race; (1) Figures cover the San Francisco-Oakland-Hayward, CA Metropolitan Statistical Area—see Appendix B for areas included
Source: U.S. Census Bureau, 2010-2014 American Community Survey 5-Year Estimates

Ancestry

Area	German	Irish	English	American	Italian	Polish	French[2]	Scottish	Dutch
City	18.1	14.1	12.7	6.0	10.5	2.4	3.6	2.1	1.6
MSA[1]	8.5	7.9	6.3	2.6	5.3	1.5	2.0	1.6	0.9
U.S.	14.9	10.8	8.0	7.1	5.5	3.0	2.7	1.7	1.4

Note: Figures are the percentage of the total population reporting a particular ancestry. The nine most commonly reported ancestries in the U.S. are shown. Figures include multiple ancestries (e.g. if a person reported being Irish and Italian, they were included in both columns); (1) Figures cover the San Francisco-Oakland-Hayward, CA Metropolitan Statistical Area—see Appendix B for areas included; (2) Excludes Basque
Source: U.S. Census Bureau, 2010-2014 American Community Survey 5-Year Estimates

Foreign-Born Population

Area	Percent of Population Born in								
	Any Foreign Country	Asia	Mexico	Europe	Carribean	Central America[2]	South America	Africa	Canada
City	12.6	7.3	0.3	3.1	0.1	0.2	0.3	0.5	0.6
MSA[1]	29.9	16.3	5.6	2.9	0.2	2.5	0.9	0.6	0.4
U.S.	13.1	3.8	3.7	1.5	1.2	1.0	0.9	0.6	0.3

Note: (1) Figures cover the San Francisco-Oakland-Hayward, CA Metropolitan Statistical Area—see Appendix B for areas included; (2) Excludes Mexico.
Source: U.S. Census Bureau, 2010-2014 American Community Survey 5-Year Estimates

Marital Status

Area	Never Married	Now Married[2]	Separated	Widowed	Divorced
City	19.6	64.4	0.6	6.1	9.3
MSA[1]	35.9	47.7	1.9	5.2	9.4
U.S.	32.5	48.4	2.2	5.9	10.9

Note: Figures are percentages and cover the population 15 years of age and older; (1) Figures cover the San Francisco-Oakland-Hayward, CA Metropolitan Statistical Area—see Appendix B for areas included; (2) Excludes separated
Source: U.S. Census Bureau, 2010-2014 American Community Survey 5-Year Estimates

Disability Status

Area	All Ages	Under 18 Years Old	18 to 64 Years Old	65 Years and Over
City	7.1	2.4	3.1	27.8
MSA[1]	9.5	2.7	6.9	33.3
U.S.	12.3	4.1	10.2	36.3

Note: Figures show percent of the civilian noninstitutionalized population that reported having a disability. Disability status is determined from from six types of difficulty: vision, hearing, cognitive, ambulatory, self-care, and independent living. For children under 5 years old, hearing and vision difficulty are used to determine disability status. For children between the ages of 5 and 14, disability status is determined from hearing, vision, cognitive, ambulatory, and self-care difficulties. For people aged 15 years and older, they are considered to have a disability if they have difficulty with any one of the six difficulty types; (1) Figures cover the San Francisco-Oakland-Hayward, CA Metropolitan Statistical Area—see Appendix B for areas included.
Source: U.S. Census Bureau, 2010-2014 American Community Survey 5-Year Estimates

Age

Area	Percent of Population									Median Age
	Under Age 5	Age 5–19	Age 20–34	Age 35–44	Age 45–54	Age 55–64	Age 65–74	Age 75–84	Age 85+	
City	5.5	23.9	8.5	12.4	18.2	15.7	8.1	5.0	2.7	44.8
MSA[1]	5.8	17.3	21.6	14.8	14.7	12.5	7.3	4.0	2.0	38.6
U.S.	6.4	19.9	20.6	13.0	14.1	12.3	7.6	4.3	1.9	37.4

Note: (1) Figures cover the San Francisco-Oakland-Hayward, CA Metropolitan Statistical Area—see Appendix B for areas included
Source: U.S. Census Bureau, 2010-2014 American Community Survey 5-Year Estimates

Gender

Area	Males	Females	Males per 100 Females
City	20,200	22,691	89.0
MSA[1]	2,202,384	2,263,867	97.3
U.S.	154,515,159	159,591,925	96.8

Note: (1) Figures cover the San Francisco-Oakland-Hayward, CA Metropolitan Statistical Area—see Appendix B for areas included
Source: U.S. Census Bureau, 2010-2014 American Community Survey 5-Year Estimates

Religious Groups by Family

Area	Catholic	Baptist	Non-Den.	Methodist[2]	Lutheran	LDS[3]	Pente-costal	Presby-terian[4]	Muslim[5]	Judaism
MSA[1]	20.7	2.5	2.4	1.9	0.5	1.5	1.2	1.1	1.2	0.8
U.S.	19.1	9.3	4.0	4.0	2.3	2.0	1.9	1.6	0.8	0.7

Note: Figures are the number of adherents as a percentage of the total population; (1) Figures cover the San Francisco-Oakland-Fremont, CA Metropolitan Statistical Area—see Appendix B for areas included; (2) Methodist/Pietist; (3) Latter Day Saints; (4) Reformed; (5) Figures are estimates
Source: Association of Statisticians of American Religious Bodies, 2010 U.S. Religion Census: Religious Congregations & Membership Study

Religious Groups by Tradition

Area	Catholic	Evangelical Protestant	Mainline Protestant	Other Tradition	Black Protestant	Orthodox
MSA[1]	20.7	6.1	3.8	5.2	1.0	0.6
U.S.	19.1	16.2	7.3	4.3	1.6	0.3

Note: Figures are the number of adherents as a percentage of the total population; (1) Figures cover the San Francisco-Oakland-Fremont, CA Metropolitan Statistical Area—see Appendix B for areas included
Source: Association of Statisticians of American Religious Bodies, 2010 U.S. Religion Census: Religious Congregations & Membership Study

ECONOMY

Gross Metropolitan Product

Area	2013	2014	2015	2016	Rank[2]
MSA[1]	388.2	408.6	426.9	451.0	7

Note: Figures are in billions of dollars; (1) Figures cover the San Francisco-Oakland-Hayward, CA Metropolitan Statistical Area—see Appendix B for areas included; (2) Rank is based on 2016 data and ranges from 1 to 381
Source: The U.S. Conference of Mayors, U.S. Metro Economies: GMP and Employment 2014-2016, June 2015

Economic Growth

Area	2011-13 (%)	2014 (%)	2015 (%)	2016 (%)	Rank[2]
MSA[1]	4.2	3.8	3.2	3.7	27
U.S.	2.2	2.4	2.3	2.9	–

Note: Figures are real gross metropolitan product (GMP) growth rates and represent annual average percent change; (1) Figures cover the San Francisco-Oakland-Hayward, CA Metropolitan Statistical Area—see Appendix B for areas included; (2) Rank is based on 2016 data and ranges from 1 to 381
Source: The U.S. Conference of Mayors, U.S. Metro Economies: GMP and Employment 2014-2016, June 2015

Metropolitan Area Exports

Area	2009	2010	2011	2012	2013	2014	Rank[2]
MSA[1]	16,040.3	21,355.4	23,573.7	23,031.6	25,305.2	26,863.6	10

Note: Figures are in millions of dollars; (1) Figures cover the San Francisco-Oakland-Hayward, CA Metropolitan Statistical Area—see Appendix B for areas included; (2) Rank is based on 2014 data and ranges from 1 to 385
Source: U.S. Department of Commerce, International Trade Administration, Office of Trade & Industry Information, Manufacturing & Services, data extracted March 10, 2016

Building Permits

Area	Single-Family			Multi-Family			Total		
	2014	2015p	Pct. Chg.	2014	2015p	Pct. Chg.	2014	2015p	Pct. Chg.
City	29	63	117.2	16	2	-87.5	45	65	44.4
MSA[1]	3,716	4,595	23.7	6,285	8,171	30.0	10,001	12,766	27.6
U.S.	640,300	690,800	7.9	411,800	487,600	18.4	1,052,100	1,178,400	12.0

Note: (1) Figures cover the San Francisco-Oakland-Hayward, CA Metropolitan Statistical Area—see Appendix B for areas included; Figures represent new, privately-owned housing units authorized (unadjusted data); All permit data are based on estimates with imputation; (p) preliminary data.
Source: U.S. Census Bureau, Manufacturing, Mining, and Construction Statistics, Building Permits, 2014, 2015

Bankruptcy Filings

Area	Business Filings			Nonbusiness Filings		
	2014	2015	% Chg.	2014	2015	% Chg.
Contra Costa County	104	93	-10.6	2,467	1,850	-25.0
U.S.	26,983	24,735	-8.3	909,812	819,760	-9.9

Note: Business filings include Chapter 7, Chapter 11, Chapter 12, and Chapter 13; Nonbusiness filings include Chapter 7, Chapter 11, and Chapter 13

Source: Administrative Office of the U.S. Courts, Business and Nonbusiness Bankruptcy, County Cases Commenced by Chapter of the Bankruptcy Code, During the 12- Month Period Ending December 31, 2014 and Business and Nonbusiness Bankruptcy, County Cases Commenced by Chapter of the Bankruptcy Code, During the 12- Month Period Ending December 31, 2015

Housing Vacancy Rates

Area	Gross Vacancy Rate[2] (%)			Year-Round Vacancy Rate[3] (%)			Rental Vacancy Rate[4] (%)			Homeowner Vacancy Rate[5] (%)		
	2013	2014	2015	2013	2014	2015	2013	2014	2015	2013	2014	2015
MSA[1]	6.5	5.9	5.7	6.4	5.9	5.7	3.9	3.2	3.6	1.1	0.4	0.7
U.S.	13.6	13.4	12.9	10.7	10.4	10.0	8.3	7.6	7.1	2.0	1.9	1.8

Note: (1) Figures cover the San Francisco-Oakland-Hayward, CA Metropolitan Statistical Area—see Appendix B for areas included; (2) The percentage of the total housing inventory that is vacant; (3) The percentage of the housing inventory (excluding seasonal units) that is year-round vacant; (4) The percentage of rental inventory that is vacant for rent; (5) The percentage of homeowner inventory that is vacant for sale

Source: U.S. Census Bureau, Housing Vacancies and Homeownership Annual Statistics: 2015

INCOME

Income

Area	Per Capita ($)	Median Household ($)	Average Household ($)
City	65,783	140,616	178,684
MSA[1]	42,540	80,008	112,073
U.S.	28,555	53,482	74,596

Note: (1) Figures cover the San Francisco-Oakland-Hayward, CA Metropolitan Statistical Area—see Appendix B for areas included

Source: U.S. Census Bureau, 2010-2014 American Community Survey 5-Year Estimates

Household Income Distribution

Area	Percent of Households Earning							
	Under $15,000	$15,000 -24,999	$25,000 -34,999	$35,000 -49,999	$50,000 -74,999	$75,000 -99,000	$100,000 -149,999	$150,000 and up
City	3.6	2.8	2.9	5.1	11.4	8.7	19.9	45.7
MSA[1]	9.2	7.2	6.7	9.6	14.8	11.8	17.5	23.3
U.S.	12.5	10.7	10.2	13.5	17.8	12.2	13.0	10.0

Note: (1) Figures cover the San Francisco-Oakland-Hayward, CA Metropolitan Statistical Area—see Appendix B for areas included

Source: U.S. Census Bureau, 2010-2014 American Community Survey 5-Year Estimates

Poverty Rate

Area	All Ages	Under 18 Years Old	18 to 64 Years Old	65 Years and Over
City	4.2	4.4	3.6	5.9
MSA[1]	11.3	13.5	11.1	9.0
U.S.	15.6	21.9	14.6	9.4

Note: Figures are percentage of people whose income during the past 12 months was below the poverty level; (1) Figures cover the San Francisco-Oakland-Hayward, CA Metropolitan Statistical Area—see Appendix B for areas included

Source: U.S. Census Bureau, 2010-2014 American Community Survey 5-Year Estimates

EMPLOYMENT

Labor Force and Employment

Area	Civilian Labor Force			Workers Employed		
	Dec. 2014	Dec. 2015	% Chg.	Dec. 2014	Dec. 2015	% Chg.
City	20,466	20,625	0.7	19,609	19,885	1.4
MD[1]	1,361,975	1,371,421	0.6	1,292,276	1,310,864	1.4
U.S.	155,521,000	157,245,000	1.1	147,190,000	149,703,000	1.7

Note: Data is not seasonally adjusted and covers workers 16 years of age and older; (1) Figures cover the Oakland-Hayward-Berkeley, CA Metropolitan Division—see Appendix B for areas included
Source: Bureau of Labor Statistics, Local Area Unemployment Statistics

Unemployment Rate

Area	2015											
	Jan.	Feb.	Mar.	Apr.	May	Jun.	Jul.	Aug.	Sep.	Oct.	Nov.	Dec.
City	4.5	4.2	4.0	3.7	3.8	3.9	4.1	3.9	3.5	3.7	3.6	3.6
MD[1]	5.5	5.1	4.8	4.5	4.7	4.7	5.1	4.8	4.3	4.6	4.5	4.4
U.S.	6.1	5.8	5.6	5.1	5.3	5.5	5.6	5.2	4.9	4.8	4.8	4.8

Note: Data is not seasonally adjusted and covers workers 16 years of age and older; (1) Figures cover the Oakland-Hayward-Berkeley, CA Metropolitan Division—see Appendix B for areas included
Source: Bureau of Labor Statistics, Local Area Unemployment Statistics

Employment by Occupation

Occupation Classification	City (%)	MSA[1] (%)	U.S. (%)
Management, Business, Science, and Arts	63.3	46.8	36.4
Natural Resources, Construction, and Maintenance	2.4	6.2	9.0
Production, Transportation, and Material Moving	2.5	7.5	12.1
Sales and Office	23.6	22.4	24.4
Service	8.2	17.2	18.2

Note: Figures cover employed civilians 16 years of age and older; (1) Figures cover the San Francisco-Oakland-Hayward, CA Metropolitan Statistical Area—see Appendix B for areas included
Source: U.S. Census Bureau, 2010-2014 American Community Survey 5-Year Estimates

Employment by Industry

Sector	MD[1]		U.S.
	Number of Employees	Percent of Total	Percent of Total
Construction	65,100	5.8	4.5
Education and Health Services	181,300	16.2	15.7
Financial Activities	49,000	4.3	5.7
Government	170,200	15.2	15.5
Information	22,900	2.0	1.9
Leisure and Hospitality	107,500	9.6	10.4
Manufacturing	88,600	7.9	8.6
Mining and Logging	900	<0.1	0.5
Other Services	38,000	3.4	3.9
Professional and Business Services	183,200	16.4	13.9
Retail Trade	120,600	10.8	11.3
Transportation, Warehousing, and Utilities	40,700	3.6	3.9
Wholesale Trade	48,500	4.3	4.1

Note: Figures are non-farm employment as of December 2015. Figures are not seasonally adjusted and include workers 16 years of age and older; (1) Figures cover the Oakland-Hayward-Berkeley, CA Metropolitan Division—see Appendix B for areas included
Source: Bureau of Labor Statistics, Current Employment Statistics, Employment, Hours, and Earnings

Occupations with Greatest Projected Employment Growth: 2012 – 2022

Occupation[1]	2012 Employment	2022 Projected Employment	Numeric Employment Change	Percent Employment Change
Personal Care Aides	386,900	587,200	200,300	51.8
Combined Food Preparation and Serving Workers, Including Fast Food	286,000	362,400	76,400	26.7
Retail Salespersons	468,400	528,100	59,700	12.7
Laborers and Freight, Stock, and Material Movers, Hand	270,500	322,300	51,800	19.1
Waiters and Waitresses	246,100	290,300	44,200	18.0
Registered Nurses	254,500	297,400	42,900	16.9
General and Operations Managers	253,800	295,700	41,900	16.5
Secretaries and Administrative Assistants, Except Legal, Medical, and Executive	212,800	250,100	37,300	17.5
Cashiers	357,800	392,600	34,800	9.7
Cooks, Restaurant	116,900	150,600	33,700	28.8

Note: Projections cover California; (1) Sorted by numeric employment change
Source: www.projectionscentral.com, State Occupational Projections, 2012–2022 Long-Term Projections

Fastest Growing Occupations: 2012 – 2022

Occupation[1]	2012 Employment	2022 Projected Employment	Numeric Employment Change	Percent Employment Change
Economists	3,100	5,100	2,000	64.5
Helpers—Brickmasons, Blockmasons, Stonemasons, and Tile and Marble Setters	2,900	4,600	1,700	58.6
Brickmasons and Blockmasons	5,100	8,000	2,900	56.9
Insulation Workers, Floor, Ceiling, and Wall	1,600	2,500	900	56.3
Stonemasons	1,100	1,700	600	54.5
Insulation Workers, Mechanical	1,100	1,700	600	54.5
Personal Care Aides	386,900	587,200	200,300	51.8
Foresters	1,200	1,800	600	50.0
Terrazzo Workers and Finishers	1,100	1,600	500	45.5
Mechanical Door Repairers	1,100	1,600	500	45.5

Note: Projections cover California; (1) Sorted by percent employment change and excludes occupations with numeric employment change less than 100
Source: www.projectionscentral.com, State Occupational Projections, 2012–2022 Long-Term Projections

Average Wages

Occupation	$/Hr.	Occupation	$/Hr.
Accountants and Auditors	41.65	Maids and Housekeeping Cleaners	15.77
Automotive Mechanics	25.00	Maintenance and Repair Workers	21.70
Bookkeepers	22.97	Marketing Managers	79.92
Carpenters	30.64	Nuclear Medicine Technologists	55.63
Cashiers	12.48	Nurses, Licensed Practical	28.78
Clerks, General Office	18.66	Nurses, Registered	60.05
Clerks, Receptionists/Information	16.89	Nursing Assistants	16.42
Clerks, Shipping/Receiving	17.62	Packers and Packagers, Hand	11.99
Computer Programmers	45.15	Physical Therapists	47.88
Computer Systems Analysts	45.26	Postal Service Mail Carriers	26.11
Computer User Support Specialists	30.35	Real Estate Brokers	44.42
Cooks, Restaurant	11.82	Retail Salespersons	14.35
Dentists	94.70	Sales Reps., Exc. Tech./Scientific	33.64
Electrical Engineers	53.69	Sales Reps., Tech./Scientific	48.56
Electricians	37.97	Secretaries, Exc. Legal/Med./Exec.	20.82
Financial Managers	72.46	Security Guards	14.78
First-Line Supervisors/Managers, Sales	23.00	Surgeons	118.49
Food Preparation Workers	11.41	Teacher Assistants*	15.50
General and Operations Managers	66.83	Teachers, Elementary School*	35.79
Hairdressers/Cosmetologists	14.25	Teachers, Secondary School*	35.54
Internists	102.30	Telemarketers	15.39
Janitors and Cleaners	15.37	Truck Drivers, Heavy/Tractor-Trailer	22.83
Landscaping/Groundskeeping Workers	15.75	Truck Drivers, Light/Delivery Svcs.	19.08
Lawyers	75.13	Waiters and Waitresses	13.20

Note: Wage data covers the Oakland-Fremont-Hayward, CA Metropolitan Division—see Appendix B for areas included; (*) Hourly wages for elementary/secondary school teachers and teacher assistants were calculated by the editors from annual wage data based on a 40 hour work week; n/a not available.
Source: Bureau of Labor Statistics, Metro Area Occupational Employment and Wage Estimates, May 2015

TAXES

State Corporate Income Tax Rates

State	Tax Rate (%)	Income Brackets ($)	Num. of Brackets	Financial Institution Tax Rate (%)[a]	Federal Income Tax Ded.
California	8.84 (c)	Flat rate	1	10.84 (c)	No

Note: Tax rates as of January 1, 2016; (a) Rates listed are the corporate income tax rate applied to financial institutions or excise taxes based on income. Some states have other taxes based upon the value of deposits or shares; (c) Minimum tax is $800 in California, $100 in District of Columbia, $50 in North Dakota (banks), $500 in Rhode Island, $200 per location in South Dakota (banks), $100 in Utah, $250 in Vermont.
Source: Federation of Tax Administrators, "State Corporate Income Tax Rates, 2016"

State Individual Income Tax Rates

State	Tax Rate (%)	Income Brackets ($)	Num. of Brackets	Personal Exempt. ($)[1]		Fed. Inc. Tax Ded.
				Single	Dependents	
California (a)	1.0 - 12.3 (f)	7,850- 526,443 (b)	9	109 (c)	337 (c)	No

Note: Tax rates as of January 1, 2016; Local- and county-level taxes are not included; n/a not applicable; (1) Married joint filers generally receive double the single exemption; (a) 18 states have statutory provision for automatically adjusting to the rate of inflation the dollar values of the income tax brackets, standard deductions, and/or personal exemptions. Massachusetts, Michigan, and Nebraska index the personal exemptiononly. Oregon does not index the income brackets for $125,000 and over. Maine has suspended indexing for 2014 and 2015; (b) For joint returns, taxes are twice the tax on half the couple's income; (c) The personal exemption takes the form of a tax credit instead of a deduction; (f) California imposes an additional 1% tax on taxable income over $1 million, making the maximum rate 13.3% over $1 million.
Source: Federation of Tax Administrators, "State Individual Income Tax Rates, 2016"

Various State and Local Tax Rates

State	State and Local Sales and Use (%)	State Sales and Use (%)	Gasoline[1] (¢/gal.)	Cigarette[2] ($/pack)	Spirits[3] ($/gal.)	Wine[4] ($/gal.)	Beer[5] ($/gal.)
California	8.50	7.50 (b)	40.62	0.87	3.30 (f)	0.20 (l)	0.08

Note: All tax rates as of January 1, 2016; (1) The American Petroleum Institute has developed a methodology for determining the average tax rate on a gallon of fuel. Rates may include any of the following: excise taxes, environmental fees, storage tank fees, other fees or taxes, general sales tax, and local taxes. In states where gasoline is subject to the general sales tax, or where the fuel tax is based on the average sale price, the average rate determined by API is sensitive to changes in the price of gasoline. States that fully or partially apply general sales taxes to gasoline: CA, CO, GA, IL, IN, MI, NY; (2) The federal excise tax of $1.0066 per pack and local taxes are not included; (3) Rates are those applicable to off-premise sales of 40% alcohol by volume (a.b.v.) distilled spirits in 750ml containers. Local excise taxes are excluded; (4) Rates are those applicable to off-premise sales of 11% a.b.v. non-carbonated wine in 750ml containers; (5) Rates are those applicable to off-premise sales of 4.7% a.b.v. beer in 12 ounce containers; (b) Three states levy mandatory, statewide local add-on sales taxes at the state level: California (1%), Utah (1.25%), and Virginia (1%). We include these in their state sales tax rates; (f) Different rates are also applicable according to alcohol content, place of production, size of container, or place purchased (on- or off-premise or onboard airlines); (l) Different rates also applicable according to alcohol content, place of production, size of container, place purchased (on- or off-premise or on board airlines) or type of wine (carbonated, vermouth, etc.).
Source: Tax Foundation, 2016 Facts & Figures: How Does Your State Compare?

State Business Tax Climate Index Rankings

State	Overall Rank	Corporate Tax Rank	Individual Income Tax Rank	Sales Tax Rank	Unemployment Insurance Tax Rank	Property Tax Rank
California	48	35	50	40	13	13

Note: The index is a measure of how each state's tax laws affect economic performance. The lower the rank, the more favorable a state's tax system is for business. States without a given tax are given a ranking of 1. The scores/rankings for the District of Columbia do not affect other states. The 2016 index represents the tax climate as of July 1, 2015 (the beginning of Fiscal Year 2016).
Source: Tax Foundation, State Business Tax Climate Index 2016

TRANSPORTATION

Means of Transportation to Work

Area	Car/Truck/Van		Public Transportation			Bicycle	Walked	Other Means	Worked at Home
	Drove Alone	Car-pooled	Bus	Subway	Railroad				
City	76.4	6.7	0.4	4.6	0.9	0.3	1.0	0.9	8.8
MSA[1]	60.6	10.1	7.6	6.1	1.0	1.9	4.4	2.3	6.1
U.S.	76.4	9.6	2.6	1.8	0.6	0.6	2.8	1.3	4.4

Note: Figures are percentages and cover workers 16 years of age and older; (1) Figures cover the San Francisco-Oakland-Hayward, CA Metropolitan Statistical Area—see Appendix B for areas included
Source: U.S. Census Bureau, 2010-2014 American Community Survey 5-Year Estimates

Travel Time to Work

Area	Less Than 10 Minutes	10 to 19 Minutes	20 to 29 Minutes	30 to 44 Minutes	45 to 59 Minutes	60 to 89 Minutes	90 Minutes or More
City	11.9	25.2	17.4	18.2	11.4	13.5	2.4
MSA[1]	7.8	24.9	19.1	24.1	11.1	10.0	3.0
U.S.	13.3	29.6	21.0	20.2	7.7	5.7	2.6

Note: Figures are percentages and include workers 16 years old and over; (1) Figures cover the San Francisco-Oakland-Hayward, CA Metropolitan Statistical Area—see Appendix B for areas included
Source: U.S. Census Bureau, 2010-2014 American Community Survey 5-Year Estimates

Freeway Travel Time Index

Area	1985	1990	1995	2000	2005	2010	2014
Urban Area Rank[1,2]	2	2	2	2	2	2	2
Urban Area Index[1]	1.30	1.32	1.36	1.38	1.40	1.38	1.41
Average Index[3]	1.09	1.11	1.14	1.17	1.20	1.19	1.20

Note: Freeway Travel Time Index—the ratio of travel time in the peak period to the travel time at free-flow conditions. For example, a value of 1.30 indicates a 20-minute free-flow trip takes 26 minutes in the peak (20 minutes x 1.30 = 26 minutes); (1) Covers the San Francisco-Oakland CA urban area; (2) Rank is based on 101 urban areas (#1 = highest travel time index); (3) Average of 101 urban areas
Source: Texas Transportation Institute, 2015 Urban Mobility Scorecard, August 2015

Freeway Commuter Stress Index

Area	1985	1990	1995	2000	2005	2010	2014
Urban Area Rank[1,2]	2	2	2	2	2	2	2
Urban Area Index[1]	1.45	1.48	1.52	1.54	1.56	1.54	1.57
Average Index[3]	1.13	1.16	1.19	1.22	1.25	1.24	1.25

Note: The Freeway Commuter Stress Index is the same as the Freeway Travel Time Index (see table above) except that it includes only the travel in the peak directions during the peak periods; the TTI includes travel in all directions during the peak period. Thus, the CSI is more indicative of the work trip experienced by each commuter on a daily basis. (1) Covers the San Francisco-Oakland CA urban area; (2) Rank is based on 101 urban areas (#1 = highest stress index); (3) Average of 101 urban areas

Source: Texas Transportation Institute, 2015 Urban Mobility Scorecard, August 2015

Living Environment

COST OF LIVING

Cost of Living Index

Composite Index	Groceries	Housing	Utilities	Trans-portation	Health Care	Misc. Goods/ Services
147.2	128.5	228.0	106.6	124.5	114.4	110.5

Note: The Cost of Living Index measures regional differences in the cost of consumer goods and services, excluding taxes and non-consumer expenditures, for professional and managerial households in the top income quintile. It is based on more than 50,000 prices covering almost 60 different items for which prices are collected three times a year by chambers of commerce, economic development organizations or university applied economic centers in each participating urban area. The numbers shown should be read as a percentage above or below the national average of 100. For example, a value of 115.4 in the groceries column indicates that grocery prices are 15.4% higher than the national average. Small differences in the index numbers should not be interpreted as significant; Figures cover the Oakland CA urban area.
Source: The Council for Community and Economic Research, ACCRA Cost of Living Index, 2015

Grocery Prices

Area[1]	T-Bone Steak ($/pound)	Frying Chicken ($/pound)	Whole Milk ($/half gal.)	Eggs ($/dozen)	Orange Juice ($/64 oz.)	Coffee ($/11.5 oz.)
City[2]	11.54	2.28	2.75	3.66	4.75	5.98
Avg.	10.99	1.43	2.25	2.26	3.58	4.48
Min.	7.16	0.98	1.30	1.35	2.88	2.98
Max.	14.13	2.43	3.85	4.81	6.39	7.56

Note: (1) Values for the local area are compared with the average, minimum and maximum values for all 292 areas in the Cost of Living Index; (2) Figures cover the Oakland CA urban area; **T-Bone Steak** *(price per pound);* **Frying Chicken** *(price per pound, whole fryer);* **Whole Milk** *(half gallon carton);* **Eggs** *(price per dozen, Grade A, large);* **Orange Juice** *(64 oz. Tropicana or Florida Natural);* **Coffee** *(11.5 oz. can, vacuum-packed, Maxwell House, Hills Bros, or Folgers).*
Source: The Council for Community and Economic Research, ACCRA Cost of Living Index, 2015

Housing and Utility Costs

Area[1]	New Home Price ($)	Apartment Rent ($/month)	All Electric ($/month)	Part Electric ($/month)	Other Energy ($/month)	Telephone ($/month)
City[2]	747,967	1,912	-	129.66	75.31	24.33
Avg.	312,874	945	179.30	95.07	72.96	28.11
Min.	178,682	479	116.28	43.14	26.46	10.01
Max.	1,472,476	3,984	504.25	189.44	421.11	43.06

Note: (1) Values for the local area are compared with the average, minimum and maximum values for all 292 areas in the Cost of Living Index; (2) Figures cover the Oakland CA urban area; **New Home Price** *(2,400 sf living area, 8,000 sf lot, in urban area with full utilities);* **Apartment Rent** *(950 sf 2 bedroom/1.5 or 2 bath, unfurnished, excluding all utilities except water);* **All Electric** *(average monthly cost for an all-electric home);* **Part Electric** *(average monthly cost for a part-electric home);* **Other Energy** *(average monthly cost for natural gas, fuel oil, coal, wood, and any other forms of energy except electricity);* **Telephone** *(price includes basic monthly rate for a private residential line plus additional local usage charges incurred by a family of four).*
Source: The Council for Community and Economic Research, ACCRA Cost of Living Index, 2015

Health Care, Transportation, and Other Costs

Area[1]	Doctor ($/visit)	Dentist ($/visit)	Optometrist ($/visit)	Gasoline ($/gallon)	Beauty Salon ($/visit)	Men's Shirt ($)
City[2]	123.63	113.02	116.21	3.13	55.17	35.17
Avg.	105.15	89.02	99.78	2.38	35.30	28.10
Min.	66.87	56.09	48.53	1.95	18.91	13.38
Max.	182.34	150.36	228.33	4.09	67.91	63.80

Note: (1) Values for the local area are compared with the average, minimum and maximum values for all 292 areas in the Cost of Living Index; (2) Figures cover the Oakland CA urban area; **Doctor** *(general practitioners routine exam of an established patient);* **Dentist** *(adult teeth cleaning and periodic oral examination);* **Optometrist** *(full vision eye exam for established adult patient);* **Gasoline** *(one gallon regular unleaded, national brand, including all taxes, cash price at self-service pump if available);* **Beauty Salon** *(woman's shampoo, trim, and blow-dry);* **Men's Shirt** *(cotton/polyester dress shirt, pinpoint weave, long sleeves).*
Source: The Council for Community and Economic Research, ACCRA Cost of Living Index, 2015

HOUSING

House Price Index (HPI)

Area	National Ranking[2]	Quarterly Change (%)	One-Year Change (%)	Five-Year Change (%)
MD[1]	13	1.20	11.70	47.60
U.S.[3]	–	1.45	5.76	22.85

Note: The HPI is a weighted repeat sales index. It measures average price changes in repeat sales or refinancings on the same properties. This information is obtained by reviewing repeat mortgage transactions on single-family properties whose mortgages have been purchased or securitized by Fannie Mae or Freddie Mac in January 1975; (1) Oakland-Hayward-Berkeley Metropolitan Division—see Appendix B for areas included; (2) Rankings are based on annual percentage change for all metro areas containing at least 15,000 transactions over the last 10 years and ranges from 1 to 266; (3) figures based on a weighted average of Census Division estimates using a seasonally adjusted, purchase-only index; all figures are for the period ending December 31, 2015

Source: Federal Housing Finance Agency, House Price Index, February 25, 2016

Median Single-Family Home Prices

Area	2013	2014	2015[p]	Percent Change 2014 to 2015
MSA[1]	643.8	715.8	782.3	9.3
U.S. Average	197.4	208.9	223.9	7.2

Note: Figures are median sales prices of existing single-family homes in thousands of dollars; (p) preliminary; n/a not available; (1) San Francisco-Oakland-Hayward, CA Metropolitan Statistical Area—see Appendix B for areas included

Source: National Association of Realtors, Median Sales Price of Existing Single-Family Homes for Metropolitan Areas, 4th Quarter 2015

Qualifying Income Based on Median Sales Price of Existing Single-Family Homes

Area	With 5% Down ($)	With 10% Down ($)	With 20% Down ($)
MSA[1]	173,852	164,701	146,401
U.S. Average	49,535	46,928	41,714

Note: Figures are preliminary; Qualifying income is based on a mortgage rate of 4.1%. Monthly principal and interest payment is limited to 25% of income; n/a not available; (1) San Francisco-Oakland-Hayward, CA Metropolitan Statistical Area—see Appendix B for areas included

Source: National Association of Realtors, Qualifying Income Based on Median Sales Price of Existing Single-Family Homes for Metropolitan Areas, 4th Quarter 2015

Median Apartment Condo-Coop Home Prices

Area	2013	2014	2015[p]	Percent Change 2014 to 2015
MSA[1]	517.4	580.1	658.9	13.6
U.S. Average	194.9	204.3	210.7	3.1

Note: Figures are median sales prices of existing apartment condo-coop homes in thousands of dollars; (p) preliminary; n/a not available; (1) San Francisco-Oakland-Hayward, CA Metropolitan Statistical Area—see Appendix B for areas included

Source: National Association of Realtors, Median Sales Price of Existing Apartment Condo-Coop Homes for Metropolitan Areas, 4th Quarter 2015

Gross Monthly Rent

Area	Under $200	$200 -299	$300 -499	$500 -749	$750 -999	$1,000 -1,499	$1,500 and up	Median ($)
City	0.0	0.0	2.5	3.5	0.6	9.7	83.6	2,000+
MSA[1]	0.9	2.8	3.5	5.2	10.4	30.6	46.6	1,446
U.S.	1.5	3.2	7.4	21.0	24.1	26.9	15.9	920

Note: Figures are percentages except for Median; Gross rent is the contract rent plus the estimated average monthly cost of utilities (electricity, gas, and water and sewer) and fuels (oil, coal, kerosene, wood, etc.) if these are paid by the renter (or paid for the renter by someone else); (1) Figures cover the San Francisco-Oakland-Hayward, CA Metropolitan Statistical Area—see Appendix B for areas included

Source: U.S. Census Bureau, 2010-2014 American Community Survey 5-Year Estimates

Homeownership Rate

Area	2008 (%)	2009 (%)	2010 (%)	2011 (%)	2012 (%)	2013 (%)	2014 (%)	2015 (%)
MSA[1]	56.4	57.3	58.0	56.1	53.2	55.2	54.6	56.3
U.S.	67.8	67.4	66.9	66.1	65.4	65.1	64.5	63.7

Note: (1) Figures cover the San Francisco-Oakland-Hayward, CA Metropolitan Statistical Area—see Appendix B for areas included
Source: U.S. Census Bureau, Housing Vacancies and Homeownership Annual Statistics: 2015

Year Housing Structure Built

Area	2010 or Later	2000 -2009	1990 -1999	1980 -1989	1970 -1979	1960 -1969	1950 -1959	1940 -1949	Before 1940	Median Year
City	1.1	5.0	23.2	15.3	31.1	14.8	7.8	1.3	0.6	1978
MSA[1]	0.6	8.3	8.0	10.8	15.4	13.4	14.4	8.6	20.5	1965
U.S.	1.0	14.9	13.9	13.8	15.8	11.0	10.8	5.4	13.3	1976

Note: Figures are percentages except for Median Year; (1) Figures cover the San Francisco-Oakland-Hayward, CA Metropolitan Statistical Area—see Appendix B for areas included
Source: U.S. Census Bureau, 2010-2014 American Community Survey 5-Year Estimates

HEALTH

Health Risk Data

Category	MSA[1] (%)	U.S. (%)
Adults aged 18–64 who have any kind of health care coverage	86.3	79.6
Adults who reported being in good or excellent health	87.0	83.1
Adults who are current smokers	11.2	19.6
Adults who are heavy drinkers[2]	7.6	6.1
Adults who are binge drinkers[3]	18.9	16.9
Adults who are overweight (BMI 25.0 - 29.9)	35.6	35.8
Adults who are obese (BMI 30.0 - 99.8)	22.6	27.6
Adults who participated in any physical activities in the past month	83.8	77.1
Adults 50+ who have ever had a sigmoidoscopy or colonoscopy	72.4	67.3
Women aged 40+ who have had a mammogram within the past two years	86.3	74.0
Men aged 40+ who have had a PSA test within the past two years	41.2	45.2
Adults aged 65+ who have had flu shot within the past year	59.2	60.1
Adults who always wear a seatbelt	n/a	93.8

Note: Data as of 2012 unless otherwise noted; n/a not available; (1) Figures cover the Oakland-Fremont-Hayward, CA—see Appendix B for areas included; (2) Heavy drinkers are classified as males having more than two drinks per day or females having more than one drink per day; (3) Binge drinkers are classified as males having five or more drinks on one occasion or females having four or more drinks on one occasion
Source: Centers for Disease Control and Prevention, Behaviorial Risk Factor Surveillance System, SMART: Selected Metropolitan/Micropolitan Area Risk Trends, 2012 (Note: the CDC has discontinued this dataset but will be releasing a replacement in mid-2016)

Chronic Health Indicators

Category	MSA[1] (%)	U.S. (%)
Adults who have ever been told they had a heart attack	2.8	4.5
Adults who have ever been told they had a stroke	n/a	2.9
Adults who have been told they currently have asthma	10.9	8.9
Adults who have ever been told they have arthritis	21.9	25.7
Adults who have ever been told they have diabetes[2]	8.6	9.7
Adults who have ever been told they had skin cancer	4.1	5.7
Adults who have ever been told they had any other types of cancer	7.9	6.5
Adults who have ever been told they have COPD	2.9	6.2
Adults who have ever been told they have kidney disease	2.1	2.5
Adults who have ever been told they have a form of depression	11.8	18.0

Note: Data as of 2012 unless otherwise noted; n/a not available; (1) Figures cover the Oakland-Fremont-Hayward, CA—see Appendix B for areas included; (2) Figures do not include pregnancy-related, borderline, or pre-diabetes
Source: Centers for Disease Control and Prevention, Behaviorial Risk Factor Surveillance System, SMART: Selected Metropolitan/Micropolitan Area Risk Trends, 2012 (Note: the CDC has discontinued this dataset but will be releasing a replacement in mid-2016)

Mortality Rates for the Top 10 Causes of Death in the U.S.

ICD-10[a] Sub-Chapter	ICD-10[a] Code	Age-Adjusted Mortality Rate[1] per 100,000 population	
		County[2]	U.S.
Malignant neoplasms	C00-C97	145.6	163.6
Ischaemic heart diseases	I20-I25	67.2	102.2
Other forms of heart disease	I30-I51	37.1	50.1
Chronic lower respiratory diseases	J40-J47	32.4	41.4
Organic, including symptomatic, mental disorders	F01-F09	28.6	38.5
Cerebrovascular diseases	I60-I69	38.8	36.5
Other external causes of accidental injury	W00-X59	18.7	27.5
Other degenerative diseases of the nervous system	G30-G31	36.2	26.3
Diabetes mellitus	E10-E14	16.2	21.1
Hypertensive diseases	I10-I15	21.8	19.7

Note: (a) ICD-10 = International Classification of Diseases 10th Revision; (1) Mortality rates are a three year average covering 2012-2014; (2) Figures cover COUNTY NOT FOUND!!!!!!.
Source: Centers for Disease Control and Prevention, National Center for Health Statistics. Underlying Cause of Death 1999-2014 on CDC WONDER Online Database, released 2015.

Mortality Rates for Selected Causes of Death

ICD-10[a] Sub-Chapter	ICD-10[a] Code	Age-Adjusted Mortality Rate[1] per 100,000 population	
		County[2]	U.S.
Assault	X85-Y09	6.1	5.1
Diseases of the liver	K70-K76	10.3	13.5
Human immunodeficiency virus (HIV) disease	B20-B24	1.0	2.1
Influenza and pneumonia	J09-J18	9.8	15.2
Intentional self-harm	X60-X84	9.4	12.7
Malnutrition	E40-E46	0.8	0.9
Obesity and other hyperalimentation	E65-E68	1.6	1.9
Renal failure	N17-N19	5.7	13.0
Transport accidents	V01-V99	6.8	11.6
Viral hepatitis	B15-B19	2.9	2.1

Note: (a) ICD-10 = International Classification of Diseases 10th Revision; (1) Mortality rates are a three year average covering 2012-2014; (2) Figures cover COUNTY NOT FOUND!!!!!!; Data are Suppressed when the data meet the criteria for confidentiality constraints; Mortality rates are flagged as Unreliable when the rate would be calculated with a numerator of 20 or less.
Source: Centers for Disease Control and Prevention, National Center for Health Statistics. Underlying Cause of Death 1999-2014 on CDC WONDER Online Database, released 2015.

Health Insurance Coverage

Area	With Health Insurance	With Private Health Insurance	With Public Health Insurance	Without Health Insurance	Population Under Age 18 Without Health Insurance
City	97.4	92.7	18.2	2.6	0.9
MSA[1]	89.2	72.5	26.5	10.8	4.7
U.S.	85.8	65.8	31.1	14.2	7.1

Note: Figures are percentages that cover the civilian noninstitutionalized population; (1) Figures cover the San Francisco-Oakland-Hayward, CA Metropolitan Statistical Area—see Appendix B for areas included
Source: U.S. Census Bureau, 2010-2014 American Community Survey 5-Year Estimates

Number of Medical Professionals

Area	MDs[3]	DOs[3,4]	Dentists	Podiatrists	Chiropractors	Optometrists
County[1] (number)	3,084	113	900	49	330	190
County[1] (rate[2])	281.4	10.3	81.0	4.4	29.7	17.1
U.S. (rate[2])	272.5	20.9	64.7	5.8	25.9	15.2

Note: Data as of 2014 unless noted; (1) Data covers Contra Costa County; (2) Rate per 100,000 population; (3) Data as of 2013 and includes all active, non-federal physicians; (4) Doctor of Osteopathic Medicine
Source: U.S. Department of Health and Human Services, Health Resources and Services Administration, Bureau of Health Professions, Area Resource File (ARF) 2014-2015

Best Hospitals

According to *U.S. News,* the Oakland-Hayward-Berkeley, CA metro area is home to three of the best hospitals in the U.S.: **John Muir Medical Center** (1 specialty); **El Camino Hospital** (1 specialty); **John Muir Medical Center** (3 specialties). The hospitals listed were nationally ranked in at least one adult specialty. Only 137 hospitals nationwide were nationally ranked in one or more specialties. Fifteen hospitals in the U.S. made the Honor Roll with high scores in at least six specialties. *U.S. News Online, "America's Best Children's Hospitals 2015-16"*

EDUCATION

Public School District Statistics

District Name	Schls	Pupils	Pupil/ Teacher Ratio	Minority Pupils[1] (%)	Free Lunch Eligible[2] (%)	IEP[3] (%)
San Ramon Valley Unified	36	31,398	24.9	51.4	3.0	7.5

Note: Table includes school districts with 100 or more students; (1) Percentage of students that are not non-Hispanic white; (2) Percentage of students that are eligible for the free lunch program; (3) Percentage of students that have an Individualized Education Program.
Source: U.S. Department of Education, National Center for Education Statistics, Common Core of Data, Local Education Agency (School District) Universe Survey: School Year 2013-2014; U.S. Department of Education, National Center for Education Statistics, Common Core of Data, Public Elementary/Secondary School Universe Survey: School Year 2013-2014

Highest Level of Education

Area	Less than H.S.	H.S. Diploma	Some College, No Deg.	Associate Degree	Bachelor's Degree	Master's Degree	Prof. School Degree	Doctorate Degree
City	2.3	9.0	17.0	7.5	41.0	16.6	3.8	2.8
MSA[1]	12.1	17.0	19.0	6.9	27.1	11.8	3.6	2.5
U.S.	13.7	28.0	21.2	7.9	18.3	7.8	2.0	1.3

Note: Figures cover persons age 25 and over; (1) Figures cover the San Francisco-Oakland-Hayward, CA Metropolitan Statistical Area—see Appendix B for areas included
Source: U.S. Census Bureau, 2010-2014 American Community Survey 5-Year Estimates

Educational Attainment by Race

Area	High School Graduate or Higher (%)					Bachelor's Degree or Higher (%)				
	Total	White	Black	Asian	Hisp.[2]	Total	White	Black	Asian	Hisp.[2]
City	97.7	98.2	97.5	94.9	91.7	64.2	63.9	39.2	70.4	53.4
MSA[1]	87.9	91.3	89.5	85.3	68.2	44.9	49.6	23.9	50.5	18.4
U.S.	86.3	88.4	83.2	85.8	64.1	29.3	30.6	19.0	50.9	13.9

Note: Figures shown cover persons 25 years old and over; (1) Figures cover the San Francisco-Oakland-Hayward, CA Metropolitan Statistical Area—see Appendix B for areas included; (2) People of Hispanic origin can be of any race
Source: U.S. Census Bureau, 2010-2014 American Community Survey 5-Year Estimates

School Enrollment by Grade and Control

Area	Preschool (%)		Kindergarten (%)		Grades 1 - 4 (%)		Grades 5 - 8 (%)		Grades 9 - 12 (%)	
	Public	Private	Public	Private	Public	Private	Public	Private	Public	Private
City	21.5	78.5	80.5	19.5	83.8	16.2	83.7	16.3	92.6	7.4
MSA[1]	40.4	59.6	83.6	16.4	85.3	14.7	85.6	14.4	88.0	12.0
U.S.	57.4	42.6	87.8	12.2	89.8	10.2	89.9	10.1	90.6	9.4

Note: Figures shown cover persons 3 years old and over; (1) Figures cover the San Francisco-Oakland-Hayward, CA Metropolitan Statistical Area—see Appendix B for areas included
Source: U.S. Census Bureau, 2010-2014 American Community Survey 5-Year Estimates

Average Salaries of Public School Classroom Teachers

Area	2013-14		2014-15		Percent Change 2013-14 to 2014-15	Percent Change 2004-05 to 2014-15
	Dollars	Rank[1]	Dollars	Rank[1]		
California	71,396	4	72,535	4	1.59	25.9
U.S. Average	56,610	–	57,379	–	1.36	20.8

Note: (1) State rank ranges from 1 to 51 where 1 indicates highest salary.
Source: National Education Association, Rankings & Estimates: Rankings of the States 2014 and Estimates of School Statistics 2015, March 2015

Higher Education

Four-Year Colleges			Two-Year Colleges			Medical Schools[1]	Law Schools[2]	Voc/ Tech[3]
Public	Private Non-profit	Private For-profit	Public	Private Non-profit	Private For-profit			
0	0	0	0	0	0	0	0	1

Note: Figures cover institutions located within the city limits and include main campuses only; (1) includes schools accredited by the Liaison Committee on Medical Education and the American Osteopathic Association's Commission on Osteopathic College Accreditation; (2) includes ABA-accredited schools, schools with provisional ABA accreditation, and state accredited schools; (3) includes all schools with programs that are less than 2 years.

Source: National Center for Education Statistics, Integrated Postsecondary Education System (IPEDS), 2014-15; Association of American Medical Colleges, Member List, March 21, 2016; American Osteopathic Association, Member List, March 21, 2016; Law School Admission Council, Official Guide to ABA-Approved Law Schools Online, March 21, 2016; Wikipedia, List of Medical Schools in the United States, March 21, 2016; Wikipedia, List of Law Schools in the United States, March 21, 2016

According to *U.S. News & World Report,* the Oakland-Hayward-Berkeley, CA metro division is home to one of the best national universities in the U.S.: **University of California–Berkeley** (#20). The indicators used to capture academic quality fall into a number of categories: assessment by administrators at peer institutions; retention of students; faculty resources; student selectivity; financial resources; alumni giving; high school counselor ratings of colleges; and graduation rate. *U.S. News & World Report, "America's Best Colleges 2016"*

According to *U.S. News & World Report,* the Oakland-Hayward-Berkeley, CA metro division is home to one of the top 100 law schools in the U.S.: **University of California–Berkeley, School of Law** (#8 tie). The rankings are based on a weighted average of 12 measures of quality: peer assessment score; assessment score by lawyers/judges; median LSAT scores; median undergrad GPA; acceptance rate; employment rates for graduates; placement success; bar passage rate; faculty resources; expenditures per student; student/faculty ratio; and library resources. *U.S. News & World Report, "America's Best Graduate Schools, Law, 2017"*

According to *U.S. News & World Report,* the Oakland-Hayward-Berkeley, CA metro division is home to one of the top 75 business schools in the U.S.: **University of California–Berkeley, Haas School of Business** (#7). The rankings are based on a weighted average of the following nine measures: quality assessment; peer assessment; recruiter assessment; placement success; mean starting salary and bonus; student selectivity; mean GMAT and GRE scores; mean undergraduate GPA; and acceptance rate. *U.S. News & World Report, "America's Best Graduate Schools, Business, 2017"*

PRESIDENTIAL ELECTION

2012 Presidential Election Results

Area	Obama (%)	Romney (%)	Other (%)
Contra Costa County	65.8	31.9	2.3
U.S.	51.0	47.2	1.8

Note: Results may not add to 100% due to rounding
Source: Dave Leip's Atlas of U.S. Presidential Elections

EMPLOYERS

Major Employers

Company Name	Industry
All Hallows Preservation	Apartment building operators
AT&T Corp.	Telephone communication, except radio
AT&T Services	Telephone communication, except radio
California Pacific Medical Center	General medical & surgical hospitals
City & County of San Francisco	General medical & surgical hospitals
City & County of San Francisco	Public welfare administration: nonoperating, govt.
Edy's Grand Ice Cream	Ice cream & ice milk
Franklin Templeton Services	Investment advice
Lawrence Berkeley National Laboratory	Noncommercial research organizations
Lawrence Berkeley National Laboratory	Supply agency, government
Lawrence Livermore National Laboratory	Noncommercial research organizations
Menlo Worldwide Forwarding	Letter delivery, private air
Oracle America	Minicomputers
Oracle Systems Corporation	Prepackaged software
Pacific Gas and Electric Company	Electric & other services combined
PACPIZZA	Pizzeria, chain
San Francisco Community College District	Colleges & universities
University of California, Berkeley	University
Veterans Health Administration	Administration of veterans' affairs
Wells Fargo Bank	National commercial banks

Note: Companies shown are located within the San Francisco-Oakland-Hayward, CA Metropolitan Statistical Area.
Source: Hoovers.com; Wikipedia

PUBLIC SAFETY

Crime Rate

Area	All Crimes	Violent Crimes				Property Crimes		
		Murder	Rape[3]	Robbery	Aggrav. Assault	Burglary	Larceny -Theft	Motor Vehicle Theft
City	1,043.8	0.0	6.9	2.3	29.8	247.2	673.0	84.7
Metro[1]	3,824.5	5.5	24.3	239.2	246.8	618.0	1,982.1	708.7
U.S.	2,961.6	4.5	26.4	102.2	232.5	542.5	1,837.3	216.2

Note: Figures are crimes per 100,000 population; (1) Figures cover the Oakland-Hayward-Berkeley, CA Metropolitan Division—see Appendix B for areas included; (3) The city and U.S. figures shown were reported using the legacy Uniform Crime Reporting (UCR) definition of rape. The suburban and metro area figures shown are an aggregate total of the data submitted using both the revised and legacy UCR definitions.
Source: FBI Uniform Crime Reports, 2014

Hate Crimes

Area	Number of Quarters Reported	Number of Incidents per Bias Motivation						
		Race	Religion	Sexual Orientation	Ethnicity	Disability	Gender	Gender Identity
City	4	0	0	0	0	0	0	0
U.S.	4	2,568	1,014	1,017	648	84	33	98

Source: Federal Bureau of Investigation, Hate Crime Statistics 2014

Identity Theft Consumer Complaints

Area	Complaints	Complaints per 100,000 Population	Rank[2]
MSA[1]	7,968	173.4	33
U.S.	490,220	152.4	-

Note: (1) Figures cover the San Francisco-Oakland-Hayward, CA Metropolitan Statistical Area—see Appendix B for areas included; (2) Rank ranges from 1 to 379 where 1 indicates greatest number of identity theft complaints per 100,000 population
Source: Federal Trade Commission, Consumer Sentinel Network Data Book for January–December 2015

Fraud and Other Consumer Complaints

Area	Complaints	Complaints per 100,000 Population	Rank[2]
MSA[1]	18,411	400.8	99
U.S.	2,593,159	806.0	-

Note: (1) Figures cover the San Francisco-Oakland-Hayward, CA Metropolitan Statistical Area—see Appendix B for areas included; (2) Rank ranges from 1 to 379 where 1 indicates greatest number of identity theft complaints per 100,000 population
Source: Federal Trade Commission, Consumer Sentinel Network Data Book for January–December 2015

RECREATION

Culture

Dance[1]	Theatre[1]	Instrumental Music[1]	Vocal Music[1]	Series and Festivals	Museums and Art Galleries[2]	Zoos and Aquariums[3]
0	0	0	0	0	0	0

Note: (1) Professional perfoming groups; (2) Based on organizations with SIC code 8412; (3) AZA-accredited
Source: The Grey House Performing Arts Directory, 2015-16; Association of Zoos & Aquariums, AZA Member Zoos & Aquariums, March 25, 2016; www.AccuLeads.com, March 29, 2016

Professional Sports Teams

Team Name	League	Year Established
Golden State Warriors	National Basketball Association (NBA)	1962
Oakland Athletics	Major League Baseball (MLB)	1968
Oakland Raiders	National Football League (NFL)	1960
San Francisco 49ers	National Football League (NFL)	1946
San Francisco Giants	Major League Baseball (MLB)	1958

Note: Includes teams located in the San Francisco-Oakland-Hayward, CA Metropolitan Statistical Area.
Source: Wikipedia, Major Professional Sports Teams of the United States and Canada, March 24, 2016

CLIMATE

Average and Extreme Temperatures

Temperature	Jan	Feb	Mar	Apr	May	Jun	Jul	Aug	Sep	Oct	Nov	Dec	Yr.
Extreme High (°F)	72	79	86	92	100	101	101	102	106	101	85	75	106
Average High (°F)	56	60	62	66	68	71	71	72	74	71	64	57	66
Average Temp. (°F)	50	54	56	58	60	63	64	65	66	63	57	51	59
Average Low (°F)	44	47	49	51	52	55	56	57	57	55	51	46	52
Extreme Low (°F)	30	32	36	38	42	47	48	40	50	44	38	27	27

Note: Figures cover the years 1945-1993
Source: National Climatic Data Center, International Station Meteorological Climate Summary, 9/96

Average Precipitation/Snowfall/Humidity

Precip./Humidity	Jan	Feb	Mar	Apr	May	Jun	Jul	Aug	Sep	Oct	Nov	Dec	Yr.
Avg. Precip. (in.)	3.7	2.7	2.7	1.1	0.4	0.1	0	0	0.3	1.1	2.3	3.1	17.6
Avg. Snowfall (in.)	Tr	Tr	0	0	0	0	0	0	0	0	0	Tr	Tr
Avg. Rel. Hum. 7am (%)	84	83	81	78	77	79	83	85	84	82	81	83	82
Avg. Rel. Hum. 4pm (%)	68	65	62	59	60	60	62	63	60	60	64	69	63

Note: Figures cover the years 1945-1993; Tr = Trace amounts (<0.05 in. of rain; <0.5 in. of snow)
Source: National Climatic Data Center, International Station Meteorological Climate Summary, 9/96

Weather Conditions

Temperature			Daytime Sky			Precipitation		
10°F & below	32°F & below	90°F & above	Clear	Partly cloudy	Cloudy	0.01 inch or more precip.	0.1 inch or more snow/ice	Thunder-storms
0	< 1	3	99	168	98	59	0	6

Note: Figures are average number of days per year and cover the years 1945-1993
Source: National Climatic Data Center, International Station Meteorological Climate Summary, 9/96

HAZARDOUS WASTE

Superfund Sites

Danville has no sites on the EPA's Superfund Final National Priorities List. There are a total of 1,323 Superfund sites on the list in the U.S. *U.S. Environmental Protection Agency, Final National Priorities List, March 18, 2016*

AIR & WATER QUALITY

Air Quality Trends: Ozone

	1990	1995	2000	2005	2010	2011	2012	2013	2014
MSA[1]	0.058	0.074	0.057	0.055	0.061	0.060	0.057	0.056	0.065

Note: (1) Data covers the San Francisco-Oakland-Hayward, CA Metropolitan Statistical Area—see Appendix B for areas included. The values shown are the composite ozone concentration averages among trend sites based on the highest fourth daily maximum 8-hour concentration in parts per million. These trends are based on sites having an adequate record of monitoring data during the trend period. Data from exceptional events are included.

Source: U.S. Environmental Protection Agency, Air Quality Monitoring Information, "Air Quality Trends by City, 1990-2014"

Air Quality Index

Area	Percent of Days when Air Quality was...[2]					AQI Statistics[2]	
	Good	Moderate	Unhealthy for Sensitive Groups	Unhealthy	Very Unhealthy	Maximum	Median
MSA[1]	57.3	39.7	3.0	0.0	0.0	124	47

Note: (1) Data covers the San Francisco-Oakland-Hayward, CA Metropolitan Statistical Area—see Appendix B for areas included; (2) Based on 365 days with AQI data in 2015. Air Quality Index (AQI) is an index for reporting daily air quality. EPA calculates the AQI for five major air pollutants regulated by the Clean Air Act: ground-level ozone, particle pollution (aka particulate matter), carbon monoxide, sulfur dioxide, and nitrogen dioxide. The AQI runs from 0 to 500. The higher the AQI value, the greater the level of air pollution and the greater the health concern. There are six AQI categories: "Good" AQI is between 0 and 50. Air quality is considered satisfactory; "Moderate" AQI is between 51 and 100. Air quality is acceptable; "Unhealthy for Sensitive Groups" When AQI values are between 101 and 150, members of sensitive groups may experience health effects; "Unhealthy" When AQI values are between 151 and 200 everyone may begin to experience health effects; "Very Unhealthy" AQI values between 201 and 300 trigger a health alert; "Hazardous" AQI values over 300 trigger warnings of emergency conditions (not shown).

Source: U.S. Environmental Protection Agency, Air Quality Index Report, 2015

Air Quality Index Pollutants

Area	Percent of Days when AQI Pollutant was...[2]					
	Carbon Monoxide	Nitrogen Dioxide	Ozone	Sulfur Dioxide	Particulate Matter 2.5	Particulate Matter 10
MSA[1]	0.0	6.3	33.4	0.0	60.3	0.0

Note: (1) Data covers the San Francisco-Oakland-Hayward, CA Metropolitan Statistical Area—see Appendix B for areas included; (2) Based on 365 days with AQI data in 2015. The Air Quality Index (AQI) is an index for reporting daily air quality. EPA calculates the AQI for five major air pollutants regulated by the Clean Air Act: ground-level ozone, particle pollution (also known as particulate matter), carbon monoxide, sulfur dioxide, and nitrogen dioxide. The AQI runs from 0 to 500. The higher the AQI value, the greater the level of air pollution and the greater the health concern.

Source: U.S. Environmental Protection Agency, Air Quality Index Report, 2015

Maximum Air Pollutant Concentrations: Particulate Matter, Ozone, CO and Lead

	Particulate Matter 10 (ug/m^3)	Particulate Matter 2.5 Wtd AM (ug/m^3)	Particulate Matter 2.5 24-Hr (ug/m^3)	Ozone (ppm)	Carbon Monoxide (ppm)	Lead (ug/m^3)
MSA[1] Level	37	10.8	26	0.076	3	n/a
NAAQS[2]	150	15	35	0.075	9	0.15
Met NAAQS[2]	Yes	Yes	Yes	No	Yes	n/a

Note: (1) Data covers the San Francisco-Oakland-Hayward, CA Metropolitan Statistical Area—see Appendix B for areas included; Data from exceptional events are included; (2) National Ambient Air Quality Standards; ppm = parts per million; ug/m³ = micrograms per cubic meter; n/a not available.
Concentrations: Particulate Matter 10 (coarse particulate)—highest second maximum 24-hour concentration; Particulate Matter 2.5 Wtd AM (fine particulate)—highest weighted annual mean concentration; Particulate Matter 2.5 24-Hour (fine particulate)—highest 98th percentile 24-hour concentration; Ozone—highest fourth daily maximum 8-hour concentration; Carbon Monoxide—highest second maximum non-overlapping 8-hour concentration; Lead—maximum running 3-month average
Source: U.S. Environmental Protection Agency, Air Quality Monitoring Information, "Air Quality Statistics by City, 2014"

Maximum Air Pollutant Concentrations: Nitrogen Dioxide and Sulfur Dioxide

	Nitrogen Dioxide AM (ppb)	Nitrogen Dioxide 1-Hr (ppb)	Sulfur Dioxide AM (ppb)	Sulfur Dioxide 1-Hr (ppb)	Sulfur Dioxide 24-Hr (ppb)
MSA[1] Level	17	58	n/a	16	n/a
NAAQS[2]	53	100	30	75	140
Met NAAQS[2]	Yes	Yes	n/a	Yes	n/a

Note: (1) Data covers the San Francisco-Oakland-Hayward, CA Metropolitan Statistical Area—see Appendix B for areas included; Data from exceptional events are included; (2) National Ambient Air Quality Standards; ppm = parts per million; ug/m³ = micrograms per cubic meter; n/a not available.
Concentrations: Nitrogen Dioxide AM—highest arithmetic mean concentration; Nitrogen Dioxide 1-Hr—highest 98th percentile 1-hour daily maximum concentration; Sulfur Dioxide AM—highest annual mean concentration; Sulfur Dioxide 1-Hr—highest 99th percentile 1-hour daily maximum concentration; Sulfur Dioxide 24-Hr—highest second maximum 24-hour concentration
Source: U.S. Environmental Protection Agency, Air Quality Monitoring Information, "Air Quality Statistics by City, 2014"

Drinking Water

Water System Name	Pop. Served	Primary Water Source Type	Violations[1] Health Based	Violations[1] Monitoring/ Reporting
East Bay MUD	1,379,000	Surface	0	0

Note: (1) Based on violation data from January 1, 2015 to December 31, 2015 (includes unresolved violations from earlier years)
Source: U.S. Environmental Protection Agency, Office of Ground Water and Drinking Water, Safe Drinking Water Information System (based on data extracted April 29, 2016)

Folsom, California

Background

Folsom is located in the Sierra-Nevada foothills, in Sacramento County, a little more than 20 miles northeast of Sacramento. Made famous by Johnny Cash's Folsom Prison Blues, the city has much more to offer than prison lore.

Folsom and its surrounding areas were part of the California Gold Rush, as gold was found in a nearby spot on the American River. Joseph Folsom, a US Army Captain, purchased the surrounding lands and his new town, Granite City, was established. Following Folsom's death in 1855, the town was renamed in his honor.

Less than a year later, every plot in the city had been sold, the railway station was completed and Folsom started to blossom. The city is proud of its railway heritage, as the first train on the first railroad in the West stopped at Folsom station in February 1856.

Construction began for Folsom Prison in 1878 and it housed its first prisoners in 1880. It was one of the first maximum security prisons and is the second oldest prison in the state, second to San Quentin. Folsom Prison was also the first prison in the country to have electricity.

The original owners of the land on which the prison stands, the Livermore family, donated the land to the state in exchange for prison labor. Using this labor force, the Livermore family built Folsom Powerhouse. Completed in 1895, the Powerhouse had the first long-distance run of electricity in the country, with 22 miles of cable running to Sacramento. In operation until 1952, the Folsom Powerhouse is now a National Historic Landmark.

Folsom Dam, a concrete structure 340 feet high and 1,400 feet long, was completed in 1955. Prior to this structure, the Livermore family had built a smaller dam a short distance away, as part of the Powerhouse. Constructed where the north and south forks of the American River connect, the Dam provides flood control, hydroelectricity, drinking water and much-needed water for irrigation.

The Dam also created Folsom Lake, now one of California's most popular. Part of the California State Park System, the Folsom Lake State Recreation Area encompasses 18,000 acres perfect for boating, fishing, swimming, hiking and camping.

The city's General Plan calls for five acres of park land for every 1,000 residents. In addition to easy access to Folsom Lake, the city has over 40 parks, with over 400 acres of park land, over 30 miles of recreational trails and numerous athletic fields, tennis courts and swimming pools.

With an easy commute to Sacramento, Folsom is enjoying both growth and popularity. The city is attracting more young families and is responding to their needs with two new shopping centers in planning stages. Folsom is also home to one of the largest antique districts in the west, with over 40 galleries and studios.

Folsom is part of the Folsom-Cordova Unified School District. Folsom residents have access to ten elementary schools, two middle schools and two high schools. In addition, the local Folsom Lake College has recently expanded.

The climate in Folsom is characterized by hot, dry and sunny summers, while winters are usually rainy, cool and foggy.

Rankings

Business/Finance Rankings

- The personal finance site NerdWallet analyzed 183 American metropolitan areas with populations over 250,000 and more than 15,000 businesses to rank where entrepreneurs find the most success. Criteria included area economy, annual income, housing cost, unemployment rate, and the success rate of area businesses. Sacramento* ranked #157. *www.nerdwallet.com, "Best Places to Start a Business," April 27, 2015*
- Based on metro area social media reviews, the employment opinion group Glassdoor surveyed 50 of the largest U.S. metro areas and equally weighed cost of living, hiring opportunity, and job satisfaction to compose a list of "25 Best Cities for Jobs." The Sacramento* metro area was ranked #14 in overall job satisfaction. *www.glassdoor.com, "Best Cities for Jobs," May 19, 2015*
- In a survey of economic confidence in the nation's 50 largest metropolitan areas conducted January–December 2014, the Sacramento* metro area placed #22, according to Gallup's 2014 Economic Confidence Index. *Gallup, "San Jose and San Francisco Lead in Economic Confidence," March 19, 2015*
- The Brookings Institution ranked the 100 largest metro areas in the U.S. based on income inequality. Sacramento* was ranked #32 (#1 = greatest ineqality). Criteria: the "95/20 ratio," a figure representing the income at which a household earns more than 95 percent of all other households, divided by the income at which a household earns more than only 20 percent of all other households. *Brookings Institution, "Income Inequality, 100 Largest U.S. Metro Areas, 2007-2014," January 14, 2016*
- The finance site *24/7 Wall St.* identified the metropolitan areas that have the smallest and largest pay disparities between men and women, comparing the median earnings for the past 12 months of both men and women working full-time in the country's 100 largest metropolitan statistical areas. Of the ten best-paying metros for women, the Sacramento* metro area ranked #3. *24/7 Wall St., "The Best (and Worst) Paying Cities for Women," March 6, 2015*
- The Sacramento* metro area appeared on the Milken Institute "2015 Best Performing Cities" list. Rank: #84 out of 200 large metro areas. Criteria: job growth; wage and salary growth; high-tech output growth. *Milken Institute, "Best-Performing Cities 2015," December 2015*
- *Forbes* ranked the 200 most populous metro areas to determine the nation's "Best Places for Business and Careers." The Sacramento* metro area was ranked #107. Criteria: costs (business and living); job growth (past and projected); income growth; educational attainment (college and high school); projected economic growth; cultural and recreational opportunities; net migration patterns; number of highly ranked colleges. *Forbes, "The Best Places for Business and Careers 2015," July 29, 2015*

Education Rankings

- Personal finance website *WalletHub* analyzed the 150 largest U.S. metropolitan statistical areas to determine where the most educated Americans are choosing to settle. Criteria: education quality and attainment gap; education levels; percentage of workers with degrees; public school rankings; quality and size of each metro area's universities. Sacramento* was ranked #41 (#1 = most educated city). *www.WalletHub.com, "2015's Most and Least Educated Cities*

Environmental Rankings

- The Sacramento* metro area came in at #121 for the relative comfort of its climate on Sperling's list of "chill cities," as measured by the Sperling Heat Index. All 361 metro areas are included. Criteria included daytime high temperatures, nighttime low temperatures, dew point, and relative humidity at the high temperatures. *www.bertsperling.com, "Sperling's Chill Cities," July 18, 2013*

- Sperling's BestPlaces assessed 379 metropolitan areas of the United States for the likelihood of dangerously extreme weather events or earthquakes. In general the Southeast and South-Central regions have the highest risk of weather extremes and earthquakes, while the Pacific Northwest enjoys the lowest risk. Of the least risky metropolitan areas, the Sacramento* metro area was ranked #47. *www.bestplaces.net, "Safest Places from Natural Disasters," April 2011*

- Sacramento* was identified as one of America's dirtiest metro areas by *Forbes*. The area ranked #12 out of 20. Criteria: air quality; water quality; toxic releases; superfund sites. *Forbes, "America's 20 Dirtiest Cities," December 10, 2012*

- The U.S. Environmental Protection Agency (EPA) released a list of U.S. metropolitan areas with the most ENERGY STAR certified buildings in 2015. The Sacramento* metro area was ranked #19 out of 25. *U.S. Environmental Protection Agency, "Top Cities With the Most ENERGY STAR Certified Buildings in 2016," March 30, 2016*

- The Sacramento* metro area was identified as one of nine cities running out of water by *24/7 Wall St.* The area ranked #8. Based on data provided by the U.S. Drought Monitor, a joint program produced by academic and government organizations, *24/7 Wall St.* identified large U.S. urban areas that have been under persistent, serious drought for months. *24/7 Wall St., "Nine Cities Running Out of Water," June 16, 2015*

- Sacramento* was highlighted as one of the 25 most ozone-polluted metro areas in the U.S. during 2011 through 2013. The area ranked #5. *American Lung Association, State of the Air 2015*

- Sacramento* was highlighted as one of the 25 metro areas most polluted by short-term particle pollution (24-hour PM 2.5) in the U.S. during 2011 through 2013. The area ranked #14. *American Lung Association, State of the Air 2015*

Health/Fitness Rankings

- For each of the 50 most populous metro areas in the United States, the American College of Sports Medicine's American Fitness Index evaluated infrastructure, community assets, and policies that encourage healthy and fit lifestyles, including preventive health behaviors, levels of chronic disease conditions, health care access, and community resources and policies that support physical activity. The Sacramento* metro area ranked #5 for "community fitness." *www.americanfitnessindex.org, "ACSM American Fitness Index Health and Community Fitness Status of the 50 Largest Metropolitan Areas," May 2015*

- The Sacramento* metro area was identified as one of the worst cities for bed bugs in America by pest control company Orkin. The area ranked #45 out of 50 based on the number of bed bug treatments Orkin performed from January to December 2015. *Orkin, "Chicago Tops Bed Bug Cities List for Fourth Year in a Row," January 13, 2016*

- Sacramento* was identified as a "2016 Spring Allergy Capital." The area ranked #89 out of 100. Three groups of factors were used to identify the most severe cities for people with allergies during the spring season: annual pollen levels; medicine utilization; access to board-certified allergists. *Asthma and Allergy Foundation of America, "Spring Allergy Capitals 2016"*

- Sacramento* was identified as a "2015 Asthma Capital." The area ranked #73 out of the nation's 100 largest metropolitan areas. Criteria: estimated prevalence; self-reported prevalence; crude death rate for asthma; annual pollen score; annual air quality; public smoking laws; number of board-certified asthma specialists; school inhaler access laws; rescue medication use; controller medication use; ER visits for asthma; uninsured rate; poverty rate. *Asthma and Allergy Foundation of America, "Asthma Capitals 2015"*

- The Sacramento* metro area ranked #87 out of 190 in The Gallup-Healthways Well-Being Index. Criteria: purpose; social well being; financial health; community and physical health. Results are based on telephone interviews with adults, aged 18 and older, living in metropolitan areas in the 50 U.S. states and the District of Columbia. *Gallup-Healthways, "State of American Well-Being," February 23, 2016*

Real Estate Rankings

- Based on the home-price forecasts compiled by the real-estate valuation firm CoreLogic Case-Shiller, CNNMoney reported that in 2016, the Sacramento* metro area is expected to be one of the hottest housing markets in the U.S. Criteria: residential real estate prices. *money.cnn.com, "The 10 Hottest Housing Markets for 2016," December 3, 2015*

- The Sacramento* metro area appeared on Realtor.com's list of the hottest housing markets to watch in 2016. The area ranked #4. Criteria: strong housing growth; affordable prices; and fast-paced sales. *Realtor.com®, "Top 10 Hot Real Estate Markets to Watch in 2016," December 2, 2015*

- The Sacramento* metro area was identified as #10 among the ten housing markets with the highest percentage of distressed property sales, based on the findings of the housing data website RealtyTrac. Criteria: short sales; income and poverty figures; and unemployment data. *247wallst.com, "Cities Selling the Most Distressed Homes," January 23, 2014*

- The Sacramento* metro area was identified as one of the nations's 20 hottest housing markets in 2016. Criteria: listing views as an indicator of demand and median days on the market as an indicator of supply. The area ranked #11. *Realtor.com, "The 20 Hottest U.S. Real Estate Markets in February 2016," February 25, 2016*

- The Sacramento* metro area was identified as one of the 20 least affordable housing markets in the U.S. in 2015. The area ranked #20 out of 179 markets. Criteria: qualification for a mortgage loan on a typical home. *National Association of Realtors®, Affordability Index of Existing Single-Family Homes for Metropolitan Areas, 2015*

- Sacramento* was ranked #201 out of 225 metro areas in terms of housing affordability in 2015 by the National Association of Home Builders (#1 = most affordable). Criteria: the share of homes sold in that area affordable to a family earning the local median income, based on standard mortgage underwriting criteria. *National Association of Home Builders®, NAHB-Wells Fargo Housing Opportunity Index, 4th Quarter 2015*

Safety Rankings

- The National Insurance Crime Bureau ranked 380 metro areas in the U.S. in terms of per capita rates of vehicle theft. The Sacramento* metro area ranked #29 (#1 = highest rate). Criteria: number of vehicle theft offenses per 100,000 inhabitants in 2014. *National Insurance Crime Bureau, "Hot Spots 2014," June 24, 2015*

Seniors/Retirement Rankings

- From its Best Cities for Successful Aging indexes, the Milken Institute generated rankings for metropolitan areas, weighing data in eight categories—health care, wellness, living arrangements, transportation, financial characteristics, education and employment opportunities, community engagement, and overall livability. The Sacramento* metro area was ranked #87 overall in the large metro area category. *Milken Institute, "Best Cities for Successful Aging, 2014"*

Women/Minorities Rankings

- *24/7 Wall St.* compared median earnings over a 12-month period for men and women who worked full-time, year-round, and employment composition by sector to identify the best-paying cities for women. Of the largest 100 U.S. metropolitan areas, Sacramento* was ranked #3 in pay disparity. *24/7 Wall St., "The Best (and Worst) Paying Cities for Women," March 6, 2015*

Miscellaneous Rankings

- Mars Chocolate North America, the makers of COMBOS®, in partnership with Sperling's BestPlaces, ranked 50 major metro areas in terms of their "manliness." The Sacramento* metro area ranked #44. Criteria: number of professional sports teams; number of nearby NASCAR tracks and racing events; manly lifestyle; concentration of manly retail stores; manly occupations per capita; salty snack sales; "Board of Manliness" rankings. *Mars Chocolate North America, "America's Manliest Cities 2012"*

- The National Alliance to End Homelessness ranked the 100 most populous metro areas with the highest rate of homelessness. The Sacramento* metro area ranked #41. Criteria: number of homeless people per 10,000 population in 2011. *National Alliance to End Homelessness, The State of Homelessness in America 2012*

Folsom is located within the Sacramento—Roseville—Arden-Arcade, CA Metropolitan Statistical Area.

Business Environment

CITY FINANCES

City Government Finances

Component	2012 ($000)	2012 ($ per capita)
Total Revenues	119,577	1,656
Total Expenditures	121,988	1,689
Debt Outstanding	237,543	3,289
Cash and Securities[1]	207,532	2,874

Note: (1) Cash and security holdings of a government at the close of its fiscal year, including those of its dependent agencies, utilities, and liquor stores.
Source: U.S Census Bureau, State & Local Government Finances 2012

City Government Revenue by Source

Source	2012 ($000)	2012 ($ per capita)
General Revenue		
From Federal Government	862	11
From State Government	3,860	53
From Local Governments	0	0
Taxes		
Property	35,329	489
Sales and Gross Receipts	18,510	256
Personal Income	0	0
Corporate Income	0	0
Motor Vehicle License	0	0
Other Taxes	7,691	106
Current Charges	35,447	490
Liquor Store	0	0
Utility	13,387	185
Employee Retirement	0	0

Source: U.S Census Bureau, State & Local Government Finances 2012

City Government Expenditures by Function

Function	2012 ($000)	2012 ($ per capita)	2012 (%)
General Direct Expenditures			
Air Transportation	0	0	0.0
Corrections	0	0	0.0
Education	0	0	0.0
Employment Security Administration	0	0	0.0
Financial Administration	2,053	28	1.6
Fire Protection	17,951	248	14.7
General Public Buildings	1,095	15	0.8
Governmental Administration, Other	12,757	176	10.4
Health	682	9	0.5
Highways	7,929	109	6.5
Hospitals	0	0	0.0
Housing and Community Development	8,232	114	6.7
Interest on General Debt	7,079	98	5.8
Judicial and Legal	1,307	18	1.0
Libraries	1,591	22	1.3
Parking	0	0	0.0
Parks and Recreation	11,108	153	9.1
Police Protection	19,271	266	15.7
Public Welfare	0	0	0.0
Sewerage	3,223	44	2.6
Solid Waste Management	7,507	103	6.1
Veterans' Services	0	0	0.0
Liquor Store	0	0	0.0
Utility	15,077	208	12.3
Employee Retirement	0	0	0.0

Source: U.S Census Bureau, State & Local Government Finances 2012

DEMOGRAPHICS

Population Growth

Area	1990 Census	2000 Census	2010 Census	2014* Estimate	Population Growth (%) 1990-2014	Population Growth (%) 2010-2014
City	29,701	51,884	72,203	73,334	146.9	1.6
MSA[1]	1,481,126	1,796,857	2,149,127	2,197,422	48.4	2.2
U.S.	248,709,873	281,421,906	308,745,538	314,107,084	26.3	1.7

Note: (1) Figures cover the Sacramento—Roseville—Arden-Arcade, CA Metropolitan Statistical Area—see Appendix B for areas included; (*) 2010-2014 5-year estimated population
Source: U.S. Census Bureau, 1990 Census, Census 2000, Census 2010, 2010-2014 American Community Survey 5-Year Estimates

Household Size

Area	Persons in Household (%) One	Two	Three	Four	Five	Six	Seven or More	Average Household Size
City	24.6	30.6	18.7	18.2	5.7	1.6	0.3	2.63
MSA[1]	25.8	32.7	15.7	14.1	6.7	2.7	2.0	2.72
U.S.	27.5	33.5	15.8	13.1	6.0	2.3	1.4	2.64

Note: (1) Figures cover the Sacramento—Roseville—Arden-Arcade, CA Metropolitan Statistical Area—see Appendix B for areas included
Source: U.S. Census Bureau, 2010-2014 American Community Survey 5-Year Estimates

Race

Area	White Alone[2] (%)	Black Alone[2] (%)	Asian Alone[2] (%)	AIAN[3] Alone[2] (%)	NHOPI[4] Alone[2] (%)	Other Race Alone[2] (%)	Two or More Races (%)
City	70.4	5.8	14.1	0.5	0.6	4.1	4.4
MSA[1]	66.6	7.2	12.4	0.8	0.8	6.4	5.9
U.S.	73.8	12.6	5.0	0.8	0.2	4.7	2.9

Note: (1) Figures cover the Sacramento—Roseville—Arden-Arcade, CA Metropolitan Statistical Area—see Appendix B for areas included; (2) Alone is defined as not being in combination with one or more other races; (3) American Indian and Alaska Native; (4) Native Hawaiian and Other Pacific Islander
Source: U.S. Census Bureau, 2010-2014 American Community Survey 5-Year Estimates

Hispanic or Latino Origin

Area	Total (%)	Mexican (%)	Puerto Rican (%)	Cuban (%)	Other (%)
City	11.8	8.9	0.4	0.1	2.4
MSA[1]	20.6	17.0	0.7	0.1	2.8
U.S.	16.9	10.8	1.6	0.6	3.8

Note: Persons of Hispanic or Latino origin can be of any race; (1) Figures cover the Sacramento—Roseville—Arden-Arcade, CA Metropolitan Statistical Area—see Appendix B for areas included
Source: U.S. Census Bureau, 2010-2014 American Community Survey 5-Year Estimates

Ancestry

Area	German	Irish	English	American	Italian	Polish	French[2]	Scottish	Dutch
City	15.9	11.1	9.6	4.4	7.3	2.2	2.8	2.1	1.3
MSA[1]	13.0	9.6	8.7	3.5	5.4	1.4	2.6	2.0	1.3
U.S.	14.9	10.8	8.0	7.1	5.5	3.0	2.7	1.7	1.4

Note: Figures are the percentage of the total population reporting a particular ancestry. The nine most commonly reported ancestries in the U.S. are shown. Figures include multiple ancestries (e.g. if a person reported being Irish and Italian, they were included in both columns); (1) Figures cover the Sacramento—Roseville—Arden-Arcade, CA Metropolitan Statistical Area—see Appendix B for areas included; (2) Excludes Basque
Source: U.S. Census Bureau, 2010-2014 American Community Survey 5-Year Estimates

Foreign-Born Population

Area	Percent of Population Born in								
	Any Foreign Country	Asia	Mexico	Europe	Carribean	Central America[2]	South America	Africa	Canada
City	15.3	10.3	1.0	2.0	0.1	0.5	0.2	0.2	0.7
MSA[1]	17.7	7.9	4.8	2.7	0.1	0.6	0.3	0.4	0.3
U.S.	13.1	3.8	3.7	1.5	1.2	1.0	0.9	0.6	0.3

Note: (1) Figures cover the Sacramento—Roseville—Arden-Arcade, CA Metropolitan Statistical Area—see Appendix B for areas included; (2) Excludes Mexico.
Source: U.S. Census Bureau, 2010-2014 American Community Survey 5-Year Estimates

Marital Status

Area	Never Married	Now Married[2]	Separated	Widowed	Divorced
City	29.1	53.8	1.6	4.2	11.3
MSA[1]	33.1	47.7	2.3	5.4	11.5
U.S.	32.5	48.4	2.2	5.9	10.9

Note: Figures are percentages and cover the population 15 years of age and older; (1) Figures cover the Sacramento—Roseville—Arden-Arcade, CA Metropolitan Statistical Area—see Appendix B for areas included; (2) Excludes separated
Source: U.S. Census Bureau, 2010-2014 American Community Survey 5-Year Estimates

Disability Status

Area	All Ages	Under 18 Years Old	18 to 64 Years Old	65 Years and Over
City	7.5	2.4	4.7	36.8
MSA[1]	12.2	4.2	10.2	37.3
U.S.	12.3	4.1	10.2	36.3

Note: Figures show percent of the civilian noninstitutionalized population that reported having a disability. Disability status is determined from from six types of difficulty: vision, hearing, cognitive, ambulatory, self-care, and independent living. For children under 5 years old, hearing and vision difficulty are used to determine disability status. For children between the ages of 5 and 14, disability status is determined from hearing, vision, cognitive, ambulatory, and self-care difficulties. For people aged 15 years and older, they are considered to have a disability if they have difficulty with any one of the six difficulty types; (1) Figures cover the Sacramento—Roseville—Arden-Arcade, CA Metropolitan Statistical Area—see Appendix B for areas included.
Source: U.S. Census Bureau, 2010-2014 American Community Survey 5-Year Estimates

Age

Area	Percent of Population									Median Age
	Under Age 5	Age 5–19	Age 20–34	Age 35–44	Age 45–54	Age 55–64	Age 65–74	Age 75–84	Age 85+	
City	6.2	19.4	18.7	17.0	16.5	11.5	5.8	3.3	1.5	38.7
MSA[1]	6.4	20.5	21.2	12.9	14.0	12.0	7.2	4.0	1.8	36.4
U.S.	6.4	19.9	20.6	13.0	14.1	12.3	7.6	4.3	1.9	37.4

Note: (1) Figures cover the Sacramento—Roseville—Arden-Arcade, CA Metropolitan Statistical Area—see Appendix B for areas included
Source: U.S. Census Bureau, 2010-2014 American Community Survey 5-Year Estimates

Gender

Area	Males	Females	Males per 100 Females
City	39,652	33,682	117.7
MSA[1]	1,076,441	1,120,981	96.0
U.S.	154,515,159	159,591,925	96.8

Note: (1) Figures cover the Sacramento—Roseville—Arden-Arcade, CA Metropolitan Statistical Area—see Appendix B for areas included
Source: U.S. Census Bureau, 2010-2014 American Community Survey 5-Year Estimates

Religious Groups by Family

Area	Catholic	Baptist	Non-Den.	Methodist[2]	Lutheran	LDS[3]	Pente-costal	Presby-terian[4]	Muslim[5]	Judaism
MSA[1]	16.1	3.1	4.0	1.7	0.7	3.3	2.0	0.8	0.8	0.2
U.S.	19.1	9.3	4.0	4.0	2.3	2.0	1.9	1.6	0.8	0.7

Note: Figures are the number of adherents as a percentage of the total population; (1) Figures cover the Sacramento—Arden-Arcade—Roseville, CA Metropolitan Statistical Area—see Appendix B for areas included; (2) Methodist/Pietist; (3) Latter Day Saints; (4) Reformed; (5) Figures are estimates
Source: Association of Statisticians of American Religious Bodies, 2010 U.S. Religion Census: Religious Congregations & Membership Study

Religious Groups by Tradition

Area	Catholic	Evangelical Protestant	Mainline Protestant	Other Tradition	Black Protestant	Orthodox
MSA[1]	16.1	11.3	2.2	5.8	0.5	0.3
U.S.	19.1	16.2	7.3	4.3	1.6	0.3

Note: Figures are the number of adherents as a percentage of the total population; (1) Figures cover the Sacramento—Arden-Arcade—Roseville, CA Metropolitan Statistical Area—see Appendix B for areas included
Source: Association of Statisticians of American Religious Bodies, 2010 U.S. Religion Census: Religious Congregations & Membership Study

ECONOMY

Gross Metropolitan Product

Area	2013	2014	2015	2016	Rank[2]
MSA[1]	108.2	113.4	117.8	124.1	32

Note: Figures are in billions of dollars; (1) Figures cover the Sacramento—Roseville—Arden-Arcade, CA Metropolitan Statistical Area—see Appendix B for areas included; (2) Rank is based on 2016 data and ranges from 1 to 381
Source: The U.S. Conference of Mayors, U.S. Metro Economies: GMP and Employment 2014-2016, June 2015

Economic Growth

Area	2011-13 (%)	2014 (%)	2015 (%)	2016 (%)	Rank[2]
MSA[1]	2.6	3.1	2.6	3.3	49
U.S.	2.2	2.4	2.3	2.9	–

Note: Figures are real gross metropolitan product (GMP) growth rates and represent annual average percent change; (1) Figures cover the Sacramento—Roseville—Arden-Arcade, CA Metropolitan Statistical Area—see Appendix B for areas included; (2) Rank is based on 2016 data and ranges from 1 to 381
Source: The U.S. Conference of Mayors, U.S. Metro Economies: GMP and Employment 2014-2016, June 2015

Metropolitan Area Exports

Area	2009	2010	2011	2012	2013	2014	Rank[2]
MSA[1]	3,502.0	4,070.4	4,685.9	5,194.5	5,777.0	7,143.9	43

Note: Figures are in millions of dollars; (1) Figures cover the Sacramento—Roseville—Arden-Arcade, CA Metropolitan Statistical Area—see Appendix B for areas included; (2) Rank is based on 2014 data and ranges from 1 to 385
Source: U.S. Department of Commerce, International Trade Administration, Office of Trade & Industry Information, Manufacturing & Services, data extracted March 10, 2016

Building Permits

Area	Single-Family			Multi-Family			Total		
	2014	2015p	Pct. Chg.	2014	2015p	Pct. Chg.	2014	2015p	Pct. Chg.
City	300	244	-18.7	0	0	-	300	244	-18.7
MSA[1]	3,694	5,174	40.1	465	1,009	117.0	4,159	6,183	48.7
U.S.	640,300	690,800	7.9	411,800	487,600	18.4	1,052,100	1,178,400	12.0

Note: (1) Figures cover the Sacramento—Roseville—Arden-Arcade, CA Metropolitan Statistical Area—see Appendix B for areas included; Figures represent new, privately-owned housing units authorized (unadjusted data); All permit data are based on estimates with imputation; (p) preliminary data.
Source: U.S. Census Bureau, Manufacturing, Mining, and Construction Statistics, Building Permits, 2014, 2015

Bankruptcy Filings

Area	Business Filings 2014	Business Filings 2015	Business Filings % Chg.	Nonbusiness Filings 2014	Nonbusiness Filings 2015	Nonbusiness Filings % Chg.
Sacramento County	128	111	-13.3	5,064	4,145	-18.1
U.S.	26,983	24,735	-8.3	909,812	819,760	-9.9

Note: Business filings include Chapter 7, Chapter 11, Chapter 12, and Chapter 13; Nonbusiness filings include Chapter 7, Chapter 11, and Chapter 13
Source: Administrative Office of the U.S. Courts, Business and Nonbusiness Bankruptcy, County Cases Commenced by Chapter of the Bankruptcy Code, During the 12- Month Period Ending December 31, 2014 and Business and Nonbusiness Bankruptcy, County Cases Commenced by Chapter of the Bankruptcy Code, During the 12- Month Period Ending December 31, 2015

Housing Vacancy Rates

Area	Gross Vacancy Rate[2] (%)			Year-Round Vacancy Rate[3] (%)			Rental Vacancy Rate[4] (%)			Homeowner Vacancy Rate[5] (%)		
	2013	2014	2015	2013	2014	2015	2013	2014	2015	2013	2014	2015
MSA[1]	9.7	10.2	8.8	8.4	7.6	6.0	7.0	6.5	5.3	1.2	1.0	1.4
U.S.	13.6	13.4	12.9	10.7	10.4	10.0	8.3	7.6	7.1	2.0	1.9	1.8

Note: (1) Figures cover the Sacramento—Roseville—Arden-Arcade, CA Metropolitan Statistical Area—see Appendix B for areas included; (2) The percentage of the total housing inventory that is vacant; (3) The percentage of the housing inventory (excluding seasonal units) that is year-round vacant; (4) The percentage of rental inventory that is vacant for rent; (5) The percentage of homeowner inventory that is vacant for sale
Source: U.S. Census Bureau, Housing Vacancies and Homeownership Annual Statistics: 2015

INCOME

Income

Area	Per Capita ($)	Median Household ($)	Average Household ($)
City	38,472	100,163	110,870
MSA[1]	29,252	59,439	78,856
U.S.	28,555	53,482	74,596

Note: (1) Figures cover the Sacramento—Roseville—Arden-Arcade, CA Metropolitan Statistical Area—see Appendix B for areas included
Source: U.S. Census Bureau, 2010-2014 American Community Survey 5-Year Estimates

Household Income Distribution

Area	Percent of Households Earning: Under $15,000	$15,000 -24,999	$25,000 -34,999	$35,000 -49,999	$50,000 -74,999	$75,000 -99,000	$100,000 -149,999	$150,000 and up
City	5.1	4.0	5.7	7.6	13.3	14.2	25.4	24.7
MSA[1]	11.2	9.4	9.3	12.9	17.6	12.7	15.1	11.9
U.S.	12.5	10.7	10.2	13.5	17.8	12.2	13.0	10.0

Note: (1) Figures cover the Sacramento—Roseville—Arden-Arcade, CA Metropolitan Statistical Area—see Appendix B for areas included
Source: U.S. Census Bureau, 2010-2014 American Community Survey 5-Year Estimates

Poverty Rate

Area	All Ages	Under 18 Years Old	18 to 64 Years Old	65 Years and Over
City	4.4	3.1	4.3	8.1
MSA[1]	16.1	21.3	15.6	8.6
U.S.	15.6	21.9	14.6	9.4

Note: Figures are percentage of people whose income during the past 12 months was below the poverty level; (1) Figures cover the Sacramento—Roseville—Arden-Arcade, CA Metropolitan Statistical Area—see Appendix B for areas included
Source: U.S. Census Bureau, 2010-2014 American Community Survey 5-Year Estimates

EMPLOYMENT

Labor Force and Employment

Area	Civilian Labor Force			Workers Employed		
	Dec. 2014	Dec. 2015	% Chg.	Dec. 2014	Dec. 2015	% Chg.
City	34,539	34,894	1.0	33,102	33,636	1.6
MSA[1]	1,046,596	1,054,618	0.7	980,489	996,693	1.6
U.S.	155,521,000	157,245,000	1.1	147,190,000	149,703,000	1.7

Note: Data is not seasonally adjusted and covers workers 16 years of age and older; (1) Figures cover the Sacramento—Roseville—Arden-Arcade, CA Metropolitan Statistical Area—see Appendix B for areas included
Source: Bureau of Labor Statistics, Local Area Unemployment Statistics

Unemployment Rate

Area	2015											
	Jan.	Feb.	Mar.	Apr.	May	Jun.	Jul.	Aug.	Sep.	Oct.	Nov.	Dec.
City	4.4	4.1	3.9	3.7	3.7	3.8	4.0	3.8	3.4	3.7	3.6	3.6
MSA[1]	6.7	6.3	5.9	5.5	5.6	5.6	6.0	5.7	5.1	5.5	5.5	5.5
U.S.	6.1	5.8	5.6	5.1	5.3	5.5	5.6	5.2	4.9	4.8	4.8	4.8

Note: Data is not seasonally adjusted and covers workers 16 years of age and older; (1) Figures cover the Sacramento—Roseville—Arden-Arcade, CA Metropolitan Statistical Area—see Appendix B for areas included
Source: Bureau of Labor Statistics, Local Area Unemployment Statistics

Employment by Occupation

Occupation Classification	City (%)	MSA[1] (%)	U.S. (%)
Management, Business, Science, and Arts	56.0	39.0	36.4
Natural Resources, Construction, and Maintenance	4.1	8.0	9.0
Production, Transportation, and Material Moving	5.0	8.3	12.1
Sales and Office	22.1	25.8	24.4
Service	12.7	18.9	18.2

Note: Figures cover employed civilians 16 years of age and older; (1) Figures cover the Sacramento—Roseville—Arden-Arcade, CA Metropolitan Statistical Area—see Appendix B for areas included
Source: U.S. Census Bureau, 2010-2014 American Community Survey 5-Year Estimates

Employment by Industry

Sector	MSA[1]		U.S.
	Number of Employees	Percent of Total	Percent of Total
Construction	52,300	5.6	4.5
Education and Health Services	142,500	15.3	15.7
Financial Activities	51,800	5.5	5.7
Government	232,600	25.0	15.5
Information	14,100	1.5	1.9
Leisure and Hospitality	94,600	10.1	10.4
Manufacturing	36,500	3.9	8.6
Mining and Logging	600	<0.1	0.5
Other Services	30,000	3.2	3.9
Professional and Business Services	120,600	12.9	13.9
Retail Trade	102,600	11.0	11.3
Transportation, Warehousing, and Utilities	25,900	2.7	3.9
Wholesale Trade	25,100	2.7	4.1

Note: Figures are non-farm employment as of December 2015. Figures are not seasonally adjusted and include workers 16 years of age and older; (1) Figures cover the Sacramento—Roseville—Arden-Arcade, CA Metropolitan Statistical Area—see Appendix B for areas included
Source: Bureau of Labor Statistics, Current Employment Statistics, Employment, Hours, and Earnings

Occupations with Greatest Projected Employment Growth: 2012 – 2022

Occupation[1]	2012 Employment	2022 Projected Employment	Numeric Employment Change	Percent Employment Change
Personal Care Aides	386,900	587,200	200,300	51.8
Combined Food Preparation and Serving Workers, Including Fast Food	286,000	362,400	76,400	26.7
Retail Salespersons	468,400	528,100	59,700	12.7
Laborers and Freight, Stock, and Material Movers, Hand	270,500	322,300	51,800	19.1
Waiters and Waitresses	246,100	290,300	44,200	18.0
Registered Nurses	254,500	297,400	42,900	16.9
General and Operations Managers	253,800	295,700	41,900	16.5
Secretaries and Administrative Assistants, Except Legal, Medical, and Executive	212,800	250,100	37,300	17.5
Cashiers	357,800	392,600	34,800	9.7
Cooks, Restaurant	116,900	150,600	33,700	28.8

Note: Projections cover California; (1) Sorted by numeric employment change
Source: www.projectionscentral.com, State Occupational Projections, 2012–2022 Long-Term Projections

Fastest Growing Occupations: 2012 – 2022

Occupation[1]	2012 Employment	2022 Projected Employment	Numeric Employment Change	Percent Employment Change
Economists	3,100	5,100	2,000	64.5
Helpers—Brickmasons, Blockmasons, Stonemasons, and Tile and Marble Setters	2,900	4,600	1,700	58.6
Brickmasons and Blockmasons	5,100	8,000	2,900	56.9
Insulation Workers, Floor, Ceiling, and Wall	1,600	2,500	900	56.3
Stonemasons	1,100	1,700	600	54.5
Insulation Workers, Mechanical	1,100	1,700	600	54.5
Personal Care Aides	386,900	587,200	200,300	51.8
Foresters	1,200	1,800	600	50.0
Terrazzo Workers and Finishers	1,100	1,600	500	45.5
Mechanical Door Repairers	1,100	1,600	500	45.5

Note: Projections cover California; (1) Sorted by percent employment change and excludes occupations with numeric employment change less than 100
Source: www.projectionscentral.com, State Occupational Projections, 2012–2022 Long-Term Projections

Average Wages

Occupation	$/Hr.	Occupation	$/Hr.
Accountants and Auditors	33.75	Maids and Housekeeping Cleaners	12.55
Automotive Mechanics	21.38	Maintenance and Repair Workers	20.05
Bookkeepers	20.18	Marketing Managers	57.90
Carpenters	23.10	Nuclear Medicine Technologists	56.48
Cashiers	11.90	Nurses, Licensed Practical	28.21
Clerks, General Office	17.08	Nurses, Registered	54.33
Clerks, Receptionists/Information	15.07	Nursing Assistants	17.78
Clerks, Shipping/Receiving	15.45	Packers and Packagers, Hand	13.37
Computer Programmers	39.27	Physical Therapists	47.23
Computer Systems Analysts	39.06	Postal Service Mail Carriers	25.32
Computer User Support Specialists	27.42	Real Estate Brokers	69.32
Cooks, Restaurant	12.24	Retail Salespersons	13.42
Dentists	78.99	Sales Reps., Exc. Tech./Scientific	32.76
Electrical Engineers	44.34	Sales Reps., Tech./Scientific	42.49
Electricians	33.30	Secretaries, Exc. Legal/Med./Exec.	18.02
Financial Managers	59.81	Security Guards	13.09
First-Line Supervisors/Managers, Sales	20.20	Surgeons	123.73
Food Preparation Workers	11.03	Teacher Assistants*	15.20
General and Operations Managers	53.98	Teachers, Elementary School*	33.21
Hairdressers/Cosmetologists	13.24	Teachers, Secondary School*	33.73
Internists	100.33	Telemarketers	13.27
Janitors and Cleaners	13.63	Truck Drivers, Heavy/Tractor-Trailer	20.21
Landscaping/Groundskeeping Workers	13.99	Truck Drivers, Light/Delivery Svcs.	18.39
Lawyers	64.01	Waiters and Waitresses	13.30

Note: Wage data covers the Sacramento—Arden-Arcade—Roseville, CA Metropolitan Statistical Area—see Appendix B for areas included; (*) Hourly wages for elementary/secondary school teachers and teacher assistants were calculated by the editors from annual wage data based on a 40 hour work week; n/a not available.
Source: Bureau of Labor Statistics, Metro Area Occupational Employment and Wage Estimates, May 2015

TAXES

State Corporate Income Tax Rates

State	Tax Rate (%)	Income Brackets ($)	Num. of Brackets	Financial Institution Tax Rate (%)[a]	Federal Income Tax Ded.
California	8.84 (c)	Flat rate	1	10.84 (c)	No

Note: Tax rates as of January 1, 2016; (a) Rates listed are the corporate income tax rate applied to financial institutions or excise taxes based on income. Some states have other taxes based upon the value of deposits or shares; (c) Minimum tax is $800 in California, $100 in District of Columbia, $50 in North Dakota (banks), $500 in Rhode Island, $200 per location in South Dakota (banks), $100 in Utah, $250 in Vermont.
Source: Federation of Tax Administrators, "State Corporate Income Tax Rates, 2016"

State Individual Income Tax Rates

State	Tax Rate (%)	Income Brackets ($)	Num. of Brackets	Personal Exempt. ($)[1]		Fed. Inc. Tax Ded.
				Single	Dependents	
California (a)	1.0 - 12.3 (f)	7,850- 526,443 (b)	9	109 (c)	337 (c)	No

Note: Tax rates as of January 1, 2016; Local- and county-level taxes are not included; n/a not applicable; (1) Married joint filers generally receive double the single exemption; (a) 18 states have statutory provision for automatically adjusting to the rate of inflation the dollar values of the income tax brackets, standard deductions, and/or personal exemptions. Massachusetts, Michigan, and Nebraska index the personal exemptiononly. Oregon does not index the income brackets for $125,000 and over. Maine has suspended indexing for 2014 and 2015; (b) For joint returns, taxes are twice the tax on half the couple's income; (c) The personal exemption takes the form of a tax credit instead of a deduction; (f) California imposes an additional 1% tax on taxable income over $1 million, making the maximum rate 13.3% over $1 million.
Source: Federation of Tax Administrators, "State Individual Income Tax Rates, 2016"

Various State and Local Tax Rates

State	State and Local Sales and Use (%)	State Sales and Use (%)	Gasoline[1] (¢/gal.)	Cigarette[2] ($/pack)	Spirits[3] ($/gal.)	Wine[4] ($/gal.)	Beer[5] ($/gal.)
California	8.00	7.50 (b)	40.62	0.87	3.30 (f)	0.20 (l)	0.08

Note: All tax rates as of January 1, 2016; (1) The American Petroleum Institute has developed a methodology for determining the average tax rate on a gallon of fuel. Rates may include any of the following: excise taxes, environmental fees, storage tank fees, other fees or taxes, general sales tax, and local taxes. In states where gasoline is subject to the general sales tax, or where the fuel tax is based on the average sale price, the average rate determined by API is sensitive to changes in the price of gasoline. States that fully or partially apply general sales taxes to gasoline: CA, CO, GA, IL, IN, MI, NY; (2) The federal excise tax of $1.0066 per pack and local taxes are not included; (3) Rates are those applicable to off-premise sales of 40% alcohol by volume (a.b.v.) distilled spirits in 750ml containers. Local excise taxes are excluded; (4) Rates are those applicable to off-premise sales of 11% a.b.v. non-carbonated wine in 750ml containers; (5) Rates are those applicable to off-premise sales of 4.7% a.b.v. beer in 12 ounce containers; (b) Three states levy mandatory, statewide local add-on sales taxes at the state level: California (1%), Utah (1.25%), and Virginia (1%). We include these in their state sales tax rates; (f) Different rates are also applicable according to alcohol content, place of production, size of container, or place purchased (on- or off-premise or onboard airlines); (l) Different rates also applicable according to alcohol content, place of production, size of container, place purchased (on- or off-premise or on board airlines) or type of wine (carbonated, vermouth, etc.).
Source: Tax Foundation, 2016 Facts & Figures: How Does Your State Compare?

State Business Tax Climate Index Rankings

State	Overall Rank	Corporate Tax Rank	Individual Income Tax Rank	Sales Tax Rank	Unemployment Insurance Tax Rank	Property Tax Rank
California	48	35	50	40	13	13

Note: The index is a measure of how each state's tax laws affect economic performance. The lower the rank, the more favorable a state's tax system is for business. States without a given tax are given a ranking of 1. The scores/rankings for the District of Columbia do not affect other states. The 2016 index represents the tax climate as of July 1, 2015 (the beginning of Fiscal Year 2016).
Source: Tax Foundation, State Business Tax Climate Index 2016

TRANSPORTATION

Means of Transportation to Work

Area	Car/Truck/Van: Drove Alone	Car/Truck/Van: Car-pooled	Public Transportation: Bus	Public Transportation: Subway	Public Transportation: Railroad	Bicycle	Walked	Other Means	Worked at Home
City	79.1	9.3	0.6	0.7	0.8	0.7	1.2	1.5	6.1
MSA[1]	75.5	11.2	1.9	0.3	0.3	1.9	2.1	1.3	5.6
U.S.	76.4	9.6	2.6	1.8	0.6	0.6	2.8	1.3	4.4

Note: Figures are percentages and cover workers 16 years of age and older; (1) Figures cover the Sacramento—Roseville—Arden-Arcade, CA Metropolitan Statistical Area—see Appendix B for areas included
Source: U.S. Census Bureau, 2010-2014 American Community Survey 5-Year Estimates

Travel Time to Work

Area	Less Than 10 Minutes	10 to 19 Minutes	20 to 29 Minutes	30 to 44 Minutes	45 to 59 Minutes	60 to 89 Minutes	90 Minutes or More
City	15.4	30.9	19.4	21.8	6.1	3.8	2.5
MSA[1]	11.8	29.7	22.6	21.7	7.0	4.0	3.1
U.S.	13.3	29.6	21.0	20.2	7.7	5.7	2.6

Note: Figures are percentages and include workers 16 years old and over; (1) Figures cover the Sacramento—Roseville—Arden-Arcade, CA Metropolitan Statistical Area—see Appendix B for areas included
Source: U.S. Census Bureau, 2010-2014 American Community Survey 5-Year Estimates

Freeway Travel Time Index

Area	1985	1990	1995	2000	2005	2010	2014
Urban Area Rank[1,2]	26	25	29	28	27	29	29
Urban Area Index[1]	1.10	1.14	1.17	1.20	1.23	1.22	1.23
Average Index[3]	1.09	1.11	1.14	1.17	1.20	1.19	1.20

Note: Freeway Travel Time Index—the ratio of travel time in the peak period to the travel time at free-flow conditions. For example, a value of 1.30 indicates a 20-minute free-flow trip takes 26 minutes in the peak (20 minutes x 1.30 = 26 minutes); (1) Covers the Sacramento CA urban area; (2) Rank is based on 101 urban areas (#1 = highest travel time index); (3) Average of 101 urban areas
Source: Texas Transportation Institute, 2015 Urban Mobility Scorecard, August 2015

Freeway Commuter Stress Index

Area	1985	1990	1995	2000	2005	2010	2014
Urban Area Rank[1,2]	36	36	37	38	35	34	36
Urban Area Index[1]	1.13	1.17	1.20	1.23	1.27	1.26	1.26
Average Index[3]	1.13	1.16	1.19	1.22	1.25	1.24	1.25

Note: The Freeway Commuter Stress Index is the same as the Freeway Travel Time Index (see table above) except that it includes only the travel in the peak directions during the peak periods; the TTI includes travel in all directions during the peak period. Thus, the CSI is more indicative of the work trip experienced by each commuter on a daily basis. (1) Covers the Sacramento CA urban area; (2) Rank is based on 101 urban areas (#1 = highest stress index); (3) Average of 101 urban areas

Source: Texas Transportation Institute, 2015 Urban Mobility Scorecard, August 2015

Living Environment

COST OF LIVING

Cost of Living Index

Composite Index	Groceries	Housing	Utilities	Trans-portation	Health Care	Misc. Goods/ Services
115.2	118.6	138.4	77.3	118.1	98.7	107.2

Note: The Cost of Living Index measures regional differences in the cost of consumer goods and services, excluding taxes and non-consumer expenditures, for professional and managerial households in the top income quintile. It is based on more than 50,000 prices covering almost 60 different items for which prices are collected three times a year by chambers of commerce, economic development organizations or university applied economic centers in each participating urban area. The numbers shown should be read as a percentage above or below the national average of 100. For example, a value of 115.4 in the groceries column indicates that grocery prices are 15.4% higher than the national average. Small differences in the index numbers should not be interpreted as significant; Figures cover the Sacramento CA urban area.
Source: The Council for Community and Economic Research, ACCRA Cost of Living Index, 2015

Grocery Prices

Area[1]	T-Bone Steak ($/pound)	Frying Chicken ($/pound)	Whole Milk ($/half gal.)	Eggs ($/dozen)	Orange Juice ($/64 oz.)	Coffee ($/11.5 oz.)
City[2]	11.32	1.96	2.75	3.31	3.48	6.83
Avg.	10.99	1.43	2.25	2.26	3.58	4.48
Min.	7.16	0.98	1.30	1.35	2.88	2.98
Max.	14.13	2.43	3.85	4.81	6.39	7.56

Note: (1) Values for the local area are compared with the average, minimum and maximum values for all 292 areas in the Cost of Living Index; (2) Figures cover the Sacramento CA urban area; **T-Bone Steak** *(price per pound);* **Frying Chicken** *(price per pound, whole fryer);* **Whole Milk** *(half gallon carton);* **Eggs** *(price per dozen, Grade A, large);* **Orange Juice** *(64 oz. Tropicana or Florida Natural);* **Coffee** *(11.5 oz. can, vacuum-packed, Maxwell House, Hills Bros, or Folgers).*
Source: The Council for Community and Economic Research, ACCRA Cost of Living Index, 2015

Housing and Utility Costs

Area[1]	New Home Price ($)	Apartment Rent ($/month)	All Electric ($/month)	Part Electric ($/month)	Other Energy ($/month)	Telephone ($/month)
City[2]	398,011	1,575	-	99.01	37.79	20.43
Avg.	312,874	945	179.30	95.07	72.96	28.11
Min.	178,682	479	116.28	43.14	26.46	10.01
Max.	1,472,476	3,984	504.25	189.44	421.11	43.06

Note: (1) Values for the local area are compared with the average, minimum and maximum values for all 292 areas in the Cost of Living Index; (2) Figures cover the Sacramento CA urban area; **New Home Price** *(2,400 sf living area, 8,000 sf lot, in urban area with full utilities);* **Apartment Rent** *(950 sf 2 bedroom/1.5 or 2 bath, unfurnished, excluding all utilities except water);* **All Electric** *(average monthly cost for an all-electric home);* **Part Electric** *(average monthly cost for a part-electric home);* **Other Energy** *(average monthly cost for natural gas, fuel oil, coal, wood, and any other forms of energy except electricity);* **Telephone** *(price includes basic monthly rate for a private residential line plus additional local usage charges incurred by a family of four).*
Source: The Council for Community and Economic Research, ACCRA Cost of Living Index, 2015

Health Care, Transportation, and Other Costs

Area[1]	Doctor ($/visit)	Dentist ($/visit)	Optometrist ($/visit)	Gasoline ($/gallon)	Beauty Salon ($/visit)	Men's Shirt ($)
City[2]	92.46	87.18	109.14	2.97	42.32	31.24
Avg.	105.15	89.02	99.78	2.38	35.30	28.10
Min.	66.87	56.09	48.53	1.95	18.91	13.38
Max.	182.34	150.36	228.33	4.09	67.91	63.80

Note: (1) Values for the local area are compared with the average, minimum and maximum values for all 292 areas in the Cost of Living Index; (2) Figures cover the Sacramento CA urban area; **Doctor** *(general practitioners routine exam of an established patient);* **Dentist** *(adult teeth cleaning and periodic oral examination);* **Optometrist** *(full vision eye exam for established adult patient);* **Gasoline** *(one gallon regular unleaded, national brand, including all taxes, cash price at self-service pump if available);* **Beauty Salon** *(woman's shampoo, trim, and blow-dry);* **Men's Shirt** *(cotton/polyester dress shirt, pinpoint weave, long sleeves).*
Source: The Council for Community and Economic Research, ACCRA Cost of Living Index, 2015

HOUSING

House Price Index (HPI)

Area	National Ranking[2]	Quarterly Change (%)	One-Year Change (%)	Five-Year Change (%)
MSA[1]	57	0.90	7.50	36.60
U.S.[3]	–	1.45	5.76	22.85

Note: The HPI is a weighted repeat sales index. It measures average price changes in repeat sales or refinancings on the same properties. This information is obtained by reviewing repeat mortgage transactions on single-family properties whose mortgages have been purchased or securitized by Fannie Mae or Freddie Mac in January 1975; (1) Sacramento—Roseville—Arden-Arcade Metropolitan Statistical Area—see Appendix B for areas included; (2) Rankings are based on annual percentage change for all metro areas containing at least 15,000 transactions over the last 10 years and ranges from 1 to 266; (3) figures based on a weighted average of Census Division estimates using a seasonally adjusted, purchase-only index; all figures are for the period ending December 31, 2015

Source: Federal Housing Finance Agency, House Price Index, February 25, 2016

Median Single-Family Home Prices

Area	2013	2014	2015^p	Percent Change 2014 to 2015
MSA[1]	239.5	268.7	289.3	7.7
U.S. Average	197.4	208.9	223.9	7.2

Note: Figures are median sales prices of existing single-family homes in thousands of dollars; (p) preliminary; n/a not available; (1) Sacramento—Roseville—Arden-Arcade, CA Metropolitan Statistical Area—see Appendix B for areas included

Source: National Association of Realtors, Median Sales Price of Existing Single-Family Homes for Metropolitan Areas, 4th Quarter 2015

Qualifying Income Based on Median Sales Price of Existing Single-Family Homes

Area	With 5% Down ($)	With 10% Down ($)	With 20% Down ($)
MSA[1]	65,417	61,974	55,088
U.S. Average	49,535	46,928	41,714

Note: Figures are preliminary; Qualifying income is based on a mortgage rate of 4.1%. Monthly principal and interest payment is limited to 25% of income; n/a not available; (1) Sacramento—Roseville—Arden-Arcade, CA Metropolitan Statistical Area—see Appendix B for areas included

Source: National Association of Realtors, Qualifying Income Based on Median Sales Price of Existing Single-Family Homes for Metropolitan Areas, 4th Quarter 2015

Median Apartment Condo-Coop Home Prices

Area	2013	2014	2015^p	Percent Change 2014 to 2015
MSA[1]	123.0	138.9	146.8	5.7
U.S. Average	194.9	204.3	210.7	3.1

Note: Figures are median sales prices of existing apartment condo-coop homes in thousands of dollars; (p) preliminary; n/a not available; (1) Sacramento—Roseville—Arden-Arcade, CA Metropolitan Statistical Area—see Appendix B for areas included

Source: National Association of Realtors, Median Sales Price of Existing Apartment Condo-Coop Homes for Metropolitan Areas, 4th Quarter 2015

Gross Monthly Rent

Area	Under $200	$200 -299	$300 -499	$500 -749	$750 -999	$1,000 -1,499	$1,500 and up	Median ($)
City	0.1	0.1	1.0	5.5	7.4	43.2	42.8	1,416
MSA[1]	0.7	1.9	2.9	12.7	26.1	34.5	21.3	1,071
U.S.	1.5	3.2	7.4	21.0	24.1	26.9	15.9	920

Note: Figures are percentages except for Median; Gross rent is the contract rent plus the estimated average monthly cost of utilities (electricity, gas, and water and sewer) and fuels (oil, coal, kerosene, wood, etc.) if these are paid by the renter (or paid for the renter by someone else); (1) Figures cover the Sacramento—Roseville—Arden-Arcade, CA Metropolitan Statistical Area—see Appendix B for areas included

Source: U.S. Census Bureau, 2010-2014 American Community Survey 5-Year Estimates

Homeownership Rate

Area	2008 (%)	2009 (%)	2010 (%)	2011 (%)	2012 (%)	2013 (%)	2014 (%)	2015 (%)
MSA[1]	61.1	64.3	61.1	57.2	58.6	60.4	60.1	60.8
U.S.	67.8	67.4	66.9	66.1	65.4	65.1	64.5	63.7

Note: (1) Figures cover the Sacramento—Roseville—Arden-Arcade, CA Metropolitan Statistical Area—see Appendix B for areas included
Source: U.S. Census Bureau, Housing Vacancies and Homeownership Annual Statistics: 2015

Year Housing Structure Built

Area	2010 or Later	2000 -2009	1990 -1999	1980 -1989	1970 -1979	1960 -1969	1950 -1959	1940 -1949	Before 1940	Median Year
City	0.9	32.4	29.9	20.1	8.2	2.6	3.2	0.9	1.9	1994
MSA[1]	0.7	18.5	14.3	16.7	19.4	11.2	10.7	4.0	4.6	1980
U.S.	1.0	14.9	13.9	13.8	15.8	11.0	10.8	5.4	13.3	1976

Note: Figures are percentages except for Median Year; (1) Figures cover the Sacramento—Roseville—Arden-Arcade, CA Metropolitan Statistical Area—see Appendix B for areas included
Source: U.S. Census Bureau, 2010-2014 American Community Survey 5-Year Estimates

HEALTH

Health Risk Data

Category	MSA[1] (%)	U.S. (%)
Adults aged 18–64 who have any kind of health care coverage	81.2	79.6
Adults who reported being in good or excellent health	85.8	83.1
Adults who are current smokers	14.7	19.6
Adults who are heavy drinkers[2]	6.2	6.1
Adults who are binge drinkers[3]	16.6	16.9
Adults who are overweight (BMI 25.0 - 29.9)	36.0	35.8
Adults who are obese (BMI 30.0 - 99.8)	25.4	27.6
Adults who participated in any physical activities in the past month	84.4	77.1
Adults 50+ who have ever had a sigmoidoscopy or colonoscopy	71.9	67.3
Women aged 40+ who have had a mammogram within the past two years	82.2	74.0
Men aged 40+ who have had a PSA test within the past two years	34.6	45.2
Adults aged 65+ who have had flu shot within the past year	61.6	60.1
Adults who always wear a seatbelt	n/a	93.8

Note: Data as of 2012 unless otherwise noted; n/a not available; (1) Figures cover the SacramentoùArden-ArcadeùRoseville, CA Metropolitan Statistical Area—see Appendix B for areas included; (2) Heavy drinkers are classified as males having more than two drinks per day or females having more than one drink per day; (3) Binge drinkers are classified as males having five or more drinks on one occasion or females having four or more drinks on one occasion
Source: Centers for Disease Control and Prevention, Behaviorial Risk Factor Surveillance System, SMART: Selected Metropolitan/Micropolitan Area Risk Trends, 2012 (Note: the CDC has discontinued this dataset but will be releasing a replacement in mid-2016)

Chronic Health Indicators

Category	MSA[1] (%)	U.S. (%)
Adults who have ever been told they had a heart attack	2.8	4.5
Adults who have ever been told they had a stroke	2.7	2.9
Adults who have been told they currently have asthma	10.0	8.9
Adults who have ever been told they have arthritis	24.5	25.7
Adults who have ever been told they have diabetes[2]	9.5	9.7
Adults who have ever been told they had skin cancer	5.2	5.7
Adults who have ever been told they had any other types of cancer	6.3	6.5
Adults who have ever been told they have COPD	4.6	6.2
Adults who have ever been told they have kidney disease	1.8	2.5
Adults who have ever been told they have a form of depression	10.6	18.0

Note: Data as of 2012 unless otherwise noted; (1) Figures cover the SacramentoùArden-ArcadeùRoseville, CA Metropolitan Statistical Area—see Appendix B for areas included; (2) Figures do not include pregnancy-related, borderline, or pre-diabetes
Source: Centers for Disease Control and Prevention, Behaviorial Risk Factor Surveillance System, SMART: Selected Metropolitan/Micropolitan Area Risk Trends, 2012 (Note: the CDC has discontinued this dataset but will be releasing a replacement in mid-2016)

Mortality Rates for the Top 10 Causes of Death in the U.S.

ICD-10[a] Sub-Chapter	ICD-10[a] Code	Age-Adjusted Mortality Rate[1] per 100,000 population	
		County[2]	U.S.
Malignant neoplasms	C00-C97	163.9	163.6
Ischaemic heart diseases	I20-I25	103.5	102.2
Other forms of heart disease	I30-I51	39.8	50.1
Chronic lower respiratory diseases	J40-J47	40.2	41.4
Organic, including symptomatic, mental disorders	F01-F09	34.4	38.5
Cerebrovascular diseases	I60-I69	38.9	36.5
Other external causes of accidental injury	W00-X59	23.8	27.5
Other degenerative diseases of the nervous system	G30-G31	30.3	26.3
Diabetes mellitus	E10-E14	23.3	21.1
Hypertensive diseases	I10-I15	27.6	19.7

Note: (a) ICD-10 = International Classification of Diseases 10th Revision; (1) Mortality rates are a three year average covering 2012-2014; (2) Figures cover COUNTY NOT FOUND!!!!!!.
Source: Centers for Disease Control and Prevention, National Center for Health Statistics. Underlying Cause of Death 1999-2014 on CDC WONDER Online Database, released 2015.

Mortality Rates for Selected Causes of Death

ICD-10[a] Sub-Chapter	ICD-10[a] Code	Age-Adjusted Mortality Rate[1] per 100,000 population	
		County[2]	U.S.
Assault	X85-Y09	6.0	5.1
Diseases of the liver	K70-K76	13.1	13.5
Human immunodeficiency virus (HIV) disease	B20-B24	1.9	2.1
Influenza and pneumonia	J09-J18	15.4	15.2
Intentional self-harm	X60-X84	13.6	12.7
Malnutrition	E40-E46	0.9	0.9
Obesity and other hyperalimentation	E65-E68	1.5	1.9
Renal failure	N17-N19	4.3	13.0
Transport accidents	V01-V99	10.0	11.6
Viral hepatitis	B15-B19	4.6	2.1

Note: (a) ICD-10 = International Classification of Diseases 10th Revision; (1) Mortality rates are a three year average covering 2012-2014; (2) Figures cover COUNTY NOT FOUND!!!!!!; Data are Suppressed when the data meet the criteria for confidentiality constraints; Mortality rates are flagged as Unreliable when the rate would be calculated with a numerator of 20 or less.
Source: Centers for Disease Control and Prevention, National Center for Health Statistics. Underlying Cause of Death 1999-2014 on CDC WONDER Online Database, released 2015.

Health Insurance Coverage

Area	With Health Insurance	With Private Health Insurance	With Public Health Insurance	Without Health Insurance	Population Under Age 18 Without Health Insurance
City	94.3	86.7	17.1	5.7	1.9
MSA[1]	87.4	67.2	31.5	12.6	5.4
U.S.	85.8	65.8	31.1	14.2	7.1

Note: Figures are percentages that cover the civilian noninstitutionalized population; (1) Figures cover the Sacramento—Roseville—Arden-Arcade, CA Metropolitan Statistical Area—see Appendix B for areas included
Source: U.S. Census Bureau, 2010-2014 American Community Survey 5-Year Estimates

Number of Medical Professionals

Area	MDs[3]	DOs[3,4]	Dentists	Podiatrists	Chiropractors	Optometrists
County[1] (number)	4,291	188	1,079	65	326	248
County[1] (rate[2])	293.3	12.8	72.8	4.4	22.0	16.7
U.S. (rate[2])	272.5	20.9	64.7	5.8	25.9	15.2

Note: Data as of 2014 unless noted; (1) Data covers Sacramento County; (2) Rate per 100,000 population; (3) Data as of 2013 and includes all active, non-federal physicians; (4) Doctor of Osteopathic Medicine
Source: U.S. Department of Health and Human Services, Health Resources and Services Administration, Bureau of Health Professions, Area Resource File (ARF) 2014-2015

Best Hospitals

According to *U.S. News,* the Sacramento—Roseville—Arden-Arcade, CA metro area is home to one of the best hospitals in the U.S.: **University of California, Davis Medical Center** (10 specialties). The hospital listed was nationally ranked in at least one adult specialty. Only 137 hospitals nationwide were nationally ranked in one or more specialties. Fifteen hospitals in the U.S. made the Honor Roll with high scores in at least six specialties. *U.S. News Online, "America's Best Children's Hospitals 2015-16"*

According to *U.S. News,* the Sacramento—Roseville—Arden-Arcade, CA metro area is home to one of the best children's hospitals in the U.S.: **University of California Davis Children's Hospital** (5 specialties). The hospital listed was highly ranked in at least one pediatric specialty. Eighty-three children's hospitals in the U.S. were nationally ranked in at least one specialty. Twelve children's hospitals in the U.S. made the Honor Roll with high scores in at least three specialties. *U.S. News Online, "America's Best Children's Hospitals 2015-16"*

EDUCATION

Public School District Statistics

District Name	Schls	Pupils	Pupil/ Teacher Ratio	Minority Pupils[1] (%)	Free Lunch Eligible[2] (%)	IEP[3] (%)
Folsom-Cordova Unified	34	19,356	26.1	44.0	30.4	11.7

Note: Table includes school districts with 100 or more students; (1) Percentage of students that are not non-Hispanic white; (2) Percentage of students that are eligible for the free lunch program; (3) Percentage of students that have an Individualized Education Program.
Source: U.S. Department of Education, National Center for Education Statistics, Common Core of Data, Local Education Agency (School District) Universe Survey: School Year 2013-2014; U.S. Department of Education, National Center for Education Statistics, Common Core of Data, Public Elementary/Secondary School Universe Survey: School Year 2013-2014

Highest Level of Education

Area	Less than H.S.	H.S. Diploma	Some College, No Deg.	Associate Degree	Bachelor's Degree	Master's Degree	Prof. School Degree	Doctorate Degree
City	8.0	17.2	19.9	9.2	28.5	12.3	3.1	1.9
MSA[1]	12.0	21.5	26.2	9.7	19.9	6.9	2.4	1.4
U.S.	13.7	28.0	21.2	7.9	18.3	7.8	2.0	1.3

Note: Figures cover persons age 25 and over; (1) Figures cover the Sacramento—Roseville—Arden-Arcade, CA Metropolitan Statistical Area—see Appendix B for areas included
Source: U.S. Census Bureau, 2010-2014 American Community Survey 5-Year Estimates

Educational Attainment by Race

Area	High School Graduate or Higher (%)					Bachelor's Degree or Higher (%)				
	Total	White	Black	Asian	Hisp.[2]	Total	White	Black	Asian	Hisp.[2]
City	92.0	95.2	68.3	94.8	80.0	45.7	45.8	9.1	73.5	31.7
MSA[1]	88.0	90.9	88.1	81.8	70.0	30.7	32.1	20.2	39.8	14.6
U.S.	86.3	88.4	83.2	85.8	64.1	29.3	30.6	19.0	50.9	13.9

Note: Figures shown cover persons 25 years old and over; (1) Figures cover the Sacramento—Roseville—Arden-Arcade, CA Metropolitan Statistical Area—see Appendix B for areas included; (2) People of Hispanic origin can be of any race
Source: U.S. Census Bureau, 2010-2014 American Community Survey 5-Year Estimates

School Enrollment by Grade and Control

Area	Preschool (%)		Kindergarten (%)		Grades 1 - 4 (%)		Grades 5 - 8 (%)		Grades 9 - 12 (%)	
	Public	Private	Public	Private	Public	Private	Public	Private	Public	Private
City	42.4	57.6	69.3	30.7	88.8	11.2	89.4	10.6	90.5	9.5
MSA[1]	53.1	46.9	88.8	11.2	91.8	8.2	92.2	7.8	91.7	8.3
U.S.	57.4	42.6	87.8	12.2	89.8	10.2	89.9	10.1	90.6	9.4

Note: Figures shown cover persons 3 years old and over; (1) Figures cover the Sacramento—Roseville—Arden-Arcade, CA Metropolitan Statistical Area—see Appendix B for areas included
Source: U.S. Census Bureau, 2010-2014 American Community Survey 5-Year Estimates

Average Salaries of Public School Classroom Teachers

Area	2013-14 Dollars	2013-14 Rank[1]	2014-15 Dollars	2014-15 Rank[1]	Percent Change 2013-14 to 2014-15	Percent Change 2004-05 to 2014-15
California	71,396	4	72,535	4	1.59	25.9
U.S. Average	56,610	–	57,379	–	1.36	20.8

Note: (1) State rank ranges from 1 to 51 where 1 indicates highest salary.
Source: National Education Association, Rankings & Estimates: Rankings of the States 2014 and Estimates of School Statistics 2015, March 2015

Higher Education

Four-Year Colleges			Two-Year Colleges			Medical Schools[1]	Law Schools[2]	Voc/ Tech[3]
Public	Private Non-profit	Private For-profit	Public	Private Non-profit	Private For-profit			
0	0	0	1	0	0	0	0	0

Note: Figures cover institutions located within the city limits and include main campuses only; (1) includes schools accredited by the Liaison Committee on Medical Education and the American Osteopathic Association's Commission on Osteopathic College Accreditation; (2) includes ABA-accredited schools, schools with provisional ABA accreditation, and state accredited schools; (3) includes all schools with programs that are less than 2 years.
Source: National Center for Education Statistics, Integrated Postsecondary Education System (IPEDS), 2014-15; Association of American Medical Colleges, Member List, March 21, 2016; American Osteopathic Association, Member List, March 21, 2016; Law School Admission Council, Official Guide to ABA-Approved Law Schools Online, March 21, 2016; Wikipedia, List of Medical Schools in the United States, March 21, 2016; Wikipedia, List of Law Schools in the United States, March 21, 2016

According to *U.S. News & World Report,* the Sacramento—Roseville—Arden-Arcade, CA metro area is home to one of the best national universities in the U.S.: **University of California–Davis** (#41 tie). The indicators used to capture academic quality fall into a number of categories: assessment by administrators at peer institutions; retention of students; faculty resources; student selectivity; financial resources; alumni giving; high school counselor ratings of colleges; and graduation rate. *U.S. News & World Report, "America's Best Colleges 2016"*

According to *U.S. News & World Report,* the Sacramento—Roseville—Arden-Arcade, CA metro area is home to one of the top 100 law schools in the U.S.: **University of California–Davis, School of Law** (#30 tie). The rankings are based on a weighted average of 12 measures of quality: peer assessment score; assessment score by lawyers/judges; median LSAT scores; median undergrad GPA; acceptance rate; employment rates for graduates; placement success; bar passage rate; faculty resources; expenditures per student; student/faculty ratio; and library resources. *U.S. News & World Report, "America's Best Graduate Schools, Law, 2017"*

According to *U.S. News & World Report,* the Sacramento—Roseville—Arden-Arcade, CA metro area is home to one of the top 75 medical schools for research in the U.S.: **University of California–Davis, School of Medicine** (#47 tie). The rankings are based on a weighted average of 11 measures of quality: quality assessment; peer assessment score; assessment score by residency directors; research activity; total research activity; average research activity per faculty member; student selectivity; median MCAT total score; median undergraduate GPA; acceptance rate; and faculty resources. *U.S. News & World Report, "America's Best Graduate Schools, Medical, 2017"*

According to *U.S. News & World Report,* the Sacramento—Roseville—Arden-Arcade, CA metro area is home to one of the top 75 business schools in the U.S.: **University of California–Davis, Graduate School of Management** (#45 tie). The rankings are based on a weighted average of the following nine measures: quality assessment; peer assessment; recruiter assessment; placement success; mean starting salary and bonus; student selectivity; mean GMAT and GRE scores; mean undergraduate GPA; and acceptance rate. *U.S. News & World Report, "America's Best Graduate Schools, Business, 2017"*

PRESIDENTIAL ELECTION

2012 Presidential Election Results

Area	Obama (%)	Romney (%)	Other (%)
Sacramento County	57.5	40.0	2.5
U.S.	51.0	47.2	1.8

Note: Results may not add to 100% due to rounding
Source: Dave Leip's Atlas of U.S. Presidential Elections

EMPLOYERS

Major Employers

Company Name	Industry
Air Resources Board Tstg Off	Engineers-environmental
C H W Mercy Healthcare	X-ray laboratory, including dental
CA Dept of Corrections and Rehab	Correctional institutions
Cache Creek Casino Resorts	Casino hotels
California Department of General Services	Building maintenance services, nec
California Department of Justice	Legal counsel & prosecution
California Department of Transportation	Regulation, administration of transportation
California Dept of Health Care Services	Administration of public health programs
California Employment Dev Dept	Administration of social & manpower programs
California State University Sacramento	Colleges & universities
CHW/Mercy Healthcare	Hospitals
Corrections Department	State government-correctional institutions
Dept of Transportation	Government offices-state
Employment Development Department	Government-job training/voc rehab svcs
Environmental Protection Agency	State government-environmental programs
Food & Agriculture, Calif. Dept of	Marketing & consumer service, government
Hewlett-Packard Co.	Computer hardware
Intel Corporation	Semiconductor devices (mfrs)
Kaiser Foundation Hospitals	Trusts, nec
Kaiser Permanente	Medical clinic
Los Rios Community College District	Colleges & universities
McClatchy Newspapers	Newspapers, publishing & printing
Mercy General Hospital	Hospitals
RaleyÆs	Grocery distribution
Red Hawk Casino	Gambling establishment
Sacramento City Unified School District	Education
Sacramento Municipal Utility District	Electrical services
SBC Telecommunications	Telecommunications
Shaw Environmental & Infrastructure	Engineering services
Sutter Health Sacramento Sierra Region	Health screening service
Sutter Medical Center	Hospitals
Sutter Roseville Medical Center	General medical & surgical hospitals
UC Davis Medical Center	Hospitals
University Enterprises	Educational services
University of California, Davis	General medical & surgical hospitals
Water Resources, California Dept of	Air, water, & solid waste management

Note: Companies shown are located within the Sacramento—Roseville—Arden-Arcade, CA Metropolitan Statistical Area.
Source: Hoovers.com; Wikipedia

PUBLIC SAFETY

Crime Rate

Area	All Crimes	Violent Crimes				Property Crimes		
		Murder	Rape[3]	Robbery	Aggrav. Assault	Burglary	Larceny -Theft	Motor Vehicle Theft
City	1,887.4	1.4	10.9	31.4	64.1	332.7	1,358.3	88.6
Metro[1]	2,885.5	4.0	24.5	115.9	266.3	552.3	1,579.4	343.2
U.S.	2,961.6	4.5	26.4	102.2	232.5	542.5	1,837.3	216.2

Note: Figures are crimes per 100,000 population; (1) Figures cover the Sacramento—Roseville—Arden-Arcade, CA Metropolitan Statistical Area—see Appendix B for areas included; (3) The city and U.S. figures shown were reported using the legacy Uniform Crime Reporting (UCR) definition of rape. The suburban and metro area figures shown are an aggregate total of the data submitted using both the revised and legacy UCR definitions.
Source: FBI Uniform Crime Reports, 2014

Hate Crimes

Area	Number of Quarters Reported	Number of Incidents per Bias Motivation: Race	Religion	Sexual Orientation	Ethnicity	Disability	Gender	Gender Identity
City	4	0	0	0	0	0	0	0
U.S.	4	2,568	1,014	1,017	648	84	33	98

Source: Federal Bureau of Investigation, Hate Crime Statistics 2014

Identity Theft Consumer Complaints

Area	Complaints	Complaints per 100,000 Population	Rank[2]
MSA[1]	3,133	139.6	70
U.S.	490,220	152.4	-

Note: (1) Figures cover the Sacramento—Roseville—Arden-Arcade, CA Metropolitan Statistical Area—see Appendix B for areas included; (2) Rank ranges from 1 to 379 where 1 indicates greatest number of identity theft complaints per 100,000 population
Source: Federal Trade Commission, Consumer Sentinel Network Data Book for January–December 2015

Fraud and Other Consumer Complaints

Area	Complaints	Complaints per 100,000 Population	Rank[2]
MSA[1]	9,923	442.1	53
U.S.	2,593,159	806.0	-

Note: (1) Figures cover the Sacramento—Roseville—Arden-Arcade, CA Metropolitan Statistical Area—see Appendix B for areas included; (2) Rank ranges from 1 to 379 where 1 indicates greatest number of identity theft complaints per 100,000 population
Source: Federal Trade Commission, Consumer Sentinel Network Data Book for January–December 2015

RECREATION

Culture

Dance[1]	Theatre[1]	Instrumental Music[1]	Vocal Music[1]	Series and Festivals	Museums and Art Galleries[2]	Zoos and Aquariums[3]
0	0	0	0	0	0	0

Note: (1) Professional perfoming groups; (2) Based on organizations with SIC code 8412; (3) AZA-accredited
Source: The Grey House Performing Arts Directory, 2015-16; Association of Zoos & Aquariums, AZA Member Zoos & Aquariums, March 25, 2016; www.AccuLeads.com, March 29, 2016

Professional Sports Teams

Team Name	League	Year Established
Sacramento Kings	National Basketball Association (NBA)	1985

Note: Includes teams located in the Sacramento—Roseville—Arden-Arcade, CA Metropolitan Statistical Area.
Source: Wikipedia, Major Professional Sports Teams of the United States and Canada, March 24, 2016

CLIMATE

Average and Extreme Temperatures

Temperature	Jan	Feb	Mar	Apr	May	Jun	Jul	Aug	Sep	Oct	Nov	Dec	Yr.
Extreme High (°F)	70	76	88	93	105	115	114	109	108	101	87	72	115
Average High (°F)	53	60	64	71	80	87	93	91	87	78	63	53	73
Average Temp. (°F)	45	51	54	59	65	72	76	75	72	64	53	46	61
Average Low (°F)	38	41	43	46	50	55	58	58	56	50	43	38	48
Extreme Low (°F)	20	23	26	32	34	41	48	48	43	35	26	18	18

Note: Figures cover the years 1947-1990
Source: National Climatic Data Center, International Station Meteorological Climate Summary, 9/96

Average Precipitation/Snowfall/Humidity

Precip./Humidity	Jan	Feb	Mar	Apr	May	Jun	Jul	Aug	Sep	Oct	Nov	Dec	Yr.
Avg. Precip. (in.)	3.6	2.8	2.4	1.3	0.4	0.1	Tr	0.1	0.3	1.0	2.4	2.8	17.3
Avg. Snowfall (in.)	Tr	Tr	Tr	Tr	0	0	0	0	0	0	0	Tr	Tr
Avg. Rel. Hum. 7am (%)	90	88	84	78	71	67	68	73	75	80	87	90	79
Avg. Rel. Hum. 4pm (%)	70	59	51	43	36	31	28	29	31	39	57	70	45

Note: Figures cover the years 1947-1990; Tr = Trace amounts (<0.05 in. of rain; <0.5 in. of snow)
Source: National Climatic Data Center, International Station Meteorological Climate Summary, 9/96

Weather Conditions

Temperature			Daytime Sky			Precipitation		
10°F & below	32°F & below	90°F & above	Clear	Partly cloudy	Cloudy	0.01 inch or more precip.	0.1 inch or more snow/ice	Thunder-storms
0	21	73	175	111	79	58	< 1	2

Note: Figures are average number of days per year and cover the years 1947-1990
Source: National Climatic Data Center, International Station Meteorological Climate Summary, 9/96

HAZARDOUS WASTE

Superfund Sites

Folsom has no sites on the EPA's Superfund Final National Priorities List. There are a total of 1,323 Superfund sites on the list in the U.S. *U.S. Environmental Protection Agency, Final National Priorities List, March 18, 2016*

AIR & WATER QUALITY

Air Quality Trends: Ozone

	1990	1995	2000	2005	2010	2011	2012	2013	2014
MSA[1]	0.088	0.093	0.087	0.087	0.074	0.074	0.079	0.070	0.073

Note: (1) Data covers the Sacramento—Roseville—Arden-Arcade, CA Metropolitan Statistical Area—see Appendix B for areas included. The values shown are the composite ozone concentration averages among trend sites based on the highest fourth daily maximum 8-hour concentration in parts per million. These trends are based on sites having an adequate record of monitoring data during the trend period. Data from exceptional events are included.
Source: U.S. Environmental Protection Agency, Air Quality Monitoring Information, "Air Quality Trends by City, 1990-2014"

Air Quality Index

Area	Percent of Days when Air Quality was...[2]					AQI Statistics[2]	
	Good	Moderate	Unhealthy for Sensitive Groups	Unhealthy	Very Unhealthy	Maximum	Median
MSA[1]	37.8	55.3	6.3	0.5	0.0	179	56

Note: (1) Data covers the Sacramento—Roseville—Arden-Arcade, CA Metropolitan Statistical Area—see Appendix B for areas included; (2) Based on 365 days with AQI data in 2015. Air Quality Index (AQI) is an index for reporting daily air quality. EPA calculates the AQI for five major air pollutants regulated by the Clean Air Act: ground-level ozone, particle pollution (aka particulate matter), carbon monoxide, sulfur dioxide, and nitrogen dioxide. The AQI runs from 0 to 500. The higher the AQI value, the greater the level of air pollution and the greater the health concern. There are six AQI categories: "Good" AQI is between 0 and 50. Air quality is considered satisfactory; "Moderate" AQI is between 51 and 100. Air quality is acceptable; "Unhealthy for Sensitive Groups" When AQI values are between 101 and 150, members of sensitive groups may experience health effects; "Unhealthy" When AQI values are between 151 and 200 everyone may begin to experience health effects; "Very Unhealthy" AQI values between 201 and 300 trigger a health alert; "Hazardous" AQI values over 300 trigger warnings of emergency conditions (not shown).
Source: U.S. Environmental Protection Agency, Air Quality Index Report, 2015

Air Quality Index Pollutants

Area	Percent of Days when AQI Pollutant was...[2]					
	Carbon Monoxide	Nitrogen Dioxide	Ozone	Sulfur Dioxide	Particulate Matter 2.5	Particulate Matter 10
MSA[1]	0.0	0.0	51.5	0.0	48.5	0.0

Note: (1) Data covers the Sacramento—Roseville—Arden-Arcade, CA Metropolitan Statistical Area—see Appendix B for areas included; (2) Based on 365 days with AQI data in 2015. The Air Quality Index (AQI) is an index for reporting daily air quality. EPA calculates the AQI for five major air pollutants regulated by the Clean Air Act: ground-level ozone, particle pollution (also known as particulate matter), carbon monoxide, sulfur dioxide, and nitrogen dioxide. The AQI runs from 0 to 500. The higher the AQI value, the greater the level of air pollution and the greater the health concern.
Source: U.S. Environmental Protection Agency, Air Quality Index Report, 2015

Maximum Air Pollutant Concentrations: Particulate Matter, Ozone, CO and Lead

	Particulate Matter 10 (ug/m^3)	Particulate Matter 2.5 Wtd AM (ug/m^3)	Particulate Matter 2.5 24-Hr (ug/m^3)	Ozone (ppm)	Carbon Monoxide (ppm)	Lead (ug/m^3)
MSA[1] Level	83	8.8	28	0.083	2	n/a
NAAQS[2]	150	15	35	0.075	9	0.15
Met NAAQS[2]	Yes	Yes	Yes	No	Yes	n/a

Note: (1) Data covers the Sacramento—Roseville—Arden-Arcade, CA Metropolitan Statistical Area—see Appendix B for areas included; Data from exceptional events are included; (2) National Ambient Air Quality Standards; ppm = parts per million; ug/m^3 = micrograms per cubic meter; n/a not available.
Concentrations: Particulate Matter 10 (coarse particulate)—highest second maximum 24-hour concentration; Particulate Matter 2.5 Wtd AM (fine particulate)—highest weighted annual mean concentration; Particulate Matter 2.5 24-Hour (fine particulate)—highest 98th percentile 24-hour concentration; Ozone—highest fourth daily maximum 8-hour concentration; Carbon Monoxide—highest second maximum non-overlapping 8-hour concentration; Lead—maximum running 3-month average
Source: U.S. Environmental Protection Agency, Air Quality Monitoring Information, "Air Quality Statistics by City, 2014"

Maximum Air Pollutant Concentrations: Nitrogen Dioxide and Sulfur Dioxide

	Nitrogen Dioxide AM (ppb)	Nitrogen Dioxide 1-Hr (ppb)	Sulfur Dioxide AM (ppb)	Sulfur Dioxide 1-Hr (ppb)	Sulfur Dioxide 24-Hr (ppb)
MSA[1] Level	11	55	n/a	5	n/a
NAAQS[2]	53	100	30	75	140
Met NAAQS[2]	Yes	Yes	n/a	Yes	n/a

Note: (1) Data covers the Sacramento—Roseville—Arden-Arcade, CA Metropolitan Statistical Area—see Appendix B for areas included; Data from exceptional events are included; (2) National Ambient Air Quality Standards; ppm = parts per million; ug/m^3 = micrograms per cubic meter; n/a not available.
Concentrations: Nitrogen Dioxide AM—highest arithmetic mean concentration; Nitrogen Dioxide 1-Hr—highest 98th percentile 1-hour daily maximum concentration; Sulfur Dioxide AM—highest annual mean concentration; Sulfur Dioxide 1-Hr—highest 99th percentile 1-hour daily maximum concentration; Sulfur Dioxide 24-Hr—highest second maximum 24-hour concentration
Source: U.S. Environmental Protection Agency, Air Quality Monitoring Information, "Air Quality Statistics by City, 2014"

Drinking Water

Water System Name	Pop. Served	Primary Water Source Type	Violations[1]	
			Health Based	Monitoring/ Reporting
City of Folsom - Main	54,871	Surface	0	0

Note: (1) Based on violation data from January 1, 2015 to December 31, 2015 (includes unresolved violations from earlier years)
Source: U.S. Environmental Protection Agency, Office of Ground Water and Drinking Water, Safe Drinking Water Information System (based on data extracted April 29, 2016)

Foster City, California

Background

Foster City is located on the San Francisco Peninsula, across San Francisco Bay from Oakland where the San Mateo-Hayward Bridge (aka California State Route 92) meets U.S. Route 101 south of San Francisco.

The planned community was launched in 1958 by T. Jack Foster, who backed the effort to build a city at Brewer's Island by putting up his own money and by persuading government officials to create a municipal improvement district that could issue bonds. A massive engineering effort went into creating buildable land, including excavating 2.5 million yards of material to create lagoons that serve as an impoundment basin. Foster City's first home was built in 1964, and the city was incorporated in 1971.

Today the city's lagoons support boating and swimming and beaches, part of the Foster City's recreational appeal. Windsurfing and kiteboarding rentals are easily accessible, as are 21 parks of all sizes, replete with basketball, cycling, a boat launch, children's play area, par course, picnic areas, tennis courts and a community building. In all, the city manages more than 160 acres with numerous walkways, bike paths, and recreational ball fields of all types.

The city also boasts a new public library, and has begun negotiations with a private company to create a senior housing and mixed-commercial use development on city-owned land. Current plans include up to 200 housing units for sale, 150 assisted living units, and 66 affordable housing units within the development.

Students attend the San Mateo-Foster City School District, 20 schools for both communities that includes a Mandarin Language Immersion elementary magnet school, a Spanish-English Two-Way Immersion magnet middle school, and year-round schools. A recent $175 million modernization program has updated schools and facilities.

Sometimes considered to be part of Silicon Valley, Foster City is home to IBM's Innovation Center Silicon Valley, and biopharmaceutical company Gilead Sciences is headquartered here. VISA also maintains a significant presence. In addition to the city's 392-acre industrial park/commercial district is the 132-acre Vintage Park, whose corporate residents include Honeywell.

With its easy access to San Francisco, Oakland, and all the Bay Area has to offer, Foster City's residents can enjoy all manner of cultural opportunities. Closer to home is the Hillbarn Theater, the country's sixth-oldest continuously operating theater, as well as activities backed by the Foster City Arts & Culture Committee that hosts everything from a writing contest to winter classical music concerts.

Abundant transportation opportunities are available, from commuter services to the Caltrain commuter trains in nearby San Mateo to the San Francisco International Airport, a 20-minute drive from Foster City.

Foster City's climate is generally mild, with average summertime highs in the 70s and low humidity with little rain. Winter sees more precipitation—which peaks in January—although temperatures average well above freezing.

Rankings

General Rankings

- The San Francisco* metro area was identified as one of America's fastest-growing areas in terms of population and economy by *Forbes*. The area ranked #7 out of 20. The 100 most populous metro areas in the U.S. were evaluated on the following criteria: estimated population growth; job growth; gross metropolitan product growth; unemployment; median salaries for college-educated workers. *Forbes, "America's Fastest-Growing Cities 2015," January 27, 2015*

Business/Finance Rankings

- The personal finance site NerdWallet analyzed 183 American metropolitan areas with populations over 250,000 and more than 15,000 businesses to rank where entrepreneurs find the most success. Criteria included area economy, annual income, housing cost, unemployment rate, and the success rate of area businesses. San Francisco* ranked #19. *www.nerdwallet.com, "Best Places to Start a Business," April 27, 2015*
- TransUnion ranked the nation's metro areas by average credit score, calculated on the VantageScore system, developed by the three major credit-reporting bureaus—TransUnion, Experian, and Equifax. The San Francisco* metro area was among the ten cities with the highest collective credit score, meaning that its residents posed the lowest average consumer credit risk. *www.usatoday.com, "Metro Areas' Average Credit Rating Revealed," February 7, 2013*
- Based on the U.S. Department of Labor's Occupational Information Network Data Collection Program, the Brookings Institution defined job opportunities for STEM workers at various levels of educational attainment. The San Francisco* metro area was one of the ten metro areas where workers in low-education-level STEM jobs earn the lowest relative wages. *www.brookings.edu, "The Hidden Stem Economy," June 10, 2013*
- 24/7 Wall Street used Brookings Institution research on 50 advanced industries to identify the proportion of workers in the nation's largest metropolitan areas that were employed in jobs requiring knowledge in the science, technology, engineering, or math (STEM) fields. The San Francisco* metro area was #5. *247wallst.com, "15 Cities with the Most High-Tech Jobs," March 13, 2015*
- Based on metro area social media reviews, the employment opinion group Glassdoor surveyed 50 of the largest U.S. metro areas and equally weighed cost of living, hiring opportunity, and job satisfaction to compose a list of "25 Best Cities for Jobs." The San Francisco* metro area was ranked #1 in overall job satisfaction. *www.glassdoor.com, "Best Cities for Jobs," May 19, 2015*
- In a survey of economic confidence in the nation's 50 largest metropolitan areas conducted January–December 2014, the San Francisco* metro area placed #2, according to Gallup's 2014 Economic Confidence Index. *Gallup, "San Jose and San Francisco Lead in Economic Confidence," March 19, 2015*
- The Brookings Institution ranked the 100 largest metro areas in the U.S. based on income inequality. San Francisco* was ranked #3 (#1 = greatest ineqality). Criteria: the "95/20 ratio," a figure representing the income at which a household earns more than 95 percent of all other households, divided by the income at which a household earns more than only 20 percent of all other households. *Brookings Institution, "Income Inequality, 100 Largest U.S. Metro Areas, 2007-2014," January 14, 2016*
- *Forbes* ranked the largest metro areas in the U.S. in terms of the "Best Cities for Young Professionals." The San Francisco* metro area ranked #15 out of 15. Criteria: job growth; unemployment rate; median salary of college graduates age 24 to 34; cost of living; number of small businesses per capita; number of large companies; percentage of population 25 years of age and older with college degrees. *Forbes.com, "America's 15 Best Cities for Young Professionals," August 18, 2014*
- Payscale.com ranked the 20 largest metro areas in terms of wage growth. The San Francisco* metro area ranked #3. Criteria: private-sector wage growth between the 1st quarter of 2015 and the 1st quarter of 2016. *PayScale, "Wage Trends by Metro Area," 1st Quarter, 2016*

- San Francisco* was identified as one of America's most frugal metro areas by *Coupons.com*. The city ranked #1 out of 25. Criteria: online coupon usage. *Coupons.com, "Top 25 Most Frugal Cities of 2014," May 11, 2015*

- The San Francisco* metro area appeared on the Milken Institute "2015 Best Performing Cities" list. Rank: #2 out of 200 large metro areas. Criteria: job growth; wage and salary growth; high-tech output growth. *Milken Institute, "Best-Performing Cities 2015," December 2015*

- *Forbes* ranked the 200 most populous metro areas to determine the nation's "Best Places for Business and Careers." The San Francisco* metro area was ranked #32. Criteria: costs (business and living); job growth (past and projected); income growth; educational attainment (college and high school); projected economic growth; cultural and recreational opportunities; net migration patterns; number of highly ranked colleges. *Forbes, "The Best Places for Business and Careers 2015," July 29, 2015*

Dating/Romance Rankings

- CreditDonkey, a financial education website, sought out the ten best U.S. cities for newlyweds, considering the number of married couples, divorce rate, average credit score, and average number of hours worked per week in metro areas with a million or more residents. The San Francisco* metro area placed #9. *www.creditdonkey.com, "Study: Best Cities for Newlyweds," November 30, 2013*

Education Rankings

- The San Francisco* metro area was selected as one of the world's most inventive cities by *Forbes*. The area was ranked #3 out of 15. Criteria: patent applications per capita. *Forbes, "World's 15 Most Inventive Cities," July 9, 2013*

- Based on a Brookings Institution study, *24/7 Wall St.* identified the ten U.S. metropolitan areas with the most average patent filings per million residents between 2007 and 2011. San Francisco* ranked #8. *24/7 Wall St., "America's Most Innovative Cities," February 1, 2013*

- The San Francisco* metro area was selected as one of America's most innovative cities" by *The Business Insider*. The metro area was ranked #8 out of 20. Criteria: patents per capita. *The Business Insider, "The 20 Most Innovative Cities in the U.S.," February 1, 2013*

- San Francisco* was identified as one of America's "smartest" metropolitan areas by *The Business Journals*. The area ranked #7 out of 10. Criteria: percentage of adults (25 and older) with high school diplomas, bachelor's degrees and graduate degrees. *The Business Journals, "Where the Brainpower Is: Exclusive U.S. Rankings, Insights," February 27, 2014*

- Personal finance website *WalletHub* analyzed the 150 largest U.S. metropolitan statistical areas to determine where the most educated Americans are choosing to settle. Criteria: education quality and attainment gap; education levels; percentage of workers with degrees; public school rankings; quality and size of each metro area's universities. San Francisco* was ranked #20 (#1 = most educated city). *www.WalletHub.com, "2015's Most and Least Educated Cities*

Environmental Rankings

- The San Francisco* metro area came in at #28 for the relative comfort of its climate on Sperling's list of "chill cities," as measured by the Sperling Heat Index. All 361 metro areas are included. Criteria included daytime high temperatures, nighttime low temperatures, dew point, and relative humidity at the high temperatures. *www.bertsperling.com, "Sperling's Chill Cities," July 18, 2013*

- Sperling's BestPlaces assessed 379 metropolitan areas of the United States for the likelihood of dangerously extreme weather events or earthquakes. In general the Southeast and South-Central regions have the highest risk of weather extremes and earthquakes, while the Pacific Northwest enjoys the lowest risk. Of the least risky metropolitan areas, the San Francisco* metro area was ranked #75. *www.bestplaces.net, "Safest Places from Natural Disasters," April 2011*

- The U.S. Environmental Protection Agency (EPA) released a list of U.S. metropolitan areas with the most ENERGY STAR certified buildings in 2015. The San Francisco* metro area was ranked #3 out of 25. *U.S. Environmental Protection Agency, "Top Cities With the Most ENERGY STAR Certified Buildings in 2016," March 30, 2016*

Health/Fitness Rankings

- Analysts who tracked obesity rates in the nation's largest metro areas (populations above one million) found that the San Francisco* metro area was one of the ten major metros where residents were least likely to be obese, defined as a BMI score of 30 or above. *www.gallup.com, "Boulder, Colo., Residents Still Least Likely to Be Obese," April 4, 2014*

- Analysts who tracked obesity rates in 100 of the nation's most populous areas found that the San Francisco* metro area was one of the ten communities where residents were least likely to be obese, defined as a BMI score of 30 or above. *www.gallup.com, "Colorado Springs Residents Least Likely to Be Obese," May 28, 2015*

- For each of the 50 most populous metro areas in the United States, the American College of Sports Medicine's American Fitness Index evaluated infrastructure, community assets, and policies that encourage healthy and fit lifestyles, including preventive health behaviors, levels of chronic disease conditions, health care access, and community resources and policies that support physical activity. The San Francisco* metro area ranked #4 for "community fitness." *www.americanfitnessindex.org, "ACSM American Fitness Index Health and Community Fitness Status of the 50 Largest Metropolitan Areas," May 2015*

- *Business Insider* reported Trulia's analysis of the 100 largest U.S. metro areas to identify the nation's best cities for weight loss, based on healthful food options, access to outdoor activities, weight-loss centers, gyms, and opportunities to bike or walk to work. San Francisco* ranked #1. *Businessinsider.com, "These Are the Best US Cities for Weight loss," January 17, 2013*

- The San Francisco* metro area was identified as one of the worst cities for bed bugs in America by pest control company Orkin. The area ranked #14 out of 50 based on the number of bed bug treatments Orkin performed from January to December 2015. *Orkin, "Chicago Tops Bed Bug Cities List for Fourth Year in a Row," January 13, 2016*

- San Francisco* was identified as a "2016 Spring Allergy Capital." The area ranked #80 out of 100. Three groups of factors were used to identify the most severe cities for people with allergies during the spring season: annual pollen levels; medicine utilization; access to board-certified allergists. *Asthma and Allergy Foundation of America, "Spring Allergy Capitals 2016"*

- San Francisco* was identified as a "2015 Asthma Capital." The area ranked #100 out of the nation's 100 largest metropolitan areas. Criteria: estimated prevalence; self-reported prevalence; crude death rate for asthma; annual pollen score; annual air quality; public smoking laws; number of board-certified asthma specialists; school inhaler access laws; rescue medication use; controller medication use; ER visits for asthma; uninsured rate; poverty rate. *Asthma and Allergy Foundation of America, "Asthma Capitals 2015"*

- The San Francisco* metro area ranked #30 out of 190 in The Gallup-Healthways Well-Being Index. Criteria: purpose; social well being; financial health; community and physical health. Results are based on telephone interviews with adults, aged 18 and older, living in metropolitan areas in the 50 U.S. states and the District of Columbia. *Gallup-Healthways, "State of American Well-Being," February 23, 2016*

Real Estate Rankings

- With data from RealtyTrac, Yahoo! Finance researchers listed the housing markets in which housing affordability is improving most, factoring in interest rates as well as median home prices. The San Francisco* metro area was among the least affordable housing markets. *news.yahoo.com, "10 Cities Where Ordinary People Can No Longer Afford Homes," March 5, 2014*

- The San Francisco* metro area was identified as one of the nations's 20 hottest housing markets in 2016. Criteria: listing views as an indicator of demand and median days on the market as an indicator of supply. The area ranked #1. *Realtor.com, "The 20 Hottest U.S. Real Estate Markets in February 2016," February 25, 2016*

- San Francisco* was ranked #4 in the top 20 out of 266 metro areas in terms of house price appreciation in 2015 (#1 = highest rate). *Federal Housing Finance Agency, House Price Index, 4th Quarter 2015*

- The San Francisco* metro area was identified as one of the 10 best condo markets in the U.S. in 2015. The area ranked #6 out of 61 markets. Criteria: year-over-year change of median sales price of existing apartment condo-coop homes between the 4th quarter of 2014 and the 4th quarter of 2015. *National Association of Realtors®, Median Sales Price of Existing Apartment Condo-Coop Homes for Metropolitan Areas, 4th Quarter 2015*

- The San Francisco* metro area was identified as one of the 20 least affordable housing markets in the U.S. in 2015. The area ranked #4 out of 179 markets. Criteria: qualification for a mortgage loan on a typical home. *National Association of Realtors®, Affordability Index of Existing Single-Family Homes for Metropolitan Areas, 2015*

- San Francisco* was ranked #225 out of 225 metro areas in terms of housing affordability in 2015 by the National Association of Home Builders (#1 = most affordable). Criteria: the share of homes sold in that area affordable to a family earning the local median income, based on standard mortgage underwriting criteria. *National Association of Home Builders®, NAHB-Wells Fargo Housing Opportunity Index, 4th Quarter 2015*

Safety Rankings

- Farmers Insurance, in partnership with Sperling's BestPlaces, ranked metro areas in the U.S. as the "Most Secure Places to Live." The San Francisco* metro area ranked #8 out of the top 20 in the large metro area category (500,000 or more residents). Criteria: economic stability; crime statistics; extreme weather; risk of natural disasters; housing depreciation; foreclosures; air quality; environmental hazards; life expectancy; motor vehicle fatalities; and employment numbers. *Farmers Insurance Group of Companies, "Most Secure U.S. Places to Live in the U.S.," June 25, 2013*

- The National Insurance Crime Bureau ranked 380 metro areas in the U.S. in terms of per capita rates of vehicle theft. The San Francisco* metro area ranked #1 (#1 = highest rate). Criteria: number of vehicle theft offenses per 100,000 inhabitants in 2014. *National Insurance Crime Bureau, "Hot Spots 2014," June 24, 2015*

Seniors/Retirement Rankings

- From its Best Cities for Successful Aging indexes, the Milken Institute generated rankings for metropolitan areas, weighing data in eight categories—health care, wellness, living arrangements, transportation, financial characteristics, education and employment opportunities, community engagement, and overall livability. The San Francisco* metro area was ranked #17 overall in the large metro area category. *Milken Institute, "Best Cities for Successful Aging, 2014"*

Sports/Recreation Rankings

- According to the personal finance website NerdWallet, the San Francisco* metro area, at #5, is one of the nation's top dozen metro areas for sports fans. Criteria included the presence of all four major sports—MLB, NFL, NHL, and NBA, fan enthusiasm (as measured by game attendance), ticket affordability, and "sports culture," that is, number of sports bars. *www.nerdwallet.com, "Best Cities for Sports Fans," May 5, 2013*

Transportation Rankings

- San Francisco* was identified as one of the most congested metro areas in the U.S. The area ranked #3 out of 10. Criteria: yearly delay per auto commuter in hours. *Texas A&M Transportation Institute, "2015 Urban Mobility Scorecard," August 2015*

- The San Francisco* metro area appeared on *Forbes* list of places with the most extreme commutes. The metro area ranked #1 out of 10. Criteria: average travel time; percentage of mega commuters. Mega-commuters travel more than 90 minutes and 50 miles each way to work. *Forbes.com, "The Cities with the Most Extreme Commutes," March 5, 2013*

Miscellaneous Rankings

- The watchdog site Charity Navigator conducts an annual study of charities in the nation's major markets both to analyze statistical differences in their financial, accountability, and transparency practices and to track year-to-year variations in individual communities. The San Francisco* metro area was ranked #9 among the 30 metro markets in the rating dimension of Overall Score. *www.charitynavigator.org, "Metro Market Study 2015," June 5, 2015*
- The Harris Poll's Happiness Index survey revealed that of the top ten U.S. markets, the San Francisco* metro area residents ranked #10 in happiness. Criteria included strong assent to positive statements and strong disagreement with negative ones, and degree of agreement with a series of statements about respondents' personal relationships and general outlook. *www.harrisinteractive.com, "Dallas/Fort Worth Is "Happiest" City among America's Top Ten Markets," September 4, 2013*
- Mars Chocolate North America, the makers of COMBOS®, in partnership with Sperling's BestPlaces, ranked 50 major metro areas in terms of their "manliness." The San Francisco* metro area ranked #49. Criteria: number of professional sports teams; number of nearby NASCAR tracks and racing events; manly lifestyle; concentration of manly retail stores; manly occupations per capita; salty snack sales; "Board of Manliness" rankings. *Mars Chocolate North America, "America's Manliest Cities 2012"*
- The National Alliance to End Homelessness ranked the 100 most populous metro areas with the highest rate of homelessness. The San Francisco* metro area ranked #12. Criteria: number of homeless people per 10,000 population in 2011. *National Alliance to End Homelessness, The State of Homelessness in America 2012*

Foster City is located within the San Francisco-Oakland-Hayward, CA Metropolitan Statistical Area.

Business Environment

CITY FINANCES

City Government Finances

Component	2012 ($000)	2012 ($ per capita)
Total Revenues	62,093	2,031
Total Expenditures	62,438	2,042
Debt Outstanding	0	0
Cash and Securities[1]	62,337	2,039

Note: (1) Cash and security holdings of a government at the close of its fiscal year, including those of its dependent agencies, utilities, and liquor stores.
Source: U.S Census Bureau, State & Local Government Finances 2012

City Government Revenue by Source

Source	2012 ($000)	2012 ($ per capita)
General Revenue		
From Federal Government	0	0
From State Government	1,891	61
From Local Governments	0	0
Taxes		
Property	29,583	967
Sales and Gross Receipts	6,735	220
Personal Income	0	0
Corporate Income	0	0
Motor Vehicle License	0	0
Other Taxes	2,357	77
Current Charges	9,407	307
Liquor Store	0	0
Utility	10,454	342
Employee Retirement	0	0

Source: U.S Census Bureau, State & Local Government Finances 2012

City Government Expenditures by Function

Function	2012 ($000)	2012 ($ per capita)	2012 (%)
General Direct Expenditures			
Air Transportation	0	0	0.0
Corrections	0	0	0.0
Education	0	0	0.0
Employment Security Administration	0	0	0.0
Financial Administration	737	24	1.1
Fire Protection	8,149	266	13.0
General Public Buildings	0	0	0.0
Governmental Administration, Other	3,574	116	5.7
Health	0	0	0.0
Highways	2,575	84	4.1
Hospitals	0	0	0.0
Housing and Community Development	2,646	86	4.2
Interest on General Debt	0	0	0.0
Judicial and Legal	340	11	0.5
Libraries	0	0	0.0
Parking	0	0	0.0
Parks and Recreation	9,576	313	15.3
Police Protection	9,186	300	14.7
Public Welfare	0	0	0.0
Sewerage	6,461	211	10.3
Solid Waste Management	0	0	0.0
Veterans' Services	0	0	0.0
Liquor Store	0	0	0.0
Utility	9,231	301	14.7
Employee Retirement	0	0	0.0

Source: U.S Census Bureau, State & Local Government Finances 2012

DEMOGRAPHICS

Population Growth

Area	1990 Census	2000 Census	2010 Census	2014* Estimate	Population Growth (%) 1990-2014	2010-2014
City	28,176	28,803	30,567	31,809	12.9	4.1
MSA[1]	3,686,592	4,123,740	4,335,391	4,466,251	21.1	3.0
U.S.	248,709,873	281,421,906	308,745,538	314,107,084	26.3	1.7

Note: (1) Figures cover the San Francisco-Oakland-Hayward, CA Metropolitan Statistical Area—see Appendix B for areas included; (*) 2010-2014 5-year estimated population
Source: U.S. Census Bureau, 1990 Census, Census 2000, Census 2010, 2010-2014 American Community Survey 5-Year Estimates

Household Size

Area	Persons in Household (%) One	Two	Three	Four	Five	Six	Seven or More	Average Household Size
City	23.9	35.4	17.2	16.8	4.4	1.6	0.4	2.63
MSA[1]	28.1	31.4	16.2	14.0	5.8	2.3	1.7	2.67
U.S.	27.5	33.5	15.8	13.1	6.0	2.3	1.4	2.64

Note: (1) Figures cover the San Francisco-Oakland-Hayward, CA Metropolitan Statistical Area—see Appendix B for areas included
Source: U.S. Census Bureau, 2010-2014 American Community Survey 5-Year Estimates

Race

Area	White Alone[2] (%)	Black Alone[2] (%)	Asian Alone[2] (%)	AIAN[3] Alone[2] (%)	NHOPI[4] Alone[2] (%)	Other Race Alone[2] (%)	Two or More Races (%)
City	45.4	1.9	45.9	0.2	0.2	1.0	5.5
MSA[1]	54.0	8.0	24.0	0.5	0.7	7.5	5.4
U.S.	73.8	12.6	5.0	0.8	0.2	4.7	2.9

Note: (1) Figures cover the San Francisco-Oakland-Hayward, CA Metropolitan Statistical Area—see Appendix B for areas included; (2) Alone is defined as not being in combination with one or more other races; (3) American Indian and Alaska Native; (4) Native Hawaiian and Other Pacific Islander
Source: U.S. Census Bureau, 2010-2014 American Community Survey 5-Year Estimates

Hispanic or Latino Origin

Area	Total (%)	Mexican (%)	Puerto Rican (%)	Cuban (%)	Other (%)
City	5.5	3.5	0.3	0.0	1.7
MSA[1]	21.8	14.8	0.6	0.2	6.2
U.S.	16.9	10.8	1.6	0.6	3.8

Note: Persons of Hispanic or Latino origin can be of any race; (1) Figures cover the San Francisco-Oakland-Hayward, CA Metropolitan Statistical Area—see Appendix B for areas included
Source: U.S. Census Bureau, 2010-2014 American Community Survey 5-Year Estimates

Ancestry

Area	German	Irish	English	American	Italian	Polish	French[2]	Scottish	Dutch
City	7.7	5.7	5.2	2.6	4.0	1.5	1.6	0.9	0.3
MSA[1]	8.5	7.9	6.3	2.6	5.3	1.5	2.0	1.6	0.9
U.S.	14.9	10.8	8.0	7.1	5.5	3.0	2.7	1.7	1.4

Note: Figures are the percentage of the total population reporting a particular ancestry. The nine most commonly reported ancestries in the U.S. are shown. Figures include multiple ancestries (e.g. if a person reported being Irish and Italian, they were included in both columns); (1) Figures cover the San Francisco-Oakland-Hayward, CA Metropolitan Statistical Area—see Appendix B for areas included; (2) Excludes Basque
Source: U.S. Census Bureau, 2010-2014 American Community Survey 5-Year Estimates

Foreign-Born Population

Area	Percent of Population Born in								
	Any Foreign Country	Asia	Mexico	Europe	Carribean	Central America[2]	South America	Africa	Canada
City	43.1	33.8	0.5	5.5	0.1	0.4	0.9	1.0	0.6
MSA[1]	29.9	16.3	5.6	2.9	0.2	2.5	0.9	0.6	0.4
U.S.	13.1	3.8	3.7	1.5	1.2	1.0	0.9	0.6	0.3

Note: (1) Figures cover the San Francisco-Oakland-Hayward, CA Metropolitan Statistical Area—see Appendix B for areas included; (2) Excludes Mexico.
Source: U.S. Census Bureau, 2010-2014 American Community Survey 5-Year Estimates

Marital Status

Area	Never Married	Now Married[2]	Separated	Widowed	Divorced
City	23.9	61.3	1.3	5.9	7.5
MSA[1]	35.9	47.7	1.9	5.2	9.4
U.S.	32.5	48.4	2.2	5.9	10.9

Note: Figures are percentages and cover the population 15 years of age and older; (1) Figures cover the San Francisco-Oakland-Hayward, CA Metropolitan Statistical Area—see Appendix B for areas included; (2) Excludes separated
Source: U.S. Census Bureau, 2010-2014 American Community Survey 5-Year Estimates

Disability Status

Area	All Ages	Under 18 Years Old	18 to 64 Years Old	65 Years and Over
City	5.2	1.0	2.6	21.1
MSA[1]	9.5	2.7	6.9	33.3
U.S.	12.3	4.1	10.2	36.3

Note: Figures show percent of the civilian noninstitutionalized population that reported having a disability. Disability status is determined from from six types of difficulty: vision, hearing, cognitive, ambulatory, self-care, and independent living. For children under 5 years old, hearing and vision difficulty are used to determine disability status. For children between the ages of 5 and 14, disability status is determined from hearing, vision, cognitive, ambulatory, and self-care difficulties. For people aged 15 years and older, they are considered to have a disability if they have difficulty with any one of the six difficulty types; (1) Figures cover the San Francisco-Oakland-Hayward, CA Metropolitan Statistical Area—see Appendix B for areas included.
Source: U.S. Census Bureau, 2010-2014 American Community Survey 5-Year Estimates

Age

Area	Percent of Population									Median Age
	Under Age 5	Age 5–19	Age 20–34	Age 35–44	Age 45–54	Age 55–64	Age 65–74	Age 75–84	Age 85+	
City	6.3	16.7	17.3	17.2	13.7	12.6	9.4	4.9	2.0	40.7
MSA[1]	5.8	17.3	21.6	14.8	14.7	12.5	7.3	4.0	2.0	38.6
U.S.	6.4	19.9	20.6	13.0	14.1	12.3	7.6	4.3	1.9	37.4

Note: (1) Figures cover the San Francisco-Oakland-Hayward, CA Metropolitan Statistical Area—see Appendix B for areas included
Source: U.S. Census Bureau, 2010-2014 American Community Survey 5-Year Estimates

Gender

Area	Males	Females	Males per 100 Females
City	15,441	16,368	94.3
MSA[1]	2,202,384	2,263,867	97.3
U.S.	154,515,159	159,591,925	96.8

Note: (1) Figures cover the San Francisco-Oakland-Hayward, CA Metropolitan Statistical Area—see Appendix B for areas included
Source: U.S. Census Bureau, 2010-2014 American Community Survey 5-Year Estimates

Religious Groups by Family

Area	Catholic	Baptist	Non-Den.	Methodist[2]	Lutheran	LDS[3]	Pente-costal	Presby-terian[4]	Muslim[5]	Judaism
MSA[1]	20.7	2.5	2.4	1.9	0.5	1.5	1.2	1.1	1.2	0.8
U.S.	19.1	9.3	4.0	4.0	2.3	2.0	1.9	1.6	0.8	0.7

Note: Figures are the number of adherents as a percentage of the total population; (1) Figures cover the San Francisco-Oakland-Fremont, CA Metropolitan Statistical Area—see Appendix B for areas included; (2) Methodist/Pietist; (3) Latter Day Saints; (4) Reformed; (5) Figures are estimates
Source: Association of Statisticians of American Religious Bodies, 2010 U.S. Religion Census: Religious Congregations & Membership Study

Religious Groups by Tradition

Area	Catholic	Evangelical Protestant	Mainline Protestant	Other Tradition	Black Protestant	Orthodox
MSA[1]	20.7	6.1	3.8	5.2	1.0	0.6
U.S.	19.1	16.2	7.3	4.3	1.6	0.3

Note: Figures are the number of adherents as a percentage of the total population; (1) Figures cover the San Francisco-Oakland-Fremont, CA Metropolitan Statistical Area—see Appendix B for areas included
Source: Association of Statisticians of American Religious Bodies, 2010 U.S. Religion Census: Religious Congregations & Membership Study

ECONOMY

Gross Metropolitan Product

Area	2013	2014	2015	2016	Rank[2]
MSA[1]	388.2	408.6	426.9	451.0	7

Note: Figures are in billions of dollars; (1) Figures cover the San Francisco-Oakland-Hayward, CA Metropolitan Statistical Area—see Appendix B for areas included; (2) Rank is based on 2016 data and ranges from 1 to 381
Source: The U.S. Conference of Mayors, U.S. Metro Economies: GMP and Employment 2014-2016, June 2015

Economic Growth

Area	2011-13 (%)	2014 (%)	2015 (%)	2016 (%)	Rank[2]
MSA[1]	4.2	3.8	3.2	3.7	27
U.S.	2.2	2.4	2.3	2.9	–

Note: Figures are real gross metropolitan product (GMP) growth rates and represent annual average percent change; (1) Figures cover the San Francisco-Oakland-Hayward, CA Metropolitan Statistical Area—see Appendix B for areas included; (2) Rank is based on 2016 data and ranges from 1 to 381
Source: The U.S. Conference of Mayors, U.S. Metro Economies: GMP and Employment 2014-2016, June 2015

Metropolitan Area Exports

Area	2009	2010	2011	2012	2013	2014	Rank[2]
MSA[1]	16,040.3	21,355.4	23,573.7	23,031.6	25,305.2	26,863.6	10

Note: Figures are in millions of dollars; (1) Figures cover the San Francisco-Oakland-Hayward, CA Metropolitan Statistical Area—see Appendix B for areas included; (2) Rank is based on 2014 data and ranges from 1 to 385
Source: U.S. Department of Commerce, International Trade Administration, Office of Trade & Industry Information, Manufacturing & Services, data extracted March 10, 2016

Building Permits

Area	Single-Family			Multi-Family			Total		
	2014	2015p	Pct. Chg.	2014	2015p	Pct. Chg.	2014	2015p	Pct. Chg.
City	0	26	-	232	320	37.9	232	346	49.1
MSA[1]	3,716	4,595	23.7	6,285	8,171	30.0	10,001	12,766	27.6
U.S.	640,300	690,800	7.9	411,800	487,600	18.4	1,052,100	1,178,400	12.0

Note: (1) Figures cover the San Francisco-Oakland-Hayward, CA Metropolitan Statistical Area—see Appendix B for areas included; Figures represent new, privately-owned housing units authorized (unadjusted data); All permit data are based on estimates with imputation; (p) preliminary data.
Source: U.S. Census Bureau, Manufacturing, Mining, and Construction Statistics, Building Permits, 2014, 2015

INCOME

Bankruptcy Filings

Area	Business Filings			Nonbusiness Filings		
	2014	2015	% Chg.	2014	2015	% Chg.
San Mateo County	73	60	-17.8	998	826	-17.2
U.S.	26,983	24,735	-8.3	909,812	819,760	-9.9

Note: Business filings include Chapter 7, Chapter 11, Chapter 12, and Chapter 13; Nonbusiness filings include Chapter 7, Chapter 11, and Chapter 13
Source: Administrative Office of the U.S. Courts, Business and Nonbusiness Bankruptcy, County Cases Commenced by Chapter of the Bankruptcy Code, During the 12- Month Period Ending December 31, 2014 and Business and Nonbusiness Bankruptcy, County Cases Commenced by Chapter of the Bankruptcy Code, During the 12- Month Period Ending December 31, 2015

Housing Vacancy Rates

Area	Gross Vacancy Rate[2] (%)			Year-Round Vacancy Rate[3] (%)			Rental Vacancy Rate[4] (%)			Homeowner Vacancy Rate[5] (%)		
	2013	2014	2015	2013	2014	2015	2013	2014	2015	2013	2014	2015
MSA[1]	6.5	5.9	5.7	6.4	5.9	5.7	3.9	3.2	3.6	1.1	0.4	0.7
U.S.	13.6	13.4	12.9	10.7	10.4	10.0	8.3	7.6	7.1	2.0	1.9	1.8

Note: (1) Figures cover the San Francisco-Oakland-Hayward, CA Metropolitan Statistical Area—see Appendix B for areas included; (2) The percentage of the total housing inventory that is vacant; (3) The percentage of the housing inventory (excluding seasonal units) that is year-round vacant; (4) The percentage of rental inventory that is vacant for rent; (5) The percentage of homeowner inventory that is vacant for sale
Source: U.S. Census Bureau, Housing Vacancies and Homeownership Annual Statistics: 2015

Income

Area	Per Capita ($)	Median Household ($)	Average Household ($)
City	55,318	114,651	142,467
MSA[1]	42,540	80,008	112,073
U.S.	28,555	53,482	74,596

Note: (1) Figures cover the San Francisco-Oakland-Hayward, CA Metropolitan Statistical Area—see Appendix B for areas included
Source: U.S. Census Bureau, 2010-2014 American Community Survey 5-Year Estimates

Household Income Distribution

Area	Percent of Households Earning							
	Under $15,000	$15,000 -24,999	$25,000 -34,999	$35,000 -49,999	$50,000 -74,999	$75,000 -99,000	$100,000 -149,999	$150,000 and up
City	4.0	3.6	3.2	5.2	11.8	13.3	21.9	36.9
MSA[1]	9.2	7.2	6.7	9.6	14.8	11.8	17.5	23.3
U.S.	12.5	10.7	10.2	13.5	17.8	12.2	13.0	10.0

Note: (1) Figures cover the San Francisco-Oakland-Hayward, CA Metropolitan Statistical Area—see Appendix B for areas included
Source: U.S. Census Bureau, 2010-2014 American Community Survey 5-Year Estimates

Poverty Rate

Area	All Ages	Under 18 Years Old	18 to 64 Years Old	65 Years and Over
City	3.9	3.8	3.5	5.7
MSA[1]	11.3	13.5	11.1	9.0
U.S.	15.6	21.9	14.6	9.4

Note: Figures are percentage of people whose income during the past 12 months was below the poverty level; (1) Figures cover the San Francisco-Oakland-Hayward, CA Metropolitan Statistical Area—see Appendix B for areas included
Source: U.S. Census Bureau, 2010-2014 American Community Survey 5-Year Estimates

EMPLOYMENT

Labor Force and Employment

Area	Civilian Labor Force			Workers Employed		
	Dec. 2014	Dec. 2015	% Chg.	Dec. 2014	Dec. 2015	% Chg.
City	18,702	19,135	2.3	18,100	18,597	2.7
MD[1]	977,381	999,542	2.2	942,144	967,640	2.7
U.S.	155,521,000	157,245,000	1.1	147,190,000	149,703,000	1.7

Note: Data is not seasonally adjusted and covers workers 16 years of age and older; (1) Figures cover the San Francisco-Redwood City-South San Francisco, CA Metropolitan Division—see Appendix B for areas included
Source: Bureau of Labor Statistics, Local Area Unemployment Statistics

Unemployment Rate

Area	2015											
	Jan.	Feb.	Mar.	Apr.	May	Jun.	Jul.	Aug.	Sep.	Oct.	Nov.	Dec.
City	3.5	3.2	3.1	2.9	3.0	3.0	3.2	3.0	2.7	2.9	2.9	2.8
MD[1]	4.0	3.7	3.5	3.3	3.4	3.4	3.7	3.4	3.1	3.3	3.2	3.2
U.S.	6.1	5.8	5.6	5.1	5.3	5.5	5.6	5.2	4.9	4.8	4.8	4.8

Note: Data is not seasonally adjusted and covers workers 16 years of age and older; (1) Figures cover the San Francisco-Redwood City-South San Francisco, CA Metropolitan Division—see Appendix B for areas included
Source: Bureau of Labor Statistics, Local Area Unemployment Statistics

Employment by Occupation

Occupation Classification	City (%)	MSA[1] (%)	U.S. (%)
Management, Business, Science, and Arts	65.6	46.8	36.4
Natural Resources, Construction, and Maintenance	2.1	6.2	9.0
Production, Transportation, and Material Moving	4.0	7.5	12.1
Sales and Office	21.2	22.4	24.4
Service	7.0	17.2	18.2

Note: Figures cover employed civilians 16 years of age and older; (1) Figures cover the San Francisco-Oakland-Hayward, CA Metropolitan Statistical Area—see Appendix B for areas included
Source: U.S. Census Bureau, 2010-2014 American Community Survey 5-Year Estimates

Employment by Industry

Sector	MD[1]		U.S.
	Number of Employees	Percent of Total	Percent of Total
Construction	42,900	3.9	4.5
Education and Health Services	133,000	12.3	15.7
Financial Activities	74,500	6.8	5.7
Government	126,500	11.7	15.5
Information	60,900	5.6	1.9
Leisure and Hospitality	137,000	12.6	10.4
Manufacturing	35,600	3.2	8.6
Mining and Logging	100	<0.1	0.5
Other Services	40,000	3.7	3.9
Professional and Business Services	272,500	25.2	13.9
Retail Trade	87,100	8.0	11.3
Transportation, Warehousing, and Utilities	43,000	3.9	3.9
Wholesale Trade	27,400	2.5	4.1

Note: Figures are non-farm employment as of December 2015. Figures are not seasonally adjusted and include workers 16 years of age and older; (1) Figures cover the San Francisco-Redwood City-South San Francisco, CA Metropolitan Division—see Appendix B for areas included
Source: Bureau of Labor Statistics, Current Employment Statistics, Employment, Hours, and Earnings

Occupations with Greatest Projected Employment Growth: 2012 – 2022

Occupation[1]	2012 Employment	2022 Projected Employment	Numeric Employment Change	Percent Employment Change
Personal Care Aides	386,900	587,200	200,300	51.8
Combined Food Preparation and Serving Workers, Including Fast Food	286,000	362,400	76,400	26.7
Retail Salespersons	468,400	528,100	59,700	12.7
Laborers and Freight, Stock, and Material Movers, Hand	270,500	322,300	51,800	19.1
Waiters and Waitresses	246,100	290,300	44,200	18.0
Registered Nurses	254,500	297,400	42,900	16.9
General and Operations Managers	253,800	295,700	41,900	16.5
Secretaries and Administrative Assistants, Except Legal, Medical, and Executive	212,800	250,100	37,300	17.5
Cashiers	357,800	392,600	34,800	9.7
Cooks, Restaurant	116,900	150,600	33,700	28.8

Note: Projections cover California; (1) Sorted by numeric employment change
Source: www.projectionscentral.com, State Occupational Projections, 2012–2022 Long-Term Projections

Fastest Growing Occupations: 2012 – 2022

Occupation[1]	2012 Employment	2022 Projected Employment	Numeric Employment Change	Percent Employment Change
Economists	3,100	5,100	2,000	64.5
Helpers—Brickmasons, Blockmasons, Stonemasons, and Tile and Marble Setters	2,900	4,600	1,700	58.6
Brickmasons and Blockmasons	5,100	8,000	2,900	56.9
Insulation Workers, Floor, Ceiling, and Wall	1,600	2,500	900	56.3
Stonemasons	1,100	1,700	600	54.5
Insulation Workers, Mechanical	1,100	1,700	600	54.5
Personal Care Aides	386,900	587,200	200,300	51.8
Foresters	1,200	1,800	600	50.0
Terrazzo Workers and Finishers	1,100	1,600	500	45.5
Mechanical Door Repairers	1,100	1,600	500	45.5

Note: Projections cover California; (1) Sorted by percent employment change and excludes occupations with numeric employment change less than 100
Source: www.projectionscentral.com, State Occupational Projections, 2012–2022 Long-Term Projections

Average Wages

Occupation	$/Hr.	Occupation	$/Hr.
Accountants and Auditors	43.70	Maids and Housekeeping Cleaners	17.69
Automotive Mechanics	27.46	Maintenance and Repair Workers	27.89
Bookkeepers	24.88	Marketing Managers	89.58
Carpenters	32.84	Nuclear Medicine Technologists	55.14
Cashiers	13.41	Nurses, Licensed Practical	29.72
Clerks, General Office	20.58	Nurses, Registered	64.26
Clerks, Receptionists/Information	17.81	Nursing Assistants	19.09
Clerks, Shipping/Receiving	19.15	Packers and Packagers, Hand	13.19
Computer Programmers	51.96	Physical Therapists	51.47
Computer Systems Analysts	55.39	Postal Service Mail Carriers	26.23
Computer User Support Specialists	35.68	Real Estate Brokers	41.41
Cooks, Restaurant	14.96	Retail Salespersons	15.57
Dentists	93.40	Sales Reps., Exc. Tech./Scientific	31.16
Electrical Engineers	55.57	Sales Reps., Tech./Scientific	53.91
Electricians	44.77	Secretaries, Exc. Legal/Med./Exec.	22.36
Financial Managers	89.78	Security Guards	16.41
First-Line Supervisors/Managers, Sales	24.32	Surgeons	92.50
Food Preparation Workers	12.28	Teacher Assistants*	17.85
General and Operations Managers	74.80	Teachers, Elementary School*	33.40
Hairdressers/Cosmetologists	16.55	Teachers, Secondary School*	36.46
Internists	90.30	Telemarketers	17.46
Janitors and Cleaners	14.30	Truck Drivers, Heavy/Tractor-Trailer	24.39
Landscaping/Groundskeeping Workers	19.61	Truck Drivers, Light/Delivery Svcs.	19.99
Lawyers	85.63	Waiters and Waitresses	15.41

Note: Wage data covers the San Francisco-San Mateo-Redwood City, CA Metropolitan Division—see Appendix B for areas included; (*) Hourly wages for elementary/secondary school teachers and teacher assistants were calculated by the editors from annual wage data based on a 40 hour work week; n/a not available.
Source: Bureau of Labor Statistics, Metro Area Occupational Employment and Wage Estimates, May 2015

TAXES

State Corporate Income Tax Rates

State	Tax Rate (%)	Income Brackets ($)	Num. of Brackets	Financial Institution Tax Rate (%)[a]	Federal Income Tax Ded.
California	8.84 (c)	Flat rate	1	10.84 (c)	No

Note: Tax rates as of January 1, 2016; (a) Rates listed are the corporate income tax rate applied to financial institutions or excise taxes based on income. Some states have other taxes based upon the value of deposits or shares; (c) Minimum tax is $800 in California, $100 in District of Columbia, $50 in North Dakota (banks), $500 in Rhode Island, $200 per location in South Dakota (banks), $100 in Utah, $250 in Vermont.
Source: Federation of Tax Administrators, "State Corporate Income Tax Rates, 2016"

State Individual Income Tax Rates

State	Tax Rate (%)	Income Brackets ($)	Num. of Brackets	Personal Exempt. ($)[1] Single	Personal Exempt. ($)[1] Dependents	Fed. Inc. Tax Ded.
California (a)	1.0 - 12.3 (f)	7,850- 526,443 (b)	9	109 (c)	337 (c)	No

Note: Tax rates as of January 1, 2016; Local- and county-level taxes are not included; n/a not applicable; (1) Married joint filers generally receive double the single exemption; (a) 18 states have statutory provision for automatically adjusting to the rate of inflation the dollar values of the income tax brackets, standard deductions, and/or personal exemptions. Massachusetts, Michigan, and Nebraska index the personal exemptiononly. Oregon does not index the income brackets for $125,000 and over. Maine has suspended indexing for 2014 and 2015; (b) For joint returns, taxes are twice the tax on half the couple's income; (c) The personal exemption takes the form of a tax credit instead of a deduction; (f) California imposes an additional 1% tax on taxable income over $1 million, making the maximum rate 13.3% over $1 million.
Source: Federation of Tax Administrators, "State Individual Income Tax Rates, 2016"

Various State and Local Tax Rates

State	State and Local Sales and Use (%)	State Sales and Use (%)	Gasoline[1] (¢/gal.)	Cigarette[2] ($/pack)	Spirits[3] ($/gal.)	Wine[4] ($/gal.)	Beer[5] ($/gal.)
California	9.00	7.50 (b)	40.62	0.87	3.30 (f)	0.20 (l)	0.08

Note: All tax rates as of January 1, 2016; (1) The American Petroleum Institute has developed a methodology for determining the average tax rate on a gallon of fuel. Rates may include any of the following: excise taxes, environmental fees, storage tank fees, other fees or taxes, general sales tax, and local taxes. In states where gasoline is subject to the general sales tax, or where the fuel tax is based on the average sale price, the average rate determined by API is sensitive to changes in the price of gasoline. States that fully or partially apply general sales taxes to gasoline: CA, CO, GA, IL, IN, MI, NY; (2) The federal excise tax of $1.0066 per pack and local taxes are not included; (3) Rates are those applicable to off-premise sales of 40% alcohol by volume (a.b.v.) distilled spirits in 750ml containers. Local excise taxes are excluded; (4) Rates are those applicable to off-premise sales of 11% a.b.v. non-carbonated wine in 750ml containers; (5) Rates are those applicable to off-premise sales of 4.7% a.b.v. beer in 12 ounce containers; (b) Three states levy mandatory, statewide local add-on sales taxes at the state level: California (1%), Utah (1.25%), and Virginia (1%). We include these in their state sales tax rates; (f) Different rates are also applicable according to alcohol content, place of production, size of container, or place purchased (on- or off-premise or onboard airlines); (l) Different rates also applicable according to alcohol content, place of production, size of container, place purchased (on- or off-premise or on board airlines) or type of wine (carbonated, vermouth, etc.).
Source: Tax Foundation, 2016 Facts & Figures: How Does Your State Compare?

State Business Tax Climate Index Rankings

State	Overall Rank	Corporate Tax Rank	Individual Income Tax Rank	Sales Tax Rank	Unemployment Insurance Tax Rank	Property Tax Rank
California	48	35	50	40	13	13

Note: The index is a measure of how each state's tax laws affect economic performance. The lower the rank, the more favorable a state's tax system is for business. States without a given tax are given a ranking of 1. The scores/rankings for the District of Columbia do not affect other states. The 2016 index represents the tax climate as of July 1, 2015 (the beginning of Fiscal Year 2016).
Source: Tax Foundation, State Business Tax Climate Index 2016

TRANSPORTATION

Means of Transportation to Work

Area	Car/Truck/Van: Drove Alone	Car/Truck/Van: Car-pooled	Public Transportation: Bus	Public Transportation: Subway	Public Transportation: Railroad	Bicycle	Walked	Other Means	Worked at Home
City	74.2	11.9	1.1	1.2	2.2	0.9	1.4	1.2	6.0
MSA[1]	60.6	10.1	7.6	6.1	1.0	1.9	4.4	2.3	6.1
U.S.	76.4	9.6	2.6	1.8	0.6	0.6	2.8	1.3	4.4

Note: Figures are percentages and cover workers 16 years of age and older; (1) Figures cover the San Francisco-Oakland-Hayward, CA Metropolitan Statistical Area—see Appendix B for areas included
Source: U.S. Census Bureau, 2010-2014 American Community Survey 5-Year Estimates

Travel Time to Work

Area	Less Than 10 Minutes	10 to 19 Minutes	20 to 29 Minutes	30 to 44 Minutes	45 to 59 Minutes	60 to 89 Minutes	90 Minutes or More
City	8.4	28.7	20.0	23.6	10.8	7.4	1.1
MSA[1]	7.8	24.9	19.1	24.1	11.1	10.0	3.0
U.S.	13.3	29.6	21.0	20.2	7.7	5.7	2.6

Note: Figures are percentages and include workers 16 years old and over; (1) Figures cover the San Francisco-Oakland-Hayward, CA Metropolitan Statistical Area—see Appendix B for areas included
Source: U.S. Census Bureau, 2010-2014 American Community Survey 5-Year Estimates

Freeway Travel Time Index

Area	1985	1990	1995	2000	2005	2010	2014
Urban Area Rank[1,2]	2	2	2	2	2	2	2
Urban Area Index[1]	1.30	1.32	1.36	1.38	1.40	1.38	1.41
Average Index[3]	1.09	1.11	1.14	1.17	1.20	1.19	1.20

Note: Freeway Travel Time Index—the ratio of travel time in the peak period to the travel time at free-flow conditions. For example, a value of 1.30 indicates a 20-minute free-flow trip takes 26 minutes in the peak (20 minutes x 1.30 = 26 minutes); (1) Covers the San Francisco-Oakland CA urban area; (2) Rank is based on 101 urban areas (#1 = highest travel time index); (3) Average of 101 urban areas
Source: Texas Transportation Institute, 2015 Urban Mobility Scorecard, August 2015

Freeway Commuter Stress Index

Area	1985	1990	1995	2000	2005	2010	2014
Urban Area Rank[1,2]	2	2	2	2	2	2	2
Urban Area Index[1]	1.45	1.48	1.52	1.54	1.56	1.54	1.57
Average Index[3]	1.13	1.16	1.19	1.22	1.25	1.24	1.25

Note: The Freeway Commuter Stress Index is the same as the Freeway Travel Time Index (see table above) except that it includes only the travel in the peak directions during the peak periods; the TTI includes travel in all directions during the peak period. Thus, the CSI is more indicative of the work trip experienced by each commuter on a daily basis. (1) Covers the San Francisco-Oakland CA urban area; (2) Rank is based on 101 urban areas (#1 = highest stress index); (3) Average of 101 urban areas
Source: Texas Transportation Institute, 2015 Urban Mobility Scorecard, August 2015

Living Environment

COST OF LIVING

Cost of Living Index

Composite Index	Groceries	Housing	Utilities	Trans-portation	Health Care	Misc. Goods/ Services
176.7	127.9	320.6	108.3	131.7	118.1	118.2

Note: The Cost of Living Index measures regional differences in the cost of consumer goods and services, excluding taxes and non-consumer expenditures, for professional and managerial households in the top income quintile. It is based on more than 50,000 prices covering almost 60 different items for which prices are collected three times a year by chambers of commerce, economic development organizations or university applied economic centers in each participating urban area. The numbers shown should be read as a percentage above or below the national average of 100. For example, a value of 115.4 in the groceries column indicates that grocery prices are 15.4% higher than the national average. Small differences in the index numbers should not be interpreted as significant; Figures cover the San Francisco CA urban area.
Source: The Council for Community and Economic Research, ACCRA Cost of Living Index, 2015

Grocery Prices

Area[1]	T-Bone Steak ($/pound)	Frying Chicken ($/pound)	Whole Milk ($/half gal.)	Eggs ($/dozen)	Orange Juice ($/64 oz.)	Coffee ($/11.5 oz.)
City[2]	11.33	1.96	2.77	3.55	4.55	5.99
Avg.	10.99	1.43	2.25	2.26	3.58	4.48
Min.	7.16	0.98	1.30	1.35	2.88	2.98
Max.	14.13	2.43	3.85	4.81	6.39	7.56

Note: (1) Values for the local area are compared with the average, minimum and maximum values for all 292 areas in the Cost of Living Index; (2) Figures cover the San Francisco CA urban area; **T-Bone Steak** *(price per pound);* **Frying Chicken** *(price per pound, whole fryer);* **Whole Milk** *(half gallon carton);* **Eggs** *(price per dozen, Grade A, large);* **Orange Juice** *(64 oz. Tropicana or Florida Natural);* **Coffee** *(11.5 oz. can, vacuum-packed, Maxwell House, Hills Bros, or Folgers).*
Source: The Council for Community and Economic Research, ACCRA Cost of Living Index, 2015

Housing and Utility Costs

Area[1]	New Home Price ($)	Apartment Rent ($/month)	All Electric ($/month)	Part Electric ($/month)	Other Energy ($/month)	Telephone ($/month)
City[2]	978,744	3,230		135.14	75.78	24.12
Avg.	312,874	945	179.30	95.07	72.96	28.11
Min.	178,682	479	116.28	43.14	26.46	10.01
Max.	1,472,476	3,984	504.25	189.44	421.11	43.06

Note: (1) Values for the local area are compared with the average, minimum and maximum values for all 292 areas in the Cost of Living Index; (2) Figures cover the San Francisco CA urban area; **New Home Price** *(2,400 sf living area, 8,000 sf lot, in urban area with full utilities);* **Apartment Rent** *(950 sf 2 bedroom/1.5 or 2 bath, unfurnished, excluding all utilities except water);* **All Electric** *(average monthly cost for an all-electric home);* **Part Electric** *(average monthly cost for a part-electric home);* **Other Energy** *(average monthly cost for natural gas, fuel oil, coal, wood, and any other forms of energy except electricity);* **Telephone** *(price includes basic monthly rate for a private residential line plus additional local usage charges incurred by a family of four).*
Source: The Council for Community and Economic Research, ACCRA Cost of Living Index, 2015

Health Care, Transportation, and Other Costs

Area[1]	Doctor ($/visit)	Dentist ($/visit)	Optometrist ($/visit)	Gasoline ($/gallon)	Beauty Salon ($/visit)	Men's Shirt ($)
City[2]	125.52	119.23	121.18	3.24	61.93	37.26
Avg.	105.15	89.02	99.78	2.38	35.30	28.10
Min.	66.87	56.09	48.53	1.95	18.91	13.38
Max.	182.34	150.36	228.33	4.09	67.91	63.80

Note: (1) Values for the local area are compared with the average, minimum and maximum values for all 292 areas in the Cost of Living Index; (2) Figures cover the San Francisco CA urban area; **Doctor** *(general practitioners routine exam of an established patient);* **Dentist** *(adult teeth cleaning and periodic oral examination);* **Optometrist** *(full vision eye exam for established adult patient);* **Gasoline** *(one gallon regular unleaded, national brand, including all taxes, cash price at self-service pump if available);* **Beauty Salon** *(woman's shampoo, trim, and blow-dry);* **Men's Shirt** *(cotton/polyester dress shirt, pinpoint weave, long sleeves).*
Source: The Council for Community and Economic Research, ACCRA Cost of Living Index, 2015

HOUSING

House Price Index (HPI)

Area	National Ranking[2]	Quarterly Change (%)	One-Year Change (%)	Five-Year Change (%)
MD[1]	4	2.90	14.10	54.90
U.S.[3]	–	1.45	5.76	22.85

Note: The HPI is a weighted repeat sales index. It measures average price changes in repeat sales or refinancings on the same properties. This information is obtained by reviewing repeat mortgage transactions on single-family properties whose mortgages have been purchased or securitized by Fannie Mae or Freddie Mac in January 1975; (1) San Francisco-Redwood City-South San Francisco Metropolitan Division—see Appendix B for areas included; (2) Rankings are based on annual percentage change for all metro areas containing at least 15,000 transactions over the last 10 years and ranges from 1 to 266; (3) figures based on a weighted average of Census Division estimates using a seasonally adjusted, purchase-only index; all figures are for the period ending December 31, 2015

Source: Federal Housing Finance Agency, House Price Index, February 25, 2016

Median Single-Family Home Prices

Area	2013	2014	2015^p	Percent Change 2014 to 2015
MSA[1]	643.8	715.8	782.3	9.3
U.S. Average	197.4	208.9	223.9	7.2

Note: Figures are median sales prices of existing single-family homes in thousands of dollars; (p) preliminary; n/a not available; (1) San Francisco-Oakland-Hayward, CA Metropolitan Statistical Area—see Appendix B for areas included

Source: National Association of Realtors, Median Sales Price of Existing Single-Family Homes for Metropolitan Areas, 4th Quarter 2015

Qualifying Income Based on Median Sales Price of Existing Single-Family Homes

Area	With 5% Down ($)	With 10% Down ($)	With 20% Down ($)
MSA[1]	173,852	164,701	146,401
U.S. Average	49,535	46,928	41,714

Note: Figures are preliminary; Qualifying income is based on a mortgage rate of 4.1%. Monthly principal and interest payment is limited to 25% of income; n/a not available; (1) San Francisco-Oakland-Hayward, CA Metropolitan Statistical Area—see Appendix B for areas included

Source: National Association of Realtors, Qualifying Income Based on Median Sales Price of Existing Single-Family Homes for Metropolitan Areas, 4th Quarter 2015

Median Apartment Condo-Coop Home Prices

Area	2013	2014	2015^p	Percent Change 2014 to 2015
MSA[1]	517.4	580.1	658.9	13.6
U.S. Average	194.9	204.3	210.7	3.1

Note: Figures are median sales prices of existing apartment condo-coop homes in thousands of dollars; (p) preliminary; n/a not available; (1) San Francisco-Oakland-Hayward, CA Metropolitan Statistical Area—see Appendix B for areas included

Source: National Association of Realtors, Median Sales Price of Existing Apartment Condo-Coop Homes for Metropolitan Areas, 4th Quarter 2015

Gross Monthly Rent

Area	Under $200	$200 -299	$300 -499	$500 -749	$750 -999	$1,000 -1,499	$1,500 and up	Median ($)
City	0.0	0.8	0.0	2.3	1.4	8.4	87.1	2,000+
MSA[1]	0.9	2.8	3.5	5.2	10.4	30.6	46.6	1,446
U.S.	1.5	3.2	7.4	21.0	24.1	26.9	15.9	920

Note: Figures are percentages except for Median; Gross rent is the contract rent plus the estimated average monthly cost of utilities (electricity, gas, and water and sewer) and fuels (oil, coal, kerosene, wood, etc.) if these are paid by the renter (or paid for the renter by someone else); (1) Figures cover the San Francisco-Oakland-Hayward, CA Metropolitan Statistical Area—see Appendix B for areas included

Source: U.S. Census Bureau, 2010-2014 American Community Survey 5-Year Estimates

HEALTH

Homeownership Rate

Area	2008 (%)	2009 (%)	2010 (%)	2011 (%)	2012 (%)	2013 (%)	2014 (%)	2015 (%)
MSA[1]	56.4	57.3	58.0	56.1	53.2	55.2	54.6	56.3
U.S.	67.8	67.4	66.9	66.1	65.4	65.1	64.5	63.7

Note: (1) Figures cover the San Francisco-Oakland-Hayward, CA Metropolitan Statistical Area—see Appendix B for areas included
Source: U.S. Census Bureau, Housing Vacancies and Homeownership Annual Statistics: 2015

Year Housing Structure Built

Area	2010 or Later	2000 -2009	1990 -1999	1980 -1989	1970 -1979	1960 -1969	1950 -1959	1940 -1949	Before 1940	Median Year
City	0.0	3.6	6.8	18.7	48.1	19.5	2.0	0.4	0.8	1976
MSA[1]	0.6	8.3	8.0	10.8	15.4	13.4	14.4	8.6	20.5	1965
U.S.	1.0	14.9	13.9	13.8	15.8	11.0	10.8	5.4	13.3	1976

Note: Figures are percentages except for Median Year; (1) Figures cover the San Francisco-Oakland-Hayward, CA Metropolitan Statistical Area—see Appendix B for areas included
Source: U.S. Census Bureau, 2010-2014 American Community Survey 5-Year Estimates

Health Risk Data

Category	MSA[1] (%)	U.S. (%)
Adults aged 18–64 who have any kind of health care coverage	84.5	79.6
Adults who reported being in good or excellent health	86.6	83.1
Adults who are current smokers	11.3	19.6
Adults who are heavy drinkers[2]	6.0	6.1
Adults who are binge drinkers[3]	18.9	16.9
Adults who are overweight (BMI 25.0 - 29.9)	30.6	35.8
Adults who are obese (BMI 30.0 - 99.8)	19.1	27.6
Adults who participated in any physical activities in the past month	82.5	77.1
Adults 50+ who have ever had a sigmoidoscopy or colonoscopy	64.6	67.3
Women aged 40+ who have had a mammogram within the past two years	78.7	74.0
Men aged 40+ who have had a PSA test within the past two years	38.4	45.2
Adults aged 65+ who have had flu shot within the past year	64.6	60.1
Adults who always wear a seatbelt	n/a	93.8

Note: Data as of 2012 unless otherwise noted; n/a not available; (1) Figures cover the San Francisco-San Mateo-Redwood City, CA—see Appendix B for areas included; (2) Heavy drinkers are classified as males having more than two drinks per day or females having more than one drink per day; (3) Binge drinkers are classified as males having five or more drinks on one occasion or females having four or more drinks on one occasion
Source: Centers for Disease Control and Prevention, Behaviorial Risk Factor Surveillance System, SMART: Selected Metropolitan/Micropolitan Area Risk Trends, 2012 (Note: the CDC has discontinued this dataset but will be releasing a replacement in mid-2016)

Chronic Health Indicators

Category	MSA[1] (%)	U.S. (%)
Adults who have ever been told they had a heart attack	n/a	4.5
Adults who have ever been told they had a stroke	n/a	2.9
Adults who have been told they currently have asthma	10.7	8.9
Adults who have ever been told they have arthritis	21.3	25.7
Adults who have ever been told they have diabetes[2]	8.2	9.7
Adults who have ever been told they had skin cancer	4.4	5.7
Adults who have ever been told they had any other types of cancer	6.6	6.5
Adults who have ever been told they have COPD	3.0	6.2
Adults who have ever been told they have kidney disease	1.5	2.5
Adults who have ever been told they have a form of depression	10.9	18.0

Note: Data as of 2012 unless otherwise noted; n/a not available; (1) Figures cover the San Francisco-San Mateo-Redwood City, CA—see Appendix B for areas included; (2) Figures do not include pregnancy-related, borderline, or pre-diabetes
Source: Centers for Disease Control and Prevention, Behaviorial Risk Factor Surveillance System, SMART: Selected Metropolitan/Micropolitan Area Risk Trends, 2012 (Note: the CDC has discontinued this dataset but will be releasing a replacement in mid-2016)

Mortality Rates for the Top 10 Causes of Death in the U.S.

ICD-10[a] Sub-Chapter	ICD-10[a] Code	Age-Adjusted Mortality Rate[1] per 100,000 population	
		County[2]	U.S.
Malignant neoplasms	C00-C97	132.6	163.6
Ischaemic heart diseases	I20-I25	66.8	102.2
Other forms of heart disease	I30-I51	37.7	50.1
Chronic lower respiratory diseases	J40-J47	22.9	41.4
Organic, including symptomatic, mental disorders	F01-F09	14.8	38.5
Cerebrovascular diseases	I60-I69	26.2	36.5
Other external causes of accidental injury	W00-X59	15.2	27.5
Other degenerative diseases of the nervous system	G30-G31	35.0	26.3
Diabetes mellitus	E10-E14	13.0	21.1
Hypertensive diseases	I10-I15	19.3	19.7

Note: (a) ICD-10 = International Classification of Diseases 10th Revision; (1) Mortality rates are a three year average covering 2012-2014; (2) Figures cover COUNTY NOT FOUND!!!!!!.
Source: Centers for Disease Control and Prevention, National Center for Health Statistics. Underlying Cause of Death 1999-2014 on CDC WONDER Online Database, released 2015.

Mortality Rates for Selected Causes of Death

ICD-10[a] Sub-Chapter	ICD-10[a] Code	Age-Adjusted Mortality Rate[1] per 100,000 population	
		County[2]	U.S.
Assault	X85-Y09	2.3	5.1
Diseases of the liver	K70-K76	10.3	13.5
Human immunodeficiency virus (HIV) disease	B20-B24	Unreliable	2.1
Influenza and pneumonia	J09-J18	14.1	15.2
Intentional self-harm	X60-X84	7.3	12.7
Malnutrition	E40-E46	Unreliable	0.9
Obesity and other hyperalimentation	E65-E68	Unreliable	1.9
Renal failure	N17-N19	4.1	13.0
Transport accidents	V01-V99	5.9	11.6
Viral hepatitis	B15-B19	1.8	2.1

Note: (a) ICD-10 = International Classification of Diseases 10th Revision; (1) Mortality rates are a three year average covering 2012-2014; (2) Figures cover COUNTY NOT FOUND!!!!!!; Data are Suppressed when the data meet the criteria for confidentiality constraints; Mortality rates are flagged as Unreliable when the rate would be calculated with a numerator of 20 or less.
Source: Centers for Disease Control and Prevention, National Center for Health Statistics. Underlying Cause of Death 1999-2014 on CDC WONDER Online Database, released 2015.

Health Insurance Coverage

Area	With Health Insurance	With Private Health Insurance	With Public Health Insurance	Without Health Insurance	Population Under Age 18 Without Health Insurance
City	96.1	87.3	19.0	3.9	1.7
MSA[1]	89.2	72.5	26.5	10.8	4.7
U.S.	85.8	65.8	31.1	14.2	7.1

Note: Figures are percentages that cover the civilian noninstitutionalized population; (1) Figures cover the San Francisco-Oakland-Hayward, CA Metropolitan Statistical Area—see Appendix B for areas included
Source: U.S. Census Bureau, 2010-2014 American Community Survey 5-Year Estimates

Number of Medical Professionals

Area	MDs[3]	DOs[3,4]	Dentists	Podiatrists	Chiropractors	Optometrists
County[1] (number)	3,242	47	745	44	245	161
County[1] (rate[2])	432.0	6.3	98.2	5.8	32.3	21.2
U.S. (rate[2])	272.5	20.9	64.7	5.8	25.9	15.2

Note: Data as of 2014 unless noted; (1) Data covers San Mateo County; (2) Rate per 100,000 population; (3) Data as of 2013 and includes all active, non-federal physicians; (4) Doctor of Osteopathic Medicine
Source: U.S. Department of Health and Human Services, Health Resources and Services Administration, Bureau of Health Professions, Area Resource File (ARF) 2014-2015

Best Hospitals

According to *U.S. News,* the San Francisco-Redwood City-South San Francisco, CA metro area is home to two of the best hospitals in the U.S.: **California Pacific Medical Center** (1 specialty); **UCSF Medical Center** (Honor Roll/14 specialties). The hospitals listed were nationally ranked in at least one adult specialty. Only 137 hospitals nationwide were nationally ranked in one or more specialties. Fifteen hospitals in the U.S. made the Honor Roll with high scores in at least six specialties. *U.S. News Online, "America's Best Children's Hospitals 2015-16"*

According to *U.S. News,* the San Francisco-Redwood City-South San Francisco, CA metro area is home to one of the best children's hospitals in the U.S.: **UCSF Benioff Children's Hospital** (9 specialties). The hospital listed was highly ranked in at least one pediatric specialty. Eighty-three children's hospitals in the U.S. were nationally ranked in at least one specialty. Twelve children's hospitals in the U.S. made the Honor Roll with high scores in at least three specialties. *U.S. News Online, "America's Best Children's Hospitals 2015-16"*

EDUCATION

Public School District Statistics

District Name	Schls	Pupils	Pupil/ Teacher Ratio	Minority Pupils[1] (%)	Free Lunch Eligible[2] (%)	IEP[3] (%)
San Mateo-foster City	21	11,705	23.3	72.3	26.8	8.0

Note: Table includes school districts with 100 or more students; (1) Percentage of students that are not non-Hispanic white; (2) Percentage of students that are eligible for the free lunch program; (3) Percentage of students that have an Individualized Education Program.
Source: U.S. Department of Education, National Center for Education Statistics, Common Core of Data, Local Education Agency (School District) Universe Survey: School Year 2013-2014; U.S. Department of Education, National Center for Education Statistics, Common Core of Data, Public Elementary/Secondary School Universe Survey: School Year 2013-2014

Highest Level of Education

Area	Less than H.S.	H.S. Diploma	Some College, No Deg.	Associate Degree	Bachelor's Degree	Master's Degree	Prof. School Degree	Doctorate Degree
City	4.1	10.2	16.2	6.5	33.4	20.1	4.4	5.1
MSA[1]	12.1	17.0	19.0	6.9	27.1	11.8	3.6	2.5
U.S.	13.7	28.0	21.2	7.9	18.3	7.8	2.0	1.3

Note: Figures cover persons age 25 and over; (1) Figures cover the San Francisco-Oakland-Hayward, CA Metropolitan Statistical Area—see Appendix B for areas included
Source: U.S. Census Bureau, 2010-2014 American Community Survey 5-Year Estimates

Educational Attainment by Race

Area	High School Graduate or Higher (%)					Bachelor's Degree or Higher (%)				
	Total	White	Black	Asian	Hisp.[2]	Total	White	Black	Asian	Hisp.[2]
City	95.9	96.4	90.8	96.1	95.2	63.0	58.8	40.0	70.7	30.8
MSA[1]	87.9	91.3	89.5	85.3	68.2	44.9	49.6	23.9	50.5	18.4
U.S.	86.3	88.4	83.2	85.8	64.1	29.3	30.6	19.0	50.9	13.9

Note: Figures shown cover persons 25 years old and over; (1) Figures cover the San Francisco-Oakland-Hayward, CA Metropolitan Statistical Area—see Appendix B for areas included; (2) People of Hispanic origin can be of any race
Source: U.S. Census Bureau, 2010-2014 American Community Survey 5-Year Estimates

School Enrollment by Grade and Control

Area	Preschool (%)		Kindergarten (%)		Grades 1 - 4 (%)		Grades 5 - 8 (%)		Grades 9 - 12 (%)	
	Public	Private	Public	Private	Public	Private	Public	Private	Public	Private
City	9.8	90.2	87.6	12.4	81.6	18.4	83.1	16.9	81.4	18.6
MSA[1]	40.4	59.6	83.6	16.4	85.3	14.7	85.6	14.4	88.0	12.0
U.S.	57.4	42.6	87.8	12.2	89.8	10.2	89.9	10.1	90.6	9.4

Note: Figures shown cover persons 3 years old and over; (1) Figures cover the San Francisco-Oakland-Hayward, CA Metropolitan Statistical Area—see Appendix B for areas included
Source: U.S. Census Bureau, 2010-2014 American Community Survey 5-Year Estimates

Average Salaries of Public School Classroom Teachers

Area	2013-14 Dollars	2013-14 Rank[1]	2014-15 Dollars	2014-15 Rank[1]	Percent Change 2013-14 to 2014-15	Percent Change 2004-05 to 2014-15
California	71,396	4	72,535	4	1.59	25.9
U.S. Average	56,610	–	57,379	–	1.36	20.8

Note: (1) State rank ranges from 1 to 51 where 1 indicates highest salary.
Source: National Education Association, Rankings & Estimates: Rankings of the States 2014 and Estimates of School Statistics 2015, March 2015

Higher Education

Four-Year Colleges			Two-Year Colleges			Medical Schools[1]	Law Schools[2]	Voc/ Tech[3]
Public	Private Non-profit	Private For-profit	Public	Private Non-profit	Private For-profit			
0	0	0	0	0	0	0	0	0

Note: Figures cover institutions located within the city limits and include main campuses only; (1) includes schools accredited by the Liaison Committee on Medical Education and the American Osteopathic Association's Commission on Osteopathic College Accreditation; (2) includes ABA-accredited schools, schools with provisional ABA accreditation, and state accredited schools; (3) includes all schools with programs that are less than 2 years.
Source: National Center for Education Statistics, Integrated Postsecondary Education System (IPEDS), 2014-15; Association of American Medical Colleges, Member List, March 21, 2016; American Osteopathic Association, Member List, March 21, 2016; Law School Admission Council, Official Guide to ABA-Approved Law Schools Online, March 21, 2016; Wikipedia, List of Medical Schools in the United States, March 21, 2016; Wikipedia, List of Law Schools in the United States, March 21, 2016

According to *U.S. News & World Report,* the San Francisco-Redwood City-South San Francisco, CA metro division is home to one of the best national universities in the U.S.: **University of San Francisco** (#108 tie). The indicators used to capture academic quality fall into a number of categories: assessment by administrators at peer institutions; retention of students; faculty resources; student selectivity; financial resources; alumni giving; high school counselor ratings of colleges; and graduation rate. *U.S. News & World Report, "America's Best Colleges 2016"*

According to *U.S. News & World Report,* the San Francisco-Redwood City-South San Francisco, CA metro division is home to one of the top 100 law schools in the U.S.: **University of California, Hastings College of the Law** (#50 tie). The rankings are based on a weighted average of 12 measures of quality: peer assessment score; assessment score by lawyers/judges; median LSAT scores; median undergrad GPA; acceptance rate; employment rates for graduates; placement success; bar passage rate; faculty resources; expenditures per student; student/faculty ratio; and library resources. *U.S. News & World Report, "America's Best Graduate Schools, Law, 2017"*

According to *U.S. News & World Report,* the San Francisco-Redwood City-South San Francisco, CA metro division is home to one of the top 75 medical schools for research in the U.S.: **University of California–San Francisco, School of Medicine** (#3 tie). The rankings are based on a weighted average of 11 measures of quality: quality assessment; peer assessment score; assessment score by residency directors; research activity; total research activity; average research activity per faculty member; student selectivity; median MCAT total score; median undergraduate GPA; acceptance rate; and faculty resources. *U.S. News & World Report, "America's Best Graduate Schools, Medical, 2017"*

PRESIDENTIAL ELECTION

2012 Presidential Election Results

Area	Obama (%)	Romney (%)	Other (%)
San Mateo County	72.1	25.7	2.2
U.S.	51.0	47.2	1.8

Note: Results may not add to 100% due to rounding
Source: Dave Leip's Atlas of U.S. Presidential Elections

EMPLOYERS

Major Employers

Company Name	Industry
All Hallows Preservation	Apartment building operators
AT&T Corp.	Telephone communication, except radio
AT&T Services	Telephone communication, except radio
California Pacific Medical Center	General medical & surgical hospitals
City & County of San Francisco	General medical & surgical hospitals
City & County of San Francisco	Public welfare administration: nonoperating, govt.
Edy's Grand Ice Cream	Ice cream & ice milk
Franklin Templeton Services	Investment advice
Lawrence Berkeley National Laboratory	Noncommercial research organizations
Lawrence Berkeley National Laboratory	Supply agency, government
Lawrence Livermore National Laboratory	Noncommercial research organizations
Menlo Worldwide Forwarding	Letter delivery, private air
Oracle America	Minicomputers
Oracle Systems Corporation	Prepackaged software
Pacific Gas and Electric Company	Electric & other services combined
PACPIZZA	Pizzeria, chain
San Francisco Community College District	Colleges & universities
University of California, Berkeley	University
Veterans Health Administration	Administration of veterans' affairs
Wells Fargo Bank	National commercial banks

Note: Companies shown are located within the San Francisco-Oakland-Hayward, CA Metropolitan Statistical Area.
Source: Hoovers.com; Wikipedia

PUBLIC SAFETY

Crime Rate

Area	All Crimes	Violent Crimes				Property Crimes		
		Murder	Rape[3]	Robbery	Aggrav. Assault	Burglary	Larceny -Theft	Motor Vehicle Theft
City	1,157.3	0.0	9.1	6.1	27.4	246.7	755.3	112.7
Metro[1]	4,257.7	3.5	35.9	232.8	248.8	523.4	2,725.5	487.8
U.S.	2,961.6	4.5	26.4	102.2	232.5	542.5	1,837.3	216.2

Note: Figures are crimes per 100,000 population; (1) Figures cover the San Francisco-Redwood City-South San Francisco, CA Metropolitan Division—see Appendix B for areas included; (3) The city and U.S. figures shown were reported using the legacy Uniform Crime Reporting (UCR) definition of rape. The suburban and metro area figures shown are an aggregate total of the data submitted using both the revised and legacy UCR definitions.
Source: FBI Uniform Crime Reports, 2014

Hate Crimes

Area	Number of Quarters Reported	Number of Incidents per Bias Motivation						
		Race	Religion	Sexual Orientation	Ethnicity	Disability	Gender	Gender Identity
City	4	0	0	0	0	0	0	0
U.S.	4	2,568	1,014	1,017	648	84	33	98

Source: Federal Bureau of Investigation, Hate Crime Statistics 2014

Identity Theft Consumer Complaints

Area	Complaints	Complaints per 100,000 Population	Rank[2]
MSA[1]	7,968	173.4	33
U.S.	490,220	152.4	-

Note: (1) Figures cover the San Francisco-Oakland-Hayward, CA Metropolitan Statistical Area—see Appendix B for areas included; (2) Rank ranges from 1 to 379 where 1 indicates greatest number of identity theft complaints per 100,000 population
Source: Federal Trade Commission, Consumer Sentinel Network Data Book for January–December 2015

Fraud and Other Consumer Complaints

Area	Complaints	Complaints per 100,000 Population	Rank[2]
MSA[1]	18,411	400.8	99
U.S.	2,593,159	806.0	-

Note: (1) Figures cover the San Francisco-Oakland-Hayward, CA Metropolitan Statistical Area—see Appendix B for areas included; (2) Rank ranges from 1 to 379 where 1 indicates greatest number of identity theft complaints per 100,000 population
Source: Federal Trade Commission, Consumer Sentinel Network Data Book for January–December 2015

RECREATION

Culture

Dance[1]	Theatre[1]	Instrumental Music[1]	Vocal Music[1]	Series and Festivals	Museums and Art Galleries[2]	Zoos and Aquariums[3]
0	0	0	0	0	0	0

Note: (1) Professional perfoming groups; (2) Based on organizations with SIC code 8412; (3) AZA-accredited
Source: The Grey House Performing Arts Directory, 2015-16; Association of Zoos & Aquariums, AZA Member Zoos & Aquariums, March 25, 2016; www.AccuLeads.com, March 29, 2016

Professional Sports Teams

Team Name	League	Year Established
Golden State Warriors	National Basketball Association (NBA)	1962
Oakland Athletics	Major League Baseball (MLB)	1968
Oakland Raiders	National Football League (NFL)	1960
San Francisco 49ers	National Football League (NFL)	1946
San Francisco Giants	Major League Baseball (MLB)	1958

Note: Includes teams located in the San Francisco-Oakland-Hayward, CA Metropolitan Statistical Area.
Source: Wikipedia, Major Professional Sports Teams of the United States and Canada, March 24, 2016

CLIMATE

Average and Extreme Temperatures

Temperature	Jan	Feb	Mar	Apr	May	Jun	Jul	Aug	Sep	Oct	Nov	Dec	Yr.
Extreme High (°F)	72	77	85	92	97	106	105	98	103	99	85	75	106
Average High (°F)	56	59	61	64	66	70	71	72	73	70	63	56	65
Average Temp. (°F)	49	52	53	56	58	61	63	63	64	61	55	50	57
Average Low (°F)	42	44	45	47	49	52	53	54	54	51	47	42	49
Extreme Low (°F)	26	30	31	36	39	43	44	45	41	37	31	24	24

Note: Figures cover the years 1948-1990
Source: National Climatic Data Center, International Station Meteorological Climate Summary, 9/96

Average Precipitation/Snowfall/Humidity

Precip./Humidity	Jan	Feb	Mar	Apr	May	Jun	Jul	Aug	Sep	Oct	Nov	Dec	Yr.
Avg. Precip. (in.)	4.3	3.1	2.9	1.4	0.3	0.1	Tr	Tr	0.2	1.0	2.5	3.4	19.3
Avg. Snowfall (in.)	Tr	Tr	Tr	0	0	0	0	0	0	0	0	Tr	Tr
Avg. Rel. Hum. 7am (%)	86	85	82	79	78	77	81	83	83	83	85	86	82
Avg. Rel. Hum. 4pm (%)	67	65	63	61	61	60	60	62	60	60	64	68	63

Note: Figures cover the years 1948-1990; Tr = Trace amounts (<0.05 in. of rain; <0.5 in. of snow)
Source: National Climatic Data Center, International Station Meteorological Climate Summary, 9/96

Weather Conditions

Temperature			Daytime Sky			Precipitation		
10°F & below	32°F & below	90°F & above	Clear	Partly cloudy	Cloudy	0.01 inch or more precip.	0.1 inch or more snow/ice	Thunder-storms
0	6	4	136	130	99	63	< 1	5

Note: Figures are average number of days per year and cover the years 1948-1990
Source: National Climatic Data Center, International Station Meteorological Climate Summary, 9/96

HAZARDOUS WASTE

Superfund Sites

Foster City has no sites on the EPA's Superfund Final National Priorities List. There are a total of 1,323 Superfund sites on the list in the U.S. *U.S. Environmental Protection Agency, Final National Priorities List, March 18, 2016*

AIR & WATER QUALITY

Air Quality Trends: Ozone

	1990	1995	2000	2005	2010	2011	2012	2013	2014
MSA[1]	0.058	0.074	0.057	0.055	0.061	0.060	0.057	0.056	0.065

Note: (1) Data covers the San Francisco-Oakland-Hayward, CA Metropolitan Statistical Area—see Appendix B for areas included. The values shown are the composite ozone concentration averages among trend sites based on the highest fourth daily maximum 8-hour concentration in parts per million. These trends are based on sites having an adequate record of monitoring data during the trend period. Data from exceptional events are included.
Source: U.S. Environmental Protection Agency, Air Quality Monitoring Information, "Air Quality Trends by City, 1990-2014"

Air Quality Index

Area	Percent of Days when Air Quality was...[2]					AQI Statistics[2]	
	Good	Moderate	Unhealthy for Sensitive Groups	Unhealthy	Very Unhealthy	Maximum	Median
MSA[1]	57.3	39.7	3.0	0.0	0.0	124	47

Note: (1) Data covers the San Francisco-Oakland-Hayward, CA Metropolitan Statistical Area—see Appendix B for areas included; (2) Based on 365 days with AQI data in 2015. Air Quality Index (AQI) is an index for reporting daily air quality. EPA calculates the AQI for five major air pollutants regulated by the Clean Air Act: ground-level ozone, particle pollution (aka particulate matter), carbon monoxide, sulfur dioxide, and nitrogen dioxide. The AQI runs from 0 to 500. The higher the AQI value, the greater the level of air pollution and the greater the health concern. There are six AQI categories: "Good" AQI is between 0 and 50. Air quality is considered satisfactory; "Moderate" AQI is between 51 and 100. Air quality is acceptable; "Unhealthy for Sensitive Groups" When AQI values are between 101 and 150, members of sensitive groups may experience health effects; "Unhealthy" When AQI values are between 151 and 200 everyone may begin to experience health effects; "Very Unhealthy" AQI values between 201 and 300 trigger a health alert; "Hazardous" AQI values over 300 trigger warnings of emergency conditions (not shown).
Source: U.S. Environmental Protection Agency, Air Quality Index Report, 2015

Air Quality Index Pollutants

Area	Percent of Days when AQI Pollutant was...[2]					
	Carbon Monoxide	Nitrogen Dioxide	Ozone	Sulfur Dioxide	Particulate Matter 2.5	Particulate Matter 10
MSA[1]	0.0	6.3	33.4	0.0	60.3	0.0

Note: (1) Data covers the San Francisco-Oakland-Hayward, CA Metropolitan Statistical Area—see Appendix B for areas included; (2) Based on 365 days with AQI data in 2015. The Air Quality Index (AQI) is an index for reporting daily air quality. EPA calculates the AQI for five major air pollutants regulated by the Clean Air Act: ground-level ozone, particle pollution (also known as particulate matter), carbon monoxide, sulfur dioxide, and nitrogen dioxide. The AQI runs from 0 to 500. The higher the AQI value, the greater the level of air pollution and the greater the health concern.
Source: U.S. Environmental Protection Agency, Air Quality Index Report, 2015

Maximum Air Pollutant Concentrations: Particulate Matter, Ozone, CO and Lead

	Particulate Matter 10 (ug/m³)	Particulate Matter 2.5 Wtd AM (ug/m³)	Particulate Matter 2.5 24-Hr (ug/m³)	Ozone (ppm)	Carbon Monoxide (ppm)	Lead (ug/m³)
MSA[1] Level	37	10.8	26	0.076	3	n/a
NAAQS[2]	150	15	35	0.075	9	0.15
Met NAAQS[2]	Yes	Yes	Yes	No	Yes	n/a

Note: (1) Data covers the San Francisco-Oakland-Hayward, CA Metropolitan Statistical Area—see Appendix B for areas included; Data from exceptional events are included; (2) National Ambient Air Quality Standards; ppm = parts per million; ug/m³ = micrograms per cubic meter; n/a not available.

Concentrations: Particulate Matter 10 (coarse particulate)—highest second maximum 24-hour concentration; Particulate Matter 2.5 Wtd AM (fine particulate)—highest weighted annual mean concentration; Particulate Matter 2.5 24-Hour (fine particulate)—highest 98th percentile 24-hour concentration; Ozone—highest fourth daily maximum 8-hour concentration; Carbon Monoxide—highest second maximum non-overlapping 8-hour concentration; Lead—maximum running 3-month average

Source: U.S. Environmental Protection Agency, Air Quality Monitoring Information, "Air Quality Statistics by City, 2014"

Maximum Air Pollutant Concentrations: Nitrogen Dioxide and Sulfur Dioxide

	Nitrogen Dioxide AM (ppb)	Nitrogen Dioxide 1-Hr (ppb)	Sulfur Dioxide AM (ppb)	Sulfur Dioxide 1-Hr (ppb)	Sulfur Dioxide 24-Hr (ppb)
MSA[1] Level	17	58	n/a	16	n/a
NAAQS[2]	53	100	30	75	140
Met NAAQS[2]	Yes	Yes	n/a	Yes	n/a

Note: (1) Data covers the San Francisco-Oakland-Hayward, CA Metropolitan Statistical Area—see Appendix B for areas included; Data from exceptional events are included; (2) National Ambient Air Quality Standards; ppm = parts per million; ug/m³ = micrograms per cubic meter; n/a not available.

Concentrations: Nitrogen Dioxide AM—highest arithmetic mean concentration; Nitrogen Dioxide 1-Hr—highest 98th percentile 1-hour daily maximum concentration; Sulfur Dioxide AM—highest annual mean concentration; Sulfur Dioxide 1-Hr—highest 99th percentile 1-hour daily maximum concentration; Sulfur Dioxide 24-Hr—highest second maximum 24-hour concentration

Source: U.S. Environmental Protection Agency, Air Quality Monitoring Information, "Air Quality Statistics by City, 2014"

Drinking Water

Water System Name	Pop. Served	Primary Water Source Type	Violations[1] Health Based	Violations[1] Monitoring/ Reporting
Estero Municipal Improvement Dist	35,000	Purchased Surface	0	0

Note: (1) Based on violation data from January 1, 2015 to December 31, 2015 (includes unresolved violations from earlier years)

Source: U.S. Environmental Protection Agency, Office of Ground Water and Drinking Water, Safe Drinking Water Information System (based on data extracted April 29, 2016)

Los Altos, California

Background

Within the heart of Silicon Valley, Los Altos is located 37 miles south of San Francisco, in Santa Clara County.

The whole of Santa Clara County was once known as the "Valley of Heart's Delight."

Up until the 1940s and 1950s, Los Altos was primarily a rural community. With its rolling hills and fertile soil, much of the area was devoted to apricot orchards. One of these orchards still surrounds the Los Altos History Museum.

Silicon Valley has seen significant growth from the 1950s through the present day. A center of the world's high-tech, venture capital and electronics industries, the area has become a major employment center. Population growth in Los Altos, however, has stayed relatively low in the last several years.

Los Altos maintains a residential atmosphere, primarily made up of tree-lined streets and quiet neighborhoods. Commercial zones are limited to the downtown area, with small office parks and shopping centers tucked away throughout the rest of the city.

Residence in this community comes at a price, however. Many Los Altos homes are valued over $2 million, making the city one of the "Most Expensive Zip Codes in America" says *Forbes.* Los Altos' notable residents have included Steve Jobs, former CEO of Apple Computer; Charles Geschke and John Warnock, Co-Founders of Adobe Systems; and Scott McNealy, Co-Founder of Sun Microsystems.

Los Altos prides itself on being a family-friendly community. There are many active youth sports organizations throughout the city, with many award-winning clubs in soccer, baseball, Pop Warner football and cheerleading, and basketball. Community events include the Los Altos Kiwanis Pet Parade, Halloween Spooktacular, Fine Art in the Park, Los Altos Fall Festival and Festival of Lights Parade.

Public schools in the Los Altos area are managed by the Los Altos School District, the Cupertino Union School District and the Mountain View-Los Altos Union High School District. Los Altos School District has the highest Academic Performance Index in the State of California. In addition, there are many highly-regarded private, parochial and charter schools in, and within a short distance from, Los Altos. Nearby institutions of higher education include Stanford University, Santa Clara University, San Jose University along with a number of community colleges.

Los Altos sits near the San Andreas Fault in an area prone to earthquakes. Los Altos, and the surrounding areas of Santa Cruz and Watsonville, saw significant damage due to earthquakes in 1906 and 1989.

Nearby airports include San Francisco International Airport, 27 miles north of the city, and San Jose International Airport, 20 miles south of the city.

Los Altos enjoys a mild, temperate climate. Warm and dry throughout the spring, summer and fall, some rain falls in winter with temperatures rarely dropping below freezing.

Rankings

General Rankings

- The San Jose* metro area was identified as one of America's fastest-growing areas in terms of population and economy by *Forbes.* The area ranked #17 out of 20. The 100 most populous metro areas in the U.S. were evaluated on the following criteria: estimated population growth; job growth; gross metropolitan product growth; unemployment; median salaries for college-educated workers. *Forbes, "America's Fastest-Growing Cities 2015," January 27, 2015*

Business/Finance Rankings

- The personal finance site NerdWallet analyzed 183 American metropolitan areas with populations over 250,000 and more than 15,000 businesses to rank where entrepreneurs find the most success. Criteria included area economy, annual income, housing cost, unemployment rate, and the success rate of area businesses. San Jose* ranked #42. *www.nerdwallet.com, "Best Places to Start a Business," April 27, 2015*

- TransUnion ranked the nation's metro areas by average credit score, calculated on the VantageScore system, developed by the three major credit-reporting bureaus—TransUnion, Experian, and Equifax. The San Jose* metro area was among the ten cities with the highest collective credit score, meaning that its residents posed the lowest average consumer credit risk. *www.usatoday.com, "Metro Areas' Average Credit Rating Revealed," February 7, 2013*

- Based on the U.S. Department of Labor's Occupational Information Network Data Collection Program, the Brookings Institution defined job opportunities for STEM workers at various levels of educational attainment. The San Jose* metro area was placed among the ten large metro areas with the highest demand for high-level STEM knowledge. *www.brookings.edu, "The Hidden Stem Economy," June 10, 2013*

- According to data by the Bureau of Economic Analysis (BEA) and the Bureau of Labor Statistics (BLS), the San Jose* metro area has the fastest-growing GDP (gross domestic product) and positive employment trends, at #9. *247wallst.com, "Cities With the Fastest Growing (and Shrinking) Economies," September 29, 2015*

- 24/7 Wall Street used Brookings Institution research on 50 advanced industries to identify the proportion of workers in the nation's largest metropolitan areas that were employed in jobs requiring knowledge in the science, technology, engineering, or math (STEM) fields. The San Jose* metro area was #1. *247wallst.com, "15 Cities with the Most High-Tech Jobs," March 13, 2015*

- Based on metro area social media reviews, the employment opinion group Glassdoor surveyed 50 of the largest U.S. metro areas and equally weighed cost of living, hiring opportunity, and job satisfaction to compose a list of "25 Best Cities for Jobs." The San Jose* metro area was ranked #2 in overall job satisfaction. *www.glassdoor.com, "Best Cities for Jobs," May 19, 2015*

- In a survey of economic confidence in the nation's 50 largest metropolitan areas conducted January–December 2014, the San Jose* metro area placed #1, according to Gallup's 2014 Economic Confidence Index. *Gallup, "San Jose and San Francisco Lead in Economic Confidence," March 19, 2015*

- The Brookings Institution ranked the 100 largest metro areas in the U.S. based on income inequality. San Jose* was ranked #17 (#1 = greatest ineqality). Criteria: the "95/20 ratio," a figure representing the income at which a household earns more than 95 percent of all other households, divided by the income at which a household earns more than only 20 percent of all other households. *Brookings Institution, "Income Inequality, 100 Largest U.S. Metro Areas, 2007-2014," January 14, 2016*

- *Forbes* ranked the largest metro areas in the U.S. in terms of the "Best Cities for Young Professionals." The San Jose* metro area ranked #11 out of 15. Criteria: job growth; unemployment rate; median salary of college graduates age 24 to 34; cost of living; number of small businesses per capita; number of large companies; percentage of population 25 years of age and older with college degrees. *Forbes.com, "America's 15 Best Cities for Young Professionals," August 18, 2014*

- The San Jose* metro area appeared on the Milken Institute "2015 Best Performing Cities" list. Rank: #1 out of 200 large metro areas. Criteria: job growth; wage and salary growth; high-tech output growth. *Milken Institute, "Best-Performing Cities 2015," December 2015*

- *Forbes* ranked the 200 most populous metro areas to determine the nation's "Best Places for Business and Careers." The San Jose* metro area was ranked #42. Criteria: costs (business and living); job growth (past and projected); income growth; educational attainment (college and high school); projected economic growth; cultural and recreational opportunities; net migration patterns; number of highly ranked colleges. *Forbes, "The Best Places for Business and Careers 2015," July 29, 2015*

Dating/Romance Rankings

- *Forbes* reports that the San Jose* metro area made Rent.com's Best Cities for Newlyweds list for 2013, based on Bureau of Labor Statistics and Census Bureau data on number of married couples, percentage of families with children under age six, average annual income, cost of living, and availability of rentals. *www.forbes.com, "The 10 Best Cities for Newlyweds to Live and Work In," May 30, 2013*

- CreditDonkey, a financial education website, sought out the ten best U.S. cities for newlyweds, considering the number of married couples, divorce rate, average credit score, and average number of hours worked per week in metro areas with a million or more residents. The San Jose* metro area placed #2. *www.creditdonkey.com, "Study: Best Cities for Newlyweds," November 30, 2013*

Education Rankings

- Based on a Brookings Institution study, *24/7 Wall St.* identified the ten U.S. metropolitan areas with the most average patent filings per million residents between 2007 and 2011. San Jose* ranked #1. *24/7 Wall St., "America's Most Innovative Cities," February 1, 2013*

- The San Jose* metro area was selected as one of America's most innovative cities" by *The Business Insider*. The metro area was ranked #1 out of 20. Criteria: patents per capita. *The Business Insider, "The 20 Most Innovative Cities in the U.S.," February 1, 2013*

- San Jose* was identified as one of America's "smartest" metropolitan areas by *The Business Journals*. The area ranked #5 out of 10. Criteria: percentage of adults (25 and older) with high school diplomas, bachelor's degrees and graduate degrees. *The Business Journals, "Where the Brainpower Is: Exclusive U.S. Rankings, Insights," February 27, 2014*

- Personal finance website *WalletHub* analyzed the 150 largest U.S. metropolitan statistical areas to determine where the most educated Americans are choosing to settle. Criteria: education quality and attainment gap; education levels; percentage of workers with degrees; public school rankings; quality and size of each metro area's universities. San Jose* was ranked #14 (#1 = most educated city). *www.WalletHub.com, "2015's Most and Least Educated Cities*

Environmental Rankings

- The San Jose* metro area came in at #48 for the relative comfort of its climate on Sperling's list of "chill cities," as measured by the Sperling Heat Index. All 361 metro areas are included. Criteria included daytime high temperatures, nighttime low temperatures, dew point, and relative humidity at the high temperatures. *www.bertsperling.com, "Sperling's Chill Cities," July 18, 2013*

- Sperling's BestPlaces assessed 379 metropolitan areas of the United States for the likelihood of dangerously extreme weather events or earthquakes. In general the Southeast and South-Central regions have the highest risk of weather extremes and earthquakes, while the Pacific Northwest enjoys the lowest risk. Of the least risky metropolitan areas, the San Jose* metro area was ranked #69. *www.bestplaces.net, "Safest Places from Natural Disasters," April 2011*

- San Jose* was identified as one of America's dirtiest metro areas by *Forbes*. The area ranked #8 out of 20. Criteria: air quality; water quality; toxic releases; superfund sites. *Forbes, "America's 20 Dirtiest Cities," December 10, 2012*

- The U.S. Environmental Protection Agency (EPA) released a list of U.S. metropolitan areas with the most ENERGY STAR certified buildings in 2015. The San Jose* metro area was ranked #17 out of 25. *U.S. Environmental Protection Agency, "Top Cities With the Most ENERGY STAR Certified Buildings in 2016," March 30, 2016*
- The U.S. Environmental Protection Agency (EPA) released a list of mid-size U.S. metropolitan areas with the most ENERGY STAR certified buildings in 2015. The San Jose* metro area was ranked #1 out of 10. *U.S. Environmental Protection Agency, "Top Cities With the Most ENERGY STAR Certified Buildings in 2016," March 30, 2016*
- San Jose* was highlighted as one of the 25 metro areas most polluted by year-round particle pollution (Annual PM 2.5) in the U.S. during 2011 through 2013. The area ranked #7. *American Lung Association, State of the Air 2015*
- San Jose* was highlighted as one of the 25 metro areas most polluted by short-term particle pollution (24-hour PM 2.5) in the U.S. during 2011 through 2013. The area ranked #6. *American Lung Association, State of the Air 2015*

Health/Fitness Rankings

- Analysts who tracked obesity rates in the nation's largest metro areas (populations above one million) found that the San Jose* metro area was one of the ten major metros where residents were least likely to be obese, defined as a BMI score of 30 or above. *www.gallup.com, "Boulder, Colo., Residents Still Least Likely to Be Obese," April 4, 2014*
- Analysts who tracked obesity rates in 100 of the nation's most populous areas found that the San Jose* metro area was one of the ten communities where residents were least likely to be obese, defined as a BMI score of 30 or above. *www.gallup.com, "Colorado Springs Residents Least Likely to Be Obese," May 28, 2015*
- For each of the 50 most populous metro areas in the United States, the American College of Sports Medicine's American Fitness Index evaluated infrastructure, community assets, and policies that encourage healthy and fit lifestyles, including preventive health behaviors, levels of chronic disease conditions, health care access, and community resources and policies that support physical activity. The San Jose* metro area ranked #10 for "community fitness." *www.americanfitnessindex.org, "ACSM American Fitness Index Health and Community Fitness Status of the 50 Largest Metropolitan Areas," May 2015*
- San Jose* was identified as a "2016 Spring Allergy Capital." The area ranked #86 out of 100. Three groups of factors were used to identify the most severe cities for people with allergies during the spring season: annual pollen levels; medicine utilization; access to board-certified allergists. *Asthma and Allergy Foundation of America, "Spring Allergy Capitals 2016"*
- San Jose* was identified as a "2015 Asthma Capital." The area ranked #97 out of the nation's 100 largest metropolitan areas. Criteria: estimated prevalence; self-reported prevalence; crude death rate for asthma; annual pollen score; annual air quality; public smoking laws; number of board-certified asthma specialists; school inhaler access laws; rescue medication use; controller medication use; ER visits for asthma; uninsured rate; poverty rate. *Asthma and Allergy Foundation of America, "Asthma Capitals 2015"*
- The San Jose* metro area ranked #15 out of 190 in The Gallup-Healthways Well-Being Index. Criteria: purpose; social well being; financial health; community and physical health. Results are based on telephone interviews with adults, aged 18 and older, living in metropolitan areas in the 50 U.S. states and the District of Columbia. *Gallup-Healthways, "State of American Well-Being," February 23, 2016*

Real Estate Rankings

- With data from RealtyTrac, Yahoo! Finance researchers listed the housing markets in which housing affordability is improving most, factoring in interest rates as well as median home prices. The San Jose* metro area was among the least affordable housing markets. *news.yahoo.com, "10 Cities Where Ordinary People Can No Longer Afford Homes," March 5, 2014*

- The San Jose* metro area was identified as one of the nations's 20 hottest housing markets in 2016. Criteria: listing views as an indicator of demand and median days on the market as an indicator of supply. The area ranked #2. *Realtor.com, "The 20 Hottest U.S. Real Estate Markets in February 2016," February 25, 2016*
- San Jose* was ranked #15 in the top 20 out of 266 metro areas in terms of house price appreciation in 2015 (#1 = highest rate). *Federal Housing Finance Agency, House Price Index, 4th Quarter 2015*
- The San Jose* metro area was identified as one of the 20 least affordable housing markets in the U.S. in 2015. The area ranked #1 out of 179 markets. Criteria: qualification for a mortgage loan on a typical home. *National Association of Realtors®, Affordability Index of Existing Single-Family Homes for Metropolitan Areas, 2015*
- San Jose* was ranked #220 out of 225 metro areas in terms of housing affordability in 2015 by the National Association of Home Builders (#1 = most affordable). Criteria: the share of homes sold in that area affordable to a family earning the local median income, based on standard mortgage underwriting criteria. *National Association of Home Builders®, NAHB-Wells Fargo Housing Opportunity Index, 4th Quarter 2015*

Safety Rankings

- Farmers Insurance, in partnership with Sperling's BestPlaces, ranked metro areas in the U.S. as the "Most Secure Places to Live." The San Jose* metro area ranked #7 out of the top 20 in the large metro area category (500,000 or more residents). Criteria: economic stability; crime statistics; extreme weather; risk of natural disasters; housing depreciation; foreclosures; air quality; environmental hazards; life expectancy; motor vehicle fatalities; and employment numbers. *Farmers Insurance Group of Companies, "Most Secure U.S. Places to Live in the U.S.," June 25, 2013*
- The National Insurance Crime Bureau ranked 380 metro areas in the U.S. in terms of per capita rates of vehicle theft. The San Jose* metro area ranked #10 (#1 = highest rate). Criteria: number of vehicle theft offenses per 100,000 inhabitants in 2014. *National Insurance Crime Bureau, "Hot Spots 2014," June 24, 2015*

Seniors/Retirement Rankings

- From its Best Cities for Successful Aging indexes, the Milken Institute generated rankings for metropolitan areas, weighing data in eight categories—health care, wellness, living arrangements, transportation, financial characteristics, education and employment opportunities, community engagement, and overall livability. The San Jose* metro area was ranked #65 overall in the large metro area category. *Milken Institute, "Best Cities for Successful Aging, 2014"*

Transportation Rankings

- San Jose* was identified as one of the most congested metro areas in the U.S. The area ranked #5 out of 10. Criteria: yearly delay per auto commuter in hours. *Texas A&M Transportation Institute, "2015 Urban Mobility Scorecard," August 2015*

Miscellaneous Rankings

- The National Alliance to End Homelessness ranked the 100 most populous metro areas with the highest rate of homelessness. The San Jose* metro area ranked #7. Criteria: number of homeless people per 10,000 population in 2011. *National Alliance to End Homelessness, The State of Homelessness in America 2012*

Los Altos is located within the San Jose-Sunnyvale-Santa Clara, CA Metropolitan Statistical Area.

Business Environment

CITY FINANCES

City Government Finances

Component	2012 ($000)	2012 ($ per capita)
Total Revenues	38,662	1,334
Total Expenditures	41,696	1,438
Debt Outstanding	1,855	64
Cash and Securities[1]	44,713	1,543

Note: (1) Cash and security holdings of a government at the close of its fiscal year, including those of its dependent agencies, utilities, and liquor stores.
Source: U.S Census Bureau, State & Local Government Finances 2012

City Government Revenue by Source

Source	2012 ($000)	2012 ($ per capita)
General Revenue		
From Federal Government	21	0
From State Government	1,252	43
From Local Governments	0	0
Taxes		
Property	13,840	477
Sales and Gross Receipts	7,932	273
Personal Income	0	0
Corporate Income	0	0
Motor Vehicle License	0	0
Other Taxes	2,698	93
Current Charges	8,766	302
Liquor Store	0	0
Utility	0	0
Employee Retirement	0	0

Source: U.S Census Bureau, State & Local Government Finances 2012

City Government Expenditures by Function

Function	2012 ($000)	2012 ($ per capita)	2012 (%)
General Direct Expenditures			
Air Transportation	0	0	0.0
Corrections	0	0	0.0
Education	0	0	0.0
Employment Security Administration	0	0	0.0
Financial Administration	977	33	2.3
Fire Protection	5,375	185	12.8
General Public Buildings	0	0	0.0
Governmental Administration, Other	7,168	247	17.1
Health	351	12	0.8
Highways	5,874	202	14.0
Hospitals	0	0	0.0
Housing and Community Development	1,064	36	2.5
Interest on General Debt	69	2	0.1
Judicial and Legal	258	8	0.6
Libraries	0	0	0.0
Parking	0	0	0.0
Parks and Recreation	2,529	87	6.0
Police Protection	9,549	329	22.9
Public Welfare	0	0	0.0
Sewerage	4,974	171	11.9
Solid Waste Management	341	11	0.8
Veterans' Services	0	0	0.0
Liquor Store	0	0	0.0
Utility	0	0	0.0
Employee Retirement	0	0	0.0

Source: U.S Census Bureau, State & Local Government Finances 2012

DEMOGRAPHICS

Population Growth

Area	1990 Census	2000 Census	2010 Census	2014* Estimate	Population Growth (%) 1990-2014	2010-2014
City	26,400	27,693	28,976	29,762	12.7	2.7
MSA[1]	1,534,280	1,735,819	1,836,911	1,898,457	23.7	3.4
U.S.	248,709,873	281,421,906	308,745,538	314,107,084	26.3	1.7

Note: (1) Figures cover the San Jose-Sunnyvale-Santa Clara, CA Metropolitan Statistical Area—see Appendix B for areas included; (*) 2010-2014 5-year estimated population
Source: U.S. Census Bureau, 1990 Census, Census 2000, Census 2010, 2010-2014 American Community Survey 5-Year Estimates

Household Size

Area	Persons in Household (%) One	Two	Three	Four	Five	Six	Seven or More	Average Household Size
City	20.3	34.4	16.4	20.8	6.6	1.2	0.1	2.70
MSA[1]	21.3	29.2	18.6	17.6	7.6	2.8	2.5	2.95
U.S.	27.5	33.5	15.8	13.1	6.0	2.3	1.4	2.64

Note: (1) Figures cover the San Jose-Sunnyvale-Santa Clara, CA Metropolitan Statistical Area—see Appendix B for areas included
Source: U.S. Census Bureau, 2010-2014 American Community Survey 5-Year Estimates

Race

Area	White Alone[2] (%)	Black Alone[2] (%)	Asian Alone[2] (%)	AIAN[3] Alone[2] (%)	NHOPI[4] Alone[2] (%)	Other Race Alone[2] (%)	Two or More Races (%)
City	69.6	0.6	24.0	0.1	0.0	0.6	5.0
MSA[1]	50.3	2.6	32.2	0.5	0.4	9.4	4.5
U.S.	73.8	12.6	5.0	0.8	0.2	4.7	2.9

Note: (1) Figures cover the San Jose-Sunnyvale-Santa Clara, CA Metropolitan Statistical Area—see Appendix B for areas included; (2) Alone is defined as not being in combination with one or more other races; (3) American Indian and Alaska Native; (4) Native Hawaiian and Other Pacific Islander
Source: U.S. Census Bureau, 2010-2014 American Community Survey 5-Year Estimates

Hispanic or Latino Origin

Area	Total (%)	Mexican (%)	Puerto Rican (%)	Cuban (%)	Other (%)
City	3.6	1.6	0.1	0.0	2.0
MSA[1]	27.7	23.5	0.4	0.1	3.6
U.S.	16.9	10.8	1.6	0.6	3.8

Note: Persons of Hispanic or Latino origin can be of any race; (1) Figures cover the San Jose-Sunnyvale-Santa Clara, CA Metropolitan Statistical Area—see Appendix B for areas included
Source: U.S. Census Bureau, 2010-2014 American Community Survey 5-Year Estimates

Ancestry

Area	German	Irish	English	American	Italian	Polish	French[2]	Scottish	Dutch
City	15.4	10.9	13.7	3.0	6.9	2.6	2.6	2.9	2.0
MSA[1]	7.2	5.5	5.2	2.0	4.5	1.2	1.6	1.2	0.8
U.S.	14.9	10.8	8.0	7.1	5.5	3.0	2.7	1.7	1.4

Note: Figures are the percentage of the total population reporting a particular ancestry. The nine most commonly reported ancestries in the U.S. are shown. Figures include multiple ancestries (e.g. if a person reported being Irish and Italian, they were included in both columns); (1) Figures cover the San Jose-Sunnyvale-Santa Clara, CA Metropolitan Statistical Area—see Appendix B for areas included; (2) Excludes Basque
Source: U.S. Census Bureau, 2010-2014 American Community Survey 5-Year Estimates

Foreign-Born Population

Area	Any Foreign Country	Asia	Mexico	Europe	Carribean	Central America[2]	South America	Africa	Canada
	Percent of Population Born in								
City	23.3	14.4	0.2	5.8	0.0	0.3	0.5	0.4	1.4
MSA[1]	36.9	22.9	8.1	2.9	0.1	1.0	0.7	0.5	0.5
U.S.	13.1	3.8	3.7	1.5	1.2	1.0	0.9	0.6	0.3

Note: (1) Figures cover the San Jose-Sunnyvale-Santa Clara, CA Metropolitan Statistical Area—see Appendix B for areas included; (2) Excludes Mexico.
Source: U.S. Census Bureau, 2010-2014 American Community Survey 5-Year Estimates

Marital Status

Area	Never Married	Now Married[2]	Separated	Widowed	Divorced
City	18.7	68.0	0.6	6.8	5.9
MSA[1]	32.5	53.2	1.7	4.5	8.2
U.S.	32.5	48.4	2.2	5.9	10.9

Note: Figures are percentages and cover the population 15 years of age and older; (1) Figures cover the San Jose-Sunnyvale-Santa Clara, CA Metropolitan Statistical Area—see Appendix B for areas included; (2) Excludes separated
Source: U.S. Census Bureau, 2010-2014 American Community Survey 5-Year Estimates

Disability Status

Area	All Ages	Under 18 Years Old	18 to 64 Years Old	65 Years and Over
City	5.5	0.6	2.8	19.6
MSA[1]	7.7	2.2	5.2	33.5
U.S.	12.3	4.1	10.2	36.3

Note: Figures show percent of the civilian noninstitutionalized population that reported having a disability. Disability status is determined from from six types of difficulty: vision, hearing, cognitive, ambulatory, self-care, and independent living. For children under 5 years old, hearing and vision difficulty are used to determine disability status. For children between the ages of 5 and 14, disability status is determined from hearing, vision, cognitive, ambulatory, and self-care difficulties. For people aged 15 years and older, they are considered to have a disability if they have difficulty with any one of the six difficulty types; (1) Figures cover the San Jose-Sunnyvale-Santa Clara, CA Metropolitan Statistical Area—see Appendix B for areas included.
Source: U.S. Census Bureau, 2010-2014 American Community Survey 5-Year Estimates

Age

Area	Under Age 5	Age 5–19	Age 20–34	Age 35–44	Age 45–54	Age 55–64	Age 65–74	Age 75–84	Age 85+	Median Age
	Percent of Population									
City	5.4	21.6	7.4	13.6	16.7	14.7	10.1	6.4	4.1	46.2
MSA[1]	6.7	19.4	21.4	15.2	14.6	10.9	6.4	3.6	1.6	36.6
U.S.	6.4	19.9	20.6	13.0	14.1	12.3	7.6	4.3	1.9	37.4

Note: (1) Figures cover the San Jose-Sunnyvale-Santa Clara, CA Metropolitan Statistical Area—see Appendix B for areas included
Source: U.S. Census Bureau, 2010-2014 American Community Survey 5-Year Estimates

Gender

Area	Males	Females	Males per 100 Females
City	14,391	15,371	93.6
MSA[1]	953,276	945,181	100.9
U.S.	154,515,159	159,591,925	96.8

Note: (1) Figures cover the San Jose-Sunnyvale-Santa Clara, CA Metropolitan Statistical Area—see Appendix B for areas included
Source: U.S. Census Bureau, 2010-2014 American Community Survey 5-Year Estimates

Religious Groups by Family

Area	Catholic	Baptist	Non-Den.	Methodist[2]	Lutheran	LDS[3]	Pente-costal	Presby-terian[4]	Muslim[5]	Judaism
MSA[1]	26.0	1.3	4.2	1.0	0.5	1.4	1.1	0.7	1.0	0.6
U.S.	19.1	9.3	4.0	4.0	2.3	2.0	1.9	1.6	0.8	0.7

Note: Figures are the number of adherents as a percentage of the total population; (1) Figures cover the San Jose-Sunnyvale-Santa Clara, CA Metropolitan Statistical Area—see Appendix B for areas included; (2) Methodist/Pietist; (3) Latter Day Saints; (4) Reformed; (5) Figures are estimates
Source: Association of Statisticians of American Religious Bodies, 2010 U.S. Religion Census: Religious Congregations & Membership Study

Religious Groups by Tradition

Area	Catholic	Evangelical Protestant	Mainline Protestant	Other Tradition	Black Protestant	Orthodox
MSA[1]	26.0	8.2	2.4	6.8	0.1	0.4
U.S.	19.1	16.2	7.3	4.3	1.6	0.3

Note: Figures are the number of adherents as a percentage of the total population; (1) Figures cover the San Jose-Sunnyvale-Santa Clara, CA Metropolitan Statistical Area—see Appendix B for areas included
Source: Association of Statisticians of American Religious Bodies, 2010 U.S. Religion Census: Religious Congregations & Membership Study

ECONOMY

Gross Metropolitan Product

Area	2013	2014	2015	2016	Rank[2]
MSA[1]	196.8	210.1	220.3	233.3	16

Note: Figures are in billions of dollars; (1) Figures cover the San Jose-Sunnyvale-Santa Clara, CA Metropolitan Statistical Area—see Appendix B for areas included; (2) Rank is based on 2016 data and ranges from 1 to 381
Source: The U.S. Conference of Mayors, U.S. Metro Economies: GMP and Employment 2014-2016, June 2015

Economic Growth

Area	2011-13 (%)	2014 (%)	2015 (%)	2016 (%)	Rank[2]
MSA[1]	3.8	3.4	3.7	4.1	9
U.S.	2.2	2.4	2.3	2.9	–

Note: Figures are real gross metropolitan product (GMP) growth rates and represent annual average percent change; (1) Figures cover the San Jose-Sunnyvale-Santa Clara, CA Metropolitan Statistical Area—see Appendix B for areas included; (2) Rank is based on 2016 data and ranges from 1 to 381
Source: The U.S. Conference of Mayors, U.S. Metro Economies: GMP and Employment 2014-2016, June 2015

Metropolitan Area Exports

Area	2009	2010	2011	2012	2013	2014	Rank[2]
MSA[1]	21,405.7	26,333.0	26,712.1	26,687.6	23,413.1	21,128.7	16

Note: Figures are in millions of dollars; (1) Figures cover the San Jose-Sunnyvale-Santa Clara, CA Metropolitan Statistical Area—see Appendix B for areas included; (2) Rank is based on 2014 data and ranges from 1 to 385
Source: U.S. Department of Commerce, International Trade Administration, Office of Trade & Industry Information, Manufacturing & Services, data extracted March 10, 2016

Building Permits

Area	Single-Family			Multi-Family			Total		
	2014	2015p	Pct. Chg.	2014	2015p	Pct. Chg.	2014	2015p	Pct. Chg.
City	35	42	20.0	182	4	-97.8	217	46	-78.8
MSA[1]	1,861	1,954	5.0	8,176	4,364	-46.6	10,037	6,318	-37.1
U.S.	640,300	690,800	7.9	411,800	487,600	18.4	1,052,100	1,178,400	12.0

Note: (1) Figures cover the San Jose-Sunnyvale-Santa Clara, CA Metropolitan Statistical Area—see Appendix B for areas included; Figures represent new, privately-owned housing units authorized (unadjusted data); All permit data are based on estimates with imputation; (p) preliminary data.
Source: U.S. Census Bureau, Manufacturing, Mining, and Construction Statistics, Building Permits, 2014, 2015

Bankruptcy Filings

Area	Business Filings			Nonbusiness Filings		
	2014	2015	% Chg.	2014	2015	% Chg.
Santa Clara County	147	124	-15.6	3,173	2,413	-24.0
U.S.	26,983	24,735	-8.3	909,812	819,760	-9.9

Note: Business filings include Chapter 7, Chapter 11, Chapter 12, and Chapter 13; Nonbusiness filings include Chapter 7, Chapter 11, and Chapter 13
Source: Administrative Office of the U.S. Courts, Business and Nonbusiness Bankruptcy, County Cases Commenced by Chapter of the Bankruptcy Code, During the 12- Month Period Ending December 31, 2014 and Business and Nonbusiness Bankruptcy, County Cases Commenced by Chapter of the Bankruptcy Code, During the 12- Month Period Ending December 31, 2015

Housing Vacancy Rates

Area	Gross Vacancy Rate[2] (%)			Year-Round Vacancy Rate[3] (%)			Rental Vacancy Rate[4] (%)			Homeowner Vacancy Rate[5] (%)		
	2013	2014	2015	2013	2014	2015	2013	2014	2015	2013	2014	2015
MSA[1]	5.0	4.7	5.7	4.9	4.5	5.6	3.0	2.9	3.5	0.6	0.6	0.9
U.S.	13.6	13.4	12.9	10.7	10.4	10.0	8.3	7.6	7.1	2.0	1.9	1.8

Note: (1) Figures cover the San Jose-Sunnyvale-Santa Clara, CA Metropolitan Statistical Area—see Appendix B for areas included; (2) The percentage of the total housing inventory that is vacant; (3) The percentage of the housing inventory (excluding seasonal units) that is year-round vacant; (4) The percentage of rental inventory that is vacant for rent; (5) The percentage of homeowner inventory that is vacant for sale
Source: U.S. Census Bureau, Housing Vacancies and Homeownership Annual Statistics: 2015

INCOME

Income

Area	Per Capita ($)	Median Household ($)	Average Household ($)
City	84,705	157,500	227,294
MSA[1]	42,176	92,960	123,393
U.S.	28,555	53,482	74,596

Note: (1) Figures cover the San Jose-Sunnyvale-Santa Clara, CA Metropolitan Statistical Area—see Appendix B for areas included
Source: U.S. Census Bureau, 2010-2014 American Community Survey 5-Year Estimates

Household Income Distribution

Area	Percent of Households Earning							
	Under $15,000	$15,000 -24,999	$25,000 -34,999	$35,000 -49,999	$50,000 -74,999	$75,000 -99,000	$100,000 -149,999	$150,000 and up
City	4.0	3.4	3.5	6.4	7.9	7.8	15.0	51.9
MSA[1]	6.9	6.1	6.1	8.8	13.4	11.8	18.6	28.2
U.S.	12.5	10.7	10.2	13.5	17.8	12.2	13.0	10.0

Note: (1) Figures cover the San Jose-Sunnyvale-Santa Clara, CA Metropolitan Statistical Area—see Appendix B for areas included
Source: U.S. Census Bureau, 2010-2014 American Community Survey 5-Year Estimates

Poverty Rate

Area	All Ages	Under 18 Years Old	18 to 64 Years Old	65 Years and Over
City	2.7	1.4	2.8	3.8
MSA[1]	10.0	11.9	9.5	8.7
U.S.	15.6	21.9	14.6	9.4

Note: Figures are percentage of people whose income during the past 12 months was below the poverty level; (1) Figures cover the San Jose-Sunnyvale-Santa Clara, CA Metropolitan Statistical Area—see Appendix B for areas included
Source: U.S. Census Bureau, 2010-2014 American Community Survey 5-Year Estimates

EMPLOYMENT

Labor Force and Employment

Area	Civilian Labor Force			Workers Employed		
	Dec. 2014	Dec. 2015	% Chg.	Dec. 2014	Dec. 2015	% Chg.
City	14,333	14,772	3.0	13,929	14,416	3.4
MSA[1]	1,039,234	1,068,398	2.8	992,810	1,027,507	3.4
U.S.	155,521,000	157,245,000	1.1	147,190,000	149,703,000	1.7

Note: Data is not seasonally adjusted and covers workers 16 years of age and older; (1) Figures cover the San Jose-Sunnyvale-Santa Clara, CA Metropolitan Statistical Area—see Appendix B for areas included
Source: Bureau of Labor Statistics, Local Area Unemployment Statistics

Unemployment Rate

Area	2015											
	Jan.	Feb.	Mar.	Apr.	May	Jun.	Jul.	Aug.	Sep.	Oct.	Nov.	Dec.
City	3.0	2.8	2.6	2.5	2.6	2.6	2.7	2.6	2.3	2.5	2.5	2.4
MSA[1]	4.8	4.4	4.2	3.9	4.0	4.0	4.3	4.1	3.7	4.0	3.9	3.8
U.S.	6.1	5.8	5.6	5.1	5.3	5.5	5.6	5.2	4.9	4.8	4.8	4.8

Note: Data is not seasonally adjusted and covers workers 16 years of age and older; (1) Figures cover the San Jose-Sunnyvale-Santa Clara, CA Metropolitan Statistical Area—see Appendix B for areas included
Source: Bureau of Labor Statistics, Local Area Unemployment Statistics

Employment by Occupation

Occupation Classification	City (%)	MSA[1] (%)	U.S. (%)
Management, Business, Science, and Arts	77.4	49.7	36.4
Natural Resources, Construction, and Maintenance	1.3	6.9	9.0
Production, Transportation, and Material Moving	1.9	8.3	12.1
Sales and Office	15.0	20.1	24.4
Service	4.4	15.1	18.2

Note: Figures cover employed civilians 16 years of age and older; (1) Figures cover the San Jose-Sunnyvale-Santa Clara, CA Metropolitan Statistical Area—see Appendix B for areas included
Source: U.S. Census Bureau, 2010-2014 American Community Survey 5-Year Estimates

Employment by Industry

Sector	MSA[1]		U.S.
	Number of Employees	Percent of Total	Percent of Total
Construction	44,500	4.1	4.5
Education and Health Services	161,400	15.1	15.7
Financial Activities	35,600	3.3	5.7
Government	94,000	8.7	15.5
Information	77,200	7.2	1.9
Leisure and Hospitality	96,900	9.0	10.4
Manufacturing	161,800	15.1	8.6
Mining and Logging	200	<0.1	0.5
Other Services	27,800	2.6	3.9
Professional and Business Services	223,400	20.9	13.9
Retail Trade	92,200	8.6	11.3
Transportation, Warehousing, and Utilities	17,100	1.6	3.9
Wholesale Trade	36,600	3.4	4.1

Note: Figures are non-farm employment as of December 2015. Figures are not seasonally adjusted and include workers 16 years of age and older; (1) Figures cover the San Jose-Sunnyvale-Santa Clara, CA Metropolitan Statistical Area—see Appendix B for areas included
Source: Bureau of Labor Statistics, Current Employment Statistics, Employment, Hours, and Earnings

Occupations with Greatest Projected Employment Growth: 2012 – 2022

Occupation[1]	2012 Employment	2022 Projected Employment	Numeric Employment Change	Percent Employment Change
Personal Care Aides	386,900	587,200	200,300	51.8
Combined Food Preparation and Serving Workers, Including Fast Food	286,000	362,400	76,400	26.7
Retail Salespersons	468,400	528,100	59,700	12.7
Laborers and Freight, Stock, and Material Movers, Hand	270,500	322,300	51,800	19.1
Waiters and Waitresses	246,100	290,300	44,200	18.0
Registered Nurses	254,500	297,400	42,900	16.9
General and Operations Managers	253,800	295,700	41,900	16.5
Secretaries and Administrative Assistants, Except Legal, Medical, and Executive	212,800	250,100	37,300	17.5
Cashiers	357,800	392,600	34,800	9.7
Cooks, Restaurant	116,900	150,600	33,700	28.8

Note: Projections cover California; (1) Sorted by numeric employment change
Source: www.projectionscentral.com, State Occupational Projections, 2012–2022 Long-Term Projections

Fastest Growing Occupations: 2012 – 2022

Occupation[1]	2012 Employment	2022 Projected Employment	Numeric Employment Change	Percent Employment Change
Economists	3,100	5,100	2,000	64.5
Helpers—Brickmasons, Blockmasons, Stonemasons, and Tile and Marble Setters	2,900	4,600	1,700	58.6
Brickmasons and Blockmasons	5,100	8,000	2,900	56.9
Insulation Workers, Floor, Ceiling, and Wall	1,600	2,500	900	56.3
Stonemasons	1,100	1,700	600	54.5
Insulation Workers, Mechanical	1,100	1,700	600	54.5
Personal Care Aides	386,900	587,200	200,300	51.8
Foresters	1,200	1,800	600	50.0
Terrazzo Workers and Finishers	1,100	1,600	500	45.5
Mechanical Door Repairers	1,100	1,600	500	45.5

Note: Projections cover California; (1) Sorted by percent employment change and excludes occupations with numeric employment change less than 100
Source: www.projectionscentral.com, State Occupational Projections, 2012–2022 Long-Term Projections

Average Wages

Occupation	$/Hr.	Occupation	$/Hr.
Accountants and Auditors	48.36	Maids and Housekeeping Cleaners	15.18
Automotive Mechanics	25.59	Maintenance and Repair Workers	23.36
Bookkeepers	23.98	Marketing Managers	94.90
Carpenters	29.24	Nuclear Medicine Technologists	57.52
Cashiers	12.25	Nurses, Licensed Practical	28.36
Clerks, General Office	19.84	Nurses, Registered	58.47
Clerks, Receptionists/Information	17.28	Nursing Assistants	15.92
Clerks, Shipping/Receiving	17.59	Packers and Packagers, Hand	12.48
Computer Programmers	45.16	Physical Therapists	47.60
Computer Systems Analysts	55.19	Postal Service Mail Carriers	26.04
Computer User Support Specialists	37.61	Real Estate Brokers	n/a
Cooks, Restaurant	13.19	Retail Salespersons	14.30
Dentists	91.18	Sales Reps., Exc. Tech./Scientific	35.36
Electrical Engineers	64.71	Sales Reps., Tech./Scientific	56.30
Electricians	36.59	Secretaries, Exc. Legal/Med./Exec.	22.03
Financial Managers	82.91	Security Guards	15.74
First-Line Supervisors/Managers, Sales	24.43	Surgeons	125.24
Food Preparation Workers	11.88	Teacher Assistants*	15.16
General and Operations Managers	76.18	Teachers, Elementary School*	36.39
Hairdressers/Cosmetologists	12.87	Teachers, Secondary School*	36.28
Internists	112.31	Telemarketers	17.42
Janitors and Cleaners	13.50	Truck Drivers, Heavy/Tractor-Trailer	20.79
Landscaping/Groundskeeping Workers	15.50	Truck Drivers, Light/Delivery Svcs.	18.60
Lawyers	98.08	Waiters and Waitresses	13.01

Note: Wage data covers the San Jose-Sunnyvale-Santa Clara, CA Metropolitan Statistical Area—see Appendix B for areas included; (*) Hourly wages for elementary/secondary school teachers and teacher assistants were calculated by the editors from annual wage data based on a 40 hour work week; n/a not available.
Source: Bureau of Labor Statistics, Metro Area Occupational Employment and Wage Estimates, May 2015

TAXES

State Corporate Income Tax Rates

State	Tax Rate (%)	Income Brackets ($)	Num. of Brackets	Financial Institution Tax Rate (%)[a]	Federal Income Tax Ded.
California	8.84 (c)	Flat rate	1	10.84 (c)	No

Note: Tax rates as of January 1, 2016; (a) Rates listed are the corporate income tax rate applied to financial institutions or excise taxes based on income. Some states have other taxes based upon the value of deposits or shares; (c) Minimum tax is $800 in California, $100 in District of Columbia, $50 in North Dakota (banks), $500 in Rhode Island, $200 per location in South Dakota (banks), $100 in Utah, $250 in Vermont.
Source: Federation of Tax Administrators, "State Corporate Income Tax Rates, 2016"

State Individual Income Tax Rates

State	Tax Rate (%)	Income Brackets ($)	Num. of Brackets	Personal Exempt. ($)[1]		Fed. Inc. Tax Ded.
				Single	Dependents	
California (a)	1.0 - 12.3 (f)	7,850- 526,443 (b)	9	109 (c)	337 (c)	No

Note: Tax rates as of January 1, 2016; Local- and county-level taxes are not included; n/a not applicable; (1) Married joint filers generally receive double the single exemption; (a) 18 states have statutory provision for automatically adjusting to the rate of inflation the dollar values of the income tax brackets, standard deductions, and/or personal exemptions. Massachusetts, Michigan, and Nebraska index the personal exemptiononly. Oregon does not index the income brackets for $125,000 and over. Maine has suspended indexing for 2014 and 2015; (b) For joint returns, taxes are twice the tax on half the couple's income; (c) The personal exemption takes the form of a tax credit instead of a deduction; (f) California imposes an additional 1% tax on taxable income over $1 million, making the maximum rate 13.3% over $1 million.
Source: Federation of Tax Administrators, "State Individual Income Tax Rates, 2016"

Various State and Local Tax Rates

State	State and Local Sales and Use (%)	State Sales and Use (%)	Gasoline[1] (¢/gal.)	Cigarette[2] ($/pack)	Spirits[3] ($/gal.)	Wine[4] ($/gal.)	Beer[5] ($/gal.)
California	8.75	7.50 (b)	40.62	0.87	3.30 (f)	0.20 (l)	0.08

Note: All tax rates as of January 1, 2016; (1) The American Petroleum Institute has developed a methodology for determining the average tax rate on a gallon of fuel. Rates may include any of the following: excise taxes, environmental fees, storage tank fees, other fees or taxes, general sales tax, and local taxes. In states where gasoline is subject to the general sales tax, or where the fuel tax is based on the average sale price, the average rate determined by API is sensitive to changes in the price of gasoline. States that fully or partially apply general sales taxes to gasoline: CA, CO, GA, IL, IN, MI, NY; (2) The federal excise tax of $1.0066 per pack and local taxes are not included; (3) Rates are those applicable to off-premise sales of 40% alcohol by volume (a.b.v.) distilled spirits in 750ml containers. Local excise taxes are excluded; (4) Rates are those applicable to off-premise sales of 11% a.b.v. non-carbonated wine in 750ml containers; (5) Rates are those applicable to off-premise sales of 4.7% a.b.v. beer in 12 ounce containers; (b) Three states levy mandatory, statewide local add-on sales taxes at the state level: California (1%), Utah (1.25%), and Virginia (1%). We include these in their state sales tax rates; (f) Different rates are also applicable according to alcohol content, place of production, size of container, or place purchased (on- or off-premise or onboard airlines); (l) Different rates also applicable according to alcohol content, place of production, size of container, place purchased (on- or off-premise or on board airlines) or type of wine (carbonated, vermouth, etc.).
Source: Tax Foundation, 2016 Facts & Figures: How Does Your State Compare?

State Business Tax Climate Index Rankings

State	Overall Rank	Corporate Tax Rank	Individual Income Tax Rank	Sales Tax Rank	Unemployment Insurance Tax Rank	Property Tax Rank
California	48	35	50	40	13	13

Note: The index is a measure of how each state's tax laws affect economic performance. The lower the rank, the more favorable a state's tax system is for business. States without a given tax are given a ranking of 1. The scores/rankings for the District of Columbia do not affect other states. The 2016 index represents the tax climate as of July 1, 2015 (the beginning of Fiscal Year 2016).
Source: Tax Foundation, State Business Tax Climate Index 2016

TRANSPORTATION

Means of Transportation to Work

Area	Car/Truck/Van: Drove Alone	Car/Truck/Van: Car-pooled	Public Transportation: Bus	Public Transportation: Subway	Public Transportation: Railroad	Bicycle	Walked	Other Means	Worked at Home
City	78.2	5.2	0.5	0.3	1.3	3.1	2.9	0.3	8.3
MSA[1]	76.5	10.5	2.2	0.2	1.1	1.8	1.9	1.4	4.6
U.S.	76.4	9.6	2.6	1.8	0.6	0.6	2.8	1.3	4.4

Note: Figures are percentages and cover workers 16 years of age and older; (1) Figures cover the San Jose-Sunnyvale-Santa Clara, CA Metropolitan Statistical Area—see Appendix B for areas included
Source: U.S. Census Bureau, 2010-2014 American Community Survey 5-Year Estimates

Travel Time to Work

Area	Less Than 10 Minutes	10 to 19 Minutes	20 to 29 Minutes	30 to 44 Minutes	45 to 59 Minutes	60 to 89 Minutes	90 Minutes or More
City	9.6	32.8	30.8	18.6	2.8	3.7	1.6
MSA[1]	8.4	29.2	25.7	22.3	7.4	5.3	1.9
U.S.	13.3	29.6	21.0	20.2	7.7	5.7	2.6

Note: Figures are percentages and include workers 16 years old and over; (1) Figures cover the San Jose-Sunnyvale-Santa Clara, CA Metropolitan Statistical Area—see Appendix B for areas included
Source: U.S. Census Bureau, 2010-2014 American Community Survey 5-Year Estimates

Freeway Travel Time Index

Area	1985	1990	1995	2000	2005	2010	2014
Urban Area Rank[1,2]	16	7	10	9	8	6	3
Urban Area Index[1]	1.15	1.21	1.23	1.28	1.32	1.34	1.38
Average Index[3]	1.09	1.11	1.14	1.17	1.20	1.19	1.20

Note: Freeway Travel Time Index—the ratio of travel time in the peak period to the travel time at free-flow conditions. For example, a value of 1.30 indicates a 20-minute free-flow trip takes 26 minutes in the peak (20 minutes x 1.30 = 26 minutes); (1) Covers the San Jose CA urban area; (2) Rank is based on 101 urban areas (#1 = highest travel time index); (3) Average of 101 urban areas
Source: Texas Transportation Institute, 2015 Urban Mobility Scorecard, August 2015

Freeway Commuter Stress Index

Area	1985	1990	1995	2000	2005	2010	2014
Urban Area Rank[1,2]	14	7	8	7	7	5	5
Urban Area Index[1]	1.24	1.31	1.33	1.39	1.43	1.45	1.50
Average Index[3]	1.13	1.16	1.19	1.22	1.25	1.24	1.25

Note: The Freeway Commuter Stress Index is the same as the Freeway Travel Time Index (see table above) except that it includes only the travel in the peak directions during the peak periods; the TTI includes travel in all directions during the peak period. Thus, the CSI is more indicative of the work trip experienced by each commuter on a daily basis. (1) Covers the San Jose CA urban area; (2) Rank is based on 101 urban areas (#1 = highest stress index); (3) Average of 101 urban areas

Source: Texas Transportation Institute, 2015 Urban Mobility Scorecard, August 2015

Living Environment

COST OF LIVING

Cost of Living Index

Composite Index	Groceries	Housing	Utilities	Transportation	Health Care	Misc. Goods/Services
n/a	n/a	n/a	n/a	n/a	n/a	n/a

Note: The Cost of Living Index measures regional differences in the cost of consumer goods and services, excluding taxes and non-consumer expenditures, for professional and managerial households in the top income quintile. It is based on more than 50,000 prices covering almost 60 different items for which prices are collected three times a year by chambers of commerce, economic development organizations or university applied economic centers in each participating urban area. The numbers shown should be read as a percentage above or below the national average of 100. For example, a value of 115.4 in the groceries column indicates that grocery prices are 15.4% higher than the national average. Small differences in the index numbers should not be interpreted as significant; n/a not available.
Source: The Council for Community and Economic Research, ACCRA Cost of Living Index, 2015

Grocery Prices

Area[1]	T-Bone Steak ($/pound)	Frying Chicken ($/pound)	Whole Milk ($/half gal.)	Eggs ($/dozen)	Orange Juice ($/64 oz.)	Coffee ($/11.5 oz.)
City[2]	n/a	n/a	n/a	n/a	n/a	n/a
Avg.	10.99	1.43	2.25	2.26	3.58	4.48
Min.	7.16	0.98	1.30	1.35	2.88	2.98
Max.	14.13	2.43	3.85	4.81	6.39	7.56

Note: (1) Values for the local area are compared with the average, minimum and maximum values for all 292 areas in the Cost of Living Index; (2) Figures cover the Los Altos CA urban area; n/a not available; **T-Bone Steak** *(price per pound);* **Frying Chicken** *(price per pound, whole fryer);* **Whole Milk** *(half gallon carton);* **Eggs** *(price per dozen, Grade A, large);* **Orange Juice** *(64 oz. Tropicana or Florida Natural);* **Coffee** *(11.5 oz. can, vacuum-packed, Maxwell House, Hills Bros, or Folgers).*
Source: The Council for Community and Economic Research, ACCRA Cost of Living Index, 2015

Housing and Utility Costs

Area[1]	New Home Price ($)	Apartment Rent ($/month)	All Electric ($/month)	Part Electric ($/month)	Other Energy ($/month)	Telephone ($/month)
City[2]	n/a	n/a	n/a	n/a	n/a	n/a
Avg.	312,874	945	179.30	95.07	72.96	28.11
Min.	178,682	479	116.28	43.14	26.46	10.01
Max.	1,472,476	3,984	504.25	189.44	421.11	43.06

Note: (1) Values for the local area are compared with the average, minimum and maximum values for all 292 areas in the Cost of Living Index; (2) Figures cover the Los Altos CA urban area; n/a not available; **New Home Price** *(2,400 sf living area, 8,000 sf lot, in urban area with full utilities);* **Apartment Rent** *(950 sf 2 bedroom/1.5 or 2 bath, unfurnished, excluding all utilities except water);* **All Electric** *(average monthly cost for an all-electric home);* **Part Electric** *(average monthly cost for a part-electric home);* **Other Energy** *(average monthly cost for natural gas, fuel oil, coal, wood, and any other forms of energy except electricity);* **Telephone** *(price includes basic monthly rate for a private residential line plus additional local usage charges incurred by a family of four).*
Source: The Council for Community and Economic Research, ACCRA Cost of Living Index, 2015

Health Care, Transportation, and Other Costs

Area[1]	Doctor ($/visit)	Dentist ($/visit)	Optometrist ($/visit)	Gasoline ($/gallon)	Beauty Salon ($/visit)	Men's Shirt ($)
City[2]	n/a	n/a	n/a	n/a	n/a	n/a
Avg.	105.15	89.02	99.78	2.38	35.30	28.10
Min.	66.87	56.09	48.53	1.95	18.91	13.38
Max.	182.34	150.36	228.33	4.09	67.91	63.80

Note: (1) Values for the local area are compared with the average, minimum and maximum values for all 292 areas in the Cost of Living Index; (2) Figures cover the Los Altos CA urban area; n/a not available; **Doctor** *(general practitioners routine exam of an established patient);* **Dentist** *(adult teeth cleaning and periodic oral examination);* **Optometrist** *(full vision eye exam for established adult patient);* **Gasoline** *(one gallon regular unleaded, national brand, including all taxes, cash price at self-service pump if available);* **Beauty Salon** *(woman's shampoo, trim, and blow-dry);* **Men's Shirt** *(cotton/polyester dress shirt, pinpoint weave, long sleeves).*
Source: The Council for Community and Economic Research, ACCRA Cost of Living Index, 2015

HOUSING

House Price Index (HPI)

Area	National Ranking[2]	Quarterly Change (%)	One-Year Change (%)	Five-Year Change (%)
MSA[1]	15	1.20	11.30	51.20
U.S.[3]	–	1.45	5.76	22.85

Note: The HPI is a weighted repeat sales index. It measures average price changes in repeat sales or refinancings on the same properties. This information is obtained by reviewing repeat mortgage transactions on single-family properties whose mortgages have been purchased or securitized by Fannie Mae or Freddie Mac in January 1975; (1) San Jose-Sunnyvale-Santa Clara Metropolitan Statistical Area—see Appendix B for areas included; (2) Rankings are based on annual percentage change for all metro areas containing at least 15,000 transactions over the last 10 years and ranges from 1 to 266; (3) figures based on a weighted average of Census Division estimates using a seasonally adjusted, purchase-only index; all figures are for the period ending December 31, 2015

Source: Federal Housing Finance Agency, House Price Index, February 25, 2016

Median Single-Family Home Prices

Area	2013	2014	2015p	Percent Change 2014 to 2015
MSA[1]	780.0	860.0	950.4	10.5
U.S. Average	197.4	208.9	223.9	7.2

Note: Figures are median sales prices of existing single-family homes in thousands of dollars; (p) preliminary; n/a not available; (1) San Jose-Sunnyvale-Santa Clara, CA Metropolitan Statistical Area—see Appendix B for areas included

Source: National Association of Realtors, Median Sales Price of Existing Single-Family Homes for Metropolitan Areas, 4th Quarter 2015

Qualifying Income Based on Median Sales Price of Existing Single-Family Homes

Area	With 5% Down ($)	With 10% Down ($)	With 20% Down ($)
MSA[1]	209,085	198,080	176,071
U.S. Average	49,535	46,928	41,714

Note: Figures are preliminary; Qualifying income is based on a mortgage rate of 4.1%. Monthly principal and interest payment is limited to 25% of income; n/a not available; (1) San Jose-Sunnyvale-Santa Clara, CA Metropolitan Statistical Area—see Appendix B for areas included

Source: National Association of Realtors, Qualifying Income Based on Median Sales Price of Existing Single-Family Homes for Metropolitan Areas, 4th Quarter 2015

Median Apartment Condo-Coop Home Prices

Area	2013	2014	2015p	Percent Change 2014 to 2015
MSA[1]	n/a	n/a	n/a	n/a
U.S. Average	194.9	204.3	210.7	3.1

Note: Figures are median sales prices of existing apartment condo-coop homes in thousands of dollars; (p) preliminary; n/a not available; (1) San Jose-Sunnyvale-Santa Clara, CA Metropolitan Statistical Area—see Appendix B for areas included

Source: National Association of Realtors, Median Sales Price of Existing Apartment Condo-Coop Homes for Metropolitan Areas, 4th Quarter 2015

Gross Monthly Rent

Area	Under $200	$200 -299	$300 -499	$500 -749	$750 -999	$1,000 -1,499	$1,500 and up	Median ($)
City	0.0	0.0	1.1	0.4	0.4	5.7	92.4	2,000+
MSA[1]	0.5	1.5	2.6	3.7	6.5	28.1	57.1	1,629
U.S.	1.5	3.2	7.4	21.0	24.1	26.9	15.9	920

Note: Figures are percentages except for Median; Gross rent is the contract rent plus the estimated average monthly cost of utilities (electricity, gas, and water and sewer) and fuels (oil, coal, kerosene, wood, etc.) if these are paid by the renter (or paid for the renter by someone else); (1) Figures cover the San Jose-Sunnyvale-Santa Clara, CA Metropolitan Statistical Area—see Appendix B for areas included

Source: U.S. Census Bureau, 2010-2014 American Community Survey 5-Year Estimates

HEALTH

Homeownership Rate

Area	2008 (%)	2009 (%)	2010 (%)	2011 (%)	2012 (%)	2013 (%)	2014 (%)	2015 (%)
MSA[1]	54.6	57.2	58.9	60.4	58.6	56.4	56.4	50.7
U.S.	67.8	67.4	66.9	66.1	65.4	65.1	64.5	63.7

Note: (1) Figures cover the San Jose-Sunnyvale-Santa Clara, CA Metropolitan Statistical Area—see Appendix B for areas included
Source: U.S. Census Bureau, Housing Vacancies and Homeownership Annual Statistics: 2015

Year Housing Structure Built

Area	2010 or Later	2000 -2009	1990 -1999	1980 -1989	1970 -1979	1960 -1969	1950 -1959	1940 -1949	Before 1940	Median Year
City	1.0	7.0	4.9	5.2	10.9	19.7	39.8	7.4	4.0	1960
MSA[1]	0.7	9.8	10.6	12.7	22.6	18.9	15.4	4.2	5.2	1973
U.S.	1.0	14.9	13.9	13.8	15.8	11.0	10.8	5.4	13.3	1976

Note: Figures are percentages except for Median Year; (1) Figures cover the San Jose-Sunnyvale-Santa Clara, CA Metropolitan Statistical Area—see Appendix B for areas included
Source: U.S. Census Bureau, 2010-2014 American Community Survey 5-Year Estimates

Health Risk Data

Category	MSA[1] (%)	U.S. (%)
Adults aged 18–64 who have any kind of health care coverage	82.5	79.6
Adults who reported being in good or excellent health	88.2	83.1
Adults who are current smokers	9.6	19.6
Adults who are heavy drinkers[2]	4.3	6.1
Adults who are binge drinkers[3]	16.4	16.9
Adults who are overweight (BMI 25.0 - 29.9)	33.0	35.8
Adults who are obese (BMI 30.0 - 99.8)	15.9	27.6
Adults who participated in any physical activities in the past month	83.6	77.1
Adults 50+ who have ever had a sigmoidoscopy or colonoscopy	72.3	67.3
Women aged 40+ who have had a mammogram within the past two years	82.7	74.0
Men aged 40+ who have had a PSA test within the past two years	31.4	45.2
Adults aged 65+ who have had flu shot within the past year	54.1	60.1
Adults who always wear a seatbelt	n/a	93.8

Note: Data as of 2012 unless otherwise noted; n/a not available; (1) Figures cover the San Jose-Sunnyvale-Santa Clara, CA Metropolitan Statistical Area—see Appendix B for areas included; (2) Heavy drinkers are classified as males having more than two drinks per day or females having more than one drink per day; (3) Binge drinkers are classified as males having five or more drinks on one occasion or females having four or more drinks on one occasion
Source: Centers for Disease Control and Prevention, Behaviorial Risk Factor Surveillance System, SMART: Selected Metropolitan/Micropolitan Area Risk Trends, 2012 (Note: the CDC has discontinued this dataset but will be releasing a replacement in mid-2016)

Chronic Health Indicators

Category	MSA[1] (%)	U.S. (%)
Adults who have ever been told they had a heart attack	3.8	4.5
Adults who have ever been told they had a stroke	n/a	2.9
Adults who have been told they currently have asthma	8.4	8.9
Adults who have ever been told they have arthritis	17.2	25.7
Adults who have ever been told they have diabetes[2]	7.4	9.7
Adults who have ever been told they had skin cancer	4.1	5.7
Adults who have ever been told they had any other types of cancer	3.9	6.5
Adults who have ever been told they have COPD	2.7	6.2
Adults who have ever been told they have kidney disease	2.9	2.5
Adults who have ever been told they have a form of depression	11.3	18.0

Note: Data as of 2012 unless otherwise noted; n/a not available; (1) Figures cover the San Jose-Sunnyvale-Santa Clara, CA Metropolitan Statistical Area—see Appendix B for areas included; (2) Figures do not include pregnancy-related, borderline, or pre-diabetes
Source: Centers for Disease Control and Prevention, Behaviorial Risk Factor Surveillance System, SMART: Selected Metropolitan/Micropolitan Area Risk Trends, 2012 (Note: the CDC has discontinued this dataset but will be releasing a replacement in mid-2016)

Mortality Rates for the Top 10 Causes of Death in the U.S.

ICD-10[a] Sub-Chapter	ICD-10[a] Code	Age-Adjusted Mortality Rate[1] per 100,000 population	
		County[2]	U.S.
Malignant neoplasms	C00-C97	129.7	163.6
Ischaemic heart diseases	I20-I25	68.0	102.2
Other forms of heart disease	I30-I51	21.9	50.1
Chronic lower respiratory diseases	J40-J47	22.8	41.4
Organic, including symptomatic, mental disorders	F01-F09	6.6	38.5
Cerebrovascular diseases	I60-I69	26.5	36.5
Other external causes of accidental injury	W00-X59	16.7	27.5
Other degenerative diseases of the nervous system	G30-G31	48.0	26.3
Diabetes mellitus	E10-E14	22.4	21.1
Hypertensive diseases	I10-I15	29.7	19.7

Note: (a) ICD-10 = International Classification of Diseases 10th Revision; (1) Mortality rates are a three year average covering 2012-2014; (2) Figures cover COUNTY NOT FOUND!!!!!!.
Source: Centers for Disease Control and Prevention, National Center for Health Statistics. Underlying Cause of Death 1999-2014 on CDC WONDER Online Database, released 2015.

Mortality Rates for Selected Causes of Death

ICD-10[a] Sub-Chapter	ICD-10[a] Code	Age-Adjusted Mortality Rate[1] per 100,000 population	
		County[2]	U.S.
Assault	X85-Y09	2.8	5.1
Diseases of the liver	K70-K76	9.6	13.5
Human immunodeficiency virus (HIV) disease	B20-B24	0.7	2.1
Influenza and pneumonia	J09-J18	12.4	15.2
Intentional self-harm	X60-X84	7.9	12.7
Malnutrition	E40-E46	Unreliable	0.9
Obesity and other hyperalimentation	E65-E68	1.0	1.9
Renal failure	N17-N19	2.5	13.0
Transport accidents	V01-V99	6.3	11.6
Viral hepatitis	B15-B19	2.3	2.1

Note: (a) ICD-10 = International Classification of Diseases 10th Revision; (1) Mortality rates are a three year average covering 2012-2014; (2) Figures cover COUNTY NOT FOUND!!!!!!; Data are Suppressed when the data meet the criteria for confidentiality constraints; Mortality rates are flagged as Unreliable when the rate would be calculated with a numerator of 20 or less.
Source: Centers for Disease Control and Prevention, National Center for Health Statistics. Underlying Cause of Death 1999-2014 on CDC WONDER Online Database, released 2015.

Health Insurance Coverage

Area	With Health Insurance	With Private Health Insurance	With Public Health Insurance	Without Health Insurance	Population Under Age 18 Without Health Insurance
City	97.8	90.7	20.8	2.2	1.2
MSA[1]	89.3	73.0	24.2	10.7	3.9
U.S.	85.8	65.8	31.1	14.2	7.1

Note: Figures are percentages that cover the civilian noninstitutionalized population; (1) Figures cover the San Jose-Sunnyvale-Santa Clara, CA Metropolitan Statistical Area—see Appendix B for areas included
Source: U.S. Census Bureau, 2010-2014 American Community Survey 5-Year Estimates

Number of Medical Professionals

Area	MDs[3]	DOs[3,4]	Dentists	Podiatrists	Chiropractors	Optometrists
County[1] (number)	7,351	153	2,028	112	738	460
County[1] (rate[2])	392.9	8.2	107.0	5.9	39.0	24.3
U.S. (rate[2])	272.5	20.9	64.7	5.8	25.9	15.2

Note: Data as of 2014 unless noted; (1) Data covers Santa Clara County; (2) Rate per 100,000 population; (3) Data as of 2013 and includes all active, non-federal physicians; (4) Doctor of Osteopathic Medicine
Source: U.S. Department of Health and Human Services, Health Resources and Services Administration, Bureau of Health Professions, Area Resource File (ARF) 2014-2015

Best Hospitals

According to *U.S. News,* the San Jose-Sunnyvale-Santa Clara, CA metro area is home to one of the best hospitals in the U.S.: **Stanford Hospital and Clinics** (Honor Roll/13 specialties). The hospital listed was nationally ranked in at least one adult specialty. Only 137 hospitals nationwide were nationally ranked in one or more specialties. Fifteen hospitals in the U.S. made the Honor Roll with high scores in at least six specialties. *U.S. News Online, "America's Best Children's Hospitals 2015-16"*

According to *U.S. News,* the San Jose-Sunnyvale-Santa Clara, CA metro area is home to one of the best children's hospitals in the U.S.: **Lucile Packard Children's Hospital at Stanford** (9 specialties). The hospital listed was highly ranked in at least one pediatric specialty. Eighty-three children's hospitals in the U.S. were nationally ranked in at least one specialty. Twelve children's hospitals in the U.S. made the Honor Roll with high scores in at least three specialties. *U.S. News Online, "America's Best Children's Hospitals 2015-16"*

EDUCATION

Public School District Statistics

District Name	Schls	Pupils	Pupil/ Teacher Ratio	Minority Pupils[1] (%)	Free Lunch Eligible[2] (%)	IEP[3] (%)
Los Altos Elementary	10	4,550	21.4	50.0	4.1	9.8
Mountain View-Los Altos Union High	3	3,753	20.3	52.9	14.7	11.7
Santa Clara Co Office of Educ	21	9,788	19.7	85.5	45.6	19.6

Note: Table includes school districts with 100 or more students; (1) Percentage of students that are not non-Hispanic white; (2) Percentage of students that are eligible for the free lunch program; (3) Percentage of students that have an Individualized Education Program.
Source: U.S. Department of Education, National Center for Education Statistics, Common Core of Data, Local Education Agency (School District) Universe Survey: School Year 2013-2014; U.S. Department of Education, National Center for Education Statistics, Common Core of Data, Public Elementary/Secondary School Universe Survey: School Year 2013-2014

Best High Schools

According to *U.S. News,* Los Altos is home to one of the best high schools in the U.S.: **Los Altos High School** (#326); Nearly 20,000 schools were ranked based on their performance on state assessments and how well they prepare students for college. Schools with the highest unrounded College Readiness Index values were numerically ranked from No. 1 to No. 500 and were the gold medal winners. *U.S. News & World Report, "Best High Schools 2015"*

Highest Level of Education

Area	Less than H.S.	H.S. Diploma	Some College, No Deg.	Associate Degree	Bachelor's Degree	Master's Degree	Prof. School Degree	Doctorate Degree
City	1.3	4.9	10.1	4.8	32.2	30.9	8.1	7.8
MSA[1]	13.5	15.7	17.2	7.1	25.7	14.9	2.7	3.3
U.S.	13.7	28.0	21.2	7.9	18.3	7.8	2.0	1.3

Note: Figures cover persons age 25 and over; (1) Figures cover the San Jose-Sunnyvale-Santa Clara, CA Metropolitan Statistical Area—see Appendix B for areas included
Source: U.S. Census Bureau, 2010-2014 American Community Survey 5-Year Estimates

Educational Attainment by Race

Area	High School Graduate or Higher (%)					Bachelor's Degree or Higher (%)				
	Total	White	Black	Asian	Hisp.[2]	Total	White	Black	Asian	Hisp.[2]
City	98.7	98.9	100.0	98.5	94.2	79.0	77.4	64.7	83.8	48.6
MSA[1]	86.5	88.4	91.8	89.2	65.6	46.5	44.1	31.5	61.2	14.3
U.S.	86.3	88.4	83.2	85.8	64.1	29.3	30.6	19.0	50.9	13.9

Note: Figures shown cover persons 25 years old and over; (1) Figures cover the San Jose-Sunnyvale-Santa Clara, CA Metropolitan Statistical Area—see Appendix B for areas included; (2) People of Hispanic origin can be of any race
Source: U.S. Census Bureau, 2010-2014 American Community Survey 5-Year Estimates

School Enrollment by Grade and Control

Area	Preschool (%)		Kindergarten (%)		Grades 1 - 4 (%)		Grades 5 - 8 (%)		Grades 9 - 12 (%)	
	Public	Private	Public	Private	Public	Private	Public	Private	Public	Private
City	23.6	76.4	82.6	17.4	83.1	16.9	76.1	23.9	72.2	27.8
MSA[1]	34.4	65.6	81.9	18.1	87.1	12.9	87.7	12.3	89.1	10.9
U.S.	57.4	42.6	87.8	12.2	89.8	10.2	89.9	10.1	90.6	9.4

Note: Figures shown cover persons 3 years old and over; (1) Figures cover the San Jose-Sunnyvale-Santa Clara, CA Metropolitan Statistical Area—see Appendix B for areas included
Source: U.S. Census Bureau, 2010-2014 American Community Survey 5-Year Estimates

Average Salaries of Public School Classroom Teachers

Area	2013-14		2014-15		Percent Change 2013-14 to 2014-15	Percent Change 2004-05 to 2014-15
	Dollars	Rank[1]	Dollars	Rank[1]		
California	71,396	4	72,535	4	1.59	25.9
U.S. Average	56,610	–	57,379	–	1.36	20.8

Note: (1) State rank ranges from 1 to 51 where 1 indicates highest salary.
Source: National Education Association, Rankings & Estimates: Rankings of the States 2014 and Estimates of School Statistics 2015, March 2015

Higher Education

Four-Year Colleges			Two-Year Colleges			Medical Schools[1]	Law Schools[2]	Voc/ Tech[3]
Public	Private Non-profit	Private For-profit	Public	Private Non-profit	Private For-profit			
0	0	0	0	0	0	0	0	0

Note: Figures cover institutions located within the city limits and include main campuses only; (1) includes schools accredited by the Liaison Committee on Medical Education and the American Osteopathic Association's Commission on Osteopathic College Accreditation; (2) includes ABA-accredited schools, schools with provisional ABA accreditation, and state accredited schools; (3) includes all schools with programs that are less than 2 years.
Source: National Center for Education Statistics, Integrated Postsecondary Education System (IPEDS), 2014-15; Association of American Medical Colleges, Member List, March 21, 2016; American Osteopathic Association, Member List, March 21, 2016; Law School Admission Council, Official Guide to ABA-Approved Law Schools Online, March 21, 2016; Wikipedia, List of Medical Schools in the United States, March 21, 2016; Wikipedia, List of Law Schools in the United States, March 21, 2016

According to *U.S. News & World Report,* the San Jose-Sunnyvale-Santa Clara, CA metro area is home to one of the best national universities in the U.S.: **Stanford University** (#4 tie). The indicators used to capture academic quality fall into a number of categories: assessment by administrators at peer institutions; retention of students; faculty resources; student selectivity; financial resources; alumni giving; high school counselor ratings of colleges; and graduation rate. *U.S. News & World Report, "America's Best Colleges 2016"*

According to *U.S. News & World Report,* the San Jose-Sunnyvale-Santa Clara, CA metro area is home to one of the top 100 law schools in the U.S.: **Stanford University, Law School** (#2 tie). The rankings are based on a weighted average of 12 measures of quality: peer assessment score; assessment score by lawyers/judges; median LSAT scores; median undergrad GPA; acceptance rate; employment rates for graduates; placement success; bar passage rate; faculty resources; expenditures per student; student/faculty ratio; and library resources. *U.S. News & World Report, "America's Best Graduate Schools, Law, 2017"*

According to *U.S. News & World Report,* the San Jose-Sunnyvale-Santa Clara, CA metro area is home to one of the top 75 medical schools for research in the U.S.: **Stanford University, School of Medicine** (#2). The rankings are based on a weighted average of 11 measures of quality: quality assessment; peer assessment score; assessment score by residency directors; research activity; total research activity; average research activity per faculty member; student selectivity; median MCAT total score; median undergraduate GPA; acceptance rate; and faculty resources. *U.S. News & World Report, "America's Best Graduate Schools, Medical, 2017"*

According to *U.S. News & World Report,* the San Jose-Sunnyvale-Santa Clara, CA metro area is home to one of the top 75 business schools in the U.S.: **Stanford University, Graduate School of Business** (#2 tie). The rankings are based on a weighted average of the following nine measures: quality assessment; peer assessment; recruiter assessment; placement success; mean starting salary and bonus; student selectivity; mean GMAT and GRE scores; mean

undergraduate GPA; and acceptance rate. *U.S. News & World Report, "America's Best Graduate Schools, Business, 2017"*

PRESIDENTIAL ELECTION

2012 Presidential Election Results

Area	Obama (%)	Romney (%)	Other (%)
Santa Clara County	69.9	27.6	2.5
U.S.	51.0	47.2	1.8

Note: Results may not add to 100% due to rounding
Source: Dave Leip's Atlas of U.S. Presidential Elections

EMPLOYERS

Major Employers

Company Name	Industry
Adobe Systems Inc	Publishers-computer software (mfrs)
Advanced Micro Devices Inc	Semiconductor devices (mfrs)
Apple Inc	Computers-electronic-manufacturers
Applied Materials Inc	Semiconductor manufacturing equip (mfrs)
Bon Appetit-Cafe Adobe	Restaurant management
California's Great America	Amusement & theme parks
Christopher Ranch	Garlic manufacturers
Cisco Systems Inc	Computer peripherals
E Bay Inc	E-commerce
Flextronics	Solar energy equipment-manufacturers
General Motors Advanced Tech	Automobile-manufacturers
Hewlett-Packard	Computers-electronic-manufacturers
Intel Corp	Semiconductor devices (mfrs)
Kaiser Permanente Med Center	Hospitals
Kaiser Permanente Medical Ctr	Hospitals
Lockheed Martin Space Systems	Satellite equipment & systems-mfrs
Microsoft Corp	Computer software-manufacturers
NASA	Government offices-us
Net App Inc	Computer storage devices

Note: Companies shown are located within the San Jose-Sunnyvale-Santa Clara, CA Metropolitan Statistical Area.
Source: Hoovers.com; Wikipedia

PUBLIC SAFETY

Crime Rate

Area	All Crimes	Violent Crimes: Murder	Violent Crimes: Rape[3]	Violent Crimes: Robbery	Violent Crimes: Aggrav. Assault	Property Crimes: Burglary	Property Crimes: Larceny -Theft	Property Crimes: Motor Vehicle Theft
City	1,087.4	0.0	6.6	9.9	6.6	390.0	637.9	36.4
Metro[1]	2,496.5	2.3	25.2	80.4	142.0	469.8	1,272.0	504.9
U.S.	2,961.6	4.5	26.4	102.2	232.5	542.5	1,837.3	216.2

Note: Figures are crimes per 100,000 population; (1) Figures cover the San Jose-Sunnyvale-Santa Clara, CA Metropolitan Statistical Area—see Appendix B for areas included; (3) The city and U.S. figures shown were reported using the legacy Uniform Crime Reporting (UCR) definition of rape. The suburban and metro area figures shown are an aggregate total of the data submitted using both the revised and legacy UCR definitions.
Source: FBI Uniform Crime Reports, 2014

Hate Crimes

Area	Number of Quarters Reported	Race	Religion	Sexual Orientation	Ethnicity	Disability	Gender	Gender Identity
City	4	0	0	0	0	0	0	0
U.S.	4	2,568	1,014	1,017	648	84	33	98

Note: columns Race through Gender Identity are Number of Incidents per Bias Motivation.

Source: Federal Bureau of Investigation, Hate Crime Statistics 2014

RECREATION

CLIMATE

Identity Theft Consumer Complaints

Area	Complaints	Complaints per 100,000 Population	Rank[2]
MSA[1]	2,693	137.9	74
U.S.	490,220	152.4	-

Note: (1) Figures cover the San Jose-Sunnyvale-Santa Clara, CA Metropolitan Statistical Area—see Appendix B for areas included; (2) Rank ranges from 1 to 379 where 1 indicates greatest number of identity theft complaints per 100,000 population
Source: Federal Trade Commission, Consumer Sentinel Network Data Book for January–December 2015

Fraud and Other Consumer Complaints

Area	Complaints	Complaints per 100,000 Population	Rank[2]
MSA[1]	6,862	351.4	213
U.S.	2,593,159	806.0	-

Note: (1) Figures cover the San Jose-Sunnyvale-Santa Clara, CA Metropolitan Statistical Area—see Appendix B for areas included; (2) Rank ranges from 1 to 379 where 1 indicates greatest number of identity theft complaints per 100,000 population
Source: Federal Trade Commission, Consumer Sentinel Network Data Book for January–December 2015

Culture

Dance[1]	Theatre[1]	Instrumental Music[1]	Vocal Music[1]	Series and Festivals	Museums and Art Galleries[2]	Zoos and Aquariums[3]
0	0	0	0	0	0	0

Note: (1) Professional perfoming groups; (2) Based on organizations with SIC code 8412; (3) AZA-accredited
Source: The Grey House Performing Arts Directory, 2015-16; Association of Zoos & Aquariums, AZA Member Zoos & Aquariums, March 25, 2016; www.AccuLeads.com, March 29, 2016

Professional Sports Teams

Team Name	League	Year Established
San Jose Earthquakes	Major League Soccer (MLS)	1996
San Jose Sharks	National Hockey League (NHL)	1991

Note: Includes teams located in the San Jose-Sunnyvale-Santa Clara, CA Metropolitan Statistical Area.
Source: Wikipedia, Major Professional Sports Teams of the United States and Canada, March 24, 2016

Average and Extreme Temperatures

Temperature	Jan	Feb	Mar	Apr	May	Jun	Jul	Aug	Sep	Oct	Nov	Dec	Yr.
Extreme High (°F)	76	82	83	95	103	104	105	101	105	100	87	76	105
Average High (°F)	57	61	63	67	70	74	75	75	76	72	65	58	68
Average Temp. (°F)	50	53	55	58	61	65	66	67	66	63	56	50	59
Average Low (°F)	42	45	46	48	51	55	57	58	57	53	47	42	50
Extreme Low (°F)	21	26	30	32	38	43	45	47	41	33	29	23	21

Note: Figures cover the years 1945-1993
Source: National Climatic Data Center, International Station Meteorological Climate Summary, 9/96

Average Precipitation/Snowfall/Humidity

Precip./Humidity	Jan	Feb	Mar	Apr	May	Jun	Jul	Aug	Sep	Oct	Nov	Dec	Yr.
Avg. Precip. (in.)	2.7	2.3	2.2	0.9	0.3	0.1	Tr	Tr	0.2	0.7	1.7	2.3	13.5
Avg. Snowfall (in.)	Tr	Tr	Tr	0	0	0	0	0	0	0	0	Tr	Tr
Avg. Rel. Hum. 7am (%)	82	82	80	76	74	73	77	79	79	79	81	82	79
Avg. Rel. Hum. 4pm (%)	62	59	56	52	53	54	58	58	55	54	59	63	57

Note: Figures cover the years 1945-1993; Tr = Trace amounts (<0.05 in. of rain; <0.5 in. of snow)
Source: National Climatic Data Center, International Station Meteorological Climate Summary, 9/96

Weather Conditions

Temperature			Daytime Sky			Precipitation		
10°F & below	32°F & below	90°F & above	Clear	Partly cloudy	Cloudy	0.01 inch or more precip.	0.1 inch or more snow/ice	Thunder-storms
0	5	5	106	180	79	57	< 1	6

Note: Figures are average number of days per year and cover the years 1945-1993
Source: National Climatic Data Center, International Station Meteorological Climate Summary, 9/96

HAZARDOUS WASTE

Superfund Sites

Los Altos has no sites on the EPA's Superfund Final National Priorities List. There are a total of 1,323 Superfund sites on the list in the U.S. *U.S. Environmental Protection Agency, Final National Priorities List, March 18, 2016*

AIR & WATER QUALITY

Air Quality Trends: Ozone

	1990	1995	2000	2005	2010	2011	2012	2013	2014
MSA[1]	0.079	0.085	0.070	0.065	0.073	0.065	0.064	0.064	0.069

Note: (1) Data covers the San Jose-Sunnyvale-Santa Clara, CA Metropolitan Statistical Area—see Appendix B for areas included. The values shown are the composite ozone concentration averages among trend sites based on the highest fourth daily maximum 8-hour concentration in parts per million. These trends are based on sites having an adequate record of monitoring data during the trend period. Data from exceptional events are included.
Source: U.S. Environmental Protection Agency, Air Quality Monitoring Information, "Air Quality Trends by City, 1990-2014"

Air Quality Index

Area	Percent of Days when Air Quality was...[2]					AQI Statistics[2]	
	Good	Moderate	Unhealthy for Sensitive Groups	Unhealthy	Very Unhealthy	Maximum	Median
MSA[1]	67.1	31.0	1.9	0.0	0.0	135	44

Note: (1) Data covers the San Jose-Sunnyvale-Santa Clara, CA Metropolitan Statistical Area—see Appendix B for areas included; (2) Based on 365 days with AQI data in 2015. Air Quality Index (AQI) is an index for reporting daily air quality. EPA calculates the AQI for five major air pollutants regulated by the Clean Air Act: ground-level ozone, particle pollution (aka particulate matter), carbon monoxide, sulfur dioxide, and nitrogen dioxide. The AQI runs from 0 to 500. The higher the AQI value, the greater the level of air pollution and the greater the health concern. There are six AQI categories: "Good" AQI is between 0 and 50. Air quality is considered satisfactory; "Moderate" AQI is between 51 and 100. Air quality is acceptable; "Unhealthy for Sensitive Groups" When AQI values are between 101 and 150, members of sensitive groups may experience health effects; "Unhealthy" When AQI values are between 151 and 200 everyone may begin to experience health effects; "Very Unhealthy" AQI values between 201 and 300 trigger a health alert; "Hazardous" AQI values over 300 trigger warnings of emergency conditions (not shown).
Source: U.S. Environmental Protection Agency, Air Quality Index Report, 2015

Air Quality Index Pollutants

Area	Percent of Days when AQI Pollutant was...[2]					
	Carbon Monoxide	Nitrogen Dioxide	Ozone	Sulfur Dioxide	Particulate Matter 2.5	Particulate Matter 10
MSA[1]	0.0	2.5	51.0	0.0	46.3	0.3

Note: (1) Data covers the San Jose-Sunnyvale-Santa Clara, CA Metropolitan Statistical Area—see Appendix B for areas included; (2) Based on 365 days with AQI data in 2015. The Air Quality Index (AQI) is an index for reporting daily air quality. EPA calculates the AQI for five major air pollutants regulated by the Clean Air Act: ground-level ozone, particle pollution (also known as particulate matter), carbon monoxide, sulfur dioxide, and nitrogen dioxide. The AQI runs from 0 to 500. The higher the AQI value, the greater the level of air pollution and the greater the health concern.
Source: U.S. Environmental Protection Agency, Air Quality Index Report, 2015

Maximum Air Pollutant Concentrations: Particulate Matter, Ozone, CO and Lead

	Particulate Matter 10 (ug/m^3)	Particulate Matter 2.5 Wtd AM (ug/m^3)	Particulate Matter 2.5 24-Hr (ug/m^3)	Ozone (ppm)	Carbon Monoxide (ppm)	Lead (ug/m^3)
MSA[1] Level	52	8.4	27	0.073	2	0.13
NAAQS[2]	150	15	35	0.075	9	0.15
Met NAAQS[2]	Yes	Yes	Yes	Yes	Yes	Yes

Note: (1) Data covers the San Jose-Sunnyvale-Santa Clara, CA Metropolitan Statistical Area—see Appendix B for areas included; Data from exceptional events are included; (2) National Ambient Air Quality Standards; ppm = parts per million; ug/m^3 = micrograms per cubic meter; n/a not available.
Concentrations: Particulate Matter 10 (coarse particulate)—highest second maximum 24-hour concentration; Particulate Matter 2.5 Wtd AM (fine particulate)—highest weighted annual mean concentration; Particulate Matter 2.5 24-Hour (fine particulate)—highest 98th percentile 24-hour concentration; Ozone—highest fourth daily maximum 8-hour concentration; Carbon Monoxide—highest second maximum non-overlapping 8-hour concentration; Lead—maximum running 3-month average
Source: U.S. Environmental Protection Agency, Air Quality Monitoring Information, "Air Quality Statistics by City, 2014"

Maximum Air Pollutant Concentrations: Nitrogen Dioxide and Sulfur Dioxide

	Nitrogen Dioxide AM (ppb)	Nitrogen Dioxide 1-Hr (ppb)	Sulfur Dioxide AM (ppb)	Sulfur Dioxide 1-Hr (ppb)	Sulfur Dioxide 24-Hr (ppb)
MSA[1] Level	13	55	n/a	2	n/a
NAAQS[2]	53	100	30	75	140
Met NAAQS[2]	Yes	Yes	n/a	Yes	n/a

Note: (1) Data covers the San Jose-Sunnyvale-Santa Clara, CA Metropolitan Statistical Area—see Appendix B for areas included; Data from exceptional events are included; (2) National Ambient Air Quality Standards; ppm = parts per million; ug/m^3 = micrograms per cubic meter; n/a not available.
Concentrations: Nitrogen Dioxide AM—highest arithmetic mean concentration; Nitrogen Dioxide 1-Hr—highest 98th percentile 1-hour daily maximum concentration; Sulfur Dioxide AM—highest annual mean concentration; Sulfur Dioxide 1-Hr—highest 99th percentile 1-hour daily maximum concentration; Sulfur Dioxide 24-Hr—highest second maximum 24-hour concentration
Source: U.S. Environmental Protection Agency, Air Quality Monitoring Information, "Air Quality Statistics by City, 2014"

Drinking Water

Water System Name	Pop. Served	Primary Water Source Type	Violations[1]	
			Health Based	Monitoring/ Reporting
CWSC Los Altos Suburban	68,404	Purchased Surface	0	0

Note: (1) Based on violation data from January 1, 2015 to December 31, 2015 (includes unresolved violations from earlier years)
Source: U.S. Environmental Protection Agency, Office of Ground Water and Drinking Water, Safe Drinking Water Information System (based on data extracted April 29, 2016)

Rancho Palos Verdes, California

Background

Rancho Palos Verdes is an affluent suburb of Los Angeles and sits atop the Palos Verdes Hills and bluffs of the Palos Verdes Peninsula. Located within Los Angeles County, the city covers approximately 13.5 square miles and is about 50 miles south of downtown Los Angeles. The city is known for its spectacular Palos Verdes Hills and cliffs with sweeping vistas of the Pacific Ocean and Santa Catalina Island. Rancho Palos Verdes is one of four municipalities that make up the Palos Verdes Peninsula.

Rancho Palos Verdes is a Spanish phrase translated as 'Ranch of Green Trees' or 'Ranch of Sticks' that refers to the willows that distinguish the Bixby Slough, known today as Machado Lake. The history of Rancho Palos Verdes dates back to the Tongva or Gabrielino Indians who were indigenous to the area before the arrival of the Portuguese explorers. Juan Rodriguez Cabrillo first navigated the California coast in 1542 and Rancho Palos Verdes was established in 1846 through a Mexican land grant. Originally part of the expansive ranchos, the Palos Verdes Peninsula was bought with the assistance of a New York investment syndicate at the turn of the 20th century. At the time, the area was an undeveloped, large swathe of land along the Pacific close to Los Angeles—a developer's dream. Development began in the Malaga Cove area in the 1920s and the famous landscape architecture firm, Olmsted Brothers, was hired to design and plan the communities. Today, Rancho Palos Verdes boasts strong architecture and development committees that have been effective in both preserving the open space and avoiding over-development.

Rancho Palos Verdes is the quintessential southern California city and offers a range of activities to complement the stunning views of the south bay. The Palos Verdes Peninsula is home to more than 30 scenic hiking trails. Bird watchers delight in the diversity of bird species against the backdrop of the Pacific Ocean. The area is known for its falconry and there is an onsite falconer who teaches residents and visitors about the birds who call the bluffs home. There are many beaches within close proximity such as Redondo, Hermosa, and Manhattan beaches for surfing, sea kayaking, and general beach activities. The area also has 5 golf courses, each with their own distinct style and views.

Preservation of the natural environment is part of what makes the Palos Verdes Peninsula special. The Point Vicente Interpretive Center is the premier site for whale watching during the annual migration of the Pacific gray whale from December to April. Established in 1984, the center opened with a mission to present and interpret the unique historical features of the peninsula, which includes the Point Vicente Lighthouse, built in 1926. Along the coast, the historical Wayfarers Chapel was designed by Lloyd Wright and built between 1949 and 1951. The Palos Verdes Nature Preserver is the largest preserve of coastal open space north of San Diego and south of Santa Barbara. The preserve is the result of successful acquisition of two square miles of open space by the Palos Verdes Peninsula Land Conservancy in 2009.

Rancho Palos Verdes has a wide range of shopping, dining, and entertainment. There is the upscale Promenade on the Peninsula mall as well as the Malaga Cove Plaza—a smaller, charming, shopping plaza. Malaga Cove is built in the Italian architectural style evoking a distinct Mediterranean feel. Both areas offer many dining options, from seafood and elegant fine dining to fresh, on the go meals with a southern California flare. There is also a farmer's market that operates each Sunday.

Rancho Palos Verdes is part of the Los Angeles Unified School District and also served by the Palos Verdes Peninsula Unified School district. There are a number of excellent public and private school options in the area. In addition, Rancho Palos Verdes is home to Marymount California University, a private liberal arts institution that offers both undergraduate and Master's degree programs.

Rancho Palos Verdes experiences a climate similar to most of southern California with sunlight and sea breezes year 'round. The Mediterranean climate brings little rain and an average annual temperature that hovers right around 75 degrees.

Rankings

General Rankings

- Los Angeles* was identified as one of America's fastest-growing major metropolitan areas in terms of population growth by CNNMoney.com. The area ranked #3 out of 10. Criteria: population growth between July 2013 and July 2014. *CNNMoney, "10 Fastest-Growing Cities," May 27, 2015*

Business/Finance Rankings

- The personal finance site NerdWallet analyzed 183 American metropolitan areas with populations over 250,000 and more than 15,000 businesses to rank where entrepreneurs find the most success. Criteria included area economy, annual income, housing cost, unemployment rate, and the success rate of area businesses. Los Angeles* ranked #109. *www.nerdwallet.com, "Best Places to Start a Business," April 27, 2015*
- Based on the U.S. Department of Labor's Occupational Information Network Data Collection Program, the Brookings Institution defined job opportunities for STEM workers at various levels of educational attainment. The Los Angeles* metro area was one of the ten metro areas where workers in low-education-level STEM jobs earn the lowest relative wages. *www.brookings.edu, "The Hidden Stem Economy," June 10, 2013*
- Based on metro area social media reviews, the employment opinion group Glassdoor surveyed 50 of the largest U.S. metro areas and equally weighed cost of living, hiring opportunity, and job satisfaction to compose a list of "25 Best Cities for Jobs." The Los Angeles* metro area was ranked #16 in overall job satisfaction. *www.glassdoor.com, "Best Cities for Jobs," May 19, 2015*
- In a survey of economic confidence in the nation's 50 largest metropolitan areas conducted January–December 2014, the Los Angeles* metro area placed #11, according to Gallup's 2014 Economic Confidence Index. *Gallup, "San Jose and San Francisco Lead in Economic Confidence," March 19, 2015*
- The Brookings Institution ranked the 100 largest metro areas in the U.S. based on income inequality. Los Angeles* was ranked #7 (#1 = greatest ineqality). Criteria: the "95/20 ratio," a figure representing the income at which a household earns more than 95 percent of all other households, divided by the income at which a household earns more than only 20 percent of all other households. *Brookings Institution, "Income Inequality, 100 Largest U.S. Metro Areas, 2007-2014," January 14, 2016*
- The finance site *24/7 Wall St.* identified the metropolitan areas that have the smallest and largest pay disparities between men and women, comparing the median earnings for the past 12 months of both men and women working full-time in the country's 100 largest metropolitan statistical areas. Of the ten best-paying metros for women, the Los Angeles* metro area ranked #2. *24/7 Wall St., "The Best (and Worst) Paying Cities for Women," March 6, 2015*
- Payscale.com ranked the 20 largest metro areas in terms of wage growth. The Los Angeles* metro area ranked #16. Criteria: private-sector wage growth between the 1st quarter of 2015 and the 1st quarter of 2016. *PayScale, "Wage Trends by Metro Area," 1st Quarter, 2016*
- The Los Angeles* metro area appeared on the Milken Institute "2015 Best Performing Cities" list. Rank: #77 out of 200 large metro areas. Criteria: job growth; wage and salary growth; high-tech output growth. *Milken Institute, "Best-Performing Cities 2015," December 2015*
- *Forbes* ranked the 200 most populous metro areas to determine the nation's "Best Places for Business and Careers." The Los Angeles* metro area was ranked #116. Criteria: costs (business and living); job growth (past and projected); income growth; educational attainment (college and high school); projected economic growth; cultural and recreational opportunities; net migration patterns; number of highly ranked colleges. *Forbes, "The Best Places for Business and Careers 2015," July 29, 2015*

Education Rankings

- Personal finance website *WalletHub* analyzed the 150 largest U.S. metropolitan statistical areas to determine where the most educated Americans are choosing to settle. Criteria: education quality and attainment gap; education levels; percentage of workers with degrees; public school rankings; quality and size of each metro area's universities. Los Angeles* was ranked #87 (#1 = most educated city). *www.WalletHub.com, "2015's Most and Least Educated Cities*

Environmental Rankings

- The Los Angeles* metro area came in at #148 for the relative comfort of its climate on Sperling's list of "chill cities," as measured by the Sperling Heat Index. All 361 metro areas are included. Criteria included daytime high temperatures, nighttime low temperatures, dew point, and relative humidity at the high temperatures. *www.bertsperling.com, "Sperling's Chill Cities," July 18, 2013*
- Sperling's BestPlaces assessed 379 metropolitan areas of the United States for the likelihood of dangerously extreme weather events or earthquakes. In general the Southeast and South-Central regions have the highest risk of weather extremes and earthquakes, while the Pacific Northwest enjoys the lowest risk. Of the least risky metropolitan areas, the Los Angeles* metro area was ranked #183. *www.bestplaces.net, "Safest Places from Natural Disasters," April 2011*
- Los Angeles* was identified as one of America's dirtiest metro areas by *Forbes.* The area ranked #17 out of 20. Criteria: air quality; water quality; toxic releases; superfund sites. *Forbes, "America's 20 Dirtiest Cities," December 10, 2012*
- The U.S. Environmental Protection Agency (EPA) released a list of U.S. metropolitan areas with the most ENERGY STAR certified buildings in 2015. The Los Angeles* metro area was ranked #2 out of 25. *U.S. Environmental Protection Agency, "Top Cities With the Most ENERGY STAR Certified Buildings in 2016," March 30, 2016*
- Los Angeles* was highlighted as one of the 25 most ozone-polluted metro areas in the U.S. during 2011 through 2013. The area ranked #1. *American Lung Association, State of the Air 2015*
- Los Angeles* was highlighted as one of the 25 metro areas most polluted by year-round particle pollution (Annual PM 2.5) in the U.S. during 2011 through 2013. The area ranked #5. *American Lung Association, State of the Air 2015*
- Los Angeles* was highlighted as one of the 25 metro areas most polluted by short-term particle pollution (24-hour PM 2.5) in the U.S. during 2011 through 2013. The area ranked #5. *American Lung Association, State of the Air 2015*

Health/Fitness Rankings

- Analysts who tracked obesity rates in the nation's largest metro areas (populations above one million) found that the Los Angeles* metro area was one of the ten major metros where residents were least likely to be obese, defined as a BMI score of 30 or above. *www.gallup.com, "Boulder, Colo., Residents Still Least Likely to Be Obese," April 4, 2014*
- For each of the 50 most populous metro areas in the United States, the American College of Sports Medicine's American Fitness Index evaluated infrastructure, community assets, and policies that encourage healthy and fit lifestyles, including preventive health behaviors, levels of chronic disease conditions, health care access, and community resources and policies that support physical activity. The Los Angeles* metro area ranked #23 for "community fitness." *www.americanfitnessindex.org, "ACSM American Fitness Index Health and Community Fitness Status of the 50 Largest Metropolitan Areas," May 2015*
- The Los Angeles* metro area was identified as one of the worst cities for bed bugs in America by pest control company Orkin. The area ranked #2 out of 50 based on the number of bed bug treatments Orkin performed from January to December 2015. *Orkin, "Chicago Tops Bed Bug Cities List for Fourth Year in a Row," January 13, 2016*

- Los Angeles* was identified as a "2016 Spring Allergy Capital." The area ranked #67 out of 100. Three groups of factors were used to identify the most severe cities for people with allergies during the spring season: annual pollen levels; medicine utilization; access to board-certified allergists. *Asthma and Allergy Foundation of America, "Spring Allergy Capitals 2016"*
- Los Angeles* was identified as a "2015 Asthma Capital." The area ranked #52 out of the nation's 100 largest metropolitan areas. Criteria: estimated prevalence; self-reported prevalence; crude death rate for asthma; annual pollen score; annual air quality; public smoking laws; number of board-certified asthma specialists; school inhaler access laws; rescue medication use; controller medication use; ER visits for asthma; uninsured rate; poverty rate. *Asthma and Allergy Foundation of America, "Asthma Capitals 2015"*
- The Los Angeles* metro area ranked #40 out of 190 in The Gallup-Healthways Well-Being Index. Criteria: purpose; social well being; financial health; community and physical health. Results are based on telephone interviews with adults, aged 18 and older, living in metropolitan areas in the 50 U.S. states and the District of Columbia. *Gallup-Healthways, "State of American Well-Being," February 23, 2016*

Real Estate Rankings

- With data from RealtyTrac, Yahoo! Finance researchers listed the housing markets in which housing affordability is improving most, factoring in interest rates as well as median home prices. The Los Angeles* metro area was among the least affordable housing markets. *news.yahoo.com, "10 Cities Where Ordinary People Can No Longer Afford Homes," March 5, 2014*
- The Los Angeles* metro area was identified as one of the nations's 20 hottest housing markets in 2016. Criteria: listing views as an indicator of demand and median days on the market as an indicator of supply. The area ranked #12. *Realtor.com, "The 20 Hottest U.S. Real Estate Markets in February 2016," February 25, 2016*
- The Los Angeles* metro area was identified as one of the 20 least affordable housing markets in the U.S. in 2015. The area ranked #5 out of 179 markets. Criteria: qualification for a mortgage loan on a typical home. *National Association of Realtors®, Affordability Index of Existing Single-Family Homes for Metropolitan Areas, 2015*
- Los Angeles* was ranked #224 out of 225 metro areas in terms of housing affordability in 2015 by the National Association of Home Builders (#1 = most affordable). Criteria: the share of homes sold in that area affordable to a family earning the local median income, based on standard mortgage underwriting criteria. *National Association of Home Builders®, NAHB-Wells Fargo Housing Opportunity Index, 4th Quarter 2015*

Safety Rankings

- The National Insurance Crime Bureau ranked 380 metro areas in the U.S. in terms of per capita rates of vehicle theft. The Los Angeles* metro area ranked #39 (#1 = highest rate). Criteria: number of vehicle theft offenses per 100,000 inhabitants in 2014. *National Insurance Crime Bureau, "Hot Spots 2014," June 24, 2015*

Seniors/Retirement Rankings

- From its Best Cities for Successful Aging indexes, the Milken Institute generated rankings for metropolitan areas, weighing data in eight categories—health care, wellness, living arrangements, transportation, financial characteristics, education and employment opportunities, community engagement, and overall livability. The Los Angeles* metro area was ranked #66 overall in the large metro area category. *Milken Institute, "Best Cities for Successful Aging, 2014"*

Sports/Recreation Rankings

- *Card Player* magazine scoured North America to identify the top five metropolitan areas where a player can access the types of games that make launching a poker career possible. The Los Angeles* metro area ranked #1. *Card Player, "The Top Five Cities to Launch Your Poker Career," April 2, 2014*

Transportation Rankings

- Los Angeles* was identified as one of the most congested metro areas in the U.S. The area ranked #2 out of 10. Criteria: yearly delay per auto commuter in hours. *Texas A&M Transportation Institute, "2015 Urban Mobility Scorecard," August 2015*
- The Los Angeles* metro area appeared on *Forbes* list of places with the most extreme commutes. The metro area ranked #5 out of 10. Criteria: average travel time; percentage of mega commuters. Mega-commuters travel more than 90 minutes and 50 miles each way to work. *Forbes.com, "The Cities with the Most Extreme Commutes," March 5, 2013*

Women/Minorities Rankings

- *24/7 Wall St.* compared median earnings over a 12-month period for men and women who worked full-time, year-round, and employment composition by sector to identify the best-paying cities for women. Of the largest 100 U.S. metropolitan areas, Los Angeles* was ranked #2 in pay disparity. *24/7 Wall St., "The Best (and Worst) Paying Cities for Women," March 6, 2015*

Miscellaneous Rankings

- The watchdog site Charity Navigator conducts an annual study of charities in the nation's major markets both to analyze statistical differences in their financial, accountability, and transparency practices and to track year-to-year variations in individual communities. The Los Angeles* metro area was ranked #4 among the 30 metro markets in the rating dimension of Overall Score. *www.charitynavigator.org, "Metro Market Study 2015," June 5, 2015*
- The Harris Poll's Happiness Index survey revealed that of the top ten U.S. markets, the Los Angeles* metro area residents ranked #5 in happiness. Criteria included strong assent to positive statements and strong disagreement with negative ones, and degree of agreement with a series of statements about respondents' personal relationships and general outlook. *www.harrisinteractive.com, "Dallas/Fort Worth Is "Happiest" City among America's Top Ten Markets," September 4, 2013*
- Energizer Personal Care, the makers of Edge® shave gel, in partnership with Sperling's BestPlaces, ranked 50 major metro areas in terms of everyday irritations. The Los Angeles* metro area ranked #6 the 50 metro area most iritating to guys. Criteria: high male-to-female ratio; poor sports team performance and high ticket prices; slow traffic; lack of job availability; unaffordable housing; extreme weather; lack of nightlife and fitness options. *Energizer Personal Care, "Most Irritatng Cities for Guys," August 26, 2013*
- Mars Chocolate North America, the makers of COMBOS®, in partnership with Sperling's BestPlaces, ranked 50 major metro areas in terms of their "manliness." The Los Angeles* metro area ranked #46. Criteria: number of professional sports teams; number of nearby NASCAR tracks and racing events; manly lifestyle; concentration of manly retail stores; manly occupations per capita; salty snack sales; "Board of Manliness" rankings. *Mars Chocolate North America, "America's Manliest Cities 2012"*
- The National Alliance to End Homelessness ranked the 100 most populous metro areas with the highest rate of homelessness. The Los Angeles* metro area ranked #6. Criteria: number of homeless people per 10,000 population in 2011. *National Alliance to End Homelessness, The State of Homelessness in America 2012*

Rancho Palos Verdes is located within the Los Angeles-Long Beach-Anaheim, CA Metropolitan Statistical Area.

Business Environment

CITY FINANCES

City Government Finances

Component	2012 ($000)	2012 ($ per capita)
Total Revenues	29,201	701
Total Expenditures	28,499	684
Debt Outstanding	24,354	584
Cash and Securities[1]	43,610	1,047

Note: (1) Cash and security holdings of a government at the close of its fiscal year, including those of its dependent agencies, utilities, and liquor stores.
Source: U.S Census Bureau, State & Local Government Finances 2012

City Government Revenue by Source

Source	2012 ($000)	2012 ($ per capita)
General Revenue		
From Federal Government	173	4
From State Government	1,385	33
From Local Governments	0	0
Taxes		
Property	11,942	286
Sales and Gross Receipts	10,410	249
Personal Income	0	0
Corporate Income	0	0
Motor Vehicle License	0	0
Other Taxes	2,081	49
Current Charges	2,392	57
Liquor Store	0	0
Utility	0	0
Employee Retirement	0	0

Source: U.S Census Bureau, State & Local Government Finances 2012

City Government Expenditures by Function

Function	2012 ($000)	2012 ($ per capita)	2012 (%)
General Direct Expenditures			
Air Transportation	0	0	0.0
Corrections	0	0	0.0
Education	0	0	0.0
Employment Security Administration	0	0	0.0
Financial Administration	1,341	32	4.7
Fire Protection	0	0	0.0
General Public Buildings	0	0	0.0
Governmental Administration, Other	9,411	225	33.0
Health	196	4	0.6
Highways	6,130	147	21.5
Hospitals	0	0	0.0
Housing and Community Development	335	8	1.1
Interest on General Debt	1,040	24	3.6
Judicial and Legal	1,057	25	3.7
Libraries	0	0	0.0
Parking	0	0	0.0
Parks and Recreation	3,289	78	11.5
Police Protection	0	0	0.0
Public Welfare	0	0	0.0
Sewerage	0	0	0.0
Solid Waste Management	462	11	1.6
Veterans' Services	0	0	0.0
Liquor Store	0	0	0.0
Utility	0	0	0.0
Employee Retirement	0	0	0.0

Source: U.S Census Bureau, State & Local Government Finances 2012

DEMOGRAPHICS

Population Growth

Area	1990 Census	2000 Census	2010 Census	2014* Estimate	Population Growth (%) 1990-2014	Population Growth (%) 2010-2014
City	42,293	41,145	41,643	42,282	0.0	1.5
MSA[1]	11,273,720	12,365,627	12,828,837	13,060,534	15.8	1.8
U.S.	248,709,873	281,421,906	308,745,538	314,107,084	26.3	1.7

Note: (1) Figures cover the Los Angeles-Long Beach-Anaheim, CA Metropolitan Statistical Area—see Appendix B for areas included; (*) 2010-2014 5-year estimated population

Source: U.S. Census Bureau, 1990 Census, Census 2000, Census 2010, 2010-2014 American Community Survey 5-Year Estimates

Household Size

Area	Persons in Household (%) One	Two	Three	Four	Five	Six	Seven or More	Average Household Size
City	20.8	39.6	16.3	15.3	5.7	1.6	0.4	2.68
MSA[1]	24.5	28.0	16.6	15.4	8.3	3.8	3.1	3.03
U.S.	27.5	33.5	15.8	13.1	6.0	2.3	1.4	2.64

Note: (1) Figures cover the Los Angeles-Long Beach-Anaheim, CA Metropolitan Statistical Area—see Appendix B for areas included

Source: U.S. Census Bureau, 2010-2014 American Community Survey 5-Year Estimates

Race

Area	White Alone[2] (%)	Black Alone[2] (%)	Asian Alone[2] (%)	AIAN[3] Alone[2] (%)	NHOPI[4] Alone[2] (%)	Other Race Alone[2] (%)	Two or More Races (%)
City	61.9	2.6	28.0	0.2	0.2	1.7	5.4
MSA[1]	55.7	6.8	15.1	0.5	0.3	17.9	3.8
U.S.	73.8	12.6	5.0	0.8	0.2	4.7	2.9

Note: (1) Figures cover the Los Angeles-Long Beach-Anaheim, CA Metropolitan Statistical Area—see Appendix B for areas included; (2) Alone is defined as not being in combination with one or more other races; (3) American Indian and Alaska Native; (4) Native Hawaiian and Other Pacific Islander

Source: U.S. Census Bureau, 2010-2014 American Community Survey 5-Year Estimates

Hispanic or Latino Origin

Area	Total (%)	Mexican (%)	Puerto Rican (%)	Cuban (%)	Other (%)
City	7.8	5.1	0.3	0.3	2.1
MSA[1]	44.8	35.0	0.5	0.4	8.9
U.S.	16.9	10.8	1.6	0.6	3.8

Note: Persons of Hispanic or Latino origin can be of any race; (1) Figures cover the Los Angeles-Long Beach-Anaheim, CA Metropolitan Statistical Area—see Appendix B for areas included

Source: U.S. Census Bureau, 2010-2014 American Community Survey 5-Year Estimates

Ancestry

Area	German	Irish	English	American	Italian	Polish	French[2]	Scottish	Dutch
City	10.9	8.1	10.3	5.0	6.5	2.3	2.2	1.9	1.2
MSA[1]	6.0	4.8	4.4	3.2	3.0	1.3	1.4	1.0	0.7
U.S.	14.9	10.8	8.0	7.1	5.5	3.0	2.7	1.7	1.4

Note: Figures are the percentage of the total population reporting a particular ancestry. The nine most commonly reported ancestries in the U.S. are shown. Figures include multiple ancestries (e.g. if a person reported being Irish and Italian, they were included in both columns); (1) Figures cover the Los Angeles-Long Beach-Anaheim, CA Metropolitan Statistical Area—see Appendix B for areas included; (2) Excludes Basque

Source: U.S. Census Bureau, 2010-2014 American Community Survey 5-Year Estimates

Foreign-Born Population

Area	Percent of Population Born in								
	Any Foreign Country	Asia	Mexico	Europe	Carribean	Central America[2]	South America	Africa	Canada
City	26.5	18.6	0.8	4.4	0.0	0.4	0.5	0.7	0.8
MSA[1]	33.8	12.3	13.3	1.7	0.3	4.3	0.9	0.5	0.3
U.S.	13.1	3.8	3.7	1.5	1.2	1.0	0.9	0.6	0.3

Note: (1) Figures cover the Los Angeles-Long Beach-Anaheim, CA Metropolitan Statistical Area—see Appendix B for areas included; (2) Excludes Mexico.
Source: U.S. Census Bureau, 2010-2014 American Community Survey 5-Year Estimates

Marital Status

Area	Never Married	Now Married[2]	Separated	Widowed	Divorced
City	20.6	63.3	1.2	7.4	7.5
MSA[1]	39.6	44.3	2.5	5.0	8.6
U.S.	32.5	48.4	2.2	5.9	10.9

Note: Figures are percentages and cover the population 15 years of age and older; (1) Figures cover the Los Angeles-Long Beach-Anaheim, CA Metropolitan Statistical Area—see Appendix B for areas included; (2) Excludes separated
Source: U.S. Census Bureau, 2010-2014 American Community Survey 5-Year Estimates

Disability Status

Area	All Ages	Under 18 Years Old	18 to 64 Years Old	65 Years and Over
City	9.6	2.4	4.4	27.7
MSA[1]	9.2	2.8	6.8	36.1
U.S.	12.3	4.1	10.2	36.3

Note: Figures show percent of the civilian noninstitutionalized population that reported having a disability. Disability status is determined from from six types of difficulty: vision, hearing, cognitive, ambulatory, self-care, and independent living. For children under 5 years old, hearing and vision difficulty are used to determine disability status. For children between the ages of 5 and 14, disability status is determined from hearing, vision, cognitive, ambulatory, and self-care difficulties. For people aged 15 years and older, they are considered to have a disability if they have difficulty with any one of the six difficulty types; (1) Figures cover the Los Angeles-Long Beach-Anaheim, CA Metropolitan Statistical Area—see Appendix B for areas included.
Source: U.S. Census Bureau, 2010-2014 American Community Survey 5-Year Estimates

Age

Area	Percent of Population									Median Age
	Under Age 5	Age 5–19	Age 20–34	Age 35–44	Age 45–54	Age 55–64	Age 65–74	Age 75–84	Age 85+	
City	3.5	19.8	9.2	10.3	18.1	13.9	12.0	9.5	3.9	49.6
MSA[1]	6.4	20.0	22.6	14.2	14.0	11.0	6.4	3.6	1.7	35.6
U.S.	6.4	19.9	20.6	13.0	14.1	12.3	7.6	4.3	1.9	37.4

Note: (1) Figures cover the Los Angeles-Long Beach-Anaheim, CA Metropolitan Statistical Area—see Appendix B for areas included
Source: U.S. Census Bureau, 2010-2014 American Community Survey 5-Year Estimates

Gender

Area	Males	Females	Males per 100 Females
City	20,139	22,143	90.9
MSA[1]	6,438,759	6,621,775	97.2
U.S.	154,515,159	159,591,925	96.8

Note: (1) Figures cover the Los Angeles-Long Beach-Anaheim, CA Metropolitan Statistical Area—see Appendix B for areas included
Source: U.S. Census Bureau, 2010-2014 American Community Survey 5-Year Estimates

Religious Groups by Family

Area	Catholic	Baptist	Non-Den.	Methodist[2]	Lutheran	LDS[3]	Pente-costal	Presby-terian[4]	Muslim[5]	Judaism
MSA[1]	33.8	2.7	3.6	1.0	0.6	1.7	1.7	0.9	0.7	0.9
U.S.	19.1	9.3	4.0	4.0	2.3	2.0	1.9	1.6	0.8	0.7

Note: Figures are the number of adherents as a percentage of the total population; (1) Figures cover the Metropolitan Statistical Area—see Appendix B for areas included; (2) Methodist/Pietist; (3) Latter Day Saints; (4) Reformed; (5) Figures are estimates
Source: Association of Statisticians of American Religious Bodies, 2010 U.S. Religion Census: Religious Congregations & Membership Study

Religious Groups by Tradition

Area	Catholic	Evangelical Protestant	Mainline Protestant	Other Tradition	Black Protestant	Orthodox
MSA[1]	33.8	9.0	2.3	4.6	0.8	0.6
U.S.	19.1	16.2	7.3	4.3	1.6	0.3

Note: Figures are the number of adherents as a percentage of the total population; (1) Figures cover the Metropolitan Statistical Area—see Appendix B for areas included
Source: Association of Statisticians of American Religious Bodies, 2010 U.S. Religion Census: Religious Congregations & Membership Study

ECONOMY

Gross Metropolitan Product

Area	2013	2014	2015	2016	Rank[2]
MSA[1]	826.8	859.7	887.9	930.8	2

Note: Figures are in billions of dollars; (1) Figures cover the Los Angeles-Long Beach-Anaheim, CA Metropolitan Statistical Area—see Appendix B for areas included; (2) Rank is based on 2016 data and ranges from 1 to 381
Source: The U.S. Conference of Mayors, U.S. Metro Economies: GMP and Employment 2014-2016, June 2015

Economic Growth

Area	2011-13 (%)	2014 (%)	2015 (%)	2016 (%)	Rank[2]
MSA[1]	1.5	2.6	2.0	3.0	83
U.S.	2.2	2.4	2.3	2.9	-

Note: Figures are real gross metropolitan product (GMP) growth rates and represent annual average percent change; (1) Figures cover the Los Angeles-Long Beach-Anaheim, CA Metropolitan Statistical Area—see Appendix B for areas included; (2) Rank is based on 2016 data and ranges from 1 to 381
Source: The U.S. Conference of Mayors, U.S. Metro Economies: GMP and Employment 2014-2016, June 2015

Metropolitan Area Exports

Area	2009	2010	2011	2012	2013	2014	Rank[2]
MSA[1]	51,528.3	62,167.6	72,688.9	75,007.5	76,305.7	75,471.2	3

Note: Figures are in millions of dollars; (1) Figures cover the Los Angeles-Long Beach-Anaheim, CA Metropolitan Statistical Area—see Appendix B for areas included; (2) Rank is based on 2014 data and ranges from 1 to 385
Source: U.S. Department of Commerce, International Trade Administration, Office of Trade & Industry Information, Manufacturing & Services, data extracted March 10, 2016

Building Permits

Area	Single-Family			Multi-Family			Total		
	2014	2015p	Pct. Chg.	2014	2015p	Pct. Chg.	2014	2015p	Pct. Chg.
City	8	28	250.0	0	0	-	8	28	250.0
MSA[1]	8,300	8,458	1.9	18,650	25,211	35.2	26,950	33,669	24.9
U.S.	640,300	690,800	7.9	411,800	487,600	18.4	1,052,100	1,178,400	12.0

Note: (1) Figures cover the Los Angeles-Long Beach-Anaheim, CA Metropolitan Statistical Area—see Appendix B for areas included; Figures represent new, privately-owned housing units authorized (unadjusted data); All permit data are based on estimates with imputation; (p) preliminary data.
Source: U.S. Census Bureau, Manufacturing, Mining, and Construction Statistics, Building Permits, 2014, 2015

Bankruptcy Filings

Area	Business Filings 2014	Business Filings 2015	Business Filings % Chg.	Nonbusiness Filings 2014	Nonbusiness Filings 2015	Nonbusiness Filings % Chg.
Los Angeles County	1,212	1,235	1.9	29,341	23,618	-19.5
U.S.	26,983	24,735	-8.3	909,812	819,760	-9.9

Note: Business filings include Chapter 7, Chapter 11, Chapter 12, and Chapter 13; Nonbusiness filings include Chapter 7, Chapter 11, and Chapter 13

Source: Administrative Office of the U.S. Courts, Business and Nonbusiness Bankruptcy, County Cases Commenced by Chapter of the Bankruptcy Code, During the 12- Month Period Ending December 31, 2014 and Business and Nonbusiness Bankruptcy, County Cases Commenced by Chapter of the Bankruptcy Code, During the 12- Month Period Ending December 31, 2015

Housing Vacancy Rates

Area	Gross Vacancy Rate[2] (%)			Year-Round Vacancy Rate[3] (%)			Rental Vacancy Rate[4] (%)			Homeowner Vacancy Rate[5] (%)		
	2013	2014	2015	2013	2014	2015	2013	2014	2015	2013	2014	2015
MSA[1]	6.2	5.8	5.4	5.7	5.5	5.0	4.2	4.6	3.3	1.2	0.8	0.8
U.S.	13.6	13.4	12.9	10.7	10.4	10.0	8.3	7.6	7.1	2.0	1.9	1.8

Note: (1) Figures cover the Los Angeles-Long Beach-Anaheim, CA Metropolitan Statistical Area—see Appendix B for areas included; (2) The percentage of the total housing inventory that is vacant; (3) The percentage of the housing inventory (excluding seasonal units) that is year-round vacant; (4) The percentage of rental inventory that is vacant for rent; (5) The percentage of homeowner inventory that is vacant for sale

Source: U.S. Census Bureau, Housing Vacancies and Homeownership Annual Statistics: 2015

INCOME

Income

Area	Per Capita ($)	Median Household ($)	Average Household ($)
City	57,201	120,697	149,400
MSA[1]	29,506	60,337	86,928
U.S.	28,555	53,482	74,596

Note: (1) Figures cover the Los Angeles-Long Beach-Anaheim, CA Metropolitan Statistical Area—see Appendix B for areas included

Source: U.S. Census Bureau, 2010-2014 American Community Survey 5-Year Estimates

Household Income Distribution

Area	Percent of Households Earning: Under $15,000	$15,000 -24,999	$25,000 -34,999	$35,000 -49,999	$50,000 -74,999	$75,000 -99,000	$100,000 -149,999	$150,000 and up
City	4.2	4.4	4.6	5.9	13.3	9.6	18.4	39.7
MSA[1]	11.3	9.8	9.1	12.2	16.6	12.1	14.5	14.4
U.S.	12.5	10.7	10.2	13.5	17.8	12.2	13.0	10.0

Note: (1) Figures cover the Los Angeles-Long Beach-Anaheim, CA Metropolitan Statistical Area—see Appendix B for areas included

Source: U.S. Census Bureau, 2010-2014 American Community Survey 5-Year Estimates

Poverty Rate

Area	All Ages	Under 18 Years Old	18 to 64 Years Old	65 Years and Over
City	4.4	4.8	4.3	4.1
MSA[1]	17.1	24.0	15.4	12.2
U.S.	15.6	21.9	14.6	9.4

Note: Figures are percentage of people whose income during the past 12 months was below the poverty level; (1) Figures cover the Los Angeles-Long Beach-Anaheim, CA Metropolitan Statistical Area—see Appendix B for areas included

Source: U.S. Census Bureau, 2010-2014 American Community Survey 5-Year Estimates

EMPLOYMENT

Labor Force and Employment

Area	Civilian Labor Force			Workers Employed		
	Dec. 2014	Dec. 2015	% Chg.	Dec. 2014	Dec. 2015	% Chg.
City	19,221	19,135	-0.4	18,522	18,600	0.4
MD[1]	5,030,364	4,991,657	-0.7	4,662,182	4,707,516	0.9
U.S.	155,521,000	157,245,000	1.1	147,190,000	149,703,000	1.7

Note: Data is not seasonally adjusted and covers workers 16 years of age and older; (1) Figures cover the Los Angeles-Long Beach-Glendale, CA Metropolitan Division—see Appendix B for areas included
Source: Bureau of Labor Statistics, Local Area Unemployment Statistics

Unemployment Rate

Area	2015											
	Jan.	Feb.	Mar.	Apr.	May	Jun.	Jul.	Aug.	Sep.	Oct.	Nov.	Dec.
City	4.0	3.7	3.5	3.4	3.6	3.6	3.6	3.4	3.0	2.8	2.7	2.8
MD[1]	7.9	7.4	7.1	6.8	6.8	6.9	7.2	6.7	6.2	6.0	5.8	5.7
U.S.	6.1	5.8	5.6	5.1	5.3	5.5	5.6	5.2	4.9	4.8	4.8	4.8

Note: Data is not seasonally adjusted and covers workers 16 years of age and older; (1) Figures cover the Los Angeles-Long Beach-Glendale, CA Metropolitan Division—see Appendix B for areas included
Source: Bureau of Labor Statistics, Local Area Unemployment Statistics

Employment by Occupation

Occupation Classification	City (%)	MSA[1] (%)	U.S. (%)
Management, Business, Science, and Arts	63.0	36.5	36.4
Natural Resources, Construction, and Maintenance	2.7	7.5	9.0
Production, Transportation, and Material Moving	5.3	12.1	12.1
Sales and Office	23.7	25.2	24.4
Service	5.4	18.6	18.2

Note: Figures cover employed civilians 16 years of age and older; (1) Figures cover the Los Angeles-Long Beach-Anaheim, CA Metropolitan Statistical Area—see Appendix B for areas included
Source: U.S. Census Bureau, 2010-2014 American Community Survey 5-Year Estimates

Employment by Industry

Sector	MD[1]		U.S.
	Number of Employees	Percent of Total	Percent of Total
Construction	127,600	2.9	4.5
Education and Health Services	766,400	17.5	15.7
Financial Activities	217,100	4.9	5.7
Government	578,100	13.2	15.5
Information	207,300	4.7	1.9
Leisure and Hospitality	497,300	11.3	10.4
Manufacturing	357,400	8.1	8.6
Mining and Logging	3,700	<0.1	0.5
Other Services	152,400	3.4	3.9
Professional and Business Services	616,200	14.0	13.9
Retail Trade	445,100	10.1	11.3
Transportation, Warehousing, and Utilities	174,900	4.0	3.9
Wholesale Trade	229,300	5.2	4.1

Note: Figures are non-farm employment as of December 2015. Figures are not seasonally adjusted and include workers 16 years of age and older; (1) Figures cover the Los Angeles-Long Beach-Glendale, CA Metropolitan Division—see Appendix B for areas included
Source: Bureau of Labor Statistics, Current Employment Statistics, Employment, Hours, and Earnings

Occupations with Greatest Projected Employment Growth: 2012 – 2022

Occupation[1]	2012 Employment	2022 Projected Employment	Numeric Employment Change	Percent Employment Change
Personal Care Aides	386,900	587,200	200,300	51.8
Combined Food Preparation and Serving Workers, Including Fast Food	286,000	362,400	76,400	26.7
Retail Salespersons	468,400	528,100	59,700	12.7
Laborers and Freight, Stock, and Material Movers, Hand	270,500	322,300	51,800	19.1
Waiters and Waitresses	246,100	290,300	44,200	18.0
Registered Nurses	254,500	297,400	42,900	16.9
General and Operations Managers	253,800	295,700	41,900	16.5
Secretaries and Administrative Assistants, Except Legal, Medical, and Executive	212,800	250,100	37,300	17.5
Cashiers	357,800	392,600	34,800	9.7
Cooks, Restaurant	116,900	150,600	33,700	28.8

Note: Projections cover California; (1) Sorted by numeric employment change
Source: www.projectionscentral.com, State Occupational Projections, 2012–2022 Long-Term Projections

Fastest Growing Occupations: 2012 – 2022

Occupation[1]	2012 Employment	2022 Projected Employment	Numeric Employment Change	Percent Employment Change
Economists	3,100	5,100	2,000	64.5
Helpers—Brickmasons, Blockmasons, Stonemasons, and Tile and Marble Setters	2,900	4,600	1,700	58.6
Brickmasons and Blockmasons	5,100	8,000	2,900	56.9
Insulation Workers, Floor, Ceiling, and Wall	1,600	2,500	900	56.3
Stonemasons	1,100	1,700	600	54.5
Insulation Workers, Mechanical	1,100	1,700	600	54.5
Personal Care Aides	386,900	587,200	200,300	51.8
Foresters	1,200	1,800	600	50.0
Terrazzo Workers and Finishers	1,100	1,600	500	45.5
Mechanical Door Repairers	1,100	1,600	500	45.5

Note: Projections cover California; (1) Sorted by percent employment change and excludes occupations with numeric employment change less than 100
Source: www.projectionscentral.com, State Occupational Projections, 2012–2022 Long-Term Projections

Average Wages

Occupation	$/Hr.	Occupation	$/Hr.
Accountants and Auditors	37.94	Maids and Housekeeping Cleaners	12.64
Automotive Mechanics	19.33	Maintenance and Repair Workers	21.34
Bookkeepers	21.13	Marketing Managers	70.61
Carpenters	25.74	Nuclear Medicine Technologists	48.58
Cashiers	10.92	Nurses, Licensed Practical	23.86
Clerks, General Office	15.88	Nurses, Registered	46.61
Clerks, Receptionists/Information	14.57	Nursing Assistants	14.67
Clerks, Shipping/Receiving	14.82	Packers and Packagers, Hand	10.74
Computer Programmers	45.98	Physical Therapists	44.29
Computer Systems Analysts	45.58	Postal Service Mail Carriers	25.56
Computer User Support Specialists	27.56	Real Estate Brokers	39.75
Cooks, Restaurant	12.17	Retail Salespersons	13.66
Dentists	83.24	Sales Reps., Exc. Tech./Scientific	29.08
Electrical Engineers	50.86	Sales Reps., Tech./Scientific	41.19
Electricians	29.84	Secretaries, Exc. Legal/Med./Exec.	19.31
Financial Managers	72.17	Security Guards	12.83
First-Line Supervisors/Managers, Sales	20.71	Surgeons	124.06
Food Preparation Workers	11.08	Teacher Assistants*	14.90
General and Operations Managers	62.25	Teachers, Elementary School*	35.30
Hairdressers/Cosmetologists	13.93	Teachers, Secondary School*	36.88
Internists	82.36	Telemarketers	13.48
Janitors and Cleaners	13.89	Truck Drivers, Heavy/Tractor-Trailer	20.54
Landscaping/Groundskeeping Workers	14.45	Truck Drivers, Light/Delivery Svcs.	17.16
Lawyers	83.22	Waiters and Waitresses	13.26

Note: Wage data covers the Los Angeles-Long Beach-Glendale, CA Metropolitan Division—see Appendix B for areas included; (*) Hourly wages for elementary/secondary school teachers and teacher assistants were calculated by the editors from annual wage data based on a 40 hour work week; n/a not available.
Source: Bureau of Labor Statistics, Metro Area Occupational Employment and Wage Estimates, May 2015

TAXES

State Corporate Income Tax Rates

State	Tax Rate (%)	Income Brackets ($)	Num. of Brackets	Financial Institution Tax Rate (%)[a]	Federal Income Tax Ded.
California	8.84 (c)	Flat rate	1	10.84 (c)	No

Note: Tax rates as of January 1, 2016; (a) Rates listed are the corporate income tax rate applied to financial institutions or excise taxes based on income. Some states have other taxes based upon the value of deposits or shares; (c) Minimum tax is $800 in California, $100 in District of Columbia, $50 in North Dakota (banks), $500 in Rhode Island, $200 per location in South Dakota (banks), $100 in Utah, $250 in Vermont.
Source: Federation of Tax Administrators, "State Corporate Income Tax Rates, 2016"

State Individual Income Tax Rates

State	Tax Rate (%)	Income Brackets ($)	Num. of Brackets	Personal Exempt. ($)[1] Single	Personal Exempt. ($)[1] Dependents	Fed. Inc. Tax Ded.
California (a)	1.0 - 12.3 (f)	7,850- 526,443 (b)	9	109 (c)	337 (c)	No

Note: Tax rates as of January 1, 2016; Local- and county-level taxes are not included; n/a not applicable; (1) Married joint filers generally receive double the single exemption; (a) 18 states have statutory provision for automatically adjusting to the rate of inflation the dollar values of the income tax brackets, standard deductions, and/or personal exemptions. Massachusetts, Michigan, and Nebraska index the personal exemptiononly. Oregon does not index the income brackets for $125,000 and over. Maine has suspended indexing for 2014 and 2015; (b) For joint returns, taxes are twice the tax on half the couple's income; (c) The personal exemption takes the form of a tax credit instead of a deduction; (f) California imposes an additional 1% tax on taxable income over $1 million, making the maximum rate 13.3% over $1 million.
Source: Federation of Tax Administrators, "State Individual Income Tax Rates, 2016"

Various State and Local Tax Rates

State	State and Local Sales and Use (%)	State Sales and Use (%)	Gasoline[1] (¢/gal.)	Cigarette[2] ($/pack)	Spirits[3] ($/gal.)	Wine[4] ($/gal.)	Beer[5] ($/gal.)
California	9.00	7.50 (b)	40.62	0.87	3.30 (f)	0.20 (l)	0.08

Note: All tax rates as of January 1, 2016; (1) The American Petroleum Institute has developed a methodology for determining the average tax rate on a gallon of fuel. Rates may include any of the following: excise taxes, environmental fees, storage tank fees, other fees or taxes, general sales tax, and local taxes. In states where gasoline is subject to the general sales tax, or where the fuel tax is based on the average sale price, the average rate determined by API is sensitive to changes in the price of gasoline. States that fully or partially apply general sales taxes to gasoline: CA, CO, GA, IL, IN, MI, NY; (2) The federal excise tax of $1.0066 per pack and local taxes are not included; (3) Rates are those applicable to off-premise sales of 40% alcohol by volume (a.b.v.) distilled spirits in 750ml containers. Local excise taxes are excluded; (4) Rates are those applicable to off-premise sales of 11% a.b.v. non-carbonated wine in 750ml containers; (5) Rates are those applicable to off-premise sales of 4.7% a.b.v. beer in 12 ounce containers; (b) Three states levy mandatory, statewide local add-on sales taxes at the state level: California (1%), Utah (1.25%), and Virginia (1%). We include these in their state sales tax rates; (f) Different rates are also applicable according to alcohol content, place of production, size of container, or place purchased (on- or off-premise or onboard airlines); (l) Different rates also applicable according to alcohol content, place of production, size of container, place purchased (on- or off-premise or on board airlines) or type of wine (carbonated, vermouth, etc.).
Source: Tax Foundation, 2016 Facts & Figures: How Does Your State Compare?

State Business Tax Climate Index Rankings

State	Overall Rank	Corporate Tax Rank	Individual Income Tax Rank	Sales Tax Rank	Unemployment Insurance Tax Rank	Property Tax Rank
California	48	35	50	40	13	13

Note: The index is a measure of how each state's tax laws affect economic performance. The lower the rank, the more favorable a state's tax system is for business. States without a given tax are given a ranking of 1. The scores/rankings for the District of Columbia do not affect other states. The 2016 index represents the tax climate as of July 1, 2015 (the beginning of Fiscal Year 2016).
Source: Tax Foundation, State Business Tax Climate Index 2016

TRANSPORTATION

Means of Transportation to Work

Area	Car/Truck/Van: Drove Alone	Car/Truck/Van: Car-pooled	Public Transportation: Bus	Public Transportation: Subway	Public Transportation: Railroad	Bicycle	Walked	Other Means	Worked at Home
City	79.6	8.7	1.2	0.2	0.0	0.3	0.4	0.8	8.9
MSA[1]	73.9	10.3	5.3	0.4	0.2	0.9	2.6	1.3	5.1
U.S.	76.4	9.6	2.6	1.8	0.6	0.6	2.8	1.3	4.4

Note: Figures are percentages and cover workers 16 years of age and older; (1) Figures cover the Los Angeles-Long Beach-Anaheim, CA Metropolitan Statistical Area—see Appendix B for areas included
Source: U.S. Census Bureau, 2010-2014 American Community Survey 5-Year Estimates

Travel Time to Work

Area	Less Than 10 Minutes	10 to 19 Minutes	20 to 29 Minutes	30 to 44 Minutes	45 to 59 Minutes	60 to 89 Minutes	90 Minutes or More
City	4.7	17.9	23.4	30.5	11.2	9.7	2.5
MSA[1]	8.1	26.1	20.5	24.9	9.2	8.2	3.0
U.S.	13.3	29.6	21.0	20.2	7.7	5.7	2.6

Note: Figures are percentages and include workers 16 years old and over; (1) Figures cover the Los Angeles-Long Beach-Anaheim, CA Metropolitan Statistical Area—see Appendix B for areas included
Source: U.S. Census Bureau, 2010-2014 American Community Survey 5-Year Estimates

Freeway Travel Time Index

Area	1985	1990	1995	2000	2005	2010	2014
Urban Area Rank[1,2]	1	1	1	1	1	1	1
Urban Area Index[1]	1.31	1.34	1.38	1.41	1.44	1.42	1.43
Average Index[3]	1.09	1.11	1.14	1.17	1.20	1.19	1.20

Note: Freeway Travel Time Index—the ratio of travel time in the peak period to the travel time at free-flow conditions. For example, a value of 1.30 indicates a 20-minute free-flow trip takes 26 minutes in the peak (20 minutes x 1.30 = 26 minutes); (1) Covers the Los Angeles-Long Beach-Anaheim CA urban area; (2) Rank is based on 101 urban areas (#1 = highest travel time index); (3) Average of 101 urban areas
Source: Texas Transportation Institute, 2015 Urban Mobility Scorecard, August 2015

Freeway Commuter Stress Index

Area	1985	1990	1995	2000	2005	2010	2014
Urban Area Rank[1,2]	1	1	1	1	1	1	1
Urban Area Index[1]	1.49	1.52	1.56	1.59	1.63	1.61	1.62
Average Index[3]	1.13	1.16	1.19	1.22	1.25	1.24	1.25

Note: The Freeway Commuter Stress Index is the same as the Freeway Travel Time Index (see table above) except that it includes only the travel in the peak directions during the peak periods; the TTI includes travel in all directions during the peak period. Thus, the CSI is more indicative of the work trip experienced by each commuter on a daily basis. (1) Covers the Los Angeles-Long Beach-Anaheim CA urban area; (2) Rank is based on 101 urban areas (#1 = highest stress index); (3) Average of 101 urban areas
Source: Texas Transportation Institute, 2015 Urban Mobility Scorecard, August 2015

Living Environment

COST OF LIVING

Cost of Living Index

Composite Index	Groceries	Housing	Utilities	Trans-portation	Health Care	Misc. Goods/ Services
140.4	106.3	214.1	115.7	132.4	109.3	106.0

Note: The Cost of Living Index measures regional differences in the cost of consumer goods and services, excluding taxes and non-consumer expenditures, for professional and managerial households in the top income quintile. It is based on more than 50,000 prices covering almost 60 different items for which prices are collected three times a year by chambers of commerce, economic development organizations or university applied economic centers in each participating urban area. The numbers shown should be read as a percentage above or below the national average of 100. For example, a value of 115.4 in the groceries column indicates that grocery prices are 15.4% higher than the national average. Small differences in the index numbers should not be interpreted as significant; Figures cover the Los Angeles-Long Beach CA urban area.
Source: The Council for Community and Economic Research, ACCRA Cost of Living Index, 2015

Grocery Prices

Area[1]	T-Bone Steak ($/pound)	Frying Chicken ($/pound)	Whole Milk ($/half gal.)	Eggs ($/dozen)	Orange Juice ($/64 oz.)	Coffee ($/11.5 oz.)
City[2]	11.05	1.56	2.35	3.38	3.54	5.27
Avg.	10.99	1.43	2.25	2.26	3.58	4.48
Min.	7.16	0.98	1.30	1.35	2.88	2.98
Max.	14.13	2.43	3.85	4.81	6.39	7.56

Note: (1) Values for the local area are compared with the average, minimum and maximum values for all 292 areas in the Cost of Living Index; (2) Figures cover the Los Angeles-Long Beach CA urban area; **T-Bone Steak** *(price per pound);* **Frying Chicken** *(price per pound, whole fryer);* **Whole Milk** *(half gallon carton);* **Eggs** *(price per dozen, Grade A, large);* **Orange Juice** *(64 oz. Tropicana or Florida Natural);* **Coffee** *(11.5 oz. can, vacuum-packed, Maxwell House, Hills Bros, or Folgers).*
Source: The Council for Community and Economic Research, ACCRA Cost of Living Index, 2015

Housing and Utility Costs

Area[1]	New Home Price ($)	Apartment Rent ($/month)	All Electric ($/month)	Part Electric ($/month)	Other Energy ($/month)	Telephone ($/month)
City[2]	617,169	2,420	-	134.81	57.31	33.57
Avg.	312,874	945	179.30	95.07	72.96	28.11
Min.	178,682	479	116.28	43.14	26.46	10.01
Max.	1,472,476	3,984	504.25	189.44	421.11	43.06

Note: (1) Values for the local area are compared with the average, minimum and maximum values for all 292 areas in the Cost of Living Index; (2) Figures cover the Los Angeles-Long Beach CA urban area; **New Home Price** *(2,400 sf living area, 8,000 sf lot, in urban area with full utilities);* **Apartment Rent** *(950 sf 2 bedroom/1.5 or 2 bath, unfurnished, excluding all utilities except water);* **All Electric** *(average monthly cost for an all-electric home);* **Part Electric** *(average monthly cost for a part-electric home);* **Other Energy** *(average monthly cost for natural gas, fuel oil, coal, wood, and any other forms of energy except electricity);* **Telephone** *(price includes basic monthly rate for a private residential line plus additional local usage charges incurred by a family of four).*
Source: The Council for Community and Economic Research, ACCRA Cost of Living Index, 2015

Health Care, Transportation, and Other Costs

Area[1]	Doctor ($/visit)	Dentist ($/visit)	Optometrist ($/visit)	Gasoline ($/gallon)	Beauty Salon ($/visit)	Men's Shirt ($)
City[2]	98.29	105.22	121.62	3.39	59.95	25.91
Avg.	105.15	89.02	99.78	2.38	35.30	28.10
Min.	66.87	56.09	48.53	1.95	18.91	13.38
Max.	182.34	150.36	228.33	4.09	67.91	63.80

Note: (1) Values for the local area are compared with the average, minimum and maximum values for all 292 areas in the Cost of Living Index; (2) Figures cover the Los Angeles-Long Beach CA urban area; **Doctor** *(general practitioners routine exam of an established patient);* **Dentist** *(adult teeth cleaning and periodic oral examination);* **Optometrist** *(full vision eye exam for established adult patient);* **Gasoline** *(one gallon regular unleaded, national brand, including all taxes, cash price at self-service pump if available);* **Beauty Salon** *(woman's shampoo, trim, and blow-dry);* **Men's Shirt** *(cotton/polyester dress shirt, pinpoint weave, long sleeves).*
Source: The Council for Community and Economic Research, ACCRA Cost of Living Index, 2015

HOUSING

House Price Index (HPI)

Area	National Ranking[2]	Quarterly Change (%)	One-Year Change (%)	Five-Year Change (%)
MD[1]	61	1.30	7.20	31.30
U.S.[3]	–	1.45	5.76	22.85

Note: The HPI is a weighted repeat sales index. It measures average price changes in repeat sales or refinancings on the same properties. This information is obtained by reviewing repeat mortgage transactions on single-family properties whose mortgages have been purchased or securitized by Fannie Mae or Freddie Mac in January 1975; (1) Los Angeles-Long Beach-Glendale Metropolitan Division—see Appendix B for areas included; (2) Rankings are based on annual percentage change for all metro areas containing at least 15,000 transactions over the last 10 years and ranges from 1 to 266; (3) figures based on a weighted average of Census Division estimates using a seasonally adjusted, purchase-only index; all figures are for the period ending December 31, 2015

Source: Federal Housing Finance Agency, House Price Index, February 25, 2016

Median Single-Family Home Prices

Area	2013	2014	2015[p]	Percent Change 2014 to 2015
MSA[1]	n/a	n/a	n/a	n/a
U.S. Average	197.4	208.9	223.9	7.2

Note: Figures are median sales prices of existing single-family homes in thousands of dollars; (p) preliminary; n/a not available; (1) Los Angeles-Long Beach-Anaheim, CA Metropolitan Statistical Area—see Appendix B for areas included

Source: National Association of Realtors, Median Sales Price of Existing Single-Family Homes for Metropolitan Areas, 4th Quarter 2015

Qualifying Income Based on Median Sales Price of Existing Single-Family Homes

Area	With 5% Down ($)	With 10% Down ($)	With 20% Down ($)
MSA[1]	n/a	n/a	n/a
U.S. Average	49,535	46,928	41,714

Note: Figures are preliminary; Qualifying income is based on a mortgage rate of 4.1%. Monthly principal and interest payment is limited to 25% of income; n/a not available; (1) Los Angeles-Long Beach-Anaheim, CA Metropolitan Statistical Area—see Appendix B for areas included

Source: National Association of Realtors, Qualifying Income Based on Median Sales Price of Existing Single-Family Homes for Metropolitan Areas, 4th Quarter 2015

Median Apartment Condo-Coop Home Prices

Area	2013	2014	2015[p]	Percent Change 2014 to 2015
MSA[1]	n/a	n/a	n/a	n/a
U.S. Average	194.9	204.3	210.7	3.1

Note: Figures are median sales prices of existing apartment condo-coop homes in thousands of dollars; (p) preliminary; n/a not available; (1) Los Angeles-Long Beach-Anaheim, CA Metropolitan Statistical Area—see Appendix B for areas included

Source: National Association of Realtors, Median Sales Price of Existing Apartment Condo-Coop Homes for Metropolitan Areas, 4th Quarter 2015

Gross Monthly Rent

Area	Under $200	$200 -299	$300 -499	$500 -749	$750 -999	$1,000 -1,499	$1,500 and up	Median ($)
City	0.0	0.0	3.2	0.3	0.9	10.8	84.8	2,000+
MSA[1]	0.5	1.9	2.5	6.4	16.4	37.2	35.0	1,284
U.S.	1.5	3.2	7.4	21.0	24.1	26.9	15.9	920

Note: Figures are percentages except for Median; Gross rent is the contract rent plus the estimated average monthly cost of utilities (electricity, gas, and water and sewer) and fuels (oil, coal, kerosene, wood, etc.) if these are paid by the renter (or paid for the renter by someone else); (1) Figures cover the Los Angeles-Long Beach-Anaheim, CA Metropolitan Statistical Area—see Appendix B for areas included

Source: U.S. Census Bureau, 2010-2014 American Community Survey 5-Year Estimates

Homeownership Rate

Area	2008 (%)	2009 (%)	2010 (%)	2011 (%)	2012 (%)	2013 (%)	2014 (%)	2015 (%)
MSA[1]	52.1	50.4	49.7	50.1	49.9	48.7	49.0	49.1
U.S.	67.8	67.4	66.9	66.1	65.4	65.1	64.5	63.7

Note: (1) Figures cover the Los Angeles-Long Beach-Anaheim, CA Metropolitan Statistical Area—see Appendix B for areas included
Source: U.S. Census Bureau, Housing Vacancies and Homeownership Annual Statistics: 2015

Year Housing Structure Built

Area	2010 or Later	2000 -2009	1990 -1999	1980 -1989	1970 -1979	1960 -1969	1950 -1959	1940 -1949	Before 1940	Median Year
City	0.3	2.6	2.4	5.9	25.0	40.8	20.5	1.1	1.4	1967
MSA[1]	0.5	6.8	7.5	12.6	16.5	16.0	19.0	8.9	12.2	1966
U.S.	1.0	14.9	13.9	13.8	15.8	11.0	10.8	5.4	13.3	1976

Note: Figures are percentages except for Median Year; (1) Figures cover the Los Angeles-Long Beach-Anaheim, CA Metropolitan Statistical Area—see Appendix B for areas included
Source: U.S. Census Bureau, 2010-2014 American Community Survey 5-Year Estimates

HEALTH

Health Risk Data

Category	MD[1] (%)	U.S. (%)
Adults aged 18–64 who have any kind of health care coverage	68.3	79.6
Adults who reported being in good or excellent health	78.4	83.1
Adults who are current smokers	11.8	19.6
Adults who are heavy drinkers[2]	5.0	6.1
Adults who are binge drinkers[3]	16.3	16.9
Adults who are overweight (BMI 25.0 - 29.9)	34.3	35.8
Adults who are obese (BMI 30.0 - 99.8)	25.0	27.6
Adults who participated in any physical activities in the past month	78.5	77.1
Adults 50+ who have ever had a sigmoidoscopy or colonoscopy	62.0	67.3
Women aged 40+ who have had a mammogram within the past two years	78.5	74.0
Men aged 40+ who have had a PSA test within the past two years	39.8	45.2
Adults aged 65+ who have had flu shot within the past year	55.6	60.1
Adults who always wear a seatbelt	96.5	93.8

Note: Data as of 2012 unless otherwise noted; (1) Figures cover the Los Angeles-Long Beach-Glendale, CA Metropolitan Division—see Appendix B for areas included; (2) Heavy drinkers are classified as males having more than two drinks per day or females having more than one drink per day; (3) Binge drinkers are classified as males having five or more drinks on one occasion or females having four or more drinks on one occasion
Source: Centers for Disease Control and Prevention, Behaviorial Risk Factor Surveillance System, SMART: Selected Metropolitan/Micropolitan Area Risk Trends, 2012 (Note: the CDC has discontinued this dataset but will be releasing a replacement in mid-2016)

Chronic Health Indicators

Category	MD[1] (%)	U.S. (%)
Adults who have ever been told they had a heart attack	3.1	4.5
Adults who have ever been told they had a stroke	2.0	2.9
Adults who have been told they currently have asthma	7.2	8.9
Adults who have ever been told they have arthritis	19.5	25.7
Adults who have ever been told they have diabetes[2]	10.6	9.7
Adults who have ever been told they had skin cancer	3.3	5.7
Adults who have ever been told they had any other types of cancer	4.4	6.5
Adults who have ever been told they have COPD	3.6	6.2
Adults who have ever been told they have kidney disease	2.6	2.5
Adults who have ever been told they have a form of depression	10.6	18.0

Note: Data as of 2012 unless otherwise noted; (1) Figures cover the Los Angeles-Long Beach-Glendale, CA Metropolitan Division—see Appendix B for areas included; (2) Figures do not include pregnancy-related, borderline, or pre-diabetes
Source: Centers for Disease Control and Prevention, Behaviorial Risk Factor Surveillance System, SMART: Selected Metropolitan/Micropolitan Area Risk Trends, 2012 (Note: the CDC has discontinued this dataset but will be releasing a replacement in mid-2016)

Mortality Rates for the Top 10 Causes of Death in the U.S.

ICD-10[a] Sub-Chapter	ICD-10[a] Code	Age-Adjusted Mortality Rate[1] per 100,000 population	
		County[2]	U.S.
Malignant neoplasms	C00-C97	142.0	163.6
Ischaemic heart diseases	I20-I25	115.2	102.2
Other forms of heart disease	I30-I51	31.1	50.1
Chronic lower respiratory diseases	J40-J47	29.2	41.4
Organic, including symptomatic, mental disorders	F01-F09	19.6	38.5
Cerebrovascular diseases	I60-I69	33.3	36.5
Other external causes of accidental injury	W00-X59	13.3	27.5
Other degenerative diseases of the nervous system	G30-G31	27.5	26.3
Diabetes mellitus	E10-E14	22.6	21.1
Hypertensive diseases	I10-I15	20.9	19.7

Note: (a) ICD-10 = International Classification of Diseases 10th Revision; (1) Mortality rates are a three year average covering 2012-2014; (2) Figures cover COUNTY NOT FOUND!!!!!!.
Source: Centers for Disease Control and Prevention, National Center for Health Statistics. Underlying Cause of Death 1999-2014 on CDC WONDER Online Database, released 2015.

Mortality Rates for Selected Causes of Death

ICD-10[a] Sub-Chapter	ICD-10[a] Code	Age-Adjusted Mortality Rate[1] per 100,000 population	
		County[2]	U.S.
Assault	X85-Y09	5.3	5.1
Diseases of the liver	K70-K76	14.5	13.5
Human immunodeficiency virus (HIV) disease	B20-B24	2.3	2.1
Influenza and pneumonia	J09-J18	21.5	15.2
Intentional self-harm	X60-X84	7.7	12.7
Malnutrition	E40-E46	0.4	0.9
Obesity and other hyperalimentation	E65-E68	1.3	1.9
Renal failure	N17-N19	9.4	13.0
Transport accidents	V01-V99	7.7	11.6
Viral hepatitis	B15-B19	2.6	2.1

Note: (a) ICD-10 = International Classification of Diseases 10th Revision; (1) Mortality rates are a three year average covering 2012-2014; (2) Figures cover COUNTY NOT FOUND!!!!!!; Data are Suppressed when the data meet the criteria for confidentiality constraints; Mortality rates are flagged as Unreliable when the rate would be calculated with a numerator of 20 or less.
Source: Centers for Disease Control and Prevention, National Center for Health Statistics. Underlying Cause of Death 1999-2014 on CDC WONDER Online Database, released 2015.

Health Insurance Coverage

Area	With Health Insurance	With Private Health Insurance	With Public Health Insurance	Without Health Insurance	Population Under Age 18 Without Health Insurance
City	95.2	86.3	27.1	4.8	2.8
MSA[1]	80.3	56.7	29.9	19.7	8.2
U.S.	85.8	65.8	31.1	14.2	7.1

Note: Figures are percentages that cover the civilian noninstitutionalized population; (1) Figures cover the Los Angeles-Long Beach-Anaheim, CA Metropolitan Statistical Area—see Appendix B for areas included
Source: U.S. Census Bureau, 2010-2014 American Community Survey 5-Year Estimates

Number of Medical Professionals

Area	MDs[3]	DOs[3,4]	Dentists	Podiatrists	Chiropractors	Optometrists
County[1] (number)	28,521	1,135	8,056	584	2,767	1,595
County[1] (rate[2])	283.7	11.3	79.6	5.8	27.4	15.8
U.S. (rate[2])	272.5	20.9	64.7	5.8	25.9	15.2

Note: Data as of 2014 unless noted; (1) Data covers Los Angeles County; (2) Rate per 100,000 population; (3) Data as of 2013 and includes all active, non-federal physicians; (4) Doctor of Osteopathic Medicine
Source: U.S. Department of Health and Human Services, Health Resources and Services Administration, Bureau of Health Professions, Area Resource File (ARF) 2014-2015

Best Hospitals

According to *U.S. News,* the Los Angeles-Long Beach-Glendale, CA metro area is home to 11 of the best hospitals in the U.S.: **City of Hope** (2 specialties); **Long Beach Memorial Medical Center** (1 specialty); **Cedars-Sinai Medical Center** (12 specialties); **Kaiser Permanente Los Angeles Medical Center** (2 specialties); **Keck Medical Center of USC** (4 specialties); **Resnick Neuropsychiatric Hospital at UCLA** (1 specialty); **Stein and Doheny Eye Institutes, UCLA Medical Center** (1 specialty); **UCLA Medical Center** (Honor Roll/15 specialties); **USC Eye Institute-Keck Medical Center of USC** (1 specialty); **USC Norris Cancer Hospital-Keck Medical Center of USC** (4 specialties); **Santa Monica-UCLA Medical Center and Orthopedic Hospital** (1 specialty). The hospitals listed were nationally ranked in at least one adult specialty. Only 137 hospitals nationwide were nationally ranked in one or more specialties. Fifteen hospitals in the U.S. made the Honor Roll with high scores in at least six specialties. *U.S. News Online, "America's Best Children's Hospitals 2015-16"*

According to *U.S. News,* the Los Angeles-Long Beach-Glendale, CA metro area is home to two of the best children's hospitals in the U.S.: **Children's Hospital Los Angeles** (Honor Roll/10 specialties); **Mattel Children's Hospital UCLA** (9 specialties). The hospitals listed were highly ranked in at least one pediatric specialty. Eighty-three children's hospitals in the U.S. were nationally ranked in at least one specialty. Twelve children's hospitals in the U.S. made the Honor Roll with high scores in at least three specialties. *U.S. News Online, "America's Best Children's Hospitals 2015-16"*

EDUCATION

Public School District Statistics

District Name	Schls	Pupils	Pupil/ Teacher Ratio	Minority Pupils[1] (%)	Free Lunch Eligible[2] (%)	IEP[3] (%)
Los Angeles Unified	983	653,826	23.6	90.7	67.9	12.5
Palos Verdes Peninsula Unified	19	11,700	25.9	46.5	2.2	8.6

Note: Table includes school districts with 100 or more students; (1) Percentage of students that are not non-Hispanic white; (2) Percentage of students that are eligible for the free lunch program; (3) Percentage of students that have an Individualized Education Program.
Source: U.S. Department of Education, National Center for Education Statistics, Common Core of Data, Local Education Agency (School District) Universe Survey: School Year 2013-2014; U.S. Department of Education, National Center for Education Statistics, Common Core of Data, Public Elementary/Secondary School Universe Survey: School Year 2013-2014

Highest Level of Education

Area	Less than H.S.	H.S. Diploma	Some College, No Deg.	Associate Degree	Bachelor's Degree	Master's Degree	Prof. School Degree	Doctorate Degree
City	2.5	9.4	16.1	7.2	33.7	17.7	8.5	4.9
MSA[1]	21.5	19.9	19.9	7.1	20.7	7.2	2.4	1.3
U.S.	13.7	28.0	21.2	7.9	18.3	7.8	2.0	1.3

Note: Figures cover persons age 25 and over; (1) Figures cover the Los Angeles-Long Beach-Anaheim, CA Metropolitan Statistical Area—see Appendix B for areas included
Source: U.S. Census Bureau, 2010-2014 American Community Survey 5-Year Estimates

Educational Attainment by Race

Area	High School Graduate or Higher (%)					Bachelor's Degree or Higher (%)				
	Total	White	Black	Asian	Hisp.[2]	Total	White	Black	Asian	Hisp.[2]
City	97.5	98.0	99.1	97.2	93.2	64.8	62.9	49.6	74.4	41.6
MSA[1]	78.5	81.1	88.5	87.2	57.4	31.7	33.6	23.9	50.0	11.1
U.S.	86.3	88.4	83.2	85.8	64.1	29.3	30.6	19.0	50.9	13.9

Note: Figures shown cover persons 25 years old and over; (1) Figures cover the Los Angeles-Long Beach-Anaheim, CA Metropolitan Statistical Area—see Appendix B for areas included; (2) People of Hispanic origin can be of any race
Source: U.S. Census Bureau, 2010-2014 American Community Survey 5-Year Estimates

School Enrollment by Grade and Control

Area	Preschool (%)		Kindergarten (%)		Grades 1 - 4 (%)		Grades 5 - 8 (%)		Grades 9 - 12 (%)	
	Public	Private	Public	Private	Public	Private	Public	Private	Public	Private
City	23.9	76.1	81.4	18.6	87.8	12.2	90.7	9.3	93.8	6.2
MSA[1]	58.3	41.7	88.2	11.8	90.3	9.7	90.6	9.4	91.8	8.2
U.S.	57.4	42.6	87.8	12.2	89.8	10.2	89.9	10.1	90.6	9.4

Note: Figures shown cover persons 3 years old and over; (1) Figures cover the Los Angeles-Long Beach-Anaheim, CA Metropolitan Statistical Area—see Appendix B for areas included
Source: U.S. Census Bureau, 2010-2014 American Community Survey 5-Year Estimates

Average Salaries of Public School Classroom Teachers

Area	2013-14		2014-15		Percent Change 2013-14 to 2014-15	Percent Change 2004-05 to 2014-15
	Dollars	Rank[1]	Dollars	Rank[1]		
California	71,396	4	72,535	4	1.59	25.9
U.S. Average	56,610	–	57,379	–	1.36	20.8

Note: (1) State rank ranges from 1 to 51 where 1 indicates highest salary.
Source: National Education Association, Rankings & Estimates: Rankings of the States 2014 and Estimates of School Statistics 2015, March 2015

Higher Education

Four-Year Colleges			Two-Year Colleges			Medical Schools[1]	Law Schools[2]	Voc/ Tech[3]
Public	Private Non-profit	Private For-profit	Public	Private Non-profit	Private For-profit			
0	1	0	0	0	0	0	0	0

Note: Figures cover institutions located within the city limits and include main campuses only; (1) includes schools accredited by the Liaison Committee on Medical Education and the American Osteopathic Association's Commission on Osteopathic College Accreditation; (2) includes ABA-accredited schools, schools with provisional ABA accreditation, and state accredited schools; (3) includes all schools with programs that are less than 2 years.
Source: National Center for Education Statistics, Integrated Postsecondary Education System (IPEDS), 2014-15; Association of American Medical Colleges, Member List, March 21, 2016; American Osteopathic Association, Member List, March 21, 2016; Law School Admission Council, Official Guide to ABA-Approved Law Schools Online, March 21, 2016; Wikipedia, List of Medical Schools in the United States, March 21, 2016; Wikipedia, List of Law Schools in the United States, March 21, 2016

According to *U.S. News & World Report,* the Los Angeles-Long Beach-Glendale, CA metro division is home to seven of the best national universities in the U.S.: **California Institute of Technology** (#10 tie); **University of California–Los Angeles** (#23 tie); **University of Southern California** (#23 tie); **Pepperdine University** (#52 tie); **University of La Verne** (#160); **Biola University** (#161 tie); **Azusa Pacific University** (#175 tie). The indicators used to capture academic quality fall into a number of categories: assessment by administrators at peer institutions; retention of students; faculty resources; student selectivity; financial resources; alumni giving; high school counselor ratings of colleges; and graduation rate. *U.S. News & World Report, "America's Best Colleges 2016"*

According to *U.S. News & World Report,* the Los Angeles-Long Beach-Glendale, CA metro division is home to seven of the best liberal arts colleges in the U.S.: **Pomona College** (#4 tie); **Claremont McKenna College** (#9 tie); **Harvey Mudd College** (#14 tie); **Scripps College** (#29 tie); **Pitzer College** (#36); **Occidental College** (#43 tie); **Whittier College** (#127 tie). The indicators used to capture academic quality fall into a number of categories: assessment by administrators at peer institutions; retention of students; faculty resources; student selectivity; financial resources; alumni giving; high school counselor ratings of colleges; and graduation rate. *U.S. News & World Report, "America's Best Colleges 2016"*

According to *U.S. News & World Report,* the Los Angeles-Long Beach-Glendale, CA metro division is home to four of the top 100 law schools in the U.S.: **University of California–Los Angeles, School of Law** (#17); **University of Southern California, Gould School of Law** (#19); **Loyola Marymount University, Loyola Law School Los Angeles** (#65 tie); **Pepperdine University, School of Law** (#65 tie). The rankings are based on a weighted average of 12 measures of quality: peer assessment score; assessment score by lawyers/judges; median LSAT scores; median undergrad GPA; acceptance rate; employment rates for graduates; placement success; bar passage rate; faculty resources; expenditures per student; student/faculty ratio; and library resources. *U.S. News & World Report, "America's Best Graduate Schools, Law, 2017"*

According to *U.S. News & World Report,* the Los Angeles-Long Beach-Glendale, CA metro division is home to two of the top 75 medical schools for research in the U.S.: **University of California–Los Angeles, David Geffen School of Medicine** (#14); **University of Southern California, Keck School of Medicine** (#31 tie). The rankings are based on a weighted average of 11 measures of quality: quality assessment; peer assessment score; assessment score by residency directors; research activity; total research activity; average research activity per faculty member; student selectivity; median MCAT total score; median undergraduate GPA; acceptance rate; and faculty resources. *U.S. News & World Report, "America's Best Graduate Schools, Medical, 2017"*

According to *U.S. News & World Report,* the Los Angeles-Long Beach-Glendale, CA metro division is home to two of the top 75 business schools in the U.S.: **University of California–Los Angeles, Anderson School of Management** (#15); **University of Southern California, Marshall School of Business** (#31 tie). The rankings are based on a weighted average of the following nine measures: quality assessment; peer assessment; recruiter assessment; placement success; mean starting salary and bonus; student selectivity; mean GMAT and GRE scores; mean undergraduate GPA; and acceptance rate. *U.S. News & World Report, "America's Best Graduate Schools, Business, 2017"*

PRESIDENTIAL ELECTION

2012 Presidential Election Results

Area	Obama (%)	Romney (%)	Other (%)
Los Angeles County	68.6	29.1	2.3
U.S.	51.0	47.2	1.8

Note: Results may not add to 100% due to rounding
Source: Dave Leip's Atlas of U.S. Presidential Elections

EMPLOYERS

Major Employers

Company Name	Industry
City of Los Angeles	General government
County of Los Angeles	General government
Decton	Employment agencies
Disney Enterprises	Motion picture production & distribution
Disney Worldwide Services	Telecommunication equipment repair (except telephones)
Electronic Arts	Home entertainment computer software
King Holding Corporation	Bolts, nuts, rivets, & washers
Securitas Security Services USA	Security guard service
Team-One Employment Specialists	Employment agencies
The Boeing Company	Aircraft
The Boeing Company	Aircraft engines & engine parts
The Walt Disney Company	Television broadcasting stations
UCLA Health System	Home health care services
UCLA Medical Group	Medical centers
University of California, Irvine	University
University of Southern California	Colleges & universities
Veterans Health Administration	Administration of veterans' affairs
Warner Bros. Entertainment	Motion picture & video production

Note: Companies shown are located within the Los Angeles-Long Beach-Anaheim, CA Metropolitan Statistical Area.
Source: Hoovers.com; Wikipedia

PUBLIC SAFETY

Crime Rate

Area	All Crimes	Violent Crimes				Property Crimes		
		Murder	Rape[3]	Robbery	Aggrav. Assault	Burglary	Larceny -Theft	Motor Vehicle Theft
City	1,163.1	0.0	11.7	18.8	25.8	424.4	614.4	68.0
Metro[1]	2,570.9	5.2	22.0	160.0	235.0	436.9	1,350.4	361.5
U.S.	2,961.6	4.5	26.4	102.2	232.5	542.5	1,837.3	216.2

Note: Figures are crimes per 100,000 population; (1) Figures cover the Los Angeles-Long Beach-Glendale, CA Metropolitan Division—see Appendix B for areas included; (3) The city and U.S. figures shown were reported using the legacy Uniform Crime Reporting (UCR) definition of rape. The suburban and metro area figures shown are an aggregate total of the data submitted using both the revised and legacy UCR definitions.
Source: FBI Uniform Crime Reports, 2014

Hate Crimes

Area	Number of Quarters Reported	Number of Incidents per Bias Motivation						
		Race	Religion	Sexual Orientation	Ethnicity	Disability	Gender	Gender Identity
City	4	0	0	0	0	0	0	0
U.S.	4	2,568	1,014	1,017	648	84	33	98

Source: Federal Bureau of Investigation, Hate Crime Statistics 2014

Identity Theft Consumer Complaints

Area	Complaints	Complaints per 100,000 Population	Rank[2]
MSA[1]	19,791	149.2	55
U.S.	490,220	152.4	-

Note: (1) Figures cover the Los Angeles-Long Beach-Anaheim, CA Metropolitan Statistical Area—see Appendix B for areas included; (2) Rank ranges from 1 to 379 where 1 indicates greatest number of identity theft complaints per 100,000 population
Source: Federal Trade Commission, Consumer Sentinel Network Data Book for January–December 2015

Fraud and Other Consumer Complaints

Area	Complaints	Complaints per 100,000 Population	Rank[2]
MSA[1]	48,981	369.3	172
U.S.	2,593,159	806.0	-

Note: (1) Figures cover the Los Angeles-Long Beach-Anaheim, CA Metropolitan Statistical Area—see Appendix B for areas included; (2) Rank ranges from 1 to 379 where 1 indicates greatest number of identity theft complaints per 100,000 population
Source: Federal Trade Commission, Consumer Sentinel Network Data Book for January–December 2015

RECREATION

Culture

Dance[1]	Theatre[1]	Instrumental Music[1]	Vocal Music[1]	Series and Festivals	Museums and Art Galleries[2]	Zoos and Aquariums[3]
0	0	0	0	0	0	0

Note: (1) Professional perfoming groups; (2) Based on organizations with SIC code 8412; (3) AZA-accredited
Source: The Grey House Performing Arts Directory, 2015-16; Association of Zoos & Aquariums, AZA Member Zoos & Aquariums, March 25, 2016; www.AccuLeads.com, March 29, 2016

Professional Sports Teams

Team Name	League	Year Established
Anaheim Ducks	National Hockey League (NHL)	1993
C.D. Chivas USA	Major League Soccer (MLS)	2004
Los Angeles Angels of Anaheim	Major League Baseball (MLB)	1961
Los Angeles Clippers	National Basketball Association (NBA)	1984
Los Angeles Dodgers	Major League Baseball (MLB)	1958
Los Angeles FC	Major League Soccer (MLS)	2018
Los Angeles Galaxy	Major League Soccer (MLS)	1996
Los Angeles Kings	National Hockey League (NHL)	1967
Los Angeles Lakers	National Basketball Association (NBA)	1960
Los Angeles Rams	National Hockey League (NHL)	2016

Note: Includes teams located in the Los Angeles-Long Beach-Anaheim, CA Metropolitan Statistical Area.
Source: Wikipedia, Major Professional Sports Teams of the United States and Canada, March 24, 2016

CLIMATE

Average and Extreme Temperatures

Temperature	Jan	Feb	Mar	Apr	May	Jun	Jul	Aug	Sep	Oct	Nov	Dec	Yr.
Extreme High (°F)	88	92	95	102	97	104	97	98	110	106	101	94	110
Average High (°F)	65	66	65	67	69	72	75	76	76	74	71	66	70
Average Temp. (°F)	56	57	58	60	63	66	69	70	70	67	62	57	63
Average Low (°F)	47	49	50	53	56	59	63	64	63	59	52	48	55
Extreme Low (°F)	27	34	37	43	45	48	52	51	47	43	38	32	27

Note: Figures cover the years 1947-1990
Source: National Climatic Data Center, International Station Meteorological Climate Summary, 9/96

Average Precipitation/Snowfall/Humidity

Precip./Humidity	Jan	Feb	Mar	Apr	May	Jun	Jul	Aug	Sep	Oct	Nov	Dec	Yr.
Avg. Precip. (in.)	2.6	2.3	1.8	0.8	0.1	Tr	Tr	0.1	0.2	0.3	1.5	1.5	11.3
Avg. Snowfall (in.)	Tr	0	0	0	0	0	0	0	0	0	0	0	Tr
Avg. Rel. Hum. 7am (%)	69	72	76	76	77	80	80	81	80	76	69	67	75
Avg. Rel. Hum. 4pm (%)	60	62	64	64	66	67	67	68	67	66	61	60	64

Note: Figures cover the years 1947-1990; Tr = Trace amounts (<0.05 in. of rain; <0.5 in. of snow)
Source: National Climatic Data Center, International Station Meteorological Climate Summary, 9/96

Weather Conditions

Temperature			Daytime Sky			Precipitation		
10°F & below	32°F & below	90°F & above	Clear	Partly cloudy	Cloudy	0.01 inch or more precip.	0.1 inch or more snow/ice	Thunder-storms
0	< 1	5	131	125	109	34	0	1

Note: Figures are average number of days per year and cover the years 1947-1990
Source: National Climatic Data Center, International Station Meteorological Climate Summary, 9/96

HAZARDOUS WASTE

Superfund Sites

Rancho Palos Verdes has no sites on the EPA's Superfund Final National Priorities List. There are a total of 1,323 Superfund sites on the list in the U.S. *U.S. Environmental Protection Agency, Final National Priorities List, March 18, 2016*

AIR & WATER QUALITY

Air Quality Trends: Ozone

	1990	1995	2000	2005	2010	2011	2012	2013	2014
MSA[1]	0.123	0.106	0.087	0.080	0.073	0.075	0.076	0.072	0.080

Note: (1) Data covers the Los Angeles-Long Beach-Anaheim, CA Metropolitan Statistical Area—see Appendix B for areas included. The values shown are the composite ozone concentration averages among trend sites based on the highest fourth daily maximum 8-hour concentration in parts per million. These trends are based on sites having an adequate record of monitoring data during the trend period. Data from exceptional events are included.
Source: U.S. Environmental Protection Agency, Air Quality Monitoring Information, "Air Quality Trends by City, 1990-2014"

Air Quality Index

Area	Percent of Days when Air Quality was...[2]					AQI Statistics[2]	
	Good	Moderate	Unhealthy for Sensitive Groups	Unhealthy	Very Unhealthy	Maximum	Median
MSA[1]	19.7	57.8	19.5	3.0	0.0	182	67

Note: (1) Data covers the Los Angeles-Long Beach-Anaheim, CA Metropolitan Statistical Area—see Appendix B for areas included; (2) Based on 365 days with AQI data in 2015. Air Quality Index (AQI) is an index for reporting daily air quality. EPA calculates the AQI for five major air pollutants regulated by the Clean Air Act: ground-level ozone, particle pollution (aka particulate matter), carbon monoxide, sulfur dioxide, and nitrogen dioxide. The AQI runs from 0 to 500. The higher the AQI value, the greater the level of air pollution and the greater the health concern. There are six AQI categories: "Good" AQI is between 0 and 50. Air quality is considered satisfactory; "Moderate" AQI is between 51 and 100. Air quality is acceptable; "Unhealthy for Sensitive Groups" When AQI values are between 101 and 150, members of sensitive groups may experience health effects; "Unhealthy" When AQI values are between 151 and 200 everyone may begin to experience health effects; "Very Unhealthy" AQI values between 201 and 300 trigger a health alert; "Hazardous" AQI values over 300 trigger warnings of emergency conditions (not shown).
Source: U.S. Environmental Protection Agency, Air Quality Index Report, 2015

Air Quality Index Pollutants

Area	Percent of Days when AQI Pollutant was...[2]					
	Carbon Monoxide	Nitrogen Dioxide	Ozone	Sulfur Dioxide	Particulate Matter 2.5	Particulate Matter 10
MSA[1]	0.0	1.9	49.0	0.0	48.5	0.5

Note: (1) Data covers the Los Angeles-Long Beach-Anaheim, CA Metropolitan Statistical Area—see Appendix B for areas included; (2) Based on 365 days with AQI data in 2015. The Air Quality Index (AQI) is an index for reporting daily air quality. EPA calculates the AQI for five major air pollutants regulated by the Clean Air Act: ground-level ozone, particle pollution (also known as particulate matter), carbon monoxide, sulfur dioxide, and nitrogen dioxide. The AQI runs from 0 to 500. The higher the AQI value, the greater the level of air pollution and the greater the health concern.
Source: U.S. Environmental Protection Agency, Air Quality Index Report, 2015

Maximum Air Pollutant Concentrations: Particulate Matter, Ozone, CO and Lead

	Particulate Matter 10 (ug/m^3)	Particulate Matter 2.5 Wtd AM (ug/m^3)	Particulate Matter 2.5 24-Hr (ug/m^3)	Ozone (ppm)	Carbon Monoxide (ppm)	Lead (ug/m^3)
MSA[1] Level	95	12.6	35	0.097	4	0.07
NAAQS[2]	150	15	35	0.075	9	0.15
Met NAAQS[2]	Yes	Yes	Yes	No	Yes	Yes

Note: (1) Data covers the Los Angeles-Long Beach-Anaheim, CA Metropolitan Statistical Area—see Appendix B for areas included; Data from exceptional events are included; (2) National Ambient Air Quality Standards; ppm = parts per million; ug/m^3 = micrograms per cubic meter; n/a not available.
Concentrations: Particulate Matter 10 (coarse particulate)—highest second maximum 24-hour concentration; Particulate Matter 2.5 Wtd AM (fine particulate)—highest weighted annual mean concentration; Particulate Matter 2.5 24-Hour (fine particulate)—highest 98th percentile 24-hour concentration; Ozone—highest fourth daily maximum 8-hour concentration; Carbon Monoxide—highest second maximum non-overlapping 8-hour concentration; Lead—maximum running 3-month average
Source: U.S. Environmental Protection Agency, Air Quality Monitoring Information, "Air Quality Statistics by City, 2014"

Maximum Air Pollutant Concentrations: Nitrogen Dioxide and Sulfur Dioxide

	Nitrogen Dioxide AM (ppb)	Nitrogen Dioxide 1-Hr (ppb)	Sulfur Dioxide AM (ppb)	Sulfur Dioxide 1-Hr (ppb)	Sulfur Dioxide 24-Hr (ppb)
MSA[1] Level	27	69	n/a	9	n/a
NAAQS[2]	53	100	30	75	140
Met NAAQS[2]	Yes	Yes	n/a	Yes	n/a

Note: (1) Data covers the Los Angeles-Long Beach-Anaheim, CA Metropolitan Statistical Area—see Appendix B for areas included; Data from exceptional events are included; (2) National Ambient Air Quality Standards; ppm = parts per million; ug/m^3 = micrograms per cubic meter; n/a not available.
Concentrations: Nitrogen Dioxide AM—highest arithmetic mean concentration; Nitrogen Dioxide 1-Hr—highest 98th percentile 1-hour daily maximum concentration; Sulfur Dioxide AM—highest annual mean concentration; Sulfur Dioxide 1-Hr—highest 99th percentile 1-hour daily maximum concentration; Sulfur Dioxide 24-Hr—highest second maximum 24-hour concentration
Source: U.S. Environmental Protection Agency, Air Quality Monitoring Information, "Air Quality Statistics by City, 2014"

Drinking Water

Water System Name	Pop. Served	Primary Water Source Type	Violations[1]	
			Health Based	Monitoring/ Reporting
CA Water Services Co.-Palos Verdes	69,883	Purchased Surface	0	0

Note: (1) Based on violation data from January 1, 2015 to December 31, 2015 (includes unresolved violations from earlier years)

Source: U.S. Environmental Protection Agency, Office of Ground Water and Drinking Water, Safe Drinking Water Information System (based on data extracted April 29, 2016)

San Ramon, California

Background

San Ramon is located in the San Francisco Bay area, in Contra Costa County, east of Oakland along Interstate 680. With its easy access and full range of services San Ramon is one of Contra Costa County's most progressive and exciting cities.

The primary focus of the city's economy from 1850 to 1950 was agriculture. Primary products included livestock, grains, fruits, vegetables, and nuts. Agriculture is still vital to the region's economy, evidenced by the popular San Ramon Farmer's Market which recently moved to the central location of Bishop Ranch. Managed and operated by Local Roots, a San Ramon non-profit, the market is certified by the Contra Costa County Agricultural Commissioner to sell fruits, vegetables, eggs, honey, and flowers. The market provides a valuable opportunity for consumers to interact with producers.

In 1797, Mission San Jose used San Ramon land for grazing. The San Ramon Creek commemorates Ramon, the Indian who cared for the mission sheep. In 1850, Joel Harlan, Minerva Fowler, and Leo and Mary Jane Norris became the area's first permanent settlers. A church was built in 1860, a general store in 1863, and a permanent post office in 1873. In 1891 the Branch Line Railroad made its first trip in the San Ramon Valley. In the 1950s, diesel locomotives replaced steam locomotives, but service ended in 1978.

The community of San Ramon celebrates its history in a number of ways: The Museum of San Ramon Valley, housed in a restored Southern Pacific Depot from 1891, rotates exhibits from various periods in the city's history; the San Ramon Historic Foundation maintains historic farms and homesteads that are open to the public; the city's Souyen Park honors the Ohlone Indian tribes of the San Ramon Valley.

The city maintains a variety of parks, some for specific purposes: Fire Truck Park recognizes the San Ramon Valley Fire Protection District; Central Park, Bishop Ranch Regional Preserve, and the Iron Horse Regional Trail offer walking, biking and hiking trails. Limerick Park commemorates the Irish settlers who came to San Ramon in the mid-1800s, and called the area Limerick. The city was also called Brevensville and Lynchville before officially becoming San Ramon.

The city's 15 minutes of fame occurred in 1993, when the movie "Mrs. Doubtfire," was filmed in San Ramon.

San Ramon is an idyllic location for vacationing. It is home to Canyon Lakes Country Club with an 18-hole golf course, several golf clubs, and San Ramon Sports, with an indoor batting cage, a soccer arena for youth and adults, and several sports fields.

Major employers in the city are AT&T, Bank of the West, and Chevron USA Inc. Bishop Ranch is a major regional employment center which is home to over 200 companies. Over 21,000 office workers commute daily to the employment center, which employs more than 25,000 people. Thousands more jobs are expected to be created in coming years.

Average summer temperatures are in the 70s, and July is the warmest month. Average winter temperatures cool to the 40s, and the chilliest month is January. San Ramon receives more rainfall during the winter than the summer, with annual average precipitation at 23.96 inches.

The three closest airports to San Ramon are Oakland International at 25 miles, San Jose International at 34 miles, and San Francisco International at 43 miles.

Rankings

General Rankings

- The San Francisco* metro area was identified as one of America's fastest-growing areas in terms of population and economy by *Forbes.* The area ranked #7 out of 20. The 100 most populous metro areas in the U.S. were evaluated on the following criteria: estimated population growth; job growth; gross metropolitan product growth; unemployment; median salaries for college-educated workers. *Forbes, "America's Fastest-Growing Cities 2015," January 27, 2015*

Business/Finance Rankings

- The personal finance site NerdWallet analyzed 183 American metropolitan areas with populations over 250,000 and more than 15,000 businesses to rank where entrepreneurs find the most success. Criteria included area economy, annual income, housing cost, unemployment rate, and the success rate of area businesses. Oakland* ranked #19. *www.nerdwallet.com, "Best Places to Start a Business," April 27, 2015*
- TransUnion ranked the nation's metro areas by average credit score, calculated on the VantageScore system, developed by the three major credit-reporting bureaus—TransUnion, Experian, and Equifax. The Oakland* metro area was among the ten cities with the highest collective credit score, meaning that its residents posed the lowest average consumer credit risk. *www.usatoday.com, "Metro Areas' Average Credit Rating Revealed," February 7, 2013*
- Based on the U.S. Department of Labor's Occupational Information Network Data Collection Program, the Brookings Institution defined job opportunities for STEM workers at various levels of educational attainment. The Oakland* metro area was one of the ten metro areas where workers in low-education-level STEM jobs earn the lowest relative wages. *www.brookings.edu, "The Hidden Stem Economy," June 10, 2013*
- 24/7 Wall Street used Brookings Institution research on 50 advanced industries to identify the proportion of workers in the nation's largest metropolitan areas that were employed in jobs requiring knowledge in the science, technology, engineering, or math (STEM) fields. The San Francisco* metro area was #5. *247wallst.com, "15 Cities with the Most High-Tech Jobs," March 13, 2015*
- Based on metro area social media reviews, the employment opinion group Glassdoor surveyed 50 of the largest U.S. metro areas and equally weighed cost of living, hiring opportunity, and job satisfaction to compose a list of "25 Best Cities for Jobs." The San Francisco* metro area was ranked #1 in overall job satisfaction. *www.glassdoor.com, "Best Cities for Jobs," May 19, 2015*
- In a survey of economic confidence in the nation's 50 largest metropolitan areas conducted January–December 2014, the San Francisco* metro area placed #2, according to Gallup's 2014 Economic Confidence Index. *Gallup, "San Jose and San Francisco Lead in Economic Confidence," March 19, 2015*
- The Brookings Institution ranked the 100 largest metro areas in the U.S. based on income inequality. San Francisco* was ranked #3 (#1 = greatest ineqality). Criteria: the "95/20 ratio," a figure representing the income at which a household earns more than 95 percent of all other households, divided by the income at which a household earns more than only 20 percent of all other households. *Brookings Institution, "Income Inequality, 100 Largest U.S. Metro Areas, 2007-2014," January 14, 2016*
- *Forbes* ranked the largest metro areas in the U.S. in terms of the "Best Cities for Young Professionals." The San Francisco* metro area ranked #15 out of 15. Criteria: job growth; unemployment rate; median salary of college graduates age 24 to 34; cost of living; number of small businesses per capita; number of large companies; percentage of population 25 years of age and older with college degrees. *Forbes.com, "America's 15 Best Cities for Young Professionals," August 18, 2014*
- Payscale.com ranked the 20 largest metro areas in terms of wage growth. The San Francisco* metro area ranked #3. Criteria: private-sector wage growth between the 1st quarter of 2015 and the 1st quarter of 2016. *PayScale, "Wage Trends by Metro Area," 1st Quarter, 2016*

- San Francisco* was identified as one of America's most frugal metro areas by *Coupons.com*. The city ranked #1 out of 25. Criteria: online coupon usage. *Coupons.com, "Top 25 Most Frugal Cities of 2014," May 11, 2015*

- The Oakland* metro area appeared on the Milken Institute "2015 Best Performing Cities" list. Rank: #39 out of 200 large metro areas. Criteria: job growth; wage and salary growth; high-tech output growth. *Milken Institute, "Best-Performing Cities 2015," December 2015*

- *Forbes* ranked the 200 most populous metro areas to determine the nation's "Best Places for Business and Careers." The Oakland* metro area was ranked #25. Criteria: costs (business and living); job growth (past and projected); income growth; educational attainment (college and high school); projected economic growth; cultural and recreational opportunities; net migration patterns; number of highly ranked colleges. *Forbes, "The Best Places for Business and Careers 2015," July 29, 2015*

Dating/Romance Rankings

- CreditDonkey, a financial education website, sought out the ten best U.S. cities for newlyweds, considering the number of married couples, divorce rate, average credit score, and average number of hours worked per week in metro areas with a million or more residents. The San Francisco* metro area placed #9. *www.creditdonkey.com, "Study: Best Cities for Newlyweds," November 30, 2013*

Education Rankings

- The San Francisco* metro area was selected as one of the world's most inventive cities by *Forbes*. The area was ranked #3 out of 15. Criteria: patent applications per capita. *Forbes, "World's 15 Most Inventive Cities," July 9, 2013*

- Based on a Brookings Institution study, *24/7 Wall St.* identified the ten U.S. metropolitan areas with the most average patent filings per million residents between 2007 and 2011. Oakland* ranked #8. *24/7 Wall St., "America's Most Innovative Cities," February 1, 2013*

- The Oakland* metro area was selected as one of America's most innovative cities" by *The Business Insider*. The metro area was ranked #8 out of 20. Criteria: patents per capita. *The Business Insider, "The 20 Most Innovative Cities in the U.S.," February 1, 2013*

- Oakland* was identified as one of America's "smartest" metropolitan areas by *The Business Journals*. The area ranked #7 out of 10. Criteria: percentage of adults (25 and older) with high school diplomas, bachelor's degrees and graduate degrees. *The Business Journals, "Where the Brainpower Is: Exclusive U.S. Rankings, Insights," February 27, 2014*

- Personal finance website *WalletHub* analyzed the 150 largest U.S. metropolitan statistical areas to determine where the most educated Americans are choosing to settle. Criteria: education quality and attainment gap; education levels; percentage of workers with degrees; public school rankings; quality and size of each metro area's universities. San Francisco* was ranked #20 (#1 = most educated city). *www.WalletHub.com, "2015's Most and Least Educated Cities*

Environmental Rankings

- The San Francisco* metro area came in at #28 for the relative comfort of its climate on Sperling's list of "chill cities," as measured by the Sperling Heat Index. All 361 metro areas are included. Criteria included daytime high temperatures, nighttime low temperatures, dew point, and relative humidity at the high temperatures. *www.bertsperling.com, "Sperling's Chill Cities," July 18, 2013*

- Sperling's BestPlaces assessed 379 metropolitan areas of the United States for the likelihood of dangerously extreme weather events or earthquakes. In general the Southeast and South-Central regions have the highest risk of weather extremes and earthquakes, while the Pacific Northwest enjoys the lowest risk. Of the least risky metropolitan areas, the Oakland* metro area was ranked #76. *www.bestplaces.net, "Safest Places from Natural Disasters," April 2011*

- The U.S. Environmental Protection Agency (EPA) released a list of U.S. metropolitan areas with the most ENERGY STAR certified buildings in 2015. The San Francisco* metro area was ranked #3 out of 25. *U.S. Environmental Protection Agency, "Top Cities With the Most ENERGY STAR Certified Buildings in 2016," March 30, 2016*

Health/Fitness Rankings

- Analysts who tracked obesity rates in the nation's largest metro areas (populations above one million) found that the Oakland* metro area was one of the ten major metros where residents were least likely to be obese, defined as a BMI score of 30 or above. *www.gallup.com, "Boulder, Colo., Residents Still Least Likely to Be Obese," April 4, 2014*
- Analysts who tracked obesity rates in 100 of the nation's most populous areas found that the San Francisco* metro area was one of the ten communities where residents were least likely to be obese, defined as a BMI score of 30 or above. *www.gallup.com, "Colorado Springs Residents Least Likely to Be Obese," May 28, 2015*
- For each of the 50 most populous metro areas in the United States, the American College of Sports Medicine's American Fitness Index evaluated infrastructure, community assets, and policies that encourage healthy and fit lifestyles, including preventive health behaviors, levels of chronic disease conditions, health care access, and community resources and policies that support physical activity. The San Francisco* metro area ranked #4 for "community fitness." *www.americanfitnessindex.org, "ACSM American Fitness Index Health and Community Fitness Status of the 50 Largest Metropolitan Areas," May 2015*
- *Business Insider* reported Trulia's analysis of the 100 largest U.S. metro areas to identify the nation's best cities for weight loss, based on healthful food options, access to outdoor activities, weight-loss centers, gyms, and opportunities to bike or walk to work. San Francisco* ranked #1. *Businessinsider.com, "These Are the Best US Cities for Weight loss," January 17, 2013*
- The San Francisco* metro area was identified as one of the worst cities for bed bugs in America by pest control company Orkin. The area ranked #14 out of 50 based on the number of bed bug treatments Orkin performed from January to December 2015. *Orkin, "Chicago Tops Bed Bug Cities List for Fourth Year in a Row," January 13, 2016*
- San Francisco* was identified as a "2016 Spring Allergy Capital." The area ranked #80 out of 100. Three groups of factors were used to identify the most severe cities for people with allergies during the spring season: annual pollen levels; medicine utilization; access to board-certified allergists. *Asthma and Allergy Foundation of America, "Spring Allergy Capitals 2016"*
- San Francisco* was identified as a "2015 Asthma Capital." The area ranked #100 out of the nation's 100 largest metropolitan areas. Criteria: estimated prevalence; self-reported prevalence; crude death rate for asthma; annual pollen score; annual air quality; public smoking laws; number of board-certified asthma specialists; school inhaler access laws; rescue medication use; controller medication use; ER visits for asthma; uninsured rate; poverty rate. *Asthma and Allergy Foundation of America, "Asthma Capitals 2015"*
- The San Francisco* metro area ranked #30 out of 190 in The Gallup-Healthways Well-Being Index. Criteria: purpose; social well being; financial health; community and physical health. Results are based on telephone interviews with adults, aged 18 and older, living in metropolitan areas in the 50 U.S. states and the District of Columbia. *Gallup-Healthways, "State of American Well-Being," February 23, 2016*

Real Estate Rankings

- With data from RealtyTrac, Yahoo! Finance researchers listed the housing markets in which housing affordability is improving most, factoring in interest rates as well as median home prices. The San Francisco* metro area was among the least affordable housing markets. *news.yahoo.com, "10 Cities Where Ordinary People Can No Longer Afford Homes," March 5, 2014*

- The San Francisco* metro area was identified as one of the nations's 20 hottest housing markets in 2016. Criteria: listing views as an indicator of demand and median days on the market as an indicator of supply. The area ranked #1. *Realtor.com, "The 20 Hottest U.S. Real Estate Markets in February 2016," February 25, 2016*

- Oakland* was ranked #13 in the top 20 out of 266 metro areas in terms of house price appreciation in 2015 (#1 = highest rate). *Federal Housing Finance Agency, House Price Index, 4th Quarter 2015*

- The San Francisco* metro area was identified as one of the 10 best condo markets in the U.S. in 2015. The area ranked #6 out of 61 markets. Criteria: year-over-year change of median sales price of existing apartment condo-coop homes between the 4th quarter of 2014 and the 4th quarter of 2015. *National Association of Realtors®, Median Sales Price of Existing Apartment Condo-Coop Homes for Metropolitan Areas, 4th Quarter 2015*

- The San Francisco* metro area was identified as one of the 20 least affordable housing markets in the U.S. in 2015. The area ranked #4 out of 179 markets. Criteria: qualification for a mortgage loan on a typical home. *National Association of Realtors®, Affordability Index of Existing Single-Family Homes for Metropolitan Areas, 2015*

- Oakland* was ranked #213 out of 225 metro areas in terms of housing affordability in 2015 by the National Association of Home Builders (#1 = most affordable). Criteria: the share of homes sold in that area affordable to a family earning the local median income, based on standard mortgage underwriting criteria. *National Association of Home Builders®, NAHB-Wells Fargo Housing Opportunity Index, 4th Quarter 2015*

Safety Rankings

- Farmers Insurance, in partnership with Sperling's BestPlaces, ranked metro areas in the U.S. as the "Most Secure Places to Live." The San Francisco* metro area ranked #8 out of the top 20 in the large metro area category (500,000 or more residents). Criteria: economic stability; crime statistics; extreme weather; risk of natural disasters; housing depreciation; foreclosures; air quality; environmental hazards; life expectancy; motor vehicle fatalities; and employment numbers. *Farmers Insurance Group of Companies, "Most Secure U.S. Places to Live in the U.S.," June 25, 2013*

- The National Insurance Crime Bureau ranked 380 metro areas in the U.S. in terms of per capita rates of vehicle theft. The San Francisco* metro area ranked #1 (#1 = highest rate). Criteria: number of vehicle theft offenses per 100,000 inhabitants in 2014. *National Insurance Crime Bureau, "Hot Spots 2014," June 24, 2015*

Seniors/Retirement Rankings

- From its Best Cities for Successful Aging indexes, the Milken Institute generated rankings for metropolitan areas, weighing data in eight categories—health care, wellness, living arrangements, transportation, financial characteristics, education and employment opportunities, community engagement, and overall livability. The Oakland* metro area was ranked #17 overall in the large metro area category. *Milken Institute, "Best Cities for Successful Aging, 2014"*

Sports/Recreation Rankings

- According to the personal finance website NerdWallet, the San Francisco* metro area, at #5, is one of the nation's top dozen metro areas for sports fans. Criteria included the presence of all four major sports—MLB, NFL, NHL, and NBA, fan enthusiasm (as measured by game attendance), ticket affordability, and "sports culture," that is, number of sports bars. *www.nerdwallet.com, "Best Cities for Sports Fans," May 5, 2013*

Transportation Rankings

- San Francisco* was identified as one of the most congested metro areas in the U.S. The area ranked #3 out of 10. Criteria: yearly delay per auto commuter in hours. *Texas A&M Transportation Institute, "2015 Urban Mobility Scorecard," August 2015*

- The San Francisco* metro area appeared on *Forbes* list of places with the most extreme commutes. The metro area ranked #1 out of 10. Criteria: average travel time; percentage of mega commuters. Mega-commuters travel more than 90 minutes and 50 miles each way to work. *Forbes.com, "The Cities with the Most Extreme Commutes," March 5, 2013*

Miscellaneous Rankings

- The watchdog site Charity Navigator conducts an annual study of charities in the nation's major markets both to analyze statistical differences in their financial, accountability, and transparency practices and to track year-to-year variations in individual communities. The San Francisco* metro area was ranked #9 among the 30 metro markets in the rating dimension of Overall Score. *www.charitynavigator.org, "Metro Market Study 2015," June 5, 2015*

- The Harris Poll's Happiness Index survey revealed that of the top ten U.S. markets, the San Francisco* metro area residents ranked #10 in happiness. Criteria included strong assent to positive statements and strong disagreement with negative ones, and degree of agreement with a series of statements about respondents' personal relationships and general outlook. *www.harrisinteractive.com, "Dallas/Fort Worth Is "Happiest" City among America's Top Ten Markets," September 4, 2013*

- Mars Chocolate North America, the makers of COMBOS®, in partnership with Sperling's BestPlaces, ranked 50 major metro areas in terms of their "manliness." The Oakland* metro area ranked #48. Criteria: number of professional sports teams; number of nearby NASCAR tracks and racing events; manly lifestyle; concentration of manly retail stores; manly occupations per capita; salty snack sales; "Board of Manliness" rankings. *Mars Chocolate North America, "America's Manliest Cities 2012"*

- The National Alliance to End Homelessness ranked the 100 most populous metro areas with the highest rate of homelessness. The San Francisco* metro area ranked #12. Criteria: number of homeless people per 10,000 population in 2011. *National Alliance to End Homelessness, The State of Homelessness in America 2012*

San Ramon is located within the San Francisco-Oakland-Hayward, CA Metropolitan Statistical Area and the Oakland-Hayward-Berkeley, CA Metropolitan Division.

Business Environment

CITY FINANCES

City Government Finances

Component	2012 ($000)	2012 ($ per capita)
Total Revenues	74,213	1,028
Total Expenditures	75,060	1,040
Debt Outstanding	108,021	1,497
Cash and Securities[1]	104,182	1,444

Note: (1) Cash and security holdings of a government at the close of its fiscal year, including those of its dependent agencies, utilities, and liquor stores.
Source: U.S Census Bureau, State & Local Government Finances 2012

City Government Revenue by Source

Source	2012 ($000)	2012 ($ per capita)
General Revenue		
From Federal Government	0	0
From State Government	3,706	51
From Local Governments	0	0
Taxes		
Property	25,331	351
Sales and Gross Receipts	14,128	195
Personal Income	0	0
Corporate Income	0	0
Motor Vehicle License	0	0
Other Taxes	1,652	22
Current Charges	21,513	298
Liquor Store	0	0
Utility	0	0
Employee Retirement	0	0

Source: U.S Census Bureau, State & Local Government Finances 2012

City Government Expenditures by Function

Function	2012 ($000)	2012 ($ per capita)	2012 (%)
General Direct Expenditures			
Air Transportation	0	0	0.0
Corrections	0	0	0.0
Education	0	0	0.0
Employment Security Administration	0	0	0.0
Financial Administration	1,324	18	1.7
Fire Protection	0	0	0.0
General Public Buildings	175	2	0.2
Governmental Administration, Other	8,775	121	11.6
Health	0	0	0.0
Highways	8,467	117	11.2
Hospitals	0	0	0.0
Housing and Community Development	5,909	81	7.8
Interest on General Debt	5,343	74	7.1
Judicial and Legal	0	0	0.0
Libraries	412	5	0.5
Parking	0	0	0.0
Parks and Recreation	15,522	215	20.6
Police Protection	16,098	223	21.4
Public Welfare	0	0	0.0
Sewerage	0	0	0.0
Solid Waste Management	0	0	0.0
Veterans' Services	0	0	0.0
Liquor Store	0	0	0.0
Utility	0	0	0.0
Employee Retirement	0	0	0.0

Source: U.S Census Bureau, State & Local Government Finances 2012

DEMOGRAPHICS

Population Growth

Area	1990 Census	2000 Census	2010 Census	2014* Estimate	Population Growth (%) 1990-2014	Population Growth (%) 2010-2014
City	35,463	44,722	72,148	73,826	108.2	2.3
MSA[1]	3,686,592	4,123,740	4,335,391	4,466,251	21.1	3.0
U.S.	248,709,873	281,421,906	308,745,538	314,107,084	26.3	1.7

Note: (1) Figures cover the San Francisco-Oakland-Hayward, CA Metropolitan Statistical Area—see Appendix B for areas included; (*) 2010-2014 5-year estimated population
Source: U.S. Census Bureau, 1990 Census, Census 2000, Census 2010, 2010-2014 American Community Survey 5-Year Estimates

Household Size

Area	Persons in Household (%)							Average Household Size
	One	Two	Three	Four	Five	Six	Seven or More	
City	18.6	26.0	19.0	27.3	5.6	2.6	0.6	2.91
MSA[1]	28.1	31.4	16.2	14.0	5.8	2.3	1.7	2.67
U.S.	27.5	33.5	15.8	13.1	6.0	2.3	1.4	2.64

Note: (1) Figures cover the San Francisco-Oakland-Hayward, CA Metropolitan Statistical Area—see Appendix B for areas included
Source: U.S. Census Bureau, 2010-2014 American Community Survey 5-Year Estimates

Race

Area	White Alone[2] (%)	Black Alone[2] (%)	Asian Alone[2] (%)	AIAN[3] Alone[2] (%)	NHOPI[4] Alone[2] (%)	Other Race Alone[2] (%)	Two or More Races (%)
City	49.3	2.3	40.5	0.3	0.4	1.8	5.5
MSA[1]	54.0	8.0	24.0	0.5	0.7	7.5	5.4
U.S.	73.8	12.6	5.0	0.8	0.2	4.7	2.9

Note: (1) Figures cover the San Francisco-Oakland-Hayward, CA Metropolitan Statistical Area—see Appendix B for areas included; (2) Alone is defined as not being in combination with one or more other races; (3) American Indian and Alaska Native; (4) Native Hawaiian and Other Pacific Islander
Source: U.S. Census Bureau, 2010-2014 American Community Survey 5-Year Estimates

Hispanic or Latino Origin

Area	Total (%)	Mexican (%)	Puerto Rican (%)	Cuban (%)	Other (%)
City	8.6	5.1	0.4	0.1	3.1
MSA[1]	21.8	14.8	0.6	0.2	6.2
U.S.	16.9	10.8	1.6	0.6	3.8

Note: Persons of Hispanic or Latino origin can be of any race; (1) Figures cover the San Francisco-Oakland-Hayward, CA Metropolitan Statistical Area—see Appendix B for areas included
Source: U.S. Census Bureau, 2010-2014 American Community Survey 5-Year Estimates

Ancestry

Area	German	Irish	English	American	Italian	Polish	French[2]	Scottish	Dutch
City	8.7	8.2	6.9	3.7	6.7	1.2	1.9	1.5	0.7
MSA[1]	8.5	7.9	6.3	2.6	5.3	1.5	2.0	1.6	0.9
U.S.	14.9	10.8	8.0	7.1	5.5	3.0	2.7	1.7	1.4

Note: Figures are the percentage of the total population reporting a particular ancestry. The nine most commonly reported ancestries in the U.S. are shown. Figures include multiple ancestries (e.g. if a person reported being Irish and Italian, they were included in both columns); (1) Figures cover the San Francisco-Oakland-Hayward, CA Metropolitan Statistical Area—see Appendix B for areas included; (2) Excludes Basque
Source: U.S. Census Bureau, 2010-2014 American Community Survey 5-Year Estimates

Foreign-Born Population

Area	Percent of Population Born in								
	Any Foreign Country	Asia	Mexico	Europe	Carribean	Central America[2]	South America	Africa	Canada
City	32.1	25.3	0.8	2.8	0.2	0.2	1.1	0.5	0.8
MSA[1]	29.9	16.3	5.6	2.9	0.2	2.5	0.9	0.6	0.4
U.S.	13.1	3.8	3.7	1.5	1.2	1.0	0.9	0.6	0.3

Note: (1) Figures cover the San Francisco-Oakland-Hayward, CA Metropolitan Statistical Area—see Appendix B for areas included; (2) Excludes Mexico.
Source: U.S. Census Bureau, 2010-2014 American Community Survey 5-Year Estimates

Marital Status

Area	Never Married	Now Married[2]	Separated	Widowed	Divorced
City	23.7	65.3	1.1	3.4	6.4
MSA[1]	35.9	47.7	1.9	5.2	9.4
U.S.	32.5	48.4	2.2	5.9	10.9

Note: Figures are percentages and cover the population 15 years of age and older; (1) Figures cover the San Francisco-Oakland-Hayward, CA Metropolitan Statistical Area—see Appendix B for areas included; (2) Excludes separated
Source: U.S. Census Bureau, 2010-2014 American Community Survey 5-Year Estimates

Disability Status

Area	All Ages	Under 18 Years Old	18 to 64 Years Old	65 Years and Over
City	4.6	1.8	2.9	30.8
MSA[1]	9.5	2.7	6.9	33.3
U.S.	12.3	4.1	10.2	36.3

Note: Figures show percent of the civilian noninstitutionalized population that reported having a disability. Disability status is determined from from six types of difficulty: vision, hearing, cognitive, ambulatory, self-care, and independent living. For children under 5 years old, hearing and vision difficulty are used to determine disability status. For children between the ages of 5 and 14, disability status is determined from hearing, vision, cognitive, ambulatory, and self-care difficulties. For people aged 15 years and older, they are considered to have a disability if they have difficulty with any one of the six difficulty types; (1) Figures cover the San Francisco-Oakland-Hayward, CA Metropolitan Statistical Area—see Appendix B for areas included.
Source: U.S. Census Bureau, 2010-2014 American Community Survey 5-Year Estimates

Age

Area	Percent of Population									Median Age
	Under Age 5	Age 5–19	Age 20–34	Age 35–44	Age 45–54	Age 55–64	Age 65–74	Age 75–84	Age 85+	
City	6.4	25.4	13.7	19.5	17.2	9.3	5.3	2.3	0.9	37.5
MSA[1]	5.8	17.3	21.6	14.8	14.7	12.5	7.3	4.0	2.0	38.6
U.S.	6.4	19.9	20.6	13.0	14.1	12.3	7.6	4.3	1.9	37.4

Note: (1) Figures cover the San Francisco-Oakland-Hayward, CA Metropolitan Statistical Area—see Appendix B for areas included
Source: U.S. Census Bureau, 2010-2014 American Community Survey 5-Year Estimates

Gender

Area	Males	Females	Males per 100 Females
City	36,512	37,314	97.9
MSA[1]	2,202,384	2,263,867	97.3
U.S.	154,515,159	159,591,925	96.8

Note: (1) Figures cover the San Francisco-Oakland-Hayward, CA Metropolitan Statistical Area—see Appendix B for areas included
Source: U.S. Census Bureau, 2010-2014 American Community Survey 5-Year Estimates

Religious Groups by Family

Area	Catholic	Baptist	Non-Den.	Methodist[2]	Lutheran	LDS[3]	Pente-costal	Presby-terian[4]	Muslim[5]	Judaism
MSA[1]	20.7	2.5	2.4	1.9	0.5	1.5	1.2	1.1	1.2	0.8
U.S.	19.1	9.3	4.0	4.0	2.3	2.0	1.9	1.6	0.8	0.7

Note: Figures are the number of adherents as a percentage of the total population; (1) Figures cover the San Francisco-Oakland-Fremont, CA Metropolitan Statistical Area—see Appendix B for areas included; (2) Methodist/Pietist; (3) Latter Day Saints; (4) Reformed; (5) Figures are estimates
Source: Association of Statisticians of American Religious Bodies, 2010 U.S. Religion Census: Religious Congregations & Membership Study

Religious Groups by Tradition

Area	Catholic	Evangelical Protestant	Mainline Protestant	Other Tradition	Black Protestant	Orthodox
MSA[1]	20.7	6.1	3.8	5.2	1.0	0.6
U.S.	19.1	16.2	7.3	4.3	1.6	0.3

Note: Figures are the number of adherents as a percentage of the total population; (1) Figures cover the San Francisco-Oakland-Fremont, CA Metropolitan Statistical Area—see Appendix B for areas included
Source: Association of Statisticians of American Religious Bodies, 2010 U.S. Religion Census: Religious Congregations & Membership Study

ECONOMY

Gross Metropolitan Product

Area	2013	2014	2015	2016	Rank[2]
MSA[1]	388.2	408.6	426.9	451.0	7

Note: Figures are in billions of dollars; (1) Figures cover the San Francisco-Oakland-Hayward, CA Metropolitan Statistical Area—see Appendix B for areas included; (2) Rank is based on 2016 data and ranges from 1 to 381
Source: The U.S. Conference of Mayors, U.S. Metro Economies: GMP and Employment 2014-2016, June 2015

Economic Growth

Area	2011-13 (%)	2014 (%)	2015 (%)	2016 (%)	Rank[2]
MSA[1]	4.2	3.8	3.2	3.7	27
U.S.	2.2	2.4	2.3	2.9	–

Note: Figures are real gross metropolitan product (GMP) growth rates and represent annual average percent change; (1) Figures cover the San Francisco-Oakland-Hayward, CA Metropolitan Statistical Area—see Appendix B for areas included; (2) Rank is based on 2016 data and ranges from 1 to 381
Source: The U.S. Conference of Mayors, U.S. Metro Economies: GMP and Employment 2014-2016, June 2015

Metropolitan Area Exports

Area	2009	2010	2011	2012	2013	2014	Rank[2]
MSA[1]	16,040.3	21,355.4	23,573.7	23,031.6	25,305.2	26,863.6	10

Note: Figures are in millions of dollars; (1) Figures cover the San Francisco-Oakland-Hayward, CA Metropolitan Statistical Area—see Appendix B for areas included; (2) Rank is based on 2014 data and ranges from 1 to 385
Source: U.S. Department of Commerce, International Trade Administration, Office of Trade & Industry Information, Manufacturing & Services, data extracted March 10, 2016

Building Permits

Area	Single-Family			Multi-Family			Total		
	2014	2015p	Pct. Chg.	2014	2015p	Pct. Chg.	2014	2015p	Pct. Chg.
City	0	7	-	48	53	10.4	48	60	25.0
MSA[1]	3,716	4,595	23.7	6,285	8,171	30.0	10,001	12,766	27.6
U.S.	640,300	690,800	7.9	411,800	487,600	18.4	1,052,100	1,178,400	12.0

Note: (1) Figures cover the San Francisco-Oakland-Hayward, CA Metropolitan Statistical Area—see Appendix B for areas included; Figures represent new, privately-owned housing units authorized (unadjusted data); All permit data are based on estimates with imputation; (p) preliminary data.
Source: U.S. Census Bureau, Manufacturing, Mining, and Construction Statistics, Building Permits, 2014, 2015

Bankruptcy Filings

Area	Business Filings			Nonbusiness Filings		
	2014	2015	% Chg.	2014	2015	% Chg.
Contra Costa County	104	93	-10.6	2,467	1,850	-25.0
U.S.	26,983	24,735	-8.3	909,812	819,760	-9.9

Note: Business filings include Chapter 7, Chapter 11, Chapter 12, and Chapter 13; Nonbusiness filings include Chapter 7, Chapter 11, and Chapter 13
Source: Administrative Office of the U.S. Courts, Business and Nonbusiness Bankruptcy, County Cases Commenced by Chapter of the Bankruptcy Code, During the 12- Month Period Ending December 31, 2014 and Business and Nonbusiness Bankruptcy, County Cases Commenced by Chapter of the Bankruptcy Code, During the 12- Month Period Ending December 31, 2015

Housing Vacancy Rates

Area	Gross Vacancy Rate[2] (%)			Year-Round Vacancy Rate[3] (%)			Rental Vacancy Rate[4] (%)			Homeowner Vacancy Rate[5] (%)		
	2013	2014	2015	2013	2014	2015	2013	2014	2015	2013	2014	2015
MSA[1]	6.5	5.9	5.7	6.4	5.9	5.7	3.9	3.2	3.6	1.1	0.4	0.7
U.S.	13.6	13.4	12.9	10.7	10.4	10.0	8.3	7.6	7.1	2.0	1.9	1.8

Note: (1) Figures cover the San Francisco-Oakland-Hayward, CA Metropolitan Statistical Area—see Appendix B for areas included; (2) The percentage of the total housing inventory that is vacant; (3) The percentage of the housing inventory (excluding seasonal units) that is year-round vacant; (4) The percentage of rental inventory that is vacant for rent; (5) The percentage of homeowner inventory that is vacant for sale
Source: U.S. Census Bureau, Housing Vacancies and Homeownership Annual Statistics: 2015

INCOME

Income

Area	Per Capita ($)	Median Household ($)	Average Household ($)
City	51,569	129,062	149,528
MSA[1]	42,540	80,008	112,073
U.S.	28,555	53,482	74,596

Note: (1) Figures cover the San Francisco-Oakland-Hayward, CA Metropolitan Statistical Area—see Appendix B for areas included
Source: U.S. Census Bureau, 2010-2014 American Community Survey 5-Year Estimates

Household Income Distribution

Area	Percent of Households Earning							
	Under $15,000	$15,000 -24,999	$25,000 -34,999	$35,000 -49,999	$50,000 -74,999	$75,000 -99,000	$100,000 -149,999	$150,000 and up
City	2.3	3.0	4.1	5.8	9.3	10.8	22.5	42.3
MSA[1]	9.2	7.2	6.7	9.6	14.8	11.8	17.5	23.3
U.S.	12.5	10.7	10.2	13.5	17.8	12.2	13.0	10.0

Note: (1) Figures cover the San Francisco-Oakland-Hayward, CA Metropolitan Statistical Area—see Appendix B for areas included
Source: U.S. Census Bureau, 2010-2014 American Community Survey 5-Year Estimates

Poverty Rate

Area	All Ages	Under 18 Years Old	18 to 64 Years Old	65 Years and Over
City	3.6	3.5	3.6	4.3
MSA[1]	11.3	13.5	11.1	9.0
U.S.	15.6	21.9	14.6	9.4

Note: Figures are percentage of people whose income during the past 12 months was below the poverty level; (1) Figures cover the San Francisco-Oakland-Hayward, CA Metropolitan Statistical Area—see Appendix B for areas included
Source: U.S. Census Bureau, 2010-2014 American Community Survey 5-Year Estimates

EMPLOYMENT

Labor Force and Employment

Area	Civilian Labor Force			Workers Employed		
	Dec. 2014	Dec. 2015	% Chg.	Dec. 2014	Dec. 2015	% Chg.
City	39,376	39,722	0.8	37,986	38,521	1.4
MD[1]	1,361,975	1,371,421	0.6	1,292,276	1,310,864	1.4
U.S.	155,521,000	157,245,000	1.1	147,190,000	149,703,000	1.7

Note: Data is not seasonally adjusted and covers workers 16 years of age and older; (1) Figures cover the Oakland-Hayward-Berkeley, CA Metropolitan Division—see Appendix B for areas included
Source: Bureau of Labor Statistics, Local Area Unemployment Statistics

Unemployment Rate

Area	2015											
	Jan.	Feb.	Mar.	Apr.	May	Jun.	Jul.	Aug.	Sep.	Oct.	Nov.	Dec.
City	3.8	3.5	3.3	3.1	3.2	3.3	3.5	3.3	2.9	3.1	3.1	3.0
MD[1]	5.5	5.1	4.8	4.5	4.7	4.7	5.1	4.8	4.3	4.6	4.5	4.4
U.S.	6.1	5.8	5.6	5.1	5.3	5.5	5.6	5.2	4.9	4.8	4.8	4.8

Note: Data is not seasonally adjusted and covers workers 16 years of age and older; (1) Figures cover the Oakland-Hayward-Berkeley, CA Metropolitan Division—see Appendix B for areas included
Source: Bureau of Labor Statistics, Local Area Unemployment Statistics

Employment by Occupation

Occupation Classification	City (%)	MSA[1] (%)	U.S. (%)
Management, Business, Science, and Arts	62.5	46.8	36.4
Natural Resources, Construction, and Maintenance	3.9	6.2	9.0
Production, Transportation, and Material Moving	3.5	7.5	12.1
Sales and Office	20.9	22.4	24.4
Service	9.1	17.2	18.2

Note: Figures cover employed civilians 16 years of age and older; (1) Figures cover the San Francisco-Oakland-Hayward, CA Metropolitan Statistical Area—see Appendix B for areas included
Source: U.S. Census Bureau, 2010-2014 American Community Survey 5-Year Estimates

Employment by Industry

Sector	MD[1]		U.S.
	Number of Employees	Percent of Total	Percent of Total
Construction	65,100	5.8	4.5
Education and Health Services	181,300	16.2	15.7
Financial Activities	49,000	4.3	5.7
Government	170,200	15.2	15.5
Information	22,900	2.0	1.9
Leisure and Hospitality	107,500	9.6	10.4
Manufacturing	88,600	7.9	8.6
Mining and Logging	900	<0.1	0.5
Other Services	38,000	3.4	3.9
Professional and Business Services	183,200	16.4	13.9
Retail Trade	120,600	10.8	11.3
Transportation, Warehousing, and Utilities	40,700	3.6	3.9
Wholesale Trade	48,500	4.3	4.1

Note: Figures are non-farm employment as of December 2015. Figures are not seasonally adjusted and include workers 16 years of age and older; (1) Figures cover the Oakland-Hayward-Berkeley, CA Metropolitan Division—see Appendix B for areas included
Source: Bureau of Labor Statistics, Current Employment Statistics, Employment, Hours, and Earnings

Occupations with Greatest Projected Employment Growth: 2012 – 2022

Occupation[1]	2012 Employment	2022 Projected Employment	Numeric Employment Change	Percent Employment Change
Personal Care Aides	386,900	587,200	200,300	51.8
Combined Food Preparation and Serving Workers, Including Fast Food	286,000	362,400	76,400	26.7
Retail Salespersons	468,400	528,100	59,700	12.7
Laborers and Freight, Stock, and Material Movers, Hand	270,500	322,300	51,800	19.1
Waiters and Waitresses	246,100	290,300	44,200	18.0
Registered Nurses	254,500	297,400	42,900	16.9
General and Operations Managers	253,800	295,700	41,900	16.5
Secretaries and Administrative Assistants, Except Legal, Medical, and Executive	212,800	250,100	37,300	17.5
Cashiers	357,800	392,600	34,800	9.7
Cooks, Restaurant	116,900	150,600	33,700	28.8

Note: Projections cover California; (1) Sorted by numeric employment change
Source: www.projectionscentral.com, State Occupational Projections, 2012–2022 Long-Term Projections

Fastest Growing Occupations: 2012 – 2022

Occupation[1]	2012 Employment	2022 Projected Employment	Numeric Employment Change	Percent Employment Change
Economists	3,100	5,100	2,000	64.5
Helpers—Brickmasons, Blockmasons, Stonemasons, and Tile and Marble Setters	2,900	4,600	1,700	58.6
Brickmasons and Blockmasons	5,100	8,000	2,900	56.9
Insulation Workers, Floor, Ceiling, and Wall	1,600	2,500	900	56.3
Stonemasons	1,100	1,700	600	54.5
Insulation Workers, Mechanical	1,100	1,700	600	54.5
Personal Care Aides	386,900	587,200	200,300	51.8
Foresters	1,200	1,800	600	50.0
Terrazzo Workers and Finishers	1,100	1,600	500	45.5
Mechanical Door Repairers	1,100	1,600	500	45.5

Note: Projections cover California; (1) Sorted by percent employment change and excludes occupations with numeric employment change less than 100
Source: www.projectionscentral.com, State Occupational Projections, 2012–2022 Long-Term Projections

Average Wages

Occupation	$/Hr.	Occupation	$/Hr.
Accountants and Auditors	41.65	Maids and Housekeeping Cleaners	15.77
Automotive Mechanics	25.00	Maintenance and Repair Workers	21.70
Bookkeepers	22.97	Marketing Managers	79.92
Carpenters	30.64	Nuclear Medicine Technologists	55.63
Cashiers	12.48	Nurses, Licensed Practical	28.78
Clerks, General Office	18.66	Nurses, Registered	60.05
Clerks, Receptionists/Information	16.89	Nursing Assistants	16.42
Clerks, Shipping/Receiving	17.62	Packers and Packagers, Hand	11.99
Computer Programmers	45.15	Physical Therapists	47.88
Computer Systems Analysts	45.26	Postal Service Mail Carriers	26.11
Computer User Support Specialists	30.35	Real Estate Brokers	44.42
Cooks, Restaurant	11.82	Retail Salespersons	14.35
Dentists	94.70	Sales Reps., Exc. Tech./Scientific	33.64
Electrical Engineers	53.69	Sales Reps., Tech./Scientific	48.56
Electricians	37.97	Secretaries, Exc. Legal/Med./Exec.	20.82
Financial Managers	72.46	Security Guards	14.78
First-Line Supervisors/Managers, Sales	23.00	Surgeons	118.49
Food Preparation Workers	11.41	Teacher Assistants*	15.50
General and Operations Managers	66.83	Teachers, Elementary School*	35.79
Hairdressers/Cosmetologists	14.25	Teachers, Secondary School*	35.54
Internists	102.30	Telemarketers	15.39
Janitors and Cleaners	15.37	Truck Drivers, Heavy/Tractor-Trailer	22.83
Landscaping/Groundskeeping Workers	15.75	Truck Drivers, Light/Delivery Svcs.	19.08
Lawyers	75.13	Waiters and Waitresses	13.20

Note: Wage data covers the Oakland-Fremont-Hayward, CA Metropolitan Division—see Appendix B for areas included; (*) Hourly wages for elementary/secondary school teachers and teacher assistants were calculated by the editors from annual wage data based on a 40 hour work week; n/a not available.
Source: Bureau of Labor Statistics, Metro Area Occupational Employment and Wage Estimates, May 2015

TAXES

State Corporate Income Tax Rates

State	Tax Rate (%)	Income Brackets ($)	Num. of Brackets	Financial Institution Tax Rate (%)[a]	Federal Income Tax Ded.
California	8.84 (c)	Flat rate	1	10.84 (c)	No

Note: Tax rates as of January 1, 2016; (a) Rates listed are the corporate income tax rate applied to financial institutions or excise taxes based on income. Some states have other taxes based upon the value of deposits or shares; (c) Minimum tax is $800 in California, $100 in District of Columbia, $50 in North Dakota (banks), $500 in Rhode Island, $200 per location in South Dakota (banks), $100 in Utah, $250 in Vermont.
Source: Federation of Tax Administrators, "State Corporate Income Tax Rates, 2016"

State Individual Income Tax Rates

State	Tax Rate (%)	Income Brackets ($)	Num. of Brackets	Personal Exempt. ($)[1]		Fed. Inc. Tax Ded.
				Single	Dependents	
California (a)	1.0 - 12.3 (f)	7,850- 526,443 (b)	9	109 (c)	337 (c)	No

Note: Tax rates as of January 1, 2016; Local- and county-level taxes are not included; n/a not applicable; (1) Married joint filers generally receive double the single exemption; (a) 18 states have statutory provision for automatically adjusting to the rate of inflation the dollar values of the income tax brackets, standard deductions, and/or personal exemptions. Massachusetts, Michigan, and Nebraska index the personal exemptiononly. Oregon does not index the income brackets for $125,000 and over. Maine has suspended indexing for 2014 and 2015; (b) For joint returns, taxes are twice the tax on half the couple's income; (c) The personal exemption takes the form of a tax credit instead of a deduction; (f) California imposes an additional 1% tax on taxable income over $1 million, making the maximum rate 13.3% over $1 million.
Source: Federation of Tax Administrators, "State Individual Income Tax Rates, 2016"

Various State and Local Tax Rates

State	State and Local Sales and Use (%)	State Sales and Use (%)	Gasoline[1] (¢/gal.)	Cigarette[2] ($/pack)	Spirits[3] ($/gal.)	Wine[4] ($/gal.)	Beer[5] ($/gal.)
California	8.50	7.50 (b)	40.62	0.87	3.30 (f)	0.20 (l)	0.08

Note: All tax rates as of January 1, 2016; (1) The American Petroleum Institute has developed a methodology for determining the average tax rate on a gallon of fuel. Rates may include any of the following: excise taxes, environmental fees, storage tank fees, other fees or taxes, general sales tax, and local taxes. In states where gasoline is subject to the general sales tax, or where the fuel tax is based on the average sale price, the average rate determined by API is sensitive to changes in the price of gasoline. States that fully or partially apply general sales taxes to gasoline: CA, CO, GA, IL, IN, MI, NY; (2) The federal excise tax of $1.0066 per pack and local taxes are not included; (3) Rates are those applicable to off-premise sales of 40% alcohol by volume (a.b.v.) distilled spirits in 750ml containers. Local excise taxes are excluded; (4) Rates are those applicable to off-premise sales of 11% a.b.v. non-carbonated wine in 750ml containers; (5) Rates are those applicable to off-premise sales of 4.7% a.b.v. beer in 12 ounce containers; (b) Three states levy mandatory, statewide local add-on sales taxes at the state level: California (1%), Utah (1.25%), and Virginia (1%). We include these in their state sales tax rates; (f) Different rates are also applicable according to alcohol content, place of production, size of container, or place purchased (on- or off-premise or onboard airlines); (l) Different rates also applicable according to alcohol content, place of production, size of container, place purchased (on- or off-premise or on board airlines) or type of wine (carbonated, vermouth, etc.).
Source: Tax Foundation, 2016 Facts & Figures: How Does Your State Compare?

State Business Tax Climate Index Rankings

State	Overall Rank	Corporate Tax Rank	Individual Income Tax Rank	Sales Tax Rank	Unemployment Insurance Tax Rank	Property Tax Rank
California	48	35	50	40	13	13

Note: The index is a measure of how each state's tax laws affect economic performance. The lower the rank, the more favorable a state's tax system is for business. States without a given tax are given a ranking of 1. The scores/rankings for the District of Columbia do not affect other states. The 2016 index represents the tax climate as of July 1, 2015 (the beginning of Fiscal Year 2016).
Source: Tax Foundation, State Business Tax Climate Index 2016

TRANSPORTATION

Means of Transportation to Work

Area	Car/Truck/Van		Public Transportation			Bicycle	Walked	Other Means	Worked at Home
	Drove Alone	Car-pooled	Bus	Subway	Railroad				
City	75.8	7.5	0.7	4.2	0.6	0.3	1.8	1.2	8.1
MSA[1]	60.6	10.1	7.6	6.1	1.0	1.9	4.4	2.3	6.1
U.S.	76.4	9.6	2.6	1.8	0.6	0.6	2.8	1.3	4.4

Note: Figures are percentages and cover workers 16 years of age and older; (1) Figures cover the San Francisco-Oakland-Hayward, CA Metropolitan Statistical Area—see Appendix B for areas included
Source: U.S. Census Bureau, 2010-2014 American Community Survey 5-Year Estimates

Travel Time to Work

Area	Less Than 10 Minutes	10 to 19 Minutes	20 to 29 Minutes	30 to 44 Minutes	45 to 59 Minutes	60 to 89 Minutes	90 Minutes or More
City	9.6	25.5	12.8	18.2	14.7	15.3	4.0
MSA[1]	7.8	24.9	19.1	24.1	11.1	10.0	3.0
U.S.	13.3	29.6	21.0	20.2	7.7	5.7	2.6

Note: Figures are percentages and include workers 16 years old and over; (1) Figures cover the San Francisco-Oakland-Hayward, CA Metropolitan Statistical Area—see Appendix B for areas included
Source: U.S. Census Bureau, 2010-2014 American Community Survey 5-Year Estimates

Freeway Travel Time Index

Area	1985	1990	1995	2000	2005	2010	2014
Urban Area Rank[1,2]	2	2	2	2	2	2	2
Urban Area Index[1]	1.30	1.32	1.36	1.38	1.40	1.38	1.41
Average Index[3]	1.09	1.11	1.14	1.17	1.20	1.19	1.20

Note: Freeway Travel Time Index—the ratio of travel time in the peak period to the travel time at free-flow conditions. For example, a value of 1.30 indicates a 20-minute free-flow trip takes 26 minutes in the peak (20 minutes x 1.30 = 26 minutes); (1) Covers the San Francisco-Oakland CA urban area; (2) Rank is based on 101 urban areas (#1 = highest travel time index); (3) Average of 101 urban areas
Source: Texas Transportation Institute, 2015 Urban Mobility Scorecard, August 2015

Freeway Commuter Stress Index

Area	1985	1990	1995	2000	2005	2010	2014
Urban Area Rank[1,2]	2	2	2	2	2	2	2
Urban Area Index[1]	1.45	1.48	1.52	1.54	1.56	1.54	1.57
Average Index[3]	1.13	1.16	1.19	1.22	1.25	1.24	1.25

Note: The Freeway Commuter Stress Index is the same as the Freeway Travel Time Index (see table above) except that it includes only the travel in the peak directions during the peak periods; the TTI includes travel in all directions during the peak period. Thus, the CSI is more indicative of the work trip experienced by each commuter on a daily basis. (1) Covers the San Francisco-Oakland CA urban area; (2) Rank is based on 101 urban areas (#1 = highest stress index); (3) Average of 101 urban areas

Source: Texas Transportation Institute, 2015 Urban Mobility Scorecard, August 2015

Living Environment

COST OF LIVING

Cost of Living Index

Composite Index	Groceries	Housing	Utilities	Trans-portation	Health Care	Misc. Goods/ Services
147.2	128.5	228.0	106.6	124.5	114.4	110.5

Note: The Cost of Living Index measures regional differences in the cost of consumer goods and services, excluding taxes and non-consumer expenditures, for professional and managerial households in the top income quintile. It is based on more than 50,000 prices covering almost 60 different items for which prices are collected three times a year by chambers of commerce, economic development organizations or university applied economic centers in each participating urban area. The numbers shown should be read as a percentage above or below the national average of 100. For example, a value of 115.4 in the groceries column indicates that grocery prices are 15.4% higher than the national average. Small differences in the index numbers should not be interpreted as significant; Figures cover the Oakland CA urban area.
Source: The Council for Community and Economic Research, ACCRA Cost of Living Index, 2015

Grocery Prices

Area[1]	T-Bone Steak ($/pound)	Frying Chicken ($/pound)	Whole Milk ($/half gal.)	Eggs ($/dozen)	Orange Juice ($/64 oz.)	Coffee ($/11.5 oz.)
City[2]	11.54	2.28	2.75	3.66	4.75	5.98
Avg.	10.99	1.43	2.25	2.26	3.58	4.48
Min.	7.16	0.98	1.30	1.35	2.88	2.98
Max.	14.13	2.43	3.85	4.81	6.39	7.56

Note: (1) Values for the local area are compared with the average, minimum and maximum values for all 292 areas in the Cost of Living Index; (2) Figures cover the Oakland CA urban area; **T-Bone Steak** *(price per pound);* **Frying Chicken** *(price per pound, whole fryer);* **Whole Milk** *(half gallon carton);* **Eggs** *(price per dozen, Grade A, large);* **Orange Juice** *(64 oz. Tropicana or Florida Natural);* **Coffee** *(11.5 oz. can, vacuum-packed, Maxwell House, Hills Bros, or Folgers).*
Source: The Council for Community and Economic Research, ACCRA Cost of Living Index, 2015

Housing and Utility Costs

Area[1]	New Home Price ($)	Apartment Rent ($/month)	All Electric ($/month)	Part Electric ($/month)	Other Energy ($/month)	Telephone ($/month)
City[2]	747,967	1,912		129.66	75.31	24.33
Avg.	312,874	945	179.30	95.07	72.96	28.11
Min.	178,682	479	116.28	43.14	26.46	10.01
Max.	1,472,476	3,984	504.25	189.44	421.11	43.06

Note: (1) Values for the local area are compared with the average, minimum and maximum values for all 292 areas in the Cost of Living Index; (2) Figures cover the Oakland CA urban area; **New Home Price** *(2,400 sf living area, 8,000 sf lot, in urban area with full utilities);* **Apartment Rent** *(950 sf 2 bedroom/1.5 or 2 bath, unfurnished, excluding all utilities except water);* **All Electric** *(average monthly cost for an all-electric home);* **Part Electric** *(average monthly cost for a part-electric home);* **Other Energy** *(average monthly cost for natural gas, fuel oil, coal, wood, and any other forms of energy except electricity);* **Telephone** *(price includes basic monthly rate for a private residential line plus additional local usage charges incurred by a family of four).*
Source: The Council for Community and Economic Research, ACCRA Cost of Living Index, 2015

Health Care, Transportation, and Other Costs

Area[1]	Doctor ($/visit)	Dentist ($/visit)	Optometrist ($/visit)	Gasoline ($/gallon)	Beauty Salon ($/visit)	Men's Shirt ($)
City[2]	123.63	113.02	116.21	3.13	55.17	35.17
Avg.	105.15	89.02	99.78	2.38	35.30	28.10
Min.	66.87	56.09	48.53	1.95	18.91	13.38
Max.	182.34	150.36	228.33	4.09	67.91	63.80

Note: (1) Values for the local area are compared with the average, minimum and maximum values for all 292 areas in the Cost of Living Index; (2) Figures cover the Oakland CA urban area; **Doctor** *(general practitioners routine exam of an established patient);* **Dentist** *(adult teeth cleaning and periodic oral examination);* **Optometrist** *(full vision eye exam for established adult patient);* **Gasoline** *(one gallon regular unleaded, national brand, including all taxes, cash price at self-service pump if available);* **Beauty Salon** *(woman's shampoo, trim, and blow-dry);* **Men's Shirt** *(cotton/polyester dress shirt, pinpoint weave, long sleeves).*
Source: The Council for Community and Economic Research, ACCRA Cost of Living Index, 2015

HOUSING

House Price Index (HPI)

Area	National Ranking[2]	Quarterly Change (%)	One-Year Change (%)	Five-Year Change (%)
MD[1]	13	1.20	11.70	47.60
U.S.[3]	–	1.45	5.76	22.85

Note: The HPI is a weighted repeat sales index. It measures average price changes in repeat sales or refinancings on the same properties. This information is obtained by reviewing repeat mortgage transactions on single-family properties whose mortgages have been purchased or securitized by Fannie Mae or Freddie Mac in January 1975; (1) Oakland-Hayward-Berkeley Metropolitan Division—see Appendix B for areas included; (2) Rankings are based on annual percentage change for all metro areas containing at least 15,000 transactions over the last 10 years and ranges from 1 to 266; (3) figures based on a weighted average of Census Division estimates using a seasonally adjusted, purchase-only index; all figures are for the period ending December 31, 2015

Source: Federal Housing Finance Agency, House Price Index, February 25, 2016

Median Single-Family Home Prices

Area	2013	2014	2015P	Percent Change 2014 to 2015
MSA[1]	643.8	715.8	782.3	9.3
U.S. Average	197.4	208.9	223.9	7.2

Note: Figures are median sales prices of existing single-family homes in thousands of dollars; (p) preliminary; n/a not available; (1) San Francisco-Oakland-Hayward, CA Metropolitan Statistical Area—see Appendix B for areas included

Source: National Association of Realtors, Median Sales Price of Existing Single-Family Homes for Metropolitan Areas, 4th Quarter 2015

Qualifying Income Based on Median Sales Price of Existing Single-Family Homes

Area	With 5% Down ($)	With 10% Down ($)	With 20% Down ($)
MSA[1]	173,852	164,701	146,401
U.S. Average	49,535	46,928	41,714

Note: Figures are preliminary; Qualifying income is based on a mortgage rate of 4.1%. Monthly principal and interest payment is limited to 25% of income; n/a not available; (1) San Francisco-Oakland-Hayward, CA Metropolitan Statistical Area—see Appendix B for areas included

Source: National Association of Realtors, Qualifying Income Based on Median Sales Price of Existing Single-Family Homes for Metropolitan Areas, 4th Quarter 2015

Median Apartment Condo-Coop Home Prices

Area	2013	2014	2015P	Percent Change 2014 to 2015
MSA[1]	517.4	580.1	658.9	13.6
U.S. Average	194.9	204.3	210.7	3.1

Note: Figures are median sales prices of existing apartment condo-coop homes in thousands of dollars; (p) preliminary; n/a not available; (1) San Francisco-Oakland-Hayward, CA Metropolitan Statistical Area—see Appendix B for areas included

Source: National Association of Realtors, Median Sales Price of Existing Apartment Condo-Coop Homes for Metropolitan Areas, 4th Quarter 2015

Gross Monthly Rent

Area	Under $200	$200 -299	$300 -499	$500 -749	$750 -999	$1,000 -1,499	$1,500 and up	Median ($)
City	0.1	0.1	0.8	1.4	4.0	26.3	67.2	1,754
MSA[1]	0.9	2.8	3.5	5.2	10.4	30.6	46.6	1,446
U.S.	1.5	3.2	7.4	21.0	24.1	26.9	15.9	920

Note: Figures are percentages except for Median; Gross rent is the contract rent plus the estimated average monthly cost of utilities (electricity, gas, and water and sewer) and fuels (oil, coal, kerosene, wood, etc.) if these are paid by the renter (or paid for the renter by someone else); (1) Figures cover the San Francisco-Oakland-Hayward, CA Metropolitan Statistical Area—see Appendix B for areas included

Source: U.S. Census Bureau, 2010-2014 American Community Survey 5-Year Estimates

Homeownership Rate

Area	2008 (%)	2009 (%)	2010 (%)	2011 (%)	2012 (%)	2013 (%)	2014 (%)	2015 (%)
MSA[1]	56.4	57.3	58.0	56.1	53.2	55.2	54.6	56.3
U.S.	67.8	67.4	66.9	66.1	65.4	65.1	64.5	63.7

Note: (1) Figures cover the San Francisco-Oakland-Hayward, CA Metropolitan Statistical Area—see Appendix B for areas included
Source: U.S. Census Bureau, Housing Vacancies and Homeownership Annual Statistics: 2015

Year Housing Structure Built

Area	2010 or Later	2000 -2009	1990 -1999	1980 -1989	1970 -1979	1960 -1969	1950 -1959	1940 -1949	Before 1940	Median Year
City	2.5	33.1	16.5	21.4	17.3	8.0	0.6	0.3	0.4	1991
MSA[1]	0.6	8.3	8.0	10.8	15.4	13.4	14.4	8.6	20.5	1965
U.S.	1.0	14.9	13.9	13.8	15.8	11.0	10.8	5.4	13.3	1976

Note: Figures are percentages except for Median Year; (1) Figures cover the San Francisco-Oakland-Hayward, CA Metropolitan Statistical Area—see Appendix B for areas included
Source: U.S. Census Bureau, 2010-2014 American Community Survey 5-Year Estimates

HEALTH

Health Risk Data

Category	MSA[1] (%)	U.S. (%)
Adults aged 18–64 who have any kind of health care coverage	86.3	79.6
Adults who reported being in good or excellent health	87.0	83.1
Adults who are current smokers	11.2	19.6
Adults who are heavy drinkers[2]	7.6	6.1
Adults who are binge drinkers[3]	18.9	16.9
Adults who are overweight (BMI 25.0 - 29.9)	35.6	35.8
Adults who are obese (BMI 30.0 - 99.8)	22.6	27.6
Adults who participated in any physical activities in the past month	83.8	77.1
Adults 50+ who have ever had a sigmoidoscopy or colonoscopy	72.4	67.3
Women aged 40+ who have had a mammogram within the past two years	86.3	74.0
Men aged 40+ who have had a PSA test within the past two years	41.2	45.2
Adults aged 65+ who have had flu shot within the past year	59.2	60.1
Adults who always wear a seatbelt	n/a	93.8

Note: Data as of 2012 unless otherwise noted; n/a not available; (1) Figures cover the Oakland-Fremont-Hayward, CA—see Appendix B for areas included; (2) Heavy drinkers are classified as males having more than two drinks per day or females having more than one drink per day; (3) Binge drinkers are classified as males having five or more drinks on one occasion or females having four or more drinks on one occasion
Source: Centers for Disease Control and Prevention, Behaviorial Risk Factor Surveillance System, SMART: Selected Metropolitan/Micropolitan Area Risk Trends, 2012 (Note: the CDC has discontinued this dataset but will be releasing a replacement in mid-2016)

Chronic Health Indicators

Category	MSA[1] (%)	U.S. (%)
Adults who have ever been told they had a heart attack	2.8	4.5
Adults who have ever been told they had a stroke	n/a	2.9
Adults who have been told they currently have asthma	10.9	8.9
Adults who have ever been told they have arthritis	21.9	25.7
Adults who have ever been told they have diabetes[2]	8.6	9.7
Adults who have ever been told they had skin cancer	4.1	5.7
Adults who have ever been told they had any other types of cancer	7.9	6.5
Adults who have ever been told they have COPD	2.9	6.2
Adults who have ever been told they have kidney disease	2.1	2.5
Adults who have ever been told they have a form of depression	11.8	18.0

Note: Data as of 2012 unless otherwise noted; n/a not available; (1) Figures cover the Oakland-Fremont-Hayward, CA—see Appendix B for areas included; (2) Figures do not include pregnancy-related, borderline, or pre-diabetes
Source: Centers for Disease Control and Prevention, Behaviorial Risk Factor Surveillance System, SMART: Selected Metropolitan/Micropolitan Area Risk Trends, 2012 (Note: the CDC has discontinued this dataset but will be releasing a replacement in mid-2016)

Mortality Rates for the Top 10 Causes of Death in the U.S.

ICD-10[a] Sub-Chapter	ICD-10[a] Code	Age-Adjusted Mortality Rate[1] per 100,000 population	
		County[2]	U.S.
Malignant neoplasms	C00-C97	145.6	163.6
Ischaemic heart diseases	I20-I25	67.2	102.2
Other forms of heart disease	I30-I51	37.1	50.1
Chronic lower respiratory diseases	J40-J47	32.4	41.4
Organic, including symptomatic, mental disorders	F01-F09	28.6	38.5
Cerebrovascular diseases	I60-I69	38.8	36.5
Other external causes of accidental injury	W00-X59	18.7	27.5
Other degenerative diseases of the nervous system	G30-G31	36.2	26.3
Diabetes mellitus	E10-E14	16.2	21.1
Hypertensive diseases	I10-I15	21.8	19.7

Note: (a) ICD-10 = International Classification of Diseases 10th Revision; (1) Mortality rates are a three year average covering 2012-2014; (2) Figures cover COUNTY NOT FOUND!!!!!!.
Source: Centers for Disease Control and Prevention, National Center for Health Statistics. Underlying Cause of Death 1999-2014 on CDC WONDER Online Database, released 2015.

Mortality Rates for Selected Causes of Death

ICD-10[a] Sub-Chapter	ICD-10[a] Code	Age-Adjusted Mortality Rate[1] per 100,000 population	
		County[2]	U.S.
Assault	X85-Y09	6.1	5.1
Diseases of the liver	K70-K76	10.3	13.5
Human immunodeficiency virus (HIV) disease	B20-B24	1.0	2.1
Influenza and pneumonia	J09-J18	9.8	15.2
Intentional self-harm	X60-X84	9.4	12.7
Malnutrition	E40-E46	0.8	0.9
Obesity and other hyperalimentation	E65-E68	1.6	1.9
Renal failure	N17-N19	5.7	13.0
Transport accidents	V01-V99	6.8	11.6
Viral hepatitis	B15-B19	2.9	2.1

Note: (a) ICD-10 = International Classification of Diseases 10th Revision; (1) Mortality rates are a three year average covering 2012-2014; (2) Figures cover COUNTY NOT FOUND!!!!!!; Data are Suppressed when the data meet the criteria for confidentiality constraints; Mortality rates are flagged as Unreliable when the rate would be calculated with a numerator of 20 or less.
Source: Centers for Disease Control and Prevention, National Center for Health Statistics. Underlying Cause of Death 1999-2014 on CDC WONDER Online Database, released 2015.

Health Insurance Coverage

Area	With Health Insurance	With Private Health Insurance	With Public Health Insurance	Without Health Insurance	Population Under Age 18 Without Health Insurance
City	95.1	90.2	11.1	4.9	2.5
MSA[1]	89.2	72.5	26.5	10.8	4.7
U.S.	85.8	65.8	31.1	14.2	7.1

Note: Figures are percentages that cover the civilian noninstitutionalized population; (1) Figures cover the San Francisco-Oakland-Hayward, CA Metropolitan Statistical Area—see Appendix B for areas included
Source: U.S. Census Bureau, 2010-2014 American Community Survey 5-Year Estimates

Number of Medical Professionals

Area	MDs[3]	DOs[3,4]	Dentists	Podiatrists	Chiropractors	Optometrists
County[1] (number)	3,084	113	900	49	330	190
County[1] (rate[2])	281.4	10.3	81.0	4.4	29.7	17.1
U.S. (rate[2])	272.5	20.9	64.7	5.8	25.9	15.2

Note: Data as of 2014 unless noted; (1) Data covers Contra Costa County; (2) Rate per 100,000 population; (3) Data as of 2013 and includes all active, non-federal physicians; (4) Doctor of Osteopathic Medicine
Source: U.S. Department of Health and Human Services, Health Resources and Services Administration, Bureau of Health Professions, Area Resource File (ARF) 2014-2015

Best Hospitals

According to *U.S. News,* the Oakland-Hayward-Berkeley, CA metro area is home to three of the best hospitals in the U.S.: **John Muir Medical Center** (1 specialty); **El Camino Hospital** (1 specialty); **John Muir Medical Center** (3 specialties). The hospitals listed were nationally ranked in at least one adult specialty. Only 137 hospitals nationwide were nationally ranked in one or more specialties. Fifteen hospitals in the U.S. made the Honor Roll with high scores in at least six specialties. *U.S. News Online, "America's Best Children's Hospitals 2015-16"*

EDUCATION

Public School District Statistics

District Name	Schls	Pupils	Pupil/ Teacher Ratio	Minority Pupils[1] (%)	Free Lunch Eligible[2] (%)	IEP[3] (%)
San Ramon Valley Unified	36	31,398	24.9	51.4	3.0	7.5

Note: Table includes school districts with 100 or more students; (1) Percentage of students that are not non-Hispanic white; (2) Percentage of students that are eligible for the free lunch program; (3) Percentage of students that have an Individualized Education Program.
Source: U.S. Department of Education, National Center for Education Statistics, Common Core of Data, Local Education Agency (School District) Universe Survey: School Year 2013-2014; U.S. Department of Education, National Center for Education Statistics, Common Core of Data, Public Elementary/Secondary School Universe Survey: School Year 2013-2014

Best High Schools

According to *U.S. News,* San Ramon is home to one of the best high schools in the U.S.: **Dougherty Valley High School** (#179); Nearly 20,000 schools were ranked based on their performance on state assessments and how well they prepare students for college. Schools with the highest unrounded College Readiness Index values were numerically ranked from No. 1 to No. 500 and were the gold medal winners. *U.S. News & World Report, "Best High Schools 2015"*

Highest Level of Education

Area	Less than H.S.	H.S. Diploma	Some College, No Deg.	Associate Degree	Bachelor's Degree	Master's Degree	Prof. School Degree	Doctorate Degree
City	2.5	8.7	15.7	8.1	39.5	18.4	3.9	3.2
MSA[1]	12.1	17.0	19.0	6.9	27.1	11.8	3.6	2.5
U.S.	13.7	28.0	21.2	7.9	18.3	7.8	2.0	1.3

Note: Figures cover persons age 25 and over; (1) Figures cover the San Francisco-Oakland-Hayward, CA Metropolitan Statistical Area—see Appendix B for areas included
Source: U.S. Census Bureau, 2010-2014 American Community Survey 5-Year Estimates

Educational Attainment by Race

Area	High School Graduate or Higher (%)					Bachelor's Degree or Higher (%)				
	Total	White	Black	Asian	Hisp.[2]	Total	White	Black	Asian	Hisp.[2]
City	97.5	98.0	99.3	97.7	93.3	65.0	56.4	62.4	78.6	39.8
MSA[1]	87.9	91.3	89.5	85.3	68.2	44.9	49.6	23.9	50.5	18.4
U.S.	86.3	88.4	83.2	85.8	64.1	29.3	30.6	19.0	50.9	13.9

Note: Figures shown cover persons 25 years old and over; (1) Figures cover the San Francisco-Oakland-Hayward, CA Metropolitan Statistical Area—see Appendix B for areas included; (2) People of Hispanic origin can be of any race
Source: U.S. Census Bureau, 2010-2014 American Community Survey 5-Year Estimates

School Enrollment by Grade and Control

Area	Preschool (%)		Kindergarten (%)		Grades 1 - 4 (%)		Grades 5 - 8 (%)		Grades 9 - 12 (%)	
	Public	Private	Public	Private	Public	Private	Public	Private	Public	Private
City	22.2	77.8	77.1	22.9	91.8	8.2	96.9	3.1	95.6	4.4
MSA[1]	40.4	59.6	83.6	16.4	85.3	14.7	85.6	14.4	88.0	12.0
U.S.	57.4	42.6	87.8	12.2	89.8	10.2	89.9	10.1	90.6	9.4

Note: Figures shown cover persons 3 years old and over; (1) Figures cover the San Francisco-Oakland-Hayward, CA Metropolitan Statistical Area—see Appendix B for areas included
Source: U.S. Census Bureau, 2010-2014 American Community Survey 5-Year Estimates

Average Salaries of Public School Classroom Teachers

Area	2013-14 Dollars	2013-14 Rank[1]	2014-15 Dollars	2014-15 Rank[1]	Percent Change 2013-14 to 2014-15	Percent Change 2004-05 to 2014-15
California	71,396	4	72,535	4	1.59	25.9
U.S. Average	56,610	–	57,379	–	1.36	20.8

Note: (1) State rank ranges from 1 to 51 where 1 indicates highest salary.
Source: National Education Association, Rankings & Estimates: Rankings of the States 2014 and Estimates of School Statistics 2015, March 2015

Higher Education

Four-Year Colleges			Two-Year Colleges			Medical Schools[1]	Law Schools[2]	Voc/ Tech[3]
Public	Private Non-profit	Private For-profit	Public	Private Non-profit	Private For-profit			
0	0	0	0	0	0	0	0	0

Note: Figures cover institutions located within the city limits and include main campuses only; (1) includes schools accredited by the Liaison Committee on Medical Education and the American Osteopathic Association's Commission on Osteopathic College Accreditation; (2) includes ABA-accredited schools, schools with provisional ABA accreditation, and state accredited schools; (3) includes all schools with programs that are less than 2 years.
Source: National Center for Education Statistics, Integrated Postsecondary Education System (IPEDS), 2014-15; Association of American Medical Colleges, Member List, March 21, 2016; American Osteopathic Association, Member List, March 21, 2016; Law School Admission Council, Official Guide to ABA-Approved Law Schools Online, March 21, 2016; Wikipedia, List of Medical Schools in the United States, March 21, 2016; Wikipedia, List of Law Schools in the United States, March 21, 2016

According to *U.S. News & World Report,* the Oakland-Hayward-Berkeley, CA metro division is home to one of the best national universities in the U.S.: **University of California–Berkeley** (#20). The indicators used to capture academic quality fall into a number of categories: assessment by administrators at peer institutions; retention of students; faculty resources; student selectivity; financial resources; alumni giving; high school counselor ratings of colleges; and graduation rate. *U.S. News & World Report, "America's Best Colleges 2016"*

According to *U.S. News & World Report,* the Oakland-Hayward-Berkeley, CA metro division is home to one of the top 100 law schools in the U.S.: **University of California–Berkeley, School of Law** (#8 tie). The rankings are based on a weighted average of 12 measures of quality: peer assessment score; assessment score by lawyers/judges; median LSAT scores; median undergrad GPA; acceptance rate; employment rates for graduates; placement success; bar passage rate; faculty resources; expenditures per student; student/faculty ratio; and library resources. *U.S. News & World Report, "America's Best Graduate Schools, Law, 2017"*

According to *U.S. News & World Report,* the Oakland-Hayward-Berkeley, CA metro division is home to one of the top 75 business schools in the U.S.: **University of California–Berkeley, Haas School of Business** (#7). The rankings are based on a weighted average of the following nine measures: quality assessment; peer assessment; recruiter assessment; placement success; mean starting salary and bonus; student selectivity; mean GMAT and GRE scores; mean undergraduate GPA; and acceptance rate. *U.S. News & World Report, "America's Best Graduate Schools, Business, 2017"*

PRESIDENTIAL ELECTION

2012 Presidential Election Results

Area	Obama (%)	Romney (%)	Other (%)
Contra Costa County	65.8	31.9	2.3
U.S.	51.0	47.2	1.8

Note: Results may not add to 100% due to rounding
Source: Dave Leip's Atlas of U.S. Presidential Elections

EMPLOYERS

Major Employers

Company Name	Industry
All Hallows Preservation	Apartment building operators
AT&T Corp.	Telephone communication, except radio
AT&T Services	Telephone communication, except radio
California Pacific Medical Center	General medical & surgical hospitals
City & County of San Francisco	General medical & surgical hospitals
City & County of San Francisco	Public welfare administration: nonoperating, govt.
Edy's Grand Ice Cream	Ice cream & ice milk
Franklin Templeton Services	Investment advice
Lawrence Berkeley National Laboratory	Noncommercial research organizations
Lawrence Berkeley National Laboratory	Supply agency, government
Lawrence Livermore National Laboratory	Noncommercial research organizations
Menlo Worldwide Forwarding	Letter delivery, private air
Oracle America	Minicomputers
Oracle Systems Corporation	Prepackaged software
Pacific Gas and Electric Company	Electric & other services combined
PACPIZZA	Pizzeria, chain
San Francisco Community College District	Colleges & universities
University of California, Berkeley	University
Veterans Health Administration	Administration of veterans' affairs
Wells Fargo Bank	National commercial banks

Note: Companies shown are located within the San Francisco-Oakland-Hayward, CA Metropolitan Statistical Area.
Source: Hoovers.com; Wikipedia

PUBLIC SAFETY

Crime Rate

Area	All Crimes	Violent Crimes: Murder	Violent Crimes: Rape[3]	Violent Crimes: Robbery	Violent Crimes: Aggrav. Assault	Property Crimes: Burglary	Property Crimes: Larceny -Theft	Property Crimes: Motor Vehicle Theft
City	1,027.3	0.0	4.0	14.7	12.0	278.5	616.9	101.3
Metro[1]	3,824.5	5.5	24.3	239.2	246.8	618.0	1,982.1	708.7
U.S.	2,971.8	4.5	36.6	102.2	232.5	542.5	1,837.3	216.2

Note: Figures are crimes per 100,000 population; (1) Figures cover the Oakland-Hayward-Berkeley, CA Metropolitan Division—see Appendix B for areas included; (3) The city and U.S. figures shown were reported using the revised Uniform Crime Reporting (UCR) definition of rape. The suburban and metro area figures shown are an aggregate total of the data submitted using both the revised and legacy UCR definitions.
Source: FBI Uniform Crime Reports, 2014

Hate Crimes

Area	Number of Quarters Reported	Race	Religion	Sexual Orientation	Ethnicity	Disability	Gender	Gender Identity
		Number of Incidents per Bias Motivation						
City	4	0	0	1	0	0	0	0
U.S.	4	2,568	1,014	1,017	648	84	33	98

Source: Federal Bureau of Investigation, Hate Crime Statistics 2014

Identity Theft Consumer Complaints

Area	Complaints	Complaints per 100,000 Population	Rank[2]
MSA[1]	7,968	173.4	33
U.S.	490,220	152.4	-

Note: (1) Figures cover the San Francisco-Oakland-Hayward, CA Metropolitan Statistical Area—see Appendix B for areas included; (2) Rank ranges from 1 to 379 where 1 indicates greatest number of identity theft complaints per 100,000 population
Source: Federal Trade Commission, Consumer Sentinel Network Data Book for January–December 2015

Fraud and Other Consumer Complaints

Area	Complaints	Complaints per 100,000 Population	Rank[2]
MSA[1]	18,411	400.8	99
U.S.	2,593,159	806.0	-

Note: (1) Figures cover the San Francisco-Oakland-Hayward, CA Metropolitan Statistical Area—see Appendix B for areas included; (2) Rank ranges from 1 to 379 where 1 indicates greatest number of identity theft complaints per 100,000 population
Source: Federal Trade Commission, Consumer Sentinel Network Data Book for January–December 2015

RECREATION

Culture

Dance[1]	Theatre[1]	Instrumental Music[1]	Vocal Music[1]	Series and Festivals	Museums and Art Galleries[2]	Zoos and Aquariums[3]
0	0	0	0	0	0	0

Note: (1) Professional perfoming groups; (2) Based on organizations with SIC code 8412; (3) AZA-accredited
Source: The Grey House Performing Arts Directory, 2015-16; Association of Zoos & Aquariums, AZA Member Zoos & Aquariums, March 25, 2016; www.AccuLeads.com, March 29, 2016

Professional Sports Teams

Team Name	League	Year Established
Golden State Warriors	National Basketball Association (NBA)	1962
Oakland Athletics	Major League Baseball (MLB)	1968
Oakland Raiders	National Football League (NFL)	1960
San Francisco 49ers	National Football League (NFL)	1946
San Francisco Giants	Major League Baseball (MLB)	1958

Note: Includes teams located in the San Francisco-Oakland-Hayward, CA Metropolitan Statistical Area.
Source: Wikipedia, Major Professional Sports Teams of the United States and Canada, March 24, 2016

CLIMATE

Average and Extreme Temperatures

Temperature	Jan	Feb	Mar	Apr	May	Jun	Jul	Aug	Sep	Oct	Nov	Dec	Yr.
Extreme High (°F)	72	79	86	92	100	101	101	102	106	101	85	75	106
Average High (°F)	56	60	62	66	68	71	71	72	74	71	64	57	66
Average Temp. (°F)	50	54	56	58	60	63	64	65	66	63	57	51	59
Average Low (°F)	44	47	49	51	52	55	56	57	57	55	51	46	52
Extreme Low (°F)	30	32	36	38	42	47	48	40	50	44	38	27	27

Note: Figures cover the years 1945-1993
Source: National Climatic Data Center, International Station Meteorological Climate Summary, 9/96

Average Precipitation/Snowfall/Humidity

Precip./Humidity	Jan	Feb	Mar	Apr	May	Jun	Jul	Aug	Sep	Oct	Nov	Dec	Yr.
Avg. Precip. (in.)	3.7	2.7	2.7	1.1	0.4	0.1	0	0	0.3	1.1	2.3	3.1	17.6
Avg. Snowfall (in.)	Tr	Tr	0	0	0	0	0	0	0	0	0	Tr	Tr
Avg. Rel. Hum. 7am (%)	84	83	81	78	77	79	83	85	84	82	81	83	82
Avg. Rel. Hum. 4pm (%)	68	65	62	59	60	60	62	63	60	60	64	69	63

Note: Figures cover the years 1945-1993; Tr = Trace amounts (<0.05 in. of rain; <0.5 in. of snow)
Source: National Climatic Data Center, International Station Meteorological Climate Summary, 9/96

Weather Conditions

Temperature			Daytime Sky			Precipitation		
10°F & below	32°F & below	90°F & above	Clear	Partly cloudy	Cloudy	0.01 inch or more precip.	0.1 inch or more snow/ice	Thunder-storms
0	< 1	3	99	168	98	59	0	6

Note: Figures are average number of days per year and cover the years 1945-1993
Source: National Climatic Data Center, International Station Meteorological Climate Summary, 9/96

HAZARDOUS WASTE

Superfund Sites

San Ramon has no sites on the EPA's Superfund Final National Priorities List. There are a total of 1,323 Superfund sites on the list in the U.S. *U.S. Environmental Protection Agency, Final National Priorities List, March 18, 2016*

AIR & WATER QUALITY

Air Quality Trends: Ozone

	1990	1995	2000	2005	2010	2011	2012	2013	2014
MSA[1]	0.058	0.074	0.057	0.055	0.061	0.060	0.057	0.056	0.065

Note: (1) Data covers the San Francisco-Oakland-Hayward, CA Metropolitan Statistical Area—see Appendix B for areas included. The values shown are the composite ozone concentration averages among trend sites based on the highest fourth daily maximum 8-hour concentration in parts per million. These trends are based on sites having an adequate record of monitoring data during the trend period. Data from exceptional events are included.

Source: U.S. Environmental Protection Agency, Air Quality Monitoring Information, "Air Quality Trends by City, 1990-2014"

Air Quality Index

Area	Percent of Days when Air Quality was...[2]					AQI Statistics[2]	
	Good	Moderate	Unhealthy for Sensitive Groups	Unhealthy	Very Unhealthy	Maximum	Median
MSA[1]	57.3	39.7	3.0	0.0	0.0	124	47

Note: (1) Data covers the San Francisco-Oakland-Hayward, CA Metropolitan Statistical Area—see Appendix B for areas included; (2) Based on 365 days with AQI data in 2015. Air Quality Index (AQI) is an index for reporting daily air quality. EPA calculates the AQI for five major air pollutants regulated by the Clean Air Act: ground-level ozone, particle pollution (aka particulate matter), carbon monoxide, sulfur dioxide, and nitrogen dioxide. The AQI runs from 0 to 500. The higher the AQI value, the greater the level of air pollution and the greater the health concern. There are six AQI categories: "Good" AQI is between 0 and 50. Air quality is considered satisfactory; "Moderate" AQI is between 51 and 100. Air quality is acceptable; "Unhealthy for Sensitive Groups" When AQI values are between 101 and 150, members of sensitive groups may experience health effects; "Unhealthy" When AQI values are between 151 and 200 everyone may begin to experience health effects; "Very Unhealthy" AQI values between 201 and 300 trigger a health alert; "Hazardous" AQI values over 300 trigger warnings of emergency conditions (not shown).

Source: U.S. Environmental Protection Agency, Air Quality Index Report, 2015

Air Quality Index Pollutants

Area	Percent of Days when AQI Pollutant was...[2]					
	Carbon Monoxide	Nitrogen Dioxide	Ozone	Sulfur Dioxide	Particulate Matter 2.5	Particulate Matter 10
MSA[1]	0.0	6.3	33.4	0.0	60.3	0.0

Note: (1) Data covers the San Francisco-Oakland-Hayward, CA Metropolitan Statistical Area—see Appendix B for areas included; (2) Based on 365 days with AQI data in 2015. The Air Quality Index (AQI) is an index for reporting daily air quality. EPA calculates the AQI for five major air pollutants regulated by the Clean Air Act: ground-level ozone, particle pollution (also known as particulate matter), carbon monoxide, sulfur dioxide, and nitrogen dioxide. The AQI runs from 0 to 500. The higher the AQI value, the greater the level of air pollution and the greater the health concern.

Source: U.S. Environmental Protection Agency, Air Quality Index Report, 2015

Maximum Air Pollutant Concentrations: Particulate Matter, Ozone, CO and Lead

	Particulate Matter 10 (ug/m^3)	Particulate Matter 2.5 Wtd AM (ug/m^3)	Particulate Matter 2.5 24-Hr (ug/m^3)	Ozone (ppm)	Carbon Monoxide (ppm)	Lead (ug/m^3)
MSA[1] Level	37	10.8	26	0.076	3	n/a
NAAQS[2]	150	15	35	0.075	9	0.15
Met NAAQS[2]	Yes	Yes	Yes	No	Yes	n/a

Note: (1) Data covers the San Francisco-Oakland-Hayward, CA Metropolitan Statistical Area—see Appendix B for areas included; Data from exceptional events are included; (2) National Ambient Air Quality Standards; ppm = parts per million; ug/m³ = micrograms per cubic meter; n/a not available.
Concentrations: Particulate Matter 10 (coarse particulate)—highest second maximum 24-hour concentration; Particulate Matter 2.5 Wtd AM (fine particulate)—highest weighted annual mean concentration; Particulate Matter 2.5 24-Hour (fine particulate)—highest 98th percentile 24-hour concentration; Ozone—highest fourth daily maximum 8-hour concentration; Carbon Monoxide—highest second maximum non-overlapping 8-hour concentration; Lead—maximum running 3-month average
Source: U.S. Environmental Protection Agency, Air Quality Monitoring Information, "Air Quality Statistics by City, 2014"

Maximum Air Pollutant Concentrations: Nitrogen Dioxide and Sulfur Dioxide

	Nitrogen Dioxide AM (ppb)	Nitrogen Dioxide 1-Hr (ppb)	Sulfur Dioxide AM (ppb)	Sulfur Dioxide 1-Hr (ppb)	Sulfur Dioxide 24-Hr (ppb)
MSA[1] Level	17	58	n/a	16	n/a
NAAQS[2]	53	100	30	75	140
Met NAAQS[2]	Yes	Yes	n/a	Yes	n/a

Note: (1) Data covers the San Francisco-Oakland-Hayward, CA Metropolitan Statistical Area—see Appendix B for areas included; Data from exceptional events are included; (2) National Ambient Air Quality Standards; ppm = parts per million; ug/m³ = micrograms per cubic meter; n/a not available.
Concentrations: Nitrogen Dioxide AM—highest arithmetic mean concentration; Nitrogen Dioxide 1-Hr—highest 98th percentile 1-hour daily maximum concentration; Sulfur Dioxide AM—highest annual mean concentration; Sulfur Dioxide 1-Hr—highest 99th percentile 1-hour daily maximum concentration; Sulfur Dioxide 24-Hr—highest second maximum 24-hour concentration
Source: U.S. Environmental Protection Agency, Air Quality Monitoring Information, "Air Quality Statistics by City, 2014"

Drinking Water

Water System Name	Pop. Served	Primary Water Source Type	Violations[1]	
			Health Based	Monitoring/ Reporting
Contra Costa Water District	198,000	Surface	0	0

Note: (1) Based on violation data from January 1, 2015 to December 31, 2015 (includes unresolved violations from earlier years)
Source: U.S. Environmental Protection Agency, Office of Ground Water and Drinking Water, Safe Drinking Water Information System (based on data extracted April 29, 2016)

Saratoga, California

Background

Saratoga is in Santa Clara County in the foothills of the Santa Cruz Mountains. At an elevation of 500 feet, Saratoga is 26 miles east of the Pacific Coast and 50 miles south of San Francisco. Artifacts suggest that the Ohlone Indians passed through the area prior to Spanish exploration.

Saratoga was originally named Toll Gate for the tolled road to the redwood sawmills built by William Campbell in 1847. The town also was called McCartysville, after Martin McCarty who surveyed the town and built a post office in 1855, and Bank Mills, when paper and flour mills were built about 1863. In 1865, the name changed to Saratoga, after Saratoga, New York, whose water springs held similar mineral content. Wild fields of wheat and poppies were cultivated into vineyards and orchards in the 1880s. Following the Second World War, Saratoga transformed from an agricultural community to a suburban community as land became more valuable for housing than orchards. Saratoga became an incorporated city in 1956.

Saratoga is a great city for residents and tourists alike. Highways 9 and 17 are close by, and the nearest airports are San Jose International Airport (8 miles) and San Francisco International Airport (31 miles). The city is home to West Valley College with such academic and career programs as accounting, digital media, and landscape architecture. The Saratoga Library, part of the Santa Clara County Library system, is open every day with reading programs for children, teens, and adults. Saratoga encourages green building, water and energy conservation, buying locally, and planting native species of vegetation. Local produce and wine are available at Saratoga Farmers' Market and Novakovich Orchards. The Saratoga Farmers' Market is open every Saturday throughout the year with over 50 producers at the West Valley College campus. Wineries in Saratoga are Clos LaChance Wines, Cooper-Garrod Estate Vineyards, Mariani Winery and Saratoga Vineyards.

Places of interest in the city include Villa Montalvo, the Mediterranean-style home of former US Senator James Duval Phelan, and a center for cultural arts, Montalvo Arts Center. Also notable is that film director Steven Spielberg graduated high school in Saratoga, and the city was the filming location for the 1998 movie, "The Horse Whisperer."

Popular outdoor activities in Saratoga include horseback riding, swimming, golfing, camping, and bicycling. The city's Hakone Gardens is the oldest Japanese-style residential garden in the country. Outdoor recreation is abundant and varied at a dozen public parks. Historical Park is a half-acre of Saratoga's past, and includes its first library building, the McWilliams House of 1865, and the Saratoga Historical Museum building, which opened in 1976, run by the Saratoga Historical Foundation.

A popular destination for residents and visitors alike is Saratoga Village, for a historical look at life with more than 20 historical buildings. The Inn at Saratoga in Saratoga Village is a popular location for weddings, receptions, business events, and leisure traveling. The Aegis Gallery of Fine Art exhibits local artists' work and hosts poetry readings, chamber music, and dramatic interpretations. The Youth Science Institute Sanborn Discovery Center is a natural history museum with displays of reptiles, amphibians, mammals, and insects.

Inspired by New York City's tree planting initiative, The Heritage Tree Society of Saratoga came up with the idea of 2015 by 2015—the City's effort to plant 2015 trees between January 1, 2010 and December 31, 2015.

Saratoga has mild temperatures throughout the year. Rainfall averages 29 inches annually between November and April with moderate to low humidity.

Rankings

General Rankings

- The San Jose* metro area was identified as one of America's fastest-growing areas in terms of population and economy by *Forbes*. The area ranked #17 out of 20. The 100 most populous metro areas in the U.S. were evaluated on the following criteria: estimated population growth; job growth; gross metropolitan product growth; unemployment; median salaries for college-educated workers. *Forbes, "America's Fastest-Growing Cities 2015," January 27, 2015*

Business/Finance Rankings

- The personal finance site NerdWallet analyzed 183 American metropolitan areas with populations over 250,000 and more than 15,000 businesses to rank where entrepreneurs find the most success. Criteria included area economy, annual income, housing cost, unemployment rate, and the success rate of area businesses. San Jose* ranked #42. *www.nerdwallet.com, "Best Places to Start a Business," April 27, 2015*
- TransUnion ranked the nation's metro areas by average credit score, calculated on the VantageScore system, developed by the three major credit-reporting bureaus—TransUnion, Experian, and Equifax. The San Jose* metro area was among the ten cities with the highest collective credit score, meaning that its residents posed the lowest average consumer credit risk. *www.usatoday.com, "Metro Areas' Average Credit Rating Revealed," February 7, 2013*
- Based on the U.S. Department of Labor's Occupational Information Network Data Collection Program, the Brookings Institution defined job opportunities for STEM workers at various levels of educational attainment. The San Jose* metro area was placed among the ten large metro areas with the highest demand for high-level STEM knowledge. *www.brookings.edu, "The Hidden Stem Economy," June 10, 2013*
- According to data by the Bureau of Economic Analysis (BEA) and the Bureau of Labor Statistics (BLS), the San Jose* metro area has the fastest-growing GDP (gross domestic product) and positive employment trends, at #9. *247wallst.com, "Cities With the Fastest Growing (and Shrinking) Economies," September 29, 2015*
- 24/7 Wall Street used Brookings Institution research on 50 advanced industries to identify the proportion of workers in the nation's largest metropolitan areas that were employed in jobs requiring knowledge in the science, technology, engineering, or math (STEM) fields. The San Jose* metro area was #1. *247wallst.com, "15 Cities with the Most High-Tech Jobs," March 13, 2015*
- Based on metro area social media reviews, the employment opinion group Glassdoor surveyed 50 of the largest U.S. metro areas and equally weighed cost of living, hiring opportunity, and job satisfaction to compose a list of "25 Best Cities for Jobs." The San Jose* metro area was ranked #2 in overall job satisfaction. *www.glassdoor.com, "Best Cities for Jobs," May 19, 2015*
- In a survey of economic confidence in the nation's 50 largest metropolitan areas conducted January–December 2014, the San Jose* metro area placed #1, according to Gallup's 2014 Economic Confidence Index. *Gallup, "San Jose and San Francisco Lead in Economic Confidence," March 19, 2015*
- The Brookings Institution ranked the 100 largest metro areas in the U.S. based on income inequality. San Jose* was ranked #17 (#1 = greatest ineqality). Criteria: the "95/20 ratio," a figure representing the income at which a household earns more than 95 percent of all other households, divided by the income at which a household earns more than only 20 percent of all other households. *Brookings Institution, "Income Inequality, 100 Largest U.S. Metro Areas, 2007-2014," January 14, 2016*
- *Forbes* ranked the largest metro areas in the U.S. in terms of the "Best Cities for Young Professionals." The San Jose* metro area ranked #11 out of 15. Criteria: job growth; unemployment rate; median salary of college graduates age 24 to 34; cost of living; number of small businesses per capita; number of large companies; percentage of population 25 years of age and older with college degrees. *Forbes.com, "America's 15 Best Cities for Young Professionals," August 18, 2014*

- The San Jose* metro area appeared on the Milken Institute "2015 Best Performing Cities" list. Rank: #1 out of 200 large metro areas. Criteria: job growth; wage and salary growth; high-tech output growth. *Milken Institute, "Best-Performing Cities 2015," December 2015*

- *Forbes* ranked the 200 most populous metro areas to determine the nation's "Best Places for Business and Careers." The San Jose* metro area was ranked #42. Criteria: costs (business and living); job growth (past and projected); income growth; educational attainment (college and high school); projected economic growth; cultural and recreational opportunities; net migration patterns; number of highly ranked colleges. *Forbes, "The Best Places for Business and Careers 2015," July 29, 2015*

Dating/Romance Rankings

- *Forbes* reports that the San Jose* metro area made Rent.com's Best Cities for Newlyweds list for 2013, based on Bureau of Labor Statistics and Census Bureau data on number of married couples, percentage of families with children under age six, average annual income, cost of living, and availability of rentals. *www.forbes.com, "The 10 Best Cities for Newlyweds to Live and Work In," May 30, 2013*

- CreditDonkey, a financial education website, sought out the ten best U.S. cities for newlyweds, considering the number of married couples, divorce rate, average credit score, and average number of hours worked per week in metro areas with a million or more residents. The San Jose* metro area placed #2. *www.creditdonkey.com, "Study: Best Cities for Newlyweds," November 30, 2013*

Education Rankings

- Based on a Brookings Institution study, *24/7 Wall St.* identified the ten U.S. metropolitan areas with the most average patent filings per million residents between 2007 and 2011. San Jose* ranked #1. *24/7 Wall St., "America's Most Innovative Cities," February 1, 2013*

- The San Jose* metro area was selected as one of America's most innovative cities" by *The Business Insider*. The metro area was ranked #1 out of 20. Criteria: patents per capita. *The Business Insider, "The 20 Most Innovative Cities in the U.S.," February 1, 2013*

- San Jose* was identified as one of America's "smartest" metropolitan areas by *The Business Journals*. The area ranked #5 out of 10. Criteria: percentage of adults (25 and older) with high school diplomas, bachelor's degrees and graduate degrees. *The Business Journals, "Where the Brainpower Is: Exclusive U.S. Rankings, Insights," February 27, 2014*

- Personal finance website *WalletHub* analyzed the 150 largest U.S. metropolitan statistical areas to determine where the most educated Americans are choosing to settle. Criteria: education quality and attainment gap; education levels; percentage of workers with degrees; public school rankings; quality and size of each metro area's universities. San Jose* was ranked #14 (#1 = most educated city). *www.WalletHub.com, "2015's Most and Least Educated Cities*

Environmental Rankings

- The San Jose* metro area came in at #48 for the relative comfort of its climate on Sperling's list of "chill cities," as measured by the Sperling Heat Index. All 361 metro areas are included. Criteria included daytime high temperatures, nighttime low temperatures, dew point, and relative humidity at the high temperatures. *www.bertsperling.com, "Sperling's Chill Cities," July 18, 2013*

- Sperling's BestPlaces assessed 379 metropolitan areas of the United States for the likelihood of dangerously extreme weather events or earthquakes. In general the Southeast and South-Central regions have the highest risk of weather extremes and earthquakes, while the Pacific Northwest enjoys the lowest risk. Of the least risky metropolitan areas, the San Jose* metro area was ranked #69. *www.bestplaces.net, "Safest Places from Natural Disasters," April 2011*

- San Jose* was identified as one of America's dirtiest metro areas by *Forbes*. The area ranked #8 out of 20. Criteria: air quality; water quality; toxic releases; superfund sites. *Forbes, "America's 20 Dirtiest Cities," December 10, 2012*

- The U.S. Environmental Protection Agency (EPA) released a list of U.S. metropolitan areas with the most ENERGY STAR certified buildings in 2015. The San Jose* metro area was ranked #17 out of 25. *U.S. Environmental Protection Agency, "Top Cities With the Most ENERGY STAR Certified Buildings in 2016," March 30, 2016*
- The U.S. Environmental Protection Agency (EPA) released a list of mid-size U.S. metropolitan areas with the most ENERGY STAR certified buildings in 2015. The San Jose* metro area was ranked #1 out of 10. *U.S. Environmental Protection Agency, "Top Cities With the Most ENERGY STAR Certified Buildings in 2016," March 30, 2016*
- San Jose* was highlighted as one of the 25 metro areas most polluted by year-round particle pollution (Annual PM 2.5) in the U.S. during 2011 through 2013. The area ranked #7. *American Lung Association, State of the Air 2015*
- San Jose* was highlighted as one of the 25 metro areas most polluted by short-term particle pollution (24-hour PM 2.5) in the U.S. during 2011 through 2013. The area ranked #6. *American Lung Association, State of the Air 2015*

Health/Fitness Rankings

- Analysts who tracked obesity rates in the nation's largest metro areas (populations above one million) found that the San Jose* metro area was one of the ten major metros where residents were least likely to be obese, defined as a BMI score of 30 or above. *www.gallup.com, "Boulder, Colo., Residents Still Least Likely to Be Obese," April 4, 2014*
- Analysts who tracked obesity rates in 100 of the nation's most populous areas found that the San Jose* metro area was one of the ten communities where residents were least likely to be obese, defined as a BMI score of 30 or above. *www.gallup.com, "Colorado Springs Residents Least Likely to Be Obese," May 28, 2015*
- For each of the 50 most populous metro areas in the United States, the American College of Sports Medicine's American Fitness Index evaluated infrastructure, community assets, and policies that encourage healthy and fit lifestyles, including preventive health behaviors, levels of chronic disease conditions, health care access, and community resources and policies that support physical activity. The San Jose* metro area ranked #10 for "community fitness." *www.americanfitnessindex.org, "ACSM American Fitness Index Health and Community Fitness Status of the 50 Largest Metropolitan Areas," May 2015*
- San Jose* was identified as a "2016 Spring Allergy Capital." The area ranked #86 out of 100. Three groups of factors were used to identify the most severe cities for people with allergies during the spring season: annual pollen levels; medicine utilization; access to board-certified allergists. *Asthma and Allergy Foundation of America, "Spring Allergy Capitals 2016"*
- San Jose* was identified as a "2015 Asthma Capital." The area ranked #97 out of the nation's 100 largest metropolitan areas. Criteria: estimated prevalence; self-reported prevalence; crude death rate for asthma; annual pollen score; annual air quality; public smoking laws; number of board-certified asthma specialists; school inhaler access laws; rescue medication use; controller medication use; ER visits for asthma; uninsured rate; poverty rate. *Asthma and Allergy Foundation of America, "Asthma Capitals 2015"*
- The San Jose* metro area ranked #15 out of 190 in The Gallup-Healthways Well-Being Index. Criteria: purpose; social well being; financial health; community and physical health. Results are based on telephone interviews with adults, aged 18 and older, living in metropolitan areas in the 50 U.S. states and the District of Columbia. *Gallup-Healthways, "State of American Well-Being," February 23, 2016*

Real Estate Rankings

- With data from RealtyTrac, Yahoo! Finance researchers listed the housing markets in which housing affordability is improving most, factoring in interest rates as well as median home prices. The San Jose* metro area was among the least affordable housing markets. *news.yahoo.com, "10 Cities Where Ordinary People Can No Longer Afford Homes," March 5, 2014*

- The San Jose* metro area was identified as one of the nations's 20 hottest housing markets in 2016. Criteria: listing views as an indicator of demand and median days on the market as an indicator of supply. The area ranked #2. *Realtor.com, "The 20 Hottest U.S. Real Estate Markets in February 2016," February 25, 2016*
- San Jose* was ranked #15 in the top 20 out of 266 metro areas in terms of house price appreciation in 2015 (#1 = highest rate). *Federal Housing Finance Agency, House Price Index, 4th Quarter 2015*
- The San Jose* metro area was identified as one of the 20 least affordable housing markets in the U.S. in 2015. The area ranked #1 out of 179 markets. Criteria: qualification for a mortgage loan on a typical home. *National Association of Realtors®, Affordability Index of Existing Single-Family Homes for Metropolitan Areas, 2015*
- San Jose* was ranked #220 out of 225 metro areas in terms of housing affordability in 2015 by the National Association of Home Builders (#1 = most affordable). Criteria: the share of homes sold in that area affordable to a family earning the local median income, based on standard mortgage underwriting criteria. *National Association of Home Builders®, NAHB-Wells Fargo Housing Opportunity Index, 4th Quarter 2015*

Safety Rankings

- Farmers Insurance, in partnership with Sperling's BestPlaces, ranked metro areas in the U.S. as the "Most Secure Places to Live." The San Jose* metro area ranked #7 out of the top 20 in the large metro area category (500,000 or more residents). Criteria: economic stability; crime statistics; extreme weather; risk of natural disasters; housing depreciation; foreclosures; air quality; environmental hazards; life expectancy; motor vehicle fatalities; and employment numbers. *Farmers Insurance Group of Companies, "Most Secure U.S. Places to Live in the U.S.," June 25, 2013*
- Saratoga was identified as one of the safest cities in America by NeighborhoodScout. The city ranked #58 out of 100. Criteria: number of violent and property crimes per 1,000 residents. The editors only considered cities with 25,000 or more residents. *NeighborhoodScout, "Safest Cities in America 2016"*
- The National Insurance Crime Bureau ranked 380 metro areas in the U.S. in terms of per capita rates of vehicle theft. The San Jose* metro area ranked #10 (#1 = highest rate). Criteria: number of vehicle theft offenses per 100,000 inhabitants in 2014. *National Insurance Crime Bureau, "Hot Spots 2014," June 24, 2015*

Seniors/Retirement Rankings

- From its Best Cities for Successful Aging indexes, the Milken Institute generated rankings for metropolitan areas, weighing data in eight categories—health care, wellness, living arrangements, transportation, financial characteristics, education and employment opportunities, community engagement, and overall livability. The San Jose* metro area was ranked #65 overall in the large metro area category. *Milken Institute, "Best Cities for Successful Aging, 2014"*

Transportation Rankings

- San Jose* was identified as one of the most congested metro areas in the U.S. The area ranked #5 out of 10. Criteria: yearly delay per auto commuter in hours. *Texas A&M Transportation Institute, "2015 Urban Mobility Scorecard," August 2015*

Miscellaneous Rankings

- The National Alliance to End Homelessness ranked the 100 most populous metro areas with the highest rate of homelessness. The San Jose* metro area ranked #7. Criteria: number of homeless people per 10,000 population in 2011. *National Alliance to End Homelessness, The State of Homelessness in America 2012*

Saratoga is located within the San Jose-Sunnyvale-Santa Clara, CA Metropolitan Statistical Area.

Business Environment

CITY FINANCES

City Government Finances

Component	2012 ($000)	2012 ($ per capita)
Total Revenues	20,944	699
Total Expenditures	22,618	755
Debt Outstanding	11,995	400
Cash and Securities[1]	14,170	473

Note: (1) Cash and security holdings of a government at the close of its fiscal year, including those of its dependent agencies, utilities, and liquor stores.
Source: U.S Census Bureau, State & Local Government Finances 2012

City Government Revenue by Source

Source	2012 ($000)	2012 ($ per capita)
General Revenue		
From Federal Government	31	1
From State Government	1,060	35
From Local Governments	0	0
Taxes		
Property	9,400	314
Sales and Gross Receipts	3,033	101
Personal Income	0	0
Corporate Income	0	0
Motor Vehicle License	0	0
Other Taxes	2,603	86
Current Charges	3,544	118
Liquor Store	0	0
Utility	0	0
Employee Retirement	0	0

Source: U.S Census Bureau, State & Local Government Finances 2012

City Government Expenditures by Function

Function	2012 ($000)	2012 ($ per capita)	2012 (%)
General Direct Expenditures			
Air Transportation	0	0	0.0
Corrections	0	0	0.0
Education	0	0	0.0
Employment Security Administration	0	0	0.0
Financial Administration	1,452	48	6.4
Fire Protection	0	0	0.0
General Public Buildings	0	0	0.0
Governmental Administration, Other	4,748	158	20.9
Health	722	24	3.1
Highways	5,313	177	23.4
Hospitals	0	0	0.0
Housing and Community Development	93	3	0.4
Interest on General Debt	540	18	2.3
Judicial and Legal	303	10	1.3
Libraries	208	6	0.9
Parking	0	0	0.0
Parks and Recreation	4,242	141	18.7
Police Protection	4,065	135	17.9
Public Welfare	0	0	0.0
Sewerage	0	0	0.0
Solid Waste Management	0	0	0.0
Veterans' Services	0	0	0.0
Liquor Store	0	0	0.0
Utility	0	0	0.0
Employee Retirement	0	0	0.0

Source: U.S Census Bureau, State & Local Government Finances 2012

DEMOGRAPHICS

Population Growth

Area	1990 Census	2000 Census	2010 Census	2014* Estimate	Population Growth (%) 1990-2014	Population Growth (%) 2010-2014
City	28,177	29,843	29,926	30,627	8.7	2.3
MSA[1]	1,534,280	1,735,819	1,836,911	1,898,457	23.7	3.4
U.S.	248,709,873	281,421,906	308,745,538	314,107,084	26.3	1.7

Note: (1) Figures cover the San Jose-Sunnyvale-Santa Clara, CA Metropolitan Statistical Area—see Appendix B for areas included; (*) 2010-2014 5-year estimated population
Source: U.S. Census Bureau, 1990 Census, Census 2000, Census 2010, 2010-2014 American Community Survey 5-Year Estimates

Household Size

Area	Persons in Household (%) One	Two	Three	Four	Five	Six	Seven or More	Average Household Size
City	14.2	35.2	18.8	24.6	5.1	1.4	0.3	2.82
MSA[1]	21.3	29.2	18.6	17.6	7.6	2.8	2.5	2.95
U.S.	27.5	33.5	15.8	13.1	6.0	2.3	1.4	2.64

Note: (1) Figures cover the San Jose-Sunnyvale-Santa Clara, CA Metropolitan Statistical Area—see Appendix B for areas included
Source: U.S. Census Bureau, 2010-2014 American Community Survey 5-Year Estimates

Race

Area	White Alone[2] (%)	Black Alone[2] (%)	Asian Alone[2] (%)	AIAN[3] Alone[2] (%)	NHOPI[4] Alone[2] (%)	Other Race Alone[2] (%)	Two or More Races (%)
City	50.5	0.4	45.1	0.2	0.0	0.4	3.3
MSA[1]	50.3	2.6	32.2	0.5	0.4	9.4	4.5
U.S.	73.8	12.6	5.0	0.8	0.2	4.7	2.9

Note: (1) Figures cover the San Jose-Sunnyvale-Santa Clara, CA Metropolitan Statistical Area—see Appendix B for areas included; (2) Alone is defined as not being in combination with one or more other races; (3) American Indian and Alaska Native; (4) Native Hawaiian and Other Pacific Islander
Source: U.S. Census Bureau, 2010-2014 American Community Survey 5-Year Estimates

Hispanic or Latino Origin

Area	Total (%)	Mexican (%)	Puerto Rican (%)	Cuban (%)	Other (%)
City	3.3	1.9	0.3	0.1	1.0
MSA[1]	27.7	23.5	0.4	0.1	3.6
U.S.	16.9	10.8	1.6	0.6	3.8

Note: Persons of Hispanic or Latino origin can be of any race; (1) Figures cover the San Jose-Sunnyvale-Santa Clara, CA Metropolitan Statistical Area—see Appendix B for areas included
Source: U.S. Census Bureau, 2010-2014 American Community Survey 5-Year Estimates

Ancestry

Area	German	Irish	English	American	Italian	Polish	French[2]	Scottish	Dutch
City	8.5	7.6	8.3	1.7	5.7	1.5	1.4	1.8	0.9
MSA[1]	7.2	5.5	5.2	2.0	4.5	1.2	1.6	1.2	0.8
U.S.	14.9	10.8	8.0	7.1	5.5	3.0	2.7	1.7	1.4

Note: Figures are the percentage of the total population reporting a particular ancestry. The nine most commonly reported ancestries in the U.S. are shown. Figures include multiple ancestries (e.g. if a person reported being Irish and Italian, they were included in both columns); (1) Figures cover the San Jose-Sunnyvale-Santa Clara, CA Metropolitan Statistical Area—see Appendix B for areas included; (2) Excludes Basque
Source: U.S. Census Bureau, 2010-2014 American Community Survey 5-Year Estimates

Foreign-Born Population

Area	Percent of Population Born in								
	Any Foreign Country	Asia	Mexico	Europe	Carribean	Central America[2]	South America	Africa	Canada
City	37.9	30.9	0.4	4.5	0.1	0.1	0.5	0.5	0.5
MSA[1]	36.9	22.9	8.1	2.9	0.1	1.0	0.7	0.5	0.5
U.S.	13.1	3.8	3.7	1.5	1.2	1.0	0.9	0.6	0.3

Note: (1) Figures cover the San Jose-Sunnyvale-Santa Clara, CA Metropolitan Statistical Area—see Appendix B for areas included; (2) Excludes Mexico.
Source: U.S. Census Bureau, 2010-2014 American Community Survey 5-Year Estimates

Marital Status

Area	Never Married	Now Married[2]	Separated	Widowed	Divorced
City	18.6	70.1	0.8	6.2	4.3
MSA[1]	32.5	53.2	1.7	4.5	8.2
U.S.	32.5	48.4	2.2	5.9	10.9

Note: Figures are percentages and cover the population 15 years of age and older; (1) Figures cover the San Jose-Sunnyvale-Santa Clara, CA Metropolitan Statistical Area—see Appendix B for areas included; (2) Excludes separated
Source: U.S. Census Bureau, 2010-2014 American Community Survey 5-Year Estimates

Disability Status

Area	All Ages	Under 18 Years Old	18 to 64 Years Old	65 Years and Over
City	6.8	1.6	2.7	25.4
MSA[1]	7.7	2.2	5.2	33.5
U.S.	12.3	4.1	10.2	36.3

Note: Figures show percent of the civilian noninstitutionalized population that reported having a disability. Disability status is determined from from six types of difficulty: vision, hearing, cognitive, ambulatory, self-care, and independent living. For children under 5 years old, hearing and vision difficulty are used to determine disability status. For children between the ages of 5 and 14, disability status is determined from hearing, vision, cognitive, ambulatory, and self-care difficulties. For people aged 15 years and older, they are considered to have a disability if they have difficulty with any one of the six difficulty types; (1) Figures cover the San Jose-Sunnyvale-Santa Clara, CA Metropolitan Statistical Area—see Appendix B for areas included.
Source: U.S. Census Bureau, 2010-2014 American Community Survey 5-Year Estimates

Age

Area	Percent of Population									Median Age
	Under Age 5	Age 5–19	Age 20–34	Age 35–44	Age 45–54	Age 55–64	Age 65–74	Age 75–84	Age 85+	
City	2.9	21.9	8.1	11.8	19.9	15.5	9.9	6.2	3.7	47.7
MSA[1]	6.7	19.4	21.4	15.2	14.6	10.9	6.4	3.6	1.6	36.6
U.S.	6.4	19.9	20.6	13.0	14.1	12.3	7.6	4.3	1.9	37.4

Note: (1) Figures cover the San Jose-Sunnyvale-Santa Clara, CA Metropolitan Statistical Area—see Appendix B for areas included
Source: U.S. Census Bureau, 2010-2014 American Community Survey 5-Year Estimates

Gender

Area	Males	Females	Males per 100 Females
City	15,022	15,605	96.3
MSA[1]	953,276	945,181	100.9
U.S.	154,515,159	159,591,925	96.8

Note: (1) Figures cover the San Jose-Sunnyvale-Santa Clara, CA Metropolitan Statistical Area—see Appendix B for areas included
Source: U.S. Census Bureau, 2010-2014 American Community Survey 5-Year Estimates

Religious Groups by Family

Area	Catholic	Baptist	Non-Den.	Methodist[2]	Lutheran	LDS[3]	Pente-costal	Presby-terian[4]	Muslim[5]	Judaism
MSA[1]	26.0	1.3	4.2	1.0	0.5	1.4	1.1	0.7	1.0	0.6
U.S.	19.1	9.3	4.0	4.0	2.3	2.0	1.9	1.6	0.8	0.7

Note: Figures are the number of adherents as a percentage of the total population; (1) Figures cover the San Jose-Sunnyvale-Santa Clara, CA Metropolitan Statistical Area—see Appendix B for areas included; (2) Methodist/Pietist; (3) Latter Day Saints; (4) Reformed; (5) Figures are estimates
Source: Association of Statisticians of American Religious Bodies, 2010 U.S. Religion Census: Religious Congregations & Membership Study

Religious Groups by Tradition

Area	Catholic	Evangelical Protestant	Mainline Protestant	Other Tradition	Black Protestant	Orthodox
MSA[1]	26.0	8.2	2.4	6.8	0.1	0.4
U.S.	19.1	16.2	7.3	4.3	1.6	0.3

Note: Figures are the number of adherents as a percentage of the total population; (1) Figures cover the San Jose-Sunnyvale-Santa Clara, CA Metropolitan Statistical Area—see Appendix B for areas included
Source: Association of Statisticians of American Religious Bodies, 2010 U.S. Religion Census: Religious Congregations & Membership Study

ECONOMY

Gross Metropolitan Product

Area	2013	2014	2015	2016	Rank[2]
MSA[1]	196.8	210.1	220.3	233.3	16

Note: Figures are in billions of dollars; (1) Figures cover the San Jose-Sunnyvale-Santa Clara, CA Metropolitan Statistical Area—see Appendix B for areas included; (2) Rank is based on 2016 data and ranges from 1 to 381
Source: The U.S. Conference of Mayors, U.S. Metro Economies: GMP and Employment 2014-2016, June 2015

Economic Growth

Area	2011-13 (%)	2014 (%)	2015 (%)	2016 (%)	Rank[2]
MSA[1]	3.8	3.4	3.7	4.1	9
U.S.	2.2	2.4	2.3	2.9	–

Note: Figures are real gross metropolitan product (GMP) growth rates and represent annual average percent change; (1) Figures cover the San Jose-Sunnyvale-Santa Clara, CA Metropolitan Statistical Area—see Appendix B for areas included; (2) Rank is based on 2016 data and ranges from 1 to 381
Source: The U.S. Conference of Mayors, U.S. Metro Economies: GMP and Employment 2014-2016, June 2015

Metropolitan Area Exports

Area	2009	2010	2011	2012	2013	2014	Rank[2]
MSA[1]	21,405.7	26,333.0	26,712.1	26,687.6	23,413.1	21,128.7	16

Note: Figures are in millions of dollars; (1) Figures cover the San Jose-Sunnyvale-Santa Clara, CA Metropolitan Statistical Area—see Appendix B for areas included; (2) Rank is based on 2014 data and ranges from 1 to 385
Source: U.S. Department of Commerce, International Trade Administration, Office of Trade & Industry Information, Manufacturing & Services, data extracted March 10, 2016

Building Permits

Area	Single-Family			Multi-Family			Total		
	2014	2015p	Pct. Chg.	2014	2015p	Pct. Chg.	2014	2015p	Pct. Chg.
City	19	14	-26.3	0	0	-	19	14	-26.3
MSA[1]	1,861	1,954	5.0	8,176	4,364	-46.6	10,037	6,318	-37.1
U.S.	640,300	690,800	7.9	411,800	487,600	18.4	1,052,100	1,178,400	12.0

Note: (1) Figures cover the San Jose-Sunnyvale-Santa Clara, CA Metropolitan Statistical Area—see Appendix B for areas included; Figures represent new, privately-owned housing units authorized (unadjusted data); All permit data are based on estimates with imputation; (p) preliminary data.
Source: U.S. Census Bureau, Manufacturing, Mining, and Construction Statistics, Building Permits, 2014, 2015

Bankruptcy Filings

Area	Business Filings			Nonbusiness Filings		
	2014	2015	% Chg.	2014	2015	% Chg.
Santa Clara County	147	124	-15.6	3,173	2,413	-24.0
U.S.	26,983	24,735	-8.3	909,812	819,760	-9.9

Note: Business filings include Chapter 7, Chapter 11, Chapter 12, and Chapter 13; Nonbusiness filings include Chapter 7, Chapter 11, and Chapter 13
Source: Administrative Office of the U.S. Courts, Business and Nonbusiness Bankruptcy, County Cases Commenced by Chapter of the Bankruptcy Code, During the 12- Month Period Ending December 31, 2014 and Business and Nonbusiness Bankruptcy, County Cases Commenced by Chapter of the Bankruptcy Code, During the 12- Month Period Ending December 31, 2015

Housing Vacancy Rates

Area	Gross Vacancy Rate[2] (%)			Year-Round Vacancy Rate[3] (%)			Rental Vacancy Rate[4] (%)			Homeowner Vacancy Rate[5] (%)		
	2013	2014	2015	2013	2014	2015	2013	2014	2015	2013	2014	2015
MSA[1]	5.0	4.7	5.7	4.9	4.5	5.6	3.0	2.9	3.5	0.6	0.6	0.9
U.S.	13.6	13.4	12.9	10.7	10.4	10.0	8.3	7.6	7.1	2.0	1.9	1.8

Note: (1) Figures cover the San Jose-Sunnyvale-Santa Clara, CA Metropolitan Statistical Area—see Appendix B for areas included; (2) The percentage of the total housing inventory that is vacant; (3) The percentage of the housing inventory (excluding seasonal units) that is year-round vacant; (4) The percentage of rental inventory that is vacant for rent; (5) The percentage of homeowner inventory that is vacant for sale
Source: U.S. Census Bureau, Housing Vacancies and Homeownership Annual Statistics: 2015

INCOME

Income

Area	Per Capita ($)	Median Household ($)	Average Household ($)
City	77,667	167,917	219,907
MSA[1]	42,176	92,960	123,393
U.S.	28,555	53,482	74,596

Note: (1) Figures cover the San Jose-Sunnyvale-Santa Clara, CA Metropolitan Statistical Area—see Appendix B for areas included
Source: U.S. Census Bureau, 2010-2014 American Community Survey 5-Year Estimates

Household Income Distribution

Area	Percent of Households Earning							
	Under $15,000	$15,000 -24,999	$25,000 -34,999	$35,000 -49,999	$50,000 -74,999	$75,000 -99,000	$100,000 -149,999	$150,000 and up
City	3.9	3.2	3.2	4.3	6.8	8.2	13.8	56.8
MSA[1]	6.9	6.1	6.1	8.8	13.4	11.8	18.6	28.2
U.S.	12.5	10.7	10.2	13.5	17.8	12.2	13.0	10.0

Note: (1) Figures cover the San Jose-Sunnyvale-Santa Clara, CA Metropolitan Statistical Area—see Appendix B for areas included
Source: U.S. Census Bureau, 2010-2014 American Community Survey 5-Year Estimates

Poverty Rate

Area	All Ages	Under 18 Years Old	18 to 64 Years Old	65 Years and Over
City	3.6	4.3	3.2	3.7
MSA[1]	10.0	11.9	9.5	8.7
U.S.	15.6	21.9	14.6	9.4

Note: Figures are percentage of people whose income during the past 12 months was below the poverty level; (1) Figures cover the San Jose-Sunnyvale-Santa Clara, CA Metropolitan Statistical Area—see Appendix B for areas included
Source: U.S. Census Bureau, 2010-2014 American Community Survey 5-Year Estimates

EMPLOYMENT

Labor Force and Employment

Area	Civilian Labor Force			Workers Employed		
	Dec. 2014	Dec. 2015	% Chg.	Dec. 2014	Dec. 2015	% Chg.
City	14,789	15,236	3.0	14,333	14,834	3.4
MSA[1]	1,039,234	1,068,398	2.8	992,810	1,027,507	3.4
U.S.	155,521,000	157,245,000	1.1	147,190,000	149,703,000	1.7

Note: Data is not seasonally adjusted and covers workers 16 years of age and older; (1) Figures cover the San Jose-Sunnyvale-Santa Clara, CA Metropolitan Statistical Area—see Appendix B for areas included
Source: Bureau of Labor Statistics, Local Area Unemployment Statistics

Unemployment Rate

Area	2015											
	Jan.	Feb.	Mar.	Apr.	May	Jun.	Jul.	Aug.	Sep.	Oct.	Nov.	Dec.
City	3.3	3.1	2.9	2.7	2.8	2.8	3.0	2.8	2.6	2.8	2.7	2.6
MSA[1]	4.8	4.4	4.2	3.9	4.0	4.0	4.3	4.1	3.7	4.0	3.9	3.8
U.S.	6.1	5.8	5.6	5.1	5.3	5.5	5.6	5.2	4.9	4.8	4.8	4.8

Note: Data is not seasonally adjusted and covers workers 16 years of age and older; (1) Figures cover the San Jose-Sunnyvale-Santa Clara, CA Metropolitan Statistical Area—see Appendix B for areas included
Source: Bureau of Labor Statistics, Local Area Unemployment Statistics

Employment by Occupation

Occupation Classification	City (%)	MSA[1] (%)	U.S. (%)
Management, Business, Science, and Arts	75.5	49.7	36.4
Natural Resources, Construction, and Maintenance	1.3	6.9	9.0
Production, Transportation, and Material Moving	1.4	8.3	12.1
Sales and Office	15.9	20.1	24.4
Service	5.8	15.1	18.2

Note: Figures cover employed civilians 16 years of age and older; (1) Figures cover the San Jose-Sunnyvale-Santa Clara, CA Metropolitan Statistical Area—see Appendix B for areas included
Source: U.S. Census Bureau, 2010-2014 American Community Survey 5-Year Estimates

Employment by Industry

Sector	MSA[1]		U.S.
	Number of Employees	Percent of Total	Percent of Total
Construction	44,500	4.1	4.5
Education and Health Services	161,400	15.1	15.7
Financial Activities	35,600	3.3	5.7
Government	94,000	8.7	15.5
Information	77,200	7.2	1.9
Leisure and Hospitality	96,900	9.0	10.4
Manufacturing	161,800	15.1	8.6
Mining and Logging	200	<0.1	0.5
Other Services	27,800	2.6	3.9
Professional and Business Services	223,400	20.9	13.9
Retail Trade	92,200	8.6	11.3
Transportation, Warehousing, and Utilities	17,100	1.6	3.9
Wholesale Trade	36,600	3.4	4.1

Note: Figures are non-farm employment as of December 2015. Figures are not seasonally adjusted and include workers 16 years of age and older; (1) Figures cover the San Jose-Sunnyvale-Santa Clara, CA Metropolitan Statistical Area—see Appendix B for areas included
Source: Bureau of Labor Statistics, Current Employment Statistics, Employment, Hours, and Earnings

Occupations with Greatest Projected Employment Growth: 2012 – 2022

Occupation[1]	2012 Employment	2022 Projected Employment	Numeric Employment Change	Percent Employment Change
Personal Care Aides	386,900	587,200	200,300	51.8
Combined Food Preparation and Serving Workers, Including Fast Food	286,000	362,400	76,400	26.7
Retail Salespersons	468,400	528,100	59,700	12.7
Laborers and Freight, Stock, and Material Movers, Hand	270,500	322,300	51,800	19.1
Waiters and Waitresses	246,100	290,300	44,200	18.0
Registered Nurses	254,500	297,400	42,900	16.9
General and Operations Managers	253,800	295,700	41,900	16.5
Secretaries and Administrative Assistants, Except Legal, Medical, and Executive	212,800	250,100	37,300	17.5
Cashiers	357,800	392,600	34,800	9.7
Cooks, Restaurant	116,900	150,600	33,700	28.8

Note: Projections cover California; (1) Sorted by numeric employment change
Source: www.projectionscentral.com, State Occupational Projections, 2012–2022 Long-Term Projections

Fastest Growing Occupations: 2012 – 2022

Occupation[1]	2012 Employment	2022 Projected Employment	Numeric Employment Change	Percent Employment Change
Economists	3,100	5,100	2,000	64.5
Helpers—Brickmasons, Blockmasons, Stonemasons, and Tile and Marble Setters	2,900	4,600	1,700	58.6
Brickmasons and Blockmasons	5,100	8,000	2,900	56.9
Insulation Workers, Floor, Ceiling, and Wall	1,600	2,500	900	56.3
Stonemasons	1,100	1,700	600	54.5
Insulation Workers, Mechanical	1,100	1,700	600	54.5
Personal Care Aides	386,900	587,200	200,300	51.8
Foresters	1,200	1,800	600	50.0
Terrazzo Workers and Finishers	1,100	1,600	500	45.5
Mechanical Door Repairers	1,100	1,600	500	45.5

Note: Projections cover California; (1) Sorted by percent employment change and excludes occupations with numeric employment change less than 100
Source: www.projectionscentral.com, State Occupational Projections, 2012–2022 Long-Term Projections

Average Wages

Occupation	$/Hr.	Occupation	$/Hr.
Accountants and Auditors	48.36	Maids and Housekeeping Cleaners	15.18
Automotive Mechanics	25.59	Maintenance and Repair Workers	23.36
Bookkeepers	23.98	Marketing Managers	94.90
Carpenters	29.24	Nuclear Medicine Technologists	57.52
Cashiers	12.25	Nurses, Licensed Practical	28.36
Clerks, General Office	19.84	Nurses, Registered	58.47
Clerks, Receptionists/Information	17.28	Nursing Assistants	15.92
Clerks, Shipping/Receiving	17.59	Packers and Packagers, Hand	12.48
Computer Programmers	45.16	Physical Therapists	47.60
Computer Systems Analysts	55.19	Postal Service Mail Carriers	26.04
Computer User Support Specialists	37.61	Real Estate Brokers	n/a
Cooks, Restaurant	13.19	Retail Salespersons	14.30
Dentists	91.18	Sales Reps., Exc. Tech./Scientific	35.36
Electrical Engineers	64.71	Sales Reps., Tech./Scientific	56.30
Electricians	36.59	Secretaries, Exc. Legal/Med./Exec.	22.03
Financial Managers	82.91	Security Guards	15.74
First-Line Supervisors/Managers, Sales	24.43	Surgeons	125.24
Food Preparation Workers	11.88	Teacher Assistants*	15.16
General and Operations Managers	76.18	Teachers, Elementary School*	36.39
Hairdressers/Cosmetologists	12.87	Teachers, Secondary School*	36.28
Internists	112.31	Telemarketers	17.42
Janitors and Cleaners	13.50	Truck Drivers, Heavy/Tractor-Trailer	20.79
Landscaping/Groundskeeping Workers	15.50	Truck Drivers, Light/Delivery Svcs.	18.60
Lawyers	98.08	Waiters and Waitresses	13.01

Note: Wage data covers the San Jose-Sunnyvale-Santa Clara, CA Metropolitan Statistical Area—see Appendix B for areas included; (*) Hourly wages for elementary/secondary school teachers and teacher assistants were calculated by the editors from annual wage data based on a 40 hour work week; n/a not available.
Source: Bureau of Labor Statistics, Metro Area Occupational Employment and Wage Estimates, May 2015

TAXES

State Corporate Income Tax Rates

State	Tax Rate (%)	Income Brackets ($)	Num. of Brackets	Financial Institution Tax Rate (%)[a]	Federal Income Tax Ded.
California	8.84 (c)	Flat rate	1	10.84 (c)	No

Note: Tax rates as of January 1, 2016; (a) Rates listed are the corporate income tax rate applied to financial institutions or excise taxes based on income. Some states have other taxes based upon the value of deposits or shares; (c) Minimum tax is $800 in California, $100 in District of Columbia, $50 in North Dakota (banks), $500 in Rhode Island, $200 per location in South Dakota (banks), $100 in Utah, $250 in Vermont.
Source: Federation of Tax Administrators, "State Corporate Income Tax Rates, 2016"

State Individual Income Tax Rates

State	Tax Rate (%)	Income Brackets ($)	Num. of Brackets	Personal Exempt. ($)[1] Single	Personal Exempt. ($)[1] Dependents	Fed. Inc. Tax Ded.
California (a)	1.0 - 12.3 (f)	7,850- 526,443 (b)	9	109 (c)	337 (c)	No

Note: Tax rates as of January 1, 2016; Local- and county-level taxes are not included; n/a not applicable; (1) Married joint filers generally receive double the single exemption; (a) 18 states have statutory provision for automatically adjusting to the rate of inflation the dollar values of the income tax brackets, standard deductions, and/or personal exemptions. Massachusetts, Michigan, and Nebraska index the personal exemptiononly. Oregon does not index the income brackets for $125,000 and over. Maine has suspended indexing for 2014 and 2015; (b) For joint returns, taxes are twice the tax on half the couple's income; (c) The personal exemption takes the form of a tax credit instead of a deduction; (f) California imposes an additional 1% tax on taxable income over $1 million, making the maximum rate 13.3% over $1 million.
Source: Federation of Tax Administrators, "State Individual Income Tax Rates, 2016"

Various State and Local Tax Rates

State	State and Local Sales and Use (%)	State Sales and Use (%)	Gasoline[1] (¢/gal.)	Cigarette[2] ($/pack)	Spirits[3] ($/gal.)	Wine[4] ($/gal.)	Beer[5] ($/gal.)
California	8.75	7.50 (b)	40.62	0.87	3.30 (f)	0.20 (l)	0.08

Note: All tax rates as of January 1, 2016; (1) The American Petroleum Institute has developed a methodology for determining the average tax rate on a gallon of fuel. Rates may include any of the following: excise taxes, environmental fees, storage tank fees, other fees or taxes, general sales tax, and local taxes. In states where gasoline is subject to the general sales tax, or where the fuel tax is based on the average sale price, the average rate determined by API is sensitive to changes in the price of gasoline. States that fully or partially apply general sales taxes to gasoline: CA, CO, GA, IL, IN, MI, NY; (2) The federal excise tax of $1.0066 per pack and local taxes are not included; (3) Rates are those applicable to off-premise sales of 40% alcohol by volume (a.b.v.) distilled spirits in 750ml containers. Local excise taxes are excluded; (4) Rates are those applicable to off-premise sales of 11% a.b.v. non-carbonated wine in 750ml containers; (5) Rates are those applicable to off-premise sales of 4.7% a.b.v. beer in 12 ounce containers; (b) Three states levy mandatory, statewide local add-on sales taxes at the state level: California (1%), Utah (1.25%), and Virginia (1%). We include these in their state sales tax rates; (f) Different rates are also applicable according to alcohol content, place of production, size of container, or place purchased (on- or off-premise or onboard airlines); (l) Different rates also applicable according to alcohol content, place of production, size of container, place purchased (on- or off-premise or on board airlines) or type of wine (carbonated, vermouth, etc.).
Source: Tax Foundation, 2016 Facts & Figures: How Does Your State Compare?

State Business Tax Climate Index Rankings

State	Overall Rank	Corporate Tax Rank	Individual Income Tax Rank	Sales Tax Rank	Unemployment Insurance Tax Rank	Property Tax Rank
California	48	35	50	40	13	13

Note: The index is a measure of how each state's tax laws affect economic performance. The lower the rank, the more favorable a state's tax system is for business. States without a given tax are given a ranking of 1. The scores/rankings for the District of Columbia do not affect other states. The 2016 index represents the tax climate as of July 1, 2015 (the beginning of Fiscal Year 2016).
Source: Tax Foundation, State Business Tax Climate Index 2016

TRANSPORTATION

Means of Transportation to Work

Area	Car/Truck/Van: Drove Alone	Car/Truck/Van: Car-pooled	Public Transportation: Bus	Public Transportation: Subway	Public Transportation: Railroad	Bicycle	Walked	Other Means	Worked at Home
City	81.5	7.4	0.3	0.1	0.5	0.4	0.4	0.2	9.2
MSA[1]	76.5	10.5	2.2	0.2	1.1	1.8	1.9	1.4	4.6
U.S.	76.4	9.6	2.6	1.8	0.6	0.6	2.8	1.3	4.4

Note: Figures are percentages and cover workers 16 years of age and older; (1) Figures cover the San Jose-Sunnyvale-Santa Clara, CA Metropolitan Statistical Area—see Appendix B for areas included
Source: U.S. Census Bureau, 2010-2014 American Community Survey 5-Year Estimates

Travel Time to Work

Area	Less Than 10 Minutes	10 to 19 Minutes	20 to 29 Minutes	30 to 44 Minutes	45 to 59 Minutes	60 to 89 Minutes	90 Minutes or More
City	3.6	21.2	28.5	33.3	7.2	4.6	1.6
MSA[1]	8.4	29.2	25.7	22.3	7.4	5.3	1.9
U.S.	13.3	29.6	21.0	20.2	7.7	5.7	2.6

Note: Figures are percentages and include workers 16 years old and over; (1) Figures cover the San Jose-Sunnyvale-Santa Clara, CA Metropolitan Statistical Area—see Appendix B for areas included
Source: U.S. Census Bureau, 2010-2014 American Community Survey 5-Year Estimates

Freeway Travel Time Index

Area	1985	1990	1995	2000	2005	2010	2014
Urban Area Rank[1,2]	16	7	10	9	8	6	3
Urban Area Index[1]	1.15	1.21	1.23	1.28	1.32	1.34	1.38
Average Index[3]	1.09	1.11	1.14	1.17	1.20	1.19	1.20

Note: Freeway Travel Time Index—the ratio of travel time in the peak period to the travel time at free-flow conditions. For example, a value of 1.30 indicates a 20-minute free-flow trip takes 26 minutes in the peak (20 minutes x 1.30 = 26 minutes); (1) Covers the San Jose CA urban area; (2) Rank is based on 101 urban areas (#1 = highest travel time index); (3) Average of 101 urban areas
Source: Texas Transportation Institute, 2015 Urban Mobility Scorecard, August 2015

Freeway Commuter Stress Index

Area	1985	1990	1995	2000	2005	2010	2014
Urban Area Rank[1,2]	14	7	8	7	7	5	5
Urban Area Index[1]	1.24	1.31	1.33	1.39	1.43	1.45	1.50
Average Index[3]	1.13	1.16	1.19	1.22	1.25	1.24	1.25

Note: The Freeway Commuter Stress Index is the same as the Freeway Travel Time Index (see table above) except that it includes only the travel in the peak directions during the peak periods; the TTI includes travel in all directions during the peak period. Thus, the CSI is more indicative of the work trip experienced by each commuter on a daily basis. (1) Covers the San Jose CA urban area; (2) Rank is based on 101 urban areas (#1 = highest stress index); (3) Average of 101 urban areas
Source: Texas Transportation Institute, 2015 Urban Mobility Scorecard, August 2015

Living Environment

COST OF LIVING

Cost of Living Index

Composite Index	Groceries	Housing	Utilities	Trans-portation	Health Care	Misc. Goods/ Services
n/a	n/a	n/a	n/a	n/a	n/a	n/a

Note: The Cost of Living Index measures regional differences in the cost of consumer goods and services, excluding taxes and non-consumer expenditures, for professional and managerial households in the top income quintile. It is based on more than 50,000 prices covering almost 60 different items for which prices are collected three times a year by chambers of commerce, economic development organizations or university applied economic centers in each participating urban area. The numbers shown should be read as a percentage above or below the national average of 100. For example, a value of 115.4 in the groceries column indicates that grocery prices are 15.4% higher than the national average. Small differences in the index numbers should not be interpreted as significant; n/a not available.
Source: The Council for Community and Economic Research, ACCRA Cost of Living Index, 2015

Grocery Prices

Area[1]	T-Bone Steak ($/pound)	Frying Chicken ($/pound)	Whole Milk ($/half gal.)	Eggs ($/dozen)	Orange Juice ($/64 oz.)	Coffee ($/11.5 oz.)
City[2]	n/a	n/a	n/a	n/a	n/a	n/a
Avg.	10.99	1.43	2.25	2.26	3.58	4.48
Min.	7.16	0.98	1.30	1.35	2.88	2.98
Max.	14.13	2.43	3.85	4.81	6.39	7.56

Note: (1) Values for the local area are compared with the average, minimum and maximum values for all 292 areas in the Cost of Living Index; (2) Figures cover the Saratoga CA urban area; n/a not available; **T-Bone Steak** *(price per pound);* **Frying Chicken** *(price per pound, whole fryer);* **Whole Milk** *(half gallon carton);* **Eggs** *(price per dozen, Grade A, large);* **Orange Juice** *(64 oz. Tropicana or Florida Natural);* **Coffee** *(11.5 oz. can, vacuum-packed, Maxwell House, Hills Bros, or Folgers).*
Source: The Council for Community and Economic Research, ACCRA Cost of Living Index, 2015

Housing and Utility Costs

Area[1]	New Home Price ($)	Apartment Rent ($/month)	All Electric ($/month)	Part Electric ($/month)	Other Energy ($/month)	Telephone ($/month)
City[2]	n/a	n/a	n/a	n/a	n/a	n/a
Avg.	312,874	945	179.30	95.07	72.96	28.11
Min.	178,682	479	116.28	43.14	26.46	10.01
Max.	1,472,476	3,984	504.25	189.44	421.11	43.06

Note: (1) Values for the local area are compared with the average, minimum and maximum values for all 292 areas in the Cost of Living Index; (2) Figures cover the Saratoga CA urban area; n/a not available; **New Home Price** *(2,400 sf living area, 8,000 sf lot, in urban area with full utilities);* **Apartment Rent** *(950 sf 2 bedroom/1.5 or 2 bath, unfurnished, excluding all utilities except water);* **All Electric** *(average monthly cost for an all-electric home);* **Part Electric** *(average monthly cost for a part-electric home);* **Other Energy** *(average monthly cost for natural gas, fuel oil, coal, wood, and any other forms of energy except electricity);* **Telephone** *(price includes basic monthly rate for a private residential line plus additional local usage charges incurred by a family of four).*
Source: The Council for Community and Economic Research, ACCRA Cost of Living Index, 2015

Health Care, Transportation, and Other Costs

Area[1]	Doctor ($/visit)	Dentist ($/visit)	Optometrist ($/visit)	Gasoline ($/gallon)	Beauty Salon ($/visit)	Men's Shirt ($)
City[2]	n/a	n/a	n/a	n/a	n/a	n/a
Avg.	105.15	89.02	99.78	2.38	35.30	28.10
Min.	66.87	56.09	48.53	1.95	18.91	13.38
Max.	182.34	150.36	228.33	4.09	67.91	63.80

Note: (1) Values for the local area are compared with the average, minimum and maximum values for all 292 areas in the Cost of Living Index; (2) Figures cover the Saratoga CA urban area; n/a not available; **Doctor** *(general practitioners routine exam of an established patient);* **Dentist** *(adult teeth cleaning and periodic oral examination);* **Optometrist** *(full vision eye exam for established adult patient);* **Gasoline** *(one gallon regular unleaded, national brand, including all taxes, cash price at self-service pump if available);* **Beauty Salon** *(woman's shampoo, trim, and blow-dry);* **Men's Shirt** *(cotton/polyester dress shirt, pinpoint weave, long sleeves).*
Source: The Council for Community and Economic Research, ACCRA Cost of Living Index, 2015

HOUSING

House Price Index (HPI)

Area	National Ranking[2]	Quarterly Change (%)	One-Year Change (%)	Five-Year Change (%)
MSA[1]	15	1.20	11.30	51.20
U.S.[3]	–	1.45	5.76	22.85

Note: The HPI is a weighted repeat sales index. It measures average price changes in repeat sales or refinancings on the same properties. This information is obtained by reviewing repeat mortgage transactions on single-family properties whose mortgages have been purchased or securitized by Fannie Mae or Freddie Mac in January 1975; (1) San Jose-Sunnyvale-Santa Clara Metropolitan Statistical Area—see Appendix B for areas included; (2) Rankings are based on annual percentage change for all metro areas containing at least 15,000 transactions over the last 10 years and ranges from 1 to 266; (3) figures based on a weighted average of Census Division estimates using a seasonally adjusted, purchase-only index; all figures are for the period ending December 31, 2015

Source: Federal Housing Finance Agency, House Price Index, February 25, 2016

Median Single-Family Home Prices

Area	2013	2014	2015[p]	Percent Change 2014 to 2015
MSA[1]	780.0	860.0	950.4	10.5
U.S. Average	197.4	208.9	223.9	7.2

Note: Figures are median sales prices of existing single-family homes in thousands of dollars; (p) preliminary; n/a not available; (1) San Jose-Sunnyvale-Santa Clara, CA Metropolitan Statistical Area—see Appendix B for areas included

Source: National Association of Realtors, Median Sales Price of Existing Single-Family Homes for Metropolitan Areas, 4th Quarter 2015

Qualifying Income Based on Median Sales Price of Existing Single-Family Homes

Area	With 5% Down ($)	With 10% Down ($)	With 20% Down ($)
MSA[1]	209,085	198,080	176,071
U.S. Average	49,535	46,928	41,714

Note: Figures are preliminary; Qualifying income is based on a mortgage rate of 4.1%. Monthly principal and interest payment is limited to 25% of income; n/a not available; (1) San Jose-Sunnyvale-Santa Clara, CA Metropolitan Statistical Area—see Appendix B for areas included

Source: National Association of Realtors, Qualifying Income Based on Median Sales Price of Existing Single-Family Homes for Metropolitan Areas, 4th Quarter 2015

Median Apartment Condo-Coop Home Prices

Area	2013	2014	2015[p]	Percent Change 2014 to 2015
MSA[1]	n/a	n/a	n/a	n/a
U.S. Average	194.9	204.3	210.7	3.1

Note: Figures are median sales prices of existing apartment condo-coop homes in thousands of dollars; (p) preliminary; n/a not available; (1) San Jose-Sunnyvale-Santa Clara, CA Metropolitan Statistical Area—see Appendix B for areas included

Source: National Association of Realtors, Median Sales Price of Existing Apartment Condo-Coop Homes for Metropolitan Areas, 4th Quarter 2015

Gross Monthly Rent

Area	Under $200	$200 -299	$300 -499	$500 -749	$750 -999	$1,000 -1,499	$1,500 and up	Median ($)
City	0.0	9.8	6.5	4.1	0.0	7.5	72.1	2,000+
MSA[1]	0.5	1.5	2.6	3.7	6.5	28.1	57.1	1,629
U.S.	1.5	3.2	7.4	21.0	24.1	26.9	15.9	920

Note: Figures are percentages except for Median; Gross rent is the contract rent plus the estimated average monthly cost of utilities (electricity, gas, and water and sewer) and fuels (oil, coal, kerosene, wood, etc.) if these are paid by the renter (or paid for the renter by someone else); (1) Figures cover the San Jose-Sunnyvale-Santa Clara, CA Metropolitan Statistical Area—see Appendix B for areas included

Source: U.S. Census Bureau, 2010-2014 American Community Survey 5-Year Estimates

Homeownership Rate

Area	2008 (%)	2009 (%)	2010 (%)	2011 (%)	2012 (%)	2013 (%)	2014 (%)	2015 (%)
MSA[1]	54.6	57.2	58.9	60.4	58.6	56.4	56.4	50.7
U.S.	67.8	67.4	66.9	66.1	65.4	65.1	64.5	63.7

Note: (1) Figures cover the San Jose-Sunnyvale-Santa Clara, CA Metropolitan Statistical Area—see Appendix B for areas included
Source: U.S. Census Bureau, Housing Vacancies and Homeownership Annual Statistics: 2015

Year Housing Structure Built

Area	2010 or Later	2000 -2009	1990 -1999	1980 -1989	1970 -1979	1960 -1969	1950 -1959	1940 -1949	Before 1940	Median Year
City	0.8	5.8	4.3	7.1	22.9	27.1	24.5	3.8	3.7	1967
MSA[1]	0.7	9.8	10.6	12.7	22.6	18.9	15.4	4.2	5.2	1973
U.S.	1.0	14.9	13.9	13.8	15.8	11.0	10.8	5.4	13.3	1976

Note: Figures are percentages except for Median Year; (1) Figures cover the San Jose-Sunnyvale-Santa Clara, CA Metropolitan Statistical Area—see Appendix B for areas included
Source: U.S. Census Bureau, 2010-2014 American Community Survey 5-Year Estimates

HEALTH

Health Risk Data

Category	MSA[1] (%)	U.S. (%)
Adults aged 18–64 who have any kind of health care coverage	82.5	79.6
Adults who reported being in good or excellent health	88.2	83.1
Adults who are current smokers	9.6	19.6
Adults who are heavy drinkers[2]	4.3	6.1
Adults who are binge drinkers[3]	16.4	16.9
Adults who are overweight (BMI 25.0 - 29.9)	33.0	35.8
Adults who are obese (BMI 30.0 - 99.8)	15.9	27.6
Adults who participated in any physical activities in the past month	83.6	77.1
Adults 50+ who have ever had a sigmoidoscopy or colonoscopy	72.3	67.3
Women aged 40+ who have had a mammogram within the past two years	82.7	74.0
Men aged 40+ who have had a PSA test within the past two years	31.4	45.2
Adults aged 65+ who have had flu shot within the past year	54.1	60.1
Adults who always wear a seatbelt	n/a	93.8

Note: Data as of 2012 unless otherwise noted; n/a not available; (1) Figures cover the San Jose-Sunnyvale-Santa Clara, CA Metropolitan Statistical Area—see Appendix B for areas included; (2) Heavy drinkers are classified as males having more than two drinks per day or females having more than one drink per day; (3) Binge drinkers are classified as males having five or more drinks on one occasion or females having four or more drinks on one occasion
Source: Centers for Disease Control and Prevention, Behaviorial Risk Factor Surveillance System, SMART: Selected Metropolitan/Micropolitan Area Risk Trends, 2012 (Note: the CDC has discontinued this dataset but will be releasing a replacement in mid-2016)

Chronic Health Indicators

Category	MSA[1] (%)	U.S. (%)
Adults who have ever been told they had a heart attack	3.8	4.5
Adults who have ever been told they had a stroke	n/a	2.9
Adults who have been told they currently have asthma	8.4	8.9
Adults who have ever been told they have arthritis	17.2	25.7
Adults who have ever been told they have diabetes[2]	7.4	9.7
Adults who have ever been told they had skin cancer	4.1	5.7
Adults who have ever been told they had any other types of cancer	3.9	6.5
Adults who have ever been told they have COPD	2.7	6.2
Adults who have ever been told they have kidney disease	2.9	2.5
Adults who have ever been told they have a form of depression	11.3	18.0

Note: Data as of 2012 unless otherwise noted; n/a not available; (1) Figures cover the San Jose-Sunnyvale-Santa Clara, CA Metropolitan Statistical Area—see Appendix B for areas included; (2) Figures do not include pregnancy-related, borderline, or pre-diabetes
Source: Centers for Disease Control and Prevention, Behaviorial Risk Factor Surveillance System, SMART: Selected Metropolitan/Micropolitan Area Risk Trends, 2012 (Note: the CDC has discontinued this dataset but will be releasing a replacement in mid-2016)

Mortality Rates for the Top 10 Causes of Death in the U.S.

ICD-10[a] Sub-Chapter	ICD-10[a] Code	Age-Adjusted Mortality Rate[1] per 100,000 population	
		County[2]	U.S.
Malignant neoplasms	C00-C97	129.7	163.6
Ischaemic heart diseases	I20-I25	68.0	102.2
Other forms of heart disease	I30-I51	21.9	50.1
Chronic lower respiratory diseases	J40-J47	22.8	41.4
Organic, including symptomatic, mental disorders	F01-F09	6.6	38.5
Cerebrovascular diseases	I60-I69	26.5	36.5
Other external causes of accidental injury	W00-X59	16.7	27.5
Other degenerative diseases of the nervous system	G30-G31	48.0	26.3
Diabetes mellitus	E10-E14	22.4	21.1
Hypertensive diseases	I10-I15	29.7	19.7

Note: (a) ICD-10 = International Classification of Diseases 10th Revision; (1) Mortality rates are a three year average covering 2012-2014; (2) Figures cover COUNTY NOT FOUND!!!!!!.
Source: Centers for Disease Control and Prevention, National Center for Health Statistics. Underlying Cause of Death 1999-2014 on CDC WONDER Online Database, released 2015.

Mortality Rates for Selected Causes of Death

ICD-10[a] Sub-Chapter	ICD-10[a] Code	Age-Adjusted Mortality Rate[1] per 100,000 population	
		County[2]	U.S.
Assault	X85-Y09	2.8	5.1
Diseases of the liver	K70-K76	9.6	13.5
Human immunodeficiency virus (HIV) disease	B20-B24	0.7	2.1
Influenza and pneumonia	J09-J18	12.4	15.2
Intentional self-harm	X60-X84	7.9	12.7
Malnutrition	E40-E46	Unreliable	0.9
Obesity and other hyperalimentation	E65-E68	1.0	1.9
Renal failure	N17-N19	2.5	13.0
Transport accidents	V01-V99	6.3	11.6
Viral hepatitis	B15-B19	2.3	2.1

Note: (a) ICD-10 = International Classification of Diseases 10th Revision; (1) Mortality rates are a three year average covering 2012-2014; (2) Figures cover COUNTY NOT FOUND!!!!!!; Data are Suppressed when the data meet the criteria for confidentiality constraints; Mortality rates are flagged as Unreliable when the rate would be calculated with a numerator of 20 or less.
Source: Centers for Disease Control and Prevention, National Center for Health Statistics. Underlying Cause of Death 1999-2014 on CDC WONDER Online Database, released 2015.

Health Insurance Coverage

Area	With Health Insurance	With Private Health Insurance	With Public Health Insurance	Without Health Insurance	Population Under Age 18 Without Health Insurance
City	97.4	90.9	20.6	2.6	1.4
MSA[1]	89.3	73.0	24.2	10.7	3.9
U.S.	85.8	65.8	31.1	14.2	7.1

Note: Figures are percentages that cover the civilian noninstitutionalized population; (1) Figures cover the San Jose-Sunnyvale-Santa Clara, CA Metropolitan Statistical Area—see Appendix B for areas included
Source: U.S. Census Bureau, 2010-2014 American Community Survey 5-Year Estimates

Number of Medical Professionals

Area	MDs[3]	DOs[3,4]	Dentists	Podiatrists	Chiropractors	Optometrists
County[1] (number)	7,351	153	2,028	112	738	460
County[1] (rate[2])	392.9	8.2	107.0	5.9	39.0	24.3
U.S. (rate[2])	272.5	20.9	64.7	5.8	25.9	15.2

Note: Data as of 2014 unless noted; (1) Data covers Santa Clara County; (2) Rate per 100,000 population; (3) Data as of 2013 and includes all active, non-federal physicians; (4) Doctor of Osteopathic Medicine
Source: U.S. Department of Health and Human Services, Health Resources and Services Administration, Bureau of Health Professions, Area Resource File (ARF) 2014-2015

Best Hospitals

According to *U.S. News,* the San Jose-Sunnyvale-Santa Clara, CA metro area is home to one of the best hospitals in the U.S.: **Stanford Hospital and Clinics** (Honor Roll/13 specialties). The hospital listed was nationally ranked in at least one adult specialty. Only 137 hospitals nationwide were nationally ranked in one or more specialties. Fifteen hospitals in the U.S. made the Honor Roll with high scores in at least six specialties. *U.S. News Online, "America's Best Children's Hospitals 2015-16"*

According to *U.S. News,* the San Jose-Sunnyvale-Santa Clara, CA metro area is home to one of the best children's hospitals in the U.S.: **Lucile Packard Children's Hospital at Stanford** (9 specialties). The hospital listed was highly ranked in at least one pediatric specialty. Eighty-three children's hospitals in the U.S. were nationally ranked in at least one specialty. Twelve children's hospitals in the U.S. made the Honor Roll with high scores in at least three specialties. *U.S. News Online, "America's Best Children's Hospitals 2015-16"*

EDUCATION

Public School District Statistics

District Name	Schls	Pupils	Pupil/ Teacher Ratio	Minority Pupils[1] (%)	Free Lunch Eligible[2] (%)	IEP[3] (%)
Campbell Union	12	7,653	22.8	72.6	41.5	8.9
Campbell Union High	7	7,353	22.7	59.5	15.4	10.0
Los Gatos-Saratoga JUH	2	3,261	21.2	46.8	1.4	8.9
Saratoga Union Elementary	4	2,111	19.7	67.4	0.8	10.5

Note: Table includes school districts with 100 or more students; (1) Percentage of students that are not non-Hispanic white; (2) Percentage of students that are eligible for the free lunch program; (3) Percentage of students that have an Individualized Education Program.
Source: U.S. Department of Education, National Center for Education Statistics, Common Core of Data, Local Education Agency (School District) Universe Survey: School Year 2013-2014; U.S. Department of Education, National Center for Education Statistics, Common Core of Data, Public Elementary/Secondary School Universe Survey: School Year 2013-2014

Best High Schools

According to *U.S. News,* Saratoga is home to one of the best high schools in the U.S.: **Saratoga High School** (#172); Nearly 20,000 schools were ranked based on their performance on state assessments and how well they prepare students for college. Schools with the highest unrounded College Readiness Index values were numerically ranked from No. 1 to No. 500 and were the gold medal winners. *U.S. News & World Report, "Best High Schools 2015"*

Highest Level of Education

Area	Less than H.S.	H.S. Diploma	Some College, No Deg.	Associate Degree	Bachelor's Degree	Master's Degree	Prof. School Degree	Doctorate Degree
City	1.8	5.1	10.4	5.1	35.7	30.1	6.4	5.4
MSA[1]	13.5	15.7	17.2	7.1	25.7	14.9	2.7	3.3
U.S.	13.7	28.0	21.2	7.9	18.3	7.8	2.0	1.3

Note: Figures cover persons age 25 and over; (1) Figures cover the San Jose-Sunnyvale-Santa Clara, CA Metropolitan Statistical Area—see Appendix B for areas included
Source: U.S. Census Bureau, 2010-2014 American Community Survey 5-Year Estimates

Educational Attainment by Race

Area	High School Graduate or Higher (%)					Bachelor's Degree or Higher (%)				
	Total	White	Black	Asian	Hisp.[2]	Total	White	Black	Asian	Hisp.[2]
City	98.2	98.4	91.1	98.1	82.5	77.6	70.5	23.6	88.1	30.3
MSA[1]	86.5	88.4	91.8	89.2	65.6	46.5	44.1	31.5	61.2	14.3
U.S.	86.3	88.4	83.2	85.8	64.1	29.3	30.6	19.0	50.9	13.9

Note: Figures shown cover persons 25 years old and over; (1) Figures cover the San Jose-Sunnyvale-Santa Clara, CA Metropolitan Statistical Area—see Appendix B for areas included; (2) People of Hispanic origin can be of any race
Source: U.S. Census Bureau, 2010-2014 American Community Survey 5-Year Estimates

School Enrollment by Grade and Control

Area	Preschool (%)		Kindergarten (%)		Grades 1 - 4 (%)		Grades 5 - 8 (%)		Grades 9 - 12 (%)	
	Public	Private	Public	Private	Public	Private	Public	Private	Public	Private
City	27.5	72.5	85.2	14.8	85.6	14.4	87.5	12.5	80.5	19.5
MSA[1]	34.4	65.6	81.9	18.1	87.1	12.9	87.7	12.3	89.1	10.9
U.S.	57.4	42.6	87.8	12.2	89.8	10.2	89.9	10.1	90.6	9.4

Note: Figures shown cover persons 3 years old and over; (1) Figures cover the San Jose-Sunnyvale-Santa Clara, CA Metropolitan Statistical Area—see Appendix B for areas included
Source: U.S. Census Bureau, 2010-2014 American Community Survey 5-Year Estimates

Average Salaries of Public School Classroom Teachers

Area	2013-14		2014-15		Percent Change 2013-14 to 2014-15	Percent Change 2004-05 to 2014-15
	Dollars	Rank[1]	Dollars	Rank[1]		
California	71,396	4	72,535	4	1.59	25.9
U.S. Average	56,610	–	57,379	–	1.36	20.8

Note: (1) State rank ranges from 1 to 51 where 1 indicates highest salary.
Source: National Education Association, Rankings & Estimates: Rankings of the States 2014 and Estimates of School Statistics 2015, March 2015

Higher Education

Four-Year Colleges			Two-Year Colleges			Medical Schools[1]	Law Schools[2]	Voc/ Tech[3]
Public	Private Non-profit	Private For-profit	Public	Private Non-profit	Private For-profit			
0	0	0	1	0	0	0	0	0

Note: Figures cover institutions located within the city limits and include main campuses only; (1) includes schools accredited by the Liaison Committee on Medical Education and the American Osteopathic Association's Commission on Osteopathic College Accreditation; (2) includes ABA-accredited schools, schools with provisional ABA accreditation, and state accredited schools; (3) includes all schools with programs that are less than 2 years.
Source: National Center for Education Statistics, Integrated Postsecondary Education System (IPEDS), 2014-15; Association of American Medical Colleges, Member List, March 21, 2016; American Osteopathic Association, Member List, March 21, 2016; Law School Admission Council, Official Guide to ABA-Approved Law Schools Online, March 21, 2016; Wikipedia, List of Medical Schools in the United States, March 21, 2016; Wikipedia, List of Law Schools in the United States, March 21, 2016

According to *U.S. News & World Report,* the San Jose-Sunnyvale-Santa Clara, CA metro area is home to one of the best national universities in the U.S.: **Stanford University** (#4 tie). The indicators used to capture academic quality fall into a number of categories: assessment by administrators at peer institutions; retention of students; faculty resources; student selectivity; financial resources; alumni giving; high school counselor ratings of colleges; and graduation rate. *U.S. News & World Report, "America's Best Colleges 2016"*

According to *U.S. News & World Report,* the San Jose-Sunnyvale-Santa Clara, CA metro area is home to one of the top 100 law schools in the U.S.: **Stanford University, Law School** (#2 tie). The rankings are based on a weighted average of 12 measures of quality: peer assessment score; assessment score by lawyers/judges; median LSAT scores; median undergrad GPA; acceptance rate; employment rates for graduates; placement success; bar passage rate; faculty resources; expenditures per student; student/faculty ratio; and library resources. *U.S. News & World Report, "America's Best Graduate Schools, Law, 2017"*

According to *U.S. News & World Report,* the San Jose-Sunnyvale-Santa Clara, CA metro area is home to one of the top 75 medical schools for research in the U.S.: **Stanford University, School of Medicine** (#2). The rankings are based on a weighted average of 11 measures of quality: quality assessment; peer assessment score; assessment score by residency directors; research activity; total research activity; average research activity per faculty member; student selectivity; median MCAT total score; median undergraduate GPA; acceptance rate; and faculty resources. *U.S. News & World Report, "America's Best Graduate Schools, Medical, 2017"*

According to *U.S. News & World Report,* the San Jose-Sunnyvale-Santa Clara, CA metro area is home to one of the top 75 business schools in the U.S.: **Stanford University, Graduate School of Business** (#2 tie). The rankings are based on a weighted average of the following nine measures: quality assessment; peer assessment; recruiter assessment; placement success; mean starting salary and bonus; student selectivity; mean GMAT and GRE scores; mean

undergraduate GPA; and acceptance rate. *U.S. News & World Report, "America's Best Graduate Schools, Business, 2017"*

PRESIDENTIAL ELECTION

2012 Presidential Election Results

Area	Obama (%)	Romney (%)	Other (%)
Santa Clara County	69.9	27.6	2.5
U.S.	51.0	47.2	1.8

Note: Results may not add to 100% due to rounding
Source: Dave Leip's Atlas of U.S. Presidential Elections

EMPLOYERS

Major Employers

Company Name	Industry
Adobe Systems Inc	Publishers-computer software (mfrs)
Advanced Micro Devices Inc	Semiconductor devices (mfrs)
Apple Inc	Computers-electronic-manufacturers
Applied Materials Inc	Semiconductor manufacturing equip (mfrs)
Bon Appetit-Cafe Adobe	Restaurant management
California's Great America	Amusement & theme parks
Christopher Ranch	Garlic manufacturers
Cisco Systems Inc	Computer peripherals
E Bay Inc	E-commerce
Flextronics	Solar energy equipment-manufacturers
General Motors Advanced Tech	Automobile-manufacturers
Hewlett-Packard	Computers-electronic-manufacturers
Intel Corp	Semiconductor devices (mfrs)
Kaiser Permanente Med Center	Hospitals
Kaiser Permanente Medical Ctr	Hospitals
Lockheed Martin Space Systems	Satellite equipment & systems-mfrs
Microsoft Corp	Computer software-manufacturers
NASA	Government offices-us
Net App Inc	Computer storage devices

Note: Companies shown are located within the San Jose-Sunnyvale-Santa Clara, CA Metropolitan Statistical Area.
Source: Hoovers.com; Wikipedia

PUBLIC SAFETY

Crime Rate

Area	All Crimes	Violent Crimes: Murder	Violent Crimes: Rape[3]	Violent Crimes: Robbery	Violent Crimes: Aggrav. Assault	Property Crimes: Burglary	Property Crimes: Larceny -Theft	Property Crimes: Motor Vehicle Theft
City	986.4	0.0	35.3	6.4	19.3	437.0	449.8	38.6
Metro[1]	2,496.5	2.3	25.2	80.4	142.0	469.8	1,272.0	504.9
U.S.	2,971.8	4.5	36.6	102.2	232.5	542.5	1,837.3	216.2

Note: Figures are crimes per 100,000 population; (1) Figures cover the San Jose-Sunnyvale-Santa Clara, CA Metropolitan Statistical Area—see Appendix B for areas included; (3) The city and U.S. figures shown were reported using the revised Uniform Crime Reporting (UCR) definition of rape. The suburban and metro area figures shown are an aggregate total of the data submitted using both the revised and legacy UCR definitions.
Source: FBI Uniform Crime Reports, 2014

Hate Crimes

Area	Number of Quarters Reported	Race	Religion	Sexual Orientation	Ethnicity	Disability	Gender	Gender Identity
		Number of Incidents per Bias Motivation						
City	4	0	0	0	0	0	0	0
U.S.	4	2,568	1,014	1,017	648	84	33	98

Source: Federal Bureau of Investigation, Hate Crime Statistics 2014

Identity Theft Consumer Complaints

Area	Complaints	Complaints per 100,000 Population	Rank[2]
MSA[1]	2,693	137.9	74
U.S.	490,220	152.4	-

Note: (1) Figures cover the San Jose-Sunnyvale-Santa Clara, CA Metropolitan Statistical Area—see Appendix B for areas included; (2) Rank ranges from 1 to 379 where 1 indicates greatest number of identity theft complaints per 100,000 population
Source: Federal Trade Commission, Consumer Sentinel Network Data Book for January–December 2015

Fraud and Other Consumer Complaints

Area	Complaints	Complaints per 100,000 Population	Rank[2]
MSA[1]	6,862	351.4	213
U.S.	2,593,159	806.0	-

Note: (1) Figures cover the San Jose-Sunnyvale-Santa Clara, CA Metropolitan Statistical Area—see Appendix B for areas included; (2) Rank ranges from 1 to 379 where 1 indicates greatest number of identity theft complaints per 100,000 population
Source: Federal Trade Commission, Consumer Sentinel Network Data Book for January–December 2015

RECREATION

Culture

Dance[1]	Theatre[1]	Instrumental Music[1]	Vocal Music[1]	Series and Festivals	Museums and Art Galleries[2]	Zoos and Aquariums[3]
0	0	0	0	0	0	0

Note: (1) Professional perfoming groups; (2) Based on organizations with SIC code 8412; (3) AZA-accredited
Source: The Grey House Performing Arts Directory, 2015-16; Association of Zoos & Aquariums, AZA Member Zoos & Aquariums, March 25, 2016; www.AccuLeads.com, March 29, 2016

Professional Sports Teams

Team Name	League	Year Established
San Jose Earthquakes	Major League Soccer (MLS)	1996
San Jose Sharks	National Hockey League (NHL)	1991

Note: Includes teams located in the San Jose-Sunnyvale-Santa Clara, CA Metropolitan Statistical Area.
Source: Wikipedia, Major Professional Sports Teams of the United States and Canada, March 24, 2016

CLIMATE

Average and Extreme Temperatures

Temperature	Jan	Feb	Mar	Apr	May	Jun	Jul	Aug	Sep	Oct	Nov	Dec	Yr.
Extreme High (°F)	76	82	83	95	103	104	105	101	105	100	87	76	105
Average High (°F)	57	61	63	67	70	74	75	75	76	72	65	58	68
Average Temp. (°F)	50	53	55	58	61	65	66	67	66	63	56	50	59
Average Low (°F)	42	45	46	48	51	55	57	58	57	53	47	42	50
Extreme Low (°F)	21	26	30	32	38	43	45	47	41	33	29	23	21

Note: Figures cover the years 1945-1993
Source: National Climatic Data Center, International Station Meteorological Climate Summary, 9/96

Average Precipitation/Snowfall/Humidity

Precip./Humidity	Jan	Feb	Mar	Apr	May	Jun	Jul	Aug	Sep	Oct	Nov	Dec	Yr.
Avg. Precip. (in.)	2.7	2.3	2.2	0.9	0.3	0.1	Tr	Tr	0.2	0.7	1.7	2.3	13.5
Avg. Snowfall (in.)	Tr	Tr	Tr	0	0	0	0	0	0	0	0	Tr	Tr
Avg. Rel. Hum. 7am (%)	82	82	80	76	74	73	77	79	79	79	81	82	79
Avg. Rel. Hum. 4pm (%)	62	59	56	52	53	54	58	58	55	54	59	63	57

Note: Figures cover the years 1945-1993; Tr = Trace amounts (<0.05 in. of rain; <0.5 in. of snow)
Source: National Climatic Data Center, International Station Meteorological Climate Summary, 9/96

Weather Conditions

Temperature			Daytime Sky			Precipitation		
10°F & below	32°F & below	90°F & above	Clear	Partly cloudy	Cloudy	0.01 inch or more precip.	0.1 inch or more snow/ice	Thunder-storms
0	5	5	106	180	79	57	< 1	6

Note: Figures are average number of days per year and cover the years 1945-1993
Source: National Climatic Data Center, International Station Meteorological Climate Summary, 9/96

HAZARDOUS WASTE

Superfund Sites

Saratoga has no sites on the EPA's Superfund Final National Priorities List. There are a total of 1,323 Superfund sites on the list in the U.S. *U.S. Environmental Protection Agency, Final National Priorities List, March 18, 2016*

AIR & WATER QUALITY

Air Quality Trends: Ozone

	1990	1995	2000	2005	2010	2011	2012	2013	2014
MSA[1]	0.079	0.085	0.070	0.065	0.073	0.065	0.064	0.064	0.069

Note: (1) Data covers the San Jose-Sunnyvale-Santa Clara, CA Metropolitan Statistical Area—see Appendix B for areas included. The values shown are the composite ozone concentration averages among trend sites based on the highest fourth daily maximum 8-hour concentration in parts per million. These trends are based on sites having an adequate record of monitoring data during the trend period. Data from exceptional events are included.
Source: U.S. Environmental Protection Agency, Air Quality Monitoring Information, "Air Quality Trends by City, 1990-2014"

Air Quality Index

Area	Percent of Days when Air Quality was...[2]					AQI Statistics[2]	
	Good	Moderate	Unhealthy for Sensitive Groups	Unhealthy	Very Unhealthy	Maximum	Median
MSA[1]	67.1	31.0	1.9	0.0	0.0	135	44

Note: (1) Data covers the San Jose-Sunnyvale-Santa Clara, CA Metropolitan Statistical Area—see Appendix B for areas included; (2) Based on 365 days with AQI data in 2015. Air Quality Index (AQI) is an index for reporting daily air quality. EPA calculates the AQI for five major air pollutants regulated by the Clean Air Act: ground-level ozone, particle pollution (aka particulate matter), carbon monoxide, sulfur dioxide, and nitrogen dioxide. The AQI runs from 0 to 500. The higher the AQI value, the greater the level of air pollution and the greater the health concern. There are six AQI categories: "Good" AQI is between 0 and 50. Air quality is considered satisfactory; "Moderate" AQI is between 51 and 100. Air quality is acceptable; "Unhealthy for Sensitive Groups" When AQI values are between 101 and 150, members of sensitive groups may experience health effects; "Unhealthy" When AQI values are between 151 and 200 everyone may begin to experience health effects; "Very Unhealthy" AQI values between 201 and 300 trigger a health alert; "Hazardous" AQI values over 300 trigger warnings of emergency conditions (not shown).
Source: U.S. Environmental Protection Agency, Air Quality Index Report, 2015

Air Quality Index Pollutants

Area	Percent of Days when AQI Pollutant was...[2]					
	Carbon Monoxide	Nitrogen Dioxide	Ozone	Sulfur Dioxide	Particulate Matter 2.5	Particulate Matter 10
MSA[1]	0.0	2.5	51.0	0.0	46.3	0.3

Note: (1) Data covers the San Jose-Sunnyvale-Santa Clara, CA Metropolitan Statistical Area—see Appendix B for areas included; (2) Based on 365 days with AQI data in 2015. The Air Quality Index (AQI) is an index for reporting daily air quality. EPA calculates the AQI for five major air pollutants regulated by the Clean Air Act: ground-level ozone, particle pollution (also known as particulate matter), carbon monoxide, sulfur dioxide, and nitrogen dioxide. The AQI runs from 0 to 500. The higher the AQI value, the greater the level of air pollution and the greater the health concern.
Source: U.S. Environmental Protection Agency, Air Quality Index Report, 2015

Maximum Air Pollutant Concentrations: Particulate Matter, Ozone, CO and Lead

	Particulate Matter 10 (ug/m^3)	Particulate Matter 2.5 Wtd AM (ug/m^3)	Particulate Matter 2.5 24-Hr (ug/m^3)	Ozone (ppm)	Carbon Monoxide (ppm)	Lead (ug/m^3)
MSA[1] Level	52	8.4	27	0.073	2	0.13
NAAQS[2]	150	15	35	0.075	9	0.15
Met NAAQS[2]	Yes	Yes	Yes	Yes	Yes	Yes

Note: (1) Data covers the San Jose-Sunnyvale-Santa Clara, CA Metropolitan Statistical Area—see Appendix B for areas included; Data from exceptional events are included; (2) National Ambient Air Quality Standards; ppm = parts per million; ug/m^3 = micrograms per cubic meter; n/a not available.
Concentrations: Particulate Matter 10 (coarse particulate)—highest second maximum 24-hour concentration; Particulate Matter 2.5 Wtd AM (fine particulate)—highest weighted annual mean concentration; Particulate Matter 2.5 24-Hour (fine particulate)—highest 98th percentile 24-hour concentration; Ozone—highest fourth daily maximum 8-hour concentration; Carbon Monoxide—highest second maximum non-overlapping 8-hour concentration; Lead—maximum running 3-month average
Source: U.S. Environmental Protection Agency, Air Quality Monitoring Information, "Air Quality Statistics by City, 2014"

Maximum Air Pollutant Concentrations: Nitrogen Dioxide and Sulfur Dioxide

	Nitrogen Dioxide AM (ppb)	Nitrogen Dioxide 1-Hr (ppb)	Sulfur Dioxide AM (ppb)	Sulfur Dioxide 1-Hr (ppb)	Sulfur Dioxide 24-Hr (ppb)
MSA[1] Level	13	55	n/a	2	n/a
NAAQS[2]	53	100	30	75	140
Met NAAQS[2]	Yes	Yes	n/a	Yes	n/a

Note: (1) Data covers the San Jose-Sunnyvale-Santa Clara, CA Metropolitan Statistical Area—see Appendix B for areas included; Data from exceptional events are included; (2) National Ambient Air Quality Standards; ppm = parts per million; ug/m^3 = micrograms per cubic meter; n/a not available.
Concentrations: Nitrogen Dioxide AM—highest arithmetic mean concentration; Nitrogen Dioxide 1-Hr—highest 98th percentile 1-hour daily maximum concentration; Sulfur Dioxide AM—highest annual mean concentration; Sulfur Dioxide 1-Hr—highest 99th percentile 1-hour daily maximum concentration; Sulfur Dioxide 24-Hr—highest second maximum 24-hour concentration
Source: U.S. Environmental Protection Agency, Air Quality Monitoring Information, "Air Quality Statistics by City, 2014"

Drinking Water

Water System Name	Pop. Served	Primary Water Source Type	Violations[1]	
			Health Based	Monitoring/ Reporting
San Jose Water Company	998,000	Surface	0	0

Note: (1) Based on violation data from January 1, 2015 to December 31, 2015 (includes unresolved violations from earlier years)
Source: U.S. Environmental Protection Agency, Office of Ground Water and Drinking Water, Safe Drinking Water Information System (based on data extracted April 29, 2016)

Yorba Linda, California

Background

Yorba Linda, incorporated in 1967 as Orange County's 25th city, is perhaps best known to Americans as the birthplace of Richard M. Nixon, the nation's 37th president. It is also a thriving residential town, only a dozen miles from Santa Ana and 40 miles from downtown Los Angeles.

The area around Yorba Linda was long inhabited by native Americans prior to the arrival of Spanish explorers in the 17th century. The town's modern history, though, begins in 1834, when Bernardo Yorba received a land grant from the then-Mexican government. Bernardo promptly built, at the center of his ranch's many thousands of acres, a grand hacienda with fifty richly appointed rooms. After Bernardo's death, the estate was divided among his heirs and, in 1907, one parcel was acquired by Jacob Stern of Fullerton, who immediately sold it—an early California real estate flip—to the Janss Investment Company in Los Angeles. The Janss Company named the area Yorba, after Bernardo, and added "Linda," which is simply Spanish for "beautiful," and sold off plots as agricultural land. Soon there were a few dozen new residents, most of them owners of orange and lemon groves. Rail links facilitated the transport of produce to Los Angeles and, in 1912, Southern California Edison installed electric lines. Richard M. Nixon was born there on January 9, 1913.

There were no paved roads in Yorba Linda until 1917 and, by 1960 the town's population had reached only just under 1,200. The main business continued to be farming. After this, however, development in Orange County picked up speed, and Yorba Linda increased its population almost ten-fold by 1967.

Today, Yorba Linda is an elegant and affluent residential city , which supports many recreational and cultural amenities. In 2001, the town opened the Black Gold Golf Club, an Orange County favorite for golf and a special events venue. The city, in conjunction with the county, now maintains 135 acres of parks and sports fields, and 30,000 square feet of gymnasium space for baseball, softball, junior basketball, soccer and more. Yorba Linda also has over 100 miles of equestrian trails throughout the community. The Nixon Library and Museum, naturally located in Yorba Linda, is a modern multi-use facility which annually schedules a range of special events, many of national importance. A Town Center Project that will harmonize business and residential interests for Yorba Linda is in the works.

Yorba Linda is served by the Placentia-Yorba Linda Unified School District, and a number of its schools have achieved state-wide distinction. Nearby colleges and universities include Santiago Canyon College and Chapman University. Medical centers convenient to Yorba Linda include the Kaiser Foundation Hospital at Anaheim, Placentia Linda Hospital, and Chapman Medical Center.

The city is served by two major airports—John Wayne-Orange County and Ontario International. The city also enjoys the service of three nearby public-use airports. The temperature is just about perfect, rarely falling below 45 degrees in January, or rising above mid-80s in July.

Rankings

General Rankings

- Los Angeles* was identified as one of America's fastest-growing major metropolitan areas in terms of population growth by CNNMoney.com. The area ranked #3 out of 10. Criteria: population growth between July 2013 and July 2014. *CNNMoney, "10 Fastest-Growing Cities," May 27, 2015*

Business/Finance Rankings

- The personal finance site NerdWallet analyzed 183 American metropolitan areas with populations over 250,000 and more than 15,000 businesses to rank where entrepreneurs find the most success. Criteria included area economy, annual income, housing cost, unemployment rate, and the success rate of area businesses. Los Angeles* ranked #109. *www.nerdwallet.com, "Best Places to Start a Business," April 27, 2015*
- Based on the U.S. Department of Labor's Occupational Information Network Data Collection Program, the Brookings Institution defined job opportunities for STEM workers at various levels of educational attainment. The Anaheim* metro area was one of the ten metro areas where workers in low-education-level STEM jobs earn the lowest relative wages. *www.brookings.edu, "The Hidden Stem Economy," June 10, 2013*
- Based on metro area social media reviews, the employment opinion group Glassdoor surveyed 50 of the largest U.S. metro areas and equally weighed cost of living, hiring opportunity, and job satisfaction to compose a list of "25 Best Cities for Jobs." The Los Angeles* metro area was ranked #16 in overall job satisfaction. *www.glassdoor.com, "Best Cities for Jobs," May 19, 2015*
- In a survey of economic confidence in the nation's 50 largest metropolitan areas conducted January–December 2014, the Los Angeles* metro area placed #11, according to Gallup's 2014 Economic Confidence Index. *Gallup, "San Jose and San Francisco Lead in Economic Confidence," March 19, 2015*
- The Brookings Institution ranked the 100 largest metro areas in the U.S. based on income inequality. Los Angeles* was ranked #7 (#1 = greatest ineqality). Criteria: the "95/20 ratio," a figure representing the income at which a household earns more than 95 percent of all other households, divided by the income at which a household earns more than only 20 percent of all other households. *Brookings Institution, "Income Inequality, 100 Largest U.S. Metro Areas, 2007-2014," January 14, 2016*
- The finance site *24/7 Wall St.* identified the metropolitan areas that have the smallest and largest pay disparities between men and women, comparing the median earnings for the past 12 months of both men and women working full-time in the country's 100 largest metropolitan statistical areas. Of the ten best-paying metros for women, the Los Angeles* metro area ranked #2. *24/7 Wall St., "The Best (and Worst) Paying Cities for Women," March 6, 2015*
- Payscale.com ranked the 20 largest metro areas in terms of wage growth. The Los Angeles* metro area ranked #16. Criteria: private-sector wage growth between the 1st quarter of 2015 and the 1st quarter of 2016. *PayScale, "Wage Trends by Metro Area," 1st Quarter, 2016*
- The Anaheim* metro area appeared on the Milken Institute "2015 Best Performing Cities" list. Rank: #46 out of 200 large metro areas. Criteria: job growth; wage and salary growth; high-tech output growth. *Milken Institute, "Best-Performing Cities 2015," December 2015*
- *Forbes* ranked the 200 most populous metro areas to determine the nation's "Best Places for Business and Careers." The Anaheim* metro area was ranked #62. Criteria: costs (business and living); job growth (past and projected); income growth; educational attainment (college and high school); projected economic growth; cultural and recreational opportunities; net migration patterns; number of highly ranked colleges. *Forbes, "The Best Places for Business and Careers 2015," July 29, 2015*

Education Rankings

- Personal finance website *WalletHub* analyzed the 150 largest U.S. metropolitan statistical areas to determine where the most educated Americans are choosing to settle. Criteria: education quality and attainment gap; education levels; percentage of workers with degrees; public school rankings; quality and size of each metro area's universities. Los Angeles* was ranked #87 (#1 = most educated city). *www.WalletHub.com, "2015's Most and Least Educated Cities*

Environmental Rankings

- The Los Angeles* metro area came in at #148 for the relative comfort of its climate on Sperling's list of "chill cities," as measured by the Sperling Heat Index. All 361 metro areas are included. Criteria included daytime high temperatures, nighttime low temperatures, dew point, and relative humidity at the high temperatures. *www.bertsperling.com, "Sperling's Chill Cities," July 18, 2013*

- Sperling's BestPlaces assessed 379 metropolitan areas of the United States for the likelihood of dangerously extreme weather events or earthquakes. In general the Southeast and South-Central regions have the highest risk of weather extremes and earthquakes, while the Pacific Northwest enjoys the lowest risk. Of the least risky metropolitan areas, the Anaheim* metro area was ranked #198. *www.bestplaces.net, "Safest Places from Natural Disasters," April 2011*

- Los Angeles* was identified as one of America's dirtiest metro areas by *Forbes.* The area ranked #17 out of 20. Criteria: air quality; water quality; toxic releases; superfund sites. *Forbes, "America's 20 Dirtiest Cities," December 10, 2012*

- The U.S. Environmental Protection Agency (EPA) released a list of U.S. metropolitan areas with the most ENERGY STAR certified buildings in 2015. The Los Angeles* metro area was ranked #2 out of 25. *U.S. Environmental Protection Agency, "Top Cities With the Most ENERGY STAR Certified Buildings in 2016," March 30, 2016*

- Los Angeles* was highlighted as one of the 25 most ozone-polluted metro areas in the U.S. during 2011 through 2013. The area ranked #1. *American Lung Association, State of the Air 2015*

- Los Angeles* was highlighted as one of the 25 metro areas most polluted by year-round particle pollution (Annual PM 2.5) in the U.S. during 2011 through 2013. The area ranked #5. *American Lung Association, State of the Air 2015*

- Los Angeles* was highlighted as one of the 25 metro areas most polluted by short-term particle pollution (24-hour PM 2.5) in the U.S. during 2011 through 2013. The area ranked #5. *American Lung Association, State of the Air 2015*

Health/Fitness Rankings

- Analysts who tracked obesity rates in the nation's largest metro areas (populations above one million) found that the Anaheim* metro area was one of the ten major metros where residents were least likely to be obese, defined as a BMI score of 30 or above. *www.gallup.com, "Boulder, Colo., Residents Still Least Likely to Be Obese," April 4, 2014*

- For each of the 50 most populous metro areas in the United States, the American College of Sports Medicine's American Fitness Index evaluated infrastructure, community assets, and policies that encourage healthy and fit lifestyles, including preventive health behaviors, levels of chronic disease conditions, health care access, and community resources and policies that support physical activity. The Los Angeles* metro area ranked #23 for "community fitness." *www.americanfitnessindex.org, "ACSM American Fitness Index Health and Community Fitness Status of the 50 Largest Metropolitan Areas," May 2015*

- The Los Angeles* metro area was identified as one of the worst cities for bed bugs in America by pest control company Orkin. The area ranked #2 out of 50 based on the number of bed bug treatments Orkin performed from January to December 2015. *Orkin, "Chicago Tops Bed Bug Cities List for Fourth Year in a Row," January 13, 2016*

- Los Angeles* was identified as a "2016 Spring Allergy Capital." The area ranked #67 out of 100. Three groups of factors were used to identify the most severe cities for people with allergies during the spring season: annual pollen levels; medicine utilization; access to board-certified allergists. *Asthma and Allergy Foundation of America, "Spring Allergy Capitals 2016"*
- Los Angeles* was identified as a "2015 Asthma Capital." The area ranked #52 out of the nation's 100 largest metropolitan areas. Criteria: estimated prevalence; self-reported prevalence; crude death rate for asthma; annual pollen score; annual air quality; public smoking laws; number of board-certified asthma specialists; school inhaler access laws; rescue medication use; controller medication use; ER visits for asthma; uninsured rate; poverty rate. *Asthma and Allergy Foundation of America, "Asthma Capitals 2015"*
- The Los Angeles* metro area ranked #40 out of 190 in The Gallup-Healthways Well-Being Index. Criteria: purpose; social well being; financial health; community and physical health. Results are based on telephone interviews with adults, aged 18 and older, living in metropolitan areas in the 50 U.S. states and the District of Columbia. *Gallup-Healthways, "State of American Well-Being," February 23, 2016*

Real Estate Rankings

- With data from RealtyTrac, Yahoo! Finance researchers listed the housing markets in which housing affordability is improving most, factoring in interest rates as well as median home prices. The Los Angeles* metro area was among the least affordable housing markets. *news.yahoo.com, "10 Cities Where Ordinary People Can No Longer Afford Homes," March 5, 2014*
- The Los Angeles* metro area was identified as one of the nations's 20 hottest housing markets in 2016. Criteria: listing views as an indicator of demand and median days on the market as an indicator of supply. The area ranked #12. *Realtor.com, "The 20 Hottest U.S. Real Estate Markets in February 2016," February 25, 2016*
- The Anaheim* metro area was identified as one of the 20 least affordable housing markets in the U.S. in 2015. The area ranked #3 out of 179 markets. Criteria: qualification for a mortgage loan on a typical home. *National Association of Realtors®, Affordability Index of Existing Single-Family Homes for Metropolitan Areas, 2015*
- Los Angeles* was ranked #224 out of 225 metro areas in terms of housing affordability in 2015 by the National Association of Home Builders (#1 = most affordable). Criteria: the share of homes sold in that area affordable to a family earning the local median income, based on standard mortgage underwriting criteria. *National Association of Home Builders®, NAHB-Wells Fargo Housing Opportunity Index, 4th Quarter 2015*

Safety Rankings

- Farmers Insurance, in partnership with Sperling's BestPlaces, ranked metro areas in the U.S. as the "Most Secure Places to Live." The Anaheim* metro area ranked #19 out of the top 20 in the large metro area category (500,000 or more residents). Criteria: economic stability; crime statistics; extreme weather; risk of natural disasters; housing depreciation; foreclosures; air quality; environmental hazards; life expectancy; motor vehicle fatalities; and employment numbers. *Farmers Insurance Group of Companies, "Most Secure U.S. Places to Live in the U.S.," June 25, 2013*
- Yorba Linda was identified as one of the safest cities in America by NeighborhoodScout. The city ranked #82 out of 100. Criteria: number of violent and property crimes per 1,000 residents. The editors only considered cities with 25,000 or more residents. *NeighborhoodScout, "Safest Cities in America 2016"*
- The National Insurance Crime Bureau ranked 380 metro areas in the U.S. in terms of per capita rates of vehicle theft. The Los Angeles* metro area ranked #39 (#1 = highest rate). Criteria: number of vehicle theft offenses per 100,000 inhabitants in 2014. *National Insurance Crime Bureau, "Hot Spots 2014," June 24, 2015*

Seniors/Retirement Rankings

- From its Best Cities for Successful Aging indexes, the Milken Institute generated rankings for metropolitan areas, weighing data in eight categories—health care, wellness, living arrangements, transportation, financial characteristics, education and employment opportunities, community engagement, and overall livability. The Los Angeles* metro area was ranked #66 overall in the large metro area category. *Milken Institute, "Best Cities for Successful Aging, 2014"*

Sports/Recreation Rankings

- *Card Player* magazine scoured North America to identify the top five metropolitan areas where a player can access the types of games that make launching a poker career possible. The Los Angeles* metro area ranked #1. *Card Player, "The Top Five Cities to Launch Your Poker Career," April 2, 2014*

Transportation Rankings

- Los Angeles* was identified as one of the most congested metro areas in the U.S. The area ranked #2 out of 10. Criteria: yearly delay per auto commuter in hours. *Texas A&M Transportation Institute, "2015 Urban Mobility Scorecard," August 2015*
- The Los Angeles* metro area appeared on *Forbes* list of places with the most extreme commutes. The metro area ranked #5 out of 10. Criteria: average travel time; percentage of mega commuters. Mega-commuters travel more than 90 minutes and 50 miles each way to work. *Forbes.com, "The Cities with the Most Extreme Commutes," March 5, 2013*

Women/Minorities Rankings

- *24/7 Wall St.* compared median earnings over a 12-month period for men and women who worked full-time, year-round, and employment composition by sector to identify the best-paying cities for women. Of the largest 100 U.S. metropolitan areas, Los Angeles* was ranked #2 in pay disparity. *24/7 Wall St., "The Best (and Worst) Paying Cities for Women," March 6, 2015*

Miscellaneous Rankings

- The watchdog site Charity Navigator conducts an annual study of charities in the nation's major markets both to analyze statistical differences in their financial, accountability, and transparency practices and to track year-to-year variations in individual communities. The Los Angeles* metro area was ranked #4 among the 30 metro markets in the rating dimension of Overall Score. *www.charitynavigator.org, "Metro Market Study 2015," June 5, 2015*
- The Harris Poll's Happiness Index survey revealed that of the top ten U.S. markets, the Los Angeles* metro area residents ranked #5 in happiness. Criteria included strong assent to positive statements and strong disagreement with negative ones, and degree of agreement with a series of statements about respondents' personal relationships and general outlook. *www.harrisinteractive.com, "Dallas/Fort Worth Is "Happiest" City among America's Top Ten Markets," September 4, 2013*
- Energizer Personal Care, the makers of Edge® shave gel, in partnership with Sperling's BestPlaces, ranked 50 major metro areas in terms of everyday irritations. The Los Angeles* metro area ranked #6 the 50 metro area most iritating to guys. Criteria: high male-to-female ratio; poor sports team performance and high ticket prices; slow traffic; lack of job availability; unaffordable housing; extreme weather; lack of nightlife and fitness options. *Energizer Personal Care, "Most Irritatng Cities for Guys," August 26, 2013*
- Mars Chocolate North America, the makers of COMBOS®, in partnership with Sperling's BestPlaces, ranked 50 major metro areas in terms of their "manliness." The Los Angeles* metro area ranked #46. Criteria: number of professional sports teams; number of nearby NASCAR tracks and racing events; manly lifestyle; concentration of manly retail stores; manly occupations per capita; salty snack sales; "Board of Manliness" rankings. *Mars Chocolate North America, "America's Manliest Cities 2012"*

- The National Alliance to End Homelessness ranked the 100 most populous metro areas with the highest rate of homelessness. The Los Angeles* metro area ranked #6. Criteria: number of homeless people per 10,000 population in 2011. *National Alliance to End Homelessness, The State of Homelessness in America 2012*

Yorba Linda is located within the Los Angeles-Long Beach-Anaheim, CA Metropolitan Statistical Area and the Anaheim-Santa Ana-Irvine, CA Metropolitan Division.

Business Environment

CITY FINANCES

City Government Finances

Component	2012 ($000)	2012 ($ per capita)
Total Revenues	62,126	967
Total Expenditures	79,907	1,243
Debt Outstanding	117,726	1,832
Cash and Securities[1]	115,814	1,803

Note: (1) Cash and security holdings of a government at the close of its fiscal year, including those of its dependent agencies, utilities, and liquor stores.
Source: U.S Census Bureau, State & Local Government Finances 2012

City Government Revenue by Source

Source	2012 ($000)	2012 ($ per capita)
General Revenue		
From Federal Government	681	10
From State Government	2,152	33
From Local Governments	1,729	26
Taxes		
Property	25,449	396
Sales and Gross Receipts	6,590	102
Personal Income	0	0
Corporate Income	0	0
Motor Vehicle License	0	0
Other Taxes	2,962	46
Current Charges	12,711	197
Liquor Store	0	0
Utility	0	0
Employee Retirement	0	0

Source: U.S Census Bureau, State & Local Government Finances 2012

City Government Expenditures by Function

Function	2012 ($000)	2012 ($ per capita)	2012 (%)
General Direct Expenditures			
Air Transportation	0	0	0.0
Corrections	0	0	0.0
Education	0	0	0.0
Employment Security Administration	0	0	0.0
Financial Administration	791	12	0.9
Fire Protection	0	0	0.0
General Public Buildings	0	0	0.0
Governmental Administration, Other	5,798	90	7.2
Health	0	0	0.0
Highways	20,484	318	25.6
Hospitals	0	0	0.0
Housing and Community Development	8,475	131	10.6
Interest on General Debt	4,962	77	6.2
Judicial and Legal	993	15	1.2
Libraries	3,436	53	4.3
Parking	0	0	0.0
Parks and Recreation	11,227	174	14.0
Police Protection	267	4	0.3
Public Welfare	0	0	0.0
Sewerage	0	0	0.0
Solid Waste Management	5,082	79	6.3
Veterans' Services	0	0	0.0
Liquor Store	0	0	0.0
Utility	0	0	0.0
Employee Retirement	0	0	0.0

Source: U.S Census Bureau, State & Local Government Finances 2012

DEMOGRAPHICS

Population Growth

Area	1990 Census	2000 Census	2010 Census	2014* Estimate	Population Growth (%) 1990-2014	Population Growth (%) 2010-2014
City	52,827	58,918	64,234	66,335	25.6	3.3
MSA[1]	11,273,720	12,365,627	12,828,837	13,060,534	15.8	1.8
U.S.	248,709,873	281,421,906	308,745,538	314,107,084	26.3	1.7

Note: (1) Figures cover the Los Angeles-Long Beach-Anaheim, CA Metropolitan Statistical Area—see Appendix B for areas included; (*) 2010-2014 5-year estimated population
Source: U.S. Census Bureau, 1990 Census, Census 2000, Census 2010, 2010-2014 American Community Survey 5-Year Estimates

Household Size

Area	Persons in Household (%) One	Two	Three	Four	Five	Six	Seven or More	Average Household Size
City	13.5	31.8	20.0	21.6	8.5	3.5	0.7	2.99
MSA[1]	24.5	28.0	16.6	15.4	8.3	3.8	3.1	3.03
U.S.	27.5	33.5	15.8	13.1	6.0	2.3	1.4	2.64

Note: (1) Figures cover the Los Angeles-Long Beach-Anaheim, CA Metropolitan Statistical Area—see Appendix B for areas included
Source: U.S. Census Bureau, 2010-2014 American Community Survey 5-Year Estimates

Race

Area	White Alone[2] (%)	Black Alone[2] (%)	Asian Alone[2] (%)	AIAN[3] Alone[2] (%)	NHOPI[4] Alone[2] (%)	Other Race Alone[2] (%)	Two or More Races (%)
City	75.2	1.0	17.0	0.3	0.1	1.5	4.8
MSA[1]	55.7	6.8	15.1	0.5	0.3	17.9	3.8
U.S.	73.8	12.6	5.0	0.8	0.2	4.7	2.9

Note: (1) Figures cover the Los Angeles-Long Beach-Anaheim, CA Metropolitan Statistical Area—see Appendix B for areas included; (2) Alone is defined as not being in combination with one or more other races; (3) American Indian and Alaska Native; (4) Native Hawaiian and Other Pacific Islander
Source: U.S. Census Bureau, 2010-2014 American Community Survey 5-Year Estimates

Hispanic or Latino Origin

Area	Total (%)	Mexican (%)	Puerto Rican (%)	Cuban (%)	Other (%)
City	17.0	12.9	0.2	0.6	3.2
MSA[1]	44.8	35.0	0.5	0.4	8.9
U.S.	16.9	10.8	1.6	0.6	3.8

Note: Persons of Hispanic or Latino origin can be of any race; (1) Figures cover the Los Angeles-Long Beach-Anaheim, CA Metropolitan Statistical Area—see Appendix B for areas included
Source: U.S. Census Bureau, 2010-2014 American Community Survey 5-Year Estimates

Ancestry

Area	German	Irish	English	American	Italian	Polish	French[2]	Scottish	Dutch
City	15.6	10.8	11.1	5.7	6.1	2.6	3.2	1.8	2.4
MSA[1]	6.0	4.8	4.4	3.2	3.0	1.3	1.4	1.0	0.7
U.S.	14.9	10.8	8.0	7.1	5.5	3.0	2.7	1.7	1.4

Note: Figures are the percentage of the total population reporting a particular ancestry. The nine most commonly reported ancestries in the U.S. are shown. Figures include multiple ancestries (e.g. if a person reported being Irish and Italian, they were included in both columns); (1) Figures cover the Los Angeles-Long Beach-Anaheim, CA Metropolitan Statistical Area—see Appendix B for areas included; (2) Excludes Basque
Source: U.S. Census Bureau, 2010-2014 American Community Survey 5-Year Estimates

Foreign-Born Population

Area	Percent of Population Born in								
	Any Foreign Country	Asia	Mexico	Europe	Carribean	Central America[2]	South America	Africa	Canada
City	18.0	11.7	2.1	1.6	0.2	0.4	0.6	0.5	0.8
MSA[1]	33.8	12.3	13.3	1.7	0.3	4.3	0.9	0.5	0.3
U.S.	13.1	3.8	3.7	1.5	1.2	1.0	0.9	0.6	0.3

Note: (1) Figures cover the Los Angeles-Long Beach-Anaheim, CA Metropolitan Statistical Area—see Appendix B for areas included; (2) Excludes Mexico.
Source: U.S. Census Bureau, 2010-2014 American Community Survey 5-Year Estimates

Marital Status

Area	Never Married	Now Married[2]	Separated	Widowed	Divorced
City	25.7	62.0	0.8	5.1	6.4
MSA[1]	39.6	44.3	2.5	5.0	8.6
U.S.	32.5	48.4	2.2	5.9	10.9

Note: Figures are percentages and cover the population 15 years of age and older; (1) Figures cover the Los Angeles-Long Beach-Anaheim, CA Metropolitan Statistical Area—see Appendix B for areas included; (2) Excludes separated
Source: U.S. Census Bureau, 2010-2014 American Community Survey 5-Year Estimates

Disability Status

Area	All Ages	Under 18 Years Old	18 to 64 Years Old	65 Years and Over
City	7.4	1.9	4.2	31.6
MSA[1]	9.2	2.8	6.8	36.1
U.S.	12.3	4.1	10.2	36.3

Note: Figures show percent of the civilian noninstitutionalized population that reported having a disability. Disability status is determined from from six types of difficulty: vision, hearing, cognitive, ambulatory, self-care, and independent living. For children under 5 years old, hearing and vision difficulty are used to determine disability status. For children between the ages of 5 and 14, disability status is determined from hearing, vision, cognitive, ambulatory, and self-care difficulties. For people aged 15 years and older, they are considered to have a disability if they have difficulty with any one of the six difficulty types; (1) Figures cover the Los Angeles-Long Beach-Anaheim, CA Metropolitan Statistical Area—see Appendix B for areas included.
Source: U.S. Census Bureau, 2010-2014 American Community Survey 5-Year Estimates

Age

Area	Percent of Population									Median Age
	Under Age 5	Age 5–19	Age 20–34	Age 35–44	Age 45–54	Age 55–64	Age 65–74	Age 75–84	Age 85+	
City	6.1	20.4	16.2	12.2	17.6	14.0	8.2	3.6	1.7	41.8
MSA[1]	6.4	20.0	22.6	14.2	14.0	11.0	6.4	3.6	1.7	35.6
U.S.	6.4	19.9	20.6	13.0	14.1	12.3	7.6	4.3	1.9	37.4

Note: (1) Figures cover the Los Angeles-Long Beach-Anaheim, CA Metropolitan Statistical Area—see Appendix B for areas included
Source: U.S. Census Bureau, 2010-2014 American Community Survey 5-Year Estimates

Gender

Area	Males	Females	Males per 100 Females
City	33,344	32,991	101.1
MSA[1]	6,438,759	6,621,775	97.2
U.S.	154,515,159	159,591,925	96.8

Note: (1) Figures cover the Los Angeles-Long Beach-Anaheim, CA Metropolitan Statistical Area—see Appendix B for areas included
Source: U.S. Census Bureau, 2010-2014 American Community Survey 5-Year Estimates

Religious Groups by Family

Area	Catholic	Baptist	Non-Den.	Methodist[2]	Lutheran	LDS[3]	Pente-costal	Presby-terian[4]	Muslim[5]	Judaism
MSA[1]	33.8	2.7	3.6	1.0	0.6	1.7	1.7	0.9	0.7	0.9
U.S.	19.1	9.3	4.0	4.0	2.3	2.0	1.9	1.6	0.8	0.7

Note: Figures are the number of adherents as a percentage of the total population; (1) Figures cover the Los Angeles-Long Beach-Santa Ana, CA Metropolitan Statistical Area—see Appendix B for areas included; (2) Methodist/Pietist; (3) Latter Day Saints; (4) Reformed; (5) Figures are estimates
Source: Association of Statisticians of American Religious Bodies, 2010 U.S. Religion Census: Religious Congregations & Membership Study

Religious Groups by Tradition

Area	Catholic	Evangelical Protestant	Mainline Protestant	Other Tradition	Black Protestant	Orthodox
MSA[1]	33.8	9.0	2.3	4.6	0.8	0.6
U.S.	19.1	16.2	7.3	4.3	1.6	0.3

Note: Figures are the number of adherents as a percentage of the total population; (1) Figures cover the Los Angeles-Long Beach-Santa Ana, CA Metropolitan Statistical Area—see Appendix B for areas included
Source: Association of Statisticians of American Religious Bodies, 2010 U.S. Religion Census: Religious Congregations & Membership Study

ECONOMY

Gross Metropolitan Product

Area	2013	2014	2015	2016	Rank[2]
MSA[1]	826.8	859.7	887.9	930.8	2

Note: Figures are in billions of dollars; (1) Figures cover the Los Angeles-Long Beach-Anaheim, CA Metropolitan Statistical Area—see Appendix B for areas included; (2) Rank is based on 2016 data and ranges from 1 to 381
Source: The U.S. Conference of Mayors, U.S. Metro Economies: GMP and Employment 2014-2016, June 2015

Economic Growth

Area	2011-13 (%)	2014 (%)	2015 (%)	2016 (%)	Rank[2]
MSA[1]	1.5	2.6	2.0	3.0	83
U.S.	2.2	2.4	2.3	2.9	–

Note: Figures are real gross metropolitan product (GMP) growth rates and represent annual average percent change; (1) Figures cover the Los Angeles-Long Beach-Anaheim, CA Metropolitan Statistical Area—see Appendix B for areas included; (2) Rank is based on 2016 data and ranges from 1 to 381
Source: The U.S. Conference of Mayors, U.S. Metro Economies: GMP and Employment 2014-2016, June 2015

Metropolitan Area Exports

Area	2009	2010	2011	2012	2013	2014	Rank[2]
MSA[1]	51,528.3	62,167.6	72,688.9	75,007.5	76,305.7	75,471.2	3

Note: Figures are in millions of dollars; (1) Figures cover the Los Angeles-Long Beach-Anaheim, CA Metropolitan Statistical Area—see Appendix B for areas included; (2) Rank is based on 2014 data and ranges from 1 to 385
Source: U.S. Department of Commerce, International Trade Administration, Office of Trade & Industry Information, Manufacturing & Services, data extracted March 10, 2016

Building Permits

Area	Single-Family			Multi-Family			Total		
	2014	2015p	Pct. Chg.	2014	2015p	Pct. Chg.	2014	2015p	Pct. Chg.
City	94	206	119.1	0	69	-	94	275	192.6
MSA[1]	8,300	8,458	1.9	18,650	25,211	35.2	26,950	33,669	24.9
U.S.	640,300	690,800	7.9	411,800	487,600	18.4	1,052,100	1,178,400	12.0

Note: (1) Figures cover the Los Angeles-Long Beach-Anaheim, CA Metropolitan Statistical Area—see Appendix B for areas included; Figures represent new, privately-owned housing units authorized (unadjusted data); All permit data are based on estimates with imputation; (p) preliminary data.
Source: U.S. Census Bureau, Manufacturing, Mining, and Construction Statistics, Building Permits, 2014, 2015

Bankruptcy Filings

Area	Business Filings			Nonbusiness Filings		
	2014	2015	% Chg.	2014	2015	% Chg.
Orange County	397	424	6.8	7,279	5,898	-19.0
U.S.	26,983	24,735	-8.3	909,812	819,760	-9.9

Note: Business filings include Chapter 7, Chapter 11, Chapter 12, and Chapter 13; Nonbusiness filings include Chapter 7, Chapter 11, and Chapter 13
Source: Administrative Office of the U.S. Courts, Business and Nonbusiness Bankruptcy, County Cases Commenced by Chapter of the Bankruptcy Code, During the 12- Month Period Ending December 31, 2014 and Business and Nonbusiness Bankruptcy, County Cases Commenced by Chapter of the Bankruptcy Code, During the 12- Month Period Ending December 31, 2015

Housing Vacancy Rates

Area	Gross Vacancy Rate[2] (%)			Year-Round Vacancy Rate[3] (%)			Rental Vacancy Rate[4] (%)			Homeowner Vacancy Rate[5] (%)		
	2013	2014	2015	2013	2014	2015	2013	2014	2015	2013	2014	2015
MSA[1]	6.2	5.8	5.4	5.7	5.5	5.0	4.2	4.6	3.3	1.2	0.8	0.8
U.S.	13.6	13.4	12.9	10.7	10.4	10.0	8.3	7.6	7.1	2.0	1.9	1.8

Note: (1) Figures cover the Los Angeles-Long Beach-Anaheim, CA Metropolitan Statistical Area—see Appendix B for areas included; (2) The percentage of the total housing inventory that is vacant; (3) The percentage of the housing inventory (excluding seasonal units) that is year-round vacant; (4) The percentage of rental inventory that is vacant for rent; (5) The percentage of homeowner inventory that is vacant for sale
Source: U.S. Census Bureau, Housing Vacancies and Homeownership Annual Statistics: 2015

INCOME

Income

Area	Per Capita ($)	Median Household ($)	Average Household ($)
City	47,852	115,994	144,599
MSA[1]	29,506	60,337	86,928
U.S.	28,555	53,482	74,596

Note: (1) Figures cover the Los Angeles-Long Beach-Anaheim, CA Metropolitan Statistical Area—see Appendix B for areas included
Source: U.S. Census Bureau, 2010-2014 American Community Survey 5-Year Estimates

Household Income Distribution

Area	Percent of Households Earning							
	Under $15,000	$15,000 -24,999	$25,000 -34,999	$35,000 -49,999	$50,000 -74,999	$75,000 -99,000	$100,000 -149,999	$150,000 and up
City	3.2	4.2	3.3	7.4	12.3	11.4	22.6	35.7
MSA[1]	11.3	9.8	9.1	12.2	16.6	12.1	14.5	14.4
U.S.	12.5	10.7	10.2	13.5	17.8	12.2	13.0	10.0

Note: (1) Figures cover the Los Angeles-Long Beach-Anaheim, CA Metropolitan Statistical Area—see Appendix B for areas included
Source: U.S. Census Bureau, 2010-2014 American Community Survey 5-Year Estimates

Poverty Rate

Area	All Ages	Under 18 Years Old	18 to 64 Years Old	65 Years and Over
City	3.0	3.2	2.8	4.0
MSA[1]	17.1	24.0	15.4	12.2
U.S.	15.6	21.9	14.6	9.4

Note: Figures are percentage of people whose income during the past 12 months was below the poverty level; (1) Figures cover the Los Angeles-Long Beach-Anaheim, CA Metropolitan Statistical Area—see Appendix B for areas included
Source: U.S. Census Bureau, 2010-2014 American Community Survey 5-Year Estimates

EMPLOYMENT

Labor Force and Employment

Area	Civilian Labor Force			Workers Employed		
	Dec. 2014	Dec. 2015	% Chg.	Dec. 2014	Dec. 2015	% Chg.
City	34,522	34,923	1.1	33,111	33,681	1.7
MD[1]	1,584,967	1,602,110	1.0	1,511,008	1,537,037	1.7
U.S.	155,521,000	157,245,000	1.1	147,190,000	149,703,000	1.7

Note: Data is not seasonally adjusted and covers workers 16 years of age and older; (1) Figures cover the Anaheim-Santa Ana-Irvine, CA Metropolitan Division—see Appendix B for areas included
Source: Bureau of Labor Statistics, Local Area Unemployment Statistics

Unemployment Rate

Area	2015											
	Jan.	Feb.	Mar.	Apr.	May	Jun.	Jul.	Aug.	Sep.	Oct.	Nov.	Dec.
City	4.4	4.0	3.8	3.6	3.7	3.8	4.1	3.9	3.5	3.8	3.7	3.6
MD[1]	5.0	4.6	4.4	4.1	4.2	4.3	4.7	4.5	4.0	4.3	4.2	4.1
U.S.	6.1	5.8	5.6	5.1	5.3	5.5	5.6	5.2	4.9	4.8	4.8	4.8

Note: Data is not seasonally adjusted and covers workers 16 years of age and older; (1) Figures cover the Anaheim-Santa Ana-Irvine, CA Metropolitan Division—see Appendix B for areas included
Source: Bureau of Labor Statistics, Local Area Unemployment Statistics

Employment by Occupation

Occupation Classification	City (%)	MSA[1] (%)	U.S. (%)
Management, Business, Science, and Arts	51.9	36.5	36.4
Natural Resources, Construction, and Maintenance	5.0	7.5	9.0
Production, Transportation, and Material Moving	5.4	12.1	12.1
Sales and Office	25.9	25.2	24.4
Service	11.8	18.6	18.2

Note: Figures cover employed civilians 16 years of age and older; (1) Figures cover the Los Angeles-Long Beach-Anaheim, CA Metropolitan Statistical Area—see Appendix B for areas included
Source: U.S. Census Bureau, 2010-2014 American Community Survey 5-Year Estimates

Employment by Industry

Sector	MD[1]		U.S.
	Number of Employees	Percent of Total	Percent of Total
Construction	96,100	6.0	4.5
Education and Health Services	203,200	12.8	15.7
Financial Activities	118,700	7.5	5.7
Government	161,200	10.2	15.5
Information	25,800	1.6	1.9
Leisure and Hospitality	209,100	13.2	10.4
Manufacturing	157,100	9.9	8.6
Mining and Logging	600	<0.1	0.5
Other Services	48,100	3.0	3.9
Professional and Business Services	290,700	18.4	13.9
Retail Trade	159,100	10.0	11.3
Transportation, Warehousing, and Utilities	28,100	1.7	3.9
Wholesale Trade	81,900	5.1	4.1

Note: Figures are non-farm employment as of December 2015. Figures are not seasonally adjusted and include workers 16 years of age and older; (1) Figures cover the Anaheim-Santa Ana-Irvine, CA Metropolitan Division—see Appendix B for areas included
Source: Bureau of Labor Statistics, Current Employment Statistics, Employment, Hours, and Earnings

Occupations with Greatest Projected Employment Growth: 2012 – 2022

Occupation[1]	2012 Employment	2022 Projected Employment	Numeric Employment Change	Percent Employment Change
Personal Care Aides	386,900	587,200	200,300	51.8
Combined Food Preparation and Serving Workers, Including Fast Food	286,000	362,400	76,400	26.7
Retail Salespersons	468,400	528,100	59,700	12.7
Laborers and Freight, Stock, and Material Movers, Hand	270,500	322,300	51,800	19.1
Waiters and Waitresses	246,100	290,300	44,200	18.0
Registered Nurses	254,500	297,400	42,900	16.9
General and Operations Managers	253,800	295,700	41,900	16.5
Secretaries and Administrative Assistants, Except Legal, Medical, and Executive	212,800	250,100	37,300	17.5
Cashiers	357,800	392,600	34,800	9.7
Cooks, Restaurant	116,900	150,600	33,700	28.8

Note: Projections cover California; (1) Sorted by numeric employment change
Source: www.projectionscentral.com, State Occupational Projections, 2012–2022 Long-Term Projections

Fastest Growing Occupations: 2012 – 2022

Occupation[1]	2012 Employment	2022 Projected Employment	Numeric Employment Change	Percent Employment Change
Economists	3,100	5,100	2,000	64.5
Helpers—Brickmasons, Blockmasons, Stonemasons, and Tile and Marble Setters	2,900	4,600	1,700	58.6
Brickmasons and Blockmasons	5,100	8,000	2,900	56.9
Insulation Workers, Floor, Ceiling, and Wall	1,600	2,500	900	56.3
Stonemasons	1,100	1,700	600	54.5
Insulation Workers, Mechanical	1,100	1,700	600	54.5
Personal Care Aides	386,900	587,200	200,300	51.8
Foresters	1,200	1,800	600	50.0
Terrazzo Workers and Finishers	1,100	1,600	500	45.5
Mechanical Door Repairers	1,100	1,600	500	45.5

Note: Projections cover California; (1) Sorted by percent employment change and excludes occupations with numeric employment change less than 100
Source: www.projectionscentral.com, State Occupational Projections, 2012–2022 Long-Term Projections

Average Wages

Occupation	$/Hr.	Occupation	$/Hr.
Accountants and Auditors	37.26	Maids and Housekeeping Cleaners	11.34
Automotive Mechanics	25.15	Maintenance and Repair Workers	19.96
Bookkeepers	21.75	Marketing Managers	65.03
Carpenters	24.95	Nuclear Medicine Technologists	52.24
Cashiers	11.29	Nurses, Licensed Practical	24.65
Clerks, General Office	16.51	Nurses, Registered	42.74
Clerks, Receptionists/Information	14.99	Nursing Assistants	13.85
Clerks, Shipping/Receiving	15.87	Packers and Packagers, Hand	11.64
Computer Programmers	39.49	Physical Therapists	45.41
Computer Systems Analysts	45.84	Postal Service Mail Carriers	25.84
Computer User Support Specialists	28.56	Real Estate Brokers	n/a
Cooks, Restaurant	12.43	Retail Salespersons	13.50
Dentists	84.50	Sales Reps., Exc. Tech./Scientific	30.76
Electrical Engineers	53.89	Sales Reps., Tech./Scientific	41.69
Electricians	25.64	Secretaries, Exc. Legal/Med./Exec.	18.85
Financial Managers	68.25	Security Guards	12.56
First-Line Supervisors/Managers, Sales	21.08	Surgeons	87.38
Food Preparation Workers	11.02	Teacher Assistants*	16.42
General and Operations Managers	66.05	Teachers, Elementary School*	36.66
Hairdressers/Cosmetologists	14.23	Teachers, Secondary School*	38.38
Internists	129.18	Telemarketers	13.81
Janitors and Cleaners	12.80	Truck Drivers, Heavy/Tractor-Trailer	20.45
Landscaping/Groundskeeping Workers	12.75	Truck Drivers, Light/Delivery Svcs.	18.28
Lawyers	76.75	Waiters and Waitresses	13.53

Note: Wage data covers the Santa Ana-Anaheim-Irvine, CA Metropolitan Division—see Appendix B for areas included; (*) Hourly wages for elementary/secondary school teachers and teacher assistants were calculated by the editors from annual wage data based on a 40 hour work week; n/a not available.
Source: Bureau of Labor Statistics, Metro Area Occupational Employment and Wage Estimates, May 2015

TAXES

State Corporate Income Tax Rates

State	Tax Rate (%)	Income Brackets ($)	Num. of Brackets	Financial Institution Tax Rate (%)[a]	Federal Income Tax Ded.
California	8.84 (c)	Flat rate	1	10.84 (c)	No

Note: Tax rates as of January 1, 2016; (a) Rates listed are the corporate income tax rate applied to financial institutions or excise taxes based on income. Some states have other taxes based upon the value of deposits or shares; (c) Minimum tax is $800 in California, $100 in District of Columbia, $50 in North Dakota (banks), $500 in Rhode Island, $200 per location in South Dakota (banks), $100 in Utah, $250 in Vermont.
Source: Federation of Tax Administrators, "State Corporate Income Tax Rates, 2016"

State Individual Income Tax Rates

State	Tax Rate (%)	Income Brackets ($)	Num. of Brackets	Personal Exempt. ($)[1]		Fed. Inc. Tax Ded.
				Single	Dependents	
California (a)	1.0 - 12.3 (f)	7,850- 526,443 (b)	9	109 (c)	337 (c)	No

Note: Tax rates as of January 1, 2016; Local- and county-level taxes are not included; n/a not applicable; (1) Married joint filers generally receive double the single exemption; (a) 18 states have statutory provision for automatically adjusting to the rate of inflation the dollar values of the income tax brackets, standard deductions, and/or personal exemptions. Massachusetts, Michigan, and Nebraska index the personal exemptiononly. Oregon does not index the income brackets for $125,000 and over. Maine has suspended indexing for 2014 and 2015; (b) For joint returns, taxes are twice the tax on half the couple's income; (c) The personal exemption takes the form of a tax credit instead of a deduction; (f) California imposes an additional 1% tax on taxable income over $1 million, making the maximum rate 13.3% over $1 million.
Source: Federation of Tax Administrators, "State Individual Income Tax Rates, 2016"

Various State and Local Tax Rates

State	State and Local Sales and Use (%)	State Sales and Use (%)	Gasoline[1] (¢/gal.)	Cigarette[2] ($/pack)	Spirits[3] ($/gal.)	Wine[4] ($/gal.)	Beer[5] ($/gal.)
California	8.00	7.50 (b)	40.62	0.87	3.30 (f)	0.20 (l)	0.08

Note: All tax rates as of January 1, 2016; (1) The American Petroleum Institute has developed a methodology for determining the average tax rate on a gallon of fuel. Rates may include any of the following: excise taxes, environmental fees, storage tank fees, other fees or taxes, general sales tax, and local taxes. In states where gasoline is subject to the general sales tax, or where the fuel tax is based on the average sale price, the average rate determined by API is sensitive to changes in the price of gasoline. States that fully or partially apply general sales taxes to gasoline: CA, CO, GA, IL, IN, MI, NY; (2) The federal excise tax of $1.0066 per pack and local taxes are not included; (3) Rates are those applicable to off-premise sales of 40% alcohol by volume (a.b.v.) distilled spirits in 750ml containers. Local excise taxes are excluded; (4) Rates are those applicable to off-premise sales of 11% a.b.v. non-carbonated wine in 750ml containers; (5) Rates are those applicable to off-premise sales of 4.7% a.b.v. beer in 12 ounce containers; (b) Three states levy mandatory, statewide local add-on sales taxes at the state level: California (1%), Utah (1.25%), and Virginia (1%). We include these in their state sales tax rates; (f) Different rates are also applicable according to alcohol content, place of production, size of container, or place purchased (on- or off-premise or onboard airlines); (l) Different rates also applicable according to alcohol content, place of production, size of container, place purchased (on- or off-premise or on board airlines) or type of wine (carbonated, vermouth, etc.).
Source: Tax Foundation, 2016 Facts & Figures: How Does Your State Compare?

State Business Tax Climate Index Rankings

State	Overall Rank	Corporate Tax Rank	Individual Income Tax Rank	Sales Tax Rank	Unemployment Insurance Tax Rank	Property Tax Rank
California	48	35	50	40	13	13

Note: The index is a measure of how each state's tax laws affect economic performance. The lower the rank, the more favorable a state's tax system is for business. States without a given tax are given a ranking of 1. The scores/rankings for the District of Columbia do not affect other states. The 2016 index represents the tax climate as of July 1, 2015 (the beginning of Fiscal Year 2016).
Source: Tax Foundation, State Business Tax Climate Index 2016

TRANSPORTATION

Means of Transportation to Work

Area	Car/Truck/Van		Public Transportation			Bicycle	Walked	Other Means	Worked at Home
	Drove Alone	Car-pooled	Bus	Subway	Railroad				
City	81.7	8.3	0.6	0.0	0.5	0.3	0.7	1.1	6.7
MSA[1]	73.9	10.3	5.3	0.4	0.2	0.9	2.6	1.3	5.1
U.S.	76.4	9.6	2.6	1.8	0.6	0.6	2.8	1.3	4.4

Note: Figures are percentages and cover workers 16 years of age and older; (1) Figures cover the Los Angeles-Long Beach-Anaheim, CA Metropolitan Statistical Area—see Appendix B for areas included
Source: U.S. Census Bureau, 2010-2014 American Community Survey 5-Year Estimates

Travel Time to Work

Area	Less Than 10 Minutes	10 to 19 Minutes	20 to 29 Minutes	30 to 44 Minutes	45 to 59 Minutes	60 to 89 Minutes	90 Minutes or More
City	8.1	20.2	18.6	30.7	10.3	7.9	4.1
MSA[1]	8.1	26.1	20.5	24.9	9.2	8.2	3.0
U.S.	13.3	29.6	21.0	20.2	7.7	5.7	2.6

Note: Figures are percentages and include workers 16 years old and over; (1) Figures cover the Los Angeles-Long Beach-Anaheim, CA Metropolitan Statistical Area—see Appendix B for areas included
Source: U.S. Census Bureau, 2010-2014 American Community Survey 5-Year Estimates

Freeway Travel Time Index

Area	1985	1990	1995	2000	2005	2010	2014
Urban Area Rank[1,2]	1	1	1	1	1	1	1
Urban Area Index[1]	1.31	1.34	1.38	1.41	1.44	1.42	1.43
Average Index[3]	1.09	1.11	1.14	1.17	1.20	1.19	1.20

Note: Freeway Travel Time Index—the ratio of travel time in the peak period to the travel time at free-flow conditions. For example, a value of 1.30 indicates a 20-minute free-flow trip takes 26 minutes in the peak (20 minutes x 1.30 = 26 minutes); (1) Covers the Los Angeles-Long Beach-Anaheim CA urban area; (2) Rank is based on 101 urban areas (#1 = highest travel time index); (3) Average of 101 urban areas
Source: Texas Transportation Institute, 2015 Urban Mobility Scorecard, August 2015

Freeway Commuter Stress Index

Area	1985	1990	1995	2000	2005	2010	2014
Urban Area Rank[1,2]	1	1	1	1	1	1	1
Urban Area Index[1]	1.49	1.52	1.56	1.59	1.63	1.61	1.62
Average Index[3]	1.13	1.16	1.19	1.22	1.25	1.24	1.25

Note: The Freeway Commuter Stress Index is the same as the Freeway Travel Time Index (see table above) except that it includes only the travel in the peak directions during the peak periods; the TTI includes travel in all directions during the peak period. Thus, the CSI is more indicative of the work trip experienced by each commuter on a daily basis. (1) Covers the Los Angeles-Long Beach-Anaheim CA urban area; (2) Rank is based on 101 urban areas (#1 = highest stress index); (3) Average of 101 urban areas

Source: Texas Transportation Institute, 2015 Urban Mobility Scorecard, August 2015

Living Environment

COST OF LIVING

Cost of Living Index

Composite Index	Groceries	Housing	Utilities	Trans-portation	Health Care	Misc. Goods/ Services
148.8	107.6	244.7	113.9	135.0	107.6	104.8

Note: The Cost of Living Index measures regional differences in the cost of consumer goods and services, excluding taxes and non-consumer expenditures, for professional and managerial households in the top income quintile. It is based on more than 50,000 prices covering almost 60 different items for which prices are collected three times a year by chambers of commerce, economic development organizations or university applied economic centers in each participating urban area. The numbers shown should be read as a percentage above or below the national average of 100. For example, a value of 115.4 in the groceries column indicates that grocery prices are 15.4% higher than the national average. Small differences in the index numbers should not be interpreted as significant; Figures cover the Orange County CA urban area.
Source: The Council for Community and Economic Research, ACCRA Cost of Living Index, 2015

Grocery Prices

Area[1]	T-Bone Steak ($/pound)	Frying Chicken ($/pound)	Whole Milk ($/half gal.)	Eggs ($/dozen)	Orange Juice ($/64 oz.)	Coffee ($/11.5 oz.)
City[2]	11.16	1.48	2.43	3.59	3.52	5.35
Avg.	10.99	1.43	2.25	2.26	3.58	4.48
Min.	7.16	0.98	1.30	1.35	2.88	2.98
Max.	14.13	2.43	3.85	4.81	6.39	7.56

Note: (1) Values for the local area are compared with the average, minimum and maximum values for all 292 areas in the Cost of Living Index; (2) Figures cover the Orange County CA urban area; **T-Bone Steak** *(price per pound);* **Frying Chicken** *(price per pound, whole fryer);* **Whole Milk** *(half gallon carton);* **Eggs** *(price per dozen, Grade A, large);* **Orange Juice** *(64 oz. Tropicana or Florida Natural);* **Coffee** *(11.5 oz. can, vacuum-packed, Maxwell House, Hills Bros, or Folgers).*
Source: The Council for Community and Economic Research, ACCRA Cost of Living Index, 2015

Housing and Utility Costs

Area[1]	New Home Price ($)	Apartment Rent ($/month)	All Electric ($/month)	Part Electric ($/month)	Other Energy ($/month)	Telephone ($/month)
City[2]	809,108	1,998	-	129.72	57.14	33.57
Avg.	312,874	945	179.30	95.07	72.96	28.11
Min.	178,682	479	116.28	43.14	26.46	10.01
Max.	1,472,476	3,984	504.25	189.44	421.11	43.06

Note: (1) Values for the local area are compared with the average, minimum and maximum values for all 292 areas in the Cost of Living Index; (2) Figures cover the Orange County CA urban area; **New Home Price** *(2,400 sf living area, 8,000 sf lot, in urban area with full utilities);* **Apartment Rent** *(950 sf 2 bedroom/1.5 or 2 bath, unfurnished, excluding all utilities except water);* **All Electric** *(average monthly cost for an all-electric home);* **Part Electric** *(average monthly cost for a part-electric home);* **Other Energy** *(average monthly cost for natural gas, fuel oil, coal, wood, and any other forms of energy except electricity);* **Telephone** *(price includes basic monthly rate for a private residential line plus additional local usage charges incurred by a family of four).*
Source: The Council for Community and Economic Research, ACCRA Cost of Living Index, 2015

Health Care, Transportation, and Other Costs

Area[1]	Doctor ($/visit)	Dentist ($/visit)	Optometrist ($/visit)	Gasoline ($/gallon)	Beauty Salon ($/visit)	Men's Shirt ($)
City[2]	96.52	104.00	101.81	3.38	59.39	26.79
Avg.	105.15	89.02	99.78	2.38	35.30	28.10
Min.	66.87	56.09	48.53	1.95	18.91	13.38
Max.	182.34	150.36	228.33	4.09	67.91	63.80

Note: (1) Values for the local area are compared with the average, minimum and maximum values for all 292 areas in the Cost of Living Index; (2) Figures cover the Orange County CA urban area; **Doctor** *(general practitioners routine exam of an established patient);* **Dentist** *(adult teeth cleaning and periodic oral examination);* **Optometrist** *(full vision eye exam for established adult patient);* **Gasoline** *(one gallon regular unleaded, national brand, including all taxes, cash price at self-service pump if available);* **Beauty Salon** *(woman's shampoo, trim, and blow-dry);* **Men's Shirt** *(cotton/polyester dress shirt, pinpoint weave, long sleeves).*
Source: The Council for Community and Economic Research, ACCRA Cost of Living Index, 2015

HOUSING

House Price Index (HPI)

Area	National Ranking[2]	Quarterly Change (%)	One-Year Change (%)	Five-Year Change (%)
MD[1]	88	1.00	6.10	29.10
U.S.[3]	–	1.45	5.76	22.85

Note: The HPI is a weighted repeat sales index. It measures average price changes in repeat sales or refinancings on the same properties. This information is obtained by reviewing repeat mortgage transactions on single-family properties whose mortgages have been purchased or securitized by Fannie Mae or Freddie Mac in January 1975; (1) Anaheim-Santa Ana-Irvine Metropolitan Division—see Appendix B for areas included; (2) Rankings are based on annual percentage change for all metro areas containing at least 15,000 transactions over the last 10 years and ranges from 1 to 266; (3) figures based on a weighted average of Census Division estimates using a seasonally adjusted, purchase-only index; all figures are for the period ending December 31, 2015

Source: Federal Housing Finance Agency, House Price Index, February 25, 2016

Median Single-Family Home Prices

Area	2013	2014	2015[p]	Percent Change 2014 to 2015
MD[1]	651.7	687.9	707.5	2.8
U.S. Average	197.4	208.9	223.9	7.2

Note: Figures are median sales prices of existing single-family homes in thousands of dollars; (p) preliminary; n/a not available; (1) Anaheim-Santa Ana-Irvine, CA Metropolitan Division—see Appendix B for areas included

Source: National Association of Realtors, Median Sales Price of Existing Single-Family Homes for Metropolitan Areas, 4th Quarter 2015

Qualifying Income Based on Median Sales Price of Existing Single-Family Homes

Area	With 5% Down ($)	With 10% Down ($)	With 20% Down ($)
MD[1]	157,636	149,340	132,746
U.S. Average	49,535	46,928	41,714

Note: Figures are preliminary; Qualifying income is based on a mortgage rate of 4.1%. Monthly principal and interest payment is limited to 25% of income; n/a not available; (1) Anaheim-Santa Ana-Irvine, CA Metropolitan Division—see Appendix B for areas included

Source: National Association of Realtors, Qualifying Income Based on Median Sales Price of Existing Single-Family Homes for Metropolitan Areas, 4th Quarter 2015

Median Apartment Condo-Coop Home Prices

Area	2013	2014	2015[p]	Percent Change 2014 to 2015
MD[1]	n/a	n/a	n/a	n/a
U.S. Average	194.9	204.3	210.7	3.1

Note: Figures are median sales prices of existing apartment condo-coop homes in thousands of dollars; (p) preliminary; n/a not available; (1) Anaheim-Santa Ana-Irvine, CA Metropolitan Division—see Appendix B for areas included

Source: National Association of Realtors, Median Sales Price of Existing Apartment Condo-Coop Homes for Metropolitan Areas, 4th Quarter 2015

Gross Monthly Rent

Area	Under $200	$200 -299	$300 -499	$500 -749	$750 -999	$1,000 -1,499	$1,500 and up	Median ($)
City	0.0	0.2	2.9	2.5	10.4	22.9	61.1	1,709
MSA[1]	0.5	1.9	2.5	6.4	16.4	37.2	35.0	1,284
U.S.	1.5	3.2	7.4	21.0	24.1	26.9	15.9	920

Note: Figures are percentages except for Median; Gross rent is the contract rent plus the estimated average monthly cost of utilities (electricity, gas, and water and sewer) and fuels (oil, coal, kerosene, wood, etc.) if these are paid by the renter (or paid for the renter by someone else); (1) Figures cover the Los Angeles-Long Beach-Anaheim, CA Metropolitan Statistical Area—see Appendix B for areas included

Source: U.S. Census Bureau, 2010-2014 American Community Survey 5-Year Estimates

Homeownership Rate

Area	2008 (%)	2009 (%)	2010 (%)	2011 (%)	2012 (%)	2013 (%)	2014 (%)	2015 (%)
MSA[1]	52.1	50.4	49.7	50.1	49.9	48.7	49.0	49.1
U.S.	67.8	67.4	66.9	66.1	65.4	65.1	64.5	63.7

Note: (1) Figures cover the Los Angeles-Long Beach-Anaheim, CA Metropolitan Statistical Area—see Appendix B for areas included
Source: U.S. Census Bureau, Housing Vacancies and Homeownership Annual Statistics: 2015

Year Housing Structure Built

Area	2010 or Later	2000 -2009	1990 -1999	1980 -1989	1970 -1979	1960 -1969	1950 -1959	1940 -1949	Before 1940	Median Year
City	1.6	14.4	12.7	31.8	22.8	12.4	3.1	0.3	1.1	1983
MSA[1]	0.5	6.8	7.5	12.6	16.5	16.0	19.0	8.9	12.2	1966
U.S.	1.0	14.9	13.9	13.8	15.8	11.0	10.8	5.4	13.3	1976

Note: Figures are percentages except for Median Year; (1) Figures cover the Los Angeles-Long Beach-Anaheim, CA Metropolitan Statistical Area—see Appendix B for areas included
Source: U.S. Census Bureau, 2010-2014 American Community Survey 5-Year Estimates

HEALTH

Health Risk Data

Category	MD[1] (%)	U.S. (%)
Adults aged 18–64 who have any kind of health care coverage	82.4	79.6
Adults who reported being in good or excellent health	87.0	83.1
Adults who are current smokers	10.0	19.6
Adults who are heavy drinkers[2]	5.3	6.1
Adults who are binge drinkers[3]	19.5	16.9
Adults who are overweight (BMI 25.0 - 29.9)	38.2	35.8
Adults who are obese (BMI 30.0 - 99.8)	21.5	27.6
Adults who participated in any physical activities in the past month	84.4	77.1
Adults 50+ who have ever had a sigmoidoscopy or colonoscopy	69.5	67.3
Women aged 40+ who have had a mammogram within the past two years	77.4	74.0
Men aged 40+ who have had a PSA test within the past two years	45.6	45.2
Adults aged 65+ who have had flu shot within the past year	65.0	60.1
Adults who always wear a seatbelt	n/a	93.8

Note: Data as of 2012 unless otherwise noted; n/a not available; (1) Figures cover the Anaheim-Santa Ana-Irvine, CA Metropolitan Division—see Appendix B for areas included; (2) Heavy drinkers are classified as males having more than two drinks per day or females having more than one drink per day; (3) Binge drinkers are classified as males having five or more drinks on one occasion or females having four or more drinks on one occasion
Source: Centers for Disease Control and Prevention, Behaviorial Risk Factor Surveillance System, SMART: Selected Metropolitan/Micropolitan Area Risk Trends, 2012 (Note: the CDC has discontinued this dataset but will be releasing a replacement in mid-2016)

Chronic Health Indicators

Category	MD[1] (%)	U.S. (%)
Adults who have ever been told they had a heart attack	2.2	4.5
Adults who have ever been told they had a stroke	n/a	2.9
Adults who have been told they currently have asthma	5.7	8.9
Adults who have ever been told they have arthritis	18.1	25.7
Adults who have ever been told they have diabetes[2]	9.4	9.7
Adults who have ever been told they had skin cancer	7.5	5.7
Adults who have ever been told they had any other types of cancer	8.4	6.5
Adults who have ever been told they have COPD	4.3	6.2
Adults who have ever been told they have kidney disease	1.9	2.5
Adults who have ever been told they have a form of depression	9.2	18.0

Note: Data as of 2012 unless otherwise noted; n/a not available; (1) Figures cover the Anaheim-Santa Ana-Irvine, CA Metropolitan Division—see Appendix B for areas included; (2) Figures do not include pregnancy-related, borderline, or pre-diabetes
Source: Centers for Disease Control and Prevention, Behaviorial Risk Factor Surveillance System, SMART: Selected Metropolitan/Micropolitan Area Risk Trends, 2012 (Note: the CDC has discontinued this dataset but will be releasing a replacement in mid-2016)

Mortality Rates for the Top 10 Causes of Death in the U.S.

ICD-10[a] Sub-Chapter	ICD-10[a] Code	Age-Adjusted Mortality Rate[1] per 100,000 population	
		County[2]	U.S.
Malignant neoplasms	C00-C97	139.1	163.6
Ischaemic heart diseases	I20-I25	92.9	102.2
Other forms of heart disease	I30-I51	38.3	50.1
Chronic lower respiratory diseases	J40-J47	28.8	41.4
Organic, including symptomatic, mental disorders	F01-F09	22.3	38.5
Cerebrovascular diseases	I60-I69	34.3	36.5
Other external causes of accidental injury	W00-X59	16.2	27.5
Other degenerative diseases of the nervous system	G30-G31	36.8	26.3
Diabetes mellitus	E10-E14	14.4	21.1
Hypertensive diseases	I10-I15	16.0	19.7

Note: (a) ICD-10 = International Classification of Diseases 10th Revision; (1) Mortality rates are a three year average covering 2012-2014; (2) Figures cover COUNTY NOT FOUND!!!!!!.
Source: Centers for Disease Control and Prevention, National Center for Health Statistics. Underlying Cause of Death 1999-2014 on CDC WONDER Online Database, released 2015.

Mortality Rates for Selected Causes of Death

ICD-10[a] Sub-Chapter	ICD-10[a] Code	Age-Adjusted Mortality Rate[1] per 100,000 population	
		County[2]	U.S.
Assault	X85-Y09	1.8	5.1
Diseases of the liver	K70-K76	11.9	13.5
Human immunodeficiency virus (HIV) disease	B20-B24	1.0	2.1
Influenza and pneumonia	J09-J18	16.4	15.2
Intentional self-harm	X60-X84	10.0	12.7
Malnutrition	E40-E46	0.2	0.9
Obesity and other hyperalimentation	E65-E68	0.7	1.9
Renal failure	N17-N19	8.0	13.0
Transport accidents	V01-V99	6.5	11.6
Viral hepatitis	B15-B19	2.1	2.1

Note: (a) ICD-10 = International Classification of Diseases 10th Revision; (1) Mortality rates are a three year average covering 2012-2014; (2) Figures cover COUNTY NOT FOUND!!!!!!; Data are Suppressed when the data meet the criteria for confidentiality constraints; Mortality rates are flagged as Unreliable when the rate would be calculated with a numerator of 20 or less.
Source: Centers for Disease Control and Prevention, National Center for Health Statistics. Underlying Cause of Death 1999-2014 on CDC WONDER Online Database, released 2015.

Health Insurance Coverage

Area	With Health Insurance	With Private Health Insurance	With Public Health Insurance	Without Health Insurance	Population Under Age 18 Without Health Insurance
City	93.9	84.7	17.6	6.1	3.8
MSA[1]	80.3	56.7	29.9	19.7	8.2
U.S.	85.8	65.8	31.1	14.2	7.1

Note: Figures are percentages that cover the civilian noninstitutionalized population; (1) Figures cover the Los Angeles-Long Beach-Anaheim, CA Metropolitan Statistical Area—see Appendix B for areas included
Source: U.S. Census Bureau, 2010-2014 American Community Survey 5-Year Estimates

Number of Medical Professionals

Area	MDs[3]	DOs[3,4]	Dentists	Podiatrists	Chiropractors	Optometrists
County[1] (number)	9,654	595	3,265	180	1,402	753
County[1] (rate[2])	309.2	19.1	103.8	5.7	44.6	23.9
U.S. (rate[2])	272.5	20.9	64.7	5.8	25.9	15.2

Note: Data as of 2014 unless noted; (1) Data covers Orange County; (2) Rate per 100,000 population; (3) Data as of 2013 and includes all active, non-federal physicians; (4) Doctor of Osteopathic Medicine
Source: U.S. Department of Health and Human Services, Health Resources and Services Administration, Bureau of Health Professions, Area Resource File (ARF) 2014-2015

Best Hospitals

According to *U.S. News,* the Anaheim-Santa Ana-Irvine, CA metro area is home to one of the best hospitals in the U.S.: **University of California, Irvine Medical Center** (2 specialties). The hospital listed was nationally ranked in at least one adult specialty. Only 137 hospitals nationwide were nationally ranked in one or more specialties. Fifteen hospitals in the U.S. made the Honor Roll with high scores in at least six specialties. *U.S. News Online, "America's Best Children's Hospitals 2015-16"*

According to *U.S. News,* the Anaheim-Santa Ana-Irvine, CA metro area is home to one of the best children's hospitals in the U.S.: **Children's Hospital of Orange County** (8 specialties). The hospital listed was highly ranked in at least one pediatric specialty. Eighty-three children's hospitals in the U.S. were nationally ranked in at least one specialty. Twelve children's hospitals in the U.S. made the Honor Roll with high scores in at least three specialties. *U.S. News Online, "America's Best Children's Hospitals 2015-16"*

EDUCATION

Public School District Statistics

District Name	Schls	Pupils	Pupil/ Teacher Ratio	Minority Pupils[1] (%)	Free Lunch Eligible[2] (%)	IEP[3] (%)
Placentia-Yorba Linda Unified	34	25,843	27.6	59.2	27.0	11.4

Note: Table includes school districts with 100 or more students; (1) Percentage of students that are not non-Hispanic white; (2) Percentage of students that are eligible for the free lunch program; (3) Percentage of students that have an Individualized Education Program.

Source: U.S. Department of Education, National Center for Education Statistics, Common Core of Data, Local Education Agency (School District) Universe Survey: School Year 2013-2014; U.S. Department of Education, National Center for Education Statistics, Common Core of Data, Public Elementary/Secondary School Universe Survey: School Year 2013-2014

Highest Level of Education

Area	Less than H.S.	H.S. Diploma	Some College, No Deg.	Associate Degree	Bachelor's Degree	Master's Degree	Prof. School Degree	Doctorate Degree
City	4.5	12.7	23.8	9.6	30.8	13.0	3.8	1.8
MSA[1]	21.5	19.9	19.9	7.1	20.7	7.2	2.4	1.3
U.S.	13.7	28.0	21.2	7.9	18.3	7.8	2.0	1.3

Note: Figures cover persons age 25 and over; (1) Figures cover the Los Angeles-Long Beach-Anaheim, CA Metropolitan Statistical Area—see Appendix B for areas included

Source: U.S. Census Bureau, 2010-2014 American Community Survey 5-Year Estimates

Educational Attainment by Race

Area	High School Graduate or Higher (%)					Bachelor's Degree or Higher (%)				
	Total	White	Black	Asian	Hisp.[2]	Total	White	Black	Asian	Hisp.[2]
City	95.5	95.8	100.0	94.6	89.3	49.4	44.9	45.1	71.0	36.7
MSA[1]	78.5	81.1	88.5	87.2	57.4	31.7	33.6	23.9	50.0	11.1
U.S.	86.3	88.4	83.2	85.8	64.1	29.3	30.6	19.0	50.9	13.9

Note: Figures shown cover persons 25 years old and over; (1) Figures cover the Los Angeles-Long Beach-Anaheim, CA Metropolitan Statistical Area—see Appendix B for areas included; (2) People of Hispanic origin can be of any race

Source: U.S. Census Bureau, 2010-2014 American Community Survey 5-Year Estimates

School Enrollment by Grade and Control

Area	Preschool (%)		Kindergarten (%)		Grades 1 - 4 (%)		Grades 5 - 8 (%)		Grades 9 - 12 (%)	
	Public	Private	Public	Private	Public	Private	Public	Private	Public	Private
City	28.9	71.1	83.7	16.3	77.7	22.3	80.5	19.5	85.3	14.7
MSA[1]	58.3	41.7	88.2	11.8	90.3	9.7	90.6	9.4	91.8	8.2
U.S.	57.4	42.6	87.8	12.2	89.8	10.2	89.9	10.1	90.6	9.4

Note: Figures shown cover persons 3 years old and over; (1) Figures cover the Los Angeles-Long Beach-Anaheim, CA Metropolitan Statistical Area—see Appendix B for areas included

Source: U.S. Census Bureau, 2010-2014 American Community Survey 5-Year Estimates

Average Salaries of Public School Classroom Teachers

Area	2013-14 Dollars	2013-14 Rank[1]	2014-15 Dollars	2014-15 Rank[1]	Percent Change 2013-14 to 2014-15	Percent Change 2004-05 to 2014-15
California	71,396	4	72,535	4	1.59	25.9
U.S. Average	56,610	–	57,379	–	1.36	20.8

Note: (1) State rank ranges from 1 to 51 where 1 indicates highest salary.
Source: National Education Association, Rankings & Estimates: Rankings of the States 2014 and Estimates of School Statistics 2015, March 2015

Higher Education

Four-Year Colleges			Two-Year Colleges			Medical Schools[1]	Law Schools[2]	Voc/ Tech[3]
Public	Private Non-profit	Private For-profit	Public	Private Non-profit	Private For-profit			
0	0	0	0	0	0	0	0	0

Note: Figures cover institutions located within the city limits and include main campuses only; (1) includes schools accredited by the Liaison Committee on Medical Education and the American Osteopathic Association's Commission on Osteopathic College Accreditation; (2) includes ABA-accredited schools, schools with provisional ABA accreditation, and state accredited schools; (3) includes all schools with programs that are less than 2 years.
Source: National Center for Education Statistics, Integrated Postsecondary Education System (IPEDS), 2014-15; Association of American Medical Colleges, Member List, March 21, 2016; American Osteopathic Association, Member List, March 21, 2016; Law School Admission Council, Official Guide to ABA-Approved Law Schools Online, March 21, 2016; Wikipedia, List of Medical Schools in the United States, March 21, 2016; Wikipedia, List of Law Schools in the United States, March 21, 2016

According to *U.S. News & World Report,* the Anaheim-Santa Ana-Irvine, CA metro division is home to one of the best national universities in the U.S.: **University of California–Irvine** (#39 tie). The indicators used to capture academic quality fall into a number of categories: assessment by administrators at peer institutions; retention of students; faculty resources; student selectivity; financial resources; alumni giving; high school counselor ratings of colleges; and graduation rate. *U.S. News & World Report, "America's Best Colleges 2016"*

According to *U.S. News & World Report,* the Anaheim-Santa Ana-Irvine, CA metro division is home to one of the best liberal arts colleges in the U.S.: **Soka University of America** (#45 tie). The indicators used to capture academic quality fall into a number of categories: assessment by administrators at peer institutions; retention of students; faculty resources; student selectivity; financial resources; alumni giving; high school counselor ratings of colleges; and graduation rate. *U.S. News & World Report, "America's Best Colleges 2016"*

According to *U.S. News & World Report,* the Anaheim-Santa Ana-Irvine, CA metro division is home to one of the top 100 law schools in the U.S.: **University of California–Irvine, School of Law** (#28 tie). The rankings are based on a weighted average of 12 measures of quality: peer assessment score; assessment score by lawyers/judges; median LSAT scores; median undergrad GPA; acceptance rate; employment rates for graduates; placement success; bar passage rate; faculty resources; expenditures per student; student/faculty ratio; and library resources. *U.S. News & World Report, "America's Best Graduate Schools, Law, 2017"*

According to *U.S. News & World Report,* the Anaheim-Santa Ana-Irvine, CA metro division is home to one of the top 75 medical schools for research in the U.S.: **University of California–Irvine, School of Medicine** (#44 tie). The rankings are based on a weighted average of 11 measures of quality: quality assessment; peer assessment score; assessment score by residency directors; research activity; total research activity; average research activity per faculty member; student selectivity; median MCAT total score; median undergraduate GPA; acceptance rate; and faculty resources. *U.S. News & World Report, "America's Best Graduate Schools, Medical, 2017"*

According to *U.S. News & World Report,* the Anaheim-Santa Ana-Irvine, CA metro division is home to one of the top 75 business schools in the U.S.: **University of California–Irvine, Paul Merage School of Business** (#48 tie). The rankings are based on a weighted average of the following nine measures: quality assessment; peer assessment; recruiter assessment; placement success; mean starting salary and bonus; student selectivity; mean GMAT and GRE scores; mean undergraduate GPA; and acceptance rate. *U.S. News & World Report, "America's Best Graduate Schools, Business, 2017"*

PRESIDENTIAL ELECTION

2012 Presidential Election Results

Area	Obama (%)	Romney (%)	Other (%)
Orange County	45.4	52.4	2.2
U.S.	51.0	47.2	1.8

Note: Results may not add to 100% due to rounding
Source: Dave Leip's Atlas of U.S. Presidential Elections

EMPLOYERS

Major Employers

Company Name	Industry
City of Los Angeles	General government
County of Los Angeles	General government
Decton	Employment agencies
Disney Enterprises	Motion picture production & distribution
Disney Worldwide Services	Telecommunication equipment repair (except telephones)
Electronic Arts	Home entertainment computer software
King Holding Corporation	Bolts, nuts, rivets, & washers
Securitas Security Services USA	Security guard service
Team-One Employment Specialists	Employment agencies
The Boeing Company	Aircraft
The Boeing Company	Aircraft engines & engine parts
The Walt Disney Company	Television broadcasting stations
UCLA Health System	Home health care services
UCLA Medical Group	Medical centers
University of California, Irvine	University
University of Southern California	Colleges & universities
Veterans Health Administration	Administration of veterans' affairs
Warner Bros. Entertainment	Motion picture & video production

Note: Companies shown are located within the Los Angeles-Long Beach-Anaheim, CA Metropolitan Statistical Area.
Source: Hoovers.com; Wikipedia

PUBLIC SAFETY

Crime Rate

Area	All Crimes	Violent Crimes				Property Crimes		
		Murder	Rape[3]	Robbery	Aggrav. Assault	Burglary	Larceny -Theft	Motor Vehicle Theft
City	1,103.4	1.5	19.2	10.3	35.4	205.3	747.4	84.2
Metro[1]	1,932.9	1.9	20.6	61.7	114.0	293.2	1,241.9	199.5
U.S.	2,971.8	4.5	36.6	102.2	232.5	542.5	1,837.3	216.2

Note: Figures are crimes per 100,000 population; (1) Figures cover the Anaheim-Santa Ana-Irvine, CA Metropolitan Division—see Appendix B for areas included; (3) The city and U.S. figures shown were reported using the revised Uniform Crime Reporting (UCR) definition of rape. The suburban and metro area figures shown are an aggregate total of the data submitted using both the revised and legacy UCR definitions.
Source: FBI Uniform Crime Reports, 2014

Hate Crimes

Area	Number of Quarters Reported	Number of Incidents per Bias Motivation						
		Race	Religion	Sexual Orientation	Ethnicity	Disability	Gender	Gender Identity
City	4	0	1	0	0	0	0	0
U.S.	4	2,568	1,014	1,017	648	84	33	98

Source: Federal Bureau of Investigation, Hate Crime Statistics 2014

Identity Theft Consumer Complaints

Area	Complaints	Complaints per 100,000 Population	Rank[2]
MSA[1]	19,791	149.2	55
U.S.	490,220	152.4	-

Note: (1) Figures cover the Los Angeles-Long Beach-Anaheim, CA Metropolitan Statistical Area—see Appendix B for areas included; (2) Rank ranges from 1 to 379 where 1 indicates greatest number of identity theft complaints per 100,000 population
Source: Federal Trade Commission, Consumer Sentinel Network Data Book for January–December 2015

Fraud and Other Consumer Complaints

Area	Complaints	Complaints per 100,000 Population	Rank[2]
MSA[1]	48,981	369.3	172
U.S.	2,593,159	806.0	-

Note: (1) Figures cover the Los Angeles-Long Beach-Anaheim, CA Metropolitan Statistical Area—see Appendix B for areas included; (2) Rank ranges from 1 to 379 where 1 indicates greatest number of identity theft complaints per 100,000 population
Source: Federal Trade Commission, Consumer Sentinel Network Data Book for January–December 2015

RECREATION

Culture

Dance[1]	Theatre[1]	Instrumental Music[1]	Vocal Music[1]	Series and Festivals	Museums and Art Galleries[2]	Zoos and Aquariums[3]
0	0	0	0	0	0	0

Note: (1) Professional perfoming groups; (2) Based on organizations with SIC code 8412; (3) AZA-accredited
Source: The Grey House Performing Arts Directory, 2015-16; Association of Zoos & Aquariums, AZA Member Zoos & Aquariums, March 25, 2016; www.AccuLeads.com, March 29, 2016

Professional Sports Teams

Team Name	League	Year Established
Anaheim Ducks	National Hockey League (NHL)	1993
C.D. Chivas USA	Major League Soccer (MLS)	2004
Los Angeles Angels of Anaheim	Major League Baseball (MLB)	1961
Los Angeles Clippers	National Basketball Association (NBA)	1984
Los Angeles Dodgers	Major League Baseball (MLB)	1958
Los Angeles FC	Major League Soccer (MLS)	2018
Los Angeles Galaxy	Major League Soccer (MLS)	1996
Los Angeles Kings	National Hockey League (NHL)	1967
Los Angeles Lakers	National Basketball Association (NBA)	1960
Los Angeles Rams	National Hockey League (NHL)	2016

Note: Includes teams located in the Los Angeles-Long Beach-Anaheim, CA Metropolitan Statistical Area.
Source: Wikipedia, Major Professional Sports Teams of the United States and Canada, March 24, 2016

CLIMATE

Average and Extreme Temperatures

Temperature	Jan	Feb	Mar	Apr	May	Jun	Jul	Aug	Sep	Oct	Nov	Dec	Yr.
Extreme High (°F)	89	91	97	108	102	107	112	104	112	105	95	93	112
Average High (°F)	68	69	69	72	73	77	82	83	83	79	73	68	75
Average Temp. (°F)	56	58	58	61	64	68	72	74	72	67	61	56	64
Average Low (°F)	44	46	48	50	55	59	62	64	61	56	48	43	53
Extreme Low (°F)	28	29	31	34	38	42	45	48	44	30	32	25	25

Note: Figures cover the years 1945-1995
Source: National Climatic Data Center, International Station Meteorological Climate Summary, 9/96

Average Precipitation/Snowfall/Humidity

Precip./Humidity	Jan	Feb	Mar	Apr	May	Jun	Jul	Aug	Sep	Oct	Nov	Dec	Yr.
Avg. Precip. (in.)	2.7	2.4	2.2	0.8	0.2	0.1	Tr	0.1	0.4	0.3	1.3	1.5	11.9
Avg. Snowfall (in.)	0	0	0	0	0	0	0	0	0	0	0	Tr	Tr
Avg. Rel. Hum. 7am (%)	78	81	82	79	77	79	80	81	81	80	79	79	80
Avg. Rel. Hum. 4pm (%)	56	57	57	55	58	59	57	57	56	57	56	57	57

Note: Figures cover the years 1945-1995; Tr = Trace amounts (<0.05 in. of rain; <0.5 in. of snow)
Source: National Climatic Data Center, International Station Meteorological Climate Summary, 9/96

Weather Conditions

Temperature			Daytime Sky			Precipitation		
10°F & below	32°F & below	90°F & above	Clear	Partly cloudy	Cloudy	0.01 inch or more precip.	0.1 inch or more snow/ice	Thunder-storms
0	2	18	95	192	78	41	0	4

Note: Figures are average number of days per year and cover the years 1945-1995
Source: National Climatic Data Center, International Station Meteorological Climate Summary, 9/96

HAZARDOUS WASTE

Superfund Sites

Yorba Linda has no sites on the EPA's Superfund Final National Priorities List. There are a total of 1,323 Superfund sites on the list in the U.S. *U.S. Environmental Protection Agency, Final National Priorities List, March 18, 2016*

AIR & WATER QUALITY

Air Quality Trends: Ozone

	1990	1995	2000	2005	2010	2011	2012	2013	2014
MSA[1]	0.123	0.106	0.087	0.080	0.073	0.075	0.076	0.072	0.080

Note: (1) Data covers the Los Angeles-Long Beach-Anaheim, CA Metropolitan Statistical Area—see Appendix B for areas included. The values shown are the composite ozone concentration averages among trend sites based on the highest fourth daily maximum 8-hour concentration in parts per million. These trends are based on sites having an adequate record of monitoring data during the trend period. Data from exceptional events are included.
Source: U.S. Environmental Protection Agency, Air Quality Monitoring Information, "Air Quality Trends by City, 1990-2014"

Air Quality Index

Area	Percent of Days when Air Quality was...[2]					AQI Statistics[2]	
	Good	Moderate	Unhealthy for Sensitive Groups	Unhealthy	Very Unhealthy	Maximum	Median
MSA[1]	19.7	57.8	19.5	3.0	0.0	182	67

Note: (1) Data covers the Los Angeles-Long Beach-Anaheim, CA Metropolitan Statistical Area—see Appendix B for areas included; (2) Based on 365 days with AQI data in 2015. Air Quality Index (AQI) is an index for reporting daily air quality. EPA calculates the AQI for five major air pollutants regulated by the Clean Air Act: ground-level ozone, particle pollution (aka particulate matter), carbon monoxide, sulfur dioxide, and nitrogen dioxide. The AQI runs from 0 to 500. The higher the AQI value, the greater the level of air pollution and the greater the health concern. There are six AQI categories: "Good" AQI is between 0 and 50. Air quality is considered satisfactory; "Moderate" AQI is between 51 and 100. Air quality is acceptable; "Unhealthy for Sensitive Groups" When AQI values are between 101 and 150, members of sensitive groups may experience health effects; "Unhealthy" When AQI values are between 151 and 200 everyone may begin to experience health effects; "Very Unhealthy" AQI values between 201 and 300 trigger a health alert; "Hazardous" AQI values over 300 trigger warnings of emergency conditions (not shown).
Source: U.S. Environmental Protection Agency, Air Quality Index Report, 2015

Air Quality Index Pollutants

Area	Percent of Days when AQI Pollutant was...[2]					
	Carbon Monoxide	Nitrogen Dioxide	Ozone	Sulfur Dioxide	Particulate Matter 2.5	Particulate Matter 10
MSA[1]	0.0	1.9	49.0	0.0	48.5	0.5

Note: (1) Data covers the Los Angeles-Long Beach-Anaheim, CA Metropolitan Statistical Area—see Appendix B for areas included; (2) Based on 365 days with AQI data in 2015. The Air Quality Index (AQI) is an index for reporting daily air quality. EPA calculates the AQI for five major air pollutants regulated by the Clean Air Act: ground-level ozone, particle pollution (also known as particulate matter), carbon monoxide, sulfur dioxide, and nitrogen dioxide. The AQI runs from 0 to 500. The higher the AQI value, the greater the level of air pollution and the greater the health concern.
Source: U.S. Environmental Protection Agency, Air Quality Index Report, 2015

Maximum Air Pollutant Concentrations: Particulate Matter, Ozone, CO and Lead

	Particulate Matter 10 (ug/m³)	Particulate Matter 2.5 Wtd AM (ug/m³)	Particulate Matter 2.5 24-Hr (ug/m³)	Ozone (ppm)	Carbon Monoxide (ppm)	Lead (ug/m³)
MSA[1] Level	95	12.6	35	0.097	4	0.07
NAAQS[2]	150	15	35	0.075	9	0.15
Met NAAQS[2]	Yes	Yes	Yes	No	Yes	Yes

Note: (1) Data covers the Los Angeles-Long Beach-Anaheim, CA Metropolitan Statistical Area—see Appendix B for areas included; Data from exceptional events are included; (2) National Ambient Air Quality Standards; ppm = parts per million; ug/m³ = micrograms per cubic meter; n/a not available.

Concentrations: Particulate Matter 10 (coarse particulate)—highest second maximum 24-hour concentration; Particulate Matter 2.5 Wtd AM (fine particulate)—highest weighted annual mean concentration; Particulate Matter 2.5 24-Hour (fine particulate)—highest 98th percentile 24-hour concentration; Ozone—highest fourth daily maximum 8-hour concentration; Carbon Monoxide—highest second maximum non-overlapping 8-hour concentration; Lead—maximum running 3-month average

Source: U.S. Environmental Protection Agency, Air Quality Monitoring Information, "Air Quality Statistics by City, 2014"

Maximum Air Pollutant Concentrations: Nitrogen Dioxide and Sulfur Dioxide

	Nitrogen Dioxide AM (ppb)	Nitrogen Dioxide 1-Hr (ppb)	Sulfur Dioxide AM (ppb)	Sulfur Dioxide 1-Hr (ppb)	Sulfur Dioxide 24-Hr (ppb)
MSA[1] Level	27	69	n/a	9	n/a
NAAQS[2]	53	100	30	75	140
Met NAAQS[2]	Yes	Yes	n/a	Yes	n/a

Note: (1) Data covers the Los Angeles-Long Beach-Anaheim, CA Metropolitan Statistical Area—see Appendix B for areas included; Data from exceptional events are included; (2) National Ambient Air Quality Standards; ppm = parts per million; ug/m³ = micrograms per cubic meter; n/a not available.

Concentrations: Nitrogen Dioxide AM—highest arithmetic mean concentration; Nitrogen Dioxide 1-Hr—highest 98th percentile 1-hour daily maximum concentration; Sulfur Dioxide AM—highest annual mean concentration; Sulfur Dioxide 1-Hr—highest 99th percentile 1-hour daily maximum concentration; Sulfur Dioxide 24-Hr—highest second maximum 24-hour concentration

Source: U.S. Environmental Protection Agency, Air Quality Monitoring Information, "Air Quality Statistics by City, 2014"

Drinking Water

Water System Name	Pop. Served	Primary Water Source Type	Violations[1] Health Based	Violations[1] Monitoring/ Reporting
Yorba Linda Water District	77,513	Purchased Surface	0	0

Note: (1) Based on violation data from January 1, 2015 to December 31, 2015 (includes unresolved violations from earlier years)

Source: U.S. Environmental Protection Agency, Office of Ground Water and Drinking Water, Safe Drinking Water Information System (based on data extracted April 29, 2016)

Broomfield, Colorado

Background

Broomfield sits on over 33 square miles at the foot of the Rocky Mountains. It's a prominent suburb within the Denver metropolitan area. Broomfield was incorporated as a city in 1961 and over the next three decades grew primarily through annexations from four surrounding counties— Adams, Boulder, Jefferson, and Weld. Due to differences between the counties, distances between the county seats, and several different court systems, the community was presented with several predicaments. The community of Broomfield sought to modify the state constitution so it could create its own county to address the predicaments. The constitution amendment passed, and in 2001 Broomfield became the 64th county in Colorado.

While Broomfield is a part of the Denver metro area and all it has to offer, Broomfield has much to offer its residents and visitors on its own. The city boasts business, cultural and recreational opportunities and currently has over 15 million square feet of commercial space. Its fine arts include a choir, festivals, and a 9/11 memorial, as well as many exceptional outdoor recreational opportunities. Broomfield offers an abundance of trails that connect the city via lakes, parks, and other scenic sites, a park system that includes tennis courts, park shelters, therapeutic sensory playgrounds, and more, and sports facilities.

In addition, a short drive to Denver offers museums, parks, and athletics, including professional sports teams in baseball, basketball, football, and hockey. For those who like the arts, Denver is home to the Denver Art Museum and the Denver Performing Arts Complex, which is the second largest performing arts center in the nation.

Due to Broomfield being previously divided among four counties, it's served by several school districts. Several higher education institutions are available in the metropolitan area, including the University of Denver, the University of Colorado at Denver and Health Sciences Center, and the University of Colorado at Boulder.

Broomfield has experienced much economic growth based around the information technology sector. Its largest employers include Ball Corporation, Level 3 Communications, Oracle Corporation, and Hunter Douglas.

Broomfield is served by the Denver International Airport, the hub to airlines such as Frontier and United. The Denver International Airport is the eleventh busiest airport in the world based on passengers and fifth busiest airport in the world based on plane movements. Additionally, the airport covers over 52 square miles of land, making it the largest international airport in the United States and third largest in the world.

Broomfield has a semi-arid climate, which is heavily influenced by the Rocky Mountains, and experiences four seasons. Temperatures range from average lows in the teens during January to average highs in the upper 80s in July. Precipitation ranges from.5 inch in January and February to over two inches in May and July. Though snow amounts can vary, wintery precipitation generally accounts for nearly 55 inches.

Rankings

General Rankings

- The Denver* metro area was identified as one of America's fastest-growing areas in terms of population and economy by *Forbes.* The area ranked #6 out of 20. The 100 most populous metro areas in the U.S. were evaluated on the following criteria: estimated population growth; job growth; gross metropolitan product growth; unemployment; median salaries for college-educated workers. *Forbes, "America's Fastest-Growing Cities 2015," January 27, 2015*

Business/Finance Rankings

- The personal finance site NerdWallet analyzed 183 American metropolitan areas with populations over 250,000 and more than 15,000 businesses to rank where entrepreneurs find the most success. Criteria included area economy, annual income, housing cost, unemployment rate, and the success rate of area businesses. Denver* ranked #24. *www.nerdwallet.com, "Best Places to Start a Business," April 27, 2015*
- The editors of *Kiplinger's Personal Finance Magazine* named Denver* to their list of ten of the best metro areas for start-ups. The area ranked #9.Criteria: well-educated workforce; low living costs for self-employed people, as measured by the Council for Community and Economic Research; a strong existing community of small business; low unemployment; low business costs. *www.kiplinger.com, "10 Great Cities for Starting a Business," October 2014*
- The finance website Wall St. Cheat Sheet ranked the nation's largest metro areas on prospects for high-wage job creation in over the next five years. Based on analysis by CareerBuilder and Economic Modeling Specialists International (EMSI), The Denver* metro area ranked #8. *wallstcheatsheet.com, "Top 10 Cities for High-Wage Job Growth," December 8, 2013*
- Based on metro area social media reviews, the employment opinion group Glassdoor surveyed 50 of the largest U.S. metro areas and equally weighed cost of living, hiring opportunity, and job satisfaction to compose a list of "25 Best Cities for Jobs." The Denver* metro area was ranked #47 in overall job satisfaction. *www.glassdoor.com, "Best Cities for Jobs," May 19, 2015*
- In a survey of economic confidence in the nation's 50 largest metropolitan areas conducted January–December 2014, the Denver* metro area placed #8, according to Gallup's 2014 Economic Confidence Index. *Gallup, "San Jose and San Francisco Lead in Economic Confidence," March 19, 2015*
- The Brookings Institution ranked the 100 largest metro areas in the U.S. based on income inequality. Denver* was ranked #74 (#1 = greatest ineqality). Criteria: the "95/20 ratio," a figure representing the income at which a household earns more than 95 percent of all other households, divided by the income at which a household earns more than only 20 percent of all other households. *Brookings Institution, "Income Inequality, 100 Largest U.S. Metro Areas, 2007-2014," January 14, 2016*
- *Forbes* ranked the largest metro areas in the U.S. in terms of the "Best Cities for Young Professionals." The Denver* metro area ranked #9 out of 15. Criteria: job growth; unemployment rate; median salary of college graduates age 24 to 34; cost of living; number of small businesses per capita; number of large companies; percentage of population 25 years of age and older with college degrees. *Forbes.com, "America's 15 Best Cities for Young Professionals," August 18, 2014*
- The Denver* metro area was identified as one of the most debt-ridden places in America by the finance site Credit.com. The metro area was ranked #7. Criteria: residents' average personal debt load and average credit scores. *Credit.com, "The Most Debt-Ridden Cities," May 1, 2014*
- Denver* was identified as one of America's most frugal metro areas by *Coupons.com.* The city ranked #9 out of 25. Criteria: online coupon usage. *Coupons.com, "Top 25 Most Frugal Cities of 2014," May 11, 2015*
- Denver* was identified as one of America's most frugal metro areas by *Coupons.com.* The city ranked #17 out of 25. Criteria: Grocery IQ and coupons.com mobile app usage. *Coupons.com, "Top 25 Most On-the-Go Frugal Cities of 2013," April 10, 2014*

- The Denver* metro area appeared on the Milken Institute "2015 Best Performing Cities" list. Rank: #16 out of 200 large metro areas. Criteria: job growth; wage and salary growth; high-tech output growth. *Milken Institute, "Best-Performing Cities 2015," December 2015*

- *Forbes* ranked the 200 most populous metro areas to determine the nation's "Best Places for Business and Careers." The Denver* metro area was ranked #1. Criteria: costs (business and living); job growth (past and projected); income growth; educational attainment (college and high school); projected economic growth; cultural and recreational opportunities; net migration patterns; number of highly ranked colleges. *Forbes, "The Best Places for Business and Careers 2015," July 29, 2015*

Education Rankings

- Personal finance website *WalletHub* analyzed the 150 largest U.S. metropolitan statistical areas to determine where the most educated Americans are choosing to settle. Criteria: education quality and attainment gap; education levels; percentage of workers with degrees; public school rankings; quality and size of each metro area's universities. Denver* was ranked #16 (#1 = most educated city). *www.WalletHub.com, "2015's Most and Least Educated Cities*

Environmental Rankings

- The Denver* metro area came in at #29 for the relative comfort of its climate on Sperling's list of "chill cities," as measured by the Sperling Heat Index. All 361 metro areas are included. Criteria included daytime high temperatures, nighttime low temperatures, dew point, and relative humidity at the high temperatures. *www.bertsperling.com, "Sperling's Chill Cities," July 18, 2013*

- Sperling's BestPlaces assessed 379 metropolitan areas of the United States for the likelihood of dangerously extreme weather events or earthquakes. In general the Southeast and South-Central regions have the highest risk of weather extremes and earthquakes, while the Pacific Northwest enjoys the lowest risk. Of the least risky metropolitan areas, the Denver* metro area was ranked #214. *www.bestplaces.net, "Safest Places from Natural Disasters," April 2011*

- The U.S. Environmental Protection Agency (EPA) released a list of U.S. metropolitan areas with the most ENERGY STAR certified buildings in 2015. The Denver* metro area was ranked #9 out of 25. *U.S. Environmental Protection Agency, "Top Cities With the Most ENERGY STAR Certified Buildings in 2016," March 30, 2016*

- Denver* was highlighted as one of the 25 most ozone-polluted metro areas in the U.S. during 2011 through 2013. The area ranked #13. *American Lung Association, State of the Air 2015*

Health/Fitness Rankings

- Analysts who tracked obesity rates in the nation's largest metro areas (populations above one million) found that the Denver* metro area was one of the ten major metros where residents were least likely to be obese, defined as a BMI score of 30 or above. *www.gallup.com, "Boulder, Colo., Residents Still Least Likely to Be Obese," April 4, 2014*

- Analysts who tracked obesity rates in 100 of the nation's most populous areas found that the Denver* metro area was one of the ten communities where residents were least likely to be obese, defined as a BMI score of 30 or above. *www.gallup.com, "Colorado Springs Residents Least Likely to Be Obese," May 28, 2015*

- For each of the 50 most populous metro areas in the United States, the American College of Sports Medicine's American Fitness Index evaluated infrastructure, community assets, and policies that encourage healthy and fit lifestyles, including preventive health behaviors, levels of chronic disease conditions, health care access, and community resources and policies that support physical activity. The Denver* metro area ranked #6 for "community fitness." *www.americanfitnessindex.org, "ACSM American Fitness Index Health and Community Fitness Status of the 50 Largest Metropolitan Areas," May 2015*

- The Denver* metro area was identified as one of the worst cities for bed bugs in America by pest control company Orkin. The area ranked #18 out of 50 based on the number of bed bug treatments Orkin performed from January to December 2015. *Orkin, "Chicago Tops Bed Bug Cities List for Fourth Year in a Row," January 13, 2016*

- Denver* was identified as a "2016 Spring Allergy Capital." The area ranked #99 out of 100. Three groups of factors were used to identify the most severe cities for people with allergies during the spring season: annual pollen levels; medicine utilization; access to board-certified allergists. *Asthma and Allergy Foundation of America, "Spring Allergy Capitals 2016"*
- Denver* was identified as a "2015 Asthma Capital." The area ranked #78 out of the nation's 100 largest metropolitan areas. Criteria: estimated prevalence; self-reported prevalence; crude death rate for asthma; annual pollen score; annual air quality; public smoking laws; number of board-certified asthma specialists; school inhaler access laws; rescue medication use; controller medication use; ER visits for asthma; uninsured rate; poverty rate. *Asthma and Allergy Foundation of America, "Asthma Capitals 2015"*
- The Denver* metro area ranked #50 out of 190 in The Gallup-Healthways Well-Being Index. Criteria: purpose; social well being; financial health; community and physical health. Results are based on telephone interviews with adults, aged 18 and older, living in metropolitan areas in the 50 U.S. states and the District of Columbia. *Gallup-Healthways, "State of American Well-Being," February 23, 2016*

Real Estate Rankings

- According to Penske Truck Rental, the Denver* metro area was named the #6 moving destination in 2015, based on one-way consumer truck rental reservations made through Penske's website and reservations call center. *blog.gopenske.com, "Penske Truck Rental's 2015 Top Moving Destinations List," February 3, 2016*
- With data from RealtyTrac, Yahoo! Finance researchers listed the housing markets in which housing affordability is improving most, factoring in interest rates as well as median home prices. The Denver* metro area was among the least affordable housing markets. *news.yahoo.com, "10 Cities Where Ordinary People Can No Longer Afford Homes," March 5, 2014*
- The Denver* metro area was identified as one of the nations's 20 hottest housing markets in 2016. Criteria: listing views as an indicator of demand and median days on the market as an indicator of supply. The area ranked #4. *Realtor.com, "The 20 Hottest U.S. Real Estate Markets in February 2016," February 25, 2016*
- The Denver* metro area was identified as one of the top 20 housing markets to invest in for 2016 by *Forbes*. The area ranked #16. Criteria: strong job and population growth; anticipated home price appreciation; and other factors. *Forbes.com, "Best Buy Cities: Where to Invest in Housing in 2016," January 27, 2016*
- Denver* was ranked #8 in the top 20 out of 266 metro areas in terms of house price appreciation in 2015 (#1 = highest rate). *Federal Housing Finance Agency, House Price Index, 4th Quarter 2015*
- The Denver* metro area was identified as one of the 15 worst housing markets for the next five years." Criteria: projected annualized change in home prices between the fourth quarter 2012 and the fourth quarter 2017. *The Business Insider, "The 15 Worst Housing Markets for the Next Five Years," May 22, 2013*
- The Denver* metro area was identified as one of the 20 best housing markets in the U.S. in 2015. The area ranked #18 out of 179 markets. Criteria: year-over-year change of median sales price of existing single-family homes between the 4th quarter of 2014 and the 4th quarter of 2015. *National Association of Realtors®, Median Sales Price of Existing Single-Family Homes for Metropolitan Areas, 4th Quarter 2015*
- The Denver* metro area was identified as one of the 20 least affordable housing markets in the U.S. in 2015. The area ranked #13 out of 179 markets. Criteria: qualification for a mortgage loan on a typical home. *National Association of Realtors®, Affordability Index of Existing Single-Family Homes for Metropolitan Areas, 2015*
- Denver* was ranked #174 out of 225 metro areas in terms of housing affordability in 2015 by the National Association of Home Builders (#1 = most affordable). Criteria: the share of homes sold in that area affordable to a family earning the local median income, based on standard mortgage underwriting criteria. *National Association of Home Builders®, NAHB-Wells Fargo Housing Opportunity Index, 4th Quarter 2015*

Safety Rankings

- The National Insurance Crime Bureau ranked 380 metro areas in the U.S. in terms of per capita rates of vehicle theft. The Denver* metro area ranked #58 (#1 = highest rate). Criteria: number of vehicle theft offenses per 100,000 inhabitants in 2014. *National Insurance Crime Bureau, "Hot Spots 2014," June 24, 2015*

Seniors/Retirement Rankings

- From its Best Cities for Successful Aging indexes, the Milken Institute generated rankings for metropolitan areas, weighing data in eight categories—health care, wellness, living arrangements, transportation, financial characteristics, education and employment opportunities, community engagement, and overall livability. The Denver* metro area was ranked #11 overall in the large metro area category. *Milken Institute, "Best Cities for Successful Aging, 2014"*

Sports/Recreation Rankings

- According to the personal finance website NerdWallet, the Denver* metro area, at #8, is one of the nation's top dozen metro areas for sports fans. Criteria included the presence of all four major sports—MLB, NFL, NHL, and NBA, fan enthusiasm (as measured by game attendance), ticket affordability, and "sports culture," that is, number of sports bars. *www.nerdwallet.com, "Best Cities for Sports Fans," May 5, 2013*
- Broomfield was selected as one of the most playful cities in the U.S. by KaBOOM! The organization's Playful City USA initiative honors cities and towns across the nation for a vision, plan and commitment to creating an agenda for play. Criteria: creating a local play commission or task force; designing an annual action plan for play; conducting a play space audit; outlining a financial investment in play for the current fiscal year; and proclaiming and celebrating an annual "play day." *KaBOOM! National Campaign for Play, "2015 Playful City USA Communities"*

Miscellaneous Rankings

- The watchdog site Charity Navigator conducts an annual study of charities in the nation's major markets both to analyze statistical differences in their financial, accountability, and transparency practices and to track year-to-year variations in individual communities. The Denver* metro area was ranked #22 among the 30 metro markets in the rating dimension of Overall Score. *www.charitynavigator.org, "Metro Market Study 2015," June 5, 2015*
- Mars Chocolate North America, the makers of COMBOS®, in partnership with Sperling's BestPlaces, ranked 50 major metro areas in terms of their "manliness." The Denver* metro area ranked #34. Criteria: number of professional sports teams; number of nearby NASCAR tracks and racing events; manly lifestyle; concentration of manly retail stores; manly occupations per capita; salty snack sales; "Board of Manliness" rankings. *Mars Chocolate North America, "America's Manliest Cities 2012"*
- The National Alliance to End Homelessness ranked the 100 most populous metro areas with the highest rate of homelessness. The Denver* metro area ranked #30. Criteria: number of homeless people per 10,000 population in 2011. *National Alliance to End Homelessness, The State of Homelessness in America 2012*

Broomfield is located within the Denver-Aurora-Lakewood, CO Metropolitan Statistical Area.

Business Environment

CITY FINANCES

City Government Finances

Component	2012 ($000)	2012 ($ per capita)
Total Revenues	164,078	2,935
Total Expenditures	128,766	2,303
Debt Outstanding	293,045	5,243
Cash and Securities[1]	228,428	4,087

Note: (1) Cash and security holdings of a government at the close of its fiscal year, including those of its dependent agencies, utilities, and liquor stores.
Source: U.S Census Bureau, State & Local Government Finances 2012

City Government Revenue by Source

Source	2012 ($000)	2012 ($ per capita)
General Revenue		
From Federal Government	8,124	145
From State Government	6,271	112
From Local Governments	1,008	18
Taxes		
Property	38,601	690
Sales and Gross Receipts	57,037	1,020
Personal Income	0	0
Corporate Income	0	0
Motor Vehicle License	496	8
Other Taxes	17,380	310
Current Charges	16,457	294
Liquor Store	0	0
Utility	14,151	253
Employee Retirement	0	0

Source: U.S Census Bureau, State & Local Government Finances 2012

City Government Expenditures by Function

Function	2012 ($000)	2012 ($ per capita)	2012 (%)
General Direct Expenditures			
Air Transportation	0	0	0.0
Corrections	4,783	85	3.7
Education	0	0	0.0
Employment Security Administration	0	0	0.0
Financial Administration	3,440	61	2.6
Fire Protection	0	0	0.0
General Public Buildings	735	13	0.5
Governmental Administration, Other	6,751	120	5.2
Health	1,724	30	1.3
Highways	8,825	157	6.8
Hospitals	0	0	0.0
Housing and Community Development	0	0	0.0
Interest on General Debt	13,814	247	10.7
Judicial and Legal	2,598	46	2.0
Libraries	2,109	37	1.6
Parking	0	0	0.0
Parks and Recreation	14,015	250	10.8
Police Protection	15,851	283	12.3
Public Welfare	11,456	204	8.8
Sewerage	5,442	97	4.2
Solid Waste Management	183	3	0.1
Veterans' Services	0	0	0.0
Liquor Store	0	0	0.0
Utility	19,062	341	14.8
Employee Retirement	0	0	0.0

Source: U.S Census Bureau, State & Local Government Finances 2012

DEMOGRAPHICS

Population Growth

Area	1990 Census	2000 Census	2010 Census	2014* Estimate	Population Growth (%) 1990-2014	2010-2014
City	24,789	38,272	55,889	59,027	138.1	5.6
MSA[1]	1,666,935	2,179,296	2,543,482	2,651,392	59.1	4.2
U.S.	248,709,873	281,421,906	308,745,538	314,107,084	26.3	1.7

Note: (1) Figures cover the Denver-Aurora-Lakewood, CO Metropolitan Statistical Area—see Appendix B for areas included; (*) 2010-2014 5-year estimated population

Source: U.S. Census Bureau, 1990 Census, Census 2000, Census 2010, 2010-2014 American Community Survey 5-Year Estimates

Household Size

Area	Persons in Household (%) One	Two	Three	Four	Five	Six	Seven or More	Average Household Size
City	25.8	32.1	15.8	16.4	7.3	1.5	0.8	2.58
MSA[1]	29.1	33.2	15.2	13.0	5.6	2.2	1.3	2.55
U.S.	27.5	33.5	15.8	13.1	6.0	2.3	1.4	2.64

Note: (1) Figures cover the Denver-Aurora-Lakewood, CO Metropolitan Statistical Area—see Appendix B for areas included

Source: U.S. Census Bureau, 2010-2014 American Community Survey 5-Year Estimates

Race

Area	White Alone[2] (%)	Black Alone[2] (%)	Asian Alone[2] (%)	AIAN[3] Alone[2] (%)	NHOPI[4] Alone[2] (%)	Other Race Alone[2] (%)	Two or More Races (%)
City	86.9	1.0	6.0	0.4	0.0	2.2	3.5
MSA[1]	81.5	5.5	3.8	0.8	0.1	4.8	3.5
U.S.	73.8	12.6	5.0	0.8	0.2	4.7	2.9

Note: (1) Figures cover the Denver-Aurora-Lakewood, CO Metropolitan Statistical Area—see Appendix B for areas included; (2) Alone is defined as not being in combination with one or more other races; (3) American Indian and Alaska Native; (4) Native Hawaiian and Other Pacific Islander

Source: U.S. Census Bureau, 2010-2014 American Community Survey 5-Year Estimates

Hispanic or Latino Origin

Area	Total (%)	Mexican (%)	Puerto Rican (%)	Cuban (%)	Other (%)
City	11.6	8.8	0.2	0.3	2.4
MSA[1]	22.7	18.0	0.5	0.1	4.0
U.S.	16.9	10.8	1.6	0.6	3.8

Note: Persons of Hispanic or Latino origin can be of any race; (1) Figures cover the Denver-Aurora-Lakewood, CO Metropolitan Statistical Area—see Appendix B for areas included

Source: U.S. Census Bureau, 2010-2014 American Community Survey 5-Year Estimates

Ancestry

Area	German	Irish	English	American	Italian	Polish	French[2]	Scottish	Dutch
City	23.4	13.4	13.4	7.1	6.3	3.9	3.0	2.7	2.1
MSA[1]	19.4	11.6	10.0	5.0	5.2	2.6	2.7	2.4	1.6
U.S.	14.9	10.8	8.0	7.1	5.5	3.0	2.7	1.7	1.4

Note: Figures are the percentage of the total population reporting a particular ancestry. The nine most commonly reported ancestries in the U.S. are shown. Figures include multiple ancestries (e.g. if a person reported being Irish and Italian, they were included in both columns); (1) Figures cover the Denver-Aurora-Lakewood, CO Metropolitan Statistical Area—see Appendix B for areas included; (2) Excludes Basque

Source: U.S. Census Bureau, 2010-2014 American Community Survey 5-Year Estimates

Foreign-Born Population

Area	Percent of Population Born in								
	Any Foreign Country	Asia	Mexico	Europe	Carribean	Central America[2]	South America	Africa	Canada
City	9.2	3.9	2.0	1.9	0.1	0.3	0.2	0.2	0.6
MSA[1]	12.2	2.9	5.5	1.5	0.1	0.5	0.4	0.9	0.3
U.S.	13.1	3.8	3.7	1.5	1.2	1.0	0.9	0.6	0.3

Note: (1) Figures cover the Denver-Aurora-Lakewood, CO Metropolitan Statistical Area—see Appendix B for areas included; (2) Excludes Mexico.
Source: U.S. Census Bureau, 2010-2014 American Community Survey 5-Year Estimates

Marital Status

Area	Never Married	Now Married[2]	Separated	Widowed	Divorced
City	26.2	58.2	1.1	4.6	9.9
MSA[1]	31.7	50.2	1.7	4.2	12.2
U.S.	32.5	48.4	2.2	5.9	10.9

Note: Figures are percentages and cover the population 15 years of age and older; (1) Figures cover the Denver-Aurora-Lakewood, CO Metropolitan Statistical Area—see Appendix B for areas included; (2) Excludes separated
Source: U.S. Census Bureau, 2010-2014 American Community Survey 5-Year Estimates

Disability Status

Area	All Ages	Under 18 Years Old	18 to 64 Years Old	65 Years and Over
City	8.2	2.9	5.5	36.2
MSA[1]	9.2	3.0	7.6	33.0
U.S.	12.3	4.1	10.2	36.3

Note: Figures show percent of the civilian noninstitutionalized population that reported having a disability. Disability status is determined from from six types of difficulty: vision, hearing, cognitive, ambulatory, self-care, and independent living. For children under 5 years old, hearing and vision difficulty are used to determine disability status. For children between the ages of 5 and 14, disability status is determined from hearing, vision, cognitive, ambulatory, and self-care difficulties. For people aged 15 years and older, they are considered to have a disability if they have difficulty with any one of the six difficulty types; (1) Figures cover the Denver-Aurora-Lakewood, CO Metropolitan Statistical Area—see Appendix B for areas included.
Source: U.S. Census Bureau, 2010-2014 American Community Survey 5-Year Estimates

Age

Area	Percent of Population									Median Age
	Under Age 5	Age 5–19	Age 20–34	Age 35–44	Age 45–54	Age 55–64	Age 65–74	Age 75–84	Age 85+	
City	6.3	20.7	19.8	15.9	14.7	11.5	6.5	2.9	1.6	37.4
MSA[1]	6.7	19.8	21.9	14.7	14.1	11.9	6.4	3.1	1.4	36.0
U.S.	6.4	19.9	20.6	13.0	14.1	12.3	7.6	4.3	1.9	37.4

Note: (1) Figures cover the Denver-Aurora-Lakewood, CO Metropolitan Statistical Area—see Appendix B for areas included
Source: U.S. Census Bureau, 2010-2014 American Community Survey 5-Year Estimates

Gender

Area	Males	Females	Males per 100 Females
City	29,245	29,782	98.2
MSA[1]	1,319,273	1,332,119	99.0
U.S.	154,515,159	159,591,925	96.8

Note: (1) Figures cover the Denver-Aurora-Lakewood, CO Metropolitan Statistical Area—see Appendix B for areas included
Source: U.S. Census Bureau, 2010-2014 American Community Survey 5-Year Estimates

Religious Groups by Family

Area	Catholic	Baptist	Non-Den.	Methodist[2]	Lutheran	LDS[3]	Pente-costal	Presby-terian[4]	Muslim[5]	Judaism
MSA[1]	16.0	2.9	4.6	1.7	2.1	2.4	1.2	1.5	0.5	0.6
U.S.	19.1	9.3	4.0	4.0	2.3	2.0	1.9	1.6	0.8	0.7

Note: Figures are the number of adherents as a percentage of the total population; (1) Figures cover the Denver-Aurora-Broomfield, CO Metropolitan Statistical Area—see Appendix B for areas included; (2) Methodist/Pietist; (3) Latter Day Saints; (4) Reformed; (5) Figures are estimates
Source: Association of Statisticians of American Religious Bodies, 2010 U.S. Religion Census: Religious Congregations & Membership Study

Religious Groups by Tradition

Area	Catholic	Evangelical Protestant	Mainline Protestant	Other Tradition	Black Protestant	Orthodox
MSA[1]	16.0	11.0	4.5	4.6	0.3	0.3
U.S.	19.1	16.2	7.3	4.3	1.6	0.3

Note: Figures are the number of adherents as a percentage of the total population; (1) Figures cover the Denver-Aurora-Broomfield, CO Metropolitan Statistical Area—see Appendix B for areas included
Source: Association of Statisticians of American Religious Bodies, 2010 U.S. Religion Census: Religious Congregations & Membership Study

ECONOMY

Gross Metropolitan Product

Area	2013	2014	2015	2016	Rank[2]
MSA[1]	178.9	188.8	194.9	205.3	18

Note: Figures are in billions of dollars; (1) Figures cover the Denver-Aurora-Lakewood, CO Metropolitan Statistical Area—see Appendix B for areas included; (2) Rank is based on 2016 data and ranges from 1 to 381
Source: The U.S. Conference of Mayors, U.S. Metro Economies: GMP and Employment 2014-2016, June 2015

Economic Growth

Area	2011-13 (%)	2014 (%)	2015 (%)	2016 (%)	Rank[2]
MSA[1]	3.9	4.7	2.9	3.2	61
U.S.	2.2	2.4	2.3	2.9	-

Note: Figures are real gross metropolitan product (GMP) growth rates and represent annual average percent change; (1) Figures cover the Denver-Aurora-Lakewood, CO Metropolitan Statistical Area—see Appendix B for areas included; (2) Rank is based on 2016 data and ranges from 1 to 381
Source: The U.S. Conference of Mayors, U.S. Metro Economies: GMP and Employment 2014-2016, June 2015

Metropolitan Area Exports

Area	2009	2010	2011	2012	2013	2014	Rank[2]
MSA[1]	4,309.7	4,990.9	3,771.3	3,355.7	3,618.3	4,958.5	59

Note: Figures are in millions of dollars; (1) Figures cover the Denver-Aurora-Lakewood, CO Metropolitan Statistical Area—see Appendix B for areas included; (2) Rank is based on 2014 data and ranges from 1 to 385
Source: U.S. Department of Commerce, International Trade Administration, Office of Trade & Industry Information, Manufacturing & Services, data extracted March 10, 2016

Building Permits

Area	Single-Family			Multi-Family			Total		
	2014	2015p	Pct. Chg.	2014	2015p	Pct. Chg.	2014	2015p	Pct. Chg.
City	439	403	-8.2	381	44	-88.5	820	447	-45.5
MSA[1]	8,064	9,288	15.2	7,703	8,569	11.2	15,767	17,857	13.3
U.S.	640,300	690,800	7.9	411,800	487,600	18.4	1,052,100	1,178,400	12.0

Note: (1) Figures cover the Denver-Aurora-Lakewood, CO Metropolitan Statistical Area—see Appendix B for areas included; Figures represent new, privately-owned housing units authorized (unadjusted data); All permit data are based on estimates with imputation; (p) preliminary data.
Source: U.S. Census Bureau, Manufacturing, Mining, and Construction Statistics, Building Permits, 2014, 2015

Bankruptcy Filings

Area	Business Filings 2014	Business Filings 2015	% Chg.	Nonbusiness Filings 2014	Nonbusiness Filings 2015	% Chg.
Broomfield County	3	5	66.7	153	131	-14.4
U.S.	26,983	24,735	-8.3	909,812	819,760	-9.9

Note: Business filings include Chapter 7, Chapter 11, Chapter 12, and Chapter 13; Nonbusiness filings include Chapter 7, Chapter 11, and Chapter 13
Source: Administrative Office of the U.S. Courts, Business and Nonbusiness Bankruptcy, County Cases Commenced by Chapter of the Bankruptcy Code, During the 12- Month Period Ending December 31, 2014 and Business and Nonbusiness Bankruptcy, County Cases Commenced by Chapter of the Bankruptcy Code, During the 12- Month Period Ending December 31, 2015

Housing Vacancy Rates

Area	Gross Vacancy Rate[2] (%)			Year-Round Vacancy Rate[3] (%)			Rental Vacancy Rate[4] (%)			Homeowner Vacancy Rate[5] (%)		
	2013	2014	2015	2013	2014	2015	2013	2014	2015	2013	2014	2015
MSA[1]	6.3	6.1	7.4	5.5	5.1	5.6	5.3	3.3	4.8	1.2	0.8	0.7
U.S.	13.6	13.4	12.9	10.7	10.4	10.0	8.3	7.6	7.1	2.0	1.9	1.8

Note: (1) Figures cover the Denver-Aurora-Lakewood, CO Metropolitan Statistical Area—see Appendix B for areas included; (2) The percentage of the total housing inventory that is vacant; (3) The percentage of the housing inventory (excluding seasonal units) that is year-round vacant; (4) The percentage of rental inventory that is vacant for rent; (5) The percentage of homeowner inventory that is vacant for sale
Source: U.S. Census Bureau, Housing Vacancies and Homeownership Annual Statistics: 2015

INCOME

Income

Area	Per Capita ($)	Median Household ($)	Average Household ($)
City	38,706	80,430	99,462
MSA[1]	34,173	64,206	86,081
U.S.	28,555	53,482	74,596

Note: (1) Figures cover the Denver-Aurora-Lakewood, CO Metropolitan Statistical Area—see Appendix B for areas included
Source: U.S. Census Bureau, 2010-2014 American Community Survey 5-Year Estimates

Household Income Distribution

Area	Percent of Households Earning							
	Under $15,000	$15,000 -24,999	$25,000 -34,999	$35,000 -49,999	$50,000 -74,999	$75,000 -99,000	$100,000 -149,999	$150,000 and up
City	6.8	6.3	7.1	9.3	16.9	15.0	21.0	17.7
MSA[1]	9.4	8.2	8.9	12.6	18.0	13.5	16.0	13.4
U.S.	12.5	10.7	10.2	13.5	17.8	12.2	13.0	10.0

Note: (1) Figures cover the Denver-Aurora-Lakewood, CO Metropolitan Statistical Area—see Appendix B for areas included
Source: U.S. Census Bureau, 2010-2014 American Community Survey 5-Year Estimates

Poverty Rate

Area	All Ages	Under 18 Years Old	18 to 64 Years Old	65 Years and Over
City	6.3	6.9	6.3	5.4
MSA[1]	12.0	16.6	11.1	7.5
U.S.	15.6	21.9	14.6	9.4

Note: Figures are percentage of people whose income during the past 12 months was below the poverty level; (1) Figures cover the Denver-Aurora-Lakewood, CO Metropolitan Statistical Area—see Appendix B for areas included
Source: U.S. Census Bureau, 2010-2014 American Community Survey 5-Year Estimates

EMPLOYMENT

Labor Force and Employment

Area	Civilian Labor Force			Workers Employed		
	Dec. 2014	Dec. 2015	% Chg.	Dec. 2014	Dec. 2015	% Chg.
City	33,660	33,572	-0.2	32,481	32,624	0.4
MSA[1]	1,497,400	1,488,871	-0.5	1,437,876	1,442,519	0.3
U.S.	155,521,000	157,245,000	1.1	147,190,000	149,703,000	1.7

Note: Data is not seasonally adjusted and covers workers 16 years of age and older; (1) Figures cover the Denver-Aurora-Lakewood, CO Metropolitan Statistical Area—see Appendix B for areas included
Source: Bureau of Labor Statistics, Local Area Unemployment Statistics

Unemployment Rate

Area	2015											
	Jan.	Feb.	Mar.	Apr.	May	Jun.	Jul.	Aug.	Sep.	Oct.	Nov.	Dec.
City	4.0	4.0	3.9	3.8	3.8	3.9	3.5	3.3	2.9	2.9	3.0	2.8
MSA[1]	4.5	4.5	4.3	4.1	4.1	4.3	3.8	3.6	3.2	3.1	3.2	3.1
U.S.	6.1	5.8	5.6	5.1	5.3	5.5	5.6	5.2	4.9	4.8	4.8	4.8

Note: Data is not seasonally adjusted and covers workers 16 years of age and older; (1) Figures cover the Denver-Aurora-Lakewood, CO Metropolitan Statistical Area—see Appendix B for areas included
Source: Bureau of Labor Statistics, Local Area Unemployment Statistics

Employment by Occupation

Occupation Classification	City (%)	MSA[1] (%)	U.S. (%)
Management, Business, Science, and Arts	49.3	41.7	36.4
Natural Resources, Construction, and Maintenance	5.9	8.4	9.0
Production, Transportation, and Material Moving	7.3	8.7	12.1
Sales and Office	26.0	25.0	24.4
Service	11.6	16.1	18.2

Note: Figures cover employed civilians 16 years of age and older; (1) Figures cover the Denver-Aurora-Lakewood, CO Metropolitan Statistical Area—see Appendix B for areas included
Source: U.S. Census Bureau, 2010-2014 American Community Survey 5-Year Estimates

Employment by Industry

Sector	MSA[1]		U.S.
	Number of Employees	Percent of Total	Percent of Total
Construction, Mining, and Logging	95,900	6.7	5.0
Education and Health Services	178,100	12.5	15.7
Financial Activities	104,700	7.3	5.7
Government	194,300	13.7	15.5
Information	46,500	3.2	1.9
Leisure and Hospitality	153,800	10.8	10.4
Manufacturing	69,500	4.9	8.6
Other Services	54,100	3.8	3.9
Professional and Business Services	255,200	18.0	13.9
Retail Trade	139,900	9.8	11.3
Transportation, Warehousing, and Utilities	53,600	3.7	3.9
Wholesale Trade	69,900	4.9	4.1

Note: Figures are non-farm employment as of December 2015. Figures are not seasonally adjusted and include workers 16 years of age and older; (1) Figures cover the Denver-Aurora-Lakewood, CO Metropolitan Statistical Area—see Appendix B for areas included; n/a not available
Source: Bureau of Labor Statistics, Current Employment Statistics, Employment, Hours, and Earnings

Occupations with Greatest Projected Employment Growth: 2012 – 2022

Occupation[1]	2012 Employment	2022 Projected Employment	Numeric Employment Change	Percent Employment Change
Combined Food Preparation and Serving Workers, Including Fast Food	60,670	77,380	16,710	27.5
Secretaries and Administrative Assistants, Except Legal, Medical, and Executive	63,150	77,880	14,730	23.3
Retail Salespersons	79,300	94,000	14,700	18.5
Customer Service Representatives	45,990	59,210	13,220	28.8
Registered Nurses	42,200	53,270	11,070	26.2
General and Operations Managers	42,170	52,340	10,170	24.1
Accountants and Auditors	33,870	43,490	9,620	28.4
Personal Care Aides	16,940	26,210	9,270	54.7
Janitors and Cleaners, Except Maids and Housekeeping Cleaners	36,300	45,470	9,170	25.3
Business Operations Specialists, All Other	42,990	51,450	8,460	19.7

Note: Projections cover Colorado; (1) Sorted by numeric employment change
Source: www.projectionscentral.com, State Occupational Projections, 2012–2022 Long-Term Projections

Fastest Growing Occupations: 2012 – 2022

Occupation[1]	2012 Employment	2022 Projected Employment	Numeric Employment Change	Percent Employment Change
Service Unit Operators, Oil, Gas, and Mining	3,520	6,290	2,770	78.4
Derrick Operators, Oil and Gas	630	1,110	480	76.0
Rotary Drill Operators, Oil and Gas	1,280	2,200	920	71.5
Roustabouts, Oil and Gas	2,770	4,710	1,940	70.2
Interpreters and Translators	1,510	2,550	1,040	68.5
Petroleum Engineers	1,500	2,500	1,000	66.9
Pump Operators, Except Wellhead Pumpers	700	1,160	460	64.9
Helpers—Brickmasons, Blockmasons, Stonemasons, and Tile and Marble Setters	200	320	120	61.3
Insulation Workers, Mechanical	420	680	260	61.2
Information Security Analysts	1,240	1,960	720	57.8

Note: Projections cover Colorado; (1) Sorted by percent employment change and excludes occupations with numeric employment change less than 100
Source: www.projectionscentral.com, State Occupational Projections, 2012–2022 Long-Term Projections

Average Wages

Occupation	$/Hr.	Occupation	$/Hr.
Accountants and Auditors	36.90	Maids and Housekeeping Cleaners	10.39
Automotive Mechanics	20.68	Maintenance and Repair Workers	19.00
Bookkeepers	19.30	Marketing Managers	70.66
Carpenters	21.18	Nuclear Medicine Technologists	36.55
Cashiers	10.49	Nurses, Licensed Practical	24.11
Clerks, General Office	18.98	Nurses, Registered	34.48
Clerks, Receptionists/Information	15.39	Nursing Assistants	15.10
Clerks, Shipping/Receiving	16.40	Packers and Packagers, Hand	11.42
Computer Programmers	43.27	Physical Therapists	36.71
Computer Systems Analysts	46.67	Postal Service Mail Carriers	24.73
Computer User Support Specialists	28.45	Real Estate Brokers	33.01
Cooks, Restaurant	11.65	Retail Salespersons	13.11
Dentists	88.30	Sales Reps., Exc. Tech./Scientific	34.35
Electrical Engineers	46.01	Sales Reps., Tech./Scientific	54.54
Electricians	23.14	Secretaries, Exc. Legal/Med./Exec.	18.54
Financial Managers	77.09	Security Guards	13.79
First-Line Supervisors/Managers, Sales	22.01	Surgeons	121.51
Food Preparation Workers	10.50	Teacher Assistants*	13.73
General and Operations Managers	66.33	Teachers, Elementary School*	25.45
Hairdressers/Cosmetologists	13.40	Teachers, Secondary School*	27.26
Internists	72.69	Telemarketers	14.15
Janitors and Cleaners	12.11	Truck Drivers, Heavy/Tractor-Trailer	23.01
Landscaping/Groundskeeping Workers	13.95	Truck Drivers, Light/Delivery Svcs.	17.39
Lawyers	68.61	Waiters and Waitresses	10.53

Note: Wage data covers the Denver-Aurora-Broomfield, CO Metropolitan Statistical Area—see Appendix B for areas included; (*) Hourly wages for elementary/secondary school teachers and teacher assistants were calculated by the editors from annual wage data based on a 40 hour work week; n/a not available.
Source: Bureau of Labor Statistics, Metro Area Occupational Employment and Wage Estimates, May 2015

TAXES

State Corporate Income Tax Rates

State	Tax Rate (%)	Income Brackets ($)	Num. of Brackets	Financial Institution Tax Rate (%)[a]	Federal Income Tax Ded.
Colorado	4.63	Flat rate	1	4.63	No

Note: Tax rates as of January 1, 2016; (a) Rates listed are the corporate income tax rate applied to financial institutions or excise taxes based on income. Some states have other taxes based upon the value of deposits or shares.
Source: Federation of Tax Administrators, "State Corporate Income Tax Rates, 2016"

State Individual Income Tax Rates

State	Tax Rate (%)	Income Brackets ($)	Num. of Brackets	Personal Exempt. ($)[1] Single	Personal Exempt. ($)[1] Dependents	Fed. Inc. Tax Ded.
Colorado	4.63	Flat rate	1	4,050 (d)	4,050 (d)	No

Note: Tax rates as of January 1, 2016; Local- and county-level taxes are not included; n/a not applicable; (1) Married joint filers generally receive double the single exemption; (d) These states use the personal exemption amounts provided in the federal Internal Revenue Code.
Source: Federation of Tax Administrators, "State Individual Income Tax Rates, 2016"

Various State and Local Tax Rates

State	State and Local Sales and Use (%)	State Sales and Use (%)	Gasoline[1] (¢/gal.)	Cigarette[2] ($/pack)	Spirits[3] ($/gal.)	Wine[4] ($/gal.)	Beer[5] ($/gal.)
Colorado	8.15	2.9	22	0.84	2.28	0.32 (l)	0.23

Note: All tax rates as of January 1, 2016; (1) The American Petroleum Institute has developed a methodology for determining the average tax rate on a gallon of fuel. Rates may include any of the following: excise taxes, environmental fees, storage tank fees, other fees or taxes, general sales tax, and local taxes. In states where gasoline is subject to the general sales tax, or where the fuel tax is based on the average sale price, the average rate determined by API is sensitive to changes in the price of gasoline. States that fully or partially apply general sales taxes to gasoline: CA, CO, GA, IL, IN, MI, NY; (2) The federal excise tax of $1.0066 per pack and local taxes are not included; (3) Rates are those applicable to off-premise sales of 40% alcohol by volume (a.b.v.) distilled spirits in 750ml containers. Local excise taxes are excluded; (4) Rates are those applicable to off-premise sales of 11% a.b.v. non-carbonated wine in 750ml containers; (5) Rates are those applicable to off-premise sales of 4.7% a.b.v. beer in 12 ounce containers; (l) Different rates also applicable according to alcohol content, place of production, size of container, place purchased (on- or off-premise or on board airlines) or type of wine (carbonated, vermouth, etc.).
Source: Tax Foundation, 2016 Facts & Figures: How Does Your State Compare?

State Business Tax Climate Index Rankings

State	Overall Rank	Corporate Tax Rank	Individual Income Tax Rank	Sales Tax Rank	Unemployment Insurance Tax Rank	Property Tax Rank
Colorado	18	15	16	44	33	12

Note: The index is a measure of how each state's tax laws affect economic performance. The lower the rank, the more favorable a state's tax system is for business. States without a given tax are given a ranking of 1. The scores/rankings for the District of Columbia do not affect other states. The 2016 index represents the tax climate as of July 1, 2015 (the beginning of Fiscal Year 2016).
Source: Tax Foundation, State Business Tax Climate Index 2016

TRANSPORTATION

Means of Transportation to Work

Area	Car/Truck/Van: Drove Alone	Car/Truck/Van: Car-pooled	Public Transportation: Bus	Public Transportation: Subway	Public Transportation: Railroad	Bicycle	Walked	Other Means	Worked at Home
City	78.3	7.0	4.2	0.0	0.0	0.3	1.0	1.4	7.9
MSA[1]	76.0	9.1	3.6	0.5	0.2	0.9	2.1	1.1	6.4
U.S.	76.4	9.6	2.6	1.8	0.6	0.6	2.8	1.3	4.4

Note: Figures are percentages and cover workers 16 years of age and older; (1) Figures cover the Denver-Aurora-Lakewood, CO Metropolitan Statistical Area—see Appendix B for areas included
Source: U.S. Census Bureau, 2010-2014 American Community Survey 5-Year Estimates

Travel Time to Work

Area	Less Than 10 Minutes	10 to 19 Minutes	20 to 29 Minutes	30 to 44 Minutes	45 to 59 Minutes	60 to 89 Minutes	90 Minutes or More
City	10.2	24.9	21.0	28.1	8.9	5.1	1.7
MSA[1]	8.9	26.0	23.6	25.5	8.9	5.1	1.9
U.S.	13.3	29.6	21.0	20.2	7.7	5.7	2.6

Note: Figures are percentages and include workers 16 years old and over; (1) Figures cover the Denver-Aurora-Lakewood, CO Metropolitan Statistical Area—see Appendix B for areas included
Source: U.S. Census Bureau, 2010-2014 American Community Survey 5-Year Estimates

Freeway Travel Time Index

Area	1985	1990	1995	2000	2005	2010	2014
Urban Area Rank[1,2]	18	25	23	11	8	12	16
Urban Area Index[1]	1.13	1.14	1.19	1.27	1.32	1.29	1.30
Average Index[3]	1.09	1.11	1.14	1.17	1.20	1.19	1.20

Note: Freeway Travel Time Index—the ratio of travel time in the peak period to the travel time at free-flow conditions. For example, a value of 1.30 indicates a 20-minute free-flow trip takes 26 minutes in the peak (20 minutes x 1.30 = 26 minutes); (1) Covers the Denver-Aurora CO urban area; (2) Rank is based on 101 urban areas (#1 = highest travel time index); (3) Average of 101 urban areas
Source: Texas Transportation Institute, 2015 Urban Mobility Scorecard, August 2015

Freeway Commuter Stress Index

Area	1985	1990	1995	2000	2005	2010	2014
Urban Area Rank[1,2]	24	28	24	15	11	16	16
Urban Area Index[1]	1.18	1.19	1.25	1.33	1.38	1.35	1.36
Average Index[3]	1.13	1.16	1.19	1.22	1.25	1.24	1.25

Note: The Freeway Commuter Stress Index is the same as the Freeway Travel Time Index (see table above) except that it includes only the travel in the peak directions during the peak periods; the TTI includes travel in all directions during the peak period. Thus, the CSI is more indicative of the work trip experienced by each commuter on a daily basis. (1) Covers the Denver-Aurora CO urban area; (2) Rank is based on 101 urban areas (#1 = highest stress index); (3) Average of 101 urban areas

Source: Texas Transportation Institute, 2015 Urban Mobility Scorecard, August 2015

Living Environment

COST OF LIVING

Cost of Living Index

Composite Index	Groceries	Housing	Utilities	Trans-portation	Health Care	Misc. Goods/ Services
109.7	99.2	130.7	94.6	98.2	107.8	104.9

Note: The Cost of Living Index measures regional differences in the cost of consumer goods and services, excluding taxes and non-consumer expenditures, for professional and managerial households in the top income quintile. It is based on more than 50,000 prices covering almost 60 different items for which prices are collected three times a year by chambers of commerce, economic development organizations or university applied economic centers in each participating urban area. The numbers shown should be read as a percentage above or below the national average of 100. For example, a value of 115.4 in the groceries column indicates that grocery prices are 15.4% higher than the national average. Small differences in the index numbers should not be interpreted as significant; Figures cover the Denver CO urban area.
Source: The Council for Community and Economic Research, ACCRA Cost of Living Index, 2015

Grocery Prices

Area[1]	T-Bone Steak ($/pound)	Frying Chicken ($/pound)	Whole Milk ($/half gal.)	Eggs ($/dozen)	Orange Juice ($/64 oz.)	Coffee ($/11.5 oz.)
City[2]	10.92	1.50	1.99	2.44	4.05	5.49
Avg.	10.99	1.43	2.25	2.26	3.58	4.48
Min.	7.16	0.98	1.30	1.35	2.88	2.98
Max.	14.13	2.43	3.85	4.81	6.39	7.56

Note: (1) Values for the local area are compared with the average, minimum and maximum values for all 292 areas in the Cost of Living Index; (2) Figures cover the Denver CO urban area; **T-Bone Steak** *(price per pound);* **Frying Chicken** *(price per pound, whole fryer);* **Whole Milk** *(half gallon carton);* **Eggs** *(price per dozen, Grade A, large);* **Orange Juice** *(64 oz. Tropicana or Florida Natural);* **Coffee** *(11.5 oz. can, vacuum-packed, Maxwell House, Hills Bros, or Folgers).*
Source: The Council for Community and Economic Research, ACCRA Cost of Living Index, 2015

Housing and Utility Costs

Area[1]	New Home Price ($)	Apartment Rent ($/month)	All Electric ($/month)	Part Electric ($/month)	Other Energy ($/month)	Telephone ($/month)
City[2]	398,144	1,306	-	92.34	59.91	28.60
Avg.	312,874	945	179.30	95.07	72.96	28.11
Min.	178,682	479	116.28	43.14	26.46	10.01
Max.	1,472,476	3,984	504.25	189.44	421.11	43.06

Note: (1) Values for the local area are compared with the average, minimum and maximum values for all 292 areas in the Cost of Living Index; (2) Figures cover the Denver CO urban area; **New Home Price** *(2,400 sf living area, 8,000 sf lot, in urban area with full utilities);* **Apartment Rent** *(950 sf 2 bedroom/1.5 or 2 bath, unfurnished, excluding all utilities except water);* **All Electric** *(average monthly cost for an all-electric home);* **Part Electric** *(average monthly cost for a part-electric home);* **Other Energy** *(average monthly cost for natural gas, fuel oil, coal, wood, and any other forms of energy except electricity);* **Telephone** *(price includes basic monthly rate for a private residential line plus additional local usage charges incurred by a family of four).*
Source: The Council for Community and Economic Research, ACCRA Cost of Living Index, 2015

Health Care, Transportation, and Other Costs

Area[1]	Doctor ($/visit)	Dentist ($/visit)	Optometrist ($/visit)	Gasoline ($/gallon)	Beauty Salon ($/visit)	Men's Shirt ($)
City[2]	125.38	97.33	101.85	2.29	35.84	29.52
Avg.	105.15	89.02	99.78	2.38	35.30	28.10
Min.	66.87	56.09	48.53	1.95	18.91	13.38
Max.	182.34	150.36	228.33	4.09	67.91	63.80

Note: (1) Values for the local area are compared with the average, minimum and maximum values for all 292 areas in the Cost of Living Index; (2) Figures cover the Denver CO urban area; **Doctor** *(general practitioners routine exam of an established patient);* **Dentist** *(adult teeth cleaning and periodic oral examination);* **Optometrist** *(full vision eye exam for established adult patient);* **Gasoline** *(one gallon regular unleaded, national brand, including all taxes, cash price at self-service pump if available);* **Beauty Salon** *(woman's shampoo, trim, and blow-dry);* **Men's Shirt** *(cotton/polyester dress shirt, pinpoint weave, long sleeves).*
Source: The Council for Community and Economic Research, ACCRA Cost of Living Index, 2015

HOUSING

House Price Index (HPI)

Area	National Ranking[2]	Quarterly Change (%)	One-Year Change (%)	Five-Year Change (%)
MSA[1]	8	1.50	13.50	41.30
U.S.[3]	–	1.45	5.76	22.85

Note: The HPI is a weighted repeat sales index. It measures average price changes in repeat sales or refinancings on the same properties. This information is obtained by reviewing repeat mortgage transactions on single-family properties whose mortgages have been purchased or securitized by Fannie Mae or Freddie Mac in January 1975; (1) Denver-Aurora-Lakewood Metropolitan Statistical Area—see Appendix B for areas included; (2) Rankings are based on annual percentage change for all metro areas containing at least 15,000 transactions over the last 10 years and ranges from 1 to 266; (3) figures based on a weighted average of Census Division estimates using a seasonally adjusted, purchase-only index; all figures are for the period ending December 31, 2015

Source: Federal Housing Finance Agency, House Price Index, February 25, 2016

Median Single-Family Home Prices

Area	2013	2014	2015[p]	Percent Change 2014 to 2015
MSA[1]	280.6	310.2	353.6	14.0
U.S. Average	197.4	208.9	223.9	7.2

Note: Figures are median sales prices of existing single-family homes in thousands of dollars; (p) preliminary; n/a not available; (1) Denver-Aurora-Lakewood, CO Metropolitan Statistical Area—see Appendix B for areas included

Source: National Association of Realtors, Median Sales Price of Existing Single-Family Homes for Metropolitan Areas, 4th Quarter 2015

Qualifying Income Based on Median Sales Price of Existing Single-Family Homes

Area	With 5% Down ($)	With 10% Down ($)	With 20% Down ($)
MSA[1]	78,629	74,491	66,214
U.S. Average	49,535	46,928	41,714

Note: Figures are preliminary; Qualifying income is based on a mortgage rate of 4.1%. Monthly principal and interest payment is limited to 25% of income; n/a not available; (1) Denver-Aurora-Lakewood, CO Metropolitan Statistical Area—see Appendix B for areas included

Source: National Association of Realtors, Qualifying Income Based on Median Sales Price of Existing Single-Family Homes for Metropolitan Areas, 4th Quarter 2015

Median Apartment Condo-Coop Home Prices

Area	2013	2014	2015[p]	Percent Change 2014 to 2015
MSA[1]	n/a	n/a	n/a	n/a
U.S. Average	194.9	204.3	210.7	3.1

Note: Figures are median sales prices of existing apartment condo-coop homes in thousands of dollars; (p) preliminary; n/a not available; (1) Denver-Aurora-Lakewood, CO Metropolitan Statistical Area—see Appendix B for areas included

Source: National Association of Realtors, Median Sales Price of Existing Apartment Condo-Coop Homes for Metropolitan Areas, 4th Quarter 2015

Gross Monthly Rent

Area	Under $200	$200 -299	$300 -499	$500 -749	$750 -999	$1,000 -1,499	$1,500 and up	Median ($)
City	0.3	2.6	1.9	13.5	13.6	37.0	31.1	1,248
MSA[1]	1.3	2.4	3.0	16.9	26.8	32.9	16.9	998
U.S.	1.5	3.2	7.4	21.0	24.1	26.9	15.9	920

Note: Figures are percentages except for Median; Gross rent is the contract rent plus the estimated average monthly cost of utilities (electricity, gas, and water and sewer) and fuels (oil, coal, kerosene, wood, etc.) if these are paid by the renter (or paid for the renter by someone else); (1) Figures cover the Denver-Aurora-Lakewood, CO Metropolitan Statistical Area—see Appendix B for areas included

Source: U.S. Census Bureau, 2010-2014 American Community Survey 5-Year Estimates

Homeownership Rate

Area	2008 (%)	2009 (%)	2010 (%)	2011 (%)	2012 (%)	2013 (%)	2014 (%)	2015 (%)
MSA[1]	66.9	65.3	65.7	63.0	61.8	61.0	61.9	61.6
U.S.	67.8	67.4	66.9	66.1	65.4	65.1	64.5	63.7

Note: (1) Figures cover the Denver-Aurora-Lakewood, CO Metropolitan Statistical Area—see Appendix B for areas included
Source: U.S. Census Bureau, Housing Vacancies and Homeownership Annual Statistics: 2015

Year Housing Structure Built

Area	2010 or Later	2000 -2009	1990 -1999	1980 -1989	1970 -1979	1960 -1969	1950 -1959	1940 -1949	Before 1940	Median Year
City	2.7	34.0	23.0	11.0	17.7	5.3	5.5	0.1	0.7	1994
MSA[1]	1.1	18.4	15.5	15.0	19.3	10.4	10.0	3.1	7.1	1980
U.S.	1.0	14.9	13.9	13.8	15.8	11.0	10.8	5.4	13.3	1976

Note: Figures are percentages except for Median Year; (1) Figures cover the Denver-Aurora-Lakewood, CO Metropolitan Statistical Area—see Appendix B for areas included
Source: U.S. Census Bureau, 2010-2014 American Community Survey 5-Year Estimates

HEALTH

Health Risk Data

Category	MSA[1] (%)	U.S. (%)
Adults aged 18–64 who have any kind of health care coverage	79.0	79.6
Adults who reported being in good or excellent health	85.0	83.1
Adults who are current smokers	18.0	19.6
Adults who are heavy drinkers[2]	7.5	6.1
Adults who are binge drinkers[3]	21.6	16.9
Adults who are overweight (BMI 25.0 - 29.9)	35.5	35.8
Adults who are obese (BMI 30.0 - 99.8)	20.1	27.6
Adults who participated in any physical activities in the past month	82.9	77.1
Adults 50+ who have ever had a sigmoidoscopy or colonoscopy	68.0	67.3
Women aged 40+ who have had a mammogram within the past two years	70.5	74.0
Men aged 40+ who have had a PSA test within the past two years	41.8	45.2
Adults aged 65+ who have had flu shot within the past year	68.3	60.1
Adults who always wear a seatbelt	94.2	93.8

Note: Data as of 2012 unless otherwise noted; (1) Figures cover the Denver-Aurora, CO Metropolitan Statistical Area—see Appendix B for areas included; (2) Heavy drinkers are classified as males having more than two drinks per day or females having more than one drink per day; (3) Binge drinkers are classified as males having five or more drinks on one occasion or females having four or more drinks on one occasion
Source: Centers for Disease Control and Prevention, Behaviorial Risk Factor Surveillance System, SMART: Selected Metropolitan/Micropolitan Area Risk Trends, 2012 (Note: the CDC has discontinued this dataset but will be releasing a replacement in mid-2016)

Chronic Health Indicators

Category	MSA[1] (%)	U.S. (%)
Adults who have ever been told they had a heart attack	3.0	4.5
Adults who have ever been told they had a stroke	1.8	2.9
Adults who have been told they currently have asthma	9.6	8.9
Adults who have ever been told they have arthritis	21.6	25.7
Adults who have ever been told they have diabetes[2]	7.4	9.7
Adults who have ever been told they had skin cancer	6.0	5.7
Adults who have ever been told they had any other types of cancer	5.9	6.5
Adults who have ever been told they have COPD	4.5	6.2
Adults who have ever been told they have kidney disease	2.0	2.5
Adults who have ever been told they have a form of depression	17.3	18.0

Note: Data as of 2012 unless otherwise noted; (1) Figures cover the Denver-Aurora, CO Metropolitan Statistical Area—see Appendix B for areas included; (2) Figures do not include pregnancy-related, borderline, or pre-diabetes
Source: Centers for Disease Control and Prevention, Behaviorial Risk Factor Surveillance System, SMART: Selected Metropolitan/Micropolitan Area Risk Trends, 2012 (Note: the CDC has discontinued this dataset but will be releasing a replacement in mid-2016)

Mortality Rates for the Top 10 Causes of Death in the U.S.

ICD-10[a] Sub-Chapter	ICD-10[a] Code	Age-Adjusted Mortality Rate[1] per 100,000 population	
		County[2]	U.S.
Malignant neoplasms	C00-C97	153.4	163.6
Ischaemic heart diseases	I20-I25	70.6	102.2
Other forms of heart disease	I30-I51	44.4	50.1
Chronic lower respiratory diseases	J40-J47	45.5	41.4
Organic, including symptomatic, mental disorders	F01-F09	36.7	38.5
Cerebrovascular diseases	I60-I69	34.2	36.5
Other external causes of accidental injury	W00-X59	25.8	27.5
Other degenerative diseases of the nervous system	G30-G31	31.8	26.3
Diabetes mellitus	E10-E14	Unreliable	21.1
Hypertensive diseases	I10-I15	Unreliable	19.7

Note: (a) ICD-10 = International Classification of Diseases 10th Revision; (1) Mortality rates are a three year average covering 2012-2014; (2) Figures cover COUNTY NOT FOUND!!!!!!.
Source: Centers for Disease Control and Prevention, National Center for Health Statistics. Underlying Cause of Death 1999-2014 on CDC WONDER Online Database, released 2015.

Mortality Rates for Selected Causes of Death

ICD-10[a] Sub-Chapter	ICD-10[a] Code	Age-Adjusted Mortality Rate[1] per 100,000 population	
		County[2]	U.S.
Assault	X85-Y09	Suppressed	5.1
Diseases of the liver	K70-K76	10.7	13.5
Human immunodeficiency virus (HIV) disease	B20-B24	Suppressed	2.1
Influenza and pneumonia	J09-J18	Unreliable	15.2
Intentional self-harm	X60-X84	15.6	12.7
Malnutrition	E40-E46	Suppressed	0.9
Obesity and other hyperalimentation	E65-E68	Suppressed	1.9
Renal failure	N17-N19	Unreliable	13.0
Transport accidents	V01-V99	Unreliable	11.6
Viral hepatitis	B15-B19	Suppressed	2.1

Note: (a) ICD-10 = International Classification of Diseases 10th Revision; (1) Mortality rates are a three year average covering 2012-2014; (2) Figures cover COUNTY NOT FOUND!!!!!!; Data are Suppressed when the data meet the criteria for confidentiality constraints; Mortality rates are flagged as Unreliable when the rate would be calculated with a numerator of 20 or less.
Source: Centers for Disease Control and Prevention, National Center for Health Statistics. Underlying Cause of Death 1999-2014 on CDC WONDER Online Database, released 2015.

Health Insurance Coverage

Area	With Health Insurance	With Private Health Insurance	With Public Health Insurance	Without Health Insurance	Population Under Age 18 Without Health Insurance
City	92.0	81.9	18.8	8.0	4.9
MSA[1]	86.2	70.1	24.7	13.8	8.3
U.S.	85.8	65.8	31.1	14.2	7.1

Note: Figures are percentages that cover the civilian noninstitutionalized population; (1) Figures cover the Denver-Aurora-Lakewood, CO Metropolitan Statistical Area—see Appendix B for areas included
Source: U.S. Census Bureau, 2010-2014 American Community Survey 5-Year Estimates

Number of Medical Professionals

Area	MDs[3]	DOs[3,4]	Dentists	Podiatrists	Chiropractors	Optometrists
County[1] (number)	114	17	59	2	35	17
County[1] (rate[2])	189.0	28.2	95.0	3.2	56.3	27.4
U.S. (rate[2])	272.5	20.9	64.7	5.8	25.9	15.2

Note: Data as of 2014 unless noted; (1) Data covers Broomfield County; (2) Rate per 100,000 population; (3) Data as of 2013 and includes all active, non-federal physicians; (4) Doctor of Osteopathic Medicine
Source: U.S. Department of Health and Human Services, Health Resources and Services Administration, Bureau of Health Professions, Area Resource File (ARF) 2014-2015

Best Hospitals

According to *U.S. News,* the Denver-Aurora-Lakewood, CO metro area is home to four of the best hospitals in the U.S.: **National Jewish Health, Denver-University of Colorado Hospital** (1 specialty); **University of Colorado Hospital** (11 specialties); **Porter Adventist Hospital** (1 specialty); **Craig Hospital** (1 specialty). The hospitals listed were nationally ranked in at least one adult specialty. Only 137 hospitals nationwide were nationally ranked in one or more specialties. Fifteen hospitals in the U.S. made the Honor Roll with high scores in at least six specialties. *U.S. News Online, "America's Best Children's Hospitals 2015-16"*

According to *U.S. News,* the Denver-Aurora-Lakewood, CO metro area is home to one of the best children's hospitals in the U.S.: **Children's Hospital Colorado** (Honor Roll/9 specialties). The hospital listed was highly ranked in at least one pediatric specialty. Eighty-three children's hospitals in the U.S. were nationally ranked in at least one specialty. Twelve children's hospitals in the U.S. made the Honor Roll with high scores in at least three specialties. *U.S. News Online, "America's Best Children's Hospitals 2015-16"*

EDUCATION

Public School District Statistics

District Name	Schls	Pupils	Pupil/ Teacher Ratio	Minority Pupils[1] (%)	Free Lunch Eligible[2] (%)	IEP[3] (%)
Adams 12 Five Star Schools	55	42,230	20.2	45.6	31.5	n/a
Boulder Valley SD No. Re2	57	30,546	18.1	29.9	16.0	n/a
Jefferson County SD No. R-1	164	86,011	18.0	32.6	25.4	n/a

Note: Table includes school districts with 100 or more students; (1) Percentage of students that are not non-Hispanic white; (2) Percentage of students that are eligible for the free lunch program; (3) Percentage of students that have an Individualized Education Program.
Source: U.S. Department of Education, National Center for Education Statistics, Common Core of Data, Local Education Agency (School District) Universe Survey: School Year 2013-2014; U.S. Department of Education, National Center for Education Statistics, Common Core of Data, Public Elementary/Secondary School Universe Survey: School Year 2013-2014

Highest Level of Education

Area	Less than H.S.	H.S. Diploma	Some College, No Deg.	Associate Degree	Bachelor's Degree	Master's Degree	Prof. School Degree	Doctorate Degree
City	5.2	15.2	22.1	8.0	31.9	13.6	2.0	2.0
MSA[1]	10.2	20.8	21.7	7.5	25.6	10.4	2.4	1.4
U.S.	13.7	28.0	21.2	7.9	18.3	7.8	2.0	1.3

Note: Figures cover persons age 25 and over; (1) Figures cover the Denver-Aurora-Lakewood, CO Metropolitan Statistical Area—see Appendix B for areas included
Source: U.S. Census Bureau, 2010-2014 American Community Survey 5-Year Estimates

Educational Attainment by Race

Area	High School Graduate or Higher (%)					Bachelor's Degree or Higher (%)				
	Total	White	Black	Asian	Hisp.[2]	Total	White	Black	Asian	Hisp.[2]
City	94.8	95.9	94.8	89.0	79.4	49.5	50.2	38.4	57.2	20.3
MSA[1]	89.8	91.5	89.6	85.0	65.9	39.8	42.1	24.3	46.9	13.3
U.S.	86.3	88.4	83.2	85.8	64.1	29.3	30.6	19.0	50.9	13.9

Note: Figures shown cover persons 25 years old and over; (1) Figures cover the Denver-Aurora-Lakewood, CO Metropolitan Statistical Area—see Appendix B for areas included; (2) People of Hispanic origin can be of any race
Source: U.S. Census Bureau, 2010-2014 American Community Survey 5-Year Estimates

School Enrollment by Grade and Control

Area	Preschool (%)		Kindergarten (%)		Grades 1 - 4 (%)		Grades 5 - 8 (%)		Grades 9 - 12 (%)	
	Public	Private	Public	Private	Public	Private	Public	Private	Public	Private
City	35.3	64.7	82.7	17.3	89.8	10.2	92.0	8.0	95.1	4.9
MSA[1]	57.0	43.0	90.1	9.9	92.2	7.8	91.9	8.1	92.5	7.5
U.S.	57.4	42.6	87.8	12.2	89.8	10.2	89.9	10.1	90.6	9.4

Note: Figures shown cover persons 3 years old and over; (1) Figures cover the Denver-Aurora-Lakewood, CO Metropolitan Statistical Area—see Appendix B for areas included
Source: U.S. Census Bureau, 2010-2014 American Community Survey 5-Year Estimates

Average Salaries of Public School Classroom Teachers

Area	2013-14 Dollars	2013-14 Rank[1]	2014-15 Dollars	2014-15 Rank[1]	Percent Change 2013-14 to 2014-15	Percent Change 2004-05 to 2014-15
Colorado	49,615	31	49,828	34	0.43	13.4
U.S. Average	56,610	–	57,379	–	1.36	20.8

Note: (1) State rank ranges from 1 to 51 where 1 indicates highest salary.
Source: National Education Association, Rankings & Estimates: Rankings of the States 2014 and Estimates of School Statistics 2015, March 2015

Higher Education

Four-Year Colleges			Two-Year Colleges			Medical Schools[1]	Law Schools[2]	Voc/ Tech[3]
Public	Private Non-profit	Private For-profit	Public	Private Non-profit	Private For-profit			
0	0	0	0	0	1	0	0	0

Note: Figures cover institutions located within the city limits and include main campuses only; (1) includes schools accredited by the Liaison Committee on Medical Education and the American Osteopathic Association's Commission on Osteopathic College Accreditation; (2) includes ABA-accredited schools, schools with provisional ABA accreditation, and state accredited schools; (3) includes all schools with programs that are less than 2 years.
Source: National Center for Education Statistics, Integrated Postsecondary Education System (IPEDS), 2014-15; Association of American Medical Colleges, Member List, March 21, 2016; American Osteopathic Association, Member List, March 21, 2016; Law School Admission Council, Official Guide to ABA-Approved Law Schools Online, March 21, 2016; Wikipedia, List of Medical Schools in the United States, March 21, 2016; Wikipedia, List of Law Schools in the United States, March 21, 2016

According to *U.S. News & World Report,* the Denver-Aurora-Lakewood, CO metro area is home to three of the best national universities in the U.S.: **Colorado School of Mines** (#75 tie); **University of Denver** (#86 tie); **University of Colorado–Denver** (#199 tie). The indicators used to capture academic quality fall into a number of categories: assessment by administrators at peer institutions; retention of students; faculty resources; student selectivity; financial resources; alumni giving; high school counselor ratings of colleges; and graduation rate. *U.S. News & World Report, "America's Best Colleges 2016"*

According to *U.S. News & World Report,* the Denver-Aurora-Lakewood, CO metro area is home to one of the top 100 law schools in the U.S.: **University of Denver, Sturm College of Law** (#72 tie). The rankings are based on a weighted average of 12 measures of quality: peer assessment score; assessment score by lawyers/judges; median LSAT scores; median undergrad GPA; acceptance rate; employment rates for graduates; placement success; bar passage rate; faculty resources; expenditures per student; student/faculty ratio; and library resources. *U.S. News & World Report, "America's Best Graduate Schools, Law, 2017"*

According to *U.S. News & World Report,* the Denver-Aurora-Lakewood, CO metro area is home to one of the top 75 medical schools for research in the U.S.: **University of Colorado, School of Medicine** (#35 tie). The rankings are based on a weighted average of 11 measures of quality: quality assessment; peer assessment score; assessment score by residency directors; research activity; total research activity; average research activity per faculty member; student selectivity; median MCAT total score; median undergraduate GPA; acceptance rate; and faculty resources. *U.S. News & World Report, "America's Best Graduate Schools, Medical, 2017"*

PRESIDENTIAL ELECTION

2012 Presidential Election Results

Area	Obama (%)	Romney (%)	Other (%)
Broomfield County	51.8	45.8	2.4
U.S.	51.0	47.2	1.8

Note: Results may not add to 100% due to rounding
Source: Dave Leip's Atlas of U.S. Presidential Elections

EMPLOYERS

Major Employers

Company Name	Industry
Arvada House Preservation	Apartment building operators
Centura Health Corporation	General medical & surgical hospitals
Colorado Department of Transportation	Regulation, administration of transportation
County of Jefferson	County commissioner
DISH Network Corporation	Cable & other pay television services
Gart Bros Sporting Goods Company	Sporting goods & bicycle shops
HCA Healthone	General medical & surgical hospitals
IBM	Printers, computer
Level 3 Communications	Telephone communication, except radio
Lockheed Martin Corporation	Aircraft
Lockheed Martin Corporation	Search & navigation equipment
Lockheed Martin Corporation	Space vehicles, complete
Mormon Church	Mormon church
MWH/Fni Joint Venture	Engineering services
Newmont Gold Company	Gold ores mining
Noodles and Company	Eating places
Strasburg Telephone Company	Telephone communication, except radio
Synergy Services	Payroll accounting service
TW Telecom Holdings	Telephone communication, except radio
Western Union Financial Services	Electronic funds transfer network, including switching

Note: Companies shown are located within the Denver-Aurora-Lakewood, CO Metropolitan Statistical Area.
Source: Hoovers.com; Wikipedia

PUBLIC SAFETY

Crime Rate

Area	All Crimes	Violent Crimes				Property Crimes		
		Murder	Rape[3]	Robbery	Aggrav. Assault	Burglary	Larceny -Theft	Motor Vehicle Theft
City	1,758.0	0.0	24.7	8.2	18.1	187.8	1,459.8	59.3
Metro[1]	n/a	2.8	54.9	75.0	198.5	n/a	1,891.6	292.5
U.S.	2,971.8	4.5	36.6	102.2	232.5	542.5	1,837.3	216.2

Note: Figures are crimes per 100,000 population; (1) Figures cover the Denver-Aurora-Lakewood, CO Metropolitan Statistical Area—see Appendix B for areas included; (3) The city and U.S. figures shown were reported using the revised Uniform Crime Reporting (UCR) definition of rape. The suburban and metro area figures shown are an aggregate total of the data submitted using both the revised and legacy UCR definitions.
Source: FBI Uniform Crime Reports, 2014

Hate Crimes

Area	Number of Quarters Reported	Number of Incidents per Bias Motivation						
		Race	Religion	Sexual Orientation	Ethnicity	Disability	Gender	Gender Identity
City	4	0	0	0	0	0	0	0
U.S.	4	2,568	1,014	1,017	648	84	33	98

Source: Federal Bureau of Investigation, Hate Crime Statistics 2014

Identity Theft Consumer Complaints

Area	Complaints	Complaints per 100,000 Population	Rank[2]
MSA[1]	3,648	132.4	90
U.S.	490,220	152.4	-

Note: (1) Figures cover the Denver-Aurora-Lakewood, CO Metropolitan Statistical Area—see Appendix B for areas included; (2) Rank ranges from 1 to 379 where 1 indicates greatest number of identity theft complaints per 100,000 population
Source: Federal Trade Commission, Consumer Sentinel Network Data Book for January–December 2015

Fraud and Other Consumer Complaints

Area	Complaints	Complaints per 100,000 Population	Rank[2]
MSA[1]	12,974	471.1	31
U.S.	2,593,159	806.0	-

Note: (1) Figures cover the Denver-Aurora-Lakewood, CO Metropolitan Statistical Area—see Appendix B for areas included; (2) Rank ranges from 1 to 379 where 1 indicates greatest number of identity theft complaints per 100,000 population
Source: Federal Trade Commission, Consumer Sentinel Network Data Book for January–December 2015

RECREATION

Culture

Dance[1]	Theatre[1]	Instrumental Music[1]	Vocal Music[1]	Series and Festivals	Museums and Art Galleries[2]	Zoos and Aquariums[3]
0	0	0	0	0	0	0

Note: (1) Professional perfoming groups; (2) Based on organizations with SIC code 8412; (3) AZA-accredited
Source: The Grey House Performing Arts Directory, 2015-16; Association of Zoos & Aquariums, AZA Member Zoos & Aquariums, March 25, 2016; www.AccuLeads.com, March 29, 2016

Professional Sports Teams

Team Name	League	Year Established
Colorado Avalanche	National Hockey League (NHL)	1995
Colorado Rapids	Major League Soccer (MLS)	1996
Colorado Rockies	Major League Baseball (MLB)	1993
Denver Broncos	National Football League (NFL)	1960
Denver Nuggets	National Basketball Association (NBA)	1967

Note: Includes teams located in the Denver-Aurora-Lakewood, CO Metropolitan Statistical Area.
Source: Wikipedia, Major Professional Sports Teams of the United States and Canada, March 24, 2016

CLIMATE

Average and Extreme Temperatures

Temperature	Jan	Feb	Mar	Apr	May	Jun	Jul	Aug	Sep	Oct	Nov	Dec	Yr.
Extreme High (°F)	73	76	84	90	93	102	103	100	97	89	79	75	103
Average High (°F)	43	47	52	62	71	81	88	86	77	67	52	45	64
Average Temp. (°F)	30	34	39	48	58	67	73	72	63	52	39	32	51
Average Low (°F)	16	20	25	34	44	53	59	57	48	37	25	18	37
Extreme Low (°F)	-25	-25	-10	-2	22	30	43	41	17	3	-8	-25	-25

Note: Figures cover the years 1948-1992
Source: National Climatic Data Center, International Station Meteorological Climate Summary, 9/96

Average Precipitation/Snowfall/Humidity

Precip./Humidity	Jan	Feb	Mar	Apr	May	Jun	Jul	Aug	Sep	Oct	Nov	Dec	Yr.
Avg. Precip. (in.)	0.6	0.6	1.3	1.7	2.5	1.7	1.9	1.5	1.1	1.0	0.9	0.6	15.5
Avg. Snowfall (in.)	9	7	14	9	2	Tr	0	0	2	4	9	8	63
Avg. Rel. Hum. 5am (%)	62	65	67	66	70	68	67	68	66	63	66	63	66
Avg. Rel. Hum. 5pm (%)	49	44	40	35	38	34	34	34	32	34	47	50	39

Note: Figures cover the years 1948-1992; Tr = Trace amounts (<0.05 in. of rain; <0.5 in. of snow)
Source: National Climatic Data Center, International Station Meteorological Climate Summary, 9/96

Weather Conditions

Temperature			Daytime Sky			Precipitation		
10°F & below	32°F & below	90°F & above	Clear	Partly cloudy	Cloudy	0.01 inch or more precip.	0.1 inch or more snow/ice	Thunder-storms
24	155	33	99	177	89	90	38	39

Note: Figures are average number of days per year and cover the years 1948-1992
Source: National Climatic Data Center, International Station Meteorological Climate Summary, 9/96

HAZARDOUS WASTE

Superfund Sites

Broomfield has no sites on the EPA's Superfund Final National Priorities List. There are a total of 1,323 Superfund sites on the list in the U.S. *U.S. Environmental Protection Agency, Final National Priorities List, March 18, 2016*

AIR & WATER QUALITY

Air Quality Trends: Ozone

	1990	1995	2000	2005	2010	2011	2012	2013	2014
MSA[1]	0.074	0.069	0.069	0.073	0.070	0.076	0.078	0.078	0.072

Note: (1) Data covers the Denver-Aurora-Lakewood, CO Metropolitan Statistical Area—see Appendix B for areas included. The values shown are the composite ozone concentration averages among trend sites based on the highest fourth daily maximum 8-hour concentration in parts per million. These trends are based on sites having an adequate record of monitoring data during the trend period. Data from exceptional events are included.
Source: U.S. Environmental Protection Agency, Air Quality Monitoring Information, "Air Quality Trends by City, 1990-2014"

Air Quality Index

Area	Percent of Days when Air Quality was...[2]					AQI Statistics[2]	
	Good	Moderate	Unhealthy for Sensitive Groups	Unhealthy	Very Unhealthy	Maximum	Median
MSA[1]	35.9	59.5	4.7	0.0	0.0	146	54

Note: (1) Data covers the Denver-Aurora-Lakewood, CO Metropolitan Statistical Area—see Appendix B for areas included; (2) Based on 365 days with AQI data in 2015. Air Quality Index (AQI) is an index for reporting daily air quality. EPA calculates the AQI for five major air pollutants regulated by the Clean Air Act: ground-level ozone, particle pollution (aka particulate matter), carbon monoxide, sulfur dioxide, and nitrogen dioxide. The AQI runs from 0 to 500. The higher the AQI value, the greater the level of air pollution and the greater the health concern. There are six AQI categories: "Good" AQI is between 0 and 50. Air quality is considered satisfactory; "Moderate" AQI is between 51 and 100. Air quality is acceptable; "Unhealthy for Sensitive Groups" When AQI values are between 101 and 150, members of sensitive groups may experience health effects; "Unhealthy" When AQI values are between 151 and 200 everyone may begin to experience health effects; "Very Unhealthy" AQI values between 201 and 300 trigger a health alert; "Hazardous" AQI values over 300 trigger warnings of emergency conditions (not shown).
Source: U.S. Environmental Protection Agency, Air Quality Index Report, 2015

Air Quality Index Pollutants

Area	Percent of Days when AQI Pollutant was...[2]					
	Carbon Monoxide	Nitrogen Dioxide	Ozone	Sulfur Dioxide	Particulate Matter 2.5	Particulate Matter 10
MSA[1]	0.0	28.2	49.6	0.0	20.0	2.2

Note: (1) Data covers the Denver-Aurora-Lakewood, CO Metropolitan Statistical Area—see Appendix B for areas included; (2) Based on 365 days with AQI data in 2015. The Air Quality Index (AQI) is an index for reporting daily air quality. EPA calculates the AQI for five major air pollutants regulated by the Clean Air Act: ground-level ozone, particle pollution (also known as particulate matter), carbon monoxide, sulfur dioxide, and nitrogen dioxide. The AQI runs from 0 to 500. The higher the AQI value, the greater the level of air pollution and the greater the health concern.
Source: U.S. Environmental Protection Agency, Air Quality Index Report, 2015

Maximum Air Pollutant Concentrations: Particulate Matter, Ozone, CO and Lead

	Particulate Matter 10 (ug/m^3)	Particulate Matter 2.5 Wtd AM (ug/m^3)	Particulate Matter 2.5 24-Hr (ug/m^3)	Ozone (ppm)	Carbon Monoxide (ppm)	Lead (ug/m^3)
MSA[1] Level	97	10	29	0.077	2	0.03
NAAQS[2]	150	15	35	0.075	9	0.15
Met NAAQS[2]	Yes	Yes	Yes	No	Yes	Yes

Note: (1) Data covers the Denver-Aurora-Lakewood, CO Metropolitan Statistical Area—see Appendix B for areas included; Data from exceptional events are included; (2) National Ambient Air Quality Standards; ppm = parts per million; ug/m^3 = micrograms per cubic meter; n/a not available.
Concentrations: Particulate Matter 10 (coarse particulate)—highest second maximum 24-hour concentration; Particulate Matter 2.5 Wtd AM (fine particulate)—highest weighted annual mean concentration; Particulate Matter 2.5 24-Hour (fine particulate)—highest 98th percentile 24-hour concentration; Ozone—highest fourth daily maximum 8-hour concentration; Carbon Monoxide—highest second maximum non-overlapping 8-hour concentration; Lead—maximum running 3-month average
Source: U.S. Environmental Protection Agency, Air Quality Monitoring Information, "Air Quality Statistics by City, 2014"

Maximum Air Pollutant Concentrations: Nitrogen Dioxide and Sulfur Dioxide

	Nitrogen Dioxide AM (ppb)	Nitrogen Dioxide 1-Hr (ppb)	Sulfur Dioxide AM (ppb)	Sulfur Dioxide 1-Hr (ppb)	Sulfur Dioxide 24-Hr (ppb)
MSA[1] Level	25	77	n/a	18	n/a
NAAQS[2]	53	100	30	75	140
Met NAAQS[2]	Yes	Yes	n/a	Yes	n/a

Note: (1) Data covers the Denver-Aurora-Lakewood, CO Metropolitan Statistical Area—see Appendix B for areas included; Data from exceptional events are included; (2) National Ambient Air Quality Standards; ppm = parts per million; ug/m^3 = micrograms per cubic meter; n/a not available.
Concentrations: Nitrogen Dioxide AM—highest arithmetic mean concentration; Nitrogen Dioxide 1-Hr—highest 98th percentile 1-hour daily maximum concentration; Sulfur Dioxide AM—highest annual mean concentration; Sulfur Dioxide 1-Hr—highest 99th percentile 1-hour daily maximum concentration; Sulfur Dioxide 24-Hr—highest second maximum 24-hour concentration
Source: U.S. Environmental Protection Agency, Air Quality Monitoring Information, "Air Quality Statistics by City, 2014"

Drinking Water

Water System Name	Pop. Served	Primary Water Source Type	Violations[1]	
			Health Based	Monitoring/ Reporting
City and County of Broomfield	87,104	Surface	0	0

Note: (1) Based on violation data from January 1, 2015 to December 31, 2015 (includes unresolved violations from earlier years)
Source: U.S. Environmental Protection Agency, Office of Ground Water and Drinking Water, Safe Drinking Water Information System (based on data extracted April 29, 2016)

Lafayette, Colorado

Background

Lafayette is in Boulder County, 18 miles from Denver. The city borders Broomfield and Louisville. Lafayette was incorporated in 1890, and is named after Lafayette Miller, though the founding of the city was actually the work of his wife, Mary. Mary and Lafayette Miller were living in Boulder when Lafayette died in 1878. Mary moved her family to the Lafayette area, where coal was found on her property in 1884. In 1888 Mary gave 150 acres to the town, which she named Lafayette in honor of her late husband. Lafayette was predominantly a coal-mining city until other forms of fuel became widely used. The last coal mine in Lafayette closed in 1956.

One of the city's current goals is to attract more of the business that is rapidly developing in the Boulder County area. Lafayette offers a prime location near Boulder City and Denver, a growing population, and a government that offers business incentives. Major industries in Lafayette include science, technology, healthcare, social services, and retail.

Lafayette is working to bring new economic development to the city while maintaining its natural beauty. Lafayette Urban Renewal Authority (LURA), founded in 1999 to help bring business to downtown, has transformed the area with visual and structural improvements to residential and commercial buildings, and developing commercial real estate areas. The Lafayette Chamber of Commerce provides marketing support and the city's Invest in Lafayette program re-invests local sales tax dollars into the community as a way to promote local business.

The city has over 19 parks, 20 miles of trails and 1,300 acres of open space. Waneka Lake Park captures the essence of Lafayette by offering both recreational activities and opportunities to view and enjoy nature. The park has trails designated for biking and running, a basketball court, baseball field and a soccer field. The lake allows fishing and has paddleboats and kayaks for rent. The park has a wildlife-viewing platform where visitors can bird-watch. Whitetail Park has facilities that cater to children, including an interpretative maze, sledding hill, playground and skate park. The Lafayette Skate Park is a 19,000-square-foot facility dedicated to ramps, rails and bowls. The city also operates Indian Peaks Golf Course, one of the top-ranked public golf courses in Colorado.

Open space and trails in Lafayette provides ample opportunities to experience wildlife in a natural setting while educating residents and visitors alike on the importance of preserving the environment. And, Wilson Community Garden is one of two community gardens that allow residents to grow vegetables.

Lafayette is serviced by the Boulder Valley School District, with some of the top-ranked schools in the state. The Peak to Peak Charter School, grades K-12, consistently ranks as one of the top high schools in Colorado, as does Centaurus High School. Escuela Bilingue Pioneer Elementary is a bi-lingual school that supports the city's Spanish-speaking community, and Justice High Charter School has a widely diverse student body. The University of Colorado at Boulder is nine miles from Lafayette.

The climate of Lafayette features a significant number of sunny days and a comfort index of 64, which is significantly higher then the national average. Both the July average high of 89 degrees and the January average low of 19 degrees fall close to national averages. Lafayette receives 14 inches of rain and 43 inches of snow a year.

Rankings

Business/Finance Rankings

- The personal finance site NerdWallet analyzed 183 American metropolitan areas with populations over 250,000 and more than 15,000 businesses to rank where entrepreneurs find the most success. Criteria included area economy, annual income, housing cost, unemployment rate, and the success rate of area businesses. Boulder* ranked #1. *www.nerdwallet.com, "Best Places to Start a Business," April 27, 2015*
- The Boulder* metro area was identified as having one of the largest percentage of home workers in the U.S. The area ranked #1, according to the business website 24/7 Wall Street, which based its conclusions on data from the U.S. Census Bureau and the Bureau of Labor Statistics. *247wallst.com, "Cities Where the Most Americans Work from Home," March 18, 2013*
- The Boulder* metro area appeared on the Milken Institute "2015 Best Performing Cities" list. Rank: #22 out of 200 large metro areas. Criteria: job growth; wage and salary growth; high-tech output growth. *Milken Institute, "Best-Performing Cities 2015," December 2015*
- *Forbes* ranked the 200 most populous metro areas to determine the nation's "Best Places for Business and Careers." The Boulder* metro area was ranked #26. Criteria: costs (business and living); job growth (past and projected); income growth; educational attainment (college and high school); projected economic growth; cultural and recreational opportunities; net migration patterns; number of highly ranked colleges. *Forbes, "The Best Places for Business and Careers 2015," July 29, 2015*

Education Rankings

- Based on a Brookings Institution study, *24/7 Wall St.* identified the ten U.S. metropolitan areas with the most average patent filings per million residents between 2007 and 2011. Boulder* ranked #5. *24/7 Wall St., "America's Most Innovative Cities," February 1, 2013*
- The Boulder* metro area was selected as one of America's most innovative cities" by *The Business Insider*. The metro area was ranked #5 out of 20. Criteria: patents per capita. *The Business Insider, "The 20 Most Innovative Cities in the U.S.," February 1, 2013*
- Boulder* was identified as one of the "Smartest Cities in America" by the brain-training website *Lumosity* using data from three million of its own users. The metro area ranked #16 out of 50. Criteria: users' brain performance index scores, considering core cognitive abilities such as memory, processing speed, flexibility, attention and problem-solving. *Lumosity, " Smartest Cities in America," June 25, 2013*

Environmental Rankings

- The Boulder* metro area came in at #6 for the relative comfort of its climate on Sperling's list of "chill cities," as measured by the Sperling Heat Index. All 361 metro areas are included. Criteria included daytime high temperatures, nighttime low temperatures, dew point, and relative humidity at the high temperatures. *www.bertsperling.com, "Sperling's Chill Cities," July 18, 2013*
- Sperling's BestPlaces assessed 379 metropolitan areas of the United States for the likelihood of dangerously extreme weather events or earthquakes. In general the Southeast and South-Central regions have the highest risk of weather extremes and earthquakes, while the Pacific Northwest enjoys the lowest risk. Of the least risky metropolitan areas, the Boulder* metro area was ranked #119. *www.bestplaces.net, "Safest Places from Natural Disasters," April 2011*

Food/Drink Rankings

- For the Gallup-Healthways Well-Being Index, researchers interviewed at least 300 adults in each of 189 metropolitan areas on residents' access to affordable fresh produce. The Boulder* metro area was found to be among the top ten communities for affordable produce accessibility. *www.gallup.com, "In Anchorage, Access to Fruits and Vegetables Remains Lowest," April 8, 2014*

Health/Fitness Rankings

- Gallup-Healthways Well-Being Index researchers asked at least 300 adult residents in each of 189 U.S. metropolitan areas how satisfied they were with the metro area in which they lived. The Boulder* metro area was among the top ten for residents' satisfaction. *www.gallup.com, "City Satisfaction Highest in Fort Collins-Loveland, Colo.," April 11, 2014*
- The Boulder* metro area ranked #7 out of 190 in The Gallup-Healthways Well-Being Index. Criteria: purpose; social well being; financial health; community and physical health. Results are based on telephone interviews with adults, aged 18 and older, living in metropolitan areas in the 50 U.S. states and the District of Columbia. *Gallup-Healthways, "State of American Well-Being," February 23, 2016*

Real Estate Rankings

- The Boulder* metro area was identified as one of the nations's 20 hottest housing markets in 2016. Criteria: listing views as an indicator of demand and median days on the market as an indicator of supply. The area ranked #13. *Realtor.com, "The 20 Hottest U.S. Real Estate Markets in February 2016," February 25, 2016*
- Boulder* was ranked #7 in the top 20 out of 266 metro areas in terms of house price appreciation in 2015 (#1 = highest rate). *Federal Housing Finance Agency, House Price Index, 4th Quarter 2015*
- The Boulder* metro area was identified as one of the 20 best housing markets in the U.S. in 2015. The area ranked #12 out of 179 markets. Criteria: year-over-year change of median sales price of existing single-family homes between the 4th quarter of 2014 and the 4th quarter of 2015. *National Association of Realtors®, Median Sales Price of Existing Single-Family Homes for Metropolitan Areas, 4th Quarter 2015*
- The Boulder* metro area was identified as one of the 10 best condo markets in the U.S. in 2015. The area ranked #3 out of 61 markets. Criteria: year-over-year change of median sales price of existing apartment condo-coop homes between the 4th quarter of 2014 and the 4th quarter of 2015. *National Association of Realtors®, Median Sales Price of Existing Apartment Condo-Coop Homes for Metropolitan Areas, 4th Quarter 2015*
- The Boulder* metro area was identified as one of the 20 least affordable housing markets in the U.S. in 2015. The area ranked #11 out of 179 markets. Criteria: qualification for a mortgage loan on a typical home. *National Association of Realtors®, Affordability Index of Existing Single-Family Homes for Metropolitan Areas, 2015*
- Boulder* was ranked #171 out of 225 metro areas in terms of housing affordability in 2015 by the National Association of Home Builders (#1 = most affordable). Criteria: the share of homes sold in that area affordable to a family earning the local median income, based on standard mortgage underwriting criteria. *National Association of Home Builders®, NAHB-Wells Fargo Housing Opportunity Index, 4th Quarter 2015*

Safety Rankings

- Farmers Insurance, in partnership with Sperling's BestPlaces, ranked metro areas in the U.S. as the "Most Secure Places to Live." The Boulder* metro area ranked #5 out of the top 20 in the mid-size city category (150,000 to 500,000 residents). Criteria: economic stability; crime statistics; extreme weather; risk of natural disasters; housing depreciation; foreclosures; air quality; environmental hazards; life expectancy; motor vehicle fatalities; and employment numbers. *Farmers Insurance Group of Companies, "Most Secure U.S. Places to Live in the U.S.," June 25, 2013*
- The National Insurance Crime Bureau ranked 380 metro areas in the U.S. in terms of per capita rates of vehicle theft. The Boulder* metro area ranked #253 (#1 = highest rate). Criteria: number of vehicle theft offenses per 100,000 inhabitants in 2014. *National Insurance Crime Bureau, "Hot Spots 2014," June 24, 2015*

Seniors/Retirement Rankings

- From its Best Cities for Successful Aging indexes, the Milken Institute generated rankings for metropolitan areas, weighing data in eight categories—health care, wellness, living arrangements, transportation, financial characteristics, education and employment opportunities, community engagement, and overall livability. The Boulder* metro area was ranked #26 overall in the small metro area category. *Milken Institute, "Best Cities for Successful Aging, 2014"*

Miscellaneous Rankings

- Of the American metro areas that allow medical or recreational use of marijuana, the Boulder* metro area was identified by CNBC editors as one of the most livable for marijuana lovers. Criteria included the Sperling's BestPlaces assessment of marijuana-friendly cities in terms of sound economy, cultural diversity, and a healthy population, plus cost-of-living index and high-quality schools. *www.cnbc.com, "The Best Cities to Live for Marijuana Lovers," February 5, 2014*
- The finance and lifestyle site NerdWallet looked for the U.S. cities that topped the list in donating money and time to good causes. The Boulder* metro area proved to be the #5-ranked metro area, judged by culture of volunteerism, depth of commitment in terms of volunteer hours per year, and monetary contributions. *www.nerdwallet.com, "Most Generous Cities," September 22, 2013*

Lafayette is located within the Boulder, CO Metropolitan Statistical Area.

Business Environment

CITY FINANCES

City Government Finances

Component	2012 ($000)	2012 ($ per capita)
Total Revenues	40,748	1,666
Total Expenditures	38,921	1,591
Debt Outstanding	52,352	2,140
Cash and Securities[1]	59,179	2,420

Note: (1) Cash and security holdings of a government at the close of its fiscal year, including those of its dependent agencies, utilities, and liquor stores.
Source: U.S Census Bureau, State & Local Government Finances 2012

City Government Revenue by Source

Source	2012 ($000)	2012 ($ per capita)
General Revenue		
From Federal Government	20	0
From State Government	1,415	57
From Local Governments	156	6
Taxes		
Property	6,209	253
Sales and Gross Receipts	12,527	512
Personal Income	0	0
Corporate Income	0	0
Motor Vehicle License	1	0
Other Taxes	510	20
Current Charges	8,941	365
Liquor Store	0	0
Utility	6,380	260
Employee Retirement	0	0

Source: U.S Census Bureau, State & Local Government Finances 2012

City Government Expenditures by Function

Function	2012 ($000)	2012 ($ per capita)	2012 (%)
General Direct Expenditures			
Air Transportation	0	0	0.0
Corrections	0	0	0.0
Education	0	0	0.0
Employment Security Administration	0	0	0.0
Financial Administration	525	21	1.3
Fire Protection	2,780	113	7.1
General Public Buildings	1,060	43	2.7
Governmental Administration, Other	3,877	158	9.9
Health	1,021	41	2.6
Highways	1,729	70	4.4
Hospitals	0	0	0.0
Housing and Community Development	534	21	1.3
Interest on General Debt	1,162	47	2.9
Judicial and Legal	333	13	0.8
Libraries	1,040	42	2.6
Parking	0	0	0.0
Parks and Recreation	6,356	259	16.3
Police Protection	5,070	207	13.0
Public Welfare	0	0	0.0
Sewerage	1,632	66	4.1
Solid Waste Management	838	34	2.1
Veterans' Services	0	0	0.0
Liquor Store	0	0	0.0
Utility	6,722	274	17.2
Employee Retirement	0	0	0.0

Source: U.S Census Bureau, State & Local Government Finances 2012

DEMOGRAPHICS

Population Growth

Area	1990 Census	2000 Census	2010 Census	2014* Estimate	Population Growth (%) 1990-2014	2010-2014
City	15,609	23,197	24,453	25,812	65.4	5.6
MSA[1]	208,898	269,758	294,567	305,166	46.1	3.6
U.S.	248,709,873	281,421,906	308,745,538	314,107,084	26.3	1.7

Note: (1) Figures cover the Boulder, CO Metropolitan Statistical Area—see Appendix B for areas included; (*) 2010-2014 5-year estimated population
Source: U.S. Census Bureau, 1990 Census, Census 2000, Census 2010, 2010-2014 American Community Survey 5-Year Estimates

Household Size

Area	Persons in Household (%) One	Two	Three	Four	Five	Six	Seven or More	Average Household Size
City	29.0	33.4	16.1	15.2	4.0	1.4	0.6	2.45
MSA[1]	27.8	36.4	15.5	13.2	4.7	1.4	0.6	2.43
U.S.	27.5	33.5	15.8	13.1	6.0	2.3	1.4	2.64

Note: (1) Figures cover the Boulder, CO Metropolitan Statistical Area—see Appendix B for areas included
Source: U.S. Census Bureau, 2010-2014 American Community Survey 5-Year Estimates

Race

Area	White Alone[2] (%)	Black Alone[2] (%)	Asian Alone[2] (%)	AIAN[3] Alone[2] (%)	NHOPI[4] Alone[2] (%)	Other Race Alone[2] (%)	Two or More Races (%)
City	86.4	0.5	5.4	0.5	0.1	3.3	3.8
MSA[1]	87.7	0.9	4.2	0.5	0.1	3.7	3.0
U.S.	73.8	12.6	5.0	0.8	0.2	4.7	2.9

Note: (1) Figures cover the Boulder, CO Metropolitan Statistical Area—see Appendix B for areas included; (2) Alone is defined as not being in combination with one or more other races; (3) American Indian and Alaska Native; (4) Native Hawaiian and Other Pacific Islander
Source: U.S. Census Bureau, 2010-2014 American Community Survey 5-Year Estimates

Hispanic or Latino Origin

Area	Total (%)	Mexican (%)	Puerto Rican (%)	Cuban (%)	Other (%)
City	14.7	11.1	0.1	0.1	3.4
MSA[1]	13.6	10.5	0.3	0.2	2.6
U.S.	16.9	10.8	1.6	0.6	3.8

Note: Persons of Hispanic or Latino origin can be of any race; (1) Figures cover the Boulder, CO Metropolitan Statistical Area—see Appendix B for areas included
Source: U.S. Census Bureau, 2010-2014 American Community Survey 5-Year Estimates

Ancestry

Area	German	Irish	English	American	Italian	Polish	French[2]	Scottish	Dutch
City	23.1	15.6	14.5	7.0	5.3	4.2	3.4	4.2	2.7
MSA[1]	22.0	13.5	13.2	4.9	5.9	3.7	3.7	3.7	2.1
U.S.	14.9	10.8	8.0	7.1	5.5	3.0	2.7	1.7	1.4

Note: Figures are the percentage of the total population reporting a particular ancestry. The nine most commonly reported ancestries in the U.S. are shown. Figures include multiple ancestries (e.g. if a person reported being Irish and Italian, they were included in both columns); (1) Figures cover the Boulder, CO Metropolitan Statistical Area—see Appendix B for areas included; (2) Excludes Basque
Source: U.S. Census Bureau, 2010-2014 American Community Survey 5-Year Estimates

Foreign-Born Population

Area	Any Foreign Country	Asia	Mexico	Europe	Carribean	Central America[2]	South America	Africa	Canada
	Percent of Population Born in								
City	10.8	3.2	2.7	2.3	0.0	1.4	0.7	0.1	0.4
MSA[1]	10.6	3.2	3.6	2.3	0.1	0.3	0.4	0.2	0.4
U.S.	13.1	3.8	3.7	1.5	1.2	1.0	0.9	0.6	0.3

Note: (1) Figures cover the Boulder, CO Metropolitan Statistical Area—see Appendix B for areas included; (2) Excludes Mexico.
Source: U.S. Census Bureau, 2010-2014 American Community Survey 5-Year Estimates

Marital Status

Area	Never Married	Now Married[2]	Separated	Widowed	Divorced
City	29.7	51.9	1.2	4.0	13.3
MSA[1]	37.1	47.7	1.1	3.5	10.6
U.S.	32.5	48.4	2.2	5.9	10.9

Note: Figures are percentages and cover the population 15 years of age and older; (1) Figures cover the Boulder, CO Metropolitan Statistical Area—see Appendix B for areas included; (2) Excludes separated
Source: U.S. Census Bureau, 2010-2014 American Community Survey 5-Year Estimates

Disability Status

Area	All Ages	Under 18 Years Old	18 to 64 Years Old	65 Years and Over
City	9.6	2.4	8.4	32.1
MSA[1]	8.1	2.7	6.6	27.9
U.S.	12.3	4.1	10.2	36.3

Note: Figures show percent of the civilian noninstitutionalized population that reported having a disability. Disability status is determined from from six types of difficulty: vision, hearing, cognitive, ambulatory, self-care, and independent living. For children under 5 years old, hearing and vision difficulty are used to determine disability status. For children between the ages of 5 and 14, disability status is determined from hearing, vision, cognitive, ambulatory, and self-care difficulties. For people aged 15 years and older, they are considered to have a disability if they have difficulty with any one of the six difficulty types; (1) Figures cover the Boulder, CO Metropolitan Statistical Area—see Appendix B for areas included.
Source: U.S. Census Bureau, 2010-2014 American Community Survey 5-Year Estimates

Age

Area	Under Age 5	Age 5–19	Age 20–34	Age 35–44	Age 45–54	Age 55–64	Age 65–74	Age 75–84	Age 85+	Median Age
	Percent of Population									
City	6.6	18.7	19.3	16.6	15.1	14.2	5.5	3.3	0.7	38.4
MSA[1]	5.3	19.9	23.8	13.4	14.1	12.5	6.5	3.1	1.5	35.7
U.S.	6.4	19.9	20.6	13.0	14.1	12.3	7.6	4.3	1.9	37.4

Note: (1) Figures cover the Boulder, CO Metropolitan Statistical Area—see Appendix B for areas included
Source: U.S. Census Bureau, 2010-2014 American Community Survey 5-Year Estimates

Gender

Area	Males	Females	Males per 100 Females
City	12,617	13,195	95.6
MSA[1]	153,300	151,866	100.9
U.S.	154,515,159	159,591,925	96.8

Note: (1) Figures cover the Boulder, CO Metropolitan Statistical Area—see Appendix B for areas included
Source: U.S. Census Bureau, 2010-2014 American Community Survey 5-Year Estimates

Religious Groups by Family

Area	Catholic	Baptist	Non-Den.	Methodist[2]	Lutheran	LDS[3]	Pentecostal	Presbyterian[4]	Muslim[5]	Judaism
MSA[1]	20.1	2.3	4.7	1.7	3.0	2.9	0.4	2.0	0.1	0.7
U.S.	19.1	9.3	4.0	4.0	2.3	2.0	1.9	1.6	0.8	0.7

Note: Figures are the number of adherents as a percentage of the total population; (1) Figures cover the Boulder, CO Metropolitan Statistical Area—see Appendix B for areas included; (2) Methodist/Pietist; (3) Latter Day Saints; (4) Reformed; (5) Figures are estimates
Source: Association of Statisticians of American Religious Bodies, 2010 U.S. Religion Census: Religious Congregations & Membership Study

Religious Groups by Tradition

Area	Catholic	Evangelical Protestant	Mainline Protestant	Other Tradition	Black Protestant	Orthodox
MSA[1]	20.1	9.7	6.4	4.8	<0.1	0.2
U.S.	19.1	16.2	7.3	4.3	1.6	0.3

Note: Figures are the number of adherents as a percentage of the total population; (1) Figures cover the Boulder, CO Metropolitan Statistical Area—see Appendix B for areas included
Source: Association of Statisticians of American Religious Bodies, 2010 U.S. Religion Census: Religious Congregations & Membership Study

ECONOMY

Gross Metropolitan Product

Area	2013	2014	2015	2016	Rank[2]
MSA[1]	21.3	22.2	22.7	23.8	108

Note: Figures are in billions of dollars; (1) Figures cover the Boulder, CO Metropolitan Statistical Area—see Appendix B for areas included; (2) Rank is based on 2016 data and ranges from 1 to 381
Source: The U.S. Conference of Mayors, U.S. Metro Economies: GMP and Employment 2014-2016, June 2015

Economic Growth

Area	2011-13 (%)	2014 (%)	2015 (%)	2016 (%)	Rank[2]
MSA[1]	3.4	2.5	1.5	2.5	178
U.S.	2.2	2.4	2.3	2.9	–

Note: Figures are real gross metropolitan product (GMP) growth rates and represent annual average percent change; (1) Figures cover the Boulder, CO Metropolitan Statistical Area—see Appendix B for areas included; (2) Rank is based on 2016 data and ranges from 1 to 381
Source: The U.S. Conference of Mayors, U.S. Metro Economies: GMP and Employment 2014-2016, June 2015

Metropolitan Area Exports

Area	2009	2010	2011	2012	2013	2014	Rank[2]
MSA[1]	727.2	1,058.6	946.7	1,128.0	1,045.9	1,016.0	159

Note: Figures are in millions of dollars; (1) Figures cover the Boulder, CO Metropolitan Statistical Area—see Appendix B for areas included; (2) Rank is based on 2014 data and ranges from 1 to 385
Source: U.S. Department of Commerce, International Trade Administration, Office of Trade & Industry Information, Manufacturing & Services, data extracted March 10, 2016

Building Permits

Area	Single-Family			Multi-Family			Total		
	2014	2015p	Pct. Chg.	2014	2015p	Pct. Chg.	2014	2015p	Pct. Chg.
City	104	123	18.3	105	133	26.7	209	256	22.5
MSA[1]	560	683	22.0	811	481	-40.7	1,371	1,164	-15.1
U.S.	640,300	690,800	7.9	411,800	487,600	18.4	1,052,100	1,178,400	12.0

Note: (1) Figures cover the Boulder, CO Metropolitan Statistical Area—see Appendix B for areas included; Figures represent new, privately-owned housing units authorized (unadjusted data); All permit data are based on estimates with imputation; (p) preliminary data.
Source: U.S. Census Bureau, Manufacturing, Mining, and Construction Statistics, Building Permits, 2014, 2015

Bankruptcy Filings

Area	Business Filings 2014	Business Filings 2015	% Chg.	Nonbusiness Filings 2014	Nonbusiness Filings 2015	% Chg.
Boulder County	33	26	-21.2	544	441	-18.9
U.S.	26,983	24,735	-8.3	909,812	819,760	-9.9

Note: Business filings include Chapter 7, Chapter 11, Chapter 12, and Chapter 13; Nonbusiness filings include Chapter 7, Chapter 11, and Chapter 13
Source: Administrative Office of the U.S. Courts, Business and Nonbusiness Bankruptcy, County Cases Commenced by Chapter of the Bankruptcy Code, During the 12- Month Period Ending December 31, 2014 and Business and Nonbusiness Bankruptcy, County Cases Commenced by Chapter of the Bankruptcy Code, During the 12- Month Period Ending December 31, 2015

Housing Vacancy Rates

Area	Gross Vacancy Rate[2] (%)			Year-Round Vacancy Rate[3] (%)			Rental Vacancy Rate[4] (%)			Homeowner Vacancy Rate[5] (%)		
	2013	2014	2015	2013	2014	2015	2013	2014	2015	2013	2014	2015
MSA[1]	n/a	n/a	n/a	n/a	n/a	n/a	n/a	n/a	n/a	n/a	n/a	n/a
U.S.	13.6	13.4	12.9	10.7	10.4	10.0	8.3	7.6	7.1	2.0	1.9	1.8

Note: (1) Figures cover the Boulder, CO Metropolitan Statistical Area—see Appendix B for areas included; (2) The percentage of the total housing inventory that is vacant; (3) The percentage of the housing inventory (excluding seasonal units) that is year-round vacant; (4) The percentage of rental inventory that is vacant for rent; (5) The percentage of homeowner inventory that is vacant for sale; n/a not available
Source: U.S. Census Bureau, Housing Vacancies and Homeownership Annual Statistics: 2015

INCOME

Income

Area	Per Capita ($)	Median Household ($)	Average Household ($)
City	39,288	71,038	95,616
MSA[1]	38,524	69,407	94,871
U.S.	28,555	53,482	74,596

Note: (1) Figures cover the Boulder, CO Metropolitan Statistical Area—see Appendix B for areas included
Source: U.S. Census Bureau, 2010-2014 American Community Survey 5-Year Estimates

Household Income Distribution

Area	Percent of Households Earning							
	Under $15,000	$15,000 -24,999	$25,000 -34,999	$35,000 -49,999	$50,000 -74,999	$75,000 -99,000	$100,000 -149,999	$150,000 and up
City	6.7	7.8	5.7	14.9	17.4	13.7	16.5	17.2
MSA[1]	10.2	8.3	8.0	11.3	15.5	12.0	16.7	18.0
U.S.	12.5	10.7	10.2	13.5	17.8	12.2	13.0	10.0

Note: (1) Figures cover the Boulder, CO Metropolitan Statistical Area—see Appendix B for areas included
Source: U.S. Census Bureau, 2010-2014 American Community Survey 5-Year Estimates

Poverty Rate

Area	All Ages	Under 18 Years Old	18 to 64 Years Old	65 Years and Over
City	9.2	15.8	7.6	5.1
MSA[1]	14.6	14.6	16.0	5.9
U.S.	15.6	21.9	14.6	9.4

Note: Figures are percentage of people whose income during the past 12 months was below the poverty level; (1) Figures cover the Boulder, CO Metropolitan Statistical Area—see Appendix B for areas included
Source: U.S. Census Bureau, 2010-2014 American Community Survey 5-Year Estimates

EMPLOYMENT

Labor Force and Employment

Area	Civilian Labor Force Dec. 2014	Civilian Labor Force Dec. 2015	% Chg.	Workers Employed Dec. 2014	Workers Employed Dec. 2015	% Chg.
City	15,655	15,472	-1.1	15,154	15,051	-0.6
MSA[1]	177,034	174,620	-1.3	171,184	170,017	-0.6
U.S.	155,521,000	157,245,000	1.1	147,190,000	149,703,000	1.7

Note: Data is not seasonally adjusted and covers workers 16 years of age and older; (1) Figures cover the Boulder, CO Metropolitan Statistical Area—see Appendix B for areas included
Source: Bureau of Labor Statistics, Local Area Unemployment Statistics

Unemployment Rate

Area	Jan.	Feb.	Mar.	Apr.	May	Jun.	Jul.	Aug.	Sep.	Oct.	Nov.	Dec.
	2015											
City	3.7	3.9	3.5	3.5	3.3	3.4	3.2	3.1	2.7	2.8	2.8	2.7
MSA[1]	3.7	3.9	3.6	3.5	3.5	3.8	3.3	3.2	2.6	2.7	2.8	2.6
U.S.	6.1	5.8	5.6	5.1	5.3	5.5	5.6	5.2	4.9	4.8	4.8	4.8

Note: Data is not seasonally adjusted and covers workers 16 years of age and older; (1) Figures cover the Boulder, CO Metropolitan Statistical Area—see Appendix B for areas included
Source: Bureau of Labor Statistics, Local Area Unemployment Statistics

Employment by Occupation

Occupation Classification	City (%)	MSA[1] (%)	U.S. (%)
Management, Business, Science, and Arts	51.1	52.6	36.4
Natural Resources, Construction, and Maintenance	6.3	5.2	9.0
Production, Transportation, and Material Moving	6.4	6.4	12.1
Sales and Office	21.7	20.0	24.4
Service	14.5	15.8	18.2

Note: Figures cover employed civilians 16 years of age and older; (1) Figures cover the Boulder, CO Metropolitan Statistical Area—see Appendix B for areas included
Source: U.S. Census Bureau, 2010-2014 American Community Survey 5-Year Estimates

Employment by Industry

Sector	MSA[1] Number of Employees	MSA[1] Percent of Total	U.S. Percent of Total
Construction, Mining, and Logging	5,500	3.0	5.0
Education and Health Services	24,000	13.1	15.7
Financial Activities	7,300	3.9	5.7
Government	37,200	20.3	15.5
Information	7,900	4.3	1.9
Leisure and Hospitality	19,600	10.7	10.4
Manufacturing	17,600	9.6	8.6
Other Services	5,900	3.2	3.9
Professional and Business Services	32,800	17.9	13.9
Retail Trade	17,300	9.4	11.3
Transportation, Warehousing, and Utilities	1,800	0.9	3.9
Wholesale Trade	5,800	3.1	4.1

Note: Figures are non-farm employment as of December 2015. Figures are not seasonally adjusted and include workers 16 years of age and older; (1) Figures cover the Boulder, CO Metropolitan Statistical Area—see Appendix B for areas included; n/a not available
Source: Bureau of Labor Statistics, Current Employment Statistics, Employment, Hours, and Earnings

Occupations with Greatest Projected Employment Growth: 2012 – 2022

Occupation[1]	2012 Employment	2022 Projected Employment	Numeric Employment Change	Percent Employment Change
Combined Food Preparation and Serving Workers, Including Fast Food	60,670	77,380	16,710	27.5
Secretaries and Administrative Assistants, Except Legal, Medical, and Executive	63,150	77,880	14,730	23.3
Retail Salespersons	79,300	94,000	14,700	18.5
Customer Service Representatives	45,990	59,210	13,220	28.8
Registered Nurses	42,200	53,270	11,070	26.2
General and Operations Managers	42,170	52,340	10,170	24.1
Accountants and Auditors	33,870	43,490	9,620	28.4
Personal Care Aides	16,940	26,210	9,270	54.7
Janitors and Cleaners, Except Maids and Housekeeping Cleaners	36,300	45,470	9,170	25.3
Business Operations Specialists, All Other	42,990	51,450	8,460	19.7

Note: Projections cover Colorado; (1) Sorted by numeric employment change
Source: www.projectionscentral.com, State Occupational Projections, 2012–2022 Long-Term Projections

Fastest Growing Occupations: 2012 – 2022

Occupation[1]	2012 Employment	2022 Projected Employment	Numeric Employment Change	Percent Employment Change
Service Unit Operators, Oil, Gas, and Mining	3,520	6,290	2,770	78.4
Derrick Operators, Oil and Gas	630	1,110	480	76.0
Rotary Drill Operators, Oil and Gas	1,280	2,200	920	71.5
Roustabouts, Oil and Gas	2,770	4,710	1,940	70.2
Interpreters and Translators	1,510	2,550	1,040	68.5
Petroleum Engineers	1,500	2,500	1,000	66.9
Pump Operators, Except Wellhead Pumpers	700	1,160	460	64.9
Helpers—Brickmasons, Blockmasons, Stonemasons, and Tile and Marble Setters	200	320	120	61.3
Insulation Workers, Mechanical	420	680	260	61.2
Information Security Analysts	1,240	1,960	720	57.8

Note: Projections cover Colorado; (1) Sorted by percent employment change and excludes occupations with numeric employment change less than 100
Source: www.projectionscentral.com, State Occupational Projections, 2012–2022 Long-Term Projections

Average Wages

Occupation	$/Hr.	Occupation	$/Hr.
Accountants and Auditors	37.93	Maids and Housekeeping Cleaners	11.06
Automotive Mechanics	24.16	Maintenance and Repair Workers	19.16
Bookkeepers	19.87	Marketing Managers	73.56
Carpenters	19.50	Nuclear Medicine Technologists	n/a
Cashiers	12.26	Nurses, Licensed Practical	22.45
Clerks, General Office	19.84	Nurses, Registered	36.29
Clerks, Receptionists/Information	14.19	Nursing Assistants	13.80
Clerks, Shipping/Receiving	16.38	Packers and Packagers, Hand	11.48
Computer Programmers	46.98	Physical Therapists	34.27
Computer Systems Analysts	41.57	Postal Service Mail Carriers	24.85
Computer User Support Specialists	27.14	Real Estate Brokers	33.53
Cooks, Restaurant	12.68	Retail Salespersons	15.79
Dentists	92.45	Sales Reps., Exc. Tech./Scientific	38.60
Electrical Engineers	47.98	Sales Reps., Tech./Scientific	37.25
Electricians	23.59	Secretaries, Exc. Legal/Med./Exec.	17.92
Financial Managers	69.87	Security Guards	13.67
First-Line Supervisors/Managers, Sales	25.94	Surgeons	132.34
Food Preparation Workers	10.75	Teacher Assistants*	15.71
General and Operations Managers	64.82	Teachers, Elementary School*	28.17
Hairdressers/Cosmetologists	17.65	Teachers, Secondary School*	28.00
Internists	103.76	Telemarketers	12.13
Janitors and Cleaners	13.35	Truck Drivers, Heavy/Tractor-Trailer	21.11
Landscaping/Groundskeeping Workers	14.44	Truck Drivers, Light/Delivery Svcs.	16.65
Lawyers	58.47	Waiters and Waitresses	12.73

Note: Wage data covers the Boulder, CO Metropolitan Statistical Area—see Appendix B for areas included; (*) Hourly wages for elementary/secondary school teachers and teacher assistants were calculated by the editors from annual wage data based on a 40 hour work week; n/a not available.
Source: Bureau of Labor Statistics, Metro Area Occupational Employment and Wage Estimates, May 2015

TAXES

State Corporate Income Tax Rates

State	Tax Rate (%)	Income Brackets ($)	Num. of Brackets	Financial Institution Tax Rate (%)[a]	Federal Income Tax Ded.
Colorado	4.63	Flat rate	1	4.63	No

Note: Tax rates as of January 1, 2016; (a) Rates listed are the corporate income tax rate applied to financial institutions or excise taxes based on income. Some states have other taxes based upon the value of deposits or shares.
Source: Federation of Tax Administrators, "State Corporate Income Tax Rates, 2016"

State Individual Income Tax Rates

State	Tax Rate (%)	Income Brackets ($)	Num. of Brackets	Personal Exempt. ($)[1] Single	Personal Exempt. ($)[1] Dependents	Fed. Inc. Tax Ded.
Colorado	4.63	Flat rate	1	4,050 (d)	4,050 (d)	No

Note: Tax rates as of January 1, 2016; Local- and county-level taxes are not included; n/a not applicable; (1) Married joint filers generally receive double the single exemption; (d) These states use the personal exemption amounts provided in the federal Internal Revenue Code.
Source: Federation of Tax Administrators, "State Individual Income Tax Rates, 2016"

Various State and Local Tax Rates

State	State and Local Sales and Use (%)	State Sales and Use (%)	Gasoline[1] (¢/gal.)	Cigarette[2] ($/pack)	Spirits[3] ($/gal.)	Wine[4] ($/gal.)	Beer[5] ($/gal.)
Colorado	8.485	2.9	22	0.84	2.28	0.32 (l)	0.23

Note: All tax rates as of January 1, 2016; (1) The American Petroleum Institute has developed a methodology for determining the average tax rate on a gallon of fuel. Rates may include any of the following: excise taxes, environmental fees, storage tank fees, other fees or taxes, general sales tax, and local taxes. In states where gasoline is subject to the general sales tax, or where the fuel tax is based on the average sale price, the average rate determined by API is sensitive to changes in the price of gasoline. States that fully or partially apply general sales taxes to gasoline: CA, CO, GA, IL, IN, MI, NY; (2) The federal excise tax of $1.0066 per pack and local taxes are not included; (3) Rates are those applicable to off-premise sales of 40% alcohol by volume (a.b.v.) distilled spirits in 750ml containers. Local excise taxes are excluded; (4) Rates are those applicable to off-premise sales of 11% a.b.v. non-carbonated wine in 750ml containers; (5) Rates are those applicable to off-premise sales of 4.7% a.b.v. beer in 12 ounce containers; (l) Different rates also applicable according to alcohol content, place of production, size of container, place purchased (on- or off-premise or on board airlines) or type of wine (carbonated, vermouth, etc.).
Source: Tax Foundation, 2016 Facts & Figures: How Does Your State Compare?

State Business Tax Climate Index Rankings

State	Overall Rank	Corporate Tax Rank	Individual Income Tax Rank	Sales Tax Rank	Unemployment Insurance Tax Rank	Property Tax Rank
Colorado	18	15	16	44	33	12

Note: The index is a measure of how each state's tax laws affect economic performance. The lower the rank, the more favorable a state's tax system is for business. States without a given tax are given a ranking of 1. The scores/rankings for the District of Columbia do not affect other states. The 2016 index represents the tax climate as of July 1, 2015 (the beginning of Fiscal Year 2016).
Source: Tax Foundation, State Business Tax Climate Index 2016

TRANSPORTATION

Means of Transportation to Work

Area	Car/Truck/Van: Drove Alone	Car/Truck/Van: Car-pooled	Public Transportation: Bus	Public Transportation: Subway	Public Transportation: Railroad	Bicycle	Walked	Other Means	Worked at Home
City	75.4	7.3	3.4	0.0	0.0	1.0	1.5	1.3	10.0
MSA[1]	64.9	8.4	5.3	0.0	0.0	4.2	4.9	1.4	10.8
U.S.	76.4	9.6	2.6	1.8	0.6	0.6	2.8	1.3	4.4

Note: Figures are percentages and cover workers 16 years of age and older; (1) Figures cover the Boulder, CO Metropolitan Statistical Area—see Appendix B for areas included
Source: U.S. Census Bureau, 2010-2014 American Community Survey 5-Year Estimates

Travel Time to Work

Area	Less Than 10 Minutes	10 to 19 Minutes	20 to 29 Minutes	30 to 44 Minutes	45 to 59 Minutes	60 to 89 Minutes	90 Minutes or More
City	10.0	25.8	31.6	20.1	6.4	4.5	1.6
MSA[1]	15.7	35.2	21.4	16.2	6.1	3.8	1.5
U.S.	13.3	29.6	21.0	20.2	7.7	5.7	2.6

Note: Figures are percentages and include workers 16 years old and over; (1) Figures cover the Boulder, CO Metropolitan Statistical Area—see Appendix B for areas included
Source: U.S. Census Bureau, 2010-2014 American Community Survey 5-Year Estimates

Freeway Travel Time Index

Area	1985	1990	1995	2000	2005	2010	2014
Urban Area Rank[1,2]	81	63	47	38	36	36	37
Urban Area Index[1]	1.04	1.08	1.13	1.17	1.20	1.20	1.20
Average Index[3]	1.09	1.11	1.14	1.17	1.20	1.19	1.20

Note: Freeway Travel Time Index—the ratio of travel time in the peak period to the travel time at free-flow conditions. For example, a value of 1.30 indicates a 20-minute free-flow trip takes 26 minutes in the peak (20 minutes x 1.30 = 26 minutes); (1) Covers the Boulder CO urban area; (2) Rank is based on 101 urban areas (#1 = highest travel time index); (3) Average of 101 urban areas
Source: Texas Transportation Institute, 2015 Urban Mobility Scorecard, August 2015

Freeway Commuter Stress Index

Area	1985	1990	1995	2000	2005	2010	2014
Urban Area Rank[1,2]	66	59	50	40	40	39	40
Urban Area Index[1]	1.07	1.11	1.16	1.21	1.24	1.24	1.24
Average Index[3]	1.13	1.16	1.19	1.22	1.25	1.24	1.25

Note: The Freeway Commuter Stress Index is the same as the Freeway Travel Time Index (see table above) except that it includes only the travel in the peak directions during the peak periods; the TTI includes travel in all directions during the peak period. Thus, the CSI is more indicative of the work trip experienced by each commuter on a daily basis. (1) Covers the Boulder CO urban area; (2) Rank is based on 101 urban areas (#1 = highest stress index); (3) Average of 101 urban areas
Source: Texas Transportation Institute, 2015 Urban Mobility Scorecard, August 2015

Living Environment

COST OF LIVING

Cost of Living Index

Composite Index	Groceries	Housing	Utilities	Trans-portation	Health Care	Misc. Goods/ Services
n/a	n/a	n/a	n/a	n/a	n/a	n/a

Note: The Cost of Living Index measures regional differences in the cost of consumer goods and services, excluding taxes and non-consumer expenditures, for professional and managerial households in the top income quintile. It is based on more than 50,000 prices covering almost 60 different items for which prices are collected three times a year by chambers of commerce, economic development organizations or university applied economic centers in each participating urban area. The numbers shown should be read as a percentage above or below the national average of 100. For example, a value of 115.4 in the groceries column indicates that grocery prices are 15.4% higher than the national average. Small differences in the index numbers should not be interpreted as significant; n/a not available.
Source: The Council for Community and Economic Research, ACCRA Cost of Living Index, 2015

Grocery Prices

Area[1]	T-Bone Steak ($/pound)	Frying Chicken ($/pound)	Whole Milk ($/half gal.)	Eggs ($/dozen)	Orange Juice ($/64 oz.)	Coffee ($/11.5 oz.)
City[2]	n/a	n/a	n/a	n/a	n/a	n/a
Avg.	10.99	1.43	2.25	2.26	3.58	4.48
Min.	7.16	0.98	1.30	1.35	2.88	2.98
Max.	14.13	2.43	3.85	4.81	6.39	7.56

Note: (1) Values for the local area are compared with the average, minimum and maximum values for all 292 areas in the Cost of Living Index; (2) Figures cover the Lafayette CO urban area; n/a not available; **T-Bone Steak** *(price per pound);* **Frying Chicken** *(price per pound, whole fryer);* **Whole Milk** *(half gallon carton);* **Eggs** *(price per dozen, Grade A, large);* **Orange Juice** *(64 oz. Tropicana or Florida Natural);* **Coffee** *(11.5 oz. can, vacuum-packed, Maxwell House, Hills Bros, or Folgers).*
Source: The Council for Community and Economic Research, ACCRA Cost of Living Index, 2015

Housing and Utility Costs

Area[1]	New Home Price ($)	Apartment Rent ($/month)	All Electric ($/month)	Part Electric ($/month)	Other Energy ($/month)	Telephone ($/month)
City[2]	n/a	n/a	n/a	n/a	n/a	n/a
Avg.	312,874	945	179.30	95.07	72.96	28.11
Min.	178,682	479	116.28	43.14	26.46	10.01
Max.	1,472,476	3,984	504.25	189.44	421.11	43.06

Note: (1) Values for the local area are compared with the average, minimum and maximum values for all 292 areas in the Cost of Living Index; (2) Figures cover the Lafayette CO urban area; n/a not available; **New Home Price** *(2,400 sf living area, 8,000 sf lot, in urban area with full utilities);* **Apartment Rent** *(950 sf 2 bedroom/1.5 or 2 bath, unfurnished, excluding all utilities except water);* **All Electric** *(average monthly cost for an all-electric home);* **Part Electric** *(average monthly cost for a part-electric home);* **Other Energy** *(average monthly cost for natural gas, fuel oil, coal, wood, and any other forms of energy except electricity);* **Telephone** *(price includes basic monthly rate for a private residential line plus additional local usage charges incurred by a family of four).*
Source: The Council for Community and Economic Research, ACCRA Cost of Living Index, 2015

Health Care, Transportation, and Other Costs

Area[1]	Doctor ($/visit)	Dentist ($/visit)	Optometrist ($/visit)	Gasoline ($/gallon)	Beauty Salon ($/visit)	Men's Shirt ($)
City[2]	n/a	n/a	n/a	n/a	n/a	n/a
Avg.	105.15	89.02	99.78	2.38	35.30	28.10
Min.	66.87	56.09	48.53	1.95	18.91	13.38
Max.	182.34	150.36	228.33	4.09	67.91	63.80

Note: (1) Values for the local area are compared with the average, minimum and maximum values for all 292 areas in the Cost of Living Index; (2) Figures cover the Lafayette CO urban area; n/a not available; **Doctor** *(general practitioners routine exam of an established patient);* **Dentist** *(adult teeth cleaning and periodic oral examination);* **Optometrist** *(full vision eye exam for established adult patient);* **Gasoline** *(one gallon regular unleaded, national brand, including all taxes, cash price at self-service pump if available);* **Beauty Salon** *(woman's shampoo, trim, and blow-dry);* **Men's Shirt** *(cotton/polyester dress shirt, pinpoint weave, long sleeves).*
Source: The Council for Community and Economic Research, ACCRA Cost of Living Index, 2015

HOUSING

House Price Index (HPI)

Area	National Ranking[2]	Quarterly Change (%)	One-Year Change (%)	Five-Year Change (%)
MSA[1]	7	2.30	13.50	35.70
U.S.[3]	–	1.45	5.76	22.85

Note: The HPI is a weighted repeat sales index. It measures average price changes in repeat sales or refinancings on the same properties. This information is obtained by reviewing repeat mortgage transactions on single-family properties whose mortgages have been purchased or securitized by Fannie Mae or Freddie Mac in January 1975; (1) Boulder Metropolitan Statistical Area—see Appendix B for areas included; (2) Rankings are based on annual percentage change for all metro areas containing at least 15,000 transactions over the last 10 years and ranges from 1 to 266; (3) figures based on a weighted average of Census Division estimates using a seasonally adjusted, purchase-only index; all figures are for the period ending December 31, 2015
Source: Federal Housing Finance Agency, House Price Index, February 25, 2016

Median Single-Family Home Prices

Area	2013	2014	2015p	Percent Change 2014 to 2015
MSA[1]	371.8	390.7	454.1	16.2
U.S. Average	197.4	208.9	223.9	7.2

Note: Figures are median sales prices of existing single-family homes in thousands of dollars; (p) preliminary; n/a not available; (1) Boulder, CO Metropolitan Statistical Area—see Appendix B for areas included
Source: National Association of Realtors, Median Sales Price of Existing Single-Family Homes for Metropolitan Areas, 4th Quarter 2015

Qualifying Income Based on Median Sales Price of Existing Single-Family Homes

Area	With 5% Down ($)	With 10% Down ($)	With 20% Down ($)
MSA[1]	104,520	99,019	88,017
U.S. Average	49,535	46,928	41,714

Note: Figures are preliminary; Qualifying income is based on a mortgage rate of 4.1%. Monthly principal and interest payment is limited to 25% of income; n/a not available; (1) Boulder, CO Metropolitan Statistical Area—see Appendix B for areas included
Source: National Association of Realtors, Qualifying Income Based on Median Sales Price of Existing Single-Family Homes for Metropolitan Areas, 4th Quarter 2015

Median Apartment Condo-Coop Home Prices

Area	2013	2014	2015p	Percent Change 2014 to 2015
MSA[1]	193.4	231.8	282.9	22.0
U.S. Average	194.9	204.3	210.7	3.1

Note: Figures are median sales prices of existing apartment condo-coop homes in thousands of dollars; (p) preliminary; n/a not available; (1) Boulder, CO Metropolitan Statistical Area—see Appendix B for areas included
Source: National Association of Realtors, Median Sales Price of Existing Apartment Condo-Coop Homes for Metropolitan Areas, 4th Quarter 2015

Gross Monthly Rent

Area	Under $200	$200 -299	$300 -499	$500 -749	$750 -999	$1,000 -1,499	$1,500 and up	Median ($)
City	1.5	0.2	3.1	7.3	18.9	46.3	22.6	1,175
MSA[1]	0.8	1.4	2.3	8.7	23.5	36.0	27.3	1,149
U.S.	1.5	3.2	7.4	21.0	24.1	26.9	15.9	920

Note: Figures are percentages except for Median; Gross rent is the contract rent plus the estimated average monthly cost of utilities (electricity, gas, and water and sewer) and fuels (oil, coal, kerosene, wood, etc.) if these are paid by the renter (or paid for the renter by someone else); (1) Figures cover the Boulder, CO Metropolitan Statistical Area—see Appendix B for areas included
Source: U.S. Census Bureau, 2010-2014 American Community Survey 5-Year Estimates

Homeownership Rate

Area	2008 (%)	2009 (%)	2010 (%)	2011 (%)	2012 (%)	2013 (%)	2014 (%)	2015 (%)
MSA[1]	n/a	n/a	n/a	n/a	n/a	n/a	n/a	n/a
U.S.	67.8	67.4	66.9	66.1	65.4	65.1	64.5	63.7

Note: (1) Figures cover the Boulder, CO Metropolitan Statistical Area—see Appendix B for areas included; n/a not available
Source: U.S. Census Bureau, Housing Vacancies and Homeownership Annual Statistics: 2015

Year Housing Structure Built

Area	2010 or Later	2000 -2009	1990 -1999	1980 -1989	1970 -1979	1960 -1969	1950 -1959	1940 -1949	Before 1940	Median Year
City	2.7	13.5	35.0	22.2	15.6	3.5	2.6	1.3	3.7	1990
MSA[1]	1.1	13.7	20.2	16.3	22.0	12.0	5.5	1.7	7.5	1981
U.S.	1.0	14.9	13.9	13.8	15.8	11.0	10.8	5.4	13.3	1976

Note: Figures are percentages except for Median Year; (1) Figures cover the Boulder, CO Metropolitan Statistical Area—see Appendix B for areas included
Source: U.S. Census Bureau, 2010-2014 American Community Survey 5-Year Estimates

HEALTH

Health Risk Data

Category	MSA[1] (%)	U.S. (%)
Adults aged 18–64 who have any kind of health care coverage	79.3	79.6
Adults who reported being in good or excellent health	90.5	83.1
Adults who are current smokers	13.5	19.6
Adults who are heavy drinkers[2]	5.8	6.1
Adults who are binge drinkers[3]	15.4	16.9
Adults who are overweight (BMI 25.0 - 29.9)	31.5	35.8
Adults who are obese (BMI 30.0 - 99.8)	14.8	27.6
Adults who participated in any physical activities in the past month	90.8	77.1
Adults 50+ who have ever had a sigmoidoscopy or colonoscopy	68.0	67.3
Women aged 40+ who have had a mammogram within the past two years	63.1	74.0
Men aged 40+ who have had a PSA test within the past two years	33.9	45.2
Adults aged 65+ who have had flu shot within the past year	72.2	60.1
Adults who always wear a seatbelt	95.3	93.8

Note: Data as of 2012 unless otherwise noted; (1) Figures cover the Boulder, CO Metropolitan Statistical Area—see Appendix B for areas included; (2) Heavy drinkers are classified as males having more than two drinks per day or females having more than one drink per day; (3) Binge drinkers are classified as males having five or more drinks on one occasion or females having four or more drinks on one occasion
Source: Centers for Disease Control and Prevention, Behaviorial Risk Factor Surveillance System, SMART: Selected Metropolitan/Micropolitan Area Risk Trends, 2012 (Note: the CDC has discontinued this dataset but will be releasing a replacement in mid-2016)

Chronic Health Indicators

Category	MSA[1] (%)	U.S. (%)
Adults who have ever been told they had a heart attack	n/a	4.5
Adults who have ever been told they had a stroke	n/a	2.9
Adults who have been told they currently have asthma	6.3	8.9
Adults who have ever been told they have arthritis	23.0	25.7
Adults who have ever been told they have diabetes[2]	3.4	9.7
Adults who have ever been told they had skin cancer	7.2	5.7
Adults who have ever been told they had any other types of cancer	6.0	6.5
Adults who have ever been told they have COPD	2.4	6.2
Adults who have ever been told they have kidney disease	n/a	2.5
Adults who have ever been told they have a form of depression	18.3	18.0

Note: Data as of 2012 unless otherwise noted; n/a not available; (1) Figures cover the Boulder, CO Metropolitan Statistical Area—see Appendix B for areas included; (2) Figures do not include pregnancy-related, borderline, or pre-diabetes
Source: Centers for Disease Control and Prevention, Behaviorial Risk Factor Surveillance System, SMART: Selected Metropolitan/Micropolitan Area Risk Trends, 2012 (Note: the CDC has discontinued this dataset but will be releasing a replacement in mid-2016)

Mortality Rates for the Top 10 Causes of Death in the U.S.

ICD-10[a] Sub-Chapter	ICD-10[a] Code	Age-Adjusted Mortality Rate[1] per 100,000 population County[2]	U.S.
Malignant neoplasms	C00-C97	119.5	163.6
Ischaemic heart diseases	I20-I25	63.8	102.2
Other forms of heart disease	I30-I51	39.8	50.1
Chronic lower respiratory diseases	J40-J47	30.8	41.4
Organic, including symptomatic, mental disorders	F01-F09	38.4	38.5
Cerebrovascular diseases	I60-I69	32.1	36.5
Other external causes of accidental injury	W00-X59	40.1	27.5
Other degenerative diseases of the nervous system	G30-G31	26.3	26.3
Diabetes mellitus	E10-E14	7.8	21.1
Hypertensive diseases	I10-I15	4.6	19.7

Note: (a) ICD-10 = International Classification of Diseases 10th Revision; (1) Mortality rates are a three year average covering 2012-2014; (2) Figures cover COUNTY NOT FOUND!!!!!!.
Source: Centers for Disease Control and Prevention, National Center for Health Statistics. Underlying Cause of Death 1999-2014 on CDC WONDER Online Database, released 2015.

Mortality Rates for Selected Causes of Death

ICD-10[a] Sub-Chapter	ICD-10[a] Code	Age-Adjusted Mortality Rate[1] per 100,000 population County[2]	U.S.
Assault	X85-Y09	Unreliable	5.1
Diseases of the liver	K70-K76	12.1	13.5
Human immunodeficiency virus (HIV) disease	B20-B24	Suppressed	2.1
Influenza and pneumonia	J09-J18	11.5	15.2
Intentional self-harm	X60-X84	16.7	12.7
Malnutrition	E40-E46	2.5	0.9
Obesity and other hyperalimentation	E65-E68	Suppressed	1.9
Renal failure	N17-N19	5.8	13.0
Transport accidents	V01-V99	6.1	11.6
Viral hepatitis	B15-B19	Unreliable	2.1

Note: (a) ICD-10 = International Classification of Diseases 10th Revision; (1) Mortality rates are a three year average covering 2012-2014; (2) Figures cover COUNTY NOT FOUND!!!!!!; Data are Suppressed when the data meet the criteria for confidentiality constraints; Mortality rates are flagged as Unreliable when the rate would be calculated with a numerator of 20 or less.
Source: Centers for Disease Control and Prevention, National Center for Health Statistics. Underlying Cause of Death 1999-2014 on CDC WONDER Online Database, released 2015.

Health Insurance Coverage

Area	With Health Insurance	With Private Health Insurance	With Public Health Insurance	Without Health Insurance	Population Under Age 18 Without Health Insurance
City	89.3	75.7	20.9	10.7	4.4
MSA[1]	89.7	78.3	20.0	10.3	6.3
U.S.	85.8	65.8	31.1	14.2	7.1

Note: Figures are percentages that cover the civilian noninstitutionalized population; (1) Figures cover the Boulder, CO Metropolitan Statistical Area—see Appendix B for areas included
Source: U.S. Census Bureau, 2010-2014 American Community Survey 5-Year Estimates

Number of Medical Professionals

Area	MDs[3]	DOs[3,4]	Dentists	Podiatrists	Chiropractors	Optometrists
County[1] (number)	1,113	72	295	15	218	75
County[1] (rate[2])	358.6	23.2	94.1	4.8	69.6	23.9
U.S. (rate[2])	272.5	20.9	64.7	5.8	25.9	15.2

Note: Data as of 2014 unless noted; (1) Data covers Boulder County; (2) Rate per 100,000 population; (3) Data as of 2013 and includes all active, non-federal physicians; (4) Doctor of Osteopathic Medicine
Source: U.S. Department of Health and Human Services, Health Resources and Services Administration, Bureau of Health Professions, Area Resource File (ARF) 2014-2015

EDUCATION

Public School District Statistics

District Name	Schls	Pupils	Pupil/ Teacher Ratio	Minority Pupils[1] (%)	Free Lunch Eligible[2] (%)	IEP[3] (%)
Boulder Valley SD No. Re2	57	30,546	18.1	29.9	16.0	n/a

Note: Table includes school districts with 100 or more students; (1) Percentage of students that are not non-Hispanic white; (2) Percentage of students that are eligible for the free lunch program; (3) Percentage of students that have an Individualized Education Program.
Source: U.S. Department of Education, National Center for Education Statistics, Common Core of Data, Local Education Agency (School District) Universe Survey: School Year 2013-2014; U.S. Department of Education, National Center for Education Statistics, Common Core of Data, Public Elementary/Secondary School Universe Survey: School Year 2013-2014

Best High Schools

According to *U.S. News,* Lafayette is home to one of the best high schools in the U.S.: **Peak to Peak Charter School** (#131); Nearly 20,000 schools were ranked based on their performance on state assessments and how well they prepare students for college. Schools with the highest unrounded College Readiness Index values were numerically ranked from No. 1 to No. 500 and were the gold medal winners. *U.S. News & World Report, "Best High Schools 2015"*

Highest Level of Education

Area	Less than H.S.	H.S. Diploma	Some College, No Deg.	Associate Degree	Bachelor's Degree	Master's Degree	Prof. School Degree	Doctorate Degree
City	5.3	14.9	16.7	7.4	33.7	16.3	2.2	3.4
MSA[1]	6.0	12.8	17.2	5.7	31.5	17.8	3.4	5.5
U.S.	13.7	28.0	21.2	7.9	18.3	7.8	2.0	1.3

Note: Figures cover persons age 25 and over; (1) Figures cover the Boulder, CO Metropolitan Statistical Area—see Appendix B for areas included
Source: U.S. Census Bureau, 2010-2014 American Community Survey 5-Year Estimates

Educational Attainment by Race

Area	High School Graduate or Higher (%)					Bachelor's Degree or Higher (%)				
	Total	White	Black	Asian	Hisp.[2]	Total	White	Black	Asian	Hisp.[2]
City	94.7	95.8	100.0	90.2	75.6	55.6	57.7	61.5	54.5	23.5
MSA[1]	94.0	95.6	85.7	91.6	64.2	58.2	60.1	38.7	65.1	21.2
U.S.	86.3	88.4	83.2	85.8	64.1	29.3	30.6	19.0	50.9	13.9

Note: Figures shown cover persons 25 years old and over; (1) Figures cover the Boulder, CO Metropolitan Statistical Area—see Appendix B for areas included; (2) People of Hispanic origin can be of any race
Source: U.S. Census Bureau, 2010-2014 American Community Survey 5-Year Estimates

School Enrollment by Grade and Control

Area	Preschool (%)		Kindergarten (%)		Grades 1 - 4 (%)		Grades 5 - 8 (%)		Grades 9 - 12 (%)	
	Public	Private	Public	Private	Public	Private	Public	Private	Public	Private
City	41.5	58.5	94.9	5.1	91.0	9.0	94.0	6.0	97.2	2.8
MSA[1]	41.9	58.1	91.9	8.1	90.1	9.9	90.7	9.3	94.7	5.3
U.S.	57.4	42.6	87.8	12.2	89.8	10.2	89.9	10.1	90.6	9.4

Note: Figures shown cover persons 3 years old and over; (1) Figures cover the Boulder, CO Metropolitan Statistical Area—see Appendix B for areas included
Source: U.S. Census Bureau, 2010-2014 American Community Survey 5-Year Estimates

Average Salaries of Public School Classroom Teachers

Area	2013-14		2014-15		Percent Change 2013-14 to 2014-15	Percent Change 2004-05 to 2014-15
	Dollars	Rank[1]	Dollars	Rank[1]		
Colorado	49,615	31	49,828	34	0.43	13.4
U.S. Average	56,610	–	57,379	–	1.36	20.8

Note: (1) State rank ranges from 1 to 51 where 1 indicates highest salary.
Source: National Education Association, Rankings & Estimates: Rankings of the States 2014 and Estimates of School Statistics 2015, March 2015

Higher Education

Four-Year Colleges			Two-Year Colleges			Medical Schools[1]	Law Schools[2]	Voc/ Tech[3]
Public	Private Non-profit	Private For-profit	Public	Private Non-profit	Private For-profit			
0	0	0	0	0	0	0	0	0

Note: Figures cover institutions located within the city limits and include main campuses only; (1) includes schools accredited by the Liaison Committee on Medical Education and the American Osteopathic Association's Commission on Osteopathic College Accreditation; (2) includes ABA-accredited schools, schools with provisional ABA accreditation, and state accredited schools; (3) includes all schools with programs that are less than 2 years.

Source: National Center for Education Statistics, Integrated Postsecondary Education System (IPEDS), 2014-15; Association of American Medical Colleges, Member List, March 21, 2016; American Osteopathic Association, Member List, March 21, 2016; Law School Admission Council, Official Guide to ABA-Approved Law Schools Online, March 21, 2016; Wikipedia, List of Medical Schools in the United States, March 21, 2016; Wikipedia, List of Law Schools in the United States, March 21, 2016

According to *U.S. News & World Report,* the Boulder, CO metro area is home to one of the best national universities in the U.S.: **University of Colorado–Boulder** (#89 tie). The indicators used to capture academic quality fall into a number of categories: assessment by administrators at peer institutions; retention of students; faculty resources; student selectivity; financial resources; alumni giving; high school counselor ratings of colleges; and graduation rate. *U.S. News & World Report, "America's Best Colleges 2016"*

According to *U.S. News & World Report,* the Boulder, CO metro area is home to one of the top 100 law schools in the U.S.: **University of Colorado–Boulder, Law School** (#40 tie). The rankings are based on a weighted average of 12 measures of quality: peer assessment score; assessment score by lawyers/judges; median LSAT scores; median undergrad GPA; acceptance rate; employment rates for graduates; placement success; bar passage rate; faculty resources; expenditures per student; student/faculty ratio; and library resources. *U.S. News & World Report, "America's Best Graduate Schools, Law, 2017"*

PRESIDENTIAL ELECTION

2012 Presidential Election Results

Area	Obama (%)	Romney (%)	Other (%)
Boulder County	69.7	27.9	2.4
U.S.	51.0	47.2	1.8

Note: Results may not add to 100% due to rounding

Source: Dave Leip's Atlas of U.S. Presidential Elections

EMPLOYERS

Major Employers

Company Name	Industry
Agilent Technologies	Instruments to measure electricity
America's Note Network	Mortgage bankers & loan correspondents
Ball Aerospace & Technologies Corp.	Search & navigation equipment
Ball Corporation	Space research & technology
Corden Pharma Colorado	Pharmaceutical preparations
County of Boulder	Sheriffs' office
Crispin Porter Bogusky	Business services at non-commercial site
Health Carechain	Medical field-related associations
IBM	Magnetic storage devices, computer
Lockheed Martin Corporation	Search & navigation equipment
Micro Motion	Liquid meters
National Oceanic and Atmospheric Admin	Environmental protection agency, government
Natl Inst of Standards & Technology	Commercial physical research
Qualcomm Incorporated	Integrated circuits, semiconductor networks
Staffing Solutions Southwest	Temporary help service
The Regents of the University of Colorado	Libraries
The Regents of the University of Colorado	Noncommercial research organizations
Tyco Healthcare Group	Medical instruments & equipment, blood & bone work
University Corp for Atmospheric Research	Noncommercial research organizations
University of Colorado	Colleges & universities
Wall Street On Demand	Financial services
Whole Foods Market	Grocery stores

Note: Companies shown are located within the Boulder, CO Metropolitan Statistical Area.
Source: Hoovers.com; Wikipedia

PUBLIC SAFETY

Crime Rate

Area	All Crimes	Violent Crimes				Property Crimes		
		Murder	Rape[3]	Robbery	Aggrav. Assault	Burglary	Larceny -Theft	Motor Vehicle Theft
City	1,840.8	3.7	40.2	21.9	29.2	233.7	1,409.8	102.3
Metro[1]	n/a	1.9	65.0	25.7	139.2	352.3	n/a	138.9
U.S.	2,971.8	4.5	36.6	102.2	232.5	542.5	1,837.3	216.2

Note: Figures are crimes per 100,000 population; (1) Figures cover the Boulder, CO Metropolitan Statistical Area—see Appendix B for areas included; (3) The city and U.S. figures shown were reported using the revised Uniform Crime Reporting (UCR) definition of rape. The suburban and metro area figures shown are an aggregate total of the data submitted using both the revised and legacy UCR definitions.
Source: FBI Uniform Crime Reports, 2014

Hate Crimes

Area	Number of Quarters Reported	Number of Incidents per Bias Motivation						
		Race	Religion	Sexual Orientation	Ethnicity	Disability	Gender	Gender Identity
City	4	0	0	0	0	0	0	0
U.S.	4	2,568	1,014	1,017	648	84	33	98

Source: Federal Bureau of Investigation, Hate Crime Statistics 2014

Identity Theft Consumer Complaints

Area	Complaints	Complaints per 100,000 Population	Rank[2]
MSA[1]	420	134.0	84
U.S.	490,220	152.4	-

Note: (1) Figures cover the Boulder, CO Metropolitan Statistical Area—see Appendix B for areas included; (2) Rank ranges from 1 to 379 where 1 indicates greatest number of identity theft complaints per 100,000 population
Source: Federal Trade Commission, Consumer Sentinel Network Data Book for January–December 2015

Fraud and Other Consumer Complaints

Area	Complaints	Complaints per 100,000 Population	Rank[2]
MSA[1]	1,251	399.3	106
U.S.	2,593,159	806.0	-

Note: (1) Figures cover the Boulder, CO Metropolitan Statistical Area—see Appendix B for areas included; (2) Rank ranges from 1 to 379 where 1 indicates greatest number of identity theft complaints per 100,000 population

Source: Federal Trade Commission, Consumer Sentinel Network Data Book for January–December 2015

RECREATION

Culture

Dance[1]	Theatre[1]	Instrumental Music[1]	Vocal Music[1]	Series and Festivals	Museums and Art Galleries[2]	Zoos and Aquariums[3]
0	0	0	0	0	0	0

Note: (1) Professional perfoming groups; (2) Based on organizations with SIC code 8412; (3) AZA-accredited

Source: The Grey House Performing Arts Directory, 2015-16; Association of Zoos & Aquariums, AZA Member Zoos & Aquariums, March 25, 2016; www.AccuLeads.com, March 29, 2016

Professional Sports Teams

Team Name	League	Year Established
No teams are located in the metro area		

Source: Wikipedia, Major Professional Sports Teams of the United States and Canada, March 24, 2016

CLIMATE

Average and Extreme Temperatures

Temperature	Jan	Feb	Mar	Apr	May	Jun	Jul	Aug	Sep	Oct	Nov	Dec	Yr.
Extreme High (°F)	73	76	84	90	93	102	103	100	97	89	79	75	103
Average High (°F)	43	47	52	62	71	81	88	86	77	67	52	45	64
Average Temp. (°F)	30	34	39	48	58	67	73	72	63	52	39	32	51
Average Low (°F)	16	20	25	34	44	53	59	57	48	37	25	18	37
Extreme Low (°F)	-25	-25	-10	-2	22	30	43	41	17	3	-8	-25	-25

Note: Figures cover the years 1948-1992

Source: National Climatic Data Center, International Station Meteorological Climate Summary, 9/96

Average Precipitation/Snowfall/Humidity

Precip./Humidity	Jan	Feb	Mar	Apr	May	Jun	Jul	Aug	Sep	Oct	Nov	Dec	Yr.
Avg. Precip. (in.)	0.6	0.6	1.3	1.7	2.5	1.7	1.9	1.5	1.1	1.0	0.9	0.6	15.5
Avg. Snowfall (in.)	9	7	14	9	2	Tr	0	0	2	4	9	8	63
Avg. Rel. Hum. 5am (%)	62	65	67	66	70	68	67	68	66	63	66	63	66
Avg. Rel. Hum. 5pm (%)	49	44	40	35	38	34	34	34	32	34	47	50	39

Note: Figures cover the years 1948-1992; Tr = Trace amounts (<0.05 in. of rain; <0.5 in. of snow)

Source: National Climatic Data Center, International Station Meteorological Climate Summary, 9/96

Weather Conditions

Temperature			Daytime Sky			Precipitation		
10°F & below	32°F & below	90°F & above	Clear	Partly cloudy	Cloudy	0.01 inch or more precip.	0.1 inch or more snow/ice	Thunderstorms
24	155	33	99	177	89	90	38	39

Note: Figures are average number of days per year and cover the years 1948-1992

Source: National Climatic Data Center, International Station Meteorological Climate Summary, 9/96

HAZARDOUS WASTE

Superfund Sites

Lafayette has no sites on the EPA's Superfund Final National Priorities List. There are a total of 1,323 Superfund sites on the list in the U.S. *U.S. Environmental Protection Agency, Final National Priorities List, March 18, 2016*

AIR & WATER QUALITY

Air Quality Trends: Ozone

	1990	1995	2000	2005	2010	2011	2012	2013	2014
MSA[1]	n/a	n/a	n/a	n/a	n/a	n/a	n/a	n/a	n/a

Note: (1) Data covers the Boulder, CO Metropolitan Statistical Area—see Appendix B for areas included; n/a not available. The values shown are the composite ozone concentration averages among trend sites based on the highest fourth daily maximum 8-hour concentration in parts per million. These trends are based on sites having an adequate record of monitoring data during the trend period. Data from exceptional events are included.
Source: U.S. Environmental Protection Agency, Air Quality Monitoring Information, "Air Quality Trends by City, 1990-2014"

Air Quality Index

Area	Percent of Days when Air Quality was...[2]					AQI Statistics[2]	
	Good	Moderate	Unhealthy for Sensitive Groups	Unhealthy	Very Unhealthy	Maximum	Median
MSA[1]	85.8	13.4	0.8	0.0	0.0	109	40

Note: (1) Data covers the Boulder, CO Metropolitan Statistical Area—see Appendix B for areas included; (2) Based on 365 days with AQI data in 2015. Air Quality Index (AQI) is an index for reporting daily air quality. EPA calculates the AQI for five major air pollutants regulated by the Clean Air Act: ground-level ozone, particle pollution (aka particulate matter), carbon monoxide, sulfur dioxide, and nitrogen dioxide. The AQI runs from 0 to 500. The higher the AQI value, the greater the level of air pollution and the greater the health concern. There are six AQI categories: "Good" AQI is between 0 and 50. Air quality is considered satisfactory; "Moderate" AQI is between 51 and 100. Air quality is acceptable; "Unhealthy for Sensitive Groups" When AQI values are between 101 and 150, members of sensitive groups may experience health effects; "Unhealthy" When AQI values are between 151 and 200 everyone may begin to experience health effects; "Very Unhealthy" AQI values between 201 and 300 trigger a health alert; "Hazardous" AQI values over 300 trigger warnings of emergency conditions (not shown).
Source: U.S. Environmental Protection Agency, Air Quality Index Report, 2015

Air Quality Index Pollutants

Area	Percent of Days when AQI Pollutant was...[2]					
	Carbon Monoxide	Nitrogen Dioxide	Ozone	Sulfur Dioxide	Particulate Matter 2.5	Particulate Matter 10
MSA[1]	0.0	0.0	90.7	0.0	8.5	0.8

Note: (1) Data covers the Boulder, CO Metropolitan Statistical Area—see Appendix B for areas included; (2) Based on 365 days with AQI data in 2015. The Air Quality Index (AQI) is an index for reporting daily air quality. EPA calculates the AQI for five major air pollutants regulated by the Clean Air Act: ground-level ozone, particle pollution (also known as particulate matter), carbon monoxide, sulfur dioxide, and nitrogen dioxide. The AQI runs from 0 to 500. The higher the AQI value, the greater the level of air pollution and the greater the health concern.
Source: U.S. Environmental Protection Agency, Air Quality Index Report, 2015

Maximum Air Pollutant Concentrations: Particulate Matter, Ozone, CO and Lead

	Particulate Matter 10 (ug/m^3)	Particulate Matter 2.5 Wtd AM (ug/m^3)	Particulate Matter 2.5 24-Hr (ug/m^3)	Ozone (ppm)	Carbon Monoxide (ppm)	Lead (ug/m^3)
MSA[1] Level	55	7.5	26	0.07	n/a	n/a
NAAQS[2]	150	15	35	0.075	9	0.15
Met NAAQS[2]	Yes	Yes	Yes	Yes	n/a	n/a

Note: (1) Data covers the Boulder, CO Metropolitan Statistical Area—see Appendix B for areas included; Data from exceptional events are included; (2) National Ambient Air Quality Standards; ppm = parts per million; ug/m^3 = micrograms per cubic meter; n/a not available.
Concentrations: Particulate Matter 10 (coarse particulate)—highest second maximum 24-hour concentration; Particulate Matter 2.5 Wtd AM (fine particulate)—highest weighted annual mean concentration; Particulate Matter 2.5 24-Hour (fine particulate)—highest 98th percentile 24-hour concentration; Ozone—highest fourth daily maximum 8-hour concentration; Carbon Monoxide—highest second maximum non-overlapping 8-hour concentration; Lead—maximum running 3-month average
Source: U.S. Environmental Protection Agency, Air Quality Monitoring Information, "Air Quality Statistics by City, 2014"

Maximum Air Pollutant Concentrations: Nitrogen Dioxide and Sulfur Dioxide

	Nitrogen Dioxide AM (ppb)	Nitrogen Dioxide 1-Hr (ppb)	Sulfur Dioxide AM (ppb)	Sulfur Dioxide 1-Hr (ppb)	Sulfur Dioxide 24-Hr (ppb)
MSA[1] Level	n/a	n/a	n/a	n/a	n/a
NAAQS[2]	53	100	30	75	140
Met NAAQS[2]	n/a	n/a	n/a	n/a	n/a

Note: (1) Data covers the Boulder, CO Metropolitan Statistical Area—see Appendix B for areas included; Data from exceptional events are included; (2) National Ambient Air Quality Standards; ppm = parts per million; ug/m³ = micrograms per cubic meter; n/a not available.
Concentrations: Nitrogen Dioxide AM—highest arithmetic mean concentration; Nitrogen Dioxide 1-Hr—highest 98th percentile 1-hour daily maximum concentration; Sulfur Dioxide AM—highest annual mean concentration; Sulfur Dioxide 1-Hr—highest 99th percentile 1-hour daily maximum concentration; Sulfur Dioxide 24-Hr—highest second maximum 24-hour concentration
Source: U.S. Environmental Protection Agency, Air Quality Monitoring Information, "Air Quality Statistics by City, 2014"

Drinking Water

Water System Name	Pop. Served	Primary Water Source Type	Violations[1]	
			Health Based	Monitoring/ Reporting
City of Lafayette	27,651	Surface	0	1

Note: (1) Based on violation data from January 1, 2015 to December 31, 2015 (includes unresolved violations from earlier years)
Source: U.S. Environmental Protection Agency, Office of Ground Water and Drinking Water, Safe Drinking Water Information System (based on data extracted April 29, 2016)

Parker, Colorado

Background

Parker, founded in 1864, sits at an elevation of 5,900 feet above sea level, 20 miles southeast of Denver. Even though it's currently one of the fastest growing cities in the United States, the town's governmental agencies and residents strive to ensure that the rolling rural hills not be spoiled by over-building and lack of planning. The community boasts new shops, low buildings, new housing developments and plenty of open space while emphasizing its small-town flavor and atmosphere.

Parker's modest history began in 1860, serving as a stage stop demarcated by a one-room shack situated 20 miles from the origination point of the Butterfield stage, in what is now downtown Denver. The shack grew into a 10-room inn, changed hands twice and finally became a major hub for the railroad in 1882 under the ownership of James Sample Parker. During the Depression in the 1930s, the local bank was robbed, railroad tracks were washed out and slipping agricultural prices almost wiped out the small village.

The town struggled to hold onto economic viability into the 1960s when the city was discovered by residents fleeing overcrowded Denver.

Parker's Chamber of Commerce sponsors many local events including Parker Country Festival and the Parker Christmas Carriage Parade. The Parker Economic Development Council works closely with businesses interested in moving or expanding to the Parker area. Large retail establishments such as Walmart and Home Depot peacefully co-exist with quaint in-town boutiques and restaurants.

Other amenities in the 14-square-mile area include an award-winning recreation center (featuring an indoor and outdoor pool), a state-of-the-art public library, a skate park, an in-town trail system, and two golf courses—Canterberry and Pinery. The town is currently involved in a 15-year plan to establish a new arboretum showcasing 200 to 300 different local tree varieties.

The Denver Airport is accessible by a 25-minute drive, and Denver's Tech Center corporate park is 15 minutes by car. Parker Adventist Hospital, a faith-based, not-for-profit, 134-bed facility provides 24-hour emergency, women's services, cardiac care and pediatric care.

The town supports three high schools, including Chaparral High School and the Ponderosa High School, which hosts Colorado's 5A State Football Champions. Parker's Arapahoe Community College, established in 1965, serves 8,000 students a semester, and is the oldest community college in the Denver metro area.

Rankings

General Rankings

- The Denver* metro area was identified as one of America's fastest-growing areas in terms of population and economy by *Forbes.* The area ranked #6 out of 20. The 100 most populous metro areas in the U.S. were evaluated on the following criteria: estimated population growth; job growth; gross metropolitan product growth; unemployment; median salaries for college-educated workers. *Forbes, "America's Fastest-Growing Cities 2015," January 27, 2015*

Business/Finance Rankings

- The personal finance site NerdWallet analyzed 183 American metropolitan areas with populations over 250,000 and more than 15,000 businesses to rank where entrepreneurs find the most success. Criteria included area economy, annual income, housing cost, unemployment rate, and the success rate of area businesses. Denver* ranked #24. *www.nerdwallet.com, "Best Places to Start a Business," April 27, 2015*
- The editors of *Kiplinger's Personal Finance Magazine* named Denver* to their list of ten of the best metro areas for start-ups. The area ranked #9.Criteria: well-educated workforce; low living costs for self-employed people, as measured by the Council for Community and Economic Research; a strong existing community of small business; low unemployment; low business costs. *www.kiplinger.com, "10 Great Cities for Starting a Business," October 2014*
- The finance website Wall St. Cheat Sheet ranked the nation's largest metro areas on prospects for high-wage job creation in over the next five years. Based on analysis by CareerBuilder and Economic Modeling Specialists International (EMSI), The Denver* metro area ranked #8. *wallstcheatsheet.com, "Top 10 Cities for High-Wage Job Growth," December 8, 2013*
- Based on metro area social media reviews, the employment opinion group Glassdoor surveyed 50 of the largest U.S. metro areas and equally weighed cost of living, hiring opportunity, and job satisfaction to compose a list of "25 Best Cities for Jobs." The Denver* metro area was ranked #47 in overall job satisfaction. *www.glassdoor.com, "Best Cities for Jobs," May 19, 2015*
- In a survey of economic confidence in the nation's 50 largest metropolitan areas conducted January–December 2014, the Denver* metro area placed #8, according to Gallup's 2014 Economic Confidence Index. *Gallup, "San Jose and San Francisco Lead in Economic Confidence," March 19, 2015*
- The Brookings Institution ranked the 100 largest metro areas in the U.S. based on income inequality. Denver* was ranked #74 (#1 = greatest ineqality). Criteria: the "95/20 ratio," a figure representing the income at which a household earns more than 95 percent of all other households, divided by the income at which a household earns more than only 20 percent of all other households. *Brookings Institution, "Income Inequality, 100 Largest U.S. Metro Areas, 2007-2014," January 14, 2016*
- *Forbes* ranked the largest metro areas in the U.S. in terms of the "Best Cities for Young Professionals." The Denver* metro area ranked #9 out of 15. Criteria: job growth; unemployment rate; median salary of college graduates age 24 to 34; cost of living; number of small businesses per capita; number of large companies; percentage of population 25 years of age and older with college degrees. *Forbes.com, "America's 15 Best Cities for Young Professionals," August 18, 2014*
- The Denver* metro area was identified as one of the most debt-ridden places in America by the finance site Credit.com. The metro area was ranked #7. Criteria: residents' average personal debt load and average credit scores. *Credit.com, "The Most Debt-Ridden Cities," May 1, 2014*
- Denver* was identified as one of America's most frugal metro areas by *Coupons.com.* The city ranked #9 out of 25. Criteria: online coupon usage. *Coupons.com, "Top 25 Most Frugal Cities of 2014," May 11, 2015*
- Denver* was identified as one of America's most frugal metro areas by *Coupons.com.* The city ranked #17 out of 25. Criteria: Grocery IQ and coupons.com mobile app usage. *Coupons.com, "Top 25 Most On-the-Go Frugal Cities of 2013," April 10, 2014*

- The Denver* metro area appeared on the Milken Institute "2015 Best Performing Cities" list. Rank: #16 out of 200 large metro areas. Criteria: job growth; wage and salary growth; high-tech output growth. *Milken Institute, "Best-Performing Cities 2015," December 2015*
- *Forbes* ranked the 200 most populous metro areas to determine the nation's "Best Places for Business and Careers." The Denver* metro area was ranked #1. Criteria: costs (business and living); job growth (past and projected); income growth; educational attainment (college and high school); projected economic growth; cultural and recreational opportunities; net migration patterns; number of highly ranked colleges. *Forbes, "The Best Places for Business and Careers 2015," July 29, 2015*

Education Rankings

- Personal finance website *WalletHub* analyzed the 150 largest U.S. metropolitan statistical areas to determine where the most educated Americans are choosing to settle. Criteria: education quality and attainment gap; education levels; percentage of workers with degrees; public school rankings; quality and size of each metro area's universities. Denver* was ranked #16 (#1 = most educated city). *www.WalletHub.com, "2015's Most and Least Educated Cities*

Environmental Rankings

- The Denver* metro area came in at #29 for the relative comfort of its climate on Sperling's list of "chill cities," as measured by the Sperling Heat Index. All 361 metro areas are included. Criteria included daytime high temperatures, nighttime low temperatures, dew point, and relative humidity at the high temperatures. *www.bertsperling.com, "Sperling's Chill Cities," July 18, 2013*
- Sperling's BestPlaces assessed 379 metropolitan areas of the United States for the likelihood of dangerously extreme weather events or earthquakes. In general the Southeast and South-Central regions have the highest risk of weather extremes and earthquakes, while the Pacific Northwest enjoys the lowest risk. Of the least risky metropolitan areas, the Denver* metro area was ranked #214. *www.bestplaces.net, "Safest Places from Natural Disasters," April 2011*
- The U.S. Environmental Protection Agency (EPA) released a list of U.S. metropolitan areas with the most ENERGY STAR certified buildings in 2015. The Denver* metro area was ranked #9 out of 25. *U.S. Environmental Protection Agency, "Top Cities With the Most ENERGY STAR Certified Buildings in 2016," March 30, 2016*
- Denver* was highlighted as one of the 25 most ozone-polluted metro areas in the U.S. during 2011 through 2013. The area ranked #13. *American Lung Association, State of the Air 2015*

Health/Fitness Rankings

- Analysts who tracked obesity rates in the nation's largest metro areas (populations above one million) found that the Denver* metro area was one of the ten major metros where residents were least likely to be obese, defined as a BMI score of 30 or above. *www.gallup.com, "Boulder, Colo., Residents Still Least Likely to Be Obese," April 4, 2014*
- Analysts who tracked obesity rates in 100 of the nation's most populous areas found that the Denver* metro area was one of the ten communities where residents were least likely to be obese, defined as a BMI score of 30 or above. *www.gallup.com, "Colorado Springs Residents Least Likely to Be Obese," May 28, 2015*
- For each of the 50 most populous metro areas in the United States, the American College of Sports Medicine's American Fitness Index evaluated infrastructure, community assets, and policies that encourage healthy and fit lifestyles, including preventive health behaviors, levels of chronic disease conditions, health care access, and community resources and policies that support physical activity. The Denver* metro area ranked #6 for "community fitness." *www.americanfitnessindex.org, "ACSM American Fitness Index Health and Community Fitness Status of the 50 Largest Metropolitan Areas," May 2015*
- The Denver* metro area was identified as one of the worst cities for bed bugs in America by pest control company Orkin. The area ranked #18 out of 50 based on the number of bed bug treatments Orkin performed from January to December 2015. *Orkin, "Chicago Tops Bed Bug Cities List for Fourth Year in a Row," January 13, 2016*

- Denver* was identified as a "2016 Spring Allergy Capital." The area ranked #99 out of 100. Three groups of factors were used to identify the most severe cities for people with allergies during the spring season: annual pollen levels; medicine utilization; access to board-certified allergists. *Asthma and Allergy Foundation of America, "Spring Allergy Capitals 2016"*
- Denver* was identified as a "2015 Asthma Capital." The area ranked #78 out of the nation's 100 largest metropolitan areas. Criteria: estimated prevalence; self-reported prevalence; crude death rate for asthma; annual pollen score; annual air quality; public smoking laws; number of board-certified asthma specialists; school inhaler access laws; rescue medication use; controller medication use; ER visits for asthma; uninsured rate; poverty rate. *Asthma and Allergy Foundation of America, "Asthma Capitals 2015"*
- The Denver* metro area ranked #50 out of 190 in The Gallup-Healthways Well-Being Index. Criteria: purpose; social well being; financial health; community and physical health. Results are based on telephone interviews with adults, aged 18 and older, living in metropolitan areas in the 50 U.S. states and the District of Columbia. *Gallup-Healthways, "State of American Well-Being," February 23, 2016*

Real Estate Rankings

- According to Penske Truck Rental, the Denver* metro area was named the #6 moving destination in 2015, based on one-way consumer truck rental reservations made through Penske's website and reservations call center. *blog.gopenske.com, "Penske Truck Rental's 2015 Top Moving Destinations List," February 3, 2016*
- With data from RealtyTrac, Yahoo! Finance researchers listed the housing markets in which housing affordability is improving most, factoring in interest rates as well as median home prices. The Denver* metro area was among the least affordable housing markets. *news.yahoo.com, "10 Cities Where Ordinary People Can No Longer Afford Homes," March 5, 2014*
- The Denver* metro area was identified as one of the nations's 20 hottest housing markets in 2016. Criteria: listing views as an indicator of demand and median days on the market as an indicator of supply. The area ranked #4. *Realtor.com, "The 20 Hottest U.S. Real Estate Markets in February 2016," February 25, 2016*
- The Denver* metro area was identified as one of the top 20 housing markets to invest in for 2016 by *Forbes*. The area ranked #16. Criteria: strong job and population growth; anticipated home price appreciation; and other factors. *Forbes.com, "Best Buy Cities: Where to Invest in Housing in 2016," January 27, 2016*
- Denver* was ranked #8 in the top 20 out of 266 metro areas in terms of house price appreciation in 2015 (#1 = highest rate). *Federal Housing Finance Agency, House Price Index, 4th Quarter 2015*
- The Denver* metro area was identified as one of the 15 worst housing markets for the next five years." Criteria: projected annualized change in home prices between the fourth quarter 2012 and the fourth quarter 2017. *The Business Insider, "The 15 Worst Housing Markets for the Next Five Years," May 22, 2013*
- The Denver* metro area was identified as one of the 20 best housing markets in the U.S. in 2015. The area ranked #18 out of 179 markets. Criteria: year-over-year change of median sales price of existing single-family homes between the 4th quarter of 2014 and the 4th quarter of 2015. *National Association of Realtors®, Median Sales Price of Existing Single-Family Homes for Metropolitan Areas, 4th Quarter 2015*
- The Denver* metro area was identified as one of the 20 least affordable housing markets in the U.S. in 2015. The area ranked #13 out of 179 markets. Criteria: qualification for a mortgage loan on a typical home. *National Association of Realtors®, Affordability Index of Existing Single-Family Homes for Metropolitan Areas, 2015*
- Denver* was ranked #174 out of 225 metro areas in terms of housing affordability in 2015 by the National Association of Home Builders (#1 = most affordable). Criteria: the share of homes sold in that area affordable to a family earning the local median income, based on standard mortgage underwriting criteria. *National Association of Home Builders®, NAHB-Wells Fargo Housing Opportunity Index, 4th Quarter 2015*

Safety Rankings

- The National Insurance Crime Bureau ranked 380 metro areas in the U.S. in terms of per capita rates of vehicle theft. The Denver* metro area ranked #58 (#1 = highest rate). Criteria: number of vehicle theft offenses per 100,000 inhabitants in 2014. *National Insurance Crime Bureau, "Hot Spots 2014," June 24, 2015*

Seniors/Retirement Rankings

- From its Best Cities for Successful Aging indexes, the Milken Institute generated rankings for metropolitan areas, weighing data in eight categories—health care, wellness, living arrangements, transportation, financial characteristics, education and employment opportunities, community engagement, and overall livability. The Denver* metro area was ranked #11 overall in the large metro area category. *Milken Institute, "Best Cities for Successful Aging, 2014"*

Sports/Recreation Rankings

- According to the personal finance website NerdWallet, the Denver* metro area, at #8, is one of the nation's top dozen metro areas for sports fans. Criteria included the presence of all four major sports—MLB, NFL, NHL, and NBA, fan enthusiasm (as measured by game attendance), ticket affordability, and "sports culture," that is, number of sports bars. *www.nerdwallet.com, "Best Cities for Sports Fans," May 5, 2013*

Miscellaneous Rankings

- The watchdog site Charity Navigator conducts an annual study of charities in the nation's major markets both to analyze statistical differences in their financial, accountability, and transparency practices and to track year-to-year variations in individual communities. The Denver* metro area was ranked #22 among the 30 metro markets in the rating dimension of Overall Score. *www.charitynavigator.org, "Metro Market Study 2015," June 5, 2015*

- Mars Chocolate North America, the makers of COMBOS®, in partnership with Sperling's BestPlaces, ranked 50 major metro areas in terms of their "manliness." The Denver* metro area ranked #34. Criteria: number of professional sports teams; number of nearby NASCAR tracks and racing events; manly lifestyle; concentration of manly retail stores; manly occupations per capita; salty snack sales; "Board of Manliness" rankings. *Mars Chocolate North America, "America's Manliest Cities 2012"*

- The National Alliance to End Homelessness ranked the 100 most populous metro areas with the highest rate of homelessness. The Denver* metro area ranked #30. Criteria: number of homeless people per 10,000 population in 2011. *National Alliance to End Homelessness, The State of Homelessness in America 2012*

Parker is located within the Denver-Aurora-Lakewood, CO Metropolitan Statistical Area.

Business Environment

CITY FINANCES

City Government Finances

Component	2012 ($000)	2012 ($ per capita)
Total Revenues	53,820	1,188
Total Expenditures	55,496	1,225
Debt Outstanding	55,930	1,234
Cash and Securities[1]	48,597	1,072

Note: (1) Cash and security holdings of a government at the close of its fiscal year, including those of its dependent agencies, utilities, and liquor stores.
Source: U.S Census Bureau, State & Local Government Finances 2012

City Government Revenue by Source

Source	2012 ($000)	2012 ($ per capita)
General Revenue		
From Federal Government	893	19
From State Government	1,842	40
From Local Governments	5,614	123
Taxes		
Property	1,644	36
Sales and Gross Receipts	28,966	639
Personal Income	0	0
Corporate Income	0	0
Motor Vehicle License	136	3
Other Taxes	2,267	50
Current Charges	9,558	211
Liquor Store	0	0
Utility	0	0
Employee Retirement	0	0

Source: U.S Census Bureau, State & Local Government Finances 2012

City Government Expenditures by Function

Function	2012 ($000)	2012 ($ per capita)	2012 (%)
General Direct Expenditures			
Air Transportation	0	0	0.0
Corrections	0	0	0.0
Education	0	0	0.0
Employment Security Administration	0	0	0.0
Financial Administration	1,917	42	3.4
Fire Protection	0	0	0.0
General Public Buildings	472	10	0.8
Governmental Administration, Other	2,281	50	4.1
Health	0	0	0.0
Highways	8,671	191	15.6
Hospitals	0	0	0.0
Housing and Community Development	1,098	24	1.9
Interest on General Debt	3,216	70	5.7
Judicial and Legal	640	14	1.1
Libraries	0	0	0.0
Parking	0	0	0.0
Parks and Recreation	20,698	456	37.2
Police Protection	9,372	206	16.8
Public Welfare	0	0	0.0
Sewerage	1,161	25	2.0
Solid Waste Management	77	1	0.1
Veterans' Services	0	0	0.0
Liquor Store	0	0	0.0
Utility	0	0	0.0
Employee Retirement	0	0	0.0

Source: U.S Census Bureau, State & Local Government Finances 2012

DEMOGRAPHICS

Population Growth

Area	1990 Census	2000 Census	2010 Census	2014* Estimate	Population Growth (%) 1990-2014	Population Growth (%) 2010-2014
City	5,562	23,558	45,297	47,515	754.3	4.9
MSA[1]	1,666,935	2,179,296	2,543,482	2,651,392	59.1	4.2
U.S.	248,709,873	281,421,906	308,745,538	314,107,084	26.3	1.7

Note: (1) Figures cover the Denver-Aurora-Lakewood, CO Metropolitan Statistical Area—see Appendix B for areas included; (*) 2010-2014 5-year estimated population
Source: U.S. Census Bureau, 1990 Census, Census 2000, Census 2010, 2010-2014 American Community Survey 5-Year Estimates

Household Size

Area	Persons in Household (%) One	Two	Three	Four	Five	Six	Seven or More	Average Household Size
City	19.2	27.3	18.8	23.0	8.1	1.5	1.8	2.88
MSA[1]	29.1	33.2	15.2	13.0	5.6	2.2	1.3	2.55
U.S.	27.5	33.5	15.8	13.1	6.0	2.3	1.4	2.64

Note: (1) Figures cover the Denver-Aurora-Lakewood, CO Metropolitan Statistical Area—see Appendix B for areas included
Source: U.S. Census Bureau, 2010-2014 American Community Survey 5-Year Estimates

Race

Area	White Alone[2] (%)	Black Alone[2] (%)	Asian Alone[2] (%)	AIAN[3] Alone[2] (%)	NHOPI[4] Alone[2] (%)	Other Race Alone[2] (%)	Two or More Races (%)
City	90.8	1.3	2.6	0.2	0.1	0.9	4.0
MSA[1]	81.5	5.5	3.8	0.8	0.1	4.8	3.5
U.S.	73.8	12.6	5.0	0.8	0.2	4.7	2.9

Note: (1) Figures cover the Denver-Aurora-Lakewood, CO Metropolitan Statistical Area—see Appendix B for areas included; (2) Alone is defined as not being in combination with one or more other races; (3) American Indian and Alaska Native; (4) Native Hawaiian and Other Pacific Islander
Source: U.S. Census Bureau, 2010-2014 American Community Survey 5-Year Estimates

Hispanic or Latino Origin

Area	Total (%)	Mexican (%)	Puerto Rican (%)	Cuban (%)	Other (%)
City	7.6	5.4	0.4	0.0	1.8
MSA[1]	22.7	18.0	0.5	0.1	4.0
U.S.	16.9	10.8	1.6	0.6	3.8

Note: Persons of Hispanic or Latino origin can be of any race; (1) Figures cover the Denver-Aurora-Lakewood, CO Metropolitan Statistical Area—see Appendix B for areas included
Source: U.S. Census Bureau, 2010-2014 American Community Survey 5-Year Estimates

Ancestry

Area	German	Irish	English	American	Italian	Polish	French[2]	Scottish	Dutch
City	27.6	17.0	13.4	6.0	6.7	3.1	3.5	3.7	1.6
MSA[1]	19.4	11.6	10.0	5.0	5.2	2.6	2.7	2.4	1.6
U.S.	14.9	10.8	8.0	7.1	5.5	3.0	2.7	1.7	1.4

Note: Figures are the percentage of the total population reporting a particular ancestry. The nine most commonly reported ancestries in the U.S. are shown. Figures include multiple ancestries (e.g. if a person reported being Irish and Italian, they were included in both columns); (1) Figures cover the Denver-Aurora-Lakewood, CO Metropolitan Statistical Area—see Appendix B for areas included; (2) Excludes Basque
Source: U.S. Census Bureau, 2010-2014 American Community Survey 5-Year Estimates

Foreign-Born Population

Area	Percent of Population Born in								
	Any Foreign Country	Asia	Mexico	Europe	Carribean	Central America[2]	South America	Africa	Canada
City	5.0	1.9	0.9	1.1	0.1	0.4	0.1	0.1	0.4
MSA[1]	12.2	2.9	5.5	1.5	0.1	0.5	0.4	0.9	0.3
U.S.	13.1	3.8	3.7	1.5	1.2	1.0	0.9	0.6	0.3

Note: (1) Figures cover the Denver-Aurora-Lakewood, CO Metropolitan Statistical Area—see Appendix B for areas included; (2) Excludes Mexico.
Source: U.S. Census Bureau, 2010-2014 American Community Survey 5-Year Estimates

Marital Status

Area	Never Married	Now Married[2]	Separated	Widowed	Divorced
City	22.9	64.6	0.9	1.8	9.9
MSA[1]	31.7	50.2	1.7	4.2	12.2
U.S.	32.5	48.4	2.2	5.9	10.9

Note: Figures are percentages and cover the population 15 years of age and older; (1) Figures cover the Denver-Aurora-Lakewood, CO Metropolitan Statistical Area—see Appendix B for areas included; (2) Excludes separated
Source: U.S. Census Bureau, 2010-2014 American Community Survey 5-Year Estimates

Disability Status

Area	All Ages	Under 18 Years Old	18 to 64 Years Old	65 Years and Over
City	6.1	4.7	4.8	27.2
MSA[1]	9.2	3.0	7.6	33.0
U.S.	12.3	4.1	10.2	36.3

Note: Figures show percent of the civilian noninstitutionalized population that reported having a disability. Disability status is determined from from six types of difficulty: vision, hearing, cognitive, ambulatory, self-care, and independent living. For children under 5 years old, hearing and vision difficulty are used to determine disability status. For children between the ages of 5 and 14, disability status is determined from hearing, vision, cognitive, ambulatory, and self-care difficulties. For people aged 15 years and older, they are considered to have a disability if they have difficulty with any one of the six difficulty types; (1) Figures cover the Denver-Aurora-Lakewood, CO Metropolitan Statistical Area—see Appendix B for areas included.
Source: U.S. Census Bureau, 2010-2014 American Community Survey 5-Year Estimates

Age

Area	Percent of Population									Median Age
	Under Age 5	Age 5–19	Age 20–34	Age 35–44	Age 45–54	Age 55–64	Age 65–74	Age 75–84	Age 85+	
City	7.5	26.7	17.1	19.6	15.5	8.2	3.8	1.2	0.4	34.0
MSA[1]	6.7	19.8	21.9	14.7	14.1	11.9	6.4	3.1	1.4	36.0
U.S.	6.4	19.9	20.6	13.0	14.1	12.3	7.6	4.3	1.9	37.4

Note: (1) Figures cover the Denver-Aurora-Lakewood, CO Metropolitan Statistical Area—see Appendix B for areas included
Source: U.S. Census Bureau, 2010-2014 American Community Survey 5-Year Estimates

Gender

Area	Males	Females	Males per 100 Females
City	23,872	23,643	101.0
MSA[1]	1,319,273	1,332,119	99.0
U.S.	154,515,159	159,591,925	96.8

Note: (1) Figures cover the Denver-Aurora-Lakewood, CO Metropolitan Statistical Area—see Appendix B for areas included
Source: U.S. Census Bureau, 2010-2014 American Community Survey 5-Year Estimates

Religious Groups by Family

Area	Catholic	Baptist	Non-Den.	Methodist[2]	Lutheran	LDS[3]	Pente-costal	Presby-terian[4]	Muslim[5]	Judaism
MSA[1]	16.0	2.9	4.6	1.7	2.1	2.4	1.2	1.5	0.5	0.6
U.S.	19.1	9.3	4.0	4.0	2.3	2.0	1.9	1.6	0.8	0.7

Note: Figures are the number of adherents as a percentage of the total population; (1) Figures cover the Denver-Aurora-Broomfield, CO Metropolitan Statistical Area—see Appendix B for areas included; (2) Methodist/Pietist; (3) Latter Day Saints; (4) Reformed; (5) Figures are estimates
Source: Association of Statisticians of American Religious Bodies, 2010 U.S. Religion Census: Religious Congregations & Membership Study

Religious Groups by Tradition

Area	Catholic	Evangelical Protestant	Mainline Protestant	Other Tradition	Black Protestant	Orthodox
MSA[1]	16.0	11.0	4.5	4.6	0.3	0.3
U.S.	19.1	16.2	7.3	4.3	1.6	0.3

Note: Figures are the number of adherents as a percentage of the total population; (1) Figures cover the Denver-Aurora-Broomfield, CO Metropolitan Statistical Area—see Appendix B for areas included
Source: Association of Statisticians of American Religious Bodies, 2010 U.S. Religion Census: Religious Congregations & Membership Study

ECONOMY

Gross Metropolitan Product

Area	2013	2014	2015	2016	Rank[2]
MSA[1]	178.9	188.8	194.9	205.3	18

Note: Figures are in billions of dollars; (1) Figures cover the Denver-Aurora-Lakewood, CO Metropolitan Statistical Area—see Appendix B for areas included; (2) Rank is based on 2016 data and ranges from 1 to 381
Source: The U.S. Conference of Mayors, U.S. Metro Economies: GMP and Employment 2014-2016, June 2015

Economic Growth

Area	2011-13 (%)	2014 (%)	2015 (%)	2016 (%)	Rank[2]
MSA[1]	3.9	4.7	2.9	3.2	61
U.S.	2.2	2.4	2.3	2.9	-

Note: Figures are real gross metropolitan product (GMP) growth rates and represent annual average percent change; (1) Figures cover the Denver-Aurora-Lakewood, CO Metropolitan Statistical Area—see Appendix B for areas included; (2) Rank is based on 2016 data and ranges from 1 to 381
Source: The U.S. Conference of Mayors, U.S. Metro Economies: GMP and Employment 2014-2016, June 2015

Metropolitan Area Exports

Area	2009	2010	2011	2012	2013	2014	Rank[2]
MSA[1]	4,309.7	4,990.9	3,771.3	3,355.7	3,618.3	4,958.5	59

Note: Figures are in millions of dollars; (1) Figures cover the Denver-Aurora-Lakewood, CO Metropolitan Statistical Area—see Appendix B for areas included; (2) Rank is based on 2014 data and ranges from 1 to 385
Source: U.S. Department of Commerce, International Trade Administration, Office of Trade & Industry Information, Manufacturing & Services, data extracted March 10, 2016

Building Permits

Area	Single-Family			Multi-Family			Total		
	2014	2015p	Pct. Chg.	2014	2015p	Pct. Chg.	2014	2015p	Pct. Chg.
City	348	325	-6.6	306	403	31.7	654	728	11.3
MSA[1]	8,064	9,288	15.2	7,703	8,569	11.2	15,767	17,857	13.3
U.S.	640,300	690,800	7.9	411,800	487,600	18.4	1,052,100	1,178,400	12.0

Note: (1) Figures cover the Denver-Aurora-Lakewood, CO Metropolitan Statistical Area—see Appendix B for areas included; Figures represent new, privately-owned housing units authorized (unadjusted data); All permit data are based on estimates with imputation; (p) preliminary data.
Source: U.S. Census Bureau, Manufacturing, Mining, and Construction Statistics, Building Permits, 2014, 2015

Bankruptcy Filings

Area	Business Filings			Nonbusiness Filings		
	2014	2015	% Chg.	2014	2015	% Chg.
Douglas County	45	45	0.0	797	670	-15.9
U.S.	26,983	24,735	-8.3	909,812	819,760	-9.9

Note: Business filings include Chapter 7, Chapter 11, Chapter 12, and Chapter 13; Nonbusiness filings include Chapter 7, Chapter 11, and Chapter 13

Source: Administrative Office of the U.S. Courts, Business and Nonbusiness Bankruptcy, County Cases Commenced by Chapter of the Bankruptcy Code, During the 12- Month Period Ending December 31, 2014 and Business and Nonbusiness Bankruptcy, County Cases Commenced by Chapter of the Bankruptcy Code, During the 12- Month Period Ending December 31, 2015

Housing Vacancy Rates

Area	Gross Vacancy Rate[2] (%)			Year-Round Vacancy Rate[3] (%)			Rental Vacancy Rate[4] (%)			Homeowner Vacancy Rate[5] (%)		
	2013	2014	2015	2013	2014	2015	2013	2014	2015	2013	2014	2015
MSA[1]	6.3	6.1	7.4	5.5	5.1	5.6	5.3	3.3	4.8	1.2	0.8	0.7
U.S.	13.6	13.4	12.9	10.7	10.4	10.0	8.3	7.6	7.1	2.0	1.9	1.8

Note: (1) Figures cover the Denver-Aurora-Lakewood, CO Metropolitan Statistical Area—see Appendix B for areas included; (2) The percentage of the total housing inventory that is vacant; (3) The percentage of the housing inventory (excluding seasonal units) that is year-round vacant; (4) The percentage of rental inventory that is vacant for rent; (5) The percentage of homeowner inventory that is vacant for sale

Source: U.S. Census Bureau, Housing Vacancies and Homeownership Annual Statistics: 2015

INCOME

Income

Area	Per Capita ($)	Median Household ($)	Average Household ($)
City	36,763	98,170	106,038
MSA[1]	34,173	64,206	86,081
U.S.	28,555	53,482	74,596

Note: (1) Figures cover the Denver-Aurora-Lakewood, CO Metropolitan Statistical Area—see Appendix B for areas included

Source: U.S. Census Bureau, 2010-2014 American Community Survey 5-Year Estimates

Household Income Distribution

Area	Percent of Households Earning							
	Under $15,000	$15,000 -24,999	$25,000 -34,999	$35,000 -49,999	$50,000 -74,999	$75,000 -99,000	$100,000 -149,999	$150,000 and up
City	4.4	3.6	4.8	8.3	15.7	14.3	27.9	20.9
MSA[1]	9.4	8.2	8.9	12.6	18.0	13.5	16.0	13.4
U.S.	12.5	10.7	10.2	13.5	17.8	12.2	13.0	10.0

Note: (1) Figures cover the Denver-Aurora-Lakewood, CO Metropolitan Statistical Area—see Appendix B for areas included

Source: U.S. Census Bureau, 2010-2014 American Community Survey 5-Year Estimates

Poverty Rate

Area	All Ages	Under 18 Years Old	18 to 64 Years Old	65 Years and Over
City	4.2	4.9	3.5	7.9
MSA[1]	12.0	16.6	11.1	7.5
U.S.	15.6	21.9	14.6	9.4

Note: Figures are percentage of people whose income during the past 12 months was below the poverty level; (1) Figures cover the Denver-Aurora-Lakewood, CO Metropolitan Statistical Area—see Appendix B for areas included

Source: U.S. Census Bureau, 2010-2014 American Community Survey 5-Year Estimates

EMPLOYMENT

Labor Force and Employment

Area	Civilian Labor Force			Workers Employed		
	Dec. 2014	Dec. 2015	% Chg.	Dec. 2014	Dec. 2015	% Chg.
City	27,813	27,674	-0.5	26,828	26,918	0.3
MSA[1]	1,497,400	1,488,871	-0.5	1,437,876	1,442,519	0.3
U.S.	155,521,000	157,245,000	1.1	147,190,000	149,703,000	1.7

Note: Data is not seasonally adjusted and covers workers 16 years of age and older; (1) Figures cover the Denver-Aurora-Lakewood, CO Metropolitan Statistical Area—see Appendix B for areas included
Source: Bureau of Labor Statistics, Local Area Unemployment Statistics

Unemployment Rate

Area	2015											
	Jan.	Feb.	Mar.	Apr.	May	Jun.	Jul.	Aug.	Sep.	Oct.	Nov.	Dec.
City	3.8	3.9	3.6	3.6	3.6	3.9	3.5	3.3	3.0	2.9	2.9	2.7
MSA[1]	4.5	4.5	4.3	4.1	4.1	4.3	3.8	3.6	3.2	3.1	3.2	3.1
U.S.	6.1	5.8	5.6	5.1	5.3	5.5	5.6	5.2	4.9	4.8	4.8	4.8

Note: Data is not seasonally adjusted and covers workers 16 years of age and older; (1) Figures cover the Denver-Aurora-Lakewood, CO Metropolitan Statistical Area—see Appendix B for areas included
Source: Bureau of Labor Statistics, Local Area Unemployment Statistics

Employment by Occupation

Occupation Classification	City (%)	MSA[1] (%)	U.S. (%)
Management, Business, Science, and Arts	50.8	41.7	36.4
Natural Resources, Construction, and Maintenance	4.9	8.4	9.0
Production, Transportation, and Material Moving	5.4	8.7	12.1
Sales and Office	26.0	25.0	24.4
Service	12.9	16.1	18.2

Note: Figures cover employed civilians 16 years of age and older; (1) Figures cover the Denver-Aurora-Lakewood, CO Metropolitan Statistical Area—see Appendix B for areas included
Source: U.S. Census Bureau, 2010-2014 American Community Survey 5-Year Estimates

Employment by Industry

Sector	MSA[1]		U.S.
	Number of Employees	Percent of Total	Percent of Total
Construction, Mining, and Logging	95,900	6.7	5.0
Education and Health Services	178,100	12.5	15.7
Financial Activities	104,700	7.3	5.7
Government	194,300	13.7	15.5
Information	46,500	3.2	1.9
Leisure and Hospitality	153,800	10.8	10.4
Manufacturing	69,500	4.9	8.6
Other Services	54,100	3.8	3.9
Professional and Business Services	255,200	18.0	13.9
Retail Trade	139,900	9.8	11.3
Transportation, Warehousing, and Utilities	53,600	3.7	3.9
Wholesale Trade	69,900	4.9	4.1

Note: Figures are non-farm employment as of December 2015. Figures are not seasonally adjusted and include workers 16 years of age and older; (1) Figures cover the Denver-Aurora-Lakewood, CO Metropolitan Statistical Area—see Appendix B for areas included; n/a not available
Source: Bureau of Labor Statistics, Current Employment Statistics, Employment, Hours, and Earnings

Occupations with Greatest Projected Employment Growth: 2012 – 2022

Occupation[1]	2012 Employment	2022 Projected Employment	Numeric Employment Change	Percent Employment Change
Combined Food Preparation and Serving Workers, Including Fast Food	60,670	77,380	16,710	27.5
Secretaries and Administrative Assistants, Except Legal, Medical, and Executive	63,150	77,880	14,730	23.3
Retail Salespersons	79,300	94,000	14,700	18.5
Customer Service Representatives	45,990	59,210	13,220	28.8
Registered Nurses	42,200	53,270	11,070	26.2
General and Operations Managers	42,170	52,340	10,170	24.1
Accountants and Auditors	33,870	43,490	9,620	28.4
Personal Care Aides	16,940	26,210	9,270	54.7
Janitors and Cleaners, Except Maids and Housekeeping Cleaners	36,300	45,470	9,170	25.3
Business Operations Specialists, All Other	42,990	51,450	8,460	19.7

Note: Projections cover Colorado; (1) Sorted by numeric employment change
Source: www.projectionscentral.com, State Occupational Projections, 2012–2022 Long-Term Projections

Fastest Growing Occupations: 2012 – 2022

Occupation[1]	2012 Employment	2022 Projected Employment	Numeric Employment Change	Percent Employment Change
Service Unit Operators, Oil, Gas, and Mining	3,520	6,290	2,770	78.4
Derrick Operators, Oil and Gas	630	1,110	480	76.0
Rotary Drill Operators, Oil and Gas	1,280	2,200	920	71.5
Roustabouts, Oil and Gas	2,770	4,710	1,940	70.2
Interpreters and Translators	1,510	2,550	1,040	68.5
Petroleum Engineers	1,500	2,500	1,000	66.9
Pump Operators, Except Wellhead Pumpers	700	1,160	460	64.9
Helpers—Brickmasons, Blockmasons, Stonemasons, and Tile and Marble Setters	200	320	120	61.3
Insulation Workers, Mechanical	420	680	260	61.2
Information Security Analysts	1,240	1,960	720	57.8

Note: Projections cover Colorado; (1) Sorted by percent employment change and excludes occupations with numeric employment change less than 100
Source: www.projectionscentral.com, State Occupational Projections, 2012–2022 Long-Term Projections

Average Wages

Occupation	$/Hr.	Occupation	$/Hr.
Accountants and Auditors	36.90	Maids and Housekeeping Cleaners	10.39
Automotive Mechanics	20.68	Maintenance and Repair Workers	19.00
Bookkeepers	19.30	Marketing Managers	70.66
Carpenters	21.18	Nuclear Medicine Technologists	36.55
Cashiers	10.49	Nurses, Licensed Practical	24.11
Clerks, General Office	18.98	Nurses, Registered	34.48
Clerks, Receptionists/Information	15.39	Nursing Assistants	15.10
Clerks, Shipping/Receiving	16.40	Packers and Packagers, Hand	11.42
Computer Programmers	43.27	Physical Therapists	36.71
Computer Systems Analysts	46.67	Postal Service Mail Carriers	24.73
Computer User Support Specialists	28.45	Real Estate Brokers	33.01
Cooks, Restaurant	11.65	Retail Salespersons	13.11
Dentists	88.30	Sales Reps., Exc. Tech./Scientific	34.35
Electrical Engineers	46.01	Sales Reps., Tech./Scientific	54.54
Electricians	23.14	Secretaries, Exc. Legal/Med./Exec.	18.54
Financial Managers	77.09	Security Guards	13.79
First-Line Supervisors/Managers, Sales	22.01	Surgeons	121.51
Food Preparation Workers	10.50	Teacher Assistants*	13.73
General and Operations Managers	66.33	Teachers, Elementary School*	25.45
Hairdressers/Cosmetologists	13.40	Teachers, Secondary School*	27.26
Internists	72.69	Telemarketers	14.15
Janitors and Cleaners	12.11	Truck Drivers, Heavy/Tractor-Trailer	23.01
Landscaping/Groundskeeping Workers	13.95	Truck Drivers, Light/Delivery Svcs.	17.39
Lawyers	68.61	Waiters and Waitresses	10.53

Note: Wage data covers the Denver-Aurora-Broomfield, CO Metropolitan Statistical Area—see Appendix B for areas included; (*) Hourly wages for elementary/secondary school teachers and teacher assistants were calculated by the editors from annual wage data based on a 40 hour work week; n/a not available.
Source: Bureau of Labor Statistics, Metro Area Occupational Employment and Wage Estimates, May 2015

TAXES

State Corporate Income Tax Rates

State	Tax Rate (%)	Income Brackets ($)	Num. of Brackets	Financial Institution Tax Rate (%)[a]	Federal Income Tax Ded.
Colorado	4.63	Flat rate	1	4.63	No

Note: Tax rates as of January 1, 2016; (a) Rates listed are the corporate income tax rate applied to financial institutions or excise taxes based on income. Some states have other taxes based upon the value of deposits or shares.
Source: Federation of Tax Administrators, "State Corporate Income Tax Rates, 2016"

State Individual Income Tax Rates

State	Tax Rate (%)	Income Brackets ($)	Num. of Brackets	Personal Exempt. ($)[1]		Fed. Inc. Tax Ded.
				Single	Dependents	
Colorado	4.63	Flat rate	1	4,050 (d)	4,050 (d)	No

Note: Tax rates as of January 1, 2016; Local- and county-level taxes are not included; n/a not applicable; (1) Married joint filers generally receive double the single exemption; (d) These states use the personal exemption amounts provided in the federal Internal Revenue Code.
Source: Federation of Tax Administrators, "State Individual Income Tax Rates, 2016"

Various State and Local Tax Rates

State	State and Local Sales and Use (%)	State Sales and Use (%)	Gasoline[1] (¢/gal.)	Cigarette[2] ($/pack)	Spirits[3] ($/gal.)	Wine[4] ($/gal.)	Beer[5] ($/gal.)
Colorado	8.00	2.9	22	0.84	2.28	0.32 (l)	0.23

Note: All tax rates as of January 1, 2016; (1) The American Petroleum Institute has developed a methodology for determining the average tax rate on a gallon of fuel. Rates may include any of the following: excise taxes, environmental fees, storage tank fees, other fees or taxes, general sales tax, and local taxes. In states where gasoline is subject to the general sales tax, or where the fuel tax is based on the average sale price, the average rate determined by API is sensitive to changes in the price of gasoline. States that fully or partially apply general sales taxes to gasoline: CA, CO, GA, IL, IN, MI, NY; (2) The federal excise tax of $1.0066 per pack and local taxes are not included; (3) Rates are those applicable to off-premise sales of 40% alcohol by volume (a.b.v.) distilled spirits in 750ml containers. Local excise taxes are excluded; (4) Rates are those applicable to off-premise sales of 11% a.b.v. non-carbonated wine in 750ml containers; (5) Rates are those applicable to off-premise sales of 4.7% a.b.v. beer in 12 ounce containers; (l) Different rates also applicable according to alcohol content, place of production, size of container, place purchased (on- or off-premise or on board airlines) or type of wine (carbonated, vermouth, etc.).
Source: Tax Foundation, 2016 Facts & Figures: How Does Your State Compare?

State Business Tax Climate Index Rankings

State	Overall Rank	Corporate Tax Rank	Individual Income Tax Rank	Sales Tax Rank	Unemployment Insurance Tax Rank	Property Tax Rank
Colorado	18	15	16	44	33	12

Note: The index is a measure of how each state's tax laws affect economic performance. The lower the rank, the more favorable a state's tax system is for business. States without a given tax are given a ranking of 1. The scores/rankings for the District of Columbia do not affect other states. The 2016 index represents the tax climate as of July 1, 2015 (the beginning of Fiscal Year 2016).
Source: Tax Foundation, State Business Tax Climate Index 2016

TRANSPORTATION

Means of Transportation to Work

Area	Car/Truck/Van		Public Transportation			Bicycle	Walked	Other Means	Worked at Home
	Drove Alone	Car-pooled	Bus	Subway	Railroad				
City	80.6	8.1	1.1	0.5	0.5	0.2	0.4	1.3	7.4
MSA[1]	76.0	9.1	3.6	0.5	0.2	0.9	2.1	1.1	6.4
U.S.	76.4	9.6	2.6	1.8	0.6	0.6	2.8	1.3	4.4

Note: Figures are percentages and cover workers 16 years of age and older; (1) Figures cover the Denver-Aurora-Lakewood, CO Metropolitan Statistical Area—see Appendix B for areas included
Source: U.S. Census Bureau, 2010-2014 American Community Survey 5-Year Estimates

Travel Time to Work

Area	Less Than 10 Minutes	10 to 19 Minutes	20 to 29 Minutes	30 to 44 Minutes	45 to 59 Minutes	60 to 89 Minutes	90 Minutes or More
City	9.7	24.5	22.8	25.7	9.6	4.6	3.0
MSA[1]	8.9	26.0	23.6	25.5	8.9	5.1	1.9
U.S.	13.3	29.6	21.0	20.2	7.7	5.7	2.6

Note: Figures are percentages and include workers 16 years old and over; (1) Figures cover the Denver-Aurora-Lakewood, CO Metropolitan Statistical Area—see Appendix B for areas included
Source: U.S. Census Bureau, 2010-2014 American Community Survey 5-Year Estimates

Freeway Travel Time Index

Area	1985	1990	1995	2000	2005	2010	2014
Urban Area Rank[1,2]	18	25	23	11	8	12	16
Urban Area Index[1]	1.13	1.14	1.19	1.27	1.32	1.29	1.30
Average Index[3]	1.09	1.11	1.14	1.17	1.20	1.19	1.20

Note: Freeway Travel Time Index—the ratio of travel time in the peak period to the travel time at free-flow conditions. For example, a value of 1.30 indicates a 20-minute free-flow trip takes 26 minutes in the peak (20 minutes x 1.30 = 26 minutes); (1) Covers the Denver-Aurora CO urban area; (2) Rank is based on 101 urban areas (#1 = highest travel time index); (3) Average of 101 urban areas
Source: Texas Transportation Institute, 2015 Urban Mobility Scorecard, August 2015

Freeway Commuter Stress Index

Area	1985	1990	1995	2000	2005	2010	2014
Urban Area Rank[1,2]	24	28	24	15	11	16	16
Urban Area Index[1]	1.18	1.19	1.25	1.33	1.38	1.35	1.36
Average Index[3]	1.13	1.16	1.19	1.22	1.25	1.24	1.25

Note: The Freeway Commuter Stress Index is the same as the Freeway Travel Time Index (see table above) except that it includes only the travel in the peak directions during the peak periods; the TTI includes travel in all directions during the peak period. Thus, the CSI is more indicative of the work trip experienced by each commuter on a daily basis. (1) Covers the Denver-Aurora CO urban area; (2) Rank is based on 101 urban areas (#1 = highest stress index); (3) Average of 101 urban areas

Source: Texas Transportation Institute, 2015 Urban Mobility Scorecard, August 2015

Living Environment

COST OF LIVING

Cost of Living Index

Composite Index	Groceries	Housing	Utilities	Trans-portation	Health Care	Misc. Goods/ Services
109.7	99.2	130.7	94.6	98.2	107.8	104.9

Note: The Cost of Living Index measures regional differences in the cost of consumer goods and services, excluding taxes and non-consumer expenditures, for professional and managerial households in the top income quintile. It is based on more than 50,000 prices covering almost 60 different items for which prices are collected three times a year by chambers of commerce, economic development organizations or university applied economic centers in each participating urban area. The numbers shown should be read as a percentage above or below the national average of 100. For example, a value of 115.4 in the groceries column indicates that grocery prices are 15.4% higher than the national average. Small differences in the index numbers should not be interpreted as significant; Figures cover the Denver CO urban area.
Source: The Council for Community and Economic Research, ACCRA Cost of Living Index, 2015

Grocery Prices

Area[1]	T-Bone Steak ($/pound)	Frying Chicken ($/pound)	Whole Milk ($/half gal.)	Eggs ($/dozen)	Orange Juice ($/64 oz.)	Coffee ($/11.5 oz.)
City[2]	10.92	1.50	1.99	2.44	4.05	5.49
Avg.	10.99	1.43	2.25	2.26	3.58	4.48
Min.	7.16	0.98	1.30	1.35	2.88	2.98
Max.	14.13	2.43	3.85	4.81	6.39	7.56

Note: (1) Values for the local area are compared with the average, minimum and maximum values for all 292 areas in the Cost of Living Index; (2) Figures cover the Denver CO urban area; **T-Bone Steak** *(price per pound);* **Frying Chicken** *(price per pound, whole fryer);* **Whole Milk** *(half gallon carton);* **Eggs** *(price per dozen, Grade A, large);* **Orange Juice** *(64 oz. Tropicana or Florida Natural);* **Coffee** *(11.5 oz. can, vacuum-packed, Maxwell House, Hills Bros, or Folgers).*
Source: The Council for Community and Economic Research, ACCRA Cost of Living Index, 2015

Housing and Utility Costs

Area[1]	New Home Price ($)	Apartment Rent ($/month)	All Electric ($/month)	Part Electric ($/month)	Other Energy ($/month)	Telephone ($/month)
City[2]	398,144	1,306	-	92.34	59.91	28.60
Avg.	312,874	945	179.30	95.07	72.96	28.11
Min.	178,682	479	116.28	43.14	26.46	10.01
Max.	1,472,476	3,984	504.25	189.44	421.11	43.06

Note: (1) Values for the local area are compared with the average, minimum and maximum values for all 292 areas in the Cost of Living Index; (2) Figures cover the Denver CO urban area; **New Home Price** *(2,400 sf living area, 8,000 sf lot, in urban area with full utilities);* **Apartment Rent** *(950 sf 2 bedroom/1.5 or 2 bath, unfurnished, excluding all utilities except water);* **All Electric** *(average monthly cost for an all-electric home);* **Part Electric** *(average monthly cost for a part-electric home);* **Other Energy** *(average monthly cost for natural gas, fuel oil, coal, wood, and any other forms of energy except electricity);* **Telephone** *(price includes basic monthly rate for a private residential line plus additional local usage charges incurred by a family of four).*
Source: The Council for Community and Economic Research, ACCRA Cost of Living Index, 2015

Health Care, Transportation, and Other Costs

Area[1]	Doctor ($/visit)	Dentist ($/visit)	Optometrist ($/visit)	Gasoline ($/gallon)	Beauty Salon ($/visit)	Men's Shirt ($)
City[2]	125.38	97.33	101.85	2.29	35.84	29.52
Avg.	105.15	89.02	99.78	2.38	35.30	28.10
Min.	66.87	56.09	48.53	1.95	18.91	13.38
Max.	182.34	150.36	228.33	4.09	67.91	63.80

Note: (1) Values for the local area are compared with the average, minimum and maximum values for all 292 areas in the Cost of Living Index; (2) Figures cover the Denver CO urban area; **Doctor** *(general practitioners routine exam of an established patient);* **Dentist** *(adult teeth cleaning and periodic oral examination);* **Optometrist** *(full vision eye exam for established adult patient);* **Gasoline** *(one gallon regular unleaded, national brand, including all taxes, cash price at self-service pump if available);* **Beauty Salon** *(woman's shampoo, trim, and blow-dry);* **Men's Shirt** *(cotton/polyester dress shirt, pinpoint weave, long sleeves).*
Source: The Council for Community and Economic Research, ACCRA Cost of Living Index, 2015

HOUSING

House Price Index (HPI)

Area	National Ranking[2]	Quarterly Change (%)	One-Year Change (%)	Five-Year Change (%)
MSA[1]	8	1.50	13.50	41.30
U.S.[3]	–	1.45	5.76	22.85

Note: The HPI is a weighted repeat sales index. It measures average price changes in repeat sales or refinancings on the same properties. This information is obtained by reviewing repeat mortgage transactions on single-family properties whose mortgages have been purchased or securitized by Fannie Mae or Freddie Mac in January 1975; (1) Denver-Aurora-Lakewood Metropolitan Statistical Area—see Appendix B for areas included; (2) Rankings are based on annual percentage change for all metro areas containing at least 15,000 transactions over the last 10 years and ranges from 1 to 266; (3) figures based on a weighted average of Census Division estimates using a seasonally adjusted, purchase-only index; all figures are for the period ending December 31, 2015

Source: Federal Housing Finance Agency, House Price Index, February 25, 2016

Median Single-Family Home Prices

Area	2013	2014	2015[p]	Percent Change 2014 to 2015
MSA[1]	280.6	310.2	353.6	14.0
U.S. Average	197.4	208.9	223.9	7.2

Note: Figures are median sales prices of existing single-family homes in thousands of dollars; (p) preliminary; n/a not available; (1) Denver-Aurora-Lakewood, CO Metropolitan Statistical Area—see Appendix B for areas included

Source: National Association of Realtors, Median Sales Price of Existing Single-Family Homes for Metropolitan Areas, 4th Quarter 2015

Qualifying Income Based on Median Sales Price of Existing Single-Family Homes

Area	With 5% Down ($)	With 10% Down ($)	With 20% Down ($)
MSA[1]	78,629	74,491	66,214
U.S. Average	49,535	46,928	41,714

Note: Figures are preliminary; Qualifying income is based on a mortgage rate of 4.1%. Monthly principal and interest payment is limited to 25% of income; n/a not available; (1) Denver-Aurora-Lakewood, CO Metropolitan Statistical Area—see Appendix B for areas included

Source: National Association of Realtors, Qualifying Income Based on Median Sales Price of Existing Single-Family Homes for Metropolitan Areas, 4th Quarter 2015

Median Apartment Condo-Coop Home Prices

Area	2013	2014	2015[p]	Percent Change 2014 to 2015
MSA[1]	n/a	n/a	n/a	n/a
U.S. Average	194.9	204.3	210.7	3.1

Note: Figures are median sales prices of existing apartment condo-coop homes in thousands of dollars; (p) preliminary; n/a not available; (1) Denver-Aurora-Lakewood, CO Metropolitan Statistical Area—see Appendix B for areas included

Source: National Association of Realtors, Median Sales Price of Existing Apartment Condo-Coop Homes for Metropolitan Areas, 4th Quarter 2015

Gross Monthly Rent

Area	Under $200	$200 -299	$300 -499	$500 -749	$750 -999	$1,000 -1,499	$1,500 and up	Median ($)
City	1.6	0.0	0.6	2.7	22.2	43.8	28.9	1,219
MSA[1]	1.3	2.4	3.0	16.9	26.8	32.9	16.9	998
U.S.	1.5	3.2	7.4	21.0	24.1	26.9	15.9	920

Note: Figures are percentages except for Median; Gross rent is the contract rent plus the estimated average monthly cost of utilities (electricity, gas, and water and sewer) and fuels (oil, coal, kerosene, wood, etc.) if these are paid by the renter (or paid for the renter by someone else); (1) Figures cover the Denver-Aurora-Lakewood, CO Metropolitan Statistical Area—see Appendix B for areas included

Source: U.S. Census Bureau, 2010-2014 American Community Survey 5-Year Estimates

Homeownership Rate

Area	2008 (%)	2009 (%)	2010 (%)	2011 (%)	2012 (%)	2013 (%)	2014 (%)	2015 (%)
MSA[1]	66.9	65.3	65.7	63.0	61.8	61.0	61.9	61.6
U.S.	67.8	67.4	66.9	66.1	65.4	65.1	64.5	63.7

Note: (1) Figures cover the Denver-Aurora-Lakewood, CO Metropolitan Statistical Area—see Appendix B for areas included
Source: U.S. Census Bureau, Housing Vacancies and Homeownership Annual Statistics: 2015

Year Housing Structure Built

Area	2010 or Later	2000 -2009	1990 -1999	1980 -1989	1970 -1979	1960 -1969	1950 -1959	1940 -1949	Before 1940	Median Year
City	1.4	42.4	37.0	15.5	1.9	0.6	0.4	0.4	0.5	1998
MSA[1]	1.1	18.4	15.5	15.0	19.3	10.4	10.0	3.1	7.1	1980
U.S.	1.0	14.9	13.9	13.8	15.8	11.0	10.8	5.4	13.3	1976

Note: Figures are percentages except for Median Year; (1) Figures cover the Denver-Aurora-Lakewood, CO Metropolitan Statistical Area—see Appendix B for areas included
Source: U.S. Census Bureau, 2010-2014 American Community Survey 5-Year Estimates

HEALTH

Health Risk Data

Category	MSA[1] (%)	U.S. (%)
Adults aged 18–64 who have any kind of health care coverage	79.0	79.6
Adults who reported being in good or excellent health	85.0	83.1
Adults who are current smokers	18.0	19.6
Adults who are heavy drinkers[2]	7.5	6.1
Adults who are binge drinkers[3]	21.6	16.9
Adults who are overweight (BMI 25.0 - 29.9)	35.5	35.8
Adults who are obese (BMI 30.0 - 99.8)	20.1	27.6
Adults who participated in any physical activities in the past month	82.9	77.1
Adults 50+ who have ever had a sigmoidoscopy or colonoscopy	68.0	67.3
Women aged 40+ who have had a mammogram within the past two years	70.5	74.0
Men aged 40+ who have had a PSA test within the past two years	41.8	45.2
Adults aged 65+ who have had flu shot within the past year	68.3	60.1
Adults who always wear a seatbelt	94.2	93.8

Note: Data as of 2012 unless otherwise noted; (1) Figures cover the Denver-Aurora, CO Metropolitan Statistical Area—see Appendix B for areas included; (2) Heavy drinkers are classified as males having more than two drinks per day or females having more than one drink per day; (3) Binge drinkers are classified as males having five or more drinks on one occasion or females having four or more drinks on one occasion
Source: Centers for Disease Control and Prevention, Behaviorial Risk Factor Surveillance System, SMART: Selected Metropolitan/Micropolitan Area Risk Trends, 2012 (Note: the CDC has discontinued this dataset but will be releasing a replacement in mid-2016)

Chronic Health Indicators

Category	MSA[1] (%)	U.S. (%)
Adults who have ever been told they had a heart attack	3.0	4.5
Adults who have ever been told they had a stroke	1.8	2.9
Adults who have been told they currently have asthma	9.6	8.9
Adults who have ever been told they have arthritis	21.6	25.7
Adults who have ever been told they have diabetes[2]	7.4	9.7
Adults who have ever been told they had skin cancer	6.0	5.7
Adults who have ever been told they had any other types of cancer	5.9	6.5
Adults who have ever been told they have COPD	4.5	6.2
Adults who have ever been told they have kidney disease	2.0	2.5
Adults who have ever been told they have a form of depression	17.3	18.0

Note: Data as of 2012 unless otherwise noted; (1) Figures cover the Denver-Aurora, CO Metropolitan Statistical Area—see Appendix B for areas included; (2) Figures do not include pregnancy-related, borderline, or pre-diabetes
Source: Centers for Disease Control and Prevention, Behaviorial Risk Factor Surveillance System, SMART: Selected Metropolitan/Micropolitan Area Risk Trends, 2012 (Note: the CDC has discontinued this dataset but will be releasing a replacement in mid-2016)

Mortality Rates for the Top 10 Causes of Death in the U.S.

ICD-10[a] Sub-Chapter	ICD-10[a] Code	Age-Adjusted Mortality Rate[1] per 100,000 population County[2]	U.S.
Malignant neoplasms	C00-C97	111.0	163.6
Ischaemic heart diseases	I20-I25	43.6	102.2
Other forms of heart disease	I30-I51	32.1	50.1
Chronic lower respiratory diseases	J40-J47	27.7	41.4
Organic, including symptomatic, mental disorders	F01-F09	27.9	38.5
Cerebrovascular diseases	I60-I69	24.3	36.5
Other external causes of accidental injury	W00-X59	27.2	27.5
Other degenerative diseases of the nervous system	G30-G31	40.4	26.3
Diabetes mellitus	E10-E14	8.1	21.1
Hypertensive diseases	I10-I15	8.8	19.7

Note: (a) ICD-10 = International Classification of Diseases 10th Revision; (1) Mortality rates are a three year average covering 2012-2014; (2) Figures cover COUNTY NOT FOUND!!!!!!.
Source: Centers for Disease Control and Prevention, National Center for Health Statistics. Underlying Cause of Death 1999-2014 on CDC WONDER Online Database, released 2015.

Mortality Rates for Selected Causes of Death

ICD-10[a] Sub-Chapter	ICD-10[a] Code	Age-Adjusted Mortality Rate[1] per 100,000 population County[2]	U.S.
Assault	X85-Y09	Suppressed	5.1
Diseases of the liver	K70-K76	8.1	13.5
Human immunodeficiency virus (HIV) disease	B20-B24	Suppressed	2.1
Influenza and pneumonia	J09-J18	9.6	15.2
Intentional self-harm	X60-X84	17.1	12.7
Malnutrition	E40-E46	Suppressed	0.9
Obesity and other hyperalimentation	E65-E68	Suppressed	1.9
Renal failure	N17-N19	8.3	13.0
Transport accidents	V01-V99	5.0	11.6
Viral hepatitis	B15-B19	Suppressed	2.1

Note: (a) ICD-10 = International Classification of Diseases 10th Revision; (1) Mortality rates are a three year average covering 2012-2014; (2) Figures cover COUNTY NOT FOUND!!!!!!; Data are Suppressed when the data meet the criteria for confidentiality constraints; Mortality rates are flagged as Unreliable when the rate would be calculated with a numerator of 20 or less.
Source: Centers for Disease Control and Prevention, National Center for Health Statistics. Underlying Cause of Death 1999-2014 on CDC WONDER Online Database, released 2015.

Health Insurance Coverage

Area	With Health Insurance	With Private Health Insurance	With Public Health Insurance	Without Health Insurance	Population Under Age 18 Without Health Insurance
City	94.5	89.5	11.2	5.5	2.7
MSA[1]	86.2	70.1	24.7	13.8	8.3
U.S.	85.8	65.8	31.1	14.2	7.1

Note: Figures are percentages that cover the civilian noninstitutionalized population; (1) Figures cover the Denver-Aurora-Lakewood, CO Metropolitan Statistical Area—see Appendix B for areas included
Source: U.S. Census Bureau, 2010-2014 American Community Survey 5-Year Estimates

Number of Medical Professionals

Area	MDs[3]	DOs[3,4]	Dentists	Podiatrists	Chiropractors	Optometrists
County[1] (number)	606	98	195	13	106	62
County[1] (rate[2])	197.8	32.0	62.0	4.1	33.7	19.7
U.S. (rate[2])	272.5	20.9	64.7	5.8	25.9	15.2

Note: Data as of 2014 unless noted; (1) Data covers Douglas County; (2) Rate per 100,000 population; (3) Data as of 2013 and includes all active, non-federal physicians; (4) Doctor of Osteopathic Medicine
Source: U.S. Department of Health and Human Services, Health Resources and Services Administration, Bureau of Health Professions, Area Resource File (ARF) 2014-2015

Best Hospitals

According to *U.S. News,* the Denver-Aurora-Lakewood, CO metro area is home to four of the best hospitals in the U.S.: **National Jewish Health, Denver-University of Colorado Hospital** (1 specialty); **University of Colorado Hospital** (11 specialties); **Porter Adventist Hospital** (1 specialty); **Craig Hospital** (1 specialty). The hospitals listed were nationally ranked in at least one adult specialty. Only 137 hospitals nationwide were nationally ranked in one or more specialties. Fifteen hospitals in the U.S. made the Honor Roll with high scores in at least six specialties. *U.S. News Online, "America's Best Children's Hospitals 2015-16"*

According to *U.S. News,* the Denver-Aurora-Lakewood, CO metro area is home to one of the best children's hospitals in the U.S.: **Children's Hospital Colorado** (Honor Roll/9 specialties). The hospital listed was highly ranked in at least one pediatric specialty. Eighty-three children's hospitals in the U.S. were nationally ranked in at least one specialty. Twelve children's hospitals in the U.S. made the Honor Roll with high scores in at least three specialties. *U.S. News Online, "America's Best Children's Hospitals 2015-16"*

EDUCATION

Public School District Statistics

District Name	Schls	Pupils	Pupil/ Teacher Ratio	Minority Pupils[1] (%)	Free Lunch Eligible[2] (%)	IEP[3] (%)
Douglas County SD No. Re 1	85	66,230	20.2	24.3	9.0	n/a
School District No. C-1	8	2,621	18.0	14.2	13.6	n/a

Note: Table includes school districts with 100 or more students; (1) Percentage of students that are not non-Hispanic white; (2) Percentage of students that are eligible for the free lunch program; (3) Percentage of students that have an Individualized Education Program.

Source: U.S. Department of Education, National Center for Education Statistics, Common Core of Data, Local Education Agency (School District) Universe Survey: School Year 2013-2014; U.S. Department of Education, National Center for Education Statistics, Common Core of Data, Public Elementary/Secondary School Universe Survey: School Year 2013-2014

Highest Level of Education

Area	Less than H.S.	H.S. Diploma	Some College, No Deg.	Associate Degree	Bachelor's Degree	Master's Degree	Prof. School Degree	Doctorate Degree
City	2.4	14.1	22.5	9.3	37.0	11.2	2.1	1.3
MSA[1]	10.2	20.8	21.7	7.5	25.6	10.4	2.4	1.4
U.S.	13.7	28.0	21.2	7.9	18.3	7.8	2.0	1.3

Note: Figures cover persons age 25 and over; (1) Figures cover the Denver-Aurora-Lakewood, CO Metropolitan Statistical Area—see Appendix B for areas included

Source: U.S. Census Bureau, 2010-2014 American Community Survey 5-Year Estimates

Educational Attainment by Race

Area	High School Graduate or Higher (%)					Bachelor's Degree or Higher (%)				
	Total	White	Black	Asian	Hisp.[2]	Total	White	Black	Asian	Hisp.[2]
City	97.6	97.9	77.5	98.0	90.7	51.6	52.2	34.5	62.9	33.4
MSA[1]	89.8	91.5	89.6	85.0	65.9	39.8	42.1	24.3	46.9	13.3
U.S.	86.3	88.4	83.2	85.8	64.1	29.3	30.6	19.0	50.9	13.9

Note: Figures shown cover persons 25 years old and over; (1) Figures cover the Denver-Aurora-Lakewood, CO Metropolitan Statistical Area—see Appendix B for areas included; (2) People of Hispanic origin can be of any race

Source: U.S. Census Bureau, 2010-2014 American Community Survey 5-Year Estimates

School Enrollment by Grade and Control

Area	Preschool (%)		Kindergarten (%)		Grades 1 - 4 (%)		Grades 5 - 8 (%)		Grades 9 - 12 (%)	
	Public	Private	Public	Private	Public	Private	Public	Private	Public	Private
City	50.7	49.3	92.5	7.5	91.8	8.2	93.1	6.9	93.8	6.2
MSA[1]	57.0	43.0	90.1	9.9	92.2	7.8	91.9	8.1	92.5	7.5
U.S.	57.4	42.6	87.8	12.2	89.8	10.2	89.9	10.1	90.6	9.4

Note: Figures shown cover persons 3 years old and over; (1) Figures cover the Denver-Aurora-Lakewood, CO Metropolitan Statistical Area—see Appendix B for areas included

Source: U.S. Census Bureau, 2010-2014 American Community Survey 5-Year Estimates

Average Salaries of Public School Classroom Teachers

Area	2013-14 Dollars	2013-14 Rank[1]	2014-15 Dollars	2014-15 Rank[1]	Percent Change 2013-14 to 2014-15	Percent Change 2004-05 to 2014-15
Colorado	49,615	31	49,828	34	0.43	13.4
U.S. Average	56,610	–	57,379	–	1.36	20.8

Note: (1) State rank ranges from 1 to 51 where 1 indicates highest salary.
Source: National Education Association, Rankings & Estimates: Rankings of the States 2014 and Estimates of School Statistics 2015, March 2015

Higher Education

Four-Year Colleges			Two-Year Colleges			Medical Schools[1]	Law Schools[2]	Voc/ Tech[3]
Public	Private Non-profit	Private For-profit	Public	Private Non-profit	Private For-profit			
0	0	1	0	0	1	1	0	0

Note: Figures cover institutions located within the city limits and include main campuses only; (1) includes schools accredited by the Liaison Committee on Medical Education and the American Osteopathic Association's Commission on Osteopathic College Accreditation; (2) includes ABA-accredited schools, schools with provisional ABA accreditation, and state accredited schools; (3) includes all schools with programs that are less than 2 years.
Source: National Center for Education Statistics, Integrated Postsecondary Education System (IPEDS), 2014-15; Association of American Medical Colleges, Member List, March 21, 2016; American Osteopathic Association, Member List, March 21, 2016; Law School Admission Council, Official Guide to ABA-Approved Law Schools Online, March 21, 2016; Wikipedia, List of Medical Schools in the United States, March 21, 2016; Wikipedia, List of Law Schools in the United States, March 21, 2016

According to *U.S. News & World Report,* the Denver-Aurora-Lakewood, CO metro area is home to three of the best national universities in the U.S.: **Colorado School of Mines** (#75 tie); **University of Denver** (#86 tie); **University of Colorado–Denver** (#199 tie). The indicators used to capture academic quality fall into a number of categories: assessment by administrators at peer institutions; retention of students; faculty resources; student selectivity; financial resources; alumni giving; high school counselor ratings of colleges; and graduation rate. *U.S. News & World Report, "America's Best Colleges 2016"*

According to *U.S. News & World Report,* the Denver-Aurora-Lakewood, CO metro area is home to one of the top 100 law schools in the U.S.: **University of Denver, Sturm College of Law** (#72 tie). The rankings are based on a weighted average of 12 measures of quality: peer assessment score; assessment score by lawyers/judges; median LSAT scores; median undergrad GPA; acceptance rate; employment rates for graduates; placement success; bar passage rate; faculty resources; expenditures per student; student/faculty ratio; and library resources. *U.S. News & World Report, "America's Best Graduate Schools, Law, 2017"*

According to *U.S. News & World Report,* the Denver-Aurora-Lakewood, CO metro area is home to one of the top 75 medical schools for research in the U.S.: **University of Colorado, School of Medicine** (#35 tie). The rankings are based on a weighted average of 11 measures of quality; quality assessment; peer assessment score; assessment score by residency directors; research activity; total research activity; average research activity per faculty member; student selectivity; median MCAT total score; median undergraduate GPA; acceptance rate; and faculty resources. *U.S. News & World Report, "America's Best Graduate Schools, Medical, 2017"*

PRESIDENTIAL ELECTION

2012 Presidential Election Results

Area	Obama (%)	Romney (%)	Other (%)
Douglas County	36.0	62.6	1.4
U.S.	51.0	47.2	1.8

Note: Results may not add to 100% due to rounding
Source: Dave Leip's Atlas of U.S. Presidential Elections

EMPLOYERS

Major Employers

Company Name	Industry
Arvada House Preservation	Apartment building operators
Centura Health Corporation	General medical & surgical hospitals
Colorado Department of Transportation	Regulation, administration of transportation
County of Jefferson	County commissioner
DISH Network Corporation	Cable & other pay television services
Gart Bros Sporting Goods Company	Sporting goods & bicycle shops
HCA Healthone	General medical & surgical hospitals
IBM	Printers, computer
Level 3 Communications	Telephone communication, except radio
Lockheed Martin Corporation	Aircraft
Lockheed Martin Corporation	Search & navigation equipment
Lockheed Martin Corporation	Space vehicles, complete
Mormon Church	Mormon church
MWH/Fni Joint Venture	Engineering services
Newmont Gold Company	Gold ores mining
Noodles and Company	Eating places
Strasburg Telephone Company	Telephone communication, except radio
Synergy Services	Payroll accounting service
TW Telecom Holdings	Telephone communication, except radio
Western Union Financial Services	Electronic funds transfer network, including switching

Note: Companies shown are located within the Denver-Aurora-Lakewood, CO Metropolitan Statistical Area.
Source: Hoovers.com; Wikipedia

PUBLIC SAFETY

Crime Rate

Area	All Crimes	Violent Crimes				Property Crimes		
		Murder	Rape[3]	Robbery	Aggrav. Assault	Burglary	Larceny -Theft	Motor Vehicle Theft
City	1,363.6	0.0	24.3	8.1	97.1	161.9	1,023.7	48.6
Metro[1]	n/a	2.8	54.9	75.0	198.5	n/a	1,891.6	292.5
U.S.	2,971.8	4.5	36.6	102.2	232.5	542.5	1,837.3	216.2

Note: Figures are crimes per 100,000 population; (1) Figures cover the Denver-Aurora-Lakewood, CO Metropolitan Statistical Area—see Appendix B for areas included; (3) The city and U.S. figures shown were reported using the revised Uniform Crime Reporting (UCR) definition of rape. The suburban and metro area figures shown are an aggregate total of the data submitted using both the revised and legacy UCR definitions.
Source: FBI Uniform Crime Reports, 2014

Hate Crimes

Area	Number of Quarters Reported	Number of Incidents per Bias Motivation						
		Race	Religion	Sexual Orientation	Ethnicity	Disability	Gender	Gender Identity
City	4	0	0	0	0	0	0	0
U.S.	4	2,568	1,014	1,017	648	84	33	98

Source: Federal Bureau of Investigation, Hate Crime Statistics 2014

Identity Theft Consumer Complaints

Area	Complaints	Complaints per 100,000 Population	Rank[2]
MSA[1]	3,648	132.4	90
U.S.	490,220	152.4	-

Note: (1) Figures cover the Denver-Aurora-Lakewood, CO Metropolitan Statistical Area—see Appendix B for areas included; (2) Rank ranges from 1 to 379 where 1 indicates greatest number of identity theft complaints per 100,000 population
Source: Federal Trade Commission, Consumer Sentinel Network Data Book for January–December 2015

Fraud and Other Consumer Complaints

Area	Complaints	Complaints per 100,000 Population	Rank[2]
MSA[1]	12,974	471.1	31
U.S.	2,593,159	806.0	-

Note: (1) Figures cover the Denver-Aurora-Lakewood, CO Metropolitan Statistical Area—see Appendix B for areas included; (2) Rank ranges from 1 to 379 where 1 indicates greatest number of identity theft complaints per 100,000 population
Source: Federal Trade Commission, Consumer Sentinel Network Data Book for January–December 2015

RECREATION

Culture

Dance[1]	Theatre[1]	Instrumental Music[1]	Vocal Music[1]	Series and Festivals	Museums and Art Galleries[2]	Zoos and Aquariums[3]
0	0	0	0	0	0	0

Note: (1) Professional perfoming groups; (2) Based on organizations with SIC code 8412; (3) AZA-accredited
Source: The Grey House Performing Arts Directory, 2015-16; Association of Zoos & Aquariums, AZA Member Zoos & Aquariums, March 25, 2016; www.AccuLeads.com, March 29, 2016

Professional Sports Teams

Team Name	League	Year Established
Colorado Avalanche	National Hockey League (NHL)	1995
Colorado Rapids	Major League Soccer (MLS)	1996
Colorado Rockies	Major League Baseball (MLB)	1993
Denver Broncos	National Football League (NFL)	1960
Denver Nuggets	National Basketball Association (NBA)	1967

Note: Includes teams located in the Denver-Aurora-Lakewood, CO Metropolitan Statistical Area.
Source: Wikipedia, Major Professional Sports Teams of the United States and Canada, March 24, 2016

CLIMATE

Average and Extreme Temperatures

Temperature	Jan	Feb	Mar	Apr	May	Jun	Jul	Aug	Sep	Oct	Nov	Dec	Yr.
Extreme High (°F)	73	76	84	90	93	102	103	100	97	89	79	75	103
Average High (°F)	43	47	52	62	71	81	88	86	77	67	52	45	64
Average Temp. (°F)	30	34	39	48	58	67	73	72	63	52	39	32	51
Average Low (°F)	16	20	25	34	44	53	59	57	48	37	25	18	37
Extreme Low (°F)	-25	-25	-10	-2	22	30	43	41	17	3	-8	-25	-25

Note: Figures cover the years 1948-1992
Source: National Climatic Data Center, International Station Meteorological Climate Summary, 9/96

Average Precipitation/Snowfall/Humidity

Precip./Humidity	Jan	Feb	Mar	Apr	May	Jun	Jul	Aug	Sep	Oct	Nov	Dec	Yr.
Avg. Precip. (in.)	0.6	0.6	1.3	1.7	2.5	1.7	1.9	1.5	1.1	1.0	0.9	0.6	15.5
Avg. Snowfall (in.)	9	7	14	9	2	Tr	0	0	2	4	9	8	63
Avg. Rel. Hum. 5am (%)	62	65	67	66	70	68	67	68	66	63	66	63	66
Avg. Rel. Hum. 5pm (%)	49	44	40	35	38	34	34	34	32	34	47	50	39

Note: Figures cover the years 1948-1992; Tr = Trace amounts (<0.05 in. of rain; <0.5 in. of snow)
Source: National Climatic Data Center, International Station Meteorological Climate Summary, 9/96

Weather Conditions

Temperature			Daytime Sky			Precipitation		
10°F & below	32°F & below	90°F & above	Clear	Partly cloudy	Cloudy	0.01 inch or more precip.	0.1 inch or more snow/ice	Thunder-storms
24	155	33	99	177	89	90	38	39

Note: Figures are average number of days per year and cover the years 1948-1992
Source: National Climatic Data Center, International Station Meteorological Climate Summary, 9/96

HAZARDOUS WASTE

Superfund Sites

Parker has no sites on the EPA's Superfund Final National Priorities List. There are a total of 1,323 Superfund sites on the list in the U.S. *U.S. Environmental Protection Agency, Final National Priorities List, March 18, 2016*

AIR & WATER QUALITY

Air Quality Trends: Ozone

	1990	1995	2000	2005	2010	2011	2012	2013	2014
MSA[1]	0.074	0.069	0.069	0.073	0.070	0.076	0.078	0.078	0.072

Note: (1) Data covers the Denver-Aurora-Lakewood, CO Metropolitan Statistical Area—see Appendix B for areas included. The values shown are the composite ozone concentration averages among trend sites based on the highest fourth daily maximum 8-hour concentration in parts per million. These trends are based on sites having an adequate record of monitoring data during the trend period. Data from exceptional events are included.

Source: U.S. Environmental Protection Agency, Air Quality Monitoring Information, "Air Quality Trends by City, 1990-2014"

Air Quality Index

Area	Percent of Days when Air Quality was...[2]					AQI Statistics[2]	
	Good	Moderate	Unhealthy for Sensitive Groups	Unhealthy	Very Unhealthy	Maximum	Median
MSA[1]	35.9	59.5	4.7	0.0	0.0	146	54

Note: (1) Data covers the Denver-Aurora-Lakewood, CO Metropolitan Statistical Area—see Appendix B for areas included; (2) Based on 365 days with AQI data in 2015. Air Quality Index (AQI) is an index for reporting daily air quality. EPA calculates the AQI for five major air pollutants regulated by the Clean Air Act: ground-level ozone, particle pollution (aka particulate matter), carbon monoxide, sulfur dioxide, and nitrogen dioxide. The AQI runs from 0 to 500. The higher the AQI value, the greater the level of air pollution and the greater the health concern. There are six AQI categories: "Good" AQI is between 0 and 50. Air quality is considered satisfactory; "Moderate" AQI is between 51 and 100. Air quality is acceptable; "Unhealthy for Sensitive Groups" When AQI values are between 101 and 150, members of sensitive groups may experience health effects; "Unhealthy" When AQI values are between 151 and 200 everyone may begin to experience health effects; "Very Unhealthy" AQI values between 201 and 300 trigger a health alert; "Hazardous" AQI values over 300 trigger warnings of emergency conditions (not shown).

Source: U.S. Environmental Protection Agency, Air Quality Index Report, 2015

Air Quality Index Pollutants

Area	Percent of Days when AQI Pollutant was...[2]					
	Carbon Monoxide	Nitrogen Dioxide	Ozone	Sulfur Dioxide	Particulate Matter 2.5	Particulate Matter 10
MSA[1]	0.0	28.2	49.6	0.0	20.0	2.2

Note: (1) Data covers the Denver-Aurora-Lakewood, CO Metropolitan Statistical Area—see Appendix B for areas included; (2) Based on 365 days with AQI data in 2015. The Air Quality Index (AQI) is an index for reporting daily air quality. EPA calculates the AQI for five major air pollutants regulated by the Clean Air Act: ground-level ozone, particle pollution (also known as particulate matter), carbon monoxide, sulfur dioxide, and nitrogen dioxide. The AQI runs from 0 to 500. The higher the AQI value, the greater the level of air pollution and the greater the health concern.

Source: U.S. Environmental Protection Agency, Air Quality Index Report, 2015

Maximum Air Pollutant Concentrations: Particulate Matter, Ozone, CO and Lead

	Particulate Matter 10 (ug/m^3)	Particulate Matter 2.5 Wtd AM (ug/m^3)	Particulate Matter 2.5 24-Hr (ug/m^3)	Ozone (ppm)	Carbon Monoxide (ppm)	Lead (ug/m^3)
MSA[1] Level	97	10	29	0.077	2	0.03
NAAQS[2]	150	15	35	0.075	9	0.15
Met NAAQS[2]	Yes	Yes	Yes	No	Yes	Yes

Note: (1) Data covers the Denver-Aurora-Lakewood, CO Metropolitan Statistical Area—see Appendix B for areas included; Data from exceptional events are included; (2) National Ambient Air Quality Standards; ppm = parts per million; ug/m^3 = micrograms per cubic meter; n/a not available.
Concentrations: Particulate Matter 10 (coarse particulate)—highest second maximum 24-hour concentration; Particulate Matter 2.5 Wtd AM (fine particulate)—highest weighted annual mean concentration; Particulate Matter 2.5 24-Hour (fine particulate)—highest 98th percentile 24-hour concentration; Ozone—highest fourth daily maximum 8-hour concentration; Carbon Monoxide—highest second maximum non-overlapping 8-hour concentration; Lead—maximum running 3-month average
Source: U.S. Environmental Protection Agency, Air Quality Monitoring Information, "Air Quality Statistics by City, 2014"

Maximum Air Pollutant Concentrations: Nitrogen Dioxide and Sulfur Dioxide

	Nitrogen Dioxide AM (ppb)	Nitrogen Dioxide 1-Hr (ppb)	Sulfur Dioxide AM (ppb)	Sulfur Dioxide 1-Hr (ppb)	Sulfur Dioxide 24-Hr (ppb)
MSA[1] Level	25	77	n/a	18	n/a
NAAQS[2]	53	100	30	75	140
Met NAAQS[2]	Yes	Yes	n/a	Yes	n/a

Note: (1) Data covers the Denver-Aurora-Lakewood, CO Metropolitan Statistical Area—see Appendix B for areas included; Data from exceptional events are included; (2) National Ambient Air Quality Standards; ppm = parts per million; ug/m^3 = micrograms per cubic meter; n/a not available.
Concentrations: Nitrogen Dioxide AM—highest arithmetic mean concentration; Nitrogen Dioxide 1-Hr—highest 98th percentile 1-hour daily maximum concentration; Sulfur Dioxide AM—highest annual mean concentration; Sulfur Dioxide 1-Hr—highest 99th percentile 1-hour daily maximum concentration; Sulfur Dioxide 24-Hr—highest second maximum 24-hour concentration
Source: U.S. Environmental Protection Agency, Air Quality Monitoring Information, "Air Quality Statistics by City, 2014"

Drinking Water

Water System Name	Pop. Served	Primary Water Source Type	Violations[1]	
			Health Based	Monitoring/ Reporting
Parker WSD	40,500	Ground	0	0

Note: (1) Based on violation data from January 1, 2015 to December 31, 2015 (includes unresolved violations from earlier years)
Source: U.S. Environmental Protection Agency, Office of Ground Water and Drinking Water, Safe Drinking Water Information System (based on data extracted April 29, 2016)

Cheshire, Connecticut

Background

Cheshire, in west central Connecticut, is fourteen miles north of New Haven, and Yale University, and twenty-five miles south of the state capital at Hartford. Europeans first came into the area in the 1680s, and settled on the Quinnipiac River. The area was considered a hamlet of nearby Wallingford until 1705, when Thomas Brooks of Cheshire, England arrived and renamed it. Brooksvale, a section of the present-day city, was named in honor of the Cheshireman. A school was established in 1719, and in 1724 a Congregational church was built. St. Peter's Episcopal Church was organized in 1760 and, in 1780 Cheshire was recognized as a separate town.

In 1794, an Episcopal Academy of Connecticut (now Cheshire Academy) was established through the efforts of Samuel Seabury, the First Bishop of Connecticut.

The town was a trade and transportation hub for many years, first along the main route between Hartford and New Haven, and then as a stop along the Farmington Canal, which linked the Connecticut River to Long Island Sound. Sections of the canal have been preserved, as have many other historic structures.

The earliest settlers were farmers, and early industry was heavily based on copper and barite mining—an important element in glass and paint manufacture. A great number of miners were from Cornwall, England, and their numbers swelled the ranks of the local Methodist Church.

The Cheshire Manufacturing Company was established in 1850. Renamed the Ball and Socket Company, it became important during the Civil War.

A number of specialty metal industries survive today in Cheshire, a testimony to the traditions of an area that gave rise to the expression "Yankee ingenuity." The town is also active in contemporary technologies, such as Alexion Pharmaceuticals, founded by scientists connected to nearby Yale University. The city also maintains a tie to its deeper agricultural past by supporting its horticultural industry, which gave Cheshire the nickname "Bedding Plant Capital."

Hospitals and medical centers near Cheshire include Gaylord Hospital, Masonicare Health Center, and the Bradley Memorial campus of Hospital of Central Connecticut. Local Schools are highly regarded, and the town is home to the private Cheshire Academy, which was one of the first ten private academies to be founded in America. Colleges and universities within 15 miles of Cheshire include Quinnipiac College, Yale University, Naugatuck Valley Community College, Gateway Community College, Southern Connecticut State University, and Central Connecticut State.

The airports most convenient to Cheshire are Tweed-New Haven to the south, and Bradley International to the north. New York City's airports are also within convenient driving distance.

Rankings

General Rankings

- Cheshire was selected as one of the best places to live in the United States by *Money* magazine. The city ranked #45 out of 50. This year's list focused on cities with populations of 10,000 to 50,000. Beginning with a pool of over 3,000 candidates, editors looked at 39 data points, from local economy and housing market to schools and healthcare—and then sent reporters to look for a sense of community and other intangibles. *Money, "Best Places to Live: America's Best Small Towns, 2015" August, 2015*

Business/Finance Rankings

- The personal finance site NerdWallet analyzed 183 American metropolitan areas with populations over 250,000 and more than 15,000 businesses to rank where entrepreneurs find the most success. Criteria included area economy, annual income, housing cost, unemployment rate, and the success rate of area businesses. New Haven* ranked #130. *www.nerdwallet.com, "Best Places to Start a Business," April 27, 2015*
- The Brookings Institution ranked the 100 largest metro areas in the U.S. based on income inequality. New Haven* was ranked #9 (#1 = greatest ineqality). Criteria: the "95/20 ratio," a figure representing the income at which a household earns more than 95 percent of all other households, divided by the income at which a household earns more than only 20 percent of all other households. *Brookings Institution, "Income Inequality, 100 Largest U.S. Metro Areas, 2007-2014," January 14, 2016*
- The New Haven* metro area appeared on the Milken Institute "2015 Best Performing Cities" list. Rank: #149 out of 200 large metro areas. Criteria: job growth; wage and salary growth; high-tech output growth. *Milken Institute, "Best-Performing Cities 2015," December 2015*
- *Forbes* ranked the 200 most populous metro areas to determine the nation's "Best Places for Business and Careers." The New Haven* metro area was ranked #162. Criteria: costs (business and living); job growth (past and projected); income growth; educational attainment (college and high school); projected economic growth; cultural and recreational opportunities; net migration patterns; number of highly ranked colleges. *Forbes, "The Best Places for Business and Careers 2015," July 29, 2015*

Education Rankings

- Personal finance website *WalletHub* analyzed the 150 largest U.S. metropolitan statistical areas to determine where the most educated Americans are choosing to settle. Criteria: education quality and attainment gap; education levels; percentage of workers with degrees; public school rankings; quality and size of each metro area's universities. New Haven* was ranked #44 (#1 = most educated city). *www.WalletHub.com, "2015's Most and Least Educated Cities*

Environmental Rankings

- The New Haven* metro area came in at #151 for the relative comfort of its climate on Sperling's list of "chill cities," as measured by the Sperling Heat Index. All 361 metro areas are included. Criteria included daytime high temperatures, nighttime low temperatures, dew point, and relative humidity at the high temperatures. *www.bertsperling.com, "Sperling's Chill Cities," July 18, 2013*
- Sperling's BestPlaces assessed 379 metropolitan areas of the United States for the likelihood of dangerously extreme weather events or earthquakes. In general the Southeast and South-Central regions have the highest risk of weather extremes and earthquakes, while the Pacific Northwest enjoys the lowest risk. Of the least risky metropolitan areas, the New Haven* metro area was ranked #170. *www.bestplaces.net, "Safest Places from Natural Disasters," April 2011*
- New Haven* was identified as one of America's dirtiest metro areas by *Forbes*. The area ranked #7 out of 20. Criteria: air quality; water quality; toxic releases; superfund sites. *Forbes, "America's 20 Dirtiest Cities," December 10, 2012*

Health/Fitness Rankings

- New Haven* was identified as a "2016 Spring Allergy Capital." The area ranked #57 out of 100. Three groups of factors were used to identify the most severe cities for people with allergies during the spring season: annual pollen levels; medicine utilization; access to board-certified allergists. *Asthma and Allergy Foundation of America, "Spring Allergy Capitals 2016"*
- New Haven* was identified as a "2015 Asthma Capital." The area ranked #12 out of the nation's 100 largest metropolitan areas. Criteria: estimated prevalence; self-reported prevalence; crude death rate for asthma; annual pollen score; annual air quality; public smoking laws; number of board-certified asthma specialists; school inhaler access laws; rescue medication use; controller medication use; ER visits for asthma; uninsured rate; poverty rate. *Asthma and Allergy Foundation of America, "Asthma Capitals 2015"*
- The New Haven* metro area ranked #85 out of 190 in The Gallup-Healthways Well-Being Index. Criteria: purpose; social well being; financial health; community and physical health. Results are based on telephone interviews with adults, aged 18 and older, living in metropolitan areas in the 50 U.S. states and the District of Columbia. *Gallup-Healthways, "State of American Well-Being," February 23, 2016*

Real Estate Rankings

- The New Haven* metro area was identified as one of the 20 worst housing markets in the U.S. in 2015. The area ranked #17 out of 179 markets. Criteria: year-over-year change of median sales price of existing single-family homes between the 4th quarter of 2014 and the 4th quarter of 2015. *National Association of Realtors®, Median Sales Price of Existing Single-Family Homes for Metropolitan Areas, 4th Quarter 2015*
- The New Haven* metro area was identified as one of the 10 worst condo markets in the U.S. in 2015. The area ranked #7 out of 61 markets. Criteria: year-over-year change of median sales price of existing apartment condo-coop homes between the 4th quarter of 2014 and the 4th quarter of 2015. *National Association of Realtors®, Median Sales Price of Existing Apartment Condo-Coop Homes for Metropolitan Areas, 4th Quarter 2015*
- New Haven* was ranked #69 out of 225 metro areas in terms of housing affordability in 2015 by the National Association of Home Builders (#1 = most affordable). Criteria: the share of homes sold in that area affordable to a family earning the local median income, based on standard mortgage underwriting criteria. *National Association of Home Builders®, NAHB-Wells Fargo Housing Opportunity Index, 4th Quarter 2015*

Safety Rankings

- Cheshire was identified as one of the safest cities in America by NeighborhoodScout. The city ranked #33 out of 100. Criteria: number of violent and property crimes per 1,000 residents. The editors only considered cities with 25,000 or more residents. *NeighborhoodScout, "Safest Cities in America 2016"*
- The National Insurance Crime Bureau ranked 380 metro areas in the U.S. in terms of per capita rates of vehicle theft. The New Haven* metro area ranked #88 (#1 = highest rate). Criteria: number of vehicle theft offenses per 100,000 inhabitants in 2014. *National Insurance Crime Bureau, "Hot Spots 2014," June 24, 2015*

Seniors/Retirement Rankings

- From its Best Cities for Successful Aging indexes, the Milken Institute generated rankings for metropolitan areas, weighing data in eight categories—health care, wellness, living arrangements, transportation, financial characteristics, education and employment opportunities, community engagement, and overall livability. The New Haven* metro area was ranked #72 overall in the large metro area category. *Milken Institute, "Best Cities for Successful Aging, 2014"*

Miscellaneous Rankings

- The National Alliance to End Homelessness ranked the 100 most populous metro areas with the highest rate of homelessness. The New Haven* metro area ranked #79. Criteria: number of homeless people per 10,000 population in 2011. *National Alliance to End Homelessness, The State of Homelessness in America 2012*

Cheshire is located within the New Haven-Milford, CT Metropolitan Statistical Area.

Business Environment

CITY FINANCES

City Government Finances

Component	2012 ($000)	2012 ($ per capita)
Total Revenues	105,594	3,608
Total Expenditures	108,994	3,724
Debt Outstanding	57,173	1,953
Cash and Securities[1]	79,815	2,727

Note: (1) Cash and security holdings of a government at the close of its fiscal year, including those of its dependent agencies, utilities, and liquor stores.
Source: U.S Census Bureau, State & Local Government Finances 2012

City Government Revenue by Source

Source	2012 ($000)	2012 ($ per capita)
General Revenue		
From Federal Government	15	0
From State Government	21,424	732
From Local Governments	435	14
Taxes		
Property	76,299	2,607
Sales and Gross Receipts	0	0
Personal Income	0	0
Corporate Income	0	0
Motor Vehicle License	0	0
Other Taxes	560	19
Current Charges	6,585	225
Liquor Store	0	0
Utility	0	0
Employee Retirement	-709	-24

Source: U.S Census Bureau, State & Local Government Finances 2012

City Government Expenditures by Function

Function	2012 ($000)	2012 ($ per capita)	2012 (%)
General Direct Expenditures			
Air Transportation	0	0	0.0
Corrections	0	0	0.0
Education	64,416	2,201	59.1
Employment Security Administration	0	0	0.0
Financial Administration	1,836	62	1.6
Fire Protection	883	30	0.8
General Public Buildings	0	0	0.0
Governmental Administration, Other	1,072	36	0.9
Health	1,157	39	1.0
Highways	5,569	190	5.1
Hospitals	0	0	0.0
Housing and Community Development	0	0	0.0
Interest on General Debt	2,269	77	2.0
Judicial and Legal	245	8	0.2
Libraries	1,699	58	1.5
Parking	0	0	0.0
Parks and Recreation	1,435	49	1.3
Police Protection	4,857	165	4.4
Public Welfare	734	25	0.6
Sewerage	2,016	68	1.8
Solid Waste Management	0	0	0.0
Veterans' Services	0	0	0.0
Liquor Store	0	0	0.0
Utility	0	0	0.0
Employee Retirement	3,168	108	2.9

Source: U.S Census Bureau, State & Local Government Finances 2012

DEMOGRAPHICS

Population Growth

Area	1990 Census	2000 Census	2010 Census	2014* Estimate	Population Growth (%) 1990-2014	Population Growth (%) 2010-2014
City	25,684	28,543	29,261	29,272	14.0	0.0
MSA[1]	804,219	824,008	862,477	863,148	7.3	0.1
U.S.	248,709,873	281,421,906	308,745,538	314,107,084	26.3	1.7

Note: (1) Figures cover the New Haven-Milford, CT Metropolitan Statistical Area—see Appendix B for areas included; (*) 2010-2014 5-year estimated population
Source: U.S. Census Bureau, 1990 Census, Census 2000, Census 2010, 2010-2014 American Community Survey 5-Year Estimates

Household Size

Area	Persons in Household (%) One	Two	Three	Four	Five	Six	Seven or More	Average Household Size
City	23.0	32.6	17.7	17.8	6.2	2.0	0.4	2.72
MSA[1]	30.2	32.0	16.5	13.2	5.4	1.7	0.8	2.55
U.S.	27.5	33.5	15.8	13.1	6.0	2.3	1.4	2.64

Note: (1) Figures cover the New Haven-Milford, CT Metropolitan Statistical Area—see Appendix B for areas included
Source: U.S. Census Bureau, 2010-2014 American Community Survey 5-Year Estimates

Race

Area	White Alone[2] (%)	Black Alone[2] (%)	Asian Alone[2] (%)	AIAN[3] Alone[2] (%)	NHOPI[4] Alone[2] (%)	Other Race Alone[2] (%)	Two or More Races (%)
City	82.1	4.7	7.7	0.1	0.0	2.8	2.6
MSA[1]	75.2	12.7	3.7	0.2	0.0	5.6	2.5
U.S.	73.8	12.6	5.0	0.8	0.2	4.7	2.9

Note: (1) Figures cover the New Haven-Milford, CT Metropolitan Statistical Area—see Appendix B for areas included; (2) Alone is defined as not being in combination with one or more other races; (3) American Indian and Alaska Native; (4) Native Hawaiian and Other Pacific Islander
Source: U.S. Census Bureau, 2010-2014 American Community Survey 5-Year Estimates

Hispanic or Latino Origin

Area	Total (%)	Mexican (%)	Puerto Rican (%)	Cuban (%)	Other (%)
City	6.8	0.9	4.2	0.1	1.6
MSA[1]	16.0	1.9	9.8	0.3	4.0
U.S.	16.9	10.8	1.6	0.6	3.8

Note: Persons of Hispanic or Latino origin can be of any race; (1) Figures cover the New Haven-Milford, CT Metropolitan Statistical Area—see Appendix B for areas included
Source: U.S. Census Bureau, 2010-2014 American Community Survey 5-Year Estimates

Ancestry

Area	German	Irish	English	American	Italian	Polish	French[2]	Scottish	Dutch
City	11.0	22.6	8.9	2.7	26.3	8.8	3.7	1.6	0.3
MSA[1]	8.4	15.9	6.9	2.8	22.8	7.2	3.8	1.4	0.6
U.S.	14.9	10.8	8.0	7.1	5.5	3.0	2.7	1.7	1.4

Note: Figures are the percentage of the total population reporting a particular ancestry. The nine most commonly reported ancestries in the U.S. are shown. Figures include multiple ancestries (e.g. if a person reported being Irish and Italian, they were included in both columns); (1) Figures cover the New Haven-Milford, CT Metropolitan Statistical Area—see Appendix B for areas included; (2) Excludes Basque
Source: U.S. Census Bureau, 2010-2014 American Community Survey 5-Year Estimates

Foreign-Born Population

Area	Percent of Population Born in								
	Any Foreign Country	Asia	Mexico	Europe	Carribean	Central America[2]	South America	Africa	Canada
City	10.2	5.2	0.4	3.2	0.1	0.1	0.5	0.3	0.5
MSA[1]	11.7	3.1	1.0	3.3	1.3	0.5	1.6	0.7	0.3
U.S.	13.1	3.8	3.7	1.5	1.2	1.0	0.9	0.6	0.3

Note: (1) Figures cover the New Haven-Milford, CT Metropolitan Statistical Area—see Appendix B for areas included; (2) Excludes Mexico.
Source: U.S. Census Bureau, 2010-2014 American Community Survey 5-Year Estimates

Marital Status

Area	Never Married	Now Married[2]	Separated	Widowed	Divorced
City	30.2	54.6	0.6	6.1	8.4
MSA[1]	36.3	45.1	1.4	6.3	10.8
U.S.	32.5	48.4	2.2	5.9	10.9

Note: Figures are percentages and cover the population 15 years of age and older; (1) Figures cover the New Haven-Milford, CT Metropolitan Statistical Area—see Appendix B for areas included; (2) Excludes separated
Source: U.S. Census Bureau, 2010-2014 American Community Survey 5-Year Estimates

Disability Status

Area	All Ages	Under 18 Years Old	18 to 64 Years Old	65 Years and Over
City	8.5	2.7	5.7	28.4
MSA[1]	11.3	3.8	8.7	33.7
U.S.	12.3	4.1	10.2	36.3

Note: Figures show percent of the civilian noninstitutionalized population that reported having a disability. Disability status is determined from from six types of difficulty: vision, hearing, cognitive, ambulatory, self-care, and independent living. For children under 5 years old, hearing and vision difficulty are used to determine disability status. For children between the ages of 5 and 14, disability status is determined from hearing, vision, cognitive, ambulatory, and self-care difficulties. For people aged 15 years and older, they are considered to have a disability if they have difficulty with any one of the six difficulty types; (1) Figures cover the New Haven-Milford, CT Metropolitan Statistical Area—see Appendix B for areas included.
Source: U.S. Census Bureau, 2010-2014 American Community Survey 5-Year Estimates

Age

Area	Percent of Population									Median Age
	Under Age 5	Age 5–19	Age 20–34	Age 35–44	Age 45–54	Age 55–64	Age 65–74	Age 75–84	Age 85+	
City	3.4	21.9	14.9	12.8	18.0	14.5	7.8	4.3	2.5	42.9
MSA[1]	5.4	19.4	19.9	12.6	15.1	12.9	7.8	4.5	2.7	39.6
U.S.	6.4	19.9	20.6	13.0	14.1	12.3	7.6	4.3	1.9	37.4

Note: (1) Figures cover the New Haven-Milford, CT Metropolitan Statistical Area—see Appendix B for areas included
Source: U.S. Census Bureau, 2010-2014 American Community Survey 5-Year Estimates

Gender

Area	Males	Females	Males per 100 Females
City	15,170	14,102	107.6
MSA[1]	416,027	447,121	93.0
U.S.	154,515,159	159,591,925	96.8

Note: (1) Figures cover the New Haven-Milford, CT Metropolitan Statistical Area—see Appendix B for areas included
Source: U.S. Census Bureau, 2010-2014 American Community Survey 5-Year Estimates

Religious Groups by Family

Area	Catholic	Baptist	Non-Den.	Methodist[2]	Lutheran	LDS[3]	Pentecostal	Presbyterian[4]	Muslim[5]	Judaism
MSA[1]	35.3	1.4	1.9	1.5	0.6	0.3	1.0	2.2	0.5	1.2
U.S.	19.1	9.3	4.0	4.0	2.3	2.0	1.9	1.6	0.8	0.7

Note: Figures are the number of adherents as a percentage of the total population; (1) Figures cover the New Haven-Milford, CT Metropolitan Statistical Area—see Appendix B for areas included; (2) Methodist/Pietist; (3) Latter Day Saints; (4) Reformed; (5) Figures are estimates
Source: Association of Statisticians of American Religious Bodies, 2010 U.S. Religion Census: Religious Congregations & Membership Study

Religious Groups by Tradition

Area	Catholic	Evangelical Protestant	Mainline Protestant	Other Tradition	Black Protestant	Orthodox
MSA[1]	35.3	3.8	6.1	2.3	0.7	0.4
U.S.	19.1	16.2	7.3	4.3	1.6	0.3

Note: Figures are the number of adherents as a percentage of the total population; (1) Figures cover the New Haven-Milford, CT Metropolitan Statistical Area—see Appendix B for areas included
Source: Association of Statisticians of American Religious Bodies, 2010 U.S. Religion Census: Religious Congregations & Membership Study

ECONOMY

Gross Metropolitan Product

Area	2013	2014	2015	2016	Rank[2]
MSA[1]	44.2	45.7	47.2	49.2	60

Note: Figures are in billions of dollars; (1) Figures cover the New Haven-Milford, CT Metropolitan Statistical Area—see Appendix B for areas included; (2) Rank is based on 2016 data and ranges from 1 to 381
Source: The U.S. Conference of Mayors, U.S. Metro Economies: GMP and Employment 2014-2016, June 2015

Economic Growth

Area	2011-13 (%)	2014 (%)	2015 (%)	2016 (%)	Rank[2]
MSA[1]	1.3	1.7	1.9	2.1	262
U.S.	2.2	2.4	2.3	2.9	–

Note: Figures are real gross metropolitan product (GMP) growth rates and represent annual average percent change; (1) Figures cover the New Haven-Milford, CT Metropolitan Statistical Area—see Appendix B for areas included; (2) Rank is based on 2016 data and ranges from 1 to 381
Source: The U.S. Conference of Mayors, U.S. Metro Economies: GMP and Employment 2014-2016, June 2015

Metropolitan Area Exports

Area	2009	2010	2011	2012	2013	2014	Rank[2]
MSA[1]	1,594.7	1,778.7	1,856.6	1,965.3	1,903.9	1,834.4	110

Note: Figures are in millions of dollars; (1) Figures cover the New Haven-Milford, CT Metropolitan Statistical Area—see Appendix B for areas included; (2) Rank is based on 2014 data and ranges from 1 to 385
Source: U.S. Department of Commerce, International Trade Administration, Office of Trade & Industry Information, Manufacturing & Services, data extracted March 10, 2016

Building Permits

Area	Single-Family			Multi-Family			Total		
	2014	2015p	Pct. Chg.	2014	2015p	Pct. Chg.	2014	2015p	Pct. Chg.
City	41	41	0.0	0	0	-	41	41	0.0
MSA[1]	484	238	-50.8	656	614	-6.4	1,140	852	-25.3
U.S.	640,300	690,800	7.9	411,800	487,600	18.4	1,052,100	1,178,400	12.0

Note: (1) Figures cover the New Haven-Milford, CT Metropolitan Statistical Area—see Appendix B for areas included; Figures represent new, privately-owned housing units authorized (unadjusted data); All permit data are based on estimates with imputation; (p) preliminary data.
Source: U.S. Census Bureau, Manufacturing, Mining, and Construction Statistics, Building Permits, 2014, 2015

Bankruptcy Filings

Area	Business Filings			Nonbusiness Filings		
	2014	2015	% Chg.	2014	2015	% Chg.
New Haven County	64	46	-28.1	1,998	1,813	-9.3
U.S.	26,983	24,735	-8.3	909,812	819,760	-9.9

Note: Business filings include Chapter 7, Chapter 11, Chapter 12, and Chapter 13; Nonbusiness filings include Chapter 7, Chapter 11, and Chapter 13
Source: Administrative Office of the U.S. Courts, Business and Nonbusiness Bankruptcy, County Cases Commenced by Chapter of the Bankruptcy Code, During the 12- Month Period Ending December 31, 2014 and Business and Nonbusiness Bankruptcy, County Cases Commenced by Chapter of the Bankruptcy Code, During the 12- Month Period Ending December 31, 2015

Housing Vacancy Rates

Area	Gross Vacancy Rate[2] (%)			Year-Round Vacancy Rate[3] (%)			Rental Vacancy Rate[4] (%)			Homeowner Vacancy Rate[5] (%)		
	2013	2014	2015	2013	2014	2015	2013	2014	2015	2013	2014	2015
MSA[1]	9.9	7.4	8.7	9.5	7.1	8.6	7.8	4.8	5.8	2.6	1.2	2.1
U.S.	13.6	13.4	12.9	10.7	10.4	10.0	8.3	7.6	7.1	2.0	1.9	1.8

Note: (1) Figures cover the New Haven-Milford, CT Metropolitan Statistical Area—see Appendix B for areas included; (2) The percentage of the total housing inventory that is vacant; (3) The percentage of the housing inventory (excluding seasonal units) that is year-round vacant; (4) The percentage of rental inventory that is vacant for rent; (5) The percentage of homeowner inventory that is vacant for sale
Source: U.S. Census Bureau, Housing Vacancies and Homeownership Annual Statistics: 2015

INCOME

Income

Area	Per Capita ($)	Median Household ($)	Average Household ($)
City	43,583	107,716	125,801
MSA[1]	32,794	61,646	83,146
U.S.	28,555	53,482	74,596

Note: (1) Figures cover the New Haven-Milford, CT Metropolitan Statistical Area—see Appendix B for areas included
Source: U.S. Census Bureau, 2010-2014 American Community Survey 5-Year Estimates

Household Income Distribution

Area	Percent of Households Earning							
	Under $15,000	$15,000 -24,999	$25,000 -34,999	$35,000 -49,999	$50,000 -74,999	$75,000 -99,000	$100,000 -149,999	$150,000 and up
City	3.2	4.6	4.3	7.3	12.7	13.4	24.0	30.4
MSA[1]	11.7	9.4	8.6	11.8	16.6	12.7	15.6	13.7
U.S.	12.5	10.7	10.2	13.5	17.8	12.2	13.0	10.0

Note: (1) Figures cover the New Haven-Milford, CT Metropolitan Statistical Area—see Appendix B for areas included
Source: U.S. Census Bureau, 2010-2014 American Community Survey 5-Year Estimates

Poverty Rate

Area	All Ages	Under 18 Years Old	18 to 64 Years Old	65 Years and Over
City	2.1	1.0	2.0	4.4
MSA[1]	12.7	18.4	11.8	7.9
U.S.	15.6	21.9	14.6	9.4

Note: Figures are percentage of people whose income during the past 12 months was below the poverty level; (1) Figures cover the New Haven-Milford, CT Metropolitan Statistical Area—see Appendix B for areas included
Source: U.S. Census Bureau, 2010-2014 American Community Survey 5-Year Estimates

EMPLOYMENT

Labor Force and Employment

Area	Civilian Labor Force			Workers Employed		
	Dec. 2014	Dec. 2015	% Chg.	Dec. 2014	Dec. 2015	% Chg.
City	15,340	15,261	-0.5	14,758	14,755	0.0
NECTA[1]	323,360	322,103	-0.3	305,248	306,200	0.3
U.S.	155,521,000	157,245,000	1.1	147,190,000	149,703,000	1.7

Note: Data is not seasonally adjusted and covers workers 16 years of age and older; (1) Figures cover the New Haven, CT New England City and Town Area—see Appendix B for areas included
Source: Bureau of Labor Statistics, Local Area Unemployment Statistics

Unemployment Rate

Area	2015											
	Jan.	Feb.	Mar.	Apr.	May	Jun.	Jul.	Aug.	Sep.	Oct.	Nov.	Dec.
City	4.5	4.5	4.3	3.8	3.8	3.7	3.8	3.7	3.4	3.3	3.2	3.3
NECTA[1]	6.7	6.8	6.4	5.8	5.6	5.5	5.8	5.6	5.1	4.9	4.9	4.9
U.S.	6.1	5.8	5.6	5.1	5.3	5.5	5.6	5.2	4.9	4.8	4.8	4.8

Note: Data is not seasonally adjusted and covers workers 16 years of age and older; (1) Figures cover the New Haven, CT New England City and Town Area—see Appendix B for areas included
Source: Bureau of Labor Statistics, Local Area Unemployment Statistics

Employment by Occupation

Occupation Classification	City (%)	MSA[1] (%)	U.S. (%)
Management, Business, Science, and Arts	56.2	39.7	36.4
Natural Resources, Construction, and Maintenance	5.4	7.0	9.0
Production, Transportation, and Material Moving	6.2	11.2	12.1
Sales and Office	23.2	24.0	24.4
Service	9.0	18.2	18.2

Note: Figures cover employed civilians 16 years of age and older; (1) Figures cover the New Haven-Milford, CT Metropolitan Statistical Area—see Appendix B for areas included
Source: U.S. Census Bureau, 2010-2014 American Community Survey 5-Year Estimates

Employment by Industry

Sector	NECTA[1]		U.S.
	Number of Employees	Percent of Total	Percent of Total
Construction, Mining, and Logging	10,600	3.7	5.0
Education and Health Services	80,500	28.2	15.7
Financial Activities	12,700	4.4	5.7
Government	36,400	12.7	15.5
Information	3,500	1.2	1.9
Leisure and Hospitality	23,500	8.2	10.4
Manufacturing	24,100	8.4	8.6
Other Services	10,800	3.7	3.9
Professional and Business Services	30,600	10.7	13.9
Retail Trade	31,300	10.9	11.3
Transportation, Warehousing, and Utilities	9,700	3.4	3.9
Wholesale Trade	11,300	3.9	4.1

Note: Figures are non-farm employment as of December 2015. Figures are not seasonally adjusted and include workers 16 years of age and older; (1) Figures cover the New Haven, CT New England City and Town Area—see Appendix B for areas included; n/a not available
Source: Bureau of Labor Statistics, Current Employment Statistics, Employment, Hours, and Earnings

Occupations with Greatest Projected Employment Growth: 2012 – 2022

Occupation[1]	2012 Employment	2022 Projected Employment	Numeric Employment Change	Percent Employment Change
Personal Care Aides	23,240	32,090	8,850	38.1
Registered Nurses	35,990	41,230	5,240	14.6
Secretaries and Administrative Assistants, Except Legal, Medical, and Executive	34,530	38,640	4,110	11.9
Combined Food Preparation and Serving Workers, Including Fast Food	26,730	30,740	4,010	15.0
Retail Salespersons	53,800	57,270	3,470	6.4
General and Operations Managers	31,160	34,420	3,260	10.5
Home Health Aides	8,250	11,450	3,200	38.7
Childcare Workers	18,300	21,170	2,870	15.7
Maids and Housekeeping Cleaners	17,800	20,560	2,760	15.5
First-Line Supervisors of Office and Administrative Support Workers	26,360	28,900	2,540	9.6

Note: Projections cover Connecticut; (1) Sorted by numeric employment change
Source: www.projectionscentral.com, State Occupational Projections, 2012–2022 Long-Term Projections

Fastest Growing Occupations: 2012 – 2022

Occupation[1]	2012 Employment	2022 Projected Employment	Numeric Employment Change	Percent Employment Change
Insulation Workers, Mechanical	210	350	140	65.6
Interpreters and Translators	460	650	190	43.1
Helpers—Electricians	270	380	110	39.4
Home Health Aides	8,250	11,450	3,200	38.7
Diagnostic Medical Sonographers	1,000	1,380	380	38.3
Personal Care Aides	23,240	32,090	8,850	38.1
Physical Therapist Assistants	540	740	200	37.4
Occupational Therapy Assistants	490	670	180	35.4
Health Specialties Teachers, Postsecondary	2,810	3,770	960	34.3
Nursing Instructors and Teachers, Postsecondary	700	940	240	34.0

Note: Projections cover Connecticut; (1) Sorted by percent employment change and excludes occupations with numeric employment change less than 100
Source: www.projectionscentral.com, State Occupational Projections, 2012–2022 Long-Term Projections

Average Wages

Occupation	$/Hr.	Occupation	$/Hr.
Accountants and Auditors	34.56	Maids and Housekeeping Cleaners	11.36
Automotive Mechanics	21.35	Maintenance and Repair Workers	22.16
Bookkeepers	22.03	Marketing Managers	61.13
Carpenters	24.84	Nuclear Medicine Technologists	37.84
Cashiers	10.84	Nurses, Licensed Practical	27.02
Clerks, General Office	17.81	Nurses, Registered	38.49
Clerks, Receptionists/Information	15.59	Nursing Assistants	16.09
Clerks, Shipping/Receiving	15.39	Packers and Packagers, Hand	12.84
Computer Programmers	36.35	Physical Therapists	40.66
Computer Systems Analysts	43.82	Postal Service Mail Carriers	25.81
Computer User Support Specialists	25.53	Real Estate Brokers	29.11
Cooks, Restaurant	12.74	Retail Salespersons	12.48
Dentists	81.31	Sales Reps., Exc. Tech./Scientific	31.05
Electrical Engineers	41.30	Sales Reps., Tech./Scientific	46.95
Electricians	28.51	Secretaries, Exc. Legal/Med./Exec.	20.12
Financial Managers	60.98	Security Guards	15.36
First-Line Supervisors/Managers, Sales	22.43	Surgeons	102.31
Food Preparation Workers	13.00	Teacher Assistants*	14.40
General and Operations Managers	66.12	Teachers, Elementary School*	35.38
Hairdressers/Cosmetologists	15.82	Teachers, Secondary School*	36.67
Internists	107.57	Telemarketers	22.18
Janitors and Cleaners	15.58	Truck Drivers, Heavy/Tractor-Trailer	22.13
Landscaping/Groundskeeping Workers	17.64	Truck Drivers, Light/Delivery Svcs.	17.77
Lawyers	60.45	Waiters and Waitresses	10.95

Note: Wage data covers the New England City and Town Area—see Appendix B for areas included; (*) Hourly wages for elementary/secondary school teachers and teacher assistants were calculated by the editors from annual wage data based on a 40 hour work week; n/a not available.
Source: Bureau of Labor Statistics, Metro Area Occupational Employment and Wage Estimates, May 2015

TAXES

State Corporate Income Tax Rates

State	Tax Rate (%)	Income Brackets ($)	Num. of Brackets	Financial Institution Tax Rate (%)[a]	Federal Income Tax Ded.
Connecticut	7.5 (d)	Flat rate	1	7.5 (d)	No

Note: Tax rates as of January 1, 2016; (a) Rates listed are the corporate income tax rate applied to financial institutions or excise taxes based on income. Some states have other taxes based upon the value of deposits or shares; (d) Connecticut's tax is the greater of the 7.5% tax on net income, a 0.31% tax on capital stock and surplus (maximum tax of $1 million), or $250 (the minimum tax). Plus, an additional 20% surtax applies for tax years 2012 and 2016.
Source: Federation of Tax Administrators, "State Corporate Income Tax Rates, 2016"

State Individual Income Tax Rates

State	Tax Rate (%)	Income Brackets ($)	Num. of Brackets	Personal Exempt. ($)[1] Single	Personal Exempt. ($)[1] Dependents	Fed. Inc. Tax Ded.
Connecticut	3.0 - 6.99	10,000 - 500,000 (b)	7	14,500 (g)	None	No

Note: Tax rates as of January 1, 2016; Local- and county-level taxes are not included; n/a not applicable; (1) Married joint filers generally receive double the single exemption; (b) For joint returns, taxes are twice the tax on half the couple's income; (g) Connecticut's personal exemption incorporates a standard deduction. An additional tax credit is allowed ranging from 75% to 0% based on state adjusted gross income. Exemption amounts are phased out for higher income taxpayers until they are eliminated for households earning over $71,000.
Source: Federation of Tax Administrators, "State Individual Income Tax Rates, 2016"

Various State and Local Tax Rates

State	State and Local Sales and Use (%)	State Sales and Use (%)	Gasoline[1] (¢/gal.)	Cigarette[2] ($/pack)	Spirits[3] ($/gal.)	Wine[4] ($/gal.)	Beer[5] ($/gal.)
Connecticut	6.35	6.35	37.51	3.65	5.40 (f)	0.72 (l)	0.16

Note: All tax rates as of January 1, 2016; (1) The American Petroleum Institute has developed a methodology for determining the average tax rate on a gallon of fuel. Rates may include any of the following: excise taxes, environmental fees, storage tank fees, other fees or taxes, general sales tax, and local taxes. In states where gasoline is subject to the general sales tax, or where the fuel tax is based on the average sale price, the average rate determined by API is sensitive to changes in the price of gasoline. States that fully or partially apply general sales taxes to gasoline: CA, CO, GA, IL, IN, MI, NY; (2) The federal excise tax of $1.0066 per pack and local taxes are not included; (3) Rates are those applicable to off-premise sales of 40% alcohol by volume (a.b.v.) distilled spirits in 750ml containers. Local excise taxes are excluded; (4) Rates are those applicable to off-premise sales of 11% a.b.v. non-carbonated wine in 750ml containers; (5) Rates are those applicable to off-premise sales of 4.7% a.b.v. beer in 12 ounce containers; (f) Different rates are also applicable according to alcohol content, place of production, size of container, or place purchased (on- or off-premise or onboard airlines); (l) Different rates also applicable according to alcohol content, place of production, size of container, place purchased (on- or off-premise or on board airlines) or type of wine (carbonated, vermouth, etc.).
Source: Tax Foundation, 2016 Facts & Figures: How Does Your State Compare?

State Business Tax Climate Index Rankings

State	Overall Rank	Corporate Tax Rank	Individual Income Tax Rank	Sales Tax Rank	Unemployment Insurance Tax Rank	Property Tax Rank
Connecticut	44	33	36	29	20	49

Note: The index is a measure of how each state's tax laws affect economic performance. The lower the rank, the more favorable a state's tax system is for business. States without a given tax are given a ranking of 1. The scores/rankings for the District of Columbia do not affect other states. The 2016 index represents the tax climate as of July 1, 2015 (the beginning of Fiscal Year 2016).
Source: Tax Foundation, State Business Tax Climate Index 2016

TRANSPORTATION

Means of Transportation to Work

Area	Car/Truck/Van		Public Transportation			Bicycle	Walked	Other Means	Worked at Home
	Drove Alone	Car-pooled	Bus	Subway	Railroad				
City	80.5	7.6	1.1	0.1	0.2	0.0	4.1	0.6	5.9
MSA[1]	79.3	8.1	3.0	0.1	1.0	0.5	3.6	0.8	3.6
U.S.	76.4	9.6	2.6	1.8	0.6	0.6	2.8	1.3	4.4

Note: Figures are percentages and cover workers 16 years of age and older; (1) Figures cover the New Haven-Milford, CT Metropolitan Statistical Area—see Appendix B for areas included
Source: U.S. Census Bureau, 2010-2014 American Community Survey 5-Year Estimates

Travel Time to Work

Area	Less Than 10 Minutes	10 to 19 Minutes	20 to 29 Minutes	30 to 44 Minutes	45 to 59 Minutes	60 to 89 Minutes	90 Minutes or More
City	16.8	21.3	21.2	27.6	8.5	2.8	1.8
MSA[1]	12.5	32.3	23.0	19.7	6.0	4.1	2.3
U.S.	13.3	29.6	21.0	20.2	7.7	5.7	2.6

Note: Figures are percentages and include workers 16 years old and over; (1) Figures cover the New Haven-Milford, CT Metropolitan Statistical Area—see Appendix B for areas included
Source: U.S. Census Bureau, 2010-2014 American Community Survey 5-Year Estimates

Freeway Travel Time Index

Area	1985	1990	1995	2000	2005	2010	2014
Urban Area Rank[1,2]	54	56	47	46	51	57	65
Urban Area Index[1]	1.06	1.09	1.13	1.16	1.17	1.16	1.16
Average Index[3]	1.09	1.11	1.14	1.17	1.20	1.19	1.20

Note: Freeway Travel Time Index—the ratio of travel time in the peak period to the travel time at free-flow conditions. For example, a value of 1.30 indicates a 20-minute free-flow trip takes 26 minutes in the peak (20 minutes x 1.30 = 26 minutes); (1) Covers the New Haven CT urban area; (2) Rank is based on 101 urban areas (#1 = highest travel time index); (3) Average of 101 urban areas
Source: Texas Transportation Institute, 2015 Urban Mobility Scorecard, August 2015

Freeway Commuter Stress Index

Area	1985	1990	1995	2000	2005	2010	2014
Urban Area Rank[1,2]	58	59	55	54	58	65	61
Urban Area Index[1]	1.08	1.11	1.15	1.18	1.19	1.18	1.19
Average Index[3]	1.13	1.16	1.19	1.22	1.25	1.24	1.25

Note: The Freeway Commuter Stress Index is the same as the Freeway Travel Time Index (see table above) except that it includes only the travel in the peak directions during the peak periods; the TTI includes travel in all directions during the peak period. Thus, the CSI is more indicative of the work trip experienced by each commuter on a daily basis. (1) Covers the New Haven CT urban area; (2) Rank is based on 101 urban areas (#1 = highest stress index); (3) Average of 101 urban areas

Source: Texas Transportation Institute, 2015 Urban Mobility Scorecard, August 2015

Living Environment

COST OF LIVING

Cost of Living Index

Composite Index	Groceries	Housing	Utilities	Trans-portation	Health Care	Misc. Goods/ Services
124.3	131.5	142.7	101.2	107.2	113.8	120.1

Note: The Cost of Living Index measures regional differences in the cost of consumer goods and services, excluding taxes and non-consumer expenditures, for professional and managerial households in the top income quintile. It is based on more than 50,000 prices covering almost 60 different items for which prices are collected three times a year by chambers of commerce, economic development organizations or university applied economic centers in each participating urban area. The numbers shown should be read as a percentage above or below the national average of 100. For example, a value of 115.4 in the groceries column indicates that grocery prices are 15.4% higher than the national average. Small differences in the index numbers should not be interpreted as significant; Figures cover the New Haven CT urban area.
Source: The Council for Community and Economic Research, ACCRA Cost of Living Index, 2015

Grocery Prices

Area[1]	T-Bone Steak ($/pound)	Frying Chicken ($/pound)	Whole Milk ($/half gal.)	Eggs ($/dozen)	Orange Juice ($/64 oz.)	Coffee ($/11.5 oz.)
City[2]	11.71	1.53	3.39	3.10	3.56	3.71
Avg.	10.99	1.43	2.25	2.26	3.58	4.48
Min.	7.16	0.98	1.30	1.35	2.88	2.98
Max.	14.13	2.43	3.85	4.81	6.39	7.56

Note: (1) Values for the local area are compared with the average, minimum and maximum values for all 292 areas in the Cost of Living Index; (2) Figures cover the New Haven CT urban area; **T-Bone Steak** *(price per pound);* **Frying Chicken** *(price per pound, whole fryer);* **Whole Milk** *(half gallon carton);* **Eggs** *(price per dozen, Grade A, large);* **Orange Juice** *(64 oz. Tropicana or Florida Natural);* **Coffee** *(11.5 oz. can, vacuum-packed, Maxwell House, Hills Bros, or Folgers).*
Source: The Council for Community and Economic Research, ACCRA Cost of Living Index, 2015

Housing and Utility Costs

Area[1]	New Home Price ($)	Apartment Rent ($/month)	All Electric ($/month)	Part Electric ($/month)	Other Energy ($/month)	Telephone ($/month)
City[2]	438,228	1,355	-	109.68	81.09	24.00
Avg.	312,874	945	179.30	95.07	72.96	28.11
Min.	178,682	479	116.28	43.14	26.46	10.01
Max.	1,472,476	3,984	504.25	189.44	421.11	43.06

Note: (1) Values for the local area are compared with the average, minimum and maximum values for all 292 areas in the Cost of Living Index; (2) Figures cover the New Haven CT urban area; **New Home Price** *(2,400 sf living area, 8,000 sf lot, in urban area with full utilities);* **Apartment Rent** *(950 sf 2 bedroom/1.5 or 2 bath, unfurnished, excluding all utilities except water);* **All Electric** *(average monthly cost for an all-electric home);* **Part Electric** *(average monthly cost for a part-electric home);* **Other Energy** *(average monthly cost for natural gas, fuel oil, coal, wood, and any other forms of energy except electricity);* **Telephone** *(price includes basic monthly rate for a private residential line plus additional local usage charges incurred by a family of four).*
Source: The Council for Community and Economic Research, ACCRA Cost of Living Index, 2015

Health Care, Transportation, and Other Costs

Area[1]	Doctor ($/visit)	Dentist ($/visit)	Optometrist ($/visit)	Gasoline ($/gallon)	Beauty Salon ($/visit)	Men's Shirt ($)
City[2]	126.59	111.48	117.01	2.52	52.93	29.98
Avg.	105.15	89.02	99.78	2.38	35.30	28.10
Min.	66.87	56.09	48.53	1.95	18.91	13.38
Max.	182.34	150.36	228.33	4.09	67.91	63.80

Note: (1) Values for the local area are compared with the average, minimum and maximum values for all 292 areas in the Cost of Living Index; (2) Figures cover the New Haven CT urban area; **Doctor** *(general practitioners routine exam of an established patient);* **Dentist** *(adult teeth cleaning and periodic oral examination);* **Optometrist** *(full vision eye exam for established adult patient);* **Gasoline** *(one gallon regular unleaded, national brand, including all taxes, cash price at self-service pump if available);* **Beauty Salon** *(woman's shampoo, trim, and blow-dry);* **Men's Shirt** *(cotton/polyester dress shirt, pinpoint weave, long sleeves).*
Source: The Council for Community and Economic Research, ACCRA Cost of Living Index, 2015

HOUSING

House Price Index (HPI)

Area	National Ranking²	Quarterly Change (%)	One-Year Change (%)	Five-Year Change (%)
MSA¹	252	-0.70	1.00	-5.30
U.S.³	–	1.45	5.76	22.85

Note: The HPI is a weighted repeat sales index. It measures average price changes in repeat sales or refinancings on the same properties. This information is obtained by reviewing repeat mortgage transactions on single-family properties whose mortgages have been purchased or securitized by Fannie Mae or Freddie Mac in January 1975; (1) New Haven-Milford Metropolitan Statistical Area—see Appendix B for areas included; (2) Rankings are based on annual percentage change for all metro areas containing at least 15,000 transactions over the last 10 years and ranges from 1 to 266; (3) figures based on a weighted average of Census Division estimates using a seasonally adjusted, purchase-only index; all figures are for the period ending December 31, 2015

Source: Federal Housing Finance Agency, House Price Index, February 25, 2016

Median Single-Family Home Prices

Area	2013	2014	2015^p	Percent Change 2014 to 2015
MSA¹	226.5	233.3	215.4	-7.7
U.S. Average	197.4	208.9	223.9	7.2

Note: Figures are median sales prices of existing single-family homes in thousands of dollars; (p) preliminary; n/a not available; (1) New Haven-Milford, CT Metropolitan Statistical Area—see Appendix B for areas included

Source: National Association of Realtors, Median Sales Price of Existing Single-Family Homes for Metropolitan Areas, 4th Quarter 2015

Qualifying Income Based on Median Sales Price of Existing Single-Family Homes

Area	With 5% Down ($)	With 10% Down ($)	With 20% Down ($)
MSA¹	45,932	43,514	38,679
U.S. Average	49,535	46,928	41,714

Note: Figures are preliminary; Qualifying income is based on a mortgage rate of 4.1%. Monthly principal and interest payment is limited to 25% of income; n/a not available; (1) New Haven-Milford, CT Metropolitan Statistical Area—see Appendix B for areas included

Source: National Association of Realtors, Qualifying Income Based on Median Sales Price of Existing Single-Family Homes for Metropolitan Areas, 4th Quarter 2015

Median Apartment Condo-Coop Home Prices

Area	2013	2014	2015^p	Percent Change 2014 to 2015
MSA¹	150.7	129.2	129.0	-0.2
U.S. Average	194.9	204.3	210.7	3.1

Note: Figures are median sales prices of existing apartment condo-coop homes in thousands of dollars; (p) preliminary; n/a not available; (1) New Haven-Milford, CT Metropolitan Statistical Area—see Appendix B for areas included

Source: National Association of Realtors, Median Sales Price of Existing Apartment Condo-Coop Homes for Metropolitan Areas, 4th Quarter 2015

Gross Monthly Rent

Area	Under $200	$200 -299	$300 -499	$500 -749	$750 -999	$1,000 -1,499	$1,500 and up	Median ($)
City	1.1	0.0	11.6	5.9	18.2	32.2	31.0	1,195
MSA¹	2.0	3.4	6.5	9.3	22.3	39.5	17.2	1,064
U.S.	1.5	3.2	7.4	21.0	24.1	26.9	15.9	920

Note: Figures are percentages except for Median; Gross rent is the contract rent plus the estimated average monthly cost of utilities (electricity, gas, and water and sewer) and fuels (oil, coal, kerosene, wood, etc.) if these are paid by the renter (or paid for the renter by someone else); (1) Figures cover the New Haven-Milford, CT Metropolitan Statistical Area—see Appendix B for areas included

Source: U.S. Census Bureau, 2010-2014 American Community Survey 5-Year Estimates

Homeownership Rate

Area	2008 (%)	2009 (%)	2010 (%)	2011 (%)	2012 (%)	2013 (%)	2014 (%)	2015 (%)
MSA[1]	65.5	64.1	65.6	66.3	62.2	62.0	62.4	64.6
U.S.	67.8	67.4	66.9	66.1	65.4	65.1	64.5	63.7

Note: (1) Figures cover the New Haven-Milford, CT Metropolitan Statistical Area—see Appendix B for areas included
Source: U.S. Census Bureau, Housing Vacancies and Homeownership Annual Statistics: 2015

Year Housing Structure Built

Area	2010 or Later	2000 -2009	1990 -1999	1980 -1989	1970 -1979	1960 -1969	1950 -1959	1940 -1949	Before 1940	Median Year
City	0.3	8.9	11.7	16.1	15.1	17.4	15.7	6.1	8.6	1971
MSA[1]	0.5	5.6	7.4	12.7	12.9	12.5	15.0	7.0	26.4	1961
U.S.	1.0	14.9	13.9	13.8	15.8	11.0	10.8	5.4	13.3	1976

Note: Figures are percentages except for Median Year; (1) Figures cover the New Haven-Milford, CT Metropolitan Statistical Area—see Appendix B for areas included
Source: U.S. Census Bureau, 2010-2014 American Community Survey 5-Year Estimates

HEALTH

Health Risk Data

Category	MSA[1] (%)	U.S. (%)
Adults aged 18–64 who have any kind of health care coverage	86.6	79.6
Adults who reported being in good or excellent health	84.2	83.1
Adults who are current smokers	18.3	19.6
Adults who are heavy drinkers[2]	6.3	6.1
Adults who are binge drinkers[3]	15.5	16.9
Adults who are overweight (BMI 25.0 - 29.9)	38.5	35.8
Adults who are obese (BMI 30.0 - 99.8)	26.0	27.6
Adults who participated in any physical activities in the past month	75.9	77.1
Adults 50+ who have ever had a sigmoidoscopy or colonoscopy	74.1	67.3
Women aged 40+ who have had a mammogram within the past two years	77.1	74.0
Men aged 40+ who have had a PSA test within the past two years	43.5	45.2
Adults aged 65+ who have had flu shot within the past year	57.3	60.1
Adults who always wear a seatbelt	94.5	93.8

Note: Data as of 2012 unless otherwise noted; (1) Figures cover the New Haven-Milford, CT Metropolitan Statistical Area—see Appendix B for areas included; (2) Heavy drinkers are classified as males having more than two drinks per day or females having more than one drink per day; (3) Binge drinkers are classified as males having five or more drinks on one occasion or females having four or more drinks on one occasion
Source: Centers for Disease Control and Prevention, Behaviorial Risk Factor Surveillance System, SMART: Selected Metropolitan/Micropolitan Area Risk Trends, 2012 (Note: the CDC has discontinued this dataset but will be releasing a replacement in mid-2016)

Chronic Health Indicators

Category	MSA[1] (%)	U.S. (%)
Adults who have ever been told they had a heart attack	3.8	4.5
Adults who have ever been told they had a stroke	2.3	2.9
Adults who have been told they currently have asthma	11.8	8.9
Adults who have ever been told they have arthritis	25.6	25.7
Adults who have ever been told they have diabetes[2]	10.2	9.7
Adults who have ever been told they had skin cancer	5.4	5.7
Adults who have ever been told they had any other types of cancer	7.5	6.5
Adults who have ever been told they have COPD	6.1	6.2
Adults who have ever been told they have kidney disease	2.3	2.5
Adults who have ever been told they have a form of depression	16.4	18.0

Note: Data as of 2012 unless otherwise noted; (1) Figures cover the New Haven-Milford, CT Metropolitan Statistical Area—see Appendix B for areas included; (2) Figures do not include pregnancy-related, borderline, or pre-diabetes
Source: Centers for Disease Control and Prevention, Behaviorial Risk Factor Surveillance System, SMART: Selected Metropolitan/Micropolitan Area Risk Trends, 2012 (Note: the CDC has discontinued this dataset but will be releasing a replacement in mid-2016)

Mortality Rates for the Top 10 Causes of Death in the U.S.

ICD-10[a] Sub-Chapter	ICD-10[a] Code	Age-Adjusted Mortality Rate[1] per 100,000 population	
		County[2]	U.S.
Malignant neoplasms	C00-C97	157.5	163.6
Ischaemic heart diseases	I20-I25	78.2	102.2
Other forms of heart disease	I30-I51	58.3	50.1
Chronic lower respiratory diseases	J40-J47	30.1	41.4
Organic, including symptomatic, mental disorders	F01-F09	45.8	38.5
Cerebrovascular diseases	I60-I69	27.8	36.5
Other external causes of accidental injury	W00-X59	31.9	27.5
Other degenerative diseases of the nervous system	G30-G31	16.8	26.3
Diabetes mellitus	E10-E14	17.7	21.1
Hypertensive diseases	I10-I15	14.0	19.7

Note: (a) ICD-10 = International Classification of Diseases 10th Revision; (1) Mortality rates are a three year average covering 2012-2014; (2) Figures cover COUNTY NOT FOUND!!!!!!.
Source: Centers for Disease Control and Prevention, National Center for Health Statistics. Underlying Cause of Death 1999-2014 on CDC WONDER Online Database, released 2015.

Mortality Rates for Selected Causes of Death

ICD-10[a] Sub-Chapter	ICD-10[a] Code	Age-Adjusted Mortality Rate[1] per 100,000 population	
		County[2]	U.S.
Assault	X85-Y09	3.7	5.1
Diseases of the liver	K70-K76	12.9	13.5
Human immunodeficiency virus (HIV) disease	B20-B24	2.2	2.1
Influenza and pneumonia	J09-J18	13.1	15.2
Intentional self-harm	X60-X84	9.1	12.7
Malnutrition	E40-E46	0.7	0.9
Obesity and other hyperalimentation	E65-E68	1.4	1.9
Renal failure	N17-N19	14.0	13.0
Transport accidents	V01-V99	8.5	11.6
Viral hepatitis	B15-B19	1.7	2.1

Note: (a) ICD-10 = International Classification of Diseases 10th Revision; (1) Mortality rates are a three year average covering 2012-2014; (2) Figures cover COUNTY NOT FOUND!!!!!!; Data are Suppressed when the data meet the criteria for confidentiality constraints; Mortality rates are flagged as Unreliable when the rate would be calculated with a numerator of 20 or less.
Source: Centers for Disease Control and Prevention, National Center for Health Statistics. Underlying Cause of Death 1999-2014 on CDC WONDER Online Database, released 2015.

Health Insurance Coverage

Area	With Health Insurance	With Private Health Insurance	With Public Health Insurance	Without Health Insurance	Population Under Age 18 Without Health Insurance
City	94.3	86.7	18.7	5.7	2.0
MSA[1]	91.7	69.9	33.0	8.3	3.1
U.S.	85.8	65.8	31.1	14.2	7.1

Note: Figures are percentages that cover the civilian noninstitutionalized population; (1) Figures cover the New Haven-Milford, CT Metropolitan Statistical Area—see Appendix B for areas included
Source: U.S. Census Bureau, 2010-2014 American Community Survey 5-Year Estimates

Number of Medical Professionals

Area	MDs[3]	DOs[3,4]	Dentists	Podiatrists	Chiropractors	Optometrists
County[1] (number)	4,737	96	634	83	213	136
County[1] (rate[2])	548.9	11.1	73.6	9.6	24.7	15.8
U.S. (rate[2])	272.5	20.9	64.7	5.8	25.9	15.2

Note: Data as of 2014 unless noted; (1) Data covers New Haven County; (2) Rate per 100,000 population; (3) Data as of 2013 and includes all active, non-federal physicians; (4) Doctor of Osteopathic Medicine
Source: U.S. Department of Health and Human Services, Health Resources and Services Administration, Bureau of Health Professions, Area Resource File (ARF) 2014-2015

Best Hospitals

According to *U.S. News,* the New Haven-Milford, CT metro area is home to one of the best hospitals in the U.S.: **Yale-New Haven Hospital** (8 specialties). The hospital listed was nationally ranked in at least one adult specialty. Only 137 hospitals nationwide were nationally ranked in one or more specialties. Fifteen hospitals in the U.S. made the Honor Roll with high scores in at least six specialties. *U.S. News Online, "America's Best Children's Hospitals 2015-16"*

According to *U.S. News,* the New Haven-Milford, CT metro area is home to one of the best children's hospitals in the U.S.: **Yale-New Haven Children's Hospital** (6 specialties). The hospital listed was highly ranked in at least one pediatric specialty. Eighty-three children's hospitals in the U.S. were nationally ranked in at least one specialty. Twelve children's hospitals in the U.S. made the Honor Roll with high scores in at least three specialties. *U.S. News Online, "America's Best Children's Hospitals 2015-16"*

EDUCATION

Public School District Statistics

District Name	Schls	Pupils	Pupil/ Teacher Ratio	Minority Pupils[1] (%)	Free Lunch Eligible[2] (%)	IEP[3] (%)
Cheshire School District	8	4,594	13.9	16.8	5.6	10.9
Unified School District #1	15	539	n/a	90.4	91.5	43.2

Note: Table includes school districts with 100 or more students; (1) Percentage of students that are not non-Hispanic white; (2) Percentage of students that are eligible for the free lunch program; (3) Percentage of students that have an Individualized Education Program.

Source: U.S. Department of Education, National Center for Education Statistics, Common Core of Data, Local Education Agency (School District) Universe Survey: School Year 2013-2014; U.S. Department of Education, National Center for Education Statistics, Common Core of Data, Public Elementary/Secondary School Universe Survey: School Year 2013-2014

Highest Level of Education

Area	Less than H.S.	H.S. Diploma	Some College, No Deg.	Associate Degree	Bachelor's Degree	Master's Degree	Prof. School Degree	Doctorate Degree
City	5.6	22.5	13.8	6.3	26.1	17.0	5.0	3.6
MSA[1]	11.1	30.5	17.9	7.1	18.0	10.4	2.8	2.1
U.S.	13.7	28.0	21.2	7.9	18.3	7.8	2.0	1.3

Note: Figures cover persons age 25 and over; (1) Figures cover the New Haven-Milford, CT Metropolitan Statistical Area—see Appendix B for areas included

Source: U.S. Census Bureau, 2010-2014 American Community Survey 5-Year Estimates

Educational Attainment by Race

Area	High School Graduate or Higher (%)					Bachelor's Degree or Higher (%)				
	Total	White	Black	Asian	Hisp.[2]	Total	White	Black	Asian	Hisp.[2]
City	94.4	96.4	79.5	89.8	84.6	51.7	53.2	8.8	75.4	24.6
MSA[1]	88.9	90.6	84.8	89.6	71.7	33.4	35.4	19.6	65.2	14.0
U.S.	86.3	88.4	83.2	85.8	64.1	29.3	30.6	19.0	50.9	13.9

Note: Figures shown cover persons 25 years old and over; (1) Figures cover the New Haven-Milford, CT Metropolitan Statistical Area—see Appendix B for areas included; (2) People of Hispanic origin can be of any race

Source: U.S. Census Bureau, 2010-2014 American Community Survey 5-Year Estimates

School Enrollment by Grade and Control

Area	Preschool (%)		Kindergarten (%)		Grades 1 - 4 (%)		Grades 5 - 8 (%)		Grades 9 - 12 (%)	
	Public	Private	Public	Private	Public	Private	Public	Private	Public	Private
City	40.7	59.3	89.7	10.3	95.3	4.7	88.6	11.4	89.3	10.7
MSA[1]	59.1	40.9	87.5	12.5	91.4	8.6	90.8	9.2	89.3	10.7
U.S.	57.4	42.6	87.8	12.2	89.8	10.2	89.9	10.1	90.6	9.4

Note: Figures shown cover persons 3 years old and over; (1) Figures cover the New Haven-Milford, CT Metropolitan Statistical Area—see Appendix B for areas included

Source: U.S. Census Bureau, 2010-2014 American Community Survey 5-Year Estimates

Average Salaries of Public School Classroom Teachers

Area	2013-14 Dollars	2013-14 Rank[1]	2014-15 Dollars	2014-15 Rank[1]	Percent Change 2013-14 to 2014-15	Percent Change 2004-05 to 2014-15
Connecticut	70,583	5	71,709	5	1.59	24.2
U.S. Average	56,610	–	57,379	–	1.36	20.8

Note: (1) State rank ranges from 1 to 51 where 1 indicates highest salary.
Source: National Education Association, Rankings & Estimates: Rankings of the States 2014 and Estimates of School Statistics 2015, March 2015

Higher Education

Four-Year Colleges			Two-Year Colleges					
Public	Private Non-profit	Private For-profit	Public	Private Non-profit	Private For-profit	Medical Schools[1]	Law Schools[2]	Voc/ Tech[3]
0	0	0	0	0	0	0	0	0

Note: Figures cover institutions located within the city limits and include main campuses only; (1) includes schools accredited by the Liaison Committee on Medical Education and the American Osteopathic Association's Commission on Osteopathic College Accreditation; (2) includes ABA-accredited schools, schools with provisional ABA accreditation, and state accredited schools; (3) includes all schools with programs that are less than 2 years.
Source: National Center for Education Statistics, Integrated Postsecondary Education System (IPEDS), 2014-15; Association of American Medical Colleges, Member List, March 21, 2016; American Osteopathic Association, Member List, March 21, 2016; Law School Admission Council, Official Guide to ABA-Approved Law Schools Online, March 21, 2016; Wikipedia, List of Medical Schools in the United States, March 21, 2016; Wikipedia, List of Law Schools in the United States, March 21, 2016

According to *U.S. News & World Report,* the New Haven-Milford, CT metro area is home to one of the best national universities in the U.S.: **Yale University** (#3). The indicators used to capture academic quality fall into a number of categories: assessment by administrators at peer institutions; retention of students; faculty resources; student selectivity; financial resources; alumni giving; high school counselor ratings of colleges; and graduation rate. *U.S. News & World Report, "America's Best Colleges 2016"*

According to *U.S. News & World Report,* the New Haven-Milford, CT metro area is home to one of the top 100 law schools in the U.S.: **Yale University, Law School** (#1). The rankings are based on a weighted average of 12 measures of quality: peer assessment score; assessment score by lawyers/judges; median LSAT scores; median undergrad GPA; acceptance rate; employment rates for graduates; placement success; bar passage rate; faculty resources; expenditures per student; student/faculty ratio; and library resources. *U.S. News & World Report, "America's Best Graduate Schools, Law, 2017"*

According to *U.S. News & World Report,* the New Haven-Milford, CT metro area is home to one of the top 75 medical schools for research in the U.S.: **Yale University, School of Medicine** (#8 tie). The rankings are based on a weighted average of 11 measures of quality: quality assessment; peer assessment score; assessment score by residency directors; research activity; total research activity; average research activity per faculty member; student selectivity; median MCAT total score; median undergraduate GPA; acceptance rate; and faculty resources. *U.S. News & World Report, "America's Best Graduate Schools, Medical, 2017"*

According to *U.S. News & World Report,* the New Haven-Milford, CT metro area is home to one of the top 75 business schools in the U.S.: **Yale University, School of Management** (#8 tie). The rankings are based on a weighted average of the following nine measures: quality assessment; peer assessment; recruiter assessment; placement success; mean starting salary and bonus; student selectivity; mean GMAT and GRE scores; mean undergraduate GPA; and acceptance rate. *U.S. News & World Report, "America's Best Graduate Schools, Business, 2017"*

PRESIDENTIAL ELECTION

2012 Presidential Election Results

Area	Obama (%)	Romney (%)	Other (%)
New Haven County	60.6	38.3	1.1
U.S.	51.0	47.2	1.8

Note: Results may not add to 100% due to rounding
Source: Dave Leip's Atlas of U.S. Presidential Elections

EMPLOYERS

Major Employers

Company Name	Industry
Alinabal	Stamping & assemblies
Bayer Healthcare Pharmaceuticals	Physicians & surgeons equip.
Bozzuto's Inc.	Distribution center
City of Milford	Government
City of Milford, Board of Ed	Government
Covidien	Hospital equipment
Grandview Adult Behavioral Health	Mental health services
Hasler Neopost	Postage equipment
Macy's	Retail
Masonicare Health Ctr.	Retirement community
Mid State Medical Center	Hospitals
Milford Hospital	Hospitals
Schick	Consumer goods
Servicom LLC	Call centers
ShopRite	Retail grocery
Southbury Training School	Schools
Southern CT State Univ.	Schools-universities
Stop & Shop	Retail grocery
Subway	Food chain
United Healthcare	Health services
Va Medical Ctr	Hospitals
Veterans Affairs CT	Hospitals
Waterbury Hospital	Hospitals
Yale New Haven Health System	Clinics
Yale University	Schools-universities

Note: Companies shown are located within the New Haven-Milford, CT Metropolitan Statistical Area.
Source: Hoovers.com; Wikipedia

PUBLIC SAFETY

Crime Rate

Area	All Crimes	Violent Crimes: Murder	Violent Crimes: Rape[3]	Violent Crimes: Robbery	Violent Crimes: Aggrav. Assault	Property Crimes: Burglary	Property Crimes: Larceny -Theft	Property Crimes: Motor Vehicle Theft
City	844.8	3.4	0.0	6.9	10.3	137.4	587.2	99.6
Metro[1]	2,993.1	3.1	21.8	135.7	166.1	406.5	1,983.3	276.8
U.S.	2,971.8	4.5	36.6	102.2	232.5	542.5	1,837.3	216.2

Note: Figures are crimes per 100,000 population; (1) Figures cover the New Haven-Milford, CT Metropolitan Statistical Area—see Appendix B for areas included; (3) The city and U.S. figures shown were reported using the revised Uniform Crime Reporting (UCR) definition of rape. The suburban and metro area figures shown are an aggregate total of the data submitted using both the revised and legacy UCR definitions.
Source: FBI Uniform Crime Reports, 2014

Hate Crimes

Area	Number of Quarters Reported	Race	Religion	Sexual Orientation	Ethnicity	Disability	Gender	Gender Identity
		Number of Incidents per Bias Motivation						
City	4	1	0	0	0	0	0	0
U.S.	4	2,568	1,014	1,017	648	84	33	98

Source: Federal Bureau of Investigation, Hate Crime Statistics 2014

Identity Theft Consumer Complaints

Area	Complaints	Complaints per 100,000 Population	Rank[2]
MSA[1]	1,776	206.2	17
U.S.	490,220	152.4	-

Note: (1) Figures cover the New Haven-Milford, CT Metropolitan Statistical Area—see Appendix B for areas included; (2) Rank ranges from 1 to 379 where 1 indicates greatest number of identity theft complaints per 100,000 population
Source: Federal Trade Commission, Consumer Sentinel Network Data Book for January–December 2015

Fraud and Other Consumer Complaints

Area	Complaints	Complaints per 100,000 Population	Rank[2]
MSA[1]	3,334	387.1	131
U.S.	2,593,159	806.0	-

Note: (1) Figures cover the New Haven-Milford, CT Metropolitan Statistical Area—see Appendix B for areas included; (2) Rank ranges from 1 to 379 where 1 indicates greatest number of identity theft complaints per 100,000 population
Source: Federal Trade Commission, Consumer Sentinel Network Data Book for January–December 2015

RECREATION

Culture

Dance[1]	Theatre[1]	Instrumental Music[1]	Vocal Music[1]	Series and Festivals	Museums and Art Galleries[2]	Zoos and Aquariums[3]
0	0	0	0	0	0	0

Note: (1) Professional perfoming groups; (2) Based on organizations with SIC code 8412; (3) AZA-accredited
Source: The Grey House Performing Arts Directory, 2015-16; Association of Zoos & Aquariums, AZA Member Zoos & Aquariums, March 25, 2016; www.AccuLeads.com, March 29, 2016

Professional Sports Teams

Team Name	League	Year Established
No teams are located in the metro area		

Source: Wikipedia, Major Professional Sports Teams of the United States and Canada, March 24, 2016

CLIMATE

Average and Extreme Temperatures

Temperature	Jan	Feb	Mar	Apr	May	Jun	Jul	Aug	Sep	Oct	Nov	Dec	Yr.
Extreme High (°F)	65	67	84	91	92	96	103	100	99	85	78	65	103
Average High (°F)	37	38	46	57	67	76	82	81	74	64	53	41	60
Average Temp. (°F)	30	32	39	49	59	68	74	73	66	56	46	35	52
Average Low (°F)	23	24	31	40	50	59	65	65	57	47	38	27	44
Extreme Low (°F)	-7	-5	4	18	31	41	49	44	36	26	16	-4	-7

Note: Figures cover the years 1948-1992
Source: National Climatic Data Center, International Station Meteorological Climate Summary, 9/96

Average Precipitation/Snowfall/Humidity

Precip./Humidity	Jan	Feb	Mar	Apr	May	Jun	Jul	Aug	Sep	Oct	Nov	Dec	Yr.
Avg. Precip. (in.)	3.2	2.9	3.7	3.7	3.7	3.1	3.7	3.8	3.0	3.2	3.8	3.5	41.4
Avg. Snowfall (in.)	7	7	5	1	Tr	0	0	0	0	Tr	1	5	25
Avg. Rel. Hum. 7am (%)	73	72	72	72	76	77	79	80	81	79	77	74	76
Avg. Rel. Hum. 4pm (%)	61	59	56	55	59	60	60	61	61	60	62	63	60

Note: Figures cover the years 1948-1992; Tr = Trace amounts (<0.05 in. of rain; <0.5 in. of snow)
Source: National Climatic Data Center, International Station Meteorological Climate Summary, 9/96

Weather Conditions

Temperature			Daytime Sky			Precipitation		
32°F & below	45°F & below	90°F & above	Clear	Partly cloudy	Cloudy	0.01 inch or more precip.	0.1 inch or more snow/ice	Thunder-storms
100	193	7	80	146	139	118	17	22

Note: Figures are average number of days per year and cover the years 1948-1992
Source: National Climatic Data Center, International Station Meteorological Climate Summary, 9/96

HAZARDOUS WASTE

Superfund Sites

Cheshire has no sites on the EPA's Superfund Final National Priorities List. There are a total of 1,323 Superfund sites on the list in the U.S. *U.S. Environmental Protection Agency, Final National Priorities List, March 18, 2016*

AIR & WATER QUALITY

Air Quality Trends: Ozone

	1990	1995	2000	2005	2010	2011	2012	2013	2014
MSA[1]	0.121	0.117	0.087	0.092	0.079	0.092	0.087	0.087	0.087

Note: (1) Data covers the New Haven-Milford, CT Metropolitan Statistical Area—see Appendix B for areas included. The values shown are the composite ozone concentration averages among trend sites based on the highest fourth daily maximum 8-hour concentration in parts per million. These trends are based on sites having an adequate record of monitoring data during the trend period. Data from exceptional events are included.
Source: U.S. Environmental Protection Agency, Air Quality Monitoring Information, "Air Quality Trends by City, 1990-2014"

Air Quality Index

Area	Percent of Days when Air Quality was...[2]					AQI Statistics[2]	
	Good	Moderate	Unhealthy for Sensitive Groups	Unhealthy	Very Unhealthy	Maximum	Median
MSA[1]	64.1	32.6	3.3	0.0	0.0	145	43

Note: (1) Data covers the New Haven-Milford, CT Metropolitan Statistical Area—see Appendix B for areas included; (2) Based on 365 days with AQI data in 2015. Air Quality Index (AQI) is an index for reporting daily air quality. EPA calculates the AQI for five major air pollutants regulated by the Clean Air Act: ground-level ozone, particle pollution (aka particulate matter), carbon monoxide, sulfur dioxide, and nitrogen dioxide. The AQI runs from 0 to 500. The higher the AQI value, the greater the level of air pollution and the greater the health concern. There are six AQI categories: "Good" AQI is between 0 and 50. Air quality is considered satisfactory; "Moderate" AQI is between 51 and 100. Air quality is acceptable; "Unhealthy for Sensitive Groups" When AQI values are between 101 and 150, members of sensitive groups may experience health effects; "Unhealthy" When AQI values are between 151 and 200 everyone may begin to experience health effects; "Very Unhealthy" AQI values between 201 and 300 trigger a health alert; "Hazardous" AQI values over 300 trigger warnings of emergency conditions (not shown).
Source: U.S. Environmental Protection Agency, Air Quality Index Report, 2015

Air Quality Index Pollutants

Area	Percent of Days when AQI Pollutant was...[2]					
	Carbon Monoxide	Nitrogen Dioxide	Ozone	Sulfur Dioxide	Particulate Matter 2.5	Particulate Matter 10
MSA[1]	0.0	3.8	44.9	0.0	51.2	0.0

Note: (1) Data covers the New Haven-Milford, CT Metropolitan Statistical Area—see Appendix B for areas included; (2) Based on 365 days with AQI data in 2015. The Air Quality Index (AQI) is an index for reporting daily air quality. EPA calculates the AQI for five major air pollutants regulated by the Clean Air Act: ground-level ozone, particle pollution (also known as particulate matter), carbon monoxide, sulfur dioxide, and nitrogen dioxide. The AQI runs from 0 to 500. The higher the AQI value, the greater the level of air pollution and the greater the health concern.
Source: U.S. Environmental Protection Agency, Air Quality Index Report, 2015

Maximum Air Pollutant Concentrations: Particulate Matter, Ozone, CO and Lead

	Particulate Matter 10 (ug/m^3)	Particulate Matter 2.5 Wtd AM (ug/m^3)	Particulate Matter 2.5 24-Hr (ug/m^3)	Ozone (ppm)	Carbon Monoxide (ppm)	Lead (ug/m^3)
MSA[1] Level	34	8.7	26	0.072	1	n/a
NAAQS[2]	150	15	35	0.075	9	0.15
Met NAAQS[2]	Yes	Yes	Yes	Yes	Yes	n/a

Note: (1) Data covers the New Haven-Milford, CT Metropolitan Statistical Area—see Appendix B for areas included; Data from exceptional events are included; (2) National Ambient Air Quality Standards; ppm = parts per million; ug/m^3 = micrograms per cubic meter; n/a not available.
Concentrations: Particulate Matter 10 (coarse particulate)—highest second maximum 24-hour concentration; Particulate Matter 2.5 Wtd AM (fine particulate)—highest weighted annual mean concentration; Particulate Matter 2.5 24-Hour (fine particulate)—highest 98th percentile 24-hour concentration; Ozone—highest fourth daily maximum 8-hour concentration; Carbon Monoxide—highest second maximum non-overlapping 8-hour concentration; Lead—maximum running 3-month average
Source: U.S. Environmental Protection Agency, Air Quality Monitoring Information, "Air Quality Statistics by City, 2014"

Maximum Air Pollutant Concentrations: Nitrogen Dioxide and Sulfur Dioxide

	Nitrogen Dioxide AM (ppb)	Nitrogen Dioxide 1-Hr (ppb)	Sulfur Dioxide AM (ppb)	Sulfur Dioxide 1-Hr (ppb)	Sulfur Dioxide 24-Hr (ppb)
MSA[1] Level	13	50	n/a	17	n/a
NAAQS[2]	53	100	30	75	140
Met NAAQS[2]	Yes	Yes	n/a	Yes	n/a

Note: (1) Data covers the New Haven-Milford, CT Metropolitan Statistical Area—see Appendix B for areas included; Data from exceptional events are included; (2) National Ambient Air Quality Standards; ppm = parts per million; ug/m^3 = micrograms per cubic meter; n/a not available.

Concentrations: Nitrogen Dioxide AM—highest arithmetic mean concentration; Nitrogen Dioxide 1-Hr—highest 98th percentile 1-hour daily maximum concentration; Sulfur Dioxide AM—highest annual mean concentration; Sulfur Dioxide 1-Hr—highest 99th percentile 1-hour daily maximum concentration; Sulfur Dioxide 24-Hr—highest second maximum 24-hour concentration

Source: U.S. Environmental Protection Agency, Air Quality Monitoring Information, "Air Quality Statistics by City, 2014"

Drinking Water

Water System Name	Pop. Served	Primary Water Source Type	Violations[1]	
			Health Based	Monitoring/ Reporting
Wallingford Water Dept	37,267	Surface	0	0

Note: (1) Based on violation data from January 1, 2015 to December 31, 2015 (includes unresolved violations from earlier years)

Source: U.S. Environmental Protection Agency, Office of Ground Water and Drinking Water, Safe Drinking Water Information System (based on data extracted April 29, 2016)

Glastonbury, Connecticut

Background

Glastonbury, in central Connecticut, east of the Connecticut River, is located less than ten miles from the state capital of Hartford. It has long been an elegant residential town, graced by tree-shaded streets, wide lawns and attractive homes. More than 300 years old, Glastonbury has successfully worked to preserve its natural and historical resources while encouraging responsible development.

The town dates its foundation to 1636, when European settlers bought a tract of land on the eastern bank of the Connecticut River, from Chief Sowheag of the local tribe, for a length of cloth. The town was initially settled as part of the town of Wethersfield, but it was formally named Glastonbury in 1693, in memory of a town in Somerset, England.

In its early days, the town was an important agricultural hub, a function which it carried into modern times, particularly in regard to growing distinctive Connecticut cigar wrapper tobacco. As the town grew, it also became an important industrial center, and by the time of the Revolutionary War, it was home to a gunpowder factory, a shipworks, sawmills, and foundries. During the war, Glastonbury's agricultural richness served it well: in 1777, when food shortages in New Haven became acute, the entire junior class of Yale College moved to Glastonbury where the students boarded at the home of William Welles, local resident and Yale tutor.

Glastonbury was ahead of the times in many ways, and by the end of the Revolution, boasted ten schools, an extraordinary number for that period. In 1780, many years before the rest of the state did so, Glastonbury decreed that all slaves be freed. The town's first hospital was formed just after the Revolution, to treat small pox and other infectious diseases, and the first library was built in 1803. This strong educational heritage is perhaps partly responsible for the fact that Glastonbury today is a highly educated community where almost one-fifth of its citizens hold either graduate or professional degrees.

By the mid-nineteenth century, Glastonbury became home to the J.B. Williams Soap Factory, the first such factory in the world, which eventually manufactured ink, shoe polish, and shaving products. The town also hosted factories that produced leather and woolen goods, feldspar products, cotton cloth, paper, silver plate, and airplanes.

Glastonbury continued to be an important agricultural center, and was the site of several important agricultural innovations, such as peaches that were cultivated extensively by John Howard Hale, the aptly named "Peach King." The city also hosted Storrs Agricultural College, which later became the University of Connecticut. The Glastonbury Chamber of Commerce's annual Apple Harvest Festival is still a town favorite.

The J.B. Williams Soap business was sold in the 1950s, though some operations continued into the 1970s. Today, some parts of the old factory complex have been converted into elegant condominiums, and also house the Glastonbury Board of Education office.

The town has been home to many famous figures, including Noah Webster, who taught in a Glastonbury school, and the artist Laurilla Aleroyia (1785-1857), whose watercolor sketches are on display at the town's Historical Society's Museum. Other noted personalities are the classics scholar Julia Evelina (1792-1886), and her sister Abby Hadassah (1797-1878). Julia and Abby, and three other sisters, had been active in the abolitionist movement and, after the war, became active in the cause of woman's suffrage, once refusing to pay their taxes on the grounds of non-representation.

Glastonbury supports a highly regarded school system and is also convenient to a range of private and parochial schools, as well as a broad range of institutions of higher learning, including Trinity College, Wesleyan University, University of Hartford, Central Connecticut State University and the University of Connecticut at Storrs, all of which are within a half hour's drive.

Nearby major health facilities include the Connecticut Children's Medical Center and Manchester Memorial Hospital. The town is served by Bradley International Airport, less than half an hour away, and by several smaller regional airports.

Rankings

Business/Finance Rankings

- The personal finance site NerdWallet analyzed 183 American metropolitan areas with populations over 250,000 and more than 15,000 businesses to rank where entrepreneurs find the most success. Criteria included area economy, annual income, housing cost, unemployment rate, and the success rate of area businesses. Hartford* ranked #20. *www.nerdwallet.com, "Best Places to Start a Business," April 27, 2015*
- Based on metro area social media reviews, the employment opinion group Glassdoor surveyed 50 of the largest U.S. metro areas and equally weighed cost of living, hiring opportunity, and job satisfaction to compose a list of "25 Best Cities for Jobs." The Hartford* metro area was ranked #43 in overall job satisfaction. *www.glassdoor.com, "Best Cities for Jobs," May 19, 2015*
- In a survey of economic confidence in the nation's 50 largest metropolitan areas conducted January–December 2014, the Hartford* metro area placed #32, according to Gallup's 2014 Economic Confidence Index. *Gallup, "San Jose and San Francisco Lead in Economic Confidence," March 19, 2015*
- The Brookings Institution ranked the 100 largest metro areas in the U.S. based on income inequality. Hartford* was ranked #27 (#1 = greatest ineqality). Criteria: the "95/20 ratio," a figure representing the income at which a household earns more than 95 percent of all other households, divided by the income at which a household earns more than only 20 percent of all other households. *Brookings Institution, "Income Inequality, 100 Largest U.S. Metro Areas, 2007-2014," January 14, 2016*
- The Hartford* metro area appeared on the Milken Institute "2015 Best Performing Cities" list. Rank: #152 out of 200 large metro areas. Criteria: job growth; wage and salary growth; high-tech output growth. *Milken Institute, "Best-Performing Cities 2015," December 2015*
- *Forbes* ranked the 200 most populous metro areas to determine the nation's "Best Places for Business and Careers." The Hartford* metro area was ranked #151. Criteria: costs (business and living); job growth (past and projected); income growth; educational attainment (college and high school); projected economic growth; cultural and recreational opportunities; net migration patterns; number of highly ranked colleges. *Forbes, "The Best Places for Business and Careers 2015," July 29, 2015*

Education Rankings

- Personal finance website *WalletHub* analyzed the 150 largest U.S. metropolitan statistical areas to determine where the most educated Americans are choosing to settle. Criteria: education quality and attainment gap; education levels; percentage of workers with degrees; public school rankings; quality and size of each metro area's universities. Hartford* was ranked #23 (#1 = most educated city). *www.WalletHub.com, "2015's Most and Least Educated Cities*

Environmental Rankings

- The Hartford* metro area came in at #122 for the relative comfort of its climate on Sperling's list of "chill cities," as measured by the Sperling Heat Index. All 361 metro areas are included. Criteria included daytime high temperatures, nighttime low temperatures, dew point, and relative humidity at the high temperatures. *www.bertsperling.com, "Sperling's Chill Cities," July 18, 2013*
- Sperling's BestPlaces assessed 379 metropolitan areas of the United States for the likelihood of dangerously extreme weather events or earthquakes. In general the Southeast and South-Central regions have the highest risk of weather extremes and earthquakes, while the Pacific Northwest enjoys the lowest risk. Of the least risky metropolitan areas, the Hartford* metro area was ranked #199. *www.bestplaces.net, "Safest Places from Natural Disasters," April 2011*

Health/Fitness Rankings

- For each of the 50 most populous metro areas in the United States, the American College of Sports Medicine's American Fitness Index evaluated infrastructure, community assets, and policies that encourage healthy and fit lifestyles, including preventive health behaviors, levels of chronic disease conditions, health care access, and community resources and policies that support physical activity. The Hartford* metro area ranked #11 for "community fitness." *www.americanfitnessindex.org, "ACSM American Fitness Index Health and Community Fitness Status of the 50 Largest Metropolitan Areas," May 2015*
- The Hartford* metro area was identified as one of the worst cities for bed bugs in America by pest control company Orkin. The area ranked #34 out of 50 based on the number of bed bug treatments Orkin performed from January to December 2015. *Orkin, "Chicago Tops Bed Bug Cities List for Fourth Year in a Row," January 13, 2016*
- Hartford* was identified as a "2016 Spring Allergy Capital." The area ranked #56 out of 100. Three groups of factors were used to identify the most severe cities for people with allergies during the spring season: annual pollen levels; medicine utilization; access to board-certified allergists. *Asthma and Allergy Foundation of America, "Spring Allergy Capitals 2016"*
- Hartford* was identified as a "2015 Asthma Capital." The area ranked #33 out of the nation's 100 largest metropolitan areas. Criteria: estimated prevalence; self-reported prevalence; crude death rate for asthma; annual pollen score; annual air quality; public smoking laws; number of board-certified asthma specialists; school inhaler access laws; rescue medication use; controller medication use; ER visits for asthma; uninsured rate; poverty rate. *Asthma and Allergy Foundation of America, "Asthma Capitals 2015"*
- The Hartford* metro area ranked #71 out of 190 in The Gallup-Healthways Well-Being Index. Criteria: purpose; social well being; financial health; community and physical health. Results are based on telephone interviews with adults, aged 18 and older, living in metropolitan areas in the 50 U.S. states and the District of Columbia. *Gallup-Healthways, "State of American Well-Being," February 23, 2016*

Real Estate Rankings

- Hartford* was ranked #61 out of 225 metro areas in terms of housing affordability in 2015 by the National Association of Home Builders (#1 = most affordable). Criteria: the share of homes sold in that area affordable to a family earning the local median income, based on standard mortgage underwriting criteria. *National Association of Home Builders®, NAHB-Wells Fargo Housing Opportunity Index, 4th Quarter 2015*

Safety Rankings

- The National Insurance Crime Bureau ranked 380 metro areas in the U.S. in terms of per capita rates of vehicle theft. The Hartford* metro area ranked #169 (#1 = highest rate). Criteria: number of vehicle theft offenses per 100,000 inhabitants in 2014. *National Insurance Crime Bureau, "Hot Spots 2014," June 24, 2015*

Seniors/Retirement Rankings

- From its Best Cities for Successful Aging indexes, the Milken Institute generated rankings for metropolitan areas, weighing data in eight categories—health care, wellness, living arrangements, transportation, financial characteristics, education and employment opportunities, community engagement, and overall livability. The Hartford* metro area was ranked #41 overall in the large metro area category. *Milken Institute, "Best Cities for Successful Aging, 2014"*

Miscellaneous Rankings

- The National Alliance to End Homelessness ranked the 100 most populous metro areas with the highest rate of homelessness. The Hartford* metro area ranked #93. Criteria: number of homeless people per 10,000 population in 2011. *National Alliance to End Homelessness, The State of Homelessness in America 2012*

Glastonbury is located within the Hartford-West Hartford-East Hartford, CT Metropolitan Statistical Area.

Business Environment

CITY FINANCES

City Government Finances

Component	2012 ($000)	2012 ($ per capita)
Total Revenues	169,573	4,925
Total Expenditures	143,739	4,175
Debt Outstanding	94,413	2,742
Cash and Securities[1]	52,356	1,520

Note: (1) Cash and security holdings of a government at the close of its fiscal year, including those of its dependent agencies, utilities, and liquor stores.
Source: U.S Census Bureau, State & Local Government Finances 2012

City Government Revenue by Source

Source	2012 ($000)	2012 ($ per capita)
General Revenue		
From Federal Government	296	8
From State Government	33,497	972
From Local Governments	783	22
Taxes		
Property	125,803	3,654
Sales and Gross Receipts	0	0
Personal Income	0	0
Corporate Income	0	0
Motor Vehicle License	0	0
Other Taxes	1,403	40
Current Charges	5,435	157
Liquor Store	0	0
Utility	0	0
Employee Retirement	0	0

Source: U.S Census Bureau, State & Local Government Finances 2012

City Government Expenditures by Function

Function	2012 ($000)	2012 ($ per capita)	2012 (%)
General Direct Expenditures			
Air Transportation	0	0	0.0
Corrections	0	0	0.0
Education	98,870	2,871	68.7
Employment Security Administration	0	0	0.0
Financial Administration	2,472	71	1.7
Fire Protection	1,300	37	0.9
General Public Buildings	1,804	52	1.2
Governmental Administration, Other	1,491	43	1.0
Health	557	16	0.3
Highways	6,558	190	4.5
Hospitals	0	0	0.0
Housing and Community Development	539	15	0.3
Interest on General Debt	3,478	101	2.4
Judicial and Legal	344	9	0.2
Libraries	1,765	51	1.2
Parking	0	0	0.0
Parks and Recreation	3,317	96	2.3
Police Protection	9,656	280	6.7
Public Welfare	2,969	86	2.0
Sewerage	1,751	50	1.2
Solid Waste Management	681	19	0.4
Veterans' Services	0	0	0.0
Liquor Store	0	0	0.0
Utility	0	0	0.0
Employee Retirement	0	0	0.0

Source: U.S Census Bureau, State & Local Government Finances 2012

DEMOGRAPHICS

Population Growth

Area	1990 Census	2000 Census	2010 Census	2014* Estimate	Population Growth (%) 1990-2014	2010-2014
City	27,901	31,876	34,427	34,661	24.2	0.7
MSA[1]	1,123,706	1,148,618	1,212,381	1,215,159	8.1	0.2
U.S.	248,709,873	281,421,906	308,745,538	314,107,084	26.3	1.7

Note: (1) Figures cover the Hartford-West Hartford-East Hartford, CT Metropolitan Statistical Area—see Appendix B for areas included; (*) 2010-2014 5-year estimated population
Source: U.S. Census Bureau, 1990 Census, Census 2000, Census 2010, 2010-2014 American Community Survey 5-Year Estimates

Household Size

Area	Persons in Household (%) One	Two	Three	Four	Five	Six	Seven or More	Average Household Size
City	23.0	35.2	16.5	16.2	6.3	1.7	0.7	2.61
MSA[1]	28.2	33.6	16.0	14.2	5.5	1.6	0.6	2.48
U.S.	27.5	33.5	15.8	13.1	6.0	2.3	1.4	2.64

Note: (1) Figures cover the Hartford-West Hartford-East Hartford, CT Metropolitan Statistical Area—see Appendix B for areas included
Source: U.S. Census Bureau, 2010-2014 American Community Survey 5-Year Estimates

Race

Area	White Alone[2] (%)	Black Alone[2] (%)	Asian Alone[2] (%)	AIAN[3] Alone[2] (%)	NHOPI[4] Alone[2] (%)	Other Race Alone[2] (%)	Two or More Races (%)
City	85.4	2.4	9.6	0.0	0.0	1.3	1.4
MSA[1]	77.2	10.8	4.3	0.2	0.0	4.5	3.0
U.S.	73.8	12.6	5.0	0.8	0.2	4.7	2.9

Note: (1) Figures cover the Hartford-West Hartford-East Hartford, CT Metropolitan Statistical Area—see Appendix B for areas included; (2) Alone is defined as not being in combination with one or more other races; (3) American Indian and Alaska Native; (4) Native Hawaiian and Other Pacific Islander
Source: U.S. Census Bureau, 2010-2014 American Community Survey 5-Year Estimates

Hispanic or Latino Origin

Area	Total (%)	Mexican (%)	Puerto Rican (%)	Cuban (%)	Other (%)
City	3.9	0.6	1.3	0.2	1.8
MSA[1]	13.3	0.9	9.0	0.3	3.0
U.S.	16.9	10.8	1.6	0.6	3.8

Note: Persons of Hispanic or Latino origin can be of any race; (1) Figures cover the Hartford-West Hartford-East Hartford, CT Metropolitan Statistical Area—see Appendix B for areas included
Source: U.S. Census Bureau, 2010-2014 American Community Survey 5-Year Estimates

Ancestry

Area	German	Irish	English	American	Italian	Polish	French[2]	Scottish	Dutch
City	12.6	21.1	12.9	5.3	19.4	10.0	6.2	2.4	0.8
MSA[1]	9.2	16.0	9.4	4.0	16.8	10.2	7.2	1.8	0.7
U.S.	14.9	10.8	8.0	7.1	5.5	3.0	2.7	1.7	1.4

Note: Figures are the percentage of the total population reporting a particular ancestry. The nine most commonly reported ancestries in the U.S. are shown. Figures include multiple ancestries (e.g. if a person reported being Irish and Italian, they were included in both columns); (1) Figures cover the Hartford-West Hartford-East Hartford, CT Metropolitan Statistical Area—see Appendix B for areas included; (2) Excludes Basque
Source: U.S. Census Bureau, 2010-2014 American Community Survey 5-Year Estimates

Foreign-Born Population

Area	Percent of Population Born in								
	Any Foreign Country	Asia	Mexico	Europe	Carribean	Central America[2]	South America	Africa	Canada
City	12.4	5.4	0.2	3.6	0.2	0.2	1.1	0.9	0.7
MSA[1]	12.8	3.3	0.4	3.9	2.2	0.4	1.4	0.6	0.6
U.S.	13.1	3.8	3.7	1.5	1.2	1.0	0.9	0.6	0.3

Note: (1) Figures cover the Hartford-West Hartford-East Hartford, CT Metropolitan Statistical Area—see Appendix B for areas included; (2) Excludes Mexico.
Source: U.S. Census Bureau, 2010-2014 American Community Survey 5-Year Estimates

Marital Status

Area	Never Married	Now Married[2]	Separated	Widowed	Divorced
City	25.6	57.0	1.0	5.8	10.6
MSA[1]	34.1	47.5	1.5	5.9	11.1
U.S.	32.5	48.4	2.2	5.9	10.9

Note: Figures are percentages and cover the population 15 years of age and older; (1) Figures cover the Hartford-West Hartford-East Hartford, CT Metropolitan Statistical Area—see Appendix B for areas included; (2) Excludes separated
Source: U.S. Census Bureau, 2010-2014 American Community Survey 5-Year Estimates

Disability Status

Area	All Ages	Under 18 Years Old	18 to 64 Years Old	65 Years and Over
City	7.3	2.8	4.7	25.7
MSA[1]	11.2	4.1	8.5	33.4
U.S.	12.3	4.1	10.2	36.3

Note: Figures show percent of the civilian noninstitutionalized population that reported having a disability. Disability status is determined from from six types of difficulty: vision, hearing, cognitive, ambulatory, self-care, and independent living. For children under 5 years old, hearing and vision difficulty are used to determine disability status. For children between the ages of 5 and 14, disability status is determined from hearing, vision, cognitive, ambulatory, and self-care difficulties. For people aged 15 years and older, they are considered to have a disability if they have difficulty with any one of the six difficulty types; (1) Figures cover the Hartford-West Hartford-East Hartford, CT Metropolitan Statistical Area—see Appendix B for areas included.
Source: U.S. Census Bureau, 2010-2014 American Community Survey 5-Year Estimates

Age

Area	Percent of Population									Median Age
	Under Age 5	Age 5–19	Age 20–34	Age 35–44	Age 45–54	Age 55–64	Age 65–74	Age 75–84	Age 85+	
City	5.5	21.8	10.3	14.1	18.2	14.8	8.6	4.3	2.5	43.9
MSA[1]	5.2	19.5	19.0	12.5	15.6	13.2	7.9	4.6	2.5	40.4
U.S.	6.4	19.9	20.6	13.0	14.1	12.3	7.6	4.3	1.9	37.4

Note: (1) Figures cover the Hartford-West Hartford-East Hartford, CT Metropolitan Statistical Area—see Appendix B for areas included
Source: U.S. Census Bureau, 2010-2014 American Community Survey 5-Year Estimates

Gender

Area	Males	Females	Males per 100 Females
City	16,872	17,789	94.8
MSA[1]	592,094	623,065	95.0
U.S.	154,515,159	159,591,925	96.8

Note: (1) Figures cover the Hartford-West Hartford-East Hartford, CT Metropolitan Statistical Area—see Appendix B for areas included
Source: U.S. Census Bureau, 2010-2014 American Community Survey 5-Year Estimates

Religious Groups by Family

Area	Catholic	Baptist	Non-Den.	Methodist[2]	Lutheran	LDS[3]	Pente-costal	Presby-terian[4]	Muslim[5]	Judaism
MSA[1]	30.3	1.9	2.1	1.9	1.3	0.3	0.9	3.6	0.2	1.2
U.S.	19.1	9.3	4.0	4.0	2.3	2.0	1.9	1.6	0.8	0.7

Note: Figures are the number of adherents as a percentage of the total population; (1) Figures cover the Hartford-West Hartford-East Hartford, CT Metropolitan Statistical Area—see Appendix B for areas included; (2) Methodist/Pietist; (3) Latter Day Saints; (4) Reformed; (5) Figures are estimates
Source: Association of Statisticians of American Religious Bodies, 2010 U.S. Religion Census: Religious Congregations & Membership Study

Religious Groups by Tradition

Area	Catholic	Evangelical Protestant	Mainline Protestant	Other Tradition	Black Protestant	Orthodox
MSA[1]	30.3	4.8	8.2	2.6	0.7	0.3
U.S.	19.1	16.2	7.3	4.3	1.6	0.3

Note: Figures are the number of adherents as a percentage of the total population; (1) Figures cover the Hartford-West Hartford-East Hartford, CT Metropolitan Statistical Area—see Appendix B for areas included
Source: Association of Statisticians of American Religious Bodies, 2010 U.S. Religion Census: Religious Congregations & Membership Study

ECONOMY

Gross Metropolitan Product

Area	2013	2014	2015	2016	Rank[2]
MSA[1]	86.6	89.9	93.0	96.5	40

Note: Figures are in billions of dollars; (1) Figures cover the Hartford-West Hartford-East Hartford, CT Metropolitan Statistical Area—see Appendix B for areas included; (2) Rank is based on 2016 data and ranges from 1 to 381
Source: The U.S. Conference of Mayors, U.S. Metro Economies: GMP and Employment 2014-2016, June 2015

Economic Growth

Area	2011-13 (%)	2014 (%)	2015 (%)	2016 (%)	Rank[2]
MSA[1]	0.8	2.0	2.0	1.9	303
U.S.	2.2	2.4	2.3	2.9	–

Note: Figures are real gross metropolitan product (GMP) growth rates and represent annual average percent change; (1) Figures cover the Hartford-West Hartford-East Hartford, CT Metropolitan Statistical Area—see Appendix B for areas included; (2) Rank is based on 2016 data and ranges from 1 to 381
Source: The U.S. Conference of Mayors, U.S. Metro Economies: GMP and Employment 2014-2016, June 2015

Metropolitan Area Exports

Area	2009	2010	2011	2012	2013	2014	Rank[2]
MSA[1]	7,542.1	7,894.2	9,321.5	9,680.3	10,152.2	10,463.9	30

Note: Figures are in millions of dollars; (1) Figures cover the Hartford-West Hartford-East Hartford, CT Metropolitan Statistical Area—see Appendix B for areas included; (2) Rank is based on 2014 data and ranges from 1 to 385
Source: U.S. Department of Commerce, International Trade Administration, Office of Trade & Industry Information, Manufacturing & Services, data extracted March 10, 2016

Building Permits

Area	Single-Family			Multi-Family			Total		
	2014	2015p	Pct. Chg.	2014	2015p	Pct. Chg.	2014	2015p	Pct. Chg.
City	25	39	56.0	0	2	-	25	41	64.0
MSA[1]	754	792	5.0	639	866	35.5	1,393	1,658	19.0
U.S.	640,300	690,800	7.9	411,800	487,600	18.4	1,052,100	1,178,400	12.0

Note: (1) Figures cover the Hartford-West Hartford-East Hartford, CT Metropolitan Statistical Area—see Appendix B for areas included; Figures represent new, privately-owned housing units authorized (unadjusted data); All permit data are based on estimates with imputation; (p) preliminary data.
Source: U.S. Census Bureau, Manufacturing, Mining, and Construction Statistics, Building Permits, 2014, 2015

Bankruptcy Filings

Area	Business Filings			Nonbusiness Filings		
	2014	2015	% Chg.	2014	2015	% Chg.
Hartford County	79	74	-6.3	1,563	1,403	-10.2
U.S.	26,983	24,735	-8.3	909,812	819,760	-9.9

Note: Business filings include Chapter 7, Chapter 11, Chapter 12, and Chapter 13; Nonbusiness filings include Chapter 7, Chapter 11, and Chapter 13
Source: Administrative Office of the U.S. Courts, Business and Nonbusiness Bankruptcy, County Cases Commenced by Chapter of the Bankruptcy Code, During the 12- Month Period Ending December 31, 2014 and Business and Nonbusiness Bankruptcy, County Cases Commenced by Chapter of the Bankruptcy Code, During the 12- Month Period Ending December 31, 2015

Housing Vacancy Rates

Area	Gross Vacancy Rate[2] (%)			Year-Round Vacancy Rate[3] (%)			Rental Vacancy Rate[4] (%)			Homeowner Vacancy Rate[5] (%)		
	2013	2014	2015	2013	2014	2015	2013	2014	2015	2013	2014	2015
MSA[1]	9.9	8.2	10.5	9.2	7.5	9.7	9.0	6.0	6.1	1.0	1.3	1.5
U.S.	13.6	13.4	12.9	10.7	10.4	10.0	8.3	7.6	7.1	2.0	1.9	1.8

Note: (1) Figures cover the Hartford-West Hartford-East Hartford, CT Metropolitan Statistical Area—see Appendix B for areas included; (2) The percentage of the total housing inventory that is vacant; (3) The percentage of the housing inventory (excluding seasonal units) that is year-round vacant; (4) The percentage of rental inventory that is vacant for rent; (5) The percentage of homeowner inventory that is vacant for sale
Source: U.S. Census Bureau, Housing Vacancies and Homeownership Annual Statistics: 2015

INCOME

Income

Area	Per Capita ($)	Median Household ($)	Average Household ($)
City	55,678	108,157	145,318
MSA[1]	35,991	68,959	90,995
U.S.	28,555	53,482	74,596

Note: (1) Figures cover the Hartford-West Hartford-East Hartford, CT Metropolitan Statistical Area—see Appendix B for areas included
Source: U.S. Census Bureau, 2010-2014 American Community Survey 5-Year Estimates

Household Income Distribution

Area	Percent of Households Earning							
	Under $15,000	$15,000 -24,999	$25,000 -34,999	$35,000 -49,999	$50,000 -74,999	$75,000 -99,000	$100,000 -149,999	$150,000 and up
City	5.0	4.5	2.9	7.1	13.9	12.7	20.4	33.4
MSA[1]	9.6	8.6	7.8	10.8	16.8	13.5	17.3	15.6
U.S.	12.5	10.7	10.2	13.5	17.8	12.2	13.0	10.0

Note: (1) Figures cover the Hartford-West Hartford-East Hartford, CT Metropolitan Statistical Area—see Appendix B for areas included
Source: U.S. Census Bureau, 2010-2014 American Community Survey 5-Year Estimates

Poverty Rate

Area	All Ages	Under 18 Years Old	18 to 64 Years Old	65 Years and Over
City	3.7	2.7	3.7	5.4
MSA[1]	10.7	14.3	10.3	7.4
U.S.	15.6	21.9	14.6	9.4

Note: Figures are percentage of people whose income during the past 12 months was below the poverty level; (1) Figures cover the Hartford-West Hartford-East Hartford, CT Metropolitan Statistical Area—see Appendix B for areas included
Source: U.S. Census Bureau, 2010-2014 American Community Survey 5-Year Estimates

EMPLOYMENT

Labor Force and Employment

Area	Civilian Labor Force			Workers Employed		
	Dec. 2014	Dec. 2015	% Chg.	Dec. 2014	Dec. 2015	% Chg.
City	18,712	18,686	-0.1	18,016	18,047	0.1
NECTA[1]	616,412	614,187	-0.3	581,558	583,499	0.3
U.S.	155,521,000	157,245,000	1.1	147,190,000	149,703,000	1.7

Note: Data is not seasonally adjusted and covers workers 16 years of age and older; (1) Figures cover the Hartford-West Hartford-East Hartford, CT New England City and Town Area—see Appendix B for areas included
Source: Bureau of Labor Statistics, Local Area Unemployment Statistics

Unemployment Rate

Area	2015											
	Jan.	Feb.	Mar.	Apr.	May	Jun.	Jul.	Aug.	Sep.	Oct.	Nov.	Dec.
City	4.4	4.4	4.1	3.7	3.7	3.8	3.8	3.7	3.5	3.4	3.2	3.4
NECTA[1]	6.8	6.8	6.5	5.8	5.5	5.4	5.7	5.6	5.0	4.8	4.8	5.0
U.S.	6.1	5.8	5.6	5.1	5.3	5.5	5.6	5.2	4.9	4.8	4.8	4.8

Note: Data is not seasonally adjusted and covers workers 16 years of age and older; (1) Figures cover the Hartford-West Hartford-East Hartford, CT New England City and Town Area—see Appendix B for areas included
Source: Bureau of Labor Statistics, Local Area Unemployment Statistics

Employment by Occupation

Occupation Classification	City (%)	MSA[1] (%)	U.S. (%)
Management, Business, Science, and Arts	60.5	42.6	36.4
Natural Resources, Construction, and Maintenance	3.6	6.9	9.0
Production, Transportation, and Material Moving	3.5	9.9	12.1
Sales and Office	22.1	23.9	24.4
Service	10.4	16.7	18.2

Note: Figures cover employed civilians 16 years of age and older; (1) Figures cover the Hartford-West Hartford-East Hartford, CT Metropolitan Statistical Area—see Appendix B for areas included
Source: U.S. Census Bureau, 2010-2014 American Community Survey 5-Year Estimates

Employment by Industry

Sector	NECTA[1]		U.S.
	Number of Employees	Percent of Total	Percent of Total
Construction, Mining, and Logging	19,500	3.3	5.0
Education and Health Services	106,000	18.4	15.7
Financial Activities	57,400	9.9	5.7
Government	91,100	15.8	15.5
Information	11,900	2.0	1.9
Leisure and Hospitality	47,300	8.2	10.4
Manufacturing	55,600	9.6	8.6
Other Services	21,800	3.7	3.9
Professional and Business Services	73,400	12.7	13.9
Retail Trade	57,100	9.9	11.3
Transportation, Warehousing, and Utilities	17,200	2.9	3.9
Wholesale Trade	17,800	3.0	4.1

Note: Figures are non-farm employment as of December 2015. Figures are not seasonally adjusted and include workers 16 years of age and older; (1) Figures cover the Hartford-West Hartford-East Hartford, CT New England City and Town Area—see Appendix B for areas included; n/a not available
Source: Bureau of Labor Statistics, Current Employment Statistics, Employment, Hours, and Earnings

Occupations with Greatest Projected Employment Growth: 2012 – 2022

Occupation[1]	2012 Employment	2022 Projected Employment	Numeric Employment Change	Percent Employment Change
Personal Care Aides	23,240	32,090	8,850	38.1
Registered Nurses	35,990	41,230	5,240	14.6
Secretaries and Administrative Assistants, Except Legal, Medical, and Executive	34,530	38,640	4,110	11.9
Combined Food Preparation and Serving Workers, Including Fast Food	26,730	30,740	4,010	15.0
Retail Salespersons	53,800	57,270	3,470	6.4
General and Operations Managers	31,160	34,420	3,260	10.5
Home Health Aides	8,250	11,450	3,200	38.7
Childcare Workers	18,300	21,170	2,870	15.7
Maids and Housekeeping Cleaners	17,800	20,560	2,760	15.5
First-Line Supervisors of Office and Administrative Support Workers	26,360	28,900	2,540	9.6

Note: Projections cover Connecticut; (1) Sorted by numeric employment change
Source: www.projectionscentral.com, State Occupational Projections, 2012–2022 Long-Term Projections

Fastest Growing Occupations: 2012 – 2022

Occupation[1]	2012 Employment	2022 Projected Employment	Numeric Employment Change	Percent Employment Change
Insulation Workers, Mechanical	210	350	140	65.6
Interpreters and Translators	460	650	190	43.1
Helpers—Electricians	270	380	110	39.4
Home Health Aides	8,250	11,450	3,200	38.7
Diagnostic Medical Sonographers	1,000	1,380	380	38.3
Personal Care Aides	23,240	32,090	8,850	38.1
Physical Therapist Assistants	540	740	200	37.4
Occupational Therapy Assistants	490	670	180	35.4
Health Specialties Teachers, Postsecondary	2,810	3,770	960	34.3
Nursing Instructors and Teachers, Postsecondary	700	940	240	34.0

Note: Projections cover Connecticut; (1) Sorted by percent employment change and excludes occupations with numeric employment change less than 100
Source: www.projectionscentral.com, State Occupational Projections, 2012–2022 Long-Term Projections

Average Wages

Occupation	$/Hr.	Occupation	$/Hr.
Accountants and Auditors	36.17	Maids and Housekeeping Cleaners	12.62
Automotive Mechanics	19.62	Maintenance and Repair Workers	20.71
Bookkeepers	20.84	Marketing Managers	64.39
Carpenters	24.27	Nuclear Medicine Technologists	39.03
Cashiers	10.82	Nurses, Licensed Practical	27.04
Clerks, General Office	17.91	Nurses, Registered	36.53
Clerks, Receptionists/Information	16.53	Nursing Assistants	14.90
Clerks, Shipping/Receiving	16.88	Packers and Packagers, Hand	14.20
Computer Programmers	36.77	Physical Therapists	39.83
Computer Systems Analysts	44.04	Postal Service Mail Carriers	24.89
Computer User Support Specialists	28.45	Real Estate Brokers	48.04
Cooks, Restaurant	12.22	Retail Salespersons	13.26
Dentists	91.66	Sales Reps., Exc. Tech./Scientific	36.73
Electrical Engineers	44.18	Sales Reps., Tech./Scientific	46.11
Electricians	25.35	Secretaries, Exc. Legal/Med./Exec.	20.92
Financial Managers	68.35	Security Guards	14.25
First-Line Supervisors/Managers, Sales	23.15	Surgeons	108.58
Food Preparation Workers	11.17	Teacher Assistants*	13.61
General and Operations Managers	61.27	Teachers, Elementary School*	35.68
Hairdressers/Cosmetologists	14.53	Teachers, Secondary School*	34.92
Internists	83.89	Telemarketers	13.44
Janitors and Cleaners	15.34	Truck Drivers, Heavy/Tractor-Trailer	22.32
Landscaping/Groundskeeping Workers	14.82	Truck Drivers, Light/Delivery Svcs.	17.04
Lawyers	65.46	Waiters and Waitresses	11.02

Note: Wage data covers the New England City and Town Area—see Appendix B for areas included; (*) Hourly wages for elementary/secondary school teachers and teacher assistants were calculated by the editors from annual wage data based on a 40 hour work week; n/a not available.
Source: Bureau of Labor Statistics, Metro Area Occupational Employment and Wage Estimates, May 2015

TAXES

State Corporate Income Tax Rates

State	Tax Rate (%)	Income Brackets ($)	Num. of Brackets	Financial Institution Tax Rate (%)[a]	Federal Income Tax Ded.
Connecticut	7.5 (d)	Flat rate	1	7.5 (d)	No

Note: Tax rates as of January 1, 2016; (a) Rates listed are the corporate income tax rate applied to financial institutions or excise taxes based on income. Some states have other taxes based upon the value of deposits or shares; (d) Connecticut's tax is the greater of the 7.5% tax on net income, a 0.31% tax on capital stock and surplus (maximum tax of $1 million), or $250 (the minimum tax). Plus, an additional 20% surtax applies for tax years 2012 and 2016.
Source: Federation of Tax Administrators, "State Corporate Income Tax Rates, 2016"

State Individual Income Tax Rates

State	Tax Rate (%)	Income Brackets ($)	Num. of Brackets	Personal Exempt. ($)[1] Single	Personal Exempt. ($)[1] Dependents	Fed. Inc. Tax Ded.
Connecticut	3.0 - 6.99	10,000 - 500,000 (b)	7	14,500 (g)	None	No

Note: Tax rates as of January 1, 2016; Local- and county-level taxes are not included; n/a not applicable; (1) Married joint filers generally receive double the single exemption; (b) For joint returns, taxes are twice the tax on half the couple's income; (g) Connecticut's personal exemption incorporates a standard deduction. An additional tax credit is allowed ranging from 75% to 0% based on state adjusted gross income. Exemption amounts are phased out for higher income taxpayers until they are eliminated for households earning over $71,000.
Source: Federation of Tax Administrators, "State Individual Income Tax Rates, 2016"

Various State and Local Tax Rates

State	State and Local Sales and Use (%)	State Sales and Use (%)	Gasoline[1] (¢/gal.)	Cigarette[2] ($/pack)	Spirits[3] ($/gal.)	Wine[4] ($/gal.)	Beer[5] ($/gal.)
Connecticut	6.35	6.35	37.51	3.65	5.40 (f)	0.72 (l)	0.16

Note: All tax rates as of January 1, 2016; (1) The American Petroleum Institute has developed a methodology for determining the average tax rate on a gallon of fuel. Rates may include any of the following: excise taxes, environmental fees, storage tank fees, other fees or taxes, general sales tax, and local taxes. In states where gasoline is subject to the general sales tax, or where the fuel tax is based on the average sale price, the average rate determined by API is sensitive to changes in the price of gasoline. States that fully or partially apply general sales taxes to gasoline: CA, CO, GA, IL, IN, MI, NY; (2) The federal excise tax of $1.0066 per pack and local taxes are not included; (3) Rates are those applicable to off-premise sales of 40% alcohol by volume (a.b.v.) distilled spirits in 750ml containers. Local excise taxes are excluded; (4) Rates are those applicable to off-premise sales of 11% a.b.v. non-carbonated wine in 750ml containers; (5) Rates are those applicable to off-premise sales of 4.7% a.b.v. beer in 12 ounce containers; (f) Different rates are also applicable according to alcohol content, place of production, size of container, or place purchased (on- or off-premise or onboard airlines); (l) Different rates also applicable according to alcohol content, place of production, size of container, place purchased (on- or off-premise or on board airlines) or type of wine (carbonated, vermouth, etc.).
Source: Tax Foundation, 2016 Facts & Figures: How Does Your State Compare?

State Business Tax Climate Index Rankings

State	Overall Rank	Corporate Tax Rank	Individual Income Tax Rank	Sales Tax Rank	Unemployment Insurance Tax Rank	Property Tax Rank
Connecticut	44	33	36	29	20	49

Note: The index is a measure of how each state's tax laws affect economic performance. The lower the rank, the more favorable a state's tax system is for business. States without a given tax are given a ranking of 1. The scores/rankings for the District of Columbia do not affect other states. The 2016 index represents the tax climate as of July 1, 2015 (the beginning of Fiscal Year 2016).
Source: Tax Foundation, State Business Tax Climate Index 2016

TRANSPORTATION

Means of Transportation to Work

Area	Car/Truck/Van		Public Transportation			Bicycle	Walked	Other Means	Worked at Home
	Drove Alone	Car-pooled	Bus	Subway	Railroad				
City	84.0	5.6	0.6	0.0	0.1	0.1	2.3	1.1	6.3
MSA[1]	81.4	7.9	3.0	0.0	0.1	0.2	2.7	1.0	3.7
U.S.	76.4	9.6	2.6	1.8	0.6	0.6	2.8	1.3	4.4

Note: Figures are percentages and cover workers 16 years of age and older; (1) Figures cover the Hartford-West Hartford-East Hartford, CT Metropolitan Statistical Area—see Appendix B for areas included
Source: U.S. Census Bureau, 2010-2014 American Community Survey 5-Year Estimates

Travel Time to Work

Area	Less Than 10 Minutes	10 to 19 Minutes	20 to 29 Minutes	30 to 44 Minutes	45 to 59 Minutes	60 to 89 Minutes	90 Minutes or More
City	12.9	30.8	25.4	21.1	5.0	2.8	1.9
MSA[1]	13.2	31.3	24.1	20.7	6.0	3.1	1.5
U.S.	13.3	29.6	21.0	20.2	7.7	5.7	2.6

Note: Figures are percentages and include workers 16 years old and over; (1) Figures cover the Hartford-West Hartford-East Hartford, CT Metropolitan Statistical Area—see Appendix B for areas included
Source: U.S. Census Bureau, 2010-2014 American Community Survey 5-Year Estimates

Freeway Travel Time Index

Area	1985	1990	1995	2000	2005	2010	2014
Urban Area Rank[1,2]	64	56	47	57	42	36	37
Urban Area Index[1]	1.05	1.09	1.13	1.15	1.18	1.20	1.20
Average Index[3]	1.09	1.11	1.14	1.17	1.20	1.19	1.20

Note: Freeway Travel Time Index—the ratio of travel time in the peak period to the travel time at free-flow conditions. For example, a value of 1.30 indicates a 20-minute free-flow trip takes 26 minutes in the peak (20 minutes x 1.30 = 26 minutes); (1) Covers the Hartford CT urban area; (2) Rank is based on 101 urban areas (#1 = highest travel time index); (3) Average of 101 urban areas
Source: Texas Transportation Institute, 2015 Urban Mobility Scorecard, August 2015

Freeway Commuter Stress Index

Area	1985	1990	1995	2000	2005	2010	2014
Urban Area Rank[1,2]	58	51	50	54	47	40	43
Urban Area Index[1]	1.08	1.12	1.16	1.18	1.21	1.23	1.23
Average Index[3]	1.13	1.16	1.19	1.22	1.25	1.24	1.25

Note: The Freeway Commuter Stress Index is the same as the Freeway Travel Time Index (see table above) except that it includes only the travel in the peak directions during the peak periods; the TTI includes travel in all directions during the peak period. Thus, the CSI is more indicative of the work trip experienced by each commuter on a daily basis. (1) Covers the Hartford CT urban area; (2) Rank is based on 101 urban areas (#1 = highest stress index); (3) Average of 101 urban areas

Source: Texas Transportation Institute, 2015 Urban Mobility Scorecard, August 2015

Living Environment

COST OF LIVING

Cost of Living Index

Composite Index	Groceries	Housing	Utilities	Trans-portation	Health Care	Misc. Goods/ Services
124.5	129.7	133.0	129.4	110.4	118.2	119.2

Note: The Cost of Living Index measures regional differences in the cost of consumer goods and services, excluding taxes and non-consumer expenditures, for professional and managerial households in the top income quintile. It is based on more than 50,000 prices covering almost 60 different items for which prices are collected three times a year by chambers of commerce, economic development organizations or university applied economic centers in each participating urban area. The numbers shown should be read as a percentage above or below the national average of 100. For example, a value of 115.4 in the groceries column indicates that grocery prices are 15.4% higher than the national average. Small differences in the index numbers should not be interpreted as significant; Figures cover the Hartford CT urban area.
Source: The Council for Community and Economic Research, ACCRA Cost of Living Index, 2015

Grocery Prices

Area[1]	T-Bone Steak ($/pound)	Frying Chicken ($/pound)	Whole Milk ($/half gal.)	Eggs ($/dozen)	Orange Juice ($/64 oz.)	Coffee ($/11.5 oz.)
City[2]	11.62	1.64	2.99	2.51	3.83	3.85
Avg.	10.99	1.43	2.25	2.26	3.58	4.48
Min.	7.16	0.98	1.30	1.35	2.88	2.98
Max.	14.13	2.43	3.85	4.81	6.39	7.56

Note: (1) Values for the local area are compared with the average, minimum and maximum values for all 292 areas in the Cost of Living Index; (2) Figures cover the Hartford CT urban area; **T-Bone Steak** *(price per pound);* **Frying Chicken** *(price per pound, whole fryer);* **Whole Milk** *(half gallon carton);* **Eggs** *(price per dozen, Grade A, large);* **Orange Juice** *(64 oz. Tropicana or Florida Natural);* **Coffee** *(11.5 oz. can, vacuum-packed, Maxwell House, Hills Bros, or Folgers).*
Source: The Council for Community and Economic Research, ACCRA Cost of Living Index, 2015

Housing and Utility Costs

Area[1]	New Home Price ($)	Apartment Rent ($/month)	All Electric ($/month)	Part Electric ($/month)	Other Energy ($/month)	Telephone ($/month)
City[2]	429,480	1,123	-	148.46	119.90	24.95
Avg.	312,874	945	179.30	95.07	72.96	28.11
Min.	178,682	479	116.28	43.14	26.46	10.01
Max.	1,472,476	3,984	504.25	189.44	421.11	43.06

Note: (1) Values for the local area are compared with the average, minimum and maximum values for all 292 areas in the Cost of Living Index; (2) Figures cover the Hartford CT urban area; **New Home Price** *(2,400 sf living area, 8,000 sf lot, in urban area with full utilities);* **Apartment Rent** *(950 sf 2 bedroom/1.5 or 2 bath, unfurnished, excluding all utilities except water);* **All Electric** *(average monthly cost for an all-electric home);* **Part Electric** *(average monthly cost for a part-electric home);* **Other Energy** *(average monthly cost for natural gas, fuel oil, coal, wood, and any other forms of energy except electricity);* **Telephone** *(price includes basic monthly rate for a private residential line plus additional local usage charges incurred by a family of four).*
Source: The Council for Community and Economic Research, ACCRA Cost of Living Index, 2015

Health Care, Transportation, and Other Costs

Area[1]	Doctor ($/visit)	Dentist ($/visit)	Optometrist ($/visit)	Gasoline ($/gallon)	Beauty Salon ($/visit)	Men's Shirt ($)
City[2]	123.77	122.94	116.73	2.57	47.06	26.88
Avg.	105.15	89.02	99.78	2.38	35.30	28.10
Min.	66.87	56.09	48.53	1.95	18.91	13.38
Max.	182.34	150.36	228.33	4.09	67.91	63.80

Note: (1) Values for the local area are compared with the average, minimum and maximum values for all 292 areas in the Cost of Living Index; (2) Figures cover the Hartford CT urban area; **Doctor** *(general practitioners routine exam of an established patient);* **Dentist** *(adult teeth cleaning and periodic oral examination);* **Optometrist** *(full vision eye exam for established adult patient);* **Gasoline** *(one gallon regular unleaded, national brand, including all taxes, cash price at self-service pump if available);* **Beauty Salon** *(woman's shampoo, trim, and blow-dry);* **Men's Shirt** *(cotton/polyester dress shirt, pinpoint weave, long sleeves).*
Source: The Council for Community and Economic Research, ACCRA Cost of Living Index, 2015

HOUSING

House Price Index (HPI)

Area	National Ranking[2]	Quarterly Change (%)	One-Year Change (%)	Five-Year Change (%)
MSA[1]	258	-0.10	0.50	-4.00
U.S.[3]	–	1.45	5.76	22.85

Note: The HPI is a weighted repeat sales index. It measures average price changes in repeat sales or refinancings on the same properties. This information is obtained by reviewing repeat mortgage transactions on single-family properties whose mortgages have been purchased or securitized by Fannie Mae or Freddie Mac in January 1975; (1) Hartford-West Hartford-East Hartford Metropolitan Statistical Area—see Appendix B for areas included; (2) Rankings are based on annual percentage change for all metro areas containing at least 15,000 transactions over the last 10 years and ranges from 1 to 266; (3) figures based on a weighted average of Census Division estimates using a seasonally adjusted, purchase-only index; all figures are for the period ending December 31, 2015

Source: Federal Housing Finance Agency, House Price Index, February 25, 2016

Median Single-Family Home Prices

Area	2013	2014	2015[p]	Percent Change 2014 to 2015
MSA[1]	227.0	220.9	221.5	0.3
U.S. Average	197.4	208.9	223.9	7.2

Note: Figures are median sales prices of existing single-family homes in thousands of dollars; (p) preliminary; n/a not available; (1) Hartford-West Hartford-East Hartford, CT Metropolitan Statistical Area—see Appendix B for areas included

Source: National Association of Realtors, Median Sales Price of Existing Single-Family Homes for Metropolitan Areas, 4th Quarter 2015

Qualifying Income Based on Median Sales Price of Existing Single-Family Homes

Area	With 5% Down ($)	With 10% Down ($)	With 20% Down ($)
MSA[1]	47,622	45,116	40,103
U.S. Average	49,535	46,928	41,714

Note: Figures are preliminary; Qualifying income is based on a mortgage rate of 4.1%. Monthly principal and interest payment is limited to 25% of income; n/a not available; (1) Hartford-West Hartford-East Hartford, CT Metropolitan Statistical Area—see Appendix B for areas included

Source: National Association of Realtors, Qualifying Income Based on Median Sales Price of Existing Single-Family Homes for Metropolitan Areas, 4th Quarter 2015

Median Apartment Condo-Coop Home Prices

Area	2013	2014	2015[p]	Percent Change 2014 to 2015
MSA[1]	150.2	149.7	148.7	-0.7
U.S. Average	194.9	204.3	210.7	3.1

Note: Figures are median sales prices of existing apartment condo-coop homes in thousands of dollars; (p) preliminary; n/a not available; (1) Hartford-West Hartford-East Hartford, CT Metropolitan Statistical Area—see Appendix B for areas included

Source: National Association of Realtors, Median Sales Price of Existing Apartment Condo-Coop Homes for Metropolitan Areas, 4th Quarter 2015

Gross Monthly Rent

Area	Under $200	$200 -299	$300 -499	$500 -749	$750 -999	$1,000 -1,499	$1,500 and up	Median ($)
City	2.2	1.6	8.5	11.1	13.3	47.0	16.3	1,172
MSA[1]	1.9	4.3	5.7	11.9	26.9	37.3	12.0	995
U.S.	1.5	3.2	7.4	21.0	24.1	26.9	15.9	920

Note: Figures are percentages except for Median; Gross rent is the contract rent plus the estimated average monthly cost of utilities (electricity, gas, and water and sewer) and fuels (oil, coal, kerosene, wood, etc.) if these are paid by the renter (or paid for the renter by someone else); (1) Figures cover the Hartford-West Hartford-East Hartford, CT Metropolitan Statistical Area—see Appendix B for areas included

Source: U.S. Census Bureau, 2010-2014 American Community Survey 5-Year Estimates

Homeownership Rate

Area	2008 (%)	2009 (%)	2010 (%)	2011 (%)	2012 (%)	2013 (%)	2014 (%)	2015 (%)
MSA[1]	70.5	72.1	71.3	71.4	70.8	69.8	68.5	66.1
U.S.	67.8	67.4	66.9	66.1	65.4	65.1	64.5	63.7

Note: (1) Figures cover the Hartford-West Hartford-East Hartford, CT Metropolitan Statistical Area—see Appendix B for areas included
Source: U.S. Census Bureau, Housing Vacancies and Homeownership Annual Statistics: 2015

Year Housing Structure Built

Area	2010 or Later	2000 -2009	1990 -1999	1980 -1989	1970 -1979	1960 -1969	1950 -1959	1940 -1949	Before 1940	Median Year
City	0.4	6.5	15.0	17.6	17.6	12.5	15.1	3.7	11.5	1974
MSA[1]	0.3	7.2	7.7	13.8	13.4	14.1	16.8	7.6	19.0	1965
U.S.	1.0	14.9	13.9	13.8	15.8	11.0	10.8	5.4	13.3	1976

Note: Figures are percentages except for Median Year; (1) Figures cover the Hartford-West Hartford-East Hartford, CT Metropolitan Statistical Area—see Appendix B for areas included
Source: U.S. Census Bureau, 2010-2014 American Community Survey 5-Year Estimates

HEALTH

Health Risk Data

Category	MSA[1] (%)	U.S. (%)
Adults aged 18–64 who have any kind of health care coverage	89.4	79.6
Adults who reported being in good or excellent health	86.3	83.1
Adults who are current smokers	15.3	19.6
Adults who are heavy drinkers[2]	6.4	6.1
Adults who are binge drinkers[3]	17.5	16.9
Adults who are overweight (BMI 25.0 - 29.9)	35.0	35.8
Adults who are obese (BMI 30.0 - 99.8)	26.7	27.6
Adults who participated in any physical activities in the past month	79.0	77.1
Adults 50+ who have ever had a sigmoidoscopy or colonoscopy	74.4	67.3
Women aged 40+ who have had a mammogram within the past two years	83.2	74.0
Men aged 40+ who have had a PSA test within the past two years	50.9	45.2
Adults aged 65+ who have had flu shot within the past year	60.9	60.1
Adults who always wear a seatbelt	95.2	93.8

Note: Data as of 2012 unless otherwise noted; (1) Figures cover the Hartford-West Hartford-East Hartford, CT Metropolitan Statistical Area—see Appendix B for areas included; (2) Heavy drinkers are classified as males having more than two drinks per day or females having more than one drink per day; (3) Binge drinkers are classified as males having five or more drinks on one occasion or females having four or more drinks on one occasion
Source: Centers for Disease Control and Prevention, Behaviorial Risk Factor Surveillance System, SMART: Selected Metropolitan/Micropolitan Area Risk Trends, 2012 (Note: the CDC has discontinued this dataset but will be releasing a replacement in mid-2016)

Chronic Health Indicators

Category	MSA[1] (%)	U.S. (%)
Adults who have ever been told they had a heart attack	3.5	4.5
Adults who have ever been told they had a stroke	2.3	2.9
Adults who have been told they currently have asthma	10.4	8.9
Adults who have ever been told they have arthritis	23.6	25.7
Adults who have ever been told they have diabetes[2]	9.4	9.7
Adults who have ever been told they had skin cancer	5.4	5.7
Adults who have ever been told they had any other types of cancer	6.8	6.5
Adults who have ever been told they have COPD	5.2	6.2
Adults who have ever been told they have kidney disease	2.3	2.5
Adults who have ever been told they have a form of depression	17.5	18.0

Note: Data as of 2012 unless otherwise noted; (1) Figures cover the Hartford-West Hartford-East Hartford, CT Metropolitan Statistical Area—see Appendix B for areas included; (2) Figures do not include pregnancy-related, borderline, or pre-diabetes
Source: Centers for Disease Control and Prevention, Behaviorial Risk Factor Surveillance System, SMART: Selected Metropolitan/Micropolitan Area Risk Trends, 2012 (Note: the CDC has discontinued this dataset but will be releasing a replacement in mid-2016)

Mortality Rates for the Top 10 Causes of Death in the U.S.

ICD-10[a] Sub-Chapter	ICD-10[a] Code	Age-Adjusted Mortality Rate[1] per 100,000 population County[2]	U.S.
Malignant neoplasms	C00-C97	150.4	163.6
Ischaemic heart diseases	I20-I25	81.8	102.2
Other forms of heart disease	I30-I51	61.3	50.1
Chronic lower respiratory diseases	J40-J47	28.9	41.4
Organic, including symptomatic, mental disorders	F01-F09	41.5	38.5
Cerebrovascular diseases	I60-I69	26.3	36.5
Other external causes of accidental injury	W00-X59	31.0	27.5
Other degenerative diseases of the nervous system	G30-G31	17.8	26.3
Diabetes mellitus	E10-E14	14.4	21.1
Hypertensive diseases	I10-I15	12.2	19.7

Note: (a) ICD-10 = International Classification of Diseases 10th Revision; (1) Mortality rates are a three year average covering 2012-2014; (2) Figures cover COUNTY NOT FOUND!!!!!!.
Source: Centers for Disease Control and Prevention, National Center for Health Statistics. Underlying Cause of Death 1999-2014 on CDC WONDER Online Database, released 2015.

Mortality Rates for Selected Causes of Death

ICD-10[a] Sub-Chapter	ICD-10[a] Code	Age-Adjusted Mortality Rate[1] per 100,000 population County[2]	U.S.
Assault	X85-Y09	4.2	5.1
Diseases of the liver	K70-K76	12.3	13.5
Human immunodeficiency virus (HIV) disease	B20-B24	2.6	2.1
Influenza and pneumonia	J09-J18	14.1	15.2
Intentional self-harm	X60-X84	8.9	12.7
Malnutrition	E40-E46	0.7	0.9
Obesity and other hyperalimentation	E65-E68	1.3	1.9
Renal failure	N17-N19	14.1	13.0
Transport accidents	V01-V99	8.5	11.6
Viral hepatitis	B15-B19	1.7	2.1

Note: (a) ICD-10 = International Classification of Diseases 10th Revision; (1) Mortality rates are a three year average covering 2012-2014; (2) Figures cover COUNTY NOT FOUND!!!!!!; Data are Suppressed when the data meet the criteria for confidentiality constraints; Mortality rates are flagged as Unreliable when the rate would be calculated with a numerator of 20 or less.
Source: Centers for Disease Control and Prevention, National Center for Health Statistics. Underlying Cause of Death 1999-2014 on CDC WONDER Online Database, released 2015.

Health Insurance Coverage

Area	With Health Insurance	With Private Health Insurance	With Public Health Insurance	Without Health Insurance	Population Under Age 18 Without Health Insurance
City	95.5	86.4	21.4	4.5	1.8
MSA[1]	92.8	73.8	30.7	7.2	2.7
U.S.	85.8	65.8	31.1	14.2	7.1

Note: Figures are percentages that cover the civilian noninstitutionalized population; (1) Figures cover the Hartford-West Hartford-East Hartford, CT Metropolitan Statistical Area—see Appendix B for areas included
Source: U.S. Census Bureau, 2010-2014 American Community Survey 5-Year Estimates

Number of Medical Professionals

Area	MDs[3]	DOs[3,4]	Dentists	Podiatrists	Chiropractors	Optometrists
County[1] (number)	3,768	202	899	56	193	162
County[1] (rate[2])	419.2	22.5	100.1	6.2	21.5	18.0
U.S. (rate[2])	272.5	20.9	64.7	5.8	25.9	15.2

Note: Data as of 2014 unless noted; (1) Data covers Hartford County; (2) Rate per 100,000 population; (3) Data as of 2013 and includes all active, non-federal physicians; (4) Doctor of Osteopathic Medicine
Source: U.S. Department of Health and Human Services, Health Resources and Services Administration, Bureau of Health Professions, Area Resource File (ARF) 2014-2015

Best Hospitals

According to *U.S. News,* the Hartford-West Hartford-East Hartford, CT metro area is home to one of the best children's hospitals in the U.S.: **Connecticut Children's Medical Center** (1 specialty). The hospital listed was highly ranked in at least one pediatric specialty. Eighty-three children's hospitals in the U.S. were nationally ranked in at least one specialty. Twelve children's hospitals in the U.S. made the Honor Roll with high scores in at least three specialties. *U.S. News Online, "America's Best Children's Hospitals 2015-16"*

EDUCATION

Public School District Statistics

District Name	Schls	Pupils	Pupil/ Teacher Ratio	Minority Pupils[1] (%)	Free Lunch Eligible[2] (%)	IEP[3] (%)
Capitol Region Education Council	24	7,178	10.3	67.3	36.0	n/a
Glastonbury School District	9	6,395	13.2	23.3	6.5	10.1

Note: Table includes school districts with 100 or more students; (1) Percentage of students that are not non-Hispanic white; (2) Percentage of students that are eligible for the free lunch program; (3) Percentage of students that have an Individualized Education Program.
Source: U.S. Department of Education, National Center for Education Statistics, Common Core of Data, Local Education Agency (School District) Universe Survey: School Year 2013-2014; U.S. Department of Education, National Center for Education Statistics, Common Core of Data, Public Elementary/Secondary School Universe Survey: School Year 2013-2014

Highest Level of Education

Area	Less than H.S.	H.S. Diploma	Some College, No Deg.	Associate Degree	Bachelor's Degree	Master's Degree	Prof. School Degree	Doctorate Degree
City	3.8	14.9	12.9	7.2	28.9	21.9	7.6	2.8
MSA[1]	10.2	27.5	17.9	8.1	20.4	11.6	2.8	1.5
U.S.	13.7	28.0	21.2	7.9	18.3	7.8	2.0	1.3

Note: Figures cover persons age 25 and over; (1) Figures cover the Hartford-West Hartford-East Hartford, CT Metropolitan Statistical Area—see Appendix B for areas included
Source: U.S. Census Bureau, 2010-2014 American Community Survey 5-Year Estimates

Educational Attainment by Race

Area	High School Graduate or Higher (%)					Bachelor's Degree or Higher (%)				
	Total	White	Black	Asian	Hisp.[2]	Total	White	Black	Asian	Hisp.[2]
City	96.2	97.0	89.8	89.3	90.3	61.2	61.5	43.4	64.5	57.4
MSA[1]	89.8	91.9	83.7	88.4	69.2	36.3	38.4	19.3	64.1	14.9
U.S.	86.3	88.4	83.2	85.8	64.1	29.3	30.6	19.0	50.9	13.9

Note: Figures shown cover persons 25 years old and over; (1) Figures cover the Hartford-West Hartford-East Hartford, CT Metropolitan Statistical Area—see Appendix B for areas included; (2) People of Hispanic origin can be of any race
Source: U.S. Census Bureau, 2010-2014 American Community Survey 5-Year Estimates

School Enrollment by Grade and Control

Area	Preschool (%)		Kindergarten (%)		Grades 1 - 4 (%)		Grades 5 - 8 (%)		Grades 9 - 12 (%)	
	Public	Private	Public	Private	Public	Private	Public	Private	Public	Private
City	31.5	68.5	90.8	9.2	98.7	1.3	89.8	10.2	93.4	6.6
MSA[1]	55.7	44.3	90.0	10.0	93.2	6.8	93.3	6.7	91.6	8.4
U.S.	57.4	42.6	87.8	12.2	89.8	10.2	89.9	10.1	90.6	9.4

Note: Figures shown cover persons 3 years old and over; (1) Figures cover the Hartford-West Hartford-East Hartford, CT Metropolitan Statistical Area—see Appendix B for areas included
Source: U.S. Census Bureau, 2010-2014 American Community Survey 5-Year Estimates

Average Salaries of Public School Classroom Teachers

Area	2013-14		2014-15		Percent Change 2013-14 to 2014-15	Percent Change 2004-05 to 2014-15
	Dollars	Rank[1]	Dollars	Rank[1]		
Connecticut	70,583	5	71,709	5	1.59	24.2
U.S. Average	56,610	–	57,379	–	1.36	20.8

Note: (1) State rank ranges from 1 to 51 where 1 indicates highest salary.
Source: National Education Association, Rankings & Estimates: Rankings of the States 2014 and Estimates of School Statistics 2015, March 2015

Higher Education

Four-Year Colleges			Two-Year Colleges			Medical Schools[1]	Law Schools[2]	Voc/ Tech[3]
Public	Private Non-profit	Private For-profit	Public	Private Non-profit	Private For-profit			
0	0	0	0	0	0	0	0	0

Note: Figures cover institutions located within the city limits and include main campuses only; (1) includes schools accredited by the Liaison Committee on Medical Education and the American Osteopathic Association's Commission on Osteopathic College Accreditation; (2) includes ABA-accredited schools, schools with provisional ABA accreditation, and state accredited schools; (3) includes all schools with programs that are less than 2 years.
Source: National Center for Education Statistics, Integrated Postsecondary Education System (IPEDS), 2014-15; Association of American Medical Colleges, Member List, March 21, 2016; American Osteopathic Association, Member List, March 21, 2016; Law School Admission Council, Official Guide to ABA-Approved Law Schools Online, March 21, 2016; Wikipedia, List of Medical Schools in the United States, March 21, 2016; Wikipedia, List of Law Schools in the United States, March 21, 2016

According to *U.S. News & World Report,* the Hartford-West Hartford-East Hartford, CT metro area is home to one of the best national universities in the U.S.: **University of Connecticut** (#57 tie). The indicators used to capture academic quality fall into a number of categories: assessment by administrators at peer institutions; retention of students; faculty resources; student selectivity; financial resources; alumni giving; high school counselor ratings of colleges; and graduation rate. *U.S. News & World Report, "America's Best Colleges 2016"*

According to *U.S. News & World Report,* the Hartford-West Hartford-East Hartford, CT metro area is home to two of the best liberal arts colleges in the U.S.: **Wesleyan University** (#14 tie); **Trinity College** (#43 tie). The indicators used to capture academic quality fall into a number of categories: assessment by administrators at peer institutions; retention of students; faculty resources; student selectivity; financial resources; alumni giving; high school counselor ratings of colleges; and graduation rate. *U.S. News & World Report, "America's Best Colleges 2016"*

According to *U.S. News & World Report,* the Hartford-West Hartford-East Hartford, CT metro area is home to one of the top 100 law schools in the U.S.: **University of Connecticut, School of Law** (#65 tie). The rankings are based on a weighted average of 12 measures of quality: peer assessment score; assessment score by lawyers/judges; median LSAT scores; median undergrad GPA; acceptance rate; employment rates for graduates; placement success; bar passage rate; faculty resources; expenditures per student; student/faculty ratio; and library resources. *U.S. News & World Report, "America's Best Graduate Schools, Law, 2017"*

According to *U.S. News & World Report,* the Hartford-West Hartford-East Hartford, CT metro area is home to one of the top 75 medical schools for research in the U.S.: **University of Connecticut, School of Medicine** (#63 tie). The rankings are based on a weighted average of 11 measures of quality: quality assessment; peer assessment score; assessment score by residency directors; research activity; total research activity; average research activity per faculty member; student selectivity; median MCAT total score; median undergraduate GPA; acceptance rate; and faculty resources. *U.S. News & World Report, "America's Best Graduate Schools, Medical, 2017"*

According to *U.S. News & World Report,* the Hartford-West Hartford-East Hartford, CT metro area is home to one of the top 75 business schools in the U.S.: **University of Connecticut, School of Business** (#68 tie). The rankings are based on a weighted average of the following nine measures: quality assessment; peer assessment; recruiter assessment; placement success; mean starting salary and bonus; student selectivity; mean GMAT and GRE scores; mean undergraduate GPA; and acceptance rate. *U.S. News & World Report, "America's Best Graduate Schools, Business, 2017"*

PRESIDENTIAL ELECTION

2012 Presidential Election Results

Area	Obama (%)	Romney (%)	Other (%)
Hartford County	62.4	36.5	1.1
U.S.	51.0	47.2	1.8

Note: Results may not add to 100% due to rounding
Source: Dave Leip's Atlas of U.S. Presidential Elections

EMPLOYERS

Major Employers

Company Name	Industry
Aetna, Inc.	Insurance
AT&T CT	Telecommunications
Athena Health Care Systems	Nursing & rehab
Bank of America	Financial services
Boehringer Ingelheim Corp.	Health care products
CIGNA	Health care
ESPN	Sports media
Foxwoods Resort Casino	Gaming & tourism
GE	Diversified tech
General Dynamics Electric Boad	Submarines
Hartford Financial Services Group, Inc.	Financial services
Hartford Hospital	Healthcare
Mohegan Sun	Gaming & tourism
Northeast Utilities	Utilities
People's Bank	Financial services
Pfizer Global R&D	Pharmaceutical
St Francis Hospital and Med Center	Health care
St Paul Travelers Cos.	Insurance
Stop & Shop Cos. Inc	Supermarket
United States Surgical	Senior health care
United Technologies Corp	Building systems & aerospace
Wal-Mart	Retail
Webster Financial Corp.	Banking, insurnace, investment
Yale University	Higher education

Note: Companies shown are located within the Hartford-West Hartford-East Hartford, CT Metropolitan Statistical Area.
Source: Hoovers.com; Wikipedia

PUBLIC SAFETY

Crime Rate

Area	All Crimes	Violent Crimes: Murder	Violent Crimes: Rape[3]	Violent Crimes: Robbery	Violent Crimes: Aggrav. Assault	Property Crimes: Burglary	Property Crimes: Larceny -Theft	Property Crimes: Motor Vehicle Theft
City	880.9	0.0	2.9	14.3	11.5	229.6	602.6	20.1
Metro[1]	2,484.4	3.8	24.2	94.0	130.2	389.5	1,664.9	177.7
U.S.	2,971.8	4.5	36.6	102.2	232.5	542.5	1,837.3	216.2

Note: Figures are crimes per 100,000 population; (1) Figures cover the Hartford-West Hartford-East Hartford, CT Metropolitan Statistical Area—see Appendix B for areas included; (3) The city and U.S. figures shown were reported using the revised Uniform Crime Reporting (UCR) definition of rape. The suburban and metro area figures shown are an aggregate total of the data submitted using both the revised and legacy UCR definitions.
Source: FBI Uniform Crime Reports, 2014

Hate Crimes

Area	Number of Quarters Reported	Race	Religion	Sexual Orientation	Ethnicity	Disability	Gender	Gender Identity
City	4	1	0	0	0	0	0	0
U.S.	4	2,568	1,014	1,017	648	84	33	98

(Race through Gender Identity: Number of Incidents per Bias Motivation)

Source: Federal Bureau of Investigation, Hate Crime Statistics 2014

Identity Theft Consumer Complaints

Area	Complaints	Complaints per 100,000 Population	Rank[2]
MSA[1]	2,865	235.9	8
U.S.	490,220	152.4	-

Note: (1) Figures cover the Hartford-West Hartford-East Hartford, CT Metropolitan Statistical Area—see Appendix B for areas included; (2) Rank ranges from 1 to 379 where 1 indicates greatest number of identity theft complaints per 100,000 population
Source: Federal Trade Commission, Consumer Sentinel Network Data Book for January–December 2015

Fraud and Other Consumer Complaints

Area	Complaints	Complaints per 100,000 Population	Rank[2]
MSA[1]	4,428	364.7	186
U.S.	2,593,159	806.0	-

Note: (1) Figures cover the Hartford-West Hartford-East Hartford, CT Metropolitan Statistical Area—see Appendix B for areas included; (2) Rank ranges from 1 to 379 where 1 indicates greatest number of identity theft complaints per 100,000 population
Source: Federal Trade Commission, Consumer Sentinel Network Data Book for January–December 2015

RECREATION

Culture

Dance[1]	Theatre[1]	Instrumental Music[1]	Vocal Music[1]	Series and Festivals	Museums and Art Galleries[2]	Zoos and Aquariums[3]
0	0	0	0	0	0	0

Note: (1) Professional perfoming groups; (2) Based on organizations with SIC code 8412; (3) AZA-accredited
Source: The Grey House Performing Arts Directory, 2015-16; Association of Zoos & Aquariums, AZA Member Zoos & Aquariums, March 25, 2016; www.AccuLeads.com, March 29, 2016

Professional Sports Teams

Team Name	League	Year Established
No teams are located in the metro area		

Source: Wikipedia, Major Professional Sports Teams of the United States and Canada, March 24, 2016

CLIMATE

Average and Extreme Temperatures

Temperature	Jan	Feb	Mar	Apr	May	Jun	Jul	Aug	Sep	Oct	Nov	Dec	Yr.
Extreme High (°F)	66	73	87	96	97	101	102	101	101	91	83	74	102
Average High (°F)	34	37	46	60	71	80	85	82	74	64	51	38	60
Average Temp. (°F)	26	28	37	49	60	69	74	72	63	53	42	30	50
Average Low (°F)	17	19	28	38	47	57	62	60	52	41	33	22	40
Extreme Low (°F)	-26	-21	-8	9	28	37	44	36	27	17	1	-14	-26

Note: Figures cover the years 1949-1995
Source: National Climatic Data Center, International Station Meteorological Climate Summary, 9/96

Average Precipitation/Snowfall/Humidity

Precip./Humidity	Jan	Feb	Mar	Apr	May	Jun	Jul	Aug	Sep	Oct	Nov	Dec	Yr.
Avg. Precip. (in.)	3.4	3.1	3.9	3.9	3.7	3.5	3.3	4.0	3.8	3.6	4.1	3.9	44.2
Avg. Snowfall (in.)	12	12	9	1	Tr	0	0	0	0	Tr	2	10	46
Avg. Rel. Hum. 7am (%)	73	73	72	70	73	77	79	83	86	84	79	76	77
Avg. Rel. Hum. 4pm (%)	58	54	51	46	48	51	52	54	55	53	58	61	53

Note: Figures cover the years 1949-1995; Tr = Trace amounts (<0.05 in. of rain; <0.5 in. of snow)
Source: National Climatic Data Center, International Station Meteorological Climate Summary, 9/96

Weather Conditions

Temperature			Daytime Sky			Precipitation		
5°F & below	32°F & below	90°F & above	Clear	Partly cloudy	Cloudy	0.01 inch or more precip.	0.1 inch or more snow/ice	Thunder-storms
11	134	18	69	151	145	126	26	20

Note: Figures are average number of days per year and cover the years 1949-1995
Source: National Climatic Data Center, International Station Meteorological Climate Summary, 9/96

HAZARDOUS WASTE

Superfund Sites

Glastonbury has no sites on the EPA's Superfund Final National Priorities List. There are a total of 1,323 Superfund sites on the list in the U.S. *U.S. Environmental Protection Agency, Final National Priorities List, March 18, 2016*

AIR & WATER QUALITY

Air Quality Trends: Ozone

	1990	1995	2000	2005	2010	2011	2012	2013	2014
MSA[1]	0.103	0.097	0.082	0.094	0.079	0.073	0.080	0.080	0.078

Note: (1) Data covers the Hartford-West Hartford-East Hartford, CT Metropolitan Statistical Area—see Appendix B for areas included. The values shown are the composite ozone concentration averages among trend sites based on the highest fourth daily maximum 8-hour concentration in parts per million. These trends are based on sites having an adequate record of monitoring data during the trend period. Data from exceptional events are included.
Source: U.S. Environmental Protection Agency, Air Quality Monitoring Information, "Air Quality Trends by City, 1990-2014"

Air Quality Index

Area	Percent of Days when Air Quality was...[2]					AQI Statistics[2]	
	Good	Moderate	Unhealthy for Sensitive Groups	Unhealthy	Very Unhealthy	Maximum	Median
MSA[1]	62.7	35.3	1.9	0.0	0.0	122	43

Note: (1) Data covers the Hartford-West Hartford-East Hartford, CT Metropolitan Statistical Area—see Appendix B for areas included; (2) Based on 365 days with AQI data in 2015. Air Quality Index (AQI) is an index for reporting daily air quality. EPA calculates the AQI for five major air pollutants regulated by the Clean Air Act: ground-level ozone, particle pollution (aka particulate matter), carbon monoxide, sulfur dioxide, and nitrogen dioxide. The AQI runs from 0 to 500. The higher the AQI value, the greater the level of air pollution and the greater the health concern. There are six AQI categories: "Good" AQI is between 0 and 50. Air quality is considered satisfactory; "Moderate" AQI is between 51 and 100. Air quality is acceptable; "Unhealthy for Sensitive Groups" When AQI values are between 101 and 150, members of sensitive groups may experience health effects; "Unhealthy" When AQI values are between 151 and 200 everyone may begin to experience health effects; "Very Unhealthy" AQI values between 201 and 300 trigger a health alert; "Hazardous" AQI values over 300 trigger warnings of emergency conditions (not shown).
Source: U.S. Environmental Protection Agency, Air Quality Index Report, 2015

Air Quality Index Pollutants

Area	Percent of Days when AQI Pollutant was...[2]					
	Carbon Monoxide	Nitrogen Dioxide	Ozone	Sulfur Dioxide	Particulate Matter 2.5	Particulate Matter 10
MSA[1]	0.0	9.0	34.5	0.0	56.4	0.0

Note: (1) Data covers the Hartford-West Hartford-East Hartford, CT Metropolitan Statistical Area—see Appendix B for areas included; (2) Based on 365 days with AQI data in 2015. The Air Quality Index (AQI) is an index for reporting daily air quality. EPA calculates the AQI for five major air pollutants regulated by the Clean Air Act: ground-level ozone, particle pollution (also known as particulate matter), carbon monoxide, sulfur dioxide, and nitrogen dioxide. The AQI runs from 0 to 500. The higher the AQI value, the greater the level of air pollution and the greater the health concern.
Source: U.S. Environmental Protection Agency, Air Quality Index Report, 2015

Maximum Air Pollutant Concentrations: Particulate Matter, Ozone, CO and Lead

	Particulate Matter 10 (ug/m^3)	Particulate Matter 2.5 Wtd AM (ug/m^3)	Particulate Matter 2.5 24-Hr (ug/m^3)	Ozone (ppm)	Carbon Monoxide (ppm)	Lead (ug/m^3)
MSA[1] Level	25	8.1	22	0.08	1	n/a
NAAQS[2]	150	15	35	0.075	9	0.15
Met NAAQS[2]	Yes	Yes	Yes	No	Yes	n/a

Note: (1) Data covers the Hartford-West Hartford-East Hartford, CT Metropolitan Statistical Area—see Appendix B for areas included; Data from exceptional events are included; (2) National Ambient Air Quality Standards; ppm = parts per million; ug/m^3 = micrograms per cubic meter; n/a not available.
Concentrations: Particulate Matter 10 (coarse particulate)—highest second maximum 24-hour concentration; Particulate Matter 2.5 Wtd AM (fine particulate)—highest weighted annual mean concentration; Particulate Matter 2.5 24-Hour (fine particulate)—highest 98th percentile 24-hour concentration; Ozone—highest fourth daily maximum 8-hour concentration; Carbon Monoxide—highest second maximum non-overlapping 8-hour concentration; Lead—maximum running 3-month average
Source: U.S. Environmental Protection Agency, Air Quality Monitoring Information, "Air Quality Statistics by City, 2014"

Maximum Air Pollutant Concentrations: Nitrogen Dioxide and Sulfur Dioxide

	Nitrogen Dioxide AM (ppb)	Nitrogen Dioxide 1-Hr (ppb)	Sulfur Dioxide AM (ppb)	Sulfur Dioxide 1-Hr (ppb)	Sulfur Dioxide 24-Hr (ppb)
MSA[1] Level	14	51	n/a	7	n/a
NAAQS[2]	53	100	30	75	140
Met NAAQS[2]	Yes	Yes	n/a	Yes	n/a

Note: (1) Data covers the Hartford-West Hartford-East Hartford, CT Metropolitan Statistical Area—see Appendix B for areas included; Data from exceptional events are included; (2) National Ambient Air Quality Standards; ppm = parts per million; ug/m^3 = micrograms per cubic meter; n/a not available.
Concentrations: Nitrogen Dioxide AM—highest arithmetic mean concentration; Nitrogen Dioxide 1-Hr—highest 98th percentile 1-hour daily maximum concentration; Sulfur Dioxide AM—highest annual mean concentration; Sulfur Dioxide 1-Hr—highest 99th percentile 1-hour daily maximum concentration; Sulfur Dioxide 24-Hr—highest second maximum 24-hour concentration
Source: U.S. Environmental Protection Agency, Air Quality Monitoring Information, "Air Quality Statistics by City, 2014"

Drinking Water

Water System Name	Pop. Served	Primary Water Source Type	Violations[1]	
			Health Based	Monitoring/ Reporting
Metropolitan District Commission	390,887	Surface	0	0

Note: (1) Based on violation data from January 1, 2015 to December 31, 2015 (includes unresolved violations from earlier years)
Source: U.S. Environmental Protection Agency, Office of Ground Water and Drinking Water, Safe Drinking Water Information System (based on data extracted April 29, 2016)

Newtown, Connecticut

Background

Bordered by the Pootatuck River, Newtown is located in Fairfield County in the Housatonic Valley, a 20-minute drive east of Danbury in southwestern Connecticut. The scenic New England-style town lies along I-84 and other major thoroughfares, giving it easy access to major locales throughout the region, including New York City, 60 miles away.

Its five neighborhoods are Sandy Hook, Hawleyville, Botsford, Dodgingtown, and the Borough of Newtown, which has its own self-governing component.

The town was established in 1711. Born an agricultural community, Newtown grew into an industrial area making products like buttons and rubber as the 19th century evolved, with mills built along and powered by local waterways. By the turn of the last century, tourists had discovered what was then becoming a resort area. And finally, like so many rural towns within driving distance of bigger cities, Newtown became a commuter's bedroom community after World War II. The town is known for its giant flagpole planted on Main Street, where a 20x30 foot American flag is flown in summer, and a smaller one in winter.

Today Newtown houses the corporate headquarters for Sonics, manufacturer of plastics, ultrasonic liquid processing products, and ultrasonic metal welding systems. Major local employers are the town of Newtown and the Board of Education, Pitney Bowes, the State of Connecticut's Dept. of Corrections, Hubbell Wiring Devices-Kellems, and Taunton Press. Local students attend the Newtown Public School District schools. Newtown High School was recently renovated, which added a 73,000 square foot addition to the gymnasium and a synthetic turf ball field.

Newtown is also within commuting distance to numerous institutions of higher education, including Yale University in New Haven, a 45-minute drive. Within Fairfield County are Western Connecticut State University, St. Vincent's College, Housatonic Community College, the University of Bridgeport, Fairfield University, Sacred Heart University, Norwalk Community College, Gibbs College, St. Basil College, and the University of Connecticut's Stamford Campus.

The town's recreational opportunities include the Ram Pasture, a centrally-located pasture with a long history as a town gathering spot, a pond, Treadwell Pool, Eichler's Cove Beach, Lake Lillinonah, both with boat launches, and Dickinson Park, with tennis courts, playground, skatepark, and dog park. Hiking trails are close at hand.

In addition, the area is full of cultural activities so residents can enjoy the performing and visual arts. The Newtown Cultural Arts Commission, Newtown Friends of Music, and the Society of Creative Arts of Newtown are among the groups that present classical music concerts, the Flagpole Radio Caf_, art shows and programs such as workshops or sketch sessions with models. The Town Players of Newtown have taken to the local stage since 1936.

Newtown's climate means cold winters with the average lows dropping to 17.6 degrees in January, July highs maxing out at an average of just under 84 degrees, and September weighing in as the soggiest month at just under five inches, average, of precipitation.

Rankings

Business/Finance Rankings

- The personal finance site NerdWallet analyzed 183 American metropolitan areas with populations over 250,000 and more than 15,000 businesses to rank where entrepreneurs find the most success. Criteria included area economy, annual income, housing cost, unemployment rate, and the success rate of area businesses. Bridgeport* ranked #3. *www.nerdwallet.com, "Best Places to Start a Business," April 27, 2015*

- TransUnion ranked the nation's metro areas by average credit score, calculated on the VantageScore system, developed by the three major credit-reporting bureaus—TransUnion, Experian, and Equifax. The Bridgeport* metro area was among the ten cities with the highest collective credit score, meaning that its residents posed the lowest average consumer credit risk. *www.usatoday.com, "Metro Areas' Average Credit Rating Revealed," February 7, 2013*

- Based on the U.S. Department of Labor's Occupational Information Network Data Collection Program, the Brookings Institution defined job opportunities for STEM workers at various levels of educational attainment. The Bridgeport* metro area was one of the ten metro areas where workers in low-education-level STEM jobs earn the lowest relative wages. *www.brookings.edu, "The Hidden Stem Economy," June 10, 2013*

- Metro areas with the largest gap in income between rich and poor residents were identified by 24/7 Wall Street using the U.S. Census Bureau's 2013 American Community Survey. The Bridgeport* metro area placed #1 among metro areas with the widest wealth gap between rich and poor. *247wallst.com, "20 Cities with the Widest Gap between the Rich and Poor," July 8, 2015*

- The Brookings Institution ranked the 100 largest metro areas in the U.S. based on income inequality. Bridgeport* was ranked #1 (#1 = greatest ineqality). Criteria: the "95/20 ratio," a figure representing the income at which a household earns more than 95 percent of all other households, divided by the income at which a household earns more than only 20 percent of all other households. *Brookings Institution, "Income Inequality, 100 Largest U.S. Metro Areas, 2007-2014," January 14, 2016*

- *Forbes* ranked the largest metro areas in the U.S. in terms of the "Best Cities for Young Professionals." The Bridgeport* metro area ranked #12 out of 15. Criteria: job growth; unemployment rate; median salary of college graduates age 24 to 34; cost of living; number of small businesses per capita; number of large companies; percentage of population 25 years of age and older with college degrees. *Forbes.com, "America's 15 Best Cities for Young Professionals," August 18, 2014*

- The finance site *24/7 Wall St.* identified the metropolitan areas that have the smallest and largest pay disparities between men and women, comparing the median earnings for the past 12 months of both men and women working full-time in the country's 100 largest metropolitan statistical areas. Of the ten worst-paying metros for women, the Bridgeport* metro area ranked #8. *24/7 Wall St., "The Best (and Worst) Paying Cities for Women," March 6, 2015*

- The Bridgeport* metro area appeared on the Milken Institute "2015 Best Performing Cities" list. Rank: #166 out of 200 large metro areas. Criteria: job growth; wage and salary growth; high-tech output growth. *Milken Institute, "Best-Performing Cities 2015," December 2015*

Education Rankings

- Bridgeport* was identified as one of America's "smartest" metropolitan areas by *The Business Journals*. The area ranked #3 out of 10. Criteria: percentage of adults (25 and older) with high school diplomas, bachelor's degrees and graduate degrees. *The Business Journals, "Where the Brainpower Is: Exclusive U.S. Rankings, Insights," February 27, 2014*

- Personal finance website *WalletHub* analyzed the 150 largest U.S. metropolitan statistical areas to determine where the most educated Americans are choosing to settle. Criteria: education quality and attainment gap; education levels; percentage of workers with degrees; public school rankings; quality and size of each metro area's universities. Bridgeport* was ranked #21 (#1 = most educated city). *www.WalletHub.com, "2015's Most and Least Educated Cities*

Environmental Rankings

- The Bridgeport* metro area came in at #152 for the relative comfort of its climate on Sperling's list of "chill cities," as measured by the Sperling Heat Index. All 361 metro areas are included. Criteria included daytime high temperatures, nighttime low temperatures, dew point, and relative humidity at the high temperatures. *www.bertsperling.com, "Sperling's Chill Cities," July 18, 2013*

- Sperling's BestPlaces assessed 379 metropolitan areas of the United States for the likelihood of dangerously extreme weather events or earthquakes. In general the Southeast and South-Central regions have the highest risk of weather extremes and earthquakes, while the Pacific Northwest enjoys the lowest risk. Of the least risky metropolitan areas, the Bridgeport* metro area was ranked #159. *www.bestplaces.net, "Safest Places from Natural Disasters," April 2011*

- Bridgeport* was identified as one of America's dirtiest metro areas by *Forbes*. The area ranked #4 out of 20. Criteria: air quality; water quality; toxic releases; superfund sites. *Forbes, "America's 20 Dirtiest Cities," December 10, 2012*

Health/Fitness Rankings

- Analysts who tracked obesity rates in 100 of the nation's most populous areas found that the Bridgeport* metro area was one of the ten communities where residents were least likely to be obese, defined as a BMI score of 30 or above. *www.gallup.com, "Colorado Springs Residents Least Likely to Be Obese," May 28, 2015*

- *Business Insider* reported Trulia's analysis of the 100 largest U.S. metro areas to identify the nation's best cities for weight loss, based on healthful food options, access to outdoor activities, weight-loss centers, gyms, and opportunities to bike or walk to work. Bridgeport* ranked #2. *Businessinsider.com, "These Are the Best US Cities for Weight loss," January 17, 2013*

- Bridgeport* was identified as a "2016 Spring Allergy Capital." The area ranked #69 out of 100. Three groups of factors were used to identify the most severe cities for people with allergies during the spring season: annual pollen levels; medicine utilization; access to board-certified allergists. *Asthma and Allergy Foundation of America, "Spring Allergy Capitals 2016"*

- Bridgeport* was identified as a "2015 Asthma Capital." The area ranked #36 out of the nation's 100 largest metropolitan areas. Criteria: estimated prevalence; self-reported prevalence; crude death rate for asthma; annual pollen score; annual air quality; public smoking laws; number of board-certified asthma specialists; school inhaler access laws; rescue medication use; controller medication use; ER visits for asthma; uninsured rate; poverty rate. *Asthma and Allergy Foundation of America, "Asthma Capitals 2015"*

- The Bridgeport* metro area ranked #29 out of 190 in The Gallup-Healthways Well-Being Index. Criteria: purpose; social well being; financial health; community and physical health. Results are based on telephone interviews with adults, aged 18 and older, living in metropolitan areas in the 50 U.S. states and the District of Columbia. *Gallup-Healthways, "State of American Well-Being," February 23, 2016*

Real Estate Rankings

- The Bridgeport* metro area was identified as one of the 20 worst housing markets in the U.S. in 2015. The area ranked #15 out of 179 markets. Criteria: year-over-year change of median sales price of existing single-family homes between the 4th quarter of 2014 and the 4th quarter of 2015. *National Association of Realtors®, Median Sales Price of Existing Single-Family Homes for Metropolitan Areas, 4th Quarter 2015*

- The Bridgeport* metro area was identified as one of the 10 worst condo markets in the U.S. in 2015. The area ranked #4 out of 61 markets. Criteria: year-over-year change of median sales price of existing apartment condo-coop homes between the 4th quarter of 2014 and the 4th quarter of 2015. *National Association of Realtors®, Median Sales Price of Existing Apartment Condo-Coop Homes for Metropolitan Areas, 4th Quarter 2015*

- Bridgeport* was ranked #192 out of 225 metro areas in terms of housing affordability in 2015 by the National Association of Home Builders (#1 = most affordable). Criteria: the share of homes sold in that area affordable to a family earning the local median income, based on standard mortgage underwriting criteria. *National Association of Home Builders®, NAHB-Wells Fargo Housing Opportunity Index, 4th Quarter 2015*

Safety Rankings

- The National Insurance Crime Bureau ranked 380 metro areas in the U.S. in terms of per capita rates of vehicle theft. The Bridgeport* metro area ranked #203 (#1 = highest rate). Criteria: number of vehicle theft offenses per 100,000 inhabitants in 2014. *National Insurance Crime Bureau, "Hot Spots 2014," June 24, 2015*

Seniors/Retirement Rankings

- From its Best Cities for Successful Aging indexes, the Milken Institute generated rankings for metropolitan areas, weighing data in eight categories—health care, wellness, living arrangements, transportation, financial characteristics, education and employment opportunities, community engagement, and overall livability. The Bridgeport* metro area was ranked #10 overall in the large metro area category. *Milken Institute, "Best Cities for Successful Aging, 2014"*

Women/Minorities Rankings

- *24/7 Wall St.* compared median earnings over a 12-month period for men and women who worked full-time, year-round, and employment composition by sector to identify the worst-paying cities for women. Of the largest 100 U.S. metropolitan areas, Bridgeport* was ranked #8 in pay disparity. *24/7 Wall St., "The Best (and Worst) Paying Cities for Women," March 6, 2015*

Miscellaneous Rankings

- The National Alliance to End Homelessness ranked the 100 most populous metro areas with the highest rate of homelessness. The Bridgeport* metro area ranked #72. Criteria: number of homeless people per 10,000 population in 2011. *National Alliance to End Homelessness, The State of Homelessness in America 2012*

Newtown is located within the Bridgeport-Stamford-Norwalk, CT Metropolitan Statistical Area.

Business Environment

CITY FINANCES

City Government Finances

Component	2012 ($000)	2012 ($ per capita)
Total Revenues	118,517	4,300
Total Expenditures	117,280	4,255
Debt Outstanding	90,325	3,277
Cash and Securities[1]	22,318	809

Note: (1) Cash and security holdings of a government at the close of its fiscal year, including those of its dependent agencies, utilities, and liquor stores.
Source: U.S Census Bureau, State & Local Government Finances 2012

City Government Revenue by Source

Source	2012 ($000)	2012 ($ per capita)
General Revenue		
From Federal Government	1,488	53
From State Government	13,071	474
From Local Governments	73	2
Taxes		
Property	94,849	3,441
Sales and Gross Receipts	0	0
Personal Income	0	0
Corporate Income	0	0
Motor Vehicle License	0	0
Other Taxes	835	30
Current Charges	6,518	236
Liquor Store	0	0
Utility	351	12
Employee Retirement	0	0

Source: U.S Census Bureau, State & Local Government Finances 2012

City Government Expenditures by Function

Function	2012 ($000)	2012 ($ per capita)	2012 (%)
General Direct Expenditures			
Air Transportation	0	0	0.0
Corrections	0	0	0.0
Education	79,544	2,886	67.8
Employment Security Administration	0	0	0.0
Financial Administration	2,015	73	1.7
Fire Protection	1,359	49	1.1
General Public Buildings	813	29	0.6
Governmental Administration, Other	2,858	103	2.4
Health	808	29	0.6
Highways	8,761	317	7.4
Hospitals	0	0	0.0
Housing and Community Development	697	25	0.5
Interest on General Debt	2,984	108	2.5
Judicial and Legal	6	< 1	< 0.1
Libraries	1,049	38	0.8
Parking	0	0	0.0
Parks and Recreation	3,574	129	3.0
Police Protection	7,506	272	6.4
Public Welfare	446	16	0.3
Sewerage	1,543	55	1.3
Solid Waste Management	1,423	51	1.2
Veterans' Services	0	0	0.0
Liquor Store	0	0	0.0
Utility	288	10	0.2
Employee Retirement	0	0	0.0

Source: U.S Census Bureau, State & Local Government Finances 2012

DEMOGRAPHICS

Population Growth

Area	1990 Census	2000 Census	2010 Census	2014* Estimate	Population Growth (%) 1990-2014	Population Growth (%) 2010-2014
City	20,779	25,031	27,560	27,960	34.6	1.5
MSA[1]	827,645	882,567	916,829	934,215	12.9	1.9
U.S.	248,709,873	281,421,906	308,745,538	314,107,084	26.3	1.7

Note: (1) Figures cover the Bridgeport-Stamford-Norwalk, CT Metropolitan Statistical Area—see Appendix B for areas included; (*) 2010-2014 5-year estimated population
Source: U.S. Census Bureau, 1990 Census, Census 2000, Census 2010, 2010-2014 American Community Survey 5-Year Estimates

Household Size

Area	Persons in Household (%) One	Two	Three	Four	Five	Six	Seven or More	Average Household Size
City	19.9	31.4	19.4	17.0	8.6	2.8	0.6	2.84
MSA[1]	25.4	30.3	16.9	16.6	7.2	2.2	1.0	2.74
U.S.	27.5	33.5	15.8	13.1	6.0	2.3	1.4	2.64

Note: (1) Figures cover the Bridgeport-Stamford-Norwalk, CT Metropolitan Statistical Area—see Appendix B for areas included
Source: U.S. Census Bureau, 2010-2014 American Community Survey 5-Year Estimates

Race

Area	White Alone[2] (%)	Black Alone[2] (%)	Asian Alone[2] (%)	AIAN[3] Alone[2] (%)	NHOPI[4] Alone[2] (%)	Other Race Alone[2] (%)	Two or More Races (%)
City	91.8	1.2	2.1	0.0	0.0	3.2	1.8
MSA[1]	74.3	11.1	4.9	0.2	0.0	7.1	2.4
U.S.	73.8	12.6	5.0	0.8	0.2	4.7	2.9

Note: (1) Figures cover the Bridgeport-Stamford-Norwalk, CT Metropolitan Statistical Area—see Appendix B for areas included; (2) Alone is defined as not being in combination with one or more other races; (3) American Indian and Alaska Native; (4) Native Hawaiian and Other Pacific Islander
Source: U.S. Census Bureau, 2010-2014 American Community Survey 5-Year Estimates

Hispanic or Latino Origin

Area	Total (%)	Mexican (%)	Puerto Rican (%)	Cuban (%)	Other (%)
City	8.1	0.8	1.6	0.4	5.3
MSA[1]	17.9	2.1	5.9	0.4	9.4
U.S.	16.9	10.8	1.6	0.6	3.8

Note: Persons of Hispanic or Latino origin can be of any race; (1) Figures cover the Bridgeport-Stamford-Norwalk, CT Metropolitan Statistical Area—see Appendix B for areas included
Source: U.S. Census Bureau, 2010-2014 American Community Survey 5-Year Estimates

Ancestry

Area	German	Irish	English	American	Italian	Polish	French[2]	Scottish	Dutch
City	17.0	20.9	11.9	5.3	24.6	6.8	3.7	2.8	1.3
MSA[1]	9.2	14.8	8.0	4.4	17.6	5.4	2.5	1.8	0.8
U.S.	14.9	10.8	8.0	7.1	5.5	3.0	2.7	1.7	1.4

Note: Figures are the percentage of the total population reporting a particular ancestry. The nine most commonly reported ancestries in the U.S. are shown. Figures include multiple ancestries (e.g. if a person reported being Irish and Italian, they were included in both columns); (1) Figures cover the Bridgeport-Stamford-Norwalk, CT Metropolitan Statistical Area—see Appendix B for areas included; (2) Excludes Basque
Source: U.S. Census Bureau, 2010-2014 American Community Survey 5-Year Estimates

Foreign-Born Population

Area	Percent of Population Born in								
	Any Foreign Country	Asia	Mexico	Europe	Carribean	Central America[2]	South America	Africa	Canada
City	8.2	1.9	0.3	3.4	0.5	0.6	1.0	0.2	0.3
MSA[1]	20.5	3.9	1.2	4.7	3.2	2.2	4.3	0.6	0.4
U.S.	13.1	3.8	3.7	1.5	1.2	1.0	0.9	0.6	0.3

Note: (1) Figures cover the Bridgeport-Stamford-Norwalk, CT Metropolitan Statistical Area—see Appendix B for areas included; (2) Excludes Mexico.
Source: U.S. Census Bureau, 2010-2014 American Community Survey 5-Year Estimates

Marital Status

Area	Never Married	Now Married[2]	Separated	Widowed	Divorced
City	25.4	60.3	0.4	5.0	8.9
MSA[1]	32.3	51.2	1.4	5.8	9.4
U.S.	32.5	48.4	2.2	5.9	10.9

Note: Figures are percentages and cover the population 15 years of age and older; (1) Figures cover the Bridgeport-Stamford-Norwalk, CT Metropolitan Statistical Area—see Appendix B for areas included; (2) Excludes separated
Source: U.S. Census Bureau, 2010-2014 American Community Survey 5-Year Estimates

Disability Status

Area	All Ages	Under 18 Years Old	18 to 64 Years Old	65 Years and Over
City	8.5	3.2	4.9	33.3
MSA[1]	8.8	3.1	6.4	30.2
U.S.	12.3	4.1	10.2	36.3

Note: Figures show percent of the civilian noninstitutionalized population that reported having a disability. Disability status is determined from from six types of difficulty: vision, hearing, cognitive, ambulatory, self-care, and independent living. For children under 5 years old, hearing and vision difficulty are used to determine disability status. For children between the ages of 5 and 14, disability status is determined from hearing, vision, cognitive, ambulatory, and self-care difficulties. For people aged 15 years and older, they are considered to have a disability if they have difficulty with any one of the six difficulty types; (1) Figures cover the Bridgeport-Stamford-Norwalk, CT Metropolitan Statistical Area—see Appendix B for areas included.
Source: U.S. Census Bureau, 2010-2014 American Community Survey 5-Year Estimates

Age

Area	Percent of Population									Median Age
	Under Age 5	Age 5–19	Age 20–34	Age 35–44	Age 45–54	Age 55–64	Age 65–74	Age 75–84	Age 85+	
City	4.2	24.3	10.9	13.1	20.2	12.8	7.5	5.3	1.7	43.8
MSA[1]	5.9	21.0	17.4	13.5	16.1	12.3	7.3	4.4	2.2	39.6
U.S.	6.4	19.9	20.6	13.0	14.1	12.3	7.6	4.3	1.9	37.4

Note: (1) Figures cover the Bridgeport-Stamford-Norwalk, CT Metropolitan Statistical Area—see Appendix B for areas included
Source: U.S. Census Bureau, 2010-2014 American Community Survey 5-Year Estimates

Gender

Area	Males	Females	Males per 100 Females
City	13,986	13,974	100.1
MSA[1]	454,762	479,453	94.9
U.S.	154,515,159	159,591,925	96.8

Note: (1) Figures cover the Bridgeport-Stamford-Norwalk, CT Metropolitan Statistical Area—see Appendix B for areas included
Source: U.S. Census Bureau, 2010-2014 American Community Survey 5-Year Estimates

Religious Groups by Family

Area	Catholic	Baptist	Non-Den.	Methodist[2]	Lutheran	LDS[3]	Pente-costal	Presby-terian[4]	Muslim[5]	Judaism
MSA[1]	44.1	1.9	2.3	2.0	0.8	0.5	1.1	3.0	0.5	1.9
U.S.	19.1	9.3	4.0	4.0	2.3	2.0	1.9	1.6	0.8	0.7

Note: Figures are the number of adherents as a percentage of the total population; (1) Figures cover the Bridgeport-Stamford-Norwalk, CT Metropolitan Statistical Area—see Appendix B for areas included; (2) Methodist/Pietist; (3) Latter Day Saints; (4) Reformed; (5) Figures are estimates
Source: Association of Statisticians of American Religious Bodies, 2010 U.S. Religion Census: Religious Congregations & Membership Study

Religious Groups by Tradition

Area	Catholic	Evangelical Protestant	Mainline Protestant	Other Tradition	Black Protestant	Orthodox
MSA[1]	44.1	5.1	9.0	3.5	0.4	1.0
U.S.	19.1	16.2	7.3	4.3	1.6	0.3

Note: Figures are the number of adherents as a percentage of the total population; (1) Figures cover the Bridgeport-Stamford-Norwalk, CT Metropolitan Statistical Area—see Appendix B for areas included
Source: Association of Statisticians of American Religious Bodies, 2010 U.S. Religion Census: Religious Congregations & Membership Study

ECONOMY

Gross Metropolitan Product

Area	2013	2014	2015	2016	Rank[2]
MSA[1]	93.5	96.7	100.5	105.1	37

Note: Figures are in billions of dollars; (1) Figures cover the Bridgeport-Stamford-Norwalk, CT Metropolitan Statistical Area—see Appendix B for areas included; (2) Rank is based on 2016 data and ranges from 1 to 381
Source: The U.S. Conference of Mayors, U.S. Metro Economies: GMP and Employment 2014-2016, June 2015

Economic Growth

Area	2011-13 (%)	2014 (%)	2015 (%)	2016 (%)	Rank[2]
MSA[1]	1.3	1.7	2.6	2.6	159
U.S.	2.2	2.4	2.3	2.9	–

Note: Figures are real gross metropolitan product (GMP) growth rates and represent annual average percent change; (1) Figures cover the Bridgeport-Stamford-Norwalk, CT Metropolitan Statistical Area—see Appendix B for areas included; (2) Rank is based on 2016 data and ranges from 1 to 381
Source: The U.S. Conference of Mayors, U.S. Metro Economies: GMP and Employment 2014-2016, June 2015

Metropolitan Area Exports

Area	2009	2010	2011	2012	2013	2014	Rank[2]
MSA[1]	8,450.9	9,339.6	11,250.4	10,332.6	11,055.1	12,103.0	26

Note: Figures are in millions of dollars; (1) Figures cover the Bridgeport-Stamford-Norwalk, CT Metropolitan Statistical Area—see Appendix B for areas included; (2) Rank is based on 2014 data and ranges from 1 to 385
Source: U.S. Department of Commerce, International Trade Administration, Office of Trade & Industry Information, Manufacturing & Services, data extracted March 10, 2016

Building Permits

Area	Single-Family			Multi-Family			Total		
	2014	2015p	Pct. Chg.	2014	2015p	Pct. Chg.	2014	2015p	Pct. Chg.
City	19	29	52.6	0	0	-	19	29	52.6
MSA[1]	987	781	-20.9	902	1,802	99.8	1,889	2,583	36.7
U.S.	640,300	690,800	7.9	411,800	487,600	18.4	1,052,100	1,178,400	12.0

Note: (1) Figures cover the Bridgeport-Stamford-Norwalk, CT Metropolitan Statistical Area—see Appendix B for areas included; Figures represent new, privately-owned housing units authorized (unadjusted data); All permit data are based on estimates with imputation; (p) preliminary data.
Source: U.S. Census Bureau, Manufacturing, Mining, and Construction Statistics, Building Permits, 2014, 2015

Bankruptcy Filings

Area	Business Filings			Nonbusiness Filings		
	2014	2015	% Chg.	2014	2015	% Chg.
Fairfield County	91	83	-8.8	1,506	1,393	-7.5
U.S.	26,983	24,735	-8.3	909,812	819,760	-9.9

Note: Business filings include Chapter 7, Chapter 11, Chapter 12, and Chapter 13; Nonbusiness filings include Chapter 7, Chapter 11, and Chapter 13
Source: Administrative Office of the U.S. Courts, Business and Nonbusiness Bankruptcy, County Cases Commenced by Chapter of the Bankruptcy Code, During the 12- Month Period Ending December 31, 2014 and Business and Nonbusiness Bankruptcy, County Cases Commenced by Chapter of the Bankruptcy Code, During the 12- Month Period Ending December 31, 2015

Housing Vacancy Rates

Area	Gross Vacancy Rate[2] (%)			Year-Round Vacancy Rate[3] (%)			Rental Vacancy Rate[4] (%)			Homeowner Vacancy Rate[5] (%)		
	2013	2014	2015	2013	2014	2015	2013	2014	2015	2013	2014	2015
MSA[1]	10.2	10.8	11.3	9.4	9.2	10.1	5.1	5.6	7.1	2.6	1.6	1.8
U.S.	13.6	13.4	12.9	10.7	10.4	10.0	8.3	7.6	7.1	2.0	1.9	1.8

Note: (1) Figures cover the Bridgeport-Stamford-Norwalk, CT Metropolitan Statistical Area—see Appendix B for areas included; (2) The percentage of the total housing inventory that is vacant; (3) The percentage of the housing inventory (excluding seasonal units) that is year-round vacant; (4) The percentage of rental inventory that is vacant for rent; (5) The percentage of homeowner inventory that is vacant for sale
Source: U.S. Census Bureau, Housing Vacancies and Homeownership Annual Statistics: 2015

INCOME

Income

Area	Per Capita ($)	Median Household ($)	Average Household ($)
City	48,740	108,667	139,282
MSA[1]	49,688	83,163	135,743
U.S.	28,555	53,482	74,596

Note: (1) Figures cover the Bridgeport-Stamford-Norwalk, CT Metropolitan Statistical Area—see Appendix B for areas included
Source: U.S. Census Bureau, 2010-2014 American Community Survey 5-Year Estimates

Household Income Distribution

Area	Percent of Households Earning							
	Under $15,000	$15,000 -24,999	$25,000 -34,999	$35,000 -49,999	$50,000 -74,999	$75,000 -99,000	$100,000 -149,999	$150,000 and up
City	4.2	4.9	5.8	7.4	9.2	15.0	18.3	35.2
MSA[1]	8.3	7.1	6.9	9.4	13.9	11.6	16.0	26.7
U.S.	12.5	10.7	10.2	13.5	17.8	12.2	13.0	10.0

Note: (1) Figures cover the Bridgeport-Stamford-Norwalk, CT Metropolitan Statistical Area—see Appendix B for areas included
Source: U.S. Census Bureau, 2010-2014 American Community Survey 5-Year Estimates

Poverty Rate

Area	All Ages	Under 18 Years Old	18 to 64 Years Old	65 Years and Over
City	5.2	5.3	5.5	3.6
MSA[1]	9.1	11.4	8.7	6.7
U.S.	15.6	21.9	14.6	9.4

Note: Figures are percentage of people whose income during the past 12 months was below the poverty level; (1) Figures cover the Bridgeport-Stamford-Norwalk, CT Metropolitan Statistical Area—see Appendix B for areas included
Source: U.S. Census Bureau, 2010-2014 American Community Survey 5-Year Estimates

EMPLOYMENT

Labor Force and Employment

Area	Civilian Labor Force			Workers Employed		
	Dec. 2014	Dec. 2015	% Chg.	Dec. 2014	Dec. 2015	% Chg.
City	14,345	14,222	-0.8	13,758	13,666	-0.6
NECTA[1]	106,905	105,885	-0.9	102,297	101,609	-0.6
U.S.	155,521,000	157,245,000	1.1	147,190,000	149,703,000	1.7

Note: Data is not seasonally adjusted and covers workers 16 years of age and older; (1) Figures cover the Danbury, CT New England City and Town Area—see Appendix B for areas included
Source: Bureau of Labor Statistics, Local Area Unemployment Statistics

Unemployment Rate

Area	2015											
	Jan.	Feb.	Mar.	Apr.	May	Jun.	Jul.	Aug.	Sep.	Oct.	Nov.	Dec.
City	4.9	5.1	4.7	4.5	4.2	4.1	4.4	4.4	3.8	3.7	3.7	3.9
NECTA[1]	5.4	5.6	5.3	4.7	4.4	4.3	4.6	4.5	4.0	3.9	3.8	4.0
U.S.	6.1	5.8	5.6	5.1	5.3	5.5	5.6	5.2	4.9	4.8	4.8	4.8

Note: Data is not seasonally adjusted and covers workers 16 years of age and older; (1) Figures cover the Danbury, CT New England City and Town Area—see Appendix B for areas included
Source: Bureau of Labor Statistics, Local Area Unemployment Statistics

Employment by Occupation

Occupation Classification	City (%)	MSA[1] (%)	U.S. (%)
Management, Business, Science, and Arts	55.0	43.4	36.4
Natural Resources, Construction, and Maintenance	6.9	7.4	9.0
Production, Transportation, and Material Moving	5.5	7.1	12.1
Sales and Office	22.6	24.5	24.4
Service	10.1	17.6	18.2

Note: Figures cover employed civilians 16 years of age and older; (1) Figures cover the Bridgeport-Stamford-Norwalk, CT Metropolitan Statistical Area—see Appendix B for areas included
Source: U.S. Census Bureau, 2010-2014 American Community Survey 5-Year Estimates

Employment by Industry

Sector	NECTA[1]		U.S.
	Number of Employees	Percent of Total	Percent of Total
Construction, Mining, and Logging	n/a	n/a	5.0
Education and Health Services	n/a	n/a	15.7
Financial Activities	n/a	n/a	5.7
Government	10,100	12.6	15.5
Information	n/a	n/a	1.9
Leisure and Hospitality	7,300	9.1	10.4
Manufacturing	n/a	n/a	8.6
Other Services	n/a	n/a	3.9
Professional and Business Services	9,400	11.8	13.9
Retail Trade	13,800	17.3	11.3
Transportation, Warehousing, and Utilities	n/a	n/a	3.9
Wholesale Trade	n/a	n/a	4.1

Note: Figures are non-farm employment as of December 2015. Figures are not seasonally adjusted and include workers 16 years of age and older; (1) Figures cover the Danbury, CT New England City and Town Area—see Appendix B for areas included; n/a not available
Source: Bureau of Labor Statistics, Current Employment Statistics, Employment, Hours, and Earnings

Occupations with Greatest Projected Employment Growth: 2012 – 2022

Occupation[1]	2012 Employment	2022 Projected Employment	Numeric Employment Change	Percent Employment Change
Personal Care Aides	23,240	32,090	8,850	38.1
Registered Nurses	35,990	41,230	5,240	14.6
Secretaries and Administrative Assistants, Except Legal, Medical, and Executive	34,530	38,640	4,110	11.9
Combined Food Preparation and Serving Workers, Including Fast Food	26,730	30,740	4,010	15.0
Retail Salespersons	53,800	57,270	3,470	6.4
General and Operations Managers	31,160	34,420	3,260	10.5
Home Health Aides	8,250	11,450	3,200	38.7
Childcare Workers	18,300	21,170	2,870	15.7
Maids and Housekeeping Cleaners	17,800	20,560	2,760	15.5
First-Line Supervisors of Office and Administrative Support Workers	26,360	28,900	2,540	9.6

Note: Projections cover Connecticut; (1) Sorted by numeric employment change
Source: www.projectionscentral.com, State Occupational Projections, 2012–2022 Long-Term Projections

Fastest Growing Occupations: 2012 – 2022

Occupation[1]	2012 Employment	2022 Projected Employment	Numeric Employment Change	Percent Employment Change
Insulation Workers, Mechanical	210	350	140	65.6
Interpreters and Translators	460	650	190	43.1
Helpers—Electricians	270	380	110	39.4
Home Health Aides	8,250	11,450	3,200	38.7
Diagnostic Medical Sonographers	1,000	1,380	380	38.3
Personal Care Aides	23,240	32,090	8,850	38.1
Physical Therapist Assistants	540	740	200	37.4
Occupational Therapy Assistants	490	670	180	35.4
Health Specialties Teachers, Postsecondary	2,810	3,770	960	34.3
Nursing Instructors and Teachers, Postsecondary	700	940	240	34.0

Note: Projections cover Connecticut; (1) Sorted by percent employment change and excludes occupations with numeric employment change less than 100
Source: www.projectionscentral.com, State Occupational Projections, 2012–2022 Long-Term Projections

Average Wages

Occupation	$/Hr.	Occupation	$/Hr.
Accountants and Auditors	35.04	Maids and Housekeeping Cleaners	11.71
Automotive Mechanics	22.49	Maintenance and Repair Workers	23.48
Bookkeepers	21.16	Marketing Managers	53.44
Carpenters	27.70	Nuclear Medicine Technologists	n/a
Cashiers	11.64	Nurses, Licensed Practical	25.51
Clerks, General Office	16.36	Nurses, Registered	38.93
Clerks, Receptionists/Information	16.17	Nursing Assistants	15.27
Clerks, Shipping/Receiving	15.19	Packers and Packagers, Hand	13.74
Computer Programmers	40.11	Physical Therapists	45.79
Computer Systems Analysts	44.53	Postal Service Mail Carriers	25.07
Computer User Support Specialists	23.12	Real Estate Brokers	n/a
Cooks, Restaurant	13.09	Retail Salespersons	13.06
Dentists	76.85	Sales Reps., Exc. Tech./Scientific	42.41
Electrical Engineers	37.34	Sales Reps., Tech./Scientific	48.57
Electricians	25.37	Secretaries, Exc. Legal/Med./Exec.	18.54
Financial Managers	60.73	Security Guards	15.69
First-Line Supervisors/Managers, Sales	21.83	Surgeons	104.90
Food Preparation Workers	11.89	Teacher Assistants*	15.61
General and Operations Managers	67.21	Teachers, Elementary School*	36.23
Hairdressers/Cosmetologists	15.58	Teachers, Secondary School*	35.93
Internists	n/a	Telemarketers	n/a
Janitors and Cleaners	15.02	Truck Drivers, Heavy/Tractor-Trailer	20.87
Landscaping/Groundskeeping Workers	15.97	Truck Drivers, Light/Delivery Svcs.	17.39
Lawyers	68.53	Waiters and Waitresses	10.86

Note: Wage data covers the New England City and Town Area—see Appendix B for areas included; (*) Hourly wages for elementary/secondary school teachers and teacher assistants were calculated by the editors from annual wage data based on a 40 hour work week; n/a not available.
Source: Bureau of Labor Statistics, Metro Area Occupational Employment and Wage Estimates, May 2015

TAXES

State Corporate Income Tax Rates

State	Tax Rate (%)	Income Brackets ($)	Num. of Brackets	Financial Institution Tax Rate (%)[a]	Federal Income Tax Ded.
Connecticut	7.5 (d)	Flat rate	1	7.5 (d)	No

Note: Tax rates as of January 1, 2016; (a) Rates listed are the corporate income tax rate applied to financial institutions or excise taxes based on income. Some states have other taxes based upon the value of deposits or shares; (d) Connecticut's tax is the greater of the 7.5% tax on net income, a 0.31% tax on capital stock and surplus (maximum tax of $1 million), or $250 (the minimum tax). Plus, an additional 20% surtax applies for tax years 2012 and 2016.
Source: Federation of Tax Administrators, "State Corporate Income Tax Rates, 2016"

State Individual Income Tax Rates

State	Tax Rate (%)	Income Brackets ($)	Num. of Brackets	Personal Exempt. ($)[1] Single	Personal Exempt. ($)[1] Dependents	Fed. Inc. Tax Ded.
Connecticut	3.0 - 6.99	10,000 - 500,000 (b)	7	14,500 (g)	None	No

Note: Tax rates as of January 1, 2016; Local- and county-level taxes are not included; n/a not applicable; (1) Married joint filers generally receive double the single exemption; (b) For joint returns, taxes are twice the tax on half the couple's income; (g) Connecticut's personal exemption incorporates a standard deduction. An additional tax credit is allowed ranging from 75% to 0% based on state adjusted gross income. Exemption amounts are phased out for higher income taxpayers until they are eliminated for households earning over $71,000.
Source: Federation of Tax Administrators, "State Individual Income Tax Rates, 2016"

Various State and Local Tax Rates

State	State and Local Sales and Use (%)	State Sales and Use (%)	Gasoline[1] (¢/gal.)	Cigarette[2] ($/pack)	Spirits[3] ($/gal.)	Wine[4] ($/gal.)	Beer[5] ($/gal.)
Connecticut	6.35	6.35	37.51	3.65	5.40 (f)	0.72 (l)	0.16

Note: All tax rates as of January 1, 2016; (1) The American Petroleum Institute has developed a methodology for determining the average tax rate on a gallon of fuel. Rates may include any of the following: excise taxes, environmental fees, storage tank fees, other fees or taxes, general sales tax, and local taxes. In states where gasoline is subject to the general sales tax, or where the fuel tax is based on the average sale price, the average rate determined by API is sensitive to changes in the price of gasoline. States that fully or partially apply general sales taxes to gasoline: CA, CO, GA, IL, IN, MI, NY; (2) The federal excise tax of $1.0066 per pack and local taxes are not included; (3) Rates are those applicable to off-premise sales of 40% alcohol by volume (a.b.v.) distilled spirits in 750ml containers. Local excise taxes are excluded; (4) Rates are those applicable to off-premise sales of 11% a.b.v. non-carbonated wine in 750ml containers; (5) Rates are those applicable to off-premise sales of 4.7% a.b.v. beer in 12 ounce containers; (f) Different rates are also applicable according to alcohol content, place of production, size of container, or place purchased (on- or off-premise or onboard airlines); (l) Different rates also applicable according to alcohol content, place of production, size of container, place purchased (on- or off-premise or on board airlines) or type of wine (carbonated, vermouth, etc.).
Source: Tax Foundation, 2016 Facts & Figures: How Does Your State Compare?

State Business Tax Climate Index Rankings

State	Overall Rank	Corporate Tax Rank	Individual Income Tax Rank	Sales Tax Rank	Unemployment Insurance Tax Rank	Property Tax Rank
Connecticut	44	33	36	29	20	49

Note: The index is a measure of how each state's tax laws affect economic performance. The lower the rank, the more favorable a state's tax system is for business. States without a given tax are given a ranking of 1. The scores/rankings for the District of Columbia do not affect other states. The 2016 index represents the tax climate as of July 1, 2015 (the beginning of Fiscal Year 2016).
Source: Tax Foundation, State Business Tax Climate Index 2016

TRANSPORTATION

Means of Transportation to Work

Area	Car/Truck/Van		Public Transportation			Bicycle	Walked	Other Means	Worked at Home
	Drove Alone	Car-pooled	Bus	Subway	Railroad				
City	82.7	6.0	0.2	0.1	1.5	0.0	1.2	0.5	7.9
MSA[1]	72.8	8.4	2.7	0.3	6.3	0.3	2.7	0.9	5.5
U.S.	76.4	9.6	2.6	1.8	0.6	0.6	2.8	1.3	4.4

Note: Figures are percentages and cover workers 16 years of age and older; (1) Figures cover the Bridgeport-Stamford-Norwalk, CT Metropolitan Statistical Area—see Appendix B for areas included
Source: U.S. Census Bureau, 2010-2014 American Community Survey 5-Year Estimates

Travel Time to Work

Area	Less Than 10 Minutes	10 to 19 Minutes	20 to 29 Minutes	30 to 44 Minutes	45 to 59 Minutes	60 to 89 Minutes	90 Minutes or More
City	10.1	20.7	18.9	24.6	12.2	9.6	3.8
MSA[1]	11.8	31.4	18.6	17.2	7.1	8.6	5.3
U.S.	13.3	29.6	21.0	20.2	7.7	5.7	2.6

Note: Figures are percentages and include workers 16 years old and over; (1) Figures cover the Bridgeport-Stamford-Norwalk, CT Metropolitan Statistical Area—see Appendix B for areas included
Source: U.S. Census Bureau, 2010-2014 American Community Survey 5-Year Estimates

Freeway Travel Time Index

Area	1985	1990	1995	2000	2005	2010	2014
Urban Area Rank[1,2]	11	9	6	4	5	6	6
Urban Area Index[1]	1.16	1.20	1.25	1.32	1.36	1.34	1.36
Average Index[3]	1.09	1.11	1.14	1.17	1.20	1.19	1.20

Note: Freeway Travel Time Index—the ratio of travel time in the peak period to the travel time at free-flow conditions. For example, a value of 1.30 indicates a 20-minute free-flow trip takes 26 minutes in the peak (20 minutes x 1.30 = 26 minutes); (1) Covers the Bridgeport-Stamford CT-NY urban area; (2) Rank is based on 101 urban areas (#1 = highest travel time index); (3) Average of 101 urban areas
Source: Texas Transportation Institute, 2015 Urban Mobility Scorecard, August 2015

Freeway Commuter Stress Index

Area	1985	1990	1995	2000	2005	2010	2014
Urban Area Rank[1,2]	17	10	8	6	5	8	7
Urban Area Index[1]	1.23	1.28	1.33	1.40	1.45	1.43	1.44
Average Index[3]	1.13	1.16	1.19	1.22	1.25	1.24	1.25

Note: The Freeway Commuter Stress Index is the same as the Freeway Travel Time Index (see table above) except that it includes only the travel in the peak directions during the peak periods; the TTI includes travel in all directions during the peak period. Thus, the CSI is more indicative of the work trip experienced by each commuter on a daily basis. (1) Covers the Bridgeport-Stamford CT-NY urban area; (2) Rank is based on 101 urban areas (#1 = highest stress index); (3) Average of 101 urban areas

Source: Texas Transportation Institute, 2015 Urban Mobility Scorecard, August 2015

Living Environment

COST OF LIVING

Cost of Living Index

Composite Index	Groceries	Housing	Utilities	Trans-portation	Health Care	Misc. Goods/ Services
147.1	130.8	209.8	132.1	106.3	114.5	123.0

Note: The Cost of Living Index measures regional differences in the cost of consumer goods and services, excluding taxes and non-consumer expenditures, for professional and managerial households in the top income quintile. It is based on more than 50,000 prices covering almost 60 different items for which prices are collected three times a year by chambers of commerce, economic development organizations or university applied economic centers in each participating urban area. The numbers shown should be read as a percentage above or below the national average of 100. For example, a value of 115.4 in the groceries column indicates that grocery prices are 15.4% higher than the national average. Small differences in the index numbers should not be interpreted as significant; Figures cover the Stamford CT urban area.
Source: The Council for Community and Economic Research, ACCRA Cost of Living Index, 2015

Grocery Prices

Area[1]	T-Bone Steak ($/pound)	Frying Chicken ($/pound)	Whole Milk ($/half gal.)	Eggs ($/dozen)	Orange Juice ($/64 oz.)	Coffee ($/11.5 oz.)
City[2]	12.44	1.35	2.89	3.05	4.21	5.49
Avg.	10.99	1.43	2.25	2.26	3.58	4.48
Min.	7.16	0.98	1.30	1.35	2.88	2.98
Max.	14.13	2.43	3.85	4.81	6.39	7.56

Note: (1) Values for the local area are compared with the average, minimum and maximum values for all 292 areas in the Cost of Living Index; (2) Figures cover the Stamford CT urban area; **T-Bone Steak** *(price per pound);* **Frying Chicken** *(price per pound, whole fryer);* **Whole Milk** *(half gallon carton);* **Eggs** *(price per dozen, Grade A, large);* **Orange Juice** *(64 oz. Tropicana or Florida Natural);* **Coffee** *(11.5 oz. can, vacuum-packed, Maxwell House, Hills Bros, or Folgers).*
Source: The Council for Community and Economic Research, ACCRA Cost of Living Index, 2015

Housing and Utility Costs

Area[1]	New Home Price ($)	Apartment Rent ($/month)	All Electric ($/month)	Part Electric ($/month)	Other Energy ($/month)	Telephone ($/month)
City[2]	626,189	2,199	-	147.95	111.00	29.01
Avg.	312,874	945	179.30	95.07	72.96	28.11
Min.	178,682	479	116.28	43.14	26.46	10.01
Max.	1,472,476	3,984	504.25	189.44	421.11	43.06

Note: (1) Values for the local area are compared with the average, minimum and maximum values for all 292 areas in the Cost of Living Index; (2) Figures cover the Stamford CT urban area; **New Home Price** *(2,400 sf living area, 8,000 sf lot, in urban area with full utilities);* **Apartment Rent** *(950 sf 2 bedroom/1.5 or 2 bath, unfurnished, excluding all utilities except water);* **All Electric** *(average monthly cost for an all-electric home);* **Part Electric** *(average monthly cost for a part-electric home);* **Other Energy** *(average monthly cost for natural gas, fuel oil, coal, wood, and any other forms of energy except electricity);* **Telephone** *(price includes basic monthly rate for a private residential line plus additional local usage charges incurred by a family of four).*
Source: The Council for Community and Economic Research, ACCRA Cost of Living Index, 2015

Health Care, Transportation, and Other Costs

Area[1]	Doctor ($/visit)	Dentist ($/visit)	Optometrist ($/visit)	Gasoline ($/gallon)	Beauty Salon ($/visit)	Men's Shirt ($)
City[2]	123.75	110.00	111.67	2.47	64.17	27.43
Avg.	105.15	89.02	99.78	2.38	35.30	28.10
Min.	66.87	56.09	48.53	1.95	18.91	13.38
Max.	182.34	150.36	228.33	4.09	67.91	63.80

Note: (1) Values for the local area are compared with the average, minimum and maximum values for all 292 areas in the Cost of Living Index; (2) Figures cover the Stamford CT urban area; **Doctor** *(general practitioners routine exam of an established patient);* **Dentist** *(adult teeth cleaning and periodic oral examination);* **Optometrist** *(full vision eye exam for established adult patient);* **Gasoline** *(one gallon regular unleaded, national brand, including all taxes, cash price at self-service pump if available);* **Beauty Salon** *(woman's shampoo, trim, and blow-dry);* **Men's Shirt** *(cotton/polyester dress shirt, pinpoint weave, long sleeves).*
Source: The Council for Community and Economic Research, ACCRA Cost of Living Index, 2015

HOUSING

House Price Index (HPI)

Area	National Ranking[2]	Quarterly Change (%)	One-Year Change (%)	Five-Year Change (%)
MSA[1]	242	-1.00	1.30	-0.70
U.S.[3]	–	1.45	5.76	22.85

Note: The HPI is a weighted repeat sales index. It measures average price changes in repeat sales or refinancings on the same properties. This information is obtained by reviewing repeat mortgage transactions on single-family properties whose mortgages have been purchased or securitized by Fannie Mae or Freddie Mac in January 1975; (1) Bridgeport-Stamford-Norwalk Metropolitan Statistical Area—see Appendix B for areas included; (2) Rankings are based on annual percentage change for all metro areas containing at least 15,000 transactions over the last 10 years and ranges from 1 to 266; (3) figures based on a weighted average of Census Division estimates using a seasonally adjusted, purchase-only index; all figures are for the period ending December 31, 2015

Source: Federal Housing Finance Agency, House Price Index, February 25, 2016

Median Single-Family Home Prices

Area	2013	2014	2015p	Percent Change 2014 to 2015
MSA[1]	403.0	397.6	377.7	-5.0
U.S. Average	197.4	208.9	223.9	7.2

Note: Figures are median sales prices of existing single-family homes in thousands of dollars; (p) preliminary; n/a not available; (1) Bridgeport-Stamford-Norwalk, CT Metropolitan Statistical Area—see Appendix B for areas included

Source: National Association of Realtors, Median Sales Price of Existing Single-Family Homes for Metropolitan Areas, 4th Quarter 2015

Qualifying Income Based on Median Sales Price of Existing Single-Family Homes

Area	With 5% Down ($)	With 10% Down ($)	With 20% Down ($)
MSA[1]	80,320	76,092	67,638
U.S. Average	49,535	46,928	41,714

Note: Figures are preliminary; Qualifying income is based on a mortgage rate of 4.1%. Monthly principal and interest payment is limited to 25% of income; n/a not available; (1) Bridgeport-Stamford-Norwalk, CT Metropolitan Statistical Area—see Appendix B for areas included

Source: National Association of Realtors, Qualifying Income Based on Median Sales Price of Existing Single-Family Homes for Metropolitan Areas, 4th Quarter 2015

Median Apartment Condo-Coop Home Prices

Area	2013	2014	2015p	Percent Change 2014 to 2015
MSA[1]	220.3	221.3	218.6	-1.2
U.S. Average	194.9	204.3	210.7	3.1

Note: Figures are median sales prices of existing apartment condo-coop homes in thousands of dollars; (p) preliminary; n/a not available; (1) Bridgeport-Stamford-Norwalk, CT Metropolitan Statistical Area—see Appendix B for areas included

Source: National Association of Realtors, Median Sales Price of Existing Apartment Condo-Coop Homes for Metropolitan Areas, 4th Quarter 2015

Gross Monthly Rent

Area	Under $200	$200 -299	$300 -499	$500 -749	$750 -999	$1,000 -1,499	$1,500 and up	Median ($)
City	0.0	2.9	2.4	7.7	12.1	32.9	42.0	1,363
MSA[1]	1.4	3.5	5.1	5.9	12.3	33.6	38.3	1,327
U.S.	1.5	3.2	7.4	21.0	24.1	26.9	15.9	920

Note: Figures are percentages except for Median; Gross rent is the contract rent plus the estimated average monthly cost of utilities (electricity, gas, and water and sewer) and fuels (oil, coal, kerosene, wood, etc.) if these are paid by the renter (or paid for the renter by someone else); (1) Figures cover the Bridgeport-Stamford-Norwalk, CT Metropolitan Statistical Area—see Appendix B for areas included

Source: U.S. Census Bureau, 2010-2014 American Community Survey 5-Year Estimates

Homeownership Rate

Area	2008 (%)	2009 (%)	2010 (%)	2011 (%)	2012 (%)	2013 (%)	2014 (%)	2015 (%)
MSA[1]	72.6	70.3	71.3	71.6	70.6	70.7	67.7	66.6
U.S.	67.8	67.4	66.9	66.1	65.4	65.1	64.5	63.7

Note: (1) Figures cover the Bridgeport-Stamford-Norwalk, CT Metropolitan Statistical Area—see Appendix B for areas included

Source: U.S. Census Bureau, Housing Vacancies and Homeownership Annual Statistics: 2015

Year Housing Structure Built

Area	2010 or Later	2000 -2009	1990 -1999	1980 -1989	1970 -1979	1960 -1969	1950 -1959	1940 -1949	Before 1940	Median Year
City	0.6	13.1	16.1	11.5	14.8	15.2	12.0	4.7	12.0	1974
MSA[1]	0.8	6.9	6.8	11.4	13.6	14.5	17.1	7.6	21.4	1963
U.S.	1.0	14.9	13.9	13.8	15.8	11.0	10.8	5.4	13.3	1976

Note: Figures are percentages except for Median Year; (1) Figures cover the Bridgeport-Stamford-Norwalk, CT Metropolitan Statistical Area—see Appendix B for areas included

Source: U.S. Census Bureau, 2010-2014 American Community Survey 5-Year Estimates

HEALTH

Health Risk Data

Category	MSA[1] (%)	U.S. (%)
Adults aged 18–64 who have any kind of health care coverage	83.5	79.6
Adults who reported being in good or excellent health	86.0	83.1
Adults who are current smokers	13.2	19.6
Adults who are heavy drinkers[2]	6.0	6.1
Adults who are binge drinkers[3]	19.5	16.9
Adults who are overweight (BMI 25.0 - 29.9)	39.1	35.8
Adults who are obese (BMI 30.0 - 99.8)	21.6	27.6
Adults who participated in any physical activities in the past month	78.5	77.1
Adults 50+ who have ever had a sigmoidoscopy or colonoscopy	73.3	67.3
Women aged 40+ who have had a mammogram within the past two years	76.7	74.0
Men aged 40+ who have had a PSA test within the past two years	49.6	45.2
Adults aged 65+ who have had flu shot within the past year	57.1	60.1
Adults who always wear a seatbelt	95.4	93.8

Note: Data as of 2012 unless otherwise noted; (1) Figures cover the Bridgeport-Stamford-Norwalk, CT Metropolitan Statistical Area—see Appendix B for areas included; (2) Heavy drinkers are classified as males having more than two drinks per day or females having more than one drink per day; (3) Binge drinkers are classified as males having five or more drinks on one occasion or females having four or more drinks on one occasion

Source: Centers for Disease Control and Prevention, Behaviorial Risk Factor Surveillance System, SMART: Selected Metropolitan/Micropolitan Area Risk Trends, 2012 (Note: the CDC has discontinued this dataset but will be releasing a replacement in mid-2016)

Chronic Health Indicators

Category	MSA[1] (%)	U.S. (%)
Adults who have ever been told they had a heart attack	3.2	4.5
Adults who have ever been told they had a stroke	1.8	2.9
Adults who have been told they currently have asthma	7.8	8.9
Adults who have ever been told they have arthritis	21.6	25.7
Adults who have ever been told they have diabetes[2]	7.4	9.7
Adults who have ever been told they had skin cancer	5.6	5.7
Adults who have ever been told they had any other types of cancer	6.4	6.5
Adults who have ever been told they have COPD	4.7	6.2
Adults who have ever been told they have kidney disease	2.2	2.5
Adults who have ever been told they have a form of depression	15.2	18.0

Note: Data as of 2012 unless otherwise noted; (1) Figures cover the Bridgeport-Stamford-Norwalk, CT Metropolitan Statistical Area—see Appendix B for areas included; (2) Figures do not include pregnancy-related, borderline, or pre-diabetes

Source: Centers for Disease Control and Prevention, Behaviorial Risk Factor Surveillance System, SMART: Selected Metropolitan/Micropolitan Area Risk Trends, 2012 (Note: the CDC has discontinued this dataset but will be releasing a replacement in mid-2016)

Mortality Rates for the Top 10 Causes of Death in the U.S.

ICD-10[a] Sub-Chapter	ICD-10[a] Code	Age-Adjusted Mortality Rate[1] per 100,000 population	
		County[2]	U.S.
Malignant neoplasms	C00-C97	136.2	163.6
Ischaemic heart diseases	I20-I25	79.1	102.2
Other forms of heart disease	I30-I51	53.4	50.1
Chronic lower respiratory diseases	J40-J47	25.0	41.4
Organic, including symptomatic, mental disorders	F01-F09	36.6	38.5
Cerebrovascular diseases	I60-I69	26.8	36.5
Other external causes of accidental injury	W00-X59	23.7	27.5
Other degenerative diseases of the nervous system	G30-G31	17.6	26.3
Diabetes mellitus	E10-E14	12.7	21.1
Hypertensive diseases	I10-I15	12.3	19.7

Note: (a) ICD-10 = International Classification of Diseases 10th Revision; (1) Mortality rates are a three year average covering 2012-2014; (2) Figures cover Fairfield County.
Source: Centers for Disease Control and Prevention, National Center for Health Statistics. Underlying Cause of Death 1999-2014 on CDC WONDER Online Database, released 2015.

Mortality Rates for Selected Causes of Death

ICD-10[a] Sub-Chapter	ICD-10[a] Code	Age-Adjusted Mortality Rate[1] per 100,000 population	
		County[2]	U.S.
Assault	X85-Y09	3.7	5.1
Diseases of the liver	K70-K76	8.3	13.5
Human immunodeficiency virus (HIV) disease	B20-B24	1.6	2.1
Influenza and pneumonia	J09-J18	10.3	15.2
Intentional self-harm	X60-X84	7.5	12.7
Malnutrition	E40-E46	0.6	0.9
Obesity and other hyperalimentation	E65-E68	1.1	1.9
Renal failure	N17-N19	8.6	13.0
Transport accidents	V01-V99	6.3	11.6
Viral hepatitis	B15-B19	0.9	2.1

Note: (a) ICD-10 = International Classification of Diseases 10th Revision; (1) Mortality rates are a three year average covering 2012-2014; (2) Figures cover Fairfield County; Data are Suppressed when the data meet the criteria for confidentiality constraints; Mortality rates are flagged as Unreliable when the rate would be calculated with a numerator of 20 or less.
Source: Centers for Disease Control and Prevention, National Center for Health Statistics. Underlying Cause of Death 1999-2014 on CDC WONDER Online Database, released 2015.

Health Insurance Coverage

Area	With Health Insurance	With Private Health Insurance	With Public Health Insurance	Without Health Insurance	Population Under Age 18 Without Health Insurance
City	96.3	85.9	20.6	3.7	0.9
MSA[1]	88.7	72.4	26.4	11.3	5.1
U.S.	85.8	65.8	31.1	14.2	7.1

Note: Figures are percentages that cover the civilian noninstitutionalized population; (1) Figures cover the Bridgeport-Stamford-Norwalk, CT Metropolitan Statistical Area—see Appendix B for areas included
Source: U.S. Census Bureau, 2010-2014 American Community Survey 5-Year Estimates

Number of Medical Professionals

Area	MDs[3]	DOs[3,4]	Dentists	Podiatrists	Chiropractors	Optometrists
County[1] (number)	3,550	133	853	85	323	114
County[1] (rate[2])	376.8	14.1	90.2	9.0	34.2	12.1
U.S. (rate[2])	272.5	20.9	64.7	5.8	25.9	15.2

Note: Data as of 2014 unless noted; (1) Data covers Fairfield County; (2) Rate per 100,000 population; (3) Data as of 2013 and includes all active, non-federal physicians; (4) Doctor of Osteopathic Medicine
Source: U.S. Department of Health and Human Services, Health Resources and Services Administration, Bureau of Health Professions, Area Resource File (ARF) 2014-2015

EDUCATION

Public School District Statistics

District Name	Schls	Pupils	Pupil/ Teacher Ratio	Minority Pupils[1] (%)	Free Lunch Eligible[2] (%)	IEP[3] (%)
Newtown School District	9	4,894	12.5	11.2	4.4	9.2

Note: Table includes school districts with 100 or more students; (1) Percentage of students that are not non-Hispanic white; (2) Percentage of students that are eligible for the free lunch program; (3) Percentage of students that have an Individualized Education Program.
Source: U.S. Department of Education, National Center for Education Statistics, Common Core of Data, Local Education Agency (School District) Universe Survey: School Year 2013-2014; U.S. Department of Education, National Center for Education Statistics, Common Core of Data, Public Elementary/Secondary School Universe Survey: School Year 2013-2014

Highest Level of Education

Area	Less than H.S.	H.S. Diploma	Some College, No Deg.	Associate Degree	Bachelor's Degree	Master's Degree	Prof. School Degree	Doctorate Degree
City	5.5	18.1	15.3	6.7	29.8	18.6	4.2	1.8
MSA[1]	10.8	22.5	15.4	5.8	25.5	14.7	3.8	1.5
U.S.	13.7	28.0	21.2	7.9	18.3	7.8	2.0	1.3

Note: Figures cover persons age 25 and over; (1) Figures cover the Bridgeport-Stamford-Norwalk, CT Metropolitan Statistical Area—see Appendix B for areas included
Source: U.S. Census Bureau, 2010-2014 American Community Survey 5-Year Estimates

Educational Attainment by Race

Area	High School Graduate or Higher (%)					Bachelor's Degree or Higher (%)				
	Total	White	Black	Asian	Hisp.[2]	Total	White	Black	Asian	Hisp.[2]
City	94.5	95.6	78.8	78.9	89.5	54.4	55.5	26.7	63.9	41.0
MSA[1]	89.2	92.2	84.2	89.6	68.7	45.4	50.4	19.7	66.7	18.1
U.S.	86.3	88.4	83.2	85.8	64.1	29.3	30.6	19.0	50.9	13.9

Note: Figures shown cover persons 25 years old and over; (1) Figures cover the Bridgeport-Stamford-Norwalk, CT Metropolitan Statistical Area—see Appendix B for areas included; (2) People of Hispanic origin can be of any race
Source: U.S. Census Bureau, 2010-2014 American Community Survey 5-Year Estimates

School Enrollment by Grade and Control

Area	Preschool (%)		Kindergarten (%)		Grades 1 - 4 (%)		Grades 5 - 8 (%)		Grades 9 - 12 (%)	
	Public	Private	Public	Private	Public	Private	Public	Private	Public	Private
City	36.0	64.0	81.1	18.9	93.8	6.2	87.1	12.9	88.3	11.7
MSA[1]	38.5	61.5	83.3	16.7	86.9	13.1	85.5	14.5	86.2	13.8
U.S.	57.4	42.6	87.8	12.2	89.8	10.2	89.9	10.1	90.6	9.4

Note: Figures shown cover persons 3 years old and over; (1) Figures cover the Bridgeport-Stamford-Norwalk, CT Metropolitan Statistical Area—see Appendix B for areas included
Source: U.S. Census Bureau, 2010-2014 American Community Survey 5-Year Estimates

Average Salaries of Public School Classroom Teachers

Area	2013-14		2014-15		Percent Change 2013-14 to 2014-15	Percent Change 2004-05 to 2014-15
	Dollars	Rank[1]	Dollars	Rank[1]		
Connecticut	70,583	5	71,709	5	1.59	24.2
U.S. Average	56,610	–	57,379	–	1.36	20.8

Note: (1) State rank ranges from 1 to 51 where 1 indicates highest salary.
Source: National Education Association, Rankings & Estimates: Rankings of the States 2014 and Estimates of School Statistics 2015, March 2015

Higher Education

Four-Year Colleges			Two-Year Colleges			Medical Schools[1]	Law Schools[2]	Voc/ Tech[3]
Public	Private Non-profit	Private For-profit	Public	Private Non-profit	Private For-profit			
0	0	0	0	0	0	0	0	1

Note: Figures cover institutions located within the city limits and include main campuses only; (1) includes schools accredited by the Liaison Committee on Medical Education and the American Osteopathic Association's Commission on Osteopathic College Accreditation; (2) includes ABA-accredited schools, schools with provisional ABA accreditation, and state accredited schools; (3) includes all schools with programs that are less than 2 years.
Source: National Center for Education Statistics, Integrated Postsecondary Education System (IPEDS), 2014-15; Association of American Medical Colleges, Member List, March 21, 2016; American Osteopathic Association, Member List, March 21, 2016; Law School Admission Council, Official Guide to ABA-Approved Law Schools Online, March 21, 2016; Wikipedia, List of Medical Schools in the United States, March 21, 2016; Wikipedia, List of Law Schools in the United States, March 21, 2016

PRESIDENTIAL ELECTION

2012 Presidential Election Results

Area	Obama (%)	Romney (%)	Other (%)
Fairfield County	55.3	43.8	0.9
U.S.	51.0	47.2	1.8

Note: Results may not add to 100% due to rounding
Source: Dave Leip's Atlas of U.S. Presidential Elections

EMPLOYERS

Major Employers

Company Name	Industry
Aptuit (scientific Operations)	Pharmaceutical preparations
Atos It Solutions and Services	Computer related maintenance services
Boehringer Ingelheim USA Corporation	Medicines, capsuled or ampuled
Bridgeport Hospital	Hospital, medical school affiliated with residency
Carter's Retail	Children's & infants' wear stores
Cartus Corporation	Relocation service
City of Bridgeport	Civil service commission, government
Commerce Connect Media	Magazines: publishing & printing
Conopco	Ice cream & ice milk
Diageo North America	Wine & distilled beverages
Greenwich Health Care Services	General medical & surgical hospitals
Pitney Bowes	Office machines
Sikorsky Aircraft Corporation	Aircraft
St Vincent's Development Corp.	Health systems agency
St Vincent's Health Services	General medical & surgical hospitals
The Danbury Hospital	Hospital, medical school affiliated with residency
Thomas J. Lipton	Tea blending
Thomson Corporation U.S.A.	Newspapers, publishing & printing
UBS Americas	Security brokers & dealers
UBS Securities	Brokers, security
Western Connecticut Healthcare	General medical & surgical hospitals
Wheelabrator Connecticut	Refuse systems

Note: Companies shown are located within the Bridgeport-Stamford-Norwalk, CT Metropolitan Statistical Area.
Source: Hoovers.com; Wikipedia

PUBLIC SAFETY

Crime Rate

Area	All Crimes	Violent Crimes				Property Crimes		
		Murder	Rape[3]	Robbery	Aggrav. Assault	Burglary	Larceny -Theft	Motor Vehicle Theft
City	647.9	0.0	17.7	3.5	17.7	230.1	357.6	21.2
Metro[1]	1,850.8	1.9	20.0	100.0	122.7	304.0	1,146.2	155.9
U.S.	2,971.8	4.5	36.6	102.2	232.5	542.5	1,837.3	216.2

Note: Figures are crimes per 100,000 population; (1) Figures cover the Bridgeport-Stamford-Norwalk, CT Metropolitan Statistical Area—see Appendix B for areas included; (3) The city and U.S. figures shown were reported using the revised Uniform Crime Reporting (UCR) definition of rape. The suburban and metro area figures shown are an aggregate total of the data submitted using both the revised and legacy UCR definitions.
Source: FBI Uniform Crime Reports, 2014

Hate Crimes

Area	Number of Quarters Reported	Number of Incidents per Bias Motivation						
		Race	Religion	Sexual Orientation	Ethnicity	Disability	Gender	Gender Identity
City	4	2	1	0	0	0	0	0
U.S.	4	2,568	1,014	1,017	648	84	33	98

Source: Federal Bureau of Investigation, Hate Crime Statistics 2014

Identity Theft Consumer Complaints

Area	Complaints	Complaints per 100,000 Population	Rank[2]
MSA[1]	2,400	253.9	5
U.S.	490,220	152.4	-

Note: (1) Figures cover the Bridgeport-Stamford-Norwalk, CT Metropolitan Statistical Area—see Appendix B for areas included; (2) Rank ranges from 1 to 379 where 1 indicates greatest number of identity theft complaints per 100,000 population
Source: Federal Trade Commission, Consumer Sentinel Network Data Book for January–December 2015

Fraud and Other Consumer Complaints

Area	Complaints	Complaints per 100,000 Population	Rank[2]
MSA[1]	3,152	333.4	242
U.S.	2,593,159	806.0	-

Note: (1) Figures cover the Bridgeport-Stamford-Norwalk, CT Metropolitan Statistical Area—see Appendix B for areas included; (2) Rank ranges from 1 to 379 where 1 indicates greatest number of identity theft complaints per 100,000 population
Source: Federal Trade Commission, Consumer Sentinel Network Data Book for January–December 2015

RECREATION

Culture

Dance[1]	Theatre[1]	Instrumental Music[1]	Vocal Music[1]	Series and Festivals	Museums and Art Galleries[2]	Zoos and Aquariums[3]
0	0	0	0	0	0	0

Note: (1) Professional perfoming groups; (2) Based on organizations with SIC code 8412; (3) AZA-accredited
Source: The Grey House Performing Arts Directory, 2015-16; Association of Zoos & Aquariums, AZA Member Zoos & Aquariums, March 25, 2016; www.AccuLeads.com, March 29, 2016

Professional Sports Teams

Team Name	League	Year Established
No teams are located in the metro area		

Source: Wikipedia, Major Professional Sports Teams of the United States and Canada, March 24, 2016

CLIMATE

Average and Extreme Temperatures

Temperature	Jan	Feb	Mar	Apr	May	Jun	Jul	Aug	Sep	Oct	Nov	Dec	Yr.
Extreme High (°F)	65	67	84	91	92	96	103	100	99	85	78	65	103
Average High (°F)	37	38	46	57	67	76	82	81	74	64	53	41	60
Average Temp. (°F)	30	32	39	49	59	68	74	73	66	56	46	35	52
Average Low (°F)	23	24	31	40	50	59	65	65	57	47	38	27	44
Extreme Low (°F)	-7	-5	4	18	31	41	49	44	36	26	16	-4	-7

Note: Figures cover the years 1948-1992
Source: National Climatic Data Center, International Station Meteorological Climate Summary, 9/96

Average Precipitation/Snowfall/Humidity

Precip./Humidity	Jan	Feb	Mar	Apr	May	Jun	Jul	Aug	Sep	Oct	Nov	Dec	Yr.
Avg. Precip. (in.)	3.2	2.9	3.7	3.7	3.7	3.1	3.7	3.8	3.0	3.2	3.8	3.5	41.4
Avg. Snowfall (in.)	7	7	5	1	Tr	0	0	0	0	Tr	1	5	25
Avg. Rel. Hum. 7am (%)	73	72	72	72	76	77	79	80	81	79	77	74	76
Avg. Rel. Hum. 4pm (%)	61	59	56	55	59	60	60	61	61	60	62	63	60

Note: Figures cover the years 1948-1992; Tr = Trace amounts (<0.05 in. of rain; <0.5 in. of snow)
Source: National Climatic Data Center, International Station Meteorological Climate Summary, 9/96

Weather Conditions

Temperature			Daytime Sky			Precipitation		
32°F & below	45°F & below	90°F & above	Clear	Partly cloudy	Cloudy	0.01 inch or more precip.	0.1 inch or more snow/ice	Thunder-storms
100	193	7	80	146	139	118	17	22

Note: Figures are average number of days per year and cover the years 1948-1992
Source: National Climatic Data Center, International Station Meteorological Climate Summary, 9/96

HAZARDOUS WASTE

Superfund Sites

Newtown has no sites on the EPA's Superfund Final National Priorities List. There are a total of 1,323 Superfund sites on the list in the U.S. *U.S. Environmental Protection Agency, Final National Priorities List, March 18, 2016*

AIR & WATER QUALITY

Air Quality Trends: Ozone

	1990	1995	2000	2005	2010	2011	2012	2013	2014
MSA[1]	0.106	0.103	0.088	0.094	0.081	0.084	0.087	0.083	0.075

Note: (1) Data covers the Bridgeport-Stamford-Norwalk, CT Metropolitan Statistical Area—see Appendix B for areas included. The values shown are the composite ozone concentration averages among trend sites based on the highest fourth daily maximum 8-hour concentration in parts per million. These trends are based on sites having an adequate record of monitoring data during the trend period. Data from exceptional events are included.
Source: U.S. Environmental Protection Agency, Air Quality Monitoring Information, "Air Quality Trends by City, 1990-2014"

Air Quality Index

Area	Percent of Days when Air Quality was...[2]					AQI Statistics[2]	
	Good	Moderate	Unhealthy for Sensitive Groups	Unhealthy	Very Unhealthy	Maximum	Median
MSA[1]	61.9	33.4	4.4	0.3	0.0	151	44

Note: (1) Data covers the Bridgeport-Stamford-Norwalk, CT Metropolitan Statistical Area—see Appendix B for areas included; (2) Based on 365 days with AQI data in 2015. Air Quality Index (AQI) is an index for reporting daily air quality. EPA calculates the AQI for five major air pollutants regulated by the Clean Air Act: ground-level ozone, particle pollution (aka particulate matter), carbon monoxide, sulfur dioxide, and nitrogen dioxide. The AQI runs from 0 to 500. The higher the AQI value, the greater the level of air pollution and the greater the health concern. There are six AQI categories: "Good" AQI is between 0 and 50. Air quality is considered satisfactory; "Moderate" AQI is between 51 and 100. Air quality is acceptable; "Unhealthy for Sensitive Groups" When AQI values are between 101 and 150, members of sensitive groups may experience health effects; "Unhealthy" When AQI values are between 151 and 200 everyone may begin to experience health effects; "Very Unhealthy" AQI values between 201 and 300 trigger a health alert; "Hazardous" AQI values over 300 trigger warnings of emergency conditions (not shown).
Source: U.S. Environmental Protection Agency, Air Quality Index Report, 2015

Air Quality Index Pollutants

Area	Percent of Days when AQI Pollutant was...[2]					
	Carbon Monoxide	Nitrogen Dioxide	Ozone	Sulfur Dioxide	Particulate Matter 2.5	Particulate Matter 10
MSA[1]	0.5	0.0	34.8	0.0	64.7	0.0

Note: (1) Data covers the Bridgeport-Stamford-Norwalk, CT Metropolitan Statistical Area—see Appendix B for areas included; (2) Based on 365 days with AQI data in 2015. The Air Quality Index (AQI) is an index for reporting daily air quality. EPA calculates the AQI for five major air pollutants regulated by the Clean Air Act: ground-level ozone, particle pollution (also known as particulate matter), carbon monoxide, sulfur dioxide, and nitrogen dioxide. The AQI runs from 0 to 500. The higher the AQI value, the greater the level of air pollution and the greater the health concern.
Source: U.S. Environmental Protection Agency, Air Quality Index Report, 2015

Maximum Air Pollutant Concentrations: Particulate Matter, Ozone, CO and Lead

	Particulate Matter 10 (ug/m^3)	Particulate Matter 2.5 Wtd AM (ug/m^3)	Particulate Matter 2.5 24-Hr (ug/m^3)	Ozone (ppm)	Carbon Monoxide (ppm)	Lead (ug/m^3)
MSA[1] Level	35	9.9	25	0.081	1	n/a
NAAQS[2]	150	15	35	0.075	9	0.15
Met NAAQS[2]	Yes	Yes	Yes	No	Yes	n/a

Note: (1) Data covers the Bridgeport-Stamford-Norwalk, CT Metropolitan Statistical Area—see Appendix B for areas included; Data from exceptional events are included; (2) National Ambient Air Quality Standards; ppm = parts per million; ug/m^3 = micrograms per cubic meter; n/a not available.
Concentrations: Particulate Matter 10 (coarse particulate)—highest second maximum 24-hour concentration; Particulate Matter 2.5 Wtd AM (fine particulate)—highest weighted annual mean concentration; Particulate Matter 2.5 24-Hour (fine particulate)—highest 98th percentile 24-hour concentration; Ozone—highest fourth daily maximum 8-hour concentration; Carbon Monoxide—highest second maximum non-overlapping 8-hour concentration; Lead—maximum running 3-month average
Source: U.S. Environmental Protection Agency, Air Quality Monitoring Information, "Air Quality Statistics by City, 2014"

Maximum Air Pollutant Concentrations: Nitrogen Dioxide and Sulfur Dioxide

	Nitrogen Dioxide AM (ppb)	Nitrogen Dioxide 1-Hr (ppb)	Sulfur Dioxide AM (ppb)	Sulfur Dioxide 1-Hr (ppb)	Sulfur Dioxide 24-Hr (ppb)
MSA[1] Level	9	48	n/a	8	n/a
NAAQS[2]	53	100	30	75	140
Met NAAQS[2]	Yes	Yes	n/a	Yes	n/a

Note: (1) Data covers the Bridgeport-Stamford-Norwalk, CT Metropolitan Statistical Area—see Appendix B for areas included; Data from exceptional events are included; (2) National Ambient Air Quality Standards; ppm = parts per million; ug/m^3 = micrograms per cubic meter; n/a not available.
Concentrations: Nitrogen Dioxide AM—highest arithmetic mean concentration; Nitrogen Dioxide 1-Hr—highest 98th percentile 1-hour daily maximum concentration; Sulfur Dioxide AM—highest annual mean concentration; Sulfur Dioxide 1-Hr—highest 99th percentile 1-hour daily maximum concentration; Sulfur Dioxide 24-Hr—highest second maximum 24-hour concentration
Source: U.S. Environmental Protection Agency, Air Quality Monitoring Information, "Air Quality Statistics by City, 2014"

Drinking Water

Water System Name	Pop. Served	Primary Water Source Type	Violations[1]	
			Health Based	Monitoring/ Reporting
Fairfield Hills	2,610	Ground	0	0
United Water CT-Newtown System	4,037	Ground	0	0

Note: (1) Based on violation data from January 1, 2015 to December 31, 2015 (includes unresolved violations from earlier years)

Source: U.S. Environmental Protection Agency, Office of Ground Water and Drinking Water, Safe Drinking Water Information System (based on data extracted April 29, 2016)

Ridgefield, Connecticut

Background

Ridgefield, a blend of quaint, New England small town charm and modern Americana, is nestled in the foothills of the Berkshire Mountains in central Fairfield County in western Connecticut. The 300-year-old colonial town covers approximately 35 square miles, bordered by New York to the west, Danbury to the north, Wilton to the south, and Redding to the east.

Ridgefield was founded in 1708 when English colonialists from Norwalk and Milford on Long Island Sound bought the land from Chief Katonah of the Ramapo tribe. The town of Ridgefield was incorporated in 1709 under a royal charter from the Connecticut General Assembly. During the Revolutionary War, Ridgefield was the site of the 1777 Battle of Ridgefield in which American Generals Wooster and Arnold attempted to hold off British troops. The battle was a tactical victory for the British and a strategic victory for the American colonials as the British would never conduct inland operations in Connecticut again, despite its strategic location near the Hudson River Valley. This is the only land battle on Connecticut soil during the Revolutionary War. Today, there are monuments and markers in the town of Ridgefield that pay tribute to the town's heritage.

Ridgefield is famed for its handsome Main Street that runs through the center of town for more than a mile, along a ridge that sits 750 feet above sea level. Main Street houses museums, shops, churches, and is lined with stately and historic homes that date back to the colonial period. Majestic oak and elm trees give the street old-world character. Today, the town's charm exists alongside more modern finishes and amenities. As part of a rapidly growing community, the historic landmarks are situated amidst the modern day improvements and markers, necessary for a vibrant, growing community.

Ridgefield is known for its high quality of life based on its excellent schools, low crime rate, and scope of services. There is a strong sense of community and a collective commitment to maintaining the qualities that make Ridgefield unique. Ridgefield's school system consistently receives high marks.

Ridgefield is a hub for arts and entertainment such as the Ridgefield Symphony Orchestra and the Western Connecticut Youth Orchestra, both of which have been internationally recognized. The Keeler Tavern Museum is a historically preserved early 18th century home that was the center for community activities in its day. The Aldrich Contemporary Art Museum is a leading venue for contemporary artists and is well known and respected in the international art community. The Ridgefield Playhouse, which opened in 2000, serves as a year-round venue for concerts and other performances. There are also opportunities to experience dance performances at the Ridgefield Conservatory of Dance which is home to three pre-professional dance troupes.

There are many public open spaces in Ridgefield such as Aldrich Park, Bennett's Pond State Park, Brewster Farm, and the Weir Farm National Historic Site, which straddles the Ridgefield-Wilton border and is named for painter J. Alden Weir. The area preserves much of the farm that belonged to Weir and includes the Weir Farm Art Center and a gallery that recognizes the legacy of the American impressionist artist. Weir Farm is one of only two official National Park Service units in the state. Overall, Ridgefield's public open spaces make up 5,200 acres of land that accounts for 23% of the overall land in the town. The parks and recreation department operates and maintains over 600 acres of parks, trails, fields, and facilities. The town also features a skatepark that is used by both skateboarders and inline skaters.

Ridgefield gets an average of 174 days of sunshine per year. It has a climate similar to that of other towns in the northeast, with cold, wet winters and hot, humid summers. Ridgefield sees about 50 inches of rain per year and an average of about 22 inches of snow. The highs in summer reach into the 80s and drop well below freezing during winter.

Rankings

Business/Finance Rankings

- The personal finance site NerdWallet analyzed 183 American metropolitan areas with populations over 250,000 and more than 15,000 businesses to rank where entrepreneurs find the most success. Criteria included area economy, annual income, housing cost, unemployment rate, and the success rate of area businesses. Bridgeport* ranked #3. *www.nerdwallet.com, "Best Places to Start a Business," April 27, 2015*
- TransUnion ranked the nation's metro areas by average credit score, calculated on the VantageScore system, developed by the three major credit-reporting bureaus—TransUnion, Experian, and Equifax. The Bridgeport* metro area was among the ten cities with the highest collective credit score, meaning that its residents posed the lowest average consumer credit risk. *www.usatoday.com, "Metro Areas' Average Credit Rating Revealed," February 7, 2013*
- Based on the U.S. Department of Labor's Occupational Information Network Data Collection Program, the Brookings Institution defined job opportunities for STEM workers at various levels of educational attainment. The Bridgeport* metro area was one of the ten metro areas where workers in low-education-level STEM jobs earn the lowest relative wages. *www.brookings.edu, "The Hidden Stem Economy," June 10, 2013*
- Metro areas with the largest gap in income between rich and poor residents were identified by 24/7 Wall Street using the U.S. Census Bureau's 2013 American Community Survey. The Bridgeport* metro area placed #1 among metro areas with the widest wealth gap between rich and poor. *247wallst.com, "20 Cities with the Widest Gap between the Rich and Poor," July 8, 2015*
- The Brookings Institution ranked the 100 largest metro areas in the U.S. based on income inequality. Bridgeport* was ranked #1 (#1 = greatest ineqality). Criteria: the "95/20 ratio," a figure representing the income at which a household earns more than 95 percent of all other households, divided by the income at which a household earns more than only 20 percent of all other households. *Brookings Institution, "Income Inequality, 100 Largest U.S. Metro Areas, 2007-2014," January 14, 2016*
- *Forbes* ranked the largest metro areas in the U.S. in terms of the "Best Cities for Young Professionals." The Bridgeport* metro area ranked #12 out of 15. Criteria: job growth; unemployment rate; median salary of college graduates age 24 to 34; cost of living; number of small businesses per capita; number of large companies; percentage of population 25 years of age and older with college degrees. *Forbes.com, "America's 15 Best Cities for Young Professionals," August 18, 2014*
- The finance site *24/7 Wall St.* identified the metropolitan areas that have the smallest and largest pay disparities between men and women, comparing the median earnings for the past 12 months of both men and women working full-time in the country's 100 largest metropolitan statistical areas. Of the ten worst-paying metros for women, the Bridgeport* metro area ranked #8. *24/7 Wall St., "The Best (and Worst) Paying Cities for Women," March 6, 2015*
- The Bridgeport* metro area appeared on the Milken Institute "2015 Best Performing Cities" list. Rank: #166 out of 200 large metro areas. Criteria: job growth; wage and salary growth; high-tech output growth. *Milken Institute, "Best-Performing Cities 2015," December 2015*

Education Rankings

- Bridgeport* was identified as one of America's "smartest" metropolitan areas by *The Business Journals*. The area ranked #3 out of 10. Criteria: percentage of adults (25 and older) with high school diplomas, bachelor's degrees and graduate degrees. *The Business Journals, "Where the Brainpower Is: Exclusive U.S. Rankings, Insights," February 27, 2014*
- Personal finance website *WalletHub* analyzed the 150 largest U.S. metropolitan statistical areas to determine where the most educated Americans are choosing to settle. Criteria: education quality and attainment gap; education levels; percentage of workers with degrees; public school rankings; quality and size of each metro area's universities. Bridgeport* was ranked #21 (#1 = most educated city). *www.WalletHub.com, "2015's Most and Least Educated Cities*

Environmental Rankings

- The Bridgeport* metro area came in at #152 for the relative comfort of its climate on Sperling's list of "chill cities," as measured by the Sperling Heat Index. All 361 metro areas are included. Criteria included daytime high temperatures, nighttime low temperatures, dew point, and relative humidity at the high temperatures. *www.bertsperling.com, "Sperling's Chill Cities," July 18, 2013*

- Sperling's BestPlaces assessed 379 metropolitan areas of the United States for the likelihood of dangerously extreme weather events or earthquakes. In general the Southeast and South-Central regions have the highest risk of weather extremes and earthquakes, while the Pacific Northwest enjoys the lowest risk. Of the least risky metropolitan areas, the Bridgeport* metro area was ranked #159. *www.bestplaces.net, "Safest Places from Natural Disasters," April 2011*

- Bridgeport* was identified as one of America's dirtiest metro areas by *Forbes.* The area ranked #4 out of 20. Criteria: air quality; water quality; toxic releases; superfund sites. *Forbes, "America's 20 Dirtiest Cities," December 10, 2012*

Health/Fitness Rankings

- Analysts who tracked obesity rates in 100 of the nation's most populous areas found that the Bridgeport* metro area was one of the ten communities where residents were least likely to be obese, defined as a BMI score of 30 or above. *www.gallup.com, "Colorado Springs Residents Least Likely to Be Obese," May 28, 2015*

- *Business Insider* reported Trulia's analysis of the 100 largest U.S. metro areas to identify the nation's best cities for weight loss, based on healthful food options, access to outdoor activities, weight-loss centers, gyms, and opportunities to bike or walk to work. Bridgeport* ranked #2. *Businessinsider.com, "These Are the Best US Cities for Weight loss," January 17, 2013*

- Bridgeport* was identified as a "2016 Spring Allergy Capital." The area ranked #69 out of 100. Three groups of factors were used to identify the most severe cities for people with allergies during the spring season: annual pollen levels; medicine utilization; access to board-certified allergists. *Asthma and Allergy Foundation of America, "Spring Allergy Capitals 2016"*

- Bridgeport* was identified as a "2015 Asthma Capital." The area ranked #36 out of the nation's 100 largest metropolitan areas. Criteria: estimated prevalence; self-reported prevalence; crude death rate for asthma; annual pollen score; annual air quality; public smoking laws; number of board-certified asthma specialists; school inhaler access laws; rescue medication use; controller medication use; ER visits for asthma; uninsured rate; poverty rate. *Asthma and Allergy Foundation of America, "Asthma Capitals 2015"*

- The Bridgeport* metro area ranked #29 out of 190 in The Gallup-Healthways Well-Being Index. Criteria: purpose; social well being; financial health; community and physical health. Results are based on telephone interviews with adults, aged 18 and older, living in metropolitan areas in the 50 U.S. states and the District of Columbia. *Gallup-Healthways, "State of American Well-Being," February 23, 2016*

Real Estate Rankings

- The Bridgeport* metro area was identified as one of the 20 worst housing markets in the U.S. in 2015. The area ranked #15 out of 179 markets. Criteria: year-over-year change of median sales price of existing single-family homes between the 4th quarter of 2014 and the 4th quarter of 2015. *National Association of Realtors®, Median Sales Price of Existing Single-Family Homes for Metropolitan Areas, 4th Quarter 2015*

- The Bridgeport* metro area was identified as one of the 10 worst condo markets in the U.S. in 2015. The area ranked #4 out of 61 markets. Criteria: year-over-year change of median sales price of existing apartment condo-coop homes between the 4th quarter of 2014 and the 4th quarter of 2015. *National Association of Realtors®, Median Sales Price of Existing Apartment Condo-Coop Homes for Metropolitan Areas, 4th Quarter 2015*

- Bridgeport* was ranked #192 out of 225 metro areas in terms of housing affordability in 2015 by the National Association of Home Builders (#1 = most affordable). Criteria: the share of homes sold in that area affordable to a family earning the local median income, based on standard mortgage underwriting criteria. *National Association of Home Builders®, NAHB-Wells Fargo Housing Opportunity Index, 4th Quarter 2015*

Safety Rankings

- The National Insurance Crime Bureau ranked 380 metro areas in the U.S. in terms of per capita rates of vehicle theft. The Bridgeport* metro area ranked #203 (#1 = highest rate). Criteria: number of vehicle theft offenses per 100,000 inhabitants in 2014. *National Insurance Crime Bureau, "Hot Spots 2014," June 24, 2015*

Seniors/Retirement Rankings

- From its Best Cities for Successful Aging indexes, the Milken Institute generated rankings for metropolitan areas, weighing data in eight categories—health care, wellness, living arrangements, transportation, financial characteristics, education and employment opportunities, community engagement, and overall livability. The Bridgeport* metro area was ranked #10 overall in the large metro area category. *Milken Institute, "Best Cities for Successful Aging, 2014"*

Women/Minorities Rankings

- *24/7 Wall St.* compared median earnings over a 12-month period for men and women who worked full-time, year-round, and employment composition by sector to identify the worst-paying cities for women. Of the largest 100 U.S. metropolitan areas, Bridgeport* was ranked #8 in pay disparity. *24/7 Wall St., "The Best (and Worst) Paying Cities for Women," March 6, 2015*

Miscellaneous Rankings

- The National Alliance to End Homelessness ranked the 100 most populous metro areas with the highest rate of homelessness. The Bridgeport* metro area ranked #72. Criteria: number of homeless people per 10,000 population in 2011. *National Alliance to End Homelessness, The State of Homelessness in America 2012*

Ridgefield is located within the Bridgeport-Stamford-Norwalk, CT Metropolitan Statistical Area.

Business Environment

CITY FINANCES

City Government Finances

Component	2012 ($000)	2012 ($ per capita)
Total Revenues	143,969	5,843
Total Expenditures	135,992	5,519
Debt Outstanding	102,267	4,150
Cash and Securities[1]	36,485	1,480

Note: (1) Cash and security holdings of a government at the close of its fiscal year, including those of its dependent agencies, utilities, and liquor stores.
Source: U.S Census Bureau, State & Local Government Finances 2012

City Government Revenue by Source

Source	2012 ($000)	2012 ($ per capita)
General Revenue		
From Federal Government	0	0
From State Government	13,929	565
From Local Governments	0	0
Taxes		
Property	113,029	4,587
Sales and Gross Receipts	0	0
Personal Income	0	0
Corporate Income	0	0
Motor Vehicle License	0	0
Other Taxes	1,758	71
Current Charges	9,277	376
Liquor Store	0	0
Utility	0	0
Employee Retirement	0	0

Source: U.S Census Bureau, State & Local Government Finances 2012

City Government Expenditures by Function

Function	2012 ($000)	2012 ($ per capita)	2012 (%)
General Direct Expenditures			
Air Transportation	0	0	0.0
Corrections	0	0	0.0
Education	82,868	3,363	60.9
Employment Security Administration	0	0	0.0
Financial Administration	1,052	42	0.7
Fire Protection	3,727	151	2.7
General Public Buildings	733	29	0.5
Governmental Administration, Other	1,047	42	0.7
Health	256	10	0.1
Highways	5,839	236	4.2
Hospitals	0	0	0.0
Housing and Community Development	0	0	0.0
Interest on General Debt	3,655	148	2.6
Judicial and Legal	294	11	0.2
Libraries	4,224	171	3.1
Parking	61	2	0.0
Parks and Recreation	5,195	210	3.8
Police Protection	4,649	188	3.4
Public Welfare	449	18	0.3
Sewerage	1,304	52	0.9
Solid Waste Management	230	9	0.1
Veterans' Services	0	0	0.0
Liquor Store	0	0	0.0
Utility	0	0	0.0
Employee Retirement	0	0	0.0

Source: U.S Census Bureau, State & Local Government Finances 2012

DEMOGRAPHICS

Population Growth

Area	1990 Census	2000 Census	2010 Census	2014* Estimate	Population Growth (%) 1990-2014	2010-2014
City	20,919	23,643	24,638	25,025	19.6	1.6
MSA[1]	827,645	882,567	916,829	934,215	12.9	1.9
U.S.	248,709,873	281,421,906	308,745,538	314,107,084	26.3	1.7

Note: (1) Figures cover the Bridgeport-Stamford-Norwalk, CT Metropolitan Statistical Area—see Appendix B for areas included; (*) 2010-2014 5-year estimated population
Source: U.S. Census Bureau, 1990 Census, Census 2000, Census 2010, 2010-2014 American Community Survey 5-Year Estimates

Household Size

Area	Persons in Household (%) One	Two	Three	Four	Five	Six	Seven or More	Average Household Size
City	18.1	32.9	16.1	22.9	8.2	0.9	0.5	2.83
MSA[1]	25.4	30.3	16.9	16.6	7.2	2.2	1.0	2.74
U.S.	27.5	33.5	15.8	13.1	6.0	2.3	1.4	2.64

Note: (1) Figures cover the Bridgeport-Stamford-Norwalk, CT Metropolitan Statistical Area—see Appendix B for areas included
Source: U.S. Census Bureau, 2010-2014 American Community Survey 5-Year Estimates

Race

Area	White Alone[2] (%)	Black Alone[2] (%)	Asian Alone[2] (%)	AIAN[3] Alone[2] (%)	NHOPI[4] Alone[2] (%)	Other Race Alone[2] (%)	Two or More Races (%)
City	95.1	0.7	2.0	0.1	0.0	0.9	1.2
MSA[1]	74.3	11.1	4.9	0.2	0.0	7.1	2.4
U.S.	73.8	12.6	5.0	0.8	0.2	4.7	2.9

Note: (1) Figures cover the Bridgeport-Stamford-Norwalk, CT Metropolitan Statistical Area—see Appendix B for areas included; (2) Alone is defined as not being in combination with one or more other races; (3) American Indian and Alaska Native; (4) Native Hawaiian and Other Pacific Islander
Source: U.S. Census Bureau, 2010-2014 American Community Survey 5-Year Estimates

Hispanic or Latino Origin

Area	Total (%)	Mexican (%)	Puerto Rican (%)	Cuban (%)	Other (%)
City	5.2	0.5	0.8	0.8	3.2
MSA[1]	17.9	2.1	5.9	0.4	9.4
U.S.	16.9	10.8	1.6	0.6	3.8

Note: Persons of Hispanic or Latino origin can be of any race; (1) Figures cover the Bridgeport-Stamford-Norwalk, CT Metropolitan Statistical Area—see Appendix B for areas included
Source: U.S. Census Bureau, 2010-2014 American Community Survey 5-Year Estimates

Ancestry

Area	German	Irish	English	American	Italian	Polish	French[2]	Scottish	Dutch
City	17.7	24.4	13.7	5.5	23.6	5.7	3.0	3.0	0.9
MSA[1]	9.2	14.8	8.0	4.4	17.6	5.4	2.5	1.8	0.8
U.S.	14.9	10.8	8.0	7.1	5.5	3.0	2.7	1.7	1.4

Note: Figures are the percentage of the total population reporting a particular ancestry. The nine most commonly reported ancestries in the U.S. are shown. Figures include multiple ancestries (e.g. if a person reported being Irish and Italian, they were included in both columns); (1) Figures cover the Bridgeport-Stamford-Norwalk, CT Metropolitan Statistical Area—see Appendix B for areas included; (2) Excludes Basque
Source: U.S. Census Bureau, 2010-2014 American Community Survey 5-Year Estimates

Foreign-Born Population

Area	Percent of Population Born in								
	Any Foreign Country	Asia	Mexico	Europe	Carribean	Central America[2]	South America	Africa	Canada
City	9.4	1.3	0.1	5.0	0.5	0.2	1.1	0.5	0.6
MSA[1]	20.5	3.9	1.2	4.7	3.2	2.2	4.3	0.6	0.4
U.S.	13.1	3.8	3.7	1.5	1.2	1.0	0.9	0.6	0.3

Note: (1) Figures cover the Bridgeport-Stamford-Norwalk, CT Metropolitan Statistical Area—see Appendix B for areas included; (2) Excludes Mexico.
Source: U.S. Census Bureau, 2010-2014 American Community Survey 5-Year Estimates

Marital Status

Area	Never Married	Now Married[2]	Separated	Widowed	Divorced
City	19.8	66.9	0.6	5.0	7.7
MSA[1]	32.3	51.2	1.4	5.8	9.4
U.S.	32.5	48.4	2.2	5.9	10.9

Note: Figures are percentages and cover the population 15 years of age and older; (1) Figures cover the Bridgeport-Stamford-Norwalk, CT Metropolitan Statistical Area—see Appendix B for areas included; (2) Excludes separated
Source: U.S. Census Bureau, 2010-2014 American Community Survey 5-Year Estimates

Disability Status

Area	All Ages	Under 18 Years Old	18 to 64 Years Old	65 Years and Over
City	6.0	2.3	3.4	25.5
MSA[1]	8.8	3.1	6.4	30.2
U.S.	12.3	4.1	10.2	36.3

Note: Figures show percent of the civilian noninstitutionalized population that reported having a disability. Disability status is determined from from six types of difficulty: vision, hearing, cognitive, ambulatory, self-care, and independent living. For children under 5 years old, hearing and vision difficulty are used to determine disability status. For children between the ages of 5 and 14, disability status is determined from hearing, vision, cognitive, ambulatory, and self-care difficulties. For people aged 15 years and older, they are considered to have a disability if they have difficulty with any one of the six difficulty types; (1) Figures cover the Bridgeport-Stamford-Norwalk, CT Metropolitan Statistical Area—see Appendix B for areas included.
Source: U.S. Census Bureau, 2010-2014 American Community Survey 5-Year Estimates

Age

Area	Percent of Population									Median Age
	Under Age 5	Age 5–19	Age 20–34	Age 35–44	Age 45–54	Age 55–64	Age 65–74	Age 75–84	Age 85+	
City	4.6	27.4	7.8	12.9	19.2	14.5	6.8	5.1	1.7	43.4
MSA[1]	5.9	21.0	17.4	13.5	16.1	12.3	7.3	4.4	2.2	39.6
U.S.	6.4	19.9	20.6	13.0	14.1	12.3	7.6	4.3	1.9	37.4

Note: (1) Figures cover the Bridgeport-Stamford-Norwalk, CT Metropolitan Statistical Area—see Appendix B for areas included
Source: U.S. Census Bureau, 2010-2014 American Community Survey 5-Year Estimates

Gender

Area	Males	Females	Males per 100 Females
City	12,250	12,775	95.9
MSA[1]	454,762	479,453	94.9
U.S.	154,515,159	159,591,925	96.8

Note: (1) Figures cover the Bridgeport-Stamford-Norwalk, CT Metropolitan Statistical Area—see Appendix B for areas included
Source: U.S. Census Bureau, 2010-2014 American Community Survey 5-Year Estimates

Religious Groups by Family

Area	Catholic	Baptist	Non-Den.	Methodist[2]	Lutheran	LDS[3]	Pente-costal	Presby-terian[4]	Muslim[5]	Judaism
MSA[1]	44.1	1.9	2.3	2.0	0.8	0.5	1.1	3.0	0.5	1.9
U.S.	19.1	9.3	4.0	4.0	2.3	2.0	1.9	1.6	0.8	0.7

Note: Figures are the number of adherents as a percentage of the total population; (1) Figures cover the Bridgeport-Stamford-Norwalk, CT Metropolitan Statistical Area—see Appendix B for areas included; (2) Methodist/Pietist; (3) Latter Day Saints; (4) Reformed; (5) Figures are estimates
Source: Association of Statisticians of American Religious Bodies, 2010 U.S. Religion Census: Religious Congregations & Membership Study

Religious Groups by Tradition

Area	Catholic	Evangelical Protestant	Mainline Protestant	Other Tradition	Black Protestant	Orthodox
MSA[1]	44.1	5.1	9.0	3.5	0.4	1.0
U.S.	19.1	16.2	7.3	4.3	1.6	0.3

Note: Figures are the number of adherents as a percentage of the total population; (1) Figures cover the Bridgeport-Stamford-Norwalk, CT Metropolitan Statistical Area—see Appendix B for areas included
Source: Association of Statisticians of American Religious Bodies, 2010 U.S. Religion Census: Religious Congregations & Membership Study

ECONOMY

Gross Metropolitan Product

Area	2013	2014	2015	2016	Rank[2]
MSA[1]	93.5	96.7	100.5	105.1	37

Note: Figures are in billions of dollars; (1) Figures cover the Bridgeport-Stamford-Norwalk, CT Metropolitan Statistical Area—see Appendix B for areas included; (2) Rank is based on 2016 data and ranges from 1 to 381
Source: The U.S. Conference of Mayors, U.S. Metro Economies: GMP and Employment 2014-2016, June 2015

Economic Growth

Area	2011-13 (%)	2014 (%)	2015 (%)	2016 (%)	Rank[2]
MSA[1]	1.3	1.7	2.6	2.6	159
U.S.	2.2	2.4	2.3	2.9	–

Note: Figures are real gross metropolitan product (GMP) growth rates and represent annual average percent change; (1) Figures cover the Bridgeport-Stamford-Norwalk, CT Metropolitan Statistical Area—see Appendix B for areas included; (2) Rank is based on 2016 data and ranges from 1 to 381
Source: The U.S. Conference of Mayors, U.S. Metro Economies: GMP and Employment 2014-2016, June 2015

Metropolitan Area Exports

Area	2009	2010	2011	2012	2013	2014	Rank[2]
MSA[1]	8,450.9	9,339.6	11,250.4	10,332.6	11,055.1	12,103.0	26

Note: Figures are in millions of dollars; (1) Figures cover the Bridgeport-Stamford-Norwalk, CT Metropolitan Statistical Area—see Appendix B for areas included; (2) Rank is based on 2014 data and ranges from 1 to 385
Source: U.S. Department of Commerce, International Trade Administration, Office of Trade & Industry Information, Manufacturing & Services, data extracted March 10, 2016

Building Permits

Area	Single-Family			Multi-Family			Total		
	2014	2015p	Pct. Chg.	2014	2015p	Pct. Chg.	2014	2015p	Pct. Chg.
City	22	16	-27.3	20	10	-50.0	42	26	-38.1
MSA[1]	987	781	-20.9	902	1,802	99.8	1,889	2,583	36.7
U.S.	640,300	690,800	7.9	411,800	487,600	18.4	1,052,100	1,178,400	12.0

Note: (1) Figures cover the Bridgeport-Stamford-Norwalk, CT Metropolitan Statistical Area—see Appendix B for areas included; Figures represent new, privately-owned housing units authorized (unadjusted data); All permit data are based on estimates with imputation; (p) preliminary data.
Source: U.S. Census Bureau, Manufacturing, Mining, and Construction Statistics, Building Permits, 2014, 2015

Bankruptcy Filings

Area	Business Filings			Nonbusiness Filings		
	2014	2015	% Chg.	2014	2015	% Chg.
Fairfield County	91	83	-8.8	1,506	1,393	-7.5
U.S.	26,983	24,735	-8.3	909,812	819,760	-9.9

Note: Business filings include Chapter 7, Chapter 11, Chapter 12, and Chapter 13; Nonbusiness filings include Chapter 7, Chapter 11, and Chapter 13
Source: Administrative Office of the U.S. Courts, Business and Nonbusiness Bankruptcy, County Cases Commenced by Chapter of the Bankruptcy Code, During the 12- Month Period Ending December 31, 2014 and Business and Nonbusiness Bankruptcy, County Cases Commenced by Chapter of the Bankruptcy Code, During the 12- Month Period Ending December 31, 2015

Housing Vacancy Rates

Area	Gross Vacancy Rate[2] (%)			Year-Round Vacancy Rate[3] (%)			Rental Vacancy Rate[4] (%)			Homeowner Vacancy Rate[5] (%)		
	2013	2014	2015	2013	2014	2015	2013	2014	2015	2013	2014	2015
MSA[1]	10.2	10.8	11.3	9.4	9.2	10.1	5.1	5.6	7.1	2.6	1.6	1.8
U.S.	13.6	13.4	12.9	10.7	10.4	10.0	8.3	7.6	7.1	2.0	1.9	1.8

Note: (1) Figures cover the Bridgeport-Stamford-Norwalk, CT Metropolitan Statistical Area—see Appendix B for areas included; (2) The percentage of the total housing inventory that is vacant; (3) The percentage of the housing inventory (excluding seasonal units) that is year-round vacant; (4) The percentage of rental inventory that is vacant for rent; (5) The percentage of homeowner inventory that is vacant for sale
Source: U.S. Census Bureau, Housing Vacancies and Homeownership Annual Statistics: 2015

INCOME

Income

Area	Per Capita ($)	Median Household ($)	Average Household ($)
City	75,716	147,936	212,297
MSA[1]	49,688	83,163	135,743
U.S.	28,555	53,482	74,596

Note: (1) Figures cover the Bridgeport-Stamford-Norwalk, CT Metropolitan Statistical Area—see Appendix B for areas included
Source: U.S. Census Bureau, 2010-2014 American Community Survey 5-Year Estimates

Household Income Distribution

Area	Percent of Households Earning							
	Under $15,000	$15,000 -24,999	$25,000 -34,999	$35,000 -49,999	$50,000 -74,999	$75,000 -99,000	$100,000 -149,999	$150,000 and up
City	4.9	4.0	2.9	5.7	9.0	9.2	14.7	49.4
MSA[1]	8.3	7.1	6.9	9.4	13.9	11.6	16.0	26.7
U.S.	12.5	10.7	10.2	13.5	17.8	12.2	13.0	10.0

Note: (1) Figures cover the Bridgeport-Stamford-Norwalk, CT Metropolitan Statistical Area—see Appendix B for areas included
Source: U.S. Census Bureau, 2010-2014 American Community Survey 5-Year Estimates

Poverty Rate

Area	All Ages	Under 18 Years Old	18 to 64 Years Old	65 Years and Over
City	3.1	2.8	2.9	4.8
MSA[1]	9.1	11.4	8.7	6.7
U.S.	15.6	21.9	14.6	9.4

Note: Figures are percentage of people whose income during the past 12 months was below the poverty level; (1) Figures cover the Bridgeport-Stamford-Norwalk, CT Metropolitan Statistical Area—see Appendix B for areas included
Source: U.S. Census Bureau, 2010-2014 American Community Survey 5-Year Estimates

EMPLOYMENT

Labor Force and Employment

Area	Civilian Labor Force			Workers Employed		
	Dec. 2014	Dec. 2015	% Chg.	Dec. 2014	Dec. 2015	% Chg.
City	11,806	11,825	0.1	11,344	11,418	0.6
NECTA[1]	462,757	463,036	0.0	437,814	440,819	0.6
U.S.	155,521,000	157,245,000	1.1	147,190,000	149,703,000	1.7

Note: Data is not seasonally adjusted and covers workers 16 years of age and older; (1) Figures cover the Bridgeport-Stamford-Norwalk, CT New England City and Town Area—see Appendix B for areas included
Source: Bureau of Labor Statistics, Local Area Unemployment Statistics

Unemployment Rate

Area	2015											
	Jan.	Feb.	Mar.	Apr.	May	Jun.	Jul.	Aug.	Sep.	Oct.	Nov.	Dec.
City	4.7	4.7	4.3	3.9	3.9	3.9	3.8	3.6	3.5	3.4	3.3	3.4
NECTA[1]	6.4	6.7	6.3	5.6	5.4	5.2	5.4	5.3	4.9	4.7	4.7	4.8
U.S.	6.1	5.8	5.6	5.1	5.3	5.5	5.6	5.2	4.9	4.8	4.8	4.8

Note: Data is not seasonally adjusted and covers workers 16 years of age and older; (1) Figures cover the Bridgeport-Stamford-Norwalk, CT New England City and Town Area—see Appendix B for areas included
Source: Bureau of Labor Statistics, Local Area Unemployment Statistics

Employment by Occupation

Occupation Classification	City (%)	MSA[1] (%)	U.S. (%)
Management, Business, Science, and Arts	63.1	43.4	36.4
Natural Resources, Construction, and Maintenance	3.7	7.4	9.0
Production, Transportation, and Material Moving	3.2	7.1	12.1
Sales and Office	22.8	24.5	24.4
Service	7.3	17.6	18.2

Note: Figures cover employed civilians 16 years of age and older; (1) Figures cover the Bridgeport-Stamford-Norwalk, CT Metropolitan Statistical Area—see Appendix B for areas included
Source: U.S. Census Bureau, 2010-2014 American Community Survey 5-Year Estimates

Employment by Industry

Sector	NECTA[1]		U.S.
	Number of Employees	Percent of Total	Percent of Total
Construction, Mining, and Logging	12,500	3.0	5.0
Education and Health Services	72,100	17.3	15.7
Financial Activities	41,000	9.8	5.7
Government	45,800	11.0	15.5
Information	12,300	2.9	1.9
Leisure and Hospitality	42,300	10.1	10.4
Manufacturing	31,300	7.5	8.6
Other Services	17,600	4.2	3.9
Professional and Business Services	66,000	15.8	13.9
Retail Trade	50,000	12.0	11.3
Transportation, Warehousing, and Utilities	10,600	2.5	3.9
Wholesale Trade	13,800	3.3	4.1

Note: Figures are non-farm employment as of December 2015. Figures are not seasonally adjusted and include workers 16 years of age and older; (1) Figures cover the Bridgeport-Stamford-Norwalk, CT New England City and Town Area—see Appendix B for areas included; n/a not available
Source: Bureau of Labor Statistics, Current Employment Statistics, Employment, Hours, and Earnings

Occupations with Greatest Projected Employment Growth: 2012 – 2022

Occupation[1]	2012 Employment	2022 Projected Employment	Numeric Employment Change	Percent Employment Change
Personal Care Aides	23,240	32,090	8,850	38.1
Registered Nurses	35,990	41,230	5,240	14.6
Secretaries and Administrative Assistants, Except Legal, Medical, and Executive	34,530	38,640	4,110	11.9
Combined Food Preparation and Serving Workers, Including Fast Food	26,730	30,740	4,010	15.0
Retail Salespersons	53,800	57,270	3,470	6.4
General and Operations Managers	31,160	34,420	3,260	10.5
Home Health Aides	8,250	11,450	3,200	38.7
Childcare Workers	18,300	21,170	2,870	15.7
Maids and Housekeeping Cleaners	17,800	20,560	2,760	15.5
First-Line Supervisors of Office and Administrative Support Workers	26,360	28,900	2,540	9.6

Note: Projections cover Connecticut; (1) Sorted by numeric employment change
Source: www.projectionscentral.com, State Occupational Projections, 2012–2022 Long-Term Projections

Fastest Growing Occupations: 2012 – 2022

Occupation[1]	2012 Employment	2022 Projected Employment	Numeric Employment Change	Percent Employment Change
Insulation Workers, Mechanical	210	350	140	65.6
Interpreters and Translators	460	650	190	43.1
Helpers—Electricians	270	380	110	39.4
Home Health Aides	8,250	11,450	3,200	38.7
Diagnostic Medical Sonographers	1,000	1,380	380	38.3
Personal Care Aides	23,240	32,090	8,850	38.1
Physical Therapist Assistants	540	740	200	37.4
Occupational Therapy Assistants	490	670	180	35.4
Health Specialties Teachers, Postsecondary	2,810	3,770	960	34.3
Nursing Instructors and Teachers, Postsecondary	700	940	240	34.0

Note: Projections cover Connecticut; (1) Sorted by percent employment change and excludes occupations with numeric employment change less than 100
Source: www.projectionscentral.com, State Occupational Projections, 2012–2022 Long-Term Projections

Average Wages

Occupation	$/Hr.	Occupation	$/Hr.
Accountants and Auditors	41.89	Maids and Housekeeping Cleaners	12.27
Automotive Mechanics	22.23	Maintenance and Repair Workers	23.42
Bookkeepers	22.17	Marketing Managers	80.11
Carpenters	25.29	Nuclear Medicine Technologists	46.76
Cashiers	11.58	Nurses, Licensed Practical	27.02
Clerks, General Office	18.19	Nurses, Registered	37.63
Clerks, Receptionists/Information	16.69	Nursing Assistants	15.94
Clerks, Shipping/Receiving	17.32	Packers and Packagers, Hand	11.75
Computer Programmers	41.64	Physical Therapists	44.15
Computer Systems Analysts	45.62	Postal Service Mail Carriers	25.24
Computer User Support Specialists	27.07	Real Estate Brokers	n/a
Cooks, Restaurant	15.17	Retail Salespersons	15.11
Dentists	93.45	Sales Reps., Exc. Tech./Scientific	36.05
Electrical Engineers	44.69	Sales Reps., Tech./Scientific	48.83
Electricians	30.15	Secretaries, Exc. Legal/Med./Exec.	20.92
Financial Managers	75.74	Security Guards	14.12
First-Line Supervisors/Managers, Sales	23.59	Surgeons	128.44
Food Preparation Workers	14.89	Teacher Assistants*	16.24
General and Operations Managers	81.02	Teachers, Elementary School*	38.04
Hairdressers/Cosmetologists	14.75	Teachers, Secondary School*	39.42
Internists	100.52	Telemarketers	18.73
Janitors and Cleaners	15.35	Truck Drivers, Heavy/Tractor-Trailer	23.76
Landscaping/Groundskeeping Workers	17.04	Truck Drivers, Light/Delivery Svcs.	17.38
Lawyers	87.43	Waiters and Waitresses	11.87

Note: Wage data covers the New England City and Town Area—see Appendix B for areas included; (*) Hourly wages for elementary/secondary school teachers and teacher assistants were calculated by the editors from annual wage data based on a 40 hour work week; n/a not available.
Source: Bureau of Labor Statistics, Metro Area Occupational Employment and Wage Estimates, May 2015

TAXES

State Corporate Income Tax Rates

State	Tax Rate (%)	Income Brackets ($)	Num. of Brackets	Financial Institution Tax Rate (%)[a]	Federal Income Tax Ded.
Connecticut	7.5 (d)	Flat rate	1	7.5 (d)	No

Note: Tax rates as of January 1, 2016; (a) Rates listed are the corporate income tax rate applied to financial institutions or excise taxes based on income. Some states have other taxes based upon the value of deposits or shares; (d) Connecticut's tax is the greater of the 7.5% tax on net income, a 0.31% tax on capital stock and surplus (maximum tax of $1 million), or $250 (the minimum tax). Plus, an additional 20% surtax applies for tax years 2012 and 2016.
Source: Federation of Tax Administrators, "State Corporate Income Tax Rates, 2016"

State Individual Income Tax Rates

State	Tax Rate (%)	Income Brackets ($)	Num. of Brackets	Personal Exempt. ($)[1]		Fed. Inc. Tax Ded.
				Single	Dependents	
Connecticut	3.0 - 6.99	10,000 - 500,000 (b)	7	14,500 (g)	None	No

Note: Tax rates as of January 1, 2016; Local- and county-level taxes are not included; n/a not applicable; (1) Married joint filers generally receive double the single exemption; (b) For joint returns, taxes are twice the tax on half the couple's income; (g) Connecticut's personal exemption incorporates a standard deduction. An additional tax credit is allowed ranging from 75% to 0% based on state adjusted gross income. Exemption amounts are phased out for higher income taxpayers until they are eliminated for households earning over $71,000.
Source: Federation of Tax Administrators, "State Individual Income Tax Rates, 2016"

Various State and Local Tax Rates

State	State and Local Sales and Use (%)	State Sales and Use (%)	Gasoline[1] (¢/gal.)	Cigarette[2] ($/pack)	Spirits[3] ($/gal.)	Wine[4] ($/gal.)	Beer[5] ($/gal.)
Connecticut	6.35	6.35	37.51	3.65	5.40 (f)	0.72 (l)	0.16

Note: All tax rates as of January 1, 2016; (1) The American Petroleum Institute has developed a methodology for determining the average tax rate on a gallon of fuel. Rates may include any of the following: excise taxes, environmental fees, storage tank fees, other fees or taxes, general sales tax, and local taxes. In states where gasoline is subject to the general sales tax, or where the fuel tax is based on the average sale price, the average rate determined by API is sensitive to changes in the price of gasoline. States that fully or partially apply general sales taxes to gasoline: CA, CO, GA, IL, IN, MI, NY; (2) The federal excise tax of $1.0066 per pack and local taxes are not included; (3) Rates are those applicable to off-premise sales of 40% alcohol by volume (a.b.v.) distilled spirits in 750ml containers. Local excise taxes are excluded; (4) Rates are those applicable to off-premise sales of 11% a.b.v. non-carbonated wine in 750ml containers; (5) Rates are those applicable to off-premise sales of 4.7% a.b.v. beer in 12 ounce containers; (f) Different rates are also applicable according to alcohol content, place of production, size of container, or place purchased (on- or off-premise or onboard airlines); (l) Different rates also applicable according to alcohol content, place of production, size of container, place purchased (on- or off-premise or on board airlines) or type of wine (carbonated, vermouth, etc.).
Source: Tax Foundation, 2016 Facts & Figures: How Does Your State Compare?

State Business Tax Climate Index Rankings

State	Overall Rank	Corporate Tax Rank	Individual Income Tax Rank	Sales Tax Rank	Unemployment Insurance Tax Rank	Property Tax Rank
Connecticut	44	33	36	29	20	49

Note: The index is a measure of how each state's tax laws affect economic performance. The lower the rank, the more favorable a state's tax system is for business. States without a given tax are given a ranking of 1. The scores/rankings for the District of Columbia do not affect other states. The 2016 index represents the tax climate as of July 1, 2015 (the beginning of Fiscal Year 2016).
Source: Tax Foundation, State Business Tax Climate Index 2016

TRANSPORTATION

Means of Transportation to Work

Area	Car/Truck/Van		Public Transportation			Bicycle	Walked	Other Means	Worked at Home
	Drove Alone	Car-pooled	Bus	Subway	Railroad				
City	78.4	4.2	0.4	0.7	3.7	0.5	1.6	0.2	10.3
MSA[1]	72.8	8.4	2.7	0.3	6.3	0.3	2.7	0.9	5.5
U.S.	76.4	9.6	2.6	1.8	0.6	0.6	2.8	1.3	4.4

Note: Figures are percentages and cover workers 16 years of age and older; (1) Figures cover the Bridgeport-Stamford-Norwalk, CT Metropolitan Statistical Area—see Appendix B for areas included
Source: U.S. Census Bureau, 2010-2014 American Community Survey 5-Year Estimates

Travel Time to Work

Area	Less Than 10 Minutes	10 to 19 Minutes	20 to 29 Minutes	30 to 44 Minutes	45 to 59 Minutes	60 to 89 Minutes	90 Minutes or More
City	13.1	18.9	15.4	25.2	13.3	6.8	7.2
MSA[1]	11.8	31.4	18.6	17.2	7.1	8.6	5.3
U.S.	13.3	29.6	21.0	20.2	7.7	5.7	2.6

Note: Figures are percentages and include workers 16 years old and over; (1) Figures cover the Bridgeport-Stamford-Norwalk, CT Metropolitan Statistical Area—see Appendix B for areas included
Source: U.S. Census Bureau, 2010-2014 American Community Survey 5-Year Estimates

Freeway Travel Time Index

Area	1985	1990	1995	2000	2005	2010	2014
Urban Area Rank[1,2]	11	9	6	4	5	6	6
Urban Area Index[1]	1.16	1.20	1.25	1.32	1.36	1.34	1.36
Average Index[3]	1.09	1.11	1.14	1.17	1.20	1.19	1.20

Note: Freeway Travel Time Index—the ratio of travel time in the peak period to the travel time at free-flow conditions. For example, a value of 1.30 indicates a 20-minute free-flow trip takes 26 minutes in the peak (20 minutes x 1.30 = 26 minutes); (1) Covers the Bridgeport-Stamford CT-NY urban area; (2) Rank is based on 101 urban areas (#1 = highest travel time index); (3) Average of 101 urban areas
Source: Texas Transportation Institute, 2015 Urban Mobility Scorecard, August 2015

Freeway Commuter Stress Index

Area	1985	1990	1995	2000	2005	2010	2014
Urban Area Rank[1,2]	17	10	8	6	5	8	7
Urban Area Index[1]	1.23	1.28	1.33	1.40	1.45	1.43	1.44
Average Index[3]	1.13	1.16	1.19	1.22	1.25	1.24	1.25

Note: The Freeway Commuter Stress Index is the same as the Freeway Travel Time Index (see table above) except that it includes only the travel in the peak directions during the peak periods; the TTI includes travel in all directions during the peak period. Thus, the CSI is more indicative of the work trip experienced by each commuter on a daily basis. (1) Covers the Bridgeport-Stamford CT-NY urban area; (2) Rank is based on 101 urban areas (#1 = highest stress index); (3) Average of 101 urban areas
Source: Texas Transportation Institute, 2015 Urban Mobility Scorecard, August 2015

Living Environment

COST OF LIVING

Cost of Living Index

Composite Index	Groceries	Housing	Utilities	Transportation	Health Care	Misc. Goods/ Services
147.1	130.8	209.8	132.1	106.3	114.5	123.0

Note: The Cost of Living Index measures regional differences in the cost of consumer goods and services, excluding taxes and non-consumer expenditures, for professional and managerial households in the top income quintile. It is based on more than 50,000 prices covering almost 60 different items for which prices are collected three times a year by chambers of commerce, economic development organizations or university applied economic centers in each participating urban area. The numbers shown should be read as a percentage above or below the national average of 100. For example, a value of 115.4 in the groceries column indicates that grocery prices are 15.4% higher than the national average. Small differences in the index numbers should not be interpreted as significant; Figures cover the Stamford CT urban area.
Source: The Council for Community and Economic Research, ACCRA Cost of Living Index, 2015

Grocery Prices

Area[1]	T-Bone Steak ($/pound)	Frying Chicken ($/pound)	Whole Milk ($/half gal.)	Eggs ($/dozen)	Orange Juice ($/64 oz.)	Coffee ($/11.5 oz.)
City[2]	12.44	1.35	2.89	3.05	4.21	5.49
Avg.	10.99	1.43	2.25	2.26	3.58	4.48
Min.	7.16	0.98	1.30	1.35	2.88	2.98
Max.	14.13	2.43	3.85	4.81	6.39	7.56

Note: (1) Values for the local area are compared with the average, minimum and maximum values for all 292 areas in the Cost of Living Index; (2) Figures cover the Stamford CT urban area; **T-Bone Steak** *(price per pound);* **Frying Chicken** *(price per pound, whole fryer);* **Whole Milk** *(half gallon carton);* **Eggs** *(price per dozen, Grade A, large);* **Orange Juice** *(64 oz. Tropicana or Florida Natural);* **Coffee** *(11.5 oz. can, vacuum-packed, Maxwell House, Hills Bros, or Folgers).*
Source: The Council for Community and Economic Research, ACCRA Cost of Living Index, 2015

Housing and Utility Costs

Area[1]	New Home Price ($)	Apartment Rent ($/month)	All Electric ($/month)	Part Electric ($/month)	Other Energy ($/month)	Telephone ($/month)
City[2]	626,189	2,199	-	147.95	111.00	29.01
Avg.	312,874	945	179.30	95.07	72.96	28.11
Min.	178,682	479	116.28	43.14	26.46	10.01
Max.	1,472,476	3,984	504.25	189.44	421.11	43.06

Note: (1) Values for the local area are compared with the average, minimum and maximum values for all 292 areas in the Cost of Living Index; (2) Figures cover the Stamford CT urban area; **New Home Price** *(2,400 sf living area, 8,000 sf lot, in urban area with full utilities);* **Apartment Rent** *(950 sf 2 bedroom/1.5 or 2 bath, unfurnished, excluding all utilities except water);* **All Electric** *(average monthly cost for an all-electric home);* **Part Electric** *(average monthly cost for a part-electric home);* **Other Energy** *(average monthly cost for natural gas, fuel oil, coal, wood, and any other forms of energy except electricity);* **Telephone** *(price includes basic monthly rate for a private residential line plus additional local usage charges incurred by a family of four).*
Source: The Council for Community and Economic Research, ACCRA Cost of Living Index, 2015

Health Care, Transportation, and Other Costs

Area[1]	Doctor ($/visit)	Dentist ($/visit)	Optometrist ($/visit)	Gasoline ($/gallon)	Beauty Salon ($/visit)	Men's Shirt ($)
City[2]	123.75	110.00	111.67	2.47	64.17	27.43
Avg.	105.15	89.02	99.78	2.38	35.30	28.10
Min.	66.87	56.09	48.53	1.95	18.91	13.38
Max.	182.34	150.36	228.33	4.09	67.91	63.80

Note: (1) Values for the local area are compared with the average, minimum and maximum values for all 292 areas in the Cost of Living Index; (2) Figures cover the Stamford CT urban area; **Doctor** *(general practitioners routine exam of an established patient);* **Dentist** *(adult teeth cleaning and periodic oral examination);* **Optometrist** *(full vision eye exam for established adult patient);* **Gasoline** *(one gallon regular unleaded, national brand, including all taxes, cash price at self-service pump if available);* **Beauty Salon** *(woman's shampoo, trim, and blow-dry);* **Men's Shirt** *(cotton/polyester dress shirt, pinpoint weave, long sleeves).*
Source: The Council for Community and Economic Research, ACCRA Cost of Living Index, 2015

HOUSING

House Price Index (HPI)

Area	National Ranking[2]	Quarterly Change (%)	One-Year Change (%)	Five-Year Change (%)
MSA[1]	242	-1.00	1.30	-0.70
U.S.[3]	–	1.45	5.76	22.85

Note: The HPI is a weighted repeat sales index. It measures average price changes in repeat sales or refinancings on the same properties. This information is obtained by reviewing repeat mortgage transactions on single-family properties whose mortgages have been purchased or securitized by Fannie Mae or Freddie Mac in January 1975; (1) Bridgeport-Stamford-Norwalk Metropolitan Statistical Area—see Appendix B for areas included; (2) Rankings are based on annual percentage change for all metro areas containing at least 15,000 transactions over the last 10 years and ranges from 1 to 266; (3) figures based on a weighted average of Census Division estimates using a seasonally adjusted, purchase-only index; all figures are for the period ending December 31, 2015

Source: Federal Housing Finance Agency, House Price Index, February 25, 2016

Median Single-Family Home Prices

Area	2013	2014	2015p	Percent Change 2014 to 2015
MSA[1]	403.0	397.6	377.7	-5.0
U.S. Average	197.4	208.9	223.9	7.2

Note: Figures are median sales prices of existing single-family homes in thousands of dollars; (p) preliminary; n/a not available; (1) Bridgeport-Stamford-Norwalk, CT Metropolitan Statistical Area—see Appendix B for areas included

Source: National Association of Realtors, Median Sales Price of Existing Single-Family Homes for Metropolitan Areas, 4th Quarter 2015

Qualifying Income Based on Median Sales Price of Existing Single-Family Homes

Area	With 5% Down ($)	With 10% Down ($)	With 20% Down ($)
MSA[1]	80,320	76,092	67,638
U.S. Average	49,535	46,928	41,714

Note: Figures are preliminary; Qualifying income is based on a mortgage rate of 4.1%. Monthly principal and interest payment is limited to 25% of income; n/a not available; (1) Bridgeport-Stamford-Norwalk, CT Metropolitan Statistical Area—see Appendix B for areas included

Source: National Association of Realtors, Qualifying Income Based on Median Sales Price of Existing Single-Family Homes for Metropolitan Areas, 4th Quarter 2015

Median Apartment Condo-Coop Home Prices

Area	2013	2014	2015p	Percent Change 2014 to 2015
MSA[1]	220.3	221.3	218.6	-1.2
U.S. Average	194.9	204.3	210.7	3.1

Note: Figures are median sales prices of existing apartment condo-coop homes in thousands of dollars; (p) preliminary; n/a not available; (1) Bridgeport-Stamford-Norwalk, CT Metropolitan Statistical Area—see Appendix B for areas included

Source: National Association of Realtors, Median Sales Price of Existing Apartment Condo-Coop Homes for Metropolitan Areas, 4th Quarter 2015

Gross Monthly Rent

Area	Under $200	$200 -299	$300 -499	$500 -749	$750 -999	$1,000 -1,499	$1,500 and up	Median ($)
City	1.6	3.6	3.0	3.0	8.3	26.1	54.4	1,595
MSA[1]	1.4	3.5	5.1	5.9	12.3	33.6	38.3	1,327
U.S.	1.5	3.2	7.4	21.0	24.1	26.9	15.9	920

Note: Figures are percentages except for Median; Gross rent is the contract rent plus the estimated average monthly cost of utilities (electricity, gas, and water and sewer) and fuels (oil, coal, kerosene, wood, etc.) if these are paid by the renter (or paid for the renter by someone else); (1) Figures cover the Bridgeport-Stamford-Norwalk, CT Metropolitan Statistical Area—see Appendix B for areas included

Source: U.S. Census Bureau, 2010-2014 American Community Survey 5-Year Estimates

Homeownership Rate

Area	2008 (%)	2009 (%)	2010 (%)	2011 (%)	2012 (%)	2013 (%)	2014 (%)	2015 (%)
MSA[1]	72.6	70.3	71.3	71.6	70.6	70.7	67.7	66.6
U.S.	67.8	67.4	66.9	66.1	65.4	65.1	64.5	63.7

Note: (1) Figures cover the Bridgeport-Stamford-Norwalk, CT Metropolitan Statistical Area—see Appendix B for areas included
Source: U.S. Census Bureau, Housing Vacancies and Homeownership Annual Statistics: 2015

Year Housing Structure Built

Area	2010 or Later	2000 -2009	1990 -1999	1980 -1989	1970 -1979	1960 -1969	1950 -1959	1940 -1949	Before 1940	Median Year
City	0.9	7.4	11.2	14.2	16.9	24.2	11.4	2.5	11.4	1970
MSA[1]	0.8	6.9	6.8	11.4	13.6	14.5	17.1	7.6	21.4	1963
U.S.	1.0	14.9	13.9	13.8	15.8	11.0	10.8	5.4	13.3	1976

Note: Figures are percentages except for Median Year; (1) Figures cover the Bridgeport-Stamford-Norwalk, CT Metropolitan Statistical Area—see Appendix B for areas included
Source: U.S. Census Bureau, 2010-2014 American Community Survey 5-Year Estimates

HEALTH

Health Risk Data

Category	MSA[1] (%)	U.S. (%)
Adults aged 18–64 who have any kind of health care coverage	83.5	79.6
Adults who reported being in good or excellent health	86.0	83.1
Adults who are current smokers	13.2	19.6
Adults who are heavy drinkers[2]	6.0	6.1
Adults who are binge drinkers[3]	19.5	16.9
Adults who are overweight (BMI 25.0 - 29.9)	39.1	35.8
Adults who are obese (BMI 30.0 - 99.8)	21.6	27.6
Adults who participated in any physical activities in the past month	78.5	77.1
Adults 50+ who have ever had a sigmoidoscopy or colonoscopy	73.3	67.3
Women aged 40+ who have had a mammogram within the past two years	76.7	74.0
Men aged 40+ who have had a PSA test within the past two years	49.6	45.2
Adults aged 65+ who have had flu shot within the past year	57.1	60.1
Adults who always wear a seatbelt	95.4	93.8

Note: Data as of 2012 unless otherwise noted; (1) Figures cover the Bridgeport-Stamford-Norwalk, CT Metropolitan Statistical Area—see Appendix B for areas included; (2) Heavy drinkers are classified as males having more than two drinks per day or females having more than one drink per day; (3) Binge drinkers are classified as males having five or more drinks on one occasion or females having four or more drinks on one occasion
Source: Centers for Disease Control and Prevention, Behaviorial Risk Factor Surveillance System, SMART: Selected Metropolitan/Micropolitan Area Risk Trends, 2012 (Note: the CDC has discontinued this dataset but will be releasing a replacement in mid-2016)

Chronic Health Indicators

Category	MSA[1] (%)	U.S. (%)
Adults who have ever been told they had a heart attack	3.2	4.5
Adults who have ever been told they had a stroke	1.8	2.9
Adults who have been told they currently have asthma	7.8	8.9
Adults who have ever been told they have arthritis	21.6	25.7
Adults who have ever been told they have diabetes[2]	7.4	9.7
Adults who have ever been told they had skin cancer	5.6	5.7
Adults who have ever been told they had any other types of cancer	6.4	6.5
Adults who have ever been told they have COPD	4.7	6.2
Adults who have ever been told they have kidney disease	2.2	2.5
Adults who have ever been told they have a form of depression	15.2	18.0

Note: Data as of 2012 unless otherwise noted; (1) Figures cover the Bridgeport-Stamford-Norwalk, CT Metropolitan Statistical Area—see Appendix B for areas included; (2) Figures do not include pregnancy-related, borderline, or pre-diabetes
Source: Centers for Disease Control and Prevention, Behaviorial Risk Factor Surveillance System, SMART: Selected Metropolitan/Micropolitan Area Risk Trends, 2012 (Note: the CDC has discontinued this dataset but will be releasing a replacement in mid-2016)

Mortality Rates for the Top 10 Causes of Death in the U.S.

ICD-10[a] Sub-Chapter	ICD-10[a] Code	Age-Adjusted Mortality Rate[1] per 100,000 population	
		County[2]	U.S.
Malignant neoplasms	C00-C97	136.2	163.6
Ischaemic heart diseases	I20-I25	79.1	102.2
Other forms of heart disease	I30-I51	53.4	50.1
Chronic lower respiratory diseases	J40-J47	25.0	41.4
Organic, including symptomatic, mental disorders	F01-F09	36.6	38.5
Cerebrovascular diseases	I60-I69	26.8	36.5
Other external causes of accidental injury	W00-X59	23.7	27.5
Other degenerative diseases of the nervous system	G30-G31	17.6	26.3
Diabetes mellitus	E10-E14	12.7	21.1
Hypertensive diseases	I10-I15	12.3	19.7

Note: (a) ICD-10 = International Classification of Diseases 10th Revision; (1) Mortality rates are a three year average covering 2012-2014; (2) Figures cover Fairfield County.
Source: Centers for Disease Control and Prevention, National Center for Health Statistics. Underlying Cause of Death 1999-2014 on CDC WONDER Online Database, released 2015.

Mortality Rates for Selected Causes of Death

ICD-10[a] Sub-Chapter	ICD-10[a] Code	Age-Adjusted Mortality Rate[1] per 100,000 population	
		County[2]	U.S.
Assault	X85-Y09	3.7	5.1
Diseases of the liver	K70-K76	8.3	13.5
Human immunodeficiency virus (HIV) disease	B20-B24	1.6	2.1
Influenza and pneumonia	J09-J18	10.3	15.2
Intentional self-harm	X60-X84	7.5	12.7
Malnutrition	E40-E46	0.6	0.9
Obesity and other hyperalimentation	E65-E68	1.1	1.9
Renal failure	N17-N19	8.6	13.0
Transport accidents	V01-V99	6.3	11.6
Viral hepatitis	B15-B19	0.9	2.1

Note: (a) ICD-10 = International Classification of Diseases 10th Revision; (1) Mortality rates are a three year average covering 2012-2014; (2) Figures cover Fairfield County; Data are Suppressed when the data meet the criteria for confidentiality constraints; Mortality rates are flagged as Unreliable when the rate would be calculated with a numerator of 20 or less.
Source: Centers for Disease Control and Prevention, National Center for Health Statistics. Underlying Cause of Death 1999-2014 on CDC WONDER Online Database, released 2015.

Health Insurance Coverage

Area	With Health Insurance	With Private Health Insurance	With Public Health Insurance	Without Health Insurance	Population Under Age 18 Without Health Insurance
City	96.0	88.4	17.2	4.0	5.2
MSA[1]	88.7	72.4	26.4	11.3	5.1
U.S.	85.8	65.8	31.1	14.2	7.1

Note: Figures are percentages that cover the civilian noninstitutionalized population; (1) Figures cover the Bridgeport-Stamford-Norwalk, CT Metropolitan Statistical Area—see Appendix B for areas included
Source: U.S. Census Bureau, 2010-2014 American Community Survey 5-Year Estimates

Number of Medical Professionals

Area	MDs[3]	DOs[3,4]	Dentists	Podiatrists	Chiropractors	Optometrists
County[1] (number)	3,550	133	853	85	323	114
County[1] (rate[2])	376.8	14.1	90.2	9.0	34.2	12.1
U.S. (rate[2])	272.5	20.9	64.7	5.8	25.9	15.2

Note: Data as of 2014 unless noted; (1) Data covers Fairfield County; (2) Rate per 100,000 population; (3) Data as of 2013 and includes all active, non-federal physicians; (4) Doctor of Osteopathic Medicine
Source: U.S. Department of Health and Human Services, Health Resources and Services Administration, Bureau of Health Professions, Area Resource File (ARF) 2014-2015

EDUCATION

Public School District Statistics

District Name	Schls	Pupils	Pupil/ Teacher Ratio	Minority Pupils[1] (%)	Free Lunch Eligible[2] (%)	IEP[3] (%)
Ridgefield School District	10	5,268	13.3	13.5	2.4	8.9

Note: Table includes school districts with 100 or more students; (1) Percentage of students that are not non-Hispanic white; (2) Percentage of students that are eligible for the free lunch program; (3) Percentage of students that have an Individualized Education Program.
Source: U.S. Department of Education, National Center for Education Statistics, Common Core of Data, Local Education Agency (School District) Universe Survey: School Year 2013-2014; U.S. Department of Education, National Center for Education Statistics, Common Core of Data, Public Elementary/Secondary School Universe Survey: School Year 2013-2014

Best High Schools

According to *U.S. News,* Ridgefield is home to one of the best high schools in the U.S.: **Ridgefield High School** (#413); Nearly 20,000 schools were ranked based on their performance on state assessments and how well they prepare students for college. Schools with the highest unrounded College Readiness Index values were numerically ranked from No. 1 to No. 500 and were the gold medal winners. *U.S. News & World Report, "Best High Schools 2015"*

Highest Level of Education

Area	Less than H.S.	H.S. Diploma	Some College, No Deg.	Associate Degree	Bachelor's Degree	Master's Degree	Prof. School Degree	Doctorate Degree
City	1.8	9.4	12.0	4.3	38.0	25.0	6.9	2.7
MSA[1]	10.8	22.5	15.4	5.8	25.5	14.7	3.8	1.5
U.S.	13.7	28.0	21.2	7.9	18.3	7.8	2.0	1.3

Note: Figures cover persons age 25 and over; (1) Figures cover the Bridgeport-Stamford-Norwalk, CT Metropolitan Statistical Area—see Appendix B for areas included
Source: U.S. Census Bureau, 2010-2014 American Community Survey 5-Year Estimates

Educational Attainment by Race

Area	High School Graduate or Higher (%)					Bachelor's Degree or Higher (%)				
	Total	White	Black	Asian	Hisp.[2]	Total	White	Black	Asian	Hisp.[2]
City	98.2	98.2	94.0	100.0	92.7	72.6	72.1	66.4	94.5	66.3
MSA[1]	89.2	92.2	84.2	89.6	68.7	45.4	50.4	19.7	66.7	18.1
U.S.	86.3	88.4	83.2	85.8	64.1	29.3	30.6	19.0	50.9	13.9

Note: Figures shown cover persons 25 years old and over; (1) Figures cover the Bridgeport-Stamford-Norwalk, CT Metropolitan Statistical Area—see Appendix B for areas included; (2) People of Hispanic origin can be of any race
Source: U.S. Census Bureau, 2010-2014 American Community Survey 5-Year Estimates

School Enrollment by Grade and Control

Area	Preschool (%)		Kindergarten (%)		Grades 1 - 4 (%)		Grades 5 - 8 (%)		Grades 9 - 12 (%)	
	Public	Private	Public	Private	Public	Private	Public	Private	Public	Private
City	10.7	89.3	84.2	15.8	94.4	5.6	94.8	5.2	92.0	8.0
MSA[1]	38.5	61.5	83.3	16.7	86.9	13.1	85.5	14.5	86.2	13.8
U.S.	57.4	42.6	87.8	12.2	89.8	10.2	89.9	10.1	90.6	9.4

Note: Figures shown cover persons 3 years old and over; (1) Figures cover the Bridgeport-Stamford-Norwalk, CT Metropolitan Statistical Area—see Appendix B for areas included
Source: U.S. Census Bureau, 2010-2014 American Community Survey 5-Year Estimates

Average Salaries of Public School Classroom Teachers

Area	2013-14		2014-15		Percent Change 2013-14 to 2014-15	Percent Change 2004-05 to 2014-15
	Dollars	Rank[1]	Dollars	Rank[1]		
Connecticut	70,583	5	71,709	5	1.59	24.2
U.S. Average	56,610	–	57,379	–	1.36	20.8

Note: (1) State rank ranges from 1 to 51 where 1 indicates highest salary.
Source: National Education Association, Rankings & Estimates: Rankings of the States 2014 and Estimates of School Statistics 2015, March 2015

Higher Education

Four-Year Colleges			Two-Year Colleges			Medical Schools[1]	Law Schools[2]	Voc/ Tech[3]
Public	Private Non-profit	Private For-profit	Public	Private Non-profit	Private For-profit			
0	0	0	0	0	0	0	0	0

Note: Figures cover institutions located within the city limits and include main campuses only; (1) includes schools accredited by the Liaison Committee on Medical Education and the American Osteopathic Association's Commission on Osteopathic College Accreditation; (2) includes ABA-accredited schools, schools with provisional ABA accreditation, and state accredited schools; (3) includes all schools with programs that are less than 2 years.
Source: National Center for Education Statistics, Integrated Postsecondary Education System (IPEDS), 2014-15; Association of American Medical Colleges, Member List, March 21, 2016; American Osteopathic Association, Member List, March 21, 2016; Law School Admission Council, Official Guide to ABA-Approved Law Schools Online, March 21, 2016; Wikipedia, List of Medical Schools in the United States, March 21, 2016; Wikipedia, List of Law Schools in the United States, March 21, 2016

PRESIDENTIAL ELECTION

2012 Presidential Election Results

Area	Obama (%)	Romney (%)	Other (%)
Fairfield County	55.3	43.8	0.9
U.S.	51.0	47.2	1.8

Note: Results may not add to 100% due to rounding
Source: Dave Leip's Atlas of U.S. Presidential Elections

EMPLOYERS

Major Employers

Company Name	Industry
Aptuit (scientific Operations)	Pharmaceutical preparations
Atos It Solutions and Services	Computer related maintenance services
Boehringer Ingelheim USA Corporation	Medicines, capsuled or ampuled
Bridgeport Hospital	Hospital, medical school affiliated with residency
Carter's Retail	Children's & infants' wear stores
Cartus Corporation	Relocation service
City of Bridgeport	Civil service commission, government
Commerce Connect Media	Magazines: publishing & printing
Conopco	Ice cream & ice milk
Diageo North America	Wine & distilled beverages
Greenwich Health Care Services	General medical & surgical hospitals
Pitney Bowes	Office machines
Sikorsky Aircraft Corporation	Aircraft
St Vincent's Development Corp.	Health systems agency
St Vincent's Health Services	General medical & surgical hospitals
The Danbury Hospital	Hospital, medical school affiliated with residency
Thomas J. Lipton	Tea blending
Thomson Corporation U.S.A.	Newspapers, publishing & printing
UBS Americas	Security brokers & dealers
UBS Securities	Brokers, security
Western Connecticut Healthcare	General medical & surgical hospitals
Wheelabrator Connecticut	Refuse systems

Note: Companies shown are located within the Bridgeport-Stamford-Norwalk, CT Metropolitan Statistical Area.
Source: Hoovers.com; Wikipedia

PUBLIC SAFETY

Crime Rate

Area	All Crimes	Violent Crimes: Murder	Violent Crimes: Rape[3]	Violent Crimes: Robbery	Violent Crimes: Aggrav. Assault	Property Crimes: Burglary	Property Crimes: Larceny -Theft	Property Crimes: Motor Vehicle Theft
City	261.0	0.0	0.0	0.0	4.0	11.9	241.2	4.0
Metro[1]	1,850.8	1.9	20.0	100.0	122.7	304.0	1,146.2	155.9
U.S.	2,971.8	4.5	36.6	102.2	232.5	542.5	1,837.3	216.2

Note: Figures are crimes per 100,000 population; (1) Figures cover the Bridgeport-Stamford-Norwalk, CT Metropolitan Statistical Area—see Appendix B for areas included; (3) The city and U.S. figures shown were reported using the revised Uniform Crime Reporting (UCR) definition of rape. The suburban and metro area figures shown are an aggregate total of the data submitted using both the revised and legacy UCR definitions.
Source: FBI Uniform Crime Reports, 2014

Hate Crimes

Area	Number of Quarters Reported	Race	Religion	Sexual Orientation	Ethnicity	Disability	Gender	Gender Identity
City	4	0	0	0	0	0	0	0
U.S.	4	2,568	1,014	1,017	648	84	33	98

(Columns Race through Gender Identity: Number of Incidents per Bias Motivation)

Source: Federal Bureau of Investigation, Hate Crime Statistics 2014

Identity Theft Consumer Complaints

Area	Complaints	Complaints per 100,000 Population	Rank[2]
MSA[1]	2,400	253.9	5
U.S.	490,220	152.4	-

Note: (1) Figures cover the Bridgeport-Stamford-Norwalk, CT Metropolitan Statistical Area—see Appendix B for areas included; (2) Rank ranges from 1 to 379 where 1 indicates greatest number of identity theft complaints per 100,000 population
Source: Federal Trade Commission, Consumer Sentinel Network Data Book for January–December 2015

Fraud and Other Consumer Complaints

Area	Complaints	Complaints per 100,000 Population	Rank[2]
MSA[1]	3,152	333.4	242
U.S.	2,593,159	806.0	-

Note: (1) Figures cover the Bridgeport-Stamford-Norwalk, CT Metropolitan Statistical Area—see Appendix B for areas included; (2) Rank ranges from 1 to 379 where 1 indicates greatest number of identity theft complaints per 100,000 population
Source: Federal Trade Commission, Consumer Sentinel Network Data Book for January–December 2015

RECREATION

Culture

Dance[1]	Theatre[1]	Instrumental Music[1]	Vocal Music[1]	Series and Festivals	Museums and Art Galleries[2]	Zoos and Aquariums[3]
0	0	0	0	0	0	0

Note: (1) Professional perfoming groups; (2) Based on organizations with SIC code 8412; (3) AZA-accredited
Source: The Grey House Performing Arts Directory, 2015-16; Association of Zoos & Aquariums, AZA Member Zoos & Aquariums, March 25, 2016; www.AccuLeads.com, March 29, 2016

Professional Sports Teams

Team Name	League	Year Established
No teams are located in the metro area		

Source: Wikipedia, Major Professional Sports Teams of the United States and Canada, March 24, 2016

CLIMATE

Average and Extreme Temperatures

Temperature	Jan	Feb	Mar	Apr	May	Jun	Jul	Aug	Sep	Oct	Nov	Dec	Yr.
Extreme High (°F)	65	67	84	91	92	96	103	100	99	85	78	65	103
Average High (°F)	37	38	46	57	67	76	82	81	74	64	53	41	60
Average Temp. (°F)	30	32	39	49	59	68	74	73	66	56	46	35	52
Average Low (°F)	23	24	31	40	50	59	65	65	57	47	38	27	44
Extreme Low (°F)	-7	-5	4	18	31	41	49	44	36	26	16	-4	-7

Note: Figures cover the years 1948-1992
Source: National Climatic Data Center, International Station Meteorological Climate Summary, 9/96

Average Precipitation/Snowfall/Humidity

Precip./Humidity	Jan	Feb	Mar	Apr	May	Jun	Jul	Aug	Sep	Oct	Nov	Dec	Yr.
Avg. Precip. (in.)	3.2	2.9	3.7	3.7	3.7	3.1	3.7	3.8	3.0	3.2	3.8	3.5	41.4
Avg. Snowfall (in.)	7	7	5	1	Tr	0	0	0	0	Tr	1	5	25
Avg. Rel. Hum. 7am (%)	73	72	72	72	76	77	79	80	81	79	77	74	76
Avg. Rel. Hum. 4pm (%)	61	59	56	55	59	60	60	61	61	60	62	63	60

Note: Figures cover the years 1948-1992; Tr = Trace amounts (<0.05 in. of rain; <0.5 in. of snow)
Source: National Climatic Data Center, International Station Meteorological Climate Summary, 9/96

Weather Conditions

Temperature			Daytime Sky			Precipitation		
32°F & below	45°F & below	90°F & above	Clear	Partly cloudy	Cloudy	0.01 inch or more precip.	0.1 inch or more snow/ice	Thunder-storms
100	193	7	80	146	139	118	17	22

Note: Figures are average number of days per year and cover the years 1948-1992
Source: National Climatic Data Center, International Station Meteorological Climate Summary, 9/96

HAZARDOUS WASTE

Superfund Sites

Ridgefield has no sites on the EPA's Superfund Final National Priorities List. There are a total of 1,323 Superfund sites on the list in the U.S. *U.S. Environmental Protection Agency, Final National Priorities List, March 18, 2016*

AIR & WATER QUALITY

Air Quality Trends: Ozone

	1990	1995	2000	2005	2010	2011	2012	2013	2014
MSA[1]	0.106	0.103	0.088	0.094	0.081	0.084	0.087	0.083	0.075

Note: (1) Data covers the Bridgeport-Stamford-Norwalk, CT Metropolitan Statistical Area—see Appendix B for areas included. The values shown are the composite ozone concentration averages among trend sites based on the highest fourth daily maximum 8-hour concentration in parts per million. These trends are based on sites having an adequate record of monitoring data during the trend period. Data from exceptional events are included.
Source: U.S. Environmental Protection Agency, Air Quality Monitoring Information, "Air Quality Trends by City, 1990-2014"

Air Quality Index

Area	Percent of Days when Air Quality was...[2]					AQI Statistics[2]	
	Good	Moderate	Unhealthy for Sensitive Groups	Unhealthy	Very Unhealthy	Maximum	Median
MSA[1]	61.9	33.4	4.4	0.3	0.0	151	44

Note: (1) Data covers the Bridgeport-Stamford-Norwalk, CT Metropolitan Statistical Area—see Appendix B for areas included; (2) Based on 365 days with AQI data in 2015. Air Quality Index (AQI) is an index for reporting daily air quality. EPA calculates the AQI for five major air pollutants regulated by the Clean Air Act: ground-level ozone, particle pollution (aka particulate matter), carbon monoxide, sulfur dioxide, and nitrogen dioxide. The AQI runs from 0 to 500. The higher the AQI value, the greater the level of air pollution and the greater the health concern. There are six AQI categories: "Good" AQI is between 0 and 50. Air quality is considered satisfactory; "Moderate" AQI is between 51 and 100. Air quality is acceptable; "Unhealthy for Sensitive Groups" When AQI values are between 101 and 150, members of sensitive groups may experience health effects; "Unhealthy" When AQI values are between 151 and 200 everyone may begin to experience health effects; "Very Unhealthy" AQI values between 201 and 300 trigger a health alert; "Hazardous" AQI values over 300 trigger warnings of emergency conditions (not shown).
Source: U.S. Environmental Protection Agency, Air Quality Index Report, 2015

Air Quality Index Pollutants

Area	Percent of Days when AQI Pollutant was...[2]					
	Carbon Monoxide	Nitrogen Dioxide	Ozone	Sulfur Dioxide	Particulate Matter 2.5	Particulate Matter 10
MSA[1]	0.5	0.0	34.8	0.0	64.7	0.0

Note: (1) Data covers the Bridgeport-Stamford-Norwalk, CT Metropolitan Statistical Area—see Appendix B for areas included; (2) Based on 365 days with AQI data in 2015. The Air Quality Index (AQI) is an index for reporting daily air quality. EPA calculates the AQI for five major air pollutants regulated by the Clean Air Act: ground-level ozone, particle pollution (also known as particulate matter), carbon monoxide, sulfur dioxide, and nitrogen dioxide. The AQI runs from 0 to 500. The higher the AQI value, the greater the level of air pollution and the greater the health concern.
Source: U.S. Environmental Protection Agency, Air Quality Index Report, 2015

Maximum Air Pollutant Concentrations: Particulate Matter, Ozone, CO and Lead

	Particulate Matter 10 (ug/m^3)	Particulate Matter 2.5 Wtd AM (ug/m^3)	Particulate Matter 2.5 24-Hr (ug/m^3)	Ozone (ppm)	Carbon Monoxide (ppm)	Lead (ug/m^3)
MSA[1] Level	35	9.9	25	0.081	1	n/a
NAAQS[2]	150	15	35	0.075	9	0.15
Met NAAQS[2]	Yes	Yes	Yes	No	Yes	n/a

Note: (1) Data covers the Bridgeport-Stamford-Norwalk, CT Metropolitan Statistical Area—see Appendix B for areas included; Data from exceptional events are included; (2) National Ambient Air Quality Standards; ppm = parts per million; ug/m^3 = micrograms per cubic meter; n/a not available.
Concentrations: Particulate Matter 10 (coarse particulate)—highest second maximum 24-hour concentration; Particulate Matter 2.5 Wtd AM (fine particulate)—highest weighted annual mean concentration; Particulate Matter 2.5 24-Hour (fine particulate)—highest 98th percentile 24-hour concentration; Ozone—highest fourth daily maximum 8-hour concentration; Carbon Monoxide—highest second maximum non-overlapping 8-hour concentration; Lead—maximum running 3-month average
Source: U.S. Environmental Protection Agency, Air Quality Monitoring Information, "Air Quality Statistics by City, 2014"

Maximum Air Pollutant Concentrations: Nitrogen Dioxide and Sulfur Dioxide

	Nitrogen Dioxide AM (ppb)	Nitrogen Dioxide 1-Hr (ppb)	Sulfur Dioxide AM (ppb)	Sulfur Dioxide 1-Hr (ppb)	Sulfur Dioxide 24-Hr (ppb)
MSA[1] Level	9	48	n/a	8	n/a
NAAQS[2]	53	100	30	75	140
Met NAAQS[2]	Yes	Yes	n/a	Yes	n/a

Note: (1) Data covers the Bridgeport-Stamford-Norwalk, CT Metropolitan Statistical Area—see Appendix B for areas included; Data from exceptional events are included; (2) National Ambient Air Quality Standards; ppm = parts per million; ug/m^3 = micrograms per cubic meter; n/a not available.
Concentrations: Nitrogen Dioxide AM—highest arithmetic mean concentration; Nitrogen Dioxide 1-Hr—highest 98th percentile 1-hour daily maximum concentration; Sulfur Dioxide AM—highest annual mean concentration; Sulfur Dioxide 1-Hr—highest 99th percentile 1-hour daily maximum concentration; Sulfur Dioxide 24-Hr—highest second maximum 24-hour concentration
Source: U.S. Environmental Protection Agency, Air Quality Monitoring Information, "Air Quality Statistics by City, 2014"

Drinking Water

Water System Name	Pop. Served	Primary Water Source Type	Violations[1]	
			Health Based	Monitoring/ Reporting
Aquarion Water Co. of CT-Ridgefield	7,902	Purchased Surface	0	0
Danbury Water Department	62,055	Surface	0	4

Note: (1) Based on violation data from January 1, 2015 to December 31, 2015 (includes unresolved violations from earlier years)

Source: U.S. Environmental Protection Agency, Office of Ground Water and Drinking Water, Safe Drinking Water Information System (based on data extracted April 29, 2016)

South Windsor, Connecticut

Background

Located in Hartford County, South Windsor is about 20 minutes from the Connecticut state capital of Hartford. A former farming community, the town saw tremendous growth in the half-century between 1950 and 2000, with the population tripling. More recently, the town has also grown commercially.

During the American Revolution, more than 200 men from South Windsor volunteered for the effort. Agriculture, shipbuilding and tobacco historically were the economic foundations of the town. South Windsor was incorporated in 1845.

The Promenade Shops at Evergreen Walk, designed to resemble a traditional New England village, includes 60-plus stores. The 1.2 million-square-foot development also includes office space, a hotel, and health club. Where tobacco fields and barns once stood, today there are office and retail projects in an area known as the Buckland Road Gateway Development Zone, designed as a mixed-used space in a village-style environment. A second area is known as the 1-291 Gateway Development Zone.

New industrial areas in South Windsor include the South Windsor Technologies Center and the Executive Business Park. In 2008, Aldi, the grocery chain, opened a $60 million, 500,000 square foot distribution center and regional headquarters, creating more than 150 jobs. The town has made major improvements to roads to accommodate and encourage commercial growth, and offers tax incentives to businesses.

The nearest airport is Bradley International Airport in Windsor Locks.

The East Windsor Hill Historic District, which contains historically significant buildings dating from 1700, is listed on the National Register of Historic Places. The earliest home in the district is the Captain May House, built in 1720. The Ebenezer Grant Mansion, built in 1757, is considered the finest example of Georgian architecture in the district. Oliver Wolcott, a signer of the Declaration of Independence, was born in South Windsor.

The town's Cultural Arts Commission promotes activities relating to fine arts, applied arts, and performing arts, including a concert series and programs in the schools. The South Windsor School system includes four elementary schools, one middle school and one high school. The student population is just over 5,000. Middle schoolers have the option of attending the Two Rivers Magnet Middle School in East Hartford.

Outdoor spaces and recreational offerings in South Windsor include the Major Michael Donnelly Land Preserve, with trails through woods and fields, a fishing dock and small pond; South Windsor Wildlife Sanctuary, where paths are maintained just enough to make them passable; Veterans Memorial Park, with a pool, basketball courts and an open field; Wapping Park, which opened in 2009; Boundless Playground, which is appropriate for children of all abilities; a ropes course designed to promote team-building and leadership; and a dog park, the Bark Park. Two golf courses are located in town, Willow Brook Golf Course and the public Topstone Golf Course.

The average high temperature in July is about 83 degrees. The average low temperature in January is 18 degrees.

Rankings

Business/Finance Rankings

- The personal finance site NerdWallet analyzed 183 American metropolitan areas with populations over 250,000 and more than 15,000 businesses to rank where entrepreneurs find the most success. Criteria included area economy, annual income, housing cost, unemployment rate, and the success rate of area businesses. Hartford* ranked #20. *www.nerdwallet.com, "Best Places to Start a Business," April 27, 2015*

- Based on metro area social media reviews, the employment opinion group Glassdoor surveyed 50 of the largest U.S. metro areas and equally weighed cost of living, hiring opportunity, and job satisfaction to compose a list of "25 Best Cities for Jobs." The Hartford* metro area was ranked #43 in overall job satisfaction. *www.glassdoor.com, "Best Cities for Jobs," May 19, 2015*

- In a survey of economic confidence in the nation's 50 largest metropolitan areas conducted January–December 2014, the Hartford* metro area placed #32, according to Gallup's 2014 Economic Confidence Index. *Gallup, "San Jose and San Francisco Lead in Economic Confidence," March 19, 2015*

- The Brookings Institution ranked the 100 largest metro areas in the U.S. based on income inequality. Hartford* was ranked #27 (#1 = greatest ineqality). Criteria: the "95/20 ratio," a figure representing the income at which a household earns more than 95 percent of all other households, divided by the income at which a household earns more than only 20 percent of all other households. *Brookings Institution, "Income Inequality, 100 Largest U.S. Metro Areas, 2007-2014," January 14, 2016*

- The Hartford* metro area appeared on the Milken Institute "2015 Best Performing Cities" list. Rank: #152 out of 200 large metro areas. Criteria: job growth; wage and salary growth; high-tech output growth. *Milken Institute, "Best-Performing Cities 2015," December 2015*

- *Forbes* ranked the 200 most populous metro areas to determine the nation's "Best Places for Business and Careers." The Hartford* metro area was ranked #151. Criteria: costs (business and living); job growth (past and projected); income growth; educational attainment (college and high school); projected economic growth; cultural and recreational opportunities; net migration patterns; number of highly ranked colleges. *Forbes, "The Best Places for Business and Careers 2015," July 29, 2015*

Education Rankings

- Personal finance website *WalletHub* analyzed the 150 largest U.S. metropolitan statistical areas to determine where the most educated Americans are choosing to settle. Criteria: education quality and attainment gap; education levels; percentage of workers with degrees; public school rankings; quality and size of each metro area's universities. Hartford* was ranked #23 (#1 = most educated city). *www.WalletHub.com, "2015's Most and Least Educated Cities*

Environmental Rankings

- The Hartford* metro area came in at #122 for the relative comfort of its climate on Sperling's list of "chill cities," as measured by the Sperling Heat Index. All 361 metro areas are included. Criteria included daytime high temperatures, nighttime low temperatures, dew point, and relative humidity at the high temperatures. *www.bertsperling.com, "Sperling's Chill Cities," July 18, 2013*

- Sperling's BestPlaces assessed 379 metropolitan areas of the United States for the likelihood of dangerously extreme weather events or earthquakes. In general the Southeast and South-Central regions have the highest risk of weather extremes and earthquakes, while the Pacific Northwest enjoys the lowest risk. Of the least risky metropolitan areas, the Hartford* metro area was ranked #199. *www.bestplaces.net, "Safest Places from Natural Disasters," April 2011*

Health/Fitness Rankings

- For each of the 50 most populous metro areas in the United States, the American College of Sports Medicine's American Fitness Index evaluated infrastructure, community assets, and policies that encourage healthy and fit lifestyles, including preventive health behaviors, levels of chronic disease conditions, health care access, and community resources and policies that support physical activity. The Hartford* metro area ranked #11 for "community fitness." *www.americanfitnessindex.org, "ACSM American Fitness Index Health and Community Fitness Status of the 50 Largest Metropolitan Areas," May 2015*
- The Hartford* metro area was identified as one of the worst cities for bed bugs in America by pest control company Orkin. The area ranked #34 out of 50 based on the number of bed bug treatments Orkin performed from January to December 2015. *Orkin, "Chicago Tops Bed Bug Cities List for Fourth Year in a Row," January 13, 2016*
- Hartford* was identified as a "2016 Spring Allergy Capital." The area ranked #56 out of 100. Three groups of factors were used to identify the most severe cities for people with allergies during the spring season: annual pollen levels; medicine utilization; access to board-certified allergists. *Asthma and Allergy Foundation of America, "Spring Allergy Capitals 2016"*
- Hartford* was identified as a "2015 Asthma Capital." The area ranked #33 out of the nation's 100 largest metropolitan areas. Criteria: estimated prevalence; self-reported prevalence; crude death rate for asthma; annual pollen score; annual air quality; public smoking laws; number of board-certified asthma specialists; school inhaler access laws; rescue medication use; controller medication use; ER visits for asthma; uninsured rate; poverty rate. *Asthma and Allergy Foundation of America, "Asthma Capitals 2015"*
- The Hartford* metro area ranked #71 out of 190 in The Gallup-Healthways Well-Being Index. Criteria: purpose; social well being; financial health; community and physical health. Results are based on telephone interviews with adults, aged 18 and older, living in metropolitan areas in the 50 U.S. states and the District of Columbia. *Gallup-Healthways, "State of American Well-Being," February 23, 2016*

Real Estate Rankings

- Hartford* was ranked #61 out of 225 metro areas in terms of housing affordability in 2015 by the National Association of Home Builders (#1 = most affordable). Criteria: the share of homes sold in that area affordable to a family earning the local median income, based on standard mortgage underwriting criteria. *National Association of Home Builders®, NAHB-Wells Fargo Housing Opportunity Index, 4th Quarter 2015*

Safety Rankings

- The National Insurance Crime Bureau ranked 380 metro areas in the U.S. in terms of per capita rates of vehicle theft. The Hartford* metro area ranked #169 (#1 = highest rate). Criteria: number of vehicle theft offenses per 100,000 inhabitants in 2014. *National Insurance Crime Bureau, "Hot Spots 2014," June 24, 2015*

Seniors/Retirement Rankings

- From its Best Cities for Successful Aging indexes, the Milken Institute generated rankings for metropolitan areas, weighing data in eight categories—health care, wellness, living arrangements, transportation, financial characteristics, education and employment opportunities, community engagement, and overall livability. The Hartford* metro area was ranked #41 overall in the large metro area category. *Milken Institute, "Best Cities for Successful Aging, 2014"*

Miscellaneous Rankings

- The National Alliance to End Homelessness ranked the 100 most populous metro areas with the highest rate of homelessness. The Hartford* metro area ranked #93. Criteria: number of homeless people per 10,000 population in 2011. *National Alliance to End Homelessness, The State of Homelessness in America 2012*

South Windsor is located within the Hartford-West Hartford-East Hartford, CT Metropolitan Statistical Area.

Business Environment

CITY FINANCES

City Government Finances

Component	2012 ($000)	2012 ($ per capita)
Total Revenues	116,334	4,525
Total Expenditures	114,165	4,440
Debt Outstanding	34,491	1,341
Cash and Securities[1]	19,952	776

Note: (1) Cash and security holdings of a government at the close of its fiscal year, including those of its dependent agencies, utilities, and liquor stores.
Source: U.S Census Bureau, State & Local Government Finances 2012

City Government Revenue by Source

Source	2012 ($000)	2012 ($ per capita)
General Revenue		
From Federal Government	0	0
From State Government	27,510	1,070
From Local Governments	212	8
Taxes		
Property	79,477	3,091
Sales and Gross Receipts	0	0
Personal Income	0	0
Corporate Income	0	0
Motor Vehicle License	0	0
Other Taxes	831	32
Current Charges	8,195	318
Liquor Store	0	0
Utility	0	0
Employee Retirement	0	0

Source: U.S Census Bureau, State & Local Government Finances 2012

City Government Expenditures by Function

Function	2012 ($000)	2012 ($ per capita)	2012 (%)
General Direct Expenditures			
Air Transportation	0	0	0.0
Corrections	0	0	0.0
Education	68,494	2,664	59.9
Employment Security Administration	0	0	0.0
Financial Administration	798	31	0.6
Fire Protection	1,398	54	1.2
General Public Buildings	1,204	46	1.0
Governmental Administration, Other	2,040	79	1.7
Health	125	4	0.1
Highways	3,705	144	3.2
Hospitals	0	0	0.0
Housing and Community Development	0	0	0.0
Interest on General Debt	1,226	47	1.0
Judicial and Legal	189	7	0.1
Libraries	1,005	39	0.8
Parking	0	0	0.0
Parks and Recreation	3,218	125	2.8
Police Protection	5,418	210	4.7
Public Welfare	827	32	0.7
Sewerage	2,842	110	2.4
Solid Waste Management	2,033	79	1.7
Veterans' Services	0	0	0.0
Liquor Store	0	0	0.0
Utility	0	0	0.0
Employee Retirement	0	0	0.0

Source: U.S Census Bureau, State & Local Government Finances 2012

DEMOGRAPHICS

Population Growth

Area	1990 Census	2000 Census	2010 Census	2014* Estimate	Population Growth (%) 1990-2014	Population Growth (%) 2010-2014
City	22,090	24,412	25,709	25,795	16.8	0.3
MSA[1]	1,123,706	1,148,618	1,212,381	1,215,159	8.1	0.2
U.S.	248,709,873	281,421,906	308,745,538	314,107,084	26.3	1.7

Note: (1) Figures cover the Hartford-West Hartford-East Hartford, CT Metropolitan Statistical Area—see Appendix B for areas included; (*) 2010-2014 5-year estimated population
Source: U.S. Census Bureau, 1990 Census, Census 2000, Census 2010, 2010-2014 American Community Survey 5-Year Estimates

Household Size

Area	Persons in Household (%) One	Two	Three	Four	Five	Six	Seven or More	Average Household Size
City	22.8	32.6	17.9	16.6	7.3	1.3	1.3	2.67
MSA[1]	28.2	33.6	16.0	14.2	5.5	1.6	0.6	2.48
U.S.	27.5	33.5	15.8	13.1	6.0	2.3	1.4	2.64

Note: (1) Figures cover the Hartford-West Hartford-East Hartford, CT Metropolitan Statistical Area—see Appendix B for areas included
Source: U.S. Census Bureau, 2010-2014 American Community Survey 5-Year Estimates

Race

Area	White Alone[2] (%)	Black Alone[2] (%)	Asian Alone[2] (%)	AIAN[3] Alone[2] (%)	NHOPI[4] Alone[2] (%)	Other Race Alone[2] (%)	Two or More Races (%)
City	81.2	5.1	10.3	0.3	0.2	1.4	1.6
MSA[1]	77.2	10.8	4.3	0.2	0.0	4.5	3.0
U.S.	73.8	12.6	5.0	0.8	0.2	4.7	2.9

Note: (1) Figures cover the Hartford-West Hartford-East Hartford, CT Metropolitan Statistical Area—see Appendix B for areas included; (2) Alone is defined as not being in combination with one or more other races; (3) American Indian and Alaska Native; (4) Native Hawaiian and Other Pacific Islander
Source: U.S. Census Bureau, 2010-2014 American Community Survey 5-Year Estimates

Hispanic or Latino Origin

Area	Total (%)	Mexican (%)	Puerto Rican (%)	Cuban (%)	Other (%)
City	5.6	0.6	1.9	1.0	2.1
MSA[1]	13.3	0.9	9.0	0.3	3.0
U.S.	16.9	10.8	1.6	0.6	3.8

Note: Persons of Hispanic or Latino origin can be of any race; (1) Figures cover the Hartford-West Hartford-East Hartford, CT Metropolitan Statistical Area—see Appendix B for areas included
Source: U.S. Census Bureau, 2010-2014 American Community Survey 5-Year Estimates

Ancestry

Area	German	Irish	English	American	Italian	Polish	French[2]	Scottish	Dutch
City	9.1	18.4	13.1	2.0	16.1	9.2	6.7	2.7	0.8
MSA[1]	9.2	16.0	9.4	4.0	16.8	10.2	7.2	1.8	0.7
U.S.	14.9	10.8	8.0	7.1	5.5	3.0	2.7	1.7	1.4

Note: Figures are the percentage of the total population reporting a particular ancestry. The nine most commonly reported ancestries in the U.S. are shown. Figures include multiple ancestries (e.g. if a person reported being Irish and Italian, they were included in both columns); (1) Figures cover the Hartford-West Hartford-East Hartford, CT Metropolitan Statistical Area—see Appendix B for areas included; (2) Excludes Basque
Source: U.S. Census Bureau, 2010-2014 American Community Survey 5-Year Estimates

Foreign-Born Population

Area	Percent of Population Born in: Any Foreign Country	Asia	Mexico	Europe	Carribean	Central America[2]	South America	Africa	Canada
City	13.9	6.5	0.0	2.9	1.2	0.2	1.4	0.8	1.0
MSA[1]	12.8	3.3	0.4	3.9	2.2	0.4	1.4	0.6	0.6
U.S.	13.1	3.8	3.7	1.5	1.2	1.0	0.9	0.6	0.3

Note: (1) Figures cover the Hartford-West Hartford-East Hartford, CT Metropolitan Statistical Area—see Appendix B for areas included; (2) Excludes Mexico.
Source: U.S. Census Bureau, 2010-2014 American Community Survey 5-Year Estimates

Marital Status

Area	Never Married	Now Married[2]	Separated	Widowed	Divorced
City	22.7	59.8	0.4	6.1	11.0
MSA[1]	34.1	47.5	1.5	5.9	11.1
U.S.	32.5	48.4	2.2	5.9	10.9

Note: Figures are percentages and cover the population 15 years of age and older; (1) Figures cover the Hartford-West Hartford-East Hartford, CT Metropolitan Statistical Area—see Appendix B for areas included; (2) Excludes separated
Source: U.S. Census Bureau, 2010-2014 American Community Survey 5-Year Estimates

Disability Status

Area	All Ages	Under 18 Years Old	18 to 64 Years Old	65 Years and Over
City	9.8	5.2	5.6	33.8
MSA[1]	11.2	4.1	8.5	33.4
U.S.	12.3	4.1	10.2	36.3

Note: Figures show percent of the civilian noninstitutionalized population that reported having a disability. Disability status is determined from from six types of difficulty: vision, hearing, cognitive, ambulatory, self-care, and independent living. For children under 5 years old, hearing and vision difficulty are used to determine disability status. For children between the ages of 5 and 14, disability status is determined from hearing, vision, cognitive, ambulatory, and self-care difficulties. For people aged 15 years and older, they are considered to have a disability if they have difficulty with any one of the six difficulty types; (1) Figures cover the Hartford-West Hartford-East Hartford, CT Metropolitan Statistical Area—see Appendix B for areas included.
Source: U.S. Census Bureau, 2010-2014 American Community Survey 5-Year Estimates

Age

Area	Percent of Population: Under Age 5	Age 5–19	Age 20–34	Age 35–44	Age 45–54	Age 55–64	Age 65–74	Age 75–84	Age 85+	Median Age
City	5.4	20.8	14.2	12.9	17.6	13.6	8.2	5.2	2.1	43.1
MSA[1]	5.2	19.5	19.0	12.5	15.6	13.2	7.9	4.6	2.5	40.4
U.S.	6.4	19.9	20.6	13.0	14.1	12.3	7.6	4.3	1.9	37.4

Note: (1) Figures cover the Hartford-West Hartford-East Hartford, CT Metropolitan Statistical Area—see Appendix B for areas included
Source: U.S. Census Bureau, 2010-2014 American Community Survey 5-Year Estimates

Gender

Area	Males	Females	Males per 100 Females
City	12,991	12,804	101.5
MSA[1]	592,094	623,065	95.0
U.S.	154,515,159	159,591,925	96.8

Note: (1) Figures cover the Hartford-West Hartford-East Hartford, CT Metropolitan Statistical Area—see Appendix B for areas included
Source: U.S. Census Bureau, 2010-2014 American Community Survey 5-Year Estimates

ECONOMY

Religious Groups by Family

Area	Catholic	Baptist	Non-Den.	Methodist[2]	Lutheran	LDS[3]	Pente-costal	Presby-terian[4]	Muslim[5]	Judaism
MSA[1]	30.3	1.9	2.1	1.9	1.3	0.3	0.9	3.6	0.2	1.2
U.S.	19.1	9.3	4.0	4.0	2.3	2.0	1.9	1.6	0.8	0.7

Note: Figures are the number of adherents as a percentage of the total population; (1) Figures cover the Hartford-West Hartford-East Hartford, CT Metropolitan Statistical Area—see Appendix B for areas included; (2) Methodist/Pietist; (3) Latter Day Saints; (4) Reformed; (5) Figures are estimates
Source: Association of Statisticians of American Religious Bodies, 2010 U.S. Religion Census: Religious Congregations & Membership Study

Religious Groups by Tradition

Area	Catholic	Evangelical Protestant	Mainline Protestant	Other Tradition	Black Protestant	Orthodox
MSA[1]	30.3	4.8	8.2	2.6	0.7	0.3
U.S.	19.1	16.2	7.3	4.3	1.6	0.3

Note: Figures are the number of adherents as a percentage of the total population; (1) Figures cover the Hartford-West Hartford-East Hartford, CT Metropolitan Statistical Area—see Appendix B for areas included
Source: Association of Statisticians of American Religious Bodies, 2010 U.S. Religion Census: Religious Congregations & Membership Study

Gross Metropolitan Product

Area	2013	2014	2015	2016	Rank[2]
MSA[1]	86.6	89.9	93.0	96.5	40

Note: Figures are in billions of dollars; (1) Figures cover the Hartford-West Hartford-East Hartford, CT Metropolitan Statistical Area—see Appendix B for areas included; (2) Rank is based on 2016 data and ranges from 1 to 381
Source: The U.S. Conference of Mayors, U.S. Metro Economies: GMP and Employment 2014-2016, June 2015

Economic Growth

Area	2011-13 (%)	2014 (%)	2015 (%)	2016 (%)	Rank[2]
MSA[1]	0.8	2.0	2.0	1.9	303
U.S.	2.2	2.4	2.3	2.9	–

Note: Figures are real gross metropolitan product (GMP) growth rates and represent annual average percent change; (1) Figures cover the Hartford-West Hartford-East Hartford, CT Metropolitan Statistical Area—see Appendix B for areas included; (2) Rank is based on 2016 data and ranges from 1 to 381
Source: The U.S. Conference of Mayors, U.S. Metro Economies: GMP and Employment 2014-2016, June 2015

Metropolitan Area Exports

Area	2009	2010	2011	2012	2013	2014	Rank[2]
MSA[1]	7,542.1	7,894.2	9,321.5	9,680.3	10,152.2	10,463.9	30

Note: Figures are in millions of dollars; (1) Figures cover the Hartford-West Hartford-East Hartford, CT Metropolitan Statistical Area—see Appendix B for areas included; (2) Rank is based on 2014 data and ranges from 1 to 385
Source: U.S. Department of Commerce, International Trade Administration, Office of Trade & Industry Information, Manufacturing & Services, data extracted March 10, 2016

Building Permits

Area	Single-Family			Multi-Family			Total		
	2014	2015p	Pct. Chg.	2014	2015p	Pct. Chg.	2014	2015p	Pct. Chg.
City	25	43	72.0	0	0	-	25	43	72.0
MSA[1]	754	792	5.0	639	866	35.5	1,393	1,658	19.0
U.S.	640,300	690,800	7.9	411,800	487,600	18.4	1,052,100	1,178,400	12.0

Note: (1) Figures cover the Hartford-West Hartford-East Hartford, CT Metropolitan Statistical Area—see Appendix B for areas included; Figures represent new, privately-owned housing units authorized (unadjusted data); All permit data are based on estimates with imputation; (p) preliminary data.
Source: U.S. Census Bureau, Manufacturing, Mining, and Construction Statistics, Building Permits, 2014, 2015

Bankruptcy Filings

Area	Business Filings 2014	Business Filings 2015	Business Filings % Chg.	Nonbusiness Filings 2014	Nonbusiness Filings 2015	Nonbusiness Filings % Chg.
Hartford County	79	74	-6.3	1,563	1,403	-10.2
U.S.	26,983	24,735	-8.3	909,812	819,760	-9.9

Note: Business filings include Chapter 7, Chapter 11, Chapter 12, and Chapter 13; Nonbusiness filings include Chapter 7, Chapter 11, and Chapter 13
Source: Administrative Office of the U.S. Courts, Business and Nonbusiness Bankruptcy, County Cases Commenced by Chapter of the Bankruptcy Code, During the 12- Month Period Ending December 31, 2014 and Business and Nonbusiness Bankruptcy, County Cases Commenced by Chapter of the Bankruptcy Code, During the 12- Month Period Ending December 31, 2015

Housing Vacancy Rates

Area	Gross Vacancy Rate² (%) 2013	2014	2015	Year-Round Vacancy Rate³ (%) 2013	2014	2015	Rental Vacancy Rate⁴ (%) 2013	2014	2015	Homeowner Vacancy Rate⁵ (%) 2013	2014	2015
MSA[1]	9.9	8.2	10.5	9.2	7.5	9.7	9.0	6.0	6.1	1.0	1.3	1.5
U.S.	13.6	13.4	12.9	10.7	10.4	10.0	8.3	7.6	7.1	2.0	1.9	1.8

Note: (1) Figures cover the Hartford-West Hartford-East Hartford, CT Metropolitan Statistical Area—see Appendix B for areas included; (2) The percentage of the total housing inventory that is vacant; (3) The percentage of the housing inventory (excluding seasonal units) that is year-round vacant; (4) The percentage of rental inventory that is vacant for rent; (5) The percentage of homeowner inventory that is vacant for sale
Source: U.S. Census Bureau, Housing Vacancies and Homeownership Annual Statistics: 2015

INCOME

Income

Area	Per Capita ($)	Median Household ($)	Average Household ($)
City	44,569	94,217	117,942
MSA[1]	35,991	68,959	90,995
U.S.	28,555	53,482	74,596

Note: (1) Figures cover the Hartford-West Hartford-East Hartford, CT Metropolitan Statistical Area—see Appendix B for areas included
Source: U.S. Census Bureau, 2010-2014 American Community Survey 5-Year Estimates

Household Income Distribution

Area	Under $15,000	$15,000 -24,999	$25,000 -34,999	$35,000 -49,999	$50,000 -74,999	$75,000 -99,000	$100,000 -149,999	$150,000 and up
	Percent of Households Earning							
City	4.0	6.0	4.4	8.3	15.3	14.1	22.8	25.0
MSA[1]	9.6	8.6	7.8	10.8	16.8	13.5	17.3	15.6
U.S.	12.5	10.7	10.2	13.5	17.8	12.2	13.0	10.0

Note: (1) Figures cover the Hartford-West Hartford-East Hartford, CT Metropolitan Statistical Area—see Appendix B for areas included
Source: U.S. Census Bureau, 2010-2014 American Community Survey 5-Year Estimates

Poverty Rate

Area	All Ages	Under 18 Years Old	18 to 64 Years Old	65 Years and Over
City	4.0	4.6	3.3	5.7
MSA[1]	10.7	14.3	10.3	7.4
U.S.	15.6	21.9	14.6	9.4

Note: Figures are percentage of people whose income during the past 12 months was below the poverty level; (1) Figures cover the Hartford-West Hartford-East Hartford, CT Metropolitan Statistical Area—see Appendix B for areas included
Source: U.S. Census Bureau, 2010-2014 American Community Survey 5-Year Estimates

EMPLOYMENT

Labor Force and Employment

Area	Civilian Labor Force			Workers Employed		
	Dec. 2014	Dec. 2015	% Chg.	Dec. 2014	Dec. 2015	% Chg.
City	13,921	13,918	0.0	13,318	13,375	0.4
NECTA[1]	616,412	614,187	-0.3	581,558	583,499	0.3
U.S.	155,521,000	157,245,000	1.1	147,190,000	149,703,000	1.7

Note: Data is not seasonally adjusted and covers workers 16 years of age and older; (1) Figures cover the Hartford-West Hartford-East Hartford, CT New England City and Town Area—see Appendix B for areas included
Source: Bureau of Labor Statistics, Local Area Unemployment Statistics

Unemployment Rate

Area	2015											
	Jan.	Feb.	Mar.	Apr.	May	Jun.	Jul.	Aug.	Sep.	Oct.	Nov.	Dec.
City	5.2	5.2	4.9	4.5	4.4	4.2	4.5	4.3	3.9	3.8	3.7	3.9
NECTA[1]	6.8	6.8	6.5	5.8	5.5	5.4	5.7	5.6	5.0	4.8	4.8	5.0
U.S.	6.1	5.8	5.6	5.1	5.3	5.5	5.6	5.2	4.9	4.8	4.8	4.8

Note: Data is not seasonally adjusted and covers workers 16 years of age and older; (1) Figures cover the Hartford-West Hartford-East Hartford, CT New England City and Town Area—see Appendix B for areas included
Source: Bureau of Labor Statistics, Local Area Unemployment Statistics

Employment by Occupation

Occupation Classification	City (%)	MSA[1] (%)	U.S. (%)
Management, Business, Science, and Arts	52.9	42.6	36.4
Natural Resources, Construction, and Maintenance	4.4	6.9	9.0
Production, Transportation, and Material Moving	7.5	9.9	12.1
Sales and Office	23.8	23.9	24.4
Service	11.4	16.7	18.2

Note: Figures cover employed civilians 16 years of age and older; (1) Figures cover the Hartford-West Hartford-East Hartford, CT Metropolitan Statistical Area—see Appendix B for areas included
Source: U.S. Census Bureau, 2010-2014 American Community Survey 5-Year Estimates

Employment by Industry

Sector	NECTA[1]		U.S.
	Number of Employees	Percent of Total	Percent of Total
Construction, Mining, and Logging	19,500	3.3	5.0
Education and Health Services	106,000	18.4	15.7
Financial Activities	57,400	9.9	5.7
Government	91,100	15.8	15.5
Information	11,900	2.0	1.9
Leisure and Hospitality	47,300	8.2	10.4
Manufacturing	55,600	9.6	8.6
Other Services	21,800	3.7	3.9
Professional and Business Services	73,400	12.7	13.9
Retail Trade	57,100	9.9	11.3
Transportation, Warehousing, and Utilities	17,200	2.9	3.9
Wholesale Trade	17,800	3.0	4.1

Note: Figures are non-farm employment as of December 2015. Figures are not seasonally adjusted and include workers 16 years of age and older; (1) Figures cover the Hartford-West Hartford-East Hartford, CT New England City and Town Area—see Appendix B for areas included; n/a not available
Source: Bureau of Labor Statistics, Current Employment Statistics, Employment, Hours, and Earnings

Occupations with Greatest Projected Employment Growth: 2012 – 2022

Occupation[1]	2012 Employment	2022 Projected Employment	Numeric Employment Change	Percent Employment Change
Personal Care Aides	23,240	32,090	8,850	38.1
Registered Nurses	35,990	41,230	5,240	14.6
Secretaries and Administrative Assistants, Except Legal, Medical, and Executive	34,530	38,640	4,110	11.9
Combined Food Preparation and Serving Workers, Including Fast Food	26,730	30,740	4,010	15.0
Retail Salespersons	53,800	57,270	3,470	6.4
General and Operations Managers	31,160	34,420	3,260	10.5
Home Health Aides	8,250	11,450	3,200	38.7
Childcare Workers	18,300	21,170	2,870	15.7
Maids and Housekeeping Cleaners	17,800	20,560	2,760	15.5
First-Line Supervisors of Office and Administrative Support Workers	26,360	28,900	2,540	9.6

Note: Projections cover Connecticut; (1) Sorted by numeric employment change
Source: www.projectionscentral.com, State Occupational Projections, 2012–2022 Long-Term Projections

Fastest Growing Occupations: 2012 – 2022

Occupation[1]	2012 Employment	2022 Projected Employment	Numeric Employment Change	Percent Employment Change
Insulation Workers, Mechanical	210	350	140	65.6
Interpreters and Translators	460	650	190	43.1
Helpers—Electricians	270	380	110	39.4
Home Health Aides	8,250	11,450	3,200	38.7
Diagnostic Medical Sonographers	1,000	1,380	380	38.3
Personal Care Aides	23,240	32,090	8,850	38.1
Physical Therapist Assistants	540	740	200	37.4
Occupational Therapy Assistants	490	670	180	35.4
Health Specialties Teachers, Postsecondary	2,810	3,770	960	34.3
Nursing Instructors and Teachers, Postsecondary	700	940	240	34.0

Note: Projections cover Connecticut; (1) Sorted by percent employment change and excludes occupations with numeric employment change less than 100
Source: www.projectionscentral.com, State Occupational Projections, 2012–2022 Long-Term Projections

Average Wages

Occupation	$/Hr.	Occupation	$/Hr.
Accountants and Auditors	36.17	Maids and Housekeeping Cleaners	12.62
Automotive Mechanics	19.62	Maintenance and Repair Workers	20.71
Bookkeepers	20.84	Marketing Managers	64.39
Carpenters	24.27	Nuclear Medicine Technologists	39.03
Cashiers	10.82	Nurses, Licensed Practical	27.04
Clerks, General Office	17.91	Nurses, Registered	36.53
Clerks, Receptionists/Information	16.53	Nursing Assistants	14.90
Clerks, Shipping/Receiving	16.88	Packers and Packagers, Hand	14.20
Computer Programmers	36.77	Physical Therapists	39.83
Computer Systems Analysts	44.04	Postal Service Mail Carriers	24.89
Computer User Support Specialists	28.45	Real Estate Brokers	48.04
Cooks, Restaurant	12.22	Retail Salespersons	13.26
Dentists	91.66	Sales Reps., Exc. Tech./Scientific	36.73
Electrical Engineers	44.18	Sales Reps., Tech./Scientific	46.11
Electricians	25.35	Secretaries, Exc. Legal/Med./Exec.	20.92
Financial Managers	68.35	Security Guards	14.25
First-Line Supervisors/Managers, Sales	23.15	Surgeons	108.58
Food Preparation Workers	11.17	Teacher Assistants*	13.61
General and Operations Managers	61.27	Teachers, Elementary School*	35.68
Hairdressers/Cosmetologists	14.53	Teachers, Secondary School*	34.92
Internists	83.89	Telemarketers	13.44
Janitors and Cleaners	15.34	Truck Drivers, Heavy/Tractor-Trailer	22.32
Landscaping/Groundskeeping Workers	14.82	Truck Drivers, Light/Delivery Svcs.	17.04
Lawyers	65.46	Waiters and Waitresses	11.02

Note: Wage data covers the New England City and Town Area—see Appendix B for areas included; (*) Hourly wages for elementary/secondary school teachers and teacher assistants were calculated by the editors from annual wage data based on a 40 hour work week; n/a not available.
Source: Bureau of Labor Statistics, Metro Area Occupational Employment and Wage Estimates, May 2015

TAXES

State Corporate Income Tax Rates

State	Tax Rate (%)	Income Brackets ($)	Num. of Brackets	Financial Institution Tax Rate (%)[a]	Federal Income Tax Ded.
Connecticut	7.5 (d)	Flat rate	1	7.5 (d)	No

Note: Tax rates as of January 1, 2016; (a) Rates listed are the corporate income tax rate applied to financial institutions or excise taxes based on income. Some states have other taxes based upon the value of deposits or shares; (d) Connecticut's tax is the greater of the 7.5% tax on net income, a 0.31% tax on capital stock and surplus (maximum tax of $1 million), or $250 (the minimum tax). Plus, an additional 20% surtax applies for tax years 2012 and 2016.
Source: Federation of Tax Administrators, "State Corporate Income Tax Rates, 2016"

State Individual Income Tax Rates

State	Tax Rate (%)	Income Brackets ($)	Num. of Brackets	Personal Exempt. ($)[1] Single	Personal Exempt. ($)[1] Dependents	Fed. Inc. Tax Ded.
Connecticut	3.0 - 6.99	10,000 - 500,000 (b)	7	14,500 (g)	None	No

Note: Tax rates as of January 1, 2016; Local- and county-level taxes are not included; n/a not applicable; (1) Married joint filers generally receive double the single exemption; (b) For joint returns, taxes are twice the tax on half the couple's income; (g) Connecticut's personal exemption incorporates a standard deduction. An additional tax credit is allowed ranging from 75% to 0% based on state adjusted gross income. Exemption amounts are phased out for higher income taxpayers until they are eliminated for households earning over $71,000.
Source: Federation of Tax Administrators, "State Individual Income Tax Rates, 2016"

Various State and Local Tax Rates

State	State and Local Sales and Use (%)	State Sales and Use (%)	Gasoline[1] (¢/gal.)	Cigarette[2] ($/pack)	Spirits[3] ($/gal.)	Wine[4] ($/gal.)	Beer[5] ($/gal.)
Connecticut	6.35	6.35	37.51	3.65	5.40 (f)	0.72 (l)	0.16

Note: All tax rates as of January 1, 2016; (1) The American Petroleum Institute has developed a methodology for determining the average tax rate on a gallon of fuel. Rates may include any of the following: excise taxes, environmental fees, storage tank fees, other fees or taxes, general sales tax, and local taxes. In states where gasoline is subject to the general sales tax, or where the fuel tax is based on the average sale price, the average rate determined by API is sensitive to changes in the price of gasoline. States that fully or partially apply general sales taxes to gasoline: CA, CO, GA, IL, IN, MI, NY; (2) The federal excise tax of $1.0066 per pack and local taxes are not included; (3) Rates are those applicable to off-premise sales of 40% alcohol by volume (a.b.v.) distilled spirits in 750ml containers. Local excise taxes are excluded; (4) Rates are those applicable to off-premise sales of 11% a.b.v. non-carbonated wine in 750ml containers; (5) Rates are those applicable to off-premise sales of 4.7% a.b.v. beer in 12 ounce containers; (f) Different rates are also applicable according to alcohol content, place of production, size of container, or place purchased (on- or off-premise or onboard airlines); (l) Different rates also applicable according to alcohol content, place of production, size of container, place purchased (on- or off-premise or on board airlines) or type of wine (carbonated, vermouth, etc.).
Source: Tax Foundation, 2016 Facts & Figures: How Does Your State Compare?

State Business Tax Climate Index Rankings

State	Overall Rank	Corporate Tax Rank	Individual Income Tax Rank	Sales Tax Rank	Unemployment Insurance Tax Rank	Property Tax Rank
Connecticut	44	33	36	29	20	49

Note: The index is a measure of how each state's tax laws affect economic performance. The lower the rank, the more favorable a state's tax system is for business. States without a given tax are given a ranking of 1. The scores/rankings for the District of Columbia do not affect other states. The 2016 index represents the tax climate as of July 1, 2015 (the beginning of Fiscal Year 2016).
Source: Tax Foundation, State Business Tax Climate Index 2016

TRANSPORTATION

Means of Transportation to Work

Area	Car/Truck/Van		Public Transportation			Bicycle	Walked	Other Means	Worked at Home
	Drove Alone	Car-pooled	Bus	Subway	Railroad				
City	85.0	7.6	1.3	0.0	0.1	0.1	0.1	0.6	5.1
MSA[1]	81.4	7.9	3.0	0.0	0.1	0.2	2.7	1.0	3.7
U.S.	76.4	9.6	2.6	1.8	0.6	0.6	2.8	1.3	4.4

Note: Figures are percentages and cover workers 16 years of age and older; (1) Figures cover the Hartford-West Hartford-East Hartford, CT Metropolitan Statistical Area—see Appendix B for areas included
Source: U.S. Census Bureau, 2010-2014 American Community Survey 5-Year Estimates

Travel Time to Work

Area	Less Than 10 Minutes	10 to 19 Minutes	20 to 29 Minutes	30 to 44 Minutes	45 to 59 Minutes	60 to 89 Minutes	90 Minutes or More
City	12.4	28.4	32.8	18.9	4.7	1.7	1.0
MSA[1]	13.2	31.3	24.1	20.7	6.0	3.1	1.5
U.S.	13.3	29.6	21.0	20.2	7.7	5.7	2.6

Note: Figures are percentages and include workers 16 years old and over; (1) Figures cover the Hartford-West Hartford-East Hartford, CT Metropolitan Statistical Area—see Appendix B for areas included
Source: U.S. Census Bureau, 2010-2014 American Community Survey 5-Year Estimates

Freeway Travel Time Index

Area	1985	1990	1995	2000	2005	2010	2014
Urban Area Rank[1,2]	64	56	47	57	42	36	37
Urban Area Index[1]	1.05	1.09	1.13	1.15	1.18	1.20	1.20
Average Index[3]	1.09	1.11	1.14	1.17	1.20	1.19	1.20

Note: Freeway Travel Time Index—the ratio of travel time in the peak period to the travel time at free-flow conditions. For example, a value of 1.30 indicates a 20-minute free-flow trip takes 26 minutes in the peak (20 minutes x 1.30 = 26 minutes); (1) Covers the Hartford CT urban area; (2) Rank is based on 101 urban areas (#1 = highest travel time index); (3) Average of 101 urban areas
Source: Texas Transportation Institute, 2015 Urban Mobility Scorecard, August 2015

Freeway Commuter Stress Index

Area	1985	1990	1995	2000	2005	2010	2014
Urban Area Rank[1,2]	58	51	50	54	47	40	43
Urban Area Index[1]	1.08	1.12	1.16	1.18	1.21	1.23	1.23
Average Index[3]	1.13	1.16	1.19	1.22	1.25	1.24	1.25

Note: The Freeway Commuter Stress Index is the same as the Freeway Travel Time Index (see table above) except that it includes only the travel in the peak directions during the peak periods; the TTI includes travel in all directions during the peak period. Thus, the CSI is more indicative of the work trip experienced by each commuter on a daily basis. (1) Covers the Hartford CT urban area; (2) Rank is based on 101 urban areas (#1 = highest stress index); (3) Average of 101 urban areas

Source: Texas Transportation Institute, 2015 Urban Mobility Scorecard, August 2015

Living Environment

COST OF LIVING

Cost of Living Index

Composite Index	Groceries	Housing	Utilities	Transportation	Health Care	Misc. Goods/ Services
124.5	129.7	133.0	129.4	110.4	118.2	119.2

Note: The Cost of Living Index measures regional differences in the cost of consumer goods and services, excluding taxes and non-consumer expenditures, for professional and managerial households in the top income quintile. It is based on more than 50,000 prices covering almost 60 different items for which prices are collected three times a year by chambers of commerce, economic development organizations or university applied economic centers in each participating urban area. The numbers shown should be read as a percentage above or below the national average of 100. For example, a value of 115.4 in the groceries column indicates that grocery prices are 15.4% higher than the national average. Small differences in the index numbers should not be interpreted as significant; Figures cover the Hartford CT urban area.
Source: The Council for Community and Economic Research, ACCRA Cost of Living Index, 2015

Grocery Prices

Area[1]	T-Bone Steak ($/pound)	Frying Chicken ($/pound)	Whole Milk ($/half gal.)	Eggs ($/dozen)	Orange Juice ($/64 oz.)	Coffee ($/11.5 oz.)
City[2]	11.62	1.64	2.99	2.51	3.83	3.85
Avg.	10.99	1.43	2.25	2.26	3.58	4.48
Min.	7.16	0.98	1.30	1.35	2.88	2.98
Max.	14.13	2.43	3.85	4.81	6.39	7.56

Note: (1) Values for the local area are compared with the average, minimum and maximum values for all 292 areas in the Cost of Living Index; (2) Figures cover the Hartford CT urban area; **T-Bone Steak** *(price per pound);* **Frying Chicken** *(price per pound, whole fryer);* **Whole Milk** *(half gallon carton);* **Eggs** *(price per dozen, Grade A, large);* **Orange Juice** *(64 oz. Tropicana or Florida Natural);* **Coffee** *(11.5 oz. can, vacuum-packed, Maxwell House, Hills Bros, or Folgers).*
Source: The Council for Community and Economic Research, ACCRA Cost of Living Index, 2015

Housing and Utility Costs

Area[1]	New Home Price ($)	Apartment Rent ($/month)	All Electric ($/month)	Part Electric ($/month)	Other Energy ($/month)	Telephone ($/month)
City[2]	429,480	1,123	-	148.46	119.90	24.95
Avg.	312,874	945	179.30	95.07	72.96	28.11
Min.	178,682	479	116.28	43.14	26.46	10.01
Max.	1,472,476	3,984	504.25	189.44	421.11	43.06

Note: (1) Values for the local area are compared with the average, minimum and maximum values for all 292 areas in the Cost of Living Index; (2) Figures cover the Hartford CT urban area; **New Home Price** *(2,400 sf living area, 8,000 sf lot, in urban area with full utilities);* **Apartment Rent** *(950 sf 2 bedroom/1.5 or 2 bath, unfurnished, excluding all utilities except water);* **All Electric** *(average monthly cost for an all-electric home);* **Part Electric** *(average monthly cost for a part-electric home);* **Other Energy** *(average monthly cost for natural gas, fuel oil, coal, wood, and any other forms of energy except electricity);* **Telephone** *(price includes basic monthly rate for a private residential line plus additional local usage charges incurred by a family of four).*
Source: The Council for Community and Economic Research, ACCRA Cost of Living Index, 2015

Health Care, Transportation, and Other Costs

Area[1]	Doctor ($/visit)	Dentist ($/visit)	Optometrist ($/visit)	Gasoline ($/gallon)	Beauty Salon ($/visit)	Men's Shirt ($)
City[2]	123.77	122.94	116.73	2.57	47.06	26.88
Avg.	105.15	89.02	99.78	2.38	35.30	28.10
Min.	66.87	56.09	48.53	1.95	18.91	13.38
Max.	182.34	150.36	228.33	4.09	67.91	63.80

Note: (1) Values for the local area are compared with the average, minimum and maximum values for all 292 areas in the Cost of Living Index; (2) Figures cover the Hartford CT urban area; **Doctor** *(general practitioners routine exam of an established patient);* **Dentist** *(adult teeth cleaning and periodic oral examination);* **Optometrist** *(full vision eye exam for established adult patient);* **Gasoline** *(one gallon regular unleaded, national brand, including all taxes, cash price at self-service pump if available);* **Beauty Salon** *(woman's shampoo, trim, and blow-dry);* **Men's Shirt** *(cotton/polyester dress shirt, pinpoint weave, long sleeves).*
Source: The Council for Community and Economic Research, ACCRA Cost of Living Index, 2015

HOUSING

House Price Index (HPI)

Area	National Ranking[2]	Quarterly Change (%)	One-Year Change (%)	Five-Year Change (%)
MSA[1]	258	-0.10	0.50	-4.00
U.S.[3]	–	1.45	5.76	22.85

Note: The HPI is a weighted repeat sales index. It measures average price changes in repeat sales or refinancings on the same properties. This information is obtained by reviewing repeat mortgage transactions on single-family properties whose mortgages have been purchased or securitized by Fannie Mae or Freddie Mac in January 1975; (1) Hartford-West Hartford-East Hartford Metropolitan Statistical Area—see Appendix B for areas included; (2) Rankings are based on annual percentage change for all metro areas containing at least 15,000 transactions over the last 10 years and ranges from 1 to 266; (3) figures based on a weighted average of Census Division estimates using a seasonally adjusted, purchase-only index; all figures are for the period ending December 31, 2015

Source: Federal Housing Finance Agency, House Price Index, February 25, 2016

Median Single-Family Home Prices

Area	2013	2014	2015p	Percent Change 2014 to 2015
MSA[1]	227.0	220.9	221.5	0.3
U.S. Average	197.4	208.9	223.9	7.2

Note: Figures are median sales prices of existing single-family homes in thousands of dollars; (p) preliminary; n/a not available; (1) Hartford-West Hartford-East Hartford, CT Metropolitan Statistical Area—see Appendix B for areas included

Source: National Association of Realtors, Median Sales Price of Existing Single-Family Homes for Metropolitan Areas, 4th Quarter 2015

Qualifying Income Based on Median Sales Price of Existing Single-Family Homes

Area	With 5% Down ($)	With 10% Down ($)	With 20% Down ($)
MSA[1]	47,622	45,116	40,103
U.S. Average	49,535	46,928	41,714

Note: Figures are preliminary; Qualifying income is based on a mortgage rate of 4.1%. Monthly principal and interest payment is limited to 25% of income; n/a not available; (1) Hartford-West Hartford-East Hartford, CT Metropolitan Statistical Area—see Appendix B for areas included

Source: National Association of Realtors, Qualifying Income Based on Median Sales Price of Existing Single-Family Homes for Metropolitan Areas, 4th Quarter 2015

Median Apartment Condo-Coop Home Prices

Area	2013	2014	2015p	Percent Change 2014 to 2015
MSA[1]	150.2	149.7	148.7	-0.7
U.S. Average	194.9	204.3	210.7	3.1

Note: Figures are median sales prices of existing apartment condo-coop homes in thousands of dollars; (p) preliminary; n/a not available; (1) Hartford-West Hartford-East Hartford, CT Metropolitan Statistical Area—see Appendix B for areas included

Source: National Association of Realtors, Median Sales Price of Existing Apartment Condo-Coop Homes for Metropolitan Areas, 4th Quarter 2015

Gross Monthly Rent

Area	Under $200	$200 -299	$300 -499	$500 -749	$750 -999	$1,000 -1,499	$1,500 and up	Median ($)
City	0.0	1.3	3.0	5.5	18.8	43.8	27.6	1,177
MSA[1]	1.9	4.3	5.7	11.9	26.9	37.3	12.0	995
U.S.	1.5	3.2	7.4	21.0	24.1	26.9	15.9	920

Note: Figures are percentages except for Median; Gross rent is the contract rent plus the estimated average monthly cost of utilities (electricity, gas, and water and sewer) and fuels (oil, coal, kerosene, wood, etc.) if these are paid by the renter (or paid for the renter by someone else); (1) Figures cover the Hartford-West Hartford-East Hartford, CT Metropolitan Statistical Area—see Appendix B for areas included

Source: U.S. Census Bureau, 2010-2014 American Community Survey 5-Year Estimates

Homeownership Rate

Area	2008 (%)	2009 (%)	2010 (%)	2011 (%)	2012 (%)	2013 (%)	2014 (%)	2015 (%)
MSA[1]	70.5	72.1	71.3	71.4	70.8	69.8	68.5	66.1
U.S.	67.8	67.4	66.9	66.1	65.4	65.1	64.5	63.7

Note: (1) Figures cover the Hartford-West Hartford-East Hartford, CT Metropolitan Statistical Area—see Appendix B for areas included
Source: U.S. Census Bureau, Housing Vacancies and Homeownership Annual Statistics: 2015

Year Housing Structure Built

Area	2010 or Later	2000 -2009	1990 -1999	1980 -1989	1970 -1979	1960 -1969	1950 -1959	1940 -1949	Before 1940	Median Year
City	1.0	8.3	12.0	26.3	13.4	13.5	15.9	2.5	7.1	1978
MSA[1]	0.3	7.2	7.7	13.8	13.4	14.1	16.8	7.6	19.0	1965
U.S.	1.0	14.9	13.9	13.8	15.8	11.0	10.8	5.4	13.3	1976

Note: Figures are percentages except for Median Year; (1) Figures cover the Hartford-West Hartford-East Hartford, CT Metropolitan Statistical Area—see Appendix B for areas included
Source: U.S. Census Bureau, 2010-2014 American Community Survey 5-Year Estimates

HEALTH

Health Risk Data

Category	MSA[1] (%)	U.S. (%)
Adults aged 18–64 who have any kind of health care coverage	89.4	79.6
Adults who reported being in good or excellent health	86.3	83.1
Adults who are current smokers	15.3	19.6
Adults who are heavy drinkers[2]	6.4	6.1
Adults who are binge drinkers[3]	17.5	16.9
Adults who are overweight (BMI 25.0 - 29.9)	35.0	35.8
Adults who are obese (BMI 30.0 - 99.8)	26.7	27.6
Adults who participated in any physical activities in the past month	79.0	77.1
Adults 50+ who have ever had a sigmoidoscopy or colonoscopy	74.4	67.3
Women aged 40+ who have had a mammogram within the past two years	83.2	74.0
Men aged 40+ who have had a PSA test within the past two years	50.9	45.2
Adults aged 65+ who have had flu shot within the past year	60.9	60.1
Adults who always wear a seatbelt	95.2	93.8

Note: Data as of 2012 unless otherwise noted; (1) Figures cover the Hartford-West Hartford-East Hartford, CT Metropolitan Statistical Area—see Appendix B for areas included; (2) Heavy drinkers are classified as males having more than two drinks per day or females having more than one drink per day; (3) Binge drinkers are classified as males having five or more drinks on one occasion or females having four or more drinks on one occasion
Source: Centers for Disease Control and Prevention, Behaviorial Risk Factor Surveillance System, SMART: Selected Metropolitan/Micropolitan Area Risk Trends, 2012 (Note: the CDC has discontinued this dataset but will be releasing a replacement in mid-2016)

Chronic Health Indicators

Category	MSA[1] (%)	U.S. (%)
Adults who have ever been told they had a heart attack	3.5	4.5
Adults who have ever been told they had a stroke	2.3	2.9
Adults who have been told they currently have asthma	10.4	8.9
Adults who have ever been told they have arthritis	23.6	25.7
Adults who have ever been told they have diabetes[2]	9.4	9.7
Adults who have ever been told they had skin cancer	5.4	5.7
Adults who have ever been told they had any other types of cancer	6.8	6.5
Adults who have ever been told they have COPD	5.2	6.2
Adults who have ever been told they have kidney disease	2.3	2.5
Adults who have ever been told they have a form of depression	17.5	18.0

Note: Data as of 2012 unless otherwise noted; (1) Figures cover the Hartford-West Hartford-East Hartford, CT Metropolitan Statistical Area—see Appendix B for areas included; (2) Figures do not include pregnancy-related, borderline, or pre-diabetes
Source: Centers for Disease Control and Prevention, Behaviorial Risk Factor Surveillance System, SMART: Selected Metropolitan/Micropolitan Area Risk Trends, 2012 (Note: the CDC has discontinued this dataset but will be releasing a replacement in mid-2016)

Mortality Rates for the Top 10 Causes of Death in the U.S.

ICD-10[a] Sub-Chapter	ICD-10[a] Code	Age-Adjusted Mortality Rate[1] per 100,000 population: County[2]	U.S.
Malignant neoplasms	C00-C97	150.4	163.6
Ischaemic heart diseases	I20-I25	81.8	102.2
Other forms of heart disease	I30-I51	61.3	50.1
Chronic lower respiratory diseases	J40-J47	28.9	41.4
Organic, including symptomatic, mental disorders	F01-F09	41.5	38.5
Cerebrovascular diseases	I60-I69	26.3	36.5
Other external causes of accidental injury	W00-X59	31.0	27.5
Other degenerative diseases of the nervous system	G30-G31	17.8	26.3
Diabetes mellitus	E10-E14	14.4	21.1
Hypertensive diseases	I10-I15	12.2	19.7

Note: (a) ICD-10 = International Classification of Diseases 10th Revision; (1) Mortality rates are a three year average covering 2012-2014; (2) Figures cover Hartford County.
Source: Centers for Disease Control and Prevention, National Center for Health Statistics. Underlying Cause of Death 1999-2014 on CDC WONDER Online Database, released 2015.

Mortality Rates for Selected Causes of Death

ICD-10[a] Sub-Chapter	ICD-10[a] Code	Age-Adjusted Mortality Rate[1] per 100,000 population: County[2]	U.S.
Assault	X85-Y09	4.2	5.1
Diseases of the liver	K70-K76	12.3	13.5
Human immunodeficiency virus (HIV) disease	B20-B24	2.6	2.1
Influenza and pneumonia	J09-J18	14.1	15.2
Intentional self-harm	X60-X84	8.9	12.7
Malnutrition	E40-E46	0.7	0.9
Obesity and other hyperalimentation	E65-E68	1.3	1.9
Renal failure	N17-N19	14.1	13.0
Transport accidents	V01-V99	8.5	11.6
Viral hepatitis	B15-B19	1.7	2.1

Note: (a) ICD-10 = International Classification of Diseases 10th Revision; (1) Mortality rates are a three year average covering 2012-2014; (2) Figures cover Hartford County; Data are Suppressed when the data meet the criteria for confidentiality constraints; Mortality rates are flagged as Unreliable when the rate would be calculated with a numerator of 20 or less.
Source: Centers for Disease Control and Prevention, National Center for Health Statistics. Underlying Cause of Death 1999-2014 on CDC WONDER Online Database, released 2015.

Health Insurance Coverage

Area	With Health Insurance	With Private Health Insurance	With Public Health Insurance	Without Health Insurance	Population Under Age 18 Without Health Insurance
City	97.9	88.1	21.5	2.1	0.9
MSA[1]	92.8	73.8	30.7	7.2	2.7
U.S.	85.8	65.8	31.1	14.2	7.1

Note: Figures are percentages that cover the civilian noninstitutionalized population; (1) Figures cover the Hartford-West Hartford-East Hartford, CT Metropolitan Statistical Area—see Appendix B for areas included
Source: U.S. Census Bureau, 2010-2014 American Community Survey 5-Year Estimates

Number of Medical Professionals

Area	MDs[3]	DOs[3,4]	Dentists	Podiatrists	Chiropractors	Optometrists
County[1] (number)	3,768	202	899	56	193	162
County[1] (rate[2])	419.2	22.5	100.1	6.2	21.5	18.0
U.S. (rate[2])	272.5	20.9	64.7	5.8	25.9	15.2

Note: Data as of 2014 unless noted; (1) Data covers Hartford County; (2) Rate per 100,000 population; (3) Data as of 2013 and includes all active, non-federal physicians; (4) Doctor of Osteopathic Medicine
Source: U.S. Department of Health and Human Services, Health Resources and Services Administration, Bureau of Health Professions, Area Resource File (ARF) 2014-2015

Best Hospitals

According to *U.S. News,* the Hartford-West Hartford-East Hartford, CT metro area is home to one of the best children's hospitals in the U.S.: **Connecticut Children's Medical Center** (1 specialty). The hospital listed was highly ranked in at least one pediatric specialty. Eighty-three children's hospitals in the U.S. were nationally ranked in at least one specialty. Twelve children's hospitals in the U.S. made the Honor Roll with high scores in at least three specialties. *U.S. News Online, "America's Best Children's Hospitals 2015-16"*

EDUCATION

Public School District Statistics

District Name	Schls	Pupils	Pupil/ Teacher Ratio	Minority Pupils[1] (%)	Free Lunch Eligible[2] (%)	IEP[3] (%)
South Windsor School District	8	4,242	12.2	29.7	8.9	14.1

Note: Table includes school districts with 100 or more students; (1) Percentage of students that are not non-Hispanic white; (2) Percentage of students that are eligible for the free lunch program; (3) Percentage of students that have an Individualized Education Program.
Source: U.S. Department of Education, National Center for Education Statistics, Common Core of Data, Local Education Agency (School District) Universe Survey: School Year 2013-2014; U.S. Department of Education, National Center for Education Statistics, Common Core of Data, Public Elementary/Secondary School Universe Survey: School Year 2013-2014

Highest Level of Education

Area	Less than H.S.	H.S. Diploma	Some College, No Deg.	Associate Degree	Bachelor's Degree	Master's Degree	Prof. School Degree	Doctorate Degree
City	5.7	21.3	14.1	8.1	28.1	16.7	4.4	1.7
MSA[1]	10.2	27.5	17.9	8.1	20.4	11.6	2.8	1.5
U.S.	13.7	28.0	21.2	7.9	18.3	7.8	2.0	1.3

Note: Figures cover persons age 25 and over; (1) Figures cover the Hartford-West Hartford-East Hartford, CT Metropolitan Statistical Area—see Appendix B for areas included
Source: U.S. Census Bureau, 2010-2014 American Community Survey 5-Year Estimates

Educational Attainment by Race

Area	High School Graduate or Higher (%)					Bachelor's Degree or Higher (%)				
	Total	White	Black	Asian	Hisp.[2]	Total	White	Black	Asian	Hisp.[2]
City	94.3	95.0	88.2	92.0	90.8	50.9	49.6	46.0	69.7	36.0
MSA[1]	89.8	91.9	83.7	88.4	69.2	36.3	38.4	19.3	64.1	14.9
U.S.	86.3	88.4	83.2	85.8	64.1	29.3	30.6	19.0	50.9	13.9

Note: Figures shown cover persons 25 years old and over; (1) Figures cover the Hartford-West Hartford-East Hartford, CT Metropolitan Statistical Area—see Appendix B for areas included; (2) People of Hispanic origin can be of any race
Source: U.S. Census Bureau, 2010-2014 American Community Survey 5-Year Estimates

School Enrollment by Grade and Control

Area	Preschool (%)		Kindergarten (%)		Grades 1 - 4 (%)		Grades 5 - 8 (%)		Grades 9 - 12 (%)	
	Public	Private	Public	Private	Public	Private	Public	Private	Public	Private
City	64.1	35.9	92.8	7.2	92.1	7.9	96.7	3.3	84.5	15.5
MSA[1]	55.7	44.3	90.0	10.0	93.2	6.8	93.3	6.7	91.6	8.4
U.S.	57.4	42.6	87.8	12.2	89.8	10.2	89.9	10.1	90.6	9.4

Note: Figures shown cover persons 3 years old and over; (1) Figures cover the Hartford-West Hartford-East Hartford, CT Metropolitan Statistical Area—see Appendix B for areas included
Source: U.S. Census Bureau, 2010-2014 American Community Survey 5-Year Estimates

Average Salaries of Public School Classroom Teachers

Area	2013-14		2014-15		Percent Change 2013-14 to 2014-15	Percent Change 2004-05 to 2014-15
	Dollars	Rank[1]	Dollars	Rank[1]		
Connecticut	70,583	5	71,709	5	1.59	24.2
U.S. Average	56,610	–	57,379	–	1.36	20.8

Note: (1) State rank ranges from 1 to 51 where 1 indicates highest salary.
Source: National Education Association, Rankings & Estimates: Rankings of the States 2014 and Estimates of School Statistics 2015, March 2015

Higher Education

Four-Year Colleges			Two-Year Colleges			Medical Schools[1]	Law Schools[2]	Voc/ Tech[3]
Public	Private Non-profit	Private For-profit	Public	Private Non-profit	Private For-profit			
0	0	0	0	0	0	0	0	0

Note: Figures cover institutions located within the city limits and include main campuses only; (1) includes schools accredited by the Liaison Committee on Medical Education and the American Osteopathic Association's Commission on Osteopathic College Accreditation; (2) includes ABA-accredited schools, schools with provisional ABA accreditation, and state accredited schools; (3) includes all schools with programs that are less than 2 years.

Source: National Center for Education Statistics, Integrated Postsecondary Education System (IPEDS), 2014-15; Association of American Medical Colleges, Member List, March 21, 2016; American Osteopathic Association, Member List, March 21, 2016; Law School Admission Council, Official Guide to ABA-Approved Law Schools Online, March 21, 2016; Wikipedia, List of Medical Schools in the United States, March 21, 2016; Wikipedia, List of Law Schools in the United States, March 21, 2016

According to *U.S. News & World Report,* the Hartford-West Hartford-East Hartford, CT metro area is home to one of the best national universities in the U.S.: **University of Connecticut** (#57 tie). The indicators used to capture academic quality fall into a number of categories: assessment by administrators at peer institutions; retention of students; faculty resources; student selectivity; financial resources; alumni giving; high school counselor ratings of colleges; and graduation rate. *U.S. News & World Report, "America's Best Colleges 2016"*

According to *U.S. News & World Report,* the Hartford-West Hartford-East Hartford, CT metro area is home to two of the best liberal arts colleges in the U.S.: **Wesleyan University** (#14 tie); **Trinity College** (#43 tie). The indicators used to capture academic quality fall into a number of categories: assessment by administrators at peer institutions; retention of students; faculty resources; student selectivity; financial resources; alumni giving; high school counselor ratings of colleges; and graduation rate. *U.S. News & World Report, "America's Best Colleges 2016"*

According to *U.S. News & World Report,* the Hartford-West Hartford-East Hartford, CT metro area is home to one of the top 100 law schools in the U.S.: **University of Connecticut, School of Law** (#65 tie). The rankings are based on a weighted average of 12 measures of quality: peer assessment score; assessment score by lawyers/judges; median LSAT scores; median undergrad GPA; acceptance rate; employment rates for graduates; placement success; bar passage rate; faculty resources; expenditures per student; student/faculty ratio; and library resources. *U.S. News & World Report, "America's Best Graduate Schools, Law, 2017"*

According to *U.S. News & World Report,* the Hartford-West Hartford-East Hartford, CT metro area is home to one of the top 75 medical schools for research in the U.S.: **University of Connecticut, School of Medicine** (#63 tie). The rankings are based on a weighted average of 11 measures of quality: quality assessment; peer assessment score; assessment score by residency directors; research activity; total research activity; average research activity per faculty member; student selectivity; median MCAT total score; median undergraduate GPA; acceptance rate; and faculty resources. *U.S. News & World Report, "America's Best Graduate Schools, Medical, 2017"*

According to *U.S. News & World Report,* the Hartford-West Hartford-East Hartford, CT metro area is home to one of the top 75 business schools in the U.S.: **University of Connecticut, School of Business** (#68 tie). The rankings are based on a weighted average of the following nine measures: quality assessment; peer assessment; recruiter assessment; placement success; mean starting salary and bonus; student selectivity; mean GMAT and GRE scores; mean undergraduate GPA; and acceptance rate. *U.S. News & World Report, "America's Best Graduate Schools, Business, 2017"*

PRESIDENTIAL ELECTION

2012 Presidential Election Results

Area	Obama (%)	Romney (%)	Other (%)
Hartford County	62.4	36.5	1.1
U.S.	51.0	47.2	1.8

Note: Results may not add to 100% due to rounding

Source: Dave Leip's Atlas of U.S. Presidential Elections

EMPLOYERS

Major Employers

Company Name	Industry
Aetna, Inc.	Insurance
AT&T CT	Telecommunications
Athena Health Care Systems	Nursing & rehab
Bank of America	Financial services
Boehringer Ingelheim Corp.	Health care products
CIGNA	Health care
ESPN	Sports media
Foxwoods Resort Casino	Gaming & tourism
GE	Diversified tech
General Dynamics Electric Boad	Submarines
Hartford Financial Services Group, Inc.	Financial services
Hartford Hospital	Healthcare
Mohegan Sun	Gaming & tourism
Northeast Utilities	Utilities
People's Bank	Financial services
Pfizer Global R&D	Pharmaceutical
St Francis Hospital and Med Center	Health care
St Paul Travelers Cos.	Insurance
Stop & Shop Cos. Inc	Supermarket
United States Surgical	Senior health care
United Technologies Corp	Building systems & aerospace
Wal-Mart	Retail
Webster Financial Corp.	Banking, insurnace, investment
Yale University	Higher education

Note: Companies shown are located within the Hartford-West Hartford-East Hartford, CT Metropolitan Statistical Area.
Source: Hoovers.com; Wikipedia

PUBLIC SAFETY

Crime Rate

Area	All Crimes	Violent Crimes				Property Crimes		
		Murder	Rape[3]	Robbery	Aggrav. Assault	Burglary	Larceny -Theft	Motor Vehicle Theft
City	1,391.2	0.0	19.3	11.6	3.9	231.9	1,066.6	58.0
Metro[1]	2,484.4	3.8	24.2	94.0	130.2	389.5	1,664.9	177.7
U.S.	2,971.8	4.5	36.6	102.2	232.5	542.5	1,837.3	216.2

Note: Figures are crimes per 100,000 population; (1) Figures cover the Hartford-West Hartford-East Hartford, CT Metropolitan Statistical Area—see Appendix B for areas included; (3) The city and U.S. figures shown were reported using the revised Uniform Crime Reporting (UCR) definition of rape. The suburban and metro area figures shown are an aggregate total of the data submitted using both the revised and legacy UCR definitions.
Source: FBI Uniform Crime Reports, 2014

Hate Crimes

Area	Number of Quarters Reported	Number of Incidents per Bias Motivation						
		Race	Religion	Sexual Orientation	Ethnicity	Disability	Gender	Gender Identity
City	n/a	n/a	n/a	n/a	n/a	n/a	n/a	n/a
U.S.	4	2,568	1,014	1,017	648	84	33	98

Note: n/a not available.
Source: Federal Bureau of Investigation, Hate Crime Statistics 2014

Identity Theft Consumer Complaints

Area	Complaints	Complaints per 100,000 Population	Rank[2]
MSA[1]	2,865	235.9	8
U.S.	490,220	152.4	-

Note: (1) Figures cover the Hartford-West Hartford-East Hartford, CT Metropolitan Statistical Area—see Appendix B for areas included; (2) Rank ranges from 1 to 379 where 1 indicates greatest number of identity theft complaints per 100,000 population
Source: Federal Trade Commission, Consumer Sentinel Network Data Book for January–December 2015

Fraud and Other Consumer Complaints

Area	Complaints	Complaints per 100,000 Population	Rank[2]
MSA[1]	4,428	364.7	186
U.S.	2,593,159	806.0	-

Note: (1) Figures cover the Hartford-West Hartford-East Hartford, CT Metropolitan Statistical Area—see Appendix B for areas included; (2) Rank ranges from 1 to 379 where 1 indicates greatest number of identity theft complaints per 100,000 population
Source: Federal Trade Commission, Consumer Sentinel Network Data Book for January–December 2015

RECREATION

Culture

Dance[1]	Theatre[1]	Instrumental Music[1]	Vocal Music[1]	Series and Festivals	Museums and Art Galleries[2]	Zoos and Aquariums[3]
0	0	0	0	0	0	0

Note: (1) Professional perfoming groups; (2) Based on organizations with SIC code 8412; (3) AZA-accredited
Source: The Grey House Performing Arts Directory, 2015-16; Association of Zoos & Aquariums, AZA Member Zoos & Aquariums, March 25, 2016; www.AccuLeads.com, March 29, 2016

Professional Sports Teams

Team Name	League	Year Established
No teams are located in the metro area		

Source: Wikipedia, Major Professional Sports Teams of the United States and Canada, March 24, 2016

CLIMATE

Average and Extreme Temperatures

Temperature	Jan	Feb	Mar	Apr	May	Jun	Jul	Aug	Sep	Oct	Nov	Dec	Yr.
Extreme High (°F)	66	73	87	96	97	101	102	101	101	91	83	74	102
Average High (°F)	34	37	46	60	71	80	85	82	74	64	51	38	60
Average Temp. (°F)	26	28	37	49	60	69	74	72	63	53	42	30	50
Average Low (°F)	17	19	28	38	47	57	62	60	52	41	33	22	40
Extreme Low (°F)	-26	-21	-8	9	28	37	44	36	27	17	1	-14	-26

Note: Figures cover the years 1949-1995
Source: National Climatic Data Center, International Station Meteorological Climate Summary, 9/96

Average Precipitation/Snowfall/Humidity

Precip./Humidity	Jan	Feb	Mar	Apr	May	Jun	Jul	Aug	Sep	Oct	Nov	Dec	Yr.
Avg. Precip. (in.)	3.4	3.1	3.9	3.9	3.7	3.5	3.3	4.0	3.8	3.6	4.1	3.9	44.2
Avg. Snowfall (in.)	12	12	9	1	Tr	0	0	0	0	Tr	2	10	46
Avg. Rel. Hum. 7am (%)	73	73	72	70	73	77	79	83	86	84	79	76	77
Avg. Rel. Hum. 4pm (%)	58	54	51	46	48	51	52	54	55	53	58	61	53

Note: Figures cover the years 1949-1995; Tr = Trace amounts (<0.05 in. of rain; <0.5 in. of snow)
Source: National Climatic Data Center, International Station Meteorological Climate Summary, 9/96

Weather Conditions

Temperature			Daytime Sky			Precipitation		
5°F & below	32°F & below	90°F & above	Clear	Partly cloudy	Cloudy	0.01 inch or more precip.	0.1 inch or more snow/ice	Thunder-storms
11	134	18	69	151	145	126	26	20

Note: Figures are average number of days per year and cover the years 1949-1995
Source: National Climatic Data Center, International Station Meteorological Climate Summary, 9/96

HAZARDOUS WASTE

Superfund Sites

South Windsor has no sites on the EPA's Superfund Final National Priorities List. There are a total of 1,323 Superfund sites on the list in the U.S. *U.S. Environmental Protection Agency, Final National Priorities List, March 18, 2016*

AIR & WATER QUALITY

Air Quality Trends: Ozone

	1990	1995	2000	2005	2010	2011	2012	2013	2014
MSA[1]	0.103	0.097	0.082	0.094	0.079	0.073	0.080	0.080	0.078

Note: (1) Data covers the Hartford-West Hartford-East Hartford, CT Metropolitan Statistical Area—see Appendix B for areas included. The values shown are the composite ozone concentration averages among trend sites based on the highest fourth daily maximum 8-hour concentration in parts per million. These trends are based on sites having an adequate record of monitoring data during the trend period. Data from exceptional events are included.

Source: U.S. Environmental Protection Agency, Air Quality Monitoring Information, "Air Quality Trends by City, 1990-2014"

Air Quality Index

Area	Percent of Days when Air Quality was...[2]					AQI Statistics[2]	
	Good	Moderate	Unhealthy for Sensitive Groups	Unhealthy	Very Unhealthy	Maximum	Median
MSA[1]	62.7	35.3	1.9	0.0	0.0	122	43

Note: (1) Data covers the Hartford-West Hartford-East Hartford, CT Metropolitan Statistical Area—see Appendix B for areas included; (2) Based on 365 days with AQI data in 2015. Air Quality Index (AQI) is an index for reporting daily air quality. EPA calculates the AQI for five major air pollutants regulated by the Clean Air Act: ground-level ozone, particle pollution (aka particulate matter), carbon monoxide, sulfur dioxide, and nitrogen dioxide. The AQI runs from 0 to 500. The higher the AQI value, the greater the level of air pollution and the greater the health concern. There are six AQI categories: "Good" AQI is between 0 and 50. Air quality is considered satisfactory; "Moderate" AQI is between 51 and 100. Air quality is acceptable; "Unhealthy for Sensitive Groups" When AQI values are between 101 and 150, members of sensitive groups may experience health effects; "Unhealthy" When AQI values are between 151 and 200 everyone may begin to experience health effects; "Very Unhealthy" AQI values between 201 and 300 trigger a health alert; "Hazardous" AQI values over 300 trigger warnings of emergency conditions (not shown).

Source: U.S. Environmental Protection Agency, Air Quality Index Report, 2015

Air Quality Index Pollutants

Area	Percent of Days when AQI Pollutant was...[2]					
	Carbon Monoxide	Nitrogen Dioxide	Ozone	Sulfur Dioxide	Particulate Matter 2.5	Particulate Matter 10
MSA[1]	0.0	9.0	34.5	0.0	56.4	0.0

Note: (1) Data covers the Hartford-West Hartford-East Hartford, CT Metropolitan Statistical Area—see Appendix B for areas included; (2) Based on 365 days with AQI data in 2015. The Air Quality Index (AQI) is an index for reporting daily air quality. EPA calculates the AQI for five major air pollutants regulated by the Clean Air Act: ground-level ozone, particle pollution (also known as particulate matter), carbon monoxide, sulfur dioxide, and nitrogen dioxide. The AQI runs from 0 to 500. The higher the AQI value, the greater the level of air pollution and the greater the health concern.

Source: U.S. Environmental Protection Agency, Air Quality Index Report, 2015

Maximum Air Pollutant Concentrations: Particulate Matter, Ozone, CO and Lead

	Particulate Matter 10 (ug/m^3)	Particulate Matter 2.5 Wtd AM (ug/m^3)	Particulate Matter 2.5 24-Hr (ug/m^3)	Ozone (ppm)	Carbon Monoxide (ppm)	Lead (ug/m^3)
MSA[1] Level	25	8.1	22	0.08	1	n/a
NAAQS[2]	150	15	35	0.075	9	0.15
Met NAAQS[2]	Yes	Yes	Yes	No	Yes	n/a

Note: (1) Data covers the Hartford-West Hartford-East Hartford, CT Metropolitan Statistical Area—see Appendix B for areas included; Data from exceptional events are included; (2) National Ambient Air Quality Standards; ppm = parts per million; ug/m^3 = micrograms per cubic meter; n/a not available.

Concentrations: Particulate Matter 10 (coarse particulate)—highest second maximum 24-hour concentration; Particulate Matter 2.5 Wtd AM (fine particulate)—highest weighted annual mean concentration; Particulate Matter 2.5 24-Hour (fine particulate)—highest 98th percentile 24-hour concentration; Ozone—highest fourth daily maximum 8-hour concentration; Carbon Monoxide—highest second maximum non-overlapping 8-hour concentration; Lead—maximum running 3-month average

Source: U.S. Environmental Protection Agency, Air Quality Monitoring Information, "Air Quality Statistics by City, 2014"

Maximum Air Pollutant Concentrations: Nitrogen Dioxide and Sulfur Dioxide

	Nitrogen Dioxide AM (ppb)	Nitrogen Dioxide 1-Hr (ppb)	Sulfur Dioxide AM (ppb)	Sulfur Dioxide 1-Hr (ppb)	Sulfur Dioxide 24-Hr (ppb)
MSA[1] Level	14	51	n/a	7	n/a
NAAQS[2]	53	100	30	75	140
Met NAAQS[2]	Yes	Yes	n/a	Yes	n/a

Note: (1) Data covers the Hartford-West Hartford-East Hartford, CT Metropolitan Statistical Area—see Appendix B for areas included; Data from exceptional events are included; (2) National Ambient Air Quality Standards; ppm = parts per million; ug/m^3 = micrograms per cubic meter; n/a not available.
Concentrations: Nitrogen Dioxide AM—highest arithmetic mean concentration; Nitrogen Dioxide 1-Hr—highest 98th percentile 1-hour daily maximum concentration; Sulfur Dioxide AM—highest annual mean concentration; Sulfur Dioxide 1-Hr—highest 99th percentile 1-hour daily maximum concentration; Sulfur Dioxide 24-Hr—highest second maximum 24-hour concentration
Source: U.S. Environmental Protection Agency, Air Quality Monitoring Information, "Air Quality Statistics by City, 2014"

Drinking Water

Water System Name	Pop. Served	Primary Water Source Type	Violations[1]	
			Health Based	Monitoring/ Reporting
CTWC-Northern Reg-Western System	85,126	Surface	0	1

Note: (1) Based on violation data from January 1, 2015 to December 31, 2015 (includes unresolved violations from earlier years)
Source: U.S. Environmental Protection Agency, Office of Ground Water and Drinking Water, Safe Drinking Water Information System (based on data extracted April 29, 2016)

Westport, Connecticut

Background

Westport is a historic coastal town located along the Long Island Sound in Fairfield County, Connecticut. With an area of 33 square miles, it's 47 miles northeast of New York City. The town is bordered by Norwalk to the west, Weston to the north, Wilton to the northwest, Fairfield to the east, and Long Island Sound sits to the south.

The earliest identified inhabitants date back 7,500 years. Archaeological data shows that during this time the Pequot tribe was living in the area, which they called Machamux. The first colonialists—the so-called Bankside Farmers, arrived in 1693, following cattle herds to the isolated area. Westport played a role in the Revolutionary War when, on April 25, 1777, British forces landed on Compo Beach in an attempt to destroy the Continental Army's military supplies at nearby Danbury. Minutemen from Westport launched a successful offensive, and today a statue on Compo Beach commemorates this attack.

As the settlement grew the name also changed. It was briefly known as Bankside, then officially named Green's Farm in 1732 in honor of Bankside farmer John Green, and finally changed to the Town of Westport when it was incorporated in 1835. At that time it included lands from Fairfield, Weston, and Norwalk. Daniel Nash led the campaign for Westport's incorporation, to take economic advantage of its seaport, instead of neighboring seaports. For many decades, Westport was a prosperous agricultural community and known as a leading onion-growing center in the United States. It was also a shipping hub for the onion industry and other agricultural goods. The collapse of Westport's onion industry due to blight led to the emergence of mills and factories as the replacement industry. Westport's industrial history can be broken into 3 distinct periods—farming, industry and manufacturing, and professional services.

Cultural expansion in Westport started significantly around 1910 as the area drew artists, musicians, and authors to the seaside, such as notable author F. Scott Fitzgerald who moved to Westport to escape the commuting demands of the business class. Westport's roots as an artists' hub and creative haven can be traced back to the early 20th century, when the industrialization in nearby New York City encouraged many of the city's artists and writers to escape to the seaside community. During this time Westport emerged from its origins as a farming community toward a suburban development catering to the creative class.

Westport continued to draw baby boomers from New York to its suburbs as its reputation as an artist's haven and cultural town grew. The 1950s to the 1970s saw tremendous growth, facilitated by how easy it was to commute from New York City to the rolling hills and natural beauty of Westport. Also during this time, Westport's commercial and retail offerings grew to accommodate chic New Yorkers and a reputable school system was developed. Today, the school district is comprised of one public high school, two middle schools, and five elementary schools. There are also several options for private school in Westport. Much of the artistic charm of early Westport is captured in the stylistic and unique shops and restaurants that are part of present-day Westport.

Westport is a quintessential seaside town in New England. Its proximity to the Atlantic Ocean coupled with its location on the Long Island Sound, allows Westport to offer land and sea activities alike. Sherwood Island State Park is on Long Island Sound and includes beach access as part of its 234-acre sprawl. Compo Beach and Burying Hill beach are municipal beaches from which, on a clear day, the New York City skyline can be seen.

Westport is home to several scientific institutions and public museums. The Rolnick Observatory, operated by the Westport Astronomical Society, is located on a former Nike missile site. Earthplace, The Nature Discovery Center, is a natural history museum, nature center, and wildlife sanctuary dedicated to public education, preservation, and conservation. It maintains a 62-acre open space wildlife sanctuary with trails, public nature education programs, a water quality monitoring program, an interactive nature discovery area, a nursery school, and a summer camp for youth.

Westport experiences a climate typical of the coastal northeastern United States. Highs in summer reach into the 80s with humidity, and winter lows drop into the teens with about 24 inches of average snowfall. Westport sees about 175 days of sunshine, and about 45 inches of rainfall, per year.

Rankings

Business/Finance Rankings

- The personal finance site NerdWallet analyzed 183 American metropolitan areas with populations over 250,000 and more than 15,000 businesses to rank where entrepreneurs find the most success. Criteria included area economy, annual income, housing cost, unemployment rate, and the success rate of area businesses. Bridgeport* ranked #3. *www.nerdwallet.com, "Best Places to Start a Business," April 27, 2015*
- TransUnion ranked the nation's metro areas by average credit score, calculated on the VantageScore system, developed by the three major credit-reporting bureaus—TransUnion, Experian, and Equifax. The Bridgeport* metro area was among the ten cities with the highest collective credit score, meaning that its residents posed the lowest average consumer credit risk. *www.usatoday.com, "Metro Areas' Average Credit Rating Revealed," February 7, 2013*
- Based on the U.S. Department of Labor's Occupational Information Network Data Collection Program, the Brookings Institution defined job opportunities for STEM workers at various levels of educational attainment. The Bridgeport* metro area was one of the ten metro areas where workers in low-education-level STEM jobs earn the lowest relative wages. *www.brookings.edu, "The Hidden Stem Economy," June 10, 2013*
- Metro areas with the largest gap in income between rich and poor residents were identified by 24/7 Wall Street using the U.S. Census Bureau's 2013 American Community Survey. The Bridgeport* metro area placed #1 among metro areas with the widest wealth gap between rich and poor. *247wallst.com, "20 Cities with the Widest Gap between the Rich and Poor," July 8, 2015*
- The Brookings Institution ranked the 100 largest metro areas in the U.S. based on income inequality. Bridgeport* was ranked #1 (#1 = greatest ineqality). Criteria: the "95/20 ratio," a figure representing the income at which a household earns more than 95 percent of all other households, divided by the income at which a household earns more than only 20 percent of all other households. *Brookings Institution, "Income Inequality, 100 Largest U.S. Metro Areas, 2007-2014," January 14, 2016*
- *Forbes* ranked the largest metro areas in the U.S. in terms of the "Best Cities for Young Professionals." The Bridgeport* metro area ranked #12 out of 15. Criteria: job growth; unemployment rate; median salary of college graduates age 24 to 34; cost of living; number of small businesses per capita; number of large companies; percentage of population 25 years of age and older with college degrees. *Forbes.com, "America's 15 Best Cities for Young Professionals," August 18, 2014*
- The finance site *24/7 Wall St.* identified the metropolitan areas that have the smallest and largest pay disparities between men and women, comparing the median earnings for the past 12 months of both men and women working full-time in the country's 100 largest metropolitan statistical areas. Of the ten worst-paying metros for women, the Bridgeport* metro area ranked #8. *24/7 Wall St., "The Best (and Worst) Paying Cities for Women," March 6, 2015*
- The Bridgeport* metro area appeared on the Milken Institute "2015 Best Performing Cities" list. Rank: #166 out of 200 large metro areas. Criteria: job growth; wage and salary growth; high-tech output growth. *Milken Institute, "Best-Performing Cities 2015," December 2015*

Education Rankings

- Bridgeport* was identified as one of America's "smartest" metropolitan areas by *The Business Journals*. The area ranked #3 out of 10. Criteria: percentage of adults (25 and older) with high school diplomas, bachelor's degrees and graduate degrees. *The Business Journals, "Where the Brainpower Is: Exclusive U.S. Rankings, Insights," February 27, 2014*
- Personal finance website *WalletHub* analyzed the 150 largest U.S. metropolitan statistical areas to determine where the most educated Americans are choosing to settle. Criteria: education quality and attainment gap; education levels; percentage of workers with degrees; public school rankings; quality and size of each metro area's universities. Bridgeport* was ranked #21 (#1 = most educated city). *www.WalletHub.com, "2015's Most and Least Educated Cities*

Environmental Rankings

- The Bridgeport* metro area came in at #152 for the relative comfort of its climate on Sperling's list of "chill cities," as measured by the Sperling Heat Index. All 361 metro areas are included. Criteria included daytime high temperatures, nighttime low temperatures, dew point, and relative humidity at the high temperatures. *www.bertsperling.com, "Sperling's Chill Cities," July 18, 2013*

- Sperling's BestPlaces assessed 379 metropolitan areas of the United States for the likelihood of dangerously extreme weather events or earthquakes. In general the Southeast and South-Central regions have the highest risk of weather extremes and earthquakes, while the Pacific Northwest enjoys the lowest risk. Of the least risky metropolitan areas, the Bridgeport* metro area was ranked #159. *www.bestplaces.net, "Safest Places from Natural Disasters," April 2011*

- Bridgeport* was identified as one of America's dirtiest metro areas by *Forbes.* The area ranked #4 out of 20. Criteria: air quality; water quality; toxic releases; superfund sites. *Forbes, "America's 20 Dirtiest Cities," December 10, 2012*

Health/Fitness Rankings

- Analysts who tracked obesity rates in 100 of the nation's most populous areas found that the Bridgeport* metro area was one of the ten communities where residents were least likely to be obese, defined as a BMI score of 30 or above. *www.gallup.com, "Colorado Springs Residents Least Likely to Be Obese," May 28, 2015*

- *Business Insider* reported Trulia's analysis of the 100 largest U.S. metro areas to identify the nation's best cities for weight loss, based on healthful food options, access to outdoor activities, weight-loss centers, gyms, and opportunities to bike or walk to work. Bridgeport* ranked #2. *Businessinsider.com, "These Are the Best US Cities for Weight loss," January 17, 2013*

- Bridgeport* was identified as a "2016 Spring Allergy Capital." The area ranked #69 out of 100. Three groups of factors were used to identify the most severe cities for people with allergies during the spring season: annual pollen levels; medicine utilization; access to board-certified allergists. *Asthma and Allergy Foundation of America, "Spring Allergy Capitals 2016"*

- Bridgeport* was identified as a "2015 Asthma Capital." The area ranked #36 out of the nation's 100 largest metropolitan areas. Criteria: estimated prevalence; self-reported prevalence; crude death rate for asthma; annual pollen score; annual air quality; public smoking laws; number of board-certified asthma specialists; school inhaler access laws; rescue medication use; controller medication use; ER visits for asthma; uninsured rate; poverty rate. *Asthma and Allergy Foundation of America, "Asthma Capitals 2015"*

- The Bridgeport* metro area ranked #29 out of 190 in The Gallup-Healthways Well-Being Index. Criteria: purpose; social well being; financial health; community and physical health. Results are based on telephone interviews with adults, aged 18 and older, living in metropolitan areas in the 50 U.S. states and the District of Columbia. *Gallup-Healthways, "State of American Well-Being," February 23, 2016*

Real Estate Rankings

- The Bridgeport* metro area was identified as one of the 20 worst housing markets in the U.S. in 2015. The area ranked #15 out of 179 markets. Criteria: year-over-year change of median sales price of existing single-family homes between the 4th quarter of 2014 and the 4th quarter of 2015. *National Association of Realtors®, Median Sales Price of Existing Single-Family Homes for Metropolitan Areas, 4th Quarter 2015*

- The Bridgeport* metro area was identified as one of the 10 worst condo markets in the U.S. in 2015. The area ranked #4 out of 61 markets. Criteria: year-over-year change of median sales price of existing apartment condo-coop homes between the 4th quarter of 2014 and the 4th quarter of 2015. *National Association of Realtors®, Median Sales Price of Existing Apartment Condo-Coop Homes for Metropolitan Areas, 4th Quarter 2015*

- Bridgeport* was ranked #192 out of 225 metro areas in terms of housing affordability in 2015 by the National Association of Home Builders (#1 = most affordable). Criteria: the share of homes sold in that area affordable to a family earning the local median income, based on standard mortgage underwriting criteria. *National Association of Home Builders®, NAHB-Wells Fargo Housing Opportunity Index, 4th Quarter 2015*

Safety Rankings

- The National Insurance Crime Bureau ranked 380 metro areas in the U.S. in terms of per capita rates of vehicle theft. The Bridgeport* metro area ranked #203 (#1 = highest rate). Criteria: number of vehicle theft offenses per 100,000 inhabitants in 2014. *National Insurance Crime Bureau, "Hot Spots 2014," June 24, 2015*

Seniors/Retirement Rankings

- From its Best Cities for Successful Aging indexes, the Milken Institute generated rankings for metropolitan areas, weighing data in eight categories—health care, wellness, living arrangements, transportation, financial characteristics, education and employment opportunities, community engagement, and overall livability. The Bridgeport* metro area was ranked #10 overall in the large metro area category. *Milken Institute, "Best Cities for Successful Aging, 2014"*

Women/Minorities Rankings

- *24/7 Wall St.* compared median earnings over a 12-month period for men and women who worked full-time, year-round, and employment composition by sector to identify the worst-paying cities for women. Of the largest 100 U.S. metropolitan areas, Bridgeport* was ranked #8 in pay disparity. *24/7 Wall St., "The Best (and Worst) Paying Cities for Women," March 6, 2015*

Miscellaneous Rankings

- The National Alliance to End Homelessness ranked the 100 most populous metro areas with the highest rate of homelessness. The Bridgeport* metro area ranked #72. Criteria: number of homeless people per 10,000 population in 2011. *National Alliance to End Homelessness, The State of Homelessness in America 2012*

Westport is located within the Bridgeport-Stamford-Norwalk, CT Metropolitan Statistical Area.

Business Environment

CITY FINANCES

City Government Finances

Component	2012 ($000)	2012 ($ per capita)
Total Revenues	231,019	8,753
Total Expenditures	183,554	6,955
Debt Outstanding	142,626	5,404
Cash and Securities[1]	350,603	13,284

Note: (1) Cash and security holdings of a government at the close of its fiscal year, including those of its dependent agencies, utilities, and liquor stores.
Source: U.S Census Bureau, State & Local Government Finances 2012

City Government Revenue by Source

Source	2012 ($000)	2012 ($ per capita)
General Revenue		
From Federal Government	408	15
From State Government	6,981	264
From Local Governments	637	24
Taxes		
Property	165,269	6,262
Sales and Gross Receipts	0	0
Personal Income	0	0
Corporate Income	0	0
Motor Vehicle License	0	0
Other Taxes	3,112	117
Current Charges	18,922	716
Liquor Store	0	0
Utility	0	0
Employee Retirement	34,166	1,294

Source: U.S Census Bureau, State & Local Government Finances 2012

City Government Expenditures by Function

Function	2012 ($000)	2012 ($ per capita)	2012 (%)
General Direct Expenditures			
Air Transportation	0	0	0.0
Corrections	0	0	0.0
Education	103,776	3,932	56.5
Employment Security Administration	0	0	0.0
Financial Administration	2,738	103	1.4
Fire Protection	10,113	383	5.5
General Public Buildings	1,444	54	0.7
Governmental Administration, Other	1,451	54	0.7
Health	1,881	71	1.0
Highways	4,665	176	2.5
Hospitals	0	0	0.0
Housing and Community Development	0	0	0.0
Interest on General Debt	6,065	229	3.3
Judicial and Legal	728	27	0.3
Libraries	5,274	199	2.8
Parking	1,776	67	0.9
Parks and Recreation	4,394	166	2.3
Police Protection	7,885	298	4.2
Public Welfare	587	22	0.3
Sewerage	2,303	87	1.2
Solid Waste Management	1,797	68	0.9
Veterans' Services	0	0	0.0
Liquor Store	0	0	0.0
Utility	241	9	0.1
Employee Retirement	15,419	584	8.4

Source: U.S Census Bureau, State & Local Government Finances 2012

DEMOGRAPHICS

Population Growth

Area	1990 Census	2000 Census	2010 Census	2014* Estimate	Population Growth (%) 1990-2014	Population Growth (%) 2010-2014
City	24,410	25,749	26,391	27,055	10.8	2.5
MSA[1]	827,645	882,567	916,829	934,215	12.9	1.9
U.S.	248,709,873	281,421,906	308,745,538	314,107,084	26.3	1.7

Note: (1) Figures cover the Bridgeport-Stamford-Norwalk, CT Metropolitan Statistical Area—see Appendix B for areas included; (*) 2010-2014 5-year estimated population
Source: U.S. Census Bureau, 1990 Census, Census 2000, Census 2010, 2010-2014 American Community Survey 5-Year Estimates

Household Size

Area	Persons in Household (%) One	Two	Three	Four	Five	Six	Seven or More	Average Household Size
City	18.9	32.9	17.7	19.5	9.1	1.0	0.5	2.81
MSA[1]	25.4	30.3	16.9	16.6	7.2	2.2	1.0	2.74
U.S.	27.5	33.5	15.8	13.1	6.0	2.3	1.4	2.64

Note: (1) Figures cover the Bridgeport-Stamford-Norwalk, CT Metropolitan Statistical Area—see Appendix B for areas included
Source: U.S. Census Bureau, 2010-2014 American Community Survey 5-Year Estimates

Race

Area	White Alone[2] (%)	Black Alone[2] (%)	Asian Alone[2] (%)	AIAN[3] Alone[2] (%)	NHOPI[4] Alone[2] (%)	Other Race Alone[2] (%)	Two or More Races (%)
City	90.0	0.8	6.0	0.1	0.0	0.8	2.2
MSA[1]	74.3	11.1	4.9	0.2	0.0	7.1	2.4
U.S.	73.8	12.6	5.0	0.8	0.2	4.7	2.9

Note: (1) Figures cover the Bridgeport-Stamford-Norwalk, CT Metropolitan Statistical Area—see Appendix B for areas included; (2) Alone is defined as not being in combination with one or more other races; (3) American Indian and Alaska Native; (4) Native Hawaiian and Other Pacific Islander
Source: U.S. Census Bureau, 2010-2014 American Community Survey 5-Year Estimates

Hispanic or Latino Origin

Area	Total (%)	Mexican (%)	Puerto Rican (%)	Cuban (%)	Other (%)
City	4.6	0.8	1.1	0.4	2.3
MSA[1]	17.9	2.1	5.9	0.4	9.4
U.S.	16.9	10.8	1.6	0.6	3.8

Note: Persons of Hispanic or Latino origin can be of any race; (1) Figures cover the Bridgeport-Stamford-Norwalk, CT Metropolitan Statistical Area—see Appendix B for areas included
Source: U.S. Census Bureau, 2010-2014 American Community Survey 5-Year Estimates

Ancestry

Area	German	Irish	English	American	Italian	Polish	French[2]	Scottish	Dutch
City	11.7	16.7	11.5	7.1	17.7	7.7	3.1	3.1	1.7
MSA[1]	9.2	14.8	8.0	4.4	17.6	5.4	2.5	1.8	0.8
U.S.	14.9	10.8	8.0	7.1	5.5	3.0	2.7	1.7	1.4

Note: Figures are the percentage of the total population reporting a particular ancestry. The nine most commonly reported ancestries in the U.S. are shown. Figures include multiple ancestries (e.g. if a person reported being Irish and Italian, they were included in both columns); (1) Figures cover the Bridgeport-Stamford-Norwalk, CT Metropolitan Statistical Area—see Appendix B for areas included; (2) Excludes Basque
Source: U.S. Census Bureau, 2010-2014 American Community Survey 5-Year Estimates

Foreign-Born Population

Area	Percent of Population Born in								
	Any Foreign Country	Asia	Mexico	Europe	Carribean	Central America[2]	South America	Africa	Canada
City	12.4	5.1	0.4	4.1	0.2	0.3	0.7	0.4	1.0
MSA[1]	20.5	3.9	1.2	4.7	3.2	2.2	4.3	0.6	0.4
U.S.	13.1	3.8	3.7	1.5	1.2	1.0	0.9	0.6	0.3

Note: (1) Figures cover the Bridgeport-Stamford-Norwalk, CT Metropolitan Statistical Area—see Appendix B for areas included; (2) Excludes Mexico.
Source: U.S. Census Bureau, 2010-2014 American Community Survey 5-Year Estimates

Marital Status

Area	Never Married	Now Married[2]	Separated	Widowed	Divorced
City	22.5	62.3	0.9	4.9	9.4
MSA[1]	32.3	51.2	1.4	5.8	9.4
U.S.	32.5	48.4	2.2	5.9	10.9

Note: Figures are percentages and cover the population 15 years of age and older; (1) Figures cover the Bridgeport-Stamford-Norwalk, CT Metropolitan Statistical Area—see Appendix B for areas included; (2) Excludes separated
Source: U.S. Census Bureau, 2010-2014 American Community Survey 5-Year Estimates

Disability Status

Area	All Ages	Under 18 Years Old	18 to 64 Years Old	65 Years and Over
City	6.4	3.1	3.7	21.3
MSA[1]	8.8	3.1	6.4	30.2
U.S.	12.3	4.1	10.2	36.3

Note: Figures show percent of the civilian noninstitutionalized population that reported having a disability. Disability status is determined from from six types of difficulty: vision, hearing, cognitive, ambulatory, self-care, and independent living. For children under 5 years old, hearing and vision difficulty are used to determine disability status. For children between the ages of 5 and 14, disability status is determined from hearing, vision, cognitive, ambulatory, and self-care difficulties. For people aged 15 years and older, they are considered to have a disability if they have difficulty with any one of the six difficulty types; (1) Figures cover the Bridgeport-Stamford-Norwalk, CT Metropolitan Statistical Area—see Appendix B for areas included.
Source: U.S. Census Bureau, 2010-2014 American Community Survey 5-Year Estimates

Age

Area	Percent of Population									Median Age
	Under Age 5	Age 5–19	Age 20–34	Age 35–44	Age 45–54	Age 55–64	Age 65–74	Age 75–84	Age 85+	
City	4.9	25.9	6.9	11.7	19.6	14.8	9.1	5.2	2.1	45.3
MSA[1]	5.9	21.0	17.4	13.5	16.1	12.3	7.3	4.4	2.2	39.6
U.S.	6.4	19.9	20.6	13.0	14.1	12.3	7.6	4.3	1.9	37.4

Note: (1) Figures cover the Bridgeport-Stamford-Norwalk, CT Metropolitan Statistical Area—see Appendix B for areas included
Source: U.S. Census Bureau, 2010-2014 American Community Survey 5-Year Estimates

Gender

Area	Males	Females	Males per 100 Females
City	12,964	14,091	92.0
MSA[1]	454,762	479,453	94.9
U.S.	154,515,159	159,591,925	96.8

Note: (1) Figures cover the Bridgeport-Stamford-Norwalk, CT Metropolitan Statistical Area—see Appendix B for areas included
Source: U.S. Census Bureau, 2010-2014 American Community Survey 5-Year Estimates

Religious Groups by Family

Area	Catholic	Baptist	Non-Den.	Methodist[2]	Lutheran	LDS[3]	Pentecostal	Presbyterian[4]	Muslim[5]	Judaism
MSA[1]	44.1	1.9	2.3	2.0	0.8	0.5	1.1	3.0	0.5	1.9
U.S.	19.1	9.3	4.0	4.0	2.3	2.0	1.9	1.6	0.8	0.7

Note: Figures are the number of adherents as a percentage of the total population; (1) Figures cover the Bridgeport-Stamford-Norwalk, CT Metropolitan Statistical Area—see Appendix B for areas included; (2) Methodist/Pietist; (3) Latter Day Saints; (4) Reformed; (5) Figures are estimates
Source: Association of Statisticians of American Religious Bodies, 2010 U.S. Religion Census: Religious Congregations & Membership Study

Religious Groups by Tradition

Area	Catholic	Evangelical Protestant	Mainline Protestant	Other Tradition	Black Protestant	Orthodox
MSA[1]	44.1	5.1	9.0	3.5	0.4	1.0
U.S.	19.1	16.2	7.3	4.3	1.6	0.3

Note: Figures are the number of adherents as a percentage of the total population; (1) Figures cover the Bridgeport-Stamford-Norwalk, CT Metropolitan Statistical Area—see Appendix B for areas included
Source: Association of Statisticians of American Religious Bodies, 2010 U.S. Religion Census: Religious Congregations & Membership Study

ECONOMY

Gross Metropolitan Product

Area	2013	2014	2015	2016	Rank[2]
MSA[1]	93.5	96.7	100.5	105.1	37

Note: Figures are in billions of dollars; (1) Figures cover the Bridgeport-Stamford-Norwalk, CT Metropolitan Statistical Area—see Appendix B for areas included; (2) Rank is based on 2016 data and ranges from 1 to 381
Source: The U.S. Conference of Mayors, U.S. Metro Economies: GMP and Employment 2014-2016, June 2015

Economic Growth

Area	2011-13 (%)	2014 (%)	2015 (%)	2016 (%)	Rank[2]
MSA[1]	1.3	1.7	2.6	2.6	159
U.S.	2.2	2.4	2.3	2.9	–

Note: Figures are real gross metropolitan product (GMP) growth rates and represent annual average percent change; (1) Figures cover the Bridgeport-Stamford-Norwalk, CT Metropolitan Statistical Area—see Appendix B for areas included; (2) Rank is based on 2016 data and ranges from 1 to 381
Source: The U.S. Conference of Mayors, U.S. Metro Economies: GMP and Employment 2014-2016, June 2015

Metropolitan Area Exports

Area	2009	2010	2011	2012	2013	2014	Rank[2]
MSA[1]	8,450.9	9,339.6	11,250.4	10,332.6	11,055.1	12,103.0	26

Note: Figures are in millions of dollars; (1) Figures cover the Bridgeport-Stamford-Norwalk, CT Metropolitan Statistical Area—see Appendix B for areas included; (2) Rank is based on 2014 data and ranges from 1 to 385
Source: U.S. Department of Commerce, International Trade Administration, Office of Trade & Industry Information, Manufacturing & Services, data extracted March 10, 2016

Building Permits

Area	Single-Family			Multi-Family			Total		
	2014	2015p	Pct. Chg.	2014	2015p	Pct. Chg.	2014	2015p	Pct. Chg.
City	109	79	-27.5	54	12	-77.8	163	91	-44.2
MSA[1]	987	781	-20.9	902	1,802	99.8	1,889	2,583	36.7
U.S.	640,300	690,800	7.9	411,800	487,600	18.4	1,052,100	1,178,400	12.0

Note: (1) Figures cover the Bridgeport-Stamford-Norwalk, CT Metropolitan Statistical Area—see Appendix B for areas included; Figures represent new, privately-owned housing units authorized (unadjusted data); All permit data are based on estimates with imputation; (p) preliminary data.
Source: U.S. Census Bureau, Manufacturing, Mining, and Construction Statistics, Building Permits, 2014, 2015

Bankruptcy Filings

Area	Business Filings 2014	Business Filings 2015	Business Filings % Chg.	Nonbusiness Filings 2014	Nonbusiness Filings 2015	Nonbusiness Filings % Chg.
Fairfield County	91	83	-8.8	1,506	1,393	-7.5
U.S.	26,983	24,735	-8.3	909,812	819,760	-9.9

Note: Business filings include Chapter 7, Chapter 11, Chapter 12, and Chapter 13; Nonbusiness filings include Chapter 7, Chapter 11, and Chapter 13
Source: Administrative Office of the U.S. Courts, Business and Nonbusiness Bankruptcy, County Cases Commenced by Chapter of the Bankruptcy Code, During the 12- Month Period Ending December 31, 2014 and Business and Nonbusiness Bankruptcy, County Cases Commenced by Chapter of the Bankruptcy Code, During the 12- Month Period Ending December 31, 2015

Housing Vacancy Rates

Area	Gross Vacancy Rate[2] (%)			Year-Round Vacancy Rate[3] (%)			Rental Vacancy Rate[4] (%)			Homeowner Vacancy Rate[5] (%)		
	2013	2014	2015	2013	2014	2015	2013	2014	2015	2013	2014	2015
MSA[1]	10.2	10.8	11.3	9.4	9.2	10.1	5.1	5.6	7.1	2.6	1.6	1.8
U.S.	13.6	13.4	12.9	10.7	10.4	10.0	8.3	7.6	7.1	2.0	1.9	1.8

Note: (1) Figures cover the Bridgeport-Stamford-Norwalk, CT Metropolitan Statistical Area—see Appendix B for areas included; (2) The percentage of the total housing inventory that is vacant; (3) The percentage of the housing inventory (excluding seasonal units) that is year-round vacant; (4) The percentage of rental inventory that is vacant for rent; (5) The percentage of homeowner inventory that is vacant for sale
Source: U.S. Census Bureau, Housing Vacancies and Homeownership Annual Statistics: 2015

INCOME

Income

Area	Per Capita ($)	Median Household ($)	Average Household ($)
City	90,945	151,771	255,021
MSA[1]	49,688	83,163	135,743
U.S.	28,555	53,482	74,596

Note: (1) Figures cover the Bridgeport-Stamford-Norwalk, CT Metropolitan Statistical Area—see Appendix B for areas included
Source: U.S. Census Bureau, 2010-2014 American Community Survey 5-Year Estimates

Household Income Distribution

Area	Percent of Households Earning: Under $15,000	$15,000 -24,999	$25,000 -34,999	$35,000 -49,999	$50,000 -74,999	$75,000 -99,000	$100,000 -149,999	$150,000 and up
City	4.9	3.2	3.9	3.9	9.7	10.5	13.4	50.3
MSA[1]	8.3	7.1	6.9	9.4	13.9	11.6	16.0	26.7
U.S.	12.5	10.7	10.2	13.5	17.8	12.2	13.0	10.0

Note: (1) Figures cover the Bridgeport-Stamford-Norwalk, CT Metropolitan Statistical Area—see Appendix B for areas included
Source: U.S. Census Bureau, 2010-2014 American Community Survey 5-Year Estimates

Poverty Rate

Area	All Ages	Under 18 Years Old	18 to 64 Years Old	65 Years and Over
City	4.3	3.3	4.8	4.1
MSA[1]	9.1	11.4	8.7	6.7
U.S.	15.6	21.9	14.6	9.4

Note: Figures are percentage of people whose income during the past 12 months was below the poverty level; (1) Figures cover the Bridgeport-Stamford-Norwalk, CT Metropolitan Statistical Area—see Appendix B for areas included
Source: U.S. Census Bureau, 2010-2014 American Community Survey 5-Year Estimates

EMPLOYMENT

Labor Force and Employment

Area	Civilian Labor Force			Workers Employed		
	Dec. 2014	Dec. 2015	% Chg.	Dec. 2014	Dec. 2015	% Chg.
City	12,374	12,337	-0.2	11,863	11,898	0.2
NECTA[1]	462,757	463,036	0.0	437,814	440,819	0.6
U.S.	155,521,000	157,245,000	1.1	147,190,000	149,703,000	1.7

Note: Data is not seasonally adjusted and covers workers 16 years of age and older; (1) Figures cover the Bridgeport-Stamford-Norwalk, CT New England City and Town Area—see Appendix B for areas included
Source: Bureau of Labor Statistics, Local Area Unemployment Statistics

Unemployment Rate

Area	2015											
	Jan.	Feb.	Mar.	Apr.	May	Jun.	Jul.	Aug.	Sep.	Oct.	Nov.	Dec.
City	4.8	4.7	4.5	4.1	4.2	4.1	4.1	3.9	3.7	3.7	3.6	3.6
NECTA[1]	6.4	6.7	6.3	5.6	5.4	5.2	5.4	5.3	4.9	4.7	4.7	4.8
U.S.	6.1	5.8	5.6	5.1	5.3	5.5	5.6	5.2	4.9	4.8	4.8	4.8

Note: Data is not seasonally adjusted and covers workers 16 years of age and older; (1) Figures cover the Bridgeport-Stamford-Norwalk, CT New England City and Town Area—see Appendix B for areas included
Source: Bureau of Labor Statistics, Local Area Unemployment Statistics

Employment by Occupation

Occupation Classification	City (%)	MSA[1] (%)	U.S. (%)
Management, Business, Science, and Arts	63.7	43.4	36.4
Natural Resources, Construction, and Maintenance	2.2	7.4	9.0
Production, Transportation, and Material Moving	3.2	7.1	12.1
Sales and Office	23.5	24.5	24.4
Service	7.3	17.6	18.2

Note: Figures cover employed civilians 16 years of age and older; (1) Figures cover the Bridgeport-Stamford-Norwalk, CT Metropolitan Statistical Area—see Appendix B for areas included
Source: U.S. Census Bureau, 2010-2014 American Community Survey 5-Year Estimates

Employment by Industry

Sector	NECTA[1]		U.S.
	Number of Employees	Percent of Total	Percent of Total
Construction, Mining, and Logging	12,500	3.0	5.0
Education and Health Services	72,100	17.3	15.7
Financial Activities	41,000	9.8	5.7
Government	45,800	11.0	15.5
Information	12,300	2.9	1.9
Leisure and Hospitality	42,300	10.1	10.4
Manufacturing	31,300	7.5	8.6
Other Services	17,600	4.2	3.9
Professional and Business Services	66,000	15.8	13.9
Retail Trade	50,000	12.0	11.3
Transportation, Warehousing, and Utilities	10,600	2.5	3.9
Wholesale Trade	13,800	3.3	4.1

Note: Figures are non-farm employment as of December 2015. Figures are not seasonally adjusted and include workers 16 years of age and older; (1) Figures cover the Bridgeport-Stamford-Norwalk, CT New England City and Town Area—see Appendix B for areas included; n/a not available
Source: Bureau of Labor Statistics, Current Employment Statistics, Employment, Hours, and Earnings

Occupations with Greatest Projected Employment Growth: 2012 – 2022

Occupation[1]	2012 Employment	2022 Projected Employment	Numeric Employment Change	Percent Employment Change
Personal Care Aides	23,240	32,090	8,850	38.1
Registered Nurses	35,990	41,230	5,240	14.6
Secretaries and Administrative Assistants, Except Legal, Medical, and Executive	34,530	38,640	4,110	11.9
Combined Food Preparation and Serving Workers, Including Fast Food	26,730	30,740	4,010	15.0
Retail Salespersons	53,800	57,270	3,470	6.4
General and Operations Managers	31,160	34,420	3,260	10.5
Home Health Aides	8,250	11,450	3,200	38.7
Childcare Workers	18,300	21,170	2,870	15.7
Maids and Housekeeping Cleaners	17,800	20,560	2,760	15.5
First-Line Supervisors of Office and Administrative Support Workers	26,360	28,900	2,540	9.6

Note: Projections cover Connecticut; (1) Sorted by numeric employment change
Source: www.projectionscentral.com, State Occupational Projections, 2012–2022 Long-Term Projections

Fastest Growing Occupations: 2012 – 2022

Occupation[1]	2012 Employment	2022 Projected Employment	Numeric Employment Change	Percent Employment Change
Insulation Workers, Mechanical	210	350	140	65.6
Interpreters and Translators	460	650	190	43.1
Helpers—Electricians	270	380	110	39.4
Home Health Aides	8,250	11,450	3,200	38.7
Diagnostic Medical Sonographers	1,000	1,380	380	38.3
Personal Care Aides	23,240	32,090	8,850	38.1
Physical Therapist Assistants	540	740	200	37.4
Occupational Therapy Assistants	490	670	180	35.4
Health Specialties Teachers, Postsecondary	2,810	3,770	960	34.3
Nursing Instructors and Teachers, Postsecondary	700	940	240	34.0

Note: Projections cover Connecticut; (1) Sorted by percent employment change and excludes occupations with numeric employment change less than 100
Source: www.projectionscentral.com, State Occupational Projections, 2012–2022 Long-Term Projections

Average Wages

Occupation	$/Hr.	Occupation	$/Hr.
Accountants and Auditors	41.89	Maids and Housekeeping Cleaners	12.27
Automotive Mechanics	22.23	Maintenance and Repair Workers	23.42
Bookkeepers	22.17	Marketing Managers	80.11
Carpenters	25.29	Nuclear Medicine Technologists	46.76
Cashiers	11.58	Nurses, Licensed Practical	27.02
Clerks, General Office	18.19	Nurses, Registered	37.63
Clerks, Receptionists/Information	16.69	Nursing Assistants	15.94
Clerks, Shipping/Receiving	17.32	Packers and Packagers, Hand	11.75
Computer Programmers	41.64	Physical Therapists	44.15
Computer Systems Analysts	45.62	Postal Service Mail Carriers	25.24
Computer User Support Specialists	27.07	Real Estate Brokers	n/a
Cooks, Restaurant	15.17	Retail Salespersons	15.11
Dentists	93.45	Sales Reps., Exc. Tech./Scientific	36.05
Electrical Engineers	44.69	Sales Reps., Tech./Scientific	48.83
Electricians	30.15	Secretaries, Exc. Legal/Med./Exec.	20.92
Financial Managers	75.74	Security Guards	14.12
First-Line Supervisors/Managers, Sales	23.59	Surgeons	128.44
Food Preparation Workers	14.89	Teacher Assistants*	16.24
General and Operations Managers	81.02	Teachers, Elementary School*	38.04
Hairdressers/Cosmetologists	14.75	Teachers, Secondary School*	39.42
Internists	100.52	Telemarketers	18.73
Janitors and Cleaners	15.35	Truck Drivers, Heavy/Tractor-Trailer	23.76
Landscaping/Groundskeeping Workers	17.04	Truck Drivers, Light/Delivery Svcs.	17.38
Lawyers	87.43	Waiters and Waitresses	11.87

Note: Wage data covers the New England City and Town Area—see Appendix B for areas included; (*) Hourly wages for elementary/secondary school teachers and teacher assistants were calculated by the editors from annual wage data based on a 40 hour work week; n/a not available.
Source: Bureau of Labor Statistics, Metro Area Occupational Employment and Wage Estimates, May 2015

TAXES

State Corporate Income Tax Rates

State	Tax Rate (%)	Income Brackets ($)	Num. of Brackets	Financial Institution Tax Rate (%)[a]	Federal Income Tax Ded.
Connecticut	7.5 (d)	Flat rate	1	7.5 (d)	No

Note: Tax rates as of January 1, 2016; (a) Rates listed are the corporate income tax rate applied to financial institutions or excise taxes based on income. Some states have other taxes based upon the value of deposits or shares; (d) Connecticut's tax is the greater of the 7.5% tax on net income, a 0.31% tax on capital stock and surplus (maximum tax of $1 million), or $250 (the minimum tax). Plus, an additional 20% surtax applies for tax years 2012 and 2016.
Source: Federation of Tax Administrators, "State Corporate Income Tax Rates, 2016"

State Individual Income Tax Rates

State	Tax Rate (%)	Income Brackets ($)	Num. of Brackets	Personal Exempt. ($)[1]		Fed. Inc. Tax Ded.
				Single	Dependents	
Connecticut	3.0 - 6.99	10,000 - 500,000 (b)	7	14,500 (g)	None	No

Note: Tax rates as of January 1, 2016; Local- and county-level taxes are not included; n/a not applicable; (1) Married joint filers generally receive double the single exemption; (b) For joint returns, taxes are twice the tax on half the couple's income; (g) Connecticut's personal exemption incorporates a standard deduction. An additional tax credit is allowed ranging from 75% to 0% based on state adjusted gross income. Exemption amounts are phased out for higher income taxpayers until they are eliminated for households earning over $71,000.
Source: Federation of Tax Administrators, "State Individual Income Tax Rates, 2016"

Various State and Local Tax Rates

State	State and Local Sales and Use (%)	State Sales and Use (%)	Gasoline[1] (¢/gal.)	Cigarette[2] ($/pack)	Spirits[3] ($/gal.)	Wine[4] ($/gal.)	Beer[5] ($/gal.)
Connecticut	6.35	6.35	37.51	3.65	5.40 (f)	0.72 (l)	0.16

Note: All tax rates as of January 1, 2016; (1) The American Petroleum Institute has developed a methodology for determining the average tax rate on a gallon of fuel. Rates may include any of the following: excise taxes, environmental fees, storage tank fees, other fees or taxes, general sales tax, and local taxes. In states where gasoline is subject to the general sales tax, or where the fuel tax is based on the average sale price, the average rate determined by API is sensitive to changes in the price of gasoline. States that fully or partially apply general sales taxes to gasoline: CA, CO, GA, IL, IN, MI, NY; (2) The federal excise tax of $1.0066 per pack and local taxes are not included; (3) Rates are those applicable to off-premise sales of 40% alcohol by volume (a.b.v.) distilled spirits in 750ml containers. Local excise taxes are excluded; (4) Rates are those applicable to off-premise sales of 11% a.b.v. non-carbonated wine in 750ml containers; (5) Rates are those applicable to off-premise sales of 4.7% a.b.v. beer in 12 ounce containers; (f) Different rates are also applicable according to alcohol content, place of production, size of container, or place purchased (on- or off-premise or onboard airlines); (l) Different rates also applicable according to alcohol content, place of production, size of container, place purchased (on- or off-premise or on board airlines) or type of wine (carbonated, vermouth, etc.).
Source: Tax Foundation, 2016 Facts & Figures: How Does Your State Compare?

State Business Tax Climate Index Rankings

State	Overall Rank	Corporate Tax Rank	Individual Income Tax Rank	Sales Tax Rank	Unemployment Insurance Tax Rank	Property Tax Rank
Connecticut	44	33	36	29	20	49

Note: The index is a measure of how each state's tax laws affect economic performance. The lower the rank, the more favorable a state's tax system is for business. States without a given tax are given a ranking of 1. The scores/rankings for the District of Columbia do not affect other states. The 2016 index represents the tax climate as of July 1, 2015 (the beginning of Fiscal Year 2016).
Source: Tax Foundation, State Business Tax Climate Index 2016

TRANSPORTATION

Means of Transportation to Work

Area	Car/Truck/Van		Public Transportation			Bicycle	Walked	Other Means	Worked at Home
	Drove Alone	Car-pooled	Bus	Subway	Railroad				
City	61.1	2.7	0.1	0.9	18.3	0.0	2.0	0.5	14.4
MSA[1]	72.8	8.4	2.7	0.3	6.3	0.3	2.7	0.9	5.5
U.S.	76.4	9.6	2.6	1.8	0.6	0.6	2.8	1.3	4.4

Note: Figures are percentages and cover workers 16 years of age and older; (1) Figures cover the Bridgeport-Stamford-Norwalk, CT Metropolitan Statistical Area—see Appendix B for areas included
Source: U.S. Census Bureau, 2010-2014 American Community Survey 5-Year Estimates

Travel Time to Work

Area	Less Than 10 Minutes	10 to 19 Minutes	20 to 29 Minutes	30 to 44 Minutes	45 to 59 Minutes	60 to 89 Minutes	90 Minutes or More
City	11.0	25.6	13.6	17.1	5.6	12.4	14.6
MSA[1]	11.8	31.4	18.6	17.2	7.1	8.6	5.3
U.S.	13.3	29.6	21.0	20.2	7.7	5.7	2.6

Note: Figures are percentages and include workers 16 years old and over; (1) Figures cover the Bridgeport-Stamford-Norwalk, CT Metropolitan Statistical Area—see Appendix B for areas included
Source: U.S. Census Bureau, 2010-2014 American Community Survey 5-Year Estimates

Freeway Travel Time Index

Area	1985	1990	1995	2000	2005	2010	2014
Urban Area Rank[1,2]	11	9	6	4	5	6	6
Urban Area Index[1]	1.16	1.20	1.25	1.32	1.36	1.34	1.36
Average Index[3]	1.09	1.11	1.14	1.17	1.20	1.19	1.20

Note: Freeway Travel Time Index—the ratio of travel time in the peak period to the travel time at free-flow conditions. For example, a value of 1.30 indicates a 20-minute free-flow trip takes 26 minutes in the peak (20 minutes x 1.30 = 26 minutes); (1) Covers the Bridgeport-Stamford CT-NY urban area; (2) Rank is based on 101 urban areas (#1 = highest travel time index); (3) Average of 101 urban areas
Source: Texas Transportation Institute, 2015 Urban Mobility Scorecard, August 2015

Freeway Commuter Stress Index

Area	1985	1990	1995	2000	2005	2010	2014
Urban Area Rank[1,2]	17	10	8	6	5	8	7
Urban Area Index[1]	1.23	1.28	1.33	1.40	1.45	1.43	1.44
Average Index[3]	1.13	1.16	1.19	1.22	1.25	1.24	1.25

Note: The Freeway Commuter Stress Index is the same as the Freeway Travel Time Index (see table above) except that it includes only the travel in the peak directions during the peak periods; the TTI includes travel in all directions during the peak period. Thus, the CSI is more indicative of the work trip experienced by each commuter on a daily basis. (1) Covers the Bridgeport-Stamford CT-NY urban area; (2) Rank is based on 101 urban areas (#1 = highest stress index); (3) Average of 101 urban areas

Source: Texas Transportation Institute, 2015 Urban Mobility Scorecard, August 2015

Living Environment

COST OF LIVING

Cost of Living Index

Composite Index	Groceries	Housing	Utilities	Transportation	Health Care	Misc. Goods/ Services
147.1	130.8	209.8	132.1	106.3	114.5	123.0

Note: The Cost of Living Index measures regional differences in the cost of consumer goods and services, excluding taxes and non-consumer expenditures, for professional and managerial households in the top income quintile. It is based on more than 50,000 prices covering almost 60 different items for which prices are collected three times a year by chambers of commerce, economic development organizations or university applied economic centers in each participating urban area. The numbers shown should be read as a percentage above or below the national average of 100. For example, a value of 115.4 in the groceries column indicates that grocery prices are 15.4% higher than the national average. Small differences in the index numbers should not be interpreted as significant; Figures cover the Stamford CT urban area.
Source: The Council for Community and Economic Research, ACCRA Cost of Living Index, 2015

Grocery Prices

Area[1]	T-Bone Steak ($/pound)	Frying Chicken ($/pound)	Whole Milk ($/half gal.)	Eggs ($/dozen)	Orange Juice ($/64 oz.)	Coffee ($/11.5 oz.)
City[2]	12.44	1.35	2.89	3.05	4.21	5.49
Avg.	10.99	1.43	2.25	2.26	3.58	4.48
Min.	7.16	0.98	1.30	1.35	2.88	2.98
Max.	14.13	2.43	3.85	4.81	6.39	7.56

Note: (1) Values for the local area are compared with the average, minimum and maximum values for all 292 areas in the Cost of Living Index; (2) Figures cover the Stamford CT urban area; **T-Bone Steak** *(price per pound);* **Frying Chicken** *(price per pound, whole fryer);* **Whole Milk** *(half gallon carton);* **Eggs** *(price per dozen, Grade A, large);* **Orange Juice** *(64 oz. Tropicana or Florida Natural);* **Coffee** *(11.5 oz. can, vacuum-packed, Maxwell House, Hills Bros, or Folgers).*
Source: The Council for Community and Economic Research, ACCRA Cost of Living Index, 2015

Housing and Utility Costs

Area[1]	New Home Price ($)	Apartment Rent ($/month)	All Electric ($/month)	Part Electric ($/month)	Other Energy ($/month)	Telephone ($/month)
City[2]	626,189	2,199	-	147.95	111.00	29.01
Avg.	312,874	945	179.30	95.07	72.96	28.11
Min.	178,682	479	116.28	43.14	26.46	10.01
Max.	1,472,476	3,984	504.25	189.44	421.11	43.06

Note: (1) Values for the local area are compared with the average, minimum and maximum values for all 292 areas in the Cost of Living Index; (2) Figures cover the Stamford CT urban area; **New Home Price** *(2,400 sf living area, 8,000 sf lot, in urban area with full utilities);* **Apartment Rent** *(950 sf 2 bedroom/1.5 or 2 bath, unfurnished, excluding all utilities except water);* **All Electric** *(average monthly cost for an all-electric home);* **Part Electric** *(average monthly cost for a part-electric home);* **Other Energy** *(average monthly cost for natural gas, fuel oil, coal, wood, and any other forms of energy except electricity);* **Telephone** *(price includes basic monthly rate for a private residential line plus additional local usage charges incurred by a family of four).*
Source: The Council for Community and Economic Research, ACCRA Cost of Living Index, 2015

Health Care, Transportation, and Other Costs

Area[1]	Doctor ($/visit)	Dentist ($/visit)	Optometrist ($/visit)	Gasoline ($/gallon)	Beauty Salon ($/visit)	Men's Shirt ($)
City[2]	123.75	110.00	111.67	2.47	64.17	27.43
Avg.	105.15	89.02	99.78	2.38	35.30	28.10
Min.	66.87	56.09	48.53	1.95	18.91	13.38
Max.	182.34	150.36	228.33	4.09	67.91	63.80

Note: (1) Values for the local area are compared with the average, minimum and maximum values for all 292 areas in the Cost of Living Index; (2) Figures cover the Stamford CT urban area; **Doctor** *(general practitioners routine exam of an established patient);* **Dentist** *(adult teeth cleaning and periodic oral examination);* **Optometrist** *(full vision eye exam for established adult patient);* **Gasoline** *(one gallon regular unleaded, national brand, including all taxes, cash price at self-service pump if available);* **Beauty Salon** *(woman's shampoo, trim, and blow-dry);* **Men's Shirt** *(cotton/polyester dress shirt, pinpoint weave, long sleeves).*
Source: The Council for Community and Economic Research, ACCRA Cost of Living Index, 2015

HOUSING

House Price Index (HPI)

Area	National Ranking[2]	Quarterly Change (%)	One-Year Change (%)	Five-Year Change (%)
MSA[1]	242	-1.00	1.30	-0.70
U.S.[3]	-	1.45	5.76	22.85

Note: The HPI is a weighted repeat sales index. It measures average price changes in repeat sales or refinancings on the same properties. This information is obtained by reviewing repeat mortgage transactions on single-family properties whose mortgages have been purchased or securitized by Fannie Mae or Freddie Mac in January 1975; (1) Bridgeport-Stamford-Norwalk Metropolitan Statistical Area—see Appendix B for areas included; (2) Rankings are based on annual percentage change for all metro areas containing at least 15,000 transactions over the last 10 years and ranges from 1 to 266; (3) figures based on a weighted average of Census Division estimates using a seasonally adjusted, purchase-only index; all figures are for the period ending December 31, 2015

Source: Federal Housing Finance Agency, House Price Index, February 25, 2016

Median Single-Family Home Prices

Area	2013	2014	2015p	Percent Change 2014 to 2015
MSA[1]	403.0	397.6	377.7	-5.0
U.S. Average	197.4	208.9	223.9	7.2

Note: Figures are median sales prices of existing single-family homes in thousands of dollars; (p) preliminary; n/a not available; (1) Bridgeport-Stamford-Norwalk, CT Metropolitan Statistical Area—see Appendix B for areas included

Source: National Association of Realtors, Median Sales Price of Existing Single-Family Homes for Metropolitan Areas, 4th Quarter 2015

Qualifying Income Based on Median Sales Price of Existing Single-Family Homes

Area	With 5% Down ($)	With 10% Down ($)	With 20% Down ($)
MSA[1]	80,320	76,092	67,638
U.S. Average	49,535	46,928	41,714

Note: Figures are preliminary; Qualifying income is based on a mortgage rate of 4.1%. Monthly principal and interest payment is limited to 25% of income; n/a not available; (1) Bridgeport-Stamford-Norwalk, CT Metropolitan Statistical Area—see Appendix B for areas included

Source: National Association of Realtors, Qualifying Income Based on Median Sales Price of Existing Single-Family Homes for Metropolitan Areas, 4th Quarter 2015

Median Apartment Condo-Coop Home Prices

Area	2013	2014	2015p	Percent Change 2014 to 2015
MSA[1]	220.3	221.3	218.6	-1.2
U.S. Average	194.9	204.3	210.7	3.1

Note: Figures are median sales prices of existing apartment condo-coop homes in thousands of dollars; (p) preliminary; n/a not available; (1) Bridgeport-Stamford-Norwalk, CT Metropolitan Statistical Area—see Appendix B for areas included

Source: National Association of Realtors, Median Sales Price of Existing Apartment Condo-Coop Homes for Metropolitan Areas, 4th Quarter 2015

Gross Monthly Rent

Area	Under $200	$200 -299	$300 -499	$500 -749	$750 -999	$1,000 -1,499	$1,500 and up	Median ($)
City	4.0	1.4	3.1	1.8	7.0	28.2	54.5	1,690
MSA[1]	1.4	3.5	5.1	5.9	12.3	33.6	38.3	1,327
U.S.	1.5	3.2	7.4	21.0	24.1	26.9	15.9	920

Note: Figures are percentages except for Median; Gross rent is the contract rent plus the estimated average monthly cost of utilities (electricity, gas, and water and sewer) and fuels (oil, coal, kerosene, wood, etc.) if these are paid by the renter (or paid for the renter by someone else); (1) Figures cover the Bridgeport-Stamford-Norwalk, CT Metropolitan Statistical Area—see Appendix B for areas included

Source: U.S. Census Bureau, 2010-2014 American Community Survey 5-Year Estimates

Homeownership Rate

Area	2008 (%)	2009 (%)	2010 (%)	2011 (%)	2012 (%)	2013 (%)	2014 (%)	2015 (%)
MSA[1]	72.6	70.3	71.3	71.6	70.6	70.7	67.7	66.6
U.S.	67.8	67.4	66.9	66.1	65.4	65.1	64.5	63.7

Note: (1) Figures cover the Bridgeport-Stamford-Norwalk, CT Metropolitan Statistical Area—see Appendix B for areas included
Source: U.S. Census Bureau, Housing Vacancies and Homeownership Annual Statistics: 2015

Year Housing Structure Built

Area	2010 or Later	2000 -2009	1990 -1999	1980 -1989	1970 -1979	1960 -1969	1950 -1959	1940 -1949	Before 1940	Median Year
City	2.8	8.2	4.9	10.6	11.0	15.3	22.6	5.8	18.7	1962
MSA[1]	0.8	6.9	6.8	11.4	13.6	14.5	17.1	7.6	21.4	1963
U.S.	1.0	14.9	13.9	13.8	15.8	11.0	10.8	5.4	13.3	1976

Note: Figures are percentages except for Median Year; (1) Figures cover the Bridgeport-Stamford-Norwalk, CT Metropolitan Statistical Area—see Appendix B for areas included
Source: U.S. Census Bureau, 2010-2014 American Community Survey 5-Year Estimates

HEALTH

Health Risk Data

Category	MSA[1] (%)	U.S. (%)
Adults aged 18–64 who have any kind of health care coverage	83.5	79.6
Adults who reported being in good or excellent health	86.0	83.1
Adults who are current smokers	13.2	19.6
Adults who are heavy drinkers[2]	6.0	6.1
Adults who are binge drinkers[3]	19.5	16.9
Adults who are overweight (BMI 25.0 - 29.9)	39.1	35.8
Adults who are obese (BMI 30.0 - 99.8)	21.6	27.6
Adults who participated in any physical activities in the past month	78.5	77.1
Adults 50+ who have ever had a sigmoidoscopy or colonoscopy	73.3	67.3
Women aged 40+ who have had a mammogram within the past two years	76.7	74.0
Men aged 40+ who have had a PSA test within the past two years	49.6	45.2
Adults aged 65+ who have had flu shot within the past year	57.1	60.1
Adults who always wear a seatbelt	95.4	93.8

Note: Data as of 2012 unless otherwise noted; (1) Figures cover the Bridgeport-Stamford-Norwalk, CT Metropolitan Statistical Area—see Appendix B for areas included; (2) Heavy drinkers are classified as males having more than two drinks per day or females having more than one drink per day; (3) Binge drinkers are classified as males having five or more drinks on one occasion or females having four or more drinks on one occasion
Source: Centers for Disease Control and Prevention, Behaviorial Risk Factor Surveillance System, SMART: Selected Metropolitan/Micropolitan Area Risk Trends, 2012 (Note: the CDC has discontinued this dataset but will be releasing a replacement in mid-2016)

Chronic Health Indicators

Category	MSA[1] (%)	U.S. (%)
Adults who have ever been told they had a heart attack	3.2	4.5
Adults who have ever been told they had a stroke	1.8	2.9
Adults who have been told they currently have asthma	7.8	8.9
Adults who have ever been told they have arthritis	21.6	25.7
Adults who have ever been told they have diabetes[2]	7.4	9.7
Adults who have ever been told they had skin cancer	5.6	5.7
Adults who have ever been told they had any other types of cancer	6.4	6.5
Adults who have ever been told they have COPD	4.7	6.2
Adults who have ever been told they have kidney disease	2.2	2.5
Adults who have ever been told they have a form of depression	15.2	18.0

Note: Data as of 2012 unless otherwise noted; (1) Figures cover the Bridgeport-Stamford-Norwalk, CT Metropolitan Statistical Area—see Appendix B for areas included; (2) Figures do not include pregnancy-related, borderline, or pre-diabetes
Source: Centers for Disease Control and Prevention, Behaviorial Risk Factor Surveillance System, SMART: Selected Metropolitan/Micropolitan Area Risk Trends, 2012 (Note: the CDC has discontinued this dataset but will be releasing a replacement in mid-2016)

Mortality Rates for the Top 10 Causes of Death in the U.S.

ICD-10[a] Sub-Chapter	ICD-10[a] Code	Age-Adjusted Mortality Rate[1] per 100,000 population	
		County[2]	U.S.
Malignant neoplasms	C00-C97	136.2	163.6
Ischaemic heart diseases	I20-I25	79.1	102.2
Other forms of heart disease	I30-I51	53.4	50.1
Chronic lower respiratory diseases	J40-J47	25.0	41.4
Organic, including symptomatic, mental disorders	F01-F09	36.6	38.5
Cerebrovascular diseases	I60-I69	26.8	36.5
Other external causes of accidental injury	W00-X59	23.7	27.5
Other degenerative diseases of the nervous system	G30-G31	17.6	26.3
Diabetes mellitus	E10-E14	12.7	21.1
Hypertensive diseases	I10-I15	12.3	19.7

Note: (a) ICD-10 = International Classification of Diseases 10th Revision; (1) Mortality rates are a three year average covering 2012-2014; (2) Figures cover Fairfield County.
Source: Centers for Disease Control and Prevention, National Center for Health Statistics. Underlying Cause of Death 1999-2014 on CDC WONDER Online Database, released 2015.

Mortality Rates for Selected Causes of Death

ICD-10[a] Sub-Chapter	ICD-10[a] Code	Age-Adjusted Mortality Rate[1] per 100,000 population	
		County[2]	U.S.
Assault	X85-Y09	3.7	5.1
Diseases of the liver	K70-K76	8.3	13.5
Human immunodeficiency virus (HIV) disease	B20-B24	1.6	2.1
Influenza and pneumonia	J09-J18	10.3	15.2
Intentional self-harm	X60-X84	7.5	12.7
Malnutrition	E40-E46	0.6	0.9
Obesity and other hyperalimentation	E65-E68	1.1	1.9
Renal failure	N17-N19	8.6	13.0
Transport accidents	V01-V99	6.3	11.6
Viral hepatitis	B15-B19	0.9	2.1

Note: (a) ICD-10 = International Classification of Diseases 10th Revision; (1) Mortality rates are a three year average covering 2012-2014; (2) Figures cover Fairfield County; Data are Suppressed when the data meet the criteria for confidentiality constraints; Mortality rates are flagged as Unreliable when the rate would be calculated with a numerator of 20 or less.
Source: Centers for Disease Control and Prevention, National Center for Health Statistics. Underlying Cause of Death 1999-2014 on CDC WONDER Online Database, released 2015.

Health Insurance Coverage

Area	With Health Insurance	With Private Health Insurance	With Public Health Insurance	Without Health Insurance	Population Under Age 18 Without Health Insurance
City	96.0	89.9	18.7	4.0	2.4
MSA[1]	88.7	72.4	26.4	11.3	5.1
U.S.	85.8	65.8	31.1	14.2	7.1

Note: Figures are percentages that cover the civilian noninstitutionalized population; (1) Figures cover the Bridgeport-Stamford-Norwalk, CT Metropolitan Statistical Area—see Appendix B for areas included
Source: U.S. Census Bureau, 2010-2014 American Community Survey 5-Year Estimates

Number of Medical Professionals

Area	MDs[3]	DOs[3,4]	Dentists	Podiatrists	Chiropractors	Optometrists
County[1] (number)	3,550	133	853	85	323	114
County[1] (rate[2])	376.8	14.1	90.2	9.0	34.2	12.1
U.S. (rate[2])	272.5	20.9	64.7	5.8	25.9	15.2

Note: Data as of 2014 unless noted; (1) Data covers Fairfield County; (2) Rate per 100,000 population; (3) Data as of 2013 and includes all active, non-federal physicians; (4) Doctor of Osteopathic Medicine
Source: U.S. Department of Health and Human Services, Health Resources and Services Administration, Bureau of Health Professions, Area Resource File (ARF) 2014-2015

EDUCATION

Public School District Statistics

District Name	Schls	Pupils	Pupil/ Teacher Ratio	Minority Pupils[1] (%)	Free Lunch Eligible[2] (%)	IEP[3] (%)
Westport School District	9	5,762	11.2	13.5	2.7	10.0

Note: Table includes school districts with 100 or more students; (1) Percentage of students that are not non-Hispanic white; (2) Percentage of students that are eligible for the free lunch program; (3) Percentage of students that have an Individualized Education Program.
Source: U.S. Department of Education, National Center for Education Statistics, Common Core of Data, Local Education Agency (School District) Universe Survey: School Year 2013-2014; U.S. Department of Education, National Center for Education Statistics, Common Core of Data, Public Elementary/Secondary School Universe Survey: School Year 2013-2014

Best High Schools

According to *U.S. News,* Westport is home to one of the best high schools in the U.S.: **Staples High School** (#329); Nearly 20,000 schools were ranked based on their performance on state assessments and how well they prepare students for college. Schools with the highest unrounded College Readiness Index values were numerically ranked from No. 1 to No. 500 and were the gold medal winners. *U.S. News & World Report, "Best High Schools 2015"*

Highest Level of Education

Area	Less than H.S.	H.S. Diploma	Some College, No Deg.	Associate Degree	Bachelor's Degree	Master's Degree	Prof. School Degree	Doctorate Degree
City	2.0	11.6	8.1	2.6	38.0	26.6	8.1	3.0
MSA[1]	10.8	22.5	15.4	5.8	25.5	14.7	3.8	1.5
U.S.	13.7	28.0	21.2	7.9	18.3	7.8	2.0	1.3

Note: Figures cover persons age 25 and over; (1) Figures cover the Bridgeport-Stamford-Norwalk, CT Metropolitan Statistical Area—see Appendix B for areas included
Source: U.S. Census Bureau, 2010-2014 American Community Survey 5-Year Estimates

Educational Attainment by Race

Area	High School Graduate or Higher (%)					Bachelor's Degree or Higher (%)				
	Total	White	Black	Asian	Hisp.[2]	Total	White	Black	Asian	Hisp.[2]
City	98.0	98.4	85.6	93.0	100.0	75.7	76.7	25.3	72.6	64.0
MSA[1]	89.2	92.2	84.2	89.6	68.7	45.4	50.4	19.7	66.7	18.1
U.S.	86.3	88.4	83.2	85.8	64.1	29.3	30.6	19.0	50.9	13.9

Note: Figures shown cover persons 25 years old and over; (1) Figures cover the Bridgeport-Stamford-Norwalk, CT Metropolitan Statistical Area—see Appendix B for areas included; (2) People of Hispanic origin can be of any race
Source: U.S. Census Bureau, 2010-2014 American Community Survey 5-Year Estimates

School Enrollment by Grade and Control

Area	Preschool (%)		Kindergarten (%)		Grades 1 - 4 (%)		Grades 5 - 8 (%)		Grades 9 - 12 (%)	
	Public	Private	Public	Private	Public	Private	Public	Private	Public	Private
City	28.4	71.6	89.5	10.5	94.8	5.2	82.5	17.5	87.3	12.7
MSA[1]	38.5	61.5	83.3	16.7	86.9	13.1	85.5	14.5	86.2	13.8
U.S.	57.4	42.6	87.8	12.2	89.8	10.2	89.9	10.1	90.6	9.4

Note: Figures shown cover persons 3 years old and over; (1) Figures cover the Bridgeport-Stamford-Norwalk, CT Metropolitan Statistical Area—see Appendix B for areas included
Source: U.S. Census Bureau, 2010-2014 American Community Survey 5-Year Estimates

Average Salaries of Public School Classroom Teachers

Area	2013-14		2014-15		Percent Change 2013-14 to 2014-15	Percent Change 2004-05 to 2014-15
	Dollars	Rank[1]	Dollars	Rank[1]		
Connecticut	70,583	5	71,709	5	1.59	24.2
U.S. Average	56,610	–	57,379	–	1.36	20.8

Note: (1) State rank ranges from 1 to 51 where 1 indicates highest salary.
Source: National Education Association, Rankings & Estimates: Rankings of the States 2014 and Estimates of School Statistics 2015, March 2015

Higher Education

Four-Year Colleges			Two-Year Colleges			Medical Schools[1]	Law Schools[2]	Voc/ Tech[3]
Public	Private Non-profit	Private For-profit	Public	Private Non-profit	Private For-profit			
0	0	0	0	0	0	0	0	1

Note: Figures cover institutions located within the city limits and include main campuses only; (1) includes schools accredited by the Liaison Committee on Medical Education and the American Osteopathic Association's Commission on Osteopathic College Accreditation; (2) includes ABA-accredited schools, schools with provisional ABA accreditation, and state accredited schools; (3) includes all schools with programs that are less than 2 years.

Source: National Center for Education Statistics, Integrated Postsecondary Education System (IPEDS), 2014-15; Association of American Medical Colleges, Member List, March 21, 2016; American Osteopathic Association, Member List, March 21, 2016; Law School Admission Council, Official Guide to ABA-Approved Law Schools Online, March 21, 2016; Wikipedia, List of Medical Schools in the United States, March 21, 2016; Wikipedia, List of Law Schools in the United States, March 21, 2016

PRESIDENTIAL ELECTION

2012 Presidential Election Results

Area	Obama (%)	Romney (%)	Other (%)
Fairfield County	55.3	43.8	0.9
U.S.	51.0	47.2	1.8

Note: Results may not add to 100% due to rounding
Source: Dave Leip's Atlas of U.S. Presidential Elections

EMPLOYERS

Major Employers

Company Name	Industry
Aptuit (scientific Operations)	Pharmaceutical preparations
Atos It Solutions and Services	Computer related maintenance services
Boehringer Ingelheim USA Corporation	Medicines, capsuled or ampuled
Bridgeport Hospital	Hospital, medical school affiliated with residency
Carter's Retail	Children's & infants' wear stores
Cartus Corporation	Relocation service
City of Bridgeport	Civil service commission, government
Commerce Connect Media	Magazines: publishing & printing
Conopco	Ice cream & ice milk
Diageo North America	Wine & distilled beverages
Greenwich Health Care Services	General medical & surgical hospitals
Pitney Bowes	Office machines
Sikorsky Aircraft Corporation	Aircraft
St Vincent's Development Corp.	Health systems agency
St Vincent's Health Services	General medical & surgical hospitals
The Danbury Hospital	Hospital, medical school affiliated with residency
Thomas J. Lipton	Tea blending
Thomson Corporation U.S.A.	Newspapers, publishing & printing
UBS Americas	Security brokers & dealers
UBS Securities	Brokers, security
Western Connecticut Healthcare	General medical & surgical hospitals
Wheelabrator Connecticut	Refuse systems

Note: Companies shown are located within the Bridgeport-Stamford-Norwalk, CT Metropolitan Statistical Area.
Source: Hoovers.com; Wikipedia

PUBLIC SAFETY

Crime Rate

Area	All Crimes	Violent Crimes: Murder	Violent Crimes: Rape[3]	Violent Crimes: Robbery	Violent Crimes: Aggrav. Assault	Property Crimes: Burglary	Property Crimes: Larceny -Theft	Property Crimes: Motor Vehicle Theft
City	1,278.7	0.0	0.0	14.5	14.5	185.3	1,038.9	25.4
Metro[1]	1,850.8	1.9	20.0	100.0	122.7	304.0	1,146.2	155.9
U.S.	2,971.8	4.5	36.6	102.2	232.5	542.5	1,837.3	216.2

Note: Figures are crimes per 100,000 population; (1) Figures cover the Bridgeport-Stamford-Norwalk, CT Metropolitan Statistical Area—see Appendix B for areas included; (3) The city and U.S. figures shown were reported using the revised Uniform Crime Reporting (UCR) definition of rape. The suburban and metro area figures shown are an aggregate total of the data submitted using both the revised and legacy UCR definitions.
Source: FBI Uniform Crime Reports, 2014

Hate Crimes

Area	Number of Quarters Reported	Number of Incidents per Bias Motivation: Race	Religion	Sexual Orientation	Ethnicity	Disability	Gender	Gender Identity
City	4	0	0	0	0	0	0	0
U.S.	4	2,568	1,014	1,017	648	84	33	98

Source: Federal Bureau of Investigation, Hate Crime Statistics 2014

Identity Theft Consumer Complaints

Area	Complaints	Complaints per 100,000 Population	Rank[2]
MSA[1]	2,400	253.9	5
U.S.	490,220	152.4	-

Note: (1) Figures cover the Bridgeport-Stamford-Norwalk, CT Metropolitan Statistical Area—see Appendix B for areas included; (2) Rank ranges from 1 to 379 where 1 indicates greatest number of identity theft complaints per 100,000 population
Source: Federal Trade Commission, Consumer Sentinel Network Data Book for January–December 2015

Fraud and Other Consumer Complaints

Area	Complaints	Complaints per 100,000 Population	Rank[2]
MSA[1]	3,152	333.4	242
U.S.	2,593,159	806.0	-

Note: (1) Figures cover the Bridgeport-Stamford-Norwalk, CT Metropolitan Statistical Area—see Appendix B for areas included; (2) Rank ranges from 1 to 379 where 1 indicates greatest number of identity theft complaints per 100,000 population
Source: Federal Trade Commission, Consumer Sentinel Network Data Book for January–December 2015

RECREATION

Culture

Dance[1]	Theatre[1]	Instrumental Music[1]	Vocal Music[1]	Series and Festivals	Museums and Art Galleries[2]	Zoos and Aquariums[3]
0	0	0	0	0	0	0

Note: (1) Professional perfoming groups; (2) Based on organizations with SIC code 8412; (3) AZA-accredited
Source: The Grey House Performing Arts Directory, 2015-16; Association of Zoos & Aquariums, AZA Member Zoos & Aquariums, March 25, 2016; www.AccuLeads.com, March 29, 2016

Professional Sports Teams

Team Name	League	Year Established
No teams are located in the metro area		

Source: Wikipedia, Major Professional Sports Teams of the United States and Canada, March 24, 2016

CLIMATE

Average and Extreme Temperatures

Temperature	Jan	Feb	Mar	Apr	May	Jun	Jul	Aug	Sep	Oct	Nov	Dec	Yr.
Extreme High (°F)	65	67	84	91	92	96	103	100	99	85	78	65	103
Average High (°F)	37	38	46	57	67	76	82	81	74	64	53	41	60
Average Temp. (°F)	30	32	39	49	59	68	74	73	66	56	46	35	52
Average Low (°F)	23	24	31	40	50	59	65	65	57	47	38	27	44
Extreme Low (°F)	-7	-5	4	18	31	41	49	44	36	26	16	-4	-7

Note: Figures cover the years 1948-1992
Source: National Climatic Data Center, International Station Meteorological Climate Summary, 9/96

Average Precipitation/Snowfall/Humidity

Precip./Humidity	Jan	Feb	Mar	Apr	May	Jun	Jul	Aug	Sep	Oct	Nov	Dec	Yr.
Avg. Precip. (in.)	3.2	2.9	3.7	3.7	3.7	3.1	3.7	3.8	3.0	3.2	3.8	3.5	41.4
Avg. Snowfall (in.)	7	7	5	1	Tr	0	0	0	0	Tr	1	5	25
Avg. Rel. Hum. 7am (%)	73	72	72	72	76	77	79	80	81	79	77	74	76
Avg. Rel. Hum. 4pm (%)	61	59	56	55	59	60	60	61	61	60	62	63	60

Note: Figures cover the years 1948-1992; Tr = Trace amounts (<0.05 in. of rain; <0.5 in. of snow)
Source: National Climatic Data Center, International Station Meteorological Climate Summary, 9/96

Weather Conditions

Temperature			Daytime Sky			Precipitation		
32°F & below	45°F & below	90°F & above	Clear	Partly cloudy	Cloudy	0.01 inch or more precip.	0.1 inch or more snow/ice	Thunder-storms
100	193	7	80	146	139	118	17	22

Note: Figures are average number of days per year and cover the years 1948-1992
Source: National Climatic Data Center, International Station Meteorological Climate Summary, 9/96

HAZARDOUS WASTE

Superfund Sites

Westport has no sites on the EPA's Superfund Final National Priorities List. There are a total of 1,323 Superfund sites on the list in the U.S. *U.S. Environmental Protection Agency, Final National Priorities List, March 18, 2016*

AIR & WATER QUALITY

Air Quality Trends: Ozone

	1990	1995	2000	2005	2010	2011	2012	2013	2014
MSA[1]	0.106	0.103	0.088	0.094	0.081	0.084	0.087	0.083	0.075

Note: (1) Data covers the Bridgeport-Stamford-Norwalk, CT Metropolitan Statistical Area—see Appendix B for areas included. The values shown are the composite ozone concentration averages among trend sites based on the highest fourth daily maximum 8-hour concentration in parts per million. These trends are based on sites having an adequate record of monitoring data during the trend period. Data from exceptional events are included.
Source: U.S. Environmental Protection Agency, Air Quality Monitoring Information, "Air Quality Trends by City, 1990-2014"

Air Quality Index

Area	Percent of Days when Air Quality was...[2]					AQI Statistics[2]	
	Good	Moderate	Unhealthy for Sensitive Groups	Unhealthy	Very Unhealthy	Maximum	Median
MSA[1]	61.9	33.4	4.4	0.3	0.0	151	44

Note: (1) Data covers the Bridgeport-Stamford-Norwalk, CT Metropolitan Statistical Area—see Appendix B for areas included; (2) Based on 365 days with AQI data in 2015. Air Quality Index (AQI) is an index for reporting daily air quality. EPA calculates the AQI for five major air pollutants regulated by the Clean Air Act: ground-level ozone, particle pollution (aka particulate matter), carbon monoxide, sulfur dioxide, and nitrogen dioxide. The AQI runs from 0 to 500. The higher the AQI value, the greater the level of air pollution and the greater the health concern. There are six AQI categories: "Good" AQI is between 0 and 50. Air quality is considered satisfactory; "Moderate" AQI is between 51 and 100. Air quality is acceptable; "Unhealthy for Sensitive Groups" When AQI values are between 101 and 150, members of sensitive groups may experience health effects; "Unhealthy" When AQI values are between 151 and 200 everyone may begin to experience health effects; "Very Unhealthy" AQI values between 201 and 300 trigger a health alert; "Hazardous" AQI values over 300 trigger warnings of emergency conditions (not shown).
Source: U.S. Environmental Protection Agency, Air Quality Index Report, 2015

Air Quality Index Pollutants

Area	Percent of Days when AQI Pollutant was...[2]					
	Carbon Monoxide	Nitrogen Dioxide	Ozone	Sulfur Dioxide	Particulate Matter 2.5	Particulate Matter 10
MSA[1]	0.5	0.0	34.8	0.0	64.7	0.0

Note: (1) Data covers the Bridgeport-Stamford-Norwalk, CT Metropolitan Statistical Area—see Appendix B for areas included; (2) Based on 365 days with AQI data in 2015. The Air Quality Index (AQI) is an index for reporting daily air quality. EPA calculates the AQI for five major air pollutants regulated by the Clean Air Act: ground-level ozone, particle pollution (also known as particulate matter), carbon monoxide, sulfur dioxide, and nitrogen dioxide. The AQI runs from 0 to 500. The higher the AQI value, the greater the level of air pollution and the greater the health concern.
Source: U.S. Environmental Protection Agency, Air Quality Index Report, 2015

Maximum Air Pollutant Concentrations: Particulate Matter, Ozone, CO and Lead

	Particulate Matter 10 (ug/m^3)	Particulate Matter 2.5 Wtd AM (ug/m^3)	Particulate Matter 2.5 24-Hr (ug/m^3)	Ozone (ppm)	Carbon Monoxide (ppm)	Lead (ug/m^3)
MSA[1] Level	35	9.9	25	0.081	1	n/a
NAAQS[2]	150	15	35	0.075	9	0.15
Met NAAQS[2]	Yes	Yes	Yes	No	Yes	n/a

Note: (1) Data covers the Bridgeport-Stamford-Norwalk, CT Metropolitan Statistical Area—see Appendix B for areas included; Data from exceptional events are included; (2) National Ambient Air Quality Standards; ppm = parts per million; ug/m^3 = micrograms per cubic meter; n/a not available.
Concentrations: Particulate Matter 10 (coarse particulate)—highest second maximum 24-hour concentration; Particulate Matter 2.5 Wtd AM (fine particulate)—highest weighted annual mean concentration; Particulate Matter 2.5 24-Hour (fine particulate)—highest 98th percentile 24-hour concentration; Ozone—highest fourth daily maximum 8-hour concentration; Carbon Monoxide—highest second maximum non-overlapping 8-hour concentration; Lead—maximum running 3-month average
Source: U.S. Environmental Protection Agency, Air Quality Monitoring Information, "Air Quality Statistics by City, 2014"

Maximum Air Pollutant Concentrations: Nitrogen Dioxide and Sulfur Dioxide

	Nitrogen Dioxide AM (ppb)	Nitrogen Dioxide 1-Hr (ppb)	Sulfur Dioxide AM (ppb)	Sulfur Dioxide 1-Hr (ppb)	Sulfur Dioxide 24-Hr (ppb)
MSA[1] Level	9	48	n/a	8	n/a
NAAQS[2]	53	100	30	75	140
Met NAAQS[2]	Yes	Yes	n/a	Yes	n/a

Note: (1) Data covers the Bridgeport-Stamford-Norwalk, CT Metropolitan Statistical Area—see Appendix B for areas included; Data from exceptional events are included; (2) National Ambient Air Quality Standards; ppm = parts per million; ug/m^3 = micrograms per cubic meter; n/a not available.
Concentrations: Nitrogen Dioxide AM—highest arithmetic mean concentration; Nitrogen Dioxide 1-Hr—highest 98th percentile 1-hour daily maximum concentration; Sulfur Dioxide AM—highest annual mean concentration; Sulfur Dioxide 1-Hr—highest 99th percentile 1-hour daily maximum concentration; Sulfur Dioxide 24-Hr—highest second maximum 24-hour concentration
Source: U.S. Environmental Protection Agency, Air Quality Monitoring Information, "Air Quality Statistics by City, 2014"

Drinking Water

Water System Name	Pop. Served	Primary Water Source Type	Violations[1]	
			Health Based	Monitoring/ Reporting
Aquarion Water Co - Main System	351,731	Surface	0	0

Note: (1) Based on violation data from January 1, 2015 to December 31, 2015 (includes unresolved violations from earlier years)

Source: U.S. Environmental Protection Agency, Office of Ground Water and Drinking Water, Safe Drinking Water Information System (based on data extracted April 29, 2016)

Oviedo, Florida

Background

Oviedo, in eastern Seminole County about fifteen miles from Orlando, provides a balanced mix of housing developments, shopping opportunities, recreation facilities and open conservation spaces.

The Oviedo area was once sparsely inhabited by Seminole Indians of the Timucua tradition but they left prior to the arrival of European settlers in the 17th century. After the Civil War, homesteaders, including many Swedes and former slaves, moved into the region to take advantage of the rich agricultural land. By the late 19th century, many farms were established, producing mainly citrus and celery, for markets in nearby Orlando and Sanford.

The town was named Lake Jessup until 1879, when Swedish-born postmaster, Andrew Aulin, decided that a Spanish name would be more in keeping with the region's early colonial history—and chose Oviedo after a famous university and cathedral town in northern Spain. Over time, the pronunciation changed from the Spanish O-vee-a-doe to O-ve-e-doe.

The Oviedo recreation department operates a range of facilities including a state-of-the-art gymnasium and aquatic facility. For skateboarders, there is Rippin' Riverside Skate Park, which is a 30,000 square-foot lighted facility adjacent to Riverside Park, which offers picnic tables and racquetball courts. Another spot, Shane Kelly Park, dedicated to the firefighter that bears its name, includes soccer fields, concession, restrooms, a playground and ample parking.

Two major annual festivals attract thousands of visitors: the craft-art-and-music centered "Great Day in the Country" in the fall; and the food-and-music centered "Taste of Oviedo" in early spring. The latter includes an "Oviedo Citrus & Celery Cook-Off," a culinary celebration of the town's agricultural past.

The town operates its own school system, with four elementary schools, two middle schools and one high school. There are also private, religiously affiliated, and Montessori schools. There are a number of colleges and universities in the area, including University of Central Florida, Seminole Community College, Rollins College, and Stetson University. The town itself is home to the Reformed Theological Seminary.

Hospitals and medical centers convenient to Oviedo include Central Florida Regional Hospital, in Sanford, as well as Florida Hospital East; and Orlando Regional Medical Center, both in Orlando.

Oviedo is convenient to Orlando International Airport and four regional and general aviation airports.

Rankings

General Rankings

- The Orlando* metro area was identified as one of America's fastest-growing areas in terms of population and economy by *Forbes*. The area ranked #13 out of 20. The 100 most populous metro areas in the U.S. were evaluated on the following criteria: estimated population growth; job growth; gross metropolitan product growth; unemployment; median salaries for college-educated workers. *Forbes, "America's Fastest-Growing Cities 2015," January 27, 2015*

Business/Finance Rankings

- The personal finance site NerdWallet analyzed 183 American metropolitan areas with populations over 250,000 and more than 15,000 businesses to rank where entrepreneurs find the most success. Criteria included area economy, annual income, housing cost, unemployment rate, and the success rate of area businesses. Orlando* ranked #132. *www.nerdwallet.com, "Best Places to Start a Business," April 27, 2015*
- The finance website Wall St. Cheat Sheet ranked the nation's largest metro areas on prospects for high-wage job creation in over the next five years. Based on analysis by CareerBuilder and Economic Modeling Specialists International (EMSI), The Orlando* metro area ranked #7. *wallstcheatsheet.com, "Top 10 Cities for High-Wage Job Growth," December 8, 2013*
- 24/7 Wall Street ranked metro areas where jobs were being added at a faster rate than the labor force was growing. The #7 metro area for gains posted in employment was Orlando*. *247wallst.com, "Cities Where Unemployment Has Fallen the Most," April 16, 2013*
- Based on metro area social media reviews, the employment opinion group Glassdoor surveyed 50 of the largest U.S. metro areas and equally weighed cost of living, hiring opportunity, and job satisfaction to compose a list of "25 Best Cities for Jobs." The Orlando* metro area was ranked #19 in overall job satisfaction. *www.glassdoor.com, "Best Cities for Jobs," May 19, 2015*
- In a survey of economic confidence in the nation's 50 largest metropolitan areas conducted January–December 2014, the Orlando* metro area placed #19, according to Gallup's 2014 Economic Confidence Index. *Gallup, "San Jose and San Francisco Lead in Economic Confidence," March 19, 2015*
- The Brookings Institution ranked the 100 largest metro areas in the U.S. based on income inequality. Orlando* was ranked #48 (#1 = greatest ineqality). Criteria: the "95/20 ratio," a figure representing the income at which a household earns more than 95 percent of all other households, divided by the income at which a household earns more than only 20 percent of all other households. *Brookings Institution, "Income Inequality, 100 Largest U.S. Metro Areas, 2007-2014," January 14, 2016*
- Orlando* was identified as one of America's most frugal metro areas by *Coupons.com.* The city ranked #3 out of 25. Criteria: online coupon usage. *Coupons.com, "Top 25 Most Frugal Cities of 2014," May 11, 2015*
- Orlando* was identified as one of America's most frugal metro areas by *Coupons.com.* The city ranked #1 out of 25. Criteria: Grocery IQ and coupons.com mobile app usage. *Coupons.com, "Top 25 Most On-the-Go Frugal Cities of 2013," April 10, 2014*
- The Orlando* metro area appeared on the Milken Institute "2015 Best Performing Cities" list. Rank: #28 out of 200 large metro areas. Criteria: job growth; wage and salary growth; high-tech output growth. *Milken Institute, "Best-Performing Cities 2015," December 2015*
- *Forbes* ranked the 200 most populous metro areas to determine the nation's "Best Places for Business and Careers." The Orlando* metro area was ranked #51. Criteria: costs (business and living); job growth (past and projected); income growth; educational attainment (college and high school); projected economic growth; cultural and recreational opportunities; net migration patterns; number of highly ranked colleges. *Forbes, "The Best Places for Business and Careers 2015," July 29, 2015*

Education Rankings

- Personal finance website *WalletHub* analyzed the 150 largest U.S. metropolitan statistical areas to determine where the most educated Americans are choosing to settle. Criteria: education quality and attainment gap; education levels; percentage of workers with degrees; public school rankings; quality and size of each metro area's universities. Orlando* was ranked #85 (#1 = most educated city). *www.WalletHub.com, "2015's Most and Least Educated Cities*

Environmental Rankings

- The Orlando* metro area came in at #333 for the relative comfort of its climate on Sperling's list of "chill cities," as measured by the Sperling Heat Index. All 361 metro areas are included. Criteria included daytime high temperatures, nighttime low temperatures, dew point, and relative humidity at the high temperatures. *www.bertsperling.com, "Sperling's Chill Cities," July 18, 2013*
- Sperling's BestPlaces assessed 379 metropolitan areas of the United States for the likelihood of dangerously extreme weather events or earthquakes. In general the Southeast and South-Central regions have the highest risk of weather extremes and earthquakes, while the Pacific Northwest enjoys the lowest risk. Of the least risky metropolitan areas, the Orlando* metro area was ranked #341. *www.bestplaces.net, "Safest Places from Natural Disasters," April 2011*
- Orlando* was highlighted as one of the top 25 cleanest metro areas for year-round particle pollution (Annual PM 2.5) in the U.S. during 2011 through 2013. The area ranked #19. *American Lung Association, State of the Air 2015*

Health/Fitness Rankings

- For each of the 50 most populous metro areas in the United States, the American College of Sports Medicine's American Fitness Index evaluated infrastructure, community assets, and policies that encourage healthy and fit lifestyles, including preventive health behaviors, levels of chronic disease conditions, health care access, and community resources and policies that support physical activity. The Orlando* metro area ranked #36 for "community fitness." *www.americanfitnessindex.org, "ACSM American Fitness Index Health and Community Fitness Status of the 50 Largest Metropolitan Areas," May 2015*
- The Orlando* metro area was identified as one of the worst cities for bed bugs in America by pest control company Orkin. The area ranked #38 out of 50 based on the number of bed bug treatments Orkin performed from January to December 2015. *Orkin, "Chicago Tops Bed Bug Cities List for Fourth Year in a Row," January 13, 2016*
- Orlando* was identified as a "2016 Spring Allergy Capital." The area ranked #87 out of 100. Three groups of factors were used to identify the most severe cities for people with allergies during the spring season: annual pollen levels; medicine utilization; access to board-certified allergists. *Asthma and Allergy Foundation of America, "Spring Allergy Capitals 2016"*
- Orlando* was identified as a "2015 Asthma Capital." The area ranked #64 out of the nation's 100 largest metropolitan areas. Criteria: estimated prevalence; self-reported prevalence; crude death rate for asthma; annual pollen score; annual air quality; public smoking laws; number of board-certified asthma specialists; school inhaler access laws; rescue medication use; controller medication use; ER visits for asthma; uninsured rate; poverty rate. *Asthma and Allergy Foundation of America, "Asthma Capitals 2015"*
- The Orlando* metro area ranked #79 out of 190 in The Gallup-Healthways Well-Being Index. Criteria: purpose; social well being; financial health; community and physical health. Results are based on telephone interviews with adults, aged 18 and older, living in metropolitan areas in the 50 U.S. states and the District of Columbia. *Gallup-Healthways, "State of American Well-Being," February 23, 2016*

Real Estate Rankings

- According to Penske Truck Rental, the Orlando* metro area was named the #5 moving destination in 2015, based on one-way consumer truck rental reservations made through Penske's website and reservations call center. *blog.gopenske.com, "Penske Truck Rental's 2015 Top Moving Destinations List," February 3, 2016*
- The Orlando* metro area was identified as #2 among the ten housing markets with the highest percentage of distressed property sales, based on the findings of the housing data website RealtyTrac. Criteria: short sales; income and poverty figures; and unemployment data. *247wallst.com, "Cities Selling the Most Distressed Homes," January 23, 2014*
- The Orlando* metro area was identified as one of the top 20 housing markets to invest in for 2016 by *Forbes*. The area ranked #2. Criteria: strong job and population growth; anticipated home price appreciation; and other factors. *Forbes.com, "Best Buy Cities: Where to Invest in Housing in 2016," January 27, 2016*
- The Orlando* metro area was identified as one of the 20 best housing markets in the U.S. in 2015. The area ranked #15 out of 179 markets. Criteria: year-over-year change of median sales price of existing single-family homes between the 4th quarter of 2014 and the 4th quarter of 2015. *National Association of Realtors®, Median Sales Price of Existing Single-Family Homes for Metropolitan Areas, 4th Quarter 2015*
- Orlando* was ranked #155 out of 225 metro areas in terms of housing affordability in 2015 by the National Association of Home Builders (#1 = most affordable). Criteria: the share of homes sold in that area affordable to a family earning the local median income, based on standard mortgage underwriting criteria. *National Association of Home Builders®, NAHB-Wells Fargo Housing Opportunity Index, 4th Quarter 2015*
- The nation's largest metro areas were analyzed in terms of the percentage of households entering some stage of foreclosure in 2015. The Orlando* metro area ranked #9 out of 20 (#1 = highest foreclosure rate). *RealtyTrac, "2015 Year-End U.S. Foreclosure Market Report™," January 12, 2016*

Safety Rankings

- The National Insurance Crime Bureau ranked 380 metro areas in the U.S. in terms of per capita rates of vehicle theft. The Orlando* metro area ranked #125 (#1 = highest rate). Criteria: number of vehicle theft offenses per 100,000 inhabitants in 2014. *National Insurance Crime Bureau, "Hot Spots 2014," June 24, 2015*

Seniors/Retirement Rankings

- From its Best Cities for Successful Aging indexes, the Milken Institute generated rankings for metropolitan areas, weighing data in eight categories—health care, wellness, living arrangements, transportation, financial characteristics, education and employment opportunities, community engagement, and overall livability. The Orlando* metro area was ranked #85 overall in the large metro area category. *Milken Institute, "Best Cities for Successful Aging, 2014"*

Miscellaneous Rankings

- The watchdog site Charity Navigator conducts an annual study of charities in the nation's major markets both to analyze statistical differences in their financial, accountability, and transparency practices and to track year-to-year variations in individual communities. The Orlando* metro area was ranked #28 among the 30 metro markets in the rating dimension of Overall Score. *www.charitynavigator.org, "Metro Market Study 2015," June 5, 2015*
- Mars Chocolate North America, the makers of COMBOS®, in partnership with Sperling's BestPlaces, ranked 50 major metro areas in terms of their "manliness." The Orlando* metro area ranked #28. Criteria: number of professional sports teams; number of nearby NASCAR tracks and racing events; manly lifestyle; concentration of manly retail stores; manly occupations per capita; salty snack sales; "Board of Manliness" rankings. *Mars Chocolate North America, "America's Manliest Cities 2012"*

- The National Alliance to End Homelessness ranked the 100 most populous metro areas with the highest rate of homelessness. The Orlando* metro area ranked #17. Criteria: number of homeless people per 10,000 population in 2011. *National Alliance to End Homelessness, The State of Homelessness in America 2012*

Oviedo is located within the Orlando-Kissimmee-Sanford, FL Metropolitan Statistical Area.

Business Environment

CITY FINANCES

City Government Finances

Component	2012 ($000)	2012 ($ per capita)
Total Revenues	43,865	1,315
Total Expenditures	46,908	1,406
Debt Outstanding	79,720	2,390
Cash and Securities[1]	38,465	1,153

Note: (1) Cash and security holdings of a government at the close of its fiscal year, including those of its dependent agencies, utilities, and liquor stores.
Source: U.S Census Bureau, State & Local Government Finances 2012

City Government Revenue by Source

Source	2012 ($000)	2012 ($ per capita)
General Revenue		
From Federal Government	341	10
From State Government	2,709	81
From Local Governments	1,129	33
Taxes		
Property	9,580	287
Sales and Gross Receipts	5,847	175
Personal Income	0	0
Corporate Income	0	0
Motor Vehicle License	0	0
Other Taxes	3,345	100
Current Charges	11,998	359
Liquor Store	0	0
Utility	5,889	176
Employee Retirement	280	8

Source: U.S Census Bureau, State & Local Government Finances 2012

City Government Expenditures by Function

Function	2012 ($000)	2012 ($ per capita)	2012 (%)
General Direct Expenditures			
Air Transportation	0	0	0.0
Corrections	0	0	0.0
Education	0	0	0.0
Employment Security Administration	0	0	0.0
Financial Administration	1,172	35	2.4
Fire Protection	5,074	152	10.8
General Public Buildings	0	0	0.0
Governmental Administration, Other	1,154	34	2.4
Health	0	0	0.0
Highways	12,607	378	26.8
Hospitals	0	0	0.0
Housing and Community Development	0	0	0.0
Interest on General Debt	1,210	36	2.5
Judicial and Legal	139	4	0.2
Libraries	0	0	0.0
Parking	0	0	0.0
Parks and Recreation	3,414	102	7.2
Police Protection	6,773	203	14.4
Public Welfare	0	0	0.0
Sewerage	3,556	106	7.5
Solid Waste Management	3,502	105	7.4
Veterans' Services	0	0	0.0
Liquor Store	0	0	0.0
Utility	5,895	176	12.5
Employee Retirement	340	10	0.7

Source: U.S Census Bureau, State & Local Government Finances 2012

DEMOGRAPHICS

Population Growth

Area	1990 Census	2000 Census	2010 Census	2014* Estimate	Population Growth (%) 1990-2014	2010-2014
City	11,588	26,316	33,342	35,602	207.2	6.8
MSA[1]	1,224,852	1,644,561	2,134,411	2,226,835	81.8	4.3
U.S.	248,709,873	281,421,906	308,745,538	314,107,084	26.3	1.7

Note: (1) Figures cover the Orlando-Kissimmee-Sanford, FL Metropolitan Statistical Area—see Appendix B for areas included; (*) 2010-2014 5-year estimated population
Source: U.S. Census Bureau, 1990 Census, Census 2000, Census 2010, 2010-2014 American Community Survey 5-Year Estimates

Household Size

Area	Persons in Household (%) One	Two	Three	Four	Five	Six	Seven or More	Average Household Size
City	14.0	30.2	20.3	24.4	6.3	3.5	0.9	3.38
MSA[1]	26.0	35.0	16.7	13.2	5.8	2.0	1.0	2.80
U.S.	27.5	33.5	15.8	13.1	6.0	2.3	1.4	2.64

Note: (1) Figures cover the Orlando-Kissimmee-Sanford, FL Metropolitan Statistical Area—see Appendix B for areas included
Source: U.S. Census Bureau, 2010-2014 American Community Survey 5-Year Estimates

Race

Area	White Alone[2] (%)	Black Alone[2] (%)	Asian Alone[2] (%)	AIAN[3] Alone[2] (%)	NHOPI[4] Alone[2] (%)	Other Race Alone[2] (%)	Two or More Races (%)
City	82.5	8.5	5.4	0.3	0.1	1.2	2.0
MSA[1]	71.9	16.2	4.1	0.3	0.1	4.5	3.0
U.S.	73.8	12.6	5.0	0.8	0.2	4.7	2.9

Note: (1) Figures cover the Orlando-Kissimmee-Sanford, FL Metropolitan Statistical Area—see Appendix B for areas included; (2) Alone is defined as not being in combination with one or more other races; (3) American Indian and Alaska Native; (4) Native Hawaiian and Other Pacific Islander
Source: U.S. Census Bureau, 2010-2014 American Community Survey 5-Year Estimates

Hispanic or Latino Origin

Area	Total (%)	Mexican (%)	Puerto Rican (%)	Cuban (%)	Other (%)
City	19.5	1.3	7.9	2.4	7.9
MSA[1]	26.7	3.1	13.5	2.0	8.1
U.S.	16.9	10.8	1.6	0.6	3.8

Note: Persons of Hispanic or Latino origin can be of any race; (1) Figures cover the Orlando-Kissimmee-Sanford, FL Metropolitan Statistical Area—see Appendix B for areas included
Source: U.S. Census Bureau, 2010-2014 American Community Survey 5-Year Estimates

Ancestry

Area	German	Irish	English	American	Italian	Polish	French[2]	Scottish	Dutch
City	14.4	11.2	8.8	7.9	8.2	3.7	2.9	2.2	2.0
MSA[1]	10.3	8.6	7.1	8.0	5.3	2.1	2.2	1.5	0.9
U.S.	14.9	10.8	8.0	7.1	5.5	3.0	2.7	1.7	1.4

Note: Figures are the percentage of the total population reporting a particular ancestry. The nine most commonly reported ancestries in the U.S. are shown. Figures include multiple ancestries (e.g. if a person reported being Irish and Italian, they were included in both columns); (1) Figures cover the Orlando-Kissimmee-Sanford, FL Metropolitan Statistical Area—see Appendix B for areas included; (2) Excludes Basque
Source: U.S. Census Bureau, 2010-2014 American Community Survey 5-Year Estimates

Foreign-Born Population

Area	Percent of Population Born in								
	Any Foreign Country	Asia	Mexico	Europe	Carribean	Central America[2]	South America	Africa	Canada
City	11.8	2.6	0.2	1.7	2.7	0.7	2.6	0.9	0.5
MSA[1]	16.3	2.8	1.3	1.6	4.9	1.0	3.8	0.5	0.3
U.S.	13.1	3.8	3.7	1.5	1.2	1.0	0.9	0.6	0.3

Note: (1) Figures cover the Orlando-Kissimmee-Sanford, FL Metropolitan Statistical Area—see Appendix B for areas included; (2) Excludes Mexico.
Source: U.S. Census Bureau, 2010-2014 American Community Survey 5-Year Estimates

Marital Status

Area	Never Married	Now Married[2]	Separated	Widowed	Divorced
City	34.4	53.8	1.3	2.9	7.6
MSA[1]	34.5	45.9	2.6	5.4	11.7
U.S.	32.5	48.4	2.2	5.9	10.9

Note: Figures are percentages and cover the population 15 years of age and older; (1) Figures cover the Orlando-Kissimmee-Sanford, FL Metropolitan Statistical Area—see Appendix B for areas included; (2) Excludes separated
Source: U.S. Census Bureau, 2010-2014 American Community Survey 5-Year Estimates

Disability Status

Area	All Ages	Under 18 Years Old	18 to 64 Years Old	65 Years and Over
City	7.5	2.5	6.6	35.5
MSA[1]	11.3	4.3	9.0	34.7
U.S.	12.3	4.1	10.2	36.3

Note: Figures show percent of the civilian noninstitutionalized population that reported having a disability. Disability status is determined from from six types of difficulty: vision, hearing, cognitive, ambulatory, self-care, and independent living. For children under 5 years old, hearing and vision difficulty are used to determine disability status. For children between the ages of 5 and 14, disability status is determined from hearing, vision, cognitive, ambulatory, and self-care difficulties. For people aged 15 years and older, they are considered to have a disability if they have difficulty with any one of the six difficulty types; (1) Figures cover the Orlando-Kissimmee-Sanford, FL Metropolitan Statistical Area—see Appendix B for areas included.
Source: U.S. Census Bureau, 2010-2014 American Community Survey 5-Year Estimates

Age

Area	Percent of Population									Median Age
	Under Age 5	Age 5–19	Age 20–34	Age 35–44	Age 45–54	Age 55–64	Age 65–74	Age 75–84	Age 85+	
City	6.1	24.7	20.8	14.7	16.0	10.5	3.9	2.0	1.3	33.8
MSA[1]	6.0	19.7	22.2	13.7	14.1	11.4	7.4	4.0	1.6	36.5
U.S.	6.4	19.9	20.6	13.0	14.1	12.3	7.6	4.3	1.9	37.4

Note: (1) Figures cover the Orlando-Kissimmee-Sanford, FL Metropolitan Statistical Area—see Appendix B for areas included
Source: U.S. Census Bureau, 2010-2014 American Community Survey 5-Year Estimates

Gender

Area	Males	Females	Males per 100 Females
City	17,361	18,241	95.2
MSA[1]	1,088,823	1,138,012	95.7
U.S.	154,515,159	159,591,925	96.8

Note: (1) Figures cover the Orlando-Kissimmee-Sanford, FL Metropolitan Statistical Area—see Appendix B for areas included
Source: U.S. Census Bureau, 2010-2014 American Community Survey 5-Year Estimates

Religious Groups by Family

Area	Catholic	Baptist	Non-Den.	Methodist[2]	Lutheran	LDS[3]	Pente-costal	Presby-terian[4]	Muslim[5]	Judaism
MSA[1]	13.2	6.9	5.6	2.9	0.9	0.9	3.2	1.3	1.3	0.2
U.S.	19.1	9.3	4.0	4.0	2.3	2.0	1.9	1.6	0.8	0.7

Note: Figures are the number of adherents as a percentage of the total population; (1) Figures cover the Orlando-Kissimmee-Sanford, FL Metropolitan Statistical Area—see Appendix B for areas included; (2) Methodist/Pietist; (3) Latter Day Saints; (4) Reformed; (5) Figures are estimates
Source: Association of Statisticians of American Religious Bodies, 2010 U.S. Religion Census: Religious Congregations & Membership Study

Religious Groups by Tradition

Area	Catholic	Evangelical Protestant	Mainline Protestant	Other Tradition	Black Protestant	Orthodox
MSA[1]	13.2	17.8	4.7	3.2	1.2	0.3
U.S.	19.1	16.2	7.3	4.3	1.6	0.3

Note: Figures are the number of adherents as a percentage of the total population; (1) Figures cover the Orlando-Kissimmee-Sanford, FL Metropolitan Statistical Area—see Appendix B for areas included
Source: Association of Statisticians of American Religious Bodies, 2010 U.S. Religion Census: Religious Congregations & Membership Study

ECONOMY

Gross Metropolitan Product

Area	2013	2014	2015	2016	Rank[2]
MSA[1]	110.4	116.5	122.9	130.4	30

Note: Figures are in billions of dollars; (1) Figures cover the Orlando-Kissimmee-Sanford, FL Metropolitan Statistical Area—see Appendix B for areas included; (2) Rank is based on 2016 data and ranges from 1 to 381
Source: The U.S. Conference of Mayors, U.S. Metro Economies: GMP and Employment 2014-2016, June 2015

Economic Growth

Area	2011-13 (%)	2014 (%)	2015 (%)	2016 (%)	Rank[2]
MSA[1]	2.1	3.6	4.0	4.1	9
U.S.	2.2	2.4	2.3	2.9	–

Note: Figures are real gross metropolitan product (GMP) growth rates and represent annual average percent change; (1) Figures cover the Orlando-Kissimmee-Sanford, FL Metropolitan Statistical Area—see Appendix B for areas included; (2) Rank is based on 2016 data and ranges from 1 to 381
Source: The U.S. Conference of Mayors, U.S. Metro Economies: GMP and Employment 2014-2016, June 2015

Metropolitan Area Exports

Area	2009	2010	2011	2012	2013	2014	Rank[2]
MSA[1]	2,947.1	3,453.6	3,229.9	3,850.6	3,227.6	3,134.8	76

Note: Figures are in millions of dollars; (1) Figures cover the Orlando-Kissimmee-Sanford, FL Metropolitan Statistical Area—see Appendix B for areas included; (2) Rank is based on 2014 data and ranges from 1 to 385
Source: U.S. Department of Commerce, International Trade Administration, Office of Trade & Industry Information, Manufacturing & Services, data extracted March 10, 2016

Building Permits

Area	Single-Family			Multi-Family			Total		
	2014	2015p	Pct. Chg.	2014	2015p	Pct. Chg.	2014	2015p	Pct. Chg.
City	42	172	309.5	0	0	-	42	172	309.5
MSA[1]	9,806	12,328	25.7	6,309	7,873	24.8	16,115	20,201	25.4
U.S.	640,300	690,800	7.9	411,800	487,600	18.4	1,052,100	1,178,400	12.0

Note: (1) Figures cover the Orlando-Kissimmee-Sanford, FL Metropolitan Statistical Area—see Appendix B for areas included; Figures represent new, privately-owned housing units authorized (unadjusted data); All permit data are based on estimates with imputation; (p) preliminary data.
Source: U.S. Census Bureau, Manufacturing, Mining, and Construction Statistics, Building Permits, 2014, 2015

Bankruptcy Filings

Area	Business Filings			Nonbusiness Filings		
	2014	2015	% Chg.	2014	2015	% Chg.
Seminole County	80	71	-11.3	1,530	1,320	-13.7
U.S.	26,983	24,735	-8.3	909,812	819,760	-9.9

Note: Business filings include Chapter 7, Chapter 11, Chapter 12, and Chapter 13; Nonbusiness filings include Chapter 7, Chapter 11, and Chapter 13
Source: Administrative Office of the U.S. Courts, Business and Nonbusiness Bankruptcy, County Cases Commenced by Chapter of the Bankruptcy Code, During the 12- Month Period Ending December 31, 2014 and Business and Nonbusiness Bankruptcy, County Cases Commenced by Chapter of the Bankruptcy Code, During the 12- Month Period Ending December 31, 2015

Housing Vacancy Rates

Area	Gross Vacancy Rate[2] (%)			Year-Round Vacancy Rate[3] (%)			Rental Vacancy Rate[4] (%)			Homeowner Vacancy Rate[5] (%)		
	2013	2014	2015	2013	2014	2015	2013	2014	2015	2013	2014	2015
MSA[1]	20.5	18.8	14.3	15.5	15.2	11.3	14.7	14.6	8.0	2.8	3.1	4.1
U.S.	13.6	13.4	12.9	10.7	10.4	10.0	8.3	7.6	7.1	2.0	1.9	1.8

Note: (1) Figures cover the Orlando-Kissimmee-Sanford, FL Metropolitan Statistical Area—see Appendix B for areas included; (2) The percentage of the total housing inventory that is vacant; (3) The percentage of the housing inventory (excluding seasonal units) that is year-round vacant; (4) The percentage of rental inventory that is vacant for rent; (5) The percentage of homeowner inventory that is vacant for sale
Source: U.S. Census Bureau, Housing Vacancies and Homeownership Annual Statistics: 2015

INCOME

Income

Area	Per Capita ($)	Median Household ($)	Average Household ($)
City	28,457	82,259	94,851
MSA[1]	24,876	48,559	66,823
U.S.	28,555	53,482	74,596

Note: (1) Figures cover the Orlando-Kissimmee-Sanford, FL Metropolitan Statistical Area—see Appendix B for areas included
Source: U.S. Census Bureau, 2010-2014 American Community Survey 5-Year Estimates

Household Income Distribution

Area	Percent of Households Earning							
	Under $15,000	$15,000 -24,999	$25,000 -34,999	$35,000 -49,999	$50,000 -74,999	$75,000 -99,000	$100,000 -149,999	$150,000 and up
City	5.1	4.0	5.6	11.8	19.0	15.4	22.3	16.8
MSA[1]	12.0	11.7	12.1	15.5	19.1	11.2	11.0	7.3
U.S.	12.5	10.7	10.2	13.5	17.8	12.2	13.0	10.0

Note: (1) Figures cover the Orlando-Kissimmee-Sanford, FL Metropolitan Statistical Area—see Appendix B for areas included
Source: U.S. Census Bureau, 2010-2014 American Community Survey 5-Year Estimates

Poverty Rate

Area	All Ages	Under 18 Years Old	18 to 64 Years Old	65 Years and Over
City	6.5	6.0	6.7	6.8
MSA[1]	16.2	23.0	15.1	9.6
U.S.	15.6	21.9	14.6	9.4

Note: Figures are percentage of people whose income during the past 12 months was below the poverty level; (1) Figures cover the Orlando-Kissimmee-Sanford, FL Metropolitan Statistical Area—see Appendix B for areas included
Source: U.S. Census Bureau, 2010-2014 American Community Survey 5-Year Estimates

EMPLOYMENT

Labor Force and Employment

Area	Civilian Labor Force			Workers Employed		
	Dec. 2014	Dec. 2015	% Chg.	Dec. 2014	Dec. 2015	% Chg.
City	20,148	20,407	1.2	19,303	19,623	1.6
MSA[1]	1,211,468	1,222,042	0.8	1,149,268	1,169,073	1.7
U.S.	155,521,000	157,245,000	1.1	147,190,000	149,703,000	1.7

Note: Data is not seasonally adjusted and covers workers 16 years of age and older; (1) Figures cover the Orlando-Kissimmee-Sanford, FL Metropolitan Statistical Area—see Appendix B for areas included
Source: Bureau of Labor Statistics, Local Area Unemployment Statistics

Unemployment Rate

Area	2015											
	Jan.	Feb.	Mar.	Apr.	May	Jun.	Jul.	Aug.	Sep.	Oct.	Nov.	Dec.
City	4.7	4.4	4.3	3.9	4.2	4.1	4.1	4.0	3.9	3.8	3.7	3.8
MSA[1]	5.6	5.4	5.2	4.9	5.2	5.1	5.3	5.1	4.9	4.7	4.5	4.3
U.S.	6.1	5.8	5.6	5.1	5.3	5.5	5.6	5.2	4.9	4.8	4.8	4.8

Note: Data is not seasonally adjusted and covers workers 16 years of age and older; (1) Figures cover the Orlando-Kissimmee-Sanford, FL Metropolitan Statistical Area—see Appendix B for areas included
Source: Bureau of Labor Statistics, Local Area Unemployment Statistics

Employment by Occupation

Occupation Classification	City (%)	MSA[1] (%)	U.S. (%)
Management, Business, Science, and Arts	45.2	34.5	36.4
Natural Resources, Construction, and Maintenance	5.6	7.5	9.0
Production, Transportation, and Material Moving	5.3	8.9	12.1
Sales and Office	29.7	28.0	24.4
Service	14.1	21.1	18.2

Note: Figures cover employed civilians 16 years of age and older; (1) Figures cover the Orlando-Kissimmee-Sanford, FL Metropolitan Statistical Area—see Appendix B for areas included
Source: U.S. Census Bureau, 2010-2014 American Community Survey 5-Year Estimates

Employment by Industry

Sector	MSA[1]		U.S.
	Number of Employees	Percent of Total	Percent of Total
Construction	63,600	5.3	4.5
Education and Health Services	145,300	12.2	15.7
Financial Activities	72,000	6.0	5.7
Government	122,400	10.2	15.5
Information	23,700	1.9	1.9
Leisure and Hospitality	245,200	20.5	10.4
Manufacturing	42,900	3.6	8.6
Mining and Logging	300	<0.1	0.5
Other Services	42,200	3.5	3.9
Professional and Business Services	201,800	16.9	13.9
Retail Trade	150,000	12.5	11.3
Transportation, Warehousing, and Utilities	37,300	3.1	3.9
Wholesale Trade	43,900	3.6	4.1

Note: Figures are non-farm employment as of December 2015. Figures are not seasonally adjusted and include workers 16 years of age and older; (1) Figures cover the Orlando-Kissimmee-Sanford, FL Metropolitan Statistical Area—see Appendix B for areas included
Source: Bureau of Labor Statistics, Current Employment Statistics, Employment, Hours, and Earnings

Occupations with Greatest Projected Employment Growth: 2012 – 2022

Occupation[1]	2012 Employment	2022 Projected Employment	Numeric Employment Change	Percent Employment Change
Retail Salespersons	326,380	380,120	53,740	16.5
Combined Food Preparation and Serving Workers, Including Fast Food	196,980	237,340	40,360	20.5
Customer Service Representatives	191,210	228,620	37,410	19.6
Registered Nurses	164,020	201,140	37,120	22.6
Waiters and Waitresses	191,370	227,810	36,440	19.0
Office Clerks, General	142,710	170,300	27,590	19.3
Cashiers	206,660	230,190	23,530	11.4
Landscaping and Groundskeeping Workers	92,510	115,540	23,030	24.9
Receptionists and Information Clerks	75,780	95,680	19,900	26.2
Nursing Assistants	86,990	106,200	19,210	22.1

Note: Projections cover Florida; (1) Sorted by numeric employment change
Source: www.projectionscentral.com, State Occupational Projections, 2012–2022 Long-Term Projections

Fastest Growing Occupations: 2012 – 2022

Occupation[1]	2012 Employment	2022 Projected Employment	Numeric Employment Change	Percent Employment Change
Helpers—Carpenters	1,280	2,450	1,170	90.7
Helpers—Brickmasons, Blockmasons, Stonemasons, and Tile and Marble Setters	1,050	1,890	840	79.5
Biomedical Engineers	760	1,300	540	70.7
Reinforcing Iron and Rebar Workers	520	870	350	67.5
Glaziers	2,890	4,710	1,820	62.8
Solar Photovoltaic Installers	170	270	100	58.7
Brickmasons and Blockmasons	2,820	4,430	1,610	57.1
Stonemasons	450	710	260	56.4
Helpers—Pipelayers, Plumbers, Pipefitters, and Steamfitters	2,420	3,750	1,330	54.8
Cement Masons and Concrete Finishers	10,390	16,050	5,660	54.4

Note: Projections cover Florida; (1) Sorted by percent employment change and excludes occupations with numeric employment change less than 100
Source: www.projectionscentral.com, State Occupational Projections, 2012–2022 Long-Term Projections

Average Wages

Occupation	$/Hr.	Occupation	$/Hr.
Accountants and Auditors	31.71	Maids and Housekeeping Cleaners	10.27
Automotive Mechanics	18.53	Maintenance and Repair Workers	16.23
Bookkeepers	17.20	Marketing Managers	53.58
Carpenters	17.84	Nuclear Medicine Technologists	35.01
Cashiers	9.69	Nurses, Licensed Practical	19.35
Clerks, General Office	13.93	Nurses, Registered	29.62
Clerks, Receptionists/Information	12.90	Nursing Assistants	11.85
Clerks, Shipping/Receiving	14.15	Packers and Packagers, Hand	10.45
Computer Programmers	35.08	Physical Therapists	41.89
Computer Systems Analysts	39.31	Postal Service Mail Carriers	24.89
Computer User Support Specialists	20.76	Real Estate Brokers	59.59
Cooks, Restaurant	12.15	Retail Salespersons	11.88
Dentists	77.38	Sales Reps., Exc. Tech./Scientific	28.91
Electrical Engineers	42.40	Sales Reps., Tech./Scientific	37.43
Electricians	18.74	Secretaries, Exc. Legal/Med./Exec.	15.84
Financial Managers	62.20	Security Guards	10.90
First-Line Supervisors/Managers, Sales	20.70	Surgeons	116.31
Food Preparation Workers	10.71	Teacher Assistants*	11.54
General and Operations Managers	58.06	Teachers, Elementary School*	22.91
Hairdressers/Cosmetologists	12.42	Teachers, Secondary School*	22.61
Internists	97.37	Telemarketers	11.25
Janitors and Cleaners	10.82	Truck Drivers, Heavy/Tractor-Trailer	19.41
Landscaping/Groundskeeping Workers	11.76	Truck Drivers, Light/Delivery Svcs.	15.62
Lawyers	78.47	Waiters and Waitresses	12.80

Note: Wage data covers the Orlando-Kissimmee-Sanford, FL Metropolitan Statistical Area—see Appendix B for areas included; (*) Hourly wages for elementary/secondary school teachers and teacher assistants were calculated by the editors from annual wage data based on a 40 hour work week; n/a not available.
Source: Bureau of Labor Statistics, Metro Area Occupational Employment and Wage Estimates, May 2015

TAXES

State Corporate Income Tax Rates

State	Tax Rate (%)	Income Brackets ($)	Num. of Brackets	Financial Institution Tax Rate (%)[a]	Federal Income Tax Ded.
Florida	5.5 (f)	Flat rate	1	5.5 (f)	No

Note: Tax rates as of January 1, 2016; (a) Rates listed are the corporate income tax rate applied to financial institutions or excise taxes based on income. Some states have other taxes based upon the value of deposits or shares; (f) An exemption of $50,000 is allowed. Florida's Alternative Minimum Tax rate is 3.3%.
Source: Federation of Tax Administrators, "State Corporate Income Tax Rates, 2016"

State Individual Income Tax Rates

State	Tax Rate (%)	Income Brackets ($)	Num. of Brackets	Personal Exempt. ($)[1]		Fed. Inc. Tax Ded.
				Single	Dependents	
Florida	None	–	–	–	–	–

Note: Tax rates as of January 1, 2016; Local- and county-level taxes are not included; n/a not applicable; (1) Married joint filers generally receive double the single exemption
Source: Federation of Tax Administrators, "State Individual Income Tax Rates, 2016"

Various State and Local Tax Rates

State	State and Local Sales and Use (%)	State Sales and Use (%)	Gasoline[1] (¢/gal.)	Cigarette[2] ($/pack)	Spirits[3] ($/gal.)	Wine[4] ($/gal.)	Beer[5] ($/gal.)
Florida	7.00	6.0	36.58	1.339	6.50 (f)	2.25 (l)	0.48 (q)

Note: All tax rates as of January 1, 2016; (1) The American Petroleum Institute has developed a methodology for determining the average tax rate on a gallon of fuel. Rates may include any of the following: excise taxes, environmental fees, storage tank fees, other fees or taxes, general sales tax, and local taxes. In states where gasoline is subject to the general sales tax, or where the fuel tax is based on the average sale price, the average rate determined by API is sensitive to changes in the price of gasoline. States that fully or partially apply general sales taxes to gasoline: CA, CO, GA, IL, IN, MI, NY; (2) The federal excise tax of $1.0066 per pack and local taxes are not included; (3) Rates are those applicable to off-premise sales of 40% alcohol by volume (a.b.v.) distilled spirits in 750ml containers. Local excise taxes are excluded; (4) Rates are those applicable to off-premise sales of 11% a.b.v. non-carbonated wine in 750ml containers; (5) Rates are those applicable to off-premise sales of 4.7% a.b.v. beer in 12 ounce containers; (f) Different rates are also applicable according to alcohol content, place of production, size of container, or place purchased (on- or off-premise or onboard airlines); (l) Different rates also applicable according to alcohol content, place of production, size of container, place purchased (on- or off-premise or on board airlines) or type of wine (carbonated, vermouth, etc.); (q) Different rates are also applicable according to alcohol content, place of production, size of container, or place purchased (on- or off-premise or onboard airlines).
Source: Tax Foundation, 2016 Facts & Figures: How Does Your State Compare?

State Business Tax Climate Index Rankings

State	Overall Rank	Corporate Tax Rank	Individual Income Tax Rank	Sales Tax Rank	Unemployment Insurance Tax Rank	Property Tax Rank
Florida	4	17	1	17	3	20

Note: The index is a measure of how each state's tax laws affect economic performance. The lower the rank, the more favorable a state's tax system is for business. States without a given tax are given a ranking of 1. The scores/rankings for the District of Columbia do not affect other states. The 2016 index represents the tax climate as of July 1, 2015 (the beginning of Fiscal Year 2016).
Source: Tax Foundation, State Business Tax Climate Index 2016

TRANSPORTATION

Means of Transportation to Work

Area	Car/Truck/Van		Public Transportation			Bicycle	Walked	Other Means	Worked at Home
	Drove Alone	Car-pooled	Bus	Subway	Railroad				
City	84.9	7.0	0.2	0.0	0.0	0.3	0.8	1.0	5.6
MSA[1]	80.9	9.5	1.9	0.0	0.0	0.5	1.1	1.4	4.7
U.S.	76.4	9.6	2.6	1.8	0.6	0.6	2.8	1.3	4.4

Note: Figures are percentages and cover workers 16 years of age and older; (1) Figures cover the Orlando-Kissimmee-Sanford, FL Metropolitan Statistical Area—see Appendix B for areas included
Source: U.S. Census Bureau, 2010-2014 American Community Survey 5-Year Estimates

Travel Time to Work

Area	Less Than 10 Minutes	10 to 19 Minutes	20 to 29 Minutes	30 to 44 Minutes	45 to 59 Minutes	60 to 89 Minutes	90 Minutes or More
City	6.4	21.4	21.5	31.1	13.8	3.6	2.1
MSA[1]	7.4	27.0	23.6	25.9	9.6	4.5	2.0
U.S.	13.3	29.6	21.0	20.2	7.7	5.7	2.6

Note: Figures are percentages and include workers 16 years old and over; (1) Figures cover the Orlando-Kissimmee-Sanford, FL Metropolitan Statistical Area—see Appendix B for areas included
Source: U.S. Census Bureau, 2010-2014 American Community Survey 5-Year Estimates

Freeway Travel Time Index

Area	1985	1990	1995	2000	2005	2010	2014
Urban Area Rank[1,2]	35	25	32	28	27	33	34
Urban Area Index[1]	1.09	1.14	1.16	1.20	1.23	1.21	1.21
Average Index[3]	1.09	1.11	1.14	1.17	1.20	1.19	1.20

Note: Freeway Travel Time Index—the ratio of travel time in the peak period to the travel time at free-flow conditions. For example, a value of 1.30 indicates a 20-minute free-flow trip takes 26 minutes in the peak (20 minutes x 1.30 = 26 minutes); (1) Covers the Orlando FL urban area; (2) Rank is based on 101 urban areas (#1 = highest travel time index); (3) Average of 101 urban areas
Source: Texas Transportation Institute, 2015 Urban Mobility Scorecard, August 2015

Freeway Commuter Stress Index

Area	1985	1990	1995	2000	2005	2010	2014
Urban Area Rank[1,2]	36	33	37	36	35	37	38
Urban Area Index[1]	1.13	1.18	1.20	1.24	1.27	1.25	1.25
Average Index[3]	1.13	1.16	1.19	1.22	1.25	1.24	1.25

Note: The Freeway Commuter Stress Index is the same as the Freeway Travel Time Index (see table above) except that it includes only the travel in the peak directions during the peak periods; the TTI includes travel in all directions during the peak period. Thus, the CSI is more indicative of the work trip experienced by each commuter on a daily basis. (1) Covers the Orlando FL urban area; (2) Rank is based on 101 urban areas (#1 = highest stress index); (3) Average of 101 urban areas

Source: Texas Transportation Institute, 2015 Urban Mobility Scorecard, August 2015

Living Environment

COST OF LIVING

Cost of Living Index

Composite Index	Groceries	Housing	Utilities	Transportation	Health Care	Misc. Goods/ Services
98.3	104.8	95.7	95.9	102.0	95.0	97.8

Note: The Cost of Living Index measures regional differences in the cost of consumer goods and services, excluding taxes and non-consumer expenditures, for professional and managerial households in the top income quintile. It is based on more than 50,000 prices covering almost 60 different items for which prices are collected three times a year by chambers of commerce, economic development organizations or university applied economic centers in each participating urban area. The numbers shown should be read as a percentage above or below the national average of 100. For example, a value of 115.4 in the groceries column indicates that grocery prices are 15.4% higher than the national average. Small differences in the index numbers should not be interpreted as significant; Figures cover the Orlando FL urban area.
Source: The Council for Community and Economic Research, ACCRA Cost of Living Index, 2015

Grocery Prices

Area[1]	T-Bone Steak ($/pound)	Frying Chicken ($/pound)	Whole Milk ($/half gal.)	Eggs ($/dozen)	Orange Juice ($/64 oz.)	Coffee ($/11.5 oz.)
City[2]	11.81	1.52	2.59	2.53	3.38	3.81
Avg.	10.99	1.43	2.25	2.26	3.58	4.48
Min.	7.16	0.98	1.30	1.35	2.88	2.98
Max.	14.13	2.43	3.85	4.81	6.39	7.56

Note: (1) Values for the local area are compared with the average, minimum and maximum values for all 292 areas in the Cost of Living Index; (2) Figures cover the Orlando FL urban area; **T-Bone Steak** *(price per pound);* **Frying Chicken** *(price per pound, whole fryer);* **Whole Milk** *(half gallon carton);* **Eggs** *(price per dozen, Grade A, large);* **Orange Juice** *(64 oz. Tropicana or Florida Natural);* **Coffee** *(11.5 oz. can, vacuum-packed, Maxwell House, Hills Bros, or Folgers).*
Source: The Council for Community and Economic Research, ACCRA Cost of Living Index, 2015

Housing and Utility Costs

Area[1]	New Home Price ($)	Apartment Rent ($/month)	All Electric ($/month)	Part Electric ($/month)	Other Energy ($/month)	Telephone ($/month)
City[2]	287,272	958	178.39	-	-	23.31
Avg.	312,874	945	179.30	95.07	72.96	28.11
Min.	178,682	479	116.28	43.14	26.46	10.01
Max.	1,472,476	3,984	504.25	189.44	421.11	43.06

Note: (1) Values for the local area are compared with the average, minimum and maximum values for all 292 areas in the Cost of Living Index; (2) Figures cover the Orlando FL urban area; **New Home Price** *(2,400 sf living area, 8,000 sf lot, in urban area with full utilities);* **Apartment Rent** *(950 sf 2 bedroom/1.5 or 2 bath, unfurnished, excluding all utilities except water);* **All Electric** *(average monthly cost for an all-electric home);* **Part Electric** *(average monthly cost for a part-electric home);* **Other Energy** *(average monthly cost for natural gas, fuel oil, coal, wood, and any other forms of energy except electricity);* **Telephone** *(price includes basic monthly rate for a private residential line plus additional local usage charges incurred by a family of four).*
Source: The Council for Community and Economic Research, ACCRA Cost of Living Index, 2015

Health Care, Transportation, and Other Costs

Area[1]	Doctor ($/visit)	Dentist ($/visit)	Optometrist ($/visit)	Gasoline ($/gallon)	Beauty Salon ($/visit)	Men's Shirt ($)
City[2]	85.45	88.74	64.24	2.41	40.70	22.40
Avg.	105.15	89.02	99.78	2.38	35.30	28.10
Min.	66.87	56.09	48.53	1.95	18.91	13.38
Max.	182.34	150.36	228.33	4.09	67.91	63.80

Note: (1) Values for the local area are compared with the average, minimum and maximum values for all 292 areas in the Cost of Living Index; (2) Figures cover the Orlando FL urban area; **Doctor** *(general practitioners routine exam of an established patient);* **Dentist** *(adult teeth cleaning and periodic oral examination);* **Optometrist** *(full vision eye exam for established adult patient);* **Gasoline** *(one gallon regular unleaded, national brand, including all taxes, cash price at self-service pump if available);* **Beauty Salon** *(woman's shampoo, trim, and blow-dry);* **Men's Shirt** *(cotton/polyester dress shirt, pinpoint weave, long sleeves).*
Source: The Council for Community and Economic Research, ACCRA Cost of Living Index, 2015

HOUSING

House Price Index (HPI)

Area	National Ranking[2]	Quarterly Change (%)	One-Year Change (%)	Five-Year Change (%)
MSA[1]	33	1.60	9.50	25.20
U.S.[3]	–	1.45	5.76	22.85

Note: The HPI is a weighted repeat sales index. It measures average price changes in repeat sales or refinancings on the same properties. This information is obtained by reviewing repeat mortgage transactions on single-family properties whose mortgages have been purchased or securitized by Fannie Mae or Freddie Mac in January 1975; (1) Orlando-Kissimmee-Sanford Metropolitan Statistical Area—see Appendix B for areas included; (2) Rankings are based on annual percentage change for all metro areas containing at least 15,000 transactions over the last 10 years and ranges from 1 to 266; (3) figures based on a weighted average of Census Division estimates using a seasonally adjusted, purchase-only index; all figures are for the period ending December 31, 2015

Source: Federal Housing Finance Agency, House Price Index, February 25, 2016

Median Single-Family Home Prices

Area	2013	2014	2015[p]	Percent Change 2014 to 2015
MSA[1]	160.4	180.0	197.6	9.8
U.S. Average	197.4	208.9	223.9	7.2

Note: Figures are median sales prices of existing single-family homes in thousands of dollars; (p) preliminary; n/a not available; (1) Orlando-Kissimmee-Sanford, FL Metropolitan Statistical Area—see Appendix B for areas included

Source: National Association of Realtors, Median Sales Price of Existing Single-Family Homes for Metropolitan Areas, 4th Quarter 2015

Qualifying Income Based on Median Sales Price of Existing Single-Family Homes

Area	With 5% Down ($)	With 10% Down ($)	With 20% Down ($)
MSA[1]	45,598	43,198	38,399
U.S. Average	49,535	46,928	41,714

Note: Figures are preliminary; Qualifying income is based on a mortgage rate of 4.1%. Monthly principal and interest payment is limited to 25% of income; n/a not available; (1) Orlando-Kissimmee-Sanford, FL Metropolitan Statistical Area—see Appendix B for areas included

Source: National Association of Realtors, Qualifying Income Based on Median Sales Price of Existing Single-Family Homes for Metropolitan Areas, 4th Quarter 2015

Median Apartment Condo-Coop Home Prices

Area	2013	2014	2015[p]	Percent Change 2014 to 2015
MSA[1]	n/a	n/a	n/a	n/a
U.S. Average	194.9	204.3	210.7	3.1

Note: Figures are median sales prices of existing apartment condo-coop homes in thousands of dollars; (p) preliminary; n/a not available; (1) Orlando-Kissimmee-Sanford, FL Metropolitan Statistical Area—see Appendix B for areas included

Source: National Association of Realtors, Median Sales Price of Existing Apartment Condo-Coop Homes for Metropolitan Areas, 4th Quarter 2015

Gross Monthly Rent

Area	Under $200	$200 -299	$300 -499	$500 -749	$750 -999	$1,000 -1,499	$1,500 and up	Median ($)
City	0.5	0.3	0.9	8.0	14.5	43.5	32.2	1,321
MSA[1]	0.4	0.9	2.4	12.5	30.5	40.5	12.9	1,032
U.S.	1.5	3.2	7.4	21.0	24.1	26.9	15.9	920

Note: Figures are percentages except for Median; Gross rent is the contract rent plus the estimated average monthly cost of utilities (electricity, gas, and water and sewer) and fuels (oil, coal, kerosene, wood, etc.) if these are paid by the renter (or paid for the renter by someone else); (1) Figures cover the Orlando-Kissimmee-Sanford, FL Metropolitan Statistical Area—see Appendix B for areas included

Source: U.S. Census Bureau, 2010-2014 American Community Survey 5-Year Estimates

Homeownership Rate

Area	2008 (%)	2009 (%)	2010 (%)	2011 (%)	2012 (%)	2013 (%)	2014 (%)	2015 (%)
MSA[1]	70.5	72.4	70.8	68.6	68.0	65.5	62.3	58.4
U.S.	67.8	67.4	66.9	66.1	65.4	65.1	64.5	63.7

Note: (1) Figures cover the Orlando-Kissimmee-Sanford, FL Metropolitan Statistical Area—see Appendix B for areas included
Source: U.S. Census Bureau, Housing Vacancies and Homeownership Annual Statistics: 2015

Year Housing Structure Built

Area	2010 or Later	2000 -2009	1990 -1999	1980 -1989	1970 -1979	1960 -1969	1950 -1959	1940 -1949	Before 1940	Median Year
City	2.2	24.3	42.8	22.3	5.0	1.3	0.7	1.1	0.4	1994
MSA[1]	1.1	27.1	21.2	21.6	13.8	6.4	5.8	1.4	1.6	1990
U.S.	1.0	14.9	13.9	13.8	15.8	11.0	10.8	5.4	13.3	1976

Note: Figures are percentages except for Median Year; (1) Figures cover the Orlando-Kissimmee-Sanford, FL Metropolitan Statistical Area—see Appendix B for areas included
Source: U.S. Census Bureau, 2010-2014 American Community Survey 5-Year Estimates

HEALTH

Health Risk Data

Category	MSA[1] (%)	U.S. (%)
Adults aged 18–64 who have any kind of health care coverage	73.0	79.6
Adults who reported being in good or excellent health	76.8	83.1
Adults who are current smokers	18.7	19.6
Adults who are heavy drinkers[2]	5.7	6.1
Adults who are binge drinkers[3]	17.6	16.9
Adults who are overweight (BMI 25.0 - 29.9)	35.7	35.8
Adults who are obese (BMI 30.0 - 99.8)	28.1	27.6
Adults who participated in any physical activities in the past month	77.7	77.1
Adults 50+ who have ever had a sigmoidoscopy or colonoscopy	72.5	67.3
Women aged 40+ who have had a mammogram within the past two years	76.9	74.0
Men aged 40+ who have had a PSA test within the past two years	53.4	45.2
Adults aged 65+ who have had flu shot within the past year	54.6	60.1
Adults who always wear a seatbelt	94.5	93.8

Note: Data as of 2012 unless otherwise noted; (1) Figures cover the Orlando-Kissimmee, FL Metropolitan Statistical Area—see Appendix B for areas included; (2) Heavy drinkers are classified as males having more than two drinks per day or females having more than one drink per day; (3) Binge drinkers are classified as males having five or more drinks on one occasion or females having four or more drinks on one occasion
Source: Centers for Disease Control and Prevention, Behaviorial Risk Factor Surveillance System, SMART: Selected Metropolitan/Micropolitan Area Risk Trends, 2012 (Note: the CDC has discontinued this dataset but will be releasing a replacement in mid-2016)

Chronic Health Indicators

Category	MSA[1] (%)	U.S. (%)
Adults who have ever been told they had a heart attack	6.6	4.5
Adults who have ever been told they had a stroke	n/a	2.9
Adults who have been told they currently have asthma	9.5	8.9
Adults who have ever been told they have arthritis	21.9	25.7
Adults who have ever been told they have diabetes[2]	10.2	9.7
Adults who have ever been told they had skin cancer	5.7	5.7
Adults who have ever been told they had any other types of cancer	7.3	6.5
Adults who have ever been told they have COPD	5.9	6.2
Adults who have ever been told they have kidney disease	2.8	2.5
Adults who have ever been told they have a form of depression	18.2	18.0

Note: Data as of 2012 unless otherwise noted; n/a not available; (1) Figures cover the Orlando-Kissimmee, FL Metropolitan Statistical Area—see Appendix B for areas included; (2) Figures do not include pregnancy-related, borderline, or pre-diabetes
Source: Centers for Disease Control and Prevention, Behaviorial Risk Factor Surveillance System, SMART: Selected Metropolitan/Micropolitan Area Risk Trends, 2012 (Note: the CDC has discontinued this dataset but will be releasing a replacement in mid-2016)

Mortality Rates for the Top 10 Causes of Death in the U.S.

ICD-10[a] Sub-Chapter	ICD-10[a] Code	Age-Adjusted Mortality Rate[1] per 100,000 population	
		County[2]	U.S.
Malignant neoplasms	C00-C97	150.6	163.6
Ischaemic heart diseases	I20-I25	86.1	102.2
Other forms of heart disease	I30-I51	33.8	50.1
Chronic lower respiratory diseases	J40-J47	39.1	41.4
Organic, including symptomatic, mental disorders	F01-F09	38.2	38.5
Cerebrovascular diseases	I60-I69	32.2	36.5
Other external causes of accidental injury	W00-X59	24.1	27.5
Other degenerative diseases of the nervous system	G30-G31	23.3	26.3
Diabetes mellitus	E10-E14	23.2	21.1
Hypertensive diseases	I10-I15	19.6	19.7

Note: (a) ICD-10 = International Classification of Diseases 10th Revision; (1) Mortality rates are a three year average covering 2012-2014; (2) Figures cover Seminole County.
Source: Centers for Disease Control and Prevention, National Center for Health Statistics. Underlying Cause of Death 1999-2014 on CDC WONDER Online Database, released 2015.

Mortality Rates for Selected Causes of Death

ICD-10[a] Sub-Chapter	ICD-10[a] Code	Age-Adjusted Mortality Rate[1] per 100,000 population	
		County[2]	U.S.
Assault	X85-Y09	3.4	5.1
Diseases of the liver	K70-K76	11.9	13.5
Human immunodeficiency virus (HIV) disease	B20-B24	2.1	2.1
Influenza and pneumonia	J09-J18	10.4	15.2
Intentional self-harm	X60-X84	12.2	12.7
Malnutrition	E40-E46	Suppressed	0.9
Obesity and other hyperalimentation	E65-E68	1.5	1.9
Renal failure	N17-N19	9.7	13.0
Transport accidents	V01-V99	9.8	11.6
Viral hepatitis	B15-B19	1.8	2.1

Note: (a) ICD-10 = International Classification of Diseases 10th Revision; (1) Mortality rates are a three year average covering 2012-2014; (2) Figures cover Seminole County; Data are Suppressed when the data meet the criteria for confidentiality constraints; Mortality rates are flagged as Unreliable when the rate would be calculated with a numerator of 20 or less.
Source: Centers for Disease Control and Prevention, National Center for Health Statistics. Underlying Cause of Death 1999-2014 on CDC WONDER Online Database, released 2015.

Health Insurance Coverage

Area	With Health Insurance	With Private Health Insurance	With Public Health Insurance	Without Health Insurance	Population Under Age 18 Without Health Insurance
City	90.2	79.0	18.2	9.8	2.3
MSA[1]	79.9	60.5	28.5	20.1	11.9
U.S.	85.8	65.8	31.1	14.2	7.1

Note: Figures are percentages that cover the civilian noninstitutionalized population; (1) Figures cover the Orlando-Kissimmee-Sanford, FL Metropolitan Statistical Area—see Appendix B for areas included
Source: U.S. Census Bureau, 2010-2014 American Community Survey 5-Year Estimates

Number of Medical Professionals

Area	MDs[3]	DOs[3,4]	Dentists	Podiatrists	Chiropractors	Optometrists
County[1] (number)	814	89	249	29	131	84
County[1] (rate[2])	186.4	20.4	56.3	6.6	29.6	19.0
U.S. (rate[2])	272.5	20.9	64.7	5.8	25.9	15.2

Note: Data as of 2014 unless noted; (1) Data covers Seminole County; (2) Rate per 100,000 population; (3) Data as of 2013 and includes all active, non-federal physicians; (4) Doctor of Osteopathic Medicine
Source: U.S. Department of Health and Human Services, Health Resources and Services Administration, Bureau of Health Professions, Area Resource File (ARF) 2014-2015

Best Hospitals

According to *U.S. News,* the Orlando-Kissimmee-Sanford, FL metro area is home to one of the best hospitals in the U.S.: **Florida Hospital Orlando** (9 specialties). The hospital listed was nationally ranked in at least one adult specialty. Only 137 hospitals nationwide were nationally ranked in one or more specialties. Fifteen hospitals in the U.S. made the Honor Roll with high scores in at least six specialties. *U.S. News Online, "America's Best Children's Hospitals 2015-16"*

According to *U.S. News,* the Orlando-Kissimmee-Sanford, FL metro area is home to one of the best children's hospitals in the U.S.: **Arnold Palmer Medical Center** (7 specialties). The hospital listed was highly ranked in at least one pediatric specialty. Eighty-three children's hospitals in the U.S. were nationally ranked in at least one specialty. Twelve children's hospitals in the U.S. made the Honor Roll with high scores in at least three specialties. *U.S. News Online, "America's Best Children's Hospitals 2015-16"*

EDUCATION

Public School District Statistics

District Name	Schls	Pupils	Pupil/ Teacher Ratio	Minority Pupils[1] (%)	Free Lunch Eligible[2] (%)	IEP[3] (%)
Seminole	76	64,851	12.9	45.5	37.7	12.4

Note: Table includes school districts with 100 or more students; (1) Percentage of students that are not non-Hispanic white; (2) Percentage of students that are eligible for the free lunch program; (3) Percentage of students that have an Individualized Education Program.

Source: U.S. Department of Education, National Center for Education Statistics, Common Core of Data, Local Education Agency (School District) Universe Survey: School Year 2013-2014; U.S. Department of Education, National Center for Education Statistics, Common Core of Data, Public Elementary/Secondary School Universe Survey: School Year 2013-2014

Best High Schools

According to *U.S. News,* Oviedo is home to one of the best high schools in the U.S.: **Hagerty High School** (#444); Nearly 20,000 schools were ranked based on their performance on state assessments and how well they prepare students for college. Schools with the highest unrounded College Readiness Index values were numerically ranked from No. 1 to No. 500 and were the gold medal winners. *U.S. News & World Report, "Best High Schools 2015"*

Highest Level of Education

Area	Less than H.S.	H.S. Diploma	Some College, No Deg.	Associate Degree	Bachelor's Degree	Master's Degree	Prof. School Degree	Doctorate Degree
City	5.2	18.6	21.3	12.3	28.1	11.1	1.8	1.6
MSA[1]	12.2	28.2	21.2	10.0	19.0	6.8	1.7	0.9
U.S.	13.7	28.0	21.2	7.9	18.3	7.8	2.0	1.3

Note: Figures cover persons age 25 and over; (1) Figures cover the Orlando-Kissimmee-Sanford, FL Metropolitan Statistical Area—see Appendix B for areas included

Source: U.S. Census Bureau, 2010-2014 American Community Survey 5-Year Estimates

Educational Attainment by Race

Area	High School Graduate or Higher (%)					Bachelor's Degree or Higher (%)				
	Total	White	Black	Asian	Hisp.[2]	Total	White	Black	Asian	Hisp.[2]
City	94.8	95.7	90.1	88.4	91.0	42.6	43.9	33.6	46.8	33.1
MSA[1]	87.8	89.7	82.8	85.6	80.4	28.4	29.8	19.5	47.4	19.5
U.S.	86.3	88.4	83.2	85.8	64.1	29.3	30.6	19.0	50.9	13.9

Note: Figures shown cover persons 25 years old and over; (1) Figures cover the Orlando-Kissimmee-Sanford, FL Metropolitan Statistical Area—see Appendix B for areas included; (2) People of Hispanic origin can be of any race

Source: U.S. Census Bureau, 2010-2014 American Community Survey 5-Year Estimates

School Enrollment by Grade and Control

Area	Preschool (%)		Kindergarten (%)		Grades 1 - 4 (%)		Grades 5 - 8 (%)		Grades 9 - 12 (%)	
	Public	Private	Public	Private	Public	Private	Public	Private	Public	Private
City	51.6	48.4	64.8	35.2	87.2	12.8	84.2	15.8	91.6	8.4
MSA[1]	50.3	49.7	84.9	15.1	88.8	11.2	88.8	11.2	90.6	9.4
U.S.	57.4	42.6	87.8	12.2	89.8	10.2	89.9	10.1	90.6	9.4

Note: Figures shown cover persons 3 years old and over; (1) Figures cover the Orlando-Kissimmee-Sanford, FL Metropolitan Statistical Area—see Appendix B for areas included
Source: U.S. Census Bureau, 2010-2014 American Community Survey 5-Year Estimates

Average Salaries of Public School Classroom Teachers

Area	2013-14		2014-15		Percent Change 2013-14 to 2014-15	Percent Change 2004-05 to 2014-15
	Dollars	Rank[1]	Dollars	Rank[1]		
Florida	47,780	39	48,992	36	2.54	17.8
U.S. Average	56,610	–	57,379	–	1.36	20.8

Note: (1) State rank ranges from 1 to 51 where 1 indicates highest salary.
Source: National Education Association, Rankings & Estimates: Rankings of the States 2014 and Estimates of School Statistics 2015, March 2015

Higher Education

Four-Year Colleges			Two-Year Colleges			Medical Schools[1]	Law Schools[2]	Voc/ Tech[3]
Public	Private Non-profit	Private For-profit	Public	Private Non-profit	Private For-profit			
0	0	0	0	0	0	0	0	1

Note: Figures cover institutions located within the city limits and include main campuses only; (1) includes schools accredited by the Liaison Committee on Medical Education and the American Osteopathic Association's Commission on Osteopathic College Accreditation; (2) includes ABA-accredited schools, schools with provisional ABA accreditation, and state accredited schools; (3) includes all schools with programs that are less than 2 years.
Source: National Center for Education Statistics, Integrated Postsecondary Education System (IPEDS), 2014-15; Association of American Medical Colleges, Member List, March 21, 2016; American Osteopathic Association, Member List, March 21, 2016; Law School Admission Council, Official Guide to ABA-Approved Law Schools Online, March 21, 2016; Wikipedia, List of Medical Schools in the United States, March 21, 2016; Wikipedia, List of Law Schools in the United States, March 21, 2016

According to *U.S. News & World Report,* the Orlando-Kissimmee-Sanford, FL metro area is home to one of the best national universities in the U.S.: **University of Central Florida** (#168 tie). The indicators used to capture academic quality fall into a number of categories: assessment by administrators at peer institutions; retention of students; faculty resources; student selectivity; financial resources; alumni giving; high school counselor ratings of colleges; and graduation rate. *U.S. News & World Report, "America's Best Colleges 2016"*

PRESIDENTIAL ELECTION

2012 Presidential Election Results

Area	Obama (%)	Romney (%)	Other (%)
Seminole County	46.2	52.7	1.1
U.S.	51.0	47.2	1.8

Note: Results may not add to 100% due to rounding
Source: Dave Leip's Atlas of U.S. Presidential Elections

EMPLOYERS

Major Employers

Company Name	Industry
Adventist Health System/Sunbelt	General medical & surgical hospitals
Airtran Airways	Air passenger carrier, scheduled
Central Florida Health Alliance	Hospital management
Children & Families, Florida Department	Individual & family services
Cnl Lifestyle Properties	Real estate agents & managers
Connextions	Communication services, nec
Florida Hospital Medical Center	General medical & surgical hospitals
Gaylord Palms Resort & Conv Ctr	Hotel franchised
Leesburg Regional Medical Center	General medical & surgical hospitals
Lockheed Martin Corporation	Aircraft
Marriott International	Hotels & motels
Orlando Health	General medical & surgical hospitals
Rosen 9939	Hotels
Sea World of Florida	Theme park, amusement
Sears Termite & Pest Control	Pest control in structures
Siemens Energy	Power plant construction
Universal City Florida Partners	Amusement parks
University of Central Florida	Colleges & universities
Winter Park Healthcare Group	Hospital affiliated with ama residency

Note: Companies shown are located within the Orlando-Kissimmee-Sanford, FL Metropolitan Statistical Area.
Source: Hoovers.com; Wikipedia

PUBLIC SAFETY

Crime Rate

Area	All Crimes	Violent Crimes				Property Crimes		
		Murder	Rape[3]	Robbery	Aggrav. Assault	Burglary	Larceny -Theft	Motor Vehicle Theft
City	1,379.9	2.7	8.0	10.7	128.1	331.0	859.4	40.0
Metro[1]	4,697.9	6.8	62.5	154.4	461.8	976.0	2,789.2	247.3
U.S.	2,971.8	4.5	36.6	102.2	232.5	542.5	1,837.3	216.2

Note: Figures are crimes per 100,000 population; (1) Figures cover the Orlando-Kissimmee-Sanford, FL Metropolitan Statistical Area—see Appendix B for areas included; (3) The city and U.S. figures shown were reported using the revised Uniform Crime Reporting (UCR) definition of rape. The suburban and metro area figures shown are an aggregate total of the data submitted using both the revised and legacy UCR definitions.
Source: FBI Uniform Crime Reports, 2014

Hate Crimes

Area	Number of Quarters Reported	Number of Incidents per Bias Motivation						
		Race	Religion	Sexual Orientation	Ethnicity	Disability	Gender	Gender Identity
City	4	1	0	0	0	0	0	0
U.S.	4	2,568	1,014	1,017	648	84	33	98

Source: Federal Bureau of Investigation, Hate Crime Statistics 2014

Identity Theft Consumer Complaints

Area	Complaints	Complaints per 100,000 Population	Rank[2]
MSA[1]	4,439	191.2	22
U.S.	490,220	152.4	-

Note: (1) Figures cover the Orlando-Kissimmee-Sanford, FL Metropolitan Statistical Area—see Appendix B for areas included; (2) Rank ranges from 1 to 379 where 1 indicates greatest number of identity theft complaints per 100,000 population
Source: Federal Trade Commission, Consumer Sentinel Network Data Book for January–December 2015

Fraud and Other Consumer Complaints

Area	Complaints	Complaints per 100,000 Population	Rank[2]
MSA[1]	10,921	470.4	32
U.S.	2,593,159	806.0	-

Note: (1) Figures cover the Orlando-Kissimmee-Sanford, FL Metropolitan Statistical Area—see Appendix B for areas included; (2) Rank ranges from 1 to 379 where 1 indicates greatest number of identity theft complaints per 100,000 population
Source: Federal Trade Commission, Consumer Sentinel Network Data Book for January–December 2015

RECREATION

Culture

Dance[1]	Theatre[1]	Instrumental Music[1]	Vocal Music[1]	Series and Festivals	Museums and Art Galleries[2]	Zoos and Aquariums[3]
0	0	0	0	0	0	0

Note: (1) Professional perfoming groups; (2) Based on organizations with SIC code 8412; (3) AZA-accredited
Source: The Grey House Performing Arts Directory, 2015-16; Association of Zoos & Aquariums, AZA Member Zoos & Aquariums, March 25, 2016; www.AccuLeads.com, March 29, 2016

Professional Sports Teams

Team Name	League	Year Established
Orlando City SC	Major League Soccer (MLS)	2015
Orlando Magic	National Basketball Association (NBA)	1989

Note: Includes teams located in the Orlando-Kissimmee-Sanford, FL Metropolitan Statistical Area.
Source: Wikipedia, Major Professional Sports Teams of the United States and Canada, March 24, 2016

CLIMATE

Average and Extreme Temperatures

Temperature	Jan	Feb	Mar	Apr	May	Jun	Jul	Aug	Sep	Oct	Nov	Dec	Yr.
Extreme High (°F)	86	89	90	95	100	100	99	100	98	95	89	90	100
Average High (°F)	70	72	77	82	87	90	91	91	89	83	78	72	82
Average Temp. (°F)	59	62	67	72	77	81	82	82	81	75	68	62	72
Average Low (°F)	48	51	56	60	66	71	73	74	72	66	58	51	62
Extreme Low (°F)	19	29	25	38	51	53	64	65	57	44	32	20	19

Note: Figures cover the years 1952-1990
Source: National Climatic Data Center, International Station Meteorological Climate Summary, 9/96

Average Precipitation/Snowfall/Humidity

Precip./Humidity	Jan	Feb	Mar	Apr	May	Jun	Jul	Aug	Sep	Oct	Nov	Dec	Yr.
Avg. Precip. (in.)	2.3	2.8	3.4	2.0	3.2	7.0	7.2	5.8	5.8	2.7	3.5	2.0	47.7
Avg. Snowfall (in.)	Tr	0	0	0	0	0	0	0	0	0	0	0	Tr
Avg. Rel. Hum. 7am (%)	87	87	88	87	88	89	90	92	92	89	89	87	89
Avg. Rel. Hum. 4pm (%)	53	51	49	47	51	61	65	66	66	59	56	55	57

Note: Figures cover the years 1952-1990; Tr = Trace amounts (<0.05 in. of rain; <0.5 in. of snow)
Source: National Climatic Data Center, International Station Meteorological Climate Summary, 9/96

Weather Conditions

Temperature			Daytime Sky			Precipitation		
32°F & below	45°F & below	90°F & above	Clear	Partly cloudy	Cloudy	0.01 inch or more precip.	0.1 inch or more snow/ice	Thunder-storms
3	35	90	76	208	81	115	0	80

Note: Figures are average number of days per year and cover the years 1952-1990
Source: National Climatic Data Center, International Station Meteorological Climate Summary, 9/96

HAZARDOUS WASTE

Superfund Sites

Oviedo has no sites on the EPA's Superfund Final National Priorities List. There are a total of 1,323 Superfund sites on the list in the U.S. *U.S. Environmental Protection Agency, Final National Priorities List, March 18, 2016*

AIR & WATER QUALITY

Air Quality Trends: Ozone

	1990	1995	2000	2005	2010	2011	2012	2013	2014
MSA[1]	0.081	0.075	0.080	0.083	0.069	0.075	0.071	0.063	0.062

Note: (1) Data covers the Orlando-Kissimmee-Sanford, FL Metropolitan Statistical Area—see Appendix B for areas included. The values shown are the composite ozone concentration averages among trend sites based on the highest fourth daily maximum 8-hour concentration in parts per million. These trends are based on sites having an adequate record of monitoring data during the trend period. Data from exceptional events are included.

Source: U.S. Environmental Protection Agency, Air Quality Monitoring Information, "Air Quality Trends by City, 1990-2014"

Air Quality Index

Area	Percent of Days when Air Quality was...[2]					AQI Statistics[2]	
	Good	Moderate	Unhealthy for Sensitive Groups	Unhealthy	Very Unhealthy	Maximum	Median
MSA[1]	87.7	12.3	0.0	0.0	0.0	87	37

Note: (1) Data covers the Orlando-Kissimmee-Sanford, FL Metropolitan Statistical Area—see Appendix B for areas included; (2) Based on 365 days with AQI data in 2015. Air Quality Index (AQI) is an index for reporting daily air quality. EPA calculates the AQI for five major air pollutants regulated by the Clean Air Act: ground-level ozone, particle pollution (aka particulate matter), carbon monoxide, sulfur dioxide, and nitrogen dioxide. The AQI runs from 0 to 500. The higher the AQI value, the greater the level of air pollution and the greater the health concern. There are six AQI categories: "Good" AQI is between 0 and 50. Air quality is considered satisfactory; "Moderate" AQI is between 51 and 100. Air quality is acceptable; "Unhealthy for Sensitive Groups" When AQI values are between 101 and 150, members of sensitive groups may experience health effects; "Unhealthy" When AQI values are between 151 and 200 everyone may begin to experience health effects; "Very Unhealthy" AQI values between 201 and 300 trigger a health alert; "Hazardous" AQI values over 300 trigger warnings of emergency conditions (not shown).

Source: U.S. Environmental Protection Agency, Air Quality Index Report, 2015

Air Quality Index Pollutants

Area	Percent of Days when AQI Pollutant was...[2]					
	Carbon Monoxide	Nitrogen Dioxide	Ozone	Sulfur Dioxide	Particulate Matter 2.5	Particulate Matter 10
MSA[1]	0.0	0.0	54.2	0.0	45.5	0.3

Note: (1) Data covers the Orlando-Kissimmee-Sanford, FL Metropolitan Statistical Area—see Appendix B for areas included; (2) Based on 365 days with AQI data in 2015. The Air Quality Index (AQI) is an index for reporting daily air quality. EPA calculates the AQI for five major air pollutants regulated by the Clean Air Act: ground-level ozone, particle pollution (also known as particulate matter), carbon monoxide, sulfur dioxide, and nitrogen dioxide. The AQI runs from 0 to 500. The higher the AQI value, the greater the level of air pollution and the greater the health concern.

Source: U.S. Environmental Protection Agency, Air Quality Index Report, 2015

Maximum Air Pollutant Concentrations: Particulate Matter, Ozone, CO and Lead

	Particulate Matter 10 (ug/m^3)	Particulate Matter 2.5 Wtd AM (ug/m^3)	Particulate Matter 2.5 24-Hr (ug/m^3)	Ozone (ppm)	Carbon Monoxide (ppm)	Lead (ug/m^3)
MSA[1] Level	43	6.4	14	0.067	2	n/a
NAAQS[2]	150	15	35	0.075	9	0.15
Met NAAQS[2]	Yes	Yes	Yes	Yes	Yes	n/a

Note: (1) Data covers the Orlando-Kissimmee-Sanford, FL Metropolitan Statistical Area—see Appendix B for areas included; Data from exceptional events are included; (2) National Ambient Air Quality Standards; ppm = parts per million; ug/m^3 = micrograms per cubic meter; n/a not available.

Concentrations: Particulate Matter 10 (coarse particulate)—highest second maximum 24-hour concentration; Particulate Matter 2.5 Wtd AM (fine particulate)—highest weighted annual mean concentration; Particulate Matter 2.5 24-Hour (fine particulate)—highest 98th percentile 24-hour concentration; Ozone—highest fourth daily maximum 8-hour concentration; Carbon Monoxide—highest second maximum non-overlapping 8-hour concentration; Lead—maximum running 3-month average

Source: U.S. Environmental Protection Agency, Air Quality Monitoring Information, "Air Quality Statistics by City, 2014"

Maximum Air Pollutant Concentrations: Nitrogen Dioxide and Sulfur Dioxide

	Nitrogen Dioxide AM (ppb)	Nitrogen Dioxide 1-Hr (ppb)	Sulfur Dioxide AM (ppb)	Sulfur Dioxide 1-Hr (ppb)	Sulfur Dioxide 24-Hr (ppb)
MSA[1] Level	5	36	n/a	7	n/a
NAAQS[2]	53	100	30	75	140
Met NAAQS[2]	Yes	Yes	n/a	Yes	n/a

Note: (1) Data covers the Orlando-Kissimmee-Sanford, FL Metropolitan Statistical Area—see Appendix B for areas included; Data from exceptional events are included; (2) National Ambient Air Quality Standards; ppm = parts per million; ug/m^3 = micrograms per cubic meter; n/a not available.
Concentrations: Nitrogen Dioxide AM—highest arithmetic mean concentration; Nitrogen Dioxide 1-Hr—highest 98th percentile 1-hour daily maximum concentration; Sulfur Dioxide AM—highest annual mean concentration; Sulfur Dioxide 1-Hr—highest 99th percentile 1-hour daily maximum concentration; Sulfur Dioxide 24-Hr—highest second maximum 24-hour concentration
Source: U.S. Environmental Protection Agency, Air Quality Monitoring Information, "Air Quality Statistics by City, 2014"

Drinking Water

Water System Name	Pop. Served	Primary Water Source Type	Violations[1]	
			Health Based	Monitoring/ Reporting
City of Oviedo	41,713	Ground	0	0

Note: (1) Based on violation data from January 1, 2015 to December 31, 2015 (includes unresolved violations from earlier years)
Source: U.S. Environmental Protection Agency, Office of Ground Water and Drinking Water, Safe Drinking Water Information System (based on data extracted April 29, 2016)

Parkland, Florida

Background

Parkland is an affluent city in Broward County, part of the Miami-Fort Lauderdale-Pompano Beach Metropolitan area. It is bordered by Palm Beach, Boca Raton, Coral Springs and the Everglades and is approximately 36 miles north of Miami.

Parkland is known, and named, for its park-like character. Situated in a lush and wooded area, Parkland is a diverse and tranquil community. It has been nicknamed the 'relaxed city' and is inviting and family-friendly. Within the community there are recreational facilities and amenities such as the famed Parkland Golf and Country Club by Toll Brothers which is an 18-hole championship golf course designed by the legendary golfer Greg Norman. Parkland stretches across 790 acres of lush woods, and caters to the active lifestyles of its residents and visitors.

Incorporated in 1963, Parkland city leaders take a conservative approach to growth in order to keep a small-town feeling. When the city was first developed there were no stores or traffic lights. As the area's popularity grew in the early 2000s, Parkland established the necessary infrastructure to accommodate the growth while also adhering to a well-maintained development plan. Today, Parkland boasts luxury houses, excellent schools, recreational activities, and is a 15-minute drive to the ocean. The city covers an area of about 13 square miles and about 4 percent of that is water. Historically, the area was known for its horse and polo community, which changed as the housing boom made its way from Miami and west from Fort Lauderdale. The Miami metropolitan area has always been the commercial and cultural center in the state of Florida with influences from the nearby Caribbean. In the past 30 years. Miami has emerged as a world class international hub and as a gateway for all of Latin America.

International business in import/export and international financial trade with Latin countries make up a large part of Parkland's economy. The area has a large banking industry and is home to many corporate headquarters. Cargo transport, logistics, and warehousing are major industries operating in the area. Although Parkland is a part of a sprawling metropolitan area, the city maintains its suburban tranquility of a smaller community.

Parkland, in close proximity to the vibrant center of Miami, benefits from being just outside the buzzing metropolis in an enclave of woodland and lush foliage. The quality of life is very high in Parkland, and there is a large amount of community involvement in development, expansion, and maintenance of the city. Its beautiful homes, restaurants, and shops contribute to a well-planned region, handling growth well. Parkland is a serene oasis amidst the cosmopolitan Miami area.

Parkland's restaurants run the gamut from take out to fine dining. The city's lifestyle tends to be casual, catering to the active lifestyle of its residents. Parkland has one of the best public school districts in Florida with easy access to excellent private schools. Many of the Parkland public schools are within walking distance to the housing communities. Parkland boasts 7 parks and recreational facilities along with a new YMCA. The city also has over 8.5 miles of bike paths, sidewalks, and multipurpose trails. Pine Trails Park, an 80-acre facility, houses Parkland's community center, three pavilions, four tee ball fields, basketball courts, a fishing peer, and boardwalk, and amphitheater. Parkland is not only one of the safest cities in Florida, but in the entire country. Parkland has its own police department through the Broward County Sheriff's Office and Public Works & Fire Department.

Parkland's south Florida climate is subtropical with long, warm, humid summers and abundant rainfall, followed by mild, dry winters. Sea breezes from the east and southeast may cause year-round temperature differences of 15 degrees or more from inland locations. Freezing conditions occur occasionally in the western suburbs. Strong thunderstorms with dangerous lightning can occur year-round and hurricanes are a risk in late summer and fall.

Rankings

Business/Finance Rankings

- The personal finance site NerdWallet analyzed 183 American metropolitan areas with populations over 250,000 and more than 15,000 businesses to rank where entrepreneurs find the most success. Criteria included area economy, annual income, housing cost, unemployment rate, and the success rate of area businesses. Fort Lauderdale* ranked #35. *www.nerdwallet.com, "Best Places to Start a Business," April 27, 2015*

- USAA and Hiring Our Heroes worked with Sperlings's BestPlaces and the Institute for Veterans and Military Families at Syracuse University to rank major metropolitan areas where military-skills-related employment is strongest. Criteria for veterans *pursuing entrepreneurship* included veteran-owned businesses per capita; percentage of small businesses; colleges; certification/license transfers; airports nearby; and accessible health resources. Metro areas with a higher than national average crime or unemployment rate were excluded. At #8, the Fort Lauderdale* metro area made the top ten. *www.usaa.com, "2015 Best Places for Veterans"*

- USAA and Hiring Our Heroes worked with Sperlings's BestPlaces and the Institute for Veterans and Military Families at Syracuse University to rank major metropolitan areas where military-skills-related employment is strongest. Criteria for *mid-career* veterans included veteran wage growth; military skills, defense contractor, and government jobs; recent job growth; stability; and accessible health resources. Metro areas with a higher than national average crime or unemployment rate were excluded. At #4, the Fort Lauderdale* metro area made the top ten. *www.usaa.com, "2015 Best Places for Veterans"*

- Based on the U.S. Department of Labor's Occupational Information Network Data Collection Program, the Brookings Institution defined job opportunities for STEM workers at various levels of educational attainment. The Fort Lauderdale* metro area was placed among the ten large metro areas with the lowest demand for high-level STEM knowledge. *www.brookings.edu, "The Hidden Stem Economy," June 10, 2013*

- Metro areas with the largest gap in income between rich and poor residents were identified by 24/7 Wall Street using the U.S. Census Bureau's 2013 American Community Survey. The Miami* metro area placed #8 among metro areas with the widest wealth gap between rich and poor. *247wallst.com, "20 Cities with the Widest Gap between the Rich and Poor," July 8, 2015*

- Based on metro area social media reviews, the employment opinion group Glassdoor surveyed 50 of the largest U.S. metro areas and equally weighed cost of living, hiring opportunity, and job satisfaction to compose a list of "25 Best Cities for Jobs." The Fort Lauderdale* metro area was ranked #25 in overall job satisfaction. *www.glassdoor.com, "Best Cities for Jobs," May 19, 2015*

- In a survey of economic confidence in the nation's 50 largest metropolitan areas conducted January–December 2014, the Miami* metro area placed #5, according to Gallup's 2014 Economic Confidence Index. *Gallup, "San Jose and San Francisco Lead in Economic Confidence," March 19, 2015*

- The Brookings Institution ranked the 100 largest metro areas in the U.S. based on income inequality. Miami* was ranked #8 (#1 = greatest ineqality). Criteria: the "95/20 ratio," a figure representing the income at which a household earns more than 95 percent of all other households, divided by the income at which a household earns more than only 20 percent of all other households. *Brookings Institution, "Income Inequality, 100 Largest U.S. Metro Areas, 2007-2014," January 14, 2016*

- The finance site *24/7 Wall St.* identified the metropolitan areas that have the smallest and largest pay disparities between men and women, comparing the median earnings for the past 12 months of both men and women working full-time in the country's 100 largest metropolitan statistical areas. Of the ten best-paying metros for women, the Miami* metro area ranked #6. *24/7 Wall St., "The Best (and Worst) Paying Cities for Women," March 6, 2015*

- Payscale.com ranked the 20 largest metro areas in terms of wage growth. The Miami* metro area ranked #9. Criteria: private-sector wage growth between the 1st quarter of 2015 and the 1st quarter of 2016. *PayScale, "Wage Trends by Metro Area," 1st Quarter, 2016*

- The Fort Lauderdale* metro area appeared on the Milken Institute "2015 Best Performing Cities" list. Rank: #41 out of 200 large metro areas. Criteria: job growth; wage and salary growth; high-tech output growth. *Milken Institute, "Best-Performing Cities 2015," December 2015*

- *Forbes* ranked the 200 most populous metro areas to determine the nation's "Best Places for Business and Careers." The Fort Lauderdale* metro area was ranked #57. Criteria: costs (business and living); job growth (past and projected); income growth; educational attainment (college and high school); projected economic growth; cultural and recreational opportunities; net migration patterns; number of highly ranked colleges. *Forbes, "The Best Places for Business and Careers 2015," July 29, 2015*

Education Rankings

- Personal finance website *WalletHub* analyzed the 150 largest U.S. metropolitan statistical areas to determine where the most educated Americans are choosing to settle. Criteria: education quality and attainment gap; education levels; percentage of workers with degrees; public school rankings; quality and size of each metro area's universities. Miami* was ranked #100 (#1 = most educated city). *www.WalletHub.com, "2015's Most and Least Educated Cities*

Environmental Rankings

- The Miami* metro area came in at #342 for the relative comfort of its climate on Sperling's list of "chill cities," as measured by the Sperling Heat Index. All 361 metro areas are included. Criteria included daytime high temperatures, nighttime low temperatures, dew point, and relative humidity at the high temperatures. *www.bertsperling.com, "Sperling's Chill Cities," July 18, 2013*

- Sperling's BestPlaces assessed 379 metropolitan areas of the United States for the likelihood of dangerously extreme weather events or earthquakes. In general the Southeast and South-Central regions have the highest risk of weather extremes and earthquakes, while the Pacific Northwest enjoys the lowest risk. Of the least risky metropolitan areas, the Fort Lauderdale* metro area was ranked #311. *www.bestplaces.net, "Safest Places from Natural Disasters," April 2011*

- The U.S. Environmental Protection Agency (EPA) released a list of U.S. metropolitan areas with the most ENERGY STAR certified buildings in 2015. The Miami* metro area was ranked #18 out of 25. *U.S. Environmental Protection Agency, "Top Cities With the Most ENERGY STAR Certified Buildings in 2016," March 30, 2016*

- Miami* was highlighted as one of the top 25 cleanest metro areas for year-round particle pollution (Annual PM 2.5) in the U.S. during 2011 through 2013. The area ranked #23. *American Lung Association, State of the Air 2015*

Health/Fitness Rankings

- Analysts who tracked obesity rates in the nation's largest metro areas (populations above one million) found that the Fort Lauderdale* metro area was one of the ten major metros where residents were least likely to be obese, defined as a BMI score of 30 or above. *www.gallup.com, "Boulder, Colo., Residents Still Least Likely to Be Obese," April 4, 2014*

- For each of the 50 most populous metro areas in the United States, the American College of Sports Medicine's American Fitness Index evaluated infrastructure, community assets, and policies that encourage healthy and fit lifestyles, including preventive health behaviors, levels of chronic disease conditions, health care access, and community resources and policies that support physical activity. The Miami* metro area ranked #30 for "community fitness." *www.americanfitnessindex.org, "ACSM American Fitness Index Health and Community Fitness Status of the 50 Largest Metropolitan Areas," May 2015*

- The Miami* metro area was identified as one of the worst cities for bed bugs in America by pest control company Orkin. The area ranked #43 out of 50 based on the number of bed bug treatments Orkin performed from January to December 2015. *Orkin, "Chicago Tops Bed Bug Cities List for Fourth Year in a Row," January 13, 2016*

- Miami* was identified as a "2016 Spring Allergy Capital." The area ranked #75 out of 100. Three groups of factors were used to identify the most severe cities for people with allergies during the spring season: annual pollen levels; medicine utilization; access to board-certified allergists. *Asthma and Allergy Foundation of America, "Spring Allergy Capitals 2016"*

- Miami* was identified as a "2015 Asthma Capital." The area ranked #61 out of the nation's 100 largest metropolitan areas. Criteria: estimated prevalence; self-reported prevalence; crude death rate for asthma; annual pollen score; annual air quality; public smoking laws; number of board-certified asthma specialists; school inhaler access laws; rescue medication use; controller medication use; ER visits for asthma; uninsured rate; poverty rate. *Asthma and Allergy Foundation of America, "Asthma Capitals 2015"*

- The Miami* metro area ranked #47 out of 190 in The Gallup-Healthways Well-Being Index. Criteria: purpose; social well being; financial health; community and physical health. Results are based on telephone interviews with adults, aged 18 and older, living in metropolitan areas in the 50 U.S. states and the District of Columbia. *Gallup-Healthways, "State of American Well-Being," February 23, 2016*

Real Estate Rankings

- The Fort Lauderdale* metro area was identified as #5 among the ten housing markets with the highest percentage of distressed property sales, based on the findings of the housing data website RealtyTrac. Criteria: short sales; income and poverty figures; and unemployment data. *247wallst.com, "Cities Selling the Most Distressed Homes," January 23, 2014*

- The Fort Lauderdale* metro area was identified as one of the top 20 housing markets to invest in for 2016 by *Forbes*. The area ranked #8. Criteria: strong job and population growth; anticipated home price appreciation; and other factors. *Forbes.com, "Best Buy Cities: Where to Invest in Housing in 2016," January 27, 2016*

- The Fort Lauderdale* metro area was identified as one of the 15 worst housing markets for the next five years." Criteria: projected annualized change in home prices between the fourth quarter 2012 and the fourth quarter 2017. *The Business Insider, "The 15 Worst Housing Markets for the Next Five Years," May 22, 2013*

- The Miami* metro area was identified as one of the 20 least affordable housing markets in the U.S. in 2015. The area ranked #10 out of 179 markets. Criteria: qualification for a mortgage loan on a typical home. *National Association of Realtors®, Affordability Index of Existing Single-Family Homes for Metropolitan Areas, 2015*

- Fort Lauderdale* was ranked #165 out of 225 metro areas in terms of housing affordability in 2015 by the National Association of Home Builders (#1 = most affordable). Criteria: the share of homes sold in that area affordable to a family earning the local median income, based on standard mortgage underwriting criteria. *National Association of Home Builders®, NAHB-Wells Fargo Housing Opportunity Index, 4th Quarter 2015*

- The nation's largest metro areas were analyzed in terms of the percentage of households entering some stage of foreclosure in 2015. The Miami* metro area ranked #5 out of 20 (#1 = highest foreclosure rate). *RealtyTrac, "2015 Year-End U.S. Foreclosure Market Report™," January 12, 2016*

Safety Rankings

- The National Insurance Crime Bureau ranked 380 metro areas in the U.S. in terms of per capita rates of vehicle theft. The Miami* metro area ranked #60 (#1 = highest rate). Criteria: number of vehicle theft offenses per 100,000 inhabitants in 2014. *National Insurance Crime Bureau, "Hot Spots 2014," June 24, 2015*

Seniors/Retirement Rankings

- From its Best Cities for Successful Aging indexes, the Milken Institute generated rankings for metropolitan areas, weighing data in eight categories—health care, wellness, living arrangements, transportation, financial characteristics, education and employment opportunities, community engagement, and overall livability. The Miami* metro area was ranked #76 overall in the large metro area category. *Milken Institute, "Best Cities for Successful Aging, 2014"*

Sports/Recreation Rankings

- According to the personal finance website NerdWallet, the Miami* metro area, at #9, is one of the nation's top dozen metro areas for sports fans. Criteria included the presence of all four major sports—MLB, NFL, NHL, and NBA, fan enthusiasm (as measured by game attendance), ticket affordability, and "sports culture," that is, number of sports bars. *www.nerdwallet.com, "Best Cities for Sports Fans," May 5, 2013*
- *Card Player* magazine scoured North America to identify the top five metropolitan areas where a player can access the types of games that make launching a poker career possible. The Fort Lauderdale* metro area ranked #2. *Card Player, "The Top Five Cities to Launch Your Poker Career," April 2, 2014*
- Parkland was selected as one of the most playful cities in the U.S. by KaBOOM! The organization's Playful City USA initiative honors cities and towns across the nation for a vision, plan and commitment to creating an agenda for play. Criteria: creating a local play commission or task force; designing an annual action plan for play; conducting a play space audit; outlining a financial investment in play for the current fiscal year; and proclaiming and celebrating an annual "play day." *KaBOOM! National Campaign for Play, "2015 Playful City USA Communities"*

Women/Minorities Rankings

- *24/7 Wall St.* compared median earnings over a 12-month period for men and women who worked full-time, year-round, and employment composition by sector to identify the best-paying cities for women. Of the largest 100 U.S. metropolitan areas, Miami* was ranked #6 in pay disparity. *24/7 Wall St., "The Best (and Worst) Paying Cities for Women," March 6, 2015*

Miscellaneous Rankings

- The watchdog site Charity Navigator conducts an annual study of charities in the nation's major markets both to analyze statistical differences in their financial, accountability, and transparency practices and to track year-to-year variations in individual communities. The Miami* metro area was ranked #5 among the 30 metro markets in the rating dimension of Overall Score. *www.charitynavigator.org, "Metro Market Study 2015," June 5, 2015*
- Mars Chocolate North America, the makers of COMBOS®, in partnership with Sperling's BestPlaces, ranked 50 major metro areas in terms of their "manliness." The Miami* metro area ranked #36. Criteria: number of professional sports teams; number of nearby NASCAR tracks and racing events; manly lifestyle; concentration of manly retail stores; manly occupations per capita; salty snack sales; "Board of Manliness" rankings. *Mars Chocolate North America, "America's Manliest Cities 2012"*
- The National Alliance to End Homelessness ranked the 100 most populous metro areas with the highest rate of homelessness. The Miami* metro area ranked #38. Criteria: number of homeless people per 10,000 population in 2011. *National Alliance to End Homelessness, The State of Homelessness in America 2012*

Parkland is located within the Miami-Fort Lauderdale-West Palm Beach, FL Metropolitan Statistical Area and the Fort Lauderdale-Pompano Beach-Deerfield Beach, FL Metropolitan Division.

Business Environment

CITY FINANCES

City Government Finances

Component	2012 ($000)	2012 ($ per capita)
Total Revenues	22,836	953
Total Expenditures	21,006	876
Debt Outstanding	10,040	418
Cash and Securities[1]	19,499	813

Note: (1) Cash and security holdings of a government at the close of its fiscal year, including those of its dependent agencies, utilities, and liquor stores.
Source: U.S Census Bureau, State & Local Government Finances 2012

City Government Revenue by Source

Source	2012 ($000)	2012 ($ per capita)
General Revenue		
From Federal Government	480	20
From State Government	1,622	67
From Local Governments	0	0
Taxes		
Property	10,916	455
Sales and Gross Receipts	3,515	146
Personal Income	0	0
Corporate Income	0	0
Motor Vehicle License	0	0
Other Taxes	2,016	84
Current Charges	958	39
Liquor Store	0	0
Utility	0	0
Employee Retirement	140	5

Source: U.S Census Bureau, State & Local Government Finances 2012

City Government Expenditures by Function

Function	2012 ($000)	2012 ($ per capita)	2012 (%)
General Direct Expenditures			
Air Transportation	0	0	0.0
Corrections	0	0	0.0
Education	0	0	0.0
Employment Security Administration	0	0	0.0
Financial Administration	795	33	3.7
Fire Protection	5,028	209	23.9
General Public Buildings	350	14	1.6
Governmental Administration, Other	1,445	60	6.8
Health	0	0	0.0
Highways	1,663	69	7.9
Hospitals	0	0	0.0
Housing and Community Development	0	0	0.0
Interest on General Debt	411	17	1.9
Judicial and Legal	307	12	1.4
Libraries	450	18	2.1
Parking	0	0	0.0
Parks and Recreation	3,246	135	15.4
Police Protection	4,880	203	23.2
Public Welfare	0	0	0.0
Sewerage	0	0	0.0
Solid Waste Management	0	0	0.0
Veterans' Services	0	0	0.0
Liquor Store	0	0	0.0
Utility	0	0	0.0
Employee Retirement	170	7	0.8

Source: U.S Census Bureau, State & Local Government Finances 2012

DEMOGRAPHICS

Population Growth

Area	1990 Census	2000 Census	2010 Census	2014* Estimate	Population Growth (%) 1990-2014	2010-2014
City	4,201	13,835	23,962	25,895	516.4	8.1
MSA[1]	4,056,100	5,007,564	5,564,635	5,775,204	42.4	3.8
U.S.	248,709,873	281,421,906	308,745,538	314,107,084	26.3	1.7

Note: (1) Figures cover the Miami-Fort Lauderdale-West Palm Beach, FL Metropolitan Statistical Area—see Appendix B for areas included; (*) 2010-2014 5-year estimated population
Source: U.S. Census Bureau, 1990 Census, Census 2000, Census 2010, 2010-2014 American Community Survey 5-Year Estimates

Household Size

Area	Persons in Household (%) One	Two	Three	Four	Five	Six	Seven or More	Average Household Size
City	9.0	26.9	25.4	27.0	8.3	2.6	0.4	3.25
MSA[1]	28.7	31.9	16.6	13.3	5.8	2.1	1.3	2.80
U.S.	27.5	33.5	15.8	13.1	6.0	2.3	1.4	2.64

Note: (1) Figures cover the Miami-Fort Lauderdale-West Palm Beach, FL Metropolitan Statistical Area—see Appendix B for areas included
Source: U.S. Census Bureau, 2010-2014 American Community Survey 5-Year Estimates

Race

Area	White Alone[2] (%)	Black Alone[2] (%)	Asian Alone[2] (%)	AIAN[3] Alone[2] (%)	NHOPI[4] Alone[2] (%)	Other Race Alone[2] (%)	Two or More Races (%)
City	83.9	6.8	6.3	0.2	0.0	1.3	1.6
MSA[1]	71.6	21.3	2.4	0.2	0.0	2.6	1.9
U.S.	73.8	12.6	5.0	0.8	0.2	4.7	2.9

Note: (1) Figures cover the Miami-Fort Lauderdale-West Palm Beach, FL Metropolitan Statistical Area—see Appendix B for areas included; (2) Alone is defined as not being in combination with one or more other races; (3) American Indian and Alaska Native; (4) Native Hawaiian and Other Pacific Islander
Source: U.S. Census Bureau, 2010-2014 American Community Survey 5-Year Estimates

Hispanic or Latino Origin

Area	Total (%)	Mexican (%)	Puerto Rican (%)	Cuban (%)	Other (%)
City	19.3	1.8	1.8	3.5	12.2
MSA[1]	42.4	2.4	3.9	18.2	17.9
U.S.	16.9	10.8	1.6	0.6	3.8

Note: Persons of Hispanic or Latino origin can be of any race; (1) Figures cover the Miami-Fort Lauderdale-West Palm Beach, FL Metropolitan Statistical Area—see Appendix B for areas included
Source: U.S. Census Bureau, 2010-2014 American Community Survey 5-Year Estimates

Ancestry

Area	German	Irish	English	American	Italian	Polish	French[2]	Scottish	Dutch
City	7.6	11.5	6.0	8.7	14.2	7.0	2.6	0.5	0.3
MSA[1]	5.3	5.1	3.3	5.8	5.4	2.2	1.4	0.7	0.5
U.S.	14.9	10.8	8.0	7.1	5.5	3.0	2.7	1.7	1.4

Note: Figures are the percentage of the total population reporting a particular ancestry. The nine most commonly reported ancestries in the U.S. are shown. Figures include multiple ancestries (e.g. if a person reported being Irish and Italian, they were included in both columns); (1) Figures cover the Miami-Fort Lauderdale-West Palm Beach, FL Metropolitan Statistical Area—see Appendix B for areas included; (2) Excludes Basque
Source: U.S. Census Bureau, 2010-2014 American Community Survey 5-Year Estimates

Foreign-Born Population

Area	Percent of Population Born in								
	Any Foreign Country	Asia	Mexico	Europe	Carribean	Central America[2]	South America	Africa	Canada
City	22.6	5.3	0.5	3.9	5.2	0.5	5.6	0.1	1.4
MSA[1]	38.7	2.0	1.1	2.3	20.4	4.2	7.8	0.4	0.6
U.S.	13.1	3.8	3.7	1.5	1.2	1.0	0.9	0.6	0.3

Note: (1) Figures cover the Miami-Fort Lauderdale-West Palm Beach, FL Metropolitan Statistical Area—see Appendix B for areas included; (2) Excludes Mexico.
Source: U.S. Census Bureau, 2010-2014 American Community Survey 5-Year Estimates

Marital Status

Area	Never Married	Now Married[2]	Separated	Widowed	Divorced
City	26.4	62.1	1.6	3.2	6.6
MSA[1]	34.1	43.2	3.0	6.9	12.8
U.S.	32.5	48.4	2.2	5.9	10.9

Note: Figures are percentages and cover the population 15 years of age and older; (1) Figures cover the Miami-Fort Lauderdale-West Palm Beach, FL Metropolitan Statistical Area—see Appendix B for areas included; (2) Excludes separated
Source: U.S. Census Bureau, 2010-2014 American Community Survey 5-Year Estimates

Disability Status

Area	All Ages	Under 18 Years Old	18 to 64 Years Old	65 Years and Over
City	5.7	2.2	3.6	32.9
MSA[1]	11.0	3.1	7.5	34.5
U.S.	12.3	4.1	10.2	36.3

Note: Figures show percent of the civilian noninstitutionalized population that reported having a disability. Disability status is determined from from six types of difficulty: vision, hearing, cognitive, ambulatory, self-care, and independent living. For children under 5 years old, hearing and vision difficulty are used to determine disability status. For children between the ages of 5 and 14, disability status is determined from hearing, vision, cognitive, ambulatory, and self-care difficulties. For people aged 15 years and older, they are considered to have a disability if they have difficulty with any one of the six difficulty types; (1) Figures cover the Miami-Fort Lauderdale-West Palm Beach, FL Metropolitan Statistical Area—see Appendix B for areas included.
Source: U.S. Census Bureau, 2010-2014 American Community Survey 5-Year Estimates

Age

Area	Percent of Population									Median Age
	Under Age 5	Age 5–19	Age 20–34	Age 35–44	Age 45–54	Age 55–64	Age 65–74	Age 75–84	Age 85+	
City	7.1	27.0	12.7	16.2	16.6	12.5	5.5	1.2	1.1	38.4
MSA[1]	5.7	17.8	19.6	13.7	14.9	11.9	8.4	5.5	2.6	40.2
U.S.	6.4	19.9	20.6	13.0	14.1	12.3	7.6	4.3	1.9	37.4

Note: (1) Figures cover the Miami-Fort Lauderdale-West Palm Beach, FL Metropolitan Statistical Area—see Appendix B for areas included
Source: U.S. Census Bureau, 2010-2014 American Community Survey 5-Year Estimates

Gender

Area	Males	Females	Males per 100 Females
City	12,629	13,266	95.2
MSA[1]	2,800,775	2,974,429	94.2
U.S.	154,515,159	159,591,925	96.8

Note: (1) Figures cover the Miami-Fort Lauderdale-West Palm Beach, FL Metropolitan Statistical Area—see Appendix B for areas included
Source: U.S. Census Bureau, 2010-2014 American Community Survey 5-Year Estimates

Religious Groups by Family

Area	Catholic	Baptist	Non-Den.	Methodist[2]	Lutheran	LDS[3]	Pente-costal	Presby-terian[4]	Muslim[5]	Judaism
MSA[1]	18.5	5.3	4.1	1.2	0.4	0.5	1.7	0.6	0.9	1.5
U.S.	19.1	9.3	4.0	4.0	2.3	2.0	1.9	1.6	0.8	0.7

Note: Figures are the number of adherents as a percentage of the total population; (1) Figures cover the Miami-Fort Lauderdale-Pompano Beach, FL Metropolitan Statistical Area—see Appendix B for areas included; (2) Methodist/Pietist; (3) Latter Day Saints; (4) Reformed; (5) Figures are estimates
Source: Association of Statisticians of American Religious Bodies, 2010 U.S. Religion Census: Religious Congregations & Membership Study

Religious Groups by Tradition

Area	Catholic	Evangelical Protestant	Mainline Protestant	Other Tradition	Black Protestant	Orthodox
MSA[1]	18.5	11.4	2.4	3.5	1.7	0.2
U.S.	19.1	16.2	7.3	4.3	1.6	0.3

Note: Figures are the number of adherents as a percentage of the total population; (1) Figures cover the Miami-Fort Lauderdale-Pompano Beach, FL Metropolitan Statistical Area—see Appendix B for areas included
Source: Association of Statisticians of American Religious Bodies, 2010 U.S. Religion Census: Religious Congregations & Membership Study

ECONOMY

Gross Metropolitan Product

Area	2013	2014	2015	2016	Rank[2]
MSA[1]	281.1	295.0	309.2	325.7	11

Note: Figures are in billions of dollars; (1) Figures cover the Miami-Fort Lauderdale-West Palm Beach, FL Metropolitan Statistical Area—see Appendix B for areas included; (2) Rank is based on 2016 data and ranges from 1 to 381
Source: The U.S. Conference of Mayors, U.S. Metro Economies: GMP and Employment 2014-2016, June 2015

Economic Growth

Area	2011-13 (%)	2014 (%)	2015 (%)	2016 (%)	Rank[2]
MSA[1]	2.8	3.2	3.3	3.4	38
U.S.	2.2	2.4	2.3	2.9	–

Note: Figures are real gross metropolitan product (GMP) growth rates and represent annual average percent change; (1) Figures cover the Miami-Fort Lauderdale-West Palm Beach, FL Metropolitan Statistical Area—see Appendix B for areas included; (2) Rank is based on 2016 data and ranges from 1 to 381
Source: The U.S. Conference of Mayors, U.S. Metro Economies: GMP and Employment 2014-2016, June 2015

Metropolitan Area Exports

Area	2009	2010	2011	2012	2013	2014	Rank[2]
MSA[1]	31,174.9	35,866.9	43,129.8	47,858.7	41,771.5	37,969.4	7

Note: Figures are in millions of dollars; (1) Figures cover the Miami-Fort Lauderdale-West Palm Beach, FL Metropolitan Statistical Area—see Appendix B for areas included; (2) Rank is based on 2014 data and ranges from 1 to 385
Source: U.S. Department of Commerce, International Trade Administration, Office of Trade & Industry Information, Manufacturing & Services, data extracted March 10, 2016

Building Permits

Area	Single-Family			Multi-Family			Total		
	2014	2015p	Pct. Chg.	2014	2015p	Pct. Chg.	2014	2015p	Pct. Chg.
City	547	430	-21.4	9	0	-100.0	556	430	-22.7
MSA[1]	5,791	7,102	22.6	9,468	15,994	68.9	15,259	23,096	51.4
U.S.	640,300	690,800	7.9	411,800	487,600	18.4	1,052,100	1,178,400	12.0

Note: (1) Figures cover the Miami-Fort Lauderdale-West Palm Beach, FL Metropolitan Statistical Area—see Appendix B for areas included; Figures represent new, privately-owned housing units authorized (unadjusted data); All permit data are based on estimates with imputation; (p) preliminary data.
Source: U.S. Census Bureau, Manufacturing, Mining, and Construction Statistics, Building Permits, 2014, 2015

Bankruptcy Filings

Area	Business Filings 2014	Business Filings 2015	% Chg.	Nonbusiness Filings 2014	Nonbusiness Filings 2015	% Chg.
Broward County	241	202	-16.2	7,870	6,714	-14.7
U.S.	26,983	24,735	-8.3	909,812	819,760	-9.9

Note: Business filings include Chapter 7, Chapter 11, Chapter 12, and Chapter 13; Nonbusiness filings include Chapter 7, Chapter 11, and Chapter 13

Source: Administrative Office of the U.S. Courts, Business and Nonbusiness Bankruptcy, County Cases Commenced by Chapter of the Bankruptcy Code, During the 12- Month Period Ending December 31, 2014 and Business and Nonbusiness Bankruptcy, County Cases Commenced by Chapter of the Bankruptcy Code, During the 12- Month Period Ending December 31, 2015

Housing Vacancy Rates

Area	Gross Vacancy Rate[2] (%)			Year-Round Vacancy Rate[3] (%)			Rental Vacancy Rate[4] (%)			Homeowner Vacancy Rate[5] (%)		
	2013	2014	2015	2013	2014	2015	2013	2014	2015	2013	2014	2015
MSA[1]	20.2	19.6	16.9	10.3	10.4	8.5	6.7	7.0	6.4	1.7	1.8	1.4
U.S.	13.6	13.4	12.9	10.7	10.4	10.0	8.3	7.6	7.1	2.0	1.9	1.8

Note: (1) Figures cover the Miami-Fort Lauderdale-West Palm Beach, FL Metropolitan Statistical Area—see Appendix B for areas included; (2) The percentage of the total housing inventory that is vacant; (3) The percentage of the housing inventory (excluding seasonal units) that is year-round vacant; (4) The percentage of rental inventory that is vacant for rent; (5) The percentage of homeowner inventory that is vacant for sale

Source: U.S. Census Bureau, Housing Vacancies and Homeownership Annual Statistics: 2015

INCOME

Income

Area	Per Capita ($)	Median Household ($)	Average Household ($)
City	49,671	126,905	161,017
MSA[1]	27,240	48,435	72,352
U.S.	28,555	53,482	74,596

Note: (1) Figures cover the Miami-Fort Lauderdale-West Palm Beach, FL Metropolitan Statistical Area—see Appendix B for areas included

Source: U.S. Census Bureau, 2010-2014 American Community Survey 5-Year Estimates

Household Income Distribution

Area	Percent of Households Earning							
	Under $15,000	$15,000 -24,999	$25,000 -34,999	$35,000 -49,999	$50,000 -74,999	$75,000 -99,000	$100,000 -149,999	$150,000 and up
City	3.2	3.7	3.6	6.0	10.7	12.5	19.4	41.1
MSA[1]	14.3	11.9	10.9	14.1	16.9	10.9	11.4	9.5
U.S.	12.5	10.7	10.2	13.5	17.8	12.2	13.0	10.0

Note: (1) Figures cover the Miami-Fort Lauderdale-West Palm Beach, FL Metropolitan Statistical Area—see Appendix B for areas included

Source: U.S. Census Bureau, 2010-2014 American Community Survey 5-Year Estimates

Poverty Rate

Area	All Ages	Under 18 Years Old	18 to 64 Years Old	65 Years and Over
City	4.3	5.4	3.4	6.5
MSA[1]	17.3	23.7	15.7	15.0
U.S.	15.6	21.9	14.6	9.4

Note: Figures are percentage of people whose income during the past 12 months was below the poverty level; (1) Figures cover the Miami-Fort Lauderdale-West Palm Beach, FL Metropolitan Statistical Area—see Appendix B for areas included

Source: U.S. Census Bureau, 2010-2014 American Community Survey 5-Year Estimates

EMPLOYMENT

Labor Force and Employment

Area	Civilian Labor Force			Workers Employed		
	Dec. 2014	Dec. 2015	% Chg.	Dec. 2014	Dec. 2015	% Chg.
City	14,282	14,396	0.7	13,783	13,939	1.1
MD[1]	995,560	999,633	0.4	945,682	956,378	1.1
U.S.	155,521,000	157,245,000	1.1	147,190,000	149,703,000	1.7

Note: Data is not seasonally adjusted and covers workers 16 years of age and older; (1) Figures cover the Fort Lauderdale-Pompano Beach-Deerfield Beach, FL Metropolitan Division—see Appendix B for areas included
Source: Bureau of Labor Statistics, Local Area Unemployment Statistics

Unemployment Rate

Area	2015											
	Jan.	Feb.	Mar.	Apr.	May	Jun.	Jul.	Aug.	Sep.	Oct.	Nov.	Dec.
City	4.1	3.8	3.7	3.6	4.0	3.9	3.9	3.9	4.0	3.6	3.3	3.2
MD[1]	5.5	5.3	5.2	4.9	5.2	5.1	5.3	5.2	4.9	4.7	4.5	4.3
U.S.	6.1	5.8	5.6	5.1	5.3	5.5	5.6	5.2	4.9	4.8	4.8	4.8

Note: Data is not seasonally adjusted and covers workers 16 years of age and older; (1) Figures cover the Fort Lauderdale-Pompano Beach-Deerfield Beach, FL Metropolitan Division—see Appendix B for areas included
Source: Bureau of Labor Statistics, Local Area Unemployment Statistics

Employment by Occupation

Occupation Classification	City (%)	MSA[1] (%)	U.S. (%)
Management, Business, Science, and Arts	54.8	33.5	36.4
Natural Resources, Construction, and Maintenance	2.8	8.7	9.0
Production, Transportation, and Material Moving	1.9	8.8	12.1
Sales and Office	30.7	28.0	24.4
Service	9.9	21.0	18.2

Note: Figures cover employed civilians 16 years of age and older; (1) Figures cover the Miami-Fort Lauderdale-West Palm Beach, FL Metropolitan Statistical Area—see Appendix B for areas included
Source: U.S. Census Bureau, 2010-2014 American Community Survey 5-Year Estimates

Employment by Industry

Sector	MD[1]		U.S.
	Number of Employees	Percent of Total	Percent of Total
Construction, Mining, and Logging	n/a	n/a	5.0
Education and Health Services	104,500	12.7	15.7
Financial Activities	58,600	7.1	5.7
Government	103,000	12.5	15.5
Information	19,400	2.3	1.9
Leisure and Hospitality	92,800	11.2	10.4
Manufacturing	28,400	3.4	8.6
Other Services	37,900	4.6	3.9
Professional and Business Services	144,800	17.6	13.9
Retail Trade	112,900	13.7	11.3
Transportation, Warehousing, and Utilities	26,400	3.2	3.9
Wholesale Trade	48,700	5.9	4.1

Note: Figures are non-farm employment as of December 2015. Figures are not seasonally adjusted and include workers 16 years of age and older; (1) Figures cover the Fort Lauderdale-Pompano Beach-Deerfield Beach, FL Metropolitan Division—see Appendix B for areas included; n/a not available
Source: Bureau of Labor Statistics, Current Employment Statistics, Employment, Hours, and Earnings

Occupations with Greatest Projected Employment Growth: 2012 – 2022

Occupation[1]	2012 Employment	2022 Projected Employment	Numeric Employment Change	Percent Employment Change
Retail Salespersons	326,380	380,120	53,740	16.5
Combined Food Preparation and Serving Workers, Including Fast Food	196,980	237,340	40,360	20.5
Customer Service Representatives	191,210	228,620	37,410	19.6
Registered Nurses	164,020	201,140	37,120	22.6
Waiters and Waitresses	191,370	227,810	36,440	19.0
Office Clerks, General	142,710	170,300	27,590	19.3
Cashiers	206,660	230,190	23,530	11.4
Landscaping and Groundskeeping Workers	92,510	115,540	23,030	24.9
Receptionists and Information Clerks	75,780	95,680	19,900	26.2
Nursing Assistants	86,990	106,200	19,210	22.1

Note: Projections cover Florida; (1) Sorted by numeric employment change
Source: www.projectionscentral.com, State Occupational Projections, 2012–2022 Long-Term Projections

Fastest Growing Occupations: 2012 – 2022

Occupation[1]	2012 Employment	2022 Projected Employment	Numeric Employment Change	Percent Employment Change
Helpers—Carpenters	1,280	2,450	1,170	90.7
Helpers—Brickmasons, Blockmasons, Stonemasons, and Tile and Marble Setters	1,050	1,890	840	79.5
Biomedical Engineers	760	1,300	540	70.7
Reinforcing Iron and Rebar Workers	520	870	350	67.5
Glaziers	2,890	4,710	1,820	62.8
Solar Photovoltaic Installers	170	270	100	58.7
Brickmasons and Blockmasons	2,820	4,430	1,610	57.1
Stonemasons	450	710	260	56.4
Helpers—Pipelayers, Plumbers, Pipefitters, and Steamfitters	2,420	3,750	1,330	54.8
Cement Masons and Concrete Finishers	10,390	16,050	5,660	54.4

Note: Projections cover Florida; (1) Sorted by percent employment change and excludes occupations with numeric employment change less than 100
Source: www.projectionscentral.com, State Occupational Projections, 2012–2022 Long-Term Projections

Average Wages

Occupation	$/Hr.	Occupation	$/Hr.
Accountants and Auditors	34.83	Maids and Housekeeping Cleaners	10.28
Automotive Mechanics	20.65	Maintenance and Repair Workers	16.53
Bookkeepers	17.61	Marketing Managers	58.89
Carpenters	18.54	Nuclear Medicine Technologists	35.89
Cashiers	9.91	Nurses, Licensed Practical	21.07
Clerks, General Office	13.55	Nurses, Registered	33.22
Clerks, Receptionists/Information	13.11	Nursing Assistants	12.03
Clerks, Shipping/Receiving	14.54	Packers and Packagers, Hand	10.17
Computer Programmers	33.95	Physical Therapists	41.56
Computer Systems Analysts	38.15	Postal Service Mail Carriers	25.26
Computer User Support Specialists	22.18	Real Estate Brokers	34.73
Cooks, Restaurant	12.85	Retail Salespersons	12.70
Dentists	59.61	Sales Reps., Exc. Tech./Scientific	27.99
Electrical Engineers	43.18	Sales Reps., Tech./Scientific	45.70
Electricians	19.45	Secretaries, Exc. Legal/Med./Exec.	16.02
Financial Managers	66.68	Security Guards	11.00
First-Line Supervisors/Managers, Sales	23.10	Surgeons	108.95
Food Preparation Workers	10.52	Teacher Assistants*	11.20
General and Operations Managers	66.56	Teachers, Elementary School*	23.89
Hairdressers/Cosmetologists	12.01	Teachers, Secondary School*	26.25
Internists	66.56	Telemarketers	12.89
Janitors and Cleaners	10.35	Truck Drivers, Heavy/Tractor-Trailer	19.25
Landscaping/Groundskeeping Workers	12.70	Truck Drivers, Light/Delivery Svcs.	17.31
Lawyers	n/a	Waiters and Waitresses	11.80

Note: Wage data covers the Fort Lauderdale-Pompano Beach-Deerfield Beach, FL Metropolitan Division—see Appendix B for areas included; (*) Hourly wages for elementary/secondary school teachers and teacher assistants were calculated by the editors from annual wage data based on a 40 hour work week; n/a not available.
Source: Bureau of Labor Statistics, Metro Area Occupational Employment and Wage Estimates, May 2015

TAXES

State Corporate Income Tax Rates

State	Tax Rate (%)	Income Brackets ($)	Num. of Brackets	Financial Institution Tax Rate (%)[a]	Federal Income Tax Ded.
Florida	5.5 (f)	Flat rate	1	5.5 (f)	No

Note: Tax rates as of January 1, 2016; (a) Rates listed are the corporate income tax rate applied to financial institutions or excise taxes based on income. Some states have other taxes based upon the value of deposits or shares; (f) An exemption of $50,000 is allowed. Florida's Alternative Minimum Tax rate is 3.3%.
Source: Federation of Tax Administrators, "State Corporate Income Tax Rates, 2016"

State Individual Income Tax Rates

State	Tax Rate (%)	Income Brackets ($)	Num. of Brackets	Personal Exempt. ($)[1]		Fed. Inc. Tax Ded.
				Single	Dependents	
Florida	None	–	–	–	–	–

Note: Tax rates as of January 1, 2016; Local- and county-level taxes are not included; n/a not applicable; (1) Married joint filers generally receive double the single exemption
Source: Federation of Tax Administrators, "State Individual Income Tax Rates, 2016"

Various State and Local Tax Rates

State	State and Local Sales and Use (%)	State Sales and Use (%)	Gasoline[1] (¢/gal.)	Cigarette[2] ($/pack)	Spirits[3] ($/gal.)	Wine[4] ($/gal.)	Beer[5] ($/gal.)
Florida	6.00	6.0	36.58	1.339	6.50 (f)	2.25 (l)	0.48 (q)

Note: All tax rates as of January 1, 2016; (1) The American Petroleum Institute has developed a methodology for determining the average tax rate on a gallon of fuel. Rates may include any of the following: excise taxes, environmental fees, storage tank fees, other fees or taxes, general sales tax, and local taxes. In states where gasoline is subject to the general sales tax, or where the fuel tax is based on the average sale price, the average rate determined by API is sensitive to changes in the price of gasoline. States that fully or partially apply general sales taxes to gasoline: CA, CO, GA, IL, IN, MI, NY; (2) The federal excise tax of $1.0066 per pack and local taxes are not included; (3) Rates are those applicable to off-premise sales of 40% alcohol by volume (a.b.v.) distilled spirits in 750ml containers. Local excise taxes are excluded; (4) Rates are those applicable to off-premise sales of 11% a.b.v. non-carbonated wine in 750ml containers; (5) Rates are those applicable to off-premise sales of 4.7% a.b.v. beer in 12 ounce containers; (f) Different rates are also applicable according to alcohol content, place of production, size of container, or place purchased (on- or off-premise or onboard airlines); (l) Different rates also applicable according to alcohol content, place of production, size of container, place purchased (on- or off-premise or on board airlines) or type of wine (carbonated, vermouth, etc.); (q) Different rates are also applicable according to alcohol content, place of production, size of container, or place purchased (on- or off-premise or onboard airlines).
Source: Tax Foundation, 2016 Facts & Figures: How Does Your State Compare?

State Business Tax Climate Index Rankings

State	Overall Rank	Corporate Tax Rank	Individual Income Tax Rank	Sales Tax Rank	Unemployment Insurance Tax Rank	Property Tax Rank
Florida	4	17	1	17	3	20

Note: The index is a measure of how each state's tax laws affect economic performance. The lower the rank, the more favorable a state's tax system is for business. States without a given tax are given a ranking of 1. The scores/rankings for the District of Columbia do not affect other states. The 2016 index represents the tax climate as of July 1, 2015 (the beginning of Fiscal Year 2016).
Source: Tax Foundation, State Business Tax Climate Index 2016

TRANSPORTATION

Means of Transportation to Work

Area	Car/Truck/Van		Public Transportation			Bicycle	Walked	Other Means	Worked at Home
	Drove Alone	Car-pooled	Bus	Subway	Railroad				
City	82.1	5.7	0.1	0.0	0.2	0.0	1.0	1.4	9.5
MSA[1]	78.2	9.5	3.4	0.2	0.2	0.6	1.8	1.4	4.7
U.S.	76.4	9.6	2.6	1.8	0.6	0.6	2.8	1.3	4.4

Note: Figures are percentages and cover workers 16 years of age and older; (1) Figures cover the Miami-Fort Lauderdale-West Palm Beach, FL Metropolitan Statistical Area—see Appendix B for areas included
Source: U.S. Census Bureau, 2010-2014 American Community Survey 5-Year Estimates

Travel Time to Work

Area	Less Than 10 Minutes	10 to 19 Minutes	20 to 29 Minutes	30 to 44 Minutes	45 to 59 Minutes	60 to 89 Minutes	90 Minutes or More
City	7.3	22.8	22.3	30.3	11.0	4.6	1.6
MSA[1]	7.5	25.0	23.3	27.0	9.0	6.1	2.0
U.S.	13.3	29.6	21.0	20.2	7.7	5.7	2.6

Note: Figures are percentages and include workers 16 years old and over; (1) Figures cover the Miami-Fort Lauderdale-West Palm Beach, FL Metropolitan Statistical Area—see Appendix B for areas included
Source: U.S. Census Bureau, 2010-2014 American Community Survey 5-Year Estimates

Freeway Travel Time Index

Area	1985	1990	1995	2000	2005	2010	2014
Urban Area Rank[1,2]	11	16	18	11	13	18	17
Urban Area Index[1]	1.16	1.18	1.21	1.27	1.29	1.27	1.29
Average Index[3]	1.09	1.11	1.14	1.17	1.20	1.19	1.20

Note: Freeway Travel Time Index—the ratio of travel time in the peak period to the travel time at free-flow conditions. For example, a value of 1.30 indicates a 20-minute free-flow trip takes 26 minutes in the peak (20 minutes x 1.30 = 26 minutes); (1) Covers the Miami FL urban area; (2) Rank is based on 101 urban areas (#1 = highest travel time index); (3) Average of 101 urban areas
Source: Texas Transportation Institute, 2015 Urban Mobility Scorecard, August 2015

Freeway Commuter Stress Index

Area	1985	1990	1995	2000	2005	2010	2014
Urban Area Rank[1,2]	28	28	31	23	28	29	29
Urban Area Index[1]	1.17	1.19	1.23	1.29	1.31	1.29	1.30
Average Index[3]	1.13	1.16	1.19	1.22	1.25	1.24	1.25

Note: The Freeway Commuter Stress Index is the same as the Freeway Travel Time Index (see table above) except that it includes only the travel in the peak directions during the peak periods; the TTI includes travel in all directions during the peak period. Thus, the CSI is more indicative of the work trip experienced by each commuter on a daily basis. (1) Covers the Miami FL urban area; (2) Rank is based on 101 urban areas (#1 = highest stress index); (3) Average of 101 urban areas

Source: Texas Transportation Institute, 2015 Urban Mobility Scorecard, August 2015

Living Environment

COST OF LIVING

Cost of Living Index

Composite Index	Groceries	Housing	Utilities	Trans-portation	Health Care	Misc. Goods/ Services
114.3	103.1	145.4	96.0	111.2	99.3	101.0

Note: The Cost of Living Index measures regional differences in the cost of consumer goods and services, excluding taxes and non-consumer expenditures, for professional and managerial households in the top income quintile. It is based on more than 50,000 prices covering almost 60 different items for which prices are collected three times a year by chambers of commerce, economic development organizations or university applied economic centers in each participating urban area. The numbers shown should be read as a percentage above or below the national average of 100. For example, a value of 115.4 in the groceries column indicates that grocery prices are 15.4% higher than the national average. Small differences in the index numbers should not be interpreted as significant; Figures cover the Fort Lauderdale FL urban area.
Source: The Council for Community and Economic Research, ACCRA Cost of Living Index, 2015

Grocery Prices

Area[1]	T-Bone Steak ($/pound)	Frying Chicken ($/pound)	Whole Milk ($/half gal.)	Eggs ($/dozen)	Orange Juice ($/64 oz.)	Coffee ($/11.5 oz.)
City[2]	12.46	1.41	2.75	2.44	3.59	2.98
Avg.	10.99	1.43	2.25	2.26	3.58	4.48
Min.	7.16	0.98	1.30	1.35	2.88	2.98
Max.	14.13	2.43	3.85	4.81	6.39	7.56

Note: (1) Values for the local area are compared with the average, minimum and maximum values for all 292 areas in the Cost of Living Index; (2) Figures cover the Fort Lauderdale FL urban area; **T-Bone Steak** *(price per pound);* **Frying Chicken** *(price per pound, whole fryer);* **Whole Milk** *(half gallon carton);* **Eggs** *(price per dozen, Grade A, large);* **Orange Juice** *(64 oz. Tropicana or Florida Natural);* **Coffee** *(11.5 oz. can, vacuum-packed, Maxwell House, Hills Bros, or Folgers).*
Source: The Council for Community and Economic Research, ACCRA Cost of Living Index, 2015

Housing and Utility Costs

Area[1]	New Home Price ($)	Apartment Rent ($/month)	All Electric ($/month)	Part Electric ($/month)	Other Energy ($/month)	Telephone ($/month)
City[2]	443,005	1,483	161.87	-	-	27.31
Avg.	312,874	945	179.30	95.07	72.96	28.11
Min.	178,682	479	116.28	43.14	26.46	10.01
Max.	1,472,476	3,984	504.25	189.44	421.11	43.06

Note: (1) Values for the local area are compared with the average, minimum and maximum values for all 292 areas in the Cost of Living Index; (2) Figures cover the Fort Lauderdale FL urban area; **New Home Price** *(2,400 sf living area, 8,000 sf lot, in urban area with full utilities);* **Apartment Rent** *(950 sf 2 bedroom/1.5 or 2 bath, unfurnished, excluding all utilities except water);* **All Electric** *(average monthly cost for an all-electric home);* **Part Electric** *(average monthly cost for a part-electric home);* **Other Energy** *(average monthly cost for natural gas, fuel oil, coal, wood, and any other forms of energy except electricity);* **Telephone** *(price includes basic monthly rate for a private residential line plus additional local usage charges incurred by a family of four).*
Source: The Council for Community and Economic Research, ACCRA Cost of Living Index, 2015

Health Care, Transportation, and Other Costs

Area[1]	Doctor ($/visit)	Dentist ($/visit)	Optometrist ($/visit)	Gasoline ($/gallon)	Beauty Salon ($/visit)	Men's Shirt ($)
City[2]	85.67	89.45	90.43	2.49	52.58	25.80
Avg.	105.15	89.02	99.78	2.38	35.30	28.10
Min.	66.87	56.09	48.53	1.95	18.91	13.38
Max.	182.34	150.36	228.33	4.09	67.91	63.80

Note: (1) Values for the local area are compared with the average, minimum and maximum values for all 292 areas in the Cost of Living Index; (2) Figures cover the Fort Lauderdale FL urban area; **Doctor** *(general practitioners routine exam of an established patient);* **Dentist** *(adult teeth cleaning and periodic oral examination);* **Optometrist** *(full vision eye exam for established adult patient);* **Gasoline** *(one gallon regular unleaded, national brand, including all taxes, cash price at self-service pump if available);* **Beauty Salon** *(woman's shampoo, trim, and blow-dry);* **Men's Shirt** *(cotton/polyester dress shirt, pinpoint weave, long sleeves).*
Source: The Council for Community and Economic Research, ACCRA Cost of Living Index, 2015

HOUSING

House Price Index (HPI)

Area	National Ranking[2]	Quarterly Change (%)	One-Year Change (%)	Five-Year Change (%)
MD[1]	41	1.60	8.60	36.30
U.S.[3]	–	1.45	5.76	22.85

Note: The HPI is a weighted repeat sales index. It measures average price changes in repeat sales or refinancings on the same properties. This information is obtained by reviewing repeat mortgage transactions on single-family properties whose mortgages have been purchased or securitized by Fannie Mae or Freddie Mac in January 1975; (1) Fort Lauderdale-Pompano Beach-Deerfield Beach Metropolitan Division—see Appendix B for areas included; (2) Rankings are based on annual percentage change for all metro areas containing at least 15,000 transactions over the last 10 years and ranges from 1 to 266; (3) figures based on a weighted average of Census Division estimates using a seasonally adjusted, purchase-only index; all figures are for the period ending December 31, 2015

Source: Federal Housing Finance Agency, House Price Index, February 25, 2016

Median Single-Family Home Prices

Area	2013	2014	2015[p]	Percent Change 2014 to 2015
MSA[1]	246.0	266.0	283.8	6.7
U.S. Average	197.4	208.9	223.9	7.2

Note: Figures are median sales prices of existing single-family homes in thousands of dollars; (p) preliminary; n/a not available; (1) Miami-Fort Lauderdale-West Palm Beach, FL Metropolitan Statistical Area—see Appendix B for areas included

Source: National Association of Realtors, Median Sales Price of Existing Single-Family Homes for Metropolitan Areas, 4th Quarter 2015

Qualifying Income Based on Median Sales Price of Existing Single-Family Homes

Area	With 5% Down ($)	With 10% Down ($)	With 20% Down ($)
MSA[1]	63,615	60,267	53,571
U.S. Average	49,535	46,928	41,714

Note: Figures are preliminary; Qualifying income is based on a mortgage rate of 4.1%. Monthly principal and interest payment is limited to 25% of income; n/a not available; (1) Miami-Fort Lauderdale-West Palm Beach, FL Metropolitan Statistical Area—see Appendix B for areas included

Source: National Association of Realtors, Qualifying Income Based on Median Sales Price of Existing Single-Family Homes for Metropolitan Areas, 4th Quarter 2015

Median Apartment Condo-Coop Home Prices

Area	2013	2014	2015[p]	Percent Change 2014 to 2015
MSA[1]	129.5	144.3	154.1	6.8
U.S. Average	194.9	204.3	210.7	3.1

Note: Figures are median sales prices of existing apartment condo-coop homes in thousands of dollars; (p) preliminary; n/a not available; (1) Miami-Fort Lauderdale-West Palm Beach, FL Metropolitan Statistical Area—see Appendix B for areas included

Source: National Association of Realtors, Median Sales Price of Existing Apartment Condo-Coop Homes for Metropolitan Areas, 4th Quarter 2015

Gross Monthly Rent

Area	Under $200	$200 -299	$300 -499	$500 -749	$750 -999	$1,000 -1,499	$1,500 and up	Median ($)
City	1.7	0.0	0.0	0.0	0.0	21.3	77.0	2,000+
MSA[1]	1.4	2.3	2.7	9.0	21.9	39.0	23.8	1,136
U.S.	1.5	3.2	7.4	21.0	24.1	26.9	15.9	920

Note: Figures are percentages except for Median; Gross rent is the contract rent plus the estimated average monthly cost of utilities (electricity, gas, and water and sewer) and fuels (oil, coal, kerosene, wood, etc.) if these are paid by the renter (or paid for the renter by someone else); (1) Figures cover the Miami-Fort Lauderdale-West Palm Beach, FL Metropolitan Statistical Area—see Appendix B for areas included

Source: U.S. Census Bureau, 2010-2014 American Community Survey 5-Year Estimates

Homeownership Rate

Area	2008 (%)	2009 (%)	2010 (%)	2011 (%)	2012 (%)	2013 (%)	2014 (%)	2015 (%)
MSA[1]	66.0	67.1	63.8	64.2	61.8	60.1	58.8	58.6
U.S.	67.8	67.4	66.9	66.1	65.4	65.1	64.5	63.7

Note: (1) Figures cover the Miami-Fort Lauderdale-West Palm Beach, FL Metropolitan Statistical Area—see Appendix B for areas included
Source: U.S. Census Bureau, Housing Vacancies and Homeownership Annual Statistics: 2015

Year Housing Structure Built

Area	2010 or Later	2000 -2009	1990 -1999	1980 -1989	1970 -1979	1960 -1969	1950 -1959	1940 -1949	Before 1940	Median Year
City	3.4	40.0	37.1	17.1	1.4	0.6	0.4	0.0	0.0	1998
MSA[1]	0.5	14.1	14.8	19.9	22.0	12.8	10.4	3.2	2.2	1980
U.S.	1.0	14.9	13.9	13.8	15.8	11.0	10.8	5.4	13.3	1976

Note: Figures are percentages except for Median Year; (1) Figures cover the Miami-Fort Lauderdale-West Palm Beach, FL Metropolitan Statistical Area—see Appendix B for areas included
Source: U.S. Census Bureau, 2010-2014 American Community Survey 5-Year Estimates

HEALTH

Health Risk Data

Category	MSA[1] (%)	U.S. (%)
Adults aged 18–64 who have any kind of health care coverage	67.9	79.6
Adults who reported being in good or excellent health	81.0	83.1
Adults who are current smokers	13.2	19.6
Adults who are heavy drinkers[2]	4.6	6.1
Adults who are binge drinkers[3]	15.4	16.9
Adults who are overweight (BMI 25.0 - 29.9)	38.8	35.8
Adults who are obese (BMI 30.0 - 99.8)	23.1	27.6
Adults who participated in any physical activities in the past month	74.7	77.1
Adults 50+ who have ever had a sigmoidoscopy or colonoscopy	61.7	67.3
Women aged 40+ who have had a mammogram within the past two years	75.7	74.0
Men aged 40+ who have had a PSA test within the past two years	51.1	45.2
Adults aged 65+ who have had flu shot within the past year	53.0	60.1
Adults who always wear a seatbelt	92.8	93.8

Note: Data as of 2012 unless otherwise noted; (1) Figures cover the Miami-Fort Lauderdale-Miami Beach, FL Metropolitan Statistical Area—see Appendix B for areas included; (2) Heavy drinkers are classified as males having more than two drinks per day or females having more than one drink per day; (3) Binge drinkers are classified as males having five or more drinks on one occasion or females having four or more drinks on one occasion
Source: Centers for Disease Control and Prevention, Behaviorial Risk Factor Surveillance System, SMART: Selected Metropolitan/Micropolitan Area Risk Trends, 2012 (Note: the CDC has discontinued this dataset but will be releasing a replacement in mid-2016)

Chronic Health Indicators

Category	MSA[1] (%)	U.S. (%)
Adults who have ever been told they had a heart attack	3.8	4.5
Adults who have ever been told they had a stroke	2.4	2.9
Adults who have been told they currently have asthma	5.3	8.9
Adults who have ever been told they have arthritis	21.4	25.7
Adults who have ever been told they have diabetes[2]	10.5	9.7
Adults who have ever been told they had skin cancer	5.9	5.7
Adults who have ever been told they had any other types of cancer	5.7	6.5
Adults who have ever been told they have COPD	6.2	6.2
Adults who have ever been told they have kidney disease	4.0	2.5
Adults who have ever been told they have a form of depression	13.4	18.0

Note: Data as of 2012 unless otherwise noted; (1) Figures cover the Miami-Fort Lauderdale-Miami Beach, FL Metropolitan Statistical Area—see Appendix B for areas included; (2) Figures do not include pregnancy-related, borderline, or pre-diabetes
Source: Centers for Disease Control and Prevention, Behaviorial Risk Factor Surveillance System, SMART: Selected Metropolitan/Micropolitan Area Risk Trends, 2012 (Note: the CDC has discontinued this dataset but will be releasing a replacement in mid-2016)

Mortality Rates for the Top 10 Causes of Death in the U.S.

ICD-10[a] Sub-Chapter	ICD-10[a] Code	Age-Adjusted Mortality Rate[1] per 100,000 population	
		County[2]	U.S.
Malignant neoplasms	C00-C97	152.2	163.6
Ischaemic heart diseases	I20-I25	94.3	102.2
Other forms of heart disease	I30-I51	47.8	50.1
Chronic lower respiratory diseases	J40-J47	30.3	41.4
Organic, including symptomatic, mental disorders	F01-F09	13.6	38.5
Cerebrovascular diseases	I60-I69	37.1	36.5
Other external causes of accidental injury	W00-X59	20.8	27.5
Other degenerative diseases of the nervous system	G30-G31	30.0	26.3
Diabetes mellitus	E10-E14	13.9	21.1
Hypertensive diseases	I10-I15	13.2	19.7

Note: (a) ICD-10 = International Classification of Diseases 10th Revision; (1) Mortality rates are a three year average covering 2012-2014; (2) Figures cover Broward County.
Source: Centers for Disease Control and Prevention, National Center for Health Statistics. Underlying Cause of Death 1999-2014 on CDC WONDER Online Database, released 2015.

Mortality Rates for Selected Causes of Death

ICD-10[a] Sub-Chapter	ICD-10[a] Code	Age-Adjusted Mortality Rate[1] per 100,000 population	
		County[2]	U.S.
Assault	X85-Y09	5.0	5.1
Diseases of the liver	K70-K76	11.3	13.5
Human immunodeficiency virus (HIV) disease	B20-B24	6.5	2.1
Influenza and pneumonia	J09-J18	8.4	15.2
Intentional self-harm	X60-X84	11.1	12.7
Malnutrition	E40-E46	0.3	0.9
Obesity and other hyperalimentation	E65-E68	1.6	1.9
Renal failure	N17-N19	13.5	13.0
Transport accidents	V01-V99	10.3	11.6
Viral hepatitis	B15-B19	1.7	2.1

Note: (a) ICD-10 = International Classification of Diseases 10th Revision; (1) Mortality rates are a three year average covering 2012-2014; (2) Figures cover Broward County; Data are Suppressed when the data meet the criteria for confidentiality constraints; Mortality rates are flagged as Unreliable when the rate would be calculated with a numerator of 20 or less.
Source: Centers for Disease Control and Prevention, National Center for Health Statistics. Underlying Cause of Death 1999-2014 on CDC WONDER Online Database, released 2015.

Health Insurance Coverage

Area	With Health Insurance	With Private Health Insurance	With Public Health Insurance	Without Health Insurance	Population Under Age 18 Without Health Insurance
City	95.0	87.3	12.6	5.0	1.2
MSA[1]	75.9	52.4	30.9	24.1	12.8
U.S.	85.8	65.8	31.1	14.2	7.1

Note: Figures are percentages that cover the civilian noninstitutionalized population; (1) Figures cover the Miami-Fort Lauderdale-West Palm Beach, FL Metropolitan Statistical Area—see Appendix B for areas included
Source: U.S. Census Bureau, 2010-2014 American Community Survey 5-Year Estimates

Number of Medical Professionals

Area	MDs[3]	DOs[3,4]	Dentists	Podiatrists	Chiropractors	Optometrists
County[1] (number)	4,455	656	1,300	198	630	391
County[1] (rate[2])	241.4	35.5	69.5	10.6	33.7	20.9
U.S. (rate[2])	272.5	20.9	64.7	5.8	25.9	15.2

Note: Data as of 2014 unless noted; (1) Data covers Broward County; (2) Rate per 100,000 population; (3) Data as of 2013 and includes all active, non-federal physicians; (4) Doctor of Osteopathic Medicine
Source: U.S. Department of Health and Human Services, Health Resources and Services Administration, Bureau of Health Professions, Area Resource File (ARF) 2014-2015

Best Hospitals

According to *U.S. News*, the Fort Lauderdale-Pompano Beach-Deerfield Beach, FL metro area is home to one of the best children's hospitals in the U.S.: **Joe DiMaggio Children's Hospital at Memorial Regional Hospital** (3 specialties). The hospital listed was highly ranked in at least one pediatric specialty. Eighty-three children's hospitals in the U.S. were nationally ranked in at least one specialty. Twelve children's hospitals in the U.S. made the Honor Roll with high scores in at least three specialties. *U.S. News Online, "America's Best Children's Hospitals 2015-16"*

EDUCATION

Public School District Statistics

District Name	Schls	Pupils	Pupil/ Teacher Ratio	Minority Pupils[1] (%)	Free Lunch Eligible[2] (%)	IEP[3] (%)
Broward	349	262,666	17.3	75.9	52.2	12.2

Note: Table includes school districts with 100 or more students; (1) Percentage of students that are not non-Hispanic white; (2) Percentage of students that are eligible for the free lunch program; (3) Percentage of students that have an Individualized Education Program.
Source: U.S. Department of Education, National Center for Education Statistics, Common Core of Data, Local Education Agency (School District) Universe Survey: School Year 2013-2014; U.S. Department of Education, National Center for Education Statistics, Common Core of Data, Public Elementary/Secondary School Universe Survey: School Year 2013-2014

Best High Schools

According to *U.S. News*, Parkland is home to one of the best high schools in the U.S.: **Marjory Stoneman Douglas High School** (#461); Nearly 20,000 schools were ranked based on their performance on state assessments and how well they prepare students for college. Schools with the highest unrounded College Readiness Index values were numerically ranked from No. 1 to No. 500 and were the gold medal winners. *U.S. News & World Report, "Best High Schools 2015"*

Highest Level of Education

Area	Less than H.S.	H.S. Diploma	Some College, No Deg.	Associate Degree	Bachelor's Degree	Master's Degree	Prof. School Degree	Doctorate Degree
City	2.8	11.6	16.3	7.5	38.1	14.8	5.8	3.1
MSA[1]	15.9	27.7	18.5	8.8	18.5	6.8	2.6	1.2
U.S.	13.7	28.0	21.2	7.9	18.3	7.8	2.0	1.3

Note: Figures cover persons age 25 and over; (1) Figures cover the Miami-Fort Lauderdale-West Palm Beach, FL Metropolitan Statistical Area—see Appendix B for areas included
Source: U.S. Census Bureau, 2010-2014 American Community Survey 5-Year Estimates

Educational Attainment by Race

Area	High School Graduate or Higher (%)					Bachelor's Degree or Higher (%)				
	Total	White	Black	Asian	Hisp.[2]	Total	White	Black	Asian	Hisp.[2]
City	97.2	98.0	97.3	88.5	96.7	61.8	61.1	71.6	65.7	50.3
MSA[1]	84.1	85.7	78.8	86.7	77.4	29.1	31.7	17.4	47.8	24.0
U.S.	86.3	88.4	83.2	85.8	64.1	29.3	30.6	19.0	50.9	13.9

Note: Figures shown cover persons 25 years old and over; (1) Figures cover the Miami-Fort Lauderdale-West Palm Beach, FL Metropolitan Statistical Area—see Appendix B for areas included; (2) People of Hispanic origin can be of any race
Source: U.S. Census Bureau, 2010-2014 American Community Survey 5-Year Estimates

School Enrollment by Grade and Control

Area	Preschool (%)		Kindergarten (%)		Grades 1 - 4 (%)		Grades 5 - 8 (%)		Grades 9 - 12 (%)	
	Public	Private	Public	Private	Public	Private	Public	Private	Public	Private
City	10.0	90.0	86.2	13.8	88.4	11.6	85.9	14.1	77.1	22.9
MSA[1]	47.6	52.4	82.9	17.1	86.8	13.2	87.5	12.5	87.8	12.2
U.S.	57.4	42.6	87.8	12.2	89.8	10.2	89.9	10.1	90.6	9.4

Note: Figures shown cover persons 3 years old and over; (1) Figures cover the Miami-Fort Lauderdale-West Palm Beach, FL Metropolitan Statistical Area—see Appendix B for areas included
Source: U.S. Census Bureau, 2010-2014 American Community Survey 5-Year Estimates

Average Salaries of Public School Classroom Teachers

Area	2013-14 Dollars	2013-14 Rank[1]	2014-15 Dollars	2014-15 Rank[1]	Percent Change 2013-14 to 2014-15	Percent Change 2004-05 to 2014-15
Florida	47,780	39	48,992	36	2.54	17.8
U.S. Average	56,610	–	57,379	–	1.36	20.8

Note: (1) State rank ranges from 1 to 51 where 1 indicates highest salary.
Source: National Education Association, Rankings & Estimates: Rankings of the States 2014 and Estimates of School Statistics 2015, March 2015

Higher Education

Four-Year Colleges: Public	Four-Year Colleges: Private Non-profit	Four-Year Colleges: Private For-profit	Two-Year Colleges: Public	Two-Year Colleges: Private Non-profit	Two-Year Colleges: Private For-profit	Medical Schools[1]	Law Schools[2]	Voc/ Tech[3]
0	0	0	0	0	0	0	0	0

Note: Figures cover institutions located within the city limits and include main campuses only; (1) includes schools accredited by the Liaison Committee on Medical Education and the American Osteopathic Association's Commission on Osteopathic College Accreditation; (2) includes ABA-accredited schools, schools with provisional ABA accreditation, and state accredited schools; (3) includes all schools with programs that are less than 2 years.
Source: National Center for Education Statistics, Integrated Postsecondary Education System (IPEDS), 2014-15; Association of American Medical Colleges, Member List, March 21, 2016; American Osteopathic Association, Member List, March 21, 2016; Law School Admission Council, Official Guide to ABA-Approved Law Schools Online, March 21, 2016; Wikipedia, List of Medical Schools in the United States, March 21, 2016; Wikipedia, List of Law Schools in the United States, March 21, 2016

PRESIDENTIAL ELECTION

2012 Presidential Election Results

Area	Obama (%)	Romney (%)	Other (%)
Broward County	67.2	32.3	0.5
U.S.	51.0	47.2	1.8

Note: Results may not add to 100% due to rounding
Source: Dave Leip's Atlas of U.S. Presidential Elections

EMPLOYERS

Major Employers

Company Name	Industry
Baptist Health South Florida	General medical & surgical hospitals
Baptist Hospital of Miami	General medical & surgical hospitals
County of Miami-Dade	Police protection, county government
County of Miami-Dade	Regulation, administration of transportation
County of, Palm Beach	County supervisors' & executives' offices
Florida International University	Colleges & universities
Intercoastal Health Systems	Management services
Miami Dade College	Community college
Mount Sinai Medical Center of Florida	General medical & surgical hospitals
North Broward Hospital District	Hospitals
Royal Caribbean Cruises Ltd.	Computer processing services
Royal Caribbean Cruises Ltd.	Deep sea passenger transportation, except ferry
School Board of Palm Beach County	Public elementary & secondary schools
Style View Products	Storm doors of windows, metal
The Answer Group	Custom computer programming services
University of Miami	Colleges & universities
Veterans Health Administration	General medical & surgical hospitals

Note: Companies shown are located within the Miami-Fort Lauderdale-West Palm Beach, FL Metropolitan Statistical Area.
Source: Hoovers.com; Wikipedia

PUBLIC SAFETY

Crime Rate

Area	All Crimes	Violent Crimes: Murder	Rape[3]	Robbery	Aggrav. Assault	Property Crimes: Burglary	Larceny -Theft	Motor Vehicle Theft
City	662.6	3.7	0.0	7.4	14.7	114.1	500.7	22.1
Metro[1]	3,521.2	4.1	33.4	141.5	239.7	637.2	2,258.8	206.5
U.S.	2,971.8	4.5	36.6	102.2	232.5	542.5	1,837.3	216.2

Note: Figures are crimes per 100,000 population; (1) Figures cover the Fort Lauderdale-Pompano Beach-Deerfield Beach, FL Metropolitan Division—see Appendix B for areas included; (3) The city and U.S. figures shown were reported using the revised Uniform Crime Reporting (UCR) definition of rape. The suburban and metro area figures shown are an aggregate total of the data submitted using both the revised and legacy UCR definitions.
Source: FBI Uniform Crime Reports, 2014

Hate Crimes

Area	Number of Quarters Reported	Number of Incidents per Bias Motivation: Race	Religion	Sexual Orientation	Ethnicity	Disability	Gender	Gender Identity
City	4	0	0	0	0	0	0	0
U.S.	4	2,568	1,014	1,017	648	84	33	98

Source: Federal Bureau of Investigation, Hate Crime Statistics 2014

Identity Theft Consumer Complaints

Area	Complaints	Complaints per 100,000 Population	Rank[2]
MSA[1]	17,832	300.7	3
U.S.	490,220	152.4	-

Note: (1) Figures cover the Miami-Fort Lauderdale-West Palm Beach, FL Metropolitan Statistical Area—see Appendix B for areas included; (2) Rank ranges from 1 to 379 where 1 indicates greatest number of identity theft complaints per 100,000 population
Source: Federal Trade Commission, Consumer Sentinel Network Data Book for January–December 2015

Fraud and Other Consumer Complaints

Area	Complaints	Complaints per 100,000 Population	Rank[2]
MSA[1]	28,598	482.3	25
U.S.	2,593,159	806.0	-

Note: (1) Figures cover the Miami-Fort Lauderdale-West Palm Beach, FL Metropolitan Statistical Area—see Appendix B for areas included; (2) Rank ranges from 1 to 379 where 1 indicates greatest number of identity theft complaints per 100,000 population
Source: Federal Trade Commission, Consumer Sentinel Network Data Book for January–December 2015

RECREATION

Culture

Dance[1]	Theatre[1]	Instrumental Music[1]	Vocal Music[1]	Series and Festivals	Museums and Art Galleries[2]	Zoos and Aquariums[3]
0	0	0	0	0	0	0

Note: (1) Professional perfoming groups; (2) Based on organizations with SIC code 8412; (3) AZA-accredited
Source: The Grey House Performing Arts Directory, 2015-16; Association of Zoos & Aquariums, AZA Member Zoos & Aquariums, March 25, 2016; www.AccuLeads.com, March 29, 2016

Professional Sports Teams

Team Name	League	Year Established
Florida Panthers	National Hockey League (NHL)	1993
Miami Dolphins	National Football League (NFL)	1966
Miami Heat	National Basketball Association (NBA)	1988
Miami Marlins	Major League Baseball (MLB)	1993

Note: Includes teams located in the Miami-Fort Lauderdale-West Palm Beach, FL Metropolitan Statistical Area.
Source: Wikipedia, Major Professional Sports Teams of the United States and Canada, March 24, 2016

CLIMATE

Average and Extreme Temperatures

Temperature	Jan	Feb	Mar	Apr	May	Jun	Jul	Aug	Sep	Oct	Nov	Dec	Yr.
Extreme High (°F)	88	89	92	96	95	98	98	98	97	95	89	87	98
Average High (°F)	75	77	79	82	85	88	89	90	88	85	80	77	83
Average Temp. (°F)	68	69	72	75	79	82	83	83	82	78	73	69	76
Average Low (°F)	59	60	64	68	72	75	76	76	76	72	66	61	69
Extreme Low (°F)	30	35	32	42	55	60	69	68	68	53	39	30	30

Note: Figures cover the years 1948-1990
Source: National Climatic Data Center, International Station Meteorological Climate Summary, 9/96

Average Precipitation/Snowfall/Humidity

Precip./Humidity	Jan	Feb	Mar	Apr	May	Jun	Jul	Aug	Sep	Oct	Nov	Dec	Yr.
Avg. Precip. (in.)	1.9	2.0	2.3	3.0	6.2	8.7	6.1	7.5	8.2	6.6	2.7	1.8	57.1
Avg. Snowfall (in.)	0	0	0	0	0	0	0	0	0	0	0	0	0
Avg. Rel. Hum. 7am (%)	84	84	82	80	81	84	84	86	88	87	85	84	84
Avg. Rel. Hum. 4pm (%)	59	57	57	57	62	68	66	67	69	65	63	60	63

Note: Figures cover the years 1948-1990; Tr = Trace amounts (<0.05 in. of rain; <0.5 in. of snow)
Source: National Climatic Data Center, International Station Meteorological Climate Summary, 9/96

Weather Conditions

Temperature			Daytime Sky			Precipitation		
32°F & below	45°F & below	90°F & above	Clear	Partly cloudy	Cloudy	0.01 inch or more precip.	0.1 inch or more snow/ice	Thunder-storms
< 1	7	55	48	263	54	128	0	74

Note: Figures are average number of days per year and cover the years 1948-1990
Source: National Climatic Data Center, International Station Meteorological Climate Summary, 9/96

HAZARDOUS WASTE

Superfund Sites

Parkland has no sites on the EPA's Superfund Final National Priorities List. There are a total of 1,323 Superfund sites on the list in the U.S. *U.S. Environmental Protection Agency, Final National Priorities List, March 18, 2016*

AIR & WATER QUALITY

Air Quality Trends: Ozone

	1990	1995	2000	2005	2010	2011	2012	2013	2014
MSA[1]	0.068	0.072	0.075	0.065	0.064	0.060	0.062	0.061	0.062

Note: (1) Data covers the Miami-Fort Lauderdale-West Palm Beach, FL Metropolitan Statistical Area—see Appendix B for areas included. The values shown are the composite ozone concentration averages among trend sites based on the highest fourth daily maximum 8-hour concentration in parts per million. These trends are based on sites having an adequate record of monitoring data during the trend period. Data from exceptional events are included.
Source: U.S. Environmental Protection Agency, Air Quality Monitoring Information, "Air Quality Trends by City, 1990-2014"

Air Quality Index

Area	Percent of Days when Air Quality was...[2]					AQI Statistics[2]	
	Good	Moderate	Unhealthy for Sensitive Groups	Unhealthy	Very Unhealthy	Maximum	Median
MSA[1]	71.2	28.8	0.0	0.0	0.0	95	42

Note: (1) Data covers the Miami-Fort Lauderdale-West Palm Beach, FL Metropolitan Statistical Area—see Appendix B for areas included; (2) Based on 365 days with AQI data in 2015. Air Quality Index (AQI) is an index for reporting daily air quality. EPA calculates the AQI for five major air pollutants regulated by the Clean Air Act: ground-level ozone, particle pollution (aka particulate matter), carbon monoxide, sulfur dioxide, and nitrogen dioxide. The AQI runs from 0 to 500. The higher the AQI value, the greater the level of air pollution and the greater the health concern. There are six AQI categories: "Good" AQI is between 0 and 50. Air quality is considered satisfactory; "Moderate" AQI is between 51 and 100. Air quality is acceptable; "Unhealthy for Sensitive Groups" When AQI values are between 101 and 150, members of sensitive groups may experience health effects; "Unhealthy" When AQI values are between 151 and 200 everyone may begin to experience health effects; "Very Unhealthy" AQI values between 201 and 300 trigger a health alert; "Hazardous" AQI values over 300 trigger warnings of emergency conditions (not shown).
Source: U.S. Environmental Protection Agency, Air Quality Index Report, 2015

Air Quality Index Pollutants

Area	Percent of Days when AQI Pollutant was...[2]					
	Carbon Monoxide	Nitrogen Dioxide	Ozone	Sulfur Dioxide	Particulate Matter 2.5	Particulate Matter 10
MSA[1]	0.0	1.1	18.1	0.3	67.1	13.4

Note: (1) Data covers the Miami-Fort Lauderdale-West Palm Beach, FL Metropolitan Statistical Area—see Appendix B for areas included; (2) Based on 365 days with AQI data in 2015. The Air Quality Index (AQI) is an index for reporting daily air quality. EPA calculates the AQI for five major air pollutants regulated by the Clean Air Act: ground-level ozone, particle pollution (also known as particulate matter), carbon monoxide, sulfur dioxide, and nitrogen dioxide. The AQI runs from 0 to 500. The higher the AQI value, the greater the level of air pollution and the greater the health concern.
Source: U.S. Environmental Protection Agency, Air Quality Index Report, 2015

Maximum Air Pollutant Concentrations: Particulate Matter, Ozone, CO and Lead

	Particulate Matter 10 (ug/m^3)	Particulate Matter 2.5 Wtd AM (ug/m^3)	Particulate Matter 2.5 24-Hr (ug/m^3)	Ozone (ppm)	Carbon Monoxide (ppm)	Lead (ug/m^3)
MSA[1] Level	61	6.3	15	0.068	2	n/a
NAAQS[2]	150	15	35	0.075	9	0.15
Met NAAQS[2]	Yes	Yes	Yes	Yes	Yes	n/a

Note: (1) Data covers the Miami-Fort Lauderdale-West Palm Beach, FL Metropolitan Statistical Area—see Appendix B for areas included; Data from exceptional events are included; (2) National Ambient Air Quality Standards; ppm = parts per million; ug/m³ = micrograms per cubic meter; n/a not available.
Concentrations: Particulate Matter 10 (coarse particulate)—highest second maximum 24-hour concentration; Particulate Matter 2.5 Wtd AM (fine particulate)—highest weighted annual mean concentration; Particulate Matter 2.5 24-Hour (fine particulate)—highest 98th percentile 24-hour concentration; Ozone—highest fourth daily maximum 8-hour concentration; Carbon Monoxide—highest second maximum non-overlapping 8-hour concentration; Lead—maximum running 3-month average
Source: U.S. Environmental Protection Agency, Air Quality Monitoring Information, "Air Quality Statistics by City, 2014"

Maximum Air Pollutant Concentrations: Nitrogen Dioxide and Sulfur Dioxide

	Nitrogen Dioxide AM (ppb)	Nitrogen Dioxide 1-Hr (ppb)	Sulfur Dioxide AM (ppb)	Sulfur Dioxide 1-Hr (ppb)	Sulfur Dioxide 24-Hr (ppb)
MSA[1] Level	9	50	n/a	5	n/a
NAAQS[2]	53	100	30	75	140
Met NAAQS[2]	Yes	Yes	n/a	Yes	n/a

Note: (1) Data covers the Miami-Fort Lauderdale-West Palm Beach, FL Metropolitan Statistical Area—see Appendix B for areas included; Data from exceptional events are included; (2) National Ambient Air Quality Standards; ppm = parts per million; ug/m³ = micrograms per cubic meter; n/a not available.
Concentrations: Nitrogen Dioxide AM—highest arithmetic mean concentration; Nitrogen Dioxide 1-Hr—highest 98th percentile 1-hour daily maximum concentration; Sulfur Dioxide AM—highest annual mean concentration; Sulfur Dioxide 1-Hr—highest 99th percentile 1-hour daily maximum concentration; Sulfur Dioxide 24-Hr—highest second maximum 24-hour concentration
Source: U.S. Environmental Protection Agency, Air Quality Monitoring Information, "Air Quality Statistics by City, 2014"

Drinking Water

Water System Name	Pop. Served	Primary Water Source Type	Violations[1]	
			Health Based	Monitoring/ Reporting
Parkland Utilities Inc.	2,590	Ground	0	0

Note: (1) Based on violation data from January 1, 2015 to December 31, 2015 (includes unresolved violations from earlier years)
Source: U.S. Environmental Protection Agency, Office of Ground Water and Drinking Water, Safe Drinking Water Information System (based on data extracted April 29, 2016)

Weston, Florida

Background

The city of Weston in Broward County was incorporated in 1996, and is one of the most ambitious planned communities in the country. It sits on 15,000 acres at the edge of the Everglades, is easily connected by interstate to the major urban areas of Tampa, Orlando and Miami, and is working to maintain a vibrant pace of development opportunities for education, recreation, and commerce. Though new, Weston has a "hometown" feel that appeals to both full and part-time residents. A strong local economy with arts festivals, concerts and golf tournaments, together with a lively South Florida ethnic mix, creates a unique excitement.

Prospects for continued prosperity are excellent. Major corporations with offices in Weston include American Express Global Mail Solutions, Hershey Foods Corporation, Office Depot, and Best Buy.

There are eleven public schools in Weston, administered by Broward County. Private and parochial schools are also available. Nearby colleges and universities include Nova Southeastern University, Keiser College, Broward Community College, and Florida Atlantic University-Boca Raton. Major hospitals in the area include the Cleveland Clinic Hospital, which is supported by more than 100 physicians in more than 40 specialties.

A network of bike and walking trails provides convenient access to all areas of the town, and the Town Center features shopping and a venue for social and cultural events. The center hosts dozens of retail shops, as well as restaurants and office suites. A park and a new amphitheater, overlooking a lake, take advantage of the site's natural beauty. Weston is minutes from the BankAtlantic Center, home to the Florida Panthers hockey team, and an arena featuring top performing artists.

Weston is served by Fort Lauderdale-Hollywood International and Miami International Airports, both within 25 miles of the city. The city enjoys the year round subtropical climate that is characteristic of South Florida.

Rankings

Business/Finance Rankings

- The personal finance site NerdWallet analyzed 183 American metropolitan areas with populations over 250,000 and more than 15,000 businesses to rank where entrepreneurs find the most success. Criteria included area economy, annual income, housing cost, unemployment rate, and the success rate of area businesses. Fort Lauderdale* ranked #35. *www.nerdwallet.com, "Best Places to Start a Business," April 27, 2015*

- USAA and Hiring Our Heroes worked with Sperlings's BestPlaces and the Institute for Veterans and Military Families at Syracuse University to rank major metropolitan areas where military-skills-related employment is strongest. Criteria for veterans *pursuing entrepreneurship* included veteran-owned businesses per capita; percentage of small businesses; colleges; certification/license transfers; airports nearby; and accessible health resources. Metro areas with a higher than national average crime or unemployment rate were excluded. At #8, the Fort Lauderdale* metro area made the top ten. *www.usaa.com, "2015 Best Places for Veterans"*

- USAA and Hiring Our Heroes worked with Sperlings's BestPlaces and the Institute for Veterans and Military Families at Syracuse University to rank major metropolitan areas where military-skills-related employment is strongest. Criteria for *mid-career* veterans included veteran wage growth; military skills, defense contractor, and government jobs; recent job growth; stability; and accessible health resources. Metro areas with a higher than national average crime or unemployment rate were excluded. At #4, the Fort Lauderdale* metro area made the top ten. *www.usaa.com, "2015 Best Places for Veterans"*

- Based on the U.S. Department of Labor's Occupational Information Network Data Collection Program, the Brookings Institution defined job opportunities for STEM workers at various levels of educational attainment. The Fort Lauderdale* metro area was placed among the ten large metro areas with the lowest demand for high-level STEM knowledge. *www.brookings.edu, "The Hidden Stem Economy," June 10, 2013*

- Metro areas with the largest gap in income between rich and poor residents were identified by 24/7 Wall Street using the U.S. Census Bureau's 2013 American Community Survey. The Miami* metro area placed #8 among metro areas with the widest wealth gap between rich and poor. *247wallst.com, "20 Cities with the Widest Gap between the Rich and Poor," July 8, 2015*

- Based on metro area social media reviews, the employment opinion group Glassdoor surveyed 50 of the largest U.S. metro areas and equally weighed cost of living, hiring opportunity, and job satisfaction to compose a list of "25 Best Cities for Jobs." The Fort Lauderdale* metro area was ranked #25 in overall job satisfaction. *www.glassdoor.com, "Best Cities for Jobs," May 19, 2015*

- In a survey of economic confidence in the nation's 50 largest metropolitan areas conducted January–December 2014, the Miami* metro area placed #5, according to Gallup's 2014 Economic Confidence Index. *Gallup, "San Jose and San Francisco Lead in Economic Confidence," March 19, 2015*

- The Brookings Institution ranked the 100 largest metro areas in the U.S. based on income inequality. Miami* was ranked #8 (#1 = greatest ineqality). Criteria: the "95/20 ratio," a figure representing the income at which a household earns more than 95 percent of all other households, divided by the income at which a household earns more than only 20 percent of all other households. *Brookings Institution, "Income Inequality, 100 Largest U.S. Metro Areas, 2007-2014," January 14, 2016*

- The finance site *24/7 Wall St.* identified the metropolitan areas that have the smallest and largest pay disparities between men and women, comparing the median earnings for the past 12 months of both men and women working full-time in the country's 100 largest metropolitan statistical areas. Of the ten best-paying metros for women, the Miami* metro area ranked #6. *24/7 Wall St., "The Best (and Worst) Paying Cities for Women," March 6, 2015*

- Payscale.com ranked the 20 largest metro areas in terms of wage growth. The Miami* metro area ranked #9. Criteria: private-sector wage growth between the 1st quarter of 2015 and the 1st quarter of 2016. *PayScale, "Wage Trends by Metro Area," 1st Quarter, 2016*

- The Fort Lauderdale* metro area appeared on the Milken Institute "2015 Best Performing Cities" list. Rank: #41 out of 200 large metro areas. Criteria: job growth; wage and salary growth; high-tech output growth. *Milken Institute, "Best-Performing Cities 2015," December 2015*

- *Forbes* ranked the 200 most populous metro areas to determine the nation's "Best Places for Business and Careers." The Fort Lauderdale* metro area was ranked #57. Criteria: costs (business and living); job growth (past and projected); income growth; educational attainment (college and high school); projected economic growth; cultural and recreational opportunities; net migration patterns; number of highly ranked colleges. *Forbes, "The Best Places for Business and Careers 2015," July 29, 2015*

Education Rankings

- Personal finance website *WalletHub* analyzed the 150 largest U.S. metropolitan statistical areas to determine where the most educated Americans are choosing to settle. Criteria: education quality and attainment gap; education levels; percentage of workers with degrees; public school rankings; quality and size of each metro area's universities. Miami* was ranked #100 (#1 = most educated city). *www.WalletHub.com, "2015's Most and Least Educated Cities*

Environmental Rankings

- The Miami* metro area came in at #342 for the relative comfort of its climate on Sperling's list of "chill cities," as measured by the Sperling Heat Index. All 361 metro areas are included. Criteria included daytime high temperatures, nighttime low temperatures, dew point, and relative humidity at the high temperatures. *www.bertsperling.com, "Sperling's Chill Cities," July 18, 2013*

- Sperling's BestPlaces assessed 379 metropolitan areas of the United States for the likelihood of dangerously extreme weather events or earthquakes. In general the Southeast and South-Central regions have the highest risk of weather extremes and earthquakes, while the Pacific Northwest enjoys the lowest risk. Of the least risky metropolitan areas, the Fort Lauderdale* metro area was ranked #311. *www.bestplaces.net, "Safest Places from Natural Disasters," April 2011*

- The U.S. Environmental Protection Agency (EPA) released a list of U.S. metropolitan areas with the most ENERGY STAR certified buildings in 2015. The Miami* metro area was ranked #18 out of 25. *U.S. Environmental Protection Agency, "Top Cities With the Most ENERGY STAR Certified Buildings in 2016," March 30, 2016*

- Miami* was highlighted as one of the top 25 cleanest metro areas for year-round particle pollution (Annual PM 2.5) in the U.S. during 2011 through 2013. The area ranked #23. *American Lung Association, State of the Air 2015*

Health/Fitness Rankings

- Analysts who tracked obesity rates in the nation's largest metro areas (populations above one million) found that the Fort Lauderdale* metro area was one of the ten major metros where residents were least likely to be obese, defined as a BMI score of 30 or above. *www.gallup.com, "Boulder, Colo., Residents Still Least Likely to Be Obese," April 4, 2014*

- For each of the 50 most populous metro areas in the United States, the American College of Sports Medicine's American Fitness Index evaluated infrastructure, community assets, and policies that encourage healthy and fit lifestyles, including preventive health behaviors, levels of chronic disease conditions, health care access, and community resources and policies that support physical activity. The Miami* metro area ranked #30 for "community fitness." *www.americanfitnessindex.org, "ACSM American Fitness Index Health and Community Fitness Status of the 50 Largest Metropolitan Areas," May 2015*

- The Miami* metro area was identified as one of the worst cities for bed bugs in America by pest control company Orkin. The area ranked #43 out of 50 based on the number of bed bug treatments Orkin performed from January to December 2015. *Orkin, "Chicago Tops Bed Bug Cities List for Fourth Year in a Row," January 13, 2016*

- Miami* was identified as a "2016 Spring Allergy Capital." The area ranked #75 out of 100. Three groups of factors were used to identify the most severe cities for people with allergies during the spring season: annual pollen levels; medicine utilization; access to board-certified allergists. *Asthma and Allergy Foundation of America, "Spring Allergy Capitals 2016"*

- Miami* was identified as a "2015 Asthma Capital." The area ranked #61 out of the nation's 100 largest metropolitan areas. Criteria: estimated prevalence; self-reported prevalence; crude death rate for asthma; annual pollen score; annual air quality; public smoking laws; number of board-certified asthma specialists; school inhaler access laws; rescue medication use; controller medication use; ER visits for asthma; uninsured rate; poverty rate. *Asthma and Allergy Foundation of America, "Asthma Capitals 2015"*

- The Miami* metro area ranked #47 out of 190 in The Gallup-Healthways Well-Being Index. Criteria: purpose; social well being; financial health; community and physical health. Results are based on telephone interviews with adults, aged 18 and older, living in metropolitan areas in the 50 U.S. states and the District of Columbia. *Gallup-Healthways, "State of American Well-Being," February 23, 2016*

Real Estate Rankings

- The Fort Lauderdale* metro area was identified as #5 among the ten housing markets with the highest percentage of distressed property sales, based on the findings of the housing data website RealtyTrac. Criteria: short sales; income and poverty figures; and unemployment data. *247wallst.com, "Cities Selling the Most Distressed Homes," January 23, 2014*

- The Fort Lauderdale* metro area was identified as one of the top 20 housing markets to invest in for 2016 by *Forbes*. The area ranked #8. Criteria: strong job and population growth; anticipated home price appreciation; and other factors. *Forbes.com, "Best Buy Cities: Where to Invest in Housing in 2016," January 27, 2016*

- The Fort Lauderdale* metro area was identified as one of the 15 worst housing markets for the next five years." Criteria: projected annualized change in home prices between the fourth quarter 2012 and the fourth quarter 2017. *The Business Insider, "The 15 Worst Housing Markets for the Next Five Years," May 22, 2013*

- The Miami* metro area was identified as one of the 20 least affordable housing markets in the U.S. in 2015. The area ranked #10 out of 179 markets. Criteria: qualification for a mortgage loan on a typical home. *National Association of Realtors®, Affordability Index of Existing Single-Family Homes for Metropolitan Areas, 2015*

- Fort Lauderdale* was ranked #165 out of 225 metro areas in terms of housing affordability in 2015 by the National Association of Home Builders (#1 = most affordable). Criteria: the share of homes sold in that area affordable to a family earning the local median income, based on standard mortgage underwriting criteria. *National Association of Home Builders®, NAHB-Wells Fargo Housing Opportunity Index, 4th Quarter 2015*

- The nation's largest metro areas were analyzed in terms of the percentage of households entering some stage of foreclosure in 2015. The Miami* metro area ranked #5 out of 20 (#1 = highest foreclosure rate). *RealtyTrac, "2015 Year-End U.S. Foreclosure Market Report™," January 12, 2016*

Safety Rankings

- Weston was identified as one of the safest cities in America by NeighborhoodScout. The city ranked #11 out of 100. Criteria: number of violent and property crimes per 1,000 residents. The editors only considered cities with 25,000 or more residents. *NeighborhoodScout, "Safest Cities in America 2016"*

- The National Insurance Crime Bureau ranked 380 metro areas in the U.S. in terms of per capita rates of vehicle theft. The Miami* metro area ranked #60 (#1 = highest rate). Criteria: number of vehicle theft offenses per 100,000 inhabitants in 2014. *National Insurance Crime Bureau, "Hot Spots 2014," June 24, 2015*

Seniors/Retirement Rankings

- From its Best Cities for Successful Aging indexes, the Milken Institute generated rankings for metropolitan areas, weighing data in eight categories—health care, wellness, living arrangements, transportation, financial characteristics, education and employment opportunities, community engagement, and overall livability. The Miami* metro area was ranked #76 overall in the large metro area category. *Milken Institute, "Best Cities for Successful Aging, 2014"*

Sports/Recreation Rankings

- According to the personal finance website NerdWallet, the Miami* metro area, at #9, is one of the nation's top dozen metro areas for sports fans. Criteria included the presence of all four major sports—MLB, NFL, NHL, and NBA, fan enthusiasm (as measured by game attendance), ticket affordability, and "sports culture," that is, number of sports bars. *www.nerdwallet.com, "Best Cities for Sports Fans," May 5, 2013*
- *Card Player* magazine scoured North America to identify the top five metropolitan areas where a player can access the types of games that make launching a poker career possible. The Fort Lauderdale* metro area ranked #2. *Card Player, "The Top Five Cities to Launch Your Poker Career," April 2, 2014*

Women/Minorities Rankings

- *24/7 Wall St.* compared median earnings over a 12-month period for men and women who worked full-time, year-round, and employment composition by sector to identify the best-paying cities for women. Of the largest 100 U.S. metropolitan areas, Miami* was ranked #6 in pay disparity. *24/7 Wall St., "The Best (and Worst) Paying Cities for Women," March 6, 2015*

Miscellaneous Rankings

- The watchdog site Charity Navigator conducts an annual study of charities in the nation's major markets both to analyze statistical differences in their financial, accountability, and transparency practices and to track year-to-year variations in individual communities. The Miami* metro area was ranked #5 among the 30 metro markets in the rating dimension of Overall Score. *www.charitynavigator.org, "Metro Market Study 2015," June 5, 2015*
- Mars Chocolate North America, the makers of COMBOS®, in partnership with Sperling's BestPlaces, ranked 50 major metro areas in terms of their "manliness." The Miami* metro area ranked #36. Criteria: number of professional sports teams; number of nearby NASCAR tracks and racing events; manly lifestyle; concentration of manly retail stores; manly occupations per capita; salty snack sales; "Board of Manliness" rankings. *Mars Chocolate North America, "America's Manliest Cities 2012"*
- The National Alliance to End Homelessness ranked the 100 most populous metro areas with the highest rate of homelessness. The Miami* metro area ranked #38. Criteria: number of homeless people per 10,000 population in 2011. *National Alliance to End Homelessness, The State of Homelessness in America 2012*

Weston is located within the Miami-Fort Lauderdale-West Palm Beach, FL Metropolitan Statistical Area and the Fort Lauderdale-Pompano Beach-Deerfield Beach, FL Metropolitan Division.

Business Environment

CITY FINANCES

City Government Finances

Component	2012 ($000)	2012 ($ per capita)
Total Revenues	103,169	1,579
Total Expenditures	100,018	1,530
Debt Outstanding	12,629	193
Cash and Securities[1]	110,735	1,694

Note: (1) Cash and security holdings of a government at the close of its fiscal year, including those of its dependent agencies, utilities, and liquor stores.
Source: U.S Census Bureau, State & Local Government Finances 2012

City Government Revenue by Source

Source	2012 ($000)	2012 ($ per capita)
General Revenue		
From Federal Government	595	9
From State Government	4,607	70
From Local Governments	0	0
Taxes		
Property	12,012	183
Sales and Gross Receipts	17,811	272
Personal Income	0	0
Corporate Income	0	0
Motor Vehicle License	0	0
Other Taxes	8,782	134
Current Charges	17,128	262
Liquor Store	0	0
Utility	13,082	200
Employee Retirement	0	0

Source: U.S Census Bureau, State & Local Government Finances 2012

City Government Expenditures by Function

Function	2012 ($000)	2012 ($ per capita)	2012 (%)
General Direct Expenditures			
Air Transportation	0	0	0.0
Corrections	0	0	0.0
Education	0	0	0.0
Employment Security Administration	0	0	0.0
Financial Administration	1,020	15	1.0
Fire Protection	18,391	281	18.3
General Public Buildings	0	0	0.0
Governmental Administration, Other	2,433	37	2.4
Health	0	0	0.0
Highways	699	10	0.6
Hospitals	0	0	0.0
Housing and Community Development	1,413	21	1.4
Interest on General Debt	506	7	0.5
Judicial and Legal	553	8	0.5
Libraries	0	0	0.0
Parking	0	0	0.0
Parks and Recreation	5,307	81	5.3
Police Protection	10,597	162	10.5
Public Welfare	0	0	0.0
Sewerage	11,505	176	11.5
Solid Waste Management	3,922	60	3.9
Veterans' Services	0	0	0.0
Liquor Store	0	0	0.0
Utility	16,762	256	16.7
Employee Retirement	0	0	0.0

Source: U.S Census Bureau, State & Local Government Finances 2012

DEMOGRAPHICS

Population Growth

Area	1990 Census	2000 Census	2010 Census	2014* Estimate	Population Growth (%)	
					1990-2014	2010-2014
City	10,099	49,286	65,333	67,567	569.0	3.4
MSA[1]	4,056,100	5,007,564	5,564,635	5,775,204	42.4	3.8
U.S.	248,709,873	281,421,906	308,745,538	314,107,084	26.3	1.7

Note: (1) Figures cover the Miami-Fort Lauderdale-West Palm Beach, FL Metropolitan Statistical Area—see Appendix B for areas included; (*) 2010-2014 5-year estimated population
Source: U.S. Census Bureau, 1990 Census, Census 2000, Census 2010, 2010-2014 American Community Survey 5-Year Estimates

Household Size

Area	Persons in Household (%)							Average Household Size
	One	Two	Three	Four	Five	Six	Seven or More	
City	12.8	29.0	19.6	27.3	8.8	1.9	0.2	3.22
MSA[1]	28.7	31.9	16.6	13.3	5.8	2.1	1.3	2.80
U.S.	27.5	33.5	15.8	13.1	6.0	2.3	1.4	2.64

Note: (1) Figures cover the Miami-Fort Lauderdale-West Palm Beach, FL Metropolitan Statistical Area—see Appendix B for areas included
Source: U.S. Census Bureau, 2010-2014 American Community Survey 5-Year Estimates

Race

Area	White Alone[2] (%)	Black Alone[2] (%)	Asian Alone[2] (%)	AIAN[3] Alone[2] (%)	NHOPI[4] Alone[2] (%)	Other Race Alone[2] (%)	Two or More Races (%)
City	85.4	4.4	4.3	0.4	0.0	3.1	2.4
MSA[1]	71.6	21.3	2.4	0.2	0.0	2.6	1.9
U.S.	73.8	12.6	5.0	0.8	0.2	4.7	2.9

Note: (1) Figures cover the Miami-Fort Lauderdale-West Palm Beach, FL Metropolitan Statistical Area—see Appendix B for areas included; (2) Alone is defined as not being in combination with one or more other races; (3) American Indian and Alaska Native; (4) Native Hawaiian and Other Pacific Islander
Source: U.S. Census Bureau, 2010-2014 American Community Survey 5-Year Estimates

Hispanic or Latino Origin

Area	Total (%)	Mexican (%)	Puerto Rican (%)	Cuban (%)	Other (%)
City	47.8	1.7	3.4	3.8	38.9
MSA[1]	42.4	2.4	3.9	18.2	17.9
U.S.	16.9	10.8	1.6	0.6	3.8

Note: Persons of Hispanic or Latino origin can be of any race; (1) Figures cover the Miami-Fort Lauderdale-West Palm Beach, FL Metropolitan Statistical Area—see Appendix B for areas included
Source: U.S. Census Bureau, 2010-2014 American Community Survey 5-Year Estimates

Ancestry

Area	German	Irish	English	American	Italian	Polish	French[2]	Scottish	Dutch
City	7.3	6.2	3.3	5.9	7.9	3.8	1.6	0.8	0.4
MSA[1]	5.3	5.1	3.3	5.8	5.4	2.2	1.4	0.7	0.5
U.S.	14.9	10.8	8.0	7.1	5.5	3.0	2.7	1.7	1.4

Note: Figures are the percentage of the total population reporting a particular ancestry. The nine most commonly reported ancestries in the U.S. are shown. Figures include multiple ancestries (e.g. if a person reported being Irish and Italian, they were included in both columns); (1) Figures cover the Miami-Fort Lauderdale-West Palm Beach, FL Metropolitan Statistical Area—see Appendix B for areas included; (2) Excludes Basque
Source: U.S. Census Bureau, 2010-2014 American Community Survey 5-Year Estimates

Foreign-Born Population

Area	Percent of Population Born in								
	Any Foreign Country	Asia	Mexico	Europe	Carribean	Central America[2]	South America	Africa	Canada
City	39.9	3.0	0.9	2.9	4.4	1.3	26.4	0.2	0.8
MSA[1]	38.7	2.0	1.1	2.3	20.4	4.2	7.8	0.4	0.6
U.S.	13.1	3.8	3.7	1.5	1.2	1.0	0.9	0.6	0.3

Note: (1) Figures cover the Miami-Fort Lauderdale-West Palm Beach, FL Metropolitan Statistical Area—see Appendix B for areas included; (2) Excludes Mexico.
Source: U.S. Census Bureau, 2010-2014 American Community Survey 5-Year Estimates

Marital Status

Area	Never Married	Now Married[2]	Separated	Widowed	Divorced
City	25.6	60.4	1.0	3.2	9.7
MSA[1]	34.1	43.2	3.0	6.9	12.8
U.S.	32.5	48.4	2.2	5.9	10.9

Note: Figures are percentages and cover the population 15 years of age and older; (1) Figures cover the Miami-Fort Lauderdale-West Palm Beach, FL Metropolitan Statistical Area—see Appendix B for areas included; (2) Excludes separated
Source: U.S. Census Bureau, 2010-2014 American Community Survey 5-Year Estimates

Disability Status

Area	All Ages	Under 18 Years Old	18 to 64 Years Old	65 Years and Over
City	4.2	0.8	3.7	19.7
MSA[1]	11.0	3.1	7.5	34.5
U.S.	12.3	4.1	10.2	36.3

Note: Figures show percent of the civilian noninstitutionalized population that reported having a disability. Disability status is determined from from six types of difficulty: vision, hearing, cognitive, ambulatory, self-care, and independent living. For children under 5 years old, hearing and vision difficulty are used to determine disability status. For children between the ages of 5 and 14, disability status is determined from hearing, vision, cognitive, ambulatory, and self-care difficulties. For people aged 15 years and older, they are considered to have a disability if they have difficulty with any one of the six difficulty types; (1) Figures cover the Miami-Fort Lauderdale-West Palm Beach, FL Metropolitan Statistical Area—see Appendix B for areas included.
Source: U.S. Census Bureau, 2010-2014 American Community Survey 5-Year Estimates

Age

Area	Percent of Population									Median Age
	Under Age 5	Age 5–19	Age 20–34	Age 35–44	Age 45–54	Age 55–64	Age 65–74	Age 75–84	Age 85+	
City	4.6	28.4	11.8	16.0	19.5	11.0	4.8	2.7	1.1	39.1
MSA[1]	5.7	17.8	19.6	13.7	14.9	11.9	8.4	5.5	2.6	40.2
U.S.	6.4	19.9	20.6	13.0	14.1	12.3	7.6	4.3	1.9	37.4

Note: (1) Figures cover the Miami-Fort Lauderdale-West Palm Beach, FL Metropolitan Statistical Area—see Appendix B for areas included
Source: U.S. Census Bureau, 2010-2014 American Community Survey 5-Year Estimates

Gender

Area	Males	Females	Males per 100 Females
City	33,506	34,061	98.4
MSA[1]	2,800,775	2,974,429	94.2
U.S.	154,515,159	159,591,925	96.8

Note: (1) Figures cover the Miami-Fort Lauderdale-West Palm Beach, FL Metropolitan Statistical Area—see Appendix B for areas included
Source: U.S. Census Bureau, 2010-2014 American Community Survey 5-Year Estimates

Religious Groups by Family

Area	Catholic	Baptist	Non-Den.	Methodist[2]	Lutheran	LDS[3]	Pente-costal	Presby-terian[4]	Muslim[5]	Judaism
MSA[1]	18.5	5.3	4.1	1.2	0.4	0.5	1.7	0.6	0.9	1.5
U.S.	19.1	9.3	4.0	4.0	2.3	2.0	1.9	1.6	0.8	0.7

Note: Figures are the number of adherents as a percentage of the total population; (1) Figures cover the Miami-Fort Lauderdale-Pompano Beach, FL Metropolitan Statistical Area—see Appendix B for areas included; (2) Methodist/Pietist; (3) Latter Day Saints; (4) Reformed; (5) Figures are estimates
Source: Association of Statisticians of American Religious Bodies, 2010 U.S. Religion Census: Religious Congregations & Membership Study

Religious Groups by Tradition

Area	Catholic	Evangelical Protestant	Mainline Protestant	Other Tradition	Black Protestant	Orthodox
MSA[1]	18.5	11.4	2.4	3.5	1.7	0.2
U.S.	19.1	16.2	7.3	4.3	1.6	0.3

Note: Figures are the number of adherents as a percentage of the total population; (1) Figures cover the Miami-Fort Lauderdale-Pompano Beach, FL Metropolitan Statistical Area—see Appendix B for areas included
Source: Association of Statisticians of American Religious Bodies, 2010 U.S. Religion Census: Religious Congregations & Membership Study

ECONOMY

Gross Metropolitan Product

Area	2013	2014	2015	2016	Rank[2]
MSA[1]	281.1	295.0	309.2	325.7	11

Note: Figures are in billions of dollars; (1) Figures cover the Miami-Fort Lauderdale-West Palm Beach, FL Metropolitan Statistical Area—see Appendix B for areas included; (2) Rank is based on 2016 data and ranges from 1 to 381
Source: The U.S. Conference of Mayors, U.S. Metro Economies: GMP and Employment 2014-2016, June 2015

Economic Growth

Area	2011-13 (%)	2014 (%)	2015 (%)	2016 (%)	Rank[2]
MSA[1]	2.8	3.2	3.3	3.4	38
U.S.	2.2	2.4	2.3	2.9	–

Note: Figures are real gross metropolitan product (GMP) growth rates and represent annual average percent change; (1) Figures cover the Miami-Fort Lauderdale-West Palm Beach, FL Metropolitan Statistical Area—see Appendix B for areas included; (2) Rank is based on 2016 data and ranges from 1 to 381
Source: The U.S. Conference of Mayors, U.S. Metro Economies: GMP and Employment 2014-2016, June 2015

Metropolitan Area Exports

Area	2009	2010	2011	2012	2013	2014	Rank[2]
MSA[1]	31,174.9	35,866.9	43,129.8	47,858.7	41,771.5	37,969.4	7

Note: Figures are in millions of dollars; (1) Figures cover the Miami-Fort Lauderdale-West Palm Beach, FL Metropolitan Statistical Area—see Appendix B for areas included; (2) Rank is based on 2014 data and ranges from 1 to 385
Source: U.S. Department of Commerce, International Trade Administration, Office of Trade & Industry Information, Manufacturing & Services, data extracted March 10, 2016

Building Permits

Area	Single-Family			Multi-Family			Total		
	2014	2015p	Pct. Chg.	2014	2015p	Pct. Chg.	2014	2015p	Pct. Chg.
City	4	2	-50.0	0	0	-	4	2	-50.0
MSA[1]	5,791	7,102	22.6	9,468	15,994	68.9	15,259	23,096	51.4
U.S.	640,300	690,800	7.9	411,800	487,600	18.4	1,052,100	1,178,400	12.0

Note: (1) Figures cover the Miami-Fort Lauderdale-West Palm Beach, FL Metropolitan Statistical Area—see Appendix B for areas included; Figures represent new, privately-owned housing units authorized (unadjusted data); All permit data are based on estimates with imputation; (p) preliminary data.
Source: U.S. Census Bureau, Manufacturing, Mining, and Construction Statistics, Building Permits, 2014, 2015

Bankruptcy Filings

Area	Business Filings			Nonbusiness Filings		
	2014	2015	% Chg.	2014	2015	% Chg.
Broward County	241	202	-16.2	7,870	6,714	-14.7
U.S.	26,983	24,735	-8.3	909,812	819,760	-9.9

Note: Business filings include Chapter 7, Chapter 11, Chapter 12, and Chapter 13; Nonbusiness filings include Chapter 7, Chapter 11, and Chapter 13
Source: Administrative Office of the U.S. Courts, Business and Nonbusiness Bankruptcy, County Cases Commenced by Chapter of the Bankruptcy Code, During the 12- Month Period Ending December 31, 2014 and Business and Nonbusiness Bankruptcy, County Cases Commenced by Chapter of the Bankruptcy Code, During the 12- Month Period Ending December 31, 2015

Housing Vacancy Rates

Area	Gross Vacancy Rate[2] (%)			Year-Round Vacancy Rate[3] (%)			Rental Vacancy Rate[4] (%)			Homeowner Vacancy Rate[5] (%)		
	2013	2014	2015	2013	2014	2015	2013	2014	2015	2013	2014	2015
MSA[1]	20.2	19.6	16.9	10.3	10.4	8.5	6.7	7.0	6.4	1.7	1.8	1.4
U.S.	13.6	13.4	12.9	10.7	10.4	10.0	8.3	7.6	7.1	2.0	1.9	1.8

Note: (1) Figures cover the Miami-Fort Lauderdale-West Palm Beach, FL Metropolitan Statistical Area—see Appendix B for areas included; (2) The percentage of the total housing inventory that is vacant; (3) The percentage of the housing inventory (excluding seasonal units) that is year-round vacant; (4) The percentage of rental inventory that is vacant for rent; (5) The percentage of homeowner inventory that is vacant for sale
Source: U.S. Census Bureau, Housing Vacancies and Homeownership Annual Statistics: 2015

INCOME

Income

Area	Per Capita ($)	Median Household ($)	Average Household ($)
City	40,452	91,613	124,595
MSA[1]	27,240	48,435	72,352
U.S.	28,555	53,482	74,596

Note: (1) Figures cover the Miami-Fort Lauderdale-West Palm Beach, FL Metropolitan Statistical Area—see Appendix B for areas included
Source: U.S. Census Bureau, 2010-2014 American Community Survey 5-Year Estimates

Household Income Distribution

Area	Percent of Households Earning							
	Under $15,000	$15,000 -24,999	$25,000 -34,999	$35,000 -49,999	$50,000 -74,999	$75,000 -99,000	$100,000 -149,999	$150,000 and up
City	6.1	4.8	6.0	8.7	15.0	12.8	18.8	27.8
MSA[1]	14.3	11.9	10.9	14.1	16.9	10.9	11.4	9.5
U.S.	12.5	10.7	10.2	13.5	17.8	12.2	13.0	10.0

Note: (1) Figures cover the Miami-Fort Lauderdale-West Palm Beach, FL Metropolitan Statistical Area—see Appendix B for areas included
Source: U.S. Census Bureau, 2010-2014 American Community Survey 5-Year Estimates

Poverty Rate

Area	All Ages	Under 18 Years Old	18 to 64 Years Old	65 Years and Over
City	7.8	8.1	7.4	9.5
MSA[1]	17.3	23.7	15.7	15.0
U.S.	15.6	21.9	14.6	9.4

Note: Figures are percentage of people whose income during the past 12 months was below the poverty level; (1) Figures cover the Miami-Fort Lauderdale-West Palm Beach, FL Metropolitan Statistical Area—see Appendix B for areas included
Source: U.S. Census Bureau, 2010-2014 American Community Survey 5-Year Estimates

EMPLOYMENT

Labor Force and Employment

Area	Civilian Labor Force			Workers Employed		
	Dec. 2014	Dec. 2015	% Chg.	Dec. 2014	Dec. 2015	% Chg.
City	35,751	36,071	0.8	34,307	34,695	1.1
MD[1]	995,560	999,633	0.4	945,682	956,378	1.1
U.S.	155,521,000	157,245,000	1.1	147,190,000	149,703,000	1.7

Note: Data is not seasonally adjusted and covers workers 16 years of age and older; (1) Figures cover the Fort Lauderdale-Pompano Beach-Deerfield Beach, FL Metropolitan Division—see Appendix B for areas included
Source: Bureau of Labor Statistics, Local Area Unemployment Statistics

Unemployment Rate

Area	2015											
	Jan.	Feb.	Mar.	Apr.	May	Jun.	Jul.	Aug.	Sep.	Oct.	Nov.	Dec.
City	4.5	4.3	4.3	4.0	4.4	4.5	4.2	4.2	4.1	3.8	3.7	3.8
MD[1]	5.5	5.3	5.2	4.9	5.2	5.1	5.3	5.2	4.9	4.7	4.5	4.3
U.S.	6.1	5.8	5.6	5.1	5.3	5.5	5.6	5.2	4.9	4.8	4.8	4.8

Note: Data is not seasonally adjusted and covers workers 16 years of age and older; (1) Figures cover the Fort Lauderdale-Pompano Beach-Deerfield Beach, FL Metropolitan Division—see Appendix B for areas included
Source: Bureau of Labor Statistics, Local Area Unemployment Statistics

Employment by Occupation

Occupation Classification	City (%)	MSA[1] (%)	U.S. (%)
Management, Business, Science, and Arts	52.4	33.5	36.4
Natural Resources, Construction, and Maintenance	3.6	8.7	9.0
Production, Transportation, and Material Moving	3.4	8.8	12.1
Sales and Office	29.5	28.0	24.4
Service	11.2	21.0	18.2

Note: Figures cover employed civilians 16 years of age and older; (1) Figures cover the Miami-Fort Lauderdale-West Palm Beach, FL Metropolitan Statistical Area—see Appendix B for areas included
Source: U.S. Census Bureau, 2010-2014 American Community Survey 5-Year Estimates

Employment by Industry

Sector	MD[1]		U.S.
	Number of Employees	Percent of Total	Percent of Total
Construction, Mining, and Logging	n/a	n/a	5.0
Education and Health Services	104,500	12.7	15.7
Financial Activities	58,600	7.1	5.7
Government	103,000	12.5	15.5
Information	19,400	2.3	1.9
Leisure and Hospitality	92,800	11.2	10.4
Manufacturing	28,400	3.4	8.6
Other Services	37,900	4.6	3.9
Professional and Business Services	144,800	17.6	13.9
Retail Trade	112,900	13.7	11.3
Transportation, Warehousing, and Utilities	26,400	3.2	3.9
Wholesale Trade	48,700	5.9	4.1

Note: Figures are non-farm employment as of December 2015. Figures are not seasonally adjusted and include workers 16 years of age and older; (1) Figures cover the Fort Lauderdale-Pompano Beach-Deerfield Beach, FL Metropolitan Division—see Appendix B for areas included; n/a not available
Source: Bureau of Labor Statistics, Current Employment Statistics, Employment, Hours, and Earnings

Occupations with Greatest Projected Employment Growth: 2012 – 2022

Occupation[1]	2012 Employment	2022 Projected Employment	Numeric Employment Change	Percent Employment Change
Retail Salespersons	326,380	380,120	53,740	16.5
Combined Food Preparation and Serving Workers, Including Fast Food	196,980	237,340	40,360	20.5
Customer Service Representatives	191,210	228,620	37,410	19.6
Registered Nurses	164,020	201,140	37,120	22.6
Waiters and Waitresses	191,370	227,810	36,440	19.0
Office Clerks, General	142,710	170,300	27,590	19.3
Cashiers	206,660	230,190	23,530	11.4
Landscaping and Groundskeeping Workers	92,510	115,540	23,030	24.9
Receptionists and Information Clerks	75,780	95,680	19,900	26.2
Nursing Assistants	86,990	106,200	19,210	22.1

Note: Projections cover Florida; (1) Sorted by numeric employment change
Source: www.projectionscentral.com, State Occupational Projections, 2012–2022 Long-Term Projections

Fastest Growing Occupations: 2012 – 2022

Occupation[1]	2012 Employment	2022 Projected Employment	Numeric Employment Change	Percent Employment Change
Helpers—Carpenters	1,280	2,450	1,170	90.7
Helpers—Brickmasons, Blockmasons, Stonemasons, and Tile and Marble Setters	1,050	1,890	840	79.5
Biomedical Engineers	760	1,300	540	70.7
Reinforcing Iron and Rebar Workers	520	870	350	67.5
Glaziers	2,890	4,710	1,820	62.8
Solar Photovoltaic Installers	170	270	100	58.7
Brickmasons and Blockmasons	2,820	4,430	1,610	57.1
Stonemasons	450	710	260	56.4
Helpers—Pipelayers, Plumbers, Pipefitters, and Steamfitters	2,420	3,750	1,330	54.8
Cement Masons and Concrete Finishers	10,390	16,050	5,660	54.4

Note: Projections cover Florida; (1) Sorted by percent employment change and excludes occupations with numeric employment change less than 100
Source: www.projectionscentral.com, State Occupational Projections, 2012–2022 Long-Term Projections

Average Wages

Occupation	$/Hr.	Occupation	$/Hr.
Accountants and Auditors	34.83	Maids and Housekeeping Cleaners	10.28
Automotive Mechanics	20.65	Maintenance and Repair Workers	16.53
Bookkeepers	17.61	Marketing Managers	58.89
Carpenters	18.54	Nuclear Medicine Technologists	35.89
Cashiers	9.91	Nurses, Licensed Practical	21.07
Clerks, General Office	13.55	Nurses, Registered	33.22
Clerks, Receptionists/Information	13.11	Nursing Assistants	12.03
Clerks, Shipping/Receiving	14.54	Packers and Packagers, Hand	10.17
Computer Programmers	33.95	Physical Therapists	41.56
Computer Systems Analysts	38.15	Postal Service Mail Carriers	25.26
Computer User Support Specialists	22.18	Real Estate Brokers	34.73
Cooks, Restaurant	12.85	Retail Salespersons	12.70
Dentists	59.61	Sales Reps., Exc. Tech./Scientific	27.99
Electrical Engineers	43.18	Sales Reps., Tech./Scientific	45.70
Electricians	19.45	Secretaries, Exc. Legal/Med./Exec.	16.02
Financial Managers	66.68	Security Guards	11.00
First-Line Supervisors/Managers, Sales	23.10	Surgeons	108.95
Food Preparation Workers	10.52	Teacher Assistants*	11.20
General and Operations Managers	66.56	Teachers, Elementary School*	23.89
Hairdressers/Cosmetologists	12.01	Teachers, Secondary School*	26.25
Internists	66.56	Telemarketers	12.89
Janitors and Cleaners	10.35	Truck Drivers, Heavy/Tractor-Trailer	19.25
Landscaping/Groundskeeping Workers	12.70	Truck Drivers, Light/Delivery Svcs.	17.31
Lawyers	n/a	Waiters and Waitresses	11.80

Note: Wage data covers the Fort Lauderdale-Pompano Beach-Deerfield Beach, FL Metropolitan Division—see Appendix B for areas included; (*) Hourly wages for elementary/secondary school teachers and teacher assistants were calculated by the editors from annual wage data based on a 40 hour work week; n/a not available.

Source: Bureau of Labor Statistics, Metro Area Occupational Employment and Wage Estimates, May 2015

TAXES

State Corporate Income Tax Rates

State	Tax Rate (%)	Income Brackets ($)	Num. of Brackets	Financial Institution Tax Rate (%)[a]	Federal Income Tax Ded.
Florida	5.5 (f)	Flat rate	1	5.5 (f)	No

Note: Tax rates as of January 1, 2016; (a) Rates listed are the corporate income tax rate applied to financial institutions or excise taxes based on income. Some states have other taxes based upon the value of deposits or shares; (f) An exemption of $50,000 is allowed. Florida's Alternative Minimum Tax rate is 3.3%.

Source: Federation of Tax Administrators, "State Corporate Income Tax Rates, 2016"

State Individual Income Tax Rates

State	Tax Rate (%)	Income Brackets ($)	Num. of Brackets	Personal Exempt. ($)[1] Single	Personal Exempt. ($)[1] Dependents	Fed. Inc. Tax Ded.
Florida	None	–	–	–	–	–

Note: Tax rates as of January 1, 2016; Local- and county-level taxes are not included; n/a not applicable; (1) Married joint filers generally receive double the single exemption

Source: Federation of Tax Administrators, "State Individual Income Tax Rates, 2016"

Various State and Local Tax Rates

State	State and Local Sales and Use (%)	State Sales and Use (%)	Gasoline[1] (¢/gal.)	Cigarette[2] ($/pack)	Spirits[3] ($/gal.)	Wine[4] ($/gal.)	Beer[5] ($/gal.)
Florida	6.00	6.0	36.58	1.339	6.50 (f)	2.25 (l)	0.48 (q)

Note: All tax rates as of January 1, 2016; (1) The American Petroleum Institute has developed a methodology for determining the average tax rate on a gallon of fuel. Rates may include any of the following: excise taxes, environmental fees, storage tank fees, other fees or taxes, general sales tax, and local taxes. In states where gasoline is subject to the general sales tax, or where the fuel tax is based on the average sale price, the average rate determined by API is sensitive to changes in the price of gasoline. States that fully or partially apply general sales taxes to gasoline: CA, CO, GA, IL, IN, MI, NY; (2) The federal excise tax of $1.0066 per pack and local taxes are not included; (3) Rates are those applicable to off-premise sales of 40% alcohol by volume (a.b.v.) distilled spirits in 750ml containers. Local excise taxes are excluded; (4) Rates are those applicable to off-premise sales of 11% a.b.v. non-carbonated wine in 750ml containers; (5) Rates are those applicable to off-premise sales of 4.7% a.b.v. beer in 12 ounce containers; (f) Different rates are also applicable according to alcohol content, place of production, size of container, or place purchased (on- or off-premise or onboard airlines); (l) Different rates also applicable according to alcohol content, place of production, size of container, place purchased (on- or off-premise or on board airlines) or type of wine (carbonated, vermouth, etc.); (q) Different rates are also applicable according to alcohol content, place of production, size of container, or place purchased (on- or off-premise or onboard airlines).
Source: Tax Foundation, 2016 Facts & Figures: How Does Your State Compare?

State Business Tax Climate Index Rankings

State	Overall Rank	Corporate Tax Rank	Individual Income Tax Rank	Sales Tax Rank	Unemployment Insurance Tax Rank	Property Tax Rank
Florida	4	17	1	17	3	20

Note: The index is a measure of how each state's tax laws affect economic performance. The lower the rank, the more favorable a state's tax system is for business. States without a given tax are given a ranking of 1. The scores/rankings for the District of Columbia do not affect other states. The 2016 index represents the tax climate as of July 1, 2015 (the beginning of Fiscal Year 2016).
Source: Tax Foundation, State Business Tax Climate Index 2016

TRANSPORTATION

Means of Transportation to Work

Area	Car/Truck/Van		Public Transportation			Bicycle	Walked	Other Means	Worked at Home
	Drove Alone	Car-pooled	Bus	Subway	Railroad				
City	80.5	7.7	0.1	0.1	0.1	0.0	1.3	1.1	9.2
MSA[1]	78.2	9.5	3.4	0.2	0.2	0.6	1.8	1.4	4.7
U.S.	76.4	9.6	2.6	1.8	0.6	0.6	2.8	1.3	4.4

Note: Figures are percentages and cover workers 16 years of age and older; (1) Figures cover the Miami-Fort Lauderdale-West Palm Beach, FL Metropolitan Statistical Area—see Appendix B for areas included
Source: U.S. Census Bureau, 2010-2014 American Community Survey 5-Year Estimates

Travel Time to Work

Area	Less Than 10 Minutes	10 to 19 Minutes	20 to 29 Minutes	30 to 44 Minutes	45 to 59 Minutes	60 to 89 Minutes	90 Minutes or More
City	9.4	23.0	18.5	25.0	14.5	7.6	2.0
MSA[1]	7.5	25.0	23.3	27.0	9.0	6.1	2.0
U.S.	13.3	29.6	21.0	20.2	7.7	5.7	2.6

Note: Figures are percentages and include workers 16 years old and over; (1) Figures cover the Miami-Fort Lauderdale-West Palm Beach, FL Metropolitan Statistical Area—see Appendix B for areas included
Source: U.S. Census Bureau, 2010-2014 American Community Survey 5-Year Estimates

Freeway Travel Time Index

Area	1985	1990	1995	2000	2005	2010	2014
Urban Area Rank[1,2]	11	16	18	11	13	18	17
Urban Area Index[1]	1.16	1.18	1.21	1.27	1.29	1.27	1.29
Average Index[3]	1.09	1.11	1.14	1.17	1.20	1.19	1.20

Note: Freeway Travel Time Index—the ratio of travel time in the peak period to the travel time at free-flow conditions. For example, a value of 1.30 indicates a 20-minute free-flow trip takes 26 minutes in the peak (20 minutes x 1.30 = 26 minutes); (1) Covers the Miami FL urban area; (2) Rank is based on 101 urban areas (#1 = highest travel time index); (3) Average of 101 urban areas
Source: Texas Transportation Institute, 2015 Urban Mobility Scorecard, August 2015

Freeway Commuter Stress Index

Area	1985	1990	1995	2000	2005	2010	2014
Urban Area Rank[1,2]	28	28	31	23	28	29	29
Urban Area Index[1]	1.17	1.19	1.23	1.29	1.31	1.29	1.30
Average Index[3]	1.13	1.16	1.19	1.22	1.25	1.24	1.25

Note: The Freeway Commuter Stress Index is the same as the Freeway Travel Time Index (see table above) except that it includes only the travel in the peak directions during the peak periods; the TTI includes travel in all directions during the peak period. Thus, the CSI is more indicative of the work trip experienced by each commuter on a daily basis. (1) Covers the Miami FL urban area; (2) Rank is based on 101 urban areas (#1 = highest stress index); (3) Average of 101 urban areas

Source: Texas Transportation Institute, 2015 Urban Mobility Scorecard, August 2015

Living Environment

COST OF LIVING

Cost of Living Index

Composite Index	Groceries	Housing	Utilities	Trans-portation	Health Care	Misc. Goods/ Services
114.3	103.1	145.4	96.0	111.2	99.3	101.0

Note: The Cost of Living Index measures regional differences in the cost of consumer goods and services, excluding taxes and non-consumer expenditures, for professional and managerial households in the top income quintile. It is based on more than 50,000 prices covering almost 60 different items for which prices are collected three times a year by chambers of commerce, economic development organizations or university applied economic centers in each participating urban area. The numbers shown should be read as a percentage above or below the national average of 100. For example, a value of 115.4 in the groceries column indicates that grocery prices are 15.4% higher than the national average. Small differences in the index numbers should not be interpreted as significant; Figures cover the Fort Lauderdale FL urban area.
Source: The Council for Community and Economic Research, ACCRA Cost of Living Index, 2015

Grocery Prices

Area[1]	T-Bone Steak ($/pound)	Frying Chicken ($/pound)	Whole Milk ($/half gal.)	Eggs ($/dozen)	Orange Juice ($/64 oz.)	Coffee ($/11.5 oz.)
City[2]	12.46	1.41	2.75	2.44	3.59	2.98
Avg.	10.99	1.43	2.25	2.26	3.58	4.48
Min.	7.16	0.98	1.30	1.35	2.88	2.98
Max.	14.13	2.43	3.85	4.81	6.39	7.56

Note: (1) Values for the local area are compared with the average, minimum and maximum values for all 292 areas in the Cost of Living Index; (2) Figures cover the Fort Lauderdale FL urban area; **T-Bone Steak** *(price per pound);* **Frying Chicken** *(price per pound, whole fryer);* **Whole Milk** *(half gallon carton);* **Eggs** *(price per dozen, Grade A, large);* **Orange Juice** *(64 oz. Tropicana or Florida Natural);* **Coffee** *(11.5 oz. can, vacuum-packed, Maxwell House, Hills Bros, or Folgers).*
Source: The Council for Community and Economic Research, ACCRA Cost of Living Index, 2015

Housing and Utility Costs

Area[1]	New Home Price ($)	Apartment Rent ($/month)	All Electric ($/month)	Part Electric ($/month)	Other Energy ($/month)	Telephone ($/month)
City[2]	443,005	1,483	161.87	-	-	27.31
Avg.	312,874	945	179.30	95.07	72.96	28.11
Min.	178,682	479	116.28	43.14	26.46	10.01
Max.	1,472,476	3,984	504.25	189.44	421.11	43.06

Note: (1) Values for the local area are compared with the average, minimum and maximum values for all 292 areas in the Cost of Living Index; (2) Figures cover the Fort Lauderdale FL urban area; **New Home Price** *(2,400 sf living area, 8,000 sf lot, in urban area with full utilities);* **Apartment Rent** *(950 sf 2 bedroom/1.5 or 2 bath, unfurnished, excluding all utilities except water);* **All Electric** *(average monthly cost for an all-electric home);* **Part Electric** *(average monthly cost for a part-electric home);* **Other Energy** *(average monthly cost for natural gas, fuel oil, coal, wood, and any other forms of energy except electricity);* **Telephone** *(price includes basic monthly rate for a private residential line plus additional local usage charges incurred by a family of four).*
Source: The Council for Community and Economic Research, ACCRA Cost of Living Index, 2015

Health Care, Transportation, and Other Costs

Area[1]	Doctor ($/visit)	Dentist ($/visit)	Optometrist ($/visit)	Gasoline ($/gallon)	Beauty Salon ($/visit)	Men's Shirt ($)
City[2]	85.67	89.45	90.43	2.49	52.58	25.80
Avg.	105.15	89.02	99.78	2.38	35.30	28.10
Min.	66.87	56.09	48.53	1.95	18.91	13.38
Max.	182.34	150.36	228.33	4.09	67.91	63.80

Note: (1) Values for the local area are compared with the average, minimum and maximum values for all 292 areas in the Cost of Living Index; (2) Figures cover the Fort Lauderdale FL urban area; **Doctor** *(general practitioners routine exam of an established patient);* **Dentist** *(adult teeth cleaning and periodic oral examination);* **Optometrist** *(full vision eye exam for established adult patient);* **Gasoline** *(one gallon regular unleaded, national brand, including all taxes, cash price at self-service pump if available);* **Beauty Salon** *(woman's shampoo, trim, and blow-dry);* **Men's Shirt** *(cotton/polyester dress shirt, pinpoint weave, long sleeves).*
Source: The Council for Community and Economic Research, ACCRA Cost of Living Index, 2015

HOUSING

House Price Index (HPI)

Area	National Ranking[2]	Quarterly Change (%)	One-Year Change (%)	Five-Year Change (%)
MD[1]	41	1.60	8.60	36.30
U.S.[3]	–	1.45	5.76	22.85

Note: The HPI is a weighted repeat sales index. It measures average price changes in repeat sales or refinancings on the same properties. This information is obtained by reviewing repeat mortgage transactions on single-family properties whose mortgages have been purchased or securitized by Fannie Mae or Freddie Mac in January 1975; (1) Fort Lauderdale-Pompano Beach-Deerfield Beach Metropolitan Division—see Appendix B for areas included; (2) Rankings are based on annual percentage change for all metro areas containing at least 15,000 transactions over the last 10 years and ranges from 1 to 266; (3) figures based on a weighted average of Census Division estimates using a seasonally adjusted, purchase-only index; all figures are for the period ending December 31, 2015

Source: Federal Housing Finance Agency, House Price Index, February 25, 2016

Median Single-Family Home Prices

Area	2013	2014	2015[p]	Percent Change 2014 to 2015
MSA[1]	246.0	266.0	283.8	6.7
U.S. Average	197.4	208.9	223.9	7.2

Note: Figures are median sales prices of existing single-family homes in thousands of dollars; (p) preliminary; n/a not available; (1) Miami-Fort Lauderdale-West Palm Beach, FL Metropolitan Statistical Area—see Appendix B for areas included

Source: National Association of Realtors, Median Sales Price of Existing Single-Family Homes for Metropolitan Areas, 4th Quarter 2015

Qualifying Income Based on Median Sales Price of Existing Single-Family Homes

Area	With 5% Down ($)	With 10% Down ($)	With 20% Down ($)
MSA[1]	63,615	60,267	53,571
U.S. Average	49,535	46,928	41,714

Note: Figures are preliminary; Qualifying income is based on a mortgage rate of 4.1%. Monthly principal and interest payment is limited to 25% of income; n/a not available; (1) Miami-Fort Lauderdale-West Palm Beach, FL Metropolitan Statistical Area—see Appendix B for areas included

Source: National Association of Realtors, Qualifying Income Based on Median Sales Price of Existing Single-Family Homes for Metropolitan Areas, 4th Quarter 2015

Median Apartment Condo-Coop Home Prices

Area	2013	2014	2015[p]	Percent Change 2014 to 2015
MSA[1]	129.5	144.3	154.1	6.8
U.S. Average	194.9	204.3	210.7	3.1

Note: Figures are median sales prices of existing apartment condo-coop homes in thousands of dollars; (p) preliminary; n/a not available; (1) Miami-Fort Lauderdale-West Palm Beach, FL Metropolitan Statistical Area—see Appendix B for areas included

Source: National Association of Realtors, Median Sales Price of Existing Apartment Condo-Coop Homes for Metropolitan Areas, 4th Quarter 2015

Gross Monthly Rent

Area	Under $200	$200 -299	$300 -499	$500 -749	$750 -999	$1,000 -1,499	$1,500 and up	Median ($)
City	0.0	0.0	0.0	2.1	0.6	20.5	76.9	1,886
MSA[1]	1.4	2.3	2.7	9.0	21.9	39.0	23.8	1,136
U.S.	1.5	3.2	7.4	21.0	24.1	26.9	15.9	920

Note: Figures are percentages except for Median; Gross rent is the contract rent plus the estimated average monthly cost of utilities (electricity, gas, and water and sewer) and fuels (oil, coal, kerosene, wood, etc.) if these are paid by the renter (or paid for the renter by someone else); (1) Figures cover the Miami-Fort Lauderdale-West Palm Beach, FL Metropolitan Statistical Area—see Appendix B for areas included

Source: U.S. Census Bureau, 2010-2014 American Community Survey 5-Year Estimates

Homeownership Rate

Area	2008 (%)	2009 (%)	2010 (%)	2011 (%)	2012 (%)	2013 (%)	2014 (%)	2015 (%)
MSA[1]	66.0	67.1	63.8	64.2	61.8	60.1	58.8	58.6
U.S.	67.8	67.4	66.9	66.1	65.4	65.1	64.5	63.7

Note: (1) Figures cover the Miami-Fort Lauderdale-West Palm Beach, FL Metropolitan Statistical Area—see Appendix B for areas included
Source: U.S. Census Bureau, Housing Vacancies and Homeownership Annual Statistics: 2015

Year Housing Structure Built

Area	2010 or Later	2000 -2009	1990 -1999	1980 -1989	1970 -1979	1960 -1969	1950 -1959	1940 -1949	Before 1940	Median Year
City	0.0	22.9	52.5	17.4	6.1	0.6	0.5	0.1	0.0	1995
MSA[1]	0.5	14.1	14.8	19.9	22.0	12.8	10.4	3.2	2.2	1980
U.S.	1.0	14.9	13.9	13.8	15.8	11.0	10.8	5.4	13.3	1976

Note: Figures are percentages except for Median Year; (1) Figures cover the Miami-Fort Lauderdale-West Palm Beach, FL Metropolitan Statistical Area—see Appendix B for areas included
Source: U.S. Census Bureau, 2010-2014 American Community Survey 5-Year Estimates

HEALTH

Health Risk Data

Category	MSA[1] (%)	U.S. (%)
Adults aged 18–64 who have any kind of health care coverage	67.9	79.6
Adults who reported being in good or excellent health	81.0	83.1
Adults who are current smokers	13.2	19.6
Adults who are heavy drinkers[2]	4.6	6.1
Adults who are binge drinkers[3]	15.4	16.9
Adults who are overweight (BMI 25.0 - 29.9)	38.8	35.8
Adults who are obese (BMI 30.0 - 99.8)	23.1	27.6
Adults who participated in any physical activities in the past month	74.7	77.1
Adults 50+ who have ever had a sigmoidoscopy or colonoscopy	61.7	67.3
Women aged 40+ who have had a mammogram within the past two years	75.7	74.0
Men aged 40+ who have had a PSA test within the past two years	51.1	45.2
Adults aged 65+ who have had flu shot within the past year	53.0	60.1
Adults who always wear a seatbelt	92.8	93.8

Note: Data as of 2012 unless otherwise noted; (1) Figures cover the Miami-Fort Lauderdale-Miami Beach, FL Metropolitan Statistical Area—see Appendix B for areas included; (2) Heavy drinkers are classified as males having more than two drinks per day or females having more than one drink per day; (3) Binge drinkers are classified as males having five or more drinks on one occasion or females having four or more drinks on one occasion
Source: Centers for Disease Control and Prevention, Behaviorial Risk Factor Surveillance System, SMART: Selected Metropolitan/Micropolitan Area Risk Trends, 2012 (Note: the CDC has discontinued this dataset but will be releasing a replacement in mid-2016)

Chronic Health Indicators

Category	MSA[1] (%)	U.S. (%)
Adults who have ever been told they had a heart attack	3.8	4.5
Adults who have ever been told they had a stroke	2.4	2.9
Adults who have been told they currently have asthma	5.3	8.9
Adults who have ever been told they have arthritis	21.4	25.7
Adults who have ever been told they have diabetes[2]	10.5	9.7
Adults who have ever been told they had skin cancer	5.9	5.7
Adults who have ever been told they had any other types of cancer	5.7	6.5
Adults who have ever been told they have COPD	6.2	6.2
Adults who have ever been told they have kidney disease	4.0	2.5
Adults who have ever been told they have a form of depression	13.4	18.0

Note: Data as of 2012 unless otherwise noted; (1) Figures cover the Miami-Fort Lauderdale-Miami Beach, FL Metropolitan Statistical Area—see Appendix B for areas included; (2) Figures do not include pregnancy-related, borderline, or pre-diabetes
Source: Centers for Disease Control and Prevention, Behaviorial Risk Factor Surveillance System, SMART: Selected Metropolitan/Micropolitan Area Risk Trends, 2012 (Note: the CDC has discontinued this dataset but will be releasing a replacement in mid-2016)

Mortality Rates for the Top 10 Causes of Death in the U.S.

ICD-10[a] Sub-Chapter	ICD-10[a] Code	Age-Adjusted Mortality Rate[1] per 100,000 population	
		County[2]	U.S.
Malignant neoplasms	C00-C97	152.2	163.6
Ischaemic heart diseases	I20-I25	94.3	102.2
Other forms of heart disease	I30-I51	47.8	50.1
Chronic lower respiratory diseases	J40-J47	30.3	41.4
Organic, including symptomatic, mental disorders	F01-F09	13.6	38.5
Cerebrovascular diseases	I60-I69	37.1	36.5
Other external causes of accidental injury	W00-X59	20.8	27.5
Other degenerative diseases of the nervous system	G30-G31	30.0	26.3
Diabetes mellitus	E10-E14	13.9	21.1
Hypertensive diseases	I10-I15	13.2	19.7

Note: (a) ICD-10 = International Classification of Diseases 10th Revision; (1) Mortality rates are a three year average covering 2012-2014; (2) Figures cover Broward County.
Source: Centers for Disease Control and Prevention, National Center for Health Statistics. Underlying Cause of Death 1999-2014 on CDC WONDER Online Database, released 2015.

Mortality Rates for Selected Causes of Death

ICD-10[a] Sub-Chapter	ICD-10[a] Code	Age-Adjusted Mortality Rate[1] per 100,000 population	
		County[2]	U.S.
Assault	X85-Y09	5.0	5.1
Diseases of the liver	K70-K76	11.3	13.5
Human immunodeficiency virus (HIV) disease	B20-B24	6.5	2.1
Influenza and pneumonia	J09-J18	8.4	15.2
Intentional self-harm	X60-X84	11.1	12.7
Malnutrition	E40-E46	0.3	0.9
Obesity and other hyperalimentation	E65-E68	1.6	1.9
Renal failure	N17-N19	13.5	13.0
Transport accidents	V01-V99	10.3	11.6
Viral hepatitis	B15-B19	1.7	2.1

Note: (a) ICD-10 = International Classification of Diseases 10th Revision; (1) Mortality rates are a three year average covering 2012-2014; (2) Figures cover Broward County; Data are Suppressed when the data meet the criteria for confidentiality constraints; Mortality rates are flagged as Unreliable when the rate would be calculated with a numerator of 20 or less.
Source: Centers for Disease Control and Prevention, National Center for Health Statistics. Underlying Cause of Death 1999-2014 on CDC WONDER Online Database, released 2015.

Health Insurance Coverage

Area	With Health Insurance	With Private Health Insurance	With Public Health Insurance	Without Health Insurance	Population Under Age 18 Without Health Insurance
City	87.8	79.1	13.6	12.2	10.2
MSA[1]	75.9	52.4	30.9	24.1	12.8
U.S.	85.8	65.8	31.1	14.2	7.1

Note: Figures are percentages that cover the civilian noninstitutionalized population; (1) Figures cover the Miami-Fort Lauderdale-West Palm Beach, FL Metropolitan Statistical Area—see Appendix B for areas included
Source: U.S. Census Bureau, 2010-2014 American Community Survey 5-Year Estimates

Number of Medical Professionals

Area	MDs[3]	DOs[3,4]	Dentists	Podiatrists	Chiropractors	Optometrists
County[1] (number)	4,455	656	1,300	198	630	391
County[1] (rate[2])	241.4	35.5	69.5	10.6	33.7	20.9
U.S. (rate[2])	272.5	20.9	64.7	5.8	25.9	15.2

Note: Data as of 2014 unless noted; (1) Data covers Broward County; (2) Rate per 100,000 population; (3) Data as of 2013 and includes all active, non-federal physicians; (4) Doctor of Osteopathic Medicine
Source: U.S. Department of Health and Human Services, Health Resources and Services Administration, Bureau of Health Professions, Area Resource File (ARF) 2014-2015

EDUCATION

Best Hospitals

According to *U.S. News,* the Fort Lauderdale-Pompano Beach-Deerfield Beach, FL metro area is home to one of the best children's hospitals in the U.S.: **Joe DiMaggio Children's Hospital at Memorial Regional Hospital** (3 specialties). The hospital listed was highly ranked in at least one pediatric specialty. Eighty-three children's hospitals in the U.S. were nationally ranked in at least one specialty. Twelve children's hospitals in the U.S. made the Honor Roll with high scores in at least three specialties. *U.S. News Online, "America's Best Children's Hospitals 2015-16"*

Public School District Statistics

District Name	Schls	Pupils	Pupil/ Teacher Ratio	Minority Pupils[1] (%)	Free Lunch Eligible[2] (%)	IEP[3] (%)
Broward	349	262,666	17.3	75.9	52.2	12.2

Note: Table includes school districts with 100 or more students; (1) Percentage of students that are not non-Hispanic white; (2) Percentage of students that are eligible for the free lunch program; (3) Percentage of students that have an Individualized Education Program.
Source: U.S. Department of Education, National Center for Education Statistics, Common Core of Data, Local Education Agency (School District) Universe Survey: School Year 2013-2014; U.S. Department of Education, National Center for Education Statistics, Common Core of Data, Public Elementary/Secondary School Universe Survey: School Year 2013-2014

Best High Schools

According to *U.S. News,* Weston is home to one of the best high schools in the U.S.: **Cypress Bay High School** (#206); Nearly 20,000 schools were ranked based on their performance on state assessments and how well they prepare students for college. Schools with the highest unrounded College Readiness Index values were numerically ranked from No. 1 to No. 500 and were the gold medal winners. *U.S. News & World Report, "Best High Schools 2015"*

Highest Level of Education

Area	Less than H.S.	H.S. Diploma	Some College, No Deg.	Associate Degree	Bachelor's Degree	Master's Degree	Prof. School Degree	Doctorate Degree
City	3.0	13.0	17.3	8.8	33.5	16.3	6.0	2.1
MSA[1]	15.9	27.7	18.5	8.8	18.5	6.8	2.6	1.2
U.S.	13.7	28.0	21.2	7.9	18.3	7.8	2.0	1.3

Note: Figures cover persons age 25 and over; (1) Figures cover the Miami-Fort Lauderdale-West Palm Beach, FL Metropolitan Statistical Area—see Appendix B for areas included
Source: U.S. Census Bureau, 2010-2014 American Community Survey 5-Year Estimates

Educational Attainment by Race

Area	High School Graduate or Higher (%)					Bachelor's Degree or Higher (%)				
	Total	White	Black	Asian	Hisp.[2]	Total	White	Black	Asian	Hisp.[2]
City	97.0	97.0	97.3	94.9	96.7	57.9	57.9	64.3	64.3	54.4
MSA[1]	84.1	85.7	78.8	86.7	77.4	29.1	31.7	17.4	47.8	24.0
U.S.	86.3	88.4	83.2	85.8	64.1	29.3	30.6	19.0	50.9	13.9

Note: Figures shown cover persons 25 years old and over; (1) Figures cover the Miami-Fort Lauderdale-West Palm Beach, FL Metropolitan Statistical Area—see Appendix B for areas included; (2) People of Hispanic origin can be of any race
Source: U.S. Census Bureau, 2010-2014 American Community Survey 5-Year Estimates

School Enrollment by Grade and Control

Area	Preschool (%)		Kindergarten (%)		Grades 1 - 4 (%)		Grades 5 - 8 (%)		Grades 9 - 12 (%)	
	Public	Private	Public	Private	Public	Private	Public	Private	Public	Private
City	34.1	65.9	79.4	20.6	79.3	20.7	88.6	11.4	84.7	15.3
MSA[1]	47.6	52.4	82.9	17.1	86.8	13.2	87.5	12.5	87.8	12.2
U.S.	57.4	42.6	87.8	12.2	89.8	10.2	89.9	10.1	90.6	9.4

Note: Figures shown cover persons 3 years old and over; (1) Figures cover the Miami-Fort Lauderdale-West Palm Beach, FL Metropolitan Statistical Area—see Appendix B for areas included
Source: U.S. Census Bureau, 2010-2014 American Community Survey 5-Year Estimates

Average Salaries of Public School Classroom Teachers

Area	2013-14 Dollars	2013-14 Rank[1]	2014-15 Dollars	2014-15 Rank[1]	Percent Change 2013-14 to 2014-15	Percent Change 2004-05 to 2014-15
Florida	47,780	39	48,992	36	2.54	17.8
U.S. Average	56,610	–	57,379	–	1.36	20.8

Note: (1) State rank ranges from 1 to 51 where 1 indicates highest salary.
Source: National Education Association, Rankings & Estimates: Rankings of the States 2014 and Estimates of School Statistics 2015, March 2015

Higher Education

Four-Year Colleges			Two-Year Colleges					
Public	Private Non-profit	Private For-profit	Public	Private Non-profit	Private For-profit	Medical Schools[1]	Law Schools[2]	Voc/ Tech[3]
0	0	1	0	0	0	0	0	0

Note: Figures cover institutions located within the city limits and include main campuses only; (1) includes schools accredited by the Liaison Committee on Medical Education and the American Osteopathic Association's Commission on Osteopathic College Accreditation; (2) includes ABA-accredited schools, schools with provisional ABA accreditation, and state accredited schools; (3) includes all schools with programs that are less than 2 years.
Source: National Center for Education Statistics, Integrated Postsecondary Education System (IPEDS), 2014-15; Association of American Medical Colleges, Member List, March 21, 2016; American Osteopathic Association, Member List, March 21, 2016; Law School Admission Council, Official Guide to ABA-Approved Law Schools Online, March 21, 2016; Wikipedia, List of Medical Schools in the United States, March 21, 2016; Wikipedia, List of Law Schools in the United States, March 21, 2016

PRESIDENTIAL ELECTION

2012 Presidential Election Results

Area	Obama (%)	Romney (%)	Other (%)
Broward County	67.2	32.3	0.5
U.S.	51.0	47.2	1.8

Note: Results may not add to 100% due to rounding
Source: Dave Leip's Atlas of U.S. Presidential Elections

EMPLOYERS

Major Employers

Company Name	Industry
Baptist Health South Florida	General medical & surgical hospitals
Baptist Hospital of Miami	General medical & surgical hospitals
County of Miami-Dade	Police protection, county government
County of Miami-Dade	Regulation, administration of transportation
County of, Palm Beach	County supervisors' & executives' offices
Florida International University	Colleges & universities
Intercoastal Health Systems	Management services
Miami Dade College	Community college
Mount Sinai Medical Center of Florida	General medical & surgical hospitals
North Broward Hospital District	Hospitals
Royal Caribbean Cruises Ltd.	Computer processing services
Royal Caribbean Cruises Ltd.	Deep sea passenger transportation, except ferry
School Board of Palm Beach County	Public elementary & secondary schools
Style View Products	Storm doors of windows, metal
The Answer Group	Custom computer programming services
University of Miami	Colleges & universities
Veterans Health Administration	General medical & surgical hospitals

Note: Companies shown are located within the Miami-Fort Lauderdale-West Palm Beach, FL Metropolitan Statistical Area.
Source: Hoovers.com; Wikipedia

PUBLIC SAFETY

Crime Rate

Area	All Crimes	Violent Crimes				Property Crimes		
		Murder	Rape[3]	Robbery	Aggrav. Assault	Burglary	Larceny -Theft	Motor Vehicle Theft
City	614.8	1.4	17.4	8.7	37.6	89.7	432.5	27.5
Metro[1]	3,521.2	4.1	33.4	141.5	239.7	637.2	2,258.8	206.5
U.S.	2,971.8	4.5	36.6	102.2	232.5	542.5	1,837.3	216.2

Note: Figures are crimes per 100,000 population; (1) Figures cover the Fort Lauderdale-Pompano Beach-Deerfield Beach, FL Metropolitan Division—see Appendix B for areas included; (3) The city and U.S. figures shown were reported using the revised Uniform Crime Reporting (UCR) definition of rape. The suburban and metro area figures shown are an aggregate total of the data submitted using both the revised and legacy UCR definitions.
Source: FBI Uniform Crime Reports, 2014

Hate Crimes

Area	Number of Quarters Reported	Number of Incidents per Bias Motivation						
		Race	Religion	Sexual Orientation	Ethnicity	Disability	Gender	Gender Identity
City	4	1	0	0	0	0	0	0
U.S.	4	2,568	1,014	1,017	648	84	33	98

Source: Federal Bureau of Investigation, Hate Crime Statistics 2014

Identity Theft Consumer Complaints

Area	Complaints	Complaints per 100,000 Population	Rank[2]
MSA[1]	17,832	300.7	3
U.S.	490,220	152.4	-

Note: (1) Figures cover the Miami-Fort Lauderdale-West Palm Beach, FL Metropolitan Statistical Area—see Appendix B for areas included; (2) Rank ranges from 1 to 379 where 1 indicates greatest number of identity theft complaints per 100,000 population
Source: Federal Trade Commission, Consumer Sentinel Network Data Book for January–December 2015

Fraud and Other Consumer Complaints

Area	Complaints	Complaints per 100,000 Population	Rank[2]
MSA[1]	28,598	482.3	25
U.S.	2,593,159	806.0	-

Note: (1) Figures cover the Miami-Fort Lauderdale-West Palm Beach, FL Metropolitan Statistical Area—see Appendix B for areas included; (2) Rank ranges from 1 to 379 where 1 indicates greatest number of identity theft complaints per 100,000 population
Source: Federal Trade Commission, Consumer Sentinel Network Data Book for January–December 2015

RECREATION

Culture

Dance[1]	Theatre[1]	Instrumental Music[1]	Vocal Music[1]	Series and Festivals	Museums and Art Galleries[2]	Zoos and Aquariums[3]
0	0	0	0	0	0	0

Note: (1) Professional perfoming groups; (2) Based on organizations with SIC code 8412; (3) AZA-accredited
Source: The Grey House Performing Arts Directory, 2015-16; Association of Zoos & Aquariums, AZA Member Zoos & Aquariums, March 25, 2016; www.AccuLeads.com, March 29, 2016

Professional Sports Teams

Team Name	League	Year Established
Florida Panthers	National Hockey League (NHL)	1993
Miami Dolphins	National Football League (NFL)	1966
Miami Heat	National Basketball Association (NBA)	1988
Miami Marlins	Major League Baseball (MLB)	1993

Note: Includes teams located in the Miami-Fort Lauderdale-West Palm Beach, FL Metropolitan Statistical Area.
Source: Wikipedia, Major Professional Sports Teams of the United States and Canada, March 24, 2016

CLIMATE

Average and Extreme Temperatures

Temperature	Jan	Feb	Mar	Apr	May	Jun	Jul	Aug	Sep	Oct	Nov	Dec	Yr.
Extreme High (°F)	88	89	92	96	95	98	98	98	97	95	89	87	98
Average High (°F)	75	77	79	82	85	88	89	90	88	85	80	77	83
Average Temp. (°F)	68	69	72	75	79	82	83	83	82	78	73	69	76
Average Low (°F)	59	60	64	68	72	75	76	76	76	72	66	61	69
Extreme Low (°F)	30	35	32	42	55	60	69	68	68	53	39	30	30

Note: Figures cover the years 1948-1990
Source: National Climatic Data Center, International Station Meteorological Climate Summary, 9/96

Average Precipitation/Snowfall/Humidity

Precip./Humidity	Jan	Feb	Mar	Apr	May	Jun	Jul	Aug	Sep	Oct	Nov	Dec	Yr.
Avg. Precip. (in.)	1.9	2.0	2.3	3.0	6.2	8.7	6.1	7.5	8.2	6.6	2.7	1.8	57.1
Avg. Snowfall (in.)	0	0	0	0	0	0	0	0	0	0	0	0	0
Avg. Rel. Hum. 7am (%)	84	84	82	80	81	84	84	86	88	87	85	84	84
Avg. Rel. Hum. 4pm (%)	59	57	57	57	62	68	66	67	69	65	63	60	63

Note: Figures cover the years 1948-1990; Tr = Trace amounts (<0.05 in. of rain; <0.5 in. of snow)
Source: National Climatic Data Center, International Station Meteorological Climate Summary, 9/96

Weather Conditions

Temperature			Daytime Sky			Precipitation		
32°F & below	45°F & below	90°F & above	Clear	Partly cloudy	Cloudy	0.01 inch or more precip.	0.1 inch or more snow/ice	Thunder-storms
< 1	7	55	48	263	54	128	0	74

Note: Figures are average number of days per year and cover the years 1948-1990
Source: National Climatic Data Center, International Station Meteorological Climate Summary, 9/96

HAZARDOUS WASTE

Superfund Sites

Weston has no sites on the EPA's Superfund Final National Priorities List. There are a total of 1,323 Superfund sites on the list in the U.S. *U.S. Environmental Protection Agency, Final National Priorities List, March 18, 2016*

AIR & WATER QUALITY

Air Quality Trends: Ozone

	1990	1995	2000	2005	2010	2011	2012	2013	2014
MSA[1]	0.068	0.072	0.075	0.065	0.064	0.060	0.062	0.061	0.062

Note: (1) Data covers the Miami-Fort Lauderdale-West Palm Beach, FL Metropolitan Statistical Area—see Appendix B for areas included. The values shown are the composite ozone concentration averages among trend sites based on the highest fourth daily maximum 8-hour concentration in parts per million. These trends are based on sites having an adequate record of monitoring data during the trend period. Data from exceptional events are included.
Source: U.S. Environmental Protection Agency, Air Quality Monitoring Information, "Air Quality Trends by City, 1990-2014"

Air Quality Index

Area	Percent of Days when Air Quality was...[2]					AQI Statistics[2]	
	Good	Moderate	Unhealthy for Sensitive Groups	Unhealthy	Very Unhealthy	Maximum	Median
MSA[1]	71.2	28.8	0.0	0.0	0.0	95	42

Note: (1) Data covers the Miami-Fort Lauderdale-West Palm Beach, FL Metropolitan Statistical Area—see Appendix B for areas included; (2) Based on 365 days with AQI data in 2015. Air Quality Index (AQI) is an index for reporting daily air quality. EPA calculates the AQI for five major air pollutants regulated by the Clean Air Act: ground-level ozone, particle pollution (aka particulate matter), carbon monoxide, sulfur dioxide, and nitrogen dioxide. The AQI runs from 0 to 500. The higher the AQI value, the greater the level of air pollution and the greater the health concern. There are six AQI categories: "Good" AQI is between 0 and 50. Air quality is considered satisfactory; "Moderate" AQI is between 51 and 100. Air quality is acceptable; "Unhealthy for Sensitive Groups" When AQI values are between 101 and 150, members of sensitive groups may experience health effects; "Unhealthy" When AQI values are between 151 and 200 everyone may begin to experience health effects; "Very Unhealthy" AQI values between 201 and 300 trigger a health alert; "Hazardous" AQI values over 300 trigger warnings of emergency conditions (not shown).
Source: U.S. Environmental Protection Agency, Air Quality Index Report, 2015

Air Quality Index Pollutants

Area	Percent of Days when AQI Pollutant was...[2]					
	Carbon Monoxide	Nitrogen Dioxide	Ozone	Sulfur Dioxide	Particulate Matter 2.5	Particulate Matter 10
MSA[1]	0.0	1.1	18.1	0.3	67.1	13.4

Note: (1) Data covers the Miami-Fort Lauderdale-West Palm Beach, FL Metropolitan Statistical Area—see Appendix B for areas included; (2) Based on 365 days with AQI data in 2015. The Air Quality Index (AQI) is an index for reporting daily air quality. EPA calculates the AQI for five major air pollutants regulated by the Clean Air Act: ground-level ozone, particle pollution (also known as particulate matter), carbon monoxide, sulfur dioxide, and nitrogen dioxide. The AQI runs from 0 to 500. The higher the AQI value, the greater the level of air pollution and the greater the health concern.
Source: U.S. Environmental Protection Agency, Air Quality Index Report, 2015

Maximum Air Pollutant Concentrations: Particulate Matter, Ozone, CO and Lead

	Particulate Matter 10 (ug/m^3)	Particulate Matter 2.5 Wtd AM (ug/m^3)	Particulate Matter 2.5 24-Hr (ug/m^3)	Ozone (ppm)	Carbon Monoxide (ppm)	Lead (ug/m^3)
MSA[1] Level	61	6.3	15	0.068	2	n/a
NAAQS[2]	150	15	35	0.075	9	0.15
Met NAAQS[2]	Yes	Yes	Yes	Yes	Yes	n/a

Note: (1) Data covers the Miami-Fort Lauderdale-West Palm Beach, FL Metropolitan Statistical Area—see Appendix B for areas included; Data from exceptional events are included; (2) National Ambient Air Quality Standards; ppm = parts per million; ug/m^3 = micrograms per cubic meter; n/a not available.
Concentrations: Particulate Matter 10 (coarse particulate)—highest second maximum 24-hour concentration; Particulate Matter 2.5 Wtd AM (fine particulate)—highest weighted annual mean concentration; Particulate Matter 2.5 24-Hour (fine particulate)—highest 98th percentile 24-hour concentration; Ozone—highest fourth daily maximum 8-hour concentration; Carbon Monoxide—highest second maximum non-overlapping 8-hour concentration; Lead—maximum running 3-month average
Source: U.S. Environmental Protection Agency, Air Quality Monitoring Information, "Air Quality Statistics by City, 2014"

Maximum Air Pollutant Concentrations: Nitrogen Dioxide and Sulfur Dioxide

	Nitrogen Dioxide AM (ppb)	Nitrogen Dioxide 1-Hr (ppb)	Sulfur Dioxide AM (ppb)	Sulfur Dioxide 1-Hr (ppb)	Sulfur Dioxide 24-Hr (ppb)
MSA[1] Level	9	50	n/a	5	n/a
NAAQS[2]	53	100	30	75	140
Met NAAQS[2]	Yes	Yes	n/a	Yes	n/a

Note: (1) Data covers the Miami-Fort Lauderdale-West Palm Beach, FL Metropolitan Statistical Area—see Appendix B for areas included; Data from exceptional events are included; (2) National Ambient Air Quality Standards; ppm = parts per million; ug/m^3 = micrograms per cubic meter; n/a not available.
Concentrations: Nitrogen Dioxide AM—highest arithmetic mean concentration; Nitrogen Dioxide 1-Hr—highest 98th percentile 1-hour daily maximum concentration; Sulfur Dioxide AM—highest annual mean concentration; Sulfur Dioxide 1-Hr—highest 99th percentile 1-hour daily maximum concentration; Sulfur Dioxide 24-Hr—highest second maximum 24-hour concentration
Source: U.S. Environmental Protection Agency, Air Quality Monitoring Information, "Air Quality Statistics by City, 2014"

Drinking Water

Water System Name	Pop. Served	Primary Water Source Type	Violations[1]	
			Health Based	Monitoring/ Reporting
City of Weston (Indian Trace)	52,300	Purchased Ground	0	0

Note: (1) Based on violation data from January 1, 2015 to December 31, 2015 (includes unresolved violations from earlier years)
Source: U.S. Environmental Protection Agency, Office of Ground Water and Drinking Water, Safe Drinking Water Information System (based on data extracted April 29, 2016)

Alpharetta, Georgia

Background

Alpharetta is located in between the North Georgia Mountains and the Chattahoochee River, in northern Fulton County, nearly 22 miles north of downtown Atlanta.

Once a small trading post where Indians and settlers bought, sold and traded goods, Alpharetta was chartered in 1858 and became the first county seat in Milton County. Translated from Greek, Alpharetta means "first city."

By the Civil War, Alpharetta boasted three hotels, a school, many mercantile shops, and several churches. The surrounding lands were of excellent quality for growing crops, cotton in particular, with many family farms in operation outside the city. With little reliance on Plantations and large numbers of small family-run farms, the Alpharetta economy fared much better than its neighbors, following the Civil War and the resulting breakdown of the "plantation" economy.

In the decades after the Civil War, growth in Alpharetta and surrounding Milton County was slow but steady. Development of the county as a whole was stunted without a working railroad, the closest railroad dead-ended in a neighboring town. Following the Great Depression, both Milton County and Fulton County were in significant economic hardship and the decision was made to merge the two counties to avoid bankruptcy.

Today, Alpharetta has blossomed into one of the most affluent, and fastest growing, cities in the state. The city prides itself as an ideal location to raise a family or build a business, with its unique combination of small town, Southern charm and big city appeal. Local attractions include Wills Park Equestrian Center; Big Creek Greenway, a 6 mile walking trail highlighting the natural beauty of the area; the Verizon Wireless Amphitheater; along with many unique shopping venues and dining options.

During the work day, the city's population more than doubles in size, with tens of thousands of commuters coming into the city each morning. In 2009, Alpharetta was named the #1 "reloville" in the United States by Forbes magazine. Alpharetta is an ideal location for technology-focused companies due to its proximity to important transportation hubs and being in the heart of the largest fiber-linked network in the nation.

Alpharetta is served by the Fulton County Public School System, with fifteen elementary schools, seven middle schools and four high schools. The Fulton County Public School System was named "One of the Top 100 School Districts in Places You Can Afford" by Money magazine. Local institutions of higher learning include the Alpharetta campuses of DeVry University, Keller Graduate School of Management, and Georgia State University along with several colleges and universities in the nearby Atlanta area.

The Northside/Alpharetta Medical Campus provides comprehensive and preventative care services for the Alpharetta community. The nearby Northside Hospital, with locations in Atlanta, Forsyth and Cherokee, provide full service and emergency care.

Alpharetta residents can expect hot and humid summers followed by cool winters. Significant amounts of rain fall in all seasons.

Rankings

Business/Finance Rankings

- The personal finance site NerdWallet analyzed 183 American metropolitan areas with populations over 250,000 and more than 15,000 businesses to rank where entrepreneurs find the most success. Criteria included area economy, annual income, housing cost, unemployment rate, and the success rate of area businesses. Atlanta* ranked #86. *www.nerdwallet.com, "Best Places to Start a Business," April 27, 2015*

- Based on metro area social media reviews, the employment opinion group Glassdoor surveyed 50 of the largest U.S. metro areas and equally weighed cost of living, hiring opportunity, and job satisfaction to compose a list of "25 Best Cities for Jobs." The Atlanta* metro area was ranked #24 in overall job satisfaction. *www.glassdoor.com, "Best Cities for Jobs," May 19, 2015*

- In a survey of economic confidence in the nation's 50 largest metropolitan areas conducted January–December 2014, the Atlanta* metro area placed #21, according to Gallup's 2014 Economic Confidence Index. *Gallup, "San Jose and San Francisco Lead in Economic Confidence," March 19, 2015*

- The Brookings Institution ranked the 100 largest metro areas in the U.S. based on income inequality. Atlanta* was ranked #36 (#1 = greatest ineqality). Criteria: the "95/20 ratio," a figure representing the income at which a household earns more than 95 percent of all other households, divided by the income at which a household earns more than only 20 percent of all other households. *Brookings Institution, "Income Inequality, 100 Largest U.S. Metro Areas, 2007-2014," January 14, 2016*

- Payscale.com ranked the 20 largest metro areas in terms of wage growth. The Atlanta* metro area ranked #5. Criteria: private-sector wage growth between the 1st quarter of 2015 and the 1st quarter of 2016. *PayScale, "Wage Trends by Metro Area," 1st Quarter, 2016*

- The Atlanta* metro area was identified as one of the most debt-ridden places in America by the finance site Credit.com. The metro area was ranked #8. Criteria: residents' average personal debt load and average credit scores. *Credit.com, "The Most Debt-Ridden Cities," May 1, 2014*

- Atlanta* was identified as one of America's most frugal metro areas by *Coupons.com.* The city ranked #6 out of 25. Criteria: online coupon usage. *Coupons.com, "Top 25 Most Frugal Cities of 2014," May 11, 2015*

- Atlanta* was identified as one of America's most frugal metro areas by *Coupons.com.* The city ranked #3 out of 25. Criteria: Grocery IQ and coupons.com mobile app usage. *Coupons.com, "Top 25 Most On-the-Go Frugal Cities of 2013," April 10, 2014*

- Atlanta* was cited as one of America's top metros for new and expanded facility projects in 2015. The area ranked #8 in the large metro area category (population over 1 million). *Site Selection, "Top Metropolitans of 2015," March 2016*

- The Atlanta* metro area appeared on the Milken Institute "2015 Best Performing Cities" list. Rank: #27 out of 200 large metro areas. Criteria: job growth; wage and salary growth; high-tech output growth. *Milken Institute, "Best-Performing Cities 2015," December 2015*

- *Forbes* ranked the 200 most populous metro areas to determine the nation's "Best Places for Business and Careers." The Atlanta* metro area was ranked #5. Criteria: costs (business and living); job growth (past and projected); income growth; educational attainment (college and high school); projected economic growth; cultural and recreational opportunities; net migration patterns; number of highly ranked colleges. *Forbes, "The Best Places for Business and Careers 2015," July 29, 2015*

Dating/Romance Rankings

- CreditDonkey, a financial education website, sought out the ten best U.S. cities for newlyweds, considering the number of married couples, divorce rate, average credit score, and average number of hours worked per week in metro areas with a million or more residents. The Atlanta* metro area placed #1. *www.creditdonkey.com, "Study: Best Cities for Newlyweds," November 30, 2013*

Education Rankings

- Personal finance website *WalletHub* analyzed the 150 largest U.S. metropolitan statistical areas to determine where the most educated Americans are choosing to settle. Criteria: education quality and attainment gap; education levels; percentage of workers with degrees; public school rankings; quality and size of each metro area's universities. Atlanta* was ranked #34 (#1 = most educated city). *www.WalletHub.com, "2015's Most and Least Educated Cities*

Environmental Rankings

- The Atlanta* metro area came in at #246 for the relative comfort of its climate on Sperling's list of "chill cities," as measured by the Sperling Heat Index. All 361 metro areas are included. Criteria included daytime high temperatures, nighttime low temperatures, dew point, and relative humidity at the high temperatures. *www.bertsperling.com, "Sperling's Chill Cities," July 18, 2013*

- Sperling's BestPlaces assessed 379 metropolitan areas of the United States for the likelihood of dangerously extreme weather events or earthquakes. In general the Southeast and South-Central regions have the highest risk of weather extremes and earthquakes, while the Pacific Northwest enjoys the lowest risk. Of the least risky metropolitan areas, the Atlanta* metro area was ranked #358. *www.bestplaces.net, "Safest Places from Natural Disasters," April 2011*

- The U.S. Environmental Protection Agency (EPA) released a list of U.S. metropolitan areas with the most ENERGY STAR certified buildings in 2015. The Atlanta* metro area was ranked #4 out of 25. *U.S. Environmental Protection Agency, "Top Cities With the Most ENERGY STAR Certified Buildings in 2016," March 30, 2016*

Health/Fitness Rankings

- For each of the 50 most populous metro areas in the United States, the American College of Sports Medicine's American Fitness Index evaluated infrastructure, community assets, and policies that encourage healthy and fit lifestyles, including preventive health behaviors, levels of chronic disease conditions, health care access, and community resources and policies that support physical activity. The Atlanta* metro area ranked #14 for "community fitness." *www.americanfitnessindex.org, "ACSM American Fitness Index Health and Community Fitness Status of the 50 Largest Metropolitan Areas," May 2015*

- The Atlanta* metro area was identified as one of the worst cities for bed bugs in America by pest control company Orkin. The area ranked #19 out of 50 based on the number of bed bug treatments Orkin performed from January to December 2015. *Orkin, "Chicago Tops Bed Bug Cities List for Fourth Year in a Row," January 13, 2016*

- Atlanta* was identified as a "2016 Spring Allergy Capital." The area ranked #70 out of 100. Three groups of factors were used to identify the most severe cities for people with allergies during the spring season: annual pollen levels; medicine utilization; access to board-certified allergists. *Asthma and Allergy Foundation of America, "Spring Allergy Capitals 2016"*

- Atlanta* was identified as a "2015 Asthma Capital." The area ranked #16 out of the nation's 100 largest metropolitan areas. Criteria: estimated prevalence; self-reported prevalence; crude death rate for asthma; annual pollen score; annual air quality; public smoking laws; number of board-certified asthma specialists; school inhaler access laws; rescue medication use; controller medication use; ER visits for asthma; uninsured rate; poverty rate. *Asthma and Allergy Foundation of America, "Asthma Capitals 2015"*

- The Atlanta* metro area ranked #100 out of 190 in The Gallup-Healthways Well-Being Index. Criteria: purpose; social well being; financial health; community and physical health. Results are based on telephone interviews with adults, aged 18 and older, living in metropolitan areas in the 50 U.S. states and the District of Columbia. *Gallup-Healthways, "State of American Well-Being," February 23, 2016*

Real Estate Rankings

- Based on the home-price forecasts compiled by the real-estate valuation firm CoreLogic Case-Shiller, CNNMoney reported that in 2016, the Atlanta* metro area is expected to be one of the hottest housing markets in the U.S. Criteria: residential real estate prices. *money.cnn.com, "The 10 Hottest Housing Markets for 2016," December 3, 2015*
- According to Penske Truck Rental, the Atlanta* metro area was named the #1 moving destination in 2015, based on one-way consumer truck rental reservations made through Penske's website and reservations call center. *blog.gopenske.com, "Penske Truck Rental's 2015 Top Moving Destinations List," February 3, 2016*
- The Atlanta* metro area appeared on Realtor.com's list of the hottest housing markets to watch in 2016. The area ranked #5. Criteria: strong housing growth; affordable prices; and fast-paced sales. *Realtor.com®, "Top 10 Hot Real Estate Markets to Watch in 2016," December 2, 2015*
- Atlanta* was ranked #127 out of 225 metro areas in terms of housing affordability in 2015 by the National Association of Home Builders (#1 = most affordable). Criteria: the share of homes sold in that area affordable to a family earning the local median income, based on standard mortgage underwriting criteria. *National Association of Home Builders®, NAHB-Wells Fargo Housing Opportunity Index, 4th Quarter 2015*

Safety Rankings

- The National Insurance Crime Bureau ranked 380 metro areas in the U.S. in terms of per capita rates of vehicle theft. The Atlanta* metro area ranked #54 (#1 = highest rate). Criteria: number of vehicle theft offenses per 100,000 inhabitants in 2014. *National Insurance Crime Bureau, "Hot Spots 2014," June 24, 2015*

Seniors/Retirement Rankings

- From its Best Cities for Successful Aging indexes, the Milken Institute generated rankings for metropolitan areas, weighing data in eight categories—health care, wellness, living arrangements, transportation, financial characteristics, education and employment opportunities, community engagement, and overall livability. The Atlanta* metro area was ranked #83 overall in the large metro area category. *Milken Institute, "Best Cities for Successful Aging, 2014"*

Transportation Rankings

- The Atlanta* metro area appeared on *Forbes* list of places with the most extreme commutes. The metro area ranked #7 out of 10. Criteria: average travel time; percentage of mega commuters. Mega-commuters travel more than 90 minutes and 50 miles each way to work. *Forbes.com, "The Cities with the Most Extreme Commutes," March 5, 2013*

Miscellaneous Rankings

- The watchdog site Charity Navigator conducts an annual study of charities in the nation's major markets both to analyze statistical differences in their financial, accountability, and transparency practices and to track year-to-year variations in individual communities. The Atlanta* metro area was ranked #23 among the 30 metro markets in the rating dimension of Overall Score. *www.charitynavigator.org, "Metro Market Study 2015," June 5, 2015*
- The Harris Poll's Happiness Index survey revealed that of the top ten U.S. markets, the Atlanta* metro area residents ranked #4 in happiness. Criteria included strong assent to positive statements and strong disagreement with negative ones, and degree of agreement with a series of statements about respondents' personal relationships and general outlook. *www.harrisinteractive.com, "Dallas/Fort Worth Is "Happiest" City among America's Top Ten Markets," September 4, 2013*

- Energizer Personal Care, the makers of Edge® shave gel, in partnership with Sperling's BestPlaces, ranked 50 major metro areas in terms of everyday irritations. The Atlanta* metro area ranked #5 the 50 metro area most iritating to guys. Criteria: high male-to-female ratio; poor sports team performance and high ticket prices; slow traffic; lack of job availability; unaffordable housing; extreme weather; lack of nightlife and fitness options. *Energizer Personal Care, "Most Irritatng Cities for Guys," August 26, 2013*
- Mars Chocolate North America, the makers of COMBOS®, in partnership with Sperling's BestPlaces, ranked 50 major metro areas in terms of their "manliness." The Atlanta* metro area ranked #17. Criteria: number of professional sports teams; number of nearby NASCAR tracks and racing events; manly lifestyle; concentration of manly retail stores; manly occupations per capita; salty snack sales; "Board of Manliness" rankings. *Mars Chocolate North America, "America's Manliest Cities 2012"*
- The Atlanta* metro area was selected as one of "America's Most Miserable Cities" by *Forbes.com.* The metro area ranked #16 out of 20. Criteria: violent crime; unemployment; foreclosures; income and property taxes; home prices; commute times; climate. *Forbes.com, "America's Most Miserable Cities" February 22, 2013*
- The National Alliance to End Homelessness ranked the 100 most populous metro areas with the highest rate of homelessness. The Atlanta* metro area ranked #61. Criteria: number of homeless people per 10,000 population in 2011. *National Alliance to End Homelessness, The State of Homelessness in America 2012*

Alpharetta is located within the Atlanta-Sandy Springs-Roswell, GA Metropolitan Statistical Area.

Business Environment

CITY FINANCES

City Government Finances

Component	2012 ($000)	2012 ($ per capita)
Total Revenues	73,106	1,270
Total Expenditures	72,253	1,255
Debt Outstanding	54,569	948
Cash and Securities[1]	66,172	1,149

Note: (1) Cash and security holdings of a government at the close of its fiscal year, including those of its dependent agencies, utilities, and liquor stores.
Source: U.S Census Bureau, State & Local Government Finances 2012

City Government Revenue by Source

Source	2012 ($000)	2012 ($ per capita)
General Revenue		
From Federal Government	2,004	34
From State Government	1,375	23
From Local Governments	12,239	212
Taxes		
Property	24,367	423
Sales and Gross Receipts	14,181	246
Personal Income	0	0
Corporate Income	0	0
Motor Vehicle License	0	0
Other Taxes	3,491	60
Current Charges	9,077	157
Liquor Store	0	0
Utility	0	0
Employee Retirement	0	0

Source: U.S Census Bureau, State & Local Government Finances 2012

City Government Expenditures by Function

Function	2012 ($000)	2012 ($ per capita)	2012 (%)
General Direct Expenditures			
Air Transportation	0	0	0.0
Corrections	0	0	0.0
Education	0	0	0.0
Employment Security Administration	0	0	0.0
Financial Administration	2,771	48	3.8
Fire Protection	8,621	149	11.9
General Public Buildings	0	0	0.0
Governmental Administration, Other	9,049	157	12.5
Health	0	0	0.0
Highways	16,976	294	23.4
Hospitals	0	0	0.0
Housing and Community Development	0	0	0.0
Interest on General Debt	1,303	22	1.8
Judicial and Legal	939	16	1.3
Libraries	0	0	0.0
Parking	0	0	0.0
Parks and Recreation	6,141	106	8.4
Police Protection	14,361	249	19.8
Public Welfare	0	0	0.0
Sewerage	0	0	0.0
Solid Waste Management	3,143	54	4.3
Veterans' Services	0	0	0.0
Liquor Store	0	0	0.0
Utility	0	0	0.0
Employee Retirement	0	0	0.0

Source: U.S Census Bureau, State & Local Government Finances 2012

DEMOGRAPHICS

Population Growth

Area	1990 Census	2000 Census	2010 Census	2014* Estimate	Population Growth (%) 1990-2014	Population Growth (%) 2010-2014
City	15,338	34,854	57,551	60,903	297.1	5.8
MSA[1]	3,069,411	4,247,981	5,268,860	5,455,053	77.7	3.5
U.S.	248,709,873	281,421,906	308,745,538	314,107,084	26.3	1.7

Note: (1) Figures cover the Atlanta-Sandy Springs-Roswell, GA Metropolitan Statistical Area—see Appendix B for areas included; (*) 2010-2014 5-year estimated population
Source: U.S. Census Bureau, 1990 Census, Census 2000, Census 2010, 2010-2014 American Community Survey 5-Year Estimates

Household Size

Area	Persons in Household (%) One	Two	Three	Four	Five	Six	Seven or More	Average Household Size
City	25.5	28.2	16.5	20.7	6.3	2.3	0.2	2.72
MSA[1]	26.5	31.3	16.8	14.7	6.5	2.4	1.4	2.77
U.S.	27.5	33.5	15.8	13.1	6.0	2.3	1.4	2.64

Note: (1) Figures cover the Atlanta-Sandy Springs-Roswell, GA Metropolitan Statistical Area—see Appendix B for areas included
Source: U.S. Census Bureau, 2010-2014 American Community Survey 5-Year Estimates

Race

Area	White Alone[2] (%)	Black Alone[2] (%)	Asian Alone[2] (%)	AIAN[3] Alone[2] (%)	NHOPI[4] Alone[2] (%)	Other Race Alone[2] (%)	Two or More Races (%)
City	68.9	10.7	15.1	0.1	0.2	1.1	3.9
MSA[1]	56.1	32.9	5.2	0.3	0.0	3.4	2.2
U.S.	73.8	12.6	5.0	0.8	0.2	4.7	2.9

Note: (1) Figures cover the Atlanta-Sandy Springs-Roswell, GA Metropolitan Statistical Area—see Appendix B for areas included; (2) Alone is defined as not being in combination with one or more other races; (3) American Indian and Alaska Native; (4) Native Hawaiian and Other Pacific Islander
Source: U.S. Census Bureau, 2010-2014 American Community Survey 5-Year Estimates

Hispanic or Latino Origin

Area	Total (%)	Mexican (%)	Puerto Rican (%)	Cuban (%)	Other (%)
City	8.2	3.4	0.8	0.3	3.6
MSA[1]	10.4	5.9	0.9	0.4	3.2
U.S.	16.9	10.8	1.6	0.6	3.8

Note: Persons of Hispanic or Latino origin can be of any race; (1) Figures cover the Atlanta-Sandy Springs-Roswell, GA Metropolitan Statistical Area—see Appendix B for areas included
Source: U.S. Census Bureau, 2010-2014 American Community Survey 5-Year Estimates

Ancestry

Area	German	Irish	English	American	Italian	Polish	French[2]	Scottish	Dutch
City	11.4	11.3	8.5	5.9	4.6	1.8	1.9	2.2	0.8
MSA[1]	7.4	7.5	7.5	9.8	2.6	1.3	1.5	1.8	0.8
U.S.	14.9	10.8	8.0	7.1	5.5	3.0	2.7	1.7	1.4

Note: Figures are the percentage of the total population reporting a particular ancestry. The nine most commonly reported ancestries in the U.S. are shown. Figures include multiple ancestries (e.g. if a person reported being Irish and Italian, they were included in both columns); (1) Figures cover the Atlanta-Sandy Springs-Roswell, GA Metropolitan Statistical Area—see Appendix B for areas included; (2) Excludes Basque
Source: U.S. Census Bureau, 2010-2014 American Community Survey 5-Year Estimates

Foreign-Born Population

Area	Percent of Population Born in								
	Any Foreign Country	Asia	Mexico	Europe	Carribean	Central America[2]	South America	Africa	Canada
City	22.0	11.8	2.1	3.5	0.8	0.4	1.8	1.0	0.5
MSA[1]	13.3	4.0	3.1	1.2	1.4	1.1	0.9	1.3	0.2
U.S.	13.1	3.8	3.7	1.5	1.2	1.0	0.9	0.6	0.3

Note: (1) Figures cover the Atlanta-Sandy Springs-Roswell, GA Metropolitan Statistical Area—see Appendix B for areas included; (2) Excludes Mexico.
Source: U.S. Census Bureau, 2010-2014 American Community Survey 5-Year Estimates

Marital Status

Area	Never Married	Now Married[2]	Separated	Widowed	Divorced
City	26.0	60.3	0.6	4.1	9.0
MSA[1]	34.1	47.8	2.3	4.7	11.1
U.S.	32.5	48.4	2.2	5.9	10.9

Note: Figures are percentages and cover the population 15 years of age and older; (1) Figures cover the Atlanta-Sandy Springs-Roswell, GA Metropolitan Statistical Area—see Appendix B for areas included; (2) Excludes separated
Source: U.S. Census Bureau, 2010-2014 American Community Survey 5-Year Estimates

Disability Status

Area	All Ages	Under 18 Years Old	18 to 64 Years Old	65 Years and Over
City	6.0	1.6	3.6	39.6
MSA[1]	9.8	3.3	8.5	35.2
U.S.	12.3	4.1	10.2	36.3

Note: Figures show percent of the civilian noninstitutionalized population that reported having a disability. Disability status is determined from from six types of difficulty: vision, hearing, cognitive, ambulatory, self-care, and independent living. For children under 5 years old, hearing and vision difficulty are used to determine disability status. For children between the ages of 5 and 14, disability status is determined from hearing, vision, cognitive, ambulatory, and self-care difficulties. For people aged 15 years and older, they are considered to have a disability if they have difficulty with any one of the six difficulty types; (1) Figures cover the Atlanta-Sandy Springs-Roswell, GA Metropolitan Statistical Area—see Appendix B for areas included.
Source: U.S. Census Bureau, 2010-2014 American Community Survey 5-Year Estimates

Age

Area	Percent of Population									Median Age
	Under Age 5	Age 5–19	Age 20–34	Age 35–44	Age 45–54	Age 55–64	Age 65–74	Age 75–84	Age 85+	
City	7.8	24.0	16.2	16.4	16.4	10.9	4.3	2.4	1.6	36.4
MSA[1]	6.9	21.7	20.7	15.2	14.6	10.9	6.1	2.8	1.0	35.4
U.S.	6.4	19.9	20.6	13.0	14.1	12.3	7.6	4.3	1.9	37.4

Note: (1) Figures cover the Atlanta-Sandy Springs-Roswell, GA Metropolitan Statistical Area—see Appendix B for areas included
Source: U.S. Census Bureau, 2010-2014 American Community Survey 5-Year Estimates

Gender

Area	Males	Females	Males per 100 Females
City	30,377	30,526	99.5
MSA[1]	2,649,723	2,805,330	94.5
U.S.	154,515,159	159,591,925	96.8

Note: (1) Figures cover the Atlanta-Sandy Springs-Roswell, GA Metropolitan Statistical Area—see Appendix B for areas included
Source: U.S. Census Bureau, 2010-2014 American Community Survey 5-Year Estimates

Religious Groups by Family

Area	Catholic	Baptist	Non-Den.	Methodist[2]	Lutheran	LDS[3]	Pente-costal	Presby-terian[4]	Muslim[5]	Judaism
MSA[1]	7.4	17.4	6.8	7.8	0.5	0.7	2.6	1.8	0.7	0.5
U.S.	19.1	9.3	4.0	4.0	2.3	2.0	1.9	1.6	0.8	0.7

Note: Figures are the number of adherents as a percentage of the total population; (1) Figures cover the Atlanta-Sandy Springs-Marietta, GA Metropolitan Statistical Area—see Appendix B for areas included; (2) Methodist/Pietist; (3) Latter Day Saints; (4) Reformed; (5) Figures are estimates
Source: Association of Statisticians of American Religious Bodies, 2010 U.S. Religion Census: Religious Congregations & Membership Study

Religious Groups by Tradition

Area	Catholic	Evangelical Protestant	Mainline Protestant	Other Tradition	Black Protestant	Orthodox
MSA[1]	7.4	26.0	9.8	2.9	3.1	0.2
U.S.	19.1	16.2	7.3	4.3	1.6	0.3

Note: Figures are the number of adherents as a percentage of the total population; (1) Figures cover the Atlanta-Sandy Springs-Marietta, GA Metropolitan Statistical Area—see Appendix B for areas included
Source: Association of Statisticians of American Religious Bodies, 2010 U.S. Religion Census: Religious Congregations & Membership Study

ECONOMY

Gross Metropolitan Product

Area	2013	2014	2015	2016	Rank[2]
MSA[1]	307.2	321.1	335.5	354.0	10

Note: Figures are in billions of dollars; (1) Figures cover the Atlanta-Sandy Springs-Roswell, GA Metropolitan Statistical Area—see Appendix B for areas included; (2) Rank is based on 2016 data and ranges from 1 to 381
Source: The U.S. Conference of Mayors, U.S. Metro Economies: GMP and Employment 2014-2016, June 2015

Economic Growth

Area	2011-13 (%)	2014 (%)	2015 (%)	2016 (%)	Rank[2]
MSA[1]	1.8	2.8	3.1	3.5	33
U.S.	2.2	2.4	2.3	2.9	-

Note: Figures are real gross metropolitan product (GMP) growth rates and represent annual average percent change; (1) Figures cover the Atlanta-Sandy Springs-Roswell, GA Metropolitan Statistical Area—see Appendix B for areas included; (2) Rank is based on 2016 data and ranges from 1 to 381
Source: The U.S. Conference of Mayors, U.S. Metro Economies: GMP and Employment 2014-2016, June 2015

Metropolitan Area Exports

Area	2009	2010	2011	2012	2013	2014	Rank[2]
MSA[1]	13,405.8	15,009.6	17,229.0	18,169.0	18,827.8	19,870.2	18

Note: Figures are in millions of dollars; (1) Figures cover the Atlanta-Sandy Springs-Roswell, GA Metropolitan Statistical Area—see Appendix B for areas included; (2) Rank is based on 2014 data and ranges from 1 to 385
Source: U.S. Department of Commerce, International Trade Administration, Office of Trade & Industry Information, Manufacturing & Services, data extracted March 10, 2016

Building Permits

Area	Single-Family			Multi-Family			Total		
	2014	2015p	Pct. Chg.	2014	2015p	Pct. Chg.	2014	2015p	Pct. Chg.
City	288	277	-3.8	0	235	-	288	512	77.8
MSA[1]	16,984	19,885	17.1	9,699	10,126	4.4	26,683	30,011	12.5
U.S.	640,300	690,800	7.9	411,800	487,600	18.4	1,052,100	1,178,400	12.0

Note: (1) Figures cover the Atlanta-Sandy Springs-Roswell, GA Metropolitan Statistical Area—see Appendix B for areas included; Figures represent new, privately-owned housing units authorized (unadjusted data); All permit data are based on estimates with imputation; (p) preliminary data.
Source: U.S. Census Bureau, Manufacturing, Mining, and Construction Statistics, Building Permits, 2014, 2015

Bankruptcy Filings

Area	Business Filings			Nonbusiness Filings		
	2014	2015	% Chg.	2014	2015	% Chg.
Fulton County	161	138	-14.3	5,080	4,863	-4.3
U.S.	26,983	24,735	-8.3	909,812	819,760	-9.9

Note: Business filings include Chapter 7, Chapter 11, Chapter 12, and Chapter 13; Nonbusiness filings include Chapter 7, Chapter 11, and Chapter 13

Source: Administrative Office of the U.S. Courts, Business and Nonbusiness Bankruptcy, County Cases Commenced by Chapter of the Bankruptcy Code, During the 12- Month Period Ending December 31, 2014 and Business and Nonbusiness Bankruptcy, County Cases Commenced by Chapter of the Bankruptcy Code, During the 12- Month Period Ending December 31, 2015

Housing Vacancy Rates

Area	Gross Vacancy Rate[2] (%)			Year-Round Vacancy Rate[3] (%)			Rental Vacancy Rate[4] (%)			Homeowner Vacancy Rate[5] (%)		
	2013	2014	2015	2013	2014	2015	2013	2014	2015	2013	2014	2015
MSA[1]	12.4	11.0	11.0	11.8	10.3	10.7	10.2	8.8	8.2	2.1	2.5	2.2
U.S.	13.6	13.4	12.9	10.7	10.4	10.0	8.3	7.6	7.1	2.0	1.9	1.8

Note: (1) Figures cover the Atlanta-Sandy Springs-Roswell, GA Metropolitan Statistical Area—see Appendix B for areas included; (2) The percentage of the total housing inventory that is vacant; (3) The percentage of the housing inventory (excluding seasonal units) that is year-round vacant; (4) The percentage of rental inventory that is vacant for rent; (5) The percentage of homeowner inventory that is vacant for sale

Source: U.S. Census Bureau, Housing Vacancies and Homeownership Annual Statistics: 2015

INCOME

Income

Area	Per Capita ($)	Median Household ($)	Average Household ($)
City	42,644	87,837	115,032
MSA[1]	28,880	56,618	78,422
U.S.	28,555	53,482	74,596

Note: (1) Figures cover the Atlanta-Sandy Springs-Roswell, GA Metropolitan Statistical Area—see Appendix B for areas included

Source: U.S. Census Bureau, 2010-2014 American Community Survey 5-Year Estimates

Household Income Distribution

Area	Percent of Households Earning							
	Under $15,000	$15,000 -24,999	$25,000 -34,999	$35,000 -49,999	$50,000 -74,999	$75,000 -99,000	$100,000 -149,999	$150,000 and up
City	5.8	5.6	4.9	8.3	17.5	14.8	19.1	23.9
MSA[1]	11.2	9.5	9.9	13.7	18.3	12.4	13.7	11.3
U.S.	12.5	10.7	10.2	13.5	17.8	12.2	13.0	10.0

Note: (1) Figures cover the Atlanta-Sandy Springs-Roswell, GA Metropolitan Statistical Area—see Appendix B for areas included

Source: U.S. Census Bureau, 2010-2014 American Community Survey 5-Year Estimates

Poverty Rate

Area	All Ages	Under 18 Years Old	18 to 64 Years Old	65 Years and Over
City	5.1	6.6	4.3	6.3
MSA[1]	15.7	22.2	14.0	9.6
U.S.	15.6	21.9	14.6	9.4

Note: Figures are percentage of people whose income during the past 12 months was below the poverty level; (1) Figures cover the Atlanta-Sandy Springs-Roswell, GA Metropolitan Statistical Area—see Appendix B for areas included

Source: U.S. Census Bureau, 2010-2014 American Community Survey 5-Year Estimates

EMPLOYMENT

Labor Force and Employment

Area	Civilian Labor Force			Workers Employed		
	Dec. 2014	Dec. 2015	% Chg.	Dec. 2014	Dec. 2015	% Chg.
City	33,497	33,937	1.3	32,027	32,607	1.8
MSA[1]	2,815,375	2,835,654	0.7	2,647,261	2,695,404	1.8
U.S.	155,521,000	157,245,000	1.1	147,190,000	149,703,000	1.7

Note: Data is not seasonally adjusted and covers workers 16 years of age and older; (1) Figures cover the Atlanta-Sandy Springs-Roswell, GA Metropolitan Statistical Area—see Appendix B for areas included
Source: Bureau of Labor Statistics, Local Area Unemployment Statistics

Unemployment Rate

Area	2015											
	Jan.	Feb.	Mar.	Apr.	May	Jun.	Jul.	Aug.	Sep.	Oct.	Nov.	Dec.
City	4.5	4.5	4.5	4.4	4.7	4.8	4.8	4.5	4.4	4.1	3.8	3.9
MSA[1]	6.2	6.1	5.9	5.6	5.9	6.0	6.1	5.6	5.5	5.4	4.9	4.9
U.S.	6.1	5.8	5.6	5.1	5.3	5.5	5.6	5.2	4.9	4.8	4.8	4.8

Note: Data is not seasonally adjusted and covers workers 16 years of age and older; (1) Figures cover the Atlanta-Sandy Springs-Roswell, GA Metropolitan Statistical Area—see Appendix B for areas included
Source: Bureau of Labor Statistics, Local Area Unemployment Statistics

Employment by Occupation

Occupation Classification	City (%)	MSA[1] (%)	U.S. (%)
Management, Business, Science, and Arts	59.1	39.4	36.4
Natural Resources, Construction, and Maintenance	2.6	8.1	9.0
Production, Transportation, and Material Moving	3.4	10.9	12.1
Sales and Office	24.7	25.6	24.4
Service	10.2	16.0	18.2

Note: Figures cover employed civilians 16 years of age and older; (1) Figures cover the Atlanta-Sandy Springs-Roswell, GA Metropolitan Statistical Area—see Appendix B for areas included
Source: U.S. Census Bureau, 2010-2014 American Community Survey 5-Year Estimates

Employment by Industry

Sector	MSA[1]		U.S.
	Number of Employees	Percent of Total	Percent of Total
Construction	111,700	4.2	4.5
Education and Health Services	323,700	12.2	15.7
Financial Activities	163,400	6.1	5.7
Government	326,200	12.3	15.5
Information	87,400	3.3	1.9
Leisure and Hospitality	275,800	10.4	10.4
Manufacturing	161,300	6.1	8.6
Mining and Logging	1,500	<0.1	0.5
Other Services	98,700	3.7	3.9
Professional and Business Services	489,600	18.5	13.9
Retail Trade	301,200	11.3	11.3
Transportation, Warehousing, and Utilities	144,200	5.4	3.9
Wholesale Trade	159,100	6.0	4.1

Note: Figures are non-farm employment as of December 2015. Figures are not seasonally adjusted and include workers 16 years of age and older; (1) Figures cover the Atlanta-Sandy Springs-Roswell, GA Metropolitan Statistical Area—see Appendix B for areas included
Source: Bureau of Labor Statistics, Current Employment Statistics, Employment, Hours, and Earnings

Occupations with Greatest Projected Employment Growth: 2012 – 2022

Occupation[1]	2012 Employment	2022 Projected Employment	Numeric Employment Change	Percent Employment Change
Combined Food Preparation and Serving Workers, Including Fast Food	169,450	192,830	23,380	13.8
Customer Service Representatives	95,900	115,410	19,510	20.3
Laborers and Freight, Stock, and Material Movers, Hand	85,460	104,150	18,690	21.9
Elementary School Teachers, Except Special Education	42,300	56,170	13,870	32.8
General and Operations Managers	71,410	84,890	13,480	18.9
Sales Representatives, Wholesale and Manufacturing, Except Technical and Scientific Products	56,220	67,450	11,230	20.0
Secretaries and Administrative Assistants, Except Legal, Medical, and Executive	51,850	63,030	11,180	21.6
Office Clerks, General	79,920	91,010	11,090	13.9
Janitors and Cleaners, Except Maids and Housekeeping Cleaners	52,860	63,600	10,740	20.3
Childcare Workers	37,650	48,280	10,630	28.2

Note: Projections cover Georgia; (1) Sorted by numeric employment change
Source: www.projectionscentral.com, State Occupational Projections, 2012–2022 Long-Term Projections

Fastest Growing Occupations: 2012 – 2022

Occupation[1]	2012 Employment	2022 Projected Employment	Numeric Employment Change	Percent Employment Change
Physician Assistants	2,820	4,740	1,920	67.9
Health Specialties Teachers, Postsecondary	4,870	8,060	3,190	65.5
Agents and Business Managers of Artists, Performers, and Athletes	430	700	270	62.6
Personal Care Aides	16,440	26,630	10,190	62.0
Interpreters and Translators	1,650	2,630	980	58.9
Nursing Instructors and Teachers, Postsecondary	1,420	2,200	780	55.5
Psychiatric Aides	1,390	2,150	760	55.3
Home Health Aides	7,950	12,340	4,390	55.1
Nurse Practitioners	3,260	5,010	1,750	53.9
Nurse Midwives	250	380	130	53.6

Note: Projections cover Georgia; (1) Sorted by percent employment change and excludes occupations with numeric employment change less than 100
Source: www.projectionscentral.com, State Occupational Projections, 2012–2022 Long-Term Projections

Average Wages

Occupation	$/Hr.	Occupation	$/Hr.
Accountants and Auditors	38.06	Maids and Housekeeping Cleaners	9.32
Automotive Mechanics	19.15	Maintenance and Repair Workers	18.24
Bookkeepers	19.46	Marketing Managers	64.91
Carpenters	19.77	Nuclear Medicine Technologists	35.79
Cashiers	9.38	Nurses, Licensed Practical	19.58
Clerks, General Office	14.20	Nurses, Registered	31.73
Clerks, Receptionists/Information	14.19	Nursing Assistants	11.41
Clerks, Shipping/Receiving	14.09	Packers and Packagers, Hand	10.96
Computer Programmers	40.72	Physical Therapists	39.70
Computer Systems Analysts	42.17	Postal Service Mail Carriers	24.82
Computer User Support Specialists	25.87	Real Estate Brokers	51.40
Cooks, Restaurant	11.38	Retail Salespersons	11.85
Dentists	83.66	Sales Reps., Exc. Tech./Scientific	32.41
Electrical Engineers	43.06	Sales Reps., Tech./Scientific	39.40
Electricians	22.23	Secretaries, Exc. Legal/Med./Exec.	17.34
Financial Managers	68.91	Security Guards	12.62
First-Line Supervisors/Managers, Sales	19.56	Surgeons	128.18
Food Preparation Workers	9.93	Teacher Assistants*	10.47
General and Operations Managers	60.10	Teachers, Elementary School*	26.05
Hairdressers/Cosmetologists	13.42	Teachers, Secondary School*	27.22
Internists	129.01	Telemarketers	14.98
Janitors and Cleaners	11.57	Truck Drivers, Heavy/Tractor-Trailer	19.95
Landscaping/Groundskeeping Workers	12.98	Truck Drivers, Light/Delivery Svcs.	17.48
Lawyers	66.05	Waiters and Waitresses	9.22

Note: Wage data covers the Atlanta-Sandy Springs-Marietta, GA Metropolitan Statistical Area—see Appendix B for areas included; (*) Hourly wages for elementary/secondary school teachers and teacher assistants were calculated by the editors from annual wage data based on a 40 hour work week; n/a not available.
Source: Bureau of Labor Statistics, Metro Area Occupational Employment and Wage Estimates, May 2015

TAXES

State Corporate Income Tax Rates

State	Tax Rate (%)	Income Brackets ($)	Num. of Brackets	Financial Institution Tax Rate (%)[a]	Federal Income Tax Ded.
Georgia	6.0	Flat rate	1	6.0	No

Note: Tax rates as of January 1, 2016; (a) Rates listed are the corporate income tax rate applied to financial institutions or excise taxes based on income. Some states have other taxes based upon the value of deposits or shares.
Source: Federation of Tax Administrators, "State Corporate Income Tax Rates, 2016"

State Individual Income Tax Rates

State	Tax Rate (%)	Income Brackets ($)	Num. of Brackets	Personal Exempt. ($)[1]		Fed. Inc. Tax Ded.
				Single	Dependents	
Georgia	1.0 - 6.0	750 - 7,001 (h)	6	2,700	3,000	No

Note: Tax rates as of January 1, 2016; Local- and county-level taxes are not included; n/a not applicable; (1) Married joint filers generally receive double the single exemption; (h) The Georgia income brackets reported are for single individuals. For married couples filing jointly, the same tax rates apply to income brackets ranging from $1,000, to $10,000.
Source: Federation of Tax Administrators, "State Individual Income Tax Rates, 2016"

Various State and Local Tax Rates

State	State and Local Sales and Use (%)	State Sales and Use (%)	Gasoline[1] (¢/gal.)	Cigarette[2] ($/pack)	Spirits[3] ($/gal.)	Wine[4] ($/gal.)	Beer[5] ($/gal.)
Georgia	7.00	4.0	31.02	0.37	3.79 (f)	1.51 (l)	0.48 (q)(r)

Note: All tax rates as of January 1, 2016; (1) The American Petroleum Institute has developed a methodology for determining the average tax rate on a gallon of fuel. Rates may include any of the following: excise taxes, environmental fees, storage tank fees, other fees or taxes, general sales tax, and local taxes. In states where gasoline is subject to the general sales tax, or where the fuel tax is based on the average sale price, the average rate determined by API is sensitive to changes in the price of gasoline. States that fully or partially apply general sales taxes to gasoline: CA, CO, GA, IL, IN, MI, NY; (2) The federal excise tax of $1.0066 per pack and local taxes are not included; (3) Rates are those applicable to off-premise sales of 40% alcohol by volume (a.b.v.) distilled spirits in 750ml containers. Local excise taxes are excluded; (4) Rates are those applicable to off-premise sales of 11% a.b.v. non-carbonated wine in 750ml containers; (5) Rates are those applicable to off-premise sales of 4.7% a.b.v. beer in 12 ounce containers; (f) Different rates are also applicable according to alcohol content, place of production, size of container, or place purchased (on- or off-premise or onboard airlines); (l) Different rates also applicable according to alcohol content, place of production, size of container, place purchased (on- or off-premise or on board airlines) or type of wine (carbonated, vermouth, etc.); (q) Different rates are also applicable according to alcohol content, place of production, size of container, or place purchased (on- or off-premise or onboard airlines); (r) Includes the statewide local rate in Alabama ($0.52) and Georgia ($0.53).
Source: Tax Foundation, 2016 Facts & Figures: How Does Your State Compare?

State Business Tax Climate Index Rankings

State	Overall Rank	Corporate Tax Rank	Individual Income Tax Rank	Sales Tax Rank	Unemployment Insurance Tax Rank	Property Tax Rank
Georgia	39	9	42	35	37	31

Note: The index is a measure of how each state's tax laws affect economic performance. The lower the rank, the more favorable a state's tax system is for business. States without a given tax are given a ranking of 1. The scores/rankings for the District of Columbia do not affect other states. The 2016 index represents the tax climate as of July 1, 2015 (the beginning of Fiscal Year 2016).
Source: Tax Foundation, State Business Tax Climate Index 2016

TRANSPORTATION

Means of Transportation to Work

Area	Car/Truck/Van: Drove Alone	Car/Truck/Van: Car-pooled	Public Transportation: Bus	Public Transportation: Subway	Public Transportation: Railroad	Bicycle	Walked	Other Means	Worked at Home
City	78.9	5.1	0.7	0.6	0.1	0.0	2.4	1.0	11.3
MSA[1]	77.9	10.4	2.2	0.7	0.1	0.2	1.4	1.4	5.8
U.S.	76.4	9.6	2.6	1.8	0.6	0.6	2.8	1.3	4.4

Note: Figures are percentages and cover workers 16 years of age and older; (1) Figures cover the Atlanta-Sandy Springs-Roswell, GA Metropolitan Statistical Area—see Appendix B for areas included
Source: U.S. Census Bureau, 2010-2014 American Community Survey 5-Year Estimates

Travel Time to Work

Area	Less Than 10 Minutes	10 to 19 Minutes	20 to 29 Minutes	30 to 44 Minutes	45 to 59 Minutes	60 to 89 Minutes	90 Minutes or More
City	11.3	34.2	17.7	17.0	10.7	6.8	2.2
MSA[1]	7.8	23.4	20.4	24.7	11.9	8.8	3.0
U.S.	13.3	29.6	21.0	20.2	7.7	5.7	2.6

Note: Figures are percentages and include workers 16 years old and over; (1) Figures cover the Atlanta-Sandy Springs-Roswell, GA Metropolitan Statistical Area—see Appendix B for areas included
Source: U.S. Census Bureau, 2010-2014 American Community Survey 5-Year Estimates

Freeway Travel Time Index

Area	1985	1990	1995	2000	2005	2010	2014
Urban Area Rank[1,2]	24	21	13	19	21	25	25
Urban Area Index[1]	1.11	1.15	1.22	1.24	1.26	1.23	1.24
Average Index[3]	1.09	1.11	1.14	1.17	1.20	1.19	1.20

Note: Freeway Travel Time Index—the ratio of travel time in the peak period to the travel time at free-flow conditions. For example, a value of 1.30 indicates a 20-minute free-flow trip takes 26 minutes in the peak (20 minutes x 1.30 = 26 minutes); (1) Covers the Atlanta GA urban area; (2) Rank is based on 101 urban areas (#1 = highest travel time index); (3) Average of 101 urban areas
Source: Texas Transportation Institute, 2015 Urban Mobility Scorecard, August 2015

Freeway Commuter Stress Index

Area	1985	1990	1995	2000	2005	2010	2014
Urban Area Rank[1,2]	24	22	13	16	18	22	23
Urban Area Index[1]	1.18	1.22	1.29	1.32	1.33	1.31	1.32
Average Index[3]	1.13	1.16	1.19	1.22	1.25	1.24	1.25

Note: The Freeway Commuter Stress Index is the same as the Freeway Travel Time Index (see table above) except that it includes only the travel in the peak directions during the peak periods; the TTI includes travel in all directions during the peak period. Thus, the CSI is more indicative of the work trip experienced by each commuter on a daily basis. (1) Covers the Atlanta GA urban area; (2) Rank is based on 101 urban areas (#1 = highest stress index); (3) Average of 101 urban areas

Source: Texas Transportation Institute, 2015 Urban Mobility Scorecard, August 2015

Living Environment

COST OF LIVING

Cost of Living Index

Composite Index	Groceries	Housing	Utilities	Trans-portation	Health Care	Misc. Goods/ Services
99.9	103.7	97.8	93.6	104.8	101.4	100.4

Note: The Cost of Living Index measures regional differences in the cost of consumer goods and services, excluding taxes and non-consumer expenditures, for professional and managerial households in the top income quintile. It is based on more than 50,000 prices covering almost 60 different items for which prices are collected three times a year by chambers of commerce, economic development organizations or university applied economic centers in each participating urban area. The numbers shown should be read as a percentage above or below the national average of 100. For example, a value of 115.4 in the groceries column indicates that grocery prices are 15.4% higher than the national average. Small differences in the index numbers should not be interpreted as significant; Figures cover the Atlanta GA urban area.
Source: The Council for Community and Economic Research, ACCRA Cost of Living Index, 2015

Grocery Prices

Area[1]	T-Bone Steak ($/pound)	Frying Chicken ($/pound)	Whole Milk ($/half gal.)	Eggs ($/dozen)	Orange Juice ($/64 oz.)	Coffee ($/11.5 oz.)
City[2]	12.83	1.42	2.30	2.07	3.75	4.58
Avg.	10.99	1.43	2.25	2.26	3.58	4.48
Min.	7.16	0.98	1.30	1.35	2.88	2.98
Max.	14.13	2.43	3.85	4.81	6.39	7.56

Note: (1) Values for the local area are compared with the average, minimum and maximum values for all 292 areas in the Cost of Living Index; (2) Figures cover the Atlanta GA urban area; **T-Bone Steak** *(price per pound);* **Frying Chicken** *(price per pound, whole fryer);* **Whole Milk** *(half gallon carton);* **Eggs** *(price per dozen, Grade A, large);* **Orange Juice** *(64 oz. Tropicana or Florida Natural);* **Coffee** *(11.5 oz. can, vacuum-packed, Maxwell House, Hills Bros, or Folgers).*
Source: The Council for Community and Economic Research, ACCRA Cost of Living Index, 2015

Housing and Utility Costs

Area[1]	New Home Price ($)	Apartment Rent ($/month)	All Electric ($/month)	Part Electric ($/month)	Other Energy ($/month)	Telephone ($/month)
City[2]	289,012	1,050	-	88.79	57.58	29.30
Avg.	312,874	945	179.30	95.07	72.96	28.11
Min.	178,682	479	116.28	43.14	26.46	10.01
Max.	1,472,476	3,984	504.25	189.44	421.11	43.06

Note: (1) Values for the local area are compared with the average, minimum and maximum values for all 292 areas in the Cost of Living Index; (2) Figures cover the Atlanta GA urban area; **New Home Price** *(2,400 sf living area, 8,000 sf lot, in urban area with full utilities);* **Apartment Rent** *(950 sf 2 bedroom/1.5 or 2 bath, unfurnished, excluding all utilities except water);* **All Electric** *(average monthly cost for an all-electric home);* **Part Electric** *(average monthly cost for a part-electric home);* **Other Energy** *(average monthly cost for natural gas, fuel oil, coal, wood, and any other forms of energy except electricity);* **Telephone** *(price includes basic monthly rate for a private residential line plus additional local usage charges incurred by a family of four).*
Source: The Council for Community and Economic Research, ACCRA Cost of Living Index, 2015

Health Care, Transportation, and Other Costs

Area[1]	Doctor ($/visit)	Dentist ($/visit)	Optometrist ($/visit)	Gasoline ($/gallon)	Beauty Salon ($/visit)	Men's Shirt ($)
City[2]	95.50	102.54	89.05	2.46	45.03	24.26
Avg.	105.15	89.02	99.78	2.38	35.30	28.10
Min.	66.87	56.09	48.53	1.95	18.91	13.38
Max.	182.34	150.36	228.33	4.09	67.91	63.80

Note: (1) Values for the local area are compared with the average, minimum and maximum values for all 292 areas in the Cost of Living Index; (2) Figures cover the Atlanta GA urban area; **Doctor** *(general practitioners routine exam of an established patient);* **Dentist** *(adult teeth cleaning and periodic oral examination);* **Optometrist** *(full vision eye exam for established adult patient);* **Gasoline** *(one gallon regular unleaded, national brand, including all taxes, cash price at self-service pump if available);* **Beauty Salon** *(woman's shampoo, trim, and blow-dry);* **Men's Shirt** *(cotton/polyester dress shirt, pinpoint weave, long sleeves).*
Source: The Council for Community and Economic Research, ACCRA Cost of Living Index, 2015

HOUSING

House Price Index (HPI)

Area	National Ranking[2]	Quarterly Change (%)	One-Year Change (%)	Five-Year Change (%)
MSA[1]	49	0.70	7.90	16.00
U.S.[3]	–	1.45	5.76	22.85

Note: The HPI is a weighted repeat sales index. It measures average price changes in repeat sales or refinancings on the same properties. This information is obtained by reviewing repeat mortgage transactions on single-family properties whose mortgages have been purchased or securitized by Fannie Mae or Freddie Mac in January 1975; (1) Atlanta-Sandy Springs-Roswell Metropolitan Statistical Area—see Appendix B for areas included; (2) Rankings are based on annual percentage change for all metro areas containing at least 15,000 transactions over the last 10 years and ranges from 1 to 266; (3) figures based on a weighted average of Census Division estimates using a seasonally adjusted, purchase-only index; all figures are for the period ending December 31, 2015

Source: Federal Housing Finance Agency, House Price Index, February 25, 2016

Median Single-Family Home Prices

Area	2013	2014	2015[p]	Percent Change 2014 to 2015
MSA[1]	139.5	159.5	173.6	8.8
U.S. Average	197.4	208.9	223.9	7.2

Note: Figures are median sales prices of existing single-family homes in thousands of dollars; (p) preliminary; n/a not available; (1) Atlanta-Sandy Springs-Roswell, GA Metropolitan Statistical Area—see Appendix B for areas included

Source: National Association of Realtors, Median Sales Price of Existing Single-Family Homes for Metropolitan Areas, 4th Quarter 2015

Qualifying Income Based on Median Sales Price of Existing Single-Family Homes

Area	With 5% Down ($)	With 10% Down ($)	With 20% Down ($)
MSA[1]	37,635	35,654	31,693
U.S. Average	49,535	46,928	41,714

Note: Figures are preliminary; Qualifying income is based on a mortgage rate of 4.1%. Monthly principal and interest payment is limited to 25% of income; n/a not available; (1) Atlanta-Sandy Springs-Roswell, GA Metropolitan Statistical Area—see Appendix B for areas included

Source: National Association of Realtors, Qualifying Income Based on Median Sales Price of Existing Single-Family Homes for Metropolitan Areas, 4th Quarter 2015

Median Apartment Condo-Coop Home Prices

Area	2013	2014	2015[p]	Percent Change 2014 to 2015
MSA[1]	117.3	136.3	156.9	15.1
U.S. Average	194.9	204.3	210.7	3.1

Note: Figures are median sales prices of existing apartment condo-coop homes in thousands of dollars; (p) preliminary; n/a not available; (1) Atlanta-Sandy Springs-Roswell, GA Metropolitan Statistical Area—see Appendix B for areas included

Source: National Association of Realtors, Median Sales Price of Existing Apartment Condo-Coop Homes for Metropolitan Areas, 4th Quarter 2015

Gross Monthly Rent

Area	Under $200	$200 -299	$300 -499	$500 -749	$750 -999	$1,000 -1,499	$1,500 and up	Median ($)
City	1.1	0.9	0.9	2.9	24.6	56.2	13.4	1,142
MSA[1]	0.9	1.6	3.0	16.1	32.2	35.8	10.2	970
U.S.	1.5	3.2	7.4	21.0	24.1	26.9	15.9	920

Note: Figures are percentages except for Median; Gross rent is the contract rent plus the estimated average monthly cost of utilities (electricity, gas, and water and sewer) and fuels (oil, coal, kerosene, wood, etc.) if these are paid by the renter (or paid for the renter by someone else); (1) Figures cover the Atlanta-Sandy Springs-Roswell, GA Metropolitan Statistical Area—see Appendix B for areas included

Source: U.S. Census Bureau, 2010-2014 American Community Survey 5-Year Estimates

HEALTH

Homeownership Rate

Area	2008 (%)	2009 (%)	2010 (%)	2011 (%)	2012 (%)	2013 (%)	2014 (%)	2015 (%)
MSA[1]	67.5	67.7	67.2	65.8	62.1	61.6	61.6	61.7
U.S.	67.8	67.4	66.9	66.1	65.4	65.1	64.5	63.7

Note: (1) Figures cover the Atlanta-Sandy Springs-Roswell, GA Metropolitan Statistical Area—see Appendix B for areas included
Source: U.S. Census Bureau, Housing Vacancies and Homeownership Annual Statistics: 2015

Year Housing Structure Built

Area	2010 or Later	2000 -2009	1990 -1999	1980 -1989	1970 -1979	1960 -1969	1950 -1959	1940 -1949	Before 1940	Median Year
City	0.7	20.5	48.7	20.9	6.6	1.4	0.5	0.2	0.5	1994
MSA[1]	0.9	26.9	22.5	18.1	13.1	8.1	5.0	2.1	3.2	1990
U.S.	1.0	14.9	13.9	13.8	15.8	11.0	10.8	5.4	13.3	1976

Note: Figures are percentages except for Median Year; (1) Figures cover the Atlanta-Sandy Springs-Roswell, GA Metropolitan Statistical Area—see Appendix B for areas included
Source: U.S. Census Bureau, 2010-2014 American Community Survey 5-Year Estimates

Health Risk Data

Category	MSA[1] (%)	U.S. (%)
Adults aged 18–64 who have any kind of health care coverage	74.3	79.6
Adults who reported being in good or excellent health	86.5	83.1
Adults who are current smokers	17.3	19.6
Adults who are heavy drinkers[2]	4.6	6.1
Adults who are binge drinkers[3]	14.6	16.9
Adults who are overweight (BMI 25.0 - 29.9)	34.4	35.8
Adults who are obese (BMI 30.0 - 99.8)	26.5	27.6
Adults who participated in any physical activities in the past month	81.0	77.1
Adults 50+ who have ever had a sigmoidoscopy or colonoscopy	70.3	67.3
Women aged 40+ who have had a mammogram within the past two years	75.7	74.0
Men aged 40+ who have had a PSA test within the past two years	54.7	45.2
Adults aged 65+ who have had flu shot within the past year	57.2	60.1
Adults who always wear a seatbelt	96.3	93.8

Note: Data as of 2012 unless otherwise noted; (1) Figures cover the Atlanta-Sandy Springs-Marietta, GA Metropolitan Statistical Area—see Appendix B for areas included; (2) Heavy drinkers are classified as males having more than two drinks per day or females having more than one drink per day; (3) Binge drinkers are classified as males having five or more drinks on one occasion or females having four or more drinks on one occasion
Source: Centers for Disease Control and Prevention, Behaviorial Risk Factor Surveillance System, SMART: Selected Metropolitan/Micropolitan Area Risk Trends, 2012 (Note: the CDC has discontinued this dataset but will be releasing a replacement in mid-2016)

Chronic Health Indicators

Category	MSA[1] (%)	U.S. (%)
Adults who have ever been told they had a heart attack	3.7	4.5
Adults who have ever been told they had a stroke	2.9	2.9
Adults who have been told they currently have asthma	8.0	8.9
Adults who have ever been told they have arthritis	20.7	25.7
Adults who have ever been told they have diabetes[2]	8.9	9.7
Adults who have ever been told they had skin cancer	5.2	5.7
Adults who have ever been told they had any other types of cancer	5.2	6.5
Adults who have ever been told they have COPD	5.2	6.2
Adults who have ever been told they have kidney disease	3.0	2.5
Adults who have ever been told they have a form of depression	14.5	18.0

Note: Data as of 2012 unless otherwise noted; (1) Figures cover the Atlanta-Sandy Springs-Marietta, GA Metropolitan Statistical Area—see Appendix B for areas included; (2) Figures do not include pregnancy-related, borderline, or pre-diabetes
Source: Centers for Disease Control and Prevention, Behaviorial Risk Factor Surveillance System, SMART: Selected Metropolitan/Micropolitan Area Risk Trends, 2012 (Note: the CDC has discontinued this dataset but will be releasing a replacement in mid-2016)

Mortality Rates for the Top 10 Causes of Death in the U.S.

ICD-10[a] Sub-Chapter	ICD-10[a] Code	Age-Adjusted Mortality Rate[1] per 100,000 population	
		County[2]	U.S.
Malignant neoplasms	C00-C97	160.6	163.6
Ischaemic heart diseases	I20-I25	64.9	102.2
Other forms of heart disease	I30-I51	60.4	50.1
Chronic lower respiratory diseases	J40-J47	26.8	41.4
Organic, including symptomatic, mental disorders	F01-F09	55.5	38.5
Cerebrovascular diseases	I60-I69	39.9	36.5
Other external causes of accidental injury	W00-X59	24.5	27.5
Other degenerative diseases of the nervous system	G30-G31	21.2	26.3
Diabetes mellitus	E10-E14	18.5	21.1
Hypertensive diseases	I10-I15	41.0	19.7

Note: (a) ICD-10 = International Classification of Diseases 10th Revision; (1) Mortality rates are a three year average covering 2012-2014; (2) Figures cover Fulton County.
Source: Centers for Disease Control and Prevention, National Center for Health Statistics. Underlying Cause of Death 1999-2014 on CDC WONDER Online Database, released 2015.

Mortality Rates for Selected Causes of Death

ICD-10[a] Sub-Chapter	ICD-10[a] Code	Age-Adjusted Mortality Rate[1] per 100,000 population	
		County[2]	U.S.
Assault	X85-Y09	10.6	5.1
Diseases of the liver	K70-K76	10.2	13.5
Human immunodeficiency virus (HIV) disease	B20-B24	9.5	2.1
Influenza and pneumonia	J09-J18	11.1	15.2
Intentional self-harm	X60-X84	11.3	12.7
Malnutrition	E40-E46	1.0	0.9
Obesity and other hyperalimentation	E65-E68	1.3	1.9
Renal failure	N17-N19	17.2	13.0
Transport accidents	V01-V99	8.7	11.6
Viral hepatitis	B15-B19	2.0	2.1

Note: (a) ICD-10 = International Classification of Diseases 10th Revision; (1) Mortality rates are a three year average covering 2012-2014; (2) Figures cover Fulton County; Data are Suppressed when the data meet the criteria for confidentiality constraints; Mortality rates are flagged as Unreliable when the rate would be calculated with a numerator of 20 or less.
Source: Centers for Disease Control and Prevention, National Center for Health Statistics. Underlying Cause of Death 1999-2014 on CDC WONDER Online Database, released 2015.

Health Insurance Coverage

Area	With Health Insurance	With Private Health Insurance	With Public Health Insurance	Without Health Insurance	Population Under Age 18 Without Health Insurance
City	91.6	84.7	12.3	8.4	4.6
MSA[1]	81.9	65.5	24.4	18.1	9.1
U.S.	85.8	65.8	31.1	14.2	7.1

Note: Figures are percentages that cover the civilian noninstitutionalized population; (1) Figures cover the Atlanta-Sandy Springs-Roswell, GA Metropolitan Statistical Area—see Appendix B for areas included
Source: U.S. Census Bureau, 2010-2014 American Community Survey 5-Year Estimates

Number of Medical Professionals

Area	MDs[3]	DOs[3,4]	Dentists	Podiatrists	Chiropractors	Optometrists
County[1] (number)	4,809	97	669	41	482	139
County[1] (rate[2])	488.4	9.9	67.1	4.1	48.4	14.0
U.S. (rate[2])	272.5	20.9	64.7	5.8	25.9	15.2

Note: Data as of 2014 unless noted; (1) Data covers Fulton County; (2) Rate per 100,000 population; (3) Data as of 2013 and includes all active, non-federal physicians; (4) Doctor of Osteopathic Medicine
Source: U.S. Department of Health and Human Services, Health Resources and Services Administration, Bureau of Health Professions, Area Resource File (ARF) 2014-2015

Best Hospitals

According to *U.S. News,* the Atlanta-Sandy Springs-Roswell, GA metro area is home to three of the best hospitals in the U.S.: **Emory University Hospital** (12 specialties); **Emory Wesley Woods Geriatric Hospital** (1 specialty); **Shepherd Center** (1 specialty). The hospitals listed were nationally ranked in at least one adult specialty. Only 137 hospitals nationwide were nationally ranked in one or more specialties. Fifteen hospitals in the U.S. made the Honor Roll with high scores in at least six specialties. *U.S. News Online, "America's Best Children's Hospitals 2015-16"*

According to *U.S. News,* the Atlanta-Sandy Springs-Roswell, GA metro area is home to one of the best children's hospitals in the U.S.: **Children's Healthcare of Atlanta** (Honor Roll/10 specialties). The hospital listed was highly ranked in at least one pediatric specialty. Eighty-three children's hospitals in the U.S. were nationally ranked in at least one specialty. Twelve children's hospitals in the U.S. made the Honor Roll with high scores in at least three specialties. *U.S. News Online, "America's Best Children's Hospitals 2015-16"*

EDUCATION

Public School District Statistics

District Name	Schls	Pupils	Pupil/ Teacher Ratio	Minority Pupils[1] (%)	Free Lunch Eligible[2] (%)	IEP[3] (%)
Forsyth County	36	40,691	17.1	28.6	16.1	12.4
Fulton County	104	95,232	15.1	69.0	41.7	10.3

Note: Table includes school districts with 100 or more students; (1) Percentage of students that are not non-Hispanic white; (2) Percentage of students that are eligible for the free lunch program; (3) Percentage of students that have an Individualized Education Program.

Source: U.S. Department of Education, National Center for Education Statistics, Common Core of Data, Local Education Agency (School District) Universe Survey: School Year 2013-2014; U.S. Department of Education, National Center for Education Statistics, Common Core of Data, Public Elementary/Secondary School Universe Survey: School Year 2013-2014

Best High Schools

According to *U.S. News,* Alpharetta is home to three of the best high schools in the U.S.: **Milton High School** (#187); **Alpharetta High School** (#286); **Chattahoochee High School** (#328); Nearly 20,000 schools were ranked based on their performance on state assessments and how well they prepare students for college. Schools with the highest unrounded College Readiness Index values were numerically ranked from No. 1 to No. 500 and were the gold medal winners. *U.S. News & World Report, "Best High Schools 2015"*

Highest Level of Education

Area	Less than H.S.	H.S. Diploma	Some College, No Deg.	Associate Degree	Bachelor's Degree	Master's Degree	Prof. School Degree	Doctorate Degree
City	3.2	10.8	16.8	6.8	39.4	17.8	3.1	2.1
MSA[1]	12.1	24.7	20.9	7.1	22.7	9.0	2.2	1.3
U.S.	13.7	28.0	21.2	7.9	18.3	7.8	2.0	1.3

Note: Figures cover persons age 25 and over; (1) Figures cover the Atlanta-Sandy Springs-Roswell, GA Metropolitan Statistical Area—see Appendix B for areas included

Source: U.S. Census Bureau, 2010-2014 American Community Survey 5-Year Estimates

Educational Attainment by Race

Area	High School Graduate or Higher (%)					Bachelor's Degree or Higher (%)				
	Total	White	Black	Asian	Hisp.[2]	Total	White	Black	Asian	Hisp.[2]
City	96.8	97.0	96.1	98.0	80.6	62.4	62.3	39.6	81.7	45.2
MSA[1]	87.9	89.3	88.5	86.4	61.4	35.3	39.0	27.1	53.3	16.5
U.S.	86.3	88.4	83.2	85.8	64.1	29.3	30.6	19.0	50.9	13.9

Note: Figures shown cover persons 25 years old and over; (1) Figures cover the Atlanta-Sandy Springs-Roswell, GA Metropolitan Statistical Area—see Appendix B for areas included; (2) People of Hispanic origin can be of any race

Source: U.S. Census Bureau, 2010-2014 American Community Survey 5-Year Estimates

School Enrollment by Grade and Control

Area	Preschool (%)		Kindergarten (%)		Grades 1 - 4 (%)		Grades 5 - 8 (%)		Grades 9 - 12 (%)	
	Public	Private	Public	Private	Public	Private	Public	Private	Public	Private
City	39.6	60.4	82.2	17.8	94.1	5.9	89.4	10.6	89.8	10.2
MSA[1]	54.2	45.8	87.7	12.3	90.2	9.8	89.5	10.5	90.3	9.7
U.S.	57.4	42.6	87.8	12.2	89.8	10.2	89.9	10.1	90.6	9.4

Note: Figures shown cover persons 3 years old and over; (1) Figures cover the Atlanta-Sandy Springs-Roswell, GA Metropolitan Statistical Area—see Appendix B for areas included
Source: U.S. Census Bureau, 2010-2014 American Community Survey 5-Year Estimates

Average Salaries of Public School Classroom Teachers

Area	2013-14		2014-15		Percent Change 2013-14 to 2014-15	Percent Change 2004-05 to 2014-15
	Dollars	Rank[1]	Dollars	Rank[1]		
Georgia	52,924	24	53,382	24	0.87	14.7
U.S. Average	56,610	–	57,379	–	1.36	20.8

Note: (1) State rank ranges from 1 to 51 where 1 indicates highest salary.
Source: National Education Association, Rankings & Estimates: Rankings of the States 2014 and Estimates of School Statistics 2015, March 2015

Higher Education

Four-Year Colleges			Two-Year Colleges			Medical Schools[1]	Law Schools[2]	Voc/ Tech[3]
Public	Private Non-profit	Private For-profit	Public	Private Non-profit	Private For-profit			
0	0	0	0	0	0	0	0	0

Note: Figures cover institutions located within the city limits and include main campuses only; (1) includes schools accredited by the Liaison Committee on Medical Education and the American Osteopathic Association's Commission on Osteopathic College Accreditation; (2) includes ABA-accredited schools, schools with provisional ABA accreditation, and state accredited schools; (3) includes all schools with programs that are less than 2 years.
Source: National Center for Education Statistics, Integrated Postsecondary Education System (IPEDS), 2014-15; Association of American Medical Colleges, Member List, March 21, 2016; American Osteopathic Association, Member List, March 21, 2016; Law School Admission Council, Official Guide to ABA-Approved Law Schools Online, March 21, 2016; Wikipedia, List of Medical Schools in the United States, March 21, 2016; Wikipedia, List of Law Schools in the United States, March 21, 2016

According to *U.S. News & World Report,* the Atlanta-Sandy Springs-Roswell, GA metro area is home to two of the best national universities in the U.S.: **Emory University** (#21 tie); **Georgia Institute of Technology** (#36). The indicators used to capture academic quality fall into a number of categories: assessment by administrators at peer institutions; retention of students; faculty resources; student selectivity; financial resources; alumni giving; high school counselor ratings of colleges; and graduation rate. *U.S. News & World Report, "America's Best Colleges 2016"*

According to *U.S. News & World Report,* the Atlanta-Sandy Springs-Roswell, GA metro area is home to four of the best liberal arts colleges in the U.S.: **Agnes Scott College** (#67 tie); **Spelman College** (#72 tie); **Morehouse College** (#148 tie); **Oglethorpe University** (#167 tie). The indicators used to capture academic quality fall into a number of categories: assessment by administrators at peer institutions; retention of students; faculty resources; student selectivity; financial resources; alumni giving; high school counselor ratings of colleges; and graduation rate. *U.S. News & World Report, "America's Best Colleges 2016"*

According to *U.S. News & World Report,* the Atlanta-Sandy Springs-Roswell, GA metro area is home to two of the top 100 law schools in the U.S.: **Emory University, School of Law** (#22 tie); **Georgia State University, College of Law** (#57 tie). The rankings are based on a weighted average of 12 measures of quality: peer assessment score; assessment score by lawyers/judges; median LSAT scores; median undergrad GPA; acceptance rate; employment rates for graduates; placement success; bar passage rate; faculty resources; expenditures per student; student/faculty ratio; and library resources. *U.S. News & World Report, "America's Best Graduate Schools, Law, 2017"*

According to *U.S. News & World Report,* the Atlanta-Sandy Springs-Roswell, GA metro area is home to one of the top 75 medical schools for research in the U.S.: **Emory University, School of Medicine** (#23). The rankings are based on a weighted average of 11 measures of quality: quality assessment; peer assessment score; assessment score by residency directors; research activity; total research activity; average research activity per faculty member; student

selectivity; median MCAT total score; median undergraduate GPA; acceptance rate; and faculty resources. *U.S. News & World Report, "America's Best Graduate Schools, Medical, 2017"*

According to *U.S. News & World Report,* the Atlanta-Sandy Springs-Roswell, GA metro area is home to two of the top 75 business schools in the U.S.: **Emory University, Goizueta Business School** (#19); **Georgia Institute of Technology, Scheller College of Business** (#34). The rankings are based on a weighted average of the following nine measures: quality assessment; peer assessment; recruiter assessment; placement success; mean starting salary and bonus; student selectivity; mean GMAT and GRE scores; mean undergraduate GPA; and acceptance rate. *U.S. News & World Report, "America's Best Graduate Schools, Business, 2017"*

PRESIDENTIAL ELECTION

2012 Presidential Election Results

Area	Obama (%)	Romney (%)	Other (%)
Fulton County	64.3	34.5	1.2
U.S.	51.0	47.2	1.8

Note: Results may not add to 100% due to rounding
Source: Dave Leip's Atlas of U.S. Presidential Elections

EMPLOYERS

Major Employers

Company Name	Industry
Apartments.Com	Apartment locating service
Aquilex Holdings	Facilities support services
AT&T Corp.	Engineering services
Behavioral Health, Georgia Department of	Administration of public health programs
Children's Healthcare of Atlanta	Healthcare
Clayton County Board of Education	Public elementary and secondary schools
County of Gwinnett	County commissioner
Delta Air Lines	Air transportation, scheduled
Georgia Department of Human Resoures	Administration of public health programs
Georgia Department of Transportation	Regulation, administration of transportation
IBM Corporation	Engineering services
Internal Revenue Service	Taxation department, government
Lockheed Martin Aeronautical Company	Aircraft
NCR Corporation	Calculating and accounting equipment
Northide Hospital	Healthcare
Progressive Logistics Services	Labor organizations
Robert Half International	Employment agencies
Saint Joseph's Hospital	Healthcare
The Army, United States Department of	Army
The Coca-Cola Company	Bottled and canned soft drinks
The Fulton-Dekalb Hospital Authority	General medical and surgical hospitals
The Home Depot	Hardware stores
WellStar Kennestone Hospital	General medical and surgical hospitals
World Travel Partners Group	Travel agencies

Note: Companies shown are located within the Atlanta-Sandy Springs-Roswell, GA Metropolitan Statistical Area.
Source: Hoovers.com; Wikipedia

PUBLIC SAFETY

Crime Rate

Area	All Crimes	Violent Crimes				Property Crimes		
		Murder	Rape[3]	Robbery	Aggrav. Assault	Burglary	Larceny -Theft	Motor Vehicle Theft
City	2,035.4	0.0	4.7	33.1	22.1	236.3	1,685.6	53.6
Metro[1]	3,629.7	6.1	20.4	154.0	217.9	725.9	2,170.4	334.9
U.S.	2,961.6	4.5	26.4	102.2	232.5	542.5	1,837.3	216.2

Note: Figures are crimes per 100,000 population; (1) Figures cover the Atlanta-Sandy Springs-Roswell, GA Metropolitan Statistical Area—see Appendix B for areas included; (3) The city and U.S. figures shown were reported using the legacy Uniform Crime Reporting (UCR) definition of rape. The suburban and metro area figures shown are an aggregate total of the data submitted using both the revised and legacy UCR definitions.
Source: FBI Uniform Crime Reports, 2014

Hate Crimes

Area	Number of Quarters Reported	Number of Incidents per Bias Motivation						
		Race	Religion	Sexual Orientation	Ethnicity	Disability	Gender	Gender Identity
City	4	0	0	0	0	0	0	0
U.S.	4	2,568	1,014	1,017	648	84	33	98

Source: Federal Bureau of Investigation, Hate Crime Statistics 2014

Identity Theft Consumer Complaints

Area	Complaints	Complaints per 100,000 Population	Rank[2]
MSA[1]	10,418	185.6	24
U.S.	490,220	152.4	-

Note: (1) Figures cover the Atlanta-Sandy Springs-Roswell, GA Metropolitan Statistical Area—see Appendix B for areas included; (2) Rank ranges from 1 to 379 where 1 indicates greatest number of identity theft complaints per 100,000 population
Source: Federal Trade Commission, Consumer Sentinel Network Data Book for January–December 2015

Fraud and Other Consumer Complaints

Area	Complaints	Complaints per 100,000 Population	Rank[2]
MSA[1]	26,684	475.3	30
U.S.	2,593,159	806.0	-

Note: (1) Figures cover the Atlanta-Sandy Springs-Roswell, GA Metropolitan Statistical Area—see Appendix B for areas included; (2) Rank ranges from 1 to 379 where 1 indicates greatest number of identity theft complaints per 100,000 population
Source: Federal Trade Commission, Consumer Sentinel Network Data Book for January–December 2015

RECREATION

Culture

Dance[1]	Theatre[1]	Instrumental Music[1]	Vocal Music[1]	Series and Festivals	Museums and Art Galleries[2]	Zoos and Aquariums[3]
0	0	0	0	0	0	0

Note: (1) Professional perfoming groups; (2) Based on organizations with SIC code 8412; (3) AZA-accredited
Source: The Grey House Performing Arts Directory, 2015-16; Association of Zoos & Aquariums, AZA Member Zoos & Aquariums, March 25, 2016; www.AccuLeads.com, March 29, 2016

Professional Sports Teams

Team Name	League	Year Established
Atlanta Braves	Major League Baseball (MLB)	1966
Atlanta Falcons	National Football League (NFL)	1966
Atlanta Hawks	National Basketball Association (NBA)	1968
Atlanta United FC	Major League Soccer (MLS)	2017

Note: Includes teams located in the Atlanta-Sandy Springs-Roswell, GA Metropolitan Statistical Area.
Source: Wikipedia, Major Professional Sports Teams of the United States and Canada, March 24, 2016

CLIMATE

Average and Extreme Temperatures

Temperature	Jan	Feb	Mar	Apr	May	Jun	Jul	Aug	Sep	Oct	Nov	Dec	Yr.
Extreme High (°F)	79	80	85	93	95	101	105	102	98	95	84	77	105
Average High (°F)	52	56	64	73	80	86	88	88	82	73	63	54	72
Average Temp. (°F)	43	46	53	62	70	77	79	79	73	63	53	45	62
Average Low (°F)	33	36	42	51	59	66	70	69	64	52	42	35	52
Extreme Low (°F)	-8	5	10	26	37	46	53	55	36	28	3	0	-8

Note: Figures cover the years 1945-1990
Source: National Climatic Data Center, International Station Meteorological Climate Summary, 9/96

Average Precipitation/Snowfall/Humidity

Precip./Humidity	Jan	Feb	Mar	Apr	May	Jun	Jul	Aug	Sep	Oct	Nov	Dec	Yr.
Avg. Precip. (in.)	4.7	4.6	5.7	4.3	4.0	3.5	5.1	3.6	3.4	2.8	3.8	4.2	49.8
Avg. Snowfall (in.)	1	1	Tr	Tr	0	0	0	0	0	0	Tr	Tr	2
Avg. Rel. Hum. 7am (%)	79	77	78	78	82	83	88	89	88	84	81	79	82
Avg. Rel. Hum. 4pm (%)	56	50	48	45	49	52	57	56	56	51	52	55	52

Note: Figures cover the years 1945-1990; Tr = Trace amounts (<0.05 in. of rain; <0.5 in. of snow)
Source: National Climatic Data Center, International Station Meteorological Climate Summary, 9/96

Weather Conditions

Temperature			Daytime Sky			Precipitation		
10°F & below	32°F & below	90°F & above	Clear	Partly cloudy	Cloudy	0.01 inch or more precip.	0.1 inch or more snow/ice	Thunder-storms
1	49	38	98	147	120	116	3	48

Note: Figures are average number of days per year and cover the years 1945-1990
Source: National Climatic Data Center, International Station Meteorological Climate Summary, 9/96

HAZARDOUS WASTE

Superfund Sites

Alpharetta has no sites on the EPA's Superfund Final National Priorities List. There are a total of 1,323 Superfund sites on the list in the U.S. *U.S. Environmental Protection Agency, Final National Priorities List, March 18, 2016*

AIR & WATER QUALITY

Air Quality Trends: Ozone

	1990	1995	2000	2005	2010	2011	2012	2013	2014
MSA[1]	0.104	0.103	0.101	0.087	0.076	0.078	0.079	0.066	0.072

Note: (1) Data covers the Atlanta-Sandy Springs-Roswell, GA Metropolitan Statistical Area—see Appendix B for areas included. The values shown are the composite ozone concentration averages among trend sites based on the highest fourth daily maximum 8-hour concentration in parts per million. These trends are based on sites having an adequate record of monitoring data during the trend period. Data from exceptional events are included.
Source: U.S. Environmental Protection Agency, Air Quality Monitoring Information, "Air Quality Trends by City, 1990-2014"

Air Quality Index

Area	Percent of Days when Air Quality was...²					AQI Statistics²	
	Good	Moderate	Unhealthy for Sensitive Groups	Unhealthy	Very Unhealthy	Maximum	Median
MSA¹	40.0	57.8	2.2	0.0	0.0	147	55

Note: (1) Data covers the Atlanta-Sandy Springs-Roswell, GA Metropolitan Statistical Area—see Appendix B for areas included; (2) Based on 365 days with AQI data in 2015. Air Quality Index (AQI) is an index for reporting daily air quality. EPA calculates the AQI for five major air pollutants regulated by the Clean Air Act: ground-level ozone, particle pollution (aka particulate matter), carbon monoxide, sulfur dioxide, and nitrogen dioxide. The AQI runs from 0 to 500. The higher the AQI value, the greater the level of air pollution and the greater the health concern. There are six AQI categories: "Good" AQI is between 0 and 50. Air quality is considered satisfactory; "Moderate" AQI is between 51 and 100. Air quality is acceptable; "Unhealthy for Sensitive Groups" When AQI values are between 101 and 150, members of sensitive groups may experience health effects; "Unhealthy" When AQI values are between 151 and 200 everyone may begin to experience health effects; "Very Unhealthy" AQI values between 201 and 300 trigger a health alert; "Hazardous" AQI values over 300 trigger warnings of emergency conditions (not shown).
Source: U.S. Environmental Protection Agency, Air Quality Index Report, 2015

Air Quality Index Pollutants

Area	Percent of Days when AQI Pollutant was...²					
	Carbon Monoxide	Nitrogen Dioxide	Ozone	Sulfur Dioxide	Particulate Matter 2.5	Particulate Matter 10
MSA¹	0.0	1.6	24.7	0.0	73.2	0.5

Note: (1) Data covers the Atlanta-Sandy Springs-Roswell, GA Metropolitan Statistical Area—see Appendix B for areas included; (2) Based on 365 days with AQI data in 2015. The Air Quality Index (AQI) is an index for reporting daily air quality. EPA calculates the AQI for five major air pollutants regulated by the Clean Air Act: ground-level ozone, particle pollution (also known as particulate matter), carbon monoxide, sulfur dioxide, and nitrogen dioxide. The AQI runs from 0 to 500. The higher the AQI value, the greater the level of air pollution and the greater the health concern.
Source: U.S. Environmental Protection Agency, Air Quality Index Report, 2015

Maximum Air Pollutant Concentrations: Particulate Matter, Ozone, CO and Lead

	Particulate Matter 10 (ug/m³)	Particulate Matter 2.5 Wtd AM (ug/m³)	Particulate Matter 2.5 24-Hr (ug/m³)	Ozone (ppm)	Carbon Monoxide (ppm)	Lead (ug/m³)
MSA¹ Level	61	11.2	22	0.079	2	0
NAAQS²	150	15	35	0.075	9	0.15
Met NAAQS²	Yes	Yes	Yes	No	Yes	Yes

Note: (1) Data covers the Atlanta-Sandy Springs-Roswell, GA Metropolitan Statistical Area—see Appendix B for areas included; Data from exceptional events are included; (2) National Ambient Air Quality Standards; ppm = parts per million; ug/m³ = micrograms per cubic meter; n/a not available.
Concentrations: Particulate Matter 10 (coarse particulate)—highest second maximum 24-hour concentration; Particulate Matter 2.5 Wtd AM (fine particulate)—highest weighted annual mean concentration; Particulate Matter 2.5 24-Hour (fine particulate)—highest 98th percentile 24-hour concentration; Ozone—highest fourth daily maximum 8-hour concentration; Carbon Monoxide—highest second maximum non-overlapping 8-hour concentration; Lead—maximum running 3-month average
Source: U.S. Environmental Protection Agency, Air Quality Monitoring Information, "Air Quality Statistics by City, 2014"

Maximum Air Pollutant Concentrations: Nitrogen Dioxide and Sulfur Dioxide

	Nitrogen Dioxide AM (ppb)	Nitrogen Dioxide 1-Hr (ppb)	Sulfur Dioxide AM (ppb)	Sulfur Dioxide 1-Hr (ppb)	Sulfur Dioxide 24-Hr (ppb)
MSA¹ Level	11	53	n/a	6	n/a
NAAQS²	53	100	30	75	140
Met NAAQS²	Yes	Yes	n/a	Yes	n/a

Note: (1) Data covers the Atlanta-Sandy Springs-Roswell, GA Metropolitan Statistical Area—see Appendix B for areas included; Data from exceptional events are included; (2) National Ambient Air Quality Standards; ppm = parts per million; ug/m³ = micrograms per cubic meter; n/a not available.
Concentrations: Nitrogen Dioxide AM—highest arithmetic mean concentration; Nitrogen Dioxide 1-Hr—highest 98th percentile 1-hour daily maximum concentration; Sulfur Dioxide AM—highest annual mean concentration; Sulfur Dioxide 1-Hr—highest 99th percentile 1-hour daily maximum concentration; Sulfur Dioxide 24-Hr—highest second maximum 24-hour concentration
Source: U.S. Environmental Protection Agency, Air Quality Monitoring Information, "Air Quality Statistics by City, 2014"

Drinking Water

Water System Name	Pop. Served	Primary Water Source Type	Violations[1]	
			Health Based	Monitoring/ Reporting
North Fulton County	172,533	Purchased Surface	0	0

Note: (1) Based on violation data from January 1, 2015 to December 31, 2015 (includes unresolved violations from earlier years)

Source: U.S. Environmental Protection Agency, Office of Ground Water and Drinking Water, Safe Drinking Water Information System (based on data extracted April 29, 2016)

Johns Creek, Georgia

Background

Johns Creek lies along the Chattahoochee River about 30 miles north of Atlanta, allowing the city to boast a slower hometown pace of life amid the bustling metro area. The city, incorporated in 2006, abuts Alpharetta and Roswell to the east with easy access to I-85 and GA 400/US 19.

Historically this was a home to the Cherokee tribe of Native Americans; settlers arrived in the region and created trading posts in what was rural country up until fairly recently. In the 1980s, Technology Park/Atlanta named their new mixed use community Technology Park/Johns Creek after seeing the name on an old map. Now the 800-acre Technology Park at Johns Creek employs more than 10,000 people from 200 companies—and many of them reside in the community that has grown up around the technology center, which was founded by Georgia Institute of Technology graduates who hoped to build Atlanta into a technology powerhouse. The community incorporated in 2006.

Today the park remains central to Johns Creek. A total of 5.8 million square feet have been developed. Fortune 500 companies in the park include State Farm Insurance, with its regional headquarters here. Also here is Ciba Vision's world headquarters, Macy's Technology Systems's national headquarters, Teradata, and Saia, Inc.

The park also houses the other elements that make a community: restaurants, stores, a hospital, houses of worship, and housing of all types, from senior housing to single-family homes.

Local students attend 11 elementary schools, four middle schools, and four high schools operated by the Fulton County School System. This includes the Johns Creek High School that opened in 2009; the other three high schools—Centennial, Northview and Chattahoochee—have consistently been ranked as an Outstanding American High School by *U.S. News & World Report.*

Residents have easy access to all of Atlanta's world-class attractions—such as the Georgia Aquarium and the High Museum of Art—but closer to home are the Johns Creek Arts Center, Performing Arts North, the North Atlanta Dance Theatre, and the professional Johns Creek Symphony Orchestra with its regular season and summer music camp.

Quality of life is further enhanced by facilities such as Park Place at Newtown School, an active adult center hosting activities ranging from yoga, Pilates and zumba to meetings of the Johns Creek Veterans Association. Two miles of trails wind through the 46-acre Autrey Mill Nature Preserve & Heritage Center, where a re-created Heritage Village shows mid-19th to mid-20th century rural life in the region. In addition, Native American dwellings including a hunting lodge and tepee can be explored on site. The city operates four additional parks, including a dog park and maintains a network of trails. The Chattahoochie National Park adjoins the city, providing kayaking, trout fishing and other recreation to local residents.

Johns Creek's climate peaks with 87-degree average highs in July, 28-degree average lows in January, with February, March and August as the wettest months.

Rankings

Business/Finance Rankings

- The personal finance site NerdWallet analyzed 183 American metropolitan areas with populations over 250,000 and more than 15,000 businesses to rank where entrepreneurs find the most success. Criteria included area economy, annual income, housing cost, unemployment rate, and the success rate of area businesses. Atlanta* ranked #86. *www.nerdwallet.com, "Best Places to Start a Business," April 27, 2015*

- Based on metro area social media reviews, the employment opinion group Glassdoor surveyed 50 of the largest U.S. metro areas and equally weighed cost of living, hiring opportunity, and job satisfaction to compose a list of "25 Best Cities for Jobs." The Atlanta* metro area was ranked #24 in overall job satisfaction. *www.glassdoor.com, "Best Cities for Jobs," May 19, 2015*

- In a survey of economic confidence in the nation's 50 largest metropolitan areas conducted January–December 2014, the Atlanta* metro area placed #21, according to Gallup's 2014 Economic Confidence Index. *Gallup, "San Jose and San Francisco Lead in Economic Confidence," March 19, 2015*

- The Brookings Institution ranked the 100 largest metro areas in the U.S. based on income inequality. Atlanta* was ranked #36 (#1 = greatest ineqality). Criteria: the "95/20 ratio," a figure representing the income at which a household earns more than 95 percent of all other households, divided by the income at which a household earns more than only 20 percent of all other households. *Brookings Institution, "Income Inequality, 100 Largest U.S. Metro Areas, 2007-2014," January 14, 2016*

- Payscale.com ranked the 20 largest metro areas in terms of wage growth. The Atlanta* metro area ranked #5. Criteria: private-sector wage growth between the 1st quarter of 2015 and the 1st quarter of 2016. *PayScale, "Wage Trends by Metro Area," 1st Quarter, 2016*

- The Atlanta* metro area was identified as one of the most debt-ridden places in America by the finance site Credit.com. The metro area was ranked #8. Criteria: residents' average personal debt load and average credit scores. *Credit.com, "The Most Debt-Ridden Cities," May 1, 2014*

- Atlanta* was identified as one of America's most frugal metro areas by *Coupons.com.* The city ranked #6 out of 25. Criteria: online coupon usage. *Coupons.com, "Top 25 Most Frugal Cities of 2014," May 11, 2015*

- Atlanta* was identified as one of America's most frugal metro areas by *Coupons.com.* The city ranked #3 out of 25. Criteria: Grocery IQ and coupons.com mobile app usage. *Coupons.com, "Top 25 Most On-the-Go Frugal Cities of 2013," April 10, 2014*

- Atlanta* was cited as one of America's top metros for new and expanded facility projects in 2015. The area ranked #8 in the large metro area category (population over 1 million). *Site Selection, "Top Metropolitans of 2015," March 2016*

- The Atlanta* metro area appeared on the Milken Institute "2015 Best Performing Cities" list. Rank: #27 out of 200 large metro areas. Criteria: job growth; wage and salary growth; high-tech output growth. *Milken Institute, "Best-Performing Cities 2015," December 2015*

- *Forbes* ranked the 200 most populous metro areas to determine the nation's "Best Places for Business and Careers." The Atlanta* metro area was ranked #5. Criteria: costs (business and living); job growth (past and projected); income growth; educational attainment (college and high school); projected economic growth; cultural and recreational opportunities; net migration patterns; number of highly ranked colleges. *Forbes, "The Best Places for Business and Careers 2015," July 29, 2015*

Dating/Romance Rankings

- CreditDonkey, a financial education website, sought out the ten best U.S. cities for newlyweds, considering the number of married couples, divorce rate, average credit score, and average number of hours worked per week in metro areas with a million or more residents. The Atlanta* metro area placed #1. *www.creditdonkey.com, "Study: Best Cities for Newlyweds," November 30, 2013*

Education Rankings

- Personal finance website *WalletHub* analyzed the 150 largest U.S. metropolitan statistical areas to determine where the most educated Americans are choosing to settle. Criteria: education quality and attainment gap; education levels; percentage of workers with degrees; public school rankings; quality and size of each metro area's universities. Atlanta* was ranked #34 (#1 = most educated city). *www.WalletHub.com, "2015's Most and Least Educated Cities*

Environmental Rankings

- The Atlanta* metro area came in at #246 for the relative comfort of its climate on Sperling's list of "chill cities," as measured by the Sperling Heat Index. All 361 metro areas are included. Criteria included daytime high temperatures, nighttime low temperatures, dew point, and relative humidity at the high temperatures. *www.bertsperling.com, "Sperling's Chill Cities," July 18, 2013*
- Sperling's BestPlaces assessed 379 metropolitan areas of the United States for the likelihood of dangerously extreme weather events or earthquakes. In general the Southeast and South-Central regions have the highest risk of weather extremes and earthquakes, while the Pacific Northwest enjoys the lowest risk. Of the least risky metropolitan areas, the Atlanta* metro area was ranked #358. *www.bestplaces.net, "Safest Places from Natural Disasters," April 2011*
- The U.S. Environmental Protection Agency (EPA) released a list of U.S. metropolitan areas with the most ENERGY STAR certified buildings in 2015. The Atlanta* metro area was ranked #4 out of 25. *U.S. Environmental Protection Agency, "Top Cities With the Most ENERGY STAR Certified Buildings in 2016," March 30, 2016*

Health/Fitness Rankings

- For each of the 50 most populous metro areas in the United States, the American College of Sports Medicine's American Fitness Index evaluated infrastructure, community assets, and policies that encourage healthy and fit lifestyles, including preventive health behaviors, levels of chronic disease conditions, health care access, and community resources and policies that support physical activity. The Atlanta* metro area ranked #14 for "community fitness." *www.americanfitnessindex.org, "ACSM American Fitness Index Health and Community Fitness Status of the 50 Largest Metropolitan Areas," May 2015*
- The Atlanta* metro area was identified as one of the worst cities for bed bugs in America by pest control company Orkin. The area ranked #19 out of 50 based on the number of bed bug treatments Orkin performed from January to December 2015. *Orkin, "Chicago Tops Bed Bug Cities List for Fourth Year in a Row," January 13, 2016*
- Atlanta* was identified as a "2016 Spring Allergy Capital." The area ranked #70 out of 100. Three groups of factors were used to identify the most severe cities for people with allergies during the spring season: annual pollen levels; medicine utilization; access to board-certified allergists. *Asthma and Allergy Foundation of America, "Spring Allergy Capitals 2016"*
- Atlanta* was identified as a "2015 Asthma Capital." The area ranked #16 out of the nation's 100 largest metropolitan areas. Criteria: estimated prevalence; self-reported prevalence; crude death rate for asthma; annual pollen score; annual air quality; public smoking laws; number of board-certified asthma specialists; school inhaler access laws; rescue medication use; controller medication use; ER visits for asthma; uninsured rate; poverty rate. *Asthma and Allergy Foundation of America, "Asthma Capitals 2015"*
- The Atlanta* metro area ranked #100 out of 190 in The Gallup-Healthways Well-Being Index. Criteria: purpose; social well being; financial health; community and physical health. Results are based on telephone interviews with adults, aged 18 and older, living in metropolitan areas in the 50 U.S. states and the District of Columbia. *Gallup-Healthways, "State of American Well-Being," February 23, 2016*

Real Estate Rankings

- Based on the home-price forecasts compiled by the real-estate valuation firm CoreLogic Case-Shiller, CNNMoney reported that in 2016, the Atlanta* metro area is expected to be one of the hottest housing markets in the U.S. Criteria: residential real estate prices. *money.cnn.com, "The 10 Hottest Housing Markets for 2016," December 3, 2015*

- According to Penske Truck Rental, the Atlanta* metro area was named the #1 moving destination in 2015, based on one-way consumer truck rental reservations made through Penske's website and reservations call center. *blog.gopenske.com, "Penske Truck Rental's 2015 Top Moving Destinations List," February 3, 2016*

- The Atlanta* metro area appeared on Realtor.com's list of the hottest housing markets to watch in 2016. The area ranked #5. Criteria: strong housing growth; affordable prices; and fast-paced sales. *Realtor.com®, "Top 10 Hot Real Estate Markets to Watch in 2016," December 2, 2015*

- Atlanta* was ranked #127 out of 225 metro areas in terms of housing affordability in 2015 by the National Association of Home Builders (#1 = most affordable). Criteria: the share of homes sold in that area affordable to a family earning the local median income, based on standard mortgage underwriting criteria. *National Association of Home Builders®, NAHB-Wells Fargo Housing Opportunity Index, 4th Quarter 2015*

Safety Rankings

- The National Insurance Crime Bureau ranked 380 metro areas in the U.S. in terms of per capita rates of vehicle theft. The Atlanta* metro area ranked #54 (#1 = highest rate). Criteria: number of vehicle theft offenses per 100,000 inhabitants in 2014. *National Insurance Crime Bureau, "Hot Spots 2014," June 24, 2015*

Seniors/Retirement Rankings

- From its Best Cities for Successful Aging indexes, the Milken Institute generated rankings for metropolitan areas, weighing data in eight categories—health care, wellness, living arrangements, transportation, financial characteristics, education and employment opportunities, community engagement, and overall livability. The Atlanta* metro area was ranked #83 overall in the large metro area category. *Milken Institute, "Best Cities for Successful Aging, 2014"*

Transportation Rankings

- The Atlanta* metro area appeared on *Forbes* list of places with the most extreme commutes. The metro area ranked #7 out of 10. Criteria: average travel time; percentage of mega commuters. Mega-commuters travel more than 90 minutes and 50 miles each way to work. *Forbes.com, "The Cities with the Most Extreme Commutes," March 5, 2013*

Miscellaneous Rankings

- The watchdog site Charity Navigator conducts an annual study of charities in the nation's major markets both to analyze statistical differences in their financial, accountability, and transparency practices and to track year-to-year variations in individual communities. The Atlanta* metro area was ranked #23 among the 30 metro markets in the rating dimension of Overall Score. *www.charitynavigator.org, "Metro Market Study 2015," June 5, 2015*

- The Harris Poll's Happiness Index survey revealed that of the top ten U.S. markets, the Atlanta* metro area residents ranked #4 in happiness. Criteria included strong assent to positive statements and strong disagreement with negative ones, and degree of agreement with a series of statements about respondents' personal relationships and general outlook. *www.harrisinteractive.com, "Dallas/Fort Worth Is "Happiest" City among America's Top Ten Markets," September 4, 2013*

- Energizer Personal Care, the makers of Edge® shave gel, in partnership with Sperling's BestPlaces, ranked 50 major metro areas in terms of everyday irritations. The Atlanta* metro area ranked #5 the 50 metro area most iritating to guys. Criteria: high male-to-female ratio; poor sports team performance and high ticket prices; slow traffic; lack of job availability; unaffordable housing; extreme weather; lack of nightlife and fitness options. *Energizer Personal Care, "Most Irritatng Cities for Guys," August 26, 2013*
- Mars Chocolate North America, the makers of COMBOS®, in partnership with Sperling's BestPlaces, ranked 50 major metro areas in terms of their "manliness." The Atlanta* metro area ranked #17. Criteria: number of professional sports teams; number of nearby NASCAR tracks and racing events; manly lifestyle; concentration of manly retail stores; manly occupations per capita; salty snack sales; "Board of Manliness" rankings. *Mars Chocolate North America, "America's Manliest Cities 2012"*
- The Atlanta* metro area was selected as one of "America's Most Miserable Cities" by *Forbes.com.* The metro area ranked #16 out of 20. Criteria: violent crime; unemployment; foreclosures; income and property taxes; home prices; commute times; climate. *Forbes.com, "America's Most Miserable Cities" February 22, 2013*
- The National Alliance to End Homelessness ranked the 100 most populous metro areas with the highest rate of homelessness. The Atlanta* metro area ranked #61. Criteria: number of homeless people per 10,000 population in 2011. *National Alliance to End Homelessness, The State of Homelessness in America 2012*

Johns Creek is located within the Atlanta-Sandy Springs-Roswell, GA Metropolitan Statistical Area.

Business Environment

CITY FINANCES

City Government Finances

Component	2012 ($000)	2012 ($ per capita)
Total Revenues	48,465	631
Total Expenditures	41,471	540
Debt Outstanding	3,181	41
Cash and Securities[1]	15,343	199

Note: (1) Cash and security holdings of a government at the close of its fiscal year, including those of its dependent agencies, utilities, and liquor stores.
Source: U.S Census Bureau, State & Local Government Finances 2012

City Government Revenue by Source

Source	2012 ($000)	2012 ($ per capita)
General Revenue		
From Federal Government	164	2
From State Government	203	2
From Local Governments	15,931	207
Taxes		
Property	16,717	217
Sales and Gross Receipts	8,976	116
Personal Income	0	0
Corporate Income	0	0
Motor Vehicle License	0	0
Other Taxes	3,310	43
Current Charges	1,607	20
Liquor Store	0	0
Utility	0	0
Employee Retirement	0	0

Source: U.S Census Bureau, State & Local Government Finances 2012

City Government Expenditures by Function

Function	2012 ($000)	2012 ($ per capita)	2012 (%)
General Direct Expenditures			
Air Transportation	0	0	0.0
Corrections	0	0	0.0
Education	0	0	0.0
Employment Security Administration	0	0	0.0
Financial Administration	1,009	13	2.4
Fire Protection	9,912	129	23.9
General Public Buildings	1,377	17	3.3
Governmental Administration, Other	5,737	74	13.8
Health	0	0	0.0
Highways	8,525	111	20.5
Hospitals	0	0	0.0
Housing and Community Development	2,879	37	6.9
Interest on General Debt	228	2	0.5
Judicial and Legal	1,047	13	2.5
Libraries	0	0	0.0
Parking	0	0	0.0
Parks and Recreation	1,513	19	3.6
Police Protection	8,690	113	20.9
Public Welfare	0	0	0.0
Sewerage	0	0	0.0
Solid Waste Management	0	0	0.0
Veterans' Services	0	0	0.0
Liquor Store	0	0	0.0
Utility	0	0	0.0
Employee Retirement	0	0	0.0

Source: U.S Census Bureau, State & Local Government Finances 2012

DEMOGRAPHICS

Population Growth

Area	1990 Census	2000 Census	2010 Census	2014* Estimate	Population Growth (%) 1990-2014	Population Growth (%) 2010-2014
City	n/a	n/a	76,728	80,979	n/a	5.5
MSA[1]	3,069,411	4,247,981	5,268,860	5,455,053	77.7	3.5
U.S.	248,709,873	281,421,906	308,745,538	314,107,084	26.3	1.7

Note: (1) Figures cover the Atlanta-Sandy Springs-Roswell, GA Metropolitan Statistical Area—see Appendix B for areas included; (*) 2010-2014 5-year estimated population
Source: U.S. Census Bureau, 1990 Census, Census 2000, Census 2010, 2010-2014 American Community Survey 5-Year Estimates

Household Size

Area	Persons in Household (%) One	Two	Three	Four	Five	Six	Seven or More	Average Household Size
City	16.9	26.8	20.5	24.3	8.0	1.9	1.1	3.10
MSA[1]	26.5	31.3	16.8	14.7	6.5	2.4	1.4	2.77
U.S.	27.5	33.5	15.8	13.1	6.0	2.3	1.4	2.64

Note: (1) Figures cover the Atlanta-Sandy Springs-Roswell, GA Metropolitan Statistical Area—see Appendix B for areas included
Source: U.S. Census Bureau, 2010-2014 American Community Survey 5-Year Estimates

Race

Area	White Alone[2] (%)	Black Alone[2] (%)	Asian Alone[2] (%)	AIAN[3] Alone[2] (%)	NHOPI[4] Alone[2] (%)	Other Race Alone[2] (%)	Two or More Races (%)
City	62.6	10.9	22.5	0.2	0.0	0.9	2.8
MSA[1]	56.1	32.9	5.2	0.3	0.0	3.4	2.2
U.S.	73.8	12.6	5.0	0.8	0.2	4.7	2.9

Note: (1) Figures cover the Atlanta-Sandy Springs-Roswell, GA Metropolitan Statistical Area—see Appendix B for areas included; (2) Alone is defined as not being in combination with one or more other races; (3) American Indian and Alaska Native; (4) Native Hawaiian and Other Pacific Islander
Source: U.S. Census Bureau, 2010-2014 American Community Survey 5-Year Estimates

Hispanic or Latino Origin

Area	Total (%)	Mexican (%)	Puerto Rican (%)	Cuban (%)	Other (%)
City	5.5	2.2	0.6	0.6	2.2
MSA[1]	10.4	5.9	0.9	0.4	3.2
U.S.	16.9	10.8	1.6	0.6	3.8

Note: Persons of Hispanic or Latino origin can be of any race; (1) Figures cover the Atlanta-Sandy Springs-Roswell, GA Metropolitan Statistical Area—see Appendix B for areas included
Source: U.S. Census Bureau, 2010-2014 American Community Survey 5-Year Estimates

Ancestry

Area	German	Irish	English	American	Italian	Polish	French[2]	Scottish	Dutch
City	10.4	9.1	9.0	5.6	4.6	2.5	2.4	1.8	1.0
MSA[1]	7.4	7.5	7.5	9.8	2.6	1.3	1.5	1.8	0.8
U.S.	14.9	10.8	8.0	7.1	5.5	3.0	2.7	1.7	1.4

Note: Figures are the percentage of the total population reporting a particular ancestry. The nine most commonly reported ancestries in the U.S. are shown. Figures include multiple ancestries (e.g. if a person reported being Irish and Italian, they were included in both columns); (1) Figures cover the Atlanta-Sandy Springs-Roswell, GA Metropolitan Statistical Area—see Appendix B for areas included; (2) Excludes Basque
Source: U.S. Census Bureau, 2010-2014 American Community Survey 5-Year Estimates

Foreign-Born Population

Area	Any Foreign Country	Asia	Mexico	Europe	Carribean	Central America[2]	South America	Africa	Canada
	Percent of Population Born in								
City	25.4	17.4	1.0	3.1	0.5	0.2	1.3	0.8	0.5
MSA[1]	13.3	4.0	3.1	1.2	1.4	1.1	0.9	1.3	0.2
U.S.	13.1	3.8	3.7	1.5	1.2	1.0	0.9	0.6	0.3

Note: (1) Figures cover the Atlanta-Sandy Springs-Roswell, GA Metropolitan Statistical Area—see Appendix B for areas included; (2) Excludes Mexico.
Source: U.S. Census Bureau, 2010-2014 American Community Survey 5-Year Estimates

Marital Status

Area	Never Married	Now Married[2]	Separated	Widowed	Divorced
City	23.3	64.6	1.3	3.4	7.4
MSA[1]	34.1	47.8	2.3	4.7	11.1
U.S.	32.5	48.4	2.2	5.9	10.9

Note: Figures are percentages and cover the population 15 years of age and older; (1) Figures cover the Atlanta-Sandy Springs-Roswell, GA Metropolitan Statistical Area—see Appendix B for areas included; (2) Excludes separated
Source: U.S. Census Bureau, 2010-2014 American Community Survey 5-Year Estimates

Disability Status

Area	All Ages	Under 18 Years Old	18 to 64 Years Old	65 Years and Over
City	4.7	4.0	3.3	18.3
MSA[1]	9.8	3.3	8.5	35.2
U.S.	12.3	4.1	10.2	36.3

Note: Figures show percent of the civilian noninstitutionalized population that reported having a disability. Disability status is determined from from six types of difficulty: vision, hearing, cognitive, ambulatory, self-care, and independent living. For children under 5 years old, hearing and vision difficulty are used to determine disability status. For children between the ages of 5 and 14, disability status is determined from hearing, vision, cognitive, ambulatory, and self-care difficulties. For people aged 15 years and older, they are considered to have a disability if they have difficulty with any one of the six difficulty types; (1) Figures cover the Atlanta-Sandy Springs-Roswell, GA Metropolitan Statistical Area—see Appendix B for areas included.
Source: U.S. Census Bureau, 2010-2014 American Community Survey 5-Year Estimates

Age

Area	Under Age 5	Age 5–19	Age 20–34	Age 35–44	Age 45–54	Age 55–64	Age 65–74	Age 75–84	Age 85+	Median Age
	Percent of Population									
City	6.3	26.1	12.5	16.3	18.7	12.1	5.2	2.0	0.8	38.7
MSA[1]	6.9	21.7	20.7	15.2	14.6	10.9	6.1	2.8	1.0	35.4
U.S.	6.4	19.9	20.6	13.0	14.1	12.3	7.6	4.3	1.9	37.4

Note: (1) Figures cover the Atlanta-Sandy Springs-Roswell, GA Metropolitan Statistical Area—see Appendix B for areas included
Source: U.S. Census Bureau, 2010-2014 American Community Survey 5-Year Estimates

Gender

Area	Males	Females	Males per 100 Females
City	39,833	41,146	96.8
MSA[1]	2,649,723	2,805,330	94.5
U.S.	154,515,159	159,591,925	96.8

Note: (1) Figures cover the Atlanta-Sandy Springs-Roswell, GA Metropolitan Statistical Area—see Appendix B for areas included
Source: U.S. Census Bureau, 2010-2014 American Community Survey 5-Year Estimates

Religious Groups by Family

Area	Catholic	Baptist	Non-Den.	Methodist²	Lutheran	LDS³	Pente-costal	Presby-terian⁴	Muslim⁵	Judaism
MSA¹	7.4	17.4	6.8	7.8	0.5	0.7	2.6	1.8	0.7	0.5
U.S.	19.1	9.3	4.0	4.0	2.3	2.0	1.9	1.6	0.8	0.7

Note: Figures are the number of adherents as a percentage of the total population; (1) Figures cover the Atlanta-Sandy Springs-Marietta, GA Metropolitan Statistical Area—see Appendix B for areas included; (2) Methodist/Pietist; (3) Latter Day Saints; (4) Reformed; (5) Figures are estimates
Source: Association of Statisticians of American Religious Bodies, 2010 U.S. Religion Census: Religious Congregations & Membership Study

Religious Groups by Tradition

Area	Catholic	Evangelical Protestant	Mainline Protestant	Other Tradition	Black Protestant	Orthodox
MSA¹	7.4	26.0	9.8	2.9	3.1	0.2
U.S.	19.1	16.2	7.3	4.3	1.6	0.3

Note: Figures are the number of adherents as a percentage of the total population; (1) Figures cover the Atlanta-Sandy Springs-Marietta, GA Metropolitan Statistical Area—see Appendix B for areas included
Source: Association of Statisticians of American Religious Bodies, 2010 U.S. Religion Census: Religious Congregations & Membership Study

ECONOMY

Gross Metropolitan Product

Area	2013	2014	2015	2016	Rank²
MSA¹	307.2	321.1	335.5	354.0	10

Note: Figures are in billions of dollars; (1) Figures cover the Atlanta-Sandy Springs-Roswell, GA Metropolitan Statistical Area—see Appendix B for areas included; (2) Rank is based on 2016 data and ranges from 1 to 381
Source: The U.S. Conference of Mayors, U.S. Metro Economies: GMP and Employment 2014-2016, June 2015

Economic Growth

Area	2011-13 (%)	2014 (%)	2015 (%)	2016 (%)	Rank²
MSA¹	1.8	2.8	3.1	3.5	33
U.S.	2.2	2.4	2.3	2.9	–

Note: Figures are real gross metropolitan product (GMP) growth rates and represent annual average percent change; (1) Figures cover the Atlanta-Sandy Springs-Roswell, GA Metropolitan Statistical Area—see Appendix B for areas included; (2) Rank is based on 2016 data and ranges from 1 to 381
Source: The U.S. Conference of Mayors, U.S. Metro Economies: GMP and Employment 2014-2016, June 2015

Metropolitan Area Exports

Area	2009	2010	2011	2012	2013	2014	Rank²
MSA¹	13,405.8	15,009.6	17,229.0	18,169.0	18,827.8	19,870.2	18

Note: Figures are in millions of dollars; (1) Figures cover the Atlanta-Sandy Springs-Roswell, GA Metropolitan Statistical Area—see Appendix B for areas included; (2) Rank is based on 2014 data and ranges from 1 to 385
Source: U.S. Department of Commerce, International Trade Administration, Office of Trade & Industry Information, Manufacturing & Services, data extracted March 10, 2016

Building Permits

Area	Single-Family			Multi-Family			Total		
	2014	2015ᵖ	Pct. Chg.	2014	2015ᵖ	Pct. Chg.	2014	2015ᵖ	Pct. Chg.
City	125	292	133.6	0	0	-	125	292	133.6
MSA¹	16,984	19,885	17.1	9,699	10,126	4.4	26,683	30,011	12.5
U.S.	640,300	690,800	7.9	411,800	487,600	18.4	1,052,100	1,178,400	12.0

Note: (1) Figures cover the Atlanta-Sandy Springs-Roswell, GA Metropolitan Statistical Area—see Appendix B for areas included; Figures represent new, privately-owned housing units authorized (unadjusted data); All permit data are based on estimates with imputation; (p) preliminary data.
Source: U.S. Census Bureau, Manufacturing, Mining, and Construction Statistics, Building Permits, 2014, 2015

Bankruptcy Filings

Area	Business Filings 2014	Business Filings 2015	Business Filings % Chg.	Nonbusiness Filings 2014	Nonbusiness Filings 2015	Nonbusiness Filings % Chg.
Fulton County	161	138	-14.3	5,080	4,863	-4.3
U.S.	26,983	24,735	-8.3	909,812	819,760	-9.9

Note: Business filings include Chapter 7, Chapter 11, Chapter 12, and Chapter 13; Nonbusiness filings include Chapter 7, Chapter 11, and Chapter 13
Source: Administrative Office of the U.S. Courts, Business and Nonbusiness Bankruptcy, County Cases Commenced by Chapter of the Bankruptcy Code, During the 12- Month Period Ending December 31, 2014 and Business and Nonbusiness Bankruptcy, County Cases Commenced by Chapter of the Bankruptcy Code, During the 12- Month Period Ending December 31, 2015

Housing Vacancy Rates

Area	Gross Vacancy Rate[2] (%)			Year-Round Vacancy Rate[3] (%)			Rental Vacancy Rate[4] (%)			Homeowner Vacancy Rate[5] (%)		
	2013	2014	2015	2013	2014	2015	2013	2014	2015	2013	2014	2015
MSA[1]	12.4	11.0	11.0	11.8	10.3	10.7	10.2	8.8	8.2	2.1	2.5	2.2
U.S.	13.6	13.4	12.9	10.7	10.4	10.0	8.3	7.6	7.1	2.0	1.9	1.8

Note: (1) Figures cover the Atlanta-Sandy Springs-Roswell, GA Metropolitan Statistical Area—see Appendix B for areas included; (2) The percentage of the total housing inventory that is vacant; (3) The percentage of the housing inventory (excluding seasonal units) that is year-round vacant; (4) The percentage of rental inventory that is vacant for rent; (5) The percentage of homeowner inventory that is vacant for sale
Source: U.S. Census Bureau, Housing Vacancies and Homeownership Annual Statistics: 2015

INCOME

Income

Area	Per Capita ($)	Median Household ($)	Average Household ($)
City	43,998	108,114	132,303
MSA[1]	28,880	56,618	78,422
U.S.	28,555	53,482	74,596

Note: (1) Figures cover the Atlanta-Sandy Springs-Roswell, GA Metropolitan Statistical Area—see Appendix B for areas included
Source: U.S. Census Bureau, 2010-2014 American Community Survey 5-Year Estimates

Household Income Distribution

Area	Percent of Households Earning							
	Under $15,000	$15,000 -24,999	$25,000 -34,999	$35,000 -49,999	$50,000 -74,999	$75,000 -99,000	$100,000 -149,999	$150,000 and up
City	4.2	4.2	3.9	7.0	15.2	11.9	21.0	32.6
MSA[1]	11.2	9.5	9.9	13.7	18.3	12.4	13.7	11.3
U.S.	12.5	10.7	10.2	13.5	17.8	12.2	13.0	10.0

Note: (1) Figures cover the Atlanta-Sandy Springs-Roswell, GA Metropolitan Statistical Area—see Appendix B for areas included
Source: U.S. Census Bureau, 2010-2014 American Community Survey 5-Year Estimates

Poverty Rate

Area	All Ages	Under 18 Years Old	18 to 64 Years Old	65 Years and Over
City	4.6	4.5	4.4	6.3
MSA[1]	15.7	22.2	14.0	9.6
U.S.	15.6	21.9	14.6	9.4

Note: Figures are percentage of people whose income during the past 12 months was below the poverty level; (1) Figures cover the Atlanta-Sandy Springs-Roswell, GA Metropolitan Statistical Area—see Appendix B for areas included
Source: U.S. Census Bureau, 2010-2014 American Community Survey 5-Year Estimates

EMPLOYMENT

Labor Force and Employment

Area	Civilian Labor Force			Workers Employed		
	Dec. 2014	Dec. 2015	% Chg.	Dec. 2014	Dec. 2015	% Chg.
City	42,889	43,443	1.2	40,992	41,735	1.8
MSA[1]	2,815,375	2,835,654	0.7	2,647,261	2,695,404	1.8
U.S.	155,521,000	157,245,000	1.1	147,190,000	149,703,000	1.7

Note: Data is not seasonally adjusted and covers workers 16 years of age and older; (1) Figures cover the Atlanta-Sandy Springs-Roswell, GA Metropolitan Statistical Area—see Appendix B for areas included
Source: Bureau of Labor Statistics, Local Area Unemployment Statistics

Unemployment Rate

Area	2015											
	Jan.	Feb.	Mar.	Apr.	May	Jun.	Jul.	Aug.	Sep.	Oct.	Nov.	Dec.
City	4.7	4.6	4.5	4.3	4.6	4.9	4.9	4.6	4.5	4.3	3.9	3.9
MSA[1]	6.2	6.1	5.9	5.6	5.9	6.0	6.1	5.6	5.5	5.4	4.9	4.9
U.S.	6.1	5.8	5.6	5.1	5.3	5.5	5.6	5.2	4.9	4.8	4.8	4.8

Note: Data is not seasonally adjusted and covers workers 16 years of age and older; (1) Figures cover the Atlanta-Sandy Springs-Roswell, GA Metropolitan Statistical Area—see Appendix B for areas included
Source: Bureau of Labor Statistics, Local Area Unemployment Statistics

Employment by Occupation

Occupation Classification	City (%)	MSA[1] (%)	U.S. (%)
Management, Business, Science, and Arts	58.9	39.4	36.4
Natural Resources, Construction, and Maintenance	3.4	8.1	9.0
Production, Transportation, and Material Moving	3.6	10.9	12.1
Sales and Office	22.2	25.6	24.4
Service	12.0	16.0	18.2

Note: Figures cover employed civilians 16 years of age and older; (1) Figures cover the Atlanta-Sandy Springs-Roswell, GA Metropolitan Statistical Area—see Appendix B for areas included
Source: U.S. Census Bureau, 2010-2014 American Community Survey 5-Year Estimates

Employment by Industry

Sector	MSA[1]		U.S.
	Number of Employees	Percent of Total	Percent of Total
Construction	111,700	4.2	4.5
Education and Health Services	323,700	12.2	15.7
Financial Activities	163,400	6.1	5.7
Government	326,200	12.3	15.5
Information	87,400	3.3	1.9
Leisure and Hospitality	275,800	10.4	10.4
Manufacturing	161,300	6.1	8.6
Mining and Logging	1,500	<0.1	0.5
Other Services	98,700	3.7	3.9
Professional and Business Services	489,600	18.5	13.9
Retail Trade	301,200	11.3	11.3
Transportation, Warehousing, and Utilities	144,200	5.4	3.9
Wholesale Trade	159,100	6.0	4.1

Note: Figures are non-farm employment as of December 2015. Figures are not seasonally adjusted and include workers 16 years of age and older; (1) Figures cover the Atlanta-Sandy Springs-Roswell, GA Metropolitan Statistical Area—see Appendix B for areas included
Source: Bureau of Labor Statistics, Current Employment Statistics, Employment, Hours, and Earnings

Occupations with Greatest Projected Employment Growth: 2012 – 2022

Occupation[1]	2012 Employment	2022 Projected Employment	Numeric Employment Change	Percent Employment Change
Combined Food Preparation and Serving Workers, Including Fast Food	169,450	192,830	23,380	13.8
Customer Service Representatives	95,900	115,410	19,510	20.3
Laborers and Freight, Stock, and Material Movers, Hand	85,460	104,150	18,690	21.9
Elementary School Teachers, Except Special Education	42,300	56,170	13,870	32.8
General and Operations Managers	71,410	84,890	13,480	18.9
Sales Representatives, Wholesale and Manufacturing, Except Technical and Scientific Products	56,220	67,450	11,230	20.0
Secretaries and Administrative Assistants, Except Legal, Medical, and Executive	51,850	63,030	11,180	21.6
Office Clerks, General	79,920	91,010	11,090	13.9
Janitors and Cleaners, Except Maids and Housekeeping Cleaners	52,860	63,600	10,740	20.3
Childcare Workers	37,650	48,280	10,630	28.2

Note: Projections cover Georgia; (1) Sorted by numeric employment change
Source: www.projectionscentral.com, State Occupational Projections, 2012–2022 Long-Term Projections

Fastest Growing Occupations: 2012 – 2022

Occupation[1]	2012 Employment	2022 Projected Employment	Numeric Employment Change	Percent Employment Change
Physician Assistants	2,820	4,740	1,920	67.9
Health Specialties Teachers, Postsecondary	4,870	8,060	3,190	65.5
Agents and Business Managers of Artists, Performers, and Athletes	430	700	270	62.6
Personal Care Aides	16,440	26,630	10,190	62.0
Interpreters and Translators	1,650	2,630	980	58.9
Nursing Instructors and Teachers, Postsecondary	1,420	2,200	780	55.5
Psychiatric Aides	1,390	2,150	760	55.3
Home Health Aides	7,950	12,340	4,390	55.1
Nurse Practitioners	3,260	5,010	1,750	53.9
Nurse Midwives	250	380	130	53.6

Note: Projections cover Georgia; (1) Sorted by percent employment change and excludes occupations with numeric employment change less than 100
Source: www.projectionscentral.com, State Occupational Projections, 2012–2022 Long-Term Projections

Average Wages

Occupation	$/Hr.	Occupation	$/Hr.
Accountants and Auditors	38.06	Maids and Housekeeping Cleaners	9.32
Automotive Mechanics	19.15	Maintenance and Repair Workers	18.24
Bookkeepers	19.46	Marketing Managers	64.91
Carpenters	19.77	Nuclear Medicine Technologists	35.79
Cashiers	9.38	Nurses, Licensed Practical	19.58
Clerks, General Office	14.20	Nurses, Registered	31.73
Clerks, Receptionists/Information	14.19	Nursing Assistants	11.41
Clerks, Shipping/Receiving	14.09	Packers and Packagers, Hand	10.96
Computer Programmers	40.72	Physical Therapists	39.70
Computer Systems Analysts	42.17	Postal Service Mail Carriers	24.82
Computer User Support Specialists	25.87	Real Estate Brokers	51.40
Cooks, Restaurant	11.38	Retail Salespersons	11.85
Dentists	83.66	Sales Reps., Exc. Tech./Scientific	32.41
Electrical Engineers	43.06	Sales Reps., Tech./Scientific	39.40
Electricians	22.23	Secretaries, Exc. Legal/Med./Exec.	17.34
Financial Managers	68.91	Security Guards	12.62
First-Line Supervisors/Managers, Sales	19.56	Surgeons	128.18
Food Preparation Workers	9.93	Teacher Assistants*	10.47
General and Operations Managers	60.10	Teachers, Elementary School*	26.05
Hairdressers/Cosmetologists	13.42	Teachers, Secondary School*	27.22
Internists	129.01	Telemarketers	14.98
Janitors and Cleaners	11.57	Truck Drivers, Heavy/Tractor-Trailer	19.95
Landscaping/Groundskeeping Workers	12.98	Truck Drivers, Light/Delivery Svcs.	17.48
Lawyers	66.05	Waiters and Waitresses	9.22

Note: Wage data covers the Atlanta-Sandy Springs-Marietta, GA Metropolitan Statistical Area—see Appendix B for areas included; (*) Hourly wages for elementary/secondary school teachers and teacher assistants were calculated by the editors from annual wage data based on a 40 hour work week; n/a not available.
Source: Bureau of Labor Statistics, Metro Area Occupational Employment and Wage Estimates, May 2015

TAXES

State Corporate Income Tax Rates

State	Tax Rate (%)	Income Brackets ($)	Num. of Brackets	Financial Institution Tax Rate (%)[a]	Federal Income Tax Ded.
Georgia	6.0	Flat rate	1	6.0	No

Note: Tax rates as of January 1, 2016; (a) Rates listed are the corporate income tax rate applied to financial institutions or excise taxes based on income. Some states have other taxes based upon the value of deposits or shares.
Source: Federation of Tax Administrators, "State Corporate Income Tax Rates, 2016"

State Individual Income Tax Rates

State	Tax Rate (%)	Income Brackets ($)	Num. of Brackets	Personal Exempt. ($)[1]		Fed. Inc. Tax Ded.
				Single	Dependents	
Georgia	1.0 - 6.0	750 - 7,001 (h)	6	2,700	3,000	No

Note: Tax rates as of January 1, 2016; Local- and county-level taxes are not included; n/a not applicable; (1) Married joint filers generally receive double the single exemption; (h) The Georgia income brackets reported are for single individuals. For married couples filing jointly, the same tax rates apply to income brackets ranging from $1,000, to $10,000.
Source: Federation of Tax Administrators, "State Individual Income Tax Rates, 2016"

Various State and Local Tax Rates

State	State and Local Sales and Use (%)	State Sales and Use (%)	Gasoline[1] (¢/gal.)	Cigarette[2] ($/pack)	Spirits[3] ($/gal.)	Wine[4] ($/gal.)	Beer[5] ($/gal.)
Georgia	7.00	4.0	31.02	0.37	3.79 (f)	1.51 (l)	0.48 (q)(r)

Note: All tax rates as of January 1, 2016; (1) The American Petroleum Institute has developed a methodology for determining the average tax rate on a gallon of fuel. Rates may include any of the following: excise taxes, environmental fees, storage tank fees, other fees or taxes, general sales tax, and local taxes. In states where gasoline is subject to the general sales tax, or where the fuel tax is based on the average sale price, the average rate determined by API is sensitive to changes in the price of gasoline. States that fully or partially apply general sales taxes to gasoline: CA, CO, GA, IL, IN, MI, NY; (2) The federal excise tax of $1.0066 per pack and local taxes are not included; (3) Rates are those applicable to off-premise sales of 40% alcohol by volume (a.b.v.) distilled spirits in 750ml containers. Local excise taxes are excluded; (4) Rates are those applicable to off-premise sales of 11% a.b.v. non-carbonated wine in 750ml containers; (5) Rates are those applicable to off-premise sales of 4.7% a.b.v. beer in 12 ounce containers; (f) Different rates are also applicable according to alcohol content, place of production, size of container, or place purchased (on- or off-premise or onboard airlines); (l) Different rates also applicable according to alcohol content, place of production, size of container, place purchased (on- or off-premise or on board airlines) or type of wine (carbonated, vermouth, etc.); (q) Different rates are also applicable according to alcohol content, place of production, size of container, or place purchased (on- or off-premise or onboard airlines); (r) Includes the statewide local rate in Alabama ($0.52) and Georgia ($0.53).
Source: Tax Foundation, 2016 Facts & Figures: How Does Your State Compare?

State Business Tax Climate Index Rankings

State	Overall Rank	Corporate Tax Rank	Individual Income Tax Rank	Sales Tax Rank	Unemployment Insurance Tax Rank	Property Tax Rank
Georgia	39	9	42	35	37	31

Note: The index is a measure of how each state's tax laws affect economic performance. The lower the rank, the more favorable a state's tax system is for business. States without a given tax are given a ranking of 1. The scores/rankings for the District of Columbia do not affect other states. The 2016 index represents the tax climate as of July 1, 2015 (the beginning of Fiscal Year 2016).
Source: Tax Foundation, State Business Tax Climate Index 2016

TRANSPORTATION

Means of Transportation to Work

Area	Car/Truck/Van		Public Transportation			Bicycle	Walked	Other Means	Worked at Home
	Drove Alone	Car-pooled	Bus	Subway	Railroad				
City	77.4	8.2	0.1	0.4	0.1	0.1	1.2	0.9	11.5
MSA[1]	77.9	10.4	2.2	0.7	0.1	0.2	1.4	1.4	5.8
U.S.	76.4	9.6	2.6	1.8	0.6	0.6	2.8	1.3	4.4

Note: Figures are percentages and cover workers 16 years of age and older; (1) Figures cover the Atlanta-Sandy Springs-Roswell, GA Metropolitan Statistical Area—see Appendix B for areas included
Source: U.S. Census Bureau, 2010-2014 American Community Survey 5-Year Estimates

Travel Time to Work

Area	Less Than 10 Minutes	10 to 19 Minutes	20 to 29 Minutes	30 to 44 Minutes	45 to 59 Minutes	60 to 89 Minutes	90 Minutes or More
City	7.8	23.2	18.9	23.6	14.3	9.2	3.1
MSA[1]	7.8	23.4	20.4	24.7	11.9	8.8	3.0
U.S.	13.3	29.6	21.0	20.2	7.7	5.7	2.6

Note: Figures are percentages and include workers 16 years old and over; (1) Figures cover the Atlanta-Sandy Springs-Roswell, GA Metropolitan Statistical Area—see Appendix B for areas included
Source: U.S. Census Bureau, 2010-2014 American Community Survey 5-Year Estimates

Freeway Travel Time Index

Area	1985	1990	1995	2000	2005	2010	2014
Urban Area Rank[1,2]	24	21	13	19	21	25	25
Urban Area Index[1]	1.11	1.15	1.22	1.24	1.26	1.23	1.24
Average Index[3]	1.09	1.11	1.14	1.17	1.20	1.19	1.20

Note: Freeway Travel Time Index—the ratio of travel time in the peak period to the travel time at free-flow conditions. For example, a value of 1.30 indicates a 20-minute free-flow trip takes 26 minutes in the peak (20 minutes x 1.30 = 26 minutes); (1) Covers the Atlanta GA urban area; (2) Rank is based on 101 urban areas (#1 = highest travel time index); (3) Average of 101 urban areas
Source: Texas Transportation Institute, 2015 Urban Mobility Scorecard, August 2015

Freeway Commuter Stress Index

Area	1985	1990	1995	2000	2005	2010	2014
Urban Area Rank[1,2]	24	22	13	16	18	22	23
Urban Area Index[1]	1.18	1.22	1.29	1.32	1.33	1.31	1.32
Average Index[3]	1.13	1.16	1.19	1.22	1.25	1.24	1.25

Note: The Freeway Commuter Stress Index is the same as the Freeway Travel Time Index (see table above) except that it includes only the travel in the peak directions during the peak periods; the TTI includes travel in all directions during the peak period. Thus, the CSI is more indicative of the work trip experienced by each commuter on a daily basis. (1) Covers the Atlanta GA urban area; (2) Rank is based on 101 urban areas (#1 = highest stress index); (3) Average of 101 urban areas

Source: Texas Transportation Institute, 2015 Urban Mobility Scorecard, August 2015

Living Environment

COST OF LIVING

Cost of Living Index

Composite Index	Groceries	Housing	Utilities	Transportation	Health Care	Misc. Goods/ Services
99.9	103.7	97.8	93.6	104.8	101.4	100.4

Note: The Cost of Living Index measures regional differences in the cost of consumer goods and services, excluding taxes and non-consumer expenditures, for professional and managerial households in the top income quintile. It is based on more than 50,000 prices covering almost 60 different items for which prices are collected three times a year by chambers of commerce, economic development organizations or university applied economic centers in each participating urban area. The numbers shown should be read as a percentage above or below the national average of 100. For example, a value of 115.4 in the groceries column indicates that grocery prices are 15.4% higher than the national average. Small differences in the index numbers should not be interpreted as significant; Figures cover the Atlanta GA urban area.
Source: The Council for Community and Economic Research, ACCRA Cost of Living Index, 2015

Grocery Prices

Area[1]	T-Bone Steak ($/pound)	Frying Chicken ($/pound)	Whole Milk ($/half gal.)	Eggs ($/dozen)	Orange Juice ($/64 oz.)	Coffee ($/11.5 oz.)
City[2]	12.83	1.42	2.30	2.07	3.75	4.58
Avg.	10.99	1.43	2.25	2.26	3.58	4.48
Min.	7.16	0.98	1.30	1.35	2.88	2.98
Max.	14.13	2.43	3.85	4.81	6.39	7.56

Note: (1) Values for the local area are compared with the average, minimum and maximum values for all 292 areas in the Cost of Living Index; (2) Figures cover the Atlanta GA urban area; **T-Bone Steak** *(price per pound);* **Frying Chicken** *(price per pound, whole fryer);* **Whole Milk** *(half gallon carton);* **Eggs** *(price per dozen, Grade A, large);* **Orange Juice** *(64 oz. Tropicana or Florida Natural);* **Coffee** *(11.5 oz. can, vacuum-packed, Maxwell House, Hills Bros, or Folgers).*
Source: The Council for Community and Economic Research, ACCRA Cost of Living Index, 2015

Housing and Utility Costs

Area[1]	New Home Price ($)	Apartment Rent ($/month)	All Electric ($/month)	Part Electric ($/month)	Other Energy ($/month)	Telephone ($/month)
City[2]	289,012	1,050	-	88.79	57.58	29.30
Avg.	312,874	945	179.30	95.07	72.96	28.11
Min.	178,682	479	116.28	43.14	26.46	10.01
Max.	1,472,476	3,984	504.25	189.44	421.11	43.06

Note: (1) Values for the local area are compared with the average, minimum and maximum values for all 292 areas in the Cost of Living Index; (2) Figures cover the Atlanta GA urban area; **New Home Price** *(2,400 sf living area, 8,000 sf lot, in urban area with full utilities);* **Apartment Rent** *(950 sf 2 bedroom/1.5 or 2 bath, unfurnished, excluding all utilities except water);* **All Electric** *(average monthly cost for an all-electric home);* **Part Electric** *(average monthly cost for a part-electric home);* **Other Energy** *(average monthly cost for natural gas, fuel oil, coal, wood, and any other forms of energy except electricity);* **Telephone** *(price includes basic monthly rate for a private residential line plus additional local usage charges incurred by a family of four).*
Source: The Council for Community and Economic Research, ACCRA Cost of Living Index, 2015

Health Care, Transportation, and Other Costs

Area[1]	Doctor ($/visit)	Dentist ($/visit)	Optometrist ($/visit)	Gasoline ($/gallon)	Beauty Salon ($/visit)	Men's Shirt ($)
City[2]	95.50	102.54	89.05	2.46	45.03	24.26
Avg.	105.15	89.02	99.78	2.38	35.30	28.10
Min.	66.87	56.09	48.53	1.95	18.91	13.38
Max.	182.34	150.36	228.33	4.09	67.91	63.80

Note: (1) Values for the local area are compared with the average, minimum and maximum values for all 292 areas in the Cost of Living Index; (2) Figures cover the Atlanta GA urban area; **Doctor** *(general practitioners routine exam of an established patient);* **Dentist** *(adult teeth cleaning and periodic oral examination);* **Optometrist** *(full vision eye exam for established adult patient);* **Gasoline** *(one gallon regular unleaded, national brand, including all taxes, cash price at self-service pump if available);* **Beauty Salon** *(woman's shampoo, trim, and blow-dry);* **Men's Shirt** *(cotton/polyester dress shirt, pinpoint weave, long sleeves).*
Source: The Council for Community and Economic Research, ACCRA Cost of Living Index, 2015

HOUSING

House Price Index (HPI)

Area	National Ranking[2]	Quarterly Change (%)	One-Year Change (%)	Five-Year Change (%)
MSA[1]	49	0.70	7.90	16.00
U.S.[3]	–	1.45	5.76	22.85

Note: The HPI is a weighted repeat sales index. It measures average price changes in repeat sales or refinancings on the same properties. This information is obtained by reviewing repeat mortgage transactions on single-family properties whose mortgages have been purchased or securitized by Fannie Mae or Freddie Mac in January 1975; (1) Atlanta-Sandy Springs-Roswell Metropolitan Statistical Area—see Appendix B for areas included; (2) Rankings are based on annual percentage change for all metro areas containing at least 15,000 transactions over the last 10 years and ranges from 1 to 266; (3) figures based on a weighted average of Census Division estimates using a seasonally adjusted, purchase-only index; all figures are for the period ending December 31, 2015

Source: Federal Housing Finance Agency, House Price Index, February 25, 2016

Median Single-Family Home Prices

Area	2013	2014	2015p	Percent Change 2014 to 2015
MSA[1]	139.5	159.5	173.6	8.8
U.S. Average	197.4	208.9	223.9	7.2

Note: Figures are median sales prices of existing single-family homes in thousands of dollars; (p) preliminary; n/a not available; (1) Atlanta-Sandy Springs-Roswell, GA Metropolitan Statistical Area—see Appendix B for areas included

Source: National Association of Realtors, Median Sales Price of Existing Single-Family Homes for Metropolitan Areas, 4th Quarter 2015

Qualifying Income Based on Median Sales Price of Existing Single-Family Homes

Area	With 5% Down ($)	With 10% Down ($)	With 20% Down ($)
MSA[1]	37,635	35,654	31,693
U.S. Average	49,535	46,928	41,714

Note: Figures are preliminary; Qualifying income is based on a mortgage rate of 4.1%. Monthly principal and interest payment is limited to 25% of income; n/a not available; (1) Atlanta-Sandy Springs-Roswell, GA Metropolitan Statistical Area—see Appendix B for areas included

Source: National Association of Realtors, Qualifying Income Based on Median Sales Price of Existing Single-Family Homes for Metropolitan Areas, 4th Quarter 2015

Median Apartment Condo-Coop Home Prices

Area	2013	2014	2015p	Percent Change 2014 to 2015
MSA[1]	117.3	136.3	156.9	15.1
U.S. Average	194.9	204.3	210.7	3.1

Note: Figures are median sales prices of existing apartment condo-coop homes in thousands of dollars; (p) preliminary; n/a not available; (1) Atlanta-Sandy Springs-Roswell, GA Metropolitan Statistical Area—see Appendix B for areas included

Source: National Association of Realtors, Median Sales Price of Existing Apartment Condo-Coop Homes for Metropolitan Areas, 4th Quarter 2015

Gross Monthly Rent

Area	Under $200	$200 -299	$300 -499	$500 -749	$750 -999	$1,000 -1,499	$1,500 and up	Median ($)
City	0.0	0.0	0.0	1.3	15.6	48.7	34.4	1,353
MSA[1]	0.9	1.6	3.0	16.1	32.2	35.8	10.2	970
U.S.	1.5	3.2	7.4	21.0	24.1	26.9	15.9	920

Note: Figures are percentages except for Median; Gross rent is the contract rent plus the estimated average monthly cost of utilities (electricity, gas, and water and sewer) and fuels (oil, coal, kerosene, wood, etc.) if these are paid by the renter (or paid for the renter by someone else); (1) Figures cover the Atlanta-Sandy Springs-Roswell, GA Metropolitan Statistical Area—see Appendix B for areas included

Source: U.S. Census Bureau, 2010-2014 American Community Survey 5-Year Estimates

Homeownership Rate

Area	2008 (%)	2009 (%)	2010 (%)	2011 (%)	2012 (%)	2013 (%)	2014 (%)	2015 (%)
MSA[1]	67.5	67.7	67.2	65.8	62.1	61.6	61.6	61.7
U.S.	67.8	67.4	66.9	66.1	65.4	65.1	64.5	63.7

Note: (1) Figures cover the Atlanta-Sandy Springs-Roswell, GA Metropolitan Statistical Area—see Appendix B for areas included
Source: U.S. Census Bureau, Housing Vacancies and Homeownership Annual Statistics: 2015

Year Housing Structure Built

Area	2010 or Later	2000 -2009	1990 -1999	1980 -1989	1970 -1979	1960 -1969	1950 -1959	1940 -1949	Before 1940	Median Year
City	1.1	20.3	49.4	25.5	2.2	0.5	0.3	0.1	0.4	1994
MSA[1]	0.9	26.9	22.5	18.1	13.1	8.1	5.0	2.1	3.2	1990
U.S.	1.0	14.9	13.9	13.8	15.8	11.0	10.8	5.4	13.3	1976

Note: Figures are percentages except for Median Year; (1) Figures cover the Atlanta-Sandy Springs-Roswell, GA Metropolitan Statistical Area—see Appendix B for areas included
Source: U.S. Census Bureau, 2010-2014 American Community Survey 5-Year Estimates

HEALTH

Health Risk Data

Category	MSA[1] (%)	U.S. (%)
Adults aged 18–64 who have any kind of health care coverage	74.3	79.6
Adults who reported being in good or excellent health	86.5	83.1
Adults who are current smokers	17.3	19.6
Adults who are heavy drinkers[2]	4.6	6.1
Adults who are binge drinkers[3]	14.6	16.9
Adults who are overweight (BMI 25.0 - 29.9)	34.4	35.8
Adults who are obese (BMI 30.0 - 99.8)	26.5	27.6
Adults who participated in any physical activities in the past month	81.0	77.1
Adults 50+ who have ever had a sigmoidoscopy or colonoscopy	70.3	67.3
Women aged 40+ who have had a mammogram within the past two years	75.7	74.0
Men aged 40+ who have had a PSA test within the past two years	54.7	45.2
Adults aged 65+ who have had flu shot within the past year	57.2	60.1
Adults who always wear a seatbelt	96.3	93.8

Note: Data as of 2012 unless otherwise noted; (1) Figures cover the Atlanta-Sandy Springs-Marietta, GA Metropolitan Statistical Area—see Appendix B for areas included; (2) Heavy drinkers are classified as males having more than two drinks per day or females having more than one drink per day; (3) Binge drinkers are classified as males having five or more drinks on one occasion or females having four or more drinks on one occasion
Source: Centers for Disease Control and Prevention, Behaviorial Risk Factor Surveillance System, SMART: Selected Metropolitan/Micropolitan Area Risk Trends, 2012 (Note: the CDC has discontinued this dataset but will be releasing a replacement in mid-2016)

Chronic Health Indicators

Category	MSA[1] (%)	U.S. (%)
Adults who have ever been told they had a heart attack	3.7	4.5
Adults who have ever been told they had a stroke	2.9	2.9
Adults who have been told they currently have asthma	8.0	8.9
Adults who have ever been told they have arthritis	20.7	25.7
Adults who have ever been told they have diabetes[2]	8.9	9.7
Adults who have ever been told they had skin cancer	5.2	5.7
Adults who have ever been told they had any other types of cancer	5.2	6.5
Adults who have ever been told they have COPD	5.2	6.2
Adults who have ever been told they have kidney disease	3.0	2.5
Adults who have ever been told they have a form of depression	14.5	18.0

Note: Data as of 2012 unless otherwise noted; (1) Figures cover the Atlanta-Sandy Springs-Marietta, GA Metropolitan Statistical Area—see Appendix B for areas included; (2) Figures do not include pregnancy-related, borderline, or pre-diabetes
Source: Centers for Disease Control and Prevention, Behaviorial Risk Factor Surveillance System, SMART: Selected Metropolitan/Micropolitan Area Risk Trends, 2012 (Note: the CDC has discontinued this dataset but will be releasing a replacement in mid-2016)

Mortality Rates for the Top 10 Causes of Death in the U.S.

ICD-10[a] Sub-Chapter	ICD-10[a] Code	Age-Adjusted Mortality Rate[1] per 100,000 population	
		County[2]	U.S.
Malignant neoplasms	C00-C97	160.6	163.6
Ischaemic heart diseases	I20-I25	64.9	102.2
Other forms of heart disease	I30-I51	60.4	50.1
Chronic lower respiratory diseases	J40-J47	26.8	41.4
Organic, including symptomatic, mental disorders	F01-F09	55.5	38.5
Cerebrovascular diseases	I60-I69	39.9	36.5
Other external causes of accidental injury	W00-X59	24.5	27.5
Other degenerative diseases of the nervous system	G30-G31	21.2	26.3
Diabetes mellitus	E10-E14	18.5	21.1
Hypertensive diseases	I10-I15	41.0	19.7

Note: (a) ICD-10 = International Classification of Diseases 10th Revision; (1) Mortality rates are a three year average covering 2012-2014; (2) Figures cover Fulton County.
Source: Centers for Disease Control and Prevention, National Center for Health Statistics. Underlying Cause of Death 1999-2014 on CDC WONDER Online Database, released 2015.

Mortality Rates for Selected Causes of Death

ICD-10[a] Sub-Chapter	ICD-10[a] Code	Age-Adjusted Mortality Rate[1] per 100,000 population	
		County[2]	U.S.
Assault	X85-Y09	10.6	5.1
Diseases of the liver	K70-K76	10.2	13.5
Human immunodeficiency virus (HIV) disease	B20-B24	9.5	2.1
Influenza and pneumonia	J09-J18	11.1	15.2
Intentional self-harm	X60-X84	11.3	12.7
Malnutrition	E40-E46	1.0	0.9
Obesity and other hyperalimentation	E65-E68	1.3	1.9
Renal failure	N17-N19	17.2	13.0
Transport accidents	V01-V99	8.7	11.6
Viral hepatitis	B15-B19	2.0	2.1

Note: (a) ICD-10 = International Classification of Diseases 10th Revision; (1) Mortality rates are a three year average covering 2012-2014; (2) Figures cover Fulton County; Data are Suppressed when the data meet the criteria for confidentiality constraints; Mortality rates are flagged as Unreliable when the rate would be calculated with a numerator of 20 or less.
Source: Centers for Disease Control and Prevention, National Center for Health Statistics. Underlying Cause of Death 1999-2014 on CDC WONDER Online Database, released 2015.

Health Insurance Coverage

Area	With Health Insurance	With Private Health Insurance	With Public Health Insurance	Without Health Insurance	Population Under Age 18 Without Health Insurance
City	89.7	84.5	11.2	10.3	5.1
MSA[1]	81.9	65.5	24.4	18.1	9.1
U.S.	85.8	65.8	31.1	14.2	7.1

Note: Figures are percentages that cover the civilian noninstitutionalized population; (1) Figures cover the Atlanta-Sandy Springs-Roswell, GA Metropolitan Statistical Area—see Appendix B for areas included
Source: U.S. Census Bureau, 2010-2014 American Community Survey 5-Year Estimates

Number of Medical Professionals

Area	MDs[3]	DOs[3,4]	Dentists	Podiatrists	Chiropractors	Optometrists
County[1] (number)	4,809	97	669	41	482	139
County[1] (rate[2])	488.4	9.9	67.1	4.1	48.4	14.0
U.S. (rate[2])	272.5	20.9	64.7	5.8	25.9	15.2

Note: Data as of 2014 unless noted; (1) Data covers Fulton County; (2) Rate per 100,000 population; (3) Data as of 2013 and includes all active, non-federal physicians; (4) Doctor of Osteopathic Medicine
Source: U.S. Department of Health and Human Services, Health Resources and Services Administration, Bureau of Health Professions, Area Resource File (ARF) 2014-2015

Best Hospitals

According to *U.S. News,* the Atlanta-Sandy Springs-Roswell, GA metro area is home to three of the best hospitals in the U.S.: **Emory University Hospital** (12 specialties); **Emory Wesley Woods Geriatric Hospital** (1 specialty); **Shepherd Center** (1 specialty). The hospitals listed were nationally ranked in at least one adult specialty. Only 137 hospitals nationwide were nationally ranked in one or more specialties. Fifteen hospitals in the U.S. made the Honor Roll with high scores in at least six specialties. *U.S. News Online, "America's Best Children's Hospitals 2015-16"*

According to *U.S. News,* the Atlanta-Sandy Springs-Roswell, GA metro area is home to one of the best children's hospitals in the U.S.: **Children's Healthcare of Atlanta** (Honor Roll/10 specialties). The hospital listed was highly ranked in at least one pediatric specialty. Eighty-three children's hospitals in the U.S. were nationally ranked in at least one specialty. Twelve children's hospitals in the U.S. made the Honor Roll with high scores in at least three specialties. *U.S. News Online, "America's Best Children's Hospitals 2015-16"*

EDUCATION

Public School District Statistics

District Name	Schls	Pupils	Pupil/ Teacher Ratio	Minority Pupils[1] (%)	Free Lunch Eligible[2] (%)	IEP[3] (%)
Fulton County	104	95,232	15.1	69.0	41.7	10.3

Note: Table includes school districts with 100 or more students; (1) Percentage of students that are not non-Hispanic white; (2) Percentage of students that are eligible for the free lunch program; (3) Percentage of students that have an Individualized Education Program.
Source: U.S. Department of Education, National Center for Education Statistics, Common Core of Data, Local Education Agency (School District) Universe Survey: School Year 2013-2014; U.S. Department of Education, National Center for Education Statistics, Common Core of Data, Public Elementary/Secondary School Universe Survey: School Year 2013-2014

Best High Schools

According to *U.S. News,* Johns Creek is home to one of the best high schools in the U.S.: **Johns Creek High School** (#277); Nearly 20,000 schools were ranked based on their performance on state assessments and how well they prepare students for college. Schools with the highest unrounded College Readiness Index values were numerically ranked from No. 1 to No. 500 and were the gold medal winners. *U.S. News & World Report, "Best High Schools 2015"*

Highest Level of Education

Area	Less than H.S.	H.S. Diploma	Some College, No Deg.	Associate Degree	Bachelor's Degree	Master's Degree	Prof. School Degree	Doctorate Degree
City	4.1	10.1	15.3	6.6	39.1	19.0	3.1	2.6
MSA[1]	12.1	24.7	20.9	7.1	22.7	9.0	2.2	1.3
U.S.	13.7	28.0	21.2	7.9	18.3	7.8	2.0	1.3

Note: Figures cover persons age 25 and over; (1) Figures cover the Atlanta-Sandy Springs-Roswell, GA Metropolitan Statistical Area—see Appendix B for areas included
Source: U.S. Census Bureau, 2010-2014 American Community Survey 5-Year Estimates

Educational Attainment by Race

Area	High School Graduate or Higher (%)					Bachelor's Degree or Higher (%)				
	Total	White	Black	Asian	Hisp.[2]	Total	White	Black	Asian	Hisp.[2]
City	95.9	97.3	96.5	92.0	84.3	63.8	63.5	47.2	72.8	37.0
MSA[1]	87.9	89.3	88.5	86.4	61.4	35.3	39.0	27.1	53.3	16.5
U.S.	86.3	88.4	83.2	85.8	64.1	29.3	30.6	19.0	50.9	13.9

Note: Figures shown cover persons 25 years old and over; (1) Figures cover the Atlanta-Sandy Springs-Roswell, GA Metropolitan Statistical Area—see Appendix B for areas included; (2) People of Hispanic origin can be of any race
Source: U.S. Census Bureau, 2010-2014 American Community Survey 5-Year Estimates

School Enrollment by Grade and Control

Area	Preschool (%)		Kindergarten (%)		Grades 1 - 4 (%)		Grades 5 - 8 (%)		Grades 9 - 12 (%)	
	Public	Private	Public	Private	Public	Private	Public	Private	Public	Private
City	38.0	62.0	87.8	12.2	91.2	8.8	92.5	7.5	91.5	8.5
MSA[1]	54.2	45.8	87.7	12.3	90.2	9.8	89.5	10.5	90.3	9.7
U.S.	57.4	42.6	87.8	12.2	89.8	10.2	89.9	10.1	90.6	9.4

Note: Figures shown cover persons 3 years old and over; (1) Figures cover the Atlanta-Sandy Springs-Roswell, GA Metropolitan Statistical Area—see Appendix B for areas included
Source: U.S. Census Bureau, 2010-2014 American Community Survey 5-Year Estimates

Average Salaries of Public School Classroom Teachers

Area	2013-14		2014-15		Percent Change 2013-14 to 2014-15	Percent Change 2004-05 to 2014-15
	Dollars	Rank[1]	Dollars	Rank[1]		
Georgia	52,924	24	53,382	24	0.87	14.7
U.S. Average	56,610	–	57,379	–	1.36	20.8

Note: (1) State rank ranges from 1 to 51 where 1 indicates highest salary.
Source: National Education Association, Rankings & Estimates: Rankings of the States 2014 and Estimates of School Statistics 2015, March 2015

Higher Education

Four-Year Colleges			Two-Year Colleges			Medical Schools[1]	Law Schools[2]	Voc/ Tech[3]
Public	Private Non-profit	Private For-profit	Public	Private Non-profit	Private For-profit			
0	0	0	0	0	0	0	0	0

Note: Figures cover institutions located within the city limits and include main campuses only; (1) includes schools accredited by the Liaison Committee on Medical Education and the American Osteopathic Association's Commission on Osteopathic College Accreditation; (2) includes ABA-accredited schools, schools with provisional ABA accreditation, and state accredited schools; (3) includes all schools with programs that are less than 2 years.
Source: National Center for Education Statistics, Integrated Postsecondary Education System (IPEDS), 2014-15; Association of American Medical Colleges, Member List, March 21, 2016; American Osteopathic Association, Member List, March 21, 2016; Law School Admission Council, Official Guide to ABA-Approved Law Schools Online, March 21, 2016; Wikipedia, List of Medical Schools in the United States, March 21, 2016; Wikipedia, List of Law Schools in the United States, March 21, 2016

According to *U.S. News & World Report,* the Atlanta-Sandy Springs-Roswell, GA metro area is home to two of the best national universities in the U.S.: **Emory University** (#21 tie); **Georgia Institute of Technology** (#36). The indicators used to capture academic quality fall into a number of categories: assessment by administrators at peer institutions; retention of students; faculty resources; student selectivity; financial resources; alumni giving; high school counselor ratings of colleges; and graduation rate. *U.S. News & World Report, "America's Best Colleges 2016"*

According to *U.S. News & World Report,* the Atlanta-Sandy Springs-Roswell, GA metro area is home to four of the best liberal arts colleges in the U.S.: **Agnes Scott College** (#67 tie); **Spelman College** (#72 tie); **Morehouse College** (#148 tie); **Oglethorpe University** (#167 tie). The indicators used to capture academic quality fall into a number of categories: assessment by administrators at peer institutions; retention of students; faculty resources; student selectivity; financial resources; alumni giving; high school counselor ratings of colleges; and graduation rate. *U.S. News & World Report, "America's Best Colleges 2016"*

According to *U.S. News & World Report,* the Atlanta-Sandy Springs-Roswell, GA metro area is home to two of the top 100 law schools in the U.S.: **Emory University, School of Law** (#22 tie); **Georgia State University, College of Law** (#57 tie). The rankings are based on a weighted average of 12 measures of quality: peer assessment score; assessment score by lawyers/judges; median LSAT scores; median undergrad GPA; acceptance rate; employment rates for graduates; placement success; bar passage rate; faculty resources; expenditures per student; student/faculty ratio; and library resources. *U.S. News & World Report, "America's Best Graduate Schools, Law, 2017"*

According to *U.S. News & World Report,* the Atlanta-Sandy Springs-Roswell, GA metro area is home to one of the top 75 medical schools for research in the U.S.: **Emory University, School of Medicine** (#23). The rankings are based on a weighted average of 11 measures of quality: quality assessment; peer assessment score; assessment score by residency directors; research activity; total research activity; average research activity per faculty member; student

selectivity; median MCAT total score; median undergraduate GPA; acceptance rate; and faculty resources. *U.S. News & World Report, "America's Best Graduate Schools, Medical, 2017"*

According to *U.S. News & World Report,* the Atlanta-Sandy Springs-Roswell, GA metro area is home to two of the top 75 business schools in the U.S.: **Emory University, Goizueta Business School** (#19); **Georgia Institute of Technology, Scheller College of Business** (#34). The rankings are based on a weighted average of the following nine measures: quality assessment; peer assessment; recruiter assessment; placement success; mean starting salary and bonus; student selectivity; mean GMAT and GRE scores; mean undergraduate GPA; and acceptance rate. *U.S. News & World Report, "America's Best Graduate Schools, Business, 2017"*

PRESIDENTIAL ELECTION

2012 Presidential Election Results

Area	Obama (%)	Romney (%)	Other (%)
Fulton County	64.3	34.5	1.2
U.S.	51.0	47.2	1.8

Note: Results may not add to 100% due to rounding
Source: Dave Leip's Atlas of U.S. Presidential Elections

EMPLOYERS

Major Employers

Company Name	Industry
Apartments.Com	Apartment locating service
Aquilex Holdings	Facilities support services
AT&T Corp.	Engineering services
Behavioral Health, Georgia Department of	Administration of public health programs
Children's Healthcare of Atlanta	Healthcare
Clayton County Board of Education	Public elementary and secondary schools
County of Gwinnett	County commissioner
Delta Air Lines	Air transportation, scheduled
Georgia Department of Human Resoures	Administration of public health programs
Georgia Department of Transportation	Regulation, administration of transportation
IBM Corporation	Engineering services
Internal Revenue Service	Taxation department, government
Lockheed Martin Aeronautical Company	Aircraft
NCR Corporation	Calculating and accounting equipment
Northide Hospital	Healthcare
Progressive Logistics Services	Labor organizations
Robert Half International	Employment agencies
Saint Joseph's Hospital	Healthcare
The Army, United States Department of	Army
The Coca-Cola Company	Bottled and canned soft drinks
The Fulton-Dekalb Hospital Authority	General medical and surgical hospitals
The Home Depot	Hardware stores
WellStar Kennestone Hospital	General medical and surgical hospitals
World Travel Partners Group	Travel agencies

Note: Companies shown are located within the Atlanta-Sandy Springs-Roswell, GA Metropolitan Statistical Area.
Source: Hoovers.com; Wikipedia

PUBLIC SAFETY

Crime Rate

Area	All Crimes	Violent Crimes				Property Crimes		
		Murder	Rape[3]	Robbery	Aggrav. Assault	Burglary	Larceny -Theft	Motor Vehicle Theft
City	738.2	0.0	3.6	9.5	20.2	109.2	581.6	14.2
Metro[1]	3,629.7	6.1	20.4	154.0	217.9	725.9	2,170.4	334.9
U.S.	2,961.6	4.5	26.4	102.2	232.5	542.5	1,837.3	216.2

Note: Figures are crimes per 100,000 population; (1) Figures cover the Atlanta-Sandy Springs-Roswell, GA Metropolitan Statistical Area—see Appendix B for areas included; (3) The city and U.S. figures shown were reported using the legacy Uniform Crime Reporting (UCR) definition of rape. The suburban and metro area figures shown are an aggregate total of the data submitted using both the revised and legacy UCR definitions.
Source: FBI Uniform Crime Reports, 2014

Hate Crimes

Area	Number of Quarters Reported	Number of Incidents per Bias Motivation						
		Race	Religion	Sexual Orientation	Ethnicity	Disability	Gender	Gender Identity
City	4	0	0	0	0	0	0	0
U.S.	4	2,568	1,014	1,017	648	84	33	98

Source: Federal Bureau of Investigation, Hate Crime Statistics 2014

Identity Theft Consumer Complaints

Area	Complaints	Complaints per 100,000 Population	Rank[2]
MSA[1]	10,418	185.6	24
U.S.	490,220	152.4	-

Note: (1) Figures cover the Atlanta-Sandy Springs-Roswell, GA Metropolitan Statistical Area—see Appendix B for areas included; (2) Rank ranges from 1 to 379 where 1 indicates greatest number of identity theft complaints per 100,000 population
Source: Federal Trade Commission, Consumer Sentinel Network Data Book for January–December 2015

Fraud and Other Consumer Complaints

Area	Complaints	Complaints per 100,000 Population	Rank[2]
MSA[1]	26,684	475.3	30
U.S.	2,593,159	806.0	-

Note: (1) Figures cover the Atlanta-Sandy Springs-Roswell, GA Metropolitan Statistical Area—see Appendix B for areas included; (2) Rank ranges from 1 to 379 where 1 indicates greatest number of identity theft complaints per 100,000 population
Source: Federal Trade Commission, Consumer Sentinel Network Data Book for January–December 2015

RECREATION

Culture

Dance[1]	Theatre[1]	Instrumental Music[1]	Vocal Music[1]	Series and Festivals	Museums and Art Galleries[2]	Zoos and Aquariums[3]
0	0	0	0	0	0	0

Note: (1) Professional perfoming groups; (2) Based on organizations with SIC code 8412; (3) AZA-accredited
Source: The Grey House Performing Arts Directory, 2015-16; Association of Zoos & Aquariums, AZA Member Zoos & Aquariums, March 25, 2016; www.AccuLeads.com, March 29, 2016

Professional Sports Teams

Team Name	League	Year Established
Atlanta Braves	Major League Baseball (MLB)	1966
Atlanta Falcons	National Football League (NFL)	1966
Atlanta Hawks	National Basketball Association (NBA)	1968
Atlanta United FC	Major League Soccer (MLS)	2017

Note: Includes teams located in the Atlanta-Sandy Springs-Roswell, GA Metropolitan Statistical Area.
Source: Wikipedia, Major Professional Sports Teams of the United States and Canada, March 24, 2016

CLIMATE

Average and Extreme Temperatures

Temperature	Jan	Feb	Mar	Apr	May	Jun	Jul	Aug	Sep	Oct	Nov	Dec	Yr.
Extreme High (°F)	79	80	85	93	95	101	105	102	98	95	84	77	105
Average High (°F)	52	56	64	73	80	86	88	88	82	73	63	54	72
Average Temp. (°F)	43	46	53	62	70	77	79	79	73	63	53	45	62
Average Low (°F)	33	36	42	51	59	66	70	69	64	52	42	35	52
Extreme Low (°F)	-8	5	10	26	37	46	53	55	36	28	3	0	-8

Note: Figures cover the years 1945-1990
Source: National Climatic Data Center, International Station Meteorological Climate Summary, 9/96

Average Precipitation/Snowfall/Humidity

Precip./Humidity	Jan	Feb	Mar	Apr	May	Jun	Jul	Aug	Sep	Oct	Nov	Dec	Yr.
Avg. Precip. (in.)	4.7	4.6	5.7	4.3	4.0	3.5	5.1	3.6	3.4	2.8	3.8	4.2	49.8
Avg. Snowfall (in.)	1	1	Tr	Tr	0	0	0	0	0	0	Tr	Tr	2
Avg. Rel. Hum. 7am (%)	79	77	78	78	82	83	88	89	88	84	81	79	82
Avg. Rel. Hum. 4pm (%)	56	50	48	45	49	52	57	56	56	51	52	55	52

Note: Figures cover the years 1945-1990; Tr = Trace amounts (<0.05 in. of rain; <0.5 in. of snow)
Source: National Climatic Data Center, International Station Meteorological Climate Summary, 9/96

Weather Conditions

Temperature			Daytime Sky			Precipitation		
10°F & below	32°F & below	90°F & above	Clear	Partly cloudy	Cloudy	0.01 inch or more precip.	0.1 inch or more snow/ice	Thunder-storms
1	49	38	98	147	120	116	3	48

Note: Figures are average number of days per year and cover the years 1945-1990
Source: National Climatic Data Center, International Station Meteorological Climate Summary, 9/96

HAZARDOUS WASTE

Superfund Sites

Johns Creek has no sites on the EPA's Superfund Final National Priorities List. There are a total of 1,323 Superfund sites on the list in the U.S. *U.S. Environmental Protection Agency, Final National Priorities List, March 18, 2016*

AIR & WATER QUALITY

Air Quality Trends: Ozone

	1990	1995	2000	2005	2010	2011	2012	2013	2014
MSA[1]	0.104	0.103	0.101	0.087	0.076	0.078	0.079	0.066	0.072

Note: (1) Data covers the Atlanta-Sandy Springs-Roswell, GA Metropolitan Statistical Area—see Appendix B for areas included. The values shown are the composite ozone concentration averages among trend sites based on the highest fourth daily maximum 8-hour concentration in parts per million. These trends are based on sites having an adequate record of monitoring data during the trend period. Data from exceptional events are included.
Source: U.S. Environmental Protection Agency, Air Quality Monitoring Information, "Air Quality Trends by City, 1990-2014"

Air Quality Index

Area	Percent of Days when Air Quality was...[2]					AQI Statistics[2]	
	Good	Moderate	Unhealthy for Sensitive Groups	Unhealthy	Very Unhealthy	Maximum	Median
MSA[1]	40.0	57.8	2.2	0.0	0.0	147	55

Note: (1) Data covers the Atlanta-Sandy Springs-Roswell, GA Metropolitan Statistical Area—see Appendix B for areas included; (2) Based on 365 days with AQI data in 2015. Air Quality Index (AQI) is an index for reporting daily air quality. EPA calculates the AQI for five major air pollutants regulated by the Clean Air Act: ground-level ozone, particle pollution (aka particulate matter), carbon monoxide, sulfur dioxide, and nitrogen dioxide. The AQI runs from 0 to 500. The higher the AQI value, the greater the level of air pollution and the greater the health concern. There are six AQI categories: "Good" AQI is between 0 and 50. Air quality is considered satisfactory; "Moderate" AQI is between 51 and 100. Air quality is acceptable; "Unhealthy for Sensitive Groups" When AQI values are between 101 and 150, members of sensitive groups may experience health effects; "Unhealthy" When AQI values are between 151 and 200 everyone may begin to experience health effects; "Very Unhealthy" AQI values between 201 and 300 trigger a health alert; "Hazardous" AQI values over 300 trigger warnings of emergency conditions (not shown).
Source: U.S. Environmental Protection Agency, Air Quality Index Report, 2015

Air Quality Index Pollutants

Area	Percent of Days when AQI Pollutant was...[2]					
	Carbon Monoxide	Nitrogen Dioxide	Ozone	Sulfur Dioxide	Particulate Matter 2.5	Particulate Matter 10
MSA[1]	0.0	1.6	24.7	0.0	73.2	0.5

Note: (1) Data covers the Atlanta-Sandy Springs-Roswell, GA Metropolitan Statistical Area—see Appendix B for areas included; (2) Based on 365 days with AQI data in 2015. The Air Quality Index (AQI) is an index for reporting daily air quality. EPA calculates the AQI for five major air pollutants regulated by the Clean Air Act: ground-level ozone, particle pollution (also known as particulate matter), carbon monoxide, sulfur dioxide, and nitrogen dioxide. The AQI runs from 0 to 500. The higher the AQI value, the greater the level of air pollution and the greater the health concern.
Source: U.S. Environmental Protection Agency, Air Quality Index Report, 2015

Maximum Air Pollutant Concentrations: Particulate Matter, Ozone, CO and Lead

	Particulate Matter 10 (ug/m^3)	Particulate Matter 2.5 Wtd AM (ug/m^3)	Particulate Matter 2.5 24-Hr (ug/m^3)	Ozone (ppm)	Carbon Monoxide (ppm)	Lead (ug/m^3)
MSA[1] Level	61	11.2	22	0.079	2	0
NAAQS[2]	150	15	35	0.075	9	0.15
Met NAAQS[2]	Yes	Yes	Yes	No	Yes	Yes

Note: (1) Data covers the Atlanta-Sandy Springs-Roswell, GA Metropolitan Statistical Area—see Appendix B for areas included; Data from exceptional events are included; (2) National Ambient Air Quality Standards; ppm = parts per million; ug/m^3 = micrograms per cubic meter; n/a not available.
Concentrations: Particulate Matter 10 (coarse particulate)—highest second maximum 24-hour concentration; Particulate Matter 2.5 Wtd AM (fine particulate)—highest weighted annual mean concentration; Particulate Matter 2.5 24-Hour (fine particulate)—highest 98th percentile 24-hour concentration; Ozone—highest fourth daily maximum 8-hour concentration; Carbon Monoxide—highest second maximum non-overlapping 8-hour concentration; Lead—maximum running 3-month average
Source: U.S. Environmental Protection Agency, Air Quality Monitoring Information, "Air Quality Statistics by City, 2014"

Maximum Air Pollutant Concentrations: Nitrogen Dioxide and Sulfur Dioxide

	Nitrogen Dioxide AM (ppb)	Nitrogen Dioxide 1-Hr (ppb)	Sulfur Dioxide AM (ppb)	Sulfur Dioxide 1-Hr (ppb)	Sulfur Dioxide 24-Hr (ppb)
MSA[1] Level	11	53	n/a	6	n/a
NAAQS[2]	53	100	30	75	140
Met NAAQS[2]	Yes	Yes	n/a	Yes	n/a

Note: (1) Data covers the Atlanta-Sandy Springs-Roswell, GA Metropolitan Statistical Area—see Appendix B for areas included; Data from exceptional events are included; (2) National Ambient Air Quality Standards; ppm = parts per million; ug/m^3 = micrograms per cubic meter; n/a not available.
Concentrations: Nitrogen Dioxide AM—highest arithmetic mean concentration; Nitrogen Dioxide 1-Hr—highest 98th percentile 1-hour daily maximum concentration; Sulfur Dioxide AM—highest annual mean concentration; Sulfur Dioxide 1-Hr—highest 99th percentile 1-hour daily maximum concentration; Sulfur Dioxide 24-Hr—highest second maximum 24-hour concentration
Source: U.S. Environmental Protection Agency, Air Quality Monitoring Information, "Air Quality Statistics by City, 2014"

Drinking Water

Water System Name	Pop. Served	Primary Water Source Type	Violations[1]	
			Health Based	Monitoring/ Reporting
North Fulton County	172,533	Purchased Surface	0	0

Note: (1) Based on violation data from January 1, 2015 to December 31, 2015 (includes unresolved violations from earlier years)

Source: U.S. Environmental Protection Agency, Office of Ground Water and Drinking Water, Safe Drinking Water Information System (based on data extracted April 29, 2016)

Peachtree City, Georgia

Background

Peachtree City is 15 miles south of Atlanta and is a planned city, established in 1959. At an elevation of from 740 to 960 feet above sea level, Peachtree City is situated in a gentle area of low hills and valleys typical of the beautiful Georgia piedmont region.

The earliest residents of the area were Native Americans—recent archaeological indications show that Creek Indians were significantly involved in the early history of the site nearly 2,000 years ago. William McIntosh, Jr., the son of a Scotsman and Creek Indian woman, was chief of the Lower Creeks, and, believing in harmonious co-existence, ceded Creek land to the Federal Government in 1821. Much of this land is now part of Fayette County. After McIntosh's death in 1825, his family settled briefly at Ware plantation, subsequently the site of Peachtree City.

Peachtree City sits on 15,000 acres of land and features 125 neighborhoods connected by 70 miles of paths, all within four "villages." These are named Aberdeen, Braelinn, Glenloch, and Kedron, in honor of William McIntosh's Scottish heritage.

Culturally and recreationally, Peachtree City offers many amenities, including a 2,000-seat amphitheater, three golf courses, two lakes, a world-class tennis center, and a swimming complex. The network of recreational paths is integral to the town's master design, and allows convenient and safe movement through tunnels, over bridges, and across major roads. It is open to pedestrians, bicycles, and golf carts, and affords access to neighborhoods, stores, churches, recreation areas, and schools. The city has always been serious about careful and long-term planning, to retain the best features of the site, and it is a member of the Atlanta Regional Commission.

Peachtree City is served by Interstates 75 and 85, as well as by state highways, and is convenient to Hartsfield-Jackson Atlanta International Airport, one of the world's busiest passenger airports. A smaller regional airport, Peachtree City Falcon Field, on the western edge of Peachtree City, is open to private and corporate executive aircraft. Businesses requiring efficient freight service can access service provided by CSX (Chessie Seaboard Railroad), a major link to the entire Southeast.

Peachtree City is served by the Fayette County School System, and a high percentage of Peachtree's students graduate and go on to institutes of higher learning.

Locally based businesses include Lawson Mardon, which operates a packaging facility in Peachtree City, Gardner Denver, with its Blower Division Headquarters, Southern Motor Carriers, and Cooper Lighting.

And, of course, Peachtree City has easy access to all of the benefits of Atlanta, from shops and restaurants in interesting neighborhoods to the notable High Museum of Art, the Atlanta Symphony Orchestra, and more.

Peachtree City is a four-season town, with fluctuations in temperature somewhat moderated by the Gulf of Mexico and Atlantic Ocean, 250 miles south and east of the city respectively. In winter, mountains to the north partially block the movement of polar air masses, preventing long spells of icy temperatures; snowfall is not heavy and snow does not remain on the ground for long. Summers are hot and humid, but prolonged periods of very hot weather are unusual.

Rankings

Business/Finance Rankings

- The personal finance site NerdWallet analyzed 183 American metropolitan areas with populations over 250,000 and more than 15,000 businesses to rank where entrepreneurs find the most success. Criteria included area economy, annual income, housing cost, unemployment rate, and the success rate of area businesses. Atlanta* ranked #86. *www.nerdwallet.com, "Best Places to Start a Business," April 27, 2015*
- Based on metro area social media reviews, the employment opinion group Glassdoor surveyed 50 of the largest U.S. metro areas and equally weighed cost of living, hiring opportunity, and job satisfaction to compose a list of "25 Best Cities for Jobs." The Atlanta* metro area was ranked #24 in overall job satisfaction. *www.glassdoor.com, "Best Cities for Jobs," May 19, 2015*
- In a survey of economic confidence in the nation's 50 largest metropolitan areas conducted January–December 2014, the Atlanta* metro area placed #21, according to Gallup's 2014 Economic Confidence Index. *Gallup, "San Jose and San Francisco Lead in Economic Confidence," March 19, 2015*
- The Brookings Institution ranked the 100 largest metro areas in the U.S. based on income inequality. Atlanta* was ranked #36 (#1 = greatest ineqality). Criteria: the "95/20 ratio," a figure representing the income at which a household earns more than 95 percent of all other households, divided by the income at which a household earns more than only 20 percent of all other households. *Brookings Institution, "Income Inequality, 100 Largest U.S. Metro Areas, 2007-2014," January 14, 2016*
- Payscale.com ranked the 20 largest metro areas in terms of wage growth. The Atlanta* metro area ranked #5. Criteria: private-sector wage growth between the 1st quarter of 2015 and the 1st quarter of 2016. *PayScale, "Wage Trends by Metro Area," 1st Quarter, 2016*
- The Atlanta* metro area was identified as one of the most debt-ridden places in America by the finance site Credit.com. The metro area was ranked #8. Criteria: residents' average personal debt load and average credit scores. *Credit.com, "The Most Debt-Ridden Cities," May 1, 2014*
- Atlanta* was identified as one of America's most frugal metro areas by *Coupons.com.* The city ranked #6 out of 25. Criteria: online coupon usage. *Coupons.com, "Top 25 Most Frugal Cities of 2014," May 11, 2015*
- Atlanta* was identified as one of America's most frugal metro areas by *Coupons.com.* The city ranked #3 out of 25. Criteria: Grocery IQ and coupons.com mobile app usage. *Coupons.com, "Top 25 Most On-the-Go Frugal Cities of 2013," April 10, 2014*
- Atlanta* was cited as one of America's top metros for new and expanded facility projects in 2015. The area ranked #8 in the large metro area category (population over 1 million). *Site Selection, "Top Metropolitans of 2015," March 2016*
- The Atlanta* metro area appeared on the Milken Institute "2015 Best Performing Cities" list. Rank: #27 out of 200 large metro areas. Criteria: job growth; wage and salary growth; high-tech output growth. *Milken Institute, "Best-Performing Cities 2015," December 2015*
- *Forbes* ranked the 200 most populous metro areas to determine the nation's "Best Places for Business and Careers." The Atlanta* metro area was ranked #5. Criteria: costs (business and living); job growth (past and projected); income growth; educational attainment (college and high school); projected economic growth; cultural and recreational opportunities; net migration patterns; number of highly ranked colleges. *Forbes, "The Best Places for Business and Careers 2015," July 29, 2015*

Dating/Romance Rankings

- CreditDonkey, a financial education website, sought out the ten best U.S. cities for newlyweds, considering the number of married couples, divorce rate, average credit score, and average number of hours worked per week in metro areas with a million or more residents. The Atlanta* metro area placed #1. *www.creditdonkey.com, "Study: Best Cities for Newlyweds," November 30, 2013*

Education Rankings

- Personal finance website *WalletHub* analyzed the 150 largest U.S. metropolitan statistical areas to determine where the most educated Americans are choosing to settle. Criteria: education quality and attainment gap; education levels; percentage of workers with degrees; public school rankings; quality and size of each metro area's universities. Atlanta* was ranked #34 (#1 = most educated city). *www.WalletHub.com, "2015's Most and Least Educated Cities*

Environmental Rankings

- The Atlanta* metro area came in at #246 for the relative comfort of its climate on Sperling's list of "chill cities," as measured by the Sperling Heat Index. All 361 metro areas are included. Criteria included daytime high temperatures, nighttime low temperatures, dew point, and relative humidity at the high temperatures. *www.bertsperling.com, "Sperling's Chill Cities," July 18, 2013*

- Sperling's BestPlaces assessed 379 metropolitan areas of the United States for the likelihood of dangerously extreme weather events or earthquakes. In general the Southeast and South-Central regions have the highest risk of weather extremes and earthquakes, while the Pacific Northwest enjoys the lowest risk. Of the least risky metropolitan areas, the Atlanta* metro area was ranked #358. *www.bestplaces.net, "Safest Places from Natural Disasters," April 2011*

- The U.S. Environmental Protection Agency (EPA) released a list of U.S. metropolitan areas with the most ENERGY STAR certified buildings in 2015. The Atlanta* metro area was ranked #4 out of 25. *U.S. Environmental Protection Agency, "Top Cities With the Most ENERGY STAR Certified Buildings in 2016," March 30, 2016*

Health/Fitness Rankings

- For each of the 50 most populous metro areas in the United States, the American College of Sports Medicine's American Fitness Index evaluated infrastructure, community assets, and policies that encourage healthy and fit lifestyles, including preventive health behaviors, levels of chronic disease conditions, health care access, and community resources and policies that support physical activity. The Atlanta* metro area ranked #14 for "community fitness." *www.americanfitnessindex.org, "ACSM American Fitness Index Health and Community Fitness Status of the 50 Largest Metropolitan Areas," May 2015*

- The Atlanta* metro area was identified as one of the worst cities for bed bugs in America by pest control company Orkin. The area ranked #19 out of 50 based on the number of bed bug treatments Orkin performed from January to December 2015. *Orkin, "Chicago Tops Bed Bug Cities List for Fourth Year in a Row," January 13, 2016*

- Atlanta* was identified as a "2016 Spring Allergy Capital." The area ranked #70 out of 100. Three groups of factors were used to identify the most severe cities for people with allergies during the spring season: annual pollen levels; medicine utilization; access to board-certified allergists. *Asthma and Allergy Foundation of America, "Spring Allergy Capitals 2016"*

- Atlanta* was identified as a "2015 Asthma Capital." The area ranked #16 out of the nation's 100 largest metropolitan areas. Criteria: estimated prevalence; self-reported prevalence; crude death rate for asthma; annual pollen score; annual air quality; public smoking laws; number of board-certified asthma specialists; school inhaler access laws; rescue medication use; controller medication use; ER visits for asthma; uninsured rate; poverty rate. *Asthma and Allergy Foundation of America, "Asthma Capitals 2015"*

- The Atlanta* metro area ranked #100 out of 190 in The Gallup-Healthways Well-Being Index. Criteria: purpose; social well being; financial health; community and physical health. Results are based on telephone interviews with adults, aged 18 and older, living in metropolitan areas in the 50 U.S. states and the District of Columbia. *Gallup-Healthways, "State of American Well-Being," February 23, 2016*

Real Estate Rankings

- Based on the home-price forecasts compiled by the real-estate valuation firm CoreLogic Case-Shiller, CNNMoney reported that in 2016, the Atlanta* metro area is expected to be one of the hottest housing markets in the U.S. Criteria: residential real estate prices. *money.cnn.com, "The 10 Hottest Housing Markets for 2016," December 3, 2015*
- According to Penske Truck Rental, the Atlanta* metro area was named the #1 moving destination in 2015, based on one-way consumer truck rental reservations made through Penske's website and reservations call center. *blog.gopenske.com, "Penske Truck Rental's 2015 Top Moving Destinations List," February 3, 2016*
- The Atlanta* metro area appeared on Realtor.com's list of the hottest housing markets to watch in 2016. The area ranked #5. Criteria: strong housing growth; affordable prices; and fast-paced sales. *Realtor.com®, "Top 10 Hot Real Estate Markets to Watch in 2016," December 2, 2015*
- Atlanta* was ranked #127 out of 225 metro areas in terms of housing affordability in 2015 by the National Association of Home Builders (#1 = most affordable). Criteria: the share of homes sold in that area affordable to a family earning the local median income, based on standard mortgage underwriting criteria. *National Association of Home Builders®, NAHB-Wells Fargo Housing Opportunity Index, 4th Quarter 2015*

Safety Rankings

- The National Insurance Crime Bureau ranked 380 metro areas in the U.S. in terms of per capita rates of vehicle theft. The Atlanta* metro area ranked #54 (#1 = highest rate). Criteria: number of vehicle theft offenses per 100,000 inhabitants in 2014. *National Insurance Crime Bureau, "Hot Spots 2014," June 24, 2015*

Seniors/Retirement Rankings

- From its Best Cities for Successful Aging indexes, the Milken Institute generated rankings for metropolitan areas, weighing data in eight categories—health care, wellness, living arrangements, transportation, financial characteristics, education and employment opportunities, community engagement, and overall livability. The Atlanta* metro area was ranked #83 overall in the large metro area category. *Milken Institute, "Best Cities for Successful Aging, 2014"*

Transportation Rankings

- The Atlanta* metro area appeared on *Forbes* list of places with the most extreme commutes. The metro area ranked #7 out of 10. Criteria: average travel time; percentage of mega commuters. Mega-commuters travel more than 90 minutes and 50 miles each way to work. *Forbes.com, "The Cities with the Most Extreme Commutes," March 5, 2013*

Miscellaneous Rankings

- The watchdog site Charity Navigator conducts an annual study of charities in the nation's major markets both to analyze statistical differences in their financial, accountability, and transparency practices and to track year-to-year variations in individual communities. The Atlanta* metro area was ranked #23 among the 30 metro markets in the rating dimension of Overall Score. *www.charitynavigator.org, "Metro Market Study 2015," June 5, 2015*
- The Harris Poll's Happiness Index survey revealed that of the top ten U.S. markets, the Atlanta* metro area residents ranked #4 in happiness. Criteria included strong assent to positive statements and strong disagreement with negative ones, and degree of agreement with a series of statements about respondents' personal relationships and general outlook. *www.harrisinteractive.com, "Dallas/Fort Worth Is "Happiest" City among America's Top Ten Markets," September 4, 2013*

- Energizer Personal Care, the makers of Edge® shave gel, in partnership with Sperling's BestPlaces, ranked 50 major metro areas in terms of everyday irritations. The Atlanta* metro area ranked #5 the 50 metro area most iritating to guys. Criteria: high male-to-female ratio; poor sports team performance and high ticket prices; slow traffic; lack of job availability; unaffordable housing; extreme weather; lack of nightlife and fitness options. *Energizer Personal Care, "Most Irritatng Cities for Guys," August 26, 2013*
- Mars Chocolate North America, the makers of COMBOS®, in partnership with Sperling's BestPlaces, ranked 50 major metro areas in terms of their "manliness." The Atlanta* metro area ranked #17. Criteria: number of professional sports teams; number of nearby NASCAR tracks and racing events; manly lifestyle; concentration of manly retail stores; manly occupations per capita; salty snack sales; "Board of Manliness" rankings. *Mars Chocolate North America, "America's Manliest Cities 2012"*
- The Atlanta* metro area was selected as one of "America's Most Miserable Cities" by *Forbes.com.* The metro area ranked #16 out of 20. Criteria: violent crime; unemployment; foreclosures; income and property taxes; home prices; commute times; climate. *Forbes.com, "America's Most Miserable Cities" February 22, 2013*
- The National Alliance to End Homelessness ranked the 100 most populous metro areas with the highest rate of homelessness. The Atlanta* metro area ranked #61. Criteria: number of homeless people per 10,000 population in 2011. *National Alliance to End Homelessness, The State of Homelessness in America 2012*

Peachtree City is located within the Atlanta-Sandy Springs-Roswell, GA Metropolitan Statistical Area.

Business Environment

CITY FINANCES

City Government Finances

Component	2012 ($000)	2012 ($ per capita)
Total Revenues	37,712	1,097
Total Expenditures	41,577	1,209
Debt Outstanding	15,834	460
Cash and Securities[1]	39,167	1,139

Note: (1) Cash and security holdings of a government at the close of its fiscal year, including those of its dependent agencies, utilities, and liquor stores.
Source: U.S Census Bureau, State & Local Government Finances 2012

City Government Revenue by Source

Source	2012 ($000)	2012 ($ per capita)
General Revenue		
From Federal Government	2,509	73
From State Government	182	5
From Local Governments	6,576	191
Taxes		
Property	12,459	362
Sales and Gross Receipts	5,729	166
Personal Income	0	0
Corporate Income	0	0
Motor Vehicle License	0	0
Other Taxes	1,176	34
Current Charges	7,489	217
Liquor Store	0	0
Utility	0	0
Employee Retirement	0	0

Source: U.S Census Bureau, State & Local Government Finances 2012

City Government Expenditures by Function

Function	2012 ($000)	2012 ($ per capita)	2012 (%)
General Direct Expenditures			
Air Transportation	9,736	283	23.4
Corrections	0	0	0.0
Education	0	0	0.0
Employment Security Administration	0	0	0.0
Financial Administration	1,032	30	2.4
Fire Protection	7,118	207	17.1
General Public Buildings	156	4	0.3
Governmental Administration, Other	2,248	65	5.4
Health	275	8	0.6
Highways	3,279	95	7.8
Hospitals	0	0	0.0
Housing and Community Development	48	1	0.1
Interest on General Debt	788	22	1.8
Judicial and Legal	670	19	1.6
Libraries	908	26	2.1
Parking	0	0	0.0
Parks and Recreation	3,620	105	8.7
Police Protection	6,669	194	16.0
Public Welfare	133	3	0.3
Sewerage	1,072	31	2.5
Solid Waste Management	0	0	0.0
Veterans' Services	0	0	0.0
Liquor Store	0	0	0.0
Utility	0	0	0.0
Employee Retirement	0	0	0.0

Source: U.S Census Bureau, State & Local Government Finances 2012

DEMOGRAPHICS

Population Growth

Area	1990 Census	2000 Census	2010 Census	2014* Estimate	Population Growth (%) 1990-2014	2010-2014
City	18,908	31,580	34,364	34,701	83.5	1.0
MSA[1]	3,069,411	4,247,981	5,268,860	5,455,053	77.7	3.5
U.S.	248,709,873	281,421,906	308,745,538	314,107,084	26.3	1.7

Note: (1) Figures cover the Atlanta-Sandy Springs-Roswell, GA Metropolitan Statistical Area—see Appendix B for areas included; (*) 2010-2014 5-year estimated population
Source: U.S. Census Bureau, 1990 Census, Census 2000, Census 2010, 2010-2014 American Community Survey 5-Year Estimates

Household Size

Area	Persons in Household (%) One	Two	Three	Four	Five	Six	Seven or More	Average Household Size
City	21.9	34.9	16.4	15.2	7.6	2.0	1.6	2.83
MSA[1]	26.5	31.3	16.8	14.7	6.5	2.4	1.4	2.77
U.S.	27.5	33.5	15.8	13.1	6.0	2.3	1.4	2.64

Note: (1) Figures cover the Atlanta-Sandy Springs-Roswell, GA Metropolitan Statistical Area—see Appendix B for areas included
Source: U.S. Census Bureau, 2010-2014 American Community Survey 5-Year Estimates

Race

Area	White Alone[2] (%)	Black Alone[2] (%)	Asian Alone[2] (%)	AIAN[3] Alone[2] (%)	NHOPI[4] Alone[2] (%)	Other Race Alone[2] (%)	Two or More Races (%)
City	83.2	8.5	4.7	0.3	0.1	1.2	2.1
MSA[1]	56.1	32.9	5.2	0.3	0.0	3.4	2.2
U.S.	73.8	12.6	5.0	0.8	0.2	4.7	2.9

Note: (1) Figures cover the Atlanta-Sandy Springs-Roswell, GA Metropolitan Statistical Area—see Appendix B for areas included; (2) Alone is defined as not being in combination with one or more other races; (3) American Indian and Alaska Native; (4) Native Hawaiian and Other Pacific Islander
Source: U.S. Census Bureau, 2010-2014 American Community Survey 5-Year Estimates

Hispanic or Latino Origin

Area	Total (%)	Mexican (%)	Puerto Rican (%)	Cuban (%)	Other (%)
City	7.9	4.4	0.8	0.6	2.0
MSA[1]	10.4	5.9	0.9	0.4	3.2
U.S.	16.9	10.8	1.6	0.6	3.8

Note: Persons of Hispanic or Latino origin can be of any race; (1) Figures cover the Atlanta-Sandy Springs-Roswell, GA Metropolitan Statistical Area—see Appendix B for areas included
Source: U.S. Census Bureau, 2010-2014 American Community Survey 5-Year Estimates

Ancestry

Area	German	Irish	English	American	Italian	Polish	French[2]	Scottish	Dutch
City	17.0	14.3	13.2	9.6	6.1	2.3	2.5	2.7	2.5
MSA[1]	7.4	7.5	7.5	9.8	2.6	1.3	1.5	1.8	0.8
U.S.	14.9	10.8	8.0	7.1	5.5	3.0	2.7	1.7	1.4

Note: Figures are the percentage of the total population reporting a particular ancestry. The nine most commonly reported ancestries in the U.S. are shown. Figures include multiple ancestries (e.g. if a person reported being Irish and Italian, they were included in both columns); (1) Figures cover the Atlanta-Sandy Springs-Roswell, GA Metropolitan Statistical Area—see Appendix B for areas included; (2) Excludes Basque
Source: U.S. Census Bureau, 2010-2014 American Community Survey 5-Year Estimates

Foreign-Born Population

Area	Percent of Population Born in								
	Any Foreign Country	Asia	Mexico	Europe	Carribean	Central America[2]	South America	Africa	Canada
City	11.6	3.9	2.8	2.0	0.8	0.2	0.9	0.6	0.4
MSA[1]	13.3	4.0	3.1	1.2	1.4	1.1	0.9	1.3	0.2
U.S.	13.1	3.8	3.7	1.5	1.2	1.0	0.9	0.6	0.3

Note: (1) Figures cover the Atlanta-Sandy Springs-Roswell, GA Metropolitan Statistical Area—see Appendix B for areas included; (2) Excludes Mexico.
Source: U.S. Census Bureau, 2010-2014 American Community Survey 5-Year Estimates

Marital Status

Area	Never Married	Now Married[2]	Separated	Widowed	Divorced
City	24.1	61.5	1.1	4.5	8.8
MSA[1]	34.1	47.8	2.3	4.7	11.1
U.S.	32.5	48.4	2.2	5.9	10.9

Note: Figures are percentages and cover the population 15 years of age and older; (1) Figures cover the Atlanta-Sandy Springs-Roswell, GA Metropolitan Statistical Area—see Appendix B for areas included; (2) Excludes separated
Source: U.S. Census Bureau, 2010-2014 American Community Survey 5-Year Estimates

Disability Status

Area	All Ages	Under 18 Years Old	18 to 64 Years Old	65 Years and Over
City	6.4	3.2	4.5	21.1
MSA[1]	9.8	3.3	8.5	35.2
U.S.	12.3	4.1	10.2	36.3

Note: Figures show percent of the civilian noninstitutionalized population that reported having a disability. Disability status is determined from from six types of difficulty: vision, hearing, cognitive, ambulatory, self-care, and independent living. For children under 5 years old, hearing and vision difficulty are used to determine disability status. For children between the ages of 5 and 14, disability status is determined from hearing, vision, cognitive, ambulatory, and self-care difficulties. For people aged 15 years and older, they are considered to have a disability if they have difficulty with any one of the six difficulty types; (1) Figures cover the Atlanta-Sandy Springs-Roswell, GA Metropolitan Statistical Area—see Appendix B for areas included.
Source: U.S. Census Bureau, 2010-2014 American Community Survey 5-Year Estimates

Age

Area	Percent of Population									Median Age
	Under Age 5	Age 5–19	Age 20–34	Age 35–44	Age 45–54	Age 55–64	Age 65–74	Age 75–84	Age 85+	
City	4.3	24.7	13.4	12.4	17.1	14.8	8.4	3.1	1.6	42.2
MSA[1]	6.9	21.7	20.7	15.2	14.6	10.9	6.1	2.8	1.0	35.4
U.S.	6.4	19.9	20.6	13.0	14.1	12.3	7.6	4.3	1.9	37.4

Note: (1) Figures cover the Atlanta-Sandy Springs-Roswell, GA Metropolitan Statistical Area—see Appendix B for areas included
Source: U.S. Census Bureau, 2010-2014 American Community Survey 5-Year Estimates

Gender

Area	Males	Females	Males per 100 Females
City	16,715	17,986	92.9
MSA[1]	2,649,723	2,805,330	94.5
U.S.	154,515,159	159,591,925	96.8

Note: (1) Figures cover the Atlanta-Sandy Springs-Roswell, GA Metropolitan Statistical Area—see Appendix B for areas included
Source: U.S. Census Bureau, 2010-2014 American Community Survey 5-Year Estimates

Religious Groups by Family

Area	Catholic	Baptist	Non-Den.	Methodist[2]	Lutheran	LDS[3]	Pente-costal	Presby-terian[4]	Muslim[5]	Judaism
MSA[1]	7.4	17.4	6.8	7.8	0.5	0.7	2.6	1.8	0.7	0.5
U.S.	19.1	9.3	4.0	4.0	2.3	2.0	1.9	1.6	0.8	0.7

Note: Figures are the number of adherents as a percentage of the total population; (1) Figures cover the Atlanta-Sandy Springs-Marietta, GA Metropolitan Statistical Area—see Appendix B for areas included; (2) Methodist/Pietist; (3) Latter Day Saints; (4) Reformed; (5) Figures are estimates
Source: Association of Statisticians of American Religious Bodies, 2010 U.S. Religion Census: Religious Congregations & Membership Study

Religious Groups by Tradition

Area	Catholic	Evangelical Protestant	Mainline Protestant	Other Tradition	Black Protestant	Orthodox
MSA[1]	7.4	26.0	9.8	2.9	3.1	0.2
U.S.	19.1	16.2	7.3	4.3	1.6	0.3

Note: Figures are the number of adherents as a percentage of the total population; (1) Figures cover the Atlanta-Sandy Springs-Marietta, GA Metropolitan Statistical Area—see Appendix B for areas included
Source: Association of Statisticians of American Religious Bodies, 2010 U.S. Religion Census: Religious Congregations & Membership Study

ECONOMY

Gross Metropolitan Product

Area	2013	2014	2015	2016	Rank[2]
MSA[1]	307.2	321.1	335.5	354.0	10

Note: Figures are in billions of dollars; (1) Figures cover the Atlanta-Sandy Springs-Roswell, GA Metropolitan Statistical Area—see Appendix B for areas included; (2) Rank is based on 2016 data and ranges from 1 to 381
Source: The U.S. Conference of Mayors, U.S. Metro Economies: GMP and Employment 2014-2016, June 2015

Economic Growth

Area	2011-13 (%)	2014 (%)	2015 (%)	2016 (%)	Rank[2]
MSA[1]	1.8	2.8	3.1	3.5	33
U.S.	2.2	2.4	2.3	2.9	–

Note: Figures are real gross metropolitan product (GMP) growth rates and represent annual average percent change; (1) Figures cover the Atlanta-Sandy Springs-Roswell, GA Metropolitan Statistical Area—see Appendix B for areas included; (2) Rank is based on 2016 data and ranges from 1 to 381
Source: The U.S. Conference of Mayors, U.S. Metro Economies: GMP and Employment 2014-2016, June 2015

Metropolitan Area Exports

Area	2009	2010	2011	2012	2013	2014	Rank[2]
MSA[1]	13,405.8	15,009.6	17,229.0	18,169.0	18,827.8	19,870.2	18

Note: Figures are in millions of dollars; (1) Figures cover the Atlanta-Sandy Springs-Roswell, GA Metropolitan Statistical Area—see Appendix B for areas included; (2) Rank is based on 2014 data and ranges from 1 to 385
Source: U.S. Department of Commerce, International Trade Administration, Office of Trade & Industry Information, Manufacturing & Services, data extracted March 10, 2016

Building Permits

Area	Single-Family			Multi-Family			Total		
	2014	2015p	Pct. Chg.	2014	2015p	Pct. Chg.	2014	2015p	Pct. Chg.
City	39	36	-7.7	0	0	-	39	36	-7.7
MSA[1]	16,984	19,885	17.1	9,699	10,126	4.4	26,683	30,011	12.5
U.S.	640,300	690,800	7.9	411,800	487,600	18.4	1,052,100	1,178,400	12.0

Note: (1) Figures cover the Atlanta-Sandy Springs-Roswell, GA Metropolitan Statistical Area—see Appendix B for areas included; Figures represent new, privately-owned housing units authorized (unadjusted data); All permit data are based on estimates with imputation; (p) preliminary data.
Source: U.S. Census Bureau, Manufacturing, Mining, and Construction Statistics, Building Permits, 2014, 2015

Bankruptcy Filings

Area	Business Filings 2014	Business Filings 2015	Business Filings % Chg.	Nonbusiness Filings 2014	Nonbusiness Filings 2015	Nonbusiness Filings % Chg.
Fayette County	13	10	-23.1	401	398	-0.7
U.S.	26,983	24,735	-8.3	909,812	819,760	-9.9

Note: Business filings include Chapter 7, Chapter 11, Chapter 12, and Chapter 13; Nonbusiness filings include Chapter 7, Chapter 11, and Chapter 13
Source: Administrative Office of the U.S. Courts, Business and Nonbusiness Bankruptcy, County Cases Commenced by Chapter of the Bankruptcy Code, During the 12- Month Period Ending December 31, 2014 and Business and Nonbusiness Bankruptcy, County Cases Commenced by Chapter of the Bankruptcy Code, During the 12- Month Period Ending December 31, 2015

Housing Vacancy Rates

Area	Gross Vacancy Rate[2] (%)			Year-Round Vacancy Rate[3] (%)			Rental Vacancy Rate[4] (%)			Homeowner Vacancy Rate[5] (%)		
	2013	2014	2015	2013	2014	2015	2013	2014	2015	2013	2014	2015
MSA[1]	12.4	11.0	11.0	11.8	10.3	10.7	10.2	8.8	8.2	2.1	2.5	2.2
U.S.	13.6	13.4	12.9	10.7	10.4	10.0	8.3	7.6	7.1	2.0	1.9	1.8

Note: (1) Figures cover the Atlanta-Sandy Springs-Roswell, GA Metropolitan Statistical Area—see Appendix B for areas included; (2) The percentage of the total housing inventory that is vacant; (3) The percentage of the housing inventory (excluding seasonal units) that is year-round vacant; (4) The percentage of rental inventory that is vacant for rent; (5) The percentage of homeowner inventory that is vacant for sale
Source: U.S. Census Bureau, Housing Vacancies and Homeownership Annual Statistics: 2015

INCOME

Income

Area	Per Capita ($)	Median Household ($)	Average Household ($)
City	38,599	86,352	104,908
MSA[1]	28,880	56,618	78,422
U.S.	28,555	53,482	74,596

Note: (1) Figures cover the Atlanta-Sandy Springs-Roswell, GA Metropolitan Statistical Area—see Appendix B for areas included
Source: U.S. Census Bureau, 2010-2014 American Community Survey 5-Year Estimates

Household Income Distribution

Area	Percent of Households Earning: Under $15,000	$15,000 -24,999	$25,000 -34,999	$35,000 -49,999	$50,000 -74,999	$75,000 -99,000	$100,000 -149,999	$150,000 and up
City	6.0	4.4	5.6	9.8	17.2	14.4	20.8	21.8
MSA[1]	11.2	9.5	9.9	13.7	18.3	12.4	13.7	11.3
U.S.	12.5	10.7	10.2	13.5	17.8	12.2	13.0	10.0

Note: (1) Figures cover the Atlanta-Sandy Springs-Roswell, GA Metropolitan Statistical Area—see Appendix B for areas included
Source: U.S. Census Bureau, 2010-2014 American Community Survey 5-Year Estimates

Poverty Rate

Area	All Ages	Under 18 Years Old	18 to 64 Years Old	65 Years and Over
City	7.7	11.1	6.8	5.1
MSA[1]	15.7	22.2	14.0	9.6
U.S.	15.6	21.9	14.6	9.4

Note: Figures are percentage of people whose income during the past 12 months was below the poverty level; (1) Figures cover the Atlanta-Sandy Springs-Roswell, GA Metropolitan Statistical Area—see Appendix B for areas included
Source: U.S. Census Bureau, 2010-2014 American Community Survey 5-Year Estimates

EMPLOYMENT

Labor Force and Employment

Area	Civilian Labor Force			Workers Employed		
	Dec. 2014	Dec. 2015	% Chg.	Dec. 2014	Dec. 2015	% Chg.
City	17,667	17,893	1.2	16,841	17,144	1.7
MSA[1]	2,815,375	2,835,654	0.7	2,647,261	2,695,404	1.8
U.S.	155,521,000	157,245,000	1.1	147,190,000	149,703,000	1.7

Note: Data is not seasonally adjusted and covers workers 16 years of age and older; (1) Figures cover the Atlanta-Sandy Springs-Roswell, GA Metropolitan Statistical Area—see Appendix B for areas included
Source: Bureau of Labor Statistics, Local Area Unemployment Statistics

Unemployment Rate

Area	2015											
	Jan.	Feb.	Mar.	Apr.	May	Jun.	Jul.	Aug.	Sep.	Oct.	Nov.	Dec.
City	5.1	5.0	4.7	4.5	5.1	5.3	5.4	4.8	4.6	4.5	3.9	4.2
MSA[1]	6.2	6.1	5.9	5.6	5.9	6.0	6.1	5.6	5.5	5.4	4.9	4.9
U.S.	6.1	5.8	5.6	5.1	5.3	5.5	5.6	5.2	4.9	4.8	4.8	4.8

Note: Data is not seasonally adjusted and covers workers 16 years of age and older; (1) Figures cover the Atlanta-Sandy Springs-Roswell, GA Metropolitan Statistical Area—see Appendix B for areas included
Source: Bureau of Labor Statistics, Local Area Unemployment Statistics

Employment by Occupation

Occupation Classification	City (%)	MSA[1] (%)	U.S. (%)
Management, Business, Science, and Arts	46.6	39.4	36.4
Natural Resources, Construction, and Maintenance	3.6	8.1	9.0
Production, Transportation, and Material Moving	11.4	10.9	12.1
Sales and Office	24.0	25.6	24.4
Service	14.4	16.0	18.2

Note: Figures cover employed civilians 16 years of age and older; (1) Figures cover the Atlanta-Sandy Springs-Roswell, GA Metropolitan Statistical Area—see Appendix B for areas included
Source: U.S. Census Bureau, 2010-2014 American Community Survey 5-Year Estimates

Employment by Industry

Sector	MSA[1]		U.S.
	Number of Employees	Percent of Total	Percent of Total
Construction	111,700	4.2	4.5
Education and Health Services	323,700	12.2	15.7
Financial Activities	163,400	6.1	5.7
Government	326,200	12.3	15.5
Information	87,400	3.3	1.9
Leisure and Hospitality	275,800	10.4	10.4
Manufacturing	161,300	6.1	8.6
Mining and Logging	1,500	<0.1	0.5
Other Services	98,700	3.7	3.9
Professional and Business Services	489,600	18.5	13.9
Retail Trade	301,200	11.3	11.3
Transportation, Warehousing, and Utilities	144,200	5.4	3.9
Wholesale Trade	159,100	6.0	4.1

Note: Figures are non-farm employment as of December 2015. Figures are not seasonally adjusted and include workers 16 years of age and older; (1) Figures cover the Atlanta-Sandy Springs-Roswell, GA Metropolitan Statistical Area—see Appendix B for areas included
Source: Bureau of Labor Statistics, Current Employment Statistics, Employment, Hours, and Earnings

Occupations with Greatest Projected Employment Growth: 2012 – 2022

Occupation[1]	2012 Employment	2022 Projected Employment	Numeric Employment Change	Percent Employment Change
Combined Food Preparation and Serving Workers, Including Fast Food	169,450	192,830	23,380	13.8
Customer Service Representatives	95,900	115,410	19,510	20.3
Laborers and Freight, Stock, and Material Movers, Hand	85,460	104,150	18,690	21.9
Elementary School Teachers, Except Special Education	42,300	56,170	13,870	32.8
General and Operations Managers	71,410	84,890	13,480	18.9
Sales Representatives, Wholesale and Manufacturing, Except Technical and Scientific Products	56,220	67,450	11,230	20.0
Secretaries and Administrative Assistants, Except Legal, Medical, and Executive	51,850	63,030	11,180	21.6
Office Clerks, General	79,920	91,010	11,090	13.9
Janitors and Cleaners, Except Maids and Housekeeping Cleaners	52,860	63,600	10,740	20.3
Childcare Workers	37,650	48,280	10,630	28.2

Note: Projections cover Georgia; (1) Sorted by numeric employment change
Source: www.projectionscentral.com, State Occupational Projections, 2012–2022 Long-Term Projections

Fastest Growing Occupations: 2012 – 2022

Occupation[1]	2012 Employment	2022 Projected Employment	Numeric Employment Change	Percent Employment Change
Physician Assistants	2,820	4,740	1,920	67.9
Health Specialties Teachers, Postsecondary	4,870	8,060	3,190	65.5
Agents and Business Managers of Artists, Performers, and Athletes	430	700	270	62.6
Personal Care Aides	16,440	26,630	10,190	62.0
Interpreters and Translators	1,650	2,630	980	58.9
Nursing Instructors and Teachers, Postsecondary	1,420	2,200	780	55.5
Psychiatric Aides	1,390	2,150	760	55.3
Home Health Aides	7,950	12,340	4,390	55.1
Nurse Practitioners	3,260	5,010	1,750	53.9
Nurse Midwives	250	380	130	53.6

Note: Projections cover Georgia; (1) Sorted by percent employment change and excludes occupations with numeric employment change less than 100
Source: www.projectionscentral.com, State Occupational Projections, 2012–2022 Long-Term Projections

Average Wages

Occupation	$/Hr.	Occupation	$/Hr.
Accountants and Auditors	38.06	Maids and Housekeeping Cleaners	9.32
Automotive Mechanics	19.15	Maintenance and Repair Workers	18.24
Bookkeepers	19.46	Marketing Managers	64.91
Carpenters	19.77	Nuclear Medicine Technologists	35.79
Cashiers	9.38	Nurses, Licensed Practical	19.58
Clerks, General Office	14.20	Nurses, Registered	31.73
Clerks, Receptionists/Information	14.19	Nursing Assistants	11.41
Clerks, Shipping/Receiving	14.09	Packers and Packagers, Hand	10.96
Computer Programmers	40.72	Physical Therapists	39.70
Computer Systems Analysts	42.17	Postal Service Mail Carriers	24.82
Computer User Support Specialists	25.87	Real Estate Brokers	51.40
Cooks, Restaurant	11.38	Retail Salespersons	11.85
Dentists	83.66	Sales Reps., Exc. Tech./Scientific	32.41
Electrical Engineers	43.06	Sales Reps., Tech./Scientific	39.40
Electricians	22.23	Secretaries, Exc. Legal/Med./Exec.	17.34
Financial Managers	68.91	Security Guards	12.62
First-Line Supervisors/Managers, Sales	19.56	Surgeons	128.18
Food Preparation Workers	9.93	Teacher Assistants*	10.47
General and Operations Managers	60.10	Teachers, Elementary School*	26.05
Hairdressers/Cosmetologists	13.42	Teachers, Secondary School*	27.22
Internists	129.01	Telemarketers	14.98
Janitors and Cleaners	11.57	Truck Drivers, Heavy/Tractor-Trailer	19.95
Landscaping/Groundskeeping Workers	12.98	Truck Drivers, Light/Delivery Svcs.	17.48
Lawyers	66.05	Waiters and Waitresses	9.22

Note: Wage data covers the Atlanta-Sandy Springs-Marietta, GA Metropolitan Statistical Area—see Appendix B for areas included; (*) Hourly wages for elementary/secondary school teachers and teacher assistants were calculated by the editors from annual wage data based on a 40 hour work week; n/a not available.
Source: Bureau of Labor Statistics, Metro Area Occupational Employment and Wage Estimates, May 2015

TAXES

State Corporate Income Tax Rates

State	Tax Rate (%)	Income Brackets ($)	Num. of Brackets	Financial Institution Tax Rate (%)[a]	Federal Income Tax Ded.
Georgia	6.0	Flat rate	1	6.0	No

Note: Tax rates as of January 1, 2016; (a) Rates listed are the corporate income tax rate applied to financial institutions or excise taxes based on income. Some states have other taxes based upon the value of deposits or shares.
Source: Federation of Tax Administrators, "State Corporate Income Tax Rates, 2016"

State Individual Income Tax Rates

State	Tax Rate (%)	Income Brackets ($)	Num. of Brackets	Personal Exempt. ($)[1]		Fed. Inc. Tax Ded.
				Single	Dependents	
Georgia	1.0 - 6.0	750 - 7,001 (h)	6	2,700	3,000	No

Note: Tax rates as of January 1, 2016; Local- and county-level taxes are not included; n/a not applicable; (1) Married joint filers generally receive double the single exemption; (h) The Georgia income brackets reported are for single individuals. For married couples filing jointly, the same tax rates apply to income brackets ranging from $1,000, to $10,000.
Source: Federation of Tax Administrators, "State Individual Income Tax Rates, 2016"

Various State and Local Tax Rates

State	State and Local Sales and Use (%)	State Sales and Use (%)	Gasoline[1] (¢/gal.)	Cigarette[2] ($/pack)	Spirits[3] ($/gal.)	Wine[4] ($/gal.)	Beer[5] ($/gal.)
Georgia	6.00	4.0	31.02	0.37	3.79 (f)	1.51 (l)	0.48 (q)(r)

Note: All tax rates as of January 1, 2016; (1) The American Petroleum Institute has developed a methodology for determining the average tax rate on a gallon of fuel. Rates may include any of the following: excise taxes, environmental fees, storage tank fees, other fees or taxes, general sales tax, and local taxes. In states where gasoline is subject to the general sales tax, or where the fuel tax is based on the average sale price, the average rate determined by API is sensitive to changes in the price of gasoline. States that fully or partially apply general sales taxes to gasoline: CA, CO, GA, IL, IN, MI, NY; (2) The federal excise tax of $1.0066 per pack and local taxes are not included; (3) Rates are those applicable to off-premise sales of 40% alcohol by volume (a.b.v.) distilled spirits in 750ml containers. Local excise taxes are excluded; (4) Rates are those applicable to off-premise sales of 11% a.b.v. non-carbonated wine in 750ml containers; (5) Rates are those applicable to off-premise sales of 4.7% a.b.v. beer in 12 ounce containers; (f) Different rates are also applicable according to alcohol content, place of production, size of container, or place purchased (on- or off-premise or onboard airlines); (l) Different rates also applicable according to alcohol content, place of production, size of container, place purchased (on- or off-premise or on board airlines) or type of wine (carbonated, vermouth, etc.); (q) Different rates are also applicable according to alcohol content, place of production, size of container, or place purchased (on- or off-premise or onboard airlines); (r) Includes the statewide local rate in Alabama ($0.52) and Georgia ($0.53).
Source: Tax Foundation, 2016 Facts & Figures: How Does Your State Compare?

State Business Tax Climate Index Rankings

State	Overall Rank	Corporate Tax Rank	Individual Income Tax Rank	Sales Tax Rank	Unemployment Insurance Tax Rank	Property Tax Rank
Georgia	39	9	42	35	37	31

Note: The index is a measure of how each state's tax laws affect economic performance. The lower the rank, the more favorable a state's tax system is for business. States without a given tax are given a ranking of 1. The scores/rankings for the District of Columbia do not affect other states. The 2016 index represents the tax climate as of July 1, 2015 (the beginning of Fiscal Year 2016).
Source: Tax Foundation, State Business Tax Climate Index 2016

TRANSPORTATION

Means of Transportation to Work

Area	Car/Truck/Van: Drove Alone	Car/Truck/Van: Car-pooled	Public Transportation: Bus	Public Transportation: Subway	Public Transportation: Railroad	Bicycle	Walked	Other Means	Worked at Home
City	78.1	9.1	0.6	0.3	0.1	0.2	0.4	3.1	8.1
MSA[1]	77.9	10.4	2.2	0.7	0.1	0.2	1.4	1.4	5.8
U.S.	76.4	9.6	2.6	1.8	0.6	0.6	2.8	1.3	4.4

Note: Figures are percentages and cover workers 16 years of age and older; (1) Figures cover the Atlanta-Sandy Springs-Roswell, GA Metropolitan Statistical Area—see Appendix B for areas included
Source: U.S. Census Bureau, 2010-2014 American Community Survey 5-Year Estimates

Travel Time to Work

Area	Less Than 10 Minutes	10 to 19 Minutes	20 to 29 Minutes	30 to 44 Minutes	45 to 59 Minutes	60 to 89 Minutes	90 Minutes or More
City	14.3	26.4	10.7	24.5	14.5	8.0	1.5
MSA[1]	7.8	23.4	20.4	24.7	11.9	8.8	3.0
U.S.	13.3	29.6	21.0	20.2	7.7	5.7	2.6

Note: Figures are percentages and include workers 16 years old and over; (1) Figures cover the Atlanta-Sandy Springs-Roswell, GA Metropolitan Statistical Area—see Appendix B for areas included
Source: U.S. Census Bureau, 2010-2014 American Community Survey 5-Year Estimates

Freeway Travel Time Index

Area	1985	1990	1995	2000	2005	2010	2014
Urban Area Rank[1,2]	24	21	13	19	21	25	25
Urban Area Index[1]	1.11	1.15	1.22	1.24	1.26	1.23	1.24
Average Index[3]	1.09	1.11	1.14	1.17	1.20	1.19	1.20

Note: Freeway Travel Time Index—the ratio of travel time in the peak period to the travel time at free-flow conditions. For example, a value of 1.30 indicates a 20-minute free-flow trip takes 26 minutes in the peak (20 minutes x 1.30 = 26 minutes); (1) Covers the Atlanta GA urban area; (2) Rank is based on 101 urban areas (#1 = highest travel time index); (3) Average of 101 urban areas
Source: Texas Transportation Institute, 2015 Urban Mobility Scorecard, August 2015

Freeway Commuter Stress Index

Area	1985	1990	1995	2000	2005	2010	2014
Urban Area Rank[1,2]	24	22	13	16	18	22	23
Urban Area Index[1]	1.18	1.22	1.29	1.32	1.33	1.31	1.32
Average Index[3]	1.13	1.16	1.19	1.22	1.25	1.24	1.25

Note: The Freeway Commuter Stress Index is the same as the Freeway Travel Time Index (see table above) except that it includes only the travel in the peak directions during the peak periods; the TTI includes travel in all directions during the peak period. Thus, the CSI is more indicative of the work trip experienced by each commuter on a daily basis. (1) Covers the Atlanta GA urban area; (2) Rank is based on 101 urban areas (#1 = highest stress index); (3) Average of 101 urban areas

Source: Texas Transportation Institute, 2015 Urban Mobility Scorecard, August 2015

Living Environment

COST OF LIVING

Cost of Living Index

Composite Index	Groceries	Housing	Utilities	Trans-portation	Health Care	Misc. Goods/ Services
99.9	103.7	97.8	93.6	104.8	101.4	100.4

Note: The Cost of Living Index measures regional differences in the cost of consumer goods and services, excluding taxes and non-consumer expenditures, for professional and managerial households in the top income quintile. It is based on more than 50,000 prices covering almost 60 different items for which prices are collected three times a year by chambers of commerce, economic development organizations or university applied economic centers in each participating urban area. The numbers shown should be read as a percentage above or below the national average of 100. For example, a value of 115.4 in the groceries column indicates that grocery prices are 15.4% higher than the national average. Small differences in the index numbers should not be interpreted as significant; Figures cover the Atlanta GA urban area.
Source: The Council for Community and Economic Research, ACCRA Cost of Living Index, 2015

Grocery Prices

Area[1]	T-Bone Steak ($/pound)	Frying Chicken ($/pound)	Whole Milk ($/half gal.)	Eggs ($/dozen)	Orange Juice ($/64 oz.)	Coffee ($/11.5 oz.)
City[2]	12.83	1.42	2.30	2.07	3.75	4.58
Avg.	10.99	1.43	2.25	2.26	3.58	4.48
Min.	7.16	0.98	1.30	1.35	2.88	2.98
Max.	14.13	2.43	3.85	4.81	6.39	7.56

Note: (1) Values for the local area are compared with the average, minimum and maximum values for all 292 areas in the Cost of Living Index; (2) Figures cover the Atlanta GA urban area; **T-Bone Steak** *(price per pound);* **Frying Chicken** *(price per pound, whole fryer);* **Whole Milk** *(half gallon carton);* **Eggs** *(price per dozen, Grade A, large);* **Orange Juice** *(64 oz. Tropicana or Florida Natural);* **Coffee** *(11.5 oz. can, vacuum-packed, Maxwell House, Hills Bros, or Folgers).*
Source: The Council for Community and Economic Research, ACCRA Cost of Living Index, 2015

Housing and Utility Costs

Area[1]	New Home Price ($)	Apartment Rent ($/month)	All Electric ($/month)	Part Electric ($/month)	Other Energy ($/month)	Telephone ($/month)
City[2]	289,012	1,050	-	88.79	57.58	29.30
Avg.	312,874	945	179.30	95.07	72.96	28.11
Min.	178,682	479	116.28	43.14	26.46	10.01
Max.	1,472,476	3,984	504.25	189.44	421.11	43.06

Note: (1) Values for the local area are compared with the average, minimum and maximum values for all 292 areas in the Cost of Living Index; (2) Figures cover the Atlanta GA urban area; **New Home Price** *(2,400 sf living area, 8,000 sf lot, in urban area with full utilities);* **Apartment Rent** *(950 sf 2 bedroom/1.5 or 2 bath, unfurnished, excluding all utilities except water);* **All Electric** *(average monthly cost for an all-electric home);* **Part Electric** *(average monthly cost for a part-electric home);* **Other Energy** *(average monthly cost for natural gas, fuel oil, coal, wood, and any other forms of energy except electricity);* **Telephone** *(price includes basic monthly rate for a private residential line plus additional local usage charges incurred by a family of four).*
Source: The Council for Community and Economic Research, ACCRA Cost of Living Index, 2015

Health Care, Transportation, and Other Costs

Area[1]	Doctor ($/visit)	Dentist ($/visit)	Optometrist ($/visit)	Gasoline ($/gallon)	Beauty Salon ($/visit)	Men's Shirt ($)
City[2]	95.50	102.54	89.05	2.46	45.03	24.26
Avg.	105.15	89.02	99.78	2.38	35.30	28.10
Min.	66.87	56.09	48.53	1.95	18.91	13.38
Max.	182.34	150.36	228.33	4.09	67.91	63.80

Note: (1) Values for the local area are compared with the average, minimum and maximum values for all 292 areas in the Cost of Living Index; (2) Figures cover the Atlanta GA urban area; **Doctor** *(general practitioners routine exam of an established patient);* **Dentist** *(adult teeth cleaning and periodic oral examination);* **Optometrist** *(full vision eye exam for established adult patient);* **Gasoline** *(one gallon regular unleaded, national brand, including all taxes, cash price at self-service pump if available);* **Beauty Salon** *(woman's shampoo, trim, and blow-dry);* **Men's Shirt** *(cotton/polyester dress shirt, pinpoint weave, long sleeves).*
Source: The Council for Community and Economic Research, ACCRA Cost of Living Index, 2015

HOUSING

House Price Index (HPI)

Area	National Ranking[2]	Quarterly Change (%)	One-Year Change (%)	Five-Year Change (%)
MSA[1]	49	0.70	7.90	16.00
U.S.[3]	–	1.45	5.76	22.85

Note: The HPI is a weighted repeat sales index. It measures average price changes in repeat sales or refinancings on the same properties. This information is obtained by reviewing repeat mortgage transactions on single-family properties whose mortgages have been purchased or securitized by Fannie Mae or Freddie Mac in January 1975; (1) Atlanta-Sandy Springs-Roswell Metropolitan Statistical Area—see Appendix B for areas included; (2) Rankings are based on annual percentage change for all metro areas containing at least 15,000 transactions over the last 10 years and ranges from 1 to 266; (3) figures based on a weighted average of Census Division estimates using a seasonally adjusted, purchase-only index; all figures are for the period ending December 31, 2015

Source: Federal Housing Finance Agency, House Price Index, February 25, 2016

Median Single-Family Home Prices

Area	2013	2014	2015p	Percent Change 2014 to 2015
MSA[1]	139.5	159.5	173.6	8.8
U.S. Average	197.4	208.9	223.9	7.2

Note: Figures are median sales prices of existing single-family homes in thousands of dollars; (p) preliminary; n/a not available; (1) Atlanta-Sandy Springs-Roswell, GA Metropolitan Statistical Area—see Appendix B for areas included

Source: National Association of Realtors, Median Sales Price of Existing Single-Family Homes for Metropolitan Areas, 4th Quarter 2015

Qualifying Income Based on Median Sales Price of Existing Single-Family Homes

Area	With 5% Down ($)	With 10% Down ($)	With 20% Down ($)
MSA[1]	37,635	35,654	31,693
U.S. Average	49,535	46,928	41,714

Note: Figures are preliminary; Qualifying income is based on a mortgage rate of 4.1%. Monthly principal and interest payment is limited to 25% of income; n/a not available; (1) Atlanta-Sandy Springs-Roswell, GA Metropolitan Statistical Area—see Appendix B for areas included

Source: National Association of Realtors, Qualifying Income Based on Median Sales Price of Existing Single-Family Homes for Metropolitan Areas, 4th Quarter 2015

Median Apartment Condo-Coop Home Prices

Area	2013	2014	2015p	Percent Change 2014 to 2015
MSA[1]	117.3	136.3	156.9	15.1
U.S. Average	194.9	204.3	210.7	3.1

Note: Figures are median sales prices of existing apartment condo-coop homes in thousands of dollars; (p) preliminary; n/a not available; (1) Atlanta-Sandy Springs-Roswell, GA Metropolitan Statistical Area—see Appendix B for areas included

Source: National Association of Realtors, Median Sales Price of Existing Apartment Condo-Coop Homes for Metropolitan Areas, 4th Quarter 2015

Gross Monthly Rent

Area	Under $200	$200 -299	$300 -499	$500 -749	$750 -999	$1,000 -1,499	$1,500 and up	Median ($)
City	3.4	0.0	3.5	1.1	26.3	36.3	29.6	1,218
MSA[1]	0.9	1.6	3.0	16.1	32.2	35.8	10.2	970
U.S.	1.5	3.2	7.4	21.0	24.1	26.9	15.9	920

Note: Figures are percentages except for Median; Gross rent is the contract rent plus the estimated average monthly cost of utilities (electricity, gas, and water and sewer) and fuels (oil, coal, kerosene, wood, etc.) if these are paid by the renter (or paid for the renter by someone else); (1) Figures cover the Atlanta-Sandy Springs-Roswell, GA Metropolitan Statistical Area—see Appendix B for areas included

Source: U.S. Census Bureau, 2010-2014 American Community Survey 5-Year Estimates

Homeownership Rate

Area	2008 (%)	2009 (%)	2010 (%)	2011 (%)	2012 (%)	2013 (%)	2014 (%)	2015 (%)
MSA[1]	67.5	67.7	67.2	65.8	62.1	61.6	61.6	61.7
U.S.	67.8	67.4	66.9	66.1	65.4	65.1	64.5	63.7

Note: (1) Figures cover the Atlanta-Sandy Springs-Roswell, GA Metropolitan Statistical Area—see Appendix B for areas included
Source: U.S. Census Bureau, Housing Vacancies and Homeownership Annual Statistics: 2015

Year Housing Structure Built

Area	2010 or Later	2000 -2009	1990 -1999	1980 -1989	1970 -1979	1960 -1969	1950 -1959	1940 -1949	Before 1940	Median Year
City	1.4	16.3	36.4	30.1	12.7	2.3	0.3	0.0	0.4	1991
MSA[1]	0.9	26.9	22.5	18.1	13.1	8.1	5.0	2.1	3.2	1990
U.S.	1.0	14.9	13.9	13.8	15.8	11.0	10.8	5.4	13.3	1976

Note: Figures are percentages except for Median Year; (1) Figures cover the Atlanta-Sandy Springs-Roswell, GA Metropolitan Statistical Area—see Appendix B for areas included
Source: U.S. Census Bureau, 2010-2014 American Community Survey 5-Year Estimates

HEALTH

Health Risk Data

Category	MSA[1] (%)	U.S. (%)
Adults aged 18–64 who have any kind of health care coverage	74.3	79.6
Adults who reported being in good or excellent health	86.5	83.1
Adults who are current smokers	17.3	19.6
Adults who are heavy drinkers[2]	4.6	6.1
Adults who are binge drinkers[3]	14.6	16.9
Adults who are overweight (BMI 25.0 - 29.9)	34.4	35.8
Adults who are obese (BMI 30.0 - 99.8)	26.5	27.6
Adults who participated in any physical activities in the past month	81.0	77.1
Adults 50+ who have ever had a sigmoidoscopy or colonoscopy	70.3	67.3
Women aged 40+ who have had a mammogram within the past two years	75.7	74.0
Men aged 40+ who have had a PSA test within the past two years	54.7	45.2
Adults aged 65+ who have had flu shot within the past year	57.2	60.1
Adults who always wear a seatbelt	96.3	93.8

Note: Data as of 2012 unless otherwise noted; (1) Figures cover the Atlanta-Sandy Springs-Marietta, GA Metropolitan Statistical Area—see Appendix B for areas included; (2) Heavy drinkers are classified as males having more than two drinks per day or females having more than one drink per day; (3) Binge drinkers are classified as males having five or more drinks on one occasion or females having four or more drinks on one occasion
Source: Centers for Disease Control and Prevention, Behaviorial Risk Factor Surveillance System, SMART: Selected Metropolitan/Micropolitan Area Risk Trends, 2012 (Note: the CDC has discontinued this dataset but will be releasing a replacement in mid-2016)

Chronic Health Indicators

Category	MSA[1] (%)	U.S. (%)
Adults who have ever been told they had a heart attack	3.7	4.5
Adults who have ever been told they had a stroke	2.9	2.9
Adults who have been told they currently have asthma	8.0	8.9
Adults who have ever been told they have arthritis	20.7	25.7
Adults who have ever been told they have diabetes[2]	8.9	9.7
Adults who have ever been told they had skin cancer	5.2	5.7
Adults who have ever been told they had any other types of cancer	5.2	6.5
Adults who have ever been told they have COPD	5.2	6.2
Adults who have ever been told they have kidney disease	3.0	2.5
Adults who have ever been told they have a form of depression	14.5	18.0

Note: Data as of 2012 unless otherwise noted; (1) Figures cover the Atlanta-Sandy Springs-Marietta, GA Metropolitan Statistical Area—see Appendix B for areas included; (2) Figures do not include pregnancy-related, borderline, or pre-diabetes
Source: Centers for Disease Control and Prevention, Behaviorial Risk Factor Surveillance System, SMART: Selected Metropolitan/Micropolitan Area Risk Trends, 2012 (Note: the CDC has discontinued this dataset but will be releasing a replacement in mid-2016)

Mortality Rates for the Top 10 Causes of Death in the U.S.

ICD-10[a] Sub-Chapter	ICD-10[a] Code	Age-Adjusted Mortality Rate[1] per 100,000 population	
		County[2]	U.S.
Malignant neoplasms	C00-C97	125.7	163.6
Ischaemic heart diseases	I20-I25	51.0	102.2
Other forms of heart disease	I30-I51	67.4	50.1
Chronic lower respiratory diseases	J40-J47	32.7	41.4
Organic, including symptomatic, mental disorders	F01-F09	45.5	38.5
Cerebrovascular diseases	I60-I69	33.9	36.5
Other external causes of accidental injury	W00-X59	24.2	27.5
Other degenerative diseases of the nervous system	G30-G31	30.2	26.3
Diabetes mellitus	E10-E14	17.2	21.1
Hypertensive diseases	I10-I15	17.5	19.7

Note: (a) ICD-10 = International Classification of Diseases 10th Revision; (1) Mortality rates are a three year average covering 2012-2014; (2) Figures cover Fayette County.
Source: Centers for Disease Control and Prevention, National Center for Health Statistics. Underlying Cause of Death 1999-2014 on CDC WONDER Online Database, released 2015.

Mortality Rates for Selected Causes of Death

ICD-10[a] Sub-Chapter	ICD-10[a] Code	Age-Adjusted Mortality Rate[1] per 100,000 population	
		County[2]	U.S.
Assault	X85-Y09	Unreliable	5.1
Diseases of the liver	K70-K76	8.7	13.5
Human immunodeficiency virus (HIV) disease	B20-B24	Suppressed	2.1
Influenza and pneumonia	J09-J18	14.7	15.2
Intentional self-harm	X60-X84	8.4	12.7
Malnutrition	E40-E46	Suppressed	0.9
Obesity and other hyperalimentation	E65-E68	Suppressed	1.9
Renal failure	N17-N19	15.8	13.0
Transport accidents	V01-V99	12.1	11.6
Viral hepatitis	B15-B19	Suppressed	2.1

Note: (a) ICD-10 = International Classification of Diseases 10th Revision; (1) Mortality rates are a three year average covering 2012-2014; (2) Figures cover Fayette County; Data are Suppressed when the data meet the criteria for confidentiality constraints; Mortality rates are flagged as Unreliable when the rate would be calculated with a numerator of 20 or less.
Source: Centers for Disease Control and Prevention, National Center for Health Statistics. Underlying Cause of Death 1999-2014 on CDC WONDER Online Database, released 2015.

Health Insurance Coverage

Area	With Health Insurance	With Private Health Insurance	With Public Health Insurance	Without Health Insurance	Population Under Age 18 Without Health Insurance
City	91.3	83.5	19.5	8.7	5.6
MSA[1]	81.9	65.5	24.4	18.1	9.1
U.S.	85.8	65.8	31.1	14.2	7.1

Note: Figures are percentages that cover the civilian noninstitutionalized population; (1) Figures cover the Atlanta-Sandy Springs-Roswell, GA Metropolitan Statistical Area—see Appendix B for areas included
Source: U.S. Census Bureau, 2010-2014 American Community Survey 5-Year Estimates

Number of Medical Professionals

Area	MDs[3]	DOs[3,4]	Dentists	Podiatrists	Chiropractors	Optometrists
County[1] (number)	324	10	101	16	51	20
County[1] (rate[2])	299.0	9.2	92.1	14.6	46.5	18.2
U.S. (rate[2])	272.5	20.9	64.7	5.8	25.9	15.2

Note: Data as of 2014 unless noted; (1) Data covers Fayette County; (2) Rate per 100,000 population; (3) Data as of 2013 and includes all active, non-federal physicians; (4) Doctor of Osteopathic Medicine
Source: U.S. Department of Health and Human Services, Health Resources and Services Administration, Bureau of Health Professions, Area Resource File (ARF) 2014-2015

Best Hospitals

According to *U.S. News,* the Atlanta-Sandy Springs-Roswell, GA metro area is home to three of the best hospitals in the U.S.: **Emory University Hospital** (12 specialties); **Emory Wesley Woods Geriatric Hospital** (1 specialty); **Shepherd Center** (1 specialty). The hospitals listed were nationally ranked in at least one adult specialty. Only 137 hospitals nationwide were nationally ranked in one or more specialties. Fifteen hospitals in the U.S. made the Honor Roll with high scores in at least six specialties. *U.S. News Online, "America's Best Children's Hospitals 2015-16"*

According to *U.S. News,* the Atlanta-Sandy Springs-Roswell, GA metro area is home to one of the best children's hospitals in the U.S.: **Children's Healthcare of Atlanta** (Honor Roll/10 specialties). The hospital listed was highly ranked in at least one pediatric specialty. Eighty-three children's hospitals in the U.S. were nationally ranked in at least one specialty. Twelve children's hospitals in the U.S. made the Honor Roll with high scores in at least three specialties. *U.S. News Online, "America's Best Children's Hospitals 2015-16"*

EDUCATION

Public School District Statistics

District Name	Schls	Pupils	Pupil/ Teacher Ratio	Minority Pupils[1] (%)	Free Lunch Eligible[2] (%)	IEP[3] (%)
Fayette County	24	20,159	15.6	46.5	21.4	9.2

Note: Table includes school districts with 100 or more students; (1) Percentage of students that are not non-Hispanic white; (2) Percentage of students that are eligible for the free lunch program; (3) Percentage of students that have an Individualized Education Program.

Source: U.S. Department of Education, National Center for Education Statistics, Common Core of Data, Local Education Agency (School District) Universe Survey: School Year 2013-2014; U.S. Department of Education, National Center for Education Statistics, Common Core of Data, Public Elementary/Secondary School Universe Survey: School Year 2013-2014

Highest Level of Education

Area	Less than H.S.	H.S. Diploma	Some College, No Deg.	Associate Degree	Bachelor's Degree	Master's Degree	Prof. School Degree	Doctorate Degree
City	5.2	14.5	18.8	8.0	35.0	13.7	2.8	2.0
MSA[1]	12.1	24.7	20.9	7.1	22.7	9.0	2.2	1.3
U.S.	13.7	28.0	21.2	7.9	18.3	7.8	2.0	1.3

Note: Figures cover persons age 25 and over; (1) Figures cover the Atlanta-Sandy Springs-Roswell, GA Metropolitan Statistical Area—see Appendix B for areas included

Source: U.S. Census Bureau, 2010-2014 American Community Survey 5-Year Estimates

Educational Attainment by Race

Area	High School Graduate or Higher (%)					Bachelor's Degree or Higher (%)				
	Total	White	Black	Asian	Hisp.[2]	Total	White	Black	Asian	Hisp.[2]
City	94.8	95.4	95.0	93.1	70.2	53.5	53.9	49.2	69.1	33.8
MSA[1]	87.9	89.3	88.5	86.4	61.4	35.3	39.0	27.1	53.3	16.5
U.S.	86.3	88.4	83.2	85.8	64.1	29.3	30.6	19.0	50.9	13.9

Note: Figures shown cover persons 25 years old and over; (1) Figures cover the Atlanta-Sandy Springs-Roswell, GA Metropolitan Statistical Area—see Appendix B for areas included; (2) People of Hispanic origin can be of any race

Source: U.S. Census Bureau, 2010-2014 American Community Survey 5-Year Estimates

School Enrollment by Grade and Control

Area	Preschool (%)		Kindergarten (%)		Grades 1 - 4 (%)		Grades 5 - 8 (%)		Grades 9 - 12 (%)	
	Public	Private	Public	Private	Public	Private	Public	Private	Public	Private
City	43.4	56.6	94.5	5.5	89.5	10.5	84.2	15.8	90.4	9.6
MSA[1]	54.2	45.8	87.7	12.3	90.2	9.8	89.5	10.5	90.3	9.7
U.S.	57.4	42.6	87.8	12.2	89.8	10.2	89.9	10.1	90.6	9.4

Note: Figures shown cover persons 3 years old and over; (1) Figures cover the Atlanta-Sandy Springs-Roswell, GA Metropolitan Statistical Area—see Appendix B for areas included

Source: U.S. Census Bureau, 2010-2014 American Community Survey 5-Year Estimates

Average Salaries of Public School Classroom Teachers

Area	2013-14 Dollars	2013-14 Rank[1]	2014-15 Dollars	2014-15 Rank[1]	Percent Change 2013-14 to 2014-15	Percent Change 2004-05 to 2014-15
Georgia	52,924	24	53,382	24	0.87	14.7
U.S. Average	56,610	–	57,379	–	1.36	20.8

Note: (1) State rank ranges from 1 to 51 where 1 indicates highest salary.
Source: National Education Association, Rankings & Estimates: Rankings of the States 2014 and Estimates of School Statistics 2015, March 2015

Higher Education

Four-Year Colleges			Two-Year Colleges			Medical Schools[1]	Law Schools[2]	Voc/ Tech[3]
Public	Private Non-profit	Private For-profit	Public	Private Non-profit	Private For-profit			
0	0	0	0	0	0	0	0	0

Note: Figures cover institutions located within the city limits and include main campuses only; (1) includes schools accredited by the Liaison Committee on Medical Education and the American Osteopathic Association's Commission on Osteopathic College Accreditation; (2) includes ABA-accredited schools, schools with provisional ABA accreditation, and state accredited schools; (3) includes all schools with programs that are less than 2 years.
Source: National Center for Education Statistics, Integrated Postsecondary Education System (IPEDS), 2014-15; Association of American Medical Colleges, Member List, March 21, 2016; American Osteopathic Association, Member List, March 21, 2016; Law School Admission Council, Official Guide to ABA-Approved Law Schools Online, March 21, 2016; Wikipedia, List of Medical Schools in the United States, March 21, 2016; Wikipedia, List of Law Schools in the United States, March 21, 2016

According to *U.S. News & World Report,* the Atlanta-Sandy Springs-Roswell, GA metro area is home to two of the best national universities in the U.S.: **Emory University** (#21 tie); **Georgia Institute of Technology** (#36). The indicators used to capture academic quality fall into a number of categories: assessment by administrators at peer institutions; retention of students; faculty resources; student selectivity; financial resources; alumni giving; high school counselor ratings of colleges; and graduation rate. *U.S. News & World Report, "America's Best Colleges 2016"*

According to *U.S. News & World Report,* the Atlanta-Sandy Springs-Roswell, GA metro area is home to four of the best liberal arts colleges in the U.S.: **Agnes Scott College** (#67 tie); **Spelman College** (#72 tie); **Morehouse College** (#148 tie); **Oglethorpe University** (#167 tie). The indicators used to capture academic quality fall into a number of categories: assessment by administrators at peer institutions; retention of students; faculty resources; student selectivity; financial resources; alumni giving; high school counselor ratings of colleges; and graduation rate. *U.S. News & World Report, "America's Best Colleges 2016"*

According to *U.S. News & World Report,* the Atlanta-Sandy Springs-Roswell, GA metro area is home to two of the top 100 law schools in the U.S.: **Emory University, School of Law** (#22 tie); **Georgia State University, College of Law** (#57 tie). The rankings are based on a weighted average of 12 measures of quality: peer assessment score; assessment score by lawyers/judges; median LSAT scores; median undergrad GPA; acceptance rate; employment rates for graduates; placement success; bar passage rate; faculty resources; expenditures per student; student/faculty ratio; and library resources. *U.S. News & World Report, "America's Best Graduate Schools, Law, 2017"*

According to *U.S. News & World Report,* the Atlanta-Sandy Springs-Roswell, GA metro area is home to one of the top 75 medical schools for research in the U.S.: **Emory University, School of Medicine** (#23). The rankings are based on a weighted average of 11 measures of quality: quality assessment; peer assessment score; assessment score by residency directors; research activity; total research activity; average research activity per faculty member; student selectivity; median MCAT total score; median undergraduate GPA; acceptance rate; and faculty resources. *U.S. News & World Report, "America's Best Graduate Schools, Medical, 2017"*

According to *U.S. News & World Report,* the Atlanta-Sandy Springs-Roswell, GA metro area is home to two of the top 75 business schools in the U.S.: **Emory University, Goizueta Business School** (#19); **Georgia Institute of Technology, Scheller College of Business** (#34). The rankings are based on a weighted average of the following nine measures: quality assessment; peer assessment; recruiter assessment; placement success; mean starting salary and bonus; student selectivity; mean GMAT and GRE scores; mean undergraduate GPA; and acceptance rate. *U.S. News & World Report, "America's Best Graduate Schools, Business, 2017"*

PRESIDENTIAL ELECTION

2012 Presidential Election Results

Area	Obama (%)	Romney (%)	Other (%)
Fayette County	33.7	65.0	1.2
U.S.	51.0	47.2	1.8

Note: Results may not add to 100% due to rounding
Source: Dave Leip's Atlas of U.S. Presidential Elections

EMPLOYERS

Major Employers

Company Name	Industry
Apartments.Com	Apartment locating service
Aquilex Holdings	Facilities support services
AT&T Corp.	Engineering services
Behavioral Health, Georgia Department of	Administration of public health programs
Children's Healthcare of Atlanta	Healthcare
Clayton County Board of Education	Public elementary and secondary schools
County of Gwinnett	County commissioner
Delta Air Lines	Air transportation, scheduled
Georgia Department of Human Resoures	Administration of public health programs
Georgia Department of Transportation	Regulation, administration of transportation
IBM Corporation	Engineering services
Internal Revenue Service	Taxation department, government
Lockheed Martin Aeronautical Company	Aircraft
NCR Corporation	Calculating and accounting equipment
Northide Hospital	Healthcare
Progressive Logistics Services	Labor organizations
Robert Half International	Employment agencies
Saint Joseph's Hospital	Healthcare
The Army, United States Department of	Army
The Coca-Cola Company	Bottled and canned soft drinks
The Fulton-Dekalb Hospital Authority	General medical and surgical hospitals
The Home Depot	Hardware stores
WellStar Kennestone Hospital	General medical and surgical hospitals
World Travel Partners Group	Travel agencies

Note: Companies shown are located within the Atlanta-Sandy Springs-Roswell, GA Metropolitan Statistical Area.
Source: Hoovers.com; Wikipedia

PUBLIC SAFETY

Crime Rate

Area	All Crimes	Violent Crimes				Property Crimes		
		Murder	Rape[3]	Robbery	Aggrav. Assault	Burglary	Larceny -Theft	Motor Vehicle Theft
City	1,294.7	0.0	2.9	14.3	11.4	77.2	1,068.9	120.0
Metro[1]	3,629.7	6.1	20.4	154.0	217.9	725.9	2,170.4	334.9
U.S.	2,961.6	4.5	26.4	102.2	232.5	542.5	1,837.3	216.2

Note: Figures are crimes per 100,000 population; (1) Figures cover the Atlanta-Sandy Springs-Roswell, GA Metropolitan Statistical Area—see Appendix B for areas included; (3) The city and U.S. figures shown were reported using the legacy Uniform Crime Reporting (UCR) definition of rape. The suburban and metro area figures shown are an aggregate total of the data submitted using both the revised and legacy UCR definitions.
Source: FBI Uniform Crime Reports, 2014

Hate Crimes

Area	Number of Quarters Reported	Number of Incidents per Bias Motivation						
		Race	Religion	Sexual Orientation	Ethnicity	Disability	Gender	Gender Identity
City	4	0	0	0	0	0	0	0
U.S.	4	2,568	1,014	1,017	648	84	33	98

Source: Federal Bureau of Investigation, Hate Crime Statistics 2014

Identity Theft Consumer Complaints

Area	Complaints	Complaints per 100,000 Population	Rank[2]
MSA[1]	10,418	185.6	24
U.S.	490,220	152.4	-

Note: (1) Figures cover the Atlanta-Sandy Springs-Roswell, GA Metropolitan Statistical Area—see Appendix B for areas included; (2) Rank ranges from 1 to 379 where 1 indicates greatest number of identity theft complaints per 100,000 population
Source: Federal Trade Commission, Consumer Sentinel Network Data Book for January–December 2015

Fraud and Other Consumer Complaints

Area	Complaints	Complaints per 100,000 Population	Rank[2]
MSA[1]	26,684	475.3	30
U.S.	2,593,159	806.0	-

Note: (1) Figures cover the Atlanta-Sandy Springs-Roswell, GA Metropolitan Statistical Area—see Appendix B for areas included; (2) Rank ranges from 1 to 379 where 1 indicates greatest number of identity theft complaints per 100,000 population
Source: Federal Trade Commission, Consumer Sentinel Network Data Book for January–December 2015

RECREATION

Culture

Dance[1]	Theatre[1]	Instrumental Music[1]	Vocal Music[1]	Series and Festivals	Museums and Art Galleries[2]	Zoos and Aquariums[3]
0	0	0	0	0	0	0

Note: (1) Professional perfoming groups; (2) Based on organizations with SIC code 8412; (3) AZA-accredited
Source: The Grey House Performing Arts Directory, 2015-16; Association of Zoos & Aquariums, AZA Member Zoos & Aquariums, March 25, 2016; www.AccuLeads.com, March 29, 2016

Professional Sports Teams

Team Name	League	Year Established
Atlanta Braves	Major League Baseball (MLB)	1966
Atlanta Falcons	National Football League (NFL)	1966
Atlanta Hawks	National Basketball Association (NBA)	1968
Atlanta United FC	Major League Soccer (MLS)	2017

Note: Includes teams located in the Atlanta-Sandy Springs-Roswell, GA Metropolitan Statistical Area.
Source: Wikipedia, Major Professional Sports Teams of the United States and Canada, March 24, 2016

CLIMATE

Average and Extreme Temperatures

Temperature	Jan	Feb	Mar	Apr	May	Jun	Jul	Aug	Sep	Oct	Nov	Dec	Yr.
Extreme High (°F)	79	80	85	93	95	101	105	102	98	95	84	77	105
Average High (°F)	52	56	64	73	80	86	88	88	82	73	63	54	72
Average Temp. (°F)	43	46	53	62	70	77	79	79	73	63	53	45	62
Average Low (°F)	33	36	42	51	59	66	70	69	64	52	42	35	52
Extreme Low (°F)	-8	5	10	26	37	46	53	55	36	28	3	0	-8

Note: Figures cover the years 1945-1990
Source: National Climatic Data Center, International Station Meteorological Climate Summary, 9/96

Average Precipitation/Snowfall/Humidity

Precip./Humidity	Jan	Feb	Mar	Apr	May	Jun	Jul	Aug	Sep	Oct	Nov	Dec	Yr.
Avg. Precip. (in.)	4.7	4.6	5.7	4.3	4.0	3.5	5.1	3.6	3.4	2.8	3.8	4.2	49.8
Avg. Snowfall (in.)	1	1	Tr	Tr	0	0	0	0	0	0	Tr	Tr	2
Avg. Rel. Hum. 7am (%)	79	77	78	78	82	83	88	89	88	84	81	79	82
Avg. Rel. Hum. 4pm (%)	56	50	48	45	49	52	57	56	56	51	52	55	52

Note: Figures cover the years 1945-1990; Tr = Trace amounts (<0.05 in. of rain; <0.5 in. of snow)
Source: National Climatic Data Center, International Station Meteorological Climate Summary, 9/96

Weather Conditions

Temperature			Daytime Sky			Precipitation		
10°F & below	32°F & below	90°F & above	Clear	Partly cloudy	Cloudy	0.01 inch or more precip.	0.1 inch or more snow/ice	Thunder-storms
1	49	38	98	147	120	116	3	48

Note: Figures are average number of days per year and cover the years 1945-1990
Source: National Climatic Data Center, International Station Meteorological Climate Summary, 9/96

HAZARDOUS WASTE

Superfund Sites

Peachtree City has no sites on the EPA's Superfund Final National Priorities List. There are a total of 1,323 Superfund sites on the list in the U.S. *U.S. Environmental Protection Agency, Final National Priorities List, March 18, 2016*

AIR & WATER QUALITY

Air Quality Trends: Ozone

	1990	1995	2000	2005	2010	2011	2012	2013	2014
MSA[1]	0.104	0.103	0.101	0.087	0.076	0.078	0.079	0.066	0.072

Note: (1) Data covers the Atlanta-Sandy Springs-Roswell, GA Metropolitan Statistical Area—see Appendix B for areas included. The values shown are the composite ozone concentration averages among trend sites based on the highest fourth daily maximum 8-hour concentration in parts per million. These trends are based on sites having an adequate record of monitoring data during the trend period. Data from exceptional events are included.
Source: U.S. Environmental Protection Agency, Air Quality Monitoring Information, "Air Quality Trends by City, 1990-2014"

Air Quality Index

Area	Percent of Days when Air Quality was...[2]					AQI Statistics[2]	
	Good	Moderate	Unhealthy for Sensitive Groups	Unhealthy	Very Unhealthy	Maximum	Median
MSA[1]	40.0	57.8	2.2	0.0	0.0	147	55

Note: (1) Data covers the Atlanta-Sandy Springs-Roswell, GA Metropolitan Statistical Area—see Appendix B for areas included; (2) Based on 365 days with AQI data in 2015. Air Quality Index (AQI) is an index for reporting daily air quality. EPA calculates the AQI for five major air pollutants regulated by the Clean Air Act: ground-level ozone, particle pollution (aka particulate matter), carbon monoxide, sulfur dioxide, and nitrogen dioxide. The AQI runs from 0 to 500. The higher the AQI value, the greater the level of air pollution and the greater the health concern. There are six AQI categories: "Good" AQI is between 0 and 50. Air quality is considered satisfactory; "Moderate" AQI is between 51 and 100. Air quality is acceptable; "Unhealthy for Sensitive Groups" When AQI values are between 101 and 150, members of sensitive groups may experience health effects; "Unhealthy" When AQI values are between 151 and 200 everyone may begin to experience health effects; "Very Unhealthy" AQI values between 201 and 300 trigger a health alert; "Hazardous" AQI values over 300 trigger warnings of emergency conditions (not shown).
Source: U.S. Environmental Protection Agency, Air Quality Index Report, 2015

Air Quality Index Pollutants

Area	Percent of Days when AQI Pollutant was...[2]					
	Carbon Monoxide	Nitrogen Dioxide	Ozone	Sulfur Dioxide	Particulate Matter 2.5	Particulate Matter 10
MSA[1]	0.0	1.6	24.7	0.0	73.2	0.5

Note: (1) Data covers the Atlanta-Sandy Springs-Roswell, GA Metropolitan Statistical Area—see Appendix B for areas included; (2) Based on 365 days with AQI data in 2015. The Air Quality Index (AQI) is an index for reporting daily air quality. EPA calculates the AQI for five major air pollutants regulated by the Clean Air Act: ground-level ozone, particle pollution (also known as particulate matter), carbon monoxide, sulfur dioxide, and nitrogen dioxide. The AQI runs from 0 to 500. The higher the AQI value, the greater the level of air pollution and the greater the health concern.
Source: U.S. Environmental Protection Agency, Air Quality Index Report, 2015

Maximum Air Pollutant Concentrations: Particulate Matter, Ozone, CO and Lead

	Particulate Matter 10 (ug/m^3)	Particulate Matter 2.5 Wtd AM (ug/m^3)	Particulate Matter 2.5 24-Hr (ug/m^3)	Ozone (ppm)	Carbon Monoxide (ppm)	Lead (ug/m^3)
MSA[1] Level	61	11.2	22	0.079	2	0
NAAQS[2]	150	15	35	0.075	9	0.15
Met NAAQS[2]	Yes	Yes	Yes	No	Yes	Yes

Note: (1) Data covers the Atlanta-Sandy Springs-Roswell, GA Metropolitan Statistical Area—see Appendix B for areas included; Data from exceptional events are included; (2) National Ambient Air Quality Standards; ppm = parts per million; ug/m^3 = micrograms per cubic meter; n/a not available.
Concentrations: Particulate Matter 10 (coarse particulate)—highest second maximum 24-hour concentration; Particulate Matter 2.5 Wtd AM (fine particulate)—highest weighted annual mean concentration; Particulate Matter 2.5 24-Hour (fine particulate)—highest 98th percentile 24-hour concentration; Ozone—highest fourth daily maximum 8-hour concentration; Carbon Monoxide—highest second maximum non-overlapping 8-hour concentration; Lead—maximum running 3-month average
Source: U.S. Environmental Protection Agency, Air Quality Monitoring Information, "Air Quality Statistics by City, 2014"

Maximum Air Pollutant Concentrations: Nitrogen Dioxide and Sulfur Dioxide

	Nitrogen Dioxide AM (ppb)	Nitrogen Dioxide 1-Hr (ppb)	Sulfur Dioxide AM (ppb)	Sulfur Dioxide 1-Hr (ppb)	Sulfur Dioxide 24-Hr (ppb)
MSA[1] Level	11	53	n/a	6	n/a
NAAQS[2]	53	100	30	75	140
Met NAAQS[2]	Yes	Yes	n/a	Yes	n/a

Note: (1) Data covers the Atlanta-Sandy Springs-Roswell, GA Metropolitan Statistical Area—see Appendix B for areas included; Data from exceptional events are included; (2) National Ambient Air Quality Standards; ppm = parts per million; ug/m^3 = micrograms per cubic meter; n/a not available.
Concentrations: Nitrogen Dioxide AM—highest arithmetic mean concentration; Nitrogen Dioxide 1-Hr—highest 98th percentile 1-hour daily maximum concentration; Sulfur Dioxide AM—highest annual mean concentration; Sulfur Dioxide 1-Hr—highest 99th percentile 1-hour daily maximum concentration; Sulfur Dioxide 24-Hr—highest second maximum 24-hour concentration
Source: U.S. Environmental Protection Agency, Air Quality Monitoring Information, "Air Quality Statistics by City, 2014"

Drinking Water

Water System Name	Pop. Served	Primary Water Source Type	Violations[1]	
			Health Based	Monitoring/ Reporting
Fayette County	74,163	Surface	0	0

Note: (1) Based on violation data from January 1, 2015 to December 31, 2015 (includes unresolved violations from earlier years)
Source: U.S. Environmental Protection Agency, Office of Ground Water and Drinking Water, Safe Drinking Water Information System (based on data extracted April 29, 2016)

Meridian, Idaho

Background

Located in southwest Idaho, about nine miles west of Boise, the state capital, Meridian lies in the fertile Snake River plain and is one of a chain of prosperous cities running from Boise northwest to the Oregon border.

The city enjoys many advantages due its location. It has seen almost explosive growth because of the influx into the capital region of people who work in government, finance, business and technical fields. The city of Meridian itself is home to the corporate headquarters of Scentsy, a candle warmer company and Bodybuilder.com. Other regional, national, and international companies are headquartered in Boise, including Boise (formerly Boise Cascade), Simplot, Albertsons, and Micron Technology. Meridian was once fertile farming country for grains, vegetables, and fruits. During the last decades of the twentieth century, however, farms yielded to residences for the expanding population. In fact, during the 1990s, the Boise area was one of the three or four fastest-growing metropolitan regions in the country, and Meridian's population alone doubled between 1990 and 2000. In spite of this growth, the region has avoided much of the crowding, crime, high prices, and long commutes that plague other major metropolitan areas.

The public schools in Meridian are generally excellent, and Boise State University in Boise offers a wide range of courses and advanced degrees.

Recreational opportunities are legion. In addition to hiking, fishing, and hunting, many enjoy kayaking or river rafting on the swift streams in the area, particularly in spring when the water is highest. Thanks to the difference in elevation between the valley floor (about 2,700 feet above sea level) and the mountains (over 7,000 feet), there is excellent skiing in the hills immediately adjacent to the city, even when the weather in the valley is too warm for snow. Bogus Basin is a popular family resort with gentle slopes for beginners, as well as steep slopes that challenge the expert.

Meridian's landmark is an impressive yellow water tower that rises high above I-84 to clearly identify downtown Meridian. Close to the tower, on Main Street, is a popular auto racetrack that features summertime drag racing. In addition to the racetrack, Main Street features a string of shops, restaurants, and offices in a range of architectural styles including Old West, Victorian, and modern chic, all of which make Meridian an interesting and charming small city.

The climate in Meridian, as elsewhere in southwest Idaho, is dry. It is influenced by winds from the Pacific, producing milder temperatures than are found elsewhere at this latitude. Winter brings only moderate snow, though heavier snowfalls occur in the nearby mountains. Spring comes early, with rains that turn the valleys and hills a rich green. By summer, the green has turned to brown, as temperatures rise by day; nights, however, are generally cool. The warm daytime temperatures persist into the fall, and it is not until October that the air is truly chilly.

Rankings

Business/Finance Rankings

- The personal finance site NerdWallet analyzed 183 American metropolitan areas with populations over 250,000 and more than 15,000 businesses to rank where entrepreneurs find the most success. Criteria included area economy, annual income, housing cost, unemployment rate, and the success rate of area businesses. Boise City* ranked #28. *www.nerdwallet.com, "Best Places to Start a Business," April 27, 2015*

- Based on the Bureau of Labor Statistics (BLS) quarterly reports on employment and wages over the fourth-quarter 2012–2013, researchers at 24/7 Wall Street listed the Boise City* metro area as the #7 metro area for wage growth. *247wallst.com, "Ten Cities Where Wages Are Soaring," July 16, 2014*

- 24/7 Wall Street ranked metro areas where jobs were being added at a faster rate than the labor force was growing. The #5 metro area for gains posted in employment was Boise City*. *247wallst.com, "Cities Where Unemployment Has Fallen the Most," April 16, 2013*

- The Boise City* metro area was identified as having one of the largest percentage of home workers in the U.S. The area ranked #9, according to the business website 24/7 Wall Street, which based its conclusions on data from the U.S. Census Bureau and the Bureau of Labor Statistics. *247wallst.com, "Cities Where the Most Americans Work from Home," March 18, 2013*

- The Brookings Institution ranked the 100 largest metro areas in the U.S. based on income inequality. Boise City* was ranked #65 (#1 = greatest ineqality). Criteria: the "95/20 ratio," a figure representing the income at which a household earns more than 95 percent of all other households, divided by the income at which a household earns more than only 20 percent of all other households. *Brookings Institution, "Income Inequality, 100 Largest U.S. Metro Areas, 2007-2014," January 14, 2016*

- *Forbes* ranked the largest metro areas in the U.S. in terms of the "Best Cities for Young Professionals." The Boise City* metro area ranked #6 out of 15. Criteria: job growth; unemployment rate; median salary of college graduates age 24 to 34; cost of living; number of small businesses per capita; number of large companies; percentage of population 25 years of age and older with college degrees. *Forbes.com, "America's 15 Best Cities for Young Professionals," August 18, 2014*

- The Boise City* metro area appeared on the Milken Institute "2015 Best Performing Cities" list. Rank: #33 out of 200 large metro areas. Criteria: job growth; wage and salary growth; high-tech output growth. *Milken Institute, "Best-Performing Cities 2015," December 2015*

- *Forbes* ranked the 200 most populous metro areas to determine the nation's "Best Places for Business and Careers." The Boise City* metro area was ranked #27. Criteria: costs (business and living); job growth (past and projected); income growth; educational attainment (college and high school); projected economic growth; cultural and recreational opportunities; net migration patterns; number of highly ranked colleges. *Forbes, "The Best Places for Business and Careers 2015," July 29, 2015*

Children/Family Rankings

- *Forbes* analyzed data on the 100 largest metropolitan areas in the United States to compile its 2014 list of the ten "Best Cities for Raising a Family." The Boise City* metro area was ranked #7. Criteria: median income; overall cost of living; housing affordability; commuting delays; percentage of families owning homes; crime rate; education quality (mainly test scores). *Forbes, "The Best Cities for Raising a Family," April 16, 2014*

Education Rankings

- Personal finance website *WalletHub* analyzed the 150 largest U.S. metropolitan statistical areas to determine where the most educated Americans are choosing to settle. Criteria: education quality and attainment gap; education levels; percentage of workers with degrees; public school rankings; quality and size of each metro area's universities. Boise City* was ranked #50 (#1 = most educated city). *www.WalletHub.com, "2015's Most and Least Educated Cities*

Environmental Rankings

- The Boise City* metro area came in at #73 for the relative comfort of its climate on Sperling's list of "chill cities," as measured by the Sperling Heat Index. All 361 metro areas are included. Criteria included daytime high temperatures, nighttime low temperatures, dew point, and relative humidity at the high temperatures. *www.bertsperling.com, "Sperling's Chill Cities," July 18, 2013*

- Sperling's BestPlaces assessed 379 metropolitan areas of the United States for the likelihood of dangerously extreme weather events or earthquakes. In general the Southeast and South-Central regions have the highest risk of weather extremes and earthquakes, while the Pacific Northwest enjoys the lowest risk. Of the least risky metropolitan areas, the Boise City* metro area was ranked #31. *www.bestplaces.net, "Safest Places from Natural Disasters," April 2011*

- Boise City* was highlighted as one of the 25 metro areas most polluted by short-term particle pollution (24-hour PM 2.5) in the U.S. during 2011 through 2013. The area ranked #23. *American Lung Association, State of the Air 2015*

Health/Fitness Rankings

- Boise City* was identified as a "2016 Spring Allergy Capital." The area ranked #94 out of 100. Three groups of factors were used to identify the most severe cities for people with allergies during the spring season: annual pollen levels; medicine utilization; access to board-certified allergists. *Asthma and Allergy Foundation of America, "Spring Allergy Capitals 2016"*

- Boise City* was identified as a "2015 Asthma Capital." The area ranked #99 out of the nation's 100 largest metropolitan areas. Criteria: estimated prevalence; self-reported prevalence; crude death rate for asthma; annual pollen score; annual air quality; public smoking laws; number of board-certified asthma specialists; school inhaler access laws; rescue medication use; controller medication use; ER visits for asthma; uninsured rate; poverty rate. *Asthma and Allergy Foundation of America, "Asthma Capitals 2015"*

- The Boise City* metro area ranked #95 out of 190 in The Gallup-Healthways Well-Being Index. Criteria: purpose; social well being; financial health; community and physical health. Results are based on telephone interviews with adults, aged 18 and older, living in metropolitan areas in the 50 U.S. states and the District of Columbia. *Gallup-Healthways, "State of American Well-Being," February 23, 2016*

Real Estate Rankings

- The Boise City* metro area was identified as one of the top 20 housing markets to invest in for 2016 by *Forbes*. The area ranked #20. Criteria: strong job and population growth; anticipated home price appreciation; and other factors. *Forbes.com, "Best Buy Cities: Where to Invest in Housing in 2016," January 27, 2016*

- Boise City* was ranked #153 out of 225 metro areas in terms of housing affordability in 2015 by the National Association of Home Builders (#1 = most affordable). Criteria: the share of homes sold in that area affordable to a family earning the local median income, based on standard mortgage underwriting criteria. *National Association of Home Builders®, NAHB-Wells Fargo Housing Opportunity Index, 4th Quarter 2015*

Safety Rankings

- Farmers Insurance, in partnership with Sperling's BestPlaces, ranked metro areas in the U.S. as the "Most Secure Places to Live." The Boise City* metro area ranked #11 out of the top 20 in the large metro area category (500,000 or more residents). Criteria: economic stability; crime statistics; extreme weather; risk of natural disasters; housing depreciation; foreclosures; air quality; environmental hazards; life expectancy; motor vehicle fatalities; and employment numbers. *Farmers Insurance Group of Companies, "Most Secure U.S. Places to Live in the U.S.," June 25, 2013*

- The National Insurance Crime Bureau ranked 380 metro areas in the U.S. in terms of per capita rates of vehicle theft. The Boise City* metro area ranked #309 (#1 = highest rate). Criteria: number of vehicle theft offenses per 100,000 inhabitants in 2014. *National Insurance Crime Bureau, "Hot Spots 2014," June 24, 2015*

Seniors/Retirement Rankings

- From its Best Cities for Successful Aging indexes, the Milken Institute generated rankings for metropolitan areas, weighing data in eight categories—health care, wellness, living arrangements, transportation, financial characteristics, education and employment opportunities, community engagement, and overall livability. The Boise City* metro area was ranked #22 overall in the large metro area category. *Milken Institute, "Best Cities for Successful Aging, 2014"*

Miscellaneous Rankings

- The finance and lifestyle site NerdWallet looked for the U.S. cities that topped the list in donating money and time to good causes. The Boise City* metro area proved to be the #9-ranked metro area, judged by culture of volunteerism, depth of commitment in terms of volunteer hours per year, and monetary contributions. *www.nerdwallet.com, "Most Generous Cities," September 22, 2013*
- The National Alliance to End Homelessness ranked the 100 most populous metro areas with the highest rate of homelessness. The Boise City* metro area ranked #58. Criteria: number of homeless people per 10,000 population in 2011. *National Alliance to End Homelessness, The State of Homelessness in America 2012*

Meridian is located within the Boise City, ID Metropolitan Statistical Area.

Business Environment

CITY FINANCES

City Government Finances

Component	2012 ($000)	2012 ($ per capita)
Total Revenues	60,834	810
Total Expenditures	50,930	678
Debt Outstanding	1,334	17
Cash and Securities[1]	61,097	813

Note: (1) Cash and security holdings of a government at the close of its fiscal year, including those of its dependent agencies, utilities, and liquor stores.
Source: U.S Census Bureau, State & Local Government Finances 2012

City Government Revenue by Source

Source	2012 ($000)	2012 ($ per capita)
General Revenue		
From Federal Government	0	0
From State Government	9,928	132
From Local Governments	0	0
Taxes		
Property	19,417	258
Sales and Gross Receipts	1,352	18
Personal Income	0	0
Corporate Income	0	0
Motor Vehicle License	0	0
Other Taxes	2,511	33
Current Charges	13,376	178
Liquor Store	0	0
Utility	6,908	91
Employee Retirement	0	0

Source: U.S Census Bureau, State & Local Government Finances 2012

City Government Expenditures by Function

Function	2012 ($000)	2012 ($ per capita)	2012 (%)
General Direct Expenditures			
Air Transportation	0	0	0.0
Corrections	0	0	0.0
Education	0	0	0.0
Employment Security Administration	0	0	0.0
Financial Administration	0	0	0.0
Fire Protection	7,985	106	15.6
General Public Buildings	0	0	0.0
Governmental Administration, Other	4,537	60	8.9
Health	0	0	0.0
Highways	0	0	0.0
Hospitals	0	0	0.0
Housing and Community Development	150	1	0.2
Interest on General Debt	123	1	0.2
Judicial and Legal	0	0	0.0
Libraries	0	0	0.0
Parking	0	0	0.0
Parks and Recreation	3,822	50	7.5
Police Protection	11,290	150	22.1
Public Welfare	0	0	0.0
Sewerage	10,016	133	19.6
Solid Waste Management	0	0	0.0
Veterans' Services	0	0	0.0
Liquor Store	0	0	0.0
Utility	8,532	113	16.7
Employee Retirement	0	0	0.0

Source: U.S Census Bureau, State & Local Government Finances 2012

DEMOGRAPHICS

Population Growth

Area	1990 Census	2000 Census	2010 Census	2014* Estimate	Population Growth (%) 1990-2014	Population Growth (%) 2010-2014
City	12,266	34,919	75,092	81,025	560.6	7.9
MSA[1]	319,596	464,840	616,561	639,616	100.1	3.7
U.S.	248,709,873	281,421,906	308,745,538	314,107,084	26.3	1.7

Note: (1) Figures cover the Boise City, ID Metropolitan Statistical Area—see Appendix B for areas included; (*) 2010-2014 5-year estimated population
Source: U.S. Census Bureau, 1990 Census, Census 2000, Census 2010, 2010-2014 American Community Survey 5-Year Estimates

Household Size

Area	Persons in Household (%) One	Two	Three	Four	Five	Six	Seven or More	Average Household Size
City	19.2	35.4	13.6	17.4	8.1	4.3	1.6	2.93
MSA[1]	24.4	34.7	14.7	14.5	6.7	2.8	1.8	2.71
U.S.	27.5	33.5	15.8	13.1	6.0	2.3	1.4	2.64

Note: (1) Figures cover the Boise City, ID Metropolitan Statistical Area—see Appendix B for areas included
Source: U.S. Census Bureau, 2010-2014 American Community Survey 5-Year Estimates

Race

Area	White Alone[2] (%)	Black Alone[2] (%)	Asian Alone[2] (%)	AIAN[3] Alone[2] (%)	NHOPI[4] Alone[2] (%)	Other Race Alone[2] (%)	Two or More Races (%)
City	94.0	0.8	2.0	0.0	0.1	0.8	2.3
MSA[1]	91.5	0.8	2.0	0.7	0.2	2.0	2.7
U.S.	73.8	12.6	5.0	0.8	0.2	4.7	2.9

Note: (1) Figures cover the Boise City, ID Metropolitan Statistical Area—see Appendix B for areas included; (2) Alone is defined as not being in combination with one or more other races; (3) American Indian and Alaska Native; (4) Native Hawaiian and Other Pacific Islander
Source: U.S. Census Bureau, 2010-2014 American Community Survey 5-Year Estimates

Hispanic or Latino Origin

Area	Total (%)	Mexican (%)	Puerto Rican (%)	Cuban (%)	Other (%)
City	7.1	5.8	0.3	0.0	0.9
MSA[1]	12.9	11.1	0.3	0.1	1.4
U.S.	16.9	10.8	1.6	0.6	3.8

Note: Persons of Hispanic or Latino origin can be of any race; (1) Figures cover the Boise City, ID Metropolitan Statistical Area—see Appendix B for areas included
Source: U.S. Census Bureau, 2010-2014 American Community Survey 5-Year Estimates

Ancestry

Area	German	Irish	English	American	Italian	Polish	French[2]	Scottish	Dutch
City	15.9	8.0	15.3	6.2	3.3	1.8	2.0	2.5	1.9
MSA[1]	16.8	8.9	14.4	9.8	3.1	1.5	2.3	3.0	1.9
U.S.	14.9	10.8	8.0	7.1	5.5	3.0	2.7	1.7	1.4

Note: Figures are the percentage of the total population reporting a particular ancestry. The nine most commonly reported ancestries in the U.S. are shown. Figures include multiple ancestries (e.g. if a person reported being Irish and Italian, they were included in both columns); (1) Figures cover the Boise City, ID Metropolitan Statistical Area—see Appendix B for areas included; (2) Excludes Basque
Source: U.S. Census Bureau, 2010-2014 American Community Survey 5-Year Estimates

Foreign-Born Population

Area	Percent of Population Born in								
	Any Foreign Country	Asia	Mexico	Europe	Carribean	Central America[2]	South America	Africa	Canada
City	4.9	1.1	0.9	1.6	0.1	0.0	0.4	0.3	0.4
MSA[1]	6.7	1.5	3.1	1.1	0.0	0.2	0.2	0.3	0.3
U.S.	13.1	3.8	3.7	1.5	1.2	1.0	0.9	0.6	0.3

Note: (1) Figures cover the Boise City, ID Metropolitan Statistical Area—see Appendix B for areas included; (2) Excludes Mexico.
Source: U.S. Census Bureau, 2010-2014 American Community Survey 5-Year Estimates

Marital Status

Area	Never Married	Now Married[2]	Separated	Widowed	Divorced
City	22.8	62.5	0.9	3.9	9.9
MSA[1]	27.3	54.5	1.3	4.7	12.1
U.S.	32.5	48.4	2.2	5.9	10.9

Note: Figures are percentages and cover the population 15 years of age and older; (1) Figures cover the Boise City, ID Metropolitan Statistical Area—see Appendix B for areas included; (2) Excludes separated
Source: U.S. Census Bureau, 2010-2014 American Community Survey 5-Year Estimates

Disability Status

Area	All Ages	Under 18 Years Old	18 to 64 Years Old	65 Years and Over
City	7.6	2.8	6.6	28.4
MSA[1]	11.3	4.2	9.7	35.7
U.S.	12.3	4.1	10.2	36.3

Note: Figures show percent of the civilian noninstitutionalized population that reported having a disability. Disability status is determined from from six types of difficulty: vision, hearing, cognitive, ambulatory, self-care, and independent living. For children under 5 years old, hearing and vision difficulty are used to determine disability status. For children between the ages of 5 and 14, disability status is determined from hearing, vision, cognitive, ambulatory, and self-care difficulties. For people aged 15 years and older, they are considered to have a disability if they have difficulty with any one of the six difficulty types; (1) Figures cover the Boise City, ID Metropolitan Statistical Area—see Appendix B for areas included.
Source: U.S. Census Bureau, 2010-2014 American Community Survey 5-Year Estimates

Age

Area	Percent of Population									Median Age
	Under Age 5	Age 5–19	Age 20–34	Age 35–44	Age 45–54	Age 55–64	Age 65–74	Age 75–84	Age 85+	
City	7.9	25.6	18.1	15.3	13.5	9.7	6.1	2.7	1.1	34.1
MSA[1]	7.1	22.6	20.4	13.6	13.1	11.3	7.0	3.4	1.5	34.9
U.S.	6.4	19.9	20.6	13.0	14.1	12.3	7.6	4.3	1.9	37.4

Note: (1) Figures cover the Boise City, ID Metropolitan Statistical Area—see Appendix B for areas included
Source: U.S. Census Bureau, 2010-2014 American Community Survey 5-Year Estimates

Gender

Area	Males	Females	Males per 100 Females
City	39,142	41,883	93.5
MSA[1]	319,467	320,149	99.8
U.S.	154,515,159	159,591,925	96.8

Note: (1) Figures cover the Boise City, ID Metropolitan Statistical Area—see Appendix B for areas included
Source: U.S. Census Bureau, 2010-2014 American Community Survey 5-Year Estimates

Religious Groups by Family

Area	Catholic	Baptist	Non-Den.	Methodist[2]	Lutheran	LDS[3]	Pente-costal	Presby-terian[4]	Muslim[5]	Judaism
MSA[1]	8.0	2.9	4.1	2.1	1.1	15.8	2.3	0.6	0.1	0.1
U.S.	19.1	9.3	4.0	4.0	2.3	2.0	1.9	1.6	0.8	0.7

Note: Figures are the number of adherents as a percentage of the total population; (1) Figures cover the Boise City-Nampa, ID Metropolitan Statistical Area—see Appendix B for areas included; (2) Methodist/Pietist; (3) Latter Day Saints; (4) Reformed; (5) Figures are estimates
Source: Association of Statisticians of American Religious Bodies, 2010 U.S. Religion Census: Religious Congregations & Membership Study

Religious Groups by Tradition

Area	Catholic	Evangelical Protestant	Mainline Protestant	Other Tradition	Black Protestant	Orthodox
MSA[1]	8.0	12.9	4.3	16.7	<0.1	<0.1
U.S.	19.1	16.2	7.3	4.3	1.6	0.3

Note: Figures are the number of adherents as a percentage of the total population; (1) Figures cover the Boise City-Nampa, ID Metropolitan Statistical Area—see Appendix B for areas included
Source: Association of Statisticians of American Religious Bodies, 2010 U.S. Religion Census: Religious Congregations & Membership Study

ECONOMY

Gross Metropolitan Product

Area	2013	2014	2015	2016	Rank[2]
MSA[1]	28.5	29.8	31.2	32.8	83

Note: Figures are in billions of dollars; (1) Figures cover the Boise City, ID Metropolitan Statistical Area—see Appendix B for areas included; (2) Rank is based on 2016 data and ranges from 1 to 381
Source: The U.S. Conference of Mayors, U.S. Metro Economies: GMP and Employment 2014-2016, June 2015

Economic Growth

Area	2011-13 (%)	2014 (%)	2015 (%)	2016 (%)	Rank[2]
MSA[1]	3.0	2.5	2.9	3.0	83
U.S.	2.2	2.4	2.3	2.9	–

Note: Figures are real gross metropolitan product (GMP) growth rates and represent annual average percent change; (1) Figures cover the Boise City, ID Metropolitan Statistical Area—see Appendix B for areas included; (2) Rank is based on 2016 data and ranges from 1 to 381
Source: The U.S. Conference of Mayors, U.S. Metro Economies: GMP and Employment 2014-2016, June 2015

Metropolitan Area Exports

Area	2009	2010	2011	2012	2013	2014	Rank[2]
MSA[1]	2,849.7	3,647.6	4,131.4	4,088.2	3,657.9	3,143.3	75

Note: Figures are in millions of dollars; (1) Figures cover the Boise City, ID Metropolitan Statistical Area—see Appendix B for areas included; (2) Rank is based on 2014 data and ranges from 1 to 385
Source: U.S. Department of Commerce, International Trade Administration, Office of Trade & Industry Information, Manufacturing & Services, data extracted March 10, 2016

Building Permits

Area	Single-Family			Multi-Family			Total		
	2014	2015p	Pct. Chg.	2014	2015p	Pct. Chg.	2014	2015p	Pct. Chg.
City	764	1,056	38.2	496	414	-16.5	1,260	1,470	16.7
MSA[1]	3,481	4,293	23.3	1,702	1,204	-29.3	5,183	5,497	6.1
U.S.	640,300	690,800	7.9	411,800	487,600	18.4	1,052,100	1,178,400	12.0

Note: (1) Figures cover the Boise City, ID Metropolitan Statistical Area—see Appendix B for areas included; Figures represent new, privately-owned housing units authorized (unadjusted data); All permit data are based on estimates with imputation; (p) preliminary data.
Source: U.S. Census Bureau, Manufacturing, Mining, and Construction Statistics, Building Permits, 2014, 2015

Bankruptcy Filings

Area	Business Filings			Nonbusiness Filings		
	2014	2015	% Chg.	2014	2015	% Chg.
Ada County	47	47	0.0	1,177	969	-17.7
U.S.	26,983	24,735	-8.3	909,812	819,760	-9.9

Note: Business filings include Chapter 7, Chapter 11, Chapter 12, and Chapter 13; Nonbusiness filings include Chapter 7, Chapter 11, and Chapter 13
Source: Administrative Office of the U.S. Courts, Business and Nonbusiness Bankruptcy, County Cases Commenced by Chapter of the Bankruptcy Code, During the 12- Month Period Ending December 31, 2014 and Business and Nonbusiness Bankruptcy, County Cases Commenced by Chapter of the Bankruptcy Code, During the 12- Month Period Ending December 31, 2015

Housing Vacancy Rates

Area	Gross Vacancy Rate[2] (%)			Year-Round Vacancy Rate[3] (%)			Rental Vacancy Rate[4] (%)			Homeowner Vacancy Rate[5] (%)		
	2013	2014	2015	2013	2014	2015	2013	2014	2015	2013	2014	2015
MSA[1]	n/a	n/a	n/a	n/a	n/a	n/a	n/a	n/a	n/a	n/a	n/a	n/a
U.S.	13.6	13.4	12.9	10.7	10.4	10.0	8.3	7.6	7.1	2.0	1.9	1.8

Note: (1) Figures cover the Boise City, ID Metropolitan Statistical Area—see Appendix B for areas included; (2) The percentage of the total housing inventory that is vacant; (3) The percentage of the housing inventory (excluding seasonal units) that is year-round vacant; (4) The percentage of rental inventory that is vacant for rent; (5) The percentage of homeowner inventory that is vacant for sale; n/a not available
Source: U.S. Census Bureau, Housing Vacancies and Homeownership Annual Statistics: 2015

INCOME

Income

Area	Per Capita ($)	Median Household ($)	Average Household ($)
City	26,738	63,225	75,177
MSA[1]	24,715	50,776	66,347
U.S.	28,555	53,482	74,596

Note: (1) Figures cover the Boise City, ID Metropolitan Statistical Area—see Appendix B for areas included
Source: U.S. Census Bureau, 2010-2014 American Community Survey 5-Year Estimates

Household Income Distribution

Area	Percent of Households Earning							
	Under $15,000	$15,000 -24,999	$25,000 -34,999	$35,000 -49,999	$50,000 -74,999	$75,000 -99,000	$100,000 -149,999	$150,000 and up
City	6.3	7.2	9.5	14.3	24.9	15.3	13.6	8.8
MSA[1]	11.6	10.8	11.4	15.3	20.3	12.5	11.1	6.9
U.S.	12.5	10.7	10.2	13.5	17.8	12.2	13.0	10.0

Note: (1) Figures cover the Boise City, ID Metropolitan Statistical Area—see Appendix B for areas included
Source: U.S. Census Bureau, 2010-2014 American Community Survey 5-Year Estimates

Poverty Rate

Area	All Ages	Under 18 Years Old	18 to 64 Years Old	65 Years and Over
City	8.6	9.6	8.3	6.9
MSA[1]	15.6	20.1	14.9	8.4
U.S.	15.6	21.9	14.6	9.4

Note: Figures are percentage of people whose income during the past 12 months was below the poverty level; (1) Figures cover the Boise City, ID Metropolitan Statistical Area—see Appendix B for areas included
Source: U.S. Census Bureau, 2010-2014 American Community Survey 5-Year Estimates

EMPLOYMENT

Labor Force and Employment

Area	Civilian Labor Force			Workers Employed		
	Dec. 2014	Dec. 2015	% Chg.	Dec. 2014	Dec. 2015	% Chg.
City	40,426	41,368	2.3	38,738	40,065	3.4
MSA[1]	313,572	323,203	3.0	300,918	311,157	3.4
U.S.	155,521,000	157,245,000	1.1	147,190,000	149,703,000	1.7

Note: Data is not seasonally adjusted and covers workers 16 years of age and older; (1) Figures cover the Boise City, ID Metropolitan Statistical Area—see Appendix B for areas included
Source: Bureau of Labor Statistics, Local Area Unemployment Statistics

Unemployment Rate

Area	2015											
	Jan.	Feb.	Mar.	Apr.	May	Jun.	Jul.	Aug.	Sep.	Oct.	Nov.	Dec.
City	4.8	4.6	4.9	4.5	3.7	4.0	4.4	4.3	3.8	3.1	3.3	3.1
MSA[1]	4.4	4.2	4.1	3.8	3.4	3.6	3.7	3.8	3.5	3.4	3.7	3.7
U.S.	6.1	5.8	5.6	5.1	5.3	5.5	5.6	5.2	4.9	4.8	4.8	4.8

Note: Data is not seasonally adjusted and covers workers 16 years of age and older; (1) Figures cover the Boise City, ID Metropolitan Statistical Area—see Appendix B for areas included
Source: Bureau of Labor Statistics, Local Area Unemployment Statistics

Employment by Occupation

Occupation Classification	City (%)	MSA[1] (%)	U.S. (%)
Management, Business, Science, and Arts	41.7	36.8	36.4
Natural Resources, Construction, and Maintenance	8.0	9.8	9.0
Production, Transportation, and Material Moving	9.3	10.6	12.1
Sales and Office	26.8	25.3	24.4
Service	14.2	17.5	18.2

Note: Figures cover employed civilians 16 years of age and older; (1) Figures cover the Boise City, ID Metropolitan Statistical Area—see Appendix B for areas included
Source: U.S. Census Bureau, 2010-2014 American Community Survey 5-Year Estimates

Employment by Industry

Sector	MSA[1]		U.S.
	Number of Employees	Percent of Total	Percent of Total
Construction, Mining, and Logging	18,500	6.2	5.0
Education and Health Services	44,900	15.1	15.7
Financial Activities	16,700	5.6	5.7
Government	46,500	15.6	15.5
Information	4,500	1.5	1.9
Leisure and Hospitality	28,300	9.5	10.4
Manufacturing	25,600	8.6	8.6
Other Services	10,600	3.5	3.9
Professional and Business Services	41,200	13.9	13.9
Retail Trade	35,900	12.1	11.3
Transportation, Warehousing, and Utilities	9,900	3.3	3.9
Wholesale Trade	13,700	4.6	4.1

Note: Figures are non-farm employment as of December 2015. Figures are not seasonally adjusted and include workers 16 years of age and older; (1) Figures cover the Boise City, ID Metropolitan Statistical Area—see Appendix B for areas included; n/a not available
Source: Bureau of Labor Statistics, Current Employment Statistics, Employment, Hours, and Earnings

Occupations with Greatest Projected Employment Growth: 2012 – 2022

Occupation[1]	2012 Employment	2022 Projected Employment	Numeric Employment Change	Percent Employment Change
Retail Salespersons	21,290	25,580	4,290	20.1
Customer Service Representatives	15,620	19,010	3,390	21.7
Registered Nurses	12,280	15,510	3,230	26.4
Combined Food Preparation and Serving Workers, Including Fast Food	9,860	13,080	3,220	32.6
Personal Care Aides	8,200	11,300	3,100	37.8
Cashiers	14,780	17,070	2,290	15.5
Waiters and Waitresses	10,000	12,160	2,160	21.6
General and Operations Managers	10,970	13,000	2,030	18.5
Nursing Assistants	7,630	9,450	1,820	23.9
Cooks, Restaurant	5,510	7,280	1,770	32.2

Note: Projections cover Idaho; (1) Sorted by numeric employment change
Source: www.projectionscentral.com, State Occupational Projections, 2012–2022 Long-Term Projections

Fastest Growing Occupations: 2012 – 2022

Occupation[1]	2012 Employment	2022 Projected Employment	Numeric Employment Change	Percent Employment Change
Insulation Workers, Floor, Ceiling, and Wall	150	250	100	74.5
Diagnostic Medical Sonographers	420	630	210	50.8
Drywall and Ceiling Tile Installers	680	990	310	45.6
Brickmasons and Blockmasons	230	330	100	43.4
Tile and Marble Setters	370	530	160	41.8
Home Health Aides	2,330	3,300	970	41.6
Cardiovascular Technologists and Technicians	270	370	100	39.8
Physical Therapist Assistants	370	510	140	37.8
Personal Care Aides	8,200	11,300	3,100	37.8
Nursing Instructors and Teachers, Postsecondary	270	370	100	37.5

Note: Projections cover Idaho; (1) Sorted by percent employment change and excludes occupations with numeric employment change less than 100
Source: www.projectionscentral.com, State Occupational Projections, 2012–2022 Long-Term Projections

Average Wages

Occupation	$/Hr.	Occupation	$/Hr.
Accountants and Auditors	32.15	Maids and Housekeeping Cleaners	10.53
Automotive Mechanics	19.11	Maintenance and Repair Workers	15.47
Bookkeepers	17.16	Marketing Managers	60.19
Carpenters	16.82	Nuclear Medicine Technologists	n/a
Cashiers	9.83	Nurses, Licensed Practical	19.34
Clerks, General Office	14.14	Nurses, Registered	30.00
Clerks, Receptionists/Information	12.82	Nursing Assistants	11.69
Clerks, Shipping/Receiving	13.94	Packers and Packagers, Hand	13.87
Computer Programmers	32.04	Physical Therapists	34.91
Computer Systems Analysts	38.55	Postal Service Mail Carriers	24.26
Computer User Support Specialists	20.80	Real Estate Brokers	24.24
Cooks, Restaurant	10.27	Retail Salespersons	13.07
Dentists	107.79	Sales Reps., Exc. Tech./Scientific	31.08
Electrical Engineers	41.19	Sales Reps., Tech./Scientific	33.56
Electricians	22.18	Secretaries, Exc. Legal/Med./Exec.	14.78
Financial Managers	46.56	Security Guards	12.78
First-Line Supervisors/Managers, Sales	18.65	Surgeons	n/a
Food Preparation Workers	9.72	Teacher Assistants*	11.76
General and Operations Managers	38.80	Teachers, Elementary School*	23.23
Hairdressers/Cosmetologists	13.23	Teachers, Secondary School*	21.61
Internists	n/a	Telemarketers	11.63
Janitors and Cleaners	11.41	Truck Drivers, Heavy/Tractor-Trailer	18.12
Landscaping/Groundskeeping Workers	12.94	Truck Drivers, Light/Delivery Svcs.	14.77
Lawyers	49.52	Waiters and Waitresses	9.49

Note: Wage data covers the Boise City-Nampa, ID Metropolitan Statistical Area—see Appendix B for areas included; (*) Hourly wages for elementary/secondary school teachers and teacher assistants were calculated by the editors from annual wage data based on a 40 hour work week; n/a not available.
Source: Bureau of Labor Statistics, Metro Area Occupational Employment and Wage Estimates, May 2015

TAXES

State Corporate Income Tax Rates

State	Tax Rate (%)	Income Brackets ($)	Num. of Brackets	Financial Institution Tax Rate (%)[a]	Federal Income Tax Ded.
Idaho	7.4 (h)	Flat rate	1	7.4 (h)	No

Note: Tax rates as of January 1, 2016; (a) Rates listed are the corporate income tax rate applied to financial institutions or excise taxes based on income. Some states have other taxes based upon the value of deposits or shares; (h) Idaho's minimum tax on a corporation is $20. The $10 Permanent Building Fund Tax must be paid by each corporation in a unitary group filing a combined return. Taxpayers with gross sales in Idaho under $100,000, and with no property or payroll in Idaho, may elect to pay 1% on such sales (instead of the tax on net income).
Source: Federation of Tax Administrators, "State Corporate Income Tax Rates, 2016"

State Individual Income Tax Rates

State	Tax Rate (%)	Income Brackets ($)	Num. of Brackets	Personal Exempt. ($)[1] Single	Personal Exempt. ($)[1] Dependents	Fed. Inc. Tax Ded.
Idaho (a)	1.6 - 7.4	1,452 - 10,890 (b)	7	4,050 (d)	4,050 (d)	No

Note: Tax rates as of January 1, 2016; Local- and county-level taxes are not included; n/a not applicable; (1) Married joint filers generally receive double the single exemption; (a) 18 states have statutory provision for automatically adjusting to the rate of inflation the dollar values of the income tax brackets, standard deductions, and/or personal exemptions. Massachusetts, Michigan, and Nebraska index the personal exemptiononly. Oregon does not index the income brackets for $125,000 and over. Maine has suspended indexing for 2014 and 2015; (b) For joint returns, taxes are twice the tax on half the couple's income; (d) These states use the personal exemption amounts provided in the federal Internal Revenue Code.
Source: Federation of Tax Administrators, "State Individual Income Tax Rates, 2016"

Various State and Local Tax Rates

State	State and Local Sales and Use (%)	State Sales and Use (%)	Gasoline[1] (¢/gal.)	Cigarette[2] ($/pack)	Spirits[3] ($/gal.)	Wine[4] ($/gal.)	Beer[5] ($/gal.)
Idaho	6.00	6.0	32	0.57	10.94 (g)	0.45 (l)	0.15 (q)

Note: All tax rates as of January 1, 2016; (1) The American Petroleum Institute has developed a methodology for determining the average tax rate on a gallon of fuel. Rates may include any of the following: excise taxes, environmental fees, storage tank fees, other fees or taxes, general sales tax, and local taxes. In states where gasoline is subject to the general sales tax, or where the fuel tax is based on the average sale price, the average rate determined by API is sensitive to changes in the price of gasoline. States that fully or partially apply general sales taxes to gasoline: CA, CO, GA, IL, IN, MI, NY; (2) The federal excise tax of $1.0066 per pack and local taxes are not included; (3) Rates are those applicable to off-premise sales of 40% alcohol by volume (a.b.v.) distilled spirits in 750ml containers. Local excise taxes are excluded; (4) Rates are those applicable to off-premise sales of 11% a.b.v. non-carbonated wine in 750ml containers; (5) Rates are those applicable to off-premise sales of 4.7% a.b.v. beer in 12 ounce containers; (g) Control states, where the government controls all sales. Products can be subject to ad valorem mark-up as well as excise taxes; (l) Different rates also applicable according to alcohol content, place of production, size of container, place purchased (on- or off-premise or on board airlines) or type of wine (carbonated, vermouth, etc.); (q) Different rates are also applicable according to alcohol content, place of production, size of container, or place purchased (on- or off-premise or onboard airlines).
Source: Tax Foundation, 2016 Facts & Figures: How Does Your State Compare?

State Business Tax Climate Index Rankings

State	Overall Rank	Corporate Tax Rank	Individual Income Tax Rank	Sales Tax Rank	Unemployment Insurance Tax Rank	Property Tax Rank
Idaho	19	24	23	20	45	4

Note: The index is a measure of how each state's tax laws affect economic performance. The lower the rank, the more favorable a state's tax system is for business. States without a given tax are given a ranking of 1. The scores/rankings for the District of Columbia do not affect other states. The 2016 index represents the tax climate as of July 1, 2015 (the beginning of Fiscal Year 2016).
Source: Tax Foundation, State Business Tax Climate Index 2016

TRANSPORTATION

Means of Transportation to Work

Area	Car/Truck/Van: Drove Alone	Car/Truck/Van: Car-pooled	Public Transportation: Bus	Public Transportation: Subway	Public Transportation: Railroad	Bicycle	Walked	Other Means	Worked at Home
City	82.3	8.8	0.2	0.0	0.0	0.4	0.7	0.6	7.2
MSA[1]	79.2	8.6	0.4	0.0	0.0	1.4	2.0	1.6	7.0
U.S.	76.4	9.6	2.6	1.8	0.6	0.6	2.8	1.3	4.4

Note: Figures are percentages and cover workers 16 years of age and older; (1) Figures cover the Boise City, ID Metropolitan Statistical Area—see Appendix B for areas included
Source: U.S. Census Bureau, 2010-2014 American Community Survey 5-Year Estimates

Travel Time to Work

Area	Less Than 10 Minutes	10 to 19 Minutes	20 to 29 Minutes	30 to 44 Minutes	45 to 59 Minutes	60 to 89 Minutes	90 Minutes or More
City	8.6	32.0	32.7	21.4	2.3	1.6	1.4
MSA[1]	14.0	34.0	25.6	19.0	4.1	2.1	1.2
U.S.	13.3	29.6	21.0	20.2	7.7	5.7	2.6

Note: Figures are percentages and include workers 16 years old and over; (1) Figures cover the Boise City, ID Metropolitan Statistical Area—see Appendix B for areas included
Source: U.S. Census Bureau, 2010-2014 American Community Survey 5-Year Estimates

Freeway Travel Time Index

Area	1985	1990	1995	2000	2005	2010	2014
Urban Area Rank[1,2]	100	94	93	80	72	76	65
Urban Area Index[1]	1.01	1.04	1.06	1.11	1.15	1.14	1.16
Average Index[3]	1.09	1.11	1.14	1.17	1.20	1.19	1.20

Note: Freeway Travel Time Index—the ratio of travel time in the peak period to the travel time at free-flow conditions. For example, a value of 1.30 indicates a 20-minute free-flow trip takes 26 minutes in the peak (20 minutes x 1.30 = 26 minutes); (1) Covers the Boise ID urban area; (2) Rank is based on 101 urban areas (#1 = highest travel time index); (3) Average of 101 urban areas
Source: Texas Transportation Institute, 2015 Urban Mobility Scorecard, August 2015

Freeway Commuter Stress Index

Area	1985	1990	1995	2000	2005	2010	2014
Urban Area Rank[1,2]	91	84	93	76	58	74	57
Urban Area Index[1]	1.05	1.08	1.09	1.15	1.19	1.17	1.20
Average Index[3]	1.13	1.16	1.19	1.22	1.25	1.24	1.25

Note: The Freeway Commuter Stress Index is the same as the Freeway Travel Time Index (see table above) except that it includes only the travel in the peak directions during the peak periods; the TTI includes travel in all directions during the peak period. Thus, the CSI is more indicative of the work trip experienced by each commuter on a daily basis. (1) Covers the Boise ID urban area; (2) Rank is based on 101 urban areas (#1 = highest stress index); (3) Average of 101 urban areas
Source: Texas Transportation Institute, 2015 Urban Mobility Scorecard, August 2015

Living Environment

COST OF LIVING

Cost of Living Index

Composite Index	Groceries	Housing	Utilities	Trans-portation	Health Care	Misc. Goods/ Services
90.9	84.5	80.1	85.2	105.3	105.5	97.5

Note: The Cost of Living Index measures regional differences in the cost of consumer goods and services, excluding taxes and non-consumer expenditures, for professional and managerial households in the top income quintile. It is based on more than 50,000 prices covering almost 60 different items for which prices are collected three times a year by chambers of commerce, economic development organizations or university applied economic centers in each participating urban area. The numbers shown should be read as a percentage above or below the national average of 100. For example, a value of 115.4 in the groceries column indicates that grocery prices are 15.4% higher than the national average. Small differences in the index numbers should not be interpreted as significant; Figures cover the Boise ID urban area.
Source: The Council for Community and Economic Research, ACCRA Cost of Living Index, 2015

Grocery Prices

Area[1]	T-Bone Steak ($/pound)	Frying Chicken ($/pound)	Whole Milk ($/half gal.)	Eggs ($/dozen)	Orange Juice ($/64 oz.)	Coffee ($/11.5 oz.)
City[2]	9.95	1.05	1.76	1.86	3.51	4.68
Avg.	10.99	1.43	2.25	2.26	3.58	4.48
Min.	7.16	0.98	1.30	1.35	2.88	2.98
Max.	14.13	2.43	3.85	4.81	6.39	7.56

Note: (1) Values for the local area are compared with the average, minimum and maximum values for all 292 areas in the Cost of Living Index; (2) Figures cover the Boise ID urban area; **T-Bone Steak** *(price per pound);* **Frying Chicken** *(price per pound, whole fryer);* **Whole Milk** *(half gallon carton);* **Eggs** *(price per dozen, Grade A, large);* **Orange Juice** *(64 oz. Tropicana or Florida Natural);* **Coffee** *(11.5 oz. can, vacuum-packed, Maxwell House, Hills Bros, or Folgers).*
Source: The Council for Community and Economic Research, ACCRA Cost of Living Index, 2015

Housing and Utility Costs

Area[1]	New Home Price ($)	Apartment Rent ($/month)	All Electric ($/month)	Part Electric ($/month)	Other Energy ($/month)	Telephone ($/month)
City[2]	258,125	700	-	70.21	70.23	24.99
Avg.	312,874	945	179.30	95.07	72.96	28.11
Min.	178,682	479	116.28	43.14	26.46	10.01
Max.	1,472,476	3,984	504.25	189.44	421.11	43.06

Note: (1) Values for the local area are compared with the average, minimum and maximum values for all 292 areas in the Cost of Living Index; (2) Figures cover the Boise ID urban area; **New Home Price** *(2,400 sf living area, 8,000 sf lot, in urban area with full utilities);* **Apartment Rent** *(950 sf 2 bedroom/1.5 or 2 bath, unfurnished, excluding all utilities except water);* **All Electric** *(average monthly cost for an all-electric home);* **Part Electric** *(average monthly cost for a part-electric home);* **Other Energy** *(average monthly cost for natural gas, fuel oil, coal, wood, and any other forms of energy except electricity);* **Telephone** *(price includes basic monthly rate for a private residential line plus additional local usage charges incurred by a family of four).*
Source: The Council for Community and Economic Research, ACCRA Cost of Living Index, 2015

Health Care, Transportation, and Other Costs

Area[1]	Doctor ($/visit)	Dentist ($/visit)	Optometrist ($/visit)	Gasoline ($/gallon)	Beauty Salon ($/visit)	Men's Shirt ($)
City[2]	128.96	87.20	117.98	2.47	30.63	25.65
Avg.	105.15	89.02	99.78	2.38	35.30	28.10
Min.	66.87	56.09	48.53	1.95	18.91	13.38
Max.	182.34	150.36	228.33	4.09	67.91	63.80

Note: (1) Values for the local area are compared with the average, minimum and maximum values for all 292 areas in the Cost of Living Index; (2) Figures cover the Boise ID urban area; **Doctor** *(general practitioners routine exam of an established patient);* **Dentist** *(adult teeth cleaning and periodic oral examination);* **Optometrist** *(full vision eye exam for established adult patient);* **Gasoline** *(one gallon regular unleaded, national brand, including all taxes, cash price at self-service pump if available);* **Beauty Salon** *(woman's shampoo, trim, and blow-dry);* **Men's Shirt** *(cotton/polyester dress shirt, pinpoint weave, long sleeves).*
Source: The Council for Community and Economic Research, ACCRA Cost of Living Index, 2015

HOUSING

House Price Index (HPI)

Area	National Ranking[2]	Quarterly Change (%)	One-Year Change (%)	Five-Year Change (%)
MSA[1]	26	2.60	10.10	33.40
U.S.[3]	–	1.45	5.76	22.85

Note: The HPI is a weighted repeat sales index. It measures average price changes in repeat sales or refinancings on the same properties. This information is obtained by reviewing repeat mortgage transactions on single-family properties whose mortgages have been purchased or securitized by Fannie Mae or Freddie Mac in January 1975; (1) Boise City Metropolitan Statistical Area—see Appendix B for areas included; (2) Rankings are based on annual percentage change for all metro areas containing at least 15,000 transactions over the last 10 years and ranges from 1 to 266; (3) figures based on a weighted average of Census Division estimates using a seasonally adjusted, purchase-only index; all figures are for the period ending December 31, 2015
Source: Federal Housing Finance Agency, House Price Index, February 25, 2016

Median Single-Family Home Prices

Area	2013	2014	2015p	Percent Change 2014 to 2015
MSA[1]	163.7	172.9	188.8	9.2
U.S. Average	197.4	208.9	223.9	7.2

Note: Figures are median sales prices of existing single-family homes in thousands of dollars; (p) preliminary; n/a not available; (1) Boise City, ID Metropolitan Statistical Area—see Appendix B for areas included
Source: National Association of Realtors, Median Sales Price of Existing Single-Family Homes for Metropolitan Areas, 4th Quarter 2015

Qualifying Income Based on Median Sales Price of Existing Single-Family Homes

Area	With 5% Down ($)	With 10% Down ($)	With 20% Down ($)
MSA[1]	42,195	39,974	35,533
U.S. Average	49,535	46,928	41,714

Note: Figures are preliminary; Qualifying income is based on a mortgage rate of 4.1%. Monthly principal and interest payment is limited to 25% of income; n/a not available; (1) Boise City, ID Metropolitan Statistical Area—see Appendix B for areas included
Source: National Association of Realtors, Qualifying Income Based on Median Sales Price of Existing Single-Family Homes for Metropolitan Areas, 4th Quarter 2015

Median Apartment Condo-Coop Home Prices

Area	2013	2014	2015p	Percent Change 2014 to 2015
MSA[1]	n/a	n/a	n/a	n/a
U.S. Average	194.9	204.3	210.7	3.1

Note: Figures are median sales prices of existing apartment condo-coop homes in thousands of dollars; (p) preliminary; n/a not available; (1) Boise City, ID Metropolitan Statistical Area—see Appendix B for areas included
Source: National Association of Realtors, Median Sales Price of Existing Apartment Condo-Coop Homes for Metropolitan Areas, 4th Quarter 2015

Gross Monthly Rent

Area	Under $200	$200 -299	$300 -499	$500 -749	$750 -999	$1,000 -1,499	$1,500 and up	Median ($)
City	1.3	1.0	2.1	18.3	25.6	45.0	6.8	1,016
MSA[1]	0.7	2.6	8.4	30.0	29.0	24.5	4.8	813
U.S.	1.5	3.2	7.4	21.0	24.1	26.9	15.9	920

Note: Figures are percentages except for Median; Gross rent is the contract rent plus the estimated average monthly cost of utilities (electricity, gas, and water and sewer) and fuels (oil, coal, kerosene, wood, etc.) if these are paid by the renter (or paid for the renter by someone else); (1) Figures cover the Boise City, ID Metropolitan Statistical Area—see Appendix B for areas included
Source: U.S. Census Bureau, 2010-2014 American Community Survey 5-Year Estimates

Homeownership Rate

Area	2008 (%)	2009 (%)	2010 (%)	2011 (%)	2012 (%)	2013 (%)	2014 (%)	2015 (%)
MSA[1]	n/a	n/a	n/a	n/a	n/a	n/a	n/a	n/a
U.S.	67.8	67.4	66.9	66.1	65.4	65.1	64.5	63.7

Note: (1) Figures cover the Boise City, ID Metropolitan Statistical Area—see Appendix B for areas included; n/a not available
Source: U.S. Census Bureau, Housing Vacancies and Homeownership Annual Statistics: 2015

Year Housing Structure Built

Area	2010 or Later	2000 -2009	1990 -1999	1980 -1989	1970 -1979	1960 -1969	1950 -1959	1940 -1949	Before 1940	Median Year
City	4.6	47.6	31.1	6.1	6.8	1.3	0.6	0.8	1.2	2000
MSA[1]	1.5	27.9	22.5	10.5	17.7	5.3	5.2	3.7	5.7	1991
U.S.	1.0	14.9	13.9	13.8	15.8	11.0	10.8	5.4	13.3	1976

Note: Figures are percentages except for Median Year; (1) Figures cover the Boise City, ID Metropolitan Statistical Area—see Appendix B for areas included
Source: U.S. Census Bureau, 2010-2014 American Community Survey 5-Year Estimates

HEALTH

Health Risk Data

Category	MSA[1] (%)	U.S. (%)
Adults aged 18–64 who have any kind of health care coverage	76.3	79.6
Adults who reported being in good or excellent health	85.9	83.1
Adults who are current smokers	16.0	19.6
Adults who are heavy drinkers[2]	5.6	6.1
Adults who are binge drinkers[3]	15.1	16.9
Adults who are overweight (BMI 25.0 - 29.9)	33.6	35.8
Adults who are obese (BMI 30.0 - 99.8)	28.1	27.6
Adults who participated in any physical activities in the past month	81.5	77.1
Adults 50+ who have ever had a sigmoidoscopy or colonoscopy	70.0	67.3
Women aged 40+ who have had a mammogram within the past two years	62.8	74.0
Men aged 40+ who have had a PSA test within the past two years	44.9	45.2
Adults aged 65+ who have had flu shot within the past year	51.1	60.1
Adults who always wear a seatbelt	91.0	93.8

Note: Data as of 2012 unless otherwise noted; (1) Figures cover the Boise City-Nampa, ID Metropolitan Statistical Area—see Appendix B for areas included; (2) Heavy drinkers are classified as males having more than two drinks per day or females having more than one drink per day; (3) Binge drinkers are classified as males having five or more drinks on one occasion or females having four or more drinks on one occasion
Source: Centers for Disease Control and Prevention, Behaviorial Risk Factor Surveillance System, SMART: Selected Metropolitan/Micropolitan Area Risk Trends, 2012 (Note: the CDC has discontinued this dataset but will be releasing a replacement in mid-2016)

Chronic Health Indicators

Category	MSA[1] (%)	U.S. (%)
Adults who have ever been told they had a heart attack	2.6	4.5
Adults who have ever been told they had a stroke	3.2	2.9
Adults who have been told they currently have asthma	7.3	8.9
Adults who have ever been told they have arthritis	24.3	25.7
Adults who have ever been told they have diabetes[2]	7.3	9.7
Adults who have ever been told they had skin cancer	7.6	5.7
Adults who have ever been told they had any other types of cancer	6.5	6.5
Adults who have ever been told they have COPD	5.1	6.2
Adults who have ever been told they have kidney disease	1.7	2.5
Adults who have ever been told they have a form of depression	20.0	18.0

Note: Data as of 2012 unless otherwise noted; (1) Figures cover the Boise City-Nampa, ID Metropolitan Statistical Area—see Appendix B for areas included; (2) Figures do not include pregnancy-related, borderline, or pre-diabetes
Source: Centers for Disease Control and Prevention, Behaviorial Risk Factor Surveillance System, SMART: Selected Metropolitan/Micropolitan Area Risk Trends, 2012 (Note: the CDC has discontinued this dataset but will be releasing a replacement in mid-2016)

Mortality Rates for the Top 10 Causes of Death in the U.S.

ICD-10[a] Sub-Chapter	ICD-10[a] Code	Age-Adjusted Mortality Rate[1] per 100,000 population	
		County[2]	U.S.
Malignant neoplasms	C00-C97	146.6	163.6
Ischaemic heart diseases	I20-I25	77.0	102.2
Other forms of heart disease	I30-I51	46.7	50.1
Chronic lower respiratory diseases	J40-J47	38.3	41.4
Organic, including symptomatic, mental disorders	F01-F09	53.6	38.5
Cerebrovascular diseases	I60-I69	30.8	36.5
Other external causes of accidental injury	W00-X59	26.0	27.5
Other degenerative diseases of the nervous system	G30-G31	28.1	26.3
Diabetes mellitus	E10-E14	17.2	21.1
Hypertensive diseases	I10-I15	16.1	19.7

Note: (a) ICD-10 = International Classification of Diseases 10th Revision; (1) Mortality rates are a three year average covering 2012-2014; (2) Figures cover Ada County.
Source: Centers for Disease Control and Prevention, National Center for Health Statistics. Underlying Cause of Death 1999-2014 on CDC WONDER Online Database, released 2015.

Mortality Rates for Selected Causes of Death

ICD-10[a] Sub-Chapter	ICD-10[a] Code	Age-Adjusted Mortality Rate[1] per 100,000 population	
		County[2]	U.S.
Assault	X85-Y09	Unreliable	5.1
Diseases of the liver	K70-K76	12.6	13.5
Human immunodeficiency virus (HIV) disease	B20-B24	Suppressed	2.1
Influenza and pneumonia	J09-J18	7.9	15.2
Intentional self-harm	X60-X84	16.5	12.7
Malnutrition	E40-E46	Unreliable	0.9
Obesity and other hyperalimentation	E65-E68	Unreliable	1.9
Renal failure	N17-N19	8.1	13.0
Transport accidents	V01-V99	9.4	11.6
Viral hepatitis	B15-B19	3.0	2.1

Note: (a) ICD-10 = International Classification of Diseases 10th Revision; (1) Mortality rates are a three year average covering 2012-2014; (2) Figures cover Ada County; Data are Suppressed when the data meet the criteria for confidentiality constraints; Mortality rates are flagged as Unreliable when the rate would be calculated with a numerator of 20 or less.
Source: Centers for Disease Control and Prevention, National Center for Health Statistics. Underlying Cause of Death 1999-2014 on CDC WONDER Online Database, released 2015.

Health Insurance Coverage

Area	With Health Insurance	With Private Health Insurance	With Public Health Insurance	Without Health Insurance	Population Under Age 18 Without Health Insurance
City	88.2	78.3	18.9	11.8	8.5
MSA[1]	85.0	68.9	26.9	15.0	8.0
U.S.	85.8	65.8	31.1	14.2	7.1

Note: Figures are percentages that cover the civilian noninstitutionalized population; (1) Figures cover the Boise City, ID Metropolitan Statistical Area—see Appendix B for areas included
Source: U.S. Census Bureau, 2010-2014 American Community Survey 5-Year Estimates

Number of Medical Professionals

Area	MDs[3]	DOs[3,4]	Dentists	Podiatrists	Chiropractors	Optometrists
County[1] (number)	1,195	99	342	15	221	75
County[1] (rate[2])	286.9	23.8	80.2	3.5	51.8	17.6
U.S. (rate[2])	272.5	20.9	64.7	5.8	25.9	15.2

Note: Data as of 2014 unless noted; (1) Data covers Ada County; (2) Rate per 100,000 population; (3) Data as of 2013 and includes all active, non-federal physicians; (4) Doctor of Osteopathic Medicine
Source: U.S. Department of Health and Human Services, Health Resources and Services Administration, Bureau of Health Professions, Area Resource File (ARF) 2014-2015

EDUCATION

Public School District Statistics

District Name	Schls	Pupils	Pupil/ Teacher Ratio	Minority Pupils[1] (%)	Free Lunch Eligible[2] (%)	IEP[3] (%)
Compass Charter School	1	568	19.1	16.5	14.1	1.8
Idaho Virtual Academy	2	3,438	53.4	10.7	35.3	8.0
Kuna Joint District	11	5,245	19.4	14.0	31.4	9.1
Meridian Joint District	55	38,006	21.4	16.3	23.5	9.2

Note: Table includes school districts with 100 or more students; (1) Percentage of students that are not non-Hispanic white; (2) Percentage of students that are eligible for the free lunch program; (3) Percentage of students that have an Individualized Education Program.
Source: U.S. Department of Education, National Center for Education Statistics, Common Core of Data, Local Education Agency (School District) Universe Survey: School Year 2013-2014; U.S. Department of Education, National Center for Education Statistics, Common Core of Data, Public Elementary/Secondary School Universe Survey: School Year 2013-2014

Highest Level of Education

Area	Less than H.S.	H.S. Diploma	Some College, No Deg.	Associate Degree	Bachelor's Degree	Master's Degree	Prof. School Degree	Doctorate Degree
City	5.1	23.9	28.7	8.9	24.3	6.3	1.8	0.8
MSA[1]	9.9	25.1	26.8	8.4	20.2	6.7	1.8	1.1
U.S.	13.7	28.0	21.2	7.9	18.3	7.8	2.0	1.3

Note: Figures cover persons age 25 and over; (1) Figures cover the Boise City, ID Metropolitan Statistical Area—see Appendix B for areas included
Source: U.S. Census Bureau, 2010-2014 American Community Survey 5-Year Estimates

Educational Attainment by Race

Area	High School Graduate or Higher (%)					Bachelor's Degree or Higher (%)				
	Total	White	Black	Asian	Hisp.[2]	Total	White	Black	Asian	Hisp.[2]
City	94.9	95.5	80.4	87.5	81.1	33.3	33.0	33.9	59.1	16.1
MSA[1]	90.1	91.0	80.5	84.4	62.1	29.8	30.1	18.7	48.0	11.4
U.S.	86.3	88.4	83.2	85.8	64.1	29.3	30.6	19.0	50.9	13.9

Note: Figures shown cover persons 25 years old and over; (1) Figures cover the Boise City, ID Metropolitan Statistical Area—see Appendix B for areas included; (2) People of Hispanic origin can be of any race
Source: U.S. Census Bureau, 2010-2014 American Community Survey 5-Year Estimates

School Enrollment by Grade and Control

Area	Preschool (%)		Kindergarten (%)		Grades 1 - 4 (%)		Grades 5 - 8 (%)		Grades 9 - 12 (%)	
	Public	Private	Public	Private	Public	Private	Public	Private	Public	Private
City	38.5	61.5	95.5	4.5	92.5	7.5	95.0	5.0	96.7	3.3
MSA[1]	43.6	56.4	91.8	8.2	92.9	7.1	94.3	5.7	93.1	6.9
U.S.	57.4	42.6	87.8	12.2	89.8	10.2	89.9	10.1	90.6	9.4

Note: Figures shown cover persons 3 years old and over; (1) Figures cover the Boise City, ID Metropolitan Statistical Area—see Appendix B for areas included
Source: U.S. Census Bureau, 2010-2014 American Community Survey 5-Year Estimates

Average Salaries of Public School Classroom Teachers

Area	2013-14		2014-15		Percent Change 2013-14 to 2014-15	Percent Change 2004-05 to 2014-15
	Dollars	Rank[1]	Dollars	Rank[1]		
Idaho	44,465	49	45,218	48	1.69	10.7
U.S. Average	56,610	–	57,379	–	1.36	20.8

Note: (1) State rank ranges from 1 to 51 where 1 indicates highest salary.
Source: National Education Association, Rankings & Estimates: Rankings of the States 2014 and Estimates of School Statistics 2015, March 2015

Higher Education

Four-Year Colleges			Two-Year Colleges			Medical Schools[1]	Law Schools[2]	Voc/ Tech[3]
Public	Private Non-profit	Private For-profit	Public	Private Non-profit	Private For-profit			
0	0	2	0	0	0	0	0	0

Note: Figures cover institutions located within the city limits and include main campuses only; (1) includes schools accredited by the Liaison Committee on Medical Education and the American Osteopathic Association's Commission on Osteopathic College Accreditation; (2) includes ABA-accredited schools, schools with provisional ABA accreditation, and state accredited schools; (3) includes all schools with programs that are less than 2 years.

Source: National Center for Education Statistics, Integrated Postsecondary Education System (IPEDS), 2014-15; Association of American Medical Colleges, Member List, March 21, 2016; American Osteopathic Association, Member List, March 21, 2016; Law School Admission Council, Official Guide to ABA-Approved Law Schools Online, March 21, 2016; Wikipedia, List of Medical Schools in the United States, March 21, 2016; Wikipedia, List of Law Schools in the United States, March 21, 2016

According to *U.S. News & World Report,* the Boise City, ID metro area is home to one of the best liberal arts colleges in the U.S.: **College of Idaho** (#169). The indicators used to capture academic quality fall into a number of categories: assessment by administrators at peer institutions; retention of students; faculty resources; student selectivity; financial resources; alumni giving; high school counselor ratings of colleges; and graduation rate. *U.S. News & World Report, "America's Best Colleges 2016"*

PRESIDENTIAL ELECTION

2012 Presidential Election Results

Area	Obama (%)	Romney (%)	Other (%)
Ada County	42.7	54.0	3.2
U.S.	51.0	47.2	1.8

Note: Results may not add to 100% due to rounding
Source: Dave Leip's Atlas of U.S. Presidential Elections

EMPLOYERS

Major Employers

Company Name	Industry
Ada County	Administration - local government
Albertsons Inc	Retail trade
Boise City ISD #1	Education - local government
Boise State University	Education - state government
City of Boise	Administration - local government
DirectTV Customer Service	Administrative & waste service
Hewlett-Packard Co	Manufacturing
Idaho Power Co	Utilities
J R Simplot Co	Manufacturing
Mcdonalds	Accommodation & food service
Meridian JSD #2	Education - local government
Micron Technology	Manufacturing
Nampa School District #13	Education - local government
St Alphonsus Regional Medical Center	Health care
St Lukes Health Systems	Health care
State of Idaho Department of Health	Administration - state government
State of Idaho Dept of Corrections	Administration - state government
U.S. Veterans Administration	Federal government - health care
US Postal Service	Transportation & warehousing
Wal-Mart Stores	Retail trade
WDS Global	Administrative & waste service
Wells Fargo Bank	Finance & insurance

Note: Companies shown are located within the Boise City, ID Metropolitan Statistical Area.
Source: Hoovers.com; Wikipedia

PUBLIC SAFETY

Crime Rate

Area	All Crimes	Violent Crimes: Murder	Violent Crimes: Rape[3]	Violent Crimes: Robbery	Violent Crimes: Aggrav. Assault	Property Crimes: Burglary	Property Crimes: Larceny -Theft	Property Crimes: Motor Vehicle Theft
City	1,465.0	2.3	22.2	1.2	54.8	220.5	1,130.3	33.8
Metro[1]	2,000.4	1.7	44.6	13.9	168.1	339.8	1,341.5	90.9
U.S.	2,971.8	4.5	36.6	102.2	232.5	542.5	1,837.3	216.2

Note: Figures are crimes per 100,000 population; (1) Figures cover the Boise City, ID Metropolitan Statistical Area—see Appendix B for areas included; (3) The city and U.S. figures shown were reported using the revised Uniform Crime Reporting (UCR) definition of rape. The suburban and metro area figures shown are an aggregate total of the data submitted using both the revised and legacy UCR definitions.
Source: FBI Uniform Crime Reports, 2014

Hate Crimes

Area	Number of Quarters Reported	Race	Religion	Sexual Orientation	Ethnicity	Disability	Gender	Gender Identity
City	4	0	0	0	0	0	0	0
U.S.	4	2,568	1,014	1,017	648	84	33	98

(Race through Gender Identity: Number of Incidents per Bias Motivation)

Source: Federal Bureau of Investigation, Hate Crime Statistics 2014

Identity Theft Consumer Complaints

Area	Complaints	Complaints per 100,000 Population	Rank[2]
MSA[1]	903	135.9	79
U.S.	490,220	152.4	-

Note: (1) Figures cover the Boise City, ID Metropolitan Statistical Area—see Appendix B for areas included; (2) Rank ranges from 1 to 379 where 1 indicates greatest number of identity theft complaints per 100,000 population
Source: Federal Trade Commission, Consumer Sentinel Network Data Book for January–December 2015

Fraud and Other Consumer Complaints

Area	Complaints	Complaints per 100,000 Population	Rank[2]
MSA[1]	2,707	407.4	94
U.S.	2,593,159	806.0	-

Note: (1) Figures cover the Boise City, ID Metropolitan Statistical Area—see Appendix B for areas included; (2) Rank ranges from 1 to 379 where 1 indicates greatest number of identity theft complaints per 100,000 population
Source: Federal Trade Commission, Consumer Sentinel Network Data Book for January–December 2015

RECREATION

Culture

Dance[1]	Theatre[1]	Instrumental Music[1]	Vocal Music[1]	Series and Festivals	Museums and Art Galleries[2]	Zoos and Aquariums[3]
0	0	0	0	0	0	0

Note: (1) Professional perfoming groups; (2) Based on organizations with SIC code 8412; (3) AZA-accredited
Source: The Grey House Performing Arts Directory, 2015-16; Association of Zoos & Aquariums, AZA Member Zoos & Aquariums, March 25, 2016; www.AccuLeads.com, March 29, 2016

Professional Sports Teams

Team Name	League	Year Established
No teams are located in the metro area		

Source: Wikipedia, Major Professional Sports Teams of the United States and Canada, March 24, 2016

CLIMATE

Average and Extreme Temperatures

Temperature	Jan	Feb	Mar	Apr	May	Jun	Jul	Aug	Sep	Oct	Nov	Dec	Yr.
Extreme High (°F)	63	70	81	92	98	105	111	110	101	94	74	65	111
Average High (°F)	36	44	53	62	71	80	90	88	78	65	48	38	63
Average Temp. (°F)	29	36	42	49	58	66	74	73	63	52	40	31	51
Average Low (°F)	22	27	31	37	44	52	58	57	48	39	30	23	39
Extreme Low (°F)	-17	-15	6	19	22	31	35	34	23	11	-3	-25	-25

Note: Figures cover the years 1948-1995
Source: National Climatic Data Center, International Station Meteorological Climate Summary, 9/96

Average Precipitation/Snowfall/Humidity

Precip./Humidity	Jan	Feb	Mar	Apr	May	Jun	Jul	Aug	Sep	Oct	Nov	Dec	Yr.
Avg. Precip. (in.)	1.4	1.1	1.2	1.2	1.2	0.9	0.3	0.3	0.6	0.7	1.4	1.4	11.8
Avg. Snowfall (in.)	7	4	2	1	Tr	Tr	0	0	0	Tr	2	6	22
Avg. Rel. Hum. 7am (%)	81	80	75	69	65	59	48	50	58	67	77	81	68
Avg. Rel. Hum. 4pm (%)	68	58	45	35	34	29	22	23	28	36	55	67	42

Note: Figures cover the years 1948-1995; Tr = Trace amounts (<0.05 in. of rain; <0.5 in. of snow)
Source: National Climatic Data Center, International Station Meteorological Climate Summary, 9/96

Weather Conditions

Temperature			Daytime Sky			Precipitation		
5°F & below	32°F & below	90°F & above	Clear	Partly cloudy	Cloudy	0.01 inch or more precip.	0.1 inch or more snow/ice	Thunder-storms
6	124	45	106	133	126	91	22	14

Note: Figures are average number of days per year and cover the years 1948-1995
Source: National Climatic Data Center, International Station Meteorological Climate Summary, 9/96

HAZARDOUS WASTE

Superfund Sites

Meridian has no sites on the EPA's Superfund Final National Priorities List. There are a total of 1,323 Superfund sites on the list in the U.S. *U.S. Environmental Protection Agency, Final National Priorities List, March 18, 2016*

AIR & WATER QUALITY

Air Quality Trends: Ozone

	1990	1995	2000	2005	2010	2011	2012	2013	2014
MSA[1]	n/a	n/a	n/a	n/a	n/a	n/a	n/a	n/a	n/a

Note: (1) Data covers the Boise City, ID Metropolitan Statistical Area—see Appendix B for areas included; n/a not available. The values shown are the composite ozone concentration averages among trend sites based on the highest fourth daily maximum 8-hour concentration in parts per million. These trends are based on sites having an adequate record of monitoring data during the trend period. Data from exceptional events are included.
Source: U.S. Environmental Protection Agency, Air Quality Monitoring Information, "Air Quality Trends by City, 1990-2014"

Air Quality Index

Area	Percent of Days when Air Quality was...[2]					AQI Statistics[2]	
	Good	Moderate	Unhealthy for Sensitive Groups	Unhealthy	Very Unhealthy	Maximum	Median
MSA[1]	80.5	15.8	3.0	0.7	0.0	155	40

Note: (1) Data covers the Boise City, ID Metropolitan Statistical Area—see Appendix B for areas included; (2) Based on 303 days with AQI data in 2015. Air Quality Index (AQI) is an index for reporting daily air quality. EPA calculates the AQI for five major air pollutants regulated by the Clean Air Act: ground-level ozone, particle pollution (aka particulate matter), carbon monoxide, sulfur dioxide, and nitrogen dioxide. The AQI runs from 0 to 500. The higher the AQI value, the greater the level of air pollution and the greater the health concern. There are six AQI categories: "Good" AQI is between 0 and 50. Air quality is considered satisfactory; "Moderate" AQI is between 51 and 100. Air quality is acceptable; "Unhealthy for Sensitive Groups" When AQI values are between 101 and 150, members of sensitive groups may experience health effects; "Unhealthy" When AQI values are between 151 and 200 everyone may begin to experience health effects; "Very Unhealthy" AQI values between 201 and 300 trigger a health alert; "Hazardous" AQI values over 300 trigger warnings of emergency conditions (not shown).
Source: U.S. Environmental Protection Agency, Air Quality Index Report, 2015

Air Quality Index Pollutants

Area	Percent of Days when AQI Pollutant was...[2]					
	Carbon Monoxide	Nitrogen Dioxide	Ozone	Sulfur Dioxide	Particulate Matter 2.5	Particulate Matter 10
MSA[1]	0.3	6.9	47.9	0.0	34.3	10.6

Note: (1) Data covers the Boise City, ID Metropolitan Statistical Area—see Appendix B for areas included; (2) Based on 303 days with AQI data in 2015. The Air Quality Index (AQI) is an index for reporting daily air quality. EPA calculates the AQI for five major air pollutants regulated by the Clean Air Act: ground-level ozone, particle pollution (also known as particulate matter), carbon monoxide, sulfur dioxide, and nitrogen dioxide. The AQI runs from 0 to 500. The higher the AQI value, the greater the level of air pollution and the greater the health concern.

Source: U.S. Environmental Protection Agency, Air Quality Index Report, 2015

Maximum Air Pollutant Concentrations: Particulate Matter, Ozone, CO and Lead

	Particulate Matter 10 (ug/m^3)	Particulate Matter 2.5 Wtd AM (ug/m^3)	Particulate Matter 2.5 24-Hr (ug/m^3)	Ozone (ppm)	Carbon Monoxide (ppm)	Lead (ug/m^3)
MSA[1] Level	61	n/a	n/a	0.065	2	n/a
NAAQS[2]	150	15	35	0.075	9	0.15
Met NAAQS[2]	Yes	n/a	n/a	Yes	Yes	n/a

Note: (1) Data covers the Boise City, ID Metropolitan Statistical Area—see Appendix B for areas included; Data from exceptional events are included; (2) National Ambient Air Quality Standards; ppm = parts per million; ug/m^3 = micrograms per cubic meter; n/a not available.

Concentrations: Particulate Matter 10 (coarse particulate)—highest second maximum 24-hour concentration; Particulate Matter 2.5 Wtd AM (fine particulate)—highest weighted annual mean concentration; Particulate Matter 2.5 24-Hour (fine particulate)—highest 98th percentile 24-hour concentration; Ozone—highest fourth daily maximum 8-hour concentration; Carbon Monoxide—highest second maximum non-overlapping 8-hour concentration; Lead—maximum running 3-month average

Source: U.S. Environmental Protection Agency, Air Quality Monitoring Information, "Air Quality Statistics by City, 2014"

Maximum Air Pollutant Concentrations: Nitrogen Dioxide and Sulfur Dioxide

	Nitrogen Dioxide AM (ppb)	Nitrogen Dioxide 1-Hr (ppb)	Sulfur Dioxide AM (ppb)	Sulfur Dioxide 1-Hr (ppb)	Sulfur Dioxide 24-Hr (ppb)
MSA[1] Level	n/a	n/a	n/a	5	n/a
NAAQS[2]	53	100	30	75	140
Met NAAQS[2]	n/a	n/a	n/a	Yes	n/a

Note: (1) Data covers the Boise City, ID Metropolitan Statistical Area—see Appendix B for areas included; Data from exceptional events are included; (2) National Ambient Air Quality Standards; ppm = parts per million; ug/m^3 = micrograms per cubic meter; n/a not available.

Concentrations: Nitrogen Dioxide AM—highest arithmetic mean concentration; Nitrogen Dioxide 1-Hr—highest 98th percentile 1-hour daily maximum concentration; Sulfur Dioxide AM—highest annual mean concentration; Sulfur Dioxide 1-Hr—highest 99th percentile 1-hour daily maximum concentration; Sulfur Dioxide 24-Hr—highest second maximum 24-hour concentration

Source: U.S. Environmental Protection Agency, Air Quality Monitoring Information, "Air Quality Statistics by City, 2014"

Drinking Water

Water System Name	Pop. Served	Primary Water Source Type	Violations[1]	
			Health Based	Monitoring/ Reporting
Meridian Water Dept	80,000	Ground	0	0

Note: (1) Based on violation data from January 1, 2015 to December 31, 2015 (includes unresolved violations from earlier years)

Source: U.S. Environmental Protection Agency, Office of Ground Water and Drinking Water, Safe Drinking Water Information System (based on data extracted April 29, 2016)

Northbrook, Illinois

Background

Northbrook is on the northern edge of Cook County along Chicago's affluent North Shore. It is about 20 miles northwest from the downtown Chicago Loop and covers approximately 13 square miles.

The area of Northbrook was originally home to the Potawatomi Indians. After they relocated to Council Bluffs, Iowa, in 1833, Joel Sterling Sherman bought 159 acres, which today is the site of the Northbrook Central Business District.

Following Sherman's purchase, businessman Frederick Schermer donated land for the town's first railroad station, and the area was named Shermerville. The area grew as a farm town with well established brick yards that were crucial to the rebuilding that followed the Great Chicago Fire of 1871. From the 1870s, the area prospered from the brick yards and its agricultural efforts. In 1923 the residents, in an attempt to change the town's image, changed its name to Northbrook, after the flow of the West Fork and North Branch of the Chicago River through the town.

Northbrook experienced rapid growth and significant subdivisions after World War II, and by 1960 its population increased substantially. The completion of a water line to bring Lake Michigan water to a new water treatment plant in Northbrook also stimulated a growth spurt during the 1960s. Northbrook continues to be governed by a council manager form of government, including a board of six trustees and the president. The board's role is to establish policies and oversee the hiring of a village manager to operate the daily business.

Northbrook benefits from its close proximity to downtown Chicago and the offerings of the North Shore. It plays host to a variety of world renowned national stores, designer boutiques, and a diversity of restaurants and dining options.

Recreational activities abound in the area, with facilities and services to match the community's needs. There are over 500 acres of land in 22 park areas within the Northbrook Park District. The district provides and maintains the area for the celebration and enjoyment of nature in parks, playgrounds, and natural areas. Within the district you will also find lakes and streams for fishing, routes to bicycle, and courses to golf. There are numerous public swimming pools, ball fields, and skate parks that provide many extra-curricular and family oriented options. For over 40 years, the Northbrook Park District skating school has offered recreational and competitive skating opportunities for residents of all ages and skill levels.

As a predominate subdivision in the greater Chicago area, Northbrook offers a robust public school system for elementary through to high school students. Northwestern University in Evanston is just a short distance to the south, and there are several excellent universities in Chicago itself. The public library in Northbrook has a unique history, going back to 1919 when the first reading room was established by the Citizens' Club. In 1970 the library received a Distinguished Building award from the Chicago chapter of the American Institute of Architects. Today, the library has expanded and gone through many renovations and is a testament to the distinct architecture that Chicago is known for. The community has been integral in creating the Northbrook Public Library as a welcoming space for all residents and visitors to share.

For those interested in the performing arts, the Northbrook Theatre Department of Performing Arts was created to support a variety of local theatrical productions. The Northbrook Theatre has been a staple in the region's performing arts scene for the past 30 years. There are a multitude of ways for residents of all ages to get involved in Northbrook's performing arts scene, including the summer performing arts workshops and Creative Companions program at the Bright Star Theatre that offers the opportunity to work in theatrical productions with professionals.

Northbrook shares a similar climate to Chicago and, due to its proximity to Lake Michigan, winters can be especially harsh with snow, ice, and cold temperatures. Northbrook experiences winter lows well below freezing, with summer highs that reach into the 80s. Spring and fall average temperatures are in the 50s and 60s.

Rankings

Business/Finance Rankings

- The personal finance site NerdWallet analyzed 183 American metropolitan areas with populations over 250,000 and more than 15,000 businesses to rank where entrepreneurs find the most success. Criteria included area economy, annual income, housing cost, unemployment rate, and the success rate of area businesses. Chicago* ranked #71. *www.nerdwallet.com, "Best Places to Start a Business," April 27, 2015*
- Based on metro area social media reviews, the employment opinion group Glassdoor surveyed 50 of the largest U.S. metro areas and equally weighed cost of living, hiring opportunity, and job satisfaction to compose a list of "25 Best Cities for Jobs." The Chicago* metro area was ranked #28 in overall job satisfaction. *www.glassdoor.com, "Best Cities for Jobs," May 19, 2015*
- In a survey of economic confidence in the nation's 50 largest metropolitan areas conducted January–December 2014, the Chicago* metro area placed #16, according to Gallup's 2014 Economic Confidence Index. *Gallup, "San Jose and San Francisco Lead in Economic Confidence," March 19, 2015*
- The Brookings Institution ranked the 100 largest metro areas in the U.S. based on income inequality. Chicago* was ranked #20 (#1 = greatest ineqality). Criteria: the "95/20 ratio," a figure representing the income at which a household earns more than 95 percent of all other households, divided by the income at which a household earns more than only 20 percent of all other households. *Brookings Institution, "Income Inequality, 100 Largest U.S. Metro Areas, 2007-2014," January 14, 2016*
- Payscale.com ranked the 20 largest metro areas in terms of wage growth. The Chicago* metro area ranked #6. Criteria: private-sector wage growth between the 1st quarter of 2015 and the 1st quarter of 2016. *PayScale, "Wage Trends by Metro Area," 1st Quarter, 2016*
- The Chicago* metro area was identified as one of the most debt-ridden places in America by the finance site Credit.com. The metro area was ranked #10. Criteria: residents' average personal debt load and average credit scores. *Credit.com, "The Most Debt-Ridden Cities," May 1, 2014*
- Chicago* was identified as one of America's most frugal metro areas by *Coupons.com.* The city ranked #24 out of 25. Criteria: online coupon usage. *Coupons.com, "Top 25 Most Frugal Cities of 2014," May 11, 2015*
- Chicago* was identified as one of America's most frugal metro areas by *Coupons.com.* The city ranked #25 out of 25. Criteria: Grocery IQ and coupons.com mobile app usage. *Coupons.com, "Top 25 Most On-the-Go Frugal Cities of 2013," April 10, 2014*
- Chicago* was cited as one of America's top metros for new and expanded facility projects in 2015. The area ranked #1 in the large metro area category (population over 1 million). *Site Selection, "Top Metropolitans of 2015," March 2016*
- The Chicago* metro area appeared on the Milken Institute "2015 Best Performing Cities" list. Rank: #122 out of 200 large metro areas. Criteria: job growth; wage and salary growth; high-tech output growth. *Milken Institute, "Best-Performing Cities 2015," December 2015*
- *Forbes* ranked the 200 most populous metro areas to determine the nation's "Best Places for Business and Careers." The Chicago* metro area was ranked #87. Criteria: costs (business and living); job growth (past and projected); income growth; educational attainment (college and high school); projected economic growth; cultural and recreational opportunities; net migration patterns; number of highly ranked colleges. *Forbes, "The Best Places for Business and Careers 2015," July 29, 2015*

Education Rankings

- Personal finance website *WalletHub* analyzed the 150 largest U.S. metropolitan statistical areas to determine where the most educated Americans are choosing to settle. Criteria: education quality and attainment gap; education levels; percentage of workers with degrees; public school rankings; quality and size of each metro area's universities. Chicago* was ranked #40 (#1 = most educated city). *www.WalletHub.com, "2015's Most and Least Educated Cities*

Environmental Rankings

- The Chicago* metro area came in at #137 for the relative comfort of its climate on Sperling's list of "chill cities," as measured by the Sperling Heat Index. All 361 metro areas are included. Criteria included daytime high temperatures, nighttime low temperatures, dew point, and relative humidity at the high temperatures. *www.bertsperling.com, "Sperling's Chill Cities," July 18, 2013*
- Sperling's BestPlaces assessed 379 metropolitan areas of the United States for the likelihood of dangerously extreme weather events or earthquakes. In general the Southeast and South-Central regions have the highest risk of weather extremes and earthquakes, while the Pacific Northwest enjoys the lowest risk. Of the least risky metropolitan areas, the Chicago* metro area was ranked #324. *www.bestplaces.net, "Safest Places from Natural Disasters," April 2011*
- The U.S. Environmental Protection Agency (EPA) released a list of U.S. metropolitan areas with the most ENERGY STAR certified buildings in 2015. The Chicago* metro area was ranked #6 out of 25. *U.S. Environmental Protection Agency, "Top Cities With the Most ENERGY STAR Certified Buildings in 2016," March 30, 2016*
- Chicago* was highlighted as one of the 25 most ozone-polluted metro areas in the U.S. during 2011 through 2013. The area ranked #19. *American Lung Association, State of the Air 2015*

Health/Fitness Rankings

- For each of the 50 most populous metro areas in the United States, the American College of Sports Medicine's American Fitness Index evaluated infrastructure, community assets, and policies that encourage healthy and fit lifestyles, including preventive health behaviors, levels of chronic disease conditions, health care access, and community resources and policies that support physical activity. The Chicago* metro area ranked #17 for "community fitness." *www.americanfitnessindex.org, "ACSM American Fitness Index Health and Community Fitness Status of the 50 Largest Metropolitan Areas," May 2015*
- The Chicago* metro area was identified as one of the worst cities for bed bugs in America by pest control company Orkin. The area ranked #1 out of 50 based on the number of bed bug treatments Orkin performed from January to December 2015. *Orkin, "Chicago Tops Bed Bug Cities List for Fourth Year in a Row," January 13, 2016*
- Chicago* was identified as a "2016 Spring Allergy Capital." The area ranked #81 out of 100. Three groups of factors were used to identify the most severe cities for people with allergies during the spring season: annual pollen levels; medicine utilization; access to board-certified allergists. *Asthma and Allergy Foundation of America, "Spring Allergy Capitals 2016"*
- Chicago* was identified as a "2015 Asthma Capital." The area ranked #10 out of the nation's 100 largest metropolitan areas. Criteria: estimated prevalence; self-reported prevalence; crude death rate for asthma; annual pollen score; annual air quality; public smoking laws; number of board-certified asthma specialists; school inhaler access laws; rescue medication use; controller medication use; ER visits for asthma; uninsured rate; poverty rate. *Asthma and Allergy Foundation of America, "Asthma Capitals 2015"*
- The Chicago* metro area ranked #105 out of 190 in The Gallup-Healthways Well-Being Index. Criteria: purpose; social well being; financial health; community and physical health. Results are based on telephone interviews with adults, aged 18 and older, living in metropolitan areas in the 50 U.S. states and the District of Columbia. *Gallup-Healthways, "State of American Well-Being," February 23, 2016*

Real Estate Rankings

- According to Penske Truck Rental, the Chicago* metro area was named the #10 moving destination in 2015, based on one-way consumer truck rental reservations made through Penske's website and reservations call center. *blog.gopenske.com, "Penske Truck Rental's 2015 Top Moving Destinations List," February 3, 2016*
- The Chicago* metro area was identified as #9 among the ten housing markets with the highest percentage of distressed property sales, based on the findings of the housing data website RealtyTrac. Criteria: short sales; income and poverty figures; and unemployment data. *247wallst.com, "Cities Selling the Most Distressed Homes," January 23, 2014*
- Chicago* was ranked #147 out of 225 metro areas in terms of housing affordability in 2015 by the National Association of Home Builders (#1 = most affordable). Criteria: the share of homes sold in that area affordable to a family earning the local median income, based on standard mortgage underwriting criteria. *National Association of Home Builders®, NAHB-Wells Fargo Housing Opportunity Index, 4th Quarter 2015*
- The nation's largest metro areas were analyzed in terms of the percentage of households entering some stage of foreclosure in 2015. The Chicago* metro area ranked #14 out of 20 (#1 = highest foreclosure rate). *RealtyTrac, "2015 Year-End U.S. Foreclosure Market Report™," January 12, 2016*

Safety Rankings

- Chicago* was identified as one of the most disaster-proof places in the U.S. in terms of its vulnerability to natural and non-natural disasters. The city ranked #3 out of 5. Rankings are based on the U.S. Center for Disease Control's Cities Readiness Initiative (CRI), which assesses local emergency-management plans, protocols and capabilities for 72 Metropolitan Statistical Areas and four non-MSA large cities. *Forbes, "America's Most and Least Disaster-Proof Cities," December 12, 2011*
- The National Insurance Crime Bureau ranked 380 metro areas in the U.S. in terms of per capita rates of vehicle theft. The Chicago* metro area ranked #109 (#1 = highest rate). Criteria: number of vehicle theft offenses per 100,000 inhabitants in 2014. *National Insurance Crime Bureau, "Hot Spots 2014," June 24, 2015*

Seniors/Retirement Rankings

- From its Best Cities for Successful Aging indexes, the Milken Institute generated rankings for metropolitan areas, weighing data in eight categories—health care, wellness, living arrangements, transportation, financial characteristics, education and employment opportunities, community engagement, and overall livability. The Chicago* metro area was ranked #64 overall in the large metro area category. *Milken Institute, "Best Cities for Successful Aging, 2014"*

Sports/Recreation Rankings

- According to the personal finance website NerdWallet, the Chicago* metro area, at #2, is one of the nation's top dozen metro areas for sports fans. Criteria included the presence of all four major sports—MLB, NFL, NHL, and NBA, fan enthusiasm (as measured by game attendance), ticket affordability, and "sports culture," that is, number of sports bars. *www.nerdwallet.com, "Best Cities for Sports Fans," May 5, 2013*

Transportation Rankings

- Chicago* was identified as one of the most congested metro areas in the U.S. The area ranked #8 out of 10. Criteria: yearly delay per auto commuter in hours. *Texas A&M Transportation Institute, "2015 Urban Mobility Scorecard," August 2015*
- The Chicago* metro area appeared on *Forbes* list of places with the most extreme commutes. The metro area ranked #8 out of 10. Criteria: average travel time; percentage of mega commuters. Mega-commuters travel more than 90 minutes and 50 miles each way to work. *Forbes.com, "The Cities with the Most Extreme Commutes," March 5, 2013*

Miscellaneous Rankings

- The watchdog site Charity Navigator conducts an annual study of charities in the nation's major markets both to analyze statistical differences in their financial, accountability, and transparency practices and to track year-to-year variations in individual communities. The Chicago* metro area was ranked #14 among the 30 metro markets in the rating dimension of Overall Score. *www.charitynavigator.org, "Metro Market Study 2015," June 5, 2015*
- The Harris Poll's Happiness Index survey revealed that of the top ten U.S. markets, the Chicago* metro area residents ranked #8 in happiness. Criteria included strong assent to positive statements and strong disagreement with negative ones, and degree of agreement with a series of statements about respondents' personal relationships and general outlook. *www.harrisinteractive.com, "Dallas/Fort Worth Is "Happiest" City among America's Top Ten Markets," September 4, 2013*
- Energizer Personal Care, the makers of Edge® shave gel, in partnership with Sperling's BestPlaces, ranked 50 major metro areas in terms of everyday irritations. The Chicago* metro area ranked #1 the 50 metro area most iritating to guys. Criteria: high male-to-female ratio; poor sports team performance and high ticket prices; slow traffic; lack of job availability; unaffordable housing; extreme weather; lack of nightlife and fitness options. *Energizer Personal Care, "Most Irritatng Cities for Guys," August 26, 2013*
- Mars Chocolate North America, the makers of COMBOS®, in partnership with Sperling's BestPlaces, ranked 50 major metro areas in terms of their "manliness." The Chicago* metro area ranked #37. Criteria: number of professional sports teams; number of nearby NASCAR tracks and racing events; manly lifestyle; concentration of manly retail stores; manly occupations per capita; salty snack sales; "Board of Manliness" rankings. *Mars Chocolate North America, "America's Manliest Cities 2012"*
- The Chicago* metro area was selected as one of "America's Most Miserable Cities" by *Forbes.com.* The metro area ranked #4 out of 20. Criteria: violent crime; unemployment; foreclosures; income and property taxes; home prices; commute times; climate. *Forbes.com, "America's Most Miserable Cities" February 22, 2013*
- The National Alliance to End Homelessness ranked the 100 most populous metro areas with the highest rate of homelessness. The Chicago* metro area ranked #75. Criteria: number of homeless people per 10,000 population in 2011. *National Alliance to End Homelessness, The State of Homelessness in America 2012*

Northbrook is located within the Chicago-Naperville-Elgin, IL-IN-WI Metropolitan Statistical Area.

Business Environment

CITY FINANCES

City Government Finances

Component	2012 ($000)	2012 ($ per capita)
Total Revenues	62,387	1,880
Total Expenditures	65,858	1,985
Debt Outstanding	72,501	2,185
Cash and Securities[1]	95,322	2,873

Note: (1) Cash and security holdings of a government at the close of its fiscal year, including those of its dependent agencies, utilities, and liquor stores.
Source: U.S Census Bureau, State & Local Government Finances 2012

City Government Revenue by Source

Source	2012 ($000)	2012 ($ per capita)
General Revenue		
From Federal Government	0	0
From State Government	18,035	543
From Local Governments	354	10
Taxes		
Property	16,119	485
Sales and Gross Receipts	3,346	100
Personal Income	0	0
Corporate Income	0	0
Motor Vehicle License	595	17
Other Taxes	3,864	116
Current Charges	7,762	234
Liquor Store	0	0
Utility	6,696	201
Employee Retirement	4,120	124

Source: U.S Census Bureau, State & Local Government Finances 2012

City Government Expenditures by Function

Function	2012 ($000)	2012 ($ per capita)	2012 (%)
General Direct Expenditures			
Air Transportation	0	0	0.0
Corrections	0	0	0.0
Education	0	0	0.0
Employment Security Administration	0	0	0.0
Financial Administration	1,196	36	1.8
Fire Protection	10,229	308	15.5
General Public Buildings	0	0	0.0
Governmental Administration, Other	3,630	109	5.5
Health	0	0	0.0
Highways	8,839	266	13.4
Hospitals	0	0	0.0
Housing and Community Development	0	0	0.0
Interest on General Debt	2,641	79	4.0
Judicial and Legal	0	0	0.0
Libraries	6,480	195	9.8
Parking	147	4	0.2
Parks and Recreation	0	0	0.0
Police Protection	13,110	395	19.9
Public Welfare	0	0	0.0
Sewerage	1,311	39	1.9
Solid Waste Management	0	0	0.0
Veterans' Services	0	0	0.0
Liquor Store	0	0	0.0
Utility	7,829	236	11.8
Employee Retirement	5,209	157	7.9

Source: U.S Census Bureau, State & Local Government Finances 2012

DEMOGRAPHICS

Population Growth

Area	1990 Census	2000 Census	2010 Census	2014* Estimate	Population Growth (%)	
					1990-2014	2010-2014
City	33,020	33,435	33,170	33,396	1.1	0.7
MSA[1]	8,182,076	9,098,316	9,461,105	9,516,448	16.3	0.6
U.S.	248,709,873	281,421,906	308,745,538	314,107,084	26.3	1.7

Note: (1) Figures cover the Chicago-Naperville-Elgin, IL-IN-WI Metropolitan Statistical Area—see Appendix B for areas included; (*) 2010-2014 5-year estimated population

Source: U.S. Census Bureau, 1990 Census, Census 2000, Census 2010, 2010-2014 American Community Survey 5-Year Estimates

Household Size

Area	Persons in Household (%)							Average Household Size
	One	Two	Three	Four	Five	Six	Seven or More	
City	21.6	35.3	16.4	16.9	7.4	2.1	0.0	2.68
MSA[1]	28.1	29.9	15.8	14.3	7.0	2.7	1.8	2.72
U.S.	27.5	33.5	15.8	13.1	6.0	2.3	1.4	2.64

Note: (1) Figures cover the Chicago-Naperville-Elgin, IL-IN-WI Metropolitan Statistical Area—see Appendix B for areas included

Source: U.S. Census Bureau, 2010-2014 American Community Survey 5-Year Estimates

Race

Area	White Alone[2] (%)	Black Alone[2] (%)	Asian Alone[2] (%)	AIAN[3] Alone[2] (%)	NHOPI[4] Alone[2] (%)	Other Race Alone[2] (%)	Two or More Races (%)
City	84.9	0.7	11.7	0.0	0.0	0.7	2.0
MSA[1]	66.6	17.0	6.0	0.2	0.0	7.9	2.2
U.S.	73.8	12.6	5.0	0.8	0.2	4.7	2.9

Note: (1) Figures cover the Chicago-Naperville-Elgin, IL-IN-WI Metropolitan Statistical Area—see Appendix B for areas included; (2) Alone is defined as not being in combination with one or more other races; (3) American Indian and Alaska Native; (4) Native Hawaiian and Other Pacific Islander

Source: U.S. Census Bureau, 2010-2014 American Community Survey 5-Year Estimates

Hispanic or Latino Origin

Area	Total (%)	Mexican (%)	Puerto Rican (%)	Cuban (%)	Other (%)
City	2.7	0.8	0.3	0.6	1.1
MSA[1]	21.2	16.8	2.1	0.2	2.0
U.S.	16.9	10.8	1.6	0.6	3.8

Note: Persons of Hispanic or Latino origin can be of any race; (1) Figures cover the Chicago-Naperville-Elgin, IL-IN-WI Metropolitan Statistical Area—see Appendix B for areas included

Source: U.S. Census Bureau, 2010-2014 American Community Survey 5-Year Estimates

Ancestry

Area	German	Irish	English	American	Italian	Polish	French[2]	Scottish	Dutch
City	17.1	11.4	5.4	6.9	6.0	10.0	1.6	1.4	0.5
MSA[1]	15.5	11.6	4.4	2.9	7.0	9.4	1.5	1.0	1.3
U.S.	14.9	10.8	8.0	7.1	5.5	3.0	2.7	1.7	1.4

Note: Figures are the percentage of the total population reporting a particular ancestry. The nine most commonly reported ancestries in the U.S. are shown. Figures include multiple ancestries (e.g. if a person reported being Irish and Italian, they were included in both columns); (1) Figures cover the Chicago-Naperville-Elgin, IL-IN-WI Metropolitan Statistical Area—see Appendix B for areas included; (2) Excludes Basque

Source: U.S. Census Bureau, 2010-2014 American Community Survey 5-Year Estimates

Foreign-Born Population

Area	Percent of Population Born in								
	Any Foreign Country	Asia	Mexico	Europe	Carribean	Central America[2]	South America	Africa	Canada
City	19.1	10.3	0.4	6.7	0.4	0.2	0.5	0.4	0.1
MSA[1]	17.6	4.8	7.0	3.8	0.3	0.5	0.6	0.5	0.2
U.S.	13.1	3.8	3.7	1.5	1.2	1.0	0.9	0.6	0.3

Note: (1) Figures cover the Chicago-Naperville-Elgin, IL-IN-WI Metropolitan Statistical Area—see Appendix B for areas included; (2) Excludes Mexico.
Source: U.S. Census Bureau, 2010-2014 American Community Survey 5-Year Estimates

Marital Status

Area	Never Married	Now Married[2]	Separated	Widowed	Divorced
City	19.2	65.4	0.9	7.4	7.1
MSA[1]	36.2	47.2	1.8	5.6	9.1
U.S.	32.5	48.4	2.2	5.9	10.9

Note: Figures are percentages and cover the population 15 years of age and older; (1) Figures cover the Chicago-Naperville-Elgin, IL-IN-WI Metropolitan Statistical Area—see Appendix B for areas included; (2) Excludes separated
Source: U.S. Census Bureau, 2010-2014 American Community Survey 5-Year Estimates

Disability Status

Area	All Ages	Under 18 Years Old	18 to 64 Years Old	65 Years and Over
City	7.9	2.2	4.6	21.9
MSA[1]	9.7	3.1	7.6	35.0
U.S.	12.3	4.1	10.2	36.3

Note: Figures show percent of the civilian noninstitutionalized population that reported having a disability. Disability status is determined from from six types of difficulty: vision, hearing, cognitive, ambulatory, self-care, and independent living. For children under 5 years old, hearing and vision difficulty are used to determine disability status. For children between the ages of 5 and 14, disability status is determined from hearing, vision, cognitive, ambulatory, and self-care difficulties. For people aged 15 years and older, they are considered to have a disability if they have difficulty with any one of the six difficulty types; (1) Figures cover the Chicago-Naperville-Elgin, IL-IN-WI Metropolitan Statistical Area—see Appendix B for areas included.
Source: U.S. Census Bureau, 2010-2014 American Community Survey 5-Year Estimates

Age

Area	Percent of Population									Median Age
	Under Age 5	Age 5–19	Age 20–34	Age 35–44	Age 45–54	Age 55–64	Age 65–74	Age 75–84	Age 85+	
City	4.6	21.2	8.3	12.4	15.8	14.2	11.6	7.9	4.1	47.8
MSA[1]	6.5	20.7	21.1	13.7	14.2	11.8	6.7	3.7	1.7	36.3
U.S.	6.4	19.9	20.6	13.0	14.1	12.3	7.6	4.3	1.9	37.4

Note: (1) Figures cover the Chicago-Naperville-Elgin, IL-IN-WI Metropolitan Statistical Area—see Appendix B for areas included
Source: U.S. Census Bureau, 2010-2014 American Community Survey 5-Year Estimates

Gender

Area	Males	Females	Males per 100 Females
City	16,172	17,224	93.9
MSA[1]	4,650,729	4,865,719	95.6
U.S.	154,515,159	159,591,925	96.8

Note: (1) Figures cover the Chicago-Naperville-Elgin, IL-IN-WI Metropolitan Statistical Area—see Appendix B for areas included
Source: U.S. Census Bureau, 2010-2014 American Community Survey 5-Year Estimates

Religious Groups by Family

Area	Catholic	Baptist	Non-Den.	Methodist[2]	Lutheran	LDS[3]	Pente-costal	Presby-terian[4]	Muslim[5]	Judaism
MSA[1]	34.2	3.2	4.4	1.9	3.0	0.3	1.2	1.9	3.2	0.8
U.S.	19.1	9.3	4.0	4.0	2.3	2.0	1.9	1.6	0.8	0.7

Note: Figures are the number of adherents as a percentage of the total population; (1) Figures cover the Chicago-Joliet-Naperville, IL-IN-WI Metropolitan Statistical Area—see Appendix B for areas included; (2) Methodist/Pietist; (3) Latter Day Saints; (4) Reformed; (5) Figures are estimates
Source: Association of Statisticians of American Religious Bodies, 2010 U.S. Religion Census: Religious Congregations & Membership Study

Religious Groups by Tradition

Area	Catholic	Evangelical Protestant	Mainline Protestant	Other Tradition	Black Protestant	Orthodox
MSA[1]	34.2	9.7	5.1	5.0	2.0	0.9
U.S.	19.1	16.2	7.3	4.3	1.6	0.3

Note: Figures are the number of adherents as a percentage of the total population; (1) Figures cover the Chicago-Joliet-Naperville, IL-IN-WI Metropolitan Statistical Area—see Appendix B for areas included
Source: Association of Statisticians of American Religious Bodies, 2010 U.S. Religion Census: Religious Congregations & Membership Study

ECONOMY

Gross Metropolitan Product

Area	2013	2014	2015	2016	Rank[2]
MSA[1]	590.2	611.0	630.3	658.6	3

Note: Figures are in billions of dollars; (1) Figures cover the Chicago-Naperville-Elgin, IL-IN-WI Metropolitan Statistical Area—see Appendix B for areas included; (2) Rank is based on 2016 data and ranges from 1 to 381
Source: The U.S. Conference of Mayors, U.S. Metro Economies: GMP and Employment 2014-2016, June 2015

Economic Growth

Area	2011-13 (%)	2014 (%)	2015 (%)	2016 (%)	Rank[2]
MSA[1]	1.6	1.9	1.7	2.6	159
U.S.	2.2	2.4	2.3	2.9	-

Note: Figures are real gross metropolitan product (GMP) growth rates and represent annual average percent change; (1) Figures cover the Chicago-Naperville-Elgin, IL-IN-WI Metropolitan Statistical Area—see Appendix B for areas included; (2) Rank is based on 2016 data and ranges from 1 to 381
Source: The U.S. Conference of Mayors, U.S. Metro Economies: GMP and Employment 2014-2016, June 2015

Metropolitan Area Exports

Area	2009	2010	2011	2012	2013	2014	Rank[2]
MSA[1]	28,196.6	33,671.9	39,522.4	40,567.9	44,910.6	47,340.1	6

Note: Figures are in millions of dollars; (1) Figures cover the Chicago-Naperville-Elgin, IL-IN-WI Metropolitan Statistical Area—see Appendix B for areas included; (2) Rank is based on 2014 data and ranges from 1 to 385
Source: U.S. Department of Commerce, International Trade Administration, Office of Trade & Industry Information, Manufacturing & Services, data extracted March 10, 2016

Building Permits

Area	Single-Family			Multi-Family			Total		
	2014	2015p	Pct. Chg.	2014	2015p	Pct. Chg.	2014	2015p	Pct. Chg.
City	46	38	-17.4	0	0	-	46	38	-17.4
MSA[1]	7,723	7,577	-1.9	7,956	8,160	2.6	15,679	15,737	0.4
U.S.	640,300	690,800	7.9	411,800	487,600	18.4	1,052,100	1,178,400	12.0

Note: (1) Figures cover the Chicago-Naperville-Elgin, IL-IN-WI Metropolitan Statistical Area—see Appendix B for areas included; Figures represent new, privately-owned housing units authorized (unadjusted data); All permit data are based on estimates with imputation; (p) preliminary data.
Source: U.S. Census Bureau, Manufacturing, Mining, and Construction Statistics, Building Permits, 2014, 2015

Bankruptcy Filings

Area	Business Filings			Nonbusiness Filings		
	2014	2015	% Chg.	2014	2015	% Chg.
Cook County	569	511	-10.2	33,968	33,318	-1.9
U.S.	26,983	24,735	-8.3	909,812	819,760	-9.9

Note: Business filings include Chapter 7, Chapter 11, Chapter 12, and Chapter 13; Nonbusiness filings include Chapter 7, Chapter 11, and Chapter 13
Source: Administrative Office of the U.S. Courts, Business and Nonbusiness Bankruptcy, County Cases Commenced by Chapter of the Bankruptcy Code, During the 12- Month Period Ending December 31, 2014 and Business and Nonbusiness Bankruptcy, County Cases Commenced by Chapter of the Bankruptcy Code, During the 12- Month Period Ending December 31, 2015

Housing Vacancy Rates

Area	Gross Vacancy Rate[2] (%)			Year-Round Vacancy Rate[3] (%)			Rental Vacancy Rate[4] (%)			Homeowner Vacancy Rate[5] (%)		
	2013	2014	2015	2013	2014	2015	2013	2014	2015	2013	2014	2015
MSA[1]	10.5	10.3	9.7	10.3	10.2	9.4	10.9	9.1	7.4	2.8	2.6	2.3
U.S.	13.6	13.4	12.9	10.7	10.4	10.0	8.3	7.6	7.1	2.0	1.9	1.8

Note: (1) Figures cover the Chicago-Naperville-Elgin, IL-IN-WI Metropolitan Statistical Area—see Appendix B for areas included; (2) The percentage of the total housing inventory that is vacant; (3) The percentage of the housing inventory (excluding seasonal units) that is year-round vacant; (4) The percentage of rental inventory that is vacant for rent; (5) The percentage of homeowner inventory that is vacant for sale
Source: U.S. Census Bureau, Housing Vacancies and Homeownership Annual Statistics: 2015

INCOME

Income

Area	Per Capita ($)	Median Household ($)	Average Household ($)
City	58,154	115,085	154,913
MSA[1]	31,488	61,497	84,504
U.S.	28,555	53,482	74,596

Note: (1) Figures cover the Chicago-Naperville-Elgin, IL-IN-WI Metropolitan Statistical Area—see Appendix B for areas included
Source: U.S. Census Bureau, 2010-2014 American Community Survey 5-Year Estimates

Household Income Distribution

Area	Percent of Households Earning							
	Under $15,000	$15,000 -24,999	$25,000 -34,999	$35,000 -49,999	$50,000 -74,999	$75,000 -99,000	$100,000 -149,999	$150,000 and up
City	4.5	6.4	6.3	7.2	10.0	9.1	18.8	37.7
MSA[1]	11.1	9.3	8.9	12.2	17.4	13.0	15.1	13.1
U.S.	12.5	10.7	10.2	13.5	17.8	12.2	13.0	10.0

Note: (1) Figures cover the Chicago-Naperville-Elgin, IL-IN-WI Metropolitan Statistical Area—see Appendix B for areas included
Source: U.S. Census Bureau, 2010-2014 American Community Survey 5-Year Estimates

Poverty Rate

Area	All Ages	Under 18 Years Old	18 to 64 Years Old	65 Years and Over
City	3.7	3.7	3.4	4.4
MSA[1]	14.1	20.3	12.6	9.2
U.S.	15.6	21.9	14.6	9.4

Note: Figures are percentage of people whose income during the past 12 months was below the poverty level; (1) Figures cover the Chicago-Naperville-Elgin, IL-IN-WI Metropolitan Statistical Area—see Appendix B for areas included
Source: U.S. Census Bureau, 2010-2014 American Community Survey 5-Year Estimates

EMPLOYMENT

Labor Force and Employment

Area	Civilian Labor Force			Workers Employed		
	Dec. 2014	Dec. 2015	% Chg.	Dec. 2014	Dec. 2015	% Chg.
City	16,194	16,224	0.1	15,595	15,552	-0.2
MD[1]	3,743,002	3,771,441	0.7	3,525,255	3,562,874	1.0
U.S.	155,521,000	157,245,000	1.1	147,190,000	149,703,000	1.7

Note: Data is not seasonally adjusted and covers workers 16 years of age and older; (1) Figures cover the Chicago-Naperville-Arlington Heights, IL Metropolitan Division—see Appendix B for areas included
Source: Bureau of Labor Statistics, Local Area Unemployment Statistics

Unemployment Rate

Area	2015											
	Jan.	Feb.	Mar.	Apr.	May	Jun.	Jul.	Aug.	Sep.	Oct.	Nov.	Dec.
City	4.4	4.8	4.6	4.3	4.4	4.6	4.5	4.3	3.7	3.8	4.1	4.1
MD[1]	6.9	6.5	6.0	5.7	5.9	6.1	6.2	5.6	5.1	5.3	5.4	5.5
U.S.	6.1	5.8	5.6	5.1	5.3	5.5	5.6	5.2	4.9	4.8	4.8	4.8

Note: Data is not seasonally adjusted and covers workers 16 years of age and older; (1) Figures cover the Chicago-Naperville-Arlington Heights, IL Metropolitan Division—see Appendix B for areas included
Source: Bureau of Labor Statistics, Local Area Unemployment Statistics

Employment by Occupation

Occupation Classification	City (%)	MSA[1] (%)	U.S. (%)
Management, Business, Science, and Arts	60.4	37.9	36.4
Natural Resources, Construction, and Maintenance	2.4	6.8	9.0
Production, Transportation, and Material Moving	2.8	13.2	12.1
Sales and Office	25.3	25.1	24.4
Service	9.0	17.0	18.2

Note: Figures cover employed civilians 16 years of age and older; (1) Figures cover the Chicago-Naperville-Elgin, IL-IN-WI Metropolitan Statistical Area—see Appendix B for areas included
Source: U.S. Census Bureau, 2010-2014 American Community Survey 5-Year Estimates

Employment by Industry

Sector	MD[1]		U.S.
	Number of Employees	Percent of Total	Percent of Total
Construction	123,700	3.3	4.5
Education and Health Services	580,900	15.7	15.7
Financial Activities	254,500	6.8	5.7
Government	430,400	11.6	15.5
Information	73,200	1.9	1.9
Leisure and Hospitality	359,200	9.7	10.4
Manufacturing	282,400	7.6	8.6
Mining and Logging	1,100	<0.1	0.5
Other Services	159,600	4.3	3.9
Professional and Business Services	679,200	18.3	13.9
Retail Trade	371,600	10.0	11.3
Transportation, Warehousing, and Utilities	190,000	5.1	3.9
Wholesale Trade	193,700	5.2	4.1

Note: Figures are non-farm employment as of December 2015. Figures are not seasonally adjusted and include workers 16 years of age and older; (1) Figures cover the Chicago-Naperville-Arlington Heights, IL Metropolitan Division—see Appendix B for areas included
Source: Bureau of Labor Statistics, Current Employment Statistics, Employment, Hours, and Earnings

Occupations with Greatest Projected Employment Growth: 2012 – 2022

Occupation[1]	2012 Employment	2022 Projected Employment	Numeric Employment Change	Percent Employment Change
Laborers and Freight, Stock, and Material Movers, Hand	127,890	148,390	20,500	16.0
Home Health Aides	40,020	56,650	16,630	41.6
Combined Food Preparation and Serving Workers, Including Fast Food	104,150	119,060	14,910	14.3
Retail Salespersons	174,910	188,030	13,120	7.5
Customer Service Representatives	111,240	123,880	12,640	11.4
Registered Nurses	113,100	124,990	11,890	10.5
Janitors and Cleaners, Except Maids and Housekeeping Cleaners	105,870	116,370	10,500	9.9
Nursing Assistants	61,430	70,820	9,390	15.3
General and Operations Managers	91,660	100,910	9,250	10.1
Construction Laborers	49,810	59,060	9,250	18.6

Note: Projections cover Illinois; (1) Sorted by numeric employment change
Source: www.projectionscentral.com, State Occupational Projections, 2012–2022 Long-Term Projections

Fastest Growing Occupations: 2012 – 2022

Occupation[1]	2012 Employment	2022 Projected Employment	Numeric Employment Change	Percent Employment Change
Home Health Aides	40,020	56,650	16,630	41.6
Skincare Specialists	1,650	2,290	640	38.2
Biomedical Engineers	540	740	200	38.0
Interpreters and Translators	1,880	2,590	710	37.6
Occupational Therapy Assistants	1,320	1,810	490	37.3
Insulation Workers, Mechanical	1,500	2,020	520	34.5
Physical Therapist Aides	2,540	3,390	850	33.5
Health Specialties Teachers, Postsecondary	3,120	4,150	1,030	32.8
Physical Therapist Assistants	3,010	3,990	980	32.5
Physical Therapists	9,320	12,340	3,020	32.4

Note: Projections cover Illinois; (1) Sorted by percent employment change and excludes occupations with numeric employment change less than 100
Source: www.projectionscentral.com, State Occupational Projections, 2012–2022 Long-Term Projections

Average Wages

Occupation	$/Hr.	Occupation	$/Hr.
Accountants and Auditors	35.11	Maids and Housekeeping Cleaners	12.44
Automotive Mechanics	22.85	Maintenance and Repair Workers	21.36
Bookkeepers	19.63	Marketing Managers	58.77
Carpenters	31.04	Nuclear Medicine Technologists	35.61
Cashiers	10.38	Nurses, Licensed Practical	24.67
Clerks, General Office	16.40	Nurses, Registered	35.96
Clerks, Receptionists/Information	14.47	Nursing Assistants	12.89
Clerks, Shipping/Receiving	16.37	Packers and Packagers, Hand	12.25
Computer Programmers	37.27	Physical Therapists	41.57
Computer Systems Analysts	42.42	Postal Service Mail Carriers	25.13
Computer User Support Specialists	26.66	Real Estate Brokers	38.44
Cooks, Restaurant	11.75	Retail Salespersons	13.08
Dentists	61.93	Sales Reps., Exc. Tech./Scientific	35.53
Electrical Engineers	45.45	Sales Reps., Tech./Scientific	36.28
Electricians	35.46	Secretaries, Exc. Legal/Med./Exec.	18.19
Financial Managers	63.54	Security Guards	14.91
First-Line Supervisors/Managers, Sales	22.18	Surgeons	122.87
Food Preparation Workers	10.44	Teacher Assistants*	14.05
General and Operations Managers	58.83	Teachers, Elementary School*	30.77
Hairdressers/Cosmetologists	13.34	Teachers, Secondary School*	36.04
Internists	83.00	Telemarketers	12.71
Janitors and Cleaners	14.23	Truck Drivers, Heavy/Tractor-Trailer	23.64
Landscaping/Groundskeeping Workers	14.34	Truck Drivers, Light/Delivery Svcs.	17.54
Lawyers	62.12	Waiters and Waitresses	10.57

Note: Wage data covers the Chicago-Joliet-Naperville, IL Metropolitan Division—see Appendix B for areas included; (*) Hourly wages for elementary/secondary school teachers and teacher assistants were calculated by the editors from annual wage data based on a 40 hour work week; n/a not available.
Source: Bureau of Labor Statistics, Metro Area Occupational Employment and Wage Estimates, May 2015

TAXES

State Corporate Income Tax Rates

State	Tax Rate (%)	Income Brackets ($)	Num. of Brackets	Financial Institution Tax Rate (%)[a]	Federal Income Tax Ded.
Illinois	7.75 (i)	Flat rate	1	7.75 (i)	No

Note: Tax rates as of January 1, 2016; (a) Rates listed are the corporate income tax rate applied to financial institutions or excise taxes based on income. Some states have other taxes based upon the value of deposits or shares; (i) The Illinois rate of 7.75% is the sum of a corporate income tax rate of 5.25% plus a replacement tax of 2.5%.
Source: Federation of Tax Administrators, "State Corporate Income Tax Rates, 2016"

State Individual Income Tax Rates

State	Tax Rate (%)	Income Brackets ($)	Num. of Brackets	Personal Exempt. ($)[1]		Fed. Inc. Tax Ded.
				Single	Dependents	
Illinois	3.75	Flat rate	1	2,000	2,000	No

Note: Tax rates as of January 1, 2016; Local- and county-level taxes are not included; n/a not applicable; (1) Married joint filers generally receive double the single exemption
Source: Federation of Tax Administrators, "State Individual Income Tax Rates, 2016"

Various State and Local Tax Rates

State	State and Local Sales and Use (%)	State Sales and Use (%)	Gasoline[1] (¢/gal.)	Cigarette[2] ($/pack)	Spirits[3] ($/gal.)	Wine[4] ($/gal.)	Beer[5] ($/gal.)
Illinois	9.75	6.25	30.18	1.98	8.55 (f)	1.39 (l)	0.23

Note: All tax rates as of January 1, 2016; (1) The American Petroleum Institute has developed a methodology for determining the average tax rate on a gallon of fuel. Rates may include any of the following: excise taxes, environmental fees, storage tank fees, other fees or taxes, general sales tax, and local taxes. In states where gasoline is subject to the general sales tax, or where the fuel tax is based on the average sale price, the average rate determined by API is sensitive to changes in the price of gasoline. States that fully or partially apply general sales taxes to gasoline: CA, CO, GA, IL, IN, MI, NY; (2) The federal excise tax of $1.0066 per pack and local taxes are not included; (3) Rates are those applicable to off-premise sales of 40% alcohol by volume (a.b.v.) distilled spirits in 750ml containers. Local excise taxes are excluded; (4) Rates are those applicable to off-premise sales of 11% a.b.v. non-carbonated wine in 750ml containers; (5) Rates are those applicable to off-premise sales of 4.7% a.b.v. beer in 12 ounce containers; (f) Different rates are also applicable according to alcohol content, place of production, size of container, or place purchased (on- or off-premise or onboard airlines); (l) Different rates also applicable according to alcohol content, place of production, size of container, place purchased (on- or off-premise or on board airlines) or type of wine (carbonated, vermouth, etc.).
Source: Tax Foundation, 2016 Facts & Figures: How Does Your State Compare?

State Business Tax Climate Index Rankings

State	Overall Rank	Corporate Tax Rank	Individual Income Tax Rank	Sales Tax Rank	Unemployment Insurance Tax Rank	Property Tax Rank
Illinois	23	36	10	33	39	45

Note: The index is a measure of how each state's tax laws affect economic performance. The lower the rank, the more favorable a state's tax system is for business. States without a given tax are given a ranking of 1. The scores/rankings for the District of Columbia do not affect other states. The 2016 index represents the tax climate as of July 1, 2015 (the beginning of Fiscal Year 2016).
Source: Tax Foundation, State Business Tax Climate Index 2016

TRANSPORTATION

Means of Transportation to Work

Area	Car/Truck/Van		Public Transportation			Bicycle	Walked	Other Means	Worked at Home
	Drove Alone	Car-pooled	Bus	Subway	Railroad				
City	69.5	6.6	0.4	0.6	10.4	0.2	2.1	0.7	9.5
MSA[1]	70.9	8.4	4.6	3.6	3.2	0.6	3.2	1.1	4.3
U.S.	76.4	9.6	2.6	1.8	0.6	0.6	2.8	1.3	4.4

Note: Figures are percentages and cover workers 16 years of age and older; (1) Figures cover the Chicago-Naperville-Elgin, IL-IN-WI Metropolitan Statistical Area—see Appendix B for areas included
Source: U.S. Census Bureau, 2010-2014 American Community Survey 5-Year Estimates

Travel Time to Work

Area	Less Than 10 Minutes	10 to 19 Minutes	20 to 29 Minutes	30 to 44 Minutes	45 to 59 Minutes	60 to 89 Minutes	90 Minutes or More
City	13.7	24.8	17.4	19.7	11.5	11.5	1.5
MSA[1]	9.0	22.4	18.7	24.7	11.8	10.1	3.2
U.S.	13.3	29.6	21.0	20.2	7.7	5.7	2.6

Note: Figures are percentages and include workers 16 years old and over; (1) Figures cover the Chicago-Naperville-Elgin, IL-IN-WI Metropolitan Statistical Area—see Appendix B for areas included
Source: U.S. Census Bureau, 2010-2014 American Community Survey 5-Year Estimates

Freeway Travel Time Index

Area	1985	1990	1995	2000	2005	2010	2014
Urban Area Rank[1,2]	9	9	8	11	13	14	14
Urban Area Index[1]	1.17	1.20	1.24	1.27	1.29	1.28	1.31
Average Index[3]	1.09	1.11	1.14	1.17	1.20	1.19	1.20

Note: Freeway Travel Time Index—the ratio of travel time in the peak period to the travel time at free-flow conditions. For example, a value of 1.30 indicates a 20-minute free-flow trip takes 26 minutes in the peak (20 minutes x 1.30 = 26 minutes); (1) Covers the Chicago IL-IN urban area; (2) Rank is based on 101 urban areas (#1 = highest travel time index); (3) Average of 101 urban areas
Source: Texas Transportation Institute, 2015 Urban Mobility Scorecard, August 2015

Freeway Commuter Stress Index

Area	1985	1990	1995	2000	2005	2010	2014
Urban Area Rank[1,2]	19	19	19	20	18	19	19
Urban Area Index[1]	1.21	1.24	1.27	1.30	1.33	1.32	1.34
Average Index[3]	1.13	1.16	1.19	1.22	1.25	1.24	1.25

Note: The Freeway Commuter Stress Index is the same as the Freeway Travel Time Index (see table above) except that it includes only the travel in the peak directions during the peak periods; the TTI includes travel in all directions during the peak period. Thus, the CSI is more indicative of the work trip experienced by each commuter on a daily basis. (1) Covers the Chicago IL-IN urban area; (2) Rank is based on 101 urban areas (#1 = highest stress index); (3) Average of 101 urban areas

Source: Texas Transportation Institute, 2015 Urban Mobility Scorecard, August 2015

Living Environment

COST OF LIVING

Cost of Living Index

Composite Index	Groceries	Housing	Utilities	Trans-portation	Health Care	Misc. Goods/Services
116.3	116.7	136.2	104.2	114.3	99.1	105.9

Note: The Cost of Living Index measures regional differences in the cost of consumer goods and services, excluding taxes and non-consumer expenditures, for professional and managerial households in the top income quintile. It is based on more than 50,000 prices covering almost 60 different items for which prices are collected three times a year by chambers of commerce, economic development organizations or university applied economic centers in each participating urban area. The numbers shown should be read as a percentage above or below the national average of 100. For example, a value of 115.4 in the groceries column indicates that grocery prices are 15.4% higher than the national average. Small differences in the index numbers should not be interpreted as significant; Figures cover the Chicago IL urban area.
Source: The Council for Community and Economic Research, ACCRA Cost of Living Index, 2015

Grocery Prices

Area[1]	T-Bone Steak ($/pound)	Frying Chicken ($/pound)	Whole Milk ($/half gal.)	Eggs ($/dozen)	Orange Juice ($/64 oz.)	Coffee ($/11.5 oz.)
City[2]	11.95	1.43	2.39	2.82	4.05	4.92
Avg.	10.99	1.43	2.25	2.26	3.58	4.48
Min.	7.16	0.98	1.30	1.35	2.88	2.98
Max.	14.13	2.43	3.85	4.81	6.39	7.56

Note: (1) Values for the local area are compared with the average, minimum and maximum values for all 292 areas in the Cost of Living Index; (2) Figures cover the Chicago IL urban area; **T-Bone Steak** *(price per pound);* **Frying Chicken** *(price per pound, whole fryer);* **Whole Milk** *(half gallon carton);* **Eggs** *(price per dozen, Grade A, large);* **Orange Juice** *(64 oz. Tropicana or Florida Natural);* **Coffee** *(11.5 oz. can, vacuum-packed, Maxwell House, Hills Bros, or Folgers).*
Source: The Council for Community and Economic Research, ACCRA Cost of Living Index, 2015

Housing and Utility Costs

Area[1]	New Home Price ($)	Apartment Rent ($/month)	All Electric ($/month)	Part Electric ($/month)	Other Energy ($/month)	Telephone ($/month)
City[2]	431,884	1,236	-	97.38	76.61	30.05
Avg.	312,874	945	179.30	95.07	72.96	28.11
Min.	178,682	479	116.28	43.14	26.46	10.01
Max.	1,472,476	3,984	504.25	189.44	421.11	43.06

Note: (1) Values for the local area are compared with the average, minimum and maximum values for all 292 areas in the Cost of Living Index; (2) Figures cover the Chicago IL urban area; **New Home Price** *(2,400 sf living area, 8,000 sf lot, in urban area with full utilities);* **Apartment Rent** *(950 sf 2 bedroom/1.5 or 2 bath, unfurnished, excluding all utilities except water);* **All Electric** *(average monthly cost for an all-electric home);* **Part Electric** *(average monthly cost for a part-electric home);* **Other Energy** *(average monthly cost for natural gas, fuel oil, coal, wood, and any other forms of energy except electricity);* **Telephone** *(price includes basic monthly rate for a private residential line plus additional local usage charges incurred by a family of four).*
Source: The Council for Community and Economic Research, ACCRA Cost of Living Index, 2015

Health Care, Transportation, and Other Costs

Area[1]	Doctor ($/visit)	Dentist ($/visit)	Optometrist ($/visit)	Gasoline ($/gallon)	Beauty Salon ($/visit)	Men's Shirt ($)
City[2]	99.17	99.44	95.00	2.70	45.00	25.27
Avg.	105.15	89.02	99.78	2.38	35.30	28.10
Min.	66.87	56.09	48.53	1.95	18.91	13.38
Max.	182.34	150.36	228.33	4.09	67.91	63.80

Note: (1) Values for the local area are compared with the average, minimum and maximum values for all 292 areas in the Cost of Living Index; (2) Figures cover the Chicago IL urban area; **Doctor** *(general practitioners routine exam of an established patient);* **Dentist** *(adult teeth cleaning and periodic oral examination);* **Optometrist** *(full vision eye exam for established adult patient);* **Gasoline** *(one gallon regular unleaded, national brand, including all taxes, cash price at self-service pump if available);* **Beauty Salon** *(woman's shampoo, trim, and blow-dry);* **Men's Shirt** *(cotton/polyester dress shirt, pinpoint weave, long sleeves).*
Source: The Council for Community and Economic Research, ACCRA Cost of Living Index, 2015

HOUSING

House Price Index (HPI)

Area	National Ranking[2]	Quarterly Change (%)	One-Year Change (%)	Five-Year Change (%)
MD[1]	146	0.80	4.30	4.70
U.S.[3]	–	1.45	5.76	22.85

Note: The HPI is a weighted repeat sales index. It measures average price changes in repeat sales or refinancings on the same properties. This information is obtained by reviewing repeat mortgage transactions on single-family properties whose mortgages have been purchased or securitized by Fannie Mae or Freddie Mac in January 1975; (1) Chicago-Naperville-Arlington Heights Metropolitan Division—see Appendix B for areas included; (2) Rankings are based on annual percentage change for all metro areas containing at least 15,000 transactions over the last 10 years and ranges from 1 to 266; (3) figures based on a weighted average of Census Division estimates using a seasonally adjusted, purchase-only index; all figures are for the period ending December 31, 2015

Source: Federal Housing Finance Agency, House Price Index, February 25, 2016

Median Single-Family Home Prices

Area	2013	2014	2015p	Percent Change 2014 to 2015
MSA[1]	191.3	205.9	218.9	6.3
U.S. Average	197.4	208.9	223.9	7.2

Note: Figures are median sales prices of existing single-family homes in thousands of dollars; (p) preliminary; n/a not available; (1) Chicago-Naperville-Elgin, IL-IN-WI Metropolitan Statistical Area—see Appendix B for areas included

Source: National Association of Realtors, Median Sales Price of Existing Single-Family Homes for Metropolitan Areas, 4th Quarter 2015

Qualifying Income Based on Median Sales Price of Existing Single-Family Homes

Area	With 5% Down ($)	With 10% Down ($)	With 20% Down ($)
MSA[1]	46,666	44,210	39,298
U.S. Average	49,535	46,928	41,714

Note: Figures are preliminary; Qualifying income is based on a mortgage rate of 4.1%. Monthly principal and interest payment is limited to 25% of income; n/a not available; (1) Chicago-Naperville-Elgin, IL-IN-WI Metropolitan Statistical Area—see Appendix B for areas included

Source: National Association of Realtors, Qualifying Income Based on Median Sales Price of Existing Single-Family Homes for Metropolitan Areas, 4th Quarter 2015

Median Apartment Condo-Coop Home Prices

Area	2013	2014	2015p	Percent Change 2014 to 2015
MSA[1]	145.5	163.6	178.2	8.9
U.S. Average	194.9	204.3	210.7	3.1

Note: Figures are median sales prices of existing apartment condo-coop homes in thousands of dollars; (p) preliminary; n/a not available; (1) Chicago-Naperville-Elgin, IL-IN-WI Metropolitan Statistical Area—see Appendix B for areas included

Source: National Association of Realtors, Median Sales Price of Existing Apartment Condo-Coop Homes for Metropolitan Areas, 4th Quarter 2015

Gross Monthly Rent

Area	Under $200	$200 -299	$300 -499	$500 -749	$750 -999	$1,000 -1,499	$1,500 and up	Median ($)
City	2.0	0.0	2.1	5.2	6.0	16.3	68.4	1,900
MSA[1]	1.6	2.6	4.3	14.5	29.6	30.8	16.6	979
U.S.	1.5	3.2	7.4	21.0	24.1	26.9	15.9	920

Note: Figures are percentages except for Median; Gross rent is the contract rent plus the estimated average monthly cost of utilities (electricity, gas, and water and sewer) and fuels (oil, coal, kerosene, wood, etc.) if these are paid by the renter (or paid for the renter by someone else); (1) Figures cover the Chicago-Naperville-Elgin, IL-IN-WI Metropolitan Statistical Area—see Appendix B for areas included

Source: U.S. Census Bureau, 2010-2014 American Community Survey 5-Year Estimates

Homeownership Rate

Area	2008 (%)	2009 (%)	2010 (%)	2011 (%)	2012 (%)	2013 (%)	2014 (%)	2015 (%)
MSA[1]	68.4	69.2	68.2	67.7	67.1	68.2	66.3	64.3
U.S.	67.8	67.4	66.9	66.1	65.4	65.1	64.5	63.7

Note: (1) Figures cover the Chicago-Naperville-Elgin, IL-IN-WI Metropolitan Statistical Area—see Appendix B for areas included
Source: U.S. Census Bureau, Housing Vacancies and Homeownership Annual Statistics: 2015

Year Housing Structure Built

Area	2010 or Later	2000 -2009	1990 -1999	1980 -1989	1970 -1979	1960 -1969	1950 -1959	1940 -1949	Before 1940	Median Year
City	0.2	9.2	8.3	11.1	25.0	23.9	13.2	5.1	4.0	1972
MSA[1]	0.4	12.0	10.8	8.8	14.0	11.9	13.6	6.1	22.4	1967
U.S.	1.0	14.9	13.9	13.8	15.8	11.0	10.8	5.4	13.3	1976

Note: Figures are percentages except for Median Year; (1) Figures cover the Chicago-Naperville-Elgin, IL-IN-WI Metropolitan Statistical Area—see Appendix B for areas included
Source: U.S. Census Bureau, 2010-2014 American Community Survey 5-Year Estimates

HEALTH

Health Risk Data

Category	MSA[1] (%)	U.S. (%)
Adults aged 18–64 who have any kind of health care coverage	78.8	79.6
Adults who reported being in good or excellent health	83.6	83.1
Adults who are current smokers	17.7	19.6
Adults who are heavy drinkers[2]	5.8	6.1
Adults who are binge drinkers[3]	21.1	16.9
Adults who are overweight (BMI 25.0 - 29.9)	35.7	35.8
Adults who are obese (BMI 30.0 - 99.8)	26.6	27.6
Adults who participated in any physical activities in the past month	79.1	77.1
Adults 50+ who have ever had a sigmoidoscopy or colonoscopy	61.4	67.3
Women aged 40+ who have had a mammogram within the past two years	72.2	74.0
Men aged 40+ who have had a PSA test within the past two years	41.8	45.2
Adults aged 65+ who have had flu shot within the past year	52.2	60.1
Adults who always wear a seatbelt	95.8	93.8

Note: Data as of 2012 unless otherwise noted; (1) Figures cover the Chicago-Naperville-Joliet, IL-IN-WI Metropolitan Statistical Area—see Appendix B for areas included; (2) Heavy drinkers are classified as males having more than two drinks per day or females having more than one drink per day; (3) Binge drinkers are classified as males having five or more drinks on one occasion or females having four or more drinks on one occasion
Source: Centers for Disease Control and Prevention, Behaviorial Risk Factor Surveillance System, SMART: Selected Metropolitan/Micropolitan Area Risk Trends, 2012 (Note: the CDC has discontinued this dataset but will be releasing a replacement in mid-2016)

Chronic Health Indicators

Category	MSA[1] (%)	U.S. (%)
Adults who have ever been told they had a heart attack	3.0	4.5
Adults who have ever been told they had a stroke	2.3	2.9
Adults who have been told they currently have asthma	8.0	8.9
Adults who have ever been told they have arthritis	23.1	25.7
Adults who have ever been told they have diabetes[2]	8.0	9.7
Adults who have ever been told they had skin cancer	3.5	5.7
Adults who have ever been told they had any other types of cancer	5.6	6.5
Adults who have ever been told they have COPD	5.1	6.2
Adults who have ever been told they have kidney disease	2.8	2.5
Adults who have ever been told they have a form of depression	14.0	18.0

Note: Data as of 2012 unless otherwise noted; (1) Figures cover the Chicago-Naperville-Joliet, IL-IN-WI Metropolitan Statistical Area—see Appendix B for areas included; (2) Figures do not include pregnancy-related, borderline, or pre-diabetes
Source: Centers for Disease Control and Prevention, Behaviorial Risk Factor Surveillance System, SMART: Selected Metropolitan/Micropolitan Area Risk Trends, 2012 (Note: the CDC has discontinued this dataset but will be releasing a replacement in mid-2016)

Mortality Rates for the Top 10 Causes of Death in the U.S.

ICD-10[a] Sub-Chapter	ICD-10[a] Code	Age-Adjusted Mortality Rate[1] per 100,000 population	
		County[2]	U.S.
Malignant neoplasms	C00-C97	172.3	163.6
Ischaemic heart diseases	I20-I25	103.9	102.2
Other forms of heart disease	I30-I51	47.4	50.1
Chronic lower respiratory diseases	J40-J47	30.8	41.4
Organic, including symptomatic, mental disorders	F01-F09	39.0	38.5
Cerebrovascular diseases	I60-I69	37.0	36.5
Other external causes of accidental injury	W00-X59	21.0	27.5
Other degenerative diseases of the nervous system	G30-G31	18.9	26.3
Diabetes mellitus	E10-E14	20.3	21.1
Hypertensive diseases	I10-I15	30.2	19.7

Note: (a) ICD-10 = International Classification of Diseases 10th Revision; (1) Mortality rates are a three year average covering 2012-2014; (2) Figures cover Cook County.
Source: Centers for Disease Control and Prevention, National Center for Health Statistics. Underlying Cause of Death 1999-2014 on CDC WONDER Online Database, released 2015.

Mortality Rates for Selected Causes of Death

ICD-10[a] Sub-Chapter	ICD-10[a] Code	Age-Adjusted Mortality Rate[1] per 100,000 population	
		County[2]	U.S.
Assault	X85-Y09	10.5	5.1
Diseases of the liver	K70-K76	12.0	13.5
Human immunodeficiency virus (HIV) disease	B20-B24	2.6	2.1
Influenza and pneumonia	J09-J18	16.6	15.2
Intentional self-harm	X60-X84	8.2	12.7
Malnutrition	E40-E46	0.8	0.9
Obesity and other hyperalimentation	E65-E68	1.8	1.9
Renal failure	N17-N19	17.0	13.0
Transport accidents	V01-V99	6.1	11.6
Viral hepatitis	B15-B19	1.4	2.1

Note: (a) ICD-10 = International Classification of Diseases 10th Revision; (1) Mortality rates are a three year average covering 2012-2014; (2) Figures cover Cook County; Data are Suppressed when the data meet the criteria for confidentiality constraints; Mortality rates are flagged as Unreliable when the rate would be calculated with a numerator of 20 or less.
Source: Centers for Disease Control and Prevention, National Center for Health Statistics. Underlying Cause of Death 1999-2014 on CDC WONDER Online Database, released 2015.

Health Insurance Coverage

Area	With Health Insurance	With Private Health Insurance	With Public Health Insurance	Without Health Insurance	Population Under Age 18 Without Health Insurance
City	96.4	87.2	25.1	3.6	1.2
MSA[1]	86.5	66.8	28.7	13.5	4.1
U.S.	85.8	65.8	31.1	14.2	7.1

Note: Figures are percentages that cover the civilian noninstitutionalized population; (1) Figures cover the Chicago-Naperville-Elgin, IL-IN-WI Metropolitan Statistical Area—see Appendix B for areas included
Source: U.S. Census Bureau, 2010-2014 American Community Survey 5-Year Estimates

Number of Medical Professionals

Area	MDs[3]	DOs[3,4]	Dentists	Podiatrists	Chiropractors	Optometrists
County[1] (number)	21,707	1,127	4,339	602	1,351	959
County[1] (rate[2])	413.7	21.5	82.7	11.5	25.8	18.3
U.S. (rate[2])	272.5	20.9	64.7	5.8	25.9	15.2

Note: Data as of 2014 unless noted; (1) Data covers Cook County; (2) Rate per 100,000 population; (3) Data as of 2013 and includes all active, non-federal physicians; (4) Doctor of Osteopathic Medicine
Source: U.S. Department of Health and Human Services, Health Resources and Services Administration, Bureau of Health Professions, Area Resource File (ARF) 2014-2015

Best Hospitals

According to *U.S. News*, the Chicago-Naperville-Arlington Heights, IL metro area is home to 13 of the best hospitals in the U.S.: **Northwest Community Healthcare** (1 specialty); **Advocate Illinois Masonic Medical Center** (1 specialty); **Northwestern Memorial Hospital** (Honor Roll/13 specialties); **Rehabilitation Institute of Chicago** (1 specialty); **Rush University Medical Center** (7 specialties); **University of Chicago Medical Center** (4 specialties); **Alexian Brothers Medical Center** (1 specialty); **NorthShore Evanston Hospital** (1 specialty); **St. Alexius Medical Center** (1 specialty); **Loyola University Medical Center** (4 specialties); **Advocate Christ Medical Center** (3 specialties); **Advocate Lutheran General Hospital** (1 specialty); **Cadence Health-Central DuPage Hospital** (1 specialty). The hospitals listed were nationally ranked in at least one adult specialty. Only 137 hospitals nationwide were nationally ranked in one or more specialties. Fifteen hospitals in the U.S. made the Honor Roll with high scores in at least six specialties. *U.S. News Online, "America's Best Children's Hospitals 2015-16"*

According to *U.S. News*, the Chicago-Naperville-Arlington Heights, IL metro area is home to three of the best children's hospitals in the U.S.: **Ann and Robert H. Lurie Children's Hospital of Chicago** (Honor Roll/10 specialties); **University of Chicago Comer Children's Hospital** (3 specialties); **Advocate Children's Hospital** (4 specialties). The hospitals listed were highly ranked in at least one pediatric specialty. Eighty-three children's hospitals in the U.S. were nationally ranked in at least one specialty. Twelve children's hospitals in the U.S. made the Honor Roll with high scores in at least three specialties. *U.S. News Online, "America's Best Children's Hospitals 2015-16"*

EDUCATION

Public School District Statistics

District Name	Schls	Pupils	Pupil/ Teacher Ratio	Minority Pupils[1] (%)	Free Lunch Eligible[2] (%)	IEP[3] (%)
Northbrook ESD 27	3	1,202	12.1	16.8	2.9	15.5
Northbrook SD 28	4	1,679	10.5	18.5	2.8	12.5
Northbrook/Glenview SD 30	3	1,127	11.7	31.3	2.8	15.8
Northfield Twp HSD 225	4	4,841	n/a	27.1	n/a	11.8
West Northfield SD 31	2	885	11.1	50.6	22.3	11.5

Note: Table includes school districts with 100 or more students; (1) Percentage of students that are not non-Hispanic white; (2) Percentage of students that are eligible for the free lunch program; (3) Percentage of students that have an Individualized Education Program.
Source: U.S. Department of Education, National Center for Education Statistics, Common Core of Data, Local Education Agency (School District) Universe Survey: School Year 2013-2014; U.S. Department of Education, National Center for Education Statistics, Common Core of Data, Public Elementary/Secondary School Universe Survey: School Year 2013-2014

Highest Level of Education

Area	Less than H.S.	H.S. Diploma	Some College, No Deg.	Associate Degree	Bachelor's Degree	Master's Degree	Prof. School Degree	Doctorate Degree
City	3.1	10.0	13.9	4.2	37.5	17.9	10.1	3.3
MSA[1]	13.1	24.8	20.2	6.9	21.5	9.8	2.5	1.3
U.S.	13.7	28.0	21.2	7.9	18.3	7.8	2.0	1.3

Note: Figures cover persons age 25 and over; (1) Figures cover the Chicago-Naperville-Elgin, IL-IN-WI Metropolitan Statistical Area—see Appendix B for areas included
Source: U.S. Census Bureau, 2010-2014 American Community Survey 5-Year Estimates

Educational Attainment by Race

Area	High School Graduate or Higher (%)					Bachelor's Degree or Higher (%)				
	Total	White	Black	Asian	Hisp.[2]	Total	White	Black	Asian	Hisp.[2]
City	96.9	97.2	89.8	98.9	84.4	68.9	69.1	1.6	74.4	58.8
MSA[1]	86.9	89.9	85.1	90.5	62.5	35.1	38.5	20.3	62.8	12.8
U.S.	86.3	88.4	83.2	85.8	64.1	29.3	30.6	19.0	50.9	13.9

Note: Figures shown cover persons 25 years old and over; (1) Figures cover the Chicago-Naperville-Elgin, IL-IN-WI Metropolitan Statistical Area—see Appendix B for areas included; (2) People of Hispanic origin can be of any race
Source: U.S. Census Bureau, 2010-2014 American Community Survey 5-Year Estimates

School Enrollment by Grade and Control

Area	Preschool (%)		Kindergarten (%)		Grades 1 - 4 (%)		Grades 5 - 8 (%)		Grades 9 - 12 (%)	
	Public	Private	Public	Private	Public	Private	Public	Private	Public	Private
City	29.2	70.8	78.3	21.7	85.7	14.3	90.6	9.4	94.9	5.1
MSA[1]	57.4	42.6	85.1	14.9	88.3	11.7	89.1	10.9	90.6	9.4
U.S.	57.4	42.6	87.8	12.2	89.8	10.2	89.9	10.1	90.6	9.4

Note: Figures shown cover persons 3 years old and over; (1) Figures cover the Chicago-Naperville-Elgin, IL-IN-WI Metropolitan Statistical Area—see Appendix B for areas included
Source: U.S. Census Bureau, 2010-2014 American Community Survey 5-Year Estimates

Average Salaries of Public School Classroom Teachers

Area	2013-14		2014-15		Percent Change 2013-14 to 2014-15	Percent Change 2004-05 to 2014-15
	Dollars	Rank[1]	Dollars	Rank[1]		
Illinois	60,124	12	61,083	12	1.59	6.2
U.S. Average	56,610	–	57,379	–	1.36	20.8

Note: (1) State rank ranges from 1 to 51 where 1 indicates highest salary.
Source: National Education Association, Rankings & Estimates: Rankings of the States 2014 and Estimates of School Statistics 2015, March 2015

Higher Education

Four-Year Colleges			Two-Year Colleges			Medical Schools[1]	Law Schools[2]	Voc/ Tech[3]
Public	Private Non-profit	Private For-profit	Public	Private Non-profit	Private For-profit			
0	0	0	0	0	0	0	0	0

Note: Figures cover institutions located within the city limits and include main campuses only; (1) includes schools accredited by the Liaison Committee on Medical Education and the American Osteopathic Association's Commission on Osteopathic College Accreditation; (2) includes ABA-accredited schools, schools with provisional ABA accreditation, and state accredited schools; (3) includes all schools with programs that are less than 2 years.
Source: National Center for Education Statistics, Integrated Postsecondary Education System (IPEDS), 2014-15; Association of American Medical Colleges, Member List, March 21, 2016; American Osteopathic Association, Member List, March 21, 2016; Law School Admission Council, Official Guide to ABA-Approved Law Schools Online, March 21, 2016; Wikipedia, List of Medical Schools in the United States, March 21, 2016; Wikipedia, List of Law Schools in the United States, March 21, 2016

According to *U.S. News & World Report,* the Chicago-Naperville-Arlington Heights, IL metro division is home to six of the best national universities in the U.S.: **University of Chicago** (#4 tie); **Northwestern University** (#12 tie); **Loyola University Chicago** (#99 tie); **Illinois Institute of Technology** (#108 tie); **DePaul University** (#123 tie); **University of Illinois–Chicago** (#129 tie). The indicators used to capture academic quality fall into a number of categories: assessment by administrators at peer institutions; retention of students; faculty resources; student selectivity; financial resources; alumni giving; high school counselor ratings of colleges; and graduation rate. *U.S. News & World Report, "America's Best Colleges 2016"*

According to *U.S. News & World Report,* the Chicago-Naperville-Arlington Heights, IL metro division is home to one of the best liberal arts colleges in the U.S.: **Wheaton College** (#57 tie). The indicators used to capture academic quality fall into a number of categories: assessment by administrators at peer institutions; retention of students; faculty resources; student selectivity; financial resources; alumni giving; high school counselor ratings of colleges; and graduation rate. *U.S. News & World Report, "America's Best Colleges 2016"*

According to *U.S. News & World Report,* the Chicago-Naperville-Arlington Heights, IL metro division is home to four of the top 100 law schools in the U.S.: **University of Chicago, Law School** (#4 tie); **Northwestern University, Pritzker School of Law** (#12); **Loyola University Chicago, School of Law** (#72 tie); **Illinois Institute of Technology, Chicago-Kent College of Law** (#86 tie). The rankings are based on a weighted average of 12 measures of quality: peer assessment score; assessment score by lawyers/judges; median LSAT scores; median undergrad GPA; acceptance rate; employment rates for graduates; placement success; bar passage rate; faculty resources; expenditures per student; student/faculty ratio; and library resources. *U.S. News & World Report, "America's Best Graduate Schools, Law, 2017"*

According to *U.S. News & World Report,* the Chicago-Naperville-Arlington Heights, IL metro division is home to three of the top 75 medical schools for research in the U.S.: **University of**

Chicago, Pritzker School of Medicine (#11 tie); **Northwestern University, Feinberg School of Medicine** (#17); **University of Illinois, College of Medicine** (#47 tie). The rankings are based on a weighted average of 11 measures of quality: quality assessment; peer assessment score; assessment score by residency directors; research activity; total research activity; average research activity per faculty member; student selectivity; median MCAT total score; median undergraduate GPA; acceptance rate; and faculty resources. *U.S. News & World Report, "America's Best Graduate Schools, Medical, 2017"*

According to *U.S. News & World Report*, the Chicago-Naperville-Arlington Heights, IL metro division is home to two of the top 75 business schools in the U.S.: **University of Chicago, Booth School of Business** (#2 tie); **Northwestern University, Kellogg School of Management** (#5 tie). The rankings are based on a weighted average of the following nine measures: quality assessment; peer assessment; recruiter assessment; placement success; mean starting salary and bonus; student selectivity; mean GMAT and GRE scores; mean undergraduate GPA; and acceptance rate. *U.S. News & World Report, "America's Best Graduate Schools, Business, 2017"*

PRESIDENTIAL ELECTION

2012 Presidential Election Results

Area	Obama (%)	Romney (%)	Other (%)
Cook County	74.0	24.6	1.3
U.S.	51.0	47.2	1.8

Note: Results may not add to 100% due to rounding
Source: Dave Leip's Atlas of U.S. Presidential Elections

EMPLOYERS

Major Employers

Company Name	Industry
Abbott Laboratories	Pharmaceutical preparations
Addus HomeCare Corporation	Home health care services
Advocate Lutheran General Hospital	General medical & surgical hospitals
BMO Bankcorp	National commercial banks
City of Chicago	General government
Cook County Bureau of Health Services	Administration of public health programs, county govt
Graphic Packaging International	Folding boxboard
Loyola University Health System	General medical & surgical hospitals
Northshore University Healthsystem	General medical & surgical hospitals
Northwestern Memorial Hospital	General medical & surgical hospitals
SCC Holding Co.	Cups, plastics, except foam
Schneider Electric Holdings	Air transportation, scheduled
SOLO Cup Company	Cups, plastics, except foam
The Allstate Corporation	Fire, marine, & casualty insurance
The University of Chicago Medical Center	General medical & surgical hospitals
United Parcel Service	Mailing & messenger services
United States Steel Corporation	Steel foundries
WM Recycle America	Material recovery

Note: Companies shown are located within the Chicago-Naperville-Elgin, IL-IN-WI Metropolitan Statistical Area.
Source: Hoovers.com; Wikipedia

PUBLIC SAFETY

Crime Rate

Area	All Crimes	Violent Crimes				Property Crimes		
		Murder	Rape[3]	Robbery	Aggrav. Assault	Burglary	Larceny -Theft	Motor Vehicle Theft
City	1,077.2	0.0	11.9	5.9	3.0	127.6	919.9	8.9
Metro[1]	2,620.4	6.9	29.9	167.9	222.2	365.2	1,641.4	186.9
U.S.	2,971.8	4.5	36.6	102.2	232.5	542.5	1,837.3	216.2

Note: Figures are crimes per 100,000 population; (1) Figures cover the Chicago-Naperville-Arlington Heights, IL Metropolitan Division—see Appendix B for areas included; (3) The city and U.S. figures shown were reported using the revised Uniform Crime Reporting (UCR) definition of rape. The suburban and metro area figures shown are an aggregate total of the data submitted using both the revised and legacy UCR definitions.
Source: FBI Uniform Crime Reports, 2014

Hate Crimes

Area	Number of Quarters Reported	Number of Incidents per Bias Motivation: Race	Religion	Sexual Orientation	Ethnicity	Disability	Gender	Gender Identity
City	4	0	0	0	0	0	0	0
U.S.	4	2,568	1,014	1,017	648	84	33	98

Source: Federal Bureau of Investigation, Hate Crime Statistics 2014

Identity Theft Consumer Complaints

Area	Complaints	Complaints per 100,000 Population	Rank[2]
MSA[1]	14,252	149.2	55
U.S.	490,220	152.4	-

Note: (1) Figures cover the Chicago-Naperville-Elgin, IL-IN-WI Metropolitan Statistical Area—see Appendix B for areas included; (2) Rank ranges from 1 to 379 where 1 indicates greatest number of identity theft complaints per 100,000 population
Source: Federal Trade Commission, Consumer Sentinel Network Data Book for January–December 2015

Fraud and Other Consumer Complaints

Area	Complaints	Complaints per 100,000 Population	Rank[2]
MSA[1]	35,300	369.5	171
U.S.	2,593,159	806.0	-

Note: (1) Figures cover the Chicago-Naperville-Elgin, IL-IN-WI Metropolitan Statistical Area—see Appendix B for areas included; (2) Rank ranges from 1 to 379 where 1 indicates greatest number of identity theft complaints per 100,000 population
Source: Federal Trade Commission, Consumer Sentinel Network Data Book for January–December 2015

RECREATION

Culture

Dance[1]	Theatre[1]	Instrumental Music[1]	Vocal Music[1]	Series and Festivals	Museums and Art Galleries[2]	Zoos and Aquariums[3]
0	0	0	0	0	0	0

Note: (1) Professional perfoming groups; (2) Based on organizations with SIC code 8412; (3) AZA-accredited
Source: The Grey House Performing Arts Directory, 2015-16; Association of Zoos & Aquariums, AZA Member Zoos & Aquariums, March 25, 2016; www.AccuLeads.com, March 29, 2016

Professional Sports Teams

Team Name	League	Year Established
Chicago Bears	National Football League (NFL)	1921
Chicago Blackhawks	National Hockey League (NHL)	1926
Chicago Bulls	National Basketball Association (NBA)	1966
Chicago Cubs	Major League Baseball (MLB)	1874
Chicago Fire	Major League Soccer (MLS)	1997
Chicago White Sox	Major League Baseball (MLB)	1900

Note: Includes teams located in the Chicago-Naperville-Elgin, IL-IN-WI Metropolitan Statistical Area.
Source: Wikipedia, Major Professional Sports Teams of the United States and Canada, March 24, 2016

CLIMATE

Average and Extreme Temperatures

Temperature	Jan	Feb	Mar	Apr	May	Jun	Jul	Aug	Sep	Oct	Nov	Dec	Yr.
Extreme High (°F)	65	71	88	91	93	104	102	100	99	91	78	71	104
Average High (°F)	29	33	45	59	70	79	84	82	75	63	48	34	59
Average Temp. (°F)	21	26	37	49	59	69	73	72	65	53	40	27	49
Average Low (°F)	13	17	28	39	48	57	63	62	54	42	32	19	40
Extreme Low (°F)	-27	-17	-8	7	24	36	40	41	28	17	1	-25	-27

Note: Figures cover the years 1958-1990
Source: National Climatic Data Center, International Station Meteorological Climate Summary, 9/96

Average Precipitation/Snowfall/Humidity

Precip./Humidity	Jan	Feb	Mar	Apr	May	Jun	Jul	Aug	Sep	Oct	Nov	Dec	Yr.
Avg. Precip. (in.)	1.6	1.4	2.7	3.6	3.3	3.7	3.7	4.1	3.7	2.4	2.8	2.3	35.4
Avg. Snowfall (in.)	11	8	7	2	Tr	0	0	0	0	1	2	9	39
Avg. Rel. Hum. 6am (%)	76	77	79	77	77	78	82	85	85	82	80	80	80
Avg. Rel. Hum. 3pm (%)	65	63	59	53	51	52	54	55	55	53	61	68	57

Note: Figures cover the years 1958-1990; Tr = Trace amounts (<0.05 in. of rain; <0.5 in. of snow)
Source: National Climatic Data Center, International Station Meteorological Climate Summary, 9/96

Weather Conditions

Temperature			Daytime Sky			Precipitation		
5°F & below	32°F & below	90°F & above	Clear	Partly cloudy	Cloudy	0.01 inch or more precip.	0.1 inch or more snow/ice	Thunder-storms
21	132	17	84	135	146	125	31	38

Note: Figures are average number of days per year and cover the years 1958-1990
Source: National Climatic Data Center, International Station Meteorological Climate Summary, 9/96

HAZARDOUS WASTE

Superfund Sites

Northbrook has no sites on the EPA's Superfund Final National Priorities List. There are a total of 1,323 Superfund sites on the list in the U.S. *U.S. Environmental Protection Agency, Final National Priorities List, March 18, 2016*

AIR & WATER QUALITY

Air Quality Trends: Ozone

	1990	1995	2000	2005	2010	2011	2012	2013	2014
MSA[1]	0.074	0.093	0.072	0.084	0.070	0.072	0.082	0.066	0.067

Note: (1) Data covers the Chicago-Naperville-Elgin, IL-IN-WI Metropolitan Statistical Area—see Appendix B for areas included. The values shown are the composite ozone concentration averages among trend sites based on the highest fourth daily maximum 8-hour concentration in parts per million. These trends are based on sites having an adequate record of monitoring data during the trend period. Data from exceptional events are included.
Source: U.S. Environmental Protection Agency, Air Quality Monitoring Information, "Air Quality Trends by City, 1990-2014"

Air Quality Index

Area	Percent of Days when Air Quality was...[2]					AQI Statistics[2]	
	Good	Moderate	Unhealthy for Sensitive Groups	Unhealthy	Very Unhealthy	Maximum	Median
MSA[1]	33.2	64.4	1.9	0.5	0.0	183	55

Note: (1) Data covers the Chicago-Naperville-Elgin, IL-IN-WI Metropolitan Statistical Area—see Appendix B for areas included; (2) Based on 365 days with AQI data in 2015. Air Quality Index (AQI) is an index for reporting daily air quality. EPA calculates the AQI for five major air pollutants regulated by the Clean Air Act: ground-level ozone, particle pollution (aka particulate matter), carbon monoxide, sulfur dioxide, and nitrogen dioxide. The AQI runs from 0 to 500. The higher the AQI value, the greater the level of air pollution and the greater the health concern. There are six AQI categories: "Good" AQI is between 0 and 50. Air quality is considered satisfactory; "Moderate" AQI is between 51 and 100. Air quality is acceptable; "Unhealthy for Sensitive Groups" When AQI values are between 101 and 150, members of sensitive groups may experience health effects; "Unhealthy" When AQI values are between 151 and 200 everyone may begin to experience health effects; "Very Unhealthy" AQI values between 201 and 300 trigger a health alert; "Hazardous" AQI values over 300 trigger warnings of emergency conditions (not shown).
Source: U.S. Environmental Protection Agency, Air Quality Index Report, 2015

Air Quality Index Pollutants

Area	Percent of Days when AQI Pollutant was...[2]					
	Carbon Monoxide	Nitrogen Dioxide	Ozone	Sulfur Dioxide	Particulate Matter 2.5	Particulate Matter 10
MSA[1]	0.0	6.8	9.9	2.5	73.2	7.7

Note: (1) Data covers the Chicago-Naperville-Elgin, IL-IN-WI Metropolitan Statistical Area—see Appendix B for areas included; (2) Based on 365 days with AQI data in 2015. The Air Quality Index (AQI) is an index for reporting daily air quality. EPA calculates the AQI for five major air pollutants regulated by the Clean Air Act: ground-level ozone, particle pollution (also known as particulate matter), carbon monoxide, sulfur dioxide, and nitrogen dioxide. The AQI runs from 0 to 500. The higher the AQI value, the greater the level of air pollution and the greater the health concern.
Source: U.S. Environmental Protection Agency, Air Quality Index Report, 2015

Maximum Air Pollutant Concentrations: Particulate Matter, Ozone, CO and Lead

	Particulate Matter 10 (ug/m^3)	Particulate Matter 2.5 Wtd AM (ug/m^3)	Particulate Matter 2.5 24-Hr (ug/m^3)	Ozone (ppm)	Carbon Monoxide (ppm)	Lead (ug/m^3)
MSA[1] Level	93	11.7	27	0.076	2	0.15
NAAQS[2]	150	15	35	0.075	9	0.15
Met NAAQS[2]	Yes	Yes	Yes	No	Yes	Yes

Note: (1) Data covers the Chicago-Naperville-Elgin, IL-IN-WI Metropolitan Statistical Area—see Appendix B for areas included; Data from exceptional events are included; (2) National Ambient Air Quality Standards; ppm = parts per million; ug/m^3 = micrograms per cubic meter; n/a not available.
Concentrations: Particulate Matter 10 (coarse particulate)—highest second maximum 24-hour concentration; Particulate Matter 2.5 Wtd AM (fine particulate)—highest weighted annual mean concentration; Particulate Matter 2.5 24-Hour (fine particulate)—highest 98th percentile 24-hour concentration; Ozone—highest fourth daily maximum 8-hour concentration; Carbon Monoxide—highest second maximum non-overlapping 8-hour concentration; Lead—maximum running 3-month average
Source: U.S. Environmental Protection Agency, Air Quality Monitoring Information, "Air Quality Statistics by City, 2014"

Maximum Air Pollutant Concentrations: Nitrogen Dioxide and Sulfur Dioxide

	Nitrogen Dioxide AM (ppb)	Nitrogen Dioxide 1-Hr (ppb)	Sulfur Dioxide AM (ppb)	Sulfur Dioxide 1-Hr (ppb)	Sulfur Dioxide 24-Hr (ppb)
MSA[1] Level	21	67	n/a	53	n/a
NAAQS[2]	53	100	30	75	140
Met NAAQS[2]	Yes	Yes	n/a	Yes	n/a

Note: (1) Data covers the Chicago-Naperville-Elgin, IL-IN-WI Metropolitan Statistical Area—see Appendix B for areas included; Data from exceptional events are included; (2) National Ambient Air Quality Standards; ppm = parts per million; ug/m^3 = micrograms per cubic meter; n/a not available.
Concentrations: Nitrogen Dioxide AM—highest arithmetic mean concentration; Nitrogen Dioxide 1-Hr—highest 98th percentile 1-hour daily maximum concentration; Sulfur Dioxide AM—highest annual mean concentration; Sulfur Dioxide 1-Hr—highest 99th percentile 1-hour daily maximum concentration; Sulfur Dioxide 24-Hr—highest second maximum 24-hour concentration
Source: U.S. Environmental Protection Agency, Air Quality Monitoring Information, "Air Quality Statistics by City, 2014"

Drinking Water

Water System Name	Pop. Served	Primary Water Source Type	Violations[1]	
			Health Based	Monitoring/ Reporting
Northbrook	33,435	Surface	0	0

Note: (1) Based on violation data from January 1, 2015 to December 31, 2015 (includes unresolved violations from earlier years)
Source: U.S. Environmental Protection Agency, Office of Ground Water and Drinking Water, Safe Drinking Water Information System (based on data extracted April 29, 2016)

O'Fallon, Illinois

Background

O'Fallon is located in southwestern Illinois, in St. Clair County, 14 miles outside of St. Louis and 5 miles from Scott Air Force Base. O'Fallon is one of the fastest growing suburbs in the St. Louis Metropolitan Area.

The Ohio & Mississippi Railroad built a station in the area in 1854 and named it O'Fallon Station, after one of St. Louis' notable businessmen. The railroad brought growth to the area, in addition to the discovery of productive coalfields nearby. O'Fallon was also a popular destination for German immigrants searching for fertile lands to farm. O'Fallon was incorporated as a village in 1874, residents later voted to change to a city form of government in 1905.

O'Fallon has seen tremendous growth over the past three decades. With its close proximity to St. Louis and the nearby Scott Air Force Base, O'Fallon has been attracting considerable numbers of new residents. Several new subdivisions have been built in recent years, and are popular among newcomers. Over 50% of O'Fallon's housing is less than 15 years old.

The O'Fallon community has much to offer its residents in the form of recreational activities. The city has an excellent community park system, offering several youth sports programs, along with a number of championship golf courses, parks, bike paths and a new indoor swimming pool.

Elementary schools in O'Fallon are managed by two districts: Central District 104 and District 90. Together, the two districts serve 3,600 students with five elementary schools and two junior high schools. The city's high school, O'Fallon Township High School, has been expanded several times over the past few decades to accommodate its growing number of students. O'Fallon also has four private schools.

O'Fallon is served by MidAmerica St. Louis Airport and Lambert St. Louis International Airport, both a short drive from the city.

The climate in O'Fallon consists of hot and humid summers, a mild fall season with some heavy rainfall, cold winters with periodic snow storms, followed by a wet spring season that can produce erratic weather, including thunderstorms, tornadoes and late winter storms. O'Fallon was hit by a tornado in 2006, causing significant property damage.

Rankings

Business/Finance Rankings

- The personal finance site NerdWallet analyzed 183 American metropolitan areas with populations over 250,000 and more than 15,000 businesses to rank where entrepreneurs find the most success. Criteria included area economy, annual income, housing cost, unemployment rate, and the success rate of area businesses. Saint Louis* ranked #47. *www.nerdwallet.com, "Best Places to Start a Business," April 27, 2015*
- USAA and Hiring Our Heroes worked with Sperlings's BestPlaces and the Institute for Veterans and Military Families at Syracuse University to rank major metropolitan areas where military-skills-related employment is strongest. Criteria for *mid-career* veterans included veteran wage growth; military skills, defense contractor, and government jobs; recent job growth; stability; and accessible health resources. Metro areas with a higher than national average crime or unemployment rate were excluded. At #6, the Saint Louis* metro area made the top ten. *www.usaa.com, "2015 Best Places for Veterans"*
- Based on metro area social media reviews, the employment opinion group Glassdoor surveyed 50 of the largest U.S. metro areas and equally weighed cost of living, hiring opportunity, and job satisfaction to compose a list of "25 Best Cities for Jobs." The Saint Louis* metro area was ranked #11 in overall job satisfaction. *www.glassdoor.com, "Best Cities for Jobs," May 19, 2015*
- In a survey of economic confidence in the nation's 50 largest metropolitan areas conducted January–December 2014, the Saint Louis* metro area placed #38, according to Gallup's 2014 Economic Confidence Index. *Gallup, "San Jose and San Francisco Lead in Economic Confidence," March 19, 2015*
- The Brookings Institution ranked the 100 largest metro areas in the U.S. based on income inequality. Saint Louis* was ranked #59 (#1 = greatest ineqality). Criteria: the "95/20 ratio," a figure representing the income at which a household earns more than 95 percent of all other households, divided by the income at which a household earns more than only 20 percent of all other households. *Brookings Institution, "Income Inequality, 100 Largest U.S. Metro Areas, 2007-2014," January 14, 2016*
- Payscale.com ranked the 20 largest metro areas in terms of wage growth. The Saint Louis* metro area ranked #14. Criteria: private-sector wage growth between the 1st quarter of 2015 and the 1st quarter of 2016. *PayScale, "Wage Trends by Metro Area," 1st Quarter, 2016*
- The Saint Louis* metro area was identified as one of the most debt-ridden places in America by the finance site Credit.com. The metro area was ranked #9. Criteria: residents' average personal debt load and average credit scores. *Credit.com, "The Most Debt-Ridden Cities," May 1, 2014*
- The Saint Louis* metro area was identified as one of the most affordable metropolitan areas in America by *Forbes.* The area ranked #7 out of 20 based on the National Association of Home Builders/Wells Fargo Housing Affordability Index and Sperling's Best Places' cost-of-living index. *Forbes.com, "America's Most Affordable Cities in 2015," March 12, 2015*
- Saint Louis* was identified as one of America's most frugal metro areas by *Coupons.com.* The city ranked #17 out of 25. Criteria: online coupon usage. *Coupons.com, "Top 25 Most Frugal Cities of 2014," May 11, 2015*
- Saint Louis* was identified as one of America's most frugal metro areas by *Coupons.com.* The city ranked #13 out of 25. Criteria: Grocery IQ and coupons.com mobile app usage. *Coupons.com, "Top 25 Most On-the-Go Frugal Cities of 2013," April 10, 2014*
- The Saint Louis* metro area appeared on the Milken Institute "2015 Best Performing Cities" list. Rank: #170 out of 200 large metro areas. Criteria: job growth; wage and salary growth; high-tech output growth. *Milken Institute, "Best-Performing Cities 2015," December 2015*

- *Forbes* ranked the 200 most populous metro areas to determine the nation's "Best Places for Business and Careers." The Saint Louis* metro area was ranked #84. Criteria: costs (business and living); job growth (past and projected); income growth; educational attainment (college and high school); projected economic growth; cultural and recreational opportunities; net migration patterns; number of highly ranked colleges. *Forbes, "The Best Places for Business and Careers 2015," July 29, 2015*

Education Rankings

- Personal finance website *WalletHub* analyzed the 150 largest U.S. metropolitan statistical areas to determine where the most educated Americans are choosing to settle. Criteria: education quality and attainment gap; education levels; percentage of workers with degrees; public school rankings; quality and size of each metro area's universities. Saint Louis* was ranked #35 (#1 = most educated city). *www.WalletHub.com, "2015's Most and Least Educated Cities*

Environmental Rankings

- The Saint Louis* metro area came in at #232 for the relative comfort of its climate on Sperling's list of "chill cities," as measured by the Sperling Heat Index. All 361 metro areas are included. Criteria included daytime high temperatures, nighttime low temperatures, dew point, and relative humidity at the high temperatures. *www.bertsperling.com, "Sperling's Chill Cities," July 18, 2013*

- Sperling's BestPlaces assessed 379 metropolitan areas of the United States for the likelihood of dangerously extreme weather events or earthquakes. In general the Southeast and South-Central regions have the highest risk of weather extremes and earthquakes, while the Pacific Northwest enjoys the lowest risk. Of the least risky metropolitan areas, the Saint Louis* metro area was ranked #327. *www.bestplaces.net, "Safest Places from Natural Disasters," April 2011*

- Saint Louis* was identified as one of America's dirtiest metro areas by *Forbes*. The area ranked #20 out of 20. Criteria: air quality; water quality; toxic releases; superfund sites. *Forbes, "America's 20 Dirtiest Cities," December 10, 2012*

- Saint Louis* was highlighted as one of the 25 most ozone-polluted metro areas in the U.S. during 2011 through 2013. The area ranked #16. *American Lung Association, State of the Air 2015*

Health/Fitness Rankings

- For each of the 50 most populous metro areas in the United States, the American College of Sports Medicine's American Fitness Index evaluated infrastructure, community assets, and policies that encourage healthy and fit lifestyles, including preventive health behaviors, levels of chronic disease conditions, health care access, and community resources and policies that support physical activity. The Saint Louis* metro area ranked #29 for "community fitness." *www.americanfitnessindex.org, "ACSM American Fitness Index Health and Community Fitness Status of the 50 Largest Metropolitan Areas," May 2015*

- The Saint Louis* metro area was identified as one of the worst cities for bed bugs in America by pest control company Orkin. The area ranked #40 out of 50 based on the number of bed bug treatments Orkin performed from January to December 2015. *Orkin, "Chicago Tops Bed Bug Cities List for Fourth Year in a Row," January 13, 2016*

- Saint Louis* was identified as a "2016 Spring Allergy Capital." The area ranked #35 out of 100. Three groups of factors were used to identify the most severe cities for people with allergies during the spring season: annual pollen levels; medicine utilization; access to board-certified allergists. *Asthma and Allergy Foundation of America, "Spring Allergy Capitals 2016"*

- Saint Louis* was identified as a "2015 Asthma Capital." The area ranked #26 out of the nation's 100 largest metropolitan areas. Criteria: estimated prevalence; self-reported prevalence; crude death rate for asthma; annual pollen score; annual air quality; public smoking laws; number of board-certified asthma specialists; school inhaler access laws; rescue medication use; controller medication use; ER visits for asthma; uninsured rate; poverty rate. *Asthma and Allergy Foundation of America, "Asthma Capitals 2015"*

- The Saint Louis* metro area ranked #162 out of 190 in The Gallup-Healthways Well-Being Index. Criteria: purpose; social well being; financial health; community and physical health. Results are based on telephone interviews with adults, aged 18 and older, living in metropolitan areas in the 50 U.S. states and the District of Columbia. *Gallup-Healthways, "State of American Well-Being," February 23, 2016*

Real Estate Rankings

- Based on the home-price forecasts compiled by the real-estate valuation firm CoreLogic Case-Shiller, CNNMoney reported that in 2016, the Saint Louis* metro area is expected to be one of the hottest housing markets in the U.S. Criteria: residential real estate prices. *money.cnn.com, "The 10 Hottest Housing Markets for 2016," December 3, 2015*

- The Saint Louis* metro area appeared on Realtor.com's list of the hottest housing markets to watch in 2016. The area ranked #2. Criteria: strong housing growth; affordable prices; and fast-paced sales. *Realtor.com®, "Top 10 Hot Real Estate Markets to Watch in 2016," December 2, 2015*

- Saint Louis* was ranked #50 out of 225 metro areas in terms of housing affordability in 2015 by the National Association of Home Builders (#1 = most affordable). Criteria: the share of homes sold in that area affordable to a family earning the local median income, based on standard mortgage underwriting criteria. *National Association of Home Builders®, NAHB-Wells Fargo Housing Opportunity Index, 4th Quarter 2015*

Safety Rankings

- The National Insurance Crime Bureau ranked 380 metro areas in the U.S. in terms of per capita rates of vehicle theft. The Saint Louis* metro area ranked #102 (#1 = highest rate). Criteria: number of vehicle theft offenses per 100,000 inhabitants in 2014. *National Insurance Crime Bureau, "Hot Spots 2014," June 24, 2015*

Seniors/Retirement Rankings

- From its Best Cities for Successful Aging indexes, the Milken Institute generated rankings for metropolitan areas, weighing data in eight categories—health care, wellness, living arrangements, transportation, financial characteristics, education and employment opportunities, community engagement, and overall livability. The Saint Louis* metro area was ranked #30 overall in the large metro area category. *Milken Institute, "Best Cities for Successful Aging, 2014"*

Miscellaneous Rankings

- The watchdog site Charity Navigator conducts an annual study of charities in the nation's major markets both to analyze statistical differences in their financial, accountability, and transparency practices and to track year-to-year variations in individual communities. The Saint Louis* metro area was ranked #16 among the 30 metro markets in the rating dimension of Overall Score. *www.charitynavigator.org, "Metro Market Study 2015," June 5, 2015*

- Mars Chocolate North America, the makers of COMBOS®, in partnership with Sperling's BestPlaces, ranked 50 major metro areas in terms of their "manliness." The Saint Louis* metro area ranked #7. Criteria: number of professional sports teams; number of nearby NASCAR tracks and racing events; manly lifestyle; concentration of manly retail stores; manly occupations per capita; salty snack sales; "Board of Manliness" rankings. *Mars Chocolate North America, "America's Manliest Cities 2012"*

- The Saint Louis* metro area was selected as one of "America's Most Miserable Cities" by *Forbes.com.* The metro area ranked #12 out of 20. Criteria: violent crime; unemployment; foreclosures; income and property taxes; home prices; commute times; climate. *Forbes.com, "America's Most Miserable Cities" February 22, 2013*

- The National Alliance to End Homelessness ranked the 100 most populous metro areas with the highest rate of homelessness. The Saint Louis* metro area ranked #64. Criteria: number of homeless people per 10,000 population in 2011. *National Alliance to End Homelessness, The State of Homelessness in America 2012*

***O'Fallon is located within the St. Louis, MO-IL Metropolitan Statistical Area.**

Business Environment

CITY FINANCES

City Government Finances

Component	2012 ($000)	2012 ($ per capita)
Total Revenues	43,059	1,522
Total Expenditures	39,109	1,382
Debt Outstanding	47,325	1,673
Cash and Securities[1]	47,971	1,696

Note: (1) Cash and security holdings of a government at the close of its fiscal year, including those of its dependent agencies, utilities, and liquor stores.
Source: U.S Census Bureau, State & Local Government Finances 2012

City Government Revenue by Source

Source	2012 ($000)	2012 ($ per capita)
General Revenue		
From Federal Government	184	6
From State Government	13,172	465
From Local Governments	0	0
Taxes		
Property	6,934	245
Sales and Gross Receipts	3,405	120
Personal Income	0	0
Corporate Income	0	0
Motor Vehicle License	0	0
Other Taxes	496	17
Current Charges	8,337	294
Liquor Store	0	0
Utility	9,557	337
Employee Retirement	344	12

Source: U.S Census Bureau, State & Local Government Finances 2012

City Government Expenditures by Function

Function	2012 ($000)	2012 ($ per capita)	2012 (%)
General Direct Expenditures			
Air Transportation	0	0	0.0
Corrections	0	0	0.0
Education	0	0	0.0
Employment Security Administration	0	0	0.0
Financial Administration	1,093	38	2.7
Fire Protection	658	23	1.6
General Public Buildings	1,402	49	3.5
Governmental Administration, Other	2,871	101	7.3
Health	0	0	0.0
Highways	4,122	145	10.5
Hospitals	0	0	0.0
Housing and Community Development	0	0	0.0
Interest on General Debt	2,827	99	7.2
Judicial and Legal	0	0	0.0
Libraries	998	35	2.5
Parking	0	0	0.0
Parks and Recreation	4,729	167	12.0
Police Protection	4,851	171	12.4
Public Welfare	18	< 1	< 0.1
Sewerage	3,266	115	8.3
Solid Waste Management	0	0	0.0
Veterans' Services	0	0	0.0
Liquor Store	0	0	0.0
Utility	7,479	264	19.1
Employee Retirement	272	9	0.6

Source: U.S Census Bureau, State & Local Government Finances 2012

DEMOGRAPHICS

Population Growth

Area	1990 Census	2000 Census	2010 Census	2014* Estimate	Population Growth (%) 1990-2014	Population Growth (%) 2010-2014
City	17,169	21,910	28,281	29,100	69.5	2.9
MSA[1]	2,580,897	2,698,687	2,812,896	2,797,737	8.4	-0.5
U.S.	248,709,873	281,421,906	308,745,538	314,107,084	26.3	1.7

Note: (1) Figures cover the St. Louis, MO-IL Metropolitan Statistical Area—see Appendix B for areas included; (*) 2010-2014 5-year estimated population
Source: U.S. Census Bureau, 1990 Census, Census 2000, Census 2010, 2010-2014 American Community Survey 5-Year Estimates

Household Size

Area	Persons in Household (%) One	Two	Three	Four	Five	Six	Seven or More	Average Household Size
City	25.0	30.0	18.0	15.9	7.1	2.2	1.4	2.73
MSA[1]	29.2	33.8	15.7	12.8	5.5	1.7	0.8	2.48
U.S.	27.5	33.5	15.8	13.1	6.0	2.3	1.4	2.64

Note: (1) Figures cover the St. Louis, MO-IL Metropolitan Statistical Area—see Appendix B for areas included
Source: U.S. Census Bureau, 2010-2014 American Community Survey 5-Year Estimates

Race

Area	White Alone[2] (%)	Black Alone[2] (%)	Asian Alone[2] (%)	AIAN[3] Alone[2] (%)	NHOPI[4] Alone[2] (%)	Other Race Alone[2] (%)	Two or More Races (%)
City	78.1	14.7	2.5	0.1	0.0	0.8	3.8
MSA[1]	76.5	18.3	2.2	0.2	0.0	0.6	2.1
U.S.	73.8	12.6	5.0	0.8	0.2	4.7	2.9

Note: (1) Figures cover the St. Louis, MO-IL Metropolitan Statistical Area—see Appendix B for areas included; (2) Alone is defined as not being in combination with one or more other races; (3) American Indian and Alaska Native; (4) Native Hawaiian and Other Pacific Islander
Source: U.S. Census Bureau, 2010-2014 American Community Survey 5-Year Estimates

Hispanic or Latino Origin

Area	Total (%)	Mexican (%)	Puerto Rican (%)	Cuban (%)	Other (%)
City	3.1	1.8	0.9	0.1	0.3
MSA[1]	2.7	1.8	0.2	0.1	0.6
U.S.	16.9	10.8	1.6	0.6	3.8

Note: Persons of Hispanic or Latino origin can be of any race; (1) Figures cover the St. Louis, MO-IL Metropolitan Statistical Area—see Appendix B for areas included
Source: U.S. Census Bureau, 2010-2014 American Community Survey 5-Year Estimates

Ancestry

Area	German	Irish	English	American	Italian	Polish	French[2]	Scottish	Dutch
City	28.4	14.2	11.8	5.2	3.1	5.0	3.8	2.2	2.0
MSA[1]	29.3	13.8	8.1	7.3	4.8	2.6	3.6	1.5	1.3
U.S.	14.9	10.8	8.0	7.1	5.5	3.0	2.7	1.7	1.4

Note: Figures are the percentage of the total population reporting a particular ancestry. The nine most commonly reported ancestries in the U.S. are shown. Figures include multiple ancestries (e.g. if a person reported being Irish and Italian, they were included in both columns); (1) Figures cover the St. Louis, MO-IL Metropolitan Statistical Area—see Appendix B for areas included; (2) Excludes Basque
Source: U.S. Census Bureau, 2010-2014 American Community Survey 5-Year Estimates

Foreign-Born Population

Area	Percent of Population Born in								
	Any Foreign Country	Asia	Mexico	Europe	Carribean	Central America[2]	South America	Africa	Canada
City	3.9	2.2	0.1	0.9	0.2	0.1	0.0	0.1	0.2
MSA[1]	4.5	1.9	0.6	1.2	0.1	0.1	0.1	0.3	0.1
U.S.	13.1	3.8	3.7	1.5	1.2	1.0	0.9	0.6	0.3

Note: (1) Figures cover the St. Louis, MO-IL Metropolitan Statistical Area—see Appendix B for areas included; (2) Excludes Mexico.
Source: U.S. Census Bureau, 2010-2014 American Community Survey 5-Year Estimates

Marital Status

Area	Never Married	Now Married[2]	Separated	Widowed	Divorced
City	28.8	54.4	2.0	4.8	10.1
MSA[1]	31.8	48.9	1.8	6.3	11.2
U.S.	32.5	48.4	2.2	5.9	10.9

Note: Figures are percentages and cover the population 15 years of age and older; (1) Figures cover the St. Louis, MO-IL Metropolitan Statistical Area—see Appendix B for areas included; (2) Excludes separated
Source: U.S. Census Bureau, 2010-2014 American Community Survey 5-Year Estimates

Disability Status

Area	All Ages	Under 18 Years Old	18 to 64 Years Old	65 Years and Over
City	9.0	3.0	6.9	36.8
MSA[1]	12.1	4.3	10.0	35.2
U.S.	12.3	4.1	10.2	36.3

Note: Figures show percent of the civilian noninstitutionalized population that reported having a disability. Disability status is determined from from six types of difficulty: vision, hearing, cognitive, ambulatory, self-care, and independent living. For children under 5 years old, hearing and vision difficulty are used to determine disability status. For children between the ages of 5 and 14, disability status is determined from hearing, vision, cognitive, ambulatory, and self-care difficulties. For people aged 15 years and older, they are considered to have a disability if they have difficulty with any one of the six difficulty types; (1) Figures cover the St. Louis, MO-IL Metropolitan Statistical Area—see Appendix B for areas included.
Source: U.S. Census Bureau, 2010-2014 American Community Survey 5-Year Estimates

Age

Area	Percent of Population									Median Age
	Under Age 5	Age 5–19	Age 20–34	Age 35–44	Age 45–54	Age 55–64	Age 65–74	Age 75–84	Age 85+	
City	6.9	23.8	17.9	16.9	14.2	10.7	5.8	3.2	0.8	35.8
MSA[1]	6.1	19.7	19.9	12.5	14.8	12.9	7.6	4.5	2.0	38.5
U.S.	6.4	19.9	20.6	13.0	14.1	12.3	7.6	4.3	1.9	37.4

Note: (1) Figures cover the St. Louis, MO-IL Metropolitan Statistical Area—see Appendix B for areas included
Source: U.S. Census Bureau, 2010-2014 American Community Survey 5-Year Estimates

Gender

Area	Males	Females	Males per 100 Females
City	14,082	15,018	93.8
MSA[1]	1,354,888	1,442,849	93.9
U.S.	154,515,159	159,591,925	96.8

Note: (1) Figures cover the St. Louis, MO-IL Metropolitan Statistical Area—see Appendix B for areas included
Source: U.S. Census Bureau, 2010-2014 American Community Survey 5-Year Estimates

Religious Groups by Family

Area	Catholic	Baptist	Non-Den.	Methodist[2]	Lutheran	LDS[3]	Pentecostal	Presbyterian[4]	Muslim[5]	Judaism
MSA[1]	19.8	10.0	3.8	3.4	4.1	0.6	1.2	3.0	0.4	0.7
U.S.	19.1	9.3	4.0	4.0	2.3	2.0	1.9	1.6	0.8	0.7

Note: Figures are the number of adherents as a percentage of the total population; (1) Figures cover the St. Louis, MO-IL Metropolitan Statistical Area—see Appendix B for areas included; (2) Methodist/Pietist; (3) Latter Day Saints; (4) Reformed; (5) Figures are estimates
Source: Association of Statisticians of American Religious Bodies, 2010 U.S. Religion Census: Religious Congregations & Membership Study

Religious Groups by Tradition

Area	Catholic	Evangelical Protestant	Mainline Protestant	Other Tradition	Black Protestant	Orthodox
MSA[1]	19.8	17.4	7.3	2.3	2.1	0.2
U.S.	19.1	16.2	7.3	4.3	1.6	0.3

Note: Figures are the number of adherents as a percentage of the total population; (1) Figures cover the St. Louis, MO-IL Metropolitan Statistical Area—see Appendix B for areas included
Source: Association of Statisticians of American Religious Bodies, 2010 U.S. Religion Census: Religious Congregations & Membership Study

ECONOMY

Gross Metropolitan Product

Area	2013	2014	2015	2016	Rank[2]
MSA[1]	146.0	150.2	154.6	161.1	22

Note: Figures are in billions of dollars; (1) Figures cover the St. Louis, MO-IL Metropolitan Statistical Area—see Appendix B for areas included; (2) Rank is based on 2016 data and ranges from 1 to 381
Source: The U.S. Conference of Mayors, U.S. Metro Economies: GMP and Employment 2014-2016, June 2015

Economic Growth

Area	2011-13 (%)	2014 (%)	2015 (%)	2016 (%)	Rank[2]
MSA[1]	0.9	1.2	1.5	2.2	236
U.S.	2.2	2.4	2.3	2.9	–

Note: Figures are real gross metropolitan product (GMP) growth rates and represent annual average percent change; (1) Figures cover the St. Louis, MO-IL Metropolitan Statistical Area—see Appendix B for areas included; (2) Rank is based on 2016 data and ranges from 1 to 381
Source: The U.S. Conference of Mayors, U.S. Metro Economies: GMP and Employment 2014-2016, June 2015

Metropolitan Area Exports

Area	2009	2010	2011	2012	2013	2014	Rank[2]
MSA[1]	9,026.6	11,239.4	12,307.5	14,642.3	12,393.6	10,359.8	31

Note: Figures are in millions of dollars; (1) Figures cover the St. Louis, MO-IL Metropolitan Statistical Area—see Appendix B for areas included; (2) Rank is based on 2014 data and ranges from 1 to 385
Source: U.S. Department of Commerce, International Trade Administration, Office of Trade & Industry Information, Manufacturing & Services, data extracted March 10, 2016

Building Permits

Area	Single-Family			Multi-Family			Total		
	2014	2015p	Pct. Chg.	2014	2015p	Pct. Chg.	2014	2015p	Pct. Chg.
City	126	120	-4.8	0	0	-	126	120	-4.8
MSA[1]	4,538	5,008	10.4	2,454	2,290	-6.7	6,992	7,298	4.4
U.S.	640,300	690,800	7.9	411,800	487,600	18.4	1,052,100	1,178,400	12.0

Note: (1) Figures cover the St. Louis, MO-IL Metropolitan Statistical Area—see Appendix B for areas included; Figures represent new, privately-owned housing units authorized (unadjusted data); All permit data are based on estimates with imputation; (p) preliminary data.
Source: U.S. Census Bureau, Manufacturing, Mining, and Construction Statistics, Building Permits, 2014, 2015

Bankruptcy Filings

Area	Business Filings			Nonbusiness Filings		
	2014	2015	% Chg.	2014	2015	% Chg.
Saint Clair County	19	18	-5.3	1,141	1,139	-0.2
U.S.	26,983	24,735	-8.3	909,812	819,760	-9.9

Note: Business filings include Chapter 7, Chapter 11, Chapter 12, and Chapter 13; Nonbusiness filings include Chapter 7, Chapter 11, and Chapter 13
Source: Administrative Office of the U.S. Courts, Business and Nonbusiness Bankruptcy, County Cases Commenced by Chapter of the Bankruptcy Code, During the 12- Month Period Ending December 31, 2014 and Business and Nonbusiness Bankruptcy, County Cases Commenced by Chapter of the Bankruptcy Code, During the 12- Month Period Ending December 31, 2015

Housing Vacancy Rates

Area	Gross Vacancy Rate[2] (%)			Year-Round Vacancy Rate[3] (%)			Rental Vacancy Rate[4] (%)			Homeowner Vacancy Rate[5] (%)		
	2013	2014	2015	2013	2014	2015	2013	2014	2015	2013	2014	2015
MSA[1]	15.1	12.3	10.7	14.9	12.0	10.3	13.2	10.3	9.7	3.5	2.4	3.1
U.S.	13.6	13.4	12.9	10.7	10.4	10.0	8.3	7.6	7.1	2.0	1.9	1.8

Note: (1) Figures cover the St. Louis, MO-IL Metropolitan Statistical Area—see Appendix B for areas included; (2) The percentage of the total housing inventory that is vacant; (3) The percentage of the housing inventory (excluding seasonal units) that is year-round vacant; (4) The percentage of rental inventory that is vacant for rent; (5) The percentage of homeowner inventory that is vacant for sale
Source: U.S. Census Bureau, Housing Vacancies and Homeownership Annual Statistics: 2015

INCOME

Income

Area	Per Capita ($)	Median Household ($)	Average Household ($)
City	36,234	79,795	98,266
MSA[1]	30,024	54,959	74,420
U.S.	28,555	53,482	74,596

Note: (1) Figures cover the St. Louis, MO-IL Metropolitan Statistical Area—see Appendix B for areas included
Source: U.S. Census Bureau, 2010-2014 American Community Survey 5-Year Estimates

Household Income Distribution

Area	Percent of Households Earning							
	Under $15,000	$15,000 -24,999	$25,000 -34,999	$35,000 -49,999	$50,000 -74,999	$75,000 -99,000	$100,000 -149,999	$150,000 and up
City	7.0	8.8	6.0	8.4	17.1	11.4	23.4	17.9
MSA[1]	11.7	10.2	10.0	13.6	18.3	12.8	13.7	9.6
U.S.	12.5	10.7	10.2	13.5	17.8	12.2	13.0	10.0

Note: (1) Figures cover the St. Louis, MO-IL Metropolitan Statistical Area—see Appendix B for areas included
Source: U.S. Census Bureau, 2010-2014 American Community Survey 5-Year Estimates

Poverty Rate

Area	All Ages	Under 18 Years Old	18 to 64 Years Old	65 Years and Over
City	7.9	9.7	7.6	4.9
MSA[1]	13.2	18.9	12.3	7.5
U.S.	15.6	21.9	14.6	9.4

Note: Figures are percentage of people whose income during the past 12 months was below the poverty level; (1) Figures cover the St. Louis, MO-IL Metropolitan Statistical Area—see Appendix B for areas included
Source: U.S. Census Bureau, 2010-2014 American Community Survey 5-Year Estimates

EMPLOYMENT

Labor Force and Employment

Area	Civilian Labor Force			Workers Employed		
	Dec. 2014	Dec. 2015	% Chg.	Dec. 2014	Dec. 2015	% Chg.
City	13,489	13,869	2.8	12,750	13,110	2.8
MSA[1]	1,448,218	1,479,973	2.1	1,372,069	1,416,204	3.2
U.S.	155,521,000	157,245,000	1.1	147,190,000	149,703,000	1.7

Note: Data is not seasonally adjusted and covers workers 16 years of age and older; (1) Figures cover the St. Louis, MO-IL Metropolitan Statistical Area—see Appendix B for areas included
Source: Bureau of Labor Statistics, Local Area Unemployment Statistics

Unemployment Rate

Area	2015											
	Jan.	Feb.	Mar.	Apr.	May	Jun.	Jul.	Aug.	Sep.	Oct.	Nov.	Dec.
City	6.2	5.6	5.5	4.5	4.7	5.2	5.4	5.1	5.1	5.4	6.2	5.5
MSA[1]	6.0	6.0	5.9	5.3	5.5	5.6	5.7	5.1	4.6	4.6	4.6	4.3
U.S.	6.1	5.8	5.6	5.1	5.3	5.5	5.6	5.2	4.9	4.8	4.8	4.8

Note: Data is not seasonally adjusted and covers workers 16 years of age and older; (1) Figures cover the St. Louis, MO-IL Metropolitan Statistical Area—see Appendix B for areas included
Source: Bureau of Labor Statistics, Local Area Unemployment Statistics

Employment by Occupation

Occupation Classification	City (%)	MSA[1] (%)	U.S. (%)
Management, Business, Science, and Arts	46.9	38.0	36.4
Natural Resources, Construction, and Maintenance	5.4	7.7	9.0
Production, Transportation, and Material Moving	6.1	11.2	12.1
Sales and Office	26.2	25.6	24.4
Service	15.4	17.5	18.2

Note: Figures cover employed civilians 16 years of age and older; (1) Figures cover the St. Louis, MO-IL Metropolitan Statistical Area—see Appendix B for areas included
Source: U.S. Census Bureau, 2010-2014 American Community Survey 5-Year Estimates

Employment by Industry

Sector	MSA[1]		U.S.
	Number of Employees	Percent of Total	Percent of Total
Construction, Mining, and Logging	63,100	4.6	5.0
Education and Health Services	243,900	17.9	15.7
Financial Activities	86,300	6.3	5.7
Government	163,900	12.0	15.5
Information	28,000	2.0	1.9
Leisure and Hospitality	143,100	10.5	10.4
Manufacturing	113,000	8.3	8.6
Other Services	48,100	3.5	3.9
Professional and Business Services	208,200	15.3	13.9
Retail Trade	146,100	10.7	11.3
Transportation, Warehousing, and Utilities	51,400	3.7	3.9
Wholesale Trade	63,400	4.6	4.1

Note: Figures are non-farm employment as of December 2015. Figures are not seasonally adjusted and include workers 16 years of age and older; (1) Figures cover the St. Louis, MO-IL Metropolitan Statistical Area—see Appendix B for areas included; n/a not available
Source: Bureau of Labor Statistics, Current Employment Statistics, Employment, Hours, and Earnings

Occupations with Greatest Projected Employment Growth: 2012 – 2022

Occupation[1]	2012 Employment	2022 Projected Employment	Numeric Employment Change	Percent Employment Change
Laborers and Freight, Stock, and Material Movers, Hand	127,890	148,390	20,500	16.0
Home Health Aides	40,020	56,650	16,630	41.6
Combined Food Preparation and Serving Workers, Including Fast Food	104,150	119,060	14,910	14.3
Retail Salespersons	174,910	188,030	13,120	7.5
Customer Service Representatives	111,240	123,880	12,640	11.4
Registered Nurses	113,100	124,990	11,890	10.5
Janitors and Cleaners, Except Maids and Housekeeping Cleaners	105,870	116,370	10,500	9.9
Nursing Assistants	61,430	70,820	9,390	15.3
General and Operations Managers	91,660	100,910	9,250	10.1
Construction Laborers	49,810	59,060	9,250	18.6

Note: Projections cover Illinois; (1) Sorted by numeric employment change
Source: www.projectionscentral.com, State Occupational Projections, 2012–2022 Long-Term Projections

Fastest Growing Occupations: 2012 – 2022

Occupation[1]	2012 Employment	2022 Projected Employment	Numeric Employment Change	Percent Employment Change
Home Health Aides	40,020	56,650	16,630	41.6
Skincare Specialists	1,650	2,290	640	38.2
Biomedical Engineers	540	740	200	38.0
Interpreters and Translators	1,880	2,590	710	37.6
Occupational Therapy Assistants	1,320	1,810	490	37.3
Insulation Workers, Mechanical	1,500	2,020	520	34.5
Physical Therapist Aides	2,540	3,390	850	33.5
Health Specialties Teachers, Postsecondary	3,120	4,150	1,030	32.8
Physical Therapist Assistants	3,010	3,990	980	32.5
Physical Therapists	9,320	12,340	3,020	32.4

Note: Projections cover Illinois; (1) Sorted by percent employment change and excludes occupations with numeric employment change less than 100
Source: www.projectionscentral.com, State Occupational Projections, 2012–2022 Long-Term Projections

Average Wages

Occupation	$/Hr.	Occupation	$/Hr.
Accountants and Auditors	37.50	Maids and Housekeeping Cleaners	10.36
Automotive Mechanics	20.95	Maintenance and Repair Workers	19.01
Bookkeepers	19.10	Marketing Managers	66.57
Carpenters	26.82	Nuclear Medicine Technologists	33.83
Cashiers	10.22	Nurses, Licensed Practical	20.33
Clerks, General Office	15.53	Nurses, Registered	29.20
Clerks, Receptionists/Information	12.44	Nursing Assistants	12.03
Clerks, Shipping/Receiving	16.25	Packers and Packagers, Hand	11.44
Computer Programmers	40.55	Physical Therapists	37.83
Computer Systems Analysts	44.34	Postal Service Mail Carriers	24.38
Computer User Support Specialists	25.26	Real Estate Brokers	15.47
Cooks, Restaurant	11.65	Retail Salespersons	13.21
Dentists	83.85	Sales Reps., Exc. Tech./Scientific	32.93
Electrical Engineers	48.11	Sales Reps., Tech./Scientific	35.44
Electricians	30.18	Secretaries, Exc. Legal/Med./Exec.	16.37
Financial Managers	63.93	Security Guards	13.13
First-Line Supervisors/Managers, Sales	21.20	Surgeons	n/a
Food Preparation Workers	10.12	Teacher Assistants*	12.99
General and Operations Managers	53.15	Teachers, Elementary School*	27.63
Hairdressers/Cosmetologists	12.87	Teachers, Secondary School*	27.07
Internists	127.15	Telemarketers	12.35
Janitors and Cleaners	11.59	Truck Drivers, Heavy/Tractor-Trailer	20.70
Landscaping/Groundskeeping Workers	13.20	Truck Drivers, Light/Delivery Svcs.	17.44
Lawyers	55.39	Waiters and Waitresses	9.46

Note: Wage data covers the St. Louis, MO-IL Metropolitan Statistical Area—see Appendix B for areas included; (*) Hourly wages for elementary/secondary school teachers and teacher assistants were calculated by the editors from annual wage data based on a 40 hour work week; n/a not available.
Source: Bureau of Labor Statistics, Metro Area Occupational Employment and Wage Estimates, May 2015

TAXES

State Corporate Income Tax Rates

State	Tax Rate (%)	Income Brackets ($)	Num. of Brackets	Financial Institution Tax Rate (%)[a]	Federal Income Tax Ded.
Illinois	7.75 (i)	Flat rate	1	7.75 (i)	No

Note: Tax rates as of January 1, 2016; (a) Rates listed are the corporate income tax rate applied to financial institutions or excise taxes based on income. Some states have other taxes based upon the value of deposits or shares; (i) The Illinois rate of 7.75% is the sum of a corporate income tax rate of 5.25% plus a replacement tax of 2.5%.
Source: Federation of Tax Administrators, "State Corporate Income Tax Rates, 2016"

State Individual Income Tax Rates

State	Tax Rate (%)	Income Brackets ($)	Num. of Brackets	Personal Exempt. ($)[1] Single	Personal Exempt. ($)[1] Dependents	Fed. Inc. Tax Ded.
Illinois	3.75	Flat rate	1	2,000	2,000	No

Note: Tax rates as of January 1, 2016; Local- and county-level taxes are not included; n/a not applicable; (1) Married joint filers generally receive double the single exemption
Source: Federation of Tax Administrators, "State Individual Income Tax Rates, 2016"

Various State and Local Tax Rates

State	State and Local Sales and Use (%)	State Sales and Use (%)	Gasoline[1] (¢/gal.)	Cigarette[2] ($/pack)	Spirits[3] ($/gal.)	Wine[4] ($/gal.)	Beer[5] ($/gal.)
Illinois	7.35	6.25	30.18	1.98	8.55 (f)	1.39 (l)	0.23

Note: All tax rates as of January 1, 2016; (1) The American Petroleum Institute has developed a methodology for determining the average tax rate on a gallon of fuel. Rates may include any of the following: excise taxes, environmental fees, storage tank fees, other fees or taxes, general sales tax, and local taxes. In states where gasoline is subject to the general sales tax, or where the fuel tax is based on the average sale price, the average rate determined by API is sensitive to changes in the price of gasoline. States that fully or partially apply general sales taxes to gasoline: CA, CO, GA, IL, IN, MI, NY; (2) The federal excise tax of $1.0066 per pack and local taxes are not included; (3) Rates are those applicable to off-premise sales of 40% alcohol by volume (a.b.v.) distilled spirits in 750ml containers. Local excise taxes are excluded; (4) Rates are those applicable to off-premise sales of 11% a.b.v. non-carbonated wine in 750ml containers; (5) Rates are those applicable to off-premise sales of 4.7% a.b.v. beer in 12 ounce containers; (f) Different rates are also applicable according to alcohol content, place of production, size of container, or place purchased (on- or off-premise or onboard airlines); (l) Different rates also applicable according to alcohol content, place of production, size of container, place purchased (on- or off-premise or on board airlines) or type of wine (carbonated, vermouth, etc.).
Source: Tax Foundation, 2016 Facts & Figures: How Does Your State Compare?

State Business Tax Climate Index Rankings

State	Overall Rank	Corporate Tax Rank	Individual Income Tax Rank	Sales Tax Rank	Unemployment Insurance Tax Rank	Property Tax Rank
Illinois	23	36	10	33	39	45

Note: The index is a measure of how each state's tax laws affect economic performance. The lower the rank, the more favorable a state's tax system is for business. States without a given tax are given a ranking of 1. The scores/rankings for the District of Columbia do not affect other states. The 2016 index represents the tax climate as of July 1, 2015 (the beginning of Fiscal Year 2016).
Source: Tax Foundation, State Business Tax Climate Index 2016

TRANSPORTATION

Means of Transportation to Work

Area	Car/Truck/Van: Drove Alone	Car/Truck/Van: Car-pooled	Public Transportation: Bus	Public Transportation: Subway	Public Transportation: Railroad	Bicycle	Walked	Other Means	Worked at Home
City	85.9	7.3	0.6	0.7	0.1	0.0	1.3	1.0	3.2
MSA[1]	83.0	7.7	2.1	0.4	0.1	0.3	1.8	0.9	3.9
U.S.	76.4	9.6	2.6	1.8	0.6	0.6	2.8	1.3	4.4

Note: Figures are percentages and cover workers 16 years of age and older; (1) Figures cover the St. Louis, MO-IL Metropolitan Statistical Area—see Appendix B for areas included
Source: U.S. Census Bureau, 2010-2014 American Community Survey 5-Year Estimates

Travel Time to Work

Area	Less Than 10 Minutes	10 to 19 Minutes	20 to 29 Minutes	30 to 44 Minutes	45 to 59 Minutes	60 to 89 Minutes	90 Minutes or More
City	14.6	30.5	22.1	21.2	8.0	2.1	1.4
MSA[1]	11.2	28.2	24.0	23.2	8.0	3.9	1.5
U.S.	13.3	29.6	21.0	20.2	7.7	5.7	2.6

Note: Figures are percentages and include workers 16 years old and over; (1) Figures cover the St. Louis, MO-IL Metropolitan Statistical Area—see Appendix B for areas included
Source: U.S. Census Bureau, 2010-2014 American Community Survey 5-Year Estimates

Freeway Travel Time Index

Area	1985	1990	1995	2000	2005	2010	2014
Urban Area Rank[1,2]	48	56	47	57	61	57	65
Urban Area Index[1]	1.07	1.09	1.13	1.15	1.16	1.16	1.16
Average Index[3]	1.09	1.11	1.14	1.17	1.20	1.19	1.20

Note: Freeway Travel Time Index—the ratio of travel time in the peak period to the travel time at free-flow conditions. For example, a value of 1.30 indicates a 20-minute free-flow trip takes 26 minutes in the peak (20 minutes x 1.30 = 26 minutes); (1) Covers the St. Louis MO-IL urban area; (2) Rank is based on 101 urban areas (#1 = highest travel time index); (3) Average of 101 urban areas

Source: Texas Transportation Institute, 2015 Urban Mobility Scorecard, August 2015

Freeway Commuter Stress Index

Area	1985	1990	1995	2000	2005	2010	2014
Urban Area Rank[1,2]	53	59	55	63	68	65	61
Urban Area Index[1]	1.09	1.11	1.15	1.17	1.18	1.18	1.19
Average Index[3]	1.13	1.16	1.19	1.22	1.25	1.24	1.25

Note: The Freeway Commuter Stress Index is the same as the Freeway Travel Time Index (see table above) except that it includes only the travel in the peak directions during the peak periods; the TTI includes travel in all directions during the peak period. Thus, the CSI is more indicative of the work trip experienced by each commuter on a daily basis. (1) Covers the St. Louis MO-IL urban area; (2) Rank is based on 101 urban areas (#1 = highest stress index); (3) Average of 101 urban areas

Source: Texas Transportation Institute, 2015 Urban Mobility Scorecard, August 2015

Living Environment

COST OF LIVING

Cost of Living Index

Composite Index	Groceries	Housing	Utilities	Trans-portation	Health Care	Misc. Goods/ Services
92.5	104.6	72.3	116.6	98.5	99.8	94.3

Note: The Cost of Living Index measures regional differences in the cost of consumer goods and services, excluding taxes and non-consumer expenditures, for professional and managerial households in the top income quintile. It is based on more than 50,000 prices covering almost 60 different items for which prices are collected three times a year by chambers of commerce, economic development organizations or university applied economic centers in each participating urban area. The numbers shown should be read as a percentage above or below the national average of 100. For example, a value of 115.4 in the groceries column indicates that grocery prices are 15.4% higher than the national average. Small differences in the index numbers should not be interpreted as significant; Figures cover the St. Louis MO-IL urban area.
Source: The Council for Community and Economic Research, ACCRA Cost of Living Index, 2015

Grocery Prices

Area[1]	T-Bone Steak ($/pound)	Frying Chicken ($/pound)	Whole Milk ($/half gal.)	Eggs ($/dozen)	Orange Juice ($/64 oz.)	Coffee ($/11.5 oz.)
City[2]	11.55	2.02	2.46	2.48	3.61	4.56
Avg.	10.99	1.43	2.25	2.26	3.58	4.48
Min.	7.16	0.98	1.30	1.35	2.88	2.98
Max.	14.13	2.43	3.85	4.81	6.39	7.56

Note: (1) Values for the local area are compared with the average, minimum and maximum values for all 292 areas in the Cost of Living Index; (2) Figures cover the St. Louis MO-IL urban area; **T-Bone Steak** *(price per pound);* **Frying Chicken** *(price per pound, whole fryer);* **Whole Milk** *(half gallon carton);* **Eggs** *(price per dozen, Grade A, large);* **Orange Juice** *(64 oz. Tropicana or Florida Natural);* **Coffee** *(11.5 oz. can, vacuum-packed, Maxwell House, Hills Bros, or Folgers).*
Source: The Council for Community and Economic Research, ACCRA Cost of Living Index, 2015

Housing and Utility Costs

Area[1]	New Home Price ($)	Apartment Rent ($/month)	All Electric ($/month)	Part Electric ($/month)	Other Energy ($/month)	Telephone ($/month)
City[2]	207,522	832	-	95.19	70.93	40.32
Avg.	312,874	945	179.30	95.07	72.96	28.11
Min.	178,682	479	116.28	43.14	26.46	10.01
Max.	1,472,476	3,984	504.25	189.44	421.11	43.06

Note: (1) Values for the local area are compared with the average, minimum and maximum values for all 292 areas in the Cost of Living Index; (2) Figures cover the St. Louis MO-IL urban area; **New Home Price** *(2,400 sf living area, 8,000 sf lot, in urban area with full utilities);* **Apartment Rent** *(950 sf 2 bedroom/1.5 or 2 bath, unfurnished, excluding all utilities except water);* **All Electric** *(average monthly cost for an all-electric home);* **Part Electric** *(average monthly cost for a part-electric home);* **Other Energy** *(average monthly cost for natural gas, fuel oil, coal, wood, and any other forms of energy except electricity);* **Telephone** *(price includes basic monthly rate for a private residential line plus additional local usage charges incurred by a family of four).*
Source: The Council for Community and Economic Research, ACCRA Cost of Living Index, 2015

Health Care, Transportation, and Other Costs

Area[1]	Doctor ($/visit)	Dentist ($/visit)	Optometrist ($/visit)	Gasoline ($/gallon)	Beauty Salon ($/visit)	Men's Shirt ($)
City[2]	94.95	91.43	83.95	2.31	35.77	23.78
Avg.	105.15	89.02	99.78	2.38	35.30	28.10
Min.	66.87	56.09	48.53	1.95	18.91	13.38
Max.	182.34	150.36	228.33	4.09	67.91	63.80

Note: (1) Values for the local area are compared with the average, minimum and maximum values for all 292 areas in the Cost of Living Index; (2) Figures cover the St. Louis MO-IL urban area; **Doctor** *(general practitioners routine exam of an established patient);* **Dentist** *(adult teeth cleaning and periodic oral examination);* **Optometrist** *(full vision eye exam for established adult patient);* **Gasoline** *(one gallon regular unleaded, national brand, including all taxes, cash price at self-service pump if available);* **Beauty Salon** *(woman's shampoo, trim, and blow-dry);* **Men's Shirt** *(cotton/polyester dress shirt, pinpoint weave, long sleeves).*
Source: The Council for Community and Economic Research, ACCRA Cost of Living Index, 2015

HOUSING

House Price Index (HPI)

Area	National Ranking[2]	Quarterly Change (%)	One-Year Change (%)	Five-Year Change (%)
MSA[1]	164	0.50	3.80	4.00
U.S.[3]	–	1.45	5.76	22.85

Note: The HPI is a weighted repeat sales index. It measures average price changes in repeat sales or refinancings on the same properties. This information is obtained by reviewing repeat mortgage transactions on single-family properties whose mortgages have been purchased or securitized by Fannie Mae or Freddie Mac in January 1975; (1) St. Louis Metropolitan Statistical Area—see Appendix B for areas included; (2) Rankings are based on annual percentage change for all metro areas containing at least 15,000 transactions over the last 10 years and ranges from 1 to 266; (3) figures based on a weighted average of Census Division estimates using a seasonally adjusted, purchase-only index; all figures are for the period ending December 31, 2015
Source: Federal Housing Finance Agency, House Price Index, February 25, 2016

Median Single-Family Home Prices

Area	2013	2014	2015[p]	Percent Change 2014 to 2015
MSA[1]	134.3	141.7	150.6	6.3
U.S. Average	197.4	208.9	223.9	7.2

Note: Figures are median sales prices of existing single-family homes in thousands of dollars; (p) preliminary; n/a not available; (1) St. Louis, MO-IL Metropolitan Statistical Area—see Appendix B for areas included
Source: National Association of Realtors, Median Sales Price of Existing Single-Family Homes for Metropolitan Areas, 4th Quarter 2015

Qualifying Income Based on Median Sales Price of Existing Single-Family Homes

Area	With 5% Down ($)	With 10% Down ($)	With 20% Down ($)
MSA[1]	31,963	30,281	26,916
U.S. Average	49,535	46,928	41,714

Note: Figures are preliminary; Qualifying income is based on a mortgage rate of 4.1%. Monthly principal and interest payment is limited to 25% of income; n/a not available; (1) St. Louis, MO-IL Metropolitan Statistical Area—see Appendix B for areas included
Source: National Association of Realtors, Qualifying Income Based on Median Sales Price of Existing Single-Family Homes for Metropolitan Areas, 4th Quarter 2015

Median Apartment Condo-Coop Home Prices

Area	2013	2014	2015[p]	Percent Change 2014 to 2015
MSA[1]	n/a	n/a	n/a	n/a
U.S. Average	194.9	204.3	210.7	3.1

Note: Figures are median sales prices of existing apartment condo-coop homes in thousands of dollars; (p) preliminary; n/a not available; (1) St. Louis, MO-IL Metropolitan Statistical Area—see Appendix B for areas included
Source: National Association of Realtors, Median Sales Price of Existing Apartment Condo-Coop Homes for Metropolitan Areas, 4th Quarter 2015

Gross Monthly Rent

Area	Under $200	$200 -299	$300 -499	$500 -749	$750 -999	$1,000 -1,499	$1,500 and up	Median ($)
City	0.6	1.8	2.3	14.4	30.2	29.4	21.2	1,009
MSA[1]	1.4	3.3	8.2	29.0	30.0	21.9	6.1	808
U.S.	1.5	3.2	7.4	21.0	24.1	26.9	15.9	920

Note: Figures are percentages except for Median; Gross rent is the contract rent plus the estimated average monthly cost of utilities (electricity, gas, and water and sewer) and fuels (oil, coal, kerosene, wood, etc.) if these are paid by the renter (or paid for the renter by someone else); (1) Figures cover the St. Louis, MO-IL Metropolitan Statistical Area—see Appendix B for areas included
Source: U.S. Census Bureau, 2010-2014 American Community Survey 5-Year Estimates

Homeownership Rate

Area	2008 (%)	2009 (%)	2010 (%)	2011 (%)	2012 (%)	2013 (%)	2014 (%)	2015 (%)
MSA[1]	72.2	72.5	72.2	71.1	72.0	72.7	71.1	68.7
U.S.	67.8	67.4	66.9	66.1	65.4	65.1	64.5	63.7

Note: (1) Figures cover the St. Louis, MO-IL Metropolitan Statistical Area—see Appendix B for areas included
Source: U.S. Census Bureau, Housing Vacancies and Homeownership Annual Statistics: 2015

Year Housing Structure Built

Area	2010 or Later	2000 -2009	1990 -1999	1980 -1989	1970 -1979	1960 -1969	1950 -1959	1940 -1949	Before 1940	Median Year
City	2.4	26.0	26.7	14.4	9.6	7.8	7.0	1.9	4.2	1992
MSA[1]	0.8	12.2	12.4	11.3	13.5	12.8	13.8	6.5	16.7	1970
U.S.	1.0	14.9	13.9	13.8	15.8	11.0	10.8	5.4	13.3	1976

Note: Figures are percentages except for Median Year; (1) Figures cover the St. Louis, MO-IL Metropolitan Statistical Area—see Appendix B for areas included
Source: U.S. Census Bureau, 2010-2014 American Community Survey 5-Year Estimates

HEALTH

Health Risk Data

Category	MSA[1] (%)	U.S. (%)
Adults aged 18–64 who have any kind of health care coverage	83.4	79.6
Adults who reported being in good or excellent health	83.6	83.1
Adults who are current smokers	20.1	19.6
Adults who are heavy drinkers[2]	6.9	6.1
Adults who are binge drinkers[3]	22.1	16.9
Adults who are overweight (BMI 25.0 - 29.9)	36.5	35.8
Adults who are obese (BMI 30.0 - 99.8)	31.1	27.6
Adults who participated in any physical activities in the past month	75.6	77.1
Adults 50+ who have ever had a sigmoidoscopy or colonoscopy	69.9	67.3
Women aged 40+ who have had a mammogram within the past two years	79.4	74.0
Men aged 40+ who have had a PSA test within the past two years	52.8	45.2
Adults aged 65+ who have had flu shot within the past year	63.6	60.1
Adults who always wear a seatbelt	90.8	93.8

Note: Data as of 2012 unless otherwise noted; (1) Figures cover the St. Louis, MO-IL Metropolitan Statistical Area—see Appendix B for areas included; (2) Heavy drinkers are classified as males having more than two drinks per day or females having more than one drink per day; (3) Binge drinkers are classified as males having five or more drinks on one occasion or females having four or more drinks on one occasion
Source: Centers for Disease Control and Prevention, Behaviorial Risk Factor Surveillance System, SMART: Selected Metropolitan/Micropolitan Area Risk Trends, 2012 (Note: the CDC has discontinued this dataset but will be releasing a replacement in mid-2016)

Chronic Health Indicators

Category	MSA[1] (%)	U.S. (%)
Adults who have ever been told they had a heart attack	5.4	4.5
Adults who have ever been told they had a stroke	3.6	2.9
Adults who have been told they currently have asthma	10.2	8.9
Adults who have ever been told they have arthritis	27.0	25.7
Adults who have ever been told they have diabetes[2]	10.6	9.7
Adults who have ever been told they had skin cancer	5.4	5.7
Adults who have ever been told they had any other types of cancer	7.0	6.5
Adults who have ever been told they have COPD	5.9	6.2
Adults who have ever been told they have kidney disease	2.9	2.5
Adults who have ever been told they have a form of depression	16.9	18.0

Note: Data as of 2012 unless otherwise noted; (1) Figures cover the St. Louis, MO-IL Metropolitan Statistical Area—see Appendix B for areas included; (2) Figures do not include pregnancy-related, borderline, or pre-diabetes
Source: Centers for Disease Control and Prevention, Behaviorial Risk Factor Surveillance System, SMART: Selected Metropolitan/Micropolitan Area Risk Trends, 2012 (Note: the CDC has discontinued this dataset but will be releasing a replacement in mid-2016)

Mortality Rates for the Top 10 Causes of Death in the U.S.

ICD-10[a] Sub-Chapter	ICD-10[a] Code	Age-Adjusted Mortality Rate[1] per 100,000 population	
		County[2]	U.S.
Malignant neoplasms	C00-C97	188.8	163.6
Ischaemic heart diseases	I20-I25	114.8	102.2
Other forms of heart disease	I30-I51	53.2	50.1
Chronic lower respiratory diseases	J40-J47	51.9	41.4
Organic, including symptomatic, mental disorders	F01-F09	43.7	38.5
Cerebrovascular diseases	I60-I69	42.3	36.5
Other external causes of accidental injury	W00-X59	36.7	27.5
Other degenerative diseases of the nervous system	G30-G31	27.8	26.3
Diabetes mellitus	E10-E14	34.9	21.1
Hypertensive diseases	I10-I15	23.7	19.7

Note: (a) ICD-10 = International Classification of Diseases 10th Revision; (1) Mortality rates are a three year average covering 2012-2014; (2) Figures cover St. Clair County.
Source: Centers for Disease Control and Prevention, National Center for Health Statistics. Underlying Cause of Death 1999-2014 on CDC WONDER Online Database, released 2015.

Mortality Rates for Selected Causes of Death

ICD-10[a] Sub-Chapter	ICD-10[a] Code	Age-Adjusted Mortality Rate[1] per 100,000 population	
		County[2]	U.S.
Assault	X85-Y09	13.9	5.1
Diseases of the liver	K70-K76	9.5	13.5
Human immunodeficiency virus (HIV) disease	B20-B24	3.5	2.1
Influenza and pneumonia	J09-J18	16.3	15.2
Intentional self-harm	X60-X84	10.5	12.7
Malnutrition	E40-E46	Suppressed	0.9
Obesity and other hyperalimentation	E65-E68	Unreliable	1.9
Renal failure	N17-N19	18.0	13.0
Transport accidents	V01-V99	15.7	11.6
Viral hepatitis	B15-B19	2.2	2.1

Note: (a) ICD-10 = International Classification of Diseases 10th Revision; (1) Mortality rates are a three year average covering 2012-2014; (2) Figures cover St. Clair County; Data are Suppressed when the data meet the criteria for confidentiality constraints; Mortality rates are flagged as Unreliable when the rate would be calculated with a numerator of 20 or less.
Source: Centers for Disease Control and Prevention, National Center for Health Statistics. Underlying Cause of Death 1999-2014 on CDC WONDER Online Database, released 2015.

Health Insurance Coverage

Area	With Health Insurance	With Private Health Insurance	With Public Health Insurance	Without Health Insurance	Population Under Age 18 Without Health Insurance
City	94.6	81.8	24.2	5.4	2.9
MSA[1]	89.6	72.6	28.0	10.4	4.4
U.S.	85.8	65.8	31.1	14.2	7.1

Note: Figures are percentages that cover the civilian noninstitutionalized population; (1) Figures cover the St. Louis, MO-IL Metropolitan Statistical Area—see Appendix B for areas included
Source: U.S. Census Bureau, 2010-2014 American Community Survey 5-Year Estimates

Number of Medical Professionals

Area	MDs[3]	DOs[3,4]	Dentists	Podiatrists	Chiropractors	Optometrists
County[1] (number)	427	43	183	15	117	48
County[1] (rate[2])	159.9	16.1	68.9	5.6	44.0	18.1
U.S. (rate[2])	272.5	20.9	64.7	5.8	25.9	15.2

Note: Data as of 2014 unless noted; (1) Data covers St. Clair County; (2) Rate per 100,000 population; (3) Data as of 2013 and includes all active, non-federal physicians; (4) Doctor of Osteopathic Medicine
Source: U.S. Department of Health and Human Services, Health Resources and Services Administration, Bureau of Health Professions, Area Resource File (ARF) 2014-2015

Best Hospitals

According to *U.S. News,* the St. Louis, MO-IL metro area is home to one of the best hospitals in the U.S.: **Barnes-Jewish Hospital/Washington University** (Honor Roll/14 specialties). The hospital listed was nationally ranked in at least one adult specialty. Only 137 hospitals nationwide were nationally ranked in one or more specialties. Fifteen hospitals in the U.S. made the Honor Roll with high scores in at least six specialties. *U.S. News Online, "America's Best Children's Hospitals 2015-16"*

According to *U.S. News,* the St. Louis, MO-IL metro area is home to three of the best children's hospitals in the U.S.: **SSM Cardinal Glennon Children's Medical Center** (2 specialties); **St. Louis Children's Hospital-Washington University** (10 specialties); **St. Louis Children's-Washington University-Shriners Hospital** (10 specialties). The hospitals listed were highly ranked in at least one pediatric specialty. Eighty-three children's hospitals in the U.S. were nationally ranked in at least one specialty. Twelve children's hospitals in the U.S. made the Honor Roll with high scores in at least three specialties. *U.S. News Online, "America's Best Children's Hospitals 2015-16"*

EDUCATION

Public School District Statistics

District Name	Schls	Pupils	Pupil/ Teacher Ratio	Minority Pupils[1] (%)	Free Lunch Eligible[2] (%)	IEP[3] (%)
Central SD 104	2	585	13.9	48.2	51.2	17.8
O'Fallon CCSD 90	7	3,484	19.8	31.7	17.7	15.1
O'Fallon Twp HSD 203	1	2,484	19.3	32.8	20.5	12.7

Note: Table includes school districts with 100 or more students; (1) Percentage of students that are not non-Hispanic white; (2) Percentage of students that are eligible for the free lunch program; (3) Percentage of students that have an Individualized Education Program.
Source: U.S. Department of Education, National Center for Education Statistics, Common Core of Data, Local Education Agency (School District) Universe Survey: School Year 2013-2014; U.S. Department of Education, National Center for Education Statistics, Common Core of Data, Public Elementary/Secondary School Universe Survey: School Year 2013-2014

Highest Level of Education

Area	Less than H.S.	H.S. Diploma	Some College, No Deg.	Associate Degree	Bachelor's Degree	Master's Degree	Prof. School Degree	Doctorate Degree
City	3.8	16.3	20.8	10.3	27.6	17.9	1.8	1.4
MSA[1]	9.7	27.2	23.2	8.3	19.3	8.9	2.0	1.3
U.S.	13.7	28.0	21.2	7.9	18.3	7.8	2.0	1.3

Note: Figures cover persons age 25 and over; (1) Figures cover the St. Louis, MO-IL Metropolitan Statistical Area—see Appendix B for areas included
Source: U.S. Census Bureau, 2010-2014 American Community Survey 5-Year Estimates

Educational Attainment by Race

Area	High School Graduate or Higher (%)					Bachelor's Degree or Higher (%)				
	Total	White	Black	Asian	Hisp.[2]	Total	White	Black	Asian	Hisp.[2]
City	96.2	96.7	93.2	91.2	95.9	48.8	49.7	40.8	54.9	42.8
MSA[1]	90.3	91.9	83.5	88.2	76.8	31.5	33.6	17.3	62.8	24.9
U.S.	86.3	88.4	83.2	85.8	64.1	29.3	30.6	19.0	50.9	13.9

Note: Figures shown cover persons 25 years old and over; (1) Figures cover the St. Louis, MO-IL Metropolitan Statistical Area—see Appendix B for areas included; (2) People of Hispanic origin can be of any race
Source: U.S. Census Bureau, 2010-2014 American Community Survey 5-Year Estimates

School Enrollment by Grade and Control

Area	Preschool (%)		Kindergarten (%)		Grades 1 - 4 (%)		Grades 5 - 8 (%)		Grades 9 - 12 (%)	
	Public	Private	Public	Private	Public	Private	Public	Private	Public	Private
City	69.3	30.7	83.0	17.0	91.0	9.0	88.2	11.8	97.5	2.5
MSA[1]	53.9	46.1	81.1	18.9	83.2	16.8	83.4	16.6	85.5	14.5
U.S.	57.4	42.6	87.8	12.2	89.8	10.2	89.9	10.1	90.6	9.4

Note: Figures shown cover persons 3 years old and over; (1) Figures cover the St. Louis, MO-IL Metropolitan Statistical Area—see Appendix B for areas included
Source: U.S. Census Bureau, 2010-2014 American Community Survey 5-Year Estimates

Average Salaries of Public School Classroom Teachers

Area	2013-14 Dollars	2013-14 Rank[1]	2014-15 Dollars	2014-15 Rank[1]	Percent Change 2013-14 to 2014-15	Percent Change 2004-05 to 2014-15
Illinois	60,124	12	61,083	12	1.59	6.2
U.S. Average	56,610	–	57,379	–	1.36	20.8

Note: (1) State rank ranges from 1 to 51 where 1 indicates highest salary.
Source: National Education Association, Rankings & Estimates: Rankings of the States 2014 and Estimates of School Statistics 2015, March 2015

Higher Education

Four-Year Colleges			Two-Year Colleges					
Public	Private Non-profit	Private For-profit	Public	Private Non-profit	Private For-profit	Medical Schools[1]	Law Schools[2]	Voc/ Tech[3]
0	0	0	0	0	0	0	0	0

Note: Figures cover institutions located within the city limits and include main campuses only; (1) includes schools accredited by the Liaison Committee on Medical Education and the American Osteopathic Association's Commission on Osteopathic College Accreditation; (2) includes ABA-accredited schools, schools with provisional ABA accreditation, and state accredited schools; (3) includes all schools with programs that are less than 2 years.
Source: National Center for Education Statistics, Integrated Postsecondary Education System (IPEDS), 2014-15; Association of American Medical Colleges, Member List, March 21, 2016; American Osteopathic Association, Member List, March 21, 2016; Law School Admission Council, Official Guide to ABA-Approved Law Schools Online, March 21, 2016; Wikipedia, List of Medical Schools in the United States, March 21, 2016; Wikipedia, List of Law Schools in the United States, March 21, 2016

According to *U.S. News & World Report,* the St. Louis, MO-IL metro area is home to three of the best national universities in the U.S.: **Washington University in St. Louis** (#15 tie); **Saint Louis University** (#96 tie); **Maryville University of St. Louis** (#161 tie). The indicators used to capture academic quality fall into a number of categories: assessment by administrators at peer institutions; retention of students; faculty resources; student selectivity; financial resources; alumni giving; high school counselor ratings of colleges; and graduation rate. *U.S. News & World Report, "America's Best Colleges 2016"*

According to *U.S. News & World Report,* the St. Louis, MO-IL metro area is home to one of the best liberal arts colleges in the U.S.: **Principia College** (#127 tie). The indicators used to capture academic quality fall into a number of categories: assessment by administrators at peer institutions; retention of students; faculty resources; student selectivity; financial resources; alumni giving; high school counselor ratings of colleges; and graduation rate. *U.S. News & World Report, "America's Best Colleges 2016"*

According to *U.S. News & World Report,* the St. Louis, MO-IL metro area is home to two of the top 100 law schools in the U.S.: **Washington University in St. Louis, School of Law** (#18); **St. Louis University, School of Law** (#82 tie). The rankings are based on a weighted average of 12 measures of quality: peer assessment score; assessment score by lawyers/judges; median LSAT scores; median undergrad GPA; acceptance rate; employment rates for graduates; placement success; bar passage rate; faculty resources; expenditures per student; student/faculty ratio; and library resources. *U.S. News & World Report, "America's Best Graduate Schools, Law, 2017"*

According to *U.S. News & World Report,* the St. Louis, MO-IL metro area is home to two of the top 75 medical schools for research in the U.S.: **Washington University in St. Louis, School of Medicine** (#6); **St. Louis University, School of Medicine** (#63 tie). The rankings are based on a weighted average of 11 measures of quality: quality assessment; peer assessment score; assessment score by residency directors; research activity; total research activity; average research activity per faculty member; student selectivity; median MCAT total score; median undergraduate GPA; acceptance rate; and faculty resources. *U.S. News & World Report, "America's Best Graduate Schools, Medical, 2017"*

According to *U.S. News & World Report,* the St. Louis, MO-IL metro area is home to one of the top 75 business schools in the U.S.: **Washington University in St. Louis, Olin Business School** (#21). The rankings are based on a weighted average of the following nine measures: quality assessment; peer assessment; recruiter assessment; placement success; mean starting salary and bonus; student selectivity; mean GMAT and GRE scores; mean undergraduate GPA; and acceptance rate. *U.S. News & World Report, "America's Best Graduate Schools, Business, 2017"*

PRESIDENTIAL ELECTION

2012 Presidential Election Results

Area	Obama (%)	Romney (%)	Other (%)
St. Clair County	56.4	41.9	1.7
U.S.	51.0	47.2	1.8

Note: Results may not add to 100% due to rounding
Source: Dave Leip's Atlas of U.S. Presidential Elections

EMPLOYERS

Major Employers

Company Name	Industry
Ameren	Utilities
Anheuser-Busch	Brewery
Archdiocese of St. Louis Catholic Church	Catholic church
BJC Healthcare Hospital System	Hospital system
Boeing Defense	Contractor
Dierbergs Markets	Grocery chain
Edward Jones	Financial services
Enterprise Holdings	Car rental
Express Scripts	Pharmacy benefit manager
McDonald's	Food service
Mercy Health Hospital	Hospital system
Monsanto Biotech	Crop producer
National Geospatial-Intelligence Agency	National security
Schnuck Markets	Grocery chain
Scott Air Force	Military installation
Special School District of St. Louis Cty.	Primary/secondary education
SSM Health Care	Hospital system
St Anthony's Medical Center	Healthcare
St Louis City	Government
St Louis Community College	Higher education
St Louis County	Government
St Louis University	Higher education
USPS	Government
Wal-Mart	Retailer
Washington University	Higher education
Wells Fargo	Financial services

Note: Companies shown are located within the St. Louis, MO-IL Metropolitan Statistical Area.
Source: Hoovers.com; Wikipedia

PUBLIC SAFETY

Crime Rate

Area	All Crimes	Violent Crimes				Property Crimes		
		Murder	Rape[3]	Robbery	Aggrav. Assault	Burglary	Larceny -Theft	Motor Vehicle Theft
City	1,616.8	0.0	41.0	10.3	88.9	232.4	1,203.2	41.0
Metro[1]	2,879.0	8.8	35.8	103.4	281.8	470.4	1,765.0	213.8
U.S.	2,971.8	4.5	36.6	102.2	232.5	542.5	1,837.3	216.2

Note: Figures are crimes per 100,000 population; (1) Figures cover the St. Louis, MO-IL Metropolitan Statistical Area—see Appendix B for areas included; (3) The city and U.S. figures shown were reported using the revised Uniform Crime Reporting (UCR) definition of rape. The suburban and metro area figures shown are an aggregate total of the data submitted using both the revised and legacy UCR definitions.
Source: FBI Uniform Crime Reports, 2014

Hate Crimes

Area	Number of Quarters Reported	Number of Incidents per Bias Motivation						
		Race	Religion	Sexual Orientation	Ethnicity	Disability	Gender	Gender Identity
City	4	1	0	0	0	0	0	0
U.S.	4	2,568	1,014	1,017	648	84	33	98

Source: Federal Bureau of Investigation, Hate Crime Statistics 2014

Identity Theft Consumer Complaints

Area	Complaints	Complaints per 100,000 Population	Rank[2]
MSA[1]	19,195	684.0	1
U.S.	490,220	152.4	-

Note: (1) Figures cover the St. Louis, MO-IL Metropolitan Statistical Area—see Appendix B for areas included; (2) Rank ranges from 1 to 379 where 1 indicates greatest number of identity theft complaints per 100,000 population
Source: Federal Trade Commission, Consumer Sentinel Network Data Book for January–December 2015

Fraud and Other Consumer Complaints

Area	Complaints	Complaints per 100,000 Population	Rank[2]
MSA[1]	10,939	389.8	126
U.S.	2,593,159	806.0	-

Note: (1) Figures cover the St. Louis, MO-IL Metropolitan Statistical Area—see Appendix B for areas included; (2) Rank ranges from 1 to 379 where 1 indicates greatest number of identity theft complaints per 100,000 population
Source: Federal Trade Commission, Consumer Sentinel Network Data Book for January–December 2015

RECREATION

Culture

Dance[1]	Theatre[1]	Instrumental Music[1]	Vocal Music[1]	Series and Festivals	Museums and Art Galleries[2]	Zoos and Aquariums[3]
0	0	0	0	0	0	0

Note: (1) Professional perfoming groups; (2) Based on organizations with SIC code 8412; (3) AZA-accredited
Source: The Grey House Performing Arts Directory, 2015-16; Association of Zoos & Aquariums, AZA Member Zoos & Aquariums, March 25, 2016; www.AccuLeads.com, March 29, 2016

Professional Sports Teams

Team Name	League	Year Established
Los Angeles Rams	National Football League (NFL)	2016
Saint Louis Blues	National Hockey League (NHL)	1967
Saint Louis Cardinals	Major League Baseball (MLB)	1882

Note: Includes teams located in the St. Louis, MO-IL Metropolitan Statistical Area.
Source: Wikipedia, Major Professional Sports Teams of the United States and Canada, March 24, 2016

CLIMATE

Average and Extreme Temperatures

Temperature	Jan	Feb	Mar	Apr	May	Jun	Jul	Aug	Sep	Oct	Nov	Dec	Yr.
Extreme High (°F)	77	83	89	93	98	105	115	107	104	94	85	76	115
Average High (°F)	39	43	54	67	76	85	89	87	80	69	54	42	66
Average Temp. (°F)	30	34	44	56	66	75	79	78	70	59	45	34	56
Average Low (°F)	21	25	34	46	55	65	69	67	59	48	36	26	46
Extreme Low (°F)	-18	-10	-5	22	31	43	51	47	36	23	1	-16	-18

Note: Figures cover the years 1945-1990
Source: National Climatic Data Center, International Station Meteorological Climate Summary, 9/96

Average Precipitation/Snowfall/Humidity

Precip./Humidity	Jan	Feb	Mar	Apr	May	Jun	Jul	Aug	Sep	Oct	Nov	Dec	Yr.
Avg. Precip. (in.)	1.9	2.2	3.4	3.4	3.8	4.0	3.8	2.9	2.9	2.8	3.0	2.6	36.8
Avg. Snowfall (in.)	6	4	4	Tr	0	0	0	0	0	Tr	1	4	20
Avg. Rel. Hum. 6am (%)	80	81	80	78	81	82	84	86	87	83	81	81	82
Avg. Rel. Hum. 3pm (%)	62	59	54	49	51	51	51	52	50	50	56	63	54

Note: Figures cover the years 1945-1990; Tr = Trace amounts (<0.05 in. of rain; <0.5 in. of snow)
Source: National Climatic Data Center, International Station Meteorological Climate Summary, 9/96

Weather Conditions

Temperature			Daytime Sky			Precipitation		
10°F & below	32°F & below	90°F & above	Clear	Partly cloudy	Cloudy	0.01 inch or more precip.	0.1 inch or more snow/ice	Thunder-storms
13	100	43	97	138	130	109	14	46

Note: Figures are average number of days per year and cover the years 1945-1990
Source: National Climatic Data Center, International Station Meteorological Climate Summary, 9/96

HAZARDOUS WASTE

Superfund Sites

O'Fallon has no sites on the EPA's Superfund Final National Priorities List. There are a total of 1,323 Superfund sites on the list in the U.S. *U.S. Environmental Protection Agency, Final National Priorities List, March 18, 2016*

AIR & WATER QUALITY

Air Quality Trends: Ozone

	1990	1995	2000	2005	2010	2011	2012	2013	2014
MSA[1]	0.085	0.092	0.082	0.087	0.075	0.078	0.085	0.069	0.068

Note: (1) Data covers the St. Louis, MO-IL Metropolitan Statistical Area—see Appendix B for areas included. The values shown are the composite ozone concentration averages among trend sites based on the highest fourth daily maximum 8-hour concentration in parts per million. These trends are based on sites having an adequate record of monitoring data during the trend period. Data from exceptional events are included.
Source: U.S. Environmental Protection Agency, Air Quality Monitoring Information, "Air Quality Trends by City, 1990-2014"

Air Quality Index

Area	Percent of Days when Air Quality was...[2]					AQI Statistics[2]	
	Good	Moderate	Unhealthy for Sensitive Groups	Unhealthy	Very Unhealthy	Maximum	Median
MSA[1]	38.6	59.2	1.6	0.5	0.0	154	55

Note: (1) Data covers the St. Louis, MO-IL Metropolitan Statistical Area—see Appendix B for areas included; (2) Based on 365 days with AQI data in 2015. Air Quality Index (AQI) is an index for reporting daily air quality. EPA calculates the AQI for five major air pollutants regulated by the Clean Air Act: ground-level ozone, particle pollution (aka particulate matter), carbon monoxide, sulfur dioxide, and nitrogen dioxide. The AQI runs from 0 to 500. The higher the AQI value, the greater the level of air pollution and the greater the health concern. There are six AQI categories: "Good" AQI is between 0 and 50. Air quality is considered satisfactory; "Moderate" AQI is between 51 and 100. Air quality is acceptable; "Unhealthy for Sensitive Groups" When AQI values are between 101 and 150, members of sensitive groups may experience health effects; "Unhealthy" When AQI values are between 151 and 200 everyone may begin to experience health effects; "Very Unhealthy" AQI values between 201 and 300 trigger a health alert; "Hazardous" AQI values over 300 trigger warnings of emergency conditions (not shown).
Source: U.S. Environmental Protection Agency, Air Quality Index Report, 2015

Air Quality Index Pollutants

Area	Percent of Days when AQI Pollutant was...[2]					
	Carbon Monoxide	Nitrogen Dioxide	Ozone	Sulfur Dioxide	Particulate Matter 2.5	Particulate Matter 10
MSA[1]	0.0	2.2	18.6	0.8	75.1	3.3

Note: (1) Data covers the St. Louis, MO-IL Metropolitan Statistical Area—see Appendix B for areas included; (2) Based on 365 days with AQI data in 2015. The Air Quality Index (AQI) is an index for reporting daily air quality. EPA calculates the AQI for five major air pollutants regulated by the Clean Air Act: ground-level ozone, particle pollution (also known as particulate matter), carbon monoxide, sulfur dioxide, and nitrogen dioxide. The AQI runs from 0 to 500. The higher the AQI value, the greater the level of air pollution and the greater the health concern.
Source: U.S. Environmental Protection Agency, Air Quality Index Report, 2015

Maximum Air Pollutant Concentrations: Particulate Matter, Ozone, CO and Lead

	Particulate Matter 10 (ug/m³)	Particulate Matter 2.5 Wtd AM (ug/m³)	Particulate Matter 2.5 24-Hr (ug/m³)	Ozone (ppm)	Carbon Monoxide (ppm)	Lead (ug/m³)
MSA[1] Level	159	11.4	29	0.072	1	0.36
NAAQS[2]	150	15	35	0.075	9	0.15
Met NAAQS[2]	No	Yes	Yes	Yes	Yes	No

Note: (1) Data covers the St. Louis, MO-IL Metropolitan Statistical Area—see Appendix B for areas included; Data from exceptional events are included; (2) National Ambient Air Quality Standards; ppm = parts per million; ug/m³ = micrograms per cubic meter; n/a not available.
Concentrations: Particulate Matter 10 (coarse particulate)—highest second maximum 24-hour concentration; Particulate Matter 2.5 Wtd AM (fine particulate)—highest weighted annual mean concentration; Particulate Matter 2.5 24-Hour (fine particulate)—highest 98th percentile 24-hour concentration; Ozone—highest fourth daily maximum 8-hour concentration; Carbon Monoxide—highest second maximum non-overlapping 8-hour concentration; Lead—maximum running 3-month average
Source: U.S. Environmental Protection Agency, Air Quality Monitoring Information, "Air Quality Statistics by City, 2014"

Maximum Air Pollutant Concentrations: Nitrogen Dioxide and Sulfur Dioxide

	Nitrogen Dioxide AM (ppb)	Nitrogen Dioxide 1-Hr (ppb)	Sulfur Dioxide AM (ppb)	Sulfur Dioxide 1-Hr (ppb)	Sulfur Dioxide 24-Hr (ppb)
MSA[1] Level	14	60	n/a	41	n/a
NAAQS[2]	53	100	30	75	140
Met NAAQS[2]	Yes	Yes	n/a	Yes	n/a

Note: (1) Data covers the St. Louis, MO-IL Metropolitan Statistical Area—see Appendix B for areas included; Data from exceptional events are included; (2) National Ambient Air Quality Standards; ppm = parts per million; ug/m³ = micrograms per cubic meter; n/a not available.
Concentrations: Nitrogen Dioxide AM—highest arithmetic mean concentration; Nitrogen Dioxide 1-Hr—highest 98th percentile 1-hour daily maximum concentration; Sulfur Dioxide AM—highest annual mean concentration; Sulfur Dioxide 1-Hr—highest 99th percentile 1-hour daily maximum concentration; Sulfur Dioxide 24-Hr—highest second maximum 24-hour concentration
Source: U.S. Environmental Protection Agency, Air Quality Monitoring Information, "Air Quality Statistics by City, 2014"

Drinking Water

Water System Name	Pop. Served	Primary Water Source Type	Violations[1]	
			Health Based	Monitoring/ Reporting
O'Fallon	43,596	Purchased Surface	0	0

Note: (1) Based on violation data from January 1, 2015 to December 31, 2015 (includes unresolved violations from earlier years)
Source: U.S. Environmental Protection Agency, Office of Ground Water and Drinking Water, Safe Drinking Water Information System (based on data extracted April 29, 2016)

Plainfield, Illinois

Background

The village of Plainfield is located in northeastern Illinois, 35 miles southwest of Chicago, in Will County.

The Plainfield area was originally settled by a large community of Potawatomi. The land was later given to the United States as part of the Treaty of St. Louis in 1816. The first Europeans in Plainfield included French fur traders along with its first permanent settler, James Walker. Walker built a sawmill in the area and the settlement of Walker's Grove expanded around the mill. The oldest community in Will County, Walker's Grove thrived because of its close proximity to the DuPage River and established routes to Ottawa and Chicago. Plainfield was nicknamed the "Mother of Chicago" because Chicago depended so heavily on Plainfield for lumber, mail and supplies. The new village of Plainfield, named for its flat expanse of prairie, was constructed just north of the original Walker's Grove settlement.

Early industries in Plainfield included a cheese factory, gristmill, tile factory, wagon manufacturing facility and foundry. Plainfield grew steadily over the years, transforming from a small rural community to what is now a thriving suburb of Chicago.

One of the fastest growing communities in Illinois, Plainfield's population has boomed in the past two decades. The population increased from 4,500 in 1990 to 13,000 in 2000 to over 39,500 in 2012. Plainfield's officials estimate that the population could grow to 120,000 by 2030. This population explosion brought some growing pains, with some traffic congestion and significant amounts of new residential construction.

Despite its growth, Plainfield seeks to maintain its original small town character and preserve its natural resources. The Village has created several initiatives that address growing environmental concerns, historic preservation and development and beautification of its Riverfront area.

Plainfield Township Park District manages 78 parks, providing its residents with fishing ponds, canoe launches, nature areas, picnic sites, outdoor ice skating areas, playgrounds, athletic fields and an outdoor swimming pool. Additionally, Plainfield's Lake Renwick Preserve is a popular spot for bird watching and other outdoor activities.

Plainfield is served by the Plainfield Community Consolidated School District #202, with fourteen elementary schools, five middle schools and three high schools. Plainfield College was founded in Plainfield in 1861. It was later moved to Naperville and renamed North Central College. Local institutions of higher learning include Lewis University and Joliet Junior College, along with the many colleges and universities in the Chicago area.

Plainfield is located 30 miles from Chicago's Midway International Airport and 40 miles from O'Hare International Airport.

Plainfield's climate consists of four distinct seasons: mild springs, hot and humid summers, crisp falls, along with cold and snowy winters. Summers are prone to thunderstorms. A tornado struck Plainfield in 1990, killing 29 people, injuring hundreds and causing devastating amounts of property damage.

Rankings

Business/Finance Rankings

- The personal finance site NerdWallet analyzed 183 American metropolitan areas with populations over 250,000 and more than 15,000 businesses to rank where entrepreneurs find the most success. Criteria included area economy, annual income, housing cost, unemployment rate, and the success rate of area businesses. Chicago* ranked #71. *www.nerdwallet.com, "Best Places to Start a Business," April 27, 2015*
- Based on metro area social media reviews, the employment opinion group Glassdoor surveyed 50 of the largest U.S. metro areas and equally weighed cost of living, hiring opportunity, and job satisfaction to compose a list of "25 Best Cities for Jobs." The Chicago* metro area was ranked #28 in overall job satisfaction. *www.glassdoor.com, "Best Cities for Jobs," May 19, 2015*
- In a survey of economic confidence in the nation's 50 largest metropolitan areas conducted January–December 2014, the Chicago* metro area placed #16, according to Gallup's 2014 Economic Confidence Index. *Gallup, "San Jose and San Francisco Lead in Economic Confidence," March 19, 2015*
- The Brookings Institution ranked the 100 largest metro areas in the U.S. based on income inequality. Chicago* was ranked #20 (#1 = greatest ineqality). Criteria: the "95/20 ratio," a figure representing the income at which a household earns more than 95 percent of all other households, divided by the income at which a household earns more than only 20 percent of all other households. *Brookings Institution, "Income Inequality, 100 Largest U.S. Metro Areas, 2007-2014," January 14, 2016*
- Payscale.com ranked the 20 largest metro areas in terms of wage growth. The Chicago* metro area ranked #6. Criteria: private-sector wage growth between the 1st quarter of 2015 and the 1st quarter of 2016. *PayScale, "Wage Trends by Metro Area," 1st Quarter, 2016*
- The Chicago* metro area was identified as one of the most debt-ridden places in America by the finance site Credit.com. The metro area was ranked #10. Criteria: residents' average personal debt load and average credit scores. *Credit.com, "The Most Debt-Ridden Cities," May 1, 2014*
- Chicago* was identified as one of America's most frugal metro areas by *Coupons.com.* The city ranked #24 out of 25. Criteria: online coupon usage. *Coupons.com, "Top 25 Most Frugal Cities of 2014," May 11, 2015*
- Chicago* was identified as one of America's most frugal metro areas by *Coupons.com.* The city ranked #25 out of 25. Criteria: Grocery IQ and coupons.com mobile app usage. *Coupons.com, "Top 25 Most On-the-Go Frugal Cities of 2013," April 10, 2014*
- Chicago* was cited as one of America's top metros for new and expanded facility projects in 2015. The area ranked #1 in the large metro area category (population over 1 million). *Site Selection, "Top Metropolitans of 2015," March 2016*
- The Chicago* metro area appeared on the Milken Institute "2015 Best Performing Cities" list. Rank: #122 out of 200 large metro areas. Criteria: job growth; wage and salary growth; high-tech output growth. *Milken Institute, "Best-Performing Cities 2015," December 2015*
- *Forbes* ranked the 200 most populous metro areas to determine the nation's "Best Places for Business and Careers." The Chicago* metro area was ranked #87. Criteria: costs (business and living); job growth (past and projected); income growth; educational attainment (college and high school); projected economic growth; cultural and recreational opportunities; net migration patterns; number of highly ranked colleges. *Forbes, "The Best Places for Business and Careers 2015," July 29, 2015*

Education Rankings

- Personal finance website *WalletHub* analyzed the 150 largest U.S. metropolitan statistical areas to determine where the most educated Americans are choosing to settle. Criteria: education quality and attainment gap; education levels; percentage of workers with degrees; public school rankings; quality and size of each metro area's universities. Chicago* was ranked #40 (#1 = most educated city). *www.WalletHub.com, "2015's Most and Least Educated Cities*

Environmental Rankings

- The Chicago* metro area came in at #137 for the relative comfort of its climate on Sperling's list of "chill cities," as measured by the Sperling Heat Index. All 361 metro areas are included. Criteria included daytime high temperatures, nighttime low temperatures, dew point, and relative humidity at the high temperatures. *www.bertsperling.com, "Sperling's Chill Cities," July 18, 2013*
- Sperling's BestPlaces assessed 379 metropolitan areas of the United States for the likelihood of dangerously extreme weather events or earthquakes. In general the Southeast and South-Central regions have the highest risk of weather extremes and earthquakes, while the Pacific Northwest enjoys the lowest risk. Of the least risky metropolitan areas, the Chicago* metro area was ranked #324. *www.bestplaces.net, "Safest Places from Natural Disasters," April 2011*
- The U.S. Environmental Protection Agency (EPA) released a list of U.S. metropolitan areas with the most ENERGY STAR certified buildings in 2015. The Chicago* metro area was ranked #6 out of 25. *U.S. Environmental Protection Agency, "Top Cities With the Most ENERGY STAR Certified Buildings in 2016," March 30, 2016*
- Chicago* was highlighted as one of the 25 most ozone-polluted metro areas in the U.S. during 2011 through 2013. The area ranked #19. *American Lung Association, State of the Air 2015*

Health/Fitness Rankings

- For each of the 50 most populous metro areas in the United States, the American College of Sports Medicine's American Fitness Index evaluated infrastructure, community assets, and policies that encourage healthy and fit lifestyles, including preventive health behaviors, levels of chronic disease conditions, health care access, and community resources and policies that support physical activity. The Chicago* metro area ranked #17 for "community fitness." *www.americanfitnessindex.org, "ACSM American Fitness Index Health and Community Fitness Status of the 50 Largest Metropolitan Areas," May 2015*
- The Chicago* metro area was identified as one of the worst cities for bed bugs in America by pest control company Orkin. The area ranked #1 out of 50 based on the number of bed bug treatments Orkin performed from January to December 2015. *Orkin, "Chicago Tops Bed Bug Cities List for Fourth Year in a Row," January 13, 2016*
- Chicago* was identified as a "2016 Spring Allergy Capital." The area ranked #81 out of 100. Three groups of factors were used to identify the most severe cities for people with allergies during the spring season: annual pollen levels; medicine utilization; access to board-certified allergists. *Asthma and Allergy Foundation of America, "Spring Allergy Capitals 2016"*
- Chicago* was identified as a "2015 Asthma Capital." The area ranked #10 out of the nation's 100 largest metropolitan areas. Criteria: estimated prevalence; self-reported prevalence; crude death rate for asthma; annual pollen score; annual air quality; public smoking laws; number of board-certified asthma specialists; school inhaler access laws; rescue medication use; controller medication use; ER visits for asthma; uninsured rate; poverty rate. *Asthma and Allergy Foundation of America, "Asthma Capitals 2015"*
- The Chicago* metro area ranked #105 out of 190 in The Gallup-Healthways Well-Being Index. Criteria: purpose; social well being; financial health; community and physical health. Results are based on telephone interviews with adults, aged 18 and older, living in metropolitan areas in the 50 U.S. states and the District of Columbia. *Gallup-Healthways, "State of American Well-Being," February 23, 2016*

Real Estate Rankings

- According to Penske Truck Rental, the Chicago* metro area was named the #10 moving destination in 2015, based on one-way consumer truck rental reservations made through Penske's website and reservations call center. *blog.gopenske.com, "Penske Truck Rental's 2015 Top Moving Destinations List," February 3, 2016*

- The Chicago* metro area was identified as #9 among the ten housing markets with the highest percentage of distressed property sales, based on the findings of the housing data website RealtyTrac. Criteria: short sales; income and poverty figures; and unemployment data. *247wallst.com, "Cities Selling the Most Distressed Homes," January 23, 2014*

- Chicago* was ranked #147 out of 225 metro areas in terms of housing affordability in 2015 by the National Association of Home Builders (#1 = most affordable). Criteria: the share of homes sold in that area affordable to a family earning the local median income, based on standard mortgage underwriting criteria. *National Association of Home Builders®, NAHB-Wells Fargo Housing Opportunity Index, 4th Quarter 2015*

- The nation's largest metro areas were analyzed in terms of the percentage of households entering some stage of foreclosure in 2015. The Chicago* metro area ranked #14 out of 20 (#1 = highest foreclosure rate). *RealtyTrac, "2015 Year-End U.S. Foreclosure Market Report™," January 12, 2016*

Safety Rankings

- Chicago* was identified as one of the most disaster-proof places in the U.S. in terms of its vulnerability to natural and non-natural disasters. The city ranked #3 out of 5. Rankings are based on the U.S. Center for Disease Control's Cities Readiness Initiative (CRI), which assesses local emergency-management plans, protocols and capabilities for 72 Metropolitan Statistical Areas and four non-MSA large cities. *Forbes, "America's Most and Least Disaster-Proof Cities," December 12, 2011*

- The National Insurance Crime Bureau ranked 380 metro areas in the U.S. in terms of per capita rates of vehicle theft. The Chicago* metro area ranked #109 (#1 = highest rate). Criteria: number of vehicle theft offenses per 100,000 inhabitants in 2014. *National Insurance Crime Bureau, "Hot Spots 2014," June 24, 2015*

Seniors/Retirement Rankings

- From its Best Cities for Successful Aging indexes, the Milken Institute generated rankings for metropolitan areas, weighing data in eight categories—health care, wellness, living arrangements, transportation, financial characteristics, education and employment opportunities, community engagement, and overall livability. The Chicago* metro area was ranked #64 overall in the large metro area category. *Milken Institute, "Best Cities for Successful Aging, 2014"*

Sports/Recreation Rankings

- According to the personal finance website NerdWallet, the Chicago* metro area, at #2, is one of the nation's top dozen metro areas for sports fans. Criteria included the presence of all four major sports—MLB, NFL, NHL, and NBA, fan enthusiasm (as measured by game attendance), ticket affordability, and "sports culture," that is, number of sports bars. *www.nerdwallet.com, "Best Cities for Sports Fans," May 5, 2013*

Transportation Rankings

- Chicago* was identified as one of the most congested metro areas in the U.S. The area ranked #8 out of 10. Criteria: yearly delay per auto commuter in hours. *Texas A&M Transportation Institute, "2015 Urban Mobility Scorecard," August 2015*

- The Chicago* metro area appeared on *Forbes* list of places with the most extreme commutes. The metro area ranked #8 out of 10. Criteria: average travel time; percentage of mega commuters. Mega-commuters travel more than 90 minutes and 50 miles each way to work. *Forbes.com, "The Cities with the Most Extreme Commutes," March 5, 2013*

Miscellaneous Rankings

- The watchdog site Charity Navigator conducts an annual study of charities in the nation's major markets both to analyze statistical differences in their financial, accountability, and transparency practices and to track year-to-year variations in individual communities. The Chicago* metro area was ranked #14 among the 30 metro markets in the rating dimension of Overall Score. *www.charitynavigator.org, "Metro Market Study 2015," June 5, 2015*

- The Harris Poll's Happiness Index survey revealed that of the top ten U.S. markets, the Chicago* metro area residents ranked #8 in happiness. Criteria included strong assent to positive statements and strong disagreement with negative ones, and degree of agreement with a series of statements about respondents' personal relationships and general outlook. *www.harrisinteractive.com, "Dallas/Fort Worth Is "Happiest" City among America's Top Ten Markets," September 4, 2013*

- Energizer Personal Care, the makers of Edge® shave gel, in partnership with Sperling's BestPlaces, ranked 50 major metro areas in terms of everyday irritations. The Chicago* metro area ranked #1 the 50 metro area most iritating to guys. Criteria: high male-to-female ratio; poor sports team performance and high ticket prices; slow traffic; lack of job availability; unaffordable housing; extreme weather; lack of nightlife and fitness options. *Energizer Personal Care, "Most Irritatng Cities for Guys," August 26, 2013*

- Mars Chocolate North America, the makers of COMBOS®, in partnership with Sperling's BestPlaces, ranked 50 major metro areas in terms of their "manliness." The Chicago* metro area ranked #37. Criteria: number of professional sports teams; number of nearby NASCAR tracks and racing events; manly lifestyle; concentration of manly retail stores; manly occupations per capita; salty snack sales; "Board of Manliness" rankings. *Mars Chocolate North America, "America's Manliest Cities 2012"*

- The Chicago* metro area was selected as one of "America's Most Miserable Cities" by *Forbes.com.* The metro area ranked #4 out of 20. Criteria: violent crime; unemployment; foreclosures; income and property taxes; home prices; commute times; climate. *Forbes.com, "America's Most Miserable Cities" February 22, 2013*

- The National Alliance to End Homelessness ranked the 100 most populous metro areas with the highest rate of homelessness. The Chicago* metro area ranked #75. Criteria: number of homeless people per 10,000 population in 2011. *National Alliance to End Homelessness, The State of Homelessness in America 2012*

Plainfield is located within the Chicago-Naperville-Elgin, IL-IN-WI Metropolitan Statistical Area.

Business Environment

CITY FINANCES

City Government Finances

Component	2012 ($000)	2012 ($ per capita)
Total Revenues	42,929	1,084
Total Expenditures	36,568	923
Debt Outstanding	63,728	1,610
Cash and Securities[1]	28,186	712

Note: (1) Cash and security holdings of a government at the close of its fiscal year, including those of its dependent agencies, utilities, and liquor stores.
Source: U.S Census Bureau, State & Local Government Finances 2012

City Government Revenue by Source

Source	2012 ($000)	2012 ($ per capita)
General Revenue		
From Federal Government	0	0
From State Government	9,069	229
From Local Governments	963	24
Taxes		
Property	6,258	158
Sales and Gross Receipts	7,200	181
Personal Income	0	0
Corporate Income	0	0
Motor Vehicle License	0	0
Other Taxes	612	15
Current Charges	8,150	205
Liquor Store	0	0
Utility	7,713	194
Employee Retirement	443	11

Source: U.S Census Bureau, State & Local Government Finances 2012

City Government Expenditures by Function

Function	2012 ($000)	2012 ($ per capita)	2012 (%)
General Direct Expenditures			
Air Transportation	0	0	0.0
Corrections	0	0	0.0
Education	0	0	0.0
Employment Security Administration	0	0	0.0
Financial Administration	0	0	0.0
Fire Protection	0	0	0.0
General Public Buildings	0	0	0.0
Governmental Administration, Other	3,080	77	8.4
Health	0	0	0.0
Highways	5,653	142	15.4
Hospitals	0	0	0.0
Housing and Community Development	0	0	0.0
Interest on General Debt	2,988	75	8.1
Judicial and Legal	0	0	0.0
Libraries	0	0	0.0
Parking	0	0	0.0
Parks and Recreation	0	0	0.0
Police Protection	10,801	272	29.5
Public Welfare	0	0	0.0
Sewerage	1,785	45	4.8
Solid Waste Management	2,766	69	7.5
Veterans' Services	0	0	0.0
Liquor Store	0	0	0.0
Utility	8,678	219	23.7
Employee Retirement	377	9	1.0

Source: U.S Census Bureau, State & Local Government Finances 2012

DEMOGRAPHICS

Population Growth

Area	1990 Census	2000 Census	2010 Census	2014* Estimate	Population Growth (%) 1990-2014	Population Growth (%) 2010-2014
City	6,409	13,038	39,581	40,641	534.1	2.7
MSA[1]	8,182,076	9,098,316	9,461,105	9,516,448	16.3	0.6
U.S.	248,709,873	281,421,906	308,745,538	314,107,084	26.3	1.7

Note: (1) Figures cover the Chicago-Naperville-Elgin, IL-IN-WI Metropolitan Statistical Area—see Appendix B for areas included; (*) 2010-2014 5-year estimated population
Source: U.S. Census Bureau, 1990 Census, Census 2000, Census 2010, 2010-2014 American Community Survey 5-Year Estimates

Household Size

Area	Persons in Household (%)							Average Household Size
	One	Two	Three	Four	Five	Six	Seven or More	
City	12.3	25.2	16.5	26.1	12.6	5.3	1.7	3.38
MSA[1]	28.1	29.9	15.8	14.3	7.0	2.7	1.8	2.72
U.S.	27.5	33.5	15.8	13.1	6.0	2.3	1.4	2.64

Note: (1) Figures cover the Chicago-Naperville-Elgin, IL-IN-WI Metropolitan Statistical Area—see Appendix B for areas included
Source: U.S. Census Bureau, 2010-2014 American Community Survey 5-Year Estimates

Race

Area	White Alone[2] (%)	Black Alone[2] (%)	Asian Alone[2] (%)	AIAN[3] Alone[2] (%)	NHOPI[4] Alone[2] (%)	Other Race Alone[2] (%)	Two or More Races (%)
City	80.2	6.0	8.4	0.0	0.0	2.8	2.6
MSA[1]	66.6	17.0	6.0	0.2	0.0	7.9	2.2
U.S.	73.8	12.6	5.0	0.8	0.2	4.7	2.9

Note: (1) Figures cover the Chicago-Naperville-Elgin, IL-IN-WI Metropolitan Statistical Area—see Appendix B for areas included; (2) Alone is defined as not being in combination with one or more other races; (3) American Indian and Alaska Native; (4) Native Hawaiian and Other Pacific Islander
Source: U.S. Census Bureau, 2010-2014 American Community Survey 5-Year Estimates

Hispanic or Latino Origin

Area	Total (%)	Mexican (%)	Puerto Rican (%)	Cuban (%)	Other (%)
City	10.5	7.6	1.1	0.3	1.4
MSA[1]	21.2	16.8	2.1	0.2	2.0
U.S.	16.9	10.8	1.6	0.6	3.8

Note: Persons of Hispanic or Latino origin can be of any race; (1) Figures cover the Chicago-Naperville-Elgin, IL-IN-WI Metropolitan Statistical Area—see Appendix B for areas included
Source: U.S. Census Bureau, 2010-2014 American Community Survey 5-Year Estimates

Ancestry

Area	German	Irish	English	American	Italian	Polish	French[2]	Scottish	Dutch
City	20.4	20.6	6.3	4.0	13.0	12.4	1.6	1.3	1.7
MSA[1]	15.5	11.6	4.4	2.9	7.0	9.4	1.5	1.0	1.3
U.S.	14.9	10.8	8.0	7.1	5.5	3.0	2.7	1.7	1.4

Note: Figures are the percentage of the total population reporting a particular ancestry. The nine most commonly reported ancestries in the U.S. are shown. Figures include multiple ancestries (e.g. if a person reported being Irish and Italian, they were included in both columns); (1) Figures cover the Chicago-Naperville-Elgin, IL-IN-WI Metropolitan Statistical Area—see Appendix B for areas included; (2) Excludes Basque
Source: U.S. Census Bureau, 2010-2014 American Community Survey 5-Year Estimates

Foreign-Born Population

Area	Any Foreign Country	Asia	Mexico	Europe	Carribean	Central America[2]	South America	Africa	Canada
	Percent of Population Born in								
City	11.5	6.7	2.0	1.8	0.0	0.2	0.4	0.3	0.1
MSA[1]	17.6	4.8	7.0	3.8	0.3	0.5	0.6	0.5	0.2
U.S.	13.1	3.8	3.7	1.5	1.2	1.0	0.9	0.6	0.3

Note: (1) Figures cover the Chicago-Naperville-Elgin, IL-IN-WI Metropolitan Statistical Area—see Appendix B for areas included; (2) Excludes Mexico.
Source: U.S. Census Bureau, 2010-2014 American Community Survey 5-Year Estimates

Marital Status

Area	Never Married	Now Married[2]	Separated	Widowed	Divorced
City	26.3	61.9	0.8	3.0	8.0
MSA[1]	36.2	47.2	1.8	5.6	9.1
U.S.	32.5	48.4	2.2	5.9	10.9

Note: Figures are percentages and cover the population 15 years of age and older; (1) Figures cover the Chicago-Naperville-Elgin, IL-IN-WI Metropolitan Statistical Area—see Appendix B for areas included; (2) Excludes separated
Source: U.S. Census Bureau, 2010-2014 American Community Survey 5-Year Estimates

Disability Status

Area	All Ages	Under 18 Years Old	18 to 64 Years Old	65 Years and Over
City	4.4	1.6	3.7	31.7
MSA[1]	9.7	3.1	7.6	35.0
U.S.	12.3	4.1	10.2	36.3

Note: Figures show percent of the civilian noninstitutionalized population that reported having a disability. Disability status is determined from from six types of difficulty: vision, hearing, cognitive, ambulatory, self-care, and independent living. For children under 5 years old, hearing and vision difficulty are used to determine disability status. For children between the ages of 5 and 14, disability status is determined from hearing, vision, cognitive, ambulatory, and self-care difficulties. For people aged 15 years and older, they are considered to have a disability if they have difficulty with any one of the six difficulty types; (1) Figures cover the Chicago-Naperville-Elgin, IL-IN-WI Metropolitan Statistical Area—see Appendix B for areas included.
Source: U.S. Census Bureau, 2010-2014 American Community Survey 5-Year Estimates

Age

Area	Under Age 5	Age 5–19	Age 20–34	Age 35–44	Age 45–54	Age 55–64	Age 65–74	Age 75–84	Age 85+	Median Age
	Percent of Population									
City	7.0	29.5	14.4	19.6	15.8	7.8	3.9	1.5	0.6	34.4
MSA[1]	6.5	20.7	21.1	13.7	14.2	11.8	6.7	3.7	1.7	36.3
U.S.	6.4	19.9	20.6	13.0	14.1	12.3	7.6	4.3	1.9	37.4

Note: (1) Figures cover the Chicago-Naperville-Elgin, IL-IN-WI Metropolitan Statistical Area—see Appendix B for areas included
Source: U.S. Census Bureau, 2010-2014 American Community Survey 5-Year Estimates

Gender

Area	Males	Females	Males per 100 Females
City	20,007	20,634	97.0
MSA[1]	4,650,729	4,865,719	95.6
U.S.	154,515,159	159,591,925	96.8

Note: (1) Figures cover the Chicago-Naperville-Elgin, IL-IN-WI Metropolitan Statistical Area—see Appendix B for areas included
Source: U.S. Census Bureau, 2010-2014 American Community Survey 5-Year Estimates

Religious Groups by Family

Area	Catholic	Baptist	Non-Den.	Methodist[2]	Lutheran	LDS[3]	Pente-costal	Presby-terian[4]	Muslim[5]	Judaism
MSA[1]	34.2	3.2	4.4	1.9	3.0	0.3	1.2	1.9	3.2	0.8
U.S.	19.1	9.3	4.0	4.0	2.3	2.0	1.9	1.6	0.8	0.7

Note: Figures are the number of adherents as a percentage of the total population; (1) Figures cover the Chicago-Joliet-Naperville, IL-IN-WI Metropolitan Statistical Area—see Appendix B for areas included; (2) Methodist/Pietist; (3) Latter Day Saints; (4) Reformed; (5) Figures are estimates
Source: Association of Statisticians of American Religious Bodies, 2010 U.S. Religion Census: Religious Congregations & Membership Study

Religious Groups by Tradition

Area	Catholic	Evangelical Protestant	Mainline Protestant	Other Tradition	Black Protestant	Orthodox
MSA[1]	34.2	9.7	5.1	5.0	2.0	0.9
U.S.	19.1	16.2	7.3	4.3	1.6	0.3

Note: Figures are the number of adherents as a percentage of the total population; (1) Figures cover the Chicago-Joliet-Naperville, IL-IN-WI Metropolitan Statistical Area—see Appendix B for areas included
Source: Association of Statisticians of American Religious Bodies, 2010 U.S. Religion Census: Religious Congregations & Membership Study

ECONOMY

Gross Metropolitan Product

Area	2013	2014	2015	2016	Rank[2]
MSA[1]	590.2	611.0	630.3	658.6	3

Note: Figures are in billions of dollars; (1) Figures cover the Chicago-Naperville-Elgin, IL-IN-WI Metropolitan Statistical Area—see Appendix B for areas included; (2) Rank is based on 2016 data and ranges from 1 to 381
Source: The U.S. Conference of Mayors, U.S. Metro Economies: GMP and Employment 2014-2016, June 2015

Economic Growth

Area	2011-13 (%)	2014 (%)	2015 (%)	2016 (%)	Rank[2]
MSA[1]	1.6	1.9	1.7	2.6	159
U.S.	2.2	2.4	2.3	2.9	-

Note: Figures are real gross metropolitan product (GMP) growth rates and represent annual average percent change; (1) Figures cover the Chicago-Naperville-Elgin, IL-IN-WI Metropolitan Statistical Area—see Appendix B for areas included; (2) Rank is based on 2016 data and ranges from 1 to 381
Source: The U.S. Conference of Mayors, U.S. Metro Economies: GMP and Employment 2014-2016, June 2015

Metropolitan Area Exports

Area	2009	2010	2011	2012	2013	2014	Rank[2]
MSA[1]	28,196.6	33,671.9	39,522.4	40,567.9	44,910.6	47,340.1	6

Note: Figures are in millions of dollars; (1) Figures cover the Chicago-Naperville-Elgin, IL-IN-WI Metropolitan Statistical Area—see Appendix B for areas included; (2) Rank is based on 2014 data and ranges from 1 to 385
Source: U.S. Department of Commerce, International Trade Administration, Office of Trade & Industry Information, Manufacturing & Services, data extracted March 10, 2016

Building Permits

Area	Single-Family			Multi-Family			Total		
	2014	2015p	Pct. Chg.	2014	2015p	Pct. Chg.	2014	2015p	Pct. Chg.
City	163	139	-14.7	0	12	-	163	151	-7.4
MSA[1]	7,723	7,577	-1.9	7,956	8,160	2.6	15,679	15,737	0.4
U.S.	640,300	690,800	7.9	411,800	487,600	18.4	1,052,100	1,178,400	12.0

Note: (1) Figures cover the Chicago-Naperville-Elgin, IL-IN-WI Metropolitan Statistical Area—see Appendix B for areas included; Figures represent new, privately-owned housing units authorized (unadjusted data); All permit data are based on estimates with imputation; (p) preliminary data.
Source: U.S. Census Bureau, Manufacturing, Mining, and Construction Statistics, Building Permits, 2014, 2015

Bankruptcy Filings

Area	Business Filings 2014	Business Filings 2015	Business Filings % Chg.	Nonbusiness Filings 2014	Nonbusiness Filings 2015	Nonbusiness Filings % Chg.
Will County	93	62	-33.3	3,522	2,987	-15.2
U.S.	26,983	24,735	-8.3	909,812	819,760	-9.9

Note: Business filings include Chapter 7, Chapter 11, Chapter 12, and Chapter 13; Nonbusiness filings include Chapter 7, Chapter 11, and Chapter 13
Source: Administrative Office of the U.S. Courts, Business and Nonbusiness Bankruptcy, County Cases Commenced by Chapter of the Bankruptcy Code, During the 12- Month Period Ending December 31, 2014 and Business and Nonbusiness Bankruptcy, County Cases Commenced by Chapter of the Bankruptcy Code, During the 12- Month Period Ending December 31, 2015

Housing Vacancy Rates

Area	Gross Vacancy Rate[2] (%)			Year-Round Vacancy Rate[3] (%)			Rental Vacancy Rate[4] (%)			Homeowner Vacancy Rate[5] (%)		
	2013	2014	2015	2013	2014	2015	2013	2014	2015	2013	2014	2015
MSA[1]	10.5	10.3	9.7	10.3	10.2	9.4	10.9	9.1	7.4	2.8	2.6	2.3
U.S.	13.6	13.4	12.9	10.7	10.4	10.0	8.3	7.6	7.1	2.0	1.9	1.8

Note: (1) Figures cover the Chicago-Naperville-Elgin, IL-IN-WI Metropolitan Statistical Area—see Appendix B for areas included; (2) The percentage of the total housing inventory that is vacant; (3) The percentage of the housing inventory (excluding seasonal units) that is year-round vacant; (4) The percentage of rental inventory that is vacant for rent; (5) The percentage of homeowner inventory that is vacant for sale
Source: U.S. Census Bureau, Housing Vacancies and Homeownership Annual Statistics: 2015

INCOME

Income

Area	Per Capita ($)	Median Household ($)	Average Household ($)
City	36,007	111,536	119,533
MSA[1]	31,488	61,497	84,504
U.S.	28,555	53,482	74,596

Note: (1) Figures cover the Chicago-Naperville-Elgin, IL-IN-WI Metropolitan Statistical Area—see Appendix B for areas included
Source: U.S. Census Bureau, 2010-2014 American Community Survey 5-Year Estimates

Household Income Distribution

Area	Percent of Households Earning: Under $15,000	$15,000 -24,999	$25,000 -34,999	$35,000 -49,999	$50,000 -74,999	$75,000 -99,000	$100,000 -149,999	$150,000 and up
City	2.6	3.1	1.6	7.4	15.9	13.2	27.1	29.1
MSA[1]	11.1	9.3	8.9	12.2	17.4	13.0	15.1	13.1
U.S.	12.5	10.7	10.2	13.5	17.8	12.2	13.0	10.0

Note: (1) Figures cover the Chicago-Naperville-Elgin, IL-IN-WI Metropolitan Statistical Area—see Appendix B for areas included
Source: U.S. Census Bureau, 2010-2014 American Community Survey 5-Year Estimates

Poverty Rate

Area	All Ages	Under 18 Years Old	18 to 64 Years Old	65 Years and Over
City	4.2	6.2	3.1	4.5
MSA[1]	14.1	20.3	12.6	9.2
U.S.	15.6	21.9	14.6	9.4

Note: Figures are percentage of people whose income during the past 12 months was below the poverty level; (1) Figures cover the Chicago-Naperville-Elgin, IL-IN-WI Metropolitan Statistical Area—see Appendix B for areas included
Source: U.S. Census Bureau, 2010-2014 American Community Survey 5-Year Estimates

EMPLOYMENT

Labor Force and Employment

Area	Civilian Labor Force			Workers Employed		
	Dec. 2014	Dec. 2015	% Chg.	Dec. 2014	Dec. 2015	% Chg.
City	21,815	21,774	-0.1	20,730	20,708	-0.1
MD[1]	3,743,002	3,771,441	0.7	3,525,255	3,562,874	1.0
U.S.	155,521,000	157,245,000	1.1	147,190,000	149,703,000	1.7

Note: Data is not seasonally adjusted and covers workers 16 years of age and older; (1) Figures cover the Chicago-Naperville-Arlington Heights, IL Metropolitan Division—see Appendix B for areas included
Source: Bureau of Labor Statistics, Local Area Unemployment Statistics

Unemployment Rate

Area	2015											
	Jan.	Feb.	Mar.	Apr.	May	Jun.	Jul.	Aug.	Sep.	Oct.	Nov.	Dec.
City	6.2	5.8	5.6	5.2	5.4	5.9	5.8	5.3	4.5	4.6	4.7	4.9
MD[1]	6.9	6.5	6.0	5.7	5.9	6.1	6.2	5.6	5.1	5.3	5.4	5.5
U.S.	6.1	5.8	5.6	5.1	5.3	5.5	5.6	5.2	4.9	4.8	4.8	4.8

Note: Data is not seasonally adjusted and covers workers 16 years of age and older; (1) Figures cover the Chicago-Naperville-Arlington Heights, IL Metropolitan Division—see Appendix B for areas included
Source: Bureau of Labor Statistics, Local Area Unemployment Statistics

Employment by Occupation

Occupation Classification	City (%)	MSA[1] (%)	U.S. (%)
Management, Business, Science, and Arts	48.0	37.9	36.4
Natural Resources, Construction, and Maintenance	4.3	6.8	9.0
Production, Transportation, and Material Moving	9.1	13.2	12.1
Sales and Office	26.5	25.1	24.4
Service	12.0	17.0	18.2

Note: Figures cover employed civilians 16 years of age and older; (1) Figures cover the Chicago-Naperville-Elgin, IL-IN-WI Metropolitan Statistical Area—see Appendix B for areas included
Source: U.S. Census Bureau, 2010-2014 American Community Survey 5-Year Estimates

Employment by Industry

Sector	MD[1]		U.S.
	Number of Employees	Percent of Total	Percent of Total
Construction	123,700	3.3	4.5
Education and Health Services	580,900	15.7	15.7
Financial Activities	254,500	6.8	5.7
Government	430,400	11.6	15.5
Information	73,200	1.9	1.9
Leisure and Hospitality	359,200	9.7	10.4
Manufacturing	282,400	7.6	8.6
Mining and Logging	1,100	<0.1	0.5
Other Services	159,600	4.3	3.9
Professional and Business Services	679,200	18.3	13.9
Retail Trade	371,600	10.0	11.3
Transportation, Warehousing, and Utilities	190,000	5.1	3.9
Wholesale Trade	193,700	5.2	4.1

Note: Figures are non-farm employment as of December 2015. Figures are not seasonally adjusted and include workers 16 years of age and older; (1) Figures cover the Chicago-Naperville-Arlington Heights, IL Metropolitan Division—see Appendix B for areas included
Source: Bureau of Labor Statistics, Current Employment Statistics, Employment, Hours, and Earnings

Occupations with Greatest Projected Employment Growth: 2012 – 2022

Occupation[1]	2012 Employment	2022 Projected Employment	Numeric Employment Change	Percent Employment Change
Laborers and Freight, Stock, and Material Movers, Hand	127,890	148,390	20,500	16.0
Home Health Aides	40,020	56,650	16,630	41.6
Combined Food Preparation and Serving Workers, Including Fast Food	104,150	119,060	14,910	14.3
Retail Salespersons	174,910	188,030	13,120	7.5
Customer Service Representatives	111,240	123,880	12,640	11.4
Registered Nurses	113,100	124,990	11,890	10.5
Janitors and Cleaners, Except Maids and Housekeeping Cleaners	105,870	116,370	10,500	9.9
Nursing Assistants	61,430	70,820	9,390	15.3
General and Operations Managers	91,660	100,910	9,250	10.1
Construction Laborers	49,810	59,060	9,250	18.6

Note: Projections cover Illinois; (1) Sorted by numeric employment change
Source: www.projectionscentral.com, State Occupational Projections, 2012–2022 Long-Term Projections

Fastest Growing Occupations: 2012 – 2022

Occupation[1]	2012 Employment	2022 Projected Employment	Numeric Employment Change	Percent Employment Change
Home Health Aides	40,020	56,650	16,630	41.6
Skincare Specialists	1,650	2,290	640	38.2
Biomedical Engineers	540	740	200	38.0
Interpreters and Translators	1,880	2,590	710	37.6
Occupational Therapy Assistants	1,320	1,810	490	37.3
Insulation Workers, Mechanical	1,500	2,020	520	34.5
Physical Therapist Aides	2,540	3,390	850	33.5
Health Specialties Teachers, Postsecondary	3,120	4,150	1,030	32.8
Physical Therapist Assistants	3,010	3,990	980	32.5
Physical Therapists	9,320	12,340	3,020	32.4

Note: Projections cover Illinois; (1) Sorted by percent employment change and excludes occupations with numeric employment change less than 100
Source: www.projectionscentral.com, State Occupational Projections, 2012–2022 Long-Term Projections

Average Wages

Occupation	$/Hr.	Occupation	$/Hr.
Accountants and Auditors	35.11	Maids and Housekeeping Cleaners	12.44
Automotive Mechanics	22.85	Maintenance and Repair Workers	21.36
Bookkeepers	19.63	Marketing Managers	58.77
Carpenters	31.04	Nuclear Medicine Technologists	35.61
Cashiers	10.38	Nurses, Licensed Practical	24.67
Clerks, General Office	16.40	Nurses, Registered	35.96
Clerks, Receptionists/Information	14.47	Nursing Assistants	12.89
Clerks, Shipping/Receiving	16.37	Packers and Packagers, Hand	12.25
Computer Programmers	37.27	Physical Therapists	41.57
Computer Systems Analysts	42.42	Postal Service Mail Carriers	25.13
Computer User Support Specialists	26.66	Real Estate Brokers	38.44
Cooks, Restaurant	11.75	Retail Salespersons	13.08
Dentists	61.93	Sales Reps., Exc. Tech./Scientific	35.53
Electrical Engineers	45.45	Sales Reps., Tech./Scientific	36.28
Electricians	35.46	Secretaries, Exc. Legal/Med./Exec.	18.19
Financial Managers	63.54	Security Guards	14.91
First-Line Supervisors/Managers, Sales	22.18	Surgeons	122.87
Food Preparation Workers	10.44	Teacher Assistants*	14.05
General and Operations Managers	58.83	Teachers, Elementary School*	30.77
Hairdressers/Cosmetologists	13.34	Teachers, Secondary School*	36.04
Internists	83.00	Telemarketers	12.71
Janitors and Cleaners	14.23	Truck Drivers, Heavy/Tractor-Trailer	23.64
Landscaping/Groundskeeping Workers	14.34	Truck Drivers, Light/Delivery Svcs.	17.54
Lawyers	62.12	Waiters and Waitresses	10.57

Note: Wage data covers the Chicago-Joliet-Naperville, IL Metropolitan Division—see Appendix B for areas included; (*) Hourly wages for elementary/secondary school teachers and teacher assistants were calculated by the editors from annual wage data based on a 40 hour work week; n/a not available.
Source: Bureau of Labor Statistics, Metro Area Occupational Employment and Wage Estimates, May 2015

TAXES

State Corporate Income Tax Rates

State	Tax Rate (%)	Income Brackets ($)	Num. of Brackets	Financial Institution Tax Rate (%)[a]	Federal Income Tax Ded.
Illinois	7.75 (i)	Flat rate	1	7.75 (i)	No

Note: Tax rates as of January 1, 2016; (a) Rates listed are the corporate income tax rate applied to financial institutions or excise taxes based on income. Some states have other taxes based upon the value of deposits or shares; (i) The Illinois rate of 7.75% is the sum of a corporate income tax rate of 5.25% plus a replacement tax of 2.5%.
Source: Federation of Tax Administrators, "State Corporate Income Tax Rates, 2016"

State Individual Income Tax Rates

State	Tax Rate (%)	Income Brackets ($)	Num. of Brackets	Personal Exempt. ($)[1] Single	Personal Exempt. ($)[1] Dependents	Fed. Inc. Tax Ded.
Illinois	3.75	Flat rate	1	2,000	2,000	No

Note: Tax rates as of January 1, 2016; Local- and county-level taxes are not included; n/a not applicable; (1) Married joint filers generally receive double the single exemption
Source: Federation of Tax Administrators, "State Individual Income Tax Rates, 2016"

Various State and Local Tax Rates

State	State and Local Sales and Use (%)	State Sales and Use (%)	Gasoline[1] (¢/gal.)	Cigarette[2] ($/pack)	Spirits[3] ($/gal.)	Wine[4] ($/gal.)	Beer[5] ($/gal.)
Illinois	8.50	6.25	30.18	1.98	8.55 (f)	1.39 (l)	0.23

Note: All tax rates as of January 1, 2016; (1) The American Petroleum Institute has developed a methodology for determining the average tax rate on a gallon of fuel. Rates may include any of the following: excise taxes, environmental fees, storage tank fees, other fees or taxes, general sales tax, and local taxes. In states where gasoline is subject to the general sales tax, or where the fuel tax is based on the average sale price, the average rate determined by API is sensitive to changes in the price of gasoline. States that fully or partially apply general sales taxes to gasoline: CA, CO, GA, IL, IN, MI, NY; (2) The federal excise tax of $1.0066 per pack and local taxes are not included; (3) Rates are those applicable to off-premise sales of 40% alcohol by volume (a.b.v.) distilled spirits in 750ml containers. Local excise taxes are excluded; (4) Rates are those applicable to off-premise sales of 11% a.b.v. non-carbonated wine in 750ml containers; (5) Rates are those applicable to off-premise sales of 4.7% a.b.v. beer in 12 ounce containers; (f) Different rates are also applicable according to alcohol content, place of production, size of container, or place purchased (on- or off-premise or onboard airlines); (l) Different rates also applicable according to alcohol content, place of production, size of container, place purchased (on- or off-premise or on board airlines) or type of wine (carbonated, vermouth, etc.).
Source: Tax Foundation, 2016 Facts & Figures: How Does Your State Compare?

State Business Tax Climate Index Rankings

State	Overall Rank	Corporate Tax Rank	Individual Income Tax Rank	Sales Tax Rank	Unemployment Insurance Tax Rank	Property Tax Rank
Illinois	23	36	10	33	39	45

Note: The index is a measure of how each state's tax laws affect economic performance. The lower the rank, the more favorable a state's tax system is for business. States without a given tax are given a ranking of 1. The scores/rankings for the District of Columbia do not affect other states. The 2016 index represents the tax climate as of July 1, 2015 (the beginning of Fiscal Year 2016).
Source: Tax Foundation, State Business Tax Climate Index 2016

TRANSPORTATION

Means of Transportation to Work

Area	Car/Truck/Van		Public Transportation			Bicycle	Walked	Other Means	Worked at Home
	Drove Alone	Car-pooled	Bus	Subway	Railroad				
City	84.1	6.6	0.8	0.0	1.8	0.0	0.9	1.3	4.5
MSA[1]	70.9	8.4	4.6	3.6	3.2	0.6	3.2	1.1	4.3
U.S.	76.4	9.6	2.6	1.8	0.6	0.6	2.8	1.3	4.4

Note: Figures are percentages and cover workers 16 years of age and older; (1) Figures cover the Chicago-Naperville-Elgin, IL-IN-WI Metropolitan Statistical Area—see Appendix B for areas included
Source: U.S. Census Bureau, 2010-2014 American Community Survey 5-Year Estimates

Travel Time to Work

Area	Less Than 10 Minutes	10 to 19 Minutes	20 to 29 Minutes	30 to 44 Minutes	45 to 59 Minutes	60 to 89 Minutes	90 Minutes or More
City	5.7	19.1	17.4	19.9	17.7	14.3	6.0
MSA[1]	9.0	22.4	18.7	24.7	11.8	10.1	3.2
U.S.	13.3	29.6	21.0	20.2	7.7	5.7	2.6

Note: Figures are percentages and include workers 16 years old and over; (1) Figures cover the Chicago-Naperville-Elgin, IL-IN-WI Metropolitan Statistical Area—see Appendix B for areas included
Source: U.S. Census Bureau, 2010-2014 American Community Survey 5-Year Estimates

Freeway Travel Time Index

Area	1985	1990	1995	2000	2005	2010	2014
Urban Area Rank[1,2]	9	9	8	11	13	14	14
Urban Area Index[1]	1.17	1.20	1.24	1.27	1.29	1.28	1.31
Average Index[3]	1.09	1.11	1.14	1.17	1.20	1.19	1.20

Note: Freeway Travel Time Index—the ratio of travel time in the peak period to the travel time at free-flow conditions. For example, a value of 1.30 indicates a 20-minute free-flow trip takes 26 minutes in the peak (20 minutes x 1.30 = 26 minutes); (1) Covers the Chicago IL-IN urban area; (2) Rank is based on 101 urban areas (#1 = highest travel time index); (3) Average of 101 urban areas
Source: Texas Transportation Institute, 2015 Urban Mobility Scorecard, August 2015

Freeway Commuter Stress Index

Area	1985	1990	1995	2000	2005	2010	2014
Urban Area Rank[1,2]	19	19	19	20	18	19	19
Urban Area Index[1]	1.21	1.24	1.27	1.30	1.33	1.32	1.34
Average Index[3]	1.13	1.16	1.19	1.22	1.25	1.24	1.25

Note: The Freeway Commuter Stress Index is the same as the Freeway Travel Time Index (see table above) except that it includes only the travel in the peak directions during the peak periods; the TTI includes travel in all directions during the peak period. Thus, the CSI is more indicative of the work trip experienced by each commuter on a daily basis. (1) Covers the Chicago IL-IN urban area; (2) Rank is based on 101 urban areas (#1 = highest stress index); (3) Average of 101 urban areas

Source: Texas Transportation Institute, 2015 Urban Mobility Scorecard, August 2015

Living Environment

COST OF LIVING

Cost of Living Index

Composite Index	Groceries	Housing	Utilities	Trans-portation	Health Care	Misc. Goods/ Services
101.0	104.5	103.4	99.9	106.9	105.5	95.2

Note: The Cost of Living Index measures regional differences in the cost of consumer goods and services, excluding taxes and non-consumer expenditures, for professional and managerial households in the top income quintile. It is based on more than 50,000 prices covering almost 60 different items for which prices are collected three times a year by chambers of commerce, economic development organizations or university applied economic centers in each participating urban area. The numbers shown should be read as a percentage above or below the national average of 100. For example, a value of 115.4 in the groceries column indicates that grocery prices are 15.4% higher than the national average. Small differences in the index numbers should not be interpreted as significant; Figures cover the Joliet-Will County IL urban area.
Source: The Council for Community and Economic Research, ACCRA Cost of Living Index, 2015

Grocery Prices

Area[1]	T-Bone Steak ($/pound)	Frying Chicken ($/pound)	Whole Milk ($/half gal.)	Eggs ($/dozen)	Orange Juice ($/64 oz.)	Coffee ($/11.5 oz.)
City[2]	10.28	1.45	2.45	1.97	3.60	6.03
Avg.	10.99	1.43	2.25	2.26	3.58	4.48
Min.	7.16	0.98	1.30	1.35	2.88	2.98
Max.	14.13	2.43	3.85	4.81	6.39	7.56

Note: (1) Values for the local area are compared with the average, minimum and maximum values for all 292 areas in the Cost of Living Index; (2) Figures cover the Joliet-Will County IL urban area; **T-Bone Steak** *(price per pound);* **Frying Chicken** *(price per pound, whole fryer);* **Whole Milk** *(half gallon carton);* **Eggs** *(price per dozen, Grade A, large);* **Orange Juice** *(64 oz. Tropicana or Florida Natural);* **Coffee** *(11.5 oz. can, vacuum-packed, Maxwell House, Hills Bros, or Folgers).*
Source: The Council for Community and Economic Research, ACCRA Cost of Living Index, 2015

Housing and Utility Costs

Area[1]	New Home Price ($)	Apartment Rent ($/month)	All Electric ($/month)	Part Electric ($/month)	Other Energy ($/month)	Telephone ($/month)
City[2]	295,329	1,196	-	98.64	78.21	26.41
Avg.	312,874	945	179.30	95.07	72.96	28.11
Min.	178,682	479	116.28	43.14	26.46	10.01
Max.	1,472,476	3,984	504.25	189.44	421.11	43.06

Note: (1) Values for the local area are compared with the average, minimum and maximum values for all 292 areas in the Cost of Living Index; (2) Figures cover the Joliet-Will County IL urban area; **New Home Price** *(2,400 sf living area, 8,000 sf lot, in urban area with full utilities);* **Apartment Rent** *(950 sf 2 bedroom/1.5 or 2 bath, unfurnished, excluding all utilities except water);* **All Electric** *(average monthly cost for an all-electric home);* **Part Electric** *(average monthly cost for a part-electric home);* **Other Energy** *(average monthly cost for natural gas, fuel oil, coal, wood, and any other forms of energy except electricity);* **Telephone** *(price includes basic monthly rate for a private residential line plus additional local usage charges incurred by a family of four).*
Source: The Council for Community and Economic Research, ACCRA Cost of Living Index, 2015

Health Care, Transportation, and Other Costs

Area[1]	Doctor ($/visit)	Dentist ($/visit)	Optometrist ($/visit)	Gasoline ($/gallon)	Beauty Salon ($/visit)	Men's Shirt ($)
City[2]	131.40	84.25	109.32	2.50	36.01	22.71
Avg.	105.15	89.02	99.78	2.38	35.30	28.10
Min.	66.87	56.09	48.53	1.95	18.91	13.38
Max.	182.34	150.36	228.33	4.09	67.91	63.80

Note: (1) Values for the local area are compared with the average, minimum and maximum values for all 292 areas in the Cost of Living Index; (2) Figures cover the Joliet-Will County IL urban area; **Doctor** *(general practitioners routine exam of an established patient);* **Dentist** *(adult teeth cleaning and periodic oral examination);* **Optometrist** *(full vision eye exam for established adult patient);* **Gasoline** *(one gallon regular unleaded, national brand, including all taxes, cash price at self-service pump if available);* **Beauty Salon** *(woman's shampoo, trim, and blow-dry);* **Men's Shirt** *(cotton/polyester dress shirt, pinpoint weave, long sleeves).*
Source: The Council for Community and Economic Research, ACCRA Cost of Living Index, 2015

HOUSING

House Price Index (HPI)

Area	National Ranking[2]	Quarterly Change (%)	One-Year Change (%)	Five-Year Change (%)
MD[1]	146	0.80	4.30	4.70
U.S.[3]	–	1.45	5.76	22.85

Note: The HPI is a weighted repeat sales index. It measures average price changes in repeat sales or refinancings on the same properties. This information is obtained by reviewing repeat mortgage transactions on single-family properties whose mortgages have been purchased or securitized by Fannie Mae or Freddie Mac in January 1975; (1) Chicago-Naperville-Arlington Heights Metropolitan Division—see Appendix B for areas included; (2) Rankings are based on annual percentage change for all metro areas containing at least 15,000 transactions over the last 10 years and ranges from 1 to 266; (3) figures based on a weighted average of Census Division estimates using a seasonally adjusted, purchase-only index; all figures are for the period ending December 31, 2015

Source: Federal Housing Finance Agency, House Price Index, February 25, 2016

Median Single-Family Home Prices

Area	2013	2014	2015[p]	Percent Change 2014 to 2015
MSA[1]	191.3	205.9	218.9	6.3
U.S. Average	197.4	208.9	223.9	7.2

Note: Figures are median sales prices of existing single-family homes in thousands of dollars; (p) preliminary; n/a not available; (1) Chicago-Naperville-Elgin, IL-IN-WI Metropolitan Statistical Area—see Appendix B for areas included

Source: National Association of Realtors, Median Sales Price of Existing Single-Family Homes for Metropolitan Areas, 4th Quarter 2015

Qualifying Income Based on Median Sales Price of Existing Single-Family Homes

Area	With 5% Down ($)	With 10% Down ($)	With 20% Down ($)
MSA[1]	46,666	44,210	39,298
U.S. Average	49,535	46,928	41,714

Note: Figures are preliminary; Qualifying income is based on a mortgage rate of 4.1%. Monthly principal and interest payment is limited to 25% of income; n/a not available; (1) Chicago-Naperville-Elgin, IL-IN-WI Metropolitan Statistical Area—see Appendix B for areas included

Source: National Association of Realtors, Qualifying Income Based on Median Sales Price of Existing Single-Family Homes for Metropolitan Areas, 4th Quarter 2015

Median Apartment Condo-Coop Home Prices

Area	2013	2014	2015[p]	Percent Change 2014 to 2015
MSA[1]	145.5	163.6	178.2	8.9
U.S. Average	194.9	204.3	210.7	3.1

Note: Figures are median sales prices of existing apartment condo-coop homes in thousands of dollars; (p) preliminary; n/a not available; (1) Chicago-Naperville-Elgin, IL-IN-WI Metropolitan Statistical Area—see Appendix B for areas included

Source: National Association of Realtors, Median Sales Price of Existing Apartment Condo-Coop Homes for Metropolitan Areas, 4th Quarter 2015

Gross Monthly Rent

Area	Under $200	$200 -299	$300 -499	$500 -749	$750 -999	$1,000 -1,499	$1,500 and up	Median ($)
City	0.8	0.0	1.0	4.1	8.6	40.0	45.4	1,465
MSA[1]	1.6	2.6	4.3	14.5	29.6	30.8	16.6	979
U.S.	1.5	3.2	7.4	21.0	24.1	26.9	15.9	920

Note: Figures are percentages except for Median; Gross rent is the contract rent plus the estimated average monthly cost of utilities (electricity, gas, and water and sewer) and fuels (oil, coal, kerosene, wood, etc.) if these are paid by the renter (or paid for the renter by someone else); (1) Figures cover the Chicago-Naperville-Elgin, IL-IN-WI Metropolitan Statistical Area—see Appendix B for areas included

Source: U.S. Census Bureau, 2010-2014 American Community Survey 5-Year Estimates

Homeownership Rate

Area	2008 (%)	2009 (%)	2010 (%)	2011 (%)	2012 (%)	2013 (%)	2014 (%)	2015 (%)
MSA[1]	68.4	69.2	68.2	67.7	67.1	68.2	66.3	64.3
U.S.	67.8	67.4	66.9	66.1	65.4	65.1	64.5	63.7

Note: (1) Figures cover the Chicago-Naperville-Elgin, IL-IN-WI Metropolitan Statistical Area—see Appendix B for areas included
Source: U.S. Census Bureau, Housing Vacancies and Homeownership Annual Statistics: 2015

Year Housing Structure Built

Area	2010 or Later	2000 -2009	1990 -1999	1980 -1989	1970 -1979	1960 -1969	1950 -1959	1940 -1949	Before 1940	Median Year
City	1.4	65.7	20.2	2.9	3.7	2.1	1.8	0.4	1.9	2003
MSA[1]	0.4	12.0	10.8	8.8	14.0	11.9	13.6	6.1	22.4	1967
U.S.	1.0	14.9	13.9	13.8	15.8	11.0	10.8	5.4	13.3	1976

Note: Figures are percentages except for Median Year; (1) Figures cover the Chicago-Naperville-Elgin, IL-IN-WI Metropolitan Statistical Area—see Appendix B for areas included
Source: U.S. Census Bureau, 2010-2014 American Community Survey 5-Year Estimates

HEALTH

Health Risk Data

Category	MSA[1] (%)	U.S. (%)
Adults aged 18–64 who have any kind of health care coverage	78.8	79.6
Adults who reported being in good or excellent health	83.6	83.1
Adults who are current smokers	17.7	19.6
Adults who are heavy drinkers[2]	5.8	6.1
Adults who are binge drinkers[3]	21.1	16.9
Adults who are overweight (BMI 25.0 - 29.9)	35.7	35.8
Adults who are obese (BMI 30.0 - 99.8)	26.6	27.6
Adults who participated in any physical activities in the past month	79.1	77.1
Adults 50+ who have ever had a sigmoidoscopy or colonoscopy	61.4	67.3
Women aged 40+ who have had a mammogram within the past two years	72.2	74.0
Men aged 40+ who have had a PSA test within the past two years	41.8	45.2
Adults aged 65+ who have had flu shot within the past year	52.2	60.1
Adults who always wear a seatbelt	95.8	93.8

Note: Data as of 2012 unless otherwise noted; (1) Figures cover the Chicago-Naperville-Joliet, IL-IN-WI Metropolitan Statistical Area—see Appendix B for areas included; (2) Heavy drinkers are classified as males having more than two drinks per day or females having more than one drink per day; (3) Binge drinkers are classified as males having five or more drinks on one occasion or females having four or more drinks on one occasion
Source: Centers for Disease Control and Prevention, Behaviorial Risk Factor Surveillance System, SMART: Selected Metropolitan/Micropolitan Area Risk Trends, 2012 (Note: the CDC has discontinued this dataset but will be releasing a replacement in mid-2016)

Chronic Health Indicators

Category	MSA[1] (%)	U.S. (%)
Adults who have ever been told they had a heart attack	3.0	4.5
Adults who have ever been told they had a stroke	2.3	2.9
Adults who have been told they currently have asthma	8.0	8.9
Adults who have ever been told they have arthritis	23.1	25.7
Adults who have ever been told they have diabetes[2]	8.0	9.7
Adults who have ever been told they had skin cancer	3.5	5.7
Adults who have ever been told they had any other types of cancer	5.6	6.5
Adults who have ever been told they have COPD	5.1	6.2
Adults who have ever been told they have kidney disease	2.8	2.5
Adults who have ever been told they have a form of depression	14.0	18.0

Note: Data as of 2012 unless otherwise noted; (1) Figures cover the Chicago-Naperville-Joliet, IL-IN-WI Metropolitan Statistical Area—see Appendix B for areas included; (2) Figures do not include pregnancy-related, borderline, or pre-diabetes
Source: Centers for Disease Control and Prevention, Behaviorial Risk Factor Surveillance System, SMART: Selected Metropolitan/Micropolitan Area Risk Trends, 2012 (Note: the CDC has discontinued this dataset but will be releasing a replacement in mid-2016)

Mortality Rates for the Top 10 Causes of Death in the U.S.

ICD-10[a] Sub-Chapter	ICD-10[a] Code	Age-Adjusted Mortality Rate[1] per 100,000 population	
		County[2]	U.S.
Malignant neoplasms	C00-C97	171.6	163.6
Ischaemic heart diseases	I20-I25	99.5	102.2
Other forms of heart disease	I30-I51	52.8	50.1
Chronic lower respiratory diseases	J40-J47	36.1	41.4
Organic, including symptomatic, mental disorders	F01-F09	43.6	38.5
Cerebrovascular diseases	I60-I69	37.7	36.5
Other external causes of accidental injury	W00-X59	20.6	27.5
Other degenerative diseases of the nervous system	G30-G31	19.0	26.3
Diabetes mellitus	E10-E14	17.2	21.1
Hypertensive diseases	I10-I15	20.0	19.7

Note: (a) ICD-10 = International Classification of Diseases 10th Revision; (1) Mortality rates are a three year average covering 2012-2014; (2) Figures cover Will County.
Source: Centers for Disease Control and Prevention, National Center for Health Statistics. Underlying Cause of Death 1999-2014 on CDC WONDER Online Database, released 2015.

Mortality Rates for Selected Causes of Death

ICD-10[a] Sub-Chapter	ICD-10[a] Code	Age-Adjusted Mortality Rate[1] per 100,000 population	
		County[2]	U.S.
Assault	X85-Y09	3.6	5.1
Diseases of the liver	K70-K76	12.6	13.5
Human immunodeficiency virus (HIV) disease	B20-B24	Unreliable	2.1
Influenza and pneumonia	J09-J18	14.1	15.2
Intentional self-harm	X60-X84	9.3	12.7
Malnutrition	E40-E46	Unreliable	0.9
Obesity and other hyperalimentation	E65-E68	1.3	1.9
Renal failure	N17-N19	17.8	13.0
Transport accidents	V01-V99	8.4	11.6
Viral hepatitis	B15-B19	Unreliable	2.1

Note: (a) ICD-10 = International Classification of Diseases 10th Revision; (1) Mortality rates are a three year average covering 2012-2014; (2) Figures cover Will County; Data are Suppressed when the data meet the criteria for confidentiality constraints; Mortality rates are flagged as Unreliable when the rate would be calculated with a numerator of 20 or less.
Source: Centers for Disease Control and Prevention, National Center for Health Statistics. Underlying Cause of Death 1999-2014 on CDC WONDER Online Database, released 2015.

Health Insurance Coverage

Area	With Health Insurance	With Private Health Insurance	With Public Health Insurance	Without Health Insurance	Population Under Age 18 Without Health Insurance
City	92.8	84.7	13.0	7.2	4.7
MSA[1]	86.5	66.8	28.7	13.5	4.1
U.S.	85.8	65.8	31.1	14.2	7.1

Note: Figures are percentages that cover the civilian noninstitutionalized population; (1) Figures cover the Chicago-Naperville-Elgin, IL-IN-WI Metropolitan Statistical Area—see Appendix B for areas included
Source: U.S. Census Bureau, 2010-2014 American Community Survey 5-Year Estimates

Number of Medical Professionals

Area	MDs[3]	DOs[3,4]	Dentists	Podiatrists	Chiropractors	Optometrists
County[1] (number)	855	142	351	40	210	85
County[1] (rate[2])	125.1	20.8	51.2	5.8	30.6	12.4
U.S. (rate[2])	272.5	20.9	64.7	5.8	25.9	15.2

Note: Data as of 2014 unless noted; (1) Data covers Will County; (2) Rate per 100,000 population; (3) Data as of 2013 and includes all active, non-federal physicians; (4) Doctor of Osteopathic Medicine
Source: U.S. Department of Health and Human Services, Health Resources and Services Administration, Bureau of Health Professions, Area Resource File (ARF) 2014-2015

Best Hospitals

According to *U.S. News,* the Chicago-Naperville-Arlington Heights, IL metro area is home to 13 of the best hospitals in the U.S.: **Northwest Community Healthcare** (1 specialty); **Advocate Illinois Masonic Medical Center** (1 specialty); **Northwestern Memorial Hospital** (Honor Roll/13 specialties); **Rehabilitation Institute of Chicago** (1 specialty); **Rush University Medical Center** (7 specialties); **University of Chicago Medical Center** (4 specialties); **Alexian Brothers Medical Center** (1 specialty); **NorthShore Evanston Hospital** (1 specialty); **St. Alexius Medical Center** (1 specialty); **Loyola University Medical Center** (4 specialties); **Advocate Christ Medical Center** (3 specialties); **Advocate Lutheran General Hospital** (1 specialty); **Cadence Health-Central DuPage Hospital** (1 specialty). The hospitals listed were nationally ranked in at least one adult specialty. Only 137 hospitals nationwide were nationally ranked in one or more specialties. Fifteen hospitals in the U.S. made the Honor Roll with high scores in at least six specialties. *U.S. News Online, "America's Best Children's Hospitals 2015-16"*

According to *U.S. News,* the Chicago-Naperville-Arlington Heights, IL metro area is home to three of the best children's hospitals in the U.S.: **Ann and Robert H. Lurie Children's Hospital of Chicago** (Honor Roll/10 specialties); **University of Chicago Comer Children's Hospital** (3 specialties); **Advocate Children's Hospital** (4 specialties). The hospitals listed were highly ranked in at least one pediatric specialty. Eighty-three children's hospitals in the U.S. were nationally ranked in at least one specialty. Twelve children's hospitals in the U.S. made the Honor Roll with high scores in at least three specialties. *U.S. News Online, "America's Best Children's Hospitals 2015-16"*

EDUCATION

Public School District Statistics

District Name	Schls	Pupils	Pupil/ Teacher Ratio	Minority Pupils[1] (%)	Free Lunch Eligible[2] (%)	IEP[3] (%)
Oswego CUSD 308	23	17,644	17.9	38.8	25.0	13.1
Plainfield SD 202	30	28,559	18.1	41.3	16.5	13.6
Troy CCSD 30C	7	4,507	15.7	42.4	34.7	11.1

Note: Table includes school districts with 100 or more students; (1) Percentage of students that are not non-Hispanic white; (2) Percentage of students that are eligible for the free lunch program; (3) Percentage of students that have an Individualized Education Program.
Source: U.S. Department of Education, National Center for Education Statistics, Common Core of Data, Local Education Agency (School District) Universe Survey: School Year 2013-2014; U.S. Department of Education, National Center for Education Statistics, Common Core of Data, Public Elementary/Secondary School Universe Survey: School Year 2013-2014

Highest Level of Education

Area	Less than H.S.	H.S. Diploma	Some College, No Deg.	Associate Degree	Bachelor's Degree	Master's Degree	Prof. School Degree	Doctorate Degree
City	4.1	17.2	19.1	10.8	30.1	16.2	1.4	1.1
MSA[1]	13.1	24.8	20.2	6.9	21.5	9.8	2.5	1.3
U.S.	13.7	28.0	21.2	7.9	18.3	7.8	2.0	1.3

Note: Figures cover persons age 25 and over; (1) Figures cover the Chicago-Naperville-Elgin, IL-IN-WI Metropolitan Statistical Area—see Appendix B for areas included
Source: U.S. Census Bureau, 2010-2014 American Community Survey 5-Year Estimates

Educational Attainment by Race

Area	High School Graduate or Higher (%)					Bachelor's Degree or Higher (%)				
	Total	White	Black	Asian	Hisp.[2]	Total	White	Black	Asian	Hisp.[2]
City	95.9	97.3	94.7	87.8	84.2	48.8	49.5	52.8	58.4	27.4
MSA[1]	86.9	89.9	85.1	90.5	62.5	35.1	38.5	20.3	62.8	12.8
U.S.	86.3	88.4	83.2	85.8	64.1	29.3	30.6	19.0	50.9	13.9

Note: Figures shown cover persons 25 years old and over; (1) Figures cover the Chicago-Naperville-Elgin, IL-IN-WI Metropolitan Statistical Area—see Appendix B for areas included; (2) People of Hispanic origin can be of any race
Source: U.S. Census Bureau, 2010-2014 American Community Survey 5-Year Estimates

School Enrollment by Grade and Control

Area	Preschool (%)		Kindergarten (%)		Grades 1 - 4 (%)		Grades 5 - 8 (%)		Grades 9 - 12 (%)	
	Public	Private	Public	Private	Public	Private	Public	Private	Public	Private
City	57.8	42.2	86.4	13.6	90.9	9.1	89.2	10.8	96.6	3.4
MSA[1]	57.4	42.6	85.1	14.9	88.3	11.7	89.1	10.9	90.6	9.4
U.S.	57.4	42.6	87.8	12.2	89.8	10.2	89.9	10.1	90.6	9.4

Note: Figures shown cover persons 3 years old and over; (1) Figures cover the Chicago-Naperville-Elgin, IL-IN-WI Metropolitan Statistical Area—see Appendix B for areas included
Source: U.S. Census Bureau, 2010-2014 American Community Survey 5-Year Estimates

Average Salaries of Public School Classroom Teachers

Area	2013-14		2014-15		Percent Change 2013-14 to 2014-15	Percent Change 2004-05 to 2014-15
	Dollars	Rank[1]	Dollars	Rank[1]		
Illinois	60,124	12	61,083	12	1.59	6.2
U.S. Average	56,610	–	57,379	–	1.36	20.8

Note: (1) State rank ranges from 1 to 51 where 1 indicates highest salary.
Source: National Education Association, Rankings & Estimates: Rankings of the States 2014 and Estimates of School Statistics 2015, March 2015

Higher Education

Four-Year Colleges			Two-Year Colleges			Medical Schools[1]	Law Schools[2]	Voc/ Tech[3]
Public	Private Non-profit	Private For-profit	Public	Private Non-profit	Private For-profit			
0	0	0	0	0	0	0	0	0

Note: Figures cover institutions located within the city limits and include main campuses only; (1) includes schools accredited by the Liaison Committee on Medical Education and the American Osteopathic Association's Commission on Osteopathic College Accreditation; (2) includes ABA-accredited schools, schools with provisional ABA accreditation, and state accredited schools; (3) includes all schools with programs that are less than 2 years.
Source: National Center for Education Statistics, Integrated Postsecondary Education System (IPEDS), 2014-15; Association of American Medical Colleges, Member List, March 21, 2016; American Osteopathic Association, Member List, March 21, 2016; Law School Admission Council, Official Guide to ABA-Approved Law Schools Online, March 21, 2016; Wikipedia, List of Medical Schools in the United States, March 21, 2016; Wikipedia, List of Law Schools in the United States, March 21, 2016

According to *U.S. News & World Report,* the Chicago-Naperville-Arlington Heights, IL metro division is home to six of the best national universities in the U.S.: **University of Chicago** (#4 tie); **Northwestern University** (#12 tie); **Loyola University Chicago** (#99 tie); **Illinois Institute of Technology** (#108 tie); **DePaul University** (#123 tie); **University of Illinois–Chicago** (#129 tie). The indicators used to capture academic quality fall into a number of categories: assessment by administrators at peer institutions; retention of students; faculty resources; student selectivity; financial resources; alumni giving; high school counselor ratings of colleges; and graduation rate. *U.S. News & World Report, "America's Best Colleges 2016"*

According to *U.S. News & World Report,* the Chicago-Naperville-Arlington Heights, IL metro division is home to one of the best liberal arts colleges in the U.S.: **Wheaton College** (#57 tie). The indicators used to capture academic quality fall into a number of categories: assessment by administrators at peer institutions; retention of students; faculty resources; student selectivity; financial resources; alumni giving; high school counselor ratings of colleges; and graduation rate. *U.S. News & World Report, "America's Best Colleges 2016"*

According to *U.S. News & World Report,* the Chicago-Naperville-Arlington Heights, IL metro division is home to four of the top 100 law schools in the U.S.: **University of Chicago, Law School** (#4 tie); **Northwestern University, Pritzker School of Law** (#12); **Loyola University Chicago, School of Law** (#72 tie); **Illinois Institute of Technology, Chicago-Kent College of Law** (#86 tie). The rankings are based on a weighted average of 12 measures of quality: peer assessment score; assessment score by lawyers/judges; median LSAT scores; median undergrad GPA; acceptance rate; employment rates for graduates; placement success; bar passage rate; faculty resources; expenditures per student; student/faculty ratio; and library resources. *U.S. News & World Report, "America's Best Graduate Schools, Law, 2017"*

According to *U.S. News & World Report,* the Chicago-Naperville-Arlington Heights, IL metro division is home to three of the top 75 medical schools for research in the U.S.: **University of**

Chicago, Pritzker School of Medicine (#11 tie); **Northwestern University, Feinberg School of Medicine** (#17); **University of Illinois, College of Medicine** (#47 tie). The rankings are based on a weighted average of 11 measures of quality: quality assessment; peer assessment score; assessment score by residency directors; research activity; total research activity; average research activity per faculty member; student selectivity; median MCAT total score; median undergraduate GPA; acceptance rate; and faculty resources. *U.S. News & World Report, "America's Best Graduate Schools, Medical, 2017"*

According to *U.S. News & World Report,* the Chicago-Naperville-Arlington Heights, IL metro division is home to two of the top 75 business schools in the U.S.: **University of Chicago, Booth School of Business** (#2 tie); **Northwestern University, Kellogg School of Management** (#5 tie). The rankings are based on a weighted average of the following nine measures: quality assessment; peer assessment; recruiter assessment; placement success; mean starting salary and bonus; student selectivity; mean GMAT and GRE scores; mean undergraduate GPA; and acceptance rate. *U.S. News & World Report, "America's Best Graduate Schools, Business, 2017"*

PRESIDENTIAL ELECTION

2012 Presidential Election Results

Area	Obama (%)	Romney (%)	Other (%)
Will County	51.1	47.4	1.5
U.S.	51.0	47.2	1.8

Note: Results may not add to 100% due to rounding
Source: Dave Leip's Atlas of U.S. Presidential Elections

EMPLOYERS

Major Employers

Company Name	Industry
Abbott Laboratories	Pharmaceutical preparations
Addus HomeCare Corporation	Home health care services
Advocate Lutheran General Hospital	General medical & surgical hospitals
BMO Bankcorp	National commercial banks
City of Chicago	General government
Cook County Bureau of Health Services	Administration of public health programs, county govt
Graphic Packaging International	Folding boxboard
Loyola University Health System	General medical & surgical hospitals
Northshore University Healthsystem	General medical & surgical hospitals
Northwestern Memorial Hospital	General medical & surgical hospitals
SCC Holding Co.	Cups, plastics, except foam
Schneider Electric Holdings	Air transportation, scheduled
SOLO Cup Company	Cups, plastics, except foam
The Allstate Corporation	Fire, marine, & casualty insurance
The University of Chicago Medical Center	General medical & surgical hospitals
United Parcel Service	Mailing & messenger services
United States Steel Corporation	Steel foundries
WM Recycle America	Material recovery

Note: Companies shown are located within the Chicago-Naperville-Elgin, IL-IN-WI Metropolitan Statistical Area.
Source: Hoovers.com; Wikipedia

PUBLIC SAFETY

Crime Rate

Area	All Crimes	Violent Crimes: Murder	Violent Crimes: Rape[3]	Violent Crimes: Robbery	Violent Crimes: Aggrav. Assault	Property Crimes: Burglary	Property Crimes: Larceny -Theft	Property Crimes: Motor Vehicle Theft
City	836.6	0.0	14.2	21.3	37.9	87.7	647.0	28.4
Metro[1]	2,620.4	6.9	29.9	167.9	222.2	365.2	1,641.4	186.9
U.S.	2,971.8	4.5	36.6	102.2	232.5	542.5	1,837.3	216.2

Note: Figures are crimes per 100,000 population; (1) Figures cover the Chicago-Naperville-Arlington Heights, IL Metropolitan Division—see Appendix B for areas included; (3) The city and U.S. figures shown were reported using the revised Uniform Crime Reporting (UCR) definition of rape. The suburban and metro area figures shown are an aggregate total of the data submitted using both the revised and legacy UCR definitions.
Source: FBI Uniform Crime Reports, 2014

Hate Crimes

Area	Number of Quarters Reported	Number of Incidents per Bias Motivation							
		Race	Religion	Sexual Orientation	Ethnicity	Disability	Gender	Gender Identity
City	4	0	0	0	0	0	0	0
U.S.	4	2,568	1,014	1,017	648	84	33	98

Source: Federal Bureau of Investigation, Hate Crime Statistics 2014

Identity Theft Consumer Complaints

Area	Complaints	Complaints per 100,000 Population	Rank[2]
MSA[1]	14,252	149.2	55
U.S.	490,220	152.4	-

Note: (1) Figures cover the Chicago-Naperville-Elgin, IL-IN-WI Metropolitan Statistical Area—see Appendix B for areas included; (2) Rank ranges from 1 to 379 where 1 indicates greatest number of identity theft complaints per 100,000 population
Source: Federal Trade Commission, Consumer Sentinel Network Data Book for January–December 2015

Fraud and Other Consumer Complaints

Area	Complaints	Complaints per 100,000 Population	Rank[2]
MSA[1]	35,300	369.5	171
U.S.	2,593,159	806.0	-

Note: (1) Figures cover the Chicago-Naperville-Elgin, IL-IN-WI Metropolitan Statistical Area—see Appendix B for areas included; (2) Rank ranges from 1 to 379 where 1 indicates greatest number of identity theft complaints per 100,000 population
Source: Federal Trade Commission, Consumer Sentinel Network Data Book for January–December 2015

RECREATION

Culture

Dance[1]	Theatre[1]	Instrumental Music[1]	Vocal Music[1]	Series and Festivals	Museums and Art Galleries[2]	Zoos and Aquariums[3]
0	0	0	0	0	0	0

Note: (1) Professional perfoming groups; (2) Based on organizations with SIC code 8412; (3) AZA-accredited
Source: The Grey House Performing Arts Directory, 2015-16; Association of Zoos & Aquariums, AZA Member Zoos & Aquariums, March 25, 2016; www.AccuLeads.com, March 29, 2016

Professional Sports Teams

Team Name	League	Year Established
Chicago Bears	National Football League (NFL)	1921
Chicago Blackhawks	National Hockey League (NHL)	1926
Chicago Bulls	National Basketball Association (NBA)	1966
Chicago Cubs	Major League Baseball (MLB)	1874
Chicago Fire	Major League Soccer (MLS)	1997
Chicago White Sox	Major League Baseball (MLB)	1900

Note: Includes teams located in the Chicago-Naperville-Elgin, IL-IN-WI Metropolitan Statistical Area.
Source: Wikipedia, Major Professional Sports Teams of the United States and Canada, March 24, 2016

CLIMATE

Average and Extreme Temperatures

Temperature	Jan	Feb	Mar	Apr	May	Jun	Jul	Aug	Sep	Oct	Nov	Dec	Yr.
Extreme High (°F)	65	71	88	91	93	104	102	100	99	91	78	71	104
Average High (°F)	29	33	45	59	70	79	84	82	75	63	48	34	59
Average Temp. (°F)	21	26	37	49	59	69	73	72	65	53	40	27	49
Average Low (°F)	13	17	28	39	48	57	63	62	54	42	32	19	40
Extreme Low (°F)	-27	-17	-8	7	24	36	40	41	28	17	1	-25	-27

Note: Figures cover the years 1958-1990
Source: National Climatic Data Center, International Station Meteorological Climate Summary, 9/96

Average Precipitation/Snowfall/Humidity

Precip./Humidity	Jan	Feb	Mar	Apr	May	Jun	Jul	Aug	Sep	Oct	Nov	Dec	Yr.
Avg. Precip. (in.)	1.6	1.4	2.7	3.6	3.3	3.7	3.7	4.1	3.7	2.4	2.8	2.3	35.4
Avg. Snowfall (in.)	11	8	7	2	Tr	0	0	0	0	1	2	9	39
Avg. Rel. Hum. 6am (%)	76	77	79	77	77	78	82	85	85	82	80	80	80
Avg. Rel. Hum. 3pm (%)	65	63	59	53	51	52	54	55	55	53	61	68	57

Note: Figures cover the years 1958-1990; Tr = Trace amounts (<0.05 in. of rain; <0.5 in. of snow)
Source: National Climatic Data Center, International Station Meteorological Climate Summary, 9/96

Weather Conditions

Temperature			Daytime Sky			Precipitation		
5°F & below	32°F & below	90°F & above	Clear	Partly cloudy	Cloudy	0.01 inch or more precip.	0.1 inch or more snow/ice	Thunder-storms
21	132	17	84	135	146	125	31	38

Note: Figures are average number of days per year and cover the years 1958-1990
Source: National Climatic Data Center, International Station Meteorological Climate Summary, 9/96

HAZARDOUS WASTE

Superfund Sites

Plainfield has no sites on the EPA's Superfund Final National Priorities List. There are a total of 1,323 Superfund sites on the list in the U.S. *U.S. Environmental Protection Agency, Final National Priorities List, March 18, 2016*

AIR & WATER QUALITY

Air Quality Trends: Ozone

	1990	1995	2000	2005	2010	2011	2012	2013	2014
MSA[1]	0.074	0.093	0.072	0.084	0.070	0.072	0.082	0.066	0.067

Note: (1) Data covers the Chicago-Naperville-Elgin, IL-IN-WI Metropolitan Statistical Area—see Appendix B for areas included. The values shown are the composite ozone concentration averages among trend sites based on the highest fourth daily maximum 8-hour concentration in parts per million. These trends are based on sites having an adequate record of monitoring data during the trend period. Data from exceptional events are included.
Source: U.S. Environmental Protection Agency, Air Quality Monitoring Information, "Air Quality Trends by City, 1990-2014"

Air Quality Index

Area	Percent of Days when Air Quality was...[2]					AQI Statistics[2]	
	Good	Moderate	Unhealthy for Sensitive Groups	Unhealthy	Very Unhealthy	Maximum	Median
MSA[1]	33.2	64.4	1.9	0.5	0.0	183	55

Note: (1) Data covers the Chicago-Naperville-Elgin, IL-IN-WI Metropolitan Statistical Area—see Appendix B for areas included; (2) Based on 365 days with AQI data in 2015. Air Quality Index (AQI) is an index for reporting daily air quality. EPA calculates the AQI for five major air pollutants regulated by the Clean Air Act: ground-level ozone, particle pollution (aka particulate matter), carbon monoxide, sulfur dioxide, and nitrogen dioxide. The AQI runs from 0 to 500. The higher the AQI value, the greater the level of air pollution and the greater the health concern. There are six AQI categories: "Good" AQI is between 0 and 50. Air quality is considered satisfactory; "Moderate" AQI is between 51 and 100. Air quality is acceptable; "Unhealthy for Sensitive Groups" When AQI values are between 101 and 150, members of sensitive groups may experience health effects; "Unhealthy" When AQI values are between 151 and 200 everyone may begin to experience health effects; "Very Unhealthy" AQI values between 201 and 300 trigger a health alert; "Hazardous" AQI values over 300 trigger warnings of emergency conditions (not shown).
Source: U.S. Environmental Protection Agency, Air Quality Index Report, 2015

Air Quality Index Pollutants

Area	Percent of Days when AQI Pollutant was...[2]					
	Carbon Monoxide	Nitrogen Dioxide	Ozone	Sulfur Dioxide	Particulate Matter 2.5	Particulate Matter 10
MSA[1]	0.0	6.8	9.9	2.5	73.2	7.7

Note: (1) Data covers the Chicago-Naperville-Elgin, IL-IN-WI Metropolitan Statistical Area—see Appendix B for areas included; (2) Based on 365 days with AQI data in 2015. The Air Quality Index (AQI) is an index for reporting daily air quality. EPA calculates the AQI for five major air pollutants regulated by the Clean Air Act: ground-level ozone, particle pollution (also known as particulate matter), carbon monoxide, sulfur dioxide, and nitrogen dioxide. The AQI runs from 0 to 500. The higher the AQI value, the greater the level of air pollution and the greater the health concern.
Source: U.S. Environmental Protection Agency, Air Quality Index Report, 2015

Maximum Air Pollutant Concentrations: Particulate Matter, Ozone, CO and Lead

	Particulate Matter 10 (ug/m^3)	Particulate Matter 2.5 Wtd AM (ug/m^3)	Particulate Matter 2.5 24-Hr (ug/m^3)	Ozone (ppm)	Carbon Monoxide (ppm)	Lead (ug/m^3)
MSA[1] Level	93	11.7	27	0.076	2	0.15
NAAQS[2]	150	15	35	0.075	9	0.15
Met NAAQS[2]	Yes	Yes	Yes	No	Yes	Yes

Note: (1) Data covers the Chicago-Naperville-Elgin, IL-IN-WI Metropolitan Statistical Area—see Appendix B for areas included; Data from exceptional events are included; (2) National Ambient Air Quality Standards; ppm = parts per million; ug/m^3 = micrograms per cubic meter; n/a not available.
Concentrations: Particulate Matter 10 (coarse particulate)—highest second maximum 24-hour concentration; Particulate Matter 2.5 Wtd AM (fine particulate)—highest weighted annual mean concentration; Particulate Matter 2.5 24-Hour (fine particulate)—highest 98th percentile 24-hour concentration; Ozone—highest fourth daily maximum 8-hour concentration; Carbon Monoxide—highest second maximum non-overlapping 8-hour concentration; Lead—maximum running 3-month average
Source: U.S. Environmental Protection Agency, Air Quality Monitoring Information, "Air Quality Statistics by City, 2014"

Maximum Air Pollutant Concentrations: Nitrogen Dioxide and Sulfur Dioxide

	Nitrogen Dioxide AM (ppb)	Nitrogen Dioxide 1-Hr (ppb)	Sulfur Dioxide AM (ppb)	Sulfur Dioxide 1-Hr (ppb)	Sulfur Dioxide 24-Hr (ppb)
MSA[1] Level	21	67	n/a	53	n/a
NAAQS[2]	53	100	30	75	140
Met NAAQS[2]	Yes	Yes	n/a	Yes	n/a

Note: (1) Data covers the Chicago-Naperville-Elgin, IL-IN-WI Metropolitan Statistical Area—see Appendix B for areas included; Data from exceptional events are included; (2) National Ambient Air Quality Standards; ppm = parts per million; ug/m^3 = micrograms per cubic meter; n/a not available.
Concentrations: Nitrogen Dioxide AM—highest arithmetic mean concentration; Nitrogen Dioxide 1-Hr—highest 98th percentile 1-hour daily maximum concentration; Sulfur Dioxide AM—highest annual mean concentration; Sulfur Dioxide 1-Hr—highest 99th percentile 1-hour daily maximum concentration; Sulfur Dioxide 24-Hr—highest second maximum 24-hour concentration
Source: U.S. Environmental Protection Agency, Air Quality Monitoring Information, "Air Quality Statistics by City, 2014"

Drinking Water

Water System Name	Pop. Served	Primary Water Source Type	Violations[1]	
			Health Based	Monitoring/ Reporting
Plainfield	39,581	Purchased Surface	0	0

Note: (1) Based on violation data from January 1, 2015 to December 31, 2015 (includes unresolved violations from earlier years)
Source: U.S. Environmental Protection Agency, Office of Ground Water and Drinking Water, Safe Drinking Water Information System (based on data extracted April 29, 2016)

Wilmette, Illinois

Background

Wilmette is in New Trier Township, Cook County. It is located approximately 14 miles north of Chicago's downtown, on the western shore of Lake Michigan and covers an area of 5.5 square miles. Wilmette consistently ranks high in terms of quality of life due to its low unemployment rate, high median income, low housing vacancy rate, excellent schools, low crime, and short commute times.

Potawatomi village occupied the area that is now Wilmette, before European settlement in the area. Along came Antoine Ouilmette, a French-Canadian fur trader who married a Potawatomi woman. For his role in assisting with the signing the second Treaty of Prairie du Chien in 1829, between local Native Americans and the U.S. government, he was awarded a parcel of land in present day Wilmette, which was named for him, and Evanston. During the 1840s, the area was settled by German Catholic farmers from the area of Trier. The Chicago and Milwaukee Railroad tracks were built in 1854 and helped to facilitate the settlement of the present day North Shore. Industry expanded with the building of pickling factories, a cooperage, brick kilns, and an icehouse. By 1869 the first train station was constructed in the area by the Chicago and Milwaukee railroad. In 1899, the North Shore Line connected Chicago, the North Shore, and Milwaukee, 27 years after the incorporation of Wilmette in 1872.

Wilmette is home to the oldest surviving Bahá'í House of Worship. Constructed between 1920 and 1953, the Bahá'í House of Worship is the only such house of worship in the United States. It serves all of North America and as the administrative offices for the Bahá'í National Spiritual Assembly. Wilmette is also known for other religious architecture, such as the First Congregational Church, built in 1909 and is the oldest existing church in Wilmette in the Tudor Revival style. The Trinity United Methodist Church, built in 1928, boasts a Neo-Gothic design and features stained glass windows by Philadelphia's Willet Studios, one of the top American stained glass studios during the 1920s. A third example is St. Joseph's Church, home to Wilmette's oldest religious congregation, and built in 1939 and lauded as one of the finest examples of Art Deco architecture on Chicago's North Shore.

Wilmette's other attractions include the Wilmette Theater for film and performances, the Plaza del Lago, one of the nation's oldest shopping centers, and the Wallace Bowl, a public theatre that offers a rich schedule of performances throughout the summer.

Outdoor activities include Gillson Park, with a marina, beach access, and an off-leash area for dogs. The shores of Lake Michigan offer several other beaches, and Wilmette maintains a public swimming pool, tennis courts, and ice skating facilities. The Wilmette Golf Course is open to the public. The residents of Wilmette pride themselves for creating a sustainable environment through energy efficiency, improved storm water management, water conservation, recycling, and continued efforts in pollution reduction.

Wilmette's public schools have an excellent reputation and there are a number of district elementary, middle, and high schools. There are also several parochial schools at both elementary and secondary levels in the area as well as a Montessori school. The Wilmette Public Library provides educational support and facilities for all ages and grade levels.

Wilmette experiences a climate similar to nearby Chicago with hot, humid summers and cold winters. Its proximity to the lake can result in the lake effect, and brutally cold temperatures. Average temperatures in summer reach into the 80s with humidity, and in winter can drop into single digits. There is an average of 190 days of sun in Wilmette.

Rankings

Business/Finance Rankings

- The personal finance site NerdWallet analyzed 183 American metropolitan areas with populations over 250,000 and more than 15,000 businesses to rank where entrepreneurs find the most success. Criteria included area economy, annual income, housing cost, unemployment rate, and the success rate of area businesses. Chicago* ranked #71. *www.nerdwallet.com, "Best Places to Start a Business," April 27, 2015*
- Based on metro area social media reviews, the employment opinion group Glassdoor surveyed 50 of the largest U.S. metro areas and equally weighed cost of living, hiring opportunity, and job satisfaction to compose a list of "25 Best Cities for Jobs." The Chicago* metro area was ranked #28 in overall job satisfaction. *www.glassdoor.com, "Best Cities for Jobs," May 19, 2015*
- In a survey of economic confidence in the nation's 50 largest metropolitan areas conducted January–December 2014, the Chicago* metro area placed #16, according to Gallup's 2014 Economic Confidence Index. *Gallup, "San Jose and San Francisco Lead in Economic Confidence," March 19, 2015*
- The Brookings Institution ranked the 100 largest metro areas in the U.S. based on income inequality. Chicago* was ranked #20 (#1 = greatest ineqality). Criteria: the "95/20 ratio," a figure representing the income at which a household earns more than 95 percent of all other households, divided by the income at which a household earns more than only 20 percent of all other households. *Brookings Institution, "Income Inequality, 100 Largest U.S. Metro Areas, 2007-2014," January 14, 2016*
- Payscale.com ranked the 20 largest metro areas in terms of wage growth. The Chicago* metro area ranked #6. Criteria: private-sector wage growth between the 1st quarter of 2015 and the 1st quarter of 2016. *PayScale, "Wage Trends by Metro Area," 1st Quarter, 2016*
- The Chicago* metro area was identified as one of the most debt-ridden places in America by the finance site Credit.com. The metro area was ranked #10. Criteria: residents' average personal debt load and average credit scores. *Credit.com, "The Most Debt-Ridden Cities," May 1, 2014*
- Chicago* was identified as one of America's most frugal metro areas by *Coupons.com.* The city ranked #24 out of 25. Criteria: online coupon usage. *Coupons.com, "Top 25 Most Frugal Cities of 2014," May 11, 2015*
- Chicago* was identified as one of America's most frugal metro areas by *Coupons.com.* The city ranked #25 out of 25. Criteria: Grocery IQ and coupons.com mobile app usage. *Coupons.com, "Top 25 Most On-the-Go Frugal Cities of 2013," April 10, 2014*
- Chicago* was cited as one of America's top metros for new and expanded facility projects in 2015. The area ranked #1 in the large metro area category (population over 1 million). *Site Selection, "Top Metropolitans of 2015," March 2016*
- The Chicago* metro area appeared on the Milken Institute "2015 Best Performing Cities" list. Rank: #122 out of 200 large metro areas. Criteria: job growth; wage and salary growth; high-tech output growth. *Milken Institute, "Best-Performing Cities 2015," December 2015*
- *Forbes* ranked the 200 most populous metro areas to determine the nation's "Best Places for Business and Careers." The Chicago* metro area was ranked #87. Criteria: costs (business and living); job growth (past and projected); income growth; educational attainment (college and high school); projected economic growth; cultural and recreational opportunities; net migration patterns; number of highly ranked colleges. *Forbes, "The Best Places for Business and Careers 2015," July 29, 2015*

Education Rankings

- Personal finance website *WalletHub* analyzed the 150 largest U.S. metropolitan statistical areas to determine where the most educated Americans are choosing to settle. Criteria: education quality and attainment gap; education levels; percentage of workers with degrees; public school rankings; quality and size of each metro area's universities. Chicago* was ranked #40 (#1 = most educated city). *www.WalletHub.com, "2015's Most and Least Educated Cities*

Environmental Rankings

- The Chicago* metro area came in at #137 for the relative comfort of its climate on Sperling's list of "chill cities," as measured by the Sperling Heat Index. All 361 metro areas are included. Criteria included daytime high temperatures, nighttime low temperatures, dew point, and relative humidity at the high temperatures. *www.bertsperling.com, "Sperling's Chill Cities," July 18, 2013*
- Sperling's BestPlaces assessed 379 metropolitan areas of the United States for the likelihood of dangerously extreme weather events or earthquakes. In general the Southeast and South-Central regions have the highest risk of weather extremes and earthquakes, while the Pacific Northwest enjoys the lowest risk. Of the least risky metropolitan areas, the Chicago* metro area was ranked #324. *www.bestplaces.net, "Safest Places from Natural Disasters," April 2011*
- The U.S. Environmental Protection Agency (EPA) released a list of U.S. metropolitan areas with the most ENERGY STAR certified buildings in 2015. The Chicago* metro area was ranked #6 out of 25. *U.S. Environmental Protection Agency, "Top Cities With the Most ENERGY STAR Certified Buildings in 2016," March 30, 2016*
- Chicago* was highlighted as one of the 25 most ozone-polluted metro areas in the U.S. during 2011 through 2013. The area ranked #19. *American Lung Association, State of the Air 2015*

Health/Fitness Rankings

- For each of the 50 most populous metro areas in the United States, the American College of Sports Medicine's American Fitness Index evaluated infrastructure, community assets, and policies that encourage healthy and fit lifestyles, including preventive health behaviors, levels of chronic disease conditions, health care access, and community resources and policies that support physical activity. The Chicago* metro area ranked #17 for "community fitness." *www.americanfitnessindex.org, "ACSM American Fitness Index Health and Community Fitness Status of the 50 Largest Metropolitan Areas," May 2015*
- The Chicago* metro area was identified as one of the worst cities for bed bugs in America by pest control company Orkin. The area ranked #1 out of 50 based on the number of bed bug treatments Orkin performed from January to December 2015. *Orkin, "Chicago Tops Bed Bug Cities List for Fourth Year in a Row," January 13, 2016*
- Chicago* was identified as a "2016 Spring Allergy Capital." The area ranked #81 out of 100. Three groups of factors were used to identify the most severe cities for people with allergies during the spring season: annual pollen levels; medicine utilization; access to board-certified allergists. *Asthma and Allergy Foundation of America, "Spring Allergy Capitals 2016"*
- Chicago* was identified as a "2015 Asthma Capital." The area ranked #10 out of the nation's 100 largest metropolitan areas. Criteria: estimated prevalence; self-reported prevalence; crude death rate for asthma; annual pollen score; annual air quality; public smoking laws; number of board-certified asthma specialists; school inhaler access laws; rescue medication use; controller medication use; ER visits for asthma; uninsured rate; poverty rate. *Asthma and Allergy Foundation of America, "Asthma Capitals 2015"*
- The Chicago* metro area ranked #105 out of 190 in The Gallup-Healthways Well-Being Index. Criteria: purpose; social well being; financial health; community and physical health. Results are based on telephone interviews with adults, aged 18 and older, living in metropolitan areas in the 50 U.S. states and the District of Columbia. *Gallup-Healthways, "State of American Well-Being," February 23, 2016*

Real Estate Rankings

- According to Penske Truck Rental, the Chicago* metro area was named the #10 moving destination in 2015, based on one-way consumer truck rental reservations made through Penske's website and reservations call center. *blog.gopenske.com, "Penske Truck Rental's 2015 Top Moving Destinations List," February 3, 2016*

- The Chicago* metro area was identified as #9 among the ten housing markets with the highest percentage of distressed property sales, based on the findings of the housing data website RealtyTrac. Criteria: short sales; income and poverty figures; and unemployment data. *247wallst.com, "Cities Selling the Most Distressed Homes," January 23, 2014*

- Chicago* was ranked #147 out of 225 metro areas in terms of housing affordability in 2015 by the National Association of Home Builders (#1 = most affordable). Criteria: the share of homes sold in that area affordable to a family earning the local median income, based on standard mortgage underwriting criteria. *National Association of Home Builders®, NAHB-Wells Fargo Housing Opportunity Index, 4th Quarter 2015*

- The nation's largest metro areas were analyzed in terms of the percentage of households entering some stage of foreclosure in 2015. The Chicago* metro area ranked #14 out of 20 (#1 = highest foreclosure rate). *RealtyTrac, "2015 Year-End U.S. Foreclosure Market Report™," January 12, 2016*

Safety Rankings

- Chicago* was identified as one of the most disaster-proof places in the U.S. in terms of its vulnerability to natural and non-natural disasters. The city ranked #3 out of 5. Rankings are based on the U.S. Center for Disease Control's Cities Readiness Initiative (CRI), which assesses local emergency-management plans, protocols and capabilities for 72 Metropolitan Statistical Areas and four non-MSA large cities. *Forbes, "America's Most and Least Disaster-Proof Cities," December 12, 2011*

- The National Insurance Crime Bureau ranked 380 metro areas in the U.S. in terms of per capita rates of vehicle theft. The Chicago* metro area ranked #109 (#1 = highest rate). Criteria: number of vehicle theft offenses per 100,000 inhabitants in 2014. *National Insurance Crime Bureau, "Hot Spots 2014," June 24, 2015*

Seniors/Retirement Rankings

- From its Best Cities for Successful Aging indexes, the Milken Institute generated rankings for metropolitan areas, weighing data in eight categories—health care, wellness, living arrangements, transportation, financial characteristics, education and employment opportunities, community engagement, and overall livability. The Chicago* metro area was ranked #64 overall in the large metro area category. *Milken Institute, "Best Cities for Successful Aging, 2014"*

Sports/Recreation Rankings

- According to the personal finance website NerdWallet, the Chicago* metro area, at #2, is one of the nation's top dozen metro areas for sports fans. Criteria included the presence of all four major sports—MLB, NFL, NHL, and NBA, fan enthusiasm (as measured by game attendance), ticket affordability, and "sports culture," that is, number of sports bars. *www.nerdwallet.com, "Best Cities for Sports Fans," May 5, 2013*

Transportation Rankings

- Chicago* was identified as one of the most congested metro areas in the U.S. The area ranked #8 out of 10. Criteria: yearly delay per auto commuter in hours. *Texas A&M Transportation Institute, "2015 Urban Mobility Scorecard," August 2015*

- The Chicago* metro area appeared on *Forbes* list of places with the most extreme commutes. The metro area ranked #8 out of 10. Criteria: average travel time; percentage of mega commuters. Mega-commuters travel more than 90 minutes and 50 miles each way to work. *Forbes.com, "The Cities with the Most Extreme Commutes," March 5, 2013*

Miscellaneous Rankings

- The watchdog site Charity Navigator conducts an annual study of charities in the nation's major markets both to analyze statistical differences in their financial, accountability, and transparency practices and to track year-to-year variations in individual communities. The Chicago* metro area was ranked #14 among the 30 metro markets in the rating dimension of Overall Score. *www.charitynavigator.org, "Metro Market Study 2015," June 5, 2015*

- The Harris Poll's Happiness Index survey revealed that of the top ten U.S. markets, the Chicago* metro area residents ranked #8 in happiness. Criteria included strong assent to positive statements and strong disagreement with negative ones, and degree of agreement with a series of statements about respondents' personal relationships and general outlook. *www.harrisinteractive.com, "Dallas/Fort Worth Is "Happiest" City among America's Top Ten Markets," September 4, 2013*

- Energizer Personal Care, the makers of Edge® shave gel, in partnership with Sperling's BestPlaces, ranked 50 major metro areas in terms of everyday irritations. The Chicago* metro area ranked #1 the 50 metro area most iritating to guys. Criteria: high male-to-female ratio; poor sports team performance and high ticket prices; slow traffic; lack of job availability; unaffordable housing; extreme weather; lack of nightlife and fitness options. *Energizer Personal Care, "Most Irritatng Cities for Guys," August 26, 2013*

- Mars Chocolate North America, the makers of COMBOS®, in partnership with Sperling's BestPlaces, ranked 50 major metro areas in terms of their "manliness." The Chicago* metro area ranked #37. Criteria: number of professional sports teams; number of nearby NASCAR tracks and racing events; manly lifestyle; concentration of manly retail stores; manly occupations per capita; salty snack sales; "Board of Manliness" rankings. *Mars Chocolate North America, "America's Manliest Cities 2012"*

- The Chicago* metro area was selected as one of "America's Most Miserable Cities" by *Forbes.com.* The metro area ranked #4 out of 20. Criteria: violent crime; unemployment; foreclosures; income and property taxes; home prices; commute times; climate. *Forbes.com, "America's Most Miserable Cities" February 22, 2013*

- The National Alliance to End Homelessness ranked the 100 most populous metro areas with the highest rate of homelessness. The Chicago* metro area ranked #75. Criteria: number of homeless people per 10,000 population in 2011. *National Alliance to End Homelessness, The State of Homelessness in America 2012*

Wilmette is located within the Chicago-Naperville-Elgin, IL-IN-WI Metropolitan Statistical Area.

Business Environment

CITY FINANCES

City Government Finances

Component	2012 ($000)	2012 ($ per capita)
Total Revenues	46,712	1,724
Total Expenditures	49,684	1,834
Debt Outstanding	76,169	2,812
Cash and Securities[1]	72,142	2,663

Note: (1) Cash and security holdings of a government at the close of its fiscal year, including those of its dependent agencies, utilities, and liquor stores.
Source: U.S Census Bureau, State & Local Government Finances 2012

City Government Revenue by Source

Source	2012 ($000)	2012 ($ per capita)
General Revenue		
From Federal Government	0	0
From State Government	6,421	237
From Local Governments	1,137	41
Taxes		
Property	13,886	512
Sales and Gross Receipts	4,781	176
Personal Income	0	0
Corporate Income	0	0
Motor Vehicle License	1,353	49
Other Taxes	2,408	88
Current Charges	7,419	273
Liquor Store	0	0
Utility	7,448	274
Employee Retirement	785	28

Source: U.S Census Bureau, State & Local Government Finances 2012

City Government Expenditures by Function

Function	2012 ($000)	2012 ($ per capita)	2012 (%)
General Direct Expenditures			
Air Transportation	0	0	0.0
Corrections	0	0	0.0
Education	0	0	0.0
Employment Security Administration	0	0	0.0
Financial Administration	1,334	49	2.6
Fire Protection	7,936	292	15.9
General Public Buildings	603	22	1.2
Governmental Administration, Other	890	32	1.7
Health	216	7	0.4
Highways	5,614	207	11.2
Hospitals	0	0	0.0
Housing and Community Development	0	0	0.0
Interest on General Debt	2,308	85	4.6
Judicial and Legal	295	10	0.5
Libraries	0	0	0.0
Parking	328	12	0.6
Parks and Recreation	0	0	0.0
Police Protection	9,590	354	19.3
Public Welfare	0	0	0.0
Sewerage	3,724	137	7.4
Solid Waste Management	2,285	84	4.5
Veterans' Services	0	0	0.0
Liquor Store	0	0	0.0
Utility	6,075	224	12.2
Employee Retirement	4,707	173	9.4

Source: U.S Census Bureau, State & Local Government Finances 2012

DEMOGRAPHICS

Population Growth

Area	1990 Census	2000 Census	2010 Census	2014* Estimate	Population Growth (%) 1990-2014	2010-2014
City	26,685	27,651	27,087	27,345	2.5	1.0
MSA[1]	8,182,076	9,098,316	9,461,105	9,516,448	16.3	0.6
U.S.	248,709,873	281,421,906	308,745,538	314,107,084	26.3	1.7

Note: (1) Figures cover the Chicago-Naperville-Elgin, IL-IN-WI Metropolitan Statistical Area—see Appendix B for areas included; (*) 2010-2014 5-year estimated population
Source: U.S. Census Bureau, 1990 Census, Census 2000, Census 2010, 2010-2014 American Community Survey 5-Year Estimates

Household Size

Area	Persons in Household (%) One	Two	Three	Four	Five	Six	Seven or More	Average Household Size
City	20.5	31.6	15.6	20.2	8.2	2.8	0.8	2.87
MSA[1]	28.1	29.9	15.8	14.3	7.0	2.7	1.8	2.72
U.S.	27.5	33.5	15.8	13.1	6.0	2.3	1.4	2.64

Note: (1) Figures cover the Chicago-Naperville-Elgin, IL-IN-WI Metropolitan Statistical Area—see Appendix B for areas included
Source: U.S. Census Bureau, 2010-2014 American Community Survey 5-Year Estimates

Race

Area	White Alone[2] (%)	Black Alone[2] (%)	Asian Alone[2] (%)	AIAN[3] Alone[2] (%)	NHOPI[4] Alone[2] (%)	Other Race Alone[2] (%)	Two or More Races (%)
City	84.2	1.1	12.7	0.2	0.0	0.4	1.3
MSA[1]	66.6	17.0	6.0	0.2	0.0	7.9	2.2
U.S.	73.8	12.6	5.0	0.8	0.2	4.7	2.9

Note: (1) Figures cover the Chicago-Naperville-Elgin, IL-IN-WI Metropolitan Statistical Area—see Appendix B for areas included; (2) Alone is defined as not being in combination with one or more other races; (3) American Indian and Alaska Native; (4) Native Hawaiian and Other Pacific Islander
Source: U.S. Census Bureau, 2010-2014 American Community Survey 5-Year Estimates

Hispanic or Latino Origin

Area	Total (%)	Mexican (%)	Puerto Rican (%)	Cuban (%)	Other (%)
City	4.6	1.8	0.6	0.7	1.6
MSA[1]	21.2	16.8	2.1	0.2	2.0
U.S.	16.9	10.8	1.6	0.6	3.8

Note: Persons of Hispanic or Latino origin can be of any race; (1) Figures cover the Chicago-Naperville-Elgin, IL-IN-WI Metropolitan Statistical Area—see Appendix B for areas included
Source: U.S. Census Bureau, 2010-2014 American Community Survey 5-Year Estimates

Ancestry

Area	German	Irish	English	American	Italian	Polish	French[2]	Scottish	Dutch
City	23.4	16.3	10.4	5.3	7.1	8.0	2.9	1.9	1.3
MSA[1]	15.5	11.6	4.4	2.9	7.0	9.4	1.5	1.0	1.3
U.S.	14.9	10.8	8.0	7.1	5.5	3.0	2.7	1.7	1.4

Note: Figures are the percentage of the total population reporting a particular ancestry. The nine most commonly reported ancestries in the U.S. are shown. Figures include multiple ancestries (e.g. if a person reported being Irish and Italian, they were included in both columns); (1) Figures cover the Chicago-Naperville-Elgin, IL-IN-WI Metropolitan Statistical Area—see Appendix B for areas included; (2) Excludes Basque
Source: U.S. Census Bureau, 2010-2014 American Community Survey 5-Year Estimates

Foreign-Born Population

Area	Percent of Population Born in: Any Foreign Country	Asia	Mexico	Europe	Carribean	Central America[2]	South America	Africa	Canada
City	17.7	10.2	0.5	5.3	0.3	0.1	0.7	0.2	0.3
MSA[1]	17.6	4.8	7.0	3.8	0.3	0.5	0.6	0.5	0.2
U.S.	13.1	3.8	3.7	1.5	1.2	1.0	0.9	0.6	0.3

Note: (1) Figures cover the Chicago-Naperville-Elgin, IL-IN-WI Metropolitan Statistical Area—see Appendix B for areas included; (2) Excludes Mexico.
Source: U.S. Census Bureau, 2010-2014 American Community Survey 5-Year Estimates

Marital Status

Area	Never Married	Now Married[2]	Separated	Widowed	Divorced
City	21.9	64.3	0.9	5.6	7.2
MSA[1]	36.2	47.2	1.8	5.6	9.1
U.S.	32.5	48.4	2.2	5.9	10.9

Note: Figures are percentages and cover the population 15 years of age and older; (1) Figures cover the Chicago-Naperville-Elgin, IL-IN-WI Metropolitan Statistical Area—see Appendix B for areas included; (2) Excludes separated
Source: U.S. Census Bureau, 2010-2014 American Community Survey 5-Year Estimates

Disability Status

Area	All Ages	Under 18 Years Old	18 to 64 Years Old	65 Years and Over
City	7.5	1.5	4.6	26.9
MSA[1]	9.7	3.1	7.6	35.0
U.S.	12.3	4.1	10.2	36.3

Note: Figures show percent of the civilian noninstitutionalized population that reported having a disability. Disability status is determined from from six types of difficulty: vision, hearing, cognitive, ambulatory, self-care, and independent living. For children under 5 years old, hearing and vision difficulty are used to determine disability status. For children between the ages of 5 and 14, disability status is determined from hearing, vision, cognitive, ambulatory, and self-care difficulties. For people aged 15 years and older, they are considered to have a disability if they have difficulty with any one of the six difficulty types; (1) Figures cover the Chicago-Naperville-Elgin, IL-IN-WI Metropolitan Statistical Area—see Appendix B for areas included.
Source: U.S. Census Bureau, 2010-2014 American Community Survey 5-Year Estimates

Age

Area	Percent of Population: Under Age 5	Age 5–19	Age 20–34	Age 35–44	Age 45–54	Age 55–64	Age 65–74	Age 75–84	Age 85+	Median Age
City	5.4	25.3	8.1	12.9	16.4	14.2	9.5	5.1	3.2	43.8
MSA[1]	6.5	20.7	21.1	13.7	14.2	11.8	6.7	3.7	1.7	36.3
U.S.	6.4	19.9	20.6	13.0	14.1	12.3	7.6	4.3	1.9	37.4

Note: (1) Figures cover the Chicago-Naperville-Elgin, IL-IN-WI Metropolitan Statistical Area—see Appendix B for areas included
Source: U.S. Census Bureau, 2010-2014 American Community Survey 5-Year Estimates

Gender

Area	Males	Females	Males per 100 Females
City	13,584	13,761	98.7
MSA[1]	4,650,729	4,865,719	95.6
U.S.	154,515,159	159,591,925	96.8

Note: (1) Figures cover the Chicago-Naperville-Elgin, IL-IN-WI Metropolitan Statistical Area—see Appendix B for areas included
Source: U.S. Census Bureau, 2010-2014 American Community Survey 5-Year Estimates

Religious Groups by Family

Area	Catholic	Baptist	Non-Den.	Methodist[2]	Lutheran	LDS[3]	Pente-costal	Presby-terian[4]	Muslim[5]	Judaism
MSA[1]	34.2	3.2	4.4	1.9	3.0	0.3	1.2	1.9	3.2	0.8
U.S.	19.1	9.3	4.0	4.0	2.3	2.0	1.9	1.6	0.8	0.7

Note: Figures are the number of adherents as a percentage of the total population; (1) Figures cover the Chicago-Joliet-Naperville, IL-IN-WI Metropolitan Statistical Area—see Appendix B for areas included; (2) Methodist/Pietist; (3) Latter Day Saints; (4) Reformed; (5) Figures are estimates
Source: Association of Statisticians of American Religious Bodies, 2010 U.S. Religion Census: Religious Congregations & Membership Study

Religious Groups by Tradition

Area	Catholic	Evangelical Protestant	Mainline Protestant	Other Tradition	Black Protestant	Orthodox
MSA[1]	34.2	9.7	5.1	5.0	2.0	0.9
U.S.	19.1	16.2	7.3	4.3	1.6	0.3

Note: Figures are the number of adherents as a percentage of the total population; (1) Figures cover the Chicago-Joliet-Naperville, IL-IN-WI Metropolitan Statistical Area—see Appendix B for areas included
Source: Association of Statisticians of American Religious Bodies, 2010 U.S. Religion Census: Religious Congregations & Membership Study

ECONOMY

Gross Metropolitan Product

Area	2013	2014	2015	2016	Rank[2]
MSA[1]	590.2	611.0	630.3	658.6	3

Note: Figures are in billions of dollars; (1) Figures cover the Chicago-Naperville-Elgin, IL-IN-WI Metropolitan Statistical Area—see Appendix B for areas included; (2) Rank is based on 2016 data and ranges from 1 to 381
Source: The U.S. Conference of Mayors, U.S. Metro Economies: GMP and Employment 2014-2016, June 2015

Economic Growth

Area	2011-13 (%)	2014 (%)	2015 (%)	2016 (%)	Rank[2]
MSA[1]	1.6	1.9	1.7	2.6	159
U.S.	2.2	2.4	2.3	2.9	-

Note: Figures are real gross metropolitan product (GMP) growth rates and represent annual average percent change; (1) Figures cover the Chicago-Naperville-Elgin, IL-IN-WI Metropolitan Statistical Area—see Appendix B for areas included; (2) Rank is based on 2016 data and ranges from 1 to 381
Source: The U.S. Conference of Mayors, U.S. Metro Economies: GMP and Employment 2014-2016, June 2015

Metropolitan Area Exports

Area	2009	2010	2011	2012	2013	2014	Rank[2]
MSA[1]	28,196.6	33,671.9	39,522.4	40,567.9	44,910.6	47,340.1	6

Note: Figures are in millions of dollars; (1) Figures cover the Chicago-Naperville-Elgin, IL-IN-WI Metropolitan Statistical Area—see Appendix B for areas included; (2) Rank is based on 2014 data and ranges from 1 to 385
Source: U.S. Department of Commerce, International Trade Administration, Office of Trade & Industry Information, Manufacturing & Services, data extracted March 10, 2016

Building Permits

Area	Single-Family			Multi-Family			Total		
	2014	2015p	Pct. Chg.	2014	2015p	Pct. Chg.	2014	2015p	Pct. Chg.
City	44	48	9.1	0	0	-	44	48	9.1
MSA[1]	7,723	7,577	-1.9	7,956	8,160	2.6	15,679	15,737	0.4
U.S.	640,300	690,800	7.9	411,800	487,600	18.4	1,052,100	1,178,400	12.0

Note: (1) Figures cover the Chicago-Naperville-Elgin, IL-IN-WI Metropolitan Statistical Area—see Appendix B for areas included; Figures represent new, privately-owned housing units authorized (unadjusted data); All permit data are based on estimates with imputation; (p) preliminary data.
Source: U.S. Census Bureau, Manufacturing, Mining, and Construction Statistics, Building Permits, 2014, 2015

Bankruptcy Filings

Area	Business Filings			Nonbusiness Filings		
	2014	2015	% Chg.	2014	2015	% Chg.
Cook County	569	511	-10.2	33,968	33,318	-1.9
U.S.	26,983	24,735	-8.3	909,812	819,760	-9.9

Note: Business filings include Chapter 7, Chapter 11, Chapter 12, and Chapter 13; Nonbusiness filings include Chapter 7, Chapter 11, and Chapter 13
Source: Administrative Office of the U.S. Courts, Business and Nonbusiness Bankruptcy, County Cases Commenced by Chapter of the Bankruptcy Code, During the 12- Month Period Ending December 31, 2014 and Business and Nonbusiness Bankruptcy, County Cases Commenced by Chapter of the Bankruptcy Code, During the 12- Month Period Ending December 31, 2015

Housing Vacancy Rates

Area	Gross Vacancy Rate[2] (%)			Year-Round Vacancy Rate[3] (%)			Rental Vacancy Rate[4] (%)			Homeowner Vacancy Rate[5] (%)		
	2013	2014	2015	2013	2014	2015	2013	2014	2015	2013	2014	2015
MSA[1]	10.5	10.3	9.7	10.3	10.2	9.4	10.9	9.1	7.4	2.8	2.6	2.3
U.S.	13.6	13.4	12.9	10.7	10.4	10.0	8.3	7.6	7.1	2.0	1.9	1.8

Note: (1) Figures cover the Chicago-Naperville-Elgin, IL-IN-WI Metropolitan Statistical Area—see Appendix B for areas included; (2) The percentage of the total housing inventory that is vacant; (3) The percentage of the housing inventory (excluding seasonal units) that is year-round vacant; (4) The percentage of rental inventory that is vacant for rent; (5) The percentage of homeowner inventory that is vacant for sale
Source: U.S. Census Bureau, Housing Vacancies and Homeownership Annual Statistics: 2015

INCOME

Income

Area	Per Capita ($)	Median Household ($)	Average Household ($)
City	67,116	126,471	188,450
MSA[1]	31,488	61,497	84,504
U.S.	28,555	53,482	74,596

Note: (1) Figures cover the Chicago-Naperville-Elgin, IL-IN-WI Metropolitan Statistical Area—see Appendix B for areas included
Source: U.S. Census Bureau, 2010-2014 American Community Survey 5-Year Estimates

Household Income Distribution

Area	Percent of Households Earning							
	Under $15,000	$15,000 -24,999	$25,000 -34,999	$35,000 -49,999	$50,000 -74,999	$75,000 -99,000	$100,000 -149,999	$150,000 and up
City	4.1	3.4	4.3	6.7	11.6	10.4	16.5	42.9
MSA[1]	11.1	9.3	8.9	12.2	17.4	13.0	15.1	13.1
U.S.	12.5	10.7	10.2	13.5	17.8	12.2	13.0	10.0

Note: (1) Figures cover the Chicago-Naperville-Elgin, IL-IN-WI Metropolitan Statistical Area—see Appendix B for areas included
Source: U.S. Census Bureau, 2010-2014 American Community Survey 5-Year Estimates

Poverty Rate

Area	All Ages	Under 18 Years Old	18 to 64 Years Old	65 Years and Over
City	3.0	2.2	2.7	5.6
MSA[1]	14.1	20.3	12.6	9.2
U.S.	15.6	21.9	14.6	9.4

Note: Figures are percentage of people whose income during the past 12 months was below the poverty level; (1) Figures cover the Chicago-Naperville-Elgin, IL-IN-WI Metropolitan Statistical Area—see Appendix B for areas included
Source: U.S. Census Bureau, 2010-2014 American Community Survey 5-Year Estimates

EMPLOYMENT

Labor Force and Employment

Area	Civilian Labor Force			Workers Employed		
	Dec. 2014	Dec. 2015	% Chg.	Dec. 2014	Dec. 2015	% Chg.
City	12,827	12,827	0.0	12,332	12,298	-0.2
MD[1]	3,743,002	3,771,441	0.7	3,525,255	3,562,874	1.0
U.S.	155,521,000	157,245,000	1.1	147,190,000	149,703,000	1.7

Note: Data is not seasonally adjusted and covers workers 16 years of age and older; (1) Figures cover the Chicago-Naperville-Arlington Heights, IL Metropolitan Division—see Appendix B for areas included
Source: Bureau of Labor Statistics, Local Area Unemployment Statistics

Unemployment Rate

Area	2015											
	Jan.	Feb.	Mar.	Apr.	May	Jun.	Jul.	Aug.	Sep.	Oct.	Nov.	Dec.
City	4.6	4.7	4.4	4.2	4.6	4.6	4.4	3.9	3.5	3.8	4.2	4.1
MD[1]	6.9	6.5	6.0	5.7	5.9	6.1	6.2	5.6	5.1	5.3	5.4	5.5
U.S.	6.1	5.8	5.6	5.1	5.3	5.5	5.6	5.2	4.9	4.8	4.8	4.8

Note: Data is not seasonally adjusted and covers workers 16 years of age and older; (1) Figures cover the Chicago-Naperville-Arlington Heights, IL Metropolitan Division—see Appendix B for areas included
Source: Bureau of Labor Statistics, Local Area Unemployment Statistics

Employment by Occupation

Occupation Classification	City (%)	MSA[1] (%)	U.S. (%)
Management, Business, Science, and Arts	70.5	37.9	36.4
Natural Resources, Construction, and Maintenance	1.4	6.8	9.0
Production, Transportation, and Material Moving	2.5	13.2	12.1
Sales and Office	19.2	25.1	24.4
Service	6.3	17.0	18.2

Note: Figures cover employed civilians 16 years of age and older; (1) Figures cover the Chicago-Naperville-Elgin, IL-IN-WI Metropolitan Statistical Area—see Appendix B for areas included
Source: U.S. Census Bureau, 2010-2014 American Community Survey 5-Year Estimates

Employment by Industry

Sector	MD[1]		U.S.
	Number of Employees	Percent of Total	Percent of Total
Construction	123,700	3.3	4.5
Education and Health Services	580,900	15.7	15.7
Financial Activities	254,500	6.8	5.7
Government	430,400	11.6	15.5
Information	73,200	1.9	1.9
Leisure and Hospitality	359,200	9.7	10.4
Manufacturing	282,400	7.6	8.6
Mining and Logging	1,100	<0.1	0.5
Other Services	159,600	4.3	3.9
Professional and Business Services	679,200	18.3	13.9
Retail Trade	371,600	10.0	11.3
Transportation, Warehousing, and Utilities	190,000	5.1	3.9
Wholesale Trade	193,700	5.2	4.1

Note: Figures are non-farm employment as of December 2015. Figures are not seasonally adjusted and include workers 16 years of age and older; (1) Figures cover the Chicago-Naperville-Arlington Heights, IL Metropolitan Division—see Appendix B for areas included
Source: Bureau of Labor Statistics, Current Employment Statistics, Employment, Hours, and Earnings

Occupations with Greatest Projected Employment Growth: 2012 – 2022

Occupation[1]	2012 Employment	2022 Projected Employment	Numeric Employment Change	Percent Employment Change
Laborers and Freight, Stock, and Material Movers, Hand	127,890	148,390	20,500	16.0
Home Health Aides	40,020	56,650	16,630	41.6
Combined Food Preparation and Serving Workers, Including Fast Food	104,150	119,060	14,910	14.3
Retail Salespersons	174,910	188,030	13,120	7.5
Customer Service Representatives	111,240	123,880	12,640	11.4
Registered Nurses	113,100	124,990	11,890	10.5
Janitors and Cleaners, Except Maids and Housekeeping Cleaners	105,870	116,370	10,500	9.9
Nursing Assistants	61,430	70,820	9,390	15.3
General and Operations Managers	91,660	100,910	9,250	10.1
Construction Laborers	49,810	59,060	9,250	18.6

Note: Projections cover Illinois; (1) Sorted by numeric employment change
Source: www.projectionscentral.com, State Occupational Projections, 2012–2022 Long-Term Projections

Fastest Growing Occupations: 2012 – 2022

Occupation[1]	2012 Employment	2022 Projected Employment	Numeric Employment Change	Percent Employment Change
Home Health Aides	40,020	56,650	16,630	41.6
Skincare Specialists	1,650	2,290	640	38.2
Biomedical Engineers	540	740	200	38.0
Interpreters and Translators	1,880	2,590	710	37.6
Occupational Therapy Assistants	1,320	1,810	490	37.3
Insulation Workers, Mechanical	1,500	2,020	520	34.5
Physical Therapist Aides	2,540	3,390	850	33.5
Health Specialties Teachers, Postsecondary	3,120	4,150	1,030	32.8
Physical Therapist Assistants	3,010	3,990	980	32.5
Physical Therapists	9,320	12,340	3,020	32.4

Note: Projections cover Illinois; (1) Sorted by percent employment change and excludes occupations with numeric employment change less than 100
Source: www.projectionscentral.com, State Occupational Projections, 2012–2022 Long-Term Projections

Average Wages

Occupation	$/Hr.	Occupation	$/Hr.
Accountants and Auditors	35.11	Maids and Housekeeping Cleaners	12.44
Automotive Mechanics	22.85	Maintenance and Repair Workers	21.36
Bookkeepers	19.63	Marketing Managers	58.77
Carpenters	31.04	Nuclear Medicine Technologists	35.61
Cashiers	10.38	Nurses, Licensed Practical	24.67
Clerks, General Office	16.40	Nurses, Registered	35.96
Clerks, Receptionists/Information	14.47	Nursing Assistants	12.89
Clerks, Shipping/Receiving	16.37	Packers and Packagers, Hand	12.25
Computer Programmers	37.27	Physical Therapists	41.57
Computer Systems Analysts	42.42	Postal Service Mail Carriers	25.13
Computer User Support Specialists	26.66	Real Estate Brokers	38.44
Cooks, Restaurant	11.75	Retail Salespersons	13.08
Dentists	61.93	Sales Reps., Exc. Tech./Scientific	35.53
Electrical Engineers	45.45	Sales Reps., Tech./Scientific	36.28
Electricians	35.46	Secretaries, Exc. Legal/Med./Exec.	18.19
Financial Managers	63.54	Security Guards	14.91
First-Line Supervisors/Managers, Sales	22.18	Surgeons	122.87
Food Preparation Workers	10.44	Teacher Assistants*	14.05
General and Operations Managers	58.83	Teachers, Elementary School*	30.77
Hairdressers/Cosmetologists	13.34	Teachers, Secondary School*	36.04
Internists	83.00	Telemarketers	12.71
Janitors and Cleaners	14.23	Truck Drivers, Heavy/Tractor-Trailer	23.64
Landscaping/Groundskeeping Workers	14.34	Truck Drivers, Light/Delivery Svcs.	17.54
Lawyers	62.12	Waiters and Waitresses	10.57

Note: Wage data covers the Chicago-Joliet-Naperville, IL Metropolitan Division—see Appendix B for areas included; (*) Hourly wages for elementary/secondary school teachers and teacher assistants were calculated by the editors from annual wage data based on a 40 hour work week; n/a not available.
Source: Bureau of Labor Statistics, Metro Area Occupational Employment and Wage Estimates, May 2015

TAXES

State Corporate Income Tax Rates

State	Tax Rate (%)	Income Brackets ($)	Num. of Brackets	Financial Institution Tax Rate (%)[a]	Federal Income Tax Ded.
Illinois	7.75 (i)	Flat rate	1	7.75 (i)	No

Note: Tax rates as of January 1, 2016; (a) Rates listed are the corporate income tax rate applied to financial institutions or excise taxes based on income. Some states have other taxes based upon the value of deposits or shares; (i) The Illinois rate of 7.75% is the sum of a corporate income tax rate of 5.25% plus a replacement tax of 2.5%.
Source: Federation of Tax Administrators, "State Corporate Income Tax Rates, 2016"

State Individual Income Tax Rates

State	Tax Rate (%)	Income Brackets ($)	Num. of Brackets	Personal Exempt. ($)[1] Single	Personal Exempt. ($)[1] Dependents	Fed. Inc. Tax Ded.
Illinois	3.75	Flat rate	1	2,000	2,000	No

Note: Tax rates as of January 1, 2016; Local- and county-level taxes are not included; n/a not applicable; (1) Married joint filers generally receive double the single exemption
Source: Federation of Tax Administrators, "State Individual Income Tax Rates, 2016"

Various State and Local Tax Rates

State	State and Local Sales and Use (%)	State Sales and Use (%)	Gasoline[1] (¢/gal.)	Cigarette[2] ($/pack)	Spirits[3] ($/gal.)	Wine[4] ($/gal.)	Beer[5] ($/gal.)
Illinois	10.00	6.25	30.18	1.98	8.55 (f)	1.39 (l)	0.23

Note: All tax rates as of January 1, 2016; (1) The American Petroleum Institute has developed a methodology for determining the average tax rate on a gallon of fuel. Rates may include any of the following: excise taxes, environmental fees, storage tank fees, other fees or taxes, general sales tax, and local taxes. In states where gasoline is subject to the general sales tax, or where the fuel tax is based on the average sale price, the average rate determined by API is sensitive to changes in the price of gasoline. States that fully or partially apply general sales taxes to gasoline: CA, CO, GA, IL, IN, MI, NY; (2) The federal excise tax of $1.0066 per pack and local taxes are not included; (3) Rates are those applicable to off-premise sales of 40% alcohol by volume (a.b.v.) distilled spirits in 750ml containers. Local excise taxes are excluded; (4) Rates are those applicable to off-premise sales of 11% a.b.v. non-carbonated wine in 750ml containers; (5) Rates are those applicable to off-premise sales of 4.7% a.b.v. beer in 12 ounce containers; (f) Different rates are also applicable according to alcohol content, place of production, size of container, or place purchased (on- or off-premise or onboard airlines); (l) Different rates also applicable according to alcohol content, place of production, size of container, place purchased (on- or off-premise or on board airlines) or type of wine (carbonated, vermouth, etc.).
Source: Tax Foundation, 2016 Facts & Figures: How Does Your State Compare?

State Business Tax Climate Index Rankings

State	Overall Rank	Corporate Tax Rank	Individual Income Tax Rank	Sales Tax Rank	Unemployment Insurance Tax Rank	Property Tax Rank
Illinois	23	36	10	33	39	45

Note: The index is a measure of how each state's tax laws affect economic performance. The lower the rank, the more favorable a state's tax system is for business. States without a given tax are given a ranking of 1. The scores/rankings for the District of Columbia do not affect other states. The 2016 index represents the tax climate as of July 1, 2015 (the beginning of Fiscal Year 2016).
Source: Tax Foundation, State Business Tax Climate Index 2016

TRANSPORTATION

Means of Transportation to Work

Area	Car/Truck/Van		Public Transportation			Bicycle	Walked	Other Means	Worked at Home
	Drove Alone	Car-pooled	Bus	Subway	Railroad				
City	57.9	6.4	1.8	2.4	17.4	0.2	2.1	0.2	11.5
MSA[1]	70.9	8.4	4.6	3.6	3.2	0.6	3.2	1.1	4.3
U.S.	76.4	9.6	2.6	1.8	0.6	0.6	2.8	1.3	4.4

Note: Figures are percentages and cover workers 16 years of age and older; (1) Figures cover the Chicago-Naperville-Elgin, IL-IN-WI Metropolitan Statistical Area—see Appendix B for areas included
Source: U.S. Census Bureau, 2010-2014 American Community Survey 5-Year Estimates

Travel Time to Work

Area	Less Than 10 Minutes	10 to 19 Minutes	20 to 29 Minutes	30 to 44 Minutes	45 to 59 Minutes	60 to 89 Minutes	90 Minutes or More
City	10.0	19.2	12.8	23.8	17.1	13.4	3.7
MSA[1]	9.0	22.4	18.7	24.7	11.8	10.1	3.2
U.S.	13.3	29.6	21.0	20.2	7.7	5.7	2.6

Note: Figures are percentages and include workers 16 years old and over; (1) Figures cover the Chicago-Naperville-Elgin, IL-IN-WI Metropolitan Statistical Area—see Appendix B for areas included
Source: U.S. Census Bureau, 2010-2014 American Community Survey 5-Year Estimates

Freeway Travel Time Index

Area	1985	1990	1995	2000	2005	2010	2014
Urban Area Rank[1,2]	9	9	8	11	13	14	14
Urban Area Index[1]	1.17	1.20	1.24	1.27	1.29	1.28	1.31
Average Index[3]	1.09	1.11	1.14	1.17	1.20	1.19	1.20

Note: Freeway Travel Time Index—the ratio of travel time in the peak period to the travel time at free-flow conditions. For example, a value of 1.30 indicates a 20-minute free-flow trip takes 26 minutes in the peak (20 minutes x 1.30 = 26 minutes); (1) Covers the Chicago IL-IN urban area; (2) Rank is based on 101 urban areas (#1 = highest travel time index); (3) Average of 101 urban areas
Source: Texas Transportation Institute, 2015 Urban Mobility Scorecard, August 2015

Freeway Commuter Stress Index

Area	1985	1990	1995	2000	2005	2010	2014
Urban Area Rank[1,2]	19	19	19	20	18	19	19
Urban Area Index[1]	1.21	1.24	1.27	1.30	1.33	1.32	1.34
Average Index[3]	1.13	1.16	1.19	1.22	1.25	1.24	1.25

Note: The Freeway Commuter Stress Index is the same as the Freeway Travel Time Index (see table above) except that it includes only the travel in the peak directions during the peak periods; the TTI includes travel in all directions during the peak period. Thus, the CSI is more indicative of the work trip experienced by each commuter on a daily basis. (1) Covers the Chicago IL-IN urban area; (2) Rank is based on 101 urban areas (#1 = highest stress index); (3) Average of 101 urban areas

Source: Texas Transportation Institute, 2015 Urban Mobility Scorecard, August 2015

Living Environment

COST OF LIVING

Cost of Living Index

Composite Index	Groceries	Housing	Utilities	Transportation	Health Care	Misc. Goods/ Services
116.3	116.7	136.2	104.2	114.3	99.1	105.9

Note: The Cost of Living Index measures regional differences in the cost of consumer goods and services, excluding taxes and non-consumer expenditures, for professional and managerial households in the top income quintile. It is based on more than 50,000 prices covering almost 60 different items for which prices are collected three times a year by chambers of commerce, economic development organizations or university applied economic centers in each participating urban area. The numbers shown should be read as a percentage above or below the national average of 100. For example, a value of 115.4 in the groceries column indicates that grocery prices are 15.4% higher than the national average. Small differences in the index numbers should not be interpreted as significant; Figures cover the Chicago IL urban area.
Source: The Council for Community and Economic Research, ACCRA Cost of Living Index, 2015

Grocery Prices

Area[1]	T-Bone Steak ($/pound)	Frying Chicken ($/pound)	Whole Milk ($/half gal.)	Eggs ($/dozen)	Orange Juice ($/64 oz.)	Coffee ($/11.5 oz.)
City[2]	11.95	1.43	2.39	2.82	4.05	4.92
Avg.	10.99	1.43	2.25	2.26	3.58	4.48
Min.	7.16	0.98	1.30	1.35	2.88	2.98
Max.	14.13	2.43	3.85	4.81	6.39	7.56

Note: (1) Values for the local area are compared with the average, minimum and maximum values for all 292 areas in the Cost of Living Index; (2) Figures cover the Chicago IL urban area; **T-Bone Steak** *(price per pound);* **Frying Chicken** *(price per pound, whole fryer);* **Whole Milk** *(half gallon carton);* **Eggs** *(price per dozen, Grade A, large);* **Orange Juice** *(64 oz. Tropicana or Florida Natural);* **Coffee** *(11.5 oz. can, vacuum-packed, Maxwell House, Hills Bros, or Folgers).*
Source: The Council for Community and Economic Research, ACCRA Cost of Living Index, 2015

Housing and Utility Costs

Area[1]	New Home Price ($)	Apartment Rent ($/month)	All Electric ($/month)	Part Electric ($/month)	Other Energy ($/month)	Telephone ($/month)
City[2]	431,884	1,236	-	97.38	76.61	30.05
Avg.	312,874	945	179.30	95.07	72.96	28.11
Min.	178,682	479	116.28	43.14	26.46	10.01
Max.	1,472,476	3,984	504.25	189.44	421.11	43.06

Note: (1) Values for the local area are compared with the average, minimum and maximum values for all 292 areas in the Cost of Living Index; (2) Figures cover the Chicago IL urban area; **New Home Price** *(2,400 sf living area, 8,000 sf lot, in urban area with full utilities);* **Apartment Rent** *(950 sf 2 bedroom/1.5 or 2 bath, unfurnished, excluding all utilities except water);* **All Electric** *(average monthly cost for an all-electric home);* **Part Electric** *(average monthly cost for a part-electric home);* **Other Energy** *(average monthly cost for natural gas, fuel oil, coal, wood, and any other forms of energy except electricity);* **Telephone** *(price includes basic monthly rate for a private residential line plus additional local usage charges incurred by a family of four).*
Source: The Council for Community and Economic Research, ACCRA Cost of Living Index, 2015

Health Care, Transportation, and Other Costs

Area[1]	Doctor ($/visit)	Dentist ($/visit)	Optometrist ($/visit)	Gasoline ($/gallon)	Beauty Salon ($/visit)	Men's Shirt ($)
City[2]	99.17	99.44	95.00	2.70	45.00	25.27
Avg.	105.15	89.02	99.78	2.38	35.30	28.10
Min.	66.87	56.09	48.53	1.95	18.91	13.38
Max.	182.34	150.36	228.33	4.09	67.91	63.80

Note: (1) Values for the local area are compared with the average, minimum and maximum values for all 292 areas in the Cost of Living Index; (2) Figures cover the Chicago IL urban area; **Doctor** *(general practitioners routine exam of an established patient);* **Dentist** *(adult teeth cleaning and periodic oral examination);* **Optometrist** *(full vision eye exam for established adult patient);* **Gasoline** *(one gallon regular unleaded, national brand, including all taxes, cash price at self-service pump if available);* **Beauty Salon** *(woman's shampoo, trim, and blow-dry);* **Men's Shirt** *(cotton/polyester dress shirt, pinpoint weave, long sleeves).*
Source: The Council for Community and Economic Research, ACCRA Cost of Living Index, 2015

HOUSING

House Price Index (HPI)

Area	National Ranking[2]	Quarterly Change (%)	One-Year Change (%)	Five-Year Change (%)
MD[1]	146	0.80	4.30	4.70
U.S.[3]	–	1.45	5.76	22.85

Note: The HPI is a weighted repeat sales index. It measures average price changes in repeat sales or refinancings on the same properties. This information is obtained by reviewing repeat mortgage transactions on single-family properties whose mortgages have been purchased or securitized by Fannie Mae or Freddie Mac in January 1975; (1) Chicago-Naperville-Arlington Heights Metropolitan Division—see Appendix B for areas included; (2) Rankings are based on annual percentage change for all metro areas containing at least 15,000 transactions over the last 10 years and ranges from 1 to 266; (3) figures based on a weighted average of Census Division estimates using a seasonally adjusted, purchase-only index; all figures are for the period ending December 31, 2015

Source: Federal Housing Finance Agency, House Price Index, February 25, 2016

Median Single-Family Home Prices

Area	2013	2014	2015p	Percent Change 2014 to 2015
MSA[1]	191.3	205.9	218.9	6.3
U.S. Average	197.4	208.9	223.9	7.2

Note: Figures are median sales prices of existing single-family homes in thousands of dollars; (p) preliminary; n/a not available; (1) Chicago-Naperville-Elgin, IL-IN-WI Metropolitan Statistical Area—see Appendix B for areas included

Source: National Association of Realtors, Median Sales Price of Existing Single-Family Homes for Metropolitan Areas, 4th Quarter 2015

Qualifying Income Based on Median Sales Price of Existing Single-Family Homes

Area	With 5% Down ($)	With 10% Down ($)	With 20% Down ($)
MSA[1]	46,666	44,210	39,298
U.S. Average	49,535	46,928	41,714

Note: Figures are preliminary; Qualifying income is based on a mortgage rate of 4.1%. Monthly principal and interest payment is limited to 25% of income; n/a not available; (1) Chicago-Naperville-Elgin, IL-IN-WI Metropolitan Statistical Area—see Appendix B for areas included

Source: National Association of Realtors, Qualifying Income Based on Median Sales Price of Existing Single-Family Homes for Metropolitan Areas, 4th Quarter 2015

Median Apartment Condo-Coop Home Prices

Area	2013	2014	2015p	Percent Change 2014 to 2015
MSA[1]	145.5	163.6	178.2	8.9
U.S. Average	194.9	204.3	210.7	3.1

Note: Figures are median sales prices of existing apartment condo-coop homes in thousands of dollars; (p) preliminary; n/a not available; (1) Chicago-Naperville-Elgin, IL-IN-WI Metropolitan Statistical Area—see Appendix B for areas included

Source: National Association of Realtors, Median Sales Price of Existing Apartment Condo-Coop Homes for Metropolitan Areas, 4th Quarter 2015

Gross Monthly Rent

Area	Under $200	$200 -299	$300 -499	$500 -749	$750 -999	$1,000 -1,499	$1,500 and up	Median ($)
City	1.4	0.0	6.7	2.9	15.2	16.0	57.9	1,779
MSA[1]	1.6	2.6	4.3	14.5	29.6	30.8	16.6	979
U.S.	1.5	3.2	7.4	21.0	24.1	26.9	15.9	920

Note: Figures are percentages except for Median; Gross rent is the contract rent plus the estimated average monthly cost of utilities (electricity, gas, and water and sewer) and fuels (oil, coal, kerosene, wood, etc.) if these are paid by the renter (or paid for the renter by someone else); (1) Figures cover the Chicago-Naperville-Elgin, IL-IN-WI Metropolitan Statistical Area—see Appendix B for areas included

Source: U.S. Census Bureau, 2010-2014 American Community Survey 5-Year Estimates

Homeownership Rate

Area	2008 (%)	2009 (%)	2010 (%)	2011 (%)	2012 (%)	2013 (%)	2014 (%)	2015 (%)
MSA[1]	68.4	69.2	68.2	67.7	67.1	68.2	66.3	64.3
U.S.	67.8	67.4	66.9	66.1	65.4	65.1	64.5	63.7

Note: (1) Figures cover the Chicago-Naperville-Elgin, IL-IN-WI Metropolitan Statistical Area—see Appendix B for areas included
Source: U.S. Census Bureau, Housing Vacancies and Homeownership Annual Statistics: 2015

Year Housing Structure Built

Area	2010 or Later	2000 -2009	1990 -1999	1980 -1989	1970 -1979	1960 -1969	1950 -1959	1940 -1949	Before 1940	Median Year
City	0.2	6.9	3.9	2.2	6.5	13.5	25.7	8.6	32.7	1953
MSA[1]	0.4	12.0	10.8	8.8	14.0	11.9	13.6	6.1	22.4	1967
U.S.	1.0	14.9	13.9	13.8	15.8	11.0	10.8	5.4	13.3	1976

Note: Figures are percentages except for Median Year; (1) Figures cover the Chicago-Naperville-Elgin, IL-IN-WI Metropolitan Statistical Area—see Appendix B for areas included
Source: U.S. Census Bureau, 2010-2014 American Community Survey 5-Year Estimates

HEALTH

Health Risk Data

Category	MSA[1] (%)	U.S. (%)
Adults aged 18–64 who have any kind of health care coverage	78.8	79.6
Adults who reported being in good or excellent health	83.6	83.1
Adults who are current smokers	17.7	19.6
Adults who are heavy drinkers[2]	5.8	6.1
Adults who are binge drinkers[3]	21.1	16.9
Adults who are overweight (BMI 25.0 - 29.9)	35.7	35.8
Adults who are obese (BMI 30.0 - 99.8)	26.6	27.6
Adults who participated in any physical activities in the past month	79.1	77.1
Adults 50+ who have ever had a sigmoidoscopy or colonoscopy	61.4	67.3
Women aged 40+ who have had a mammogram within the past two years	72.2	74.0
Men aged 40+ who have had a PSA test within the past two years	41.8	45.2
Adults aged 65+ who have had flu shot within the past year	52.2	60.1
Adults who always wear a seatbelt	95.8	93.8

Note: Data as of 2012 unless otherwise noted; (1) Figures cover the Chicago-Naperville-Joliet, IL-IN-WI Metropolitan Statistical Area—see Appendix B for areas included; (2) Heavy drinkers are classified as males having more than two drinks per day or females having more than one drink per day; (3) Binge drinkers are classified as males having five or more drinks on one occasion or females having four or more drinks on one occasion
Source: Centers for Disease Control and Prevention, Behaviorial Risk Factor Surveillance System, SMART: Selected Metropolitan/Micropolitan Area Risk Trends, 2012 (Note: the CDC has discontinued this dataset but will be releasing a replacement in mid-2016)

Chronic Health Indicators

Category	MSA[1] (%)	U.S. (%)
Adults who have ever been told they had a heart attack	3.0	4.5
Adults who have ever been told they had a stroke	2.3	2.9
Adults who have been told they currently have asthma	8.0	8.9
Adults who have ever been told they have arthritis	23.1	25.7
Adults who have ever been told they have diabetes[2]	8.0	9.7
Adults who have ever been told they had skin cancer	3.5	5.7
Adults who have ever been told they had any other types of cancer	5.6	6.5
Adults who have ever been told they have COPD	5.1	6.2
Adults who have ever been told they have kidney disease	2.8	2.5
Adults who have ever been told they have a form of depression	14.0	18.0

Note: Data as of 2012 unless otherwise noted; (1) Figures cover the Chicago-Naperville-Joliet, IL-IN-WI Metropolitan Statistical Area—see Appendix B for areas included; (2) Figures do not include pregnancy-related, borderline, or pre-diabetes
Source: Centers for Disease Control and Prevention, Behaviorial Risk Factor Surveillance System, SMART: Selected Metropolitan/Micropolitan Area Risk Trends, 2012 (Note: the CDC has discontinued this dataset but will be releasing a replacement in mid-2016)

Mortality Rates for the Top 10 Causes of Death in the U.S.

ICD-10[a] Sub-Chapter	ICD-10[a] Code	Age-Adjusted Mortality Rate[1] per 100,000 population	
		County[2]	U.S.
Malignant neoplasms	C00-C97	172.3	163.6
Ischaemic heart diseases	I20-I25	103.9	102.2
Other forms of heart disease	I30-I51	47.4	50.1
Chronic lower respiratory diseases	J40-J47	30.8	41.4
Organic, including symptomatic, mental disorders	F01-F09	39.0	38.5
Cerebrovascular diseases	I60-I69	37.0	36.5
Other external causes of accidental injury	W00-X59	21.0	27.5
Other degenerative diseases of the nervous system	G30-G31	18.9	26.3
Diabetes mellitus	E10-E14	20.3	21.1
Hypertensive diseases	I10-I15	30.2	19.7

Note: (a) ICD-10 = International Classification of Diseases 10th Revision; (1) Mortality rates are a three year average covering 2012-2014; (2) Figures cover Cook County.
Source: Centers for Disease Control and Prevention, National Center for Health Statistics. Underlying Cause of Death 1999-2014 on CDC WONDER Online Database, released 2015.

Mortality Rates for Selected Causes of Death

ICD-10[a] Sub-Chapter	ICD-10[a] Code	Age-Adjusted Mortality Rate[1] per 100,000 population	
		County[2]	U.S.
Assault	X85-Y09	10.5	5.1
Diseases of the liver	K70-K76	12.0	13.5
Human immunodeficiency virus (HIV) disease	B20-B24	2.6	2.1
Influenza and pneumonia	J09-J18	16.6	15.2
Intentional self-harm	X60-X84	8.2	12.7
Malnutrition	E40-E46	0.8	0.9
Obesity and other hyperalimentation	E65-E68	1.8	1.9
Renal failure	N17-N19	17.0	13.0
Transport accidents	V01-V99	6.1	11.6
Viral hepatitis	B15-B19	1.4	2.1

Note: (a) ICD-10 = International Classification of Diseases 10th Revision; (1) Mortality rates are a three year average covering 2012-2014; (2) Figures cover Cook County; Data are Suppressed when the data meet the criteria for confidentiality constraints; Mortality rates are flagged as Unreliable when the rate would be calculated with a numerator of 20 or less.
Source: Centers for Disease Control and Prevention, National Center for Health Statistics. Underlying Cause of Death 1999-2014 on CDC WONDER Online Database, released 2015.

Health Insurance Coverage

Area	With Health Insurance	With Private Health Insurance	With Public Health Insurance	Without Health Insurance	Population Under Age 18 Without Health Insurance
City	95.9	89.5	18.8	4.1	4.0
MSA[1]	86.5	66.8	28.7	13.5	4.1
U.S.	85.8	65.8	31.1	14.2	7.1

Note: Figures are percentages that cover the civilian noninstitutionalized population; (1) Figures cover the Chicago-Naperville-Elgin, IL-IN-WI Metropolitan Statistical Area—see Appendix B for areas included
Source: U.S. Census Bureau, 2010-2014 American Community Survey 5-Year Estimates

Number of Medical Professionals

Area	MDs[3]	DOs[3,4]	Dentists	Podiatrists	Chiropractors	Optometrists
County[1] (number)	21,707	1,127	4,339	602	1,351	959
County[1] (rate[2])	413.7	21.5	82.7	11.5	25.8	18.3
U.S. (rate[2])	272.5	20.9	64.7	5.8	25.9	15.2

Note: Data as of 2014 unless noted; (1) Data covers Cook County; (2) Rate per 100,000 population; (3) Data as of 2013 and includes all active, non-federal physicians; (4) Doctor of Osteopathic Medicine
Source: U.S. Department of Health and Human Services, Health Resources and Services Administration, Bureau of Health Professions, Area Resource File (ARF) 2014-2015

Best Hospitals

According to *U.S. News,* the Chicago-Naperville-Arlington Heights, IL metro area is home to 13 of the best hospitals in the U.S.: **Northwest Community Healthcare** (1 specialty); **Advocate Illinois Masonic Medical Center** (1 specialty); **Northwestern Memorial Hospital** (Honor Roll/13 specialties); **Rehabilitation Institute of Chicago** (1 specialty); **Rush University Medical Center** (7 specialties); **University of Chicago Medical Center** (4 specialties); **Alexian Brothers Medical Center** (1 specialty); **NorthShore Evanston Hospital** (1 specialty); **St. Alexius Medical Center** (1 specialty); **Loyola University Medical Center** (4 specialties); **Advocate Christ Medical Center** (3 specialties); **Advocate Lutheran General Hospital** (1 specialty); **Cadence Health-Central DuPage Hospital** (1 specialty). The hospitals listed were nationally ranked in at least one adult specialty. Only 137 hospitals nationwide were nationally ranked in one or more specialties. Fifteen hospitals in the U.S. made the Honor Roll with high scores in at least six specialties. *U.S. News Online, "America's Best Children's Hospitals 2015-16"*

According to *U.S. News,* the Chicago-Naperville-Arlington Heights, IL metro area is home to three of the best children's hospitals in the U.S.: **Ann and Robert H. Lurie Children's Hospital of Chicago** (Honor Roll/10 specialties); **University of Chicago Comer Children's Hospital** (3 specialties); **Advocate Children's Hospital** (4 specialties). The hospitals listed were highly ranked in at least one pediatric specialty. Eighty-three children's hospitals in the U.S. were nationally ranked in at least one specialty. Twelve children's hospitals in the U.S. made the Honor Roll with high scores in at least three specialties. *U.S. News Online, "America's Best Children's Hospitals 2015-16"*

EDUCATION

Public School District Statistics

District Name	Schls	Pupils	Pupil/ Teacher Ratio	Minority Pupils[1] (%)	Free Lunch Eligible[2] (%)	IEP[3] (%)
Avoca SD 37	2	711	9.7	40.5	7.8	11.3
Wilmette SD 39	6	3,702	13.2	22.0	3.0	11.6

Note: Table includes school districts with 100 or more students; (1) Percentage of students that are not non-Hispanic white; (2) Percentage of students that are eligible for the free lunch program; (3) Percentage of students that have an Individualized Education Program.
Source: U.S. Department of Education, National Center for Education Statistics, Common Core of Data, Local Education Agency (School District) Universe Survey: School Year 2013-2014; U.S. Department of Education, National Center for Education Statistics, Common Core of Data, Public Elementary/Secondary School Universe Survey: School Year 2013-2014

Highest Level of Education

Area	Less than H.S.	H.S. Diploma	Some College, No Deg.	Associate Degree	Bachelor's Degree	Master's Degree	Prof. School Degree	Doctorate Degree
City	1.2	5.7	8.9	3.0	35.1	25.6	14.3	6.2
MSA[1]	13.1	24.8	20.2	6.9	21.5	9.8	2.5	1.3
U.S.	13.7	28.0	21.2	7.9	18.3	7.8	2.0	1.3

Note: Figures cover persons age 25 and over; (1) Figures cover the Chicago-Naperville-Elgin, IL-IN-WI Metropolitan Statistical Area—see Appendix B for areas included
Source: U.S. Census Bureau, 2010-2014 American Community Survey 5-Year Estimates

Educational Attainment by Race

Area	High School Graduate or Higher (%)					Bachelor's Degree or Higher (%)				
	Total	White	Black	Asian	Hisp.[2]	Total	White	Black	Asian	Hisp.[2]
City	98.8	99.1	97.0	97.8	100.0	81.1	81.9	56.2	79.6	81.1
MSA[1]	86.9	89.9	85.1	90.5	62.5	35.1	38.5	20.3	62.8	12.8
U.S.	86.3	88.4	83.2	85.8	64.1	29.3	30.6	19.0	50.9	13.9

Note: Figures shown cover persons 25 years old and over; (1) Figures cover the Chicago-Naperville-Elgin, IL-IN-WI Metropolitan Statistical Area—see Appendix B for areas included; (2) People of Hispanic origin can be of any race
Source: U.S. Census Bureau, 2010-2014 American Community Survey 5-Year Estimates

School Enrollment by Grade and Control

Area	Preschool (%)		Kindergarten (%)		Grades 1 - 4 (%)		Grades 5 - 8 (%)		Grades 9 - 12 (%)	
	Public	Private	Public	Private	Public	Private	Public	Private	Public	Private
City	20.5	79.5	83.7	16.3	80.8	19.2	83.6	16.4	89.0	11.0
MSA[1]	57.4	42.6	85.1	14.9	88.3	11.7	89.1	10.9	90.6	9.4
U.S.	57.4	42.6	87.8	12.2	89.8	10.2	89.9	10.1	90.6	9.4

Note: Figures shown cover persons 3 years old and over; (1) Figures cover the Chicago-Naperville-Elgin, IL-IN-WI Metropolitan Statistical Area—see Appendix B for areas included
Source: U.S. Census Bureau, 2010-2014 American Community Survey 5-Year Estimates

Average Salaries of Public School Classroom Teachers

Area	2013-14		2014-15		Percent Change 2013-14 to 2014-15	Percent Change 2004-05 to 2014-15
	Dollars	Rank[1]	Dollars	Rank[1]		
Illinois	60,124	12	61,083	12	1.59	6.2
U.S. Average	56,610	–	57,379	–	1.36	20.8

Note: (1) State rank ranges from 1 to 51 where 1 indicates highest salary.
Source: National Education Association, Rankings & Estimates: Rankings of the States 2014 and Estimates of School Statistics 2015, March 2015

Higher Education

Four-Year Colleges			Two-Year Colleges			Medical Schools[1]	Law Schools[2]	Voc/ Tech[3]
Public	Private Non-profit	Private For-profit	Public	Private Non-profit	Private For-profit			
0	0	0	0	0	0	0	0	0

Note: Figures cover institutions located within the city limits and include main campuses only; (1) includes schools accredited by the Liaison Committee on Medical Education and the American Osteopathic Association's Commission on Osteopathic College Accreditation; (2) includes ABA-accredited schools, schools with provisional ABA accreditation, and state accredited schools; (3) includes all schools with programs that are less than 2 years.
Source: National Center for Education Statistics, Integrated Postsecondary Education System (IPEDS), 2014-15; Association of American Medical Colleges, Member List, March 21, 2016; American Osteopathic Association, Member List, March 21, 2016; Law School Admission Council, Official Guide to ABA-Approved Law Schools Online, March 21, 2016; Wikipedia, List of Medical Schools in the United States, March 21, 2016; Wikipedia, List of Law Schools in the United States, March 21, 2016

According to *U.S. News & World Report,* the Chicago-Naperville-Arlington Heights, IL metro division is home to six of the best national universities in the U.S.: **University of Chicago** (#4 tie); **Northwestern University** (#12 tie); **Loyola University Chicago** (#99 tie); **Illinois Institute of Technology** (#108 tie); **DePaul University** (#123 tie); **University of Illinois–Chicago** (#129 tie). The indicators used to capture academic quality fall into a number of categories: assessment by administrators at peer institutions; retention of students; faculty resources; student selectivity; financial resources; alumni giving; high school counselor ratings of colleges; and graduation rate. *U.S. News & World Report, "America's Best Colleges 2016"*

According to *U.S. News & World Report,* the Chicago-Naperville-Arlington Heights, IL metro division is home to one of the best liberal arts colleges in the U.S.: **Wheaton College** (#57 tie). The indicators used to capture academic quality fall into a number of categories: assessment by administrators at peer institutions; retention of students; faculty resources; student selectivity; financial resources; alumni giving; high school counselor ratings of colleges; and graduation rate. *U.S. News & World Report, "America's Best Colleges 2016"*

According to *U.S. News & World Report,* the Chicago-Naperville-Arlington Heights, IL metro division is home to four of the top 100 law schools in the U.S.: **University of Chicago, Law School** (#4 tie); **Northwestern University, Pritzker School of Law** (#12); **Loyola University Chicago, School of Law** (#72 tie); **Illinois Institute of Technology, Chicago-Kent College of Law** (#86 tie). The rankings are based on a weighted average of 12 measures of quality: peer assessment score; assessment score by lawyers/judges; median LSAT scores; median undergrad GPA; acceptance rate; employment rates for graduates; placement success; bar passage rate; faculty resources; expenditures per student; student/faculty ratio; and library resources. *U.S. News & World Report, "America's Best Graduate Schools, Law, 2017"*

According to *U.S. News & World Report,* the Chicago-Naperville-Arlington Heights, IL metro division is home to three of the top 75 medical schools for research in the U.S.: **University of**

Chicago, Pritzker School of Medicine (#11 tie); **Northwestern University, Feinberg School of Medicine** (#17); **University of Illinois, College of Medicine** (#47 tie). The rankings are based on a weighted average of 11 measures of quality: quality assessment; peer assessment score; assessment score by residency directors; research activity; total research activity; average research activity per faculty member; student selectivity; median MCAT total score; median undergraduate GPA; acceptance rate; and faculty resources. *U.S. News & World Report, "America's Best Graduate Schools, Medical, 2017"*

According to *U.S. News & World Report,* the Chicago-Naperville-Arlington Heights, IL metro division is home to two of the top 75 business schools in the U.S.: **University of Chicago, Booth School of Business** (#2 tie); **Northwestern University, Kellogg School of Management** (#5 tie). The rankings are based on a weighted average of the following nine measures: quality assessment; peer assessment; recruiter assessment; placement success; mean starting salary and bonus; student selectivity; mean GMAT and GRE scores; mean undergraduate GPA; and acceptance rate. *U.S. News & World Report, "America's Best Graduate Schools, Business, 2017"*

PRESIDENTIAL ELECTION

2012 Presidential Election Results

Area	Obama (%)	Romney (%)	Other (%)
Cook County	74.0	24.6	1.3
U.S.	51.0	47.2	1.8

Note: Results may not add to 100% due to rounding
Source: Dave Leip's Atlas of U.S. Presidential Elections

EMPLOYERS

Major Employers

Company Name	Industry
Abbott Laboratories	Pharmaceutical preparations
Addus HomeCare Corporation	Home health care services
Advocate Lutheran General Hospital	General medical & surgical hospitals
BMO Bankcorp	National commercial banks
City of Chicago	General government
Cook County Bureau of Health Services	Administration of public health programs, county govt
Graphic Packaging International	Folding boxboard
Loyola University Health System	General medical & surgical hospitals
Northshore University Healthsystem	General medical & surgical hospitals
Northwestern Memorial Hospital	General medical & surgical hospitals
SCC Holding Co.	Cups, plastics, except foam
Schneider Electric Holdings	Air transportation, scheduled
SOLO Cup Company	Cups, plastics, except foam
The Allstate Corporation	Fire, marine, & casualty insurance
The University of Chicago Medical Center	General medical & surgical hospitals
United Parcel Service	Mailing & messenger services
United States Steel Corporation	Steel foundries
WM Recycle America	Material recovery

Note: Companies shown are located within the Chicago-Naperville-Elgin, IL-IN-WI Metropolitan Statistical Area.
Source: Hoovers.com; Wikipedia

PUBLIC SAFETY

Crime Rate

Area	All Crimes	Violent Crimes				Property Crimes		
		Murder	Rape[3]	Robbery	Aggrav. Assault	Burglary	Larceny -Theft	Motor Vehicle Theft
City	1,319.9	0.0	10.9	7.3	18.2	207.8	1,057.4	18.2
Metro[1]	2,620.4	6.9	29.9	167.9	222.2	365.2	1,641.4	186.9
U.S.	2,971.8	4.5	36.6	102.2	232.5	542.5	1,837.3	216.2

Note: Figures are crimes per 100,000 population; (1) Figures cover the Chicago-Naperville-Arlington Heights, IL Metropolitan Division—see Appendix B for areas included; (3) The city and U.S. figures shown were reported using the revised Uniform Crime Reporting (UCR) definition of rape. The suburban and metro area figures shown are an aggregate total of the data submitted using both the revised and legacy UCR definitions.
Source: FBI Uniform Crime Reports, 2014

Hate Crimes

Area	Number of Quarters Reported	Number of Incidents per Bias Motivation							
		Race	Religion	Sexual Orientation	Ethnicity	Disability	Gender	Gender Identity
City	3	0	0	0	0	0	0	0
U.S.	4	2,568	1,014	1,017	648	84	33	98

Source: Federal Bureau of Investigation, Hate Crime Statistics 2014

Identity Theft Consumer Complaints

Area	Complaints	Complaints per 100,000 Population	Rank[2]
MSA[1]	14,252	149.2	55
U.S.	490,220	152.4	-

Note: (1) Figures cover the Chicago-Naperville-Elgin, IL-IN-WI Metropolitan Statistical Area—see Appendix B for areas included; (2) Rank ranges from 1 to 379 where 1 indicates greatest number of identity theft complaints per 100,000 population
Source: Federal Trade Commission, Consumer Sentinel Network Data Book for January–December 2015

Fraud and Other Consumer Complaints

Area	Complaints	Complaints per 100,000 Population	Rank[2]
MSA[1]	35,300	369.5	171
U.S.	2,593,159	806.0	-

Note: (1) Figures cover the Chicago-Naperville-Elgin, IL-IN-WI Metropolitan Statistical Area—see Appendix B for areas included; (2) Rank ranges from 1 to 379 where 1 indicates greatest number of identity theft complaints per 100,000 population
Source: Federal Trade Commission, Consumer Sentinel Network Data Book for January–December 2015

RECREATION

Culture

Dance[1]	Theatre[1]	Instrumental Music[1]	Vocal Music[1]	Series and Festivals	Museums and Art Galleries[2]	Zoos and Aquariums[3]
0	0	0	0	0	0	0

Note: (1) Professional perfoming groups; (2) Based on organizations with SIC code 8412; (3) AZA-accredited
Source: The Grey House Performing Arts Directory, 2015-16; Association of Zoos & Aquariums, AZA Member Zoos & Aquariums, March 25, 2016; www.AccuLeads.com, March 29, 2016

Professional Sports Teams

Team Name	League	Year Established
Chicago Bears	National Football League (NFL)	1921
Chicago Blackhawks	National Hockey League (NHL)	1926
Chicago Bulls	National Basketball Association (NBA)	1966
Chicago Cubs	Major League Baseball (MLB)	1874
Chicago Fire	Major League Soccer (MLS)	1997
Chicago White Sox	Major League Baseball (MLB)	1900

Note: Includes teams located in the Chicago-Naperville-Elgin, IL-IN-WI Metropolitan Statistical Area.
Source: Wikipedia, Major Professional Sports Teams of the United States and Canada, March 24, 2016

CLIMATE

Average and Extreme Temperatures

Temperature	Jan	Feb	Mar	Apr	May	Jun	Jul	Aug	Sep	Oct	Nov	Dec	Yr.
Extreme High (°F)	65	71	88	91	93	104	102	100	99	91	78	71	104
Average High (°F)	29	33	45	59	70	79	84	82	75	63	48	34	59
Average Temp. (°F)	21	26	37	49	59	69	73	72	65	53	40	27	49
Average Low (°F)	13	17	28	39	48	57	63	62	54	42	32	19	40
Extreme Low (°F)	-27	-17	-8	7	24	36	40	41	28	17	1	-25	-27

Note: Figures cover the years 1958-1990
Source: National Climatic Data Center, International Station Meteorological Climate Summary, 9/96

Average Precipitation/Snowfall/Humidity

Precip./Humidity	Jan	Feb	Mar	Apr	May	Jun	Jul	Aug	Sep	Oct	Nov	Dec	Yr.
Avg. Precip. (in.)	1.6	1.4	2.7	3.6	3.3	3.7	3.7	4.1	3.7	2.4	2.8	2.3	35.4
Avg. Snowfall (in.)	11	8	7	2	Tr	0	0	0	0	1	2	9	39
Avg. Rel. Hum. 6am (%)	76	77	79	77	77	78	82	85	85	82	80	80	80
Avg. Rel. Hum. 3pm (%)	65	63	59	53	51	52	54	55	55	53	61	68	57

Note: Figures cover the years 1958-1990; Tr = Trace amounts (<0.05 in. of rain; <0.5 in. of snow)
Source: National Climatic Data Center, International Station Meteorological Climate Summary, 9/96

Weather Conditions

Temperature			Daytime Sky			Precipitation		
5°F & below	32°F & below	90°F & above	Clear	Partly cloudy	Cloudy	0.01 inch or more precip.	0.1 inch or more snow/ice	Thunder-storms
21	132	17	84	135	146	125	31	38

Note: Figures are average number of days per year and cover the years 1958-1990
Source: National Climatic Data Center, International Station Meteorological Climate Summary, 9/96

HAZARDOUS WASTE

Superfund Sites

Wilmette has no sites on the EPA's Superfund Final National Priorities List. There are a total of 1,323 Superfund sites on the list in the U.S. *U.S. Environmental Protection Agency, Final National Priorities List, March 18, 2016*

AIR & WATER QUALITY

Air Quality Trends: Ozone

	1990	1995	2000	2005	2010	2011	2012	2013	2014
MSA[1]	0.074	0.093	0.072	0.084	0.070	0.072	0.082	0.066	0.067

Note: (1) Data covers the Chicago-Naperville-Elgin, IL-IN-WI Metropolitan Statistical Area—see Appendix B for areas included. The values shown are the composite ozone concentration averages among trend sites based on the highest fourth daily maximum 8-hour concentration in parts per million. These trends are based on sites having an adequate record of monitoring data during the trend period. Data from exceptional events are included.
Source: U.S. Environmental Protection Agency, Air Quality Monitoring Information, "Air Quality Trends by City, 1990-2014"

Air Quality Index

Area	Percent of Days when Air Quality was...[2]					AQI Statistics[2]	
	Good	Moderate	Unhealthy for Sensitive Groups	Unhealthy	Very Unhealthy	Maximum	Median
MSA[1]	33.2	64.4	1.9	0.5	0.0	183	55

Note: (1) Data covers the Chicago-Naperville-Elgin, IL-IN-WI Metropolitan Statistical Area—see Appendix B for areas included; (2) Based on 365 days with AQI data in 2015. Air Quality Index (AQI) is an index for reporting daily air quality. EPA calculates the AQI for five major air pollutants regulated by the Clean Air Act: ground-level ozone, particle pollution (aka particulate matter), carbon monoxide, sulfur dioxide, and nitrogen dioxide. The AQI runs from 0 to 500. The higher the AQI value, the greater the level of air pollution and the greater the health concern. There are six AQI categories: "Good" AQI is between 0 and 50. Air quality is considered satisfactory; "Moderate" AQI is between 51 and 100. Air quality is acceptable; "Unhealthy for Sensitive Groups" When AQI values are between 101 and 150, members of sensitive groups may experience health effects; "Unhealthy" When AQI values are between 151 and 200 everyone may begin to experience health effects; "Very Unhealthy" AQI values between 201 and 300 trigger a health alert; "Hazardous" AQI values over 300 trigger warnings of emergency conditions (not shown).
Source: U.S. Environmental Protection Agency, Air Quality Index Report, 2015

Air Quality Index Pollutants

Area	Percent of Days when AQI Pollutant was...[2]					
	Carbon Monoxide	Nitrogen Dioxide	Ozone	Sulfur Dioxide	Particulate Matter 2.5	Particulate Matter 10
MSA[1]	0.0	6.8	9.9	2.5	73.2	7.7

Note: (1) Data covers the Chicago-Naperville-Elgin, IL-IN-WI Metropolitan Statistical Area—see Appendix B for areas included; (2) Based on 365 days with AQI data in 2015. The Air Quality Index (AQI) is an index for reporting daily air quality. EPA calculates the AQI for five major air pollutants regulated by the Clean Air Act: ground-level ozone, particle pollution (also known as particulate matter), carbon monoxide, sulfur dioxide, and nitrogen dioxide. The AQI runs from 0 to 500. The higher the AQI value, the greater the level of air pollution and the greater the health concern.
Source: U.S. Environmental Protection Agency, Air Quality Index Report, 2015

Maximum Air Pollutant Concentrations: Particulate Matter, Ozone, CO and Lead

	Particulate Matter 10 (ug/m³)	Particulate Matter 2.5 Wtd AM (ug/m³)	Particulate Matter 2.5 24-Hr (ug/m³)	Ozone (ppm)	Carbon Monoxide (ppm)	Lead (ug/m³)
MSA[1] Level	93	11.7	27	0.076	2	0.15
NAAQS[2]	150	15	35	0.075	9	0.15
Met NAAQS[2]	Yes	Yes	Yes	No	Yes	Yes

Note: (1) Data covers the Chicago-Naperville-Elgin, IL-IN-WI Metropolitan Statistical Area—see Appendix B for areas included; Data from exceptional events are included; (2) National Ambient Air Quality Standards; ppm = parts per million; ug/m³ = micrograms per cubic meter; n/a not available.
Concentrations: Particulate Matter 10 (coarse particulate)—highest second maximum 24-hour concentration; Particulate Matter 2.5 Wtd AM (fine particulate)—highest weighted annual mean concentration; Particulate Matter 2.5 24-Hour (fine particulate)—highest 98th percentile 24-hour concentration; Ozone—highest fourth daily maximum 8-hour concentration; Carbon Monoxide—highest second maximum non-overlapping 8-hour concentration; Lead—maximum running 3-month average
Source: U.S. Environmental Protection Agency, Air Quality Monitoring Information, "Air Quality Statistics by City, 2014"

Maximum Air Pollutant Concentrations: Nitrogen Dioxide and Sulfur Dioxide

	Nitrogen Dioxide AM (ppb)	Nitrogen Dioxide 1-Hr (ppb)	Sulfur Dioxide AM (ppb)	Sulfur Dioxide 1-Hr (ppb)	Sulfur Dioxide 24-Hr (ppb)
MSA[1] Level	21	67	n/a	53	n/a
NAAQS[2]	53	100	30	75	140
Met NAAQS[2]	Yes	Yes	n/a	Yes	n/a

Note: (1) Data covers the Chicago-Naperville-Elgin, IL-IN-WI Metropolitan Statistical Area—see Appendix B for areas included; Data from exceptional events are included; (2) National Ambient Air Quality Standards; ppm = parts per million; ug/m³ = micrograms per cubic meter; n/a not available.
Concentrations: Nitrogen Dioxide AM—highest arithmetic mean concentration; Nitrogen Dioxide 1-Hr—highest 98th percentile 1-hour daily maximum concentration; Sulfur Dioxide AM—highest annual mean concentration; Sulfur Dioxide 1-Hr—highest 99th percentile 1-hour daily maximum concentration; Sulfur Dioxide 24-Hr—highest second maximum 24-hour concentration
Source: U.S. Environmental Protection Agency, Air Quality Monitoring Information, "Air Quality Statistics by City, 2014"

Drinking Water

Water System Name	Pop. Served	Primary Water Source Type	Violations[1]	
			Health Based	Monitoring/ Reporting
Wilmette	27,087	Surface	0	0

Note: (1) Based on violation data from January 1, 2015 to December 31, 2015 (includes unresolved violations from earlier years)
Source: U.S. Environmental Protection Agency, Office of Ground Water and Drinking Water, Safe Drinking Water Information System (based on data extracted April 29, 2016)

Carmel, Indiana

Background

Carmel, located in Clay Township, Hamilton County, just north of Indianapolis, is a city of more than 120 family-oriented neighborhoods. Carmel homes, from custom-designed show houses to turn-of-the-century bungalows, have increased steadily in value as the town continues to attract new residents. It is one of the fastest growing communities in the state.

Primarily an agricultural region throughout the nineteenth century, Carmel has, in recent decades, been tied to the urban Indianapolis area. Indianapolis itself, which suffered considerable economic hardship in the 1960s, has since rebounded dramatically, and the economy of Carmel has grown even more robustly. Carmel enjoys a stable and varied business and employment climate.

Particularly since the 1960s, townspeople have been concerned about maintaining and expanding a viable and attractive system of parks and recreational resources for Carmel and Clay Township, and in the past decade this has resulted in an increase of park land from 46 to 507 acres. This effort has been recognized in the form of five awards from Indiana Park and Recreation Association, one from the Indiana Association of Landscape Architects, and one from the National Park and Recreation Association.

The Carmel Arts Council was formed in 1993 in order to support the fine arts in the city, and it provides a gallery for the display of locally created works. Also established in 1993 was a theater group, the Carmel Community Players, which stages dramatic musical presentations. The city hosts its own Symphony Orchestra that performs both classical and pops concerts throughout the year. The Carmel Clay Historical Society Museum houses a collection of materials and objects of interest to regional researchers and genealogists, and the town is home to a unique Museum of Miniature Houses.

Recreational resources in Carmel are rich and varied, with its own community swimming pool, and year-round ice-skating at the Carmel Ice Skadium. Tennis is available at the Carmel Racquet Club, and the town also supports baseball, basketball and soccer facilities for all ages. There are five public golf courses in town. The city has received special mention as a bicycle-friendly city from the League of American Bicyclists.

Carmel City Center, a complex of retail, dining, and entertainment establishments in the center of the city, includes the Carmel Performing Arts Center, with a 1,600 seat world-class concert hall, and a 500 seat theater. The City Center, adjacent to the Monon Trail Park, provides a network of facilities where professionals can lunch during the day, enjoy brisk walks on the Monon Trail at any time, and dine in the evenings with family or friends. Elsewhere in the city, the Old Town district has been redeveloped to include the Arts & Design District, a premier Midwest destination for art galleries, interior designers, antique stores, showrooms, specialty shops and restaurants. The 161-acre Central Park features the new Monon Community Center and Waterpark.

Carmel Clay Schools achieve consistently high ratings in standardized tests. Carmel students routinely win state or regional music and drama championships, and the Science Olympiad Team has achieved the highest ranking at state and national levels. Sports achievements are also dramatic, and Carmel High has won 119 state championships in 17 different sports. The school system includes Carmel High School, three middle schools and eleven elementary schools.

Carmel enjoys a four-season temperate climate, with tropical air from the Gulf of Mexico bringing warm temperatures and moderate humidity in summer, and polar air from the north producing cold winters.

Rankings

General Rankings

- The U.S. Conference of Mayors and Waste Management sponsor the City Livability Awards Program, which recognize mayors for exemplary leadership in developing and implementing specific programs that improve the quality of life in America's cities. Carmel was one of 15 second round finalists in the small cities (population under 100,000) category. *U.S. Conference of Mayors, "2016 City Livability Awards"*

Business/Finance Rankings

- The personal finance site NerdWallet analyzed 183 American metropolitan areas with populations over 250,000 and more than 15,000 businesses to rank where entrepreneurs find the most success. Criteria included area economy, annual income, housing cost, unemployment rate, and the success rate of area businesses. Indianapolis* ranked #95. *www.nerdwallet.com, "Best Places to Start a Business," April 27, 2015*
- The editors of *Kiplinger's Personal Finance Magazine* named Indianapolis* to their list of ten of the best metro areas for start-ups. The area ranked #8.Criteria: well-educated workforce; low living costs for self-employed people, as measured by the Council for Community and Economic Research; a strong existing community of small business; low unemployment; low business costs. *www.kiplinger.com, "10 Great Cities for Starting a Business," October 2014*
- Based on metro area social media reviews, the employment opinion group Glassdoor surveyed 50 of the largest U.S. metro areas and equally weighed cost of living, hiring opportunity, and job satisfaction to compose a list of "25 Best Cities for Jobs." The Indianapolis* metro area was ranked #30 in overall job satisfaction. *www.glassdoor.com, "Best Cities for Jobs," May 19, 2015*
- In a survey of economic confidence in the nation's 50 largest metropolitan areas conducted January–December 2014, the Indianapolis* metro area placed #42, according to Gallup's 2014 Economic Confidence Index. *Gallup, "San Jose and San Francisco Lead in Economic Confidence," March 19, 2015*
- The Brookings Institution ranked the 100 largest metro areas in the U.S. based on income inequality. Indianapolis* was ranked #64 (#1 = greatest ineqality). Criteria: the "95/20 ratio," a figure representing the income at which a household earns more than 95 percent of all other households, divided by the income at which a household earns more than only 20 percent of all other households. *Brookings Institution, "Income Inequality, 100 Largest U.S. Metro Areas, 2007-2014," January 14, 2016*
- The Indianapolis* metro area was identified as one of the most affordable metropolitan areas in America by *Forbes*. The area ranked #9 out of 20 based on the National Association of Home Builders/Wells Fargo Housing Affordability Index and Sperling's Best Places' cost-of-living index. *Forbes.com, "America's Most Affordable Cities in 2015," March 12, 2015*
- Indianapolis* was identified as one of America's most frugal metro areas by *Coupons.com*. The city ranked #16 out of 25. Criteria: online coupon usage. *Coupons.com, "Top 25 Most Frugal Cities of 2014," May 11, 2015*
- Indianapolis* was identified as one of America's most frugal metro areas by *Coupons.com*. The city ranked #9 out of 25. Criteria: Grocery IQ and coupons.com mobile app usage. *Coupons.com, "Top 25 Most On-the-Go Frugal Cities of 2013," April 10, 2014*
- The Indianapolis* metro area appeared on the Milken Institute "2015 Best Performing Cities" list. Rank: #48 out of 200 large metro areas. Criteria: job growth; wage and salary growth; high-tech output growth. *Milken Institute, "Best-Performing Cities 2015," December 2015*
- *Forbes* ranked the 200 most populous metro areas to determine the nation's "Best Places for Business and Careers." The Indianapolis* metro area was ranked #8. Criteria: costs (business and living); job growth (past and projected); income growth; educational attainment (college and high school); projected economic growth; cultural and recreational opportunities; net migration patterns; number of highly ranked colleges. *Forbes, "The Best Places for Business and Careers 2015," July 29, 2015*

Education Rankings

- Personal finance website *WalletHub* analyzed the 150 largest U.S. metropolitan statistical areas to determine where the most educated Americans are choosing to settle. Criteria: education quality and attainment gap; education levels; percentage of workers with degrees; public school rankings; quality and size of each metro area's universities. Indianapolis* was ranked #65 (#1 = most educated city). *www.WalletHub.com, "2015's Most and Least Educated Cities*

Environmental Rankings

- The Indianapolis* metro area came in at #163 for the relative comfort of its climate on Sperling's list of "chill cities," as measured by the Sperling Heat Index. All 361 metro areas are included. Criteria included daytime high temperatures, nighttime low temperatures, dew point, and relative humidity at the high temperatures. *www.bertsperling.com, "Sperling's Chill Cities," July 18, 2013*
- Sperling's BestPlaces assessed 379 metropolitan areas of the United States for the likelihood of dangerously extreme weather events or earthquakes. In general the Southeast and South-Central regions have the highest risk of weather extremes and earthquakes, while the Pacific Northwest enjoys the lowest risk. Of the least risky metropolitan areas, the Indianapolis* metro area was ranked #283. *www.bestplaces.net, "Safest Places from Natural Disasters," April 2011*
- The U.S. Environmental Protection Agency (EPA) released a list of U.S. metropolitan areas with the most ENERGY STAR certified buildings in 2015. The Indianapolis* metro area was ranked #24 out of 25. *U.S. Environmental Protection Agency, "Top Cities With the Most ENERGY STAR Certified Buildings in 2016," March 30, 2016*
- The U.S. Environmental Protection Agency (EPA) released a list of mid-size U.S. metropolitan areas with the most ENERGY STAR certified buildings in 2015. The Indianapolis* metro area was ranked #4 out of 10. *U.S. Environmental Protection Agency, "Top Cities With the Most ENERGY STAR Certified Buildings in 2016," March 30, 2016*
- Indianapolis* was highlighted as one of the 25 metro areas most polluted by year-round particle pollution (Annual PM 2.5) in the U.S. during 2011 through 2013. The area ranked #17. *American Lung Association, State of the Air 2015*
- Indianapolis* was highlighted as one of the 25 metro areas most polluted by short-term particle pollution (24-hour PM 2.5) in the U.S. during 2011 through 2013. The area ranked #23. *American Lung Association, State of the Air 2015*

Health/Fitness Rankings

- Analysts who tracked obesity rates in 100 of the nation's most populous areas found that the Indianapolis* metro area was one of the ten communities where residents were most likely to be obese, defined as a BMI score of 30 or above. *www.gallup.com, "Colorado Springs Residents Least Likely to Be Obese," May 28, 2015*
- For each of the 50 most populous metro areas in the United States, the American College of Sports Medicine's American Fitness Index evaluated infrastructure, community assets, and policies that encourage healthy and fit lifestyles, including preventive health behaviors, levels of chronic disease conditions, health care access, and community resources and policies that support physical activity. The Indianapolis* metro area ranked #50 for "community fitness." *www.americanfitnessindex.org, "ACSM American Fitness Index Health and Community Fitness Status of the 50 Largest Metropolitan Areas," May 2015*
- The Indianapolis* metro area was identified as one of the worst cities for bed bugs in America by pest control company Orkin. The area ranked #15 out of 50 based on the number of bed bug treatments Orkin performed from January to December 2015. *Orkin, "Chicago Tops Bed Bug Cities List for Fourth Year in a Row," January 13, 2016*
- Indianapolis* was identified as a "2016 Spring Allergy Capital." The area ranked #65 out of 100. Three groups of factors were used to identify the most severe cities for people with allergies during the spring season: annual pollen levels; medicine utilization; access to board-certified allergists. *Asthma and Allergy Foundation of America, "Spring Allergy Capitals 2016"*

- Indianapolis* was identified as a "2015 Asthma Capital." The area ranked #11 out of the nation's 100 largest metropolitan areas. Criteria: estimated prevalence; self-reported prevalence; crude death rate for asthma; annual pollen score; annual air quality; public smoking laws; number of board-certified asthma specialists; school inhaler access laws; rescue medication use; controller medication use; ER visits for asthma; uninsured rate; poverty rate. *Asthma and Allergy Foundation of America, "Asthma Capitals 2015"*
- The Indianapolis* metro area ranked #176 out of 190 in The Gallup-Healthways Well-Being Index. Criteria: purpose; social well being; financial health; community and physical health. Results are based on telephone interviews with adults, aged 18 and older, living in metropolitan areas in the 50 U.S. states and the District of Columbia. *Gallup-Healthways, "State of American Well-Being," February 23, 2016*

Real Estate Rankings

- The Indianapolis* metro area was identified as one of the top 20 housing markets to invest in for 2016 by *Forbes*. The area ranked #11. Criteria: strong job and population growth; anticipated home price appreciation; and other factors. *Forbes.com, "Best Buy Cities: Where to Invest in Housing in 2016," January 27, 2016*
- The Indianapolis* metro area was identified as one of the 10 worst condo markets in the U.S. in 2015. The area ranked #9 out of 61 markets. Criteria: year-over-year change of median sales price of existing apartment condo-coop homes between the 4th quarter of 2014 and the 4th quarter of 2015. *National Association of Realtors®, Median Sales Price of Existing Apartment Condo-Coop Homes for Metropolitan Areas, 4th Quarter 2015*
- Indianapolis* was ranked #31 out of 225 metro areas in terms of housing affordability in 2015 by the National Association of Home Builders (#1 = most affordable). Criteria: the share of homes sold in that area affordable to a family earning the local median income, based on standard mortgage underwriting criteria. *National Association of Home Builders®, NAHB-Wells Fargo Housing Opportunity Index, 4th Quarter 2015*

Safety Rankings

- Carmel was identified as one of the safest cities in America by NeighborhoodScout. The city ranked #49 out of 100. Criteria: number of violent and property crimes per 1,000 residents. The editors only considered cities with 25,000 or more residents. *NeighborhoodScout, "Safest Cities in America 2016"*
- The National Insurance Crime Bureau ranked 380 metro areas in the U.S. in terms of per capita rates of vehicle theft. The Indianapolis* metro area ranked #31 (#1 = highest rate). Criteria: number of vehicle theft offenses per 100,000 inhabitants in 2014. *National Insurance Crime Bureau, "Hot Spots 2014," June 24, 2015*

Seniors/Retirement Rankings

- From its Best Cities for Successful Aging indexes, the Milken Institute generated rankings for metropolitan areas, weighing data in eight categories—health care, wellness, living arrangements, transportation, financial characteristics, education and employment opportunities, community engagement, and overall livability. The Indianapolis* metro area was ranked #49 overall in the large metro area category. *Milken Institute, "Best Cities for Successful Aging, 2014"*

Miscellaneous Rankings

- The watchdog site Charity Navigator conducts an annual study of charities in the nation's major markets both to analyze statistical differences in their financial, accountability, and transparency practices and to track year-to-year variations in individual communities. The Indianapolis* metro area was ranked #6 among the 30 metro markets in the rating dimension of Overall Score. *www.charitynavigator.org, "Metro Market Study 2015," June 5, 2015*

- Mars Chocolate North America, the makers of COMBOS®, in partnership with Sperling's BestPlaces, ranked 50 major metro areas in terms of their "manliness." The Indianapolis* metro area ranked #13. Criteria: number of professional sports teams; number of nearby NASCAR tracks and racing events; manly lifestyle; concentration of manly retail stores; manly occupations per capita; salty snack sales; "Board of Manliness" rankings. *Mars Chocolate North America, "America's Manliest Cities 2012"*
- The National Alliance to End Homelessness ranked the 100 most populous metro areas with the highest rate of homelessness. The Indianapolis* metro area ranked #86. Criteria: number of homeless people per 10,000 population in 2011. *National Alliance to End Homelessness, The State of Homelessness in America 2012*

Carmel is located within the Indianapolis-Carmel-Anderson, IN Metropolitan Statistical Area.

Business Environment

CITY FINANCES

City Government Finances

Component	2012 ($000)	2012 ($ per capita)
Total Revenues	130,157	1,643
Total Expenditures	119,497	1,508
Debt Outstanding	367,804	4,644
Cash and Securities[1]	44,136	557

Note: (1) Cash and security holdings of a government at the close of its fiscal year, including those of its dependent agencies, utilities, and liquor stores.
Source: U.S Census Bureau, State & Local Government Finances 2012

City Government Revenue by Source

Source	2012 ($000)	2012 ($ per capita)
General Revenue		
From Federal Government	377	4
From State Government	11,849	149
From Local Governments	5,647	71
Taxes		
Property	49,941	630
Sales and Gross Receipts	2,053	25
Personal Income	18,452	233
Corporate Income	0	0
Motor Vehicle License	0	0
Other Taxes	2,402	30
Current Charges	16,494	208
Liquor Store	0	0
Utility	17,945	226
Employee Retirement	311	3

Source: U.S Census Bureau, State & Local Government Finances 2012

City Government Expenditures by Function

Function	2012 ($000)	2012 ($ per capita)	2012 (%)
General Direct Expenditures			
Air Transportation	0	0	0.0
Corrections	0	0	0.0
Education	0	0	0.0
Employment Security Administration	0	0	0.0
Financial Administration	718	9	0.6
Fire Protection	17,382	219	14.5
General Public Buildings	0	0	0.0
Governmental Administration, Other	5,142	64	4.3
Health	0	0	0.0
Highways	8,657	109	7.2
Hospitals	0	0	0.0
Housing and Community Development	6,405	80	5.3
Interest on General Debt	11,115	140	9.3
Judicial and Legal	645	8	0.5
Libraries	0	0	0.0
Parking	0	0	0.0
Parks and Recreation	3,628	45	3.0
Police Protection	15,059	190	12.6
Public Welfare	0	0	0.0
Sewerage	5,428	68	4.5
Solid Waste Management	0	0	0.0
Veterans' Services	0	0	0.0
Liquor Store	0	0	0.0
Utility	25,134	317	21.0
Employee Retirement	564	7	0.4

Source: U.S Census Bureau, State & Local Government Finances 2012

DEMOGRAPHICS

Population Growth

Area	1990 Census	2000 Census	2010 Census	2014* Estimate	Population Growth (%) 1990-2014	Population Growth (%) 2010-2014
City	27,705	37,733	79,191	83,474	201.3	5.4
MSA[1]	1,294,217	1,525,104	1,756,241	1,931,182	49.2	10.0
U.S.	248,709,873	281,421,906	308,745,538	314,107,084	26.3	1.7

Note: (1) Figures cover the Indianapolis-Carmel-Anderson, IN Metropolitan Statistical Area—see Appendix B for areas included; (*) 2010-2014 5-year estimated population
Source: U.S. Census Bureau, 1990 Census, Census 2000, Census 2010, 2010-2014 American Community Survey 5-Year Estimates

Household Size

Area	Persons in Household (%) One	Two	Three	Four	Five	Six	Seven or More	Average Household Size
City	20.2	35.8	16.1	17.3	7.7	1.6	0.9	2.72
MSA[1]	28.4	33.4	15.8	13.1	6.0	2.0	1.0	2.57
U.S.	27.5	33.5	15.8	13.1	6.0	2.3	1.4	2.64

Note: (1) Figures cover the Indianapolis-Carmel-Anderson, IN Metropolitan Statistical Area—see Appendix B for areas included
Source: U.S. Census Bureau, 2010-2014 American Community Survey 5-Year Estimates

Race

Area	White Alone[2] (%)	Black Alone[2] (%)	Asian Alone[2] (%)	AIAN[3] Alone[2] (%)	NHOPI[4] Alone[2] (%)	Other Race Alone[2] (%)	Two or More Races (%)
City	84.1	2.7	9.7	0.1	0.0	1.0	2.4
MSA[1]	77.9	14.6	2.3	0.2	0.0	2.6	2.3
U.S.	73.8	12.6	5.0	0.8	0.2	4.7	2.9

Note: (1) Figures cover the Indianapolis-Carmel-Anderson, IN Metropolitan Statistical Area—see Appendix B for areas included; (2) Alone is defined as not being in combination with one or more other races; (3) American Indian and Alaska Native; (4) Native Hawaiian and Other Pacific Islander
Source: U.S. Census Bureau, 2010-2014 American Community Survey 5-Year Estimates

Hispanic or Latino Origin

Area	Total (%)	Mexican (%)	Puerto Rican (%)	Cuban (%)	Other (%)
City	3.5	2.0	0.1	0.2	1.3
MSA[1]	6.2	4.5	0.3	0.1	1.3
U.S.	16.9	10.8	1.6	0.6	3.8

Note: Persons of Hispanic or Latino origin can be of any race; (1) Figures cover the Indianapolis-Carmel-Anderson, IN Metropolitan Statistical Area—see Appendix B for areas included
Source: U.S. Census Bureau, 2010-2014 American Community Survey 5-Year Estimates

Ancestry

Area	German	Irish	English	American	Italian	Polish	French[2]	Scottish	Dutch
City	25.9	13.2	11.1	7.7	3.9	3.4	2.3	2.6	2.4
MSA[1]	20.6	11.7	9.3	9.5	2.7	1.9	2.1	2.0	1.6
U.S.	14.9	10.8	8.0	7.1	5.5	3.0	2.7	1.7	1.4

Note: Figures are the percentage of the total population reporting a particular ancestry. The nine most commonly reported ancestries in the U.S. are shown. Figures include multiple ancestries (e.g. if a person reported being Irish and Italian, they were included in both columns); (1) Figures cover the Indianapolis-Carmel-Anderson, IN Metropolitan Statistical Area—see Appendix B for areas included; (2) Excludes Basque
Source: U.S. Census Bureau, 2010-2014 American Community Survey 5-Year Estimates

Foreign-Born Population

Area	Percent of Population Born in								
	Any Foreign Country	Asia	Mexico	Europe	Carribean	Central America[2]	South America	Africa	Canada
City	11.9	7.3	0.7	1.8	0.2	0.2	0.4	0.7	0.5
MSA[1]	6.2	2.0	2.0	0.6	0.2	0.4	0.2	0.7	0.1
U.S.	13.1	3.8	3.7	1.5	1.2	1.0	0.9	0.6	0.3

Note: (1) Figures cover the Indianapolis-Carmel-Anderson, IN Metropolitan Statistical Area—see Appendix B for areas included; (2) Excludes Mexico.
Source: U.S. Census Bureau, 2010-2014 American Community Survey 5-Year Estimates

Marital Status

Area	Never Married	Now Married[2]	Separated	Widowed	Divorced
City	22.6	66.3	0.6	3.6	6.9
MSA[1]	31.2	49.0	1.8	5.3	12.8
U.S.	32.5	48.4	2.2	5.9	10.9

Note: Figures are percentages and cover the population 15 years of age and older; (1) Figures cover the Indianapolis-Carmel-Anderson, IN Metropolitan Statistical Area—see Appendix B for areas included; (2) Excludes separated
Source: U.S. Census Bureau, 2010-2014 American Community Survey 5-Year Estimates

Disability Status

Area	All Ages	Under 18 Years Old	18 to 64 Years Old	65 Years and Over
City	6.3	2.6	4.0	28.4
MSA[1]	12.0	4.6	10.6	36.3
U.S.	12.3	4.1	10.2	36.3

Note: Figures show percent of the civilian noninstitutionalized population that reported having a disability. Disability status is determined from from six types of difficulty: vision, hearing, cognitive, ambulatory, self-care, and independent living. For children under 5 years old, hearing and vision difficulty are used to determine disability status. For children between the ages of 5 and 14, disability status is determined from hearing, vision, cognitive, ambulatory, and self-care difficulties. For people aged 15 years and older, they are considered to have a disability if they have difficulty with any one of the six difficulty types; (1) Figures cover the Indianapolis-Carmel-Anderson, IN Metropolitan Statistical Area—see Appendix B for areas included.
Source: U.S. Census Bureau, 2010-2014 American Community Survey 5-Year Estimates

Age

Area	Percent of Population									Median Age
	Under Age 5	Age 5–19	Age 20–34	Age 35–44	Age 45–54	Age 55–64	Age 65–74	Age 75–84	Age 85+	
City	6.3	24.4	13.2	15.2	16.6	12.6	7.0	3.0	1.5	39.3
MSA[1]	7.0	21.1	20.5	13.7	14.3	11.6	6.6	3.6	1.6	36.0
U.S.	6.4	19.9	20.6	13.0	14.1	12.3	7.6	4.3	1.9	37.4

Note: (1) Figures cover the Indianapolis-Carmel-Anderson, IN Metropolitan Statistical Area—see Appendix B for areas included
Source: U.S. Census Bureau, 2010-2014 American Community Survey 5-Year Estimates

Gender

Area	Males	Females	Males per 100 Females
City	40,238	43,236	93.1
MSA[1]	943,352	987,830	95.5
U.S.	154,515,159	159,591,925	96.8

Note: (1) Figures cover the Indianapolis-Carmel-Anderson, IN Metropolitan Statistical Area—see Appendix B for areas included
Source: U.S. Census Bureau, 2010-2014 American Community Survey 5-Year Estimates

Religious Groups by Family

Area	Catholic	Baptist	Non-Den.	Methodist[2]	Lutheran	LDS[3]	Pente-costal	Presby-terian[4]	Muslim[5]	Judaism
MSA[1]	10.5	10.2	7.1	4.9	1.6	0.7	1.6	1.6	0.2	0.3
U.S.	19.1	9.3	4.0	4.0	2.3	2.0	1.9	1.6	0.8	0.7

Note: Figures are the number of adherents as a percentage of the total population; (1) Figures cover the Indianapolis-Carmel, IN Metropolitan Statistical Area—see Appendix B for areas included; (2) Methodist/Pietist; (3) Latter Day Saints; (4) Reformed; (5) Figures are estimates
Source: Association of Statisticians of American Religious Bodies, 2010 U.S. Religion Census: Religious Congregations & Membership Study

Religious Groups by Tradition

Area	Catholic	Evangelical Protestant	Mainline Protestant	Other Tradition	Black Protestant	Orthodox
MSA[1]	10.5	18.2	9.6	1.6	1.8	0.2
U.S.	19.1	16.2	7.3	4.3	1.6	0.3

Note: Figures are the number of adherents as a percentage of the total population; (1) Figures cover the Indianapolis-Carmel, IN Metropolitan Statistical Area—see Appendix B for areas included
Source: Association of Statisticians of American Religious Bodies, 2010 U.S. Religion Census: Religious Congregations & Membership Study

ECONOMY

Gross Metropolitan Product

Area	2013	2014	2015	2016	Rank[2]
MSA[1]	126.5	132.3	138.0	144.6	25

Note: Figures are in billions of dollars; (1) Figures cover the Indianapolis-Carmel-Anderson, IN Metropolitan Statistical Area—see Appendix B for areas included; (2) Rank is based on 2016 data and ranges from 1 to 381
Source: The U.S. Conference of Mayors, U.S. Metro Economies: GMP and Employment 2014-2016, June 2015

Economic Growth

Area	2011-13 (%)	2014 (%)	2015 (%)	2016 (%)	Rank[2]
MSA[1]	3.0	3.3	2.8	2.9	99
U.S.	2.2	2.4	2.3	2.9	-

Note: Figures are real gross metropolitan product (GMP) growth rates and represent annual average percent change; (1) Figures cover the Indianapolis-Carmel-Anderson, IN Metropolitan Statistical Area—see Appendix B for areas included; (2) Rank is based on 2016 data and ranges from 1 to 381
Source: The U.S. Conference of Mayors, U.S. Metro Economies: GMP and Employment 2014-2016, June 2015

Metropolitan Area Exports

Area	2009	2010	2011	2012	2013	2014	Rank[2]
MSA[1]	8,030.8	9,446.7	9,560.6	10,436.0	9,747.4	9,539.3	34

Note: Figures are in millions of dollars; (1) Figures cover the Indianapolis-Carmel-Anderson, IN Metropolitan Statistical Area—see Appendix B for areas included; (2) Rank is based on 2014 data and ranges from 1 to 385
Source: U.S. Department of Commerce, International Trade Administration, Office of Trade & Industry Information, Manufacturing & Services, data extracted March 10, 2016

Building Permits

Area	Single-Family			Multi-Family			Total		
	2014	2015p	Pct. Chg.	2014	2015p	Pct. Chg.	2014	2015p	Pct. Chg.
City	352	275	-21.9	714	1,368	91.6	1,066	1,643	54.1
MSA[1]	4,965	5,054	1.8	3,041	3,647	19.9	8,006	8,701	8.7
U.S.	640,300	690,800	7.9	411,800	487,600	18.4	1,052,100	1,178,400	12.0

Note: (1) Figures cover the Indianapolis-Carmel-Anderson, IN Metropolitan Statistical Area—see Appendix B for areas included; Figures represent new, privately-owned housing units authorized (unadjusted data); All permit data are based on estimates with imputation; (p) preliminary data.
Source: U.S. Census Bureau, Manufacturing, Mining, and Construction Statistics, Building Permits, 2014, 2015

Bankruptcy Filings

Area	Business Filings			Nonbusiness Filings		
	2014	2015	% Chg.	2014	2015	% Chg.
Hamilton County	52	54	3.8	889	766	-13.8
U.S.	26,983	24,735	-8.3	909,812	819,760	-9.9

Note: Business filings include Chapter 7, Chapter 11, Chapter 12, and Chapter 13; Nonbusiness filings include Chapter 7, Chapter 11, and Chapter 13
Source: Administrative Office of the U.S. Courts, Business and Nonbusiness Bankruptcy, County Cases Commenced by Chapter of the Bankruptcy Code, During the 12- Month Period Ending December 31, 2014 and Business and Nonbusiness Bankruptcy, County Cases Commenced by Chapter of the Bankruptcy Code, During the 12- Month Period Ending December 31, 2015

Housing Vacancy Rates

Area	Gross Vacancy Rate[2] (%)			Year-Round Vacancy Rate[3] (%)			Rental Vacancy Rate[4] (%)			Homeowner Vacancy Rate[5] (%)		
	2013	2014	2015	2013	2014	2015	2013	2014	2015	2013	2014	2015
MSA[1]	9.2	8.8	7.4	8.7	8.7	7.4	10.9	10.9	8.4	1.5	2.2	1.0
U.S.	13.6	13.4	12.9	10.7	10.4	10.0	8.3	7.6	7.1	2.0	1.9	1.8

Note: (1) Figures cover the Indianapolis-Carmel-Anderson, IN Metropolitan Statistical Area—see Appendix B for areas included; (2) The percentage of the total housing inventory that is vacant; (3) The percentage of the housing inventory (excluding seasonal units) that is year-round vacant; (4) The percentage of rental inventory that is vacant for rent; (5) The percentage of homeowner inventory that is vacant for sale
Source: U.S. Census Bureau, Housing Vacancies and Homeownership Annual Statistics: 2015

INCOME

Income

Area	Per Capita ($)	Median Household ($)	Average Household ($)
City	52,207	107,916	141,596
MSA[1]	27,778	52,434	71,052
U.S.	28,555	53,482	74,596

Note: (1) Figures cover the Indianapolis-Carmel-Anderson, IN Metropolitan Statistical Area—see Appendix B for areas included
Source: U.S. Census Bureau, 2010-2014 American Community Survey 5-Year Estimates

Household Income Distribution

Area	Percent of Households Earning							
	Under $15,000	$15,000 -24,999	$25,000 -34,999	$35,000 -49,999	$50,000 -74,999	$75,000 -99,000	$100,000 -149,999	$150,000 and up
City	4.3	4.1	5.1	7.1	12.8	12.0	23.9	30.7
MSA[1]	11.7	10.5	10.7	14.6	18.6	12.6	12.9	8.3
U.S.	12.5	10.7	10.2	13.5	17.8	12.2	13.0	10.0

Note: (1) Figures cover the Indianapolis-Carmel-Anderson, IN Metropolitan Statistical Area—see Appendix B for areas included
Source: U.S. Census Bureau, 2010-2014 American Community Survey 5-Year Estimates

Poverty Rate

Area	All Ages	Under 18 Years Old	18 to 64 Years Old	65 Years and Over
City	3.6	4.1	3.7	2.3
MSA[1]	14.6	20.8	13.5	7.0
U.S.	15.6	21.9	14.6	9.4

Note: Figures are percentage of people whose income during the past 12 months was below the poverty level; (1) Figures cover the Indianapolis-Carmel-Anderson, IN Metropolitan Statistical Area—see Appendix B for areas included
Source: U.S. Census Bureau, 2010-2014 American Community Survey 5-Year Estimates

EMPLOYMENT

Labor Force and Employment

Area	Civilian Labor Force			Workers Employed		
	Dec. 2014	Dec. 2015	% Chg.	Dec. 2014	Dec. 2015	% Chg.
City	45,598	46,885	2.8	43,824	45,476	3.7
MSA[1]	996,479	1,020,083	2.3	942,497	978,074	3.7
U.S.	155,521,000	157,245,000	1.1	147,190,000	149,703,000	1.7

Note: Data is not seasonally adjusted and covers workers 16 years of age and older; (1) Figures cover the Indianapolis-Carmel-Anderson, IN Metropolitan Statistical Area—see Appendix B for areas included
Source: Bureau of Labor Statistics, Local Area Unemployment Statistics

Unemployment Rate

Area	2015											
	Jan.	Feb.	Mar.	Apr.	May	Jun.	Jul.	Aug.	Sep.	Oct.	Nov.	Dec.
City	4.3	3.8	3.7	2.9	3.3	3.5	3.4	3.0	2.9	3.0	3.2	3.0
MSA[1]	6.2	5.7	5.5	4.3	4.5	4.5	4.4	4.2	3.8	4.0	4.2	4.1
U.S.	6.1	5.8	5.6	5.1	5.3	5.5	5.6	5.2	4.9	4.8	4.8	4.8

Note: Data is not seasonally adjusted and covers workers 16 years of age and older; (1) Figures cover the Indianapolis-Carmel-Anderson, IN Metropolitan Statistical Area—see Appendix B for areas included
Source: Bureau of Labor Statistics, Local Area Unemployment Statistics

Employment by Occupation

Occupation Classification	City (%)	MSA[1] (%)	U.S. (%)
Management, Business, Science, and Arts	60.1	37.0	36.4
Natural Resources, Construction, and Maintenance	2.8	7.8	9.0
Production, Transportation, and Material Moving	4.7	13.3	12.1
Sales and Office	23.4	25.4	24.4
Service	9.0	16.5	18.2

Note: Figures cover employed civilians 16 years of age and older; (1) Figures cover the Indianapolis-Carmel-Anderson, IN Metropolitan Statistical Area—see Appendix B for areas included
Source: U.S. Census Bureau, 2010-2014 American Community Survey 5-Year Estimates

Employment by Industry

Sector	MSA[1]		U.S.
	Number of Employees	Percent of Total	Percent of Total
Construction	45,400	4.3	4.5
Education and Health Services	150,200	14.4	15.7
Financial Activities	63,200	6.0	5.7
Government	132,300	12.7	15.5
Information	16,100	1.5	1.9
Leisure and Hospitality	104,000	10.0	10.4
Manufacturing	90,200	8.6	8.6
Mining and Logging	600	<0.1	0.5
Other Services	44,300	4.2	3.9
Professional and Business Services	165,200	15.9	13.9
Retail Trade	112,200	10.8	11.3
Transportation, Warehousing, and Utilities	68,100	6.5	3.9
Wholesale Trade	46,300	4.4	4.1

Note: Figures are non-farm employment as of December 2015. Figures are not seasonally adjusted and include workers 16 years of age and older; (1) Figures cover the Indianapolis-Carmel-Anderson, IN Metropolitan Statistical Area—see Appendix B for areas included
Source: Bureau of Labor Statistics, Current Employment Statistics, Employment, Hours, and Earnings

Occupations with Greatest Projected Employment Growth: 2012 – 2022

Occupation[1]	2012 Employment	2022 Projected Employment	Numeric Employment Change	Percent Employment Change
Registered Nurses	59,270	69,750	10,480	17.7
Laborers and Freight, Stock, and Material Movers, Hand	58,300	67,220	8,920	15.3
Retail Salespersons	88,940	97,570	8,630	9.7
Combined Food Preparation and Serving Workers, Including Fast Food	79,310	87,710	8,400	10.6
Office Clerks, General	52,850	59,940	7,090	13.4
Team Assemblers	64,220	70,850	6,630	10.3
Nursing Assistants	31,570	37,490	5,920	18.8
Janitors and Cleaners, Except Maids and Housekeeping Cleaners	42,560	48,450	5,890	13.8
Waiters and Waitresses	49,630	54,920	5,290	10.7
Personal Care Aides	20,120	25,260	5,140	25.6

Note: Projections cover Indiana; (1) Sorted by numeric employment change
Source: www.projectionscentral.com, State Occupational Projections, 2012–2022 Long-Term Projections

Fastest Growing Occupations: 2012 – 2022

Occupation[1]	2012 Employment	2022 Projected Employment	Numeric Employment Change	Percent Employment Change
Chiropractors	640	860	220	35.0
Dental Hygienists	4,780	6,440	1,660	34.7
Ophthalmic Medical Technicians	800	1,080	280	34.7
Dentists, General	1,670	2,250	580	34.4
Anesthesiologists	950	1,270	320	34.1
Dental Assistants	5,800	7,770	1,970	34.0
Optometrists	710	960	250	33.9
Surgeons	780	1,030	250	31.8
Physician Assistants	950	1,230	280	30.4
Internists, General	590	760	170	29.5

Note: Projections cover Indiana; (1) Sorted by percent employment change and excludes occupations with numeric employment change less than 100
Source: www.projectionscentral.com, State Occupational Projections, 2012–2022 Long-Term Projections

Average Wages

Occupation	$/Hr.	Occupation	$/Hr.
Accountants and Auditors	32.87	Maids and Housekeeping Cleaners	9.80
Automotive Mechanics	22.25	Maintenance and Repair Workers	18.60
Bookkeepers	18.90	Marketing Managers	53.84
Carpenters	21.12	Nuclear Medicine Technologists	34.81
Cashiers	9.33	Nurses, Licensed Practical	19.97
Clerks, General Office	14.92	Nurses, Registered	29.83
Clerks, Receptionists/Information	13.67	Nursing Assistants	12.31
Clerks, Shipping/Receiving	14.60	Packers and Packagers, Hand	11.36
Computer Programmers	34.28	Physical Therapists	40.48
Computer Systems Analysts	37.67	Postal Service Mail Carriers	24.57
Computer User Support Specialists	25.88	Real Estate Brokers	20.52
Cooks, Restaurant	11.08	Retail Salespersons	12.16
Dentists	57.12	Sales Reps., Exc. Tech./Scientific	32.46
Electrical Engineers	39.11	Sales Reps., Tech./Scientific	47.36
Electricians	27.05	Secretaries, Exc. Legal/Med./Exec.	17.08
Financial Managers	54.70	Security Guards	12.36
First-Line Supervisors/Managers, Sales	19.41	Surgeons	n/a
Food Preparation Workers	9.58	Teacher Assistants*	11.56
General and Operations Managers	55.69	Teachers, Elementary School*	24.21
Hairdressers/Cosmetologists	13.07	Teachers, Secondary School*	26.14
Internists	125.04	Telemarketers	13.23
Janitors and Cleaners	11.89	Truck Drivers, Heavy/Tractor-Trailer	21.79
Landscaping/Groundskeeping Workers	12.22	Truck Drivers, Light/Delivery Svcs.	16.94
Lawyers	59.31	Waiters and Waitresses	10.14

Note: Wage data covers the Indianapolis-Carmel, IN Metropolitan Statistical Area—see Appendix B for areas included; (*) Hourly wages for elementary/secondary school teachers and teacher assistants were calculated by the editors from annual wage data based on a 40 hour work week; n/a not available.
Source: Bureau of Labor Statistics, Metro Area Occupational Employment and Wage Estimates, May 2015

TAXES

State Corporate Income Tax Rates

State	Tax Rate (%)	Income Brackets ($)	Num. of Brackets	Financial Institution Tax Rate (%)[a]	Federal Income Tax Ded.
Indiana	6.5 (j)	Flat rate	1	8.5 (j)	No

Note: Tax rates as of January 1, 2016; (a) Rates listed are the corporate income tax rate applied to financial institutions or excise taxes based on income. Some states have other taxes based upon the value of deposits or shares; (j) The Indiana tax rate is scheduled to decrease to 6.25% on July 1, 2016.
Source: Federation of Tax Administrators, "State Corporate Income Tax Rates, 2016"

State Individual Income Tax Rates

State	Tax Rate (%)	Income Brackets ($)	Num. of Brackets	Personal Exempt. ($)[1]		Fed. Inc. Tax Ded.
				Single	Dependents	
Indiana	3.3	Flat rate	1	1,000	2,500 (i)	No

Note: Tax rates as of January 1, 2016; Local- and county-level taxes are not included; n/a not applicable; (1) Married joint filers generally receive double the single exemption; (i) In Indiana, includes an additional exemption of $1,500 for each dependent child.
Source: Federation of Tax Administrators, "State Individual Income Tax Rates, 2016"

Various State and Local Tax Rates

State	State and Local Sales and Use (%)	State Sales and Use (%)	Gasoline[1] (¢/gal.)	Cigarette[2] ($/pack)	Spirits[3] ($/gal.)	Wine[4] ($/gal.)	Beer[5] ($/gal.)
Indiana	7.00	7.0	29.89	0.995	2.68 (f)	0.47 (l)	0.12

Note: All tax rates as of January 1, 2016; (1) The American Petroleum Institute has developed a methodology for determining the average tax rate on a gallon of fuel. Rates may include any of the following: excise taxes, environmental fees, storage tank fees, other fees or taxes, general sales tax, and local taxes. In states where gasoline is subject to the general sales tax, or where the fuel tax is based on the average sale price, the average rate determined by API is sensitive to changes in the price of gasoline. States that fully or partially apply general sales taxes to gasoline: CA, CO, GA, IL, IN, MI, NY; (2) The federal excise tax of $1.0066 per pack and local taxes are not included; (3) Rates are those applicable to off-premise sales of 40% alcohol by volume (a.b.v.) distilled spirits in 750ml containers. Local excise taxes are excluded; (4) Rates are those applicable to off-premise sales of 11% a.b.v. non-carbonated wine in 750ml containers; (5) Rates are those applicable to off-premise sales of 4.7% a.b.v. beer in 12 ounce containers; (f) Different rates are also applicable according to alcohol content, place of production, size of container, or place purchased (on- or off-premise or onboard airlines); (l) Different rates also applicable according to alcohol content, place of production, size of container, place purchased (on- or off-premise or on board airlines) or type of wine (carbonated, vermouth, etc.).
Source: Tax Foundation, 2016 Facts & Figures: How Does Your State Compare?

State Business Tax Climate Index Rankings

State	Overall Rank	Corporate Tax Rank	Individual Income Tax Rank	Sales Tax Rank	Unemployment Insurance Tax Rank	Property Tax Rank
Indiana	8	20	11	11	14	5

Note: The index is a measure of how each state's tax laws affect economic performance. The lower the rank, the more favorable a state's tax system is for business. States without a given tax are given a ranking of 1. The scores/rankings for the District of Columbia do not affect other states. The 2016 index represents the tax climate as of July 1, 2015 (the beginning of Fiscal Year 2016).
Source: Tax Foundation, State Business Tax Climate Index 2016

TRANSPORTATION

Means of Transportation to Work

Area	Car/Truck/Van: Drove Alone	Car/Truck/Van: Car-pooled	Public Transportation: Bus	Public Transportation: Subway	Public Transportation: Railroad	Bicycle	Walked	Other Means	Worked at Home
City	83.5	7.4	0.2	0.1	0.0	0.4	0.8	0.6	7.1
MSA[1]	83.8	8.7	1.0	0.0	0.0	0.3	1.6	0.9	3.7
U.S.	76.4	9.6	2.6	1.8	0.6	0.6	2.8	1.3	4.4

Note: Figures are percentages and cover workers 16 years of age and older; (1) Figures cover the Indianapolis-Carmel-Anderson, IN Metropolitan Statistical Area—see Appendix B for areas included
Source: U.S. Census Bureau, 2010-2014 American Community Survey 5-Year Estimates

Travel Time to Work

Area	Less Than 10 Minutes	10 to 19 Minutes	20 to 29 Minutes	30 to 44 Minutes	45 to 59 Minutes	60 to 89 Minutes	90 Minutes or More
City	11.6	29.0	19.9	27.3	8.8	2.5	1.1
MSA[1]	12.0	27.7	24.5	23.6	7.4	3.5	1.4
U.S.	13.3	29.6	21.0	20.2	7.7	5.7	2.6

Note: Figures are percentages and include workers 16 years old and over; (1) Figures cover the Indianapolis-Carmel-Anderson, IN Metropolitan Statistical Area—see Appendix B for areas included
Source: U.S. Census Bureau, 2010-2014 American Community Survey 5-Year Estimates

Freeway Travel Time Index

Area	1985	1990	1995	2000	2005	2010	2014
Urban Area Rank[1,2]	35	41	41	38	51	42	46
Urban Area Index[1]	1.09	1.11	1.14	1.17	1.17	1.18	1.18
Average Index[3]	1.09	1.11	1.14	1.17	1.20	1.19	1.20

Note: Freeway Travel Time Index—the ratio of travel time in the peak period to the travel time at free-flow conditions. For example, a value of 1.30 indicates a 20-minute free-flow trip takes 26 minutes in the peak (20 minutes x 1.30 = 26 minutes); (1) Covers the Indianapolis IN urban area; (2) Rank is based on 101 urban areas (#1 = highest travel time index); (3) Average of 101 urban areas
Source: Texas Transportation Institute, 2015 Urban Mobility Scorecard, August 2015

Freeway Commuter Stress Index

Area	1985	1990	1995	2000	2005	2010	2014
Urban Area Rank[1,2]	48	47	50	54	58	58	61
Urban Area Index[1]	1.10	1.13	1.16	1.18	1.19	1.19	1.19
Average Index[3]	1.13	1.16	1.19	1.22	1.25	1.24	1.25

Note: The Freeway Commuter Stress Index is the same as the Freeway Travel Time Index (see table above) except that it includes only the travel in the peak directions during the peak periods; the TTI includes travel in all directions during the peak period. Thus, the CSI is more indicative of the work trip experienced by each commuter on a daily basis. (1) Covers the Indianapolis IN urban area; (2) Rank is based on 101 urban areas (#1 = highest stress index); (3) Average of 101 urban areas

Source: Texas Transportation Institute, 2015 Urban Mobility Scorecard, August 2015

Living Environment

COST OF LIVING

Cost of Living Index

Composite Index	Groceries	Housing	Utilities	Trans-portation	Health Care	Misc. Goods/ Services
91.2	92.9	82.4	90.9	91.8	99.3	96.8

Note: The Cost of Living Index measures regional differences in the cost of consumer goods and services, excluding taxes and non-consumer expenditures, for professional and managerial households in the top income quintile. It is based on more than 50,000 prices covering almost 60 different items for which prices are collected three times a year by chambers of commerce, economic development organizations or university applied economic centers in each participating urban area. The numbers shown should be read as a percentage above or below the national average of 100. For example, a value of 115.4 in the groceries column indicates that grocery prices are 15.4% higher than the national average. Small differences in the index numbers should not be interpreted as significant; Figures cover the Indianapolis IN urban area.
Source: The Council for Community and Economic Research, ACCRA Cost of Living Index, 2015

Grocery Prices

Area[1]	T-Bone Steak ($/pound)	Frying Chicken ($/pound)	Whole Milk ($/half gal.)	Eggs ($/dozen)	Orange Juice ($/64 oz.)	Coffee ($/11.5 oz.)
City[2]	10.31	1.17	1.90	2.07	3.54	4.18
Avg.	10.99	1.43	2.25	2.26	3.58	4.48
Min.	7.16	0.98	1.30	1.35	2.88	2.98
Max.	14.13	2.43	3.85	4.81	6.39	7.56

Note: (1) Values for the local area are compared with the average, minimum and maximum values for all 292 areas in the Cost of Living Index; (2) Figures cover the Indianapolis IN urban area; **T-Bone Steak** *(price per pound);* **Frying Chicken** *(price per pound, whole fryer);* **Whole Milk** *(half gallon carton);* **Eggs** *(price per dozen, Grade A, large);* **Orange Juice** *(64 oz. Tropicana or Florida Natural);* **Coffee** *(11.5 oz. can, vacuum-packed, Maxwell House, Hills Bros, or Folgers).*
Source: The Council for Community and Economic Research, ACCRA Cost of Living Index, 2015

Housing and Utility Costs

Area[1]	New Home Price ($)	Apartment Rent ($/month)	All Electric ($/month)	Part Electric ($/month)	Other Energy ($/month)	Telephone ($/month)
City[2]	236,995	950	-	78.56	75.38	25.68
Avg.	312,874	945	179.30	95.07	72.96	28.11
Min.	178,682	479	116.28	43.14	26.46	10.01
Max.	1,472,476	3,984	504.25	189.44	421.11	43.06

Note: (1) Values for the local area are compared with the average, minimum and maximum values for all 292 areas in the Cost of Living Index; (2) Figures cover the Indianapolis IN urban area; **New Home Price** *(2,400 sf living area, 8,000 sf lot, in urban area with full utilities);* **Apartment Rent** *(950 sf 2 bedroom/1.5 or 2 bath, unfurnished, excluding all utilities except water);* **All Electric** *(average monthly cost for an all-electric home);* **Part Electric** *(average monthly cost for a part-electric home);* **Other Energy** *(average monthly cost for natural gas, fuel oil, coal, wood, and any other forms of energy except electricity);* **Telephone** *(price includes basic monthly rate for a private residential line plus additional local usage charges incurred by a family of four).*
Source: The Council for Community and Economic Research, ACCRA Cost of Living Index, 2015

Health Care, Transportation, and Other Costs

Area[1]	Doctor ($/visit)	Dentist ($/visit)	Optometrist ($/visit)	Gasoline ($/gallon)	Beauty Salon ($/visit)	Men's Shirt ($)
City[2]	95.01	90.00	87.83	2.28	28.73	37.94
Avg.	105.15	89.02	99.78	2.38	35.30	28.10
Min.	66.87	56.09	48.53	1.95	18.91	13.38
Max.	182.34	150.36	228.33	4.09	67.91	63.80

Note: (1) Values for the local area are compared with the average, minimum and maximum values for all 292 areas in the Cost of Living Index; (2) Figures cover the Indianapolis IN urban area; **Doctor** *(general practitioners routine exam of an established patient);* **Dentist** *(adult teeth cleaning and periodic oral examination);* **Optometrist** *(full vision eye exam for established adult patient);* **Gasoline** *(one gallon regular unleaded, national brand, including all taxes, cash price at self-service pump if available);* **Beauty Salon** *(woman's shampoo, trim, and blow-dry);* **Men's Shirt** *(cotton/polyester dress shirt, pinpoint weave, long sleeves).*
Source: The Council for Community and Economic Research, ACCRA Cost of Living Index, 2015

HOUSING

House Price Index (HPI)

Area	National Ranking[2]	Quarterly Change (%)	One-Year Change (%)	Five-Year Change (%)
MSA[1]	129	0.30	4.70	9.30
U.S.[3]	–	1.45	5.76	22.85

Note: The HPI is a weighted repeat sales index. It measures average price changes in repeat sales or refinancings on the same properties. This information is obtained by reviewing repeat mortgage transactions on single-family properties whose mortgages have been purchased or securitized by Fannie Mae or Freddie Mac in January 1975; (1) Indianapolis-Carmel-Anderson Metropolitan Statistical Area—see Appendix B for areas included; (2) Rankings are based on annual percentage change for all metro areas containing at least 15,000 transactions over the last 10 years and ranges from 1 to 266; (3) figures based on a weighted average of Census Division estimates using a seasonally adjusted, purchase-only index; all figures are for the period ending December 31, 2015

Source: Federal Housing Finance Agency, House Price Index, February 25, 2016

Median Single-Family Home Prices

Area	2013	2014	2015p	Percent Change 2014 to 2015
MSA[1]	136.7	144.6	153.2	5.9
U.S. Average	197.4	208.9	223.9	7.2

Note: Figures are median sales prices of existing single-family homes in thousands of dollars; (p) preliminary; n/a not available; (1) Indianapolis-Carmel-Anderson, IN Metropolitan Statistical Area—see Appendix B for areas included

Source: National Association of Realtors, Median Sales Price of Existing Single-Family Homes for Metropolitan Areas, 4th Quarter 2015

Qualifying Income Based on Median Sales Price of Existing Single-Family Homes

Area	With 5% Down ($)	With 10% Down ($)	With 20% Down ($)
MSA[1]	33,253	31,503	28,003
U.S. Average	49,535	46,928	41,714

Note: Figures are preliminary; Qualifying income is based on a mortgage rate of 4.1%. Monthly principal and interest payment is limited to 25% of income; n/a not available; (1) Indianapolis-Carmel-Anderson, IN Metropolitan Statistical Area—see Appendix B for areas included

Source: National Association of Realtors, Qualifying Income Based on Median Sales Price of Existing Single-Family Homes for Metropolitan Areas, 4th Quarter 2015

Median Apartment Condo-Coop Home Prices

Area	2013	2014	2015p	Percent Change 2014 to 2015
MSA[1]	118.2	124.7	128.0	2.6
U.S. Average	194.9	204.3	210.7	3.1

Note: Figures are median sales prices of existing apartment condo-coop homes in thousands of dollars; (p) preliminary; n/a not available; (1) Indianapolis-Carmel-Anderson, IN Metropolitan Statistical Area—see Appendix B for areas included

Source: National Association of Realtors, Median Sales Price of Existing Apartment Condo-Coop Homes for Metropolitan Areas, 4th Quarter 2015

Gross Monthly Rent

Area	Under $200	$200 -299	$300 -499	$500 -749	$750 -999	$1,000 -1,499	$1,500 and up	Median ($)
City	0.0	0.2	0.6	8.4	29.8	39.8	21.2	1,118
MSA[1]	1.1	2.3	6.3	32.4	32.9	20.4	4.6	800
U.S.	1.5	3.2	7.4	21.0	24.1	26.9	15.9	920

Note: Figures are percentages except for Median; Gross rent is the contract rent plus the estimated average monthly cost of utilities (electricity, gas, and water and sewer) and fuels (oil, coal, kerosene, wood, etc.) if these are paid by the renter (or paid for the renter by someone else); (1) Figures cover the Indianapolis-Carmel-Anderson, IN Metropolitan Statistical Area—see Appendix B for areas included

Source: U.S. Census Bureau, 2010-2014 American Community Survey 5-Year Estimates

Homeownership Rate

Area	2008 (%)	2009 (%)	2010 (%)	2011 (%)	2012 (%)	2013 (%)	2014 (%)	2015 (%)
MSA[1]	75.0	71.0	68.8	68.3	67.1	67.5	66.9	64.6
U.S.	67.8	67.4	66.9	66.1	65.4	65.1	64.5	63.7

Note: (1) Figures cover the Indianapolis-Carmel-Anderson, IN Metropolitan Statistical Area—see Appendix B for areas included
Source: U.S. Census Bureau, Housing Vacancies and Homeownership Annual Statistics: 2015

Year Housing Structure Built

Area	2010 or Later	2000 -2009	1990 -1999	1980 -1989	1970 -1979	1960 -1969	1950 -1959	1940 -1949	Before 1940	Median Year
City	3.2	29.0	26.4	14.7	15.6	6.8	2.8	0.7	0.9	1993
MSA[1]	1.4	17.3	16.5	10.6	13.3	11.8	11.0	5.0	13.1	1977
U.S.	1.0	14.9	13.9	13.8	15.8	11.0	10.8	5.4	13.3	1976

Note: Figures are percentages except for Median Year; (1) Figures cover the Indianapolis-Carmel-Anderson, IN Metropolitan Statistical Area—see Appendix B for areas included
Source: U.S. Census Bureau, 2010-2014 American Community Survey 5-Year Estimates

HEALTH

Health Risk Data

Category	MSA[1] (%)	U.S. (%)
Adults aged 18–64 who have any kind of health care coverage	82.6	79.6
Adults who reported being in good or excellent health	81.0	83.1
Adults who are current smokers	21.8	19.6
Adults who are heavy drinkers[2]	4.5	6.1
Adults who are binge drinkers[3]	15.8	16.9
Adults who are overweight (BMI 25.0 - 29.9)	34.8	35.8
Adults who are obese (BMI 30.0 - 99.8)	30.1	27.6
Adults who participated in any physical activities in the past month	75.9	77.1
Adults 50+ who have ever had a sigmoidoscopy or colonoscopy	68.6	67.3
Women aged 40+ who have had a mammogram within the past two years	71.6	74.0
Men aged 40+ who have had a PSA test within the past two years	47.0	45.2
Adults aged 65+ who have had flu shot within the past year	61.5	60.1
Adults who always wear a seatbelt	96.1	93.8

Note: Data as of 2012 unless otherwise noted; (1) Figures cover the Indianapolis-Carmel, IN Metropolitan Statistical Area—see Appendix B for areas included; (2) Heavy drinkers are classified as males having more than two drinks per day or females having more than one drink per day; (3) Binge drinkers are classified as males having five or more drinks on one occasion or females having four or more drinks on one occasion
Source: Centers for Disease Control and Prevention, Behaviorial Risk Factor Surveillance System, SMART: Selected Metropolitan/Micropolitan Area Risk Trends, 2012 (Note: the CDC has discontinued this dataset but will be releasing a replacement in mid-2016)

Chronic Health Indicators

Category	MSA[1] (%)	U.S. (%)
Adults who have ever been told they had a heart attack	4.2	4.5
Adults who have ever been told they had a stroke	3.0	2.9
Adults who have been told they currently have asthma	9.5	8.9
Adults who have ever been told they have arthritis	25.3	25.7
Adults who have ever been told they have diabetes[2]	9.8	9.7
Adults who have ever been told they had skin cancer	5.1	5.7
Adults who have ever been told they had any other types of cancer	6.5	6.5
Adults who have ever been told they have COPD	7.1	6.2
Adults who have ever been told they have kidney disease	2.4	2.5
Adults who have ever been told they have a form of depression	19.6	18.0

Note: Data as of 2012 unless otherwise noted; (1) Figures cover the Indianapolis-Carmel, IN Metropolitan Statistical Area—see Appendix B for areas included; (2) Figures do not include pregnancy-related, borderline, or pre-diabetes
Source: Centers for Disease Control and Prevention, Behaviorial Risk Factor Surveillance System, SMART: Selected Metropolitan/Micropolitan Area Risk Trends, 2012 (Note: the CDC has discontinued this dataset but will be releasing a replacement in mid-2016)

Mortality Rates for the Top 10 Causes of Death in the U.S.

ICD-10[a] Sub-Chapter	ICD-10[a] Code	Age-Adjusted Mortality Rate[1] per 100,000 population	
		County[2]	U.S.
Malignant neoplasms	C00-C97	140.7	163.6
Ischaemic heart diseases	I20-I25	72.2	102.2
Other forms of heart disease	I30-I51	46.0	50.1
Chronic lower respiratory diseases	J40-J47	36.1	41.4
Organic, including symptomatic, mental disorders	F01-F09	45.9	38.5
Cerebrovascular diseases	I60-I69	32.6	36.5
Other external causes of accidental injury	W00-X59	19.0	27.5
Other degenerative diseases of the nervous system	G30-G31	35.5	26.3
Diabetes mellitus	E10-E14	16.5	21.1
Hypertensive diseases	I10-I15	7.3	19.7

Note: (a) ICD-10 = International Classification of Diseases 10th Revision; (1) Mortality rates are a three year average covering 2012-2014; (2) Figures cover Hamilton County.
Source: Centers for Disease Control and Prevention, National Center for Health Statistics. Underlying Cause of Death 1999-2014 on CDC WONDER Online Database, released 2015.

Mortality Rates for Selected Causes of Death

ICD-10[a] Sub-Chapter	ICD-10[a] Code	Age-Adjusted Mortality Rate[1] per 100,000 population	
		County[2]	U.S.
Assault	X85-Y09	Unreliable	5.1
Diseases of the liver	K70-K76	7.9	13.5
Human immunodeficiency virus (HIV) disease	B20-B24	Suppressed	2.1
Influenza and pneumonia	J09-J18	13.2	15.2
Intentional self-harm	X60-X84	9.8	12.7
Malnutrition	E40-E46	Unreliable	0.9
Obesity and other hyperalimentation	E65-E68	Suppressed	1.9
Renal failure	N17-N19	12.0	13.0
Transport accidents	V01-V99	5.1	11.6
Viral hepatitis	B15-B19	Suppressed	2.1

Note: (a) ICD-10 = International Classification of Diseases 10th Revision; (1) Mortality rates are a three year average covering 2012-2014; (2) Figures cover Hamilton County; Data are Suppressed when the data meet the criteria for confidentiality constraints; Mortality rates are flagged as Unreliable when the rate would be calculated with a numerator of 20 or less.
Source: Centers for Disease Control and Prevention, National Center for Health Statistics. Underlying Cause of Death 1999-2014 on CDC WONDER Online Database, released 2015.

Health Insurance Coverage

Area	With Health Insurance	With Private Health Insurance	With Public Health Insurance	Without Health Insurance	Population Under Age 18 Without Health Insurance
City	95.2	90.1	14.1	4.8	3.0
MSA[1]	86.7	69.0	27.9	13.3	6.9
U.S.	85.8	65.8	31.1	14.2	7.1

Note: Figures are percentages that cover the civilian noninstitutionalized population; (1) Figures cover the Indianapolis-Carmel-Anderson, IN Metropolitan Statistical Area—see Appendix B for areas included
Source: U.S. Census Bureau, 2010-2014 American Community Survey 5-Year Estimates

Number of Medical Professionals

Area	MDs[3]	DOs[3,4]	Dentists	Podiatrists	Chiropractors	Optometrists
County[1] (number)	1,678	69	221	10	105	66
County[1] (rate[2])	565.3	23.2	73.0	3.3	34.7	21.8
U.S. (rate[2])	272.5	20.9	64.7	5.8	25.9	15.2

Note: Data as of 2014 unless noted; (1) Data covers Hamilton County; (2) Rate per 100,000 population; (3) Data as of 2013 and includes all active, non-federal physicians; (4) Doctor of Osteopathic Medicine
Source: U.S. Department of Health and Human Services, Health Resources and Services Administration, Bureau of Health Professions, Area Resource File (ARF) 2014-2015

Best Hospitals

According to *U.S. News,* the Indianapolis-Carmel-Anderson, IN metro area is home to two of the best hospitals in the U.S.: **IU Health Academic Health Center** (10 specialties); **St. Vincent Hospital and Health Center** (2 specialties). The hospitals listed were nationally ranked in at least one adult specialty. Only 137 hospitals nationwide were nationally ranked in one or more specialties. Fifteen hospitals in the U.S. made the Honor Roll with high scores in at least six specialties. *U.S. News Online, "America's Best Children's Hospitals 2015-16"*

According to *U.S. News,* the Indianapolis-Carmel-Anderson, IN metro area is home to one of the best children's hospitals in the U.S.: **Riley Hospital for Children at IU Health** (10 specialties). The hospital listed was highly ranked in at least one pediatric specialty. Eighty-three children's hospitals in the U.S. were nationally ranked in at least one specialty. Twelve children's hospitals in the U.S. made the Honor Roll with high scores in at least three specialties. *U.S. News Online, "America's Best Children's Hospitals 2015-16"*

EDUCATION

Public School District Statistics

District Name	Schls	Pupils	Pupil/ Teacher Ratio	Minority Pupils[1] (%)	Free Lunch Eligible[2] (%)	IEP[3] (%)
Carmel Clay Schools	15	15,912	19.2	23.6	7.6	10.0
Options Charter School - Carmel	1	170	26.2	23.5	30.0	25.3

Note: Table includes school districts with 100 or more students; (1) Percentage of students that are not non-Hispanic white; (2) Percentage of students that are eligible for the free lunch program; (3) Percentage of students that have an Individualized Education Program.
Source: U.S. Department of Education, National Center for Education Statistics, Common Core of Data, Local Education Agency (School District) Universe Survey: School Year 2013-2014; U.S. Department of Education, National Center for Education Statistics, Common Core of Data, Public Elementary/Secondary School Universe Survey: School Year 2013-2014

Highest Level of Education

Area	Less than H.S.	H.S. Diploma	Some College, No Deg.	Associate Degree	Bachelor's Degree	Master's Degree	Prof. School Degree	Doctorate Degree
City	1.9	10.2	14.4	4.7	38.6	18.9	6.8	4.6
MSA[1]	11.3	29.6	20.7	7.7	20.1	7.6	2.0	1.1
U.S.	13.7	28.0	21.2	7.9	18.3	7.8	2.0	1.3

Note: Figures cover persons age 25 and over; (1) Figures cover the Indianapolis-Carmel-Anderson, IN Metropolitan Statistical Area—see Appendix B for areas included
Source: U.S. Census Bureau, 2010-2014 American Community Survey 5-Year Estimates

Educational Attainment by Race

Area	High School Graduate or Higher (%)					Bachelor's Degree or Higher (%)				
	Total	White	Black	Asian	Hisp.[2]	Total	White	Black	Asian	Hisp.[2]
City	98.1	98.6	98.8	94.8	89.7	68.8	68.4	61.6	77.8	52.5
MSA[1]	88.7	90.4	84.6	86.1	57.7	30.8	32.7	17.6	58.4	13.6
U.S.	86.3	88.4	83.2	85.8	64.1	29.3	30.6	19.0	50.9	13.9

Note: Figures shown cover persons 25 years old and over; (1) Figures cover the Indianapolis-Carmel-Anderson, IN Metropolitan Statistical Area—see Appendix B for areas included; (2) People of Hispanic origin can be of any race
Source: U.S. Census Bureau, 2010-2014 American Community Survey 5-Year Estimates

School Enrollment by Grade and Control

Area	Preschool (%)		Kindergarten (%)		Grades 1 - 4 (%)		Grades 5 - 8 (%)		Grades 9 - 12 (%)	
	Public	Private	Public	Private	Public	Private	Public	Private	Public	Private
City	28.5	71.5	80.7	19.3	83.8	16.2	90.0	10.0	83.4	16.6
MSA[1]	46.7	53.3	84.7	15.3	88.9	11.1	89.9	10.1	89.2	10.8
U.S.	57.4	42.6	87.8	12.2	89.8	10.2	89.9	10.1	90.6	9.4

Note: Figures shown cover persons 3 years old and over; (1) Figures cover the Indianapolis-Carmel-Anderson, IN Metropolitan Statistical Area—see Appendix B for areas included
Source: U.S. Census Bureau, 2010-2014 American Community Survey 5-Year Estimates

Average Salaries of Public School Classroom Teachers

Area	2013-14 Dollars	2013-14 Rank[1]	2014-15 Dollars	2014-15 Rank[1]	Percent Change 2013-14 to 2014-15	Percent Change 2004-05 to 2014-15
Indiana	50,289	27	50,502	30	0.42	8.4
U.S. Average	56,610	–	57,379	–	1.36	20.8

Note: (1) State rank ranges from 1 to 51 where 1 indicates highest salary.
Source: National Education Association, Rankings & Estimates: Rankings of the States 2014 and Estimates of School Statistics 2015, March 2015

Higher Education

Four-Year Colleges			Two-Year Colleges					
Public	Private Non-profit	Private For-profit	Public	Private Non-profit	Private For-profit	Medical Schools[1]	Law Schools[2]	Voc/ Tech[3]
0	0	0	0	0	0	0	0	0

Note: Figures cover institutions located within the city limits and include main campuses only; (1) includes schools accredited by the Liaison Committee on Medical Education and the American Osteopathic Association's Commission on Osteopathic College Accreditation; (2) includes ABA-accredited schools, schools with provisional ABA accreditation, and state accredited schools; (3) includes all schools with programs that are less than 2 years.
Source: National Center for Education Statistics, Integrated Postsecondary Education System (IPEDS), 2014-15; Association of American Medical Colleges, Member List, March 21, 2016; American Osteopathic Association, Member List, March 21, 2016; Law School Admission Council, Official Guide to ABA-Approved Law Schools Online, March 21, 2016; Wikipedia, List of Medical Schools in the United States, March 21, 2016; Wikipedia, List of Law Schools in the United States, March 21, 2016

According to *U.S. News & World Report,* the Indianapolis-Carmel-Anderson, IN metro area is home to one of the best national universities in the U.S.: **Indiana University-?Purdue University–Indianapolis** (#199 tie). The indicators used to capture academic quality fall into a number of categories: assessment by administrators at peer institutions; retention of students; faculty resources; student selectivity; financial resources; alumni giving; high school counselor ratings of colleges; and graduation rate. *U.S. News & World Report, "America's Best Colleges 2016"*

According to *U.S. News & World Report,* the Indianapolis-Carmel-Anderson, IN metro area is home to one of the best liberal arts colleges in the U.S.: **DePauw University** (#51 tie). The indicators used to capture academic quality fall into a number of categories: assessment by administrators at peer institutions; retention of students; faculty resources; student selectivity; financial resources; alumni giving; high school counselor ratings of colleges; and graduation rate. *U.S. News & World Report, "America's Best Colleges 2016"*

According to *U.S. News & World Report,* the Indianapolis-Carmel-Anderson, IN metro area is home to one of the top 100 law schools in the U.S.: **Indiana University–Indianapolis, Robert H. McKinney School of Law** (#100 tie). The rankings are based on a weighted average of 12 measures of quality: peer assessment score; assessment score by lawyers/judges; median LSAT scores; median undergrad GPA; acceptance rate; employment rates for graduates; placement success; bar passage rate; faculty resources; expenditures per student; student/faculty ratio; and library resources. *U.S. News & World Report, "America's Best Graduate Schools, Law, 2017"*

According to *U.S. News & World Report,* the Indianapolis-Carmel-Anderson, IN metro area is home to one of the top 75 medical schools for research in the U.S.: **Indiana University–Indianapolis, School of Medicine** (#47 tie). The rankings are based on a weighted average of 11 measures of quality: quality assessment; peer assessment score; assessment score by residency directors; research activity; total research activity; average research activity per faculty member; student selectivity; median MCAT total score; median undergraduate GPA; acceptance rate; and faculty resources. *U.S. News & World Report, "America's Best Graduate Schools, Medical, 2017"*

PRESIDENTIAL ELECTION

2012 Presidential Election Results

Area	Obama (%)	Romney (%)	Other (%)
Hamilton County	32.0	66.3	1.7
U.S.	51.0	47.2	1.8

Note: Results may not add to 100% due to rounding
Source: Dave Leip's Atlas of U.S. Presidential Elections

EMPLOYERS

Major Employers

Company Name	Industry
Allison Transmission	Motor vehicle parts/accessories
Ameritech	Local and long distance telephone
Apple American Indiana	Restaurant/family chain
Automotive Components Holdings	Steering mechanisms/motor vehicle
Celadon Trucking Service	Trucking/except local
CNO Financial Group	Insurance services
Communikty Hospitals of Indiana	General medical/surgical hospitals
Conseco Variable Ins Company	Life insurance carriers
Defense Finance and Accounting Services	Accounting/auditing and bookkeeping
Eli Lilly and Company	Pharmaceutical preparations
Family & Social Svcs Admin	Administration of social and human resources
Federal Express Corporation	Air cargo carrier
GEICO	Auto insurance
Hewlett Packard Company	Computer terminals
Indiana Department of Transportation	Regulation administration of transportation
Indiana Police State	General government/state government
Liberty Mutual	Insurance services
Meridian Citizens Mutual Ins Company	Assessment associations: fire, marine & casualty ins
Methodist Hospital	General medical/surgical hospitals
Navient (formerly Sallie Mae)	Headquarters; financial services
Rolls Royce Corporation	Aircraft engines/parts
St Vincent Hospital and Healthcare Center	General medical/surgical hospitals
The Health Hospital of Marion County	General medical/surgical hospitals
Trustees of indiana University	University
United States Postal Service	Postal service

Note: Companies shown are located within the Indianapolis-Carmel-Anderson, IN Metropolitan Statistical Area.
Source: Hoovers.com; Wikipedia

PUBLIC SAFETY

Crime Rate

Area	All Crimes	Violent Crimes				Property Crimes		
		Murder	Rape[3]	Robbery	Aggrav. Assault	Burglary	Larceny -Theft	Motor Vehicle Theft
City	945.7	1.1	2.3	6.9	3.4	82.2	786.9	62.8
Metro[1]	3,889.8	7.9	38.7	209.4	390.3	783.5	2,118.1	341.8
U.S.	2,971.8	4.5	36.6	102.2	232.5	542.5	1,837.3	216.2

Note: Figures are crimes per 100,000 population; (1) Figures cover the Indianapolis-Carmel-Anderson, IN Metropolitan Statistical Area—see Appendix B for areas included; (3) The city and U.S. figures shown were reported using the revised Uniform Crime Reporting (UCR) definition of rape. The suburban and metro area figures shown are an aggregate total of the data submitted using both the revised and legacy UCR definitions.
Source: FBI Uniform Crime Reports, 2014

Hate Crimes

Area	Number of Quarters Reported	Number of Incidents per Bias Motivation						
		Race	Religion	Sexual Orientation	Ethnicity	Disability	Gender	Gender Identity
City	4	0	0	0	0	0	0	0
U.S.	4	2,568	1,014	1,017	648	84	33	98

Source: Federal Bureau of Investigation, Hate Crime Statistics 2014

Identity Theft Consumer Complaints

Area	Complaints	Complaints per 100,000 Population	Rank[2]
MSA[1]	2,277	115.5	141
U.S.	490,220	152.4	-

Note: (1) Figures cover the Indianapolis-Carmel-Anderson, IN Metropolitan Statistical Area—see Appendix B for areas included; (2) Rank ranges from 1 to 379 where 1 indicates greatest number of identity theft complaints per 100,000 population
Source: Federal Trade Commission, Consumer Sentinel Network Data Book for January–December 2015

Fraud and Other Consumer Complaints

Area	Complaints	Complaints per 100,000 Population	Rank[2]
MSA[1]	7,750	393.1	119
U.S.	2,593,159	806.0	-

Note: (1) Figures cover the Indianapolis-Carmel-Anderson, IN Metropolitan Statistical Area—see Appendix B for areas included; (2) Rank ranges from 1 to 379 where 1 indicates greatest number of identity theft complaints per 100,000 population
Source: Federal Trade Commission, Consumer Sentinel Network Data Book for January–December 2015

RECREATION

Culture

Dance[1]	Theatre[1]	Instrumental Music[1]	Vocal Music[1]	Series and Festivals	Museums and Art Galleries[2]	Zoos and Aquariums[3]
0	0	0	0	0	0	0

Note: (1) Professional perfoming groups; (2) Based on organizations with SIC code 8412; (3) AZA-accredited
Source: The Grey House Performing Arts Directory, 2015-16; Association of Zoos & Aquariums, AZA Member Zoos & Aquariums, March 25, 2016; www.AccuLeads.com, March 29, 2016

Professional Sports Teams

Team Name	League	Year Established
Indiana Pacers	National Basketball Association (NBA)	1967
Indianapolis Colts	National Football League (NFL)	1984

Note: Includes teams located in the Indianapolis-Carmel-Anderson, IN Metropolitan Statistical Area.
Source: Wikipedia, Major Professional Sports Teams of the United States and Canada, March 24, 2016

CLIMATE

Average and Extreme Temperatures

Temperature	Jan	Feb	Mar	Apr	May	Jun	Jul	Aug	Sep	Oct	Nov	Dec	Yr.
Extreme High (°F)	71	72	85	89	93	102	104	102	100	90	81	74	104
Average High (°F)	35	39	50	63	73	82	85	84	78	66	51	39	62
Average Temp. (°F)	27	31	41	52	63	72	76	73	67	55	43	31	53
Average Low (°F)	18	22	31	41	52	61	65	63	55	44	33	23	42
Extreme Low (°F)	-22	-21	-7	18	28	39	48	41	34	20	-2	-23	-23

Note: Figures cover the years 1948-1990
Source: National Climatic Data Center, International Station Meteorological Climate Summary, 9/96

Average Precipitation/Snowfall/Humidity

Precip./Humidity	Jan	Feb	Mar	Apr	May	Jun	Jul	Aug	Sep	Oct	Nov	Dec	Yr.
Avg. Precip. (in.)	2.8	2.5	3.6	3.6	4.0	3.9	4.3	3.4	2.9	2.6	3.3	3.3	40.2
Avg. Snowfall (in.)	7	6	4	1	Tr	0	0	0	0	Tr	2	5	25
Avg. Rel. Hum. 7am (%)	81	81	79	77	79	80	84	87	87	85	83	83	82
Avg. Rel. Hum. 4pm (%)	68	64	59	53	53	53	56	56	53	53	63	70	59

Note: Figures cover the years 1948-1990; Tr = Trace amounts (<0.05 in. of rain; <0.5 in. of snow)
Source: National Climatic Data Center, International Station Meteorological Climate Summary, 9/96

Weather Conditions

Temperature			Daytime Sky			Precipitation		
10°F & below	32°F & below	90°F & above	Clear	Partly cloudy	Cloudy	0.01 inch or more precip.	0.1 inch or more snow/ice	Thunder-storms
19	119	19	83	128	154	127	24	43

Note: Figures are average number of days per year and cover the years 1948-1990
Source: National Climatic Data Center, International Station Meteorological Climate Summary, 9/96

HAZARDOUS WASTE

Superfund Sites

Carmel has no sites on the EPA's Superfund Final National Priorities List. There are a total of 1,323 Superfund sites on the list in the U.S. *U.S. Environmental Protection Agency, Final National Priorities List, March 18, 2016*

AIR & WATER QUALITY

Air Quality Trends: Ozone

	1990	1995	2000	2005	2010	2011	2012	2013	2014
MSA[1]	0.086	0.095	0.082	0.080	0.069	0.072	0.074	0.062	0.063

Note: (1) Data covers the Indianapolis-Carmel-Anderson, IN Metropolitan Statistical Area—see Appendix B for areas included. The values shown are the composite ozone concentration averages among trend sites based on the highest fourth daily maximum 8-hour concentration in parts per million. These trends are based on sites having an adequate record of monitoring data during the trend period. Data from exceptional events are included.
Source: U.S. Environmental Protection Agency, Air Quality Monitoring Information, "Air Quality Trends by City, 1990-2014"

Air Quality Index

Area	Percent of Days when Air Quality was...[2]					AQI Statistics[2]	
	Good	Moderate	Unhealthy for Sensitive Groups	Unhealthy	Very Unhealthy	Maximum	Median
MSA[1]	46.8	52.3	0.5	0.3	0.0	157	52

Note: (1) Data covers the Indianapolis-Carmel-Anderson, IN Metropolitan Statistical Area—see Appendix B for areas included; (2) Based on 365 days with AQI data in 2015. Air Quality Index (AQI) is an index for reporting daily air quality. EPA calculates the AQI for five major air pollutants regulated by the Clean Air Act: ground-level ozone, particle pollution (aka particulate matter), carbon monoxide, sulfur dioxide, and nitrogen dioxide. The AQI runs from 0 to 500. The higher the AQI value, the greater the level of air pollution and the greater the health concern. There are six AQI categories: "Good" AQI is between 0 and 50. Air quality is considered satisfactory; "Moderate" AQI is between 51 and 100. Air quality is acceptable; "Unhealthy for Sensitive Groups" When AQI values are between 101 and 150, members of sensitive groups may experience health effects; "Unhealthy" When AQI values are between 151 and 200 everyone may begin to experience health effects; "Very Unhealthy" AQI values between 201 and 300 trigger a health alert; "Hazardous" AQI values over 300 trigger warnings of emergency conditions (not shown).
Source: U.S. Environmental Protection Agency, Air Quality Index Report, 2015

Air Quality Index Pollutants

Area	Percent of Days when AQI Pollutant was...[2]					
	Carbon Monoxide	Nitrogen Dioxide	Ozone	Sulfur Dioxide	Particulate Matter 2.5	Particulate Matter 10
MSA[1]	0.0	1.6	24.7	9.0	63.8	0.8

Note: (1) Data covers the Indianapolis-Carmel-Anderson, IN Metropolitan Statistical Area—see Appendix B for areas included; (2) Based on 365 days with AQI data in 2015. The Air Quality Index (AQI) is an index for reporting daily air quality. EPA calculates the AQI for five major air pollutants regulated by the Clean Air Act: ground-level ozone, particle pollution (also known as particulate matter), carbon monoxide, sulfur dioxide, and nitrogen dioxide. The AQI runs from 0 to 500. The higher the AQI value, the greater the level of air pollution and the greater the health concern.
Source: U.S. Environmental Protection Agency, Air Quality Index Report, 2015

Maximum Air Pollutant Concentrations: Particulate Matter, Ozone, CO and Lead

	Particulate Matter 10 (ug/m^3)	Particulate Matter 2.5 Wtd AM (ug/m^3)	Particulate Matter 2.5 24-Hr (ug/m^3)	Ozone (ppm)	Carbon Monoxide (ppm)	Lead (ug/m^3)
MSA[1] Level	58	12.8	31	0.066	3	0.02
NAAQS[2]	150	15	35	0.075	9	0.15
Met NAAQS[2]	Yes	Yes	Yes	Yes	Yes	Yes

Note: (1) Data covers the Indianapolis-Carmel-Anderson, IN Metropolitan Statistical Area—see Appendix B for areas included; Data from exceptional events are included; (2) National Ambient Air Quality Standards; ppm = parts per million; ug/m^3 = micrograms per cubic meter; n/a not available.
Concentrations: Particulate Matter 10 (coarse particulate)—highest second maximum 24-hour concentration; Particulate Matter 2.5 Wtd AM (fine particulate)—highest weighted annual mean concentration; Particulate Matter 2.5 24-Hour (fine particulate)—highest 98th percentile 24-hour concentration; Ozone—highest fourth daily maximum 8-hour concentration; Carbon Monoxide—highest second maximum non-overlapping 8-hour concentration; Lead—maximum running 3-month average
Source: U.S. Environmental Protection Agency, Air Quality Monitoring Information, "Air Quality Statistics by City, 2014"

Maximum Air Pollutant Concentrations: Nitrogen Dioxide and Sulfur Dioxide

	Nitrogen Dioxide AM (ppb)	Nitrogen Dioxide 1-Hr (ppb)	Sulfur Dioxide AM (ppb)	Sulfur Dioxide 1-Hr (ppb)	Sulfur Dioxide 24-Hr (ppb)
MSA[1] Level	17	46	n/a	106	n/a
NAAQS[2]	53	100	30	75	140
Met NAAQS[2]	Yes	Yes	n/a	No	n/a

Note: (1) Data covers the Indianapolis-Carmel-Anderson, IN Metropolitan Statistical Area—see Appendix B for areas included; Data from exceptional events are included; (2) National Ambient Air Quality Standards; ppm = parts per million; ug/m³ = micrograms per cubic meter; n/a not available.
Concentrations: Nitrogen Dioxide AM—highest arithmetic mean concentration; Nitrogen Dioxide 1-Hr—highest 98th percentile 1-hour daily maximum concentration; Sulfur Dioxide AM—highest annual mean concentration; Sulfur Dioxide 1-Hr—highest 99th percentile 1-hour daily maximum concentration; Sulfur Dioxide 24-Hr—highest second maximum 24-hour concentration
Source: U.S. Environmental Protection Agency, Air Quality Monitoring Information, "Air Quality Statistics by City, 2014"

Drinking Water

Water System Name	Pop. Served	Primary Water Source Type	Violations[1]	
			Health Based	Monitoring/ Reporting
Carmel Water Dept	80,800	(2)	0	0

Note: (1) Based on violation data from January 1, 2015 to December 31, 2015 (includes unresolved violations from earlier years); (2) Ground water under direct influence of surface water
Source: U.S. Environmental Protection Agency, Office of Ground Water and Drinking Water, Safe Drinking Water Information System (based on data extracted April 29, 2016)

Fishers, Indiana

Background

Fishers is just northeast of Indianapolis, and within several hours drive of Cincinnati, Louisville and Chicago. It is a half an hour from Indianapolis International Airport. Business has grown with Fishers itself in recent decades, and the town enjoys the benefits that flow from a friendly business community. The corporate employers based in Fishers have operated in harmony with the town's needs and historic character. Though economically thriving and centrally located, Fishers has also been successful in maintaining and expanding its park facilities and green spaces.

Fishers was listed on *Family Circle's* 2012 list of "10 Best Towns for Families" and ranked 11th on *Forbes* "Best Place to Move."

Fishers was first settled by William Conner, in 1802, when he built a log cabin and a trading post along the banks of the White River. This cabin became briefly famous eighteen years later when a commission from the state of Indiana met there to consider where the capital of the state should be: present-day Indianapolis, very close to Fishers, was the choice.

For some years, Fishers remained a trading post, with few permanent settlers and little public infrastructure, but by 1827 it had grown big enough to establish its first school by 1840, when threshing machines were first introduced. The surrounding area was becoming a major agricultural site, drawing more farmers and farm-related industries. The construction of new rail lines, beginning in 1849, drove this development farther. In fact, the railroads were so influential in the growth of the town that they affected the very name: first Fisher's Switch, the town then became known as Fisher's Station, and this was the name until 1908, when the local post office finally became simply Fishers—with no apostrophe.

Fishers maintained its rural small-town character for a long time. In 1972 its population was only about 700, and by 1980 this had risen only to 2,000. There has been considerable, but controlled growth thereafter, with careful attention to the preservation and maintenance of green spaces and public amenities. In 1998, Fishers was incorporated as a city.

The town mandate includes: providing residents with safe, progressive park facilities driven by the wise use of green space; offering recreational activities and events through public and private partnerships; and enhancing the quality of family life, the feeling of neighborliness, and the sense of community in accordance with what have come to be the very high expectations of Fishers residents.

Fishers is served by the Hamilton Southeastern School District, 12 elementary, three intermediate, three junior high and two senior high schools, many receiving the highest Four Star rating from Indiana Department of Education. Academically superior, Fishers' schools have also consistently achieved high ratings in sports, music, arts, and other extracurricular activities. The town is also served by some religiously affiliated schools.

The town operates 14 parks, with many walking paths and golf courses, community pools, and a thriving youth sports organization. Nearby Geist and Morse Reservoirs provide convenient access to water recreation. The Fishers Heritage Park at White River is dedicated to hiking, birding, sledding, and bicycling. Another park, Billericay, offers lighted baseball diamonds, wooded areas, a playground, and picnic tables. Fishers boasts, in total, 451 acres of parkland and 83 miles of multi-purpose trail.

Health resources include Community Hospital North, Riverview Hospital, and St. Vincent Hospital-Carmel. The town and its immediate surrounding area host some forty different churches.

Fishers is served by a seven-member Town Council, which operates as the Town's executive and legislative body.

Rankings

Business/Finance Rankings

- The personal finance site NerdWallet analyzed 183 American metropolitan areas with populations over 250,000 and more than 15,000 businesses to rank where entrepreneurs find the most success. Criteria included area economy, annual income, housing cost, unemployment rate, and the success rate of area businesses. Indianapolis* ranked #95. *www.nerdwallet.com, "Best Places to Start a Business," April 27, 2015*
- The editors of *Kiplinger's Personal Finance Magazine* named Indianapolis* to their list of ten of the best metro areas for start-ups. The area ranked #8.Criteria: well-educated workforce; low living costs for self-employed people, as measured by the Council for Community and Economic Research; a strong existing community of small business; low unemployment; low business costs. *www.kiplinger.com, "10 Great Cities for Starting a Business," October 2014*
- Based on metro area social media reviews, the employment opinion group Glassdoor surveyed 50 of the largest U.S. metro areas and equally weighed cost of living, hiring opportunity, and job satisfaction to compose a list of "25 Best Cities for Jobs." The Indianapolis* metro area was ranked #30 in overall job satisfaction. *www.glassdoor.com, "Best Cities for Jobs," May 19, 2015*
- In a survey of economic confidence in the nation's 50 largest metropolitan areas conducted January–December 2014, the Indianapolis* metro area placed #42, according to Gallup's 2014 Economic Confidence Index. *Gallup, "San Jose and San Francisco Lead in Economic Confidence," March 19, 2015*
- The Brookings Institution ranked the 100 largest metro areas in the U.S. based on income inequality. Indianapolis* was ranked #64 (#1 = greatest ineqality). Criteria: the "95/20 ratio," a figure representing the income at which a household earns more than 95 percent of all other households, divided by the income at which a household earns more than only 20 percent of all other households. *Brookings Institution, "Income Inequality, 100 Largest U.S. Metro Areas, 2007-2014," January 14, 2016*
- The Indianapolis* metro area was identified as one of the most affordable metropolitan areas in America by *Forbes.* The area ranked #9 out of 20 based on the National Association of Home Builders/Wells Fargo Housing Affordability Index and Sperling's Best Places' cost-of-living index. *Forbes.com, "America's Most Affordable Cities in 2015," March 12, 2015*
- Indianapolis* was identified as one of America's most frugal metro areas by *Coupons.com.* The city ranked #16 out of 25. Criteria: online coupon usage. *Coupons.com, "Top 25 Most Frugal Cities of 2014," May 11, 2015*
- Indianapolis* was identified as one of America's most frugal metro areas by *Coupons.com.* The city ranked #9 out of 25. Criteria: Grocery IQ and coupons.com mobile app usage. *Coupons.com, "Top 25 Most On-the-Go Frugal Cities of 2013," April 10, 2014*
- The Indianapolis* metro area appeared on the Milken Institute "2015 Best Performing Cities" list. Rank: #48 out of 200 large metro areas. Criteria: job growth; wage and salary growth; high-tech output growth. *Milken Institute, "Best-Performing Cities 2015," December 2015*
- *Forbes* ranked the 200 most populous metro areas to determine the nation's "Best Places for Business and Careers." The Indianapolis* metro area was ranked #8. Criteria: costs (business and living); job growth (past and projected); income growth; educational attainment (college and high school); projected economic growth; cultural and recreational opportunities; net migration patterns; number of highly ranked colleges. *Forbes, "The Best Places for Business and Careers 2015," July 29, 2015*

Education Rankings

- Personal finance website *WalletHub* analyzed the 150 largest U.S. metropolitan statistical areas to determine where the most educated Americans are choosing to settle. Criteria: education quality and attainment gap; education levels; percentage of workers with degrees; public school rankings; quality and size of each metro area's universities. Indianapolis* was ranked #65 (#1 = most educated city). *www.WalletHub.com, "2015's Most and Least Educated Cities*

Environmental Rankings

- The Indianapolis* metro area came in at #163 for the relative comfort of its climate on Sperling's list of "chill cities," as measured by the Sperling Heat Index. All 361 metro areas are included. Criteria included daytime high temperatures, nighttime low temperatures, dew point, and relative humidity at the high temperatures. *www.bertsperling.com, "Sperling's Chill Cities," July 18, 2013*

- Sperling's BestPlaces assessed 379 metropolitan areas of the United States for the likelihood of dangerously extreme weather events or earthquakes. In general the Southeast and South-Central regions have the highest risk of weather extremes and earthquakes, while the Pacific Northwest enjoys the lowest risk. Of the least risky metropolitan areas, the Indianapolis* metro area was ranked #283. *www.bestplaces.net, "Safest Places from Natural Disasters," April 2011*

- The U.S. Environmental Protection Agency (EPA) released a list of U.S. metropolitan areas with the most ENERGY STAR certified buildings in 2015. The Indianapolis* metro area was ranked #24 out of 25. *U.S. Environmental Protection Agency, "Top Cities With the Most ENERGY STAR Certified Buildings in 2016," March 30, 2016*

- The U.S. Environmental Protection Agency (EPA) released a list of mid-size U.S. metropolitan areas with the most ENERGY STAR certified buildings in 2015. The Indianapolis* metro area was ranked #4 out of 10. *U.S. Environmental Protection Agency, "Top Cities With the Most ENERGY STAR Certified Buildings in 2016," March 30, 2016*

- Indianapolis* was highlighted as one of the 25 metro areas most polluted by year-round particle pollution (Annual PM 2.5) in the U.S. during 2011 through 2013. The area ranked #17. *American Lung Association, State of the Air 2015*

- Indianapolis* was highlighted as one of the 25 metro areas most polluted by short-term particle pollution (24-hour PM 2.5) in the U.S. during 2011 through 2013. The area ranked #23. *American Lung Association, State of the Air 2015*

Health/Fitness Rankings

- Analysts who tracked obesity rates in 100 of the nation's most populous areas found that the Indianapolis* metro area was one of the ten communities where residents were most likely to be obese, defined as a BMI score of 30 or above. *www.gallup.com, "Colorado Springs Residents Least Likely to Be Obese," May 28, 2015*

- For each of the 50 most populous metro areas in the United States, the American College of Sports Medicine's American Fitness Index evaluated infrastructure, community assets, and policies that encourage healthy and fit lifestyles, including preventive health behaviors, levels of chronic disease conditions, health care access, and community resources and policies that support physical activity. The Indianapolis* metro area ranked #50 for "community fitness." *www.americanfitnessindex.org, "ACSM American Fitness Index Health and Community Fitness Status of the 50 Largest Metropolitan Areas," May 2015*

- The Indianapolis* metro area was identified as one of the worst cities for bed bugs in America by pest control company Orkin. The area ranked #15 out of 50 based on the number of bed bug treatments Orkin performed from January to December 2015. *Orkin, "Chicago Tops Bed Bug Cities List for Fourth Year in a Row," January 13, 2016*

- Indianapolis* was identified as a "2016 Spring Allergy Capital." The area ranked #65 out of 100. Three groups of factors were used to identify the most severe cities for people with allergies during the spring season: annual pollen levels; medicine utilization; access to board-certified allergists. *Asthma and Allergy Foundation of America, "Spring Allergy Capitals 2016"*

- Indianapolis* was identified as a "2015 Asthma Capital." The area ranked #11 out of the nation's 100 largest metropolitan areas. Criteria: estimated prevalence; self-reported prevalence; crude death rate for asthma; annual pollen score; annual air quality; public smoking laws; number of board-certified asthma specialists; school inhaler access laws; rescue medication use; controller medication use; ER visits for asthma; uninsured rate; poverty rate. *Asthma and Allergy Foundation of America, "Asthma Capitals 2015"*

- The Indianapolis* metro area ranked #176 out of 190 in The Gallup-Healthways Well-Being Index. Criteria: purpose; social well being; financial health; community and physical health. Results are based on telephone interviews with adults, aged 18 and older, living in metropolitan areas in the 50 U.S. states and the District of Columbia. *Gallup-Healthways, "State of American Well-Being," February 23, 2016*

Real Estate Rankings

- The Indianapolis* metro area was identified as one of the top 20 housing markets to invest in for 2016 by *Forbes*. The area ranked #11. Criteria: strong job and population growth; anticipated home price appreciation; and other factors. *Forbes.com, "Best Buy Cities: Where to Invest in Housing in 2016," January 27, 2016*

- The Indianapolis* metro area was identified as one of the 10 worst condo markets in the U.S. in 2015. The area ranked #9 out of 61 markets. Criteria: year-over-year change of median sales price of existing apartment condo-coop homes between the 4th quarter of 2014 and the 4th quarter of 2015. *National Association of Realtors®, Median Sales Price of Existing Apartment Condo-Coop Homes for Metropolitan Areas, 4th Quarter 2015*

- Indianapolis* was ranked #31 out of 225 metro areas in terms of housing affordability in 2015 by the National Association of Home Builders (#1 = most affordable). Criteria: the share of homes sold in that area affordable to a family earning the local median income, based on standard mortgage underwriting criteria. *National Association of Home Builders®, NAHB-Wells Fargo Housing Opportunity Index, 4th Quarter 2015*

Safety Rankings

- Fishers was identified as one of the safest cities in America by NeighborhoodScout. The city ranked #53 out of 100. Criteria: number of violent and property crimes per 1,000 residents. The editors only considered cities with 25,000 or more residents. *NeighborhoodScout, "Safest Cities in America 2016"*

- The National Insurance Crime Bureau ranked 380 metro areas in the U.S. in terms of per capita rates of vehicle theft. The Indianapolis* metro area ranked #31 (#1 = highest rate). Criteria: number of vehicle theft offenses per 100,000 inhabitants in 2014. *National Insurance Crime Bureau, "Hot Spots 2014," June 24, 2015*

Seniors/Retirement Rankings

- From its Best Cities for Successful Aging indexes, the Milken Institute generated rankings for metropolitan areas, weighing data in eight categories—health care, wellness, living arrangements, transportation, financial characteristics, education and employment opportunities, community engagement, and overall livability. The Indianapolis* metro area was ranked #49 overall in the large metro area category. *Milken Institute, "Best Cities for Successful Aging, 2014"*

Sports/Recreation Rankings

- Fishers was selected as one of the most playful cities in the U.S. by KaBOOM! The organization's Playful City USA initiative honors cities and towns across the nation for a vision, plan and commitment to creating an agenda for play. Criteria: creating a local play commission or task force; designing an annual action plan for play; conducting a play space audit; outlining a financial investment in play for the current fiscal year; and proclaiming and celebrating an annual "play day." *KaBOOM! National Campaign for Play, "2015 Playful City USA Communities"*

Miscellaneous Rankings

- The watchdog site Charity Navigator conducts an annual study of charities in the nation's major markets both to analyze statistical differences in their financial, accountability, and transparency practices and to track year-to-year variations in individual communities. The Indianapolis* metro area was ranked #6 among the 30 metro markets in the rating dimension of Overall Score. *www.charitynavigator.org, "Metro Market Study 2015," June 5, 2015*

- Mars Chocolate North America, the makers of COMBOS®, in partnership with Sperling's BestPlaces, ranked 50 major metro areas in terms of their "manliness." The Indianapolis* metro area ranked #13. Criteria: number of professional sports teams; number of nearby NASCAR tracks and racing events; manly lifestyle; concentration of manly retail stores; manly occupations per capita; salty snack sales; "Board of Manliness" rankings. *Mars Chocolate North America, "America's Manliest Cities 2012"*
- The National Alliance to End Homelessness ranked the 100 most populous metro areas with the highest rate of homelessness. The Indianapolis* metro area ranked #86. Criteria: number of homeless people per 10,000 population in 2011. *National Alliance to End Homelessness, The State of Homelessness in America 2012*

Fishers is located within the Indianapolis-Carmel-Anderson, IN Metropolitan Statistical Area.

Business Environment

CITY FINANCES

City Government Finances

Component	2012 ($000)	2012 ($ per capita)
Total Revenues	58,228	758
Total Expenditures	55,305	720
Debt Outstanding	131,127	1,707
Cash and Securities[1]	88,477	1,152

Note: (1) Cash and security holdings of a government at the close of its fiscal year, including those of its dependent agencies, utilities, and liquor stores.
Source: U.S Census Bureau, State & Local Government Finances 2012

City Government Revenue by Source

Source	2012 ($000)	2012 ($ per capita)
General Revenue		
From Federal Government	174	2
From State Government	5,440	70
From Local Governments	1,709	22
Taxes		
Property	23,423	305
Sales and Gross Receipts	352	4
Personal Income	9,759	127
Corporate Income	0	0
Motor Vehicle License	0	0
Other Taxes	1,670	21
Current Charges	12,947	168
Liquor Store	0	0
Utility	0	0
Employee Retirement	0	0

Source: U.S Census Bureau, State & Local Government Finances 2012

City Government Expenditures by Function

Function	2012 ($000)	2012 ($ per capita)	2012 (%)
General Direct Expenditures			
Air Transportation	0	0	0.0
Corrections	0	0	0.0
Education	0	0	0.0
Employment Security Administration	0	0	0.0
Financial Administration	212	2	0.3
Fire Protection	8,212	106	14.8
General Public Buildings	1,188	15	2.1
Governmental Administration, Other	3,547	46	6.4
Health	0	0	0.0
Highways	8,577	111	15.5
Hospitals	0	0	0.0
Housing and Community Development	0	0	0.0
Interest on General Debt	4,172	54	7.5
Judicial and Legal	0	0	0.0
Libraries	0	0	0.0
Parking	0	0	0.0
Parks and Recreation	686	8	1.2
Police Protection	7,032	91	12.7
Public Welfare	0	0	0.0
Sewerage	8,306	108	15.0
Solid Waste Management	0	0	0.0
Veterans' Services	0	0	0.0
Liquor Store	0	0	0.0
Utility	0	0	0.0
Employee Retirement	0	0	0.0

Source: U.S Census Bureau, State & Local Government Finances 2012

DEMOGRAPHICS

Population Growth

Area	1990 Census	2000 Census	2010 Census	2014* Estimate	Population Growth (%) 1990-2014	2010-2014
City	12,437	37,835	76,794	81,060	551.8	5.6
MSA[1]	1,294,217	1,525,104	1,756,241	1,931,182	49.2	10.0
U.S.	248,709,873	281,421,906	308,745,538	314,107,084	26.3	1.7

Note: (1) Figures cover the Indianapolis-Carmel-Anderson, IN Metropolitan Statistical Area—see Appendix B for areas included; (*) 2010-2014 5-year estimated population
Source: U.S. Census Bureau, 1990 Census, Census 2000, Census 2010, 2010-2014 American Community Survey 5-Year Estimates

Household Size

Area	Persons in Household (%) One	Two	Three	Four	Five	Six	Seven or More	Average Household Size
City	21.0	28.5	18.3	19.1	9.0	3.0	0.7	2.92
MSA[1]	28.4	33.4	15.8	13.1	6.0	2.0	1.0	2.57
U.S.	27.5	33.5	15.8	13.1	6.0	2.3	1.4	2.64

Note: (1) Figures cover the Indianapolis-Carmel-Anderson, IN Metropolitan Statistical Area—see Appendix B for areas included
Source: U.S. Census Bureau, 2010-2014 American Community Survey 5-Year Estimates

Race

Area	White Alone[2] (%)	Black Alone[2] (%)	Asian Alone[2] (%)	AIAN[3] Alone[2] (%)	NHOPI[4] Alone[2] (%)	Other Race Alone[2] (%)	Two or More Races (%)
City	86.7	4.6	5.4	0.1	0.0	0.5	2.8
MSA[1]	77.9	14.6	2.3	0.2	0.0	2.6	2.3
U.S.	73.8	12.6	5.0	0.8	0.2	4.7	2.9

Note: (1) Figures cover the Indianapolis-Carmel-Anderson, IN Metropolitan Statistical Area—see Appendix B for areas included; (2) Alone is defined as not being in combination with one or more other races; (3) American Indian and Alaska Native; (4) Native Hawaiian and Other Pacific Islander
Source: U.S. Census Bureau, 2010-2014 American Community Survey 5-Year Estimates

Hispanic or Latino Origin

Area	Total (%)	Mexican (%)	Puerto Rican (%)	Cuban (%)	Other (%)
City	3.3	1.8	0.1	0.0	1.3
MSA[1]	6.2	4.5	0.3	0.1	1.3
U.S.	16.9	10.8	1.6	0.6	3.8

Note: Persons of Hispanic or Latino origin can be of any race; (1) Figures cover the Indianapolis-Carmel-Anderson, IN Metropolitan Statistical Area—see Appendix B for areas included
Source: U.S. Census Bureau, 2010-2014 American Community Survey 5-Year Estimates

Ancestry

Area	German	Irish	English	American	Italian	Polish	French[2]	Scottish	Dutch
City	26.4	14.5	10.3	8.4	3.6	4.0	4.4	2.7	1.7
MSA[1]	20.6	11.7	9.3	9.5	2.7	1.9	2.1	2.0	1.6
U.S.	14.9	10.8	8.0	7.1	5.5	3.0	2.7	1.7	1.4

Note: Figures are the percentage of the total population reporting a particular ancestry. The nine most commonly reported ancestries in the U.S. are shown. Figures include multiple ancestries (e.g. if a person reported being Irish and Italian, they were included in both columns); (1) Figures cover the Indianapolis-Carmel-Anderson, IN Metropolitan Statistical Area—see Appendix B for areas included; (2) Excludes Basque
Source: U.S. Census Bureau, 2010-2014 American Community Survey 5-Year Estimates

Foreign-Born Population

Area	Percent of Population Born in								
	Any Foreign Country	Asia	Mexico	Europe	Carribean	Central America[2]	South America	Africa	Canada
City	7.9	4.9	0.6	0.8	0.2	0.2	0.6	0.4	0.1
MSA[1]	6.2	2.0	2.0	0.6	0.2	0.4	0.2	0.7	0.1
U.S.	13.1	3.8	3.7	1.5	1.2	1.0	0.9	0.6	0.3

Note: (1) Figures cover the Indianapolis-Carmel-Anderson, IN Metropolitan Statistical Area—see Appendix B for areas included; (2) Excludes Mexico.
Source: U.S. Census Bureau, 2010-2014 American Community Survey 5-Year Estimates

Marital Status

Area	Never Married	Now Married[2]	Separated	Widowed	Divorced
City	24.5	62.4	1.1	2.3	9.7
MSA[1]	31.2	49.0	1.8	5.3	12.8
U.S.	32.5	48.4	2.2	5.9	10.9

Note: Figures are percentages and cover the population 15 years of age and older; (1) Figures cover the Indianapolis-Carmel-Anderson, IN Metropolitan Statistical Area—see Appendix B for areas included; (2) Excludes separated
Source: U.S. Census Bureau, 2010-2014 American Community Survey 5-Year Estimates

Disability Status

Area	All Ages	Under 18 Years Old	18 to 64 Years Old	65 Years and Over
City	5.4	4.6	3.7	26.8
MSA[1]	12.0	4.6	10.6	36.3
U.S.	12.3	4.1	10.2	36.3

Note: Figures show percent of the civilian noninstitutionalized population that reported having a disability. Disability status is determined from from six types of difficulty: vision, hearing, cognitive, ambulatory, self-care, and independent living. For children under 5 years old, hearing and vision difficulty are used to determine disability status. For children between the ages of 5 and 14, disability status is determined from hearing, vision, cognitive, ambulatory, and self-care difficulties. For people aged 15 years and older, they are considered to have a disability if they have difficulty with any one of the six difficulty types; (1) Figures cover the Indianapolis-Carmel-Anderson, IN Metropolitan Statistical Area—see Appendix B for areas included.
Source: U.S. Census Bureau, 2010-2014 American Community Survey 5-Year Estimates

Age

Area	Percent of Population									Median Age
	Under Age 5	Age 5–19	Age 20–34	Age 35–44	Age 45–54	Age 55–64	Age 65–74	Age 75–84	Age 85+	
City	8.2	26.3	17.8	18.2	15.2	7.8	3.9	2.0	0.6	33.9
MSA[1]	7.0	21.1	20.5	13.7	14.3	11.6	6.6	3.6	1.6	36.0
U.S.	6.4	19.9	20.6	13.0	14.1	12.3	7.6	4.3	1.9	37.4

Note: (1) Figures cover the Indianapolis-Carmel-Anderson, IN Metropolitan Statistical Area—see Appendix B for areas included
Source: U.S. Census Bureau, 2010-2014 American Community Survey 5-Year Estimates

Gender

Area	Males	Females	Males per 100 Females
City	39,351	41,709	94.3
MSA[1]	943,352	987,830	95.5
U.S.	154,515,159	159,591,925	96.8

Note: (1) Figures cover the Indianapolis-Carmel-Anderson, IN Metropolitan Statistical Area—see Appendix B for areas included
Source: U.S. Census Bureau, 2010-2014 American Community Survey 5-Year Estimates

Religious Groups by Family

Area	Catholic	Baptist	Non-Den.	Methodist[2]	Lutheran	LDS[3]	Pente-costal	Presby-terian[4]	Muslim[5]	Judaism
MSA[1]	10.5	10.2	7.1	4.9	1.6	0.7	1.6	1.6	0.2	0.3
U.S.	19.1	9.3	4.0	4.0	2.3	2.0	1.9	1.6	0.8	0.7

Note: Figures are the number of adherents as a percentage of the total population; (1) Figures cover the Indianapolis-Carmel, IN Metropolitan Statistical Area—see Appendix B for areas included; (2) Methodist/Pietist; (3) Latter Day Saints; (4) Reformed; (5) Figures are estimates
Source: Association of Statisticians of American Religious Bodies, 2010 U.S. Religion Census: Religious Congregations & Membership Study

Religious Groups by Tradition

Area	Catholic	Evangelical Protestant	Mainline Protestant	Other Tradition	Black Protestant	Orthodox
MSA[1]	10.5	18.2	9.6	1.6	1.8	0.2
U.S.	19.1	16.2	7.3	4.3	1.6	0.3

Note: Figures are the number of adherents as a percentage of the total population; (1) Figures cover the Indianapolis-Carmel, IN Metropolitan Statistical Area—see Appendix B for areas included
Source: Association of Statisticians of American Religious Bodies, 2010 U.S. Religion Census: Religious Congregations & Membership Study

ECONOMY

Gross Metropolitan Product

Area	2013	2014	2015	2016	Rank[2]
MSA[1]	126.5	132.3	138.0	144.6	25

Note: Figures are in billions of dollars; (1) Figures cover the Indianapolis-Carmel-Anderson, IN Metropolitan Statistical Area—see Appendix B for areas included; (2) Rank is based on 2016 data and ranges from 1 to 381
Source: The U.S. Conference of Mayors, U.S. Metro Economies: GMP and Employment 2014-2016, June 2015

Economic Growth

Area	2011-13 (%)	2014 (%)	2015 (%)	2016 (%)	Rank[2]
MSA[1]	3.0	3.3	2.8	2.9	99
U.S.	2.2	2.4	2.3	2.9	-

Note: Figures are real gross metropolitan product (GMP) growth rates and represent annual average percent change; (1) Figures cover the Indianapolis-Carmel-Anderson, IN Metropolitan Statistical Area—see Appendix B for areas included; (2) Rank is based on 2016 data and ranges from 1 to 381
Source: The U.S. Conference of Mayors, U.S. Metro Economies: GMP and Employment 2014-2016, June 2015

Metropolitan Area Exports

Area	2009	2010	2011	2012	2013	2014	Rank[2]
MSA[1]	8,030.8	9,446.7	9,560.6	10,436.0	9,747.4	9,539.3	34

Note: Figures are in millions of dollars; (1) Figures cover the Indianapolis-Carmel-Anderson, IN Metropolitan Statistical Area—see Appendix B for areas included; (2) Rank is based on 2014 data and ranges from 1 to 385
Source: U.S. Department of Commerce, International Trade Administration, Office of Trade & Industry Information, Manufacturing & Services, data extracted March 10, 2016

Building Permits

Area	Single-Family			Multi-Family			Total		
	2014	2015p	Pct. Chg.	2014	2015p	Pct. Chg.	2014	2015p	Pct. Chg.
City	564	498	-11.7	548	375	-31.6	1,112	873	-21.5
MSA[1]	4,965	5,054	1.8	3,041	3,647	19.9	8,006	8,701	8.7
U.S.	640,300	690,800	7.9	411,800	487,600	18.4	1,052,100	1,178,400	12.0

Note: (1) Figures cover the Indianapolis-Carmel-Anderson, IN Metropolitan Statistical Area—see Appendix B for areas included; Figures represent new, privately-owned housing units authorized (unadjusted data); All permit data are based on estimates with imputation; (p) preliminary data.
Source: U.S. Census Bureau, Manufacturing, Mining, and Construction Statistics, Building Permits, 2014, 2015

Bankruptcy Filings

Area	Business Filings 2014	Business Filings 2015	Business Filings % Chg.	Nonbusiness Filings 2014	Nonbusiness Filings 2015	Nonbusiness Filings % Chg.
Hamilton County	52	54	3.8	889	766	-13.8
U.S.	26,983	24,735	-8.3	909,812	819,760	-9.9

Note: Business filings include Chapter 7, Chapter 11, Chapter 12, and Chapter 13; Nonbusiness filings include Chapter 7, Chapter 11, and Chapter 13
Source: Administrative Office of the U.S. Courts, Business and Nonbusiness Bankruptcy, County Cases Commenced by Chapter of the Bankruptcy Code, During the 12- Month Period Ending December 31, 2014 and Business and Nonbusiness Bankruptcy, County Cases Commenced by Chapter of the Bankruptcy Code, During the 12- Month Period Ending December 31, 2015

Housing Vacancy Rates

Area	Gross Vacancy Rate[2] (%)			Year-Round Vacancy Rate[3] (%)			Rental Vacancy Rate[4] (%)			Homeowner Vacancy Rate[5] (%)		
	2013	2014	2015	2013	2014	2015	2013	2014	2015	2013	2014	2015
MSA[1]	9.2	8.8	7.4	8.7	8.7	7.4	10.9	10.9	8.4	1.5	2.2	1.0
U.S.	13.6	13.4	12.9	10.7	10.4	10.0	8.3	7.6	7.1	2.0	1.9	1.8

Note: (1) Figures cover the Indianapolis-Carmel-Anderson, IN Metropolitan Statistical Area—see Appendix B for areas included; (2) The percentage of the total housing inventory that is vacant; (3) The percentage of the housing inventory (excluding seasonal units) that is year-round vacant; (4) The percentage of rental inventory that is vacant for rent; (5) The percentage of homeowner inventory that is vacant for sale
Source: U.S. Census Bureau, Housing Vacancies and Homeownership Annual Statistics: 2015

INCOME

Income

Area	Per Capita ($)	Median Household ($)	Average Household ($)
City	38,600	91,646	110,153
MSA[1]	27,778	52,434	71,052
U.S.	28,555	53,482	74,596

Note: (1) Figures cover the Indianapolis-Carmel-Anderson, IN Metropolitan Statistical Area—see Appendix B for areas included
Source: U.S. Census Bureau, 2010-2014 American Community Survey 5-Year Estimates

Household Income Distribution

Area	Percent of Households Earning: Under $15,000	$15,000 -24,999	$25,000 -34,999	$35,000 -49,999	$50,000 -74,999	$75,000 -99,000	$100,000 -149,999	$150,000 and up
City	2.5	3.9	5.4	9.8	17.6	16.3	23.1	21.3
MSA[1]	11.7	10.5	10.7	14.6	18.6	12.6	12.9	8.3
U.S.	12.5	10.7	10.2	13.5	17.8	12.2	13.0	10.0

Note: (1) Figures cover the Indianapolis-Carmel-Anderson, IN Metropolitan Statistical Area—see Appendix B for areas included
Source: U.S. Census Bureau, 2010-2014 American Community Survey 5-Year Estimates

Poverty Rate

Area	All Ages	Under 18 Years Old	18 to 64 Years Old	65 Years and Over
City	3.3	3.4	3.3	2.4
MSA[1]	14.6	20.8	13.5	7.0
U.S.	15.6	21.9	14.6	9.4

Note: Figures are percentage of people whose income during the past 12 months was below the poverty level; (1) Figures cover the Indianapolis-Carmel-Anderson, IN Metropolitan Statistical Area—see Appendix B for areas included
Source: U.S. Census Bureau, 2010-2014 American Community Survey 5-Year Estimates

EMPLOYMENT

Labor Force and Employment

Area	Civilian Labor Force			Workers Employed		
	Dec. 2014	Dec. 2015	% Chg.	Dec. 2014	Dec. 2015	% Chg.
City	45,650	47,050	3.0	43,975	45,633	3.7
MSA[1]	996,479	1,020,083	2.3	942,497	978,074	3.7
U.S.	155,521,000	157,245,000	1.1	147,190,000	149,703,000	1.7

Note: Data is not seasonally adjusted and covers workers 16 years of age and older; (1) Figures cover the Indianapolis-Carmel-Anderson, IN Metropolitan Statistical Area—see Appendix B for areas included
Source: Bureau of Labor Statistics, Local Area Unemployment Statistics

Unemployment Rate

Area	2015											
	Jan.	Feb.	Mar.	Apr.	May	Jun.	Jul.	Aug.	Sep.	Oct.	Nov.	Dec.
City	4.1	3.7	3.7	2.9	3.3	3.4	3.4	3.1	2.8	3.0	3.2	3.0
MSA[1]	6.2	5.7	5.5	4.3	4.5	4.5	4.4	4.2	3.8	4.0	4.2	4.1
U.S.	6.1	5.8	5.6	5.1	5.3	5.5	5.6	5.2	4.9	4.8	4.8	4.8

Note: Data is not seasonally adjusted and covers workers 16 years of age and older; (1) Figures cover the Indianapolis-Carmel-Anderson, IN Metropolitan Statistical Area—see Appendix B for areas included
Source: Bureau of Labor Statistics, Local Area Unemployment Statistics

Employment by Occupation

Occupation Classification	City (%)	MSA[1] (%)	U.S. (%)
Management, Business, Science, and Arts	56.3	37.0	36.4
Natural Resources, Construction, and Maintenance	3.5	7.8	9.0
Production, Transportation, and Material Moving	2.9	13.3	12.1
Sales and Office	26.9	25.4	24.4
Service	10.4	16.5	18.2

Note: Figures cover employed civilians 16 years of age and older; (1) Figures cover the Indianapolis-Carmel-Anderson, IN Metropolitan Statistical Area—see Appendix B for areas included
Source: U.S. Census Bureau, 2010-2014 American Community Survey 5-Year Estimates

Employment by Industry

Sector	MSA[1]		U.S.
	Number of Employees	Percent of Total	Percent of Total
Construction	45,400	4.3	4.5
Education and Health Services	150,200	14.4	15.7
Financial Activities	63,200	6.0	5.7
Government	132,300	12.7	15.5
Information	16,100	1.5	1.9
Leisure and Hospitality	104,000	10.0	10.4
Manufacturing	90,200	8.6	8.6
Mining and Logging	600	<0.1	0.5
Other Services	44,300	4.2	3.9
Professional and Business Services	165,200	15.9	13.9
Retail Trade	112,200	10.8	11.3
Transportation, Warehousing, and Utilities	68,100	6.5	3.9
Wholesale Trade	46,300	4.4	4.1

Note: Figures are non-farm employment as of December 2015. Figures are not seasonally adjusted and include workers 16 years of age and older; (1) Figures cover the Indianapolis-Carmel-Anderson, IN Metropolitan Statistical Area—see Appendix B for areas included
Source: Bureau of Labor Statistics, Current Employment Statistics, Employment, Hours, and Earnings

Occupations with Greatest Projected Employment Growth: 2012 – 2022

Occupation[1]	2012 Employment	2022 Projected Employment	Numeric Employment Change	Percent Employment Change
Registered Nurses	59,270	69,750	10,480	17.7
Laborers and Freight, Stock, and Material Movers, Hand	58,300	67,220	8,920	15.3
Retail Salespersons	88,940	97,570	8,630	9.7
Combined Food Preparation and Serving Workers, Including Fast Food	79,310	87,710	8,400	10.6
Office Clerks, General	52,850	59,940	7,090	13.4
Team Assemblers	64,220	70,850	6,630	10.3
Nursing Assistants	31,570	37,490	5,920	18.8
Janitors and Cleaners, Except Maids and Housekeeping Cleaners	42,560	48,450	5,890	13.8
Waiters and Waitresses	49,630	54,920	5,290	10.7
Personal Care Aides	20,120	25,260	5,140	25.6

Note: Projections cover Indiana; (1) Sorted by numeric employment change
Source: www.projectionscentral.com, State Occupational Projections, 2012–2022 Long-Term Projections

Fastest Growing Occupations: 2012 – 2022

Occupation[1]	2012 Employment	2022 Projected Employment	Numeric Employment Change	Percent Employment Change
Chiropractors	640	860	220	35.0
Dental Hygienists	4,780	6,440	1,660	34.7
Ophthalmic Medical Technicians	800	1,080	280	34.7
Dentists, General	1,670	2,250	580	34.4
Anesthesiologists	950	1,270	320	34.1
Dental Assistants	5,800	7,770	1,970	34.0
Optometrists	710	960	250	33.9
Surgeons	780	1,030	250	31.8
Physician Assistants	950	1,230	280	30.4
Internists, General	590	760	170	29.5

Note: Projections cover Indiana; (1) Sorted by percent employment change and excludes occupations with numeric employment change less than 100
Source: www.projectionscentral.com, State Occupational Projections, 2012–2022 Long-Term Projections

Average Wages

Occupation	$/Hr.	Occupation	$/Hr.
Accountants and Auditors	32.87	Maids and Housekeeping Cleaners	9.80
Automotive Mechanics	22.25	Maintenance and Repair Workers	18.60
Bookkeepers	18.90	Marketing Managers	53.84
Carpenters	21.12	Nuclear Medicine Technologists	34.81
Cashiers	9.33	Nurses, Licensed Practical	19.97
Clerks, General Office	14.92	Nurses, Registered	29.83
Clerks, Receptionists/Information	13.67	Nursing Assistants	12.31
Clerks, Shipping/Receiving	14.60	Packers and Packagers, Hand	11.36
Computer Programmers	34.28	Physical Therapists	40.48
Computer Systems Analysts	37.67	Postal Service Mail Carriers	24.57
Computer User Support Specialists	25.88	Real Estate Brokers	20.52
Cooks, Restaurant	11.08	Retail Salespersons	12.16
Dentists	57.12	Sales Reps., Exc. Tech./Scientific	32.46
Electrical Engineers	39.11	Sales Reps., Tech./Scientific	47.36
Electricians	27.05	Secretaries, Exc. Legal/Med./Exec.	17.08
Financial Managers	54.70	Security Guards	12.36
First-Line Supervisors/Managers, Sales	19.41	Surgeons	n/a
Food Preparation Workers	9.58	Teacher Assistants*	11.56
General and Operations Managers	55.69	Teachers, Elementary School*	24.21
Hairdressers/Cosmetologists	13.07	Teachers, Secondary School*	26.14
Internists	125.04	Telemarketers	13.23
Janitors and Cleaners	11.89	Truck Drivers, Heavy/Tractor-Trailer	21.79
Landscaping/Groundskeeping Workers	12.22	Truck Drivers, Light/Delivery Svcs.	16.94
Lawyers	59.31	Waiters and Waitresses	10.14

Note: Wage data covers the Indianapolis-Carmel, IN Metropolitan Statistical Area—see Appendix B for areas included; (*) Hourly wages for elementary/secondary school teachers and teacher assistants were calculated by the editors from annual wage data based on a 40 hour work week; n/a not available.
Source: Bureau of Labor Statistics, Metro Area Occupational Employment and Wage Estimates, May 2015

TAXES

State Corporate Income Tax Rates

State	Tax Rate (%)	Income Brackets ($)	Num. of Brackets	Financial Institution Tax Rate (%)[a]	Federal Income Tax Ded.
Indiana	6.5 (j)	Flat rate	1	8.5 (j)	No

Note: Tax rates as of January 1, 2016; (a) Rates listed are the corporate income tax rate applied to financial institutions or excise taxes based on income. Some states have other taxes based upon the value of deposits or shares; (j) The Indiana tax rate is scheduled to decrease to 6.25% on July 1, 2016.
Source: Federation of Tax Administrators, "State Corporate Income Tax Rates, 2016"

State Individual Income Tax Rates

State	Tax Rate (%)	Income Brackets ($)	Num. of Brackets	Personal Exempt. ($)[1] Single	Personal Exempt. ($)[1] Dependents	Fed. Inc. Tax Ded.
Indiana	3.3	Flat rate	1	1,000	2,500 (i)	No

Note: Tax rates as of January 1, 2016; Local- and county-level taxes are not included; n/a not applicable; (1) Married joint filers generally receive double the single exemption; (i) In Indiana, includes an additional exemption of $1,500 for each dependent child.
Source: Federation of Tax Administrators, "State Individual Income Tax Rates, 2016"

Various State and Local Tax Rates

State	State and Local Sales and Use (%)	State Sales and Use (%)	Gasoline[1] (¢/gal.)	Cigarette[2] ($/pack)	Spirits[3] ($/gal.)	Wine[4] ($/gal.)	Beer[5] ($/gal.)
Indiana	7.00	7.0	29.89	0.995	2.68 (f)	0.47 (l)	0.12

Note: All tax rates as of January 1, 2016; (1) The American Petroleum Institute has developed a methodology for determining the average tax rate on a gallon of fuel. Rates may include any of the following: excise taxes, environmental fees, storage tank fees, other fees or taxes, general sales tax, and local taxes. In states where gasoline is subject to the general sales tax, or where the fuel tax is based on the average sale price, the average rate determined by API is sensitive to changes in the price of gasoline. States that fully or partially apply general sales taxes to gasoline: CA, CO, GA, IL, IN, MI, NY; (2) The federal excise tax of $1.0066 per pack and local taxes are not included; (3) Rates are those applicable to off-premise sales of 40% alcohol by volume (a.b.v.) distilled spirits in 750ml containers. Local excise taxes are excluded; (4) Rates are those applicable to off-premise sales of 11% a.b.v. non-carbonated wine in 750ml containers; (5) Rates are those applicable to off-premise sales of 4.7% a.b.v. beer in 12 ounce containers; (f) Different rates are also applicable according to alcohol content, place of production, size of container, or place purchased (on- or off-premise or onboard airlines); (l) Different rates also applicable according to alcohol content, place of production, size of container, place purchased (on- or off-premise or on board airlines) or type of wine (carbonated, vermouth, etc.).
Source: Tax Foundation, 2016 Facts & Figures: How Does Your State Compare?

State Business Tax Climate Index Rankings

State	Overall Rank	Corporate Tax Rank	Individual Income Tax Rank	Sales Tax Rank	Unemployment Insurance Tax Rank	Property Tax Rank
Indiana	8	20	11	11	14	5

Note: The index is a measure of how each state's tax laws affect economic performance. The lower the rank, the more favorable a state's tax system is for business. States without a given tax are given a ranking of 1. The scores/rankings for the District of Columbia do not affect other states. The 2016 index represents the tax climate as of July 1, 2015 (the beginning of Fiscal Year 2016).
Source: Tax Foundation, State Business Tax Climate Index 2016

TRANSPORTATION

Means of Transportation to Work

Area	Car/Truck/Van		Public Transportation			Bicycle	Walked	Other Means	Worked at Home
	Drove Alone	Car-pooled	Bus	Subway	Railroad				
City	84.6	7.6	0.1	0.0	0.0	0.2	0.4	0.8	6.2
MSA[1]	83.8	8.7	1.0	0.0	0.0	0.3	1.6	0.9	3.7
U.S.	76.4	9.6	2.6	1.8	0.6	0.6	2.8	1.3	4.4

Note: Figures are percentages and cover workers 16 years of age and older; (1) Figures cover the Indianapolis-Carmel-Anderson, IN Metropolitan Statistical Area—see Appendix B for areas included
Source: U.S. Census Bureau, 2010-2014 American Community Survey 5-Year Estimates

Travel Time to Work

Area	Less Than 10 Minutes	10 to 19 Minutes	20 to 29 Minutes	30 to 44 Minutes	45 to 59 Minutes	60 to 89 Minutes	90 Minutes or More
City	8.5	22.3	22.8	31.8	9.4	3.0	2.2
MSA[1]	12.0	27.7	24.5	23.6	7.4	3.5	1.4
U.S.	13.3	29.6	21.0	20.2	7.7	5.7	2.6

Note: Figures are percentages and include workers 16 years old and over; (1) Figures cover the Indianapolis-Carmel-Anderson, IN Metropolitan Statistical Area—see Appendix B for areas included
Source: U.S. Census Bureau, 2010-2014 American Community Survey 5-Year Estimates

Freeway Travel Time Index

Area	1985	1990	1995	2000	2005	2010	2014
Urban Area Rank[1,2]	35	41	41	38	51	42	46
Urban Area Index[1]	1.09	1.11	1.14	1.17	1.17	1.18	1.18
Average Index[3]	1.09	1.11	1.14	1.17	1.20	1.19	1.20

Note: Freeway Travel Time Index—the ratio of travel time in the peak period to the travel time at free-flow conditions. For example, a value of 1.30 indicates a 20-minute free-flow trip takes 26 minutes in the peak (20 minutes x 1.30 = 26 minutes); (1) Covers the Indianapolis IN urban area; (2) Rank is based on 101 urban areas (#1 = highest travel time index); (3) Average of 101 urban areas
Source: Texas Transportation Institute, 2015 Urban Mobility Scorecard, August 2015

Freeway Commuter Stress Index

Area	1985	1990	1995	2000	2005	2010	2014
Urban Area Rank[1,2]	48	47	50	54	58	58	61
Urban Area Index[1]	1.10	1.13	1.16	1.18	1.19	1.19	1.19
Average Index[3]	1.13	1.16	1.19	1.22	1.25	1.24	1.25

Note: The Freeway Commuter Stress Index is the same as the Freeway Travel Time Index (see table above) except that it includes only the travel in the peak directions during the peak periods; the TTI includes travel in all directions during the peak period. Thus, the CSI is more indicative of the work trip experienced by each commuter on a daily basis. (1) Covers the Indianapolis IN urban area; (2) Rank is based on 101 urban areas (#1 = highest stress index); (3) Average of 101 urban areas

Source: Texas Transportation Institute, 2015 Urban Mobility Scorecard, August 2015

Living Environment

COST OF LIVING

Cost of Living Index

Composite Index	Groceries	Housing	Utilities	Transportation	Health Care	Misc. Goods/ Services
91.2	92.9	82.4	90.9	91.8	99.3	96.8

Note: The Cost of Living Index measures regional differences in the cost of consumer goods and services, excluding taxes and non-consumer expenditures, for professional and managerial households in the top income quintile. It is based on more than 50,000 prices covering almost 60 different items for which prices are collected three times a year by chambers of commerce, economic development organizations or university applied economic centers in each participating urban area. The numbers shown should be read as a percentage above or below the national average of 100. For example, a value of 115.4 in the groceries column indicates that grocery prices are 15.4% higher than the national average. Small differences in the index numbers should not be interpreted as significant; Figures cover the Indianapolis IN urban area.
Source: The Council for Community and Economic Research, ACCRA Cost of Living Index, 2015

Grocery Prices

Area[1]	T-Bone Steak ($/pound)	Frying Chicken ($/pound)	Whole Milk ($/half gal.)	Eggs ($/dozen)	Orange Juice ($/64 oz.)	Coffee ($/11.5 oz.)
City[2]	10.31	1.17	1.90	2.07	3.54	4.18
Avg.	10.99	1.43	2.25	2.26	3.58	4.48
Min.	7.16	0.98	1.30	1.35	2.88	2.98
Max.	14.13	2.43	3.85	4.81	6.39	7.56

Note: (1) Values for the local area are compared with the average, minimum and maximum values for all 292 areas in the Cost of Living Index; (2) Figures cover the Indianapolis IN urban area; **T-Bone Steak** *(price per pound);* **Frying Chicken** *(price per pound, whole fryer);* **Whole Milk** *(half gallon carton);* **Eggs** *(price per dozen, Grade A, large);* **Orange Juice** *(64 oz. Tropicana or Florida Natural);* **Coffee** *(11.5 oz. can, vacuum-packed, Maxwell House, Hills Bros, or Folgers).*
Source: The Council for Community and Economic Research, ACCRA Cost of Living Index, 2015

Housing and Utility Costs

Area[1]	New Home Price ($)	Apartment Rent ($/month)	All Electric ($/month)	Part Electric ($/month)	Other Energy ($/month)	Telephone ($/month)
City[2]	236,995	950	-	78.56	75.38	25.68
Avg.	312,874	945	179.30	95.07	72.96	28.11
Min.	178,682	479	116.28	43.14	26.46	10.01
Max.	1,472,476	3,984	504.25	189.44	421.11	43.06

Note: (1) Values for the local area are compared with the average, minimum and maximum values for all 292 areas in the Cost of Living Index; (2) Figures cover the Indianapolis IN urban area; **New Home Price** *(2,400 sf living area, 8,000 sf lot, in urban area with full utilities);* **Apartment Rent** *(950 sf 2 bedroom/1.5 or 2 bath, unfurnished, excluding all utilities except water);* **All Electric** *(average monthly cost for an all-electric home);* **Part Electric** *(average monthly cost for a part-electric home);* **Other Energy** *(average monthly cost for natural gas, fuel oil, coal, wood, and any other forms of energy except electricity);* **Telephone** *(price includes basic monthly rate for a private residential line plus additional local usage charges incurred by a family of four).*
Source: The Council for Community and Economic Research, ACCRA Cost of Living Index, 2015

Health Care, Transportation, and Other Costs

Area[1]	Doctor ($/visit)	Dentist ($/visit)	Optometrist ($/visit)	Gasoline ($/gallon)	Beauty Salon ($/visit)	Men's Shirt ($)
City[2]	95.01	90.00	87.83	2.28	28.73	37.94
Avg.	105.15	89.02	99.78	2.38	35.30	28.10
Min.	66.87	56.09	48.53	1.95	18.91	13.38
Max.	182.34	150.36	228.33	4.09	67.91	63.80

Note: (1) Values for the local area are compared with the average, minimum and maximum values for all 292 areas in the Cost of Living Index; (2) Figures cover the Indianapolis IN urban area; **Doctor** *(general practitioners routine exam of an established patient);* **Dentist** *(adult teeth cleaning and periodic oral examination);* **Optometrist** *(full vision eye exam for established adult patient);* **Gasoline** *(one gallon regular unleaded, national brand, including all taxes, cash price at self-service pump if available);* **Beauty Salon** *(woman's shampoo, trim, and blow-dry);* **Men's Shirt** *(cotton/polyester dress shirt, pinpoint weave, long sleeves).*
Source: The Council for Community and Economic Research, ACCRA Cost of Living Index, 2015

HOUSING

House Price Index (HPI)

Area	National Ranking[2]	Quarterly Change (%)	One-Year Change (%)	Five-Year Change (%)
MSA[1]	129	0.30	4.70	9.30
U.S.[3]	–	1.45	5.76	22.85

Note: The HPI is a weighted repeat sales index. It measures average price changes in repeat sales or refinancings on the same properties. This information is obtained by reviewing repeat mortgage transactions on single-family properties whose mortgages have been purchased or securitized by Fannie Mae or Freddie Mac in January 1975; (1) Indianapolis-Carmel-Anderson Metropolitan Statistical Area—see Appendix B for areas included; (2) Rankings are based on annual percentage change for all metro areas containing at least 15,000 transactions over the last 10 years and ranges from 1 to 266; (3) figures based on a weighted average of Census Division estimates using a seasonally adjusted, purchase-only index; all figures are for the period ending December 31, 2015

Source: Federal Housing Finance Agency, House Price Index, February 25, 2016

Median Single-Family Home Prices

Area	2013	2014	2015p	Percent Change 2014 to 2015
MSA[1]	136.7	144.6	153.2	5.9
U.S. Average	197.4	208.9	223.9	7.2

Note: Figures are median sales prices of existing single-family homes in thousands of dollars; (p) preliminary; n/a not available; (1) Indianapolis-Carmel-Anderson, IN Metropolitan Statistical Area—see Appendix B for areas included

Source: National Association of Realtors, Median Sales Price of Existing Single-Family Homes for Metropolitan Areas, 4th Quarter 2015

Qualifying Income Based on Median Sales Price of Existing Single-Family Homes

Area	With 5% Down ($)	With 10% Down ($)	With 20% Down ($)
MSA[1]	33,253	31,503	28,003
U.S. Average	49,535	46,928	41,714

Note: Figures are preliminary; Qualifying income is based on a mortgage rate of 4.1%. Monthly principal and interest payment is limited to 25% of income; n/a not available; (1) Indianapolis-Carmel-Anderson, IN Metropolitan Statistical Area—see Appendix B for areas included

Source: National Association of Realtors, Qualifying Income Based on Median Sales Price of Existing Single-Family Homes for Metropolitan Areas, 4th Quarter 2015

Median Apartment Condo-Coop Home Prices

Area	2013	2014	2015p	Percent Change 2014 to 2015
MSA[1]	118.2	124.7	128.0	2.6
U.S. Average	194.9	204.3	210.7	3.1

Note: Figures are median sales prices of existing apartment condo-coop homes in thousands of dollars; (p) preliminary; n/a not available; (1) Indianapolis-Carmel-Anderson, IN Metropolitan Statistical Area—see Appendix B for areas included

Source: National Association of Realtors, Median Sales Price of Existing Apartment Condo-Coop Homes for Metropolitan Areas, 4th Quarter 2015

Gross Monthly Rent

Area	Under $200	$200 -299	$300 -499	$500 -749	$750 -999	$1,000 -1,499	$1,500 and up	Median ($)
City	0.0	0.0	1.9	4.1	35.9	41.3	16.8	1,071
MSA[1]	1.1	2.3	6.3	32.4	32.9	20.4	4.6	800
U.S.	1.5	3.2	7.4	21.0	24.1	26.9	15.9	920

Note: Figures are percentages except for Median; Gross rent is the contract rent plus the estimated average monthly cost of utilities (electricity, gas, and water and sewer) and fuels (oil, coal, kerosene, wood, etc.) if these are paid by the renter (or paid for the renter by someone else); (1) Figures cover the Indianapolis-Carmel-Anderson, IN Metropolitan Statistical Area—see Appendix B for areas included

Source: U.S. Census Bureau, 2010-2014 American Community Survey 5-Year Estimates

Homeownership Rate

Area	2008 (%)	2009 (%)	2010 (%)	2011 (%)	2012 (%)	2013 (%)	2014 (%)	2015 (%)
MSA[1]	75.0	71.0	68.8	68.3	67.1	67.5	66.9	64.6
U.S.	67.8	67.4	66.9	66.1	65.4	65.1	64.5	63.7

Note: (1) Figures cover the Indianapolis-Carmel-Anderson, IN Metropolitan Statistical Area—see Appendix B for areas included

Source: U.S. Census Bureau, Housing Vacancies and Homeownership Annual Statistics: 2015

Year Housing Structure Built

Area	2010 or Later	2000 -2009	1990 -1999	1980 -1989	1970 -1979	1960 -1969	1950 -1959	1940 -1949	Before 1940	Median Year
City	3.5	40.9	35.8	14.0	2.8	1.6	0.8	0.3	0.3	1998
MSA[1]	1.4	17.3	16.5	10.6	13.3	11.8	11.0	5.0	13.1	1977
U.S.	1.0	14.9	13.9	13.8	15.8	11.0	10.8	5.4	13.3	1976

Note: Figures are percentages except for Median Year; (1) Figures cover the Indianapolis-Carmel-Anderson, IN Metropolitan Statistical Area—see Appendix B for areas included

Source: U.S. Census Bureau, 2010-2014 American Community Survey 5-Year Estimates

HEALTH

Health Risk Data

Category	MSA[1] (%)	U.S. (%)
Adults aged 18–64 who have any kind of health care coverage	82.6	79.6
Adults who reported being in good or excellent health	81.0	83.1
Adults who are current smokers	21.8	19.6
Adults who are heavy drinkers[2]	4.5	6.1
Adults who are binge drinkers[3]	15.8	16.9
Adults who are overweight (BMI 25.0 - 29.9)	34.8	35.8
Adults who are obese (BMI 30.0 - 99.8)	30.1	27.6
Adults who participated in any physical activities in the past month	75.9	77.1
Adults 50+ who have ever had a sigmoidoscopy or colonoscopy	68.6	67.3
Women aged 40+ who have had a mammogram within the past two years	71.6	74.0
Men aged 40+ who have had a PSA test within the past two years	47.0	45.2
Adults aged 65+ who have had flu shot within the past year	61.5	60.1
Adults who always wear a seatbelt	96.1	93.8

Note: Data as of 2012 unless otherwise noted; (1) Figures cover the Indianapolis-Carmel, IN Metropolitan Statistical Area—see Appendix B for areas included; (2) Heavy drinkers are classified as males having more than two drinks per day or females having more than one drink per day; (3) Binge drinkers are classified as males having five or more drinks on one occasion or females having four or more drinks on one occasion

Source: Centers for Disease Control and Prevention, Behaviorial Risk Factor Surveillance System, SMART: Selected Metropolitan/Micropolitan Area Risk Trends, 2012 (Note: the CDC has discontinued this dataset but will be releasing a replacement in mid-2016)

Chronic Health Indicators

Category	MSA[1] (%)	U.S. (%)
Adults who have ever been told they had a heart attack	4.2	4.5
Adults who have ever been told they had a stroke	3.0	2.9
Adults who have been told they currently have asthma	9.5	8.9
Adults who have ever been told they have arthritis	25.3	25.7
Adults who have ever been told they have diabetes[2]	9.8	9.7
Adults who have ever been told they had skin cancer	5.1	5.7
Adults who have ever been told they had any other types of cancer	6.5	6.5
Adults who have ever been told they have COPD	7.1	6.2
Adults who have ever been told they have kidney disease	2.4	2.5
Adults who have ever been told they have a form of depression	19.6	18.0

Note: Data as of 2012 unless otherwise noted; (1) Figures cover the Indianapolis-Carmel, IN Metropolitan Statistical Area—see Appendix B for areas included; (2) Figures do not include pregnancy-related, borderline, or pre-diabetes

Source: Centers for Disease Control and Prevention, Behaviorial Risk Factor Surveillance System, SMART: Selected Metropolitan/Micropolitan Area Risk Trends, 2012 (Note: the CDC has discontinued this dataset but will be releasing a replacement in mid-2016)

Mortality Rates for the Top 10 Causes of Death in the U.S.

ICD-10[a] Sub-Chapter	ICD-10[a] Code	Age-Adjusted Mortality Rate[1] per 100,000 population	
		County[2]	U.S.
Malignant neoplasms	C00-C97	140.7	163.6
Ischaemic heart diseases	I20-I25	72.2	102.2
Other forms of heart disease	I30-I51	46.0	50.1
Chronic lower respiratory diseases	J40-J47	36.1	41.4
Organic, including symptomatic, mental disorders	F01-F09	45.9	38.5
Cerebrovascular diseases	I60-I69	32.6	36.5
Other external causes of accidental injury	W00-X59	19.0	27.5
Other degenerative diseases of the nervous system	G30-G31	35.5	26.3
Diabetes mellitus	E10-E14	16.5	21.1
Hypertensive diseases	I10-I15	7.3	19.7

Note: (a) ICD-10 = International Classification of Diseases 10th Revision; (1) Mortality rates are a three year average covering 2012-2014; (2) Figures cover Hamilton County.
Source: Centers for Disease Control and Prevention, National Center for Health Statistics. Underlying Cause of Death 1999-2014 on CDC WONDER Online Database, released 2015.

Mortality Rates for Selected Causes of Death

ICD-10[a] Sub-Chapter	ICD-10[a] Code	Age-Adjusted Mortality Rate[1] per 100,000 population	
		County[2]	U.S.
Assault	X85-Y09	Unreliable	5.1
Diseases of the liver	K70-K76	7.9	13.5
Human immunodeficiency virus (HIV) disease	B20-B24	Suppressed	2.1
Influenza and pneumonia	J09-J18	13.2	15.2
Intentional self-harm	X60-X84	9.8	12.7
Malnutrition	E40-E46	Unreliable	0.9
Obesity and other hyperalimentation	E65-E68	Suppressed	1.9
Renal failure	N17-N19	12.0	13.0
Transport accidents	V01-V99	5.1	11.6
Viral hepatitis	B15-B19	Suppressed	2.1

Note: (a) ICD-10 = International Classification of Diseases 10th Revision; (1) Mortality rates are a three year average covering 2012-2014; (2) Figures cover Hamilton County; Data are Suppressed when the data meet the criteria for confidentiality constraints; Mortality rates are flagged as Unreliable when the rate would be calculated with a numerator of 20 or less.
Source: Centers for Disease Control and Prevention, National Center for Health Statistics. Underlying Cause of Death 1999-2014 on CDC WONDER Online Database, released 2015.

Health Insurance Coverage

Area	With Health Insurance	With Private Health Insurance	With Public Health Insurance	Without Health Insurance	Population Under Age 18 Without Health Insurance
City	94.1	89.7	9.3	5.9	2.7
MSA[1]	86.7	69.0	27.9	13.3	6.9
U.S.	85.8	65.8	31.1	14.2	7.1

Note: Figures are percentages that cover the civilian noninstitutionalized population; (1) Figures cover the Indianapolis-Carmel-Anderson, IN Metropolitan Statistical Area—see Appendix B for areas included
Source: U.S. Census Bureau, 2010-2014 American Community Survey 5-Year Estimates

Number of Medical Professionals

Area	MDs[3]	DOs[3,4]	Dentists	Podiatrists	Chiropractors	Optometrists
County[1] (number)	1,678	69	221	10	105	66
County[1] (rate[2])	565.3	23.2	73.0	3.3	34.7	21.8
U.S. (rate[2])	272.5	20.9	64.7	5.8	25.9	15.2

Note: Data as of 2014 unless noted; (1) Data covers Hamilton County; (2) Rate per 100,000 population; (3) Data as of 2013 and includes all active, non-federal physicians; (4) Doctor of Osteopathic Medicine
Source: U.S. Department of Health and Human Services, Health Resources and Services Administration, Bureau of Health Professions, Area Resource File (ARF) 2014-2015

Best Hospitals

According to *U.S. News,* the Indianapolis-Carmel-Anderson, IN metro area is home to two of the best hospitals in the U.S.: **IU Health Academic Health Center** (10 specialties); **St. Vincent Hospital and Health Center** (2 specialties). The hospitals listed were nationally ranked in at least one adult specialty. Only 137 hospitals nationwide were nationally ranked in one or more specialties. Fifteen hospitals in the U.S. made the Honor Roll with high scores in at least six specialties. *U.S. News Online, "America's Best Children's Hospitals 2015-16"*

According to *U.S. News,* the Indianapolis-Carmel-Anderson, IN metro area is home to one of the best children's hospitals in the U.S.: **Riley Hospital for Children at IU Health** (10 specialties). The hospital listed was highly ranked in at least one pediatric specialty. Eighty-three children's hospitals in the U.S. were nationally ranked in at least one specialty. Twelve children's hospitals in the U.S. made the Honor Roll with high scores in at least three specialties. *U.S. News Online, "America's Best Children's Hospitals 2015-16"*

EDUCATION

Public School District Statistics

District Name	Schls	Pupils	Pupil/ Teacher Ratio	Minority Pupils[1] (%)	Free Lunch Eligible[2] (%)	IEP[3] (%)
Hamilton Southeastern Schools	21	20,524	19.8	22.9	9.4	10.8

Note: Table includes school districts with 100 or more students; (1) Percentage of students that are not non-Hispanic white; (2) Percentage of students that are eligible for the free lunch program; (3) Percentage of students that have an Individualized Education Program.
Source: U.S. Department of Education, National Center for Education Statistics, Common Core of Data, Local Education Agency (School District) Universe Survey: School Year 2013-2014; U.S. Department of Education, National Center for Education Statistics, Common Core of Data, Public Elementary/Secondary School Universe Survey: School Year 2013-2014

Highest Level of Education

Area	Less than H.S.	H.S. Diploma	Some College, No Deg.	Associate Degree	Bachelor's Degree	Master's Degree	Prof. School Degree	Doctorate Degree
City	2.3	11.7	18.1	6.8	40.4	14.8	3.9	2.1
MSA[1]	11.3	29.6	20.7	7.7	20.1	7.6	2.0	1.1
U.S.	13.7	28.0	21.2	7.9	18.3	7.8	2.0	1.3

Note: Figures cover persons age 25 and over; (1) Figures cover the Indianapolis-Carmel-Anderson, IN Metropolitan Statistical Area—see Appendix B for areas included
Source: U.S. Census Bureau, 2010-2014 American Community Survey 5-Year Estimates

Educational Attainment by Race

Area	High School Graduate or Higher (%)					Bachelor's Degree or Higher (%)				
	Total	White	Black	Asian	Hisp.[2]	Total	White	Black	Asian	Hisp.[2]
City	97.7	98.3	93.5	94.1	78.5	61.1	61.1	48.2	74.8	35.7
MSA[1]	88.7	90.4	84.6	86.1	57.7	30.8	32.7	17.6	58.4	13.6
U.S.	86.3	88.4	83.2	85.8	64.1	29.3	30.6	19.0	50.9	13.9

Note: Figures shown cover persons 25 years old and over; (1) Figures cover the Indianapolis-Carmel-Anderson, IN Metropolitan Statistical Area—see Appendix B for areas included; (2) People of Hispanic origin can be of any race
Source: U.S. Census Bureau, 2010-2014 American Community Survey 5-Year Estimates

School Enrollment by Grade and Control

Area	Preschool (%)		Kindergarten (%)		Grades 1 - 4 (%)		Grades 5 - 8 (%)		Grades 9 - 12 (%)	
	Public	Private	Public	Private	Public	Private	Public	Private	Public	Private
City	38.8	61.2	78.2	21.8	88.5	11.5	92.6	7.4	86.6	13.4
MSA[1]	46.7	53.3	84.7	15.3	88.9	11.1	89.9	10.1	89.2	10.8
U.S.	57.4	42.6	87.8	12.2	89.8	10.2	89.9	10.1	90.6	9.4

Note: Figures shown cover persons 3 years old and over; (1) Figures cover the Indianapolis-Carmel-Anderson, IN Metropolitan Statistical Area—see Appendix B for areas included
Source: U.S. Census Bureau, 2010-2014 American Community Survey 5-Year Estimates

Average Salaries of Public School Classroom Teachers

Area	2013-14 Dollars	2013-14 Rank[1]	2014-15 Dollars	2014-15 Rank[1]	Percent Change 2013-14 to 2014-15	Percent Change 2004-05 to 2014-15
Indiana	50,289	27	50,502	30	0.42	8.4
U.S. Average	56,610	–	57,379	–	1.36	20.8

Note: (1) State rank ranges from 1 to 51 where 1 indicates highest salary.
Source: National Education Association, Rankings & Estimates: Rankings of the States 2014 and Estimates of School Statistics 2015, March 2015

Higher Education

Four-Year Colleges			Two-Year Colleges			Medical Schools[1]	Law Schools[2]	Voc/ Tech[3]
Public	Private Non-profit	Private For-profit	Public	Private Non-profit	Private For-profit			
0	0	0	0	0	0	0	0	0

Note: Figures cover institutions located within the city limits and include main campuses only; (1) includes schools accredited by the Liaison Committee on Medical Education and the American Osteopathic Association's Commission on Osteopathic College Accreditation; (2) includes ABA-accredited schools, schools with provisional ABA accreditation, and state accredited schools; (3) includes all schools with programs that are less than 2 years.
Source: National Center for Education Statistics, Integrated Postsecondary Education System (IPEDS), 2014-15; Association of American Medical Colleges, Member List, March 21, 2016; American Osteopathic Association, Member List, March 21, 2016; Law School Admission Council, Official Guide to ABA-Approved Law Schools Online, March 21, 2016; Wikipedia, List of Medical Schools in the United States, March 21, 2016; Wikipedia, List of Law Schools in the United States, March 21, 2016

According to *U.S. News & World Report,* the Indianapolis-Carmel-Anderson, IN metro area is home to one of the best national universities in the U.S.: **Indiana University-?Purdue University–Indianapolis** (#199 tie). The indicators used to capture academic quality fall into a number of categories: assessment by administrators at peer institutions; retention of students; faculty resources; student selectivity; financial resources; alumni giving; high school counselor ratings of colleges; and graduation rate. *U.S. News & World Report, "America's Best Colleges 2016"*

According to *U.S. News & World Report,* the Indianapolis-Carmel-Anderson, IN metro area is home to one of the best liberal arts colleges in the U.S.: **DePauw University** (#51 tie). The indicators used to capture academic quality fall into a number of categories: assessment by administrators at peer institutions; retention of students; faculty resources; student selectivity; financial resources; alumni giving; high school counselor ratings of colleges; and graduation rate. *U.S. News & World Report, "America's Best Colleges 2016"*

According to *U.S. News & World Report,* the Indianapolis-Carmel-Anderson, IN metro area is home to one of the top 100 law schools in the U.S.: **Indiana University–Indianapolis, Robert H. McKinney School of Law** (#100 tie). The rankings are based on a weighted average of 12 measures of quality: peer assessment score; assessment score by lawyers/judges; median LSAT scores; median undergrad GPA; acceptance rate; employment rates for graduates; placement success; bar passage rate; faculty resources; expenditures per student; student/faculty ratio; and library resources. *U.S. News & World Report, "America's Best Graduate Schools, Law, 2017"*

According to *U.S. News & World Report,* the Indianapolis-Carmel-Anderson, IN metro area is home to one of the top 75 medical schools for research in the U.S.: **Indiana University–Indianapolis, School of Medicine** (#47 tie). The rankings are based on a weighted average of 11 measures of quality: quality assessment; peer assessment score; assessment score by residency directors; research activity; total research activity; average research activity per faculty member; student selectivity; median MCAT total score; median undergraduate GPA; acceptance rate; and faculty resources. *U.S. News & World Report, "America's Best Graduate Schools, Medical, 2017"*

PRESIDENTIAL ELECTION

2012 Presidential Election Results

Area	Obama (%)	Romney (%)	Other (%)
Hamilton County	32.0	66.3	1.7
U.S.	51.0	47.2	1.8

Note: Results may not add to 100% due to rounding
Source: Dave Leip's Atlas of U.S. Presidential Elections

EMPLOYERS

Major Employers

Company Name	Industry
Allison Transmission	Motor vehicle parts/accessories
Ameritech	Local and long distance telephone
Apple American Indiana	Restaurant/family chain
Automotive Components Holdings	Steering mechanisms/motor vehicle
Celadon Trucking Service	Trucking/except local
CNO Financial Group	Insurance services
Communikty Hospitals of Indiana	General medical/surgical hospitals
Conseco Variable Ins Company	Life insurance carriers
Defense Finance and Accounting Services	Accounting/auditing and bookkeeping
Eli Lilly and Company	Pharmaceutical preparations
Family & Social Svcs Admin	Administration of social and human resources
Federal Express Corporation	Air cargo carrier
GEICO	Auto insurance
Hewlett Packard Company	Computer terminals
Indiana Department of Transportation	Regulation administration of transportation
Indiana Police State	General government/state government
Liberty Mutual	Insurance services
Meridian Citizens Mutual Ins Company	Assessment associations: fire, marine & casualty ins
Methodist Hospital	General medical/surgical hospitals
Navient (formerly Sallie Mae)	Headquarters; financial services
Rolls Royce Corporation	Aircraft engines/parts
St Vincent Hospital and Healthcare Center	General medical/surgical hospitals
The Health Hospital of Marion County	General medical/surgical hospitals
Trustees of indiana University	University
United States Postal Service	Postal service

Note: Companies shown are located within the Indianapolis-Carmel-Anderson, IN Metropolitan Statistical Area.
Source: Hoovers.com; Wikipedia

PUBLIC SAFETY

Crime Rate

Area	All Crimes	Violent Crimes				Property Crimes		
		Murder	Rape[3]	Robbery	Aggrav. Assault	Burglary	Larceny -Theft	Motor Vehicle Theft
City	972.0	2.3	2.3	5.8	10.5	58.4	848.2	44.4
Metro[1]	3,889.8	7.9	38.7	209.4	390.3	783.5	2,118.1	341.8
U.S.	2,971.8	4.5	36.6	102.2	232.5	542.5	1,837.3	216.2

Note: Figures are crimes per 100,000 population; (1) Figures cover the Indianapolis-Carmel-Anderson, IN Metropolitan Statistical Area—see Appendix B for areas included; (3) The city and U.S. figures shown were reported using the revised Uniform Crime Reporting (UCR) definition of rape. The suburban and metro area figures shown are an aggregate total of the data submitted using both the revised and legacy UCR definitions.
Source: FBI Uniform Crime Reports, 2014

Hate Crimes

Area	Number of Quarters Reported	Number of Incidents per Bias Motivation						
		Race	Religion	Sexual Orientation	Ethnicity	Disability	Gender	Gender Identity
City	4	0	1	0	0	0	0	0
U.S.	4	2,568	1,014	1,017	648	84	33	98

Source: Federal Bureau of Investigation, Hate Crime Statistics 2014

Identity Theft Consumer Complaints

Area	Complaints	Complaints per 100,000 Population	Rank[2]
MSA[1]	2,277	115.5	141
U.S.	490,220	152.4	-

Note: (1) Figures cover the Indianapolis-Carmel-Anderson, IN Metropolitan Statistical Area—see Appendix B for areas included; (2) Rank ranges from 1 to 379 where 1 indicates greatest number of identity theft complaints per 100,000 population
Source: Federal Trade Commission, Consumer Sentinel Network Data Book for January–December 2015

Fraud and Other Consumer Complaints

Area	Complaints	Complaints per 100,000 Population	Rank[2]
MSA[1]	7,750	393.1	119
U.S.	2,593,159	806.0	-

Note: (1) Figures cover the Indianapolis-Carmel-Anderson, IN Metropolitan Statistical Area—see Appendix B for areas included; (2) Rank ranges from 1 to 379 where 1 indicates greatest number of identity theft complaints per 100,000 population
Source: Federal Trade Commission, Consumer Sentinel Network Data Book for January–December 2015

RECREATION

Culture

Dance[1]	Theatre[1]	Instrumental Music[1]	Vocal Music[1]	Series and Festivals	Museums and Art Galleries[2]	Zoos and Aquariums[3]
0	0	0	0	0	0	0

Note: (1) Professional perfoming groups; (2) Based on organizations with SIC code 8412; (3) AZA-accredited
Source: The Grey House Performing Arts Directory, 2015-16; Association of Zoos & Aquariums, AZA Member Zoos & Aquariums, March 25, 2016; www.AccuLeads.com, March 29, 2016

Professional Sports Teams

Team Name	League	Year Established
Indiana Pacers	National Basketball Association (NBA)	1967
Indianapolis Colts	National Football League (NFL)	1984

Note: Includes teams located in the Indianapolis-Carmel-Anderson, IN Metropolitan Statistical Area.
Source: Wikipedia, Major Professional Sports Teams of the United States and Canada, March 24, 2016

CLIMATE

Average and Extreme Temperatures

Temperature	Jan	Feb	Mar	Apr	May	Jun	Jul	Aug	Sep	Oct	Nov	Dec	Yr.
Extreme High (°F)	71	72	85	89	93	102	104	102	100	90	81	74	104
Average High (°F)	35	39	50	63	73	82	85	84	78	66	51	39	62
Average Temp. (°F)	27	31	41	52	63	72	76	73	67	55	43	31	53
Average Low (°F)	18	22	31	41	52	61	65	63	55	44	33	23	42
Extreme Low (°F)	-22	-21	-7	18	28	39	48	41	34	20	-2	-23	-23

Note: Figures cover the years 1948-1990
Source: National Climatic Data Center, International Station Meteorological Climate Summary, 9/96

Average Precipitation/Snowfall/Humidity

Precip./Humidity	Jan	Feb	Mar	Apr	May	Jun	Jul	Aug	Sep	Oct	Nov	Dec	Yr.
Avg. Precip. (in.)	2.8	2.5	3.6	3.6	4.0	3.9	4.3	3.4	2.9	2.6	3.3	3.3	40.2
Avg. Snowfall (in.)	7	6	4	1	Tr	0	0	0	0	Tr	2	5	25
Avg. Rel. Hum. 7am (%)	81	81	79	77	79	80	84	87	87	85	83	83	82
Avg. Rel. Hum. 4pm (%)	68	64	59	53	53	53	56	56	53	53	63	70	59

Note: Figures cover the years 1948-1990; Tr = Trace amounts (<0.05 in. of rain; <0.5 in. of snow)
Source: National Climatic Data Center, International Station Meteorological Climate Summary, 9/96

Weather Conditions

Temperature			Daytime Sky			Precipitation		
10°F & below	32°F & below	90°F & above	Clear	Partly cloudy	Cloudy	0.01 inch or more precip.	0.1 inch or more snow/ice	Thunder-storms
19	119	19	83	128	154	127	24	43

Note: Figures are average number of days per year and cover the years 1948-1990
Source: National Climatic Data Center, International Station Meteorological Climate Summary, 9/96

HAZARDOUS WASTE

Superfund Sites

Fishers has no sites on the EPA's Superfund Final National Priorities List. There are a total of 1,323 Superfund sites on the list in the U.S. *U.S. Environmental Protection Agency, Final National Priorities List, March 18, 2016*

AIR & WATER QUALITY

Air Quality Trends: Ozone

	1990	1995	2000	2005	2010	2011	2012	2013	2014
MSA[1]	0.086	0.095	0.082	0.080	0.069	0.072	0.074	0.062	0.063

Note: (1) Data covers the Indianapolis-Carmel-Anderson, IN Metropolitan Statistical Area—see Appendix B for areas included. The values shown are the composite ozone concentration averages among trend sites based on the highest fourth daily maximum 8-hour concentration in parts per million. These trends are based on sites having an adequate record of monitoring data during the trend period. Data from exceptional events are included.

Source: U.S. Environmental Protection Agency, Air Quality Monitoring Information, "Air Quality Trends by City, 1990-2014"

Air Quality Index

Area	Percent of Days when Air Quality was...[2]					AQI Statistics[2]	
	Good	Moderate	Unhealthy for Sensitive Groups	Unhealthy	Very Unhealthy	Maximum	Median
MSA[1]	46.8	52.3	0.5	0.3	0.0	157	52

Note: (1) Data covers the Indianapolis-Carmel-Anderson, IN Metropolitan Statistical Area—see Appendix B for areas included; (2) Based on 365 days with AQI data in 2015. Air Quality Index (AQI) is an index for reporting daily air quality. EPA calculates the AQI for five major air pollutants regulated by the Clean Air Act: ground-level ozone, particle pollution (aka particulate matter), carbon monoxide, sulfur dioxide, and nitrogen dioxide. The AQI runs from 0 to 500. The higher the AQI value, the greater the level of air pollution and the greater the health concern. There are six AQI categories: "Good" AQI is between 0 and 50. Air quality is considered satisfactory; "Moderate" AQI is between 51 and 100. Air quality is acceptable; "Unhealthy for Sensitive Groups" When AQI values are between 101 and 150, members of sensitive groups may experience health effects; "Unhealthy" When AQI values are between 151 and 200 everyone may begin to experience health effects; "Very Unhealthy" AQI values between 201 and 300 trigger a health alert; "Hazardous" AQI values over 300 trigger warnings of emergency conditions (not shown).

Source: U.S. Environmental Protection Agency, Air Quality Index Report, 2015

Air Quality Index Pollutants

Area	Percent of Days when AQI Pollutant was...[2]					
	Carbon Monoxide	Nitrogen Dioxide	Ozone	Sulfur Dioxide	Particulate Matter 2.5	Particulate Matter 10
MSA[1]	0.0	1.6	24.7	9.0	63.8	0.8

Note: (1) Data covers the Indianapolis-Carmel-Anderson, IN Metropolitan Statistical Area—see Appendix B for areas included; (2) Based on 365 days with AQI data in 2015. The Air Quality Index (AQI) is an index for reporting daily air quality. EPA calculates the AQI for five major air pollutants regulated by the Clean Air Act: ground-level ozone, particle pollution (also known as particulate matter), carbon monoxide, sulfur dioxide, and nitrogen dioxide. The AQI runs from 0 to 500. The higher the AQI value, the greater the level of air pollution and the greater the health concern.

Source: U.S. Environmental Protection Agency, Air Quality Index Report, 2015

Maximum Air Pollutant Concentrations: Particulate Matter, Ozone, CO and Lead

	Particulate Matter 10 (ug/m^3)	Particulate Matter 2.5 Wtd AM (ug/m^3)	Particulate Matter 2.5 24-Hr (ug/m^3)	Ozone (ppm)	Carbon Monoxide (ppm)	Lead (ug/m^3)
MSA[1] Level	58	12.8	31	0.066	3	0.02
NAAQS[2]	150	15	35	0.075	9	0.15
Met NAAQS[2]	Yes	Yes	Yes	Yes	Yes	Yes

Note: (1) Data covers the Indianapolis-Carmel-Anderson, IN Metropolitan Statistical Area—see Appendix B for areas included; Data from exceptional events are included; (2) National Ambient Air Quality Standards; ppm = parts per million; ug/m^3 = micrograms per cubic meter; n/a not available.

Concentrations: Particulate Matter 10 (coarse particulate)—highest second maximum 24-hour concentration; Particulate Matter 2.5 Wtd AM (fine particulate)—highest weighted annual mean concentration; Particulate Matter 2.5 24-Hour (fine particulate)—highest 98th percentile 24-hour concentration; Ozone—highest fourth daily maximum 8-hour concentration; Carbon Monoxide—highest second maximum non-overlapping 8-hour concentration; Lead—maximum running 3-month average

Source: U.S. Environmental Protection Agency, Air Quality Monitoring Information, "Air Quality Statistics by City, 2014"

Maximum Air Pollutant Concentrations: Nitrogen Dioxide and Sulfur Dioxide

	Nitrogen Dioxide AM (ppb)	Nitrogen Dioxide 1-Hr (ppb)	Sulfur Dioxide AM (ppb)	Sulfur Dioxide 1-Hr (ppb)	Sulfur Dioxide 24-Hr (ppb)
MSA[1] Level	17	46	n/a	106	n/a
NAAQS[2]	53	100	30	75	140
Met NAAQS[2]	Yes	Yes	n/a	No	n/a

Note: (1) Data covers the Indianapolis-Carmel-Anderson, IN Metropolitan Statistical Area—see Appendix B for areas included; Data from exceptional events are included; (2) National Ambient Air Quality Standards; ppm = parts per million; ug/m^3 = micrograms per cubic meter; n/a not available.
Concentrations: Nitrogen Dioxide AM—highest arithmetic mean concentration; Nitrogen Dioxide 1-Hr—highest 98th percentile 1-hour daily maximum concentration; Sulfur Dioxide AM—highest annual mean concentration; Sulfur Dioxide 1-Hr—highest 99th percentile 1-hour daily maximum concentration; Sulfur Dioxide 24-Hr—highest second maximum 24-hour concentration
Source: U.S. Environmental Protection Agency, Air Quality Monitoring Information, "Air Quality Statistics by City, 2014"

Drinking Water

Water System Name	Pop. Served	Primary Water Source Type	Violations[1]	
			Health Based	Monitoring/ Reporting
Citizens Water - Indianapolis	782,838	Surface	0	0

Note: (1) Based on violation data from January 1, 2015 to December 31, 2015 (includes unresolved violations from earlier years)
Source: U.S. Environmental Protection Agency, Office of Ground Water and Drinking Water, Safe Drinking Water Information System (based on data extracted April 29, 2016)

Ankeny, Iowa

Background

Ankeny sits on 26 square miles of fertile Midwest land east of the Saylorville Reservoir within Polk County. It's just north of Des Moines, the state capital. In Ankeny you can experience a small town atmosphere with big town amenities. Ankeny's close proximity to Des Moines offers many business, recreational, and cultural opportunities.

John Fletcher Ankeny founded Ankeny as a farming community on April 22, 1875 on 80 acres of land. Initial plans for the community were developed by Ankeny and his wife, who together, constructed the first buildings. Ankeny was officially incorporated as a town on February 28, 1903 on one square mile of land. Just seven years later the town had grown to 445. Ankeny suffered from four major fires that nearly destroyed all of the uptown business areas between 1932 and 1940. Many of the businesses rebuilt.

Ankeny remained a small town until Deere and Company opened a factory in 1947. In 1961 Ankeny was officially declared a city as its population swelled to 2,964 residents. Throughout the second half of the 20th century and into the 21st century Ankeny continued to grow. As of the 2010 census the population in Ankeny had risen to 45,600.

The community of Ankeny is heavily influenced by the city of Des Moines, the John Deere factory, and Casey's General Stores. Casey's is a convenience store chain with more than 1,600 locations headquartered in Ankeny. Ankeny is its own community, however, with its own unique attractions such as the annual Ankeny SummerFest and its outdoor recreation opportunities, including parks, 40 miles of hiking/biking trails, sporting areas and more. Ankeny's proximity to Des Moines enhances the area's offerings, namely the Blank Park Zoo, Science Center of Iowa, and minor league sports venues. Cultural opportunities are also offered by the bigger city, such as the Des Moines Art Festival and Blues on Grand.

Two times Ankeny has made the top 100 Best Places to Live list from CNN and *Money* magazine.Ankeny prides itself in forward thinking. Its design of Prairie Trail, Iowa's largest "new urbanist community" focuses on sustainable development, smart growth, green community, and reduction of vehicular traffic. Prairie Trail is a community within a community, offering residential, business, recreational, and entertainment opportunities generally within walking distance of each other.

Ankeny and the surrounding areas offer many educational opportunities. In addition to its exceptional public school district, higher education opportunities within the city are available at the Des Moines Area Community College whose main campus is in Ankeny, along with several colleges that operate satellite classrooms in the area. Plus, Drake University and Iowa State University are a short drive from Ankeny. In addition to formal post-secondary education are many opportunities to learn through classes, seminars, festivals, museums, and many events throughout the greater Des Moines-West Des Moines metropolitan area.

Several small airports serve the area; however, Des Moines International Airport is the primary air traffic hub for the area with connections to 19 major airlines across the nation. Ankeny sits near the interchange of Interstates 80 and 35, allowing for easy vehicular travel to the North, South, East, or West. Additional transportation options are available via The Ankeny Express, which offers several daily trips from within the Ankeny city limits to Des Moines and the Des Moines Area Rapid Transit which offers bus service in Des Moines and the surrounding areas.

Ankeny has a continental climate, hot and humid summers and cold and snowy winters. Average temperatures range from the teens and 20s in the winter to the upper 80s in the summer. Extremes with lows well below zero and triple digit highs are not uncommon. High humidity in the spring and summer may bring afternoon thunderstorms, annual rainfall averages 34.7 inches and annual snowfall average 36.4 inches.

Rankings

Business/Finance Rankings

- The personal finance site NerdWallet analyzed 183 American metropolitan areas with populations over 250,000 and more than 15,000 businesses to rank where entrepreneurs find the most success. Criteria included area economy, annual income, housing cost, unemployment rate, and the success rate of area businesses. Des Moines* ranked #11. *www.nerdwallet.com, "Best Places to Start a Business," April 27, 2015*
- The editors of *Kiplinger's Personal Finance Magazine* named Des Moines* to their list of ten of the best metro areas for start-ups. The area ranked #7.Criteria: well-educated workforce; low living costs for self-employed people, as measured by the Council for Community and Economic Research; a strong existing community of small business; low unemployment; low business costs. *www.kiplinger.com, "10 Great Cities for Starting a Business," October 2014*
- The Brookings Institution ranked the 100 largest metro areas in the U.S. based on income inequality. Des Moines* was ranked #88 (#1 = greatest ineqality). Criteria: the "95/20 ratio," a figure representing the income at which a household earns more than 95 percent of all other households, divided by the income at which a household earns more than only 20 percent of all other households. *Brookings Institution, "Income Inequality, 100 Largest U.S. Metro Areas, 2007-2014," January 14, 2016*
- *Forbes* ranked the largest metro areas in the U.S. in terms of the "Best Cities for Young Professionals." The Des Moines* metro area ranked #1 out of 15. Criteria: job growth; unemployment rate; median salary of college graduates age 24 to 34; cost of living; number of small businesses per capita; number of large companies; percentage of population 25 years of age and older with college degrees. *Forbes.com, "America's 15 Best Cities for Young Professionals," August 18, 2014*
- The Des Moines* metro area appeared on the Milken Institute "2015 Best Performing Cities" list. Rank: #45 out of 200 large metro areas. Criteria: job growth; wage and salary growth; high-tech output growth. *Milken Institute, "Best-Performing Cities 2015," December 2015*
- *Forbes* ranked the 200 most populous metro areas to determine the nation's "Best Places for Business and Careers." The Des Moines* metro area was ranked #13. Criteria: costs (business and living); job growth (past and projected); income growth; educational attainment (college and high school); projected economic growth; cultural and recreational opportunities; net migration patterns; number of highly ranked colleges. *Forbes, "The Best Places for Business and Careers 2015," July 29, 2015*

Children/Family Rankings

- *Forbes* analyzed data on the 100 largest metropolitan areas in the United States to compile its 2014 list of the ten "Best Cities for Raising a Family." The Des Moines* metro area was ranked #6. Criteria: median income; overall cost of living; housing affordability; commuting delays; percentage of families owning homes; crime rate; education quality (mainly test scores). *Forbes, "The Best Cities for Raising a Family," April 16, 2014*

Education Rankings

- Personal finance website *WalletHub* analyzed the 150 largest U.S. metropolitan statistical areas to determine where the most educated Americans are choosing to settle. Criteria: education quality and attainment gap; education levels; percentage of workers with degrees; public school rankings; quality and size of each metro area's universities. Des Moines* was ranked #27 (#1 = most educated city). *www.WalletHub.com, "2015's Most and Least Educated Cities*

Environmental Rankings

- The Des Moines* metro area came in at #177 for the relative comfort of its climate on Sperling's list of "chill cities," as measured by the Sperling Heat Index. All 361 metro areas are included. Criteria included daytime high temperatures, nighttime low temperatures, dew point, and relative humidity at the high temperatures. *www.bertsperling.com, "Sperling's Chill Cities," July 18, 2013*

- Sperling's BestPlaces assessed 379 metropolitan areas of the United States for the likelihood of dangerously extreme weather events or earthquakes. In general the Southeast and South-Central regions have the highest risk of weather extremes and earthquakes, while the Pacific Northwest enjoys the lowest risk. Of the least risky metropolitan areas, the Des Moines* metro area was ranked #227. *www.bestplaces.net, "Safest Places from Natural Disasters," April 2011*

- The U.S. Environmental Protection Agency (EPA) released a list of mid-size U.S. metropolitan areas with the most ENERGY STAR certified buildings in 2015. The Des Moines* metro area was ranked #8 out of 10. *U.S. Environmental Protection Agency, "Top Cities With the Most ENERGY STAR Certified Buildings in 2016," March 30, 2016*

- Des Moines* was highlighted as one of the cleanest metro areas for ozone air pollution in the U.S. during 2011 through 2013. The list represents cities with no monitored ozone air pollution in unhealthful ranges. *American Lung Association, State of the Air 2015*

- Des Moines* was highlighted as one of the top 25 cleanest metro areas for short-term particle pollution (24-hour PM 2.5) in the U.S. during 2011 through 2013. Monitors in these cities reported no days with unhealthful PM 2.5 levels. *American Lung Association, State of the Air 2015*

Health/Fitness Rankings

- The Gallup-Healthways Well-Being Index tracks Americans' optimism about their communities and satisfaction with the metro areas in which they live. At least 300 adult residents in each of 189 U.S. metropolitan areas were asked whether their metro was improving and the Des Moines* metro area placed among the top ten in the percentage of residents who were optimistic about their metro area. *www.gallup.com, "City Satisfaction Highest in Fort Collins-Loveland, Colo.," April 11, 2014*

- Gallup-Healthways Well-Being Index researchers asked at least 300 adult residents in each of 189 U.S. metropolitan areas how satisfied they were with the metro area in which they lived. The Des Moines* metro area was among the top ten for residents' satisfaction. *www.gallup.com, "City Satisfaction Highest in Fort Collins-Loveland, Colo.," April 11, 2014*

- Des Moines* was identified as a "2016 Spring Allergy Capital." The area ranked #44 out of 100. Three groups of factors were used to identify the most severe cities for people with allergies during the spring season: annual pollen levels; medicine utilization; access to board-certified allergists. *Asthma and Allergy Foundation of America, "Spring Allergy Capitals 2016"*

- Des Moines* was identified as a "2015 Asthma Capital." The area ranked #86 out of the nation's 100 largest metropolitan areas. Criteria: estimated prevalence; self-reported prevalence; crude death rate for asthma; annual pollen score; annual air quality; public smoking laws; number of board-certified asthma specialists; school inhaler access laws; rescue medication use; controller medication use; ER visits for asthma; uninsured rate; poverty rate. *Asthma and Allergy Foundation of America, "Asthma Capitals 2015"*

- The Des Moines* metro area ranked #48 out of 190 in The Gallup-Healthways Well-Being Index. Criteria: purpose; social well being; financial health; community and physical health. Results are based on telephone interviews with adults, aged 18 and older, living in metropolitan areas in the 50 U.S. states and the District of Columbia. *Gallup-Healthways, "State of American Well-Being," February 23, 2016*

Real Estate Rankings

- The Des Moines* metro area was identified as one of the 20 best housing markets in the U.S. in 2015. The area ranked #20 out of 179 markets. Criteria: year-over-year change of median sales price of existing single-family homes between the 4th quarter of 2014 and the 4th quarter of 2015. *National Association of Realtors®, Median Sales Price of Existing Single-Family Homes for Metropolitan Areas, 4th Quarter 2015*

Safety Rankings

- Farmers Insurance, in partnership with Sperling's BestPlaces, ranked metro areas in the U.S. as the "Most Secure Places to Live." The Des Moines* metro area ranked #20 out of the top 20 in the large metro area category (500,000 or more residents). Criteria: economic stability; crime statistics; extreme weather; risk of natural disasters; housing depreciation; foreclosures; air quality; environmental hazards; life expectancy; motor vehicle fatalities; and employment numbers. *Farmers Insurance Group of Companies, "Most Secure U.S. Places to Live in the U.S.," June 25, 2013*

- The National Insurance Crime Bureau ranked 380 metro areas in the U.S. in terms of per capita rates of vehicle theft. The Des Moines* metro area ranked #129 (#1 = highest rate). Criteria: number of vehicle theft offenses per 100,000 inhabitants in 2014. *National Insurance Crime Bureau, "Hot Spots 2014," June 24, 2015*

Seniors/Retirement Rankings

- From its Best Cities for Successful Aging indexes, the Milken Institute generated rankings for metropolitan areas, weighing data in eight categories—health care, wellness, living arrangements, transportation, financial characteristics, education and employment opportunities, community engagement, and overall livability. The Des Moines* metro area was ranked #7 overall in the large metro area category. *Milken Institute, "Best Cities for Successful Aging, 2014"*

- *Forbes* selected the Des Moines* metro area as one of 25 "Best Places for a Working Retirement." Criteria: affordability; improving, above-average economies and job prospects; and a favorable tax climate for retirees. *Forbes.com, "Best Places for a Working Retirement in 2013," February 4, 2013*

Sports/Recreation Rankings

- Ankeny was selected as one of the most playful cities in the U.S. by KaBOOM! The organization's Playful City USA initiative honors cities and towns across the nation for a vision, plan and commitment to creating an agenda for play. Criteria: creating a local play commission or task force; designing an annual action plan for play; conducting a play space audit; outlining a financial investment in play for the current fiscal year; and proclaiming and celebrating an annual "play day." *KaBOOM! National Campaign for Play, "2015 Playful City USA Communities"*

Miscellaneous Rankings

- The finance and lifestyle site NerdWallet looked for the U.S. cities that topped the list in donating money and time to good causes. The Des Moines* metro area proved to be the #15-ranked metro area, judged by culture of volunteerism, depth of commitment in terms of volunteer hours per year, and monetary contributions. *www.nerdwallet.com, "Most Generous Cities," September 22, 2013*

- The National Alliance to End Homelessness ranked the 100 most populous metro areas with the highest rate of homelessness. The Des Moines* metro area ranked #39. Criteria: number of homeless people per 10,000 population in 2011. *National Alliance to End Homelessness, The State of Homelessness in America 2012*

Ankeny is located within the Des Moines-West Des Moines, IA Metropolitan Statistical Area.

Business Environment

CITY FINANCES

City Government Finances

Component	2012 ($000)	2012 ($ per capita)
Total Revenues	64,874	1,423
Total Expenditures	77,797	1,706
Debt Outstanding	178,274	3,911
Cash and Securities[1]	52,779	1,157

Note: (1) Cash and security holdings of a government at the close of its fiscal year, including those of its dependent agencies, utilities, and liquor stores.
Source: U.S Census Bureau, State & Local Government Finances 2012

City Government Revenue by Source

Source	2012 ($000)	2012 ($ per capita)
General Revenue		
From Federal Government	582	12
From State Government	4,770	104
From Local Governments	659	14
Taxes		
Property	28,638	628
Sales and Gross Receipts	2,469	54
Personal Income	0	0
Corporate Income	0	0
Motor Vehicle License	0	0
Other Taxes	1,174	25
Current Charges	14,532	318
Liquor Store	0	0
Utility	7,238	158
Employee Retirement	0	0

Source: U.S Census Bureau, State & Local Government Finances 2012

City Government Expenditures by Function

Function	2012 ($000)	2012 ($ per capita)	2012 (%)
General Direct Expenditures			
Air Transportation	304	6	0.3
Corrections	0	0	0.0
Education	0	0	0.0
Employment Security Administration	0	0	0.0
Financial Administration	721	15	0.9
Fire Protection	994	21	1.2
General Public Buildings	87	1	0.1
Governmental Administration, Other	1,440	31	1.8
Health	2,692	59	3.4
Highways	18,814	412	24.1
Hospitals	0	0	0.0
Housing and Community Development	25	< 1	< 0.1
Interest on General Debt	4,987	109	6.4
Judicial and Legal	16	< 1	< 0.1
Libraries	1,306	28	1.6
Parking	0	0	0.0
Parks and Recreation	6,149	134	7.9
Police Protection	6,720	147	8.6
Public Welfare	309	6	0.3
Sewerage	14,245	312	18.3
Solid Waste Management	554	12	0.7
Veterans' Services	0	0	0.0
Liquor Store	0	0	0.0
Utility	8,064	176	10.3
Employee Retirement	0	0	0.0

Source: U.S Census Bureau, State & Local Government Finances 2012

DEMOGRAPHICS

Population Growth

Area	1990 Census	2000 Census	2010 Census	2014* Estimate	Population Growth (%) 1990-2014	2010-2014
City	19,065	27,117	45,582	49,488	159.6	8.6
MSA[1]	416,346	481,394	569,633	590,741	41.9	3.7
U.S.	248,709,873	281,421,906	308,745,538	314,107,084	26.3	1.7

Note: (1) Figures cover the Des Moines-West Des Moines, IA Metropolitan Statistical Area—see Appendix B for areas included; (*) 2010-2014 5-year estimated population
Source: U.S. Census Bureau, 1990 Census, Census 2000, Census 2010, 2010-2014 American Community Survey 5-Year Estimates

Household Size

Area	Persons in Household (%) One	Two	Three	Four	Five	Six	Seven or More	Average Household Size
City	23.5	35.5	17.0	16.0	5.0	2.0	0.6	2.53
MSA[1]	26.7	34.3	15.8	13.6	6.2	2.1	1.0	2.52
U.S.	27.5	33.5	15.8	13.1	6.0	2.3	1.4	2.64

Note: (1) Figures cover the Des Moines-West Des Moines, IA Metropolitan Statistical Area—see Appendix B for areas included
Source: U.S. Census Bureau, 2010-2014 American Community Survey 5-Year Estimates

Race

Area	White Alone[2] (%)	Black Alone[2] (%)	Asian Alone[2] (%)	AIAN[3] Alone[2] (%)	NHOPI[4] Alone[2] (%)	Other Race Alone[2] (%)	Two or More Races (%)
City	93.7	0.9	2.3	0.0	0.0	0.6	2.5
MSA[1]	87.6	4.8	3.3	0.2	0.1	1.6	2.3
U.S.	73.8	12.6	5.0	0.8	0.2	4.7	2.9

Note: (1) Figures cover the Des Moines-West Des Moines, IA Metropolitan Statistical Area—see Appendix B for areas included; (2) Alone is defined as not being in combination with one or more other races; (3) American Indian and Alaska Native; (4) Native Hawaiian and Other Pacific Islander
Source: U.S. Census Bureau, 2010-2014 American Community Survey 5-Year Estimates

Hispanic or Latino Origin

Area	Total (%)	Mexican (%)	Puerto Rican (%)	Cuban (%)	Other (%)
City	2.0	1.5	0.0	0.0	0.5
MSA[1]	6.9	5.3	0.2	0.1	1.3
U.S.	16.9	10.8	1.6	0.6	3.8

Note: Persons of Hispanic or Latino origin can be of any race; (1) Figures cover the Des Moines-West Des Moines, IA Metropolitan Statistical Area—see Appendix B for areas included
Source: U.S. Census Bureau, 2010-2014 American Community Survey 5-Year Estimates

Ancestry

Area	German	Irish	English	American	Italian	Polish	French[2]	Scottish	Dutch
City	38.3	14.2	11.5	4.8	3.1	1.5	2.4	1.3	4.4
MSA[1]	29.4	13.7	9.4	5.4	3.2	1.4	2.3	1.7	3.9
U.S.	14.9	10.8	8.0	7.1	5.5	3.0	2.7	1.7	1.4

Note: Figures are the percentage of the total population reporting a particular ancestry. The nine most commonly reported ancestries in the U.S. are shown. Figures include multiple ancestries (e.g. if a person reported being Irish and Italian, they were included in both columns); (1) Figures cover the Des Moines-West Des Moines, IA Metropolitan Statistical Area—see Appendix B for areas included; (2) Excludes Basque
Source: U.S. Census Bureau, 2010-2014 American Community Survey 5-Year Estimates

Foreign-Born Population

Area	Any Foreign Country	Asia	Mexico	Europe	Carribean	Central America[2]	South America	Africa	Canada
	Percent of Population Born in								
City	3.4	1.2	0.0	1.5	0.0	0.3	0.0	0.3	0.1
MSA[1]	7.5	2.6	1.8	1.3	0.0	0.5	0.2	0.9	0.1
U.S.	13.1	3.8	3.7	1.5	1.2	1.0	0.9	0.6	0.3

Note: (1) Figures cover the Des Moines-West Des Moines, IA Metropolitan Statistical Area—see Appendix B for areas included; (2) Excludes Mexico.
Source: U.S. Census Bureau, 2010-2014 American Community Survey 5-Year Estimates

Marital Status

Area	Never Married	Now Married[2]	Separated	Widowed	Divorced
City	25.5	60.3	1.2	3.8	9.2
MSA[1]	28.6	53.7	1.5	5.0	11.2
U.S.	32.5	48.4	2.2	5.9	10.9

Note: Figures are percentages and cover the population 15 years of age and older; (1) Figures cover the Des Moines-West Des Moines, IA Metropolitan Statistical Area—see Appendix B for areas included; (2) Excludes separated
Source: U.S. Census Bureau, 2010-2014 American Community Survey 5-Year Estimates

Disability Status

Area	All Ages	Under 18 Years Old	18 to 64 Years Old	65 Years and Over
City	6.9	1.9	5.4	33.6
MSA[1]	10.2	3.2	9.2	31.8
U.S.	12.3	4.1	10.2	36.3

Note: Figures show percent of the civilian noninstitutionalized population that reported having a disability. Disability status is determined from from six types of difficulty: vision, hearing, cognitive, ambulatory, self-care, and independent living. For children under 5 years old, hearing and vision difficulty are used to determine disability status. For children between the ages of 5 and 14, disability status is determined from hearing, vision, cognitive, ambulatory, and self-care difficulties. For people aged 15 years and older, they are considered to have a disability if they have difficulty with any one of the six difficulty types; (1) Figures cover the Des Moines-West Des Moines, IA Metropolitan Statistical Area—see Appendix B for areas included.
Source: U.S. Census Bureau, 2010-2014 American Community Survey 5-Year Estimates

Age

Area	Under Age 5	Age 5–19	Age 20–34	Age 35–44	Age 45–54	Age 55–64	Age 65–74	Age 75–84	Age 85+	Median Age
	Percent of Population									
City	8.4	20.5	26.1	14.6	11.5	9.6	5.4	2.8	1.0	32.9
MSA[1]	7.3	20.9	21.3	13.7	13.7	11.4	6.4	3.5	1.7	35.4
U.S.	6.4	19.9	20.6	13.0	14.1	12.3	7.6	4.3	1.9	37.4

Note: (1) Figures cover the Des Moines-West Des Moines, IA Metropolitan Statistical Area—see Appendix B for areas included
Source: U.S. Census Bureau, 2010-2014 American Community Survey 5-Year Estimates

Gender

Area	Males	Females	Males per 100 Females
City	25,101	24,387	102.9
MSA[1]	290,553	300,188	96.8
U.S.	154,515,159	159,591,925	96.8

Note: (1) Figures cover the Des Moines-West Des Moines, IA Metropolitan Statistical Area—see Appendix B for areas included
Source: U.S. Census Bureau, 2010-2014 American Community Survey 5-Year Estimates

Religious Groups by Family

Area	Catholic	Baptist	Non-Den.	Methodist[2]	Lutheran	LDS[3]	Pente-costal	Presby-terian[4]	Muslim[5]	Judaism
MSA[1]	13.6	4.7	3.3	6.9	8.2	0.9	2.3	2.9	0.3	0.3
U.S.	19.1	9.3	4.0	4.0	2.3	2.0	1.9	1.6	0.8	0.7

Note: Figures are the number of adherents as a percentage of the total population; (1) Figures cover the Des Moines-West Des Moines, IA Metropolitan Statistical Area—see Appendix B for areas included; (2) Methodist/Pietist; (3) Latter Day Saints; (4) Reformed; (5) Figures are estimates
Source: Association of Statisticians of American Religious Bodies, 2010 U.S. Religion Census: Religious Congregations & Membership Study

Religious Groups by Tradition

Area	Catholic	Evangelical Protestant	Mainline Protestant	Other Tradition	Black Protestant	Orthodox
MSA[1]	13.6	12.3	16.8	1.8	0.9	0.1
U.S.	19.1	16.2	7.3	4.3	1.6	0.3

Note: Figures are the number of adherents as a percentage of the total population; (1) Figures cover the Des Moines-West Des Moines, IA Metropolitan Statistical Area—see Appendix B for areas included
Source: Association of Statisticians of American Religious Bodies, 2010 U.S. Religion Census: Religious Congregations & Membership Study

ECONOMY

Gross Metropolitan Product

Area	2013	2014	2015	2016	Rank[2]
MSA[1]	42.7	44.0	45.6	47.9	63

Note: Figures are in billions of dollars; (1) Figures cover the Des Moines-West Des Moines, IA Metropolitan Statistical Area—see Appendix B for areas included; (2) Rank is based on 2016 data and ranges from 1 to 381
Source: The U.S. Conference of Mayors, U.S. Metro Economies: GMP and Employment 2014-2016, June 2015

Economic Growth

Area	2011-13 (%)	2014 (%)	2015 (%)	2016 (%)	Rank[2]
MSA[1]	3.7	1.2	2.4	3.0	83
U.S.	2.2	2.4	2.3	2.9	–

Note: Figures are real gross metropolitan product (GMP) growth rates and represent annual average percent change; (1) Figures cover the Des Moines-West Des Moines, IA Metropolitan Statistical Area—see Appendix B for areas included; (2) Rank is based on 2016 data and ranges from 1 to 381
Source: The U.S. Conference of Mayors, U.S. Metro Economies: GMP and Employment 2014-2016, June 2015

Metropolitan Area Exports

Area	2009	2010	2011	2012	2013	2014	Rank[2]
MSA[1]	782.3	767.8	970.0	1,183.2	1,279.3	1,361.8	131

Note: Figures are in millions of dollars; (1) Figures cover the Des Moines-West Des Moines, IA Metropolitan Statistical Area—see Appendix B for areas included; (2) Rank is based on 2014 data and ranges from 1 to 385
Source: U.S. Department of Commerce, International Trade Administration, Office of Trade & Industry Information, Manufacturing & Services, data extracted March 10, 2016

Building Permits

Area	Single-Family			Multi-Family			Total		
	2014	2015p	Pct. Chg.	2014	2015p	Pct. Chg.	2014	2015p	Pct. Chg.
City	974	890	-8.6	206	171	-17.0	1,180	1,061	-10.1
MSA[1]	2,952	3,495	18.4	1,484	1,949	31.3	4,436	5,444	22.7
U.S.	640,300	690,800	7.9	411,800	487,600	18.4	1,052,100	1,178,400	12.0

Note: (1) Figures cover the Des Moines-West Des Moines, IA Metropolitan Statistical Area—see Appendix B for areas included; Figures represent new, privately-owned housing units authorized (unadjusted data); All permit data are based on estimates with imputation; (p) preliminary data.
Source: U.S. Census Bureau, Manufacturing, Mining, and Construction Statistics, Building Permits, 2014, 2015

Bankruptcy Filings

Area	Business Filings			Nonbusiness Filings		
	2014	2015	% Chg.	2014	2015	% Chg.
Polk County	39	24	-38.5	978	822	-16.0
U.S.	26,983	24,735	-8.3	909,812	819,760	-9.9

Note: Business filings include Chapter 7, Chapter 11, Chapter 12, and Chapter 13; Nonbusiness filings include Chapter 7, Chapter 11, and Chapter 13
Source: Administrative Office of the U.S. Courts, Business and Nonbusiness Bankruptcy, County Cases Commenced by Chapter of the Bankruptcy Code, During the 12- Month Period Ending December 31, 2014 and Business and Nonbusiness Bankruptcy, County Cases Commenced by Chapter of the Bankruptcy Code, During the 12- Month Period Ending December 31, 2015

Housing Vacancy Rates

Area	Gross Vacancy Rate[2] (%)			Year-Round Vacancy Rate[3] (%)			Rental Vacancy Rate[4] (%)			Homeowner Vacancy Rate[5] (%)		
	2013	2014	2015	2013	2014	2015	2013	2014	2015	2013	2014	2015
MSA[1]	n/a	n/a	n/a	n/a	n/a	n/a	n/a	n/a	n/a	n/a	n/a	n/a
U.S.	13.6	13.4	12.9	10.7	10.4	10.0	8.3	7.6	7.1	2.0	1.9	1.8

Note: (1) Figures cover the Des Moines-West Des Moines, IA Metropolitan Statistical Area—see Appendix B for areas included; (2) The percentage of the total housing inventory that is vacant; (3) The percentage of the housing inventory (excluding seasonal units) that is year-round vacant; (4) The percentage of rental inventory that is vacant for rent; (5) The percentage of homeowner inventory that is vacant for sale; n/a not available
Source: U.S. Census Bureau, Housing Vacancies and Homeownership Annual Statistics: 2015

INCOME

Income

Area	Per Capita ($)	Median Household ($)	Average Household ($)
City	33,555	75,069	84,761
MSA[1]	31,342	61,640	79,073
U.S.	28,555	53,482	74,596

Note: (1) Figures cover the Des Moines-West Des Moines, IA Metropolitan Statistical Area—see Appendix B for areas included
Source: U.S. Census Bureau, 2010-2014 American Community Survey 5-Year Estimates

Household Income Distribution

Area	Percent of Households Earning							
	Under $15,000	$15,000 -24,999	$25,000 -34,999	$35,000 -49,999	$50,000 -74,999	$75,000 -99,000	$100,000 -149,999	$150,000 and up
City	5.4	5.3	7.4	11.5	20.2	17.6	21.6	10.8
MSA[1]	9.0	8.5	9.4	13.3	19.7	14.3	15.6	10.2
U.S.	12.5	10.7	10.2	13.5	17.8	12.2	13.0	10.0

Note: (1) Figures cover the Des Moines-West Des Moines, IA Metropolitan Statistical Area—see Appendix B for areas included
Source: U.S. Census Bureau, 2010-2014 American Community Survey 5-Year Estimates

Poverty Rate

Area	All Ages	Under 18 Years Old	18 to 64 Years Old	65 Years and Over
City	6.5	6.3	7.2	2.1
MSA[1]	11.2	15.2	10.4	6.6
U.S.	15.6	21.9	14.6	9.4

Note: Figures are percentage of people whose income during the past 12 months was below the poverty level; (1) Figures cover the Des Moines-West Des Moines, IA Metropolitan Statistical Area—see Appendix B for areas included
Source: U.S. Census Bureau, 2010-2014 American Community Survey 5-Year Estimates

EMPLOYMENT

Labor Force and Employment

Area	Civilian Labor Force			Workers Employed		
	Dec. 2014	Dec. 2015	% Chg.	Dec. 2014	Dec. 2015	% Chg.
City	30,371	30,657	0.9	29,610	30,033	1.4
MSA[1]	340,970	342,746	0.5	326,880	331,881	1.5
U.S.	155,521,000	157,245,000	1.1	147,190,000	149,703,000	1.7

Note: Data is not seasonally adjusted and covers workers 16 years of age and older; (1) Figures cover the Des Moines-West Des Moines, IA Metropolitan Statistical Area—see Appendix B for areas included
Source: Bureau of Labor Statistics, Local Area Unemployment Statistics

Unemployment Rate

Area	2015											
	Jan.	Feb.	Mar.	Apr.	May	Jun.	Jul.	Aug.	Sep.	Oct.	Nov.	Dec.
City	2.7	2.5	2.2	2.2	2.3	2.6	2.4	2.2	2.3	2.1	2.0	2.0
MSA[1]	4.6	4.4	4.0	3.5	3.3	3.4	3.2	3.1	3.1	3.0	2.9	3.2
U.S.	6.1	5.8	5.6	5.1	5.3	5.5	5.6	5.2	4.9	4.8	4.8	4.8

Note: Data is not seasonally adjusted and covers workers 16 years of age and older; (1) Figures cover the Des Moines-West Des Moines, IA Metropolitan Statistical Area—see Appendix B for areas included
Source: Bureau of Labor Statistics, Local Area Unemployment Statistics

Employment by Occupation

Occupation Classification	City (%)	MSA[1] (%)	U.S. (%)
Management, Business, Science, and Arts	47.2	40.3	36.4
Natural Resources, Construction, and Maintenance	5.9	7.6	9.0
Production, Transportation, and Material Moving	8.8	10.4	12.1
Sales and Office	26.5	26.1	24.4
Service	11.5	15.6	18.2

Note: Figures cover employed civilians 16 years of age and older; (1) Figures cover the Des Moines-West Des Moines, IA Metropolitan Statistical Area—see Appendix B for areas included
Source: U.S. Census Bureau, 2010-2014 American Community Survey 5-Year Estimates

Employment by Industry

Sector	MSA[1]		U.S.
	Number of Employees	Percent of Total	Percent of Total
Construction, Mining, and Logging	17,400	4.9	5.0
Education and Health Services	47,700	13.6	15.7
Financial Activities	55,800	15.9	5.7
Government	43,200	12.3	15.5
Information	6,500	1.8	1.9
Leisure and Hospitality	29,200	8.3	10.4
Manufacturing	20,000	5.7	8.6
Other Services	13,700	3.9	3.9
Professional and Business Services	47,600	13.5	13.9
Retail Trade	41,100	11.7	11.3
Transportation, Warehousing, and Utilities	10,800	3.0	3.9
Wholesale Trade	17,600	5.0	4.1

Note: Figures are non-farm employment as of December 2015. Figures are not seasonally adjusted and include workers 16 years of age and older; (1) Figures cover the Des Moines-West Des Moines, IA Metropolitan Statistical Area—see Appendix B for areas included; n/a not available
Source: Bureau of Labor Statistics, Current Employment Statistics, Employment, Hours, and Earnings

Occupations with Greatest Projected Employment Growth: 2012 – 2022

Occupation[1]	2012 Employment	2022 Projected Employment	Numeric Employment Change	Percent Employment Change
Heavy and Tractor-Trailer Truck Drivers	42,680	50,720	8,040	18.8
Registered Nurses	32,490	38,130	5,640	17.3
Combined Food Preparation and Serving Workers, Including Fast Food	32,200	37,220	5,020	15.6
Retail Salespersons	47,020	51,680	4,660	9.9
Customer Service Representatives	24,670	28,850	4,180	17.0
Laborers and Freight, Stock, and Material Movers, Hand	24,870	28,420	3,550	14.3
Childcare Workers	17,050	20,550	3,500	20.5
Home Health Aides	10,310	13,720	3,410	33.1
Janitors and Cleaners, Except Maids and Housekeeping Cleaners	26,870	30,230	3,360	12.5
Cashiers	42,590	45,940	3,350	7.9

Note: Projections cover Iowa; (1) Sorted by numeric employment change
Source: www.projectionscentral.com, State Occupational Projections, 2012–2022 Long-Term Projections

Fastest Growing Occupations: 2012 – 2022

Occupation[1]	2012 Employment	2022 Projected Employment	Numeric Employment Change	Percent Employment Change
Interpreters and Translators	520	770	250	48.1
Diagnostic Medical Sonographers	540	780	240	44.9
Occupational Therapy Assistants	360	520	160	44.3
Information Security Analysts	1,950	2,800	850	43.7
Insulation Workers, Mechanical	360	510	150	41.7
Actuaries	540	750	210	39.1
Meeting, Convention, and Event Planners	440	610	170	38.8
Physical Therapist Assistants	800	1,110	310	38.0
Personal Care Aides	6,050	8,320	2,270	37.4
Health Specialties Teachers, Postsecondary	1,830	2,480	650	35.6

Note: Projections cover Iowa; (1) Sorted by percent employment change and excludes occupations with numeric employment change less than 100
Source: www.projectionscentral.com, State Occupational Projections, 2012–2022 Long-Term Projections

Average Wages

Occupation	$/Hr.	Occupation	$/Hr.
Accountants and Auditors	32.25	Maids and Housekeeping Cleaners	10.24
Automotive Mechanics	21.01	Maintenance and Repair Workers	18.66
Bookkeepers	18.02	Marketing Managers	57.84
Carpenters	21.46	Nuclear Medicine Technologists	33.84
Cashiers	9.89	Nurses, Licensed Practical	20.06
Clerks, General Office	16.54	Nurses, Registered	27.44
Clerks, Receptionists/Information	13.93	Nursing Assistants	13.34
Clerks, Shipping/Receiving	17.24	Packers and Packagers, Hand	10.34
Computer Programmers	35.63	Physical Therapists	38.76
Computer Systems Analysts	40.00	Postal Service Mail Carriers	24.61
Computer User Support Specialists	22.49	Real Estate Brokers	n/a
Cooks, Restaurant	10.63	Retail Salespersons	13.58
Dentists	85.33	Sales Reps., Exc. Tech./Scientific	34.68
Electrical Engineers	35.79	Sales Reps., Tech./Scientific	33.82
Electricians	27.48	Secretaries, Exc. Legal/Med./Exec.	17.33
Financial Managers	59.93	Security Guards	14.01
First-Line Supervisors/Managers, Sales	19.84	Surgeons	111.55
Food Preparation Workers	9.77	Teacher Assistants*	11.04
General and Operations Managers	52.60	Teachers, Elementary School*	26.25
Hairdressers/Cosmetologists	16.42	Teachers, Secondary School*	27.57
Internists	97.55	Telemarketers	13.73
Janitors and Cleaners	11.85	Truck Drivers, Heavy/Tractor-Trailer	21.84
Landscaping/Groundskeeping Workers	14.18	Truck Drivers, Light/Delivery Svcs.	16.44
Lawyers	58.64	Waiters and Waitresses	9.18

Note: Wage data covers the Des Moines-West Des Moines, IA Metropolitan Statistical Area—see Appendix B for areas included; (*) Hourly wages for elementary/secondary school teachers and teacher assistants were calculated by the editors from annual wage data based on a 40 hour work week; n/a not available.
Source: Bureau of Labor Statistics, Metro Area Occupational Employment and Wage Estimates, May 2015

TAXES

State Corporate Income Tax Rates

State	Tax Rate (%)	Income Brackets ($)	Num. of Brackets	Financial Institution Tax Rate (%)[a]	Federal Income Tax Ded.
Iowa	6.0 - 12.0	25,000 - 250,001	4	5.0	Yes (k)

Note: Tax rates as of January 1, 2016; (a) Rates listed are the corporate income tax rate applied to financial institutions or excise taxes based on income. Some states have other taxes based upon the value of deposits or shares; (k) 50% of the federal income tax is deductible.
Source: Federation of Tax Administrators, "State Corporate Income Tax Rates, 2016"

State Individual Income Tax Rates

State	Tax Rate (%)	Income Brackets ($)	Num. of Brackets	Personal Exempt. ($)[1] Single	Personal Exempt. ($)[1] Dependents	Fed. Inc. Tax Ded.
Iowa (a)	0.36 - 8.98	1,554 - 69,930	9	40 (c)	40 (c)	Yes

Note: Tax rates as of January 1, 2016; Local- and county-level taxes are not included; n/a not applicable; (1) Married joint filers generally receive double the single exemption; (a) 18 states have statutory provision for automatically adjusting to the rate of inflation the dollar values of the income tax brackets, standard deductions, and/or personal exemptions. Massachusetts, Michigan, and Nebraska index the personal exemptiononly. Oregon does not index the income brackets for $125,000 and over. Maine has suspended indexing for 2014 and 2015; (c) The personal exemption takes the form of a tax credit instead of a deduction
Source: Federation of Tax Administrators, "State Individual Income Tax Rates, 2016"

Various State and Local Tax Rates

State	State and Local Sales and Use (%)	State Sales and Use (%)	Gasoline[1] (¢/gal.)	Cigarette[2] ($/pack)	Spirits[3] ($/gal.)	Wine[4] ($/gal.)	Beer[5] ($/gal.)
Iowa	6.00	6.0	32	1.36	12.52 (g)	1.75 (l)	0.19 (q)

Note: All tax rates as of January 1, 2016; (1) The American Petroleum Institute has developed a methodology for determining the average tax rate on a gallon of fuel. Rates may include any of the following: excise taxes, environmental fees, storage tank fees, other fees or taxes, general sales tax, and local taxes. In states where gasoline is subject to the general sales tax, or where the fuel tax is based on the average sale price, the average rate determined by API is sensitive to changes in the price of gasoline. States that fully or partially apply general sales taxes to gasoline: CA, CO, GA, IL, IN, MI, NY; (2) The federal excise tax of $1.0066 per pack and local taxes are not included; (3) Rates are those applicable to off-premise sales of 40% alcohol by volume (a.b.v.) distilled spirits in 750ml containers. Local excise taxes are excluded; (4) Rates are those applicable to off-premise sales of 11% a.b.v. non-carbonated wine in 750ml containers; (5) Rates are those applicable to off-premise sales of 4.7% a.b.v. beer in 12 ounce containers; (g) Control states, where the government controls all sales. Products can be subject to ad valorem mark-up as well as excise taxes; (l) Different rates also applicable according to alcohol content, place of production, size of container, place purchased (on- or off-premise or on board airlines) or type of wine (carbonated, vermouth, etc.); (q) Different rates are also applicable according to alcohol content, place of production, size of container, or place purchased (on- or off-premise or onboard airlines).
Source: Tax Foundation, 2016 Facts & Figures: How Does Your State Compare?

State Business Tax Climate Index Rankings

State	Overall Rank	Corporate Tax Rank	Individual Income Tax Rank	Sales Tax Rank	Unemployment Insurance Tax Rank	Property Tax Rank
Iowa	40	49	32	24	34	40

Note: The index is a measure of how each state's tax laws affect economic performance. The lower the rank, the more favorable a state's tax system is for business. States without a given tax are given a ranking of 1. The scores/rankings for the District of Columbia do not affect other states. The 2016 index represents the tax climate as of July 1, 2015 (the beginning of Fiscal Year 2016).
Source: Tax Foundation, State Business Tax Climate Index 2016

TRANSPORTATION

Means of Transportation to Work

Area	Car/Truck/Van		Public Transportation			Bicycle	Walked	Other Means	Worked at Home
	Drove Alone	Car-pooled	Bus	Subway	Railroad				
City	87.5	6.6	0.6	0.0	0.0	0.4	0.7	0.7	3.5
MSA[1]	83.3	9.0	0.9	0.0	0.0	0.2	1.6	0.7	4.2
U.S.	76.4	9.6	2.6	1.8	0.6	0.6	2.8	1.3	4.4

Note: Figures are percentages and cover workers 16 years of age and older; (1) Figures cover the Des Moines-West Des Moines, IA Metropolitan Statistical Area—see Appendix B for areas included
Source: U.S. Census Bureau, 2010-2014 American Community Survey 5-Year Estimates

Travel Time to Work

Area	Less Than 10 Minutes	10 to 19 Minutes	20 to 29 Minutes	30 to 44 Minutes	45 to 59 Minutes	60 to 89 Minutes	90 Minutes or More
City	16.9	27.4	32.4	19.8	1.3	1.0	1.3
MSA[1]	15.6	36.5	27.4	14.6	3.1	1.6	1.1
U.S.	13.3	29.6	21.0	20.2	7.7	5.7	2.6

Note: Figures are percentages and include workers 16 years old and over; (1) Figures cover the Des Moines-West Des Moines, IA Metropolitan Statistical Area—see Appendix B for areas included
Source: U.S. Census Bureau, 2010-2014 American Community Survey 5-Year Estimates

Freeway Travel Time Index

Area	1985	1990	1995	2000	2005	2010	2014
Urban Area Rank[1,2]	n/a	n/a	n/a	n/a	n/a	n/a	n/a
Urban Area Index[1]	n/a	n/a	n/a	n/a	n/a	n/a	n/a
Average Index[3]	1.09	1.11	1.14	1.17	1.20	1.19	1.20

Note: Freeway Travel Time Index—the ratio of travel time in the peak period to the travel time at free-flow conditions. For example, a value of 1.30 indicates a 20-minute free-flow trip takes 26 minutes in the peak (20 minutes x 1.30 = 26 minutes); (1) Data for the Des Moines-West Des Moines, IA urban area was not available; (2) Rank is based on 101 urban areas (#1 = highest travel time index); (3) Average of 101 urban areas
Source: Texas Transportation Institute, 2015 Urban Mobility Scorecard, August 2015

Freeway Commuter Stress Index

Area	1985	1990	1995	2000	2005	2010	2014
Urban Area Rank[1,2]	n/a	n/a	n/a	n/a	n/a	n/a	n/a
Urban Area Index[1]	n/a	n/a	n/a	n/a	n/a	n/a	n/a
Average Index[3]	1.13	1.16	1.19	1.22	1.25	1.24	1.25

Note: The Freeway Commuter Stress Index is the same as the Freeway Travel Time Index (see table above) except that it includes only the travel in the peak directions during the peak periods; the TTI includes travel in all directions during the peak period. Thus, the CSI is more indicative of the work trip experienced by each commuter on a daily basis. (1) Data for the Des Moines-West Des Moines, IA urban area was not available; (2) Rank is based on 101 urban areas (#1 = highest stress index); (3) Average of 101 urban areas
Source: Texas Transportation Institute, 2015 Urban Mobility Scorecard, August 2015

Living Environment

COST OF LIVING

Cost of Living Index

Composite Index	Groceries	Housing	Utilities	Trans-portation	Health Care	Misc. Goods/ Services
89.8	92.0	83.7	89.8	95.1	96.6	91.4

Note: The Cost of Living Index measures regional differences in the cost of consumer goods and services, excluding taxes and non-consumer expenditures, for professional and managerial households in the top income quintile. It is based on more than 50,000 prices covering almost 60 different items for which prices are collected three times a year by chambers of commerce, economic development organizations or university applied economic centers in each participating urban area. The numbers shown should be read as a percentage above or below the national average of 100. For example, a value of 115.4 in the groceries column indicates that grocery prices are 15.4% higher than the national average. Small differences in the index numbers should not be interpreted as significant; Figures cover the Des Moines IA urban area.
Source: The Council for Community and Economic Research, ACCRA Cost of Living Index, 2015

Grocery Prices

Area[1]	T-Bone Steak ($/pound)	Frying Chicken ($/pound)	Whole Milk ($/half gal.)	Eggs ($/dozen)	Orange Juice ($/64 oz.)	Coffee ($/11.5 oz.)
City[2]	9.63	1.57	1.85	2.13	3.18	4.24
Avg.	10.99	1.43	2.25	2.26	3.58	4.48
Min.	7.16	0.98	1.30	1.35	2.88	2.98
Max.	14.13	2.43	3.85	4.81	6.39	7.56

Note: (1) Values for the local area are compared with the average, minimum and maximum values for all 292 areas in the Cost of Living Index; (2) Figures cover the Des Moines IA urban area; **T-Bone Steak** *(price per pound);* **Frying Chicken** *(price per pound, whole fryer);* **Whole Milk** *(half gallon carton);* **Eggs** *(price per dozen, Grade A, large);* **Orange Juice** *(64 oz. Tropicana or Florida Natural);* **Coffee** *(11.5 oz. can, vacuum-packed, Maxwell House, Hills Bros, or Folgers).*
Source: The Council for Community and Economic Research, ACCRA Cost of Living Index, 2015

Housing and Utility Costs

Area[1]	New Home Price ($)	Apartment Rent ($/month)	All Electric ($/month)	Part Electric ($/month)	Other Energy ($/month)	Telephone ($/month)
City[2]	288,831	651	-	75.11	60.31	29.30
Avg.	312,874	945	179.30	95.07	72.96	28.11
Min.	178,682	479	116.28	43.14	26.46	10.01
Max.	1,472,476	3,984	504.25	189.44	421.11	43.06

Note: (1) Values for the local area are compared with the average, minimum and maximum values for all 292 areas in the Cost of Living Index; (2) Figures cover the Des Moines IA urban area; **New Home Price** *(2,400 sf living area, 8,000 sf lot, in urban area with full utilities);* **Apartment Rent** *(950 sf 2 bedroom/1.5 or 2 bath, unfurnished, excluding all utilities except water);* **All Electric** *(average monthly cost for an all-electric home);* **Part Electric** *(average monthly cost for a part-electric home);* **Other Energy** *(average monthly cost for natural gas, fuel oil, coal, wood, and any other forms of energy except electricity);* **Telephone** *(price includes basic monthly rate for a private residential line plus additional local usage charges incurred by a family of four).*
Source: The Council for Community and Economic Research, ACCRA Cost of Living Index, 2015

Health Care, Transportation, and Other Costs

Area[1]	Doctor ($/visit)	Dentist ($/visit)	Optometrist ($/visit)	Gasoline ($/gallon)	Beauty Salon ($/visit)	Men's Shirt ($)
City[2]	122.87	76.90	95.35	2.20	27.14	18.18
Avg.	105.15	89.02	99.78	2.38	35.30	28.10
Min.	66.87	56.09	48.53	1.95	18.91	13.38
Max.	182.34	150.36	228.33	4.09	67.91	63.80

Note: (1) Values for the local area are compared with the average, minimum and maximum values for all 292 areas in the Cost of Living Index; (2) Figures cover the Des Moines IA urban area; **Doctor** *(general practitioners routine exam of an established patient);* **Dentist** *(adult teeth cleaning and periodic oral examination);* **Optometrist** *(full vision eye exam for established adult patient);* **Gasoline** *(one gallon regular unleaded, national brand, including all taxes, cash price at self-service pump if available);* **Beauty Salon** *(woman's shampoo, trim, and blow-dry);* **Men's Shirt** *(cotton/polyester dress shirt, pinpoint weave, long sleeves).*
Source: The Council for Community and Economic Research, ACCRA Cost of Living Index, 2015

HOUSING

House Price Index (HPI)

Area	National Ranking[2]	Quarterly Change (%)	One-Year Change (%)	Five-Year Change (%)
MSA[1]	148	0.20	4.30	9.70
U.S.[3]	–	1.45	5.76	22.85

Note: The HPI is a weighted repeat sales index. It measures average price changes in repeat sales or refinancings on the same properties. This information is obtained by reviewing repeat mortgage transactions on single-family properties whose mortgages have been purchased or securitized by Fannie Mae or Freddie Mac in January 1975; (1) Des Moines-West Des Moines Metropolitan Statistical Area—see Appendix B for areas included; (2) Rankings are based on annual percentage change for all metro areas containing at least 15,000 transactions over the last 10 years and ranges from 1 to 266; (3) figures based on a weighted average of Census Division estimates using a seasonally adjusted, purchase-only index; all figures are for the period ending December 31, 2015

Source: Federal Housing Finance Agency, House Price Index, February 25, 2016

Median Single-Family Home Prices

Area	2013	2014	2015p	Percent Change 2014 to 2015
MSA[1]	170.4	171.5	181.3	5.7
U.S. Average	197.4	208.9	223.9	7.2

Note: Figures are median sales prices of existing single-family homes in thousands of dollars; (p) preliminary; n/a not available; (1) Des Moines-West Des Moines, IA Metropolitan Statistical Area—see Appendix B for areas included

Source: National Association of Realtors, Median Sales Price of Existing Single-Family Homes for Metropolitan Areas, 4th Quarter 2015

Qualifying Income Based on Median Sales Price of Existing Single-Family Homes

Area	With 5% Down ($)	With 10% Down ($)	With 20% Down ($)
MSA[1]	41,528	39,342	34,971
U.S. Average	49,535	46,928	41,714

Note: Figures are preliminary; Qualifying income is based on a mortgage rate of 4.1%. Monthly principal and interest payment is limited to 25% of income; n/a not available; (1) Des Moines-West Des Moines, IA Metropolitan Statistical Area—see Appendix B for areas included

Source: National Association of Realtors, Qualifying Income Based on Median Sales Price of Existing Single-Family Homes for Metropolitan Areas, 4th Quarter 2015

Median Apartment Condo-Coop Home Prices

Area	2013	2014	2015p	Percent Change 2014 to 2015
MSA[1]	n/a	n/a	n/a	n/a
U.S. Average	194.9	204.3	210.7	3.1

Note: Figures are median sales prices of existing apartment condo-coop homes in thousands of dollars; (p) preliminary; n/a not available; (1) Des Moines-West Des Moines, IA Metropolitan Statistical Area—see Appendix B for areas included

Source: National Association of Realtors, Median Sales Price of Existing Apartment Condo-Coop Homes for Metropolitan Areas, 4th Quarter 2015

Gross Monthly Rent

Area	Under $200	$200 -299	$300 -499	$500 -749	$750 -999	$1,000 -1,499	$1,500 and up	Median ($)
City	0.7	0.3	5.1	35.5	23.0	33.0	2.5	822
MSA[1]	1.2	2.3	7.3	32.6	30.4	21.8	4.3	793
U.S.	1.5	3.2	7.4	21.0	24.1	26.9	15.9	920

Note: Figures are percentages except for Median; Gross rent is the contract rent plus the estimated average monthly cost of utilities (electricity, gas, and water and sewer) and fuels (oil, coal, kerosene, wood, etc.) if these are paid by the renter (or paid for the renter by someone else); (1) Figures cover the Des Moines-West Des Moines, IA Metropolitan Statistical Area—see Appendix B for areas included

Source: U.S. Census Bureau, 2010-2014 American Community Survey 5-Year Estimates

HEALTH

Homeownership Rate

Area	2008 (%)	2009 (%)	2010 (%)	2011 (%)	2012 (%)	2013 (%)	2014 (%)	2015 (%)
MSA[1]	n/a	n/a	n/a	n/a	n/a	n/a	n/a	n/a
U.S.	67.8	67.4	66.9	66.1	65.4	65.1	64.5	63.7

Note: (1) Figures cover the Des Moines-West Des Moines, IA Metropolitan Statistical Area—see Appendix B for areas included; n/a not available
Source: U.S. Census Bureau, Housing Vacancies and Homeownership Annual Statistics: 2015

Year Housing Structure Built

Area	2010 or Later	2000 -2009	1990 -1999	1980 -1989	1970 -1979	1960 -1969	1950 -1959	1940 -1949	Before 1940	Median Year
City	5.8	37.1	19.1	8.7	13.5	8.8	3.6	1.4	2.0	1996
MSA[1]	2.3	18.9	14.4	9.4	14.1	9.0	10.1	4.7	17.1	1976
U.S.	1.0	14.9	13.9	13.8	15.8	11.0	10.8	5.4	13.3	1976

Note: Figures are percentages except for Median Year; (1) Figures cover the Des Moines-West Des Moines, IA Metropolitan Statistical Area—see Appendix B for areas included
Source: U.S. Census Bureau, 2010-2014 American Community Survey 5-Year Estimates

Health Risk Data

Category	MSA[1] (%)	U.S. (%)
Adults aged 18–64 who have any kind of health care coverage	89.5	79.6
Adults who reported being in good or excellent health	87.0	83.1
Adults who are current smokers	18.7	19.6
Adults who are heavy drinkers[2]	6.3	6.1
Adults who are binge drinkers[3]	23.1	16.9
Adults who are overweight (BMI 25.0 - 29.9)	33.7	35.8
Adults who are obese (BMI 30.0 - 99.8)	29.1	27.6
Adults who participated in any physical activities in the past month	78.3	77.1
Adults 50+ who have ever had a sigmoidoscopy or colonoscopy	68.5	67.3
Women aged 40+ who have had a mammogram within the past two years	70.5	74.0
Men aged 40+ who have had a PSA test within the past two years	42.0	45.2
Adults aged 65+ who have had flu shot within the past year	72.2	60.1
Adults who always wear a seatbelt	96.6	93.8

Note: Data as of 2012 unless otherwise noted; (1) Figures cover the Des Moines-West Des Moines, IA Metropolitan Statistical Area—see Appendix B for areas included; (2) Heavy drinkers are classified as males having more than two drinks per day or females having more than one drink per day; (3) Binge drinkers are classified as males having five or more drinks on one occasion or females having four or more drinks on one occasion
Source: Centers for Disease Control and Prevention, Behaviorial Risk Factor Surveillance System, SMART: Selected Metropolitan/Micropolitan Area Risk Trends, 2012 (Note: the CDC has discontinued this dataset but will be releasing a replacement in mid-2016)

Chronic Health Indicators

Category	MSA[1] (%)	U.S. (%)
Adults who have ever been told they had a heart attack	3.9	4.5
Adults who have ever been told they had a stroke	2.5	2.9
Adults who have been told they currently have asthma	8.4	8.9
Adults who have ever been told they have arthritis	24.3	25.7
Adults who have ever been told they have diabetes[2]	8.9	9.7
Adults who have ever been told they had skin cancer	4.9	5.7
Adults who have ever been told they had any other types of cancer	6.8	6.5
Adults who have ever been told they have COPD	7.0	6.2
Adults who have ever been told they have kidney disease	1.9	2.5
Adults who have ever been told they have a form of depression	19.4	18.0

Note: Data as of 2012 unless otherwise noted; (1) Figures cover the Des Moines-West Des Moines, IA Metropolitan Statistical Area—see Appendix B for areas included; (2) Figures do not include pregnancy-related, borderline, or pre-diabetes
Source: Centers for Disease Control and Prevention, Behaviorial Risk Factor Surveillance System, SMART: Selected Metropolitan/Micropolitan Area Risk Trends, 2012 (Note: the CDC has discontinued this dataset but will be releasing a replacement in mid-2016)

Mortality Rates for the Top 10 Causes of Death in the U.S.

ICD-10[a] Sub-Chapter	ICD-10[a] Code	Age-Adjusted Mortality Rate[1] per 100,000 population	
		County[2]	U.S.
Malignant neoplasms	C00-C97	179.8	163.6
Ischaemic heart diseases	I20-I25	106.7	102.2
Other forms of heart disease	I30-I51	36.2	50.1
Chronic lower respiratory diseases	J40-J47	55.9	41.4
Organic, including symptomatic, mental disorders	F01-F09	30.3	38.5
Cerebrovascular diseases	I60-I69	32.2	36.5
Other external causes of accidental injury	W00-X59	34.1	27.5
Other degenerative diseases of the nervous system	G30-G31	37.8	26.3
Diabetes mellitus	E10-E14	21.6	21.1
Hypertensive diseases	I10-I15	13.9	19.7

Note: (a) ICD-10 = International Classification of Diseases 10th Revision; (1) Mortality rates are a three year average covering 2012-2014; (2) Figures cover Polk County.
Source: Centers for Disease Control and Prevention, National Center for Health Statistics. Underlying Cause of Death 1999-2014 on CDC WONDER Online Database, released 2015.

Mortality Rates for Selected Causes of Death

ICD-10[a] Sub-Chapter	ICD-10[a] Code	Age-Adjusted Mortality Rate[1] per 100,000 population	
		County[2]	U.S.
Assault	X85-Y09	2.6	5.1
Diseases of the liver	K70-K76	13.0	13.5
Human immunodeficiency virus (HIV) disease	B20-B24	1.4	2.1
Influenza and pneumonia	J09-J18	18.2	15.2
Intentional self-harm	X60-X84	12.2	12.7
Malnutrition	E40-E46	1.9	0.9
Obesity and other hyperalimentation	E65-E68	2.4	1.9
Renal failure	N17-N19	7.1	13.0
Transport accidents	V01-V99	6.5	11.6
Viral hepatitis	B15-B19	1.4	2.1

Note: (a) ICD-10 = International Classification of Diseases 10th Revision; (1) Mortality rates are a three year average covering 2012-2014; (2) Figures cover Polk County; Data are Suppressed when the data meet the criteria for confidentiality constraints; Mortality rates are flagged as Unreliable when the rate would be calculated with a numerator of 20 or less.
Source: Centers for Disease Control and Prevention, National Center for Health Statistics. Underlying Cause of Death 1999-2014 on CDC WONDER Online Database, released 2015.

Health Insurance Coverage

Area	With Health Insurance	With Private Health Insurance	With Public Health Insurance	Without Health Insurance	Population Under Age 18 Without Health Insurance
City	96.3	88.7	17.5	3.7	2.1
MSA[1]	92.6	76.7	27.4	7.4	3.1
U.S.	85.8	65.8	31.1	14.2	7.1

Note: Figures are percentages that cover the civilian noninstitutionalized population; (1) Figures cover the Des Moines-West Des Moines, IA Metropolitan Statistical Area—see Appendix B for areas included
Source: U.S. Census Bureau, 2010-2014 American Community Survey 5-Year Estimates

Number of Medical Professionals

Area	MDs[3]	DOs[3,4]	Dentists	Podiatrists	Chiropractors	Optometrists
County[1] (number)	960	485	300	45	213	104
County[1] (rate[2])	212.5	107.3	65.2	9.8	46.3	22.6
U.S. (rate[2])	272.5	20.9	64.7	5.8	25.9	15.2

Note: Data as of 2014 unless noted; (1) Data covers Polk County; (2) Rate per 100,000 population; (3) Data as of 2013 and includes all active, non-federal physicians; (4) Doctor of Osteopathic Medicine
Source: U.S. Department of Health and Human Services, Health Resources and Services Administration, Bureau of Health Professions, Area Resource File (ARF) 2014-2015

EDUCATION

Public School District Statistics

District Name	Schls	Pupils	Pupil/ Teacher Ratio	Minority Pupils[1] (%)	Free Lunch Eligible[2] (%)	IEP[3] (%)
Ankeny Comm School District	15	10,179	16.8	10.9	10.6	7.9

Note: Table includes school districts with 100 or more students; (1) Percentage of students that are not non-Hispanic white; (2) Percentage of students that are eligible for the free lunch program; (3) Percentage of students that have an Individualized Education Program.
Source: U.S. Department of Education, National Center for Education Statistics, Common Core of Data, Local Education Agency (School District) Universe Survey: School Year 2013-2014; U.S. Department of Education, National Center for Education Statistics, Common Core of Data, Public Elementary/Secondary School Universe Survey: School Year 2013-2014

Highest Level of Education

Area	Less than H.S.	H.S. Diploma	Some College, No Deg.	Associate Degree	Bachelor's Degree	Master's Degree	Prof. School Degree	Doctorate Degree
City	2.5	17.4	20.2	14.7	32.7	9.6	1.6	1.3
MSA[1]	7.4	26.4	20.9	10.1	24.8	7.2	2.1	1.1
U.S.	13.7	28.0	21.2	7.9	18.3	7.8	2.0	1.3

Note: Figures cover persons age 25 and over; (1) Figures cover the Des Moines-West Des Moines, IA Metropolitan Statistical Area—see Appendix B for areas included
Source: U.S. Census Bureau, 2010-2014 American Community Survey 5-Year Estimates

Educational Attainment by Race

Area	High School Graduate or Higher (%)					Bachelor's Degree or Higher (%)				
	Total	White	Black	Asian	Hisp.[2]	Total	White	Black	Asian	Hisp.[2]
City	97.5	97.6	99.5	97.7	89.5	45.2	45.4	28.8	46.4	41.1
MSA[1]	92.6	94.1	84.4	80.1	59.7	35.1	36.2	18.2	44.4	13.7
U.S.	86.3	88.4	83.2	85.8	64.1	29.3	30.6	19.0	50.9	13.9

Note: Figures shown cover persons 25 years old and over; (1) Figures cover the Des Moines-West Des Moines, IA Metropolitan Statistical Area—see Appendix B for areas included; (2) People of Hispanic origin can be of any race
Source: U.S. Census Bureau, 2010-2014 American Community Survey 5-Year Estimates

School Enrollment by Grade and Control

Area	Preschool (%)		Kindergarten (%)		Grades 1 - 4 (%)		Grades 5 - 8 (%)		Grades 9 - 12 (%)	
	Public	Private	Public	Private	Public	Private	Public	Private	Public	Private
City	48.8	51.2	93.8	6.2	92.3	7.7	97.4	2.6	96.2	3.8
MSA[1]	61.2	38.8	89.4	10.6	90.4	9.6	90.8	9.2	91.0	9.0
U.S.	57.4	42.6	87.8	12.2	89.8	10.2	89.9	10.1	90.6	9.4

Note: Figures shown cover persons 3 years old and over; (1) Figures cover the Des Moines-West Des Moines, IA Metropolitan Statistical Area—see Appendix B for areas included
Source: U.S. Census Bureau, 2010-2014 American Community Survey 5-Year Estimates

Average Salaries of Public School Classroom Teachers

Area	2013-14		2014-15		Percent Change 2013-14 to 2014-15	Percent Change 2004-05 to 2014-15
	Dollars	Rank[1]	Dollars	Rank[1]		
Iowa	52,032	25	52,862	25	1.60	34.6
U.S. Average	56,610	–	57,379	–	1.36	20.8

Note: (1) State rank ranges from 1 to 51 where 1 indicates highest salary.
Source: National Education Association, Rankings & Estimates: Rankings of the States 2014 and Estimates of School Statistics 2015, March 2015

Higher Education

Four-Year Colleges			Two-Year Colleges			Medical Schools[1]	Law Schools[2]	Voc/ Tech[3]
Public	Private Non-profit	Private For-profit	Public	Private Non-profit	Private For-profit			
0	1	0	1	0	0	0	0	0

Note: Figures cover institutions located within the city limits and include main campuses only; (1) includes schools accredited by the Liaison Committee on Medical Education and the American Osteopathic Association's Commission on Osteopathic College Accreditation; (2) includes ABA-accredited schools, schools with provisional ABA accreditation, and state accredited schools; (3) includes all schools with programs that are less than 2 years.
Source: National Center for Education Statistics, Integrated Postsecondary Education System (IPEDS), 2014-15; Association of American Medical Colleges, Member List, March 21, 2016; American Osteopathic Association, Member List, March 21, 2016; Law School Admission Council, Official Guide to ABA-Approved Law Schools Online, March 21, 2016; Wikipedia, List of Medical Schools in the United States, March 21, 2016; Wikipedia, List of Law Schools in the United States, March 21, 2016

According to *U.S. News & World Report,* the Des Moines-West Des Moines, IA metro area is home to one of the best liberal arts colleges in the U.S.: **Simpson College** (#143 tie). The indicators used to capture academic quality fall into a number of categories: assessment by administrators at peer institutions; retention of students; faculty resources; student selectivity; financial resources; alumni giving; high school counselor ratings of colleges; and graduation rate. *U.S. News & World Report, "America's Best Colleges 2016"*

PRESIDENTIAL ELECTION

2012 Presidential Election Results

Area	Obama (%)	Romney (%)	Other (%)
Polk County	56.1	42.0	1.9
U.S.	51.0	47.2	1.8

Note: Results may not add to 100% due to rounding
Source: Dave Leip's Atlas of U.S. Presidential Elections

EMPLOYERS

Major Employers

Company Name	Industry
Bridgestone Americas Tire Operations	Global distribution center for tires
DuPont Pioneer	Crop inputs for worldwide agribusiness
Emerson Process Management Fisher Div	Control valves & systems, divisional headquarters
Grinnell Mutual Reinsurance Company	Reinsurance
Hy-Vee	Retail grocery & drugstore chain
JBS USA	Pork processing & packaging
John Deere companies	Agricultural machinery, consumer financial services
Lennox Manufacturing	Heating & air conditioners
Mercer	Insurance
Mercy Medical Center	Healthcare
Meredith Corporation	Magazine, book publishing, tv, integrated marketing
Nationwide	Insurance
Principal Financial Group	Financial services
UnityPoint Health	Healthcare
UPS	Logistics, distribution, transportation, freight
Vermeer Manufacturing Company	Manufacturing
Wellmark	Health insurance
Wells Fargo & Co.	Financial services & home mortgage

Note: Companies shown are located within the Des Moines-West Des Moines, IA Metropolitan Statistical Area.
Source: Hoovers.com; Wikipedia

PUBLIC SAFETY

Crime Rate

Area	All Crimes	Violent Crimes: Murder	Violent Crimes: Rape[3]	Violent Crimes: Robbery	Violent Crimes: Aggrav. Assault	Property Crimes: Burglary	Property Crimes: Larceny -Theft	Property Crimes: Motor Vehicle Theft
City	1,393.6	0.0	20.7	0.0	88.5	203.4	1,007.6	73.4
Metro[1]	2,815.4	1.8	32.2	49.2	233.6	478.4	1,812.2	208.0
U.S.	2,971.8	4.5	36.6	102.2	232.5	542.5	1,837.3	216.2

Note: Figures are crimes per 100,000 population; (1) Figures cover the Des Moines-West Des Moines, IA Metropolitan Statistical Area—see Appendix B for areas included; (3) The city and U.S. figures shown were reported using the revised Uniform Crime Reporting (UCR) definition of rape. The suburban and metro area figures shown are an aggregate total of the data submitted using both the revised and legacy UCR definitions.
Source: FBI Uniform Crime Reports, 2014

Hate Crimes

Area	Number of Quarters Reported	Race	Religion	Sexual Orientation	Ethnicity	Disability	Gender	Gender Identity
		Number of Incidents per Bias Motivation						
City	4	0	0	0	0	0	0	0
U.S.	4	2,568	1,014	1,017	648	84	33	98

Source: Federal Bureau of Investigation, Hate Crime Statistics 2014

Identity Theft Consumer Complaints

Area	Complaints	Complaints per 100,000 Population	Rank[2]
MSA[1]	645	105.5	180
U.S.	490,220	152.4	-

Note: (1) Figures cover the Des Moines-West Des Moines, IA Metropolitan Statistical Area—see Appendix B for areas included; (2) Rank ranges from 1 to 379 where 1 indicates greatest number of identity theft complaints per 100,000 population
Source: Federal Trade Commission, Consumer Sentinel Network Data Book for January–December 2015

Fraud and Other Consumer Complaints

Area	Complaints	Complaints per 100,000 Population	Rank[2]
MSA[1]	1,843	301.4	309
U.S.	2,593,159	806.0	-

Note: (1) Figures cover the Des Moines-West Des Moines, IA Metropolitan Statistical Area—see Appendix B for areas included; (2) Rank ranges from 1 to 379 where 1 indicates greatest number of identity theft complaints per 100,000 population
Source: Federal Trade Commission, Consumer Sentinel Network Data Book for January–December 2015

RECREATION

Culture

Dance[1]	Theatre[1]	Instrumental Music[1]	Vocal Music[1]	Series and Festivals	Museums and Art Galleries[2]	Zoos and Aquariums[3]
0	0	0	0	0	0	0

Note: (1) Professional perfoming groups; (2) Based on organizations with SIC code 8412; (3) AZA-accredited
Source: The Grey House Performing Arts Directory, 2015-16; Association of Zoos & Aquariums, AZA Member Zoos & Aquariums, March 25, 2016; www.AccuLeads.com, March 29, 2016

Professional Sports Teams

Team Name	League	Year Established
No teams are located in the metro area		

Source: Wikipedia, Major Professional Sports Teams of the United States and Canada, March 24, 2016

CLIMATE

Average and Extreme Temperatures

Temperature	Jan	Feb	Mar	Apr	May	Jun	Jul	Aug	Sep	Oct	Nov	Dec	Yr.
Extreme High (°F)	65	70	91	93	98	103	105	108	99	95	76	69	108
Average High (°F)	29	34	45	61	72	82	86	84	76	65	48	33	60
Average Temp. (°F)	20	25	36	51	62	72	76	74	65	54	39	25	50
Average Low (°F)	11	16	27	40	51	61	66	64	54	43	29	17	40
Extreme Low (°F)	-24	-20	-22	9	28	42	47	40	28	14	-3	-22	-24

Note: Figures cover the years 1945-1990
Source: National Climatic Data Center, International Station Meteorological Climate Summary, 9/96

Average Precipitation/Snowfall/Humidity

Precip./Humidity	Jan	Feb	Mar	Apr	May	Jun	Jul	Aug	Sep	Oct	Nov	Dec	Yr.
Avg. Precip. (in.)	1.1	1.1	2.3	3.1	3.8	4.4	3.5	3.9	3.1	2.4	1.7	1.2	31.8
Avg. Snowfall (in.)	8	7	7	2	Tr	0	0	0	Tr	Tr	3	7	33
Avg. Rel. Hum. 6am (%)	77	79	79	78	78	81	83	86	85	80	79	80	80
Avg. Rel. Hum. 3pm (%)	65	63	57	50	51	52	52	54	52	50	58	66	56

Note: Figures cover the years 1945-1990; Tr = Trace amounts (<0.05 in. of rain; <0.5 in. of snow)
Source: National Climatic Data Center, International Station Meteorological Climate Summary, 9/96

Weather Conditions

Temperature			Daytime Sky			Precipitation		
5°F & below	32°F & below	90°F & above	Clear	Partly cloudy	Cloudy	0.01 inch or more precip.	0.1 inch or more snow/ice	Thunder-storms
25	137	26	99	128	138	106	25	46

Note: Figures are average number of days per year and cover the years 1945-1990
Source: National Climatic Data Center, International Station Meteorological Climate Summary, 9/96

HAZARDOUS WASTE

Superfund Sites

Ankeny has no sites on the EPA's Superfund Final National Priorities List. There are a total of 1,323 Superfund sites on the list in the U.S. *U.S. Environmental Protection Agency, Final National Priorities List, March 18, 2016*

AIR & WATER QUALITY

Air Quality Trends: Ozone

	1990	1995	2000	2005	2010	2011	2012	2013	2014
MSA[1]	n/a	n/a	n/a	n/a	n/a	n/a	n/a	n/a	n/a

Note: (1) Data covers the Des Moines-West Des Moines, IA Metropolitan Statistical Area—see Appendix B for areas included; n/a not available. The values shown are the composite ozone concentration averages among trend sites based on the highest fourth daily maximum 8-hour concentration in parts per million. These trends are based on sites having an adequate record of monitoring data during the trend period. Data from exceptional events are included.
Source: U.S. Environmental Protection Agency, Air Quality Monitoring Information, "Air Quality Trends by City, 1990-2014"

Air Quality Index

Area	Percent of Days when Air Quality was...[2]					AQI Statistics[2]	
	Good	Moderate	Unhealthy for Sensitive Groups	Unhealthy	Very Unhealthy	Maximum	Median
MSA[1]	83.3	16.7	0.0	0.0	0.0	98	36

Note: (1) Data covers the Des Moines-West Des Moines, IA Metropolitan Statistical Area—see Appendix B for areas included; (2) Based on 365 days with AQI data in 2015. Air Quality Index (AQI) is an index for reporting daily air quality. EPA calculates the AQI for five major air pollutants regulated by the Clean Air Act: ground-level ozone, particle pollution (aka particulate matter), carbon monoxide, sulfur dioxide, and nitrogen dioxide. The AQI runs from 0 to 500. The higher the AQI value, the greater the level of air pollution and the greater the health concern. There are six AQI categories: "Good" AQI is between 0 and 50. Air quality is considered satisfactory; "Moderate" AQI is between 51 and 100. Air quality is acceptable; "Unhealthy for Sensitive Groups" When AQI values are between 101 and 150, members of sensitive groups may experience health effects; "Unhealthy" When AQI values are between 151 and 200 everyone may begin to experience health effects; "Very Unhealthy" AQI values between 201 and 300 trigger a health alert; "Hazardous" AQI values over 300 trigger warnings of emergency conditions (not shown).
Source: U.S. Environmental Protection Agency, Air Quality Index Report, 2015

Air Quality Index Pollutants

Area	Percent of Days when AQI Pollutant was...[2]					
	Carbon Monoxide	Nitrogen Dioxide	Ozone	Sulfur Dioxide	Particulate Matter 2.5	Particulate Matter 10
MSA[1]	0.0	3.0	33.2	0.0	63.0	0.8

Note: (1) Data covers the Des Moines-West Des Moines, IA Metropolitan Statistical Area—see Appendix B for areas included; (2) Based on 365 days with AQI data in 2015. The Air Quality Index (AQI) is an index for reporting daily air quality. EPA calculates the AQI for five major air pollutants regulated by the Clean Air Act: ground-level ozone, particle pollution (also known as particulate matter), carbon monoxide, sulfur dioxide, and nitrogen dioxide. The AQI runs from 0 to 500. The higher the AQI value, the greater the level of air pollution and the greater the health concern.
Source: U.S. Environmental Protection Agency, Air Quality Index Report, 2015

Maximum Air Pollutant Concentrations: Particulate Matter, Ozone, CO and Lead

	Particulate Matter 10 (ug/m³)	Particulate Matter 2.5 Wtd AM (ug/m³)	Particulate Matter 2.5 24-Hr (ug/m³)	Ozone (ppm)	Carbon Monoxide (ppm)	Lead (ug/m³)
MSA[1] Level	43	8.6	21	0.061	1	n/a
NAAQS[2]	150	15	35	0.075	9	0.15
Met NAAQS[2]	Yes	Yes	Yes	Yes	Yes	n/a

Note: (1) Data covers the Des Moines-West Des Moines, IA Metropolitan Statistical Area—see Appendix B for areas included; Data from exceptional events are included; (2) National Ambient Air Quality Standards; ppm = parts per million; ug/m³ = micrograms per cubic meter; n/a not available.
Concentrations: Particulate Matter 10 (coarse particulate)—highest second maximum 24-hour concentration; Particulate Matter 2.5 Wtd AM (fine particulate)—highest weighted annual mean concentration; Particulate Matter 2.5 24-Hour (fine particulate)—highest 98th percentile 24-hour concentration; Ozone—highest fourth daily maximum 8-hour concentration; Carbon Monoxide—highest second maximum non-overlapping 8-hour concentration; Lead—maximum running 3-month average
Source: U.S. Environmental Protection Agency, Air Quality Monitoring Information, "Air Quality Statistics by City, 2014"

Maximum Air Pollutant Concentrations: Nitrogen Dioxide and Sulfur Dioxide

	Nitrogen Dioxide AM (ppb)	Nitrogen Dioxide 1-Hr (ppb)	Sulfur Dioxide AM (ppb)	Sulfur Dioxide 1-Hr (ppb)	Sulfur Dioxide 24-Hr (ppb)
MSA[1] Level	9	35	n/a	1	n/a
NAAQS[2]	53	100	30	75	140
Met NAAQS[2]	Yes	Yes	n/a	Yes	n/a

Note: (1) Data covers the Des Moines-West Des Moines, IA Metropolitan Statistical Area—see Appendix B for areas included; Data from exceptional events are included; (2) National Ambient Air Quality Standards; ppm = parts per million; ug/m³ = micrograms per cubic meter; n/a not available.
Concentrations: Nitrogen Dioxide AM—highest arithmetic mean concentration; Nitrogen Dioxide 1-Hr—highest 98th percentile 1-hour daily maximum concentration; Sulfur Dioxide AM—highest annual mean concentration; Sulfur Dioxide 1-Hr—highest 99th percentile 1-hour daily maximum concentration; Sulfur Dioxide 24-Hr—highest second maximum 24-hour concentration
Source: U.S. Environmental Protection Agency, Air Quality Monitoring Information, "Air Quality Statistics by City, 2014"

Drinking Water

Water System Name	Pop. Served	Primary Water Source Type	Violations[1]	
			Health Based	Monitoring/ Reporting
City of Ankeny	54,598	Purchased Surface	0	0

Note: (1) Based on violation data from January 1, 2015 to December 31, 2015 (includes unresolved violations from earlier years)

Source: U.S. Environmental Protection Agency, Office of Ground Water and Drinking Water, Safe Drinking Water Information System (based on data extracted April 29, 2016)

Marion, Iowa

Background

Marion is located in Linn County in eastern central Iowa, 10 miles northeast of Cedar Rapids and its big-city convenience.

Present-day Marion was founded in 1839. Its name was chosen as a tribute to General Marion, a popular figure in American literature. By 1840, numerous merchants, professional offices, and tradesmen were establishing businesses in the community. Many homes were also being constructed during the decade. Residents purchased their property through lot auctions with proceeds being used to finance the construction of county buildings. New industry to the area was jumpstarted by the building of a water-powered sawmill on Indian Creek, which employed many residents and allowed for a significant lumber industry. By the end of the 1840s, Marion had a blacksmith, a tavern, a hotel, and a population of 2,700.

During the early 1900s the railroad was a major employer for Marion. The Chicago, Milwaukee, St. Paul and Pacific Railroads all built lines through the community, and the city served as an important distribution hub between the cities of Chicago and Omaha. Passenger trains also made frequent scheduled stops. At the railroads' peak, nearly 50 trains stopped in Marion each day.

Marion is committed to the of education if its youth, which is served by two school districts. To fulfill the need for higher education, Kirkwood Community College has a satellite campus located in the community, with the main campus in nearby Cedar Rapids.

The area boasts many historical sites that are open to the public including The Granger House—a fully restored 1870s brick home and carriage house, The African American Historical Museum, and the National Czech and Slovak Museum and Library. There are also a number of Marion's buildings listed on the National Register of Historical Places due to their architectural significance.

The many recreational opportunities in Marion include over fifteen public parks with playgrounds, baseball diamonds, soccer fields sand volleyball courts, and picnic areas; a municipal swimming pool; a historical cemetery; and many hiking, biking, and nature trails. Five public golf courses and two private courses are located in the immediate vicinity of Marion, as is a farmers market that operates seasonally from late spring to early fall and offers a variety of local products.

In 2008, major flooding in the state of Iowa destroyed many communities and damaged numerous others. While Marion fared better than some, many historical buildings, homes, and businesses were damaged or destroyed. While the recovery effort is ongoing, reconstruction of city facilities is expected to be complete by 2018, and of housing and businesses by 2020. Construction of permanent flood walls will be complete by 2024.

Marion is served by the Eastern Iowa Airport in nearby Cedar Rapids, and a smaller, privately owned airport located in Marion.

Rankings

Business/Finance Rankings

- The personal finance site NerdWallet analyzed 183 American metropolitan areas with populations over 250,000 and more than 15,000 businesses to rank where entrepreneurs find the most success. Criteria included area economy, annual income, housing cost, unemployment rate, and the success rate of area businesses. Cedar Rapids* ranked #6. *www.nerdwallet.com, "Best Places to Start a Business," April 27, 2015*
- The Cedar Rapids* metro area appeared on the Milken Institute "2015 Best Performing Cities" list. Rank: #142 out of 200 large metro areas. Criteria: job growth; wage and salary growth; high-tech output growth. *Milken Institute, "Best-Performing Cities 2015," December 2015*
- *Forbes* ranked the 200 most populous metro areas to determine the nation's "Best Places for Business and Careers." The Cedar Rapids* metro area was ranked #164. Criteria: costs (business and living); job growth (past and projected); income growth; educational attainment (college and high school); projected economic growth; cultural and recreational opportunities; net migration patterns; number of highly ranked colleges. *Forbes, "The Best Places for Business and Careers 2015," July 29, 2015*

Education Rankings

- Cedar Rapids* was identified as one of the "Smartest Cities in America" by the brain-training website *Lumosity* using data from three million of its own users. The metro area ranked #30 out of 50. Criteria: users' brain performance index scores, considering core cognitive abilities such as memory, processing speed, flexibility, attention and problem-solving. *Lumosity, " Smartest Cities in America," June 25, 2013*

Environmental Rankings

- The Cedar Rapids* metro area came in at #145 for the relative comfort of its climate on Sperling's list of "chill cities," as measured by the Sperling Heat Index. All 361 metro areas are included. Criteria included daytime high temperatures, nighttime low temperatures, dew point, and relative humidity at the high temperatures. *www.bertsperling.com, "Sperling's Chill Cities," July 18, 2013*
- Sperling's BestPlaces assessed 379 metropolitan areas of the United States for the likelihood of dangerously extreme weather events or earthquakes. In general the Southeast and South-Central regions have the highest risk of weather extremes and earthquakes, while the Pacific Northwest enjoys the lowest risk. Of the least risky metropolitan areas, the Cedar Rapids* metro area was ranked #182. *www.bestplaces.net, "Safest Places from Natural Disasters," April 2011*

Health/Fitness Rankings

- The Cedar Rapids* metro area was identified as one of the worst cities for bed bugs in America by pest control company Orkin. The area ranked #41 out of 50 based on the number of bed bug treatments Orkin performed from January to December 2015. *Orkin, "Chicago Tops Bed Bug Cities List for Fourth Year in a Row," January 13, 2016*
- The Cedar Rapids* metro area ranked #145 out of 190 in The Gallup-Healthways Well-Being Index. Criteria: purpose; social well being; financial health; community and physical health. Results are based on telephone interviews with adults, aged 18 and older, living in metropolitan areas in the 50 U.S. states and the District of Columbia. *Gallup-Healthways, "State of American Well-Being," February 23, 2016*

Safety Rankings

- The National Insurance Crime Bureau ranked 380 metro areas in the U.S. in terms of per capita rates of vehicle theft. The Cedar Rapids* metro area ranked #166 (#1 = highest rate). Criteria: number of vehicle theft offenses per 100,000 inhabitants in 2014. *National Insurance Crime Bureau, "Hot Spots 2014," June 24, 2015*

Seniors/Retirement Rankings

- From its Best Cities for Successful Aging indexes, the Milken Institute generated rankings for metropolitan areas, weighing data in eight categories—health care, wellness, living arrangements, transportation, financial characteristics, education and employment opportunities, community engagement, and overall livability. The Cedar Rapids* metro area was ranked #67 overall in the small metro area category. *Milken Institute, "Best Cities for Successful Aging, 2014"*

Miscellaneous Rankings

- The finance and lifestyle site NerdWallet looked for the U.S. cities that topped the list in donating money and time to good causes. The Cedar Rapids* metro area proved to be the #18-ranked metro area, judged by culture of volunteerism, depth of commitment in terms of volunteer hours per year, and monetary contributions. *www.nerdwallet.com, "Most Generous Cities," September 22, 2013*

Marion is located within the Cedar Rapids, IA Metropolitan Statistical Area.

Business Environment

CITY FINANCES

City Government Finances

Component	2012 ($000)	2012 ($ per capita)
Total Revenues	39,779	1,144
Total Expenditures	43,599	1,253
Debt Outstanding	67,415	1,938
Cash and Securities[1]	91,753	2,639

Note: (1) Cash and security holdings of a government at the close of its fiscal year, including those of its dependent agencies, utilities, and liquor stores.
Source: U.S Census Bureau, State & Local Government Finances 2012

City Government Revenue by Source

Source	2012 ($000)	2012 ($ per capita)
General Revenue		
From Federal Government	851	24
From State Government	4,457	128
From Local Governments	150	4
Taxes		
Property	16,990	488
Sales and Gross Receipts	5,076	145
Personal Income	0	0
Corporate Income	0	0
Motor Vehicle License	0	0
Other Taxes	517	14
Current Charges	5,973	171
Liquor Store	0	0
Utility	3,279	94
Employee Retirement	0	0

Source: U.S Census Bureau, State & Local Government Finances 2012

City Government Expenditures by Function

Function	2012 ($000)	2012 ($ per capita)	2012 (%)
General Direct Expenditures			
Air Transportation	0	0	0.0
Corrections	0	0	0.0
Education	0	0	0.0
Employment Security Administration	0	0	0.0
Financial Administration	411	11	0.9
Fire Protection	2,986	85	6.8
General Public Buildings	150	4	0.3
Governmental Administration, Other	1,299	37	2.9
Health	35	1	0.0
Highways	2,812	80	6.4
Hospitals	0	0	0.0
Housing and Community Development	715	20	1.6
Interest on General Debt	2,003	57	4.5
Judicial and Legal	167	4	0.3
Libraries	1,683	48	3.8
Parking	0	0	0.0
Parks and Recreation	1,743	50	3.9
Police Protection	5,215	149	11.9
Public Welfare	0	0	0.0
Sewerage	1,366	39	3.1
Solid Waste Management	1,367	39	3.1
Veterans' Services	0	0	0.0
Liquor Store	0	0	0.0
Utility	5,745	165	13.1
Employee Retirement	0	0	0.0

Source: U.S Census Bureau, State & Local Government Finances 2012

DEMOGRAPHICS

Population Growth

Area	1990 Census	2000 Census	2010 Census	2014* Estimate	Population Growth (%) 1990-2014	2010-2014
City	21,274	26,294	34,768	35,809	68.3	3.0
MSA[1]	210,640	237,230	257,940	261,429	24.1	1.4
U.S.	248,709,873	281,421,906	308,745,538	314,107,084	26.3	1.7

Note: (1) Figures cover the Cedar Rapids, IA Metropolitan Statistical Area—see Appendix B for areas included; (*) 2010-2014 5-year estimated population
Source: U.S. Census Bureau, 1990 Census, Census 2000, Census 2010, 2010-2014 American Community Survey 5-Year Estimates

Household Size

Area	Persons in Household (%) One	Two	Three	Four	Five	Six	Seven or More	Average Household Size
City	28.6	34.3	15.8	13.0	5.7	1.5	0.7	2.46
MSA[1]	28.4	36.3	14.4	13.0	4.8	1.9	0.9	2.42
U.S.	27.5	33.5	15.8	13.1	6.0	2.3	1.4	2.64

Note: (1) Figures cover the Cedar Rapids, IA Metropolitan Statistical Area—see Appendix B for areas included
Source: U.S. Census Bureau, 2010-2014 American Community Survey 5-Year Estimates

Race

Area	White Alone[2] (%)	Black Alone[2] (%)	Asian Alone[2] (%)	AIAN[3] Alone[2] (%)	NHOPI[4] Alone[2] (%)	Other Race Alone[2] (%)	Two or More Races (%)
City	93.6	1.9	2.0	0.2	0.0	0.7	1.6
MSA[1]	91.2	3.8	1.6	0.3	0.0	0.9	2.1
U.S.	73.8	12.6	5.0	0.8	0.2	4.7	2.9

Note: (1) Figures cover the Cedar Rapids, IA Metropolitan Statistical Area—see Appendix B for areas included; (2) Alone is defined as not being in combination with one or more other races; (3) American Indian and Alaska Native; (4) Native Hawaiian and Other Pacific Islander
Source: U.S. Census Bureau, 2010-2014 American Community Survey 5-Year Estimates

Hispanic or Latino Origin

Area	Total (%)	Mexican (%)	Puerto Rican (%)	Cuban (%)	Other (%)
City	1.5	0.7	0.1	0.1	0.7
MSA[1]	2.5	1.9	0.1	0.0	0.5
U.S.	16.9	10.8	1.6	0.6	3.8

Note: Persons of Hispanic or Latino origin can be of any race; (1) Figures cover the Cedar Rapids, IA Metropolitan Statistical Area—see Appendix B for areas included
Source: U.S. Census Bureau, 2010-2014 American Community Survey 5-Year Estimates

Ancestry

Area	German	Irish	English	American	Italian	Polish	French[2]	Scottish	Dutch
City	39.4	16.9	11.1	5.7	2.9	2.0	2.4	2.3	2.7
MSA[1]	40.5	16.3	9.2	5.9	1.8	1.4	2.6	1.7	2.5
U.S.	14.9	10.8	8.0	7.1	5.5	3.0	2.7	1.7	1.4

Note: Figures are the percentage of the total population reporting a particular ancestry. The nine most commonly reported ancestries in the U.S. are shown. Figures include multiple ancestries (e.g. if a person reported being Irish and Italian, they were included in both columns); (1) Figures cover the Cedar Rapids, IA Metropolitan Statistical Area—see Appendix B for areas included; (2) Excludes Basque
Source: U.S. Census Bureau, 2010-2014 American Community Survey 5-Year Estimates

Foreign-Born Population

Area	Percent of Population Born in								
	Any Foreign Country	Asia	Mexico	Europe	Carribean	Central America[2]	South America	Africa	Canada
City	3.9	1.7	0.3	0.4	0.3	0.3	0.1	0.4	0.4
MSA[1]	2.9	1.3	0.4	0.4	0.1	0.1	0.1	0.3	0.2
U.S.	13.1	3.8	3.7	1.5	1.2	1.0	0.9	0.6	0.3

Note: (1) Figures cover the Cedar Rapids, IA Metropolitan Statistical Area—see Appendix B for areas included; (2) Excludes Mexico.
Source: U.S. Census Bureau, 2010-2014 American Community Survey 5-Year Estimates

Marital Status

Area	Never Married	Now Married[2]	Separated	Widowed	Divorced
City	24.7	54.1	1.5	4.8	14.8
MSA[1]	28.4	52.8	1.5	5.7	11.5
U.S.	32.5	48.4	2.2	5.9	10.9

Note: Figures are percentages and cover the population 15 years of age and older; (1) Figures cover the Cedar Rapids, IA Metropolitan Statistical Area—see Appendix B for areas included; (2) Excludes separated
Source: U.S. Census Bureau, 2010-2014 American Community Survey 5-Year Estimates

Disability Status

Area	All Ages	Under 18 Years Old	18 to 64 Years Old	65 Years and Over
City	7.5	2.9	6.6	20.8
MSA[1]	10.3	4.1	8.4	29.8
U.S.	12.3	4.1	10.2	36.3

Note: Figures show percent of the civilian noninstitutionalized population that reported having a disability. Disability status is determined from from six types of difficulty: vision, hearing, cognitive, ambulatory, self-care, and independent living. For children under 5 years old, hearing and vision difficulty are used to determine disability status. For children between the ages of 5 and 14, disability status is determined from hearing, vision, cognitive, ambulatory, and self-care difficulties. For people aged 15 years and older, they are considered to have a disability if they have difficulty with any one of the six difficulty types; (1) Figures cover the Cedar Rapids, IA Metropolitan Statistical Area—see Appendix B for areas included.
Source: U.S. Census Bureau, 2010-2014 American Community Survey 5-Year Estimates

Age

Area	Percent of Population									Median Age
	Under Age 5	Age 5–19	Age 20–34	Age 35–44	Age 45–54	Age 55–64	Age 65–74	Age 75–84	Age 85+	
City	5.9	21.7	20.1	14.1	14.3	10.5	7.4	4.4	1.7	37.1
MSA[1]	6.3	20.4	19.8	12.9	14.2	12.3	7.5	4.7	2.0	37.8
U.S.	6.4	19.9	20.6	13.0	14.1	12.3	7.6	4.3	1.9	37.4

Note: (1) Figures cover the Cedar Rapids, IA Metropolitan Statistical Area—see Appendix B for areas included
Source: U.S. Census Bureau, 2010-2014 American Community Survey 5-Year Estimates

Gender

Area	Males	Females	Males per 100 Females
City	17,767	18,042	98.5
MSA[1]	129,625	131,804	98.3
U.S.	154,515,159	159,591,925	96.8

Note: (1) Figures cover the Cedar Rapids, IA Metropolitan Statistical Area—see Appendix B for areas included
Source: U.S. Census Bureau, 2010-2014 American Community Survey 5-Year Estimates

Religious Groups by Family

Area	Catholic	Baptist	Non-Den.	Methodist[2]	Lutheran	LDS[3]	Pente-costal	Presby-terian[4]	Muslim[5]	Judaism
MSA[1]	18.8	2.3	3.0	7.3	11.3	0.8	1.8	3.2	0.5	0.1
U.S.	19.1	9.3	4.0	4.0	2.3	2.0	1.9	1.6	0.8	0.7

Note: Figures are the number of adherents as a percentage of the total population; (1) Figures cover the Cedar Rapids, IA Metropolitan Statistical Area—see Appendix B for areas included; (2) Methodist/Pietist; (3) Latter Day Saints; (4) Reformed; (5) Figures are estimates
Source: Association of Statisticians of American Religious Bodies, 2010 U.S. Religion Census: Religious Congregations & Membership Study

Religious Groups by Tradition

Area	Catholic	Evangelical Protestant	Mainline Protestant	Other Tradition	Black Protestant	Orthodox
MSA[1]	18.8	13.7	17.5	1.9	0.1	0.2
U.S.	19.1	16.2	7.3	4.3	1.6	0.3

Note: Figures are the number of adherents as a percentage of the total population; (1) Figures cover the Cedar Rapids, IA Metropolitan Statistical Area—see Appendix B for areas included
Source: Association of Statisticians of American Religious Bodies, 2010 U.S. Religion Census: Religious Congregations & Membership Study

ECONOMY

Gross Metropolitan Product

Area	2013	2014	2015	2016	Rank[2]
MSA[1]	17.2	17.7	18.2	19.0	128

Note: Figures are in billions of dollars; (1) Figures cover the Cedar Rapids, IA Metropolitan Statistical Area—see Appendix B for areas included; (2) Rank is based on 2016 data and ranges from 1 to 381
Source: The U.S. Conference of Mayors, U.S. Metro Economies: GMP and Employment 2014-2016, June 2015

Economic Growth

Area	2011-13 (%)	2014 (%)	2015 (%)	2016 (%)	Rank[2]
MSA[1]	1.3	1.1	1.4	2.7	135
U.S.	2.2	2.4	2.3	2.9	–

Note: Figures are real gross metropolitan product (GMP) growth rates and represent annual average percent change; (1) Figures cover the Cedar Rapids, IA Metropolitan Statistical Area—see Appendix B for areas included; (2) Rank is based on 2016 data and ranges from 1 to 381
Source: The U.S. Conference of Mayors, U.S. Metro Economies: GMP and Employment 2014-2016, June 2015

Metropolitan Area Exports

Area	2009	2010	2011	2012	2013	2014	Rank[2]
MSA[1]	734.7	749.4	880.8	889.1	930.2	878.9	172

Note: Figures are in millions of dollars; (1) Figures cover the Cedar Rapids, IA Metropolitan Statistical Area—see Appendix B for areas included; (2) Rank is based on 2014 data and ranges from 1 to 385
Source: U.S. Department of Commerce, International Trade Administration, Office of Trade & Industry Information, Manufacturing & Services, data extracted March 10, 2016

Building Permits

Area	Single-Family			Multi-Family			Total		
	2014	2015p	Pct. Chg.	2014	2015p	Pct. Chg.	2014	2015p	Pct. Chg.
City	146	180	23.3	75	261	248.0	221	441	99.5
MSA[1]	644	489	-24.1	237	332	40.1	881	821	-6.8
U.S.	640,300	690,800	7.9	411,800	487,600	18.4	1,052,100	1,178,400	12.0

Note: (1) Figures cover the Cedar Rapids, IA Metropolitan Statistical Area—see Appendix B for areas included; Figures represent new, privately-owned housing units authorized (unadjusted data); All permit data are based on estimates with imputation; (p) preliminary data.
Source: U.S. Census Bureau, Manufacturing, Mining, and Construction Statistics, Building Permits, 2014, 2015

Bankruptcy Filings

Area	Business Filings 2014	Business Filings 2015	Business Filings % Chg.	Nonbusiness Filings 2014	Nonbusiness Filings 2015	Nonbusiness Filings % Chg.
Linn County	5	8	60.0	347	315	-9.2
U.S.	26,983	24,735	-8.3	909,812	819,760	-9.9

Note: Business filings include Chapter 7, Chapter 11, Chapter 12, and Chapter 13; Nonbusiness filings include Chapter 7, Chapter 11, and Chapter 13
Source: Administrative Office of the U.S. Courts, Business and Nonbusiness Bankruptcy, County Cases Commenced by Chapter of the Bankruptcy Code, During the 12- Month Period Ending December 31, 2014 and Business and Nonbusiness Bankruptcy, County Cases Commenced by Chapter of the Bankruptcy Code, During the 12- Month Period Ending December 31, 2015

Housing Vacancy Rates

Area	Gross Vacancy Rate[2] (%)			Year-Round Vacancy Rate[3] (%)			Rental Vacancy Rate[4] (%)			Homeowner Vacancy Rate[5] (%)		
	2013	2014	2015	2013	2014	2015	2013	2014	2015	2013	2014	2015
MSA[1]	n/a	n/a	n/a	n/a	n/a	n/a	n/a	n/a	n/a	n/a	n/a	n/a
U.S.	13.6	13.4	12.9	10.7	10.4	10.0	8.3	7.6	7.1	2.0	1.9	1.8

Note: (1) Figures cover the Cedar Rapids, IA Metropolitan Statistical Area—see Appendix B for areas included; (2) The percentage of the total housing inventory that is vacant; (3) The percentage of the housing inventory (excluding seasonal units) that is year-round vacant; (4) The percentage of rental inventory that is vacant for rent; (5) The percentage of homeowner inventory that is vacant for sale; n/a not available
Source: U.S. Census Bureau, Housing Vacancies and Homeownership Annual Statistics: 2015

INCOME

Income

Area	Per Capita ($)	Median Household ($)	Average Household ($)
City	31,037	62,532	75,025
MSA[1]	30,337	59,000	73,992
U.S.	28,555	53,482	74,596

Note: (1) Figures cover the Cedar Rapids, IA Metropolitan Statistical Area—see Appendix B for areas included
Source: U.S. Census Bureau, 2010-2014 American Community Survey 5-Year Estimates

Household Income Distribution

Area	Percent of Households Earning: Under $15,000	$15,000 -24,999	$25,000 -34,999	$35,000 -49,999	$50,000 -74,999	$75,000 -99,000	$100,000 -149,999	$150,000 and up
City	7.5	10.2	9.1	13.3	19.1	16.4	16.0	8.3
MSA[1]	9.3	9.5	9.7	13.3	20.1	15.2	14.8	8.2
U.S.	12.5	10.7	10.2	13.5	17.8	12.2	13.0	10.0

Note: (1) Figures cover the Cedar Rapids, IA Metropolitan Statistical Area—see Appendix B for areas included
Source: U.S. Census Bureau, 2010-2014 American Community Survey 5-Year Estimates

Poverty Rate

Area	All Ages	Under 18 Years Old	18 to 64 Years Old	65 Years and Over
City	6.3	6.4	6.4	5.2
MSA[1]	9.5	11.2	9.7	5.8
U.S.	15.6	21.9	14.6	9.4

Note: Figures are percentage of people whose income during the past 12 months was below the poverty level; (1) Figures cover the Cedar Rapids, IA Metropolitan Statistical Area—see Appendix B for areas included
Source: U.S. Census Bureau, 2010-2014 American Community Survey 5-Year Estimates

EMPLOYMENT

Labor Force and Employment

Area	Civilian Labor Force Dec. 2014	Civilian Labor Force Dec. 2015	Civilian Labor Force % Chg.	Workers Employed Dec. 2014	Workers Employed Dec. 2015	Workers Employed % Chg.
City	19,548	19,424	-0.6	18,807	18,820	0.0
MSA[1]	144,082	143,099	-0.6	137,538	137,950	0.3
U.S.	155,521,000	157,245,000	1.1	147,190,000	149,703,000	1.7

Note: Data is not seasonally adjusted and covers workers 16 years of age and older; (1) Figures cover the Cedar Rapids, IA Metropolitan Statistical Area—see Appendix B for areas included
Source: Bureau of Labor Statistics, Local Area Unemployment Statistics

Unemployment Rate

Area	2015											
	Jan.	Feb.	Mar.	Apr.	May	Jun.	Jul.	Aug.	Sep.	Oct.	Nov.	Dec.
City	4.1	3.8	3.6	3.0	3.0	3.0	2.9	2.8	2.9	2.7	2.9	3.1
MSA[1]	5.1	4.8	4.4	3.7	3.5	3.7	3.6	3.6	3.5	3.3	3.3	3.6
U.S.	6.1	5.8	5.6	5.1	5.3	5.5	5.6	5.2	4.9	4.8	4.8	4.8

Note: Data is not seasonally adjusted and covers workers 16 years of age and older; (1) Figures cover the Cedar Rapids, IA Metropolitan Statistical Area—see Appendix B for areas included
Source: Bureau of Labor Statistics, Local Area Unemployment Statistics

Employment by Occupation

Occupation Classification	City (%)	MSA[1] (%)	U.S. (%)
Management, Business, Science, and Arts	42.2	36.9	36.4
Natural Resources, Construction, and Maintenance	8.2	9.0	9.0
Production, Transportation, and Material Moving	10.8	14.0	12.1
Sales and Office	22.8	25.4	24.4
Service	15.9	14.7	18.2

Note: Figures cover employed civilians 16 years of age and older; (1) Figures cover the Cedar Rapids, IA Metropolitan Statistical Area—see Appendix B for areas included
Source: U.S. Census Bureau, 2010-2014 American Community Survey 5-Year Estimates

Employment by Industry

Sector	MSA[1]		U.S.
	Number of Employees	Percent of Total	Percent of Total
Construction, Mining, and Logging	7,800	5.4	5.0
Education and Health Services	20,400	14.1	15.7
Financial Activities	10,900	7.5	5.7
Government	16,500	11.4	15.5
Information	4,300	2.9	1.9
Leisure and Hospitality	11,700	8.1	10.4
Manufacturing	20,300	14.1	8.6
Other Services	5,400	3.7	3.9
Professional and Business Services	13,300	9.2	13.9
Retail Trade	15,600	10.8	11.3
Transportation, Warehousing, and Utilities	11,900	8.2	3.9
Wholesale Trade	5,700	3.9	4.1

Note: Figures are non-farm employment as of December 2015. Figures are not seasonally adjusted and include workers 16 years of age and older; (1) Figures cover the Cedar Rapids, IA Metropolitan Statistical Area—see Appendix B for areas included; n/a not available
Source: Bureau of Labor Statistics, Current Employment Statistics, Employment, Hours, and Earnings

Occupations with Greatest Projected Employment Growth: 2012 – 2022

Occupation[1]	2012 Employment	2022 Projected Employment	Numeric Employment Change	Percent Employment Change
Heavy and Tractor-Trailer Truck Drivers	42,680	50,720	8,040	18.8
Registered Nurses	32,490	38,130	5,640	17.3
Combined Food Preparation and Serving Workers, Including Fast Food	32,200	37,220	5,020	15.6
Retail Salespersons	47,020	51,680	4,660	9.9
Customer Service Representatives	24,670	28,850	4,180	17.0
Laborers and Freight, Stock, and Material Movers, Hand	24,870	28,420	3,550	14.3
Childcare Workers	17,050	20,550	3,500	20.5
Home Health Aides	10,310	13,720	3,410	33.1
Janitors and Cleaners, Except Maids and Housekeeping Cleaners	26,870	30,230	3,360	12.5
Cashiers	42,590	45,940	3,350	7.9

Note: Projections cover Iowa; (1) Sorted by numeric employment change
Source: www.projectionscentral.com, State Occupational Projections, 2012–2022 Long-Term Projections

Fastest Growing Occupations: 2012 – 2022

Occupation[1]	2012 Employment	2022 Projected Employment	Numeric Employment Change	Percent Employment Change
Interpreters and Translators	520	770	250	48.1
Diagnostic Medical Sonographers	540	780	240	44.9
Occupational Therapy Assistants	360	520	160	44.3
Information Security Analysts	1,950	2,800	850	43.7
Insulation Workers, Mechanical	360	510	150	41.7
Actuaries	540	750	210	39.1
Meeting, Convention, and Event Planners	440	610	170	38.8
Physical Therapist Assistants	800	1,110	310	38.0
Personal Care Aides	6,050	8,320	2,270	37.4
Health Specialties Teachers, Postsecondary	1,830	2,480	650	35.6

Note: Projections cover Iowa; (1) Sorted by percent employment change and excludes occupations with numeric employment change less than 100
Source: www.projectionscentral.com, State Occupational Projections, 2012–2022 Long-Term Projections

Average Wages

Occupation	$/Hr.	Occupation	$/Hr.
Accountants and Auditors	30.76	Maids and Housekeeping Cleaners	10.08
Automotive Mechanics	18.00	Maintenance and Repair Workers	21.72
Bookkeepers	17.27	Marketing Managers	59.45
Carpenters	19.92	Nuclear Medicine Technologists	n/a
Cashiers	9.25	Nurses, Licensed Practical	19.32
Clerks, General Office	16.58	Nurses, Registered	25.92
Clerks, Receptionists/Information	13.95	Nursing Assistants	12.06
Clerks, Shipping/Receiving	16.70	Packers and Packagers, Hand	9.55
Computer Programmers	32.35	Physical Therapists	35.19
Computer Systems Analysts	36.78	Postal Service Mail Carriers	24.78
Computer User Support Specialists	20.74	Real Estate Brokers	n/a
Cooks, Restaurant	10.31	Retail Salespersons	11.59
Dentists	105.89	Sales Reps., Exc. Tech./Scientific	31.01
Electrical Engineers	41.67	Sales Reps., Tech./Scientific	39.26
Electricians	28.69	Secretaries, Exc. Legal/Med./Exec.	14.45
Financial Managers	55.29	Security Guards	n/a
First-Line Supervisors/Managers, Sales	17.28	Surgeons	n/a
Food Preparation Workers	9.88	Teacher Assistants*	13.25
General and Operations Managers	45.25	Teachers, Elementary School*	25.40
Hairdressers/Cosmetologists	9.64	Teachers, Secondary School*	25.06
Internists	n/a	Telemarketers	10.08
Janitors and Cleaners	14.53	Truck Drivers, Heavy/Tractor-Trailer	19.66
Landscaping/Groundskeeping Workers	13.78	Truck Drivers, Light/Delivery Svcs.	16.43
Lawyers	50.42	Waiters and Waitresses	9.44

Note: Wage data covers the Cedar Rapids, IA Metropolitan Statistical Area—see Appendix B for areas included; (*) Hourly wages for elementary/secondary school teachers and teacher assistants were calculated by the editors from annual wage data based on a 40 hour work week; n/a not available.
Source: Bureau of Labor Statistics, Metro Area Occupational Employment and Wage Estimates, May 2015

TAXES

State Corporate Income Tax Rates

State	Tax Rate (%)	Income Brackets ($)	Num. of Brackets	Financial Institution Tax Rate (%)[a]	Federal Income Tax Ded.
Iowa	6.0 - 12.0	25,000 - 250,001	4	5.0	Yes (k)

Note: Tax rates as of January 1, 2016; (a) Rates listed are the corporate income tax rate applied to financial institutions or excise taxes based on income. Some states have other taxes based upon the value of deposits or shares; (k) 50% of the federal income tax is deductible.
Source: Federation of Tax Administrators, "State Corporate Income Tax Rates, 2016"

State Individual Income Tax Rates

State	Tax Rate (%)	Income Brackets ($)	Num. of Brackets	Personal Exempt. ($)[1] Single	Personal Exempt. ($)[1] Dependents	Fed. Inc. Tax Ded.
Iowa (a)	0.36 - 8.98	1,554 - 69,930	9	40 (c)	40 (c)	Yes

Note: Tax rates as of January 1, 2016; Local- and county-level taxes are not included; n/a not applicable; (1) Married joint filers generally receive double the single exemption; (a) 18 states have statutory provision for automatically adjusting to the rate of inflation the dollar values of the income tax brackets, standard deductions, and/or personal exemptions. Massachusetts, Michigan, and Nebraska index the personal exemptiononly. Oregon does not index the income brackets for $125,000 and over. Maine has suspended indexing for 2014 and 2015; (c) The personal exemption takes the form of a tax credit instead of a deduction
Source: Federation of Tax Administrators, "State Individual Income Tax Rates, 2016"

Various State and Local Tax Rates

State	State and Local Sales and Use (%)	State Sales and Use (%)	Gasoline[1] (¢/gal.)	Cigarette[2] ($/pack)	Spirits[3] ($/gal.)	Wine[4] ($/gal.)	Beer[5] ($/gal.)
Iowa	7.00	6.0	32	1.36	12.52 (g)	1.75 (l)	0.19 (q)

Note: All tax rates as of January 1, 2016; (1) The American Petroleum Institute has developed a methodology for determining the average tax rate on a gallon of fuel. Rates may include any of the following: excise taxes, environmental fees, storage tank fees, other fees or taxes, general sales tax, and local taxes. In states where gasoline is subject to the general sales tax, or where the fuel tax is based on the average sale price, the average rate determined by API is sensitive to changes in the price of gasoline. States that fully or partially apply general sales taxes to gasoline: CA, CO, GA, IL, IN, MI, NY; (2) The federal excise tax of $1.0066 per pack and local taxes are not included; (3) Rates are those applicable to off-premise sales of 40% alcohol by volume (a.b.v.) distilled spirits in 750ml containers. Local excise taxes are excluded; (4) Rates are those applicable to off-premise sales of 11% a.b.v. non-carbonated wine in 750ml containers; (5) Rates are those applicable to off-premise sales of 4.7% a.b.v. beer in 12 ounce containers; (g) Control states, where the government controls all sales. Products can be subject to ad valorem mark-up as well as excise taxes; (l) Different rates also applicable according to alcohol content, place of production, size of container, place purchased (on- or off-premise or on board airlines) or type of wine (carbonated, vermouth, etc.); (q) Different rates are also applicable according to alcohol content, place of production, size of container, or place purchased (on- or off-premise or onboard airlines).
Source: Tax Foundation, 2016 Facts & Figures: How Does Your State Compare?

State Business Tax Climate Index Rankings

State	Overall Rank	Corporate Tax Rank	Individual Income Tax Rank	Sales Tax Rank	Unemployment Insurance Tax Rank	Property Tax Rank
Iowa	40	49	32	24	34	40

Note: The index is a measure of how each state's tax laws affect economic performance. The lower the rank, the more favorable a state's tax system is for business. States without a given tax are given a ranking of 1. The scores/rankings for the District of Columbia do not affect other states. The 2016 index represents the tax climate as of July 1, 2015 (the beginning of Fiscal Year 2016).
Source: Tax Foundation, State Business Tax Climate Index 2016

TRANSPORTATION

Means of Transportation to Work

Area	Car/Truck/Van: Drove Alone	Car/Truck/Van: Car-pooled	Public Transportation: Bus	Public Transportation: Subway	Public Transportation: Railroad	Bicycle	Walked	Other Means	Worked at Home
City	85.8	8.1	0.9	0.0	0.0	0.3	1.1	0.8	3.0
MSA[1]	82.4	8.9	0.8	0.0	0.0	0.4	2.5	1.0	3.9
U.S.	76.4	9.6	2.6	1.8	0.6	0.6	2.8	1.3	4.4

Note: Figures are percentages and cover workers 16 years of age and older; (1) Figures cover the Cedar Rapids, IA Metropolitan Statistical Area—see Appendix B for areas included
Source: U.S. Census Bureau, 2010-2014 American Community Survey 5-Year Estimates

Travel Time to Work

Area	Less Than 10 Minutes	10 to 19 Minutes	20 to 29 Minutes	30 to 44 Minutes	45 to 59 Minutes	60 to 89 Minutes	90 Minutes or More
City	16.5	37.5	29.5	9.7	3.8	2.2	0.7
MSA[1]	19.3	38.8	21.0	13.6	4.1	2.1	1.2
U.S.	13.3	29.6	21.0	20.2	7.7	5.7	2.6

Note: Figures are percentages and include workers 16 years old and over; (1) Figures cover the Cedar Rapids, IA Metropolitan Statistical Area—see Appendix B for areas included
Source: U.S. Census Bureau, 2010-2014 American Community Survey 5-Year Estimates

Freeway Travel Time Index

Area	1985	1990	1995	2000	2005	2010	2014
Urban Area Rank[1,2]	n/a	n/a	n/a	n/a	n/a	n/a	n/a
Urban Area Index[1]	n/a	n/a	n/a	n/a	n/a	n/a	n/a
Average Index[3]	1.09	1.11	1.14	1.17	1.20	1.19	1.20

Note: Freeway Travel Time Index—the ratio of travel time in the peak period to the travel time at free-flow conditions. For example, a value of 1.30 indicates a 20-minute free-flow trip takes 26 minutes in the peak (20 minutes x 1.30 = 26 minutes); (1) Data for the Cedar Rapids, IA urban area was not available; (2) Rank is based on 101 urban areas (#1 = highest travel time index); (3) Average of 101 urban areas
Source: Texas Transportation Institute, 2015 Urban Mobility Scorecard, August 2015

Freeway Commuter Stress Index

Area	1985	1990	1995	2000	2005	2010	2014
Urban Area Rank[1,2]	n/a	n/a	n/a	n/a	n/a	n/a	n/a
Urban Area Index[1]	n/a	n/a	n/a	n/a	n/a	n/a	n/a
Average Index[3]	1.13	1.16	1.19	1.22	1.25	1.24	1.25

Note: The Freeway Commuter Stress Index is the same as the Freeway Travel Time Index (see table above) except that it includes only the travel in the peak directions during the peak periods; the TTI includes travel in all directions during the peak period. Thus, the CSI is more indicative of the work trip experienced by each commuter on a daily basis. (1) Data for the Cedar Rapids, IA urban area was not available; (2) Rank is based on 101 urban areas (#1 = highest stress index); (3) Average of 101 urban areas
Source: Texas Transportation Institute, 2015 Urban Mobility Scorecard, August 2015

Living Environment

COST OF LIVING

Cost of Living Index

Composite Index	Groceries	Housing	Utilities	Transportation	Health Care	Misc. Goods/ Services
94.7	95.6	85.2	105.9	95.1	100.6	97.9

Note: The Cost of Living Index measures regional differences in the cost of consumer goods and services, excluding taxes and non-consumer expenditures, for professional and managerial households in the top income quintile. It is based on more than 50,000 prices covering almost 60 different items for which prices are collected three times a year by chambers of commerce, economic development organizations or university applied economic centers in each participating urban area. The numbers shown should be read as a percentage above or below the national average of 100. For example, a value of 115.4 in the groceries column indicates that grocery prices are 15.4% higher than the national average. Small differences in the index numbers should not be interpreted as significant; Figures cover the Cedar Rapids IA urban area.
Source: The Council for Community and Economic Research, ACCRA Cost of Living Index, 2015

Grocery Prices

Area[1]	T-Bone Steak ($/pound)	Frying Chicken ($/pound)	Whole Milk ($/half gal.)	Eggs ($/dozen)	Orange Juice ($/64 oz.)	Coffee ($/11.5 oz.)
City[2]	9.22	1.79	2.28	2.16	3.58	4.00
Avg.	10.99	1.43	2.25	2.26	3.58	4.48
Min.	7.16	0.98	1.30	1.35	2.88	2.98
Max.	14.13	2.43	3.85	4.81	6.39	7.56

Note: (1) Values for the local area are compared with the average, minimum and maximum values for all 292 areas in the Cost of Living Index; (2) Figures cover the Cedar Rapids IA urban area; **T-Bone Steak** *(price per pound);* **Frying Chicken** *(price per pound, whole fryer);* **Whole Milk** *(half gallon carton);* **Eggs** *(price per dozen, Grade A, large);* **Orange Juice** *(64 oz. Tropicana or Florida Natural);* **Coffee** *(11.5 oz. can, vacuum-packed, Maxwell House, Hills Bros, or Folgers).*
Source: The Council for Community and Economic Research, ACCRA Cost of Living Index, 2015

Housing and Utility Costs

Area[1]	New Home Price ($)	Apartment Rent ($/month)	All Electric ($/month)	Part Electric ($/month)	Other Energy ($/month)	Telephone ($/month)
City[2]	267,450	776	-	125.54	57.75	29.00
Avg.	312,874	945	179.30	95.07	72.96	28.11
Min.	178,682	479	116.28	43.14	26.46	10.01
Max.	1,472,476	3,984	504.25	189.44	421.11	43.06

Note: (1) Values for the local area are compared with the average, minimum and maximum values for all 292 areas in the Cost of Living Index; (2) Figures cover the Cedar Rapids IA urban area; **New Home Price** *(2,400 sf living area, 8,000 sf lot, in urban area with full utilities);* **Apartment Rent** *(950 sf 2 bedroom/1.5 or 2 bath, unfurnished, excluding all utilities except water);* **All Electric** *(average monthly cost for an all-electric home);* **Part Electric** *(average monthly cost for a part-electric home);* **Other Energy** *(average monthly cost for natural gas, fuel oil, coal, wood, and any other forms of energy except electricity);* **Telephone** *(price includes basic monthly rate for a private residential line plus additional local usage charges incurred by a family of four).*
Source: The Council for Community and Economic Research, ACCRA Cost of Living Index, 2015

Health Care, Transportation, and Other Costs

Area[1]	Doctor ($/visit)	Dentist ($/visit)	Optometrist ($/visit)	Gasoline ($/gallon)	Beauty Salon ($/visit)	Men's Shirt ($)
City[2]	131.25	73.83	126.22	2.25	35.73	22.57
Avg.	105.15	89.02	99.78	2.38	35.30	28.10
Min.	66.87	56.09	48.53	1.95	18.91	13.38
Max.	182.34	150.36	228.33	4.09	67.91	63.80

Note: (1) Values for the local area are compared with the average, minimum and maximum values for all 292 areas in the Cost of Living Index; (2) Figures cover the Cedar Rapids IA urban area; **Doctor** *(general practitioners routine exam of an established patient);* **Dentist** *(adult teeth cleaning and periodic oral examination);* **Optometrist** *(full vision eye exam for established adult patient);* **Gasoline** *(one gallon regular unleaded, national brand, including all taxes, cash price at self-service pump if available);* **Beauty Salon** *(woman's shampoo, trim, and blow-dry);* **Men's Shirt** *(cotton/polyester dress shirt, pinpoint weave, long sleeves).*
Source: The Council for Community and Economic Research, ACCRA Cost of Living Index, 2015

HOUSING

House Price Index (HPI)

Area	National Ranking[2]	Quarterly Change (%)	One-Year Change (%)	Five-Year Change (%)
MSA[1]	234	0.40	1.60	4.30
U.S.[3]	-	1.45	5.76	22.85

Note: The HPI is a weighted repeat sales index. It measures average price changes in repeat sales or refinancings on the same properties. This information is obtained by reviewing repeat mortgage transactions on single-family properties whose mortgages have been purchased or securitized by Fannie Mae or Freddie Mac in January 1975; (1) Cedar Rapids Metropolitan Statistical Area—see Appendix B for areas included; (2) Rankings are based on annual percentage change for all metro areas containing at least 15,000 transactions over the last 10 years and ranges from 1 to 266; (3) figures based on a weighted average of Census Division estimates using a seasonally adjusted, purchase-only index; all figures are for the period ending December 31, 2015

Source: Federal Housing Finance Agency, House Price Index, February 25, 2016

Median Single-Family Home Prices

Area	2013	2014	2015p	Percent Change 2014 to 2015
MSA[1]	155.8	151.6	161.9	6.8
U.S. Average	197.4	208.9	223.9	7.2

Note: Figures are median sales prices of existing single-family homes in thousands of dollars; (p) preliminary; n/a not available; (1) Cedar Rapids, IA Metropolitan Statistical Area—see Appendix B for areas included

Source: National Association of Realtors, Median Sales Price of Existing Single-Family Homes for Metropolitan Areas, 4th Quarter 2015

Qualifying Income Based on Median Sales Price of Existing Single-Family Homes

Area	With 5% Down ($)	With 10% Down ($)	With 20% Down ($)
MSA[1]	35,033	33,189	29,501
U.S. Average	49,535	46,928	41,714

Note: Figures are preliminary; Qualifying income is based on a mortgage rate of 4.1%. Monthly principal and interest payment is limited to 25% of income; n/a not available; (1) Cedar Rapids, IA Metropolitan Statistical Area—see Appendix B for areas included

Source: National Association of Realtors, Qualifying Income Based on Median Sales Price of Existing Single-Family Homes for Metropolitan Areas, 4th Quarter 2015

Median Apartment Condo-Coop Home Prices

Area	2013	2014	2015p	Percent Change 2014 to 2015
MSA[1]	n/a	n/a	n/a	n/a
U.S. Average	194.9	204.3	210.7	3.1

Note: Figures are median sales prices of existing apartment condo-coop homes in thousands of dollars; (p) preliminary; n/a not available; (1) Cedar Rapids, IA Metropolitan Statistical Area—see Appendix B for areas included

Source: National Association of Realtors, Median Sales Price of Existing Apartment Condo-Coop Homes for Metropolitan Areas, 4th Quarter 2015

Gross Monthly Rent

Area	Under $200	$200 -299	$300 -499	$500 -749	$750 -999	$1,000 -1,499	$1,500 and up	Median ($)
City	1.4	3.4	23.0	36.5	17.2	14.0	4.4	625
MSA[1]	1.9	3.4	18.4	37.2	24.3	11.9	3.0	676
U.S.	1.5	3.2	7.4	21.0	24.1	26.9	15.9	920

Note: Figures are percentages except for Median; Gross rent is the contract rent plus the estimated average monthly cost of utilities (electricity, gas, and water and sewer) and fuels (oil, coal, kerosene, wood, etc.) if these are paid by the renter (or paid for the renter by someone else); (1) Figures cover the Cedar Rapids, IA Metropolitan Statistical Area—see Appendix B for areas included

Source: U.S. Census Bureau, 2010-2014 American Community Survey 5-Year Estimates

Homeownership Rate

Area	2008 (%)	2009 (%)	2010 (%)	2011 (%)	2012 (%)	2013 (%)	2014 (%)	2015 (%)
MSA[1]	n/a	n/a	n/a	n/a	n/a	n/a	n/a	n/a
U.S.	67.8	67.4	66.9	66.1	65.4	65.1	64.5	63.7

Note: (1) Figures cover the Cedar Rapids, IA Metropolitan Statistical Area—see Appendix B for areas included; n/a not available
Source: U.S. Census Bureau, Housing Vacancies and Homeownership Annual Statistics: 2015

Year Housing Structure Built

Area	2010 or Later	2000 -2009	1990 -1999	1980 -1989	1970 -1979	1960 -1969	1950 -1959	1940 -1949	Before 1940	Median Year
City	1.9	24.5	22.0	8.6	12.8	11.5	9.1	1.8	7.8	1988
MSA[1]	1.3	16.0	15.4	6.7	14.2	12.2	11.0	4.5	18.7	1973
U.S.	1.0	14.9	13.9	13.8	15.8	11.0	10.8	5.4	13.3	1976

Note: Figures are percentages except for Median Year; (1) Figures cover the Cedar Rapids, IA Metropolitan Statistical Area—see Appendix B for areas included
Source: U.S. Census Bureau, 2010-2014 American Community Survey 5-Year Estimates

HEALTH

Health Risk Data

Category	MSA[1] (%)	U.S. (%)
Adults aged 18–64 who have any kind of health care coverage	89.5	79.6
Adults who reported being in good or excellent health	87.3	83.1
Adults who are current smokers	19.1	19.6
Adults who are heavy drinkers[2]	7.0	6.1
Adults who are binge drinkers[3]	17.2	16.9
Adults who are overweight (BMI 25.0 - 29.9)	33.1	35.8
Adults who are obese (BMI 30.0 - 99.8)	30.3	27.6
Adults who participated in any physical activities in the past month	78.8	77.1
Adults 50+ who have ever had a sigmoidoscopy or colonoscopy	73.4	67.3
Women aged 40+ who have had a mammogram within the past two years	85.1	74.0
Men aged 40+ who have had a PSA test within the past two years	49.7	45.2
Adults aged 65+ who have had flu shot within the past year	71.2	60.1
Adults who always wear a seatbelt	95.1	93.8

Note: Data as of 2012 unless otherwise noted; (1) Figures cover the Cedar Rapids, IA Metropolitan Statistical Area—see Appendix B for areas included; (2) Heavy drinkers are classified as males having more than two drinks per day or females having more than one drink per day; (3) Binge drinkers are classified as males having five or more drinks on one occasion or females having four or more drinks on one occasion
Source: Centers for Disease Control and Prevention, Behaviorial Risk Factor Surveillance System, SMART: Selected Metropolitan/Micropolitan Area Risk Trends, 2012 (Note: the CDC has discontinued this dataset but will be releasing a replacement in mid-2016)

Chronic Health Indicators

Category	MSA[1] (%)	U.S. (%)
Adults who have ever been told they had a heart attack	3.1	4.5
Adults who have ever been told they had a stroke	1.9	2.9
Adults who have been told they currently have asthma	9.8	8.9
Adults who have ever been told they have arthritis	23.9	25.7
Adults who have ever been told they have diabetes[2]	9.8	9.7
Adults who have ever been told they had skin cancer	5.1	5.7
Adults who have ever been told they had any other types of cancer	7.0	6.5
Adults who have ever been told they have COPD	5.4	6.2
Adults who have ever been told they have kidney disease	n/a	2.5
Adults who have ever been told they have a form of depression	15.4	18.0

Note: Data as of 2012 unless otherwise noted; n/a not available; (1) Figures cover the Cedar Rapids, IA Metropolitan Statistical Area—see Appendix B for areas included; (2) Figures do not include pregnancy-related, borderline, or pre-diabetes
Source: Centers for Disease Control and Prevention, Behaviorial Risk Factor Surveillance System, SMART: Selected Metropolitan/Micropolitan Area Risk Trends, 2012 (Note: the CDC has discontinued this dataset but will be releasing a replacement in mid-2016)

Mortality Rates for the Top 10 Causes of Death in the U.S.

ICD-10[a] Sub-Chapter	ICD-10[a] Code	Age-Adjusted Mortality Rate[1] per 100,000 population	
		County[2]	U.S.
Malignant neoplasms	C00-C97	162.3	163.6
Ischaemic heart diseases	I20-I25	102.0	102.2
Other forms of heart disease	I30-I51	38.7	50.1
Chronic lower respiratory diseases	J40-J47	50.1	41.4
Organic, including symptomatic, mental disorders	F01-F09	31.7	38.5
Cerebrovascular diseases	I60-I69	29.2	36.5
Other external causes of accidental injury	W00-X59	31.7	27.5
Other degenerative diseases of the nervous system	G30-G31	26.7	26.3
Diabetes mellitus	E10-E14	16.5	21.1
Hypertensive diseases	I10-I15	12.4	19.7

Note: (a) ICD-10 = International Classification of Diseases 10th Revision; (1) Mortality rates are a three year average covering 2012-2014; (2) Figures cover Linn County.
Source: Centers for Disease Control and Prevention, National Center for Health Statistics. Underlying Cause of Death 1999-2014 on CDC WONDER Online Database, released 2015.

Mortality Rates for Selected Causes of Death

ICD-10[a] Sub-Chapter	ICD-10[a] Code	Age-Adjusted Mortality Rate[1] per 100,000 population	
		County[2]	U.S.
Assault	X85-Y09	Unreliable	5.1
Diseases of the liver	K70-K76	14.4	13.5
Human immunodeficiency virus (HIV) disease	B20-B24	Suppressed	2.1
Influenza and pneumonia	J09-J18	12.6	15.2
Intentional self-harm	X60-X84	13.3	12.7
Malnutrition	E40-E46	Suppressed	0.9
Obesity and other hyperalimentation	E65-E68	Unreliable	1.9
Renal failure	N17-N19	7.8	13.0
Transport accidents	V01-V99	9.2	11.6
Viral hepatitis	B15-B19	Suppressed	2.1

Note: (a) ICD-10 = International Classification of Diseases 10th Revision; (1) Mortality rates are a three year average covering 2012-2014; (2) Figures cover Linn County; Data are Suppressed when the data meet the criteria for confidentiality constraints; Mortality rates are flagged as Unreliable when the rate would be calculated with a numerator of 20 or less.
Source: Centers for Disease Control and Prevention, National Center for Health Statistics. Underlying Cause of Death 1999-2014 on CDC WONDER Online Database, released 2015.

Health Insurance Coverage

Area	With Health Insurance	With Private Health Insurance	With Public Health Insurance	Without Health Insurance	Population Under Age 18 Without Health Insurance
City	92.9	78.8	26.6	7.1	1.6
MSA[1]	93.3	78.5	27.9	6.7	2.8
U.S.	85.8	65.8	31.1	14.2	7.1

Note: Figures are percentages that cover the civilian noninstitutionalized population; (1) Figures cover the Cedar Rapids, IA Metropolitan Statistical Area—see Appendix B for areas included
Source: U.S. Census Bureau, 2010-2014 American Community Survey 5-Year Estimates

Number of Medical Professionals

Area	MDs[3]	DOs[3,4]	Dentists	Podiatrists	Chiropractors	Optometrists
County[1] (number)	411	41	151	17	120	34
County[1] (rate[2])	190.2	19.0	69.3	7.8	55.1	15.6
U.S. (rate[2])	272.5	20.9	64.7	5.8	25.9	15.2

Note: Data as of 2014 unless noted; (1) Data covers Linn County; (2) Rate per 100,000 population; (3) Data as of 2013 and includes all active, non-federal physicians; (4) Doctor of Osteopathic Medicine
Source: U.S. Department of Health and Human Services, Health Resources and Services Administration, Bureau of Health Professions, Area Resource File (ARF) 2014-2015

EDUCATION

Public School District Statistics

District Name	Schls	Pupils	Pupil/ Teacher Ratio	Minority Pupils[1] (%)	Free Lunch Eligible[2] (%)	IEP[3] (%)
Linn-Mar Comm School District	10	7,063	15.9	16.2	15.7	9.7
Marion ISD	6	1,904	11.4	13.1	22.5	12.3

Note: Table includes school districts with 100 or more students; (1) Percentage of students that are not non-Hispanic white; (2) Percentage of students that are eligible for the free lunch program; (3) Percentage of students that have an Individualized Education Program.
Source: U.S. Department of Education, National Center for Education Statistics, Common Core of Data, Local Education Agency (School District) Universe Survey: School Year 2013-2014; U.S. Department of Education, National Center for Education Statistics, Common Core of Data, Public Elementary/Secondary School Universe Survey: School Year 2013-2014

Highest Level of Education

Area	Less than H.S.	H.S. Diploma	Some College, No Deg.	Associate Degree	Bachelor's Degree	Master's Degree	Prof. School Degree	Doctorate Degree
City	4.3	25.9	22.4	13.8	23.9	7.6	1.7	0.5
MSA[1]	6.3	29.4	23.3	11.9	20.4	6.6	1.5	0.8
U.S.	13.7	28.0	21.2	7.9	18.3	7.8	2.0	1.3

Note: Figures cover persons age 25 and over; (1) Figures cover the Cedar Rapids, IA Metropolitan Statistical Area—see Appendix B for areas included
Source: U.S. Census Bureau, 2010-2014 American Community Survey 5-Year Estimates

Educational Attainment by Race

Area	High School Graduate or Higher (%)					Bachelor's Degree or Higher (%)				
	Total	White	Black	Asian	Hisp.[2]	Total	White	Black	Asian	Hisp.[2]
City	95.7	96.2	89.4	87.9	78.1	33.7	33.6	17.0	61.9	32.4
MSA[1]	93.7	94.3	82.8	92.2	72.4	29.2	29.1	16.7	58.3	20.3
U.S.	86.3	88.4	83.2	85.8	64.1	29.3	30.6	19.0	50.9	13.9

Note: Figures shown cover persons 25 years old and over; (1) Figures cover the Cedar Rapids, IA Metropolitan Statistical Area—see Appendix B for areas included; (2) People of Hispanic origin can be of any race
Source: U.S. Census Bureau, 2010-2014 American Community Survey 5-Year Estimates

School Enrollment by Grade and Control

Area	Preschool (%)		Kindergarten (%)		Grades 1 - 4 (%)		Grades 5 - 8 (%)		Grades 9 - 12 (%)	
	Public	Private	Public	Private	Public	Private	Public	Private	Public	Private
City	56.0	44.0	83.8	16.2	85.3	14.7	90.7	9.3	94.8	5.2
MSA[1]	61.9	38.1	86.3	13.7	86.0	14.0	88.9	11.1	91.5	8.5
U.S.	57.4	42.6	87.8	12.2	89.8	10.2	89.9	10.1	90.6	9.4

Note: Figures shown cover persons 3 years old and over; (1) Figures cover the Cedar Rapids, IA Metropolitan Statistical Area—see Appendix B for areas included
Source: U.S. Census Bureau, 2010-2014 American Community Survey 5-Year Estimates

Average Salaries of Public School Classroom Teachers

Area	2013-14		2014-15		Percent Change 2013-14 to 2014-15	Percent Change 2004-05 to 2014-15
	Dollars	Rank[1]	Dollars	Rank[1]		
Iowa	52,032	25	52,862	25	1.60	34.6
U.S. Average	56,610	–	57,379	–	1.36	20.8

Note: (1) State rank ranges from 1 to 51 where 1 indicates highest salary.
Source: National Education Association, Rankings & Estimates: Rankings of the States 2014 and Estimates of School Statistics 2015, March 2015

Higher Education

Four-Year Colleges			Two-Year Colleges			Medical Schools[1]	Law Schools[2]	Voc/ Tech[3]
Public	Private Non-profit	Private For-profit	Public	Private Non-profit	Private For-profit			
0	0	0	0	0	0	0	0	0

Note: Figures cover institutions located within the city limits and include main campuses only; (1) includes schools accredited by the Liaison Committee on Medical Education and the American Osteopathic Association's Commission on Osteopathic College Accreditation; (2) includes ABA-accredited schools, schools with provisional ABA accreditation, and state accredited schools; (3) includes all schools with programs that are less than 2 years.
Source: National Center for Education Statistics, Integrated Postsecondary Education System (IPEDS), 2014-15; Association of American Medical Colleges, Member List, March 21, 2016; American Osteopathic Association, Member List, March 21, 2016; Law School Admission Council, Official Guide to ABA-Approved Law Schools Online, March 21, 2016; Wikipedia, List of Medical Schools in the United States, March 21, 2016; Wikipedia, List of Law Schools in the United States, March 21, 2016

According to *U.S. News & World Report,* the Cedar Rapids, IA metro area is home to two of the best liberal arts colleges in the U.S.: **Cornell College** (#93 tie); **Coe College** (#116 tie). The indicators used to capture academic quality fall into a number of categories: assessment by administrators at peer institutions; retention of students; faculty resources; student selectivity; financial resources; alumni giving; high school counselor ratings of colleges; and graduation rate. *U.S. News & World Report, "America's Best Colleges 2016"*

PRESIDENTIAL ELECTION

2012 Presidential Election Results

Area	Obama (%)	Romney (%)	Other (%)
Linn County	57.9	40.2	1.9
U.S.	51.0	47.2	1.8

Note: Results may not add to 100% due to rounding
Source: Dave Leip's Atlas of U.S. Presidential Elections

EMPLOYERS

Major Employers

Company Name	Industry
AEGON USA	Insurance
Alliant Energy	Energy
Amana Refrigeration Products	Appliances
Cedar Rapids Community School District	Education
City of Cedar Rapids	Government
Gazette Communications	Publishing
General Mills	Food products
Hy-Vee Food Stores	Grocery stores
Kirkwood Community College	Education
Linn County Offices	Government
Linn-Mar Community Schools	Education
Maytag Appliances	Appliances
MCI	Communications
McLeodUSA Incorporated	Communications
Mercy Medical Center	Healthcare
Nash Finch Company	Retail
Rockwell Collins	Aerospace/defense
St. Luke's Hospital	Education
Wal-Mart Stores	Retail
Yellowbook USA	Publisher

Note: Companies shown are located within the Cedar Rapids, IA Metropolitan Statistical Area.
Source: Hoovers.com; Wikipedia

PUBLIC SAFETY

Crime Rate

Area	All Crimes	Violent Crimes: Murder	Violent Crimes: Rape[3]	Violent Crimes: Robbery	Violent Crimes: Aggrav. Assault	Property Crimes: Burglary	Property Crimes: Larceny -Theft	Property Crimes: Motor Vehicle Theft
City	1,576.2	0.0	30.2	21.9	82.2	309.8	1,085.5	46.6
Metro[1]	2,659.7	3.8	27.7	54.5	123.1	519.7	1,789.2	141.7
U.S.	2,971.8	4.5	36.6	102.2	232.5	542.5	1,837.3	216.2

Note: Figures are crimes per 100,000 population; (1) Figures cover the Cedar Rapids, IA Metropolitan Statistical Area—see Appendix B for areas included; (3) The city and U.S. figures shown were reported using the revised Uniform Crime Reporting (UCR) definition of rape. The suburban and metro area figures shown are an aggregate total of the data submitted using both the revised and legacy UCR definitions.
Source: FBI Uniform Crime Reports, 2014

Hate Crimes

Area	Number of Quarters Reported	Number of Incidents per Bias Motivation: Race	Religion	Sexual Orientation	Ethnicity	Disability	Gender	Gender Identity
City	4	0	0	0	0	0	0	0
U.S.	4	2,568	1,014	1,017	648	84	33	98

Source: Federal Bureau of Investigation, Hate Crime Statistics 2014

Identity Theft Consumer Complaints

Area	Complaints	Complaints per 100,000 Population	Rank[2]
MSA[1]	249	94.4	234
U.S.	490,220	152.4	-

Note: (1) Figures cover the Cedar Rapids, IA Metropolitan Statistical Area—see Appendix B for areas included; (2) Rank ranges from 1 to 379 where 1 indicates greatest number of identity theft complaints per 100,000 population
Source: Federal Trade Commission, Consumer Sentinel Network Data Book for January–December 2015

Fraud and Other Consumer Complaints

Area	Complaints	Complaints per 100,000 Population	Rank[2]
MSA[1]	802	303.9	304
U.S.	2,593,159	806.0	

Note: (1) Figures cover the Cedar Rapids, IA Metropolitan Statistical Area—see Appendix B for areas included; (2) Rank ranges from 1 to 379 where 1 indicates greatest number of identity theft complaints per 100,000 population
Source: Federal Trade Commission, Consumer Sentinel Network Data Book for January–December 2015

RECREATION

Culture

Dance[1]	Theatre[1]	Instrumental Music[1]	Vocal Music[1]	Series and Festivals	Museums and Art Galleries[2]	Zoos and Aquariums[3]
0	0	0	0	0	0	0

Note: (1) Professional perfoming groups; (2) Based on organizations with SIC code 8412; (3) AZA-accredited
Source: The Grey House Performing Arts Directory, 2015-16; Association of Zoos & Aquariums, AZA Member Zoos & Aquariums, March 25, 2016; www.AccuLeads.com, March 29, 2016

Professional Sports Teams

Team Name	League	Year Established
No teams are located in the metro area		

Source: Wikipedia, Major Professional Sports Teams of the United States and Canada, March 24, 2016

CLIMATE

Average and Extreme Temperatures

Temperature	Jan	Feb	Mar	Apr	May	Jun	Jul	Aug	Sep	Oct	Nov	Dec	Yr.
Extreme High (°F)	58	66	87	100	94	103	105	105	97	95	76	65	105
Average High (°F)	24	30	43	59	71	81	84	82	73	62	45	29	57
Average Temp. (°F)	15	21	34	48	60	69	73	71	62	50	36	21	47
Average Low (°F)	6	11	24	36	48	58	62	59	50	39	26	12	36
Extreme Low (°F)	-33	-29	-34	-4	25	38	42	38	22	11	-17	-27	-34

Note: Figures cover the years 1960-1995
Source: National Climatic Data Center, International Station Meteorological Climate Summary, 9/96

Average Precipitation/Snowfall/Humidity

Precip./Humidity	Jan	Feb	Mar	Apr	May	Jun	Jul	Aug	Sep	Oct	Nov	Dec	Yr.
Avg. Precip. (in.)	0.8	1.0	2.3	3.6	4.1	4.5	4.8	4.0	3.5	2.5	1.9	1.3	34.4
Avg. Snowfall (in.)	7	7	6	2	Tr	0	0	0	0	Tr	4	8	33
Avg. Rel. Hum. 6am (%)	77	80	82	81	81	83	87	90	89	84	83	82	83
Avg. Rel. Hum. 3pm (%)	68	66	62	52	51	51	55	55	55	52	62	70	58

Note: Figures cover the years 1960-1995; Tr = Trace amounts (<0.05 in. of rain; <0.5 in. of snow)
Source: National Climatic Data Center, International Station Meteorological Climate Summary, 9/96

Weather Conditions

Temperature			Daytime Sky			Precipitation		
5°F & below	32°F & below	90°F & above	Clear	Partly cloudy	Cloudy	0.01 inch or more precip.	0.1 inch or more snow/ice	Thunder-storms
38	156	16	89	132	144	109	28	42

Note: Figures are average number of days per year and cover the years 1960-1995
Source: National Climatic Data Center, International Station Meteorological Climate Summary, 9/96

HAZARDOUS WASTE

Superfund Sites

Marion has no sites on the EPA's Superfund Final National Priorities List. There are a total of 1,323 Superfund sites on the list in the U.S. *U.S. Environmental Protection Agency, Final National Priorities List, March 18, 2016*

AIR & WATER QUALITY

Air Quality Trends: Ozone

	1990	1995	2000	2005	2010	2011	2012	2013	2014
MSA[1]	n/a	n/a	n/a	n/a	n/a	n/a	n/a	n/a	n/a

Note: (1) Data covers the Cedar Rapids, IA Metropolitan Statistical Area—see Appendix B for areas included; n/a not available. The values shown are the composite ozone concentration averages among trend sites based on the highest fourth daily maximum 8-hour concentration in parts per million. These trends are based on sites having an adequate record of monitoring data during the trend period. Data from exceptional events are included.
Source: U.S. Environmental Protection Agency, Air Quality Monitoring Information, "Air Quality Trends by City, 1990-2014"

Air Quality Index

Area	Percent of Days when Air Quality was...[2]					AQI Statistics[2]	
	Good	Moderate	Unhealthy for Sensitive Groups	Unhealthy	Very Unhealthy	Maximum	Median
MSA[1]	75.1	24.7	0.3	0.0	0.0	112	41

Note: (1) Data covers the Cedar Rapids, IA Metropolitan Statistical Area—see Appendix B for areas included; (2) Based on 365 days with AQI data in 2015. Air Quality Index (AQI) is an index for reporting daily air quality. EPA calculates the AQI for five major air pollutants regulated by the Clean Air Act: ground-level ozone, particle pollution (aka particulate matter), carbon monoxide, sulfur dioxide, and nitrogen dioxide. The AQI runs from 0 to 500. The higher the AQI value, the greater the level of air pollution and the greater the health concern. There are six AQI categories: "Good" AQI is between 0 and 50. Air quality is considered satisfactory; "Moderate" AQI is between 51 and 100. Air quality is acceptable; "Unhealthy for Sensitive Groups" When AQI values are between 101 and 150, members of sensitive groups may experience health effects; "Unhealthy" When AQI values are between 151 and 200 everyone may begin to experience health effects; "Very Unhealthy" AQI values between 201 and 300 trigger a health alert; "Hazardous" AQI values over 300 trigger warnings of emergency conditions (not shown).
Source: U.S. Environmental Protection Agency, Air Quality Index Report, 2015

Air Quality Index Pollutants

Area	Percent of Days when AQI Pollutant was...[2]					
	Carbon Monoxide	Nitrogen Dioxide	Ozone	Sulfur Dioxide	Particulate Matter 2.5	Particulate Matter 10
MSA[1]	0.0	0.0	28.2	5.2	65.8	0.8

Note: (1) Data covers the Cedar Rapids, IA Metropolitan Statistical Area—see Appendix B for areas included; (2) Based on 365 days with AQI data in 2015. The Air Quality Index (AQI) is an index for reporting daily air quality. EPA calculates the AQI for five major air pollutants regulated by the Clean Air Act: ground-level ozone, particle pollution (also known as particulate matter), carbon monoxide, sulfur dioxide, and nitrogen dioxide. The AQI runs from 0 to 500. The higher the AQI value, the greater the level of air pollution and the greater the health concern.
Source: U.S. Environmental Protection Agency, Air Quality Index Report, 2015

Maximum Air Pollutant Concentrations: Particulate Matter, Ozone, CO and Lead

	Particulate Matter 10 (ug/m^3)	Particulate Matter 2.5 Wtd AM (ug/m^3)	Particulate Matter 2.5 24-Hr (ug/m^3)	Ozone (ppm)	Carbon Monoxide (ppm)	Lead (ug/m^3)
MSA[1] Level	52	9.7	24	0.061	1	n/a
NAAQS[2]	150	15	35	0.075	9	0.15
Met NAAQS[2]	Yes	Yes	Yes	Yes	Yes	n/a

Note: (1) Data covers the Cedar Rapids, IA Metropolitan Statistical Area—see Appendix B for areas included; Data from exceptional events are included; (2) National Ambient Air Quality Standards; ppm = parts per million; ug/m^3 = micrograms per cubic meter; n/a not available.
Concentrations: Particulate Matter 10 (coarse particulate)—highest second maximum 24-hour concentration; Particulate Matter 2.5 Wtd AM (fine particulate)—highest weighted annual mean concentration; Particulate Matter 2.5 24-Hour (fine particulate)—highest 98th percentile 24-hour concentration; Ozone—highest fourth daily maximum 8-hour concentration; Carbon Monoxide—highest second maximum non-overlapping 8-hour concentration; Lead—maximum running 3-month average
Source: U.S. Environmental Protection Agency, Air Quality Monitoring Information, "Air Quality Statistics by City, 2014"

Maximum Air Pollutant Concentrations: Nitrogen Dioxide and Sulfur Dioxide

	Nitrogen Dioxide AM (ppb)	Nitrogen Dioxide 1-Hr (ppb)	Sulfur Dioxide AM (ppb)	Sulfur Dioxide 1-Hr (ppb)	Sulfur Dioxide 24-Hr (ppb)
MSA[1] Level	n/a	n/a	n/a	113	n/a
NAAQS[2]	53	100	30	75	140
Met NAAQS[2]	n/a	n/a	n/a	No	n/a

Note: (1) Data covers the Cedar Rapids, IA Metropolitan Statistical Area—see Appendix B for areas included; Data from exceptional events are included; (2) National Ambient Air Quality Standards; ppm = parts per million; ug/m^3 = micrograms per cubic meter; n/a not available.
Concentrations: Nitrogen Dioxide AM—highest arithmetic mean concentration; Nitrogen Dioxide 1-Hr—highest 98th percentile 1-hour daily maximum concentration; Sulfur Dioxide AM—highest annual mean concentration; Sulfur Dioxide 1-Hr—highest 99th percentile 1-hour daily maximum concentration; Sulfur Dioxide 24-Hr—highest second maximum 24-hour concentration
Source: U.S. Environmental Protection Agency, Air Quality Monitoring Information, "Air Quality Statistics by City, 2014"

Drinking Water

Water System Name	Pop. Served	Primary Water Source Type	Violations[1]	
			Health Based	Monitoring/ Reporting
Marion Municipal Water Dept	34,610	Ground	1	1

Note: (1) Based on violation data from January 1, 2015 to December 31, 2015 (includes unresolved violations from earlier years)

Source: U.S. Environmental Protection Agency, Office of Ground Water and Drinking Water, Safe Drinking Water Information System (based on data extracted April 29, 2016)

Leawood, Kansas

Background

Leawood is all about community, its people, and the search for the American dream. First incorporated in 1948, it is one of the fastest growing cities in Kansas. Oscar G. Lee is credited with founding Leawood in the 1920s after he moved from Oklahoma. Leawood's true growth began after World War II, thanks to the help of the Kroh Brothers housing development, designed to help veterans returning from the war find a home with a sense of community to raise their family. The Kroh Brothers built the first 500 homes in Leawood, and also provided help in developing police and fire departments, and even street repair. Leawood has continued the careful planning started by the Kroh Brothers providing a community that is welcoming both to residents and businesses.

Present day Leawood is situated just south of Kansas City off of Interstate 435. It is a prime location in the Midwest and the country. Virtually any location in the Kansas City area is within a 30 minute drive of Leawood, whose residents value hard work and a strong education.

Dining out opportunities are abundant, as are the recreational choices. World-class parks with trails for hiking and biking, camping, and live concerts are popular with Leawood's residents. Ironwoods Park is home to the Prairie Oak Nature Center, providing hands on environmental learning experiences with a well-equipped activity room. For large groups the Lodge at Ironwoods is the ideal setting, from business meetings to wedding receptions. Its vaulted ceiling and large patio overlooking the surrounding woods is perfect too, for the variety of organized activities provided for residents of all ages.

An anticipated annual event is A Taste of Leawood. This celebration brings together samplings from the area's finest establishments while listening to the hottest local musical acts and is held at the Leawood City Hall Courtyard in June.

Health and safety is a priority for the residents of Leawood, with top-notch medical centers and citizen safety programs sponsored by the local police, including Women's Self Awareness Program, DARE and the Citizens Police Academy.

A 30-minute drive from Leawood brings you to the cultural and metropolitan center of the area—Kansas City, home to the University of Kansas medical center and various private colleges. Sports fans can take in a Kansas City Chiefs football game at Arrowhead Stadium or a Kansas City Royals baseball game at the Kauffman Stadium. Additionally, a major league soccer team calls Kansas City and its Sporting Park home, the Sporting Kansas City (formerly Kansas City Wizards). Kansas Speedway hosts the stars of NASCAR, as well as local racing. For those that like a different type of horsepower the American Royal Livestock Horse Show and Rodeo takes place in Kemper Arena each year. A parade and international barbecue contest are anticipated components of the show.

For those who appreciate the fine arts, Leawood and Kansas City have many offerings. The Nelson-Atkins Museum of Arts has an internationally renowned exhibit of Asian art. The Kansas City Symphony, Lyric Opera, Missouri Reparatory Theater and Theatre in the Park are sure to please.

Leawood is served by a number of small local and executive airports and by Kansas City International Airport, 35 miles away.

Rankings

Business/Finance Rankings

- The personal finance site NerdWallet analyzed 183 American metropolitan areas with populations over 250,000 and more than 15,000 businesses to rank where entrepreneurs find the most success. Criteria included area economy, annual income, housing cost, unemployment rate, and the success rate of area businesses. Kansas City* ranked #36. *www.nerdwallet.com, "Best Places to Start a Business," April 27, 2015*

- Based on metro area social media reviews, the employment opinion group Glassdoor surveyed 50 of the largest U.S. metro areas and equally weighed cost of living, hiring opportunity, and job satisfaction to compose a list of "25 Best Cities for Jobs." The Kansas City* metro area was ranked #23 in overall job satisfaction. *www.glassdoor.com, "Best Cities for Jobs," May 19, 2015*

- In a survey of economic confidence in the nation's 50 largest metropolitan areas conducted January–December 2014, the Kansas City* metro area placed #44, according to Gallup's 2014 Economic Confidence Index. *Gallup, "San Jose and San Francisco Lead in Economic Confidence," March 19, 2015*

- The Brookings Institution ranked the 100 largest metro areas in the U.S. based on income inequality. Kansas City* was ranked #67 (#1 = greatest ineqality). Criteria: the "95/20 ratio," a figure representing the income at which a household earns more than 95 percent of all other households, divided by the income at which a household earns more than only 20 percent of all other households. *Brookings Institution, "Income Inequality, 100 Largest U.S. Metro Areas, 2007-2014," January 14, 2016*

- Kansas City* was identified as one of America's most frugal metro areas by *Coupons.com.* The city ranked #11 out of 25. Criteria: online coupon usage. *Coupons.com, "Top 25 Most Frugal Cities of 2014," May 11, 2015*

- Kansas City* was cited as one of America's top metros for new and expanded facility projects in 2015. The area ranked #10 in the large metro area category (population over 1 million). *Site Selection, "Top Metropolitans of 2015," March 2016*

- The Kansas City* metro area appeared on the Milken Institute "2015 Best Performing Cities" list. Rank: #103 out of 200 large metro areas. Criteria: job growth; wage and salary growth; high-tech output growth. *Milken Institute, "Best-Performing Cities 2015," December 2015*

- *Forbes* ranked the 200 most populous metro areas to determine the nation's "Best Places for Business and Careers." The Kansas City* metro area was ranked #61. Criteria: costs (business and living); job growth (past and projected); income growth; educational attainment (college and high school); projected economic growth; cultural and recreational opportunities; net migration patterns; number of highly ranked colleges. *Forbes, "The Best Places for Business and Careers 2015," July 29, 2015*

Education Rankings

- Personal finance website *WalletHub* analyzed the 150 largest U.S. metropolitan statistical areas to determine where the most educated Americans are choosing to settle. Criteria: education quality and attainment gap; education levels; percentage of workers with degrees; public school rankings; quality and size of each metro area's universities. Kansas City* was ranked #28 (#1 = most educated city). *www.WalletHub.com, "2015's Most and Least Educated Cities*

Environmental Rankings

- The Kansas City* metro area came in at #238 for the relative comfort of its climate on Sperling's list of "chill cities," as measured by the Sperling Heat Index. All 361 metro areas are included. Criteria included daytime high temperatures, nighttime low temperatures, dew point, and relative humidity at the high temperatures. *www.bertsperling.com, "Sperling's Chill Cities," July 18, 2013*

- Sperling's BestPlaces assessed 379 metropolitan areas of the United States for the likelihood of dangerously extreme weather events or earthquakes. In general the Southeast and South-Central regions have the highest risk of weather extremes and earthquakes, while the Pacific Northwest enjoys the lowest risk. Of the least risky metropolitan areas, the Kansas City* metro area was ranked #254. *www.bestplaces.net, "Safest Places from Natural Disasters," April 2011*
- Kansas City* was highlighted as one of the 25 most ozone-polluted metro areas in the U.S. during 2011 through 2013. The area ranked #24. *American Lung Association, State of the Air 2015*

Health/Fitness Rankings

- For each of the 50 most populous metro areas in the United States, the American College of Sports Medicine's American Fitness Index evaluated infrastructure, community assets, and policies that encourage healthy and fit lifestyles, including preventive health behaviors, levels of chronic disease conditions, health care access, and community resources and policies that support physical activity. The Kansas City* metro area ranked #26 for "community fitness." *www.americanfitnessindex.org, "ACSM American Fitness Index Health and Community Fitness Status of the 50 Largest Metropolitan Areas," May 2015*
- The Kansas City* metro area was identified as one of the worst cities for bed bugs in America by pest control company Orkin. The area ranked #44 out of 50 based on the number of bed bug treatments Orkin performed from January to December 2015. *Orkin, "Chicago Tops Bed Bug Cities List for Fourth Year in a Row," January 13, 2016*
- Kansas City* was identified as a "2016 Spring Allergy Capital." The area ranked #64 out of 100. Three groups of factors were used to identify the most severe cities for people with allergies during the spring season: annual pollen levels; medicine utilization; access to board-certified allergists. *Asthma and Allergy Foundation of America, "Spring Allergy Capitals 2016"*
- Kansas City* was identified as a "2015 Asthma Capital." The area ranked #72 out of the nation's 100 largest metropolitan areas. Criteria: estimated prevalence; self-reported prevalence; crude death rate for asthma; annual pollen score; annual air quality; public smoking laws; number of board-certified asthma specialists; school inhaler access laws; rescue medication use; controller medication use; ER visits for asthma; uninsured rate; poverty rate. *Asthma and Allergy Foundation of America, "Asthma Capitals 2015"*
- The Kansas City* metro area ranked #111 out of 190 in The Gallup-Healthways Well-Being Index. Criteria: purpose; social well being; financial health; community and physical health. Results are based on telephone interviews with adults, aged 18 and older, living in metropolitan areas in the 50 U.S. states and the District of Columbia. *Gallup-Healthways, "State of American Well-Being," February 23, 2016*

Safety Rankings

- The National Insurance Crime Bureau ranked 380 metro areas in the U.S. in terms of per capita rates of vehicle theft. The Kansas City* metro area ranked #37 (#1 = highest rate). Criteria: number of vehicle theft offenses per 100,000 inhabitants in 2014. *National Insurance Crime Bureau, "Hot Spots 2014," June 24, 2015*

Seniors/Retirement Rankings

- From its Best Cities for Successful Aging indexes, the Milken Institute generated rankings for metropolitan areas, weighing data in eight categories—health care, wellness, living arrangements, transportation, financial characteristics, education and employment opportunities, community engagement, and overall livability. The Kansas City* metro area was ranked #26 overall in the large metro area category. *Milken Institute, "Best Cities for Successful Aging, 2014"*

Miscellaneous Rankings

- The watchdog site Charity Navigator conducts an annual study of charities in the nation's major markets both to analyze statistical differences in their financial, accountability, and transparency practices and to track year-to-year variations in individual communities. The Kansas City* metro area was ranked #25 among the 30 metro markets in the rating dimension of Overall Score. *www.charitynavigator.org, "Metro Market Study 2015," June 5, 2015*

- Mars Chocolate North America, the makers of COMBOS®, in partnership with Sperling's BestPlaces, ranked 50 major metro areas in terms of their "manliness." The Kansas City* metro area ranked #20. Criteria: number of professional sports teams; number of nearby NASCAR tracks and racing events; manly lifestyle; concentration of manly retail stores; manly occupations per capita; salty snack sales; "Board of Manliness" rankings. *Mars Chocolate North America, "America's Manliest Cities 2012"*

- The National Alliance to End Homelessness ranked the 100 most populous metro areas with the highest rate of homelessness. The Kansas City* metro area ranked #49. Criteria: number of homeless people per 10,000 population in 2011. *National Alliance to End Homelessness, The State of Homelessness in America 2012*

Leawood is located within the Kansas City, MO-KS Metropolitan Statistical Area.

Business Environment

CITY FINANCES

City Government Finances

Component	2012 ($000)	2012 ($ per capita)
Total Revenues	52,437	1,645
Total Expenditures	38,181	1,198
Debt Outstanding	60,637	1,902
Cash and Securities[1]	57,139	1,793

Note: (1) Cash and security holdings of a government at the close of its fiscal year, including those of its dependent agencies, utilities, and liquor stores.
Source: U.S Census Bureau, State & Local Government Finances 2012

City Government Revenue by Source

Source	2012 ($000)	2012 ($ per capita)
General Revenue		
From Federal Government	0	0
From State Government	2,419	75
From Local Governments	6,758	212
Taxes		
Property	16,844	528
Sales and Gross Receipts	17,802	558
Personal Income	0	0
Corporate Income	0	0
Motor Vehicle License	0	0
Other Taxes	1,849	58
Current Charges	2,508	78
Liquor Store	0	0
Utility	0	0
Employee Retirement	0	0

Source: U.S Census Bureau, State & Local Government Finances 2012

City Government Expenditures by Function

Function	2012 ($000)	2012 ($ per capita)	2012 (%)
General Direct Expenditures			
Air Transportation	0	0	0.0
Corrections	0	0	0.0
Education	0	0	0.0
Employment Security Administration	0	0	0.0
Financial Administration	648	20	1.6
Fire Protection	6,003	188	15.7
General Public Buildings	0	0	0.0
Governmental Administration, Other	4,851	152	12.7
Health	0	0	0.0
Highways	8,404	263	22.0
Hospitals	0	0	0.0
Housing and Community Development	0	0	0.0
Interest on General Debt	2,500	78	6.5
Judicial and Legal	881	27	2.3
Libraries	0	0	0.0
Parking	0	0	0.0
Parks and Recreation	6,733	211	17.6
Police Protection	8,161	256	21.3
Public Welfare	0	0	0.0
Sewerage	0	0	0.0
Solid Waste Management	0	0	0.0
Veterans' Services	0	0	0.0
Liquor Store	0	0	0.0
Utility	0	0	0.0
Employee Retirement	0	0	0.0

Source: U.S Census Bureau, State & Local Government Finances 2012

DEMOGRAPHICS

Population Growth

Area	1990 Census	2000 Census	2010 Census	2014* Estimate	Population Growth (%) 1990-2014	Population Growth (%) 2010-2014
City	19,683	27,656	31,867	32,842	66.9	3.1
MSA[1]	1,636,528	1,836,038	2,035,334	2,040,869	24.7	0.3
U.S.	248,709,873	281,421,906	308,745,538	314,107,084	26.3	1.7

Note: (1) Figures cover the Kansas City, MO-KS Metropolitan Statistical Area—see Appendix B for areas included; (*) 2010-2014 5-year estimated population
Source: U.S. Census Bureau, 1990 Census, Census 2000, Census 2010, 2010-2014 American Community Survey 5-Year Estimates

Household Size

Area	Persons in Household (%) One	Two	Three	Four	Five	Six	Seven or More	Average Household Size
City	19.5	39.5	13.2	17.4	7.4	1.6	1.2	2.61
MSA[1]	28.8	33.6	15.3	13.0	5.8	2.0	1.1	2.54
U.S.	27.5	33.5	15.8	13.1	6.0	2.3	1.4	2.64

Note: (1) Figures cover the Kansas City, MO-KS Metropolitan Statistical Area—see Appendix B for areas included
Source: U.S. Census Bureau, 2010-2014 American Community Survey 5-Year Estimates

Race

Area	White Alone[2] (%)	Black Alone[2] (%)	Asian Alone[2] (%)	AIAN[3] Alone[2] (%)	NHOPI[4] Alone[2] (%)	Other Race Alone[2] (%)	Two or More Races (%)
City	92.5	1.4	3.6	0.3	0.0	0.3	1.8
MSA[1]	79.1	12.5	2.5	0.4	0.1	2.4	2.9
U.S.	73.8	12.6	5.0	0.8	0.2	4.7	2.9

Note: (1) Figures cover the Kansas City, MO-KS Metropolitan Statistical Area—see Appendix B for areas included; (2) Alone is defined as not being in combination with one or more other races; (3) American Indian and Alaska Native; (4) Native Hawaiian and Other Pacific Islander
Source: U.S. Census Bureau, 2010-2014 American Community Survey 5-Year Estimates

Hispanic or Latino Origin

Area	Total (%)	Mexican (%)	Puerto Rican (%)	Cuban (%)	Other (%)
City	1.9	0.8	0.1	0.4	0.6
MSA[1]	8.5	6.5	0.3	0.2	1.5
U.S.	16.9	10.8	1.6	0.6	3.8

Note: Persons of Hispanic or Latino origin can be of any race; (1) Figures cover the Kansas City, MO-KS Metropolitan Statistical Area—see Appendix B for areas included
Source: U.S. Census Bureau, 2010-2014 American Community Survey 5-Year Estimates

Ancestry

Area	German	Irish	English	American	Italian	Polish	French[2]	Scottish	Dutch
City	33.0	18.6	16.3	6.5	6.9	2.7	3.3	3.2	1.6
MSA[1]	23.2	13.3	10.2	8.1	3.5	1.7	2.6	2.0	1.6
U.S.	14.9	10.8	8.0	7.1	5.5	3.0	2.7	1.7	1.4

Note: Figures are the percentage of the total population reporting a particular ancestry. The nine most commonly reported ancestries in the U.S. are shown. Figures include multiple ancestries (e.g. if a person reported being Irish and Italian, they were included in both columns); (1) Figures cover the Kansas City, MO-KS Metropolitan Statistical Area—see Appendix B for areas included; (2) Excludes Basque
Source: U.S. Census Bureau, 2010-2014 American Community Survey 5-Year Estimates

Foreign-Born Population

Area	Percent of Population Born in								
	Any Foreign Country	Asia	Mexico	Europe	Carribean	Central America[2]	South America	Africa	Canada
City	5.2	2.6	0.1	1.5	0.2	0.0	0.4	0.3	0.2
MSA[1]	6.4	2.0	2.2	0.6	0.2	0.4	0.2	0.6	0.1
U.S.	13.1	3.8	3.7	1.5	1.2	1.0	0.9	0.6	0.3

Note: (1) Figures cover the Kansas City, MO-KS Metropolitan Statistical Area—see Appendix B for areas included; (2) Excludes Mexico.
Source: U.S. Census Bureau, 2010-2014 American Community Survey 5-Year Estimates

Marital Status

Area	Never Married	Now Married[2]	Separated	Widowed	Divorced
City	18.3	69.7	0.2	5.0	6.7
MSA[1]	29.7	50.8	1.8	5.5	12.2
U.S.	32.5	48.4	2.2	5.9	10.9

Note: Figures are percentages and cover the population 15 years of age and older; (1) Figures cover the Kansas City, MO-KS Metropolitan Statistical Area—see Appendix B for areas included; (2) Excludes separated
Source: U.S. Census Bureau, 2010-2014 American Community Survey 5-Year Estimates

Disability Status

Area	All Ages	Under 18 Years Old	18 to 64 Years Old	65 Years and Over
City	6.6	1.4	3.1	25.0
MSA[1]	11.6	3.7	10.2	35.5
U.S.	12.3	4.1	10.2	36.3

Note: Figures show percent of the civilian noninstitutionalized population that reported having a disability. Disability status is determined from from six types of difficulty: vision, hearing, cognitive, ambulatory, self-care, and independent living. For children under 5 years old, hearing and vision difficulty are used to determine disability status. For children between the ages of 5 and 14, disability status is determined from hearing, vision, cognitive, ambulatory, and self-care difficulties. For people aged 15 years and older, they are considered to have a disability if they have difficulty with any one of the six difficulty types; (1) Figures cover the Kansas City, MO-KS Metropolitan Statistical Area—see Appendix B for areas included.
Source: U.S. Census Bureau, 2010-2014 American Community Survey 5-Year Estimates

Age

Area	Percent of Population									Median Age
	Under Age 5	Age 5–19	Age 20–34	Age 35–44	Age 45–54	Age 55–64	Age 65–74	Age 75–84	Age 85+	
City	5.3	24.0	7.5	14.2	16.5	16.1	9.2	4.8	2.4	44.2
MSA[1]	6.9	20.7	20.0	13.3	14.3	12.2	7.0	3.8	1.8	36.7
U.S.	6.4	19.9	20.6	13.0	14.1	12.3	7.6	4.3	1.9	37.4

Note: (1) Figures cover the Kansas City, MO-KS Metropolitan Statistical Area—see Appendix B for areas included
Source: U.S. Census Bureau, 2010-2014 American Community Survey 5-Year Estimates

Gender

Area	Males	Females	Males per 100 Females
City	16,377	16,465	99.5
MSA[1]	1,000,049	1,040,820	96.1
U.S.	154,515,159	159,591,925	96.8

Note: (1) Figures cover the Kansas City, MO-KS Metropolitan Statistical Area—see Appendix B for areas included
Source: U.S. Census Bureau, 2010-2014 American Community Survey 5-Year Estimates

Religious Groups by Family

Area	Catholic	Baptist	Non-Den.	Methodist[2]	Lutheran	LDS[3]	Pentecostal	Presbyterian[4]	Muslim[5]	Judaism
MSA[1]	12.6	13.1	5.2	5.8	2.2	2.4	2.6	1.6	0.3	0.4
U.S.	19.1	9.3	4.0	4.0	2.3	2.0	1.9	1.6	0.8	0.7

Note: Figures are the number of adherents as a percentage of the total population; (1) Figures cover the Kansas City, MO-KS Metropolitan Statistical Area—see Appendix B for areas included; (2) Methodist/Pietist; (3) Latter Day Saints; (4) Reformed; (5) Figures are estimates
Source: Association of Statisticians of American Religious Bodies, 2010 U.S. Religion Census: Religious Congregations & Membership Study

Religious Groups by Tradition

Area	Catholic	Evangelical Protestant	Mainline Protestant	Other Tradition	Black Protestant	Orthodox
MSA[1]	12.6	20.5	9.9	3.6	2.6	0.1
U.S.	19.1	16.2	7.3	4.3	1.6	0.3

Note: Figures are the number of adherents as a percentage of the total population; (1) Figures cover the Kansas City, MO-KS Metropolitan Statistical Area—see Appendix B for areas included
Source: Association of Statisticians of American Religious Bodies, 2010 U.S. Religion Census: Religious Congregations & Membership Study

ECONOMY

Gross Metropolitan Product

Area	2013	2014	2015	2016	Rank[2]
MSA[1]	117.3	121.8	126.4	132.3	29

Note: Figures are in billions of dollars; (1) Figures cover the Kansas City, MO-KS Metropolitan Statistical Area—see Appendix B for areas included; (2) Rank is based on 2016 data and ranges from 1 to 381
Source: The U.S. Conference of Mayors, U.S. Metro Economies: GMP and Employment 2014-2016, June 2015

Economic Growth

Area	2011-13 (%)	2014 (%)	2015 (%)	2016 (%)	Rank[2]
MSA[1]	1.5	2.2	2.4	2.7	135
U.S.	2.2	2.4	2.3	2.9	–

Note: Figures are real gross metropolitan product (GMP) growth rates and represent annual average percent change; (1) Figures cover the Kansas City, MO-KS Metropolitan Statistical Area—see Appendix B for areas included; (2) Rank is based on 2016 data and ranges from 1 to 381
Source: The U.S. Conference of Mayors, U.S. Metro Economies: GMP and Employment 2014-2016, June 2015

Metropolitan Area Exports

Area	2009	2010	2011	2012	2013	2014	Rank[2]
MSA[1]	5,888.8	7,374.1	7,958.9	7,880.7	8,012.0	8,262.8	40

Note: Figures are in millions of dollars; (1) Figures cover the Kansas City, MO-KS Metropolitan Statistical Area—see Appendix B for areas included; (2) Rank is based on 2014 data and ranges from 1 to 385
Source: U.S. Department of Commerce, International Trade Administration, Office of Trade & Industry Information, Manufacturing & Services, data extracted March 10, 2016

Building Permits

Area	Single-Family			Multi-Family			Total		
	2014	2015p	Pct. Chg.	2014	2015p	Pct. Chg.	2014	2015p	Pct. Chg.
City	73	62	-15.1	8	0	-100.0	81	62	-23.5
MSA[1]	4,170	4,507	8.1	4,031	4,488	11.3	8,201	8,995	9.7
U.S.	640,300	690,800	7.9	411,800	487,600	18.4	1,052,100	1,178,400	12.0

Note: (1) Figures cover the Kansas City, MO-KS Metropolitan Statistical Area—see Appendix B for areas included; Figures represent new, privately-owned housing units authorized (unadjusted data); All permit data are based on estimates with imputation; (p) preliminary data.
Source: U.S. Census Bureau, Manufacturing, Mining, and Construction Statistics, Building Permits, 2014, 2015

Bankruptcy Filings

Area	Business Filings 2014	Business Filings 2015	Business Filings % Chg.	Nonbusiness Filings 2014	Nonbusiness Filings 2015	Nonbusiness Filings % Chg.
Johnson County	80	75	-6.3	1,369	1,121	-18.1
U.S.	26,983	24,735	-8.3	909,812	819,760	-9.9

Note: Business filings include Chapter 7, Chapter 11, Chapter 12, and Chapter 13; Nonbusiness filings include Chapter 7, Chapter 11, and Chapter 13
Source: Administrative Office of the U.S. Courts, Business and Nonbusiness Bankruptcy, County Cases Commenced by Chapter of the Bankruptcy Code, During the 12- Month Period Ending December 31, 2014 and Business and Nonbusiness Bankruptcy, County Cases Commenced by Chapter of the Bankruptcy Code, During the 12- Month Period Ending December 31, 2015

Housing Vacancy Rates

Area	Gross Vacancy Rate[2] (%)			Year-Round Vacancy Rate[3] (%)			Rental Vacancy Rate[4] (%)			Homeowner Vacancy Rate[5] (%)		
	2013	2014	2015	2013	2014	2015	2013	2014	2015	2013	2014	2015
MSA[1]	10.8	9.0	7.3	10.4	8.6	7.1	10.1	9.5	7.9	2.0	1.5	1.3
U.S.	13.6	13.4	12.9	10.7	10.4	10.0	8.3	7.6	7.1	2.0	1.9	1.8

Note: (1) Figures cover the Kansas City, MO-KS Metropolitan Statistical Area—see Appendix B for areas included; (2) The percentage of the total housing inventory that is vacant; (3) The percentage of the housing inventory (excluding seasonal units) that is year-round vacant; (4) The percentage of rental inventory that is vacant for rent; (5) The percentage of homeowner inventory that is vacant for sale
Source: U.S. Census Bureau, Housing Vacancies and Homeownership Annual Statistics: 2015

INCOME

Income

Area	Per Capita ($)	Median Household ($)	Average Household ($)
City	76,304	133,702	201,273
MSA[1]	30,101	57,056	75,695
U.S.	28,555	53,482	74,596

Note: (1) Figures cover the Kansas City, MO-KS Metropolitan Statistical Area—see Appendix B for areas included
Source: U.S. Census Bureau, 2010-2014 American Community Survey 5-Year Estimates

Household Income Distribution

Area	Percent of Households Earning							
	Under $15,000	$15,000 -24,999	$25,000 -34,999	$35,000 -49,999	$50,000 -74,999	$75,000 -99,000	$100,000 -149,999	$150,000 and up
City	4.1	3.9	4.9	6.4	9.2	7.9	18.0	45.6
MSA[1]	10.9	9.5	9.9	13.7	18.6	13.4	14.4	9.6
U.S.	12.5	10.7	10.2	13.5	17.8	12.2	13.0	10.0

Note: (1) Figures cover the Kansas City, MO-KS Metropolitan Statistical Area—see Appendix B for areas included
Source: U.S. Census Bureau, 2010-2014 American Community Survey 5-Year Estimates

Poverty Rate

Area	All Ages	Under 18 Years Old	18 to 64 Years Old	65 Years and Over
City	3.3	2.9	3.2	4.5
MSA[1]	12.6	18.0	11.6	6.8
U.S.	15.6	21.9	14.6	9.4

Note: Figures are percentage of people whose income during the past 12 months was below the poverty level; (1) Figures cover the Kansas City, MO-KS Metropolitan Statistical Area—see Appendix B for areas included
Source: U.S. Census Bureau, 2010-2014 American Community Survey 5-Year Estimates

EMPLOYMENT

Labor Force and Employment

Area	Civilian Labor Force			Workers Employed		
	Dec. 2014	Dec. 2015	% Chg.	Dec. 2014	Dec. 2015	% Chg.
City	16,713	16,835	0.7	16,238	16,405	1.0
MSA[1]	1,107,078	1,118,856	1.0	1,055,730	1,076,324	1.9
U.S.	155,521,000	157,245,000	1.1	147,190,000	149,703,000	1.7

Note: Data is not seasonally adjusted and covers workers 16 years of age and older; (1) Figures cover the Kansas City, MO-KS Metropolitan Statistical Area—see Appendix B for areas included
Source: Bureau of Labor Statistics, Local Area Unemployment Statistics

Unemployment Rate

Area	2015											
	Jan.	Feb.	Mar.	Apr.	May	Jun.	Jul.	Aug.	Sep.	Oct.	Nov.	Dec.
City	3.1	3.0	3.1	3.3	3.4	3.4	3.6	3.2	2.7	2.6	2.5	2.6
MSA[1]	5.9	5.9	5.3	5.1	5.3	5.3	5.5	5.2	4.4	4.2	3.9	3.8
U.S.	6.1	5.8	5.6	5.1	5.3	5.5	5.6	5.2	4.9	4.8	4.8	4.8

Note: Data is not seasonally adjusted and covers workers 16 years of age and older; (1) Figures cover the Kansas City, MO-KS Metropolitan Statistical Area—see Appendix B for areas included
Source: Bureau of Labor Statistics, Local Area Unemployment Statistics

Employment by Occupation

Occupation Classification	City (%)	MSA[1] (%)	U.S. (%)
Management, Business, Science, and Arts	62.8	38.9	36.4
Natural Resources, Construction, and Maintenance	2.3	7.6	9.0
Production, Transportation, and Material Moving	3.2	11.5	12.1
Sales and Office	26.3	25.7	24.4
Service	5.4	16.3	18.2

Note: Figures cover employed civilians 16 years of age and older; (1) Figures cover the Kansas City, MO-KS Metropolitan Statistical Area—see Appendix B for areas included
Source: U.S. Census Bureau, 2010-2014 American Community Survey 5-Year Estimates

Employment by Industry

Sector	MSA[1]		U.S.
	Number of Employees	Percent of Total	Percent of Total
Construction, Mining, and Logging	46,200	4.3	5.0
Education and Health Services	149,700	14.2	15.7
Financial Activities	74,900	7.1	5.7
Government	148,100	14.0	15.5
Information	19,500	1.8	1.9
Leisure and Hospitality	100,600	9.5	10.4
Manufacturing	76,200	7.2	8.6
Other Services	41,200	3.9	3.9
Professional and Business Services	183,300	17.4	13.9
Retail Trade	112,500	10.6	11.3
Transportation, Warehousing, and Utilities	48,600	4.6	3.9
Wholesale Trade	50,700	4.8	4.1

Note: Figures are non-farm employment as of December 2015. Figures are not seasonally adjusted and include workers 16 years of age and older; (1) Figures cover the Kansas City, MO-KS Metropolitan Statistical Area—see Appendix B for areas included; n/a not available
Source: Bureau of Labor Statistics, Current Employment Statistics, Employment, Hours, and Earnings

Occupations with Greatest Projected Employment Growth: 2012 – 2022

Occupation[1]	2012 Employment	2022 Projected Employment	Numeric Employment Change	Percent Employment Change
Personal Care Aides	19,670	28,280	8,610	43.7
Registered Nurses	28,440	33,460	5,020	17.7
Customer Service Representatives	26,680	31,400	4,720	17.7
Nursing Assistants	19,840	23,710	3,870	19.5
Secretaries and Administrative Assistants, Except Legal, Medical, and Executive	28,240	32,070	3,830	13.6
Laborers and Freight, Stock, and Material Movers, Hand	22,110	25,700	3,590	16.3
Combined Food Preparation and Serving Workers, Including Fast Food	21,700	24,930	3,230	14.9
Janitors and Cleaners, Except Maids and Housekeeping Cleaners	23,330	26,500	3,170	13.6
Heavy and Tractor-Trailer Truck Drivers	21,040	23,640	2,600	12.3
Retail Salespersons	38,930	41,510	2,580	6.6

Note: Projections cover Kansas; (1) Sorted by numeric employment change
Source: www.projectionscentral.com, State Occupational Projections, 2012–2022 Long-Term Projections

Fastest Growing Occupations: 2012 – 2022

Occupation[1]	2012 Employment	2022 Projected Employment	Numeric Employment Change	Percent Employment Change
Interpreters and Translators	830	1,220	390	47.9
Personal Care Aides	19,670	28,280	8,610	43.7
Diagnostic Medical Sonographers	610	870	260	41.0
Health Specialties Teachers, Postsecondary	740	1,040	300	40.3
Nursing Instructors and Teachers, Postsecondary	480	670	190	39.7
Information Security Analysts	570	780	210	38.1
Occupational Therapy Assistants	400	540	140	37.7
Home Health Aides	6,670	9,150	2,480	37.2
Computer Numerically Controlled Machine Tool Programmers, Metal and Plastic	480	650	170	34.9
Insulation Workers, Mechanical	390	520	130	33.8

Note: Projections cover Kansas; (1) Sorted by percent employment change and excludes occupations with numeric employment change less than 100
Source: www.projectionscentral.com, State Occupational Projections, 2012–2022 Long-Term Projections

Average Wages

Occupation	$/Hr.	Occupation	$/Hr.
Accountants and Auditors	33.45	Maids and Housekeeping Cleaners	10.01
Automotive Mechanics	18.68	Maintenance and Repair Workers	17.76
Bookkeepers	18.37	Marketing Managers	61.85
Carpenters	24.09	Nuclear Medicine Technologists	32.84
Cashiers	9.86	Nurses, Licensed Practical	19.56
Clerks, General Office	15.39	Nurses, Registered	30.45
Clerks, Receptionists/Information	14.08	Nursing Assistants	12.30
Clerks, Shipping/Receiving	15.42	Packers and Packagers, Hand	11.13
Computer Programmers	36.37	Physical Therapists	37.13
Computer Systems Analysts	40.43	Postal Service Mail Carriers	24.23
Computer User Support Specialists	24.12	Real Estate Brokers	n/a
Cooks, Restaurant	10.81	Retail Salespersons	11.65
Dentists	78.43	Sales Reps., Exc. Tech./Scientific	32.40
Electrical Engineers	44.86	Sales Reps., Tech./Scientific	44.34
Electricians	28.55	Secretaries, Exc. Legal/Med./Exec.	16.32
Financial Managers	62.77	Security Guards	13.51
First-Line Supervisors/Managers, Sales	19.02	Surgeons	123.07
Food Preparation Workers	10.13	Teacher Assistants*	11.75
General and Operations Managers	53.31	Teachers, Elementary School*	23.84
Hairdressers/Cosmetologists	13.36	Teachers, Secondary School*	22.74
Internists	92.96	Telemarketers	14.09
Janitors and Cleaners	12.82	Truck Drivers, Heavy/Tractor-Trailer	21.09
Landscaping/Groundskeeping Workers	12.89	Truck Drivers, Light/Delivery Svcs.	17.22
Lawyers	57.35	Waiters and Waitresses	9.56

Note: Wage data covers the Kansas City, MO-KS Metropolitan Statistical Area—see Appendix B for areas included; (*) Hourly wages for elementary/secondary school teachers and teacher assistants were calculated by the editors from annual wage data based on a 40 hour work week; n/a not available.
Source: Bureau of Labor Statistics, Metro Area Occupational Employment and Wage Estimates, May 2015

TAXES

State Corporate Income Tax Rates

State	Tax Rate (%)	Income Brackets ($)	Num. of Brackets	Financial Institution Tax Rate (%)[a]	Federal Income Tax Ded.
Kansas	4.0 (l)	Flat rate	1	2.25 (l)	No

Note: Tax rates as of January 1, 2016; (a) Rates listed are the corporate income tax rate applied to financial institutions or excise taxes based on income. Some states have other taxes based upon the value of deposits or shares; (l) In addition to the flat 4% corporate income tax, Kansas levies a 3.0% surtax on taxable income over $50,000. Banks pay a privilege tax of 2.25% of net income, plus a surtax of 2.125% (2.25% for savings and loans, trust companies, and federally chartered savings banks) on net income in excess of $25,000.
Source: Federation of Tax Administrators, "State Corporate Income Tax Rates, 2016"

State Individual Income Tax Rates

State	Tax Rate (%)	Income Brackets ($)	Num. of Brackets	Personal Exempt. ($)[1]		Fed. Inc. Tax Ded.
				Single	Dependents	
Kansas	2.7 - 4.6	15,000 (b)	2	2,250	2,250	No

Note: Tax rates as of January 1, 2016; Local- and county-level taxes are not included; n/a not applicable; (1) Married joint filers generally receive double the single exemption; (b) For joint returns, taxes are twice the tax on half the couple's income.
Source: Federation of Tax Administrators, "State Individual Income Tax Rates, 2016"

Various State and Local Tax Rates

State	State and Local Sales and Use (%)	State Sales and Use (%)	Gasoline[1] (¢/gal.)	Cigarette[2] ($/pack)	Spirits[3] ($/gal.)	Wine[4] ($/gal.)	Beer[5] ($/gal.)
Kansas	8.85	6.5	24.03	1.29	2.50	0.30 (l)	0.18

Note: All tax rates as of January 1, 2016; (1) The American Petroleum Institute has developed a methodology for determining the average tax rate on a gallon of fuel. Rates may include any of the following: excise taxes, environmental fees, storage tank fees, other fees or taxes, general sales tax, and local taxes. In states where gasoline is subject to the general sales tax, or where the fuel tax is based on the average sale price, the average rate determined by API is sensitive to changes in the price of gasoline. States that fully or partially apply general sales taxes to gasoline: CA, CO, GA, IL, IN, MI, NY; (2) The federal excise tax of $1.0066 per pack and local taxes are not included; (3) Rates are those applicable to off-premise sales of 40% alcohol by volume (a.b.v.) distilled spirits in 750ml containers. Local excise taxes are excluded; (4) Rates are those applicable to off-premise sales of 11% a.b.v. non-carbonated wine in 750ml containers; (5) Rates are those applicable to off-premise sales of 4.7% a.b.v. beer in 12 ounce containers; (l) Different rates also applicable according to alcohol content, place of production, size of container, place purchased (on- or off-premise or on board airlines) or type of wine (carbonated, vermouth, etc.).
Source: Tax Foundation, 2016 Facts & Figures: How Does Your State Compare?

State Business Tax Climate Index Rankings

State	Overall Rank	Corporate Tax Rank	Individual Income Tax Rank	Sales Tax Rank	Unemployment Insurance Tax Rank	Property Tax Rank
Kansas	22	40	18	32	10	19

Note: The index is a measure of how each state's tax laws affect economic performance. The lower the rank, the more favorable a state's tax system is for business. States without a given tax are given a ranking of 1. The scores/rankings for the District of Columbia do not affect other states. The 2016 index represents the tax climate as of July 1, 2015 (the beginning of Fiscal Year 2016).
Source: Tax Foundation, State Business Tax Climate Index 2016

TRANSPORTATION

Means of Transportation to Work

Area	Car/Truck/Van		Public Transportation			Bicycle	Walked	Other Means	Worked at Home
	Drove Alone	Car-pooled	Bus	Subway	Railroad				
City	86.8	3.5	0.1	0.0	0.0	0.1	0.4	0.9	8.2
MSA[1]	83.3	8.9	1.1	0.0	0.0	0.2	1.3	1.0	4.3
U.S.	76.4	9.6	2.6	1.8	0.6	0.6	2.8	1.3	4.4

Note: Figures are percentages and cover workers 16 years of age and older; (1) Figures cover the Kansas City, MO-KS Metropolitan Statistical Area—see Appendix B for areas included
Source: U.S. Census Bureau, 2010-2014 American Community Survey 5-Year Estimates

Travel Time to Work

Area	Less Than 10 Minutes	10 to 19 Minutes	20 to 29 Minutes	30 to 44 Minutes	45 to 59 Minutes	60 to 89 Minutes	90 Minutes or More
City	12.7	38.1	26.7	18.0	2.7	0.5	1.3
MSA[1]	13.1	31.4	25.3	20.7	5.9	2.3	1.2
U.S.	13.3	29.6	21.0	20.2	7.7	5.7	2.6

Note: Figures are percentages and include workers 16 years old and over; (1) Figures cover the Kansas City, MO-KS Metropolitan Statistical Area—see Appendix B for areas included
Source: U.S. Census Bureau, 2010-2014 American Community Survey 5-Year Estimates

Freeway Travel Time Index

Area	1985	1990	1995	2000	2005	2010	2014
Urban Area Rank[1,2]	54	46	68	72	77	76	76
Urban Area Index[1]	1.06	1.10	1.11	1.13	1.14	1.14	1.15
Average Index[3]	1.09	1.11	1.14	1.17	1.20	1.19	1.20

Note: Freeway Travel Time Index—the ratio of travel time in the peak period to the travel time at free-flow conditions. For example, a value of 1.30 indicates a 20-minute free-flow trip takes 26 minutes in the peak (20 minutes x 1.30 = 26 minutes); (1) Covers the Kansas City MO-KS urban area; (2) Rank is based on 101 urban areas (#1 = highest travel time index); (3) Average of 101 urban areas
Source: Texas Transportation Institute, 2015 Urban Mobility Scorecard, August 2015

Freeway Commuter Stress Index

Area	1985	1990	1995	2000	2005	2010	2014
Urban Area Rank[1,2]	66	51	71	76	81	82	79
Urban Area Index[1]	1.07	1.12	1.13	1.15	1.16	1.16	1.17
Average Index[3]	1.13	1.16	1.19	1.22	1.25	1.24	1.25

Note: The Freeway Commuter Stress Index is the same as the Freeway Travel Time Index (see table above) except that it includes only the travel in the peak directions during the peak periods; the TTI includes travel in all directions during the peak period. Thus, the CSI is more indicative of the work trip experienced by each commuter on a daily basis. (1) Covers the Kansas City MO-KS urban area; (2) Rank is based on 101 urban areas (#1 = highest stress index); (3) Average of 101 urban areas
Source: Texas Transportation Institute, 2015 Urban Mobility Scorecard, August 2015

Living Environment

COST OF LIVING

Cost of Living Index

Composite Index	Groceries	Housing	Utilities	Transportation	Health Care	Misc. Goods/ Services
94.2	91.1	91.7	90.5	93.4	95.4	98.8

Note: The Cost of Living Index measures regional differences in the cost of consumer goods and services, excluding taxes and non-consumer expenditures, for professional and managerial households in the top income quintile. It is based on more than 50,000 prices covering almost 60 different items for which prices are collected three times a year by chambers of commerce, economic development organizations or university applied economic centers in each participating urban area. The numbers shown should be read as a percentage above or below the national average of 100. For example, a value of 115.4 in the groceries column indicates that grocery prices are 15.4% higher than the national average. Small differences in the index numbers should not be interpreted as significant; Figures cover the Kansas City MO-KS urban area.
Source: The Council for Community and Economic Research, ACCRA Cost of Living Index, 2015

Grocery Prices

Area[1]	T-Bone Steak ($/pound)	Frying Chicken ($/pound)	Whole Milk ($/half gal.)	Eggs ($/dozen)	Orange Juice ($/64 oz.)	Coffee ($/11.5 oz.)
City[2]	10.00	1.19	2.17	2.15	3.06	4.46
Avg.	10.99	1.43	2.25	2.26	3.58	4.48
Min.	7.16	0.98	1.30	1.35	2.88	2.98
Max.	14.13	2.43	3.85	4.81	6.39	7.56

Note: (1) Values for the local area are compared with the average, minimum and maximum values for all 292 areas in the Cost of Living Index; (2) Figures cover the Kansas City MO-KS urban area; **T-Bone Steak** *(price per pound);* **Frying Chicken** *(price per pound, whole fryer);* **Whole Milk** *(half gallon carton);* **Eggs** *(price per dozen, Grade A, large);* **Orange Juice** *(64 oz. Tropicana or Florida Natural);* **Coffee** *(11.5 oz. can, vacuum-packed, Maxwell House, Hills Bros, or Folgers).*
Source: The Council for Community and Economic Research, ACCRA Cost of Living Index, 2015

Housing and Utility Costs

Area[1]	New Home Price ($)	Apartment Rent ($/month)	All Electric ($/month)	Part Electric ($/month)	Other Energy ($/month)	Telephone ($/month)
City[2]	291,595	835	-	85.41	77.39	23.34
Avg.	312,874	945	179.30	95.07	72.96	28.11
Min.	178,682	479	116.28	43.14	26.46	10.01
Max.	1,472,476	3,984	504.25	189.44	421.11	43.06

Note: (1) Values for the local area are compared with the average, minimum and maximum values for all 292 areas in the Cost of Living Index; (2) Figures cover the Kansas City MO-KS urban area; **New Home Price** *(2,400 sf living area, 8,000 sf lot, in urban area with full utilities);* **Apartment Rent** *(950 sf 2 bedroom/1.5 or 2 bath, unfurnished, excluding all utilities except water);* **All Electric** *(average monthly cost for an all-electric home);* **Part Electric** *(average monthly cost for a part-electric home);* **Other Energy** *(average monthly cost for natural gas, fuel oil, coal, wood, and any other forms of energy except electricity);* **Telephone** *(price includes basic monthly rate for a private residential line plus additional local usage charges incurred by a family of four).*
Source: The Council for Community and Economic Research, ACCRA Cost of Living Index, 2015

Health Care, Transportation, and Other Costs

Area[1]	Doctor ($/visit)	Dentist ($/visit)	Optometrist ($/visit)	Gasoline ($/gallon)	Beauty Salon ($/visit)	Men's Shirt ($)
City[2]	93.36	87.39	94.68	2.16	31.21	28.60
Avg.	105.15	89.02	99.78	2.38	35.30	28.10
Min.	66.87	56.09	48.53	1.95	18.91	13.38
Max.	182.34	150.36	228.33	4.09	67.91	63.80

Note: (1) Values for the local area are compared with the average, minimum and maximum values for all 292 areas in the Cost of Living Index; (2) Figures cover the Kansas City MO-KS urban area; **Doctor** *(general practitioners routine exam of an established patient);* **Dentist** *(adult teeth cleaning and periodic oral examination);* **Optometrist** *(full vision eye exam for established adult patient);* **Gasoline** *(one gallon regular unleaded, national brand, including all taxes, cash price at self-service pump if available);* **Beauty Salon** *(woman's shampoo, trim, and blow-dry);* **Men's Shirt** *(cotton/polyester dress shirt, pinpoint weave, long sleeves).*
Source: The Council for Community and Economic Research, ACCRA Cost of Living Index, 2015

HOUSING

House Price Index (HPI)

Area	National Ranking[2]	Quarterly Change (%)	One-Year Change (%)	Five-Year Change (%)
MSA[1]	79	1.80	6.40	8.50
U.S.[3]	–	1.45	5.76	22.85

Note: The HPI is a weighted repeat sales index. It measures average price changes in repeat sales or refinancings on the same properties. This information is obtained by reviewing repeat mortgage transactions on single-family properties whose mortgages have been purchased or securitized by Fannie Mae or Freddie Mac in January 1975; (1) Kansas City Metropolitan Statistical Area—see Appendix B for areas included; (2) Rankings are based on annual percentage change for all metro areas containing at least 15,000 transactions over the last 10 years and ranges from 1 to 266; (3) figures based on a weighted average of Census Division estimates using a seasonally adjusted, purchase-only index; all figures are for the period ending December 31, 2015
Source: Federal Housing Finance Agency, House Price Index, February 25, 2016

Median Single-Family Home Prices

Area	2013	2014	2015[p]	Percent Change 2014 to 2015
MSA[1]	154.8	158.8	170.4	7.3
U.S. Average	197.4	208.9	223.9	7.2

Note: Figures are median sales prices of existing single-family homes in thousands of dollars; (p) preliminary; n/a not available; (1) Kansas City, MO-KS Metropolitan Statistical Area—see Appendix B for areas included
Source: National Association of Realtors, Median Sales Price of Existing Single-Family Homes for Metropolitan Areas, 4th Quarter 2015

Qualifying Income Based on Median Sales Price of Existing Single-Family Homes

Area	With 5% Down ($)	With 10% Down ($)	With 20% Down ($)
MSA[1]	37,257	35,296	31,374
U.S. Average	49,535	46,928	41,714

Note: Figures are preliminary; Qualifying income is based on a mortgage rate of 4.1%. Monthly principal and interest payment is limited to 25% of income; n/a not available; (1) Kansas City, MO-KS Metropolitan Statistical Area—see Appendix B for areas included
Source: National Association of Realtors, Qualifying Income Based on Median Sales Price of Existing Single-Family Homes for Metropolitan Areas, 4th Quarter 2015

Median Apartment Condo-Coop Home Prices

Area	2013	2014	2015[p]	Percent Change 2014 to 2015
MSA[1]	n/a	n/a	n/a	n/a
U.S. Average	194.9	204.3	210.7	3.1

Note: Figures are median sales prices of existing apartment condo-coop homes in thousands of dollars; (p) preliminary; n/a not available; (1) Kansas City, MO-KS Metropolitan Statistical Area—see Appendix B for areas included
Source: National Association of Realtors, Median Sales Price of Existing Apartment Condo-Coop Homes for Metropolitan Areas, 4th Quarter 2015

Gross Monthly Rent

Area	Under $200	$200 -299	$300 -499	$500 -749	$750 -999	$1,000 -1,499	$1,500 and up	Median ($)
City	0.0	0.6	1.8	13.2	21.6	26.3	36.5	1,161
MSA[1]	1.3	2.8	6.5	27.1	31.0	24.6	6.7	839
U.S.	1.5	3.2	7.4	21.0	24.1	26.9	15.9	920

Note: Figures are percentages except for Median; Gross rent is the contract rent plus the estimated average monthly cost of utilities (electricity, gas, and water and sewer) and fuels (oil, coal, kerosene, wood, etc.) if these are paid by the renter (or paid for the renter by someone else); (1) Figures cover the Kansas City, MO-KS Metropolitan Statistical Area—see Appendix B for areas included
Source: U.S. Census Bureau, 2010-2014 American Community Survey 5-Year Estimates

Homeownership Rate

Area	2008 (%)	2009 (%)	2010 (%)	2011 (%)	2012 (%)	2013 (%)	2014 (%)	2015 (%)
MSA[1]	70.2	69.5	68.8	68.5	65.1	65.6	66.1	65.0
U.S.	67.8	67.4	66.9	66.1	65.4	65.1	64.5	63.7

Note: (1) Figures cover the Kansas City, MO-KS Metropolitan Statistical Area—see Appendix B for areas included
Source: U.S. Census Bureau, Housing Vacancies and Homeownership Annual Statistics: 2015

Year Housing Structure Built

Area	2010 or Later	2000 -2009	1990 -1999	1980 -1989	1970 -1979	1960 -1969	1950 -1959	1940 -1949	Before 1940	Median Year
City	0.2	18.8	21.4	22.7	10.4	7.9	14.9	2.3	1.4	1986
MSA[1]	0.7	15.0	14.3	12.6	15.9	12.5	12.2	4.9	11.9	1975
U.S.	1.0	14.9	13.9	13.8	15.8	11.0	10.8	5.4	13.3	1976

Note: Figures are percentages except for Median Year; (1) Figures cover the Kansas City, MO-KS Metropolitan Statistical Area—see Appendix B for areas included
Source: U.S. Census Bureau, 2010-2014 American Community Survey 5-Year Estimates

HEALTH

Health Risk Data

Category	MSA[1] (%)	U.S. (%)
Adults aged 18–64 who have any kind of health care coverage	83.7	79.6
Adults who reported being in good or excellent health	84.0	83.1
Adults who are current smokers	22.0	19.6
Adults who are heavy drinkers[2]	6.2	6.1
Adults who are binge drinkers[3]	17.3	16.9
Adults who are overweight (BMI 25.0 - 29.9)	35.7	35.8
Adults who are obese (BMI 30.0 - 99.8)	28.3	27.6
Adults who participated in any physical activities in the past month	79.5	77.1
Adults 50+ who have ever had a sigmoidoscopy or colonoscopy	72.8	67.3
Women aged 40+ who have had a mammogram within the past two years	76.1	74.0
Men aged 40+ who have had a PSA test within the past two years	50.8	45.2
Adults aged 65+ who have had flu shot within the past year	66.5	60.1
Adults who always wear a seatbelt	90.3	93.8

Note: Data as of 2012 unless otherwise noted; (1) Figures cover the Kansas City, MO-KS Metropolitan Statistical Area—see Appendix B for areas included; (2) Heavy drinkers are classified as males having more than two drinks per day or females having more than one drink per day; (3) Binge drinkers are classified as males having five or more drinks on one occasion or females having four or more drinks on one occasion
Source: Centers for Disease Control and Prevention, Behaviorial Risk Factor Surveillance System, SMART: Selected Metropolitan/Micropolitan Area Risk Trends, 2012 (Note: the CDC has discontinued this dataset but will be releasing a replacement in mid-2016)

Chronic Health Indicators

Category	MSA[1] (%)	U.S. (%)
Adults who have ever been told they had a heart attack	4.0	4.5
Adults who have ever been told they had a stroke	3.3	2.9
Adults who have been told they currently have asthma	9.7	8.9
Adults who have ever been told they have arthritis	25.8	25.7
Adults who have ever been told they have diabetes[2]	10.4	9.7
Adults who have ever been told they had skin cancer	5.8	5.7
Adults who have ever been told they had any other types of cancer	6.1	6.5
Adults who have ever been told they have COPD	7.4	6.2
Adults who have ever been told they have kidney disease	2.2	2.5
Adults who have ever been told they have a form of depression	16.7	18.0

Note: Data as of 2012 unless otherwise noted; (1) Figures cover the Kansas City, MO-KS Metropolitan Statistical Area—see Appendix B for areas included; (2) Figures do not include pregnancy-related, borderline, or pre-diabetes
Source: Centers for Disease Control and Prevention, Behaviorial Risk Factor Surveillance System, SMART: Selected Metropolitan/Micropolitan Area Risk Trends, 2012 (Note: the CDC has discontinued this dataset but will be releasing a replacement in mid-2016)

Mortality Rates for the Top 10 Causes of Death in the U.S.

ICD-10[a] Sub-Chapter	ICD-10[a] Code	Age-Adjusted Mortality Rate[1] per 100,000 population	
		County[2]	U.S.
Malignant neoplasms	C00-C97	142.0	163.6
Ischaemic heart diseases	I20-I25	57.0	102.2
Other forms of heart disease	I30-I51	44.1	50.1
Chronic lower respiratory diseases	J40-J47	32.9	41.4
Organic, including symptomatic, mental disorders	F01-F09	42.2	38.5
Cerebrovascular diseases	I60-I69	32.4	36.5
Other external causes of accidental injury	W00-X59	18.9	27.5
Other degenerative diseases of the nervous system	G30-G31	21.4	26.3
Diabetes mellitus	E10-E14	10.1	21.1
Hypertensive diseases	I10-I15	5.8	19.7

Note: (a) ICD-10 = International Classification of Diseases 10th Revision; (1) Mortality rates are a three year average covering 2012-2014; (2) Figures cover Johnson County.
Source: Centers for Disease Control and Prevention, National Center for Health Statistics. Underlying Cause of Death 1999-2014 on CDC WONDER Online Database, released 2015.

Mortality Rates for Selected Causes of Death

ICD-10[a] Sub-Chapter	ICD-10[a] Code	Age-Adjusted Mortality Rate[1] per 100,000 population	
		County[2]	U.S.
Assault	X85-Y09	2.0	5.1
Diseases of the liver	K70-K76	9.4	13.5
Human immunodeficiency virus (HIV) disease	B20-B24	Suppressed	2.1
Influenza and pneumonia	J09-J18	12.6	15.2
Intentional self-harm	X60-X84	14.4	12.7
Malnutrition	E40-E46	1.1	0.9
Obesity and other hyperalimentation	E65-E68	1.7	1.9
Renal failure	N17-N19	14.0	13.0
Transport accidents	V01-V99	6.1	11.6
Viral hepatitis	B15-B19	Unreliable	2.1

Note: (a) ICD-10 = International Classification of Diseases 10th Revision; (1) Mortality rates are a three year average covering 2012-2014; (2) Figures cover Johnson County; Data are Suppressed when the data meet the criteria for confidentiality constraints; Mortality rates are flagged as Unreliable when the rate would be calculated with a numerator of 20 or less.
Source: Centers for Disease Control and Prevention, National Center for Health Statistics. Underlying Cause of Death 1999-2014 on CDC WONDER Online Database, released 2015.

Health Insurance Coverage

Area	With Health Insurance	With Private Health Insurance	With Public Health Insurance	Without Health Insurance	Population Under Age 18 Without Health Insurance
City	97.8	92.2	18.0	2.2	1.6
MSA[1]	87.5	73.2	25.1	12.5	6.5
U.S.	85.8	65.8	31.1	14.2	7.1

Note: Figures are percentages that cover the civilian noninstitutionalized population; (1) Figures cover the Kansas City, MO-KS Metropolitan Statistical Area—see Appendix B for areas included
Source: U.S. Census Bureau, 2010-2014 American Community Survey 5-Year Estimates

Number of Medical Professionals

Area	MDs[3]	DOs[3,4]	Dentists	Podiatrists	Chiropractors	Optometrists
County[1] (number)	2,721	253	449	20	337	140
County[1] (rate[2])	479.6	44.6	78.2	3.5	58.7	24.4
U.S. (rate[2])	272.5	20.9	64.7	5.8	25.9	15.2

Note: Data as of 2014 unless noted; (1) Data covers Johnson County; (2) Rate per 100,000 population; (3) Data as of 2013 and includes all active, non-federal physicians; (4) Doctor of Osteopathic Medicine
Source: U.S. Department of Health and Human Services, Health Resources and Services Administration, Bureau of Health Professions, Area Resource File (ARF) 2014-2015

Best Hospitals

According to *U.S. News,* the Kansas City, MO-KS metro area is home to two of the best hospitals in the U.S.: **St. Luke's Hospital** (7 specialties); **University of Kansas Hospital** (12 specialties). The hospitals listed were nationally ranked in at least one adult specialty. Only 137 hospitals nationwide were nationally ranked in one or more specialties. Fifteen hospitals in the U.S. made the Honor Roll with high scores in at least six specialties. *U.S. News Online, "America's Best Children's Hospitals 2015-16"*

According to *U.S. News,* the Kansas City, MO-KS metro area is home to one of the best children's hospitals in the U.S.: **Children's Mercy Hospitals and Clinics** (10 specialties). The hospital listed was highly ranked in at least one pediatric specialty. Eighty-three children's hospitals in the U.S. were nationally ranked in at least one specialty. Twelve children's hospitals in the U.S. made the Honor Roll with high scores in at least three specialties. *U.S. News Online, "America's Best Children's Hospitals 2015-16"*

EDUCATION

Public School District Statistics

District Name	Schls	Pupils	Pupil/ Teacher Ratio	Minority Pupils[1] (%)	Free Lunch Eligible[2] (%)	IEP[3] (%)
Blue Valley	34	22,400	15.4	22.6	5.9	10.0

Note: Table includes school districts with 100 or more students; (1) Percentage of students that are not non-Hispanic white; (2) Percentage of students that are eligible for the free lunch program; (3) Percentage of students that have an Individualized Education Program.
Source: U.S. Department of Education, National Center for Education Statistics, Common Core of Data, Local Education Agency (School District) Universe Survey: School Year 2013-2014; U.S. Department of Education, National Center for Education Statistics, Common Core of Data, Public Elementary/Secondary School Universe Survey: School Year 2013-2014

Highest Level of Education

Area	Less than H.S.	H.S. Diploma	Some College, No Deg.	Associate Degree	Bachelor's Degree	Master's Degree	Prof. School Degree	Doctorate Degree
City	0.8	6.5	14.4	4.0	41.7	18.1	11.6	3.0
MSA[1]	9.2	26.5	23.4	7.4	21.5	8.9	2.2	1.1
U.S.	13.7	28.0	21.2	7.9	18.3	7.8	2.0	1.3

Note: Figures cover persons age 25 and over; (1) Figures cover the Kansas City, MO-KS Metropolitan Statistical Area—see Appendix B for areas included
Source: U.S. Census Bureau, 2010-2014 American Community Survey 5-Year Estimates

Educational Attainment by Race

Area	High School Graduate or Higher (%)					Bachelor's Degree or Higher (%)				
	Total	White	Black	Asian	Hisp.[2]	Total	White	Black	Asian	Hisp.[2]
City	99.2	99.3	96.7	98.6	100.0	74.3	74.4	60.8	91.8	82.9
MSA[1]	90.8	92.5	86.1	84.1	65.5	33.6	36.1	17.9	52.6	15.2
U.S.	86.3	88.4	83.2	85.8	64.1	29.3	30.6	19.0	50.9	13.9

Note: Figures shown cover persons 25 years old and over; (1) Figures cover the Kansas City, MO-KS Metropolitan Statistical Area—see Appendix B for areas included; (2) People of Hispanic origin can be of any race
Source: U.S. Census Bureau, 2010-2014 American Community Survey 5-Year Estimates

School Enrollment by Grade and Control

Area	Preschool (%)		Kindergarten (%)		Grades 1 - 4 (%)		Grades 5 - 8 (%)		Grades 9 - 12 (%)	
	Public	Private	Public	Private	Public	Private	Public	Private	Public	Private
City	35.4	64.6	61.4	38.6	67.3	32.7	63.8	36.2	66.5	33.5
MSA[1]	51.5	48.5	86.7	13.3	88.7	11.3	88.6	11.4	89.7	10.3
U.S.	57.4	42.6	87.8	12.2	89.8	10.2	89.9	10.1	90.6	9.4

Note: Figures shown cover persons 3 years old and over; (1) Figures cover the Kansas City, MO-KS Metropolitan Statistical Area—see Appendix B for areas included
Source: U.S. Census Bureau, 2010-2014 American Community Survey 5-Year Estimates

Average Salaries of Public School Classroom Teachers

Area	2013-14 Dollars	2013-14 Rank[1]	2014-15 Dollars	2014-15 Rank[1]	Percent Change 2013-14 to 2014-15	Percent Change 2004-05 to 2014-15
Kansas	48,221	38	48,990	37	1.59	24.5
U.S. Average	56,610	–	57,379	–	1.36	20.8

Note: (1) State rank ranges from 1 to 51 where 1 indicates highest salary.
Source: National Education Association, Rankings & Estimates: Rankings of the States 2014 and Estimates of School Statistics 2015, March 2015

Higher Education

Four-Year Colleges			Two-Year Colleges			Medical Schools[1]	Law Schools[2]	Voc/ Tech[3]
Public	Private Non-profit	Private For-profit	Public	Private Non-profit	Private For-profit			
0	1	0	0	0	0	0	0	0

Note: Figures cover institutions located within the city limits and include main campuses only; (1) includes schools accredited by the Liaison Committee on Medical Education and the American Osteopathic Association's Commission on Osteopathic College Accreditation; (2) includes ABA-accredited schools, schools with provisional ABA accreditation, and state accredited schools; (3) includes all schools with programs that are less than 2 years.
Source: National Center for Education Statistics, Integrated Postsecondary Education System (IPEDS), 2014-15; Association of American Medical Colleges, Member List, March 21, 2016; American Osteopathic Association, Member List, March 21, 2016; Law School Admission Council, Official Guide to ABA-Approved Law Schools Online, March 21, 2016; Wikipedia, List of Medical Schools in the United States, March 21, 2016; Wikipedia, List of Law Schools in the United States, March 21, 2016

According to *U.S. News & World Report,* the Kansas City, MO-KS metro area is home to one of the best national universities in the U.S.: **University of Missouri–Kansas City** (#194 tie). The indicators used to capture academic quality fall into a number of categories: assessment by administrators at peer institutions; retention of students; faculty resources; student selectivity; financial resources; alumni giving; high school counselor ratings of colleges; and graduation rate. *U.S. News & World Report, "America's Best Colleges 2016"*

According to *U.S. News & World Report,* the Kansas City, MO-KS metro area is home to one of the best liberal arts colleges in the U.S.: **William Jewell College** (#158 tie). The indicators used to capture academic quality fall into a number of categories: assessment by administrators at peer institutions; retention of students; faculty resources; student selectivity; financial resources; alumni giving; high school counselor ratings of colleges; and graduation rate. *U.S. News & World Report, "America's Best Colleges 2016"*

According to *U.S. News & World Report,* the Kansas City, MO-KS metro area is home to one of the top 75 medical schools for research in the U.S.: **University of Kansas Medical Center, School of Medicine** (#69 tie). The rankings are based on a weighted average of 11 measures of quality: quality assessment; peer assessment score; assessment score by residency directors; research activity; total research activity; average research activity per faculty member; student selectivity; median MCAT total score; median undergraduate GPA; acceptance rate; and faculty resources. *U.S. News & World Report, "America's Best Graduate Schools, Medical, 2017"*

PRESIDENTIAL ELECTION

2012 Presidential Election Results

Area	Obama (%)	Romney (%)	Other (%)
Johnson County	40.1	58.0	1.9
U.S.	51.0	47.2	1.8

Note: Results may not add to 100% due to rounding
Source: Dave Leip's Atlas of U.S. Presidential Elections

EMPLOYERS

Major Employers

Company Name	Industry
B&V Baker Guam JV	Consulting engineer
B&V Baker Guam JV	Engineering services
Black and Veatch Corp	Engineering services
DST Systems	Data processing
Embarq Corporation	Telephone communications
Ford Motor Company	Automobile assembly
Hallmark Cardsorporated	Greeting cards
HCA Midwest Division	Hospital management
Honeywell International	Search & navigation equipment
Internal Revenue Service	Taxation, department/government
North Kansas City Hospital	General medical/surgical hospitals
Park University	Colleges, except junior
Performance Contracting	Drywall
St Lukes Hospital of Kansas	General medical/surgical hospitals
United Auto Workers	Labor union
University of Kansas	Charitable trust management
University of Kansas	Medical centers
University of Missouri System	General medical/surgical hospitals

Note: Companies shown are located within the Kansas City, MO-KS Metropolitan Statistical Area.
Source: Hoovers.com; Wikipedia

PUBLIC SAFETY

Crime Rate

Area	All Crimes	Violent Crimes: Murder	Violent Crimes: Rape[3]	Violent Crimes: Robbery	Violent Crimes: Aggrav. Assault	Property Crimes: Burglary	Property Crimes: Larceny -Theft	Property Crimes: Motor Vehicle Theft
City	1,295.6	0.0	6.0	3.0	60.1	216.4	971.0	39.1
Metro[1]	3,499.3	6.6	54.4	113.2	307.9	627.9	1,991.0	398.3
U.S.	2,971.8	4.5	36.6	102.2	232.5	542.5	1,837.3	216.2

Note: Figures are crimes per 100,000 population; (1) Figures cover the Kansas City, MO-KS Metropolitan Statistical Area—see Appendix B for areas included; (3) The city and U.S. figures shown were reported using the revised Uniform Crime Reporting (UCR) definition of rape. The suburban and metro area figures shown are an aggregate total of the data submitted using both the revised and legacy UCR definitions.
Source: FBI Uniform Crime Reports, 2014

Hate Crimes

Area	Number of Quarters Reported	Race	Religion	Sexual Orientation	Ethnicity	Disability	Gender	Gender Identity
		Number of Incidents per Bias Motivation						
City	4	0	1	0	0	0	0	0
U.S.	4	2,568	1,014	1,017	648	84	33	98

Source: Federal Bureau of Investigation, Hate Crime Statistics 2014

Identity Theft Consumer Complaints

Area	Complaints	Complaints per 100,000 Population	Rank[2]
MSA[1]	3,348	161.7	46
U.S.	490,220	152.4	-

Note: (1) Figures cover the Kansas City, MO-KS Metropolitan Statistical Area—see Appendix B for areas included; (2) Rank ranges from 1 to 379 where 1 indicates greatest number of identity theft complaints per 100,000 population
Source: Federal Trade Commission, Consumer Sentinel Network Data Book for January–December 2015

Fraud and Other Consumer Complaints

Area	Complaints	Complaints per 100,000 Population	Rank[2]
MSA[1]	8,239	397.8	108
U.S.	2,593,159	806.0	-

Note: (1) Figures cover the Kansas City, MO-KS Metropolitan Statistical Area—see Appendix B for areas included; (2) Rank ranges from 1 to 379 where 1 indicates greatest number of identity theft complaints per 100,000 population
Source: Federal Trade Commission, Consumer Sentinel Network Data Book for January–December 2015

RECREATION

Culture

Dance[1]	Theatre[1]	Instrumental Music[1]	Vocal Music[1]	Series and Festivals	Museums and Art Galleries[2]	Zoos and Aquariums[3]
0	0	0	0	0	0	0

Note: (1) Professional perfoming groups; (2) Based on organizations with SIC code 8412; (3) AZA-accredited
Source: The Grey House Performing Arts Directory, 2015-16; Association of Zoos & Aquariums, AZA Member Zoos & Aquariums, March 25, 2016; www.AccuLeads.com, March 29, 2016

Professional Sports Teams

Team Name	League	Year Established
Kansas City Chiefs	National Football League (NFL)	1963
Kansas City Royals	Major League Baseball (MLB)	1969
Sporting Kansas City	Major League Soccer (MLS)	1996

Note: Includes teams located in the Kansas City, MO-KS Metropolitan Statistical Area.
Source: Wikipedia, Major Professional Sports Teams of the United States and Canada, March 24, 2016

CLIMATE

Average and Extreme Temperatures

Temperature	Jan	Feb	Mar	Apr	May	Jun	Jul	Aug	Sep	Oct	Nov	Dec	Yr.
Extreme High (°F)	69	76	86	93	92	105	107	109	102	92	82	70	109
Average High (°F)	35	40	54	65	74	84	90	87	79	66	52	39	64
Average Temp. (°F)	26	31	44	55	64	74	79	77	68	56	43	30	54
Average Low (°F)	17	22	34	44	54	63	69	66	58	45	34	21	44
Extreme Low (°F)	-17	-19	-10	12	30	42	54	43	33	21	1	-23	-23

Note: Figures cover the years 1972-1990
Source: National Climatic Data Center, International Station Meteorological Climate Summary, 9/96

Average Precipitation/Snowfall/Humidity

Precip./Humidity	Jan	Feb	Mar	Apr	May	Jun	Jul	Aug	Sep	Oct	Nov	Dec	Yr.
Avg. Precip. (in.)	1.1	1.2	2.8	3.0	5.5	4.1	3.8	4.1	4.9	3.6	2.1	1.6	38.1
Avg. Snowfall (in.)	6	5	3	1	0	0	0	0	0	Tr	1	5	21
Avg. Rel. Hum. 6am (%)	76	77	78	77	82	84	84	86	86	80	79	78	80
Avg. Rel. Hum. 3pm (%)	58	59	54	50	54	54	51	53	53	51	57	60	54

Note: Figures cover the years 1972-1990; Tr = Trace amounts (<0.05 in. of rain; <0.5 in. of snow)
Source: National Climatic Data Center, International Station Meteorological Climate Summary, 9/96

Weather Conditions

Temperature			Daytime Sky			Precipitation		
10°F & below	32°F & below	90°F & above	Clear	Partly cloudy	Cloudy	0.01 inch or more precip.	0.1 inch or more snow/ice	Thunder-storms
22	110	39	112	134	119	103	17	51

Note: Figures are average number of days per year and cover the years 1972-1990
Source: National Climatic Data Center, International Station Meteorological Climate Summary, 9/96

HAZARDOUS WASTE

Superfund Sites

Leawood has no sites on the EPA's Superfund Final National Priorities List. There are a total of 1,323 Superfund sites on the list in the U.S. *U.S. Environmental Protection Agency, Final National Priorities List, March 18, 2016*

AIR & WATER QUALITY

Air Quality Trends: Ozone

	1990	1995	2000	2005	2010	2011	2012	2013	2014
MSA[1]	0.075	0.098	0.088	0.084	0.072	0.080	0.085	0.067	0.066

Note: (1) Data covers the Kansas City, MO-KS Metropolitan Statistical Area—see Appendix B for areas included. The values shown are the composite ozone concentration averages among trend sites based on the highest fourth daily maximum 8-hour concentration in parts per million. These trends are based on sites having an adequate record of monitoring data during the trend period. Data from exceptional events are included.
Source: U.S. Environmental Protection Agency, Air Quality Monitoring Information, "Air Quality Trends by City, 1990-2014"

Air Quality Index

Area	Percent of Days when Air Quality was...[2]					AQI Statistics[2]	
	Good	Moderate	Unhealthy for Sensitive Groups	Unhealthy	Very Unhealthy	Maximum	Median
MSA[1]	44.9	44.7	10.4	0.0	0.0	134	53

Note: (1) Data covers the Kansas City, MO-KS Metropolitan Statistical Area—see Appendix B for areas included; (2) Based on 365 days with AQI data in 2015. Air Quality Index (AQI) is an index for reporting daily air quality. EPA calculates the AQI for five major air pollutants regulated by the Clean Air Act: ground-level ozone, particle pollution (aka particulate matter), carbon monoxide, sulfur dioxide, and nitrogen dioxide. The AQI runs from 0 to 500. The higher the AQI value, the greater the level of air pollution and the greater the health concern. There are six AQI categories: "Good" AQI is between 0 and 50. Air quality is considered satisfactory; "Moderate" AQI is between 51 and 100. Air quality is acceptable; "Unhealthy for Sensitive Groups" When AQI values are between 101 and 150, members of sensitive groups may experience health effects; "Unhealthy" When AQI values are between 151 and 200 everyone may begin to experience health effects; "Very Unhealthy" AQI values between 201 and 300 trigger a health alert; "Hazardous" AQI values over 300 trigger warnings of emergency conditions (not shown).
Source: U.S. Environmental Protection Agency, Air Quality Index Report, 2015

Air Quality Index Pollutants

Area	Percent of Days when AQI Pollutant was...[2]					
	Carbon Monoxide	Nitrogen Dioxide	Ozone	Sulfur Dioxide	Particulate Matter 2.5	Particulate Matter 10
MSA[1]	0.0	3.8	19.5	20.3	46.8	9.6

Note: (1) Data covers the Kansas City, MO-KS Metropolitan Statistical Area—see Appendix B for areas included; (2) Based on 365 days with AQI data in 2015. The Air Quality Index (AQI) is an index for reporting daily air quality. EPA calculates the AQI for five major air pollutants regulated by the Clean Air Act: ground-level ozone, particle pollution (also known as particulate matter), carbon monoxide, sulfur dioxide, and nitrogen dioxide. The AQI runs from 0 to 500. The higher the AQI value, the greater the level of air pollution and the greater the health concern.
Source: U.S. Environmental Protection Agency, Air Quality Index Report, 2015

Maximum Air Pollutant Concentrations: Particulate Matter, Ozone, CO and Lead

	Particulate Matter 10 (ug/m^3)	Particulate Matter 2.5 Wtd AM (ug/m^3)	Particulate Matter 2.5 24-Hr (ug/m^3)	Ozone (ppm)	Carbon Monoxide (ppm)	Lead (ug/m^3)
MSA[1] Level	90	9.5	22	0.068	1	0.01
NAAQS[2]	150	15	35	0.075	9	0.15
Met NAAQS[2]	Yes	Yes	Yes	Yes	Yes	Yes

Note: (1) Data covers the Kansas City, MO-KS Metropolitan Statistical Area—see Appendix B for areas included; Data from exceptional events are included; (2) National Ambient Air Quality Standards; ppm = parts per million; ug/m^3 = micrograms per cubic meter; n/a not available.
Concentrations: Particulate Matter 10 (coarse particulate)—highest second maximum 24-hour concentration; Particulate Matter 2.5 Wtd AM (fine particulate)—highest weighted annual mean concentration; Particulate Matter 2.5 24-Hour (fine particulate)—highest 98th percentile 24-hour concentration; Ozone—highest fourth daily maximum 8-hour concentration; Carbon Monoxide—highest second maximum non-overlapping 8-hour concentration; Lead—maximum running 3-month average
Source: U.S. Environmental Protection Agency, Air Quality Monitoring Information, "Air Quality Statistics by City, 2014"

Maximum Air Pollutant Concentrations: Nitrogen Dioxide and Sulfur Dioxide

	Nitrogen Dioxide AM (ppb)	Nitrogen Dioxide 1-Hr (ppb)	Sulfur Dioxide AM (ppb)	Sulfur Dioxide 1-Hr (ppb)	Sulfur Dioxide 24-Hr (ppb)
MSA[1] Level	13	53	n/a	125	n/a
NAAQS[2]	53	100	30	75	140
Met NAAQS[2]	Yes	Yes	n/a	No	n/a

Note: (1) Data covers the Kansas City, MO-KS Metropolitan Statistical Area—see Appendix B for areas included; Data from exceptional events are included; (2) National Ambient Air Quality Standards; ppm = parts per million; ug/m³ = micrograms per cubic meter; n/a not available.

Concentrations: Nitrogen Dioxide AM—highest arithmetic mean concentration; Nitrogen Dioxide 1-Hr—highest 98th percentile 1-hour daily maximum concentration; Sulfur Dioxide AM—highest annual mean concentration; Sulfur Dioxide 1-Hr—highest 99th percentile 1-hour daily maximum concentration; Sulfur Dioxide 24-Hr—highest second maximum 24-hour concentration

Source: U.S. Environmental Protection Agency, Air Quality Monitoring Information, "Air Quality Statistics by City, 2014"

Drinking Water

Water System Name	Pop. Served	Primary Water Source Type	Violations[1] Health Based	Violations[1] Monitoring/ Reporting
Water Dist 1 of Johnson Co	331,900	Surface	0	0

Note: (1) Based on violation data from January 1, 2015 to December 31, 2015 (includes unresolved violations from earlier years)

Source: U.S. Environmental Protection Agency, Office of Ground Water and Drinking Water, Safe Drinking Water Information System (based on data extracted April 29, 2016)

Lenexa, Kansas

Background

Lenexa, in Johnson County, is located 12 miles southwest of Kansas City and borders Overland Park. Lenexa is just inside I-435, the highway that circles Kansas City.

Originally Shawnee Tribe land, the city's name is believed to come from the Shawnee Chief Thomas Blackhoof's wife's name—which was Na-Nex-Se or Len-Ag-See. The tribal land could not be sold without the permission of the U.S. President, but after the Civil War the Shawnees wanted to sell and move to the Oklahoma Indian Territories, according to the Lenexa Historical Society. Enter Charles A. Bradshaw, who purchased 160 acres after the war and negotiated a railroad right-of-way, with the stipulation that a depot was maintained on the land. Lenexa was created in 1869—replete with a post office—and incorporated in 1907. Settlers arrived and took up farming, including well-regarded crops of spinach.

Growth started in the 1980s and today, the "Old Town" where this community was first settled remains part of Lenexa's appeal, replete with shops and restaurants and an annual Lenexa Community Days Parade. The city also boasts the Lenexa City Center, a mixed-use urban development under construction in the center of town. When finished, it will become a 200-acre neighborhood with shopping, homes, parks, plazas, restaurants, offices, hotels and all the amenities designed to draw residents to its four quadrants. The site will be home to Perceptive Software's world headquarters, B.E. Smith full service healthcare executive search firm, a six-story Hyatt Place hotel and conference center, and a high-end apartment complex.

Lenexa also is home to a U.S. National Archives Records Center that services and warehouses federal records in Iowa, Kansas, Missouri and Nebraska, as well as the Ogden IRS. The city's major employers include Alliance Data Systems, B/E Aerospace, CVS Caremark, Quest Diagnostics, J.C. Penney Logistics Center, and UPS. The Lenexa Conference Center within a historic renovated barn replete with state-of-the-art technology is also in the city; the Thompson Barn stands on the Lackman-Thompson Estate, which was built by German immigrants in 1887.

Students attend schools operated by three districts: the De Soto, Olathe, and the Shawnee Mission School districts, the latter being Missouri's third-largest with a graduation rate close to 91 percent. De Soto reports a 93.4 percent graduation rate, and the Olathe schools come in at 89 percent. Institutions of higher education close to Lenexa include Johnson County Community College, the University of Kansas Edwards Campus, Kansas State Innovation Campus, and The Art Institutes International—Kansas City.

The city's recreational facilities include Lake Lenexa at Black Hoof Park, a clever storm water drainage project that operates under the city's "Rain to Recreation" program. The city operates numerous parks with basketball, tennis and volleyball courts, fishing and boating opportunities, and hiking and biking trails. The Lenexa Community Center provides a variety of programs, and the city believes in its food festivals, including the Lenexa Spinach Festival, the Great Lenexa Barbeque Battle (for the official Kansas State Championship), and the Lenexa Chili Challenge.

Lenexa's midwestern climate means hot summers with high temperatures around 90 degrees, cold winters and relatively moderate amounts of precipitation.

Rankings

Business/Finance Rankings

- The personal finance site NerdWallet analyzed 183 American metropolitan areas with populations over 250,000 and more than 15,000 businesses to rank where entrepreneurs find the most success. Criteria included area economy, annual income, housing cost, unemployment rate, and the success rate of area businesses. Kansas City* ranked #36. *www.nerdwallet.com, "Best Places to Start a Business," April 27, 2015*
- Based on metro area social media reviews, the employment opinion group Glassdoor surveyed 50 of the largest U.S. metro areas and equally weighed cost of living, hiring opportunity, and job satisfaction to compose a list of "25 Best Cities for Jobs." The Kansas City* metro area was ranked #23 in overall job satisfaction. *www.glassdoor.com, "Best Cities for Jobs," May 19, 2015*
- In a survey of economic confidence in the nation's 50 largest metropolitan areas conducted January–December 2014, the Kansas City* metro area placed #44, according to Gallup's 2014 Economic Confidence Index. *Gallup, "San Jose and San Francisco Lead in Economic Confidence," March 19, 2015*
- The Brookings Institution ranked the 100 largest metro areas in the U.S. based on income inequality. Kansas City* was ranked #67 (#1 = greatest ineqality). Criteria: the "95/20 ratio," a figure representing the income at which a household earns more than 95 percent of all other households, divided by the income at which a household earns more than only 20 percent of all other households. *Brookings Institution, "Income Inequality, 100 Largest U.S. Metro Areas, 2007-2014," January 14, 2016*
- Kansas City* was identified as one of America's most frugal metro areas by *Coupons.com.* The city ranked #11 out of 25. Criteria: online coupon usage. *Coupons.com, "Top 25 Most Frugal Cities of 2014," May 11, 2015*
- Kansas City* was cited as one of America's top metros for new and expanded facility projects in 2015. The area ranked #10 in the large metro area category (population over 1 million). *Site Selection, "Top Metropolitans of 2015," March 2016*
- The Kansas City* metro area appeared on the Milken Institute "2015 Best Performing Cities" list. Rank: #103 out of 200 large metro areas. Criteria: job growth; wage and salary growth; high-tech output growth. *Milken Institute, "Best-Performing Cities 2015," December 2015*
- *Forbes* ranked the 200 most populous metro areas to determine the nation's "Best Places for Business and Careers." The Kansas City* metro area was ranked #61. Criteria: costs (business and living); job growth (past and projected); income growth; educational attainment (college and high school); projected economic growth; cultural and recreational opportunities; net migration patterns; number of highly ranked colleges. *Forbes, "The Best Places for Business and Careers 2015," July 29, 2015*

Education Rankings

- Personal finance website *WalletHub* analyzed the 150 largest U.S. metropolitan statistical areas to determine where the most educated Americans are choosing to settle. Criteria: education quality and attainment gap; education levels; percentage of workers with degrees; public school rankings; quality and size of each metro area's universities. Kansas City* was ranked #28 (#1 = most educated city). *www.WalletHub.com, "2015's Most and Least Educated Cities*

Environmental Rankings

- The Kansas City* metro area came in at #238 for the relative comfort of its climate on Sperling's list of "chill cities," as measured by the Sperling Heat Index. All 361 metro areas are included. Criteria included daytime high temperatures, nighttime low temperatures, dew point, and relative humidity at the high temperatures. *www.bertsperling.com, "Sperling's Chill Cities," July 18, 2013*

- Sperling's BestPlaces assessed 379 metropolitan areas of the United States for the likelihood of dangerously extreme weather events or earthquakes. In general the Southeast and South-Central regions have the highest risk of weather extremes and earthquakes, while the Pacific Northwest enjoys the lowest risk. Of the least risky metropolitan areas, the Kansas City* metro area was ranked #254. *www.bestplaces.net, "Safest Places from Natural Disasters," April 2011*

- Kansas City* was highlighted as one of the 25 most ozone-polluted metro areas in the U.S. during 2011 through 2013. The area ranked #24. *American Lung Association, State of the Air 2015*

Health/Fitness Rankings

- For each of the 50 most populous metro areas in the United States, the American College of Sports Medicine's American Fitness Index evaluated infrastructure, community assets, and policies that encourage healthy and fit lifestyles, including preventive health behaviors, levels of chronic disease conditions, health care access, and community resources and policies that support physical activity. The Kansas City* metro area ranked #26 for "community fitness." *www.americanfitnessindex.org, "ACSM American Fitness Index Health and Community Fitness Status of the 50 Largest Metropolitan Areas," May 2015*

- The Kansas City* metro area was identified as one of the worst cities for bed bugs in America by pest control company Orkin. The area ranked #44 out of 50 based on the number of bed bug treatments Orkin performed from January to December 2015. *Orkin, "Chicago Tops Bed Bug Cities List for Fourth Year in a Row," January 13, 2016*

- Kansas City* was identified as a "2016 Spring Allergy Capital." The area ranked #64 out of 100. Three groups of factors were used to identify the most severe cities for people with allergies during the spring season: annual pollen levels; medicine utilization; access to board-certified allergists. *Asthma and Allergy Foundation of America, "Spring Allergy Capitals 2016"*

- Kansas City* was identified as a "2015 Asthma Capital." The area ranked #72 out of the nation's 100 largest metropolitan areas. Criteria: estimated prevalence; self-reported prevalence; crude death rate for asthma; annual pollen score; annual air quality; public smoking laws; number of board-certified asthma specialists; school inhaler access laws; rescue medication use; controller medication use; ER visits for asthma; uninsured rate; poverty rate. *Asthma and Allergy Foundation of America, "Asthma Capitals 2015"*

- The Kansas City* metro area ranked #111 out of 190 in The Gallup-Healthways Well-Being Index. Criteria: purpose; social well being; financial health; community and physical health. Results are based on telephone interviews with adults, aged 18 and older, living in metropolitan areas in the 50 U.S. states and the District of Columbia. *Gallup-Healthways, "State of American Well-Being," February 23, 2016*

Safety Rankings

- The National Insurance Crime Bureau ranked 380 metro areas in the U.S. in terms of per capita rates of vehicle theft. The Kansas City* metro area ranked #37 (#1 = highest rate). Criteria: number of vehicle theft offenses per 100,000 inhabitants in 2014. *National Insurance Crime Bureau, "Hot Spots 2014," June 24, 2015*

Seniors/Retirement Rankings

- From its Best Cities for Successful Aging indexes, the Milken Institute generated rankings for metropolitan areas, weighing data in eight categories—health care, wellness, living arrangements, transportation, financial characteristics, education and employment opportunities, community engagement, and overall livability. The Kansas City* metro area was ranked #26 overall in the large metro area category. *Milken Institute, "Best Cities for Successful Aging, 2014"*

Miscellaneous Rankings

- The watchdog site Charity Navigator conducts an annual study of charities in the nation's major markets both to analyze statistical differences in their financial, accountability, and transparency practices and to track year-to-year variations in individual communities. The Kansas City* metro area was ranked #25 among the 30 metro markets in the rating dimension of Overall Score. *www.charitynavigator.org, "Metro Market Study 2015," June 5, 2015*
- Mars Chocolate North America, the makers of COMBOS®, in partnership with Sperling's BestPlaces, ranked 50 major metro areas in terms of their "manliness." The Kansas City* metro area ranked #20. Criteria: number of professional sports teams; number of nearby NASCAR tracks and racing events; manly lifestyle; concentration of manly retail stores; manly occupations per capita; salty snack sales; "Board of Manliness" rankings. *Mars Chocolate North America, "America's Manliest Cities 2012"*
- The National Alliance to End Homelessness ranked the 100 most populous metro areas with the highest rate of homelessness. The Kansas City* metro area ranked #49. Criteria: number of homeless people per 10,000 population in 2011. *National Alliance to End Homelessness, The State of Homelessness in America 2012*

***Lenexa is located within the Kansas City, MO-KS Metropolitan Statistical Area.**

Business Environment

CITY FINANCES

City Government Finances

Component	2012 ($000)	2012 ($ per capita)
Total Revenues	84,064	1,744
Total Expenditures	101,539	2,107
Debt Outstanding	280,094	5,812
Cash and Securities[1]	205,332	4,260

Note: (1) Cash and security holdings of a government at the close of its fiscal year, including those of its dependent agencies, utilities, and liquor stores.
Source: U.S Census Bureau, State & Local Government Finances 2012

City Government Revenue by Source

Source	2012 ($000)	2012 ($ per capita)
General Revenue		
From Federal Government	0	0
From State Government	8,102	168
From Local Governments	7,047	146
Taxes		
Property	26,538	550
Sales and Gross Receipts	20,768	430
Personal Income	0	0
Corporate Income	0	0
Motor Vehicle License	0	0
Other Taxes	1,065	22
Current Charges	5,955	123
Liquor Store	0	0
Utility	0	0
Employee Retirement	0	0

Source: U.S Census Bureau, State & Local Government Finances 2012

City Government Expenditures by Function

Function	2012 ($000)	2012 ($ per capita)	2012 (%)
General Direct Expenditures			
Air Transportation	0	0	0.0
Corrections	0	0	0.0
Education	0	0	0.0
Employment Security Administration	0	0	0.0
Financial Administration	1,439	29	1.4
Fire Protection	8,221	170	8.0
General Public Buildings	12,182	252	11.9
Governmental Administration, Other	992	20	0.9
Health	0	0	0.0
Highways	20,335	421	20.0
Hospitals	0	0	0.0
Housing and Community Development	47	< 1	< 0.1
Interest on General Debt	17,174	356	16.9
Judicial and Legal	1,132	23	1.1
Libraries	0	0	0.0
Parking	0	0	0.0
Parks and Recreation	8,615	178	8.4
Police Protection	12,352	256	12.1
Public Welfare	0	0	0.0
Sewerage	3,868	80	3.8
Solid Waste Management	0	0	0.0
Veterans' Services	0	0	0.0
Liquor Store	0	0	0.0
Utility	0	0	0.0
Employee Retirement	0	0	0.0

Source: U.S Census Bureau, State & Local Government Finances 2012

DEMOGRAPHICS

Population Growth

Area	1990 Census	2000 Census	2010 Census	2014* Estimate	Population Growth (%) 1990-2014	2010-2014
City	34,268	40,238	48,190	49,573	44.7	2.9
MSA[1]	1,636,528	1,836,038	2,035,334	2,040,869	24.7	0.3
U.S.	248,709,873	281,421,906	308,745,538	314,107,084	26.3	1.7

Note: (1) Figures cover the Kansas City, MO-KS Metropolitan Statistical Area—see Appendix B for areas included; (*) 2010-2014 5-year estimated population
Source: U.S. Census Bureau, 1990 Census, Census 2000, Census 2010, 2010-2014 American Community Survey 5-Year Estimates

Household Size

Area	Persons in Household (%) One	Two	Three	Four	Five	Six	Seven or More	Average Household Size
City	25.7	37.4	15.2	13.5	5.4	2.0	0.5	2.49
MSA[1]	28.8	33.6	15.3	13.0	5.8	2.0	1.1	2.54
U.S.	27.5	33.5	15.8	13.1	6.0	2.3	1.4	2.64

Note: (1) Figures cover the Kansas City, MO-KS Metropolitan Statistical Area—see Appendix B for areas included
Source: U.S. Census Bureau, 2010-2014 American Community Survey 5-Year Estimates

Race

Area	White Alone[2] (%)	Black Alone[2] (%)	Asian Alone[2] (%)	AIAN[3] Alone[2] (%)	NHOPI[4] Alone[2] (%)	Other Race Alone[2] (%)	Two or More Races (%)
City	86.5	5.7	3.9	0.2	0.1	0.9	2.8
MSA[1]	79.1	12.5	2.5	0.4	0.1	2.4	2.9
U.S.	73.8	12.6	5.0	0.8	0.2	4.7	2.9

Note: (1) Figures cover the Kansas City, MO-KS Metropolitan Statistical Area—see Appendix B for areas included; (2) Alone is defined as not being in combination with one or more other races; (3) American Indian and Alaska Native; (4) Native Hawaiian and Other Pacific Islander
Source: U.S. Census Bureau, 2010-2014 American Community Survey 5-Year Estimates

Hispanic or Latino Origin

Area	Total (%)	Mexican (%)	Puerto Rican (%)	Cuban (%)	Other (%)
City	8.0	5.4	0.0	0.2	2.3
MSA[1]	8.5	6.5	0.3	0.2	1.5
U.S.	16.9	10.8	1.6	0.6	3.8

Note: Persons of Hispanic or Latino origin can be of any race; (1) Figures cover the Kansas City, MO-KS Metropolitan Statistical Area—see Appendix B for areas included
Source: U.S. Census Bureau, 2010-2014 American Community Survey 5-Year Estimates

Ancestry

Area	German	Irish	English	American	Italian	Polish	French[2]	Scottish	Dutch
City	29.8	15.1	12.9	5.2	3.0	2.4	3.1	2.0	1.4
MSA[1]	23.2	13.3	10.2	8.1	3.5	1.7	2.6	2.0	1.6
U.S.	14.9	10.8	8.0	7.1	5.5	3.0	2.7	1.7	1.4

Note: Figures are the percentage of the total population reporting a particular ancestry. The nine most commonly reported ancestries in the U.S. are shown. Figures include multiple ancestries (e.g. if a person reported being Irish and Italian, they were included in both columns); (1) Figures cover the Kansas City, MO-KS Metropolitan Statistical Area—see Appendix B for areas included; (2) Excludes Basque
Source: U.S. Census Bureau, 2010-2014 American Community Survey 5-Year Estimates

Foreign-Born Population

Area	Percent of Population Born in								
	Any Foreign Country	Asia	Mexico	Europe	Carribean	Central America[2]	South America	Africa	Canada
City	8.8	3.4	1.8	0.7	0.1	0.9	0.7	1.0	0.2
MSA[1]	6.4	2.0	2.2	0.6	0.2	0.4	0.2	0.6	0.1
U.S.	13.1	3.8	3.7	1.5	1.2	1.0	0.9	0.6	0.3

Note: (1) Figures cover the Kansas City, MO-KS Metropolitan Statistical Area—see Appendix B for areas included; (2) Excludes Mexico.
Source: U.S. Census Bureau, 2010-2014 American Community Survey 5-Year Estimates

Marital Status

Area	Never Married	Now Married[2]	Separated	Widowed	Divorced
City	28.6	55.5	1.3	4.3	10.3
MSA[1]	29.7	50.8	1.8	5.5	12.2
U.S.	32.5	48.4	2.2	5.9	10.9

Note: Figures are percentages and cover the population 15 years of age and older; (1) Figures cover the Kansas City, MO-KS Metropolitan Statistical Area—see Appendix B for areas included; (2) Excludes separated
Source: U.S. Census Bureau, 2010-2014 American Community Survey 5-Year Estimates

Disability Status

Area	All Ages	Under 18 Years Old	18 to 64 Years Old	65 Years and Over
City	8.0	3.9	6.2	28.5
MSA[1]	11.6	3.7	10.2	35.5
U.S.	12.3	4.1	10.2	36.3

Note: Figures show percent of the civilian noninstitutionalized population that reported having a disability. Disability status is determined from from six types of difficulty: vision, hearing, cognitive, ambulatory, self-care, and independent living. For children under 5 years old, hearing and vision difficulty are used to determine disability status. For children between the ages of 5 and 14, disability status is determined from hearing, vision, cognitive, ambulatory, and self-care difficulties. For people aged 15 years and older, they are considered to have a disability if they have difficulty with any one of the six difficulty types; (1) Figures cover the Kansas City, MO-KS Metropolitan Statistical Area—see Appendix B for areas included.
Source: U.S. Census Bureau, 2010-2014 American Community Survey 5-Year Estimates

Age

Area	Percent of Population									Median Age
	Under Age 5	Age 5–19	Age 20–34	Age 35–44	Age 45–54	Age 55–64	Age 65–74	Age 75–84	Age 85+	
City	6.9	19.4	21.3	13.7	12.6	14.8	6.1	2.9	2.4	36.6
MSA[1]	6.9	20.7	20.0	13.3	14.3	12.2	7.0	3.8	1.8	36.7
U.S.	6.4	19.9	20.6	13.0	14.1	12.3	7.6	4.3	1.9	37.4

Note: (1) Figures cover the Kansas City, MO-KS Metropolitan Statistical Area—see Appendix B for areas included
Source: U.S. Census Bureau, 2010-2014 American Community Survey 5-Year Estimates

Gender

Area	Males	Females	Males per 100 Females
City	24,055	25,518	94.3
MSA[1]	1,000,049	1,040,820	96.1
U.S.	154,515,159	159,591,925	96.8

Note: (1) Figures cover the Kansas City, MO-KS Metropolitan Statistical Area—see Appendix B for areas included
Source: U.S. Census Bureau, 2010-2014 American Community Survey 5-Year Estimates

Religious Groups by Family

Area	Catholic	Baptist	Non-Den.	Methodist[2]	Lutheran	LDS[3]	Pentecostal	Presbyterian[4]	Muslim[5]	Judaism
MSA[1]	12.6	13.1	5.2	5.8	2.2	2.4	2.6	1.6	0.3	0.4
U.S.	19.1	9.3	4.0	4.0	2.3	2.0	1.9	1.6	0.8	0.7

Note: Figures are the number of adherents as a percentage of the total population; (1) Figures cover the Kansas City, MO-KS Metropolitan Statistical Area—see Appendix B for areas included; (2) Methodist/Pietist; (3) Latter Day Saints; (4) Reformed; (5) Figures are estimates
Source: Association of Statisticians of American Religious Bodies, 2010 U.S. Religion Census: Religious Congregations & Membership Study

Religious Groups by Tradition

Area	Catholic	Evangelical Protestant	Mainline Protestant	Other Tradition	Black Protestant	Orthodox
MSA[1]	12.6	20.5	9.9	3.6	2.6	0.1
U.S.	19.1	16.2	7.3	4.3	1.6	0.3

Note: Figures are the number of adherents as a percentage of the total population; (1) Figures cover the Kansas City, MO-KS Metropolitan Statistical Area—see Appendix B for areas included
Source: Association of Statisticians of American Religious Bodies, 2010 U.S. Religion Census: Religious Congregations & Membership Study

ECONOMY

Gross Metropolitan Product

Area	2013	2014	2015	2016	Rank[2]
MSA[1]	117.3	121.8	126.4	132.3	29

Note: Figures are in billions of dollars; (1) Figures cover the Kansas City, MO-KS Metropolitan Statistical Area—see Appendix B for areas included; (2) Rank is based on 2016 data and ranges from 1 to 381
Source: The U.S. Conference of Mayors, U.S. Metro Economies: GMP and Employment 2014-2016, June 2015

Economic Growth

Area	2011-13 (%)	2014 (%)	2015 (%)	2016 (%)	Rank[2]
MSA[1]	1.5	2.2	2.4	2.7	135
U.S.	2.2	2.4	2.3	2.9	–

Note: Figures are real gross metropolitan product (GMP) growth rates and represent annual average percent change; (1) Figures cover the Kansas City, MO-KS Metropolitan Statistical Area—see Appendix B for areas included; (2) Rank is based on 2016 data and ranges from 1 to 381
Source: The U.S. Conference of Mayors, U.S. Metro Economies: GMP and Employment 2014-2016, June 2015

Metropolitan Area Exports

Area	2009	2010	2011	2012	2013	2014	Rank[2]
MSA[1]	5,888.8	7,374.1	7,958.9	7,880.7	8,012.0	8,262.8	40

Note: Figures are in millions of dollars; (1) Figures cover the Kansas City, MO-KS Metropolitan Statistical Area—see Appendix B for areas included; (2) Rank is based on 2014 data and ranges from 1 to 385
Source: U.S. Department of Commerce, International Trade Administration, Office of Trade & Industry Information, Manufacturing & Services, data extracted March 10, 2016

Building Permits

Area	Single-Family			Multi-Family			Total		
	2014	2015p	Pct. Chg.	2014	2015p	Pct. Chg.	2014	2015p	Pct. Chg.
City	193	249	29.0	446	40	-91.0	639	289	-54.8
MSA[1]	4,170	4,507	8.1	4,031	4,488	11.3	8,201	8,995	9.7
U.S.	640,300	690,800	7.9	411,800	487,600	18.4	1,052,100	1,178,400	12.0

Note: (1) Figures cover the Kansas City, MO-KS Metropolitan Statistical Area—see Appendix B for areas included; Figures represent new, privately-owned housing units authorized (unadjusted data); All permit data are based on estimates with imputation; (p) preliminary data.
Source: U.S. Census Bureau, Manufacturing, Mining, and Construction Statistics, Building Permits, 2014, 2015

Bankruptcy Filings

Area	Business Filings			Nonbusiness Filings		
	2014	2015	% Chg.	2014	2015	% Chg.
Johnson County	80	75	-6.3	1,369	1,121	-18.1
U.S.	26,983	24,735	-8.3	909,812	819,760	-9.9

Note: Business filings include Chapter 7, Chapter 11, Chapter 12, and Chapter 13; Nonbusiness filings include Chapter 7, Chapter 11, and Chapter 13
Source: Administrative Office of the U.S. Courts, Business and Nonbusiness Bankruptcy, County Cases Commenced by Chapter of the Bankruptcy Code, During the 12- Month Period Ending December 31, 2014 and Business and Nonbusiness Bankruptcy, County Cases Commenced by Chapter of the Bankruptcy Code, During the 12- Month Period Ending December 31, 2015

Housing Vacancy Rates

Area	Gross Vacancy Rate[2] (%)			Year-Round Vacancy Rate[3] (%)			Rental Vacancy Rate[4] (%)			Homeowner Vacancy Rate[5] (%)		
	2013	2014	2015	2013	2014	2015	2013	2014	2015	2013	2014	2015
MSA[1]	10.8	9.0	7.3	10.4	8.6	7.1	10.1	9.5	7.9	2.0	1.5	1.3
U.S.	13.6	13.4	12.9	10.7	10.4	10.0	8.3	7.6	7.1	2.0	1.9	1.8

Note: (1) Figures cover the Kansas City, MO-KS Metropolitan Statistical Area—see Appendix B for areas included; (2) The percentage of the total housing inventory that is vacant; (3) The percentage of the housing inventory (excluding seasonal units) that is year-round vacant; (4) The percentage of rental inventory that is vacant for rent; (5) The percentage of homeowner inventory that is vacant for sale
Source: U.S. Census Bureau, Housing Vacancies and Homeownership Annual Statistics: 2015

INCOME

Income

Area	Per Capita ($)	Median Household ($)	Average Household ($)
City	38,390	75,400	94,694
MSA[1]	30,101	57,056	75,695
U.S.	28,555	53,482	74,596

Note: (1) Figures cover the Kansas City, MO-KS Metropolitan Statistical Area—see Appendix B for areas included
Source: U.S. Census Bureau, 2010-2014 American Community Survey 5-Year Estimates

Household Income Distribution

Area	Percent of Households Earning							
	Under $15,000	$15,000 -24,999	$25,000 -34,999	$35,000 -49,999	$50,000 -74,999	$75,000 -99,000	$100,000 -149,999	$150,000 and up
City	5.0	7.4	7.3	12.2	17.8	14.6	20.0	15.7
MSA[1]	10.9	9.5	9.9	13.7	18.6	13.4	14.4	9.6
U.S.	12.5	10.7	10.2	13.5	17.8	12.2	13.0	10.0

Note: (1) Figures cover the Kansas City, MO-KS Metropolitan Statistical Area—see Appendix B for areas included
Source: U.S. Census Bureau, 2010-2014 American Community Survey 5-Year Estimates

Poverty Rate

Area	All Ages	Under 18 Years Old	18 to 64 Years Old	65 Years and Over
City	7.6	10.6	6.9	5.2
MSA[1]	12.6	18.0	11.6	6.8
U.S.	15.6	21.9	14.6	9.4

Note: Figures are percentage of people whose income during the past 12 months was below the poverty level; (1) Figures cover the Kansas City, MO-KS Metropolitan Statistical Area—see Appendix B for areas included
Source: U.S. Census Bureau, 2010-2014 American Community Survey 5-Year Estimates

EMPLOYMENT

Labor Force and Employment

Area	Civilian Labor Force			Workers Employed		
	Dec. 2014	Dec. 2015	% Chg.	Dec. 2014	Dec. 2015	% Chg.
City	29,595	29,797	0.6	28,605	28,898	1.0
MSA[1]	1,107,078	1,118,856	1.0	1,055,730	1,076,324	1.9
U.S.	155,521,000	157,245,000	1.1	147,190,000	149,703,000	1.7

Note: Data is not seasonally adjusted and covers workers 16 years of age and older; (1) Figures cover the Kansas City, MO-KS Metropolitan Statistical Area—see Appendix B for areas included
Source: Bureau of Labor Statistics, Local Area Unemployment Statistics

Unemployment Rate

Area	2015											
	Jan.	Feb.	Mar.	Apr.	May	Jun.	Jul.	Aug.	Sep.	Oct.	Nov.	Dec.
City	3.9	3.7	3.6	3.6	3.7	3.8	4.1	3.8	3.2	3.4	3.0	3.0
MSA[1]	5.9	5.9	5.3	5.1	5.3	5.3	5.5	5.2	4.4	4.2	3.9	3.8
U.S.	6.1	5.8	5.6	5.1	5.3	5.5	5.6	5.2	4.9	4.8	4.8	4.8

Note: Data is not seasonally adjusted and covers workers 16 years of age and older; (1) Figures cover the Kansas City, MO-KS Metropolitan Statistical Area—see Appendix B for areas included
Source: Bureau of Labor Statistics, Local Area Unemployment Statistics

Employment by Occupation

Occupation Classification	City (%)	MSA[1] (%)	U.S. (%)
Management, Business, Science, and Arts	49.3	38.9	36.4
Natural Resources, Construction, and Maintenance	4.9	7.6	9.0
Production, Transportation, and Material Moving	5.1	11.5	12.1
Sales and Office	26.9	25.7	24.4
Service	13.7	16.3	18.2

Note: Figures cover employed civilians 16 years of age and older; (1) Figures cover the Kansas City, MO-KS Metropolitan Statistical Area—see Appendix B for areas included
Source: U.S. Census Bureau, 2010-2014 American Community Survey 5-Year Estimates

Employment by Industry

Sector	MSA[1]		U.S.
	Number of Employees	Percent of Total	Percent of Total
Construction, Mining, and Logging	46,200	4.3	5.0
Education and Health Services	149,700	14.2	15.7
Financial Activities	74,900	7.1	5.7
Government	148,100	14.0	15.5
Information	19,500	1.8	1.9
Leisure and Hospitality	100,600	9.5	10.4
Manufacturing	76,200	7.2	8.6
Other Services	41,200	3.9	3.9
Professional and Business Services	183,300	17.4	13.9
Retail Trade	112,500	10.6	11.3
Transportation, Warehousing, and Utilities	48,600	4.6	3.9
Wholesale Trade	50,700	4.8	4.1

Note: Figures are non-farm employment as of December 2015. Figures are not seasonally adjusted and include workers 16 years of age and older; (1) Figures cover the Kansas City, MO-KS Metropolitan Statistical Area—see Appendix B for areas included; n/a not available
Source: Bureau of Labor Statistics, Current Employment Statistics, Employment, Hours, and Earnings

Occupations with Greatest Projected Employment Growth: 2012 – 2022

Occupation[1]	2012 Employment	2022 Projected Employment	Numeric Employment Change	Percent Employment Change
Personal Care Aides	19,670	28,280	8,610	43.7
Registered Nurses	28,440	33,460	5,020	17.7
Customer Service Representatives	26,680	31,400	4,720	17.7
Nursing Assistants	19,840	23,710	3,870	19.5
Secretaries and Administrative Assistants, Except Legal, Medical, and Executive	28,240	32,070	3,830	13.6
Laborers and Freight, Stock, and Material Movers, Hand	22,110	25,700	3,590	16.3
Combined Food Preparation and Serving Workers, Including Fast Food	21,700	24,930	3,230	14.9
Janitors and Cleaners, Except Maids and Housekeeping Cleaners	23,330	26,500	3,170	13.6
Heavy and Tractor-Trailer Truck Drivers	21,040	23,640	2,600	12.3
Retail Salespersons	38,930	41,510	2,580	6.6

Note: Projections cover Kansas; (1) Sorted by numeric employment change
Source: www.projectionscentral.com, State Occupational Projections, 2012–2022 Long-Term Projections

Fastest Growing Occupations: 2012 – 2022

Occupation[1]	2012 Employment	2022 Projected Employment	Numeric Employment Change	Percent Employment Change
Interpreters and Translators	830	1,220	390	47.9
Personal Care Aides	19,670	28,280	8,610	43.7
Diagnostic Medical Sonographers	610	870	260	41.0
Health Specialties Teachers, Postsecondary	740	1,040	300	40.3
Nursing Instructors and Teachers, Postsecondary	480	670	190	39.7
Information Security Analysts	570	780	210	38.1
Occupational Therapy Assistants	400	540	140	37.7
Home Health Aides	6,670	9,150	2,480	37.2
Computer Numerically Controlled Machine Tool Programmers, Metal and Plastic	480	650	170	34.9
Insulation Workers, Mechanical	390	520	130	33.8

Note: Projections cover Kansas; (1) Sorted by percent employment change and excludes occupations with numeric employment change less than 100
Source: www.projectionscentral.com, State Occupational Projections, 2012–2022 Long-Term Projections

Average Wages

Occupation	$/Hr.	Occupation	$/Hr.
Accountants and Auditors	33.45	Maids and Housekeeping Cleaners	10.01
Automotive Mechanics	18.68	Maintenance and Repair Workers	17.76
Bookkeepers	18.37	Marketing Managers	61.85
Carpenters	24.09	Nuclear Medicine Technologists	32.84
Cashiers	9.86	Nurses, Licensed Practical	19.56
Clerks, General Office	15.39	Nurses, Registered	30.45
Clerks, Receptionists/Information	14.08	Nursing Assistants	12.30
Clerks, Shipping/Receiving	15.42	Packers and Packagers, Hand	11.13
Computer Programmers	36.37	Physical Therapists	37.13
Computer Systems Analysts	40.43	Postal Service Mail Carriers	24.23
Computer User Support Specialists	24.12	Real Estate Brokers	n/a
Cooks, Restaurant	10.81	Retail Salespersons	11.65
Dentists	78.43	Sales Reps., Exc. Tech./Scientific	32.40
Electrical Engineers	44.86	Sales Reps., Tech./Scientific	44.34
Electricians	28.55	Secretaries, Exc. Legal/Med./Exec.	16.32
Financial Managers	62.77	Security Guards	13.51
First-Line Supervisors/Managers, Sales	19.02	Surgeons	123.07
Food Preparation Workers	10.13	Teacher Assistants*	11.75
General and Operations Managers	53.31	Teachers, Elementary School*	23.84
Hairdressers/Cosmetologists	13.36	Teachers, Secondary School*	22.74
Internists	92.96	Telemarketers	14.09
Janitors and Cleaners	12.82	Truck Drivers, Heavy/Tractor-Trailer	21.09
Landscaping/Groundskeeping Workers	12.89	Truck Drivers, Light/Delivery Svcs.	17.22
Lawyers	57.35	Waiters and Waitresses	9.56

Note: Wage data covers the Kansas City, MO-KS Metropolitan Statistical Area—see Appendix B for areas included; (*) Hourly wages for elementary/secondary school teachers and teacher assistants were calculated by the editors from annual wage data based on a 40 hour work week; n/a not available.
Source: Bureau of Labor Statistics, Metro Area Occupational Employment and Wage Estimates, May 2015

TAXES

State Corporate Income Tax Rates

State	Tax Rate (%)	Income Brackets ($)	Num. of Brackets	Financial Institution Tax Rate (%)[a]	Federal Income Tax Ded.
Kansas	4.0 (l)	Flat rate	1	2.25 (l)	No

Note: Tax rates as of January 1, 2016; (a) Rates listed are the corporate income tax rate applied to financial institutions or excise taxes based on income. Some states have other taxes based upon the value of deposits or shares; (l) In addition to the flat 4% corporate income tax, Kansas levies a 3.0% surtax on taxable income over $50,000. Banks pay a privilege tax of 2.25% of net income, plus a surtax of 2.125% (2.25% for savings and loans, trust companies, and federally chartered savings banks) on net income in excess of $25,000.
Source: Federation of Tax Administrators, "State Corporate Income Tax Rates, 2016"

State Individual Income Tax Rates

State	Tax Rate (%)	Income Brackets ($)	Num. of Brackets	Personal Exempt. ($)[1] Single	Personal Exempt. ($)[1] Dependents	Fed. Inc. Tax Ded.
Kansas	2.7 - 4.6	15,000 (b)	2	2,250	2,250	No

Note: Tax rates as of January 1, 2016; Local- and county-level taxes are not included; n/a not applicable; (1) Married joint filers generally receive double the single exemption; (b) For joint returns, taxes are twice the tax on half the couple's income.
Source: Federation of Tax Administrators, "State Individual Income Tax Rates, 2016"

Various State and Local Tax Rates

State	State and Local Sales and Use (%)	State Sales and Use (%)	Gasoline[1] (¢/gal.)	Cigarette[2] ($/pack)	Spirits[3] ($/gal.)	Wine[4] ($/gal.)	Beer[5] ($/gal.)
Kansas	9.10	6.5	24.03	1.29	2.50	0.30 (l)	0.18

Note: All tax rates as of January 1, 2016; (1) The American Petroleum Institute has developed a methodology for determining the average tax rate on a gallon of fuel. Rates may include any of the following: excise taxes, environmental fees, storage tank fees, other fees or taxes, general sales tax, and local taxes. In states where gasoline is subject to the general sales tax, or where the fuel tax is based on the average sale price, the average rate determined by API is sensitive to changes in the price of gasoline. States that fully or partially apply general sales taxes to gasoline: CA, CO, GA, IL, IN, MI, NY; (2) The federal excise tax of $1.0066 per pack and local taxes are not included; (3) Rates are those applicable to off-premise sales of 40% alcohol by volume (a.b.v.) distilled spirits in 750ml containers. Local excise taxes are excluded; (4) Rates are those applicable to off-premise sales of 11% a.b.v. non-carbonated wine in 750ml containers; (5) Rates are those applicable to off-premise sales of 4.7% a.b.v. beer in 12 ounce containers; (l) Different rates also applicable according to alcohol content, place of production, size of container, place purchased (on- or off-premise or on board airlines) or type of wine (carbonated, vermouth, etc.).
Source: Tax Foundation, 2016 Facts & Figures: How Does Your State Compare?

State Business Tax Climate Index Rankings

State	Overall Rank	Corporate Tax Rank	Individual Income Tax Rank	Sales Tax Rank	Unemployment Insurance Tax Rank	Property Tax Rank
Kansas	22	40	18	32	10	19

Note: The index is a measure of how each state's tax laws affect economic performance. The lower the rank, the more favorable a state's tax system is for business. States without a given tax are given a ranking of 1. The scores/rankings for the District of Columbia do not affect other states. The 2016 index represents the tax climate as of July 1, 2015 (the beginning of Fiscal Year 2016).
Source: Tax Foundation, State Business Tax Climate Index 2016

TRANSPORTATION

Means of Transportation to Work

Area	Car/Truck/Van		Public Transportation			Bicycle	Walked	Other Means	Worked at Home
	Drove Alone	Car-pooled	Bus	Subway	Railroad				
City	86.6	6.5	0.3	0.0	0.0	0.2	0.8	0.4	5.2
MSA[1]	83.3	8.9	1.1	0.0	0.0	0.2	1.3	1.0	4.3
U.S.	76.4	9.6	2.6	1.8	0.6	0.6	2.8	1.3	4.4

Note: Figures are percentages and cover workers 16 years of age and older; (1) Figures cover the Kansas City, MO-KS Metropolitan Statistical Area—see Appendix B for areas included
Source: U.S. Census Bureau, 2010-2014 American Community Survey 5-Year Estimates

Travel Time to Work

Area	Less Than 10 Minutes	10 to 19 Minutes	20 to 29 Minutes	30 to 44 Minutes	45 to 59 Minutes	60 to 89 Minutes	90 Minutes or More
City	13.0	38.4	27.1	17.7	1.9	0.9	0.9
MSA[1]	13.1	31.4	25.3	20.7	5.9	2.3	1.2
U.S.	13.3	29.6	21.0	20.2	7.7	5.7	2.6

Note: Figures are percentages and include workers 16 years old and over; (1) Figures cover the Kansas City, MO-KS Metropolitan Statistical Area—see Appendix B for areas included
Source: U.S. Census Bureau, 2010-2014 American Community Survey 5-Year Estimates

Freeway Travel Time Index

Area	1985	1990	1995	2000	2005	2010	2014
Urban Area Rank[1,2]	54	46	68	72	77	76	76
Urban Area Index[1]	1.06	1.10	1.11	1.13	1.14	1.14	1.15
Average Index[3]	1.09	1.11	1.14	1.17	1.20	1.19	1.20

Note: Freeway Travel Time Index—the ratio of travel time in the peak period to the travel time at free-flow conditions. For example, a value of 1.30 indicates a 20-minute free-flow trip takes 26 minutes in the peak (20 minutes x 1.30 = 26 minutes); (1) Covers the Kansas City MO-KS urban area; (2) Rank is based on 101 urban areas (#1 = highest travel time index); (3) Average of 101 urban areas
Source: Texas Transportation Institute, 2015 Urban Mobility Scorecard, August 2015

Freeway Commuter Stress Index

Area	1985	1990	1995	2000	2005	2010	2014
Urban Area Rank[1,2]	66	51	71	76	81	82	79
Urban Area Index[1]	1.07	1.12	1.13	1.15	1.16	1.16	1.17
Average Index[3]	1.13	1.16	1.19	1.22	1.25	1.24	1.25

Note: The Freeway Commuter Stress Index is the same as the Freeway Travel Time Index (see table above) except that it includes only the travel in the peak directions during the peak periods; the TTI includes travel in all directions during the peak period. Thus, the CSI is more indicative of the work trip experienced by each commuter on a daily basis. (1) Covers the Kansas City MO-KS urban area; (2) Rank is based on 101 urban areas (#1 = highest stress index); (3) Average of 101 urban areas

Source: Texas Transportation Institute, 2015 Urban Mobility Scorecard, August 2015

Living Environment

COST OF LIVING

Cost of Living Index

Composite Index	Groceries	Housing	Utilities	Transportation	Health Care	Misc. Goods/ Services
n/a	n/a	n/a	n/a	n/a	n/a	n/a

Note: The Cost of Living Index measures regional differences in the cost of consumer goods and services, excluding taxes and non-consumer expenditures, for professional and managerial households in the top income quintile. It is based on more than 50,000 prices covering almost 60 different items for which prices are collected three times a year by chambers of commerce, economic development organizations or university applied economic centers in each participating urban area. The numbers shown should be read as a percentage above or below the national average of 100. For example, a value of 115.4 in the groceries column indicates that grocery prices are 15.4% higher than the national average. Small differences in the index numbers should not be interpreted as significant; n/a not available.
Source: The Council for Community and Economic Research, ACCRA Cost of Living Index, 2015

Grocery Prices

Area[1]	T-Bone Steak ($/pound)	Frying Chicken ($/pound)	Whole Milk ($/half gal.)	Eggs ($/dozen)	Orange Juice ($/64 oz.)	Coffee ($/11.5 oz.)
City[2]	n/a	n/a	n/a	n/a	n/a	n/a
Avg.	10.99	1.43	2.25	2.26	3.58	4.48
Min.	7.16	0.98	1.30	1.35	2.88	2.98
Max.	14.13	2.43	3.85	4.81	6.39	7.56

Note: (1) Values for the local area are compared with the average, minimum and maximum values for all 292 areas in the Cost of Living Index; (2) Figures cover the Lenexa KS urban area; n/a not available; **T-Bone Steak** *(price per pound);* **Frying Chicken** *(price per pound, whole fryer);* **Whole Milk** *(half gallon carton);* **Eggs** *(price per dozen, Grade A, large);* **Orange Juice** *(64 oz. Tropicana or Florida Natural);* **Coffee** *(11.5 oz. can, vacuum-packed, Maxwell House, Hills Bros, or Folgers).*
Source: The Council for Community and Economic Research, ACCRA Cost of Living Index, 2015

Housing and Utility Costs

Area[1]	New Home Price ($)	Apartment Rent ($/month)	All Electric ($/month)	Part Electric ($/month)	Other Energy ($/month)	Telephone ($/month)
City[2]	n/a	n/a	n/a	n/a	n/a	n/a
Avg.	312,874	945	179.30	95.07	72.96	28.11
Min.	178,682	479	116.28	43.14	26.46	10.01
Max.	1,472,476	3,984	504.25	189.44	421.11	43.06

Note: (1) Values for the local area are compared with the average, minimum and maximum values for all 292 areas in the Cost of Living Index; (2) Figures cover the Lenexa KS urban area; n/a not available; **New Home Price** *(2,400 sf living area, 8,000 sf lot, in urban area with full utilities);* **Apartment Rent** *(950 sf 2 bedroom/1.5 or 2 bath, unfurnished, excluding all utilities except water);* **All Electric** *(average monthly cost for an all-electric home);* **Part Electric** *(average monthly cost for a part-electric home);* **Other Energy** *(average monthly cost for natural gas, fuel oil, coal, wood, and any other forms of energy except electricity);* **Telephone** *(price includes basic monthly rate for a private residential line plus additional local usage charges incurred by a family of four).*
Source: The Council for Community and Economic Research, ACCRA Cost of Living Index, 2015

Health Care, Transportation, and Other Costs

Area[1]	Doctor ($/visit)	Dentist ($/visit)	Optometrist ($/visit)	Gasoline ($/gallon)	Beauty Salon ($/visit)	Men's Shirt ($)
City[2]	n/a	n/a	n/a	n/a	n/a	n/a
Avg.	105.15	89.02	99.78	2.38	35.30	28.10
Min.	66.87	56.09	48.53	1.95	18.91	13.38
Max.	182.34	150.36	228.33	4.09	67.91	63.80

Note: (1) Values for the local area are compared with the average, minimum and maximum values for all 292 areas in the Cost of Living Index; (2) Figures cover the Lenexa KS urban area; n/a not available; **Doctor** *(general practitioners routine exam of an established patient);* **Dentist** *(adult teeth cleaning and periodic oral examination);* **Optometrist** *(full vision eye exam for established adult patient);* **Gasoline** *(one gallon regular unleaded, national brand, including all taxes, cash price at self-service pump if available);* **Beauty Salon** *(woman's shampoo, trim, and blow-dry);* **Men's Shirt** *(cotton/polyester dress shirt, pinpoint weave, long sleeves).*
Source: The Council for Community and Economic Research, ACCRA Cost of Living Index, 2015

HOUSING

House Price Index (HPI)

Area	National Ranking[2]	Quarterly Change (%)	One-Year Change (%)	Five-Year Change (%)
MSA[1]	79	1.80	6.40	8.50
U.S.[3]	–	1.45	5.76	22.85

Note: The HPI is a weighted repeat sales index. It measures average price changes in repeat sales or refinancings on the same properties. This information is obtained by reviewing repeat mortgage transactions on single-family properties whose mortgages have been purchased or securitized by Fannie Mae or Freddie Mac in January 1975; (1) Kansas City Metropolitan Statistical Area—see Appendix B for areas included; (2) Rankings are based on annual percentage change for all metro areas containing at least 15,000 transactions over the last 10 years and ranges from 1 to 266; (3) figures based on a weighted average of Census Division estimates using a seasonally adjusted, purchase-only index; all figures are for the period ending December 31, 2015
Source: Federal Housing Finance Agency, House Price Index, February 25, 2016

Median Single-Family Home Prices

Area	2013	2014	2015p	Percent Change 2014 to 2015
MSA[1]	154.8	158.8	170.4	7.3
U.S. Average	197.4	208.9	223.9	7.2

Note: Figures are median sales prices of existing single-family homes in thousands of dollars; (p) preliminary; n/a not available; (1) Kansas City, MO-KS Metropolitan Statistical Area—see Appendix B for areas included
Source: National Association of Realtors, Median Sales Price of Existing Single-Family Homes for Metropolitan Areas, 4th Quarter 2015

Qualifying Income Based on Median Sales Price of Existing Single-Family Homes

Area	With 5% Down ($)	With 10% Down ($)	With 20% Down ($)
MSA[1]	37,257	35,296	31,374
U.S. Average	49,535	46,928	41,714

Note: Figures are preliminary; Qualifying income is based on a mortgage rate of 4.1%. Monthly principal and interest payment is limited to 25% of income; n/a not available; (1) Kansas City, MO-KS Metropolitan Statistical Area—see Appendix B for areas included
Source: National Association of Realtors, Qualifying Income Based on Median Sales Price of Existing Single-Family Homes for Metropolitan Areas, 4th Quarter 2015

Median Apartment Condo-Coop Home Prices

Area	2013	2014	2015p	Percent Change 2014 to 2015
MSA[1]	n/a	n/a	n/a	n/a
U.S. Average	194.9	204.3	210.7	3.1

Note: Figures are median sales prices of existing apartment condo-coop homes in thousands of dollars; (p) preliminary; n/a not available; (1) Kansas City, MO-KS Metropolitan Statistical Area—see Appendix B for areas included
Source: National Association of Realtors, Median Sales Price of Existing Apartment Condo-Coop Homes for Metropolitan Areas, 4th Quarter 2015

Gross Monthly Rent

Area	Under $200	$200 -299	$300 -499	$500 -749	$750 -999	$1,000 -1,499	$1,500 and up	Median ($)
City	0.1	0.1	1.3	13.7	39.4	33.0	12.4	960
MSA[1]	1.3	2.8	6.5	27.1	31.0	24.6	6.7	839
U.S.	1.5	3.2	7.4	21.0	24.1	26.9	15.9	920

Note: Figures are percentages except for Median; Gross rent is the contract rent plus the estimated average monthly cost of utilities (electricity, gas, and water and sewer) and fuels (oil, coal, kerosene, wood, etc.) if these are paid by the renter (or paid for the renter by someone else); (1) Figures cover the Kansas City, MO-KS Metropolitan Statistical Area—see Appendix B for areas included
Source: U.S. Census Bureau, 2010-2014 American Community Survey 5-Year Estimates

Homeownership Rate

Area	2008 (%)	2009 (%)	2010 (%)	2011 (%)	2012 (%)	2013 (%)	2014 (%)	2015 (%)
MSA[1]	70.2	69.5	68.8	68.5	65.1	65.6	66.1	65.0
U.S.	67.8	67.4	66.9	66.1	65.4	65.1	64.5	63.7

Note: (1) Figures cover the Kansas City, MO-KS Metropolitan Statistical Area—see Appendix B for areas included
Source: U.S. Census Bureau, Housing Vacancies and Homeownership Annual Statistics: 2015

Year Housing Structure Built

Area	2010 or Later	2000 -2009	1990 -1999	1980 -1989	1970 -1979	1960 -1969	1950 -1959	1940 -1949	Before 1940	Median Year
City	1.0	20.0	16.5	25.5	26.2	5.8	3.2	0.8	1.0	1985
MSA[1]	0.7	15.0	14.3	12.6	15.9	12.5	12.2	4.9	11.9	1975
U.S.	1.0	14.9	13.9	13.8	15.8	11.0	10.8	5.4	13.3	1976

Note: Figures are percentages except for Median Year; (1) Figures cover the Kansas City, MO-KS Metropolitan Statistical Area—see Appendix B for areas included
Source: U.S. Census Bureau, 2010-2014 American Community Survey 5-Year Estimates

HEALTH

Health Risk Data

Category	MSA[1] (%)	U.S. (%)
Adults aged 18–64 who have any kind of health care coverage	83.7	79.6
Adults who reported being in good or excellent health	84.0	83.1
Adults who are current smokers	22.0	19.6
Adults who are heavy drinkers[2]	6.2	6.1
Adults who are binge drinkers[3]	17.3	16.9
Adults who are overweight (BMI 25.0 - 29.9)	35.7	35.8
Adults who are obese (BMI 30.0 - 99.8)	28.3	27.6
Adults who participated in any physical activities in the past month	79.5	77.1
Adults 50+ who have ever had a sigmoidoscopy or colonoscopy	72.8	67.3
Women aged 40+ who have had a mammogram within the past two years	76.1	74.0
Men aged 40+ who have had a PSA test within the past two years	50.8	45.2
Adults aged 65+ who have had flu shot within the past year	66.5	60.1
Adults who always wear a seatbelt	90.3	93.8

Note: Data as of 2012 unless otherwise noted; (1) Figures cover the Kansas City, MO-KS Metropolitan Statistical Area—see Appendix B for areas included; (2) Heavy drinkers are classified as males having more than two drinks per day or females having more than one drink per day; (3) Binge drinkers are classified as males having five or more drinks on one occasion or females having four or more drinks on one occasion
Source: Centers for Disease Control and Prevention, Behaviorial Risk Factor Surveillance System, SMART: Selected Metropolitan/Micropolitan Area Risk Trends, 2012 (Note: the CDC has discontinued this dataset but will be releasing a replacement in mid-2016)

Chronic Health Indicators

Category	MSA[1] (%)	U.S. (%)
Adults who have ever been told they had a heart attack	4.0	4.5
Adults who have ever been told they had a stroke	3.3	2.9
Adults who have been told they currently have asthma	9.7	8.9
Adults who have ever been told they have arthritis	25.8	25.7
Adults who have ever been told they have diabetes[2]	10.4	9.7
Adults who have ever been told they had skin cancer	5.8	5.7
Adults who have ever been told they had any other types of cancer	6.1	6.5
Adults who have ever been told they have COPD	7.4	6.2
Adults who have ever been told they have kidney disease	2.2	2.5
Adults who have ever been told they have a form of depression	16.7	18.0

Note: Data as of 2012 unless otherwise noted; (1) Figures cover the Kansas City, MO-KS Metropolitan Statistical Area—see Appendix B for areas included; (2) Figures do not include pregnancy-related, borderline, or pre-diabetes
Source: Centers for Disease Control and Prevention, Behaviorial Risk Factor Surveillance System, SMART: Selected Metropolitan/Micropolitan Area Risk Trends, 2012 (Note: the CDC has discontinued this dataset but will be releasing a replacement in mid-2016)

Mortality Rates for the Top 10 Causes of Death in the U.S.

ICD-10[a] Sub-Chapter	ICD-10[a] Code	Age-Adjusted Mortality Rate[1] per 100,000 population	
		County[2]	U.S.
Malignant neoplasms	C00-C97	142.0	163.6
Ischaemic heart diseases	I20-I25	57.0	102.2
Other forms of heart disease	I30-I51	44.1	50.1
Chronic lower respiratory diseases	J40-J47	32.9	41.4
Organic, including symptomatic, mental disorders	F01-F09	42.2	38.5
Cerebrovascular diseases	I60-I69	32.4	36.5
Other external causes of accidental injury	W00-X59	18.9	27.5
Other degenerative diseases of the nervous system	G30-G31	21.4	26.3
Diabetes mellitus	E10-E14	10.1	21.1
Hypertensive diseases	I10-I15	5.8	19.7

Note: (a) ICD-10 = International Classification of Diseases 10th Revision; (1) Mortality rates are a three year average covering 2012-2014; (2) Figures cover Johnson County.
Source: Centers for Disease Control and Prevention, National Center for Health Statistics. Underlying Cause of Death 1999-2014 on CDC WONDER Online Database, released 2015.

Mortality Rates for Selected Causes of Death

ICD-10[a] Sub-Chapter	ICD-10[a] Code	Age-Adjusted Mortality Rate[1] per 100,000 population	
		County[2]	U.S.
Assault	X85-Y09	2.0	5.1
Diseases of the liver	K70-K76	9.4	13.5
Human immunodeficiency virus (HIV) disease	B20-B24	Suppressed	2.1
Influenza and pneumonia	J09-J18	12.6	15.2
Intentional self-harm	X60-X84	14.4	12.7
Malnutrition	E40-E46	1.1	0.9
Obesity and other hyperalimentation	E65-E68	1.7	1.9
Renal failure	N17-N19	14.0	13.0
Transport accidents	V01-V99	6.1	11.6
Viral hepatitis	B15-B19	Unreliable	2.1

Note: (a) ICD-10 = International Classification of Diseases 10th Revision; (1) Mortality rates are a three year average covering 2012-2014; (2) Figures cover Johnson County; Data are Suppressed when the data meet the criteria for confidentiality constraints; Mortality rates are flagged as Unreliable when the rate would be calculated with a numerator of 20 or less.
Source: Centers for Disease Control and Prevention, National Center for Health Statistics. Underlying Cause of Death 1999-2014 on CDC WONDER Online Database, released 2015.

Health Insurance Coverage

Area	With Health Insurance	With Private Health Insurance	With Public Health Insurance	Without Health Insurance	Population Under Age 18 Without Health Insurance
City	90.8	82.6	18.2	9.2	4.9
MSA[1]	87.5	73.2	25.1	12.5	6.5
U.S.	85.8	65.8	31.1	14.2	7.1

Note: Figures are percentages that cover the civilian noninstitutionalized population; (1) Figures cover the Kansas City, MO-KS Metropolitan Statistical Area—see Appendix B for areas included
Source: U.S. Census Bureau, 2010-2014 American Community Survey 5-Year Estimates

Number of Medical Professionals

Area	MDs[3]	DOs[3,4]	Dentists	Podiatrists	Chiropractors	Optometrists
County[1] (number)	2,721	253	449	20	337	140
County[1] (rate[2])	479.6	44.6	78.2	3.5	58.7	24.4
U.S. (rate[2])	272.5	20.9	64.7	5.8	25.9	15.2

Note: Data as of 2014 unless noted; (1) Data covers Johnson County; (2) Rate per 100,000 population; (3) Data as of 2013 and includes all active, non-federal physicians; (4) Doctor of Osteopathic Medicine
Source: U.S. Department of Health and Human Services, Health Resources and Services Administration, Bureau of Health Professions, Area Resource File (ARF) 2014-2015

Best Hospitals

According to *U.S. News,* the Kansas City, MO-KS metro area is home to two of the best hospitals in the U.S.: **St. Luke's Hospital** (7 specialties); **University of Kansas Hospital** (12 specialties). The hospitals listed were nationally ranked in at least one adult specialty. Only 137 hospitals nationwide were nationally ranked in one or more specialties. Fifteen hospitals in the U.S. made the Honor Roll with high scores in at least six specialties. *U.S. News Online, "America's Best Children's Hospitals 2015-16"*

According to *U.S. News,* the Kansas City, MO-KS metro area is home to one of the best children's hospitals in the U.S.: **Children's Mercy Hospitals and Clinics** (10 specialties). The hospital listed was highly ranked in at least one pediatric specialty. Eighty-three children's hospitals in the U.S. were nationally ranked in at least one specialty. Twelve children's hospitals in the U.S. made the Honor Roll with high scores in at least three specialties. *U.S. News Online, "America's Best Children's Hospitals 2015-16"*

EDUCATION

Public School District Statistics

District Name	Schls	Pupils	Pupil/ Teacher Ratio	Minority Pupils[1] (%)	Free Lunch Eligible[2] (%)	IEP[3] (%)
De Soto	12	7,063	14.3	17.7	11.0	7.0
Olathe	47	29,080	13.8	29.4	21.9	12.1

Note: Table includes school districts with 100 or more students; (1) Percentage of students that are not non-Hispanic white; (2) Percentage of students that are eligible for the free lunch program; (3) Percentage of students that have an Individualized Education Program.
Source: U.S. Department of Education, National Center for Education Statistics, Common Core of Data, Local Education Agency (School District) Universe Survey: School Year 2013-2014; U.S. Department of Education, National Center for Education Statistics, Common Core of Data, Public Elementary/Secondary School Universe Survey: School Year 2013-2014

Highest Level of Education

Area	Less than H.S.	H.S. Diploma	Some College, No Deg.	Associate Degree	Bachelor's Degree	Master's Degree	Prof. School Degree	Doctorate Degree
City	4.0	13.8	20.9	6.9	34.2	14.4	3.8	2.0
MSA[1]	9.2	26.5	23.4	7.4	21.5	8.9	2.2	1.1
U.S.	13.7	28.0	21.2	7.9	18.3	7.8	2.0	1.3

Note: Figures cover persons age 25 and over; (1) Figures cover the Kansas City, MO-KS Metropolitan Statistical Area—see Appendix B for areas included
Source: U.S. Census Bureau, 2010-2014 American Community Survey 5-Year Estimates

Educational Attainment by Race

Area	High School Graduate or Higher (%)					Bachelor's Degree or Higher (%)				
	Total	White	Black	Asian	Hisp.[2]	Total	White	Black	Asian	Hisp.[2]
City	96.0	96.4	96.4	94.3	74.6	54.3	54.7	43.1	69.6	21.1
MSA[1]	90.8	92.5	86.1	84.1	65.5	33.6	36.1	17.9	52.6	15.2
U.S.	86.3	88.4	83.2	85.8	64.1	29.3	30.6	19.0	50.9	13.9

Note: Figures shown cover persons 25 years old and over; (1) Figures cover the Kansas City, MO-KS Metropolitan Statistical Area—see Appendix B for areas included; (2) People of Hispanic origin can be of any race
Source: U.S. Census Bureau, 2010-2014 American Community Survey 5-Year Estimates

School Enrollment by Grade and Control

Area	Preschool (%)		Kindergarten (%)		Grades 1 - 4 (%)		Grades 5 - 8 (%)		Grades 9 - 12 (%)	
	Public	Private	Public	Private	Public	Private	Public	Private	Public	Private
City	32.1	67.9	80.1	19.9	82.1	17.9	75.6	24.4	78.5	21.5
MSA[1]	51.5	48.5	86.7	13.3	88.7	11.3	88.6	11.4	89.7	10.3
U.S.	57.4	42.6	87.8	12.2	89.8	10.2	89.9	10.1	90.6	9.4

Note: Figures shown cover persons 3 years old and over; (1) Figures cover the Kansas City, MO-KS Metropolitan Statistical Area—see Appendix B for areas included
Source: U.S. Census Bureau, 2010-2014 American Community Survey 5-Year Estimates

Average Salaries of Public School Classroom Teachers

Area	2013-14 Dollars	2013-14 Rank[1]	2014-15 Dollars	2014-15 Rank[1]	Percent Change 2013-14 to 2014-15	Percent Change 2004-05 to 2014-15
Kansas	48,221	38	48,990	37	1.59	24.5
U.S. Average	56,610	–	57,379	–	1.36	20.8

Note: (1) State rank ranges from 1 to 51 where 1 indicates highest salary.
Source: National Education Association, Rankings & Estimates: Rankings of the States 2014 and Estimates of School Statistics 2015, March 2015

Higher Education

Four-Year Colleges Public	Four-Year Colleges Private Non-profit	Four-Year Colleges Private For-profit	Two-Year Colleges Public	Two-Year Colleges Private Non-profit	Two-Year Colleges Private For-profit	Medical Schools[1]	Law Schools[2]	Voc/ Tech[3]
0	0	3	0	0	0	0	0	1

Note: Figures cover institutions located within the city limits and include main campuses only; (1) includes schools accredited by the Liaison Committee on Medical Education and the American Osteopathic Association's Commission on Osteopathic College Accreditation; (2) includes ABA-accredited schools, schools with provisional ABA accreditation, and state accredited schools; (3) includes all schools with programs that are less than 2 years.
Source: National Center for Education Statistics, Integrated Postsecondary Education System (IPEDS), 2014-15; Association of American Medical Colleges, Member List, March 21, 2016; American Osteopathic Association, Member List, March 21, 2016; Law School Admission Council, Official Guide to ABA-Approved Law Schools Online, March 21, 2016; Wikipedia, List of Medical Schools in the United States, March 21, 2016; Wikipedia, List of Law Schools in the United States, March 21, 2016

According to *U.S. News & World Report,* the Kansas City, MO-KS metro area is home to one of the best national universities in the U.S.: **University of Missouri–Kansas City** (#194 tie). The indicators used to capture academic quality fall into a number of categories: assessment by administrators at peer institutions; retention of students; faculty resources; student selectivity; financial resources; alumni giving; high school counselor ratings of colleges; and graduation rate. *U.S. News & World Report, "America's Best Colleges 2016"*

According to *U.S. News & World Report,* the Kansas City, MO-KS metro area is home to one of the best liberal arts colleges in the U.S.: **William Jewell College** (#158 tie). The indicators used to capture academic quality fall into a number of categories: assessment by administrators at peer institutions; retention of students; faculty resources; student selectivity; financial resources; alumni giving; high school counselor ratings of colleges; and graduation rate. *U.S. News & World Report, "America's Best Colleges 2016"*

According to *U.S. News & World Report,* the Kansas City, MO-KS metro area is home to one of the top 75 medical schools for research in the U.S.: **University of Kansas Medical Center, School of Medicine** (#69 tie). The rankings are based on a weighted average of 11 measures of quality: quality assessment; peer assessment score; assessment score by residency directors; research activity; total research activity; average research activity per faculty member; student selectivity; median MCAT total score; median undergraduate GPA; acceptance rate; and faculty resources. *U.S. News & World Report, "America's Best Graduate Schools, Medical, 2017"*

PRESIDENTIAL ELECTION

2012 Presidential Election Results

Area	Obama (%)	Romney (%)	Other (%)
Johnson County	40.1	58.0	1.9
U.S.	51.0	47.2	1.8

Note: Results may not add to 100% due to rounding
Source: Dave Leip's Atlas of U.S. Presidential Elections

EMPLOYERS

Major Employers

Company Name	Industry
B&V Baker Guam JV	Consulting engineer
B&V Baker Guam JV	Engineering services
Black and Veatch Corp	Engineering services
DST Systems	Data processing
Embarq Corporation	Telephone communications
Ford Motor Company	Automobile assembly
Hallmark Cardsorporated	Greeting cards
HCA Midwest Division	Hospital management
Honeywell International	Search & navigation equipment
Internal Revenue Service	Taxation, department/government
North Kansas City Hospital	General medical/surgical hospitals
Park University	Colleges, except junior
Performance Contracting	Drywall
St Lukes Hospital of Kansas	General medical/surgical hospitals
United Auto Workers	Labor union
University of Kansas	Charitable trust management
University of Kansas	Medical centers
University of Missouri System	General medical/surgical hospitals

Note: Companies shown are located within the Kansas City, MO-KS Metropolitan Statistical Area.
Source: Hoovers.com; Wikipedia

PUBLIC SAFETY

Crime Rate

Area	All Crimes	Violent Crimes				Property Crimes		
		Murder	Rape[3]	Robbery	Aggrav. Assault	Burglary	Larceny -Theft	Motor Vehicle Theft
City	1,696.3	3.9	15.7	11.8	78.6	165.1	1,240.3	180.8
Metro[1]	3,499.3	6.6	54.4	113.2	307.9	627.9	1,991.0	398.3
U.S.	2,971.8	4.5	36.6	102.2	232.5	542.5	1,837.3	216.2

Note: Figures are crimes per 100,000 population; (1) Figures cover the Kansas City, MO-KS Metropolitan Statistical Area—see Appendix B for areas included; (3) The city and U.S. figures shown were reported using the revised Uniform Crime Reporting (UCR) definition of rape. The suburban and metro area figures shown are an aggregate total of the data submitted using both the revised and legacy UCR definitions.
Source: FBI Uniform Crime Reports, 2014

Hate Crimes

Area	Number of Quarters Reported	Number of Incidents per Bias Motivation						
		Race	Religion	Sexual Orientation	Ethnicity	Disability	Gender	Gender Identity
City	4	0	0	0	0	0	0	0
U.S.	4	2,568	1,014	1,017	648	84	33	98

Source: Federal Bureau of Investigation, Hate Crime Statistics 2014

Identity Theft Consumer Complaints

Area	Complaints	Complaints per 100,000 Population	Rank[2]
MSA[1]	3,348	161.7	46
U.S.	490,220	152.4	-

Note: (1) Figures cover the Kansas City, MO-KS Metropolitan Statistical Area—see Appendix B for areas included; (2) Rank ranges from 1 to 379 where 1 indicates greatest number of identity theft complaints per 100,000 population
Source: Federal Trade Commission, Consumer Sentinel Network Data Book for January–December 2015

Fraud and Other Consumer Complaints

Area	Complaints	Complaints per 100,000 Population	Rank[2]
MSA[1]	8,239	397.8	108
U.S.	2,593,159	806.0	-

Note: (1) Figures cover the Kansas City, MO-KS Metropolitan Statistical Area—see Appendix B for areas included; (2) Rank ranges from 1 to 379 where 1 indicates greatest number of identity theft complaints per 100,000 population
Source: Federal Trade Commission, Consumer Sentinel Network Data Book for January–December 2015

RECREATION

Culture

Dance[1]	Theatre[1]	Instrumental Music[1]	Vocal Music[1]	Series and Festivals	Museums and Art Galleries[2]	Zoos and Aquariums[3]
0	0	0	0	0	0	0

Note: (1) Professional perfoming groups; (2) Based on organizations with SIC code 8412; (3) AZA-accredited
Source: The Grey House Performing Arts Directory, 2015-16; Association of Zoos & Aquariums, AZA Member Zoos & Aquariums, March 25, 2016; www.AccuLeads.com, March 29, 2016

Professional Sports Teams

Team Name	League	Year Established
Kansas City Chiefs	National Football League (NFL)	1963
Kansas City Royals	Major League Baseball (MLB)	1969
Sporting Kansas City	Major League Soccer (MLS)	1996

Note: Includes teams located in the Kansas City, MO-KS Metropolitan Statistical Area.
Source: Wikipedia, Major Professional Sports Teams of the United States and Canada, March 24, 2016

CLIMATE

Average and Extreme Temperatures

Temperature	Jan	Feb	Mar	Apr	May	Jun	Jul	Aug	Sep	Oct	Nov	Dec	Yr.
Extreme High (°F)	69	76	86	93	92	105	107	109	102	92	82	70	109
Average High (°F)	35	40	54	65	74	84	90	87	79	66	52	39	64
Average Temp. (°F)	26	31	44	55	64	74	79	77	68	56	43	30	54
Average Low (°F)	17	22	34	44	54	63	69	66	58	45	34	21	44
Extreme Low (°F)	-17	-19	-10	12	30	42	54	43	33	21	1	-23	-23

Note: Figures cover the years 1972-1990
Source: National Climatic Data Center, International Station Meteorological Climate Summary, 9/96

Average Precipitation/Snowfall/Humidity

Precip./Humidity	Jan	Feb	Mar	Apr	May	Jun	Jul	Aug	Sep	Oct	Nov	Dec	Yr.
Avg. Precip. (in.)	1.1	1.2	2.8	3.0	5.5	4.1	3.8	4.1	4.9	3.6	2.1	1.6	38.1
Avg. Snowfall (in.)	6	5	3	1	0	0	0	0	0	Tr	1	5	21
Avg. Rel. Hum. 6am (%)	76	77	78	77	82	84	84	86	86	80	79	78	80
Avg. Rel. Hum. 3pm (%)	58	59	54	50	54	54	51	53	53	51	57	60	54

Note: Figures cover the years 1972-1990; Tr = Trace amounts (<0.05 in. of rain; <0.5 in. of snow)
Source: National Climatic Data Center, International Station Meteorological Climate Summary, 9/96

Weather Conditions

Temperature			Daytime Sky			Precipitation		
10°F & below	32°F & below	90°F & above	Clear	Partly cloudy	Cloudy	0.01 inch or more precip.	0.1 inch or more snow/ice	Thunderstorms
22	110	39	112	134	119	103	17	51

Note: Figures are average number of days per year and cover the years 1972-1990
Source: National Climatic Data Center, International Station Meteorological Climate Summary, 9/96

HAZARDOUS WASTE

Superfund Sites

Lenexa has no sites on the EPA's Superfund Final National Priorities List. There are a total of 1,323 Superfund sites on the list in the U.S. *U.S. Environmental Protection Agency, Final National Priorities List, March 18, 2016*

AIR & WATER QUALITY

Air Quality Trends: Ozone

	1990	1995	2000	2005	2010	2011	2012	2013	2014
MSA[1]	0.075	0.098	0.088	0.084	0.072	0.080	0.085	0.067	0.066

Note: (1) Data covers the Kansas City, MO-KS Metropolitan Statistical Area—see Appendix B for areas included. The values shown are the composite ozone concentration averages among trend sites based on the highest fourth daily maximum 8-hour concentration in parts per million. These trends are based on sites having an adequate record of monitoring data during the trend period. Data from exceptional events are included.
Source: U.S. Environmental Protection Agency, Air Quality Monitoring Information, "Air Quality Trends by City, 1990-2014"

Air Quality Index

Area	Percent of Days when Air Quality was...[2]					AQI Statistics[2]	
	Good	Moderate	Unhealthy for Sensitive Groups	Unhealthy	Very Unhealthy	Maximum	Median
MSA[1]	44.9	44.7	10.4	0.0	0.0	134	53

Note: (1) Data covers the Kansas City, MO-KS Metropolitan Statistical Area—see Appendix B for areas included; (2) Based on 365 days with AQI data in 2015. Air Quality Index (AQI) is an index for reporting daily air quality. EPA calculates the AQI for five major air pollutants regulated by the Clean Air Act: ground-level ozone, particle pollution (aka particulate matter), carbon monoxide, sulfur dioxide, and nitrogen dioxide. The AQI runs from 0 to 500. The higher the AQI value, the greater the level of air pollution and the greater the health concern. There are six AQI categories: "Good" AQI is between 0 and 50. Air quality is considered satisfactory; "Moderate" AQI is between 51 and 100. Air quality is acceptable; "Unhealthy for Sensitive Groups" When AQI values are between 101 and 150, members of sensitive groups may experience health effects; "Unhealthy" When AQI values are between 151 and 200 everyone may begin to experience health effects; "Very Unhealthy" AQI values between 201 and 300 trigger a health alert; "Hazardous" AQI values over 300 trigger warnings of emergency conditions (not shown).
Source: U.S. Environmental Protection Agency, Air Quality Index Report, 2015

Air Quality Index Pollutants

Area	Percent of Days when AQI Pollutant was...[2]					
	Carbon Monoxide	Nitrogen Dioxide	Ozone	Sulfur Dioxide	Particulate Matter 2.5	Particulate Matter 10
MSA[1]	0.0	3.8	19.5	20.3	46.8	9.6

Note: (1) Data covers the Kansas City, MO-KS Metropolitan Statistical Area—see Appendix B for areas included; (2) Based on 365 days with AQI data in 2015. The Air Quality Index (AQI) is an index for reporting daily air quality. EPA calculates the AQI for five major air pollutants regulated by the Clean Air Act: ground-level ozone, particle pollution (also known as particulate matter), carbon monoxide, sulfur dioxide, and nitrogen dioxide. The AQI runs from 0 to 500. The higher the AQI value, the greater the level of air pollution and the greater the health concern.
Source: U.S. Environmental Protection Agency, Air Quality Index Report, 2015

Maximum Air Pollutant Concentrations: Particulate Matter, Ozone, CO and Lead

	Particulate Matter 10 (ug/m^3)	Particulate Matter 2.5 Wtd AM (ug/m^3)	Particulate Matter 2.5 24-Hr (ug/m^3)	Ozone (ppm)	Carbon Monoxide (ppm)	Lead (ug/m^3)
MSA[1] Level	90	9.5	22	0.068	1	0.01
NAAQS[2]	150	15	35	0.075	9	0.15
Met NAAQS[2]	Yes	Yes	Yes	Yes	Yes	Yes

Note: (1) Data covers the Kansas City, MO-KS Metropolitan Statistical Area—see Appendix B for areas included; Data from exceptional events are included; (2) National Ambient Air Quality Standards; ppm = parts per million; ug/m^3 = micrograms per cubic meter; n/a not available.
Concentrations: Particulate Matter 10 (coarse particulate)—highest second maximum 24-hour concentration; Particulate Matter 2.5 Wtd AM (fine particulate)—highest weighted annual mean concentration; Particulate Matter 2.5 24-Hour (fine particulate)—highest 98th percentile 24-hour concentration; Ozone—highest fourth daily maximum 8-hour concentration; Carbon Monoxide—highest second maximum non-overlapping 8-hour concentration; Lead—maximum running 3-month average
Source: U.S. Environmental Protection Agency, Air Quality Monitoring Information, "Air Quality Statistics by City, 2014"

Maximum Air Pollutant Concentrations: Nitrogen Dioxide and Sulfur Dioxide

	Nitrogen Dioxide AM (ppb)	Nitrogen Dioxide 1-Hr (ppb)	Sulfur Dioxide AM (ppb)	Sulfur Dioxide 1-Hr (ppb)	Sulfur Dioxide 24-Hr (ppb)
MSA[1] Level	13	53	n/a	125	n/a
NAAQS[2]	53	100	30	75	140
Met NAAQS[2]	Yes	Yes	n/a	No	n/a

Note: (1) Data covers the Kansas City, MO-KS Metropolitan Statistical Area—see Appendix B for areas included; Data from exceptional events are included; (2) National Ambient Air Quality Standards; ppm = parts per million; ug/m³ = micrograms per cubic meter; n/a not available.

Concentrations: Nitrogen Dioxide AM—highest arithmetic mean concentration; Nitrogen Dioxide 1-Hr—highest 98th percentile 1-hour daily maximum concentration; Sulfur Dioxide AM—highest annual mean concentration; Sulfur Dioxide 1-Hr—highest 99th percentile 1-hour daily maximum concentration; Sulfur Dioxide 24-Hr—highest second maximum 24-hour concentration

Source: U.S. Environmental Protection Agency, Air Quality Monitoring Information, "Air Quality Statistics by City, 2014"

Drinking Water

Water System Name	Pop. Served	Primary Water Source Type	Violations[1] Health Based	Violations[1] Monitoring/ Reporting
Water Dist 1 of Johnson Co	331,900	Surface	0	0

Note: (1) Based on violation data from January 1, 2015 to December 31, 2015 (includes unresolved violations from earlier years)

Source: U.S. Environmental Protection Agency, Office of Ground Water and Drinking Water, Safe Drinking Water Information System (based on data extracted April 29, 2016)

Independence, Kentucky

Background

Independence is in Kenton County approximately 13 miles south of Cincinnati, Ohio. It is one of two county seats and also serves as a suburb of Cincinnati. Independence was incorporated in 1842.

A post office built in 1837 was the first building in the town. Isaac Everett originally named the small community that sprung up around the post office Everett's Creek. The city was renamed Independence in 1840 to commemorate the creation of Kenton County, resulting from the division of Campbell County.

The city of Independence is one of the fastest growing cities in Kentucky and, due to its 23 square miles of land, growth is likely to continue. The city's downtown has always been the center of business, though its leaders have taken care to see that industry is developed throughout the entire city to accommodate the booming population. The city is enticing potential businesses with favorable zoning and low property and payroll taxes. The largest industries in Independence are manufacturing, healthcare, social assistance, and retail trade.

The natural beauty of the area makes living in Independence a highly desirable alternative to Cincinnati. Even with the recent population spike the city strives to maintain a close knit community by hosting recreation programs, including kids sports camps, art classes, adult athletic leagues and a Halloween dog costume contest. Memorial Park has activities to suit people of all ages whether they desire to play sports on the fields or walk along the trails. The Independence Senior Citizen's Center is located in the park and gives its residents a chance to connect with the community and nature. The city uses the amphitheater at Memorial Park to host concerts, movies and shows for the local citizens. With 78 acres of land, Lincoln Ridge Park has a wide range of fun outdoor activities. Visitors looking to enjoy nature can walk along the hiking trails, fish at one of the ponds or relax at the picnic areas. Sports lovers can enjoy soccer, baseball and a 24-hole disc golf course.

Independence is home to three Kenton County Golf Courses. The Kenton County School District includes four elementary schools, two middle schools and one high school. Independence has three private schools: St Cecilia, Community Christian Academy and Calvary Christian. Both the public and private schools in Independence have excellent academic reputations. There are several colleges within 15 miles from Independence, including Northern Kentucky University and the University of Cincinnati.

Independence is conveniently located near two major airports, both less than 20 miles away—Cincinnati/Northern Kentucky International and Cincinnati Municipal Lunken Airport.

Summers in Independence average a high of 86 degrees, and winter's average low is 22 degrees. The city receives 41 inches of rainfall and 23 inches of snowfall annually.

Rankings

Business/Finance Rankings

- The personal finance site NerdWallet analyzed 183 American metropolitan areas with populations over 250,000 and more than 15,000 businesses to rank where entrepreneurs find the most success. Criteria included area economy, annual income, housing cost, unemployment rate, and the success rate of area businesses. Cincinnati* ranked #67. *www.nerdwallet.com, "Best Places to Start a Business," April 27, 2015*
- Based on metro area social media reviews, the employment opinion group Glassdoor surveyed 50 of the largest U.S. metro areas and equally weighed cost of living, hiring opportunity, and job satisfaction to compose a list of "25 Best Cities for Jobs." The Cincinnati* metro area was ranked #33 in overall job satisfaction. *www.glassdoor.com, "Best Cities for Jobs," May 19, 2015*
- In a survey of economic confidence in the nation's 50 largest metropolitan areas conducted January–December 2014, the Cincinnati* metro area placed #43, according to Gallup's 2014 Economic Confidence Index. *Gallup, "San Jose and San Francisco Lead in Economic Confidence," March 19, 2015*
- The Brookings Institution ranked the 100 largest metro areas in the U.S. based on income inequality. Cincinnati* was ranked #29 (#1 = greatest ineqality). Criteria: the "95/20 ratio," a figure representing the income at which a household earns more than 95 percent of all other households, divided by the income at which a household earns more than only 20 percent of all other households. *Brookings Institution, "Income Inequality, 100 Largest U.S. Metro Areas, 2007-2014," January 14, 2016*
- The Cincinnati* metro area was identified as one of the most affordable metropolitan areas in America by *Forbes*. The area ranked #5 out of 20 based on the National Association of Home Builders/Wells Fargo Housing Affordability Index and Sperling's Best Places' cost-of-living index. *Forbes.com, "America's Most Affordable Cities in 2015," March 12, 2015*
- Cincinnati* was identified as one of America's most frugal metro areas by *Coupons.com*. The city ranked #21 out of 25. Criteria: online coupon usage. *Coupons.com, "Top 25 Most Frugal Cities of 2014," May 11, 2015*
- Cincinnati* was identified as one of America's most frugal metro areas by *Coupons.com*. The city ranked #24 out of 25. Criteria: Grocery IQ and coupons.com mobile app usage. *Coupons.com, "Top 25 Most On-the-Go Frugal Cities of 2013," April 10, 2014*
- Cincinnati* was cited as one of America's top metros for new and expanded facility projects in 2015. The area ranked #4 in the large metro area category (population over 1 million). *Site Selection, "Top Metropolitans of 2015," March 2016*
- The Cincinnati* metro area appeared on the Milken Institute "2015 Best Performing Cities" list. Rank: #94 out of 200 large metro areas. Criteria: job growth; wage and salary growth; high-tech output growth. *Milken Institute, "Best-Performing Cities 2015," December 2015*
- *Forbes* ranked the 200 most populous metro areas to determine the nation's "Best Places for Business and Careers." The Cincinnati* metro area was ranked #75. Criteria: costs (business and living); job growth (past and projected); income growth; educational attainment (college and high school); projected economic growth; cultural and recreational opportunities; net migration patterns; number of highly ranked colleges. *Forbes, "The Best Places for Business and Careers 2015," July 29, 2015*

Children/Family Rankings

- *Forbes* analyzed data on the 100 largest metropolitan areas in the United States to compile its 2014 list of the ten "Best Cities for Raising a Family." The Cincinnati* metro area was ranked #9. Criteria: median income; overall cost of living; housing affordability; commuting delays; percentage of families owning homes; crime rate; education quality (mainly test scores). *Forbes, "The Best Cities for Raising a Family," April 16, 2014*

Education Rankings

- Personal finance website *WalletHub* analyzed the 150 largest U.S. metropolitan statistical areas to determine where the most educated Americans are choosing to settle. Criteria: education quality and attainment gap; education levels; percentage of workers with degrees; public school rankings; quality and size of each metro area's universities. Cincinnati* was ranked #66 (#1 = most educated city). *www.WalletHub.com, "2015's Most and Least Educated Cities*

Environmental Rankings

- The Cincinnati* metro area came in at #184 for the relative comfort of its climate on Sperling's list of "chill cities," as measured by the Sperling Heat Index. All 361 metro areas are included. Criteria included daytime high temperatures, nighttime low temperatures, dew point, and relative humidity at the high temperatures. *www.bertsperling.com, "Sperling's Chill Cities," July 18, 2013*

- Sperling's BestPlaces assessed 379 metropolitan areas of the United States for the likelihood of dangerously extreme weather events or earthquakes. In general the Southeast and South-Central regions have the highest risk of weather extremes and earthquakes, while the Pacific Northwest enjoys the lowest risk. Of the least risky metropolitan areas, the Cincinnati* metro area was ranked #249. *www.bestplaces.net, "Safest Places from Natural Disasters," April 2011*

- Cincinnati* was highlighted as one of the 25 most ozone-polluted metro areas in the U.S. during 2011 through 2013. The area ranked #23. *American Lung Association, State of the Air 2015*

- Cincinnati* was highlighted as one of the 25 metro areas most polluted by year-round particle pollution (Annual PM 2.5) in the U.S. during 2011 through 2013. The area ranked #8. *American Lung Association, State of the Air 2015*

- Cincinnati* was highlighted as one of the top 25 cleanest metro areas for short-term particle pollution (24-hour PM 2.5) in the U.S. during 2011 through 2013. Monitors in these cities reported no days with unhealthful PM 2.5 levels. *American Lung Association, State of the Air 2015*

Health/Fitness Rankings

- For each of the 50 most populous metro areas in the United States, the American College of Sports Medicine's American Fitness Index evaluated infrastructure, community assets, and policies that encourage healthy and fit lifestyles, including preventive health behaviors, levels of chronic disease conditions, health care access, and community resources and policies that support physical activity. The Cincinnati* metro area ranked #16 for "community fitness." *www.americanfitnessindex.org, "ACSM American Fitness Index Health and Community Fitness Status of the 50 Largest Metropolitan Areas," May 2015*

- The Cincinnati* metro area was identified as one of the worst cities for bed bugs in America by pest control company Orkin. The area ranked #8 out of 50 based on the number of bed bug treatments Orkin performed from January to December 2015. *Orkin, "Chicago Tops Bed Bug Cities List for Fourth Year in a Row," January 13, 2016*

- Cincinnati* was identified as a "2016 Spring Allergy Capital." The area ranked #74 out of 100. Three groups of factors were used to identify the most severe cities for people with allergies during the spring season: annual pollen levels; medicine utilization; access to board-certified allergists. *Asthma and Allergy Foundation of America, "Spring Allergy Capitals 2016"*

- Cincinnati* was identified as a "2015 Asthma Capital." The area ranked #34 out of the nation's 100 largest metropolitan areas. Criteria: estimated prevalence; self-reported prevalence; crude death rate for asthma; annual pollen score; annual air quality; public smoking laws; number of board-certified asthma specialists; school inhaler access laws; rescue medication use; controller medication use; ER visits for asthma; uninsured rate; poverty rate. *Asthma and Allergy Foundation of America, "Asthma Capitals 2015"*

- The Cincinnati* metro area ranked #165 out of 190 in The Gallup-Healthways Well-Being Index. Criteria: purpose; social well being; financial health; community and physical health. Results are based on telephone interviews with adults, aged 18 and older, living in metropolitan areas in the 50 U.S. states and the District of Columbia. *Gallup-Healthways, "State of American Well-Being," February 23, 2016*

Real Estate Rankings

- The Cincinnati* metro area was identified as one of the 10 worst condo markets in the U.S. in 2015. The area ranked #10 out of 61 markets. Criteria: year-over-year change of median sales price of existing apartment condo-coop homes between the 4th quarter of 2014 and the 4th quarter of 2015. *National Association of Realtors®, Median Sales Price of Existing Apartment Condo-Coop Homes for Metropolitan Areas, 4th Quarter 2015*
- Cincinnati* was ranked #40 out of 225 metro areas in terms of housing affordability in 2015 by the National Association of Home Builders (#1 = most affordable). Criteria: the share of homes sold in that area affordable to a family earning the local median income, based on standard mortgage underwriting criteria. *National Association of Home Builders®, NAHB-Wells Fargo Housing Opportunity Index, 4th Quarter 2015*

Safety Rankings

- The National Insurance Crime Bureau ranked 380 metro areas in the U.S. in terms of per capita rates of vehicle theft. The Cincinnati* metro area ranked #200 (#1 = highest rate). Criteria: number of vehicle theft offenses per 100,000 inhabitants in 2014. *National Insurance Crime Bureau, "Hot Spots 2014," June 24, 2015*

Seniors/Retirement Rankings

- From its Best Cities for Successful Aging indexes, the Milken Institute generated rankings for metropolitan areas, weighing data in eight categories—health care, wellness, living arrangements, transportation, financial characteristics, education and employment opportunities, community engagement, and overall livability. The Cincinnati* metro area was ranked #43 overall in the large metro area category. *Milken Institute, "Best Cities for Successful Aging, 2014"*

Miscellaneous Rankings

- The watchdog site Charity Navigator conducts an annual study of charities in the nation's major markets both to analyze statistical differences in their financial, accountability, and transparency practices and to track year-to-year variations in individual communities. The Cincinnati* metro area was ranked #7 among the 30 metro markets in the rating dimension of Overall Score. *www.charitynavigator.org, "Metro Market Study 2015," June 5, 2015*
- Mars Chocolate North America, the makers of COMBOS®, in partnership with Sperling's BestPlaces, ranked 50 major metro areas in terms of their "manliness." The Cincinnati* metro area ranked #12. Criteria: number of professional sports teams; number of nearby NASCAR tracks and racing events; manly lifestyle; concentration of manly retail stores; manly occupations per capita; salty snack sales; "Board of Manliness" rankings. *Mars Chocolate North America, "America's Manliest Cities 2012"*
- The National Alliance to End Homelessness ranked the 100 most populous metro areas with the highest rate of homelessness. The Cincinnati* metro area ranked #96. Criteria: number of homeless people per 10,000 population in 2011. *National Alliance to End Homelessness, The State of Homelessness in America 2012*

Independence is located within the Cincinnati, OH-KY-IN Metropolitan Statistical Area.

Business Environment

CITY FINANCES

City Government Finances

Component	2012 ($000)	2012 ($ per capita)
Total Revenues	8,317	335
Total Expenditures	6,645	268
Debt Outstanding	8,165	329
Cash and Securities[1]	3,172	128

Note: (1) Cash and security holdings of a government at the close of its fiscal year, including those of its dependent agencies, utilities, and liquor stores.
Source: U.S Census Bureau, State & Local Government Finances 2012

City Government Revenue by Source

Source	2012 ($000)	2012 ($ per capita)
General Revenue		
From Federal Government	137	5
From State Government	580	23
From Local Governments	65	2
Taxes		
Property	3,372	136
Sales and Gross Receipts	333	13
Personal Income	1,935	78
Corporate Income	0	0
Motor Vehicle License	0	0
Other Taxes	185	7
Current Charges	920	37
Liquor Store	0	0
Utility	0	0
Employee Retirement	0	0

Source: U.S Census Bureau, State & Local Government Finances 2012

City Government Expenditures by Function

Function	2012 ($000)	2012 ($ per capita)	2012 (%)
General Direct Expenditures			
Air Transportation	0	0	0.0
Corrections	0	0	0.0
Education	0	0	0.0
Employment Security Administration	0	0	0.0
Financial Administration	0	0	0.0
Fire Protection	0	0	0.0
General Public Buildings	0	0	0.0
Governmental Administration, Other	1,233	49	18.5
Health	0	0	0.0
Highways	1,544	62	23.2
Hospitals	0	0	0.0
Housing and Community Development	0	0	0.0
Interest on General Debt	340	13	5.1
Judicial and Legal	0	0	0.0
Libraries	0	0	0.0
Parking	0	0	0.0
Parks and Recreation	245	9	3.6
Police Protection	2,316	93	34.8
Public Welfare	0	0	0.0
Sewerage	0	0	0.0
Solid Waste Management	917	37	13.8
Veterans' Services	0	0	0.0
Liquor Store	0	0	0.0
Utility	0	0	0.0
Employee Retirement	0	0	0.0

Source: U.S Census Bureau, State & Local Government Finances 2012

DEMOGRAPHICS

Population Growth

Area	1990 Census	2000 Census	2010 Census	2014* Estimate	Population Growth (%) 1990-2014	Population Growth (%) 2010-2014
City	10,645	14,982	24,757	25,638	140.8	3.6
MSA[1]	1,844,917	2,009,632	2,130,151	2,131,793	15.5	0.1
U.S.	248,709,873	281,421,906	308,745,538	314,107,084	26.3	1.7

Note: (1) Figures cover the Cincinnati, OH-KY-IN Metropolitan Statistical Area—see Appendix B for areas included; (*) 2010-2014 5-year estimated population
Source: U.S. Census Bureau, 1990 Census, Census 2000, Census 2010, 2010-2014 American Community Survey 5-Year Estimates

Household Size

Area	Persons in Household (%) One	Two	Three	Four	Five	Six	Seven or More	Average Household Size
City	15.7	29.7	22.3	17.6	10.2	2.5	1.7	3.04
MSA[1]	28.2	33.9	15.6	13.2	5.8	2.0	1.0	2.55
U.S.	27.5	33.5	15.8	13.1	6.0	2.3	1.4	2.64

Note: (1) Figures cover the Cincinnati, OH-KY-IN Metropolitan Statistical Area—see Appendix B for areas included
Source: U.S. Census Bureau, 2010-2014 American Community Survey 5-Year Estimates

Race

Area	White Alone[2] (%)	Black Alone[2] (%)	Asian Alone[2] (%)	AIAN[3] Alone[2] (%)	NHOPI[4] Alone[2] (%)	Other Race Alone[2] (%)	Two or More Races (%)
City	95.2	1.6	0.9	0.0	0.2	0.4	1.7
MSA[1]	82.8	12.2	2.1	0.2	0.0	0.8	1.9
U.S.	73.8	12.6	5.0	0.8	0.2	4.7	2.9

Note: (1) Figures cover the Cincinnati, OH-KY-IN Metropolitan Statistical Area—see Appendix B for areas included; (2) Alone is defined as not being in combination with one or more other races; (3) American Indian and Alaska Native; (4) Native Hawaiian and Other Pacific Islander
Source: U.S. Census Bureau, 2010-2014 American Community Survey 5-Year Estimates

Hispanic or Latino Origin

Area	Total (%)	Mexican (%)	Puerto Rican (%)	Cuban (%)	Other (%)
City	2.1	0.5	0.1	0.0	1.5
MSA[1]	2.8	1.4	0.3	0.1	1.0
U.S.	16.9	10.8	1.6	0.6	3.8

Note: Persons of Hispanic or Latino origin can be of any race; (1) Figures cover the Cincinnati, OH-KY-IN Metropolitan Statistical Area—see Appendix B for areas included
Source: U.S. Census Bureau, 2010-2014 American Community Survey 5-Year Estimates

Ancestry

Area	German	Irish	English	American	Italian	Polish	French[2]	Scottish	Dutch
City	39.6	18.7	9.4	10.0	2.8	2.1	2.1	2.0	1.1
MSA[1]	29.7	14.3	8.8	10.4	4.2	1.5	2.0	1.7	1.2
U.S.	14.9	10.8	8.0	7.1	5.5	3.0	2.7	1.7	1.4

Note: Figures are the percentage of the total population reporting a particular ancestry. The nine most commonly reported ancestries in the U.S. are shown. Figures include multiple ancestries (e.g. if a person reported being Irish and Italian, they were included in both columns); (1) Figures cover the Cincinnati, OH-KY-IN Metropolitan Statistical Area—see Appendix B for areas included; (2) Excludes Basque
Source: U.S. Census Bureau, 2010-2014 American Community Survey 5-Year Estimates

Foreign-Born Population

Area	Any Foreign Country	Asia	Mexico	Europe	Carribean	Central America[2]	South America	Africa	Canada
	Percent of Population Born in								
City	2.2	0.9	0.1	0.2	0.1	0.3	0.4	0.1	0.2
MSA[1]	4.2	1.8	0.5	0.7	0.1	0.3	0.2	0.5	0.1
U.S.	13.1	3.8	3.7	1.5	1.2	1.0	0.9	0.6	0.3

Note: (1) Figures cover the Cincinnati, OH-KY-IN Metropolitan Statistical Area—see Appendix B for areas included; (2) Excludes Mexico.
Source: U.S. Census Bureau, 2010-2014 American Community Survey 5-Year Estimates

Marital Status

Area	Never Married	Now Married[2]	Separated	Widowed	Divorced
City	23.9	57.8	2.0	3.6	12.7
MSA[1]	31.3	49.5	1.8	5.8	11.5
U.S.	32.5	48.4	2.2	5.9	10.9

Note: Figures are percentages and cover the population 15 years of age and older; (1) Figures cover the Cincinnati, OH-KY-IN Metropolitan Statistical Area—see Appendix B for areas included; (2) Excludes separated
Source: U.S. Census Bureau, 2010-2014 American Community Survey 5-Year Estimates

Disability Status

Area	All Ages	Under 18 Years Old	18 to 64 Years Old	65 Years and Over
City	11.0	4.9	11.8	33.3
MSA[1]	12.1	4.2	10.6	35.3
U.S.	12.3	4.1	10.2	36.3

Note: Figures show percent of the civilian noninstitutionalized population that reported having a disability. Disability status is determined from from six types of difficulty: vision, hearing, cognitive, ambulatory, self-care, and independent living. For children under 5 years old, hearing and vision difficulty are used to determine disability status. For children between the ages of 5 and 14, disability status is determined from hearing, vision, cognitive, ambulatory, and self-care difficulties. For people aged 15 years and older, they are considered to have a disability if they have difficulty with any one of the six difficulty types; (1) Figures cover the Cincinnati, OH-KY-IN Metropolitan Statistical Area—see Appendix B for areas included.
Source: U.S. Census Bureau, 2010-2014 American Community Survey 5-Year Estimates

Age

Area	Under Age 5	Age 5–19	Age 20–34	Age 35–44	Age 45–54	Age 55–64	Age 65–74	Age 75–84	Age 85+	Median Age
	Percent of Population									
City	10.6	23.5	20.2	16.1	12.2	10.2	4.8	1.7	0.7	32.1
MSA[1]	6.6	20.6	19.8	12.8	14.7	12.6	7.1	4.0	1.8	37.4
U.S.	6.4	19.9	20.6	13.0	14.1	12.3	7.6	4.3	1.9	37.4

Note: (1) Figures cover the Cincinnati, OH-KY-IN Metropolitan Statistical Area—see Appendix B for areas included
Source: U.S. Census Bureau, 2010-2014 American Community Survey 5-Year Estimates

Gender

Area	Males	Females	Males per 100 Females
City	12,407	13,231	93.8
MSA[1]	1,042,464	1,089,329	95.7
U.S.	154,515,159	159,591,925	96.8

Note: (1) Figures cover the Cincinnati, OH-KY-IN Metropolitan Statistical Area—see Appendix B for areas included
Source: U.S. Census Bureau, 2010-2014 American Community Survey 5-Year Estimates

Religious Groups by Family

Area	Catholic	Baptist	Non-Den.	Methodist[2]	Lutheran	LDS[3]	Pente-costal	Presby-terian[4]	Muslim[5]	Judaism
MSA[1]	19.0	9.5	3.6	3.8	1.1	0.5	2.2	1.5	0.2	0.5
U.S.	19.1	9.3	4.0	4.0	2.3	2.0	1.9	1.6	0.8	0.7

Note: Figures are the number of adherents as a percentage of the total population; (1) Figures cover the Cincinnati-Middletown, OH-KY-IN Metropolitan Statistical Area—see Appendix B for areas included; (2) Methodist/Pietist; (3) Latter Day Saints; (4) Reformed; (5) Figures are estimates
Source: Association of Statisticians of American Religious Bodies, 2010 U.S. Religion Census: Religious Congregations & Membership Study

Religious Groups by Tradition

Area	Catholic	Evangelical Protestant	Mainline Protestant	Other Tradition	Black Protestant	Orthodox
MSA[1]	19.0	15.5	7.1	1.5	1.1	0.1
U.S.	19.1	16.2	7.3	4.3	1.6	0.3

Note: Figures are the number of adherents as a percentage of the total population; (1) Figures cover the Cincinnati-Middletown, OH-KY-IN Metropolitan Statistical Area—see Appendix B for areas included
Source: Association of Statisticians of American Religious Bodies, 2010 U.S. Religion Census: Religious Congregations & Membership Study

ECONOMY

Gross Metropolitan Product

Area	2013	2014	2015	2016	Rank[2]
MSA[1]	119.1	122.9	127.3	133.2	28

Note: Figures are in billions of dollars; (1) Figures cover the Cincinnati, OH-KY-IN Metropolitan Statistical Area—see Appendix B for areas included; (2) Rank is based on 2016 data and ranges from 1 to 381
Source: The U.S. Conference of Mayors, U.S. Metro Economies: GMP and Employment 2014-2016, June 2015

Economic Growth

Area	2011-13 (%)	2014 (%)	2015 (%)	2016 (%)	Rank[2]
MSA[1]	2.8	1.6	2.2	2.7	135
U.S.	2.2	2.4	2.3	2.9	-

Note: Figures are real gross metropolitan product (GMP) growth rates and represent annual average percent change; (1) Figures cover the Cincinnati, OH-KY-IN Metropolitan Statistical Area—see Appendix B for areas included; (2) Rank is based on 2016 data and ranges from 1 to 381
Source: The U.S. Conference of Mayors, U.S. Metro Economies: GMP and Employment 2014-2016, June 2015

Metropolitan Area Exports

Area	2009	2010	2011	2012	2013	2014	Rank[2]
MSA[1]	15,488.6	17,598.5	18,744.2	19,966.7	20,976.3	22,280.7	14

Note: Figures are in millions of dollars; (1) Figures cover the Cincinnati, OH-KY-IN Metropolitan Statistical Area—see Appendix B for areas included; (2) Rank is based on 2014 data and ranges from 1 to 385
Source: U.S. Department of Commerce, International Trade Administration, Office of Trade & Industry Information, Manufacturing & Services, data extracted March 10, 2016

Building Permits

Area	Single-Family			Multi-Family			Total		
	2014	2015p	Pct. Chg.	2014	2015p	Pct. Chg.	2014	2015p	Pct. Chg.
City	107	108	0.9	24	0	-100.0	131	108	-17.6
MSA[1]	3,218	3,481	8.2	1,988	1,182	-40.5	5,206	4,663	-10.4
U.S.	640,300	690,800	7.9	411,800	487,600	18.4	1,052,100	1,178,400	12.0

Note: (1) Figures cover the Cincinnati, OH-KY-IN Metropolitan Statistical Area—see Appendix B for areas included; Figures represent new, privately-owned housing units authorized (unadjusted data); All permit data are based on estimates with imputation; (p) preliminary data.
Source: U.S. Census Bureau, Manufacturing, Mining, and Construction Statistics, Building Permits, 2014, 2015

Bankruptcy Filings

Area	Business Filings 2014	Business Filings 2015	Business Filings % Chg.	Nonbusiness Filings 2014	Nonbusiness Filings 2015	Nonbusiness Filings % Chg.
Kenton County	13	10	-23.1	719	660	-8.2
U.S.	26,983	24,735	-8.3	909,812	819,760	-9.9

Note: Business filings include Chapter 7, Chapter 11, Chapter 12, and Chapter 13; Nonbusiness filings include Chapter 7, Chapter 11, and Chapter 13
Source: Administrative Office of the U.S. Courts, Business and Nonbusiness Bankruptcy, County Cases Commenced by Chapter of the Bankruptcy Code, During the 12- Month Period Ending December 31, 2014 and Business and Nonbusiness Bankruptcy, County Cases Commenced by Chapter of the Bankruptcy Code, During the 12- Month Period Ending December 31, 2015

Housing Vacancy Rates

Area	Gross Vacancy Rate[2] (%)			Year-Round Vacancy Rate[3] (%)			Rental Vacancy Rate[4] (%)			Homeowner Vacancy Rate[5] (%)		
	2013	2014	2015	2013	2014	2015	2013	2014	2015	2013	2014	2015
MSA[1]	11.2	10.1	10.5	10.0	9.3	10.0	8.9	7.9	10.1	2.6	2.2	2.2
U.S.	13.6	13.4	12.9	10.7	10.4	10.0	8.3	7.6	7.1	2.0	1.9	1.8

Note: (1) Figures cover the Cincinnati, OH-KY-IN Metropolitan Statistical Area—see Appendix B for areas included; (2) The percentage of the total housing inventory that is vacant; (3) The percentage of the housing inventory (excluding seasonal units) that is year-round vacant; (4) The percentage of rental inventory that is vacant for rent; (5) The percentage of homeowner inventory that is vacant for sale
Source: U.S. Census Bureau, Housing Vacancies and Homeownership Annual Statistics: 2015

INCOME

Income

Area	Per Capita ($)	Median Household ($)	Average Household ($)
City	24,821	65,776	73,401
MSA[1]	29,008	55,204	73,857
U.S.	28,555	53,482	74,596

Note: (1) Figures cover the Cincinnati, OH-KY-IN Metropolitan Statistical Area—see Appendix B for areas included
Source: U.S. Census Bureau, 2010-2014 American Community Survey 5-Year Estimates

Household Income Distribution

Area	Percent of Households Earning							
	Under $15,000	$15,000 -24,999	$25,000 -34,999	$35,000 -49,999	$50,000 -74,999	$75,000 -99,000	$100,000 -149,999	$150,000 and up
City	6.6	6.5	6.5	13.1	25.5	18.5	18.3	5.1
MSA[1]	12.5	10.2	9.7	13.2	18.5	12.6	13.5	9.8
U.S.	12.5	10.7	10.2	13.5	17.8	12.2	13.0	10.0

Note: (1) Figures cover the Cincinnati, OH-KY-IN Metropolitan Statistical Area—see Appendix B for areas included
Source: U.S. Census Bureau, 2010-2014 American Community Survey 5-Year Estimates

Poverty Rate

Area	All Ages	Under 18 Years Old	18 to 64 Years Old	65 Years and Over
City	9.4	15.2	7.0	3.9
MSA[1]	14.1	19.9	13.2	7.7
U.S.	15.6	21.9	14.6	9.4

Note: Figures are percentage of people whose income during the past 12 months was below the poverty level; (1) Figures cover the Cincinnati, OH-KY-IN Metropolitan Statistical Area—see Appendix B for areas included
Source: U.S. Census Bureau, 2010-2014 American Community Survey 5-Year Estimates

EMPLOYMENT

Labor Force and Employment

Area	Civilian Labor Force			Workers Employed		
	Dec. 2014	Dec. 2015	% Chg.	Dec. 2014	Dec. 2015	% Chg.
City	13,223	13,150	-0.5	12,750	12,637	-0.8
MSA[1]	1,069,102	1,071,770	0.2	1,022,870	1,026,072	0.3
U.S.	155,521,000	157,245,000	1.1	147,190,000	149,703,000	1.7

Note: Data is not seasonally adjusted and covers workers 16 years of age and older; (1) Figures cover the Cincinnati, OH-KY-IN Metropolitan Statistical Area—see Appendix B for areas included
Source: Bureau of Labor Statistics, Local Area Unemployment Statistics

Unemployment Rate

Area	2015											
	Jan.	Feb.	Mar.	Apr.	May	Jun.	Jul.	Aug.	Sep.	Oct.	Nov.	Dec.
City	4.4	4.2	4.1	3.8	4.2	4.0	4.0	3.4	3.5	3.2	3.6	3.9
MSA[1]	5.5	4.9	4.8	4.1	4.3	4.6	4.6	3.9	3.9	3.8	4.2	4.3
U.S.	6.1	5.8	5.6	5.1	5.3	5.5	5.6	5.2	4.9	4.8	4.8	4.8

Note: Data is not seasonally adjusted and covers workers 16 years of age and older; (1) Figures cover the Cincinnati, OH-KY-IN Metropolitan Statistical Area—see Appendix B for areas included
Source: Bureau of Labor Statistics, Local Area Unemployment Statistics

Employment by Occupation

Occupation Classification	City (%)	MSA[1] (%)	U.S. (%)
Management, Business, Science, and Arts	36.9	37.7	36.4
Natural Resources, Construction, and Maintenance	8.0	7.0	9.0
Production, Transportation, and Material Moving	14.8	13.0	12.1
Sales and Office	26.2	25.5	24.4
Service	14.1	16.8	18.2

Note: Figures cover employed civilians 16 years of age and older; (1) Figures cover the Cincinnati, OH-KY-IN Metropolitan Statistical Area—see Appendix B for areas included
Source: U.S. Census Bureau, 2010-2014 American Community Survey 5-Year Estimates

Employment by Industry

Sector	MSA[1]		U.S.
	Number of Employees	Percent of Total	Percent of Total
Construction, Mining, and Logging	43,000	4.0	5.0
Education and Health Services	165,100	15.3	15.7
Financial Activities	69,500	6.4	5.7
Government	131,400	12.2	15.5
Information	13,800	1.2	1.9
Leisure and Hospitality	108,200	10.0	10.4
Manufacturing	115,600	10.7	8.6
Other Services	38,600	3.6	3.9
Professional and Business Services	170,000	15.8	13.9
Retail Trade	112,800	10.5	11.3
Transportation, Warehousing, and Utilities	43,200	4.0	3.9
Wholesale Trade	61,100	5.6	4.1

Note: Figures are non-farm employment as of December 2015. Figures are not seasonally adjusted and include workers 16 years of age and older; (1) Figures cover the Cincinnati, OH-KY-IN Metropolitan Statistical Area—see Appendix B for areas included; n/a not available
Source: Bureau of Labor Statistics, Current Employment Statistics, Employment, Hours, and Earnings

Occupations with Greatest Projected Employment Growth: 2012 – 2022

Occupation[1]	2012 Employment	2022 Projected Employment	Numeric Employment Change	Percent Employment Change
Registered Nurses	49,640	59,620	9,980	20.1
Combined Food Preparation and Serving Workers, Including Fast Food	52,330	59,420	7,090	13.5
Customer Service Representatives	32,720	37,130	4,410	13.5
Bookkeeping, Accounting, and Auditing Clerks	30,510	34,780	4,270	14.0
Retail Salespersons	56,420	60,400	3,980	7.0
Orderlies	25,350	29,250	3,900	15.3
General and Operations Managers	26,320	29,990	3,670	14.0
First-Line Supervisors of Office and Administrative Support Workers	21,700	24,810	3,110	14.3
Personal Care Aides	7,340	10,340	3,000	40.8
Medical Assistants	7,920	10,850	2,930	37.0

Note: Projections cover Kentucky; (1) Sorted by numeric employment change
Source: www.projectionscentral.com, State Occupational Projections, 2012–2022 Long-Term Projections

Fastest Growing Occupations: 2012 – 2022

Occupation[1]	2012 Employment	2022 Projected Employment	Numeric Employment Change	Percent Employment Change
Commercial Pilots	240	400	160	63.8
Reservation and Transportation Ticket Agents and Travel Clerks	1,340	2,140	800	59.2
Home Health Aides	3,870	5,940	2,070	53.3
Medical Equipment Repairers	1,090	1,660	570	51.8
Helpers—Brickmasons, Blockmasons, Stonemasons, and Tile and Marble Setters	640	960	320	49.1
Occupational Therapy Assistants	370	550	180	48.5
Athletic Trainers	460	670	210	45.7
Physician Assistants	820	1,190	370	45.3
Diagnostic Medical Sonographers	580	840	260	45.3
Physical Therapist Assistants	1,430	2,050	620	43.4

Note: Projections cover Kentucky; (1) Sorted by percent employment change and excludes occupations with numeric employment change less than 100
Source: www.projectionscentral.com, State Occupational Projections, 2012–2022 Long-Term Projections

Average Wages

Occupation	$/Hr.	Occupation	$/Hr.
Accountants and Auditors	33.20	Maids and Housekeeping Cleaners	10.49
Automotive Mechanics	17.61	Maintenance and Repair Workers	19.40
Bookkeepers	17.59	Marketing Managers	61.36
Carpenters	20.71	Nuclear Medicine Technologists	32.60
Cashiers	9.72	Nurses, Licensed Practical	20.65
Clerks, General Office	15.30	Nurses, Registered	30.76
Clerks, Receptionists/Information	12.80	Nursing Assistants	12.47
Clerks, Shipping/Receiving	16.31	Packers and Packagers, Hand	10.97
Computer Programmers	32.03	Physical Therapists	41.41
Computer Systems Analysts	43.40	Postal Service Mail Carriers	24.88
Computer User Support Specialists	24.77	Real Estate Brokers	73.93
Cooks, Restaurant	11.41	Retail Salespersons	12.41
Dentists	81.77	Sales Reps., Exc. Tech./Scientific	35.53
Electrical Engineers	37.40	Sales Reps., Tech./Scientific	40.93
Electricians	23.11	Secretaries, Exc. Legal/Med./Exec.	16.83
Financial Managers	60.83	Security Guards	12.87
First-Line Supervisors/Managers, Sales	18.86	Surgeons	84.18
Food Preparation Workers	10.86	Teacher Assistants*	13.25
General and Operations Managers	54.76	Teachers, Elementary School*	27.50
Hairdressers/Cosmetologists	12.00	Teachers, Secondary School*	28.06
Internists	69.49	Telemarketers	13.26
Janitors and Cleaners	11.88	Truck Drivers, Heavy/Tractor-Trailer	20.87
Landscaping/Groundskeeping Workers	12.16	Truck Drivers, Light/Delivery Svcs.	16.51
Lawyers	58.49	Waiters and Waitresses	9.50

Note: Wage data covers the Cincinnati-Middletown, OH-KY-IN Metropolitan Statistical Area—see Appendix B for areas included; (*) Hourly wages for elementary/secondary school teachers and teacher assistants were calculated by the editors from annual wage data based on a 40 hour work week; n/a not available.
Source: Bureau of Labor Statistics, Metro Area Occupational Employment and Wage Estimates, May 2015

TAXES

State Corporate Income Tax Rates

State	Tax Rate (%)	Income Brackets ($)	Num. of Brackets	Financial Institution Tax Rate (%)[a]	Federal Income Tax Ded.
Kentucky	4.0 - 6.0	50,000 - 100,001	3	(a)	No

Note: Tax rates as of January 1, 2016; (a) Rates listed are the corporate income tax rate applied to financial institutions or excise taxes based on income. Some states have other taxes based upon the value of deposits or shares.
Source: Federation of Tax Administrators, "State Corporate Income Tax Rates, 2016"

State Individual Income Tax Rates

State	Tax Rate (%)	Income Brackets ($)	Num. of Brackets	Personal Exempt. ($)[1] Single	Personal Exempt. ($)[1] Dependents	Fed. Inc. Tax Ded.
Kentucky	2.0 - 6.0	3,000 - 75,001	6	20 (c)	20 (c)	No

Note: Tax rates as of January 1, 2016; Local- and county-level taxes are not included; n/a not applicable; (1) Married joint filers generally receive double the single exemption; (c) The personal exemption takes the form of a tax credit instead of a deduction
Source: Federation of Tax Administrators, "State Individual Income Tax Rates, 2016"

Various State and Local Tax Rates

State	State and Local Sales and Use (%)	State Sales and Use (%)	Gasoline[1] (¢/gal.)	Cigarette[2] ($/pack)	Spirits[3] ($/gal.)	Wine[4] ($/gal.)	Beer[5] ($/gal.)
Kentucky	6.00	6.0	26	0.60	7.54 (h)	3.30 (n)	0.84

Note: All tax rates as of January 1, 2016; (1) The American Petroleum Institute has developed a methodology for determining the average tax rate on a gallon of fuel. Rates may include any of the following: excise taxes, environmental fees, storage tank fees, other fees or taxes, general sales tax, and local taxes. In states where gasoline is subject to the general sales tax, or where the fuel tax is based on the average sale price, the average rate determined by API is sensitive to changes in the price of gasoline. States that fully or partially apply general sales taxes to gasoline: CA, CO, GA, IL, IN, MI, NY; (2) The federal excise tax of $1.0066 per pack and local taxes are not included; (3) Rates are those applicable to off-premise sales of 40% alcohol by volume (a.b.v.) distilled spirits in 750ml containers. Local excise taxes are excluded; (4) Rates are those applicable to off-premise sales of 11% a.b.v. non-carbonated wine in 750ml containers; (5) Rates are those applicable to off-premise sales of 4.7% a.b.v. beer in 12 ounce containers; (h) Includes the wholesale tax rate of 11%, converted to a gallonage excise tax rate; (n) Includes the wholesale tax rate of 11%, converted to a gallonage excise tax rate.
Source: Tax Foundation, 2016 Facts & Figures: How Does Your State Compare?

State Business Tax Climate Index Rankings

State	Overall Rank	Corporate Tax Rank	Individual Income Tax Rank	Sales Tax Rank	Unemployment Insurance Tax Rank	Property Tax Rank
Kentucky	28	29	30	9	46	23

Note: The index is a measure of how each state's tax laws affect economic performance. The lower the rank, the more favorable a state's tax system is for business. States without a given tax are given a ranking of 1. The scores/rankings for the District of Columbia do not affect other states. The 2016 index represents the tax climate as of July 1, 2015 (the beginning of Fiscal Year 2016).
Source: Tax Foundation, State Business Tax Climate Index 2016

TRANSPORTATION

Means of Transportation to Work

Area	Car/Truck/Van		Public Transportation			Bicycle	Walked	Other Means	Worked at Home
	Drove Alone	Car-pooled	Bus	Subway	Railroad				
City	84.8	11.1	0.8	0.0	0.0	0.1	0.3	0.2	2.6
MSA[1]	83.2	8.1	2.0	0.0	0.0	0.2	2.1	0.7	3.8
U.S.	76.4	9.6	2.6	1.8	0.6	0.6	2.8	1.3	4.4

Note: Figures are percentages and cover workers 16 years of age and older; (1) Figures cover the Cincinnati, OH-KY-IN Metropolitan Statistical Area—see Appendix B for areas included
Source: U.S. Census Bureau, 2010-2014 American Community Survey 5-Year Estimates

Travel Time to Work

Area	Less Than 10 Minutes	10 to 19 Minutes	20 to 29 Minutes	30 to 44 Minutes	45 to 59 Minutes	60 to 89 Minutes	90 Minutes or More
City	7.3	27.2	30.4	20.7	8.1	4.5	1.7
MSA[1]	11.2	29.1	25.3	22.8	7.0	3.3	1.4
U.S.	13.3	29.6	21.0	20.2	7.7	5.7	2.6

Note: Figures are percentages and include workers 16 years old and over; (1) Figures cover the Cincinnati, OH-KY-IN Metropolitan Statistical Area—see Appendix B for areas included
Source: U.S. Census Bureau, 2010-2014 American Community Survey 5-Year Estimates

Freeway Travel Time Index

Area	1985	1990	1995	2000	2005	2010	2014
Urban Area Rank[1,2]	54	41	36	38	51	57	46
Urban Area Index[1]	1.06	1.11	1.15	1.17	1.17	1.16	1.18
Average Index[3]	1.09	1.11	1.14	1.17	1.20	1.19	1.20

Note: Freeway Travel Time Index—the ratio of travel time in the peak period to the travel time at free-flow conditions. For example, a value of 1.30 indicates a 20-minute free-flow trip takes 26 minutes in the peak (20 minutes x 1.30 = 26 minutes); (1) Covers the Cincinnati OH-KY-IN urban area; (2) Rank is based on 101 urban areas (#1 = highest travel time index); (3) Average of 101 urban areas
Source: Texas Transportation Institute, 2015 Urban Mobility Scorecard, August 2015

Freeway Commuter Stress Index

Area	1985	1990	1995	2000	2005	2010	2014
Urban Area Rank[1,2]	58	45	43	46	53	58	52
Urban Area Index[1]	1.08	1.14	1.18	1.20	1.20	1.19	1.21
Average Index[3]	1.13	1.16	1.19	1.22	1.25	1.24	1.25

Note: The Freeway Commuter Stress Index is the same as the Freeway Travel Time Index (see table above) except that it includes only the travel in the peak directions during the peak periods; the TTI includes travel in all directions during the peak period. Thus, the CSI is more indicative of the work trip experienced by each commuter on a daily basis. (1) Covers the Cincinnati OH-KY-IN urban area; (2) Rank is based on 101 urban areas (#1 = highest stress index); (3) Average of 101 urban areas

Source: Texas Transportation Institute, 2015 Urban Mobility Scorecard, August 2015

Living Environment

COST OF LIVING

Cost of Living Index

Composite Index	Groceries	Housing	Utilities	Trans-portation	Health Care	Misc. Goods/ Services
87.6	89.1	72.4	93.8	101.9	101.4	91.3

Note: The Cost of Living Index measures regional differences in the cost of consumer goods and services, excluding taxes and non-consumer expenditures, for professional and managerial households in the top income quintile. It is based on more than 50,000 prices covering almost 60 different items for which prices are collected three times a year by chambers of commerce, economic development organizations or university applied economic centers in each participating urban area. The numbers shown should be read as a percentage above or below the national average of 100. For example, a value of 115.4 in the groceries column indicates that grocery prices are 15.4% higher than the national average. Small differences in the index numbers should not be interpreted as significant; Figures cover the Covington KY urban area.
Source: The Council for Community and Economic Research, ACCRA Cost of Living Index, 2015

Grocery Prices

Area[1]	T-Bone Steak ($/pound)	Frying Chicken ($/pound)	Whole Milk ($/half gal.)	Eggs ($/dozen)	Orange Juice ($/64 oz.)	Coffee ($/11.5 oz.)
City[2]	10.69	1.28	2.07	2.03	3.35	3.76
Avg.	10.99	1.43	2.25	2.26	3.58	4.48
Min.	7.16	0.98	1.30	1.35	2.88	2.98
Max.	14.13	2.43	3.85	4.81	6.39	7.56

Note: (1) Values for the local area are compared with the average, minimum and maximum values for all 292 areas in the Cost of Living Index; (2) Figures cover the Covington KY urban area; **T-Bone Steak** *(price per pound);* **Frying Chicken** *(price per pound, whole fryer);* **Whole Milk** *(half gallon carton);* **Eggs** *(price per dozen, Grade A, large);* **Orange Juice** *(64 oz. Tropicana or Florida Natural);* **Coffee** *(11.5 oz. can, vacuum-packed, Maxwell House, Hills Bros, or Folgers).*
Source: The Council for Community and Economic Research, ACCRA Cost of Living Index, 2015

Housing and Utility Costs

Area[1]	New Home Price ($)	Apartment Rent ($/month)	All Electric ($/month)	Part Electric ($/month)	Other Energy ($/month)	Telephone ($/month)
City[2]	224,020	725	-	64.47	79.49	30.01
Avg.	312,874	945	179.30	95.07	72.96	28.11
Min.	178,682	479	116.28	43.14	26.46	10.01
Max.	1,472,476	3,984	504.25	189.44	421.11	43.06

Note: (1) Values for the local area are compared with the average, minimum and maximum values for all 292 areas in the Cost of Living Index; (2) Figures cover the Covington KY urban area; **New Home Price** *(2,400 sf living area, 8,000 sf lot, in urban area with full utilities);* **Apartment Rent** *(950 sf 2 bedroom/1.5 or 2 bath, unfurnished, excluding all utilities except water);* **All Electric** *(average monthly cost for an all-electric home);* **Part Electric** *(average monthly cost for a part-electric home);* **Other Energy** *(average monthly cost for natural gas, fuel oil, coal, wood, and any other forms of energy except electricity);* **Telephone** *(price includes basic monthly rate for a private residential line plus additional local usage charges incurred by a family of four).*
Source: The Council for Community and Economic Research, ACCRA Cost of Living Index, 2015

Health Care, Transportation, and Other Costs

Area[1]	Doctor ($/visit)	Dentist ($/visit)	Optometrist ($/visit)	Gasoline ($/gallon)	Beauty Salon ($/visit)	Men's Shirt ($)
City[2]	92.47	101.64	101.00	2.40	31.88	21.32
Avg.	105.15	89.02	99.78	2.38	35.30	28.10
Min.	66.87	56.09	48.53	1.95	18.91	13.38
Max.	182.34	150.36	228.33	4.09	67.91	63.80

Note: (1) Values for the local area are compared with the average, minimum and maximum values for all 292 areas in the Cost of Living Index; (2) Figures cover the Covington KY urban area; **Doctor** *(general practitioners routine exam of an established patient);* **Dentist** *(adult teeth cleaning and periodic oral examination);* **Optometrist** *(full vision eye exam for established adult patient);* **Gasoline** *(one gallon regular unleaded, national brand, including all taxes, cash price at self-service pump if available);* **Beauty Salon** *(woman's shampoo, trim, and blow-dry);* **Men's Shirt** *(cotton/polyester dress shirt, pinpoint weave, long sleeves).*
Source: The Council for Community and Economic Research, ACCRA Cost of Living Index, 2015

HOUSING

House Price Index (HPI)

Area	National Ranking[2]	Quarterly Change (%)	One-Year Change (%)	Five-Year Change (%)
MSA[1]	165	-0.10	3.80	4.30
U.S.[3]	–	1.45	5.76	22.85

Note: The HPI is a weighted repeat sales index. It measures average price changes in repeat sales or refinancings on the same properties. This information is obtained by reviewing repeat mortgage transactions on single-family properties whose mortgages have been purchased or securitized by Fannie Mae or Freddie Mac in January 1975; (1) Cincinnati Metropolitan Statistical Area—see Appendix B for areas included; (2) Rankings are based on annual percentage change for all metro areas containing at least 15,000 transactions over the last 10 years and ranges from 1 to 266; (3) figures based on a weighted average of Census Division estimates using a seasonally adjusted, purchase-only index; all figures are for the period ending December 31, 2015
Source: Federal Housing Finance Agency, House Price Index, February 25, 2016

Median Single-Family Home Prices

Area	2013	2014	2015p	Percent Change 2014 to 2015
MSA[1]	135.5	140.6	145.4	3.4
U.S. Average	197.4	208.9	223.9	7.2

Note: Figures are median sales prices of existing single-family homes in thousands of dollars; (p) preliminary; n/a not available; (1) Cincinnati, OH-KY-IN Metropolitan Statistical Area—see Appendix B for areas included
Source: National Association of Realtors, Median Sales Price of Existing Single-Family Homes for Metropolitan Areas, 4th Quarter 2015

Qualifying Income Based on Median Sales Price of Existing Single-Family Homes

Area	With 5% Down ($)	With 10% Down ($)	With 20% Down ($)
MSA[1]	30,384	28,785	25,587
U.S. Average	49,535	46,928	41,714

Note: Figures are preliminary; Qualifying income is based on a mortgage rate of 4.1%. Monthly principal and interest payment is limited to 25% of income; n/a not available; (1) Cincinnati, OH-KY-IN Metropolitan Statistical Area—see Appendix B for areas included
Source: National Association of Realtors, Qualifying Income Based on Median Sales Price of Existing Single-Family Homes for Metropolitan Areas, 4th Quarter 2015

Median Apartment Condo-Coop Home Prices

Area	2013	2014	2015p	Percent Change 2014 to 2015
MSA[1]	109.4	111.0	109.3	-1.5
U.S. Average	194.9	204.3	210.7	3.1

Note: Figures are median sales prices of existing apartment condo-coop homes in thousands of dollars; (p) preliminary; n/a not available; (1) Cincinnati, OH-KY-IN Metropolitan Statistical Area—see Appendix B for areas included
Source: National Association of Realtors, Median Sales Price of Existing Apartment Condo-Coop Homes for Metropolitan Areas, 4th Quarter 2015

Gross Monthly Rent

Area	Under $200	$200 -299	$300 -499	$500 -749	$750 -999	$1,000 -1,499	$1,500 and up	Median ($)
City	2.2	0.0	9.1	13.3	39.2	25.2	10.9	944
MSA[1]	2.4	3.6	10.5	33.5	25.5	19.0	5.4	750
U.S.	1.5	3.2	7.4	21.0	24.1	26.9	15.9	920

Note: Figures are percentages except for Median; Gross rent is the contract rent plus the estimated average monthly cost of utilities (electricity, gas, and water and sewer) and fuels (oil, coal, kerosene, wood, etc.) if these are paid by the renter (or paid for the renter by someone else); (1) Figures cover the Cincinnati, OH-KY-IN Metropolitan Statistical Area—see Appendix B for areas included
Source: U.S. Census Bureau, 2010-2014 American Community Survey 5-Year Estimates

Homeownership Rate

Area	2008 (%)	2009 (%)	2010 (%)	2011 (%)	2012 (%)	2013 (%)	2014 (%)	2015 (%)
MSA[1]	64.7	62.4	62.8	65.2	63.4	63.3	65.5	65.9
U.S.	67.8	67.4	66.9	66.1	65.4	65.1	64.5	63.7

Note: (1) Figures cover the Cincinnati, OH-KY-IN Metropolitan Statistical Area—see Appendix B for areas included
Source: U.S. Census Bureau, Housing Vacancies and Homeownership Annual Statistics: 2015

Year Housing Structure Built

Area	2010 or Later	2000 -2009	1990 -1999	1980 -1989	1970 -1979	1960 -1969	1950 -1959	1940 -1949	Before 1940	Median Year
City	4.2	38.4	18.0	6.0	18.0	9.0	3.3	1.1	2.1	1996
MSA[1]	0.9	12.6	14.7	10.7	13.3	11.2	12.7	5.4	18.5	1972
U.S.	1.0	14.9	13.9	13.8	15.8	11.0	10.8	5.4	13.3	1976

Note: Figures are percentages except for Median Year; (1) Figures cover the Cincinnati, OH-KY-IN Metropolitan Statistical Area—see Appendix B for areas included
Source: U.S. Census Bureau, 2010-2014 American Community Survey 5-Year Estimates

HEALTH

Health Risk Data

Category	MSA[1] (%)	U.S. (%)
Adults aged 18–64 who have any kind of health care coverage	84.5	79.6
Adults who reported being in good or excellent health	82.3	83.1
Adults who are current smokers	23.3	19.6
Adults who are heavy drinkers[2]	5.8	6.1
Adults who are binge drinkers[3]	19.4	16.9
Adults who are overweight (BMI 25.0 - 29.9)	35.3	35.8
Adults who are obese (BMI 30.0 - 99.8)	28.3	27.6
Adults who participated in any physical activities in the past month	75.9	77.1
Adults 50+ who have ever had a sigmoidoscopy or colonoscopy	66.7	67.3
Women aged 40+ who have had a mammogram within the past two years	72.4	74.0
Men aged 40+ who have had a PSA test within the past two years	47.1	45.2
Adults aged 65+ who have had flu shot within the past year	63.3	60.1
Adults who always wear a seatbelt	92.4	93.8

Note: Data as of 2012 unless otherwise noted; (1) Figures cover the Cincinnati-Middletown, OH-KY-IN Metropolitan Statistical Area—see Appendix B for areas included; (2) Heavy drinkers are classified as males having more than two drinks per day or females having more than one drink per day; (3) Binge drinkers are classified as males having five or more drinks on one occasion or females having four or more drinks on one occasion
Source: Centers for Disease Control and Prevention, Behaviorial Risk Factor Surveillance System, SMART: Selected Metropolitan/Micropolitan Area Risk Trends, 2012 (Note: the CDC has discontinued this dataset but will be releasing a replacement in mid-2016)

Chronic Health Indicators

Category	MSA[1] (%)	U.S. (%)
Adults who have ever been told they had a heart attack	5.2	4.5
Adults who have ever been told they had a stroke	4.1	2.9
Adults who have been told they currently have asthma	10.3	8.9
Adults who have ever been told they have arthritis	27.6	25.7
Adults who have ever been told they have diabetes[2]	11.9	9.7
Adults who have ever been told they had skin cancer	6.1	5.7
Adults who have ever been told they had any other types of cancer	6.8	6.5
Adults who have ever been told they have COPD	7.5	6.2
Adults who have ever been told they have kidney disease	2.8	2.5
Adults who have ever been told they have a form of depression	20.2	18.0

Note: Data as of 2012 unless otherwise noted; (1) Figures cover the Cincinnati-Middletown, OH-KY-IN Metropolitan Statistical Area—see Appendix B for areas included; (2) Figures do not include pregnancy-related, borderline, or pre-diabetes
Source: Centers for Disease Control and Prevention, Behaviorial Risk Factor Surveillance System, SMART: Selected Metropolitan/Micropolitan Area Risk Trends, 2012 (Note: the CDC has discontinued this dataset but will be releasing a replacement in mid-2016)

Mortality Rates for the Top 10 Causes of Death in the U.S.

ICD-10[a] Sub-Chapter	ICD-10[a] Code	Age-Adjusted Mortality Rate[1] per 100,000 population	
		County[2]	U.S.
Malignant neoplasms	C00-C97	190.8	163.6
Ischaemic heart diseases	I20-I25	96.3	102.2
Other forms of heart disease	I30-I51	72.1	50.1
Chronic lower respiratory diseases	J40-J47	65.0	41.4
Organic, including symptomatic, mental disorders	F01-F09	59.5	38.5
Cerebrovascular diseases	I60-I69	35.4	36.5
Other external causes of accidental injury	W00-X59	49.5	27.5
Other degenerative diseases of the nervous system	G30-G31	27.8	26.3
Diabetes mellitus	E10-E14	28.9	21.1
Hypertensive diseases	I10-I15	23.8	19.7

Note: (a) ICD-10 = International Classification of Diseases 10th Revision; (1) Mortality rates are a three year average covering 2012-2014; (2) Figures cover Kenton County.
Source: Centers for Disease Control and Prevention, National Center for Health Statistics. Underlying Cause of Death 1999-2014 on CDC WONDER Online Database, released 2015.

Mortality Rates for Selected Causes of Death

ICD-10[a] Sub-Chapter	ICD-10[a] Code	Age-Adjusted Mortality Rate[1] per 100,000 population	
		County[2]	U.S.
Assault	X85-Y09	Unreliable	5.1
Diseases of the liver	K70-K76	16.6	13.5
Human immunodeficiency virus (HIV) disease	B20-B24	Suppressed	2.1
Influenza and pneumonia	J09-J18	16.3	15.2
Intentional self-harm	X60-X84	12.0	12.7
Malnutrition	E40-E46	Suppressed	0.9
Obesity and other hyperalimentation	E65-E68	Unreliable	1.9
Renal failure	N17-N19	12.0	13.0
Transport accidents	V01-V99	5.6	11.6
Viral hepatitis	B15-B19	Unreliable	2.1

Note: (a) ICD-10 = International Classification of Diseases 10th Revision; (1) Mortality rates are a three year average covering 2012-2014; (2) Figures cover Kenton County; Data are Suppressed when the data meet the criteria for confidentiality constraints; Mortality rates are flagged as Unreliable when the rate would be calculated with a numerator of 20 or less.
Source: Centers for Disease Control and Prevention, National Center for Health Statistics. Underlying Cause of Death 1999-2014 on CDC WONDER Online Database, released 2015.

Health Insurance Coverage

Area	With Health Insurance	With Private Health Insurance	With Public Health Insurance	Without Health Insurance	Population Under Age 18 Without Health Insurance
City	92.1	79.3	20.9	7.9	5.6
MSA[1]	89.8	72.5	27.7	10.2	4.7
U.S.	85.8	65.8	31.1	14.2	7.1

Note: Figures are percentages that cover the civilian noninstitutionalized population; (1) Figures cover the Cincinnati, OH-KY-IN Metropolitan Statistical Area—see Appendix B for areas included
Source: U.S. Census Bureau, 2010-2014 American Community Survey 5-Year Estimates

Number of Medical Professionals

Area	MDs[3]	DOs[3,4]	Dentists	Podiatrists	Chiropractors	Optometrists
County[1] (number)	432	23	77	9	32	21
County[1] (rate[2])	264.4	14.1	47.0	5.5	19.5	12.8
U.S. (rate[2])	272.5	20.9	64.7	5.8	25.9	15.2

Note: Data as of 2014 unless noted; (1) Data covers Kenton County; (2) Rate per 100,000 population; (3) Data as of 2013 and includes all active, non-federal physicians; (4) Doctor of Osteopathic Medicine
Source: U.S. Department of Health and Human Services, Health Resources and Services Administration, Bureau of Health Professions, Area Resource File (ARF) 2014-2015

Best Hospitals

According to *U.S. News,* the Cincinnati, OH-KY-IN metro area is home to four of the best hospitals in the U.S.: **Bethesda North Hospital** (2 specialties); **Christ Hospital** (4 specialties); **Good Samaritan Hospital** (2 specialties); **University of Cincinnati Medical Center** (1 specialty). The hospitals listed were nationally ranked in at least one adult specialty. Only 137 hospitals nationwide were nationally ranked in one or more specialties. Fifteen hospitals in the U.S. made the Honor Roll with high scores in at least six specialties. *U.S. News Online, "America's Best Children's Hospitals 2015-16"*

According to *U.S. News,* the Cincinnati, OH-KY-IN metro area is home to one of the best children's hospitals in the U.S.: **Cincinnati Children's Hospital Medical Center** (Honor Roll/10 specialties). The hospital listed was highly ranked in at least one pediatric specialty. Eighty-three children's hospitals in the U.S. were nationally ranked in at least one specialty. Twelve children's hospitals in the U.S. made the Honor Roll with high scores in at least three specialties. *U.S. News Online, "America's Best Children's Hospitals 2015-16"*

EDUCATION

Public School District Statistics

District Name	Schls	Pupils	Pupil/ Teacher Ratio	Minority Pupils[1] (%)	Free Lunch Eligible[2] (%)	IEP[3] (%)
Kenton County	25	14,698	17.7	11.9	30.8	13.8

Note: Table includes school districts with 100 or more students; (1) Percentage of students that are not non-Hispanic white; (2) Percentage of students that are eligible for the free lunch program; (3) Percentage of students that have an Individualized Education Program.
Source: U.S. Department of Education, National Center for Education Statistics, Common Core of Data, Local Education Agency (School District) Universe Survey: School Year 2013-2014; U.S. Department of Education, National Center for Education Statistics, Common Core of Data, Public Elementary/Secondary School Universe Survey: School Year 2013-2014

Highest Level of Education

Area	Less than H.S.	H.S. Diploma	Some College, No Deg.	Associate Degree	Bachelor's Degree	Master's Degree	Prof. School Degree	Doctorate Degree
City	10.0	30.9	22.1	7.9	20.1	6.3	2.2	0.5
MSA[1]	10.7	30.9	20.0	8.0	19.3	8.2	1.8	1.2
U.S.	13.7	28.0	21.2	7.9	18.3	7.8	2.0	1.3

Note: Figures cover persons age 25 and over; (1) Figures cover the Cincinnati, OH-KY-IN Metropolitan Statistical Area—see Appendix B for areas included
Source: U.S. Census Bureau, 2010-2014 American Community Survey 5-Year Estimates

Educational Attainment by Race

Area	High School Graduate or Higher (%)					Bachelor's Degree or Higher (%)				
	Total	White	Black	Asian	Hisp.[2]	Total	White	Black	Asian	Hisp.[2]
City	90.0	90.1	88.1	100.0	88.0	29.1	29.0	43.3	36.4	5.9
MSA[1]	89.3	90.2	83.8	90.9	70.7	30.5	31.6	16.5	65.7	23.7
U.S.	86.3	88.4	83.2	85.8	64.1	29.3	30.6	19.0	50.9	13.9

Note: Figures shown cover persons 25 years old and over; (1) Figures cover the Cincinnati, OH-KY-IN Metropolitan Statistical Area—see Appendix B for areas included; (2) People of Hispanic origin can be of any race
Source: U.S. Census Bureau, 2010-2014 American Community Survey 5-Year Estimates

School Enrollment by Grade and Control

Area	Preschool (%)		Kindergarten (%)		Grades 1 - 4 (%)		Grades 5 - 8 (%)		Grades 9 - 12 (%)	
	Public	Private	Public	Private	Public	Private	Public	Private	Public	Private
City	42.2	57.8	89.1	10.9	87.3	12.7	81.5	18.5	89.0	11.0
MSA[1]	51.6	48.4	83.1	16.9	83.6	16.4	82.7	17.3	83.3	16.7
U.S.	57.4	42.6	87.8	12.2	89.8	10.2	89.9	10.1	90.6	9.4

Note: Figures shown cover persons 3 years old and over; (1) Figures cover the Cincinnati, OH-KY-IN Metropolitan Statistical Area—see Appendix B for areas included
Source: U.S. Census Bureau, 2010-2014 American Community Survey 5-Year Estimates

Average Salaries of Public School Classroom Teachers

Area	2013-14 Dollars	2013-14 Rank[1]	2014-15 Dollars	2014-15 Rank[1]	Percent Change 2013-14 to 2014-15	Percent Change 2004-05 to 2014-15
Kentucky	50,560	26	51,093	26	1.05	24.7
U.S. Average	56,610	–	57,379	–	1.36	20.8

Note: (1) State rank ranges from 1 to 51 where 1 indicates highest salary.
Source: National Education Association, Rankings & Estimates: Rankings of the States 2014 and Estimates of School Statistics 2015, March 2015

Higher Education

Four-Year Colleges			Two-Year Colleges			Medical Schools[1]	Law Schools[2]	Voc/ Tech[3]
Public	Private Non-profit	Private For-profit	Public	Private Non-profit	Private For-profit			
0	0	0	0	0	0	0	0	0

Note: Figures cover institutions located within the city limits and include main campuses only; (1) includes schools accredited by the Liaison Committee on Medical Education and the American Osteopathic Association's Commission on Osteopathic College Accreditation; (2) includes ABA-accredited schools, schools with provisional ABA accreditation, and state accredited schools; (3) includes all schools with programs that are less than 2 years.
Source: National Center for Education Statistics, Integrated Postsecondary Education System (IPEDS), 2014-15; Association of American Medical Colleges, Member List, March 21, 2016; American Osteopathic Association, Member List, March 21, 2016; Law School Admission Council, Official Guide to ABA-Approved Law Schools Online, March 21, 2016; Wikipedia, List of Medical Schools in the United States, March 21, 2016; Wikipedia, List of Law Schools in the United States, March 21, 2016

According to *U.S. News & World Report,* the Cincinnati, OH-KY-IN metro area is home to two of the best national universities in the U.S.: **Miami University–Oxford** (#82 tie); **University of Cincinnati** (#140 tie). The indicators used to capture academic quality fall into a number of categories: assessment by administrators at peer institutions; retention of students; faculty resources; student selectivity; financial resources; alumni giving; high school counselor ratings of colleges; and graduation rate. *U.S. News & World Report, "America's Best Colleges 2016"*

According to *U.S. News & World Report,* the Cincinnati, OH-KY-IN metro area is home to one of the top 100 law schools in the U.S.: **University of Cincinnati, College of Law** (#60 tie). The rankings are based on a weighted average of 12 measures of quality: peer assessment score; assessment score by lawyers/judges; median LSAT scores; median undergrad GPA; acceptance rate; employment rates for graduates; placement success; bar passage rate; faculty resources; expenditures per student; student/faculty ratio; and library resources. *U.S. News & World Report, "America's Best Graduate Schools, Law, 2017"*

According to *U.S. News & World Report,* the Cincinnati, OH-KY-IN metro area is home to one of the top 75 medical schools for research in the U.S.: **University of Cincinnati, College of Medicine** (#40 tie). The rankings are based on a weighted average of 11 measures of quality: quality assessment; peer assessment score; assessment score by residency directors; research activity; total research activity; average research activity per faculty member; student selectivity; median MCAT total score; median undergraduate GPA; acceptance rate; and faculty resources. *U.S. News & World Report, "America's Best Graduate Schools, Medical, 2017"*

According to *U.S. News & World Report,* the Cincinnati, OH-KY-IN metro area is home to one of the top 75 business schools in the U.S.: **University of Cincinnati, Carl H. Lindner College of Business** (#63 tie). The rankings are based on a weighted average of the following nine measures: quality assessment; peer assessment; recruiter assessment; placement success; mean starting salary and bonus; student selectivity; mean GMAT and GRE scores; mean undergraduate GPA; and acceptance rate. *U.S. News & World Report, "America's Best Graduate Schools, Business, 2017"*

PRESIDENTIAL ELECTION

2012 Presidential Election Results

Area	Obama (%)	Romney (%)	Other (%)
Kenton County	36.8	61.2	2.0
U.S.	51.0	47.2	1.8

Note: Results may not add to 100% due to rounding
Source: Dave Leip's Atlas of U.S. Presidential Elections

EMPLOYERS

Major Employers

Company Name	Industry
Archdiocese of Cincinnati	Religious
Christ Hospital	Medical
Cincinnati Children's Hospital Med Ctr	Medical
Cincinnati Public Schools	Education
City of Cincinnati	Government
Fifth Third Bancorp	Banking
Frisch's Restaurants	Restaurant
GE Aviation	Aviation
Hamilton County	Government
Internal Revenue Service	Government
Kroger Company	Supermarket
Macy's	Retail
Mercy Health Partners	Medical
Miami University	Education
Procter & Gamble Company	Consumer products
St. Elizabeth Healthcare	Medical
TriHealth	Medical
University of Cincinnati	Education
US Postal Service	Government
Wal-Mart Stores	Retail

Note: Companies shown are located within the Cincinnati, OH-KY-IN Metropolitan Statistical Area.
Source: Hoovers.com; Wikipedia

PUBLIC SAFETY

Crime Rate

Area	All Crimes	Violent Crimes				Property Crimes		
		Murder	Rape[3]	Robbery	Aggrav. Assault	Burglary	Larceny -Theft	Motor Vehicle Theft
City	817.2	3.8	22.7	11.3	11.3	177.8	559.9	30.3
Metro[1]	3,225.2	4.6	36.7	112.6	113.4	637.6	2,187.7	132.6
U.S.	2,971.8	4.5	36.6	102.2	232.5	542.5	1,837.3	216.2

Note: Figures are crimes per 100,000 population; (1) Figures cover the Cincinnati, OH-KY-IN Metropolitan Statistical Area—see Appendix B for areas included; (3) The city and U.S. figures shown were reported using the revised Uniform Crime Reporting (UCR) definition of rape. The suburban and metro area figures shown are an aggregate total of the data submitted using both the revised and legacy UCR definitions.
Source: FBI Uniform Crime Reports, 2014

Hate Crimes

Area	Number of Quarters Reported	Number of Incidents per Bias Motivation						
		Race	Religion	Sexual Orientation	Ethnicity	Disability	Gender	Gender Identity
City	4	0	0	0	0	0	0	0
U.S.	4	2,568	1,014	1,017	648	84	33	98

Source: Federal Bureau of Investigation, Hate Crime Statistics 2014

Identity Theft Consumer Complaints

Area	Complaints	Complaints per 100,000 Population	Rank[2]
MSA[1]	2,692	125.2	110
U.S.	490,220	152.4	-

Note: (1) Figures cover the Cincinnati, OH-KY-IN Metropolitan Statistical Area—see Appendix B for areas included; (2) Rank ranges from 1 to 379 where 1 indicates greatest number of identity theft complaints per 100,000 population
Source: Federal Trade Commission, Consumer Sentinel Network Data Book for January–December 2015

Fraud and Other Consumer Complaints

Area	Complaints	Complaints per 100,000 Population	Rank[2]
MSA[1]	8,175	380.3	147
U.S.	2,593,159	806.0	-

Note: (1) Figures cover the Cincinnati, OH-KY-IN Metropolitan Statistical Area—see Appendix B for areas included; (2) Rank ranges from 1 to 379 where 1 indicates greatest number of identity theft complaints per 100,000 population
Source: Federal Trade Commission, Consumer Sentinel Network Data Book for January–December 2015

RECREATION

Culture

Dance[1]	Theatre[1]	Instrumental Music[1]	Vocal Music[1]	Series and Festivals	Museums and Art Galleries[2]	Zoos and Aquariums[3]
0	0	0	0	0	0	0

Note: (1) Professional perfoming groups; (2) Based on organizations with SIC code 8412; (3) AZA-accredited
Source: The Grey House Performing Arts Directory, 2015-16; Association of Zoos & Aquariums, AZA Member Zoos & Aquariums, March 25, 2016; www.AccuLeads.com, March 29, 2016

Professional Sports Teams

Team Name	League	Year Established
Cincinnati Bengals	National Football League (NFL)	1968
Cincinnati Reds	Major League Baseball (MLB)	1882

Note: Includes teams located in the Cincinnati, OH-KY-IN Metropolitan Statistical Area.
Source: Wikipedia, Major Professional Sports Teams of the United States and Canada, March 24, 2016

CLIMATE

Average and Extreme Temperatures

Temperature	Jan	Feb	Mar	Apr	May	Jun	Jul	Aug	Sep	Oct	Nov	Dec	Yr.
Extreme High (°F)	74	72	84	89	93	102	103	102	102	89	81	75	103
Average High (°F)	38	42	52	64	74	82	86	85	78	67	53	42	64
Average Temp. (°F)	30	33	43	54	63	72	76	74	68	56	44	34	54
Average Low (°F)	21	24	33	43	52	61	65	63	56	45	35	26	44
Extreme Low (°F)	-25	-15	-11	17	27	39	47	43	33	16	0	-20	-25

Note: Figures cover the years 1948-1990
Source: National Climatic Data Center, International Station Meteorological Climate Summary, 9/96

Average Precipitation/Snowfall/Humidity

Precip./Humidity	Jan	Feb	Mar	Apr	May	Jun	Jul	Aug	Sep	Oct	Nov	Dec	Yr.
Avg. Precip. (in.)	3.2	2.9	3.9	3.5	4.0	3.9	4.2	3.1	2.8	2.8	3.4	3.1	40.9
Avg. Snowfall (in.)	7	5	4	1	Tr	0	0	0	0	Tr	2	4	23
Avg. Rel. Hum. 7am (%)	79	78	77	76	79	82	85	87	87	83	79	79	81
Avg. Rel. Hum. 4pm (%)	65	60	55	50	51	53	54	52	52	51	58	65	55

Note: Figures cover the years 1948-1990; Tr = Trace amounts (<0.05 in. of rain; <0.5 in. of snow)
Source: National Climatic Data Center, International Station Meteorological Climate Summary, 9/96

Weather Conditions

Temperature			Daytime Sky			Precipitation		
10°F & below	32°F & below	90°F & above	Clear	Partly cloudy	Cloudy	0.01 inch or more precip.	0.1 inch or more snow/ice	Thunderstorms
14	107	23	80	126	159	127	25	39

Note: Figures are average number of days per year and cover the years 1948-1990
Source: National Climatic Data Center, International Station Meteorological Climate Summary, 9/96

HAZARDOUS WASTE

Superfund Sites

Independence has no sites on the EPA's Superfund Final National Priorities List. There are a total of 1,323 Superfund sites on the list in the U.S. *U.S. Environmental Protection Agency, Final National Priorities List, March 18, 2016*

AIR & WATER QUALITY

Air Quality Trends: Ozone

	1990	1995	2000	2005	2010	2011	2012	2013	2014
MSA[1]	0.092	0.090	0.082	0.086	0.076	0.079	0.082	0.065	0.069

Note: (1) Data covers the Cincinnati, OH-KY-IN Metropolitan Statistical Area—see Appendix B for areas included. The values shown are the composite ozone concentration averages among trend sites based on the highest fourth daily maximum 8-hour concentration in parts per million. These trends are based on sites having an adequate record of monitoring data during the trend period. Data from exceptional events are included.
Source: U.S. Environmental Protection Agency, Air Quality Monitoring Information, "Air Quality Trends by City, 1990-2014"

Air Quality Index

Area	Percent of Days when Air Quality was...[2]					AQI Statistics[2]	
	Good	Moderate	Unhealthy for Sensitive Groups	Unhealthy	Very Unhealthy	Maximum	Median
MSA[1]	46.6	51.5	1.9	0.0	0.0	127	51

Note: (1) Data covers the Cincinnati, OH-KY-IN Metropolitan Statistical Area—see Appendix B for areas included; (2) Based on 365 days with AQI data in 2015. Air Quality Index (AQI) is an index for reporting daily air quality. EPA calculates the AQI for five major air pollutants regulated by the Clean Air Act: ground-level ozone, particle pollution (aka particulate matter), carbon monoxide, sulfur dioxide, and nitrogen dioxide. The AQI runs from 0 to 500. The higher the AQI value, the greater the level of air pollution and the greater the health concern. There are six AQI categories: "Good" AQI is between 0 and 50. Air quality is considered satisfactory; "Moderate" AQI is between 51 and 100. Air quality is acceptable; "Unhealthy for Sensitive Groups" When AQI values are between 101 and 150, members of sensitive groups may experience health effects; "Unhealthy" When AQI values are between 151 and 200 everyone may begin to experience health effects; "Very Unhealthy" AQI values between 201 and 300 trigger a health alert; "Hazardous" AQI values over 300 trigger warnings of emergency conditions (not shown).
Source: U.S. Environmental Protection Agency, Air Quality Index Report, 2015

Air Quality Index Pollutants

Area	Percent of Days when AQI Pollutant was...[2]					
	Carbon Monoxide	Nitrogen Dioxide	Ozone	Sulfur Dioxide	Particulate Matter 2.5	Particulate Matter 10
MSA[1]	0.0	10.4	23.0	5.5	59.7	1.4

Note: (1) Data covers the Cincinnati, OH-KY-IN Metropolitan Statistical Area—see Appendix B for areas included; (2) Based on 365 days with AQI data in 2015. The Air Quality Index (AQI) is an index for reporting daily air quality. EPA calculates the AQI for five major air pollutants regulated by the Clean Air Act: ground-level ozone, particle pollution (also known as particulate matter), carbon monoxide, sulfur dioxide, and nitrogen dioxide. The AQI runs from 0 to 500. The higher the AQI value, the greater the level of air pollution and the greater the health concern.
Source: U.S. Environmental Protection Agency, Air Quality Index Report, 2015

Maximum Air Pollutant Concentrations: Particulate Matter, Ozone, CO and Lead

	Particulate Matter 10 (ug/m^3)	Particulate Matter 2.5 Wtd AM (ug/m^3)	Particulate Matter 2.5 24-Hr (ug/m^3)	Ozone (ppm)	Carbon Monoxide (ppm)	Lead (ug/m^3)
MSA[1] Level	75	12.9	28	0.073	1	0.01
NAAQS[2]	150	15	35	0.075	9	0.15
Met NAAQS[2]	Yes	Yes	Yes	Yes	Yes	Yes

Note: (1) Data covers the Cincinnati, OH-KY-IN Metropolitan Statistical Area—see Appendix B for areas included; Data from exceptional events are included; (2) National Ambient Air Quality Standards; ppm = parts per million; ug/m^3 = micrograms per cubic meter; n/a not available.
Concentrations: Particulate Matter 10 (coarse particulate)—highest second maximum 24-hour concentration; Particulate Matter 2.5 Wtd AM (fine particulate)—highest weighted annual mean concentration; Particulate Matter 2.5 24-Hour (fine particulate)—highest 98th percentile 24-hour concentration; Ozone—highest fourth daily maximum 8-hour concentration; Carbon Monoxide—highest second maximum non-overlapping 8-hour concentration; Lead—maximum running 3-month average
Source: U.S. Environmental Protection Agency, Air Quality Monitoring Information, "Air Quality Statistics by City, 2014"

Maximum Air Pollutant Concentrations: Nitrogen Dioxide and Sulfur Dioxide

	Nitrogen Dioxide AM (ppb)	Nitrogen Dioxide 1-Hr (ppb)	Sulfur Dioxide AM (ppb)	Sulfur Dioxide 1-Hr (ppb)	Sulfur Dioxide 24-Hr (ppb)
MSA[1] Level	23	59	n/a	71	n/a
NAAQS[2]	53	100	30	75	140
Met NAAQS[2]	Yes	Yes	n/a	Yes	n/a

Note: (1) Data covers the Cincinnati, OH-KY-IN Metropolitan Statistical Area—see Appendix B for areas included; Data from exceptional events are included; (2) National Ambient Air Quality Standards; ppm = parts per million; ug/m³ = micrograms per cubic meter; n/a not available.

Concentrations: Nitrogen Dioxide AM—highest arithmetic mean concentration; Nitrogen Dioxide 1-Hr—highest 98th percentile 1-hour daily maximum concentration; Sulfur Dioxide AM—highest annual mean concentration; Sulfur Dioxide 1-Hr—highest 99th percentile 1-hour daily maximum concentration; Sulfur Dioxide 24-Hr—highest second maximum 24-hour concentration

Source: U.S. Environmental Protection Agency, Air Quality Monitoring Information, "Air Quality Statistics by City, 2014"

Drinking Water

Water System Name	Pop. Served	Primary Water Source Type	Violations[1]	
			Health Based	Monitoring/ Reporting
Northern Kentucky Water District	199,460	Surface	0	0

Note: (1) Based on violation data from January 1, 2015 to December 31, 2015 (includes unresolved violations from earlier years)

Source: U.S. Environmental Protection Agency, Office of Ground Water and Drinking Water, Safe Drinking Water Information System (based on data extracted April 29, 2016)

Bowie, Maryland

Background

Bowie encompasses approximately eighteen square miles in the northeast corner of Prince George's County, thirty miles southwest of Baltimore and convenient to Annapolis and Washington DC.

Originally part of a 10,000-acre estate owned by Lord Calvert, the Belair estate, upon which Bowie now stands, was purchased by Samuel Ogle in 1737. A horseracing enthusiast, Ogle was intent on building his stables and growing his thoroughbred racing stock.

With rolling hills and fertile soil, the area was as suitable for raising racing stock as it was for raising crops. Agriculture, tobacco farming in particular, made up the primary economy of the region, with several large plantations stretching across the county.

In 1869, the Baltimore & Potomac Railroad Company, headed by William Duckett Bowie, began construction of a railroad, connecting Baltimore to southern Maryland, with a spur to Washington, DC. The city of Bowie, named in honor of Oden Bowie, William Duckett Bowie's son, rose up out of the junction of those railways.

The Baltimore & Potomac Railroad Company was purchased by the Pennsylvania Railroad in the early 1900s, bringing more cars, more people and more money into the area. Shortly afterwards, the Bowie Race Track was built, allowing the Belair Stud & Stable to become one of the top racing stables and thoroughbred breeders. At its closing in 1957, Belair was one of the oldest continuously operating horse farms in the country. The Belair Mansion and Stables can still be seen today, and are listed on the National Register of Historic Places.

The Belair Estate was acquired in 1957 and was incorporated into the city of Bowie in 1963. Many of Bowie's current residents live in the area formerly occupied by the Belair Estate. Growing from a small 500-plot railroad town, to one of the largest cities in the state, Bowie has much to offer its residents.

The Bowie Center for the Performing Arts, The Bowie Playhouse, four art galleries, and three museums support the cultural needs of the community.

Sports also play an important role in Bowie. The Bowie Baysox, an affiliate of the Baltimore Orioles, play out of Prince George's Stadium. Several parks, an ice arena, gymnasium, and golf course offer residents additional recreational options.

Bowie is part of the Prince George's County Public School System, with nine elementary schools, two middle schools, one high school, along with two special education centers. The city also has several private and parochial schools. Bowie State University, a former African-American college, has been in operation since the early 20th century.

Bowie is served by the Baltimore-Washington International Thurgood Marshall, Ronald Reagan Washington National and Washington Dulles International Airports.

Healthcare services are provided to the Bowie area by Anne Arundel Medical Center, Bowie Health Center, Doctors Community Hospital, Laurel Regional Hospital, and Prince George's Hospital Center.

Rankings

Business/Finance Rankings

- The personal finance site NerdWallet analyzed 183 American metropolitan areas with populations over 250,000 and more than 15,000 businesses to rank where entrepreneurs find the most success. Criteria included area economy, annual income, housing cost, unemployment rate, and the success rate of area businesses. Washington* ranked #81. *www.nerdwallet.com, "Best Places to Start a Business," April 27, 2015*

- Based on the U.S. Department of Labor's Occupational Information Network Data Collection Program, the Brookings Institution defined job opportunities for STEM workers at various levels of educational attainment. The Washington* metro area was one of the ten metro areas where workers in low-education-level STEM jobs earn the lowest relative wages. *www.brookings.edu, "The Hidden Stem Economy," June 10, 2013*

- Based on the U.S. Department of Labor's Occupational Information Network Data Collection Program, the Brookings Institution defined job opportunities for STEM workers at various levels of educational attainment. The Washington* metro area was placed among the ten large metro areas with the highest demand for high-level STEM knowledge. *www.brookings.edu, "The Hidden Stem Economy," June 10, 2013*

- 24/7 Wall Street used Brookings Institution research on 50 advanced industries to identify the proportion of workers in the nation's largest metropolitan areas that were employed in jobs requiring knowledge in the science, technology, engineering, or math (STEM) fields. The Washington* metro area was #6. *247wallst.com, "15 Cities with the Most High-Tech Jobs," March 13, 2015*

- Based on metro area social media reviews, the employment opinion group Glassdoor surveyed 50 of the largest U.S. metro areas and equally weighed cost of living, hiring opportunity, and job satisfaction to compose a list of "25 Best Cities for Jobs." The Washington* metro area was ranked #5 in overall job satisfaction. *www.glassdoor.com, "Best Cities for Jobs," May 19, 2015*

- In a survey of economic confidence in the nation's 50 largest metropolitan areas conducted January–December 2014, the Washington* metro area placed #3, according to Gallup's 2014 Economic Confidence Index. *Gallup, "San Jose and San Francisco Lead in Economic Confidence," March 19, 2015*

- The Brookings Institution ranked the 100 largest metro areas in the U.S. based on income inequality. Washington* was ranked #82 (#1 = greatest ineqality). Criteria: the "95/20 ratio," a figure representing the income at which a household earns more than 95 percent of all other households, divided by the income at which a household earns more than only 20 percent of all other households. *Brookings Institution, "Income Inequality, 100 Largest U.S. Metro Areas, 2007-2014," January 14, 2016*

- Payscale.com ranked the 20 largest metro areas in terms of wage growth. The Washington* metro area ranked #9. Criteria: private-sector wage growth between the 1st quarter of 2015 and the 1st quarter of 2016. *PayScale, "Wage Trends by Metro Area," 1st Quarter, 2016*

- The Washington* metro area was identified as one of the most debt-ridden places in America by the finance site Credit.com. The metro area was ranked #3. Criteria: residents' average personal debt load and average credit scores. *Credit.com, "The Most Debt-Ridden Cities," May 1, 2014*

- Washington* was identified as one of America's most frugal metro areas by *Coupons.com.* The city ranked #2 out of 25. Criteria: online coupon usage. *Coupons.com, "Top 25 Most Frugal Cities of 2014," May 11, 2015*

- Washington* was identified as one of America's most frugal metro areas by *Coupons.com.* The city ranked #6 out of 25. Criteria: Grocery IQ and coupons.com mobile app usage. *Coupons.com, "Top 25 Most On-the-Go Frugal Cities of 2013," April 10, 2014*

- The Washington* metro area appeared on the Milken Institute "2015 Best Performing Cities" list. Rank: #115 out of 200 large metro areas. Criteria: job growth; wage and salary growth; high-tech output growth. *Milken Institute, "Best-Performing Cities 2015," December 2015*

- *Forbes* ranked the 200 most populous metro areas to determine the nation's "Best Places for Business and Careers." The Washington* metro area was ranked #54. Criteria: costs (business and living); job growth (past and projected); income growth; educational attainment (college and high school); projected economic growth; cultural and recreational opportunities; net migration patterns; number of highly ranked colleges. *Forbes, "The Best Places for Business and Careers 2015," July 29, 2015*

Dating/Romance Rankings

- *Forbes* reports that the Washington* metro area made Rent.com's Best Cities for Newlyweds list for 2013, based on Bureau of Labor Statistics and Census Bureau data on number of married couples, percentage of families with children under age six, average annual income, cost of living, and availability of rentals. *www.forbes.com, "The 10 Best Cities for Newlyweds to Live and Work In," May 30, 2013*

- CreditDonkey, a financial education website, sought out the ten best U.S. cities for newlyweds, considering the number of married couples, divorce rate, average credit score, and average number of hours worked per week in metro areas with a million or more residents. The Washington* metro area placed #7. *www.creditdonkey.com, "Study: Best Cities for Newlyweds," November 30, 2013*

Education Rankings

- Washington* was identified as one of America's "smartest" metropolitan areas by *The Business Journals*. The area ranked #1 out of 10. Criteria: percentage of adults (25 and older) with high school diplomas, bachelor's degrees and graduate degrees. *The Business Journals, "Where the Brainpower Is: Exclusive U.S. Rankings, Insights," February 27, 2014*

- Personal finance website *WalletHub* analyzed the 150 largest U.S. metropolitan statistical areas to determine where the most educated Americans are choosing to settle. Criteria: education quality and attainment gap; education levels; percentage of workers with degrees; public school rankings; quality and size of each metro area's universities. Washington* was ranked #2 (#1 = most educated city). *www.WalletHub.com, "2015's Most and Least Educated Cities*

Environmental Rankings

- The Washington* metro area came in at #206 for the relative comfort of its climate on Sperling's list of "chill cities," as measured by the Sperling Heat Index. All 361 metro areas are included. Criteria included daytime high temperatures, nighttime low temperatures, dew point, and relative humidity at the high temperatures. *www.bertsperling.com, "Sperling's Chill Cities," July 18, 2013*

- Sperling's BestPlaces assessed 379 metropolitan areas of the United States for the likelihood of dangerously extreme weather events or earthquakes. In general the Southeast and South-Central regions have the highest risk of weather extremes and earthquakes, while the Pacific Northwest enjoys the lowest risk. Of the least risky metropolitan areas, the Washington* metro area was ranked #212. *www.bestplaces.net, "Safest Places from Natural Disasters," April 2011*

- The U.S. Environmental Protection Agency (EPA) released a list of U.S. metropolitan areas with the most ENERGY STAR certified buildings in 2015. The Washington* metro area was ranked #1 out of 25. *U.S. Environmental Protection Agency, "Top Cities With the Most ENERGY STAR Certified Buildings in 2016," March 30, 2016*

- Washington* was highlighted as one of the 25 most ozone-polluted metro areas in the U.S. during 2011 through 2013. The area ranked #22. *American Lung Association, State of the Air 2015*

Health/Fitness Rankings

- Analysts who tracked obesity rates in the nation's largest metro areas (populations above one million) found that the Washington* metro area was one of the ten major metros where residents were least likely to be obese, defined as a BMI score of 30 or above. *www.gallup.com, "Boulder, Colo., Residents Still Least Likely to Be Obese," April 4, 2014*

- For each of the 50 most populous metro areas in the United States, the American College of Sports Medicine's American Fitness Index evaluated infrastructure, community assets, and policies that encourage healthy and fit lifestyles, including preventive health behaviors, levels of chronic disease conditions, health care access, and community resources and policies that support physical activity. The Washington* metro area ranked #1 for "community fitness." *www.americanfitnessindex.org, "ACSM American Fitness Index Health and Community Fitness Status of the 50 Largest Metropolitan Areas," May 2015*

- The Washington* metro area was identified as one of the worst cities for bed bugs in America by pest control company Orkin. The area ranked #3 out of 50 based on the number of bed bug treatments Orkin performed from January to December 2015. *Orkin, "Chicago Tops Bed Bug Cities List for Fourth Year in a Row," January 13, 2016*

- Washington* was identified as a "2016 Spring Allergy Capital." The area ranked #84 out of 100. Three groups of factors were used to identify the most severe cities for people with allergies during the spring season: annual pollen levels; medicine utilization; access to board-certified allergists. *Asthma and Allergy Foundation of America, "Spring Allergy Capitals 2016"*

- Washington* was identified as a "2015 Asthma Capital." The area ranked #48 out of the nation's 100 largest metropolitan areas. Criteria: estimated prevalence; self-reported prevalence; crude death rate for asthma; annual pollen score; annual air quality; public smoking laws; number of board-certified asthma specialists; school inhaler access laws; rescue medication use; controller medication use; ER visits for asthma; uninsured rate; poverty rate. *Asthma and Allergy Foundation of America, "Asthma Capitals 2015"*

- The Washington* metro area ranked #38 out of 190 in The Gallup-Healthways Well-Being Index. Criteria: purpose; social well being; financial health; community and physical health. Results are based on telephone interviews with adults, aged 18 and older, living in metropolitan areas in the 50 U.S. states and the District of Columbia. *Gallup-Healthways, "State of American Well-Being," February 23, 2016*

Real Estate Rankings

- Washington* was ranked #143 out of 225 metro areas in terms of housing affordability in 2015 by the National Association of Home Builders (#1 = most affordable). Criteria: the share of homes sold in that area affordable to a family earning the local median income, based on standard mortgage underwriting criteria. *National Association of Home Builders®, NAHB-Wells Fargo Housing Opportunity Index, 4th Quarter 2015*

Safety Rankings

- Washington* was identified as one of the most disaster-proof places in the U.S. in terms of its vulnerability to natural and non-natural disasters. The city ranked #5 out of 5. Rankings are based on the U.S. Center for Disease Control's Cities Readiness Initiative (CRI), which assesses local emergency-management plans, protocols and capabilities for 72 Metropolitan Statistical Areas and four non-MSA large cities. *Forbes, "America's Most and Least Disaster-Proof Cities," December 12, 2011*

- The National Insurance Crime Bureau ranked 380 metro areas in the U.S. in terms of per capita rates of vehicle theft. The Washington* metro area ranked #148 (#1 = highest rate). Criteria: number of vehicle theft offenses per 100,000 inhabitants in 2014. *National Insurance Crime Bureau, "Hot Spots 2014," June 24, 2015*

Seniors/Retirement Rankings

- From its Best Cities for Successful Aging indexes, the Milken Institute generated rankings for metropolitan areas, weighing data in eight categories—health care, wellness, living arrangements, transportation, financial characteristics, education and employment opportunities, community engagement, and overall livability. The Washington* metro area was ranked #20 overall in the large metro area category. *Milken Institute, "Best Cities for Successful Aging, 2014"*

Sports/Recreation Rankings

- According to the personal finance website NerdWallet, the Washington* metro area, at #12, is one of the nation's top dozen metro areas for sports fans. Criteria included the presence of all four major sports—MLB, NFL, NHL, and NBA, fan enthusiasm (as measured by game attendance), ticket affordability, and "sports culture," that is, number of sports bars. *www.nerdwallet.com, "Best Cities for Sports Fans," May 5, 2013*

Transportation Rankings

- Washington* was identified as one of the most congested metro areas in the U.S. The area ranked #1 out of 10. Criteria: yearly delay per auto commuter in hours. *Texas A&M Transportation Institute, "2015 Urban Mobility Scorecard," August 2015*
- The Washington* metro area appeared on *Forbes* list of places with the most extreme commutes. The metro area ranked #3 out of 10. Criteria: average travel time; percentage of mega commuters. Mega-commuters travel more than 90 minutes and 50 miles each way to work. *Forbes.com, "The Cities with the Most Extreme Commutes," March 5, 2013*

Miscellaneous Rankings

- The watchdog site Charity Navigator conducts an annual study of charities in the nation's major markets both to analyze statistical differences in their financial, accountability, and transparency practices and to track year-to-year variations in individual communities. The Washington* metro area was ranked #20 among the 30 metro markets in the rating dimension of Overall Score. *www.charitynavigator.org, "Metro Market Study 2015," June 5, 2015*
- The finance and lifestyle site NerdWallet looked for the U.S. cities that topped the list in donating money and time to good causes. The Washington* metro area proved to be the #17-ranked metro area, judged by culture of volunteerism, depth of commitment in terms of volunteer hours per year, and monetary contributions. *www.nerdwallet.com, "Most Generous Cities," September 22, 2013*
- The Harris Poll's Happiness Index survey revealed that of the top ten U.S. markets, the Washington* metro area residents ranked #7 in happiness. Criteria included strong assent to positive statements and strong disagreement with negative ones, and degree of agreement with a series of statements about respondents' personal relationships and general outlook. *www.harrisinteractive.com, "Dallas/Fort Worth Is "Happiest" City among America's Top Ten Markets," September 4, 2013*
- Energizer Personal Care, the makers of Edge® shave gel, in partnership with Sperling's BestPlaces, ranked 50 major metro areas in terms of everyday irritations. The Washington* metro area ranked #9 the 50 metro area most iritating to guys. Criteria: high male-to-female ratio; poor sports team performance and high ticket prices; slow traffic; lack of job availability; unaffordable housing; extreme weather; lack of nightlife and fitness options. *Energizer Personal Care, "Most Irritatng Cities for Guys," August 26, 2013*
- Mars Chocolate North America, the makers of COMBOS®, in partnership with Sperling's BestPlaces, ranked 50 major metro areas in terms of their "manliness." The Washington* metro area ranked #43. Criteria: number of professional sports teams; number of nearby NASCAR tracks and racing events; manly lifestyle; concentration of manly retail stores; manly occupations per capita; salty snack sales; "Board of Manliness" rankings. *Mars Chocolate North America, "America's Manliest Cities 2012"*
- The National Alliance to End Homelessness ranked the 100 most populous metro areas with the highest rate of homelessness. The Washington* metro area ranked #21. Criteria: number of homeless people per 10,000 population in 2011. *National Alliance to End Homelessness, The State of Homelessness in America 2012*

Bowie is located within the Washington-Arlington-Alexandria, DC-VA-MD-WV Metropolitan Statistical Area.

Business Environment

CITY FINANCES

City Government Finances

Component	2012 ($000)	2012 ($ per capita)
Total Revenues	49,092	897
Total Expenditures	44,128	806
Debt Outstanding	18,009	329
Cash and Securities[1]	52,951	967

Note: (1) Cash and security holdings of a government at the close of its fiscal year, including those of its dependent agencies, utilities, and liquor stores.
Source: U.S Census Bureau, State & Local Government Finances 2012

City Government Revenue by Source

Source	2012 ($000)	2012 ($ per capita)
General Revenue		
From Federal Government	636	11
From State Government	1,811	33
From Local Governments	8,365	152
Taxes		
Property	24,980	456
Sales and Gross Receipts	963	17
Personal Income	0	0
Corporate Income	0	0
Motor Vehicle License	0	0
Other Taxes	1,676	30
Current Charges	4,222	77
Liquor Store	0	0
Utility	2,279	41
Employee Retirement	0	0

Source: U.S Census Bureau, State & Local Government Finances 2012

City Government Expenditures by Function

Function	2012 ($000)	2012 ($ per capita)	2012 (%)
General Direct Expenditures			
Air Transportation	0	0	0.0
Corrections	0	0	0.0
Education	0	0	0.0
Employment Security Administration	0	0	0.0
Financial Administration	2,142	39	4.8
Fire Protection	126	2	0.2
General Public Buildings	934	17	2.1
Governmental Administration, Other	2,432	44	5.5
Health	217	3	0.4
Highways	4,819	88	10.9
Hospitals	0	0	0.0
Housing and Community Development	38	< 1	< 0.1
Interest on General Debt	631	11	1.4
Judicial and Legal	133	2	0.3
Libraries	0	0	0.0
Parking	0	0	0.0
Parks and Recreation	6,902	126	15.6
Police Protection	7,431	135	16.8
Public Welfare	0	0	0.0
Sewerage	3,034	55	6.8
Solid Waste Management	6,820	124	15.4
Veterans' Services	0	0	0.0
Liquor Store	0	0	0.0
Utility	1,998	36	4.5
Employee Retirement	0	0	0.0

Source: U.S Census Bureau, State & Local Government Finances 2012

DEMOGRAPHICS

Population Growth

Area	1990 Census	2000 Census	2010 Census	2014* Estimate	Population Growth (%) 1990-2014	Population Growth (%) 2010-2014
City	39,831	50,269	54,727	56,335	41.4	2.9
MSA[1]	4,122,914	4,796,183	5,582,170	5,863,608	42.2	5.0
U.S.	248,709,873	281,421,906	308,745,538	314,107,084	26.3	1.7

Note: (1) Figures cover the Washington-Arlington-Alexandria, DC-VA-MD-WV Metropolitan Statistical Area—see Appendix B for areas included; (*) 2010-2014 5-year estimated population
Source: U.S. Census Bureau, 1990 Census, Census 2000, Census 2010, 2010-2014 American Community Survey 5-Year Estimates

Household Size

Area	Persons in Household (%) One	Two	Three	Four	Five	Six	Seven or More	Average Household Size
City	23.4	31.0	18.0	15.1	7.7	3.5	0.9	2.82
MSA[1]	27.1	30.6	16.7	14.7	6.5	2.6	1.5	2.73
U.S.	27.5	33.5	15.8	13.1	6.0	2.3	1.4	2.64

Note: (1) Figures cover the Washington-Arlington-Alexandria, DC-VA-MD-WV Metropolitan Statistical Area—see Appendix B for areas included
Source: U.S. Census Bureau, 2010-2014 American Community Survey 5-Year Estimates

Race

Area	White Alone[2] (%)	Black Alone[2] (%)	Asian Alone[2] (%)	AIAN[3] Alone[2] (%)	NHOPI[4] Alone[2] (%)	Other Race Alone[2] (%)	Two or More Races (%)
City	42.2	47.6	4.0	0.3	0.0	1.9	4.0
MSA[1]	55.9	25.4	9.5	0.3	0.1	5.1	3.7
U.S.	73.8	12.6	5.0	0.8	0.2	4.7	2.9

Note: (1) Figures cover the Washington-Arlington-Alexandria, DC-VA-MD-WV Metropolitan Statistical Area—see Appendix B for areas included; (2) Alone is defined as not being in combination with one or more other races; (3) American Indian and Alaska Native; (4) Native Hawaiian and Other Pacific Islander
Source: U.S. Census Bureau, 2010-2014 American Community Survey 5-Year Estimates

Hispanic or Latino Origin

Area	Total (%)	Mexican (%)	Puerto Rican (%)	Cuban (%)	Other (%)
City	6.7	0.9	1.0	0.6	4.3
MSA[1]	14.5	2.2	1.0	0.3	11.0
U.S.	16.9	10.8	1.6	0.6	3.8

Note: Persons of Hispanic or Latino origin can be of any race; (1) Figures cover the Washington-Arlington-Alexandria, DC-VA-MD-WV Metropolitan Statistical Area—see Appendix B for areas included
Source: U.S. Census Bureau, 2010-2014 American Community Survey 5-Year Estimates

Ancestry

Area	German	Irish	English	American	Italian	Polish	French[2]	Scottish	Dutch
City	9.9	9.4	6.0	3.7	4.2	2.3	1.2	1.8	0.6
MSA[1]	10.7	9.3	7.6	4.7	4.4	2.3	1.7	1.8	0.8
U.S.	14.9	10.8	8.0	7.1	5.5	3.0	2.7	1.7	1.4

Note: Figures are the percentage of the total population reporting a particular ancestry. The nine most commonly reported ancestries in the U.S. are shown. Figures include multiple ancestries (e.g. if a person reported being Irish and Italian, they were included in both columns); (1) Figures cover the Washington-Arlington-Alexandria, DC-VA-MD-WV Metropolitan Statistical Area—see Appendix B for areas included; (2) Excludes Basque
Source: U.S. Census Bureau, 2010-2014 American Community Survey 5-Year Estimates

Foreign-Born Population

Area	Percent of Population Born in								
	Any Foreign Country	Asia	Mexico	Europe	Carribean	Central America[2]	South America	Africa	Canada
City	13.0	3.4	0.2	1.1	1.9	1.8	0.6	3.8	0.2
MSA[1]	21.9	7.8	0.9	1.9	1.0	4.6	2.3	3.0	0.2
U.S.	13.1	3.8	3.7	1.5	1.2	1.0	0.9	0.6	0.3

Note: (1) Figures cover the Washington-Arlington-Alexandria, DC-VA-MD-WV Metropolitan Statistical Area—see Appendix B for areas included; (2) Excludes Mexico.
Source: U.S. Census Bureau, 2010-2014 American Community Survey 5-Year Estimates

Marital Status

Area	Never Married	Now Married[2]	Separated	Widowed	Divorced
City	33.3	48.4	1.8	6.5	10.0
MSA[1]	36.0	48.5	2.2	4.4	8.8
U.S.	32.5	48.4	2.2	5.9	10.9

Note: Figures are percentages and cover the population 15 years of age and older; (1) Figures cover the Washington-Arlington-Alexandria, DC-VA-MD-WV Metropolitan Statistical Area—see Appendix B for areas included; (2) Excludes separated
Source: U.S. Census Bureau, 2010-2014 American Community Survey 5-Year Estimates

Disability Status

Area	All Ages	Under 18 Years Old	18 to 64 Years Old	65 Years and Over
City	8.2	2.2	6.5	29.7
MSA[1]	8.0	2.8	6.2	30.3
U.S.	12.3	4.1	10.2	36.3

Note: Figures show percent of the civilian noninstitutionalized population that reported having a disability. Disability status is determined from from six types of difficulty: vision, hearing, cognitive, ambulatory, self-care, and independent living. For children under 5 years old, hearing and vision difficulty are used to determine disability status. For children between the ages of 5 and 14, disability status is determined from hearing, vision, cognitive, ambulatory, and self-care difficulties. For people aged 15 years and older, they are considered to have a disability if they have difficulty with any one of the six difficulty types; (1) Figures cover the Washington-Arlington-Alexandria, DC-VA-MD-WV Metropolitan Statistical Area—see Appendix B for areas included.
Source: U.S. Census Bureau, 2010-2014 American Community Survey 5-Year Estimates

Age

Area	Percent of Population									Median Age
	Under Age 5	Age 5–19	Age 20–34	Age 35–44	Age 45–54	Age 55–64	Age 65–74	Age 75–84	Age 85+	
City	6.7	19.6	18.1	14.5	17.4	12.0	6.5	3.5	1.7	39.6
MSA[1]	6.7	19.4	22.0	14.7	14.9	11.6	6.3	3.0	1.4	36.2
U.S.	6.4	19.9	20.6	13.0	14.1	12.3	7.6	4.3	1.9	37.4

Note: (1) Figures cover the Washington-Arlington-Alexandria, DC-VA-MD-WV Metropolitan Statistical Area—see Appendix B for areas included
Source: U.S. Census Bureau, 2010-2014 American Community Survey 5-Year Estimates

Gender

Area	Males	Females	Males per 100 Females
City	27,119	29,216	92.8
MSA[1]	2,859,981	3,003,627	95.2
U.S.	154,515,159	159,591,925	96.8

Note: (1) Figures cover the Washington-Arlington-Alexandria, DC-VA-MD-WV Metropolitan Statistical Area—see Appendix B for areas included
Source: U.S. Census Bureau, 2010-2014 American Community Survey 5-Year Estimates

Religious Groups by Family

Area	Catholic	Baptist	Non-Den.	Methodist[2]	Lutheran	LDS[3]	Pente-costal	Presby-terian[4]	Muslim[5]	Judaism
MSA[1]	14.5	7.3	4.8	4.5	1.2	1.1	1.0	1.3	2.3	1.1
U.S.	19.1	9.3	4.0	4.0	2.3	2.0	1.9	1.6	0.8	0.7

Note: Figures are the number of adherents as a percentage of the total population; (1) Figures cover the Washington-Arlington-Alexandria, DC-VA-MD-WV Metropolitan Statistical Area—see Appendix B for areas included; (2) Methodist/Pietist; (3) Latter Day Saints; (4) Reformed; (5) Figures are estimates
Source: Association of Statisticians of American Religious Bodies, 2010 U.S. Religion Census: Religious Congregations & Membership Study

Religious Groups by Tradition

Area	Catholic	Evangelical Protestant	Mainline Protestant	Other Tradition	Black Protestant	Orthodox
MSA[1]	14.5	12.4	8.7	5.9	2.3	0.6
U.S.	19.1	16.2	7.3	4.3	1.6	0.3

Note: Figures are the number of adherents as a percentage of the total population; (1) Figures cover the Washington-Arlington-Alexandria, DC-VA-MD-WV Metropolitan Statistical Area—see Appendix B for areas included
Source: Association of Statisticians of American Religious Bodies, 2010 U.S. Religion Census: Religious Congregations & Membership Study

ECONOMY

Gross Metropolitan Product

Area	2013	2014	2015	2016	Rank[2]
MSA[1]	463.9	477.0	495.8	523.2	5

Note: Figures are in billions of dollars; (1) Figures cover the Washington-Arlington-Alexandria, DC-VA-MD-WV Metropolitan Statistical Area—see Appendix B for areas included; (2) Rank is based on 2016 data and ranges from 1 to 381
Source: The U.S. Conference of Mayors, U.S. Metro Economies: GMP and Employment 2014-2016, June 2015

Economic Growth

Area	2011-13 (%)	2014 (%)	2015 (%)	2016 (%)	Rank[2]
MSA[1]	-0.1	1.0	2.4	3.4	38
U.S.	2.2	2.4	2.3	2.9	–

Note: Figures are real gross metropolitan product (GMP) growth rates and represent annual average percent change; (1) Figures cover the Washington-Arlington-Alexandria, DC-VA-MD-WV Metropolitan Statistical Area—see Appendix B for areas included; (2) Rank is based on 2016 data and ranges from 1 to 381
Source: The U.S. Conference of Mayors, U.S. Metro Economies: GMP and Employment 2014-2016, June 2015

Metropolitan Area Exports

Area	2009	2010	2011	2012	2013	2014	Rank[2]
MSA[1]	9,226.1	11,082.8	10,237.9	14,609.7	16,224.9	13,053.6	23

Note: Figures are in millions of dollars; (1) Figures cover the Washington-Arlington-Alexandria, DC-VA-MD-WV Metropolitan Statistical Area—see Appendix B for areas included; (2) Rank is based on 2014 data and ranges from 1 to 385
Source: U.S. Department of Commerce, International Trade Administration, Office of Trade & Industry Information, Manufacturing & Services, data extracted March 10, 2016

Building Permits

Area	Single-Family			Multi-Family			Total		
	2014	2015p	Pct. Chg.	2014	2015p	Pct. Chg.	2014	2015p	Pct. Chg.
City	n/a	n/a	n/a	n/a	n/a	n/a	n/a	n/a	n/a
MSA[1]	12,411	12,418	0.1	12,393	10,376	-16.3	24,804	22,794	-8.1
U.S.	640,300	690,800	7.9	411,800	487,600	18.4	1,052,100	1,178,400	12.0

Note: (1) Figures cover the Washington-Arlington-Alexandria, DC-VA-MD-WV Metropolitan Statistical Area—see Appendix B for areas included; Figures represent new, privately-owned housing units authorized (unadjusted data); All permit data are based on estimates with imputation; (p) preliminary data.
Source: U.S. Census Bureau, Manufacturing, Mining, and Construction Statistics, Building Permits, 2014, 2015

Bankruptcy Filings

Area	Business Filings 2014	Business Filings 2015	Business Filings % Chg.	Nonbusiness Filings 2014	Nonbusiness Filings 2015	Nonbusiness Filings % Chg.
Prince George's County	58	74	27.6	4,443	4,032	-9.3
U.S.	26,983	24,735	-8.3	909,812	819,760	-9.9

Note: Business filings include Chapter 7, Chapter 11, Chapter 12, and Chapter 13; Nonbusiness filings include Chapter 7, Chapter 11, and Chapter 13
Source: Administrative Office of the U.S. Courts, Business and Nonbusiness Bankruptcy, County Cases Commenced by Chapter of the Bankruptcy Code, During the 12- Month Period Ending December 31, 2014 and Business and Nonbusiness Bankruptcy, County Cases Commenced by Chapter of the Bankruptcy Code, During the 12- Month Period Ending December 31, 2015

Housing Vacancy Rates

Area	Gross Vacancy Rate[2] (%)			Year-Round Vacancy Rate[3] (%)			Rental Vacancy Rate[4] (%)			Homeowner Vacancy Rate[5] (%)		
	2013	2014	2015	2013	2014	2015	2013	2014	2015	2013	2014	2015
MSA[1]	8.3	7.8	7.7	8.2	7.5	7.4	7.2	6.7	5.7	1.3	1.4	0.9
U.S.	13.6	13.4	12.9	10.7	10.4	10.0	8.3	7.6	7.1	2.0	1.9	1.8

Note: (1) Figures cover the Washington-Arlington-Alexandria, DC-VA-MD-WV Metropolitan Statistical Area—see Appendix B for areas included; (2) The percentage of the total housing inventory that is vacant; (3) The percentage of the housing inventory (excluding seasonal units) that is year-round vacant; (4) The percentage of rental inventory that is vacant for rent; (5) The percentage of homeowner inventory that is vacant for sale
Source: U.S. Census Bureau, Housing Vacancies and Homeownership Annual Statistics: 2015

INCOME

Income

Area	Per Capita ($)	Median Household ($)	Average Household ($)
City	42,544	106,396	119,456
MSA[1]	43,884	91,756	117,989
U.S.	28,555	53,482	74,596

Note: (1) Figures cover the Washington-Arlington-Alexandria, DC-VA-MD-WV Metropolitan Statistical Area—see Appendix B for areas included
Source: U.S. Census Bureau, 2010-2014 American Community Survey 5-Year Estimates

Household Income Distribution

Area	Percent of Households Earning: Under $15,000	$15,000 -24,999	$25,000 -34,999	$35,000 -49,999	$50,000 -74,999	$75,000 -99,000	$100,000 -149,999	$150,000 and up
City	2.9	2.9	4.4	7.5	13.1	14.5	28.2	26.5
MSA[1]	6.3	5.0	5.4	8.9	15.3	13.1	20.1	25.9
U.S.	12.5	10.7	10.2	13.5	17.8	12.2	13.0	10.0

Note: (1) Figures cover the Washington-Arlington-Alexandria, DC-VA-MD-WV Metropolitan Statistical Area—see Appendix B for areas included
Source: U.S. Census Bureau, 2010-2014 American Community Survey 5-Year Estimates

Poverty Rate

Area	All Ages	Under 18 Years Old	18 to 64 Years Old	65 Years and Over
City	3.3	2.8	3.6	3.1
MSA[1]	8.4	10.8	7.8	6.8
U.S.	15.6	21.9	14.6	9.4

Note: Figures are percentage of people whose income during the past 12 months was below the poverty level; (1) Figures cover the Washington-Arlington-Alexandria, DC-VA-MD-WV Metropolitan Statistical Area—see Appendix B for areas included
Source: U.S. Census Bureau, 2010-2014 American Community Survey 5-Year Estimates

EMPLOYMENT

Labor Force and Employment

Area	Civilian Labor Force			Workers Employed		
	Dec. 2014	Dec. 2015	% Chg.	Dec. 2014	Dec. 2015	% Chg.
City	32,304	33,027	2.2	30,955	31,836	2.8
MD[1]	2,576,993	2,610,615	1.3	2,459,715	2,507,911	1.9
U.S.	155,521,000	157,245,000	1.1	147,190,000	149,703,000	1.7

Note: Data is not seasonally adjusted and covers workers 16 years of age and older; (1) Figures cover the Washington-Arlington-Alexandria, DC-VA-MD-WV Metropolitan Division—see Appendix B for areas included
Source: Bureau of Labor Statistics, Local Area Unemployment Statistics

Unemployment Rate

Area	2015											
	Jan.	Feb.	Mar.	Apr.	May	Jun.	Jul.	Aug.	Sep.	Oct.	Nov.	Dec.
City	4.6	4.2	4.1	3.9	4.4	4.6	4.4	4.2	4.4	4.4	4.1	3.6
MD[1]	5.0	5.0	4.8	4.4	4.7	4.9	4.7	4.4	4.3	4.3	4.2	3.9
U.S.	6.1	5.8	5.6	5.1	5.3	5.5	5.6	5.2	4.9	4.8	4.8	4.8

Note: Data is not seasonally adjusted and covers workers 16 years of age and older; (1) Figures cover the Washington-Arlington-Alexandria, DC-VA-MD-WV Metropolitan Division—see Appendix B for areas included
Source: Bureau of Labor Statistics, Local Area Unemployment Statistics

Employment by Occupation

Occupation Classification	City (%)	MSA[1] (%)	U.S. (%)
Management, Business, Science, and Arts	54.4	51.0	36.4
Natural Resources, Construction, and Maintenance	6.3	6.8	9.0
Production, Transportation, and Material Moving	4.8	5.6	12.1
Sales and Office	21.1	20.5	24.4
Service	13.4	16.0	18.2

Note: Figures cover employed civilians 16 years of age and older; (1) Figures cover the Washington-Arlington-Alexandria, DC-VA-MD-WV Metropolitan Statistical Area—see Appendix B for areas included
Source: U.S. Census Bureau, 2010-2014 American Community Survey 5-Year Estimates

Employment by Industry

Sector	MD[1]		U.S.
	Number of Employees	Percent of Total	Percent of Total
Construction, Mining, and Logging	118,500	4.5	5.0
Education and Health Services	331,900	12.6	15.7
Financial Activities	116,000	4.4	5.7
Government	592,300	22.5	15.5
Information	61,600	2.3	1.9
Leisure and Hospitality	257,600	9.8	10.4
Manufacturing	36,400	1.3	8.6
Other Services	168,000	6.3	3.9
Professional and Business Services	605,600	23.0	13.9
Retail Trade	228,600	8.7	11.3
Transportation, Warehousing, and Utilities	60,200	2.2	3.9
Wholesale Trade	50,800	1.9	4.1

Note: Figures are non-farm employment as of December 2015. Figures are not seasonally adjusted and include workers 16 years of age and older; (1) Figures cover the Washington-Arlington-Alexandria, DC-VA-MD-WV Metropolitan Division—see Appendix B for areas included; n/a not available
Source: Bureau of Labor Statistics, Current Employment Statistics, Employment, Hours, and Earnings

Occupations with Greatest Projected Employment Growth: 2012 – 2022

Occupation[1]	2012 Employment	2022 Projected Employment	Numeric Employment Change	Percent Employment Change
Combined Food Preparation and Serving Workers, Including Fast Food	45,480	52,430	6,950	15.3
Registered Nurses	48,340	54,570	6,230	12.9
Retail Salespersons	75,780	80,350	4,570	6.0
General and Operations Managers	50,600	54,800	4,200	8.3
Secretaries and Administrative Assistants, Except Legal, Medical, and Executive	54,990	58,640	3,650	6.6
Customer Service Representatives	42,250	45,870	3,620	8.6
Janitors and Cleaners, Except Maids and Housekeeping Cleaners	39,760	43,080	3,320	8.3
Nursing Assistants	29,510	32,660	3,150	10.7
Software Developers, Systems Software	14,020	17,120	3,100	22.1
Elementary School Teachers, Except Special Education	24,760	27,760	3,000	12.1

Note: Projections cover Maryland; (1) Sorted by numeric employment change
Source: www.projectionscentral.com, State Occupational Projections, 2012–2022 Long-Term Projections

Fastest Growing Occupations: 2012 – 2022

Occupation[1]	2012 Employment	2022 Projected Employment	Numeric Employment Change	Percent Employment Change
Information Security Analysts	3,380	4,760	1,380	41.2
Interpreters and Translators	1,070	1,470	400	36.9
Nursing Instructors and Teachers, Postsecondary	800	1,080	280	35.0
Diagnostic Medical Sonographers	1,210	1,610	400	32.7
Meeting, Convention, and Event Planners	2,150	2,830	680	31.7
Market Research Analysts and Marketing Specialists	7,430	9,490	2,060	27.8
Occupational Therapy Assistants	550	690	140	26.6
Operations Research Analysts	2,850	3,580	730	25.5
Cardiovascular Technologists and Technicians	1,090	1,360	270	24.9
Logisticians	4,670	5,800	1,130	24.4

Note: Projections cover Maryland; (1) Sorted by percent employment change and excludes occupations with numeric employment change less than 100
Source: www.projectionscentral.com, State Occupational Projections, 2012–2022 Long-Term Projections

Average Wages

Occupation	$/Hr.	Occupation	$/Hr.
Accountants and Auditors	43.03	Maids and Housekeeping Cleaners	12.55
Automotive Mechanics	23.59	Maintenance and Repair Workers	21.71
Bookkeepers	21.96	Marketing Managers	75.26
Carpenters	22.16	Nuclear Medicine Technologists	39.84
Cashiers	10.63	Nurses, Licensed Practical	23.74
Clerks, General Office	18.51	Nurses, Registered	37.41
Clerks, Receptionists/Information	15.29	Nursing Assistants	13.90
Clerks, Shipping/Receiving	17.38	Packers and Packagers, Hand	11.06
Computer Programmers	47.38	Physical Therapists	41.93
Computer Systems Analysts	49.66	Postal Service Mail Carriers	24.56
Computer User Support Specialists	29.48	Real Estate Brokers	45.36
Cooks, Restaurant	12.68	Retail Salespersons	12.25
Dentists	77.21	Sales Reps., Exc. Tech./Scientific	37.76
Electrical Engineers	55.22	Sales Reps., Tech./Scientific	54.87
Electricians	26.93	Secretaries, Exc. Legal/Med./Exec.	20.99
Financial Managers	74.37	Security Guards	18.56
First-Line Supervisors/Managers, Sales	22.57	Surgeons	99.71
Food Preparation Workers	11.70	Teacher Assistants*	15.41
General and Operations Managers	70.62	Teachers, Elementary School*	33.75
Hairdressers/Cosmetologists	17.08	Teachers, Secondary School*	35.25
Internists	71.81	Telemarketers	12.83
Janitors and Cleaners	13.08	Truck Drivers, Heavy/Tractor-Trailer	20.66
Landscaping/Groundskeeping Workers	13.95	Truck Drivers, Light/Delivery Svcs.	18.42
Lawyers	80.09	Waiters and Waitresses	12.66

Note: Wage data covers the Washington-Arlington-Alexandria, DC-VA-MD-WV Metropolitan Division—see Appendix B for areas included; (*) Hourly wages for elementary/secondary school teachers and teacher assistants were calculated by the editors from annual wage data based on a 40 hour work week; n/a not available.
Source: Bureau of Labor Statistics, Metro Area Occupational Employment and Wage Estimates, May 2015

TAXES

State Corporate Income Tax Rates

State	Tax Rate (%)	Income Brackets ($)	Num. of Brackets	Financial Institution Tax Rate (%)[a]	Federal Income Tax Ded.
Maryland	8.25	Flat rate	1	8.25	No

Note: Tax rates as of January 1, 2016; (a) Rates listed are the corporate income tax rate applied to financial institutions or excise taxes based on income. Some states have other taxes based upon the value of deposits or shares.
Source: Federation of Tax Administrators, "State Corporate Income Tax Rates, 2016"

State Individual Income Tax Rates

State	Tax Rate (%)	Income Brackets ($)	Num. of Brackets	Personal Exempt. ($)[1] Single	Personal Exempt. ($)[1] Dependents	Fed. Inc. Tax Ded.
Maryland	2.0 - 5.75	1,000 - 250,000 (k)	8	3,200	3,200	No

Note: Tax rates as of January 1, 2016; Local- and county-level taxes are not included; n/a not applicable; (1) Married joint filers generally receive double the single exemption; (k) The income brackets reported for Maryland are for single individuals. For married couples filing jointly, the same tax rates apply to income brackets ranging from $1,000, to $300,000.
Source: Federation of Tax Administrators, "State Individual Income Tax Rates, 2016"

Various State and Local Tax Rates

State	State and Local Sales and Use (%)	State Sales and Use (%)	Gasoline[1] (¢/gal.)	Cigarette[2] ($/pack)	Spirits[3] ($/gal.)	Wine[4] ($/gal.)	Beer[5] ($/gal.)
Maryland	6.00	6.0	32.6	2.00	4.64 (f)(j)	1.35 (p)	0.49 (s)

Note: All tax rates as of January 1, 2016; (1) The American Petroleum Institute has developed a methodology for determining the average tax rate on a gallon of fuel. Rates may include any of the following: excise taxes, environmental fees, storage tank fees, other fees or taxes, general sales tax, and local taxes. In states where gasoline is subject to the general sales tax, or where the fuel tax is based on the average sale price, the average rate determined by API is sensitive to changes in the price of gasoline. States that fully or partially apply general sales taxes to gasoline: CA, CO, GA, IL, IN, MI, NY; (2) The federal excise tax of $1.0066 per pack and local taxes are not included; (3) Rates are those applicable to off-premise sales of 40% alcohol by volume (a.b.v.) distilled spirits in 750ml containers. Local excise taxes are excluded; (4) Rates are those applicable to off-premise sales of 11% a.b.v. non-carbonated wine in 750ml containers; (5) Rates are those applicable to off-premise sales of 4.7% a.b.v. beer in 12 ounce containers; (f) Different rates are also applicable according to alcohol content, place of production, size of container, or place purchased (on- or off-premise or onboard airlines); (j) Includes sales taxes specific to alcoholic beverages; (p) Includes sales taxes specific to alcoholic beverages; (s) Includes sales taxes specific to alcoholic beverages.
Source: Tax Foundation, 2016 Facts & Figures: How Does Your State Compare?

State Business Tax Climate Index Rankings

State	Overall Rank	Corporate Tax Rank	Individual Income Tax Rank	Sales Tax Rank	Unemployment Insurance Tax Rank	Property Tax Rank
Maryland	41	19	45	8	28	42

Note: The index is a measure of how each state's tax laws affect economic performance. The lower the rank, the more favorable a state's tax system is for business. States without a given tax are given a ranking of 1. The scores/rankings for the District of Columbia do not affect other states. The 2016 index represents the tax climate as of July 1, 2015 (the beginning of Fiscal Year 2016).
Source: Tax Foundation, State Business Tax Climate Index 2016

TRANSPORTATION

Means of Transportation to Work

Area	Car/Truck/Van		Public Transportation			Bicycle	Walked	Other Means	Worked at Home
	Drove Alone	Car-pooled	Bus	Subway	Railroad				
City	73.1	10.6	1.6	7.4	0.7	0.1	1.9	0.7	3.9
MSA[1]	66.0	10.1	5.5	7.9	0.7	0.7	3.2	1.0	4.9
U.S.	76.4	9.6	2.6	1.8	0.6	0.6	2.8	1.3	4.4

Note: Figures are percentages and cover workers 16 years of age and older; (1) Figures cover the Washington-Arlington-Alexandria, DC-VA-MD-WV Metropolitan Statistical Area—see Appendix B for areas included
Source: U.S. Census Bureau, 2010-2014 American Community Survey 5-Year Estimates

Travel Time to Work

Area	Less Than 10 Minutes	10 to 19 Minutes	20 to 29 Minutes	30 to 44 Minutes	45 to 59 Minutes	60 to 89 Minutes	90 Minutes or More
City	7.0	14.5	16.4	26.5	15.5	16.3	3.9
MSA[1]	6.3	19.2	18.0	25.8	13.7	12.6	4.4
U.S.	13.3	29.6	21.0	20.2	7.7	5.7	2.6

Note: Figures are percentages and include workers 16 years old and over; (1) Figures cover the Washington-Arlington-Alexandria, DC-VA-MD-WV Metropolitan Statistical Area—see Appendix B for areas included
Source: U.S. Census Bureau, 2010-2014 American Community Survey 5-Year Estimates

Freeway Travel Time Index

Area	1985	1990	1995	2000	2005	2010	2014
Urban Area Rank[1,2]	6	5	5	7	6	5	8
Urban Area Index[1]	1.19	1.22	1.27	1.29	1.34	1.35	1.34
Average Index[3]	1.09	1.11	1.14	1.17	1.20	1.19	1.20

Note: Freeway Travel Time Index—the ratio of travel time in the peak period to the travel time at free-flow conditions. For example, a value of 1.30 indicates a 20-minute free-flow trip takes 26 minutes in the peak (20 minutes x 1.30 = 26 minutes); (1) Covers the Washington DC-VA-MD urban area; (2) Rank is based on 101 urban areas (#1 = highest travel time index); (3) Average of 101 urban areas
Source: Texas Transportation Institute, 2015 Urban Mobility Scorecard, August 2015

Freeway Commuter Stress Index

Area	1985	1990	1995	2000	2005	2010	2014
Urban Area Rank[1,2]	8	8	6	8	9	7	9
Urban Area Index[1]	1.26	1.30	1.35	1.37	1.42	1.44	1.43
Average Index[3]	1.13	1.16	1.19	1.22	1.25	1.24	1.25

Note: The Freeway Commuter Stress Index is the same as the Freeway Travel Time Index (see table above) except that it includes only the travel in the peak directions during the peak periods; the TTI includes travel in all directions during the peak period. Thus, the CSI is more indicative of the work trip experienced by each commuter on a daily basis. (1) Covers the Washington DC-VA-MD urban area; (2) Rank is based on 101 urban areas (#1 = highest stress index); (3) Average of 101 urban areas

Source: Texas Transportation Institute, 2015 Urban Mobility Scorecard, August 2015

Living Environment

COST OF LIVING

Cost of Living Index

Composite Index	Groceries	Housing	Utilities	Transportation	Health Care	Misc. Goods/ Services
129.5	108.6	201.6	101.8	109.2	88.5	97.5

Note: The Cost of Living Index measures regional differences in the cost of consumer goods and services, excluding taxes and non-consumer expenditures, for professional and managerial households in the top income quintile. It is based on more than 50,000 prices covering almost 60 different items for which prices are collected three times a year by chambers of commerce, economic development organizations or university applied economic centers in each participating urban area. The numbers shown should be read as a percentage above or below the national average of 100. For example, a value of 115.4 in the groceries column indicates that grocery prices are 15.4% higher than the national average. Small differences in the index numbers should not be interpreted as significant; Figures cover the Bethesda-Gaithersburg-Frederick MD urban area.
Source: The Council for Community and Economic Research, ACCRA Cost of Living Index, 2015

Grocery Prices

Area[1]	T-Bone Steak ($/pound)	Frying Chicken ($/pound)	Whole Milk ($/half gal.)	Eggs ($/dozen)	Orange Juice ($/64 oz.)	Coffee ($/11.5 oz.)
City[2]	11.56	1.66	2.44	2.17	3.53	4.34
Avg.	10.99	1.43	2.25	2.26	3.58	4.48
Min.	7.16	0.98	1.30	1.35	2.88	2.98
Max.	14.13	2.43	3.85	4.81	6.39	7.56

Note: (1) Values for the local area are compared with the average, minimum and maximum values for all 292 areas in the Cost of Living Index; (2) Figures cover the Bethesda-Gaithersburg-Frederick MD urban area; **T-Bone Steak** *(price per pound);* **Frying Chicken** *(price per pound, whole fryer);* **Whole Milk** *(half gallon carton);* **Eggs** *(price per dozen, Grade A, large);* **Orange Juice** *(64 oz. Tropicana or Florida Natural);* **Coffee** *(11.5 oz. can, vacuum-packed, Maxwell House, Hills Bros, or Folgers).*
Source: The Council for Community and Economic Research, ACCRA Cost of Living Index, 2015

Housing and Utility Costs

Area[1]	New Home Price ($)	Apartment Rent ($/month)	All Electric ($/month)	Part Electric ($/month)	Other Energy ($/month)	Telephone ($/month)
City[2]	652,136	1,732	-	106.79	73.56	26.86
Avg.	312,874	945	179.30	95.07	72.96	28.11
Min.	178,682	479	116.28	43.14	26.46	10.01
Max.	1,472,476	3,984	504.25	189.44	421.11	43.06

Note: (1) Values for the local area are compared with the average, minimum and maximum values for all 292 areas in the Cost of Living Index; (2) Figures cover the Bethesda-Gaithersburg-Frederick MD urban area; **New Home Price** *(2,400 sf living area, 8,000 sf lot, in urban area with full utilities);* **Apartment Rent** *(950 sf 2 bedroom/1.5 or 2 bath, unfurnished, excluding all utilities except water);* **All Electric** *(average monthly cost for an all-electric home);* **Part Electric** *(average monthly cost for a part-electric home);* **Other Energy** *(average monthly cost for natural gas, fuel oil, coal, wood, and any other forms of energy except electricity);* **Telephone** *(price includes basic monthly rate for a private residential line plus additional local usage charges incurred by a family of four).*
Source: The Council for Community and Economic Research, ACCRA Cost of Living Index, 2015

Health Care, Transportation, and Other Costs

Area[1]	Doctor ($/visit)	Dentist ($/visit)	Optometrist ($/visit)	Gasoline ($/gallon)	Beauty Salon ($/visit)	Men's Shirt ($)
City[2]	70.27	81.75	72.39	2.58	47.00	32.38
Avg.	105.15	89.02	99.78	2.38	35.30	28.10
Min.	66.87	56.09	48.53	1.95	18.91	13.38
Max.	182.34	150.36	228.33	4.09	67.91	63.80

Note: (1) Values for the local area are compared with the average, minimum and maximum values for all 292 areas in the Cost of Living Index; (2) Figures cover the Bethesda-Gaithersburg-Frederick MD urban area; **Doctor** *(general practitioners routine exam of an established patient);* **Dentist** *(adult teeth cleaning and periodic oral examination);* **Optometrist** *(full vision eye exam for established adult patient);* **Gasoline** *(one gallon regular unleaded, national brand, including all taxes, cash price at self-service pump if available);* **Beauty Salon** *(woman's shampoo, trim, and blow-dry);* **Men's Shirt** *(cotton/polyester dress shirt, pinpoint weave, long sleeves).*
Source: The Council for Community and Economic Research, ACCRA Cost of Living Index, 2015

HOUSING

House Price Index (HPI)

Area	National Ranking[2]	Quarterly Change (%)	One-Year Change (%)	Five-Year Change (%)
MD[1]	180	0.30	3.20	17.20
U.S.[3]	–	1.45	5.76	22.85

Note: The HPI is a weighted repeat sales index. It measures average price changes in repeat sales or refinancings on the same properties. This information is obtained by reviewing repeat mortgage transactions on single-family properties whose mortgages have been purchased or securitized by Fannie Mae or Freddie Mac in January 1975; (1) Washington-Arlington-Alexandria Metropolitan Division—see Appendix B for areas included; (2) Rankings are based on annual percentage change for all metro areas containing at least 15,000 transactions over the last 10 years and ranges from 1 to 266; (3) figures based on a weighted average of Census Division estimates using a seasonally adjusted, purchase-only index; all figures are for the period ending December 31, 2015

Source: Federal Housing Finance Agency, House Price Index, February 25, 2016

Median Single-Family Home Prices

Area	2013	2014	2015p	Percent Change 2014 to 2015
MSA[1]	381.9	383.8	385.2	0.4
U.S. Average	197.4	208.9	223.9	7.2

Note: Figures are median sales prices of existing single-family homes in thousands of dollars; (p) preliminary; n/a not available; (1) Washington-Arlington-Alexandria, DC-VA-MD-WV Metropolitan Statistical Area—see Appendix B for areas included

Source: National Association of Realtors, Median Sales Price of Existing Single-Family Homes for Metropolitan Areas, 4th Quarter 2015

Qualifying Income Based on Median Sales Price of Existing Single-Family Homes

Area	With 5% Down ($)	With 10% Down ($)	With 20% Down ($)
MSA[1]	82,655	78,305	69,604
U.S. Average	49,535	46,928	41,714

Note: Figures are preliminary; Qualifying income is based on a mortgage rate of 4.1%. Monthly principal and interest payment is limited to 25% of income; n/a not available; (1) Washington-Arlington-Alexandria, DC-VA-MD-WV Metropolitan Statistical Area—see Appendix B for areas included

Source: National Association of Realtors, Qualifying Income Based on Median Sales Price of Existing Single-Family Homes for Metropolitan Areas, 4th Quarter 2015

Median Apartment Condo-Coop Home Prices

Area	2013	2014	2015p	Percent Change 2014 to 2015
MSA[1]	272.2	275.7	274.8	-0.3
U.S. Average	194.9	204.3	210.7	3.1

Note: Figures are median sales prices of existing apartment condo-coop homes in thousands of dollars; (p) preliminary; n/a not available; (1) Washington-Arlington-Alexandria, DC-VA-MD-WV Metropolitan Statistical Area—see Appendix B for areas included

Source: National Association of Realtors, Median Sales Price of Existing Apartment Condo-Coop Homes for Metropolitan Areas, 4th Quarter 2015

Gross Monthly Rent

Area	Under $200	$200 -299	$300 -499	$500 -749	$750 -999	$1,000 -1,499	$1,500 and up	Median ($)
City	0.6	0.8	0.0	1.1	3.0	25.9	68.6	1,764
MSA[1]	1.2	1.8	2.0	3.9	9.2	33.4	48.5	1,479
U.S.	1.5	3.2	7.4	21.0	24.1	26.9	15.9	920

Note: Figures are percentages except for Median; Gross rent is the contract rent plus the estimated average monthly cost of utilities (electricity, gas, and water and sewer) and fuels (oil, coal, kerosene, wood, etc.) if these are paid by the renter (or paid for the renter by someone else); (1) Figures cover the Washington-Arlington-Alexandria, DC-VA-MD-WV Metropolitan Statistical Area—see Appendix B for areas included

Source: U.S. Census Bureau, 2010-2014 American Community Survey 5-Year Estimates

Homeownership Rate

Area	2008 (%)	2009 (%)	2010 (%)	2011 (%)	2012 (%)	2013 (%)	2014 (%)	2015 (%)
MSA[1]	68.1	67.2	67.3	67.6	66.9	66.0	65.0	64.6
U.S.	67.8	67.4	66.9	66.1	65.4	65.1	64.5	63.7

Note: (1) Figures cover the Washington-Arlington-Alexandria, DC-VA-MD-WV Metropolitan Statistical Area—see Appendix B for areas included
Source: U.S. Census Bureau, Housing Vacancies and Homeownership Annual Statistics: 2015

Year Housing Structure Built

Area	2010 or Later	2000 -2009	1990 -1999	1980 -1989	1970 -1979	1960 -1969	1950 -1959	1940 -1949	Before 1940	Median Year
City	0.2	9.9	26.0	16.3	8.5	35.2	2.1	1.0	0.8	1981
MSA[1]	1.2	15.7	14.4	16.5	15.0	12.9	10.0	5.6	8.7	1979
U.S.	1.0	14.9	13.9	13.8	15.8	11.0	10.8	5.4	13.3	1976

Note: Figures are percentages except for Median Year; (1) Figures cover the Washington-Arlington-Alexandria, DC-VA-MD-WV Metropolitan Statistical Area—see Appendix B for areas included
Source: U.S. Census Bureau, 2010-2014 American Community Survey 5-Year Estimates

HEALTH

Health Risk Data

Category	MD[1] (%)	U.S. (%)
Adults aged 18–64 who have any kind of health care coverage	84.5	79.6
Adults who reported being in good or excellent health	86.5	83.1
Adults who are current smokers	14.6	19.6
Adults who are heavy drinkers[2]	5.6	6.1
Adults who are binge drinkers[3]	17.4	16.9
Adults who are overweight (BMI 25.0 - 29.9)	36.7	35.8
Adults who are obese (BMI 30.0 - 99.8)	24.2	27.6
Adults who participated in any physical activities in the past month	80.8	77.1
Adults 50+ who have ever had a sigmoidoscopy or colonoscopy	70.6	67.3
Women aged 40+ who have had a mammogram within the past two years	80.5	74.0
Men aged 40+ who have had a PSA test within the past two years	45.1	45.2
Adults aged 65+ who have had flu shot within the past year	58.7	60.1
Adults who always wear a seatbelt	95.7	93.8

Note: Data as of 2012 unless otherwise noted; (1) Figures cover the Washington-Arlington-Alexandria, DC-VA-MD-WV Metropolitan Division—see Appendix B for areas included; (2) Heavy drinkers are classified as males having more than two drinks per day or females having more than one drink per day; (3) Binge drinkers are classified as males having five or more drinks on one occasion or females having four or more drinks on one occasion
Source: Centers for Disease Control and Prevention, Behaviorial Risk Factor Surveillance System, SMART: Selected Metropolitan/Micropolitan Area Risk Trends, 2012 (Note: the CDC has discontinued this dataset but will be releasing a replacement in mid-2016)

Chronic Health Indicators

Category	MD[1] (%)	U.S. (%)
Adults who have ever been told they had a heart attack	2.8	4.5
Adults who have ever been told they had a stroke	2.3	2.9
Adults who have been told they currently have asthma	8.0	8.9
Adults who have ever been told they have arthritis	18.6	25.7
Adults who have ever been told they have diabetes[2]	8.7	9.7
Adults who have ever been told they had skin cancer	3.9	5.7
Adults who have ever been told they had any other types of cancer	4.6	6.5
Adults who have ever been told they have COPD	4.1	6.2
Adults who have ever been told they have kidney disease	2.0	2.5
Adults who have ever been told they have a form of depression	13.3	18.0

Note: Data as of 2012 unless otherwise noted; (1) Figures cover the Washington-Arlington-Alexandria, DC-VA-MD-WV Metropolitan Division—see Appendix B for areas included; (2) Figures do not include pregnancy-related, borderline, or pre-diabetes
Source: Centers for Disease Control and Prevention, Behaviorial Risk Factor Surveillance System, SMART: Selected Metropolitan/Micropolitan Area Risk Trends, 2012 (Note: the CDC has discontinued this dataset but will be releasing a replacement in mid-2016)

Mortality Rates for the Top 10 Causes of Death in the U.S.

ICD-10[a] Sub-Chapter	ICD-10[a] Code	Age-Adjusted Mortality Rate[1] per 100,000 population	
		County[2]	U.S.
Malignant neoplasms	C00-C97	166.4	163.6
Ischaemic heart diseases	I20-I25	110.0	102.2
Other forms of heart disease	I30-I51	51.0	50.1
Chronic lower respiratory diseases	J40-J47	21.0	41.4
Organic, including symptomatic, mental disorders	F01-F09	47.3	38.5
Cerebrovascular diseases	I60-I69	37.8	36.5
Other external causes of accidental injury	W00-X59	15.6	27.5
Other degenerative diseases of the nervous system	G30-G31	15.2	26.3
Diabetes mellitus	E10-E14	29.4	21.1
Hypertensive diseases	I10-I15	27.9	19.7

Note: (a) ICD-10 = International Classification of Diseases 10th Revision; (1) Mortality rates are a three year average covering 2012-2014; (2) Figures cover Prince George's County.
Source: Centers for Disease Control and Prevention, National Center for Health Statistics. Underlying Cause of Death 1999-2014 on CDC WONDER Online Database, released 2015.

Mortality Rates for Selected Causes of Death

ICD-10[a] Sub-Chapter	ICD-10[a] Code	Age-Adjusted Mortality Rate[1] per 100,000 population	
		County[2]	U.S.
Assault	X85-Y09	7.7	5.1
Diseases of the liver	K70-K76	8.7	13.5
Human immunodeficiency virus (HIV) disease	B20-B24	4.3	2.1
Influenza and pneumonia	J09-J18	15.0	15.2
Intentional self-harm	X60-X84	6.0	12.7
Malnutrition	E40-E46	Suppressed	0.9
Obesity and other hyperalimentation	E65-E68	1.8	1.9
Renal failure	N17-N19	13.6	13.0
Transport accidents	V01-V99	10.6	11.6
Viral hepatitis	B15-B19	2.0	2.1

Note: (a) ICD-10 = International Classification of Diseases 10th Revision; (1) Mortality rates are a three year average covering 2012-2014; (2) Figures cover Prince George's County; Data are Suppressed when the data meet the criteria for confidentiality constraints; Mortality rates are flagged as Unreliable when the rate would be calculated with a numerator of 20 or less.
Source: Centers for Disease Control and Prevention, National Center for Health Statistics. Underlying Cause of Death 1999-2014 on CDC WONDER Online Database, released 2015.

Health Insurance Coverage

Area	With Health Insurance	With Private Health Insurance	With Public Health Insurance	Without Health Insurance	Population Under Age 18 Without Health Insurance
City	92.7	85.4	18.8	7.3	2.5
MSA[1]	88.8	77.1	21.4	11.2	5.0
U.S.	85.8	65.8	31.1	14.2	7.1

Note: Figures are percentages that cover the civilian noninstitutionalized population; (1) Figures cover the Washington-Arlington-Alexandria, DC-VA-MD-WV Metropolitan Statistical Area—see Appendix B for areas included
Source: U.S. Census Bureau, 2010-2014 American Community Survey 5-Year Estimates

Number of Medical Professionals

Area	MDs[3]	DOs[3,4]	Dentists	Podiatrists	Chiropractors	Optometrists
County[1] (number)	1,493	39	539	55	83	78
County[1] (rate[2])	167.0	4.4	59.6	6.1	9.2	8.6
U.S. (rate[2])	272.5	20.9	64.7	5.8	25.9	15.2

Note: Data as of 2014 unless noted; (1) Data covers Prince George's County; (2) Rate per 100,000 population; (3) Data as of 2013 and includes all active, non-federal physicians; (4) Doctor of Osteopathic Medicine
Source: U.S. Department of Health and Human Services, Health Resources and Services Administration, Bureau of Health Professions, Area Resource File (ARF) 2014-2015

Best Hospitals

According to *U.S. News,* the Washington-Arlington-Alexandria, DC-VA-MD-WV metro area is home to three of the best hospitals in the U.S.: **Inova Fairfax Hospital** (3 specialties); **MedStar National Rehabilitation Hospital** (1 specialty); **MedStar Washington Hospital Center** (1 specialty). The hospitals listed were nationally ranked in at least one adult specialty. Only 137 hospitals nationwide were nationally ranked in one or more specialties. Fifteen hospitals in the U.S. made the Honor Roll with high scores in at least six specialties. *U.S. News Online, "America's Best Children's Hospitals 2015-16"*

According to *U.S. News,* the Washington-Arlington-Alexandria, DC-VA-MD-WV metro area is home to two of the best children's hospitals in the U.S.: **Inova Children's Hospital** (2 specialties); **Children's National Medical Center** (Honor Roll/10 specialties). The hospitals listed were highly ranked in at least one pediatric specialty. Eighty-three children's hospitals in the U.S. were nationally ranked in at least one specialty. Twelve children's hospitals in the U.S. made the Honor Roll with high scores in at least three specialties. *U.S. News Online, "America's Best Children's Hospitals 2015-16"*

EDUCATION

Public School District Statistics

District Name	Schls	Pupils	Pupil/ Teacher Ratio	Minority Pupils[1] (%)	Free Lunch Eligible[2] (%)	IEP[3] (%)
Prince George's County Pub Schls	209	125,136	15.0	95.5	53.1	11.5

Note: Table includes school districts with 100 or more students; (1) Percentage of students that are not non-Hispanic white; (2) Percentage of students that are eligible for the free lunch program; (3) Percentage of students that have an Individualized Education Program.
Source: U.S. Department of Education, National Center for Education Statistics, Common Core of Data, Local Education Agency (School District) Universe Survey: School Year 2013-2014; U.S. Department of Education, National Center for Education Statistics, Common Core of Data, Public Elementary/Secondary School Universe Survey: School Year 2013-2014

Highest Level of Education

Area	Less than H.S.	H.S. Diploma	Some College, No Deg.	Associate Degree	Bachelor's Degree	Master's Degree	Prof. School Degree	Doctorate Degree
City	4.7	18.5	23.0	5.8	27.5	15.6	2.3	2.6
MSA[1]	9.8	19.1	17.2	5.6	25.1	16.0	4.3	3.0
U.S.	13.7	28.0	21.2	7.9	18.3	7.8	2.0	1.3

Note: Figures cover persons age 25 and over; (1) Figures cover the Washington-Arlington-Alexandria, DC-VA-MD-WV Metropolitan Statistical Area—see Appendix B for areas included
Source: U.S. Census Bureau, 2010-2014 American Community Survey 5-Year Estimates

Educational Attainment by Race

Area	High School Graduate or Higher (%)					Bachelor's Degree or Higher (%)				
	Total	White	Black	Asian	Hisp.[2]	Total	White	Black	Asian	Hisp.[2]
City	95.3	94.5	97.1	91.6	80.8	48.0	45.9	50.0	68.9	24.9
MSA[1]	90.2	92.9	89.9	90.5	65.8	48.3	55.8	31.3	62.7	23.6
U.S.	86.3	88.4	83.2	85.8	64.1	29.3	30.6	19.0	50.9	13.9

Note: Figures shown cover persons 25 years old and over; (1) Figures cover the Washington-Arlington-Alexandria, DC-VA-MD-WV Metropolitan Statistical Area—see Appendix B for areas included; (2) People of Hispanic origin can be of any race
Source: U.S. Census Bureau, 2010-2014 American Community Survey 5-Year Estimates

School Enrollment by Grade and Control

Area	Preschool (%)		Kindergarten (%)		Grades 1 - 4 (%)		Grades 5 - 8 (%)		Grades 9 - 12 (%)	
	Public	Private	Public	Private	Public	Private	Public	Private	Public	Private
City	28.9	71.1	79.2	20.8	74.4	25.6	73.3	26.7	72.9	27.1
MSA[1]	41.1	58.9	84.5	15.5	88.0	12.0	87.6	12.4	88.8	11.2
U.S.	57.4	42.6	87.8	12.2	89.8	10.2	89.9	10.1	90.6	9.4

Note: Figures shown cover persons 3 years old and over; (1) Figures cover the Washington-Arlington-Alexandria, DC-VA-MD-WV Metropolitan Statistical Area—see Appendix B for areas included
Source: U.S. Census Bureau, 2010-2014 American Community Survey 5-Year Estimates

Average Salaries of Public School Classroom Teachers

Area	2013-14		2014-15		Percent Change 2013-14 to 2014-15	Percent Change 2004-05 to 2014-15
	Dollars	Rank[1]	Dollars	Rank[1]		
Maryland	64,546	9	64,845	9	0.46	23.9
U.S. Average	56,610	–	57,379	–	1.36	20.8

Note: (1) State rank ranges from 1 to 51 where 1 indicates highest salary.
Source: National Education Association, Rankings & Estimates: Rankings of the States 2014 and Estimates of School Statistics 2015, March 2015

Higher Education

Four-Year Colleges			Two-Year Colleges			Medical Schools[1]	Law Schools[2]	Voc/ Tech[3]
Public	Private Non-profit	Private For-profit	Public	Private Non-profit	Private For-profit			
1	0	0	0	0	0	0	0	0

Note: Figures cover institutions located within the city limits and include main campuses only; (1) includes schools accredited by the Liaison Committee on Medical Education and the American Osteopathic Association's Commission on Osteopathic College Accreditation; (2) includes ABA-accredited schools, schools with provisional ABA accreditation, and state accredited schools; (3) includes all schools with programs that are less than 2 years.
Source: National Center for Education Statistics, Integrated Postsecondary Education System (IPEDS), 2014-15; Association of American Medical Colleges, Member List, March 21, 2016; American Osteopathic Association, Member List, March 21, 2016; Law School Admission Council, Official Guide to ABA-Approved Law Schools Online, March 21, 2016; Wikipedia, List of Medical Schools in the United States, March 21, 2016; Wikipedia, List of Law Schools in the United States, March 21, 2016

According to *U.S. News & World Report,* the Washington-Arlington-Alexandria, DC-VA-MD-WV metro division is home to seven of the best national universities in the U.S.: **Georgetown University** (#21 tie); **George Washington University** (#57 tie); **University of Maryland–College Park** (#57 tie); **American University** (#72 tie); **The Catholic University of America** (#123 tie); **George Mason University** (#135 tie); **Howard University** (#135 tie). The indicators used to capture academic quality fall into a number of categories: assessment by administrators at peer institutions; retention of students; faculty resources; student selectivity; financial resources; alumni giving; high school counselor ratings of colleges; and graduation rate. *U.S. News & World Report, "America's Best Colleges 2016"*

According to *U.S. News & World Report,* the Washington-Arlington-Alexandria, DC-VA-MD-WV metro division is home to four of the top 100 law schools in the U.S.: **Georgetown University, Law Center** (#14); **George Washington University, Law School** (#25 tie); **George Mason University, School of Law** (#45 tie); **American University, Washington College of Law** (#78 tie). The rankings are based on a weighted average of 12 measures of quality: peer assessment score; assessment score by lawyers/judges; median LSAT scores; median undergrad GPA; acceptance rate; employment rates for graduates; placement success; bar passage rate; faculty resources; expenditures per student; student/faculty ratio; and library resources. *U.S. News & World Report, "America's Best Graduate Schools, Law, 2017"*

According to *U.S. News & World Report,* the Washington-Arlington-Alexandria, DC-VA-MD-WV metro division is home to two of the top 75 medical schools for research in the U.S.: **Georgetown University, School of Medicine** (#47 tie); **George Washington University, School of Medicine and Health Sciences** (#63 tie). The rankings are based on a weighted average of 11 measures of quality: quality assessment; peer assessment score; assessment score by residency directors; research activity; total research activity; average research activity per faculty member; student selectivity; median MCAT total score; median undergraduate GPA; acceptance rate; and faculty resources. *U.S. News & World Report, "America's Best Graduate Schools, Medical, 2017"*

According to *U.S. News & World Report,* the Washington-Arlington-Alexandria, DC-VA-MD-WV metro division is home to three of the top 75 business schools in the U.S.: **Georgetown University, Robert Emmett McDonough School of Business** (#22 tie); **University of Maryland–College Park, Robert H. Smith School of Business** (#41 tie); **George Washington University, School of Business** (#51). The rankings are based on a weighted average of the following nine measures: quality assessment; peer assessment; recruiter assessment; placement success; mean starting salary and bonus; student selectivity; mean GMAT and GRE scores; mean undergraduate GPA; and acceptance rate. *U.S. News & World Report, "America's Best Graduate Schools, Business, 2017"*

PRESIDENTIAL ELECTION

2012 Presidential Election Results

Area	Obama (%)	Romney (%)	Other (%)
Prince George's County	89.6	9.3	1.0
U.S.	51.0	47.2	1.8

Note: Results may not add to 100% due to rounding
Source: Dave Leip's Atlas of U.S. Presidential Elections

EMPLOYERS

Major Employers

Company Name	Industry
Adventist HealthCare	General medical & surgical hospitals
Bechtel National	Engineering services
Computer Sciences Corporation	Computer related consulting services
Federal Aviation Administration	Air traffic control operations, government
Federal Bureau of Investigation	Police protection
Fish and Wildlife Service, United States	Fish & wildlife conservation agency, government
Howard University	Colleges & universities
HR Solutions	Human resource consulting services
Internal Revenue Service	Finance, taxation, & monetary policy
Intl Bank for Recons. & Dev.	Foreign trade & international banks
Natl Inst of Standards & Technology	Administration of general economic programs
Office of the Secretary of Defense	National security
US Department of Agriculture	Regulation of agricultural marketing
US Department of Commerce	Regulation, miscellaneous commercial sectors
US Department of Labor	Administration of social & manpower programs
US Department of the Army	National security
US Department of the Navy	National security
US Department of Transportation	Regulation, administration of transportation
US Environmental Protection Agency	Land, mineral, & wildlife conservation
Washington Hospital Center Corporation	General medical & surgical hospitals

Note: Companies shown are located within the Washington-Arlington-Alexandria, DC-VA-MD-WV Metropolitan Statistical Area.
Source: Hoovers.com; Wikipedia

PUBLIC SAFETY

Crime Rate

Area	All Crimes	Violent Crimes				Property Crimes		
		Murder	Rape[3]	Robbery	Aggrav. Assault	Burglary	Larceny -Theft	Motor Vehicle Theft
City	1,610.5	1.7	1.7	54.2	75.2	236.1	1,124.4	117.2
Metro[1]	2,598.3	4.3	26.4	139.9	181.4	265.1	1,764.2	217.0
U.S.	2,961.6	4.5	26.4	102.2	232.5	542.5	1,837.3	216.2

Note: Figures are crimes per 100,000 population; (1) Figures cover the Washington-Arlington-Alexandria, DC-VA-MD-WV Metropolitan Division—see Appendix B for areas included; (3) The city and U.S. figures shown were reported using the legacy Uniform Crime Reporting (UCR) definition of rape. The suburban and metro area figures shown are an aggregate total of the data submitted using both the revised and legacy UCR definitions.
Source: FBI Uniform Crime Reports, 2014

Hate Crimes

Area	Number of Quarters Reported	Number of Incidents per Bias Motivation						
		Race	Religion	Sexual Orientation	Ethnicity	Disability	Gender	Gender Identity
City	4	0	0	0	0	0	0	0
U.S.	4	2,568	1,014	1,017	648	84	33	98

Source: Federal Bureau of Investigation, Hate Crime Statistics 2014

Identity Theft Consumer Complaints

Area	Complaints	Complaints per 100,000 Population	Rank[2]
MSA[1]	10,597	175.6	30
U.S.	490,220	152.4	-

Note: (1) Figures cover the Washington-Arlington-Alexandria, DC-VA-MD-WV Metropolitan Statistical Area—see Appendix B for areas included; (2) Rank ranges from 1 to 379 where 1 indicates greatest number of identity theft complaints per 100,000 population
Source: Federal Trade Commission, Consumer Sentinel Network Data Book for January–December 2015

Fraud and Other Consumer Complaints

Area	Complaints	Complaints per 100,000 Population	Rank[2]
MSA[1]	34,185	566.6	6
U.S.	2,593,159	806.0	-

Note: (1) Figures cover the Washington-Arlington-Alexandria, DC-VA-MD-WV Metropolitan Statistical Area—see Appendix B for areas included; (2) Rank ranges from 1 to 379 where 1 indicates greatest number of identity theft complaints per 100,000 population
Source: Federal Trade Commission, Consumer Sentinel Network Data Book for January–December 2015

RECREATION

Culture

Dance[1]	Theatre[1]	Instrumental Music[1]	Vocal Music[1]	Series and Festivals	Museums and Art Galleries[2]	Zoos and Aquariums[3]
0	0	0	0	0	0	0

Note: (1) Professional perfoming groups; (2) Based on organizations with SIC code 8412; (3) AZA-accredited
Source: The Grey House Performing Arts Directory, 2015-16; Association of Zoos & Aquariums, AZA Member Zoos & Aquariums, March 25, 2016; www.AccuLeads.com, March 29, 2016

Professional Sports Teams

Team Name	League	Year Established
D.C. United	Major League Soccer (MLS)	1996
Washington Capitals	National Hockey League (NHL)	1974
Washington Nationals	Major League Baseball (MLB)	2005
Washington Redskins	National Football League (NFL)	1937
Washington Wizards	National Basketball Association (NBA)	1973

Note: Includes teams located in the Washington-Arlington-Alexandria, DC-VA-MD-WV Metropolitan Statistical Area.
Source: Wikipedia, Major Professional Sports Teams of the United States and Canada, March 24, 2016

CLIMATE

Average and Extreme Temperatures

Temperature	Jan	Feb	Mar	Apr	May	Jun	Jul	Aug	Sep	Oct	Nov	Dec	Yr.
Extreme High (°F)	79	82	89	95	97	101	104	103	101	94	86	75	104
Average High (°F)	43	46	55	67	76	84	88	86	80	69	58	47	67
Average Temp. (°F)	36	38	46	57	66	75	79	78	71	60	49	39	58
Average Low (°F)	28	30	37	46	56	65	70	69	62	50	40	31	49
Extreme Low (°F)	-5	4	14	24	34	47	54	49	39	29	16	3	-5

Note: Figures cover the years 1945-1990
Source: National Climatic Data Center, International Station Meteorological Climate Summary, 9/96

Average Precipitation/Snowfall/Humidity

Precip./Humidity	Jan	Feb	Mar	Apr	May	Jun	Jul	Aug	Sep	Oct	Nov	Dec	Yr.
Avg. Precip. (in.)	2.8	2.6	3.3	2.9	4.0	3.4	4.1	4.2	3.3	2.9	3.0	3.1	39.5
Avg. Snowfall (in.)	6	6	2	Tr	0	0	0	0	0	Tr	1	3	18
Avg. Rel. Hum. 7am (%)	71	70	70	70	74	75	77	80	82	80	76	72	75
Avg. Rel. Hum. 4pm (%)	54	50	46	45	51	52	53	54	54	53	53	55	52

Note: Figures cover the years 1945-1990; Tr = Trace amounts (<0.05 in. of rain; <0.5 in. of snow)
Source: National Climatic Data Center, International Station Meteorological Climate Summary, 9/96

Weather Conditions

Temperature			Daytime Sky			Precipitation		
10°F & below	32°F & below	90°F & above	Clear	Partly cloudy	Cloudy	0.01 inch or more precip.	0.1 inch or more snow/ice	Thunder-storms
2	71	34	84	143	138	112	9	30

Note: Figures are average number of days per year and cover the years 1945-1990
Source: National Climatic Data Center, International Station Meteorological Climate Summary, 9/96

HAZARDOUS WASTE

Superfund Sites

Bowie has no sites on the EPA's Superfund Final National Priorities List. There are a total of 1,323 Superfund sites on the list in the U.S. *U.S. Environmental Protection Agency, Final National Priorities List, March 18, 2016*

AIR & WATER QUALITY

Air Quality Trends: Ozone

	1990	1995	2000	2005	2010	2011	2012	2013	2014
MSA[1]	0.087	0.093	0.081	0.081	0.078	0.079	0.077	0.069	0.068

Note: (1) Data covers the Washington-Arlington-Alexandria, DC-VA-MD-WV Metropolitan Statistical Area—see Appendix B for areas included. The values shown are the composite ozone concentration averages among trend sites based on the highest fourth daily maximum 8-hour concentration in parts per million. These trends are based on sites having an adequate record of monitoring data during the trend period. Data from exceptional events are included.
Source: U.S. Environmental Protection Agency, Air Quality Monitoring Information, "Air Quality Trends by City, 1990-2014"

Air Quality Index

Area	Percent of Days when Air Quality was...[2]					AQI Statistics[2]	
	Good	Moderate	Unhealthy for Sensitive Groups	Unhealthy	Very Unhealthy	Maximum	Median
MSA[1]	47.9	50.7	1.4	0.0	0.0	132	51

Note: (1) Data covers the Washington-Arlington-Alexandria, DC-VA-MD-WV Metropolitan Statistical Area—see Appendix B for areas included; (2) Based on 365 days with AQI data in 2015. Air Quality Index (AQI) is an index for reporting daily air quality. EPA calculates the AQI for five major air pollutants regulated by the Clean Air Act: ground-level ozone, particle pollution (aka particulate matter), carbon monoxide, sulfur dioxide, and nitrogen dioxide. The AQI runs from 0 to 500. The higher the AQI value, the greater the level of air pollution and the greater the health concern. There are six AQI categories: "Good" AQI is between 0 and 50. Air quality is considered satisfactory; "Moderate" AQI is between 51 and 100. Air quality is acceptable; "Unhealthy for Sensitive Groups" When AQI values are between 101 and 150, members of sensitive groups may experience health effects; "Unhealthy" When AQI values are between 151 and 200 everyone may begin to experience health effects; "Very Unhealthy" AQI values between 201 and 300 trigger a health alert; "Hazardous" AQI values over 300 trigger warnings of emergency conditions (not shown).
Source: U.S. Environmental Protection Agency, Air Quality Index Report, 2015

Air Quality Index Pollutants

Area	Percent of Days when AQI Pollutant was...[2]					
	Carbon Monoxide	Nitrogen Dioxide	Ozone	Sulfur Dioxide	Particulate Matter 2.5	Particulate Matter 10
MSA[1]	0.0	7.4	30.4	0.0	62.2	0.0

Note: (1) Data covers the Washington-Arlington-Alexandria, DC-VA-MD-WV Metropolitan Statistical Area—see Appendix B for areas included; (2) Based on 365 days with AQI data in 2015. The Air Quality Index (AQI) is an index for reporting daily air quality. EPA calculates the AQI for five major air pollutants regulated by the Clean Air Act: ground-level ozone, particle pollution (also known as particulate matter), carbon monoxide, sulfur dioxide, and nitrogen dioxide. The AQI runs from 0 to 500. The higher the AQI value, the greater the level of air pollution and the greater the health concern.
Source: U.S. Environmental Protection Agency, Air Quality Index Report, 2015

Maximum Air Pollutant Concentrations: Particulate Matter, Ozone, CO and Lead

	Particulate Matter 10 (ug/m^3)	Particulate Matter 2.5 Wtd AM (ug/m^3)	Particulate Matter 2.5 24-Hr (ug/m^3)	Ozone (ppm)	Carbon Monoxide (ppm)	Lead (ug/m^3)
MSA[1] Level	43	9.3	21	0.071	2	0
NAAQS[2]	150	15	35	0.075	9	0.15
Met NAAQS[2]	Yes	Yes	Yes	Yes	Yes	Yes

Note: (1) Data covers the Washington-Arlington-Alexandria, DC-VA-MD-WV Metropolitan Statistical Area—see Appendix B for areas included; Data from exceptional events are included; (2) National Ambient Air Quality Standards; ppm = parts per million; ug/m^3 = micrograms per cubic meter; n/a not available. Concentrations: Particulate Matter 10 (coarse particulate)—highest second maximum 24-hour concentration; Particulate Matter 2.5 Wtd AM (fine particulate)—highest weighted annual mean concentration; Particulate Matter 2.5 24-Hour (fine particulate)—highest 98th percentile 24-hour concentration; Ozone—highest fourth daily maximum 8-hour concentration; Carbon Monoxide—highest second maximum non-overlapping 8-hour concentration; Lead—maximum running 3-month average

Source: U.S. Environmental Protection Agency, Air Quality Monitoring Information, "Air Quality Statistics by City, 2014"

Maximum Air Pollutant Concentrations: Nitrogen Dioxide and Sulfur Dioxide

	Nitrogen Dioxide AM (ppb)	Nitrogen Dioxide 1-Hr (ppb)	Sulfur Dioxide AM (ppb)	Sulfur Dioxide 1-Hr (ppb)	Sulfur Dioxide 24-Hr (ppb)
MSA[1] Level	11	47	n/a	16	n/a
NAAQS[2]	53	100	30	75	140
Met NAAQS[2]	Yes	Yes	n/a	Yes	n/a

Note: (1) Data covers the Washington-Arlington-Alexandria, DC-VA-MD-WV Metropolitan Statistical Area—see Appendix B for areas included; Data from exceptional events are included; (2) National Ambient Air Quality Standards; ppm = parts per million; ug/m^3 = micrograms per cubic meter; n/a not available. Concentrations: Nitrogen Dioxide AM—highest arithmetic mean concentration; Nitrogen Dioxide 1-Hr—highest 98th percentile 1-hour daily maximum concentration; Sulfur Dioxide AM—highest annual mean concentration; Sulfur Dioxide 1-Hr—highest 99th percentile 1-hour daily maximum concentration; Sulfur Dioxide 24-Hr—highest second maximum 24-hour concentration

Source: U.S. Environmental Protection Agency, Air Quality Monitoring Information, "Air Quality Statistics by City, 2014"

Drinking Water

Water System Name	Pop. Served	Primary Water Source Type	Violations[1]	
			Health Based	Monitoring/ Reporting
City of Bowie	25,000	Ground	0	0

Note: (1) Based on violation data from January 1, 2015 to December 31, 2015 (includes unresolved violations from earlier years)

Source: U.S. Environmental Protection Agency, Office of Ground Water and Drinking Water, Safe Drinking Water Information System (based on data extracted April 29, 2016)

Lexington, Massachusetts

Background

Lexington, in Middlesex County, is about 11 miles northwest of Boston. The town is known for the first battle of the American Revolution in 1775, between the American Colonists and British Army.

Originally settled in 1642, Lexington was known as Cambridge Farms until its incorporation in 1713. It was primarily a farming community until the 1960s, when the spike in high-tech industry occurred along Route 128, which runs through Boston. The result was a dramatic increase in Lexington's population, size and per capita wealth.

The historical events that took place in Lexington made the town a major tourist attraction. Home to the first Historical Districts Commission in the United States and the Lexington Visitors Centre, the town has extensive resources available for tourists to get the most out of their visit. A trolley tour of historical sites includes the Lexington Battle Green, Buckman Tavern, Hancock-Clarke House and Minuteman National Park. The Lexington Battle Green—the premiere tourist spot—is where 77 local-militia fought against the British Army in the Battle of Lexington and Concord, the first armed conflict in the Revolutionary War. The men who died in the battle are buried at the Revolutionary Monument, the oldest war memorial in America. The historic site has guided tours from spring to fall, but the site is open to visitors year-round.

Lexington continues to grow its business districts. With tourism the staple of the community, the town works hard to maintain its historical sites, provide knowledgeable staff, and run the Lexington Visitors Center. With close access to Boston, Cambridge and major universities such as MIT and Harvard, the biology technology industry has taken root in Lexington. Hartwell and Hayden Avenues are home to many life science companies. Lexington's top employer is MIT Lincoln Laboratory, and 27 biotech and pharmaceutical companies call Lexington home.

The town has historical and recreational parks and facilities that capture the beauty of the area. Minuteman National Historical Park offers visitors a chance to visit historical sites that cover over 900 acres. Minuteman Visitors Center has educational exhibits and shows about the events of the Revolutionary War. The Battle Road Trail in the park takes visitors back to April 19th, 1775, as they follow in the footsteps of the colonists across original pieces of the road that connects Lexington and Concord. The Old Reservoir offers outdoor swimming, swimming lessons and kayak and boat rentals. The Center Recreation Complex is the major sports facility in Lexington with a skate park, baseball fields, soccer field, basketball courts, and swimming pool. Pine Meadows Golf Course is Lexington's 9-hole public golf course.

Still under construction, ACROSS Lexington is a program designed to build trails around the town that connect its center with surrounding areas. When completed, there will be over 40 miles of walking and biking trails. Completed trails in Lexington include the Teresa & Roberta Lee Fitness Path, the Battle Road Trail, the Western Greenway Trail and the Minuteman Bikeway.

Lexington belongs to the Lexington Public Schools district, recognized as one of the top districts in the state. Lexington High School consistently ranks among the top high schools in the country, reaching 19th in the nation in a 2014 *Newsweek* study. Minuteman Career and Technical High School, open to surrounding towns, offer specific, career-based curriculums. The Lexington Chinese School focuses on the Chinese language. Due to the town's proximity to Boston, many institutions of higher learning are within a 12-mile radius, including MIT, Harvard, Bentley, Boston College, Boston University and Tufts University.

The nearest major airport is Boston Logan International, 17 miles from Lexington, and several local airports are even closer, including Waltham Airport, Laurence G. Hanscom Field and Woburn Airport.

The climate of Lexington features plenty of precipitation and temperatures that fall bellow national averages. The July average high is 83 degrees and the average January low is 16 degrees, both about four degrees cooler then the national averages. Lexington receives 46 inches of rain and 56 inches of snow yearly, which significantly exceeds national averages.

Rankings

General Rankings

- The Cambridge* metro area was identified as one of America's fastest-growing areas in terms of population and economy by *Forbes.* The area ranked #14 out of 20. The 100 most populous metro areas in the U.S. were evaluated on the following criteria: estimated population growth; job growth; gross metropolitan product growth; unemployment; median salaries for college-educated workers. *Forbes, "America's Fastest-Growing Cities 2015," January 27, 2015*

Business/Finance Rankings

- The personal finance site NerdWallet analyzed 183 American metropolitan areas with populations over 250,000 and more than 15,000 businesses to rank where entrepreneurs find the most success. Criteria included area economy, annual income, housing cost, unemployment rate, and the success rate of area businesses. Cambridge* ranked #30. *www.nerdwallet.com, "Best Places to Start a Business," April 27, 2015*
- TransUnion ranked the nation's metro areas by average credit score, calculated on the VantageScore system, developed by the three major credit-reporting bureaus—TransUnion, Experian, and Equifax. The Cambridge* metro area was among the ten cities with the highest collective credit score, meaning that its residents posed the lowest average consumer credit risk. *www.usatoday.com, "Metro Areas' Average Credit Rating Revealed," February 7, 2013*
- Based on the U.S. Department of Labor's Occupational Information Network Data Collection Program, the Brookings Institution defined job opportunities for STEM workers at various levels of educational attainment. The Cambridge* metro area was placed among the ten large metro areas with the highest demand for high-level STEM knowledge. *www.brookings.edu, "The Hidden Stem Economy," June 10, 2013*
- 24/7 Wall Street used Brookings Institution research on 50 advanced industries to identify the proportion of workers in the nation's largest metropolitan areas that were employed in jobs requiring knowledge in the science, technology, engineering, or math (STEM) fields. The Boston* metro area was #8. *247wallst.com, "15 Cities with the Most High-Tech Jobs," March 13, 2015*
- Based on metro area social media reviews, the employment opinion group Glassdoor surveyed 50 of the largest U.S. metro areas and equally weighed cost of living, hiring opportunity, and job satisfaction to compose a list of "25 Best Cities for Jobs." The Boston* metro area was ranked #6 in overall job satisfaction. *www.glassdoor.com, "Best Cities for Jobs," May 19, 2015*
- In a survey of economic confidence in the nation's 50 largest metropolitan areas conducted January–December 2014, the Boston* metro area placed #13, according to Gallup's 2014 Economic Confidence Index. *Gallup, "San Jose and San Francisco Lead in Economic Confidence," March 19, 2015*
- The Brookings Institution ranked the 100 largest metro areas in the U.S. based on income inequality. Boston* was ranked #6 (#1 = greatest ineqality). Criteria: the "95/20 ratio," a figure representing the income at which a household earns more than 95 percent of all other households, divided by the income at which a household earns more than only 20 percent of all other households. *Brookings Institution, "Income Inequality, 100 Largest U.S. Metro Areas, 2007-2014," January 14, 2016*
- Payscale.com ranked the 20 largest metro areas in terms of wage growth. The Boston* metro area ranked #6. Criteria: private-sector wage growth between the 1st quarter of 2015 and the 1st quarter of 2016. *PayScale, "Wage Trends by Metro Area," 1st Quarter, 2016*
- Boston* was identified as one of America's most frugal metro areas by *Coupons.com.* The city ranked #20 out of 25. Criteria: online coupon usage. *Coupons.com, "Top 25 Most Frugal Cities of 2014," May 11, 2015*
- The Cambridge* metro area appeared on the Milken Institute "2015 Best Performing Cities" list. Rank: #35 out of 200 large metro areas. Criteria: job growth; wage and salary growth; high-tech output growth. *Milken Institute, "Best-Performing Cities 2015," December 2015*

- *Forbes* ranked the 200 most populous metro areas to determine the nation's "Best Places for Business and Careers." The Cambridge* metro area was ranked #47. Criteria: costs (business and living); job growth (past and projected); income growth; educational attainment (college and high school); projected economic growth; cultural and recreational opportunities; net migration patterns; number of highly ranked colleges. *Forbes, "The Best Places for Business and Careers 2015," July 29, 2015*

Dating/Romance Rankings

- CreditDonkey, a financial education website, sought out the ten best U.S. cities for newlyweds, considering the number of married couples, divorce rate, average credit score, and average number of hours worked per week in metro areas with a million or more residents. The Boston* metro area placed #3. *www.creditdonkey.com, "Study: Best Cities for Newlyweds," November 30, 2013*

Education Rankings

- The Boston* metro area was selected as one of the world's most inventive cities by *Forbes*. The area was ranked #7 out of 15. Criteria: patent applications per capita. *Forbes, "World's 15 Most Inventive Cities," July 9, 2013*

- Boston* was identified as one of America's "smartest" metropolitan areas by *The Business Journals*. The area ranked #4 out of 10. Criteria: percentage of adults (25 and older) with high school diplomas, bachelor's degrees and graduate degrees. *The Business Journals, "Where the Brainpower Is: Exclusive U.S. Rankings, Insights," February 27, 2014*

- Personal finance website *WalletHub* analyzed the 150 largest U.S. metropolitan statistical areas to determine where the most educated Americans are choosing to settle. Criteria: education quality and attainment gap; education levels; percentage of workers with degrees; public school rankings; quality and size of each metro area's universities. Cambridge* was ranked #7 (#1 = most educated city). *www.WalletHub.com, "2015's Most and Least Educated Cities"*

- Boston* was identified as one of the "Smartest Cities in America" by the brain-training website *Lumosity* using data from three million of its own users. The metro area ranked #49 out of 50. Criteria: users' brain performance index scores, considering core cognitive abilities such as memory, processing speed, flexibility, attention and problem-solving. *Lumosity, " Smartest Cities in America," June 25, 2013*

Environmental Rankings

- The Boston* metro area came in at #107 for the relative comfort of its climate on Sperling's list of "chill cities," as measured by the Sperling Heat Index. All 361 metro areas are included. Criteria included daytime high temperatures, nighttime low temperatures, dew point, and relative humidity at the high temperatures. *www.bertsperling.com, "Sperling's Chill Cities," July 18, 2013*

- Sperling's BestPlaces assessed 379 metropolitan areas of the United States for the likelihood of dangerously extreme weather events or earthquakes. In general the Southeast and South-Central regions have the highest risk of weather extremes and earthquakes, while the Pacific Northwest enjoys the lowest risk. Of the least risky metropolitan areas, the Cambridge* metro area was ranked #257. *www.bestplaces.net, "Safest Places from Natural Disasters," April 2011*

- The U.S. Environmental Protection Agency (EPA) released a list of U.S. metropolitan areas with the most ENERGY STAR certified buildings in 2015. The Boston* metro area was ranked #11 out of 25. *U.S. Environmental Protection Agency, "Top Cities With the Most ENERGY STAR Certified Buildings in 2016," March 30, 2016*

Health/Fitness Rankings

- Analysts who tracked obesity rates in the nation's largest metro areas (populations above one million) found that the Cambridge* metro area was one of the ten major metros where residents were least likely to be obese, defined as a BMI score of 30 or above. *www.gallup.com, "Boulder, Colo., Residents Still Least Likely to Be Obese," April 4, 2014*

- Analysts who tracked obesity rates in 100 of the nation's most populous areas found that the Boston* metro area was one of the ten communities where residents were least likely to be obese, defined as a BMI score of 30 or above. *www.gallup.com, "Colorado Springs Residents Least Likely to Be Obese," May 28, 2015*

- For each of the 50 most populous metro areas in the United States, the American College of Sports Medicine's American Fitness Index evaluated infrastructure, community assets, and policies that encourage healthy and fit lifestyles, including preventive health behaviors, levels of chronic disease conditions, health care access, and community resources and policies that support physical activity. The Boston* metro area ranked #9 for "community fitness." *www.americanfitnessindex.org, "ACSM American Fitness Index Health and Community Fitness Status of the 50 Largest Metropolitan Areas," May 2015*

- *Business Insider* reported Trulia's analysis of the 100 largest U.S. metro areas to identify the nation's best cities for weight loss, based on healthful food options, access to outdoor activities, weight-loss centers, gyms, and opportunities to bike or walk to work. Boston* ranked #4. *Businessinsider.com, "These Are the Best US Cities for Weight loss," January 17, 2013*

- The Boston* metro area was identified as one of the worst cities for bed bugs in America by pest control company Orkin. The area ranked #25 out of 50 based on the number of bed bug treatments Orkin performed from January to December 2015. *Orkin, "Chicago Tops Bed Bug Cities List for Fourth Year in a Row," January 13, 2016*

- Boston* was identified as a "2016 Spring Allergy Capital." The area ranked #77 out of 100. Three groups of factors were used to identify the most severe cities for people with allergies during the spring season: annual pollen levels; medicine utilization; access to board-certified allergists. *Asthma and Allergy Foundation of America, "Spring Allergy Capitals 2016"*

- Boston* was identified as a "2015 Asthma Capital." The area ranked #74 out of the nation's 100 largest metropolitan areas. Criteria: estimated prevalence; self-reported prevalence; crude death rate for asthma; annual pollen score; annual air quality; public smoking laws; number of board-certified asthma specialists; school inhaler access laws; rescue medication use; controller medication use; ER visits for asthma; uninsured rate; poverty rate. *Asthma and Allergy Foundation of America, "Asthma Capitals 2015"*

- The Boston* metro area ranked #63 out of 190 in The Gallup-Healthways Well-Being Index. Criteria: purpose; social well being; financial health; community and physical health. Results are based on telephone interviews with adults, aged 18 and older, living in metropolitan areas in the 50 U.S. states and the District of Columbia. *Gallup-Healthways, "State of American Well-Being," February 23, 2016*

Real Estate Rankings

- Based on the home-price forecasts compiled by the real-estate valuation firm CoreLogic Case-Shiller, CNNMoney reported that in 2016, the Boston* metro area is expected to be one of the hottest housing markets in the U.S. Criteria: residential real estate prices. *money.cnn.com, "The 10 Hottest Housing Markets for 2016," December 3, 2015*

- The Boston* metro area appeared on Realtor.com's list of the hottest housing markets to watch in 2016. The area ranked #10. Criteria: strong housing growth; affordable prices; and fast-paced sales. *Realtor.com®, "Top 10 Hot Real Estate Markets to Watch in 2016," December 2, 2015*

- The Boston* metro area was identified as one of the 20 least affordable housing markets in the U.S. in 2015. The area ranked #17 out of 179 markets. Criteria: qualification for a mortgage loan on a typical home. *National Association of Realtors®, Affordability Index of Existing Single-Family Homes for Metropolitan Areas, 2015*

- Cambridge* was ranked #191 out of 225 metro areas in terms of housing affordability in 2015 by the National Association of Home Builders (#1 = most affordable). Criteria: the share of homes sold in that area affordable to a family earning the local median income, based on standard mortgage underwriting criteria. *National Association of Home Builders®, NAHB-Wells Fargo Housing Opportunity Index, 4th Quarter 2015*

Safety Rankings

- Farmers Insurance, in partnership with Sperling's BestPlaces, ranked metro areas in the U.S. as the "Most Secure Places to Live." The Cambridge* metro area ranked #5 out of the top 20 in the large metro area category (500,000 or more residents). Criteria: economic stability; crime statistics; extreme weather; risk of natural disasters; housing depreciation; foreclosures; air quality; environmental hazards; life expectancy; motor vehicle fatalities; and employment numbers. *Farmers Insurance Group of Companies, "Most Secure U.S. Places to Live in the U.S.," June 25, 2013*

- The National Insurance Crime Bureau ranked 380 metro areas in the U.S. in terms of per capita rates of vehicle theft. The Boston* metro area ranked #246 (#1 = highest rate). Criteria: number of vehicle theft offenses per 100,000 inhabitants in 2014. *National Insurance Crime Bureau, "Hot Spots 2014," June 24, 2015*

Seniors/Retirement Rankings

- From its Best Cities for Successful Aging indexes, the Milken Institute generated rankings for metropolitan areas, weighing data in eight categories—health care, wellness, living arrangements, transportation, financial characteristics, education and employment opportunities, community engagement, and overall livability. The Cambridge* metro area was ranked #4 overall in the large metro area category. *Milken Institute, "Best Cities for Successful Aging, 2014"*

Sports/Recreation Rankings

- According to the personal finance website NerdWallet, the Boston* metro area, at #11, is one of the nation's top dozen metro areas for sports fans. Criteria included the presence of all four major sports—MLB, NFL, NHL, and NBA, fan enthusiasm (as measured by game attendance), ticket affordability, and "sports culture," that is, number of sports bars. *www.nerdwallet.com, "Best Cities for Sports Fans," May 5, 2013*

Transportation Rankings

- Boston* was identified as one of the most congested metro areas in the U.S. The area ranked #6 out of 10. Criteria: yearly delay per auto commuter in hours. *Texas A&M Transportation Institute, "2015 Urban Mobility Scorecard," August 2015*

- The Boston* metro area appeared on *Forbes* list of places with the most extreme commutes. The metro area ranked #6 out of 10. Criteria: average travel time; percentage of mega commuters. Mega-commuters travel more than 90 minutes and 50 miles each way to work. *Forbes.com, "The Cities with the Most Extreme Commutes," March 5, 2013*

Miscellaneous Rankings

- The watchdog site Charity Navigator conducts an annual study of charities in the nation's major markets both to analyze statistical differences in their financial, accountability, and transparency practices and to track year-to-year variations in individual communities. The Boston* metro area was ranked #3 among the 30 metro markets in the rating dimension of Overall Score. *www.charitynavigator.org, "Metro Market Study 2015," June 5, 2015*

- The Harris Poll's Happiness Index survey revealed that of the top ten U.S. markets, the Boston* metro area residents ranked #9 in happiness. Criteria included strong assent to positive statements and strong disagreement with negative ones, and degree of agreement with a series of statements about respondents' personal relationships and general outlook. *www.harrisinteractive.com, "Dallas/Fort Worth Is "Happiest" City among America's Top Ten Markets," September 4, 2013*

- Energizer Personal Care, the makers of Edge® shave gel, in partnership with Sperling's BestPlaces, ranked 50 major metro areas in terms of everyday irritations. The Boston* metro area ranked #10 the 50 metro area most iritating to guys. Criteria: high male-to-female ratio; poor sports team performance and high ticket prices; slow traffic; lack of job availability; unaffordable housing; extreme weather; lack of nightlife and fitness options. *Energizer Personal Care, "Most Irritatng Cities for Guys," August 26, 2013*

- Mars Chocolate North America, the makers of COMBOS®, in partnership with Sperling's BestPlaces, ranked 50 major metro areas in terms of their "manliness." The Boston* metro area ranked #47. Criteria: number of professional sports teams; number of nearby NASCAR tracks and racing events; manly lifestyle; concentration of manly retail stores; manly occupations per capita; salty snack sales; "Board of Manliness" rankings. *Mars Chocolate North America, "America's Manliest Cities 2012"*
- The National Alliance to End Homelessness ranked the 100 most populous metro areas with the highest rate of homelessness. The Boston* metro area ranked #20. Criteria: number of homeless people per 10,000 population in 2011. *National Alliance to End Homelessness, The State of Homelessness in America 2012*

Lexington is located within the Boston-Cambridge-Newton, MA-NH Metropolitan Statistical Area and the Cambridge-Newton-Framingham, MA Metropolitan Division.

Business Environment

CITY FINANCES

City Government Finances

Component	2012 ($000)	2012 ($ per capita)
Total Revenues	190,439	6,066
Total Expenditures	191,480	6,099
Debt Outstanding	86,012	2,739
Cash and Securities[1]	215,302	6,858

Note: (1) Cash and security holdings of a government at the close of its fiscal year, including those of its dependent agencies, utilities, and liquor stores.
Source: U.S Census Bureau, State & Local Government Finances 2012

City Government Revenue by Source

Source	2012 ($000)	2012 ($ per capita)
General Revenue		
From Federal Government	67	2
From State Government	20,420	650
From Local Governments	0	0
Taxes		
Property	136,832	4,358
Sales and Gross Receipts	1,866	59
Personal Income	0	0
Corporate Income	0	0
Motor Vehicle License	0	0
Other Taxes	1,514	48
Current Charges	15,171	483
Liquor Store	0	0
Utility	7,722	245
Employee Retirement	3,508	111

Source: U.S Census Bureau, State & Local Government Finances 2012

City Government Expenditures by Function

Function	2012 ($000)	2012 ($ per capita)	2012 (%)
General Direct Expenditures			
Air Transportation	0	0	0.0
Corrections	0	0	0.0
Education	86,914	2,768	45.3
Employment Security Administration	0	0	0.0
Financial Administration	1,519	48	0.7
Fire Protection	5,159	164	2.6
General Public Buildings	11,481	365	5.9
Governmental Administration, Other	752	23	0.3
Health	225	7	0.1
Highways	5,017	159	2.6
Hospitals	0	0	0.0
Housing and Community Development	0	0	0.0
Interest on General Debt	2,287	72	1.1
Judicial and Legal	340	10	0.1
Libraries	1,997	63	1.0
Parking	144	4	0.0
Parks and Recreation	2,684	85	1.4
Police Protection	5,777	184	3.0
Public Welfare	230	7	0.1
Sewerage	1,668	53	0.8
Solid Waste Management	1,333	42	0.6
Veterans' Services	0	0	0.0
Liquor Store	0	0	0.0
Utility	2,930	93	1.5
Employee Retirement	10,475	333	5.4

Source: U.S Census Bureau, State & Local Government Finances 2012

DEMOGRAPHICS

Population Growth

Area	1990 Census	2000 Census	2010 Census	2014* Estimate	Population Growth (%) 1990-2014	2010-2014
City	28,974	30,355	31,394	32,306	11.5	2.9
MSA[1]	4,133,895	4,391,344	4,552,402	4,650,876	12.5	2.2
U.S.	248,709,873	281,421,906	308,745,538	314,107,084	26.3	1.7

Note: (1) Figures cover the Boston-Cambridge-Newton, MA-NH Metropolitan Statistical Area—see Appendix B for areas included; (*) 2010-2014 5-year estimated population
Source: U.S. Census Bureau, 1990 Census, Census 2000, Census 2010, 2010-2014 American Community Survey 5-Year Estimates

Household Size

Area	Persons in Household (%) One	Two	Three	Four	Five	Six	Seven or More	Average Household Size
City	20.6	32.2	16.8	19.5	8.6	1.4	0.6	2.74
MSA[1]	28.3	32.3	16.4	14.5	5.7	1.7	0.8	2.54
U.S.	27.5	33.5	15.8	13.1	6.0	2.3	1.4	2.64

Note: (1) Figures cover the Boston-Cambridge-Newton, MA-NH Metropolitan Statistical Area—see Appendix B for areas included
Source: U.S. Census Bureau, 2010-2014 American Community Survey 5-Year Estimates

Race

Area	White Alone[2] (%)	Black Alone[2] (%)	Asian Alone[2] (%)	AIAN[3] Alone[2] (%)	NHOPI[4] Alone[2] (%)	Other Race Alone[2] (%)	Two or More Races (%)
City	73.3	1.1	21.9	0.2	0.0	0.3	3.1
MSA[1]	78.1	7.7	7.0	0.2	0.0	4.1	3.0
U.S.	73.8	12.6	5.0	0.8	0.2	4.7	2.9

Note: (1) Figures cover the Boston-Cambridge-Newton, MA-NH Metropolitan Statistical Area—see Appendix B for areas included; (2) Alone is defined as not being in combination with one or more other races; (3) American Indian and Alaska Native; (4) Native Hawaiian and Other Pacific Islander
Source: U.S. Census Bureau, 2010-2014 American Community Survey 5-Year Estimates

Hispanic or Latino Origin

Area	Total (%)	Mexican (%)	Puerto Rican (%)	Cuban (%)	Other (%)
City	1.8	0.5	0.0	0.1	1.3
MSA[1]	9.7	0.6	2.7	0.2	6.2
U.S.	16.9	10.8	1.6	0.6	3.8

Note: Persons of Hispanic or Latino origin can be of any race; (1) Figures cover the Boston-Cambridge-Newton, MA-NH Metropolitan Statistical Area—see Appendix B for areas included
Source: U.S. Census Bureau, 2010-2014 American Community Survey 5-Year Estimates

Ancestry

Area	German	Irish	English	American	Italian	Polish	French[2]	Scottish	Dutch
City	7.3	15.5	11.1	4.2	12.3	3.2	2.2	2.5	0.9
MSA[1]	6.3	23.4	10.5	4.5	14.6	3.7	5.6	2.5	0.6
U.S.	14.9	10.8	8.0	7.1	5.5	3.0	2.7	1.7	1.4

Note: Figures are the percentage of the total population reporting a particular ancestry. The nine most commonly reported ancestries in the U.S. are shown. Figures include multiple ancestries (e.g. if a person reported being Irish and Italian, they were included in both columns); (1) Figures cover the Boston-Cambridge-Newton, MA-NH Metropolitan Statistical Area—see Appendix B for areas included; (2) Excludes Basque
Source: U.S. Census Bureau, 2010-2014 American Community Survey 5-Year Estimates

Foreign-Born Population

Area	Percent of Population Born in: Any Foreign Country	Asia	Mexico	Europe	Carribean	Central America[2]	South America	Africa	Canada
City	24.4	16.4	0.1	5.5	0.1	0.1	0.5	0.7	0.8
MSA[1]	17.1	5.4	0.2	3.2	3.0	1.4	1.8	1.4	0.5
U.S.	13.1	3.8	3.7	1.5	1.2	1.0	0.9	0.6	0.3

Note: (1) Figures cover the Boston-Cambridge-Newton, MA-NH Metropolitan Statistical Area—see Appendix B for areas included; (2) Excludes Mexico.
Source: U.S. Census Bureau, 2010-2014 American Community Survey 5-Year Estimates

Marital Status

Area	Never Married	Now Married[2]	Separated	Widowed	Divorced
City	23.3	63.7	0.3	6.4	6.2
MSA[1]	36.4	47.4	1.8	5.4	8.9
U.S.	32.5	48.4	2.2	5.9	10.9

Note: Figures are percentages and cover the population 15 years of age and older; (1) Figures cover the Boston-Cambridge-Newton, MA-NH Metropolitan Statistical Area—see Appendix B for areas included; (2) Excludes separated
Source: U.S. Census Bureau, 2010-2014 American Community Survey 5-Year Estimates

Disability Status

Area	All Ages	Under 18 Years Old	18 to 64 Years Old	65 Years and Over
City	6.7	1.8	3.4	24.7
MSA[1]	10.3	3.8	7.9	33.0
U.S.	12.3	4.1	10.2	36.3

Note: Figures show percent of the civilian noninstitutionalized population that reported having a disability. Disability status is determined from from six types of difficulty: vision, hearing, cognitive, ambulatory, self-care, and independent living. For children under 5 years old, hearing and vision difficulty are used to determine disability status. For children between the ages of 5 and 14, disability status is determined from hearing, vision, cognitive, ambulatory, and self-care difficulties. For people aged 15 years and older, they are considered to have a disability if they have difficulty with any one of the six difficulty types; (1) Figures cover the Boston-Cambridge-Newton, MA-NH Metropolitan Statistical Area—see Appendix B for areas included.
Source: U.S. Census Bureau, 2010-2014 American Community Survey 5-Year Estimates

Age

Area	Percent of Population: Under Age 5	Age 5–19	Age 20–34	Age 35–44	Age 45–54	Age 55–64	Age 65–74	Age 75–84	Age 85+	Median Age
City	5.3	23.6	8.0	12.5	17.6	14.7	9.0	6.0	3.3	45.4
MSA[1]	5.5	18.6	21.4	13.2	15.1	12.5	7.3	4.3	2.1	38.7
U.S.	6.4	19.9	20.6	13.0	14.1	12.3	7.6	4.3	1.9	37.4

Note: (1) Figures cover the Boston-Cambridge-Newton, MA-NH Metropolitan Statistical Area—see Appendix B for areas included
Source: U.S. Census Bureau, 2010-2014 American Community Survey 5-Year Estimates

Gender

Area	Males	Females	Males per 100 Females
City	15,634	16,672	93.8
MSA[1]	2,254,371	2,396,505	94.1
U.S.	154,515,159	159,591,925	96.8

Note: (1) Figures cover the Boston-Cambridge-Newton, MA-NH Metropolitan Statistical Area—see Appendix B for areas included
Source: U.S. Census Bureau, 2010-2014 American Community Survey 5-Year Estimates

Religious Groups by Family

Area	Catholic	Baptist	Non-Den.	Methodist[2]	Lutheran	LDS[3]	Pentecostal	Presbyterian[4]	Muslim[5]	Judaism
MSA[1]	44.3	1.1	1.0	0.9	0.3	0.4	0.6	1.6	0.4	1.4
U.S.	19.1	9.3	4.0	4.0	2.3	2.0	1.9	1.6	0.8	0.7

Note: Figures are the number of adherents as a percentage of the total population; (1) Figures cover the Boston-Cambridge-Quincy, MA-NH Metropolitan Statistical Area—see Appendix B for areas included; (2) Methodist/Pietist; (3) Latter Day Saints; (4) Reformed; (5) Figures are estimates
Source: Association of Statisticians of American Religious Bodies, 2010 U.S. Religion Census: Religious Congregations & Membership Study

Religious Groups by Tradition

Area	Catholic	Evangelical Protestant	Mainline Protestant	Other Tradition	Black Protestant	Orthodox
MSA[1]	44.3	3.2	4.5	3.4	0.1	1.0
U.S.	19.1	16.2	7.3	4.3	1.6	0.3

Note: Figures are the number of adherents as a percentage of the total population; (1) Figures cover the Boston-Cambridge-Quincy, MA-NH Metropolitan Statistical Area—see Appendix B for areas included
Source: Association of Statisticians of American Religious Bodies, 2010 U.S. Religion Census: Religious Congregations & Membership Study

ECONOMY

Gross Metropolitan Product

Area	2013	2014	2015	2016	Rank[2]
MSA[1]	370.8	384.4	398.4	418.3	9

Note: Figures are in billions of dollars; (1) Figures cover the Boston-Cambridge-Newton, MA-NH Metropolitan Statistical Area—see Appendix B for areas included; (2) Rank is based on 2016 data and ranges from 1 to 381
Source: The U.S. Conference of Mayors, U.S. Metro Economies: GMP and Employment 2014-2016, June 2015

Economic Growth

Area	2011-13 (%)	2014 (%)	2015 (%)	2016 (%)	Rank[2]
MSA[1]	2.0	1.9	2.1	3.0	83
U.S.	2.2	2.4	2.3	2.9	–

Note: Figures are real gross metropolitan product (GMP) growth rates and represent annual average percent change; (1) Figures cover the Boston-Cambridge-Newton, MA-NH Metropolitan Statistical Area—see Appendix B for areas included; (2) Rank is based on 2016 data and ranges from 1 to 381
Source: The U.S. Conference of Mayors, U.S. Metro Economies: GMP and Employment 2014-2016, June 2015

Metropolitan Area Exports

Area	2009	2010	2011	2012	2013	2014	Rank[2]
MSA[1]	18,972.6	21,804.5	22,292.8	21,234.7	22,212.8	23,378.4	13

Note: Figures are in millions of dollars; (1) Figures cover the Boston-Cambridge-Newton, MA-NH Metropolitan Statistical Area—see Appendix B for areas included; (2) Rank is based on 2014 data and ranges from 1 to 385
Source: U.S. Department of Commerce, International Trade Administration, Office of Trade & Industry Information, Manufacturing & Services, data extracted March 10, 2016

Building Permits

Area	Single-Family			Multi-Family			Total		
	2014	2015p	Pct. Chg.	2014	2015p	Pct. Chg.	2014	2015p	Pct. Chg.
City	99	87	-12.1	0	0	-	99	87	-12.1
MSA[1]	4,991	4,779	-4.2	7,033	10,469	48.9	12,024	15,248	26.8
U.S.	640,300	690,800	7.9	411,800	487,600	18.4	1,052,100	1,178,400	12.0

Note: (1) Figures cover the Boston-Cambridge-Newton, MA-NH Metropolitan Statistical Area—see Appendix B for areas included; Figures represent new, privately-owned housing units authorized (unadjusted data); All permit data are based on estimates with imputation; (p) preliminary data.
Source: U.S. Census Bureau, Manufacturing, Mining, and Construction Statistics, Building Permits, 2014, 2015

Bankruptcy Filings

Area	Business Filings			Nonbusiness Filings		
	2014	2015	% Chg.	2014	2015	% Chg.
Middlesex County	96	111	15.6	1,591	1,330	-16.4
U.S.	26,983	24,735	-8.3	909,812	819,760	-9.9

Note: Business filings include Chapter 7, Chapter 11, Chapter 12, and Chapter 13; Nonbusiness filings include Chapter 7, Chapter 11, and Chapter 13
Source: Administrative Office of the U.S. Courts, Business and Nonbusiness Bankruptcy, County Cases Commenced by Chapter of the Bankruptcy Code, During the 12- Month Period Ending December 31, 2014 and Business and Nonbusiness Bankruptcy, County Cases Commenced by Chapter of the Bankruptcy Code, During the 12- Month Period Ending December 31, 2015

Housing Vacancy Rates

Area	Gross Vacancy Rate[2] (%)			Year-Round Vacancy Rate[3] (%)			Rental Vacancy Rate[4] (%)			Homeowner Vacancy Rate[5] (%)		
	2013	2014	2015	2013	2014	2015	2013	2014	2015	2013	2014	2015
MSA[1]	7.8	9.2	9.9	6.2	6.4	6.3	6.8	4.9	3.3	1.1	0.8	1.1
U.S.	13.6	13.4	12.9	10.7	10.4	10.0	8.3	7.6	7.1	2.0	1.9	1.8

Note: (1) Figures cover the Boston-Cambridge-Newton, MA-NH Metropolitan Statistical Area—see Appendix B for areas included; (2) The percentage of the total housing inventory that is vacant; (3) The percentage of the housing inventory (excluding seasonal units) that is year-round vacant; (4) The percentage of rental inventory that is vacant for rent; (5) The percentage of homeowner inventory that is vacant for sale
Source: U.S. Census Bureau, Housing Vacancies and Homeownership Annual Statistics: 2015

INCOME

Income

Area	Per Capita ($)	Median Household ($)	Average Household ($)
City	69,064	137,456	189,916
MSA[1]	39,572	74,494	101,462
U.S.	28,555	53,482	74,596

Note: (1) Figures cover the Boston-Cambridge-Newton, MA-NH Metropolitan Statistical Area—see Appendix B for areas included
Source: U.S. Census Bureau, 2010-2014 American Community Survey 5-Year Estimates

Household Income Distribution

Area	Percent of Households Earning							
	Under $15,000	$15,000 -24,999	$25,000 -34,999	$35,000 -49,999	$50,000 -74,999	$75,000 -99,000	$100,000 -149,999	$150,000 and up
City	5.4	3.8	4.4	5.5	7.1	9.0	18.1	46.6
MSA[1]	10.2	7.7	7.1	9.9	15.4	12.7	17.7	19.3
U.S.	12.5	10.7	10.2	13.5	17.8	12.2	13.0	10.0

Note: (1) Figures cover the Boston-Cambridge-Newton, MA-NH Metropolitan Statistical Area—see Appendix B for areas included
Source: U.S. Census Bureau, 2010-2014 American Community Survey 5-Year Estimates

Poverty Rate

Area	All Ages	Under 18 Years Old	18 to 64 Years Old	65 Years and Over
City	4.4	3.4	4.4	5.5
MSA[1]	10.4	12.8	9.9	8.8
U.S.	15.6	21.9	14.6	9.4

Note: Figures are percentage of people whose income during the past 12 months was below the poverty level; (1) Figures cover the Boston-Cambridge-Newton, MA-NH Metropolitan Statistical Area—see Appendix B for areas included
Source: U.S. Census Bureau, 2010-2014 American Community Survey 5-Year Estimates

EMPLOYMENT

Labor Force and Employment

Area	Civilian Labor Force			Workers Employed		
	Dec. 2014	Dec. 2015	% Chg.	Dec. 2014	Dec. 2015	% Chg.
City	15,648	15,544	-0.6	15,149	15,034	-0.7
NECTAD[1]	2,627,900	2,607,376	-0.7	2,512,440	2,500,406	-0.4
U.S.	155,521,000	157,245,000	1.1	147,190,000	149,703,000	1.7

Note: Data is not seasonally adjusted and covers workers 16 years of age and older; (1) Figures cover the Boston-Cambridge-Newton, MA New England City and Town Area Division—see Appendix B for areas included
Source: Bureau of Labor Statistics, Local Area Unemployment Statistics

Unemployment Rate

Area	2015											
	Jan.	Feb.	Mar.	Apr.	May	Jun.	Jul.	Aug.	Sep.	Oct.	Nov.	Dec.
City	3.5	3.3	3.2	2.9	3.4	4.0	3.7	3.2	3.4	3.4	3.4	3.3
NECTAD[1]	4.9	4.8	4.4	3.8	4.0	4.5	4.5	4.1	4.1	4.1	4.1	4.1
U.S.	6.1	5.8	5.6	5.1	5.3	5.5	5.6	5.2	4.9	4.8	4.8	4.8

Note: Data is not seasonally adjusted and covers workers 16 years of age and older; (1) Figures cover the Boston-Cambridge-Newton, MA New England City and Town Area Division—see Appendix B for areas included
Source: Bureau of Labor Statistics, Local Area Unemployment Statistics

Employment by Occupation

Occupation Classification	City (%)	MSA[1] (%)	U.S. (%)
Management, Business, Science, and Arts	76.7	46.6	36.4
Natural Resources, Construction, and Maintenance	1.7	6.4	9.0
Production, Transportation, and Material Moving	1.7	7.8	12.1
Sales and Office	12.7	22.6	24.4
Service	7.3	16.6	18.2

Note: Figures cover employed civilians 16 years of age and older; (1) Figures cover the Boston-Cambridge-Newton, MA-NH Metropolitan Statistical Area—see Appendix B for areas included
Source: U.S. Census Bureau, 2010-2014 American Community Survey 5-Year Estimates

Employment by Industry

Sector	NECTAD[1]		U.S.
	Number of Employees	Percent of Total	Percent of Total
Construction, Mining, and Logging	65,500	3.6	5.0
Education and Health Services	407,300	22.6	15.7
Financial Activities	152,500	8.4	5.7
Government	197,800	11.0	15.5
Information	57,000	3.1	1.9
Leisure and Hospitality	170,300	9.4	10.4
Manufacturing	82,100	4.5	8.6
Other Services	69,100	3.8	3.9
Professional and Business Services	342,600	19.0	13.9
Retail Trade	148,800	8.2	11.3
Transportation, Warehousing, and Utilities	43,500	2.4	3.9
Wholesale Trade	57,900	3.2	4.1

Note: Figures are non-farm employment as of December 2015. Figures are not seasonally adjusted and include workers 16 years of age and older; (1) Figures cover the Boston-Cambridge-Newton, MA New England City and Town Area Division—see Appendix B for areas included; n/a not available
Source: Bureau of Labor Statistics, Current Employment Statistics, Employment, Hours, and Earnings

Occupations with Greatest Projected Employment Growth: 2012 – 2022

Occupation[1]	2012 Employment	2022 Projected Employment	Numeric Employment Change	Percent Employment Change
Registered Nurses	78,750	93,310	14,560	18.5
Combined Food Preparation and Serving Workers, Including Fast Food	58,250	70,750	12,500	21.4
Retail Salespersons	109,830	119,160	9,330	8.5
Waiters and Waitresses	58,570	66,840	8,270	14.1
Personal Care Aides	21,690	29,940	8,250	38.1
Home Health Aides	19,760	27,740	7,980	40.4
Nursing Assistants	39,170	45,940	6,770	17.3
General and Operations Managers	55,960	62,610	6,650	11.9
Software Developers, Systems Software	30,030	36,290	6,260	20.8
Management Analysts	27,100	33,070	5,970	22.0

Note: Projections cover Massachusetts; (1) Sorted by numeric employment change
Source: www.projectionscentral.com, State Occupational Projections, 2012–2022 Long-Term Projections

Fastest Growing Occupations: 2012 – 2022

Occupation[1]	2012 Employment	2022 Projected Employment	Numeric Employment Change	Percent Employment Change
Skincare Specialists	2,520	3,840	1,320	52.6
Insulation Workers, Mechanical	240	350	110	49.4
Helpers—Brickmasons, Blockmasons, Stonemasons, and Tile and Marble Setters	550	790	240	44.0
Interpreters and Translators	2,200	3,130	930	42.1
Diagnostic Medical Sonographers	1,460	2,080	620	42.1
Animal Trainers	360	500	140	42.0
Home Health Aides	19,760	27,740	7,980	40.4
Information Security Analysts	2,640	3,660	1,020	39.1
Personal Care Aides	21,690	29,940	8,250	38.1
Helpers—Electricians	920	1,270	350	37.7

Note: Projections cover Massachusetts; (1) Sorted by percent employment change and excludes occupations with numeric employment change less than 100
Source: www.projectionscentral.com, State Occupational Projections, 2012–2022 Long-Term Projections

Average Wages

Occupation	$/Hr.	Occupation	$/Hr.
Accountants and Auditors	41.34	Maids and Housekeeping Cleaners	14.49
Automotive Mechanics	23.83	Maintenance and Repair Workers	22.61
Bookkeepers	22.55	Marketing Managers	68.56
Carpenters	31.66	Nuclear Medicine Technologists	36.73
Cashiers	11.36	Nurses, Licensed Practical	26.51
Clerks, General Office	18.73	Nurses, Registered	46.05
Clerks, Receptionists/Information	16.16	Nursing Assistants	14.83
Clerks, Shipping/Receiving	17.83	Packers and Packagers, Hand	12.24
Computer Programmers	48.37	Physical Therapists	40.26
Computer Systems Analysts	44.94	Postal Service Mail Carriers	25.82
Computer User Support Specialists	31.22	Real Estate Brokers	59.92
Cooks, Restaurant	14.10	Retail Salespersons	13.15
Dentists	82.28	Sales Reps., Exc. Tech./Scientific	40.34
Electrical Engineers	52.77	Sales Reps., Tech./Scientific	50.17
Electricians	33.33	Secretaries, Exc. Legal/Med./Exec.	22.35
Financial Managers	68.75	Security Guards	14.81
First-Line Supervisors/Managers, Sales	22.66	Surgeons	106.45
Food Preparation Workers	12.90	Teacher Assistants*	15.07
General and Operations Managers	71.11	Teachers, Elementary School*	35.84
Hairdressers/Cosmetologists	17.84	Teachers, Secondary School*	36.26
Internists	112.54	Telemarketers	16.27
Janitors and Cleaners	16.71	Truck Drivers, Heavy/Tractor-Trailer	24.97
Landscaping/Groundskeeping Workers	16.71	Truck Drivers, Light/Delivery Svcs.	17.56
Lawyers	78.96	Waiters and Waitresses	13.95

Note: Wage data covers the New England City and Town Area Division—see Appendix B for areas included; (*) Hourly wages for elementary/secondary school teachers and teacher assistants were calculated by the editors from annual wage data based on a 40 hour work week; n/a not available.
Source: Bureau of Labor Statistics, Metro Area Occupational Employment and Wage Estimates, May 2015

TAXES

State Corporate Income Tax Rates

State	Tax Rate (%)	Income Brackets ($)	Num. of Brackets	Financial Institution Tax Rate (%)[a]	Federal Income Tax Ded.
Massachusetts	8.0 (n)	Flat rate	1	9.0 (n)	No

Note: Tax rates as of January 1, 2016; (a) Rates listed are the corporate income tax rate applied to financial institutions or excise taxes based on income. Some states have other taxes based upon the value of deposits or shares; (n) Business and manufacturing corporations pay an additional tax of $2.60 per $1,000 on either taxable Massachusetts tangible property or taxable net worth allocable to the state (for intangible property corporations). The minimum tax for both corporations and financial institutions is $456.
Source: Federation of Tax Administrators, "State Corporate Income Tax Rates, 2016"

State Individual Income Tax Rates

State	Tax Rate (%)	Income Brackets ($)	Num. of Brackets	Personal Exempt. ($)[1]		Fed. Inc. Tax Ded.
				Single	Dependents	
Massachusetts	5.10	Flat rate	1	4,400	1,000	No

Note: Tax rates as of January 1, 2016; Local- and county-level taxes are not included; n/a not applicable; (1) Married joint filers generally receive double the single exemption
Source: Federation of Tax Administrators, "State Individual Income Tax Rates, 2016"

Various State and Local Tax Rates

State	State and Local Sales and Use (%)	State Sales and Use (%)	Gasoline[1] (¢/gal.)	Cigarette[2] ($/pack)	Spirits[3] ($/gal.)	Wine[4] ($/gal.)	Beer[5] ($/gal.)
Massachusetts	6.25	6.25	26.54	3.51	4.05 (f)	0.55 (l)	0.11

Note: All tax rates as of January 1, 2016; (1) The American Petroleum Institute has developed a methodology for determining the average tax rate on a gallon of fuel. Rates may include any of the following: excise taxes, environmental fees, storage tank fees, other fees or taxes, general sales tax, and local taxes. In states where gasoline is subject to the general sales tax, or where the fuel tax is based on the average sale price, the average rate determined by API is sensitive to changes in the price of gasoline. States that fully or partially apply general sales taxes to gasoline: CA, CO, GA, IL, IN, MI, NY; (2) The federal excise tax of $1.0066 per pack and local taxes are not included; (3) Rates are those applicable to off-premise sales of 40% alcohol by volume (a.b.v.) distilled spirits in 750ml containers. Local excise taxes are excluded; (4) Rates are those applicable to off-premise sales of 11% a.b.v. non-carbonated wine in 750ml containers; (5) Rates are those applicable to off-premise sales of 4.7% a.b.v. beer in 12 ounce containers; (f) Different rates are also applicable according to alcohol content, place of production, size of container, or place purchased (on- or off-premise or onboard airlines); (l) Different rates also applicable according to alcohol content, place of production, size of container, place purchased (on- or off-premise or on board airlines) or type of wine (carbonated, vermouth, etc.).
Source: Tax Foundation, 2016 Facts & Figures: How Does Your State Compare?

State Business Tax Climate Index Rankings

State	Overall Rank	Corporate Tax Rank	Individual Income Tax Rank	Sales Tax Rank	Unemployment Insurance Tax Rank	Property Tax Rank
Massachusetts	25	39	13	18	47	46

Note: The index is a measure of how each state's tax laws affect economic performance. The lower the rank, the more favorable a state's tax system is for business. States without a given tax are given a ranking of 1. The scores/rankings for the District of Columbia do not affect other states. The 2016 index represents the tax climate as of July 1, 2015 (the beginning of Fiscal Year 2016).
Source: Tax Foundation, State Business Tax Climate Index 2016

TRANSPORTATION

Means of Transportation to Work

Area	Car/Truck/Van		Public Transportation			Bicycle	Walked	Other Means	Worked at Home
	Drove Alone	Car-pooled	Bus	Subway	Railroad				
City	74.3	6.6	2.3	4.3	0.6	1.3	1.2	0.8	8.6
MSA[1]	68.5	7.4	4.1	5.8	2.0	0.9	5.3	1.4	4.6
U.S.	76.4	9.6	2.6	1.8	0.6	0.6	2.8	1.3	4.4

Note: Figures are percentages and cover workers 16 years of age and older; (1) Figures cover the Boston-Cambridge-Newton, MA-NH Metropolitan Statistical Area—see Appendix B for areas included
Source: U.S. Census Bureau, 2010-2014 American Community Survey 5-Year Estimates

Travel Time to Work

Area	Less Than 10 Minutes	10 to 19 Minutes	20 to 29 Minutes	30 to 44 Minutes	45 to 59 Minutes	60 to 89 Minutes	90 Minutes or More
City	8.8	20.3	18.9	26.7	15.1	8.4	1.8
MSA[1]	10.2	23.8	18.8	23.9	11.2	9.3	2.9
U.S.	13.3	29.6	21.0	20.2	7.7	5.7	2.6

Note: Figures are percentages and include workers 16 years old and over; (1) Figures cover the Boston-Cambridge-Newton, MA-NH Metropolitan Statistical Area—see Appendix B for areas included
Source: U.S. Census Bureau, 2010-2014 American Community Survey 5-Year Estimates

Freeway Travel Time Index

Area	1985	1990	1995	2000	2005	2010	2014
Urban Area Rank[1,2]	11	9	13	9	13	14	17
Urban Area Index[1]	1.16	1.20	1.22	1.28	1.29	1.28	1.29
Average Index[3]	1.09	1.11	1.14	1.17	1.20	1.19	1.20

Note: Freeway Travel Time Index—the ratio of travel time in the peak period to the travel time at free-flow conditions. For example, a value of 1.30 indicates a 20-minute free-flow trip takes 26 minutes in the peak (20 minutes x 1.30 = 26 minutes); (1) Covers the Boston MA-NH-RI urban area; (2) Rank is based on 101 urban areas (#1 = highest travel time index); (3) Average of 101 urban areas
Source: Texas Transportation Institute, 2015 Urban Mobility Scorecard, August 2015

Freeway Commuter Stress Index

Area	1985	1990	1995	2000	2005	2010	2014
Urban Area Rank[1,2]	12	9	10	8	11	12	14
Urban Area Index[1]	1.25	1.29	1.31	1.37	1.38	1.37	1.38
Average Index[3]	1.13	1.16	1.19	1.22	1.25	1.24	1.25

Note: The Freeway Commuter Stress Index is the same as the Freeway Travel Time Index (see table above) except that it includes only the travel in the peak directions during the peak periods; the TTI includes travel in all directions during the peak period. Thus, the CSI is more indicative of the work trip experienced by each commuter on a daily basis. (1) Covers the Boston MA-NH-RI urban area; (2) Rank is based on 101 urban areas (#1 = highest stress index); (3) Average of 101 urban areas

Source: Texas Transportation Institute, 2015 Urban Mobility Scorecard, August 2015

Living Environment

COST OF LIVING

Cost of Living Index

Composite Index	Groceries	Housing	Utilities	Transportation	Health Care	Misc. Goods/ Services
136.8	111.7	192.6	102.8	109.0	123.3	121.3

Note: The Cost of Living Index measures regional differences in the cost of consumer goods and services, excluding taxes and non-consumer expenditures, for professional and managerial households in the top income quintile. It is based on more than 50,000 prices covering almost 60 different items for which prices are collected three times a year by chambers of commerce, economic development organizations or university applied economic centers in each participating urban area. The numbers shown should be read as a percentage above or below the national average of 100. For example, a value of 115.4 in the groceries column indicates that grocery prices are 15.4% higher than the national average. Small differences in the index numbers should not be interpreted as significant; Figures cover the Framingham-Natick MA urban area.
Source: The Council for Community and Economic Research, ACCRA Cost of Living Index, 2015

Grocery Prices

Area[1]	T-Bone Steak ($/pound)	Frying Chicken ($/pound)	Whole Milk ($/half gal.)	Eggs ($/dozen)	Orange Juice ($/64 oz.)	Coffee ($/11.5 oz.)
City[2]	11.86	1.66	2.61	2.81	3.46	4.04
Avg.	10.99	1.43	2.25	2.26	3.58	4.48
Min.	7.16	0.98	1.30	1.35	2.88	2.98
Max.	14.13	2.43	3.85	4.81	6.39	7.56

Note: (1) Values for the local area are compared with the average, minimum and maximum values for all 292 areas in the Cost of Living Index; (2) Figures cover the Framingham-Natick MA urban area; **T-Bone Steak** *(price per pound);* **Frying Chicken** *(price per pound, whole fryer);* **Whole Milk** *(half gallon carton);* **Eggs** *(price per dozen, Grade A, large);* **Orange Juice** *(64 oz. Tropicana or Florida Natural);* **Coffee** *(11.5 oz. can, vacuum-packed, Maxwell House, Hills Bros, or Folgers).*
Source: The Council for Community and Economic Research, ACCRA Cost of Living Index, 2015

Housing and Utility Costs

Area[1]	New Home Price ($)	Apartment Rent ($/month)	All Electric ($/month)	Part Electric ($/month)	Other Energy ($/month)	Telephone ($/month)
City[2]	592,300	1,888	-	57.91	106.18	31.39
Avg.	312,874	945	179.30	95.07	72.96	28.11
Min.	178,682	479	116.28	43.14	26.46	10.01
Max.	1,472,476	3,984	504.25	189.44	421.11	43.06

Note: (1) Values for the local area are compared with the average, minimum and maximum values for all 292 areas in the Cost of Living Index; (2) Figures cover the Framingham-Natick MA urban area; **New Home Price** *(2,400 sf living area, 8,000 sf lot, in urban area with full utilities);* **Apartment Rent** *(950 sf 2 bedroom/1.5 or 2 bath, unfurnished, excluding all utilities except water);* **All Electric** *(average monthly cost for an all-electric home);* **Part Electric** *(average monthly cost for a part-electric home);* **Other Energy** *(average monthly cost for natural gas, fuel oil, coal, wood, and any other forms of energy except electricity);* **Telephone** *(price includes basic monthly rate for a private residential line plus additional local usage charges incurred by a family of four).*
Source: The Council for Community and Economic Research, ACCRA Cost of Living Index, 2015

Health Care, Transportation, and Other Costs

Area[1]	Doctor ($/visit)	Dentist ($/visit)	Optometrist ($/visit)	Gasoline ($/gallon)	Beauty Salon ($/visit)	Men's Shirt ($)
City[2]	163.83	108.44	119.59	2.47	48.68	45.26
Avg.	105.15	89.02	99.78	2.38	35.30	28.10
Min.	66.87	56.09	48.53	1.95	18.91	13.38
Max.	182.34	150.36	228.33	4.09	67.91	63.80

Note: (1) Values for the local area are compared with the average, minimum and maximum values for all 292 areas in the Cost of Living Index; (2) Figures cover the Framingham-Natick MA urban area; **Doctor** *(general practitioners routine exam of an established patient);* **Dentist** *(adult teeth cleaning and periodic oral examination);* **Optometrist** *(full vision eye exam for established adult patient);* **Gasoline** *(one gallon regular unleaded, national brand, including all taxes, cash price at self-service pump if available);* **Beauty Salon** *(woman's shampoo, trim, and blow-dry);* **Men's Shirt** *(cotton/polyester dress shirt, pinpoint weave, long sleeves).*
Source: The Council for Community and Economic Research, ACCRA Cost of Living Index, 2015

HOUSING

House Price Index (HPI)

Area	National Ranking[2]	Quarterly Change (%)	One-Year Change (%)	Five-Year Change (%)
MD[1]	100	0.50	5.50	16.70
U.S.[3]	–	1.45	5.76	22.85

Note: The HPI is a weighted repeat sales index. It measures average price changes in repeat sales or refinancings on the same properties. This information is obtained by reviewing repeat mortgage transactions on single-family properties whose mortgages have been purchased or securitized by Fannie Mae or Freddie Mac in January 1975; (1) Cambridge-Newton-Framingham Metropolitan Division—see Appendix B for areas included; (2) Rankings are based on annual percentage change for all metro areas containing at least 15,000 transactions over the last 10 years and ranges from 1 to 266; (3) figures based on a weighted average of Census Division estimates using a seasonally adjusted, purchase-only index; all figures are for the period ending December 31, 2015

Source: Federal Housing Finance Agency, House Price Index, February 25, 2016

Median Single-Family Home Prices

Area	2013	2014	2015p	Percent Change 2014 to 2015
MSA[1]	375.9	389.8	403.9	3.6
U.S. Average	197.4	208.9	223.9	7.2

Note: Figures are median sales prices of existing single-family homes in thousands of dollars; (p) preliminary; n/a not available; (1) Boston-Cambridge-Newton, MA-NH Metropolitan Statistical Area—see Appendix B for areas included

Source: National Association of Realtors, Median Sales Price of Existing Single-Family Homes for Metropolitan Areas, 4th Quarter 2015

Qualifying Income Based on Median Sales Price of Existing Single-Family Homes

Area	With 5% Down ($)	With 10% Down ($)	With 20% Down ($)
MSA[1]	87,549	82,941	73,725
U.S. Average	49,535	46,928	41,714

Note: Figures are preliminary; Qualifying income is based on a mortgage rate of 4.1%. Monthly principal and interest payment is limited to 25% of income; n/a not available; (1) Boston-Cambridge-Newton, MA-NH Metropolitan Statistical Area—see Appendix B for areas included

Source: National Association of Realtors, Qualifying Income Based on Median Sales Price of Existing Single-Family Homes for Metropolitan Areas, 4th Quarter 2015

Median Apartment Condo-Coop Home Prices

Area	2013	2014	2015p	Percent Change 2014 to 2015
MSA[1]	327.5	339.2	352.6	4.0
U.S. Average	194.9	204.3	210.7	3.1

Note: Figures are median sales prices of existing apartment condo-coop homes in thousands of dollars; (p) preliminary; n/a not available; (1) Boston-Cambridge-Newton, MA-NH Metropolitan Statistical Area—see Appendix B for areas included

Source: National Association of Realtors, Median Sales Price of Existing Apartment Condo-Coop Homes for Metropolitan Areas, 4th Quarter 2015

Gross Monthly Rent

Area	Under $200	$200 -299	$300 -499	$500 -749	$750 -999	$1,000 -1,499	$1,500 and up	Median ($)
City	0.9	3.7	11.7	2.9	4.4	16.3	60.1	1,714
MSA[1]	2.0	5.3	6.5	7.1	13.0	33.9	32.1	1,219
U.S.	1.5	3.2	7.4	21.0	24.1	26.9	15.9	920

Note: Figures are percentages except for Median; Gross rent is the contract rent plus the estimated average monthly cost of utilities (electricity, gas, and water and sewer) and fuels (oil, coal, kerosene, wood, etc.) if these are paid by the renter (or paid for the renter by someone else); (1) Figures cover the Boston-Cambridge-Newton, MA-NH Metropolitan Statistical Area—see Appendix B for areas included

Source: U.S. Census Bureau, 2010-2014 American Community Survey 5-Year Estimates

Homeownership Rate

Area	2008 (%)	2009 (%)	2010 (%)	2011 (%)	2012 (%)	2013 (%)	2014 (%)	2015 (%)
MSA[1]	66.2	65.5	66.0	65.5	66.0	66.3	62.8	59.3
U.S.	67.8	67.4	66.9	66.1	65.4	65.1	64.5	63.7

Note: (1) Figures cover the Boston-Cambridge-Newton, MA-NH Metropolitan Statistical Area—see Appendix B for areas included
Source: U.S. Census Bureau, Housing Vacancies and Homeownership Annual Statistics: 2015

Year Housing Structure Built

Area	2010 or Later	2000 -2009	1990 -1999	1980 -1989	1970 -1979	1960 -1969	1950 -1959	1940 -1949	Before 1940	Median Year
City	1.3	12.0	4.4	7.3	7.1	14.3	21.8	8.3	23.4	1958
MSA[1]	0.7	8.0	7.2	10.7	11.0	10.5	11.1	5.6	35.1	1958
U.S.	1.0	14.9	13.9	13.8	15.8	11.0	10.8	5.4	13.3	1976

Note: Figures are percentages except for Median Year; (1) Figures cover the Boston-Cambridge-Newton, MA-NH Metropolitan Statistical Area—see Appendix B for areas included
Source: U.S. Census Bureau, 2010-2014 American Community Survey 5-Year Estimates

HEALTH

Health Risk Data

Category	MD[1] (%)	U.S. (%)
Adults aged 18–64 who have any kind of health care coverage	93.7	79.6
Adults who reported being in good or excellent health	88.0	83.1
Adults who are current smokers	13.7	19.6
Adults who are heavy drinkers[2]	6.7	6.1
Adults who are binge drinkers[3]	19.0	16.9
Adults who are overweight (BMI 25.0 - 29.9)	37.1	35.8
Adults who are obese (BMI 30.0 - 99.8)	20.1	27.6
Adults who participated in any physical activities in the past month	81.2	77.1
Adults 50+ who have ever had a sigmoidoscopy or colonoscopy	77.5	67.3
Women aged 40+ who have had a mammogram within the past two years	83.9	74.0
Men aged 40+ who have had a PSA test within the past two years	43.0	45.2
Adults aged 65+ who have had flu shot within the past year	67.0	60.1
Adults who always wear a seatbelt	89.9	93.8

Note: Data as of 2012 unless otherwise noted; (1) Figures cover the Cambridge-Newton-Framingham, MA Metropolitan Division—see Appendix B for areas included; (2) Heavy drinkers are classified as males having more than two drinks per day or females having more than one drink per day; (3) Binge drinkers are classified as males having five or more drinks on one occasion or females having four or more drinks on one occasion
Source: Centers for Disease Control and Prevention, Behaviorial Risk Factor Surveillance System, SMART: Selected Metropolitan/Micropolitan Area Risk Trends, 2012 (Note: the CDC has discontinued this dataset but will be releasing a replacement in mid-2016)

Chronic Health Indicators

Category	MD[1] (%)	U.S. (%)
Adults who have ever been told they had a heart attack	3.6	4.5
Adults who have ever been told they had a stroke	1.9	2.9
Adults who have been told they currently have asthma	9.9	8.9
Adults who have ever been told they have arthritis	21.1	25.7
Adults who have ever been told they have diabetes[2]	7.9	9.7
Adults who have ever been told they had skin cancer	5.0	5.7
Adults who have ever been told they had any other types of cancer	6.6	6.5
Adults who have ever been told they have COPD	4.9	6.2
Adults who have ever been told they have kidney disease	1.7	2.5
Adults who have ever been told they have a form of depression	17.4	18.0

Note: Data as of 2012 unless otherwise noted; (1) Figures cover the Cambridge-Newton-Framingham, MA Metropolitan Division—see Appendix B for areas included; (2) Figures do not include pregnancy-related, borderline, or pre-diabetes
Source: Centers for Disease Control and Prevention, Behaviorial Risk Factor Surveillance System, SMART: Selected Metropolitan/Micropolitan Area Risk Trends, 2012 (Note: the CDC has discontinued this dataset but will be releasing a replacement in mid-2016)

Mortality Rates for the Top 10 Causes of Death in the U.S.

ICD-10[a] Sub-Chapter	ICD-10[a] Code	Age-Adjusted Mortality Rate[1] per 100,000 population	
		County[2]	U.S.
Malignant neoplasms	C00-C97	150.4	163.6
Ischaemic heart diseases	I20-I25	70.8	102.2
Other forms of heart disease	I30-I51	42.9	50.1
Chronic lower respiratory diseases	J40-J47	26.6	41.4
Organic, including symptomatic, mental disorders	F01-F09	49.1	38.5
Cerebrovascular diseases	I60-I69	25.0	36.5
Other external causes of accidental injury	W00-X59	23.7	27.5
Other degenerative diseases of the nervous system	G30-G31	20.4	26.3
Diabetes mellitus	E10-E14	11.8	21.1
Hypertensive diseases	I10-I15	10.3	19.7

Note: (a) ICD-10 = International Classification of Diseases 10th Revision; (1) Mortality rates are a three year average covering 2012-2014; (2) Figures cover Middlesex County.
Source: Centers for Disease Control and Prevention, National Center for Health Statistics. Underlying Cause of Death 1999-2014 on CDC WONDER Online Database, released 2015.

Mortality Rates for Selected Causes of Death

ICD-10[a] Sub-Chapter	ICD-10[a] Code	Age-Adjusted Mortality Rate[1] per 100,000 population	
		County[2]	U.S.
Assault	X85-Y09	1.0	5.1
Diseases of the liver	K70-K76	9.3	13.5
Human immunodeficiency virus (HIV) disease	B20-B24	0.7	2.1
Influenza and pneumonia	J09-J18	15.1	15.2
Intentional self-harm	X60-X84	7.2	12.7
Malnutrition	E40-E46	0.5	0.9
Obesity and other hyperalimentation	E65-E68	1.1	1.9
Renal failure	N17-N19	14.3	13.0
Transport accidents	V01-V99	3.8	11.6
Viral hepatitis	B15-B19	1.0	2.1

Note: (a) ICD-10 = International Classification of Diseases 10th Revision; (1) Mortality rates are a three year average covering 2012-2014; (2) Figures cover Middlesex County; Data are Suppressed when the data meet the criteria for confidentiality constraints; Mortality rates are flagged as Unreliable when the rate would be calculated with a numerator of 20 or less.
Source: Centers for Disease Control and Prevention, National Center for Health Statistics. Underlying Cause of Death 1999-2014 on CDC WONDER Online Database, released 2015.

Health Insurance Coverage

Area	With Health Insurance	With Private Health Insurance	With Public Health Insurance	Without Health Insurance	Population Under Age 18 Without Health Insurance
City	98.5	90.6	21.4	1.5	0.3
MSA[1]	95.7	77.0	30.0	4.3	1.7
U.S.	85.8	65.8	31.1	14.2	7.1

Note: Figures are percentages that cover the civilian noninstitutionalized population; (1) Figures cover the Boston-Cambridge-Newton, MA-NH Metropolitan Statistical Area—see Appendix B for areas included
Source: U.S. Census Bureau, 2010-2014 American Community Survey 5-Year Estimates

Number of Medical Professionals

Area	MDs[3]	DOs[3,4]	Dentists	Podiatrists	Chiropractors	Optometrists
County[1] (number)	8,105	146	1,424	113	341	277
County[1] (rate[2])	520.2	9.4	90.7	7.2	21.7	17.6
U.S. (rate[2])	272.5	20.9	64.7	5.8	25.9	15.2

Note: Data as of 2014 unless noted; (1) Data covers Middlesex County; (2) Rate per 100,000 population; (3) Data as of 2013 and includes all active, non-federal physicians; (4) Doctor of Osteopathic Medicine
Source: U.S. Department of Health and Human Services, Health Resources and Services Administration, Bureau of Health Professions, Area Resource File (ARF) 2014-2015

Best Hospitals

According to *U.S. News,* the Cambridge-Newton-Framingham, MA metro area is home to one of the best hospitals in the U.S.: **McLean Hospital** (1 specialty). The hospital listed was nationally ranked in at least one adult specialty. Only 137 hospitals nationwide were nationally ranked in one or more specialties. Fifteen hospitals in the U.S. made the Honor Roll with high scores in at least six specialties. *U.S. News Online, "America's Best Children's Hospitals 2015-16"*

EDUCATION

Public School District Statistics

District Name	Schls	Pupils	Pupil/ Teacher Ratio	Minority Pupils[1] (%)	Free Lunch Eligible[2] (%)	IEP[3] (%)
Lexington	9	6,610	12.1	44.4	5.6	15.0
Minuteman Regional Voc Techl	1	715	9.0	22.0	25.5	46.6

Note: Table includes school districts with 100 or more students; (1) Percentage of students that are not non-Hispanic white; (2) Percentage of students that are eligible for the free lunch program; (3) Percentage of students that have an Individualized Education Program.
Source: U.S. Department of Education, National Center for Education Statistics, Common Core of Data, Local Education Agency (School District) Universe Survey: School Year 2013-2014; U.S. Department of Education, National Center for Education Statistics, Common Core of Data, Public Elementary/Secondary School Universe Survey: School Year 2013-2014

Best High Schools

According to *U.S. News,* Lexington is home to one of the best high schools in the U.S.: **Lexington High School** (#194); Nearly 20,000 schools were ranked based on their performance on state assessments and how well they prepare students for college. Schools with the highest unrounded College Readiness Index values were numerically ranked from No. 1 to No. 500 and were the gold medal winners. *U.S. News & World Report, "Best High Schools 2015"*

Highest Level of Education

Area	Less than H.S.	H.S. Diploma	Some College, No Deg.	Associate Degree	Bachelor's Degree	Master's Degree	Prof. School Degree	Doctorate Degree
City	3.2	8.6	7.3	4.2	27.0	28.7	8.0	13.1
MSA[1]	9.2	24.0	15.5	7.2	24.5	13.5	3.2	2.8
U.S.	13.7	28.0	21.2	7.9	18.3	7.8	2.0	1.3

Note: Figures cover persons age 25 and over; (1) Figures cover the Boston-Cambridge-Newton, MA-NH Metropolitan Statistical Area—see Appendix B for areas included
Source: U.S. Census Bureau, 2010-2014 American Community Survey 5-Year Estimates

Educational Attainment by Race

Area	High School Graduate or Higher (%)					Bachelor's Degree or Higher (%)				
	Total	White	Black	Asian	Hisp.[2]	Total	White	Black	Asian	Hisp.[2]
City	96.8	97.3	76.3	97.4	95.8	76.7	76.2	37.5	82.2	87.8
MSA[1]	90.8	93.5	82.3	84.2	69.1	44.0	46.2	23.8	58.2	19.7
U.S.	86.3	88.4	83.2	85.8	64.1	29.3	30.6	19.0	50.9	13.9

Note: Figures shown cover persons 25 years old and over; (1) Figures cover the Boston-Cambridge-Newton, MA-NH Metropolitan Statistical Area—see Appendix B for areas included; (2) People of Hispanic origin can be of any race
Source: U.S. Census Bureau, 2010-2014 American Community Survey 5-Year Estimates

School Enrollment by Grade and Control

Area	Preschool (%)		Kindergarten (%)		Grades 1 - 4 (%)		Grades 5 - 8 (%)		Grades 9 - 12 (%)	
	Public	Private	Public	Private	Public	Private	Public	Private	Public	Private
City	19.8	80.2	90.6	9.4	93.6	6.4	87.7	12.3	86.7	13.3
MSA[1]	42.8	57.2	86.5	13.5	90.9	9.1	89.4	10.6	86.9	13.1
U.S.	57.4	42.6	87.8	12.2	89.8	10.2	89.9	10.1	90.6	9.4

Note: Figures shown cover persons 3 years old and over; (1) Figures cover the Boston-Cambridge-Newton, MA-NH Metropolitan Statistical Area—see Appendix B for areas included
Source: U.S. Census Bureau, 2010-2014 American Community Survey 5-Year Estimates

Average Salaries of Public School Classroom Teachers

Area	2013-14 Dollars	2013-14 Rank[1]	2014-15 Dollars	2014-15 Rank[1]	Percent Change 2013-14 to 2014-15	Percent Change 2004-05 to 2014-15
Massachusetts	73,195	2	74,805	3	2.20	36.8
U.S. Average	56,610	–	57,379	–	1.36	20.8

Note: (1) State rank ranges from 1 to 51 where 1 indicates highest salary.
Source: National Education Association, Rankings & Estimates: Rankings of the States 2014 and Estimates of School Statistics 2015, March 2015

Higher Education

Four-Year Colleges			Two-Year Colleges			Medical Schools[1]	Law Schools[2]	Voc/ Tech[3]
Public	Private Non-profit	Private For-profit	Public	Private Non-profit	Private For-profit			
0	0	0	0	0	0	0	0	0

Note: Figures cover institutions located within the city limits and include main campuses only; (1) includes schools accredited by the Liaison Committee on Medical Education and the American Osteopathic Association's Commission on Osteopathic College Accreditation; (2) includes ABA-accredited schools, schools with provisional ABA accreditation, and state accredited schools; (3) includes all schools with programs that are less than 2 years.
Source: National Center for Education Statistics, Integrated Postsecondary Education System (IPEDS), 2014-15; Association of American Medical Colleges, Member List, March 21, 2016; American Osteopathic Association, Member List, March 21, 2016; Law School Admission Council, Official Guide to ABA-Approved Law Schools Online, March 21, 2016; Wikipedia, List of Medical Schools in the United States, March 21, 2016; Wikipedia, List of Law Schools in the United States, March 21, 2016

According to *U.S. News & World Report,* the Cambridge-Newton-Framingham, MA metro division is home to five of the best national universities in the U.S.: **Harvard University** (#2); **Massachusetts Institute of Technology** (#7); **Tufts University** (#27 tie); **Brandeis University** (#34 tie); **University of Massachusetts–Lowell** (#156 tie). The indicators used to capture academic quality fall into a number of categories: assessment by administrators at peer institutions; retention of students; faculty resources; student selectivity; financial resources; alumni giving; high school counselor ratings of colleges; and graduation rate. *U.S. News & World Report, "America's Best Colleges 2016"*

According to *U.S. News & World Report,* the Cambridge-Newton-Framingham, MA metro division is home to one of the best liberal arts colleges in the U.S.: **Gordon College** (#158 tie). The indicators used to capture academic quality fall into a number of categories: assessment by administrators at peer institutions; retention of students; faculty resources; student selectivity; financial resources; alumni giving; high school counselor ratings of colleges; and graduation rate. *U.S. News & World Report, "America's Best Colleges 2016"*

According to *U.S. News & World Report,* the Cambridge-Newton-Framingham, MA metro division is home to two of the top 100 law schools in the U.S.: **Harvard University** (#2 tie); **Boston College, Law School** (#30 tie). The rankings are based on a weighted average of 12 measures of quality: peer assessment score; assessment score by lawyers/judges; median LSAT scores; median undergrad GPA; acceptance rate; employment rates for graduates; placement success; bar passage rate; faculty resources; expenditures per student; student/faculty ratio; and library resources. *U.S. News & World Report, "America's Best Graduate Schools, Law, 2017"*

According to *U.S. News & World Report,* the Cambridge-Newton-Framingham, MA metro division is home to one of the top 75 business schools in the U.S.: **Massachusetts Institute of Technology, Sloan School of Management** (#5 tie). The rankings are based on a weighted average of the following nine measures: quality assessment; peer assessment; recruiter assessment; placement success; mean starting salary and bonus; student selectivity; mean GMAT and GRE scores; mean undergraduate GPA; and acceptance rate. *U.S. News & World Report, "America's Best Graduate Schools, Business, 2017"*

PRESIDENTIAL ELECTION

2012 Presidential Election Results

Area	Obama (%)	Romney (%)	Other (%)
Middlesex County	62.6	35.7	1.8
U.S.	51.0	47.2	1.8

Note: Results may not add to 100% due to rounding
Source: Dave Leip's Atlas of U.S. Presidential Elections

EMPLOYERS

Major Employers

Company Name	Industry
Beth Israel Deaconess Medical Center	General medical and surgical hospitals
Blue Cross Blue Shield of Massachusetts	Health insurance
Boston University	Colleges and universities
Children's Hospital Corporation	Specialty hospitals, except psychiatric
City of Lowell	City and town managers' office
EMC Corp.	Data management
Federal Deposit Insurance Corporation	Federal deposit insurance corporation (FDIC)
General Electric Company	Aircraft engines and engine parts
Harvard University	Colleges and universities
Internal Revenue Service	Taxation department, government
John Hancock Corp Tax Credit Fund I	Personal service agents, brokers & bureaus
Lahey Clinic	General medical and surgical hospitals
Massachusetts General Hospital	Health care
Massachusetts Institute of Technology	Colleges and universities
MassMutual Financial Group	Life insurance, annuities, & retirement investment
Roche Bros. Supermarkets	Food/grocery
State Street Bank and Trust Company	State trust companies accepting deposits, commercial
Sun Healthcare Group	Accident and health insurance
The Admins of the Tulane Educational Fund	Hospital, medical school affiliation
Tufts Medical Center	Hospital management

Note: Companies shown are located within the Boston-Cambridge-Newton, MA-NH Metropolitan Statistical Area.
Source: Hoovers.com; Wikipedia

PUBLIC SAFETY

Crime Rate

Area	All Crimes	Violent Crimes				Property Crimes		
		Murder	Rape[3]	Robbery	Aggrav. Assault	Burglary	Larceny -Theft	Motor Vehicle Theft
City	696.0	0.0	0.0	9.1	21.2	102.9	547.7	15.1
Metro[1]	n/a	n/a	n/a	n/a	n/a	n/a	n/a	n/a
U.S.	2,971.8	4.5	36.6	102.2	232.5	542.5	1,837.3	216.2

Note: Figures are crimes per 100,000 population; (1) Figures cover the Cambridge-Newton-Framingham, MA Metropolitan Division—see Appendix B for areas included; n/a not available; (3) The city and U.S. figures shown were reported using the revised Uniform Crime Reporting (UCR) definition of rape. The suburban and metro area figures shown are an aggregate total of the data submitted using both the revised and legacy UCR definitions.
Source: FBI Uniform Crime Reports, 2014

Hate Crimes

Area	Number of Quarters Reported	Number of Incidents per Bias Motivation						
		Race	Religion	Sexual Orientation	Ethnicity	Disability	Gender	Gender Identity
City	4	0	0	0	0	0	0	0
U.S.	4	2,568	1,014	1,017	648	84	33	98

Source: Federal Bureau of Investigation, Hate Crime Statistics 2014

Identity Theft Consumer Complaints

Area	Complaints	Complaints per 100,000 Population	Rank[2]
MSA[1]	6,507	137.5	75
U.S.	490,220	152.4	-

Note: (1) Figures cover the Boston-Cambridge-Newton, MA-NH Metropolitan Statistical Area—see Appendix B for areas included; (2) Rank ranges from 1 to 379 where 1 indicates greatest number of identity theft complaints per 100,000 population
Source: Federal Trade Commission, Consumer Sentinel Network Data Book for January–December 2015

Fraud and Other Consumer Complaints

Area	Complaints	Complaints per 100,000 Population	Rank[2]
MSA[1]	16,631	351.4	213
U.S.	2,593,159	806.0	-

Note: (1) Figures cover the Boston-Cambridge-Newton, MA-NH Metropolitan Statistical Area—see Appendix B for areas included; (2) Rank ranges from 1 to 379 where 1 indicates greatest number of identity theft complaints per 100,000 population
Source: Federal Trade Commission, Consumer Sentinel Network Data Book for January–December 2015

RECREATION

Culture

Dance[1]	Theatre[1]	Instrumental Music[1]	Vocal Music[1]	Series and Festivals	Museums and Art Galleries[2]	Zoos and Aquariums[3]
0	0	0	0	0	0	0

Note: (1) Professional perfoming groups; (2) Based on organizations with SIC code 8412; (3) AZA-accredited
Source: The Grey House Performing Arts Directory, 2015-16; Association of Zoos & Aquariums, AZA Member Zoos & Aquariums, March 25, 2016; www.AccuLeads.com, March 29, 2016

Professional Sports Teams

Team Name	League	Year Established
Boston Bruins	National Hockey League (NHL)	1924
Boston Celtics	National Basketball Association (NBA)	1946
Boston Red Sox	Major League Baseball (MLB)	1901
New England Patriots	National Football League (NFL)	1960
New England Revolution	Major League Soccer (MLS)	1996

Note: Includes teams located in the Boston-Cambridge-Newton, MA-NH Metropolitan Statistical Area.
Source: Wikipedia, Major Professional Sports Teams of the United States and Canada, March 24, 2016

CLIMATE

Average and Extreme Temperatures

Temperature	Jan	Feb	Mar	Apr	May	Jun	Jul	Aug	Sep	Oct	Nov	Dec	Yr.
Extreme High (°F)	72	70	85	94	95	100	102	102	100	90	83	73	102
Average High (°F)	36	38	46	56	67	76	82	80	73	63	52	41	59
Average Temp. (°F)	30	31	39	48	58	68	74	72	65	55	45	34	52
Average Low (°F)	22	23	31	40	50	59	65	64	57	47	38	27	44
Extreme Low (°F)	-12	-4	1	16	34	45	50	47	37	28	15	-7	-12

Note: Figures cover the years 1945-1990
Source: National Climatic Data Center, International Station Meteorological Climate Summary, 9/96

Average Precipitation/Snowfall/Humidity

Precip./Humidity	Jan	Feb	Mar	Apr	May	Jun	Jul	Aug	Sep	Oct	Nov	Dec	Yr.
Avg. Precip. (in.)	3.8	3.6	3.8	3.7	3.5	3.1	2.9	3.6	3.1	3.3	4.4	4.1	42.9
Avg. Snowfall (in.)	12	12	8	1	Tr	0	0	0	0	Tr	1	8	41
Avg. Rel. Hum. 7am (%)	68	68	69	68	71	72	73	76	79	77	74	70	72
Avg. Rel. Hum. 4pm (%)	58	57	56	56	58	58	58	61	61	59	61	60	59

Note: Figures cover the years 1945-1990; Tr = Trace amounts (<0.05 in. of rain; <0.5 in. of snow)
Source: National Climatic Data Center, International Station Meteorological Climate Summary, 9/96

Weather Conditions

Temperature			Daytime Sky			Precipitation		
5°F & below	32°F & below	90°F & above	Clear	Partly cloudy	Cloudy	0.01 inch or more precip.	0.1 inch or more snow/ice	Thunder-storms
4	97	12	88	127	150	253	48	18

Note: Figures are average number of days per year and cover the years 1945-1990
Source: National Climatic Data Center, International Station Meteorological Climate Summary, 9/96

HAZARDOUS WASTE

Superfund Sites

Lexington has no sites on the EPA's Superfund Final National Priorities List. There are a total of 1,323 Superfund sites on the list in the U.S. *U.S. Environmental Protection Agency, Final National Priorities List, March 18, 2016*

AIR & WATER QUALITY

Air Quality Trends: Ozone

	1990	1995	2000	2005	2010	2011	2012	2013	2014
MSA[1]	n/a	n/a	n/a	n/a	n/a	n/a	n/a	n/a	n/a

Note: (1) Data covers the Boston-Cambridge-Newton, MA-NH Metropolitan Statistical Area—see Appendix B for areas included; n/a not available. The values shown are the composite ozone concentration averages among trend sites based on the highest fourth daily maximum 8-hour concentration in parts per million. These trends are based on sites having an adequate record of monitoring data during the trend period. Data from exceptional events are included.
Source: U.S. Environmental Protection Agency, Air Quality Monitoring Information, "Air Quality Trends by City, 1990-2014"

Air Quality Index

Area	Percent of Days when Air Quality was...[2]					AQI Statistics[2]	
	Good	Moderate	Unhealthy for Sensitive Groups	Unhealthy	Very Unhealthy	Maximum	Median
MSA[1]	61.6	37.8	0.3	0.0	0.3	615	46

Note: (1) Data covers the Boston-Cambridge-Newton, MA-NH Metropolitan Statistical Area—see Appendix B for areas included; (2) Based on 365 days with AQI data in 2015. Air Quality Index (AQI) is an index for reporting daily air quality. EPA calculates the AQI for five major air pollutants regulated by the Clean Air Act: ground-level ozone, particle pollution (aka particulate matter), carbon monoxide, sulfur dioxide, and nitrogen dioxide. The AQI runs from 0 to 500. The higher the AQI value, the greater the level of air pollution and the greater the health concern. There are six AQI categories: "Good" AQI is between 0 and 50. Air quality is considered satisfactory; "Moderate" AQI is between 51 and 100. Air quality is acceptable; "Unhealthy for Sensitive Groups" When AQI values are between 101 and 150, members of sensitive groups may experience health effects; "Unhealthy" When AQI values are between 151 and 200 everyone may begin to experience health effects; "Very Unhealthy" AQI values between 201 and 300 trigger a health alert; "Hazardous" AQI values over 300 trigger warnings of emergency conditions (not shown).
Source: U.S. Environmental Protection Agency, Air Quality Index Report, 2015

Air Quality Index Pollutants

Area	Percent of Days when AQI Pollutant was...[2]					
	Carbon Monoxide	Nitrogen Dioxide	Ozone	Sulfur Dioxide	Particulate Matter 2.5	Particulate Matter 10
MSA[1]	0.0	3.3	27.9	0.0	68.5	0.3

Note: (1) Data covers the Boston-Cambridge-Newton, MA-NH Metropolitan Statistical Area—see Appendix B for areas included; (2) Based on 365 days with AQI data in 2015. The Air Quality Index (AQI) is an index for reporting daily air quality. EPA calculates the AQI for five major air pollutants regulated by the Clean Air Act: ground-level ozone, particle pollution (also known as particulate matter), carbon monoxide, sulfur dioxide, and nitrogen dioxide. The AQI runs from 0 to 500. The higher the AQI value, the greater the level of air pollution and the greater the health concern.
Source: U.S. Environmental Protection Agency, Air Quality Index Report, 2015

Maximum Air Pollutant Concentrations: Particulate Matter, Ozone, CO and Lead

	Particulate Matter 10 (ug/m^3)	Particulate Matter 2.5 Wtd AM (ug/m^3)	Particulate Matter 2.5 24-Hr (ug/m^3)	Ozone (ppm)	Carbon Monoxide (ppm)	Lead (ug/m^3)
MSA[1] Level	66	10.1	19	0.07	1	n/a
NAAQS[2]	150	15	35	0.075	9	0.15
Met NAAQS[2]	Yes	Yes	Yes	Yes	Yes	n/a

Note: (1) Data covers the Boston-Cambridge-Newton, MA-NH Metropolitan Statistical Area—see Appendix B for areas included; Data from exceptional events are included; (2) National Ambient Air Quality Standards; ppm = parts per million; ug/m^3 = micrograms per cubic meter; n/a not available.

Concentrations: Particulate Matter 10 (coarse particulate)—highest second maximum 24-hour concentration; Particulate Matter 2.5 Wtd AM (fine particulate)—highest weighted annual mean concentration; Particulate Matter 2.5 24-Hour (fine particulate)—highest 98th percentile 24-hour concentration; Ozone—highest fourth daily maximum 8-hour concentration; Carbon Monoxide—highest second maximum non-overlapping 8-hour concentration; Lead—maximum running 3-month average

Source: U.S. Environmental Protection Agency, Air Quality Monitoring Information, "Air Quality Statistics by City, 2014"

Maximum Air Pollutant Concentrations: Nitrogen Dioxide and Sulfur Dioxide

	Nitrogen Dioxide AM (ppb)	Nitrogen Dioxide 1-Hr (ppb)	Sulfur Dioxide AM (ppb)	Sulfur Dioxide 1-Hr (ppb)	Sulfur Dioxide 24-Hr (ppb)
MSA[1] Level	17	53	n/a	32	n/a
NAAQS[2]	53	100	30	75	140
Met NAAQS[2]	Yes	Yes	n/a	Yes	n/a

Note: (1) Data covers the Boston-Cambridge-Newton, MA-NH Metropolitan Statistical Area—see Appendix B for areas included; Data from exceptional events are included; (2) National Ambient Air Quality Standards; ppm = parts per million; ug/m^3 = micrograms per cubic meter; n/a not available.

Concentrations: Nitrogen Dioxide AM—highest arithmetic mean concentration; Nitrogen Dioxide 1-Hr—highest 98th percentile 1-hour daily maximum concentration; Sulfur Dioxide AM—highest annual mean concentration; Sulfur Dioxide 1-Hr—highest 99th percentile 1-hour daily maximum concentration; Sulfur Dioxide 24-Hr—highest second maximum 24-hour concentration

Source: U.S. Environmental Protection Agency, Air Quality Monitoring Information, "Air Quality Statistics by City, 2014"

Drinking Water

Water System Name	Pop. Served	Primary Water Source Type	Violations[1] Health Based	Violations[1] Monitoring/ Reporting
Lexington Water Dept (MWRA)	30,355	Purchased Surface	0	0

Note: (1) Based on violation data from January 1, 2015 to December 31, 2015 (includes unresolved violations from earlier years)

Source: U.S. Environmental Protection Agency, Office of Ground Water and Drinking Water, Safe Drinking Water Information System (based on data extracted April 29, 2016)

Needham, Massachusetts

Background

Needham, in Norfolk County, is approximately ten miles southwest of Boston. This suburb was incorporated in 1711, and is now a pleasant mix of residential and commercial areas along the Charles River.

Needham has undergone a series of changes since the town's first settlers began developing the land in the 1640s. Purchased from Native American Chief William Nehoiden in 1681, the land was originally part of the town of Dedham. Residents petitioned for a separation from Dedham, which was granted by Governor Dudley in 1711, and the town of Needham was born. The town experienced its own split in 1881, when its western section became the town of Wellesley. Agriculture gave way to industry in the 18th and 19th centuries as saw mills sprang up along the Charles River, and railroads made the town more accessible. In the 20th century, Route 128 was constructed and the entire Boston area experienced a rapid growth in high-tech industry. To support this growth, Needham created its own industrial, high-tech park in 1950.

Home to several distinct industries, Needham is an important economic center. Needham Crossing is the heart of Needham's industry, and home to life science and technology companies. Current expansion plans will grow this area to over three million square feet of new development, and easier access to Route 128. Technological companies in Needham Crossing include travel website Trip Advisor, computer software company PTC, life science companies Celldex Therapeutics and Verastem, and Coca-Cola has a bottling plant in Needham.

The media industry also has a large presence in Needham, with television stations WCVB and WUNI, as well as several local radio stations. The Needham Community Television Development Corporation operates three local public access channels—Municipal Channel, Community Channel, and Education Channel, all available on Verizon, RCN, Comcast and the Needham Channel website. Needham residents are encouraged to pitch their own ideas, volunteer and intern at the corporation.

Needham has several large parks and miles of trails that capture the beauty of the town. DeFazzio Park is the place for athletics and features two lighted turf fields, two grass fields, three baseball diamonds and a track. The park also has a picnic area and playground. Nature lovers enjoy Cutler Park Reservation, with access to the Charles River and Kendrick's Pond and canoeing and fishing. Cutler Park also has trails for walking and mountain biking—both a great way to see the extensive wildlife in the reservation. Centrally located, Memorial Park is where many of the town's events are hosted, including outdoor concerts, a Fourth of July celebration and the Needham-Wellesley Annual Thanksgiving football game. The Needham Golf Club was founded in 1923 and has a private 9-hole golf course.

Needham is served by the Needham School district and has an excellent academic reputation. Needham High School is one of the top 15 schools in the state, with a solid athletics program highlighted by the Boys & Girls Indoor Track Team, which recently won the state championship for their division. Saint Joseph Elementary School and Monsignor Haddad Middle School are two of Needham's private schools, and the Connecticut School of Broadcasting is a technical school for students looking to enter the broadcasting industry. Also in Needham is the Franklin W. Olin College of Engineering, a small private institution with 370 students, nationally recognized as one of one of the top engineering schools in the nation with rigorous entrance requirements.

Needham is served by Boston Logan International Airport, 21 miles away. Several local airports within a 10-mile radius include Route 128 Airport, Cambridge Airport and Norwood Memorial Airport.

The climate of Needham sees temperatures very close to national averages, with a July average high of 84 degrees and a January average low of 19 degrees. Needham receives slightly more rainfall then the national average at 45 inches a year, and almost double the average snowfall—48 inches annually.

Rankings

Business/Finance Rankings

- The personal finance site NerdWallet analyzed 183 American metropolitan areas with populations over 250,000 and more than 15,000 businesses to rank where entrepreneurs find the most success. Criteria included area economy, annual income, housing cost, unemployment rate, and the success rate of area businesses. Boston* ranked #30. *www.nerdwallet.com, "Best Places to Start a Business," April 27, 2015*
- TransUnion ranked the nation's metro areas by average credit score, calculated on the VantageScore system, developed by the three major credit-reporting bureaus—TransUnion, Experian, and Equifax. The Boston* metro area was among the ten cities with the highest collective credit score, meaning that its residents posed the lowest average consumer credit risk. *www.usatoday.com, "Metro Areas' Average Credit Rating Revealed," February 7, 2013*
- Based on the U.S. Department of Labor's Occupational Information Network Data Collection Program, the Brookings Institution defined job opportunities for STEM workers at various levels of educational attainment. The Boston* metro area was placed among the ten large metro areas with the highest demand for high-level STEM knowledge. *www.brookings.edu, "The Hidden Stem Economy," June 10, 2013*
- 24/7 Wall Street used Brookings Institution research on 50 advanced industries to identify the proportion of workers in the nation's largest metropolitan areas that were employed in jobs requiring knowledge in the science, technology, engineering, or math (STEM) fields. The Boston* metro area was #8. *247wallst.com, "15 Cities with the Most High-Tech Jobs," March 13, 2015*
- Based on metro area social media reviews, the employment opinion group Glassdoor surveyed 50 of the largest U.S. metro areas and equally weighed cost of living, hiring opportunity, and job satisfaction to compose a list of "25 Best Cities for Jobs." The Boston* metro area was ranked #6 in overall job satisfaction. *www.glassdoor.com, "Best Cities for Jobs," May 19, 2015*
- In a survey of economic confidence in the nation's 50 largest metropolitan areas conducted January–December 2014, the Boston* metro area placed #13, according to Gallup's 2014 Economic Confidence Index. *Gallup, "San Jose and San Francisco Lead in Economic Confidence," March 19, 2015*
- The Brookings Institution ranked the 100 largest metro areas in the U.S. based on income inequality. Boston* was ranked #6 (#1 = greatest ineqality). Criteria: the "95/20 ratio," a figure representing the income at which a household earns more than 95 percent of all other households, divided by the income at which a household earns more than only 20 percent of all other households. *Brookings Institution, "Income Inequality, 100 Largest U.S. Metro Areas, 2007-2014," January 14, 2016*
- Payscale.com ranked the 20 largest metro areas in terms of wage growth. The Boston* metro area ranked #6. Criteria: private-sector wage growth between the 1st quarter of 2015 and the 1st quarter of 2016. *PayScale, "Wage Trends by Metro Area," 1st Quarter, 2016*
- Boston* was identified as one of America's most frugal metro areas by *Coupons.com.* The city ranked #20 out of 25. Criteria: online coupon usage. *Coupons.com, "Top 25 Most Frugal Cities of 2014," May 11, 2015*
- The Boston* metro area appeared on the Milken Institute "2015 Best Performing Cities" list. Rank: #51 out of 200 large metro areas. Criteria: job growth; wage and salary growth; high-tech output growth. *Milken Institute, "Best-Performing Cities 2015," December 2015*
- *Forbes* ranked the 200 most populous metro areas to determine the nation's "Best Places for Business and Careers." The Boston* metro area was ranked #55. Criteria: costs (business and living); job growth (past and projected); income growth; educational attainment (college and high school); projected economic growth; cultural and recreational opportunities; net migration patterns; number of highly ranked colleges. *Forbes, "The Best Places for Business and Careers 2015," July 29, 2015*

Dating/Romance Rankings

- CreditDonkey, a financial education website, sought out the ten best U.S. cities for newlyweds, considering the number of married couples, divorce rate, average credit score, and average number of hours worked per week in metro areas with a million or more residents. The Boston* metro area placed #3. *www.creditdonkey.com, "Study: Best Cities for Newlyweds," November 30, 2013*

Education Rankings

- The Boston* metro area was selected as one of the world's most inventive cities by *Forbes*. The area was ranked #7 out of 15. Criteria: patent applications per capita. *Forbes, "World's 15 Most Inventive Cities," July 9, 2013*

- Boston* was identified as one of America's "smartest" metropolitan areas by *The Business Journals*. The area ranked #4 out of 10. Criteria: percentage of adults (25 and older) with high school diplomas, bachelor's degrees and graduate degrees. *The Business Journals, "Where the Brainpower Is: Exclusive U.S. Rankings, Insights," February 27, 2014*

- Personal finance website *WalletHub* analyzed the 150 largest U.S. metropolitan statistical areas to determine where the most educated Americans are choosing to settle. Criteria: education quality and attainment gap; education levels; percentage of workers with degrees; public school rankings; quality and size of each metro area's universities. Boston* was ranked #7 (#1 = most educated city). *www.WalletHub.com, "2015's Most and Least Educated Cities*

- Boston* was identified as one of the "Smartest Cities in America" by the brain-training website *Lumosity* using data from three million of its own users. The metro area ranked #49 out of 50. Criteria: users' brain performance index scores, considering core cognitive abilities such as memory, processing speed, flexibility, attention and problem-solving. *Lumosity, " Smartest Cities in America," June 25, 2013*

Environmental Rankings

- The Boston* metro area came in at #107 for the relative comfort of its climate on Sperling's list of "chill cities," as measured by the Sperling Heat Index. All 361 metro areas are included. Criteria included daytime high temperatures, nighttime low temperatures, dew point, and relative humidity at the high temperatures. *www.bertsperling.com, "Sperling's Chill Cities," July 18, 2013*

- Sperling's BestPlaces assessed 379 metropolitan areas of the United States for the likelihood of dangerously extreme weather events or earthquakes. In general the Southeast and South-Central regions have the highest risk of weather extremes and earthquakes, while the Pacific Northwest enjoys the lowest risk. Of the least risky metropolitan areas, the Boston* metro area was ranked #243. *www.bestplaces.net, "Safest Places from Natural Disasters," April 2011*

- The U.S. Environmental Protection Agency (EPA) released a list of U.S. metropolitan areas with the most ENERGY STAR certified buildings in 2015. The Boston* metro area was ranked #11 out of 25. *U.S. Environmental Protection Agency, "Top Cities With the Most ENERGY STAR Certified Buildings in 2016," March 30, 2016*

Health/Fitness Rankings

- Analysts who tracked obesity rates in the nation's largest metro areas (populations above one million) found that the Boston* metro area was one of the ten major metros where residents were least likely to be obese, defined as a BMI score of 30 or above. *www.gallup.com, "Boulder, Colo., Residents Still Least Likely to Be Obese," April 4, 2014*

- Analysts who tracked obesity rates in 100 of the nation's most populous areas found that the Boston* metro area was one of the ten communities where residents were least likely to be obese, defined as a BMI score of 30 or above. *www.gallup.com, "Colorado Springs Residents Least Likely to Be Obese," May 28, 2015*

- For each of the 50 most populous metro areas in the United States, the American College of Sports Medicine's American Fitness Index evaluated infrastructure, community assets, and policies that encourage healthy and fit lifestyles, including preventive health behaviors, levels of chronic disease conditions, health care access, and community resources and policies that support physical activity. The Boston* metro area ranked #9 for "community fitness." *www.americanfitnessindex.org, "ACSM American Fitness Index Health and Community Fitness Status of the 50 Largest Metropolitan Areas," May 2015*

- *Business Insider* reported Trulia's analysis of the 100 largest U.S. metro areas to identify the nation's best cities for weight loss, based on healthful food options, access to outdoor activities, weight-loss centers, gyms, and opportunities to bike or walk to work. Boston* ranked #4. *Businessinsider.com, "These Are the Best US Cities for Weight loss," January 17, 2013*

- The Boston* metro area was identified as one of the worst cities for bed bugs in America by pest control company Orkin. The area ranked #25 out of 50 based on the number of bed bug treatments Orkin performed from January to December 2015. *Orkin, "Chicago Tops Bed Bug Cities List for Fourth Year in a Row," January 13, 2016*

- Boston* was identified as a "2016 Spring Allergy Capital." The area ranked #77 out of 100. Three groups of factors were used to identify the most severe cities for people with allergies during the spring season: annual pollen levels; medicine utilization; access to board-certified allergists. *Asthma and Allergy Foundation of America, "Spring Allergy Capitals 2016"*

- Boston* was identified as a "2015 Asthma Capital." The area ranked #74 out of the nation's 100 largest metropolitan areas. Criteria: estimated prevalence; self-reported prevalence; crude death rate for asthma; annual pollen score; annual air quality; public smoking laws; number of board-certified asthma specialists; school inhaler access laws; rescue medication use; controller medication use; ER visits for asthma; uninsured rate; poverty rate. *Asthma and Allergy Foundation of America, "Asthma Capitals 2015"*

- The Boston* metro area ranked #63 out of 190 in The Gallup-Healthways Well-Being Index. Criteria: purpose; social well being; financial health; community and physical health. Results are based on telephone interviews with adults, aged 18 and older, living in metropolitan areas in the 50 U.S. states and the District of Columbia. *Gallup-Healthways, "State of American Well-Being," February 23, 2016*

Real Estate Rankings

- Based on the home-price forecasts compiled by the real-estate valuation firm CoreLogic Case-Shiller, CNNMoney reported that in 2016, the Boston* metro area is expected to be one of the hottest housing markets in the U.S. Criteria: residential real estate prices. *money.cnn.com, "The 10 Hottest Housing Markets for 2016," December 3, 2015*

- The Boston* metro area appeared on Realtor.com's list of the hottest housing markets to watch in 2016. The area ranked #10. Criteria: strong housing growth; affordable prices; and fast-paced sales. *Realtor.com®, "Top 10 Hot Real Estate Markets to Watch in 2016," December 2, 2015*

- The Boston* metro area was identified as one of the 20 least affordable housing markets in the U.S. in 2015. The area ranked #17 out of 179 markets. Criteria: qualification for a mortgage loan on a typical home. *National Association of Realtors®, Affordability Index of Existing Single-Family Homes for Metropolitan Areas, 2015*

- Boston* was ranked #198 out of 225 metro areas in terms of housing affordability in 2015 by the National Association of Home Builders (#1 = most affordable). Criteria: the share of homes sold in that area affordable to a family earning the local median income, based on standard mortgage underwriting criteria. *National Association of Home Builders®, NAHB-Wells Fargo Housing Opportunity Index, 4th Quarter 2015*

Safety Rankings

- The National Insurance Crime Bureau ranked 380 metro areas in the U.S. in terms of per capita rates of vehicle theft. The Boston* metro area ranked #246 (#1 = highest rate). Criteria: number of vehicle theft offenses per 100,000 inhabitants in 2014. *National Insurance Crime Bureau, "Hot Spots 2014," June 24, 2015*

Seniors/Retirement Rankings

- From its Best Cities for Successful Aging indexes, the Milken Institute generated rankings for metropolitan areas, weighing data in eight categories—health care, wellness, living arrangements, transportation, financial characteristics, education and employment opportunities, community engagement, and overall livability. The Boston* metro area was ranked #4 overall in the large metro area category. *Milken Institute, "Best Cities for Successful Aging, 2014"*

Sports/Recreation Rankings

- According to the personal finance website NerdWallet, the Boston* metro area, at #11, is one of the nation's top dozen metro areas for sports fans. Criteria included the presence of all four major sports—MLB, NFL, NHL, and NBA, fan enthusiasm (as measured by game attendance), ticket affordability, and "sports culture," that is, number of sports bars. *www.nerdwallet.com, "Best Cities for Sports Fans," May 5, 2013*

Transportation Rankings

- Boston* was identified as one of the most congested metro areas in the U.S. The area ranked #6 out of 10. Criteria: yearly delay per auto commuter in hours. *Texas A&M Transportation Institute, "2015 Urban Mobility Scorecard," August 2015*
- The Boston* metro area appeared on *Forbes* list of places with the most extreme commutes. The metro area ranked #6 out of 10. Criteria: average travel time; percentage of mega commuters. Mega-commuters travel more than 90 minutes and 50 miles each way to work. *Forbes.com, "The Cities with the Most Extreme Commutes," March 5, 2013*

Miscellaneous Rankings

- The watchdog site Charity Navigator conducts an annual study of charities in the nation's major markets both to analyze statistical differences in their financial, accountability, and transparency practices and to track year-to-year variations in individual communities. The Boston* metro area was ranked #3 among the 30 metro markets in the rating dimension of Overall Score. *www.charitynavigator.org, "Metro Market Study 2015," June 5, 2015*
- The Harris Poll's Happiness Index survey revealed that of the top ten U.S. markets, the Boston* metro area residents ranked #9 in happiness. Criteria included strong assent to positive statements and strong disagreement with negative ones, and degree of agreement with a series of statements about respondents' personal relationships and general outlook. *www.harrisinteractive.com, "Dallas/Fort Worth Is "Happiest" City among America's Top Ten Markets," September 4, 2013*
- Energizer Personal Care, the makers of Edge® shave gel, in partnership with Sperling's BestPlaces, ranked 50 major metro areas in terms of everyday irritations. The Boston* metro area ranked #10 the 50 metro area most iritating to guys. Criteria: high male-to-female ratio; poor sports team performance and high ticket prices; slow traffic; lack of job availability; unaffordable housing; extreme weather; lack of nightlife and fitness options. *Energizer Personal Care, "Most Irritatng Cities for Guys," August 26, 2013*
- Mars Chocolate North America, the makers of COMBOS®, in partnership with Sperling's BestPlaces, ranked 50 major metro areas in terms of their "manliness." The Boston* metro area ranked #47. Criteria: number of professional sports teams; number of nearby NASCAR tracks and racing events; manly lifestyle; concentration of manly retail stores; manly occupations per capita; salty snack sales; "Board of Manliness" rankings. *Mars Chocolate North America, "America's Manliest Cities 2012"*
- The National Alliance to End Homelessness ranked the 100 most populous metro areas with the highest rate of homelessness. The Boston* metro area ranked #20. Criteria: number of homeless people per 10,000 population in 2011. *National Alliance to End Homelessness, The State of Homelessness in America 2012*

Needham is located within the Boston-Cambridge-Newton, MA-NH Metropolitan Statistical Area.

Business Environment

CITY FINANCES

City Government Finances

Component	2012 ($000)	2012 ($ per capita)
Total Revenues	152,229	5,269
Total Expenditures	162,183	5,614
Debt Outstanding	99,785	3,454
Cash and Securities[1]	155,792	5,393

Note: (1) Cash and security holdings of a government at the close of its fiscal year, including those of its dependent agencies, utilities, and liquor stores.
Source: U.S Census Bureau, State & Local Government Finances 2012

City Government Revenue by Source

Source	2012 ($000)	2012 ($ per capita)
General Revenue		
From Federal Government	435	15
From State Government	22,714	786
From Local Governments	0	0
Taxes		
Property	100,084	3,464
Sales and Gross Receipts	1,130	39
Personal Income	0	0
Corporate Income	0	0
Motor Vehicle License	0	0
Other Taxes	1,951	67
Current Charges	15,136	523
Liquor Store	0	0
Utility	5,443	188
Employee Retirement	3,475	120

Source: U.S Census Bureau, State & Local Government Finances 2012

City Government Expenditures by Function

Function	2012 ($000)	2012 ($ per capita)	2012 (%)
General Direct Expenditures			
Air Transportation	0	0	0.0
Corrections	0	0	0.0
Education	82,407	2,852	50.8
Employment Security Administration	0	0	0.0
Financial Administration	1,543	53	0.9
Fire Protection	5,886	203	3.6
General Public Buildings	7,976	276	4.9
Governmental Administration, Other	539	18	0.3
Health	502	17	0.3
Highways	3,393	117	2.0
Hospitals	0	0	0.0
Housing and Community Development	0	0	0.0
Interest on General Debt	2,878	99	1.7
Judicial and Legal	342	11	0.2
Libraries	1,366	47	0.8
Parking	155	5	0.0
Parks and Recreation	537	18	0.3
Police Protection	4,967	171	3.0
Public Welfare	60	2	0.0
Sewerage	3,692	127	2.2
Solid Waste Management	1,650	57	1.0
Veterans' Services	0	0	0.0
Liquor Store	0	0	0.0
Utility	3,406	117	2.1
Employee Retirement	10,077	348	6.2

Source: U.S Census Bureau, State & Local Government Finances 2012

DEMOGRAPHICS

Population Growth

Area	1990 Census	2000 Census	2010 Census	2014* Estimate	Population Growth (%) 1990-2014	Population Growth (%) 2010-2014
City	27,557	28,911	28,886	29,540	7.2	2.3
MSA[1]	4,133,895	4,391,344	4,552,402	4,650,876	12.5	2.2
U.S.	248,709,873	281,421,906	308,745,538	314,107,084	26.3	1.7

Note: (1) Figures cover the Boston-Cambridge-Newton, MA-NH Metropolitan Statistical Area—see Appendix B for areas included; (*) 2010-2014 5-year estimated population

Source: U.S. Census Bureau, 1990 Census, Census 2000, Census 2010, 2010-2014 American Community Survey 5-Year Estimates

Household Size

Area	Persons in Household (%) One	Two	Three	Four	Five	Six	Seven or More	Average Household Size
City	22.5	30.0	16.6	20.9	7.9	1.8	0.1	2.72
MSA[1]	28.3	32.3	16.4	14.5	5.7	1.7	0.8	2.54
U.S.	27.5	33.5	15.8	13.1	6.0	2.3	1.4	2.64

Note: (1) Figures cover the Boston-Cambridge-Newton, MA-NH Metropolitan Statistical Area—see Appendix B for areas included

Source: U.S. Census Bureau, 2010-2014 American Community Survey 5-Year Estimates

Race

Area	White Alone[2] (%)	Black Alone[2] (%)	Asian Alone[2] (%)	AIAN[3] Alone[2] (%)	NHOPI[4] Alone[2] (%)	Other Race Alone[2] (%)	Two or More Races (%)
City	88.4	2.1	6.7	0.0	0.0	0.2	2.5
MSA[1]	78.1	7.7	7.0	0.2	0.0	4.1	3.0
U.S.	73.8	12.6	5.0	0.8	0.2	4.7	2.9

Note: (1) Figures cover the Boston-Cambridge-Newton, MA-NH Metropolitan Statistical Area—see Appendix B for areas included; (2) Alone is defined as not being in combination with one or more other races; (3) American Indian and Alaska Native; (4) Native Hawaiian and Other Pacific Islander

Source: U.S. Census Bureau, 2010-2014 American Community Survey 5-Year Estimates

Hispanic or Latino Origin

Area	Total (%)	Mexican (%)	Puerto Rican (%)	Cuban (%)	Other (%)
City	2.5	0.3	0.7	0.3	1.3
MSA[1]	9.7	0.6	2.7	0.2	6.2
U.S.	16.9	10.8	1.6	0.6	3.8

Note: Persons of Hispanic or Latino origin can be of any race; (1) Figures cover the Boston-Cambridge-Newton, MA-NH Metropolitan Statistical Area—see Appendix B for areas included

Source: U.S. Census Bureau, 2010-2014 American Community Survey 5-Year Estimates

Ancestry

Area	German	Irish	English	American	Italian	Polish	French[2]	Scottish	Dutch
City	8.6	25.0	11.7	5.4	12.3	5.1	1.9	2.4	0.7
MSA[1]	6.3	23.4	10.5	4.5	14.6	3.7	5.6	2.5	0.6
U.S.	14.9	10.8	8.0	7.1	5.5	3.0	2.7	1.7	1.4

Note: Figures are the percentage of the total population reporting a particular ancestry. The nine most commonly reported ancestries in the U.S. are shown. Figures include multiple ancestries (e.g. if a person reported being Irish and Italian, they were included in both columns); (1) Figures cover the Boston-Cambridge-Newton, MA-NH Metropolitan Statistical Area—see Appendix B for areas included; (2) Excludes Basque

Source: U.S. Census Bureau, 2010-2014 American Community Survey 5-Year Estimates

Foreign-Born Population

Area	Percent of Population Born in								
	Any Foreign Country	Asia	Mexico	Europe	Carribean	Central America[2]	South America	Africa	Canada
City	12.7	5.3	0.3	4.8	0.3	0.2	0.6	0.4	0.8
MSA[1]	17.1	5.4	0.2	3.2	3.0	1.4	1.8	1.4	0.5
U.S.	13.1	3.8	3.7	1.5	1.2	1.0	0.9	0.6	0.3

Note: (1) Figures cover the Boston-Cambridge-Newton, MA-NH Metropolitan Statistical Area—see Appendix B for areas included; (2) Excludes Mexico.
Source: U.S. Census Bureau, 2010-2014 American Community Survey 5-Year Estimates

Marital Status

Area	Never Married	Now Married[2]	Separated	Widowed	Divorced
City	23.0	62.6	0.9	7.1	6.4
MSA[1]	36.4	47.4	1.8	5.4	8.9
U.S.	32.5	48.4	2.2	5.9	10.9

Note: Figures are percentages and cover the population 15 years of age and older; (1) Figures cover the Boston-Cambridge-Newton, MA-NH Metropolitan Statistical Area—see Appendix B for areas included; (2) Excludes separated
Source: U.S. Census Bureau, 2010-2014 American Community Survey 5-Year Estimates

Disability Status

Area	All Ages	Under 18 Years Old	18 to 64 Years Old	65 Years and Over
City	7.6	2.2	4.4	28.1
MSA[1]	10.3	3.8	7.9	33.0
U.S.	12.3	4.1	10.2	36.3

Note: Figures show percent of the civilian noninstitutionalized population that reported having a disability. Disability status is determined from from six types of difficulty: vision, hearing, cognitive, ambulatory, self-care, and independent living. For children under 5 years old, hearing and vision difficulty are used to determine disability status. For children between the ages of 5 and 14, disability status is determined from hearing, vision, cognitive, ambulatory, and self-care difficulties. For people aged 15 years and older, they are considered to have a disability if they have difficulty with any one of the six difficulty types; (1) Figures cover the Boston-Cambridge-Newton, MA-NH Metropolitan Statistical Area—see Appendix B for areas included.
Source: U.S. Census Bureau, 2010-2014 American Community Survey 5-Year Estimates

Age

Area	Percent of Population									Median Age
	Under Age 5	Age 5–19	Age 20–34	Age 35–44	Age 45–54	Age 55–64	Age 65–74	Age 75–84	Age 85+	
City	7.0	22.4	10.2	13.5	15.5	14.1	8.2	4.5	4.6	42.9
MSA[1]	5.5	18.6	21.4	13.2	15.1	12.5	7.3	4.3	2.1	38.7
U.S.	6.4	19.9	20.6	13.0	14.1	12.3	7.6	4.3	1.9	37.4

Note: (1) Figures cover the Boston-Cambridge-Newton, MA-NH Metropolitan Statistical Area—see Appendix B for areas included
Source: U.S. Census Bureau, 2010-2014 American Community Survey 5-Year Estimates

Gender

Area	Males	Females	Males per 100 Females
City	14,295	15,245	93.8
MSA[1]	2,254,371	2,396,505	94.1
U.S.	154,515,159	159,591,925	96.8

Note: (1) Figures cover the Boston-Cambridge-Newton, MA-NH Metropolitan Statistical Area—see Appendix B for areas included
Source: U.S. Census Bureau, 2010-2014 American Community Survey 5-Year Estimates

Religious Groups by Family

Area	Catholic	Baptist	Non-Den.	Methodist[2]	Lutheran	LDS[3]	Pente-costal	Presby-terian[4]	Muslim[5]	Judaism
MSA[1]	44.3	1.1	1.0	0.9	0.3	0.4	0.6	1.6	0.4	1.4
U.S.	19.1	9.3	4.0	4.0	2.3	2.0	1.9	1.6	0.8	0.7

Note: Figures are the number of adherents as a percentage of the total population; (1) Figures cover the Boston-Cambridge-Quincy, MA-NH Metropolitan Statistical Area—see Appendix B for areas included; (2) Methodist/Pietist; (3) Latter Day Saints; (4) Reformed; (5) Figures are estimates
Source: Association of Statisticians of American Religious Bodies, 2010 U.S. Religion Census: Religious Congregations & Membership Study

Religious Groups by Tradition

Area	Catholic	Evangelical Protestant	Mainline Protestant	Other Tradition	Black Protestant	Orthodox
MSA[1]	44.3	3.2	4.5	3.4	0.1	1.0
U.S.	19.1	16.2	7.3	4.3	1.6	0.3

Note: Figures are the number of adherents as a percentage of the total population; (1) Figures cover the Boston-Cambridge-Quincy, MA-NH Metropolitan Statistical Area—see Appendix B for areas included
Source: Association of Statisticians of American Religious Bodies, 2010 U.S. Religion Census: Religious Congregations & Membership Study

ECONOMY

Gross Metropolitan Product

Area	2013	2014	2015	2016	Rank[2]
MSA[1]	370.8	384.4	398.4	418.3	9

Note: Figures are in billions of dollars; (1) Figures cover the Boston-Cambridge-Newton, MA-NH Metropolitan Statistical Area—see Appendix B for areas included; (2) Rank is based on 2016 data and ranges from 1 to 381
Source: The U.S. Conference of Mayors, U.S. Metro Economies: GMP and Employment 2014-2016, June 2015

Economic Growth

Area	2011-13 (%)	2014 (%)	2015 (%)	2016 (%)	Rank[2]
MSA[1]	2.0	1.9	2.1	3.0	83
U.S.	2.2	2.4	2.3	2.9	–

Note: Figures are real gross metropolitan product (GMP) growth rates and represent annual average percent change; (1) Figures cover the Boston-Cambridge-Newton, MA-NH Metropolitan Statistical Area—see Appendix B for areas included; (2) Rank is based on 2016 data and ranges from 1 to 381
Source: The U.S. Conference of Mayors, U.S. Metro Economies: GMP and Employment 2014-2016, June 2015

Metropolitan Area Exports

Area	2009	2010	2011	2012	2013	2014	Rank[2]
MSA[1]	18,972.6	21,804.5	22,292.8	21,234.7	22,212.8	23,378.4	13

Note: Figures are in millions of dollars; (1) Figures cover the Boston-Cambridge-Newton, MA-NH Metropolitan Statistical Area—see Appendix B for areas included; (2) Rank is based on 2014 data and ranges from 1 to 385
Source: U.S. Department of Commerce, International Trade Administration, Office of Trade & Industry Information, Manufacturing & Services, data extracted March 10, 2016

Building Permits

Area	Single-Family			Multi-Family			Total		
	2014	2015p	Pct. Chg.	2014	2015p	Pct. Chg.	2014	2015p	Pct. Chg.
City	106	95	-10.4	0	0	-	106	95	-10.4
MSA[1]	4,991	4,779	-4.2	7,033	10,469	48.9	12,024	15,248	26.8
U.S.	640,300	690,800	7.9	411,800	487,600	18.4	1,052,100	1,178,400	12.0

Note: (1) Figures cover the Boston-Cambridge-Newton, MA-NH Metropolitan Statistical Area—see Appendix B for areas included; Figures represent new, privately-owned housing units authorized (unadjusted data); All permit data are based on estimates with imputation; (p) preliminary data.
Source: U.S. Census Bureau, Manufacturing, Mining, and Construction Statistics, Building Permits, 2014, 2015

Bankruptcy Filings

Area	Business Filings 2014	Business Filings 2015	Business Filings % Chg.	Nonbusiness Filings 2014	Nonbusiness Filings 2015	Nonbusiness Filings % Chg.
Norfolk County	42	45	7.1	778	699	-10.2
U.S.	26,983	24,735	-8.3	909,812	819,760	-9.9

Note: Business filings include Chapter 7, Chapter 11, Chapter 12, and Chapter 13; Nonbusiness filings include Chapter 7, Chapter 11, and Chapter 13
Source: Administrative Office of the U.S. Courts, Business and Nonbusiness Bankruptcy, County Cases Commenced by Chapter of the Bankruptcy Code, During the 12- Month Period Ending December 31, 2014 and Business and Nonbusiness Bankruptcy, County Cases Commenced by Chapter of the Bankruptcy Code, During the 12- Month Period Ending December 31, 2015

Housing Vacancy Rates

Area	Gross Vacancy Rate[2] (%)			Year-Round Vacancy Rate[3] (%)			Rental Vacancy Rate[4] (%)			Homeowner Vacancy Rate[5] (%)		
	2013	2014	2015	2013	2014	2015	2013	2014	2015	2013	2014	2015
MSA[1]	7.8	9.2	9.9	6.2	6.4	6.3	6.8	4.9	3.3	1.1	0.8	1.1
U.S.	13.6	13.4	12.9	10.7	10.4	10.0	8.3	7.6	7.1	2.0	1.9	1.8

Note: (1) Figures cover the Boston-Cambridge-Newton, MA-NH Metropolitan Statistical Area—see Appendix B for areas included; (2) The percentage of the total housing inventory that is vacant; (3) The percentage of the housing inventory (excluding seasonal units) that is year-round vacant; (4) The percentage of rental inventory that is vacant for rent; (5) The percentage of homeowner inventory that is vacant for sale
Source: U.S. Census Bureau, Housing Vacancies and Homeownership Annual Statistics: 2015

INCOME

Income

Area	Per Capita ($)	Median Household ($)	Average Household ($)
City	62,497	129,154	173,737
MSA[1]	39,572	74,494	101,462
U.S.	28,555	53,482	74,596

Note: (1) Figures cover the Boston-Cambridge-Newton, MA-NH Metropolitan Statistical Area—see Appendix B for areas included
Source: U.S. Census Bureau, 2010-2014 American Community Survey 5-Year Estimates

Household Income Distribution

Area	Percent of Households Earning							
	Under $15,000	$15,000 -24,999	$25,000 -34,999	$35,000 -49,999	$50,000 -74,999	$75,000 -99,000	$100,000 -149,999	$150,000 and up
City	6.3	2.7	2.5	5.8	10.2	11.7	17.1	43.8
MSA[1]	10.2	7.7	7.1	9.9	15.4	12.7	17.7	19.3
U.S.	12.5	10.7	10.2	13.5	17.8	12.2	13.0	10.0

Note: (1) Figures cover the Boston-Cambridge-Newton, MA-NH Metropolitan Statistical Area—see Appendix B for areas included
Source: U.S. Census Bureau, 2010-2014 American Community Survey 5-Year Estimates

Poverty Rate

Area	All Ages	Under 18 Years Old	18 to 64 Years Old	65 Years and Over
City	3.2	2.5	2.4	6.7
MSA[1]	10.4	12.8	9.9	8.8
U.S.	15.6	21.9	14.6	9.4

Note: Figures are percentage of people whose income during the past 12 months was below the poverty level; (1) Figures cover the Boston-Cambridge-Newton, MA-NH Metropolitan Statistical Area—see Appendix B for areas included
Source: U.S. Census Bureau, 2010-2014 American Community Survey 5-Year Estimates

EMPLOYMENT

Labor Force and Employment

Area	Civilian Labor Force			Workers Employed		
	Dec. 2014	Dec. 2015	% Chg.	Dec. 2014	Dec. 2015	% Chg.
City	15,071	14,915	-1.0	14,594	14,462	-0.9
NECTAD[1]	2,627,900	2,607,376	-0.7	2,512,440	2,500,406	-0.4
U.S.	155,521,000	157,245,000	1.1	147,190,000	149,703,000	1.7

Note: Data is not seasonally adjusted and covers workers 16 years of age and older; (1) Figures cover the Boston-Cambridge-Newton, MA New England City and Town Area Division—see Appendix B for areas included
Source: Bureau of Labor Statistics, Local Area Unemployment Statistics

Unemployment Rate

Area	2015											
	Jan.	Feb.	Mar.	Apr.	May	Jun.	Jul.	Aug.	Sep.	Oct.	Nov.	Dec.
City	3.5	3.3	3.1	2.7	3.1	3.5	3.4	3.1	3.2	3.2	3.2	3.0
NECTAD[1]	4.9	4.8	4.4	3.8	4.0	4.5	4.5	4.1	4.1	4.1	4.1	4.1
U.S.	6.1	5.8	5.6	5.1	5.3	5.5	5.6	5.2	4.9	4.8	4.8	4.8

Note: Data is not seasonally adjusted and covers workers 16 years of age and older; (1) Figures cover the Boston-Cambridge-Newton, MA New England City and Town Area Division—see Appendix B for areas included
Source: Bureau of Labor Statistics, Local Area Unemployment Statistics

Employment by Occupation

Occupation Classification	City (%)	MSA[1] (%)	U.S. (%)
Management, Business, Science, and Arts	65.4	46.6	36.4
Natural Resources, Construction, and Maintenance	2.3	6.4	9.0
Production, Transportation, and Material Moving	3.3	7.8	12.1
Sales and Office	19.9	22.6	24.4
Service	9.1	16.6	18.2

Note: Figures cover employed civilians 16 years of age and older; (1) Figures cover the Boston-Cambridge-Newton, MA-NH Metropolitan Statistical Area—see Appendix B for areas included
Source: U.S. Census Bureau, 2010-2014 American Community Survey 5-Year Estimates

Employment by Industry

Sector	NECTAD[1]		U.S.
	Number of Employees	Percent of Total	Percent of Total
Construction, Mining, and Logging	65,500	3.6	5.0
Education and Health Services	407,300	22.6	15.7
Financial Activities	152,500	8.4	5.7
Government	197,800	11.0	15.5
Information	57,000	3.1	1.9
Leisure and Hospitality	170,300	9.4	10.4
Manufacturing	82,100	4.5	8.6
Other Services	69,100	3.8	3.9
Professional and Business Services	342,600	19.0	13.9
Retail Trade	148,800	8.2	11.3
Transportation, Warehousing, and Utilities	43,500	2.4	3.9
Wholesale Trade	57,900	3.2	4.1

Note: Figures are non-farm employment as of December 2015. Figures are not seasonally adjusted and include workers 16 years of age and older; (1) Figures cover the Boston-Cambridge-Newton, MA New England City and Town Area Division—see Appendix B for areas included; n/a not available
Source: Bureau of Labor Statistics, Current Employment Statistics, Employment, Hours, and Earnings

Occupations with Greatest Projected Employment Growth: 2012 – 2022

Occupation[1]	2012 Employment	2022 Projected Employment	Numeric Employment Change	Percent Employment Change
Registered Nurses	78,750	93,310	14,560	18.5
Combined Food Preparation and Serving Workers, Including Fast Food	58,250	70,750	12,500	21.4
Retail Salespersons	109,830	119,160	9,330	8.5
Waiters and Waitresses	58,570	66,840	8,270	14.1
Personal Care Aides	21,690	29,940	8,250	38.1
Home Health Aides	19,760	27,740	7,980	40.4
Nursing Assistants	39,170	45,940	6,770	17.3
General and Operations Managers	55,960	62,610	6,650	11.9
Software Developers, Systems Software	30,030	36,290	6,260	20.8
Management Analysts	27,100	33,070	5,970	22.0

Note: Projections cover Massachusetts; (1) Sorted by numeric employment change
Source: www.projectionscentral.com, State Occupational Projections, 2012–2022 Long-Term Projections

Fastest Growing Occupations: 2012 – 2022

Occupation[1]	2012 Employment	2022 Projected Employment	Numeric Employment Change	Percent Employment Change
Skincare Specialists	2,520	3,840	1,320	52.6
Insulation Workers, Mechanical	240	350	110	49.4
Helpers—Brickmasons, Blockmasons, Stonemasons, and Tile and Marble Setters	550	790	240	44.0
Interpreters and Translators	2,200	3,130	930	42.1
Diagnostic Medical Sonographers	1,460	2,080	620	42.1
Animal Trainers	360	500	140	42.0
Home Health Aides	19,760	27,740	7,980	40.4
Information Security Analysts	2,640	3,660	1,020	39.1
Personal Care Aides	21,690	29,940	8,250	38.1
Helpers—Electricians	920	1,270	350	37.7

Note: Projections cover Massachusetts; (1) Sorted by percent employment change and excludes occupations with numeric employment change less than 100
Source: www.projectionscentral.com, State Occupational Projections, 2012–2022 Long-Term Projections

Average Wages

Occupation	$/Hr.	Occupation	$/Hr.
Accountants and Auditors	41.34	Maids and Housekeeping Cleaners	14.49
Automotive Mechanics	23.83	Maintenance and Repair Workers	22.61
Bookkeepers	22.55	Marketing Managers	68.56
Carpenters	31.66	Nuclear Medicine Technologists	36.73
Cashiers	11.36	Nurses, Licensed Practical	26.51
Clerks, General Office	18.73	Nurses, Registered	46.05
Clerks, Receptionists/Information	16.16	Nursing Assistants	14.83
Clerks, Shipping/Receiving	17.83	Packers and Packagers, Hand	12.24
Computer Programmers	48.37	Physical Therapists	40.26
Computer Systems Analysts	44.94	Postal Service Mail Carriers	25.82
Computer User Support Specialists	31.22	Real Estate Brokers	59.92
Cooks, Restaurant	14.10	Retail Salespersons	13.15
Dentists	82.28	Sales Reps., Exc. Tech./Scientific	40.34
Electrical Engineers	52.77	Sales Reps., Tech./Scientific	50.17
Electricians	33.33	Secretaries, Exc. Legal/Med./Exec.	22.35
Financial Managers	68.75	Security Guards	14.81
First-Line Supervisors/Managers, Sales	22.66	Surgeons	106.45
Food Preparation Workers	12.90	Teacher Assistants*	15.07
General and Operations Managers	71.11	Teachers, Elementary School*	35.84
Hairdressers/Cosmetologists	17.84	Teachers, Secondary School*	36.26
Internists	112.54	Telemarketers	16.27
Janitors and Cleaners	16.71	Truck Drivers, Heavy/Tractor-Trailer	24.97
Landscaping/Groundskeeping Workers	16.71	Truck Drivers, Light/Delivery Svcs.	17.56
Lawyers	78.96	Waiters and Waitresses	13.95

Note: Wage data covers the New England City and Town Area Division—see Appendix B for areas included; (*) Hourly wages for elementary/secondary school teachers and teacher assistants were calculated by the editors from annual wage data based on a 40 hour work week; n/a not available.
Source: Bureau of Labor Statistics, Metro Area Occupational Employment and Wage Estimates, May 2015

TAXES

State Corporate Income Tax Rates

State	Tax Rate (%)	Income Brackets ($)	Num. of Brackets	Financial Institution Tax Rate (%)[a]	Federal Income Tax Ded.
Massachusetts	8.0 (n)	Flat rate	1	9.0 (n)	No

Note: Tax rates as of January 1, 2016; (a) Rates listed are the corporate income tax rate applied to financial institutions or excise taxes based on income. Some states have other taxes based upon the value of deposits or shares; (n) Business and manufacturing corporations pay an additional tax of $2.60 per $1,000 on either taxable Massachusetts tangible property or taxable net worth allocable to the state (for intangible property corporations). The minimum tax for both corporations and financial institutions is $456.
Source: Federation of Tax Administrators, "State Corporate Income Tax Rates, 2016"

State Individual Income Tax Rates

State	Tax Rate (%)	Income Brackets ($)	Num. of Brackets	Personal Exempt. ($)[1] Single	Personal Exempt. ($)[1] Dependents	Fed. Inc. Tax Ded.
Massachusetts	5.10	Flat rate	1	4,400	1,000	No

Note: Tax rates as of January 1, 2016; Local- and county-level taxes are not included; n/a not applicable; (1) Married joint filers generally receive double the single exemption
Source: Federation of Tax Administrators, "State Individual Income Tax Rates, 2016"

Various State and Local Tax Rates

State	State and Local Sales and Use (%)	State Sales and Use (%)	Gasoline[1] (¢/gal.)	Cigarette[2] ($/pack)	Spirits[3] ($/gal.)	Wine[4] ($/gal.)	Beer[5] ($/gal.)
Massachusetts	6.25	6.25	26.54	3.51	4.05 (f)	0.55 (l)	0.11

Note: All tax rates as of January 1, 2016; (1) The American Petroleum Institute has developed a methodology for determining the average tax rate on a gallon of fuel. Rates may include any of the following: excise taxes, environmental fees, storage tank fees, other fees or taxes, general sales tax, and local taxes. In states where gasoline is subject to the general sales tax, or where the fuel tax is based on the average sale price, the average rate determined by API is sensitive to changes in the price of gasoline. States that fully or partially apply general sales taxes to gasoline: CA, CO, GA, IL, IN, MI, NY; (2) The federal excise tax of $1.0066 per pack and local taxes are not included; (3) Rates are those applicable to off-premise sales of 40% alcohol by volume (a.b.v.) distilled spirits in 750ml containers. Local excise taxes are excluded; (4) Rates are those applicable to off-premise sales of 11% a.b.v. non-carbonated wine in 750ml containers; (5) Rates are those applicable to off-premise sales of 4.7% a.b.v. beer in 12 ounce containers; (f) Different rates are also applicable according to alcohol content, place of production, size of container, or place purchased (on- or off-premise or onboard airlines); (l) Different rates also applicable according to alcohol content, place of production, size of container, place purchased (on- or off-premise or on board airlines) or type of wine (carbonated, vermouth, etc.).
Source: Tax Foundation, 2016 Facts & Figures: How Does Your State Compare?

State Business Tax Climate Index Rankings

State	Overall Rank	Corporate Tax Rank	Individual Income Tax Rank	Sales Tax Rank	Unemployment Insurance Tax Rank	Property Tax Rank
Massachusetts	25	39	13	18	47	46

Note: The index is a measure of how each state's tax laws affect economic performance. The lower the rank, the more favorable a state's tax system is for business. States without a given tax are given a ranking of 1. The scores/rankings for the District of Columbia do not affect other states. The 2016 index represents the tax climate as of July 1, 2015 (the beginning of Fiscal Year 2016).
Source: Tax Foundation, State Business Tax Climate Index 2016

TRANSPORTATION

Means of Transportation to Work

Area	Car/Truck/Van		Public Transportation			Bicycle	Walked	Other Means	Worked at Home
	Drove Alone	Car-pooled	Bus	Subway	Railroad				
City	72.5	6.6	0.4	1.3	8.5	0.4	1.9	0.8	7.7
MSA[1]	68.5	7.4	4.1	5.8	2.0	0.9	5.3	1.4	4.6
U.S.	76.4	9.6	2.6	1.8	0.6	0.6	2.8	1.3	4.4

Note: Figures are percentages and cover workers 16 years of age and older; (1) Figures cover the Boston-Cambridge-Newton, MA-NH Metropolitan Statistical Area—see Appendix B for areas included
Source: U.S. Census Bureau, 2010-2014 American Community Survey 5-Year Estimates

Travel Time to Work

Area	Less Than 10 Minutes	10 to 19 Minutes	20 to 29 Minutes	30 to 44 Minutes	45 to 59 Minutes	60 to 89 Minutes	90 Minutes or More
City	9.2	23.7	17.6	25.4	15.4	6.9	1.8
MSA[1]	10.2	23.8	18.8	23.9	11.2	9.3	2.9
U.S.	13.3	29.6	21.0	20.2	7.7	5.7	2.6

Note: Figures are percentages and include workers 16 years old and over; (1) Figures cover the Boston-Cambridge-Newton, MA-NH Metropolitan Statistical Area—see Appendix B for areas included
Source: U.S. Census Bureau, 2010-2014 American Community Survey 5-Year Estimates

Freeway Travel Time Index

Area	1985	1990	1995	2000	2005	2010	2014
Urban Area Rank[1,2]	11	9	13	9	13	14	17
Urban Area Index[1]	1.16	1.20	1.22	1.28	1.29	1.28	1.29
Average Index[3]	1.09	1.11	1.14	1.17	1.20	1.19	1.20

Note: Freeway Travel Time Index—the ratio of travel time in the peak period to the travel time at free-flow conditions. For example, a value of 1.30 indicates a 20-minute free-flow trip takes 26 minutes in the peak (20 minutes x 1.30 = 26 minutes); (1) Covers the Boston MA-NH-RI urban area; (2) Rank is based on 101 urban areas (#1 = highest travel time index); (3) Average of 101 urban areas
Source: Texas Transportation Institute, 2015 Urban Mobility Scorecard, August 2015

Freeway Commuter Stress Index

Area	1985	1990	1995	2000	2005	2010	2014
Urban Area Rank[1,2]	12	9	10	8	11	12	14
Urban Area Index[1]	1.25	1.29	1.31	1.37	1.38	1.37	1.38
Average Index[3]	1.13	1.16	1.19	1.22	1.25	1.24	1.25

Note: The Freeway Commuter Stress Index is the same as the Freeway Travel Time Index (see table above) except that it includes only the travel in the peak directions during the peak periods; the TTI includes travel in all directions during the peak period. Thus, the CSI is more indicative of the work trip experienced by each commuter on a daily basis. (1) Covers the Boston MA-NH-RI urban area; (2) Rank is based on 101 urban areas (#1 = highest stress index); (3) Average of 101 urban areas

Source: Texas Transportation Institute, 2015 Urban Mobility Scorecard, August 2015

Living Environment

COST OF LIVING

Cost of Living Index

Composite Index	Groceries	Housing	Utilities	Trans-portation	Health Care	Misc. Goods/ Services
144.5	105.0	194.5	151.8	109.8	130.4	129.1

Note: The Cost of Living Index measures regional differences in the cost of consumer goods and services, excluding taxes and non-consumer expenditures, for professional and managerial households in the top income quintile. It is based on more than 50,000 prices covering almost 60 different items for which prices are collected three times a year by chambers of commerce, economic development organizations or university applied economic centers in each participating urban area. The numbers shown should be read as a percentage above or below the national average of 100. For example, a value of 115.4 in the groceries column indicates that grocery prices are 15.4% higher than the national average. Small differences in the index numbers should not be interpreted as significant; Figures cover the Boston MA urban area.
Source: The Council for Community and Economic Research, ACCRA Cost of Living Index, 2015

Grocery Prices

Area[1]	T-Bone Steak ($/pound)	Frying Chicken ($/pound)	Whole Milk ($/half gal.)	Eggs ($/dozen)	Orange Juice ($/64 oz.)	Coffee ($/11.5 oz.)
City[2]	10.99	1.78	2.21	2.39	3.63	4.46
Avg.	10.99	1.43	2.25	2.26	3.58	4.48
Min.	7.16	0.98	1.30	1.35	2.88	2.98
Max.	14.13	2.43	3.85	4.81	6.39	7.56

Note: (1) Values for the local area are compared with the average, minimum and maximum values for all 292 areas in the Cost of Living Index; (2) Figures cover the Boston MA urban area; **T-Bone Steak** *(price per pound);* **Frying Chicken** *(price per pound, whole fryer);* **Whole Milk** *(half gallon carton);* **Eggs** *(price per dozen, Grade A, large);* **Orange Juice** *(64 oz. Tropicana or Florida Natural);* **Coffee** *(11.5 oz. can, vacuum-packed, Maxwell House, Hills Bros, or Folgers).*
Source: The Council for Community and Economic Research, ACCRA Cost of Living Index, 2015

Housing and Utility Costs

Area[1]	New Home Price ($)	Apartment Rent ($/month)	All Electric ($/month)	Part Electric ($/month)	Other Energy ($/month)	Telephone ($/month)
City[2]	553,220	2,262	-	151.70	140.48	34.64
Avg.	312,874	945	179.30	95.07	72.96	28.11
Min.	178,682	479	116.28	43.14	26.46	10.01
Max.	1,472,476	3,984	504.25	189.44	421.11	43.06

Note: (1) Values for the local area are compared with the average, minimum and maximum values for all 292 areas in the Cost of Living Index; (2) Figures cover the Boston MA urban area; **New Home Price** *(2,400 sf living area, 8,000 sf lot, in urban area with full utilities);* **Apartment Rent** *(950 sf 2 bedroom/1.5 or 2 bath, unfurnished, excluding all utilities except water);* **All Electric** *(average monthly cost for an all-electric home);* **Part Electric** *(average monthly cost for a part-electric home);* **Other Energy** *(average monthly cost for natural gas, fuel oil, coal, wood, and any other forms of energy except electricity);* **Telephone** *(price includes basic monthly rate for a private residential line plus additional local usage charges incurred by a family of four).*
Source: The Council for Community and Economic Research, ACCRA Cost of Living Index, 2015

Health Care, Transportation, and Other Costs

Area[1]	Doctor ($/visit)	Dentist ($/visit)	Optometrist ($/visit)	Gasoline ($/gallon)	Beauty Salon ($/visit)	Men's Shirt ($)
City[2]	165.53	120.84	109.50	2.42	51.60	31.55
Avg.	105.15	89.02	99.78	2.38	35.30	28.10
Min.	66.87	56.09	48.53	1.95	18.91	13.38
Max.	182.34	150.36	228.33	4.09	67.91	63.80

Note: (1) Values for the local area are compared with the average, minimum and maximum values for all 292 areas in the Cost of Living Index; (2) Figures cover the Boston MA urban area; **Doctor** *(general practitioners routine exam of an established patient);* **Dentist** *(adult teeth cleaning and periodic oral examination);* **Optometrist** *(full vision eye exam for established adult patient);* **Gasoline** *(one gallon regular unleaded, national brand, including all taxes, cash price at self-service pump if available);* **Beauty Salon** *(woman's shampoo, trim, and blow-dry);* **Men's Shirt** *(cotton/polyester dress shirt, pinpoint weave, long sleeves).*
Source: The Council for Community and Economic Research, ACCRA Cost of Living Index, 2015

HOUSING

House Price Index (HPI)

Area	National Ranking[2]	Quarterly Change (%)	One-Year Change (%)	Five-Year Change (%)
MD[1]	109	1.10	5.20	14.80
U.S.[3]	–	1.45	5.76	22.85

Note: The HPI is a weighted repeat sales index. It measures average price changes in repeat sales or refinancings on the same properties. This information is obtained by reviewing repeat mortgage transactions on single-family properties whose mortgages have been purchased or securitized by Fannie Mae or Freddie Mac in January 1975; (1) Boston Metropolitan Division—see Appendix B for areas included; (2) Rankings are based on annual percentage change for all metro areas containing at least 15,000 transactions over the last 10 years and ranges from 1 to 266; (3) figures based on a weighted average of Census Division estimates using a seasonally adjusted, purchase-only index; all figures are for the period ending December 31, 2015
Source: Federal Housing Finance Agency, House Price Index, February 25, 2016

Median Single-Family Home Prices

Area	2013	2014	2015[p]	Percent Change 2014 to 2015
MSA[1]	375.9	389.8	403.9	3.6
U.S. Average	197.4	208.9	223.9	7.2

Note: Figures are median sales prices of existing single-family homes in thousands of dollars; (p) preliminary; n/a not available; (1) Boston-Cambridge-Newton, MA-NH Metropolitan Statistical Area—see Appendix B for areas included
Source: National Association of Realtors, Median Sales Price of Existing Single-Family Homes for Metropolitan Areas, 4th Quarter 2015

Qualifying Income Based on Median Sales Price of Existing Single-Family Homes

Area	With 5% Down ($)	With 10% Down ($)	With 20% Down ($)
MSA[1]	87,549	82,941	73,725
U.S. Average	49,535	46,928	41,714

Note: Figures are preliminary; Qualifying income is based on a mortgage rate of 4.1%. Monthly principal and interest payment is limited to 25% of income; n/a not available; (1) Boston-Cambridge-Newton, MA-NH Metropolitan Statistical Area—see Appendix B for areas included
Source: National Association of Realtors, Qualifying Income Based on Median Sales Price of Existing Single-Family Homes for Metropolitan Areas, 4th Quarter 2015

Median Apartment Condo-Coop Home Prices

Area	2013	2014	2015[p]	Percent Change 2014 to 2015
MSA[1]	327.5	339.2	352.6	4.0
U.S. Average	194.9	204.3	210.7	3.1

Note: Figures are median sales prices of existing apartment condo-coop homes in thousands of dollars; (p) preliminary; n/a not available; (1) Boston-Cambridge-Newton, MA-NH Metropolitan Statistical Area—see Appendix B for areas included
Source: National Association of Realtors, Median Sales Price of Existing Apartment Condo-Coop Homes for Metropolitan Areas, 4th Quarter 2015

Gross Monthly Rent

Area	Under $200	$200 -299	$300 -499	$500 -749	$750 -999	$1,000 -1,499	$1,500 and up	Median ($)
City	3.0	9.4	11.3	2.9	4.8	22.1	46.5	1,432
MSA[1]	2.0	5.3	6.5	7.1	13.0	33.9	32.1	1,219
U.S.	1.5	3.2	7.4	21.0	24.1	26.9	15.9	920

Note: Figures are percentages except for Median; Gross rent is the contract rent plus the estimated average monthly cost of utilities (electricity, gas, and water and sewer) and fuels (oil, coal, kerosene, wood, etc.) if these are paid by the renter (or paid for the renter by someone else); (1) Figures cover the Boston-Cambridge-Newton, MA-NH Metropolitan Statistical Area—see Appendix B for areas included
Source: U.S. Census Bureau, 2010-2014 American Community Survey 5-Year Estimates

Homeownership Rate

Area	2008 (%)	2009 (%)	2010 (%)	2011 (%)	2012 (%)	2013 (%)	2014 (%)	2015 (%)
MSA[1]	66.2	65.5	66.0	65.5	66.0	66.3	62.8	59.3
U.S.	67.8	67.4	66.9	66.1	65.4	65.1	64.5	63.7

Note: (1) Figures cover the Boston-Cambridge-Newton, MA-NH Metropolitan Statistical Area—see Appendix B for areas included
Source: U.S. Census Bureau, Housing Vacancies and Homeownership Annual Statistics: 2015

Year Housing Structure Built

Area	2010 or Later	2000 -2009	1990 -1999	1980 -1989	1970 -1979	1960 -1969	1950 -1959	1940 -1949	Before 1940	Median Year
City	1.7	10.5	4.2	8.6	7.6	11.3	20.6	9.5	26.1	1957
MSA[1]	0.7	8.0	7.2	10.7	11.0	10.5	11.1	5.6	35.1	1958
U.S.	1.0	14.9	13.9	13.8	15.8	11.0	10.8	5.4	13.3	1976

Note: Figures are percentages except for Median Year; (1) Figures cover the Boston-Cambridge-Newton, MA-NH Metropolitan Statistical Area—see Appendix B for areas included
Source: U.S. Census Bureau, 2010-2014 American Community Survey 5-Year Estimates

HEALTH

Health Risk Data

Category	MD[1] (%)	U.S. (%)
Adults aged 18–64 who have any kind of health care coverage	93.4	79.6
Adults who reported being in good or excellent health	87.1	83.1
Adults who are current smokers	14.9	19.6
Adults who are heavy drinkers[2]	8.1	6.1
Adults who are binge drinkers[3]	20.5	16.9
Adults who are overweight (BMI 25.0 - 29.9)	35.1	35.8
Adults who are obese (BMI 30.0 - 99.8)	21.1	27.6
Adults who participated in any physical activities in the past month	80.1	77.1
Adults 50+ who have ever had a sigmoidoscopy or colonoscopy	74.8	67.3
Women aged 40+ who have had a mammogram within the past two years	85.3	74.0
Men aged 40+ who have had a PSA test within the past two years	43.3	45.2
Adults aged 65+ who have had flu shot within the past year	61.9	60.1
Adults who always wear a seatbelt	89.1	93.8

Note: Data as of 2012 unless otherwise noted; (1) Figures cover the Boston, MA Metropolitan Division—see Appendix B for areas included; (2) Heavy drinkers are classified as males having more than two drinks per day or females having more than one drink per day; (3) Binge drinkers are classified as males having five or more drinks on one occasion or females having four or more drinks on one occasion
Source: Centers for Disease Control and Prevention, Behaviorial Risk Factor Surveillance System, SMART: Selected Metropolitan/Micropolitan Area Risk Trends, 2012 (Note: the CDC has discontinued this dataset but will be releasing a replacement in mid-2016)

Chronic Health Indicators

Category	MD[1] (%)	U.S. (%)
Adults who have ever been told they had a heart attack	3.6	4.5
Adults who have ever been told they had a stroke	1.5	2.9
Adults who have been told they currently have asthma	9.2	8.9
Adults who have ever been told they have arthritis	21.1	25.7
Adults who have ever been told they have diabetes[2]	7.3	9.7
Adults who have ever been told they had skin cancer	5.1	5.7
Adults who have ever been told they had any other types of cancer	5.8	6.5
Adults who have ever been told they have COPD	4.4	6.2
Adults who have ever been told they have kidney disease	1.5	2.5
Adults who have ever been told they have a form of depression	16.6	18.0

Note: Data as of 2012 unless otherwise noted; (1) Figures cover the Boston, MA Metropolitan Division—see Appendix B for areas included; (2) Figures do not include pregnancy-related, borderline, or pre-diabetes
Source: Centers for Disease Control and Prevention, Behaviorial Risk Factor Surveillance System, SMART: Selected Metropolitan/Micropolitan Area Risk Trends, 2012 (Note: the CDC has discontinued this dataset but will be releasing a replacement in mid-2016)

Mortality Rates for the Top 10 Causes of Death in the U.S.

ICD-10[a] Sub-Chapter	ICD-10[a] Code	Age-Adjusted Mortality Rate[1] per 100,000 population	
		County[2]	U.S.
Malignant neoplasms	C00-C97	154.9	163.6
Ischaemic heart diseases	I20-I25	78.4	102.2
Other forms of heart disease	I30-I51	44.2	50.1
Chronic lower respiratory diseases	J40-J47	27.4	41.4
Organic, including symptomatic, mental disorders	F01-F09	52.8	38.5
Cerebrovascular diseases	I60-I69	24.2	36.5
Other external causes of accidental injury	W00-X59	25.2	27.5
Other degenerative diseases of the nervous system	G30-G31	18.4	26.3
Diabetes mellitus	E10-E14	12.5	21.1
Hypertensive diseases	I10-I15	10.2	19.7

Note: (a) ICD-10 = International Classification of Diseases 10th Revision; (1) Mortality rates are a three year average covering 2012-2014; (2) Figures cover Norfolk County.
Source: Centers for Disease Control and Prevention, National Center for Health Statistics. Underlying Cause of Death 1999-2014 on CDC WONDER Online Database, released 2015.

Mortality Rates for Selected Causes of Death

ICD-10[a] Sub-Chapter	ICD-10[a] Code	Age-Adjusted Mortality Rate[1] per 100,000 population	
		County[2]	U.S.
Assault	X85-Y09	1.2	5.1
Diseases of the liver	K70-K76	10.0	13.5
Human immunodeficiency virus (HIV) disease	B20-B24	0.8	2.1
Influenza and pneumonia	J09-J18	14.6	15.2
Intentional self-harm	X60-X84	8.0	12.7
Malnutrition	E40-E46	Unreliable	0.9
Obesity and other hyperalimentation	E65-E68	1.4	1.9
Renal failure	N17-N19	12.8	13.0
Transport accidents	V01-V99	5.3	11.6
Viral hepatitis	B15-B19	1.1	2.1

Note: (a) ICD-10 = International Classification of Diseases 10th Revision; (1) Mortality rates are a three year average covering 2012-2014; (2) Figures cover Norfolk County; Data are Suppressed when the data meet the criteria for confidentiality constraints; Mortality rates are flagged as Unreliable when the rate would be calculated with a numerator of 20 or less.
Source: Centers for Disease Control and Prevention, National Center for Health Statistics. Underlying Cause of Death 1999-2014 on CDC WONDER Online Database, released 2015.

Health Insurance Coverage

Area	With Health Insurance	With Private Health Insurance	With Public Health Insurance	Without Health Insurance	Population Under Age 18 Without Health Insurance
City	98.7	92.1	20.6	1.3	0.3
MSA[1]	95.7	77.0	30.0	4.3	1.7
U.S.	85.8	65.8	31.1	14.2	7.1

Note: Figures are percentages that cover the civilian noninstitutionalized population; (1) Figures cover the Boston-Cambridge-Newton, MA-NH Metropolitan Statistical Area—see Appendix B for areas included
Source: U.S. Census Bureau, 2010-2014 American Community Survey 5-Year Estimates

Number of Medical Professionals

Area	MDs[3]	DOs[3,4]	Dentists	Podiatrists	Chiropractors	Optometrists
County[1] (number)	4,626	73	790	48	173	137
County[1] (rate[2])	671.7	10.6	114.1	6.9	25.0	19.8
U.S. (rate[2])	272.5	20.9	64.7	5.8	25.9	15.2

Note: Data as of 2014 unless noted; (1) Data covers Norfolk County; (2) Rate per 100,000 population; (3) Data as of 2013 and includes all active, non-federal physicians; (4) Doctor of Osteopathic Medicine
Source: U.S. Department of Health and Human Services, Health Resources and Services Administration, Bureau of Health Professions, Area Resource File (ARF) 2014-2015

Best Hospitals

According to *U.S. News,* the Boston, MA metro area is home to seven of the best hospitals in the U.S.: **Beth Israel Deaconess Medical Center** (1 specialty); **Brigham and Women's Hospital** (Honor Roll/13 specialties); **Dana-Farber/Brigham and Women's Cancer Center** (13 specialties); **Massachusetts Eye and Ear Infirmary, Massachusetts General Hospital** (2 specialties); **Massachusetts General Hospital** (Honor Roll/16 specialties); **New England Baptist Hospital** (1 specialty); **Spaulding Rehabilitation Hospital, Massachusetts General Hospital** (1 specialty). The hospitals listed were nationally ranked in at least one adult specialty. Only 137 hospitals nationwide were nationally ranked in one or more specialties. Fifteen hospitals in the U.S. made the Honor Roll with high scores in at least six specialties. *U.S. News Online, "America's Best Children's Hospitals 2015-16"*

According to *U.S. News,* the Boston, MA metro area is home to three of the best children's hospitals in the U.S.: **Boston Children's Hospital** (Honor Roll/10 specialties); **Dana-Farber Boston Children's Cancer and Blood Disorders Ctr** (10 specialties); **Massachusetts General Hospital for Children** (3 specialties). The hospitals listed were highly ranked in at least one pediatric specialty. Eighty-three children's hospitals in the U.S. were nationally ranked in at least one specialty. Twelve children's hospitals in the U.S. made the Honor Roll with high scores in at least three specialties. *U.S. News Online, "America's Best Children's Hospitals 2015-16"*

EDUCATION

Public School District Statistics

District Name	Schls	Pupils	Pupil/ Teacher Ratio	Minority Pupils[1] (%)	Free Lunch Eligible[2] (%)	IEP[3] (%)
Needham	8	5,523	15.5	18.4	5.1	14.9

Note: Table includes school districts with 100 or more students; (1) Percentage of students that are not non-Hispanic white; (2) Percentage of students that are eligible for the free lunch program; (3) Percentage of students that have an Individualized Education Program.

Source: U.S. Department of Education, National Center for Education Statistics, Common Core of Data, Local Education Agency (School District) Universe Survey: School Year 2013-2014; U.S. Department of Education, National Center for Education Statistics, Common Core of Data, Public Elementary/Secondary School Universe Survey: School Year 2013-2014

Best High Schools

According to *U.S. News,* Needham is home to one of the best high schools in the U.S.: **Needham High School** (#324); Nearly 20,000 schools were ranked based on their performance on state assessments and how well they prepare students for college. Schools with the highest unrounded College Readiness Index values were numerically ranked from No. 1 to No. 500 and were the gold medal winners. *U.S. News & World Report, "Best High Schools 2015"*

Highest Level of Education

Area	Less than H.S.	H.S. Diploma	Some College, No Deg.	Associate Degree	Bachelor's Degree	Master's Degree	Prof. School Degree	Doctorate Degree
City	2.1	9.9	8.8	5.1	32.4	26.4	10.0	5.3
MSA[1]	9.2	24.0	15.5	7.2	24.5	13.5	3.2	2.8
U.S.	13.7	28.0	21.2	7.9	18.3	7.8	2.0	1.3

Note: Figures cover persons age 25 and over; (1) Figures cover the Boston-Cambridge-Newton, MA-NH Metropolitan Statistical Area—see Appendix B for areas included

Source: U.S. Census Bureau, 2010-2014 American Community Survey 5-Year Estimates

Educational Attainment by Race

Area	High School Graduate or Higher (%)					Bachelor's Degree or Higher (%)				
	Total	White	Black	Asian	Hisp.[2]	Total	White	Black	Asian	Hisp.[2]
City	97.9	98.3	91.8	96.7	94.0	74.1	74.9	26.5	79.1	65.5
MSA[1]	90.8	93.5	82.3	84.2	69.1	44.0	46.2	23.8	58.2	19.7
U.S.	86.3	88.4	83.2	85.8	64.1	29.3	30.6	19.0	50.9	13.9

Note: Figures shown cover persons 25 years old and over; (1) Figures cover the Boston-Cambridge-Newton, MA-NH Metropolitan Statistical Area—see Appendix B for areas included; (2) People of Hispanic origin can be of any race

Source: U.S. Census Bureau, 2010-2014 American Community Survey 5-Year Estimates

School Enrollment by Grade and Control

Area	Preschool (%)		Kindergarten (%)		Grades 1 - 4 (%)		Grades 5 - 8 (%)		Grades 9 - 12 (%)	
	Public	Private	Public	Private	Public	Private	Public	Private	Public	Private
City	20.0	80.0	100.0	0.0	82.3	17.7	79.4	20.6	79.7	20.3
MSA[1]	42.8	57.2	86.5	13.5	90.9	9.1	89.4	10.6	86.9	13.1
U.S.	57.4	42.6	87.8	12.2	89.8	10.2	89.9	10.1	90.6	9.4

Note: Figures shown cover persons 3 years old and over; (1) Figures cover the Boston-Cambridge-Newton, MA-NH Metropolitan Statistical Area—see Appendix B for areas included
Source: U.S. Census Bureau, 2010-2014 American Community Survey 5-Year Estimates

Average Salaries of Public School Classroom Teachers

Area	2013-14		2014-15		Percent Change 2013-14 to 2014-15	Percent Change 2004-05 to 2014-15
	Dollars	Rank[1]	Dollars	Rank[1]		
Massachusetts	73,195	2	74,805	3	2.20	36.8
U.S. Average	56,610	–	57,379	–	1.36	20.8

Note: (1) State rank ranges from 1 to 51 where 1 indicates highest salary.
Source: National Education Association, Rankings & Estimates: Rankings of the States 2014 and Estimates of School Statistics 2015, March 2015

Higher Education

Four-Year Colleges			Two-Year Colleges			Medical Schools[1]	Law Schools[2]	Voc/ Tech[3]
Public	Private Non-profit	Private For-profit	Public	Private Non-profit	Private For-profit			
0	1	0	0	0	0	0	0	0

Note: Figures cover institutions located within the city limits and include main campuses only; (1) includes schools accredited by the Liaison Committee on Medical Education and the American Osteopathic Association's Commission on Osteopathic College Accreditation; (2) includes ABA-accredited schools, schools with provisional ABA accreditation, and state accredited schools; (3) includes all schools with programs that are less than 2 years.
Source: National Center for Education Statistics, Integrated Postsecondary Education System (IPEDS), 2014-15; Association of American Medical Colleges, Member List, March 21, 2016; American Osteopathic Association, Member List, March 21, 2016; Law School Admission Council, Official Guide to ABA-Approved Law Schools Online, March 21, 2016; Wikipedia, List of Medical Schools in the United States, March 21, 2016; Wikipedia, List of Law Schools in the United States, March 21, 2016

According to *U.S. News & World Report,* the Boston, MA metro division is home to three of the best national universities in the U.S.: **Boston College** (#30 tie); **Boston University** (#41 tie); **Northeastern University** (#47 tie). The indicators used to capture academic quality fall into a number of categories: assessment by administrators at peer institutions; retention of students; faculty resources; student selectivity; financial resources; alumni giving; high school counselor ratings of colleges; and graduation rate. *U.S. News & World Report, "America's Best Colleges 2016"*

According to *U.S. News & World Report,* the Boston, MA metro division is home to one of the best liberal arts colleges in the U.S.: **Wellesley College** (#4 tie). The indicators used to capture academic quality fall into a number of categories: assessment by administrators at peer institutions; retention of students; faculty resources; student selectivity; financial resources; alumni giving; high school counselor ratings of colleges; and graduation rate. *U.S. News & World Report, "America's Best Colleges 2016"*

According to *U.S. News & World Report,* the Boston, MA metro division is home to two of the top 100 law schools in the U.S.: **Boston University, School of Law** (#20 tie); **Northeastern University, School of Law** (#82 tie). The rankings are based on a weighted average of 12 measures of quality: peer assessment score; assessment score by lawyers/judges; median LSAT scores; median undergrad GPA; acceptance rate; employment rates for graduates; placement success; bar passage rate; faculty resources; expenditures per student; student/faculty ratio; and library resources. *U.S. News & World Report, "America's Best Graduate Schools, Law, 2017"*

According to *U.S. News & World Report,* the Boston, MA metro division is home to three of the top 75 medical schools for research in the U.S.: **Harvard University, Medical School** (#1); **Boston University, School of Medicine** (#29 tie); **Tufts University, School of Medicine** (#47 tie). The rankings are based on a weighted average of 11 measures of quality: quality assessment; peer assessment score; assessment score by residency directors; research activity; total research activity; average research activity per faculty member; student

selectivity; median MCAT total score; median undergraduate GPA; acceptance rate; and faculty resources. *U.S. News & World Report, "America's Best Graduate Schools, Medical, 2017"*

According to *U.S. News & World Report,* the Boston, MA metro division is home to five of the top 75 business schools in the U.S.: **Harvard University, Business School** (#1); **Boston University, Questrom School of Business** (#41 tie); **Boston College, Carroll School of Management** (#50); **Northeastern University, D'Amore-McKim School of Business** (#57 tie); **Babson College, F.W. Olin Graduate School of Business** (#60 tie). The rankings are based on a weighted average of the following nine measures: quality assessment; peer assessment; recruiter assessment; placement success; mean starting salary and bonus; student selectivity; mean GMAT and GRE scores; mean undergraduate GPA; and acceptance rate. *U.S. News & World Report, "America's Best Graduate Schools, Business, 2017"*

PRESIDENTIAL ELECTION

2012 Presidential Election Results

Area	Obama (%)	Romney (%)	Other (%)
Norfolk County	57.4	41.3	1.3
U.S.	51.0	47.2	1.8

Note: Results may not add to 100% due to rounding
Source: Dave Leip's Atlas of U.S. Presidential Elections

EMPLOYERS

Major Employers

Company Name	Industry
Beth Israel Deaconess Medical Center	General medical and surgical hospitals
Blue Cross Blue Shield of Massachusetts	Health insurance
Boston University	Colleges and universities
Children's Hospital Corporation	Specialty hospitals, except psychiatric
City of Lowell	City and town managers' office
EMC Corp.	Data management
Federal Deposit Insurance Corporation	Federal deposit insurance corporation (FDIC)
General Electric Company	Aircraft engines and engine parts
Harvard University	Colleges and universities
Internal Revenue Service	Taxation department, government
John Hancock Corp Tax Credit Fund I	Personal service agents, brokers & bureaus
Lahey Clinic	General medical and surgical hospitals
Massachusetts General Hospital	Health care
Massachusetts Institute of Technology	Colleges and universities
MassMutual Financial Group	Life insurance, annuities, & retirement investment
Roche Bros. Supermarkets	Food/grocery
State Street Bank and Trust Company	State trust companies accepting deposits, commercial
Sun Healthcare Group	Accident and health insurance
The Admins of the Tulane Educational Fund	Hospital, medical school affiliation
Tufts Medical Center	Hospital management

Note: Companies shown are located within the Boston-Cambridge-Newton, MA-NH Metropolitan Statistical Area.
Source: Hoovers.com; Wikipedia

PUBLIC SAFETY

Crime Rate

Area	All Crimes	Violent Crimes				Property Crimes		
		Murder	Rape[3]	Robbery	Aggrav. Assault	Burglary	Larceny -Theft	Motor Vehicle Theft
City	663.6	0.0	0.0	0.0	13.3	106.7	523.5	20.0
Metro[1]	n/a	n/a	n/a	n/a	n/a	n/a	n/a	n/a
U.S.	2,971.8	4.5	36.6	102.2	232.5	542.5	1,837.3	216.2

Note: Figures are crimes per 100,000 population; (1) Figures cover the Boston, MA Metropolitan Division—see Appendix B for areas included; n/a not available; (3) The city and U.S. figures shown were reported using the revised Uniform Crime Reporting (UCR) definition of rape. The suburban and metro area figures shown are an aggregate total of the data submitted using both the revised and legacy UCR definitions.
Source: FBI Uniform Crime Reports, 2014

Hate Crimes

Area	Number of Quarters Reported	Number of Incidents per Bias Motivation						
		Race	Religion	Sexual Orientation	Ethnicity	Disability	Gender	Gender Identity
City	4	1	0	0	0	0	0	0
U.S.	4	2,568	1,014	1,017	648	84	33	98

Source: Federal Bureau of Investigation, Hate Crime Statistics 2014

Identity Theft Consumer Complaints

Area	Complaints	Complaints per 100,000 Population	Rank[2]
MSA[1]	6,507	137.5	75
U.S.	490,220	152.4	-

Note: (1) Figures cover the Boston-Cambridge-Newton, MA-NH Metropolitan Statistical Area—see Appendix B for areas included; (2) Rank ranges from 1 to 379 where 1 indicates greatest number of identity theft complaints per 100,000 population
Source: Federal Trade Commission, Consumer Sentinel Network Data Book for January–December 2015

Fraud and Other Consumer Complaints

Area	Complaints	Complaints per 100,000 Population	Rank[2]
MSA[1]	16,631	351.4	213
U.S.	2,593,159	806.0	-

Note: (1) Figures cover the Boston-Cambridge-Newton, MA-NH Metropolitan Statistical Area—see Appendix B for areas included; (2) Rank ranges from 1 to 379 where 1 indicates greatest number of identity theft complaints per 100,000 population
Source: Federal Trade Commission, Consumer Sentinel Network Data Book for January–December 2015

RECREATION

Culture

Dance[1]	Theatre[1]	Instrumental Music[1]	Vocal Music[1]	Series and Festivals	Museums and Art Galleries[2]	Zoos and Aquariums[3]
0	0	0	0	0	0	0

Note: (1) Professional perfoming groups; (2) Based on organizations with SIC code 8412; (3) AZA-accredited
Source: The Grey House Performing Arts Directory, 2015-16; Association of Zoos & Aquariums, AZA Member Zoos & Aquariums, March 25, 2016; www.AccuLeads.com, March 29, 2016

Professional Sports Teams

Team Name	League	Year Established
Boston Bruins	National Hockey League (NHL)	1924
Boston Celtics	National Basketball Association (NBA)	1946
Boston Red Sox	Major League Baseball (MLB)	1901
New England Patriots	National Football League (NFL)	1960
New England Revolution	Major League Soccer (MLS)	1996

Note: Includes teams located in the Boston-Cambridge-Newton, MA-NH Metropolitan Statistical Area.
Source: Wikipedia, Major Professional Sports Teams of the United States and Canada, March 24, 2016

CLIMATE

Average and Extreme Temperatures

Temperature	Jan	Feb	Mar	Apr	May	Jun	Jul	Aug	Sep	Oct	Nov	Dec	Yr.
Extreme High (°F)	72	70	85	94	95	100	102	102	100	90	83	73	102
Average High (°F)	36	38	46	56	67	76	82	80	73	63	52	41	59
Average Temp. (°F)	30	31	39	48	58	68	74	72	65	55	45	34	52
Average Low (°F)	22	23	31	40	50	59	65	64	57	47	38	27	44
Extreme Low (°F)	-12	-4	1	16	34	45	50	47	37	28	15	-7	-12

Note: Figures cover the years 1945-1990
Source: National Climatic Data Center, International Station Meteorological Climate Summary, 9/96

Average Precipitation/Snowfall/Humidity

Precip./Humidity	Jan	Feb	Mar	Apr	May	Jun	Jul	Aug	Sep	Oct	Nov	Dec	Yr.
Avg. Precip. (in.)	3.8	3.6	3.8	3.7	3.5	3.1	2.9	3.6	3.1	3.3	4.4	4.1	42.9
Avg. Snowfall (in.)	12	12	8	1	Tr	0	0	0	0	Tr	1	8	41
Avg. Rel. Hum. 7am (%)	68	68	69	68	71	72	73	76	79	77	74	70	72
Avg. Rel. Hum. 4pm (%)	58	57	56	56	58	58	58	61	61	59	61	60	59

Note: Figures cover the years 1945-1990; Tr = Trace amounts (<0.05 in. of rain; <0.5 in. of snow)
Source: National Climatic Data Center, International Station Meteorological Climate Summary, 9/96

Weather Conditions

Temperature			Daytime Sky			Precipitation		
5°F & below	32°F & below	90°F & above	Clear	Partly cloudy	Cloudy	0.01 inch or more precip.	0.1 inch or more snow/ice	Thunder-storms
4	97	12	88	127	150	253	48	18

Note: Figures are average number of days per year and cover the years 1945-1990
Source: National Climatic Data Center, International Station Meteorological Climate Summary, 9/96

HAZARDOUS WASTE

Superfund Sites

Needham has no sites on the EPA's Superfund Final National Priorities List. There are a total of 1,323 Superfund sites on the list in the U.S. *U.S. Environmental Protection Agency, Final National Priorities List, March 18, 2016*

AIR & WATER QUALITY

Air Quality Trends: Ozone

	1990	1995	2000	2005	2010	2011	2012	2013	2014
MSA[1]	n/a	n/a	n/a	n/a	n/a	n/a	n/a	n/a	n/a

Note: (1) Data covers the Boston-Cambridge-Newton, MA-NH Metropolitan Statistical Area—see Appendix B for areas included; n/a not available. The values shown are the composite ozone concentration averages among trend sites based on the highest fourth daily maximum 8-hour concentration in parts per million. These trends are based on sites having an adequate record of monitoring data during the trend period. Data from exceptional events are included.
Source: U.S. Environmental Protection Agency, Air Quality Monitoring Information, "Air Quality Trends by City, 1990-2014"

Air Quality Index

Area	Percent of Days when Air Quality was...[2]					AQI Statistics[2]	
	Good	Moderate	Unhealthy for Sensitive Groups	Unhealthy	Very Unhealthy	Maximum	Median
MSA[1]	61.6	37.8	0.3	0.0	0.3	615	46

Note: (1) Data covers the Boston-Cambridge-Newton, MA-NH Metropolitan Statistical Area—see Appendix B for areas included; (2) Based on 365 days with AQI data in 2015. Air Quality Index (AQI) is an index for reporting daily air quality. EPA calculates the AQI for five major air pollutants regulated by the Clean Air Act: ground-level ozone, particle pollution (aka particulate matter), carbon monoxide, sulfur dioxide, and nitrogen dioxide. The AQI runs from 0 to 500. The higher the AQI value, the greater the level of air pollution and the greater the health concern. There are six AQI categories: "Good" AQI is between 0 and 50. Air quality is considered satisfactory; "Moderate" AQI is between 51 and 100. Air quality is acceptable; "Unhealthy for Sensitive Groups" When AQI values are between 101 and 150, members of sensitive groups may experience health effects; "Unhealthy" When AQI values are between 151 and 200 everyone may begin to experience health effects; "Very Unhealthy" AQI values between 201 and 300 trigger a health alert; "Hazardous" AQI values over 300 trigger warnings of emergency conditions (not shown).
Source: U.S. Environmental Protection Agency, Air Quality Index Report, 2015

Air Quality Index Pollutants

Area	Percent of Days when AQI Pollutant was...[2]					
	Carbon Monoxide	Nitrogen Dioxide	Ozone	Sulfur Dioxide	Particulate Matter 2.5	Particulate Matter 10
MSA[1]	0.0	3.3	27.9	0.0	68.5	0.3

Note: (1) Data covers the Boston-Cambridge-Newton, MA-NH Metropolitan Statistical Area—see Appendix B for areas included; (2) Based on 365 days with AQI data in 2015. The Air Quality Index (AQI) is an index for reporting daily air quality. EPA calculates the AQI for five major air pollutants regulated by the Clean Air Act: ground-level ozone, particle pollution (also known as particulate matter), carbon monoxide, sulfur dioxide, and nitrogen dioxide. The AQI runs from 0 to 500. The higher the AQI value, the greater the level of air pollution and the greater the health concern.
Source: U.S. Environmental Protection Agency, Air Quality Index Report, 2015

Maximum Air Pollutant Concentrations: Particulate Matter, Ozone, CO and Lead

	Particulate Matter 10 (ug/m^3)	Particulate Matter 2.5 Wtd AM (ug/m^3)	Particulate Matter 2.5 24-Hr (ug/m^3)	Ozone (ppm)	Carbon Monoxide (ppm)	Lead (ug/m^3)
MSA[1] Level	66	10.1	19	0.07	1	n/a
NAAQS[2]	150	15	35	0.075	9	0.15
Met NAAQS[2]	Yes	Yes	Yes	Yes	Yes	n/a

Note: (1) Data covers the Boston-Cambridge-Newton, MA-NH Metropolitan Statistical Area—see Appendix B for areas included; Data from exceptional events are included; (2) National Ambient Air Quality Standards; ppm = parts per million; ug/m^3 = micrograms per cubic meter; n/a not available.
Concentrations: Particulate Matter 10 (coarse particulate)—highest second maximum 24-hour concentration; Particulate Matter 2.5 Wtd AM (fine particulate)—highest weighted annual mean concentration; Particulate Matter 2.5 24-Hour (fine particulate)—highest 98th percentile 24-hour concentration; Ozone—highest fourth daily maximum 8-hour concentration; Carbon Monoxide—highest second maximum non-overlapping 8-hour concentration; Lead—maximum running 3-month average
Source: U.S. Environmental Protection Agency, Air Quality Monitoring Information, "Air Quality Statistics by City, 2014"

Maximum Air Pollutant Concentrations: Nitrogen Dioxide and Sulfur Dioxide

	Nitrogen Dioxide AM (ppb)	Nitrogen Dioxide 1-Hr (ppb)	Sulfur Dioxide AM (ppb)	Sulfur Dioxide 1-Hr (ppb)	Sulfur Dioxide 24-Hr (ppb)
MSA[1] Level	17	53	n/a	32	n/a
NAAQS[2]	53	100	30	75	140
Met NAAQS[2]	Yes	Yes	n/a	Yes	n/a

Note: (1) Data covers the Boston-Cambridge-Newton, MA-NH Metropolitan Statistical Area—see Appendix B for areas included; Data from exceptional events are included; (2) National Ambient Air Quality Standards; ppm = parts per million; ug/m^3 = micrograms per cubic meter; n/a not available.
Concentrations: Nitrogen Dioxide AM—highest arithmetic mean concentration; Nitrogen Dioxide 1-Hr—highest 98th percentile 1-hour daily maximum concentration; Sulfur Dioxide AM—highest annual mean concentration; Sulfur Dioxide 1-Hr—highest 99th percentile 1-hour daily maximum concentration; Sulfur Dioxide 24-Hr—highest second maximum 24-hour concentration
Source: U.S. Environmental Protection Agency, Air Quality Monitoring Information, "Air Quality Statistics by City, 2014"

Drinking Water

Water System Name	Pop. Served	Primary Water Source Type	Violations[1]	
			Health Based	Monitoring/ Reporting
Needham Water Dept	31,446	Purchased Surface	0	0

Note: (1) Based on violation data from January 1, 2015 to December 31, 2015 (includes unresolved violations from earlier years)
Source: U.S. Environmental Protection Agency, Office of Ground Water and Drinking Water, Safe Drinking Water Information System (based on data extracted April 29, 2016)

Shrewsbury, Massachusetts

Background

Shrewsbury is located in Central Massachusetts in Worcester County. It is 34 miles from Boston and 15 miles from Worcester, separated from the latter city by Lake Quinsigamond to its west. The city was named after The Duke of Shrewsbury, namesake of Shrewsbury, England.

Shrewsbury is a suburban community with a hilly, uneven landscape cut by several streams. In the early seventeenth century, these streams provided water flow to power several waterpower sites. In the mid- 1600s, state land grants (named as "farms" by their recipients) were parceled out to support settlement in central Massachusetts. They were, in order of acreage, Hayne's Farm at 3,200 acres, Sewall's Farm at 1500 acres, Malden Farm at 1000 acres, Davenport's Farm at 650 acres, and Rawson's Farm at 500 acres. These land grants later combined to become the city of Shrewsbury. In 1720, Gersham Wheelock became the first permanent settler. Shrewsbury was officially settled in 1722, and incorporated in 1727.

Following the Revolutionary War, Shrewsbury's economy spiraled into a depression resulting in tremendous hardships for the community. The government was raising taxes to fund the war debt. Creditors and tax collectors were pressing financially stressed farmers. Bartering was no longer an accepted form of payment and many individuals found themselves bankrupt. On September 4, 1786, over 400 residents marched from Shrewsbury to the courthouse in Worchester. Known as Shay's Rebellion, this public outcry attempted to close the courthouses to prevent collection of debt and mortgage foreclosures. The rebellion brought to light the inequalities the new nation was experiencing in the aftermath of the Revolution, and directly influenced Massachusetts's ratification of the U.S. Constitution.

In the late 1700s, settlers established an agricultural economy farming rye, oats, Indian corn and hay. Nearly all the farms had apple orchards and produced cider. From 1820 to 1845, regular weekly wagons would run between Boston and Shrewsbury bringing in dry goods and shipping out fresh produce. Soon after 1845, trade shifted to Worcester because it was closer and more economical, eliminating the middleman and his commissions.

As the economy slowly shifted, Shrewsbury changed its focus from agriculture to leather. Emerging industries were varied and included gunsmithing, watchmaking, and lumber.

In the early 1900s, streetcar routes were developed which in turn, once again, brought a change in Shrewsbury's economy to include summer resorts at Lake Quinsigamond and single-family houses. This new population of residents and vacationers re-energized the local economy. The city's population doubled between 1915 and 1940. Shrewsbury again found itself a resort community with lakeside cottages and recreational area serving Worcester and other nearby larger cities.

Today, Shrewsbury continues to offer an extensive list of parks in and around the city that are vital to its resort industry, including Quinsigamond State Park, Upton State Forest, Rutland State Park, Hopkinton State Park, and Wachusett Mountain State Reservation. These areas offer beaches for swimming, lakes for boating and fishing, hiking, walking trails, and mountain biking, all with beautiful natural scenery.

Among Shrewsbury's rich history are landmarks such as The General Artemas Ward Homestead, a 300-year-old public patriotic museum that was gifted to Harvard University in 1925 along with five million dollars to establish the reputation of Artemas Ward and maintain the house and grounds. The Shrewsbury Historic District opened in 2001 at the 1830 Brick School, featuring artifacts, photographs and clothing illustrating Shrewsbury's history. Other attractions include the Joseph Lothrop House, on the National Registry of Historic Places.

The weather in Shrewsbury averages high temperatures of 79.3 degrees in the month of July and low temperatures of 18.8 degrees in the month of January. The average annual rainfall is approximately 49.05 inches.

Rankings

Business/Finance Rankings

- The personal finance site NerdWallet analyzed 183 American metropolitan areas with populations over 250,000 and more than 15,000 businesses to rank where entrepreneurs find the most success. Criteria included area economy, annual income, housing cost, unemployment rate, and the success rate of area businesses. Worcester* ranked #143. *www.nerdwallet.com, "Best Places to Start a Business," April 27, 2015*

- The Brookings Institution ranked the 100 largest metro areas in the U.S. based on income inequality. Worcester* was ranked #49 (#1 = greatest ineqality). Criteria: the "95/20 ratio," a figure representing the income at which a household earns more than 95 percent of all other households, divided by the income at which a household earns more than only 20 percent of all other households. *Brookings Institution, "Income Inequality, 100 Largest U.S. Metro Areas, 2007-2014," January 14, 2016*

- The Worcester* metro area appeared on the Milken Institute "2015 Best Performing Cities" list. Rank: #37 out of 200 large metro areas. Criteria: job growth; wage and salary growth; high-tech output growth. *Milken Institute, "Best-Performing Cities 2015," December 2015*

- *Forbes* ranked the 200 most populous metro areas to determine the nation's "Best Places for Business and Careers." The Worcester* metro area was ranked #104. Criteria: costs (business and living); job growth (past and projected); income growth; educational attainment (college and high school); projected economic growth; cultural and recreational opportunities; net migration patterns; number of highly ranked colleges. *Forbes, "The Best Places for Business and Careers 2015," July 29, 2015*

Education Rankings

- Personal finance website *WalletHub* analyzed the 150 largest U.S. metropolitan statistical areas to determine where the most educated Americans are choosing to settle. Criteria: education quality and attainment gap; education levels; percentage of workers with degrees; public school rankings; quality and size of each metro area's universities. Worcester* was ranked #41 (#1 = most educated city). *www.WalletHub.com, "2015's Most and Least Educated Cities*

Environmental Rankings

- The Worcester* metro area came in at #60 for the relative comfort of its climate on Sperling's list of "chill cities," as measured by the Sperling Heat Index. All 361 metro areas are included. Criteria included daytime high temperatures, nighttime low temperatures, dew point, and relative humidity at the high temperatures. *www.bertsperling.com, "Sperling's Chill Cities," July 18, 2013*

- Sperling's BestPlaces assessed 379 metropolitan areas of the United States for the likelihood of dangerously extreme weather events or earthquakes. In general the Southeast and South-Central regions have the highest risk of weather extremes and earthquakes, while the Pacific Northwest enjoys the lowest risk. Of the least risky metropolitan areas, the Worcester* metro area was ranked #223. *www.bestplaces.net, "Safest Places from Natural Disasters," April 2011*

Health/Fitness Rankings

- Analysts who tracked obesity rates in 100 of the nation's most populous areas found that the Worcester* metro area was one of the ten communities where residents were most likely to be obese, defined as a BMI score of 30 or above. *www.gallup.com, "Colorado Springs Residents Least Likely to Be Obese," May 28, 2015*

- Worcester* was identified as a "2016 Spring Allergy Capital." The area ranked #63 out of 100. Three groups of factors were used to identify the most severe cities for people with allergies during the spring season: annual pollen levels; medicine utilization; access to board-certified allergists. *Asthma and Allergy Foundation of America, "Spring Allergy Capitals 2016"*

- Worcester* was identified as a "2015 Asthma Capital." The area ranked #79 out of the nation's 100 largest metropolitan areas. Criteria: estimated prevalence; self-reported prevalence; crude death rate for asthma; annual pollen score; annual air quality; public smoking laws; number of board-certified asthma specialists; school inhaler access laws; rescue medication use; controller medication use; ER visits for asthma; uninsured rate; poverty rate. *Asthma and Allergy Foundation of America, "Asthma Capitals 2015"*
- The Worcester* metro area ranked #183 out of 190 in The Gallup-Healthways Well-Being Index. Criteria: purpose; social well being; financial health; community and physical health. Results are based on telephone interviews with adults, aged 18 and older, living in metropolitan areas in the 50 U.S. states and the District of Columbia. *Gallup-Healthways, "State of American Well-Being," February 23, 2016*

Real Estate Rankings

- Worcester* was ranked #65 out of 225 metro areas in terms of housing affordability in 2015 by the National Association of Home Builders (#1 = most affordable). Criteria: the share of homes sold in that area affordable to a family earning the local median income, based on standard mortgage underwriting criteria. *National Association of Home Builders®, NAHB-Wells Fargo Housing Opportunity Index, 4th Quarter 2015*

Safety Rankings

- Shrewsbury was identified as one of the safest cities in America by NeighborhoodScout. The city ranked #7 out of 100. Criteria: number of violent and property crimes per 1,000 residents. The editors only considered cities with 25,000 or more residents. *NeighborhoodScout, "Safest Cities in America 2016"*
- The National Insurance Crime Bureau ranked 380 metro areas in the U.S. in terms of per capita rates of vehicle theft. The Worcester* metro area ranked #323 (#1 = highest rate). Criteria: number of vehicle theft offenses per 100,000 inhabitants in 2014. *National Insurance Crime Bureau, "Hot Spots 2014," June 24, 2015*

Seniors/Retirement Rankings

- From its Best Cities for Successful Aging indexes, the Milken Institute generated rankings for metropolitan areas, weighing data in eight categories—health care, wellness, living arrangements, transportation, financial characteristics, education and employment opportunities, community engagement, and overall livability. The Worcester* metro area was ranked #52 overall in the large metro area category. *Milken Institute, "Best Cities for Successful Aging, 2014"*

Miscellaneous Rankings

- The National Alliance to End Homelessness ranked the 100 most populous metro areas with the highest rate of homelessness. The Worcester* metro area ranked #44. Criteria: number of homeless people per 10,000 population in 2011. *National Alliance to End Homelessness, The State of Homelessness in America 2012*

Shrewsbury is located within the Worcester, MA-CT Metropolitan Statistical Area.

Business Environment

CITY FINANCES

City Government Finances

Component	2012 ($000)	2012 ($ per capita)
Total Revenues	173,565	4,874
Total Expenditures	172,212	4,836
Debt Outstanding	78,659	2,209
Cash and Securities[1]	131,213	3,684

Note: (1) Cash and security holdings of a government at the close of its fiscal year, including those of its dependent agencies, utilities, and liquor stores.
Source: U.S Census Bureau, State & Local Government Finances 2012

City Government Revenue by Source

Source	2012 ($000)	2012 ($ per capita)
General Revenue		
From Federal Government	639	17
From State Government	44,290	1,243
From Local Governments	0	0
Taxes		
Property	57,625	1,618
Sales and Gross Receipts	698	19
Personal Income	0	0
Corporate Income	0	0
Motor Vehicle License	0	0
Other Taxes	800	22
Current Charges	26,878	754
Liquor Store	0	0
Utility	38,205	1,072
Employee Retirement	2,297	64

Source: U.S Census Bureau, State & Local Government Finances 2012

City Government Expenditures by Function

Function	2012 ($000)	2012 ($ per capita)	2012 (%)
General Direct Expenditures			
Air Transportation	0	0	0.0
Corrections	0	0	0.0
Education	77,827	2,185	45.1
Employment Security Administration	0	0	0.0
Financial Administration	1,087	30	0.6
Fire Protection	2,926	82	1.6
General Public Buildings	3,102	87	1.8
Governmental Administration, Other	727	20	0.4
Health	240	6	0.1
Highways	2,650	74	1.5
Hospitals	0	0	0.0
Housing and Community Development	0	0	0.0
Interest on General Debt	2,878	80	1.6
Judicial and Legal	49	1	0.0
Libraries	1,165	32	0.6
Parking	0	0	0.0
Parks and Recreation	440	12	0.2
Police Protection	4,060	114	2.3
Public Welfare	99	2	0.0
Sewerage	5,466	153	3.1
Solid Waste Management	1,765	49	1.0
Veterans' Services	0	0	0.0
Liquor Store	0	0	0.0
Utility	34,509	969	20.0
Employee Retirement	4,877	136	2.8

Source: U.S Census Bureau, State & Local Government Finances 2012

DEMOGRAPHICS

Population Growth

Area	1990 Census	2000 Census	2010 Census	2014* Estimate	Population Growth (%)	
					1990-2014	2010-2014
City	24,146	31,640	35,608	36,114	49.6	1.4
MSA[1]	709,728	750,963	798,552	924,722	30.3	15.8
U.S.	248,709,873	281,421,906	308,745,538	314,107,084	26.3	1.7

Note: (1) Figures cover the Worcester, MA-CT Metropolitan Statistical Area—see Appendix B for areas included; (*) 2010-2014 5-year estimated population
Source: U.S. Census Bureau, 1990 Census, Census 2000, Census 2010, 2010-2014 American Community Survey 5-Year Estimates

Household Size

Area	Persons in Household (%)							Average Household Size
	One	Two	Three	Four	Five	Six	Seven or More	
City	23.0	29.4	17.3	21.7	6.5	1.0	0.9	2.75
MSA[1]	26.5	32.6	16.9	15.1	6.0	1.8	0.7	2.59
U.S.	27.5	33.5	15.8	13.1	6.0	2.3	1.4	2.64

Note: (1) Figures cover the Worcester, MA-CT Metropolitan Statistical Area—see Appendix B for areas included
Source: U.S. Census Bureau, 2010-2014 American Community Survey 5-Year Estimates

Race

Area	White Alone[2] (%)	Black Alone[2] (%)	Asian Alone[2] (%)	AIAN[3] Alone[2] (%)	NHOPI[4] Alone[2] (%)	Other Race Alone[2] (%)	Two or More Races (%)
City	77.1	2.8	16.4	0.1	0.0	1.0	2.6
MSA[1]	86.2	4.1	3.9	0.2	0.0	2.8	2.7
U.S.	73.8	12.6	5.0	0.8	0.2	4.7	2.9

Note: (1) Figures cover the Worcester, MA-CT Metropolitan Statistical Area—see Appendix B for areas included; (2) Alone is defined as not being in combination with one or more other races; (3) American Indian and Alaska Native; (4) Native Hawaiian and Other Pacific Islander
Source: U.S. Census Bureau, 2010-2014 American Community Survey 5-Year Estimates

Hispanic or Latino Origin

Area	Total (%)	Mexican (%)	Puerto Rican (%)	Cuban (%)	Other (%)
City	3.5	0.3	1.6	0.0	1.6
MSA[1]	10.0	0.7	5.8	0.1	3.4
U.S.	16.9	10.8	1.6	0.6	3.8

Note: Persons of Hispanic or Latino origin can be of any race; (1) Figures cover the Worcester, MA-CT Metropolitan Statistical Area—see Appendix B for areas included
Source: U.S. Census Bureau, 2010-2014 American Community Survey 5-Year Estimates

Ancestry

Area	German	Irish	English	American	Italian	Polish	French[2]	Scottish	Dutch
City	5.7	21.5	8.9	4.4	17.1	5.3	10.3	1.8	0.2
MSA[1]	6.6	20.3	10.6	4.1	13.3	6.5	14.4	2.2	0.8
U.S.	14.9	10.8	8.0	7.1	5.5	3.0	2.7	1.7	1.4

Note: Figures are the percentage of the total population reporting a particular ancestry. The nine most commonly reported ancestries in the U.S. are shown. Figures include multiple ancestries (e.g. if a person reported being Irish and Italian, they were included in both columns); (1) Figures cover the Worcester, MA-CT Metropolitan Statistical Area—see Appendix B for areas included; (2) Excludes Basque
Source: U.S. Census Bureau, 2010-2014 American Community Survey 5-Year Estimates

Foreign-Born Population

Area	Percent of Population Born in: Any Foreign Country	Asia	Mexico	Europe	Carribean	Central America[2]	South America	Africa	Canada
City	21.2	12.5	0.0	3.7	0.4	0.4	2.0	1.5	0.5
MSA[1]	10.7	3.3	0.3	2.2	1.0	0.5	1.5	1.4	0.6
U.S.	13.1	3.8	3.7	1.5	1.2	1.0	0.9	0.6	0.3

Note: (1) Figures cover the Worcester, MA-CT Metropolitan Statistical Area—see Appendix B for areas included; (2) Excludes Mexico.
Source: U.S. Census Bureau, 2010-2014 American Community Survey 5-Year Estimates

Marital Status

Area	Never Married	Now Married[2]	Separated	Widowed	Divorced
City	27.7	58.7	0.8	5.1	7.7
MSA[1]	33.0	48.8	1.7	5.8	10.6
U.S.	32.5	48.4	2.2	5.9	10.9

Note: Figures are percentages and cover the population 15 years of age and older; (1) Figures cover the Worcester, MA-CT Metropolitan Statistical Area—see Appendix B for areas included; (2) Excludes separated
Source: U.S. Census Bureau, 2010-2014 American Community Survey 5-Year Estimates

Disability Status

Area	All Ages	Under 18 Years Old	18 to 64 Years Old	65 Years and Over
City	8.4	3.1	5.3	32.7
MSA[1]	11.6	4.7	9.4	34.5
U.S.	12.3	4.1	10.2	36.3

Note: Figures show percent of the civilian noninstitutionalized population that reported having a disability. Disability status is determined from from six types of difficulty: vision, hearing, cognitive, ambulatory, self-care, and independent living. For children under 5 years old, hearing and vision difficulty are used to determine disability status. For children between the ages of 5 and 14, disability status is determined from hearing, vision, cognitive, ambulatory, and self-care difficulties. For people aged 15 years and older, they are considered to have a disability if they have difficulty with any one of the six difficulty types; (1) Figures cover the Worcester, MA-CT Metropolitan Statistical Area—see Appendix B for areas included.
Source: U.S. Census Bureau, 2010-2014 American Community Survey 5-Year Estimates

Age

Area	Percent of Population: Under Age 5	Age 5–19	Age 20–34	Age 35–44	Age 45–54	Age 55–64	Age 65–74	Age 75–84	Age 85+	Median Age
City	5.6	22.9	15.0	14.7	16.9	11.2	7.5	4.1	1.9	39.7
MSA[1]	5.6	20.0	18.8	13.2	16.0	12.9	7.2	4.0	2.2	39.7
U.S.	6.4	19.9	20.6	13.0	14.1	12.3	7.6	4.3	1.9	37.4

Note: (1) Figures cover the Worcester, MA-CT Metropolitan Statistical Area—see Appendix B for areas included
Source: U.S. Census Bureau, 2010-2014 American Community Survey 5-Year Estimates

Gender

Area	Males	Females	Males per 100 Females
City	17,729	18,385	96.4
MSA[1]	456,142	468,580	97.3
U.S.	154,515,159	159,591,925	96.8

Note: (1) Figures cover the Worcester, MA-CT Metropolitan Statistical Area—see Appendix B for areas included
Source: U.S. Census Bureau, 2010-2014 American Community Survey 5-Year Estimates

Religious Groups by Family

Area	Catholic	Baptist	Non-Den.	Methodist[2]	Lutheran	LDS[3]	Pente-costal	Presby-terian[4]	Muslim[5]	Judaism
MSA[1]	38.4	1.1	1.7	0.9	0.9	0.3	1.0	2.0	<0.1	0.5
U.S.	19.1	9.3	4.0	4.0	2.3	2.0	1.9	1.6	0.8	0.7

Note: Figures are the number of adherents as a percentage of the total population; (1) Figures cover the Worcester, MA Metropolitan Statistical Area—see Appendix B for areas included; (2) Methodist/Pietist; (3) Latter Day Saints; (4) Reformed; (5) Figures are estimates
Source: Association of Statisticians of American Religious Bodies, 2010 U.S. Religion Census: Religious Congregations & Membership Study

Religious Groups by Tradition

Area	Catholic	Evangelical Protestant	Mainline Protestant	Other Tradition	Black Protestant	Orthodox
MSA[1]	38.4	4.6	5.4	2.3	<0.1	0.9
U.S.	19.1	16.2	7.3	4.3	1.6	0.3

Note: Figures are the number of adherents as a percentage of the total population; (1) Figures cover the Worcester, MA Metropolitan Statistical Area—see Appendix B for areas included
Source: Association of Statisticians of American Religious Bodies, 2010 U.S. Religion Census: Religious Congregations & Membership Study

ECONOMY

Gross Metropolitan Product

Area	2013	2014	2015	2016	Rank[2]
MSA[1]	37.1	38.5	39.7	41.4	69

Note: Figures are in billions of dollars; (1) Figures cover the Worcester, MA-CT Metropolitan Statistical Area—see Appendix B for areas included; (2) Rank is based on 2016 data and ranges from 1 to 381
Source: The U.S. Conference of Mayors, U.S. Metro Economies: GMP and Employment 2014-2016, June 2015

Economic Growth

Area	2011-13 (%)	2014 (%)	2015 (%)	2016 (%)	Rank[2]
MSA[1]	1.6	2.0	1.8	2.2	236
U.S.	2.2	2.4	2.3	2.9	–

Note: Figures are real gross metropolitan product (GMP) growth rates and represent annual average percent change; (1) Figures cover the Worcester, MA-CT Metropolitan Statistical Area—see Appendix B for areas included; (2) Rank is based on 2016 data and ranges from 1 to 381
Source: The U.S. Conference of Mayors, U.S. Metro Economies: GMP and Employment 2014-2016, June 2015

Metropolitan Area Exports

Area	2009	2010	2011	2012	2013	2014	Rank[2]
MSA[1]	2,035.8	2,355.6	2,396.9	2,966.1	3,393.5	3,126.5	77

Note: Figures are in millions of dollars; (1) Figures cover the Worcester, MA-CT Metropolitan Statistical Area—see Appendix B for areas included; (2) Rank is based on 2014 data and ranges from 1 to 385
Source: U.S. Department of Commerce, International Trade Administration, Office of Trade & Industry Information, Manufacturing & Services, data extracted March 10, 2016

Building Permits

Area	Single-Family			Multi-Family			Total		
	2014	2015p	Pct. Chg.	2014	2015p	Pct. Chg.	2014	2015p	Pct. Chg.
City	57	4	-93.0	0	0	-	57	4	-93.0
MSA[1]	1,274	149	-88.3	110	24	-78.2	1,384	173	-87.5
U.S.	640,300	690,800	7.9	411,800	487,600	18.4	1,052,100	1,178,400	12.0

Note: (1) Figures cover the Worcester, MA-CT Metropolitan Statistical Area—see Appendix B for areas included; Figures represent new, privately-owned housing units authorized (unadjusted data); All permit data are based on estimates with imputation; (p) preliminary data.
Source: U.S. Census Bureau, Manufacturing, Mining, and Construction Statistics, Building Permits, 2014, 2015

Bankruptcy Filings

Area	Business Filings			Nonbusiness Filings		
	2014	2015	% Chg.	2014	2015	% Chg.
Worcester County	52	44	-15.4	1,561	1,380	-11.6
U.S.	26,983	24,735	-8.3	909,812	819,760	-9.9

Note: Business filings include Chapter 7, Chapter 11, Chapter 12, and Chapter 13; Nonbusiness filings include Chapter 7, Chapter 11, and Chapter 13
Source: Administrative Office of the U.S. Courts, Business and Nonbusiness Bankruptcy, County Cases Commenced by Chapter of the Bankruptcy Code, During the 12- Month Period Ending December 31, 2014 and Business and Nonbusiness Bankruptcy, County Cases Commenced by Chapter of the Bankruptcy Code, During the 12- Month Period Ending December 31, 2015

Housing Vacancy Rates

Area	Gross Vacancy Rate[2] (%)			Year-Round Vacancy Rate[3] (%)			Rental Vacancy Rate[4] (%)			Homeowner Vacancy Rate[5] (%)		
	2013	2014	2015	2013	2014	2015	2013	2014	2015	2013	2014	2015
MSA[1]	10.8	11.0	10.1	8.6	6.8	7.8	6.4	4.5	2.9	3.1	1.9	1.9
U.S.	13.6	13.4	12.9	10.7	10.4	10.0	8.3	7.6	7.1	2.0	1.9	1.8

Note: (1) Figures cover the Worcester, MA-CT Metropolitan Statistical Area—see Appendix B for areas included; (2) The percentage of the total housing inventory that is vacant; (3) The percentage of the housing inventory (excluding seasonal units) that is year-round vacant; (4) The percentage of rental inventory that is vacant for rent; (5) The percentage of homeowner inventory that is vacant for sale
Source: U.S. Census Bureau, Housing Vacancies and Homeownership Annual Statistics: 2015

INCOME

Income

Area	Per Capita ($)	Median Household ($)	Average Household ($)
City	41,521	97,365	113,750
MSA[1]	31,558	64,629	82,290
U.S.	28,555	53,482	74,596

Note: (1) Figures cover the Worcester, MA-CT Metropolitan Statistical Area—see Appendix B for areas included
Source: U.S. Census Bureau, 2010-2014 American Community Survey 5-Year Estimates

Household Income Distribution

Area	Percent of Households Earning							
	Under $15,000	$15,000 -24,999	$25,000 -34,999	$35,000 -49,999	$50,000 -74,999	$75,000 -99,000	$100,000 -149,999	$150,000 and up
City	5.0	4.6	5.8	9.6	12.5	14.2	22.8	25.7
MSA[1]	10.7	9.3	8.5	11.3	16.8	13.7	16.8	12.9
U.S.	12.5	10.7	10.2	13.5	17.8	12.2	13.0	10.0

Note: (1) Figures cover the Worcester, MA-CT Metropolitan Statistical Area—see Appendix B for areas included
Source: U.S. Census Bureau, 2010-2014 American Community Survey 5-Year Estimates

Poverty Rate

Area	All Ages	Under 18 Years Old	18 to 64 Years Old	65 Years and Over
City	5.0	4.7	4.7	6.9
MSA[1]	11.5	15.5	10.8	8.3
U.S.	15.6	21.9	14.6	9.4

Note: Figures are percentage of people whose income during the past 12 months was below the poverty level; (1) Figures cover the Worcester, MA-CT Metropolitan Statistical Area—see Appendix B for areas included
Source: U.S. Census Bureau, 2010-2014 American Community Survey 5-Year Estimates

EMPLOYMENT

Labor Force and Employment

Area	Civilian Labor Force			Workers Employed		
	Dec. 2014	Dec. 2015	% Chg.	Dec. 2014	Dec. 2015	% Chg.
City	19,750	19,658	-0.4	19,018	18,959	-0.3
NECTA[1]	348,073	345,834	-0.6	329,698	329,149	-0.1
U.S.	155,521,000	157,245,000	1.1	147,190,000	149,703,000	1.7

Note: Data is not seasonally adjusted and covers workers 16 years of age and older; (1) Figures cover the Worcester, MA-CT New England City and Town Area—see Appendix B for areas included
Source: Bureau of Labor Statistics, Local Area Unemployment Statistics

Unemployment Rate

Area	2015											
	Jan.	Feb.	Mar.	Apr.	May	Jun.	Jul.	Aug.	Sep.	Oct.	Nov.	Dec.
City	4.1	4.0	3.7	3.2	3.4	3.9	3.8	3.5	3.5	3.6	3.6	3.6
NECTA[1]	5.9	5.8	5.4	4.6	4.7	5.2	5.3	4.9	4.8	4.7	4.7	4.8
U.S.	6.1	5.8	5.6	5.1	5.3	5.5	5.6	5.2	4.9	4.8	4.8	4.8

Note: Data is not seasonally adjusted and covers workers 16 years of age and older; (1) Figures cover the Worcester, MA-CT New England City and Town Area—see Appendix B for areas included
Source: Bureau of Labor Statistics, Local Area Unemployment Statistics

Employment by Occupation

Occupation Classification	City (%)	MSA[1] (%)	U.S. (%)
Management, Business, Science, and Arts	55.4	39.6	36.4
Natural Resources, Construction, and Maintenance	3.4	7.8	9.0
Production, Transportation, and Material Moving	6.7	11.4	12.1
Sales and Office	20.7	23.6	24.4
Service	13.9	17.7	18.2

Note: Figures cover employed civilians 16 years of age and older; (1) Figures cover the Worcester, MA-CT Metropolitan Statistical Area—see Appendix B for areas included
Source: U.S. Census Bureau, 2010-2014 American Community Survey 5-Year Estimates

Employment by Industry

Sector	NECTA[1]		U.S.
	Number of Employees	Percent of Total	Percent of Total
Construction, Mining, and Logging	10,400	3.6	5.0
Education and Health Services	67,100	23.7	15.7
Financial Activities	15,500	5.4	5.7
Government	44,300	15.6	15.5
Information	3,500	1.2	1.9
Leisure and Hospitality	23,100	8.1	10.4
Manufacturing	27,700	9.8	8.6
Other Services	10,600	3.7	3.9
Professional and Business Services	26,100	9.2	13.9
Retail Trade	30,700	10.8	11.3
Transportation, Warehousing, and Utilities	12,900	4.5	3.9
Wholesale Trade	10,400	3.6	4.1

Note: Figures are non-farm employment as of December 2015. Figures are not seasonally adjusted and include workers 16 years of age and older; (1) Figures cover the Worcester, MA-CT New England City and Town Area—see Appendix B for areas included; n/a not available
Source: Bureau of Labor Statistics, Current Employment Statistics, Employment, Hours, and Earnings

Occupations with Greatest Projected Employment Growth: 2012 – 2022

Occupation[1]	2012 Employment	2022 Projected Employment	Numeric Employment Change	Percent Employment Change
Registered Nurses	78,750	93,310	14,560	18.5
Combined Food Preparation and Serving Workers, Including Fast Food	58,250	70,750	12,500	21.4
Retail Salespersons	109,830	119,160	9,330	8.5
Waiters and Waitresses	58,570	66,840	8,270	14.1
Personal Care Aides	21,690	29,940	8,250	38.1
Home Health Aides	19,760	27,740	7,980	40.4
Nursing Assistants	39,170	45,940	6,770	17.3
General and Operations Managers	55,960	62,610	6,650	11.9
Software Developers, Systems Software	30,030	36,290	6,260	20.8
Management Analysts	27,100	33,070	5,970	22.0

Note: Projections cover Massachusetts; (1) Sorted by numeric employment change
Source: www.projectionscentral.com, State Occupational Projections, 2012–2022 Long-Term Projections

Fastest Growing Occupations: 2012 – 2022

Occupation[1]	2012 Employment	2022 Projected Employment	Numeric Employment Change	Percent Employment Change
Skincare Specialists	2,520	3,840	1,320	52.6
Insulation Workers, Mechanical	240	350	110	49.4
Helpers—Brickmasons, Blockmasons, Stonemasons, and Tile and Marble Setters	550	790	240	44.0
Interpreters and Translators	2,200	3,130	930	42.1
Diagnostic Medical Sonographers	1,460	2,080	620	42.1
Animal Trainers	360	500	140	42.0
Home Health Aides	19,760	27,740	7,980	40.4
Information Security Analysts	2,640	3,660	1,020	39.1
Personal Care Aides	21,690	29,940	8,250	38.1
Helpers—Electricians	920	1,270	350	37.7

Note: Projections cover Massachusetts; (1) Sorted by percent employment change and excludes occupations with numeric employment change less than 100
Source: www.projectionscentral.com, State Occupational Projections, 2012–2022 Long-Term Projections

Average Wages

Occupation	$/Hr.	Occupation	$/Hr.
Accountants and Auditors	35.33	Maids and Housekeeping Cleaners	11.86
Automotive Mechanics	20.49	Maintenance and Repair Workers	20.44
Bookkeepers	19.45	Marketing Managers	59.80
Carpenters	23.98	Nuclear Medicine Technologists	n/a
Cashiers	10.81	Nurses, Licensed Practical	25.97
Clerks, General Office	15.94	Nurses, Registered	43.25
Clerks, Receptionists/Information	15.05	Nursing Assistants	14.81
Clerks, Shipping/Receiving	17.44	Packers and Packagers, Hand	12.16
Computer Programmers	38.53	Physical Therapists	38.08
Computer Systems Analysts	43.64	Postal Service Mail Carriers	24.03
Computer User Support Specialists	26.51	Real Estate Brokers	n/a
Cooks, Restaurant	12.80	Retail Salespersons	12.27
Dentists	106.87	Sales Reps., Exc. Tech./Scientific	36.85
Electrical Engineers	46.38	Sales Reps., Tech./Scientific	42.11
Electricians	33.90	Secretaries, Exc. Legal/Med./Exec.	19.80
Financial Managers	52.49	Security Guards	14.18
First-Line Supervisors/Managers, Sales	21.18	Surgeons	n/a
Food Preparation Workers	11.07	Teacher Assistants*	15.05
General and Operations Managers	57.60	Teachers, Elementary School*	33.07
Hairdressers/Cosmetologists	16.75	Teachers, Secondary School*	33.97
Internists	n/a	Telemarketers	16.06
Janitors and Cleaners	15.29	Truck Drivers, Heavy/Tractor-Trailer	24.12
Landscaping/Groundskeeping Workers	15.39	Truck Drivers, Light/Delivery Svcs.	17.67
Lawyers	50.62	Waiters and Waitresses	12.38

Note: Wage data covers the New England City and Town Area—see Appendix B for areas included; (*) Hourly wages for elementary/secondary school teachers and teacher assistants were calculated by the editors from annual wage data based on a 40 hour work week; n/a not available.
Source: Bureau of Labor Statistics, Metro Area Occupational Employment and Wage Estimates, May 2015

TAXES

State Corporate Income Tax Rates

State	Tax Rate (%)	Income Brackets ($)	Num. of Brackets	Financial Institution Tax Rate (%)[a]	Federal Income Tax Ded.
Massachusetts	8.0 (n)	Flat rate	1	9.0 (n)	No

Note: Tax rates as of January 1, 2016; (a) Rates listed are the corporate income tax rate applied to financial institutions or excise taxes based on income. Some states have other taxes based upon the value of deposits or shares; (n) Business and manufacturing corporations pay an additional tax of $2.60 per $1,000 on either taxable Massachusetts tangible property or taxable net worth allocable to the state (for intangible property corporations). The minimum tax for both corporations and financial institutions is $456.
Source: Federation of Tax Administrators, "State Corporate Income Tax Rates, 2016"

State Individual Income Tax Rates

State	Tax Rate (%)	Income Brackets ($)	Num. of Brackets	Personal Exempt. ($)[1] Single	Personal Exempt. ($)[1] Dependents	Fed. Inc. Tax Ded.
Massachusetts	5.10	Flat rate	1	4,400	1,000	No

Note: Tax rates as of January 1, 2016; Local- and county-level taxes are not included; n/a not applicable; (1) Married joint filers generally receive double the single exemption
Source: Federation of Tax Administrators, "State Individual Income Tax Rates, 2016"

Various State and Local Tax Rates

State	State and Local Sales and Use (%)	State Sales and Use (%)	Gasoline[1] (¢/gal.)	Cigarette[2] ($/pack)	Spirits[3] ($/gal.)	Wine[4] ($/gal.)	Beer[5] ($/gal.)
Massachusetts	6.25	6.25	26.54	3.51	4.05 (f)	0.55 (l)	0.11

Note: All tax rates as of January 1, 2016; (1) The American Petroleum Institute has developed a methodology for determining the average tax rate on a gallon of fuel. Rates may include any of the following: excise taxes, environmental fees, storage tank fees, other fees or taxes, general sales tax, and local taxes. In states where gasoline is subject to the general sales tax, or where the fuel tax is based on the average sale price, the average rate determined by API is sensitive to changes in the price of gasoline. States that fully or partially apply general sales taxes to gasoline: CA, CO, GA, IL, IN, MI, NY; (2) The federal excise tax of $1.0066 per pack and local taxes are not included; (3) Rates are those applicable to off-premise sales of 40% alcohol by volume (a.b.v.) distilled spirits in 750ml containers. Local excise taxes are excluded; (4) Rates are those applicable to off-premise sales of 11% a.b.v. non-carbonated wine in 750ml containers; (5) Rates are those applicable to off-premise sales of 4.7% a.b.v. beer in 12 ounce containers; (f) Different rates are also applicable according to alcohol content, place of production, size of container, or place purchased (on- or off-premise or onboard airlines); (l) Different rates also applicable according to alcohol content, place of production, size of container, place purchased (on- or off-premise or on board airlines) or type of wine (carbonated, vermouth, etc.).
Source: Tax Foundation, 2016 Facts & Figures: How Does Your State Compare?

State Business Tax Climate Index Rankings

State	Overall Rank	Corporate Tax Rank	Individual Income Tax Rank	Sales Tax Rank	Unemployment Insurance Tax Rank	Property Tax Rank
Massachusetts	25	39	13	18	47	46

Note: The index is a measure of how each state's tax laws affect economic performance. The lower the rank, the more favorable a state's tax system is for business. States without a given tax are given a ranking of 1. The scores/rankings for the District of Columbia do not affect other states. The 2016 index represents the tax climate as of July 1, 2015 (the beginning of Fiscal Year 2016).
Source: Tax Foundation, State Business Tax Climate Index 2016

TRANSPORTATION

Means of Transportation to Work

Area	Car/Truck/Van: Drove Alone	Car/Truck/Van: Car-pooled	Public Transportation: Bus	Public Transportation: Subway	Public Transportation: Railroad	Bicycle	Walked	Other Means	Worked at Home
City	82.4	9.0	0.2	0.1	1.3	0.2	1.8	0.5	4.5
MSA[1]	82.0	8.9	0.7	0.1	0.6	0.1	2.8	0.8	4.0
U.S.	76.4	9.6	2.6	1.8	0.6	0.6	2.8	1.3	4.4

Note: Figures are percentages and cover workers 16 years of age and older; (1) Figures cover the Worcester, MA-CT Metropolitan Statistical Area—see Appendix B for areas included
Source: U.S. Census Bureau, 2010-2014 American Community Survey 5-Year Estimates

Travel Time to Work

Area	Less Than 10 Minutes	10 to 19 Minutes	20 to 29 Minutes	30 to 44 Minutes	45 to 59 Minutes	60 to 89 Minutes	90 Minutes or More
City	8.1	31.0	21.0	16.9	10.2	9.9	3.0
MSA[1]	12.5	27.7	19.2	20.1	9.5	8.1	2.8
U.S.	13.3	29.6	21.0	20.2	7.7	5.7	2.6

Note: Figures are percentages and include workers 16 years old and over; (1) Figures cover the Worcester, MA-CT Metropolitan Statistical Area—see Appendix B for areas included
Source: U.S. Census Bureau, 2010-2014 American Community Survey 5-Year Estimates

Freeway Travel Time Index

Area	1985	1990	1995	2000	2005	2010	2014
Urban Area Rank[1,2]	81	76	77	80	86	89	91
Urban Area Index[1]	1.04	1.07	1.09	1.11	1.12	1.12	1.12
Average Index[3]	1.09	1.11	1.14	1.17	1.20	1.19	1.20

Note: Freeway Travel Time Index—the ratio of travel time in the peak period to the travel time at free-flow conditions. For example, a value of 1.30 indicates a 20-minute free-flow trip takes 26 minutes in the peak (20 minutes x 1.30 = 26 minutes); (1) Covers the Worcester MA-CT urban area; (2) Rank is based on 101 urban areas (#1 = highest travel time index); (3) Average of 101 urban areas
Source: Texas Transportation Institute, 2015 Urban Mobility Scorecard, August 2015

Freeway Commuter Stress Index

Area	1985	1990	1995	2000	2005	2010	2014
Urban Area Rank[1,2]	66	75	81	85	88	89	90
Urban Area Index[1]	1.07	1.09	1.11	1.13	1.15	1.14	1.15
Average Index[3]	1.13	1.16	1.19	1.22	1.25	1.24	1.25

Note: The Freeway Commuter Stress Index is the same as the Freeway Travel Time Index (see table above) except that it includes only the travel in the peak directions during the peak periods; the TTI includes travel in all directions during the peak period. Thus, the CSI is more indicative of the work trip experienced by each commuter on a daily basis. (1) Covers the Worcester MA-CT urban area; (2) Rank is based on 101 urban areas (#1 = highest stress index); (3) Average of 101 urban areas
Source: Texas Transportation Institute, 2015 Urban Mobility Scorecard, August 2015

Living Environment

COST OF LIVING

Cost of Living Index

Composite Index	Groceries	Housing	Utilities	Trans-portation	Health Care	Misc. Goods/ Services
n/a	n/a	n/a	n/a	n/a	n/a	n/a

Note: The Cost of Living Index measures regional differences in the cost of consumer goods and services, excluding taxes and non-consumer expenditures, for professional and managerial households in the top income quintile. It is based on more than 50,000 prices covering almost 60 different items for which prices are collected three times a year by chambers of commerce, economic development organizations or university applied economic centers in each participating urban area. The numbers shown should be read as a percentage above or below the national average of 100. For example, a value of 115.4 in the groceries column indicates that grocery prices are 15.4% higher than the national average. Small differences in the index numbers should not be interpreted as significant; n/a not available.

Source: The Council for Community and Economic Research, ACCRA Cost of Living Index, 2015

Grocery Prices

Area[1]	T-Bone Steak ($/pound)	Frying Chicken ($/pound)	Whole Milk ($/half gal.)	Eggs ($/dozen)	Orange Juice ($/64 oz.)	Coffee ($/11.5 oz.)
City[2]	n/a	n/a	n/a	n/a	n/a	n/a
Avg.	10.99	1.43	2.25	2.26	3.58	4.48
Min.	7.16	0.98	1.30	1.35	2.88	2.98
Max.	14.13	2.43	3.85	4.81	6.39	7.56

Note: (1) Values for the local area are compared with the average, minimum and maximum values for all 292 areas in the Cost of Living Index; (2) Figures cover the Shrewsbury MA urban area; n/a not available; **T-Bone Steak** *(price per pound);* **Frying Chicken** *(price per pound, whole fryer);* **Whole Milk** *(half gallon carton);* **Eggs** *(price per dozen, Grade A, large);* **Orange Juice** *(64 oz. Tropicana or Florida Natural);* **Coffee** *(11.5 oz. can, vacuum-packed, Maxwell House, Hills Bros, or Folgers).*

Source: The Council for Community and Economic Research, ACCRA Cost of Living Index, 2015

Housing and Utility Costs

Area[1]	New Home Price ($)	Apartment Rent ($/month)	All Electric ($/month)	Part Electric ($/month)	Other Energy ($/month)	Telephone ($/month)
City[2]	n/a	n/a	n/a	n/a	n/a	n/a
Avg.	312,874	945	179.30	95.07	72.96	28.11
Min.	178,682	479	116.28	43.14	26.46	10.01
Max.	1,472,476	3,984	504.25	189.44	421.11	43.06

Note: (1) Values for the local area are compared with the average, minimum and maximum values for all 292 areas in the Cost of Living Index; (2) Figures cover the Shrewsbury MA urban area; n/a not available; **New Home Price** *(2,400 sf living area, 8,000 sf lot, in urban area with full utilities);* **Apartment Rent** *(950 sf 2 bedroom/1.5 or 2 bath, unfurnished, excluding all utilities except water);* **All Electric** *(average monthly cost for an all-electric home);* **Part Electric** *(average monthly cost for a part-electric home);* **Other Energy** *(average monthly cost for natural gas, fuel oil, coal, wood, and any other forms of energy except electricity);* **Telephone** *(price includes basic monthly rate for a private residential line plus additional local usage charges incurred by a family of four).*

Source: The Council for Community and Economic Research, ACCRA Cost of Living Index, 2015

Health Care, Transportation, and Other Costs

Area[1]	Doctor ($/visit)	Dentist ($/visit)	Optometrist ($/visit)	Gasoline ($/gallon)	Beauty Salon ($/visit)	Men's Shirt ($)
City[2]	n/a	n/a	n/a	n/a	n/a	n/a
Avg.	105.15	89.02	99.78	2.38	35.30	28.10
Min.	66.87	56.09	48.53	1.95	18.91	13.38
Max.	182.34	150.36	228.33	4.09	67.91	63.80

Note: (1) Values for the local area are compared with the average, minimum and maximum values for all 292 areas in the Cost of Living Index; (2) Figures cover the Shrewsbury MA urban area; n/a not available; **Doctor** *(general practitioners routine exam of an established patient);* **Dentist** *(adult teeth cleaning and periodic oral examination);* **Optometrist** *(full vision eye exam for established adult patient);* **Gasoline** *(one gallon regular unleaded, national brand, including all taxes, cash price at self-service pump if available);* **Beauty Salon** *(woman's shampoo, trim, and blow-dry);* **Men's Shirt** *(cotton/polyester dress shirt, pinpoint weave, long sleeves).*

Source: The Council for Community and Economic Research, ACCRA Cost of Living Index, 2015

HOUSING

House Price Index (HPI)

Area	National Ranking[2]	Quarterly Change (%)	One-Year Change (%)	Five-Year Change (%)
MSA[1]	160	0.80	3.90	4.90
U.S.[3]	–	1.45	5.76	22.85

Note: The HPI is a weighted repeat sales index. It measures average price changes in repeat sales or refinancings on the same properties. This information is obtained by reviewing repeat mortgage transactions on single-family properties whose mortgages have been purchased or securitized by Fannie Mae or Freddie Mac in January 1975; (1) Worcester Metropolitan Statistical Area—see Appendix B for areas included; (2) Rankings are based on annual percentage change for all metro areas containing at least 15,000 transactions over the last 10 years and ranges from 1 to 266; (3) figures based on a weighted average of Census Division estimates using a seasonally adjusted, purchase-only index; all figures are for the period ending December 31, 2015
Source: Federal Housing Finance Agency, House Price Index, February 25, 2016

Median Single-Family Home Prices

Area	2013	2014	2015p	Percent Change 2014 to 2015
MSA[1]	231.3	236.1	243.8	3.3
U.S. Average	197.4	208.9	223.9	7.2

Note: Figures are median sales prices of existing single-family homes in thousands of dollars; (p) preliminary; n/a not available; (1) Worcester, MA-CT Metropolitan Statistical Area—see Appendix B for areas included
Source: National Association of Realtors, Median Sales Price of Existing Single-Family Homes for Metropolitan Areas, 4th Quarter 2015

Qualifying Income Based on Median Sales Price of Existing Single-Family Homes

Area	With 5% Down ($)	With 10% Down ($)	With 20% Down ($)
MSA[1]	53,005	50,215	44,636
U.S. Average	49,535	46,928	41,714

Note: Figures are preliminary; Qualifying income is based on a mortgage rate of 4.1%. Monthly principal and interest payment is limited to 25% of income; n/a not available; (1) Worcester, MA-CT Metropolitan Statistical Area—see Appendix B for areas included
Source: National Association of Realtors, Qualifying Income Based on Median Sales Price of Existing Single-Family Homes for Metropolitan Areas, 4th Quarter 2015

Median Apartment Condo-Coop Home Prices

Area	2013	2014	2015p	Percent Change 2014 to 2015
MSA[1]	182.5	186.7	191.6	2.6
U.S. Average	194.9	204.3	210.7	3.1

Note: Figures are median sales prices of existing apartment condo-coop homes in thousands of dollars; (p) preliminary; n/a not available; (1) Worcester, MA-CT Metropolitan Statistical Area—see Appendix B for areas included
Source: National Association of Realtors, Median Sales Price of Existing Apartment Condo-Coop Homes for Metropolitan Areas, 4th Quarter 2015

Gross Monthly Rent

Area	Under $200	$200 -299	$300 -499	$500 -749	$750 -999	$1,000 -1,499	$1,500 and up	Median ($)
City	0.4	2.1	5.4	2.7	17.3	51.6	20.6	1,232
MSA[1]	1.5	5.5	8.6	15.8	28.6	31.1	8.9	920
U.S.	1.5	3.2	7.4	21.0	24.1	26.9	15.9	920

Note: Figures are percentages except for Median; Gross rent is the contract rent plus the estimated average monthly cost of utilities (electricity, gas, and water and sewer) and fuels (oil, coal, kerosene, wood, etc.) if these are paid by the renter (or paid for the renter by someone else); (1) Figures cover the Worcester, MA-CT Metropolitan Statistical Area—see Appendix B for areas included
Source: U.S. Census Bureau, 2010-2014 American Community Survey 5-Year Estimates

Homeownership Rate

Area	2008 (%)	2009 (%)	2010 (%)	2011 (%)	2012 (%)	2013 (%)	2014 (%)	2015 (%)
MSA[1]	68.5	64.4	64.1	65.8	61.9	63.3	62.5	64.2
U.S.	67.8	67.4	66.9	66.1	65.4	65.1	64.5	63.7

Note: (1) Figures cover the Worcester, MA-CT Metropolitan Statistical Area—see Appendix B for areas included
Source: U.S. Census Bureau, Housing Vacancies and Homeownership Annual Statistics: 2015

Year Housing Structure Built

Area	2010 or Later	2000 -2009	1990 -1999	1980 -1989	1970 -1979	1960 -1969	1950 -1959	1940 -1949	Before 1940	Median Year
City	0.7	11.8	17.4	11.3	14.2	7.7	15.0	7.0	14.9	1974
MSA[1]	0.6	9.1	9.1	12.6	11.7	8.5	10.5	5.8	32.1	1962
U.S.	1.0	14.9	13.9	13.8	15.8	11.0	10.8	5.4	13.3	1976

Note: Figures are percentages except for Median Year; (1) Figures cover the Worcester, MA-CT Metropolitan Statistical Area—see Appendix B for areas included
Source: U.S. Census Bureau, 2010-2014 American Community Survey 5-Year Estimates

HEALTH

Health Risk Data

Category	MSA[1] (%)	U.S. (%)
Adults aged 18–64 who have any kind of health care coverage	91.8	79.6
Adults who reported being in good or excellent health	87.3	83.1
Adults who are current smokers	17.6	19.6
Adults who are heavy drinkers[2]	7.4	6.1
Adults who are binge drinkers[3]	19.6	16.9
Adults who are overweight (BMI 25.0 - 29.9)	33.5	35.8
Adults who are obese (BMI 30.0 - 99.8)	28.5	27.6
Adults who participated in any physical activities in the past month	79.7	77.1
Adults 50+ who have ever had a sigmoidoscopy or colonoscopy	76.4	67.3
Women aged 40+ who have had a mammogram within the past two years	83.5	74.0
Men aged 40+ who have had a PSA test within the past two years	40.8	45.2
Adults aged 65+ who have had flu shot within the past year	63.8	60.1
Adults who always wear a seatbelt	90.4	93.8

Note: Data as of 2012 unless otherwise noted; (1) Figures cover the Worcester, MA Metropolitan Statistical Area—see Appendix B for areas included; (2) Heavy drinkers are classified as males having more than two drinks per day or females having more than one drink per day; (3) Binge drinkers are classified as males having five or more drinks on one occasion or females having four or more drinks on one occasion
Source: Centers for Disease Control and Prevention, Behaviorial Risk Factor Surveillance System, SMART: Selected Metropolitan/Micropolitan Area Risk Trends, 2012 (Note: the CDC has discontinued this dataset but will be releasing a replacement in mid-2016)

Chronic Health Indicators

Category	MSA[1] (%)	U.S. (%)
Adults who have ever been told they had a heart attack	4.3	4.5
Adults who have ever been told they had a stroke	2.4	2.9
Adults who have been told they currently have asthma	11.8	8.9
Adults who have ever been told they have arthritis	24.5	25.7
Adults who have ever been told they have diabetes[2]	9.0	9.7
Adults who have ever been told they had skin cancer	5.0	5.7
Adults who have ever been told they had any other types of cancer	5.7	6.5
Adults who have ever been told they have COPD	6.7	6.2
Adults who have ever been told they have kidney disease	2.0	2.5
Adults who have ever been told they have a form of depression	19.3	18.0

Note: Data as of 2012 unless otherwise noted; (1) Figures cover the Worcester, MA Metropolitan Statistical Area—see Appendix B for areas included; (2) Figures do not include pregnancy-related, borderline, or pre-diabetes
Source: Centers for Disease Control and Prevention, Behaviorial Risk Factor Surveillance System, SMART: Selected Metropolitan/Micropolitan Area Risk Trends, 2012 (Note: the CDC has discontinued this dataset but will be releasing a replacement in mid-2016)

Mortality Rates for the Top 10 Causes of Death in the U.S.

ICD-10[a] Sub-Chapter	ICD-10[a] Code	Age-Adjusted Mortality Rate[1] per 100,000 population	
		County[2]	U.S.
Malignant neoplasms	C00-C97	166.2	163.6
Ischaemic heart diseases	I20-I25	87.3	102.2
Other forms of heart disease	I30-I51	50.0	50.1
Chronic lower respiratory diseases	J40-J47	38.1	41.4
Organic, including symptomatic, mental disorders	F01-F09	52.9	38.5
Cerebrovascular diseases	I60-I69	34.0	36.5
Other external causes of accidental injury	W00-X59	27.1	27.5
Other degenerative diseases of the nervous system	G30-G31	24.9	26.3
Diabetes mellitus	E10-E14	17.2	21.1
Hypertensive diseases	I10-I15	12.4	19.7

Note: (a) ICD-10 = International Classification of Diseases 10th Revision; (1) Mortality rates are a three year average covering 2012-2014; (2) Figures cover Worcester County.
Source: Centers for Disease Control and Prevention, National Center for Health Statistics. Underlying Cause of Death 1999-2014 on CDC WONDER Online Database, released 2015.

Mortality Rates for Selected Causes of Death

ICD-10[a] Sub-Chapter	ICD-10[a] Code	Age-Adjusted Mortality Rate[1] per 100,000 population	
		County[2]	U.S.
Assault	X85-Y09	1.4	5.1
Diseases of the liver	K70-K76	10.7	13.5
Human immunodeficiency virus (HIV) disease	B20-B24	1.1	2.1
Influenza and pneumonia	J09-J18	19.4	15.2
Intentional self-harm	X60-X84	9.2	12.7
Malnutrition	E40-E46	0.8	0.9
Obesity and other hyperalimentation	E65-E68	1.4	1.9
Renal failure	N17-N19	14.1	13.0
Transport accidents	V01-V99	6.8	11.6
Viral hepatitis	B15-B19	1.4	2.1

Note: (a) ICD-10 = International Classification of Diseases 10th Revision; (1) Mortality rates are a three year average covering 2012-2014; (2) Figures cover Worcester County; Data are Suppressed when the data meet the criteria for confidentiality constraints; Mortality rates are flagged as Unreliable when the rate would be calculated with a numerator of 20 or less.
Source: Centers for Disease Control and Prevention, National Center for Health Statistics. Underlying Cause of Death 1999-2014 on CDC WONDER Online Database, released 2015.

Health Insurance Coverage

Area	With Health Insurance	With Private Health Insurance	With Public Health Insurance	Without Health Insurance	Population Under Age 18 Without Health Insurance
City	97.5	87.2	22.3	2.5	2.1
MSA[1]	95.9	74.7	33.1	4.1	1.5
U.S.	85.8	65.8	31.1	14.2	7.1

Note: Figures are percentages that cover the civilian noninstitutionalized population; (1) Figures cover the Worcester, MA-CT Metropolitan Statistical Area—see Appendix B for areas included
Source: U.S. Census Bureau, 2010-2014 American Community Survey 5-Year Estimates

Number of Medical Professionals

Area	MDs[3]	DOs[3,4]	Dentists	Podiatrists	Chiropractors	Optometrists
County[1] (number)	2,892	150	542	51	166	140
County[1] (rate[2])	356.9	18.5	66.6	6.3	20.4	17.2
U.S. (rate[2])	272.5	20.9	64.7	5.8	25.9	15.2

Note: Data as of 2014 unless noted; (1) Data covers Worcester County; (2) Rate per 100,000 population; (3) Data as of 2013 and includes all active, non-federal physicians; (4) Doctor of Osteopathic Medicine
Source: U.S. Department of Health and Human Services, Health Resources and Services Administration, Bureau of Health Professions, Area Resource File (ARF) 2014-2015

EDUCATION

Public School District Statistics

District Name	Schls	Pupils	Pupil/ Teacher Ratio	Minority Pupils[1] (%)	Free Lunch Eligible[2] (%)	IEP[3] (%)
Shrewsbury	9	6,011	17.6	33.2	9.9	13.9

Note: Table includes school districts with 100 or more students; (1) Percentage of students that are not non-Hispanic white; (2) Percentage of students that are eligible for the free lunch program; (3) Percentage of students that have an Individualized Education Program.
Source: U.S. Department of Education, National Center for Education Statistics, Common Core of Data, Local Education Agency (School District) Universe Survey: School Year 2013-2014; U.S. Department of Education, National Center for Education Statistics, Common Core of Data, Public Elementary/Secondary School Universe Survey: School Year 2013-2014

Highest Level of Education

Area	Less than H.S.	H.S. Diploma	Some College, No Deg.	Associate Degree	Bachelor's Degree	Master's Degree	Prof. School Degree	Doctorate Degree
City	5.2	18.4	12.8	8.4	28.2	18.5	4.1	4.3
MSA[1]	10.6	29.6	18.1	9.0	20.2	9.3	1.7	1.5
U.S.	13.7	28.0	21.2	7.9	18.3	7.8	2.0	1.3

Note: Figures cover persons age 25 and over; (1) Figures cover the Worcester, MA-CT Metropolitan Statistical Area—see Appendix B for areas included
Source: U.S. Census Bureau, 2010-2014 American Community Survey 5-Year Estimates

Educational Attainment by Race

Area	High School Graduate or Higher (%)					Bachelor's Degree or Higher (%)				
	Total	White	Black	Asian	Hisp.[2]	Total	White	Black	Asian	Hisp.[2]
City	94.8	95.4	97.9	93.0	80.9	55.2	51.6	53.1	76.3	33.2
MSA[1]	89.4	90.7	87.0	82.8	67.7	32.7	33.1	23.3	53.4	14.7
U.S.	86.3	88.4	83.2	85.8	64.1	29.3	30.6	19.0	50.9	13.9

Note: Figures shown cover persons 25 years old and over; (1) Figures cover the Worcester, MA-CT Metropolitan Statistical Area—see Appendix B for areas included; (2) People of Hispanic origin can be of any race
Source: U.S. Census Bureau, 2010-2014 American Community Survey 5-Year Estimates

School Enrollment by Grade and Control

Area	Preschool (%)		Kindergarten (%)		Grades 1 - 4 (%)		Grades 5 - 8 (%)		Grades 9 - 12 (%)	
	Public	Private	Public	Private	Public	Private	Public	Private	Public	Private
City	52.7	47.3	82.8	17.2	88.6	11.4	87.5	12.5	87.7	12.3
MSA[1]	58.2	41.8	90.2	9.8	92.2	7.8	91.7	8.3	90.8	9.2
U.S.	57.4	42.6	87.8	12.2	89.8	10.2	89.9	10.1	90.6	9.4

Note: Figures shown cover persons 3 years old and over; (1) Figures cover the Worcester, MA-CT Metropolitan Statistical Area—see Appendix B for areas included
Source: U.S. Census Bureau, 2010-2014 American Community Survey 5-Year Estimates

Average Salaries of Public School Classroom Teachers

Area	2013-14		2014-15		Percent Change 2013-14 to 2014-15	Percent Change 2004-05 to 2014-15
	Dollars	Rank[1]	Dollars	Rank[1]		
Massachusetts	73,195	2	74,805	3	2.20	36.8
U.S. Average	56,610	–	57,379	–	1.36	20.8

Note: (1) State rank ranges from 1 to 51 where 1 indicates highest salary.
Source: National Education Association, Rankings & Estimates: Rankings of the States 2014 and Estimates of School Statistics 2015, March 2015

Higher Education

Four-Year Colleges			Two-Year Colleges			Medical Schools[1]	Law Schools[2]	Voc/ Tech[3]
Public	Private Non-profit	Private For-profit	Public	Private Non-profit	Private For-profit			
0	0	0	0	0	0	0	0	0

Note: Figures cover institutions located within the city limits and include main campuses only; (1) includes schools accredited by the Liaison Committee on Medical Education and the American Osteopathic Association's Commission on Osteopathic College Accreditation; (2) includes ABA-accredited schools, schools with provisional ABA accreditation, and state accredited schools; (3) includes all schools with programs that are less than 2 years.

Source: National Center for Education Statistics, Integrated Postsecondary Education System (IPEDS), 2014-15; Association of American Medical Colleges, Member List, March 21, 2016; American Osteopathic Association, Member List, March 21, 2016; Law School Admission Council, Official Guide to ABA-Approved Law Schools Online, March 21, 2016; Wikipedia, List of Medical Schools in the United States, March 21, 2016; Wikipedia, List of Law Schools in the United States, March 21, 2016

According to *U.S. News & World Report,* the Worcester, MA-CT metro area is home to two of the best national universities in the U.S.: **Worcester Polytechnic Institute** (#57 tie); **Clark University** (#75 tie). The indicators used to capture academic quality fall into a number of categories: assessment by administrators at peer institutions; retention of students; faculty resources; student selectivity; financial resources; alumni giving; high school counselor ratings of colleges; and graduation rate. *U.S. News & World Report, "America's Best Colleges 2016"*

According to *U.S. News & World Report,* the Worcester, MA-CT metro area is home to one of the best liberal arts colleges in the U.S.: **College of the Holy Cross** (#32 tie). The indicators used to capture academic quality fall into a number of categories: assessment by administrators at peer institutions; retention of students; faculty resources; student selectivity; financial resources; alumni giving; high school counselor ratings of colleges; and graduation rate. *U.S. News & World Report, "America's Best Colleges 2016"*

According to *U.S. News & World Report,* the Worcester, MA-CT metro area is home to one of the top 75 medical schools for research in the U.S.: **University of Massachusetts–Worcester, School of Medicine** (#52 tie). The rankings are based on a weighted average of 11 measures of quality: quality assessment; peer assessment score; assessment score by residency directors; research activity; total research activity; average research activity per faculty member; student selectivity; median MCAT total score; median undergraduate GPA; acceptance rate; and faculty resources. *U.S. News & World Report, "America's Best Graduate Schools, Medical, 2017"*

PRESIDENTIAL ELECTION

2012 Presidential Election Results

Area	Obama (%)	Romney (%)	Other (%)
Worcester County	53.7	44.5	1.8
U.S.	51.0	47.2	1.8

Note: Results may not add to 100% due to rounding
Source: Dave Leip's Atlas of U.S. Presidential Elections

EMPLOYERS

Major Employers

Company Name	Industry
3M Co	Manufacturer
Abb Vie Bioresearch Center	Pharmaceutical research & development
Abrasives Marketing Group	Marketing
Affiliated Podiatrists	Healthcare
Allegro Micro Systems Inc	Manufacturer
Amica Mutual Insurance Co	Insurance
Assumption College	Education
Astra Zeneca	Pharmaceutical research & development
Babcock Power Environmental	Utility
Bj's Wholesale Club	Retail
Bny Mellon Wealth Management	Finance
College of the Holy Cross	Education
Commerce Insurance Co	Insurance
Community Healthlink	Healthcare
Hanover Insurance Co	Insurance
Hanover Insurance Group	Insurance
Integrated Genetics	Lab testing
Mapfre USA Corp	Insurance
Mt Wachusett Ski Area	Ski resort
P F Pc Inc	Finance
Saint-Gobain Abrasives	Manufacturer
Saint-Gobain Ceramic Materials	Manufacturer
St Vincent Hospital	Healthcare
Vna Care Network	Healthcare
Wachusett Mountain	Ski resort

Note: Companies shown are located within the Worcester, MA-CT Metropolitan Statistical Area.
Source: Hoovers.com; Wikipedia

PUBLIC SAFETY

Crime Rate

Area	All Crimes	Violent Crimes: Murder	Violent Crimes: Rape[3]	Violent Crimes: Robbery	Violent Crimes: Aggrav. Assault	Property Crimes: Burglary	Property Crimes: Larceny -Theft	Property Crimes: Motor Vehicle Theft
City	576.8	0.0	2.7	2.7	0.0	142.2	415.6	13.7
Metro[1]	2,295.2	0.9	25.1	74.1	320.9	438.9	1,338.7	96.6
U.S.	2,971.8	4.5	36.6	102.2	232.5	542.5	1,837.3	216.2

Note: Figures are crimes per 100,000 population; (1) Figures cover the Worcester, MA-CT Metropolitan Statistical Area—see Appendix B for areas included; (3) The city and U.S. figures shown were reported using the revised Uniform Crime Reporting (UCR) definition of rape. The suburban and metro area figures shown are an aggregate total of the data submitted using both the revised and legacy UCR definitions.
Source: FBI Uniform Crime Reports, 2014

Hate Crimes

Area	Number of Quarters Reported	Race	Religion	Sexual Orientation	Ethnicity	Disability	Gender	Gender Identity
		Number of Incidents per Bias Motivation						
City	4	0	0	0	0	0	0	0
U.S.	4	2,568	1,014	1,017	648	84	33	98

Source: Federal Bureau of Investigation, Hate Crime Statistics 2014

Identity Theft Consumer Complaints

Area	Complaints	Complaints per 100,000 Population	Rank[2]
MSA[1]	1,082	116.3	137
U.S.	490,220	152.4	-

Note: (1) Figures cover the Worcester, MA-CT Metropolitan Statistical Area—see Appendix B for areas included; (2) Rank ranges from 1 to 379 where 1 indicates greatest number of identity theft complaints per 100,000 population
Source: Federal Trade Commission, Consumer Sentinel Network Data Book for January–December 2015

Fraud and Other Consumer Complaints

Area	Complaints	Complaints per 100,000 Population	Rank[2]
MSA[1]	3,255	349.8	216
U.S.	2,593,159	806.0	-

Note: (1) Figures cover the Worcester, MA-CT Metropolitan Statistical Area—see Appendix B for areas included; (2) Rank ranges from 1 to 379 where 1 indicates greatest number of identity theft complaints per 100,000 population
Source: Federal Trade Commission, Consumer Sentinel Network Data Book for January–December 2015

RECREATION

Culture

Dance[1]	Theatre[1]	Instrumental Music[1]	Vocal Music[1]	Series and Festivals	Museums and Art Galleries[2]	Zoos and Aquariums[3]
0	0	0	0	0	0	0

Note: (1) Professional perfoming groups; (2) Based on organizations with SIC code 8412; (3) AZA-accredited
Source: The Grey House Performing Arts Directory, 2015-16; Association of Zoos & Aquariums, AZA Member Zoos & Aquariums, March 25, 2016; www.AccuLeads.com, March 29, 2016

Professional Sports Teams

Team Name	League	Year Established
No teams are located in the metro area		

Source: Wikipedia, Major Professional Sports Teams of the United States and Canada, March 24, 2016

CLIMATE

Average and Extreme Temperatures

Temperature	Jan	Feb	Mar	Apr	May	Jun	Jul	Aug	Sep	Oct	Nov	Dec	Yr.
Extreme High (°F)	67	67	81	91	92	98	96	97	99	85	79	70	99
Average High (°F)	32	34	42	55	66	75	79	77	69	59	47	35	56
Average Temp. (°F)	24	26	34	45	56	65	70	68	60	51	40	28	47
Average Low (°F)	16	18	25	35	46	55	61	59	51	41	32	21	38
Extreme Low (°F)	-13	-12	-6	11	28	36	43	38	30	20	6	-13	-13

Note: Figures cover the years 1949-1992
Source: National Climatic Data Center, International Station Meteorological Climate Summary, 9/96

Average Precipitation/Snowfall/Humidity

Precip./Humidity	Jan	Feb	Mar	Apr	May	Jun	Jul	Aug	Sep	Oct	Nov	Dec	Yr.
Avg. Precip. (in.)	3.6	3.4	4.1	4.0	4.3	3.7	3.7	4.1	4.0	4.1	4.5	4.1	47.6
Avg. Snowfall (in.)	16	16	11	3	Tr	0	0	0	Tr	1	4	13	62
Avg. Rel. Hum. 7am (%)	72	73	71	69	70	73	76	79	81	78	78	75	75
Avg. Rel. Hum. 4pm (%)	61	58	55	50	52	57	58	61	62	58	63	65	58

Note: Figures cover the years 1949-1992; Tr = Trace amounts (<0.05 in. of rain; <0.5 in. of snow)
Source: National Climatic Data Center, International Station Meteorological Climate Summary, 9/96

Weather Conditions

Temperature			Daytime Sky			Precipitation		
5°F & below	32°F & below	90°F & above	Clear	Partly cloudy	Cloudy	0.01 inch or more precip.	0.1 inch or more snow/ice	Thunder-storms
12	141	4	81	144	140	131	32	23

Note: Figures are average number of days per year and cover the years 1949-1992
Source: National Climatic Data Center, International Station Meteorological Climate Summary, 9/96

HAZARDOUS WASTE

Superfund Sites

Shrewsbury has no sites on the EPA's Superfund Final National Priorities List. There are a total of 1,323 Superfund sites on the list in the U.S. *U.S. Environmental Protection Agency, Final National Priorities List, March 18, 2016*

AIR & WATER QUALITY

Air Quality Trends: Ozone

	1990	1995	2000	2005	2010	2011	2012	2013	2014
MSA[1]	0.097	0.096	0.076	0.085	0.070	0.065	0.070	0.067	0.065

Note: (1) Data covers the Worcester, MA-CT Metropolitan Statistical Area—see Appendix B for areas included. The values shown are the composite ozone concentration averages among trend sites based on the highest fourth daily maximum 8-hour concentration in parts per million. These trends are based on sites having an adequate record of monitoring data during the trend period. Data from exceptional events are included.
Source: U.S. Environmental Protection Agency, Air Quality Monitoring Information, "Air Quality Trends by City, 1990-2014"

Air Quality Index

Area	Percent of Days when Air Quality was...[2]					AQI Statistics[2]	
	Good	Moderate	Unhealthy for Sensitive Groups	Unhealthy	Very Unhealthy	Maximum	Median
MSA[1]	85.8	14.0	0.3	0.0	0.0	109	36

Note: (1) Data covers the Worcester, MA-CT Metropolitan Statistical Area—see Appendix B for areas included; (2) Based on 365 days with AQI data in 2015. Air Quality Index (AQI) is an index for reporting daily air quality. EPA calculates the AQI for five major air pollutants regulated by the Clean Air Act: ground-level ozone, particle pollution (aka particulate matter), carbon monoxide, sulfur dioxide, and nitrogen dioxide. The AQI runs from 0 to 500. The higher the AQI value, the greater the level of air pollution and the greater the health concern. There are six AQI categories: "Good" AQI is between 0 and 50. Air quality is considered satisfactory; "Moderate" AQI is between 51 and 100. Air quality is acceptable; "Unhealthy for Sensitive Groups" When AQI values are between 101 and 150, members of sensitive groups may experience health effects; "Unhealthy" When AQI values are between 151 and 200 everyone may begin to experience health effects; "Very Unhealthy" AQI values between 201 and 300 trigger a health alert; "Hazardous" AQI values over 300 trigger warnings of emergency conditions (not shown).
Source: U.S. Environmental Protection Agency, Air Quality Index Report, 2015

Air Quality Index Pollutants

Area	Percent of Days when AQI Pollutant was...[2]					
	Carbon Monoxide	Nitrogen Dioxide	Ozone	Sulfur Dioxide	Particulate Matter 2.5	Particulate Matter 10
MSA[1]	0.0	8.2	70.4	0.0	21.4	0.0

Note: (1) Data covers the Worcester, MA-CT Metropolitan Statistical Area—see Appendix B for areas included; (2) Based on 365 days with AQI data in 2015. The Air Quality Index (AQI) is an index for reporting daily air quality. EPA calculates the AQI for five major air pollutants regulated by the Clean Air Act: ground-level ozone, particle pollution (also known as particulate matter), carbon monoxide, sulfur dioxide, and nitrogen dioxide. The AQI runs from 0 to 500. The higher the AQI value, the greater the level of air pollution and the greater the health concern.
Source: U.S. Environmental Protection Agency, Air Quality Index Report, 2015

Maximum Air Pollutant Concentrations: Particulate Matter, Ozone, CO and Lead

	Particulate Matter 10 (ug/m^3)	Particulate Matter 2.5 Wtd AM (ug/m^3)	Particulate Matter 2.5 24-Hr (ug/m^3)	Ozone (ppm)	Carbon Monoxide (ppm)	Lead (ug/m^3)
MSA[1] Level	67	7.1	18	0.065	1	n/a
NAAQS[2]	150	15	35	0.075	9	0.15
Met NAAQS[2]	Yes	Yes	Yes	Yes	Yes	n/a

Note: (1) Data covers the Worcester, MA-CT Metropolitan Statistical Area—see Appendix B for areas included; Data from exceptional events are included; (2) National Ambient Air Quality Standards; ppm = parts per million; ug/m^3 = micrograms per cubic meter; n/a not available.
Concentrations: Particulate Matter 10 (coarse particulate)—highest second maximum 24-hour concentration; Particulate Matter 2.5 Wtd AM (fine particulate)—highest weighted annual mean concentration; Particulate Matter 2.5 24-Hour (fine particulate)—highest 98th percentile 24-hour concentration; Ozone—highest fourth daily maximum 8-hour concentration; Carbon Monoxide—highest second maximum non-overlapping 8-hour concentration; Lead—maximum running 3-month average
Source: U.S. Environmental Protection Agency, Air Quality Monitoring Information, "Air Quality Statistics by City, 2014"

Maximum Air Pollutant Concentrations: Nitrogen Dioxide and Sulfur Dioxide

	Nitrogen Dioxide AM (ppb)	Nitrogen Dioxide 1-Hr (ppb)	Sulfur Dioxide AM (ppb)	Sulfur Dioxide 1-Hr (ppb)	Sulfur Dioxide 24-Hr (ppb)
MSA[1] Level	13	49	n/a	9	n/a
NAAQS[2]	53	100	30	75	140
Met NAAQS[2]	Yes	Yes	n/a	Yes	n/a

Note: (1) Data covers the Worcester, MA-CT Metropolitan Statistical Area—see Appendix B for areas included; Data from exceptional events are included; (2) National Ambient Air Quality Standards; ppm = parts per million; ug/m³ = micrograms per cubic meter; n/a not available.
Concentrations: Nitrogen Dioxide AM—highest arithmetic mean concentration; Nitrogen Dioxide 1-Hr—highest 98th percentile 1-hour daily maximum concentration; Sulfur Dioxide AM—highest annual mean concentration; Sulfur Dioxide 1-Hr—highest 99th percentile 1-hour daily maximum concentration; Sulfur Dioxide 24-Hr—highest second maximum 24-hour concentration
Source: U.S. Environmental Protection Agency, Air Quality Monitoring Information, "Air Quality Statistics by City, 2014"

Drinking Water

Water System Name	Pop. Served	Primary Water Source Type	Violations[1]	
			Health Based	Monitoring/ Reporting
Shrewsbury Water Dept	35,608	Ground	0	0

Note: (1) Based on violation data from January 1, 2015 to December 31, 2015 (includes unresolved violations from earlier years)
Source: U.S. Environmental Protection Agency, Office of Ground Water and Drinking Water, Safe Drinking Water Information System (based on data extracted April 29, 2016)

Wellesley, Massachusetts

Background

Wellesley, about 15 miles west of Boston, has long been one of the most attractive towns in the greater Boston area. It is a quiet residential town, but it has many attractions, diverse businesses, and a highly educated and professional population.

In 1681, the site of present-day Needham and Wellesley was acquired from Native Americans who lived on the land. In 1771, the town was incorporated as Needham. In 1881, however, citizens in the western part of Needham became dissatisfied with the administration of town affairs and broke away to form the town of Wellesley. Today Wellesley is governed by town meeting, with day-to-day operations in the hands of an elected town clerk and a five-member board of selectmen whose terms of service are staggered.

Wellesley is a town devoted to higher education. Wellesley College, founded in 1870, is internationally known as one of America's best institutions of higher learning. In an age when many former women's colleges have become coeducational, Wellesley continues to admit women only, adhering to the goals and advantages of a college with a single-sex student body. Enjoying an endowment of over a billion dollars, the college admits a multicultural student body on a need-blind basis: Anyone who requires financial aid receives it, and approximately half the students today get some sort of assistance.

Also located in Wellesley is Babson College, founded in 1919, a leading coeducational business school granting undergraduate and graduate degrees. Babson has many programs for future entrepreneurs as well as businessmen, and it is recipient of many "best of" citations. Nearly all of its graduates find quick employment, and many rise to positions of leadership.

The Massachusetts Bay Community College maintains a campus in Wellesley, and the city is also home to the prestigious Dana Hall School, enrolling girls from grades six through twelve. Dana Hall's Music School, serving the community as well as Dana Hall students, has earned a nationwide reputation in its own right.

Today the town flourishes, blessed by its educational and cultural riches. Many of its citizens commute to Boston and other communities, but a fair number of important commercial and service operations are located within the town itself.

The weather in Wellesley is the same as elsewhere in the greater Boston area—generally warmer in summer than areas to the north and west and milder in winter. Snow is moderate, though occasional winters see especially heavy snowfalls during "Nor'easters" that blow up the coast.

Rankings

Business/Finance Rankings

- The personal finance site NerdWallet analyzed 183 American metropolitan areas with populations over 250,000 and more than 15,000 businesses to rank where entrepreneurs find the most success. Criteria included area economy, annual income, housing cost, unemployment rate, and the success rate of area businesses. Boston* ranked #30. *www.nerdwallet.com, "Best Places to Start a Business," April 27, 2015*

- TransUnion ranked the nation's metro areas by average credit score, calculated on the VantageScore system, developed by the three major credit-reporting bureaus—TransUnion, Experian, and Equifax. The Boston* metro area was among the ten cities with the highest collective credit score, meaning that its residents posed the lowest average consumer credit risk. *www.usatoday.com, "Metro Areas' Average Credit Rating Revealed," February 7, 2013*

- Based on the U.S. Department of Labor's Occupational Information Network Data Collection Program, the Brookings Institution defined job opportunities for STEM workers at various levels of educational attainment. The Boston* metro area was placed among the ten large metro areas with the highest demand for high-level STEM knowledge. *www.brookings.edu, "The Hidden Stem Economy," June 10, 2013*

- 24/7 Wall Street used Brookings Institution research on 50 advanced industries to identify the proportion of workers in the nation's largest metropolitan areas that were employed in jobs requiring knowledge in the science, technology, engineering, or math (STEM) fields. The Boston* metro area was #8. *247wallst.com, "15 Cities with the Most High-Tech Jobs," March 13, 2015*

- Based on metro area social media reviews, the employment opinion group Glassdoor surveyed 50 of the largest U.S. metro areas and equally weighed cost of living, hiring opportunity, and job satisfaction to compose a list of "25 Best Cities for Jobs." The Boston* metro area was ranked #6 in overall job satisfaction. *www.glassdoor.com, "Best Cities for Jobs," May 19, 2015*

- In a survey of economic confidence in the nation's 50 largest metropolitan areas conducted January–December 2014, the Boston* metro area placed #13, according to Gallup's 2014 Economic Confidence Index. *Gallup, "San Jose and San Francisco Lead in Economic Confidence," March 19, 2015*

- The Brookings Institution ranked the 100 largest metro areas in the U.S. based on income inequality. Boston* was ranked #6 (#1 = greatest ineqality). Criteria: the "95/20 ratio," a figure representing the income at which a household earns more than 95 percent of all other households, divided by the income at which a household earns more than only 20 percent of all other households. *Brookings Institution, "Income Inequality, 100 Largest U.S. Metro Areas, 2007-2014," January 14, 2016*

- Payscale.com ranked the 20 largest metro areas in terms of wage growth. The Boston* metro area ranked #6. Criteria: private-sector wage growth between the 1st quarter of 2015 and the 1st quarter of 2016. *PayScale, "Wage Trends by Metro Area," 1st Quarter, 2016*

- Boston* was identified as one of America's most frugal metro areas by *Coupons.com.* The city ranked #20 out of 25. Criteria: online coupon usage. *Coupons.com, "Top 25 Most Frugal Cities of 2014," May 11, 2015*

- The Boston* metro area appeared on the Milken Institute "2015 Best Performing Cities" list. Rank: #51 out of 200 large metro areas. Criteria: job growth; wage and salary growth; high-tech output growth. *Milken Institute, "Best-Performing Cities 2015," December 2015*

- *Forbes* ranked the 200 most populous metro areas to determine the nation's "Best Places for Business and Careers." The Boston* metro area was ranked #55. Criteria: costs (business and living); job growth (past and projected); income growth; educational attainment (college and high school); projected economic growth; cultural and recreational opportunities; net migration patterns; number of highly ranked colleges. *Forbes, "The Best Places for Business and Careers 2015," July 29, 2015*

Dating/Romance Rankings

- CreditDonkey, a financial education website, sought out the ten best U.S. cities for newlyweds, considering the number of married couples, divorce rate, average credit score, and average number of hours worked per week in metro areas with a million or more residents. The Boston* metro area placed #3. *www.creditdonkey.com, "Study: Best Cities for Newlyweds," November 30, 2013*

Education Rankings

- The Boston* metro area was selected as one of the world's most inventive cities by *Forbes*. The area was ranked #7 out of 15. Criteria: patent applications per capita. *Forbes, "World's 15 Most Inventive Cities," July 9, 2013*

- Boston* was identified as one of America's "smartest" metropolitan areas by *The Business Journals*. The area ranked #4 out of 10. Criteria: percentage of adults (25 and older) with high school diplomas, bachelor's degrees and graduate degrees. *The Business Journals, "Where the Brainpower Is: Exclusive U.S. Rankings, Insights," February 27, 2014*

- Personal finance website *WalletHub* analyzed the 150 largest U.S. metropolitan statistical areas to determine where the most educated Americans are choosing to settle. Criteria: education quality and attainment gap; education levels; percentage of workers with degrees; public school rankings; quality and size of each metro area's universities. Boston* was ranked #7 (#1 = most educated city). *www.WalletHub.com, "2015's Most and Least Educated Cities*

- Boston* was identified as one of the "Smartest Cities in America" by the brain-training website *Lumosity* using data from three million of its own users. The metro area ranked #49 out of 50. Criteria: users' brain performance index scores, considering core cognitive abilities such as memory, processing speed, flexibility, attention and problem-solving. *Lumosity, " Smartest Cities in America," June 25, 2013*

Environmental Rankings

- The Boston* metro area came in at #107 for the relative comfort of its climate on Sperling's list of "chill cities," as measured by the Sperling Heat Index. All 361 metro areas are included. Criteria included daytime high temperatures, nighttime low temperatures, dew point, and relative humidity at the high temperatures. *www.bertsperling.com, "Sperling's Chill Cities," July 18, 2013*

- Sperling's BestPlaces assessed 379 metropolitan areas of the United States for the likelihood of dangerously extreme weather events or earthquakes. In general the Southeast and South-Central regions have the highest risk of weather extremes and earthquakes, while the Pacific Northwest enjoys the lowest risk. Of the least risky metropolitan areas, the Boston* metro area was ranked #243. *www.bestplaces.net, "Safest Places from Natural Disasters," April 2011*

- The U.S. Environmental Protection Agency (EPA) released a list of U.S. metropolitan areas with the most ENERGY STAR certified buildings in 2015. The Boston* metro area was ranked #11 out of 25. *U.S. Environmental Protection Agency, "Top Cities With the Most ENERGY STAR Certified Buildings in 2016," March 30, 2016*

Health/Fitness Rankings

- Analysts who tracked obesity rates in the nation's largest metro areas (populations above one million) found that the Boston* metro area was one of the ten major metros where residents were least likely to be obese, defined as a BMI score of 30 or above. *www.gallup.com, "Boulder, Colo., Residents Still Least Likely to Be Obese," April 4, 2014*

- Analysts who tracked obesity rates in 100 of the nation's most populous areas found that the Boston* metro area was one of the ten communities where residents were least likely to be obese, defined as a BMI score of 30 or above. *www.gallup.com, "Colorado Springs Residents Least Likely to Be Obese," May 28, 2015*

- For each of the 50 most populous metro areas in the United States, the American College of Sports Medicine's American Fitness Index evaluated infrastructure, community assets, and policies that encourage healthy and fit lifestyles, including preventive health behaviors, levels of chronic disease conditions, health care access, and community resources and policies that support physical activity. The Boston* metro area ranked #9 for "community fitness." *www.americanfitnessindex.org, "ACSM American Fitness Index Health and Community Fitness Status of the 50 Largest Metropolitan Areas," May 2015*

- *Business Insider* reported Trulia's analysis of the 100 largest U.S. metro areas to identify the nation's best cities for weight loss, based on healthful food options, access to outdoor activities, weight-loss centers, gyms, and opportunities to bike or walk to work. Boston* ranked #4. *Businessinsider.com, "These Are the Best US Cities for Weight loss," January 17, 2013*

- The Boston* metro area was identified as one of the worst cities for bed bugs in America by pest control company Orkin. The area ranked #25 out of 50 based on the number of bed bug treatments Orkin performed from January to December 2015. *Orkin, "Chicago Tops Bed Bug Cities List for Fourth Year in a Row," January 13, 2016*

- Boston* was identified as a "2016 Spring Allergy Capital." The area ranked #77 out of 100. Three groups of factors were used to identify the most severe cities for people with allergies during the spring season: annual pollen levels; medicine utilization; access to board-certified allergists. *Asthma and Allergy Foundation of America, "Spring Allergy Capitals 2016"*

- Boston* was identified as a "2015 Asthma Capital." The area ranked #74 out of the nation's 100 largest metropolitan areas. Criteria: estimated prevalence; self-reported prevalence; crude death rate for asthma; annual pollen score; annual air quality; public smoking laws; number of board-certified asthma specialists; school inhaler access laws; rescue medication use; controller medication use; ER visits for asthma; uninsured rate; poverty rate. *Asthma and Allergy Foundation of America, "Asthma Capitals 2015"*

- The Boston* metro area ranked #63 out of 190 in The Gallup-Healthways Well-Being Index. Criteria: purpose; social well being; financial health; community and physical health. Results are based on telephone interviews with adults, aged 18 and older, living in metropolitan areas in the 50 U.S. states and the District of Columbia. *Gallup-Healthways, "State of American Well-Being," February 23, 2016*

Real Estate Rankings

- Based on the home-price forecasts compiled by the real-estate valuation firm CoreLogic Case-Shiller, CNNMoney reported that in 2016, the Boston* metro area is expected to be one of the hottest housing markets in the U.S. Criteria: residential real estate prices. *money.cnn.com, "The 10 Hottest Housing Markets for 2016," December 3, 2015*

- The Boston* metro area appeared on Realtor.com's list of the hottest housing markets to watch in 2016. The area ranked #10. Criteria: strong housing growth; affordable prices; and fast-paced sales. *Realtor.com®, "Top 10 Hot Real Estate Markets to Watch in 2016," December 2, 2015*

- The Boston* metro area was identified as one of the 20 least affordable housing markets in the U.S. in 2015. The area ranked #17 out of 179 markets. Criteria: qualification for a mortgage loan on a typical home. *National Association of Realtors®, Affordability Index of Existing Single-Family Homes for Metropolitan Areas, 2015*

- Boston* was ranked #198 out of 225 metro areas in terms of housing affordability in 2015 by the National Association of Home Builders (#1 = most affordable). Criteria: the share of homes sold in that area affordable to a family earning the local median income, based on standard mortgage underwriting criteria. *National Association of Home Builders®, NAHB-Wells Fargo Housing Opportunity Index, 4th Quarter 2015*

Safety Rankings

- The National Insurance Crime Bureau ranked 380 metro areas in the U.S. in terms of per capita rates of vehicle theft. The Boston* metro area ranked #246 (#1 = highest rate). Criteria: number of vehicle theft offenses per 100,000 inhabitants in 2014. *National Insurance Crime Bureau, "Hot Spots 2014," June 24, 2015*

Seniors/Retirement Rankings

- From its Best Cities for Successful Aging indexes, the Milken Institute generated rankings for metropolitan areas, weighing data in eight categories—health care, wellness, living arrangements, transportation, financial characteristics, education and employment opportunities, community engagement, and overall livability. The Boston* metro area was ranked #4 overall in the large metro area category. *Milken Institute, "Best Cities for Successful Aging, 2014"*

Sports/Recreation Rankings

- According to the personal finance website NerdWallet, the Boston* metro area, at #11, is one of the nation's top dozen metro areas for sports fans. Criteria included the presence of all four major sports—MLB, NFL, NHL, and NBA, fan enthusiasm (as measured by game attendance), ticket affordability, and "sports culture," that is, number of sports bars. *www.nerdwallet.com, "Best Cities for Sports Fans," May 5, 2013*

Transportation Rankings

- Boston* was identified as one of the most congested metro areas in the U.S. The area ranked #6 out of 10. Criteria: yearly delay per auto commuter in hours. *Texas A&M Transportation Institute, "2015 Urban Mobility Scorecard," August 2015*

- The Boston* metro area appeared on *Forbes* list of places with the most extreme commutes. The metro area ranked #6 out of 10. Criteria: average travel time; percentage of mega commuters. Mega-commuters travel more than 90 minutes and 50 miles each way to work. *Forbes.com, "The Cities with the Most Extreme Commutes," March 5, 2013*

Miscellaneous Rankings

- The watchdog site Charity Navigator conducts an annual study of charities in the nation's major markets both to analyze statistical differences in their financial, accountability, and transparency practices and to track year-to-year variations in individual communities. The Boston* metro area was ranked #3 among the 30 metro markets in the rating dimension of Overall Score. *www.charitynavigator.org, "Metro Market Study 2015," June 5, 2015*

- The Harris Poll's Happiness Index survey revealed that of the top ten U.S. markets, the Boston* metro area residents ranked #9 in happiness. Criteria included strong assent to positive statements and strong disagreement with negative ones, and degree of agreement with a series of statements about respondents' personal relationships and general outlook. *www.harrisinteractive.com, "Dallas/Fort Worth Is "Happiest" City among America's Top Ten Markets," September 4, 2013*

- Energizer Personal Care, the makers of Edge® shave gel, in partnership with Sperling's BestPlaces, ranked 50 major metro areas in terms of everyday irritations. The Boston* metro area ranked #10 the 50 metro area most iritating to guys. Criteria: high male-to-female ratio; poor sports team performance and high ticket prices; slow traffic; lack of job availability; unaffordable housing; extreme weather; lack of nightlife and fitness options. *Energizer Personal Care, "Most Irritatng Cities for Guys," August 26, 2013*

- Mars Chocolate North America, the makers of COMBOS®, in partnership with Sperling's BestPlaces, ranked 50 major metro areas in terms of their "manliness." The Boston* metro area ranked #47. Criteria: number of professional sports teams; number of nearby NASCAR tracks and racing events; manly lifestyle; concentration of manly retail stores; manly occupations per capita; salty snack sales; "Board of Manliness" rankings. *Mars Chocolate North America, "America's Manliest Cities 2012"*

- The National Alliance to End Homelessness ranked the 100 most populous metro areas with the highest rate of homelessness. The Boston* metro area ranked #20. Criteria: number of homeless people per 10,000 population in 2011. *National Alliance to End Homelessness, The State of Homelessness in America 2012*

Wellesley is located within the Boston-Cambridge-Newton, MA-NH Metropolitan Statistical Area.

Business Environment

CITY FINANCES

City Government Finances

Component	2012 ($000)	2012 ($ per capita)
Total Revenues	199,352	7,124
Total Expenditures	216,439	7,734
Debt Outstanding	115,405	4,124
Cash and Securities[1]	181,457	6,484

Note: (1) Cash and security holdings of a government at the close of its fiscal year, including those of its dependent agencies, utilities, and liquor stores.
Source: U.S Census Bureau, State & Local Government Finances 2012

City Government Revenue by Source

Source	2012 ($000)	2012 ($ per capita)
General Revenue		
From Federal Government	106	3
From State Government	28,083	1,003
From Local Governments	0	0
Taxes		
Property	108,848	3,889
Sales and Gross Receipts	577	20
Personal Income	0	0
Corporate Income	0	0
Motor Vehicle License	0	0
Other Taxes	1,767	63
Current Charges	11,842	423
Liquor Store	0	0
Utility	39,874	1,424
Employee Retirement	6,504	232

Source: U.S Census Bureau, State & Local Government Finances 2012

City Government Expenditures by Function

Function	2012 ($000)	2012 ($ per capita)	2012 (%)
General Direct Expenditures			
Air Transportation	0	0	0.0
Corrections	0	0	0.0
Education	108,297	3,870	50.0
Employment Security Administration	0	0	0.0
Financial Administration	1,534	54	0.7
Fire Protection	4,724	168	2.1
General Public Buildings	1,213	43	0.5
Governmental Administration, Other	661	23	0.3
Health	564	20	0.2
Highways	2,848	101	1.3
Hospitals	0	0	0.0
Housing and Community Development	0	0	0.0
Interest on General Debt	4,470	159	2.0
Judicial and Legal	269	9	0.1
Libraries	2,486	88	1.1
Parking	541	19	0.2
Parks and Recreation	319	11	0.1
Police Protection	5,295	189	2.4
Public Welfare	85	3	0.0
Sewerage	1,310	46	0.6
Solid Waste Management	2,227	79	1.0
Veterans' Services	0	0	0.0
Liquor Store	0	0	0.0
Utility	33,636	1,202	15.5
Employee Retirement	10,071	359	4.6

Source: U.S Census Bureau, State & Local Government Finances 2012

DEMOGRAPHICS

Population Growth

Area	1990 Census	2000 Census	2010 Census	2014* Estimate	Population Growth (%) 1990-2014	Population Growth (%) 2010-2014
City	26,615	26,613	27,982	28,858	8.4	3.1
MSA[1]	4,133,895	4,391,344	4,552,402	4,650,876	12.5	2.2
U.S.	248,709,873	281,421,906	308,745,538	314,107,084	26.3	1.7

Note: (1) Figures cover the Boston-Cambridge-Newton, MA-NH Metropolitan Statistical Area—see Appendix B for areas included; (*) 2010-2014 5-year estimated population
Source: U.S. Census Bureau, 1990 Census, Census 2000, Census 2010, 2010-2014 American Community Survey 5-Year Estimates

Household Size

Area	Persons in Household (%) One	Two	Three	Four	Five	Six	Seven or More	Average Household Size
City	20.4	31.3	14.5	19.7	11.0	2.7	0.2	2.82
MSA[1]	28.3	32.3	16.4	14.5	5.7	1.7	0.8	2.54
U.S.	27.5	33.5	15.8	13.1	6.0	2.3	1.4	2.64

Note: (1) Figures cover the Boston-Cambridge-Newton, MA-NH Metropolitan Statistical Area—see Appendix B for areas included
Source: U.S. Census Bureau, 2010-2014 American Community Survey 5-Year Estimates

Race

Area	White Alone[2] (%)	Black Alone[2] (%)	Asian Alone[2] (%)	AIAN[3] Alone[2] (%)	NHOPI[4] Alone[2] (%)	Other Race Alone[2] (%)	Two or More Races (%)
City	83.5	2.0	10.8	0.1	0.0	1.2	2.4
MSA[1]	78.1	7.7	7.0	0.2	0.0	4.1	3.0
U.S.	73.8	12.6	5.0	0.8	0.2	4.7	2.9

Note: (1) Figures cover the Boston-Cambridge-Newton, MA-NH Metropolitan Statistical Area—see Appendix B for areas included; (2) Alone is defined as not being in combination with one or more other races; (3) American Indian and Alaska Native; (4) Native Hawaiian and Other Pacific Islander
Source: U.S. Census Bureau, 2010-2014 American Community Survey 5-Year Estimates

Hispanic or Latino Origin

Area	Total (%)	Mexican (%)	Puerto Rican (%)	Cuban (%)	Other (%)
City	4.9	0.9	0.9	0.5	2.6
MSA[1]	9.7	0.6	2.7	0.2	6.2
U.S.	16.9	10.8	1.6	0.6	3.8

Note: Persons of Hispanic or Latino origin can be of any race; (1) Figures cover the Boston-Cambridge-Newton, MA-NH Metropolitan Statistical Area—see Appendix B for areas included
Source: U.S. Census Bureau, 2010-2014 American Community Survey 5-Year Estimates

Ancestry

Area	German	Irish	English	American	Italian	Polish	French[2]	Scottish	Dutch
City	10.6	22.4	13.9	4.4	12.9	3.9	2.5	2.7	1.7
MSA[1]	6.3	23.4	10.5	4.5	14.6	3.7	5.6	2.5	0.6
U.S.	14.9	10.8	8.0	7.1	5.5	3.0	2.7	1.7	1.4

Note: Figures are the percentage of the total population reporting a particular ancestry. The nine most commonly reported ancestries in the U.S. are shown. Figures include multiple ancestries (e.g. if a person reported being Irish and Italian, they were included in both columns); (1) Figures cover the Boston-Cambridge-Newton, MA-NH Metropolitan Statistical Area—see Appendix B for areas included; (2) Excludes Basque
Source: U.S. Census Bureau, 2010-2014 American Community Survey 5-Year Estimates

Foreign-Born Population

Area	Any Foreign Country	Asia	Mexico	Europe	Carribean	Central America[2]	South America	Africa	Canada
	Percent of Population Born in								
City	14.0	7.4	0.1	3.5	0.3	0.1	0.9	0.6	0.8
MSA[1]	17.1	5.4	0.2	3.2	3.0	1.4	1.8	1.4	0.5
U.S.	13.1	3.8	3.7	1.5	1.2	1.0	0.9	0.6	0.3

Note: (1) Figures cover the Boston-Cambridge-Newton, MA-NH Metropolitan Statistical Area—see Appendix B for areas included; (2) Excludes Mexico.
Source: U.S. Census Bureau, 2010-2014 American Community Survey 5-Year Estimates

Marital Status

Area	Never Married	Now Married[2]	Separated	Widowed	Divorced
City	35.1	54.6	0.9	4.1	5.2
MSA[1]	36.4	47.4	1.8	5.4	8.9
U.S.	32.5	48.4	2.2	5.9	10.9

Note: Figures are percentages and cover the population 15 years of age and older; (1) Figures cover the Boston-Cambridge-Newton, MA-NH Metropolitan Statistical Area—see Appendix B for areas included; (2) Excludes separated
Source: U.S. Census Bureau, 2010-2014 American Community Survey 5-Year Estimates

Disability Status

Area	All Ages	Under 18 Years Old	18 to 64 Years Old	65 Years and Over
City	6.6	1.7	4.7	25.6
MSA[1]	10.3	3.8	7.9	33.0
U.S.	12.3	4.1	10.2	36.3

Note: Figures show percent of the civilian noninstitutionalized population that reported having a disability. Disability status is determined from from six types of difficulty: vision, hearing, cognitive, ambulatory, self-care, and independent living. For children under 5 years old, hearing and vision difficulty are used to determine disability status. For children between the ages of 5 and 14, disability status is determined from hearing, vision, cognitive, ambulatory, and self-care difficulties. For people aged 15 years and older, they are considered to have a disability if they have difficulty with any one of the six difficulty types; (1) Figures cover the Boston-Cambridge-Newton, MA-NH Metropolitan Statistical Area—see Appendix B for areas included.
Source: U.S. Census Bureau, 2010-2014 American Community Survey 5-Year Estimates

Age

Area	Under Age 5	Age 5–19	Age 20–34	Age 35–44	Age 45–54	Age 55–64	Age 65–74	Age 75–84	Age 85+	Median Age
	Percent of Population									
City	5.1	30.2	13.3	11.3	15.4	10.9	7.0	4.5	2.2	37.0
MSA[1]	5.5	18.6	21.4	13.2	15.1	12.5	7.3	4.3	2.1	38.7
U.S.	6.4	19.9	20.6	13.0	14.1	12.3	7.6	4.3	1.9	37.4

Note: (1) Figures cover the Boston-Cambridge-Newton, MA-NH Metropolitan Statistical Area—see Appendix B for areas included
Source: U.S. Census Bureau, 2010-2014 American Community Survey 5-Year Estimates

Gender

Area	Males	Females	Males per 100 Females
City	12,563	16,295	77.1
MSA[1]	2,254,371	2,396,505	94.1
U.S.	154,515,159	159,591,925	96.8

Note: (1) Figures cover the Boston-Cambridge-Newton, MA-NH Metropolitan Statistical Area—see Appendix B for areas included
Source: U.S. Census Bureau, 2010-2014 American Community Survey 5-Year Estimates

Religious Groups by Family

Area	Catholic	Baptist	Non-Den.	Methodist[2]	Lutheran	LDS[3]	Pente-costal	Presby-terian[4]	Muslim[5]	Judaism
MSA[1]	44.3	1.1	1.0	0.9	0.3	0.4	0.6	1.6	0.4	1.4
U.S.	19.1	9.3	4.0	4.0	2.3	2.0	1.9	1.6	0.8	0.7

Note: Figures are the number of adherents as a percentage of the total population; (1) Figures cover the Boston-Cambridge-Quincy, MA-NH Metropolitan Statistical Area—see Appendix B for areas included; (2) Methodist/Pietist; (3) Latter Day Saints; (4) Reformed; (5) Figures are estimates
Source: Association of Statisticians of American Religious Bodies, 2010 U.S. Religion Census: Religious Congregations & Membership Study

Religious Groups by Tradition

Area	Catholic	Evangelical Protestant	Mainline Protestant	Other Tradition	Black Protestant	Orthodox
MSA[1]	44.3	3.2	4.5	3.4	0.1	1.0
U.S.	19.1	16.2	7.3	4.3	1.6	0.3

Note: Figures are the number of adherents as a percentage of the total population; (1) Figures cover the Boston-Cambridge-Quincy, MA-NH Metropolitan Statistical Area—see Appendix B for areas included
Source: Association of Statisticians of American Religious Bodies, 2010 U.S. Religion Census: Religious Congregations & Membership Study

ECONOMY

Gross Metropolitan Product

Area	2013	2014	2015	2016	Rank[2]
MSA[1]	370.8	384.4	398.4	418.3	9

Note: Figures are in billions of dollars; (1) Figures cover the Boston-Cambridge-Newton, MA-NH Metropolitan Statistical Area—see Appendix B for areas included; (2) Rank is based on 2016 data and ranges from 1 to 381
Source: The U.S. Conference of Mayors, U.S. Metro Economies: GMP and Employment 2014-2016, June 2015

Economic Growth

Area	2011-13 (%)	2014 (%)	2015 (%)	2016 (%)	Rank[2]
MSA[1]	2.0	1.9	2.1	3.0	83
U.S.	2.2	2.4	2.3	2.9	-

Note: Figures are real gross metropolitan product (GMP) growth rates and represent annual average percent change; (1) Figures cover the Boston-Cambridge-Newton, MA-NH Metropolitan Statistical Area—see Appendix B for areas included; (2) Rank is based on 2016 data and ranges from 1 to 381
Source: The U.S. Conference of Mayors, U.S. Metro Economies: GMP and Employment 2014-2016, June 2015

Metropolitan Area Exports

Area	2009	2010	2011	2012	2013	2014	Rank[2]
MSA[1]	18,972.6	21,804.5	22,292.8	21,234.7	22,212.8	23,378.4	13

Note: Figures are in millions of dollars; (1) Figures cover the Boston-Cambridge-Newton, MA-NH Metropolitan Statistical Area—see Appendix B for areas included; (2) Rank is based on 2014 data and ranges from 1 to 385
Source: U.S. Department of Commerce, International Trade Administration, Office of Trade & Industry Information, Manufacturing & Services, data extracted March 10, 2016

Building Permits

Area	Single-Family			Multi-Family			Total		
	2014	2015p	Pct. Chg.	2014	2015p	Pct. Chg.	2014	2015p	Pct. Chg.
City	66	95	43.9	0	0	-	66	95	43.9
MSA[1]	4,991	4,779	-4.2	7,033	10,469	48.9	12,024	15,248	26.8
U.S.	640,300	690,800	7.9	411,800	487,600	18.4	1,052,100	1,178,400	12.0

Note: (1) Figures cover the Boston-Cambridge-Newton, MA-NH Metropolitan Statistical Area—see Appendix B for areas included; Figures represent new, privately-owned housing units authorized (unadjusted data); All permit data are based on estimates with imputation; (p) preliminary data.
Source: U.S. Census Bureau, Manufacturing, Mining, and Construction Statistics, Building Permits, 2014, 2015

Bankruptcy Filings

Area	Business Filings			Nonbusiness Filings		
	2014	2015	% Chg.	2014	2015	% Chg.
Norfolk County	42	45	7.1	778	699	-10.2
U.S.	26,983	24,735	-8.3	909,812	819,760	-9.9

Note: Business filings include Chapter 7, Chapter 11, Chapter 12, and Chapter 13; Nonbusiness filings include Chapter 7, Chapter 11, and Chapter 13
Source: Administrative Office of the U.S. Courts, Business and Nonbusiness Bankruptcy, County Cases Commenced by Chapter of the Bankruptcy Code, During the 12- Month Period Ending December 31, 2014 and Business and Nonbusiness Bankruptcy, County Cases Commenced by Chapter of the Bankruptcy Code, During the 12- Month Period Ending December 31, 2015

Housing Vacancy Rates

Area	Gross Vacancy Rate[2] (%)			Year-Round Vacancy Rate[3] (%)			Rental Vacancy Rate[4] (%)			Homeowner Vacancy Rate[5] (%)		
	2013	2014	2015	2013	2014	2015	2013	2014	2015	2013	2014	2015
MSA[1]	7.8	9.2	9.9	6.2	6.4	6.3	6.8	4.9	3.3	1.1	0.8	1.1
U.S.	13.6	13.4	12.9	10.7	10.4	10.0	8.3	7.6	7.1	2.0	1.9	1.8

Note: (1) Figures cover the Boston-Cambridge-Newton, MA-NH Metropolitan Statistical Area—see Appendix B for areas included; (2) The percentage of the total housing inventory that is vacant; (3) The percentage of the housing inventory (excluding seasonal units) that is year-round vacant; (4) The percentage of rental inventory that is vacant for rent; (5) The percentage of homeowner inventory that is vacant for sale
Source: U.S. Census Bureau, Housing Vacancies and Homeownership Annual Statistics: 2015

INCOME

Income

Area	Per Capita ($)	Median Household ($)	Average Household ($)
City	71,733	159,615	237,462
MSA[1]	39,572	74,494	101,462
U.S.	28,555	53,482	74,596

Note: (1) Figures cover the Boston-Cambridge-Newton, MA-NH Metropolitan Statistical Area—see Appendix B for areas included
Source: U.S. Census Bureau, 2010-2014 American Community Survey 5-Year Estimates

Household Income Distribution

Area	Percent of Households Earning							
	Under $15,000	$15,000 -24,999	$25,000 -34,999	$35,000 -49,999	$50,000 -74,999	$75,000 -99,000	$100,000 -149,999	$150,000 and up
City	3.2	5.8	2.4	3.6	8.6	8.7	14.0	53.9
MSA[1]	10.2	7.7	7.1	9.9	15.4	12.7	17.7	19.3
U.S.	12.5	10.7	10.2	13.5	17.8	12.2	13.0	10.0

Note: (1) Figures cover the Boston-Cambridge-Newton, MA-NH Metropolitan Statistical Area—see Appendix B for areas included
Source: U.S. Census Bureau, 2010-2014 American Community Survey 5-Year Estimates

Poverty Rate

Area	All Ages	Under 18 Years Old	18 to 64 Years Old	65 Years and Over
City	3.5	3.2	3.8	2.8
MSA[1]	10.4	12.8	9.9	8.8
U.S.	15.6	21.9	14.6	9.4

Note: Figures are percentage of people whose income during the past 12 months was below the poverty level; (1) Figures cover the Boston-Cambridge-Newton, MA-NH Metropolitan Statistical Area—see Appendix B for areas included
Source: U.S. Census Bureau, 2010-2014 American Community Survey 5-Year Estimates

EMPLOYMENT

Labor Force and Employment

Area	Civilian Labor Force			Workers Employed		
	Dec. 2014	Dec. 2015	% Chg.	Dec. 2014	Dec. 2015	% Chg.
City	13,115	13,056	-0.4	12,678	12,626	-0.4
NECTAD[1]	2,627,900	2,607,376	-0.7	2,512,440	2,500,406	-0.4
U.S.	155,521,000	157,245,000	1.1	147,190,000	149,703,000	1.7

Note: Data is not seasonally adjusted and covers workers 16 years of age and older; (1) Figures cover the Boston-Cambridge-Newton, MA New England City and Town Area Division—see Appendix B for areas included
Source: Bureau of Labor Statistics, Local Area Unemployment Statistics

Unemployment Rate

Area	2015											
	Jan.	Feb.	Mar.	Apr.	May	Jun.	Jul.	Aug.	Sep.	Oct.	Nov.	Dec.
City	3.7	3.2	3.1	3.0	3.4	4.2	3.9	3.3	3.4	3.4	3.6	3.3
NECTAD[1]	4.9	4.8	4.4	3.8	4.0	4.5	4.5	4.1	4.1	4.1	4.1	4.1
U.S.	6.1	5.8	5.6	5.1	5.3	5.5	5.6	5.2	4.9	4.8	4.8	4.8

Note: Data is not seasonally adjusted and covers workers 16 years of age and older; (1) Figures cover the Boston-Cambridge-Newton, MA New England City and Town Area Division—see Appendix B for areas included
Source: Bureau of Labor Statistics, Local Area Unemployment Statistics

Employment by Occupation

Occupation Classification	City (%)	MSA[1] (%)	U.S. (%)
Management, Business, Science, and Arts	66.2	46.6	36.4
Natural Resources, Construction, and Maintenance	0.7	6.4	9.0
Production, Transportation, and Material Moving	2.1	7.8	12.1
Sales and Office	21.7	22.6	24.4
Service	9.2	16.6	18.2

Note: Figures cover employed civilians 16 years of age and older; (1) Figures cover the Boston-Cambridge-Newton, MA-NH Metropolitan Statistical Area—see Appendix B for areas included
Source: U.S. Census Bureau, 2010-2014 American Community Survey 5-Year Estimates

Employment by Industry

Sector	NECTAD[1]		U.S.
	Number of Employees	Percent of Total	Percent of Total
Construction, Mining, and Logging	65,500	3.6	5.0
Education and Health Services	407,300	22.6	15.7
Financial Activities	152,500	8.4	5.7
Government	197,800	11.0	15.5
Information	57,000	3.1	1.9
Leisure and Hospitality	170,300	9.4	10.4
Manufacturing	82,100	4.5	8.6
Other Services	69,100	3.8	3.9
Professional and Business Services	342,600	19.0	13.9
Retail Trade	148,800	8.2	11.3
Transportation, Warehousing, and Utilities	43,500	2.4	3.9
Wholesale Trade	57,900	3.2	4.1

Note: Figures are non-farm employment as of December 2015. Figures are not seasonally adjusted and include workers 16 years of age and older; (1) Figures cover the Boston-Cambridge-Newton, MA New England City and Town Area Division—see Appendix B for areas included; n/a not available
Source: Bureau of Labor Statistics, Current Employment Statistics, Employment, Hours, and Earnings

Occupations with Greatest Projected Employment Growth: 2012 – 2022

Occupation[1]	2012 Employment	2022 Projected Employment	Numeric Employment Change	Percent Employment Change
Registered Nurses	78,750	93,310	14,560	18.5
Combined Food Preparation and Serving Workers, Including Fast Food	58,250	70,750	12,500	21.4
Retail Salespersons	109,830	119,160	9,330	8.5
Waiters and Waitresses	58,570	66,840	8,270	14.1
Personal Care Aides	21,690	29,940	8,250	38.1
Home Health Aides	19,760	27,740	7,980	40.4
Nursing Assistants	39,170	45,940	6,770	17.3
General and Operations Managers	55,960	62,610	6,650	11.9
Software Developers, Systems Software	30,030	36,290	6,260	20.8
Management Analysts	27,100	33,070	5,970	22.0

Note: Projections cover Massachusetts; (1) Sorted by numeric employment change
Source: www.projectionscentral.com, State Occupational Projections, 2012–2022 Long-Term Projections

Fastest Growing Occupations: 2012 – 2022

Occupation[1]	2012 Employment	2022 Projected Employment	Numeric Employment Change	Percent Employment Change
Skincare Specialists	2,520	3,840	1,320	52.6
Insulation Workers, Mechanical	240	350	110	49.4
Helpers—Brickmasons, Blockmasons, Stonemasons, and Tile and Marble Setters	550	790	240	44.0
Interpreters and Translators	2,200	3,130	930	42.1
Diagnostic Medical Sonographers	1,460	2,080	620	42.1
Animal Trainers	360	500	140	42.0
Home Health Aides	19,760	27,740	7,980	40.4
Information Security Analysts	2,640	3,660	1,020	39.1
Personal Care Aides	21,690	29,940	8,250	38.1
Helpers—Electricians	920	1,270	350	37.7

Note: Projections cover Massachusetts; (1) Sorted by percent employment change and excludes occupations with numeric employment change less than 100
Source: www.projectionscentral.com, State Occupational Projections, 2012–2022 Long-Term Projections

Average Wages

Occupation	$/Hr.	Occupation	$/Hr.
Accountants and Auditors	41.34	Maids and Housekeeping Cleaners	14.49
Automotive Mechanics	23.83	Maintenance and Repair Workers	22.61
Bookkeepers	22.55	Marketing Managers	68.56
Carpenters	31.66	Nuclear Medicine Technologists	36.73
Cashiers	11.36	Nurses, Licensed Practical	26.51
Clerks, General Office	18.73	Nurses, Registered	46.05
Clerks, Receptionists/Information	16.16	Nursing Assistants	14.83
Clerks, Shipping/Receiving	17.83	Packers and Packagers, Hand	12.24
Computer Programmers	48.37	Physical Therapists	40.26
Computer Systems Analysts	44.94	Postal Service Mail Carriers	25.82
Computer User Support Specialists	31.22	Real Estate Brokers	59.92
Cooks, Restaurant	14.10	Retail Salespersons	13.15
Dentists	82.28	Sales Reps., Exc. Tech./Scientific	40.34
Electrical Engineers	52.77	Sales Reps., Tech./Scientific	50.17
Electricians	33.33	Secretaries, Exc. Legal/Med./Exec.	22.35
Financial Managers	68.75	Security Guards	14.81
First-Line Supervisors/Managers, Sales	22.66	Surgeons	106.45
Food Preparation Workers	12.90	Teacher Assistants*	15.07
General and Operations Managers	71.11	Teachers, Elementary School*	35.84
Hairdressers/Cosmetologists	17.84	Teachers, Secondary School*	36.26
Internists	112.54	Telemarketers	16.27
Janitors and Cleaners	16.71	Truck Drivers, Heavy/Tractor-Trailer	24.97
Landscaping/Groundskeeping Workers	16.71	Truck Drivers, Light/Delivery Svcs.	17.56
Lawyers	78.96	Waiters and Waitresses	13.95

Note: Wage data covers the New England City and Town Area Division—see Appendix B for areas included; (*) Hourly wages for elementary/secondary school teachers and teacher assistants were calculated by the editors from annual wage data based on a 40 hour work week; n/a not available.
Source: Bureau of Labor Statistics, Metro Area Occupational Employment and Wage Estimates, May 2015

TAXES

State Corporate Income Tax Rates

State	Tax Rate (%)	Income Brackets ($)	Num. of Brackets	Financial Institution Tax Rate (%)[a]	Federal Income Tax Ded.
Massachusetts	8.0 (n)	Flat rate	1	9.0 (n)	No

Note: Tax rates as of January 1, 2016; (a) Rates listed are the corporate income tax rate applied to financial institutions or excise taxes based on income. Some states have other taxes based upon the value of deposits or shares; (n) Business and manufacturing corporations pay an additional tax of $2.60 per $1,000 on either taxable Massachusetts tangible property or taxable net worth allocable to the state (for intangible property corporations). The minimum tax for both corporations and financial institutions is $456.
Source: Federation of Tax Administrators, "State Corporate Income Tax Rates, 2016"

State Individual Income Tax Rates

State	Tax Rate (%)	Income Brackets ($)	Num. of Brackets	Personal Exempt. ($)[1] Single	Personal Exempt. ($)[1] Dependents	Fed. Inc. Tax Ded.
Massachusetts	5.10	Flat rate	1	4,400	1,000	No

Note: Tax rates as of January 1, 2016; Local- and county-level taxes are not included; n/a not applicable; (1) Married joint filers generally receive double the single exemption
Source: Federation of Tax Administrators, "State Individual Income Tax Rates, 2016"

Various State and Local Tax Rates

State	State and Local Sales and Use (%)	State Sales and Use (%)	Gasoline[1] (¢/gal.)	Cigarette[2] ($/pack)	Spirits[3] ($/gal.)	Wine[4] ($/gal.)	Beer[5] ($/gal.)
Massachusetts	6.25	6.25	26.54	3.51	4.05 (f)	0.55 (l)	0.11

Note: All tax rates as of January 1, 2016; (1) The American Petroleum Institute has developed a methodology for determining the average tax rate on a gallon of fuel. Rates may include any of the following: excise taxes, environmental fees, storage tank fees, other fees or taxes, general sales tax, and local taxes. In states where gasoline is subject to the general sales tax, or where the fuel tax is based on the average sale price, the average rate determined by API is sensitive to changes in the price of gasoline. States that fully or partially apply general sales taxes to gasoline: CA, CO, GA, IL, IN, MI, NY; (2) The federal excise tax of $1.0066 per pack and local taxes are not included; (3) Rates are those applicable to off-premise sales of 40% alcohol by volume (a.b.v.) distilled spirits in 750ml containers. Local excise taxes are excluded; (4) Rates are those applicable to off-premise sales of 11% a.b.v. non-carbonated wine in 750ml containers; (5) Rates are those applicable to off-premise sales of 4.7% a.b.v. beer in 12 ounce containers; (f) Different rates are also applicable according to alcohol content, place of production, size of container, or place purchased (on- or off-premise or onboard airlines); (l) Different rates also applicable according to alcohol content, place of production, size of container, place purchased (on- or off-premise or on board airlines) or type of wine (carbonated, vermouth, etc.).
Source: Tax Foundation, 2016 Facts & Figures: How Does Your State Compare?

State Business Tax Climate Index Rankings

State	Overall Rank	Corporate Tax Rank	Individual Income Tax Rank	Sales Tax Rank	Unemployment Insurance Tax Rank	Property Tax Rank
Massachusetts	25	39	13	18	47	46

Note: The index is a measure of how each state's tax laws affect economic performance. The lower the rank, the more favorable a state's tax system is for business. States without a given tax are given a ranking of 1. The scores/rankings for the District of Columbia do not affect other states. The 2016 index represents the tax climate as of July 1, 2015 (the beginning of Fiscal Year 2016).
Source: Tax Foundation, State Business Tax Climate Index 2016

TRANSPORTATION

Means of Transportation to Work

Area	Car/Truck/Van		Public Transportation			Bicycle	Walked	Other Means	Worked at Home
	Drove Alone	Car-pooled	Bus	Subway	Railroad				
City	61.0	5.4	0.8	1.8	6.5	0.6	13.1	1.2	9.6
MSA[1]	68.5	7.4	4.1	5.8	2.0	0.9	5.3	1.4	4.6
U.S.	76.4	9.6	2.6	1.8	0.6	0.6	2.8	1.3	4.4

Note: Figures are percentages and cover workers 16 years of age and older; (1) Figures cover the Boston-Cambridge-Newton, MA-NH Metropolitan Statistical Area—see Appendix B for areas included
Source: U.S. Census Bureau, 2010-2014 American Community Survey 5-Year Estimates

Travel Time to Work

Area	Less Than 10 Minutes	10 to 19 Minutes	20 to 29 Minutes	30 to 44 Minutes	45 to 59 Minutes	60 to 89 Minutes	90 Minutes or More
City	15.6	22.1	15.6	25.1	13.2	7.1	1.4
MSA[1]	10.2	23.8	18.8	23.9	11.2	9.3	2.9
U.S.	13.3	29.6	21.0	20.2	7.7	5.7	2.6

Note: Figures are percentages and include workers 16 years old and over; (1) Figures cover the Boston-Cambridge-Newton, MA-NH Metropolitan Statistical Area—see Appendix B for areas included
Source: U.S. Census Bureau, 2010-2014 American Community Survey 5-Year Estimates

Freeway Travel Time Index

Area	1985	1990	1995	2000	2005	2010	2014
Urban Area Rank[1,2]	11	9	13	9	13	14	17
Urban Area Index[1]	1.16	1.20	1.22	1.28	1.29	1.28	1.29
Average Index[3]	1.09	1.11	1.14	1.17	1.20	1.19	1.20

Note: Freeway Travel Time Index—the ratio of travel time in the peak period to the travel time at free-flow conditions. For example, a value of 1.30 indicates a 20-minute free-flow trip takes 26 minutes in the peak (20 minutes x 1.30 = 26 minutes); (1) Covers the Boston MA-NH-RI urban area; (2) Rank is based on 101 urban areas (#1 = highest travel time index); (3) Average of 101 urban areas
Source: Texas Transportation Institute, 2015 Urban Mobility Scorecard, August 2015

Freeway Commuter Stress Index

Area	1985	1990	1995	2000	2005	2010	2014
Urban Area Rank[1,2]	12	9	10	8	11	12	14
Urban Area Index[1]	1.25	1.29	1.31	1.37	1.38	1.37	1.38
Average Index[3]	1.13	1.16	1.19	1.22	1.25	1.24	1.25

Note: The Freeway Commuter Stress Index is the same as the Freeway Travel Time Index (see table above) except that it includes only the travel in the peak directions during the peak periods; the TTI includes travel in all directions during the peak period. Thus, the CSI is more indicative of the work trip experienced by each commuter on a daily basis. (1) Covers the Boston MA-NH-RI urban area; (2) Rank is based on 101 urban areas (#1 = highest stress index); (3) Average of 101 urban areas

Source: Texas Transportation Institute, 2015 Urban Mobility Scorecard, August 2015

Living Environment

COST OF LIVING

Cost of Living Index

Composite Index	Groceries	Housing	Utilities	Trans-portation	Health Care	Misc. Goods/ Services
136.8	111.7	192.6	102.8	109.0	123.3	121.3

Note: The Cost of Living Index measures regional differences in the cost of consumer goods and services, excluding taxes and non-consumer expenditures, for professional and managerial households in the top income quintile. It is based on more than 50,000 prices covering almost 60 different items for which prices are collected three times a year by chambers of commerce, economic development organizations or university applied economic centers in each participating urban area. The numbers shown should be read as a percentage above or below the national average of 100. For example, a value of 115.4 in the groceries column indicates that grocery prices are 15.4% higher than the national average. Small differences in the index numbers should not be interpreted as significant; Figures cover the Framingham-Natick MA urban area.
Source: The Council for Community and Economic Research, ACCRA Cost of Living Index, 2015

Grocery Prices

Area[1]	T-Bone Steak ($/pound)	Frying Chicken ($/pound)	Whole Milk ($/half gal.)	Eggs ($/dozen)	Orange Juice ($/64 oz.)	Coffee ($/11.5 oz.)
City[2]	11.86	1.66	2.61	2.81	3.46	4.04
Avg.	10.99	1.43	2.25	2.26	3.58	4.48
Min.	7.16	0.98	1.30	1.35	2.88	2.98
Max.	14.13	2.43	3.85	4.81	6.39	7.56

Note: (1) Values for the local area are compared with the average, minimum and maximum values for all 292 areas in the Cost of Living Index; (2) Figures cover the Framingham-Natick MA urban area; **T-Bone Steak** *(price per pound);* **Frying Chicken** *(price per pound, whole fryer);* **Whole Milk** *(half gallon carton);* **Eggs** *(price per dozen, Grade A, large);* **Orange Juice** *(64 oz. Tropicana or Florida Natural);* **Coffee** *(11.5 oz. can, vacuum-packed, Maxwell House, Hills Bros, or Folgers).*
Source: The Council for Community and Economic Research, ACCRA Cost of Living Index, 2015

Housing and Utility Costs

Area[1]	New Home Price ($)	Apartment Rent ($/month)	All Electric ($/month)	Part Electric ($/month)	Other Energy ($/month)	Telephone ($/month)
City[2]	592,300	1,888	-	57.91	106.18	31.39
Avg.	312,874	945	179.30	95.07	72.96	28.11
Min.	178,682	479	116.28	43.14	26.46	10.01
Max.	1,472,476	3,984	504.25	189.44	421.11	43.06

Note: (1) Values for the local area are compared with the average, minimum and maximum values for all 292 areas in the Cost of Living Index; (2) Figures cover the Framingham-Natick MA urban area; **New Home Price** *(2,400 sf living area, 8,000 sf lot, in urban area with full utilities);* **Apartment Rent** *(950 sf 2 bedroom/1.5 or 2 bath, unfurnished, excluding all utilities except water);* **All Electric** *(average monthly cost for an all-electric home);* **Part Electric** *(average monthly cost for a part-electric home);* **Other Energy** *(average monthly cost for natural gas, fuel oil, coal, wood, and any other forms of energy except electricity);* **Telephone** *(price includes basic monthly rate for a private residential line plus additional local usage charges incurred by a family of four).*
Source: The Council for Community and Economic Research, ACCRA Cost of Living Index, 2015

Health Care, Transportation, and Other Costs

Area[1]	Doctor ($/visit)	Dentist ($/visit)	Optometrist ($/visit)	Gasoline ($/gallon)	Beauty Salon ($/visit)	Men's Shirt ($)
City[2]	163.83	108.44	119.59	2.47	48.68	45.26
Avg.	105.15	89.02	99.78	2.38	35.30	28.10
Min.	66.87	56.09	48.53	1.95	18.91	13.38
Max.	182.34	150.36	228.33	4.09	67.91	63.80

Note: (1) Values for the local area are compared with the average, minimum and maximum values for all 292 areas in the Cost of Living Index; (2) Figures cover the Framingham-Natick MA urban area; **Doctor** *(general practitioners routine exam of an established patient);* **Dentist** *(adult teeth cleaning and periodic oral examination);* **Optometrist** *(full vision eye exam for established adult patient);* **Gasoline** *(one gallon regular unleaded, national brand, including all taxes, cash price at self-service pump if available);* **Beauty Salon** *(woman's shampoo, trim, and blow-dry);* **Men's Shirt** *(cotton/polyester dress shirt, pinpoint weave, long sleeves).*
Source: The Council for Community and Economic Research, ACCRA Cost of Living Index, 2015

HOUSING

House Price Index (HPI)

Area	National Ranking[2]	Quarterly Change (%)	One-Year Change (%)	Five-Year Change (%)
MD[1]	109	1.10	5.20	14.80
U.S.[3]	–	1.45	5.76	22.85

Note: The HPI is a weighted repeat sales index. It measures average price changes in repeat sales or refinancings on the same properties. This information is obtained by reviewing repeat mortgage transactions on single-family properties whose mortgages have been purchased or securitized by Fannie Mae or Freddie Mac in January 1975; (1) Boston Metropolitan Division—see Appendix B for areas included; (2) Rankings are based on annual percentage change for all metro areas containing at least 15,000 transactions over the last 10 years and ranges from 1 to 266; (3) figures based on a weighted average of Census Division estimates using a seasonally adjusted, purchase-only index; all figures are for the period ending December 31, 2015
Source: Federal Housing Finance Agency, House Price Index, February 25, 2016

Median Single-Family Home Prices

Area	2013	2014	2015p	Percent Change 2014 to 2015
MSA[1]	375.9	389.8	403.9	3.6
U.S. Average	197.4	208.9	223.9	7.2

Note: Figures are median sales prices of existing single-family homes in thousands of dollars; (p) preliminary; n/a not available; (1) Boston-Cambridge-Newton, MA-NH Metropolitan Statistical Area—see Appendix B for areas included
Source: National Association of Realtors, Median Sales Price of Existing Single-Family Homes for Metropolitan Areas, 4th Quarter 2015

Qualifying Income Based on Median Sales Price of Existing Single-Family Homes

Area	With 5% Down ($)	With 10% Down ($)	With 20% Down ($)
MSA[1]	87,549	82,941	73,725
U.S. Average	49,535	46,928	41,714

Note: Figures are preliminary; Qualifying income is based on a mortgage rate of 4.1%. Monthly principal and interest payment is limited to 25% of income; n/a not available; (1) Boston-Cambridge-Newton, MA-NH Metropolitan Statistical Area—see Appendix B for areas included
Source: National Association of Realtors, Qualifying Income Based on Median Sales Price of Existing Single-Family Homes for Metropolitan Areas, 4th Quarter 2015

Median Apartment Condo-Coop Home Prices

Area	2013	2014	2015p	Percent Change 2014 to 2015
MSA[1]	327.5	339.2	352.6	4.0
U.S. Average	194.9	204.3	210.7	3.1

Note: Figures are median sales prices of existing apartment condo-coop homes in thousands of dollars; (p) preliminary; n/a not available; (1) Boston-Cambridge-Newton, MA-NH Metropolitan Statistical Area—see Appendix B for areas included
Source: National Association of Realtors, Median Sales Price of Existing Apartment Condo-Coop Homes for Metropolitan Areas, 4th Quarter 2015

Gross Monthly Rent

Area	Under $200	$200 -299	$300 -499	$500 -749	$750 -999	$1,000 -1,499	$1,500 and up	Median ($)
City	0.6	5.8	9.8	3.7	3.4	22.3	54.4	1,651
MSA[1]	2.0	5.3	6.5	7.1	13.0	33.9	32.1	1,219
U.S.	1.5	3.2	7.4	21.0	24.1	26.9	15.9	920

Note: Figures are percentages except for Median; Gross rent is the contract rent plus the estimated average monthly cost of utilities (electricity, gas, and water and sewer) and fuels (oil, coal, kerosene, wood, etc.) if these are paid by the renter (or paid for the renter by someone else); (1) Figures cover the Boston-Cambridge-Newton, MA-NH Metropolitan Statistical Area—see Appendix B for areas included
Source: U.S. Census Bureau, 2010-2014 American Community Survey 5-Year Estimates

Homeownership Rate

Area	2008 (%)	2009 (%)	2010 (%)	2011 (%)	2012 (%)	2013 (%)	2014 (%)	2015 (%)
MSA[1]	66.2	65.5	66.0	65.5	66.0	66.3	62.8	59.3
U.S.	67.8	67.4	66.9	66.1	65.4	65.1	64.5	63.7

Note: (1) Figures cover the Boston-Cambridge-Newton, MA-NH Metropolitan Statistical Area—see Appendix B for areas included
Source: U.S. Census Bureau, Housing Vacancies and Homeownership Annual Statistics: 2015

Year Housing Structure Built

Area	2010 or Later	2000 -2009	1990 -1999	1980 -1989	1970 -1979	1960 -1969	1950 -1959	1940 -1949	Before 1940	Median Year
City	1.9	7.0	3.8	5.2	7.2	8.4	17.4	12.8	36.3	1951
MSA[1]	0.7	8.0	7.2	10.7	11.0	10.5	11.1	5.6	35.1	1958
U.S.	1.0	14.9	13.9	13.8	15.8	11.0	10.8	5.4	13.3	1976

Note: Figures are percentages except for Median Year; (1) Figures cover the Boston-Cambridge-Newton, MA-NH Metropolitan Statistical Area—see Appendix B for areas included
Source: U.S. Census Bureau, 2010-2014 American Community Survey 5-Year Estimates

HEALTH

Health Risk Data

Category	MD[1] (%)	U.S. (%)
Adults aged 18–64 who have any kind of health care coverage	93.4	79.6
Adults who reported being in good or excellent health	87.1	83.1
Adults who are current smokers	14.9	19.6
Adults who are heavy drinkers[2]	8.1	6.1
Adults who are binge drinkers[3]	20.5	16.9
Adults who are overweight (BMI 25.0 - 29.9)	35.1	35.8
Adults who are obese (BMI 30.0 - 99.8)	21.1	27.6
Adults who participated in any physical activities in the past month	80.1	77.1
Adults 50+ who have ever had a sigmoidoscopy or colonoscopy	74.8	67.3
Women aged 40+ who have had a mammogram within the past two years	85.3	74.0
Men aged 40+ who have had a PSA test within the past two years	43.3	45.2
Adults aged 65+ who have had flu shot within the past year	61.9	60.1
Adults who always wear a seatbelt	89.1	93.8

Note: Data as of 2012 unless otherwise noted; (1) Figures cover the Boston, MA Metropolitan Division—see Appendix B for areas included; (2) Heavy drinkers are classified as males having more than two drinks per day or females having more than one drink per day; (3) Binge drinkers are classified as males having five or more drinks on one occasion or females having four or more drinks on one occasion
Source: Centers for Disease Control and Prevention, Behaviorial Risk Factor Surveillance System, SMART: Selected Metropolitan/Micropolitan Area Risk Trends, 2012 (Note: the CDC has discontinued this dataset but will be releasing a replacement in mid-2016)

Chronic Health Indicators

Category	MD[1] (%)	U.S. (%)
Adults who have ever been told they had a heart attack	3.6	4.5
Adults who have ever been told they had a stroke	1.5	2.9
Adults who have been told they currently have asthma	9.2	8.9
Adults who have ever been told they have arthritis	21.1	25.7
Adults who have ever been told they have diabetes[2]	7.3	9.7
Adults who have ever been told they had skin cancer	5.1	5.7
Adults who have ever been told they had any other types of cancer	5.8	6.5
Adults who have ever been told they have COPD	4.4	6.2
Adults who have ever been told they have kidney disease	1.5	2.5
Adults who have ever been told they have a form of depression	16.6	18.0

Note: Data as of 2012 unless otherwise noted; (1) Figures cover the Boston, MA Metropolitan Division—see Appendix B for areas included; (2) Figures do not include pregnancy-related, borderline, or pre-diabetes
Source: Centers for Disease Control and Prevention, Behaviorial Risk Factor Surveillance System, SMART: Selected Metropolitan/Micropolitan Area Risk Trends, 2012 (Note: the CDC has discontinued this dataset but will be releasing a replacement in mid-2016)

Mortality Rates for the Top 10 Causes of Death in the U.S.

ICD-10[a] Sub-Chapter	ICD-10[a] Code	Age-Adjusted Mortality Rate[1] per 100,000 population	
		County[2]	U.S.
Malignant neoplasms	C00-C97	154.9	163.6
Ischaemic heart diseases	I20-I25	78.4	102.2
Other forms of heart disease	I30-I51	44.2	50.1
Chronic lower respiratory diseases	J40-J47	27.4	41.4
Organic, including symptomatic, mental disorders	F01-F09	52.8	38.5
Cerebrovascular diseases	I60-I69	24.2	36.5
Other external causes of accidental injury	W00-X59	25.2	27.5
Other degenerative diseases of the nervous system	G30-G31	18.4	26.3
Diabetes mellitus	E10-E14	12.5	21.1
Hypertensive diseases	I10-I15	10.2	19.7

Note: (a) ICD-10 = International Classification of Diseases 10th Revision; (1) Mortality rates are a three year average covering 2012-2014; (2) Figures cover Norfolk County.
Source: Centers for Disease Control and Prevention, National Center for Health Statistics. Underlying Cause of Death 1999-2014 on CDC WONDER Online Database, released 2015.

Mortality Rates for Selected Causes of Death

ICD-10[a] Sub-Chapter	ICD-10[a] Code	Age-Adjusted Mortality Rate[1] per 100,000 population	
		County[2]	U.S.
Assault	X85-Y09	1.2	5.1
Diseases of the liver	K70-K76	10.0	13.5
Human immunodeficiency virus (HIV) disease	B20-B24	0.8	2.1
Influenza and pneumonia	J09-J18	14.6	15.2
Intentional self-harm	X60-X84	8.0	12.7
Malnutrition	E40-E46	Unreliable	0.9
Obesity and other hyperalimentation	E65-E68	1.4	1.9
Renal failure	N17-N19	12.8	13.0
Transport accidents	V01-V99	5.3	11.6
Viral hepatitis	B15-B19	1.1	2.1

Note: (a) ICD-10 = International Classification of Diseases 10th Revision; (1) Mortality rates are a three year average covering 2012-2014; (2) Figures cover Norfolk County; Data are Suppressed when the data meet the criteria for confidentiality constraints; Mortality rates are flagged as Unreliable when the rate would be calculated with a numerator of 20 or less.
Source: Centers for Disease Control and Prevention, National Center for Health Statistics. Underlying Cause of Death 1999-2014 on CDC WONDER Online Database, released 2015.

Health Insurance Coverage

Area	With Health Insurance	With Private Health Insurance	With Public Health Insurance	Without Health Insurance	Population Under Age 18 Without Health Insurance
City	98.5	92.9	17.2	1.5	1.4
MSA[1]	95.7	77.0	30.0	4.3	1.7
U.S.	85.8	65.8	31.1	14.2	7.1

Note: Figures are percentages that cover the civilian noninstitutionalized population; (1) Figures cover the Boston-Cambridge-Newton, MA-NH Metropolitan Statistical Area—see Appendix B for areas included
Source: U.S. Census Bureau, 2010-2014 American Community Survey 5-Year Estimates

Number of Medical Professionals

Area	MDs[3]	DOs[3,4]	Dentists	Podiatrists	Chiropractors	Optometrists
County[1] (number)	4,626	73	790	48	173	137
County[1] (rate[2])	671.7	10.6	114.1	6.9	25.0	19.8
U.S. (rate[2])	272.5	20.9	64.7	5.8	25.9	15.2

Note: Data as of 2014 unless noted; (1) Data covers Norfolk County; (2) Rate per 100,000 population; (3) Data as of 2013 and includes all active, non-federal physicians; (4) Doctor of Osteopathic Medicine
Source: U.S. Department of Health and Human Services, Health Resources and Services Administration, Bureau of Health Professions, Area Resource File (ARF) 2014-2015

Best Hospitals

According to *U.S. News,* the Boston, MA metro area is home to seven of the best hospitals in the U.S.: **Beth Israel Deaconess Medical Center** (1 specialty); **Brigham and Women's Hospital** (Honor Roll/13 specialties); **Dana-Farber/Brigham and Women's Cancer Center** (13 specialties); **Massachusetts Eye and Ear Infirmary, Massachusetts General Hospital** (2 specialties); **Massachusetts General Hospital** (Honor Roll/16 specialties); **New England Baptist Hospital** (1 specialty); **Spaulding Rehabilitation Hospital, Massachusetts General Hospital** (1 specialty). The hospitals listed were nationally ranked in at least one adult specialty. Only 137 hospitals nationwide were nationally ranked in one or more specialties. Fifteen hospitals in the U.S. made the Honor Roll with high scores in at least six specialties. *U.S. News Online, "America's Best Children's Hospitals 2015-16"*

According to *U.S. News,* the Boston, MA metro area is home to three of the best children's hospitals in the U.S.: **Boston Children's Hospital** (Honor Roll/10 specialties); **Dana-Farber Boston Children's Cancer and Blood Disorders Ctr** (10 specialties); **Massachusetts General Hospital for Children** (3 specialties). The hospitals listed were highly ranked in at least one pediatric specialty. Eighty-three children's hospitals in the U.S. were nationally ranked in at least one specialty. Twelve children's hospitals in the U.S. made the Honor Roll with high scores in at least three specialties. *U.S. News Online, "America's Best Children's Hospitals 2015-16"*

EDUCATION

Public School District Statistics

District Name	Schls	Pupils	Pupil/ Teacher Ratio	Minority Pupils[1] (%)	Free Lunch Eligible[2] (%)	IEP[3] (%)
Wellesley	9	5,033	13.2	23.8	4.7	17.4

Note: Table includes school districts with 100 or more students; (1) Percentage of students that are not non-Hispanic white; (2) Percentage of students that are eligible for the free lunch program; (3) Percentage of students that have an Individualized Education Program.
Source: U.S. Department of Education, National Center for Education Statistics, Common Core of Data, Local Education Agency (School District) Universe Survey: School Year 2013-2014; U.S. Department of Education, National Center for Education Statistics, Common Core of Data, Public Elementary/Secondary School Universe Survey: School Year 2013-2014

Best High Schools

According to *U.S. News,* Wellesley is home to one of the best high schools in the U.S.: **Wellesley High School** (#285); Nearly 20,000 schools were ranked based on their performance on state assessments and how well they prepare students for college. Schools with the highest unrounded College Readiness Index values were numerically ranked from No. 1 to No. 500 and were the gold medal winners. *U.S. News & World Report, "Best High Schools 2015"*

Highest Level of Education

Area	Less than H.S.	H.S. Diploma	Some College, No Deg.	Associate Degree	Bachelor's Degree	Master's Degree	Prof. School Degree	Doctorate Degree
City	1.9	6.7	5.6	3.6	33.6	29.5	11.2	7.9
MSA[1]	9.2	24.0	15.5	7.2	24.5	13.5	3.2	2.8
U.S.	13.7	28.0	21.2	7.9	18.3	7.8	2.0	1.3

Note: Figures cover persons age 25 and over; (1) Figures cover the Boston-Cambridge-Newton, MA-NH Metropolitan Statistical Area—see Appendix B for areas included
Source: U.S. Census Bureau, 2010-2014 American Community Survey 5-Year Estimates

Educational Attainment by Race

Area	High School Graduate or Higher (%)					Bachelor's Degree or Higher (%)				
	Total	White	Black	Asian	Hisp.[2]	Total	White	Black	Asian	Hisp.[2]
City	98.1	98.5	94.3	97.2	95.9	82.2	83.0	39.0	80.8	70.2
MSA[1]	90.8	93.5	82.3	84.2	69.1	44.0	46.2	23.8	58.2	19.7
U.S.	86.3	88.4	83.2	85.8	64.1	29.3	30.6	19.0	50.9	13.9

Note: Figures shown cover persons 25 years old and over; (1) Figures cover the Boston-Cambridge-Newton, MA-NH Metropolitan Statistical Area—see Appendix B for areas included; (2) People of Hispanic origin can be of any race
Source: U.S. Census Bureau, 2010-2014 American Community Survey 5-Year Estimates

School Enrollment by Grade and Control

Area	Preschool (%)		Kindergarten (%)		Grades 1 - 4 (%)		Grades 5 - 8 (%)		Grades 9 - 12 (%)	
	Public	Private	Public	Private	Public	Private	Public	Private	Public	Private
City	23.3	76.7	66.4	33.6	82.6	17.4	79.4	20.6	82.4	17.6
MSA[1]	42.8	57.2	86.5	13.5	90.9	9.1	89.4	10.6	86.9	13.1
U.S.	57.4	42.6	87.8	12.2	89.8	10.2	89.9	10.1	90.6	9.4

Note: Figures shown cover persons 3 years old and over; (1) Figures cover the Boston-Cambridge-Newton, MA-NH Metropolitan Statistical Area—see Appendix B for areas included
Source: U.S. Census Bureau, 2010-2014 American Community Survey 5-Year Estimates

Average Salaries of Public School Classroom Teachers

Area	2013-14		2014-15		Percent Change 2013-14 to 2014-15	Percent Change 2004-05 to 2014-15
	Dollars	Rank[1]	Dollars	Rank[1]		
Massachusetts	73,195	2	74,805	3	2.20	36.8
U.S. Average	56,610	–	57,379	–	1.36	20.8

Note: (1) State rank ranges from 1 to 51 where 1 indicates highest salary.
Source: National Education Association, Rankings & Estimates: Rankings of the States 2014 and Estimates of School Statistics 2015, March 2015

Higher Education

Four-Year Colleges			Two-Year Colleges			Medical Schools[1]	Law Schools[2]	Voc/ Tech[3]
Public	Private Non-profit	Private For-profit	Public	Private Non-profit	Private For-profit			
0	2	0	0	0	0	0	0	0

Note: Figures cover institutions located within the city limits and include main campuses only; (1) includes schools accredited by the Liaison Committee on Medical Education and the American Osteopathic Association's Commission on Osteopathic College Accreditation; (2) includes ABA-accredited schools, schools with provisional ABA accreditation, and state accredited schools; (3) includes all schools with programs that are less than 2 years.
Source: National Center for Education Statistics, Integrated Postsecondary Education System (IPEDS), 2014-15; Association of American Medical Colleges, Member List, March 21, 2016; American Osteopathic Association, Member List, March 21, 2016; Law School Admission Council, Official Guide to ABA-Approved Law Schools Online, March 21, 2016; Wikipedia, List of Medical Schools in the United States, March 21, 2016; Wikipedia, List of Law Schools in the United States, March 21, 2016

According to *U.S. News & World Report,* the Boston, MA metro division is home to three of the best national universities in the U.S.: **Boston College** (#30 tie); **Boston University** (#41 tie); **Northeastern University** (#47 tie). The indicators used to capture academic quality fall into a number of categories: assessment by administrators at peer institutions; retention of students; faculty resources; student selectivity; financial resources; alumni giving; high school counselor ratings of colleges; and graduation rate. *U.S. News & World Report, "America's Best Colleges 2016"*

According to *U.S. News & World Report,* the Boston, MA metro division is home to one of the best liberal arts colleges in the U.S.: **Wellesley College** (#4 tie). The indicators used to capture academic quality fall into a number of categories: assessment by administrators at peer institutions; retention of students; faculty resources; student selectivity; financial resources; alumni giving; high school counselor ratings of colleges; and graduation rate. *U.S. News & World Report, "America's Best Colleges 2016"*

According to *U.S. News & World Report,* the Boston, MA metro division is home to two of the top 100 law schools in the U.S.: **Boston University, School of Law** (#20 tie); **Northeastern University, School of Law** (#82 tie). The rankings are based on a weighted average of 12 measures of quality: peer assessment score; assessment score by lawyers/judges; median LSAT scores; median undergrad GPA; acceptance rate; employment rates for graduates; placement success; bar passage rate; faculty resources; expenditures per student; student/faculty ratio; and library resources. *U.S. News & World Report, "America's Best Graduate Schools, Law, 2017"*

According to *U.S. News & World Report,* the Boston, MA metro division is home to three of the top 75 medical schools for research in the U.S.: **Harvard University, Medical School** (#1); **Boston University, School of Medicine** (#29 tie); **Tufts University, School of Medicine** (#47 tie). The rankings are based on a weighted average of 11 measures of quality: quality assessment; peer assessment score; assessment score by residency directors; research activity; total research activity; average research activity per faculty member; student

selectivity; median MCAT total score; median undergraduate GPA; acceptance rate; and faculty resources. *U.S. News & World Report, "America's Best Graduate Schools, Medical, 2017"*

According to *U.S. News & World Report,* the Boston, MA metro division is home to five of the top 75 business schools in the U.S.: **Harvard University, Business School** (#1); **Boston University, Questrom School of Business** (#41 tie); **Boston College, Carroll School of Management** (#50); **Northeastern University, D'Amore-McKim School of Business** (#57 tie); **Babson College, F.W. Olin Graduate School of Business** (#60 tie). The rankings are based on a weighted average of the following nine measures: quality assessment; peer assessment; recruiter assessment; placement success; mean starting salary and bonus; student selectivity; mean GMAT and GRE scores; mean undergraduate GPA; and acceptance rate. *U.S. News & World Report, "America's Best Graduate Schools, Business, 2017"*

PRESIDENTIAL ELECTION

2012 Presidential Election Results

Area	Obama (%)	Romney (%)	Other (%)
Norfolk County	57.4	41.3	1.3
U.S.	51.0	47.2	1.8

Note: Results may not add to 100% due to rounding
Source: Dave Leip's Atlas of U.S. Presidential Elections

EMPLOYERS

Major Employers

Company Name	Industry
Beth Israel Deaconess Medical Center	General medical and surgical hospitals
Blue Cross Blue Shield of Massachusetts	Health insurance
Boston University	Colleges and universities
Children's Hospital Corporation	Specialty hospitals, except psychiatric
City of Lowell	City and town managers' office
EMC Corp.	Data management
Federal Deposit Insurance Corporation	Federal deposit insurance corporation (FDIC)
General Electric Company	Aircraft engines and engine parts
Harvard University	Colleges and universities
Internal Revenue Service	Taxation department, government
John Hancock Corp Tax Credit Fund I	Personal service agents, brokers & bureaus
Lahey Clinic	General medical and surgical hospitals
Massachusetts General Hospital	Health care
Massachusetts Institute of Technology	Colleges and universities
MassMutual Financial Group	Life insurance, annuities, & retirement investment
Roche Bros. Supermarkets	Food/grocery
State Street Bank and Trust Company	State trust companies accepting deposits, commercial
Sun Healthcare Group	Accident and health insurance
The Admins of the Tulane Educational Fund	Hospital, medical school affiliation
Tufts Medical Center	Hospital management

Note: Companies shown are located within the Boston-Cambridge-Newton, MA-NH Metropolitan Statistical Area.
Source: Hoovers.com; Wikipedia

PUBLIC SAFETY

Crime Rate

Area	All Crimes	Violent Crimes				Property Crimes		
		Murder	Rape[3]	Robbery	Aggrav. Assault	Burglary	Larceny -Theft	Motor Vehicle Theft
City	652.8	0.0	3.4	13.6	30.6	132.6	459.0	13.6
Metro[1]	n/a	n/a	n/a	n/a	n/a	n/a	n/a	n/a
U.S.	2,971.8	4.5	36.6	102.2	232.5	542.5	1,837.3	216.2

Note: Figures are crimes per 100,000 population; (1) Figures cover the Boston, MA Metropolitan Division—see Appendix B for areas included; n/a not available; (3) The city and U.S. figures shown were reported using the revised Uniform Crime Reporting (UCR) definition of rape. The suburban and metro area figures shown are an aggregate total of the data submitted using both the revised and legacy UCR definitions.
Source: FBI Uniform Crime Reports, 2014

Hate Crimes

Area	Number of Quarters Reported	Number of Incidents per Bias Motivation: Race	Religion	Sexual Orientation	Ethnicity	Disability	Gender	Gender Identity
City	4	0	0	0	0	0	0	0
U.S.	4	2,568	1,014	1,017	648	84	33	98

Source: Federal Bureau of Investigation, Hate Crime Statistics 2014

Identity Theft Consumer Complaints

Area	Complaints	Complaints per 100,000 Population	Rank[2]
MSA[1]	6,507	137.5	75
U.S.	490,220	152.4	-

Note: (1) Figures cover the Boston-Cambridge-Newton, MA-NH Metropolitan Statistical Area—see Appendix B for areas included; (2) Rank ranges from 1 to 379 where 1 indicates greatest number of identity theft complaints per 100,000 population
Source: Federal Trade Commission, Consumer Sentinel Network Data Book for January–December 2015

Fraud and Other Consumer Complaints

Area	Complaints	Complaints per 100,000 Population	Rank[2]
MSA[1]	16,631	351.4	213
U.S.	2,593,159	806.0	-

Note: (1) Figures cover the Boston-Cambridge-Newton, MA-NH Metropolitan Statistical Area—see Appendix B for areas included; (2) Rank ranges from 1 to 379 where 1 indicates greatest number of identity theft complaints per 100,000 population
Source: Federal Trade Commission, Consumer Sentinel Network Data Book for January–December 2015

RECREATION

Culture

Dance[1]	Theatre[1]	Instrumental Music[1]	Vocal Music[1]	Series and Festivals	Museums and Art Galleries[2]	Zoos and Aquariums[3]
0	0	0	0	0	0	0

Note: (1) Professional perfoming groups; (2) Based on organizations with SIC code 8412; (3) AZA-accredited
Source: The Grey House Performing Arts Directory, 2015-16; Association of Zoos & Aquariums, AZA Member Zoos & Aquariums, March 25, 2016; www.AccuLeads.com, March 29, 2016

Professional Sports Teams

Team Name	League	Year Established
Boston Bruins	National Hockey League (NHL)	1924
Boston Celtics	National Basketball Association (NBA)	1946
Boston Red Sox	Major League Baseball (MLB)	1901
New England Patriots	National Football League (NFL)	1960
New England Revolution	Major League Soccer (MLS)	1996

Note: Includes teams located in the Boston-Cambridge-Newton, MA-NH Metropolitan Statistical Area.
Source: Wikipedia, Major Professional Sports Teams of the United States and Canada, March 24, 2016

CLIMATE

Average and Extreme Temperatures

Temperature	Jan	Feb	Mar	Apr	May	Jun	Jul	Aug	Sep	Oct	Nov	Dec	Yr.
Extreme High (°F)	72	70	85	94	95	100	102	102	100	90	83	73	102
Average High (°F)	36	38	46	56	67	76	82	80	73	63	52	41	59
Average Temp. (°F)	30	31	39	48	58	68	74	72	65	55	45	34	52
Average Low (°F)	22	23	31	40	50	59	65	64	57	47	38	27	44
Extreme Low (°F)	-12	-4	1	16	34	45	50	47	37	28	15	-7	-12

Note: Figures cover the years 1945-1990
Source: National Climatic Data Center, International Station Meteorological Climate Summary, 9/96

Average Precipitation/Snowfall/Humidity

Precip./Humidity	Jan	Feb	Mar	Apr	May	Jun	Jul	Aug	Sep	Oct	Nov	Dec	Yr.
Avg. Precip. (in.)	3.8	3.6	3.8	3.7	3.5	3.1	2.9	3.6	3.1	3.3	4.4	4.1	42.9
Avg. Snowfall (in.)	12	12	8	1	Tr	0	0	0	0	Tr	1	8	41
Avg. Rel. Hum. 7am (%)	68	68	69	68	71	72	73	76	79	77	74	70	72
Avg. Rel. Hum. 4pm (%)	58	57	56	56	58	58	58	61	61	59	61	60	59

Note: Figures cover the years 1945-1990; Tr = Trace amounts (<0.05 in. of rain; <0.5 in. of snow)
Source: National Climatic Data Center, International Station Meteorological Climate Summary, 9/96

Weather Conditions

Temperature			Daytime Sky			Precipitation		
5°F & below	32°F & below	90°F & above	Clear	Partly cloudy	Cloudy	0.01 inch or more precip.	0.1 inch or more snow/ice	Thunder-storms
4	97	12	88	127	150	253	48	18

Note: Figures are average number of days per year and cover the years 1945-1990
Source: National Climatic Data Center, International Station Meteorological Climate Summary, 9/96

HAZARDOUS WASTE

Superfund Sites

Wellesley has no sites on the EPA's Superfund Final National Priorities List. There are a total of 1,323 Superfund sites on the list in the U.S. *U.S. Environmental Protection Agency, Final National Priorities List, March 18, 2016*

AIR & WATER QUALITY

Air Quality Trends: Ozone

	1990	1995	2000	2005	2010	2011	2012	2013	2014
MSA[1]	n/a	n/a	n/a	n/a	n/a	n/a	n/a	n/a	n/a

Note: (1) Data covers the Boston-Cambridge-Newton, MA-NH Metropolitan Statistical Area—see Appendix B for areas included; n/a not available. The values shown are the composite ozone concentration averages among trend sites based on the highest fourth daily maximum 8-hour concentration in parts per million. These trends are based on sites having an adequate record of monitoring data during the trend period. Data from exceptional events are included.
Source: U.S. Environmental Protection Agency, Air Quality Monitoring Information, "Air Quality Trends by City, 1990-2014"

Air Quality Index

Area	Percent of Days when Air Quality was...[2]					AQI Statistics[2]	
	Good	Moderate	Unhealthy for Sensitive Groups	Unhealthy	Very Unhealthy	Maximum	Median
MSA[1]	61.6	37.8	0.3	0.0	0.3	615	46

Note: (1) Data covers the Boston-Cambridge-Newton, MA-NH Metropolitan Statistical Area—see Appendix B for areas included; (2) Based on 365 days with AQI data in 2015. Air Quality Index (AQI) is an index for reporting daily air quality. EPA calculates the AQI for five major air pollutants regulated by the Clean Air Act: ground-level ozone, particle pollution (aka particulate matter), carbon monoxide, sulfur dioxide, and nitrogen dioxide. The AQI runs from 0 to 500. The higher the AQI value, the greater the level of air pollution and the greater the health concern. There are six AQI categories: "Good" AQI is between 0 and 50. Air quality is considered satisfactory; "Moderate" AQI is between 51 and 100. Air quality is acceptable; "Unhealthy for Sensitive Groups" When AQI values are between 101 and 150, members of sensitive groups may experience health effects; "Unhealthy" When AQI values are between 151 and 200 everyone may begin to experience health effects; "Very Unhealthy" AQI values between 201 and 300 trigger a health alert; "Hazardous" AQI values over 300 trigger warnings of emergency conditions (not shown).
Source: U.S. Environmental Protection Agency, Air Quality Index Report, 2015

Air Quality Index Pollutants

Area	Percent of Days when AQI Pollutant was...[2]					
	Carbon Monoxide	Nitrogen Dioxide	Ozone	Sulfur Dioxide	Particulate Matter 2.5	Particulate Matter 10
MSA[1]	0.0	3.3	27.9	0.0	68.5	0.3

Note: (1) Data covers the Boston-Cambridge-Newton, MA-NH Metropolitan Statistical Area—see Appendix B for areas included; (2) Based on 365 days with AQI data in 2015. The Air Quality Index (AQI) is an index for reporting daily air quality. EPA calculates the AQI for five major air pollutants regulated by the Clean Air Act: ground-level ozone, particle pollution (also known as particulate matter), carbon monoxide, sulfur dioxide, and nitrogen dioxide. The AQI runs from 0 to 500. The higher the AQI value, the greater the level of air pollution and the greater the health concern.
Source: U.S. Environmental Protection Agency, Air Quality Index Report, 2015

Maximum Air Pollutant Concentrations: Particulate Matter, Ozone, CO and Lead

	Particulate Matter 10 (ug/m^3)	Particulate Matter 2.5 Wtd AM (ug/m^3)	Particulate Matter 2.5 24-Hr (ug/m^3)	Ozone (ppm)	Carbon Monoxide (ppm)	Lead (ug/m^3)
MSA[1] Level	66	10.1	19	0.07	1	n/a
NAAQS[2]	150	15	35	0.075	9	0.15
Met NAAQS[2]	Yes	Yes	Yes	Yes	Yes	n/a

Note: (1) Data covers the Boston-Cambridge-Newton, MA-NH Metropolitan Statistical Area—see Appendix B for areas included; Data from exceptional events are included; (2) National Ambient Air Quality Standards; ppm = parts per million; ug/m^3 = micrograms per cubic meter; n/a not available.
Concentrations: Particulate Matter 10 (coarse particulate)—highest second maximum 24-hour concentration; Particulate Matter 2.5 Wtd AM (fine particulate)—highest weighted annual mean concentration; Particulate Matter 2.5 24-Hour (fine particulate)—highest 98th percentile 24-hour concentration; Ozone—highest fourth daily maximum 8-hour concentration; Carbon Monoxide—highest second maximum non-overlapping 8-hour concentration; Lead—maximum running 3-month average
Source: U.S. Environmental Protection Agency, Air Quality Monitoring Information, "Air Quality Statistics by City, 2014"

Maximum Air Pollutant Concentrations: Nitrogen Dioxide and Sulfur Dioxide

	Nitrogen Dioxide AM (ppb)	Nitrogen Dioxide 1-Hr (ppb)	Sulfur Dioxide AM (ppb)	Sulfur Dioxide 1-Hr (ppb)	Sulfur Dioxide 24-Hr (ppb)
MSA[1] Level	17	53	n/a	32	n/a
NAAQS[2]	53	100	30	75	140
Met NAAQS[2]	Yes	Yes	n/a	Yes	n/a

Note: (1) Data covers the Boston-Cambridge-Newton, MA-NH Metropolitan Statistical Area—see Appendix B for areas included; Data from exceptional events are included; (2) National Ambient Air Quality Standards; ppm = parts per million; ug/m^3 = micrograms per cubic meter; n/a not available.
Concentrations: Nitrogen Dioxide AM—highest arithmetic mean concentration; Nitrogen Dioxide 1-Hr—highest 98th percentile 1-hour daily maximum concentration; Sulfur Dioxide AM—highest annual mean concentration; Sulfur Dioxide 1-Hr—highest 99th percentile 1-hour daily maximum concentration; Sulfur Dioxide 24-Hr—highest second maximum 24-hour concentration
Source: U.S. Environmental Protection Agency, Air Quality Monitoring Information, "Air Quality Statistics by City, 2014"

Drinking Water

Water System Name	Pop. Served	Primary Water Source Type	Violations[1]	
			Health Based	Monitoring/ Reporting
Wellesley Water Division	28,535	Purchased Surface	0	0

Note: (1) Based on violation data from January 1, 2015 to December 31, 2015 (includes unresolved violations from earlier years)
Source: U.S. Environmental Protection Agency, Office of Ground Water and Drinking Water, Safe Drinking Water Information System (based on data extracted April 29, 2016)

Bloomfield, Michigan

Background

Bloomfield is in Oakland County, approximately 20 miles from Detroit. It shares a border with Pontiac and Auburn Hills to the north, Troy to the east and Birmingham to the southeast.

During the late 18th century the U. S. government created a systematic method to divide the Northwest Territory, which included Michigan. Known as the Northwest Ordinance, it implemented processes for surveying and purchasing land. The Northwest Ordinance created the first organized territory in the United States, establishing the Ohio River as the divider between free and slave states, and formatting political boundaries.

Bloomfield is one of several communities in Oakland County boasting a median household income of over $100,000. Education is a top priority in Bloomfield and the town has four school districts, which also serve Bloomfield's neighboring communities—Bloomfield Hills Public Schools, Pontiac Public Schools, Avondale Public Schools, and Birmingham Public Schools. Bloomfield's International Academy, a public high school with three campuses, offers students a top ranked education. Bloomfield also has seven private schools, and Oakland Community College is located in neighboring Bloomfield Hills.

Bloomfield's Safety Path Program, founded in 1999, was designed to develop and maintain paths that connect the communities' schools, natural wooded areas, shopping centers and town features. Through this program, Bloomfield now has over 50 miles of safe, concrete paths for citizens to walk, jog or bike at their leisure.

Bloomfield caters to its diverse population with many houses of worship, including Kirk in the Hills, modeled after Melrose Abbey in Scotland and known for its 77-bell carillon.

Oakland County International Airport is 11 miles from Bloomfield, which is also serviced by Coleman A. Young International Airport, Detroit Metropolitan Wayne Count Airport and Windsor International Airport, all less than 40 miles from Bloomfield.

Bloomfield has four distinct seasons, with average temperatures below national averages. The July average high is 83 degrees and the January average low is 16 degrees. Bloomfield receives 30 inches of rainfall, and 32 inches of snow per year, which exceeds the national average.

Rankings

Business/Finance Rankings

- The personal finance site NerdWallet analyzed 183 American metropolitan areas with populations over 250,000 and more than 15,000 businesses to rank where entrepreneurs find the most success. Criteria included area economy, annual income, housing cost, unemployment rate, and the success rate of area businesses. Warren* ranked #91. *www.nerdwallet.com, "Best Places to Start a Business," April 27, 2015*
- 24/7 Wall Street used Brookings Institution research on 50 advanced industries to identify the proportion of workers in the nation's largest metropolitan areas that were employed in jobs requiring knowledge in the science, technology, engineering, or math (STEM) fields. The Detroit* metro area was #4. *247wallst.com, "15 Cities with the Most High-Tech Jobs," March 13, 2015*
- Based on metro area social media reviews, the employment opinion group Glassdoor surveyed 50 of the largest U.S. metro areas and equally weighed cost of living, hiring opportunity, and job satisfaction to compose a list of "25 Best Cities for Jobs." The Detroit* metro area was ranked #42 in overall job satisfaction. *www.glassdoor.com, "Best Cities for Jobs," May 19, 2015*
- In a survey of economic confidence in the nation's 50 largest metropolitan areas conducted January–December 2014, the Detroit* metro area placed #34, according to Gallup's 2014 Economic Confidence Index. *Gallup, "San Jose and San Francisco Lead in Economic Confidence," March 19, 2015*
- The Brookings Institution ranked the 100 largest metro areas in the U.S. based on income inequality. Detroit* was ranked #24 (#1 = greatest ineqality). Criteria: the "95/20 ratio," a figure representing the income at which a household earns more than 95 percent of all other households, divided by the income at which a household earns more than only 20 percent of all other households. *Brookings Institution, "Income Inequality, 100 Largest U.S. Metro Areas, 2007-2014," January 14, 2016*
- Payscale.com ranked the 20 largest metro areas in terms of wage growth. The Detroit* metro area ranked #3. Criteria: private-sector wage growth between the 1st quarter of 2015 and the 1st quarter of 2016. *PayScale, "Wage Trends by Metro Area," 1st Quarter, 2016*
- The Warren* metro area was identified as one of the most affordable metropolitan areas in America by *Forbes*. The area ranked #14 out of 20 based on the National Association of Home Builders/Wells Fargo Housing Affordability Index and Sperling's Best Places' cost-of-living index. *Forbes.com, "America's Most Affordable Cities in 2015," March 12, 2015*
- Warren* was cited as one of America's top metros for new and expanded facility projects in 2015. The area ranked #6 in the large metro area category (population over 1 million). *Site Selection, "Top Metropolitans of 2015," March 2016*
- The Warren* metro area appeared on the Milken Institute "2015 Best Performing Cities" list. Rank: #55 out of 200 large metro areas. Criteria: job growth; wage and salary growth; high-tech output growth. *Milken Institute, "Best-Performing Cities 2015," December 2015*
- *Forbes* ranked the 200 most populous metro areas to determine the nation's "Best Places for Business and Careers." The Warren* metro area was ranked #9. Criteria: costs (business and living); job growth (past and projected); income growth; educational attainment (college and high school); projected economic growth; cultural and recreational opportunities; net migration patterns; number of highly ranked colleges. *Forbes, "The Best Places for Business and Careers 2015," July 29, 2015*

Education Rankings

- Personal finance website *WalletHub* analyzed the 150 largest U.S. metropolitan statistical areas to determine where the most educated Americans are choosing to settle. Criteria: education quality and attainment gap; education levels; percentage of workers with degrees; public school rankings; quality and size of each metro area's universities. Detroit* was ranked #70 (#1 = most educated city). *www.WalletHub.com, "2015's Most and Least Educated Cities*

Environmental Rankings

- The Detroit* metro area came in at #103 for the relative comfort of its climate on Sperling's list of "chill cities," as measured by the Sperling Heat Index. All 361 metro areas are included. Criteria included daytime high temperatures, nighttime low temperatures, dew point, and relative humidity at the high temperatures. *www.bertsperling.com, "Sperling's Chill Cities," July 18, 2013*

- Sperling's BestPlaces assessed 379 metropolitan areas of the United States for the likelihood of dangerously extreme weather events or earthquakes. In general the Southeast and South-Central regions have the highest risk of weather extremes and earthquakes, while the Pacific Northwest enjoys the lowest risk. Of the least risky metropolitan areas, the Warren* metro area was ranked #156. *www.bestplaces.net, "Safest Places from Natural Disasters," April 2011*

Health/Fitness Rankings

- Analysts who tracked obesity rates in the nation's largest metro areas (populations above one million) found that the Detroit* metro area was one of the ten major metros where residents were most likely to be obese, defined as a BMI score of 30 or above. *www.gallup.com, "Boulder, Colo., Residents Still Least Likely to Be Obese," April 4, 2014*

- For each of the 50 most populous metro areas in the United States, the American College of Sports Medicine's American Fitness Index evaluated infrastructure, community assets, and policies that encourage healthy and fit lifestyles, including preventive health behaviors, levels of chronic disease conditions, health care access, and community resources and policies that support physical activity. The Detroit* metro area ranked #40 for "community fitness." *www.americanfitnessindex.org, "ACSM American Fitness Index Health and Community Fitness Status of the 50 Largest Metropolitan Areas," May 2015*

- The Detroit* metro area was identified as one of the worst cities for bed bugs in America by pest control company Orkin. The area ranked #7 out of 50 based on the number of bed bug treatments Orkin performed from January to December 2015. *Orkin, "Chicago Tops Bed Bug Cities List for Fourth Year in a Row," January 13, 2016*

- Detroit* was identified as a "2016 Spring Allergy Capital." The area ranked #39 out of 100. Three groups of factors were used to identify the most severe cities for people with allergies during the spring season: annual pollen levels; medicine utilization; access to board-certified allergists. *Asthma and Allergy Foundation of America, "Spring Allergy Capitals 2016"*

- Detroit* was identified as a "2015 Asthma Capital." The area ranked #4 out of the nation's 100 largest metropolitan areas. Criteria: estimated prevalence; self-reported prevalence; crude death rate for asthma; annual pollen score; annual air quality; public smoking laws; number of board-certified asthma specialists; school inhaler access laws; rescue medication use; controller medication use; ER visits for asthma; uninsured rate; poverty rate. *Asthma and Allergy Foundation of America, "Asthma Capitals 2015"*

- The Detroit* metro area ranked #174 out of 190 in The Gallup-Healthways Well-Being Index. Criteria: purpose; social well being; financial health; community and physical health. Results are based on telephone interviews with adults, aged 18 and older, living in metropolitan areas in the 50 U.S. states and the District of Columbia. *Gallup-Healthways, "State of American Well-Being," February 23, 2016*

Real Estate Rankings

- The Detroit* metro area was identified as #3 among the ten housing markets with the highest percentage of distressed property sales, based on the findings of the housing data website RealtyTrac. Criteria: short sales; income and poverty figures; and unemployment data. *247wallst.com, "Cities Selling the Most Distressed Homes," January 23, 2014*

- Warren* was ranked #72 out of 225 metro areas in terms of housing affordability in 2015 by the National Association of Home Builders (#1 = most affordable). Criteria: the share of homes sold in that area affordable to a family earning the local median income, based on standard mortgage underwriting criteria. *National Association of Home Builders®, NAHB-Wells Fargo Housing Opportunity Index, 4th Quarter 2015*

Safety Rankings

- The National Insurance Crime Bureau ranked 380 metro areas in the U.S. in terms of per capita rates of vehicle theft. The Detroit* metro area ranked #35 (#1 = highest rate). Criteria: number of vehicle theft offenses per 100,000 inhabitants in 2014. *National Insurance Crime Bureau, "Hot Spots 2014," June 24, 2015*

Seniors/Retirement Rankings

- From its Best Cities for Successful Aging indexes, the Milken Institute generated rankings for metropolitan areas, weighing data in eight categories—health care, wellness, living arrangements, transportation, financial characteristics, education and employment opportunities, community engagement, and overall livability. The Detroit* metro area was ranked #80 overall in the large metro area category. *Milken Institute, "Best Cities for Successful Aging, 2014"*

Sports/Recreation Rankings

- According to the personal finance website NerdWallet, the Detroit* metro area, at #3, is one of the nation's top dozen metro areas for sports fans. Criteria included the presence of all four major sports—MLB, NFL, NHL, and NBA, fan enthusiasm (as measured by game attendance), ticket affordability, and "sports culture," that is, number of sports bars. *www.nerdwallet.com, "Best Cities for Sports Fans," May 5, 2013*

Miscellaneous Rankings

- The watchdog site Charity Navigator conducts an annual study of charities in the nation's major markets both to analyze statistical differences in their financial, accountability, and transparency practices and to track year-to-year variations in individual communities. The Detroit* metro area was ranked #18 among the 30 metro markets in the rating dimension of Overall Score. *www.charitynavigator.org, "Metro Market Study 2015," June 5, 2015*
- Energizer Personal Care, the makers of Edge® shave gel, in partnership with Sperling's BestPlaces, ranked 50 major metro areas in terms of everyday irritations. The Detroit* metro area ranked #7 the 50 metro area most iritating to guys. Criteria: high male-to-female ratio; poor sports team performance and high ticket prices; slow traffic; lack of job availability; unaffordable housing; extreme weather; lack of nightlife and fitness options. *Energizer Personal Care, "Most Irritatng Cities for Guys," August 26, 2013*
- Mars Chocolate North America, the makers of COMBOS®, in partnership with Sperling's BestPlaces, ranked 50 major metro areas in terms of their "manliness." The Detroit* metro area ranked #31. Criteria: number of professional sports teams; number of nearby NASCAR tracks and racing events; manly lifestyle; concentration of manly retail stores; manly occupations per capita; salty snack sales; "Board of Manliness" rankings. *Mars Chocolate North America, "America's Manliest Cities 2012"*
- The Warren* metro area was selected as one of "America's Most Miserable Cities" by *Forbes.com.* The metro area ranked #7 out of 20. Criteria: violent crime; unemployment; foreclosures; income and property taxes; home prices; commute times; climate. *Forbes.com, "America's Most Miserable Cities" February 22, 2013*
- The National Alliance to End Homelessness ranked the 100 most populous metro areas with the highest rate of homelessness. The Detroit* metro area ranked #71. Criteria: number of homeless people per 10,000 population in 2011. *National Alliance to End Homelessness, The State of Homelessness in America 2012*

Bloomfield is located within the Detroit-Warren-Dearborn, MI Metropolitan Statistical Area and the Warren-Troy-Farmington Hills, MI Metropolitan Division.

Business Environment

CITY FINANCES

City Government Finances

Component	2012 ($000)	2012 ($ per capita)
Total Revenues	71,562	1,742
Total Expenditures	63,196	1,538
Debt Outstanding	64,981	1,582
Cash and Securities[1]	58,466	1,423

Note: (1) Cash and security holdings of a government at the close of its fiscal year, including those of its dependent agencies, utilities, and liquor stores.
Source: U.S Census Bureau, State & Local Government Finances 2012

City Government Revenue by Source

Source	2012 ($000)	2012 ($ per capita)
General Revenue		
From Federal Government	380	9
From State Government	2,923	71
From Local Governments	682	16
Taxes		
Property	39,902	971
Sales and Gross Receipts	1,641	39
Personal Income	0	0
Corporate Income	0	0
Motor Vehicle License	0	0
Other Taxes	1,273	30
Current Charges	10,681	260
Liquor Store	0	0
Utility	9,263	225
Employee Retirement	0	0

Source: U.S Census Bureau, State & Local Government Finances 2012

City Government Expenditures by Function

Function	2012 ($000)	2012 ($ per capita)	2012 (%)
General Direct Expenditures			
Air Transportation	0	0	0.0
Corrections	0	0	0.0
Education	0	0	0.0
Employment Security Administration	0	0	0.0
Financial Administration	3,312	80	5.2
Fire Protection	11,845	288	18.7
General Public Buildings	2,337	56	3.6
Governmental Administration, Other	1,548	37	2.4
Health	0	0	0.0
Highways	4,691	114	7.4
Hospitals	0	0	0.0
Housing and Community Development	0	0	0.0
Interest on General Debt	2,903	70	4.5
Judicial and Legal	1,886	45	2.9
Libraries	6,327	154	10.0
Parking	0	0	0.0
Parks and Recreation	0	0	0.0
Police Protection	12,178	296	19.2
Public Welfare	0	0	0.0
Sewerage	450	10	0.7
Solid Waste Management	0	0	0.0
Veterans' Services	0	0	0.0
Liquor Store	0	0	0.0
Utility	6,450	157	10.2
Employee Retirement	0	0	0.0

Source: U.S Census Bureau, State & Local Government Finances 2012

DEMOGRAPHICS

Population Growth

Area	1990 Census	2000 Census	2010 Census	2014* Estimate	Population Growth (%) 1990-2014	Population Growth (%) 2010-2014
City	42,137	43,021	41,070	41,571	-1.3	1.2
MSA[1]	4,248,699	4,452,557	4,296,250	4,292,647	1.0	-0.1
U.S.	248,709,873	281,421,906	308,745,538	314,107,084	26.3	1.7

Note: (1) Figures cover the Detroit-Warren-Dearborn, MI Metropolitan Statistical Area—see Appendix B for areas included; (*) 2010-2014 5-year estimated population
Source: U.S. Census Bureau, 1990 Census, Census 2000, Census 2010, 2010-2014 American Community Survey 5-Year Estimates

Household Size

Area	Persons in Household (%) One	Two	Three	Four	Five	Six	Seven or More	Average Household Size
City	23.6	40.5	12.7	13.7	6.1	2.8	0.2	2.52
MSA[1]	29.9	31.9	15.6	13.2	5.7	2.2	1.2	2.56
U.S.	27.5	33.5	15.8	13.1	6.0	2.3	1.4	2.64

Note: (1) Figures cover the Detroit-Warren-Dearborn, MI Metropolitan Statistical Area—see Appendix B for areas included
Source: U.S. Census Bureau, 2010-2014 American Community Survey 5-Year Estimates

Race

Area	White Alone[2] (%)	Black Alone[2] (%)	Asian Alone[2] (%)	AIAN[3] Alone[2] (%)	NHOPI[4] Alone[2] (%)	Other Race Alone[2] (%)	Two or More Races (%)
City	80.7	7.6	8.5	0.2	0.2	0.3	2.5
MSA[1]	70.2	22.5	3.6	0.3	0.0	1.1	2.3
U.S.	73.8	12.6	5.0	0.8	0.2	4.7	2.9

Note: (1) Figures cover the Detroit-Warren-Dearborn, MI Metropolitan Statistical Area—see Appendix B for areas included; (2) Alone is defined as not being in combination with one or more other races; (3) American Indian and Alaska Native; (4) Native Hawaiian and Other Pacific Islander
Source: U.S. Census Bureau, 2010-2014 American Community Survey 5-Year Estimates

Hispanic or Latino Origin

Area	Total (%)	Mexican (%)	Puerto Rican (%)	Cuban (%)	Other (%)
City	1.2	0.7	0.1	0.1	0.4
MSA[1]	4.1	2.9	0.5	0.1	0.6
U.S.	16.9	10.8	1.6	0.6	3.8

Note: Persons of Hispanic or Latino origin can be of any race; (1) Figures cover the Detroit-Warren-Dearborn, MI Metropolitan Statistical Area—see Appendix B for areas included
Source: U.S. Census Bureau, 2010-2014 American Community Survey 5-Year Estimates

Ancestry

Area	German	Irish	English	American	Italian	Polish	French[2]	Scottish	Dutch
City	17.2	13.2	10.3	5.6	6.6	8.8	3.5	3.0	1.7
MSA[1]	16.5	10.2	7.3	5.4	6.4	10.6	3.8	2.2	1.3
U.S.	14.9	10.8	8.0	7.1	5.5	3.0	2.7	1.7	1.4

Note: Figures are the percentage of the total population reporting a particular ancestry. The nine most commonly reported ancestries in the U.S. are shown. Figures include multiple ancestries (e.g. if a person reported being Irish and Italian, they were included in both columns); (1) Figures cover the Detroit-Warren-Dearborn, MI Metropolitan Statistical Area—see Appendix B for areas included; (2) Excludes Basque
Source: U.S. Census Bureau, 2010-2014 American Community Survey 5-Year Estimates

Foreign-Born Population

Area	Percent of Population Born in								
	Any Foreign Country	Asia	Mexico	Europe	Carribean	Central America[2]	South America	Africa	Canada
City	15.2	9.2	0.3	3.1	0.2	0.1	0.2	0.7	1.3
MSA[1]	8.9	4.6	0.8	2.2	0.1	0.1	0.1	0.3	0.6
U.S.	13.1	3.8	3.7	1.5	1.2	1.0	0.9	0.6	0.3

Note: (1) Figures cover the Detroit-Warren-Dearborn, MI Metropolitan Statistical Area—see Appendix B for areas included; (2) Excludes Mexico.
Source: U.S. Census Bureau, 2010-2014 American Community Survey 5-Year Estimates

Marital Status

Area	Never Married	Now Married[2]	Separated	Widowed	Divorced
City	21.8	63.6	0.4	6.4	7.9
MSA[1]	33.9	46.6	1.6	6.5	11.4
U.S.	32.5	48.4	2.2	5.9	10.9

Note: Figures are percentages and cover the population 15 years of age and older; (1) Figures cover the Detroit-Warren-Dearborn, MI Metropolitan Statistical Area—see Appendix B for areas included; (2) Excludes separated
Source: U.S. Census Bureau, 2010-2014 American Community Survey 5-Year Estimates

Disability Status

Area	All Ages	Under 18 Years Old	18 to 64 Years Old	65 Years and Over
City	9.1	3.2	5.3	24.4
MSA[1]	13.9	4.8	12.2	37.4
U.S.	12.3	4.1	10.2	36.3

Note: Figures show percent of the civilian noninstitutionalized population that reported having a disability. Disability status is determined from from six types of difficulty: vision, hearing, cognitive, ambulatory, self-care, and independent living. For children under 5 years old, hearing and vision difficulty are used to determine disability status. For children between the ages of 5 and 14, disability status is determined from hearing, vision, cognitive, ambulatory, and self-care difficulties. For people aged 15 years and older, they are considered to have a disability if they have difficulty with any one of the six difficulty types; (1) Figures cover the Detroit-Warren-Dearborn, MI Metropolitan Statistical Area—see Appendix B for areas included.
Source: U.S. Census Bureau, 2010-2014 American Community Survey 5-Year Estimates

Age

Area	Percent of Population									Median Age
	Under Age 5	Age 5–19	Age 20–34	Age 35–44	Age 45–54	Age 55–64	Age 65–74	Age 75–84	Age 85+	
City	4.6	19.4	11.1	10.6	15.5	16.6	12.7	6.3	3.2	48.0
MSA[1]	5.9	20.1	18.3	13.1	15.3	13.3	7.6	4.3	2.0	39.7
U.S.	6.4	19.9	20.6	13.0	14.1	12.3	7.6	4.3	1.9	37.4

Note: (1) Figures cover the Detroit-Warren-Dearborn, MI Metropolitan Statistical Area—see Appendix B for areas included
Source: U.S. Census Bureau, 2010-2014 American Community Survey 5-Year Estimates

Gender

Area	Males	Females	Males per 100 Females
City	19,702	21,869	90.1
MSA[1]	2,081,346	2,211,301	94.1
U.S.	154,515,159	159,591,925	96.8

Note: (1) Figures cover the Detroit-Warren-Dearborn, MI Metropolitan Statistical Area—see Appendix B for areas included
Source: U.S. Census Bureau, 2010-2014 American Community Survey 5-Year Estimates

Religious Groups by Family

Area	Catholic	Baptist	Non-Den.	Methodist[2]	Lutheran	LDS[3]	Pente-costal	Presby-terian[4]	Muslim[5]	Judaism
MSA[1]	21.3	4.5	4.9	2.1	3.1	0.3	1.2	1.3	1.8	0.8
U.S.	19.1	9.3	4.0	4.0	2.3	2.0	1.9	1.6	0.8	0.7

Note: Figures are the number of adherents as a percentage of the total population; (1) Figures cover the Detroit-Warren-Livonia, MI Metropolitan Statistical Area—see Appendix B for areas included; (2) Methodist/Pietist; (3) Latter Day Saints; (4) Reformed; (5) Figures are estimates
Source: Association of Statisticians of American Religious Bodies, 2010 U.S. Religion Census: Religious Congregations & Membership Study

Religious Groups by Tradition

Area	Catholic	Evangelical Protestant	Mainline Protestant	Other Tradition	Black Protestant	Orthodox
MSA[1]	21.3	10.6	4.7	3.5	3.3	0.9
U.S.	19.1	16.2	7.3	4.3	1.6	0.3

Note: Figures are the number of adherents as a percentage of the total population; (1) Figures cover the Detroit-Warren-Livonia, MI Metropolitan Statistical Area—see Appendix B for areas included
Source: Association of Statisticians of American Religious Bodies, 2010 U.S. Religion Census: Religious Congregations & Membership Study

ECONOMY

Gross Metropolitan Product

Area	2013	2014	2015	2016	Rank[2]
MSA[1]	224.7	231.1	239.2	248.9	14

Note: Figures are in billions of dollars; (1) Figures cover the Detroit-Warren-Dearborn, MI Metropolitan Statistical Area—see Appendix B for areas included; (2) Rank is based on 2016 data and ranges from 1 to 381
Source: The U.S. Conference of Mayors, U.S. Metro Economies: GMP and Employment 2014-2016, June 2015

Economic Growth

Area	2011-13 (%)	2014 (%)	2015 (%)	2016 (%)	Rank[2]
MSA[1]	1.7	1.2	2.1	2.2	236
U.S.	2.2	2.4	2.3	2.9	–

Note: Figures are real gross metropolitan product (GMP) growth rates and represent annual average percent change; (1) Figures cover the Detroit-Warren-Dearborn, MI Metropolitan Statistical Area—see Appendix B for areas included; (2) Rank is based on 2016 data and ranges from 1 to 381
Source: The U.S. Conference of Mayors, U.S. Metro Economies: GMP and Employment 2014-2016, June 2015

Metropolitan Area Exports

Area	2009	2010	2011	2012	2013	2014	Rank[2]
MSA[1]	28,405.1	43,964.7	49,422.7	55,387.3	53,906.4	50,279.3	5

Note: Figures are in millions of dollars; (1) Figures cover the Detroit-Warren-Dearborn, MI Metropolitan Statistical Area—see Appendix B for areas included; (2) Rank is based on 2014 data and ranges from 1 to 385
Source: U.S. Department of Commerce, International Trade Administration, Office of Trade & Industry Information, Manufacturing & Services, data extracted March 10, 2016

Building Permits

Area	Single-Family			Multi-Family			Total		
	2014	2015p	Pct. Chg.	2014	2015p	Pct. Chg.	2014	2015p	Pct. Chg.
City	61	64	4.9	0	0	-	61	64	4.9
MSA[1]	4,830	5,197	7.6	1,465	2,020	37.9	6,295	7,217	14.6
U.S.	640,300	690,800	7.9	411,800	487,600	18.4	1,052,100	1,178,400	12.0

Note: (1) Figures cover the Detroit-Warren-Dearborn, MI Metropolitan Statistical Area—see Appendix B for areas included; Figures represent new, privately-owned housing units authorized (unadjusted data); All permit data are based on estimates with imputation; (p) preliminary data.
Source: U.S. Census Bureau, Manufacturing, Mining, and Construction Statistics, Building Permits, 2014, 2015

Bankruptcy Filings

Area	Business Filings			Nonbusiness Filings		
	2014	2015	% Chg.	2014	2015	% Chg.
Oakland County	162	163	0.6	4,091	3,721	-9.0
U.S.	26,983	24,735	-8.3	909,812	819,760	-9.9

Note: Business filings include Chapter 7, Chapter 11, Chapter 12, and Chapter 13; Nonbusiness filings include Chapter 7, Chapter 11, and Chapter 13
Source: Administrative Office of the U.S. Courts, Business and Nonbusiness Bankruptcy, County Cases Commenced by Chapter of the Bankruptcy Code, During the 12- Month Period Ending December 31, 2014 and Business and Nonbusiness Bankruptcy, County Cases Commenced by Chapter of the Bankruptcy Code, During the 12- Month Period Ending December 31, 2015

Housing Vacancy Rates

Area	Gross Vacancy Rate[2] (%)			Year-Round Vacancy Rate[3] (%)			Rental Vacancy Rate[4] (%)			Homeowner Vacancy Rate[5] (%)		
	2013	2014	2015	2013	2014	2015	2013	2014	2015	2013	2014	2015
MSA[1]	11.6	11.1	9.7	11.4	10.7	9.5	12.1	9.5	6.8	1.7	1.2	1.1
U.S.	13.6	13.4	12.9	10.7	10.4	10.0	8.3	7.6	7.1	2.0	1.9	1.8

Note: (1) Figures cover the Detroit-Warren-Dearborn, MI Metropolitan Statistical Area—see Appendix B for areas included; (2) The percentage of the total housing inventory that is vacant; (3) The percentage of the housing inventory (excluding seasonal units) that is year-round vacant; (4) The percentage of rental inventory that is vacant for rent; (5) The percentage of homeowner inventory that is vacant for sale
Source: U.S. Census Bureau, Housing Vacancies and Homeownership Annual Statistics: 2015

INCOME

Income

Area	Per Capita ($)	Median Household ($)	Average Household ($)
City	63,030	108,235	158,104
MSA[1]	28,182	52,305	71,184
U.S.	28,555	53,482	74,596

Note: (1) Figures cover the Detroit-Warren-Dearborn, MI Metropolitan Statistical Area—see Appendix B for areas included
Source: U.S. Census Bureau, 2010-2014 American Community Survey 5-Year Estimates

Household Income Distribution

Area	Percent of Households Earning							
	Under $15,000	$15,000 -24,999	$25,000 -34,999	$35,000 -49,999	$50,000 -74,999	$75,000 -99,000	$100,000 -149,999	$150,000 and up
City	5.0	4.4	5.7	7.7	12.2	10.3	18.5	36.1
MSA[1]	13.7	10.8	10.1	13.4	17.5	12.2	13.1	9.2
U.S.	12.5	10.7	10.2	13.5	17.8	12.2	13.0	10.0

Note: (1) Figures cover the Detroit-Warren-Dearborn, MI Metropolitan Statistical Area—see Appendix B for areas included
Source: U.S. Census Bureau, 2010-2014 American Community Survey 5-Year Estimates

Poverty Rate

Area	All Ages	Under 18 Years Old	18 to 64 Years Old	65 Years and Over
City	6.0	6.0	6.0	6.1
MSA[1]	16.9	24.6	15.7	9.1
U.S.	15.6	21.9	14.6	9.4

Note: Figures are percentage of people whose income during the past 12 months was below the poverty level; (1) Figures cover the Detroit-Warren-Dearborn, MI Metropolitan Statistical Area—see Appendix B for areas included
Source: U.S. Census Bureau, 2010-2014 American Community Survey 5-Year Estimates

EMPLOYMENT

Labor Force and Employment

Area	Civilian Labor Force			Workers Employed		
	Dec. 2014	Dec. 2015	% Chg.	Dec. 2014	Dec. 2015	% Chg.
City	20,210	20,384	0.8	19,486	19,791	1.5
MD[1]	1,245,341	1,252,111	0.5	1,173,548	1,191,493	1.5
U.S.	155,521,000	157,245,000	1.1	147,190,000	149,703,000	1.7

Note: Data is not seasonally adjusted and covers workers 16 years of age and older; (1) Figures cover the Warren-Troy-Farmington Hills, MI Metropolitan Division—see Appendix B for areas included
Source: Bureau of Labor Statistics, Local Area Unemployment Statistics

Unemployment Rate

Area	2015											
	Jan.	Feb.	Mar.	Apr.	May	Jun.	Jul.	Aug.	Sep.	Oct.	Nov.	Dec.
City	4.1	3.5	3.4	2.8	3.8	3.7	4.0	3.5	3.2	3.5	2.9	2.9
MD[1]	6.7	5.7	5.5	4.5	5.9	5.9	6.3	5.5	5.0	5.5	4.6	4.8
U.S.	6.1	5.8	5.6	5.1	5.3	5.5	5.6	5.2	4.9	4.8	4.8	4.8

Note: Data is not seasonally adjusted and covers workers 16 years of age and older; (1) Figures cover the Warren-Troy-Farmington Hills, MI Metropolitan Division—see Appendix B for areas included
Source: Bureau of Labor Statistics, Local Area Unemployment Statistics

Employment by Occupation

Occupation Classification	City (%)	MSA[1] (%)	U.S. (%)
Management, Business, Science, and Arts	64.5	37.1	36.4
Natural Resources, Construction, and Maintenance	1.8	6.7	9.0
Production, Transportation, and Material Moving	3.8	13.6	12.1
Sales and Office	21.6	24.7	24.4
Service	8.3	17.8	18.2

Note: Figures cover employed civilians 16 years of age and older; (1) Figures cover the Detroit-Warren-Dearborn, MI Metropolitan Statistical Area—see Appendix B for areas included
Source: U.S. Census Bureau, 2010-2014 American Community Survey 5-Year Estimates

Employment by Industry

Sector	MD[1]		U.S.
	Number of Employees	Percent of Total	Percent of Total
Construction, Mining, and Logging	44,600	3.6	5.0
Education and Health Services	175,700	14.4	15.7
Financial Activities	74,800	6.1	5.7
Government	98,500	8.0	15.5
Information	20,100	1.6	1.9
Leisure and Hospitality	114,500	9.3	10.4
Manufacturing	149,200	12.2	8.6
Other Services	48,600	3.9	3.9
Professional and Business Services	267,200	21.9	13.9
Retail Trade	143,100	11.7	11.3
Transportation, Warehousing, and Utilities	25,500	2.0	3.9
Wholesale Trade	57,200	4.6	4.1

Note: Figures are non-farm employment as of December 2015. Figures are not seasonally adjusted and include workers 16 years of age and older; (1) Figures cover the Warren-Troy-Farmington Hills, MI Metropolitan Division—see Appendix B for areas included; n/a not available
Source: Bureau of Labor Statistics, Current Employment Statistics, Employment, Hours, and Earnings

Occupations with Greatest Projected Employment Growth: 2010 – 2020

Occupation[1]	2010 Employment	2020 Projected Employment	Numeric Employment Change	Percent Employment Change
Home Health Aides	35,400	54,310	18,910	53.4
Registered Nurses	87,170	104,000	16,820	19.3
Office Clerks, General	112,620	123,920	11,300	10.0
Retail Salespersons	127,580	137,710	10,140	8.0
Combined Food Preparation and Serving Workers, Including Fast Food	70,020	78,610	8,590	12.3
Nursing Aides, Orderlies, and Attendants	50,400	57,320	6,920	13.7
Personal Care Aides	14,720	20,900	6,180	42.0
Landscaping and Groundskeeping Workers	28,350	34,370	6,020	21.2
Customer Service Representatives	61,310	67,240	5,930	9.7
Heavy and Tractor-Trailer Truck Drivers	48,610	54,070	5,460	11.2

Note: Projections cover Michigan; (1) Sorted by numeric employment change
Source: www.projectionscentral.com, State Occupational Projections, 2010–2020 Long-Term Projections

Fastest Growing Occupations: 2010 – 2020

Occupation[1]	2010 Employment	2020 Projected Employment	Numeric Employment Change	Percent Employment Change
Biomedical Engineers	200	310	110	54.0
Home Health Aides	35,400	54,310	18,910	53.4
Personal Care Aides	14,720	20,900	6,180	42.0
Veterinary Technologists and Technicians	1,810	2,570	760	42.0
Meeting, Convention, and Event Planners	1,540	2,140	600	39.1
Market Research Analysts and Marketing Specialists	6,920	9,500	2,590	37.4
Software Developers, Systems Software	6,550	8,960	2,420	36.9
Marriage and Family Therapists	300	400	110	36.6
Helpers—Carpenters	300	410	110	36.5
Bicycle Repairers	570	770	200	36.0

Note: Projections cover Michigan; (1) Sorted by percent employment change and excludes occupations with numeric employment change less than 100
Source: www.projectionscentral.com, State Occupational Projections, 2010–2020 Long-Term Projections

Average Wages

Occupation	$/Hr.	Occupation	$/Hr.
Accountants and Auditors	38.84	Maids and Housekeeping Cleaners	11.00
Automotive Mechanics	20.93	Maintenance and Repair Workers	17.36
Bookkeepers	18.98	Marketing Managers	58.43
Carpenters	23.50	Nuclear Medicine Technologists	33.31
Cashiers	10.66	Nurses, Licensed Practical	23.80
Clerks, General Office	15.98	Nurses, Registered	37.09
Clerks, Receptionists/Information	13.16	Nursing Assistants	13.69
Clerks, Shipping/Receiving	16.11	Packers and Packagers, Hand	13.40
Computer Programmers	35.12	Physical Therapists	44.15
Computer Systems Analysts	41.45	Postal Service Mail Carriers	25.14
Computer User Support Specialists	25.16	Real Estate Brokers	30.04
Cooks, Restaurant	11.58	Retail Salespersons	12.66
Dentists	77.55	Sales Reps., Exc. Tech./Scientific	32.88
Electrical Engineers	41.86	Sales Reps., Tech./Scientific	43.24
Electricians	31.88	Secretaries, Exc. Legal/Med./Exec.	16.88
Financial Managers	60.90	Security Guards	12.90
First-Line Supervisors/Managers, Sales	22.50	Surgeons	121.74
Food Preparation Workers	11.79	Teacher Assistants*	13.01
General and Operations Managers	57.93	Teachers, Elementary School*	32.81
Hairdressers/Cosmetologists	13.62	Teachers, Secondary School*	30.56
Internists	90.64	Telemarketers	14.67
Janitors and Cleaners	12.22	Truck Drivers, Heavy/Tractor-Trailer	20.22
Landscaping/Groundskeeping Workers	13.36	Truck Drivers, Light/Delivery Svcs.	15.80
Lawyers	57.37	Waiters and Waitresses	10.50

Note: Wage data covers the Metropolitan Division—see Appendix B for areas included; (*) Hourly wages for elementary/secondary school teachers and teacher assistants were calculated by the editors from annual wage data based on a 40 hour work week; n/a not available.
Source: Bureau of Labor Statistics, Metro Area Occupational Employment and Wage Estimates, May 2015

TAXES

State Corporate Income Tax Rates

State	Tax Rate (%)	Income Brackets ($)	Num. of Brackets	Financial Institution Tax Rate (%)[a]	Federal Income Tax Ded.
Michigan	6.0	Flat rate	1	(a)	No

Note: Tax rates as of January 1, 2016; (a) Rates listed are the corporate income tax rate applied to financial institutions or excise taxes based on income. Some states have other taxes based upon the value of deposits or shares.
Source: Federation of Tax Administrators, "State Corporate Income Tax Rates, 2016"

State Individual Income Tax Rates

State	Tax Rate (%)	Income Brackets ($)	Num. of Brackets	Personal Exempt. ($)[1]		Fed. Inc. Tax Ded.
				Single	Dependents	
Michigan (a)	4.25	Flat rate	1	3,950	3,950	No

Note: Tax rates as of January 1, 2016; Local- and county-level taxes are not included; n/a not applicable; (1) Married joint filers generally receive double the single exemption; (a) 18 states have statutory provision for automatically adjusting to the rate of inflation the dollar values of the income tax brackets, standard deductions, and/or personal exemptions. Massachusetts, Michigan, and Nebraska index the personal exemptiononly. Oregon does not index the income brackets for $125,000 and over. Maine has suspended indexing for 2014 and 2015.
Source: Federation of Tax Administrators, "State Individual Income Tax Rates, 2016"

Various State and Local Tax Rates

State	State and Local Sales and Use (%)	State Sales and Use (%)	Gasoline[1] (¢/gal.)	Cigarette[2] ($/pack)	Spirits[3] ($/gal.)	Wine[4] ($/gal.)	Beer[5] ($/gal.)
Michigan	6.00	6.0	30.54	2.00	11.94 (g)	0.51 (l)	0.20

Note: All tax rates as of January 1, 2016; (1) The American Petroleum Institute has developed a methodology for determining the average tax rate on a gallon of fuel. Rates may include any of the following: excise taxes, environmental fees, storage tank fees, other fees or taxes, general sales tax, and local taxes. In states where gasoline is subject to the general sales tax, or where the fuel tax is based on the average sale price, the average rate determined by API is sensitive to changes in the price of gasoline. States that fully or partially apply general sales taxes to gasoline: CA, CO, GA, IL, IN, MI, NY; (2) The federal excise tax of $1.0066 per pack and local taxes are not included; (3) Rates are those applicable to off-premise sales of 40% alcohol by volume (a.b.v.) distilled spirits in 750ml containers. Local excise taxes are excluded; (4) Rates are those applicable to off-premise sales of 11% a.b.v. non-carbonated wine in 750ml containers; (5) Rates are those applicable to off-premise sales of 4.7% a.b.v. beer in 12 ounce containers; (g) Control states, where the government controls all sales. Products can be subject to ad valorem mark-up as well as excise taxes; (l) Different rates also applicable according to alcohol content, place of production, size of container, place purchased (on- or off-premise or on board airlines) or type of wine (carbonated, vermouth, etc.).
Source: Tax Foundation, 2016 Facts & Figures: How Does Your State Compare?

State Business Tax Climate Index Rankings

State	Overall Rank	Corporate Tax Rank	Individual Income Tax Rank	Sales Tax Rank	Unemployment Insurance Tax Rank	Property Tax Rank
Michigan	13	11	15	7	48	26

Note: The index is a measure of how each state's tax laws affect economic performance. The lower the rank, the more favorable a state's tax system is for business. States without a given tax are given a ranking of 1. The scores/rankings for the District of Columbia do not affect other states. The 2016 index represents the tax climate as of July 1, 2015 (the beginning of Fiscal Year 2016).
Source: Tax Foundation, State Business Tax Climate Index 2016

TRANSPORTATION

Means of Transportation to Work

Area	Car/Truck/Van		Public Transportation			Bicycle	Walked	Other Means	Worked at Home
	Drove Alone	Car-pooled	Bus	Subway	Railroad				
City	86.1	5.5	0.4	0.0	0.0	0.1	0.5	0.7	6.7
MSA[1]	84.1	8.7	1.6	0.0	0.0	0.2	1.3	0.8	3.2
U.S.	76.4	9.6	2.6	1.8	0.6	0.6	2.8	1.3	4.4

Note: Figures are percentages and cover workers 16 years of age and older; (1) Figures cover the Detroit-Warren-Dearborn, MI Metropolitan Statistical Area—see Appendix B for areas included
Source: U.S. Census Bureau, 2010-2014 American Community Survey 5-Year Estimates

Travel Time to Work

Area	Less Than 10 Minutes	10 to 19 Minutes	20 to 29 Minutes	30 to 44 Minutes	45 to 59 Minutes	60 to 89 Minutes	90 Minutes or More
City	9.2	31.0	23.9	25.0	6.7	3.3	0.9
MSA[1]	10.0	26.9	23.1	24.2	9.0	5.0	1.8
U.S.	13.3	29.6	21.0	20.2	7.7	5.7	2.6

Note: Figures are percentages and include workers 16 years old and over; (1) Figures cover the Detroit-Warren-Dearborn, MI Metropolitan Statistical Area—see Appendix B for areas included
Source: U.S. Census Bureau, 2010-2014 American Community Survey 5-Year Estimates

Freeway Travel Time Index

Area	1985	1990	1995	2000	2005	2010	2014
Urban Area Rank[1,2]	9	9	10	19	24	29	25
Urban Area Index[1]	1.17	1.20	1.23	1.24	1.25	1.22	1.24
Average Index[3]	1.09	1.11	1.14	1.17	1.20	1.19	1.20

Note: Freeway Travel Time Index—the ratio of travel time in the peak period to the travel time at free-flow conditions. For example, a value of 1.30 indicates a 20-minute free-flow trip takes 26 minutes in the peak (20 minutes x 1.30 = 26 minutes); (1) Covers the Detroit MI urban area; (2) Rank is based on 101 urban areas (#1 = highest travel time index); (3) Average of 101 urban areas
Source: Texas Transportation Institute, 2015 Urban Mobility Scorecard, August 2015

Freeway Commuter Stress Index

Area	1985	1990	1995	2000	2005	2010	2014
Urban Area Rank[1,2]	22	22	24	27	35	37	33
Urban Area Index[1]	1.19	1.22	1.25	1.27	1.27	1.25	1.27
Average Index[3]	1.13	1.16	1.19	1.22	1.25	1.24	1.25

Note: The Freeway Commuter Stress Index is the same as the Freeway Travel Time Index (see table above) except that it includes only the travel in the peak directions during the peak periods; the TTI includes travel in all directions during the peak period. Thus, the CSI is more indicative of the work trip experienced by each commuter on a daily basis. (1) Covers the Detroit MI urban area; (2) Rank is based on 101 urban areas (#1 = highest stress index); (3) Average of 101 urban areas
Source: Texas Transportation Institute, 2015 Urban Mobility Scorecard, August 2015

Living Environment

COST OF LIVING

Cost of Living Index

Composite Index	Groceries	Housing	Utilities	Transportation	Health Care	Misc. Goods/ Services
95.4	88.8	91.1	104.5	104.8	96.4	95.5

Note: The Cost of Living Index measures regional differences in the cost of consumer goods and services, excluding taxes and non-consumer expenditures, for professional and managerial households in the top income quintile. It is based on more than 50,000 prices covering almost 60 different items for which prices are collected three times a year by chambers of commerce, economic development organizations or university applied economic centers in each participating urban area. The numbers shown should be read as a percentage above or below the national average of 100. For example, a value of 115.4 in the groceries column indicates that grocery prices are 15.4% higher than the national average. Small differences in the index numbers should not be interpreted as significant; Figures cover the Detroit MI urban area.
Source: The Council for Community and Economic Research, ACCRA Cost of Living Index, 2015

Grocery Prices

Area[1]	T-Bone Steak ($/pound)	Frying Chicken ($/pound)	Whole Milk ($/half gal.)	Eggs ($/dozen)	Orange Juice ($/64 oz.)	Coffee ($/11.5 oz.)
City[2]	10.81	1.20	1.85	1.98	3.00	4.06
Avg.	10.99	1.43	2.25	2.26	3.58	4.48
Min.	7.16	0.98	1.30	1.35	2.88	2.98
Max.	14.13	2.43	3.85	4.81	6.39	7.56

Note: (1) Values for the local area are compared with the average, minimum and maximum values for all 292 areas in the Cost of Living Index; (2) Figures cover the Detroit MI urban area; **T-Bone Steak** *(price per pound);* **Frying Chicken** *(price per pound, whole fryer);* **Whole Milk** *(half gallon carton);* **Eggs** *(price per dozen, Grade A, large);* **Orange Juice** *(64 oz. Tropicana or Florida Natural);* **Coffee** *(11.5 oz. can, vacuum-packed, Maxwell House, Hills Bros, or Folgers).*
Source: The Council for Community and Economic Research, ACCRA Cost of Living Index, 2015

Housing and Utility Costs

Area[1]	New Home Price ($)	Apartment Rent ($/month)	All Electric ($/month)	Part Electric ($/month)	Other Energy ($/month)	Telephone ($/month)
City[2]	269,215	955	-	108.88	66.14	30.00
Avg.	312,874	945	179.30	95.07	72.96	28.11
Min.	178,682	479	116.28	43.14	26.46	10.01
Max.	1,472,476	3,984	504.25	189.44	421.11	43.06

Note: (1) Values for the local area are compared with the average, minimum and maximum values for all 292 areas in the Cost of Living Index; (2) Figures cover the Detroit MI urban area; **New Home Price** *(2,400 sf living area, 8,000 sf lot, in urban area with full utilities);* **Apartment Rent** *(950 sf 2 bedroom/1.5 or 2 bath, unfurnished, excluding all utilities except water);* **All Electric** *(average monthly cost for an all-electric home);* **Part Electric** *(average monthly cost for a part-electric home);* **Other Energy** *(average monthly cost for natural gas, fuel oil, coal, wood, and any other forms of energy except electricity);* **Telephone** *(price includes basic monthly rate for a private residential line plus additional local usage charges incurred by a family of four).*
Source: The Council for Community and Economic Research, ACCRA Cost of Living Index, 2015

Health Care, Transportation, and Other Costs

Area[1]	Doctor ($/visit)	Dentist ($/visit)	Optometrist ($/visit)	Gasoline ($/gallon)	Beauty Salon ($/visit)	Men's Shirt ($)
City[2]	100.13	86.47	79.43	2.44	47.83	21.95
Avg.	105.15	89.02	99.78	2.38	35.30	28.10
Min.	66.87	56.09	48.53	1.95	18.91	13.38
Max.	182.34	150.36	228.33	4.09	67.91	63.80

Note: (1) Values for the local area are compared with the average, minimum and maximum values for all 292 areas in the Cost of Living Index; (2) Figures cover the Detroit MI urban area; **Doctor** *(general practitioners routine exam of an established patient);* **Dentist** *(adult teeth cleaning and periodic oral examination);* **Optometrist** *(full vision eye exam for established adult patient);* **Gasoline** *(one gallon regular unleaded, national brand, including all taxes, cash price at self-service pump if available);* **Beauty Salon** *(woman's shampoo, trim, and blow-dry);* **Men's Shirt** *(cotton/polyester dress shirt, pinpoint weave, long sleeves).*
Source: The Council for Community and Economic Research, ACCRA Cost of Living Index, 2015

HOUSING

House Price Index (HPI)

Area	National Ranking[2]	Quarterly Change (%)	One-Year Change (%)	Five-Year Change (%)
MD[1]	107	-0.20	5.30	33.30
U.S.[3]	–	1.45	5.76	22.85

Note: The HPI is a weighted repeat sales index. It measures average price changes in repeat sales or refinancings on the same properties. This information is obtained by reviewing repeat mortgage transactions on single-family properties whose mortgages have been purchased or securitized by Fannie Mae or Freddie Mac in January 1975; (1) Warren-Troy-Farmington Hills Metropolitan Division—see Appendix B for areas included; (2) Rankings are based on annual percentage change for all metro areas containing at least 15,000 transactions over the last 10 years and ranges from 1 to 266; (3) figures based on a weighted average of Census Division estimates using a seasonally adjusted, purchase-only index; all figures are for the period ending December 31, 2015

Source: Federal Housing Finance Agency, House Price Index, February 25, 2016

Median Single-Family Home Prices

Area	2013	2014	2015[p]	Percent Change 2014 to 2015
MSA[1]	n/a	n/a	n/a	n/a
U.S. Average	197.4	208.9	223.9	7.2

Note: Figures are median sales prices of existing single-family homes in thousands of dollars; (p) preliminary; n/a not available; (1) Detroit-Warren-Dearborn, MI Metropolitan Statistical Area—see Appendix B for areas included

Source: National Association of Realtors, Median Sales Price of Existing Single-Family Homes for Metropolitan Areas, 4th Quarter 2015

Qualifying Income Based on Median Sales Price of Existing Single-Family Homes

Area	With 5% Down ($)	With 10% Down ($)	With 20% Down ($)
MSA[1]	n/a	n/a	n/a
U.S. Average	49,535	46,928	41,714

Note: Figures are preliminary; Qualifying income is based on a mortgage rate of 4.1%. Monthly principal and interest payment is limited to 25% of income; n/a not available; (1) Detroit-Warren-Dearborn, MI Metropolitan Statistical Area—see Appendix B for areas included

Source: National Association of Realtors, Qualifying Income Based on Median Sales Price of Existing Single-Family Homes for Metropolitan Areas, 4th Quarter 2015

Median Apartment Condo-Coop Home Prices

Area	2013	2014	2015[p]	Percent Change 2014 to 2015
MSA[1]	n/a	n/a	n/a	n/a
U.S. Average	194.9	204.3	210.7	3.1

Note: Figures are median sales prices of existing apartment condo-coop homes in thousands of dollars; (p) preliminary; n/a not available; (1) Detroit-Warren-Dearborn, MI Metropolitan Statistical Area—see Appendix B for areas included

Source: National Association of Realtors, Median Sales Price of Existing Apartment Condo-Coop Homes for Metropolitan Areas, 4th Quarter 2015

Gross Monthly Rent

Area	Under $200	$200 -299	$300 -499	$500 -749	$750 -999	$1,000 -1,499	$1,500 and up	Median ($)
City	0.7	0.3	0.7	10.3	31.6	27.3	29.1	1,088
MSA[1]	1.7	3.4	7.0	26.0	28.5	25.6	7.7	846
U.S.	1.5	3.2	7.4	21.0	24.1	26.9	15.9	920

Note: Figures are percentages except for Median; Gross rent is the contract rent plus the estimated average monthly cost of utilities (electricity, gas, and water and sewer) and fuels (oil, coal, kerosene, wood, etc.) if these are paid by the renter (or paid for the renter by someone else); (1) Figures cover the Detroit-Warren-Dearborn, MI Metropolitan Statistical Area—see Appendix B for areas included

Source: U.S. Census Bureau, 2010-2014 American Community Survey 5-Year Estimates

Homeownership Rate

Area	2008 (%)	2009 (%)	2010 (%)	2011 (%)	2012 (%)	2013 (%)	2014 (%)	2015 (%)
MSA[1]	75.5	73.9	73.6	73.5	73.4	71.7	71.2	74.0
U.S.	67.8	67.4	66.9	66.1	65.4	65.1	64.5	63.7

Note: (1) Figures cover the Detroit-Warren-Dearborn, MI Metropolitan Statistical Area—see Appendix B for areas included
Source: U.S. Census Bureau, Housing Vacancies and Homeownership Annual Statistics: 2015

Year Housing Structure Built

Area	2010 or Later	2000 -2009	1990 -1999	1980 -1989	1970 -1979	1960 -1969	1950 -1959	1940 -1949	Before 1940	Median Year
City	0.3	4.0	8.9	11.9	19.3	27.1	23.3	2.4	2.8	1968
MSA[1]	0.3	8.8	11.1	9.0	14.4	12.7	19.8	10.6	13.3	1965
U.S.	1.0	14.9	13.9	13.8	15.8	11.0	10.8	5.4	13.3	1976

Note: Figures are percentages except for Median Year; (1) Figures cover the Detroit-Warren-Dearborn, MI Metropolitan Statistical Area—see Appendix B for areas included
Source: U.S. Census Bureau, 2010-2014 American Community Survey 5-Year Estimates

HEALTH

Health Risk Data

Category	MSA[1] (%)	U.S. (%)
Adults aged 18–64 who have any kind of health care coverage	n/a	79.6
Adults who reported being in good or excellent health	n/a	83.1
Adults who are current smokers	n/a	19.6
Adults who are heavy drinkers[2]	n/a	6.1
Adults who are binge drinkers[3]	n/a	16.9
Adults who are overweight (BMI 25.0 - 29.9)	n/a	35.8
Adults who are obese (BMI 30.0 - 99.8)	n/a	27.6
Adults who participated in any physical activities in the past month	n/a	77.1
Adults 50+ who have ever had a sigmoidoscopy or colonoscopy	n/a	67.3
Women aged 40+ who have had a mammogram within the past two years	n/a	74.0
Men aged 40+ who have had a PSA test within the past two years	n/a	45.2
Adults aged 65+ who have had flu shot within the past year	n/a	60.1
Adults who always wear a seatbelt	n/a	93.8

Note: Data as of 2012 unless otherwise noted; n/a not available; (1) Figures cover the Detroit-Warren-Dearborn, MI Metropolitan Statistical Area—see Appendix B for areas included; (2) Heavy drinkers are classified as males having more than two drinks per day or females having more than one drink per day; (3) Binge drinkers are classified as males having five or more drinks on one occasion or females having four or more drinks on one occasion
Source: Centers for Disease Control and Prevention, Behaviorial Risk Factor Surveillance System, SMART: Selected Metropolitan/Micropolitan Area Risk Trends, 2012 (Note: the CDC has discontinued this dataset but will be releasing a replacement in mid-2016)

Chronic Health Indicators

Category	MSA[1] (%)	U.S. (%)
Adults who have ever been told they had a heart attack	n/a	4.5
Adults who have ever been told they had a stroke	n/a	2.9
Adults who have been told they currently have asthma	n/a	8.9
Adults who have ever been told they have arthritis	n/a	25.7
Adults who have ever been told they have diabetes[2]	n/a	9.7
Adults who have ever been told they had skin cancer	n/a	5.7
Adults who have ever been told they had any other types of cancer	n/a	6.5
Adults who have ever been told they have COPD	n/a	6.2
Adults who have ever been told they have kidney disease	n/a	2.5
Adults who have ever been told they have a form of depression	n/a	18.0

Note: Data as of 2012 unless otherwise noted; n/a not available; (1) Figures cover the Detroit-Warren-Dearborn, MI Metropolitan Statistical Area—see Appendix B for areas included; (2) Figures do not include pregnancy-related, borderline, or pre-diabetes
Source: Centers for Disease Control and Prevention, Behaviorial Risk Factor Surveillance System, SMART: Selected Metropolitan/Micropolitan Area Risk Trends, 2012 (Note: the CDC has discontinued this dataset but will be releasing a replacement in mid-2016)

Mortality Rates for the Top 10 Causes of Death in the U.S.

ICD-10[a] Sub-Chapter	ICD-10[a] Code	Age-Adjusted Mortality Rate[1] per 100,000 population	
		County[2]	U.S.
Malignant neoplasms	C00-C97	154.2	163.6
Ischaemic heart diseases	I20-I25	116.4	102.2
Other forms of heart disease	I30-I51	47.6	50.1
Chronic lower respiratory diseases	J40-J47	35.7	41.4
Organic, including symptomatic, mental disorders	F01-F09	34.3	38.5
Cerebrovascular diseases	I60-I69	35.3	36.5
Other external causes of accidental injury	W00-X59	18.4	27.5
Other degenerative diseases of the nervous system	G30-G31	24.5	26.3
Diabetes mellitus	E10-E14	18.9	21.1
Hypertensive diseases	I10-I15	17.3	19.7

Note: (a) ICD-10 = International Classification of Diseases 10th Revision; (1) Mortality rates are a three year average covering 2012-2014; (2) Figures cover Oakland County.
Source: Centers for Disease Control and Prevention, National Center for Health Statistics. Underlying Cause of Death 1999-2014 on CDC WONDER Online Database, released 2015.

Mortality Rates for Selected Causes of Death

ICD-10[a] Sub-Chapter	ICD-10[a] Code	Age-Adjusted Mortality Rate[1] per 100,000 population	
		County[2]	U.S.
Assault	X85-Y09	3.3	5.1
Diseases of the liver	K70-K76	11.7	13.5
Human immunodeficiency virus (HIV) disease	B20-B24	0.9	2.1
Influenza and pneumonia	J09-J18	12.4	15.2
Intentional self-harm	X60-X84	12.8	12.7
Malnutrition	E40-E46	1.4	0.9
Obesity and other hyperalimentation	E65-E68	1.0	1.9
Renal failure	N17-N19	12.3	13.0
Transport accidents	V01-V99	6.6	11.6
Viral hepatitis	B15-B19	1.2	2.1

Note: (a) ICD-10 = International Classification of Diseases 10th Revision; (1) Mortality rates are a three year average covering 2012-2014; (2) Figures cover Oakland County; Data are Suppressed when the data meet the criteria for confidentiality constraints; Mortality rates are flagged as Unreliable when the rate would be calculated with a numerator of 20 or less.
Source: Centers for Disease Control and Prevention, National Center for Health Statistics. Underlying Cause of Death 1999-2014 on CDC WONDER Online Database, released 2015.

Health Insurance Coverage

Area	With Health Insurance	With Private Health Insurance	With Public Health Insurance	Without Health Insurance	Population Under Age 18 Without Health Insurance
City	96.1	88.9	26.0	3.9	2.4
MSA[1]	88.5	68.7	33.3	11.5	3.9
U.S.	85.8	65.8	31.1	14.2	7.1

Note: Figures are percentages that cover the civilian noninstitutionalized population; (1) Figures cover the Detroit-Warren-Dearborn, MI Metropolitan Statistical Area—see Appendix B for areas included
Source: U.S. Census Bureau, 2010-2014 American Community Survey 5-Year Estimates

Number of Medical Professionals

Area	MDs[3]	DOs[3,4]	Dentists	Podiatrists	Chiropractors	Optometrists
County[1] (number)	6,664	1,292	1,262	217	383	221
County[1] (rate[2])	541.0	104.9	101.9	17.5	30.9	17.9
U.S. (rate[2])	272.5	20.9	64.7	5.8	25.9	15.2

Note: Data as of 2014 unless noted; (1) Data covers Oakland County; (2) Rate per 100,000 population; (3) Data as of 2013 and includes all active, non-federal physicians; (4) Doctor of Osteopathic Medicine
Source: U.S. Department of Health and Human Services, Health Resources and Services Administration, Bureau of Health Professions, Area Resource File (ARF) 2014-2015

Best Hospitals

According to *U.S. News,* the Warren-Troy-Farmington Hills, MI metro area is home to two of the best hospitals in the U.S.: **Beaumont Hospital** (9 specialties); **Beaumont Hospital** (3 specialties). The hospitals listed were nationally ranked in at least one adult specialty. Only 137 hospitals nationwide were nationally ranked in one or more specialties. Fifteen hospitals in the U.S. made the Honor Roll with high scores in at least six specialties. *U.S. News Online, "America's Best Children's Hospitals 2015-16"*

EDUCATION

Public School District Statistics

District Name	Schls	Pupils	Pupil/ Teacher Ratio	Minority Pupils[1] (%)	Free Lunch Eligible[2] (%)	IEP[3] (%)
Birmingham Public Schools	13	8,253	14.8	19.8	6.0	11.1
Bloomfield Hills Schools	10	5,455	13.0	28.6	6.9	15.9

Note: Table includes school districts with 100 or more students; (1) Percentage of students that are not non-Hispanic white; (2) Percentage of students that are eligible for the free lunch program; (3) Percentage of students that have an Individualized Education Program.
Source: U.S. Department of Education, National Center for Education Statistics, Common Core of Data, Local Education Agency (School District) Universe Survey: School Year 2013-2014; U.S. Department of Education, National Center for Education Statistics, Common Core of Data, Public Elementary/Secondary School Universe Survey: School Year 2013-2014

Best High Schools

According to *U.S. News,* Bloomfield is home to two of the best high schools in the U.S.: **International Academy** (#97); **Bloomfield Hills Andover High School** (#428); Nearly 20,000 schools were ranked based on their performance on state assessments and how well they prepare students for college. Schools with the highest unrounded College Readiness Index values were numerically ranked from No. 1 to No. 500 and were the gold medal winners. *U.S. News & World Report, "Best High Schools 2015"*

Highest Level of Education

Area	Less than H.S.	H.S. Diploma	Some College, No Deg.	Associate Degree	Bachelor's Degree	Master's Degree	Prof. School Degree	Doctorate Degree
City	2.8	9.5	13.2	5.1	34.8	20.7	11.1	2.9
MSA[1]	11.5	27.7	23.8	8.4	17.3	8.5	1.9	0.9
U.S.	13.7	28.0	21.2	7.9	18.3	7.8	2.0	1.3

Note: Figures cover persons age 25 and over; (1) Figures cover the Detroit-Warren-Dearborn, MI Metropolitan Statistical Area—see Appendix B for areas included
Source: U.S. Census Bureau, 2010-2014 American Community Survey 5-Year Estimates

Educational Attainment by Race

Area	High School Graduate or Higher (%)					Bachelor's Degree or Higher (%)				
	Total	White	Black	Asian	Hisp.[2]	Total	White	Black	Asian	Hisp.[2]
City	97.2	97.8	96.1	92.9	97.6	69.4	70.4	43.5	80.8	75.6
MSA[1]	88.5	90.2	83.9	88.7	68.6	28.6	30.4	17.1	63.9	17.3
U.S.	86.3	88.4	83.2	85.8	64.1	29.3	30.6	19.0	50.9	13.9

Note: Figures shown cover persons 25 years old and over; (1) Figures cover the Detroit-Warren-Dearborn, MI Metropolitan Statistical Area—see Appendix B for areas included; (2) People of Hispanic origin can be of any race
Source: U.S. Census Bureau, 2010-2014 American Community Survey 5-Year Estimates

School Enrollment by Grade and Control

Area	Preschool (%)		Kindergarten (%)		Grades 1 - 4 (%)		Grades 5 - 8 (%)		Grades 9 - 12 (%)	
	Public	Private	Public	Private	Public	Private	Public	Private	Public	Private
City	32.6	67.4	65.1	34.9	80.0	20.0	71.8	28.2	75.3	24.7
MSA[1]	65.2	34.8	88.2	11.8	89.7	10.3	90.5	9.5	91.4	8.6
U.S.	57.4	42.6	87.8	12.2	89.8	10.2	89.9	10.1	90.6	9.4

Note: Figures shown cover persons 3 years old and over; (1) Figures cover the Detroit-Warren-Dearborn, MI Metropolitan Statistical Area—see Appendix B for areas included
Source: U.S. Census Bureau, 2010-2014 American Community Survey 5-Year Estimates

Average Salaries of Public School Classroom Teachers

Area	2013-14 Dollars	2013-14 Rank[1]	2014-15 Dollars	2014-15 Rank[1]	Percent Change 2013-14 to 2014-15	Percent Change 2004-05 to 2014-15
Michigan	62,166	11	62,778	11	0.98	16.3
U.S. Average	56,610	–	57,379	–	1.36	20.8

Note: (1) State rank ranges from 1 to 51 where 1 indicates highest salary.
Source: National Education Association, Rankings & Estimates: Rankings of the States 2014 and Estimates of School Statistics 2015, March 2015

Higher Education

Four-Year Colleges			Two-Year Colleges			Medical Schools[1]	Law Schools[2]	Voc/ Tech[3]
Public	Private Non-profit	Private For-profit	Public	Private Non-profit	Private For-profit			
0	0	0	0	0	0	0	0	0

Note: Figures cover institutions located within the city limits and include main campuses only; (1) includes schools accredited by the Liaison Committee on Medical Education and the American Osteopathic Association's Commission on Osteopathic College Accreditation; (2) includes ABA-accredited schools, schools with provisional ABA accreditation, and state accredited schools; (3) includes all schools with programs that are less than 2 years.
Source: National Center for Education Statistics, Integrated Postsecondary Education System (IPEDS), 2014-15; Association of American Medical Colleges, Member List, March 21, 2016; American Osteopathic Association, Member List, March 21, 2016; Law School Admission Council, Official Guide to ABA-Approved Law Schools Online, March 21, 2016; Wikipedia, List of Medical Schools in the United States, March 21, 2016; Wikipedia, List of Law Schools in the United States, March 21, 2016

PRESIDENTIAL ELECTION

2012 Presidential Election Results

Area	Obama (%)	Romney (%)	Other (%)
Oakland County	53.4	45.4	1.2
U.S.	51.0	47.2	1.8

Note: Results may not add to 100% due to rounding
Source: Dave Leip's Atlas of U.S. Presidential Elections

EMPLOYERS

Major Employers

Company Name	Industry
CEI Liquidation Estates	Mobile homes
Chrysler Group	Motor vehicles & car bodies
Detroit Diesel Corporation	Motor vehicle parts & accessories
Dph-Das	Motor vehicle parts & accessories
Eagle Ottawa	Leather tanning & finishing
Employees Only	Management consulting services
Ford Motor Company	Drive shafts, motor vehicle
General Motors	Motor vehicles & car bodies
General Motors Company	Automobile assembly, including specialty automobiles
Oakwood Healthcare	General medical & surgical hospitals
St Joseph Mercy Oakland Foundation	General medical & surgical hospitals
The Army, United States Department of	Army
The Chrysler Group	Truck & tractor truck assembly
Tower Automotive	Automotive stampings
Wayne State University	Colleges & universities

Note: Companies shown are located within the Detroit-Warren-Dearborn, MI Metropolitan Statistical Area.
Source: Hoovers.com; Wikipedia

PUBLIC SAFETY

Crime Rate

Area	All Crimes	Violent Crimes				Property Crimes		
		Murder	Rape[3]	Robbery	Aggrav. Assault	Burglary	Larceny -Theft	Motor Vehicle Theft
City	824.0	2.4	7.1	16.6	14.2	159.1	588.9	35.6
Metro[1]	1,685.3	1.5	36.6	39.5	136.1	250.4	1,090.9	130.3
U.S.	2,971.8	4.5	36.6	102.2	232.5	542.5	1,837.3	216.2

Note: Figures are crimes per 100,000 population; (1) Figures cover the Warren-Troy-Farmington Hills, MI Metropolitan Division—see Appendix B for areas included; (3) The city and U.S. figures shown were reported using the revised Uniform Crime Reporting (UCR) definition of rape. The suburban and metro area figures shown are an aggregate total of the data submitted using both the revised and legacy UCR definitions.
Source: FBI Uniform Crime Reports, 2014

Hate Crimes

Area	Number of Quarters Reported	Number of Incidents per Bias Motivation						
		Race	Religion	Sexual Orientation	Ethnicity	Disability	Gender	Gender Identity
City	4	0	0	0	0	0	0	0
U.S.	4	2,568	1,014	1,017	648	84	33	98

Source: Federal Bureau of Investigation, Hate Crime Statistics 2014

Identity Theft Consumer Complaints

Area	Complaints	Complaints per 100,000 Population	Rank[2]
MSA[1]	9,468	220.4	10
U.S.	490,220	152.4	-

Note: (1) Figures cover the Detroit-Warren-Dearborn, MI Metropolitan Statistical Area—see Appendix B for areas included; (2) Rank ranges from 1 to 379 where 1 indicates greatest number of identity theft complaints per 100,000 population
Source: Federal Trade Commission, Consumer Sentinel Network Data Book for January–December 2015

Fraud and Other Consumer Complaints

Area	Complaints	Complaints per 100,000 Population	Rank[2]
MSA[1]	16,371	381.0	145
U.S.	2,593,159	806.0	-

Note: (1) Figures cover the Detroit-Warren-Dearborn, MI Metropolitan Statistical Area—see Appendix B for areas included; (2) Rank ranges from 1 to 379 where 1 indicates greatest number of identity theft complaints per 100,000 population
Source: Federal Trade Commission, Consumer Sentinel Network Data Book for January–December 2015

RECREATION

Culture

Dance[1]	Theatre[1]	Instrumental Music[1]	Vocal Music[1]	Series and Festivals	Museums and Art Galleries[2]	Zoos and Aquariums[3]
0	0	0	0	0	0	0

Note: (1) Professional perfoming groups; (2) Based on organizations with SIC code 8412; (3) AZA-accredited
Source: The Grey House Performing Arts Directory, 2015-16; Association of Zoos & Aquariums, AZA Member Zoos & Aquariums, March 25, 2016; www.AccuLeads.com, March 29, 2016

Professional Sports Teams

Team Name	League	Year Established
Detroit Lions	National Football League (NFL)	1934
Detroit Pistons	National Basketball Association (NBA)	1957
Detroit Red Wings	National Hockey League (NHL)	1926
Detroit Tigers	Major League Baseball (MLB)	1901

Note: Includes teams located in the Detroit-Warren-Dearborn, MI Metropolitan Statistical Area.
Source: Wikipedia, Major Professional Sports Teams of the United States and Canada, March 24, 2016

CLIMATE

Average and Extreme Temperatures

Temperature	Jan	Feb	Mar	Apr	May	Jun	Jul	Aug	Sep	Oct	Nov	Dec	Yr.
Extreme High (°F)	62	65	81	89	93	104	102	100	98	91	77	68	104
Average High (°F)	30	33	44	58	70	79	83	81	74	61	48	35	58
Average Temp. (°F)	23	26	36	48	59	68	72	71	64	52	40	29	49
Average Low (°F)	16	18	27	37	47	56	61	60	53	41	32	21	39
Extreme Low (°F)	-21	-15	-4	10	25	36	41	38	29	17	9	-10	-21

Note: Figures cover the years 1958-1990
Source: National Climatic Data Center, International Station Meteorological Climate Summary, 9/96

Average Precipitation/Snowfall/Humidity

Precip./Humidity	Jan	Feb	Mar	Apr	May	Jun	Jul	Aug	Sep	Oct	Nov	Dec	Yr.
Avg. Precip. (in.)	1.8	1.8	2.5	3.0	2.9	3.6	3.1	3.4	2.8	2.2	2.6	2.7	32.4
Avg. Snowfall (in.)	10	9	7	2	Tr	0	0	0	0	Tr	3	11	41
Avg. Rel. Hum. 7am (%)	80	79	79	78	78	79	82	86	87	84	82	81	81
Avg. Rel. Hum. 4pm (%)	67	63	59	53	51	52	52	54	55	55	64	70	58

Note: Figures cover the years 1958-1990; Tr = Trace amounts (<0.05 in. of rain; <0.5 in. of snow)
Source: National Climatic Data Center, International Station Meteorological Climate Summary, 9/96

Weather Conditions

Temperature			Daytime Sky			Precipitation		
5°F & below	32°F & below	90°F & above	Clear	Partly cloudy	Cloudy	0.01 inch or more precip.	0.1 inch or more snow/ice	Thunder-storms
15	136	12	74	134	157	135	38	32

Note: Figures are average number of days per year and cover the years 1958-1990
Source: National Climatic Data Center, International Station Meteorological Climate Summary, 9/96

HAZARDOUS WASTE

Superfund Sites

Bloomfield has no sites on the EPA's Superfund Final National Priorities List. There are a total of 1,323 Superfund sites on the list in the U.S. *U.S. Environmental Protection Agency, Final National Priorities List, March 18, 2016*

AIR & WATER QUALITY

Air Quality Trends: Ozone

	1990	1995	2000	2005	2010	2011	2012	2013	2014
MSA[1]	0.083	0.088	0.076	0.083	0.074	0.079	0.081	0.068	0.069

Note: (1) Data covers the Detroit-Warren-Dearborn, MI Metropolitan Statistical Area—see Appendix B for areas included. The values shown are the composite ozone concentration averages among trend sites based on the highest fourth daily maximum 8-hour concentration in parts per million. These trends are based on sites having an adequate record of monitoring data during the trend period. Data from exceptional events are included.
Source: U.S. Environmental Protection Agency, Air Quality Monitoring Information, "Air Quality Trends by City, 1990-2014"

Air Quality Index

Area	Percent of Days when Air Quality was...[2]					AQI Statistics[2]	
	Good	Moderate	Unhealthy for Sensitive Groups	Unhealthy	Very Unhealthy	Maximum	Median
MSA[1]	41.1	55.6	3.0	0.3	0.0	165	54

Note: (1) Data covers the Detroit-Warren-Dearborn, MI Metropolitan Statistical Area—see Appendix B for areas included; (2) Based on 365 days with AQI data in 2015. Air Quality Index (AQI) is an index for reporting daily air quality. EPA calculates the AQI for five major air pollutants regulated by the Clean Air Act: ground-level ozone, particle pollution (aka particulate matter), carbon monoxide, sulfur dioxide, and nitrogen dioxide. The AQI runs from 0 to 500. The higher the AQI value, the greater the level of air pollution and the greater the health concern. There are six AQI categories: "Good" AQI is between 0 and 50. Air quality is considered satisfactory; "Moderate" AQI is between 51 and 100. Air quality is acceptable; "Unhealthy for Sensitive Groups" When AQI values are between 101 and 150, members of sensitive groups may experience health effects; "Unhealthy" When AQI values are between 151 and 200 everyone may begin to experience health effects; "Very Unhealthy" AQI values between 201 and 300 trigger a health alert; "Hazardous" AQI values over 300 trigger warnings of emergency conditions (not shown).
Source: U.S. Environmental Protection Agency, Air Quality Index Report, 2015

Air Quality Index Pollutants

Area	Percent of Days when AQI Pollutant was...[2]					
	Carbon Monoxide	Nitrogen Dioxide	Ozone	Sulfur Dioxide	Particulate Matter 2.5	Particulate Matter 10
MSA[1]	0.0	2.5	15.6	14.2	58.9	8.8

Note: (1) Data covers the Detroit-Warren-Dearborn, MI Metropolitan Statistical Area—see Appendix B for areas included; (2) Based on 365 days with AQI data in 2015. The Air Quality Index (AQI) is an index for reporting daily air quality. EPA calculates the AQI for five major air pollutants regulated by the Clean Air Act: ground-level ozone, particle pollution (also known as particulate matter), carbon monoxide, sulfur dioxide, and nitrogen dioxide. The AQI runs from 0 to 500. The higher the AQI value, the greater the level of air pollution and the greater the health concern.
Source: U.S. Environmental Protection Agency, Air Quality Index Report, 2015

Maximum Air Pollutant Concentrations: Particulate Matter, Ozone, CO and Lead

	Particulate Matter 10 (ug/m^3)	Particulate Matter 2.5 Wtd AM (ug/m^3)	Particulate Matter 2.5 24-Hr (ug/m^3)	Ozone (ppm)	Carbon Monoxide (ppm)	Lead (ug/m^3)
MSA[1] Level	150	11.7	27	0.073	2	0.03
NAAQS[2]	150	15	35	0.075	9	0.15
Met NAAQS[2]	Yes	Yes	Yes	Yes	Yes	Yes

Note: (1) Data covers the Detroit-Warren-Dearborn, MI Metropolitan Statistical Area—see Appendix B for areas included; Data from exceptional events are included; (2) National Ambient Air Quality Standards; ppm = parts per million; ug/m^3 = micrograms per cubic meter; n/a not available.
Concentrations: Particulate Matter 10 (coarse particulate)—highest second maximum 24-hour concentration; Particulate Matter 2.5 Wtd AM (fine particulate)—highest weighted annual mean concentration; Particulate Matter 2.5 24-Hour (fine particulate)—highest 98th percentile 24-hour concentration; Ozone—highest fourth daily maximum 8-hour concentration; Carbon Monoxide—highest second maximum non-overlapping 8-hour concentration; Lead—maximum running 3-month average
Source: U.S. Environmental Protection Agency, Air Quality Monitoring Information, "Air Quality Statistics by City, 2014"

Maximum Air Pollutant Concentrations: Nitrogen Dioxide and Sulfur Dioxide

	Nitrogen Dioxide AM (ppb)	Nitrogen Dioxide 1-Hr (ppb)	Sulfur Dioxide AM (ppb)	Sulfur Dioxide 1-Hr (ppb)	Sulfur Dioxide 24-Hr (ppb)
MSA[1] Level	16	52	n/a	72	n/a
NAAQS[2]	53	100	30	75	140
Met NAAQS[2]	Yes	Yes	n/a	Yes	n/a

Note: (1) Data covers the Detroit-Warren-Dearborn, MI Metropolitan Statistical Area—see Appendix B for areas included; Data from exceptional events are included; (2) National Ambient Air Quality Standards; ppm = parts per million; ug/m^3 = micrograms per cubic meter; n/a not available.
Concentrations: Nitrogen Dioxide AM—highest arithmetic mean concentration; Nitrogen Dioxide 1-Hr—highest 98th percentile 1-hour daily maximum concentration; Sulfur Dioxide AM—highest annual mean concentration; Sulfur Dioxide 1-Hr—highest 99th percentile 1-hour daily maximum concentration; Sulfur Dioxide 24-Hr—highest second maximum 24-hour concentration
Source: U.S. Environmental Protection Agency, Air Quality Monitoring Information, "Air Quality Statistics by City, 2014"

Drinking Water

Water System Name	Pop. Served	Primary Water Source Type	Violations[1]	
			Health Based	Monitoring/ Reporting
Bloomfield Township	41,070	Purchased Surface	0	0

Note: (1) Based on violation data from January 1, 2015 to December 31, 2015 (includes unresolved violations from earlier years)

Source: U.S. Environmental Protection Agency, Office of Ground Water and Drinking Water, Safe Drinking Water Information System (based on data extracted April 29, 2016)

Grand Blanc, Michigan

Background

Grand Blanc is located in southeast Genesee County 60 miles north of Detroit and less than 10 miles from Flint. It covers approximately four square miles.

Originally a Chippewa Indians camping ground, Grand Blanc (then called Grumlaw, meaning Great White), was first settled by Frenchman Jacob Stevens in 1823. In 1826, his son Rufus started a trading post. Soon after, pioneer families began buying up the region's abundant land for $1.25 per acre, and a farming community was born.

In 1862 the railroad came to Grand Blanc, transforming the town from a farming community to a lumber town. The railroad was a major contributor to the growth of this small community, which officially became a city on March 4, 1930.

Today, Grand Blanc is known as a premier living community. The city boasts many exceptional golf courses, both private and public, and beautiful housing developments continue to be constructed among them. The Warwick Hills Country Club hosts the annual Buick Open Golf Tournament, the only PGA event in the state. In addition to golf, Grand Blanc offers beautifully maintained parks, beaches and recreational areas. Hiking, biking and equestrian trails, waterfalls, water and downhill skiing, and snowmobiling are easily found. If you enjoy fishing, boating, and canoeing, Buell Lake and the Flint River are places to visit. For a more relaxing experience, the For-Mar Nature Preserve and Arboretum is the way to go.

Downtown Grand Blanc is graced by sunburst locust trees that were planted in 1988 using community donations. Glowing streetlamps and park benches line the sidewalks, inviting residents to frequently enjoy the gracefully restored downtown area, which epitomizes Grand Blanc's approach to development—look toward the future while striving to preserve history and heritage.

A popular attraction is the Mayor's Memorial Clock, located in the heart of downtown—a dream come true for the city's beloved Mayor Paul T. Galuszka, who served from 1989 to 1992. On May 21,1994 with contributions of over 200 local residents, the Mayor's Clock was officially dedicated.

The major employers of Grand Blanc include General Motors HQ of Service Parts and Operations, and Genesys Regional Weld Tool Center. Heritage Park is the area's major shopping center, comprised of many super stores including Wal-Mart, Sam's Club, Kohl's, and Staples.

Trillium Circle lifestyle center, scheduled for completion in 2018, will bring hundreds of jobs to the city. When complete, this outdoor, 275,000 square foot center will house a state-of-the-art IMAX theater featuring 14 screens, Buffalo Wild Wings restaurant (one of at least five eateries), and a variety of retail stores, coffee shops and boutiques.

Today, both the city and township governments cooperate to provide services for the community, including parks and recreational facilities, senior citizens' services, the Grand Blanc Heritage Museum, McFarlen Public Library, and Grand Blanc Community Schools—the oldest and one of the highest-rated public school districts in Michigan, formed in 1904.

Speaking of education, Grand Blanc is known for its well-educated population, served by the University of Michigan-Flint, Baker College of Flint, Mott Community College, Kettering University, and the Michigan School for the Deaf and Blind.

The township government is made up of seven elected members who serve as Board of Trustees—supervisor, treasurer, clerk, and four members who take care of business with the help of residents at the well-attended public meetings every second Thursday of the month.

Grand Blanc has an average high temperature in July of 82 degrees and a low in January of 13 degrees with as much as a foot of snowfall. Annual rainfall is approximately 31.5 inches.

The closest airport is Bishop International Airport, which is about 5 miles away.

Rankings

Business/Finance Rankings

- The personal finance site NerdWallet analyzed 183 American metropolitan areas with populations over 250,000 and more than 15,000 businesses to rank where entrepreneurs find the most success. Criteria included area economy, annual income, housing cost, unemployment rate, and the success rate of area businesses. Flint* ranked #163. *www.nerdwallet.com, "Best Places to Start a Business," April 27, 2015*
- The Flint* metro area appeared on the Milken Institute "2015 Best Performing Cities" list. Rank: #156 out of 200 large metro areas. Criteria: job growth; wage and salary growth; high-tech output growth. *Milken Institute, "Best-Performing Cities 2015," December 2015*
- *Forbes* ranked the 200 most populous metro areas to determine the nation's "Best Places for Business and Careers." The Flint* metro area was ranked #192. Criteria: costs (business and living); job growth (past and projected); income growth; educational attainment (college and high school); projected economic growth; cultural and recreational opportunities; net migration patterns; number of highly ranked colleges. *Forbes, "The Best Places for Business and Careers 2015," July 29, 2015*

Education Rankings

- Personal finance website *WalletHub* analyzed the 150 largest U.S. metropolitan statistical areas to determine where the most educated Americans are choosing to settle. Criteria: education quality and attainment gap; education levels; percentage of workers with degrees; public school rankings; quality and size of each metro area's universities. Flint* was ranked #116 (#1 = most educated city). *www.WalletHub.com, "2015's Most and Least Educated Cities*

Environmental Rankings

- The Flint* metro area came in at #72 for the relative comfort of its climate on Sperling's list of "chill cities," as measured by the Sperling Heat Index. All 361 metro areas are included. Criteria included daytime high temperatures, nighttime low temperatures, dew point, and relative humidity at the high temperatures. *www.bertsperling.com, "Sperling's Chill Cities," July 18, 2013*
- Sperling's BestPlaces assessed 379 metropolitan areas of the United States for the likelihood of dangerously extreme weather events or earthquakes. In general the Southeast and South-Central regions have the highest risk of weather extremes and earthquakes, while the Pacific Northwest enjoys the lowest risk. Of the least risky metropolitan areas, the Flint* metro area was ranked #172. *www.bestplaces.net, "Safest Places from Natural Disasters," April 2011*

Health/Fitness Rankings

- The Gallup-Healthways Well-Being Index tracks Americans' optimism about their communities and satisfaction with the metro areas in which they live. At least 300 adult residents in each of 189 U.S. metropolitan areas were asked whether their metro was improving and the Flint* metro area was one of the ten communities where residents were least optimistic. *www.gallup.com, "City Satisfaction Highest in Fort Collins-Loveland, Colo.," April 11, 2014*
- Gallup-Healthways Well-Being Index researchers asked at least 300 adult residents in each of 189 U.S. metropolitan areas how satisfied they were with the metro area in which they lived. The Flint* metro area was one of the ten metros where residents were least likely to be satisfied. *www.gallup.com, "City Satisfaction Highest in Fort Collins-Loveland, Colo.," April 11, 2014*
- The Flint* metro area ranked #178 out of 190 in The Gallup-Healthways Well-Being Index. Criteria: purpose; social well being; financial health; community and physical health. Results are based on telephone interviews with adults, aged 18 and older, living in metropolitan areas in the 50 U.S. states and the District of Columbia. *Gallup-Healthways, "State of American Well-Being," February 23, 2016*

Real Estate Rankings

- With data from RealtyTrac, Yahoo! Finance researchers listed the housing markets in which housing affordability is improving most, factoring in interest rates as well as median home prices. The Flint* metro area was among the most affordable housing markets. *news.yahoo.com, "10 Cities Where Ordinary People Can No Longer Afford Homes," March 5, 2014*
- Flint* was ranked #54 out of 225 metro areas in terms of housing affordability in 2015 by the National Association of Home Builders (#1 = most affordable). Criteria: the share of homes sold in that area affordable to a family earning the local median income, based on standard mortgage underwriting criteria. *National Association of Home Builders®, NAHB-Wells Fargo Housing Opportunity Index, 4th Quarter 2015*

Safety Rankings

- The National Insurance Crime Bureau ranked 380 metro areas in the U.S. in terms of per capita rates of vehicle theft. The Flint* metro area ranked #212 (#1 = highest rate). Criteria: number of vehicle theft offenses per 100,000 inhabitants in 2014. *National Insurance Crime Bureau, "Hot Spots 2014," June 24, 2015*

Seniors/Retirement Rankings

- From its Best Cities for Successful Aging indexes, the Milken Institute generated rankings for metropolitan areas, weighing data in eight categories—health care, wellness, living arrangements, transportation, financial characteristics, education and employment opportunities, community engagement, and overall livability. The Flint* metro area was ranked #187 overall in the small metro area category. *Milken Institute, "Best Cities for Successful Aging, 2014"*

Miscellaneous Rankings

- The Flint* metro area was selected as one of "America's Most Miserable Cities" by *Forbes.com.* The metro area ranked #2 out of 20. Criteria: violent crime; unemployment; foreclosures; income and property taxes; home prices; commute times; climate. *Forbes.com, "America's Most Miserable Cities" February 22, 2013*

Grand Blanc is located within the Flint, MI Metropolitan Statistical Area.

Business Environment

CITY FINANCES

City Government Finances

Component	2012 ($000)	2012 ($ per capita)
Total Revenues	28,355	755
Total Expenditures	29,195	778
Debt Outstanding	11,856	316
Cash and Securities[1]	14,439	384

Note: (1) Cash and security holdings of a government at the close of its fiscal year, including those of its dependent agencies, utilities, and liquor stores.
Source: U.S Census Bureau, State & Local Government Finances 2012

City Government Revenue by Source

Source	2012 ($000)	2012 ($ per capita)
General Revenue		
From Federal Government	4	0
From State Government	3,124	83
From Local Governments	0	0
Taxes		
Property	7,887	210
Sales and Gross Receipts	554	14
Personal Income	0	0
Corporate Income	0	0
Motor Vehicle License	0	0
Other Taxes	413	11
Current Charges	8,173	217
Liquor Store	0	0
Utility	5,472	145
Employee Retirement	0	0

Source: U.S Census Bureau, State & Local Government Finances 2012

City Government Expenditures by Function

Function	2012 ($000)	2012 ($ per capita)	2012 (%)
General Direct Expenditures			
Air Transportation	0	0	0.0
Corrections	0	0	0.0
Education	0	0	0.0
Employment Security Administration	0	0	0.0
Financial Administration	1,173	31	4.0
Fire Protection	0	0	0.0
General Public Buildings	147	3	0.5
Governmental Administration, Other	1,228	32	4.2
Health	0	0	0.0
Highways	774	20	2.6
Hospitals	0	0	0.0
Housing and Community Development	0	0	0.0
Interest on General Debt	529	14	1.8
Judicial and Legal	0	0	0.0
Libraries	13	< 1	< 0.1
Parking	0	0	0.0
Parks and Recreation	372	9	1.2
Police Protection	5,581	148	19.1
Public Welfare	0	0	0.0
Sewerage	5,943	158	20.3
Solid Waste Management	1,252	33	4.2
Veterans' Services	0	0	0.0
Liquor Store	0	0	0.0
Utility	4,862	129	16.6
Employee Retirement	0	0	0.0

Source: U.S Census Bureau, State & Local Government Finances 2012

DEMOGRAPHICS

Population Growth

Area	1990 Census	2000 Census	2010 Census	2014* Estimate	Population Growth (%) 1990-2014	Population Growth (%) 2010-2014
City	25,180	29,827	37,508	37,019	47.0	-1.3
MSA[1]	430,459	436,141	425,790	418,654	-2.7	-1.7
U.S.	248,709,873	281,421,906	308,745,538	314,107,084	26.3	1.7

Note: (1) Figures cover the Flint, MI Metropolitan Statistical Area—see Appendix B for areas included; (*) 2010-2014 5-year estimated population

Source: U.S. Census Bureau, 1990 Census, Census 2000, Census 2010, 2010-2014 American Community Survey 5-Year Estimates

Household Size

Area	Persons in Household (%) One	Two	Three	Four	Five	Six	Seven or More	Average Household Size
City	26.7	35.0	14.2	12.6	8.7	1.9	0.5	2.56
MSA[1]	29.7	33.9	15.9	11.9	5.6	1.8	0.8	2.49
U.S.	27.5	33.5	15.8	13.1	6.0	2.3	1.4	2.64

Note: (1) Figures cover the Flint, MI Metropolitan Statistical Area—see Appendix B for areas included

Source: U.S. Census Bureau, 2010-2014 American Community Survey 5-Year Estimates

Race

Area	White Alone[2] (%)	Black Alone[2] (%)	Asian Alone[2] (%)	AIAN[3] Alone[2] (%)	NHOPI[4] Alone[2] (%)	Other Race Alone[2] (%)	Two or More Races (%)
City	81.1	11.6	4.2	0.0	0.1	0.4	2.6
MSA[1]	74.7	20.4	1.0	0.5	0.0	0.5	2.9
U.S.	73.8	12.6	5.0	0.8	0.2	4.7	2.9

Note: (1) Figures cover the Flint, MI Metropolitan Statistical Area—see Appendix B for areas included; (2) Alone is defined as not being in combination with one or more other races; (3) American Indian and Alaska Native; (4) Native Hawaiian and Other Pacific Islander

Source: U.S. Census Bureau, 2010-2014 American Community Survey 5-Year Estimates

Hispanic or Latino Origin

Area	Total (%)	Mexican (%)	Puerto Rican (%)	Cuban (%)	Other (%)
City	2.2	1.6	0.1	0.2	0.2
MSA[1]	3.1	2.5	0.2	0.1	0.3
U.S.	16.9	10.8	1.6	0.6	3.8

Note: Persons of Hispanic or Latino origin can be of any race; (1) Figures cover the Flint, MI Metropolitan Statistical Area—see Appendix B for areas included

Source: U.S. Census Bureau, 2010-2014 American Community Survey 5-Year Estimates

Ancestry

Area	German	Irish	English	American	Italian	Polish	French[2]	Scottish	Dutch
City	18.4	10.5	10.7	7.3	3.9	7.3	3.6	2.8	2.0
MSA[1]	16.7	10.3	9.3	6.8	2.8	5.5	4.3	2.2	1.9
U.S.	14.9	10.8	8.0	7.1	5.5	3.0	2.7	1.7	1.4

Note: Figures are the percentage of the total population reporting a particular ancestry. The nine most commonly reported ancestries in the U.S. are shown. Figures include multiple ancestries (e.g. if a person reported being Irish and Italian, they were included in both columns); (1) Figures cover the Flint, MI Metropolitan Statistical Area—see Appendix B for areas included; (2) Excludes Basque

Source: U.S. Census Bureau, 2010-2014 American Community Survey 5-Year Estimates

Foreign-Born Population

Area	Percent of Population Born in: Any Foreign Country	Asia	Mexico	Europe	Carribean	Central America[2]	South America	Africa	Canada
City	6.4	4.3	0.1	0.8	0.1	0.0	0.5	0.3	0.4
MSA[1]	2.3	1.2	0.1	0.5	0.0	0.0	0.1	0.1	0.2
U.S.	13.1	3.8	3.7	1.5	1.2	1.0	0.9	0.6	0.3

Note: (1) Figures cover the Flint, MI Metropolitan Statistical Area—see Appendix B for areas included; (2) Excludes Mexico.
Source: U.S. Census Bureau, 2010-2014 American Community Survey 5-Year Estimates

Marital Status

Area	Never Married	Now Married[2]	Separated	Widowed	Divorced
City	26.3	55.6	2.0	5.6	10.5
MSA[1]	33.0	44.8	2.0	6.6	13.5
U.S.	32.5	48.4	2.2	5.9	10.9

Note: Figures are percentages and cover the population 15 years of age and older; (1) Figures cover the Flint, MI Metropolitan Statistical Area—see Appendix B for areas included; (2) Excludes separated
Source: U.S. Census Bureau, 2010-2014 American Community Survey 5-Year Estimates

Disability Status

Area	All Ages	Under 18 Years Old	18 to 64 Years Old	65 Years and Over
City	9.6	3.4	7.3	32.5
MSA[1]	16.1	5.9	15.0	38.0
U.S.	12.3	4.1	10.2	36.3

Note: Figures show percent of the civilian noninstitutionalized population that reported having a disability. Disability status is determined from from six types of difficulty: vision, hearing, cognitive, ambulatory, self-care, and independent living. For children under 5 years old, hearing and vision difficulty are used to determine disability status. For children between the ages of 5 and 14, disability status is determined from hearing, vision, cognitive, ambulatory, and self-care difficulties. For people aged 15 years and older, they are considered to have a disability if they have difficulty with any one of the six difficulty types; (1) Figures cover the Flint, MI Metropolitan Statistical Area—see Appendix B for areas included.
Source: U.S. Census Bureau, 2010-2014 American Community Survey 5-Year Estimates

Age

Area	Percent of Population: Under Age 5	Age 5–19	Age 20–34	Age 35–44	Age 45–54	Age 55–64	Age 65–74	Age 75–84	Age 85+	Median Age
City	6.0	22.4	18.7	14.4	13.6	11.5	7.8	3.6	2.1	37.3
MSA[1]	6.2	20.7	18.1	12.5	14.7	13.2	8.0	4.8	1.8	39.1
U.S.	6.4	19.9	20.6	13.0	14.1	12.3	7.6	4.3	1.9	37.4

Note: (1) Figures cover the Flint, MI Metropolitan Statistical Area—see Appendix B for areas included
Source: U.S. Census Bureau, 2010-2014 American Community Survey 5-Year Estimates

Gender

Area	Males	Females	Males per 100 Females
City	18,169	18,850	96.4
MSA[1]	201,815	216,839	93.1
U.S.	154,515,159	159,591,925	96.8

Note: (1) Figures cover the Flint, MI Metropolitan Statistical Area—see Appendix B for areas included
Source: U.S. Census Bureau, 2010-2014 American Community Survey 5-Year Estimates

Religious Groups by Family

Area	Catholic	Baptist	Non-Den.	Methodist[2]	Lutheran	LDS[3]	Pente-costal	Presby-terian[4]	Muslim[5]	Judaism
MSA[1]	10.7	6.9	3.4	3.0	3.2	0.5	2.9	1.4	2.5	0.1
U.S.	19.1	9.3	4.0	4.0	2.3	2.0	1.9	1.6	0.8	0.7

Note: Figures are the number of adherents as a percentage of the total population; (1) Figures cover the Flint, MI Metropolitan Statistical Area—see Appendix B for areas included; (2) Methodist/Pietist; (3) Latter Day Saints; (4) Reformed; (5) Figures are estimates
Source: Association of Statisticians of American Religious Bodies, 2010 U.S. Religion Census: Religious Congregations & Membership Study

Religious Groups by Tradition

Area	Catholic	Evangelical Protestant	Mainline Protestant	Other Tradition	Black Protestant	Orthodox
MSA[1]	10.7	14.0	5.3	4.1	4.8	0.3
U.S.	19.1	16.2	7.3	4.3	1.6	0.3

Note: Figures are the number of adherents as a percentage of the total population; (1) Figures cover the Flint, MI Metropolitan Statistical Area—see Appendix B for areas included
Source: Association of Statisticians of American Religious Bodies, 2010 U.S. Religion Census: Religious Congregations & Membership Study

ECONOMY

Gross Metropolitan Product

Area	2013	2014	2015	2016	Rank[2]
MSA[1]	12.6	12.8	13.3	13.8	169

Note: Figures are in billions of dollars; (1) Figures cover the Flint, MI Metropolitan Statistical Area—see Appendix B for areas included; (2) Rank is based on 2016 data and ranges from 1 to 381
Source: The U.S. Conference of Mayors, U.S. Metro Economies: GMP and Employment 2014-2016, June 2015

Economic Growth

Area	2011-13 (%)	2014 (%)	2015 (%)	2016 (%)	Rank[2]
MSA[1]	0.6	0.4	2.1	1.9	303
U.S.	2.2	2.4	2.3	2.9	–

Note: Figures are real gross metropolitan product (GMP) growth rates and represent annual average percent change; (1) Figures cover the Flint, MI Metropolitan Statistical Area—see Appendix B for areas included; (2) Rank is based on 2016 data and ranges from 1 to 381
Source: The U.S. Conference of Mayors, U.S. Metro Economies: GMP and Employment 2014-2016, June 2015

Metropolitan Area Exports

Area	2009	2010	2011	2012	2013	2014	Rank[2]
MSA[1]	354.0	367.1	367.5	399.2	474.5	561.3	209

Note: Figures are in millions of dollars; (1) Figures cover the Flint, MI Metropolitan Statistical Area—see Appendix B for areas included; (2) Rank is based on 2014 data and ranges from 1 to 385
Source: U.S. Department of Commerce, International Trade Administration, Office of Trade & Industry Information, Manufacturing & Services, data extracted March 10, 2016

Building Permits

Area	Single-Family			Multi-Family			Total		
	2014	2015p	Pct. Chg.	2014	2015p	Pct. Chg.	2014	2015p	Pct. Chg.
City	111	118	6.3	0	0	-	111	118	6.3
MSA[1]	271	103	-62.0	72	24	-66.7	343	127	-63.0
U.S.	640,300	690,800	7.9	411,800	487,600	18.4	1,052,100	1,178,400	12.0

Note: (1) Figures cover the Flint, MI Metropolitan Statistical Area—see Appendix B for areas included; Figures represent new, privately-owned housing units authorized (unadjusted data); All permit data are based on estimates with imputation; (p) preliminary data.
Source: U.S. Census Bureau, Manufacturing, Mining, and Construction Statistics, Building Permits, 2014, 2015

Bankruptcy Filings

Area	Business Filings 2014	Business Filings 2015	% Chg.	Nonbusiness Filings 2014	Nonbusiness Filings 2015	% Chg.
Genesee County	24	26	8.3	2,490	2,362	-5.1
U.S.	26,983	24,735	-8.3	909,812	819,760	-9.9

Note: Business filings include Chapter 7, Chapter 11, Chapter 12, and Chapter 13; Nonbusiness filings include Chapter 7, Chapter 11, and Chapter 13
Source: Administrative Office of the U.S. Courts, Business and Nonbusiness Bankruptcy, County Cases Commenced by Chapter of the Bankruptcy Code, During the 12- Month Period Ending December 31, 2014 and Business and Nonbusiness Bankruptcy, County Cases Commenced by Chapter of the Bankruptcy Code, During the 12- Month Period Ending December 31, 2015

Housing Vacancy Rates

Area	Gross Vacancy Rate[2] (%)			Year-Round Vacancy Rate[3] (%)			Rental Vacancy Rate[4] (%)			Homeowner Vacancy Rate[5] (%)		
	2013	2014	2015	2013	2014	2015	2013	2014	2015	2013	2014	2015
MSA[1]	n/a	n/a	n/a	n/a	n/a	n/a	n/a	n/a	n/a	n/a	n/a	n/a
U.S.	13.6	13.4	12.9	10.7	10.4	10.0	8.3	7.6	7.1	2.0	1.9	1.8

Note: (1) Figures cover the Flint, MI Metropolitan Statistical Area—see Appendix B for areas included; (2) The percentage of the total housing inventory that is vacant; (3) The percentage of the housing inventory (excluding seasonal units) that is year-round vacant; (4) The percentage of rental inventory that is vacant for rent; (5) The percentage of homeowner inventory that is vacant for sale; n/a not available
Source: U.S. Census Bureau, Housing Vacancies and Homeownership Annual Statistics: 2015

INCOME

Income

Area	Per Capita ($)	Median Household ($)	Average Household ($)
City	30,476	58,392	77,817
MSA[1]	22,536	41,879	55,656
U.S.	28,555	53,482	74,596

Note: (1) Figures cover the Flint, MI Metropolitan Statistical Area—see Appendix B for areas included
Source: U.S. Census Bureau, 2010-2014 American Community Survey 5-Year Estimates

Household Income Distribution

Area	Percent of Households Earning							
	Under $15,000	$15,000 -24,999	$25,000 -34,999	$35,000 -49,999	$50,000 -74,999	$75,000 -99,000	$100,000 -149,999	$150,000 and up
City	8.4	7.1	12.2	15.3	16.3	15.8	14.1	10.8
MSA[1]	17.0	12.8	12.5	15.3	18.2	10.6	9.2	4.5
U.S.	12.5	10.7	10.2	13.5	17.8	12.2	13.0	10.0

Note: (1) Figures cover the Flint, MI Metropolitan Statistical Area—see Appendix B for areas included
Source: U.S. Census Bureau, 2010-2014 American Community Survey 5-Year Estimates

Poverty Rate

Area	All Ages	Under 18 Years Old	18 to 64 Years Old	65 Years and Over
City	10.4	11.5	11.4	3.9
MSA[1]	21.2	32.1	20.3	7.2
U.S.	15.6	21.9	14.6	9.4

Note: Figures are percentage of people whose income during the past 12 months was below the poverty level; (1) Figures cover the Flint, MI Metropolitan Statistical Area—see Appendix B for areas included
Source: U.S. Census Bureau, 2010-2014 American Community Survey 5-Year Estimates

EMPLOYMENT

Labor Force and Employment

Area	Civilian Labor Force Dec. 2014	Civilian Labor Force Dec. 2015	% Chg.	Workers Employed Dec. 2014	Workers Employed Dec. 2015	% Chg.
City	18,456	18,524	0.3	17,784	17,990	1.1
MSA[1]	184,709	184,534	0.0	174,034	176,047	1.1
U.S.	155,521,000	157,245,000	1.1	147,190,000	149,703,000	1.7

Note: Data is not seasonally adjusted and covers workers 16 years of age and older; (1) Figures cover the Flint, MI Metropolitan Statistical Area—see Appendix B for areas included
Source: Bureau of Labor Statistics, Local Area Unemployment Statistics

Unemployment Rate

Area	2015											
	Jan.	Feb.	Mar.	Apr.	May	Jun.	Jul.	Aug.	Sep.	Oct.	Nov.	Dec.
City	4.5	3.9	4.0	3.4	4.0	4.0	4.3	3.4	3.1	3.1	3.0	2.9
MSA[1]	7.1	6.2	6.3	5.4	6.4	6.3	6.8	5.4	5.0	5.0	4.8	4.6
U.S.	6.1	5.8	5.6	5.1	5.3	5.5	5.6	5.2	4.9	4.8	4.8	4.8

Note: Data is not seasonally adjusted and covers workers 16 years of age and older; (1) Figures cover the Flint, MI Metropolitan Statistical Area—see Appendix B for areas included
Source: Bureau of Labor Statistics, Local Area Unemployment Statistics

Employment by Occupation

Occupation Classification	City (%)	MSA[1] (%)	U.S. (%)
Management, Business, Science, and Arts	44.7	30.2	36.4
Natural Resources, Construction, and Maintenance	5.2	7.9	9.0
Production, Transportation, and Material Moving	9.8	16.3	12.1
Sales and Office	24.3	25.3	24.4
Service	16.0	20.4	18.2

Note: Figures cover employed civilians 16 years of age and older; (1) Figures cover the Flint, MI Metropolitan Statistical Area—see Appendix B for areas included
Source: U.S. Census Bureau, 2010-2014 American Community Survey 5-Year Estimates

Employment by Industry

Sector	MSA[1]		U.S.
	Number of Employees	Percent of Total	Percent of Total
Construction, Mining, and Logging	4,600	3.2	5.0
Education and Health Services	28,700	20.3	15.7
Financial Activities	6,200	4.4	5.7
Government	19,300	13.7	15.5
Information	4,100	2.9	1.9
Leisure and Hospitality	15,000	10.6	10.4
Manufacturing	12,100	8.5	8.6
Other Services	5,500	3.9	3.9
Professional and Business Services	15,400	10.9	13.9
Retail Trade	20,500	14.5	11.3
Transportation, Warehousing, and Utilities	3,900	2.7	3.9
Wholesale Trade	5,500	3.9	4.1

Note: Figures are non-farm employment as of December 2015. Figures are not seasonally adjusted and include workers 16 years of age and older; (1) Figures cover the Flint, MI Metropolitan Statistical Area—see Appendix B for areas included; n/a not available
Source: Bureau of Labor Statistics, Current Employment Statistics, Employment, Hours, and Earnings

Occupations with Greatest Projected Employment Growth: 2010 – 2020

Occupation[1]	2010 Employment	2020 Projected Employment	Numeric Employment Change	Percent Employment Change
Home Health Aides	35,400	54,310	18,910	53.4
Registered Nurses	87,170	104,000	16,820	19.3
Office Clerks, General	112,620	123,920	11,300	10.0
Retail Salespersons	127,580	137,710	10,140	8.0
Combined Food Preparation and Serving Workers, Including Fast Food	70,020	78,610	8,590	12.3
Nursing Aides, Orderlies, and Attendants	50,400	57,320	6,920	13.7
Personal Care Aides	14,720	20,900	6,180	42.0
Landscaping and Groundskeeping Workers	28,350	34,370	6,020	21.2
Customer Service Representatives	61,310	67,240	5,930	9.7
Heavy and Tractor-Trailer Truck Drivers	48,610	54,070	5,460	11.2

Note: Projections cover Michigan; (1) Sorted by numeric employment change
Source: www.projectionscentral.com, State Occupational Projections, 2010–2020 Long-Term Projections

Fastest Growing Occupations: 2010 – 2020

Occupation[1]	2010 Employment	2020 Projected Employment	Numeric Employment Change	Percent Employment Change
Biomedical Engineers	200	310	110	54.0
Home Health Aides	35,400	54,310	18,910	53.4
Personal Care Aides	14,720	20,900	6,180	42.0
Veterinary Technologists and Technicians	1,810	2,570	760	42.0
Meeting, Convention, and Event Planners	1,540	2,140	600	39.1
Market Research Analysts and Marketing Specialists	6,920	9,500	2,590	37.4
Software Developers, Systems Software	6,550	8,960	2,420	36.9
Marriage and Family Therapists	300	400	110	36.6
Helpers—Carpenters	300	410	110	36.5
Bicycle Repairers	570	770	200	36.0

Note: Projections cover Michigan; (1) Sorted by percent employment change and excludes occupations with numeric employment change less than 100
Source: www.projectionscentral.com, State Occupational Projections, 2010–2020 Long-Term Projections

Average Wages

Occupation	$/Hr.	Occupation	$/Hr.
Accountants and Auditors	32.50	Maids and Housekeeping Cleaners	11.19
Automotive Mechanics	18.20	Maintenance and Repair Workers	15.35
Bookkeepers	17.31	Marketing Managers	51.67
Carpenters	23.74	Nuclear Medicine Technologists	30.03
Cashiers	10.04	Nurses, Licensed Practical	21.95
Clerks, General Office	15.33	Nurses, Registered	31.88
Clerks, Receptionists/Information	13.41	Nursing Assistants	12.70
Clerks, Shipping/Receiving	14.27	Packers and Packagers, Hand	13.23
Computer Programmers	n/a	Physical Therapists	39.55
Computer Systems Analysts	39.90	Postal Service Mail Carriers	24.88
Computer User Support Specialists	24.04	Real Estate Brokers	n/a
Cooks, Restaurant	10.85	Retail Salespersons	11.27
Dentists	92.88	Sales Reps., Exc. Tech./Scientific	24.51
Electrical Engineers	n/a	Sales Reps., Tech./Scientific	70.77
Electricians	29.93	Secretaries, Exc. Legal/Med./Exec.	15.44
Financial Managers	52.11	Security Guards	10.70
First-Line Supervisors/Managers, Sales	18.47	Surgeons	n/a
Food Preparation Workers	12.02	Teacher Assistants*	12.55
General and Operations Managers	47.48	Teachers, Elementary School*	29.67
Hairdressers/Cosmetologists	12.05	Teachers, Secondary School*	29.24
Internists	46.45	Telemarketers	11.43
Janitors and Cleaners	12.45	Truck Drivers, Heavy/Tractor-Trailer	18.64
Landscaping/Groundskeeping Workers	12.40	Truck Drivers, Light/Delivery Svcs.	14.84
Lawyers	45.59	Waiters and Waitresses	10.18

Note: Wage data covers the Flint, MI Metropolitan Statistical Area—see Appendix B for areas included; (*) Hourly wages for elementary/secondary school teachers and teacher assistants were calculated by the editors from annual wage data based on a 40 hour work week; n/a not available.
Source: Bureau of Labor Statistics, Metro Area Occupational Employment and Wage Estimates, May 2015

TAXES

State Corporate Income Tax Rates

State	Tax Rate (%)	Income Brackets ($)	Num. of Brackets	Financial Institution Tax Rate (%)[a]	Federal Income Tax Ded.
Michigan	6.0	Flat rate	1	(a)	No

Note: Tax rates as of January 1, 2016; (a) Rates listed are the corporate income tax rate applied to financial institutions or excise taxes based on income. Some states have other taxes based upon the value of deposits or shares.
Source: Federation of Tax Administrators, "State Corporate Income Tax Rates, 2016"

State Individual Income Tax Rates

State	Tax Rate (%)	Income Brackets ($)	Num. of Brackets	Personal Exempt. ($)[1]		Fed. Inc. Tax Ded.
				Single	Dependents	
Michigan (a)	4.25	Flat rate	1	3,950	3,950	No

Note: Tax rates as of January 1, 2016; Local- and county-level taxes are not included; n/a not applicable; (1) Married joint filers generally receive double the single exemption; (a) 18 states have statutory provision for automatically adjusting to the rate of inflation the dollar values of the income tax brackets, standard deductions, and/or personal exemptions. Massachusetts, Michigan, and Nebraska index the personal exemptiononly. Oregon does not index the income brackets for $125,000 and over. Maine has suspended indexing for 2014 and 2015.
Source: Federation of Tax Administrators, "State Individual Income Tax Rates, 2016"

Various State and Local Tax Rates

State	State and Local Sales and Use (%)	State Sales and Use (%)	Gasoline[1] (¢/gal.)	Cigarette[2] ($/pack)	Spirits[3] ($/gal.)	Wine[4] ($/gal.)	Beer[5] ($/gal.)
Michigan	6.00	6.0	30.54	2.00	11.94 (g)	0.51 (l)	0.20

Note: All tax rates as of January 1, 2016; (1) The American Petroleum Institute has developed a methodology for determining the average tax rate on a gallon of fuel. Rates may include any of the following: excise taxes, environmental fees, storage tank fees, other fees or taxes, general sales tax, and local taxes. In states where gasoline is subject to the general sales tax, or where the fuel tax is based on the average sale price, the average rate determined by API is sensitive to changes in the price of gasoline. States that fully or partially apply general sales taxes to gasoline: CA, CO, GA, IL, IN, MI, NY; (2) The federal excise tax of $1.0066 per pack and local taxes are not included; (3) Rates are those applicable to off-premise sales of 40% alcohol by volume (a.b.v.) distilled spirits in 750ml containers. Local excise taxes are excluded; (4) Rates are those applicable to off-premise sales of 11% a.b.v. non-carbonated wine in 750ml containers; (5) Rates are those applicable to off-premise sales of 4.7% a.b.v. beer in 12 ounce containers; (g) Control states, where the government controls all sales. Products can be subject to ad valorem mark-up as well as excise taxes; (l) Different rates also applicable according to alcohol content, place of production, size of container, place purchased (on- or off-premise or on board airlines) or type of wine (carbonated, vermouth, etc.).
Source: Tax Foundation, 2016 Facts & Figures: How Does Your State Compare?

State Business Tax Climate Index Rankings

State	Overall Rank	Corporate Tax Rank	Individual Income Tax Rank	Sales Tax Rank	Unemployment Insurance Tax Rank	Property Tax Rank
Michigan	13	11	15	7	48	26

Note: The index is a measure of how each state's tax laws affect economic performance. The lower the rank, the more favorable a state's tax system is for business. States without a given tax are given a ranking of 1. The scores/rankings for the District of Columbia do not affect other states. The 2016 index represents the tax climate as of July 1, 2015 (the beginning of Fiscal Year 2016).
Source: Tax Foundation, State Business Tax Climate Index 2016

TRANSPORTATION

Means of Transportation to Work

Area	Car/Truck/Van		Public Transportation			Bicycle	Walked	Other Means	Worked at Home
	Drove Alone	Car-pooled	Bus	Subway	Railroad				
City	89.3	6.3	0.1	0.0	0.0	0.1	0.4	0.3	3.6
MSA[1]	85.1	8.9	1.2	0.0	0.0	0.1	1.2	0.6	2.9
U.S.	76.4	9.6	2.6	1.8	0.6	0.6	2.8	1.3	4.4

Note: Figures are percentages and cover workers 16 years of age and older; (1) Figures cover the Flint, MI Metropolitan Statistical Area—see Appendix B for areas included
Source: U.S. Census Bureau, 2010-2014 American Community Survey 5-Year Estimates

Travel Time to Work

Area	Less Than 10 Minutes	10 to 19 Minutes	20 to 29 Minutes	30 to 44 Minutes	45 to 59 Minutes	60 to 89 Minutes	90 Minutes or More
City	13.9	33.4	20.0	13.0	7.9	10.1	1.7
MSA[1]	13.2	32.8	22.5	14.0	7.8	7.2	2.5
U.S.	13.3	29.6	21.0	20.2	7.7	5.7	2.6

Note: Figures are percentages and include workers 16 years old and over; (1) Figures cover the Flint, MI Metropolitan Statistical Area—see Appendix B for areas included
Source: U.S. Census Bureau, 2010-2014 American Community Survey 5-Year Estimates

Freeway Travel Time Index

Area	1985	1990	1995	2000	2005	2010	2014
Urban Area Rank[1,2]	n/a	n/a	n/a	n/a	n/a	n/a	n/a
Urban Area Index[1]	n/a	n/a	n/a	n/a	n/a	n/a	n/a
Average Index[3]	1.09	1.11	1.14	1.17	1.20	1.19	1.20

Note: Freeway Travel Time Index—the ratio of travel time in the peak period to the travel time at free-flow conditions. For example, a value of 1.30 indicates a 20-minute free-flow trip takes 26 minutes in the peak (20 minutes x 1.30 = 26 minutes); (1) Data for the Flint, MI urban area was not available; (2) Rank is based on 101 urban areas (#1 = highest travel time index); (3) Average of 101 urban areas

Source: Texas Transportation Institute, 2015 Urban Mobility Scorecard, August 2015

Freeway Commuter Stress Index

Area	1985	1990	1995	2000	2005	2010	2014
Urban Area Rank[1,2]	n/a	n/a	n/a	n/a	n/a	n/a	n/a
Urban Area Index[1]	n/a	n/a	n/a	n/a	n/a	n/a	n/a
Average Index[3]	1.13	1.16	1.19	1.22	1.25	1.24	1.25

Note: The Freeway Commuter Stress Index is the same as the Freeway Travel Time Index (see table above) except that it includes only the travel in the peak directions during the peak periods; the TTI includes travel in all directions during the peak period. Thus, the CSI is more indicative of the work trip experienced by each commuter on a daily basis. (1) Data for the Flint, MI urban area was not available; (2) Rank is based on 101 urban areas (#1 = highest stress index); (3) Average of 101 urban areas

Source: Texas Transportation Institute, 2015 Urban Mobility Scorecard, August 2015

Living Environment

COST OF LIVING

Cost of Living Index

Composite Index	Groceries	Housing	Utilities	Trans-portation	Health Care	Misc. Goods/ Services
n/a	n/a	n/a	n/a	n/a	n/a	n/a

Note: The Cost of Living Index measures regional differences in the cost of consumer goods and services, excluding taxes and non-consumer expenditures, for professional and managerial households in the top income quintile. It is based on more than 50,000 prices covering almost 60 different items for which prices are collected three times a year by chambers of commerce, economic development organizations or university applied economic centers in each participating urban area. The numbers shown should be read as a percentage above or below the national average of 100. For example, a value of 115.4 in the groceries column indicates that grocery prices are 15.4% higher than the national average. Small differences in the index numbers should not be interpreted as significant; n/a not available.

Source: The Council for Community and Economic Research, ACCRA Cost of Living Index, 2015

Grocery Prices

Area[1]	T-Bone Steak ($/pound)	Frying Chicken ($/pound)	Whole Milk ($/half gal.)	Eggs ($/dozen)	Orange Juice ($/64 oz.)	Coffee ($/11.5 oz.)
City[2]	n/a	n/a	n/a	n/a	n/a	n/a
Avg.	10.99	1.43	2.25	2.26	3.58	4.48
Min.	7.16	0.98	1.30	1.35	2.88	2.98
Max.	14.13	2.43	3.85	4.81	6.39	7.56

Note: (1) Values for the local area are compared with the average, minimum and maximum values for all 292 areas in the Cost of Living Index; (2) Figures cover the Grand Blanc MI urban area; n/a not available; **T-Bone Steak** *(price per pound);* **Frying Chicken** *(price per pound, whole fryer);* **Whole Milk** *(half gallon carton);* **Eggs** *(price per dozen, Grade A, large);* **Orange Juice** *(64 oz. Tropicana or Florida Natural);* **Coffee** *(11.5 oz. can, vacuum-packed, Maxwell House, Hills Bros, or Folgers).*

Source: The Council for Community and Economic Research, ACCRA Cost of Living Index, 2015

Housing and Utility Costs

Area[1]	New Home Price ($)	Apartment Rent ($/month)	All Electric ($/month)	Part Electric ($/month)	Other Energy ($/month)	Telephone ($/month)
City[2]	n/a	n/a	n/a	n/a	n/a	n/a
Avg.	312,874	945	179.30	95.07	72.96	28.11
Min.	178,682	479	116.28	43.14	26.46	10.01
Max.	1,472,476	3,984	504.25	189.44	421.11	43.06

Note: (1) Values for the local area are compared with the average, minimum and maximum values for all 292 areas in the Cost of Living Index; (2) Figures cover the Grand Blanc MI urban area; n/a not available; **New Home Price** *(2,400 sf living area, 8,000 sf lot, in urban area with full utilities);* **Apartment Rent** *(950 sf 2 bedroom/1.5 or 2 bath, unfurnished, excluding all utilities except water);* **All Electric** *(average monthly cost for an all-electric home);* **Part Electric** *(average monthly cost for a part-electric home);* **Other Energy** *(average monthly cost for natural gas, fuel oil, coal, wood, and any other forms of energy except electricity);* **Telephone** *(price includes basic monthly rate for a private residential line plus additional local usage charges incurred by a family of four).*

Source: The Council for Community and Economic Research, ACCRA Cost of Living Index, 2015

Health Care, Transportation, and Other Costs

Area[1]	Doctor ($/visit)	Dentist ($/visit)	Optometrist ($/visit)	Gasoline ($/gallon)	Beauty Salon ($/visit)	Men's Shirt ($)
City[2]	n/a	n/a	n/a	n/a	n/a	n/a
Avg.	105.15	89.02	99.78	2.38	35.30	28.10
Min.	66.87	56.09	48.53	1.95	18.91	13.38
Max.	182.34	150.36	228.33	4.09	67.91	63.80

Note: (1) Values for the local area are compared with the average, minimum and maximum values for all 292 areas in the Cost of Living Index; (2) Figures cover the Grand Blanc MI urban area; n/a not available; **Doctor** *(general practitioners routine exam of an established patient);* **Dentist** *(adult teeth cleaning and periodic oral examination);* **Optometrist** *(full vision eye exam for established adult patient);* **Gasoline** *(one gallon regular unleaded, national brand, including all taxes, cash price at self-service pump if available);* **Beauty Salon** *(woman's shampoo, trim, and blow-dry);* **Men's Shirt** *(cotton/polyester dress shirt, pinpoint weave, long sleeves).*

Source: The Council for Community and Economic Research, ACCRA Cost of Living Index, 2015

HOUSING

House Price Index (HPI)

Area	National Ranking[2]	Quarterly Change (%)	One-Year Change (%)	Five-Year Change (%)
MSA[1]	135	0.80	4.60	19.10
U.S.[3]	–	1.45	5.76	22.85

Note: The HPI is a weighted repeat sales index. It measures average price changes in repeat sales or refinancings on the same properties. This information is obtained by reviewing repeat mortgage transactions on single-family properties whose mortgages have been purchased or securitized by Fannie Mae or Freddie Mac in January 1975; (1) Flint Metropolitan Statistical Area—see Appendix B for areas included; (2) Rankings are based on annual percentage change for all metro areas containing at least 15,000 transactions over the last 10 years and ranges from 1 to 266; (3) figures based on a weighted average of Census Division estimates using a seasonally adjusted, purchase-only index; all figures are for the period ending December 31, 2015
Source: Federal Housing Finance Agency, House Price Index, February 25, 2016

Median Single-Family Home Prices

Area	2013	2014	2015p	Percent Change 2014 to 2015
MSA[1]	n/a	n/a	n/a	n/a
U.S. Average	197.4	208.9	223.9	7.2

Note: Figures are median sales prices of existing single-family homes in thousands of dollars; (p) preliminary; n/a not available; (1) Flint, MI Metropolitan Statistical Area—see Appendix B for areas included
Source: National Association of Realtors, Median Sales Price of Existing Single-Family Homes for Metropolitan Areas, 4th Quarter 2015

Qualifying Income Based on Median Sales Price of Existing Single-Family Homes

Area	With 5% Down ($)	With 10% Down ($)	With 20% Down ($)
MSA[1]	n/a	n/a	n/a
U.S. Average	49,535	46,928	41,714

Note: Figures are preliminary; Qualifying income is based on a mortgage rate of 4.1%. Monthly principal and interest payment is limited to 25% of income; n/a not available; (1) Flint, MI Metropolitan Statistical Area—see Appendix B for areas included
Source: National Association of Realtors, Qualifying Income Based on Median Sales Price of Existing Single-Family Homes for Metropolitan Areas, 4th Quarter 2015

Median Apartment Condo-Coop Home Prices

Area	2013	2014	2015p	Percent Change 2014 to 2015
MSA[1]	n/a	n/a	n/a	n/a
U.S. Average	194.9	204.3	210.7	3.1

Note: Figures are median sales prices of existing apartment condo-coop homes in thousands of dollars; (p) preliminary; n/a not available; (1) Flint, MI Metropolitan Statistical Area—see Appendix B for areas included
Source: National Association of Realtors, Median Sales Price of Existing Apartment Condo-Coop Homes for Metropolitan Areas, 4th Quarter 2015

Gross Monthly Rent

Area	Under $200	$200 -299	$300 -499	$500 -749	$750 -999	$1,000 -1,499	$1,500 and up	Median ($)
City	0.0	0.6	6.4	39.0	34.3	17.0	2.7	767
MSA[1]	1.8	3.7	13.0	36.7	28.1	13.8	3.0	718
U.S.	1.5	3.2	7.4	21.0	24.1	26.9	15.9	920

Note: Figures are percentages except for Median; Gross rent is the contract rent plus the estimated average monthly cost of utilities (electricity, gas, and water and sewer) and fuels (oil, coal, kerosene, wood, etc.) if these are paid by the renter (or paid for the renter by someone else); (1) Figures cover the Flint, MI Metropolitan Statistical Area—see Appendix B for areas included
Source: U.S. Census Bureau, 2010-2014 American Community Survey 5-Year Estimates

Homeownership Rate

Area	2008 (%)	2009 (%)	2010 (%)	2011 (%)	2012 (%)	2013 (%)	2014 (%)	2015 (%)
MSA[1]	n/a	n/a	n/a	n/a	n/a	n/a	n/a	n/a
U.S.	67.8	67.4	66.9	66.1	65.4	65.1	64.5	63.7

Note: (1) Figures cover the Flint, MI Metropolitan Statistical Area—see Appendix B for areas included; n/a not available
Source: U.S. Census Bureau, Housing Vacancies and Homeownership Annual Statistics: 2015

Year Housing Structure Built

Area	2010 or Later	2000 -2009	1990 -1999	1980 -1989	1970 -1979	1960 -1969	1950 -1959	1940 -1949	Before 1940	Median Year
City	0.5	24.0	16.4	11.6	16.4	15.0	10.2	3.1	2.8	1982
MSA[1]	0.1	10.4	11.3	7.5	16.1	16.0	18.8	8.0	11.9	1967
U.S.	1.0	14.9	13.9	13.8	15.8	11.0	10.8	5.4	13.3	1976

Note: Figures are percentages except for Median Year; (1) Figures cover the Flint, MI Metropolitan Statistical Area—see Appendix B for areas included
Source: U.S. Census Bureau, 2010-2014 American Community Survey 5-Year Estimates

HEALTH

Health Risk Data

Category	MSA[1] (%)	U.S. (%)
Adults aged 18–64 who have any kind of health care coverage	n/a	79.6
Adults who reported being in good or excellent health	n/a	83.1
Adults who are current smokers	n/a	19.6
Adults who are heavy drinkers[2]	n/a	6.1
Adults who are binge drinkers[3]	n/a	16.9
Adults who are overweight (BMI 25.0 - 29.9)	n/a	35.8
Adults who are obese (BMI 30.0 - 99.8)	n/a	27.6
Adults who participated in any physical activities in the past month	n/a	77.1
Adults 50+ who have ever had a sigmoidoscopy or colonoscopy	n/a	67.3
Women aged 40+ who have had a mammogram within the past two years	n/a	74.0
Men aged 40+ who have had a PSA test within the past two years	n/a	45.2
Adults aged 65+ who have had flu shot within the past year	n/a	60.1
Adults who always wear a seatbelt	n/a	93.8

Note: Data as of 2012 unless otherwise noted; n/a not available; (1) Figures cover the Flint, MI Metropolitan Statistical Area—see Appendix B for areas included; (2) Heavy drinkers are classified as males having more than two drinks per day or females having more than one drink per day; (3) Binge drinkers are classified as males having five or more drinks on one occasion or females having four or more drinks on one occasion
Source: Centers for Disease Control and Prevention, Behaviorial Risk Factor Surveillance System, SMART: Selected Metropolitan/Micropolitan Area Risk Trends, 2012 (Note: the CDC has discontinued this dataset but will be releasing a replacement in mid-2016)

Chronic Health Indicators

Category	MSA[1] (%)	U.S. (%)
Adults who have ever been told they had a heart attack	n/a	4.5
Adults who have ever been told they had a stroke	n/a	2.9
Adults who have been told they currently have asthma	n/a	8.9
Adults who have ever been told they have arthritis	n/a	25.7
Adults who have ever been told they have diabetes[2]	n/a	9.7
Adults who have ever been told they had skin cancer	n/a	5.7
Adults who have ever been told they had any other types of cancer	n/a	6.5
Adults who have ever been told they have COPD	n/a	6.2
Adults who have ever been told they have kidney disease	n/a	2.5
Adults who have ever been told they have a form of depression	n/a	18.0

Note: Data as of 2012 unless otherwise noted; n/a not available; (1) Figures cover the Flint, MI Metropolitan Statistical Area—see Appendix B for areas included; (2) Figures do not include pregnancy-related, borderline, or pre-diabetes
Source: Centers for Disease Control and Prevention, Behaviorial Risk Factor Surveillance System, SMART: Selected Metropolitan/Micropolitan Area Risk Trends, 2012 (Note: the CDC has discontinued this dataset but will be releasing a replacement in mid-2016)

Mortality Rates for the Top 10 Causes of Death in the U.S.

ICD-10[a] Sub-Chapter	ICD-10[a] Code	Age-Adjusted Mortality Rate[1] per 100,000 population	
		County[2]	U.S.
Malignant neoplasms	C00-C97	191.1	163.6
Ischaemic heart diseases	I20-I25	132.2	102.2
Other forms of heart disease	I30-I51	65.9	50.1
Chronic lower respiratory diseases	J40-J47	55.6	41.4
Organic, including symptomatic, mental disorders	F01-F09	38.5	38.5
Cerebrovascular diseases	I60-I69	51.5	36.5
Other external causes of accidental injury	W00-X59	26.8	27.5
Other degenerative diseases of the nervous system	G30-G31	33.6	26.3
Diabetes mellitus	E10-E14	33.4	21.1
Hypertensive diseases	I10-I15	33.1	19.7

Note: (a) ICD-10 = International Classification of Diseases 10th Revision; (1) Mortality rates are a three year average covering 2012-2014; (2) Figures cover Genesee County.
Source: Centers for Disease Control and Prevention, National Center for Health Statistics. Underlying Cause of Death 1999-2014 on CDC WONDER Online Database, released 2015.

Mortality Rates for Selected Causes of Death

ICD-10[a] Sub-Chapter	ICD-10[a] Code	Age-Adjusted Mortality Rate[1] per 100,000 population	
		County[2]	U.S.
Assault	X85-Y09	13.5	5.1
Diseases of the liver	K70-K76	16.9	13.5
Human immunodeficiency virus (HIV) disease	B20-B24	Unreliable	2.1
Influenza and pneumonia	J09-J18	14.4	15.2
Intentional self-harm	X60-X84	14.3	12.7
Malnutrition	E40-E46	Unreliable	0.9
Obesity and other hyperalimentation	E65-E68	2.4	1.9
Renal failure	N17-N19	22.1	13.0
Transport accidents	V01-V99	10.2	11.6
Viral hepatitis	B15-B19	1.9	2.1

Note: (a) ICD-10 = International Classification of Diseases 10th Revision; (1) Mortality rates are a three year average covering 2012-2014; (2) Figures cover Genesee County; Data are Suppressed when the data meet the criteria for confidentiality constraints; Mortality rates are flagged as Unreliable when the rate would be calculated with a numerator of 20 or less.
Source: Centers for Disease Control and Prevention, National Center for Health Statistics. Underlying Cause of Death 1999-2014 on CDC WONDER Online Database, released 2015.

Health Insurance Coverage

Area	With Health Insurance	With Private Health Insurance	With Public Health Insurance	Without Health Insurance	Population Under Age 18 Without Health Insurance
City	93.2	78.8	27.8	6.8	1.6
MSA[1]	90.5	63.2	43.1	9.5	3.0
U.S.	85.8	65.8	31.1	14.2	7.1

Note: Figures are percentages that cover the civilian noninstitutionalized population; (1) Figures cover the Flint, MI Metropolitan Statistical Area—see Appendix B for areas included
Source: U.S. Census Bureau, 2010-2014 American Community Survey 5-Year Estimates

Number of Medical Professionals

Area	MDs[3]	DOs[3,4]	Dentists	Podiatrists	Chiropractors	Optometrists
County[1] (number)	923	260	278	31	100	71
County[1] (rate[2])	222.1	62.6	67.3	7.5	24.2	17.2
U.S. (rate[2])	272.5	20.9	64.7	5.8	25.9	15.2

Note: Data as of 2014 unless noted; (1) Data covers Genesee County; (2) Rate per 100,000 population; (3) Data as of 2013 and includes all active, non-federal physicians; (4) Doctor of Osteopathic Medicine
Source: U.S. Department of Health and Human Services, Health Resources and Services Administration, Bureau of Health Professions, Area Resource File (ARF) 2014-2015

EDUCATION

Public School District Statistics

District Name	Schls	Pupils	Pupil/ Teacher Ratio	Minority Pupils[1] (%)	Free Lunch Eligible[2] (%)	IEP[3] (%)
Grand Blanc Academy	1	370	13.3	78.6	93.5	13.8
Grand Blanc Community Schools	13	8,475	19.4	25.0	24.5	9.8
Woodland Park Academy	1	427	15.0	61.8	76.1	11.0

Note: Table includes school districts with 100 or more students; (1) Percentage of students that are not non-Hispanic white; (2) Percentage of students that are eligible for the free lunch program; (3) Percentage of students that have an Individualized Education Program.
Source: U.S. Department of Education, National Center for Education Statistics, Common Core of Data, Local Education Agency (School District) Universe Survey: School Year 2013-2014; U.S. Department of Education, National Center for Education Statistics, Common Core of Data, Public Elementary/Secondary School Universe Survey: School Year 2013-2014

Highest Level of Education

Area	Less than H.S.	H.S. Diploma	Some College, No Deg.	Associate Degree	Bachelor's Degree	Master's Degree	Prof. School Degree	Doctorate Degree
City	5.0	23.7	24.2	12.1	20.5	10.4	2.8	1.3
MSA[1]	11.0	33.1	27.1	9.7	12.0	5.5	1.1	0.6
U.S.	13.7	28.0	21.2	7.9	18.3	7.8	2.0	1.3

Note: Figures cover persons age 25 and over; (1) Figures cover the Flint, MI Metropolitan Statistical Area—see Appendix B for areas included
Source: U.S. Census Bureau, 2010-2014 American Community Survey 5-Year Estimates

Educational Attainment by Race

Area	High School Graduate or Higher (%)					Bachelor's Degree or Higher (%)				
	Total	White	Black	Asian	Hisp.[2]	Total	White	Black	Asian	Hisp.[2]
City	95.0	95.1	94.7	96.2	88.9	35.0	34.4	28.7	64.7	30.9
MSA[1]	89.0	90.0	85.3	91.8	84.8	19.2	20.3	12.7	54.2	16.4
U.S.	86.3	88.4	83.2	85.8	64.1	29.3	30.6	19.0	50.9	13.9

Note: Figures shown cover persons 25 years old and over; (1) Figures cover the Flint, MI Metropolitan Statistical Area—see Appendix B for areas included; (2) People of Hispanic origin can be of any race
Source: U.S. Census Bureau, 2010-2014 American Community Survey 5-Year Estimates

School Enrollment by Grade and Control

Area	Preschool (%)		Kindergarten (%)		Grades 1 - 4 (%)		Grades 5 - 8 (%)		Grades 9 - 12 (%)	
	Public	Private	Public	Private	Public	Private	Public	Private	Public	Private
City	82.0	18.0	83.4	16.6	92.5	7.5	88.6	11.4	95.2	4.8
MSA[1]	80.2	19.8	92.3	7.7	92.8	7.2	92.2	7.8	93.9	6.1
U.S.	57.4	42.6	87.8	12.2	89.8	10.2	89.9	10.1	90.6	9.4

Note: Figures shown cover persons 3 years old and over; (1) Figures cover the Flint, MI Metropolitan Statistical Area—see Appendix B for areas included
Source: U.S. Census Bureau, 2010-2014 American Community Survey 5-Year Estimates

Average Salaries of Public School Classroom Teachers

Area	2013-14		2014-15		Percent Change 2013-14 to 2014-15	Percent Change 2004-05 to 2014-15
	Dollars	Rank[1]	Dollars	Rank[1]		
Michigan	62,166	11	62,778	11	0.98	16.3
U.S. Average	56,610	–	57,379	–	1.36	20.8

Note: (1) State rank ranges from 1 to 51 where 1 indicates highest salary.
Source: National Education Association, Rankings & Estimates: Rankings of the States 2014 and Estimates of School Statistics 2015, March 2015

Higher Education

Four-Year Colleges			Two-Year Colleges			Medical Schools[1]	Law Schools[2]	Voc/ Tech[3]
Public	Private Non-profit	Private For-profit	Public	Private Non-profit	Private For-profit			
0	0	0	0	0	0	0	0	1

Note: Figures cover institutions located within the city limits and include main campuses only; (1) includes schools accredited by the Liaison Committee on Medical Education and the American Osteopathic Association's Commission on Osteopathic College Accreditation; (2) includes ABA-accredited schools, schools with provisional ABA accreditation, and state accredited schools; (3) includes all schools with programs that are less than 2 years.
Source: National Center for Education Statistics, Integrated Postsecondary Education System (IPEDS), 2014-15; Association of American Medical Colleges, Member List, March 21, 2016; American Osteopathic Association, Member List, March 21, 2016; Law School Admission Council, Official Guide to ABA-Approved Law Schools Online, March 21, 2016; Wikipedia, List of Medical Schools in the United States, March 21, 2016; Wikipedia, List of Law Schools in the United States, March 21, 2016

PRESIDENTIAL ELECTION

2012 Presidential Election Results

Area	Obama (%)	Romney (%)	Other (%)
Genesee County	63.3	35.2	1.5
U.S.	51.0	47.2	1.8

Note: Results may not add to 100% due to rounding
Source: Dave Leip's Atlas of U.S. Presidential Elections

EMPLOYERS

Major Employers

Company Name	Industry
A I Flint	LLC
Baker College	Schools-universities & colleges academic
Beecher Community Schools	Schools
Carman Ainsworth Community Schools	Schools
Charles Stewart Mott Community College	Schools-universities & colleges academic
Citizens Bank	Banking
City of Flint	Government offices-city
Delphi	Motor vehicle parts and accessories
Flint Community Schools	Schools
General Motors	Automobile assembly, including specialty automobiles
Genesee County	Government offices-county
Genesee Intermediate School District	School district
Genesys Health System	Health care services
Hurley Medical Center	General medical and surgical hospitals
McLaren Medical Center	General medical and surgical hospitals
Meijers	Supermarket
Miller Apple LTD Partnership	Full-service chain bar & grill

Note: Companies shown are located within the Flint, MI Metropolitan Statistical Area.
Source: Hoovers.com; Wikipedia

PUBLIC SAFETY

Crime Rate

Area	All Crimes	Violent Crimes				Property Crimes		
		Murder	Rape[3]	Robbery	Aggrav. Assault	Burglary	Larceny -Theft	Motor Vehicle Theft
City	1,742.6	2.7	57.4	10.9	90.1	314.1	1,226.3	41.0
Metro[1]	3,386.0	7.7	69.9	117.1	457.5	880.1	1,718.0	135.7
U.S.	2,971.8	4.5	36.6	102.2	232.5	542.5	1,837.3	216.2

Note: Figures are crimes per 100,000 population; (1) Figures cover the Flint, MI Metropolitan Statistical Area—see Appendix B for areas included; (3) The city and U.S. figures shown were reported using the revised Uniform Crime Reporting (UCR) definition of rape. The suburban and metro area figures shown are an aggregate total of the data submitted using both the revised and legacy UCR definitions.
Source: FBI Uniform Crime Reports, 2014

Hate Crimes

Area	Number of Quarters Reported	Number of Incidents per Bias Motivation: Race	Religion	Sexual Orientation	Ethnicity	Disability	Gender	Gender Identity
City	4	0	0	0	0	0	0	0
U.S.	4	2,568	1,014	1,017	648	84	33	98

Source: Federal Bureau of Investigation, Hate Crime Statistics 2014

Identity Theft Consumer Complaints

Area	Complaints	Complaints per 100,000 Population	Rank[2]
MSA[1]	589	142.7	65
U.S.	490,220	152.4	-

Note: (1) Figures cover the Flint, MI Metropolitan Statistical Area—see Appendix B for areas included; (2) Rank ranges from 1 to 379 where 1 indicates greatest number of identity theft complaints per 100,000 population
Source: Federal Trade Commission, Consumer Sentinel Network Data Book for January–December 2015

Fraud and Other Consumer Complaints

Area	Complaints	Complaints per 100,000 Population	Rank[2]
MSA[1]	1,477	357.7	200
U.S.	2,593,159	806.0	-

Note: (1) Figures cover the Flint, MI Metropolitan Statistical Area—see Appendix B for areas included; (2) Rank ranges from 1 to 379 where 1 indicates greatest number of identity theft complaints per 100,000 population
Source: Federal Trade Commission, Consumer Sentinel Network Data Book for January–December 2015

RECREATION

Culture

Dance[1]	Theatre[1]	Instrumental Music[1]	Vocal Music[1]	Series and Festivals	Museums and Art Galleries[2]	Zoos and Aquariums[3]
0	0	0	0	0	0	0

Note: (1) Professional perfoming groups; (2) Based on organizations with SIC code 8412; (3) AZA-accredited
Source: The Grey House Performing Arts Directory, 2015-16; Association of Zoos & Aquariums, AZA Member Zoos & Aquariums, March 25, 2016; www.AccuLeads.com, March 29, 2016

Professional Sports Teams

Team Name	League	Year Established
No teams are located in the metro area		

Source: Wikipedia, Major Professional Sports Teams of the United States and Canada, March 24, 2016

CLIMATE

Average and Extreme Temperatures

Temperature	Jan	Feb	Mar	Apr	May	Jun	Jul	Aug	Sep	Oct	Nov	Dec	Yr.
Extreme High (°F)	65	63	78	87	93	101	101	98	97	89	79	67	101
Average High (°F)	29	32	42	56	68	77	82	80	72	60	46	34	57
Average Temp. (°F)	22	24	33	46	57	66	71	69	61	51	39	27	47
Average Low (°F)	15	16	25	36	45	55	59	58	51	41	31	20	38
Extreme Low (°F)	-25	-22	-12	6	22	33	40	37	27	19	-7	-12	-25

Note: Figures cover the years 1948-1990
Source: National Climatic Data Center, International Station Meteorological Climate Summary, 9/96

Average Precipitation/Snowfall/Humidity

Precip./Humidity	Jan	Feb	Mar	Apr	May	Jun	Jul	Aug	Sep	Oct	Nov	Dec	Yr.
Avg. Precip. (in.)	1.6	1.5	2.1	3.0	2.8	3.2	2.9	3.5	3.2	2.2	2.5	2.0	30.5
Avg. Snowfall (in.)	12	10	8	2	Tr	0	0	0	Tr	Tr	4	10	47
Avg. Rel. Hum. 7am (%)	81	80	80	78	77	80	83	88	89	85	83	82	82
Avg. Rel. Hum. 4pm (%)	70	66	60	53	51	53	52	55	57	57	66	72	59

Note: Figures cover the years 1948-1990; Tr = Trace amounts (<0.05 in. of rain; <0.5 in. of snow)
Source: National Climatic Data Center, International Station Meteorological Climate Summary, 9/96

Weather Conditions

Temperature			Daytime Sky			Precipitation		
5°F & below	32°F & below	90°F & above	Clear	Partly cloudy	Cloudy	0.01 inch or more precip.	0.1 inch or more snow/ice	Thunder-storms
19	143	8	74	122	169	133	47	33

Note: Figures are average number of days per year and cover the years 1948-1990
Source: National Climatic Data Center, International Station Meteorological Climate Summary, 9/96

HAZARDOUS WASTE

Superfund Sites

Grand Blanc has no sites on the EPA's Superfund Final National Priorities List. There are a total of 1,323 Superfund sites on the list in the U.S. *U.S. Environmental Protection Agency, Final National Priorities List, March 18, 2016*

AIR & WATER QUALITY

Air Quality Trends: Ozone

	1990	1995	2000	2005	2010	2011	2012	2013	2014
MSA[1]	0.076	0.081	0.073	0.080	0.068	0.073	0.084	0.066	0.068

Note: (1) Data covers the Flint, MI Metropolitan Statistical Area—see Appendix B for areas included. The values shown are the composite ozone concentration averages among trend sites based on the highest fourth daily maximum 8-hour concentration in parts per million. These trends are based on sites having an adequate record of monitoring data during the trend period. Data from exceptional events are included.
Source: U.S. Environmental Protection Agency, Air Quality Monitoring Information, "Air Quality Trends by City, 1990-2014"

Air Quality Index

Area	Percent of Days when Air Quality was...[2]					AQI Statistics[2]	
	Good	Moderate	Unhealthy for Sensitive Groups	Unhealthy	Very Unhealthy	Maximum	Median
MSA[1]	77.9	21.8	0.3	0.0	0.0	131	38

Note: (1) Data covers the Flint, MI Metropolitan Statistical Area—see Appendix B for areas included; (2) Based on 357 days with AQI data in 2015. Air Quality Index (AQI) is an index for reporting daily air quality. EPA calculates the AQI for five major air pollutants regulated by the Clean Air Act: ground-level ozone, particle pollution (aka particulate matter), carbon monoxide, sulfur dioxide, and nitrogen dioxide. The AQI runs from 0 to 500. The higher the AQI value, the greater the level of air pollution and the greater the health concern. There are six AQI categories: "Good" AQI is between 0 and 50. Air quality is considered satisfactory; "Moderate" AQI is between 51 and 100. Air quality is acceptable; "Unhealthy for Sensitive Groups" When AQI values are between 101 and 150, members of sensitive groups may experience health effects; "Unhealthy" When AQI values are between 151 and 200 everyone may begin to experience health effects; "Very Unhealthy" AQI values between 201 and 300 trigger a health alert; "Hazardous" AQI values over 300 trigger warnings of emergency conditions (not shown).
Source: U.S. Environmental Protection Agency, Air Quality Index Report, 2015

Air Quality Index Pollutants

Area	Percent of Days when AQI Pollutant was...[2]					
	Carbon Monoxide	Nitrogen Dioxide	Ozone	Sulfur Dioxide	Particulate Matter 2.5	Particulate Matter 10
MSA[1]	0.0	0.0	31.4	0.0	68.6	0.0

Note: (1) Data covers the Flint, MI Metropolitan Statistical Area—see Appendix B for areas included; (2) Based on 357 days with AQI data in 2015. The Air Quality Index (AQI) is an index for reporting daily air quality. EPA calculates the AQI for five major air pollutants regulated by the Clean Air Act: ground-level ozone, particle pollution (also known as particulate matter), carbon monoxide, sulfur dioxide, and nitrogen dioxide. The AQI runs from 0 to 500. The higher the AQI value, the greater the level of air pollution and the greater the health concern.
Source: U.S. Environmental Protection Agency, Air Quality Index Report, 2015

Maximum Air Pollutant Concentrations: Particulate Matter, Ozone, CO and Lead

	Particulate Matter 10 (ug/m^3)	Particulate Matter 2.5 Wtd AM (ug/m^3)	Particulate Matter 2.5 24-Hr (ug/m^3)	Ozone (ppm)	Carbon Monoxide (ppm)	Lead (ug/m^3)
MSA[1] Level	n/a	8.9	24	0.068	n/a	n/a
NAAQS[2]	150	15	35	0.075	9	0.15
Met NAAQS[2]	n/a	Yes	Yes	Yes	n/a	n/a

Note: (1) Data covers the Flint, MI Metropolitan Statistical Area—see Appendix B for areas included; Data from exceptional events are included; (2) National Ambient Air Quality Standards; ppm = parts per million; ug/m^3 = micrograms per cubic meter; n/a not available.
Concentrations: Particulate Matter 10 (coarse particulate)—highest second maximum 24-hour concentration; Particulate Matter 2.5 Wtd AM (fine particulate)—highest weighted annual mean concentration; Particulate Matter 2.5 24-Hour (fine particulate)—highest 98th percentile 24-hour concentration; Ozone—highest fourth daily maximum 8-hour concentration; Carbon Monoxide—highest second maximum non-overlapping 8-hour concentration; Lead—maximum running 3-month average
Source: U.S. Environmental Protection Agency, Air Quality Monitoring Information, "Air Quality Statistics by City, 2014"

Maximum Air Pollutant Concentrations: Nitrogen Dioxide and Sulfur Dioxide

	Nitrogen Dioxide AM (ppb)	Nitrogen Dioxide 1-Hr (ppb)	Sulfur Dioxide AM (ppb)	Sulfur Dioxide 1-Hr (ppb)	Sulfur Dioxide 24-Hr (ppb)
MSA[1] Level	n/a	n/a	n/a	n/a	n/a
NAAQS[2]	53	100	30	75	140
Met NAAQS[2]	n/a	n/a	n/a	n/a	n/a

Note: (1) Data covers the Flint, MI Metropolitan Statistical Area—see Appendix B for areas included; Data from exceptional events are included; (2) National Ambient Air Quality Standards; ppm = parts per million; ug/m^3 = micrograms per cubic meter; n/a not available.
Concentrations: Nitrogen Dioxide AM—highest arithmetic mean concentration; Nitrogen Dioxide 1-Hr—highest 98th percentile 1-hour daily maximum concentration; Sulfur Dioxide AM—highest annual mean concentration; Sulfur Dioxide 1-Hr—highest 99th percentile 1-hour daily maximum concentration; Sulfur Dioxide 24-Hr—highest second maximum 24-hour concentration
Source: U.S. Environmental Protection Agency, Air Quality Monitoring Information, "Air Quality Statistics by City, 2014"

Drinking Water

Water System Name	Pop. Served	Primary Water Source Type	Violations[1]	
			Health Based	Monitoring/ Reporting
Grand Blanc Township	18,000	Purchased Surface	0	0

Note: (1) Based on violation data from January 1, 2015 to December 31, 2015 (includes unresolved violations from earlier years)
Source: U.S. Environmental Protection Agency, Office of Ground Water and Drinking Water, Safe Drinking Water Information System (based on data extracted April 29, 2016)

Northville, Michigan

Background

Northville sits in both Wayne and Oakland Counties, equidistant (at about 25 miles) from Detroit and Ann Arbor, and 3 miles from Novi. It is currently one of the most affluent cities in Wayne County, whose population is likely to remain stable and small because there is very little land left to develop.

A fairly new city, Northville was incorporated in 1955, with most of its homes built after 1970. Nevertheless, Northville maintains a distinctive Victorian charm. The city boasts many historic buildings, and streets lined with old-fashioned lamps and benches. At the town center stands its landmark four-sided clock.

During warm months, Main Street comes alive with colorful umbrellas, flower boxes and a water fountain at Town Square. Numerous summer events, such as Summer Friday Night Concerts, offer everything from blues to big band to swing, and Tunes on Tuesdays Children's Concerts.

A popular attraction in Northville is the Mill Race Historical Village. This living museum, created in 1972 on land donated by the Ford Motor Company, includes significant historic buildings that were moved from the surrounding area to this site and carefully restored by the Northville Historical Society. Also popular is the Northville water wheel and duck pond, developed on an old Ford Motor Company valve plant. A refreshing drink of cold well water can still be had at the Northville well.

The Marquis Theatre, a favorite venue for major theater productions, is housed in a fully restored, 80-year-old Victorian building. Renovators discovered original doors and brass handles under sheets of plywood, and a black walnut ticket booth under eight coats of paint. Originally an opera house, then used for vaudeville acts, the Marquis stage hosted such notables as Charlie Chaplin and Mary Pickford. Today this local treasure has plush upholstered seats in wrought iron framework to remind theater-goers of its original Victorian roots. Although it no longer costs a nickel to enjoy its entertainment, the Marquis continues to offer productions such as Camelot, Peter Pan, Gypsy and Annie, to packed houses.

Northville's unique location provides its residents with natural beauty and the benefits of small town living, while being conveniently located to several big cities. Practically next door to Novi, and a short drive to Detroit and Ann Arbor offers easy access to Detroit Metro Airport and a number of colleges and universities, including Eastern Michigan University-Livonia Center, Northwood University, Madonna University, University of Phoenix, Michigan Theological Seminary, Schoolcraft College, Birkram's Yoga College of India and Lawrence Tech Executive Education Center.

Maybury State Park offers Northville's residents 900 acres of open space for walking, hiking and biking. A family friendly community, the city is located around several lakes, with many opportunities for boating, swimming and water sports. Silver Springs Lake is noted as being the only natural lake in the county.

Northville has an average high temperature in July of 83 degrees F and a low in January of 17 degrees F. An average of 33 inches of snow falls annually.

Rankings

Business/Finance Rankings

- The personal finance site NerdWallet analyzed 183 American metropolitan areas with populations over 250,000 and more than 15,000 businesses to rank where entrepreneurs find the most success. Criteria included area economy, annual income, housing cost, unemployment rate, and the success rate of area businesses. Detroit* ranked #91. *www.nerdwallet.com, "Best Places to Start a Business," April 27, 2015*

- 24/7 Wall Street used Brookings Institution research on 50 advanced industries to identify the proportion of workers in the nation's largest metropolitan areas that were employed in jobs requiring knowledge in the science, technology, engineering, or math (STEM) fields. The Detroit* metro area was #4. *247wallst.com, "15 Cities with the Most High-Tech Jobs," March 13, 2015*

- Based on metro area social media reviews, the employment opinion group Glassdoor surveyed 50 of the largest U.S. metro areas and equally weighed cost of living, hiring opportunity, and job satisfaction to compose a list of "25 Best Cities for Jobs." The Detroit* metro area was ranked #42 in overall job satisfaction. *www.glassdoor.com, "Best Cities for Jobs," May 19, 2015*

- In a survey of economic confidence in the nation's 50 largest metropolitan areas conducted January–December 2014, the Detroit* metro area placed #34, according to Gallup's 2014 Economic Confidence Index. *Gallup, "San Jose and San Francisco Lead in Economic Confidence," March 19, 2015*

- The Brookings Institution ranked the 100 largest metro areas in the U.S. based on income inequality. Detroit* was ranked #24 (#1 = greatest ineqality). Criteria: the "95/20 ratio," a figure representing the income at which a household earns more than 95 percent of all other households, divided by the income at which a household earns more than only 20 percent of all other households. *Brookings Institution, "Income Inequality, 100 Largest U.S. Metro Areas, 2007-2014," January 14, 2016*

- Payscale.com ranked the 20 largest metro areas in terms of wage growth. The Detroit* metro area ranked #3. Criteria: private-sector wage growth between the 1st quarter of 2015 and the 1st quarter of 2016. *PayScale, "Wage Trends by Metro Area," 1st Quarter, 2016*

- The Detroit* metro area was identified as one of the most affordable metropolitan areas in America by *Forbes*. The area ranked #10 out of 20 based on the National Association of Home Builders/Wells Fargo Housing Affordability Index and Sperling's Best Places' cost-of-living index. *Forbes.com, "America's Most Affordable Cities in 2015," March 12, 2015*

- Detroit* was cited as one of America's top metros for new and expanded facility projects in 2015. The area ranked #6 in the large metro area category (population over 1 million). *Site Selection, "Top Metropolitans of 2015," March 2016*

- The Detroit* metro area appeared on the Milken Institute "2015 Best Performing Cities" list. Rank: #155 out of 200 large metro areas. Criteria: job growth; wage and salary growth; high-tech output growth. *Milken Institute, "Best-Performing Cities 2015," December 2015*

- *Forbes* ranked the 200 most populous metro areas to determine the nation's "Best Places for Business and Careers." The Detroit* metro area was ranked #160. Criteria: costs (business and living); job growth (past and projected); income growth; educational attainment (college and high school); projected economic growth; cultural and recreational opportunities; net migration patterns; number of highly ranked colleges. *Forbes, "The Best Places for Business and Careers 2015," July 29, 2015*

Education Rankings

- Personal finance website *WalletHub* analyzed the 150 largest U.S. metropolitan statistical areas to determine where the most educated Americans are choosing to settle. Criteria: education quality and attainment gap; education levels; percentage of workers with degrees; public school rankings; quality and size of each metro area's universities. Detroit* was ranked #70 (#1 = most educated city). *www.WalletHub.com, "2015's Most and Least Educated Cities*

Environmental Rankings

- The Detroit* metro area came in at #103 for the relative comfort of its climate on Sperling's list of "chill cities," as measured by the Sperling Heat Index. All 361 metro areas are included. Criteria included daytime high temperatures, nighttime low temperatures, dew point, and relative humidity at the high temperatures. *www.bertsperling.com, "Sperling's Chill Cities," July 18, 2013*

- Sperling's BestPlaces assessed 379 metropolitan areas of the United States for the likelihood of dangerously extreme weather events or earthquakes. In general the Southeast and South-Central regions have the highest risk of weather extremes and earthquakes, while the Pacific Northwest enjoys the lowest risk. Of the least risky metropolitan areas, the Detroit* metro area was ranked #178. *www.bestplaces.net, "Safest Places from Natural Disasters," April 2011*

Health/Fitness Rankings

- Analysts who tracked obesity rates in the nation's largest metro areas (populations above one million) found that the Detroit* metro area was one of the ten major metros where residents were most likely to be obese, defined as a BMI score of 30 or above. *www.gallup.com, "Boulder, Colo., Residents Still Least Likely to Be Obese," April 4, 2014*

- For each of the 50 most populous metro areas in the United States, the American College of Sports Medicine's American Fitness Index evaluated infrastructure, community assets, and policies that encourage healthy and fit lifestyles, including preventive health behaviors, levels of chronic disease conditions, health care access, and community resources and policies that support physical activity. The Detroit* metro area ranked #40 for "community fitness." *www.americanfitnessindex.org, "ACSM American Fitness Index Health and Community Fitness Status of the 50 Largest Metropolitan Areas," May 2015*

- The Detroit* metro area was identified as one of the worst cities for bed bugs in America by pest control company Orkin. The area ranked #7 out of 50 based on the number of bed bug treatments Orkin performed from January to December 2015. *Orkin, "Chicago Tops Bed Bug Cities List for Fourth Year in a Row," January 13, 2016*

- Detroit* was identified as a "2016 Spring Allergy Capital." The area ranked #39 out of 100. Three groups of factors were used to identify the most severe cities for people with allergies during the spring season: annual pollen levels; medicine utilization; access to board-certified allergists. *Asthma and Allergy Foundation of America, "Spring Allergy Capitals 2016"*

- Detroit* was identified as a "2015 Asthma Capital." The area ranked #4 out of the nation's 100 largest metropolitan areas. Criteria: estimated prevalence; self-reported prevalence; crude death rate for asthma; annual pollen score; annual air quality; public smoking laws; number of board-certified asthma specialists; school inhaler access laws; rescue medication use; controller medication use; ER visits for asthma; uninsured rate; poverty rate. *Asthma and Allergy Foundation of America, "Asthma Capitals 2015"*

- The Detroit* metro area ranked #174 out of 190 in The Gallup-Healthways Well-Being Index. Criteria: purpose; social well being; financial health; community and physical health. Results are based on telephone interviews with adults, aged 18 and older, living in metropolitan areas in the 50 U.S. states and the District of Columbia. *Gallup-Healthways, "State of American Well-Being," February 23, 2016*

Real Estate Rankings

- The Detroit* metro area was identified as #3 among the ten housing markets with the highest percentage of distressed property sales, based on the findings of the housing data website RealtyTrac. Criteria: short sales; income and poverty figures; and unemployment data. *247wallst.com, "Cities Selling the Most Distressed Homes," January 23, 2014*

- Detroit* was ranked #98 out of 225 metro areas in terms of housing affordability in 2015 by the National Association of Home Builders (#1 = most affordable). Criteria: the share of homes sold in that area affordable to a family earning the local median income, based on standard mortgage underwriting criteria. *National Association of Home Builders®, NAHB-Wells Fargo Housing Opportunity Index, 4th Quarter 2015*

Safety Rankings

- The National Insurance Crime Bureau ranked 380 metro areas in the U.S. in terms of per capita rates of vehicle theft. The Detroit* metro area ranked #35 (#1 = highest rate). Criteria: number of vehicle theft offenses per 100,000 inhabitants in 2014. *National Insurance Crime Bureau, "Hot Spots 2014," June 24, 2015*

Seniors/Retirement Rankings

- From its Best Cities for Successful Aging indexes, the Milken Institute generated rankings for metropolitan areas, weighing data in eight categories—health care, wellness, living arrangements, transportation, financial characteristics, education and employment opportunities, community engagement, and overall livability. The Detroit* metro area was ranked #80 overall in the large metro area category. *Milken Institute, "Best Cities for Successful Aging, 2014"*

Sports/Recreation Rankings

- According to the personal finance website NerdWallet, the Detroit* metro area, at #3, is one of the nation's top dozen metro areas for sports fans. Criteria included the presence of all four major sports—MLB, NFL, NHL, and NBA, fan enthusiasm (as measured by game attendance), ticket affordability, and "sports culture," that is, number of sports bars. *www.nerdwallet.com, "Best Cities for Sports Fans," May 5, 2013*

Miscellaneous Rankings

- The watchdog site Charity Navigator conducts an annual study of charities in the nation's major markets both to analyze statistical differences in their financial, accountability, and transparency practices and to track year-to-year variations in individual communities. The Detroit* metro area was ranked #18 among the 30 metro markets in the rating dimension of Overall Score. *www.charitynavigator.org, "Metro Market Study 2015," June 5, 2015*

- Energizer Personal Care, the makers of Edge® shave gel, in partnership with Sperling's BestPlaces, ranked 50 major metro areas in terms of everyday irritations. The Detroit* metro area ranked #7 the 50 metro area most iritating to guys. Criteria: high male-to-female ratio; poor sports team performance and high ticket prices; slow traffic; lack of job availability; unaffordable housing; extreme weather; lack of nightlife and fitness options. *Energizer Personal Care, "Most Irritatng Cities for Guys," August 26, 2013*

- Mars Chocolate North America, the makers of COMBOS®, in partnership with Sperling's BestPlaces, ranked 50 major metro areas in terms of their "manliness." The Detroit* metro area ranked #31. Criteria: number of professional sports teams; number of nearby NASCAR tracks and racing events; manly lifestyle; concentration of manly retail stores; manly occupations per capita; salty snack sales; "Board of Manliness" rankings. *Mars Chocolate North America, "America's Manliest Cities 2012"*

- The Detroit* metro area was selected as one of "America's Most Miserable Cities" by *Forbes.com.* The metro area ranked #1 out of 20. Criteria: violent crime; unemployment; foreclosures; income and property taxes; home prices; commute times; climate. *Forbes.com, "America's Most Miserable Cities" February 22, 2013*

- The National Alliance to End Homelessness ranked the 100 most populous metro areas with the highest rate of homelessness. The Detroit* metro area ranked #71. Criteria: number of homeless people per 10,000 population in 2011. *National Alliance to End Homelessness, The State of Homelessness in America 2012*

Northville is located within the Detroit-Warren-Dearborn, MI Metropolitan Statistical Area.

Business Environment

CITY FINANCES

City Government Finances

Component	2012 ($000)	2012 ($ per capita)
Total Revenues	33,604	1,179
Total Expenditures	29,129	1,022
Debt Outstanding	39,935	1,401
Cash and Securities[1]	52,176	1,830

Note: (1) Cash and security holdings of a government at the close of its fiscal year, including those of its dependent agencies, utilities, and liquor stores.
Source: U.S Census Bureau, State & Local Government Finances 2012

City Government Revenue by Source

Source	2012 ($000)	2012 ($ per capita)
General Revenue		
From Federal Government	485	17
From State Government	2,600	91
From Local Governments	0	0
Taxes		
Property	12,456	437
Sales and Gross Receipts	0	0
Personal Income	0	0
Corporate Income	0	0
Motor Vehicle License	0	0
Other Taxes	328	11
Current Charges	7,062	247
Liquor Store	0	0
Utility	5,113	179
Employee Retirement	0	0

Source: U.S Census Bureau, State & Local Government Finances 2012

City Government Expenditures by Function

Function	2012 ($000)	2012 ($ per capita)	2012 (%)
General Direct Expenditures			
Air Transportation	0	0	0.0
Corrections	0	0	0.0
Education	0	0	0.0
Employment Security Administration	0	0	0.0
Financial Administration	1,061	37	3.6
Fire Protection	3,548	124	12.1
General Public Buildings	431	15	1.4
Governmental Administration, Other	1,892	66	6.4
Health	0	0	0.0
Highways	0	0	0.0
Hospitals	0	0	0.0
Housing and Community Development	61	2	0.2
Interest on General Debt	719	25	2.4
Judicial and Legal	0	0	0.0
Libraries	0	0	0.0
Parking	0	0	0.0
Parks and Recreation	0	0	0.0
Police Protection	6,054	212	20.7
Public Welfare	0	0	0.0
Sewerage	6,472	227	22.2
Solid Waste Management	1,021	35	3.5
Veterans' Services	0	0	0.0
Liquor Store	0	0	0.0
Utility	5,420	190	18.6
Employee Retirement	0	0	0.0

Source: U.S Census Bureau, State & Local Government Finances 2012

DEMOGRAPHICS

Population Growth

Area	1990 Census	2000 Census	2010 Census	2014* Estimate	Population Growth (%) 1990-2014	2010-2014
City	17,300	21,036	28,497	28,682	65.8	0.6
MSA[1]	4,248,699	4,452,557	4,296,250	4,292,647	1.0	-0.1
U.S.	248,709,873	281,421,906	308,745,538	314,107,084	26.3	1.7

Note: (1) Figures cover the Detroit-Warren-Dearborn, MI Metropolitan Statistical Area—see Appendix B for areas included; (*) 2010-2014 5-year estimated population
Source: U.S. Census Bureau, 1990 Census, Census 2000, Census 2010, 2010-2014 American Community Survey 5-Year Estimates

Household Size

Area	Persons in Household (%) One	Two	Three	Four	Five	Six	Seven or More	Average Household Size
City	28.7	30.3	16.6	15.8	5.5	2.9	0.0	2.57
MSA[1]	29.9	31.9	15.6	13.2	5.7	2.2	1.2	2.56
U.S.	27.5	33.5	15.8	13.1	6.0	2.3	1.4	2.64

Note: (1) Figures cover the Detroit-Warren-Dearborn, MI Metropolitan Statistical Area—see Appendix B for areas included
Source: U.S. Census Bureau, 2010-2014 American Community Survey 5-Year Estimates

Race

Area	White Alone[2] (%)	Black Alone[2] (%)	Asian Alone[2] (%)	AIAN[3] Alone[2] (%)	NHOPI[4] Alone[2] (%)	Other Race Alone[2] (%)	Two or More Races (%)
City	79.9	3.0	14.7	0.1	0.1	0.2	1.9
MSA[1]	70.2	22.5	3.6	0.3	0.0	1.1	2.3
U.S.	73.8	12.6	5.0	0.8	0.2	4.7	2.9

Note: (1) Figures cover the Detroit-Warren-Dearborn, MI Metropolitan Statistical Area—see Appendix B for areas included; (2) Alone is defined as not being in combination with one or more other races; (3) American Indian and Alaska Native; (4) Native Hawaiian and Other Pacific Islander
Source: U.S. Census Bureau, 2010-2014 American Community Survey 5-Year Estimates

Hispanic or Latino Origin

Area	Total (%)	Mexican (%)	Puerto Rican (%)	Cuban (%)	Other (%)
City	4.2	2.9	0.1	0.0	1.2
MSA[1]	4.1	2.9	0.5	0.1	0.6
U.S.	16.9	10.8	1.6	0.6	3.8

Note: Persons of Hispanic or Latino origin can be of any race; (1) Figures cover the Detroit-Warren-Dearborn, MI Metropolitan Statistical Area—see Appendix B for areas included
Source: U.S. Census Bureau, 2010-2014 American Community Survey 5-Year Estimates

Ancestry

Area	German	Irish	English	American	Italian	Polish	French[2]	Scottish	Dutch
City	19.0	10.2	10.9	5.5	8.3	13.1	3.5	2.8	1.5
MSA[1]	16.5	10.2	7.3	5.4	6.4	10.6	3.8	2.2	1.3
U.S.	14.9	10.8	8.0	7.1	5.5	3.0	2.7	1.7	1.4

Note: Figures are the percentage of the total population reporting a particular ancestry. The nine most commonly reported ancestries in the U.S. are shown. Figures include multiple ancestries (e.g. if a person reported being Irish and Italian, they were included in both columns); (1) Figures cover the Detroit-Warren-Dearborn, MI Metropolitan Statistical Area—see Appendix B for areas included; (2) Excludes Basque
Source: U.S. Census Bureau, 2010-2014 American Community Survey 5-Year Estimates

Foreign-Born Population

Area	Percent of Population Born in								
	Any Foreign Country	Asia	Mexico	Europe	Carribean	Central America[2]	South America	Africa	Canada
City	16.2	11.2	0.4	3.2	0.0	0.1	0.5	0.1	0.8
MSA[1]	8.9	4.6	0.8	2.2	0.1	0.1	0.1	0.3	0.6
U.S.	13.1	3.8	3.7	1.5	1.2	1.0	0.9	0.6	0.3

Note: (1) Figures cover the Detroit-Warren-Dearborn, MI Metropolitan Statistical Area—see Appendix B for areas included; (2) Excludes Mexico.
Source: U.S. Census Bureau, 2010-2014 American Community Survey 5-Year Estimates

Marital Status

Area	Never Married	Now Married[2]	Separated	Widowed	Divorced
City	24.0	61.6	0.5	5.6	8.3
MSA[1]	33.9	46.6	1.6	6.5	11.4
U.S.	32.5	48.4	2.2	5.9	10.9

Note: Figures are percentages and cover the population 15 years of age and older; (1) Figures cover the Detroit-Warren-Dearborn, MI Metropolitan Statistical Area—see Appendix B for areas included; (2) Excludes separated
Source: U.S. Census Bureau, 2010-2014 American Community Survey 5-Year Estimates

Disability Status

Area	All Ages	Under 18 Years Old	18 to 64 Years Old	65 Years and Over
City	8.6	2.1	5.0	29.9
MSA[1]	13.9	4.8	12.2	37.4
U.S.	12.3	4.1	10.2	36.3

Note: Figures show percent of the civilian noninstitutionalized population that reported having a disability. Disability status is determined from from six types of difficulty: vision, hearing, cognitive, ambulatory, self-care, and independent living. For children under 5 years old, hearing and vision difficulty are used to determine disability status. For children between the ages of 5 and 14, disability status is determined from hearing, vision, cognitive, ambulatory, and self-care difficulties. For people aged 15 years and older, they are considered to have a disability if they have difficulty with any one of the six difficulty types; (1) Figures cover the Detroit-Warren-Dearborn, MI Metropolitan Statistical Area—see Appendix B for areas included.
Source: U.S. Census Bureau, 2010-2014 American Community Survey 5-Year Estimates

Age

Area	Percent of Population									Median Age
	Under Age 5	Age 5–19	Age 20–34	Age 35–44	Age 45–54	Age 55–64	Age 65–74	Age 75–84	Age 85+	
City	4.6	21.0	13.1	14.0	17.9	12.3	8.9	5.3	2.9	43.1
MSA[1]	5.9	20.1	18.3	13.1	15.3	13.3	7.6	4.3	2.0	39.7
U.S.	6.4	19.9	20.6	13.0	14.1	12.3	7.6	4.3	1.9	37.4

Note: (1) Figures cover the Detroit-Warren-Dearborn, MI Metropolitan Statistical Area—see Appendix B for areas included
Source: U.S. Census Bureau, 2010-2014 American Community Survey 5-Year Estimates

Gender

Area	Males	Females	Males per 100 Females
City	13,674	15,008	91.1
MSA[1]	2,081,346	2,211,301	94.1
U.S.	154,515,159	159,591,925	96.8

Note: (1) Figures cover the Detroit-Warren-Dearborn, MI Metropolitan Statistical Area—see Appendix B for areas included
Source: U.S. Census Bureau, 2010-2014 American Community Survey 5-Year Estimates

Religious Groups by Family

Area	Catholic	Baptist	Non-Den.	Methodist[2]	Lutheran	LDS[3]	Pente-costal	Presby-terian[4]	Muslim[5]	Judaism
MSA[1]	21.3	4.5	4.9	2.1	3.1	0.3	1.2	1.3	1.8	0.8
U.S.	19.1	9.3	4.0	4.0	2.3	2.0	1.9	1.6	0.8	0.7

Note: Figures are the number of adherents as a percentage of the total population; (1) Figures cover the Detroit-Warren-Livonia, MI Metropolitan Statistical Area—see Appendix B for areas included; (2) Methodist/Pietist; (3) Latter Day Saints; (4) Reformed; (5) Figures are estimates
Source: Association of Statisticians of American Religious Bodies, 2010 U.S. Religion Census: Religious Congregations & Membership Study

Religious Groups by Tradition

Area	Catholic	Evangelical Protestant	Mainline Protestant	Other Tradition	Black Protestant	Orthodox
MSA[1]	21.3	10.6	4.7	3.5	3.3	0.9
U.S.	19.1	16.2	7.3	4.3	1.6	0.3

Note: Figures are the number of adherents as a percentage of the total population; (1) Figures cover the Detroit-Warren-Livonia, MI Metropolitan Statistical Area—see Appendix B for areas included
Source: Association of Statisticians of American Religious Bodies, 2010 U.S. Religion Census: Religious Congregations & Membership Study

ECONOMY

Gross Metropolitan Product

Area	2013	2014	2015	2016	Rank[2]
MSA[1]	224.7	231.1	239.2	248.9	14

Note: Figures are in billions of dollars; (1) Figures cover the Detroit-Warren-Dearborn, MI Metropolitan Statistical Area—see Appendix B for areas included; (2) Rank is based on 2016 data and ranges from 1 to 381
Source: The U.S. Conference of Mayors, U.S. Metro Economies: GMP and Employment 2014-2016, June 2015

Economic Growth

Area	2011-13 (%)	2014 (%)	2015 (%)	2016 (%)	Rank[2]
MSA[1]	1.7	1.2	2.1	2.2	236
U.S.	2.2	2.4	2.3	2.9	–

Note: Figures are real gross metropolitan product (GMP) growth rates and represent annual average percent change; (1) Figures cover the Detroit-Warren-Dearborn, MI Metropolitan Statistical Area—see Appendix B for areas included; (2) Rank is based on 2016 data and ranges from 1 to 381
Source: The U.S. Conference of Mayors, U.S. Metro Economies: GMP and Employment 2014-2016, June 2015

Metropolitan Area Exports

Area	2009	2010	2011	2012	2013	2014	Rank[2]
MSA[1]	28,405.1	43,964.7	49,422.7	55,387.3	53,906.4	50,279.3	5

Note: Figures are in millions of dollars; (1) Figures cover the Detroit-Warren-Dearborn, MI Metropolitan Statistical Area—see Appendix B for areas included; (2) Rank is based on 2014 data and ranges from 1 to 385
Source: U.S. Department of Commerce, International Trade Administration, Office of Trade & Industry Information, Manufacturing & Services, data extracted March 10, 2016

Building Permits

Area	Single-Family			Multi-Family			Total		
	2014	2015p	Pct. Chg.	2014	2015p	Pct. Chg.	2014	2015p	Pct. Chg.
City	57	43	-24.6	0	0	-	57	43	-24.6
MSA[1]	4,830	5,197	7.6	1,465	2,020	37.9	6,295	7,217	14.6
U.S.	640,300	690,800	7.9	411,800	487,600	18.4	1,052,100	1,178,400	12.0

Note: (1) Figures cover the Detroit-Warren-Dearborn, MI Metropolitan Statistical Area—see Appendix B for areas included; Figures represent new, privately-owned housing units authorized (unadjusted data); All permit data are based on estimates with imputation; (p) preliminary data.
Source: U.S. Census Bureau, Manufacturing, Mining, and Construction Statistics, Building Permits, 2014, 2015

Bankruptcy Filings

Area	Business Filings			Nonbusiness Filings		
	2014	2015	% Chg.	2014	2015	% Chg.
Wayne County	109	107	-1.8	9,516	9,339	-1.9
U.S.	26,983	24,735	-8.3	909,812	819,760	-9.9

Note: Business filings include Chapter 7, Chapter 11, Chapter 12, and Chapter 13; Nonbusiness filings include Chapter 7, Chapter 11, and Chapter 13
Source: Administrative Office of the U.S. Courts, Business and Nonbusiness Bankruptcy, County Cases Commenced by Chapter of the Bankruptcy Code, During the 12- Month Period Ending December 31, 2014 and Business and Nonbusiness Bankruptcy, County Cases Commenced by Chapter of the Bankruptcy Code, During the 12- Month Period Ending December 31, 2015

Housing Vacancy Rates

Area	Gross Vacancy Rate[2] (%)			Year-Round Vacancy Rate[3] (%)			Rental Vacancy Rate[4] (%)			Homeowner Vacancy Rate[5] (%)		
	2013	2014	2015	2013	2014	2015	2013	2014	2015	2013	2014	2015
MSA[1]	11.6	11.1	9.7	11.4	10.7	9.5	12.1	9.5	6.8	1.7	1.2	1.1
U.S.	13.6	13.4	12.9	10.7	10.4	10.0	8.3	7.6	7.1	2.0	1.9	1.8

Note: (1) Figures cover the Detroit-Warren-Dearborn, MI Metropolitan Statistical Area—see Appendix B for areas included; (2) The percentage of the total housing inventory that is vacant; (3) The percentage of the housing inventory (excluding seasonal units) that is year-round vacant; (4) The percentage of rental inventory that is vacant for rent; (5) The percentage of homeowner inventory that is vacant for sale
Source: U.S. Census Bureau, Housing Vacancies and Homeownership Annual Statistics: 2015

INCOME

Income

Area	Per Capita ($)	Median Household ($)	Average Household ($)
City	54,794	101,949	139,451
MSA[1]	28,182	52,305	71,184
U.S.	28,555	53,482	74,596

Note: (1) Figures cover the Detroit-Warren-Dearborn, MI Metropolitan Statistical Area—see Appendix B for areas included
Source: U.S. Census Bureau, 2010-2014 American Community Survey 5-Year Estimates

Household Income Distribution

Area	Percent of Households Earning							
	Under $15,000	$15,000 -24,999	$25,000 -34,999	$35,000 -49,999	$50,000 -74,999	$75,000 -99,000	$100,000 -149,999	$150,000 and up
City	4.9	6.7	5.7	7.6	13.4	11.3	17.2	33.2
MSA[1]	13.7	10.8	10.1	13.4	17.5	12.2	13.1	9.2
U.S.	12.5	10.7	10.2	13.5	17.8	12.2	13.0	10.0

Note: (1) Figures cover the Detroit-Warren-Dearborn, MI Metropolitan Statistical Area—see Appendix B for areas included
Source: U.S. Census Bureau, 2010-2014 American Community Survey 5-Year Estimates

Poverty Rate

Area	All Ages	Under 18 Years Old	18 to 64 Years Old	65 Years and Over
City	3.1	1.9	3.1	4.8
MSA[1]	16.9	24.6	15.7	9.1
U.S.	15.6	21.9	14.6	9.4

Note: Figures are percentage of people whose income during the past 12 months was below the poverty level; (1) Figures cover the Detroit-Warren-Dearborn, MI Metropolitan Statistical Area—see Appendix B for areas included
Source: U.S. Census Bureau, 2010-2014 American Community Survey 5-Year Estimates

EMPLOYMENT

Labor Force and Employment

Area	Civilian Labor Force			Workers Employed		
	Dec. 2014	Dec. 2015	% Chg.	Dec. 2014	Dec. 2015	% Chg.
City	14,456	14,493	0.2	14,135	14,226	0.6
MD[1]	758,003	752,875	-0.6	700,376	704,860	0.6
U.S.	155,521,000	157,245,000	1.1	147,190,000	149,703,000	1.7

Note: Data is not seasonally adjusted and covers workers 16 years of age and older; (1) Figures cover the Detroit-Dearborn-Livonia, MI Metropolitan Division—see Appendix B for areas included
Source: Bureau of Labor Statistics, Local Area Unemployment Statistics

Unemployment Rate

Area	2015											
	Jan.	Feb.	Mar.	Apr.	May	Jun.	Jul.	Aug.	Sep.	Oct.	Nov.	Dec.
City	2.5	2.1	2.0	1.7	2.3	2.3	2.4	2.2	2.0	2.3	1.8	1.8
MD[1]	8.5	7.3	6.9	5.9	7.7	7.7	8.2	7.5	6.7	7.7	6.2	6.4
U.S.	6.1	5.8	5.6	5.1	5.3	5.5	5.6	5.2	4.9	4.8	4.8	4.8

Note: Data is not seasonally adjusted and covers workers 16 years of age and older; (1) Figures cover the Detroit-Dearborn-Livonia, MI Metropolitan Division—see Appendix B for areas included
Source: Bureau of Labor Statistics, Local Area Unemployment Statistics

Employment by Occupation

Occupation Classification	City (%)	MSA[1] (%)	U.S. (%)
Management, Business, Science, and Arts	65.8	37.1	36.4
Natural Resources, Construction, and Maintenance	2.7	6.7	9.0
Production, Transportation, and Material Moving	4.2	13.6	12.1
Sales and Office	17.1	24.7	24.4
Service	10.3	17.8	18.2

Note: Figures cover employed civilians 16 years of age and older; (1) Figures cover the Detroit-Warren-Dearborn, MI Metropolitan Statistical Area—see Appendix B for areas included
Source: U.S. Census Bureau, 2010-2014 American Community Survey 5-Year Estimates

Employment by Industry

Sector	MD[1]		U.S.
	Number of Employees	Percent of Total	Percent of Total
Construction, Mining, and Logging	19,100	2.5	5.0
Education and Health Services	134,600	18.0	15.7
Financial Activities	34,800	4.6	5.7
Government	86,000	11.5	15.5
Information	7,500	1.0	1.9
Leisure and Hospitality	74,500	9.9	10.4
Manufacturing	90,700	12.1	8.6
Other Services	29,500	3.9	3.9
Professional and Business Services	125,900	16.8	13.9
Retail Trade	71,000	9.5	11.3
Transportation, Warehousing, and Utilities	41,400	5.5	3.9
Wholesale Trade	30,400	4.0	4.1

Note: Figures are non-farm employment as of December 2015. Figures are not seasonally adjusted and include workers 16 years of age and older; (1) Figures cover the Detroit-Dearborn-Livonia, MI Metropolitan Division—see Appendix B for areas included; n/a not available
Source: Bureau of Labor Statistics, Current Employment Statistics, Employment, Hours, and Earnings

Occupations with Greatest Projected Employment Growth: 2010 – 2020

Occupation[1]	2010 Employment	2020 Projected Employment	Numeric Employment Change	Percent Employment Change
Home Health Aides	35,400	54,310	18,910	53.4
Registered Nurses	87,170	104,000	16,820	19.3
Office Clerks, General	112,620	123,920	11,300	10.0
Retail Salespersons	127,580	137,710	10,140	8.0
Combined Food Preparation and Serving Workers, Including Fast Food	70,020	78,610	8,590	12.3
Nursing Aides, Orderlies, and Attendants	50,400	57,320	6,920	13.7
Personal Care Aides	14,720	20,900	6,180	42.0
Landscaping and Groundskeeping Workers	28,350	34,370	6,020	21.2
Customer Service Representatives	61,310	67,240	5,930	9.7
Heavy and Tractor-Trailer Truck Drivers	48,610	54,070	5,460	11.2

Note: Projections cover Michigan; (1) Sorted by numeric employment change
Source: www.projectionscentral.com, State Occupational Projections, 2010–2020 Long-Term Projections

Fastest Growing Occupations: 2010 – 2020

Occupation[1]	2010 Employment	2020 Projected Employment	Numeric Employment Change	Percent Employment Change
Biomedical Engineers	200	310	110	54.0
Home Health Aides	35,400	54,310	18,910	53.4
Personal Care Aides	14,720	20,900	6,180	42.0
Veterinary Technologists and Technicians	1,810	2,570	760	42.0
Meeting, Convention, and Event Planners	1,540	2,140	600	39.1
Market Research Analysts and Marketing Specialists	6,920	9,500	2,590	37.4
Software Developers, Systems Software	6,550	8,960	2,420	36.9
Marriage and Family Therapists	300	400	110	36.6
Helpers—Carpenters	300	410	110	36.5
Bicycle Repairers	570	770	200	36.0

Note: Projections cover Michigan; (1) Sorted by percent employment change and excludes occupations with numeric employment change less than 100
Source: www.projectionscentral.com, State Occupational Projections, 2010–2020 Long-Term Projections

Average Wages

Occupation	$/Hr.	Occupation	$/Hr.
Accountants and Auditors	34.91	Maids and Housekeeping Cleaners	11.87
Automotive Mechanics	19.00	Maintenance and Repair Workers	18.83
Bookkeepers	19.34	Marketing Managers	71.40
Carpenters	25.46	Nuclear Medicine Technologists	30.26
Cashiers	10.71	Nurses, Licensed Practical	23.40
Clerks, General Office	16.30	Nurses, Registered	32.23
Clerks, Receptionists/Information	13.67	Nursing Assistants	13.44
Clerks, Shipping/Receiving	17.91	Packers and Packagers, Hand	11.94
Computer Programmers	38.39	Physical Therapists	40.69
Computer Systems Analysts	45.88	Postal Service Mail Carriers	25.31
Computer User Support Specialists	21.55	Real Estate Brokers	36.14
Cooks, Restaurant	12.17	Retail Salespersons	12.62
Dentists	72.86	Sales Reps., Exc. Tech./Scientific	33.87
Electrical Engineers	45.78	Sales Reps., Tech./Scientific	41.29
Electricians	31.99	Secretaries, Exc. Legal/Med./Exec.	16.79
Financial Managers	58.52	Security Guards	13.11
First-Line Supervisors/Managers, Sales	18.59	Surgeons	92.00
Food Preparation Workers	12.30	Teacher Assistants*	13.22
General and Operations Managers	57.48	Teachers, Elementary School*	29.44
Hairdressers/Cosmetologists	13.85	Teachers, Secondary School*	30.57
Internists	75.38	Telemarketers	12.87
Janitors and Cleaners	12.80	Truck Drivers, Heavy/Tractor-Trailer	21.95
Landscaping/Groundskeeping Workers	13.17	Truck Drivers, Light/Delivery Svcs.	18.58
Lawyers	52.07	Waiters and Waitresses	10.39

Note: Wage data covers the Detroit-Livonia-Dearborn, MI Metropolitan Division—see Appendix B for areas included; (*) Hourly wages for elementary/secondary school teachers and teacher assistants were calculated by the editors from annual wage data based on a 40 hour work week; n/a not available.
Source: Bureau of Labor Statistics, Metro Area Occupational Employment and Wage Estimates, May 2015

TAXES

State Corporate Income Tax Rates

State	Tax Rate (%)	Income Brackets ($)	Num. of Brackets	Financial Institution Tax Rate (%)[a]	Federal Income Tax Ded.
Michigan	6.0	Flat rate	1	(a)	No

Note: Tax rates as of January 1, 2016; (a) Rates listed are the corporate income tax rate applied to financial institutions or excise taxes based on income. Some states have other taxes based upon the value of deposits or shares.
Source: Federation of Tax Administrators, "State Corporate Income Tax Rates, 2016"

State Individual Income Tax Rates

State	Tax Rate (%)	Income Brackets ($)	Num. of Brackets	Personal Exempt. ($)[1]		Fed. Inc. Tax Ded.
				Single	Dependents	
Michigan (a)	4.25	Flat rate	1	3,950	3,950	No

Note: Tax rates as of January 1, 2016; Local- and county-level taxes are not included; n/a not applicable; (1) Married joint filers generally receive double the single exemption; (a) 18 states have statutory provision for automatically adjusting to the rate of inflation the dollar values of the income tax brackets, standard deductions, and/or personal exemptions. Massachusetts, Michigan, and Nebraska index the personal exemptiononly. Oregon does not index the income brackets for $125,000 and over. Maine has suspended indexing for 2014 and 2015.
Source: Federation of Tax Administrators, "State Individual Income Tax Rates, 2016"

Various State and Local Tax Rates

State	State and Local Sales and Use (%)	State Sales and Use (%)	Gasoline[1] (¢/gal.)	Cigarette[2] ($/pack)	Spirits[3] ($/gal.)	Wine[4] ($/gal.)	Beer[5] ($/gal.)
Michigan	6.00	6.0	30.54	2.00	11.94 (g)	0.51 (l)	0.20

Note: All tax rates as of January 1, 2016; (1) The American Petroleum Institute has developed a methodology for determining the average tax rate on a gallon of fuel. Rates may include any of the following: excise taxes, environmental fees, storage tank fees, other fees or taxes, general sales tax, and local taxes. In states where gasoline is subject to the general sales tax, or where the fuel tax is based on the average sale price, the average rate determined by API is sensitive to changes in the price of gasoline. States that fully or partially apply general sales taxes to gasoline: CA, CO, GA, IL, IN, MI, NY; (2) The federal excise tax of $1.0066 per pack and local taxes are not included; (3) Rates are those applicable to off-premise sales of 40% alcohol by volume (a.b.v.) distilled spirits in 750ml containers. Local excise taxes are excluded; (4) Rates are those applicable to off-premise sales of 11% a.b.v. non-carbonated wine in 750ml containers; (5) Rates are those applicable to off-premise sales of 4.7% a.b.v. beer in 12 ounce containers; (g) Control states, where the government controls all sales. Products can be subject to ad valorem mark-up as well as excise taxes; (l) Different rates also applicable according to alcohol content, place of production, size of container, place purchased (on- or off-premise or on board airlines) or type of wine (carbonated, vermouth, etc.).
Source: Tax Foundation, 2016 Facts & Figures: How Does Your State Compare?

State Business Tax Climate Index Rankings

State	Overall Rank	Corporate Tax Rank	Individual Income Tax Rank	Sales Tax Rank	Unemployment Insurance Tax Rank	Property Tax Rank
Michigan	13	11	15	7	48	26

Note: The index is a measure of how each state's tax laws affect economic performance. The lower the rank, the more favorable a state's tax system is for business. States without a given tax are given a ranking of 1. The scores/rankings for the District of Columbia do not affect other states. The 2016 index represents the tax climate as of July 1, 2015 (the beginning of Fiscal Year 2016).
Source: Tax Foundation, State Business Tax Climate Index 2016

TRANSPORTATION

Means of Transportation to Work

Area	Car/Truck/Van		Public Transportation			Bicycle	Walked	Other Means	Worked at Home
	Drove Alone	Car-pooled	Bus	Subway	Railroad				
City	90.0	4.4	0.3	0.0	0.0	0.2	0.6	0.2	4.3
MSA[1]	84.1	8.7	1.6	0.0	0.0	0.2	1.3	0.8	3.2
U.S.	76.4	9.6	2.6	1.8	0.6	0.6	2.8	1.3	4.4

Note: Figures are percentages and cover workers 16 years of age and older; (1) Figures cover the Detroit-Warren-Dearborn, MI Metropolitan Statistical Area—see Appendix B for areas included
Source: U.S. Census Bureau, 2010-2014 American Community Survey 5-Year Estimates

Travel Time to Work

Area	Less Than 10 Minutes	10 to 19 Minutes	20 to 29 Minutes	30 to 44 Minutes	45 to 59 Minutes	60 to 89 Minutes	90 Minutes or More
City	7.5	22.8	21.2	33.5	9.3	4.2	1.4
MSA[1]	10.0	26.9	23.1	24.2	9.0	5.0	1.8
U.S.	13.3	29.6	21.0	20.2	7.7	5.7	2.6

Note: Figures are percentages and include workers 16 years old and over; (1) Figures cover the Detroit-Warren-Dearborn, MI Metropolitan Statistical Area—see Appendix B for areas included
Source: U.S. Census Bureau, 2010-2014 American Community Survey 5-Year Estimates

Freeway Travel Time Index

Area	1985	1990	1995	2000	2005	2010	2014
Urban Area Rank[1,2]	9	9	10	19	24	29	25
Urban Area Index[1]	1.17	1.20	1.23	1.24	1.25	1.22	1.24
Average Index[3]	1.09	1.11	1.14	1.17	1.20	1.19	1.20

Note: Freeway Travel Time Index—the ratio of travel time in the peak period to the travel time at free-flow conditions. For example, a value of 1.30 indicates a 20-minute free-flow trip takes 26 minutes in the peak (20 minutes x 1.30 = 26 minutes); (1) Covers the Detroit MI urban area; (2) Rank is based on 101 urban areas (#1 = highest travel time index); (3) Average of 101 urban areas
Source: Texas Transportation Institute, 2015 Urban Mobility Scorecard, August 2015

Freeway Commuter Stress Index

Area	1985	1990	1995	2000	2005	2010	2014
Urban Area Rank[1,2]	22	22	24	27	35	37	33
Urban Area Index[1]	1.19	1.22	1.25	1.27	1.27	1.25	1.27
Average Index[3]	1.13	1.16	1.19	1.22	1.25	1.24	1.25

Note: The Freeway Commuter Stress Index is the same as the Freeway Travel Time Index (see table above) except that it includes only the travel in the peak directions during the peak periods; the TTI includes travel in all directions during the peak period. Thus, the CSI is more indicative of the work trip experienced by each commuter on a daily basis. (1) Covers the Detroit MI urban area; (2) Rank is based on 101 urban areas (#1 = highest stress index); (3) Average of 101 urban areas

Source: Texas Transportation Institute, 2015 Urban Mobility Scorecard, August 2015

Living Environment

COST OF LIVING

Cost of Living Index

Composite Index	Groceries	Housing	Utilities	Trans-portation	Health Care	Misc. Goods/ Services
95.4	88.8	91.1	104.5	104.8	96.4	95.5

Note: The Cost of Living Index measures regional differences in the cost of consumer goods and services, excluding taxes and non-consumer expenditures, for professional and managerial households in the top income quintile. It is based on more than 50,000 prices covering almost 60 different items for which prices are collected three times a year by chambers of commerce, economic development organizations or university applied economic centers in each participating urban area. The numbers shown should be read as a percentage above or below the national average of 100. For example, a value of 115.4 in the groceries column indicates that grocery prices are 15.4% higher than the national average. Small differences in the index numbers should not be interpreted as significant; Figures cover the Detroit MI urban area.
Source: The Council for Community and Economic Research, ACCRA Cost of Living Index, 2015

Grocery Prices

Area[1]	T-Bone Steak ($/pound)	Frying Chicken ($/pound)	Whole Milk ($/half gal.)	Eggs ($/dozen)	Orange Juice ($/64 oz.)	Coffee ($/11.5 oz.)
City[2]	10.81	1.20	1.85	1.98	3.00	4.06
Avg.	10.99	1.43	2.25	2.26	3.58	4.48
Min.	7.16	0.98	1.30	1.35	2.88	2.98
Max.	14.13	2.43	3.85	4.81	6.39	7.56

Note: (1) Values for the local area are compared with the average, minimum and maximum values for all 292 areas in the Cost of Living Index; (2) Figures cover the Detroit MI urban area; **T-Bone Steak** *(price per pound);* **Frying Chicken** *(price per pound, whole fryer);* **Whole Milk** *(half gallon carton);* **Eggs** *(price per dozen, Grade A, large);* **Orange Juice** *(64 oz. Tropicana or Florida Natural);* **Coffee** *(11.5 oz. can, vacuum-packed, Maxwell House, Hills Bros, or Folgers).*
Source: The Council for Community and Economic Research, ACCRA Cost of Living Index, 2015

Housing and Utility Costs

Area[1]	New Home Price ($)	Apartment Rent ($/month)	All Electric ($/month)	Part Electric ($/month)	Other Energy ($/month)	Telephone ($/month)
City[2]	269,215	955	-	108.88	66.14	30.00
Avg.	312,874	945	179.30	95.07	72.96	28.11
Min.	178,682	479	116.28	43.14	26.46	10.01
Max.	1,472,476	3,984	504.25	189.44	421.11	43.06

Note: (1) Values for the local area are compared with the average, minimum and maximum values for all 292 areas in the Cost of Living Index; (2) Figures cover the Detroit MI urban area; **New Home Price** *(2,400 sf living area, 8,000 sf lot, in urban area with full utilities);* **Apartment Rent** *(950 sf 2 bedroom/1.5 or 2 bath, unfurnished, excluding all utilities except water);* **All Electric** *(average monthly cost for an all-electric home);* **Part Electric** *(average monthly cost for a part-electric home);* **Other Energy** *(average monthly cost for natural gas, fuel oil, coal, wood, and any other forms of energy except electricity);* **Telephone** *(price includes basic monthly rate for a private residential line plus additional local usage charges incurred by a family of four).*
Source: The Council for Community and Economic Research, ACCRA Cost of Living Index, 2015

Health Care, Transportation, and Other Costs

Area[1]	Doctor ($/visit)	Dentist ($/visit)	Optometrist ($/visit)	Gasoline ($/gallon)	Beauty Salon ($/visit)	Men's Shirt ($)
City[2]	100.13	86.47	79.43	2.44	47.83	21.95
Avg.	105.15	89.02	99.78	2.38	35.30	28.10
Min.	66.87	56.09	48.53	1.95	18.91	13.38
Max.	182.34	150.36	228.33	4.09	67.91	63.80

Note: (1) Values for the local area are compared with the average, minimum and maximum values for all 292 areas in the Cost of Living Index; (2) Figures cover the Detroit MI urban area; **Doctor** *(general practitioners routine exam of an established patient);* **Dentist** *(adult teeth cleaning and periodic oral examination);* **Optometrist** *(full vision eye exam for established adult patient);* **Gasoline** *(one gallon regular unleaded, national brand, including all taxes, cash price at self-service pump if available);* **Beauty Salon** *(woman's shampoo, trim, and blow-dry);* **Men's Shirt** *(cotton/polyester dress shirt, pinpoint weave, long sleeves).*
Source: The Council for Community and Economic Research, ACCRA Cost of Living Index, 2015

HOUSING

House Price Index (HPI)

Area	National Ranking[2]	Quarterly Change (%)	One-Year Change (%)	Five-Year Change (%)
MD[1]	75	1.30	6.50	28.40
U.S.[3]	–	1.45	5.76	22.85

Note: The HPI is a weighted repeat sales index. It measures average price changes in repeat sales or refinancings on the same properties. This information is obtained by reviewing repeat mortgage transactions on single-family properties whose mortgages have been purchased or securitized by Fannie Mae or Freddie Mac in January 1975; (1) Detroit-Dearborn-Livonia Metropolitan Division—see Appendix B for areas included; (2) Rankings are based on annual percentage change for all metro areas containing at least 15,000 transactions over the last 10 years and ranges from 1 to 266; (3) figures based on a weighted average of Census Division estimates using a seasonally adjusted, purchase-only index; all figures are for the period ending December 31, 2015

Source: Federal Housing Finance Agency, House Price Index, February 25, 2016

Median Single-Family Home Prices

Area	2013	2014	2015^p	Percent Change 2014 to 2015
MSA[1]	n/a	n/a	n/a	n/a
U.S. Average	197.4	208.9	223.9	7.2

Note: Figures are median sales prices of existing single-family homes in thousands of dollars; (p) preliminary; n/a not available; (1) Detroit-Warren-Dearborn, MI Metropolitan Statistical Area—see Appendix B for areas included

Source: National Association of Realtors, Median Sales Price of Existing Single-Family Homes for Metropolitan Areas, 4th Quarter 2015

Qualifying Income Based on Median Sales Price of Existing Single-Family Homes

Area	With 5% Down ($)	With 10% Down ($)	With 20% Down ($)
MSA[1]	n/a	n/a	n/a
U.S. Average	49,535	46,928	41,714

Note: Figures are preliminary; Qualifying income is based on a mortgage rate of 4.1%. Monthly principal and interest payment is limited to 25% of income; n/a not available; (1) Detroit-Warren-Dearborn, MI Metropolitan Statistical Area—see Appendix B for areas included

Source: National Association of Realtors, Qualifying Income Based on Median Sales Price of Existing Single-Family Homes for Metropolitan Areas, 4th Quarter 2015

Median Apartment Condo-Coop Home Prices

Area	2013	2014	2015^p	Percent Change 2014 to 2015
MSA[1]	n/a	n/a	n/a	n/a
U.S. Average	194.9	204.3	210.7	3.1

Note: Figures are median sales prices of existing apartment condo-coop homes in thousands of dollars; (p) preliminary; n/a not available; (1) Detroit-Warren-Dearborn, MI Metropolitan Statistical Area—see Appendix B for areas included

Source: National Association of Realtors, Median Sales Price of Existing Apartment Condo-Coop Homes for Metropolitan Areas, 4th Quarter 2015

Gross Monthly Rent

Area	Under $200	$200 -299	$300 -499	$500 -749	$750 -999	$1,000 -1,499	$1,500 and up	Median ($)
City	0.0	0.0	0.0	6.6	32.2	38.9	22.3	1,118
MSA[1]	1.7	3.4	7.0	26.0	28.5	25.6	7.7	846
U.S.	1.5	3.2	7.4	21.0	24.1	26.9	15.9	920

Note: Figures are percentages except for Median; Gross rent is the contract rent plus the estimated average monthly cost of utilities (electricity, gas, and water and sewer) and fuels (oil, coal, kerosene, wood, etc.) if these are paid by the renter (or paid for the renter by someone else); (1) Figures cover the Detroit-Warren-Dearborn, MI Metropolitan Statistical Area—see Appendix B for areas included

Source: U.S. Census Bureau, 2010-2014 American Community Survey 5-Year Estimates

Homeownership Rate

Area	2008 (%)	2009 (%)	2010 (%)	2011 (%)	2012 (%)	2013 (%)	2014 (%)	2015 (%)
MSA[1]	75.5	73.9	73.6	73.5	73.4	71.7	71.2	74.0
U.S.	67.8	67.4	66.9	66.1	65.4	65.1	64.5	63.7

Note: (1) Figures cover the Detroit-Warren-Dearborn, MI Metropolitan Statistical Area—see Appendix B for areas included
Source: U.S. Census Bureau, Housing Vacancies and Homeownership Annual Statistics: 2015

Year Housing Structure Built

Area	2010 or Later	2000 -2009	1990 -1999	1980 -1989	1970 -1979	1960 -1969	1950 -1959	1940 -1949	Before 1940	Median Year
City	1.5	26.6	19.6	20.2	19.6	6.1	3.4	0.8	2.2	1989
MSA[1]	0.3	8.8	11.1	9.0	14.4	12.7	19.8	10.6	13.3	1965
U.S.	1.0	14.9	13.9	13.8	15.8	11.0	10.8	5.4	13.3	1976

Note: Figures are percentages except for Median Year; (1) Figures cover the Detroit-Warren-Dearborn, MI Metropolitan Statistical Area—see Appendix B for areas included
Source: U.S. Census Bureau, 2010-2014 American Community Survey 5-Year Estimates

HEALTH

Health Risk Data

Category	MD[1] (%)	U.S. (%)
Adults aged 18–64 who have any kind of health care coverage	77.9	79.6
Adults who reported being in good or excellent health	78.1	83.1
Adults who are current smokers	24.4	19.6
Adults who are heavy drinkers[2]	5.7	6.1
Adults who are binge drinkers[3]	18.9	16.9
Adults who are overweight (BMI 25.0 - 29.9)	32.5	35.8
Adults who are obese (BMI 30.0 - 99.8)	34.2	27.6
Adults who participated in any physical activities in the past month	71.8	77.1
Adults 50+ who have ever had a sigmoidoscopy or colonoscopy	67.0	67.3
Women aged 40+ who have had a mammogram within the past two years	77.3	74.0
Men aged 40+ who have had a PSA test within the past two years	47.4	45.2
Adults aged 65+ who have had flu shot within the past year	46.5	60.1
Adults who always wear a seatbelt	93.6	93.8

Note: Data as of 2012 unless otherwise noted; (1) Figures cover the Detroit-Livonia-Dearborn, MI Metropolitan Division—see Appendix B for areas included; (2) Heavy drinkers are classified as males having more than two drinks per day or females having more than one drink per day; (3) Binge drinkers are classified as males having five or more drinks on one occasion or females having four or more drinks on one occasion
Source: Centers for Disease Control and Prevention, Behaviorial Risk Factor Surveillance System, SMART: Selected Metropolitan/Micropolitan Area Risk Trends, 2012 (Note: the CDC has discontinued this dataset but will be releasing a replacement in mid-2016)

Chronic Health Indicators

Category	MD[1] (%)	U.S. (%)
Adults who have ever been told they had a heart attack	5.7	4.5
Adults who have ever been told they had a stroke	3.6	2.9
Adults who have been told they currently have asthma	11.8	8.9
Adults who have ever been told they have arthritis	32.7	25.7
Adults who have ever been told they have diabetes[2]	12.6	9.7
Adults who have ever been told they had skin cancer	4.1	5.7
Adults who have ever been told they had any other types of cancer	7.3	6.5
Adults who have ever been told they have COPD	7.9	6.2
Adults who have ever been told they have kidney disease	4.2	2.5
Adults who have ever been told they have a form of depression	19.9	18.0

Note: Data as of 2012 unless otherwise noted; (1) Figures cover the Detroit-Livonia-Dearborn, MI Metropolitan Division—see Appendix B for areas included; (2) Figures do not include pregnancy-related, borderline, or pre-diabetes
Source: Centers for Disease Control and Prevention, Behaviorial Risk Factor Surveillance System, SMART: Selected Metropolitan/Micropolitan Area Risk Trends, 2012 (Note: the CDC has discontinued this dataset but will be releasing a replacement in mid-2016)

Mortality Rates for the Top 10 Causes of Death in the U.S.

ICD-10[a] Sub-Chapter	ICD-10[a] Code	Age-Adjusted Mortality Rate[1] per 100,000 population	
		County[2]	U.S.
Malignant neoplasms	C00-C97	191.6	163.6
Ischaemic heart diseases	I20-I25	168.9	102.2
Other forms of heart disease	I30-I51	57.3	50.1
Chronic lower respiratory diseases	J40-J47	44.9	41.4
Organic, including symptomatic, mental disorders	F01-F09	31.3	38.5
Cerebrovascular diseases	I60-I69	39.2	36.5
Other external causes of accidental injury	W00-X59	34.7	27.5
Other degenerative diseases of the nervous system	G30-G31	24.3	26.3
Diabetes mellitus	E10-E14	26.8	21.1
Hypertensive diseases	I10-I15	36.4	19.7

Note: (a) ICD-10 = International Classification of Diseases 10th Revision; (1) Mortality rates are a three year average covering 2012-2014; (2) Figures cover Wayne County.
Source: Centers for Disease Control and Prevention, National Center for Health Statistics. Underlying Cause of Death 1999-2014 on CDC WONDER Online Database, released 2015.

Mortality Rates for Selected Causes of Death

ICD-10[a] Sub-Chapter	ICD-10[a] Code	Age-Adjusted Mortality Rate[1] per 100,000 population	
		County[2]	U.S.
Assault	X85-Y09	21.5	5.1
Diseases of the liver	K70-K76	14.3	13.5
Human immunodeficiency virus (HIV) disease	B20-B24	3.2	2.1
Influenza and pneumonia	J09-J18	19.1	15.2
Intentional self-harm	X60-X84	11.6	12.7
Malnutrition	E40-E46	1.9	0.9
Obesity and other hyperalimentation	E65-E68	2.4	1.9
Renal failure	N17-N19	17.9	13.0
Transport accidents	V01-V99	10.6	11.6
Viral hepatitis	B15-B19	2.5	2.1

Note: (a) ICD-10 = International Classification of Diseases 10th Revision; (1) Mortality rates are a three year average covering 2012-2014; (2) Figures cover Wayne County; Data are Suppressed when the data meet the criteria for confidentiality constraints; Mortality rates are flagged as Unreliable when the rate would be calculated with a numerator of 20 or less.
Source: Centers for Disease Control and Prevention, National Center for Health Statistics. Underlying Cause of Death 1999-2014 on CDC WONDER Online Database, released 2015.

Health Insurance Coverage

Area	With Health Insurance	With Private Health Insurance	With Public Health Insurance	Without Health Insurance	Population Under Age 18 Without Health Insurance
City	95.0	89.9	20.9	5.0	2.4
MSA[1]	88.5	68.7	33.3	11.5	3.9
U.S.	85.8	65.8	31.1	14.2	7.1

Note: Figures are percentages that cover the civilian noninstitutionalized population; (1) Figures cover the Detroit-Warren-Dearborn, MI Metropolitan Statistical Area—see Appendix B for areas included
Source: U.S. Census Bureau, 2010-2014 American Community Survey 5-Year Estimates

Number of Medical Professionals

Area	MDs[3]	DOs[3,4]	Dentists	Podiatrists	Chiropractors	Optometrists
County[1] (number)	5,163	624	1,091	157	301	163
County[1] (rate[2])	290.8	35.1	61.8	8.9	17.1	9.2
U.S. (rate[2])	272.5	20.9	64.7	5.8	25.9	15.2

Note: Data as of 2014 unless noted; (1) Data covers Wayne County; (2) Rate per 100,000 population; (3) Data as of 2013 and includes all active, non-federal physicians; (4) Doctor of Osteopathic Medicine
Source: U.S. Department of Health and Human Services, Health Resources and Services Administration, Bureau of Health Professions, Area Resource File (ARF) 2014-2015

Best Hospitals

According to *U.S. News,* the Detroit-Dearborn-Livonia, MI metro area is home to one of the best hospitals in the U.S.: **Harper University Hospital** (1 specialty). The hospital listed was nationally ranked in at least one adult specialty. Only 137 hospitals nationwide were nationally ranked in one or more specialties. Fifteen hospitals in the U.S. made the Honor Roll with high scores in at least six specialties. *U.S. News Online, "America's Best Children's Hospitals 2015-16"*

According to *U.S. News,* the Detroit-Dearborn-Livonia, MI metro area is home to one of the best children's hospitals in the U.S.: **Children's Hospital of Michigan** (8 specialties). The hospital listed was highly ranked in at least one pediatric specialty. Eighty-three children's hospitals in the U.S. were nationally ranked in at least one specialty. Twelve children's hospitals in the U.S. made the Honor Roll with high scores in at least three specialties. *U.S. News Online, "America's Best Children's Hospitals 2015-16"*

EDUCATION

Public School District Statistics

District Name	Schls	Pupils	Pupil/ Teacher Ratio	Minority Pupils[1] (%)	Free Lunch Eligible[2] (%)	IEP[3] (%)
Northville Public Schools	11	7,323	19.0	25.6	5.1	8.7
South Lyon Community Schools	11	7,430	19.8	11.1	16.6	13.2

Note: Table includes school districts with 100 or more students; (1) Percentage of students that are not non-Hispanic white; (2) Percentage of students that are eligible for the free lunch program; (3) Percentage of students that have an Individualized Education Program.
Source: U.S. Department of Education, National Center for Education Statistics, Common Core of Data, Local Education Agency (School District) Universe Survey: School Year 2013-2014; U.S. Department of Education, National Center for Education Statistics, Common Core of Data, Public Elementary/Secondary School Universe Survey: School Year 2013-2014

Highest Level of Education

Area	Less than H.S.	H.S. Diploma	Some College, No Deg.	Associate Degree	Bachelor's Degree	Master's Degree	Prof. School Degree	Doctorate Degree
City	3.1	13.3	15.6	7.5	29.4	22.9	5.6	2.6
MSA[1]	11.5	27.7	23.8	8.4	17.3	8.5	1.9	0.9
U.S.	13.7	28.0	21.2	7.9	18.3	7.8	2.0	1.3

Note: Figures cover persons age 25 and over; (1) Figures cover the Detroit-Warren-Dearborn, MI Metropolitan Statistical Area—see Appendix B for areas included
Source: U.S. Census Bureau, 2010-2014 American Community Survey 5-Year Estimates

Educational Attainment by Race

Area	High School Graduate or Higher (%)					Bachelor's Degree or Higher (%)				
	Total	White	Black	Asian	Hisp.[2]	Total	White	Black	Asian	Hisp.[2]
City	96.9	98.0	90.3	93.2	95.9	60.5	58.3	53.8	77.1	51.8
MSA[1]	88.5	90.2	83.9	88.7	68.6	28.6	30.4	17.1	63.9	17.3
U.S.	86.3	88.4	83.2	85.8	64.1	29.3	30.6	19.0	50.9	13.9

Note: Figures shown cover persons 25 years old and over; (1) Figures cover the Detroit-Warren-Dearborn, MI Metropolitan Statistical Area—see Appendix B for areas included; (2) People of Hispanic origin can be of any race
Source: U.S. Census Bureau, 2010-2014 American Community Survey 5-Year Estimates

School Enrollment by Grade and Control

Area	Preschool (%)		Kindergarten (%)		Grades 1 - 4 (%)		Grades 5 - 8 (%)		Grades 9 - 12 (%)	
	Public	Private	Public	Private	Public	Private	Public	Private	Public	Private
City	29.2	70.8	80.3	19.7	80.8	19.2	90.7	9.3	81.5	18.5
MSA[1]	65.2	34.8	88.2	11.8	89.7	10.3	90.5	9.5	91.4	8.6
U.S.	57.4	42.6	87.8	12.2	89.8	10.2	89.9	10.1	90.6	9.4

Note: Figures shown cover persons 3 years old and over; (1) Figures cover the Detroit-Warren-Dearborn, MI Metropolitan Statistical Area—see Appendix B for areas included
Source: U.S. Census Bureau, 2010-2014 American Community Survey 5-Year Estimates

Average Salaries of Public School Classroom Teachers

Area	2013-14 Dollars	2013-14 Rank[1]	2014-15 Dollars	2014-15 Rank[1]	Percent Change 2013-14 to 2014-15	Percent Change 2004-05 to 2014-15
Michigan	62,166	11	62,778	11	0.98	16.3
U.S. Average	56,610	–	57,379	–	1.36	20.8

Note: (1) State rank ranges from 1 to 51 where 1 indicates highest salary.
Source: National Education Association, Rankings & Estimates: Rankings of the States 2014 and Estimates of School Statistics 2015, March 2015

Higher Education

Four-Year Colleges			Two-Year Colleges			Medical Schools[1]	Law Schools[2]	Voc/ Tech[3]
Public	Private Non-profit	Private For-profit	Public	Private Non-profit	Private For-profit			
0	0	0	0	0	0	0	0	0

Note: Figures cover institutions located within the city limits and include main campuses only; (1) includes schools accredited by the Liaison Committee on Medical Education and the American Osteopathic Association's Commission on Osteopathic College Accreditation; (2) includes ABA-accredited schools, schools with provisional ABA accreditation, and state accredited schools; (3) includes all schools with programs that are less than 2 years.
Source: National Center for Education Statistics, Integrated Postsecondary Education System (IPEDS), 2014-15; Association of American Medical Colleges, Member List, March 21, 2016; American Osteopathic Association, Member List, March 21, 2016; Law School Admission Council, Official Guide to ABA-Approved Law Schools Online, March 21, 2016; Wikipedia, List of Medical Schools in the United States, March 21, 2016; Wikipedia, List of Law Schools in the United States, March 21, 2016

According to *U.S. News & World Report,* the Detroit-Dearborn-Livonia, MI metro division is home to one of the top 100 law schools in the U.S.: **Wayne State University, Law School** (#97 tie). The rankings are based on a weighted average of 12 measures of quality: peer assessment score; assessment score by lawyers/judges; median LSAT scores; median undergrad GPA; acceptance rate; employment rates for graduates; placement success; bar passage rate; faculty resources; expenditures per student; student/faculty ratio; and library resources. *U.S. News & World Report, "America's Best Graduate Schools, Law, 2017"*

According to *U.S. News & World Report,* the Detroit-Dearborn-Livonia, MI metro division is home to one of the top 75 medical schools for research in the U.S.: **Wayne State University, School of Medicine** (#69 tie). The rankings are based on a weighted average of 11 measures of quality: quality assessment; peer assessment score; assessment score by residency directors; research activity; total research activity; average research activity per faculty member; student selectivity; median MCAT total score; median undergraduate GPA; acceptance rate; and faculty resources. *U.S. News & World Report, "America's Best Graduate Schools, Medical, 2017"*

PRESIDENTIAL ELECTION

2012 Presidential Election Results

Area	Obama (%)	Romney (%)	Other (%)
Wayne County	72.8	26.1	1.0
U.S.	51.0	47.2	1.8

Note: Results may not add to 100% due to rounding
Source: Dave Leip's Atlas of U.S. Presidential Elections

EMPLOYERS

Major Employers

Company Name	Industry
CEI Liquidation Estates	Mobile homes
Chrysler Group	Motor vehicles & car bodies
Detroit Diesel Corporation	Motor vehicle parts & accessories
Dph-Das	Motor vehicle parts & accessories
Eagle Ottawa	Leather tanning & finishing
Employees Only	Management consulting services
Ford Motor Company	Drive shafts, motor vehicle
General Motors	Motor vehicles & car bodies
General Motors Company	Automobile assembly, including specialty automobiles
Oakwood Healthcare	General medical & surgical hospitals
St Joseph Mercy Oakland Foundation	General medical & surgical hospitals
The Army, United States Department of	Army
The Chrysler Group	Truck & tractor truck assembly
Tower Automotive	Automotive stampings
Wayne State University	Colleges & universities

Note: Companies shown are located within the Detroit-Warren-Dearborn, MI Metropolitan Statistical Area.
Source: Hoovers.com; Wikipedia

PUBLIC SAFETY

Crime Rate

Area	All Crimes	Violent Crimes				Property Crimes		
		Murder	Rape[3]	Robbery	Aggrav. Assault	Burglary	Larceny -Theft	Motor Vehicle Theft
City	1,312.5	0.0	20.8	6.9	52.1	131.9	1,024.3	76.4
Metro[1]	4,235.3	19.0	56.7	248.9	657.4	777.9	1,728.8	746.6
U.S.	2,971.8	4.5	36.6	102.2	232.5	542.5	1,837.3	216.2

Note: Figures are crimes per 100,000 population; (1) Figures cover the Detroit-Dearborn-Livonia, MI Metropolitan Division—see Appendix B for areas included; (3) The city and U.S. figures shown were reported using the revised Uniform Crime Reporting (UCR) definition of rape. The suburban and metro area figures shown are an aggregate total of the data submitted using both the revised and legacy UCR definitions.
Source: FBI Uniform Crime Reports, 2014

Hate Crimes

Area	Number of Quarters Reported	Number of Incidents per Bias Motivation						
		Race	Religion	Sexual Orientation	Ethnicity	Disability	Gender	Gender Identity
City	4	0	0	0	0	0	0	0
U.S.	4	2,568	1,014	1,017	648	84	33	98

Source: Federal Bureau of Investigation, Hate Crime Statistics 2014

Identity Theft Consumer Complaints

Area	Complaints	Complaints per 100,000 Population	Rank[2]
MSA[1]	9,468	220.4	10
U.S.	490,220	152.4	-

Note: (1) Figures cover the Detroit-Warren-Dearborn, MI Metropolitan Statistical Area—see Appendix B for areas included; (2) Rank ranges from 1 to 379 where 1 indicates greatest number of identity theft complaints per 100,000 population
Source: Federal Trade Commission, Consumer Sentinel Network Data Book for January–December 2015

Fraud and Other Consumer Complaints

Area	Complaints	Complaints per 100,000 Population	Rank[2]
MSA[1]	16,371	381.0	145
U.S.	2,593,159	806.0	-

Note: (1) Figures cover the Detroit-Warren-Dearborn, MI Metropolitan Statistical Area—see Appendix B for areas included; (2) Rank ranges from 1 to 379 where 1 indicates greatest number of identity theft complaints per 100,000 population
Source: Federal Trade Commission, Consumer Sentinel Network Data Book for January–December 2015

RECREATION

Culture

Dance[1]	Theatre[1]	Instrumental Music[1]	Vocal Music[1]	Series and Festivals	Museums and Art Galleries[2]	Zoos and Aquariums[3]
0	0	0	0	0	0	0

Note: (1) Professional perfoming groups; (2) Based on organizations with SIC code 8412; (3) AZA-accredited
Source: The Grey House Performing Arts Directory, 2015-16; Association of Zoos & Aquariums, AZA Member Zoos & Aquariums, March 25, 2016; www.AccuLeads.com, March 29, 2016

Professional Sports Teams

Team Name	League	Year Established
Detroit Lions	National Football League (NFL)	1934
Detroit Pistons	National Basketball Association (NBA)	1957
Detroit Red Wings	National Hockey League (NHL)	1926
Detroit Tigers	Major League Baseball (MLB)	1901

Note: Includes teams located in the Detroit-Warren-Dearborn, MI Metropolitan Statistical Area.
Source: Wikipedia, Major Professional Sports Teams of the United States and Canada, March 24, 2016

CLIMATE

Average and Extreme Temperatures

Temperature	Jan	Feb	Mar	Apr	May	Jun	Jul	Aug	Sep	Oct	Nov	Dec	Yr.
Extreme High (°F)	62	65	81	89	93	104	102	100	98	91	77	68	104
Average High (°F)	30	33	44	58	70	79	83	81	74	61	48	35	58
Average Temp. (°F)	23	26	36	48	59	68	72	71	64	52	40	29	49
Average Low (°F)	16	18	27	37	47	56	61	60	53	41	32	21	39
Extreme Low (°F)	-21	-15	-4	10	25	36	41	38	29	17	9	-10	-21

Note: Figures cover the years 1958-1990
Source: National Climatic Data Center, International Station Meteorological Climate Summary, 9/96

Average Precipitation/Snowfall/Humidity

Precip./Humidity	Jan	Feb	Mar	Apr	May	Jun	Jul	Aug	Sep	Oct	Nov	Dec	Yr.
Avg. Precip. (in.)	1.8	1.8	2.5	3.0	2.9	3.6	3.1	3.4	2.8	2.2	2.6	2.7	32.4
Avg. Snowfall (in.)	10	9	7	2	Tr	0	0	0	0	Tr	3	11	41
Avg. Rel. Hum. 7am (%)	80	79	79	78	78	79	82	86	87	84	82	81	81
Avg. Rel. Hum. 4pm (%)	67	63	59	53	51	52	52	54	55	55	64	70	58

Note: Figures cover the years 1958-1990; Tr = Trace amounts (<0.05 in. of rain; <0.5 in. of snow)
Source: National Climatic Data Center, International Station Meteorological Climate Summary, 9/96

Weather Conditions

Temperature			Daytime Sky			Precipitation		
5°F & below	32°F & below	90°F & above	Clear	Partly cloudy	Cloudy	0.01 inch or more precip.	0.1 inch or more snow/ice	Thunder-storms
15	136	12	74	134	157	135	38	32

Note: Figures are average number of days per year and cover the years 1958-1990
Source: National Climatic Data Center, International Station Meteorological Climate Summary, 9/96

HAZARDOUS WASTE

Superfund Sites

Northville has no sites on the EPA's Superfund Final National Priorities List. There are a total of 1,323 Superfund sites on the list in the U.S. *U.S. Environmental Protection Agency, Final National Priorities List, March 18, 2016*

AIR & WATER QUALITY

Air Quality Trends: Ozone

	1990	1995	2000	2005	2010	2011	2012	2013	2014
MSA[1]	0.083	0.088	0.076	0.083	0.074	0.079	0.081	0.068	0.069

Note: (1) Data covers the Detroit-Warren-Dearborn, MI Metropolitan Statistical Area—see Appendix B for areas included. The values shown are the composite ozone concentration averages among trend sites based on the highest fourth daily maximum 8-hour concentration in parts per million. These trends are based on sites having an adequate record of monitoring data during the trend period. Data from exceptional events are included.
Source: U.S. Environmental Protection Agency, Air Quality Monitoring Information, "Air Quality Trends by City, 1990-2014"

Air Quality Index

Area	Percent of Days when Air Quality was...[2]					AQI Statistics[2]	
	Good	Moderate	Unhealthy for Sensitive Groups	Unhealthy	Very Unhealthy	Maximum	Median
MSA[1]	41.1	55.6	3.0	0.3	0.0	165	54

Note: (1) Data covers the Detroit-Warren-Dearborn, MI Metropolitan Statistical Area—see Appendix B for areas included; (2) Based on 365 days with AQI data in 2015. Air Quality Index (AQI) is an index for reporting daily air quality. EPA calculates the AQI for five major air pollutants regulated by the Clean Air Act: ground-level ozone, particle pollution (aka particulate matter), carbon monoxide, sulfur dioxide, and nitrogen dioxide. The AQI runs from 0 to 500. The higher the AQI value, the greater the level of air pollution and the greater the health concern. There are six AQI categories: "Good" AQI is between 0 and 50. Air quality is considered satisfactory; "Moderate" AQI is between 51 and 100. Air quality is acceptable; "Unhealthy for Sensitive Groups" When AQI values are between 101 and 150, members of sensitive groups may experience health effects; "Unhealthy" When AQI values are between 151 and 200 everyone may begin to experience health effects; "Very Unhealthy" AQI values between 201 and 300 trigger a health alert; "Hazardous" AQI values over 300 trigger warnings of emergency conditions (not shown).
Source: U.S. Environmental Protection Agency, Air Quality Index Report, 2015

Air Quality Index Pollutants

Area	Percent of Days when AQI Pollutant was...[2]					
	Carbon Monoxide	Nitrogen Dioxide	Ozone	Sulfur Dioxide	Particulate Matter 2.5	Particulate Matter 10
MSA[1]	0.0	2.5	15.6	14.2	58.9	8.8

Note: (1) Data covers the Detroit-Warren-Dearborn, MI Metropolitan Statistical Area—see Appendix B for areas included; (2) Based on 365 days with AQI data in 2015. The Air Quality Index (AQI) is an index for reporting daily air quality. EPA calculates the AQI for five major air pollutants regulated by the Clean Air Act: ground-level ozone, particle pollution (also known as particulate matter), carbon monoxide, sulfur dioxide, and nitrogen dioxide. The AQI runs from 0 to 500. The higher the AQI value, the greater the level of air pollution and the greater the health concern.
Source: U.S. Environmental Protection Agency, Air Quality Index Report, 2015

Maximum Air Pollutant Concentrations: Particulate Matter, Ozone, CO and Lead

	Particulate Matter 10 (ug/m^3)	Particulate Matter 2.5 Wtd AM (ug/m^3)	Particulate Matter 2.5 24-Hr (ug/m^3)	Ozone (ppm)	Carbon Monoxide (ppm)	Lead (ug/m^3)
MSA[1] Level	150	11.7	27	0.073	2	0.03
NAAQS[2]	150	15	35	0.075	9	0.15
Met NAAQS[2]	Yes	Yes	Yes	Yes	Yes	Yes

Note: (1) Data covers the Detroit-Warren-Dearborn, MI Metropolitan Statistical Area—see Appendix B for areas included; Data from exceptional events are included; (2) National Ambient Air Quality Standards; ppm = parts per million; ug/m^3 = micrograms per cubic meter; n/a not available.
Concentrations: Particulate Matter 10 (coarse particulate)—highest second maximum 24-hour concentration; Particulate Matter 2.5 Wtd AM (fine particulate)—highest weighted annual mean concentration; Particulate Matter 2.5 24-Hour (fine particulate)—highest 98th percentile 24-hour concentration; Ozone—highest fourth daily maximum 8-hour concentration; Carbon Monoxide—highest second maximum non-overlapping 8-hour concentration; Lead—maximum running 3-month average
Source: U.S. Environmental Protection Agency, Air Quality Monitoring Information, "Air Quality Statistics by City, 2014"

Maximum Air Pollutant Concentrations: Nitrogen Dioxide and Sulfur Dioxide

	Nitrogen Dioxide AM (ppb)	Nitrogen Dioxide 1-Hr (ppb)	Sulfur Dioxide AM (ppb)	Sulfur Dioxide 1-Hr (ppb)	Sulfur Dioxide 24-Hr (ppb)
MSA[1] Level	16	52	n/a	72	n/a
NAAQS[2]	53	100	30	75	140
Met NAAQS[2]	Yes	Yes	n/a	Yes	n/a

Note: (1) Data covers the Detroit-Warren-Dearborn, MI Metropolitan Statistical Area—see Appendix B for areas included; Data from exceptional events are included; (2) National Ambient Air Quality Standards; ppm = parts per million; ug/m^3 = micrograms per cubic meter; n/a not available.

Concentrations: Nitrogen Dioxide AM—highest arithmetic mean concentration; Nitrogen Dioxide 1-Hr—highest 98th percentile 1-hour daily maximum concentration; Sulfur Dioxide AM—highest annual mean concentration; Sulfur Dioxide 1-Hr—highest 99th percentile 1-hour daily maximum concentration; Sulfur Dioxide 24-Hr—highest second maximum 24-hour concentration

Source: U.S. Environmental Protection Agency, Air Quality Monitoring Information, "Air Quality Statistics by City, 2014"

Drinking Water

Water System Name	Pop. Served	Primary Water Source Type	Violations[1]	
			Health Based	Monitoring/ Reporting
Northville Township	26,655	Purchased Surface	0	0

Note: (1) Based on violation data from January 1, 2015 to December 31, 2015 (includes unresolved violations from earlier years)

Source: U.S. Environmental Protection Agency, Office of Ground Water and Drinking Water, Safe Drinking Water Information System (based on data extracted April 29, 2016)

Novi, Michigan

Background

Novi is located in Oakland County in southeastern Michigan. It is 25 minutes from downtown Detroit, with the Great Lakes nearby. Despite attempts to incorporate in 1959, the city was not established until 1969, helped by the Novi Jaycees and the Willowbrook Community Association and their door-to-door campaigns and community-unifying open meetings.

Of historical significance is Novi's Grand River Avenue Bridge, constructed along the Chesapeake and Ohio Railroad in 1925. It is one of the largest concrete "camelback" girder bridges left in Michigan.

Novi is home to six major medical centers, four public schools, three colleges and a growing business district that houses the headquarters of ITC Transmission and Brembo North America. The city is a member of Automation Alley, a group of technology firms and institutions in southeast Michigan which provides a forum for networking, recruiting, and promoting the growth of the interactive technology industries throughout the Great Lakes Region.

A variety of parks, wetland and woodland protected areas, structured outdoor activity and cultural attractions can all be found in Novi. The Suburban Collection Showplace and the Novi Ice Arena are all modern, multi-use facilities.

Novi has convenient access to several nearby expressways, is connected to the CSX Railway, and the Detroit Metropolitan Airport and Oakland County International Airport are less than an hour away.

Novi's climate, with four distinct seasons, is perfect for outdoor recreation any time of year. Winter snowfalls are a big support of winter sports, while the warm summer breezes encourage boating, biking and outdoor sports of all varieties.

Rankings

Business/Finance Rankings

- The personal finance site NerdWallet analyzed 183 American metropolitan areas with populations over 250,000 and more than 15,000 businesses to rank where entrepreneurs find the most success. Criteria included area economy, annual income, housing cost, unemployment rate, and the success rate of area businesses. Warren* ranked #91. *www.nerdwallet.com, "Best Places to Start a Business," April 27, 2015*
- 24/7 Wall Street used Brookings Institution research on 50 advanced industries to identify the proportion of workers in the nation's largest metropolitan areas that were employed in jobs requiring knowledge in the science, technology, engineering, or math (STEM) fields. The Detroit* metro area was #4. *247wallst.com, "15 Cities with the Most High-Tech Jobs," March 13, 2015*
- Based on metro area social media reviews, the employment opinion group Glassdoor surveyed 50 of the largest U.S. metro areas and equally weighed cost of living, hiring opportunity, and job satisfaction to compose a list of "25 Best Cities for Jobs." The Detroit* metro area was ranked #42 in overall job satisfaction. *www.glassdoor.com, "Best Cities for Jobs," May 19, 2015*
- In a survey of economic confidence in the nation's 50 largest metropolitan areas conducted January–December 2014, the Detroit* metro area placed #34, according to Gallup's 2014 Economic Confidence Index. *Gallup, "San Jose and San Francisco Lead in Economic Confidence," March 19, 2015*
- The Brookings Institution ranked the 100 largest metro areas in the U.S. based on income inequality. Detroit* was ranked #24 (#1 = greatest ineqality). Criteria: the "95/20 ratio," a figure representing the income at which a household earns more than 95 percent of all other households, divided by the income at which a household earns more than only 20 percent of all other households. *Brookings Institution, "Income Inequality, 100 Largest U.S. Metro Areas, 2007-2014," January 14, 2016*
- Payscale.com ranked the 20 largest metro areas in terms of wage growth. The Detroit* metro area ranked #3. Criteria: private-sector wage growth between the 1st quarter of 2015 and the 1st quarter of 2016. *PayScale, "Wage Trends by Metro Area," 1st Quarter, 2016*
- The Warren* metro area was identified as one of the most affordable metropolitan areas in America by *Forbes.* The area ranked #14 out of 20 based on the National Association of Home Builders/Wells Fargo Housing Affordability Index and Sperling's Best Places' cost-of-living index. *Forbes.com, "America's Most Affordable Cities in 2015," March 12, 2015*
- Warren* was cited as one of America's top metros for new and expanded facility projects in 2015. The area ranked #6 in the large metro area category (population over 1 million). *Site Selection, "Top Metropolitans of 2015," March 2016*
- The Warren* metro area appeared on the Milken Institute "2015 Best Performing Cities" list. Rank: #55 out of 200 large metro areas. Criteria: job growth; wage and salary growth; high-tech output growth. *Milken Institute, "Best-Performing Cities 2015," December 2015*
- *Forbes* ranked the 200 most populous metro areas to determine the nation's "Best Places for Business and Careers." The Warren* metro area was ranked #9. Criteria: costs (business and living); job growth (past and projected); income growth; educational attainment (college and high school); projected economic growth; cultural and recreational opportunities; net migration patterns; number of highly ranked colleges. *Forbes, "The Best Places for Business and Careers 2015," July 29, 2015*

Education Rankings

- Personal finance website *WalletHub* analyzed the 150 largest U.S. metropolitan statistical areas to determine where the most educated Americans are choosing to settle. Criteria: education quality and attainment gap; education levels; percentage of workers with degrees; public school rankings; quality and size of each metro area's universities. Detroit* was ranked #70 (#1 = most educated city). *www.WalletHub.com, "2015's Most and Least Educated Cities*

Environmental Rankings

- The Detroit* metro area came in at #103 for the relative comfort of its climate on Sperling's list of "chill cities," as measured by the Sperling Heat Index. All 361 metro areas are included. Criteria included daytime high temperatures, nighttime low temperatures, dew point, and relative humidity at the high temperatures. *www.bertsperling.com, "Sperling's Chill Cities," July 18, 2013*

- Sperling's BestPlaces assessed 379 metropolitan areas of the United States for the likelihood of dangerously extreme weather events or earthquakes. In general the Southeast and South-Central regions have the highest risk of weather extremes and earthquakes, while the Pacific Northwest enjoys the lowest risk. Of the least risky metropolitan areas, the Warren* metro area was ranked #156. *www.bestplaces.net, "Safest Places from Natural Disasters," April 2011*

Health/Fitness Rankings

- Analysts who tracked obesity rates in the nation's largest metro areas (populations above one million) found that the Detroit* metro area was one of the ten major metros where residents were most likely to be obese, defined as a BMI score of 30 or above. *www.gallup.com, "Boulder, Colo., Residents Still Least Likely to Be Obese," April 4, 2014*

- For each of the 50 most populous metro areas in the United States, the American College of Sports Medicine's American Fitness Index evaluated infrastructure, community assets, and policies that encourage healthy and fit lifestyles, including preventive health behaviors, levels of chronic disease conditions, health care access, and community resources and policies that support physical activity. The Detroit* metro area ranked #40 for "community fitness." *www.americanfitnessindex.org, "ACSM American Fitness Index Health and Community Fitness Status of the 50 Largest Metropolitan Areas," May 2015*

- The Detroit* metro area was identified as one of the worst cities for bed bugs in America by pest control company Orkin. The area ranked #7 out of 50 based on the number of bed bug treatments Orkin performed from January to December 2015. *Orkin, "Chicago Tops Bed Bug Cities List for Fourth Year in a Row," January 13, 2016*

- Detroit* was identified as a "2016 Spring Allergy Capital." The area ranked #39 out of 100. Three groups of factors were used to identify the most severe cities for people with allergies during the spring season: annual pollen levels; medicine utilization; access to board-certified allergists. *Asthma and Allergy Foundation of America, "Spring Allergy Capitals 2016"*

- Detroit* was identified as a "2015 Asthma Capital." The area ranked #4 out of the nation's 100 largest metropolitan areas. Criteria: estimated prevalence; self-reported prevalence; crude death rate for asthma; annual pollen score; annual air quality; public smoking laws; number of board-certified asthma specialists; school inhaler access laws; rescue medication use; controller medication use; ER visits for asthma; uninsured rate; poverty rate. *Asthma and Allergy Foundation of America, "Asthma Capitals 2015"*

- The Detroit* metro area ranked #174 out of 190 in The Gallup-Healthways Well-Being Index. Criteria: purpose; social well being; financial health; community and physical health. Results are based on telephone interviews with adults, aged 18 and older, living in metropolitan areas in the 50 U.S. states and the District of Columbia. *Gallup-Healthways, "State of American Well-Being," February 23, 2016*

Real Estate Rankings

- The Detroit* metro area was identified as #3 among the ten housing markets with the highest percentage of distressed property sales, based on the findings of the housing data website RealtyTrac. Criteria: short sales; income and poverty figures; and unemployment data. *247wallst.com, "Cities Selling the Most Distressed Homes," January 23, 2014*

- Warren* was ranked #72 out of 225 metro areas in terms of housing affordability in 2015 by the National Association of Home Builders (#1 = most affordable). Criteria: the share of homes sold in that area affordable to a family earning the local median income, based on standard mortgage underwriting criteria. *National Association of Home Builders®, NAHB-Wells Fargo Housing Opportunity Index, 4th Quarter 2015*

Safety Rankings

- The National Insurance Crime Bureau ranked 380 metro areas in the U.S. in terms of per capita rates of vehicle theft. The Detroit* metro area ranked #35 (#1 = highest rate). Criteria: number of vehicle theft offenses per 100,000 inhabitants in 2014. *National Insurance Crime Bureau, "Hot Spots 2014," June 24, 2015*

Seniors/Retirement Rankings

- From its Best Cities for Successful Aging indexes, the Milken Institute generated rankings for metropolitan areas, weighing data in eight categories—health care, wellness, living arrangements, transportation, financial characteristics, education and employment opportunities, community engagement, and overall livability. The Detroit* metro area was ranked #80 overall in the large metro area category. *Milken Institute, "Best Cities for Successful Aging, 2014"*

Sports/Recreation Rankings

- According to the personal finance website NerdWallet, the Detroit* metro area, at #3, is one of the nation's top dozen metro areas for sports fans. Criteria included the presence of all four major sports—MLB, NFL, NHL, and NBA, fan enthusiasm (as measured by game attendance), ticket affordability, and "sports culture," that is, number of sports bars. *www.nerdwallet.com, "Best Cities for Sports Fans," May 5, 2013*

Miscellaneous Rankings

- The watchdog site Charity Navigator conducts an annual study of charities in the nation's major markets both to analyze statistical differences in their financial, accountability, and transparency practices and to track year-to-year variations in individual communities. The Detroit* metro area was ranked #18 among the 30 metro markets in the rating dimension of Overall Score. *www.charitynavigator.org, "Metro Market Study 2015," June 5, 2015*

- Energizer Personal Care, the makers of Edge® shave gel, in partnership with Sperling's BestPlaces, ranked 50 major metro areas in terms of everyday irritations. The Detroit* metro area ranked #7 the 50 metro area most iritating to guys. Criteria: high male-to-female ratio; poor sports team performance and high ticket prices; slow traffic; lack of job availability; unaffordable housing; extreme weather; lack of nightlife and fitness options. *Energizer Personal Care, "Most Irritatng Cities for Guys," August 26, 2013*

- Mars Chocolate North America, the makers of COMBOS®, in partnership with Sperling's BestPlaces, ranked 50 major metro areas in terms of their "manliness." The Detroit* metro area ranked #31. Criteria: number of professional sports teams; number of nearby NASCAR tracks and racing events; manly lifestyle; concentration of manly retail stores; manly occupations per capita; salty snack sales; "Board of Manliness" rankings. *Mars Chocolate North America, "America's Manliest Cities 2012"*

- The Warren* metro area was selected as one of "America's Most Miserable Cities" by *Forbes.com.* The metro area ranked #7 out of 20. Criteria: violent crime; unemployment; foreclosures; income and property taxes; home prices; commute times; climate. *Forbes.com, "America's Most Miserable Cities" February 22, 2013*

- The National Alliance to End Homelessness ranked the 100 most populous metro areas with the highest rate of homelessness. The Detroit* metro area ranked #71. Criteria: number of homeless people per 10,000 population in 2011. *National Alliance to End Homelessness, The State of Homelessness in America 2012*

Novi is located within the Detroit-Warren-Dearborn, MI Metropolitan Statistical Area and the Warren-Troy-Farmington Hills, MI Metropolitan Division.

Business Environment

CITY FINANCES

City Government Finances

Component	2012 ($000)	2012 ($ per capita)
Total Revenues	74,563	1,350
Total Expenditures	69,044	1,250
Debt Outstanding	48,023	869
Cash and Securities[1]	107,113	1,939

Note: (1) Cash and security holdings of a government at the close of its fiscal year, including those of its dependent agencies, utilities, and liquor stores.
Source: U.S Census Bureau, State & Local Government Finances 2012

City Government Revenue by Source

Source	2012 ($000)	2012 ($ per capita)
General Revenue		
From Federal Government	133	2
From State Government	7,455	134
From Local Governments	0	0
Taxes		
Property	30,176	546
Sales and Gross Receipts	0	0
Personal Income	0	0
Corporate Income	0	0
Motor Vehicle License	0	0
Other Taxes	1,482	26
Current Charges	16,142	292
Liquor Store	0	0
Utility	10,438	189
Employee Retirement	0	0

Source: U.S Census Bureau, State & Local Government Finances 2012

City Government Expenditures by Function

Function	2012 ($000)	2012 ($ per capita)	2012 (%)
General Direct Expenditures			
Air Transportation	0	0	0.0
Corrections	0	0	0.0
Education	0	0	0.0
Employment Security Administration	0	0	0.0
Financial Administration	2,466	44	3.5
Fire Protection	4,540	82	6.5
General Public Buildings	688	12	0.9
Governmental Administration, Other	1,432	25	2.0
Health	0	0	0.0
Highways	9,714	175	14.0
Hospitals	0	0	0.0
Housing and Community Development	0	0	0.0
Interest on General Debt	2,337	42	3.3
Judicial and Legal	0	0	0.0
Libraries	2,650	47	3.8
Parking	0	0	0.0
Parks and Recreation	3,978	72	5.7
Police Protection	11,270	204	16.3
Public Welfare	0	0	0.0
Sewerage	9,979	180	14.4
Solid Waste Management	0	0	0.0
Veterans' Services	0	0	0.0
Liquor Store	0	0	0.0
Utility	10,222	185	14.8
Employee Retirement	0	0	0.0

Source: U.S Census Bureau, State & Local Government Finances 2012

DEMOGRAPHICS

Population Growth

Area	1990 Census	2000 Census	2010 Census	2014* Estimate	Population Growth (%) 1990-2014	Population Growth (%) 2010-2014
City	33,103	47,386	55,224	56,887	71.8	3.0
MSA[1]	4,248,699	4,452,557	4,296,250	4,292,647	1.0	-0.1
U.S.	248,709,873	281,421,906	308,745,538	314,107,084	26.3	1.7

Note: (1) Figures cover the Detroit-Warren-Dearborn, MI Metropolitan Statistical Area—see Appendix B for areas included; (*) 2010-2014 5-year estimated population
Source: U.S. Census Bureau, 1990 Census, Census 2000, Census 2010, 2010-2014 American Community Survey 5-Year Estimates

Household Size

Area	Persons in Household (%) One	Two	Three	Four	Five	Six	Seven or More	Average Household Size
City	31.8	29.0	15.0	16.2	5.9	1.3	0.5	2.43
MSA[1]	29.9	31.9	15.6	13.2	5.7	2.2	1.2	2.56
U.S.	27.5	33.5	15.8	13.1	6.0	2.3	1.4	2.64

Note: (1) Figures cover the Detroit-Warren-Dearborn, MI Metropolitan Statistical Area—see Appendix B for areas included
Source: U.S. Census Bureau, 2010-2014 American Community Survey 5-Year Estimates

Race

Area	White Alone[2] (%)	Black Alone[2] (%)	Asian Alone[2] (%)	AIAN[3] Alone[2] (%)	NHOPI[4] Alone[2] (%)	Other Race Alone[2] (%)	Two or More Races (%)
City	71.7	7.4	17.6	0.1	0.0	0.8	2.4
MSA[1]	70.2	22.5	3.6	0.3	0.0	1.1	2.3
U.S.	73.8	12.6	5.0	0.8	0.2	4.7	2.9

Note: (1) Figures cover the Detroit-Warren-Dearborn, MI Metropolitan Statistical Area—see Appendix B for areas included; (2) Alone is defined as not being in combination with one or more other races; (3) American Indian and Alaska Native; (4) Native Hawaiian and Other Pacific Islander
Source: U.S. Census Bureau, 2010-2014 American Community Survey 5-Year Estimates

Hispanic or Latino Origin

Area	Total (%)	Mexican (%)	Puerto Rican (%)	Cuban (%)	Other (%)
City	2.8	1.9	0.2	0.0	0.7
MSA[1]	4.1	2.9	0.5	0.1	0.6
U.S.	16.9	10.8	1.6	0.6	3.8

Note: Persons of Hispanic or Latino origin can be of any race; (1) Figures cover the Detroit-Warren-Dearborn, MI Metropolitan Statistical Area—see Appendix B for areas included
Source: U.S. Census Bureau, 2010-2014 American Community Survey 5-Year Estimates

Ancestry

Area	German	Irish	English	American	Italian	Polish	French[2]	Scottish	Dutch
City	18.2	11.9	8.9	4.7	8.0	9.8	3.1	2.2	1.3
MSA[1]	16.5	10.2	7.3	5.4	6.4	10.6	3.8	2.2	1.3
U.S.	14.9	10.8	8.0	7.1	5.5	3.0	2.7	1.7	1.4

Note: Figures are the percentage of the total population reporting a particular ancestry. The nine most commonly reported ancestries in the U.S. are shown. Figures include multiple ancestries (e.g. if a person reported being Irish and Italian, they were included in both columns); (1) Figures cover the Detroit-Warren-Dearborn, MI Metropolitan Statistical Area—see Appendix B for areas included; (2) Excludes Basque
Source: U.S. Census Bureau, 2010-2014 American Community Survey 5-Year Estimates

Foreign-Born Population

Area	Percent of Population Born in								
	Any Foreign Country	Asia	Mexico	Europe	Carribean	Central America[2]	South America	Africa	Canada
City	18.8	13.5	0.8	2.7	0.1	0.2	0.2	0.2	0.9
MSA[1]	8.9	4.6	0.8	2.2	0.1	0.1	0.1	0.3	0.6
U.S.	13.1	3.8	3.7	1.5	1.2	1.0	0.9	0.6	0.3

Note: (1) Figures cover the Detroit-Warren-Dearborn, MI Metropolitan Statistical Area—see Appendix B for areas included; (2) Excludes Mexico.
Source: U.S. Census Bureau, 2010-2014 American Community Survey 5-Year Estimates

Marital Status

Area	Never Married	Now Married[2]	Separated	Widowed	Divorced
City	26.6	57.0	1.1	5.9	9.3
MSA[1]	33.9	46.6	1.6	6.5	11.4
U.S.	32.5	48.4	2.2	5.9	10.9

Note: Figures are percentages and cover the population 15 years of age and older; (1) Figures cover the Detroit-Warren-Dearborn, MI Metropolitan Statistical Area—see Appendix B for areas included; (2) Excludes separated
Source: U.S. Census Bureau, 2010-2014 American Community Survey 5-Year Estimates

Disability Status

Area	All Ages	Under 18 Years Old	18 to 64 Years Old	65 Years and Over
City	7.3	2.1	5.0	28.4
MSA[1]	13.9	4.8	12.2	37.4
U.S.	12.3	4.1	10.2	36.3

Note: Figures show percent of the civilian noninstitutionalized population that reported having a disability. Disability status is determined from from six types of difficulty: vision, hearing, cognitive, ambulatory, self-care, and independent living. For children under 5 years old, hearing and vision difficulty are used to determine disability status. For children between the ages of 5 and 14, disability status is determined from hearing, vision, cognitive, ambulatory, and self-care difficulties. For people aged 15 years and older, they are considered to have a disability if they have difficulty with any one of the six difficulty types; (1) Figures cover the Detroit-Warren-Dearborn, MI Metropolitan Statistical Area—see Appendix B for areas included.
Source: U.S. Census Bureau, 2010-2014 American Community Survey 5-Year Estimates

Age

Area	Percent of Population									Median Age
	Under Age 5	Age 5–19	Age 20–34	Age 35–44	Age 45–54	Age 55–64	Age 65–74	Age 75–84	Age 85+	
City	5.6	20.8	17.1	15.1	16.1	12.1	5.9	4.3	2.9	39.8
MSA[1]	5.9	20.1	18.3	13.1	15.3	13.3	7.6	4.3	2.0	39.7
U.S.	6.4	19.9	20.6	13.0	14.1	12.3	7.6	4.3	1.9	37.4

Note: (1) Figures cover the Detroit-Warren-Dearborn, MI Metropolitan Statistical Area—see Appendix B for areas included
Source: U.S. Census Bureau, 2010-2014 American Community Survey 5-Year Estimates

Gender

Area	Males	Females	Males per 100 Females
City	27,809	29,078	95.6
MSA[1]	2,081,346	2,211,301	94.1
U.S.	154,515,159	159,591,925	96.8

Note: (1) Figures cover the Detroit-Warren-Dearborn, MI Metropolitan Statistical Area—see Appendix B for areas included
Source: U.S. Census Bureau, 2010-2014 American Community Survey 5-Year Estimates

Religious Groups by Family

Area	Catholic	Baptist	Non-Den.	Methodist[2]	Lutheran	LDS[3]	Pentecostal	Presbyterian[4]	Muslim[5]	Judaism
MSA[1]	21.3	4.5	4.9	2.1	3.1	0.3	1.2	1.3	1.8	0.8
U.S.	19.1	9.3	4.0	4.0	2.3	2.0	1.9	1.6	0.8	0.7

Note: Figures are the number of adherents as a percentage of the total population; (1) Figures cover the Detroit-Warren-Livonia, MI Metropolitan Statistical Area—see Appendix B for areas included; (2) Methodist/Pietist; (3) Latter Day Saints; (4) Reformed; (5) Figures are estimates
Source: Association of Statisticians of American Religious Bodies, 2010 U.S. Religion Census: Religious Congregations & Membership Study

Religious Groups by Tradition

Area	Catholic	Evangelical Protestant	Mainline Protestant	Other Tradition	Black Protestant	Orthodox
MSA[1]	21.3	10.6	4.7	3.5	3.3	0.9
U.S.	19.1	16.2	7.3	4.3	1.6	0.3

Note: Figures are the number of adherents as a percentage of the total population; (1) Figures cover the Detroit-Warren-Livonia, MI Metropolitan Statistical Area—see Appendix B for areas included
Source: Association of Statisticians of American Religious Bodies, 2010 U.S. Religion Census: Religious Congregations & Membership Study

ECONOMY

Gross Metropolitan Product

Area	2013	2014	2015	2016	Rank[2]
MSA[1]	224.7	231.1	239.2	248.9	14

Note: Figures are in billions of dollars; (1) Figures cover the Detroit-Warren-Dearborn, MI Metropolitan Statistical Area—see Appendix B for areas included; (2) Rank is based on 2016 data and ranges from 1 to 381
Source: The U.S. Conference of Mayors, U.S. Metro Economies: GMP and Employment 2014-2016, June 2015

Economic Growth

Area	2011-13 (%)	2014 (%)	2015 (%)	2016 (%)	Rank[2]
MSA[1]	1.7	1.2	2.1	2.2	236
U.S.	2.2	2.4	2.3	2.9	–

Note: Figures are real gross metropolitan product (GMP) growth rates and represent annual average percent change; (1) Figures cover the Detroit-Warren-Dearborn, MI Metropolitan Statistical Area—see Appendix B for areas included; (2) Rank is based on 2016 data and ranges from 1 to 381
Source: The U.S. Conference of Mayors, U.S. Metro Economies: GMP and Employment 2014-2016, June 2015

Metropolitan Area Exports

Area	2009	2010	2011	2012	2013	2014	Rank[2]
MSA[1]	28,405.1	43,964.7	49,422.7	55,387.3	53,906.4	50,279.3	5

Note: Figures are in millions of dollars; (1) Figures cover the Detroit-Warren-Dearborn, MI Metropolitan Statistical Area—see Appendix B for areas included; (2) Rank is based on 2014 data and ranges from 1 to 385
Source: U.S. Department of Commerce, International Trade Administration, Office of Trade & Industry Information, Manufacturing & Services, data extracted March 10, 2016

Building Permits

Area	Single-Family			Multi-Family			Total		
	2014	2015p	Pct. Chg.	2014	2015p	Pct. Chg.	2014	2015p	Pct. Chg.
City	198	173	-12.6	5	116	2,220.0	203	289	42.4
MSA[1]	4,830	5,197	7.6	1,465	2,020	37.9	6,295	7,217	14.6
U.S.	640,300	690,800	7.9	411,800	487,600	18.4	1,052,100	1,178,400	12.0

Note: (1) Figures cover the Detroit-Warren-Dearborn, MI Metropolitan Statistical Area—see Appendix B for areas included; Figures represent new, privately-owned housing units authorized (unadjusted data); All permit data are based on estimates with imputation; (p) preliminary data.
Source: U.S. Census Bureau, Manufacturing, Mining, and Construction Statistics, Building Permits, 2014, 2015

Bankruptcy Filings

Area	Business Filings			Nonbusiness Filings		
	2014	2015	% Chg.	2014	2015	% Chg.
Oakland County	162	163	0.6	4,091	3,721	-9.0
U.S.	26,983	24,735	-8.3	909,812	819,760	-9.9

Note: Business filings include Chapter 7, Chapter 11, Chapter 12, and Chapter 13; Nonbusiness filings include Chapter 7, Chapter 11, and Chapter 13
Source: Administrative Office of the U.S. Courts, Business and Nonbusiness Bankruptcy, County Cases Commenced by Chapter of the Bankruptcy Code, During the 12- Month Period Ending December 31, 2014 and Business and Nonbusiness Bankruptcy, County Cases Commenced by Chapter of the Bankruptcy Code, During the 12- Month Period Ending December 31, 2015

Housing Vacancy Rates

Area	Gross Vacancy Rate[2] (%)			Year-Round Vacancy Rate[3] (%)			Rental Vacancy Rate[4] (%)			Homeowner Vacancy Rate[5] (%)		
	2013	2014	2015	2013	2014	2015	2013	2014	2015	2013	2014	2015
MSA[1]	11.6	11.1	9.7	11.4	10.7	9.5	12.1	9.5	6.8	1.7	1.2	1.1
U.S.	13.6	13.4	12.9	10.7	10.4	10.0	8.3	7.6	7.1	2.0	1.9	1.8

Note: (1) Figures cover the Detroit-Warren-Dearborn, MI Metropolitan Statistical Area—see Appendix B for areas included; (2) The percentage of the total housing inventory that is vacant; (3) The percentage of the housing inventory (excluding seasonal units) that is year-round vacant; (4) The percentage of rental inventory that is vacant for rent; (5) The percentage of homeowner inventory that is vacant for sale
Source: U.S. Census Bureau, Housing Vacancies and Homeownership Annual Statistics: 2015

INCOME

Income

Area	Per Capita ($)	Median Household ($)	Average Household ($)
City	44,800	80,299	109,602
MSA[1]	28,182	52,305	71,184
U.S.	28,555	53,482	74,596

Note: (1) Figures cover the Detroit-Warren-Dearborn, MI Metropolitan Statistical Area—see Appendix B for areas included
Source: U.S. Census Bureau, 2010-2014 American Community Survey 5-Year Estimates

Household Income Distribution

Area	Percent of Households Earning							
	Under $15,000	$15,000 -24,999	$25,000 -34,999	$35,000 -49,999	$50,000 -74,999	$75,000 -99,000	$100,000 -149,999	$150,000 and up
City	6.0	5.5	7.2	10.8	17.7	11.9	17.6	23.3
MSA[1]	13.7	10.8	10.1	13.4	17.5	12.2	13.1	9.2
U.S.	12.5	10.7	10.2	13.5	17.8	12.2	13.0	10.0

Note: (1) Figures cover the Detroit-Warren-Dearborn, MI Metropolitan Statistical Area—see Appendix B for areas included
Source: U.S. Census Bureau, 2010-2014 American Community Survey 5-Year Estimates

Poverty Rate

Area	All Ages	Under 18 Years Old	18 to 64 Years Old	65 Years and Over
City	6.4	8.5	6.1	4.3
MSA[1]	16.9	24.6	15.7	9.1
U.S.	15.6	21.9	14.6	9.4

Note: Figures are percentage of people whose income during the past 12 months was below the poverty level; (1) Figures cover the Detroit-Warren-Dearborn, MI Metropolitan Statistical Area—see Appendix B for areas included
Source: U.S. Census Bureau, 2010-2014 American Community Survey 5-Year Estimates

EMPLOYMENT

Labor Force and Employment

Area	Civilian Labor Force			Workers Employed		
	Dec. 2014	Dec. 2015	% Chg.	Dec. 2014	Dec. 2015	% Chg.
City	30,485	30,755	0.8	29,427	29,888	1.5
MD[1]	1,245,341	1,252,111	0.5	1,173,548	1,191,493	1.5
U.S.	155,521,000	157,245,000	1.1	147,190,000	149,703,000	1.7

Note: Data is not seasonally adjusted and covers workers 16 years of age and older; (1) Figures cover the Warren-Troy-Farmington Hills, MI Metropolitan Division—see Appendix B for areas included
Source: Bureau of Labor Statistics, Local Area Unemployment Statistics

Unemployment Rate

Area	2015											
	Jan.	Feb.	Mar.	Apr.	May	Jun.	Jul.	Aug.	Sep.	Oct.	Nov.	Dec.
City	3.9	3.4	3.3	2.7	3.7	3.6	3.9	3.4	3.1	3.4	2.8	2.8
MD[1]	6.7	5.7	5.5	4.5	5.9	5.9	6.3	5.5	5.0	5.5	4.6	4.8
U.S.	6.1	5.8	5.6	5.1	5.3	5.5	5.6	5.2	4.9	4.8	4.8	4.8

Note: Data is not seasonally adjusted and covers workers 16 years of age and older; (1) Figures cover the Warren-Troy-Farmington Hills, MI Metropolitan Division—see Appendix B for areas included
Source: Bureau of Labor Statistics, Local Area Unemployment Statistics

Employment by Occupation

Occupation Classification	City (%)	MSA[1] (%)	U.S. (%)
Management, Business, Science, and Arts	54.4	37.1	36.4
Natural Resources, Construction, and Maintenance	2.6	6.7	9.0
Production, Transportation, and Material Moving	6.3	13.6	12.1
Sales and Office	25.3	24.7	24.4
Service	11.4	17.8	18.2

Note: Figures cover employed civilians 16 years of age and older; (1) Figures cover the Detroit-Warren-Dearborn, MI Metropolitan Statistical Area—see Appendix B for areas included
Source: U.S. Census Bureau, 2010-2014 American Community Survey 5-Year Estimates

Employment by Industry

Sector	MD[1]		U.S.
	Number of Employees	Percent of Total	Percent of Total
Construction, Mining, and Logging	44,600	3.6	5.0
Education and Health Services	175,700	14.4	15.7
Financial Activities	74,800	6.1	5.7
Government	98,500	8.0	15.5
Information	20,100	1.6	1.9
Leisure and Hospitality	114,500	9.3	10.4
Manufacturing	149,200	12.2	8.6
Other Services	48,600	3.9	3.9
Professional and Business Services	267,200	21.9	13.9
Retail Trade	143,100	11.7	11.3
Transportation, Warehousing, and Utilities	25,500	2.0	3.9
Wholesale Trade	57,200	4.6	4.1

Note: Figures are non-farm employment as of December 2015. Figures are not seasonally adjusted and include workers 16 years of age and older; (1) Figures cover the Warren-Troy-Farmington Hills, MI Metropolitan Division—see Appendix B for areas included; n/a not available
Source: Bureau of Labor Statistics, Current Employment Statistics, Employment, Hours, and Earnings

Occupations with Greatest Projected Employment Growth: 2010 – 2020

Occupation[1]	2010 Employment	2020 Projected Employment	Numeric Employment Change	Percent Employment Change
Home Health Aides	35,400	54,310	18,910	53.4
Registered Nurses	87,170	104,000	16,820	19.3
Office Clerks, General	112,620	123,920	11,300	10.0
Retail Salespersons	127,580	137,710	10,140	8.0
Combined Food Preparation and Serving Workers, Including Fast Food	70,020	78,610	8,590	12.3
Nursing Aides, Orderlies, and Attendants	50,400	57,320	6,920	13.7
Personal Care Aides	14,720	20,900	6,180	42.0
Landscaping and Groundskeeping Workers	28,350	34,370	6,020	21.2
Customer Service Representatives	61,310	67,240	5,930	9.7
Heavy and Tractor-Trailer Truck Drivers	48,610	54,070	5,460	11.2

Note: Projections cover Michigan; (1) Sorted by numeric employment change
Source: www.projectionscentral.com, State Occupational Projections, 2010–2020 Long-Term Projections

Fastest Growing Occupations: 2010 – 2020

Occupation[1]	2010 Employment	2020 Projected Employment	Numeric Employment Change	Percent Employment Change
Biomedical Engineers	200	310	110	54.0
Home Health Aides	35,400	54,310	18,910	53.4
Personal Care Aides	14,720	20,900	6,180	42.0
Veterinary Technologists and Technicians	1,810	2,570	760	42.0
Meeting, Convention, and Event Planners	1,540	2,140	600	39.1
Market Research Analysts and Marketing Specialists	6,920	9,500	2,590	37.4
Software Developers, Systems Software	6,550	8,960	2,420	36.9
Marriage and Family Therapists	300	400	110	36.6
Helpers—Carpenters	300	410	110	36.5
Bicycle Repairers	570	770	200	36.0

Note: Projections cover Michigan; (1) Sorted by percent employment change and excludes occupations with numeric employment change less than 100
Source: www.projectionscentral.com, State Occupational Projections, 2010–2020 Long-Term Projections

TAXES

Average Wages

Occupation	$/Hr.	Occupation	$/Hr.
Accountants and Auditors	38.84	Maids and Housekeeping Cleaners	11.00
Automotive Mechanics	20.93	Maintenance and Repair Workers	17.36
Bookkeepers	18.98	Marketing Managers	58.43
Carpenters	23.50	Nuclear Medicine Technologists	33.31
Cashiers	10.66	Nurses, Licensed Practical	23.80
Clerks, General Office	15.98	Nurses, Registered	37.09
Clerks, Receptionists/Information	13.16	Nursing Assistants	13.69
Clerks, Shipping/Receiving	16.11	Packers and Packagers, Hand	13.40
Computer Programmers	35.12	Physical Therapists	44.15
Computer Systems Analysts	41.45	Postal Service Mail Carriers	25.14
Computer User Support Specialists	25.16	Real Estate Brokers	30.04
Cooks, Restaurant	11.58	Retail Salespersons	12.66
Dentists	77.55	Sales Reps., Exc. Tech./Scientific	32.88
Electrical Engineers	41.86	Sales Reps., Tech./Scientific	43.24
Electricians	31.88	Secretaries, Exc. Legal/Med./Exec.	16.88
Financial Managers	60.90	Security Guards	12.90
First-Line Supervisors/Managers, Sales	22.50	Surgeons	121.74
Food Preparation Workers	11.79	Teacher Assistants*	13.01
General and Operations Managers	57.93	Teachers, Elementary School*	32.81
Hairdressers/Cosmetologists	13.62	Teachers, Secondary School*	30.56
Internists	90.64	Telemarketers	14.67
Janitors and Cleaners	12.22	Truck Drivers, Heavy/Tractor-Trailer	20.22
Landscaping/Groundskeeping Workers	13.36	Truck Drivers, Light/Delivery Svcs.	15.80
Lawyers	57.37	Waiters and Waitresses	10.50

Note: Wage data covers the Metropolitan Division—see Appendix B for areas included; (*) Hourly wages for elementary/secondary school teachers and teacher assistants were calculated by the editors from annual wage data based on a 40 hour work week; n/a not available.
Source: Bureau of Labor Statistics, Metro Area Occupational Employment and Wage Estimates, May 2015

State Corporate Income Tax Rates

State	Tax Rate (%)	Income Brackets ($)	Num. of Brackets	Financial Institution Tax Rate (%)[a]	Federal Income Tax Ded.
Michigan	6.0	Flat rate	1	(a)	No

Note: Tax rates as of January 1, 2016; (a) Rates listed are the corporate income tax rate applied to financial institutions or excise taxes based on income. Some states have other taxes based upon the value of deposits or shares.
Source: Federation of Tax Administrators, "State Corporate Income Tax Rates, 2016"

State Individual Income Tax Rates

State	Tax Rate (%)	Income Brackets ($)	Num. of Brackets	Personal Exempt. ($)[1]		Fed. Inc. Tax Ded.
				Single	Dependents	
Michigan (a)	4.25	Flat rate	1	3,950	3,950	No

Note: Tax rates as of January 1, 2016; Local- and county-level taxes are not included; n/a not applicable; (1) Married joint filers generally receive double the single exemption; (a) 18 states have statutory provision for automatically adjusting to the rate of inflation the dollar values of the income tax brackets, standard deductions, and/or personal exemptions. Massachusetts, Michigan, and Nebraska index the personal exemptiononly. Oregon does not index the income brackets for $125,000 and over. Maine has suspended indexing for 2014 and 2015.
Source: Federation of Tax Administrators, "State Individual Income Tax Rates, 2016"

Various State and Local Tax Rates

State	State and Local Sales and Use (%)	State Sales and Use (%)	Gasoline[1] (¢/gal.)	Cigarette[2] ($/pack)	Spirits[3] ($/gal.)	Wine[4] ($/gal.)	Beer[5] ($/gal.)
Michigan	6.00	6.0	30.54	2.00	11.94 (g)	0.51 (l)	0.20

Note: All tax rates as of January 1, 2016; (1) The American Petroleum Institute has developed a methodology for determining the average tax rate on a gallon of fuel. Rates may include any of the following: excise taxes, environmental fees, storage tank fees, other fees or taxes, general sales tax, and local taxes. In states where gasoline is subject to the general sales tax, or where the fuel tax is based on the average sale price, the average rate determined by API is sensitive to changes in the price of gasoline. States that fully or partially apply general sales taxes to gasoline: CA, CO, GA, IL, IN, MI, NY; (2) The federal excise tax of $1.0066 per pack and local taxes are not included; (3) Rates are those applicable to off-premise sales of 40% alcohol by volume (a.b.v.) distilled spirits in 750ml containers. Local excise taxes are excluded; (4) Rates are those applicable to off-premise sales of 11% a.b.v. non-carbonated wine in 750ml containers; (5) Rates are those applicable to off-premise sales of 4.7% a.b.v. beer in 12 ounce containers; (g) Control states, where the government controls all sales. Products can be subject to ad valorem mark-up as well as excise taxes; (l) Different rates also applicable according to alcohol content, place of production, size of container, place purchased (on- or off-premise or on board airlines) or type of wine (carbonated, vermouth, etc.).
Source: Tax Foundation, 2016 Facts & Figures: How Does Your State Compare?

State Business Tax Climate Index Rankings

State	Overall Rank	Corporate Tax Rank	Individual Income Tax Rank	Sales Tax Rank	Unemployment Insurance Tax Rank	Property Tax Rank
Michigan	13	11	15	7	48	26

Note: The index is a measure of how each state's tax laws affect economic performance. The lower the rank, the more favorable a state's tax system is for business. States without a given tax are given a ranking of 1. The scores/rankings for the District of Columbia do not affect other states. The 2016 index represents the tax climate as of July 1, 2015 (the beginning of Fiscal Year 2016).
Source: Tax Foundation, State Business Tax Climate Index 2016

TRANSPORTATION

Means of Transportation to Work

Area	Car/Truck/Van		Public Transportation			Bicycle	Walked	Other Means	Worked at Home
	Drove Alone	Car-pooled	Bus	Subway	Railroad				
City	89.2	6.0	0.3	0.1	0.0	0.2	0.4	0.5	3.4
MSA[1]	84.1	8.7	1.6	0.0	0.0	0.2	1.3	0.8	3.2
U.S.	76.4	9.6	2.6	1.8	0.6	0.6	2.8	1.3	4.4

Note: Figures are percentages and cover workers 16 years of age and older; (1) Figures cover the Detroit-Warren-Dearborn, MI Metropolitan Statistical Area—see Appendix B for areas included
Source: U.S. Census Bureau, 2010-2014 American Community Survey 5-Year Estimates

Travel Time to Work

Area	Less Than 10 Minutes	10 to 19 Minutes	20 to 29 Minutes	30 to 44 Minutes	45 to 59 Minutes	60 to 89 Minutes	90 Minutes or More
City	10.0	24.8	21.7	27.3	11.4	4.1	0.6
MSA[1]	10.0	26.9	23.1	24.2	9.0	5.0	1.8
U.S.	13.3	29.6	21.0	20.2	7.7	5.7	2.6

Note: Figures are percentages and include workers 16 years old and over; (1) Figures cover the Detroit-Warren-Dearborn, MI Metropolitan Statistical Area—see Appendix B for areas included
Source: U.S. Census Bureau, 2010-2014 American Community Survey 5-Year Estimates

Freeway Travel Time Index

Area	1985	1990	1995	2000	2005	2010	2014
Urban Area Rank[1,2]	9	9	10	19	24	29	25
Urban Area Index[1]	1.17	1.20	1.23	1.24	1.25	1.22	1.24
Average Index[3]	1.09	1.11	1.14	1.17	1.20	1.19	1.20

Note: Freeway Travel Time Index—the ratio of travel time in the peak period to the travel time at free-flow conditions. For example, a value of 1.30 indicates a 20-minute free-flow trip takes 26 minutes in the peak (20 minutes x 1.30 = 26 minutes); (1) Covers the Detroit MI urban area; (2) Rank is based on 101 urban areas (#1 = highest travel time index); (3) Average of 101 urban areas
Source: Texas Transportation Institute, 2015 Urban Mobility Scorecard, August 2015

Freeway Commuter Stress Index

Area	1985	1990	1995	2000	2005	2010	2014
Urban Area Rank[1,2]	22	22	24	27	35	37	33
Urban Area Index[1]	1.19	1.22	1.25	1.27	1.27	1.25	1.27
Average Index[3]	1.13	1.16	1.19	1.22	1.25	1.24	1.25

Note: The Freeway Commuter Stress Index is the same as the Freeway Travel Time Index (see table above) except that it includes only the travel in the peak directions during the peak periods; the TTI includes travel in all directions during the peak period. Thus, the CSI is more indicative of the work trip experienced by each commuter on a daily basis. (1) Covers the Detroit MI urban area; (2) Rank is based on 101 urban areas (#1 = highest stress index); (3) Average of 101 urban areas

Source: Texas Transportation Institute, 2015 Urban Mobility Scorecard, August 2015

Living Environment

COST OF LIVING

Cost of Living Index

Composite Index	Groceries	Housing	Utilities	Trans-portation	Health Care	Misc. Goods/ Services
95.4	88.8	91.1	104.5	104.8	96.4	95.5

Note: The Cost of Living Index measures regional differences in the cost of consumer goods and services, excluding taxes and non-consumer expenditures, for professional and managerial households in the top income quintile. It is based on more than 50,000 prices covering almost 60 different items for which prices are collected three times a year by chambers of commerce, economic development organizations or university applied economic centers in each participating urban area. The numbers shown should be read as a percentage above or below the national average of 100. For example, a value of 115.4 in the groceries column indicates that grocery prices are 15.4% higher than the national average. Small differences in the index numbers should not be interpreted as significant; Figures cover the Detroit MI urban area.
Source: The Council for Community and Economic Research, ACCRA Cost of Living Index, 2015

Grocery Prices

Area[1]	T-Bone Steak ($/pound)	Frying Chicken ($/pound)	Whole Milk ($/half gal.)	Eggs ($/dozen)	Orange Juice ($/64 oz.)	Coffee ($/11.5 oz.)
City[2]	10.81	1.20	1.85	1.98	3.00	4.06
Avg.	10.99	1.43	2.25	2.26	3.58	4.48
Min.	7.16	0.98	1.30	1.35	2.88	2.98
Max.	14.13	2.43	3.85	4.81	6.39	7.56

Note: (1) Values for the local area are compared with the average, minimum and maximum values for all 292 areas in the Cost of Living Index; (2) Figures cover the Detroit MI urban area; **T-Bone Steak** *(price per pound);* **Frying Chicken** *(price per pound, whole fryer);* **Whole Milk** *(half gallon carton);* **Eggs** *(price per dozen, Grade A, large);* **Orange Juice** *(64 oz. Tropicana or Florida Natural);* **Coffee** *(11.5 oz. can, vacuum-packed, Maxwell House, Hills Bros, or Folgers).*
Source: The Council for Community and Economic Research, ACCRA Cost of Living Index, 2015

Housing and Utility Costs

Area[1]	New Home Price ($)	Apartment Rent ($/month)	All Electric ($/month)	Part Electric ($/month)	Other Energy ($/month)	Telephone ($/month)
City[2]	269,215	955	-	108.88	66.14	30.00
Avg.	312,874	945	179.30	95.07	72.96	28.11
Min.	178,682	479	116.28	43.14	26.46	10.01
Max.	1,472,476	3,984	504.25	189.44	421.11	43.06

Note: (1) Values for the local area are compared with the average, minimum and maximum values for all 292 areas in the Cost of Living Index; (2) Figures cover the Detroit MI urban area; **New Home Price** *(2,400 sf living area, 8,000 sf lot, in urban area with full utilities);* **Apartment Rent** *(950 sf 2 bedroom/1.5 or 2 bath, unfurnished, excluding all utilities except water);* **All Electric** *(average monthly cost for an all-electric home);* **Part Electric** *(average monthly cost for a part-electric home);* **Other Energy** *(average monthly cost for natural gas, fuel oil, coal, wood, and any other forms of energy except electricity);* **Telephone** *(price includes basic monthly rate for a private residential line plus additional local usage charges incurred by a family of four).*
Source: The Council for Community and Economic Research, ACCRA Cost of Living Index, 2015

Health Care, Transportation, and Other Costs

Area[1]	Doctor ($/visit)	Dentist ($/visit)	Optometrist ($/visit)	Gasoline ($/gallon)	Beauty Salon ($/visit)	Men's Shirt ($)
City[2]	100.13	86.47	79.43	2.44	47.83	21.95
Avg.	105.15	89.02	99.78	2.38	35.30	28.10
Min.	66.87	56.09	48.53	1.95	18.91	13.38
Max.	182.34	150.36	228.33	4.09	67.91	63.80

Note: (1) Values for the local area are compared with the average, minimum and maximum values for all 292 areas in the Cost of Living Index; (2) Figures cover the Detroit MI urban area; **Doctor** *(general practitioners routine exam of an established patient);* **Dentist** *(adult teeth cleaning and periodic oral examination);* **Optometrist** *(full vision eye exam for established adult patient);* **Gasoline** *(one gallon regular unleaded, national brand, including all taxes, cash price at self-service pump if available);* **Beauty Salon** *(woman's shampoo, trim, and blow-dry);* **Men's Shirt** *(cotton/polyester dress shirt, pinpoint weave, long sleeves).*
Source: The Council for Community and Economic Research, ACCRA Cost of Living Index, 2015

HOUSING

House Price Index (HPI)

Area	National Ranking[2]	Quarterly Change (%)	One-Year Change (%)	Five-Year Change (%)
MD[1]	107	-0.20	5.30	33.30
U.S.[3]	–	1.45	5.76	22.85

Note: The HPI is a weighted repeat sales index. It measures average price changes in repeat sales or refinancings on the same properties. This information is obtained by reviewing repeat mortgage transactions on single-family properties whose mortgages have been purchased or securitized by Fannie Mae or Freddie Mac in January 1975; (1) Warren-Troy-Farmington Hills Metropolitan Division—see Appendix B for areas included; (2) Rankings are based on annual percentage change for all metro areas containing at least 15,000 transactions over the last 10 years and ranges from 1 to 266; (3) figures based on a weighted average of Census Division estimates using a seasonally adjusted, purchase-only index; all figures are for the period ending December 31, 2015

Source: Federal Housing Finance Agency, House Price Index, February 25, 2016

Median Single-Family Home Prices

Area	2013	2014	2015p	Percent Change 2014 to 2015
MSA[1]	n/a	n/a	n/a	n/a
U.S. Average	197.4	208.9	223.9	7.2

Note: Figures are median sales prices of existing single-family homes in thousands of dollars; (p) preliminary; n/a not available; (1) Detroit-Warren-Dearborn, MI Metropolitan Statistical Area—see Appendix B for areas included

Source: National Association of Realtors, Median Sales Price of Existing Single-Family Homes for Metropolitan Areas, 4th Quarter 2015

Qualifying Income Based on Median Sales Price of Existing Single-Family Homes

Area	With 5% Down ($)	With 10% Down ($)	With 20% Down ($)
MSA[1]	n/a	n/a	n/a
U.S. Average	49,535	46,928	41,714

Note: Figures are preliminary; Qualifying income is based on a mortgage rate of 4.1%. Monthly principal and interest payment is limited to 25% of income; n/a not available; (1) Detroit-Warren-Dearborn, MI Metropolitan Statistical Area—see Appendix B for areas included

Source: National Association of Realtors, Qualifying Income Based on Median Sales Price of Existing Single-Family Homes for Metropolitan Areas, 4th Quarter 2015

Median Apartment Condo-Coop Home Prices

Area	2013	2014	2015p	Percent Change 2014 to 2015
MSA[1]	n/a	n/a	n/a	n/a
U.S. Average	194.9	204.3	210.7	3.1

Note: Figures are median sales prices of existing apartment condo-coop homes in thousands of dollars; (p) preliminary; n/a not available; (1) Detroit-Warren-Dearborn, MI Metropolitan Statistical Area—see Appendix B for areas included

Source: National Association of Realtors, Median Sales Price of Existing Apartment Condo-Coop Homes for Metropolitan Areas, 4th Quarter 2015

Gross Monthly Rent

Area	Under $200	$200 -299	$300 -499	$500 -749	$750 -999	$1,000 -1,499	$1,500 and up	Median ($)
City	0.0	0.0	1.7	13.1	31.8	26.3	27.1	1,053
MSA[1]	1.7	3.4	7.0	26.0	28.5	25.6	7.7	846
U.S.	1.5	3.2	7.4	21.0	24.1	26.9	15.9	920

Note: Figures are percentages except for Median; Gross rent is the contract rent plus the estimated average monthly cost of utilities (electricity, gas, and water and sewer) and fuels (oil, coal, kerosene, wood, etc.) if these are paid by the renter (or paid for the renter by someone else); (1) Figures cover the Detroit-Warren-Dearborn, MI Metropolitan Statistical Area—see Appendix B for areas included

Source: U.S. Census Bureau, 2010-2014 American Community Survey 5-Year Estimates

Homeownership Rate

Area	2008 (%)	2009 (%)	2010 (%)	2011 (%)	2012 (%)	2013 (%)	2014 (%)	2015 (%)
MSA[1]	75.5	73.9	73.6	73.5	73.4	71.7	71.2	74.0
U.S.	67.8	67.4	66.9	66.1	65.4	65.1	64.5	63.7

Note: (1) Figures cover the Detroit-Warren-Dearborn, MI Metropolitan Statistical Area—see Appendix B for areas included
Source: U.S. Census Bureau, Housing Vacancies and Homeownership Annual Statistics: 2015

Year Housing Structure Built

Area	2010 or Later	2000 -2009	1990 -1999	1980 -1989	1970 -1979	1960 -1969	1950 -1959	1940 -1949	Before 1940	Median Year
City	1.3	22.0	25.4	19.8	20.6	4.7	3.9	0.3	2.0	1989
MSA[1]	0.3	8.8	11.1	9.0	14.4	12.7	19.8	10.6	13.3	1965
U.S.	1.0	14.9	13.9	13.8	15.8	11.0	10.8	5.4	13.3	1976

Note: Figures are percentages except for Median Year; (1) Figures cover the Detroit-Warren-Dearborn, MI Metropolitan Statistical Area—see Appendix B for areas included
Source: U.S. Census Bureau, 2010-2014 American Community Survey 5-Year Estimates

HEALTH

Health Risk Data

Category	MSA[1] (%)	U.S. (%)
Adults aged 18–64 who have any kind of health care coverage	n/a	79.6
Adults who reported being in good or excellent health	n/a	83.1
Adults who are current smokers	n/a	19.6
Adults who are heavy drinkers[2]	n/a	6.1
Adults who are binge drinkers[3]	n/a	16.9
Adults who are overweight (BMI 25.0 - 29.9)	n/a	35.8
Adults who are obese (BMI 30.0 - 99.8)	n/a	27.6
Adults who participated in any physical activities in the past month	n/a	77.1
Adults 50+ who have ever had a sigmoidoscopy or colonoscopy	n/a	67.3
Women aged 40+ who have had a mammogram within the past two years	n/a	74.0
Men aged 40+ who have had a PSA test within the past two years	n/a	45.2
Adults aged 65+ who have had flu shot within the past year	n/a	60.1
Adults who always wear a seatbelt	n/a	93.8

Note: Data as of 2012 unless otherwise noted; n/a not available; (1) Figures cover the Detroit-Warren-Dearborn, MI Metropolitan Statistical Area—see Appendix B for areas included; (2) Heavy drinkers are classified as males having more than two drinks per day or females having more than one drink per day; (3) Binge drinkers are classified as males having five or more drinks on one occasion or females having four or more drinks on one occasion
Source: Centers for Disease Control and Prevention, Behaviorial Risk Factor Surveillance System, SMART: Selected Metropolitan/Micropolitan Area Risk Trends, 2012 (Note: the CDC has discontinued this dataset but will be releasing a replacement in mid-2016)

Chronic Health Indicators

Category	MSA[1] (%)	U.S. (%)
Adults who have ever been told they had a heart attack	n/a	4.5
Adults who have ever been told they had a stroke	n/a	2.9
Adults who have been told they currently have asthma	n/a	8.9
Adults who have ever been told they have arthritis	n/a	25.7
Adults who have ever been told they have diabetes[2]	n/a	9.7
Adults who have ever been told they had skin cancer	n/a	5.7
Adults who have ever been told they had any other types of cancer	n/a	6.5
Adults who have ever been told they have COPD	n/a	6.2
Adults who have ever been told they have kidney disease	n/a	2.5
Adults who have ever been told they have a form of depression	n/a	18.0

Note: Data as of 2012 unless otherwise noted; n/a not available; (1) Figures cover the Detroit-Warren-Dearborn, MI Metropolitan Statistical Area—see Appendix B for areas included; (2) Figures do not include pregnancy-related, borderline, or pre-diabetes
Source: Centers for Disease Control and Prevention, Behaviorial Risk Factor Surveillance System, SMART: Selected Metropolitan/Micropolitan Area Risk Trends, 2012 (Note: the CDC has discontinued this dataset but will be releasing a replacement in mid-2016)

Mortality Rates for the Top 10 Causes of Death in the U.S.

ICD-10[a] Sub-Chapter	ICD-10[a] Code	Age-Adjusted Mortality Rate[1] per 100,000 population	
		County[2]	U.S.
Malignant neoplasms	C00-C97	154.2	163.6
Ischaemic heart diseases	I20-I25	116.4	102.2
Other forms of heart disease	I30-I51	47.6	50.1
Chronic lower respiratory diseases	J40-J47	35.7	41.4
Organic, including symptomatic, mental disorders	F01-F09	34.3	38.5
Cerebrovascular diseases	I60-I69	35.3	36.5
Other external causes of accidental injury	W00-X59	18.4	27.5
Other degenerative diseases of the nervous system	G30-G31	24.5	26.3
Diabetes mellitus	E10-E14	18.9	21.1
Hypertensive diseases	I10-I15	17.3	19.7

Note: (a) ICD-10 = International Classification of Diseases 10th Revision; (1) Mortality rates are a three year average covering 2012-2014; (2) Figures cover Oakland County.
Source: Centers for Disease Control and Prevention, National Center for Health Statistics. Underlying Cause of Death 1999-2014 on CDC WONDER Online Database, released 2015.

Mortality Rates for Selected Causes of Death

ICD-10[a] Sub-Chapter	ICD-10[a] Code	Age-Adjusted Mortality Rate[1] per 100,000 population	
		County[2]	U.S.
Assault	X85-Y09	3.3	5.1
Diseases of the liver	K70-K76	11.7	13.5
Human immunodeficiency virus (HIV) disease	B20-B24	0.9	2.1
Influenza and pneumonia	J09-J18	12.4	15.2
Intentional self-harm	X60-X84	12.8	12.7
Malnutrition	E40-E46	1.4	0.9
Obesity and other hyperalimentation	E65-E68	1.0	1.9
Renal failure	N17-N19	12.3	13.0
Transport accidents	V01-V99	6.6	11.6
Viral hepatitis	B15-B19	1.2	2.1

Note: (a) ICD-10 = International Classification of Diseases 10th Revision; (1) Mortality rates are a three year average covering 2012-2014; (2) Figures cover Oakland County; Data are Suppressed when the data meet the criteria for confidentiality constraints; Mortality rates are flagged as Unreliable when the rate would be calculated with a numerator of 20 or less.
Source: Centers for Disease Control and Prevention, National Center for Health Statistics. Underlying Cause of Death 1999-2014 on CDC WONDER Online Database, released 2015.

Health Insurance Coverage

Area	With Health Insurance	With Private Health Insurance	With Public Health Insurance	Without Health Insurance	Population Under Age 18 Without Health Insurance
City	93.3	85.4	19.9	6.7	1.9
MSA[1]	88.5	68.7	33.3	11.5	3.9
U.S.	85.8	65.8	31.1	14.2	7.1

Note: Figures are percentages that cover the civilian noninstitutionalized population; (1) Figures cover the Detroit-Warren-Dearborn, MI Metropolitan Statistical Area—see Appendix B for areas included
Source: U.S. Census Bureau, 2010-2014 American Community Survey 5-Year Estimates

Number of Medical Professionals

Area	MDs[3]	DOs[3,4]	Dentists	Podiatrists	Chiropractors	Optometrists
County[1] (number)	6,664	1,292	1,262	217	383	221
County[1] (rate[2])	541.0	104.9	101.9	17.5	30.9	17.9
U.S. (rate[2])	272.5	20.9	64.7	5.8	25.9	15.2

Note: Data as of 2014 unless noted; (1) Data covers Oakland County; (2) Rate per 100,000 population; (3) Data as of 2013 and includes all active, non-federal physicians; (4) Doctor of Osteopathic Medicine
Source: U.S. Department of Health and Human Services, Health Resources and Services Administration, Bureau of Health Professions, Area Resource File (ARF) 2014-2015

Best Hospitals

According to *U.S. News*, the Warren-Troy-Farmington Hills, MI metro area is home to two of the best hospitals in the U.S.: **Beaumont Hospital** (9 specialties); **Beaumont Hospital** (3 specialties). The hospitals listed were nationally ranked in at least one adult specialty. Only 137 hospitals nationwide were nationally ranked in one or more specialties. Fifteen hospitals in the U.S. made the Honor Roll with high scores in at least six specialties. *U.S. News Online, "America's Best Children's Hospitals 2015-16"*

EDUCATION

Public School District Statistics

District Name	Schls	Pupils	Pupil/ Teacher Ratio	Minority Pupils[1] (%)	Free Lunch Eligible[2] (%)	IEP[3] (%)
Novi Community School District	10	6,345	16.0	47.8	6.4	8.8
Walled Lake Consolidated Schools	20	14,944	19.4	21.2	22.0	11.2

Note: Table includes school districts with 100 or more students; (1) Percentage of students that are not non-Hispanic white; (2) Percentage of students that are eligible for the free lunch program; (3) Percentage of students that have an Individualized Education Program.
Source: U.S. Department of Education, National Center for Education Statistics, Common Core of Data, Local Education Agency (School District) Universe Survey: School Year 2013-2014; U.S. Department of Education, National Center for Education Statistics, Common Core of Data, Public Elementary/Secondary School Universe Survey: School Year 2013-2014

Highest Level of Education

Area	Less than H.S.	H.S. Diploma	Some College, No Deg.	Associate Degree	Bachelor's Degree	Master's Degree	Prof. School Degree	Doctorate Degree
City	5.1	14.7	17.4	6.8	31.2	18.9	3.8	1.9
MSA[1]	11.5	27.7	23.8	8.4	17.3	8.5	1.9	0.9
U.S.	13.7	28.0	21.2	7.9	18.3	7.8	2.0	1.3

Note: Figures cover persons age 25 and over; (1) Figures cover the Detroit-Warren-Dearborn, MI Metropolitan Statistical Area—see Appendix B for areas included
Source: U.S. Census Bureau, 2010-2014 American Community Survey 5-Year Estimates

Educational Attainment by Race

Area	High School Graduate or Higher (%)					Bachelor's Degree or Higher (%)				
	Total	White	Black	Asian	Hisp.[2]	Total	White	Black	Asian	Hisp.[2]
City	94.9	95.0	93.0	96.2	85.0	55.9	52.2	35.4	81.7	38.9
MSA[1]	88.5	90.2	83.9	88.7	68.6	28.6	30.4	17.1	63.9	17.3
U.S.	86.3	88.4	83.2	85.8	64.1	29.3	30.6	19.0	50.9	13.9

Note: Figures shown cover persons 25 years old and over; (1) Figures cover the Detroit-Warren-Dearborn, MI Metropolitan Statistical Area—see Appendix B for areas included; (2) People of Hispanic origin can be of any race
Source: U.S. Census Bureau, 2010-2014 American Community Survey 5-Year Estimates

School Enrollment by Grade and Control

Area	Preschool (%)		Kindergarten (%)		Grades 1 - 4 (%)		Grades 5 - 8 (%)		Grades 9 - 12 (%)	
	Public	Private	Public	Private	Public	Private	Public	Private	Public	Private
City	54.1	45.9	88.8	11.2	89.6	10.4	92.6	7.4	87.9	12.1
MSA[1]	65.2	34.8	88.2	11.8	89.7	10.3	90.5	9.5	91.4	8.6
U.S.	57.4	42.6	87.8	12.2	89.8	10.2	89.9	10.1	90.6	9.4

Note: Figures shown cover persons 3 years old and over; (1) Figures cover the Detroit-Warren-Dearborn, MI Metropolitan Statistical Area—see Appendix B for areas included
Source: U.S. Census Bureau, 2010-2014 American Community Survey 5-Year Estimates

Average Salaries of Public School Classroom Teachers

Area	2013-14		2014-15		Percent Change 2013-14 to 2014-15	Percent Change 2004-05 to 2014-15
	Dollars	Rank[1]	Dollars	Rank[1]		
Michigan	62,166	11	62,778	11	0.98	16.3
U.S. Average	56,610	–	57,379	–	1.36	20.8

Note: (1) State rank ranges from 1 to 51 where 1 indicates highest salary.
Source: National Education Association, Rankings & Estimates: Rankings of the States 2014 and Estimates of School Statistics 2015, March 2015

Higher Education

Four-Year Colleges			Two-Year Colleges			Medical Schools[1]	Law Schools[2]	Voc/ Tech[3]
Public	Private Non-profit	Private For-profit	Public	Private Non-profit	Private For-profit			
0	0	2	0	0	0	0	0	0

Note: Figures cover institutions located within the city limits and include main campuses only; (1) includes schools accredited by the Liaison Committee on Medical Education and the American Osteopathic Association's Commission on Osteopathic College Accreditation; (2) includes ABA-accredited schools, schools with provisional ABA accreditation, and state accredited schools; (3) includes all schools with programs that are less than 2 years.

Source: National Center for Education Statistics, Integrated Postsecondary Education System (IPEDS), 2014-15; Association of American Medical Colleges, Member List, March 21, 2016; American Osteopathic Association, Member List, March 21, 2016; Law School Admission Council, Official Guide to ABA-Approved Law Schools Online, March 21, 2016; Wikipedia, List of Medical Schools in the United States, March 21, 2016; Wikipedia, List of Law Schools in the United States, March 21, 2016

PRESIDENTIAL ELECTION

2012 Presidential Election Results

Area	Obama (%)	Romney (%)	Other (%)
Oakland County	53.4	45.4	1.2
U.S.	51.0	47.2	1.8

Note: Results may not add to 100% due to rounding
Source: Dave Leip's Atlas of U.S. Presidential Elections

EMPLOYERS

Major Employers

Company Name	Industry
CEI Liquidation Estates	Mobile homes
Chrysler Group	Motor vehicles & car bodies
Detroit Diesel Corporation	Motor vehicle parts & accessories
Dph-Das	Motor vehicle parts & accessories
Eagle Ottawa	Leather tanning & finishing
Employees Only	Management consulting services
Ford Motor Company	Drive shafts, motor vehicle
General Motors	Motor vehicles & car bodies
General Motors Company	Automobile assembly, including specialty automobiles
Oakwood Healthcare	General medical & surgical hospitals
St Joseph Mercy Oakland Foundation	General medical & surgical hospitals
The Army, United States Department of	Army
The Chrysler Group	Truck & tractor truck assembly
Tower Automotive	Automotive stampings
Wayne State University	Colleges & universities

Note: Companies shown are located within the Detroit-Warren-Dearborn, MI Metropolitan Statistical Area.
Source: Hoovers.com; Wikipedia

PUBLIC SAFETY

Crime Rate

Area	All Crimes	Violent Crimes				Property Crimes		
		Murder	Rape[3]	Robbery	Aggrav. Assault	Burglary	Larceny -Theft	Motor Vehicle Theft
City	1,534.4	1.7	22.2	11.9	44.3	90.4	1,295.7	68.2
Metro[1]	1,685.3	1.5	36.6	39.5	136.1	250.4	1,090.9	130.3
U.S.	2,971.8	4.5	36.6	102.2	232.5	542.5	1,837.3	216.2

Note: Figures are crimes per 100,000 population; (1) Figures cover the Warren-Troy-Farmington Hills, MI Metropolitan Division—see Appendix B for areas included; (3) The city and U.S. figures shown were reported using the revised Uniform Crime Reporting (UCR) definition of rape. The suburban and metro area figures shown are an aggregate total of the data submitted using both the revised and legacy UCR definitions.
Source: FBI Uniform Crime Reports, 2014

Hate Crimes

Area	Number of Quarters Reported	Number of Incidents per Bias Motivation						
		Race	Religion	Sexual Orientation	Ethnicity	Disability	Gender	Gender Identity
City	4	0	0	0	0	0	0	0
U.S.	4	2,568	1,014	1,017	648	84	33	98

Source: Federal Bureau of Investigation, Hate Crime Statistics 2014

Identity Theft Consumer Complaints

Area	Complaints	Complaints per 100,000 Population	Rank[2]
MSA[1]	9,468	220.4	10
U.S.	490,220	152.4	-

Note: (1) Figures cover the Detroit-Warren-Dearborn, MI Metropolitan Statistical Area—see Appendix B for areas included; (2) Rank ranges from 1 to 379 where 1 indicates greatest number of identity theft complaints per 100,000 population
Source: Federal Trade Commission, Consumer Sentinel Network Data Book for January–December 2015

Fraud and Other Consumer Complaints

Area	Complaints	Complaints per 100,000 Population	Rank[2]
MSA[1]	16,371	381.0	145
U.S.	2,593,159	806.0	-

Note: (1) Figures cover the Detroit-Warren-Dearborn, MI Metropolitan Statistical Area—see Appendix B for areas included; (2) Rank ranges from 1 to 379 where 1 indicates greatest number of identity theft complaints per 100,000 population
Source: Federal Trade Commission, Consumer Sentinel Network Data Book for January–December 2015

RECREATION

Culture

Dance[1]	Theatre[1]	Instrumental Music[1]	Vocal Music[1]	Series and Festivals	Museums and Art Galleries[2]	Zoos and Aquariums[3]
0	0	0	0	0	0	0

Note: (1) Professional perfoming groups; (2) Based on organizations with SIC code 8412; (3) AZA-accredited
Source: The Grey House Performing Arts Directory, 2015-16; Association of Zoos & Aquariums, AZA Member Zoos & Aquariums, March 25, 2016; www.AccuLeads.com, March 29, 2016

Professional Sports Teams

Team Name	League	Year Established
Detroit Lions	National Football League (NFL)	1934
Detroit Pistons	National Basketball Association (NBA)	1957
Detroit Red Wings	National Hockey League (NHL)	1926
Detroit Tigers	Major League Baseball (MLB)	1901

Note: Includes teams located in the Detroit-Warren-Dearborn, MI Metropolitan Statistical Area.
Source: Wikipedia, Major Professional Sports Teams of the United States and Canada, March 24, 2016

CLIMATE

Average and Extreme Temperatures

Temperature	Jan	Feb	Mar	Apr	May	Jun	Jul	Aug	Sep	Oct	Nov	Dec	Yr.
Extreme High (°F)	62	65	81	89	93	104	102	100	98	91	77	68	104
Average High (°F)	30	33	44	58	70	79	83	81	74	61	48	35	58
Average Temp. (°F)	23	26	36	48	59	68	72	71	64	52	40	29	49
Average Low (°F)	16	18	27	37	47	56	61	60	53	41	32	21	39
Extreme Low (°F)	-21	-15	-4	10	25	36	41	38	29	17	9	-10	-21

Note: Figures cover the years 1958-1990
Source: National Climatic Data Center, International Station Meteorological Climate Summary, 9/96

Average Precipitation/Snowfall/Humidity

Precip./Humidity	Jan	Feb	Mar	Apr	May	Jun	Jul	Aug	Sep	Oct	Nov	Dec	Yr.
Avg. Precip. (in.)	1.8	1.8	2.5	3.0	2.9	3.6	3.1	3.4	2.8	2.2	2.6	2.7	32.4
Avg. Snowfall (in.)	10	9	7	2	Tr	0	0	0	0	Tr	3	11	41
Avg. Rel. Hum. 7am (%)	80	79	79	78	78	79	82	86	87	84	82	81	81
Avg. Rel. Hum. 4pm (%)	67	63	59	53	51	52	52	54	55	55	64	70	58

Note: Figures cover the years 1958-1990; Tr = Trace amounts (<0.05 in. of rain; <0.5 in. of snow)
Source: National Climatic Data Center, International Station Meteorological Climate Summary, 9/96

Weather Conditions

Temperature			Daytime Sky			Precipitation		
5°F & below	32°F & below	90°F & above	Clear	Partly cloudy	Cloudy	0.01 inch or more precip.	0.1 inch or more snow/ice	Thunder-storms
15	136	12	74	134	157	135	38	32

Note: Figures are average number of days per year and cover the years 1958-1990
Source: National Climatic Data Center, International Station Meteorological Climate Summary, 9/96

HAZARDOUS WASTE

Superfund Sites

Novi has no sites on the EPA's Superfund Final National Priorities List. There are a total of 1,323 Superfund sites on the list in the U.S. *U.S. Environmental Protection Agency, Final National Priorities List, March 18, 2016*

AIR & WATER QUALITY

Air Quality Trends: Ozone

	1990	1995	2000	2005	2010	2011	2012	2013	2014
MSA[1]	0.083	0.088	0.076	0.083	0.074	0.079	0.081	0.068	0.069

Note: (1) Data covers the Detroit-Warren-Dearborn, MI Metropolitan Statistical Area—see Appendix B for areas included. The values shown are the composite ozone concentration averages among trend sites based on the highest fourth daily maximum 8-hour concentration in parts per million. These trends are based on sites having an adequate record of monitoring data during the trend period. Data from exceptional events are included.
Source: U.S. Environmental Protection Agency, Air Quality Monitoring Information, "Air Quality Trends by City, 1990-2014"

Air Quality Index

Area	Percent of Days when Air Quality was...[2]					AQI Statistics[2]	
	Good	Moderate	Unhealthy for Sensitive Groups	Unhealthy	Very Unhealthy	Maximum	Median
MSA[1]	41.1	55.6	3.0	0.3	0.0	165	54

Note: (1) Data covers the Detroit-Warren-Dearborn, MI Metropolitan Statistical Area—see Appendix B for areas included; (2) Based on 365 days with AQI data in 2015. Air Quality Index (AQI) is an index for reporting daily air quality. EPA calculates the AQI for five major air pollutants regulated by the Clean Air Act: ground-level ozone, particle pollution (aka particulate matter), carbon monoxide, sulfur dioxide, and nitrogen dioxide. The AQI runs from 0 to 500. The higher the AQI value, the greater the level of air pollution and the greater the health concern. There are six AQI categories: "Good" AQI is between 0 and 50. Air quality is considered satisfactory; "Moderate" AQI is between 51 and 100. Air quality is acceptable; "Unhealthy for Sensitive Groups" When AQI values are between 101 and 150, members of sensitive groups may experience health effects; "Unhealthy" When AQI values are between 151 and 200 everyone may begin to experience health effects; "Very Unhealthy" AQI values between 201 and 300 trigger a health alert; "Hazardous" AQI values over 300 trigger warnings of emergency conditions (not shown).
Source: U.S. Environmental Protection Agency, Air Quality Index Report, 2015

Air Quality Index Pollutants

Area	Percent of Days when AQI Pollutant was...[2]					
	Carbon Monoxide	Nitrogen Dioxide	Ozone	Sulfur Dioxide	Particulate Matter 2.5	Particulate Matter 10
MSA[1]	0.0	2.5	15.6	14.2	58.9	8.8

Note: (1) Data covers the Detroit-Warren-Dearborn, MI Metropolitan Statistical Area—see Appendix B for areas included; (2) Based on 365 days with AQI data in 2015. The Air Quality Index (AQI) is an index for reporting daily air quality. EPA calculates the AQI for five major air pollutants regulated by the Clean Air Act: ground-level ozone, particle pollution (also known as particulate matter), carbon monoxide, sulfur dioxide, and nitrogen dioxide. The AQI runs from 0 to 500. The higher the AQI value, the greater the level of air pollution and the greater the health concern.
Source: U.S. Environmental Protection Agency, Air Quality Index Report, 2015

Maximum Air Pollutant Concentrations: Particulate Matter, Ozone, CO and Lead

	Particulate Matter 10 (ug/m^3)	Particulate Matter 2.5 Wtd AM (ug/m^3)	Particulate Matter 2.5 24-Hr (ug/m^3)	Ozone (ppm)	Carbon Monoxide (ppm)	Lead (ug/m^3)
MSA[1] Level	150	11.7	27	0.073	2	0.03
NAAQS[2]	150	15	35	0.075	9	0.15
Met NAAQS[2]	Yes	Yes	Yes	Yes	Yes	Yes

Note: (1) Data covers the Detroit-Warren-Dearborn, MI Metropolitan Statistical Area—see Appendix B for areas included; Data from exceptional events are included; (2) National Ambient Air Quality Standards; ppm = parts per million; ug/m^3 = micrograms per cubic meter; n/a not available.
Concentrations: Particulate Matter 10 (coarse particulate)—highest second maximum 24-hour concentration; Particulate Matter 2.5 Wtd AM (fine particulate)—highest weighted annual mean concentration; Particulate Matter 2.5 24-Hour (fine particulate)—highest 98th percentile 24-hour concentration; Ozone—highest fourth daily maximum 8-hour concentration; Carbon Monoxide—highest second maximum non-overlapping 8-hour concentration; Lead—maximum running 3-month average
Source: U.S. Environmental Protection Agency, Air Quality Monitoring Information, "Air Quality Statistics by City, 2014"

Maximum Air Pollutant Concentrations: Nitrogen Dioxide and Sulfur Dioxide

	Nitrogen Dioxide AM (ppb)	Nitrogen Dioxide 1-Hr (ppb)	Sulfur Dioxide AM (ppb)	Sulfur Dioxide 1-Hr (ppb)	Sulfur Dioxide 24-Hr (ppb)
MSA[1] Level	16	52	n/a	72	n/a
NAAQS[2]	53	100	30	75	140
Met NAAQS[2]	Yes	Yes	n/a	Yes	n/a

Note: (1) Data covers the Detroit-Warren-Dearborn, MI Metropolitan Statistical Area—see Appendix B for areas included; Data from exceptional events are included; (2) National Ambient Air Quality Standards; ppm = parts per million; ug/m^3 = micrograms per cubic meter; n/a not available.
Concentrations: Nitrogen Dioxide AM—highest arithmetic mean concentration; Nitrogen Dioxide 1-Hr—highest 98th percentile 1-hour daily maximum concentration; Sulfur Dioxide AM—highest annual mean concentration; Sulfur Dioxide 1-Hr—highest 99th percentile 1-hour daily maximum concentration; Sulfur Dioxide 24-Hr—highest second maximum 24-hour concentration
Source: U.S. Environmental Protection Agency, Air Quality Monitoring Information, "Air Quality Statistics by City, 2014"

Drinking Water

Water System Name	Pop. Served	Primary Water Source Type	Violations[1]	
			Health Based	Monitoring/ Reporting
City of Novi	44,000	Purchased Surface	0	0

Note: (1) Based on violation data from January 1, 2015 to December 31, 2015 (includes unresolved violations from earlier years)
Source: U.S. Environmental Protection Agency, Office of Ground Water and Drinking Water, Safe Drinking Water Information System (based on data extracted April 29, 2016)

Eden Prairie, Minnesota

Background

Eden Prairie, in Hennepin County, is approximately 11 miles from Minneapolis and consistently ranks among the top suburbs to live in America. Eden Prairie's entire southern border is the Minnesota River.

Native American tribes Ojibwa and Dakota fought for control of the region until the first pioneers settled in Eden Prairie in 1852. Even then, the two tribes continued their feuding until the late 1960s.

Eden Prairie became a township in 1858. In 1942, Flying Cloud Airport was built, and by the 1960s it was one of the busiest airports in the mid-west. Though it now serves mostly as an aviation reliever airport, its construction was the catalyst that began Eden Prairie's rapid urbanization. The town became a village in 1962, when the population significantly increased, and then incorporated as a city in 1974.

Accessibility is a major draw of Eden Prairie. Tourists and residents alike have the option of flying corporate or private aircraft out of Flying Cloud Airport, using major highways Minnesota State 5 or Interstate 494, or the Southwest Light Rail transit, a train that runs into Minneapolis.

Eden Prairie Center mall opened in 1976 and has since become a staple of the Eden Prairie community. It is a major tourist attraction that draws millions of visitors annually and boasts over 100 stores, a movie theatre and an indoor play area.

With over 2,800 business in the city, Eden Prairie is one of Minnesota's premiere business centers. Lifetouch, MTS and Optum are just a few of the companies that are headquartered there. The National Football League's Minnesota Vikings has operated out of Eden Prairie for over 30 years, with their headquarters and practice facility located in the city.

Students in Eden Prairie attend schools in Independent School District, Hopkins Independent School District, or the Minnetonka Independent School District. The city offers both public and private school options to best serve its population. Eden Prairie High School is one of the largest high schools in the state, with highly ranked programs and a state-recognized athletics department. Educational options for students grades K-12 include the Eagle Ridge Academy Charter School, and the International School of Minnesota.

There are two colleges in Eden Prairie—ITT and Hennepin Technical College. ITT Technical School has a small campus in Eden Prairie, with 400 students enrolled full time. Hennepin has over 9,000 students between the two main campuses in Eden Prairie and nearby Brooklyn Park.

The natural beauty of Eden Prairie is evident in its 37 parks, over 100 miles of trails, and multiple sports facilities. Bryant Lake Park offers lake swimming, biking, hiking and an 18-hole disc golf course. Eden Prairie is proud to offer non-mobile children and adults an opportunity to enjoy a barrier-free playground at Miller Park, which also has an ice skating rink and ice castle in the winter season.

In addition to Flying Cloud Airport, Eden Prairie is served by Minneapolis-Saint Paul International Airport located in Minneapolis 17 miles away.

The average high temperature in Eden Prairie in July is close to the national average at 85 degrees. Winters in Eden Prairie are cold, with the average low temperature in January less than 3 degrees, well below the national average. Eden Prairie averages 42 inches of snow and 29 inches of rain.

Rankings

Business/Finance Rankings

- The personal finance site NerdWallet analyzed 183 American metropolitan areas with populations over 250,000 and more than 15,000 businesses to rank where entrepreneurs find the most success. Criteria included area economy, annual income, housing cost, unemployment rate, and the success rate of area businesses. Minneapolis* ranked #14. *www.nerdwallet.com, "Best Places to Start a Business," April 27, 2015*
- TransUnion ranked the nation's metro areas by average credit score, calculated on the VantageScore system, developed by the three major credit-reporting bureaus—TransUnion, Experian, and Equifax. The Minneapolis* metro area was among the ten cities with the highest collective credit score, meaning that its residents posed the lowest average consumer credit risk. *www.usatoday.com, "Metro Areas' Average Credit Rating Revealed," February 7, 2013*
- Based on metro area social media reviews, the employment opinion group Glassdoor surveyed 50 of the largest U.S. metro areas and equally weighed cost of living, hiring opportunity, and job satisfaction to compose a list of "25 Best Cities for Jobs." The Minneapolis* metro area was ranked #18 in overall job satisfaction. *www.glassdoor.com, "Best Cities for Jobs," May 19, 2015*
- In a survey of economic confidence in the nation's 50 largest metropolitan areas conducted January–December 2014, the Minneapolis* metro area placed #4, according to Gallup's 2014 Economic Confidence Index. *Gallup, "San Jose and San Francisco Lead in Economic Confidence," March 19, 2015*
- The Brookings Institution ranked the 100 largest metro areas in the U.S. based on income inequality. Minneapolis* was ranked #79 (#1 = greatest ineqality). Criteria: the "95/20 ratio," a figure representing the income at which a household earns more than 95 percent of all other households, divided by the income at which a household earns more than only 20 percent of all other households. *Brookings Institution, "Income Inequality, 100 Largest U.S. Metro Areas, 2007-2014," January 14, 2016*
- *Forbes* ranked the largest metro areas in the U.S. in terms of the "Best Cities for Young Professionals." The Minneapolis* metro area ranked #10 out of 15. Criteria: job growth; unemployment rate; median salary of college graduates age 24 to 34; cost of living; number of small businesses per capita; number of large companies; percentage of population 25 years of age and older with college degrees. *Forbes.com, "America's 15 Best Cities for Young Professionals," August 18, 2014*
- Payscale.com ranked the 20 largest metro areas in terms of wage growth. The Minneapolis* metro area ranked #2. Criteria: private-sector wage growth between the 1st quarter of 2015 and the 1st quarter of 2016. *PayScale, "Wage Trends by Metro Area," 1st Quarter, 2016*
- The Minneapolis* metro area appeared on the Milken Institute "2015 Best Performing Cities" list. Rank: #59 out of 200 large metro areas. Criteria: job growth; wage and salary growth; high-tech output growth. *Milken Institute, "Best-Performing Cities 2015," December 2015*
- *Forbes* ranked the 200 most populous metro areas to determine the nation's "Best Places for Business and Careers." The Minneapolis* metro area was ranked #39. Criteria: costs (business and living); job growth (past and projected); income growth; educational attainment (college and high school); projected economic growth; cultural and recreational opportunities; net migration patterns; number of highly ranked colleges. *Forbes, "The Best Places for Business and Careers 2015," July 29, 2015*

Dating/Romance Rankings

- *Forbes* reports that the Minneapolis* metro area made Rent.com's Best Cities for Newlyweds list for 2013, based on Bureau of Labor Statistics and Census Bureau data on number of married couples, percentage of families with children under age six, average annual income, cost of living, and availability of rentals. *www.forbes.com, "The 10 Best Cities for Newlyweds to Live and Work In," May 30, 2013*

- CreditDonkey, a financial education website, sought out the ten best U.S. cities for newlyweds, considering the number of married couples, divorce rate, average credit score, and average number of hours worked per week in metro areas with a million or more residents. The Minneapolis* metro area placed #10. *www.creditdonkey.com, "Study: Best Cities for Newlyweds," November 30, 2013*

Education Rankings

- The Minneapolis* metro area was selected as one of the world's most inventive cities by *Forbes*. The area was ranked #9 out of 15. Criteria: patent applications per capita. *Forbes, "World's 15 Most Inventive Cities," July 9, 2013*
- The Minneapolis* metro area was selected as one of America's most innovative cities" by *The Business Insider*. The metro area was ranked #20 out of 20. Criteria: patents per capita. *The Business Insider, "The 20 Most Innovative Cities in the U.S.," February 1, 2013*
- Minneapolis* was identified as one of America's "smartest" metropolitan areas by *The Business Journals*. The area ranked #9 out of 10. Criteria: percentage of adults (25 and older) with high school diplomas, bachelor's degrees and graduate degrees. *The Business Journals, "Where the Brainpower Is: Exclusive U.S. Rankings, Insights," February 27, 2014*
- Personal finance website *WalletHub* analyzed the 150 largest U.S. metropolitan statistical areas to determine where the most educated Americans are choosing to settle. Criteria: education quality and attainment gap; education levels; percentage of workers with degrees; public school rankings; quality and size of each metro area's universities. Minneapolis* was ranked #9 (#1 = most educated city). *www.WalletHub.com, "2015's Most and Least Educated Cities*
- Minneapolis* was identified as one of the "Smartest Cities in America" by the brain-training website *Lumosity* using data from three million of its own users. The metro area ranked #33 out of 50. Criteria: users' brain performance index scores, considering core cognitive abilities such as memory, processing speed, flexibility, attention and problem-solving. *Lumosity, " Smartest Cities in America," June 25, 2013*

Environmental Rankings

- The Minneapolis* metro area came in at #118 for the relative comfort of its climate on Sperling's list of "chill cities," as measured by the Sperling Heat Index. All 361 metro areas are included. Criteria included daytime high temperatures, nighttime low temperatures, dew point, and relative humidity at the high temperatures. *www.bertsperling.com, "Sperling's Chill Cities," July 18, 2013*
- Sperling's BestPlaces assessed 379 metropolitan areas of the United States for the likelihood of dangerously extreme weather events or earthquakes. In general the Southeast and South-Central regions have the highest risk of weather extremes and earthquakes, while the Pacific Northwest enjoys the lowest risk. Of the least risky metropolitan areas, the Minneapolis* metro area was ranked #99. *www.bestplaces.net, "Safest Places from Natural Disasters," April 2011*
- The U.S. Environmental Protection Agency (EPA) released a list of U.S. metropolitan areas with the most ENERGY STAR certified buildings in 2015. The Minneapolis* metro area was ranked #13 out of 25. *U.S. Environmental Protection Agency, "Top Cities With the Most ENERGY STAR Certified Buildings in 2016," March 30, 2016*

Health/Fitness Rankings

- Analysts who tracked obesity rates in the nation's largest metro areas (populations above one million) found that the Minneapolis* metro area was one of the ten major metros where residents were least likely to be obese, defined as a BMI score of 30 or above. *www.gallup.com, "Boulder, Colo., Residents Still Least Likely to Be Obese," April 4, 2014*

- For each of the 50 most populous metro areas in the United States, the American College of Sports Medicine's American Fitness Index evaluated infrastructure, community assets, and policies that encourage healthy and fit lifestyles, including preventive health behaviors, levels of chronic disease conditions, health care access, and community resources and policies that support physical activity. The Minneapolis* metro area ranked #2 for "community fitness." *www.americanfitnessindex.org, "ACSM American Fitness Index Health and Community Fitness Status of the 50 Largest Metropolitan Areas," May 2015*

- Minneapolis* was identified as a "2016 Spring Allergy Capital." The area ranked #71 out of 100. Three groups of factors were used to identify the most severe cities for people with allergies during the spring season: annual pollen levels; medicine utilization; access to board-certified allergists. *Asthma and Allergy Foundation of America, "Spring Allergy Capitals 2016"*

- Minneapolis* was identified as a "2015 Asthma Capital." The area ranked #87 out of the nation's 100 largest metropolitan areas. Criteria: estimated prevalence; self-reported prevalence; crude death rate for asthma; annual pollen score; annual air quality; public smoking laws; number of board-certified asthma specialists; school inhaler access laws; rescue medication use; controller medication use; ER visits for asthma; uninsured rate; poverty rate. *Asthma and Allergy Foundation of America, "Asthma Capitals 2015"*

- The Minneapolis* metro area ranked #27 out of 190 in The Gallup-Healthways Well-Being Index. Criteria: purpose; social well being; financial health; community and physical health. Results are based on telephone interviews with adults, aged 18 and older, living in metropolitan areas in the 50 U.S. states and the District of Columbia. *Gallup-Healthways, "State of American Well-Being," February 23, 2016*

Real Estate Rankings

- Minneapolis* was ranked #77 out of 225 metro areas in terms of housing affordability in 2015 by the National Association of Home Builders (#1 = most affordable). Criteria: the share of homes sold in that area affordable to a family earning the local median income, based on standard mortgage underwriting criteria. *National Association of Home Builders®, NAHB-Wells Fargo Housing Opportunity Index, 4th Quarter 2015*

Safety Rankings

- Farmers Insurance, in partnership with Sperling's BestPlaces, ranked metro areas in the U.S. as the "Most Secure Places to Live." The Minneapolis* metro area ranked #13 out of the top 20 in the large metro area category (500,000 or more residents). Criteria: economic stability; crime statistics; extreme weather; risk of natural disasters; housing depreciation; foreclosures; air quality; environmental hazards; life expectancy; motor vehicle fatalities; and employment numbers. *Farmers Insurance Group of Companies, "Most Secure U.S. Places to Live in the U.S.," June 25, 2013*

- The National Insurance Crime Bureau ranked 380 metro areas in the U.S. in terms of per capita rates of vehicle theft. The Minneapolis* metro area ranked #134 (#1 = highest rate). Criteria: number of vehicle theft offenses per 100,000 inhabitants in 2014. *National Insurance Crime Bureau, "Hot Spots 2014," June 24, 2015*

Seniors/Retirement Rankings

- From its Best Cities for Successful Aging indexes, the Milken Institute generated rankings for metropolitan areas, weighing data in eight categories—health care, wellness, living arrangements, transportation, financial characteristics, education and employment opportunities, community engagement, and overall livability. The Minneapolis* metro area was ranked #16 overall in the large metro area category. *Milken Institute, "Best Cities for Successful Aging, 2014"*

Sports/Recreation Rankings

- According to the personal finance website NerdWallet, the Minneapolis* metro area, at #6, is one of the nation's top dozen metro areas for sports fans. Criteria included the presence of all four major sports—MLB, NFL, NHL, and NBA, fan enthusiasm (as measured by game attendance), ticket affordability, and "sports culture," that is, number of sports bars. *www.nerdwallet.com, "Best Cities for Sports Fans," May 5, 2013*

Miscellaneous Rankings

- The watchdog site Charity Navigator conducts an annual study of charities in the nation's major markets both to analyze statistical differences in their financial, accountability, and transparency practices and to track year-to-year variations in individual communities. The Minneapolis* metro area was ranked #12 among the 30 metro markets in the rating dimension of Overall Score. *www.charitynavigator.org, "Metro Market Study 2015," June 5, 2015*
- Mars Chocolate North America, the makers of COMBOS®, in partnership with Sperling's BestPlaces, ranked 50 major metro areas in terms of their "manliness." The Minneapolis* metro area ranked #40. Criteria: number of professional sports teams; number of nearby NASCAR tracks and racing events; manly lifestyle; concentration of manly retail stores; manly occupations per capita; salty snack sales; "Board of Manliness" rankings. *Mars Chocolate North America, "America's Manliest Cities 2012"*
- The National Alliance to End Homelessness ranked the 100 most populous metro areas with the highest rate of homelessness. The Minneapolis* metro area ranked #48. Criteria: number of homeless people per 10,000 population in 2011. *National Alliance to End Homelessness, The State of Homelessness in America 2012*

Eden Prairie is located within the Minneapolis-St. Paul-Bloomington, MN-WI Metropolitan Statistical Area.

Business Environment

CITY FINANCES

City Government Finances

Component	2012 ($000)	2012 ($ per capita)
Total Revenues	88,899	1,462
Total Expenditures	85,306	1,403
Debt Outstanding	202,695	3,333
Cash and Securities[1]	227,819	3,747

Note: (1) Cash and security holdings of a government at the close of its fiscal year, including those of its dependent agencies, utilities, and liquor stores.
Source: U.S Census Bureau, State & Local Government Finances 2012

City Government Revenue by Source

Source	2012 ($000)	2012 ($ per capita)
General Revenue		
From Federal Government	645	10
From State Government	4,188	68
From Local Governments	386	6
Taxes		
Property	34,562	568
Sales and Gross Receipts	775	12
Personal Income	0	0
Corporate Income	0	0
Motor Vehicle License	0	0
Other Taxes	2,588	42
Current Charges	22,054	362
Liquor Store	11,676	192
Utility	7,182	118
Employee Retirement	0	0

Source: U.S Census Bureau, State & Local Government Finances 2012

City Government Expenditures by Function

Function	2012 ($000)	2012 ($ per capita)	2012 (%)
General Direct Expenditures			
Air Transportation	0	0	0.0
Corrections	0	0	0.0
Education	0	0	0.0
Employment Security Administration	0	0	0.0
Financial Administration	1,609	26	1.8
Fire Protection	2,825	46	3.3
General Public Buildings	3,547	58	4.1
Governmental Administration, Other	2,184	35	2.5
Health	154	2	0.1
Highways	8,426	138	9.8
Hospitals	0	0	0.0
Housing and Community Development	3,298	54	3.8
Interest on General Debt	8,066	132	9.4
Judicial and Legal	0	0	0.0
Libraries	0	0	0.0
Parking	0	0	0.0
Parks and Recreation	10,663	175	12.5
Police Protection	11,852	194	13.8
Public Welfare	824	13	0.9
Sewerage	6,469	106	7.5
Solid Waste Management	3,171	52	3.7
Veterans' Services	0	0	0.0
Liquor Store	10,888	179	12.7
Utility	7,290	119	8.5
Employee Retirement	0	0	0.0

Source: U.S Census Bureau, State & Local Government Finances 2012

DEMOGRAPHICS

Population Growth

Area	1990 Census	2000 Census	2010 Census	2014* Estimate	Population Growth (%) 1990-2014	2010-2014
City	39,311	54,901	60,797	62,096	58.0	2.1
MSA[1]	2,538,834	2,968,806	3,279,833	3,424,786	34.9	4.4
U.S.	248,709,873	281,421,906	308,745,538	314,107,084	26.3	1.7

Note: (1) Figures cover the Minneapolis-St. Paul-Bloomington, MN-WI Metropolitan Statistical Area—see Appendix B for areas included; (*) 2010-2014 5-year estimated population
Source: U.S. Census Bureau, 1990 Census, Census 2000, Census 2010, 2010-2014 American Community Survey 5-Year Estimates

Household Size

Area	Persons in Household (%) One	Two	Three	Four	Five	Six	Seven or More	Average Household Size
City	24.3	33.8	17.6	15.2	5.8	2.5	0.4	2.54
MSA[1]	27.8	33.7	15.0	14.0	5.9	2.0	1.3	2.54
U.S.	27.5	33.5	15.8	13.1	6.0	2.3	1.4	2.64

Note: (1) Figures cover the Minneapolis-St. Paul-Bloomington, MN-WI Metropolitan Statistical Area—see Appendix B for areas included
Source: U.S. Census Bureau, 2010-2014 American Community Survey 5-Year Estimates

Race

Area	White Alone[2] (%)	Black Alone[2] (%)	Asian Alone[2] (%)	AIAN[3] Alone[2] (%)	NHOPI[4] Alone[2] (%)	Other Race Alone[2] (%)	Two or More Races (%)
City	79.8	5.5	10.6	0.3	0.1	0.9	2.8
MSA[1]	81.2	7.4	5.9	0.6	0.0	1.8	3.0
U.S.	73.8	12.6	5.0	0.8	0.2	4.7	2.9

Note: (1) Figures cover the Minneapolis-St. Paul-Bloomington, MN-WI Metropolitan Statistical Area—see Appendix B for areas included; (2) Alone is defined as not being in combination with one or more other races; (3) American Indian and Alaska Native; (4) Native Hawaiian and Other Pacific Islander
Source: U.S. Census Bureau, 2010-2014 American Community Survey 5-Year Estimates

Hispanic or Latino Origin

Area	Total (%)	Mexican (%)	Puerto Rican (%)	Cuban (%)	Other (%)
City	3.1	1.8	0.2	0.0	1.1
MSA[1]	5.5	3.7	0.3	0.1	1.4
U.S.	16.9	10.8	1.6	0.6	3.8

Note: Persons of Hispanic or Latino origin can be of any race; (1) Figures cover the Minneapolis-St. Paul-Bloomington, MN-WI Metropolitan Statistical Area—see Appendix B for areas included
Source: U.S. Census Bureau, 2010-2014 American Community Survey 5-Year Estimates

Ancestry

Area	German	Irish	English	American	Italian	Polish	French[2]	Scottish	Dutch
City	32.1	11.4	7.1	2.7	3.1	3.6	2.7	1.7	1.8
MSA[1]	32.4	11.8	6.0	3.3	2.8	4.6	3.7	1.4	1.6
U.S.	14.9	10.8	8.0	7.1	5.5	3.0	2.7	1.7	1.4

Note: Figures are the percentage of the total population reporting a particular ancestry. The nine most commonly reported ancestries in the U.S. are shown. Figures include multiple ancestries (e.g. if a person reported being Irish and Italian, they were included in both columns); (1) Figures cover the Minneapolis-St. Paul-Bloomington, MN-WI Metropolitan Statistical Area—see Appendix B for areas included; (2) Excludes Basque
Source: U.S. Census Bureau, 2010-2014 American Community Survey 5-Year Estimates

Foreign-Born Population

Area	Percent of Population Born in								
	Any Foreign Country	Asia	Mexico	Europe	Carribean	Central America[2]	South America	Africa	Canada
City	13.9	8.4	0.8	1.6	0.1	0.2	0.7	1.7	0.3
MSA[1]	9.7	3.9	1.4	1.1	0.1	0.3	0.5	2.1	0.2
U.S.	13.1	3.8	3.7	1.5	1.2	1.0	0.9	0.6	0.3

Note: (1) Figures cover the Minneapolis-St. Paul-Bloomington, MN-WI Metropolitan Statistical Area—see Appendix B for areas included; (2) Excludes Mexico.
Source: U.S. Census Bureau, 2010-2014 American Community Survey 5-Year Estimates

Marital Status

Area	Never Married	Now Married[2]	Separated	Widowed	Divorced
City	26.5	60.3	1.4	3.3	8.5
MSA[1]	32.9	51.5	1.3	4.4	10.0
U.S.	32.5	48.4	2.2	5.9	10.9

Note: Figures are percentages and cover the population 15 years of age and older; (1) Figures cover the Minneapolis-St. Paul-Bloomington, MN-WI Metropolitan Statistical Area—see Appendix B for areas included; (2) Excludes separated
Source: U.S. Census Bureau, 2010-2014 American Community Survey 5-Year Estimates

Disability Status

Area	All Ages	Under 18 Years Old	18 to 64 Years Old	65 Years and Over
City	6.3	4.7	4.2	26.7
MSA[1]	9.2	3.6	7.6	30.8
U.S.	12.3	4.1	10.2	36.3

Note: Figures show percent of the civilian noninstitutionalized population that reported having a disability. Disability status is determined from from six types of difficulty: vision, hearing, cognitive, ambulatory, self-care, and independent living. For children under 5 years old, hearing and vision difficulty are used to determine disability status. For children between the ages of 5 and 14, disability status is determined from hearing, vision, cognitive, ambulatory, and self-care difficulties. For people aged 15 years and older, they are considered to have a disability if they have difficulty with any one of the six difficulty types; (1) Figures cover the Minneapolis-St. Paul-Bloomington, MN-WI Metropolitan Statistical Area—see Appendix B for areas included.
Source: U.S. Census Bureau, 2010-2014 American Community Survey 5-Year Estimates

Age

Area	Percent of Population									Median Age
	Under Age 5	Age 5–19	Age 20–34	Age 35–44	Age 45–54	Age 55–64	Age 65–74	Age 75–84	Age 85+	
City	6.7	21.2	18.3	13.7	17.7	13.2	5.6	2.4	1.3	37.9
MSA[1]	6.7	20.3	21.0	13.4	15.0	12.1	6.4	3.5	1.6	36.4
U.S.	6.4	19.9	20.6	13.0	14.1	12.3	7.6	4.3	1.9	37.4

Note: (1) Figures cover the Minneapolis-St. Paul-Bloomington, MN-WI Metropolitan Statistical Area—see Appendix B for areas included
Source: U.S. Census Bureau, 2010-2014 American Community Survey 5-Year Estimates

Gender

Area	Males	Females	Males per 100 Females
City	31,185	30,911	100.9
MSA[1]	1,692,444	1,732,342	97.7
U.S.	154,515,159	159,591,925	96.8

Note: (1) Figures cover the Minneapolis-St. Paul-Bloomington, MN-WI Metropolitan Statistical Area—see Appendix B for areas included
Source: U.S. Census Bureau, 2010-2014 American Community Survey 5-Year Estimates

Religious Groups by Family

Area	Catholic	Baptist	Non-Den.	Methodist[2]	Lutheran	LDS[3]	Pente-costal	Presby-terian[4]	Muslim[5]	Judaism
MSA[1]	21.7	2.4	2.9	2.7	14.4	0.6	1.7	1.8	0.4	0.7
U.S.	19.1	9.3	4.0	4.0	2.3	2.0	1.9	1.6	0.8	0.7

Note: Figures are the number of adherents as a percentage of the total population; (1) Figures cover the Minneapolis-St. Paul-Bloomington, MN-WI Metropolitan Statistical Area—see Appendix B for areas included; (2) Methodist/Pietist; (3) Latter Day Saints; (4) Reformed; (5) Figures are estimates
Source: Association of Statisticians of American Religious Bodies, 2010 U.S. Religion Census: Religious Congregations & Membership Study

Religious Groups by Tradition

Area	Catholic	Evangelical Protestant	Mainline Protestant	Other Tradition	Black Protestant	Orthodox
MSA[1]	21.7	12.8	14.5	2.2	0.4	0.2
U.S.	19.1	16.2	7.3	4.3	1.6	0.3

Note: Figures are the number of adherents as a percentage of the total population; (1) Figures cover the Minneapolis-St. Paul-Bloomington, MN-WI Metropolitan Statistical Area—see Appendix B for areas included
Source: Association of Statisticians of American Religious Bodies, 2010 U.S. Religion Census: Religious Congregations & Membership Study

ECONOMY

Gross Metropolitan Product

Area	2013	2014	2015	2016	Rank[2]
MSA[1]	227.8	236.7	246.4	258.6	13

Note: Figures are in billions of dollars; (1) Figures cover the Minneapolis-St. Paul-Bloomington, MN-WI Metropolitan Statistical Area—see Appendix B for areas included; (2) Rank is based on 2016 data and ranges from 1 to 381
Source: The U.S. Conference of Mayors, U.S. Metro Economies: GMP and Employment 2014-2016, June 2015

Economic Growth

Area	2011-13 (%)	2014 (%)	2015 (%)	2016 (%)	Rank[2]
MSA[1]	2.0	2.4	2.7	3.0	83
U.S.	2.2	2.4	2.3	2.9	–

Note: Figures are real gross metropolitan product (GMP) growth rates and represent annual average percent change; (1) Figures cover the Minneapolis-St. Paul-Bloomington, MN-WI Metropolitan Statistical Area—see Appendix B for areas included; (2) Rank is based on 2016 data and ranges from 1 to 381
Source: The U.S. Conference of Mayors, U.S. Metro Economies: GMP and Employment 2014-2016, June 2015

Metropolitan Area Exports

Area	2009	2010	2011	2012	2013	2014	Rank[2]
MSA[1]	20,096.7	23,192.7	26,189.0	25,155.7	23,747.4	21,198.2	15

Note: Figures are in millions of dollars; (1) Figures cover the Minneapolis-St. Paul-Bloomington, MN-WI Metropolitan Statistical Area—see Appendix B for areas included; (2) Rank is based on 2014 data and ranges from 1 to 385
Source: U.S. Department of Commerce, International Trade Administration, Office of Trade & Industry Information, Manufacturing & Services, data extracted March 10, 2016

Building Permits

Area	Single-Family			Multi-Family			Total		
	2014	2015p	Pct. Chg.	2014	2015p	Pct. Chg.	2014	2015p	Pct. Chg.
City	61	73	19.7	0	0	-	61	73	19.7
MSA[1]	6,689	6,786	1.5	4,736	4,927	4.0	11,425	11,713	2.5
U.S.	640,300	690,800	7.9	411,800	487,600	18.4	1,052,100	1,178,400	12.0

Note: (1) Figures cover the Minneapolis-St. Paul-Bloomington, MN-WI Metropolitan Statistical Area—see Appendix B for areas included; Figures represent new, privately-owned housing units authorized (unadjusted data); All permit data are based on estimates with imputation; (p) preliminary data.
Source: U.S. Census Bureau, Manufacturing, Mining, and Construction Statistics, Building Permits, 2014, 2015

Bankruptcy Filings

Area	Business Filings			Nonbusiness Filings		
	2014	2015	% Chg.	2014	2015	% Chg.
Hennepin County	110	99	-10.0	2,625	2,330	-11.2
U.S.	26,983	24,735	-8.3	909,812	819,760	-9.9

Note: Business filings include Chapter 7, Chapter 11, Chapter 12, and Chapter 13; Nonbusiness filings include Chapter 7, Chapter 11, and Chapter 13
Source: Administrative Office of the U.S. Courts, Business and Nonbusiness Bankruptcy, County Cases Commenced by Chapter of the Bankruptcy Code, During the 12- Month Period Ending December 31, 2014 and Business and Nonbusiness Bankruptcy, County Cases Commenced by Chapter of the Bankruptcy Code, During the 12- Month Period Ending December 31, 2015

Housing Vacancy Rates

Area	Gross Vacancy Rate² (%)			Year-Round Vacancy Rate³ (%)			Rental Vacancy Rate⁴ (%)			Homeowner Vacancy Rate⁵ (%)		
	2013	2014	2015	2013	2014	2015	2013	2014	2015	2013	2014	2015
MSA[1]	5.7	5.7	6.4	5.1	5.3	6.0	5.4	4.4	4.9	0.9	1.4	0.8
U.S.	13.6	13.4	12.9	10.7	10.4	10.0	8.3	7.6	7.1	2.0	1.9	1.8

Note: (1) Figures cover the Minneapolis-St. Paul-Bloomington, MN-WI Metropolitan Statistical Area—see Appendix B for areas included; (2) The percentage of the total housing inventory that is vacant; (3) The percentage of the housing inventory (excluding seasonal units) that is year-round vacant; (4) The percentage of rental inventory that is vacant for rent; (5) The percentage of homeowner inventory that is vacant for sale
Source: U.S. Census Bureau, Housing Vacancies and Homeownership Annual Statistics: 2015

INCOME

Income

Area	Per Capita ($)	Median Household ($)	Average Household ($)
City	50,435	95,697	129,002
MSA[1]	34,593	68,019	88,061
U.S.	28,555	53,482	74,596

Note: (1) Figures cover the Minneapolis-St. Paul-Bloomington, MN-WI Metropolitan Statistical Area—see Appendix B for areas included
Source: U.S. Census Bureau, 2010-2014 American Community Survey 5-Year Estimates

Household Income Distribution

Area	Percent of Households Earning							
	Under $15,000	$15,000 -24,999	$25,000 -34,999	$35,000 -49,999	$50,000 -74,999	$75,000 -99,000	$100,000 -149,999	$150,000 and up
City	5.0	4.2	5.5	7.6	16.6	13.2	20.0	28.0
MSA[1]	8.6	7.8	8.1	12.0	18.2	14.5	17.5	13.4
U.S.	12.5	10.7	10.2	13.5	17.8	12.2	13.0	10.0

Note: (1) Figures cover the Minneapolis-St. Paul-Bloomington, MN-WI Metropolitan Statistical Area—see Appendix B for areas included
Source: U.S. Census Bureau, 2010-2014 American Community Survey 5-Year Estimates

Poverty Rate

Area	All Ages	Under 18 Years Old	18 to 64 Years Old	65 Years and Over
City	5.2	6.7	4.5	5.7
MSA[1]	10.6	13.9	9.9	7.1
U.S.	15.6	21.9	14.6	9.4

Note: Figures are percentage of people whose income during the past 12 months was below the poverty level; (1) Figures cover the Minneapolis-St. Paul-Bloomington, MN-WI Metropolitan Statistical Area—see Appendix B for areas included
Source: U.S. Census Bureau, 2010-2014 American Community Survey 5-Year Estimates

EMPLOYMENT

Labor Force and Employment

Area	Civilian Labor Force			Workers Employed		
	Dec. 2014	Dec. 2015	% Chg.	Dec. 2014	Dec. 2015	% Chg.
City	35,211	35,891	1.9	34,359	35,055	2.0
MSA[1]	1,905,506	1,942,269	1.9	1,843,783	1,881,640	2.0
U.S.	155,521,000	157,245,000	1.1	147,190,000	149,703,000	1.7

Note: Data is not seasonally adjusted and covers workers 16 years of age and older; (1) Figures cover the Minneapolis-St. Paul-Bloomington, MN-WI Metropolitan Statistical Area—see Appendix B for areas included
Source: Bureau of Labor Statistics, Local Area Unemployment Statistics

Unemployment Rate

Area	2015											
	Jan.	Feb.	Mar.	Apr.	May	Jun.	Jul.	Aug.	Sep.	Oct.	Nov.	Dec.
City	3.1	2.9	3.1	2.8	3.0	3.1	3.2	2.9	2.7	2.6	2.2	2.3
MSA[1]	4.1	4.0	4.1	3.5	3.5	3.8	3.7	3.4	3.1	2.9	2.8	3.1
U.S.	6.1	5.8	5.6	5.1	5.3	5.5	5.6	5.2	4.9	4.8	4.8	4.8

Note: Data is not seasonally adjusted and covers workers 16 years of age and older; (1) Figures cover the Minneapolis-St. Paul-Bloomington, MN-WI Metropolitan Statistical Area—see Appendix B for areas included
Source: Bureau of Labor Statistics, Local Area Unemployment Statistics

Employment by Occupation

Occupation Classification	City (%)	MSA[1] (%)	U.S. (%)
Management, Business, Science, and Arts	57.9	42.6	36.4
Natural Resources, Construction, and Maintenance	2.8	6.4	9.0
Production, Transportation, and Material Moving	5.9	11.3	12.1
Sales and Office	23.6	24.1	24.4
Service	9.7	15.6	18.2

Note: Figures cover employed civilians 16 years of age and older; (1) Figures cover the Minneapolis-St. Paul-Bloomington, MN-WI Metropolitan Statistical Area—see Appendix B for areas included
Source: U.S. Census Bureau, 2010-2014 American Community Survey 5-Year Estimates

Employment by Industry

Sector	MSA[1]		U.S.
	Number of Employees	Percent of Total	Percent of Total
Construction, Mining, and Logging	71,100	3.6	5.0
Education and Health Services	321,100	16.4	15.7
Financial Activities	148,800	7.6	5.7
Government	254,400	13.0	15.5
Information	39,400	2.0	1.9
Leisure and Hospitality	174,900	8.9	10.4
Manufacturing	194,800	10.0	8.6
Other Services	81,200	4.1	3.9
Professional and Business Services	305,100	15.6	13.9
Retail Trade	189,400	9.7	11.3
Transportation, Warehousing, and Utilities	69,100	3.5	3.9
Wholesale Trade	97,300	4.9	4.1

Note: Figures are non-farm employment as of December 2015. Figures are not seasonally adjusted and include workers 16 years of age and older; (1) Figures cover the Minneapolis-St. Paul-Bloomington, MN-WI Metropolitan Statistical Area—see Appendix B for areas included; n/a not available
Source: Bureau of Labor Statistics, Current Employment Statistics, Employment, Hours, and Earnings

Occupations with Greatest Projected Employment Growth: 2012 – 2022

Occupation[1]	2012 Employment	2022 Projected Employment	Numeric Employment Change	Percent Employment Change
Personal Care Aides	50,550	73,150	22,600	44.7
Home Health Aides	34,520	44,660	10,140	29.3
Registered Nurses	55,950	65,430	9,480	16.9
Retail Salespersons	85,800	92,450	6,650	7.8
Combined Food Preparation and Serving Workers, Including Fast Food	56,120	61,580	5,460	9.7
Carpenters	19,610	24,100	4,490	22.9
Childcare Workers	30,870	34,870	4,000	13.0
Janitors and Cleaners, Except Maids and Housekeeping Cleaners	46,140	49,920	3,780	8.2
Licensed Practical and Licensed Vocational Nurses	17,420	20,660	3,240	18.6
Customer Service Representatives	48,000	51,210	3,210	6.7

Note: Projections cover Minnesota; (1) Sorted by numeric employment change
Source: www.projectionscentral.com, State Occupational Projections, 2012–2022 Long-Term Projections

Fastest Growing Occupations: 2012 – 2022

Occupation[1]	2012 Employment	2022 Projected Employment	Numeric Employment Change	Percent Employment Change
Personal Care Aides	50,550	73,150	22,600	44.7
Insulation Workers, Mechanical	470	660	190	40.6
Physician Assistants	1,650	2,220	570	34.5
Computer Numerically Controlled Machine Tool Programmers, Metal and Plastic	810	1,080	270	33.3
Helpers—Carpenters	510	680	170	32.9
Brickmasons and Blockmasons	1,370	1,810	440	31.9
Interpreters and Translators	1,490	1,960	470	31.4
Diagnostic Medical Sonographers	1,380	1,810	430	31.1
Cement Masons and Concrete Finishers	2,930	3,830	900	30.7
Meeting, Convention, and Event Planners	1,950	2,540	590	29.8

Note: Projections cover Minnesota; (1) Sorted by percent employment change and excludes occupations with numeric employment change less than 100
Source: www.projectionscentral.com, State Occupational Projections, 2012–2022 Long-Term Projections

Average Wages

Occupation	$/Hr.	Occupation	$/Hr.
Accountants and Auditors	34.30	Maids and Housekeeping Cleaners	11.42
Automotive Mechanics	20.89	Maintenance and Repair Workers	21.64
Bookkeepers	19.75	Marketing Managers	66.76
Carpenters	26.22	Nuclear Medicine Technologists	37.32
Cashiers	10.43	Nurses, Licensed Practical	21.42
Clerks, General Office	16.68	Nurses, Registered	37.00
Clerks, Receptionists/Information	14.44	Nursing Assistants	14.83
Clerks, Shipping/Receiving	16.89	Packers and Packagers, Hand	12.13
Computer Programmers	38.85	Physical Therapists	36.96
Computer Systems Analysts	43.76	Postal Service Mail Carriers	24.43
Computer User Support Specialists	26.27	Real Estate Brokers	n/a
Cooks, Restaurant	12.47	Retail Salespersons	12.38
Dentists	90.82	Sales Reps., Exc. Tech./Scientific	37.53
Electrical Engineers	44.95	Sales Reps., Tech./Scientific	58.26
Electricians	30.25	Secretaries, Exc. Legal/Med./Exec.	19.51
Financial Managers	68.00	Security Guards	16.78
First-Line Supervisors/Managers, Sales	20.97	Surgeons	129.05
Food Preparation Workers	12.51	Teacher Assistants*	15.40
General and Operations Managers	55.19	Teachers, Elementary School*	30.58
Hairdressers/Cosmetologists	13.88	Teachers, Secondary School*	32.31
Internists	119.37	Telemarketers	14.42
Janitors and Cleaners	13.40	Truck Drivers, Heavy/Tractor-Trailer	21.24
Landscaping/Groundskeeping Workers	14.32	Truck Drivers, Light/Delivery Svcs.	18.30
Lawyers	64.64	Waiters and Waitresses	10.29

Note: Wage data covers the Minneapolis-St. Paul-Bloomington, MN-WI Metropolitan Statistical Area—see Appendix B for areas included; (*) Hourly wages for elementary/secondary school teachers and teacher assistants were calculated by the editors from annual wage data based on a 40 hour work week; n/a not available.
Source: Bureau of Labor Statistics, Metro Area Occupational Employment and Wage Estimates, May 2015

TAXES

State Corporate Income Tax Rates

State	Tax Rate (%)	Income Brackets ($)	Num. of Brackets	Financial Institution Tax Rate (%)[a]	Federal Income Tax Ded.
Minnesota	9.8 (o)	Flat rate	1	9.8 (o)	No

Note: Tax rates as of January 1, 2016; (a) Rates listed are the corporate income tax rate applied to financial institutions or excise taxes based on income. Some states have other taxes based upon the value of deposits or shares; (o) In addition, Minnesota levies a 5.8% tentative minimum tax on Alternative Minimum Taxable Income.
Source: Federation of Tax Administrators, "State Corporate Income Tax Rates, 2016"

State Individual Income Tax Rates

State	Tax Rate (%)	Income Brackets ($)	Num. of Brackets	Personal Exempt. ($)[1] Single	Personal Exempt. ($)[1] Dependents	Fed. Inc. Tax Ded.
Minnesota (a)	5.35 - 9.85	25,070 - 154,951 (l)	4	4,050 (d)	4,000 (d)	No

Note: Tax rates as of January 1, 2016; Local- and county-level taxes are not included; n/a not applicable; (1) Married joint filers generally receive double the single exemption; (a) 18 states have statutory provision for automatically adjusting to the rate of inflation the dollar values of the income tax brackets, standard deductions, and/or personal exemptions. Massachusetts, Michigan, and Nebraska index the personal exemptiononly. Oregon does not index the income brackets for $125,000 and over. Maine has suspended indexing for 2014 and 2015; (d) These states use the personal exemption amounts provided in the federal Internal Revenue Code; (l) The income brackets reported for Minnesota are for single individuals. For married couples filing jointly, the same tax rates apply to income brackets ranging from $36,820 to $259,421.
Source: Federation of Tax Administrators, "State Individual Income Tax Rates, 2016"

Various State and Local Tax Rates

State	State and Local Sales and Use (%)	State Sales and Use (%)	Gasoline[1] (¢/gal.)	Cigarette[2] ($/pack)	Spirits[3] ($/gal.)	Wine[4] ($/gal.)	Beer[5] ($/gal.)
Minnesota	7.275	6.875	28.6	3.00	8.67 (i)(j)	1.18 (o)(p)	0.47 (q)(s)

Note: All tax rates as of January 1, 2016; (1) The American Petroleum Institute has developed a methodology for determining the average tax rate on a gallon of fuel. Rates may include any of the following: excise taxes, environmental fees, storage tank fees, other fees or taxes, general sales tax, and local taxes. In states where gasoline is subject to the general sales tax, or where the fuel tax is based on the average sale price, the average rate determined by API is sensitive to changes in the price of gasoline. States that fully or partially apply general sales taxes to gasoline: CA, CO, GA, IL, IN, MI, NY; (2) The federal excise tax of $1.0066 per pack and local taxes are not included; (3) Rates are those applicable to off-premise sales of 40% alcohol by volume (a.b.v.) distilled spirits in 750ml containers. Local excise taxes are excluded; (4) Rates are those applicable to off-premise sales of 11% a.b.v. non-carbonated wine in 750ml containers; (5) Rates are those applicable to off-premise sales of 4.7% a.b.v. beer in 12 ounce containers; (i) Includes case fees and/or bottle fees which may vary with size of container; (j) Includes sales taxes specific to alcoholic beverages; (o) Includes case fees and/or bottle fees which may vary with size of container; (p) Includes sales taxes specific to alcoholic beverages; (q) Different rates are also applicable according to alcohol content, place of production, size of container, or place purchased (on- or off-premise or onboard airlines); (s) Includes sales taxes specific to alcoholic beverages.
Source: Tax Foundation, 2016 Facts & Figures: How Does Your State Compare?

State Business Tax Climate Index Rankings

State	Overall Rank	Corporate Tax Rank	Individual Income Tax Rank	Sales Tax Rank	Unemployment Insurance Tax Rank	Property Tax Rank
Minnesota	47	46	46	36	29	30

Note: The index is a measure of how each state's tax laws affect economic performance. The lower the rank, the more favorable a state's tax system is for business. States without a given tax are given a ranking of 1. The scores/rankings for the District of Columbia do not affect other states. The 2016 index represents the tax climate as of July 1, 2015 (the beginning of Fiscal Year 2016).
Source: Tax Foundation, State Business Tax Climate Index 2016

TRANSPORTATION

Means of Transportation to Work

Area	Car/Truck/Van		Public Transportation			Bicycle	Walked	Other Means	Worked at Home
	Drove Alone	Car-pooled	Bus	Subway	Railroad				
City	81.6	6.6	2.9	0.0	0.0	0.2	1.4	0.9	6.4
MSA[1]	78.2	8.4	4.3	0.1	0.1	0.9	2.3	0.9	4.9
U.S.	76.4	9.6	2.6	1.8	0.6	0.6	2.8	1.3	4.4

Note: Figures are percentages and cover workers 16 years of age and older; (1) Figures cover the Minneapolis-St. Paul-Bloomington, MN-WI Metropolitan Statistical Area—see Appendix B for areas included
Source: U.S. Census Bureau, 2010-2014 American Community Survey 5-Year Estimates

Travel Time to Work

Area	Less Than 10 Minutes	10 to 19 Minutes	20 to 29 Minutes	30 to 44 Minutes	45 to 59 Minutes	60 to 89 Minutes	90 Minutes or More
City	11.2	36.2	25.2	19.0	5.3	2.1	1.1
MSA[1]	10.9	28.1	24.8	23.0	7.8	4.1	1.3
U.S.	13.3	29.6	21.0	20.2	7.7	5.7	2.6

Note: Figures are percentages and include workers 16 years old and over; (1) Figures cover the Minneapolis-St. Paul-Bloomington, MN-WI Metropolitan Statistical Area—see Appendix B for areas included
Source: U.S. Census Bureau, 2010-2014 American Community Survey 5-Year Estimates

Freeway Travel Time Index

Area	1985	1990	1995	2000	2005	2010	2014
Urban Area Rank[1,2]	26	25	18	11	17	21	21
Urban Area Index[1]	1.10	1.14	1.21	1.27	1.28	1.25	1.26
Average Index[3]	1.09	1.11	1.14	1.17	1.20	1.19	1.20

Note: Freeway Travel Time Index—the ratio of travel time in the peak period to the travel time at free-flow conditions. For example, a value of 1.30 indicates a 20-minute free-flow trip takes 26 minutes in the peak (20 minutes x 1.30 = 26 minutes); (1) Covers the Minneapolis-St. Paul MN-WI urban area; (2) Rank is based on 101 urban areas (#1 = highest travel time index); (3) Average of 101 urban areas
Source: Texas Transportation Institute, 2015 Urban Mobility Scorecard, August 2015

Freeway Commuter Stress Index

Area	1985	1990	1995	2000	2005	2010	2014
Urban Area Rank[1,2]	33	33	23	17	18	25	27
Urban Area Index[1]	1.14	1.18	1.26	1.31	1.33	1.30	1.31
Average Index[3]	1.13	1.16	1.19	1.22	1.25	1.24	1.25

Note: The Freeway Commuter Stress Index is the same as the Freeway Travel Time Index (see table above) except that it includes only the travel in the peak directions during the peak periods; the TTI includes travel in all directions during the peak period. Thus, the CSI is more indicative of the work trip experienced by each commuter on a daily basis. (1) Covers the Minneapolis-St. Paul MN-WI urban area; (2) Rank is based on 101 urban areas (#1 = highest stress index); (3) Average of 101 urban areas
Source: Texas Transportation Institute, 2015 Urban Mobility Scorecard, August 2015

Living Environment

COST OF LIVING

Cost of Living Index

Composite Index	Groceries	Housing	Utilities	Trans-portation	Health Care	Misc. Goods/ Services
108.3	108.0	112.3	93.1	111.9	105.5	108.8

Note: The Cost of Living Index measures regional differences in the cost of consumer goods and services, excluding taxes and non-consumer expenditures, for professional and managerial households in the top income quintile. It is based on more than 50,000 prices covering almost 60 different items for which prices are collected three times a year by chambers of commerce, economic development organizations or university applied economic centers in each participating urban area. The numbers shown should be read as a percentage above or below the national average of 100. For example, a value of 115.4 in the groceries column indicates that grocery prices are 15.4% higher than the national average. Small differences in the index numbers should not be interpreted as significant; Figures cover the Minneapolis MN urban area.
Source: The Council for Community and Economic Research, ACCRA Cost of Living Index, 2015

Grocery Prices

Area[1]	T-Bone Steak ($/pound)	Frying Chicken ($/pound)	Whole Milk ($/half gal.)	Eggs ($/dozen)	Orange Juice ($/64 oz.)	Coffee ($/11.5 oz.)
City[2]	14.13	1.90	2.26	1.92	3.78	4.64
Avg.	10.99	1.43	2.25	2.26	3.58	4.48
Min.	7.16	0.98	1.30	1.35	2.88	2.98
Max.	14.13	2.43	3.85	4.81	6.39	7.56

Note: (1) Values for the local area are compared with the average, minimum and maximum values for all 292 areas in the Cost of Living Index; (2) Figures cover the Minneapolis MN urban area; **T-Bone Steak** *(price per pound);* **Frying Chicken** *(price per pound, whole fryer);* **Whole Milk** *(half gallon carton);* **Eggs** *(price per dozen, Grade A, large);* **Orange Juice** *(64 oz. Tropicana or Florida Natural);* **Coffee** *(11.5 oz. can, vacuum-packed, Maxwell House, Hills Bros, or Folgers).*
Source: The Council for Community and Economic Research, ACCRA Cost of Living Index, 2015

Housing and Utility Costs

Area[1]	New Home Price ($)	Apartment Rent ($/month)	All Electric ($/month)	Part Electric ($/month)	Other Energy ($/month)	Telephone ($/month)
City[2]	345,759	1,098	-	93.62	69.52	24.99
Avg.	312,874	945	179.30	95.07	72.96	28.11
Min.	178,682	479	116.28	43.14	26.46	10.01
Max.	1,472,476	3,984	504.25	189.44	421.11	43.06

Note: (1) Values for the local area are compared with the average, minimum and maximum values for all 292 areas in the Cost of Living Index; (2) Figures cover the Minneapolis MN urban area; **New Home Price** *(2,400 sf living area, 8,000 sf lot, in urban area with full utilities);* **Apartment Rent** *(950 sf 2 bedroom/1.5 or 2 bath, unfurnished, excluding all utilities except water);* **All Electric** *(average monthly cost for an all-electric home);* **Part Electric** *(average monthly cost for a part-electric home);* **Other Energy** *(average monthly cost for natural gas, fuel oil, coal, wood, and any other forms of energy except electricity);* **Telephone** *(price includes basic monthly rate for a private residential line plus additional local usage charges incurred by a family of four).*
Source: The Council for Community and Economic Research, ACCRA Cost of Living Index, 2015

Health Care, Transportation, and Other Costs

Area[1]	Doctor ($/visit)	Dentist ($/visit)	Optometrist ($/visit)	Gasoline ($/gallon)	Beauty Salon ($/visit)	Men's Shirt ($)
City[2]	133.87	84.35	82.36	2.62	33.40	30.95
Avg.	105.15	89.02	99.78	2.38	35.30	28.10
Min.	66.87	56.09	48.53	1.95	18.91	13.38
Max.	182.34	150.36	228.33	4.09	67.91	63.80

Note: (1) Values for the local area are compared with the average, minimum and maximum values for all 292 areas in the Cost of Living Index; (2) Figures cover the Minneapolis MN urban area; **Doctor** *(general practitioners routine exam of an established patient);* **Dentist** *(adult teeth cleaning and periodic oral examination);* **Optometrist** *(full vision eye exam for established adult patient);* **Gasoline** *(one gallon regular unleaded, national brand, including all taxes, cash price at self-service pump if available);* **Beauty Salon** *(woman's shampoo, trim, and blow-dry);* **Men's Shirt** *(cotton/polyester dress shirt, pinpoint weave, long sleeves).*
Source: The Council for Community and Economic Research, ACCRA Cost of Living Index, 2015

HOUSING

House Price Index (HPI)

Area	National Ranking[2]	Quarterly Change (%)	One-Year Change (%)	Five-Year Change (%)
MSA[1]	112	0.20	5.20	13.00
U.S.[3]	–	1.45	5.76	22.85

Note: The HPI is a weighted repeat sales index. It measures average price changes in repeat sales or refinancings on the same properties. This information is obtained by reviewing repeat mortgage transactions on single-family properties whose mortgages have been purchased or securitized by Fannie Mae or Freddie Mac in January 1975; (1) Minneapolis-St. Paul-Bloomington Metropolitan Statistical Area—see Appendix B for areas included; (2) Rankings are based on annual percentage change for all metro areas containing at least 15,000 transactions over the last 10 years and ranges from 1 to 266; (3) figures based on a weighted average of Census Division estimates using a seasonally adjusted, purchase-only index; all figures are for the period ending December 31, 2015

Source: Federal Housing Finance Agency, House Price Index, February 25, 2016

Median Single-Family Home Prices

Area	2013	2014	2015p	Percent Change 2014 to 2015
MSA[1]	196.2	210.1	225.1	7.1
U.S. Average	197.4	208.9	223.9	7.2

Note: Figures are median sales prices of existing single-family homes in thousands of dollars; (p) preliminary; n/a not available; (1) Minneapolis-St. Paul-Bloomington, MN-WI Metropolitan Statistical Area—see Appendix B for areas included

Source: National Association of Realtors, Median Sales Price of Existing Single-Family Homes for Metropolitan Areas, 4th Quarter 2015

Qualifying Income Based on Median Sales Price of Existing Single-Family Homes

Area	With 5% Down ($)	With 10% Down ($)	With 20% Down ($)
MSA[1]	49,758	47,139	41,901
U.S. Average	49,535	46,928	41,714

Note: Figures are preliminary; Qualifying income is based on a mortgage rate of 4.1%. Monthly principal and interest payment is limited to 25% of income; n/a not available; (1) Minneapolis-St. Paul-Bloomington, MN-WI Metropolitan Statistical Area—see Appendix B for areas included

Source: National Association of Realtors, Qualifying Income Based on Median Sales Price of Existing Single-Family Homes for Metropolitan Areas, 4th Quarter 2015

Median Apartment Condo-Coop Home Prices

Area	2013	2014	2015p	Percent Change 2014 to 2015
MSA[1]	n/a	n/a	n/a	n/a
U.S. Average	194.9	204.3	210.7	3.1

Note: Figures are median sales prices of existing apartment condo-coop homes in thousands of dollars; (p) preliminary; n/a not available; (1) Minneapolis-St. Paul-Bloomington, MN-WI Metropolitan Statistical Area—see Appendix B for areas included

Source: National Association of Realtors, Median Sales Price of Existing Apartment Condo-Coop Homes for Metropolitan Areas, 4th Quarter 2015

Gross Monthly Rent

Area	Under $200	$200 -299	$300 -499	$500 -749	$750 -999	$1,000 -1,499	$1,500 and up	Median ($)
City	0.8	1.1	2.1	3.3	24.0	47.3	21.4	1,154
MSA[1]	1.9	3.8	5.3	18.2	29.7	28.8	12.3	916
U.S.	1.5	3.2	7.4	21.0	24.1	26.9	15.9	920

Note: Figures are percentages except for Median; Gross rent is the contract rent plus the estimated average monthly cost of utilities (electricity, gas, and water and sewer) and fuels (oil, coal, kerosene, wood, etc.) if these are paid by the renter (or paid for the renter by someone else); (1) Figures cover the Minneapolis-St. Paul-Bloomington, MN-WI Metropolitan Statistical Area—see Appendix B for areas included

Source: U.S. Census Bureau, 2010-2014 American Community Survey 5-Year Estimates

Homeownership Rate

Area	2008 (%)	2009 (%)	2010 (%)	2011 (%)	2012 (%)	2013 (%)	2014 (%)	2015 (%)
MSA[1]	69.9	70.9	71.2	69.1	70.8	71.7	69.7	67.9
U.S.	67.8	67.4	66.9	66.1	65.4	65.1	64.5	63.7

Note: (1) Figures cover the Minneapolis-St. Paul-Bloomington, MN-WI Metropolitan Statistical Area—see Appendix B for areas included
Source: U.S. Census Bureau, Housing Vacancies and Homeownership Annual Statistics: 2015

Year Housing Structure Built

Area	2010 or Later	2000 -2009	1990 -1999	1980 -1989	1970 -1979	1960 -1969	1950 -1959	1940 -1949	Before 1940	Median Year
City	0.4	16.0	24.7	35.4	15.9	3.7	2.5	0.3	1.1	1987
MSA[1]	0.8	15.2	14.6	14.8	15.4	10.0	10.1	4.1	15.0	1977
U.S.	1.0	14.9	13.9	13.8	15.8	11.0	10.8	5.4	13.3	1976

Note: Figures are percentages except for Median Year; (1) Figures cover the Minneapolis-St. Paul-Bloomington, MN-WI Metropolitan Statistical Area—see Appendix B for areas included
Source: U.S. Census Bureau, 2010-2014 American Community Survey 5-Year Estimates

HEALTH

Health Risk Data

Category	MSA[1] (%)	U.S. (%)
Adults aged 18–64 who have any kind of health care coverage	87.3	79.6
Adults who reported being in good or excellent health	89.2	83.1
Adults who are current smokers	18.0	19.6
Adults who are heavy drinkers[2]	6.6	6.1
Adults who are binge drinkers[3]	21.4	16.9
Adults who are overweight (BMI 25.0 - 29.9)	37.0	35.8
Adults who are obese (BMI 30.0 - 99.8)	23.9	27.6
Adults who participated in any physical activities in the past month	83.5	77.1
Adults 50+ who have ever had a sigmoidoscopy or colonoscopy	74.4	67.3
Women aged 40+ who have had a mammogram within the past two years	78.6	74.0
Men aged 40+ who have had a PSA test within the past two years	38.5	45.2
Adults aged 65+ who have had flu shot within the past year	67.6	60.1
Adults who always wear a seatbelt	96.6	93.8

Note: Data as of 2012 unless otherwise noted; (1) Figures cover the Minneapolis-St. Paul-Bloomington, MN-WI Metropolitan Statistical Area—see Appendix B for areas included; (2) Heavy drinkers are classified as males having more than two drinks per day or females having more than one drink per day; (3) Binge drinkers are classified as males having five or more drinks on one occasion or females having four or more drinks on one occasion
Source: Centers for Disease Control and Prevention, Behaviorial Risk Factor Surveillance System, SMART: Selected Metropolitan/Micropolitan Area Risk Trends, 2012 (Note: the CDC has discontinued this dataset but will be releasing a replacement in mid-2016)

Chronic Health Indicators

Category	MSA[1] (%)	U.S. (%)
Adults who have ever been told they had a heart attack	3.6	4.5
Adults who have ever been told they had a stroke	2.5	2.9
Adults who have been told they currently have asthma	8.7	8.9
Adults who have ever been told they have arthritis	19.6	25.7
Adults who have ever been told they have diabetes[2]	6.7	9.7
Adults who have ever been told they had skin cancer	5.0	5.7
Adults who have ever been told they had any other types of cancer	5.7	6.5
Adults who have ever been told they have COPD	3.9	6.2
Adults who have ever been told they have kidney disease	2.1	2.5
Adults who have ever been told they have a form of depression	16.5	18.0

Note: Data as of 2012 unless otherwise noted; (1) Figures cover the Minneapolis-St. Paul-Bloomington, MN-WI Metropolitan Statistical Area—see Appendix B for areas included; (2) Figures do not include pregnancy-related, borderline, or pre-diabetes
Source: Centers for Disease Control and Prevention, Behaviorial Risk Factor Surveillance System, SMART: Selected Metropolitan/Micropolitan Area Risk Trends, 2012 (Note: the CDC has discontinued this dataset but will be releasing a replacement in mid-2016)

Mortality Rates for the Top 10 Causes of Death in the U.S.

ICD-10[a] Sub-Chapter	ICD-10[a] Code	Age-Adjusted Mortality Rate[1] per 100,000 population	
		County[2]	U.S.
Malignant neoplasms	C00-C97	149.6	163.6
Ischaemic heart diseases	I20-I25	48.8	102.2
Other forms of heart disease	I30-I51	41.7	50.1
Chronic lower respiratory diseases	J40-J47	34.0	41.4
Organic, including symptomatic, mental disorders	F01-F09	61.6	38.5
Cerebrovascular diseases	I60-I69	32.1	36.5
Other external causes of accidental injury	W00-X59	36.1	27.5
Other degenerative diseases of the nervous system	G30-G31	22.7	26.3
Diabetes mellitus	E10-E14	16.8	21.1
Hypertensive diseases	I10-I15	11.2	19.7

Note: (a) ICD-10 = International Classification of Diseases 10th Revision; (1) Mortality rates are a three year average covering 2012-2014; (2) Figures cover Hennepin County.
Source: Centers for Disease Control and Prevention, National Center for Health Statistics. Underlying Cause of Death 1999-2014 on CDC WONDER Online Database, released 2015.

Mortality Rates for Selected Causes of Death

ICD-10[a] Sub-Chapter	ICD-10[a] Code	Age-Adjusted Mortality Rate[1] per 100,000 population	
		County[2]	U.S.
Assault	X85-Y09	3.5	5.1
Diseases of the liver	K70-K76	12.3	13.5
Human immunodeficiency virus (HIV) disease	B20-B24	1.4	2.1
Influenza and pneumonia	J09-J18	8.9	15.2
Intentional self-harm	X60-X84	10.4	12.7
Malnutrition	E40-E46	0.6	0.9
Obesity and other hyperalimentation	E65-E68	1.6	1.9
Renal failure	N17-N19	10.0	13.0
Transport accidents	V01-V99	4.5	11.6
Viral hepatitis	B15-B19	1.9	2.1

Note: (a) ICD-10 = International Classification of Diseases 10th Revision; (1) Mortality rates are a three year average covering 2012-2014; (2) Figures cover Hennepin County; Data are Suppressed when the data meet the criteria for confidentiality constraints; Mortality rates are flagged as Unreliable when the rate would be calculated with a numerator of 20 or less.
Source: Centers for Disease Control and Prevention, National Center for Health Statistics. Underlying Cause of Death 1999-2014 on CDC WONDER Online Database, released 2015.

Health Insurance Coverage

Area	With Health Insurance	With Private Health Insurance	With Public Health Insurance	Without Health Insurance	Population Under Age 18 Without Health Insurance
City	94.0	85.5	16.7	6.0	3.2
MSA[1]	92.2	77.7	25.1	7.8	4.9
U.S.	85.8	65.8	31.1	14.2	7.1

Note: Figures are percentages that cover the civilian noninstitutionalized population; (1) Figures cover the Minneapolis-St. Paul-Bloomington, MN-WI Metropolitan Statistical Area—see Appendix B for areas included
Source: U.S. Census Bureau, 2010-2014 American Community Survey 5-Year Estimates

Number of Medical Professionals

Area	MDs[3]	DOs[3,4]	Dentists	Podiatrists	Chiropractors	Optometrists
County[1] (number)	5,783	197	1,085	43	806	220
County[1] (rate[2])	481.9	16.4	89.5	3.5	66.5	18.2
U.S. (rate[2])	272.5	20.9	64.7	5.8	25.9	15.2

Note: Data as of 2014 unless noted; (1) Data covers Hennepin County; (2) Rate per 100,000 population; (3) Data as of 2013 and includes all active, non-federal physicians; (4) Doctor of Osteopathic Medicine
Source: U.S. Department of Health and Human Services, Health Resources and Services Administration, Bureau of Health Professions, Area Resource File (ARF) 2014-2015

Best Hospitals

According to *U.S. News,* the Minneapolis-St. Paul-Bloomington, MN-WI metro area is home to three of the best hospitals in the U.S.: **MercyHospital** (1 specialty); **Abbott Northwestern Hospital** (5 specialties); **Minneapolis Heart Institute at Abbott Northwestern Hospital** (1 specialty). The hospitals listed were nationally ranked in at least one adult specialty. Only 137 hospitals nationwide were nationally ranked in one or more specialties. Fifteen hospitals in the U.S. made the Honor Roll with high scores in at least six specialties. *U.S. News Online, "America's Best Children's Hospitals 2015-16"*

According to *U.S. News,* the Minneapolis-St. Paul-Bloomington, MN-WI metro area is home to three of the best children's hospitals in the U.S.: **Children's Hospitals and Clinics of Minnesota** (1 specialties); **University of Minnesota Masonic Children's Hospital** (5 specialties); **Gillette Children's Specialty Healthcare** (1 specialty). The hospitals listed were highly ranked in at least one pediatric specialty. Eighty-three children's hospitals in the U.S. were nationally ranked in at least one specialty. Twelve children's hospitals in the U.S. made the Honor Roll with high scores in at least three specialties. *U.S. News Online, "America's Best Children's Hospitals 2015-16"*

EDUCATION

Public School District Statistics

District Name	Schls	Pupils	Pupil/ Teacher Ratio	Minority Pupils[1] (%)	Free Lunch Eligible[2] (%)	IEP[3] (%)
Eagle Ridge Academy Charter	2	823	15.7	32.2	9.0	8.1
Eden Prairie Public School District	13	9,275	16.9	34.5	16.8	12.6
Intermediate School District 287	82	473	1.7	68.7	n/a	n/a

Note: Table includes school districts with 100 or more students; (1) Percentage of students that are not non-Hispanic white; (2) Percentage of students that are eligible for the free lunch program; (3) Percentage of students that have an Individualized Education Program.
Source: U.S. Department of Education, National Center for Education Statistics, Common Core of Data, Local Education Agency (School District) Universe Survey: School Year 2013-2014; U.S. Department of Education, National Center for Education Statistics, Common Core of Data, Public Elementary/Secondary School Universe Survey: School Year 2013-2014

Highest Level of Education

Area	Less than H.S.	H.S. Diploma	Some College, No Deg.	Associate Degree	Bachelor's Degree	Master's Degree	Prof. School Degree	Doctorate Degree
City	2.7	10.6	17.3	8.7	39.1	15.6	3.5	2.4
MSA[1]	6.9	22.8	21.4	9.9	25.9	9.2	2.4	1.4
U.S.	13.7	28.0	21.2	7.9	18.3	7.8	2.0	1.3

Note: Figures cover persons age 25 and over; (1) Figures cover the Minneapolis-St. Paul-Bloomington, MN-WI Metropolitan Statistical Area—see Appendix B for areas included
Source: U.S. Census Bureau, 2010-2014 American Community Survey 5-Year Estimates

Educational Attainment by Race

Area	High School Graduate or Higher (%)					Bachelor's Degree or Higher (%)				
	Total	White	Black	Asian	Hisp.[2]	Total	White	Black	Asian	Hisp.[2]
City	97.3	98.8	83.0	92.6	82.2	60.7	60.9	28.9	76.5	45.4
MSA[1]	93.1	95.3	81.8	79.8	65.7	39.0	40.7	20.2	44.0	17.6
U.S.	86.3	88.4	83.2	85.8	64.1	29.3	30.6	19.0	50.9	13.9

Note: Figures shown cover persons 25 years old and over; (1) Figures cover the Minneapolis-St. Paul-Bloomington, MN-WI Metropolitan Statistical Area—see Appendix B for areas included; (2) People of Hispanic origin can be of any race
Source: U.S. Census Bureau, 2010-2014 American Community Survey 5-Year Estimates

School Enrollment by Grade and Control

Area	Preschool (%)		Kindergarten (%)		Grades 1 - 4 (%)		Grades 5 - 8 (%)		Grades 9 - 12 (%)	
	Public	Private	Public	Private	Public	Private	Public	Private	Public	Private
City	52.4	47.6	86.1	13.9	84.4	15.6	81.6	18.4	88.8	11.2
MSA[1]	55.6	44.4	86.8	13.2	87.9	12.1	88.6	11.4	90.9	9.1
U.S.	57.4	42.6	87.8	12.2	89.8	10.2	89.9	10.1	90.6	9.4

Note: Figures shown cover persons 3 years old and over; (1) Figures cover the Minneapolis-St. Paul-Bloomington, MN-WI Metropolitan Statistical Area—see Appendix B for areas included
Source: U.S. Census Bureau, 2010-2014 American Community Survey 5-Year Estimates

Average Salaries of Public School Classroom Teachers

Area	2013-14		2014-15		Percent Change 2013-14 to 2014-15	Percent Change 2004-05 to 2014-15
	Dollars	Rank[1]	Dollars	Rank[1]		
Minnesota	54,752	21	56,670	20	3.50	19.5
U.S. Average	56,610	–	57,379	–	1.36	20.8

Note: (1) State rank ranges from 1 to 51 where 1 indicates highest salary.
Source: National Education Association, Rankings & Estimates: Rankings of the States 2014 and Estimates of School Statistics 2015, March 2015

Higher Education

Four-Year Colleges			Two-Year Colleges			Medical Schools[1]	Law Schools[2]	Voc/ Tech[3]
Public	Private Non-profit	Private For-profit	Public	Private Non-profit	Private For-profit			
0	0	1	0	0	0	0	0	1

Note: Figures cover institutions located within the city limits and include main campuses only; (1) includes schools accredited by the Liaison Committee on Medical Education and the American Osteopathic Association's Commission on Osteopathic College Accreditation; (2) includes ABA-accredited schools, schools with provisional ABA accreditation, and state accredited schools; (3) includes all schools with programs that are less than 2 years.
Source: National Center for Education Statistics, Integrated Postsecondary Education System (IPEDS), 2014-15; Association of American Medical Colleges, Member List, March 21, 2016; American Osteopathic Association, Member List, March 21, 2016; Law School Admission Council, Official Guide to ABA-Approved Law Schools Online, March 21, 2016; Wikipedia, List of Medical Schools in the United States, March 21, 2016; Wikipedia, List of Law Schools in the United States, March 21, 2016

According to *U.S. News & World Report,* the Minneapolis-St. Paul-Bloomington, MN-WI metro area is home to two of the best national universities in the U.S.: **University of Minnesota–Twin Cities** (#69); **University of St. Thomas** (#115 tie). The indicators used to capture academic quality fall into a number of categories: assessment by administrators at peer institutions; retention of students; faculty resources; student selectivity; financial resources; alumni giving; high school counselor ratings of colleges; and graduation rate. *U.S. News & World Report, "America's Best Colleges 2016"*

According to *U.S. News & World Report,* the Minneapolis-St. Paul-Bloomington, MN-WI metro area is home to two of the best liberal arts colleges in the U.S.: **Macalester College** (#23 tie); **Gustavus Adolphus College** (#79 tie). The indicators used to capture academic quality fall into a number of categories: assessment by administrators at peer institutions; retention of students; faculty resources; student selectivity; financial resources; alumni giving; high school counselor ratings of colleges; and graduation rate. *U.S. News & World Report, "America's Best Colleges 2016"*

According to *U.S. News & World Report,* the Minneapolis-St. Paul-Bloomington, MN-WI metro area is home to one of the top 100 law schools in the U.S.: **University of Minnesota, Law School** (#22 tie). The rankings are based on a weighted average of 12 measures of quality: peer assessment score; assessment score by lawyers/judges; median LSAT scores; median undergrad GPA; acceptance rate; employment rates for graduates; placement success; bar passage rate; faculty resources; expenditures per student; student/faculty ratio; and library resources. *U.S. News & World Report, "America's Best Graduate Schools, Law, 2017"*

According to *U.S. News & World Report,* the Minneapolis-St. Paul-Bloomington, MN-WI metro area is home to one of the top 75 medical schools for research in the U.S.: **University of Minnesota, Medical School** (#35 tie). The rankings are based on a weighted average of 11 measures of quality: quality assessment; peer assessment score; assessment score by residency directors; research activity; total research activity; average research activity per faculty member; student selectivity; median MCAT total score; median undergraduate GPA;

acceptance rate; and faculty resources. *U.S. News & World Report, "America's Best Graduate Schools, Medical, 2017"*

According to *U.S. News & World Report,* the Minneapolis-St. Paul-Bloomington, MN-WI metro area is home to one of the top 75 business schools in the U.S.: **University of Minnesota–Twin Cities, Carlson School of Management** (#27 tie). The rankings are based on a weighted average of the following nine measures: quality assessment; peer assessment; recruiter assessment; placement success; mean starting salary and bonus; student selectivity; mean GMAT and GRE scores; mean undergraduate GPA; and acceptance rate. *U.S. News & World Report, "America's Best Graduate Schools, Business, 2017"*

PRESIDENTIAL ELECTION

2012 Presidential Election Results

Area	Obama (%)	Romney (%)	Other (%)
Hennepin County	62.3	35.3	2.4
U.S.	51.0	47.2	1.8

Note: Results may not add to 100% due to rounding
Source: Dave Leip's Atlas of U.S. Presidential Elections

EMPLOYERS

Major Employers

Company Name	Industry
3M Company	Adhesives, sealants
Ameriprise Financial	Investment advice
Anderson Corporation	Millwork
Aware Integrated	Hospital & medical services plans
Bethesda Healtheast Hospital	General medical/surgical hospitals
Carlson Holdings	Hotels/motels
City of Minneapolis	General government, local government
County of Hennepin	General government, county government
Hennepin County	County supervisors' & executives' offices
Honeywell International	Aircraft engines & engine parts
Lawson Software	Application computer software
Medtronic	Electromedical equipment
Minnesota Department of Human Services	Family services agency
Minnesota Department of Transportation	Regulation, administration of transportation
North Memorial Hospital	General medical/surgical hospitals
Regents of the University of Minnesota	Specialty outpatient clinics
Rosemount Apple Valley and Eagan	Personal service agents, brokers, & bureaus
St Paul Fire and marine Insurance Company	Fire, marine, & casualty insurance
Thomson Legal Regulatory	Books, publishing & printing
United Parcel Service	Package delivery vehicular
Wells Fargo Bank	Mortgage bankers
West Publishing Corporation	Data base information retrieval

Note: Companies shown are located within the Minneapolis-St. Paul-Bloomington, MN-WI Metropolitan Statistical Area.
Source: Hoovers.com; Wikipedia

PUBLIC SAFETY

Crime Rate

Area	All Crimes	Violent Crimes				Property Crimes		
		Murder	Rape[3]	Robbery	Aggrav. Assault	Burglary	Larceny -Theft	Motor Vehicle Theft
City	1,381.8	0.0	17.5	6.3	11.1	155.5	1,166.0	25.4
Metro[1]	2,758.2	1.8	33.7	94.3	131.9	402.3	1,915.8	178.4
U.S.	2,971.8	4.5	36.6	102.2	232.5	542.5	1,837.3	216.2

Note: Figures are crimes per 100,000 population; (1) Figures cover the Minneapolis-St. Paul-Bloomington, MN-WI Metropolitan Statistical Area—see Appendix B for areas included; (3) The city and U.S. figures shown were reported using the revised Uniform Crime Reporting (UCR) definition of rape. The suburban and metro area figures shown are an aggregate total of the data submitted using both the revised and legacy UCR definitions.
Source: FBI Uniform Crime Reports, 2014

Hate Crimes

Area	Number of Quarters Reported	Number of Incidents per Bias Motivation: Race	Religion	Sexual Orientation	Ethnicity	Disability	Gender	Gender Identity
City	4	0	0	0	0	0	0	0
U.S.	4	2,568	1,014	1,017	648	84	33	98

Source: Federal Bureau of Investigation, Hate Crime Statistics 2014

Identity Theft Consumer Complaints

Area	Complaints	Complaints per 100,000 Population	Rank[2]
MSA[1]	3,988	114.1	149
U.S.	490,220	152.4	-

Note: (1) Figures cover the Minneapolis-St. Paul-Bloomington, MN-WI Metropolitan Statistical Area—see Appendix B for areas included; (2) Rank ranges from 1 to 379 where 1 indicates greatest number of identity theft complaints per 100,000 population
Source: Federal Trade Commission, Consumer Sentinel Network Data Book for January–December 2015

Fraud and Other Consumer Complaints

Area	Complaints	Complaints per 100,000 Population	Rank[2]
MSA[1]	13,758	393.6	116
U.S.	2,593,159	806.0	-

Note: (1) Figures cover the Minneapolis-St. Paul-Bloomington, MN-WI Metropolitan Statistical Area—see Appendix B for areas included; (2) Rank ranges from 1 to 379 where 1 indicates greatest number of identity theft complaints per 100,000 population
Source: Federal Trade Commission, Consumer Sentinel Network Data Book for January–December 2015

RECREATION

Culture

Dance[1]	Theatre[1]	Instrumental Music[1]	Vocal Music[1]	Series and Festivals	Museums and Art Galleries[2]	Zoos and Aquariums[3]
0	0	0	0	0	0	0

Note: (1) Professional perfoming groups; (2) Based on organizations with SIC code 8412; (3) AZA-accredited
Source: The Grey House Performing Arts Directory, 2015-16; Association of Zoos & Aquariums, AZA Member Zoos & Aquariums, March 25, 2016; www.AccuLeads.com, March 29, 2016

Professional Sports Teams

Team Name	League	Year Established
Minnesota Timberwolves	National Basketball Association (NBA)	1989
Minnesota Twins	Major League Baseball (MLB)	1961
Minnesota United FC	Major League Soccer (MLS)	2018
Minnesota Vikings	National Football League (NFL)	1961
Minnesota Wild	National Hockey League (NHL)	2000

Note: Includes teams located in the Minneapolis-St. Paul-Bloomington, MN-WI Metropolitan Statistical Area.
Source: Wikipedia, Major Professional Sports Teams of the United States and Canada, March 24, 2016

CLIMATE

Average and Extreme Temperatures

Temperature	Jan	Feb	Mar	Apr	May	Jun	Jul	Aug	Sep	Oct	Nov	Dec	Yr.
Extreme High (°F)	57	60	83	95	96	102	105	101	98	89	74	63	105
Average High (°F)	21	27	38	56	69	79	84	81	71	59	41	26	54
Average Temp. (°F)	12	18	30	46	59	69	74	71	61	50	33	19	45
Average Low (°F)	3	9	21	36	48	58	63	61	50	39	25	11	35
Extreme Low (°F)	-34	-28	-32	2	18	37	43	39	26	15	-17	-29	-34

Note: Figures cover the years 1948-1990
Source: National Climatic Data Center, International Station Meteorological Climate Summary, 9/96

Average Precipitation/Snowfall/Humidity

Precip./Humidity	Jan	Feb	Mar	Apr	May	Jun	Jul	Aug	Sep	Oct	Nov	Dec	Yr.
Avg. Precip. (in.)	0.8	0.8	1.9	2.2	3.1	4.0	3.8	3.6	2.5	1.9	1.4	1.0	27.1
Avg. Snowfall (in.)	11	9	12	3	Tr	0	0	0	Tr	Tr	7	10	52
Avg. Rel. Hum. 6am (%)	75	76	77	75	75	79	81	84	85	81	80	79	79
Avg. Rel. Hum. 3pm (%)	64	62	58	48	47	50	50	52	53	52	62	68	55

Note: Figures cover the years 1948-1990; Tr = Trace amounts (<0.05 in. of rain; <0.5 in. of snow)
Source: National Climatic Data Center, International Station Meteorological Climate Summary, 9/96

Weather Conditions

Temperature			Daytime Sky			Precipitation		
5°F & below	32°F & below	90°F & above	Clear	Partly cloudy	Cloudy	0.01 inch or more precip.	0.1 inch or more snow/ice	Thunder-storms
45	156	16	93	125	147	113	41	37

Note: Figures are average number of days per year and cover the years 1948-1990
Source: National Climatic Data Center, International Station Meteorological Climate Summary, 9/96

HAZARDOUS WASTE

Superfund Sites

Eden Prairie has no sites on the EPA's Superfund Final National Priorities List. There are a total of 1,323 Superfund sites on the list in the U.S. *U.S. Environmental Protection Agency, Final National Priorities List, March 18, 2016*

AIR & WATER QUALITY

Air Quality Trends: Ozone

	1990	1995	2000	2005	2010	2011	2012	2013	2014
MSA[1]	0.068	0.084	0.065	0.074	0.066	0.064	0.073	0.066	0.063

Note: (1) Data covers the Minneapolis-St. Paul-Bloomington, MN-WI Metropolitan Statistical Area—see Appendix B for areas included. The values shown are the composite ozone concentration averages among trend sites based on the highest fourth daily maximum 8-hour concentration in parts per million. These trends are based on sites having an adequate record of monitoring data during the trend period. Data from exceptional events are included.
Source: U.S. Environmental Protection Agency, Air Quality Monitoring Information, "Air Quality Trends by City, 1990-2014"

Air Quality Index

Area	Percent of Days when Air Quality was...[2]					AQI Statistics[2]	
	Good	Moderate	Unhealthy for Sensitive Groups	Unhealthy	Very Unhealthy	Maximum	Median
MSA[1]	54.5	44.1	1.4	0.0	0.0	137	48

Note: (1) Data covers the Minneapolis-St. Paul-Bloomington, MN-WI Metropolitan Statistical Area—see Appendix B for areas included; (2) Based on 365 days with AQI data in 2015. Air Quality Index (AQI) is an index for reporting daily air quality. EPA calculates the AQI for five major air pollutants regulated by the Clean Air Act: ground-level ozone, particle pollution (aka particulate matter), carbon monoxide, sulfur dioxide, and nitrogen dioxide. The AQI runs from 0 to 500. The higher the AQI value, the greater the level of air pollution and the greater the health concern. There are six AQI categories: "Good" AQI is between 0 and 50. Air quality is considered satisfactory; "Moderate" AQI is between 51 and 100. Air quality is acceptable; "Unhealthy for Sensitive Groups" When AQI values are between 101 and 150, members of sensitive groups may experience health effects; "Unhealthy" When AQI values are between 151 and 200 everyone may begin to experience health effects; "Very Unhealthy" AQI values between 201 and 300 trigger a health alert; "Hazardous" AQI values over 300 trigger warnings of emergency conditions (not shown).
Source: U.S. Environmental Protection Agency, Air Quality Index Report, 2015

Air Quality Index Pollutants

Area	Percent of Days when AQI Pollutant was...[2]					
	Carbon Monoxide	Nitrogen Dioxide	Ozone	Sulfur Dioxide	Particulate Matter 2.5	Particulate Matter 10
MSA[1]	0.0	1.9	18.6	0.0	51.0	28.5

Note: (1) Data covers the Minneapolis-St. Paul-Bloomington, MN-WI Metropolitan Statistical Area—see Appendix B for areas included; (2) Based on 365 days with AQI data in 2015. The Air Quality Index (AQI) is an index for reporting daily air quality. EPA calculates the AQI for five major air pollutants regulated by the Clean Air Act: ground-level ozone, particle pollution (also known as particulate matter), carbon monoxide, sulfur dioxide, and nitrogen dioxide. The AQI runs from 0 to 500. The higher the AQI value, the greater the level of air pollution and the greater the health concern.
Source: U.S. Environmental Protection Agency, Air Quality Index Report, 2015

Maximum Air Pollutant Concentrations: Particulate Matter, Ozone, CO and Lead

	Particulate Matter 10 (ug/m^3)	Particulate Matter 2.5 Wtd AM (ug/m^3)	Particulate Matter 2.5 24-Hr (ug/m^3)	Ozone (ppm)	Carbon Monoxide (ppm)	Lead (ug/m^3)
MSA[1] Level	76	9.9	28	0.064	2	0.12
NAAQS[2]	150	15	35	0.075	9	0.15
Met NAAQS[2]	Yes	Yes	Yes	Yes	Yes	Yes

Note: (1) Data covers the Minneapolis-St. Paul-Bloomington, MN-WI Metropolitan Statistical Area—see Appendix B for areas included; Data from exceptional events are included; (2) National Ambient Air Quality Standards; ppm = parts per million; ug/m^3 = micrograms per cubic meter; n/a not available.
Concentrations: Particulate Matter 10 (coarse particulate)—highest second maximum 24-hour concentration; Particulate Matter 2.5 Wtd AM (fine particulate)—highest weighted annual mean concentration; Particulate Matter 2.5 24-Hour (fine particulate)—highest 98th percentile 24-hour concentration; Ozone—highest fourth daily maximum 8-hour concentration; Carbon Monoxide—highest second maximum non-overlapping 8-hour concentration; Lead—maximum running 3-month average
Source: U.S. Environmental Protection Agency, Air Quality Monitoring Information, "Air Quality Statistics by City, 2014"

Maximum Air Pollutant Concentrations: Nitrogen Dioxide and Sulfur Dioxide

	Nitrogen Dioxide AM (ppb)	Nitrogen Dioxide 1-Hr (ppb)	Sulfur Dioxide AM (ppb)	Sulfur Dioxide 1-Hr (ppb)	Sulfur Dioxide 24-Hr (ppb)
MSA[1] Level	16	50	n/a	12	n/a
NAAQS[2]	53	100	30	75	140
Met NAAQS[2]	Yes	Yes	n/a	Yes	n/a

Note: (1) Data covers the Minneapolis-St. Paul-Bloomington, MN-WI Metropolitan Statistical Area—see Appendix B for areas included; Data from exceptional events are included; (2) National Ambient Air Quality Standards; ppm = parts per million; ug/m^3 = micrograms per cubic meter; n/a not available.
Concentrations: Nitrogen Dioxide AM—highest arithmetic mean concentration; Nitrogen Dioxide 1-Hr—highest 98th percentile 1-hour daily maximum concentration; Sulfur Dioxide AM—highest annual mean concentration; Sulfur Dioxide 1-Hr—highest 99th percentile 1-hour daily maximum concentration; Sulfur Dioxide 24-Hr—highest second maximum 24-hour concentration
Source: U.S. Environmental Protection Agency, Air Quality Monitoring Information, "Air Quality Statistics by City, 2014"

Drinking Water

Water System Name	Pop. Served	Primary Water Source Type	Violations[1]	
			Health Based	Monitoring/ Reporting
Eden Prairie	62,004	Ground	0	0

Note: (1) Based on violation data from January 1, 2015 to December 31, 2015 (includes unresolved violations from earlier years)
Source: U.S. Environmental Protection Agency, Office of Ground Water and Drinking Water, Safe Drinking Water Information System (based on data extracted April 29, 2016)

Maple Grove, Minnesota

Background

Maple Grove in Hennepin County is approximately 11 miles from Minneapolis. It became a city in 1974. In 1851, Louis Gervais and Pierre Bottineau settled the area, then controlled by Winnebago Native Americans. By 1855, a small town developed with no significant growth until the mid 20th century.

In the 1970s, Maple Grove's population exploded due to a variety of factors, including construction of the I-94, upgrades to other roadways, developing industry, and the area's natural beauty.

Today, Maple Grove is one of the fastest growing cities in Minnesota and, like many cities in the area, an important industrial area. The city has over 1,000 businesses anchored by three main industries: healthcare, retail, and manufacturing. The city is the second largest retail center in the state. Grove Drive North has a large concentration of shopping areas, Grove Square Mall, Grove Square, Grove Shops and Homestead Corners. Arbor Lakes, one of the newly developed downtown areas in Maple Grove, was developed from a former gravel mine, with retail and healthcare centers, and more than 260 stores and businesses in three unique assortments of shops, restaurants and entertainment—Arbor Lakes Main Street, The Fountains at Arbor Lakes and The Shoppes at Arbor Lakes.

It is hard to imagine that, with so many retail and industrial centers, Maple Grove has over 1000 acres of parkland and 55 miles of biking and hiking trails that are located among seven lakes, two regional park reserves and an arboretum. Central Park of Maple Grove offers an ice-skating loop, botanical garden, children's playground, 120 foot climbing wall and trails with access to other parks. The 2.5-acre Great Lawn at the park is perfect for picnics and relaxation. The Weaver Lake Community Park features a beach, fishing, boating, ball fields and sand volleyball. The beach is open to the public and has lifeguards on duty. The Maple Grove Arboretum is located along Elm Creek and hosts events at its pavilion. The trails in the park expose hikers to over 100 local tree varieties.

Maple Grove also has several sports facilities used to host youth and adult athletic leagues, recreational play, and encourage fitness. The Community Center and Sports Dome are the two premiere facilities in the city that accommodate a wide range of sports activities. The Sports Dome is an indoor facility with a turf field. The Community Center provides swimming pools, gymnasiums, sand volleyball, ice arena, skate park, and playhouse, and a wide range of programs for all ages. The Center also hosts a Farmers Market in the summer with over 50 vendors selling local produce.

Maple Grove is served by Independent School District 279 and Wayzata Independent School District 284. Maple Grove Senior High School is ranked in the top 50 Minnesota high schools. The city also has several charter and private school options, including Heritage Christian Academy grades K-12, Ava Marie Academy grades K-8, Parnassus Preparatory School and Beacon Academy Charter School. Several colleges are within 15 miles of the city, including Hennepin Technical College, North Hennepin Community College and the University of Minnesota Twin Cities.

Maple Grove is 26 miles from the Minneapolis-Saint Paul International Airport, and six miles from local Crystal Airport.

The climate of Maple Grove is significantly colder then the national average, with cold winters and lots of snow. The July average high is 81 degrees, and the January average low is 6 degrees. While Maple Grove receives average rainfall at 35 inches a year, its 55 inches of snowfall is more than double the national average.

Rankings

Business/Finance Rankings

- The personal finance site NerdWallet analyzed 183 American metropolitan areas with populations over 250,000 and more than 15,000 businesses to rank where entrepreneurs find the most success. Criteria included area economy, annual income, housing cost, unemployment rate, and the success rate of area businesses. Minneapolis* ranked #14. *www.nerdwallet.com, "Best Places to Start a Business," April 27, 2015*

- TransUnion ranked the nation's metro areas by average credit score, calculated on the VantageScore system, developed by the three major credit-reporting bureaus—TransUnion, Experian, and Equifax. The Minneapolis* metro area was among the ten cities with the highest collective credit score, meaning that its residents posed the lowest average consumer credit risk. *www.usatoday.com, "Metro Areas' Average Credit Rating Revealed," February 7, 2013*

- Based on metro area social media reviews, the employment opinion group Glassdoor surveyed 50 of the largest U.S. metro areas and equally weighed cost of living, hiring opportunity, and job satisfaction to compose a list of "25 Best Cities for Jobs." The Minneapolis* metro area was ranked #18 in overall job satisfaction. *www.glassdoor.com, "Best Cities for Jobs," May 19, 2015*

- In a survey of economic confidence in the nation's 50 largest metropolitan areas conducted January–December 2014, the Minneapolis* metro area placed #4, according to Gallup's 2014 Economic Confidence Index. *Gallup, "San Jose and San Francisco Lead in Economic Confidence," March 19, 2015*

- The Brookings Institution ranked the 100 largest metro areas in the U.S. based on income inequality. Minneapolis* was ranked #79 (#1 = greatest ineqality). Criteria: the "95/20 ratio," a figure representing the income at which a household earns more than 95 percent of all other households, divided by the income at which a household earns more than only 20 percent of all other households. *Brookings Institution, "Income Inequality, 100 Largest U.S. Metro Areas, 2007-2014," January 14, 2016*

- *Forbes* ranked the largest metro areas in the U.S. in terms of the "Best Cities for Young Professionals." The Minneapolis* metro area ranked #10 out of 15. Criteria: job growth; unemployment rate; median salary of college graduates age 24 to 34; cost of living; number of small businesses per capita; number of large companies; percentage of population 25 years of age and older with college degrees. *Forbes.com, "America's 15 Best Cities for Young Professionals," August 18, 2014*

- Payscale.com ranked the 20 largest metro areas in terms of wage growth. The Minneapolis* metro area ranked #2. Criteria: private-sector wage growth between the 1st quarter of 2015 and the 1st quarter of 2016. *PayScale, "Wage Trends by Metro Area," 1st Quarter, 2016*

- The Minneapolis* metro area appeared on the Milken Institute "2015 Best Performing Cities" list. Rank: #59 out of 200 large metro areas. Criteria: job growth; wage and salary growth; high-tech output growth. *Milken Institute, "Best-Performing Cities 2015," December 2015*

- *Forbes* ranked the 200 most populous metro areas to determine the nation's "Best Places for Business and Careers." The Minneapolis* metro area was ranked #39. Criteria: costs (business and living); job growth (past and projected); income growth; educational attainment (college and high school); projected economic growth; cultural and recreational opportunities; net migration patterns; number of highly ranked colleges. *Forbes, "The Best Places for Business and Careers 2015," July 29, 2015*

Dating/Romance Rankings

- *Forbes* reports that the Minneapolis* metro area made Rent.com's Best Cities for Newlyweds list for 2013, based on Bureau of Labor Statistics and Census Bureau data on number of married couples, percentage of families with children under age six, average annual income, cost of living, and availability of rentals. *www.forbes.com, "The 10 Best Cities for Newlyweds to Live and Work In," May 30, 2013*

- CreditDonkey, a financial education website, sought out the ten best U.S. cities for newlyweds, considering the number of married couples, divorce rate, average credit score, and average number of hours worked per week in metro areas with a million or more residents. The Minneapolis* metro area placed #10. *www.creditdonkey.com, "Study: Best Cities for Newlyweds," November 30, 2013*

Education Rankings

- The Minneapolis* metro area was selected as one of the world's most inventive cities by *Forbes*. The area was ranked #9 out of 15. Criteria: patent applications per capita. *Forbes, "World's 15 Most Inventive Cities," July 9, 2013*
- The Minneapolis* metro area was selected as one of America's most innovative cities" by *The Business Insider*. The metro area was ranked #20 out of 20. Criteria: patents per capita. *The Business Insider, "The 20 Most Innovative Cities in the U.S.," February 1, 2013*
- Minneapolis* was identified as one of America's "smartest" metropolitan areas by *The Business Journals*. The area ranked #9 out of 10. Criteria: percentage of adults (25 and older) with high school diplomas, bachelor's degrees and graduate degrees. *The Business Journals, "Where the Brainpower Is: Exclusive U.S. Rankings, Insights," February 27, 2014*
- Personal finance website *WalletHub* analyzed the 150 largest U.S. metropolitan statistical areas to determine where the most educated Americans are choosing to settle. Criteria: education quality and attainment gap; education levels; percentage of workers with degrees; public school rankings; quality and size of each metro area's universities. Minneapolis* was ranked #9 (#1 = most educated city). *www.WalletHub.com, "2015's Most and Least Educated Cities*
- Minneapolis* was identified as one of the "Smartest Cities in America" by the brain-training website *Lumosity* using data from three million of its own users. The metro area ranked #33 out of 50. Criteria: users' brain performance index scores, considering core cognitive abilities such as memory, processing speed, flexibility, attention and problem-solving. *Lumosity, " Smartest Cities in America," June 25, 2013*

Environmental Rankings

- The Minneapolis* metro area came in at #118 for the relative comfort of its climate on Sperling's list of "chill cities," as measured by the Sperling Heat Index. All 361 metro areas are included. Criteria included daytime high temperatures, nighttime low temperatures, dew point, and relative humidity at the high temperatures. *www.bertsperling.com, "Sperling's Chill Cities," July 18, 2013*
- Sperling's BestPlaces assessed 379 metropolitan areas of the United States for the likelihood of dangerously extreme weather events or earthquakes. In general the Southeast and South-Central regions have the highest risk of weather extremes and earthquakes, while the Pacific Northwest enjoys the lowest risk. Of the least risky metropolitan areas, the Minneapolis* metro area was ranked #99. *www.bestplaces.net, "Safest Places from Natural Disasters," April 2011*
- The U.S. Environmental Protection Agency (EPA) released a list of U.S. metropolitan areas with the most ENERGY STAR certified buildings in 2015. The Minneapolis* metro area was ranked #13 out of 25. *U.S. Environmental Protection Agency, "Top Cities With the Most ENERGY STAR Certified Buildings in 2016," March 30, 2016*

Health/Fitness Rankings

- Analysts who tracked obesity rates in the nation's largest metro areas (populations above one million) found that the Minneapolis* metro area was one of the ten major metros where residents were least likely to be obese, defined as a BMI score of 30 or above. *www.gallup.com, "Boulder, Colo., Residents Still Least Likely to Be Obese," April 4, 2014*

- For each of the 50 most populous metro areas in the United States, the American College of Sports Medicine's American Fitness Index evaluated infrastructure, community assets, and policies that encourage healthy and fit lifestyles, including preventive health behaviors, levels of chronic disease conditions, health care access, and community resources and policies that support physical activity. The Minneapolis* metro area ranked #2 for "community fitness." *www.americanfitnessindex.org, "ACSM American Fitness Index Health and Community Fitness Status of the 50 Largest Metropolitan Areas," May 2015*
- Minneapolis* was identified as a "2016 Spring Allergy Capital." The area ranked #71 out of 100. Three groups of factors were used to identify the most severe cities for people with allergies during the spring season: annual pollen levels; medicine utilization; access to board-certified allergists. *Asthma and Allergy Foundation of America, "Spring Allergy Capitals 2016"*
- Minneapolis* was identified as a "2015 Asthma Capital." The area ranked #87 out of the nation's 100 largest metropolitan areas. Criteria: estimated prevalence; self-reported prevalence; crude death rate for asthma; annual pollen score; annual air quality; public smoking laws; number of board-certified asthma specialists; school inhaler access laws; rescue medication use; controller medication use; ER visits for asthma; uninsured rate; poverty rate. *Asthma and Allergy Foundation of America, "Asthma Capitals 2015"*
- The Minneapolis* metro area ranked #27 out of 190 in The Gallup-Healthways Well-Being Index. Criteria: purpose; social well being; financial health; community and physical health. Results are based on telephone interviews with adults, aged 18 and older, living in metropolitan areas in the 50 U.S. states and the District of Columbia. *Gallup-Healthways, "State of American Well-Being," February 23, 2016*

Real Estate Rankings

- Minneapolis* was ranked #77 out of 225 metro areas in terms of housing affordability in 2015 by the National Association of Home Builders (#1 = most affordable). Criteria: the share of homes sold in that area affordable to a family earning the local median income, based on standard mortgage underwriting criteria. *National Association of Home Builders®, NAHB-Wells Fargo Housing Opportunity Index, 4th Quarter 2015*

Safety Rankings

- Farmers Insurance, in partnership with Sperling's BestPlaces, ranked metro areas in the U.S. as the "Most Secure Places to Live." The Minneapolis* metro area ranked #13 out of the top 20 in the large metro area category (500,000 or more residents). Criteria: economic stability; crime statistics; extreme weather; risk of natural disasters; housing depreciation; foreclosures; air quality; environmental hazards; life expectancy; motor vehicle fatalities; and employment numbers. *Farmers Insurance Group of Companies, "Most Secure U.S. Places to Live in the U.S.," June 25, 2013*
- The National Insurance Crime Bureau ranked 380 metro areas in the U.S. in terms of per capita rates of vehicle theft. The Minneapolis* metro area ranked #134 (#1 = highest rate). Criteria: number of vehicle theft offenses per 100,000 inhabitants in 2014. *National Insurance Crime Bureau, "Hot Spots 2014," June 24, 2015*

Seniors/Retirement Rankings

- From its Best Cities for Successful Aging indexes, the Milken Institute generated rankings for metropolitan areas, weighing data in eight categories—health care, wellness, living arrangements, transportation, financial characteristics, education and employment opportunities, community engagement, and overall livability. The Minneapolis* metro area was ranked #16 overall in the large metro area category. *Milken Institute, "Best Cities for Successful Aging, 2014"*

Sports/Recreation Rankings

- According to the personal finance website NerdWallet, the Minneapolis* metro area, at #6, is one of the nation's top dozen metro areas for sports fans. Criteria included the presence of all four major sports—MLB, NFL, NHL, and NBA, fan enthusiasm (as measured by game attendance), ticket affordability, and "sports culture," that is, number of sports bars. *www.nerdwallet.com, "Best Cities for Sports Fans," May 5, 2013*

Miscellaneous Rankings

- The watchdog site Charity Navigator conducts an annual study of charities in the nation's major markets both to analyze statistical differences in their financial, accountability, and transparency practices and to track year-to-year variations in individual communities. The Minneapolis* metro area was ranked #12 among the 30 metro markets in the rating dimension of Overall Score. *www.charitynavigator.org, "Metro Market Study 2015," June 5, 2015*
- Mars Chocolate North America, the makers of COMBOS®, in partnership with Sperling's BestPlaces, ranked 50 major metro areas in terms of their "manliness." The Minneapolis* metro area ranked #40. Criteria: number of professional sports teams; number of nearby NASCAR tracks and racing events; manly lifestyle; concentration of manly retail stores; manly occupations per capita; salty snack sales; "Board of Manliness" rankings. *Mars Chocolate North America, "America's Manliest Cities 2012"*
- The National Alliance to End Homelessness ranked the 100 most populous metro areas with the highest rate of homelessness. The Minneapolis* metro area ranked #48. Criteria: number of homeless people per 10,000 population in 2011. *National Alliance to End Homelessness, The State of Homelessness in America 2012*

Maple Grove is located within the Minneapolis-St. Paul-Bloomington, MN-WI Metropolitan Statistical Area.

Business Environment

CITY FINANCES

City Government Finances

Component	2012 ($000)	2012 ($ per capita)
Total Revenues	100,256	1,628
Total Expenditures	95,915	1,557
Debt Outstanding	207,772	3,374
Cash and Securities[1]	282,098	4,581

Note: (1) Cash and security holdings of a government at the close of its fiscal year, including those of its dependent agencies, utilities, and liquor stores.
Source: U.S Census Bureau, State & Local Government Finances 2012

City Government Revenue by Source

Source	2012 ($000)	2012 ($ per capita)
General Revenue		
From Federal Government	138	2
From State Government	6,615	107
From Local Governments	0	0
Taxes		
Property	31,806	516
Sales and Gross Receipts	38	0
Personal Income	0	0
Corporate Income	0	0
Motor Vehicle License	0	0
Other Taxes	2,568	41
Current Charges	13,455	218
Liquor Store	0	0
Utility	6,250	101
Employee Retirement	0	0

Source: U.S Census Bureau, State & Local Government Finances 2012

City Government Expenditures by Function

Function	2012 ($000)	2012 ($ per capita)	2012 (%)
General Direct Expenditures			
Air Transportation	0	0	0.0
Corrections	241	3	0.2
Education	0	0	0.0
Employment Security Administration	0	0	0.0
Financial Administration	3,475	56	3.6
Fire Protection	3,645	59	3.8
General Public Buildings	963	15	1.0
Governmental Administration, Other	929	15	0.9
Health	0	0	0.0
Highways	34,083	553	35.5
Hospitals	0	0	0.0
Housing and Community Development	1,278	20	1.3
Interest on General Debt	4,385	71	4.5
Judicial and Legal	433	7	0.4
Libraries	0	0	0.0
Parking	0	0	0.0
Parks and Recreation	13,307	216	13.8
Police Protection	9,545	155	9.9
Public Welfare	0	0	0.0
Sewerage	6,319	102	6.5
Solid Waste Management	1,218	19	1.2
Veterans' Services	0	0	0.0
Liquor Store	0	0	0.0
Utility	8,169	132	8.5
Employee Retirement	0	0	0.0

Source: U.S Census Bureau, State & Local Government Finances 2012

DEMOGRAPHICS

Population Growth

Area	1990 Census	2000 Census	2010 Census	2014* Estimate	Population Growth (%) 1990-2014	Population Growth (%) 2010-2014
City	38,868	50,365	61,567	64,364	65.6	4.5
MSA[1]	2,538,834	2,968,806	3,279,833	3,424,786	34.9	4.4
U.S.	248,709,873	281,421,906	308,745,538	314,107,084	26.3	1.7

Note: (1) Figures cover the Minneapolis-St. Paul-Bloomington, MN-WI Metropolitan Statistical Area—see Appendix B for areas included; (*) 2010-2014 5-year estimated population
Source: U.S. Census Bureau, 1990 Census, Census 2000, Census 2010, 2010-2014 American Community Survey 5-Year Estimates

Household Size

Area	Persons in Household (%) One	Two	Three	Four	Five	Six	Seven or More	Average Household Size
City	20.6	36.0	17.4	17.3	6.6	1.3	0.6	2.68
MSA[1]	27.8	33.7	15.0	14.0	5.9	2.0	1.3	2.54
U.S.	27.5	33.5	15.8	13.1	6.0	2.3	1.4	2.64

Note: (1) Figures cover the Minneapolis-St. Paul-Bloomington, MN-WI Metropolitan Statistical Area—see Appendix B for areas included
Source: U.S. Census Bureau, 2010-2014 American Community Survey 5-Year Estimates

Race

Area	White Alone[2] (%)	Black Alone[2] (%)	Asian Alone[2] (%)	AIAN[3] Alone[2] (%)	NHOPI[4] Alone[2] (%)	Other Race Alone[2] (%)	Two or More Races (%)
City	87.0	3.8	6.6	0.1	0.0	0.3	2.2
MSA[1]	81.2	7.4	5.9	0.6	0.0	1.8	3.0
U.S.	73.8	12.6	5.0	0.8	0.2	4.7	2.9

Note: (1) Figures cover the Minneapolis-St. Paul-Bloomington, MN-WI Metropolitan Statistical Area—see Appendix B for areas included; (2) Alone is defined as not being in combination with one or more other races; (3) American Indian and Alaska Native; (4) Native Hawaiian and Other Pacific Islander
Source: U.S. Census Bureau, 2010-2014 American Community Survey 5-Year Estimates

Hispanic or Latino Origin

Area	Total (%)	Mexican (%)	Puerto Rican (%)	Cuban (%)	Other (%)
City	2.1	0.9	0.1	0.1	1.1
MSA[1]	5.5	3.7	0.3	0.1	1.4
U.S.	16.9	10.8	1.6	0.6	3.8

Note: Persons of Hispanic or Latino origin can be of any race; (1) Figures cover the Minneapolis-St. Paul-Bloomington, MN-WI Metropolitan Statistical Area—see Appendix B for areas included
Source: U.S. Census Bureau, 2010-2014 American Community Survey 5-Year Estimates

Ancestry

Area	German	Irish	English	American	Italian	Polish	French[2]	Scottish	Dutch
City	32.3	12.2	5.4	4.0	2.8	5.1	5.4	1.5	1.6
MSA[1]	32.4	11.8	6.0	3.3	2.8	4.6	3.7	1.4	1.6
U.S.	14.9	10.8	8.0	7.1	5.5	3.0	2.7	1.7	1.4

Note: Figures are the percentage of the total population reporting a particular ancestry. The nine most commonly reported ancestries in the U.S. are shown. Figures include multiple ancestries (e.g. if a person reported being Irish and Italian, they were included in both columns); (1) Figures cover the Minneapolis-St. Paul-Bloomington, MN-WI Metropolitan Statistical Area—see Appendix B for areas included; (2) Excludes Basque
Source: U.S. Census Bureau, 2010-2014 American Community Survey 5-Year Estimates

Foreign-Born Population

Area	Any Foreign Country	Asia	Mexico	Europe	Carribean	Central America[2]	South America	Africa	Canada
	Percent of Population Born in								
City	9.1	5.0	0.2	2.2	0.1	0.0	0.5	0.6	0.3
MSA[1]	9.7	3.9	1.4	1.1	0.1	0.3	0.5	2.1	0.2
U.S.	13.1	3.8	3.7	1.5	1.2	1.0	0.9	0.6	0.3

Note: (1) Figures cover the Minneapolis-St. Paul-Bloomington, MN-WI Metropolitan Statistical Area—see Appendix B for areas included; (2) Excludes Mexico.
Source: U.S. Census Bureau, 2010-2014 American Community Survey 5-Year Estimates

Marital Status

Area	Never Married	Now Married[2]	Separated	Widowed	Divorced
City	23.0	63.4	0.9	3.1	9.5
MSA[1]	32.9	51.5	1.3	4.4	10.0
U.S.	32.5	48.4	2.2	5.9	10.9

Note: Figures are percentages and cover the population 15 years of age and older; (1) Figures cover the Minneapolis-St. Paul-Bloomington, MN-WI Metropolitan Statistical Area—see Appendix B for areas included; (2) Excludes separated
Source: U.S. Census Bureau, 2010-2014 American Community Survey 5-Year Estimates

Disability Status

Area	All Ages	Under 18 Years Old	18 to 64 Years Old	65 Years and Over
City	5.2	1.3	4.2	24.1
MSA[1]	9.2	3.6	7.6	30.8
U.S.	12.3	4.1	10.2	36.3

Note: Figures show percent of the civilian noninstitutionalized population that reported having a disability. Disability status is determined from from six types of difficulty: vision, hearing, cognitive, ambulatory, self-care, and independent living. For children under 5 years old, hearing and vision difficulty are used to determine disability status. For children between the ages of 5 and 14, disability status is determined from hearing, vision, cognitive, ambulatory, and self-care difficulties. For people aged 15 years and older, they are considered to have a disability if they have difficulty with any one of the six difficulty types; (1) Figures cover the Minneapolis-St. Paul-Bloomington, MN-WI Metropolitan Statistical Area—see Appendix B for areas included.
Source: U.S. Census Bureau, 2010-2014 American Community Survey 5-Year Estimates

Age

Area	Under Age 5	Age 5–19	Age 20–34	Age 35–44	Age 45–54	Age 55–64	Age 65–74	Age 75–84	Age 85+	Median Age
	Percent of Population									
City	6.8	21.6	16.8	15.9	16.2	14.1	5.8	2.0	0.9	38.2
MSA[1]	6.7	20.3	21.0	13.4	15.0	12.1	6.4	3.5	1.6	36.4
U.S.	6.4	19.9	20.6	13.0	14.1	12.3	7.6	4.3	1.9	37.4

Note: (1) Figures cover the Minneapolis-St. Paul-Bloomington, MN-WI Metropolitan Statistical Area—see Appendix B for areas included
Source: U.S. Census Bureau, 2010-2014 American Community Survey 5-Year Estimates

Gender

Area	Males	Females	Males per 100 Females
City	31,044	33,320	93.2
MSA[1]	1,692,444	1,732,342	97.7
U.S.	154,515,159	159,591,925	96.8

Note: (1) Figures cover the Minneapolis-St. Paul-Bloomington, MN-WI Metropolitan Statistical Area—see Appendix B for areas included
Source: U.S. Census Bureau, 2010-2014 American Community Survey 5-Year Estimates

Religious Groups by Family

Area	Catholic	Baptist	Non-Den.	Methodist[2]	Lutheran	LDS[3]	Pente-costal	Presby-terian[4]	Muslim[5]	Judaism
MSA[1]	21.7	2.4	2.9	2.7	14.4	0.6	1.7	1.8	0.4	0.7
U.S.	19.1	9.3	4.0	4.0	2.3	2.0	1.9	1.6	0.8	0.7

Note: Figures are the number of adherents as a percentage of the total population; (1) Figures cover the Minneapolis-St. Paul-Bloomington, MN-WI Metropolitan Statistical Area—see Appendix B for areas included; (2) Methodist/Pietist; (3) Latter Day Saints; (4) Reformed; (5) Figures are estimates
Source: Association of Statisticians of American Religious Bodies, 2010 U.S. Religion Census: Religious Congregations & Membership Study

Religious Groups by Tradition

Area	Catholic	Evangelical Protestant	Mainline Protestant	Other Tradition	Black Protestant	Orthodox
MSA[1]	21.7	12.8	14.5	2.2	0.4	0.2
U.S.	19.1	16.2	7.3	4.3	1.6	0.3

Note: Figures are the number of adherents as a percentage of the total population; (1) Figures cover the Minneapolis-St. Paul-Bloomington, MN-WI Metropolitan Statistical Area—see Appendix B for areas included
Source: Association of Statisticians of American Religious Bodies, 2010 U.S. Religion Census: Religious Congregations & Membership Study

ECONOMY

Gross Metropolitan Product

Area	2013	2014	2015	2016	Rank[2]
MSA[1]	227.8	236.7	246.4	258.6	13

Note: Figures are in billions of dollars; (1) Figures cover the Minneapolis-St. Paul-Bloomington, MN-WI Metropolitan Statistical Area—see Appendix B for areas included; (2) Rank is based on 2016 data and ranges from 1 to 381
Source: The U.S. Conference of Mayors, U.S. Metro Economies: GMP and Employment 2014-2016, June 2015

Economic Growth

Area	2011-13 (%)	2014 (%)	2015 (%)	2016 (%)	Rank[2]
MSA[1]	2.0	2.4	2.7	3.0	83
U.S.	2.2	2.4	2.3	2.9	–

Note: Figures are real gross metropolitan product (GMP) growth rates and represent annual average percent change; (1) Figures cover the Minneapolis-St. Paul-Bloomington, MN-WI Metropolitan Statistical Area—see Appendix B for areas included; (2) Rank is based on 2016 data and ranges from 1 to 381
Source: The U.S. Conference of Mayors, U.S. Metro Economies: GMP and Employment 2014-2016, June 2015

Metropolitan Area Exports

Area	2009	2010	2011	2012	2013	2014	Rank[2]
MSA[1]	20,096.7	23,192.7	26,189.0	25,155.7	23,747.4	21,198.2	15

Note: Figures are in millions of dollars; (1) Figures cover the Minneapolis-St. Paul-Bloomington, MN-WI Metropolitan Statistical Area—see Appendix B for areas included; (2) Rank is based on 2014 data and ranges from 1 to 385
Source: U.S. Department of Commerce, International Trade Administration, Office of Trade & Industry Information, Manufacturing & Services, data extracted March 10, 2016

Building Permits

Area	Single-Family			Multi-Family			Total		
	2014	2015p	Pct. Chg.	2014	2015p	Pct. Chg.	2014	2015p	Pct. Chg.
City	306	192	-37.3	196	205	4.6	502	397	-20.9
MSA[1]	6,689	6,786	1.5	4,736	4,927	4.0	11,425	11,713	2.5
U.S.	640,300	690,800	7.9	411,800	487,600	18.4	1,052,100	1,178,400	12.0

Note: (1) Figures cover the Minneapolis-St. Paul-Bloomington, MN-WI Metropolitan Statistical Area—see Appendix B for areas included; Figures represent new, privately-owned housing units authorized (unadjusted data); All permit data are based on estimates with imputation; (p) preliminary data.
Source: U.S. Census Bureau, Manufacturing, Mining, and Construction Statistics, Building Permits, 2014, 2015

Bankruptcy Filings

Area	Business Filings			Nonbusiness Filings		
	2014	2015	% Chg.	2014	2015	% Chg.
Hennepin County	110	99	-10.0	2,625	2,330	-11.2
U.S.	26,983	24,735	-8.3	909,812	819,760	-9.9

Note: Business filings include Chapter 7, Chapter 11, Chapter 12, and Chapter 13; Nonbusiness filings include Chapter 7, Chapter 11, and Chapter 13
Source: Administrative Office of the U.S. Courts, Business and Nonbusiness Bankruptcy, County Cases Commenced by Chapter of the Bankruptcy Code, During the 12- Month Period Ending December 31, 2014 and Business and Nonbusiness Bankruptcy, County Cases Commenced by Chapter of the Bankruptcy Code, During the 12- Month Period Ending December 31, 2015

Housing Vacancy Rates

Area	Gross Vacancy Rate[2] (%)			Year-Round Vacancy Rate[3] (%)			Rental Vacancy Rate[4] (%)			Homeowner Vacancy Rate[5] (%)		
	2013	2014	2015	2013	2014	2015	2013	2014	2015	2013	2014	2015
MSA[1]	5.7	5.7	6.4	5.1	5.3	6.0	5.4	4.4	4.9	0.9	1.4	0.8
U.S.	13.6	13.4	12.9	10.7	10.4	10.0	8.3	7.6	7.1	2.0	1.9	1.8

Note: (1) Figures cover the Minneapolis-St. Paul-Bloomington, MN-WI Metropolitan Statistical Area—see Appendix B for areas included; (2) The percentage of the total housing inventory that is vacant; (3) The percentage of the housing inventory (excluding seasonal units) that is year-round vacant; (4) The percentage of rental inventory that is vacant for rent; (5) The percentage of homeowner inventory that is vacant for sale
Source: U.S. Census Bureau, Housing Vacancies and Homeownership Annual Statistics: 2015

INCOME

Income

Area	Per Capita ($)	Median Household ($)	Average Household ($)
City	43,833	92,267	114,692
MSA[1]	34,593	68,019	88,061
U.S.	28,555	53,482	74,596

Note: (1) Figures cover the Minneapolis-St. Paul-Bloomington, MN-WI Metropolitan Statistical Area—see Appendix B for areas included
Source: U.S. Census Bureau, 2010-2014 American Community Survey 5-Year Estimates

Household Income Distribution

Area	Percent of Households Earning							
	Under $15,000	$15,000 -24,999	$25,000 -34,999	$35,000 -49,999	$50,000 -74,999	$75,000 -99,000	$100,000 -149,999	$150,000 and up
City	4.3	4.2	5.1	7.8	17.1	15.0	24.0	22.6
MSA[1]	8.6	7.8	8.1	12.0	18.2	14.5	17.5	13.4
U.S.	12.5	10.7	10.2	13.5	17.8	12.2	13.0	10.0

Note: (1) Figures cover the Minneapolis-St. Paul-Bloomington, MN-WI Metropolitan Statistical Area—see Appendix B for areas included
Source: U.S. Census Bureau, 2010-2014 American Community Survey 5-Year Estimates

Poverty Rate

Area	All Ages	Under 18 Years Old	18 to 64 Years Old	65 Years and Over
City	5.1	8.4	3.5	6.9
MSA[1]	10.6	13.9	9.9	7.1
U.S.	15.6	21.9	14.6	9.4

Note: Figures are percentage of people whose income during the past 12 months was below the poverty level; (1) Figures cover the Minneapolis-St. Paul-Bloomington, MN-WI Metropolitan Statistical Area—see Appendix B for areas included
Source: U.S. Census Bureau, 2010-2014 American Community Survey 5-Year Estimates

EMPLOYMENT

Labor Force and Employment

Area	Civilian Labor Force			Workers Employed		
	Dec. 2014	Dec. 2015	% Chg.	Dec. 2014	Dec. 2015	% Chg.
City	37,785	38,498	1.8	36,822	37,567	2.0
MSA[1]	1,905,506	1,942,269	1.9	1,843,783	1,881,640	2.0
U.S.	155,521,000	157,245,000	1.1	147,190,000	149,703,000	1.7

Note: Data is not seasonally adjusted and covers workers 16 years of age and older; (1) Figures cover the Minneapolis-St. Paul-Bloomington, MN-WI Metropolitan Statistical Area—see Appendix B for areas included
Source: Bureau of Labor Statistics, Local Area Unemployment Statistics

Unemployment Rate

Area	2015											
	Jan.	Feb.	Mar.	Apr.	May	Jun.	Jul.	Aug.	Sep.	Oct.	Nov.	Dec.
City	3.1	3.1	3.3	3.0	3.0	3.3	3.2	3.0	2.8	2.6	2.4	2.4
MSA[1]	4.1	4.0	4.1	3.5	3.5	3.8	3.7	3.4	3.1	2.9	2.8	3.1
U.S.	6.1	5.8	5.6	5.1	5.3	5.5	5.6	5.2	4.9	4.8	4.8	4.8

Note: Data is not seasonally adjusted and covers workers 16 years of age and older; (1) Figures cover the Minneapolis-St. Paul-Bloomington, MN-WI Metropolitan Statistical Area—see Appendix B for areas included
Source: Bureau of Labor Statistics, Local Area Unemployment Statistics

Employment by Occupation

Occupation Classification	City (%)	MSA[1] (%)	U.S. (%)
Management, Business, Science, and Arts	51.1	42.6	36.4
Natural Resources, Construction, and Maintenance	4.4	6.4	9.0
Production, Transportation, and Material Moving	8.6	11.3	12.1
Sales and Office	26.8	24.1	24.4
Service	9.1	15.6	18.2

Note: Figures cover employed civilians 16 years of age and older; (1) Figures cover the Minneapolis-St. Paul-Bloomington, MN-WI Metropolitan Statistical Area—see Appendix B for areas included
Source: U.S. Census Bureau, 2010-2014 American Community Survey 5-Year Estimates

Employment by Industry

Sector	MSA[1]		U.S.
	Number of Employees	Percent of Total	Percent of Total
Construction, Mining, and Logging	71,100	3.6	5.0
Education and Health Services	321,100	16.4	15.7
Financial Activities	148,800	7.6	5.7
Government	254,400	13.0	15.5
Information	39,400	2.0	1.9
Leisure and Hospitality	174,900	8.9	10.4
Manufacturing	194,800	10.0	8.6
Other Services	81,200	4.1	3.9
Professional and Business Services	305,100	15.6	13.9
Retail Trade	189,400	9.7	11.3
Transportation, Warehousing, and Utilities	69,100	3.5	3.9
Wholesale Trade	97,300	4.9	4.1

Note: Figures are non-farm employment as of December 2015. Figures are not seasonally adjusted and include workers 16 years of age and older; (1) Figures cover the Minneapolis-St. Paul-Bloomington, MN-WI Metropolitan Statistical Area—see Appendix B for areas included; n/a not available
Source: Bureau of Labor Statistics, Current Employment Statistics, Employment, Hours, and Earnings

Occupations with Greatest Projected Employment Growth: 2012 – 2022

Occupation[1]	2012 Employment	2022 Projected Employment	Numeric Employment Change	Percent Employment Change
Personal Care Aides	50,550	73,150	22,600	44.7
Home Health Aides	34,520	44,660	10,140	29.3
Registered Nurses	55,950	65,430	9,480	16.9
Retail Salespersons	85,800	92,450	6,650	7.8
Combined Food Preparation and Serving Workers, Including Fast Food	56,120	61,580	5,460	9.7
Carpenters	19,610	24,100	4,490	22.9
Childcare Workers	30,870	34,870	4,000	13.0
Janitors and Cleaners, Except Maids and Housekeeping Cleaners	46,140	49,920	3,780	8.2
Licensed Practical and Licensed Vocational Nurses	17,420	20,660	3,240	18.6
Customer Service Representatives	48,000	51,210	3,210	6.7

Note: Projections cover Minnesota; (1) Sorted by numeric employment change
Source: www.projectionscentral.com, State Occupational Projections, 2012–2022 Long-Term Projections

Fastest Growing Occupations: 2012 – 2022

Occupation[1]	2012 Employment	2022 Projected Employment	Numeric Employment Change	Percent Employment Change
Personal Care Aides	50,550	73,150	22,600	44.7
Insulation Workers, Mechanical	470	660	190	40.6
Physician Assistants	1,650	2,220	570	34.5
Computer Numerically Controlled Machine Tool Programmers, Metal and Plastic	810	1,080	270	33.3
Helpers—Carpenters	510	680	170	32.9
Brickmasons and Blockmasons	1,370	1,810	440	31.9
Interpreters and Translators	1,490	1,960	470	31.4
Diagnostic Medical Sonographers	1,380	1,810	430	31.1
Cement Masons and Concrete Finishers	2,930	3,830	900	30.7
Meeting, Convention, and Event Planners	1,950	2,540	590	29.8

Note: Projections cover Minnesota; (1) Sorted by percent employment change and excludes occupations with numeric employment change less than 100
Source: www.projectionscentral.com, State Occupational Projections, 2012–2022 Long-Term Projections

Average Wages

Occupation	$/Hr.	Occupation	$/Hr.
Accountants and Auditors	34.30	Maids and Housekeeping Cleaners	11.42
Automotive Mechanics	20.89	Maintenance and Repair Workers	21.64
Bookkeepers	19.75	Marketing Managers	66.76
Carpenters	26.22	Nuclear Medicine Technologists	37.32
Cashiers	10.43	Nurses, Licensed Practical	21.42
Clerks, General Office	16.68	Nurses, Registered	37.00
Clerks, Receptionists/Information	14.44	Nursing Assistants	14.83
Clerks, Shipping/Receiving	16.89	Packers and Packagers, Hand	12.13
Computer Programmers	38.85	Physical Therapists	36.96
Computer Systems Analysts	43.76	Postal Service Mail Carriers	24.43
Computer User Support Specialists	26.27	Real Estate Brokers	n/a
Cooks, Restaurant	12.47	Retail Salespersons	12.38
Dentists	90.82	Sales Reps., Exc. Tech./Scientific	37.53
Electrical Engineers	44.95	Sales Reps., Tech./Scientific	58.26
Electricians	30.25	Secretaries, Exc. Legal/Med./Exec.	19.51
Financial Managers	68.00	Security Guards	16.78
First-Line Supervisors/Managers, Sales	20.97	Surgeons	129.05
Food Preparation Workers	12.51	Teacher Assistants*	15.40
General and Operations Managers	55.19	Teachers, Elementary School*	30.58
Hairdressers/Cosmetologists	13.88	Teachers, Secondary School*	32.31
Internists	119.37	Telemarketers	14.42
Janitors and Cleaners	13.40	Truck Drivers, Heavy/Tractor-Trailer	21.24
Landscaping/Groundskeeping Workers	14.32	Truck Drivers, Light/Delivery Svcs.	18.30
Lawyers	64.64	Waiters and Waitresses	10.29

Note: Wage data covers the Minneapolis-St. Paul-Bloomington, MN-WI Metropolitan Statistical Area—see Appendix B for areas included; (*) Hourly wages for elementary/secondary school teachers and teacher assistants were calculated by the editors from annual wage data based on a 40 hour work week; n/a not available.

Source: Bureau of Labor Statistics, Metro Area Occupational Employment and Wage Estimates, May 2015

TAXES

State Corporate Income Tax Rates

State	Tax Rate (%)	Income Brackets ($)	Num. of Brackets	Financial Institution Tax Rate (%)[a]	Federal Income Tax Ded.
Minnesota	9.8 (o)	Flat rate	1	9.8 (o)	No

Note: Tax rates as of January 1, 2016; (a) Rates listed are the corporate income tax rate applied to financial institutions or excise taxes based on income. Some states have other taxes based upon the value of deposits or shares; (o) In addition, Minnesota levies a 5.8% tentative minimum tax on Alternative Minimum Taxable Income.

Source: Federation of Tax Administrators, "State Corporate Income Tax Rates, 2016"

State Individual Income Tax Rates

State	Tax Rate (%)	Income Brackets ($)	Num. of Brackets	Personal Exempt. ($)[1] Single	Personal Exempt. ($)[1] Dependents	Fed. Inc. Tax Ded.
Minnesota (a)	5.35 - 9.85	25,070 - 154,951 (l)	4	4,050 (d)	4,000 (d)	No

Note: Tax rates as of January 1, 2016; Local- and county-level taxes are not included; n/a not applicable; (1) Married joint filers generally receive double the single exemption; (a) 18 states have statutory provision for automatically adjusting to the rate of inflation the dollar values of the income tax brackets, standard deductions, and/or personal exemptions. Massachusetts, Michigan, and Nebraska index the personal exemptiononly. Oregon does not index the income brackets for $125,000 and over. Maine has suspended indexing for 2014 and 2015; (d) These states use the personal exemption amounts provided in the federal Internal Revenue Code; (l) The income brackets reported for Minnesota are for single individuals. For married couples filing jointly, the same tax rates apply to income brackets ranging from $36,820 to $259,421.

Source: Federation of Tax Administrators, "State Individual Income Tax Rates, 2016"

Various State and Local Tax Rates

State	State and Local Sales and Use (%)	State Sales and Use (%)	Gasoline[1] (¢/gal.)	Cigarette[2] ($/pack)	Spirits[3] ($/gal.)	Wine[4] ($/gal.)	Beer[5] ($/gal.)
Minnesota	7.275	6.875	28.6	3.00	8.67 (i)(j)	1.18 (o)(p)	0.47 (q)(s)

Note: All tax rates as of January 1, 2016; (1) The American Petroleum Institute has developed a methodology for determining the average tax rate on a gallon of fuel. Rates may include any of the following: excise taxes, environmental fees, storage tank fees, other fees or taxes, general sales tax, and local taxes. In states where gasoline is subject to the general sales tax, or where the fuel tax is based on the average sale price, the average rate determined by API is sensitive to changes in the price of gasoline. States that fully or partially apply general sales taxes to gasoline: CA, CO, GA, IL, IN, MI, NY; (2) The federal excise tax of $1.0066 per pack and local taxes are not included; (3) Rates are those applicable to off-premise sales of 40% alcohol by volume (a.b.v.) distilled spirits in 750ml containers. Local excise taxes are excluded; (4) Rates are those applicable to off-premise sales of 11% a.b.v. non-carbonated wine in 750ml containers; (5) Rates are those applicable to off-premise sales of 4.7% a.b.v. beer in 12 ounce containers; (i) Includes case fees and/or bottle fees which may vary with size of container; (j) Includes sales taxes specific to alcoholic beverages; (o) Includes case fees and/or bottle fees which may vary with size of container; (p) Includes sales taxes specific to alcoholic beverages; (q) Different rates are also applicable according to alcohol content, place of production, size of container, or place purchased (on- or off-premise or onboard airlines); (s) Includes sales taxes specific to alcoholic beverages.
Source: Tax Foundation, 2016 Facts & Figures: How Does Your State Compare?

State Business Tax Climate Index Rankings

State	Overall Rank	Corporate Tax Rank	Individual Income Tax Rank	Sales Tax Rank	Unemployment Insurance Tax Rank	Property Tax Rank
Minnesota	47	46	46	36	29	30

Note: The index is a measure of how each state's tax laws affect economic performance. The lower the rank, the more favorable a state's tax system is for business. States without a given tax are given a ranking of 1. The scores/rankings for the District of Columbia do not affect other states. The 2016 index represents the tax climate as of July 1, 2015 (the beginning of Fiscal Year 2016).
Source: Tax Foundation, State Business Tax Climate Index 2016

TRANSPORTATION

Means of Transportation to Work

Area	Car/Truck/Van: Drove Alone	Car/Truck/Van: Car-pooled	Public Transportation: Bus	Public Transportation: Subway	Public Transportation: Railroad	Bicycle	Walked	Other Means	Worked at Home
City	83.9	6.2	3.9	0.0	0.0	0.1	0.5	0.5	4.9
MSA[1]	78.2	8.4	4.3	0.1	0.1	0.9	2.3	0.9	4.9
U.S.	76.4	9.6	2.6	1.8	0.6	0.6	2.8	1.3	4.4

Note: Figures are percentages and cover workers 16 years of age and older; (1) Figures cover the Minneapolis-St. Paul-Bloomington, MN-WI Metropolitan Statistical Area—see Appendix B for areas included
Source: U.S. Census Bureau, 2010-2014 American Community Survey 5-Year Estimates

Travel Time to Work

Area	Less Than 10 Minutes	10 to 19 Minutes	20 to 29 Minutes	30 to 44 Minutes	45 to 59 Minutes	60 to 89 Minutes	90 Minutes or More
City	8.4	23.8	26.4	29.5	7.8	3.7	0.5
MSA[1]	10.9	28.1	24.8	23.0	7.8	4.1	1.3
U.S.	13.3	29.6	21.0	20.2	7.7	5.7	2.6

Note: Figures are percentages and include workers 16 years old and over; (1) Figures cover the Minneapolis-St. Paul-Bloomington, MN-WI Metropolitan Statistical Area—see Appendix B for areas included
Source: U.S. Census Bureau, 2010-2014 American Community Survey 5-Year Estimates

Freeway Travel Time Index

Area	1985	1990	1995	2000	2005	2010	2014
Urban Area Rank[1,2]	26	25	18	11	17	21	21
Urban Area Index[1]	1.10	1.14	1.21	1.27	1.28	1.25	1.26
Average Index[3]	1.09	1.11	1.14	1.17	1.20	1.19	1.20

Note: Freeway Travel Time Index—the ratio of travel time in the peak period to the travel time at free-flow conditions. For example, a value of 1.30 indicates a 20-minute free-flow trip takes 26 minutes in the peak (20 minutes x 1.30 = 26 minutes); (1) Covers the Minneapolis-St. Paul MN-WI urban area; (2) Rank is based on 101 urban areas (#1 = highest travel time index); (3) Average of 101 urban areas
Source: Texas Transportation Institute, 2015 Urban Mobility Scorecard, August 2015

Freeway Commuter Stress Index

Area	1985	1990	1995	2000	2005	2010	2014
Urban Area Rank[1,2]	33	33	23	17	18	25	27
Urban Area Index[1]	1.14	1.18	1.26	1.31	1.33	1.30	1.31
Average Index[3]	1.13	1.16	1.19	1.22	1.25	1.24	1.25

Note: The Freeway Commuter Stress Index is the same as the Freeway Travel Time Index (see table above) except that it includes only the travel in the peak directions during the peak periods; the TTI includes travel in all directions during the peak period. Thus, the CSI is more indicative of the work trip experienced by each commuter on a daily basis. (1) Covers the Minneapolis-St. Paul MN-WI urban area; (2) Rank is based on 101 urban areas (#1 = highest stress index); (3) Average of 101 urban areas
Source: Texas Transportation Institute, 2015 Urban Mobility Scorecard, August 2015

Living Environment

COST OF LIVING

Cost of Living Index

Composite Index	Groceries	Housing	Utilities	Trans-portation	Health Care	Misc. Goods/ Services
108.3	108.0	112.3	93.1	111.9	105.5	108.8

Note: The Cost of Living Index measures regional differences in the cost of consumer goods and services, excluding taxes and non-consumer expenditures, for professional and managerial households in the top income quintile. It is based on more than 50,000 prices covering almost 60 different items for which prices are collected three times a year by chambers of commerce, economic development organizations or university applied economic centers in each participating urban area. The numbers shown should be read as a percentage above or below the national average of 100. For example, a value of 115.4 in the groceries column indicates that grocery prices are 15.4% higher than the national average. Small differences in the index numbers should not be interpreted as significant; Figures cover the Minneapolis MN urban area.
Source: The Council for Community and Economic Research, ACCRA Cost of Living Index, 2015

Grocery Prices

Area[1]	T-Bone Steak ($/pound)	Frying Chicken ($/pound)	Whole Milk ($/half gal.)	Eggs ($/dozen)	Orange Juice ($/64 oz.)	Coffee ($/11.5 oz.)
City[2]	14.13	1.90	2.26	1.92	3.78	4.64
Avg.	10.99	1.43	2.25	2.26	3.58	4.48
Min.	7.16	0.98	1.30	1.35	2.88	2.98
Max.	14.13	2.43	3.85	4.81	6.39	7.56

Note: (1) Values for the local area are compared with the average, minimum and maximum values for all 292 areas in the Cost of Living Index; (2) Figures cover the Minneapolis MN urban area; **T-Bone Steak** *(price per pound);* **Frying Chicken** *(price per pound, whole fryer);* **Whole Milk** *(half gallon carton);* **Eggs** *(price per dozen, Grade A, large);* **Orange Juice** *(64 oz. Tropicana or Florida Natural);* **Coffee** *(11.5 oz. can, vacuum-packed, Maxwell House, Hills Bros, or Folgers).*
Source: The Council for Community and Economic Research, ACCRA Cost of Living Index, 2015

Housing and Utility Costs

Area[1]	New Home Price ($)	Apartment Rent ($/month)	All Electric ($/month)	Part Electric ($/month)	Other Energy ($/month)	Telephone ($/month)
City[2]	345,759	1,098	-	93.62	69.52	24.99
Avg.	312,874	945	179.30	95.07	72.96	28.11
Min.	178,682	479	116.28	43.14	26.46	10.01
Max.	1,472,476	3,984	504.25	189.44	421.11	43.06

Note: (1) Values for the local area are compared with the average, minimum and maximum values for all 292 areas in the Cost of Living Index; (2) Figures cover the Minneapolis MN urban area; **New Home Price** *(2,400 sf living area, 8,000 sf lot, in urban area with full utilities);* **Apartment Rent** *(950 sf 2 bedroom/1.5 or 2 bath, unfurnished, excluding all utilities except water);* **All Electric** *(average monthly cost for an all-electric home);* **Part Electric** *(average monthly cost for a part-electric home);* **Other Energy** *(average monthly cost for natural gas, fuel oil, coal, wood, and any other forms of energy except electricity);* **Telephone** *(price includes basic monthly rate for a private residential line plus additional local usage charges incurred by a family of four).*
Source: The Council for Community and Economic Research, ACCRA Cost of Living Index, 2015

Health Care, Transportation, and Other Costs

Area[1]	Doctor ($/visit)	Dentist ($/visit)	Optometrist ($/visit)	Gasoline ($/gallon)	Beauty Salon ($/visit)	Men's Shirt ($)
City[2]	133.87	84.35	82.36	2.62	33.40	30.95
Avg.	105.15	89.02	99.78	2.38	35.30	28.10
Min.	66.87	56.09	48.53	1.95	18.91	13.38
Max.	182.34	150.36	228.33	4.09	67.91	63.80

Note: (1) Values for the local area are compared with the average, minimum and maximum values for all 292 areas in the Cost of Living Index; (2) Figures cover the Minneapolis MN urban area; **Doctor** *(general practitioners routine exam of an established patient);* **Dentist** *(adult teeth cleaning and periodic oral examination);* **Optometrist** *(full vision eye exam for established adult patient);* **Gasoline** *(one gallon regular unleaded, national brand, including all taxes, cash price at self-service pump if available);* **Beauty Salon** *(woman's shampoo, trim, and blow-dry);* **Men's Shirt** *(cotton/polyester dress shirt, pinpoint weave, long sleeves).*
Source: The Council for Community and Economic Research, ACCRA Cost of Living Index, 2015

HOUSING

House Price Index (HPI)

Area	National Ranking[2]	Quarterly Change (%)	One-Year Change (%)	Five-Year Change (%)
MSA[1]	112	0.20	5.20	13.00
U.S.[3]	–	1.45	5.76	22.85

Note: The HPI is a weighted repeat sales index. It measures average price changes in repeat sales or refinancings on the same properties. This information is obtained by reviewing repeat mortgage transactions on single-family properties whose mortgages have been purchased or securitized by Fannie Mae or Freddie Mac in January 1975; (1) Minneapolis-St. Paul-Bloomington Metropolitan Statistical Area—see Appendix B for areas included; (2) Rankings are based on annual percentage change for all metro areas containing at least 15,000 transactions over the last 10 years and ranges from 1 to 266; (3) figures based on a weighted average of Census Division estimates using a seasonally adjusted, purchase-only index; all figures are for the period ending December 31, 2015

Source: Federal Housing Finance Agency, House Price Index, February 25, 2016

Median Single-Family Home Prices

Area	2013	2014	2015p	Percent Change 2014 to 2015
MSA[1]	196.2	210.1	225.1	7.1
U.S. Average	197.4	208.9	223.9	7.2

Note: Figures are median sales prices of existing single-family homes in thousands of dollars; (p) preliminary; n/a not available; (1) Minneapolis-St. Paul-Bloomington, MN-WI Metropolitan Statistical Area—see Appendix B for areas included

Source: National Association of Realtors, Median Sales Price of Existing Single-Family Homes for Metropolitan Areas, 4th Quarter 2015

Qualifying Income Based on Median Sales Price of Existing Single-Family Homes

Area	With 5% Down ($)	With 10% Down ($)	With 20% Down ($)
MSA[1]	49,758	47,139	41,901
U.S. Average	49,535	46,928	41,714

Note: Figures are preliminary; Qualifying income is based on a mortgage rate of 4.1%. Monthly principal and interest payment is limited to 25% of income; n/a not available; (1) Minneapolis-St. Paul-Bloomington, MN-WI Metropolitan Statistical Area—see Appendix B for areas included

Source: National Association of Realtors, Qualifying Income Based on Median Sales Price of Existing Single-Family Homes for Metropolitan Areas, 4th Quarter 2015

Median Apartment Condo-Coop Home Prices

Area	2013	2014	2015p	Percent Change 2014 to 2015
MSA[1]	n/a	n/a	n/a	n/a
U.S. Average	194.9	204.3	210.7	3.1

Note: Figures are median sales prices of existing apartment condo-coop homes in thousands of dollars; (p) preliminary; n/a not available; (1) Minneapolis-St. Paul-Bloomington, MN-WI Metropolitan Statistical Area—see Appendix B for areas included

Source: National Association of Realtors, Median Sales Price of Existing Apartment Condo-Coop Homes for Metropolitan Areas, 4th Quarter 2015

Gross Monthly Rent

Area	Under $200	$200 -299	$300 -499	$500 -749	$750 -999	$1,000 -1,499	$1,500 and up	Median ($)
City	0.3	1.1	0.3	5.7	12.6	49.7	30.3	1,286
MSA[1]	1.9	3.8	5.3	18.2	29.7	28.8	12.3	916
U.S.	1.5	3.2	7.4	21.0	24.1	26.9	15.9	920

Note: Figures are percentages except for Median; Gross rent is the contract rent plus the estimated average monthly cost of utilities (electricity, gas, and water and sewer) and fuels (oil, coal, kerosene, wood, etc.) if these are paid by the renter (or paid for the renter by someone else); (1) Figures cover the Minneapolis-St. Paul-Bloomington, MN-WI Metropolitan Statistical Area—see Appendix B for areas included

Source: U.S. Census Bureau, 2010-2014 American Community Survey 5-Year Estimates

Homeownership Rate

Area	2008 (%)	2009 (%)	2010 (%)	2011 (%)	2012 (%)	2013 (%)	2014 (%)	2015 (%)
MSA[1]	69.9	70.9	71.2	69.1	70.8	71.7	69.7	67.9
U.S.	67.8	67.4	66.9	66.1	65.4	65.1	64.5	63.7

Note: (1) Figures cover the Minneapolis-St. Paul-Bloomington, MN-WI Metropolitan Statistical Area—see Appendix B for areas included
Source: U.S. Census Bureau, Housing Vacancies and Homeownership Annual Statistics: 2015

Year Housing Structure Built

Area	2010 or Later	2000 -2009	1990 -1999	1980 -1989	1970 -1979	1960 -1969	1950 -1959	1940 -1949	Before 1940	Median Year
City	2.0	23.8	22.3	24.2	20.0	3.7	1.9	0.9	1.2	1989
MSA[1]	0.8	15.2	14.6	14.8	15.4	10.0	10.1	4.1	15.0	1977
U.S.	1.0	14.9	13.9	13.8	15.8	11.0	10.8	5.4	13.3	1976

Note: Figures are percentages except for Median Year; (1) Figures cover the Minneapolis-St. Paul-Bloomington, MN-WI Metropolitan Statistical Area—see Appendix B for areas included
Source: U.S. Census Bureau, 2010-2014 American Community Survey 5-Year Estimates

HEALTH

Health Risk Data

Category	MSA[1] (%)	U.S. (%)
Adults aged 18–64 who have any kind of health care coverage	87.3	79.6
Adults who reported being in good or excellent health	89.2	83.1
Adults who are current smokers	18.0	19.6
Adults who are heavy drinkers[2]	6.6	6.1
Adults who are binge drinkers[3]	21.4	16.9
Adults who are overweight (BMI 25.0 - 29.9)	37.0	35.8
Adults who are obese (BMI 30.0 - 99.8)	23.9	27.6
Adults who participated in any physical activities in the past month	83.5	77.1
Adults 50+ who have ever had a sigmoidoscopy or colonoscopy	74.4	67.3
Women aged 40+ who have had a mammogram within the past two years	78.6	74.0
Men aged 40+ who have had a PSA test within the past two years	38.5	45.2
Adults aged 65+ who have had flu shot within the past year	67.6	60.1
Adults who always wear a seatbelt	96.6	93.8

Note: Data as of 2012 unless otherwise noted; (1) Figures cover the Minneapolis-St. Paul-Bloomington, MN-WI Metropolitan Statistical Area—see Appendix B for areas included; (2) Heavy drinkers are classified as males having more than two drinks per day or females having more than one drink per day; (3) Binge drinkers are classified as males having five or more drinks on one occasion or females having four or more drinks on one occasion
Source: Centers for Disease Control and Prevention, Behaviorial Risk Factor Surveillance System, SMART: Selected Metropolitan/Micropolitan Area Risk Trends, 2012 (Note: the CDC has discontinued this dataset but will be releasing a replacement in mid-2016)

Chronic Health Indicators

Category	MSA[1] (%)	U.S. (%)
Adults who have ever been told they had a heart attack	3.6	4.5
Adults who have ever been told they had a stroke	2.5	2.9
Adults who have been told they currently have asthma	8.7	8.9
Adults who have ever been told they have arthritis	19.6	25.7
Adults who have ever been told they have diabetes[2]	6.7	9.7
Adults who have ever been told they had skin cancer	5.0	5.7
Adults who have ever been told they had any other types of cancer	5.7	6.5
Adults who have ever been told they have COPD	3.9	6.2
Adults who have ever been told they have kidney disease	2.1	2.5
Adults who have ever been told they have a form of depression	16.5	18.0

Note: Data as of 2012 unless otherwise noted; (1) Figures cover the Minneapolis-St. Paul-Bloomington, MN-WI Metropolitan Statistical Area—see Appendix B for areas included; (2) Figures do not include pregnancy-related, borderline, or pre-diabetes
Source: Centers for Disease Control and Prevention, Behaviorial Risk Factor Surveillance System, SMART: Selected Metropolitan/Micropolitan Area Risk Trends, 2012 (Note: the CDC has discontinued this dataset but will be releasing a replacement in mid-2016)

Mortality Rates for the Top 10 Causes of Death in the U.S.

ICD-10[a] Sub-Chapter	ICD-10[a] Code	Age-Adjusted Mortality Rate[1] per 100,000 population	
		County[2]	U.S.
Malignant neoplasms	C00-C97	149.6	163.6
Ischaemic heart diseases	I20-I25	48.8	102.2
Other forms of heart disease	I30-I51	41.7	50.1
Chronic lower respiratory diseases	J40-J47	34.0	41.4
Organic, including symptomatic, mental disorders	F01-F09	61.6	38.5
Cerebrovascular diseases	I60-I69	32.1	36.5
Other external causes of accidental injury	W00-X59	36.1	27.5
Other degenerative diseases of the nervous system	G30-G31	22.7	26.3
Diabetes mellitus	E10-E14	16.8	21.1
Hypertensive diseases	I10-I15	11.2	19.7

Note: (a) ICD-10 = International Classification of Diseases 10th Revision; (1) Mortality rates are a three year average covering 2012-2014; (2) Figures cover Hennepin County.
Source: Centers for Disease Control and Prevention, National Center for Health Statistics. Underlying Cause of Death 1999-2014 on CDC WONDER Online Database, released 2015.

Mortality Rates for Selected Causes of Death

ICD-10[a] Sub-Chapter	ICD-10[a] Code	Age-Adjusted Mortality Rate[1] per 100,000 population	
		County[2]	U.S.
Assault	X85-Y09	3.5	5.1
Diseases of the liver	K70-K76	12.3	13.5
Human immunodeficiency virus (HIV) disease	B20-B24	1.4	2.1
Influenza and pneumonia	J09-J18	8.9	15.2
Intentional self-harm	X60-X84	10.4	12.7
Malnutrition	E40-E46	0.6	0.9
Obesity and other hyperalimentation	E65-E68	1.6	1.9
Renal failure	N17-N19	10.0	13.0
Transport accidents	V01-V99	4.5	11.6
Viral hepatitis	B15-B19	1.9	2.1

Note: (a) ICD-10 = International Classification of Diseases 10th Revision; (1) Mortality rates are a three year average covering 2012-2014; (2) Figures cover Hennepin County; Data are Suppressed when the data meet the criteria for confidentiality constraints; Mortality rates are flagged as Unreliable when the rate would be calculated with a numerator of 20 or less.
Source: Centers for Disease Control and Prevention, National Center for Health Statistics. Underlying Cause of Death 1999-2014 on CDC WONDER Online Database, released 2015.

Health Insurance Coverage

Area	With Health Insurance	With Private Health Insurance	With Public Health Insurance	Without Health Insurance	Population Under Age 18 Without Health Insurance
City	96.1	88.4	16.0	3.9	3.0
MSA[1]	92.2	77.7	25.1	7.8	4.9
U.S.	85.8	65.8	31.1	14.2	7.1

Note: Figures are percentages that cover the civilian noninstitutionalized population; (1) Figures cover the Minneapolis-St. Paul-Bloomington, MN-WI Metropolitan Statistical Area—see Appendix B for areas included
Source: U.S. Census Bureau, 2010-2014 American Community Survey 5-Year Estimates

Number of Medical Professionals

Area	MDs[3]	DOs[3,4]	Dentists	Podiatrists	Chiropractors	Optometrists
County[1] (number)	5,783	197	1,085	43	806	220
County[1] (rate[2])	481.9	16.4	89.5	3.5	66.5	18.2
U.S. (rate[2])	272.5	20.9	64.7	5.8	25.9	15.2

Note: Data as of 2014 unless noted; (1) Data covers Hennepin County; (2) Rate per 100,000 population; (3) Data as of 2013 and includes all active, non-federal physicians; (4) Doctor of Osteopathic Medicine
Source: U.S. Department of Health and Human Services, Health Resources and Services Administration, Bureau of Health Professions, Area Resource File (ARF) 2014-2015

Best Hospitals

According to *U.S. News,* the Minneapolis-St. Paul-Bloomington, MN-WI metro area is home to three of the best hospitals in the U.S.: **MercyHospital** (1 specialty); **Abbott Northwestern Hospital** (5 specialties); **Minneapolis Heart Institute at Abbott Northwestern Hospital** (1 specialty). The hospitals listed were nationally ranked in at least one adult specialty. Only 137 hospitals nationwide were nationally ranked in one or more specialties. Fifteen hospitals in the U.S. made the Honor Roll with high scores in at least six specialties. *U.S. News Online, "America's Best Children's Hospitals 2015-16"*

According to *U.S. News,* the Minneapolis-St. Paul-Bloomington, MN-WI metro area is home to three of the best children's hospitals in the U.S.: **Children's Hospitals and Clinics of Minnesota** (1 specialties); **University of Minnesota Masonic Children's Hospital** (5 specialties); **Gillette Children's Specialty Healthcare** (1 specialty). The hospitals listed were highly ranked in at least one pediatric specialty. Eighty-three children's hospitals in the U.S. were nationally ranked in at least one specialty. Twelve children's hospitals in the U.S. made the Honor Roll with high scores in at least three specialties. *U.S. News Online, "America's Best Children's Hospitals 2015-16"*

EDUCATION

Public School District Statistics

District Name	Schls	Pupils	Pupil/ Teacher Ratio	Minority Pupils[1] (%)	Free Lunch Eligible[2] (%)	IEP[3] (%)
Beacon Academy	1	412	12.5	18.2	13.3	13.6
Osseo Public School District	34	20,913	17.1	52.4	32.9	14.2
Parnassus Preparatory Charter	1	760	21.9	33.9	14.6	4.7

Note: Table includes school districts with 100 or more students; (1) Percentage of students that are not non-Hispanic white; (2) Percentage of students that are eligible for the free lunch program; (3) Percentage of students that have an Individualized Education Program.
Source: U.S. Department of Education, National Center for Education Statistics, Common Core of Data, Local Education Agency (School District) Universe Survey: School Year 2013-2014; U.S. Department of Education, National Center for Education Statistics, Common Core of Data, Public Elementary/Secondary School Universe Survey: School Year 2013-2014

Highest Level of Education

Area	Less than H.S.	H.S. Diploma	Some College, No Deg.	Associate Degree	Bachelor's Degree	Master's Degree	Prof. School Degree	Doctorate Degree
City	2.7	17.3	20.2	10.4	33.8	12.2	2.2	1.2
MSA[1]	6.9	22.8	21.4	9.9	25.9	9.2	2.4	1.4
U.S.	13.7	28.0	21.2	7.9	18.3	7.8	2.0	1.3

Note: Figures cover persons age 25 and over; (1) Figures cover the Minneapolis-St. Paul-Bloomington, MN-WI Metropolitan Statistical Area—see Appendix B for areas included
Source: U.S. Census Bureau, 2010-2014 American Community Survey 5-Year Estimates

Educational Attainment by Race

Area	High School Graduate or Higher (%)					Bachelor's Degree or Higher (%)				
	Total	White	Black	Asian	Hisp.[2]	Total	White	Black	Asian	Hisp.[2]
City	97.3	98.0	84.3	93.2	87.7	49.4	48.6	42.1	61.9	42.4
MSA[1]	93.1	95.3	81.8	79.8	65.7	39.0	40.7	20.2	44.0	17.6
U.S.	86.3	88.4	83.2	85.8	64.1	29.3	30.6	19.0	50.9	13.9

Note: Figures shown cover persons 25 years old and over; (1) Figures cover the Minneapolis-St. Paul-Bloomington, MN-WI Metropolitan Statistical Area—see Appendix B for areas included; (2) People of Hispanic origin can be of any race
Source: U.S. Census Bureau, 2010-2014 American Community Survey 5-Year Estimates

School Enrollment by Grade and Control

Area	Preschool (%)		Kindergarten (%)		Grades 1 - 4 (%)		Grades 5 - 8 (%)		Grades 9 - 12 (%)	
	Public	Private	Public	Private	Public	Private	Public	Private	Public	Private
City	50.7	49.3	86.7	13.3	81.9	18.1	91.4	8.6	91.6	8.4
MSA[1]	55.6	44.4	86.8	13.2	87.9	12.1	88.6	11.4	90.9	9.1
U.S.	57.4	42.6	87.8	12.2	89.8	10.2	89.9	10.1	90.6	9.4

Note: Figures shown cover persons 3 years old and over; (1) Figures cover the Minneapolis-St. Paul-Bloomington, MN-WI Metropolitan Statistical Area—see Appendix B for areas included
Source: U.S. Census Bureau, 2010-2014 American Community Survey 5-Year Estimates

Average Salaries of Public School Classroom Teachers

Area	2013-14		2014-15		Percent Change 2013-14 to 2014-15	Percent Change 2004-05 to 2014-15
	Dollars	Rank[1]	Dollars	Rank[1]		
Minnesota	54,752	21	56,670	20	3.50	19.5
U.S. Average	56,610	–	57,379	–	1.36	20.8

Note: (1) State rank ranges from 1 to 51 where 1 indicates highest salary.
Source: National Education Association, Rankings & Estimates: Rankings of the States 2014 and Estimates of School Statistics 2015, March 2015

Higher Education

Four-Year Colleges			Two-Year Colleges			Medical Schools[1]	Law Schools[2]	Voc/ Tech[3]
Public	Private Non-profit	Private For-profit	Public	Private Non-profit	Private For-profit			
0	0	0	0	0	0	0	0	0

Note: Figures cover institutions located within the city limits and include main campuses only; (1) includes schools accredited by the Liaison Committee on Medical Education and the American Osteopathic Association's Commission on Osteopathic College Accreditation; (2) includes ABA-accredited schools, schools with provisional ABA accreditation, and state accredited schools; (3) includes all schools with programs that are less than 2 years.
Source: National Center for Education Statistics, Integrated Postsecondary Education System (IPEDS), 2014-15; Association of American Medical Colleges, Member List, March 21, 2016; American Osteopathic Association, Member List, March 21, 2016; Law School Admission Council, Official Guide to ABA-Approved Law Schools Online, March 21, 2016; Wikipedia, List of Medical Schools in the United States, March 21, 2016; Wikipedia, List of Law Schools in the United States, March 21, 2016

According to *U.S. News & World Report,* the Minneapolis-St. Paul-Bloomington, MN-WI metro area is home to two of the best national universities in the U.S.: **University of Minnesota–Twin Cities** (#69); **University of St. Thomas** (#115 tie). The indicators used to capture academic quality fall into a number of categories: assessment by administrators at peer institutions; retention of students; faculty resources; student selectivity; financial resources; alumni giving; high school counselor ratings of colleges; and graduation rate. *U.S. News & World Report, "America's Best Colleges 2016"*

According to *U.S. News & World Report,* the Minneapolis-St. Paul-Bloomington, MN-WI metro area is home to two of the best liberal arts colleges in the U.S.: **Macalester College** (#23 tie); **Gustavus Adolphus College** (#79 tie). The indicators used to capture academic quality fall into a number of categories: assessment by administrators at peer institutions; retention of students; faculty resources; student selectivity; financial resources; alumni giving; high school counselor ratings of colleges; and graduation rate. *U.S. News & World Report, "America's Best Colleges 2016"*

According to *U.S. News & World Report,* the Minneapolis-St. Paul-Bloomington, MN-WI metro area is home to one of the top 100 law schools in the U.S.: **University of Minnesota, Law School** (#22 tie). The rankings are based on a weighted average of 12 measures of quality: peer assessment score; assessment score by lawyers/judges; median LSAT scores; median undergrad GPA; acceptance rate; employment rates for graduates; placement success; bar passage rate; faculty resources; expenditures per student; student/faculty ratio; and library resources. *U.S. News & World Report, "America's Best Graduate Schools, Law, 2017"*

According to *U.S. News & World Report,* the Minneapolis-St. Paul-Bloomington, MN-WI metro area is home to one of the top 75 medical schools for research in the U.S.: **University of Minnesota, Medical School** (#35 tie). The rankings are based on a weighted average of 11 measures of quality: quality assessment; peer assessment score; assessment score by residency directors; research activity; total research activity; average research activity per faculty member; student selectivity; median MCAT total score; median undergraduate GPA;

acceptance rate; and faculty resources. *U.S. News & World Report, "America's Best Graduate Schools, Medical, 2017"*

According to *U.S. News & World Report,* the Minneapolis-St. Paul-Bloomington, MN-WI metro area is home to one of the top 75 business schools in the U.S.: **University of Minnesota–Twin Cities, Carlson School of Management** (#27 tie). The rankings are based on a weighted average of the following nine measures: quality assessment; peer assessment; recruiter assessment; placement success; mean starting salary and bonus; student selectivity; mean GMAT and GRE scores; mean undergraduate GPA; and acceptance rate. *U.S. News & World Report, "America's Best Graduate Schools, Business, 2017"*

PRESIDENTIAL ELECTION

2012 Presidential Election Results

Area	Obama (%)	Romney (%)	Other (%)
Hennepin County	62.3	35.3	2.4
U.S.	51.0	47.2	1.8

Note: Results may not add to 100% due to rounding
Source: Dave Leip's Atlas of U.S. Presidential Elections

EMPLOYERS

Major Employers

Company Name	Industry
3M Company	Adhesives, sealants
Ameriprise Financial	Investment advice
Anderson Corporation	Millwork
Aware Integrated	Hospital & medical services plans
Bethesda Healtheast Hospital	General medical/surgical hospitals
Carlson Holdings	Hotels/motels
City of Minneapolis	General government, local government
County of Hennepin	General government, county government
Hennepin County	County supervisors' & executives' offices
Honeywell International	Aircraft engines & engine parts
Lawson Software	Application computer software
Medtronic	Electromedical equipment
Minnesota Department of Human Services	Family services agency
Minnesota Department of Transportation	Regulation, administration of transportation
North Memorial Hospital	General medical/surgical hospitals
Regents of the University of Minnesota	Specialty outpatient clinics
Rosemount Apple Valley and Eagan	Personal service agents, brokers, & bureaus
St Paul Fire and marine Insurance Company	Fire, marine, & casualty insurance
Thomson Legal Regulatory	Books, publishing & printing
United Parcel Service	Package delivery vehicular
Wells Fargo Bank	Mortgage bankers
West Publishing Corporation	Data base information retrieval

Note: Companies shown are located within the Minneapolis-St. Paul-Bloomington, MN-WI Metropolitan Statistical Area.
Source: Hoovers.com; Wikipedia

PUBLIC SAFETY

Crime Rate

Area	All Crimes	Violent Crimes				Property Crimes		
		Murder	Rape[3]	Robbery	Aggrav. Assault	Burglary	Larceny -Theft	Motor Vehicle Theft
City	1,814.5	3.0	4.5	13.6	13.6	179.3	1,562.8	37.7
Metro[1]	2,758.2	1.8	33.7	94.3	131.9	402.3	1,915.8	178.4
U.S.	2,971.8	4.5	36.6	102.2	232.5	542.5	1,837.3	216.2

Note: Figures are crimes per 100,000 population; (1) Figures cover the Minneapolis-St. Paul-Bloomington, MN-WI Metropolitan Statistical Area—see Appendix B for areas included; (3) The city and U.S. figures shown were reported using the revised Uniform Crime Reporting (UCR) definition of rape. The suburban and metro area figures shown are an aggregate total of the data submitted using both the revised and legacy UCR definitions.
Source: FBI Uniform Crime Reports, 2014

Hate Crimes

Area	Number of Quarters Reported	Number of Incidents per Bias Motivation						
		Race	Religion	Sexual Orientation	Ethnicity	Disability	Gender	Gender Identity
City	4	0	0	0	0	0	0	0
U.S.	4	2,568	1,014	1,017	648	84	33	98

Source: Federal Bureau of Investigation, Hate Crime Statistics 2014

Identity Theft Consumer Complaints

Area	Complaints	Complaints per 100,000 Population	Rank[2]
MSA[1]	3,988	114.1	149
U.S.	490,220	152.4	-

Note: (1) Figures cover the Minneapolis-St. Paul-Bloomington, MN-WI Metropolitan Statistical Area—see Appendix B for areas included; (2) Rank ranges from 1 to 379 where 1 indicates greatest number of identity theft complaints per 100,000 population
Source: Federal Trade Commission, Consumer Sentinel Network Data Book for January–December 2015

Fraud and Other Consumer Complaints

Area	Complaints	Complaints per 100,000 Population	Rank[2]
MSA[1]	13,758	393.6	116
U.S.	2,593,159	806.0	-

Note: (1) Figures cover the Minneapolis-St. Paul-Bloomington, MN-WI Metropolitan Statistical Area—see Appendix B for areas included; (2) Rank ranges from 1 to 379 where 1 indicates greatest number of identity theft complaints per 100,000 population
Source: Federal Trade Commission, Consumer Sentinel Network Data Book for January–December 2015

RECREATION

Culture

Dance[1]	Theatre[1]	Instrumental Music[1]	Vocal Music[1]	Series and Festivals	Museums and Art Galleries[2]	Zoos and Aquariums[3]
0	0	0	0	0	0	0

Note: (1) Professional perfoming groups; (2) Based on organizations with SIC code 8412; (3) AZA-accredited
Source: The Grey House Performing Arts Directory, 2015-16; Association of Zoos & Aquariums, AZA Member Zoos & Aquariums, March 25, 2016; www.AccuLeads.com, March 29, 2016

Professional Sports Teams

Team Name	League	Year Established
Minnesota Timberwolves	National Basketball Association (NBA)	1989
Minnesota Twins	Major League Baseball (MLB)	1961
Minnesota United FC	Major League Soccer (MLS)	2018
Minnesota Vikings	National Football League (NFL)	1961
Minnesota Wild	National Hockey League (NHL)	2000

Note: Includes teams located in the Minneapolis-St. Paul-Bloomington, MN-WI Metropolitan Statistical Area.
Source: Wikipedia, Major Professional Sports Teams of the United States and Canada, March 24, 2016

CLIMATE

Average and Extreme Temperatures

Temperature	Jan	Feb	Mar	Apr	May	Jun	Jul	Aug	Sep	Oct	Nov	Dec	Yr.
Extreme High (°F)	57	60	83	95	96	102	105	101	98	89	74	63	105
Average High (°F)	21	27	38	56	69	79	84	81	71	59	41	26	54
Average Temp. (°F)	12	18	30	46	59	69	74	71	61	50	33	19	45
Average Low (°F)	3	9	21	36	48	58	63	61	50	39	25	11	35
Extreme Low (°F)	-34	-28	-32	2	18	37	43	39	26	15	-17	-29	-34

Note: Figures cover the years 1948-1990
Source: National Climatic Data Center, International Station Meteorological Climate Summary, 9/96

Average Precipitation/Snowfall/Humidity

Precip./Humidity	Jan	Feb	Mar	Apr	May	Jun	Jul	Aug	Sep	Oct	Nov	Dec	Yr.
Avg. Precip. (in.)	0.8	0.8	1.9	2.2	3.1	4.0	3.8	3.6	2.5	1.9	1.4	1.0	27.1
Avg. Snowfall (in.)	11	9	12	3	Tr	0	0	0	Tr	Tr	7	10	52
Avg. Rel. Hum. 6am (%)	75	76	77	75	75	79	81	84	85	81	80	79	79
Avg. Rel. Hum. 3pm (%)	64	62	58	48	47	50	50	52	53	52	62	68	55

Note: Figures cover the years 1948-1990; Tr = Trace amounts (<0.05 in. of rain; <0.5 in. of snow)
Source: National Climatic Data Center, International Station Meteorological Climate Summary, 9/96

Weather Conditions

Temperature			Daytime Sky			Precipitation		
5°F & below	32°F & below	90°F & above	Clear	Partly cloudy	Cloudy	0.01 inch or more precip.	0.1 inch or more snow/ice	Thunder-storms
45	156	16	93	125	147	113	41	37

Note: Figures are average number of days per year and cover the years 1948-1990
Source: National Climatic Data Center, International Station Meteorological Climate Summary, 9/96

HAZARDOUS WASTE

Superfund Sites

Maple Grove has no sites on the EPA's Superfund Final National Priorities List. There are a total of 1,323 Superfund sites on the list in the U.S. *U.S. Environmental Protection Agency, Final National Priorities List, March 18, 2016*

AIR & WATER QUALITY

Air Quality Trends: Ozone

	1990	1995	2000	2005	2010	2011	2012	2013	2014
MSA[1]	0.068	0.084	0.065	0.074	0.066	0.064	0.073	0.066	0.063

Note: (1) Data covers the Minneapolis-St. Paul-Bloomington, MN-WI Metropolitan Statistical Area—see Appendix B for areas included. The values shown are the composite ozone concentration averages among trend sites based on the highest fourth daily maximum 8-hour concentration in parts per million. These trends are based on sites having an adequate record of monitoring data during the trend period. Data from exceptional events are included.
Source: U.S. Environmental Protection Agency, Air Quality Monitoring Information, "Air Quality Trends by City, 1990-2014"

Air Quality Index

Area	Percent of Days when Air Quality was...[2]					AQI Statistics[2]	
	Good	Moderate	Unhealthy for Sensitive Groups	Unhealthy	Very Unhealthy	Maximum	Median
MSA[1]	54.5	44.1	1.4	0.0	0.0	137	48

Note: (1) Data covers the Minneapolis-St. Paul-Bloomington, MN-WI Metropolitan Statistical Area—see Appendix B for areas included; (2) Based on 365 days with AQI data in 2015. Air Quality Index (AQI) is an index for reporting daily air quality. EPA calculates the AQI for five major air pollutants regulated by the Clean Air Act: ground-level ozone, particle pollution (aka particulate matter), carbon monoxide, sulfur dioxide, and nitrogen dioxide. The AQI runs from 0 to 500. The higher the AQI value, the greater the level of air pollution and the greater the health concern. There are six AQI categories: "Good" AQI is between 0 and 50. Air quality is considered satisfactory; "Moderate" AQI is between 51 and 100. Air quality is acceptable; "Unhealthy for Sensitive Groups" When AQI values are between 101 and 150, members of sensitive groups may experience health effects; "Unhealthy" When AQI values are between 151 and 200 everyone may begin to experience health effects; "Very Unhealthy" AQI values between 201 and 300 trigger a health alert; "Hazardous" AQI values over 300 trigger warnings of emergency conditions (not shown).
Source: U.S. Environmental Protection Agency, Air Quality Index Report, 2015

Air Quality Index Pollutants

Area	Percent of Days when AQI Pollutant was...[2]					
	Carbon Monoxide	Nitrogen Dioxide	Ozone	Sulfur Dioxide	Particulate Matter 2.5	Particulate Matter 10
MSA[1]	0.0	1.9	18.6	0.0	51.0	28.5

Note: (1) Data covers the Minneapolis-St. Paul-Bloomington, MN-WI Metropolitan Statistical Area—see Appendix B for areas included; (2) Based on 365 days with AQI data in 2015. The Air Quality Index (AQI) is an index for reporting daily air quality. EPA calculates the AQI for five major air pollutants regulated by the Clean Air Act: ground-level ozone, particle pollution (also known as particulate matter), carbon monoxide, sulfur dioxide, and nitrogen dioxide. The AQI runs from 0 to 500. The higher the AQI value, the greater the level of air pollution and the greater the health concern.
Source: U.S. Environmental Protection Agency, Air Quality Index Report, 2015

Maximum Air Pollutant Concentrations: Particulate Matter, Ozone, CO and Lead

	Particulate Matter 10 (ug/m^3)	Particulate Matter 2.5 Wtd AM (ug/m^3)	Particulate Matter 2.5 24-Hr (ug/m^3)	Ozone (ppm)	Carbon Monoxide (ppm)	Lead (ug/m^3)
MSA[1] Level	76	9.9	28	0.064	2	0.12
NAAQS[2]	150	15	35	0.075	9	0.15
Met NAAQS[2]	Yes	Yes	Yes	Yes	Yes	Yes

Note: (1) Data covers the Minneapolis-St. Paul-Bloomington, MN-WI Metropolitan Statistical Area—see Appendix B for areas included; Data from exceptional events are included; (2) National Ambient Air Quality Standards; ppm = parts per million; ug/m^3 = micrograms per cubic meter; n/a not available.
Concentrations: Particulate Matter 10 (coarse particulate)—highest second maximum 24-hour concentration; Particulate Matter 2.5 Wtd AM (fine particulate)—highest weighted annual mean concentration; Particulate Matter 2.5 24-Hour (fine particulate)—highest 98th percentile 24-hour concentration; Ozone—highest fourth daily maximum 8-hour concentration; Carbon Monoxide—highest second maximum non-overlapping 8-hour concentration; Lead—maximum running 3-month average
Source: U.S. Environmental Protection Agency, Air Quality Monitoring Information, "Air Quality Statistics by City, 2014"

Maximum Air Pollutant Concentrations: Nitrogen Dioxide and Sulfur Dioxide

	Nitrogen Dioxide AM (ppb)	Nitrogen Dioxide 1-Hr (ppb)	Sulfur Dioxide AM (ppb)	Sulfur Dioxide 1-Hr (ppb)	Sulfur Dioxide 24-Hr (ppb)
MSA[1] Level	16	50	n/a	12	n/a
NAAQS[2]	53	100	30	75	140
Met NAAQS[2]	Yes	Yes	n/a	Yes	n/a

Note: (1) Data covers the Minneapolis-St. Paul-Bloomington, MN-WI Metropolitan Statistical Area—see Appendix B for areas included; Data from exceptional events are included; (2) National Ambient Air Quality Standards; ppm = parts per million; ug/m^3 = micrograms per cubic meter; n/a not available.
Concentrations: Nitrogen Dioxide AM—highest arithmetic mean concentration; Nitrogen Dioxide 1-Hr—highest 98th percentile 1-hour daily maximum concentration; Sulfur Dioxide AM—highest annual mean concentration; Sulfur Dioxide 1-Hr—highest 99th percentile 1-hour daily maximum concentration; Sulfur Dioxide 24-Hr—highest second maximum 24-hour concentration
Source: U.S. Environmental Protection Agency, Air Quality Monitoring Information, "Air Quality Statistics by City, 2014"

Drinking Water

Water System Name	Pop. Served	Primary Water Source Type	Violations[1]	
			Health Based	Monitoring/ Reporting
Maple Grove	62,000	Ground	0	0

Note: (1) Based on violation data from January 1, 2015 to December 31, 2015 (includes unresolved violations from earlier years)
Source: U.S. Environmental Protection Agency, Office of Ground Water and Drinking Water, Safe Drinking Water Information System (based on data extracted April 29, 2016)

Woodbury, Minnesota

Background

Woodbury, a southeastern suburb of the Minneapolis-St. Paul "Twin Cities" metropolitan area, is one of Minnesota's fastest-growing cities. Woodbury is a thoughtfully designed city with eight small lakes, 3,000 acres of community and neighborhood parks, a swimming beach, and over 100 miles of multi-use trails. It's 12 miles west of the St. Croix River, the border between Minnesota and Wisconsin, and nine miles east of St. Paul, Minnesota's state capital.

Woodbury was originally named Red Rock after a sacred rock painted by Dakota Chief Little Crow. Settlers from eastern states first came to the forested area in 1844, along with immigrants from Germany, Ireland, Sweden, Switzerland, Scotland, and Denmark bringing with them their rich culture. They cleared timber and farmed the land with wheat, corn, barley, and potatoes. The rolling hills were also conducive for dairy farming. In 1859, Red Rock was renamed Woodbury Township, after Judge Levi Woodbury from New Hampshire, a friend of one of the city leaders.

Agriculture continued to play an important part in the local economy through the 1950s. Woodbury Heights, the community's first housing development, was started in 1955, and urban development has since continued to replace farmland. But, with a core value of open spaces and natural resources, the city has taken steps to acquire and maintain hundreds of undeveloped acres.

Woodbury was incorporated in 1967, installed a mayor and city council, and formed planning and park commissions. At that time, a comprehensive land use plan was developed to manage construction and development. The city has demonstrated a commitment to environmental preservation with the hiring of an environmental planner and environmental resources coordinator. Other activities that emphasize Woodbury's emphasis on the environment include their participation in the National Pollutant Discharge Elimination System program, maintenance of a Garbage and Recycling website, organization of an Environmental Advisory Commission and Energy Conservation Task Force.

The corporate headquarters for 3M, one of Minnesota's largest employers, is six miles from Woodbury. The University of Minnesota, St. Paul campus is 11 miles from Woodbury and the Mall of America in Bloomington, the nation's largest shopping mall, is 24 miles away. With its theme of "The Best Place to Do Business," the city recruits firms to its two business parks, which are strategically located on Interstate 94. Woodbury is currently home to The Hartford, Target.com, EcoWater Systems, and Dean Foods/Land O' Lakes.

Woodbury offers numerous recreational opportunities including a municipal golf course, Eagle Valley, The Bielenberg Sports Center, with two indoor ice rinks and a field house with a walking/running track. The city also maintains an outdoor sports complex with 18 athletic fields, picnic areas, a sand volleyball court and playground equipment. The Central Park facility, located in the City Center, includes an indoor park linked to a local library, a YMCA, an indoor playground, and an Early Childhood Family Education program. The Woodbury Parks and Recreation Department and local organizations sponsor recreational programs such as the annual Fourth of July celebration, Minnesota Night to Unite activities, Woodbury Days, Curbside Recycling, and Buckthorn Busting.

The proximity to the St. Croix River Valley and Minnesota's 10,000 lakes offers fishing, swimming, and boating opportunities. The Twin Cities provide a variety of recreational, entertainment, sports, cultural, and business opportunities. They are home to Minnesota Twins baseball, the Minnesota Vikings football, Timberwolves basketball, and Minnesota Wild hockey. Other favorites include the Minnesota Public Radio's A Prairie Home Companion show, the Minnesota Orchestra, the Chanhassen Dinner Theatres, the Guthrie Theater, the Walker Art Center, the American Swedish Institute with its new Nelson Cultural Center, and the St. Paul Farmers' Market.

Dozens of private and public colleges and universities are located within a 50-mile radius of Woodbury on both the Minnesota and Wisconsin side of the St. Croix River, including the University of Minnesota, Bethel University, and the University of Wisconsin—River Falls.

The city enjoys an average of 193 sunny days per year, and receives ample moisture with an average of 31 inches of rain and 49 inches of snow per year. The temperatures range from average highs in July around 83 degrees and average lows in January around 5 degrees. Sunshine and moisture are ideal for attractive landscapes and for four-season recreational activities.

Rankings

Business/Finance Rankings

- The personal finance site NerdWallet analyzed 183 American metropolitan areas with populations over 250,000 and more than 15,000 businesses to rank where entrepreneurs find the most success. Criteria included area economy, annual income, housing cost, unemployment rate, and the success rate of area businesses. Minneapolis* ranked #14. *www.nerdwallet.com, "Best Places to Start a Business," April 27, 2015*

- TransUnion ranked the nation's metro areas by average credit score, calculated on the VantageScore system, developed by the three major credit-reporting bureaus—TransUnion, Experian, and Equifax. The Minneapolis* metro area was among the ten cities with the highest collective credit score, meaning that its residents posed the lowest average consumer credit risk. *www.usatoday.com, "Metro Areas' Average Credit Rating Revealed," February 7, 2013*

- Based on metro area social media reviews, the employment opinion group Glassdoor surveyed 50 of the largest U.S. metro areas and equally weighed cost of living, hiring opportunity, and job satisfaction to compose a list of "25 Best Cities for Jobs." The Minneapolis* metro area was ranked #18 in overall job satisfaction. *www.glassdoor.com, "Best Cities for Jobs," May 19, 2015*

- In a survey of economic confidence in the nation's 50 largest metropolitan areas conducted January–December 2014, the Minneapolis* metro area placed #4, according to Gallup's 2014 Economic Confidence Index. *Gallup, "San Jose and San Francisco Lead in Economic Confidence," March 19, 2015*

- The Brookings Institution ranked the 100 largest metro areas in the U.S. based on income inequality. Minneapolis* was ranked #79 (#1 = greatest ineqality). Criteria: the "95/20 ratio," a figure representing the income at which a household earns more than 95 percent of all other households, divided by the income at which a household earns more than only 20 percent of all other households. *Brookings Institution, "Income Inequality, 100 Largest U.S. Metro Areas, 2007-2014," January 14, 2016*

- *Forbes* ranked the largest metro areas in the U.S. in terms of the "Best Cities for Young Professionals." The Minneapolis* metro area ranked #10 out of 15. Criteria: job growth; unemployment rate; median salary of college graduates age 24 to 34; cost of living; number of small businesses per capita; number of large companies; percentage of population 25 years of age and older with college degrees. *Forbes.com, "America's 15 Best Cities for Young Professionals," August 18, 2014*

- Payscale.com ranked the 20 largest metro areas in terms of wage growth. The Minneapolis* metro area ranked #2. Criteria: private-sector wage growth between the 1st quarter of 2015 and the 1st quarter of 2016. *PayScale, "Wage Trends by Metro Area," 1st Quarter, 2016*

- The Minneapolis* metro area appeared on the Milken Institute "2015 Best Performing Cities" list. Rank: #59 out of 200 large metro areas. Criteria: job growth; wage and salary growth; high-tech output growth. *Milken Institute, "Best-Performing Cities 2015," December 2015*

- *Forbes* ranked the 200 most populous metro areas to determine the nation's "Best Places for Business and Careers." The Minneapolis* metro area was ranked #39. Criteria: costs (business and living); job growth (past and projected); income growth; educational attainment (college and high school); projected economic growth; cultural and recreational opportunities; net migration patterns; number of highly ranked colleges. *Forbes, "The Best Places for Business and Careers 2015," July 29, 2015*

Dating/Romance Rankings

- *Forbes* reports that the Minneapolis* metro area made Rent.com's Best Cities for Newlyweds list for 2013, based on Bureau of Labor Statistics and Census Bureau data on number of married couples, percentage of families with children under age six, average annual income, cost of living, and availability of rentals. *www.forbes.com, "The 10 Best Cities for Newlyweds to Live and Work In," May 30, 2013*

- CreditDonkey, a financial education website, sought out the ten best U.S. cities for newlyweds, considering the number of married couples, divorce rate, average credit score, and average number of hours worked per week in metro areas with a million or more residents. The Minneapolis* metro area placed #10. *www.creditdonkey.com, "Study: Best Cities for Newlyweds," November 30, 2013*

Education Rankings

- The Minneapolis* metro area was selected as one of the world's most inventive cities by *Forbes*. The area was ranked #9 out of 15. Criteria: patent applications per capita. *Forbes, "World's 15 Most Inventive Cities," July 9, 2013*
- The Minneapolis* metro area was selected as one of America's most innovative cities" by *The Business Insider*. The metro area was ranked #20 out of 20. Criteria: patents per capita. *The Business Insider, "The 20 Most Innovative Cities in the U.S.," February 1, 2013*
- Minneapolis* was identified as one of America's "smartest" metropolitan areas by *The Business Journals*. The area ranked #9 out of 10. Criteria: percentage of adults (25 and older) with high school diplomas, bachelor's degrees and graduate degrees. *The Business Journals, "Where the Brainpower Is: Exclusive U.S. Rankings, Insights," February 27, 2014*
- Personal finance website *WalletHub* analyzed the 150 largest U.S. metropolitan statistical areas to determine where the most educated Americans are choosing to settle. Criteria: education quality and attainment gap; education levels; percentage of workers with degrees; public school rankings; quality and size of each metro area's universities. Minneapolis* was ranked #9 (#1 = most educated city). *www.WalletHub.com, "2015's Most and Least Educated Cities*
- Minneapolis* was identified as one of the "Smartest Cities in America" by the brain-training website *Lumosity* using data from three million of its own users. The metro area ranked #33 out of 50. Criteria: users' brain performance index scores, considering core cognitive abilities such as memory, processing speed, flexibility, attention and problem-solving. *Lumosity, " Smartest Cities in America," June 25, 2013*

Environmental Rankings

- The Minneapolis* metro area came in at #118 for the relative comfort of its climate on Sperling's list of "chill cities," as measured by the Sperling Heat Index. All 361 metro areas are included. Criteria included daytime high temperatures, nighttime low temperatures, dew point, and relative humidity at the high temperatures. *www.bertsperling.com, "Sperling's Chill Cities," July 18, 2013*
- Sperling's BestPlaces assessed 379 metropolitan areas of the United States for the likelihood of dangerously extreme weather events or earthquakes. In general the Southeast and South-Central regions have the highest risk of weather extremes and earthquakes, while the Pacific Northwest enjoys the lowest risk. Of the least risky metropolitan areas, the Minneapolis* metro area was ranked #99. *www.bestplaces.net, "Safest Places from Natural Disasters," April 2011*
- The U.S. Environmental Protection Agency (EPA) released a list of U.S. metropolitan areas with the most ENERGY STAR certified buildings in 2015. The Minneapolis* metro area was ranked #13 out of 25. *U.S. Environmental Protection Agency, "Top Cities With the Most ENERGY STAR Certified Buildings in 2016," March 30, 2016*

Health/Fitness Rankings

- Analysts who tracked obesity rates in the nation's largest metro areas (populations above one million) found that the Minneapolis* metro area was one of the ten major metros where residents were least likely to be obese, defined as a BMI score of 30 or above. *www.gallup.com, "Boulder, Colo., Residents Still Least Likely to Be Obese," April 4, 2014*

- For each of the 50 most populous metro areas in the United States, the American College of Sports Medicine's American Fitness Index evaluated infrastructure, community assets, and policies that encourage healthy and fit lifestyles, including preventive health behaviors, levels of chronic disease conditions, health care access, and community resources and policies that support physical activity. The Minneapolis* metro area ranked #2 for "community fitness." *www.americanfitnessindex.org, "ACSM American Fitness Index Health and Community Fitness Status of the 50 Largest Metropolitan Areas," May 2015*
- Minneapolis* was identified as a "2016 Spring Allergy Capital." The area ranked #71 out of 100. Three groups of factors were used to identify the most severe cities for people with allergies during the spring season: annual pollen levels; medicine utilization; access to board-certified allergists. *Asthma and Allergy Foundation of America, "Spring Allergy Capitals 2016"*
- Minneapolis* was identified as a "2015 Asthma Capital." The area ranked #87 out of the nation's 100 largest metropolitan areas. Criteria: estimated prevalence; self-reported prevalence; crude death rate for asthma; annual pollen score; annual air quality; public smoking laws; number of board-certified asthma specialists; school inhaler access laws; rescue medication use; controller medication use; ER visits for asthma; uninsured rate; poverty rate. *Asthma and Allergy Foundation of America, "Asthma Capitals 2015"*
- The Minneapolis* metro area ranked #27 out of 190 in The Gallup-Healthways Well-Being Index. Criteria: purpose; social well being; financial health; community and physical health. Results are based on telephone interviews with adults, aged 18 and older, living in metropolitan areas in the 50 U.S. states and the District of Columbia. *Gallup-Healthways, "State of American Well-Being," February 23, 2016*

Real Estate Rankings

- Minneapolis* was ranked #77 out of 225 metro areas in terms of housing affordability in 2015 by the National Association of Home Builders (#1 = most affordable). Criteria: the share of homes sold in that area affordable to a family earning the local median income, based on standard mortgage underwriting criteria. *National Association of Home Builders®, NAHB-Wells Fargo Housing Opportunity Index, 4th Quarter 2015*

Safety Rankings

- Farmers Insurance, in partnership with Sperling's BestPlaces, ranked metro areas in the U.S. as the "Most Secure Places to Live." The Minneapolis* metro area ranked #13 out of the top 20 in the large metro area category (500,000 or more residents). Criteria: economic stability; crime statistics; extreme weather; risk of natural disasters; housing depreciation; foreclosures; air quality; environmental hazards; life expectancy; motor vehicle fatalities; and employment numbers. *Farmers Insurance Group of Companies, "Most Secure U.S. Places to Live in the U.S.," June 25, 2013*
- The National Insurance Crime Bureau ranked 380 metro areas in the U.S. in terms of per capita rates of vehicle theft. The Minneapolis* metro area ranked #134 (#1 = highest rate). Criteria: number of vehicle theft offenses per 100,000 inhabitants in 2014. *National Insurance Crime Bureau, "Hot Spots 2014," June 24, 2015*

Seniors/Retirement Rankings

- From its Best Cities for Successful Aging indexes, the Milken Institute generated rankings for metropolitan areas, weighing data in eight categories—health care, wellness, living arrangements, transportation, financial characteristics, education and employment opportunities, community engagement, and overall livability. The Minneapolis* metro area was ranked #16 overall in the large metro area category. *Milken Institute, "Best Cities for Successful Aging, 2014"*

Sports/Recreation Rankings

- According to the personal finance website NerdWallet, the Minneapolis* metro area, at #6, is one of the nation's top dozen metro areas for sports fans. Criteria included the presence of all four major sports—MLB, NFL, NHL, and NBA, fan enthusiasm (as measured by game attendance), ticket affordability, and "sports culture," that is, number of sports bars. *www.nerdwallet.com, "Best Cities for Sports Fans," May 5, 2013*

Miscellaneous Rankings

- The watchdog site Charity Navigator conducts an annual study of charities in the nation's major markets both to analyze statistical differences in their financial, accountability, and transparency practices and to track year-to-year variations in individual communities. The Minneapolis* metro area was ranked #12 among the 30 metro markets in the rating dimension of Overall Score. *www.charitynavigator.org, "Metro Market Study 2015," June 5, 2015*

- Mars Chocolate North America, the makers of COMBOS®, in partnership with Sperling's BestPlaces, ranked 50 major metro areas in terms of their "manliness." The Minneapolis* metro area ranked #40. Criteria: number of professional sports teams; number of nearby NASCAR tracks and racing events; manly lifestyle; concentration of manly retail stores; manly occupations per capita; salty snack sales; "Board of Manliness" rankings. *Mars Chocolate North America, "America's Manliest Cities 2012"*

- The National Alliance to End Homelessness ranked the 100 most populous metro areas with the highest rate of homelessness. The Minneapolis* metro area ranked #48. Criteria: number of homeless people per 10,000 population in 2011. *National Alliance to End Homelessness, The State of Homelessness in America 2012*

Woodbury is located within the Minneapolis-St. Paul-Bloomington, MN-WI Metropolitan Statistical Area.

Business Environment

CITY FINANCES

City Government Finances

Component	2012 ($000)	2012 ($ per capita)
Total Revenues	64,921	1,047
Total Expenditures	58,045	936
Debt Outstanding	92,035	1,485
Cash and Securities[1]	164,727	2,658

Note: (1) Cash and security holdings of a government at the close of its fiscal year, including those of its dependent agencies, utilities, and liquor stores.
Source: U.S Census Bureau, State & Local Government Finances 2012

City Government Revenue by Source

Source	2012 ($000)	2012 ($ per capita)
General Revenue		
From Federal Government	280	4
From State Government	2,802	45
From Local Governments	616	9
Taxes		
Property	27,839	449
Sales and Gross Receipts	0	0
Personal Income	0	0
Corporate Income	0	0
Motor Vehicle License	0	0
Other Taxes	2,829	45
Current Charges	14,028	226
Liquor Store	0	0
Utility	3,785	61
Employee Retirement	0	0

Source: U.S Census Bureau, State & Local Government Finances 2012

City Government Expenditures by Function

Function	2012 ($000)	2012 ($ per capita)	2012 (%)
General Direct Expenditures			
Air Transportation	0	0	0.0
Corrections	0	0	0.0
Education	0	0	0.0
Employment Security Administration	0	0	0.0
Financial Administration	1,842	29	3.1
Fire Protection	4,120	66	7.0
General Public Buildings	1,011	16	1.7
Governmental Administration, Other	1,716	27	2.9
Health	1,679	27	2.8
Highways	12,257	197	21.1
Hospitals	0	0	0.0
Housing and Community Development	1,780	28	3.0
Interest on General Debt	2,041	32	3.5
Judicial and Legal	0	0	0.0
Libraries	0	0	0.0
Parking	1,621	26	2.7
Parks and Recreation	6,506	105	11.2
Police Protection	11,516	185	19.8
Public Welfare	0	0	0.0
Sewerage	6,630	107	11.4
Solid Waste Management	0	0	0.0
Veterans' Services	0	0	0.0
Liquor Store	0	0	0.0
Utility	2,369	38	4.0
Employee Retirement	0	0	0.0

Source: U.S Census Bureau, State & Local Government Finances 2012

DEMOGRAPHICS

Population Growth

Area	1990 Census	2000 Census	2010 Census	2014* Estimate	Population Growth (%) 1990-2014	Population Growth (%) 2010-2014
City	20,075	46,463	61,961	64,544	221.5	4.2
MSA[1]	2,538,834	2,968,806	3,279,833	3,424,786	34.9	4.4
U.S.	248,709,873	281,421,906	308,745,538	314,107,084	26.3	1.7

Note: (1) Figures cover the Minneapolis-St. Paul-Bloomington, MN-WI Metropolitan Statistical Area—see Appendix B for areas included; (*) 2010-2014 5-year estimated population
Source: U.S. Census Bureau, 1990 Census, Census 2000, Census 2010, 2010-2014 American Community Survey 5-Year Estimates

Household Size

Area	Persons in Household (%) One	Two	Three	Four	Five	Six	Seven or More	Average Household Size
City	20.5	33.9	16.7	18.7	6.8	1.9	1.2	2.73
MSA[1]	27.8	33.7	15.0	14.0	5.9	2.0	1.3	2.54
U.S.	27.5	33.5	15.8	13.1	6.0	2.3	1.4	2.64

Note: (1) Figures cover the Minneapolis-St. Paul-Bloomington, MN-WI Metropolitan Statistical Area—see Appendix B for areas included
Source: U.S. Census Bureau, 2010-2014 American Community Survey 5-Year Estimates

Race

Area	White Alone[2] (%)	Black Alone[2] (%)	Asian Alone[2] (%)	AIAN[3] Alone[2] (%)	NHOPI[4] Alone[2] (%)	Other Race Alone[2] (%)	Two or More Races (%)
City	81.2	5.5	8.9	0.2	0.1	0.7	3.2
MSA[1]	81.2	7.4	5.9	0.6	0.0	1.8	3.0
U.S.	73.8	12.6	5.0	0.8	0.2	4.7	2.9

Note: (1) Figures cover the Minneapolis-St. Paul-Bloomington, MN-WI Metropolitan Statistical Area—see Appendix B for areas included; (2) Alone is defined as not being in combination with one or more other races; (3) American Indian and Alaska Native; (4) Native Hawaiian and Other Pacific Islander
Source: U.S. Census Bureau, 2010-2014 American Community Survey 5-Year Estimates

Hispanic or Latino Origin

Area	Total (%)	Mexican (%)	Puerto Rican (%)	Cuban (%)	Other (%)
City	4.6	3.1	0.1	0.0	1.4
MSA[1]	5.5	3.7	0.3	0.1	1.4
U.S.	16.9	10.8	1.6	0.6	3.8

Note: Persons of Hispanic or Latino origin can be of any race; (1) Figures cover the Minneapolis-St. Paul-Bloomington, MN-WI Metropolitan Statistical Area—see Appendix B for areas included
Source: U.S. Census Bureau, 2010-2014 American Community Survey 5-Year Estimates

Ancestry

Area	German	Irish	English	American	Italian	Polish	French[2]	Scottish	Dutch
City	33.5	13.0	7.8	2.3	5.0	4.9	4.0	1.9	1.1
MSA[1]	32.4	11.8	6.0	3.3	2.8	4.6	3.7	1.4	1.6
U.S.	14.9	10.8	8.0	7.1	5.5	3.0	2.7	1.7	1.4

Note: Figures are the percentage of the total population reporting a particular ancestry. The nine most commonly reported ancestries in the U.S. are shown. Figures include multiple ancestries (e.g. if a person reported being Irish and Italian, they were included in both columns); (1) Figures cover the Minneapolis-St. Paul-Bloomington, MN-WI Metropolitan Statistical Area—see Appendix B for areas included; (2) Excludes Basque
Source: U.S. Census Bureau, 2010-2014 American Community Survey 5-Year Estimates

Foreign-Born Population

Area	Percent of Population Born in								
	Any Foreign Country	Asia	Mexico	Europe	Carribean	Central America[2]	South America	Africa	Canada
City	10.5	5.9	0.7	0.9	0.1	0.1	0.5	1.7	0.5
MSA[1]	9.7	3.9	1.4	1.1	0.1	0.3	0.5	2.1	0.2
U.S.	13.1	3.8	3.7	1.5	1.2	1.0	0.9	0.6	0.3

Note: (1) Figures cover the Minneapolis-St. Paul-Bloomington, MN-WI Metropolitan Statistical Area—see Appendix B for areas included; (2) Excludes Mexico.
Source: U.S. Census Bureau, 2010-2014 American Community Survey 5-Year Estimates

Marital Status

Area	Never Married	Now Married[2]	Separated	Widowed	Divorced
City	25.3	62.0	0.9	3.2	8.5
MSA[1]	32.9	51.5	1.3	4.4	10.0
U.S.	32.5	48.4	2.2	5.9	10.9

Note: Figures are percentages and cover the population 15 years of age and older; (1) Figures cover the Minneapolis-St. Paul-Bloomington, MN-WI Metropolitan Statistical Area—see Appendix B for areas included; (2) Excludes separated
Source: U.S. Census Bureau, 2010-2014 American Community Survey 5-Year Estimates

Disability Status

Area	All Ages	Under 18 Years Old	18 to 64 Years Old	65 Years and Over
City	5.5	2.5	3.8	26.2
MSA[1]	9.2	3.6	7.6	30.8
U.S.	12.3	4.1	10.2	36.3

Note: Figures show percent of the civilian noninstitutionalized population that reported having a disability. Disability status is determined from from six types of difficulty: vision, hearing, cognitive, ambulatory, self-care, and independent living. For children under 5 years old, hearing and vision difficulty are used to determine disability status. For children between the ages of 5 and 14, disability status is determined from hearing, vision, cognitive, ambulatory, and self-care difficulties. For people aged 15 years and older, they are considered to have a disability if they have difficulty with any one of the six difficulty types; (1) Figures cover the Minneapolis-St. Paul-Bloomington, MN-WI Metropolitan Statistical Area—see Appendix B for areas included.
Source: U.S. Census Bureau, 2010-2014 American Community Survey 5-Year Estimates

Age

Area	Percent of Population									Median Age
	Under Age 5	Age 5–19	Age 20–34	Age 35–44	Age 45–54	Age 55–64	Age 65–74	Age 75–84	Age 85+	
City	7.1	23.0	18.0	15.3	16.1	10.9	5.7	2.7	1.1	36.2
MSA[1]	6.7	20.3	21.0	13.4	15.0	12.1	6.4	3.5	1.6	36.4
U.S.	6.4	19.9	20.6	13.0	14.1	12.3	7.6	4.3	1.9	37.4

Note: (1) Figures cover the Minneapolis-St. Paul-Bloomington, MN-WI Metropolitan Statistical Area—see Appendix B for areas included
Source: U.S. Census Bureau, 2010-2014 American Community Survey 5-Year Estimates

Gender

Area	Males	Females	Males per 100 Females
City	30,863	33,681	91.6
MSA[1]	1,692,444	1,732,342	97.7
U.S.	154,515,159	159,591,925	96.8

Note: (1) Figures cover the Minneapolis-St. Paul-Bloomington, MN-WI Metropolitan Statistical Area—see Appendix B for areas included
Source: U.S. Census Bureau, 2010-2014 American Community Survey 5-Year Estimates

Religious Groups by Family

Area	Catholic	Baptist	Non-Den.	Methodist[2]	Lutheran	LDS[3]	Pentecostal	Presbyterian[4]	Muslim[5]	Judaism
MSA[1]	21.7	2.4	2.9	2.7	14.4	0.6	1.7	1.8	0.4	0.7
U.S.	19.1	9.3	4.0	4.0	2.3	2.0	1.9	1.6	0.8	0.7

Note: Figures are the number of adherents as a percentage of the total population; (1) Figures cover the Minneapolis-St. Paul-Bloomington, MN-WI Metropolitan Statistical Area—see Appendix B for areas included; (2) Methodist/Pietist; (3) Latter Day Saints; (4) Reformed; (5) Figures are estimates
Source: Association of Statisticians of American Religious Bodies, 2010 U.S. Religion Census: Religious Congregations & Membership Study

Religious Groups by Tradition

Area	Catholic	Evangelical Protestant	Mainline Protestant	Other Tradition	Black Protestant	Orthodox
MSA[1]	21.7	12.8	14.5	2.2	0.4	0.2
U.S.	19.1	16.2	7.3	4.3	1.6	0.3

Note: Figures are the number of adherents as a percentage of the total population; (1) Figures cover the Minneapolis-St. Paul-Bloomington, MN-WI Metropolitan Statistical Area—see Appendix B for areas included
Source: Association of Statisticians of American Religious Bodies, 2010 U.S. Religion Census: Religious Congregations & Membership Study

ECONOMY

Gross Metropolitan Product

Area	2013	2014	2015	2016	Rank[2]
MSA[1]	227.8	236.7	246.4	258.6	13

Note: Figures are in billions of dollars; (1) Figures cover the Minneapolis-St. Paul-Bloomington, MN-WI Metropolitan Statistical Area—see Appendix B for areas included; (2) Rank is based on 2016 data and ranges from 1 to 381
Source: The U.S. Conference of Mayors, U.S. Metro Economies: GMP and Employment 2014-2016, June 2015

Economic Growth

Area	2011-13 (%)	2014 (%)	2015 (%)	2016 (%)	Rank[2]
MSA[1]	2.0	2.4	2.7	3.0	83
U.S.	2.2	2.4	2.3	2.9	-

Note: Figures are real gross metropolitan product (GMP) growth rates and represent annual average percent change; (1) Figures cover the Minneapolis-St. Paul-Bloomington, MN-WI Metropolitan Statistical Area—see Appendix B for areas included; (2) Rank is based on 2016 data and ranges from 1 to 381
Source: The U.S. Conference of Mayors, U.S. Metro Economies: GMP and Employment 2014-2016, June 2015

Metropolitan Area Exports

Area	2009	2010	2011	2012	2013	2014	Rank[2]
MSA[1]	20,096.7	23,192.7	26,189.0	25,155.7	23,747.4	21,198.2	15

Note: Figures are in millions of dollars; (1) Figures cover the Minneapolis-St. Paul-Bloomington, MN-WI Metropolitan Statistical Area—see Appendix B for areas included; (2) Rank is based on 2014 data and ranges from 1 to 385
Source: U.S. Department of Commerce, International Trade Administration, Office of Trade & Industry Information, Manufacturing & Services, data extracted March 10, 2016

Building Permits

Area	Single-Family			Multi-Family			Total		
	2014	2015p	Pct. Chg.	2014	2015p	Pct. Chg.	2014	2015p	Pct. Chg.
City	297	257	-13.5	45	160	255.6	342	417	21.9
MSA[1]	6,689	6,786	1.5	4,736	4,927	4.0	11,425	11,713	2.5
U.S.	640,300	690,800	7.9	411,800	487,600	18.4	1,052,100	1,178,400	12.0

Note: (1) Figures cover the Minneapolis-St. Paul-Bloomington, MN-WI Metropolitan Statistical Area—see Appendix B for areas included; Figures represent new, privately-owned housing units authorized (unadjusted data); All permit data are based on estimates with imputation; (p) preliminary data.
Source: U.S. Census Bureau, Manufacturing, Mining, and Construction Statistics, Building Permits, 2014, 2015

Bankruptcy Filings

Area	Business Filings 2014	Business Filings 2015	Business Filings % Chg.	Nonbusiness Filings 2014	Nonbusiness Filings 2015	Nonbusiness Filings % Chg.
Washington County	32	30	-6.3	639	572	-10.5
U.S.	26,983	24,735	-8.3	909,812	819,760	-9.9

Note: Business filings include Chapter 7, Chapter 11, Chapter 12, and Chapter 13; Nonbusiness filings include Chapter 7, Chapter 11, and Chapter 13
Source: Administrative Office of the U.S. Courts, Business and Nonbusiness Bankruptcy, County Cases Commenced by Chapter of the Bankruptcy Code, During the 12- Month Period Ending December 31, 2014 and Business and Nonbusiness Bankruptcy, County Cases Commenced by Chapter of the Bankruptcy Code, During the 12- Month Period Ending December 31, 2015

Housing Vacancy Rates

Area	Gross Vacancy Rate[2] (%)			Year-Round Vacancy Rate[3] (%)			Rental Vacancy Rate[4] (%)			Homeowner Vacancy Rate[5] (%)		
	2013	2014	2015	2013	2014	2015	2013	2014	2015	2013	2014	2015
MSA[1]	5.7	5.7	6.4	5.1	5.3	6.0	5.4	4.4	4.9	0.9	1.4	0.8
U.S.	13.6	13.4	12.9	10.7	10.4	10.0	8.3	7.6	7.1	2.0	1.9	1.8

Note: (1) Figures cover the Minneapolis-St. Paul-Bloomington, MN-WI Metropolitan Statistical Area—see Appendix B for areas included; (2) The percentage of the total housing inventory that is vacant; (3) The percentage of the housing inventory (excluding seasonal units) that is year-round vacant; (4) The percentage of rental inventory that is vacant for rent; (5) The percentage of homeowner inventory that is vacant for sale
Source: U.S. Census Bureau, Housing Vacancies and Homeownership Annual Statistics: 2015

INCOME

Income

Area	Per Capita ($)	Median Household ($)	Average Household ($)
City	44,047	98,974	119,421
MSA[1]	34,593	68,019	88,061
U.S.	28,555	53,482	74,596

Note: (1) Figures cover the Minneapolis-St. Paul-Bloomington, MN-WI Metropolitan Statistical Area—see Appendix B for areas included
Source: U.S. Census Bureau, 2010-2014 American Community Survey 5-Year Estimates

Household Income Distribution

Area	Percent of Households Earning							
	Under $15,000	$15,000 -24,999	$25,000 -34,999	$35,000 -49,999	$50,000 -74,999	$75,000 -99,000	$100,000 -149,999	$150,000 and up
City	2.9	5.0	3.9	8.0	16.5	14.3	23.6	25.7
MSA[1]	8.6	7.8	8.1	12.0	18.2	14.5	17.5	13.4
U.S.	12.5	10.7	10.2	13.5	17.8	12.2	13.0	10.0

Note: (1) Figures cover the Minneapolis-St. Paul-Bloomington, MN-WI Metropolitan Statistical Area—see Appendix B for areas included
Source: U.S. Census Bureau, 2010-2014 American Community Survey 5-Year Estimates

Poverty Rate

Area	All Ages	Under 18 Years Old	18 to 64 Years Old	65 Years and Over
City	3.5	3.1	3.4	5.0
MSA[1]	10.6	13.9	9.9	7.1
U.S.	15.6	21.9	14.6	9.4

Note: Figures are percentage of people whose income during the past 12 months was below the poverty level; (1) Figures cover the Minneapolis-St. Paul-Bloomington, MN-WI Metropolitan Statistical Area—see Appendix B for areas included
Source: U.S. Census Bureau, 2010-2014 American Community Survey 5-Year Estimates

EMPLOYMENT

Labor Force and Employment

Area	Civilian Labor Force			Workers Employed		
	Dec. 2014	Dec. 2015	% Chg.	Dec. 2014	Dec. 2015	% Chg.
City	36,651	37,451	2.1	35,824	36,560	2.0
MSA[1]	1,905,506	1,942,269	1.9	1,843,783	1,881,640	2.0
U.S.	155,521,000	157,245,000	1.1	147,190,000	149,703,000	1.7

Note: Data is not seasonally adjusted and covers workers 16 years of age and older; (1) Figures cover the Minneapolis-St. Paul-Bloomington, MN-WI Metropolitan Statistical Area—see Appendix B for areas included
Source: Bureau of Labor Statistics, Local Area Unemployment Statistics

Unemployment Rate

Area	2015											
	Jan.	Feb.	Mar.	Apr.	May	Jun.	Jul.	Aug.	Sep.	Oct.	Nov.	Dec.
City	2.9	2.7	2.7	2.6	2.8	3.0	3.0	2.7	2.6	2.5	2.3	2.4
MSA[1]	4.1	4.0	4.1	3.5	3.5	3.8	3.7	3.4	3.1	2.9	2.8	3.1
U.S.	6.1	5.8	5.6	5.1	5.3	5.5	5.6	5.2	4.9	4.8	4.8	4.8

Note: Data is not seasonally adjusted and covers workers 16 years of age and older; (1) Figures cover the Minneapolis-St. Paul-Bloomington, MN-WI Metropolitan Statistical Area—see Appendix B for areas included
Source: Bureau of Labor Statistics, Local Area Unemployment Statistics

Employment by Occupation

Occupation Classification	City (%)	MSA[1] (%)	U.S. (%)
Management, Business, Science, and Arts	54.6	42.6	36.4
Natural Resources, Construction, and Maintenance	2.9	6.4	9.0
Production, Transportation, and Material Moving	7.1	11.3	12.1
Sales and Office	23.4	24.1	24.4
Service	12.1	15.6	18.2

Note: Figures cover employed civilians 16 years of age and older; (1) Figures cover the Minneapolis-St. Paul-Bloomington, MN-WI Metropolitan Statistical Area—see Appendix B for areas included
Source: U.S. Census Bureau, 2010-2014 American Community Survey 5-Year Estimates

Employment by Industry

Sector	MSA[1]		U.S.
	Number of Employees	Percent of Total	Percent of Total
Construction, Mining, and Logging	71,100	3.6	5.0
Education and Health Services	321,100	16.4	15.7
Financial Activities	148,800	7.6	5.7
Government	254,400	13.0	15.5
Information	39,400	2.0	1.9
Leisure and Hospitality	174,900	8.9	10.4
Manufacturing	194,800	10.0	8.6
Other Services	81,200	4.1	3.9
Professional and Business Services	305,100	15.6	13.9
Retail Trade	189,400	9.7	11.3
Transportation, Warehousing, and Utilities	69,100	3.5	3.9
Wholesale Trade	97,300	4.9	4.1

Note: Figures are non-farm employment as of December 2015. Figures are not seasonally adjusted and include workers 16 years of age and older; (1) Figures cover the Minneapolis-St. Paul-Bloomington, MN-WI Metropolitan Statistical Area—see Appendix B for areas included; n/a not available
Source: Bureau of Labor Statistics, Current Employment Statistics, Employment, Hours, and Earnings

Occupations with Greatest Projected Employment Growth: 2012 – 2022

Occupation[1]	2012 Employment	2022 Projected Employment	Numeric Employment Change	Percent Employment Change
Personal Care Aides	50,550	73,150	22,600	44.7
Home Health Aides	34,520	44,660	10,140	29.3
Registered Nurses	55,950	65,430	9,480	16.9
Retail Salespersons	85,800	92,450	6,650	7.8
Combined Food Preparation and Serving Workers, Including Fast Food	56,120	61,580	5,460	9.7
Carpenters	19,610	24,100	4,490	22.9
Childcare Workers	30,870	34,870	4,000	13.0
Janitors and Cleaners, Except Maids and Housekeeping Cleaners	46,140	49,920	3,780	8.2
Licensed Practical and Licensed Vocational Nurses	17,420	20,660	3,240	18.6
Customer Service Representatives	48,000	51,210	3,210	6.7

Note: Projections cover Minnesota; (1) Sorted by numeric employment change
Source: www.projectionscentral.com, State Occupational Projections, 2012–2022 Long-Term Projections

Fastest Growing Occupations: 2012 – 2022

Occupation[1]	2012 Employment	2022 Projected Employment	Numeric Employment Change	Percent Employment Change
Personal Care Aides	50,550	73,150	22,600	44.7
Insulation Workers, Mechanical	470	660	190	40.6
Physician Assistants	1,650	2,220	570	34.5
Computer Numerically Controlled Machine Tool Programmers, Metal and Plastic	810	1,080	270	33.3
Helpers—Carpenters	510	680	170	32.9
Brickmasons and Blockmasons	1,370	1,810	440	31.9
Interpreters and Translators	1,490	1,960	470	31.4
Diagnostic Medical Sonographers	1,380	1,810	430	31.1
Cement Masons and Concrete Finishers	2,930	3,830	900	30.7
Meeting, Convention, and Event Planners	1,950	2,540	590	29.8

Note: Projections cover Minnesota; (1) Sorted by percent employment change and excludes occupations with numeric employment change less than 100
Source: www.projectionscentral.com, State Occupational Projections, 2012–2022 Long-Term Projections

Average Wages

Occupation	$/Hr.	Occupation	$/Hr.
Accountants and Auditors	34.30	Maids and Housekeeping Cleaners	11.42
Automotive Mechanics	20.89	Maintenance and Repair Workers	21.64
Bookkeepers	19.75	Marketing Managers	66.76
Carpenters	26.22	Nuclear Medicine Technologists	37.32
Cashiers	10.43	Nurses, Licensed Practical	21.42
Clerks, General Office	16.68	Nurses, Registered	37.00
Clerks, Receptionists/Information	14.44	Nursing Assistants	14.83
Clerks, Shipping/Receiving	16.89	Packers and Packagers, Hand	12.13
Computer Programmers	38.85	Physical Therapists	36.96
Computer Systems Analysts	43.76	Postal Service Mail Carriers	24.43
Computer User Support Specialists	26.27	Real Estate Brokers	n/a
Cooks, Restaurant	12.47	Retail Salespersons	12.38
Dentists	90.82	Sales Reps., Exc. Tech./Scientific	37.53
Electrical Engineers	44.95	Sales Reps., Tech./Scientific	58.26
Electricians	30.25	Secretaries, Exc. Legal/Med./Exec.	19.51
Financial Managers	68.00	Security Guards	16.78
First-Line Supervisors/Managers, Sales	20.97	Surgeons	129.05
Food Preparation Workers	12.51	Teacher Assistants*	15.40
General and Operations Managers	55.19	Teachers, Elementary School*	30.58
Hairdressers/Cosmetologists	13.88	Teachers, Secondary School*	32.31
Internists	119.37	Telemarketers	14.42
Janitors and Cleaners	13.40	Truck Drivers, Heavy/Tractor-Trailer	21.24
Landscaping/Groundskeeping Workers	14.32	Truck Drivers, Light/Delivery Svcs.	18.30
Lawyers	64.64	Waiters and Waitresses	10.29

Note: Wage data covers the Minneapolis-St. Paul-Bloomington, MN-WI Metropolitan Statistical Area—see Appendix B for areas included; (*) Hourly wages for elementary/secondary school teachers and teacher assistants were calculated by the editors from annual wage data based on a 40 hour work week; n/a not available.
Source: Bureau of Labor Statistics, Metro Area Occupational Employment and Wage Estimates, May 2015

TAXES

State Corporate Income Tax Rates

State	Tax Rate (%)	Income Brackets ($)	Num. of Brackets	Financial Institution Tax Rate (%)[a]	Federal Income Tax Ded.
Minnesota	9.8 (o)	Flat rate	1	9.8 (o)	No

Note: Tax rates as of January 1, 2016; (a) Rates listed are the corporate income tax rate applied to financial institutions or excise taxes based on income. Some states have other taxes based upon the value of deposits or shares; (o) In addition, Minnesota levies a 5.8% tentative minimum tax on Alternative Minimum Taxable Income.
Source: Federation of Tax Administrators, "State Corporate Income Tax Rates, 2016"

State Individual Income Tax Rates

State	Tax Rate (%)	Income Brackets ($)	Num. of Brackets	Personal Exempt. ($)[1]		Fed. Inc. Tax Ded.
				Single	Dependents	
Minnesota (a)	5.35 - 9.85	25,070 - 154,951 (l)	4	4,050 (d)	4,000 (d)	No

Note: Tax rates as of January 1, 2016; Local- and county-level taxes are not included; n/a not applicable; (1) Married joint filers generally receive double the single exemption; (a) 18 states have statutory provision for automatically adjusting to the rate of inflation the dollar values of the income tax brackets, standard deductions, and/or personal exemptions. Massachusetts, Michigan, and Nebraska index the personal exemptiononly. Oregon does not index the income brackets for $125,000 and over. Maine has suspended indexing for 2014 and 2015; (d) These states use the personal exemption amounts provided in the federal Internal Revenue Code; (l) The income brackets reported for Minnesota are for single individuals. For married couples filing jointly, the same tax rates apply to income brackets ranging from $36,820 to $259,421.
Source: Federation of Tax Administrators, "State Individual Income Tax Rates, 2016"

Various State and Local Tax Rates

State	State and Local Sales and Use (%)	State Sales and Use (%)	Gasoline[1] (¢/gal.)	Cigarette[2] ($/pack)	Spirits[3] ($/gal.)	Wine[4] ($/gal.)	Beer[5] ($/gal.)
Minnesota	7.125	6.875	28.6	3.00	8.67 (i)(j)	1.18 (o)(p)	0.47 (q)(s)

Note: All tax rates as of January 1, 2016; (1) The American Petroleum Institute has developed a methodology for determining the average tax rate on a gallon of fuel. Rates may include any of the following: excise taxes, environmental fees, storage tank fees, other fees or taxes, general sales tax, and local taxes. In states where gasoline is subject to the general sales tax, or where the fuel tax is based on the average sale price, the average rate determined by API is sensitive to changes in the price of gasoline. States that fully or partially apply general sales taxes to gasoline: CA, CO, GA, IL, IN, MI, NY; (2) The federal excise tax of $1.0066 per pack and local taxes are not included; (3) Rates are those applicable to off-premise sales of 40% alcohol by volume (a.b.v.) distilled spirits in 750ml containers. Local excise taxes are excluded; (4) Rates are those applicable to off-premise sales of 11% a.b.v. non-carbonated wine in 750ml containers; (5) Rates are those applicable to off-premise sales of 4.7% a.b.v. beer in 12 ounce containers; (i) Includes case fees and/or bottle fees which may vary with size of container; (j) Includes sales taxes specific to alcoholic beverages; (o) Includes case fees and/or bottle fees which may vary with size of container; (p) Includes sales taxes specific to alcoholic beverages; (q) Different rates are also applicable according to alcohol content, place of production, size of container, or place purchased (on- or off-premise or onboard airlines); (s) Includes sales taxes specific to alcoholic beverages.
Source: Tax Foundation, 2016 Facts & Figures: How Does Your State Compare?

State Business Tax Climate Index Rankings

State	Overall Rank	Corporate Tax Rank	Individual Income Tax Rank	Sales Tax Rank	Unemployment Insurance Tax Rank	Property Tax Rank
Minnesota	47	46	46	36	29	30

Note: The index is a measure of how each state's tax laws affect economic performance. The lower the rank, the more favorable a state's tax system is for business. States without a given tax are given a ranking of 1. The scores/rankings for the District of Columbia do not affect other states. The 2016 index represents the tax climate as of July 1, 2015 (the beginning of Fiscal Year 2016).
Source: Tax Foundation, State Business Tax Climate Index 2016

TRANSPORTATION

Means of Transportation to Work

Area	Car/Truck/Van		Public Transportation			Bicycle	Walked	Other Means	Worked at Home
	Drove Alone	Car-pooled	Bus	Subway	Railroad				
City	82.9	7.7	3.4	0.0	0.0	0.2	0.7	0.2	4.9
MSA[1]	78.2	8.4	4.3	0.1	0.1	0.9	2.3	0.9	4.9
U.S.	76.4	9.6	2.6	1.8	0.6	0.6	2.8	1.3	4.4

Note: Figures are percentages and cover workers 16 years of age and older; (1) Figures cover the Minneapolis-St. Paul-Bloomington, MN-WI Metropolitan Statistical Area—see Appendix B for areas included
Source: U.S. Census Bureau, 2010-2014 American Community Survey 5-Year Estimates

Travel Time to Work

Area	Less Than 10 Minutes	10 to 19 Minutes	20 to 29 Minutes	30 to 44 Minutes	45 to 59 Minutes	60 to 89 Minutes	90 Minutes or More
City	10.8	26.6	26.4	23.0	8.9	3.4	0.9
MSA[1]	10.9	28.1	24.8	23.0	7.8	4.1	1.3
U.S.	13.3	29.6	21.0	20.2	7.7	5.7	2.6

Note: Figures are percentages and include workers 16 years old and over; (1) Figures cover the Minneapolis-St. Paul-Bloomington, MN-WI Metropolitan Statistical Area—see Appendix B for areas included
Source: U.S. Census Bureau, 2010-2014 American Community Survey 5-Year Estimates

Freeway Travel Time Index

Area	1985	1990	1995	2000	2005	2010	2014
Urban Area Rank[1,2]	26	25	18	11	17	21	21
Urban Area Index[1]	1.10	1.14	1.21	1.27	1.28	1.25	1.26
Average Index[3]	1.09	1.11	1.14	1.17	1.20	1.19	1.20

Note: Freeway Travel Time Index—the ratio of travel time in the peak period to the travel time at free-flow conditions. For example, a value of 1.30 indicates a 20-minute free-flow trip takes 26 minutes in the peak (20 minutes x 1.30 = 26 minutes); (1) Covers the Minneapolis-St. Paul MN-WI urban area; (2) Rank is based on 101 urban areas (#1 = highest travel time index); (3) Average of 101 urban areas
Source: Texas Transportation Institute, 2015 Urban Mobility Scorecard, August 2015

Freeway Commuter Stress Index

Area	1985	1990	1995	2000	2005	2010	2014
Urban Area Rank[1,2]	33	33	23	17	18	25	27
Urban Area Index[1]	1.14	1.18	1.26	1.31	1.33	1.30	1.31
Average Index[3]	1.13	1.16	1.19	1.22	1.25	1.24	1.25

Note: The Freeway Commuter Stress Index is the same as the Freeway Travel Time Index (see table above) except that it includes only the travel in the peak directions during the peak periods; the TTI includes travel in all directions during the peak period. Thus, the CSI is more indicative of the work trip experienced by each commuter on a daily basis. (1) Covers the Minneapolis-St. Paul MN-WI urban area; (2) Rank is based on 101 urban areas (#1 = highest stress index); (3) Average of 101 urban areas

Source: Texas Transportation Institute, 2015 Urban Mobility Scorecard, August 2015

Living Environment

COST OF LIVING

Cost of Living Index

Composite Index	Groceries	Housing	Utilities	Trans-portation	Health Care	Misc. Goods/ Services
108.3	108.0	112.3	93.1	111.9	105.5	108.8

Note: The Cost of Living Index measures regional differences in the cost of consumer goods and services, excluding taxes and non-consumer expenditures, for professional and managerial households in the top income quintile. It is based on more than 50,000 prices covering almost 60 different items for which prices are collected three times a year by chambers of commerce, economic development organizations or university applied economic centers in each participating urban area. The numbers shown should be read as a percentage above or below the national average of 100. For example, a value of 115.4 in the groceries column indicates that grocery prices are 15.4% higher than the national average. Small differences in the index numbers should not be interpreted as significant; Figures cover the Minneapolis MN urban area.
Source: The Council for Community and Economic Research, ACCRA Cost of Living Index, 2015

Grocery Prices

Area[1]	T-Bone Steak ($/pound)	Frying Chicken ($/pound)	Whole Milk ($/half gal.)	Eggs ($/dozen)	Orange Juice ($/64 oz.)	Coffee ($/11.5 oz.)
City[2]	14.13	1.90	2.26	1.92	3.78	4.64
Avg.	10.99	1.43	2.25	2.26	3.58	4.48
Min.	7.16	0.98	1.30	1.35	2.88	2.98
Max.	14.13	2.43	3.85	4.81	6.39	7.56

Note: (1) Values for the local area are compared with the average, minimum and maximum values for all 292 areas in the Cost of Living Index; (2) Figures cover the Minneapolis MN urban area; **T-Bone Steak** *(price per pound);* **Frying Chicken** *(price per pound, whole fryer);* **Whole Milk** *(half gallon carton);* **Eggs** *(price per dozen, Grade A, large);* **Orange Juice** *(64 oz. Tropicana or Florida Natural);* **Coffee** *(11.5 oz. can, vacuum-packed, Maxwell House, Hills Bros, or Folgers).*
Source: The Council for Community and Economic Research, ACCRA Cost of Living Index, 2015

Housing and Utility Costs

Area[1]	New Home Price ($)	Apartment Rent ($/month)	All Electric ($/month)	Part Electric ($/month)	Other Energy ($/month)	Telephone ($/month)
City[2]	345,759	1,098	-	93.62	69.52	24.99
Avg.	312,874	945	179.30	95.07	72.96	28.11
Min.	178,682	479	116.28	43.14	26.46	10.01
Max.	1,472,476	3,984	504.25	189.44	421.11	43.06

Note: (1) Values for the local area are compared with the average, minimum and maximum values for all 292 areas in the Cost of Living Index; (2) Figures cover the Minneapolis MN urban area; **New Home Price** *(2,400 sf living area, 8,000 sf lot, in urban area with full utilities);* **Apartment Rent** *(950 sf 2 bedroom/1.5 or 2 bath, unfurnished, excluding all utilities except water);* **All Electric** *(average monthly cost for an all-electric home);* **Part Electric** *(average monthly cost for a part-electric home);* **Other Energy** *(average monthly cost for natural gas, fuel oil, coal, wood, and any other forms of energy except electricity);* **Telephone** *(price includes basic monthly rate for a private residential line plus additional local usage charges incurred by a family of four).*
Source: The Council for Community and Economic Research, ACCRA Cost of Living Index, 2015

Health Care, Transportation, and Other Costs

Area[1]	Doctor ($/visit)	Dentist ($/visit)	Optometrist ($/visit)	Gasoline ($/gallon)	Beauty Salon ($/visit)	Men's Shirt ($)
City[2]	133.87	84.35	82.36	2.62	33.40	30.95
Avg.	105.15	89.02	99.78	2.38	35.30	28.10
Min.	66.87	56.09	48.53	1.95	18.91	13.38
Max.	182.34	150.36	228.33	4.09	67.91	63.80

Note: (1) Values for the local area are compared with the average, minimum and maximum values for all 292 areas in the Cost of Living Index; (2) Figures cover the Minneapolis MN urban area; **Doctor** *(general practitioners routine exam of an established patient);* **Dentist** *(adult teeth cleaning and periodic oral examination);* **Optometrist** *(full vision eye exam for established adult patient);* **Gasoline** *(one gallon regular unleaded, national brand, including all taxes, cash price at self-service pump if available);* **Beauty Salon** *(woman's shampoo, trim, and blow-dry);* **Men's Shirt** *(cotton/polyester dress shirt, pinpoint weave, long sleeves).*
Source: The Council for Community and Economic Research, ACCRA Cost of Living Index, 2015

HOUSING

House Price Index (HPI)

Area	National Ranking[2]	Quarterly Change (%)	One-Year Change (%)	Five-Year Change (%)
MSA[1]	112	0.20	5.20	13.00
U.S.[3]	–	1.45	5.76	22.85

Note: The HPI is a weighted repeat sales index. It measures average price changes in repeat sales or refinancings on the same properties. This information is obtained by reviewing repeat mortgage transactions on single-family properties whose mortgages have been purchased or securitized by Fannie Mae or Freddie Mac in January 1975; (1) Minneapolis-St. Paul-Bloomington Metropolitan Statistical Area—see Appendix B for areas included; (2) Rankings are based on annual percentage change for all metro areas containing at least 15,000 transactions over the last 10 years and ranges from 1 to 266; (3) figures based on a weighted average of Census Division estimates using a seasonally adjusted, purchase-only index; all figures are for the period ending December 31, 2015

Source: Federal Housing Finance Agency, House Price Index, February 25, 2016

Median Single-Family Home Prices

Area	2013	2014	2015p	Percent Change 2014 to 2015
MSA[1]	196.2	210.1	225.1	7.1
U.S. Average	197.4	208.9	223.9	7.2

Note: Figures are median sales prices of existing single-family homes in thousands of dollars; (p) preliminary; n/a not available; (1) Minneapolis-St. Paul-Bloomington, MN-WI Metropolitan Statistical Area—see Appendix B for areas included

Source: National Association of Realtors, Median Sales Price of Existing Single-Family Homes for Metropolitan Areas, 4th Quarter 2015

Qualifying Income Based on Median Sales Price of Existing Single-Family Homes

Area	With 5% Down ($)	With 10% Down ($)	With 20% Down ($)
MSA[1]	49,758	47,139	41,901
U.S. Average	49,535	46,928	41,714

Note: Figures are preliminary; Qualifying income is based on a mortgage rate of 4.1%. Monthly principal and interest payment is limited to 25% of income; n/a not available; (1) Minneapolis-St. Paul-Bloomington, MN-WI Metropolitan Statistical Area—see Appendix B for areas included

Source: National Association of Realtors, Qualifying Income Based on Median Sales Price of Existing Single-Family Homes for Metropolitan Areas, 4th Quarter 2015

Median Apartment Condo-Coop Home Prices

Area	2013	2014	2015p	Percent Change 2014 to 2015
MSA[1]	n/a	n/a	n/a	n/a
U.S. Average	194.9	204.3	210.7	3.1

Note: Figures are median sales prices of existing apartment condo-coop homes in thousands of dollars; (p) preliminary; n/a not available; (1) Minneapolis-St. Paul-Bloomington, MN-WI Metropolitan Statistical Area—see Appendix B for areas included

Source: National Association of Realtors, Median Sales Price of Existing Apartment Condo-Coop Homes for Metropolitan Areas, 4th Quarter 2015

Gross Monthly Rent

Area	Under $200	$200 -299	$300 -499	$500 -749	$750 -999	$1,000 -1,499	$1,500 and up	Median ($)
City	0.0	0.0	0.4	3.0	13.4	46.2	36.9	1,344
MSA[1]	1.9	3.8	5.3	18.2	29.7	28.8	12.3	916
U.S.	1.5	3.2	7.4	21.0	24.1	26.9	15.9	920

Note: Figures are percentages except for Median; Gross rent is the contract rent plus the estimated average monthly cost of utilities (electricity, gas, and water and sewer) and fuels (oil, coal, kerosene, wood, etc.) if these are paid by the renter (or paid for the renter by someone else); (1) Figures cover the Minneapolis-St. Paul-Bloomington, MN-WI Metropolitan Statistical Area—see Appendix B for areas included

Source: U.S. Census Bureau, 2010-2014 American Community Survey 5-Year Estimates

Homeownership Rate

Area	2008 (%)	2009 (%)	2010 (%)	2011 (%)	2012 (%)	2013 (%)	2014 (%)	2015 (%)
MSA[1]	69.9	70.9	71.2	69.1	70.8	71.7	69.7	67.9
U.S.	67.8	67.4	66.9	66.1	65.4	65.1	64.5	63.7

Note: (1) Figures cover the Minneapolis-St. Paul-Bloomington, MN-WI Metropolitan Statistical Area—see Appendix B for areas included
Source: U.S. Census Bureau, Housing Vacancies and Homeownership Annual Statistics: 2015

Year Housing Structure Built

Area	2010 or Later	2000 -2009	1990 -1999	1980 -1989	1970 -1979	1960 -1969	1950 -1959	1940 -1949	Before 1940	Median Year
City	2.6	28.5	39.2	15.7	8.1	3.7	1.5	0.2	0.6	1995
MSA[1]	0.8	15.2	14.6	14.8	15.4	10.0	10.1	4.1	15.0	1977
U.S.	1.0	14.9	13.9	13.8	15.8	11.0	10.8	5.4	13.3	1976

Note: Figures are percentages except for Median Year; (1) Figures cover the Minneapolis-St. Paul-Bloomington, MN-WI Metropolitan Statistical Area—see Appendix B for areas included
Source: U.S. Census Bureau, 2010-2014 American Community Survey 5-Year Estimates

HEALTH

Health Risk Data

Category	MSA[1] (%)	U.S. (%)
Adults aged 18–64 who have any kind of health care coverage	87.3	79.6
Adults who reported being in good or excellent health	89.2	83.1
Adults who are current smokers	18.0	19.6
Adults who are heavy drinkers[2]	6.6	6.1
Adults who are binge drinkers[3]	21.4	16.9
Adults who are overweight (BMI 25.0 - 29.9)	37.0	35.8
Adults who are obese (BMI 30.0 - 99.8)	23.9	27.6
Adults who participated in any physical activities in the past month	83.5	77.1
Adults 50+ who have ever had a sigmoidoscopy or colonoscopy	74.4	67.3
Women aged 40+ who have had a mammogram within the past two years	78.6	74.0
Men aged 40+ who have had a PSA test within the past two years	38.5	45.2
Adults aged 65+ who have had flu shot within the past year	67.6	60.1
Adults who always wear a seatbelt	96.6	93.8

Note: Data as of 2012 unless otherwise noted; (1) Figures cover the Minneapolis-St. Paul-Bloomington, MN-WI Metropolitan Statistical Area—see Appendix B for areas included; (2) Heavy drinkers are classified as males having more than two drinks per day or females having more than one drink per day; (3) Binge drinkers are classified as males having five or more drinks on one occasion or females having four or more drinks on one occasion
Source: Centers for Disease Control and Prevention, Behaviorial Risk Factor Surveillance System, SMART: Selected Metropolitan/Micropolitan Area Risk Trends, 2012 (Note: the CDC has discontinued this dataset but will be releasing a replacement in mid-2016)

Chronic Health Indicators

Category	MSA[1] (%)	U.S. (%)
Adults who have ever been told they had a heart attack	3.6	4.5
Adults who have ever been told they had a stroke	2.5	2.9
Adults who have been told they currently have asthma	8.7	8.9
Adults who have ever been told they have arthritis	19.6	25.7
Adults who have ever been told they have diabetes[2]	6.7	9.7
Adults who have ever been told they had skin cancer	5.0	5.7
Adults who have ever been told they had any other types of cancer	5.7	6.5
Adults who have ever been told they have COPD	3.9	6.2
Adults who have ever been told they have kidney disease	2.1	2.5
Adults who have ever been told they have a form of depression	16.5	18.0

Note: Data as of 2012 unless otherwise noted; (1) Figures cover the Minneapolis-St. Paul-Bloomington, MN-WI Metropolitan Statistical Area—see Appendix B for areas included; (2) Figures do not include pregnancy-related, borderline, or pre-diabetes
Source: Centers for Disease Control and Prevention, Behaviorial Risk Factor Surveillance System, SMART: Selected Metropolitan/Micropolitan Area Risk Trends, 2012 (Note: the CDC has discontinued this dataset but will be releasing a replacement in mid-2016)

Mortality Rates for the Top 10 Causes of Death in the U.S.

ICD-10[a] Sub-Chapter	ICD-10[a] Code	Age-Adjusted Mortality Rate[1] per 100,000 population County[2]	U.S.
Malignant neoplasms	C00-C97	145.3	163.6
Ischaemic heart diseases	I20-I25	52.0	102.2
Other forms of heart disease	I30-I51	44.0	50.1
Chronic lower respiratory diseases	J40-J47	36.5	41.4
Organic, including symptomatic, mental disorders	F01-F09	32.1	38.5
Cerebrovascular diseases	I60-I69	29.1	36.5
Other external causes of accidental injury	W00-X59	22.4	27.5
Other degenerative diseases of the nervous system	G30-G31	48.7	26.3
Diabetes mellitus	E10-E14	15.5	21.1
Hypertensive diseases	I10-I15	10.7	19.7

Note: (a) ICD-10 = International Classification of Diseases 10th Revision; (1) Mortality rates are a three year average covering 2012-2014; (2) Figures cover Washington County.
Source: Centers for Disease Control and Prevention, National Center for Health Statistics. Underlying Cause of Death 1999-2014 on CDC WONDER Online Database, released 2015.

Mortality Rates for Selected Causes of Death

ICD-10[a] Sub-Chapter	ICD-10[a] Code	Age-Adjusted Mortality Rate[1] per 100,000 population County[2]	U.S.
Assault	X85-Y09	Suppressed	5.1
Diseases of the liver	K70-K76	8.4	13.5
Human immunodeficiency virus (HIV) disease	B20-B24	Suppressed	2.1
Influenza and pneumonia	J09-J18	6.1	15.2
Intentional self-harm	X60-X84	10.5	12.7
Malnutrition	E40-E46	Suppressed	0.9
Obesity and other hyperalimentation	E65-E68	Suppressed	1.9
Renal failure	N17-N19	8.4	13.0
Transport accidents	V01-V99	7.4	11.6
Viral hepatitis	B15-B19	Suppressed	2.1

Note: (a) ICD-10 = International Classification of Diseases 10th Revision; (1) Mortality rates are a three year average covering 2012-2014; (2) Figures cover Washington County; Data are Suppressed when the data meet the criteria for confidentiality constraints; Mortality rates are flagged as Unreliable when the rate would be calculated with a numerator of 20 or less.
Source: Centers for Disease Control and Prevention, National Center for Health Statistics. Underlying Cause of Death 1999-2014 on CDC WONDER Online Database, released 2015.

Health Insurance Coverage

Area	With Health Insurance	With Private Health Insurance	With Public Health Insurance	Without Health Insurance	Population Under Age 18 Without Health Insurance
City	96.0	90.4	14.4	4.0	3.0
MSA[1]	92.2	77.7	25.1	7.8	4.9
U.S.	85.8	65.8	31.1	14.2	7.1

Note: Figures are percentages that cover the civilian noninstitutionalized population; (1) Figures cover the Minneapolis-St. Paul-Bloomington, MN-WI Metropolitan Statistical Area—see Appendix B for areas included
Source: U.S. Census Bureau, 2010-2014 American Community Survey 5-Year Estimates

Number of Medical Professionals

Area	MDs[3]	DOs[3,4]	Dentists	Podiatrists	Chiropractors	Optometrists
County[1] (number)	674	28	168	7	154	54
County[1] (rate[2])	273.2	11.4	67.4	2.8	61.8	21.7
U.S. (rate[2])	272.5	20.9	64.7	5.8	25.9	15.2

Note: Data as of 2014 unless noted; (1) Data covers Washington County; (2) Rate per 100,000 population; (3) Data as of 2013 and includes all active, non-federal physicians; (4) Doctor of Osteopathic Medicine
Source: U.S. Department of Health and Human Services, Health Resources and Services Administration, Bureau of Health Professions, Area Resource File (ARF) 2014-2015

Best Hospitals

According to *U.S. News,* the Minneapolis-St. Paul-Bloomington, MN-WI metro area is home to three of the best hospitals in the U.S.: **MercyHospital** (1 specialty); **Abbott Northwestern Hospital** (5 specialties); **Minneapolis Heart Institute at Abbott Northwestern Hospital** (1 specialty). The hospitals listed were nationally ranked in at least one adult specialty. Only 137 hospitals nationwide were nationally ranked in one or more specialties. Fifteen hospitals in the U.S. made the Honor Roll with high scores in at least six specialties. *U.S. News Online, "America's Best Children's Hospitals 2015-16"*

According to *U.S. News,* the Minneapolis-St. Paul-Bloomington, MN-WI metro area is home to three of the best children's hospitals in the U.S.: **Children's Hospitals and Clinics of Minnesota** (1 specialties); **University of Minnesota Masonic Children's Hospital** (5 specialties); **Gillette Children's Specialty Healthcare** (1 specialty). The hospitals listed were highly ranked in at least one pediatric specialty. Eighty-three children's hospitals in the U.S. were nationally ranked in at least one specialty. Twelve children's hospitals in the U.S. made the Honor Roll with high scores in at least three specialties. *U.S. News Online, "America's Best Children's Hospitals 2015-16"*

EDUCATION

Public School District Statistics

District Name	Schls	Pupils	Pupil/ Teacher Ratio	Minority Pupils[1] (%)	Free Lunch Eligible[2] (%)	IEP[3] (%)
East Metro Integration District	2	105	2.4	60.0	51.4	n/a
Math And Science Academy	1	442	15.9	32.8	0.9	5.7
North St Paul-Maplewood Oakdale	21	10,742	16.4	47.1	39.0	17.2
Northeast Metro 916	18	235	1.9	63.8	48.8	n/a
South Washington County SD	27	18,137	16.1	28.7	14.4	12.7

Note: Table includes school districts with 100 or more students; (1) Percentage of students that are not non-Hispanic white; (2) Percentage of students that are eligible for the free lunch program; (3) Percentage of students that have an Individualized Education Program.
Source: U.S. Department of Education, National Center for Education Statistics, Common Core of Data, Local Education Agency (School District) Universe Survey: School Year 2013-2014; U.S. Department of Education, National Center for Education Statistics, Common Core of Data, Public Elementary/Secondary School Universe Survey: School Year 2013-2014

Highest Level of Education

Area	Less than H.S.	H.S. Diploma	Some College, No Deg.	Associate Degree	Bachelor's Degree	Master's Degree	Prof. School Degree	Doctorate Degree
City	2.7	14.2	16.9	9.0	36.1	14.8	3.2	3.0
MSA[1]	6.9	22.8	21.4	9.9	25.9	9.2	2.4	1.4
U.S.	13.7	28.0	21.2	7.9	18.3	7.8	2.0	1.3

Note: Figures cover persons age 25 and over; (1) Figures cover the Minneapolis-St. Paul-Bloomington, MN-WI Metropolitan Statistical Area—see Appendix B for areas included
Source: U.S. Census Bureau, 2010-2014 American Community Survey 5-Year Estimates

Educational Attainment by Race

Area	High School Graduate or Higher (%)					Bachelor's Degree or Higher (%)				
	Total	White	Black	Asian	Hisp.[2]	Total	White	Black	Asian	Hisp.[2]
City	97.3	97.9	90.2	97.2	87.1	57.2	55.9	44.1	77.2	33.2
MSA[1]	93.1	95.3	81.8	79.8	65.7	39.0	40.7	20.2	44.0	17.6
U.S.	86.3	88.4	83.2	85.8	64.1	29.3	30.6	19.0	50.9	13.9

Note: Figures shown cover persons 25 years old and over; (1) Figures cover the Minneapolis-St. Paul-Bloomington, MN-WI Metropolitan Statistical Area—see Appendix B for areas included; (2) People of Hispanic origin can be of any race
Source: U.S. Census Bureau, 2010-2014 American Community Survey 5-Year Estimates

School Enrollment by Grade and Control

Area	Preschool (%)		Kindergarten (%)		Grades 1 - 4 (%)		Grades 5 - 8 (%)		Grades 9 - 12 (%)	
	Public	Private	Public	Private	Public	Private	Public	Private	Public	Private
City	32.8	67.2	83.3	16.7	89.4	10.6	86.4	13.6	89.3	10.7
MSA[1]	55.6	44.4	86.8	13.2	87.9	12.1	88.6	11.4	90.9	9.1
U.S.	57.4	42.6	87.8	12.2	89.8	10.2	89.9	10.1	90.6	9.4

Note: Figures shown cover persons 3 years old and over; (1) Figures cover the Minneapolis-St. Paul-Bloomington, MN-WI Metropolitan Statistical Area—see Appendix B for areas included
Source: U.S. Census Bureau, 2010-2014 American Community Survey 5-Year Estimates

Average Salaries of Public School Classroom Teachers

Area	2013-14		2014-15		Percent Change 2013-14 to 2014-15	Percent Change 2004-05 to 2014-15
	Dollars	Rank[1]	Dollars	Rank[1]		
Minnesota	54,752	21	56,670	20	3.50	19.5
U.S. Average	56,610	–	57,379	–	1.36	20.8

Note: (1) State rank ranges from 1 to 51 where 1 indicates highest salary.
Source: National Education Association, Rankings & Estimates: Rankings of the States 2014 and Estimates of School Statistics 2015, March 2015

Higher Education

Four-Year Colleges			Two-Year Colleges			Medical Schools[1]	Law Schools[2]	Voc/ Tech[3]
Public	Private Non-profit	Private For-profit	Public	Private Non-profit	Private For-profit			
0	0	1	0	0	0	0	0	1

Note: Figures cover institutions located within the city limits and include main campuses only; (1) includes schools accredited by the Liaison Committee on Medical Education and the American Osteopathic Association's Commission on Osteopathic College Accreditation; (2) includes ABA-accredited schools, schools with provisional ABA accreditation, and state accredited schools; (3) includes all schools with programs that are less than 2 years.
Source: National Center for Education Statistics, Integrated Postsecondary Education System (IPEDS), 2014-15; Association of American Medical Colleges, Member List, March 21, 2016; American Osteopathic Association, Member List, March 21, 2016; Law School Admission Council, Official Guide to ABA-Approved Law Schools Online, March 21, 2016; Wikipedia, List of Medical Schools in the United States, March 21, 2016; Wikipedia, List of Law Schools in the United States, March 21, 2016

According to *U.S. News & World Report,* the Minneapolis-St. Paul-Bloomington, MN-WI metro area is home to two of the best national universities in the U.S.: **University of Minnesota–Twin Cities** (#69); **University of St. Thomas** (#115 tie). The indicators used to capture academic quality fall into a number of categories: assessment by administrators at peer institutions; retention of students; faculty resources; student selectivity; financial resources; alumni giving; high school counselor ratings of colleges; and graduation rate. *U.S. News & World Report, "America's Best Colleges 2016"*

According to *U.S. News & World Report,* the Minneapolis-St. Paul-Bloomington, MN-WI metro area is home to two of the best liberal arts colleges in the U.S.: **Macalester College** (#23 tie); **Gustavus Adolphus College** (#79 tie). The indicators used to capture academic quality fall into a number of categories: assessment by administrators at peer institutions; retention of students; faculty resources; student selectivity; financial resources; alumni giving; high school counselor ratings of colleges; and graduation rate. *U.S. News & World Report, "America's Best Colleges 2016"*

According to *U.S. News & World Report,* the Minneapolis-St. Paul-Bloomington, MN-WI metro area is home to one of the top 100 law schools in the U.S.: **University of Minnesota, Law School** (#22 tie). The rankings are based on a weighted average of 12 measures of quality: peer assessment score; assessment score by lawyers/judges; median LSAT scores; median undergrad GPA; acceptance rate; employment rates for graduates; placement success; bar passage rate; faculty resources; expenditures per student; student/faculty ratio; and library resources. *U.S. News & World Report, "America's Best Graduate Schools, Law, 2017"*

According to *U.S. News & World Report,* the Minneapolis-St. Paul-Bloomington, MN-WI metro area is home to one of the top 75 medical schools for research in the U.S.: **University of Minnesota, Medical School** (#35 tie). The rankings are based on a weighted average of 11 measures of quality: quality assessment; peer assessment score; assessment score by residency directors; research activity; total research activity; average research activity per faculty member; student selectivity; median MCAT total score; median undergraduate GPA;

acceptance rate; and faculty resources. *U.S. News & World Report, "America's Best Graduate Schools, Medical, 2017"*

According to *U.S. News & World Report,* the Minneapolis-St. Paul-Bloomington, MN-WI metro area is home to one of the top 75 business schools in the U.S.: **University of Minnesota–Twin Cities, Carlson School of Management** (#27 tie). The rankings are based on a weighted average of the following nine measures: quality assessment; peer assessment; recruiter assessment; placement success; mean starting salary and bonus; student selectivity; mean GMAT and GRE scores; mean undergraduate GPA; and acceptance rate. *U.S. News & World Report, "America's Best Graduate Schools, Business, 2017"*

PRESIDENTIAL ELECTION

2012 Presidential Election Results

Area	Obama (%)	Romney (%)	Other (%)
Washington County	49.4	48.6	2.0
U.S.	51.0	47.2	1.8

Note: Results may not add to 100% due to rounding
Source: Dave Leip's Atlas of U.S. Presidential Elections

EMPLOYERS

Major Employers

Company Name	Industry
3M Company	Adhesives, sealants
Ameriprise Financial	Investment advice
Anderson Corporation	Millwork
Aware Integrated	Hospital & medical services plans
Bethesda Healtheast Hospital	General medical/surgical hospitals
Carlson Holdings	Hotels/motels
City of Minneapolis	General government, local government
County of Hennepin	General government, county government
Hennepin County	County supervisors' & executives' offices
Honeywell International	Aircraft engines & engine parts
Lawson Software	Application computer software
Medtronic	Electromedical equipment
Minnesota Department of Human Services	Family services agency
Minnesota Department of Transportation	Regulation, administration of transportation
North Memorial Hospital	General medical/surgical hospitals
Regents of the University of Minnesota	Specialty outpatient clinics
Rosemount Apple Valley and Eagan	Personal service agents, brokers, & bureaus
St Paul Fire and marine Insurance Company	Fire, marine, & casualty insurance
Thomson Legal Regulatory	Books, publishing & printing
United Parcel Service	Package delivery vehicular
Wells Fargo Bank	Mortgage bankers
West Publishing Corporation	Data base information retrieval

Note: Companies shown are located within the Minneapolis-St. Paul-Bloomington, MN-WI Metropolitan Statistical Area.
Source: Hoovers.com; Wikipedia

PUBLIC SAFETY

Crime Rate

Area	All Crimes	Violent Crimes				Property Crimes		
		Murder	Rape[3]	Robbery	Aggrav. Assault	Burglary	Larceny -Theft	Motor Vehicle Theft
City	1,823.0	0.0	13.5	10.5	30.1	220.9	1,487.8	60.1
Metro[1]	2,758.2	1.8	33.7	94.3	131.9	402.3	1,915.8	178.4
U.S.	2,971.8	4.5	36.6	102.2	232.5	542.5	1,837.3	216.2

Note: Figures are crimes per 100,000 population; (1) Figures cover the Minneapolis-St. Paul-Bloomington, MN-WI Metropolitan Statistical Area—see Appendix B for areas included; (3) The city and U.S. figures shown were reported using the revised Uniform Crime Reporting (UCR) definition of rape. The suburban and metro area figures shown are an aggregate total of the data submitted using both the revised and legacy UCR definitions.
Source: FBI Uniform Crime Reports, 2014

Hate Crimes

Area	Number of Quarters Reported	Number of Incidents per Bias Motivation: Race	Religion	Sexual Orientation	Ethnicity	Disability	Gender	Gender Identity
City	3	0	0	0	0	0	0	0
U.S.	4	2,568	1,014	1,017	648	84	33	98

Source: Federal Bureau of Investigation, Hate Crime Statistics 2014

Identity Theft Consumer Complaints

Area	Complaints	Complaints per 100,000 Population	Rank[2]
MSA[1]	3,988	114.1	149
U.S.	490,220	152.4	-

Note: (1) Figures cover the Minneapolis-St. Paul-Bloomington, MN-WI Metropolitan Statistical Area—see Appendix B for areas included; (2) Rank ranges from 1 to 379 where 1 indicates greatest number of identity theft complaints per 100,000 population
Source: Federal Trade Commission, Consumer Sentinel Network Data Book for January–December 2015

Fraud and Other Consumer Complaints

Area	Complaints	Complaints per 100,000 Population	Rank[2]
MSA[1]	13,758	393.6	116
U.S.	2,593,159	806.0	-

Note: (1) Figures cover the Minneapolis-St. Paul-Bloomington, MN-WI Metropolitan Statistical Area—see Appendix B for areas included; (2) Rank ranges from 1 to 379 where 1 indicates greatest number of identity theft complaints per 100,000 population
Source: Federal Trade Commission, Consumer Sentinel Network Data Book for January–December 2015

RECREATION

Culture

Dance[1]	Theatre[1]	Instrumental Music[1]	Vocal Music[1]	Series and Festivals	Museums and Art Galleries[2]	Zoos and Aquariums[3]
0	0	0	0	0	0	0

Note: (1) Professional perfoming groups; (2) Based on organizations with SIC code 8412; (3) AZA-accredited
Source: The Grey House Performing Arts Directory, 2015-16; Association of Zoos & Aquariums, AZA Member Zoos & Aquariums, March 25, 2016; www.AccuLeads.com, March 29, 2016

Professional Sports Teams

Team Name	League	Year Established
Minnesota Timberwolves	National Basketball Association (NBA)	1989
Minnesota Twins	Major League Baseball (MLB)	1961
Minnesota United FC	Major League Soccer (MLS)	2018
Minnesota Vikings	National Football League (NFL)	1961
Minnesota Wild	National Hockey League (NHL)	2000

Note: Includes teams located in the Minneapolis-St. Paul-Bloomington, MN-WI Metropolitan Statistical Area.
Source: Wikipedia, Major Professional Sports Teams of the United States and Canada, March 24, 2016

CLIMATE

Average and Extreme Temperatures

Temperature	Jan	Feb	Mar	Apr	May	Jun	Jul	Aug	Sep	Oct	Nov	Dec	Yr.
Extreme High (°F)	57	60	83	95	96	102	105	101	98	89	74	63	105
Average High (°F)	21	27	38	56	69	79	84	81	71	59	41	26	54
Average Temp. (°F)	12	18	30	46	59	69	74	71	61	50	33	19	45
Average Low (°F)	3	9	21	36	48	58	63	61	50	39	25	11	35
Extreme Low (°F)	-34	-28	-32	2	18	37	43	39	26	15	-17	-29	-34

Note: Figures cover the years 1948-1990
Source: National Climatic Data Center, International Station Meteorological Climate Summary, 9/96

Average Precipitation/Snowfall/Humidity

Precip./Humidity	Jan	Feb	Mar	Apr	May	Jun	Jul	Aug	Sep	Oct	Nov	Dec	Yr.
Avg. Precip. (in.)	0.8	0.8	1.9	2.2	3.1	4.0	3.8	3.6	2.5	1.9	1.4	1.0	27.1
Avg. Snowfall (in.)	11	9	12	3	Tr	0	0	0	Tr	Tr	7	10	52
Avg. Rel. Hum. 6am (%)	75	76	77	75	75	79	81	84	85	81	80	79	79
Avg. Rel. Hum. 3pm (%)	64	62	58	48	47	50	50	52	53	52	62	68	55

Note: Figures cover the years 1948-1990; Tr = Trace amounts (<0.05 in. of rain; <0.5 in. of snow)
Source: National Climatic Data Center, International Station Meteorological Climate Summary, 9/96

Weather Conditions

Temperature			Daytime Sky			Precipitation		
5°F & below	32°F & below	90°F & above	Clear	Partly cloudy	Cloudy	0.01 inch or more precip.	0.1 inch or more snow/ice	Thunder-storms
45	156	16	93	125	147	113	41	37

Note: Figures are average number of days per year and cover the years 1948-1990
Source: National Climatic Data Center, International Station Meteorological Climate Summary, 9/96

HAZARDOUS WASTE

Superfund Sites

Woodbury has no sites on the EPA's Superfund Final National Priorities List. There are a total of 1,323 Superfund sites on the list in the U.S. *U.S. Environmental Protection Agency, Final National Priorities List, March 18, 2016*

AIR & WATER QUALITY

Air Quality Trends: Ozone

	1990	1995	2000	2005	2010	2011	2012	2013	2014
MSA[1]	0.068	0.084	0.065	0.074	0.066	0.064	0.073	0.066	0.063

Note: (1) Data covers the Minneapolis-St. Paul-Bloomington, MN-WI Metropolitan Statistical Area—see Appendix B for areas included. The values shown are the composite ozone concentration averages among trend sites based on the highest fourth daily maximum 8-hour concentration in parts per million. These trends are based on sites having an adequate record of monitoring data during the trend period. Data from exceptional events are included.
Source: U.S. Environmental Protection Agency, Air Quality Monitoring Information, "Air Quality Trends by City, 1990-2014"

Air Quality Index

Area	Percent of Days when Air Quality was...[2]						AQI Statistics[2]	
	Good	Moderate	Unhealthy for Sensitive Groups	Unhealthy	Very Unhealthy		Maximum	Median
MSA[1]	54.5	44.1	1.4	0.0	0.0		137	48

Note: (1) Data covers the Minneapolis-St. Paul-Bloomington, MN-WI Metropolitan Statistical Area—see Appendix B for areas included; (2) Based on 365 days with AQI data in 2015. Air Quality Index (AQI) is an index for reporting daily air quality. EPA calculates the AQI for five major air pollutants regulated by the Clean Air Act: ground-level ozone, particle pollution (aka particulate matter), carbon monoxide, sulfur dioxide, and nitrogen dioxide. The AQI runs from 0 to 500. The higher the AQI value, the greater the level of air pollution and the greater the health concern. There are six AQI categories: "Good" AQI is between 0 and 50. Air quality is considered satisfactory; "Moderate" AQI is between 51 and 100. Air quality is acceptable; "Unhealthy for Sensitive Groups" When AQI values are between 101 and 150, members of sensitive groups may experience health effects; "Unhealthy" When AQI values are between 151 and 200 everyone may begin to experience health effects; "Very Unhealthy" AQI values between 201 and 300 trigger a health alert; "Hazardous" AQI values over 300 trigger warnings of emergency conditions (not shown).
Source: U.S. Environmental Protection Agency, Air Quality Index Report, 2015

Air Quality Index Pollutants

Area	Percent of Days when AQI Pollutant was...[2]					
	Carbon Monoxide	Nitrogen Dioxide	Ozone	Sulfur Dioxide	Particulate Matter 2.5	Particulate Matter 10
MSA[1]	0.0	1.9	18.6	0.0	51.0	28.5

Note: (1) Data covers the Minneapolis-St. Paul-Bloomington, MN-WI Metropolitan Statistical Area—see Appendix B for areas included; (2) Based on 365 days with AQI data in 2015. The Air Quality Index (AQI) is an index for reporting daily air quality. EPA calculates the AQI for five major air pollutants regulated by the Clean Air Act: ground-level ozone, particle pollution (also known as particulate matter), carbon monoxide, sulfur dioxide, and nitrogen dioxide. The AQI runs from 0 to 500. The higher the AQI value, the greater the level of air pollution and the greater the health concern.
Source: U.S. Environmental Protection Agency, Air Quality Index Report, 2015

Maximum Air Pollutant Concentrations: Particulate Matter, Ozone, CO and Lead

	Particulate Matter 10 (ug/m³)	Particulate Matter 2.5 Wtd AM (ug/m³)	Particulate Matter 2.5 24-Hr (ug/m³)	Ozone (ppm)	Carbon Monoxide (ppm)	Lead (ug/m³)
MSA[1] Level	76	9.9	28	0.064	2	0.12
NAAQS[2]	150	15	35	0.075	9	0.15
Met NAAQS[2]	Yes	Yes	Yes	Yes	Yes	Yes

Note: (1) Data covers the Minneapolis-St. Paul-Bloomington, MN-WI Metropolitan Statistical Area—see Appendix B for areas included; Data from exceptional events are included; (2) National Ambient Air Quality Standards; ppm = parts per million; ug/m³ = micrograms per cubic meter; n/a not available.
Concentrations: Particulate Matter 10 (coarse particulate)—highest second maximum 24-hour concentration; Particulate Matter 2.5 Wtd AM (fine particulate)—highest weighted annual mean concentration; Particulate Matter 2.5 24-Hour (fine particulate)—highest 98th percentile 24-hour concentration; Ozone—highest fourth daily maximum 8-hour concentration; Carbon Monoxide—highest second maximum non-overlapping 8-hour concentration; Lead—maximum running 3-month average
Source: U.S. Environmental Protection Agency, Air Quality Monitoring Information, "Air Quality Statistics by City, 2014"

Maximum Air Pollutant Concentrations: Nitrogen Dioxide and Sulfur Dioxide

	Nitrogen Dioxide AM (ppb)	Nitrogen Dioxide 1-Hr (ppb)	Sulfur Dioxide AM (ppb)	Sulfur Dioxide 1-Hr (ppb)	Sulfur Dioxide 24-Hr (ppb)
MSA[1] Level	16	50	n/a	12	n/a
NAAQS[2]	53	100	30	75	140
Met NAAQS[2]	Yes	Yes	n/a	Yes	n/a

Note: (1) Data covers the Minneapolis-St. Paul-Bloomington, MN-WI Metropolitan Statistical Area—see Appendix B for areas included; Data from exceptional events are included; (2) National Ambient Air Quality Standards; ppm = parts per million; ug/m³ = micrograms per cubic meter; n/a not available.
Concentrations: Nitrogen Dioxide AM—highest arithmetic mean concentration; Nitrogen Dioxide 1-Hr—highest 98th percentile 1-hour daily maximum concentration; Sulfur Dioxide AM—highest annual mean concentration; Sulfur Dioxide 1-Hr—highest 99th percentile 1-hour daily maximum concentration; Sulfur Dioxide 24-Hr—highest second maximum 24-hour concentration
Source: U.S. Environmental Protection Agency, Air Quality Monitoring Information, "Air Quality Statistics by City, 2014"

Drinking Water

Water System Name	Pop. Served	Primary Water Source Type	Violations[1]	
			Health Based	Monitoring/ Reporting
Woodbury	64,350	Ground	0	0

Note: (1) Based on violation data from January 1, 2015 to December 31, 2015 (includes unresolved violations from earlier years)
Source: U.S. Environmental Protection Agency, Office of Ground Water and Drinking Water, Safe Drinking Water Information System (based on data extracted April 29, 2016)

Ballwin, Missouri

Background

Settler John Ball moved to what is now known as West St. Louis County in the late 18th century and by 1800 had laid formal claim to 400 acres. Soon after came the Louisiana Purchase, thereby entangling the property on Grand Glaize Creek in ownership questions that took a decade to resolve. In 1826, with the coming of a new road to support the mail, Ball laid out a town that became Ballwin. The city was incorporated on December 29, 1950, and today is a thriving St. Louis suburb known for its good schools and fine, city-backed recreational facilities.

The city, which has no municipal property tax, lies west of Interstate 270—which circles St. Louis—and also has easy access to east-west Interstates 64 and 44. Ballwin lies within a half-hour's drive of five major universities and colleges, as well as St. Louis-Lambert International Airport.

Ballwin's students attend the Parkway and Rockwood School districts. The Parkway schools include 14 federal Blue Ribbon schools of excellence and 17 Missouri Gold Star schools. In a recent school year, 2011, the district saw a 99 percent participation rate among its high school students who took the ACT exam. The Rockwood schools saw students achieve an average ACT score of 23.5, compared to 21.6 for students across Missouri, and 20.9 nationally. On the Missouri Assessment Program tests, Rockwood saw 71.1 percent of its students score in the top two levels in mathematics, and 74.3 score in the top levels for Communication Arts.

The city's recreational facilities are top-notch: its The Point at Ballwin Commons includes an indoor pool, an indoor track, two full gyms, and a circuit weight system. The North Pointe Family Aquatic Center likewise looks after the community's fitness, with a ten-lane pool and a 910-foot "Lazy River" which features two, two-story water slides. The community's golfers can hit the greens at its public nine-hole course, and five community parks include amenities such as those found at Vlasis Park, with tennis courts, sand volleyball, trail and two baseball diamonds.

In addition to hospitals in St. Louis, nearby Chesterfield is home to St. Luke's Hospital.

Ballwin residents have easy access to the cultural assets of St. Louis, as well as the city's professional sports teams, MLB's St. Louis Cardinals, the NFL's St. Louis Rams, and the NHL's St. Louis Blues.

Every year, Ballwin residents gather for Ballwin Days, replete with a five-mile parade and talent show, to celebrate the community.

The four-season climate here means hot and humid summers with winters averaging lows below 20 degrees.

Rankings

Business/Finance Rankings

- The personal finance site NerdWallet analyzed 183 American metropolitan areas with populations over 250,000 and more than 15,000 businesses to rank where entrepreneurs find the most success. Criteria included area economy, annual income, housing cost, unemployment rate, and the success rate of area businesses. Saint Louis* ranked #47. *www.nerdwallet.com, "Best Places to Start a Business," April 27, 2015*

- USAA and Hiring Our Heroes worked with Sperlings's BestPlaces and the Institute for Veterans and Military Families at Syracuse University to rank major metropolitan areas where military-skills-related employment is strongest. Criteria for *mid-career* veterans included veteran wage growth; military skills, defense contractor, and government jobs; recent job growth; stability; and accessible health resources. Metro areas with a higher than national average crime or unemployment rate were excluded. At #6, the Saint Louis* metro area made the top ten. *www.usaa.com, "2015 Best Places for Veterans"*

- Based on metro area social media reviews, the employment opinion group Glassdoor surveyed 50 of the largest U.S. metro areas and equally weighed cost of living, hiring opportunity, and job satisfaction to compose a list of "25 Best Cities for Jobs." The Saint Louis* metro area was ranked #11 in overall job satisfaction. *www.glassdoor.com, "Best Cities for Jobs," May 19, 2015*

- In a survey of economic confidence in the nation's 50 largest metropolitan areas conducted January–December 2014, the Saint Louis* metro area placed #38, according to Gallup's 2014 Economic Confidence Index. *Gallup, "San Jose and San Francisco Lead in Economic Confidence," March 19, 2015*

- The Brookings Institution ranked the 100 largest metro areas in the U.S. based on income inequality. Saint Louis* was ranked #59 (#1 = greatest ineqality). Criteria: the "95/20 ratio," a figure representing the income at which a household earns more than 95 percent of all other households, divided by the income at which a household earns more than only 20 percent of all other households. *Brookings Institution, "Income Inequality, 100 Largest U.S. Metro Areas, 2007-2014," January 14, 2016*

- Payscale.com ranked the 20 largest metro areas in terms of wage growth. The Saint Louis* metro area ranked #14. Criteria: private-sector wage growth between the 1st quarter of 2015 and the 1st quarter of 2016. *PayScale, "Wage Trends by Metro Area," 1st Quarter, 2016*

- The Saint Louis* metro area was identified as one of the most debt-ridden places in America by the finance site Credit.com. The metro area was ranked #9. Criteria: residents' average personal debt load and average credit scores. *Credit.com, "The Most Debt-Ridden Cities," May 1, 2014*

- The Saint Louis* metro area was identified as one of the most affordable metropolitan areas in America by *Forbes*. The area ranked #7 out of 20 based on the National Association of Home Builders/Wells Fargo Housing Affordability Index and Sperling's Best Places' cost-of-living index. *Forbes.com, "America's Most Affordable Cities in 2015," March 12, 2015*

- Saint Louis* was identified as one of America's most frugal metro areas by *Coupons.com*. The city ranked #17 out of 25. Criteria: online coupon usage. *Coupons.com, "Top 25 Most Frugal Cities of 2014," May 11, 2015*

- Saint Louis* was identified as one of America's most frugal metro areas by *Coupons.com*. The city ranked #13 out of 25. Criteria: Grocery IQ and coupons.com mobile app usage. *Coupons.com, "Top 25 Most On-the-Go Frugal Cities of 2013," April 10, 2014*

- The Saint Louis* metro area appeared on the Milken Institute "2015 Best Performing Cities" list. Rank: #170 out of 200 large metro areas. Criteria: job growth; wage and salary growth; high-tech output growth. *Milken Institute, "Best-Performing Cities 2015," December 2015*

- *Forbes* ranked the 200 most populous metro areas to determine the nation's "Best Places for Business and Careers." The Saint Louis* metro area was ranked #84. Criteria: costs (business and living); job growth (past and projected); income growth; educational attainment (college and high school); projected economic growth; cultural and recreational opportunities; net migration patterns; number of highly ranked colleges. *Forbes, "The Best Places for Business and Careers 2015," July 29, 2015*

Education Rankings

- Personal finance website *WalletHub* analyzed the 150 largest U.S. metropolitan statistical areas to determine where the most educated Americans are choosing to settle. Criteria: education quality and attainment gap; education levels; percentage of workers with degrees; public school rankings; quality and size of each metro area's universities. Saint Louis* was ranked #35 (#1 = most educated city). *www.WalletHub.com, "2015's Most and Least Educated Cities*

Environmental Rankings

- The Saint Louis* metro area came in at #232 for the relative comfort of its climate on Sperling's list of "chill cities," as measured by the Sperling Heat Index. All 361 metro areas are included. Criteria included daytime high temperatures, nighttime low temperatures, dew point, and relative humidity at the high temperatures. *www.bertsperling.com, "Sperling's Chill Cities," July 18, 2013*

- Sperling's BestPlaces assessed 379 metropolitan areas of the United States for the likelihood of dangerously extreme weather events or earthquakes. In general the Southeast and South-Central regions have the highest risk of weather extremes and earthquakes, while the Pacific Northwest enjoys the lowest risk. Of the least risky metropolitan areas, the Saint Louis* metro area was ranked #327. *www.bestplaces.net, "Safest Places from Natural Disasters," April 2011*

- Saint Louis* was identified as one of America's dirtiest metro areas by *Forbes.* The area ranked #20 out of 20. Criteria: air quality; water quality; toxic releases; superfund sites. *Forbes, "America's 20 Dirtiest Cities," December 10, 2012*

- Saint Louis* was highlighted as one of the 25 most ozone-polluted metro areas in the U.S. during 2011 through 2013. The area ranked #16. *American Lung Association, State of the Air 2015*

Health/Fitness Rankings

- For each of the 50 most populous metro areas in the United States, the American College of Sports Medicine's American Fitness Index evaluated infrastructure, community assets, and policies that encourage healthy and fit lifestyles, including preventive health behaviors, levels of chronic disease conditions, health care access, and community resources and policies that support physical activity. The Saint Louis* metro area ranked #29 for "community fitness." *www.americanfitnessindex.org, "ACSM American Fitness Index Health and Community Fitness Status of the 50 Largest Metropolitan Areas," May 2015*

- The Saint Louis* metro area was identified as one of the worst cities for bed bugs in America by pest control company Orkin. The area ranked #40 out of 50 based on the number of bed bug treatments Orkin performed from January to December 2015. *Orkin, "Chicago Tops Bed Bug Cities List for Fourth Year in a Row," January 13, 2016*

- Saint Louis* was identified as a "2016 Spring Allergy Capital." The area ranked #35 out of 100. Three groups of factors were used to identify the most severe cities for people with allergies during the spring season: annual pollen levels; medicine utilization; access to board-certified allergists. *Asthma and Allergy Foundation of America, "Spring Allergy Capitals 2016"*

- Saint Louis* was identified as a "2015 Asthma Capital." The area ranked #26 out of the nation's 100 largest metropolitan areas. Criteria: estimated prevalence; self-reported prevalence; crude death rate for asthma; annual pollen score; annual air quality; public smoking laws; number of board-certified asthma specialists; school inhaler access laws; rescue medication use; controller medication use; ER visits for asthma; uninsured rate; poverty rate. *Asthma and Allergy Foundation of America, "Asthma Capitals 2015"*

- The Saint Louis* metro area ranked #162 out of 190 in The Gallup-Healthways Well-Being Index. Criteria: purpose; social well being; financial health; community and physical health. Results are based on telephone interviews with adults, aged 18 and older, living in metropolitan areas in the 50 U.S. states and the District of Columbia. *Gallup-Healthways, "State of American Well-Being," February 23, 2016*

Real Estate Rankings

- Based on the home-price forecasts compiled by the real-estate valuation firm CoreLogic Case-Shiller, CNNMoney reported that in 2016, the Saint Louis* metro area is expected to be one of the hottest housing markets in the U.S. Criteria: residential real estate prices. *money.cnn.com, "The 10 Hottest Housing Markets for 2016," December 3, 2015*
- The Saint Louis* metro area appeared on Realtor.com's list of the hottest housing markets to watch in 2016. The area ranked #2. Criteria: strong housing growth; affordable prices; and fast-paced sales. *Realtor.com®, "Top 10 Hot Real Estate Markets to Watch in 2016," December 2, 2015*
- Saint Louis* was ranked #50 out of 225 metro areas in terms of housing affordability in 2015 by the National Association of Home Builders (#1 = most affordable). Criteria: the share of homes sold in that area affordable to a family earning the local median income, based on standard mortgage underwriting criteria. *National Association of Home Builders®, NAHB-Wells Fargo Housing Opportunity Index, 4th Quarter 2015*

Safety Rankings

- Ballwin was identified as one of the safest cities in America by NeighborhoodScout. The city ranked #17 out of 100. Criteria: number of violent and property crimes per 1,000 residents. The editors only considered cities with 25,000 or more residents. *NeighborhoodScout, "Safest Cities in America 2016"*
- The National Insurance Crime Bureau ranked 380 metro areas in the U.S. in terms of per capita rates of vehicle theft. The Saint Louis* metro area ranked #102 (#1 = highest rate). Criteria: number of vehicle theft offenses per 100,000 inhabitants in 2014. *National Insurance Crime Bureau, "Hot Spots 2014," June 24, 2015*

Seniors/Retirement Rankings

- From its Best Cities for Successful Aging indexes, the Milken Institute generated rankings for metropolitan areas, weighing data in eight categories—health care, wellness, living arrangements, transportation, financial characteristics, education and employment opportunities, community engagement, and overall livability. The Saint Louis* metro area was ranked #30 overall in the large metro area category. *Milken Institute, "Best Cities for Successful Aging, 2014"*

Miscellaneous Rankings

- The watchdog site Charity Navigator conducts an annual study of charities in the nation's major markets both to analyze statistical differences in their financial, accountability, and transparency practices and to track year-to-year variations in individual communities. The Saint Louis* metro area was ranked #16 among the 30 metro markets in the rating dimension of Overall Score. *www.charitynavigator.org, "Metro Market Study 2015," June 5, 2015*
- Mars Chocolate North America, the makers of COMBOS®, in partnership with Sperling's BestPlaces, ranked 50 major metro areas in terms of their "manliness." The Saint Louis* metro area ranked #7. Criteria: number of professional sports teams; number of nearby NASCAR tracks and racing events; manly lifestyle; concentration of manly retail stores; manly occupations per capita; salty snack sales; "Board of Manliness" rankings. *Mars Chocolate North America, "America's Manliest Cities 2012"*
- The Saint Louis* metro area was selected as one of "America's Most Miserable Cities" by *Forbes.com.* The metro area ranked #12 out of 20. Criteria: violent crime; unemployment; foreclosures; income and property taxes; home prices; commute times; climate. *Forbes.com, "America's Most Miserable Cities" February 22, 2013*

- The National Alliance to End Homelessness ranked the 100 most populous metro areas with the highest rate of homelessness. The Saint Louis* metro area ranked #64. Criteria: number of homeless people per 10,000 population in 2011. *National Alliance to End Homelessness, The State of Homelessness in America 2012*

***Ballwin is located within the St. Louis, MO-IL Metropolitan Statistical Area.**

Business Environment

CITY FINANCES

City Government Finances

Component	2012 ($000)	2012 ($ per capita)
Total Revenues	18,735	616
Total Expenditures	18,683	614
Debt Outstanding	17,147	563
Cash and Securities[1]	9,992	328

Note: (1) Cash and security holdings of a government at the close of its fiscal year, including those of its dependent agencies, utilities, and liquor stores.
Source: U.S Census Bureau, State & Local Government Finances 2012

City Government Revenue by Source

Source	2012 ($000)	2012 ($ per capita)
General Revenue		
From Federal Government	0	0
From State Government	174	5
From Local Governments	9,191	302
Taxes		
Property	448	14
Sales and Gross Receipts	3,790	124
Personal Income	0	0
Corporate Income	0	0
Motor Vehicle License	136	4
Other Taxes	903	29
Current Charges	2,846	93
Liquor Store	0	0
Utility	0	0
Employee Retirement	0	0

Source: U.S Census Bureau, State & Local Government Finances 2012

City Government Expenditures by Function

Function	2012 ($000)	2012 ($ per capita)	2012 (%)
General Direct Expenditures			
Air Transportation	0	0	0.0
Corrections	0	0	0.0
Education	0	0	0.0
Employment Security Administration	0	0	0.0
Financial Administration	684	22	3.6
Fire Protection	0	0	0.0
General Public Buildings	0	0	0.0
Governmental Administration, Other	950	31	5.0
Health	3	< 1	< 0.1
Highways	5,013	164	26.8
Hospitals	0	0	0.0
Housing and Community Development	0	0	0.0
Interest on General Debt	1,183	38	6.3
Judicial and Legal	158	5	0.8
Libraries	0	0	0.0
Parking	0	0	0.0
Parks and Recreation	3,890	127	20.8
Police Protection	4,721	155	25.2
Public Welfare	0	0	0.0
Sewerage	293	9	1.5
Solid Waste Management	0	0	0.0
Veterans' Services	0	0	0.0
Liquor Store	0	0	0.0
Utility	0	0	0.0
Employee Retirement	0	0	0.0

Source: U.S Census Bureau, State & Local Government Finances 2012

DEMOGRAPHICS

Population Growth

Area	1990 Census	2000 Census	2010 Census	2014* Estimate	Population Growth (%) 1990-2014	Population Growth (%) 2010-2014
City	29,423	31,283	30,404	30,478	3.6	0.2
MSA[1]	2,580,897	2,698,687	2,812,896	2,797,737	8.4	-0.5
U.S.	248,709,873	281,421,906	308,745,538	314,107,084	26.3	1.7

Note: (1) Figures cover the St. Louis, MO-IL Metropolitan Statistical Area—see Appendix B for areas included; (*) 2010-2014 5-year estimated population
Source: U.S. Census Bureau, 1990 Census, Census 2000, Census 2010, 2010-2014 American Community Survey 5-Year Estimates

Household Size

Area	Persons in Household (%) One	Two	Three	Four	Five	Six	Seven or More	Average Household Size
City	18.4	37.4	19.3	17.8	5.5	0.9	0.4	2.76
MSA[1]	29.2	33.8	15.7	12.8	5.5	1.7	0.8	2.48
U.S.	27.5	33.5	15.8	13.1	6.0	2.3	1.4	2.64

Note: (1) Figures cover the St. Louis, MO-IL Metropolitan Statistical Area—see Appendix B for areas included
Source: U.S. Census Bureau, 2010-2014 American Community Survey 5-Year Estimates

Race

Area	White Alone[2] (%)	Black Alone[2] (%)	Asian Alone[2] (%)	AIAN[3] Alone[2] (%)	NHOPI[4] Alone[2] (%)	Other Race Alone[2] (%)	Two or More Races (%)
City	88.8	2.3	5.7	0.1	0.0	0.3	2.9
MSA[1]	76.5	18.3	2.2	0.2	0.0	0.6	2.1
U.S.	73.8	12.6	5.0	0.8	0.2	4.7	2.9

Note: (1) Figures cover the St. Louis, MO-IL Metropolitan Statistical Area—see Appendix B for areas included; (2) Alone is defined as not being in combination with one or more other races; (3) American Indian and Alaska Native; (4) Native Hawaiian and Other Pacific Islander
Source: U.S. Census Bureau, 2010-2014 American Community Survey 5-Year Estimates

Hispanic or Latino Origin

Area	Total (%)	Mexican (%)	Puerto Rican (%)	Cuban (%)	Other (%)
City	1.8	0.6	0.2	0.1	0.9
MSA[1]	2.7	1.8	0.2	0.1	0.6
U.S.	16.9	10.8	1.6	0.6	3.8

Note: Persons of Hispanic or Latino origin can be of any race; (1) Figures cover the St. Louis, MO-IL Metropolitan Statistical Area—see Appendix B for areas included
Source: U.S. Census Bureau, 2010-2014 American Community Survey 5-Year Estimates

Ancestry

Area	German	Irish	English	American	Italian	Polish	French[2]	Scottish	Dutch
City	33.8	20.3	11.4	6.6	6.9	4.3	3.5	2.3	1.5
MSA[1]	29.3	13.8	8.1	7.3	4.8	2.6	3.6	1.5	1.3
U.S.	14.9	10.8	8.0	7.1	5.5	3.0	2.7	1.7	1.4

Note: Figures are the percentage of the total population reporting a particular ancestry. The nine most commonly reported ancestries in the U.S. are shown. Figures include multiple ancestries (e.g. if a person reported being Irish and Italian, they were included in both columns); (1) Figures cover the St. Louis, MO-IL Metropolitan Statistical Area—see Appendix B for areas included; (2) Excludes Basque
Source: U.S. Census Bureau, 2010-2014 American Community Survey 5-Year Estimates

Foreign-Born Population

Area	Percent of Population Born in								
	Any Foreign Country	Asia	Mexico	Europe	Carribean	Central America[2]	South America	Africa	Canada
City	7.3	4.5	0.1	2.1	0.0	0.2	0.1	0.1	0.1
MSA[1]	4.5	1.9	0.6	1.2	0.1	0.1	0.1	0.3	0.1
U.S.	13.1	3.8	3.7	1.5	1.2	1.0	0.9	0.6	0.3

Note: (1) Figures cover the St. Louis, MO-IL Metropolitan Statistical Area—see Appendix B for areas included; (2) Excludes Mexico.
Source: U.S. Census Bureau, 2010-2014 American Community Survey 5-Year Estimates

Marital Status

Area	Never Married	Now Married[2]	Separated	Widowed	Divorced
City	23.5	62.4	0.8	5.0	8.3
MSA[1]	31.8	48.9	1.8	6.3	11.2
U.S.	32.5	48.4	2.2	5.9	10.9

Note: Figures are percentages and cover the population 15 years of age and older; (1) Figures cover the St. Louis, MO-IL Metropolitan Statistical Area—see Appendix B for areas included; (2) Excludes separated
Source: U.S. Census Bureau, 2010-2014 American Community Survey 5-Year Estimates

Disability Status

Area	All Ages	Under 18 Years Old	18 to 64 Years Old	65 Years and Over
City	8.0	0.8	6.2	27.3
MSA[1]	12.1	4.3	10.0	35.2
U.S.	12.3	4.1	10.2	36.3

Note: Figures show percent of the civilian noninstitutionalized population that reported having a disability. Disability status is determined from from six types of difficulty: vision, hearing, cognitive, ambulatory, self-care, and independent living. For children under 5 years old, hearing and vision difficulty are used to determine disability status. For children between the ages of 5 and 14, disability status is determined from hearing, vision, cognitive, ambulatory, and self-care difficulties. For people aged 15 years and older, they are considered to have a disability if they have difficulty with any one of the six difficulty types; (1) Figures cover the St. Louis, MO-IL Metropolitan Statistical Area—see Appendix B for areas included.
Source: U.S. Census Bureau, 2010-2014 American Community Survey 5-Year Estimates

Age

Area	Percent of Population									Median Age
	Under Age 5	Age 5–19	Age 20–34	Age 35–44	Age 45–54	Age 55–64	Age 65–74	Age 75–84	Age 85+	
City	5.0	20.4	15.7	13.2	14.5	15.0	9.7	5.1	1.4	41.8
MSA[1]	6.1	19.7	19.9	12.5	14.8	12.9	7.6	4.5	2.0	38.5
U.S.	6.4	19.9	20.6	13.0	14.1	12.3	7.6	4.3	1.9	37.4

Note: (1) Figures cover the St. Louis, MO-IL Metropolitan Statistical Area—see Appendix B for areas included
Source: U.S. Census Bureau, 2010-2014 American Community Survey 5-Year Estimates

Gender

Area	Males	Females	Males per 100 Females
City	14,436	16,042	90.0
MSA[1]	1,354,888	1,442,849	93.9
U.S.	154,515,159	159,591,925	96.8

Note: (1) Figures cover the St. Louis, MO-IL Metropolitan Statistical Area—see Appendix B for areas included
Source: U.S. Census Bureau, 2010-2014 American Community Survey 5-Year Estimates

Religious Groups by Family

Area	Catholic	Baptist	Non-Den.	Methodist[2]	Lutheran	LDS[3]	Pente-costal	Presby-terian[4]	Muslim[5]	Judaism
MSA[1]	19.8	10.0	3.8	3.4	4.1	0.6	1.2	3.0	0.4	0.7
U.S.	19.1	9.3	4.0	4.0	2.3	2.0	1.9	1.6	0.8	0.7

Note: Figures are the number of adherents as a percentage of the total population; (1) Figures cover the St. Louis, MO-IL Metropolitan Statistical Area—see Appendix B for areas included; (2) Methodist/Pietist; (3) Latter Day Saints; (4) Reformed; (5) Figures are estimates
Source: Association of Statisticians of American Religious Bodies, 2010 U.S. Religion Census: Religious Congregations & Membership Study

Religious Groups by Tradition

Area	Catholic	Evangelical Protestant	Mainline Protestant	Other Tradition	Black Protestant	Orthodox
MSA[1]	19.8	17.4	7.3	2.3	2.1	0.2
U.S.	19.1	16.2	7.3	4.3	1.6	0.3

Note: Figures are the number of adherents as a percentage of the total population; (1) Figures cover the St. Louis, MO-IL Metropolitan Statistical Area—see Appendix B for areas included
Source: Association of Statisticians of American Religious Bodies, 2010 U.S. Religion Census: Religious Congregations & Membership Study

ECONOMY

Gross Metropolitan Product

Area	2013	2014	2015	2016	Rank[2]
MSA[1]	146.0	150.2	154.6	161.1	22

Note: Figures are in billions of dollars; (1) Figures cover the St. Louis, MO-IL Metropolitan Statistical Area—see Appendix B for areas included; (2) Rank is based on 2016 data and ranges from 1 to 381
Source: The U.S. Conference of Mayors, U.S. Metro Economies: GMP and Employment 2014-2016, June 2015

Economic Growth

Area	2011-13 (%)	2014 (%)	2015 (%)	2016 (%)	Rank[2]
MSA[1]	0.9	1.2	1.5	2.2	236
U.S.	2.2	2.4	2.3	2.9	–

Note: Figures are real gross metropolitan product (GMP) growth rates and represent annual average percent change; (1) Figures cover the St. Louis, MO-IL Metropolitan Statistical Area—see Appendix B for areas included; (2) Rank is based on 2016 data and ranges from 1 to 381
Source: The U.S. Conference of Mayors, U.S. Metro Economies: GMP and Employment 2014-2016, June 2015

Metropolitan Area Exports

Area	2009	2010	2011	2012	2013	2014	Rank[2]
MSA[1]	9,026.6	11,239.4	12,307.5	14,642.3	12,393.6	10,359.8	31

Note: Figures are in millions of dollars; (1) Figures cover the St. Louis, MO-IL Metropolitan Statistical Area—see Appendix B for areas included; (2) Rank is based on 2014 data and ranges from 1 to 385
Source: U.S. Department of Commerce, International Trade Administration, Office of Trade & Industry Information, Manufacturing & Services, data extracted March 10, 2016

Building Permits

Area	Single-Family			Multi-Family			Total		
	2014	2015p	Pct. Chg.	2014	2015p	Pct. Chg.	2014	2015p	Pct. Chg.
City	37	17	-54.1	0	0	-	37	17	-54.1
MSA[1]	4,538	5,008	10.4	2,454	2,290	-6.7	6,992	7,298	4.4
U.S.	640,300	690,800	7.9	411,800	487,600	18.4	1,052,100	1,178,400	12.0

Note: (1) Figures cover the St. Louis, MO-IL Metropolitan Statistical Area—see Appendix B for areas included; Figures represent new, privately-owned housing units authorized (unadjusted data); All permit data are based on estimates with imputation; (p) preliminary data.
Source: U.S. Census Bureau, Manufacturing, Mining, and Construction Statistics, Building Permits, 2014, 2015

Bankruptcy Filings

Area	Business Filings			Nonbusiness Filings		
	2014	2015	% Chg.	2014	2015	% Chg.
Saint Louis County	43	68	58.1	4,418	3,924	-11.2
U.S.	26,983	24,735	-8.3	909,812	819,760	-9.9

Note: Business filings include Chapter 7, Chapter 11, Chapter 12, and Chapter 13; Nonbusiness filings include Chapter 7, Chapter 11, and Chapter 13

Source: Administrative Office of the U.S. Courts, Business and Nonbusiness Bankruptcy, County Cases Commenced by Chapter of the Bankruptcy Code, During the 12- Month Period Ending December 31, 2014 and Business and Nonbusiness Bankruptcy, County Cases Commenced by Chapter of the Bankruptcy Code, During the 12- Month Period Ending December 31, 2015

Housing Vacancy Rates

Area	Gross Vacancy Rate[2] (%)			Year-Round Vacancy Rate[3] (%)			Rental Vacancy Rate[4] (%)			Homeowner Vacancy Rate[5] (%)		
	2013	2014	2015	2013	2014	2015	2013	2014	2015	2013	2014	2015
MSA[1]	15.1	12.3	10.7	14.9	12.0	10.3	13.2	10.3	9.7	3.5	2.4	3.1
U.S.	13.6	13.4	12.9	10.7	10.4	10.0	8.3	7.6	7.1	2.0	1.9	1.8

Note: (1) Figures cover the St. Louis, MO-IL Metropolitan Statistical Area—see Appendix B for areas included; (2) The percentage of the total housing inventory that is vacant; (3) The percentage of the housing inventory (excluding seasonal units) that is year-round vacant; (4) The percentage of rental inventory that is vacant for rent; (5) The percentage of homeowner inventory that is vacant for sale

Source: U.S. Census Bureau, Housing Vacancies and Homeownership Annual Statistics: 2015

INCOME

Income

Area	Per Capita ($)	Median Household ($)	Average Household ($)
City	40,300	82,685	105,277
MSA[1]	30,024	54,959	74,420
U.S.	28,555	53,482	74,596

Note: (1) Figures cover the St. Louis, MO-IL Metropolitan Statistical Area—see Appendix B for areas included

Source: U.S. Census Bureau, 2010-2014 American Community Survey 5-Year Estimates

Household Income Distribution

Area	Percent of Households Earning							
	Under $15,000	$15,000 -24,999	$25,000 -34,999	$35,000 -49,999	$50,000 -74,999	$75,000 -99,000	$100,000 -149,999	$150,000 and up
City	3.8	6.5	8.6	10.9	16.8	14.1	20.2	19.2
MSA[1]	11.7	10.2	10.0	13.6	18.3	12.8	13.7	9.6
U.S.	12.5	10.7	10.2	13.5	17.8	12.2	13.0	10.0

Note: (1) Figures cover the St. Louis, MO-IL Metropolitan Statistical Area—see Appendix B for areas included

Source: U.S. Census Bureau, 2010-2014 American Community Survey 5-Year Estimates

Poverty Rate

Area	All Ages	Under 18 Years Old	18 to 64 Years Old	65 Years and Over
City	3.5	2.3	4.4	2.0
MSA[1]	13.2	18.9	12.3	7.5
U.S.	15.6	21.9	14.6	9.4

Note: Figures are percentage of people whose income during the past 12 months was below the poverty level; (1) Figures cover the St. Louis, MO-IL Metropolitan Statistical Area—see Appendix B for areas included

Source: U.S. Census Bureau, 2010-2014 American Community Survey 5-Year Estimates

EMPLOYMENT

Labor Force and Employment

Area	Civilian Labor Force			Workers Employed		
	Dec. 2014	Dec. 2015	% Chg.	Dec. 2014	Dec. 2015	% Chg.
City	16,910	17,328	2.4	16,326	16,874	3.3
MSA[1]	1,448,218	1,479,973	2.1	1,372,069	1,416,204	3.2
U.S.	155,521,000	157,245,000	1.1	147,190,000	149,703,000	1.7

Note: Data is not seasonally adjusted and covers workers 16 years of age and older; (1) Figures cover the St. Louis, MO-IL Metropolitan Statistical Area—see Appendix B for areas included

Source: Bureau of Labor Statistics, Local Area Unemployment Statistics

Unemployment Rate

Area	2015 Jan.	Feb.	Mar.	Apr.	May	Jun.	Jul.	Aug.	Sep.	Oct.	Nov.	Dec.
City	3.9	4.0	4.2	4.1	4.1	4.0	4.0	3.4	3.3	3.1	2.8	2.6
MSA[1]	6.0	6.0	5.9	5.3	5.5	5.6	5.7	5.1	4.6	4.6	4.6	4.3
U.S.	6.1	5.8	5.6	5.1	5.3	5.5	5.6	5.2	4.9	4.8	4.8	4.8

Note: Data is not seasonally adjusted and covers workers 16 years of age and older; (1) Figures cover the St. Louis, MO-IL Metropolitan Statistical Area—see Appendix B for areas included
Source: Bureau of Labor Statistics, Local Area Unemployment Statistics

Employment by Occupation

Occupation Classification	City (%)	MSA[1] (%)	U.S. (%)
Management, Business, Science, and Arts	49.7	38.0	36.4
Natural Resources, Construction, and Maintenance	5.8	7.7	9.0
Production, Transportation, and Material Moving	6.1	11.2	12.1
Sales and Office	27.1	25.6	24.4
Service	11.3	17.5	18.2

Note: Figures cover employed civilians 16 years of age and older; (1) Figures cover the St. Louis, MO-IL Metropolitan Statistical Area—see Appendix B for areas included
Source: U.S. Census Bureau, 2010-2014 American Community Survey 5-Year Estimates

Employment by Industry

Sector	MSA[1] Number of Employees	MSA[1] Percent of Total	U.S. Percent of Total
Construction, Mining, and Logging	63,100	4.6	5.0
Education and Health Services	243,900	17.9	15.7
Financial Activities	86,300	6.3	5.7
Government	163,900	12.0	15.5
Information	28,000	2.0	1.9
Leisure and Hospitality	143,100	10.5	10.4
Manufacturing	113,000	8.3	8.6
Other Services	48,100	3.5	3.9
Professional and Business Services	208,200	15.3	13.9
Retail Trade	146,100	10.7	11.3
Transportation, Warehousing, and Utilities	51,400	3.7	3.9
Wholesale Trade	63,400	4.6	4.1

Note: Figures are non-farm employment as of December 2015. Figures are not seasonally adjusted and include workers 16 years of age and older; (1) Figures cover the St. Louis, MO-IL Metropolitan Statistical Area—see Appendix B for areas included; n/a not available
Source: Bureau of Labor Statistics, Current Employment Statistics, Employment, Hours, and Earnings

Occupations with Greatest Projected Employment Growth: 2012 – 2022

Occupation[1]	2012 Employment	2022 Projected Employment	Numeric Employment Change	Percent Employment Change
Combined Food Preparation and Serving Workers, Including Fast Food	71,840	81,660	9,820	13.7
Personal Care Aides	31,360	40,430	9,070	28.9
Registered Nurses	66,970	74,990	8,020	12.0
Customer Service Representatives	49,990	56,010	6,020	12.0
Retail Salespersons	81,140	86,700	5,560	6.8
Nursing Assistants	42,320	47,470	5,150	12.2
General and Operations Managers	53,130	58,220	5,090	9.6
Secretaries and Administrative Assistants, Except Legal, Medical, and Executive	52,290	56,860	4,570	8.7
Carpenters	21,880	26,280	4,400	20.1
Heavy and Tractor-Trailer Truck Drivers	42,720	47,030	4,310	10.1

Note: Projections cover Missouri; (1) Sorted by numeric employment change
Source: www.projectionscentral.com, State Occupational Projections, 2012–2022 Long-Term Projections

Fastest Growing Occupations: 2012 – 2022

Occupation[1]	2012 Employment	2022 Projected Employment	Numeric Employment Change	Percent Employment Change
Insulation Workers, Mechanical	490	730	240	48.8
Helpers—Brickmasons, Blockmasons, Stonemasons, and Tile and Marble Setters	470	660	190	40.4
Helpers—Electricians	370	510	140	37.9
Insulation Workers, Floor, Ceiling, and Wall	490	680	190	37.5
Diagnostic Medical Sonographers	1,120	1,520	400	35.5
Interpreters and Translators	960	1,270	310	32.7
Brickmasons and Blockmasons	2,370	3,130	760	32.0
Nursing Instructors and Teachers, Postsecondary	1,350	1,780	430	31.9
Health Specialties Teachers, Postsecondary	3,370	4,420	1,050	31.1
Skincare Specialists	1,430	1,860	430	30.5

Note: Projections cover Missouri; (1) Sorted by percent employment change and excludes occupations with numeric employment change less than 100
Source: www.projectionscentral.com, State Occupational Projections, 2012–2022 Long-Term Projections

Average Wages

Occupation	$/Hr.	Occupation	$/Hr.
Accountants and Auditors	37.50	Maids and Housekeeping Cleaners	10.36
Automotive Mechanics	20.95	Maintenance and Repair Workers	19.01
Bookkeepers	19.10	Marketing Managers	66.57
Carpenters	26.82	Nuclear Medicine Technologists	33.83
Cashiers	10.22	Nurses, Licensed Practical	20.33
Clerks, General Office	15.53	Nurses, Registered	29.20
Clerks, Receptionists/Information	12.44	Nursing Assistants	12.03
Clerks, Shipping/Receiving	16.25	Packers and Packagers, Hand	11.44
Computer Programmers	40.55	Physical Therapists	37.83
Computer Systems Analysts	44.34	Postal Service Mail Carriers	24.38
Computer User Support Specialists	25.26	Real Estate Brokers	15.47
Cooks, Restaurant	11.65	Retail Salespersons	13.21
Dentists	83.85	Sales Reps., Exc. Tech./Scientific	32.93
Electrical Engineers	48.11	Sales Reps., Tech./Scientific	35.44
Electricians	30.18	Secretaries, Exc. Legal/Med./Exec.	16.37
Financial Managers	63.93	Security Guards	13.13
First-Line Supervisors/Managers, Sales	21.20	Surgeons	n/a
Food Preparation Workers	10.12	Teacher Assistants*	12.99
General and Operations Managers	53.15	Teachers, Elementary School*	27.63
Hairdressers/Cosmetologists	12.87	Teachers, Secondary School*	27.07
Internists	127.15	Telemarketers	12.35
Janitors and Cleaners	11.59	Truck Drivers, Heavy/Tractor-Trailer	20.70
Landscaping/Groundskeeping Workers	13.20	Truck Drivers, Light/Delivery Svcs.	17.44
Lawyers	55.39	Waiters and Waitresses	9.46

Note: Wage data covers the St. Louis, MO-IL Metropolitan Statistical Area—see Appendix B for areas included; (*) Hourly wages for elementary/secondary school teachers and teacher assistants were calculated by the editors from annual wage data based on a 40 hour work week; n/a not available.
Source: Bureau of Labor Statistics, Metro Area Occupational Employment and Wage Estimates, May 2015

TAXES

State Corporate Income Tax Rates

State	Tax Rate (%)	Income Brackets ($)	Num. of Brackets	Financial Institution Tax Rate (%)[a]	Federal Income Tax Ded.
Missouri	6.25	Flat rate	1	7.0	Yes (k)

Note: Tax rates as of January 1, 2016; (a) Rates listed are the corporate income tax rate applied to financial institutions or excise taxes based on income. Some states have other taxes based upon the value of deposits or shares; (k) 50% of the federal income tax is deductible.
Source: Federation of Tax Administrators, "State Corporate Income Tax Rates, 2016"

State Individual Income Tax Rates

State	Tax Rate (%)	Income Brackets ($)	Num. of Brackets	Personal Exempt. ($)[1] Single	Personal Exempt. ($)[1] Dependents	Fed. Inc. Tax Ded.
Missouri	1.5 - 6.0	1,000 - 9,001	10	2,100	1,200	Yes (m)

Note: Tax rates as of January 1, 2016; Local- and county-level taxes are not included; n/a not applicable; (1) Married joint filers generally receive double the single exemption; (m) The deduction for federal income tax is limited to $5,000 for individuals and $10,000 for joint returns in Missouri and Montana, and to $6,350 for all filers in Oregon.

Source: Federation of Tax Administrators, "State Individual Income Tax Rates, 2016"

Various State and Local Tax Rates

State	State and Local Sales and Use (%)	State Sales and Use (%)	Gasoline[1] (¢/gal.)	Cigarette[2] ($/pack)	Spirits[3] ($/gal.)	Wine[4] ($/gal.)	Beer[5] ($/gal.)
Missouri	8.113	4.225	17.3	0.17	2.00	0.42	0.06

Note: All tax rates as of January 1, 2016; (1) The American Petroleum Institute has developed a methodology for determining the average tax rate on a gallon of fuel. Rates may include any of the following: excise taxes, environmental fees, storage tank fees, other fees or taxes, general sales tax, and local taxes. In states where gasoline is subject to the general sales tax, or where the fuel tax is based on the average sale price, the average rate determined by API is sensitive to changes in the price of gasoline. States that fully or partially apply general sales taxes to gasoline: CA, CO, GA, IL, IN, MI, NY; (2) The federal excise tax of $1.0066 per pack and local taxes are not included; (3) Rates are those applicable to off-premise sales of 40% alcohol by volume (a.b.v.) distilled spirits in 750ml containers. Local excise taxes are excluded; (4) Rates are those applicable to off-premise sales of 11% a.b.v. non-carbonated wine in 750ml containers; (5) Rates are those applicable to off-premise sales of 4.7% a.b.v. beer in 12 ounce containers.

Source: Tax Foundation, 2016 Facts & Figures: How Does Your State Compare?

State Business Tax Climate Index Rankings

State	Overall Rank	Corporate Tax Rank	Individual Income Tax Rank	Sales Tax Rank	Unemployment Insurance Tax Rank	Property Tax Rank
Missouri	17	3	28	23	12	8

Note: The index is a measure of how each state's tax laws affect economic performance. The lower the rank, the more favorable a state's tax system is for business. States without a given tax are given a ranking of 1. The scores/rankings for the District of Columbia do not affect other states. The 2016 index represents the tax climate as of July 1, 2015 (the beginning of Fiscal Year 2016).

Source: Tax Foundation, State Business Tax Climate Index 2016

TRANSPORTATION

Means of Transportation to Work

Area	Car/Truck/Van: Drove Alone	Car/Truck/Van: Car-pooled	Public Transportation: Bus	Public Transportation: Subway	Public Transportation: Railroad	Bicycle	Walked	Other Means	Worked at Home
City	86.2	4.2	0.2	0.1	0.0	0.0	1.8	0.4	7.2
MSA[1]	83.0	7.7	2.1	0.4	0.1	0.3	1.8	0.9	3.9
U.S.	76.4	9.6	2.6	1.8	0.6	0.6	2.8	1.3	4.4

Note: Figures are percentages and cover workers 16 years of age and older; (1) Figures cover the St. Louis, MO-IL Metropolitan Statistical Area—see Appendix B for areas included

Source: U.S. Census Bureau, 2010-2014 American Community Survey 5-Year Estimates

Travel Time to Work

Area	Less Than 10 Minutes	10 to 19 Minutes	20 to 29 Minutes	30 to 44 Minutes	45 to 59 Minutes	60 to 89 Minutes	90 Minutes or More
City	9.6	24.3	25.7	30.1	8.3	1.1	0.8
MSA[1]	11.2	28.2	24.0	23.2	8.0	3.9	1.5
U.S.	13.3	29.6	21.0	20.2	7.7	5.7	2.6

Note: Figures are percentages and include workers 16 years old and over; (1) Figures cover the St. Louis, MO-IL Metropolitan Statistical Area—see Appendix B for areas included

Source: U.S. Census Bureau, 2010-2014 American Community Survey 5-Year Estimates

Freeway Travel Time Index

Area	1985	1990	1995	2000	2005	2010	2014
Urban Area Rank[1,2]	48	56	47	57	61	57	65
Urban Area Index[1]	1.07	1.09	1.13	1.15	1.16	1.16	1.16
Average Index[3]	1.09	1.11	1.14	1.17	1.20	1.19	1.20

Note: Freeway Travel Time Index—the ratio of travel time in the peak period to the travel time at free-flow conditions. For example, a value of 1.30 indicates a 20-minute free-flow trip takes 26 minutes in the peak (20 minutes x 1.30 = 26 minutes); (1) Covers the St. Louis MO-IL urban area; (2) Rank is based on 101 urban areas (#1 = highest travel time index); (3) Average of 101 urban areas

Source: Texas Transportation Institute, 2015 Urban Mobility Scorecard, August 2015

Freeway Commuter Stress Index

Area	1985	1990	1995	2000	2005	2010	2014
Urban Area Rank[1,2]	53	59	55	63	68	65	61
Urban Area Index[1]	1.09	1.11	1.15	1.17	1.18	1.18	1.19
Average Index[3]	1.13	1.16	1.19	1.22	1.25	1.24	1.25

Note: The Freeway Commuter Stress Index is the same as the Freeway Travel Time Index (see table above) except that it includes only the travel in the peak directions during the peak periods; the TTI includes travel in all directions during the peak period. Thus, the CSI is more indicative of the work trip experienced by each commuter on a daily basis. (1) Covers the St. Louis MO-IL urban area; (2) Rank is based on 101 urban areas (#1 = highest stress index); (3) Average of 101 urban areas

Source: Texas Transportation Institute, 2015 Urban Mobility Scorecard, August 2015

Living Environment

COST OF LIVING

Cost of Living Index

Composite Index	Groceries	Housing	Utilities	Trans-portation	Health Care	Misc. Goods/ Services
92.5	104.6	72.3	116.6	98.5	99.8	94.3

Note: The Cost of Living Index measures regional differences in the cost of consumer goods and services, excluding taxes and non-consumer expenditures, for professional and managerial households in the top income quintile. It is based on more than 50,000 prices covering almost 60 different items for which prices are collected three times a year by chambers of commerce, economic development organizations or university applied economic centers in each participating urban area. The numbers shown should be read as a percentage above or below the national average of 100. For example, a value of 115.4 in the groceries column indicates that grocery prices are 15.4% higher than the national average. Small differences in the index numbers should not be interpreted as significant; Figures cover the St. Louis MO-IL urban area.
Source: The Council for Community and Economic Research, ACCRA Cost of Living Index, 2015

Grocery Prices

Area[1]	T-Bone Steak ($/pound)	Frying Chicken ($/pound)	Whole Milk ($/half gal.)	Eggs ($/dozen)	Orange Juice ($/64 oz.)	Coffee ($/11.5 oz.)
City[2]	11.55	2.02	2.46	2.48	3.61	4.56
Avg.	10.99	1.43	2.25	2.26	3.58	4.48
Min.	7.16	0.98	1.30	1.35	2.88	2.98
Max.	14.13	2.43	3.85	4.81	6.39	7.56

Note: (1) Values for the local area are compared with the average, minimum and maximum values for all 292 areas in the Cost of Living Index; (2) Figures cover the St. Louis MO-IL urban area; **T-Bone Steak** *(price per pound);* **Frying Chicken** *(price per pound, whole fryer);* **Whole Milk** *(half gallon carton);* **Eggs** *(price per dozen, Grade A, large);* **Orange Juice** *(64 oz. Tropicana or Florida Natural);* **Coffee** *(11.5 oz. can, vacuum-packed, Maxwell House, Hills Bros, or Folgers).*
Source: The Council for Community and Economic Research, ACCRA Cost of Living Index, 2015

Housing and Utility Costs

Area[1]	New Home Price ($)	Apartment Rent ($/month)	All Electric ($/month)	Part Electric ($/month)	Other Energy ($/month)	Telephone ($/month)
City[2]	207,522	832	-	95.19	70.93	40.32
Avg.	312,874	945	179.30	95.07	72.96	28.11
Min.	178,682	479	116.28	43.14	26.46	10.01
Max.	1,472,476	3,984	504.25	189.44	421.11	43.06

Note: (1) Values for the local area are compared with the average, minimum and maximum values for all 292 areas in the Cost of Living Index; (2) Figures cover the St. Louis MO-IL urban area; **New Home Price** *(2,400 sf living area, 8,000 sf lot, in urban area with full utilities);* **Apartment Rent** *(950 sf 2 bedroom/1.5 or 2 bath, unfurnished, excluding all utilities except water);* **All Electric** *(average monthly cost for an all-electric home);* **Part Electric** *(average monthly cost for a part-electric home);* **Other Energy** *(average monthly cost for natural gas, fuel oil, coal, wood, and any other forms of energy except electricity);* **Telephone** *(price includes basic monthly rate for a private residential line plus additional local usage charges incurred by a family of four).*
Source: The Council for Community and Economic Research, ACCRA Cost of Living Index, 2015

Health Care, Transportation, and Other Costs

Area[1]	Doctor ($/visit)	Dentist ($/visit)	Optometrist ($/visit)	Gasoline ($/gallon)	Beauty Salon ($/visit)	Men's Shirt ($)
City[2]	94.95	91.43	83.95	2.31	35.77	23.78
Avg.	105.15	89.02	99.78	2.38	35.30	28.10
Min.	66.87	56.09	48.53	1.95	18.91	13.38
Max.	182.34	150.36	228.33	4.09	67.91	63.80

Note: (1) Values for the local area are compared with the average, minimum and maximum values for all 292 areas in the Cost of Living Index; (2) Figures cover the St. Louis MO-IL urban area; **Doctor** *(general practitioners routine exam of an established patient);* **Dentist** *(adult teeth cleaning and periodic oral examination);* **Optometrist** *(full vision eye exam for established adult patient);* **Gasoline** *(one gallon regular unleaded, national brand, including all taxes, cash price at self-service pump if available);* **Beauty Salon** *(woman's shampoo, trim, and blow-dry);* **Men's Shirt** *(cotton/polyester dress shirt, pinpoint weave, long sleeves).*
Source: The Council for Community and Economic Research, ACCRA Cost of Living Index, 2015

HOUSING

House Price Index (HPI)

Area	National Ranking[2]	Quarterly Change (%)	One-Year Change (%)	Five-Year Change (%)
MSA[1]	164	0.50	3.80	4.00
U.S.[3]	–	1.45	5.76	22.85

Note: The HPI is a weighted repeat sales index. It measures average price changes in repeat sales or refinancings on the same properties. This information is obtained by reviewing repeat mortgage transactions on single-family properties whose mortgages have been purchased or securitized by Fannie Mae or Freddie Mac in January 1975; (1) St. Louis Metropolitan Statistical Area—see Appendix B for areas included; (2) Rankings are based on annual percentage change for all metro areas containing at least 15,000 transactions over the last 10 years and ranges from 1 to 266; (3) figures based on a weighted average of Census Division estimates using a seasonally adjusted, purchase-only index; all figures are for the period ending December 31, 2015
Source: Federal Housing Finance Agency, House Price Index, February 25, 2016

Median Single-Family Home Prices

Area	2013	2014	2015p	Percent Change 2014 to 2015
MSA[1]	134.3	141.7	150.6	6.3
U.S. Average	197.4	208.9	223.9	7.2

Note: Figures are median sales prices of existing single-family homes in thousands of dollars; (p) preliminary; n/a not available; (1) St. Louis, MO-IL Metropolitan Statistical Area—see Appendix B for areas included
Source: National Association of Realtors, Median Sales Price of Existing Single-Family Homes for Metropolitan Areas, 4th Quarter 2015

Qualifying Income Based on Median Sales Price of Existing Single-Family Homes

Area	With 5% Down ($)	With 10% Down ($)	With 20% Down ($)
MSA[1]	31,963	30,281	26,916
U.S. Average	49,535	46,928	41,714

Note: Figures are preliminary; Qualifying income is based on a mortgage rate of 4.1%. Monthly principal and interest payment is limited to 25% of income; n/a not available; (1) St. Louis, MO-IL Metropolitan Statistical Area—see Appendix B for areas included
Source: National Association of Realtors, Qualifying Income Based on Median Sales Price of Existing Single-Family Homes for Metropolitan Areas, 4th Quarter 2015

Median Apartment Condo-Coop Home Prices

Area	2013	2014	2015p	Percent Change 2014 to 2015
MSA[1]	n/a	n/a	n/a	n/a
U.S. Average	194.9	204.3	210.7	3.1

Note: Figures are median sales prices of existing apartment condo-coop homes in thousands of dollars; (p) preliminary; n/a not available; (1) St. Louis, MO-IL Metropolitan Statistical Area—see Appendix B for areas included
Source: National Association of Realtors, Median Sales Price of Existing Apartment Condo-Coop Homes for Metropolitan Areas, 4th Quarter 2015

Gross Monthly Rent

Area	Under $200	$200 -299	$300 -499	$500 -749	$750 -999	$1,000 -1,499	$1,500 and up	Median ($)
City	0.0	0.5	1.4	12.7	32.9	33.2	19.2	1,030
MSA[1]	1.4	3.3	8.2	29.0	30.0	21.9	6.1	808
U.S.	1.5	3.2	7.4	21.0	24.1	26.9	15.9	920

Note: Figures are percentages except for Median; Gross rent is the contract rent plus the estimated average monthly cost of utilities (electricity, gas, and water and sewer) and fuels (oil, coal, kerosene, wood, etc.) if these are paid by the renter (or paid for the renter by someone else); (1) Figures cover the St. Louis, MO-IL Metropolitan Statistical Area—see Appendix B for areas included
Source: U.S. Census Bureau, 2010-2014 American Community Survey 5-Year Estimates

Homeownership Rate

Area	2008 (%)	2009 (%)	2010 (%)	2011 (%)	2012 (%)	2013 (%)	2014 (%)	2015 (%)
MSA[1]	72.2	72.5	72.2	71.1	72.0	72.7	71.1	68.7
U.S.	67.8	67.4	66.9	66.1	65.4	65.1	64.5	63.7

Note: (1) Figures cover the St. Louis, MO-IL Metropolitan Statistical Area—see Appendix B for areas included
Source: U.S. Census Bureau, Housing Vacancies and Homeownership Annual Statistics: 2015

Year Housing Structure Built

Area	2010 or Later	2000 -2009	1990 -1999	1980 -1989	1970 -1979	1960 -1969	1950 -1959	1940 -1949	Before 1940	Median Year
City	0.1	5.0	15.7	12.2	29.4	25.6	9.8	1.1	1.1	1974
MSA[1]	0.8	12.2	12.4	11.3	13.5	12.8	13.8	6.5	16.7	1970
U.S.	1.0	14.9	13.9	13.8	15.8	11.0	10.8	5.4	13.3	1976

Note: Figures are percentages except for Median Year; (1) Figures cover the St. Louis, MO-IL Metropolitan Statistical Area—see Appendix B for areas included
Source: U.S. Census Bureau, 2010-2014 American Community Survey 5-Year Estimates

HEALTH

Health Risk Data

Category	MSA[1] (%)	U.S. (%)
Adults aged 18–64 who have any kind of health care coverage	83.4	79.6
Adults who reported being in good or excellent health	83.6	83.1
Adults who are current smokers	20.1	19.6
Adults who are heavy drinkers[2]	6.9	6.1
Adults who are binge drinkers[3]	22.1	16.9
Adults who are overweight (BMI 25.0 - 29.9)	36.5	35.8
Adults who are obese (BMI 30.0 - 99.8)	31.1	27.6
Adults who participated in any physical activities in the past month	75.6	77.1
Adults 50+ who have ever had a sigmoidoscopy or colonoscopy	69.9	67.3
Women aged 40+ who have had a mammogram within the past two years	79.4	74.0
Men aged 40+ who have had a PSA test within the past two years	52.8	45.2
Adults aged 65+ who have had flu shot within the past year	63.6	60.1
Adults who always wear a seatbelt	90.8	93.8

Note: Data as of 2012 unless otherwise noted; (1) Figures cover the St. Louis, MO-IL Metropolitan Statistical Area—see Appendix B for areas included; (2) Heavy drinkers are classified as males having more than two drinks per day or females having more than one drink per day; (3) Binge drinkers are classified as males having five or more drinks on one occasion or females having four or more drinks on one occasion
Source: Centers for Disease Control and Prevention, Behaviorial Risk Factor Surveillance System, SMART: Selected Metropolitan/Micropolitan Area Risk Trends, 2012 (Note: the CDC has discontinued this dataset but will be releasing a replacement in mid-2016)

Chronic Health Indicators

Category	MSA[1] (%)	U.S. (%)
Adults who have ever been told they had a heart attack	5.4	4.5
Adults who have ever been told they had a stroke	3.6	2.9
Adults who have been told they currently have asthma	10.2	8.9
Adults who have ever been told they have arthritis	27.0	25.7
Adults who have ever been told they have diabetes[2]	10.6	9.7
Adults who have ever been told they had skin cancer	5.4	5.7
Adults who have ever been told they had any other types of cancer	7.0	6.5
Adults who have ever been told they have COPD	5.9	6.2
Adults who have ever been told they have kidney disease	2.9	2.5
Adults who have ever been told they have a form of depression	16.9	18.0

Note: Data as of 2012 unless otherwise noted; (1) Figures cover the St. Louis, MO-IL Metropolitan Statistical Area—see Appendix B for areas included; (2) Figures do not include pregnancy-related, borderline, or pre-diabetes
Source: Centers for Disease Control and Prevention, Behaviorial Risk Factor Surveillance System, SMART: Selected Metropolitan/Micropolitan Area Risk Trends, 2012 (Note: the CDC has discontinued this dataset but will be releasing a replacement in mid-2016)

Mortality Rates for the Top 10 Causes of Death in the U.S.

ICD-10[a] Sub-Chapter	ICD-10[a] Code	Age-Adjusted Mortality Rate[1] per 100,000 population	
		County[2]	U.S.
Malignant neoplasms	C00-C97	164.6	163.6
Ischaemic heart diseases	I20-I25	119.6	102.2
Other forms of heart disease	I30-I51	43.2	50.1
Chronic lower respiratory diseases	J40-J47	34.0	41.4
Organic, including symptomatic, mental disorders	F01-F09	42.8	38.5
Cerebrovascular diseases	I60-I69	36.5	36.5
Other external causes of accidental injury	W00-X59	33.5	27.5
Other degenerative diseases of the nervous system	G30-G31	22.9	26.3
Diabetes mellitus	E10-E14	15.6	21.1
Hypertensive diseases	I10-I15	12.4	19.7

Note: (a) ICD-10 = International Classification of Diseases 10th Revision; (1) Mortality rates are a three year average covering 2012-2014; (2) Figures cover St. Louis County.
Source: Centers for Disease Control and Prevention, National Center for Health Statistics. Underlying Cause of Death 1999-2014 on CDC WONDER Online Database, released 2015.

Mortality Rates for Selected Causes of Death

ICD-10[a] Sub-Chapter	ICD-10[a] Code	Age-Adjusted Mortality Rate[1] per 100,000 population	
		County[2]	U.S.
Assault	X85-Y09	9.2	5.1
Diseases of the liver	K70-K76	10.1	13.5
Human immunodeficiency virus (HIV) disease	B20-B24	1.2	2.1
Influenza and pneumonia	J09-J18	17.1	15.2
Intentional self-harm	X60-X84	13.5	12.7
Malnutrition	E40-E46	0.8	0.9
Obesity and other hyperalimentation	E65-E68	1.2	1.9
Renal failure	N17-N19	16.6	13.0
Transport accidents	V01-V99	7.1	11.6
Viral hepatitis	B15-B19	1.3	2.1

Note: (a) ICD-10 = International Classification of Diseases 10th Revision; (1) Mortality rates are a three year average covering 2012-2014; (2) Figures cover St. Louis County; Data are Suppressed when the data meet the criteria for confidentiality constraints; Mortality rates are flagged as Unreliable when the rate would be calculated with a numerator of 20 or less.
Source: Centers for Disease Control and Prevention, National Center for Health Statistics. Underlying Cause of Death 1999-2014 on CDC WONDER Online Database, released 2015.

Health Insurance Coverage

Area	With Health Insurance	With Private Health Insurance	With Public Health Insurance	Without Health Insurance	Population Under Age 18 Without Health Insurance
City	92.7	85.0	20.3	7.3	5.1
MSA[1]	89.6	72.6	28.0	10.4	4.4
U.S.	85.8	65.8	31.1	14.2	7.1

Note: Figures are percentages that cover the civilian noninstitutionalized population; (1) Figures cover the St. Louis, MO-IL Metropolitan Statistical Area—see Appendix B for areas included
Source: U.S. Census Bureau, 2010-2014 American Community Survey 5-Year Estimates

Number of Medical Professionals

Area	MDs[3]	DOs[3,4]	Dentists	Podiatrists	Chiropractors	Optometrists
County[1] (number)	5,040	270	833	93	509	262
County[1] (rate[2])	503.2	27.0	83.1	9.3	50.8	26.2
U.S. (rate[2])	272.5	20.9	64.7	5.8	25.9	15.2

Note: Data as of 2014 unless noted; (1) Data covers St. Louis County; (2) Rate per 100,000 population; (3) Data as of 2013 and includes all active, non-federal physicians; (4) Doctor of Osteopathic Medicine
Source: U.S. Department of Health and Human Services, Health Resources and Services Administration, Bureau of Health Professions, Area Resource File (ARF) 2014-2015

Best Hospitals

According to *U.S. News,* the St. Louis, MO-IL metro area is home to one of the best hospitals in the U.S.: **Barnes-Jewish Hospital/Washington University** (Honor Roll/14 specialties). The hospital listed was nationally ranked in at least one adult specialty. Only 137 hospitals nationwide were nationally ranked in one or more specialties. Fifteen hospitals in the U.S. made the Honor Roll with high scores in at least six specialties. *U.S. News Online, "America's Best Children's Hospitals 2015-16"*

According to *U.S. News,* the St. Louis, MO-IL metro area is home to three of the best children's hospitals in the U.S.: **SSM Cardinal Glennon Children's Medical Center** (2 specialties); **St. Louis Children's Hospital-Washington University** (10 specialties); **St. Louis Children's-Washington University-Shriners Hospital** (10 specialties). The hospitals listed were highly ranked in at least one pediatric specialty. Eighty-three children's hospitals in the U.S. were nationally ranked in at least one specialty. Twelve children's hospitals in the U.S. made the Honor Roll with high scores in at least three specialties. *U.S. News Online, "America's Best Children's Hospitals 2015-16"*

EDUCATION

Public School District Statistics

District Name	Schls	Pupils	Pupil/ Teacher Ratio	Minority Pupils[1] (%)	Free Lunch Eligible[2] (%)	IEP[3] (%)
Parkway C-2	28	17,955	15.2	35.4	16.9	15.5
Rockwood R-VI	31	21,883	15.1	20.6	13.2	15.6

Note: Table includes school districts with 100 or more students; (1) Percentage of students that are not non-Hispanic white; (2) Percentage of students that are eligible for the free lunch program; (3) Percentage of students that have an Individualized Education Program.
Source: U.S. Department of Education, National Center for Education Statistics, Common Core of Data, Local Education Agency (School District) Universe Survey: School Year 2013-2014; U.S. Department of Education, National Center for Education Statistics, Common Core of Data, Public Elementary/Secondary School Universe Survey: School Year 2013-2014

Highest Level of Education

Area	Less than H.S.	H.S. Diploma	Some College, No Deg.	Associate Degree	Bachelor's Degree	Master's Degree	Prof. School Degree	Doctorate Degree
City	3.0	15.8	21.4	6.1	33.9	14.7	3.5	1.5
MSA[1]	9.7	27.2	23.2	8.3	19.3	8.9	2.0	1.3
U.S.	13.7	28.0	21.2	7.9	18.3	7.8	2.0	1.3

Note: Figures cover persons age 25 and over; (1) Figures cover the St. Louis, MO-IL Metropolitan Statistical Area—see Appendix B for areas included
Source: U.S. Census Bureau, 2010-2014 American Community Survey 5-Year Estimates

Educational Attainment by Race

Area	High School Graduate or Higher (%)					Bachelor's Degree or Higher (%)				
	Total	White	Black	Asian	Hisp.[2]	Total	White	Black	Asian	Hisp.[2]
City	97.0	97.2	100.0	91.7	100.0	53.6	52.6	28.5	80.7	28.8
MSA[1]	90.3	91.9	83.5	88.2	76.8	31.5	33.6	17.3	62.8	24.9
U.S.	86.3	88.4	83.2	85.8	64.1	29.3	30.6	19.0	50.9	13.9

Note: Figures shown cover persons 25 years old and over; (1) Figures cover the St. Louis, MO-IL Metropolitan Statistical Area—see Appendix B for areas included; (2) People of Hispanic origin can be of any race
Source: U.S. Census Bureau, 2010-2014 American Community Survey 5-Year Estimates

School Enrollment by Grade and Control

Area	Preschool (%)		Kindergarten (%)		Grades 1 - 4 (%)		Grades 5 - 8 (%)		Grades 9 - 12 (%)	
	Public	Private	Public	Private	Public	Private	Public	Private	Public	Private
City	43.5	56.5	72.0	28.0	78.3	21.7	77.6	22.4	78.2	21.8
MSA[1]	53.9	46.1	81.1	18.9	83.2	16.8	83.4	16.6	85.5	14.5
U.S.	57.4	42.6	87.8	12.2	89.8	10.2	89.9	10.1	90.6	9.4

Note: Figures shown cover persons 3 years old and over; (1) Figures cover the St. Louis, MO-IL Metropolitan Statistical Area—see Appendix B for areas included
Source: U.S. Census Bureau, 2010-2014 American Community Survey 5-Year Estimates

Average Salaries of Public School Classroom Teachers

Area	2013-14 Dollars	2013-14 Rank[1]	2014-15 Dollars	2014-15 Rank[1]	Percent Change 2013-14 to 2014-15	Percent Change 2004-05 to 2014-15
Missouri	46,750	42	47,394	43	1.38	21.3
U.S. Average	56,610	–	57,379	–	1.36	20.8

Note: (1) State rank ranges from 1 to 51 where 1 indicates highest salary.
Source: National Education Association, Rankings & Estimates: Rankings of the States 2014 and Estimates of School Statistics 2015, March 2015

Higher Education

Four-Year Colleges			Two-Year Colleges			Medical Schools[1]	Law Schools[2]	Voc/ Tech[3]
Public	Private Non-profit	Private For-profit	Public	Private Non-profit	Private For-profit			
0	0	0	0	0	0	0	0	0

Note: Figures cover institutions located within the city limits and include main campuses only; (1) includes schools accredited by the Liaison Committee on Medical Education and the American Osteopathic Association's Commission on Osteopathic College Accreditation; (2) includes ABA-accredited schools, schools with provisional ABA accreditation, and state accredited schools; (3) includes all schools with programs that are less than 2 years.
Source: National Center for Education Statistics, Integrated Postsecondary Education System (IPEDS), 2014-15; Association of American Medical Colleges, Member List, March 21, 2016; American Osteopathic Association, Member List, March 21, 2016; Law School Admission Council, Official Guide to ABA-Approved Law Schools Online, March 21, 2016; Wikipedia, List of Medical Schools in the United States, March 21, 2016; Wikipedia, List of Law Schools in the United States, March 21, 2016

According to *U.S. News & World Report,* the St. Louis, MO-IL metro area is home to three of the best national universities in the U.S.: **Washington University in St. Louis** (#15 tie); **Saint Louis University** (#96 tie); **Maryville University of St. Louis** (#161 tie). The indicators used to capture academic quality fall into a number of categories: assessment by administrators at peer institutions; retention of students; faculty resources; student selectivity; financial resources; alumni giving; high school counselor ratings of colleges; and graduation rate. *U.S. News & World Report, "America's Best Colleges 2016"*

According to *U.S. News & World Report,* the St. Louis, MO-IL metro area is home to one of the best liberal arts colleges in the U.S.: **Principia College** (#127 tie). The indicators used to capture academic quality fall into a number of categories: assessment by administrators at peer institutions; retention of students; faculty resources; student selectivity; financial resources; alumni giving; high school counselor ratings of colleges; and graduation rate. *U.S. News & World Report, "America's Best Colleges 2016"*

According to *U.S. News & World Report,* the St. Louis, MO-IL metro area is home to two of the top 100 law schools in the U.S.: **Washington University in St. Louis, School of Law** (#18); **St. Louis University, School of Law** (#82 tie). The rankings are based on a weighted average of 12 measures of quality: peer assessment score; assessment score by lawyers/judges; median LSAT scores; median undergrad GPA; acceptance rate; employment rates for graduates; placement success; bar passage rate; faculty resources; expenditures per student; student/faculty ratio; and library resources. *U.S. News & World Report, "America's Best Graduate Schools, Law, 2017"*

According to *U.S. News & World Report,* the St. Louis, MO-IL metro area is home to two of the top 75 medical schools for research in the U.S.: **Washington University in St. Louis, School of Medicine** (#6); **St. Louis University, School of Medicine** (#63 tie). The rankings are based on a weighted average of 11 measures of quality: quality assessment; peer assessment score; assessment score by residency directors; research activity; total research activity; average research activity per faculty member; student selectivity; median MCAT total score; median undergraduate GPA; acceptance rate; and faculty resources. *U.S. News & World Report, "America's Best Graduate Schools, Medical, 2017"*

According to *U.S. News & World Report,* the St. Louis, MO-IL metro area is home to one of the top 75 business schools in the U.S.: **Washington University in St. Louis, Olin Business School** (#21). The rankings are based on a weighted average of the following nine measures: quality assessment; peer assessment; recruiter assessment; placement success; mean starting salary and bonus; student selectivity; mean GMAT and GRE scores; mean undergraduate GPA; and acceptance rate. *U.S. News & World Report, "America's Best Graduate Schools, Business, 2017"*

PRESIDENTIAL ELECTION

2012 Presidential Election Results

Area	Obama (%)	Romney (%)	Other (%)
St. Louis County	56.2	42.5	1.3
U.S.	51.0	47.2	1.8

Note: Results may not add to 100% due to rounding
Source: Dave Leip's Atlas of U.S. Presidential Elections

EMPLOYERS

Major Employers

Company Name	Industry
Ameren	Utilities
Anheuser-Busch	Brewery
Archdiocese of St. Louis Catholic Church	Catholic church
BJC Healthcare Hospital System	Hospital system
Boeing Defense	Contractor
Dierbergs Markets	Grocery chain
Edward Jones	Financial services
Enterprise Holdings	Car rental
Express Scripts	Pharmacy benefit manager
McDonald's	Food service
Mercy Health Hospital	Hospital system
Monsanto Biotech	Crop producer
National Geospatial-Intelligence Agency	National security
Schnuck Markets	Grocery chain
Scott Air Force	Military installation
Special School District of St. Louis Cty.	Primary/secondary education
SSM Health Care	Hospital system
St Anthony's Medical Center	Healthcare
St Louis City	Government
St Louis Community College	Higher education
St Louis County	Government
St Louis University	Higher education
USPS	Government
Wal-Mart	Retailer
Washington University	Higher education
Wells Fargo	Financial services

Note: Companies shown are located within the St. Louis, MO-IL Metropolitan Statistical Area.
Source: Hoovers.com; Wikipedia

PUBLIC SAFETY

Crime Rate

Area	All Crimes	Violent Crimes				Property Crimes		
		Murder	Rape[3]	Robbery	Aggrav. Assault	Burglary	Larceny -Theft	Motor Vehicle Theft
City	714.4	0.0	16.4	6.6	3.3	59.0	602.9	26.2
Metro[1]	2,879.0	8.8	35.8	103.4	281.8	470.4	1,765.0	213.8
U.S.	2,971.8	4.5	36.6	102.2	232.5	542.5	1,837.3	216.2

Note: Figures are crimes per 100,000 population; (1) Figures cover the St. Louis, MO-IL Metropolitan Statistical Area—see Appendix B for areas included; (3) The city and U.S. figures shown were reported using the revised Uniform Crime Reporting (UCR) definition of rape. The suburban and metro area figures shown are an aggregate total of the data submitted using both the revised and legacy UCR definitions.
Source: FBI Uniform Crime Reports, 2014

Hate Crimes

Area	Number of Quarters Reported	Number of Incidents per Bias Motivation						
		Race	Religion	Sexual Orientation	Ethnicity	Disability	Gender	Gender Identity
City	4	0	0	0	0	0	0	0
U.S.	4	2,568	1,014	1,017	648	84	33	98

Source: Federal Bureau of Investigation, Hate Crime Statistics 2014

Identity Theft Consumer Complaints

Area	Complaints	Complaints per 100,000 Population	Rank[2]
MSA[1]	19,195	684.0	1
U.S.	490,220	152.4	-

Note: (1) Figures cover the St. Louis, MO-IL Metropolitan Statistical Area—see Appendix B for areas included; (2) Rank ranges from 1 to 379 where 1 indicates greatest number of identity theft complaints per 100,000 population
Source: Federal Trade Commission, Consumer Sentinel Network Data Book for January–December 2015

Fraud and Other Consumer Complaints

Area	Complaints	Complaints per 100,000 Population	Rank[2]
MSA[1]	10,939	389.8	126
U.S.	2,593,159	806.0	-

Note: (1) Figures cover the St. Louis, MO-IL Metropolitan Statistical Area—see Appendix B for areas included; (2) Rank ranges from 1 to 379 where 1 indicates greatest number of identity theft complaints per 100,000 population
Source: Federal Trade Commission, Consumer Sentinel Network Data Book for January–December 2015

RECREATION

Culture

Dance[1]	Theatre[1]	Instrumental Music[1]	Vocal Music[1]	Series and Festivals	Museums and Art Galleries[2]	Zoos and Aquariums[3]
0	0	0	0	0	0	0

Note: (1) Professional perfoming groups; (2) Based on organizations with SIC code 8412; (3) AZA-accredited
Source: The Grey House Performing Arts Directory, 2015-16; Association of Zoos & Aquariums, AZA Member Zoos & Aquariums, March 25, 2016; www.AccuLeads.com, March 29, 2016

Professional Sports Teams

Team Name	League	Year Established
Los Angeles Rams	National Football League (NFL)	2016
Saint Louis Blues	National Hockey League (NHL)	1967
Saint Louis Cardinals	Major League Baseball (MLB)	1882

Note: Includes teams located in the St. Louis, MO-IL Metropolitan Statistical Area.
Source: Wikipedia, Major Professional Sports Teams of the United States and Canada, March 24, 2016

CLIMATE

Average and Extreme Temperatures

Temperature	Jan	Feb	Mar	Apr	May	Jun	Jul	Aug	Sep	Oct	Nov	Dec	Yr.
Extreme High (°F)	77	83	89	93	98	105	115	107	104	94	85	76	115
Average High (°F)	39	43	54	67	76	85	89	87	80	69	54	42	66
Average Temp. (°F)	30	34	44	56	66	75	79	78	70	59	45	34	56
Average Low (°F)	21	25	34	46	55	65	69	67	59	48	36	26	46
Extreme Low (°F)	-18	-10	-5	22	31	43	51	47	36	23	1	-16	-18

Note: Figures cover the years 1945-1990
Source: National Climatic Data Center, International Station Meteorological Climate Summary, 9/96

Average Precipitation/Snowfall/Humidity

Precip./Humidity	Jan	Feb	Mar	Apr	May	Jun	Jul	Aug	Sep	Oct	Nov	Dec	Yr.
Avg. Precip. (in.)	1.9	2.2	3.4	3.4	3.8	4.0	3.8	2.9	2.9	2.8	3.0	2.6	36.8
Avg. Snowfall (in.)	6	4	4	Tr	0	0	0	0	0	Tr	1	4	20
Avg. Rel. Hum. 6am (%)	80	81	80	78	81	82	84	86	87	83	81	81	82
Avg. Rel. Hum. 3pm (%)	62	59	54	49	51	51	51	52	50	50	56	63	54

Note: Figures cover the years 1945-1990; Tr = Trace amounts (<0.05 in. of rain; <0.5 in. of snow)
Source: National Climatic Data Center, International Station Meteorological Climate Summary, 9/96

Weather Conditions

Temperature			Daytime Sky			Precipitation		
10°F & below	32°F & below	90°F & above	Clear	Partly cloudy	Cloudy	0.01 inch or more precip.	0.1 inch or more snow/ice	Thunder-storms
13	100	43	97	138	130	109	14	46

Note: Figures are average number of days per year and cover the years 1945-1990
Source: National Climatic Data Center, International Station Meteorological Climate Summary, 9/96

HAZARDOUS WASTE

Superfund Sites

Ballwin has no sites on the EPA's Superfund Final National Priorities List. There are a total of 1,323 Superfund sites on the list in the U.S. *U.S. Environmental Protection Agency, Final National Priorities List, March 18, 2016*

AIR & WATER QUALITY

Air Quality Trends: Ozone

	1990	1995	2000	2005	2010	2011	2012	2013	2014
MSA[1]	0.085	0.092	0.082	0.087	0.075	0.078	0.085	0.069	0.068

Note: (1) Data covers the St. Louis, MO-IL Metropolitan Statistical Area—see Appendix B for areas included. The values shown are the composite ozone concentration averages among trend sites based on the highest fourth daily maximum 8-hour concentration in parts per million. These trends are based on sites having an adequate record of monitoring data during the trend period. Data from exceptional events are included.
Source: U.S. Environmental Protection Agency, Air Quality Monitoring Information, "Air Quality Trends by City, 1990-2014"

Air Quality Index

Area	Percent of Days when Air Quality was...[2]					AQI Statistics[2]	
	Good	Moderate	Unhealthy for Sensitive Groups	Unhealthy	Very Unhealthy	Maximum	Median
MSA[1]	38.6	59.2	1.6	0.5	0.0	154	55

Note: (1) Data covers the St. Louis, MO-IL Metropolitan Statistical Area—see Appendix B for areas included; (2) Based on 365 days with AQI data in 2015. Air Quality Index (AQI) is an index for reporting daily air quality. EPA calculates the AQI for five major air pollutants regulated by the Clean Air Act: ground-level ozone, particle pollution (aka particulate matter), carbon monoxide, sulfur dioxide, and nitrogen dioxide. The AQI runs from 0 to 500. The higher the AQI value, the greater the level of air pollution and the greater the health concern. There are six AQI categories: "Good" AQI is between 0 and 50. Air quality is considered satisfactory; "Moderate" AQI is between 51 and 100. Air quality is acceptable; "Unhealthy for Sensitive Groups" When AQI values are between 101 and 150, members of sensitive groups may experience health effects; "Unhealthy" When AQI values are between 151 and 200 everyone may begin to experience health effects; "Very Unhealthy" AQI values between 201 and 300 trigger a health alert; "Hazardous" AQI values over 300 trigger warnings of emergency conditions (not shown).
Source: U.S. Environmental Protection Agency, Air Quality Index Report, 2015

Air Quality Index Pollutants

Area	Percent of Days when AQI Pollutant was...[2]					
	Carbon Monoxide	Nitrogen Dioxide	Ozone	Sulfur Dioxide	Particulate Matter 2.5	Particulate Matter 10
MSA[1]	0.0	2.2	18.6	0.8	75.1	3.3

Note: (1) Data covers the St. Louis, MO-IL Metropolitan Statistical Area—see Appendix B for areas included; (2) Based on 365 days with AQI data in 2015. The Air Quality Index (AQI) is an index for reporting daily air quality. EPA calculates the AQI for five major air pollutants regulated by the Clean Air Act: ground-level ozone, particle pollution (also known as particulate matter), carbon monoxide, sulfur dioxide, and nitrogen dioxide. The AQI runs from 0 to 500. The higher the AQI value, the greater the level of air pollution and the greater the health concern.
Source: U.S. Environmental Protection Agency, Air Quality Index Report, 2015

Maximum Air Pollutant Concentrations: Particulate Matter, Ozone, CO and Lead

	Particulate Matter 10 (ug/m^3)	Particulate Matter 2.5 Wtd AM (ug/m^3)	Particulate Matter 2.5 24-Hr (ug/m^3)	Ozone (ppm)	Carbon Monoxide (ppm)	Lead (ug/m^3)
MSA[1] Level	159	11.4	29	0.072	1	0.36
NAAQS[2]	150	15	35	0.075	9	0.15
Met NAAQS[2]	No	Yes	Yes	Yes	Yes	No

Note: (1) Data covers the St. Louis, MO-IL Metropolitan Statistical Area—see Appendix B for areas included; Data from exceptional events are included; (2) National Ambient Air Quality Standards; ppm = parts per million; ug/m^3 = micrograms per cubic meter; n/a not available.

Concentrations: Particulate Matter 10 (coarse particulate)—highest second maximum 24-hour concentration; Particulate Matter 2.5 Wtd AM (fine particulate)—highest weighted annual mean concentration; Particulate Matter 2.5 24-Hour (fine particulate)—highest 98th percentile 24-hour concentration; Ozone—highest fourth daily maximum 8-hour concentration; Carbon Monoxide—highest second maximum non-overlapping 8-hour concentration; Lead—maximum running 3-month average

Source: U.S. Environmental Protection Agency, Air Quality Monitoring Information, "Air Quality Statistics by City, 2014"

Maximum Air Pollutant Concentrations: Nitrogen Dioxide and Sulfur Dioxide

	Nitrogen Dioxide AM (ppb)	Nitrogen Dioxide 1-Hr (ppb)	Sulfur Dioxide AM (ppb)	Sulfur Dioxide 1-Hr (ppb)	Sulfur Dioxide 24-Hr (ppb)
MSA[1] Level	14	60	n/a	41	n/a
NAAQS[2]	53	100	30	75	140
Met NAAQS[2]	Yes	Yes	n/a	Yes	n/a

Note: (1) Data covers the St. Louis, MO-IL Metropolitan Statistical Area—see Appendix B for areas included; Data from exceptional events are included; (2) National Ambient Air Quality Standards; ppm = parts per million; ug/m^3 = micrograms per cubic meter; n/a not available.

Concentrations: Nitrogen Dioxide AM—highest arithmetic mean concentration; Nitrogen Dioxide 1-Hr—highest 98th percentile 1-hour daily maximum concentration; Sulfur Dioxide AM—highest annual mean concentration; Sulfur Dioxide 1-Hr—highest 99th percentile 1-hour daily maximum concentration; Sulfur Dioxide 24-Hr—highest second maximum 24-hour concentration

Source: U.S. Environmental Protection Agency, Air Quality Monitoring Information, "Air Quality Statistics by City, 2014"

Drinking Water

Water System Name	Pop. Served	Primary Water Source Type	Violations[1]	
			Health Based	Monitoring/ Reporting
Missouri American Water	1,100,000	Surface	0	0

Note: (1) Based on violation data from January 1, 2015 to December 31, 2015 (includes unresolved violations from earlier years)

Source: U.S. Environmental Protection Agency, Office of Ground Water and Drinking Water, Safe Drinking Water Information System (based on data extracted April 29, 2016)

Chesterfield, Missouri

Background

Chesterfield is only 25 years old and located a half-hour's drive west of downtown St. Louis along the Interstate 64/U.S. Highway 40 corridor. The city calls itself the "City of Volunteers" and is improving its community life via projects such as augmenting walking and biking trails and a master plan for public art to visually enhance the community.

Formed from a collection of six communities settled throughout the mid-to-late 1800s, the community of Chesterfield began in 1816 when a Vermonter named Justus Post arrived and purchased land to start a settlement. Over time, the original Chesterfield re-located. In 1988, the city incorporated; today the city's oldest commercial building is its 1914 bank.

The city sits in the Chesterfield Valley in the Missouri River floodplain, and most recently suffered a major flood in 1993 when the river, at nineteen feet above flood stage, burst through a levee. The community banded together to rebuild, and rallied to boost its levee and flood protection.

Given its suburban proximity to St. Louis, Chesterfield residents benefit from the economic and cultural activities there. However, Chesterfield is home to a Fortune Top 500 company, the Reinsurance Group of America. Other major corporate residents include Abengoa Bioenergy (a division of Abengoa SA of Spain). Major employers within St. Louis County include Boeing Defense Space and Security and Washington University.

Chesterfield's youth attend school in one of two public school systems, the Parkway School District or the Rockwood School District. The former is "Accredited with Distinction" by the Missouri Department of Elementary and Secondary Education, and the latter has been honored for "Distinction in Performance with High Achievement" from the same department. Parkway schools boast a 91.9 percent graduation rate, Rockwood boasts 94.4 percent. A number of private and parochial schools also serve the area.

Higher education based in town includes the Logan College of Chiropractic/University Programs, which in 2012 dedicated a $4.9 million, 13,000-square foot educational wing at its 112-acre campus. The school is one of the continent's largest chiropractic colleges or universities, which also offers two MS degrees (Sports Science and Rehabilitation, and Nutrition and Human Performance) as well as undergraduate degrees.

The city's quality of life is further enhanced by six parks and various public lands. New football and soccer fields and a "lazy river" recently opened at the Chesterfield Family Aquatic Center in 38-acre Central Park—which is also home to the Chesterfield Amphitheater, the Chesterfield Pavilion, the Chesterfield Gazebo, a lake and a hiking trail.

Another city jewel is Faust Park, which includes Thornhill, the original estate of the state's second governor, Frederick Bates. Also onsite is a historic village recreated to represent the different types of architecture found in the region during its 19th century history. Finally, the circa-1920 St. Louis Carousel is here, as well as a Butterfly House affiliated with the Missouri Botanical Garden. Chesterfield's climate is like that of nearby St. Louis, where July's average maximum temperature is 89.3 and January's average minimum temperature is 20.8. Average annual snowfall is 19.5 inches.

Rankings

Business/Finance Rankings

- The personal finance site NerdWallet analyzed 183 American metropolitan areas with populations over 250,000 and more than 15,000 businesses to rank where entrepreneurs find the most success. Criteria included area economy, annual income, housing cost, unemployment rate, and the success rate of area businesses. Saint Louis* ranked #47. *www.nerdwallet.com, "Best Places to Start a Business," April 27, 2015*

- USAA and Hiring Our Heroes worked with Sperlings's BestPlaces and the Institute for Veterans and Military Families at Syracuse University to rank major metropolitan areas where military-skills-related employment is strongest. Criteria for *mid-career* veterans included veteran wage growth; military skills, defense contractor, and government jobs; recent job growth; stability; and accessible health resources. Metro areas with a higher than national average crime or unemployment rate were excluded. At #6, the Saint Louis* metro area made the top ten. *www.usaa.com, "2015 Best Places for Veterans"*

- Based on metro area social media reviews, the employment opinion group Glassdoor surveyed 50 of the largest U.S. metro areas and equally weighed cost of living, hiring opportunity, and job satisfaction to compose a list of "25 Best Cities for Jobs." The Saint Louis* metro area was ranked #11 in overall job satisfaction. *www.glassdoor.com, "Best Cities for Jobs," May 19, 2015*

- In a survey of economic confidence in the nation's 50 largest metropolitan areas conducted January–December 2014, the Saint Louis* metro area placed #38, according to Gallup's 2014 Economic Confidence Index. *Gallup, "San Jose and San Francisco Lead in Economic Confidence," March 19, 2015*

- The Brookings Institution ranked the 100 largest metro areas in the U.S. based on income inequality. Saint Louis* was ranked #59 (#1 = greatest ineqality). Criteria: the "95/20 ratio," a figure representing the income at which a household earns more than 95 percent of all other households, divided by the income at which a household earns more than only 20 percent of all other households. *Brookings Institution, "Income Inequality, 100 Largest U.S. Metro Areas, 2007-2014," January 14, 2016*

- Payscale.com ranked the 20 largest metro areas in terms of wage growth. The Saint Louis* metro area ranked #14. Criteria: private-sector wage growth between the 1st quarter of 2015 and the 1st quarter of 2016. *PayScale, "Wage Trends by Metro Area," 1st Quarter, 2016*

- The Saint Louis* metro area was identified as one of the most debt-ridden places in America by the finance site Credit.com. The metro area was ranked #9. Criteria: residents' average personal debt load and average credit scores. *Credit.com, "The Most Debt-Ridden Cities," May 1, 2014*

- The Saint Louis* metro area was identified as one of the most affordable metropolitan areas in America by *Forbes.* The area ranked #7 out of 20 based on the National Association of Home Builders/Wells Fargo Housing Affordability Index and Sperling's Best Places' cost-of-living index. *Forbes.com, "America's Most Affordable Cities in 2015," March 12, 2015*

- Saint Louis* was identified as one of America's most frugal metro areas by *Coupons.com.* The city ranked #17 out of 25. Criteria: online coupon usage. *Coupons.com, "Top 25 Most Frugal Cities of 2014," May 11, 2015*

- Saint Louis* was identified as one of America's most frugal metro areas by *Coupons.com.* The city ranked #13 out of 25. Criteria: Grocery IQ and coupons.com mobile app usage. *Coupons.com, "Top 25 Most On-the-Go Frugal Cities of 2013," April 10, 2014*

- The Saint Louis* metro area appeared on the Milken Institute "2015 Best Performing Cities" list. Rank: #170 out of 200 large metro areas. Criteria: job growth; wage and salary growth; high-tech output growth. *Milken Institute, "Best-Performing Cities 2015," December 2015*

- *Forbes* ranked the 200 most populous metro areas to determine the nation's "Best Places for Business and Careers." The Saint Louis* metro area was ranked #84. Criteria: costs (business and living); job growth (past and projected); income growth; educational attainment (college and high school); projected economic growth; cultural and recreational opportunities; net migration patterns; number of highly ranked colleges. *Forbes, "The Best Places for Business and Careers 2015," July 29, 2015*

Education Rankings

- Personal finance website *WalletHub* analyzed the 150 largest U.S. metropolitan statistical areas to determine where the most educated Americans are choosing to settle. Criteria: education quality and attainment gap; education levels; percentage of workers with degrees; public school rankings; quality and size of each metro area's universities. Saint Louis* was ranked #35 (#1 = most educated city). *www.WalletHub.com, "2015's Most and Least Educated Cities*

Environmental Rankings

- The Saint Louis* metro area came in at #232 for the relative comfort of its climate on Sperling's list of "chill cities," as measured by the Sperling Heat Index. All 361 metro areas are included. Criteria included daytime high temperatures, nighttime low temperatures, dew point, and relative humidity at the high temperatures. *www.bertsperling.com, "Sperling's Chill Cities," July 18, 2013*

- Sperling's BestPlaces assessed 379 metropolitan areas of the United States for the likelihood of dangerously extreme weather events or earthquakes. In general the Southeast and South-Central regions have the highest risk of weather extremes and earthquakes, while the Pacific Northwest enjoys the lowest risk. Of the least risky metropolitan areas, the Saint Louis* metro area was ranked #327. *www.bestplaces.net, "Safest Places from Natural Disasters," April 2011*

- Saint Louis* was identified as one of America's dirtiest metro areas by *Forbes*. The area ranked #20 out of 20. Criteria: air quality; water quality; toxic releases; superfund sites. *Forbes, "America's 20 Dirtiest Cities," December 10, 2012*

- Saint Louis* was highlighted as one of the 25 most ozone-polluted metro areas in the U.S. during 2011 through 2013. The area ranked #16. *American Lung Association, State of the Air 2015*

Health/Fitness Rankings

- For each of the 50 most populous metro areas in the United States, the American College of Sports Medicine's American Fitness Index evaluated infrastructure, community assets, and policies that encourage healthy and fit lifestyles, including preventive health behaviors, levels of chronic disease conditions, health care access, and community resources and policies that support physical activity. The Saint Louis* metro area ranked #29 for "community fitness." *www.americanfitnessindex.org, "ACSM American Fitness Index Health and Community Fitness Status of the 50 Largest Metropolitan Areas," May 2015*

- The Saint Louis* metro area was identified as one of the worst cities for bed bugs in America by pest control company Orkin. The area ranked #40 out of 50 based on the number of bed bug treatments Orkin performed from January to December 2015. *Orkin, "Chicago Tops Bed Bug Cities List for Fourth Year in a Row," January 13, 2016*

- Saint Louis* was identified as a "2016 Spring Allergy Capital." The area ranked #35 out of 100. Three groups of factors were used to identify the most severe cities for people with allergies during the spring season: annual pollen levels; medicine utilization; access to board-certified allergists. *Asthma and Allergy Foundation of America, "Spring Allergy Capitals 2016"*

- Saint Louis* was identified as a "2015 Asthma Capital." The area ranked #26 out of the nation's 100 largest metropolitan areas. Criteria: estimated prevalence; self-reported prevalence; crude death rate for asthma; annual pollen score; annual air quality; public smoking laws; number of board-certified asthma specialists; school inhaler access laws; rescue medication use; controller medication use; ER visits for asthma; uninsured rate; poverty rate. *Asthma and Allergy Foundation of America, "Asthma Capitals 2015"*

- The Saint Louis* metro area ranked #162 out of 190 in The Gallup-Healthways Well-Being Index. Criteria: purpose; social well being; financial health; community and physical health. Results are based on telephone interviews with adults, aged 18 and older, living in metropolitan areas in the 50 U.S. states and the District of Columbia. *Gallup-Healthways, "State of American Well-Being," February 23, 2016*

Real Estate Rankings

- Based on the home-price forecasts compiled by the real-estate valuation firm CoreLogic Case-Shiller, CNNMoney reported that in 2016, the Saint Louis* metro area is expected to be one of the hottest housing markets in the U.S. Criteria: residential real estate prices. *money.cnn.com, "The 10 Hottest Housing Markets for 2016," December 3, 2015*
- The Saint Louis* metro area appeared on Realtor.com's list of the hottest housing markets to watch in 2016. The area ranked #2. Criteria: strong housing growth; affordable prices; and fast-paced sales. *Realtor.com®, "Top 10 Hot Real Estate Markets to Watch in 2016," December 2, 2015*
- Saint Louis* was ranked #50 out of 225 metro areas in terms of housing affordability in 2015 by the National Association of Home Builders (#1 = most affordable). Criteria: the share of homes sold in that area affordable to a family earning the local median income, based on standard mortgage underwriting criteria. *National Association of Home Builders®, NAHB-Wells Fargo Housing Opportunity Index, 4th Quarter 2015*

Safety Rankings

- The National Insurance Crime Bureau ranked 380 metro areas in the U.S. in terms of per capita rates of vehicle theft. The Saint Louis* metro area ranked #102 (#1 = highest rate). Criteria: number of vehicle theft offenses per 100,000 inhabitants in 2014. *National Insurance Crime Bureau, "Hot Spots 2014," June 24, 2015*

Seniors/Retirement Rankings

- From its Best Cities for Successful Aging indexes, the Milken Institute generated rankings for metropolitan areas, weighing data in eight categories—health care, wellness, living arrangements, transportation, financial characteristics, education and employment opportunities, community engagement, and overall livability. The Saint Louis* metro area was ranked #30 overall in the large metro area category. *Milken Institute, "Best Cities for Successful Aging, 2014"*

Miscellaneous Rankings

- The watchdog site Charity Navigator conducts an annual study of charities in the nation's major markets both to analyze statistical differences in their financial, accountability, and transparency practices and to track year-to-year variations in individual communities. The Saint Louis* metro area was ranked #16 among the 30 metro markets in the rating dimension of Overall Score. *www.charitynavigator.org, "Metro Market Study 2015," June 5, 2015*
- Mars Chocolate North America, the makers of COMBOS®, in partnership with Sperling's BestPlaces, ranked 50 major metro areas in terms of their "manliness." The Saint Louis* metro area ranked #7. Criteria: number of professional sports teams; number of nearby NASCAR tracks and racing events; manly lifestyle; concentration of manly retail stores; manly occupations per capita; salty snack sales; "Board of Manliness" rankings. *Mars Chocolate North America, "America's Manliest Cities 2012"*
- The Saint Louis* metro area was selected as one of "America's Most Miserable Cities" by *Forbes.com.* The metro area ranked #12 out of 20. Criteria: violent crime; unemployment; foreclosures; income and property taxes; home prices; commute times; climate. *Forbes.com, "America's Most Miserable Cities" February 22, 2013*
- The National Alliance to End Homelessness ranked the 100 most populous metro areas with the highest rate of homelessness. The Saint Louis* metro area ranked #64. Criteria: number of homeless people per 10,000 population in 2011. *National Alliance to End Homelessness, The State of Homelessness in America 2012*

Chesterfield is located within the St. Louis, MO-IL Metropolitan Statistical Area.

Business Environment

CITY FINANCES

City Government Finances

Component	2012 ($000)	2012 ($ per capita)
Total Revenues	34,660	729
Total Expenditures	34,462	725
Debt Outstanding	69,906	1,472
Cash and Securities[1]	23,647	498

Note: (1) Cash and security holdings of a government at the close of its fiscal year, including those of its dependent agencies, utilities, and liquor stores.
Source: U.S Census Bureau, State & Local Government Finances 2012

City Government Revenue by Source

Source	2012 ($000)	2012 ($ per capita)
General Revenue		
From Federal Government	284	5
From State Government	1,983	41
From Local Governments	19,692	414
Taxes		
Property	953	20
Sales and Gross Receipts	7,223	152
Personal Income	0	0
Corporate Income	0	0
Motor Vehicle License	0	0
Other Taxes	1,429	30
Current Charges	1,306	27
Liquor Store	0	0
Utility	0	0
Employee Retirement	0	0

Source: U.S Census Bureau, State & Local Government Finances 2012

City Government Expenditures by Function

Function	2012 ($000)	2012 ($ per capita)	2012 (%)
General Direct Expenditures			
Air Transportation	0	0	0.0
Corrections	0	0	0.0
Education	0	0	0.0
Employment Security Administration	0	0	0.0
Financial Administration	543	11	1.5
Fire Protection	0	0	0.0
General Public Buildings	717	15	2.0
Governmental Administration, Other	2,234	47	6.4
Health	0	0	0.0
Highways	7,190	151	20.8
Hospitals	0	0	0.0
Housing and Community Development	0	0	0.0
Interest on General Debt	2,996	63	8.6
Judicial and Legal	238	5	0.6
Libraries	0	0	0.0
Parking	0	0	0.0
Parks and Recreation	9,671	203	28.0
Police Protection	7,561	159	21.9
Public Welfare	0	0	0.0
Sewerage	283	5	0.8
Solid Waste Management	0	0	0.0
Veterans' Services	0	0	0.0
Liquor Store	0	0	0.0
Utility	0	0	0.0
Employee Retirement	0	0	0.0

Source: U.S Census Bureau, State & Local Government Finances 2012

DEMOGRAPHICS

Population Growth

Area	1990 Census	2000 Census	2010 Census	2014* Estimate	Population Growth (%) 1990-2014	Population Growth (%) 2010-2014
City	41,843	46,802	47,484	47,651	13.9	0.4
MSA[1]	2,580,897	2,698,687	2,812,896	2,797,737	8.4	-0.5
U.S.	248,709,873	281,421,906	308,745,538	314,107,084	26.3	1.7

Note: (1) Figures cover the St. Louis, MO-IL Metropolitan Statistical Area—see Appendix B for areas included; (*) 2010-2014 5-year estimated population
Source: U.S. Census Bureau, 1990 Census, Census 2000, Census 2010, 2010-2014 American Community Survey 5-Year Estimates

Household Size

Area	Persons in Household (%) One	Two	Three	Four	Five	Six	Seven or More	Average Household Size
City	25.2	38.6	15.8	14.0	4.6	1.1	0.3	2.50
MSA[1]	29.2	33.8	15.7	12.8	5.5	1.7	0.8	2.48
U.S.	27.5	33.5	15.8	13.1	6.0	2.3	1.4	2.64

Note: (1) Figures cover the St. Louis, MO-IL Metropolitan Statistical Area—see Appendix B for areas included
Source: U.S. Census Bureau, 2010-2014 American Community Survey 5-Year Estimates

Race

Area	White Alone[2] (%)	Black Alone[2] (%)	Asian Alone[2] (%)	AIAN[3] Alone[2] (%)	NHOPI[4] Alone[2] (%)	Other Race Alone[2] (%)	Two or More Races (%)
City	84.7	3.6	9.3	0.1	0.0	0.8	1.5
MSA[1]	76.5	18.3	2.2	0.2	0.0	0.6	2.1
U.S.	73.8	12.6	5.0	0.8	0.2	4.7	2.9

Note: (1) Figures cover the St. Louis, MO-IL Metropolitan Statistical Area—see Appendix B for areas included; (2) Alone is defined as not being in combination with one or more other races; (3) American Indian and Alaska Native; (4) Native Hawaiian and Other Pacific Islander
Source: U.S. Census Bureau, 2010-2014 American Community Survey 5-Year Estimates

Hispanic or Latino Origin

Area	Total (%)	Mexican (%)	Puerto Rican (%)	Cuban (%)	Other (%)
City	3.5	1.7	0.5	0.3	1.0
MSA[1]	2.7	1.8	0.2	0.1	0.6
U.S.	16.9	10.8	1.6	0.6	3.8

Note: Persons of Hispanic or Latino origin can be of any race; (1) Figures cover the St. Louis, MO-IL Metropolitan Statistical Area—see Appendix B for areas included
Source: U.S. Census Bureau, 2010-2014 American Community Survey 5-Year Estimates

Ancestry

Area	German	Irish	English	American	Italian	Polish	French[2]	Scottish	Dutch
City	28.9	14.9	11.1	6.9	4.5	3.5	3.5	1.9	1.3
MSA[1]	29.3	13.8	8.1	7.3	4.8	2.6	3.6	1.5	1.3
U.S.	14.9	10.8	8.0	7.1	5.5	3.0	2.7	1.7	1.4

Note: Figures are the percentage of the total population reporting a particular ancestry. The nine most commonly reported ancestries in the U.S. are shown. Figures include multiple ancestries (e.g. if a person reported being Irish and Italian, they were included in both columns); (1) Figures cover the St. Louis, MO-IL Metropolitan Statistical Area—see Appendix B for areas included; (2) Excludes Basque
Source: U.S. Census Bureau, 2010-2014 American Community Survey 5-Year Estimates

Foreign-Born Population

Area	Percent of Population Born in								
	Any Foreign Country	Asia	Mexico	Europe	Carribean	Central America[2]	South America	Africa	Canada
City	11.3	7.1	0.5	2.1	0.2	0.1	0.6	0.2	0.3
MSA[1]	4.5	1.9	0.6	1.2	0.1	0.1	0.1	0.3	0.1
U.S.	13.1	3.8	3.7	1.5	1.2	1.0	0.9	0.6	0.3

Note: (1) Figures cover the St. Louis, MO-IL Metropolitan Statistical Area—see Appendix B for areas included; (2) Excludes Mexico.
Source: U.S. Census Bureau, 2010-2014 American Community Survey 5-Year Estimates

Marital Status

Area	Never Married	Now Married[2]	Separated	Widowed	Divorced
City	21.1	61.7	0.8	6.7	9.8
MSA[1]	31.8	48.9	1.8	6.3	11.2
U.S.	32.5	48.4	2.2	5.9	10.9

Note: Figures are percentages and cover the population 15 years of age and older; (1) Figures cover the St. Louis, MO-IL Metropolitan Statistical Area—see Appendix B for areas included; (2) Excludes separated
Source: U.S. Census Bureau, 2010-2014 American Community Survey 5-Year Estimates

Disability Status

Area	All Ages	Under 18 Years Old	18 to 64 Years Old	65 Years and Over
City	8.5	4.4	4.4	25.5
MSA[1]	12.1	4.3	10.0	35.2
U.S.	12.3	4.1	10.2	36.3

Note: Figures show percent of the civilian noninstitutionalized population that reported having a disability. Disability status is determined from from six types of difficulty: vision, hearing, cognitive, ambulatory, self-care, and independent living. For children under 5 years old, hearing and vision difficulty are used to determine disability status. For children between the ages of 5 and 14, disability status is determined from hearing, vision, cognitive, ambulatory, and self-care difficulties. For people aged 15 years and older, they are considered to have a disability if they have difficulty with any one of the six difficulty types; (1) Figures cover the St. Louis, MO-IL Metropolitan Statistical Area—see Appendix B for areas included.
Source: U.S. Census Bureau, 2010-2014 American Community Survey 5-Year Estimates

Age

Area	Percent of Population									Median Age
	Under Age 5	Age 5–19	Age 20–34	Age 35–44	Age 45–54	Age 55–64	Age 65–74	Age 75–84	Age 85+	
City	4.7	19.0	13.2	10.5	16.9	13.7	11.7	6.9	3.5	46.6
MSA[1]	6.1	19.7	19.9	12.5	14.8	12.9	7.6	4.5	2.0	38.5
U.S.	6.4	19.9	20.6	13.0	14.1	12.3	7.6	4.3	1.9	37.4

Note: (1) Figures cover the St. Louis, MO-IL Metropolitan Statistical Area—see Appendix B for areas included
Source: U.S. Census Bureau, 2010-2014 American Community Survey 5-Year Estimates

Gender

Area	Males	Females	Males per 100 Females
City	22,225	25,426	87.4
MSA[1]	1,354,888	1,442,849	93.9
U.S.	154,515,159	159,591,925	96.8

Note: (1) Figures cover the St. Louis, MO-IL Metropolitan Statistical Area—see Appendix B for areas included
Source: U.S. Census Bureau, 2010-2014 American Community Survey 5-Year Estimates

Religious Groups by Family

Area	Catholic	Baptist	Non-Den.	Methodist[2]	Lutheran	LDS[3]	Pentecostal	Presbyterian[4]	Muslim[5]	Judaism
MSA[1]	19.8	10.0	3.8	3.4	4.1	0.6	1.2	3.0	0.4	0.7
U.S.	19.1	9.3	4.0	4.0	2.3	2.0	1.9	1.6	0.8	0.7

Note: Figures are the number of adherents as a percentage of the total population; (1) Figures cover the St. Louis, MO-IL Metropolitan Statistical Area—see Appendix B for areas included; (2) Methodist/Pietist; (3) Latter Day Saints; (4) Reformed; (5) Figures are estimates
Source: Association of Statisticians of American Religious Bodies, 2010 U.S. Religion Census: Religious Congregations & Membership Study

Religious Groups by Tradition

Area	Catholic	Evangelical Protestant	Mainline Protestant	Other Tradition	Black Protestant	Orthodox
MSA[1]	19.8	17.4	7.3	2.3	2.1	0.2
U.S.	19.1	16.2	7.3	4.3	1.6	0.3

Note: Figures are the number of adherents as a percentage of the total population; (1) Figures cover the St. Louis, MO-IL Metropolitan Statistical Area—see Appendix B for areas included
Source: Association of Statisticians of American Religious Bodies, 2010 U.S. Religion Census: Religious Congregations & Membership Study

ECONOMY

Gross Metropolitan Product

Area	2013	2014	2015	2016	Rank[2]
MSA[1]	146.0	150.2	154.6	161.1	22

Note: Figures are in billions of dollars; (1) Figures cover the St. Louis, MO-IL Metropolitan Statistical Area—see Appendix B for areas included; (2) Rank is based on 2016 data and ranges from 1 to 381
Source: The U.S. Conference of Mayors, U.S. Metro Economies: GMP and Employment 2014-2016, June 2015

Economic Growth

Area	2011-13 (%)	2014 (%)	2015 (%)	2016 (%)	Rank[2]
MSA[1]	0.9	1.2	1.5	2.2	236
U.S.	2.2	2.4	2.3	2.9	–

Note: Figures are real gross metropolitan product (GMP) growth rates and represent annual average percent change; (1) Figures cover the St. Louis, MO-IL Metropolitan Statistical Area—see Appendix B for areas included; (2) Rank is based on 2016 data and ranges from 1 to 381
Source: The U.S. Conference of Mayors, U.S. Metro Economies: GMP and Employment 2014-2016, June 2015

Metropolitan Area Exports

Area	2009	2010	2011	2012	2013	2014	Rank[2]
MSA[1]	9,026.6	11,239.4	12,307.5	14,642.3	12,393.6	10,359.8	31

Note: Figures are in millions of dollars; (1) Figures cover the St. Louis, MO-IL Metropolitan Statistical Area—see Appendix B for areas included; (2) Rank is based on 2014 data and ranges from 1 to 385
Source: U.S. Department of Commerce, International Trade Administration, Office of Trade & Industry Information, Manufacturing & Services, data extracted March 10, 2016

Building Permits

Area	Single-Family			Multi-Family			Total		
	2014	2015p	Pct. Chg.	2014	2015p	Pct. Chg.	2014	2015p	Pct. Chg.
City	n/a	n/a	n/a	n/a	n/a	n/a	n/a	n/a	n/a
MSA[1]	4,538	5,008	10.4	2,454	2,290	-6.7	6,992	7,298	4.4
U.S.	640,300	690,800	7.9	411,800	487,600	18.4	1,052,100	1,178,400	12.0

Note: (1) Figures cover the St. Louis, MO-IL Metropolitan Statistical Area—see Appendix B for areas included; Figures represent new, privately-owned housing units authorized (unadjusted data); All permit data are based on estimates with imputation; (p) preliminary data.
Source: U.S. Census Bureau, Manufacturing, Mining, and Construction Statistics, Building Permits, 2014, 2015

Bankruptcy Filings

Area	Business Filings 2014	Business Filings 2015	Business Filings % Chg.	Nonbusiness Filings 2014	Nonbusiness Filings 2015	Nonbusiness Filings % Chg.
Saint Louis County	43	68	58.1	4,418	3,924	-11.2
U.S.	26,983	24,735	-8.3	909,812	819,760	-9.9

Note: Business filings include Chapter 7, Chapter 11, Chapter 12, and Chapter 13; Nonbusiness filings include Chapter 7, Chapter 11, and Chapter 13
Source: Administrative Office of the U.S. Courts, Business and Nonbusiness Bankruptcy, County Cases Commenced by Chapter of the Bankruptcy Code, During the 12- Month Period Ending December 31, 2014 and Business and Nonbusiness Bankruptcy, County Cases Commenced by Chapter of the Bankruptcy Code, During the 12- Month Period Ending December 31, 2015

Housing Vacancy Rates

Area	Gross Vacancy Rate[2] (%)			Year-Round Vacancy Rate[3] (%)			Rental Vacancy Rate[4] (%)			Homeowner Vacancy Rate[5] (%)		
	2013	2014	2015	2013	2014	2015	2013	2014	2015	2013	2014	2015
MSA[1]	15.1	12.3	10.7	14.9	12.0	10.3	13.2	10.3	9.7	3.5	2.4	3.1
U.S.	13.6	13.4	12.9	10.7	10.4	10.0	8.3	7.6	7.1	2.0	1.9	1.8

Note: (1) Figures cover the St. Louis, MO-IL Metropolitan Statistical Area—see Appendix B for areas included; (2) The percentage of the total housing inventory that is vacant; (3) The percentage of the housing inventory (excluding seasonal units) that is year-round vacant; (4) The percentage of rental inventory that is vacant for rent; (5) The percentage of homeowner inventory that is vacant for sale
Source: U.S. Census Bureau, Housing Vacancies and Homeownership Annual Statistics: 2015

INCOME

Income

Area	Per Capita ($)	Median Household ($)	Average Household ($)
City	52,010	94,263	127,077
MSA[1]	30,024	54,959	74,420
U.S.	28,555	53,482	74,596

Note: (1) Figures cover the St. Louis, MO-IL Metropolitan Statistical Area—see Appendix B for areas included
Source: U.S. Census Bureau, 2010-2014 American Community Survey 5-Year Estimates

Household Income Distribution

Area	Percent of Households Earning: Under $15,000	$15,000 -24,999	$25,000 -34,999	$35,000 -49,999	$50,000 -74,999	$75,000 -99,000	$100,000 -149,999	$150,000 and up
City	4.7	6.7	5.8	9.0	14.4	12.5	17.9	29.0
MSA[1]	11.7	10.2	10.0	13.6	18.3	12.8	13.7	9.6
U.S.	12.5	10.7	10.2	13.5	17.8	12.2	13.0	10.0

Note: (1) Figures cover the St. Louis, MO-IL Metropolitan Statistical Area—see Appendix B for areas included
Source: U.S. Census Bureau, 2010-2014 American Community Survey 5-Year Estimates

Poverty Rate

Area	All Ages	Under 18 Years Old	18 to 64 Years Old	65 Years and Over
City	4.8	5.9	5.0	3.3
MSA[1]	13.2	18.9	12.3	7.5
U.S.	15.6	21.9	14.6	9.4

Note: Figures are percentage of people whose income during the past 12 months was below the poverty level; (1) Figures cover the St. Louis, MO-IL Metropolitan Statistical Area—see Appendix B for areas included
Source: U.S. Census Bureau, 2010-2014 American Community Survey 5-Year Estimates

EMPLOYMENT

Labor Force and Employment

Area	Civilian Labor Force Dec. 2014	Civilian Labor Force Dec. 2015	Civilian Labor Force % Chg.	Workers Employed Dec. 2014	Workers Employed Dec. 2015	Workers Employed % Chg.
City	24,675	25,312	2.5	23,847	24,648	3.3
MSA[1]	1,448,218	1,479,973	2.1	1,372,069	1,416,204	3.2
U.S.	155,521,000	157,245,000	1.1	147,190,000	149,703,000	1.7

Note: Data is not seasonally adjusted and covers workers 16 years of age and older; (1) Figures cover the St. Louis, MO-IL Metropolitan Statistical Area—see Appendix B for areas included
Source: Bureau of Labor Statistics, Local Area Unemployment Statistics

Unemployment Rate

Area	2015											
	Jan.	Feb.	Mar.	Apr.	May	Jun.	Jul.	Aug.	Sep.	Oct.	Nov.	Dec.
City	3.9	4.0	4.1	3.9	4.3	4.1	4.0	3.4	3.2	3.0	2.8	2.6
MSA[1]	6.0	6.0	5.9	5.3	5.5	5.6	5.7	5.1	4.6	4.6	4.6	4.3
U.S.	6.1	5.8	5.6	5.1	5.3	5.5	5.6	5.2	4.9	4.8	4.8	4.8

Note: Data is not seasonally adjusted and covers workers 16 years of age and older; (1) Figures cover the St. Louis, MO-IL Metropolitan Statistical Area—see Appendix B for areas included
Source: Bureau of Labor Statistics, Local Area Unemployment Statistics

Employment by Occupation

Occupation Classification	City (%)	MSA[1] (%)	U.S. (%)
Management, Business, Science, and Arts	59.2	38.0	36.4
Natural Resources, Construction, and Maintenance	1.8	7.7	9.0
Production, Transportation, and Material Moving	3.7	11.2	12.1
Sales and Office	25.5	25.6	24.4
Service	9.8	17.5	18.2

Note: Figures cover employed civilians 16 years of age and older; (1) Figures cover the St. Louis, MO-IL Metropolitan Statistical Area—see Appendix B for areas included
Source: U.S. Census Bureau, 2010-2014 American Community Survey 5-Year Estimates

Employment by Industry

Sector	MSA[1]		U.S.
	Number of Employees	Percent of Total	Percent of Total
Construction, Mining, and Logging	63,100	4.6	5.0
Education and Health Services	243,900	17.9	15.7
Financial Activities	86,300	6.3	5.7
Government	163,900	12.0	15.5
Information	28,000	2.0	1.9
Leisure and Hospitality	143,100	10.5	10.4
Manufacturing	113,000	8.3	8.6
Other Services	48,100	3.5	3.9
Professional and Business Services	208,200	15.3	13.9
Retail Trade	146,100	10.7	11.3
Transportation, Warehousing, and Utilities	51,400	3.7	3.9
Wholesale Trade	63,400	4.6	4.1

Note: Figures are non-farm employment as of December 2015. Figures are not seasonally adjusted and include workers 16 years of age and older; (1) Figures cover the St. Louis, MO-IL Metropolitan Statistical Area—see Appendix B for areas included; n/a not available
Source: Bureau of Labor Statistics, Current Employment Statistics, Employment, Hours, and Earnings

Occupations with Greatest Projected Employment Growth: 2012 – 2022

Occupation[1]	2012 Employment	2022 Projected Employment	Numeric Employment Change	Percent Employment Change
Combined Food Preparation and Serving Workers, Including Fast Food	71,840	81,660	9,820	13.7
Personal Care Aides	31,360	40,430	9,070	28.9
Registered Nurses	66,970	74,990	8,020	12.0
Customer Service Representatives	49,990	56,010	6,020	12.0
Retail Salespersons	81,140	86,700	5,560	6.8
Nursing Assistants	42,320	47,470	5,150	12.2
General and Operations Managers	53,130	58,220	5,090	9.6
Secretaries and Administrative Assistants, Except Legal, Medical, and Executive	52,290	56,860	4,570	8.7
Carpenters	21,880	26,280	4,400	20.1
Heavy and Tractor-Trailer Truck Drivers	42,720	47,030	4,310	10.1

Note: Projections cover Missouri; (1) Sorted by numeric employment change
Source: www.projectionscentral.com, State Occupational Projections, 2012–2022 Long-Term Projections

Fastest Growing Occupations: 2012 – 2022

Occupation[1]	2012 Employment	2022 Projected Employment	Numeric Employment Change	Percent Employment Change
Insulation Workers, Mechanical	490	730	240	48.8
Helpers—Brickmasons, Blockmasons, Stonemasons, and Tile and Marble Setters	470	660	190	40.4
Helpers—Electricians	370	510	140	37.9
Insulation Workers, Floor, Ceiling, and Wall	490	680	190	37.5
Diagnostic Medical Sonographers	1,120	1,520	400	35.5
Interpreters and Translators	960	1,270	310	32.7
Brickmasons and Blockmasons	2,370	3,130	760	32.0
Nursing Instructors and Teachers, Postsecondary	1,350	1,780	430	31.9
Health Specialties Teachers, Postsecondary	3,370	4,420	1,050	31.1
Skincare Specialists	1,430	1,860	430	30.5

Note: Projections cover Missouri; (1) Sorted by percent employment change and excludes occupations with numeric employment change less than 100
Source: www.projectionscentral.com, State Occupational Projections, 2012–2022 Long-Term Projections

Average Wages

Occupation	$/Hr.	Occupation	$/Hr.
Accountants and Auditors	37.50	Maids and Housekeeping Cleaners	10.36
Automotive Mechanics	20.95	Maintenance and Repair Workers	19.01
Bookkeepers	19.10	Marketing Managers	66.57
Carpenters	26.82	Nuclear Medicine Technologists	33.83
Cashiers	10.22	Nurses, Licensed Practical	20.33
Clerks, General Office	15.53	Nurses, Registered	29.20
Clerks, Receptionists/Information	12.44	Nursing Assistants	12.03
Clerks, Shipping/Receiving	16.25	Packers and Packagers, Hand	11.44
Computer Programmers	40.55	Physical Therapists	37.83
Computer Systems Analysts	44.34	Postal Service Mail Carriers	24.38
Computer User Support Specialists	25.26	Real Estate Brokers	15.47
Cooks, Restaurant	11.65	Retail Salespersons	13.21
Dentists	83.85	Sales Reps., Exc. Tech./Scientific	32.93
Electrical Engineers	48.11	Sales Reps., Tech./Scientific	35.44
Electricians	30.18	Secretaries, Exc. Legal/Med./Exec.	16.37
Financial Managers	63.93	Security Guards	13.13
First-Line Supervisors/Managers, Sales	21.20	Surgeons	n/a
Food Preparation Workers	10.12	Teacher Assistants*	12.99
General and Operations Managers	53.15	Teachers, Elementary School*	27.63
Hairdressers/Cosmetologists	12.87	Teachers, Secondary School*	27.07
Internists	127.15	Telemarketers	12.35
Janitors and Cleaners	11.59	Truck Drivers, Heavy/Tractor-Trailer	20.70
Landscaping/Groundskeeping Workers	13.20	Truck Drivers, Light/Delivery Svcs.	17.44
Lawyers	55.39	Waiters and Waitresses	9.46

Note: Wage data covers the St. Louis, MO-IL Metropolitan Statistical Area—see Appendix B for areas included; (*) Hourly wages for elementary/secondary school teachers and teacher assistants were calculated by the editors from annual wage data based on a 40 hour work week; n/a not available.
Source: Bureau of Labor Statistics, Metro Area Occupational Employment and Wage Estimates, May 2015

TAXES

State Corporate Income Tax Rates

State	Tax Rate (%)	Income Brackets ($)	Num. of Brackets	Financial Institution Tax Rate (%)[a]	Federal Income Tax Ded.
Missouri	6.25	Flat rate	1	7.0	Yes (k)

Note: Tax rates as of January 1, 2016; (a) Rates listed are the corporate income tax rate applied to financial institutions or excise taxes based on income. Some states have other taxes based upon the value of deposits or shares; (k) 50% of the federal income tax is deductible.
Source: Federation of Tax Administrators, "State Corporate Income Tax Rates, 2016"

State Individual Income Tax Rates

State	Tax Rate (%)	Income Brackets ($)	Num. of Brackets	Personal Exempt. ($)[1] Single	Personal Exempt. ($)[1] Dependents	Fed. Inc. Tax Ded.
Missouri	1.5 - 6.0	1,000 - 9,001	10	2,100	1,200	Yes (m)

Note: Tax rates as of January 1, 2016; Local- and county-level taxes are not included; n/a not applicable; (1) Married joint filers generally receive double the single exemption; (m) The deduction for federal income tax is limited to $5,000 for individuals and $10,000 for joint returns in Missouri and Montana, and to $6,350 for all filers in Oregon.
Source: Federation of Tax Administrators, "State Individual Income Tax Rates, 2016"

Various State and Local Tax Rates

State	State and Local Sales and Use (%)	State Sales and Use (%)	Gasoline[1] (¢/gal.)	Cigarette[2] ($/pack)	Spirits[3] ($/gal.)	Wine[4] ($/gal.)	Beer[5] ($/gal.)
Missouri	8.113	4.225	17.3	0.17	2.00	0.42	0.06

Note: All tax rates as of January 1, 2016; (1) The American Petroleum Institute has developed a methodology for determining the average tax rate on a gallon of fuel. Rates may include any of the following: excise taxes, environmental fees, storage tank fees, other fees or taxes, general sales tax, and local taxes. In states where gasoline is subject to the general sales tax, or where the fuel tax is based on the average sale price, the average rate determined by API is sensitive to changes in the price of gasoline. States that fully or partially apply general sales taxes to gasoline: CA, CO, GA, IL, IN, MI, NY; (2) The federal excise tax of $1.0066 per pack and local taxes are not included; (3) Rates are those applicable to off-premise sales of 40% alcohol by volume (a.b.v.) distilled spirits in 750ml containers. Local excise taxes are excluded; (4) Rates are those applicable to off-premise sales of 11% a.b.v. non-carbonated wine in 750ml containers; (5) Rates are those applicable to off-premise sales of 4.7% a.b.v. beer in 12 ounce containers.
Source: Tax Foundation, 2016 Facts & Figures: How Does Your State Compare?

State Business Tax Climate Index Rankings

State	Overall Rank	Corporate Tax Rank	Individual Income Tax Rank	Sales Tax Rank	Unemployment Insurance Tax Rank	Property Tax Rank
Missouri	17	3	28	23	12	8

Note: The index is a measure of how each state's tax laws affect economic performance. The lower the rank, the more favorable a state's tax system is for business. States without a given tax are given a ranking of 1. The scores/rankings for the District of Columbia do not affect other states. The 2016 index represents the tax climate as of July 1, 2015 (the beginning of Fiscal Year 2016).
Source: Tax Foundation, State Business Tax Climate Index 2016

TRANSPORTATION

Means of Transportation to Work

Area	Car/Truck/Van: Drove Alone	Car/Truck/Van: Car-pooled	Public Transportation: Bus	Public Transportation: Subway	Public Transportation: Railroad	Bicycle	Walked	Other Means	Worked at Home
City	86.6	5.3	0.3	0.0	0.0	0.1	0.7	0.7	6.3
MSA[1]	83.0	7.7	2.1	0.4	0.1	0.3	1.8	0.9	3.9
U.S.	76.4	9.6	2.6	1.8	0.6	0.6	2.8	1.3	4.4

Note: Figures are percentages and cover workers 16 years of age and older; (1) Figures cover the St. Louis, MO-IL Metropolitan Statistical Area—see Appendix B for areas included
Source: U.S. Census Bureau, 2010-2014 American Community Survey 5-Year Estimates

Travel Time to Work

Area	Less Than 10 Minutes	10 to 19 Minutes	20 to 29 Minutes	30 to 44 Minutes	45 to 59 Minutes	60 to 89 Minutes	90 Minutes or More
City	10.6	31.1	27.4	24.5	4.9	0.7	0.9
MSA[1]	11.2	28.2	24.0	23.2	8.0	3.9	1.5
U.S.	13.3	29.6	21.0	20.2	7.7	5.7	2.6

Note: Figures are percentages and include workers 16 years old and over; (1) Figures cover the St. Louis, MO-IL Metropolitan Statistical Area—see Appendix B for areas included
Source: U.S. Census Bureau, 2010-2014 American Community Survey 5-Year Estimates

Freeway Travel Time Index

Area	1985	1990	1995	2000	2005	2010	2014
Urban Area Rank[1,2]	48	56	47	57	61	57	65
Urban Area Index[1]	1.07	1.09	1.13	1.15	1.16	1.16	1.16
Average Index[3]	1.09	1.11	1.14	1.17	1.20	1.19	1.20

Note: Freeway Travel Time Index—the ratio of travel time in the peak period to the travel time at free-flow conditions. For example, a value of 1.30 indicates a 20-minute free-flow trip takes 26 minutes in the peak (20 minutes x 1.30 = 26 minutes); (1) Covers the St. Louis MO-IL urban area; (2) Rank is based on 101 urban areas (#1 = highest travel time index); (3) Average of 101 urban areas

Source: Texas Transportation Institute, 2015 Urban Mobility Scorecard, August 2015

Freeway Commuter Stress Index

Area	1985	1990	1995	2000	2005	2010	2014
Urban Area Rank[1,2]	53	59	55	63	68	65	61
Urban Area Index[1]	1.09	1.11	1.15	1.17	1.18	1.18	1.19
Average Index[3]	1.13	1.16	1.19	1.22	1.25	1.24	1.25

Note: The Freeway Commuter Stress Index is the same as the Freeway Travel Time Index (see table above) except that it includes only the travel in the peak directions during the peak periods; the TTI includes travel in all directions during the peak period. Thus, the CSI is more indicative of the work trip experienced by each commuter on a daily basis. (1) Covers the St. Louis MO-IL urban area; (2) Rank is based on 101 urban areas (#1 = highest stress index); (3) Average of 101 urban areas

Source: Texas Transportation Institute, 2015 Urban Mobility Scorecard, August 2015

Living Environment

COST OF LIVING

Cost of Living Index

Composite Index	Groceries	Housing	Utilities	Trans-portation	Health Care	Misc. Goods/ Services
92.5	104.6	72.3	116.6	98.5	99.8	94.3

Note: The Cost of Living Index measures regional differences in the cost of consumer goods and services, excluding taxes and non-consumer expenditures, for professional and managerial households in the top income quintile. It is based on more than 50,000 prices covering almost 60 different items for which prices are collected three times a year by chambers of commerce, economic development organizations or university applied economic centers in each participating urban area. The numbers shown should be read as a percentage above or below the national average of 100. For example, a value of 115.4 in the groceries column indicates that grocery prices are 15.4% higher than the national average. Small differences in the index numbers should not be interpreted as significant; Figures cover the St. Louis MO-IL urban area.
Source: The Council for Community and Economic Research, ACCRA Cost of Living Index, 2015

Grocery Prices

Area[1]	T-Bone Steak ($/pound)	Frying Chicken ($/pound)	Whole Milk ($/half gal.)	Eggs ($/dozen)	Orange Juice ($/64 oz.)	Coffee ($/11.5 oz.)
City[2]	11.55	2.02	2.46	2.48	3.61	4.56
Avg.	10.99	1.43	2.25	2.26	3.58	4.48
Min.	7.16	0.98	1.30	1.35	2.88	2.98
Max.	14.13	2.43	3.85	4.81	6.39	7.56

Note: (1) Values for the local area are compared with the average, minimum and maximum values for all 292 areas in the Cost of Living Index; (2) Figures cover the St. Louis MO-IL urban area; **T-Bone Steak** *(price per pound);* **Frying Chicken** *(price per pound, whole fryer);* **Whole Milk** *(half gallon carton);* **Eggs** *(price per dozen, Grade A, large);* **Orange Juice** *(64 oz. Tropicana or Florida Natural);* **Coffee** *(11.5 oz. can, vacuum-packed, Maxwell House, Hills Bros, or Folgers).*
Source: The Council for Community and Economic Research, ACCRA Cost of Living Index, 2015

Housing and Utility Costs

Area[1]	New Home Price ($)	Apartment Rent ($/month)	All Electric ($/month)	Part Electric ($/month)	Other Energy ($/month)	Telephone ($/month)
City[2]	207,522	832	-	95.19	70.93	40.32
Avg.	312,874	945	179.30	95.07	72.96	28.11
Min.	178,682	479	116.28	43.14	26.46	10.01
Max.	1,472,476	3,984	504.25	189.44	421.11	43.06

Note: (1) Values for the local area are compared with the average, minimum and maximum values for all 292 areas in the Cost of Living Index; (2) Figures cover the St. Louis MO-IL urban area; **New Home Price** *(2,400 sf living area, 8,000 sf lot, in urban area with full utilities);* **Apartment Rent** *(950 sf 2 bedroom/1.5 or 2 bath, unfurnished, excluding all utilities except water);* **All Electric** *(average monthly cost for an all-electric home);* **Part Electric** *(average monthly cost for a part-electric home);* **Other Energy** *(average monthly cost for natural gas, fuel oil, coal, wood, and any other forms of energy except electricity);* **Telephone** *(price includes basic monthly rate for a private residential line plus additional local usage charges incurred by a family of four).*
Source: The Council for Community and Economic Research, ACCRA Cost of Living Index, 2015

Health Care, Transportation, and Other Costs

Area[1]	Doctor ($/visit)	Dentist ($/visit)	Optometrist ($/visit)	Gasoline ($/gallon)	Beauty Salon ($/visit)	Men's Shirt ($)
City[2]	94.95	91.43	83.95	2.31	35.77	23.78
Avg.	105.15	89.02	99.78	2.38	35.30	28.10
Min.	66.87	56.09	48.53	1.95	18.91	13.38
Max.	182.34	150.36	228.33	4.09	67.91	63.80

Note: (1) Values for the local area are compared with the average, minimum and maximum values for all 292 areas in the Cost of Living Index; (2) Figures cover the St. Louis MO-IL urban area; **Doctor** *(general practitioners routine exam of an established patient);* **Dentist** *(adult teeth cleaning and periodic oral examination);* **Optometrist** *(full vision eye exam for established adult patient);* **Gasoline** *(one gallon regular unleaded, national brand, including all taxes, cash price at self-service pump if available);* **Beauty Salon** *(woman's shampoo, trim, and blow-dry);* **Men's Shirt** *(cotton/polyester dress shirt, pinpoint weave, long sleeves).*
Source: The Council for Community and Economic Research, ACCRA Cost of Living Index, 2015

HOUSING

House Price Index (HPI)

Area	National Ranking[2]	Quarterly Change (%)	One-Year Change (%)	Five-Year Change (%)
MSA[1]	164	0.50	3.80	4.00
U.S.[3]	–	1.45	5.76	22.85

Note: The HPI is a weighted repeat sales index. It measures average price changes in repeat sales or refinancings on the same properties. This information is obtained by reviewing repeat mortgage transactions on single-family properties whose mortgages have been purchased or securitized by Fannie Mae or Freddie Mac in January 1975; (1) St. Louis Metropolitan Statistical Area—see Appendix B for areas included; (2) Rankings are based on annual percentage change for all metro areas containing at least 15,000 transactions over the last 10 years and ranges from 1 to 266; (3) figures based on a weighted average of Census Division estimates using a seasonally adjusted, purchase-only index; all figures are for the period ending December 31, 2015
Source: Federal Housing Finance Agency, House Price Index, February 25, 2016

Median Single-Family Home Prices

Area	2013	2014	2015[p]	Percent Change 2014 to 2015
MSA[1]	134.3	141.7	150.6	6.3
U.S. Average	197.4	208.9	223.9	7.2

Note: Figures are median sales prices of existing single-family homes in thousands of dollars; (p) preliminary; n/a not available; (1) St. Louis, MO-IL Metropolitan Statistical Area—see Appendix B for areas included
Source: National Association of Realtors, Median Sales Price of Existing Single-Family Homes for Metropolitan Areas, 4th Quarter 2015

Qualifying Income Based on Median Sales Price of Existing Single-Family Homes

Area	With 5% Down ($)	With 10% Down ($)	With 20% Down ($)
MSA[1]	31,963	30,281	26,916
U.S. Average	49,535	46,928	41,714

Note: Figures are preliminary; Qualifying income is based on a mortgage rate of 4.1%. Monthly principal and interest payment is limited to 25% of income; n/a not available; (1) St. Louis, MO-IL Metropolitan Statistical Area—see Appendix B for areas included
Source: National Association of Realtors, Qualifying Income Based on Median Sales Price of Existing Single-Family Homes for Metropolitan Areas, 4th Quarter 2015

Median Apartment Condo-Coop Home Prices

Area	2013	2014	2015[p]	Percent Change 2014 to 2015
MSA[1]	n/a	n/a	n/a	n/a
U.S. Average	194.9	204.3	210.7	3.1

Note: Figures are median sales prices of existing apartment condo-coop homes in thousands of dollars; (p) preliminary; n/a not available; (1) St. Louis, MO-IL Metropolitan Statistical Area—see Appendix B for areas included
Source: National Association of Realtors, Median Sales Price of Existing Apartment Condo-Coop Homes for Metropolitan Areas, 4th Quarter 2015

Gross Monthly Rent

Area	Under $200	$200 -299	$300 -499	$500 -749	$750 -999	$1,000 -1,499	$1,500 and up	Median ($)
City	0.0	0.8	1.0	7.1	35.7	36.8	18.6	1,050
MSA[1]	1.4	3.3	8.2	29.0	30.0	21.9	6.1	808
U.S.	1.5	3.2	7.4	21.0	24.1	26.9	15.9	920

Note: Figures are percentages except for Median; Gross rent is the contract rent plus the estimated average monthly cost of utilities (electricity, gas, and water and sewer) and fuels (oil, coal, kerosene, wood, etc.) if these are paid by the renter (or paid for the renter by someone else); (1) Figures cover the St. Louis, MO-IL Metropolitan Statistical Area—see Appendix B for areas included
Source: U.S. Census Bureau, 2010-2014 American Community Survey 5-Year Estimates

Homeownership Rate

Area	2008 (%)	2009 (%)	2010 (%)	2011 (%)	2012 (%)	2013 (%)	2014 (%)	2015 (%)
MSA[1]	72.2	72.5	72.2	71.1	72.0	72.7	71.1	68.7
U.S.	67.8	67.4	66.9	66.1	65.4	65.1	64.5	63.7

Note: (1) Figures cover the St. Louis, MO-IL Metropolitan Statistical Area—see Appendix B for areas included
Source: U.S. Census Bureau, Housing Vacancies and Homeownership Annual Statistics: 2015

Year Housing Structure Built

Area	2010 or Later	2000 -2009	1990 -1999	1980 -1989	1970 -1979	1960 -1969	1950 -1959	1940 -1949	Before 1940	Median Year
City	0.7	9.3	18.1	24.4	33.2	11.9	1.7	0.2	0.5	1981
MSA[1]	0.8	12.2	12.4	11.3	13.5	12.8	13.8	6.5	16.7	1970
U.S.	1.0	14.9	13.9	13.8	15.8	11.0	10.8	5.4	13.3	1976

Note: Figures are percentages except for Median Year; (1) Figures cover the St. Louis, MO-IL Metropolitan Statistical Area—see Appendix B for areas included
Source: U.S. Census Bureau, 2010-2014 American Community Survey 5-Year Estimates

HEALTH

Health Risk Data

Category	MSA[1] (%)	U.S. (%)
Adults aged 18–64 who have any kind of health care coverage	83.4	79.6
Adults who reported being in good or excellent health	83.6	83.1
Adults who are current smokers	20.1	19.6
Adults who are heavy drinkers[2]	6.9	6.1
Adults who are binge drinkers[3]	22.1	16.9
Adults who are overweight (BMI 25.0 - 29.9)	36.5	35.8
Adults who are obese (BMI 30.0 - 99.8)	31.1	27.6
Adults who participated in any physical activities in the past month	75.6	77.1
Adults 50+ who have ever had a sigmoidoscopy or colonoscopy	69.9	67.3
Women aged 40+ who have had a mammogram within the past two years	79.4	74.0
Men aged 40+ who have had a PSA test within the past two years	52.8	45.2
Adults aged 65+ who have had flu shot within the past year	63.6	60.1
Adults who always wear a seatbelt	90.8	93.8

Note: Data as of 2012 unless otherwise noted; (1) Figures cover the St. Louis, MO-IL Metropolitan Statistical Area—see Appendix B for areas included; (2) Heavy drinkers are classified as males having more than two drinks per day or females having more than one drink per day; (3) Binge drinkers are classified as males having five or more drinks on one occasion or females having four or more drinks on one occasion
Source: Centers for Disease Control and Prevention, Behaviorial Risk Factor Surveillance System, SMART: Selected Metropolitan/Micropolitan Area Risk Trends, 2012 (Note: the CDC has discontinued this dataset but will be releasing a replacement in mid-2016)

Chronic Health Indicators

Category	MSA[1] (%)	U.S. (%)
Adults who have ever been told they had a heart attack	5.4	4.5
Adults who have ever been told they had a stroke	3.6	2.9
Adults who have been told they currently have asthma	10.2	8.9
Adults who have ever been told they have arthritis	27.0	25.7
Adults who have ever been told they have diabetes[2]	10.6	9.7
Adults who have ever been told they had skin cancer	5.4	5.7
Adults who have ever been told they had any other types of cancer	7.0	6.5
Adults who have ever been told they have COPD	5.9	6.2
Adults who have ever been told they have kidney disease	2.9	2.5
Adults who have ever been told they have a form of depression	16.9	18.0

Note: Data as of 2012 unless otherwise noted; (1) Figures cover the St. Louis, MO-IL Metropolitan Statistical Area—see Appendix B for areas included; (2) Figures do not include pregnancy-related, borderline, or pre-diabetes
Source: Centers for Disease Control and Prevention, Behaviorial Risk Factor Surveillance System, SMART: Selected Metropolitan/Micropolitan Area Risk Trends, 2012 (Note: the CDC has discontinued this dataset but will be releasing a replacement in mid-2016)

Mortality Rates for the Top 10 Causes of Death in the U.S.

ICD-10[a] Sub-Chapter	ICD-10[a] Code	Age-Adjusted Mortality Rate[1] per 100,000 population	
		County[2]	U.S.
Malignant neoplasms	C00-C97	164.6	163.6
Ischaemic heart diseases	I20-I25	119.6	102.2
Other forms of heart disease	I30-I51	43.2	50.1
Chronic lower respiratory diseases	J40-J47	34.0	41.4
Organic, including symptomatic, mental disorders	F01-F09	42.8	38.5
Cerebrovascular diseases	I60-I69	36.5	36.5
Other external causes of accidental injury	W00-X59	33.5	27.5
Other degenerative diseases of the nervous system	G30-G31	22.9	26.3
Diabetes mellitus	E10-E14	15.6	21.1
Hypertensive diseases	I10-I15	12.4	19.7

Note: (a) ICD-10 = International Classification of Diseases 10th Revision; (1) Mortality rates are a three year average covering 2012-2014; (2) Figures cover St. Louis County.
Source: Centers for Disease Control and Prevention, National Center for Health Statistics. Underlying Cause of Death 1999-2014 on CDC WONDER Online Database, released 2015.

Mortality Rates for Selected Causes of Death

ICD-10[a] Sub-Chapter	ICD-10[a] Code	Age-Adjusted Mortality Rate[1] per 100,000 population	
		County[2]	U.S.
Assault	X85-Y09	9.2	5.1
Diseases of the liver	K70-K76	10.1	13.5
Human immunodeficiency virus (HIV) disease	B20-B24	1.2	2.1
Influenza and pneumonia	J09-J18	17.1	15.2
Intentional self-harm	X60-X84	13.5	12.7
Malnutrition	E40-E46	0.8	0.9
Obesity and other hyperalimentation	E65-E68	1.2	1.9
Renal failure	N17-N19	16.6	13.0
Transport accidents	V01-V99	7.1	11.6
Viral hepatitis	B15-B19	1.3	2.1

Note: (a) ICD-10 = International Classification of Diseases 10th Revision; (1) Mortality rates are a three year average covering 2012-2014; (2) Figures cover St. Louis County; Data are Suppressed when the data meet the criteria for confidentiality constraints; Mortality rates are flagged as Unreliable when the rate would be calculated with a numerator of 20 or less.
Source: Centers for Disease Control and Prevention, National Center for Health Statistics. Underlying Cause of Death 1999-2014 on CDC WONDER Online Database, released 2015.

Health Insurance Coverage

Area	With Health Insurance	With Private Health Insurance	With Public Health Insurance	Without Health Insurance	Population Under Age 18 Without Health Insurance
City	95.5	88.8	22.4	4.5	3.1
MSA[1]	89.6	72.6	28.0	10.4	4.4
U.S.	85.8	65.8	31.1	14.2	7.1

Note: Figures are percentages that cover the civilian noninstitutionalized population; (1) Figures cover the St. Louis, MO-IL Metropolitan Statistical Area—see Appendix B for areas included
Source: U.S. Census Bureau, 2010-2014 American Community Survey 5-Year Estimates

Number of Medical Professionals

Area	MDs[3]	DOs[3,4]	Dentists	Podiatrists	Chiropractors	Optometrists
County[1] (number)	5,040	270	833	93	509	262
County[1] (rate[2])	503.2	27.0	83.1	9.3	50.8	26.2
U.S. (rate[2])	272.5	20.9	64.7	5.8	25.9	15.2

Note: Data as of 2014 unless noted; (1) Data covers St. Louis County; (2) Rate per 100,000 population; (3) Data as of 2013 and includes all active, non-federal physicians; (4) Doctor of Osteopathic Medicine
Source: U.S. Department of Health and Human Services, Health Resources and Services Administration, Bureau of Health Professions, Area Resource File (ARF) 2014-2015

Best Hospitals

According to *U.S. News,* the St. Louis, MO-IL metro area is home to one of the best hospitals in the U.S.: **Barnes-Jewish Hospital/Washington University** (Honor Roll/14 specialties). The hospital listed was nationally ranked in at least one adult specialty. Only 137 hospitals nationwide were nationally ranked in one or more specialties. Fifteen hospitals in the U.S. made the Honor Roll with high scores in at least six specialties. *U.S. News Online, "America's Best Children's Hospitals 2015-16"*

According to *U.S. News,* the St. Louis, MO-IL metro area is home to three of the best children's hospitals in the U.S.: **SSM Cardinal Glennon Children's Medical Center** (2 specialties); **St. Louis Children's Hospital-Washington University** (10 specialties); **St. Louis Children's-Washington University-Shriners Hospital** (10 specialties). The hospitals listed were highly ranked in at least one pediatric specialty. Eighty-three children's hospitals in the U.S. were nationally ranked in at least one specialty. Twelve children's hospitals in the U.S. made the Honor Roll with high scores in at least three specialties. *U.S. News Online, "America's Best Children's Hospitals 2015-16"*

EDUCATION

Public School District Statistics

District Name	Schls	Pupils	Pupil/ Teacher Ratio	Minority Pupils[1] (%)	Free Lunch Eligible[2] (%)	IEP[3] (%)
Division Of Youth Service	42	875	7.2	38.9	86.6	31.5

Note: Table includes school districts with 100 or more students; (1) Percentage of students that are not non-Hispanic white; (2) Percentage of students that are eligible for the free lunch program; (3) Percentage of students that have an Individualized Education Program.
Source: U.S. Department of Education, National Center for Education Statistics, Common Core of Data, Local Education Agency (School District) Universe Survey: School Year 2013-2014; U.S. Department of Education, National Center for Education Statistics, Common Core of Data, Public Elementary/Secondary School Universe Survey: School Year 2013-2014

Highest Level of Education

Area	Less than H.S.	H.S. Diploma	Some College, No Deg.	Associate Degree	Bachelor's Degree	Master's Degree	Prof. School Degree	Doctorate Degree
City	2.3	11.6	16.7	5.4	35.2	19.2	6.4	3.2
MSA[1]	9.7	27.2	23.2	8.3	19.3	8.9	2.0	1.3
U.S.	13.7	28.0	21.2	7.9	18.3	7.8	2.0	1.3

Note: Figures cover persons age 25 and over; (1) Figures cover the St. Louis, MO-IL Metropolitan Statistical Area—see Appendix B for areas included
Source: U.S. Census Bureau, 2010-2014 American Community Survey 5-Year Estimates

Educational Attainment by Race

Area	High School Graduate or Higher (%)					Bachelor's Degree or Higher (%)				
	Total	White	Black	Asian	Hisp.[2]	Total	White	Black	Asian	Hisp.[2]
City	97.7	98.1	91.4	97.1	93.3	64.0	64.1	34.4	76.4	48.7
MSA[1]	90.3	91.9	83.5	88.2	76.8	31.5	33.6	17.3	62.8	24.9
U.S.	86.3	88.4	83.2	85.8	64.1	29.3	30.6	19.0	50.9	13.9

Note: Figures shown cover persons 25 years old and over; (1) Figures cover the St. Louis, MO-IL Metropolitan Statistical Area—see Appendix B for areas included; (2) People of Hispanic origin can be of any race
Source: U.S. Census Bureau, 2010-2014 American Community Survey 5-Year Estimates

School Enrollment by Grade and Control

Area	Preschool (%)		Kindergarten (%)		Grades 1 - 4 (%)		Grades 5 - 8 (%)		Grades 9 - 12 (%)	
	Public	Private	Public	Private	Public	Private	Public	Private	Public	Private
City	38.8	61.2	64.6	35.4	83.2	16.8	81.5	18.5	76.2	23.8
MSA[1]	53.9	46.1	81.1	18.9	83.2	16.8	83.4	16.6	85.5	14.5
U.S.	57.4	42.6	87.8	12.2	89.8	10.2	89.9	10.1	90.6	9.4

Note: Figures shown cover persons 3 years old and over; (1) Figures cover the St. Louis, MO-IL Metropolitan Statistical Area—see Appendix B for areas included
Source: U.S. Census Bureau, 2010-2014 American Community Survey 5-Year Estimates

Average Salaries of Public School Classroom Teachers

Area	2013-14 Dollars	2013-14 Rank[1]	2014-15 Dollars	2014-15 Rank[1]	Percent Change 2013-14 to 2014-15	Percent Change 2004-05 to 2014-15
Missouri	46,750	42	47,394	43	1.38	21.3
U.S. Average	56,610	–	57,379	–	1.36	20.8

Note: (1) State rank ranges from 1 to 51 where 1 indicates highest salary.
Source: National Education Association, Rankings & Estimates: Rankings of the States 2014 and Estimates of School Statistics 2015, March 2015

Higher Education

Four-Year Colleges			Two-Year Colleges			Medical Schools[1]	Law Schools[2]	Voc/ Tech[3]
Public	Private Non-profit	Private For-profit	Public	Private Non-profit	Private For-profit			
0	1	0	0	0	0	0	0	0

Note: Figures cover institutions located within the city limits and include main campuses only; (1) includes schools accredited by the Liaison Committee on Medical Education and the American Osteopathic Association's Commission on Osteopathic College Accreditation; (2) includes ABA-accredited schools, schools with provisional ABA accreditation, and state accredited schools; (3) includes all schools with programs that are less than 2 years.
Source: National Center for Education Statistics, Integrated Postsecondary Education System (IPEDS), 2014-15; Association of American Medical Colleges, Member List, March 21, 2016; American Osteopathic Association, Member List, March 21, 2016; Law School Admission Council, Official Guide to ABA-Approved Law Schools Online, March 21, 2016; Wikipedia, List of Medical Schools in the United States, March 21, 2016; Wikipedia, List of Law Schools in the United States, March 21, 2016

According to *U.S. News & World Report,* the St. Louis, MO-IL metro area is home to three of the best national universities in the U.S.: **Washington University in St. Louis** (#15 tie); **Saint Louis University** (#96 tie); **Maryville University of St. Louis** (#161 tie). The indicators used to capture academic quality fall into a number of categories: assessment by administrators at peer institutions; retention of students; faculty resources; student selectivity; financial resources; alumni giving; high school counselor ratings of colleges; and graduation rate. *U.S. News & World Report, "America's Best Colleges 2016"*

According to *U.S. News & World Report,* the St. Louis, MO-IL metro area is home to one of the best liberal arts colleges in the U.S.: **Principia College** (#127 tie). The indicators used to capture academic quality fall into a number of categories: assessment by administrators at peer institutions; retention of students; faculty resources; student selectivity; financial resources; alumni giving; high school counselor ratings of colleges; and graduation rate. *U.S. News & World Report, "America's Best Colleges 2016"*

According to *U.S. News & World Report,* the St. Louis, MO-IL metro area is home to two of the top 100 law schools in the U.S.: **Washington University in St. Louis, School of Law** (#18); **St. Louis University, School of Law** (#82 tie). The rankings are based on a weighted average of 12 measures of quality: peer assessment score; assessment score by lawyers/judges; median LSAT scores; median undergrad GPA; acceptance rate; employment rates for graduates; placement success; bar passage rate; faculty resources; expenditures per student; student/faculty ratio; and library resources. *U.S. News & World Report, "America's Best Graduate Schools, Law, 2017"*

According to *U.S. News & World Report,* the St. Louis, MO-IL metro area is home to two of the top 75 medical schools for research in the U.S.: **Washington University in St. Louis, School of Medicine** (#6); **St. Louis University, School of Medicine** (#63 tie). The rankings are based on a weighted average of 11 measures of quality: quality assessment; peer assessment score; assessment score by residency directors; research activity; total research activity; average research activity per faculty member; student selectivity; median MCAT total score; median undergraduate GPA; acceptance rate; and faculty resources. *U.S. News & World Report, "America's Best Graduate Schools, Medical, 2017"*

According to *U.S. News & World Report,* the St. Louis, MO-IL metro area is home to one of the top 75 business schools in the U.S.: **Washington University in St. Louis, Olin Business School** (#21). The rankings are based on a weighted average of the following nine measures: quality assessment; peer assessment; recruiter assessment; placement success; mean starting salary and bonus; student selectivity; mean GMAT and GRE scores; mean undergraduate GPA; and acceptance rate. *U.S. News & World Report, "America's Best Graduate Schools, Business, 2017"*

PRESIDENTIAL ELECTION

2012 Presidential Election Results

Area	Obama (%)	Romney (%)	Other (%)
St. Louis County	56.2	42.5	1.3
U.S.	51.0	47.2	1.8

Note: Results may not add to 100% due to rounding
Source: Dave Leip's Atlas of U.S. Presidential Elections

EMPLOYERS

Major Employers

Company Name	Industry
Ameren	Utilities
Anheuser-Busch	Brewery
Archdiocese of St. Louis Catholic Church	Catholic church
BJC Healthcare Hospital System	Hospital system
Boeing Defense	Contractor
Dierbergs Markets	Grocery chain
Edward Jones	Financial services
Enterprise Holdings	Car rental
Express Scripts	Pharmacy benefit manager
McDonald's	Food service
Mercy Health Hospital	Hospital system
Monsanto Biotech	Crop producer
National Geospatial-Intelligence Agency	National security
Schnuck Markets	Grocery chain
Scott Air Force	Military installation
Special School District of St. Louis Cty.	Primary/secondary education
SSM Health Care	Hospital system
St Anthony's Medical Center	Healthcare
St Louis City	Government
St Louis Community College	Higher education
St Louis County	Government
St Louis University	Higher education
USPS	Government
Wal-Mart	Retailer
Washington University	Higher education
Wells Fargo	Financial services

Note: Companies shown are located within the St. Louis, MO-IL Metropolitan Statistical Area.
Source: Hoovers.com; Wikipedia

PUBLIC SAFETY

Crime Rate

Area	All Crimes	Violent Crimes				Property Crimes		
		Murder	Rape[3]	Robbery	Aggrav. Assault	Burglary	Larceny -Theft	Motor Vehicle Theft
City	1,598.0	0.0	8.4	10.5	52.3	87.8	1,416.0	23.0
Metro[1]	2,879.0	8.8	35.8	103.4	281.8	470.4	1,765.0	213.8
U.S.	2,971.8	4.5	36.6	102.2	232.5	542.5	1,837.3	216.2

Note: Figures are crimes per 100,000 population; (1) Figures cover the St. Louis, MO-IL Metropolitan Statistical Area—see Appendix B for areas included; (3) The city and U.S. figures shown were reported using the revised Uniform Crime Reporting (UCR) definition of rape. The suburban and metro area figures shown are an aggregate total of the data submitted using both the revised and legacy UCR definitions.
Source: FBI Uniform Crime Reports, 2014

Hate Crimes

Area	Number of Quarters Reported	Number of Incidents per Bias Motivation						
		Race	Religion	Sexual Orientation	Ethnicity	Disability	Gender	Gender Identity
City	4	0	0	0	0	0	0	0
U.S.	4	2,568	1,014	1,017	648	84	33	98

Source: Federal Bureau of Investigation, Hate Crime Statistics 2014

Identity Theft Consumer Complaints

Area	Complaints	Complaints per 100,000 Population	Rank[2]
MSA[1]	19,195	684.0	1
U.S.	490,220	152.4	-

Note: (1) Figures cover the St. Louis, MO-IL Metropolitan Statistical Area—see Appendix B for areas included; (2) Rank ranges from 1 to 379 where 1 indicates greatest number of identity theft complaints per 100,000 population
Source: Federal Trade Commission, Consumer Sentinel Network Data Book for January–December 2015

Fraud and Other Consumer Complaints

Area	Complaints	Complaints per 100,000 Population	Rank[2]
MSA[1]	10,939	389.8	126
U.S.	2,593,159	806.0	-

Note: (1) Figures cover the St. Louis, MO-IL Metropolitan Statistical Area—see Appendix B for areas included; (2) Rank ranges from 1 to 379 where 1 indicates greatest number of identity theft complaints per 100,000 population
Source: Federal Trade Commission, Consumer Sentinel Network Data Book for January–December 2015

RECREATION

Culture

Dance[1]	Theatre[1]	Instrumental Music[1]	Vocal Music[1]	Series and Festivals	Museums and Art Galleries[2]	Zoos and Aquariums[3]
0	0	0	0	0	0	0

Note: (1) Professional perfoming groups; (2) Based on organizations with SIC code 8412; (3) AZA-accredited
Source: The Grey House Performing Arts Directory, 2015-16; Association of Zoos & Aquariums, AZA Member Zoos & Aquariums, March 25, 2016; www.AccuLeads.com, March 29, 2016

Professional Sports Teams

Team Name	League	Year Established
Los Angeles Rams	National Football League (NFL)	2016
Saint Louis Blues	National Hockey League (NHL)	1967
Saint Louis Cardinals	Major League Baseball (MLB)	1882

Note: Includes teams located in the St. Louis, MO-IL Metropolitan Statistical Area.
Source: Wikipedia, Major Professional Sports Teams of the United States and Canada, March 24, 2016

CLIMATE

Average and Extreme Temperatures

Temperature	Jan	Feb	Mar	Apr	May	Jun	Jul	Aug	Sep	Oct	Nov	Dec	Yr.
Extreme High (°F)	77	83	89	93	98	105	115	107	104	94	85	76	115
Average High (°F)	39	43	54	67	76	85	89	87	80	69	54	42	66
Average Temp. (°F)	30	34	44	56	66	75	79	78	70	59	45	34	56
Average Low (°F)	21	25	34	46	55	65	69	67	59	48	36	26	46
Extreme Low (°F)	-18	-10	-5	22	31	43	51	47	36	23	1	-16	-18

Note: Figures cover the years 1945-1990
Source: National Climatic Data Center, International Station Meteorological Climate Summary, 9/96

Average Precipitation/Snowfall/Humidity

Precip./Humidity	Jan	Feb	Mar	Apr	May	Jun	Jul	Aug	Sep	Oct	Nov	Dec	Yr.
Avg. Precip. (in.)	1.9	2.2	3.4	3.4	3.8	4.0	3.8	2.9	2.9	2.8	3.0	2.6	36.8
Avg. Snowfall (in.)	6	4	4	Tr	0	0	0	0	0	Tr	1	4	20
Avg. Rel. Hum. 6am (%)	80	81	80	78	81	82	84	86	87	83	81	81	82
Avg. Rel. Hum. 3pm (%)	62	59	54	49	51	51	51	52	50	50	56	63	54

Note: Figures cover the years 1945-1990; Tr = Trace amounts (<0.05 in. of rain; <0.5 in. of snow)
Source: National Climatic Data Center, International Station Meteorological Climate Summary, 9/96

Weather Conditions

Temperature			Daytime Sky			Precipitation		
10°F & below	32°F & below	90°F & above	Clear	Partly cloudy	Cloudy	0.01 inch or more precip.	0.1 inch or more snow/ice	Thunder-storms
13	100	43	97	138	130	109	14	46

Note: Figures are average number of days per year and cover the years 1945-1990
Source: National Climatic Data Center, International Station Meteorological Climate Summary, 9/96

HAZARDOUS WASTE

Superfund Sites

Chesterfield has no sites on the EPA's Superfund Final National Priorities List. There are a total of 1,323 Superfund sites on the list in the U.S. *U.S. Environmental Protection Agency, Final National Priorities List, March 18, 2016*

AIR & WATER QUALITY

Air Quality Trends: Ozone

	1990	1995	2000	2005	2010	2011	2012	2013	2014
MSA[1]	0.085	0.092	0.082	0.087	0.075	0.078	0.085	0.069	0.068

Note: (1) Data covers the St. Louis, MO-IL Metropolitan Statistical Area—see Appendix B for areas included. The values shown are the composite ozone concentration averages among trend sites based on the highest fourth daily maximum 8-hour concentration in parts per million. These trends are based on sites having an adequate record of monitoring data during the trend period. Data from exceptional events are included.
Source: U.S. Environmental Protection Agency, Air Quality Monitoring Information, "Air Quality Trends by City, 1990-2014"

Air Quality Index

Area	Percent of Days when Air Quality was...[2]					AQI Statistics[2]	
	Good	Moderate	Unhealthy for Sensitive Groups	Unhealthy	Very Unhealthy	Maximum	Median
MSA[1]	38.6	59.2	1.6	0.5	0.0	154	55

Note: (1) Data covers the St. Louis, MO-IL Metropolitan Statistical Area—see Appendix B for areas included; (2) Based on 365 days with AQI data in 2015. Air Quality Index (AQI) is an index for reporting daily air quality. EPA calculates the AQI for five major air pollutants regulated by the Clean Air Act: ground-level ozone, particle pollution (aka particulate matter), carbon monoxide, sulfur dioxide, and nitrogen dioxide. The AQI runs from 0 to 500. The higher the AQI value, the greater the level of air pollution and the greater the health concern. There are six AQI categories: "Good" AQI is between 0 and 50. Air quality is considered satisfactory; "Moderate" AQI is between 51 and 100. Air quality is acceptable; "Unhealthy for Sensitive Groups" When AQI values are between 101 and 150, members of sensitive groups may experience health effects; "Unhealthy" When AQI values are between 151 and 200 everyone may begin to experience health effects; "Very Unhealthy" AQI values between 201 and 300 trigger a health alert; "Hazardous" AQI values over 300 trigger warnings of emergency conditions (not shown).
Source: U.S. Environmental Protection Agency, Air Quality Index Report, 2015

Air Quality Index Pollutants

Area	Percent of Days when AQI Pollutant was...[2]					
	Carbon Monoxide	Nitrogen Dioxide	Ozone	Sulfur Dioxide	Particulate Matter 2.5	Particulate Matter 10
MSA[1]	0.0	2.2	18.6	0.8	75.1	3.3

Note: (1) Data covers the St. Louis, MO-IL Metropolitan Statistical Area—see Appendix B for areas included; (2) Based on 365 days with AQI data in 2015. The Air Quality Index (AQI) is an index for reporting daily air quality. EPA calculates the AQI for five major air pollutants regulated by the Clean Air Act: ground-level ozone, particle pollution (also known as particulate matter), carbon monoxide, sulfur dioxide, and nitrogen dioxide. The AQI runs from 0 to 500. The higher the AQI value, the greater the level of air pollution and the greater the health concern.
Source: U.S. Environmental Protection Agency, Air Quality Index Report, 2015

Maximum Air Pollutant Concentrations: Particulate Matter, Ozone, CO and Lead

	Particulate Matter 10 (ug/m^3)	Particulate Matter 2.5 Wtd AM (ug/m^3)	Particulate Matter 2.5 24-Hr (ug/m^3)	Ozone (ppm)	Carbon Monoxide (ppm)	Lead (ug/m^3)
MSA[1] Level	159	11.4	29	0.072	1	0.36
NAAQS[2]	150	15	35	0.075	9	0.15
Met NAAQS[2]	No	Yes	Yes	Yes	Yes	No

Note: (1) Data covers the St. Louis, MO-IL Metropolitan Statistical Area—see Appendix B for areas included; Data from exceptional events are included; (2) National Ambient Air Quality Standards; ppm = parts per million; ug/m^3 = micrograms per cubic meter; n/a not available.
Concentrations: Particulate Matter 10 (coarse particulate)—highest second maximum 24-hour concentration; Particulate Matter 2.5 Wtd AM (fine particulate)—highest weighted annual mean concentration; Particulate Matter 2.5 24-Hour (fine particulate)—highest 98th percentile 24-hour concentration; Ozone—highest fourth daily maximum 8-hour concentration; Carbon Monoxide—highest second maximum non-overlapping 8-hour concentration; Lead—maximum running 3-month average
Source: U.S. Environmental Protection Agency, Air Quality Monitoring Information, "Air Quality Statistics by City, 2014"

Maximum Air Pollutant Concentrations: Nitrogen Dioxide and Sulfur Dioxide

	Nitrogen Dioxide AM (ppb)	Nitrogen Dioxide 1-Hr (ppb)	Sulfur Dioxide AM (ppb)	Sulfur Dioxide 1-Hr (ppb)	Sulfur Dioxide 24-Hr (ppb)
MSA[1] Level	14	60	n/a	41	n/a
NAAQS[2]	53	100	30	75	140
Met NAAQS[2]	Yes	Yes	n/a	Yes	n/a

Note: (1) Data covers the St. Louis, MO-IL Metropolitan Statistical Area—see Appendix B for areas included; Data from exceptional events are included; (2) National Ambient Air Quality Standards; ppm = parts per million; ug/m^3 = micrograms per cubic meter; n/a not available.
Concentrations: Nitrogen Dioxide AM—highest arithmetic mean concentration; Nitrogen Dioxide 1-Hr—highest 98th percentile 1-hour daily maximum concentration; Sulfur Dioxide AM—highest annual mean concentration; Sulfur Dioxide 1-Hr—highest 99th percentile 1-hour daily maximum concentration; Sulfur Dioxide 24-Hr—highest second maximum 24-hour concentration
Source: U.S. Environmental Protection Agency, Air Quality Monitoring Information, "Air Quality Statistics by City, 2014"

Drinking Water

Water System Name	Pop. Served	Primary Water Source Type	Violations[1]	
			Health Based	Monitoring/ Reporting
Missouri American Water	1,100,000	Surface	0	0

Note: (1) Based on violation data from January 1, 2015 to December 31, 2015 (includes unresolved violations from earlier years)
Source: U.S. Environmental Protection Agency, Office of Ground Water and Drinking Water, Safe Drinking Water Information System (based on data extracted April 29, 2016)

Lee's Summit, Missouri

Background

Lee's Summit, located in Jackson County 16 miles southeast of downtown Kansas City, has watched its population grow significantly in recent years.

In spite of this growth, Lee's Summit maintains a strong sense of community because of its vital, pedestrian-oriented downtown. The city offers residents and businesses the feel of a quiet suburb with high-quality employment and commerce. It boasts state and national award-winning schools, diverse housing, parks, lakes, and other recreational opportunities.

Lee's Summit was founded in 1865 by William B. Howard, a successful farmer and stockman, as the town of Strother, after his wife's maiden name. However, at the request of the United States Post Office, the town's name was changed because a town already existed called Strother. The community was incorporated in 1867 as the Town of Lee's Summit, though the origin of the town's name is disputed: some claim it is dedicated to Confederate General Robert E. Lee, while others say the spelling is a corruption of "Lea's Summit," in honor of respected citizen Dr. Pleasant Lea who was killed during the Civil War. "Summit" refers to the fact that the city is the highest point on the railroad line between Kansas City and St. Louis.

The city is graced with attractive neighborhoods and excellent schools. Students are served by the Lee's Summit R-7 School District, which has received the state's first-ever Governor's Choice Award, and the Blue Springs School District, recently recognized by the Missouri Department of Elementary & Secondary Education for distinction in performance.

Major employers include AT&T, CVS Caremark, and the Government Employees Hospital Association.

The Lee's Summit business district surrounds Howard Station Park. The original depot still stands as a reminder of how far the city has come, with its high-tech industrial parks, modern retail businesses, and lovely residential districts. In recent years, the city has invested heavily in the revitalization of its downtown area, renovating buildings, installing park benches and wrought iron fences along the railroad, and improving parking areas. A city hall complex was completed in spring of 2006, unifying an area which now features over 90 retail and service businesses, including restaurants, antique shops, and furniture stores.

Within an eight-mile radius of downtown Lee's Summit are four private and three public lakes. The city is also home to the Legacy Park Community Center, with its two leisure pools, racquetball courts, gymnasium, childcare, and more. Also nearby is Longview Farm, which was built as a gentleman's summer home by lumber baron Robert A. Long. Another nearby attraction is Powell Gardens, a 915-acre botanical garden that also houses a butterfly collection, a rock and waterfall garden, and a wildflower meadow. Rock the Green is a new summer concert series.

Lee's Summit has the modified continental climate of the greater Kansas City area. With the gently rolling terrain, there are no impediments to winds from all directions, and the air is dry or humid, depending on whether the wind is from the arid Southwest or from the Gulf of Mexico. Cold air from the northwest occasionally sweeps down, meeting warm air from the Gulf to create unsettled conditions. Winters are generally mild, summers relatively hot, with moderate humidity.

Rankings

Business/Finance Rankings

- The personal finance site NerdWallet analyzed 183 American metropolitan areas with populations over 250,000 and more than 15,000 businesses to rank where entrepreneurs find the most success. Criteria included area economy, annual income, housing cost, unemployment rate, and the success rate of area businesses. Kansas City* ranked #36. *www.nerdwallet.com, "Best Places to Start a Business," April 27, 2015*
- Based on metro area social media reviews, the employment opinion group Glassdoor surveyed 50 of the largest U.S. metro areas and equally weighed cost of living, hiring opportunity, and job satisfaction to compose a list of "25 Best Cities for Jobs." The Kansas City* metro area was ranked #23 in overall job satisfaction. *www.glassdoor.com, "Best Cities for Jobs," May 19, 2015*
- In a survey of economic confidence in the nation's 50 largest metropolitan areas conducted January–December 2014, the Kansas City* metro area placed #44, according to Gallup's 2014 Economic Confidence Index. *Gallup, "San Jose and San Francisco Lead in Economic Confidence," March 19, 2015*
- The Brookings Institution ranked the 100 largest metro areas in the U.S. based on income inequality. Kansas City* was ranked #67 (#1 = greatest ineqality). Criteria: the "95/20 ratio," a figure representing the income at which a household earns more than 95 percent of all other households, divided by the income at which a household earns more than only 20 percent of all other households. *Brookings Institution, "Income Inequality, 100 Largest U.S. Metro Areas, 2007-2014," January 14, 2016*
- Kansas City* was identified as one of America's most frugal metro areas by *Coupons.com.* The city ranked #11 out of 25. Criteria: online coupon usage. *Coupons.com, "Top 25 Most Frugal Cities of 2014," May 11, 2015*
- Kansas City* was cited as one of America's top metros for new and expanded facility projects in 2015. The area ranked #10 in the large metro area category (population over 1 million). *Site Selection, "Top Metropolitans of 2015," March 2016*
- The Kansas City* metro area appeared on the Milken Institute "2015 Best Performing Cities" list. Rank: #103 out of 200 large metro areas. Criteria: job growth; wage and salary growth; high-tech output growth. *Milken Institute, "Best-Performing Cities 2015," December 2015*
- *Forbes* ranked the 200 most populous metro areas to determine the nation's "Best Places for Business and Careers." The Kansas City* metro area was ranked #61. Criteria: costs (business and living); job growth (past and projected); income growth; educational attainment (college and high school); projected economic growth; cultural and recreational opportunities; net migration patterns; number of highly ranked colleges. *Forbes, "The Best Places for Business and Careers 2015," July 29, 2015*

Education Rankings

- Personal finance website *WalletHub* analyzed the 150 largest U.S. metropolitan statistical areas to determine where the most educated Americans are choosing to settle. Criteria: education quality and attainment gap; education levels; percentage of workers with degrees; public school rankings; quality and size of each metro area's universities. Kansas City* was ranked #28 (#1 = most educated city). *www.WalletHub.com, "2015's Most and Least Educated Cities*

Environmental Rankings

- The Kansas City* metro area came in at #238 for the relative comfort of its climate on Sperling's list of "chill cities," as measured by the Sperling Heat Index. All 361 metro areas are included. Criteria included daytime high temperatures, nighttime low temperatures, dew point, and relative humidity at the high temperatures. *www.bertsperling.com, "Sperling's Chill Cities," July 18, 2013*

- Sperling's BestPlaces assessed 379 metropolitan areas of the United States for the likelihood of dangerously extreme weather events or earthquakes. In general the Southeast and South-Central regions have the highest risk of weather extremes and earthquakes, while the Pacific Northwest enjoys the lowest risk. Of the least risky metropolitan areas, the Kansas City* metro area was ranked #254. *www.bestplaces.net, "Safest Places from Natural Disasters," April 2011*
- Kansas City* was highlighted as one of the 25 most ozone-polluted metro areas in the U.S. during 2011 through 2013. The area ranked #24. *American Lung Association, State of the Air 2015*

Health/Fitness Rankings

- For each of the 50 most populous metro areas in the United States, the American College of Sports Medicine's American Fitness Index evaluated infrastructure, community assets, and policies that encourage healthy and fit lifestyles, including preventive health behaviors, levels of chronic disease conditions, health care access, and community resources and policies that support physical activity. The Kansas City* metro area ranked #26 for "community fitness." *www.americanfitnessindex.org, "ACSM American Fitness Index Health and Community Fitness Status of the 50 Largest Metropolitan Areas," May 2015*
- The Kansas City* metro area was identified as one of the worst cities for bed bugs in America by pest control company Orkin. The area ranked #44 out of 50 based on the number of bed bug treatments Orkin performed from January to December 2015. *Orkin, "Chicago Tops Bed Bug Cities List for Fourth Year in a Row," January 13, 2016*
- Kansas City* was identified as a "2016 Spring Allergy Capital." The area ranked #64 out of 100. Three groups of factors were used to identify the most severe cities for people with allergies during the spring season: annual pollen levels; medicine utilization; access to board-certified allergists. *Asthma and Allergy Foundation of America, "Spring Allergy Capitals 2016"*
- Kansas City* was identified as a "2015 Asthma Capital." The area ranked #72 out of the nation's 100 largest metropolitan areas. Criteria: estimated prevalence; self-reported prevalence; crude death rate for asthma; annual pollen score; annual air quality; public smoking laws; number of board-certified asthma specialists; school inhaler access laws; rescue medication use; controller medication use; ER visits for asthma; uninsured rate; poverty rate. *Asthma and Allergy Foundation of America, "Asthma Capitals 2015"*
- The Kansas City* metro area ranked #111 out of 190 in The Gallup-Healthways Well-Being Index. Criteria: purpose; social well being; financial health; community and physical health. Results are based on telephone interviews with adults, aged 18 and older, living in metropolitan areas in the 50 U.S. states and the District of Columbia. *Gallup-Healthways, "State of American Well-Being," February 23, 2016*

Safety Rankings

- The National Insurance Crime Bureau ranked 380 metro areas in the U.S. in terms of per capita rates of vehicle theft. The Kansas City* metro area ranked #37 (#1 = highest rate). Criteria: number of vehicle theft offenses per 100,000 inhabitants in 2014. *National Insurance Crime Bureau, "Hot Spots 2014," June 24, 2015*

Seniors/Retirement Rankings

- From its Best Cities for Successful Aging indexes, the Milken Institute generated rankings for metropolitan areas, weighing data in eight categories—health care, wellness, living arrangements, transportation, financial characteristics, education and employment opportunities, community engagement, and overall livability. The Kansas City* metro area was ranked #26 overall in the large metro area category. *Milken Institute, "Best Cities for Successful Aging, 2014"*

Miscellaneous Rankings

- The watchdog site Charity Navigator conducts an annual study of charities in the nation's major markets both to analyze statistical differences in their financial, accountability, and transparency practices and to track year-to-year variations in individual communities. The Kansas City* metro area was ranked #25 among the 30 metro markets in the rating dimension of Overall Score. *www.charitynavigator.org, "Metro Market Study 2015," June 5, 2015*
- Mars Chocolate North America, the makers of COMBOS®, in partnership with Sperling's BestPlaces, ranked 50 major metro areas in terms of their "manliness." The Kansas City* metro area ranked #20. Criteria: number of professional sports teams; number of nearby NASCAR tracks and racing events; manly lifestyle; concentration of manly retail stores; manly occupations per capita; salty snack sales; "Board of Manliness" rankings. *Mars Chocolate North America, "America's Manliest Cities 2012"*
- The National Alliance to End Homelessness ranked the 100 most populous metro areas with the highest rate of homelessness. The Kansas City* metro area ranked #49. Criteria: number of homeless people per 10,000 population in 2011. *National Alliance to End Homelessness, The State of Homelessness in America 2012*

***Lee's Summit is located within the Kansas City, MO-KS Metropolitan Statistical Area.**

Business Environment

CITY FINANCES

City Government Finances

Component	2012 ($000)	2012 ($ per capita)
Total Revenues	140,128	1,533
Total Expenditures	130,896	1,432
Debt Outstanding	98,345	1,076
Cash and Securities[1]	129,611	1,418

Note: (1) Cash and security holdings of a government at the close of its fiscal year, including those of its dependent agencies, utilities, and liquor stores.
Source: U.S Census Bureau, State & Local Government Finances 2012

City Government Revenue by Source

Source	2012 ($000)	2012 ($ per capita)
General Revenue		
From Federal Government	1,255	13
From State Government	2,181	23
From Local Governments	2,933	32
Taxes		
Property	26,802	293
Sales and Gross Receipts	44,665	488
Personal Income	0	0
Corporate Income	0	0
Motor Vehicle License	358	3
Other Taxes	1,055	11
Current Charges	25,083	274
Liquor Store	0	0
Utility	13,577	148
Employee Retirement	0	0

Source: U.S Census Bureau, State & Local Government Finances 2012

City Government Expenditures by Function

Function	2012 ($000)	2012 ($ per capita)	2012 (%)
General Direct Expenditures			
Air Transportation	2,146	23	1.6
Corrections	0	0	0.0
Education	0	0	0.0
Employment Security Administration	0	0	0.0
Financial Administration	4,252	46	3.2
Fire Protection	15,437	168	11.7
General Public Buildings	0	0	0.0
Governmental Administration, Other	4,645	50	3.5
Health	0	0	0.0
Highways	17,753	194	13.5
Hospitals	0	0	0.0
Housing and Community Development	1,459	15	1.1
Interest on General Debt	3,805	41	2.9
Judicial and Legal	2,203	24	1.6
Libraries	0	0	0.0
Parking	0	0	0.0
Parks and Recreation	7,634	83	5.8
Police Protection	18,233	199	13.9
Public Welfare	0	0	0.0
Sewerage	10,165	111	7.7
Solid Waste Management	3,206	35	2.4
Veterans' Services	0	0	0.0
Liquor Store	0	0	0.0
Utility	14,163	155	10.8
Employee Retirement	0	0	0.0

Source: U.S Census Bureau, State & Local Government Finances 2012

DEMOGRAPHICS

Population Growth

Area	1990 Census	2000 Census	2010 Census	2014* Estimate	Population Growth (%) 1990-2014	Population Growth (%) 2010-2014
City	46,585	70,700	91,364	92,813	99.2	1.6
MSA[1]	1,636,528	1,836,038	2,035,334	2,040,869	24.7	0.3
U.S.	248,709,873	281,421,906	308,745,538	314,107,084	26.3	1.7

Note: (1) Figures cover the Kansas City, MO-KS Metropolitan Statistical Area—see Appendix B for areas included; (*) 2010-2014 5-year estimated population
Source: U.S. Census Bureau, 1990 Census, Census 2000, Census 2010, 2010-2014 American Community Survey 5-Year Estimates

Household Size

Area	Persons in Household (%) One	Two	Three	Four	Five	Six	Seven or More	Average Household Size
City	21.9	33.7	17.5	16.7	7.1	1.6	1.1	2.75
MSA[1]	28.8	33.6	15.3	13.0	5.8	2.0	1.1	2.54
U.S.	27.5	33.5	15.8	13.1	6.0	2.3	1.4	2.64

Note: (1) Figures cover the Kansas City, MO-KS Metropolitan Statistical Area—see Appendix B for areas included
Source: U.S. Census Bureau, 2010-2014 American Community Survey 5-Year Estimates

Race

Area	White Alone[2] (%)	Black Alone[2] (%)	Asian Alone[2] (%)	AIAN[3] Alone[2] (%)	NHOPI[4] Alone[2] (%)	Other Race Alone[2] (%)	Two or More Races (%)
City	84.2	8.8	2.3	0.1	0.4	1.5	2.7
MSA[1]	79.1	12.5	2.5	0.4	0.1	2.4	2.9
U.S.	73.8	12.6	5.0	0.8	0.2	4.7	2.9

Note: (1) Figures cover the Kansas City, MO-KS Metropolitan Statistical Area—see Appendix B for areas included; (2) Alone is defined as not being in combination with one or more other races; (3) American Indian and Alaska Native; (4) Native Hawaiian and Other Pacific Islander
Source: U.S. Census Bureau, 2010-2014 American Community Survey 5-Year Estimates

Hispanic or Latino Origin

Area	Total (%)	Mexican (%)	Puerto Rican (%)	Cuban (%)	Other (%)
City	3.9	2.8	0.4	0.1	0.7
MSA[1]	8.5	6.5	0.3	0.2	1.5
U.S.	16.9	10.8	1.6	0.6	3.8

Note: Persons of Hispanic or Latino origin can be of any race; (1) Figures cover the Kansas City, MO-KS Metropolitan Statistical Area—see Appendix B for areas included
Source: U.S. Census Bureau, 2010-2014 American Community Survey 5-Year Estimates

Ancestry

Area	German	Irish	English	American	Italian	Polish	French[2]	Scottish	Dutch
City	24.9	12.8	12.8	6.8	4.3	1.7	2.7	2.2	1.5
MSA[1]	23.2	13.3	10.2	8.1	3.5	1.7	2.6	2.0	1.6
U.S.	14.9	10.8	8.0	7.1	5.5	3.0	2.7	1.7	1.4

Note: Figures are the percentage of the total population reporting a particular ancestry. The nine most commonly reported ancestries in the U.S. are shown. Figures include multiple ancestries (e.g. if a person reported being Irish and Italian, they were included in both columns); (1) Figures cover the Kansas City, MO-KS Metropolitan Statistical Area—see Appendix B for areas included; (2) Excludes Basque
Source: U.S. Census Bureau, 2010-2014 American Community Survey 5-Year Estimates

Foreign-Born Population

Area	Percent of Population Born in: Any Foreign Country	Asia	Mexico	Europe	Carribean	Central America[2]	South America	Africa	Canada
City	3.8	1.8	0.3	0.6	0.1	0.2	0.2	0.2	0.2
MSA[1]	6.4	2.0	2.2	0.6	0.2	0.4	0.2	0.6	0.1
U.S.	13.1	3.8	3.7	1.5	1.2	1.0	0.9	0.6	0.3

Note: (1) Figures cover the Kansas City, MO-KS Metropolitan Statistical Area—see Appendix B for areas included; (2) Excludes Mexico.
Source: U.S. Census Bureau, 2010-2014 American Community Survey 5-Year Estimates

Marital Status

Area	Never Married	Now Married[2]	Separated	Widowed	Divorced
City	24.2	59.2	1.2	4.9	10.5
MSA[1]	29.7	50.8	1.8	5.5	12.2
U.S.	32.5	48.4	2.2	5.9	10.9

Note: Figures are percentages and cover the population 15 years of age and older; (1) Figures cover the Kansas City, MO-KS Metropolitan Statistical Area—see Appendix B for areas included; (2) Excludes separated
Source: U.S. Census Bureau, 2010-2014 American Community Survey 5-Year Estimates

Disability Status

Area	All Ages	Under 18 Years Old	18 to 64 Years Old	65 Years and Over
City	8.6	2.6	6.5	34.9
MSA[1]	11.6	3.7	10.2	35.5
U.S.	12.3	4.1	10.2	36.3

Note: Figures show percent of the civilian noninstitutionalized population that reported having a disability. Disability status is determined from from six types of difficulty: vision, hearing, cognitive, ambulatory, self-care, and independent living. For children under 5 years old, hearing and vision difficulty are used to determine disability status. For children between the ages of 5 and 14, disability status is determined from hearing, vision, cognitive, ambulatory, and self-care difficulties. For people aged 15 years and older, they are considered to have a disability if they have difficulty with any one of the six difficulty types; (1) Figures cover the Kansas City, MO-KS Metropolitan Statistical Area—see Appendix B for areas included.
Source: U.S. Census Bureau, 2010-2014 American Community Survey 5-Year Estimates

Age

Area	Percent of Population: Under Age 5	Age 5–19	Age 20–34	Age 35–44	Age 45–54	Age 55–64	Age 65–74	Age 75–84	Age 85+	Median Age
City	7.2	22.8	17.0	13.7	15.3	11.8	6.4	3.6	2.0	37.2
MSA[1]	6.9	20.7	20.0	13.3	14.3	12.2	7.0	3.8	1.8	36.7
U.S.	6.4	19.9	20.6	13.0	14.1	12.3	7.6	4.3	1.9	37.4

Note: (1) Figures cover the Kansas City, MO-KS Metropolitan Statistical Area—see Appendix B for areas included
Source: U.S. Census Bureau, 2010-2014 American Community Survey 5-Year Estimates

Gender

Area	Males	Females	Males per 100 Females
City	44,641	48,172	92.7
MSA[1]	1,000,049	1,040,820	96.1
U.S.	154,515,159	159,591,925	96.8

Note: (1) Figures cover the Kansas City, MO-KS Metropolitan Statistical Area—see Appendix B for areas included
Source: U.S. Census Bureau, 2010-2014 American Community Survey 5-Year Estimates

Religious Groups by Family

Area	Catholic	Baptist	Non-Den.	Methodist[2]	Lutheran	LDS[3]	Pente-costal	Presby-terian[4]	Muslim[5]	Judaism
MSA[1]	12.6	13.1	5.2	5.8	2.2	2.4	2.6	1.6	0.3	0.4
U.S.	19.1	9.3	4.0	4.0	2.3	2.0	1.9	1.6	0.8	0.7

Note: Figures are the number of adherents as a percentage of the total population; (1) Figures cover the Kansas City, MO-KS Metropolitan Statistical Area—see Appendix B for areas included; (2) Methodist/Pietist; (3) Latter Day Saints; (4) Reformed; (5) Figures are estimates
Source: Association of Statisticians of American Religious Bodies, 2010 U.S. Religion Census: Religious Congregations & Membership Study

Religious Groups by Tradition

Area	Catholic	Evangelical Protestant	Mainline Protestant	Other Tradition	Black Protestant	Orthodox
MSA[1]	12.6	20.5	9.9	3.6	2.6	0.1
U.S.	19.1	16.2	7.3	4.3	1.6	0.3

Note: Figures are the number of adherents as a percentage of the total population; (1) Figures cover the Kansas City, MO-KS Metropolitan Statistical Area—see Appendix B for areas included
Source: Association of Statisticians of American Religious Bodies, 2010 U.S. Religion Census: Religious Congregations & Membership Study

ECONOMY

Gross Metropolitan Product

Area	2013	2014	2015	2016	Rank[2]
MSA[1]	117.3	121.8	126.4	132.3	29

Note: Figures are in billions of dollars; (1) Figures cover the Kansas City, MO-KS Metropolitan Statistical Area—see Appendix B for areas included; (2) Rank is based on 2016 data and ranges from 1 to 381
Source: The U.S. Conference of Mayors, U.S. Metro Economies: GMP and Employment 2014-2016, June 2015

Economic Growth

Area	2011-13 (%)	2014 (%)	2015 (%)	2016 (%)	Rank[2]
MSA[1]	1.5	2.2	2.4	2.7	135
U.S.	2.2	2.4	2.3	2.9	-

Note: Figures are real gross metropolitan product (GMP) growth rates and represent annual average percent change; (1) Figures cover the Kansas City, MO-KS Metropolitan Statistical Area—see Appendix B for areas included; (2) Rank is based on 2016 data and ranges from 1 to 381
Source: The U.S. Conference of Mayors, U.S. Metro Economies: GMP and Employment 2014-2016, June 2015

Metropolitan Area Exports

Area	2009	2010	2011	2012	2013	2014	Rank[2]
MSA[1]	5,888.8	7,374.1	7,958.9	7,880.7	8,012.0	8,262.8	40

Note: Figures are in millions of dollars; (1) Figures cover the Kansas City, MO-KS Metropolitan Statistical Area—see Appendix B for areas included; (2) Rank is based on 2014 data and ranges from 1 to 385
Source: U.S. Department of Commerce, International Trade Administration, Office of Trade & Industry Information, Manufacturing & Services, data extracted March 10, 2016

Building Permits

Area	Single-Family			Multi-Family			Total		
	2014	2015p	Pct. Chg.	2014	2015p	Pct. Chg.	2014	2015p	Pct. Chg.
City	321	313	-2.5	250	209	-16.4	571	522	-8.6
MSA[1]	4,170	4,507	8.1	4,031	4,488	11.3	8,201	8,995	9.7
U.S.	640,300	690,800	7.9	411,800	487,600	18.4	1,052,100	1,178,400	12.0

Note: (1) Figures cover the Kansas City, MO-KS Metropolitan Statistical Area—see Appendix B for areas included; Figures represent new, privately-owned housing units authorized (unadjusted data); All permit data are based on estimates with imputation; (p) preliminary data.
Source: U.S. Census Bureau, Manufacturing, Mining, and Construction Statistics, Building Permits, 2014, 2015

Bankruptcy Filings

Area	Business Filings			Nonbusiness Filings		
	2014	2015	% Chg.	2014	2015	% Chg.
Jackson County	45	45	0.0	2,916	2,533	-13.1
U.S.	26,983	24,735	-8.3	909,812	819,760	-9.9

Note: Business filings include Chapter 7, Chapter 11, Chapter 12, and Chapter 13; Nonbusiness filings include Chapter 7, Chapter 11, and Chapter 13
Source: Administrative Office of the U.S. Courts, Business and Nonbusiness Bankruptcy, County Cases Commenced by Chapter of the Bankruptcy Code, During the 12- Month Period Ending December 31, 2014 and Business and Nonbusiness Bankruptcy, County Cases Commenced by Chapter of the Bankruptcy Code, During the 12- Month Period Ending December 31, 2015

Housing Vacancy Rates

Area	Gross Vacancy Rate[2] (%)			Year-Round Vacancy Rate[3] (%)			Rental Vacancy Rate[4] (%)			Homeowner Vacancy Rate[5] (%)		
	2013	2014	2015	2013	2014	2015	2013	2014	2015	2013	2014	2015
MSA[1]	10.8	9.0	7.3	10.4	8.6	7.1	10.1	9.5	7.9	2.0	1.5	1.3
U.S.	13.6	13.4	12.9	10.7	10.4	10.0	8.3	7.6	7.1	2.0	1.9	1.8

Note: (1) Figures cover the Kansas City, MO-KS Metropolitan Statistical Area—see Appendix B for areas included; (2) The percentage of the total housing inventory that is vacant; (3) The percentage of the housing inventory (excluding seasonal units) that is year-round vacant; (4) The percentage of rental inventory that is vacant for rent; (5) The percentage of homeowner inventory that is vacant for sale
Source: U.S. Census Bureau, Housing Vacancies and Homeownership Annual Statistics: 2015

INCOME

Income

Area	Per Capita ($)	Median Household ($)	Average Household ($)
City	34,153	78,186	92,467
MSA[1]	30,101	57,056	75,695
U.S.	28,555	53,482	74,596

Note: (1) Figures cover the Kansas City, MO-KS Metropolitan Statistical Area—see Appendix B for areas included
Source: U.S. Census Bureau, 2010-2014 American Community Survey 5-Year Estimates

Household Income Distribution

Area	Percent of Households Earning							
	Under $15,000	$15,000 -24,999	$25,000 -34,999	$35,000 -49,999	$50,000 -74,999	$75,000 -99,000	$100,000 -149,999	$150,000 and up
City	6.2	6.7	6.4	10.8	18.0	15.3	21.5	15.3
MSA[1]	10.9	9.5	9.9	13.7	18.6	13.4	14.4	9.6
U.S.	12.5	10.7	10.2	13.5	17.8	12.2	13.0	10.0

Note: (1) Figures cover the Kansas City, MO-KS Metropolitan Statistical Area—see Appendix B for areas included
Source: U.S. Census Bureau, 2010-2014 American Community Survey 5-Year Estimates

Poverty Rate

Area	All Ages	Under 18 Years Old	18 to 64 Years Old	65 Years and Over
City	6.6	9.6	5.7	3.9
MSA[1]	12.6	18.0	11.6	6.8
U.S.	15.6	21.9	14.6	9.4

Note: Figures are percentage of people whose income during the past 12 months was below the poverty level; (1) Figures cover the Kansas City, MO-KS Metropolitan Statistical Area—see Appendix B for areas included
Source: U.S. Census Bureau, 2010-2014 American Community Survey 5-Year Estimates

EMPLOYMENT

Labor Force and Employment

Area	Civilian Labor Force			Workers Employed		
	Dec. 2014	Dec. 2015	% Chg.	Dec. 2014	Dec. 2015	% Chg.
City	53,279	54,137	1.6	51,244	52,566	2.5
MSA[1]	1,107,078	1,118,856	1.0	1,055,730	1,076,324	1.9
U.S.	155,521,000	157,245,000	1.1	147,190,000	149,703,000	1.7

Note: Data is not seasonally adjusted and covers workers 16 years of age and older; (1) Figures cover the Kansas City, MO-KS Metropolitan Statistical Area—see Appendix B for areas included
Source: Bureau of Labor Statistics, Local Area Unemployment Statistics

Unemployment Rate

Area	2015											
	Jan.	Feb.	Mar.	Apr.	May	Jun.	Jul.	Aug.	Sep.	Oct.	Nov.	Dec.
City	4.5	4.8	4.6	4.3	4.4	4.2	4.3	4.0	3.6	3.5	3.1	2.9
MSA[1]	5.9	5.9	5.3	5.1	5.3	5.3	5.5	5.2	4.4	4.2	3.9	3.8
U.S.	6.1	5.8	5.6	5.1	5.3	5.5	5.6	5.2	4.9	4.8	4.8	4.8

Note: Data is not seasonally adjusted and covers workers 16 years of age and older; (1) Figures cover the Kansas City, MO-KS Metropolitan Statistical Area—see Appendix B for areas included
Source: Bureau of Labor Statistics, Local Area Unemployment Statistics

Employment by Occupation

Occupation Classification	City (%)	MSA[1] (%)	U.S. (%)
Management, Business, Science, and Arts	46.2	38.9	36.4
Natural Resources, Construction, and Maintenance	5.5	7.6	9.0
Production, Transportation, and Material Moving	8.2	11.5	12.1
Sales and Office	27.0	25.7	24.4
Service	13.3	16.3	18.2

Note: Figures cover employed civilians 16 years of age and older; (1) Figures cover the Kansas City, MO-KS Metropolitan Statistical Area—see Appendix B for areas included
Source: U.S. Census Bureau, 2010-2014 American Community Survey 5-Year Estimates

Employment by Industry

Sector	MSA[1]		U.S.
	Number of Employees	Percent of Total	Percent of Total
Construction, Mining, and Logging	46,200	4.3	5.0
Education and Health Services	149,700	14.2	15.7
Financial Activities	74,900	7.1	5.7
Government	148,100	14.0	15.5
Information	19,500	1.8	1.9
Leisure and Hospitality	100,600	9.5	10.4
Manufacturing	76,200	7.2	8.6
Other Services	41,200	3.9	3.9
Professional and Business Services	183,300	17.4	13.9
Retail Trade	112,500	10.6	11.3
Transportation, Warehousing, and Utilities	48,600	4.6	3.9
Wholesale Trade	50,700	4.8	4.1

Note: Figures are non-farm employment as of December 2015. Figures are not seasonally adjusted and include workers 16 years of age and older; (1) Figures cover the Kansas City, MO-KS Metropolitan Statistical Area—see Appendix B for areas included; n/a not available
Source: Bureau of Labor Statistics, Current Employment Statistics, Employment, Hours, and Earnings

Occupations with Greatest Projected Employment Growth: 2012 – 2022

Occupation[1]	2012 Employment	2022 Projected Employment	Numeric Employment Change	Percent Employment Change
Combined Food Preparation and Serving Workers, Including Fast Food	71,840	81,660	9,820	13.7
Personal Care Aides	31,360	40,430	9,070	28.9
Registered Nurses	66,970	74,990	8,020	12.0
Customer Service Representatives	49,990	56,010	6,020	12.0
Retail Salespersons	81,140	86,700	5,560	6.8
Nursing Assistants	42,320	47,470	5,150	12.2
General and Operations Managers	53,130	58,220	5,090	9.6
Secretaries and Administrative Assistants, Except Legal, Medical, and Executive	52,290	56,860	4,570	8.7
Carpenters	21,880	26,280	4,400	20.1
Heavy and Tractor-Trailer Truck Drivers	42,720	47,030	4,310	10.1

Note: Projections cover Missouri; (1) Sorted by numeric employment change
Source: www.projectionscentral.com, State Occupational Projections, 2012–2022 Long-Term Projections

Fastest Growing Occupations: 2012 – 2022

Occupation[1]	2012 Employment	2022 Projected Employment	Numeric Employment Change	Percent Employment Change
Insulation Workers, Mechanical	490	730	240	48.8
Helpers—Brickmasons, Blockmasons, Stonemasons, and Tile and Marble Setters	470	660	190	40.4
Helpers—Electricians	370	510	140	37.9
Insulation Workers, Floor, Ceiling, and Wall	490	680	190	37.5
Diagnostic Medical Sonographers	1,120	1,520	400	35.5
Interpreters and Translators	960	1,270	310	32.7
Brickmasons and Blockmasons	2,370	3,130	760	32.0
Nursing Instructors and Teachers, Postsecondary	1,350	1,780	430	31.9
Health Specialties Teachers, Postsecondary	3,370	4,420	1,050	31.1
Skincare Specialists	1,430	1,860	430	30.5

Note: Projections cover Missouri; (1) Sorted by percent employment change and excludes occupations with numeric employment change less than 100
Source: www.projectionscentral.com, State Occupational Projections, 2012–2022 Long-Term Projections

Average Wages

Occupation	$/Hr.	Occupation	$/Hr.
Accountants and Auditors	33.45	Maids and Housekeeping Cleaners	10.01
Automotive Mechanics	18.68	Maintenance and Repair Workers	17.76
Bookkeepers	18.37	Marketing Managers	61.85
Carpenters	24.09	Nuclear Medicine Technologists	32.84
Cashiers	9.86	Nurses, Licensed Practical	19.56
Clerks, General Office	15.39	Nurses, Registered	30.45
Clerks, Receptionists/Information	14.08	Nursing Assistants	12.30
Clerks, Shipping/Receiving	15.42	Packers and Packagers, Hand	11.13
Computer Programmers	36.37	Physical Therapists	37.13
Computer Systems Analysts	40.43	Postal Service Mail Carriers	24.23
Computer User Support Specialists	24.12	Real Estate Brokers	n/a
Cooks, Restaurant	10.81	Retail Salespersons	11.65
Dentists	78.43	Sales Reps., Exc. Tech./Scientific	32.40
Electrical Engineers	44.86	Sales Reps., Tech./Scientific	44.34
Electricians	28.55	Secretaries, Exc. Legal/Med./Exec.	16.32
Financial Managers	62.77	Security Guards	13.51
First-Line Supervisors/Managers, Sales	19.02	Surgeons	123.07
Food Preparation Workers	10.13	Teacher Assistants*	11.75
General and Operations Managers	53.31	Teachers, Elementary School*	23.84
Hairdressers/Cosmetologists	13.36	Teachers, Secondary School*	22.74
Internists	92.96	Telemarketers	14.09
Janitors and Cleaners	12.82	Truck Drivers, Heavy/Tractor-Trailer	21.09
Landscaping/Groundskeeping Workers	12.89	Truck Drivers, Light/Delivery Svcs.	17.22
Lawyers	57.35	Waiters and Waitresses	9.56

Note: Wage data covers the Kansas City, MO-KS Metropolitan Statistical Area—see Appendix B for areas included; (*) Hourly wages for elementary/secondary school teachers and teacher assistants were calculated by the editors from annual wage data based on a 40 hour work week; n/a not available.
Source: Bureau of Labor Statistics, Metro Area Occupational Employment and Wage Estimates, May 2015

TAXES

State Corporate Income Tax Rates

State	Tax Rate (%)	Income Brackets ($)	Num. of Brackets	Financial Institution Tax Rate (%)[a]	Federal Income Tax Ded.
Missouri	6.25	Flat rate	1	7.0	Yes (k)

Note: Tax rates as of January 1, 2016; (a) Rates listed are the corporate income tax rate applied to financial institutions or excise taxes based on income. Some states have other taxes based upon the value of deposits or shares; (k) 50% of the federal income tax is deductible.
Source: Federation of Tax Administrators, "State Corporate Income Tax Rates, 2016"

State Individual Income Tax Rates

State	Tax Rate (%)	Income Brackets ($)	Num. of Brackets	Personal Exempt. ($)[1] Single	Personal Exempt. ($)[1] Dependents	Fed. Inc. Tax Ded.
Missouri	1.5 - 6.0	1,000 - 9,001	10	2,100	1,200	Yes (m)

Note: Tax rates as of January 1, 2016; Local- and county-level taxes are not included; n/a not applicable; (1) Married joint filers generally receive double the single exemption; (m) The deduction for federal income tax is limited to $5,000 for individuals and $10,000 for joint returns in Missouri and Montana, and to $6,350 for all filers in Oregon.
Source: Federation of Tax Administrators, "State Individual Income Tax Rates, 2016"

Various State and Local Tax Rates

State	State and Local Sales and Use (%)	State Sales and Use (%)	Gasoline[1] (¢/gal.)	Cigarette[2] ($/pack)	Spirits[3] ($/gal.)	Wine[4] ($/gal.)	Beer[5] ($/gal.)
Missouri	5.475	4.225	17.3	0.17	2.00	0.42	0.06

Note: All tax rates as of January 1, 2016; (1) The American Petroleum Institute has developed a methodology for determining the average tax rate on a gallon of fuel. Rates may include any of the following: excise taxes, environmental fees, storage tank fees, other fees or taxes, general sales tax, and local taxes. In states where gasoline is subject to the general sales tax, or where the fuel tax is based on the average sale price, the average rate determined by API is sensitive to changes in the price of gasoline. States that fully or partially apply general sales taxes to gasoline: CA, CO, GA, IL, IN, MI, NY; (2) The federal excise tax of $1.0066 per pack and local taxes are not included; (3) Rates are those applicable to off-premise sales of 40% alcohol by volume (a.b.v.) distilled spirits in 750ml containers. Local excise taxes are excluded; (4) Rates are those applicable to off-premise sales of 11% a.b.v. non-carbonated wine in 750ml containers; (5) Rates are those applicable to off-premise sales of 4.7% a.b.v. beer in 12 ounce containers.
Source: Tax Foundation, 2016 Facts & Figures: How Does Your State Compare?

State Business Tax Climate Index Rankings

State	Overall Rank	Corporate Tax Rank	Individual Income Tax Rank	Sales Tax Rank	Unemployment Insurance Tax Rank	Property Tax Rank
Missouri	17	3	28	23	12	8

Note: The index is a measure of how each state's tax laws affect economic performance. The lower the rank, the more favorable a state's tax system is for business. States without a given tax are given a ranking of 1. The scores/rankings for the District of Columbia do not affect other states. The 2016 index represents the tax climate as of July 1, 2015 (the beginning of Fiscal Year 2016).
Source: Tax Foundation, State Business Tax Climate Index 2016

TRANSPORTATION

Means of Transportation to Work

Area	Car/Truck/Van		Public Transportation			Bicycle	Walked	Other Means	Worked at Home
	Drove Alone	Car-pooled	Bus	Subway	Railroad				
City	86.4	6.2	0.3	0.1	0.0	0.0	0.4	0.9	5.8
MSA[1]	83.3	8.9	1.1	0.0	0.0	0.2	1.3	1.0	4.3
U.S.	76.4	9.6	2.6	1.8	0.6	0.6	2.8	1.3	4.4

Note: Figures are percentages and cover workers 16 years of age and older; (1) Figures cover the Kansas City, MO-KS Metropolitan Statistical Area—see Appendix B for areas included
Source: U.S. Census Bureau, 2010-2014 American Community Survey 5-Year Estimates

Travel Time to Work

Area	Less Than 10 Minutes	10 to 19 Minutes	20 to 29 Minutes	30 to 44 Minutes	45 to 59 Minutes	60 to 89 Minutes	90 Minutes or More
City	14.2	24.3	21.5	28.8	8.8	1.6	0.7
MSA[1]	13.1	31.4	25.3	20.7	5.9	2.3	1.2
U.S.	13.3	29.6	21.0	20.2	7.7	5.7	2.6

Note: Figures are percentages and include workers 16 years old and over; (1) Figures cover the Kansas City, MO-KS Metropolitan Statistical Area—see Appendix B for areas included
Source: U.S. Census Bureau, 2010-2014 American Community Survey 5-Year Estimates

Freeway Travel Time Index

Area	1985	1990	1995	2000	2005	2010	2014
Urban Area Rank[1,2]	54	46	68	72	77	76	76
Urban Area Index[1]	1.06	1.10	1.11	1.13	1.14	1.14	1.15
Average Index[3]	1.09	1.11	1.14	1.17	1.20	1.19	1.20

Note: Freeway Travel Time Index—the ratio of travel time in the peak period to the travel time at free-flow conditions. For example, a value of 1.30 indicates a 20-minute free-flow trip takes 26 minutes in the peak (20 minutes x 1.30 = 26 minutes); (1) Covers the Kansas City MO-KS urban area; (2) Rank is based on 101 urban areas (#1 = highest travel time index); (3) Average of 101 urban areas
Source: Texas Transportation Institute, 2015 Urban Mobility Scorecard, August 2015

Freeway Commuter Stress Index

Area	1985	1990	1995	2000	2005	2010	2014
Urban Area Rank[1,2]	66	51	71	76	81	82	79
Urban Area Index[1]	1.07	1.12	1.13	1.15	1.16	1.16	1.17
Average Index[3]	1.13	1.16	1.19	1.22	1.25	1.24	1.25

Note: The Freeway Commuter Stress Index is the same as the Freeway Travel Time Index (see table above) except that it includes only the travel in the peak directions during the peak periods; the TTI includes travel in all directions during the peak period. Thus, the CSI is more indicative of the work trip experienced by each commuter on a daily basis. (1) Covers the Kansas City MO-KS urban area; (2) Rank is based on 101 urban areas (#1 = highest stress index); (3) Average of 101 urban areas

Source: Texas Transportation Institute, 2015 Urban Mobility Scorecard, August 2015

Living Environment

COST OF LIVING

Cost of Living Index

Composite Index	Groceries	Housing	Utilities	Trans-portation	Health Care	Misc. Goods/ Services
94.2	91.1	91.7	90.5	93.4	95.4	98.8

Note: The Cost of Living Index measures regional differences in the cost of consumer goods and services, excluding taxes and non-consumer expenditures, for professional and managerial households in the top income quintile. It is based on more than 50,000 prices covering almost 60 different items for which prices are collected three times a year by chambers of commerce, economic development organizations or university applied economic centers in each participating urban area. The numbers shown should be read as a percentage above or below the national average of 100. For example, a value of 115.4 in the groceries column indicates that grocery prices are 15.4% higher than the national average. Small differences in the index numbers should not be interpreted as significant; Figures cover the Kansas City MO-KS urban area.
Source: The Council for Community and Economic Research, ACCRA Cost of Living Index, 2015

Grocery Prices

Area[1]	T-Bone Steak ($/pound)	Frying Chicken ($/pound)	Whole Milk ($/half gal.)	Eggs ($/dozen)	Orange Juice ($/64 oz.)	Coffee ($/11.5 oz.)
City[2]	10.00	1.19	2.17	2.15	3.06	4.46
Avg.	10.99	1.43	2.25	2.26	3.58	4.48
Min.	7.16	0.98	1.30	1.35	2.88	2.98
Max.	14.13	2.43	3.85	4.81	6.39	7.56

Note: (1) Values for the local area are compared with the average, minimum and maximum values for all 292 areas in the Cost of Living Index; (2) Figures cover the Kansas City MO-KS urban area; **T-Bone Steak** *(price per pound);* **Frying Chicken** *(price per pound, whole fryer);* **Whole Milk** *(half gallon carton);* **Eggs** *(price per dozen, Grade A, large);* **Orange Juice** *(64 oz. Tropicana or Florida Natural);* **Coffee** *(11.5 oz. can, vacuum-packed, Maxwell House, Hills Bros, or Folgers).*
Source: The Council for Community and Economic Research, ACCRA Cost of Living Index, 2015

Housing and Utility Costs

Area[1]	New Home Price ($)	Apartment Rent ($/month)	All Electric ($/month)	Part Electric ($/month)	Other Energy ($/month)	Telephone ($/month)
City[2]	291,595	835	-	85.41	77.39	23.34
Avg.	312,874	945	179.30	95.07	72.96	28.11
Min.	178,682	479	116.28	43.14	26.46	10.01
Max.	1,472,476	3,984	504.25	189.44	421.11	43.06

Note: (1) Values for the local area are compared with the average, minimum and maximum values for all 292 areas in the Cost of Living Index; (2) Figures cover the Kansas City MO-KS urban area; **New Home Price** *(2,400 sf living area, 8,000 sf lot, in urban area with full utilities);* **Apartment Rent** *(950 sf 2 bedroom/1.5 or 2 bath, unfurnished, excluding all utilities except water);* **All Electric** *(average monthly cost for an all-electric home);* **Part Electric** *(average monthly cost for a part-electric home);* **Other Energy** *(average monthly cost for natural gas, fuel oil, coal, wood, and any other forms of energy except electricity);* **Telephone** *(price includes basic monthly rate for a private residential line plus additional local usage charges incurred by a family of four).*
Source: The Council for Community and Economic Research, ACCRA Cost of Living Index, 2015

Health Care, Transportation, and Other Costs

Area[1]	Doctor ($/visit)	Dentist ($/visit)	Optometrist ($/visit)	Gasoline ($/gallon)	Beauty Salon ($/visit)	Men's Shirt ($)
City[2]	93.36	87.39	94.68	2.16	31.21	28.60
Avg.	105.15	89.02	99.78	2.38	35.30	28.10
Min.	66.87	56.09	48.53	1.95	18.91	13.38
Max.	182.34	150.36	228.33	4.09	67.91	63.80

Note: (1) Values for the local area are compared with the average, minimum and maximum values for all 292 areas in the Cost of Living Index; (2) Figures cover the Kansas City MO-KS urban area; **Doctor** *(general practitioners routine exam of an established patient);* **Dentist** *(adult teeth cleaning and periodic oral examination);* **Optometrist** *(full vision eye exam for established adult patient);* **Gasoline** *(one gallon regular unleaded, national brand, including all taxes, cash price at self-service pump if available);* **Beauty Salon** *(woman's shampoo, trim, and blow-dry);* **Men's Shirt** *(cotton/polyester dress shirt, pinpoint weave, long sleeves).*
Source: The Council for Community and Economic Research, ACCRA Cost of Living Index, 2015

HOUSING

House Price Index (HPI)

Area	National Ranking[2]	Quarterly Change (%)	One-Year Change (%)	Five-Year Change (%)
MSA[1]	79	1.80	6.40	8.50
U.S.[3]	–	1.45	5.76	22.85

Note: The HPI is a weighted repeat sales index. It measures average price changes in repeat sales or refinancings on the same properties. This information is obtained by reviewing repeat mortgage transactions on single-family properties whose mortgages have been purchased or securitized by Fannie Mae or Freddie Mac in January 1975; (1) Kansas City Metropolitan Statistical Area—see Appendix B for areas included; (2) Rankings are based on annual percentage change for all metro areas containing at least 15,000 transactions over the last 10 years and ranges from 1 to 266; (3) figures based on a weighted average of Census Division estimates using a seasonally adjusted, purchase-only index; all figures are for the period ending December 31, 2015
Source: Federal Housing Finance Agency, House Price Index, February 25, 2016

Median Single-Family Home Prices

Area	2013	2014	2015p	Percent Change 2014 to 2015
MSA[1]	154.8	158.8	170.4	7.3
U.S. Average	197.4	208.9	223.9	7.2

Note: Figures are median sales prices of existing single-family homes in thousands of dollars; (p) preliminary; n/a not available; (1) Kansas City, MO-KS Metropolitan Statistical Area—see Appendix B for areas included
Source: National Association of Realtors, Median Sales Price of Existing Single-Family Homes for Metropolitan Areas, 4th Quarter 2015

Qualifying Income Based on Median Sales Price of Existing Single-Family Homes

Area	With 5% Down ($)	With 10% Down ($)	With 20% Down ($)
MSA[1]	37,257	35,296	31,374
U.S. Average	49,535	46,928	41,714

Note: Figures are preliminary; Qualifying income is based on a mortgage rate of 4.1%. Monthly principal and interest payment is limited to 25% of income; n/a not available; (1) Kansas City, MO-KS Metropolitan Statistical Area—see Appendix B for areas included
Source: National Association of Realtors, Qualifying Income Based on Median Sales Price of Existing Single-Family Homes for Metropolitan Areas, 4th Quarter 2015

Median Apartment Condo-Coop Home Prices

Area	2013	2014	2015p	Percent Change 2014 to 2015
MSA[1]	n/a	n/a	n/a	n/a
U.S. Average	194.9	204.3	210.7	3.1

Note: Figures are median sales prices of existing apartment condo-coop homes in thousands of dollars; (p) preliminary; n/a not available; (1) Kansas City, MO-KS Metropolitan Statistical Area—see Appendix B for areas included
Source: National Association of Realtors, Median Sales Price of Existing Apartment Condo-Coop Homes for Metropolitan Areas, 4th Quarter 2015

Gross Monthly Rent

Area	Under $200	$200 -299	$300 -499	$500 -749	$750 -999	$1,000 -1,499	$1,500 and up	Median ($)
City	0.2	1.2	4.9	13.7	30.5	34.4	15.2	997
MSA[1]	1.3	2.8	6.5	27.1	31.0	24.6	6.7	839
U.S.	1.5	3.2	7.4	21.0	24.1	26.9	15.9	920

Note: Figures are percentages except for Median; Gross rent is the contract rent plus the estimated average monthly cost of utilities (electricity, gas, and water and sewer) and fuels (oil, coal, kerosene, wood, etc.) if these are paid by the renter (or paid for the renter by someone else); (1) Figures cover the Kansas City, MO-KS Metropolitan Statistical Area—see Appendix B for areas included
Source: U.S. Census Bureau, 2010-2014 American Community Survey 5-Year Estimates

Homeownership Rate

Area	2008 (%)	2009 (%)	2010 (%)	2011 (%)	2012 (%)	2013 (%)	2014 (%)	2015 (%)
MSA[1]	70.2	69.5	68.8	68.5	65.1	65.6	66.1	65.0
U.S.	67.8	67.4	66.9	66.1	65.4	65.1	64.5	63.7

Note: (1) Figures cover the Kansas City, MO-KS Metropolitan Statistical Area—see Appendix B for areas included
Source: U.S. Census Bureau, Housing Vacancies and Homeownership Annual Statistics: 2015

Year Housing Structure Built

Area	2010 or Later	2000 -2009	1990 -1999	1980 -1989	1970 -1979	1960 -1969	1950 -1959	1940 -1949	Before 1940	Median Year
City	0.9	24.9	26.8	18.8	14.9	6.9	3.8	0.8	2.2	1991
MSA[1]	0.7	15.0	14.3	12.6	15.9	12.5	12.2	4.9	11.9	1975
U.S.	1.0	14.9	13.9	13.8	15.8	11.0	10.8	5.4	13.3	1976

Note: Figures are percentages except for Median Year; (1) Figures cover the Kansas City, MO-KS Metropolitan Statistical Area—see Appendix B for areas included
Source: U.S. Census Bureau, 2010-2014 American Community Survey 5-Year Estimates

HEALTH

Health Risk Data

Category	MSA[1] (%)	U.S. (%)
Adults aged 18–64 who have any kind of health care coverage	83.7	79.6
Adults who reported being in good or excellent health	84.0	83.1
Adults who are current smokers	22.0	19.6
Adults who are heavy drinkers[2]	6.2	6.1
Adults who are binge drinkers[3]	17.3	16.9
Adults who are overweight (BMI 25.0 - 29.9)	35.7	35.8
Adults who are obese (BMI 30.0 - 99.8)	28.3	27.6
Adults who participated in any physical activities in the past month	79.5	77.1
Adults 50+ who have ever had a sigmoidoscopy or colonoscopy	72.8	67.3
Women aged 40+ who have had a mammogram within the past two years	76.1	74.0
Men aged 40+ who have had a PSA test within the past two years	50.8	45.2
Adults aged 65+ who have had flu shot within the past year	66.5	60.1
Adults who always wear a seatbelt	90.3	93.8

Note: Data as of 2012 unless otherwise noted; (1) Figures cover the Kansas City, MO-KS Metropolitan Statistical Area—see Appendix B for areas included; (2) Heavy drinkers are classified as males having more than two drinks per day or females having more than one drink per day; (3) Binge drinkers are classified as males having five or more drinks on one occasion or females having four or more drinks on one occasion
Source: Centers for Disease Control and Prevention, Behaviorial Risk Factor Surveillance System, SMART: Selected Metropolitan/Micropolitan Area Risk Trends, 2012 (Note: the CDC has discontinued this dataset but will be releasing a replacement in mid-2016)

Chronic Health Indicators

Category	MSA[1] (%)	U.S. (%)
Adults who have ever been told they had a heart attack	4.0	4.5
Adults who have ever been told they had a stroke	3.3	2.9
Adults who have been told they currently have asthma	9.7	8.9
Adults who have ever been told they have arthritis	25.8	25.7
Adults who have ever been told they have diabetes[2]	10.4	9.7
Adults who have ever been told they had skin cancer	5.8	5.7
Adults who have ever been told they had any other types of cancer	6.1	6.5
Adults who have ever been told they have COPD	7.4	6.2
Adults who have ever been told they have kidney disease	2.2	2.5
Adults who have ever been told they have a form of depression	16.7	18.0

Note: Data as of 2012 unless otherwise noted; (1) Figures cover the Kansas City, MO-KS Metropolitan Statistical Area—see Appendix B for areas included; (2) Figures do not include pregnancy-related, borderline, or pre-diabetes
Source: Centers for Disease Control and Prevention, Behaviorial Risk Factor Surveillance System, SMART: Selected Metropolitan/Micropolitan Area Risk Trends, 2012 (Note: the CDC has discontinued this dataset but will be releasing a replacement in mid-2016)

Mortality Rates for the Top 10 Causes of Death in the U.S.

ICD-10[a] Sub-Chapter	ICD-10[a] Code	Age-Adjusted Mortality Rate[1] per 100,000 population: County[2]	Age-Adjusted Mortality Rate[1] per 100,000 population: U.S.
Malignant neoplasms	C00-C97	185.2	163.6
Ischaemic heart diseases	I20-I25	88.1	102.2
Other forms of heart disease	I30-I51	69.0	50.1
Chronic lower respiratory diseases	J40-J47	53.8	41.4
Organic, including symptomatic, mental disorders	F01-F09	45.7	38.5
Cerebrovascular diseases	I60-I69	41.8	36.5
Other external causes of accidental injury	W00-X59	32.9	27.5
Other degenerative diseases of the nervous system	G30-G31	30.3	26.3
Diabetes mellitus	E10-E14	21.8	21.1
Hypertensive diseases	I10-I15	21.2	19.7

Note: (a) ICD-10 = International Classification of Diseases 10th Revision; (1) Mortality rates are a three year average covering 2012-2014; (2) Figures cover Jackson County.
Source: Centers for Disease Control and Prevention, National Center for Health Statistics. Underlying Cause of Death 1999-2014 on CDC WONDER Online Database, released 2015.

Mortality Rates for Selected Causes of Death

ICD-10[a] Sub-Chapter	ICD-10[a] Code	Age-Adjusted Mortality Rate[1] per 100,000 population: County[2]	Age-Adjusted Mortality Rate[1] per 100,000 population: U.S.
Assault	X85-Y09	15.0	5.1
Diseases of the liver	K70-K76	14.8	13.5
Human immunodeficiency virus (HIV) disease	B20-B24	2.9	2.1
Influenza and pneumonia	J09-J18	15.9	15.2
Intentional self-harm	X60-X84	16.1	12.7
Malnutrition	E40-E46	1.5	0.9
Obesity and other hyperalimentation	E65-E68	1.8	1.9
Renal failure	N17-N19	21.0	13.0
Transport accidents	V01-V99	10.5	11.6
Viral hepatitis	B15-B19	2.8	2.1

Note: (a) ICD-10 = International Classification of Diseases 10th Revision; (1) Mortality rates are a three year average covering 2012-2014; (2) Figures cover Jackson County; Data are Suppressed when the data meet the criteria for confidentiality constraints; Mortality rates are flagged as Unreliable when the rate would be calculated with a numerator of 20 or less.
Source: Centers for Disease Control and Prevention, National Center for Health Statistics. Underlying Cause of Death 1999-2014 on CDC WONDER Online Database, released 2015.

Health Insurance Coverage

Area	With Health Insurance	With Private Health Insurance	With Public Health Insurance	Without Health Insurance	Population Under Age 18 Without Health Insurance
City	93.8	84.9	18.6	6.2	3.3
MSA[1]	87.5	73.2	25.1	12.5	6.5
U.S.	85.8	65.8	31.1	14.2	7.1

Note: Figures are percentages that cover the civilian noninstitutionalized population; (1) Figures cover the Kansas City, MO-KS Metropolitan Statistical Area—see Appendix B for areas included
Source: U.S. Census Bureau, 2010-2014 American Community Survey 5-Year Estimates

Number of Medical Professionals

Area	MDs[3]	DOs[3,4]	Dentists	Podiatrists	Chiropractors	Optometrists
County[1] (number)	1,970	374	544	41	269	124
County[1] (rate[2])	289.7	55.0	79.6	6.0	39.4	18.2
U.S. (rate[2])	272.5	20.9	64.7	5.8	25.9	15.2

Note: Data as of 2014 unless noted; (1) Data covers Jackson County; (2) Rate per 100,000 population; (3) Data as of 2013 and includes all active, non-federal physicians; (4) Doctor of Osteopathic Medicine
Source: U.S. Department of Health and Human Services, Health Resources and Services Administration, Bureau of Health Professions, Area Resource File (ARF) 2014-2015

Best Hospitals

According to *U.S. News,* the Kansas City, MO-KS metro area is home to two of the best hospitals in the U.S.: **St. Luke's Hospital** (7 specialties); **University of Kansas Hospital** (12 specialties). The hospitals listed were nationally ranked in at least one adult specialty. Only 137 hospitals nationwide were nationally ranked in one or more specialties. Fifteen hospitals in the U.S. made the Honor Roll with high scores in at least six specialties. *U.S. News Online, "America's Best Children's Hospitals 2015-16"*

According to *U.S. News,* the Kansas City, MO-KS metro area is home to one of the best children's hospitals in the U.S.: **Children's Mercy Hospitals and Clinics** (10 specialties). The hospital listed was highly ranked in at least one pediatric specialty. Eighty-three children's hospitals in the U.S. were nationally ranked in at least one specialty. Twelve children's hospitals in the U.S. made the Honor Roll with high scores in at least three specialties. *U.S. News Online, "America's Best Children's Hospitals 2015-16"*

EDUCATION

Public School District Statistics

District Name	Schls	Pupils	Pupil/ Teacher Ratio	Minority Pupils[1] (%)	Free Lunch Eligible[2] (%)	IEP[3] (%)
Blue Springs R-IV	22	14,382	16.0	24.6	22.6	9.8
Lee's Summit R-VII	27	17,844	15.6	23.8	15.8	9.3
MO Schls for the Severly Disabled	35	892	5.5	24.6	56.6	99.9

Note: Table includes school districts with 100 or more students; (1) Percentage of students that are not non-Hispanic white; (2) Percentage of students that are eligible for the free lunch program; (3) Percentage of students that have an Individualized Education Program.
Source: U.S. Department of Education, National Center for Education Statistics, Common Core of Data, Local Education Agency (School District) Universe Survey: School Year 2013-2014; U.S. Department of Education, National Center for Education Statistics, Common Core of Data, Public Elementary/Secondary School Universe Survey: School Year 2013-2014

Highest Level of Education

Area	Less than H.S.	H.S. Diploma	Some College, No Deg.	Associate Degree	Bachelor's Degree	Master's Degree	Prof. School Degree	Doctorate Degree
City	3.6	21.2	23.6	9.0	27.6	11.0	2.4	1.6
MSA[1]	9.2	26.5	23.4	7.4	21.5	8.9	2.2	1.1
U.S.	13.7	28.0	21.2	7.9	18.3	7.8	2.0	1.3

Note: Figures cover persons age 25 and over; (1) Figures cover the Kansas City, MO-KS Metropolitan Statistical Area—see Appendix B for areas included
Source: U.S. Census Bureau, 2010-2014 American Community Survey 5-Year Estimates

Educational Attainment by Race

Area	High School Graduate or Higher (%)					Bachelor's Degree or Higher (%)				
	Total	White	Black	Asian	Hisp.[2]	Total	White	Black	Asian	Hisp.[2]
City	96.4	96.7	94.7	96.2	80.1	42.6	43.8	34.5	40.2	36.3
MSA[1]	90.8	92.5	86.1	84.1	65.5	33.6	36.1	17.9	52.6	15.2
U.S.	86.3	88.4	83.2	85.8	64.1	29.3	30.6	19.0	50.9	13.9

Note: Figures shown cover persons 25 years old and over; (1) Figures cover the Kansas City, MO-KS Metropolitan Statistical Area—see Appendix B for areas included; (2) People of Hispanic origin can be of any race
Source: U.S. Census Bureau, 2010-2014 American Community Survey 5-Year Estimates

School Enrollment by Grade and Control

Area	Preschool (%)		Kindergarten (%)		Grades 1 - 4 (%)		Grades 5 - 8 (%)		Grades 9 - 12 (%)	
	Public	Private	Public	Private	Public	Private	Public	Private	Public	Private
City	35.2	64.8	87.8	12.2	90.3	9.7	94.4	5.6	91.3	8.7
MSA[1]	51.5	48.5	86.7	13.3	88.7	11.3	88.6	11.4	89.7	10.3
U.S.	57.4	42.6	87.8	12.2	89.8	10.2	89.9	10.1	90.6	9.4

Note: Figures shown cover persons 3 years old and over; (1) Figures cover the Kansas City, MO-KS Metropolitan Statistical Area—see Appendix B for areas included
Source: U.S. Census Bureau, 2010-2014 American Community Survey 5-Year Estimates

Average Salaries of Public School Classroom Teachers

Area	2013-14 Dollars	2013-14 Rank[1]	2014-15 Dollars	2014-15 Rank[1]	Percent Change 2013-14 to 2014-15	Percent Change 2004-05 to 2014-15
Missouri	46,750	42	47,394	43	1.38	21.3
U.S. Average	56,610	–	57,379	–	1.36	20.8

Note: (1) State rank ranges from 1 to 51 where 1 indicates highest salary.
Source: National Education Association, Rankings & Estimates: Rankings of the States 2014 and Estimates of School Statistics 2015, March 2015

Higher Education

Four-Year Colleges			Two-Year Colleges			Medical Schools[1]	Law Schools[2]	Voc/ Tech[3]
Public	Private Non-profit	Private For-profit	Public	Private Non-profit	Private For-profit			
0	0	1	0	0	0	0	0	0

Note: Figures cover institutions located within the city limits and include main campuses only; (1) includes schools accredited by the Liaison Committee on Medical Education and the American Osteopathic Association's Commission on Osteopathic College Accreditation; (2) includes ABA-accredited schools, schools with provisional ABA accreditation, and state accredited schools; (3) includes all schools with programs that are less than 2 years.
Source: National Center for Education Statistics, Integrated Postsecondary Education System (IPEDS), 2014-15; Association of American Medical Colleges, Member List, March 21, 2016; American Osteopathic Association, Member List, March 21, 2016; Law School Admission Council, Official Guide to ABA-Approved Law Schools Online, March 21, 2016; Wikipedia, List of Medical Schools in the United States, March 21, 2016; Wikipedia, List of Law Schools in the United States, March 21, 2016

According to *U.S. News & World Report,* the Kansas City, MO-KS metro area is home to one of the best national universities in the U.S.: **University of Missouri–Kansas City** (#194 tie). The indicators used to capture academic quality fall into a number of categories: assessment by administrators at peer institutions; retention of students; faculty resources; student selectivity; financial resources; alumni giving; high school counselor ratings of colleges; and graduation rate. *U.S. News & World Report, "America's Best Colleges 2016"*

According to *U.S. News & World Report,* the Kansas City, MO-KS metro area is home to one of the best liberal arts colleges in the U.S.: **William Jewell College** (#158 tie). The indicators used to capture academic quality fall into a number of categories: assessment by administrators at peer institutions; retention of students; faculty resources; student selectivity; financial resources; alumni giving; high school counselor ratings of colleges; and graduation rate. *U.S. News & World Report, "America's Best Colleges 2016"*

According to *U.S. News & World Report,* the Kansas City, MO-KS metro area is home to one of the top 75 medical schools for research in the U.S.: **University of Kansas Medical Center, School of Medicine** (#69 tie). The rankings are based on a weighted average of 11 measures of quality: quality assessment; peer assessment score; assessment score by residency directors; research activity; total research activity; average research activity per faculty member; student selectivity; median MCAT total score; median undergraduate GPA; acceptance rate; and faculty resources. *U.S. News & World Report, "America's Best Graduate Schools, Medical, 2017"*

PRESIDENTIAL ELECTION

2012 Presidential Election Results

Area	Obama (%)	Romney (%)	Other (%)
Jackson County	58.7	39.7	1.6
U.S.	51.0	47.2	1.8

Note: Results may not add to 100% due to rounding
Source: Dave Leip's Atlas of U.S. Presidential Elections

EMPLOYERS

Major Employers

Company Name	Industry
B&V Baker Guam JV	Consulting engineer
B&V Baker Guam JV	Engineering services
Black and Veatch Corp	Engineering services
DST Systems	Data processing
Embarq Corporation	Telephone communications
Ford Motor Company	Automobile assembly
Hallmark Cardsorporated	Greeting cards
HCA Midwest Division	Hospital management
Honeywell International	Search & navigation equipment
Internal Revenue Service	Taxation, department/government
North Kansas City Hospital	General medical/surgical hospitals
Park University	Colleges, except junior
Performance Contracting	Drywall
St Lukes Hospital of Kansas	General medical/surgical hospitals
United Auto Workers	Labor union
University of Kansas	Charitable trust management
University of Kansas	Medical centers
University of Missouri System	General medical/surgical hospitals

Note: Companies shown are located within the Kansas City, MO-KS Metropolitan Statistical Area.
Source: Hoovers.com; Wikipedia

PUBLIC SAFETY

Crime Rate

Area	All Crimes	Violent Crimes				Property Crimes		
		Murder	Rape[3]	Robbery	Aggrav. Assault	Burglary	Larceny -Theft	Motor Vehicle Theft
City	2,007.6	2.1	20.3	20.3	44.9	261.8	1,547.1	111.1
Metro[1]	3,499.3	6.6	54.4	113.2	307.9	627.9	1,991.0	398.3
U.S.	2,971.8	4.5	36.6	102.2	232.5	542.5	1,837.3	216.2

Note: Figures are crimes per 100,000 population; (1) Figures cover the Kansas City, MO-KS Metropolitan Statistical Area—see Appendix B for areas included; (3) The city and U.S. figures shown were reported using the revised Uniform Crime Reporting (UCR) definition of rape. The suburban and metro area figures shown are an aggregate total of the data submitted using both the revised and legacy UCR definitions.
Source: FBI Uniform Crime Reports, 2014

Hate Crimes

Area	Number of Quarters Reported	Number of Incidents per Bias Motivation						
		Race	Religion	Sexual Orientation	Ethnicity	Disability	Gender	Gender Identity
City	4	2	0	0	0	0	0	0
U.S.	4	2,568	1,014	1,017	648	84	33	98

Source: Federal Bureau of Investigation, Hate Crime Statistics 2014

Identity Theft Consumer Complaints

Area	Complaints	Complaints per 100,000 Population	Rank[2]
MSA[1]	3,348	161.7	46
U.S.	490,220	152.4	-

Note: (1) Figures cover the Kansas City, MO-KS Metropolitan Statistical Area—see Appendix B for areas included; (2) Rank ranges from 1 to 379 where 1 indicates greatest number of identity theft complaints per 100,000 population
Source: Federal Trade Commission, Consumer Sentinel Network Data Book for January–December 2015

Fraud and Other Consumer Complaints

Area	Complaints	Complaints per 100,000 Population	Rank[2]
MSA[1]	8,239	397.8	108
U.S.	2,593,159	806.0	-

Note: (1) Figures cover the Kansas City, MO-KS Metropolitan Statistical Area—see Appendix B for areas included; (2) Rank ranges from 1 to 379 where 1 indicates greatest number of identity theft complaints per 100,000 population
Source: Federal Trade Commission, Consumer Sentinel Network Data Book for January–December 2015

RECREATION

Culture

Dance[1]	Theatre[1]	Instrumental Music[1]	Vocal Music[1]	Series and Festivals	Museums and Art Galleries[2]	Zoos and Aquariums[3]
0	0	0	0	0	0	0

Note: (1) Professional perfoming groups; (2) Based on organizations with SIC code 8412; (3) AZA-accredited
Source: The Grey House Performing Arts Directory, 2015-16; Association of Zoos & Aquariums, AZA Member Zoos & Aquariums, March 25, 2016; www.AccuLeads.com, March 29, 2016

Professional Sports Teams

Team Name	League	Year Established
Kansas City Chiefs	National Football League (NFL)	1963
Kansas City Royals	Major League Baseball (MLB)	1969
Sporting Kansas City	Major League Soccer (MLS)	1996

Note: Includes teams located in the Kansas City, MO-KS Metropolitan Statistical Area.
Source: Wikipedia, Major Professional Sports Teams of the United States and Canada, March 24, 2016

CLIMATE

Average and Extreme Temperatures

Temperature	Jan	Feb	Mar	Apr	May	Jun	Jul	Aug	Sep	Oct	Nov	Dec	Yr.
Extreme High (°F)	69	76	86	93	92	105	107	109	102	92	82	70	109
Average High (°F)	35	40	54	65	74	84	90	87	79	66	52	39	64
Average Temp. (°F)	26	31	44	55	64	74	79	77	68	56	43	30	54
Average Low (°F)	17	22	34	44	54	63	69	66	58	45	34	21	44
Extreme Low (°F)	-17	-19	-10	12	30	42	54	43	33	21	1	-23	-23

Note: Figures cover the years 1972-1990
Source: National Climatic Data Center, International Station Meteorological Climate Summary, 9/96

Average Precipitation/Snowfall/Humidity

Precip./Humidity	Jan	Feb	Mar	Apr	May	Jun	Jul	Aug	Sep	Oct	Nov	Dec	Yr.
Avg. Precip. (in.)	1.1	1.2	2.8	3.0	5.5	4.1	3.8	4.1	4.9	3.6	2.1	1.6	38.1
Avg. Snowfall (in.)	6	5	3	1	0	0	0	0	0	Tr	1	5	21
Avg. Rel. Hum. 6am (%)	76	77	78	77	82	84	84	86	86	80	79	78	80
Avg. Rel. Hum. 3pm (%)	58	59	54	50	54	54	51	53	53	51	57	60	54

Note: Figures cover the years 1972-1990; Tr = Trace amounts (<0.05 in. of rain; <0.5 in. of snow)
Source: National Climatic Data Center, International Station Meteorological Climate Summary, 9/96

Weather Conditions

Temperature			Daytime Sky			Precipitation		
10°F & below	32°F & below	90°F & above	Clear	Partly cloudy	Cloudy	0.01 inch or more precip.	0.1 inch or more snow/ice	Thunder-storms
22	110	39	112	134	119	103	17	51

Note: Figures are average number of days per year and cover the years 1972-1990
Source: National Climatic Data Center, International Station Meteorological Climate Summary, 9/96

HAZARDOUS WASTE

Superfund Sites

Lee's Summit has no sites on the EPA's Superfund Final National Priorities List. There are a total of 1,323 Superfund sites on the list in the U.S. *U.S. Environmental Protection Agency, Final National Priorities List, March 18, 2016*

AIR & WATER QUALITY

Air Quality Trends: Ozone

	1990	1995	2000	2005	2010	2011	2012	2013	2014
MSA[1]	0.075	0.098	0.088	0.084	0.072	0.080	0.085	0.067	0.066

Note: (1) Data covers the Kansas City, MO-KS Metropolitan Statistical Area—see Appendix B for areas included. The values shown are the composite ozone concentration averages among trend sites based on the highest fourth daily maximum 8-hour concentration in parts per million. These trends are based on sites having an adequate record of monitoring data during the trend period. Data from exceptional events are included.
Source: U.S. Environmental Protection Agency, Air Quality Monitoring Information, "Air Quality Trends by City, 1990-2014"

Air Quality Index

Area	Percent of Days when Air Quality was...[2]					AQI Statistics[2]	
	Good	Moderate	Unhealthy for Sensitive Groups	Unhealthy	Very Unhealthy	Maximum	Median
MSA[1]	44.9	44.7	10.4	0.0	0.0	134	53

Note: (1) Data covers the Kansas City, MO-KS Metropolitan Statistical Area—see Appendix B for areas included; (2) Based on 365 days with AQI data in 2015. Air Quality Index (AQI) is an index for reporting daily air quality. EPA calculates the AQI for five major air pollutants regulated by the Clean Air Act: ground-level ozone, particle pollution (aka particulate matter), carbon monoxide, sulfur dioxide, and nitrogen dioxide. The AQI runs from 0 to 500. The higher the AQI value, the greater the level of air pollution and the greater the health concern. There are six AQI categories: "Good" AQI is between 0 and 50. Air quality is considered satisfactory; "Moderate" AQI is between 51 and 100. Air quality is acceptable; "Unhealthy for Sensitive Groups" When AQI values are between 101 and 150, members of sensitive groups may experience health effects; "Unhealthy" When AQI values are between 151 and 200 everyone may begin to experience health effects; "Very Unhealthy" AQI values between 201 and 300 trigger a health alert; "Hazardous" AQI values over 300 trigger warnings of emergency conditions (not shown).
Source: U.S. Environmental Protection Agency, Air Quality Index Report, 2015

Air Quality Index Pollutants

Area	Percent of Days when AQI Pollutant was...[2]					
	Carbon Monoxide	Nitrogen Dioxide	Ozone	Sulfur Dioxide	Particulate Matter 2.5	Particulate Matter 10
MSA[1]	0.0	3.8	19.5	20.3	46.8	9.6

Note: (1) Data covers the Kansas City, MO-KS Metropolitan Statistical Area—see Appendix B for areas included; (2) Based on 365 days with AQI data in 2015. The Air Quality Index (AQI) is an index for reporting daily air quality. EPA calculates the AQI for five major air pollutants regulated by the Clean Air Act: ground-level ozone, particle pollution (also known as particulate matter), carbon monoxide, sulfur dioxide, and nitrogen dioxide. The AQI runs from 0 to 500. The higher the AQI value, the greater the level of air pollution and the greater the health concern.
Source: U.S. Environmental Protection Agency, Air Quality Index Report, 2015

Maximum Air Pollutant Concentrations: Particulate Matter, Ozone, CO and Lead

	Particulate Matter 10 (ug/m^3)	Particulate Matter 2.5 Wtd AM (ug/m^3)	Particulate Matter 2.5 24-Hr (ug/m^3)	Ozone (ppm)	Carbon Monoxide (ppm)	Lead (ug/m^3)
MSA[1] Level	90	9.5	22	0.068	1	0.01
NAAQS[2]	150	15	35	0.075	9	0.15
Met NAAQS[2]	Yes	Yes	Yes	Yes	Yes	Yes

Note: (1) Data covers the Kansas City, MO-KS Metropolitan Statistical Area—see Appendix B for areas included; Data from exceptional events are included; (2) National Ambient Air Quality Standards; ppm = parts per million; ug/m^3 = micrograms per cubic meter; n/a not available.
Concentrations: Particulate Matter 10 (coarse particulate)—highest second maximum 24-hour concentration; Particulate Matter 2.5 Wtd AM (fine particulate)—highest weighted annual mean concentration; Particulate Matter 2.5 24-Hour (fine particulate)—highest 98th percentile 24-hour concentration; Ozone—highest fourth daily maximum 8-hour concentration; Carbon Monoxide—highest second maximum non-overlapping 8-hour concentration; Lead—maximum running 3-month average
Source: U.S. Environmental Protection Agency, Air Quality Monitoring Information, "Air Quality Statistics by City, 2014"

Maximum Air Pollutant Concentrations: Nitrogen Dioxide and Sulfur Dioxide

	Nitrogen Dioxide AM (ppb)	Nitrogen Dioxide 1-Hr (ppb)	Sulfur Dioxide AM (ppb)	Sulfur Dioxide 1-Hr (ppb)	Sulfur Dioxide 24-Hr (ppb)
MSA[1] Level	13	53	n/a	125	n/a
NAAQS[2]	53	100	30	75	140
Met NAAQS[2]	Yes	Yes	n/a	No	n/a

Note: (1) Data covers the Kansas City, MO-KS Metropolitan Statistical Area—see Appendix B for areas included; Data from exceptional events are included; (2) National Ambient Air Quality Standards; ppm = parts per million; ug/m^3 = micrograms per cubic meter; n/a not available.
Concentrations: Nitrogen Dioxide AM—highest arithmetic mean concentration; Nitrogen Dioxide 1-Hr—highest 98th percentile 1-hour daily maximum concentration; Sulfur Dioxide AM—highest annual mean concentration; Sulfur Dioxide 1-Hr—highest 99th percentile 1-hour daily maximum concentration; Sulfur Dioxide 24-Hr—highest second maximum 24-hour concentration
Source: U.S. Environmental Protection Agency, Air Quality Monitoring Information, "Air Quality Statistics by City, 2014"

Drinking Water

Water System Name	Pop. Served	Primary Water Source Type	Violations[1]	
			Health Based	Monitoring/ Reporting
Lee's Summit	87,000	Purchased Surface	0	0

Note: (1) Based on violation data from January 1, 2015 to December 31, 2015 (includes unresolved violations from earlier years)
Source: U.S. Environmental Protection Agency, Office of Ground Water and Drinking Water, Safe Drinking Water Information System (based on data extracted April 29, 2016)

O'Fallon, Missouri

Background

O'Fallon is located along Interstate 70 between Wentzville and St. Charles in St. Charles County. It is 34 miles northwest of St. Louis.

The area that is now O'Fallon originally belonged to a local judge and politician named Arnold Krekel. In 1854, Krekel granted permission to North Missouri Railroad to build a new depot on his land, which was finished in 1856 and named O'Fallon Station. Also in 1856, Krekel's younger brother Nicholas built the city's first houses. The territory was called the "Krekel Addition" until 1860 when it was renamed O'Fallon. The city was incorporated in 1912. In the mid-1950s, the construction of Interstate 70 linked O'Fallon to St. Louis and other major metropolitan areas.

For most of the twentieth century, O'Fallon was a quiet, small community. During the early 1980s, its population began to rise dramatically. Between 1990 and 2007, it grew from 17,000 to 79,000.

Two of O'Fallon's largest employers are Citigroup, a New York-based banking and insurance company, and Mastercard.

One of the city's major attractions is the T. R. Hughes Ballpark, which was built in 1999 near downtown. The park is home to the River City Rascals, a minor league baseball team of the Independent Frontier League. The Fort Zumwalt Park offers visitors 48 wooded acres and a fishing lake. Additionally, the O'Fallon Veterans Memorial Walk and the Dames Park Vietnam War Memorial are especially popular with history buffs and veterans.

O'Fallon is also home to a 72-bed BJC Progress West Healthcare Center and a $40 million Caledonia shopping center.

Median summer temperatures in O'Fallon average 70 degrees, while winter averages fall to 10 degrees during the months of December and January. The city averages 3.5 inches of rainfall per month from April to October and 8.5 inches of snowfall per month from December to March.

Rankings

Business/Finance Rankings

- The personal finance site NerdWallet analyzed 183 American metropolitan areas with populations over 250,000 and more than 15,000 businesses to rank where entrepreneurs find the most success. Criteria included area economy, annual income, housing cost, unemployment rate, and the success rate of area businesses. Saint Louis* ranked #47. *www.nerdwallet.com, "Best Places to Start a Business," April 27, 2015*
- USAA and Hiring Our Heroes worked with Sperlings's BestPlaces and the Institute for Veterans and Military Families at Syracuse University to rank major metropolitan areas where military-skills-related employment is strongest. Criteria for *mid-career* veterans included veteran wage growth; military skills, defense contractor, and government jobs; recent job growth; stability; and accessible health resources. Metro areas with a higher than national average crime or unemployment rate were excluded. At #6, the Saint Louis* metro area made the top ten. *www.usaa.com, "2015 Best Places for Veterans"*
- Based on metro area social media reviews, the employment opinion group Glassdoor surveyed 50 of the largest U.S. metro areas and equally weighed cost of living, hiring opportunity, and job satisfaction to compose a list of "25 Best Cities for Jobs." The Saint Louis* metro area was ranked #11 in overall job satisfaction. *www.glassdoor.com, "Best Cities for Jobs," May 19, 2015*
- In a survey of economic confidence in the nation's 50 largest metropolitan areas conducted January–December 2014, the Saint Louis* metro area placed #38, according to Gallup's 2014 Economic Confidence Index. *Gallup, "San Jose and San Francisco Lead in Economic Confidence," March 19, 2015*
- The Brookings Institution ranked the 100 largest metro areas in the U.S. based on income inequality. Saint Louis* was ranked #59 (#1 = greatest ineqality). Criteria: the "95/20 ratio," a figure representing the income at which a household earns more than 95 percent of all other households, divided by the income at which a household earns more than only 20 percent of all other households. *Brookings Institution, "Income Inequality, 100 Largest U.S. Metro Areas, 2007-2014," January 14, 2016*
- Payscale.com ranked the 20 largest metro areas in terms of wage growth. The Saint Louis* metro area ranked #14. Criteria: private-sector wage growth between the 1st quarter of 2015 and the 1st quarter of 2016. *PayScale, "Wage Trends by Metro Area," 1st Quarter, 2016*
- The Saint Louis* metro area was identified as one of the most debt-ridden places in America by the finance site Credit.com. The metro area was ranked #9. Criteria: residents' average personal debt load and average credit scores. *Credit.com, "The Most Debt-Ridden Cities," May 1, 2014*
- The Saint Louis* metro area was identified as one of the most affordable metropolitan areas in America by *Forbes.* The area ranked #7 out of 20 based on the National Association of Home Builders/Wells Fargo Housing Affordability Index and Sperling's Best Places' cost-of-living index. *Forbes.com, "America's Most Affordable Cities in 2015," March 12, 2015*
- Saint Louis* was identified as one of America's most frugal metro areas by *Coupons.com.* The city ranked #17 out of 25. Criteria: online coupon usage. *Coupons.com, "Top 25 Most Frugal Cities of 2014," May 11, 2015*
- Saint Louis* was identified as one of America's most frugal metro areas by *Coupons.com.* The city ranked #13 out of 25. Criteria: Grocery IQ and coupons.com mobile app usage. *Coupons.com, "Top 25 Most On-the-Go Frugal Cities of 2013," April 10, 2014*
- The Saint Louis* metro area appeared on the Milken Institute "2015 Best Performing Cities" list. Rank: #170 out of 200 large metro areas. Criteria: job growth; wage and salary growth; high-tech output growth. *Milken Institute, "Best-Performing Cities 2015," December 2015*

- *Forbes* ranked the 200 most populous metro areas to determine the nation's "Best Places for Business and Careers." The Saint Louis* metro area was ranked #84. Criteria: costs (business and living); job growth (past and projected); income growth; educational attainment (college and high school); projected economic growth; cultural and recreational opportunities; net migration patterns; number of highly ranked colleges. *Forbes, "The Best Places for Business and Careers 2015," July 29, 2015*

Education Rankings

- Personal finance website *WalletHub* analyzed the 150 largest U.S. metropolitan statistical areas to determine where the most educated Americans are choosing to settle. Criteria: education quality and attainment gap; education levels; percentage of workers with degrees; public school rankings; quality and size of each metro area's universities. Saint Louis* was ranked #35 (#1 = most educated city). *www.WalletHub.com, "2015's Most and Least Educated Cities*

Environmental Rankings

- The Saint Louis* metro area came in at #232 for the relative comfort of its climate on Sperling's list of "chill cities," as measured by the Sperling Heat Index. All 361 metro areas are included. Criteria included daytime high temperatures, nighttime low temperatures, dew point, and relative humidity at the high temperatures. *www.bertsperling.com, "Sperling's Chill Cities," July 18, 2013*

- Sperling's BestPlaces assessed 379 metropolitan areas of the United States for the likelihood of dangerously extreme weather events or earthquakes. In general the Southeast and South-Central regions have the highest risk of weather extremes and earthquakes, while the Pacific Northwest enjoys the lowest risk. Of the least risky metropolitan areas, the Saint Louis* metro area was ranked #327. *www.bestplaces.net, "Safest Places from Natural Disasters," April 2011*

- Saint Louis* was identified as one of America's dirtiest metro areas by *Forbes*. The area ranked #20 out of 20. Criteria: air quality; water quality; toxic releases; superfund sites. *Forbes, "America's 20 Dirtiest Cities," December 10, 2012*

- Saint Louis* was highlighted as one of the 25 most ozone-polluted metro areas in the U.S. during 2011 through 2013. The area ranked #16. *American Lung Association, State of the Air 2015*

Health/Fitness Rankings

- For each of the 50 most populous metro areas in the United States, the American College of Sports Medicine's American Fitness Index evaluated infrastructure, community assets, and policies that encourage healthy and fit lifestyles, including preventive health behaviors, levels of chronic disease conditions, health care access, and community resources and policies that support physical activity. The Saint Louis* metro area ranked #29 for "community fitness." *www.americanfitnessindex.org, "ACSM American Fitness Index Health and Community Fitness Status of the 50 Largest Metropolitan Areas," May 2015*

- The Saint Louis* metro area was identified as one of the worst cities for bed bugs in America by pest control company Orkin. The area ranked #40 out of 50 based on the number of bed bug treatments Orkin performed from January to December 2015. *Orkin, "Chicago Tops Bed Bug Cities List for Fourth Year in a Row," January 13, 2016*

- Saint Louis* was identified as a "2016 Spring Allergy Capital." The area ranked #35 out of 100. Three groups of factors were used to identify the most severe cities for people with allergies during the spring season: annual pollen levels; medicine utilization; access to board-certified allergists. *Asthma and Allergy Foundation of America, "Spring Allergy Capitals 2016"*

- Saint Louis* was identified as a "2015 Asthma Capital." The area ranked #26 out of the nation's 100 largest metropolitan areas. Criteria: estimated prevalence; self-reported prevalence; crude death rate for asthma; annual pollen score; annual air quality; public smoking laws; number of board-certified asthma specialists; school inhaler access laws; rescue medication use; controller medication use; ER visits for asthma; uninsured rate; poverty rate. *Asthma and Allergy Foundation of America, "Asthma Capitals 2015"*

- The Saint Louis* metro area ranked #162 out of 190 in The Gallup-Healthways Well-Being Index. Criteria: purpose; social well being; financial health; community and physical health. Results are based on telephone interviews with adults, aged 18 and older, living in metropolitan areas in the 50 U.S. states and the District of Columbia. *Gallup-Healthways, "State of American Well-Being," February 23, 2016*

Real Estate Rankings

- Based on the home-price forecasts compiled by the real-estate valuation firm CoreLogic Case-Shiller, CNNMoney reported that in 2016, the Saint Louis* metro area is expected to be one of the hottest housing markets in the U.S. Criteria: residential real estate prices. *money.cnn.com, "The 10 Hottest Housing Markets for 2016," December 3, 2015*

- The Saint Louis* metro area appeared on Realtor.com's list of the hottest housing markets to watch in 2016. The area ranked #2. Criteria: strong housing growth; affordable prices; and fast-paced sales. *Realtor.com®, "Top 10 Hot Real Estate Markets to Watch in 2016," December 2, 2015*

- Saint Louis* was ranked #50 out of 225 metro areas in terms of housing affordability in 2015 by the National Association of Home Builders (#1 = most affordable). Criteria: the share of homes sold in that area affordable to a family earning the local median income, based on standard mortgage underwriting criteria. *National Association of Home Builders®, NAHB-Wells Fargo Housing Opportunity Index, 4th Quarter 2015*

Safety Rankings

- The National Insurance Crime Bureau ranked 380 metro areas in the U.S. in terms of per capita rates of vehicle theft. The Saint Louis* metro area ranked #102 (#1 = highest rate). Criteria: number of vehicle theft offenses per 100,000 inhabitants in 2014. *National Insurance Crime Bureau, "Hot Spots 2014," June 24, 2015*

Seniors/Retirement Rankings

- From its Best Cities for Successful Aging indexes, the Milken Institute generated rankings for metropolitan areas, weighing data in eight categories—health care, wellness, living arrangements, transportation, financial characteristics, education and employment opportunities, community engagement, and overall livability. The Saint Louis* metro area was ranked #30 overall in the large metro area category. *Milken Institute, "Best Cities for Successful Aging, 2014"*

Miscellaneous Rankings

- The watchdog site Charity Navigator conducts an annual study of charities in the nation's major markets both to analyze statistical differences in their financial, accountability, and transparency practices and to track year-to-year variations in individual communities. The Saint Louis* metro area was ranked #16 among the 30 metro markets in the rating dimension of Overall Score. *www.charitynavigator.org, "Metro Market Study 2015," June 5, 2015*

- Mars Chocolate North America, the makers of COMBOS®, in partnership with Sperling's BestPlaces, ranked 50 major metro areas in terms of their "manliness." The Saint Louis* metro area ranked #7. Criteria: number of professional sports teams; number of nearby NASCAR tracks and racing events; manly lifestyle; concentration of manly retail stores; manly occupations per capita; salty snack sales; "Board of Manliness" rankings. *Mars Chocolate North America, "America's Manliest Cities 2012"*

- The Saint Louis* metro area was selected as one of "America's Most Miserable Cities" by *Forbes.com.* The metro area ranked #12 out of 20. Criteria: violent crime; unemployment; foreclosures; income and property taxes; home prices; commute times; climate. *Forbes.com, "America's Most Miserable Cities" February 22, 2013*

- The National Alliance to End Homelessness ranked the 100 most populous metro areas with the highest rate of homelessness. The Saint Louis* metro area ranked #64. Criteria: number of homeless people per 10,000 population in 2011. *National Alliance to End Homelessness, The State of Homelessness in America 2012*

***O'Fallon is located within the St. Louis, MO-IL Metropolitan Statistical Area.**

Business Environment

CITY FINANCES

City Government Finances

Component	2012 ($000)	2012 ($ per capita)
Total Revenues	69,343	874
Total Expenditures	62,339	785
Debt Outstanding	231,011	2,912
Cash and Securities[1]	158,644	1,999

Note: (1) Cash and security holdings of a government at the close of its fiscal year, including those of its dependent agencies, utilities, and liquor stores.
Source: U.S Census Bureau, State & Local Government Finances 2012

City Government Revenue by Source

Source	2012 ($000)	2012 ($ per capita)
General Revenue		
From Federal Government	175	2
From State Government	5,574	70
From Local Governments	0	0
Taxes		
Property	7,975	100
Sales and Gross Receipts	30,431	383
Personal Income	0	0
Corporate Income	0	0
Motor Vehicle License	0	0
Other Taxes	788	9
Current Charges	16,381	206
Liquor Store	0	0
Utility	4,335	54
Employee Retirement	0	0

Source: U.S Census Bureau, State & Local Government Finances 2012

City Government Expenditures by Function

Function	2012 ($000)	2012 ($ per capita)	2012 (%)
General Direct Expenditures			
Air Transportation	0	0	0.0
Corrections	0	0	0.0
Education	0	0	0.0
Employment Security Administration	0	0	0.0
Financial Administration	2,076	26	3.3
Fire Protection	0	0	0.0
General Public Buildings	1,727	21	2.7
Governmental Administration, Other	5,856	73	9.3
Health	0	0	0.0
Highways	9,820	123	15.7
Hospitals	0	0	0.0
Housing and Community Development	174	2	0.2
Interest on General Debt	4,327	54	6.9
Judicial and Legal	727	9	1.1
Libraries	0	0	0.0
Parking	0	0	0.0
Parks and Recreation	7,876	99	12.6
Police Protection	11,792	148	18.9
Public Welfare	0	0	0.0
Sewerage	4,722	59	7.5
Solid Waste Management	3,281	41	5.2
Veterans' Services	0	0	0.0
Liquor Store	0	0	0.0
Utility	4,109	51	6.5
Employee Retirement	0	0	0.0

Source: U.S Census Bureau, State & Local Government Finances 2012

DEMOGRAPHICS

Population Growth

Area	1990 Census	2000 Census	2010 Census	2014* Estimate	Population Growth (%) 1990-2014	Population Growth (%) 2010-2014
City	21,851	46,169	79,329	81,978	275.2	3.3
MSA[1]	2,580,897	2,698,687	2,812,896	2,797,737	8.4	-0.5
U.S.	248,709,873	281,421,906	308,745,538	314,107,084	26.3	1.7

Note: (1) Figures cover the St. Louis, MO-IL Metropolitan Statistical Area—see Appendix B for areas included; (*) 2010-2014 5-year estimated population
Source: U.S. Census Bureau, 1990 Census, Census 2000, Census 2010, 2010-2014 American Community Survey 5-Year Estimates

Household Size

Area	Persons in Household (%) One	Two	Three	Four	Five	Six	Seven or More	Average Household Size
City	20.6	29.5	17.8	19.8	8.4	2.6	0.8	2.78
MSA[1]	29.2	33.8	15.7	12.8	5.5	1.7	0.8	2.48
U.S.	27.5	33.5	15.8	13.1	6.0	2.3	1.4	2.64

Note: (1) Figures cover the St. Louis, MO-IL Metropolitan Statistical Area—see Appendix B for areas included
Source: U.S. Census Bureau, 2010-2014 American Community Survey 5-Year Estimates

Race

Area	White Alone[2] (%)	Black Alone[2] (%)	Asian Alone[2] (%)	AIAN[3] Alone[2] (%)	NHOPI[4] Alone[2] (%)	Other Race Alone[2] (%)	Two or More Races (%)
City	90.0	4.3	3.5	0.1	0.0	0.3	1.7
MSA[1]	76.5	18.3	2.2	0.2	0.0	0.6	2.1
U.S.	73.8	12.6	5.0	0.8	0.2	4.7	2.9

Note: (1) Figures cover the St. Louis, MO-IL Metropolitan Statistical Area—see Appendix B for areas included; (2) Alone is defined as not being in combination with one or more other races; (3) American Indian and Alaska Native; (4) Native Hawaiian and Other Pacific Islander
Source: U.S. Census Bureau, 2010-2014 American Community Survey 5-Year Estimates

Hispanic or Latino Origin

Area	Total (%)	Mexican (%)	Puerto Rican (%)	Cuban (%)	Other (%)
City	2.0	1.4	0.2	0.0	0.4
MSA[1]	2.7	1.8	0.2	0.1	0.6
U.S.	16.9	10.8	1.6	0.6	3.8

Note: Persons of Hispanic or Latino origin can be of any race; (1) Figures cover the St. Louis, MO-IL Metropolitan Statistical Area—see Appendix B for areas included
Source: U.S. Census Bureau, 2010-2014 American Community Survey 5-Year Estimates

Ancestry

Area	German	Irish	English	American	Italian	Polish	French[2]	Scottish	Dutch
City	39.3	18.0	9.2	6.7	7.2	4.2	4.8	1.5	1.4
MSA[1]	29.3	13.8	8.1	7.3	4.8	2.6	3.6	1.5	1.3
U.S.	14.9	10.8	8.0	7.1	5.5	3.0	2.7	1.7	1.4

Note: Figures are the percentage of the total population reporting a particular ancestry. The nine most commonly reported ancestries in the U.S. are shown. Figures include multiple ancestries (e.g. if a person reported being Irish and Italian, they were included in both columns); (1) Figures cover the St. Louis, MO-IL Metropolitan Statistical Area—see Appendix B for areas included; (2) Excludes Basque
Source: U.S. Census Bureau, 2010-2014 American Community Survey 5-Year Estimates

Foreign-Born Population

Area	Percent of Population Born in								
	Any Foreign Country	Asia	Mexico	Europe	Carribean	Central America[2]	South America	Africa	Canada
City	3.7	2.5	0.2	0.6	0.0	0.0	0.1	0.2	0.1
MSA[1]	4.5	1.9	0.6	1.2	0.1	0.1	0.1	0.3	0.1
U.S.	13.1	3.8	3.7	1.5	1.2	1.0	0.9	0.6	0.3

Note: (1) Figures cover the St. Louis, MO-IL Metropolitan Statistical Area—see Appendix B for areas included; (2) Excludes Mexico.
Source: U.S. Census Bureau, 2010-2014 American Community Survey 5-Year Estimates

Marital Status

Area	Never Married	Now Married[2]	Separated	Widowed	Divorced
City	25.6	59.3	1.3	4.2	9.5
MSA[1]	31.8	48.9	1.8	6.3	11.2
U.S.	32.5	48.4	2.2	5.9	10.9

Note: Figures are percentages and cover the population 15 years of age and older; (1) Figures cover the St. Louis, MO-IL Metropolitan Statistical Area—see Appendix B for areas included; (2) Excludes separated
Source: U.S. Census Bureau, 2010-2014 American Community Survey 5-Year Estimates

Disability Status

Area	All Ages	Under 18 Years Old	18 to 64 Years Old	65 Years and Over
City	8.2	4.6	5.5	37.9
MSA[1]	12.1	4.3	10.0	35.2
U.S.	12.3	4.1	10.2	36.3

Note: Figures show percent of the civilian noninstitutionalized population that reported having a disability. Disability status is determined from from six types of difficulty: vision, hearing, cognitive, ambulatory, self-care, and independent living. For children under 5 years old, hearing and vision difficulty are used to determine disability status. For children between the ages of 5 and 14, disability status is determined from hearing, vision, cognitive, ambulatory, and self-care difficulties. For people aged 15 years and older, they are considered to have a disability if they have difficulty with any one of the six difficulty types; (1) Figures cover the St. Louis, MO-IL Metropolitan Statistical Area—see Appendix B for areas included.
Source: U.S. Census Bureau, 2010-2014 American Community Survey 5-Year Estimates

Age

Area	Percent of Population									Median Age
	Under Age 5	Age 5–19	Age 20–34	Age 35–44	Age 45–54	Age 55–64	Age 65–74	Age 75–84	Age 85+	
City	7.3	24.2	18.3	16.1	14.7	9.4	5.2	3.2	1.4	35.0
MSA[1]	6.1	19.7	19.9	12.5	14.8	12.9	7.6	4.5	2.0	38.5
U.S.	6.4	19.9	20.6	13.0	14.1	12.3	7.6	4.3	1.9	37.4

Note: (1) Figures cover the St. Louis, MO-IL Metropolitan Statistical Area—see Appendix B for areas included
Source: U.S. Census Bureau, 2010-2014 American Community Survey 5-Year Estimates

Gender

Area	Males	Females	Males per 100 Females
City	40,556	41,422	97.9
MSA[1]	1,354,888	1,442,849	93.9
U.S.	154,515,159	159,591,925	96.8

Note: (1) Figures cover the St. Louis, MO-IL Metropolitan Statistical Area—see Appendix B for areas included
Source: U.S. Census Bureau, 2010-2014 American Community Survey 5-Year Estimates

Religious Groups by Family

Area	Catholic	Baptist	Non-Den.	Methodist[2]	Lutheran	LDS[3]	Pente-costal	Presby-terian[4]	Muslim[5]	Judaism
MSA[1]	19.8	10.0	3.8	3.4	4.1	0.6	1.2	3.0	0.4	0.7
U.S.	19.1	9.3	4.0	4.0	2.3	2.0	1.9	1.6	0.8	0.7

Note: Figures are the number of adherents as a percentage of the total population; (1) Figures cover the St. Louis, MO-IL Metropolitan Statistical Area—see Appendix B for areas included; (2) Methodist/Pietist; (3) Latter Day Saints; (4) Reformed; (5) Figures are estimates
Source: Association of Statisticians of American Religious Bodies, 2010 U.S. Religion Census: Religious Congregations & Membership Study

Religious Groups by Tradition

Area	Catholic	Evangelical Protestant	Mainline Protestant	Other Tradition	Black Protestant	Orthodox
MSA[1]	19.8	17.4	7.3	2.3	2.1	0.2
U.S.	19.1	16.2	7.3	4.3	1.6	0.3

Note: Figures are the number of adherents as a percentage of the total population; (1) Figures cover the St. Louis, MO-IL Metropolitan Statistical Area—see Appendix B for areas included
Source: Association of Statisticians of American Religious Bodies, 2010 U.S. Religion Census: Religious Congregations & Membership Study

ECONOMY

Gross Metropolitan Product

Area	2013	2014	2015	2016	Rank[2]
MSA[1]	146.0	150.2	154.6	161.1	22

Note: Figures are in billions of dollars; (1) Figures cover the St. Louis, MO-IL Metropolitan Statistical Area—see Appendix B for areas included; (2) Rank is based on 2016 data and ranges from 1 to 381
Source: The U.S. Conference of Mayors, U.S. Metro Economies: GMP and Employment 2014-2016, June 2015

Economic Growth

Area	2011-13 (%)	2014 (%)	2015 (%)	2016 (%)	Rank[2]
MSA[1]	0.9	1.2	1.5	2.2	236
U.S.	2.2	2.4	2.3	2.9	–

Note: Figures are real gross metropolitan product (GMP) growth rates and represent annual average percent change; (1) Figures cover the St. Louis, MO-IL Metropolitan Statistical Area—see Appendix B for areas included; (2) Rank is based on 2016 data and ranges from 1 to 381
Source: The U.S. Conference of Mayors, U.S. Metro Economies: GMP and Employment 2014-2016, June 2015

Metropolitan Area Exports

Area	2009	2010	2011	2012	2013	2014	Rank[2]
MSA[1]	9,026.6	11,239.4	12,307.5	14,642.3	12,393.6	10,359.8	31

Note: Figures are in millions of dollars; (1) Figures cover the St. Louis, MO-IL Metropolitan Statistical Area—see Appendix B for areas included; (2) Rank is based on 2014 data and ranges from 1 to 385
Source: U.S. Department of Commerce, International Trade Administration, Office of Trade & Industry Information, Manufacturing & Services, data extracted March 10, 2016

Building Permits

Area	Single-Family			Multi-Family			Total		
	2014	2015p	Pct. Chg.	2014	2015p	Pct. Chg.	2014	2015p	Pct. Chg.
City	344	378	9.9	98	172	75.5	442	550	24.4
MSA[1]	4,538	5,008	10.4	2,454	2,290	-6.7	6,992	7,298	4.4
U.S.	640,300	690,800	7.9	411,800	487,600	18.4	1,052,100	1,178,400	12.0

Note: (1) Figures cover the St. Louis, MO-IL Metropolitan Statistical Area—see Appendix B for areas included; Figures represent new, privately-owned housing units authorized (unadjusted data); All permit data are based on estimates with imputation; (p) preliminary data.
Source: U.S. Census Bureau, Manufacturing, Mining, and Construction Statistics, Building Permits, 2014, 2015

Bankruptcy Filings

Area	Business Filings 2014	Business Filings 2015	Business Filings % Chg.	Nonbusiness Filings 2014	Nonbusiness Filings 2015	Nonbusiness Filings % Chg.
Saint Charles County	28	16	-42.9	1,311	1,242	-5.3
U.S.	26,983	24,735	-8.3	909,812	819,760	-9.9

Note: Business filings include Chapter 7, Chapter 11, Chapter 12, and Chapter 13; Nonbusiness filings include Chapter 7, Chapter 11, and Chapter 13
Source: Administrative Office of the U.S. Courts, Business and Nonbusiness Bankruptcy, County Cases Commenced by Chapter of the Bankruptcy Code, During the 12- Month Period Ending December 31, 2014 and Business and Nonbusiness Bankruptcy, County Cases Commenced by Chapter of the Bankruptcy Code, During the 12- Month Period Ending December 31, 2015

Housing Vacancy Rates

Area	Gross Vacancy Rate[2] (%)			Year-Round Vacancy Rate[3] (%)			Rental Vacancy Rate[4] (%)			Homeowner Vacancy Rate[5] (%)		
	2013	2014	2015	2013	2014	2015	2013	2014	2015	2013	2014	2015
MSA[1]	15.1	12.3	10.7	14.9	12.0	10.3	13.2	10.3	9.7	3.5	2.4	3.1
U.S.	13.6	13.4	12.9	10.7	10.4	10.0	8.3	7.6	7.1	2.0	1.9	1.8

Note: (1) Figures cover the St. Louis, MO-IL Metropolitan Statistical Area—see Appendix B for areas included; (2) The percentage of the total housing inventory that is vacant; (3) The percentage of the housing inventory (excluding seasonal units) that is year-round vacant; (4) The percentage of rental inventory that is vacant for rent; (5) The percentage of homeowner inventory that is vacant for sale
Source: U.S. Census Bureau, Housing Vacancies and Homeownership Annual Statistics: 2015

INCOME

Income

Area	Per Capita ($)	Median Household ($)	Average Household ($)
City	31,809	78,634	88,857
MSA[1]	30,024	54,959	74,420
U.S.	28,555	53,482	74,596

Note: (1) Figures cover the St. Louis, MO-IL Metropolitan Statistical Area—see Appendix B for areas included
Source: U.S. Census Bureau, 2010-2014 American Community Survey 5-Year Estimates

Household Income Distribution

Area	Percent of Households Earning: Under $15,000	$15,000 -24,999	$25,000 -34,999	$35,000 -49,999	$50,000 -74,999	$75,000 -99,000	$100,000 -149,999	$150,000 and up
City	4.4	6.1	6.9	11.7	18.2	17.2	22.3	13.2
MSA[1]	11.7	10.2	10.0	13.6	18.3	12.8	13.7	9.6
U.S.	12.5	10.7	10.2	13.5	17.8	12.2	13.0	10.0

Note: (1) Figures cover the St. Louis, MO-IL Metropolitan Statistical Area—see Appendix B for areas included
Source: U.S. Census Bureau, 2010-2014 American Community Survey 5-Year Estimates

Poverty Rate

Area	All Ages	Under 18 Years Old	18 to 64 Years Old	65 Years and Over
City	4.9	5.5	4.5	5.4
MSA[1]	13.2	18.9	12.3	7.5
U.S.	15.6	21.9	14.6	9.4

Note: Figures are percentage of people whose income during the past 12 months was below the poverty level; (1) Figures cover the St. Louis, MO-IL Metropolitan Statistical Area—see Appendix B for areas included
Source: U.S. Census Bureau, 2010-2014 American Community Survey 5-Year Estimates

EMPLOYMENT

Labor Force and Employment

Area	Civilian Labor Force Dec. 2014	Civilian Labor Force Dec. 2015	Civilian Labor Force % Chg.	Workers Employed Dec. 2014	Workers Employed Dec. 2015	Workers Employed % Chg.
City	46,014	47,250	2.6	44,461	46,000	3.4
MSA[1]	1,448,218	1,479,973	2.1	1,372,069	1,416,204	3.2
U.S.	155,521,000	157,245,000	1.1	147,190,000	149,703,000	1.7

Note: Data is not seasonally adjusted and covers workers 16 years of age and older; (1) Figures cover the St. Louis, MO-IL Metropolitan Statistical Area—see Appendix B for areas included
Source: Bureau of Labor Statistics, Local Area Unemployment Statistics

Unemployment Rate

Area	2015											
	Jan.	Feb.	Mar.	Apr.	May	Jun.	Jul.	Aug.	Sep.	Oct.	Nov.	Dec.
City	4.0	4.1	4.1	3.9	3.9	3.9	3.8	3.4	3.1	2.9	2.7	2.6
MSA[1]	6.0	6.0	5.9	5.3	5.5	5.6	5.7	5.1	4.6	4.6	4.6	4.3
U.S.	6.1	5.8	5.6	5.1	5.3	5.5	5.6	5.2	4.9	4.8	4.8	4.8

Note: Data is not seasonally adjusted and covers workers 16 years of age and older; (1) Figures cover the St. Louis, MO-IL Metropolitan Statistical Area—see Appendix B for areas included
Source: Bureau of Labor Statistics, Local Area Unemployment Statistics

Employment by Occupation

Occupation Classification	City (%)	MSA[1] (%)	U.S. (%)
Management, Business, Science, and Arts	43.0	38.0	36.4
Natural Resources, Construction, and Maintenance	6.6	7.7	9.0
Production, Transportation, and Material Moving	8.5	11.2	12.1
Sales and Office	26.4	25.6	24.4
Service	15.5	17.5	18.2

Note: Figures cover employed civilians 16 years of age and older; (1) Figures cover the St. Louis, MO-IL Metropolitan Statistical Area—see Appendix B for areas included
Source: U.S. Census Bureau, 2010-2014 American Community Survey 5-Year Estimates

Employment by Industry

Sector	MSA[1]		U.S.
	Number of Employees	Percent of Total	Percent of Total
Construction, Mining, and Logging	63,100	4.6	5.0
Education and Health Services	243,900	17.9	15.7
Financial Activities	86,300	6.3	5.7
Government	163,900	12.0	15.5
Information	28,000	2.0	1.9
Leisure and Hospitality	143,100	10.5	10.4
Manufacturing	113,000	8.3	8.6
Other Services	48,100	3.5	3.9
Professional and Business Services	208,200	15.3	13.9
Retail Trade	146,100	10.7	11.3
Transportation, Warehousing, and Utilities	51,400	3.7	3.9
Wholesale Trade	63,400	4.6	4.1

Note: Figures are non-farm employment as of December 2015. Figures are not seasonally adjusted and include workers 16 years of age and older; (1) Figures cover the St. Louis, MO-IL Metropolitan Statistical Area—see Appendix B for areas included; n/a not available
Source: Bureau of Labor Statistics, Current Employment Statistics, Employment, Hours, and Earnings

Occupations with Greatest Projected Employment Growth: 2012 – 2022

Occupation[1]	2012 Employment	2022 Projected Employment	Numeric Employment Change	Percent Employment Change
Combined Food Preparation and Serving Workers, Including Fast Food	71,840	81,660	9,820	13.7
Personal Care Aides	31,360	40,430	9,070	28.9
Registered Nurses	66,970	74,990	8,020	12.0
Customer Service Representatives	49,990	56,010	6,020	12.0
Retail Salespersons	81,140	86,700	5,560	6.8
Nursing Assistants	42,320	47,470	5,150	12.2
General and Operations Managers	53,130	58,220	5,090	9.6
Secretaries and Administrative Assistants, Except Legal, Medical, and Executive	52,290	56,860	4,570	8.7
Carpenters	21,880	26,280	4,400	20.1
Heavy and Tractor-Trailer Truck Drivers	42,720	47,030	4,310	10.1

Note: Projections cover Missouri; (1) Sorted by numeric employment change
Source: www.projectionscentral.com, State Occupational Projections, 2012–2022 Long-Term Projections

Fastest Growing Occupations: 2012 – 2022

Occupation[1]	2012 Employment	2022 Projected Employment	Numeric Employment Change	Percent Employment Change
Insulation Workers, Mechanical	490	730	240	48.8
Helpers—Brickmasons, Blockmasons, Stonemasons, and Tile and Marble Setters	470	660	190	40.4
Helpers—Electricians	370	510	140	37.9
Insulation Workers, Floor, Ceiling, and Wall	490	680	190	37.5
Diagnostic Medical Sonographers	1,120	1,520	400	35.5
Interpreters and Translators	960	1,270	310	32.7
Brickmasons and Blockmasons	2,370	3,130	760	32.0
Nursing Instructors and Teachers, Postsecondary	1,350	1,780	430	31.9
Health Specialties Teachers, Postsecondary	3,370	4,420	1,050	31.1
Skincare Specialists	1,430	1,860	430	30.5

Note: Projections cover Missouri; (1) Sorted by percent employment change and excludes occupations with numeric employment change less than 100
Source: www.projectionscentral.com, State Occupational Projections, 2012–2022 Long-Term Projections

Average Wages

Occupation	$/Hr.	Occupation	$/Hr.
Accountants and Auditors	37.50	Maids and Housekeeping Cleaners	10.36
Automotive Mechanics	20.95	Maintenance and Repair Workers	19.01
Bookkeepers	19.10	Marketing Managers	66.57
Carpenters	26.82	Nuclear Medicine Technologists	33.83
Cashiers	10.22	Nurses, Licensed Practical	20.33
Clerks, General Office	15.53	Nurses, Registered	29.20
Clerks, Receptionists/Information	12.44	Nursing Assistants	12.03
Clerks, Shipping/Receiving	16.25	Packers and Packagers, Hand	11.44
Computer Programmers	40.55	Physical Therapists	37.83
Computer Systems Analysts	44.34	Postal Service Mail Carriers	24.38
Computer User Support Specialists	25.26	Real Estate Brokers	15.47
Cooks, Restaurant	11.65	Retail Salespersons	13.21
Dentists	83.85	Sales Reps., Exc. Tech./Scientific	32.93
Electrical Engineers	48.11	Sales Reps., Tech./Scientific	35.44
Electricians	30.18	Secretaries, Exc. Legal/Med./Exec.	16.37
Financial Managers	63.93	Security Guards	13.13
First-Line Supervisors/Managers, Sales	21.20	Surgeons	n/a
Food Preparation Workers	10.12	Teacher Assistants*	12.99
General and Operations Managers	53.15	Teachers, Elementary School*	27.63
Hairdressers/Cosmetologists	12.87	Teachers, Secondary School*	27.07
Internists	127.15	Telemarketers	12.35
Janitors and Cleaners	11.59	Truck Drivers, Heavy/Tractor-Trailer	20.70
Landscaping/Groundskeeping Workers	13.20	Truck Drivers, Light/Delivery Svcs.	17.44
Lawyers	55.39	Waiters and Waitresses	9.46

Note: Wage data covers the St. Louis, MO-IL Metropolitan Statistical Area—see Appendix B for areas included; (*) Hourly wages for elementary/secondary school teachers and teacher assistants were calculated by the editors from annual wage data based on a 40 hour work week; n/a not available.
Source: Bureau of Labor Statistics, Metro Area Occupational Employment and Wage Estimates, May 2015

TAXES

State Corporate Income Tax Rates

State	Tax Rate (%)	Income Brackets ($)	Num. of Brackets	Financial Institution Tax Rate (%)[a]	Federal Income Tax Ded.
Missouri	6.25	Flat rate	1	7.0	Yes (k)

Note: Tax rates as of January 1, 2016; (a) Rates listed are the corporate income tax rate applied to financial institutions or excise taxes based on income. Some states have other taxes based upon the value of deposits or shares; (k) 50% of the federal income tax is deductible.
Source: Federation of Tax Administrators, "State Corporate Income Tax Rates, 2016"

State Individual Income Tax Rates

State	Tax Rate (%)	Income Brackets ($)	Num. of Brackets	Personal Exempt. ($)[1] Single	Personal Exempt. ($)[1] Dependents	Fed. Inc. Tax Ded.
Missouri	1.5 - 6.0	1,000 - 9,001	10	2,100	1,200	Yes (m)

Note: Tax rates as of January 1, 2016; Local- and county-level taxes are not included; n/a not applicable; (1) Married joint filers generally receive double the single exemption; (m) The deduction for federal income tax is limited to $5,000 for individuals and $10,000 for joint returns in Missouri and Montana, and to $6,350 for all filers in Oregon.
Source: Federation of Tax Administrators, "State Individual Income Tax Rates, 2016"

Various State and Local Tax Rates

State	State and Local Sales and Use (%)	State Sales and Use (%)	Gasoline[1] (¢/gal.)	Cigarette[2] ($/pack)	Spirits[3] ($/gal.)	Wine[4] ($/gal.)	Beer[5] ($/gal.)
Missouri	7.95	4.225	17.3	0.17	2.00	0.42	0.06

Note: All tax rates as of January 1, 2016; (1) The American Petroleum Institute has developed a methodology for determining the average tax rate on a gallon of fuel. Rates may include any of the following: excise taxes, environmental fees, storage tank fees, other fees or taxes, general sales tax, and local taxes. In states where gasoline is subject to the general sales tax, or where the fuel tax is based on the average sale price, the average rate determined by API is sensitive to changes in the price of gasoline. States that fully or partially apply general sales taxes to gasoline: CA, CO, GA, IL, IN, MI, NY; (2) The federal excise tax of $1.0066 per pack and local taxes are not included; (3) Rates are those applicable to off-premise sales of 40% alcohol by volume (a.b.v.) distilled spirits in 750ml containers. Local excise taxes are excluded; (4) Rates are those applicable to off-premise sales of 11% a.b.v. non-carbonated wine in 750ml containers; (5) Rates are those applicable to off-premise sales of 4.7% a.b.v. beer in 12 ounce containers.
Source: Tax Foundation, 2016 Facts & Figures: How Does Your State Compare?

State Business Tax Climate Index Rankings

State	Overall Rank	Corporate Tax Rank	Individual Income Tax Rank	Sales Tax Rank	Unemployment Insurance Tax Rank	Property Tax Rank
Missouri	17	3	28	23	12	8

Note: The index is a measure of how each state's tax laws affect economic performance. The lower the rank, the more favorable a state's tax system is for business. States without a given tax are given a ranking of 1. The scores/rankings for the District of Columbia do not affect other states. The 2016 index represents the tax climate as of July 1, 2015 (the beginning of Fiscal Year 2016).
Source: Tax Foundation, State Business Tax Climate Index 2016

TRANSPORTATION

Means of Transportation to Work

Area	Car/Truck/Van: Drove Alone	Car/Truck/Van: Car-pooled	Public Transportation: Bus	Public Transportation: Subway	Public Transportation: Railroad	Bicycle	Walked	Other Means	Worked at Home
City	87.6	5.9	0.0	0.1	0.0	0.1	0.7	0.8	4.9
MSA[1]	83.0	7.7	2.1	0.4	0.1	0.3	1.8	0.9	3.9
U.S.	76.4	9.6	2.6	1.8	0.6	0.6	2.8	1.3	4.4

Note: Figures are percentages and cover workers 16 years of age and older; (1) Figures cover the St. Louis, MO-IL Metropolitan Statistical Area—see Appendix B for areas included
Source: U.S. Census Bureau, 2010-2014 American Community Survey 5-Year Estimates

Travel Time to Work

Area	Less Than 10 Minutes	10 to 19 Minutes	20 to 29 Minutes	30 to 44 Minutes	45 to 59 Minutes	60 to 89 Minutes	90 Minutes or More
City	9.9	25.3	21.5	28.7	10.5	3.0	1.2
MSA[1]	11.2	28.2	24.0	23.2	8.0	3.9	1.5
U.S.	13.3	29.6	21.0	20.2	7.7	5.7	2.6

Note: Figures are percentages and include workers 16 years old and over; (1) Figures cover the St. Louis, MO-IL Metropolitan Statistical Area—see Appendix B for areas included
Source: U.S. Census Bureau, 2010-2014 American Community Survey 5-Year Estimates

Freeway Travel Time Index

Area	1985	1990	1995	2000	2005	2010	2014
Urban Area Rank[1,2]	48	56	47	57	61	57	65
Urban Area Index[1]	1.07	1.09	1.13	1.15	1.16	1.16	1.16
Average Index[3]	1.09	1.11	1.14	1.17	1.20	1.19	1.20

Note: Freeway Travel Time Index—the ratio of travel time in the peak period to the travel time at free-flow conditions. For example, a value of 1.30 indicates a 20-minute free-flow trip takes 26 minutes in the peak (20 minutes x 1.30 = 26 minutes); (1) Covers the St. Louis MO-IL urban area; (2) Rank is based on 101 urban areas (#1 = highest travel time index); (3) Average of 101 urban areas

Source: Texas Transportation Institute, 2015 Urban Mobility Scorecard, August 2015

Freeway Commuter Stress Index

Area	1985	1990	1995	2000	2005	2010	2014
Urban Area Rank[1,2]	53	59	55	63	68	65	61
Urban Area Index[1]	1.09	1.11	1.15	1.17	1.18	1.18	1.19
Average Index[3]	1.13	1.16	1.19	1.22	1.25	1.24	1.25

Note: The Freeway Commuter Stress Index is the same as the Freeway Travel Time Index (see table above) except that it includes only the travel in the peak directions during the peak periods; the TTI includes travel in all directions during the peak period. Thus, the CSI is more indicative of the work trip experienced by each commuter on a daily basis. (1) Covers the St. Louis MO-IL urban area; (2) Rank is based on 101 urban areas (#1 = highest stress index); (3) Average of 101 urban areas

Source: Texas Transportation Institute, 2015 Urban Mobility Scorecard, August 2015

Living Environment

COST OF LIVING

Cost of Living Index

Composite Index	Groceries	Housing	Utilities	Transportation	Health Care	Misc. Goods/ Services
92.5	104.6	72.3	116.6	98.5	99.8	94.3

Note: The Cost of Living Index measures regional differences in the cost of consumer goods and services, excluding taxes and non-consumer expenditures, for professional and managerial households in the top income quintile. It is based on more than 50,000 prices covering almost 60 different items for which prices are collected three times a year by chambers of commerce, economic development organizations or university applied economic centers in each participating urban area. The numbers shown should be read as a percentage above or below the national average of 100. For example, a value of 115.4 in the groceries column indicates that grocery prices are 15.4% higher than the national average. Small differences in the index numbers should not be interpreted as significant; Figures cover the St. Louis MO-IL urban area.
Source: The Council for Community and Economic Research, ACCRA Cost of Living Index, 2015

Grocery Prices

Area[1]	T-Bone Steak ($/pound)	Frying Chicken ($/pound)	Whole Milk ($/half gal.)	Eggs ($/dozen)	Orange Juice ($/64 oz.)	Coffee ($/11.5 oz.)
City[2]	11.55	2.02	2.46	2.48	3.61	4.56
Avg.	10.99	1.43	2.25	2.26	3.58	4.48
Min.	7.16	0.98	1.30	1.35	2.88	2.98
Max.	14.13	2.43	3.85	4.81	6.39	7.56

Note: (1) Values for the local area are compared with the average, minimum and maximum values for all 292 areas in the Cost of Living Index; (2) Figures cover the St. Louis MO-IL urban area; **T-Bone Steak** *(price per pound);* **Frying Chicken** *(price per pound, whole fryer);* **Whole Milk** *(half gallon carton);* **Eggs** *(price per dozen, Grade A, large);* **Orange Juice** *(64 oz. Tropicana or Florida Natural);* **Coffee** *(11.5 oz. can, vacuum-packed, Maxwell House, Hills Bros, or Folgers).*
Source: The Council for Community and Economic Research, ACCRA Cost of Living Index, 2015

Housing and Utility Costs

Area[1]	New Home Price ($)	Apartment Rent ($/month)	All Electric ($/month)	Part Electric ($/month)	Other Energy ($/month)	Telephone ($/month)
City[2]	207,522	832	-	95.19	70.93	40.32
Avg.	312,874	945	179.30	95.07	72.96	28.11
Min.	178,682	479	116.28	43.14	26.46	10.01
Max.	1,472,476	3,984	504.25	189.44	421.11	43.06

Note: (1) Values for the local area are compared with the average, minimum and maximum values for all 292 areas in the Cost of Living Index; (2) Figures cover the St. Louis MO-IL urban area; **New Home Price** *(2,400 sf living area, 8,000 sf lot, in urban area with full utilities);* **Apartment Rent** *(950 sf 2 bedroom/1.5 or 2 bath, unfurnished, excluding all utilities except water);* **All Electric** *(average monthly cost for an all-electric home);* **Part Electric** *(average monthly cost for a part-electric home);* **Other Energy** *(average monthly cost for natural gas, fuel oil, coal, wood, and any other forms of energy except electricity);* **Telephone** *(price includes basic monthly rate for a private residential line plus additional local usage charges incurred by a family of four).*
Source: The Council for Community and Economic Research, ACCRA Cost of Living Index, 2015

Health Care, Transportation, and Other Costs

Area[1]	Doctor ($/visit)	Dentist ($/visit)	Optometrist ($/visit)	Gasoline ($/gallon)	Beauty Salon ($/visit)	Men's Shirt ($)
City[2]	94.95	91.43	83.95	2.31	35.77	23.78
Avg.	105.15	89.02	99.78	2.38	35.30	28.10
Min.	66.87	56.09	48.53	1.95	18.91	13.38
Max.	182.34	150.36	228.33	4.09	67.91	63.80

Note: (1) Values for the local area are compared with the average, minimum and maximum values for all 292 areas in the Cost of Living Index; (2) Figures cover the St. Louis MO-IL urban area; **Doctor** *(general practitioners routine exam of an established patient);* **Dentist** *(adult teeth cleaning and periodic oral examination);* **Optometrist** *(full vision eye exam for established adult patient);* **Gasoline** *(one gallon regular unleaded, national brand, including all taxes, cash price at self-service pump if available);* **Beauty Salon** *(woman's shampoo, trim, and blow-dry);* **Men's Shirt** *(cotton/polyester dress shirt, pinpoint weave, long sleeves).*
Source: The Council for Community and Economic Research, ACCRA Cost of Living Index, 2015

HOUSING

House Price Index (HPI)

Area	National Ranking[2]	Quarterly Change (%)	One-Year Change (%)	Five-Year Change (%)
MSA[1]	164	0.50	3.80	4.00
U.S.[3]	–	1.45	5.76	22.85

Note: The HPI is a weighted repeat sales index. It measures average price changes in repeat sales or refinancings on the same properties. This information is obtained by reviewing repeat mortgage transactions on single-family properties whose mortgages have been purchased or securitized by Fannie Mae or Freddie Mac in January 1975; (1) St. Louis Metropolitan Statistical Area—see Appendix B for areas included; (2) Rankings are based on annual percentage change for all metro areas containing at least 15,000 transactions over the last 10 years and ranges from 1 to 266; (3) figures based on a weighted average of Census Division estimates using a seasonally adjusted, purchase-only index; all figures are for the period ending December 31, 2015
Source: Federal Housing Finance Agency, House Price Index, February 25, 2016

Median Single-Family Home Prices

Area	2013	2014	2015p	Percent Change 2014 to 2015
MSA[1]	134.3	141.7	150.6	6.3
U.S. Average	197.4	208.9	223.9	7.2

Note: Figures are median sales prices of existing single-family homes in thousands of dollars; (p) preliminary; n/a not available; (1) St. Louis, MO-IL Metropolitan Statistical Area—see Appendix B for areas included
Source: National Association of Realtors, Median Sales Price of Existing Single-Family Homes for Metropolitan Areas, 4th Quarter 2015

Qualifying Income Based on Median Sales Price of Existing Single-Family Homes

Area	With 5% Down ($)	With 10% Down ($)	With 20% Down ($)
MSA[1]	31,963	30,281	26,916
U.S. Average	49,535	46,928	41,714

Note: Figures are preliminary; Qualifying income is based on a mortgage rate of 4.1%. Monthly principal and interest payment is limited to 25% of income; n/a not available; (1) St. Louis, MO-IL Metropolitan Statistical Area—see Appendix B for areas included
Source: National Association of Realtors, Qualifying Income Based on Median Sales Price of Existing Single-Family Homes for Metropolitan Areas, 4th Quarter 2015

Median Apartment Condo-Coop Home Prices

Area	2013	2014	2015p	Percent Change 2014 to 2015
MSA[1]	n/a	n/a	n/a	n/a
U.S. Average	194.9	204.3	210.7	3.1

Note: Figures are median sales prices of existing apartment condo-coop homes in thousands of dollars; (p) preliminary; n/a not available; (1) St. Louis, MO-IL Metropolitan Statistical Area—see Appendix B for areas included
Source: National Association of Realtors, Median Sales Price of Existing Apartment Condo-Coop Homes for Metropolitan Areas, 4th Quarter 2015

Gross Monthly Rent

Area	Under $200	$200 -299	$300 -499	$500 -749	$750 -999	$1,000 -1,499	$1,500 and up	Median ($)
City	0.5	0.9	4.0	19.4	30.0	30.3	14.9	965
MSA[1]	1.4	3.3	8.2	29.0	30.0	21.9	6.1	808
U.S.	1.5	3.2	7.4	21.0	24.1	26.9	15.9	920

Note: Figures are percentages except for Median; Gross rent is the contract rent plus the estimated average monthly cost of utilities (electricity, gas, and water and sewer) and fuels (oil, coal, kerosene, wood, etc.) if these are paid by the renter (or paid for the renter by someone else); (1) Figures cover the St. Louis, MO-IL Metropolitan Statistical Area—see Appendix B for areas included
Source: U.S. Census Bureau, 2010-2014 American Community Survey 5-Year Estimates

Homeownership Rate

Area	2008 (%)	2009 (%)	2010 (%)	2011 (%)	2012 (%)	2013 (%)	2014 (%)	2015 (%)
MSA[1]	72.2	72.5	72.2	71.1	72.0	72.7	71.1	68.7
U.S.	67.8	67.4	66.9	66.1	65.4	65.1	64.5	63.7

Note: (1) Figures cover the St. Louis, MO-IL Metropolitan Statistical Area—see Appendix B for areas included
Source: U.S. Census Bureau, Housing Vacancies and Homeownership Annual Statistics: 2015

Year Housing Structure Built

Area	2010 or Later	2000 -2009	1990 -1999	1980 -1989	1970 -1979	1960 -1969	1950 -1959	1940 -1949	Before 1940	Median Year
City	2.4	42.4	34.1	10.1	4.0	3.6	1.5	0.6	1.3	1998
MSA[1]	0.8	12.2	12.4	11.3	13.5	12.8	13.8	6.5	16.7	1970
U.S.	1.0	14.9	13.9	13.8	15.8	11.0	10.8	5.4	13.3	1976

Note: Figures are percentages except for Median Year; (1) Figures cover the St. Louis, MO-IL Metropolitan Statistical Area—see Appendix B for areas included
Source: U.S. Census Bureau, 2010-2014 American Community Survey 5-Year Estimates

HEALTH

Health Risk Data

Category	MSA[1] (%)	U.S. (%)
Adults aged 18–64 who have any kind of health care coverage	83.4	79.6
Adults who reported being in good or excellent health	83.6	83.1
Adults who are current smokers	20.1	19.6
Adults who are heavy drinkers[2]	6.9	6.1
Adults who are binge drinkers[3]	22.1	16.9
Adults who are overweight (BMI 25.0 - 29.9)	36.5	35.8
Adults who are obese (BMI 30.0 - 99.8)	31.1	27.6
Adults who participated in any physical activities in the past month	75.6	77.1
Adults 50+ who have ever had a sigmoidoscopy or colonoscopy	69.9	67.3
Women aged 40+ who have had a mammogram within the past two years	79.4	74.0
Men aged 40+ who have had a PSA test within the past two years	52.8	45.2
Adults aged 65+ who have had flu shot within the past year	63.6	60.1
Adults who always wear a seatbelt	90.8	93.8

Note: Data as of 2012 unless otherwise noted; (1) Figures cover the St. Louis, MO-IL Metropolitan Statistical Area—see Appendix B for areas included; (2) Heavy drinkers are classified as males having more than two drinks per day or females having more than one drink per day; (3) Binge drinkers are classified as males having five or more drinks on one occasion or females having four or more drinks on one occasion
Source: Centers for Disease Control and Prevention, Behaviorial Risk Factor Surveillance System, SMART: Selected Metropolitan/Micropolitan Area Risk Trends, 2012 (Note: the CDC has discontinued this dataset but will be releasing a replacement in mid-2016)

Chronic Health Indicators

Category	MSA[1] (%)	U.S. (%)
Adults who have ever been told they had a heart attack	5.4	4.5
Adults who have ever been told they had a stroke	3.6	2.9
Adults who have been told they currently have asthma	10.2	8.9
Adults who have ever been told they have arthritis	27.0	25.7
Adults who have ever been told they have diabetes[2]	10.6	9.7
Adults who have ever been told they had skin cancer	5.4	5.7
Adults who have ever been told they had any other types of cancer	7.0	6.5
Adults who have ever been told they have COPD	5.9	6.2
Adults who have ever been told they have kidney disease	2.9	2.5
Adults who have ever been told they have a form of depression	16.9	18.0

Note: Data as of 2012 unless otherwise noted; (1) Figures cover the St. Louis, MO-IL Metropolitan Statistical Area—see Appendix B for areas included; (2) Figures do not include pregnancy-related, borderline, or pre-diabetes
Source: Centers for Disease Control and Prevention, Behaviorial Risk Factor Surveillance System, SMART: Selected Metropolitan/Micropolitan Area Risk Trends, 2012 (Note: the CDC has discontinued this dataset but will be releasing a replacement in mid-2016)

Mortality Rates for the Top 10 Causes of Death in the U.S.

ICD-10[a] Sub-Chapter	ICD-10[a] Code	Age-Adjusted Mortality Rate[1] per 100,000 population	
		County[2]	U.S.
Malignant neoplasms	C00-C97	163.6	163.6
Ischaemic heart diseases	I20-I25	92.0	102.2
Other forms of heart disease	I30-I51	46.3	50.1
Chronic lower respiratory diseases	J40-J47	35.5	41.4
Organic, including symptomatic, mental disorders	F01-F09	43.8	38.5
Cerebrovascular diseases	I60-I69	30.2	36.5
Other external causes of accidental injury	W00-X59	36.2	27.5
Other degenerative diseases of the nervous system	G30-G31	19.1	26.3
Diabetes mellitus	E10-E14	13.6	21.1
Hypertensive diseases	I10-I15	10.6	19.7

Note: (a) ICD-10 = International Classification of Diseases 10th Revision; (1) Mortality rates are a three year average covering 2012-2014; (2) Figures cover St. Charles County.
Source: Centers for Disease Control and Prevention, National Center for Health Statistics. Underlying Cause of Death 1999-2014 on CDC WONDER Online Database, released 2015.

Mortality Rates for Selected Causes of Death

ICD-10[a] Sub-Chapter	ICD-10[a] Code	Age-Adjusted Mortality Rate[1] per 100,000 population	
		County[2]	U.S.
Assault	X85-Y09	Unreliable	5.1
Diseases of the liver	K70-K76	9.5	13.5
Human immunodeficiency virus (HIV) disease	B20-B24	Suppressed	2.1
Influenza and pneumonia	J09-J18	16.0	15.2
Intentional self-harm	X60-X84	12.3	12.7
Malnutrition	E40-E46	Suppressed	0.9
Obesity and other hyperalimentation	E65-E68	Unreliable	1.9
Renal failure	N17-N19	12.0	13.0
Transport accidents	V01-V99	6.3	11.6
Viral hepatitis	B15-B19	Unreliable	2.1

Note: (a) ICD-10 = International Classification of Diseases 10th Revision; (1) Mortality rates are a three year average covering 2012-2014; (2) Figures cover St. Charles County; Data are Suppressed when the data meet the criteria for confidentiality constraints; Mortality rates are flagged as Unreliable when the rate would be calculated with a numerator of 20 or less.
Source: Centers for Disease Control and Prevention, National Center for Health Statistics. Underlying Cause of Death 1999-2014 on CDC WONDER Online Database, released 2015.

Health Insurance Coverage

Area	With Health Insurance	With Private Health Insurance	With Public Health Insurance	Without Health Insurance	Population Under Age 18 Without Health Insurance
City	93.2	86.1	15.5	6.8	4.8
MSA[1]	89.6	72.6	28.0	10.4	4.4
U.S.	85.8	65.8	31.1	14.2	7.1

Note: Figures are percentages that cover the civilian noninstitutionalized population; (1) Figures cover the St. Louis, MO-IL Metropolitan Statistical Area—see Appendix B for areas included
Source: U.S. Census Bureau, 2010-2014 American Community Survey 5-Year Estimates

Number of Medical Professionals

Area	MDs[3]	DOs[3,4]	Dentists	Podiatrists	Chiropractors	Optometrists
County[1] (number)	376	68	203	19	213	62
County[1] (rate[2])	100.6	18.2	53.5	5.0	56.1	16.3
U.S. (rate[2])	272.5	20.9	64.7	5.8	25.9	15.2

Note: Data as of 2014 unless noted; (1) Data covers St. Charles County; (2) Rate per 100,000 population; (3) Data as of 2013 and includes all active, non-federal physicians; (4) Doctor of Osteopathic Medicine
Source: U.S. Department of Health and Human Services, Health Resources and Services Administration, Bureau of Health Professions, Area Resource File (ARF) 2014-2015

Best Hospitals

According to *U.S. News*, the St. Louis, MO-IL metro area is home to one of the best hospitals in the U.S.: **Barnes-Jewish Hospital/Washington University** (Honor Roll/14 specialties). The hospital listed was nationally ranked in at least one adult specialty. Only 137 hospitals nationwide were nationally ranked in one or more specialties. Fifteen hospitals in the U.S. made the Honor Roll with high scores in at least six specialties. *U.S. News Online, "America's Best Children's Hospitals 2015-16"*

According to *U.S. News*, the St. Louis, MO-IL metro area is home to three of the best children's hospitals in the U.S.: **SSM Cardinal Glennon Children's Medical Center** (2 specialties); **St. Louis Children's Hospital-Washington University** (10 specialties); **St. Louis Children's-Washington University-Shriners Hospital** (10 specialties). The hospitals listed were highly ranked in at least one pediatric specialty. Eighty-three children's hospitals in the U.S. were nationally ranked in at least one specialty. Twelve children's hospitals in the U.S. made the Honor Roll with high scores in at least three specialties. *U.S. News Online, "America's Best Children's Hospitals 2015-16"*

EDUCATION

Public School District Statistics

District Name	Schls	Pupils	Pupil/ Teacher Ratio	Minority Pupils[1] (%)	Free Lunch Eligible[2] (%)	IEP[3] (%)
Fort. Zumwalt R-II	24	18,654	16.3	16.5	19.4	16.1
Wentzville R-IV	17	14,549	16.4	14.9	21.0	13.3

Note: Table includes school districts with 100 or more students; (1) Percentage of students that are not non-Hispanic white; (2) Percentage of students that are eligible for the free lunch program; (3) Percentage of students that have an Individualized Education Program.
Source: U.S. Department of Education, National Center for Education Statistics, Common Core of Data, Local Education Agency (School District) Universe Survey: School Year 2013-2014; U.S. Department of Education, National Center for Education Statistics, Common Core of Data, Public Elementary/Secondary School Universe Survey: School Year 2013-2014

Highest Level of Education

Area	Less than H.S.	H.S. Diploma	Some College, No Deg.	Associate Degree	Bachelor's Degree	Master's Degree	Prof. School Degree	Doctorate Degree
City	5.6	24.9	23.7	8.3	24.9	10.8	0.9	0.8
MSA[1]	9.7	27.2	23.2	8.3	19.3	8.9	2.0	1.3
U.S.	13.7	28.0	21.2	7.9	18.3	7.8	2.0	1.3

Note: Figures cover persons age 25 and over; (1) Figures cover the St. Louis, MO-IL Metropolitan Statistical Area—see Appendix B for areas included
Source: U.S. Census Bureau, 2010-2014 American Community Survey 5-Year Estimates

Educational Attainment by Race

Area	High School Graduate or Higher (%)					Bachelor's Degree or Higher (%)				
	Total	White	Black	Asian	Hisp.[2]	Total	White	Black	Asian	Hisp.[2]
City	94.4	94.4	96.9	95.4	83.4	37.5	35.9	42.3	74.6	29.4
MSA[1]	90.3	91.9	83.5	88.2	76.8	31.5	33.6	17.3	62.8	24.9
U.S.	86.3	88.4	83.2	85.8	64.1	29.3	30.6	19.0	50.9	13.9

Note: Figures shown cover persons 25 years old and over; (1) Figures cover the St. Louis, MO-IL Metropolitan Statistical Area—see Appendix B for areas included; (2) People of Hispanic origin can be of any race
Source: U.S. Census Bureau, 2010-2014 American Community Survey 5-Year Estimates

School Enrollment by Grade and Control

Area	Preschool (%)		Kindergarten (%)		Grades 1 - 4 (%)		Grades 5 - 8 (%)		Grades 9 - 12 (%)	
	Public	Private	Public	Private	Public	Private	Public	Private	Public	Private
City	35.2	64.8	89.4	10.6	83.2	16.8	88.1	11.9	85.5	14.5
MSA[1]	53.9	46.1	81.1	18.9	83.2	16.8	83.4	16.6	85.5	14.5
U.S.	57.4	42.6	87.8	12.2	89.8	10.2	89.9	10.1	90.6	9.4

Note: Figures shown cover persons 3 years old and over; (1) Figures cover the St. Louis, MO-IL Metropolitan Statistical Area—see Appendix B for areas included
Source: U.S. Census Bureau, 2010-2014 American Community Survey 5-Year Estimates

Average Salaries of Public School Classroom Teachers

Area	2013-14 Dollars	2013-14 Rank[1]	2014-15 Dollars	2014-15 Rank[1]	Percent Change 2013-14 to 2014-15	Percent Change 2004-05 to 2014-15
Missouri	46,750	42	47,394	43	1.38	21.3
U.S. Average	56,610	–	57,379	–	1.36	20.8

Note: (1) State rank ranges from 1 to 51 where 1 indicates highest salary.
Source: National Education Association, Rankings & Estimates: Rankings of the States 2014 and Estimates of School Statistics 2015, March 2015

Higher Education

Four-Year Colleges			Two-Year Colleges			Medical Schools[1]	Law Schools[2]	Voc/ Tech[3]
Public	Private Non-profit	Private For-profit	Public	Private Non-profit	Private For-profit			
0	0	0	0	0	0	0	0	0

Note: Figures cover institutions located within the city limits and include main campuses only; (1) includes schools accredited by the Liaison Committee on Medical Education and the American Osteopathic Association's Commission on Osteopathic College Accreditation; (2) includes ABA-accredited schools, schools with provisional ABA accreditation, and state accredited schools; (3) includes all schools with programs that are less than 2 years.
Source: National Center for Education Statistics, Integrated Postsecondary Education System (IPEDS), 2014-15; Association of American Medical Colleges, Member List, March 21, 2016; American Osteopathic Association, Member List, March 21, 2016; Law School Admission Council, Official Guide to ABA-Approved Law Schools Online, March 21, 2016; Wikipedia, List of Medical Schools in the United States, March 21, 2016; Wikipedia, List of Law Schools in the United States, March 21, 2016

According to *U.S. News & World Report,* the St. Louis, MO-IL metro area is home to three of the best national universities in the U.S.: **Washington University in St. Louis** (#15 tie); **Saint Louis University** (#96 tie); **Maryville University of St. Louis** (#161 tie). The indicators used to capture academic quality fall into a number of categories: assessment by administrators at peer institutions; retention of students; faculty resources; student selectivity; financial resources; alumni giving; high school counselor ratings of colleges; and graduation rate. *U.S. News & World Report, "America's Best Colleges 2016"*

According to *U.S. News & World Report,* the St. Louis, MO-IL metro area is home to one of the best liberal arts colleges in the U.S.: **Principia College** (#127 tie). The indicators used to capture academic quality fall into a number of categories: assessment by administrators at peer institutions; retention of students; faculty resources; student selectivity; financial resources; alumni giving; high school counselor ratings of colleges; and graduation rate. *U.S. News & World Report, "America's Best Colleges 2016"*

According to *U.S. News & World Report,* the St. Louis, MO-IL metro area is home to two of the top 100 law schools in the U.S.: **Washington University in St. Louis, School of Law** (#18); **St. Louis University, School of Law** (#82 tie). The rankings are based on a weighted average of 12 measures of quality: peer assessment score; assessment score by lawyers/judges; median LSAT scores; median undergrad GPA; acceptance rate; employment rates for graduates; placement success; bar passage rate; faculty resources; expenditures per student; student/faculty ratio; and library resources. *U.S. News & World Report, "America's Best Graduate Schools, Law, 2017"*

According to *U.S. News & World Report,* the St. Louis, MO-IL metro area is home to two of the top 75 medical schools for research in the U.S.: **Washington University in St. Louis, School of Medicine** (#6); **St. Louis University, School of Medicine** (#63 tie). The rankings are based on a weighted average of 11 measures of quality: quality assessment; peer assessment score; assessment score by residency directors; research activity; total research activity; average research activity per faculty member; student selectivity; median MCAT total score; median undergraduate GPA; acceptance rate; and faculty resources. *U.S. News & World Report, "America's Best Graduate Schools, Medical, 2017"*

According to *U.S. News & World Report,* the St. Louis, MO-IL metro area is home to one of the top 75 business schools in the U.S.: **Washington University in St. Louis, Olin Business School** (#21). The rankings are based on a weighted average of the following nine measures: quality assessment; peer assessment; recruiter assessment; placement success; mean starting salary and bonus; student selectivity; mean GMAT and GRE scores; mean undergraduate GPA; and acceptance rate. *U.S. News & World Report, "America's Best Graduate Schools, Business, 2017"*

PRESIDENTIAL ELECTION

2012 Presidential Election Results

Area	Obama (%)	Romney (%)	Other (%)
St. Charles County	38.7	59.7	1.7
U.S.	51.0	47.2	1.8

Note: Results may not add to 100% due to rounding
Source: Dave Leip's Atlas of U.S. Presidential Elections

EMPLOYERS

Major Employers

Company Name	Industry
Ameren	Utilities
Anheuser-Busch	Brewery
Archdiocese of St. Louis Catholic Church	Catholic church
BJC Healthcare Hospital System	Hospital system
Boeing Defense	Contractor
Dierbergs Markets	Grocery chain
Edward Jones	Financial services
Enterprise Holdings	Car rental
Express Scripts	Pharmacy benefit manager
McDonald's	Food service
Mercy Health Hospital	Hospital system
Monsanto Biotech	Crop producer
National Geospatial-Intelligence Agency	National security
Schnuck Markets	Grocery chain
Scott Air Force	Military installation
Special School District of St. Louis Cty.	Primary/secondary education
SSM Health Care	Hospital system
St Anthony's Medical Center	Healthcare
St Louis City	Government
St Louis Community College	Higher education
St Louis County	Government
St Louis University	Higher education
USPS	Government
Wal-Mart	Retailer
Washington University	Higher education
Wells Fargo	Financial services

Note: Companies shown are located within the St. Louis, MO-IL Metropolitan Statistical Area.
Source: Hoovers.com; Wikipedia

PUBLIC SAFETY

Crime Rate

Area	All Crimes	Violent Crimes				Property Crimes		
		Murder	Rape[3]	Robbery	Aggrav. Assault	Burglary	Larceny -Theft	Motor Vehicle Theft
City	1,363.3	0.0	10.8	10.8	50.3	120.9	1,141.8	28.7
Metro[1]	2,879.0	8.8	35.8	103.4	281.8	470.4	1,765.0	213.8
U.S.	2,971.8	4.5	36.6	102.2	232.5	542.5	1,837.3	216.2

Note: Figures are crimes per 100,000 population; (1) Figures cover the St. Louis, MO-IL Metropolitan Statistical Area—see Appendix B for areas included; (3) The city and U.S. figures shown were reported using the revised Uniform Crime Reporting (UCR) definition of rape. The suburban and metro area figures shown are an aggregate total of the data submitted using both the revised and legacy UCR definitions.
Source: FBI Uniform Crime Reports, 2014

Hate Crimes

Area	Number of Quarters Reported	Number of Incidents per Bias Motivation						
		Race	Religion	Sexual Orientation	Ethnicity	Disability	Gender	Gender Identity
City	4	0	0	0	0	0	0	0
U.S.	4	2,568	1,014	1,017	648	84	33	98

Source: Federal Bureau of Investigation, Hate Crime Statistics 2014

Identity Theft Consumer Complaints

Area	Complaints	Complaints per 100,000 Population	Rank[2]
MSA[1]	19,195	684.0	1
U.S.	490,220	152.4	-

Note: (1) Figures cover the St. Louis, MO-IL Metropolitan Statistical Area—see Appendix B for areas included; (2) Rank ranges from 1 to 379 where 1 indicates greatest number of identity theft complaints per 100,000 population
Source: Federal Trade Commission, Consumer Sentinel Network Data Book for January–December 2015

Fraud and Other Consumer Complaints

Area	Complaints	Complaints per 100,000 Population	Rank[2]
MSA[1]	10,939	389.8	126
U.S.	2,593,159	806.0	-

Note: (1) Figures cover the St. Louis, MO-IL Metropolitan Statistical Area—see Appendix B for areas included; (2) Rank ranges from 1 to 379 where 1 indicates greatest number of identity theft complaints per 100,000 population
Source: Federal Trade Commission, Consumer Sentinel Network Data Book for January–December 2015

RECREATION

Culture

Dance[1]	Theatre[1]	Instrumental Music[1]	Vocal Music[1]	Series and Festivals	Museums and Art Galleries[2]	Zoos and Aquariums[3]
0	0	0	0	0	0	0

Note: (1) Professional perfoming groups; (2) Based on organizations with SIC code 8412; (3) AZA-accredited
Source: The Grey House Performing Arts Directory, 2015-16; Association of Zoos & Aquariums, AZA Member Zoos & Aquariums, March 25, 2016; www.AccuLeads.com, March 29, 2016

Professional Sports Teams

Team Name	League	Year Established
Los Angeles Rams	National Football League (NFL)	2016
Saint Louis Blues	National Hockey League (NHL)	1967
Saint Louis Cardinals	Major League Baseball (MLB)	1882

Note: Includes teams located in the St. Louis, MO-IL Metropolitan Statistical Area.
Source: Wikipedia, Major Professional Sports Teams of the United States and Canada, March 24, 2016

CLIMATE

Average and Extreme Temperatures

Temperature	Jan	Feb	Mar	Apr	May	Jun	Jul	Aug	Sep	Oct	Nov	Dec	Yr.
Extreme High (°F)	77	83	89	93	98	105	115	107	104	94	85	76	115
Average High (°F)	39	43	54	67	76	85	89	87	80	69	54	42	66
Average Temp. (°F)	30	34	44	56	66	75	79	78	70	59	45	34	56
Average Low (°F)	21	25	34	46	55	65	69	67	59	48	36	26	46
Extreme Low (°F)	-18	-10	-5	22	31	43	51	47	36	23	1	-16	-18

Note: Figures cover the years 1945-1990
Source: National Climatic Data Center, International Station Meteorological Climate Summary, 9/96

Average Precipitation/Snowfall/Humidity

Precip./Humidity	Jan	Feb	Mar	Apr	May	Jun	Jul	Aug	Sep	Oct	Nov	Dec	Yr.
Avg. Precip. (in.)	1.9	2.2	3.4	3.4	3.8	4.0	3.8	2.9	2.9	2.8	3.0	2.6	36.8
Avg. Snowfall (in.)	6	4	4	Tr	0	0	0	0	0	Tr	1	4	20
Avg. Rel. Hum. 6am (%)	80	81	80	78	81	82	84	86	87	83	81	81	82
Avg. Rel. Hum. 3pm (%)	62	59	54	49	51	51	51	52	50	50	56	63	54

Note: Figures cover the years 1945-1990; Tr = Trace amounts (<0.05 in. of rain; <0.5 in. of snow)
Source: National Climatic Data Center, International Station Meteorological Climate Summary, 9/96

Weather Conditions

Temperature			Daytime Sky			Precipitation		
10°F & below	32°F & below	90°F & above	Clear	Partly cloudy	Cloudy	0.01 inch or more precip.	0.1 inch or more snow/ice	Thunder-storms
13	100	43	97	138	130	109	14	46

Note: Figures are average number of days per year and cover the years 1945-1990
Source: National Climatic Data Center, International Station Meteorological Climate Summary, 9/96

HAZARDOUS WASTE

Superfund Sites

O'Fallon has no sites on the EPA's Superfund Final National Priorities List. There are a total of 1,323 Superfund sites on the list in the U.S. *U.S. Environmental Protection Agency, Final National Priorities List, March 18, 2016*

AIR & WATER QUALITY

Air Quality Trends: Ozone

	1990	1995	2000	2005	2010	2011	2012	2013	2014
MSA[1]	0.085	0.092	0.082	0.087	0.075	0.078	0.085	0.069	0.068

Note: (1) Data covers the St. Louis, MO-IL Metropolitan Statistical Area—see Appendix B for areas included. The values shown are the composite ozone concentration averages among trend sites based on the highest fourth daily maximum 8-hour concentration in parts per million. These trends are based on sites having an adequate record of monitoring data during the trend period. Data from exceptional events are included.
Source: U.S. Environmental Protection Agency, Air Quality Monitoring Information, "Air Quality Trends by City, 1990-2014"

Air Quality Index

Area	Percent of Days when Air Quality was...[2]					AQI Statistics[2]	
	Good	Moderate	Unhealthy for Sensitive Groups	Unhealthy	Very Unhealthy	Maximum	Median
MSA[1]	38.6	59.2	1.6	0.5	0.0	154	55

Note: (1) Data covers the St. Louis, MO-IL Metropolitan Statistical Area—see Appendix B for areas included; (2) Based on 365 days with AQI data in 2015. Air Quality Index (AQI) is an index for reporting daily air quality. EPA calculates the AQI for five major air pollutants regulated by the Clean Air Act: ground-level ozone, particle pollution (aka particulate matter), carbon monoxide, sulfur dioxide, and nitrogen dioxide. The AQI runs from 0 to 500. The higher the AQI value, the greater the level of air pollution and the greater the health concern. There are six AQI categories: "Good" AQI is between 0 and 50. Air quality is considered satisfactory; "Moderate" AQI is between 51 and 100. Air quality is acceptable; "Unhealthy for Sensitive Groups" When AQI values are between 101 and 150, members of sensitive groups may experience health effects; "Unhealthy" When AQI values are between 151 and 200 everyone may begin to experience health effects; "Very Unhealthy" AQI values between 201 and 300 trigger a health alert; "Hazardous" AQI values over 300 trigger warnings of emergency conditions (not shown).
Source: U.S. Environmental Protection Agency, Air Quality Index Report, 2015

Air Quality Index Pollutants

Area	Percent of Days when AQI Pollutant was...[2]					
	Carbon Monoxide	Nitrogen Dioxide	Ozone	Sulfur Dioxide	Particulate Matter 2.5	Particulate Matter 10
MSA[1]	0.0	2.2	18.6	0.8	75.1	3.3

Note: (1) Data covers the St. Louis, MO-IL Metropolitan Statistical Area—see Appendix B for areas included; (2) Based on 365 days with AQI data in 2015. The Air Quality Index (AQI) is an index for reporting daily air quality. EPA calculates the AQI for five major air pollutants regulated by the Clean Air Act: ground-level ozone, particle pollution (also known as particulate matter), carbon monoxide, sulfur dioxide, and nitrogen dioxide. The AQI runs from 0 to 500. The higher the AQI value, the greater the level of air pollution and the greater the health concern.
Source: U.S. Environmental Protection Agency, Air Quality Index Report, 2015

Maximum Air Pollutant Concentrations: Particulate Matter, Ozone, CO and Lead

	Particulate Matter 10 (ug/m^3)	Particulate Matter 2.5 Wtd AM (ug/m^3)	Particulate Matter 2.5 24-Hr (ug/m^3)	Ozone (ppm)	Carbon Monoxide (ppm)	Lead (ug/m^3)
MSA[1] Level	159	11.4	29	0.072	1	0.36
NAAQS[2]	150	15	35	0.075	9	0.15
Met NAAQS[2]	No	Yes	Yes	Yes	Yes	No

Note: (1) Data covers the St. Louis, MO-IL Metropolitan Statistical Area—see Appendix B for areas included; Data from exceptional events are included; (2) National Ambient Air Quality Standards; ppm = parts per million; ug/m^3 = micrograms per cubic meter; n/a not available.
Concentrations: Particulate Matter 10 (coarse particulate)—highest second maximum 24-hour concentration; Particulate Matter 2.5 Wtd AM (fine particulate)—highest weighted annual mean concentration; Particulate Matter 2.5 24-Hour (fine particulate)—highest 98th percentile 24-hour concentration; Ozone—highest fourth daily maximum 8-hour concentration; Carbon Monoxide—highest second maximum non-overlapping 8-hour concentration; Lead—maximum running 3-month average
Source: U.S. Environmental Protection Agency, Air Quality Monitoring Information, "Air Quality Statistics by City, 2014"

Maximum Air Pollutant Concentrations: Nitrogen Dioxide and Sulfur Dioxide

	Nitrogen Dioxide AM (ppb)	Nitrogen Dioxide 1-Hr (ppb)	Sulfur Dioxide AM (ppb)	Sulfur Dioxide 1-Hr (ppb)	Sulfur Dioxide 24-Hr (ppb)
MSA[1] Level	14	60	n/a	41	n/a
NAAQS[2]	53	100	30	75	140
Met NAAQS[2]	Yes	Yes	n/a	Yes	n/a

Note: (1) Data covers the St. Louis, MO-IL Metropolitan Statistical Area—see Appendix B for areas included; Data from exceptional events are included; (2) National Ambient Air Quality Standards; ppm = parts per million; ug/m^3 = micrograms per cubic meter; n/a not available.
Concentrations: Nitrogen Dioxide AM—highest arithmetic mean concentration; Nitrogen Dioxide 1-Hr—highest 98th percentile 1-hour daily maximum concentration; Sulfur Dioxide AM—highest annual mean concentration; Sulfur Dioxide 1-Hr—highest 99th percentile 1-hour daily maximum concentration; Sulfur Dioxide 24-Hr—highest second maximum 24-hour concentration
Source: U.S. Environmental Protection Agency, Air Quality Monitoring Information, "Air Quality Statistics by City, 2014"

Drinking Water

Water System Name	Pop. Served	Primary Water Source Type	Violations[1]	
			Health Based	Monitoring/ Reporting
O'Fallon	27,000	Purchased Surface	0	0

Note: (1) Based on violation data from January 1, 2015 to December 31, 2015 (includes unresolved violations from earlier years)
Source: U.S. Environmental Protection Agency, Office of Ground Water and Drinking Water, Safe Drinking Water Information System (based on data extracted April 29, 2016)

Bozeman, Montana

Background

Bozeman is located in the Gallatin Valley between the Bridger Mountains to the east, the Tobacco Root Mountains to the west, the Big Belt Mountains to the north, and the Spanish Peaks to the south. The city is 127 miles south of Great Falls.

Bozeman was named for John Bozeman who, in 1863, with his partner John Jacobs, opened the Bozeman Trail that passed through future territory of the city. The trail was an offshoot from the Oregon Trail and led to the mining town of Virginia City until it was closed 1868 due to fighting with Native American tribes. The city was established in 1864 by Bozeman, Daniel Rouse and William Beall. Nelson Story arrived with 3,000 head of longhorn cattle, which formed the first herd in Montana's cattle industry. In 1868, Fort Ellis was constructed three miles east of the city after the mysterious death of John Bozeman and rumors of attacks by Native Americans led to security concerns. In 1883, the Northern Pacific Railway reached Bozeman and by 1900, the city had 3,500 residents.

Today Gallatin County is the fastest growing county in Montana.

Much of the city's economy is centered around Montana State University at Bozeman, which is the university's flagship campus. The university has over 10,000 full time students and employs approximately 2,200. Technology firms employ another large number.

Bozeman boasts three major museums, the Museum of the Rockies, the American Computer Museum, and the Pioneer Museum. The Bridger Bowl Ski Resort is located in the city and the Big Sky Ski and Summer Resort is in nearby Big Sky.

Bozeman is home to the 83,000-square-foot Kenyon Noble Lumber and Hardware store warehouse, one of the largest locally owned stores in the city's history, as well as several Hilton and Marriott hotels in the Gallatin Center complex.

Bozeman has a moderate climate with hot summers and cold winters. Median summer temperatures average 65 degrees, while winter averages are as low as 5 degrees during December and January. The city averages 2 inches of rainfall per month from April to August and 8 inches of snowfall per month from December to March.

Rankings

General Rankings

- Bozeman was selected as one of the "The 10 Best Places to Live Now" by *Men's Journal*. Bozeman ranked #10. *Men's Journal, "The 10 Best Places to Live Now," March 2015*
- In their third annual survey, Livability.com looked at data for more than 2,000 U.S. cities to determine the rankings for Livability's "Top 100 Best Places to Live" in 2016. Bozeman ranked #34. Criteria: vibrant economy; low cost of living; education, health care & transportation options; abundant lifestyle amenities. *Livability.com, "Top 100 Best Places to Live 2016"*

Business/Finance Rankings

- Using data from the Council for Community and Economic Research's 2014 cost of living index, NerdWallet ranked the 100 most affordable cities in America. Median income was compared with cost of living to find truly affordable places. Bozeman ranked #77. *NerdWallet.com, "America's Most Affordable Places," May 18, 2015*
- Using data from the Council for Community and Economic Research's 2013 Annual Report, NerdWallet ranked the 100 U.S. cities with the most expensive cost of living. Cities in California and in the Northeast topped the list. Of the cities with the highest cost of living, Bozeman ranked #74. *NerdWallet.com, "Most Expensive Cities in America," June 4, 2014*

Miscellaneous Rankings

- Bustle.com, a news, entertainment, and lifestyle site for women, studied binge- and heavy drinking rates among nonalcoholics to determine the nation's ten "drunkest" cities. Bozeman made the list, at #9. *www.bustle.com, "38 Million Americans Have a Problem with Alcohol: The 10 Drunkest American Cities," January 2014*

Business Environment

CITY FINANCES

City Government Finances

Component	2012 ($000)	2012 ($ per capita)
Total Revenues	54,108	1,451
Total Expenditures	61,904	1,660
Debt Outstanding	35,062	940
Cash and Securities[1]	59,243	1,589

Note: (1) Cash and security holdings of a government at the close of its fiscal year, including those of its dependent agencies, utilities, and liquor stores.
Source: U.S Census Bureau, State & Local Government Finances 2012

City Government Revenue by Source

Source	2012 ($000)	2012 ($ per capita)
General Revenue		
From Federal Government	0	0
From State Government	7,702	206
From Local Governments	0	0
Taxes		
Property	16,057	430
Sales and Gross Receipts	0	0
Personal Income	0	0
Corporate Income	0	0
Motor Vehicle License	0	0
Other Taxes	1,215	32
Current Charges	16,290	436
Liquor Store	0	0
Utility	6,887	184
Employee Retirement	0	0

Source: U.S Census Bureau, State & Local Government Finances 2012

City Government Expenditures by Function

Function	2012 ($000)	2012 ($ per capita)	2012 (%)
General Direct Expenditures			
Air Transportation	0	0	0.0
Corrections	0	0	0.0
Education	0	0	0.0
Employment Security Administration	0	0	0.0
Financial Administration	1,000	26	1.6
Fire Protection	2,278	61	3.6
General Public Buildings	359	9	0.5
Governmental Administration, Other	2,984	80	4.8
Health	0	0	0.0
Highways	4,882	130	7.8
Hospitals	0	0	0.0
Housing and Community Development	84	2	0.1
Interest on General Debt	1,524	40	2.4
Judicial and Legal	593	15	0.9
Libraries	1,331	35	2.1
Parking	392	10	0.6
Parks and Recreation	429	11	0.6
Police Protection	9,410	252	15.2
Public Welfare	5,204	139	8.4
Sewerage	11,494	308	18.5
Solid Waste Management	2,349	63	3.7
Veterans' Services	0	0	0.0
Liquor Store	0	0	0.0
Utility	14,784	396	23.8
Employee Retirement	0	0	0.0

Source: U.S Census Bureau, State & Local Government Finances 2012

DEMOGRAPHICS

Population Growth

Area	1990 Census	2000 Census	2010 Census	2014* Estimate	Population Growth (%) 1990-2014	Population Growth (%) 2010-2014
City	23,499	27,509	37,280	39,123	66.5	4.9
MSA[1]	50,491	67,831	89,513	93,108	84.4	4.0
U.S.	248,709,873	281,421,906	308,745,538	314,107,084	26.3	1.7

Note: (1) Figures cover the Bozeman, MT Micropolitan Statistical Area—see Appendix B for areas included; (*) 2010-2014 5-year estimated population
Source: U.S. Census Bureau, 1990 Census, Census 2000, Census 2010, 2010-2014 American Community Survey 5-Year Estimates

Household Size

Area	Persons in Household (%) One	Two	Three	Four	Five	Six	Seven or More	Average Household Size
City	33.0	38.1	14.9	9.7	3.5	0.3	0.3	2.21
MSA[1]	27.0	38.8	15.9	12.2	4.2	1.1	0.5	2.38
U.S.	27.5	33.5	15.8	13.1	6.0	2.3	1.4	2.64

Note: (1) Figures cover the Bozeman, MT Micropolitan Statistical Area—see Appendix B for areas included
Source: U.S. Census Bureau, 2010-2014 American Community Survey 5-Year Estimates

Race

Area	White Alone[2] (%)	Black Alone[2] (%)	Asian Alone[2] (%)	AIAN[3] Alone[2] (%)	NHOPI[4] Alone[2] (%)	Other Race Alone[2] (%)	Two or More Races (%)
City	92.7	0.5	2.2	1.6	0.0	0.3	2.7
MSA[1]	95.2	0.3	1.1	1.0	0.1	0.3	2.1
U.S.	73.8	12.6	5.0	0.8	0.2	4.7	2.9

Note: (1) Figures cover the Bozeman, MT Micropolitan Statistical Area—see Appendix B for areas included; (2) Alone is defined as not being in combination with one or more other races; (3) American Indian and Alaska Native; (4) Native Hawaiian and Other Pacific Islander
Source: U.S. Census Bureau, 2010-2014 American Community Survey 5-Year Estimates

Hispanic or Latino Origin

Area	Total (%)	Mexican (%)	Puerto Rican (%)	Cuban (%)	Other (%)
City	3.0	1.9	0.1	0.1	0.9
MSA[1]	2.9	2.1	0.1	0.1	0.7
U.S.	16.9	10.8	1.6	0.6	3.8

Note: Persons of Hispanic or Latino origin can be of any race; (1) Figures cover the Bozeman, MT Micropolitan Statistical Area—see Appendix B for areas included
Source: U.S. Census Bureau, 2010-2014 American Community Survey 5-Year Estimates

Ancestry

Area	German	Irish	English	American	Italian	Polish	French[2]	Scottish	Dutch
City	26.3	14.9	13.2	4.0	5.7	3.2	4.0	3.7	3.1
MSA[1]	28.5	15.4	13.5	4.6	5.2	2.7	4.2	3.4	4.5
U.S.	14.9	10.8	8.0	7.1	5.5	3.0	2.7	1.7	1.4

Note: Figures are the percentage of the total population reporting a particular ancestry. The nine most commonly reported ancestries in the U.S. are shown. Figures include multiple ancestries (e.g. if a person reported being Irish and Italian, they were included in both columns); (1) Figures cover the Bozeman, MT Micropolitan Statistical Area—see Appendix B for areas included; (2) Excludes Basque
Source: U.S. Census Bureau, 2010-2014 American Community Survey 5-Year Estimates

Foreign-Born Population

Area	Percent of Population Born in								
	Any Foreign Country	Asia	Mexico	Europe	Carribean	Central America[2]	South America	Africa	Canada
City	4.3	2.2	0.3	0.7	0.0	0.1	0.2	0.2	0.4
MSA[1]	2.9	1.1	0.4	0.8	0.0	0.1	0.1	0.1	0.3
U.S.	13.1	3.8	3.7	1.5	1.2	1.0	0.9	0.6	0.3

Note: (1) Figures cover the Bozeman, MT Micropolitan Statistical Area—see Appendix B for areas included; (2) Excludes Mexico.
Source: U.S. Census Bureau, 2010-2014 American Community Survey 5-Year Estimates

Marital Status

Area	Never Married	Now Married[2]	Separated	Widowed	Divorced
City	53.3	35.0	1.0	3.3	7.4
MSA[1]	36.4	50.1	1.1	3.4	8.9
U.S.	32.5	48.4	2.2	5.9	10.9

Note: Figures are percentages and cover the population 15 years of age and older; (1) Figures cover the Bozeman, MT Micropolitan Statistical Area—see Appendix B for areas included; (2) Excludes separated
Source: U.S. Census Bureau, 2010-2014 American Community Survey 5-Year Estimates

Disability Status

Area	All Ages	Under 18 Years Old	18 to 64 Years Old	65 Years and Over
City	7.5	2.4	5.3	40.6
MSA[1]	7.8	2.7	5.9	31.1
U.S.	12.3	4.1	10.2	36.3

Note: Figures show percent of the civilian noninstitutionalized population that reported having a disability. Disability status is determined from from six types of difficulty: vision, hearing, cognitive, ambulatory, self-care, and independent living. For children under 5 years old, hearing and vision difficulty are used to determine disability status. For children between the ages of 5 and 14, disability status is determined from hearing, vision, cognitive, ambulatory, and self-care difficulties. For people aged 15 years and older, they are considered to have a disability if they have difficulty with any one of the six difficulty types; (1) Figures cover the Bozeman, MT Micropolitan Statistical Area—see Appendix B for areas included.
Source: U.S. Census Bureau, 2010-2014 American Community Survey 5-Year Estimates

Age

Area	Percent of Population									Median Age
	Under Age 5	Age 5–19	Age 20–34	Age 35–44	Age 45–54	Age 55–64	Age 65–74	Age 75–84	Age 85+	
City	5.1	17.6	40.9	12.3	8.3	7.7	4.0	2.2	1.9	27.5
MSA[1]	6.1	18.5	28.5	12.6	12.3	11.6	6.0	2.9	1.4	33.0
U.S.	6.4	19.9	20.6	13.0	14.1	12.3	7.6	4.3	1.9	37.4

Note: (1) Figures cover the Bozeman, MT Micropolitan Statistical Area—see Appendix B for areas included
Source: U.S. Census Bureau, 2010-2014 American Community Survey 5-Year Estimates

Gender

Area	Males	Females	Males per 100 Females
City	20,408	18,715	109.0
MSA[1]	47,971	45,137	106.3
U.S.	154,515,159	159,591,925	96.8

Note: (1) Figures cover the Bozeman, MT Micropolitan Statistical Area—see Appendix B for areas included
Source: U.S. Census Bureau, 2010-2014 American Community Survey 5-Year Estimates

Religious Groups by Family

Area	Catholic	Baptist	Non-Den.	Methodist[2]	Lutheran	LDS[3]	Pente-costal	Presby-terian[4]	Muslim[5]	Judaism
MSA[1]	7.1	2.0	3.9	2.8	3.6	4.0	1.6	3.2	0.3	0.3
U.S.	19.1	9.3	4.0	4.0	2.3	2.0	1.9	1.6	0.8	0.7

Note: Figures are the number of adherents as a percentage of the total population; (1) Figures cover the Bozeman, MT Micropolitan Statistical Area—see Appendix B for areas included; (2) Methodist/Pietist; (3) Latter Day Saints; (4) Reformed; (5) Figures are estimates
Source: Association of Statisticians of American Religious Bodies, 2010 U.S. Religion Census: Religious Congregations & Membership Study

Religious Groups by Tradition

Area	Catholic	Evangelical Protestant	Mainline Protestant	Other Tradition	Black Protestant	Orthodox
MSA[1]	7.1	13.5	6.5	4.9	0.1	<0.1
U.S.	19.1	16.2	7.3	4.3	1.6	0.3

Note: Figures are the number of adherents as a percentage of the total population; (1) Figures cover the Bozeman, MT Micropolitan Statistical Area—see Appendix B for areas included
Source: Association of Statisticians of American Religious Bodies, 2010 U.S. Religion Census: Religious Congregations & Membership Study

ECONOMY

Gross Metropolitan Product

Area	2013	2014	2015	2016	Rank[2]
MSA[1]	n/a	n/a	n/a	n/a	n/a

Note: Figures are in billions of dollars; (1) Figures cover the Bozeman, MT Micropolitan Statistical Area—see Appendix B for areas included; (2) Rank is based on 2016 data and ranges from 1 to 381
Source: The U.S. Conference of Mayors, U.S. Metro Economies: GMP and Employment 2014-2016, June 2015

Economic Growth

Area	2011-13 (%)	2014 (%)	2015 (%)	2016 (%)	Rank[2]
MSA[1]	n/a	n/a	n/a	n/a	n/a
U.S.	2.2	2.4	2.3	2.9	–

Note: Figures are real gross metropolitan product (GMP) growth rates and represent annual average percent change; (1) Figures cover the Bozeman, MT Micropolitan Statistical Area—see Appendix B for areas included; (2) Rank is based on 2016 data and ranges from 1 to 381
Source: The U.S. Conference of Mayors, U.S. Metro Economies: GMP and Employment 2014-2016, June 2015

Metropolitan Area Exports

Area	2009	2010	2011	2012	2013	2014	Rank[2]
MSA[1]	n/a	n/a	n/a	n/a	n/a	n/a	n/a

Note: Figures are in millions of dollars; (1) Figures cover the Bozeman, MT Micropolitan Statistical Area—see Appendix B for areas included; (2) Rank is based on 2014 data and ranges from 1 to 385
Source: U.S. Department of Commerce, International Trade Administration, Office of Trade & Industry Information, Manufacturing & Services, data extracted March 10, 2016

Building Permits

Area	Single-Family			Multi-Family			Total		
	2014	2015p	Pct. Chg.	2014	2015p	Pct. Chg.	2014	2015p	Pct. Chg.
City	295	287	-2.7	376	493	31.1	671	780	16.2
MSA[1]	701	872	24.4	490	624	27.3	1,191	1,496	25.6
U.S.	640,300	690,800	7.9	411,800	487,600	18.4	1,052,100	1,178,400	12.0

Note: (1) Figures cover the Bozeman, MT Micropolitan Statistical Area—see Appendix B for areas included; Figures represent new, privately-owned housing units authorized (unadjusted data); All permit data are based on estimates with imputation; (p) preliminary data.
Source: U.S. Census Bureau, Manufacturing, Mining, and Construction Statistics, Building Permits, 2014, 2015

Bankruptcy Filings

Area	Business Filings			Nonbusiness Filings		
	2014	2015	% Chg.	2014	2015	% Chg.
Gallatin County	8	6	-25.0	145	123	-15.2
U.S.	26,983	24,735	-8.3	909,812	819,760	-9.9

Note: Business filings include Chapter 7, Chapter 11, Chapter 12, and Chapter 13; Nonbusiness filings include Chapter 7, Chapter 11, and Chapter 13
Source: Administrative Office of the U.S. Courts, Business and Nonbusiness Bankruptcy, County Cases Commenced by Chapter of the Bankruptcy Code, During the 12- Month Period Ending December 31, 2014 and Business and Nonbusiness Bankruptcy, County Cases Commenced by Chapter of the Bankruptcy Code, During the 12- Month Period Ending December 31, 2015

Housing Vacancy Rates

Area	Gross Vacancy Rate[2] (%)			Year-Round Vacancy Rate[3] (%)			Rental Vacancy Rate[4] (%)			Homeowner Vacancy Rate[5] (%)		
	2013	2014	2015	2013	2014	2015	2013	2014	2015	2013	2014	2015
MSA[1]	n/a	n/a	n/a	n/a	n/a	n/a	n/a	n/a	n/a	n/a	n/a	n/a
U.S.	13.6	13.4	12.9	10.7	10.4	10.0	8.3	7.6	7.1	2.0	1.9	1.8

Note: (1) Figures cover the Bozeman, MT Micropolitan Statistical Area—see Appendix B for areas included; (2) The percentage of the total housing inventory that is vacant; (3) The percentage of the housing inventory (excluding seasonal units) that is year-round vacant; (4) The percentage of rental inventory that is vacant for rent; (5) The percentage of homeowner inventory that is vacant for sale; n/a not available
Source: U.S. Census Bureau, Housing Vacancies and Homeownership Annual Statistics: 2015

INCOME

Income

Area	Per Capita ($)	Median Household ($)	Average Household ($)
City	26,350	46,422	62,333
MSA[1]	29,468	54,298	71,625
U.S.	28,555	53,482	74,596

Note: (1) Figures cover the Bozeman, MT Micropolitan Statistical Area—see Appendix B for areas included
Source: U.S. Census Bureau, 2010-2014 American Community Survey 5-Year Estimates

Household Income Distribution

Area	Percent of Households Earning							
	Under $15,000	$15,000 -24,999	$25,000 -34,999	$35,000 -49,999	$50,000 -74,999	$75,000 -99,000	$100,000 -149,999	$150,000 and up
City	14.6	13.5	11.0	13.8	19.3	13.3	8.9	5.5
MSA[1]	11.1	10.2	10.9	14.0	19.9	13.9	12.3	7.8
U.S.	12.5	10.7	10.2	13.5	17.8	12.2	13.0	10.0

Note: (1) Figures cover the Bozeman, MT Micropolitan Statistical Area—see Appendix B for areas included
Source: U.S. Census Bureau, 2010-2014 American Community Survey 5-Year Estimates

Poverty Rate

Area	All Ages	Under 18 Years Old	18 to 64 Years Old	65 Years and Over
City	21.0	10.8	24.9	6.0
MSA[1]	13.9	11.3	16.2	4.6
U.S.	15.6	21.9	14.6	9.4

Note: Figures are percentage of people whose income during the past 12 months was below the poverty level; (1) Figures cover the Bozeman, MT Micropolitan Statistical Area—see Appendix B for areas included
Source: U.S. Census Bureau, 2010-2014 American Community Survey 5-Year Estimates

EMPLOYMENT

Labor Force and Employment

Area	Civilian Labor Force			Workers Employed		
	Dec. 2014	Dec. 2015	% Chg.	Dec. 2014	Dec. 2015	% Chg.
City	24,691	25,656	3.9	23,975	25,027	4.3
MSA[1]	56,832	59,093	3.9	54,968	57,381	4.3
U.S.	155,521,000	157,245,000	1.1	147,190,000	149,703,000	1.7

Note: Data is not seasonally adjusted and covers workers 16 years of age and older; (1) Figures cover the Bozeman, MT Micropolitan Statistical Area—see Appendix B for areas included
Source: Bureau of Labor Statistics, Local Area Unemployment Statistics

Unemployment Rate

Area	2015											
	Jan.	Feb.	Mar.	Apr.	May	Jun.	Jul.	Aug.	Sep.	Oct.	Nov.	Dec.
City	3.3	2.9	3.0	2.6	2.3	2.6	2.5	2.4	2.2	2.5	2.6	2.5
MSA[1]	3.6	3.3	3.3	2.9	2.8	2.8	2.5	2.3	2.3	3.0	3.4	2.9
U.S.	6.1	5.8	5.6	5.1	5.3	5.5	5.6	5.2	4.9	4.8	4.8	4.8

Note: Data is not seasonally adjusted and covers workers 16 years of age and older; (1) Figures cover the Bozeman, MT Micropolitan Statistical Area—see Appendix B for areas included
Source: Bureau of Labor Statistics, Local Area Unemployment Statistics

Employment by Occupation

Occupation Classification	City (%)	MSA[1] (%)	U.S. (%)
Management, Business, Science, and Arts	40.4	39.7	36.4
Natural Resources, Construction, and Maintenance	8.5	11.7	9.0
Production, Transportation, and Material Moving	7.1	8.5	12.1
Sales and Office	23.4	22.0	24.4
Service	20.6	18.1	18.2

Note: Figures cover employed civilians 16 years of age and older; (1) Figures cover the Bozeman, MT Micropolitan Statistical Area—see Appendix B for areas included
Source: U.S. Census Bureau, 2010-2014 American Community Survey 5-Year Estimates

Employment by Industry

Sector	MSA[1]		U.S.
	Number of Employees	Percent of Total	Percent of Total
Construction, Mining, and Logging	n/a	n/a	5.0
Education and Health Services	n/a	n/a	15.7
Financial Activities	n/a	n/a	5.7
Government	n/a	n/a	15.5
Information	n/a	n/a	1.9
Leisure and Hospitality	n/a	n/a	10.4
Manufacturing	n/a	n/a	8.6
Other Services	n/a	n/a	3.9
Professional and Business Services	n/a	n/a	13.9
Retail Trade	n/a	n/a	11.3
Transportation, Warehousing, and Utilities	n/a	n/a	3.9
Wholesale Trade	n/a	n/a	4.1

Note: Figures are non-farm employment as of December 2015. Figures are not seasonally adjusted and include workers 16 years of age and older; (1) Figures cover the Bozeman, MT Micropolitan Statistical Area—see Appendix B for areas included; n/a not available
Source: Bureau of Labor Statistics, Current Employment Statistics, Employment, Hours, and Earnings

Occupations with Greatest Projected Employment Growth: 2012 – 2022

Occupation[1]	2012 Employment	2022 Projected Employment	Numeric Employment Change	Percent Employment Change
Retail Salespersons	13,950	16,680	2,730	19.6
Combined Food Preparation and Serving Workers, Including Fast Food	10,650	12,940	2,290	21.5
Bookkeeping, Accounting, and Auditing Clerks	11,340	13,350	2,010	17.7
Registered Nurses	8,780	10,560	1,780	20.4
Secretaries and Administrative Assistants, Except Legal, Medical, and Executive	10,500	12,210	1,710	16.3
Waiters and Waitresses	8,960	10,440	1,480	16.5
Cashiers	14,680	16,130	1,450	9.8
Personal Care Aides	6,350	7,680	1,330	20.8
Maids and Housekeeping Cleaners	5,930	7,250	1,320	22.2
Heavy and Tractor-Trailer Truck Drivers	7,070	8,320	1,250	17.7

Note: Projections cover Montana; (1) Sorted by numeric employment change
Source: www.projectionscentral.com, State Occupational Projections, 2012–2022 Long-Term Projections

Fastest Growing Occupations: 2012 – 2022

Occupation[1]	2012 Employment	2022 Projected Employment	Numeric Employment Change	Percent Employment Change
Veterinary Technologists and Technicians	410	580	170	38.9
Roustabouts, Oil and Gas	700	960	260	36.8
Rotary Drill Operators, Oil and Gas	290	400	110	36.4
Aircraft Mechanics and Service Technicians	360	480	120	33.4
Software Developers, Systems Software	410	550	140	33.2
Medical Secretaries	2,160	2,850	690	32.2
Surgical Technologists	410	540	130	32.1
Physician Assistants	430	560	130	31.7
Market Research Analysts and Marketing Specialists	570	750	180	31.4
Wellhead Pumpers	590	780	190	31.4

Note: Projections cover Montana; (1) Sorted by percent employment change and excludes occupations with numeric employment change less than 100
Source: www.projectionscentral.com, State Occupational Projections, 2012–2022 Long-Term Projections

Average Wages

Occupation	$/Hr.	Occupation	$/Hr.
Accountants and Auditors	n/a	Maids and Housekeeping Cleaners	n/a
Automotive Mechanics	n/a	Maintenance and Repair Workers	n/a
Bookkeepers	n/a	Marketing Managers	n/a
Carpenters	n/a	Nuclear Medicine Technologists	n/a
Cashiers	n/a	Nurses, Licensed Practical	n/a
Clerks, General Office	n/a	Nurses, Registered	n/a
Clerks, Receptionists/Information	n/a	Nursing Assistants	n/a
Clerks, Shipping/Receiving	n/a	Packers and Packagers, Hand	n/a
Computer Programmers	n/a	Physical Therapists	n/a
Computer Systems Analysts	n/a	Postal Service Mail Carriers	n/a
Computer User Support Specialists	n/a	Real Estate Brokers	n/a
Cooks, Restaurant	n/a	Retail Salespersons	n/a
Dentists	n/a	Sales Reps., Exc. Tech./Scientific	n/a
Electrical Engineers	n/a	Sales Reps., Tech./Scientific	n/a
Electricians	n/a	Secretaries, Exc. Legal/Med./Exec.	n/a
Financial Managers	n/a	Security Guards	n/a
First-Line Supervisors/Managers, Sales	n/a	Surgeons	n/a
Food Preparation Workers	n/a	Teacher Assistants*	n/a
General and Operations Managers	n/a	Teachers, Elementary School*	n/a
Hairdressers/Cosmetologists	n/a	Teachers, Secondary School*	n/a
Internists	n/a	Telemarketers	n/a
Janitors and Cleaners	n/a	Truck Drivers, Heavy/Tractor-Trailer	n/a
Landscaping/Groundskeeping Workers	n/a	Truck Drivers, Light/Delivery Svcs.	n/a
Lawyers	n/a	Waiters and Waitresses	n/a

Note: Wage data was not available.
Source: Bureau of Labor Statistics, Metro Area Occupational Employment and Wage Estimates, May 2015

TAXES

State Corporate Income Tax Rates

State	Tax Rate (%)	Income Brackets ($)	Num. of Brackets	Financial Institution Tax Rate (%)[a]	Federal Income Tax Ded.
Montana	6.75 (p)	Flat rate	1	6.75 (p)	No

Note: Tax rates as of January 1, 2016; (a) Rates listed are the corporate income tax rate applied to financial institutions or excise taxes based on income. Some states have other taxes based upon the value of deposits or shares; (p) Montana levies a 7% tax on taxpayers using water's edge combination. The minimum tax per corporation is $50; the $50 minimum applies to each corporation included on a combined tax return. Taxpayers with gross sales in Montana of $100,000 or less maypay an alternative tax of 0.5% on such sales, instead of the net income tax.
Source: Federation of Tax Administrators, "State Corporate Income Tax Rates, 2016"

State Individual Income Tax Rates

State	Tax Rate (%)	Income Brackets ($)	Num. of Brackets	Personal Exempt. ($)[1] Single	Personal Exempt. ($)[1] Dependents	Fed. Inc. Tax Ded.
Montana (a)	1.0 - 6.9	2,800 - 17,100	7	2,280	2,330	Yes (m)

Note: Tax rates as of January 1, 2016; Local- and county-level taxes are not included; n/a not applicable; (1) Married joint filers generally receive double the single exemption; (a) 18 states have statutory provision for automatically adjusting to the rate of inflation the dollar values of the income tax brackets, standard deductions, and/or personal exemptions. Massachusetts, Michigan, and Nebraska index the personal exemptiononly. Oregon does not index the income brackets for $125,000 and over. Maine has suspended indexing for 2014 and 2015; (m) The deduction for federal income tax is limited to $5,000 for individuals and $10,000 for joint returns in Missouri and Montana, and to $6,350 for all filers in Oregon.
Source: Federation of Tax Administrators, "State Individual Income Tax Rates, 2016"

Various State and Local Tax Rates

State	State and Local Sales and Use (%)	State Sales and Use (%)	Gasoline[1] (¢/gal.)	Cigarette[2] ($/pack)	Spirits[3] ($/gal.)	Wine[4] ($/gal.)	Beer[5] ($/gal.)
Montana	None	None (d)	27.75	1.70	9.77 (g)	1.06 (l)	0.14

Note: All tax rates as of January 1, 2016; (1) The American Petroleum Institute has developed a methodology for determining the average tax rate on a gallon of fuel. Rates may include any of the following: excise taxes, environmental fees, storage tank fees, other fees or taxes, general sales tax, and local taxes. In states where gasoline is subject to the general sales tax, or where the fuel tax is based on the average sale price, the average rate determined by API is sensitive to changes in the price of gasoline. States that fully or partially apply general sales taxes to gasoline: CA, CO, GA, IL, IN, MI, NY; (2) The federal excise tax of $1.0066 per pack and local taxes are not included; (3) Rates are those applicable to off-premise sales of 40% alcohol by volume (a.b.v.) distilled spirits in 750ml containers. Local excise taxes are excluded; (4) Rates are those applicable to off-premise sales of 11% a.b.v. non-carbonated wine in 750ml containers; (5) Rates are those applicable to off-premise sales of 4.7% a.b.v. beer in 12 ounce containers; (d) Due to data limitations, the table does not include sales taxes in local resort areas in Montana; (g) Control states, where the government controls all sales. Products can be subject to ad valorem mark-up as well as excise taxes; (l) Different rates also applicable according to alcohol content, place of production, size of container, place purchased (on- or off-premise or on board airlines) or type of wine (carbonated, vermouth, etc.).
Source: Tax Foundation, 2016 Facts & Figures: How Does Your State Compare?

State Business Tax Climate Index Rankings

State	Overall Rank	Corporate Tax Rank	Individual Income Tax Rank	Sales Tax Rank	Unemployment Insurance Tax Rank	Property Tax Rank
Montana	6	23	20	3	18	9

Note: The index is a measure of how each state's tax laws affect economic performance. The lower the rank, the more favorable a state's tax system is for business. States without a given tax are given a ranking of 1. The scores/rankings for the District of Columbia do not affect other states. The 2016 index represents the tax climate as of July 1, 2015 (the beginning of Fiscal Year 2016).
Source: Tax Foundation, State Business Tax Climate Index 2016

TRANSPORTATION

Means of Transportation to Work

Area	Car/Truck/Van Drove Alone	Car/Truck/Van Car-pooled	Public Transportation Bus	Public Transportation Subway	Public Transportation Railroad	Bicycle	Walked	Other Means	Worked at Home
City	71.3	6.6	1.0	0.2	0.0	5.5	9.5	0.7	5.1
MSA[1]	73.1	8.6	0.8	0.1	0.0	3.0	6.0	1.2	7.2
U.S.	76.4	9.6	2.6	1.8	0.6	0.6	2.8	1.3	4.4

Note: Figures are percentages and cover workers 16 years of age and older; (1) Figures cover the Bozeman, MT Micropolitan Statistical Area—see Appendix B for areas included
Source: U.S. Census Bureau, 2010-2014 American Community Survey 5-Year Estimates

Travel Time to Work

Area	Less Than 10 Minutes	10 to 19 Minutes	20 to 29 Minutes	30 to 44 Minutes	45 to 59 Minutes	60 to 89 Minutes	90 Minutes or More
City	33.6	47.6	10.1	4.6	1.2	1.9	1.0
MSA[1]	24.7	43.8	18.1	8.2	1.7	1.9	1.6
U.S.	13.3	29.6	21.0	20.2	7.7	5.7	2.6

Note: Figures are percentages and include workers 16 years old and over; (1) Figures cover the Bozeman, MT Micropolitan Statistical Area—see Appendix B for areas included
Source: U.S. Census Bureau, 2010-2014 American Community Survey 5-Year Estimates

Freeway Travel Time Index

Area	1985	1990	1995	2000	2005	2010	2014
Urban Area Rank[1,2]	n/a	n/a	n/a	n/a	n/a	n/a	n/a
Urban Area Index[1]	n/a	n/a	n/a	n/a	n/a	n/a	n/a
Average Index[3]	1.09	1.11	1.14	1.17	1.20	1.19	1.20

Note: Freeway Travel Time Index—the ratio of travel time in the peak period to the travel time at free-flow conditions. For example, a value of 1.30 indicates a 20-minute free-flow trip takes 26 minutes in the peak (20 minutes x 1.30 = 26 minutes); (1) Data for the Bozeman, MT urban area was not available; (2) Rank is based on 101 urban areas (#1 = highest travel time index); (3) Average of 101 urban areas

Source: Texas Transportation Institute, 2015 Urban Mobility Scorecard, August 2015

Freeway Commuter Stress Index

Area	1985	1990	1995	2000	2005	2010	2014
Urban Area Rank[1,2]	n/a	n/a	n/a	n/a	n/a	n/a	n/a
Urban Area Index[1]	n/a	n/a	n/a	n/a	n/a	n/a	n/a
Average Index[3]	1.13	1.16	1.19	1.22	1.25	1.24	1.25

Note: The Freeway Commuter Stress Index is the same as the Freeway Travel Time Index (see table above) except that it includes only the travel in the peak directions during the peak periods; the TTI includes travel in all directions during the peak period. Thus, the CSI is more indicative of the work trip experienced by each commuter on a daily basis. (1) Data for the Bozeman, MT urban area was not available; (2) Rank is based on 101 urban areas (#1 = highest stress index); (3) Average of 101 urban areas

Source: Texas Transportation Institute, 2015 Urban Mobility Scorecard, August 2015

Living Environment

COST OF LIVING

Cost of Living Index

Composite Index	Groceries	Housing	Utilities	Trans-portation	Health Care	Misc. Goods/ Services
102.8	103.8	113.3	85.5	97.7	104.8	100.2

Note: The Cost of Living Index measures regional differences in the cost of consumer goods and services, excluding taxes and non-consumer expenditures, for professional and managerial households in the top income quintile. It is based on more than 50,000 prices covering almost 60 different items for which prices are collected three times a year by chambers of commerce, economic development organizations or university applied economic centers in each participating urban area. The numbers shown should be read as a percentage above or below the national average of 100. For example, a value of 115.4 in the groceries column indicates that grocery prices are 15.4% higher than the national average. Small differences in the index numbers should not be interpreted as significant; Figures cover the Bozeman MT urban area.
Source: The Council for Community and Economic Research, ACCRA Cost of Living Index, 2015

Grocery Prices

Area[1]	T-Bone Steak ($/pound)	Frying Chicken ($/pound)	Whole Milk ($/half gal.)	Eggs ($/dozen)	Orange Juice ($/64 oz.)	Coffee ($/11.5 oz.)
City[2]	9.08	1.48	2.13	1.95	3.35	5.26
Avg.	10.99	1.43	2.25	2.26	3.58	4.48
Min.	7.16	0.98	1.30	1.35	2.88	2.98
Max.	14.13	2.43	3.85	4.81	6.39	7.56

Note: (1) Values for the local area are compared with the average, minimum and maximum values for all 292 areas in the Cost of Living Index; (2) Figures cover the Bozeman MT urban area; **T-Bone Steak** *(price per pound);* **Frying Chicken** *(price per pound, whole fryer);* **Whole Milk** *(half gallon carton);* **Eggs** *(price per dozen, Grade A, large);* **Orange Juice** *(64 oz. Tropicana or Florida Natural);* **Coffee** *(11.5 oz. can, vacuum-packed, Maxwell House, Hills Bros, or Folgers).*
Source: The Council for Community and Economic Research, ACCRA Cost of Living Index, 2015

Housing and Utility Costs

Area[1]	New Home Price ($)	Apartment Rent ($/month)	All Electric ($/month)	Part Electric ($/month)	Other Energy ($/month)	Telephone ($/month)
City[2]	363,664	995	-	80.72	88.31	18.46
Avg.	312,874	945	179.30	95.07	72.96	28.11
Min.	178,682	479	116.28	43.14	26.46	10.01
Max.	1,472,476	3,984	504.25	189.44	421.11	43.06

Note: (1) Values for the local area are compared with the average, minimum and maximum values for all 292 areas in the Cost of Living Index; (2) Figures cover the Bozeman MT urban area; **New Home Price** *(2,400 sf living area, 8,000 sf lot, in urban area with full utilities);* **Apartment Rent** *(950 sf 2 bedroom/1.5 or 2 bath, unfurnished, excluding all utilities except water);* **All Electric** *(average monthly cost for an all-electric home);* **Part Electric** *(average monthly cost for a part-electric home);* **Other Energy** *(average monthly cost for natural gas, fuel oil, coal, wood, and any other forms of energy except electricity);* **Telephone** *(price includes basic monthly rate for a private residential line plus additional local usage charges incurred by a family of four).*
Source: The Council for Community and Economic Research, ACCRA Cost of Living Index, 2015

Health Care, Transportation, and Other Costs

Area[1]	Doctor ($/visit)	Dentist ($/visit)	Optometrist ($/visit)	Gasoline ($/gallon)	Beauty Salon ($/visit)	Men's Shirt ($)
City[2]	132.50	81.41	99.01	2.42	35.60	19.66
Avg.	105.15	89.02	99.78	2.38	35.30	28.10
Min.	66.87	56.09	48.53	1.95	18.91	13.38
Max.	182.34	150.36	228.33	4.09	67.91	63.80

Note: (1) Values for the local area are compared with the average, minimum and maximum values for all 292 areas in the Cost of Living Index; (2) Figures cover the Bozeman MT urban area; **Doctor** *(general practitioners routine exam of an established patient);* **Dentist** *(adult teeth cleaning and periodic oral examination);* **Optometrist** *(full vision eye exam for established adult patient);* **Gasoline** *(one gallon regular unleaded, national brand, including all taxes, cash price at self-service pump if available);* **Beauty Salon** *(woman's shampoo, trim, and blow-dry);* **Men's Shirt** *(cotton/polyester dress shirt, pinpoint weave, long sleeves).*
Source: The Council for Community and Economic Research, ACCRA Cost of Living Index, 2015

HOUSING

House Price Index (HPI)

Area	National Ranking[2]	Quarterly Change (%)	One-Year Change (%)	Five-Year Change (%)
MSA[1]	n/a	n/a	n/a	n/a
U.S.[3]	–	1.45	5.76	22.85

Note: The HPI is a weighted repeat sales index. It measures average price changes in repeat sales or refinancings on the same properties. This information is obtained by reviewing repeat mortgage transactions on single-family properties whose mortgages have been purchased or securitized by Fannie Mae or Freddie Mac in January 1975; (1) Micropolitan Statistical Area—see Appendix B for areas included; (2) Rankings are based on annual percentage change for all metro areas containing at least 15,000 transactions over the last 10 years and ranges from 1 to 266; (3) figures based on a weighted average of Census Division estimates using a seasonally adjusted, purchase-only index; all figures are for the period ending December 31, 2015; n/a not available

Source: Federal Housing Finance Agency, House Price Index, February 25, 2016

Median Single-Family Home Prices

Area	2013	2014	2015p	Percent Change 2014 to 2015
MSA[1]	n/a	n/a	n/a	n/a
U.S. Average	197.4	208.9	223.9	7.2

Note: Figures are median sales prices of existing single-family homes in thousands of dollars; (p) preliminary; n/a not available; (1) Bozeman, MT Micropolitan Statistical Area—see Appendix B for areas included

Source: National Association of Realtors, Median Sales Price of Existing Single-Family Homes for Metropolitan Areas, 4th Quarter 2015

Qualifying Income Based on Median Sales Price of Existing Single-Family Homes

Area	With 5% Down ($)	With 10% Down ($)	With 20% Down ($)
MSA[1]	n/a	n/a	n/a
U.S. Average	49,535	46,928	41,714

Note: Figures are preliminary; Qualifying income is based on a mortgage rate of 4.1%. Monthly principal and interest payment is limited to 25% of income; n/a not available; (1) Bozeman, MT Micropolitan Statistical Area—see Appendix B for areas included

Source: National Association of Realtors, Qualifying Income Based on Median Sales Price of Existing Single-Family Homes for Metropolitan Areas, 4th Quarter 2015

Median Apartment Condo-Coop Home Prices

Area	2013	2014	2015p	Percent Change 2014 to 2015
MSA[1]	n/a	n/a	n/a	n/a
U.S. Average	194.9	204.3	210.7	3.1

Note: Figures are median sales prices of existing apartment condo-coop homes in thousands of dollars; (p) preliminary; n/a not available; (1) Bozeman, MT Micropolitan Statistical Area—see Appendix B for areas included

Source: National Association of Realtors, Median Sales Price of Existing Apartment Condo-Coop Homes for Metropolitan Areas, 4th Quarter 2015

Gross Monthly Rent

Area	Under $200	$200 -299	$300 -499	$500 -749	$750 -999	$1,000 -1,499	$1,500 and up	Median ($)
City	2.1	0.9	6.3	28.4	27.5	26.9	7.7	849
MSA[1]	1.6	1.3	6.6	27.8	27.9	25.8	9.0	850
U.S.	1.5	3.2	7.4	21.0	24.1	26.9	15.9	920

Note: Figures are percentages except for Median; Gross rent is the contract rent plus the estimated average monthly cost of utilities (electricity, gas, and water and sewer) and fuels (oil, coal, kerosene, wood, etc.) if these are paid by the renter (or paid for the renter by someone else); (1) Figures cover the Bozeman, MT Micropolitan Statistical Area—see Appendix B for areas included

Source: U.S. Census Bureau, 2010-2014 American Community Survey 5-Year Estimates

Homeownership Rate

Area	2008 (%)	2009 (%)	2010 (%)	2011 (%)	2012 (%)	2013 (%)	2014 (%)	2015 (%)
MSA[1]	n/a	n/a	n/a	n/a	n/a	n/a	n/a	n/a
U.S.	67.8	67.4	66.9	66.1	65.4	65.1	64.5	63.7

Note: (1) Figures cover the Bozeman, MT Micropolitan Statistical Area—see Appendix B for areas included; n/a not available
Source: U.S. Census Bureau, Housing Vacancies and Homeownership Annual Statistics: 2015

Year Housing Structure Built

Area	2010 or Later	2000 -2009	1990 -1999	1980 -1989	1970 -1979	1960 -1969	1950 -1959	1940 -1949	Before 1940	Median Year
City	3.4	30.7	15.3	9.4	14.4	8.1	5.2	3.1	10.5	1989
MSA[1]	2.0	30.0	19.5	11.8	15.9	6.0	3.8	2.3	8.7	1991
U.S.	1.0	14.9	13.9	13.8	15.8	11.0	10.8	5.4	13.3	1976

Note: Figures are percentages except for Median Year; (1) Figures cover the Bozeman, MT Micropolitan Statistical Area—see Appendix B for areas included
Source: U.S. Census Bureau, 2010-2014 American Community Survey 5-Year Estimates

HEALTH

Health Risk Data

Category	MSA[1] (%)	U.S. (%)
Adults aged 18–64 who have any kind of health care coverage	n/a	79.6
Adults who reported being in good or excellent health	n/a	83.1
Adults who are current smokers	n/a	19.6
Adults who are heavy drinkers[2]	n/a	6.1
Adults who are binge drinkers[3]	n/a	16.9
Adults who are overweight (BMI 25.0 - 29.9)	n/a	35.8
Adults who are obese (BMI 30.0 - 99.8)	n/a	27.6
Adults who participated in any physical activities in the past month	n/a	77.1
Adults 50+ who have ever had a sigmoidoscopy or colonoscopy	n/a	67.3
Women aged 40+ who have had a mammogram within the past two years	n/a	74.0
Men aged 40+ who have had a PSA test within the past two years	n/a	45.2
Adults aged 65+ who have had flu shot within the past year	n/a	60.1
Adults who always wear a seatbelt	n/a	93.8

Note: Data as of 2012 unless otherwise noted; n/a not available; (1) Figures cover the Bozeman, MT Micropolitan Statistical Area—see Appendix B for areas included; (2) Heavy drinkers are classified as males having more than two drinks per day or females having more than one drink per day; (3) Binge drinkers are classified as males having five or more drinks on one occasion or females having four or more drinks on one occasion
Source: Centers for Disease Control and Prevention, Behaviorial Risk Factor Surveillance System, SMART: Selected Metropolitan/Micropolitan Area Risk Trends, 2012 (Note: the CDC has discontinued this dataset but will be releasing a replacement in mid-2016)

Chronic Health Indicators

Category	MSA[1] (%)	U.S. (%)
Adults who have ever been told they had a heart attack	n/a	4.5
Adults who have ever been told they had a stroke	n/a	2.9
Adults who have been told they currently have asthma	n/a	8.9
Adults who have ever been told they have arthritis	n/a	25.7
Adults who have ever been told they have diabetes[2]	n/a	9.7
Adults who have ever been told they had skin cancer	n/a	5.7
Adults who have ever been told they had any other types of cancer	n/a	6.5
Adults who have ever been told they have COPD	n/a	6.2
Adults who have ever been told they have kidney disease	n/a	2.5
Adults who have ever been told they have a form of depression	n/a	18.0

Note: Data as of 2012 unless otherwise noted; n/a not available; (1) Figures cover the Bozeman, MT Micropolitan Statistical Area—see Appendix B for areas included; (2) Figures do not include pregnancy-related, borderline, or pre-diabetes
Source: Centers for Disease Control and Prevention, Behaviorial Risk Factor Surveillance System, SMART: Selected Metropolitan/Micropolitan Area Risk Trends, 2012 (Note: the CDC has discontinued this dataset but will be releasing a replacement in mid-2016)

Mortality Rates for the Top 10 Causes of Death in the U.S.

ICD-10[a] Sub-Chapter	ICD-10[a] Code	Age-Adjusted Mortality Rate[1] per 100,000 population	
		County[2]	U.S.
Malignant neoplasms	C00-C97	125.6	163.6
Ischaemic heart diseases	I20-I25	68.7	102.2
Other forms of heart disease	I30-I51	48.8	50.1
Chronic lower respiratory diseases	J40-J47	35.1	41.4
Organic, including symptomatic, mental disorders	F01-F09	73.8	38.5
Cerebrovascular diseases	I60-I69	32.7	36.5
Other external causes of accidental injury	W00-X59	21.6	27.5
Other degenerative diseases of the nervous system	G30-G31	13.8	26.3
Diabetes mellitus	E10-E14	Suppressed	21.1
Hypertensive diseases	I10-I15	Unreliable	19.7

Note: (a) ICD-10 = International Classification of Diseases 10th Revision; (1) Mortality rates are a three year average covering 2012-2014; (2) Figures cover Gallatin County.
Source: Centers for Disease Control and Prevention, National Center for Health Statistics. Underlying Cause of Death 1999-2014 on CDC WONDER Online Database, released 2015.

Mortality Rates for Selected Causes of Death

ICD-10[a] Sub-Chapter	ICD-10[a] Code	Age-Adjusted Mortality Rate[1] per 100,000 population	
		County[2]	U.S.
Assault	X85-Y09	Suppressed	5.1
Diseases of the liver	K70-K76	7.6	13.5
Human immunodeficiency virus (HIV) disease	B20-B24	Suppressed	2.1
Influenza and pneumonia	J09-J18	15.7	15.2
Intentional self-harm	X60-X84	15.0	12.7
Malnutrition	E40-E46	Suppressed	0.9
Obesity and other hyperalimentation	E65-E68	Suppressed	1.9
Renal failure	N17-N19	Unreliable	13.0
Transport accidents	V01-V99	16.0	11.6
Viral hepatitis	B15-B19	Suppressed	2.1

Note: (a) ICD-10 = International Classification of Diseases 10th Revision; (1) Mortality rates are a three year average covering 2012-2014; (2) Figures cover Gallatin County; Data are Suppressed when the data meet the criteria for confidentiality constraints; Mortality rates are flagged as Unreliable when the rate would be calculated with a numerator of 20 or less.
Source: Centers for Disease Control and Prevention, National Center for Health Statistics. Underlying Cause of Death 1999-2014 on CDC WONDER Online Database, released 2015.

Health Insurance Coverage

Area	With Health Insurance	With Private Health Insurance	With Public Health Insurance	Without Health Insurance	Population Under Age 18 Without Health Insurance
City	90.2	82.1	15.1	9.8	4.1
MSA[1]	87.5	76.9	18.6	12.5	8.2
U.S.	85.8	65.8	31.1	14.2	7.1

Note: Figures are percentages that cover the civilian noninstitutionalized population; (1) Figures cover the Bozeman, MT Micropolitan Statistical Area—see Appendix B for areas included
Source: U.S. Census Bureau, 2010-2014 American Community Survey 5-Year Estimates

Number of Medical Professionals

Area	MDs[3]	DOs[3,4]	Dentists	Podiatrists	Chiropractors	Optometrists
County[1] (number)	212	10	69	3	53	16
County[1] (rate[2])	223.9	10.6	70.9	3.1	54.5	16.4
U.S. (rate[2])	272.5	20.9	64.7	5.8	25.9	15.2

Note: Data as of 2014 unless noted; (1) Data covers Gallatin County; (2) Rate per 100,000 population; (3) Data as of 2013 and includes all active, non-federal physicians; (4) Doctor of Osteopathic Medicine
Source: U.S. Department of Health and Human Services, Health Resources and Services Administration, Bureau of Health Professions, Area Resource File (ARF) 2014-2015

EDUCATION

Public School District Statistics

District Name	Schls	Pupils	Pupil/ Teacher Ratio	Minority Pupils[1] (%)	Free Lunch Eligible[2] (%)	IEP[3] (%)
Anderson Elem	2	204	16.1	9.3	6.4	6.4
Bozeman Elem	10	4,254	16.1	12.4	21.3	9.2
Bozeman H S	1	1,951	16.6	10.8	15.8	9.2
Monforton Elem	3	314	14.8	8.9	17.8	10.5

Note: Table includes school districts with 100 or more students; (1) Percentage of students that are not non-Hispanic white; (2) Percentage of students that are eligible for the free lunch program; (3) Percentage of students that have an Individualized Education Program.
Source: U.S. Department of Education, National Center for Education Statistics, Common Core of Data, Local Education Agency (School District) Universe Survey: School Year 2013-2014; U.S. Department of Education, National Center for Education Statistics, Common Core of Data, Public Elementary/Secondary School Universe Survey: School Year 2013-2014

Highest Level of Education

Area	Less than H.S.	H.S. Diploma	Some College, No Deg.	Associate Degree	Bachelor's Degree	Master's Degree	Prof. School Degree	Doctorate Degree
City	2.5	11.8	24.6	6.6	35.6	12.4	2.1	4.3
MSA[1]	3.6	19.6	24.1	6.0	31.2	9.8	2.4	3.2
U.S.	13.7	28.0	21.2	7.9	18.3	7.8	2.0	1.3

Note: Figures cover persons age 25 and over; (1) Figures cover the Bozeman, MT Micropolitan Statistical Area—see Appendix B for areas included
Source: U.S. Census Bureau, 2010-2014 American Community Survey 5-Year Estimates

Educational Attainment by Race

Area	High School Graduate or Higher (%)					Bachelor's Degree or Higher (%)				
	Total	White	Black	Asian	Hisp.[2]	Total	White	Black	Asian	Hisp.[2]
City	97.5	97.5	100.0	100.0	94.1	54.4	55.1	74.1	61.3	33.5
MSA[1]	96.4	96.5	92.6	100.0	86.6	46.7	47.1	47.2	62.5	29.5
U.S.	86.3	88.4	83.2	85.8	64.1	29.3	30.6	19.0	50.9	13.9

Note: Figures shown cover persons 25 years old and over; (1) Figures cover the Bozeman, MT Micropolitan Statistical Area—see Appendix B for areas included; (2) People of Hispanic origin can be of any race
Source: U.S. Census Bureau, 2010-2014 American Community Survey 5-Year Estimates

School Enrollment by Grade and Control

Area	Preschool (%)		Kindergarten (%)		Grades 1 - 4 (%)		Grades 5 - 8 (%)		Grades 9 - 12 (%)	
	Public	Private	Public	Private	Public	Private	Public	Private	Public	Private
City	33.0	67.0	88.0	12.0	92.9	7.1	85.9	14.1	88.9	11.1
MSA[1]	33.1	66.9	84.9	15.1	84.8	15.2	88.6	11.4	87.0	13.0
U.S.	57.4	42.6	87.8	12.2	89.8	10.2	89.9	10.1	90.6	9.4

Note: Figures shown cover persons 3 years old and over; (1) Figures cover the Bozeman, MT Micropolitan Statistical Area—see Appendix B for areas included
Source: U.S. Census Bureau, 2010-2014 American Community Survey 5-Year Estimates

Average Salaries of Public School Classroom Teachers

Area	2013-14		2014-15		Percent Change 2013-14 to 2014-15	Percent Change 2004-05 to 2014-15
	Dollars	Rank[1]	Dollars	Rank[1]		
Montana	49,893	28	50,999	27	2.22	32.5
U.S. Average	56,610	–	57,379	–	1.36	20.8

Note: (1) State rank ranges from 1 to 51 where 1 indicates highest salary.
Source: National Education Association, Rankings & Estimates: Rankings of the States 2014 and Estimates of School Statistics 2015, March 2015

Higher Education

Four-Year Colleges: Public	Four-Year Colleges: Private Non-profit	Four-Year Colleges: Private For-profit	Two-Year Colleges: Public	Two-Year Colleges: Private Non-profit	Two-Year Colleges: Private For-profit	Medical Schools[1]	Law Schools[2]	Voc/ Tech[3]
1	1	0	0	0	1	0	0	1

Note: Figures cover institutions located within the city limits and include main campuses only; (1) includes schools accredited by the Liaison Committee on Medical Education and the American Osteopathic Association's Commission on Osteopathic College Accreditation; (2) includes ABA-accredited schools, schools with provisional ABA accreditation, and state accredited schools; (3) includes all schools with programs that are less than 2 years.

Source: National Center for Education Statistics, Integrated Postsecondary Education System (IPEDS), 2014-15; Association of American Medical Colleges, Member List, March 21, 2016; American Osteopathic Association, Member List, March 21, 2016; Law School Admission Council, Official Guide to ABA-Approved Law Schools Online, March 21, 2016; Wikipedia, List of Medical Schools in the United States, March 21, 2016; Wikipedia, List of Law Schools in the United States, March 21, 2016

PRESIDENTIAL ELECTION

2012 Presidential Election Results

Area	Obama (%)	Romney (%)	Other (%)
Gallatin County	45.9	50.9	3.3
U.S.	51.0	47.2	1.8

Note: Results may not add to 100% due to rounding

Source: Dave Leip's Atlas of U.S. Presidential Elections

EMPLOYERS

Major Employers

Company Name	Industry
Big Sky Resort	Resorts
Bozeman Deaconess Hospital	General medical and surgical hospitals
Gallatin County	Government offices-county
Montana State University	Schools-universities & colleges academic
Oracle America	Software
Walmart	Department stores, discount

Note: Companies shown are located within the Bozeman, MT Micropolitan Statistical Area.

Source: Hoovers.com; Wikipedia

PUBLIC SAFETY

Crime Rate

Area	All Crimes	Violent Crimes: Murder	Violent Crimes: Rape[3]	Violent Crimes: Robbery	Violent Crimes: Aggrav. Assault	Property Crimes: Burglary	Property Crimes: Larceny -Theft	Property Crimes: Motor Vehicle Theft
City	2,934.0	0.0	76.5	7.4	98.7	175.2	2,433.1	143.1
Metro[1]	n/a	n/a	n/a	n/a	n/a	n/a	n/a	n/a
U.S.	2,971.8	4.5	36.6	102.2	232.5	542.5	1,837.3	216.2

Note: Figures are crimes per 100,000 population; (1) Figures cover the Bozeman, MT Micropolitan Statistical Area—see Appendix B for areas included; n/a not available; (3) The city and U.S. figures shown were reported using the revised Uniform Crime Reporting (UCR) definition of rape. The suburban and metro area figures shown are an aggregate total of the data submitted using both the revised and legacy UCR definitions.

Source: FBI Uniform Crime Reports, 2014

Hate Crimes

Area	Number of Quarters Reported	Number of Incidents per Bias Motivation: Race	Religion	Sexual Orientation	Ethnicity	Disability	Gender	Gender Identity
City	4	0	0	0	0	0	0	0
U.S.	4	2,568	1,014	1,017	648	84	33	98

Source: Federal Bureau of Investigation, Hate Crime Statistics 2014

Identity Theft Consumer Complaints

Area	Complaints	Complaints per 100,000 Population	Rank[2]
MSA[1]	n/a	n/a	n/a
U.S.	490,220	152.4	-

Note: (1) Figures cover the Bozeman, MT Micropolitan Statistical Area—see Appendix B for areas included; (2) Rank ranges from 1 to 379 where 1 indicates greatest number of identity theft complaints per 100,000 population
Source: Federal Trade Commission, Consumer Sentinel Network Data Book for January–December 2015

Fraud and Other Consumer Complaints

Area	Complaints	Complaints per 100,000 Population	Rank[2]
MSA[1]	n/a	n/a	n/a
U.S.	2,593,159	806.0	-

Note: (1) Figures cover the Bozeman, MT Micropolitan Statistical Area—see Appendix B for areas included; (2) Rank ranges from 1 to 379 where 1 indicates greatest number of identity theft complaints per 100,000 population
Source: Federal Trade Commission, Consumer Sentinel Network Data Book for January–December 2015

RECREATION

Culture

Dance[1]	Theatre[1]	Instrumental Music[1]	Vocal Music[1]	Series and Festivals	Museums and Art Galleries[2]	Zoos and Aquariums[3]
0	0	0	0	0	0	0

Note: (1) Professional perfoming groups; (2) Based on organizations with SIC code 8412; (3) AZA-accredited
Source: The Grey House Performing Arts Directory, 2015-16; Association of Zoos & Aquariums, AZA Member Zoos & Aquariums, March 25, 2016; www.AccuLeads.com, March 29, 2016

Professional Sports Teams

Team Name	League	Year Established
No teams are located in the metro area		

Source: Wikipedia, Major Professional Sports Teams of the United States and Canada, March 24, 2016

CLIMATE

Average and Extreme Temperatures

Temperature	Jan	Feb	Mar	Apr	May	Jun	Jul	Aug	Sep	Oct	Nov	Dec	Yr.
Extreme High (°F)	68	72	79	90	95	105	105	105	103	90	77	69	105
Average High (°F)	32	38	45	57	67	77	86	85	72	61	45	36	59
Average Temp. (°F)	23	29	35	46	56	65	72	71	60	49	36	27	47
Average Low (°F)	14	19	25	34	44	52	58	57	47	37	26	18	36
Extreme Low (°F)	-28	-28	-19	9	14	32	41	35	22	-7	-22	-32	-32

Note: Figures cover the years 1948-1995
Source: National Climatic Data Center, International Station Meteorological Climate Summary, 9/96

Average Precipitation/Snowfall/Humidity

Precip./Humidity	Jan	Feb	Mar	Apr	May	Jun	Jul	Aug	Sep	Oct	Nov	Dec	Yr.
Avg. Precip. (in.)	0.8	0.6	1.1	1.8	2.4	2.1	1.1	0.9	1.3	1.1	0.8	0.7	14.6
Avg. Snowfall (in.)	10	7	10	9	2	Tr	0	Tr	1	4	7	9	59
Avg. Rel. Hum. 5am (%)	64	66	69	68	71	72	64	61	64	63	65	64	66
Avg. Rel. Hum. 5pm (%)	56	53	48	42	42	41	32	30	37	42	53	56	44

Note: Figures cover the years 1948-1995; Tr = Trace amounts (<0.05 in. of rain; <0.5 in. of snow)
Source: National Climatic Data Center, International Station Meteorological Climate Summary, 9/96

Weather Conditions

Temperature			Daytime Sky			Precipitation		
5°F & below	32°F & below	90°F & above	Clear	Partly cloudy	Cloudy	0.01 inch or more precip.	0.1 inch or more snow/ice	Thunder-storms
25	149	29	75	163	127	97	41	27

Note: Figures are average number of days per year and cover the years 1948-1995
Source: National Climatic Data Center, International Station Meteorological Climate Summary, 9/96

HAZARDOUS WASTE

Superfund Sites

Bozeman has one hazardous waste site on the EPA's Superfund Final National Priorities List: **Idaho Pole Co.** There are a total of 1,323 Superfund sites on the list in the U.S. *U.S. Environmental Protection Agency, Final National Priorities List, March 18, 2016*

AIR & WATER QUALITY

Air Quality Trends: Ozone

	1990	1995	2000	2005	2010	2011	2012	2013	2014
MSA[1]	n/a	n/a	n/a	n/a	n/a	n/a	n/a	n/a	n/a

Note: (1) Data covers the Bozeman, MT Micropolitan Statistical Area—see Appendix B for areas included; n/a not available. The values shown are the composite ozone concentration averages among trend sites based on the highest fourth daily maximum 8-hour concentration in parts per million. These trends are based on sites having an adequate record of monitoring data during the trend period. Data from exceptional events are included.
Source: U.S. Environmental Protection Agency, Air Quality Monitoring Information, "Air Quality Trends by City, 1990-2014"

Air Quality Index

Area	Percent of Days when Air Quality was...[2]					AQI Statistics[2]	
	Good	Moderate	Unhealthy for Sensitive Groups	Unhealthy	Very Unhealthy	Maximum	Median
MSA[1]	87.4	11.8	0.5	0.3	0.0	174	22

Note: (1) Data covers the Bozeman, MT Micropolitan Statistical Area—see Appendix B for areas included; (2) Based on 365 days with AQI data in 2015. Air Quality Index (AQI) is an index for reporting daily air quality. EPA calculates the AQI for five major air pollutants regulated by the Clean Air Act: ground-level ozone, particle pollution (aka particulate matter), carbon monoxide, sulfur dioxide, and nitrogen dioxide. The AQI runs from 0 to 500. The higher the AQI value, the greater the level of air pollution and the greater the health concern. There are six AQI categories: "Good" AQI is between 0 and 50. Air quality is considered satisfactory; "Moderate" AQI is between 51 and 100. Air quality is acceptable; "Unhealthy for Sensitive Groups" When AQI values are between 101 and 150, members of sensitive groups may experience health effects; "Unhealthy" When AQI values are between 151 and 200 everyone may begin to experience health effects; "Very Unhealthy" AQI values between 201 and 300 trigger a health alert; "Hazardous" AQI values over 300 trigger warnings of emergency conditions (not shown).
Source: U.S. Environmental Protection Agency, Air Quality Index Report, 2015

Air Quality Index Pollutants

Area	Percent of Days when AQI Pollutant was...[2]					
	Carbon Monoxide	Nitrogen Dioxide	Ozone	Sulfur Dioxide	Particulate Matter 2.5	Particulate Matter 10
MSA[1]	1.6	9.6	0.0	0.0	88.8	0.0

Note: (1) Data covers the Bozeman, MT Micropolitan Statistical Area—see Appendix B for areas included; (2) Based on 365 days with AQI data in 2015. The Air Quality Index (AQI) is an index for reporting daily air quality. EPA calculates the AQI for five major air pollutants regulated by the Clean Air Act: ground-level ozone, particle pollution (also known as particulate matter), carbon monoxide, sulfur dioxide, and nitrogen dioxide. The AQI runs from 0 to 500. The higher the AQI value, the greater the level of air pollution and the greater the health concern.
Source: U.S. Environmental Protection Agency, Air Quality Index Report, 2015

Maximum Air Pollutant Concentrations: Particulate Matter, Ozone, CO and Lead

	Particulate Matter 10 (ug/m^3)	Particulate Matter 2.5 Wtd AM (ug/m^3)	Particulate Matter 2.5 24-Hr (ug/m^3)	Ozone (ppm)	Carbon Monoxide (ppm)	Lead (ug/m^3)
MSA[1] Level	n/a	n/a	n/a	n/a	1	n/a
NAAQS[2]	150	15	35	0.075	9	0.15
Met NAAQS[2]	n/a	n/a	n/a	n/a	Yes	n/a

Note: (1) Data covers the Bozeman, MT Micropolitan Statistical Area—see Appendix B for areas included; Data from exceptional events are included; (2) National Ambient Air Quality Standards; ppm = parts per million; ug/m^3 = micrograms per cubic meter; n/a not available.

Concentrations: Particulate Matter 10 (coarse particulate)—highest second maximum 24-hour concentration; Particulate Matter 2.5 Wtd AM (fine particulate)—highest weighted annual mean concentration; Particulate Matter 2.5 24-Hour (fine particulate)—highest 98th percentile 24-hour concentration; Ozone—highest fourth daily maximum 8-hour concentration; Carbon Monoxide—highest second maximum non-overlapping 8-hour concentration; Lead—maximum running 3-month average

Source: U.S. Environmental Protection Agency, Air Quality Monitoring Information, "Air Quality Statistics by City, 2014"

Maximum Air Pollutant Concentrations: Nitrogen Dioxide and Sulfur Dioxide

	Nitrogen Dioxide AM (ppb)	Nitrogen Dioxide 1-Hr (ppb)	Sulfur Dioxide AM (ppb)	Sulfur Dioxide 1-Hr (ppb)	Sulfur Dioxide 24-Hr (ppb)
MSA[1] Level	2	28	n/a	n/a	n/a
NAAQS[2]	53	100	30	75	140
Met NAAQS[2]	Yes	Yes	n/a	n/a	n/a

Note: (1) Data covers the Bozeman, MT Micropolitan Statistical Area—see Appendix B for areas included; Data from exceptional events are included; (2) National Ambient Air Quality Standards; ppm = parts per million; ug/m^3 = micrograms per cubic meter; n/a not available.

Concentrations: Nitrogen Dioxide AM—highest arithmetic mean concentration; Nitrogen Dioxide 1-Hr—highest 98th percentile 1-hour daily maximum concentration; Sulfur Dioxide AM—highest annual mean concentration; Sulfur Dioxide 1-Hr—highest 99th percentile 1-hour daily maximum concentration; Sulfur Dioxide 24-Hr—highest second maximum 24-hour concentration

Source: U.S. Environmental Protection Agency, Air Quality Monitoring Information, "Air Quality Statistics by City, 2014"

Drinking Water

Water System Name	Pop. Served	Primary Water Source Type	Violations[1]	
			Health Based	Monitoring/ Reporting
City of Bozeman	32,000	Surface	0	0

Note: (1) Based on violation data from January 1, 2015 to December 31, 2015 (includes unresolved violations from earlier years)

Source: U.S. Environmental Protection Agency, Office of Ground Water and Drinking Water, Safe Drinking Water Information System (based on data extracted April 29, 2016)

Merrimack, New Hampshire

Background

The town of Merrimack is located in southern New Hampshire, just north and adjacent to Nashua along the west bank of the Merrimack River. The township includes four villages: Reeds Ferry in the north; Merrimack Village (originally Souhegan Village) near the Souhegan River; and Thornton's Ferry and South Merrimack in the southern border. Thornton's Ferry was named after Matthew Thornton, a signer of the Declaration of Independence.

Originally the town was in Massachusetts: In 1734, the Commonwealth of Massachusetts granted the town organization under the name Naticook. In 1746, after the border between Massachusetts and New Hampshire was redrawn to its present line, Governor Wentworth of New Hampshire signed a charter awarding the lands between the Pennichuck and Souhegan Rivers to the town of "Merrymac." In 1750 the charter was ratified with the addition of lands north of the Souhegan River.

At first the four villages were fairly autonomous, each with its own schools, stores, and social life. Most of the people were farmers; what industry there was consisted of sawmills and grist mills. Later on, a central meetinghouse was built. In the nineteenth century, sawmills and grist mills gave way to brickyards: Bricks were floated down the Merrimack River on barges, to the city of Lowell.

In 1839, when Henry David Thoreau and his brother passed by Merrimack on the journey described in *A Week on the Concord and Merrimack Rivers*, the town was placid and rural, and it retained its character well into the twentieth century. After the 1950s, the pace of life picked up and the town grew quickly, as the Everett Turnpike was built and travel to and from Nashua, Lowell, and Boston became easier. During the 1960s, and later during the prosperous 1980s, the town became more and more of a bedroom community for Nashua and cities in Massachusetts, as hundreds of high-tech firms sprang up, especially along Route 128 and I-495 around Boston. Merrimack, along with southeastern New Hampshire in general, was among the fastest-growing areas in the nation. New roads and housing developments now occupied what had once been farm or woodland.

In addition, major businesses moved to town. The Anheuser-Busch Company built a bottling plant and moved its famous Clydesdale horses to Merrimack, where they remain a popular attraction for visitors. PC Connection, a leading provider of electronics and computer equipment, has its headquarters in Merrimack, as does Brookstone, the specialty retailer.

To serve this knowledgeable and sophisticated work force, the town has gourmet restaurants, specialty shops, and other features.

Merrimack, like the rest of New England, enjoys a four-season climate, with pleasant summers and falls, cold winters, and late springs. Located in the low-lying Merrimack River valley, the town enjoys warmer temperatures than the hills and mountains of western and northern New Hampshire; its climate more closely resembles that of northeastern Massachusetts and Boston. Snow can begin in late November and December, but consistent ground cover is not expected until January.

Rankings

Business/Finance Rankings

- The personal finance site NerdWallet analyzed 183 American metropolitan areas with populations over 250,000 and more than 15,000 businesses to rank where entrepreneurs find the most success. Criteria included area economy, annual income, housing cost, unemployment rate, and the success rate of area businesses. Manchester* ranked #46. *www.nerdwallet.com, "Best Places to Start a Business," April 27, 2015*
- The Manchester* metro area appeared on the Milken Institute "2015 Best Performing Cities" list. Rank: #109 out of 200 large metro areas. Criteria: job growth; wage and salary growth; high-tech output growth. *Milken Institute, "Best-Performing Cities 2015," December 2015*
- *Forbes* ranked the 200 most populous metro areas to determine the nation's "Best Places for Business and Careers." The Manchester* metro area was ranked #161. Criteria: costs (business and living); job growth (past and projected); income growth; educational attainment (college and high school); projected economic growth; cultural and recreational opportunities; net migration patterns; number of highly ranked colleges. *Forbes, "The Best Places for Business and Careers 2015," July 29, 2015*

Education Rankings

- Personal finance website *WalletHub* analyzed the 150 largest U.S. metropolitan statistical areas to determine where the most educated Americans are choosing to settle. Criteria: education quality and attainment gap; education levels; percentage of workers with degrees; public school rankings; quality and size of each metro area's universities. Manchester* was ranked #22 (#1 = most educated city). *www.WalletHub.com, "2015's Most and Least Educated Cities*

Environmental Rankings

- The Manchester* metro area came in at #68 for the relative comfort of its climate on Sperling's list of "chill cities," as measured by the Sperling Heat Index. All 361 metro areas are included. Criteria included daytime high temperatures, nighttime low temperatures, dew point, and relative humidity at the high temperatures. *www.bertsperling.com, "Sperling's Chill Cities," July 18, 2013*
- Sperling's BestPlaces assessed 379 metropolitan areas of the United States for the likelihood of dangerously extreme weather events or earthquakes. In general the Southeast and South-Central regions have the highest risk of weather extremes and earthquakes, while the Pacific Northwest enjoys the lowest risk. Of the least risky metropolitan areas, the Manchester* metro area was ranked #273. *www.bestplaces.net, "Safest Places from Natural Disasters," April 2011*

Health/Fitness Rankings

- The Manchester* metro area ranked #49 out of 190 in The Gallup-Healthways Well-Being Index. Criteria: purpose; social well being; financial health; community and physical health. Results are based on telephone interviews with adults, aged 18 and older, living in metropolitan areas in the 50 U.S. states and the District of Columbia. *Gallup-Healthways, "State of American Well-Being," February 23, 2016*

Real Estate Rankings

- Manchester* was ranked #107 out of 225 metro areas in terms of housing affordability in 2015 by the National Association of Home Builders (#1 = most affordable). Criteria: the share of homes sold in that area affordable to a family earning the local median income, based on standard mortgage underwriting criteria. *National Association of Home Builders®, NAHB-Wells Fargo Housing Opportunity Index, 4th Quarter 2015*

Safety Rankings

- Merrimack was identified as one of the safest cities in America by NeighborhoodScout. The city ranked #24 out of 100. Criteria: number of violent and property crimes per 1,000 residents. The editors only considered cities with 25,000 or more residents. *NeighborhoodScout, "Safest Cities in America 2016"*
- The National Insurance Crime Bureau ranked 380 metro areas in the U.S. in terms of per capita rates of vehicle theft. The Manchester* metro area ranked #329 (#1 = highest rate). Criteria: number of vehicle theft offenses per 100,000 inhabitants in 2014. *National Insurance Crime Bureau, "Hot Spots 2014," June 24, 2015*

Seniors/Retirement Rankings

- From its Best Cities for Successful Aging indexes, the Milken Institute generated rankings for metropolitan areas, weighing data in eight categories—health care, wellness, living arrangements, transportation, financial characteristics, education and employment opportunities, community engagement, and overall livability. The Manchester* metro area was ranked #117 overall in the small metro area category. *Milken Institute, "Best Cities for Successful Aging, 2014"*

Merrimack is located within the Manchester-Nashua, NH Metropolitan Statistical Area.

Business Environment

CITY FINANCES

City Government Finances

Component	2012 ($000)	2012 ($ per capita)
Total Revenues	31,674	1,242
Total Expenditures	30,740	1,205
Debt Outstanding	4,463	175
Cash and Securities[1]	39,117	1,534

Note: (1) Cash and security holdings of a government at the close of its fiscal year, including those of its dependent agencies, utilities, and liquor stores.
Source: U.S Census Bureau, State & Local Government Finances 2012

City Government Revenue by Source

Source	2012 ($000)	2012 ($ per capita)
General Revenue		
From Federal Government	463	18
From State Government	3,272	128
From Local Governments	0	0
Taxes		
Property	18,238	715
Sales and Gross Receipts	0	0
Personal Income	0	0
Corporate Income	0	0
Motor Vehicle License	0	0
Other Taxes	472	18
Current Charges	6,165	241
Liquor Store	0	0
Utility	0	0
Employee Retirement	0	0

Source: U.S Census Bureau, State & Local Government Finances 2012

City Government Expenditures by Function

Function	2012 ($000)	2012 ($ per capita)	2012 (%)
General Direct Expenditures			
Air Transportation	0	0	0.0
Corrections	0	0	0.0
Education	0	0	0.0
Employment Security Administration	0	0	0.0
Financial Administration	357	14	1.1
Fire Protection	5,060	198	16.4
General Public Buildings	233	9	0.7
Governmental Administration, Other	220	8	0.7
Health	0	0	0.0
Highways	7,363	288	23.9
Hospitals	0	0	0.0
Housing and Community Development	0	0	0.0
Interest on General Debt	213	8	0.6
Judicial and Legal	0	0	0.0
Libraries	1,085	42	3.5
Parking	0	0	0.0
Parks and Recreation	487	19	1.5
Police Protection	5,414	212	17.6
Public Welfare	150	5	0.4
Sewerage	4,356	170	14.1
Solid Waste Management	1,220	47	3.9
Veterans' Services	0	0	0.0
Liquor Store	0	0	0.0
Utility	0	0	0.0
Employee Retirement	0	0	0.0

Source: U.S Census Bureau, State & Local Government Finances 2012

DEMOGRAPHICS

Population Growth

Area	1990 Census	2000 Census	2010 Census	2014* Estimate	Population Growth (%) 1990-2014	Population Growth (%) 2010-2014
City	22,156	25,119	25,494	25,563	15.4	0.3
MSA[1]	336,073	380,841	400,721	402,776	19.8	0.5
U.S.	248,709,873	281,421,906	308,745,538	314,107,084	26.3	1.7

Note: (1) Figures cover the Manchester-Nashua, NH Metropolitan Statistical Area—see Appendix B for areas included; (*) 2010-2014 5-year estimated population
Source: U.S. Census Bureau, 1990 Census, Census 2000, Census 2010, 2010-2014 American Community Survey 5-Year Estimates

Household Size

Area	Persons in Household (%) One	Two	Three	Four	Five	Six	Seven or More	Average Household Size
City	19.1	41.7	14.0	16.0	6.5	1.3	1.0	2.65
MSA[1]	24.5	36.0	16.3	14.8	5.7	1.5	0.9	2.56
U.S.	27.5	33.5	15.8	13.1	6.0	2.3	1.4	2.64

Note: (1) Figures cover the Manchester-Nashua, NH Metropolitan Statistical Area—see Appendix B for areas included
Source: U.S. Census Bureau, 2010-2014 American Community Survey 5-Year Estimates

Race

Area	White Alone[2] (%)	Black Alone[2] (%)	Asian Alone[2] (%)	AIAN[3] Alone[2] (%)	NHOPI[4] Alone[2] (%)	Other Race Alone[2] (%)	Two or More Races (%)
City	95.8	0.1	2.0	0.1	0.0	0.8	1.3
MSA[1]	90.8	2.2	3.5	0.1	0.0	1.1	2.2
U.S.	73.8	12.6	5.0	0.8	0.2	4.7	2.9

Note: (1) Figures cover the Manchester-Nashua, NH Metropolitan Statistical Area—see Appendix B for areas included; (2) Alone is defined as not being in combination with one or more other races; (3) American Indian and Alaska Native; (4) Native Hawaiian and Other Pacific Islander
Source: U.S. Census Bureau, 2010-2014 American Community Survey 5-Year Estimates

Hispanic or Latino Origin

Area	Total (%)	Mexican (%)	Puerto Rican (%)	Cuban (%)	Other (%)
City	2.6	0.7	0.7	0.3	1.0
MSA[1]	5.6	1.7	1.7	0.1	2.1
U.S.	16.9	10.8	1.6	0.6	3.8

Note: Persons of Hispanic or Latino origin can be of any race; (1) Figures cover the Manchester-Nashua, NH Metropolitan Statistical Area—see Appendix B for areas included
Source: U.S. Census Bureau, 2010-2014 American Community Survey 5-Year Estimates

Ancestry

Area	German	Irish	English	American	Italian	Polish	French[2]	Scottish	Dutch
City	8.0	22.6	16.2	3.5	10.9	4.3	16.9	3.7	1.0
MSA[1]	8.1	21.2	13.8	4.2	10.1	4.7	15.5	3.3	0.9
U.S.	14.9	10.8	8.0	7.1	5.5	3.0	2.7	1.7	1.4

Note: Figures are the percentage of the total population reporting a particular ancestry. The nine most commonly reported ancestries in the U.S. are shown. Figures include multiple ancestries (e.g. if a person reported being Irish and Italian, they were included in both columns); (1) Figures cover the Manchester-Nashua, NH Metropolitan Statistical Area—see Appendix B for areas included; (2) Excludes Basque
Source: U.S. Census Bureau, 2010-2014 American Community Survey 5-Year Estimates

Foreign-Born Population

Area	Any Foreign Country	Asia	Mexico	Europe	Carribean	Central America[2]	South America	Africa	Canada
	Percent of Population Born in								
City	4.7	1.7	0.0	1.6	0.1	0.0	0.5	0.0	0.8
MSA[1]	8.7	2.9	0.6	1.7	0.7	0.3	0.8	0.6	1.0
U.S.	13.1	3.8	3.7	1.5	1.2	1.0	0.9	0.6	0.3

Note: (1) Figures cover the Manchester-Nashua, NH Metropolitan Statistical Area—see Appendix B for areas included; (2) Excludes Mexico.
Source: U.S. Census Bureau, 2010-2014 American Community Survey 5-Year Estimates

Marital Status

Area	Never Married	Now Married[2]	Separated	Widowed	Divorced
City	25.6	60.7	1.0	3.6	9.2
MSA[1]	29.9	52.1	1.4	5.1	11.5
U.S.	32.5	48.4	2.2	5.9	10.9

Note: Figures are percentages and cover the population 15 years of age and older; (1) Figures cover the Manchester-Nashua, NH Metropolitan Statistical Area—see Appendix B for areas included; (2) Excludes separated
Source: U.S. Census Bureau, 2010-2014 American Community Survey 5-Year Estimates

Disability Status

Area	All Ages	Under 18 Years Old	18 to 64 Years Old	65 Years and Over
City	8.1	3.9	6.0	26.9
MSA[1]	10.7	4.7	8.8	32.2
U.S.	12.3	4.1	10.2	36.3

Note: Figures show percent of the civilian noninstitutionalized population that reported having a disability. Disability status is determined from from six types of difficulty: vision, hearing, cognitive, ambulatory, self-care, and independent living. For children under 5 years old, hearing and vision difficulty are used to determine disability status. For children between the ages of 5 and 14, disability status is determined from hearing, vision, cognitive, ambulatory, and self-care difficulties. For people aged 15 years and older, they are considered to have a disability if they have difficulty with any one of the six difficulty types; (1) Figures cover the Manchester-Nashua, NH Metropolitan Statistical Area—see Appendix B for areas included.
Source: U.S. Census Bureau, 2010-2014 American Community Survey 5-Year Estimates

Age

Area	Under Age 5	Age 5–19	Age 20–34	Age 35–44	Age 45–54	Age 55–64	Age 65–74	Age 75–84	Age 85+	Median Age
	Percent of Population									
City	5.4	18.8	15.2	13.9	19.5	15.0	7.0	3.5	1.5	42.5
MSA[1]	5.7	19.4	18.7	13.5	16.7	13.2	7.2	3.9	1.7	39.9
U.S.	6.4	19.9	20.6	13.0	14.1	12.3	7.6	4.3	1.9	37.4

Note: (1) Figures cover the Manchester-Nashua, NH Metropolitan Statistical Area—see Appendix B for areas included
Source: U.S. Census Bureau, 2010-2014 American Community Survey 5-Year Estimates

Gender

Area	Males	Females	Males per 100 Females
City	12,416	13,147	94.4
MSA[1]	199,502	203,274	98.1
U.S.	154,515,159	159,591,925	96.8

Note: (1) Figures cover the Manchester-Nashua, NH Metropolitan Statistical Area—see Appendix B for areas included
Source: U.S. Census Bureau, 2010-2014 American Community Survey 5-Year Estimates

Religious Groups by Family

Area	Catholic	Baptist	Non-Den.	Methodist[2]	Lutheran	LDS[3]	Pente-costal	Presby-terian[4]	Muslim[5]	Judaism
MSA[1]	31.1	1.3	2.3	1.1	0.5	0.6	0.4	2.0	0.3	0.5
U.S.	19.1	9.3	4.0	4.0	2.3	2.0	1.9	1.6	0.8	0.7

Note: Figures are the number of adherents as a percentage of the total population; (1) Figures cover the Manchester-Nashua, NH Metropolitan Statistical Area—see Appendix B for areas included; (2) Methodist/Pietist; (3) Latter Day Saints; (4) Reformed; (5) Figures are estimates
Source: Association of Statisticians of American Religious Bodies, 2010 U.S. Religion Census: Religious Congregations & Membership Study

Religious Groups by Tradition

Area	Catholic	Evangelical Protestant	Mainline Protestant	Other Tradition	Black Protestant	Orthodox
MSA[1]	31.1	5.1	4.4	1.8	<0.1	0.7
U.S.	19.1	16.2	7.3	4.3	1.6	0.3

Note: Figures are the number of adherents as a percentage of the total population; (1) Figures cover the Manchester-Nashua, NH Metropolitan Statistical Area—see Appendix B for areas included
Source: Association of Statisticians of American Religious Bodies, 2010 U.S. Religion Census: Religious Congregations & Membership Study

ECONOMY

Gross Metropolitan Product

Area	2013	2014	2015	2016	Rank[2]
MSA[1]	23.6	24.2	25.1	26.4	99

Note: Figures are in billions of dollars; (1) Figures cover the Manchester-Nashua, NH Metropolitan Statistical Area—see Appendix B for areas included; (2) Rank is based on 2016 data and ranges from 1 to 381
Source: The U.S. Conference of Mayors, U.S. Metro Economies: GMP and Employment 2014-2016, June 2015

Economic Growth

Area	2011-13 (%)	2014 (%)	2015 (%)	2016 (%)	Rank[2]
MSA[1]	0.3	0.8	2.3	3.0	83
U.S.	2.2	2.4	2.3	2.9	–

Note: Figures are real gross metropolitan product (GMP) growth rates and represent annual average percent change; (1) Figures cover the Manchester-Nashua, NH Metropolitan Statistical Area—see Appendix B for areas included; (2) Rank is based on 2016 data and ranges from 1 to 381
Source: The U.S. Conference of Mayors, U.S. Metro Economies: GMP and Employment 2014-2016, June 2015

Metropolitan Area Exports

Area	2009	2010	2011	2012	2013	2014	Rank[2]
MSA[1]	1,743.0	2,612.1	2,494.0	1,634.8	1,445.7	1,575.3	119

Note: Figures are in millions of dollars; (1) Figures cover the Manchester-Nashua, NH Metropolitan Statistical Area—see Appendix B for areas included; (2) Rank is based on 2014 data and ranges from 1 to 385
Source: U.S. Department of Commerce, International Trade Administration, Office of Trade & Industry Information, Manufacturing & Services, data extracted March 10, 2016

Building Permits

Area	Single-Family			Multi-Family			Total		
	2014	2015p	Pct. Chg.	2014	2015p	Pct. Chg.	2014	2015p	Pct. Chg.
City	23	25	8.7	0	0	-	23	25	8.7
MSA[1]	464	353	-23.9	504	322	-36.1	968	675	-30.3
U.S.	640,300	690,800	7.9	411,800	487,600	18.4	1,052,100	1,178,400	12.0

Note: (1) Figures cover the Manchester-Nashua, NH Metropolitan Statistical Area—see Appendix B for areas included; Figures represent new, privately-owned housing units authorized (unadjusted data); All permit data are based on estimates with imputation; (p) preliminary data.
Source: U.S. Census Bureau, Manufacturing, Mining, and Construction Statistics, Building Permits, 2014, 2015

Bankruptcy Filings

Area	Business Filings			Nonbusiness Filings		
	2014	2015	% Chg.	2014	2015	% Chg.
Hillsborough County	78	32	-59.0	750	570	-24.0
U.S.	26,983	24,735	-8.3	909,812	819,760	-9.9

Note: Business filings include Chapter 7, Chapter 11, Chapter 12, and Chapter 13; Nonbusiness filings include Chapter 7, Chapter 11, and Chapter 13
Source: Administrative Office of the U.S. Courts, Business and Nonbusiness Bankruptcy, County Cases Commenced by Chapter of the Bankruptcy Code, During the 12- Month Period Ending December 31, 2014 and Business and Nonbusiness Bankruptcy, County Cases Commenced by Chapter of the Bankruptcy Code, During the 12- Month Period Ending December 31, 2015

Housing Vacancy Rates

Area	Gross Vacancy Rate[2] (%)			Year-Round Vacancy Rate[3] (%)			Rental Vacancy Rate[4] (%)			Homeowner Vacancy Rate[5] (%)		
	2013	2014	2015	2013	2014	2015	2013	2014	2015	2013	2014	2015
MSA[1]	n/a	n/a	n/a	n/a	n/a	n/a	n/a	n/a	n/a	n/a	n/a	n/a
U.S.	13.6	13.4	12.9	10.7	10.4	10.0	8.3	7.6	7.1	2.0	1.9	1.8

Note: (1) Figures cover the Manchester-Nashua, NH Metropolitan Statistical Area—see Appendix B for areas included; (2) The percentage of the total housing inventory that is vacant; (3) The percentage of the housing inventory (excluding seasonal units) that is year-round vacant; (4) The percentage of rental inventory that is vacant for rent; (5) The percentage of homeowner inventory that is vacant for sale; n/a not available
Source: U.S. Census Bureau, Housing Vacancies and Homeownership Annual Statistics: 2015

INCOME

Income

Area	Per Capita ($)	Median Household ($)	Average Household ($)
City	39,833	91,429	104,710
MSA[1]	34,767	70,906	89,012
U.S.	28,555	53,482	74,596

Note: (1) Figures cover the Manchester-Nashua, NH Metropolitan Statistical Area—see Appendix B for areas included
Source: U.S. Census Bureau, 2010-2014 American Community Survey 5-Year Estimates

Household Income Distribution

Area	Percent of Households Earning							
	Under $15,000	$15,000 -24,999	$25,000 -34,999	$35,000 -49,999	$50,000 -74,999	$75,000 -99,000	$100,000 -149,999	$150,000 and up
City	3.4	3.8	4.4	8.8	17.2	17.6	25.2	19.5
MSA[1]	7.5	8.0	8.0	11.2	17.9	14.4	18.8	14.4
U.S.	12.5	10.7	10.2	13.5	17.8	12.2	13.0	10.0

Note: (1) Figures cover the Manchester-Nashua, NH Metropolitan Statistical Area—see Appendix B for areas included
Source: U.S. Census Bureau, 2010-2014 American Community Survey 5-Year Estimates

Poverty Rate

Area	All Ages	Under 18 Years Old	18 to 64 Years Old	65 Years and Over
City	3.8	4.9	3.3	4.7
MSA[1]	8.6	11.9	8.0	5.9
U.S.	15.6	21.9	14.6	9.4

Note: Figures are percentage of people whose income during the past 12 months was below the poverty level; (1) Figures cover the Manchester-Nashua, NH Metropolitan Statistical Area—see Appendix B for areas included
Source: U.S. Census Bureau, 2010-2014 American Community Survey 5-Year Estimates

EMPLOYMENT

Labor Force and Employment

Area	Civilian Labor Force			Workers Employed		
	Dec. 2014	Dec. 2015	% Chg.	Dec. 2014	Dec. 2015	% Chg.
City	15,723	15,551	-1.0	15,167	15,102	-0.4
NECTAD[1]	2,627,900	2,607,376	-0.7	2,512,440	2,500,406	-0.4
U.S.	155,521,000	157,245,000	1.1	147,190,000	149,703,000	1.7

Note: Data is not seasonally adjusted and covers workers 16 years of age and older; (1) Figures cover the Nashua, NH-MA New England City and Town Area Division—see Appendix B for areas included
Source: Bureau of Labor Statistics, Local Area Unemployment Statistics

Unemployment Rate

Area	2015											
	Jan.	Feb.	Mar.	Apr.	May	Jun.	Jul.	Aug.	Sep.	Oct.	Nov.	Dec.
City	4.1	4.2	3.8	3.5	3.5	3.6	3.7	3.5	3.1	3.2	3.1	2.9
NECTAD[1]	4.9	4.8	4.4	3.8	4.0	4.5	4.5	4.1	4.1	4.1	4.1	4.1
U.S.	6.1	5.8	5.6	5.1	5.3	5.5	5.6	5.2	4.9	4.8	4.8	4.8

Note: Data is not seasonally adjusted and covers workers 16 years of age and older; (1) Figures cover the Nashua, NH-MA New England City and Town Area Division—see Appendix B for areas included
Source: Bureau of Labor Statistics, Local Area Unemployment Statistics

Employment by Occupation

Occupation Classification	City (%)	MSA[1] (%)	U.S. (%)
Management, Business, Science, and Arts	47.5	41.0	36.4
Natural Resources, Construction, and Maintenance	7.6	8.3	9.0
Production, Transportation, and Material Moving	8.0	11.2	12.1
Sales and Office	26.9	25.1	24.4
Service	10.0	14.4	18.2

Note: Figures cover employed civilians 16 years of age and older; (1) Figures cover the Manchester-Nashua, NH Metropolitan Statistical Area—see Appendix B for areas included
Source: U.S. Census Bureau, 2010-2014 American Community Survey 5-Year Estimates

Employment by Industry

Sector	NECTAD[1]		U.S.
	Number of Employees	Percent of Total	Percent of Total
Construction, Mining, and Logging	4,900	3.8	5.0
Education and Health Services	18,300	14.2	15.7
Financial Activities	7,800	6.0	5.7
Government	13,500	10.5	15.5
Information	1,900	1.4	1.9
Leisure and Hospitality	11,000	8.5	10.4
Manufacturing	19,700	15.3	8.6
Other Services	5,400	4.2	3.9
Professional and Business Services	15,400	11.9	13.9
Retail Trade	21,900	17.0	11.3
Transportation, Warehousing, and Utilities	3,100	2.4	3.9
Wholesale Trade	5,500	4.2	4.1

Note: Figures are non-farm employment as of December 2015. Figures are not seasonally adjusted and include workers 16 years of age and older; (1) Figures cover the Nashua, NH-MA New England City and Town Area Division—see Appendix B for areas included; n/a not available
Source: Bureau of Labor Statistics, Current Employment Statistics, Employment, Hours, and Earnings

Occupations with Greatest Projected Employment Growth: 2012 – 2022

Occupation[1]	2012 Employment	2022 Projected Employment	Numeric Employment Change	Percent Employment Change
Registered Nurses	12,580	15,000	2,420	19.2
Personal Care Aides	5,160	7,390	2,230	43.3
Combined Food Preparation and Serving Workers, Including Fast Food	11,560	13,370	1,810	15.6
Nursing Assistants	8,490	10,290	1,800	21.2
Retail Salespersons	25,170	26,780	1,610	6.4
Software Developers, Applications	4,820	6,170	1,350	27.9
Customer Service Representatives	8,920	10,210	1,290	14.4
Home Health Aides	2,590	3,850	1,260	48.4
Secretaries and Administrative Assistants, Except Legal, Medical, and Executive	11,010	12,210	1,200	10.9
Janitors and Cleaners, Except Maids and Housekeeping Cleaners	9,870	10,930	1,060	10.8

Note: Projections cover New Hampshire; (1) Sorted by numeric employment change
Source: www.projectionscentral.com, State Occupational Projections, 2012–2022 Long-Term Projections

Fastest Growing Occupations: 2012 – 2022

Occupation[1]	2012 Employment	2022 Projected Employment	Numeric Employment Change	Percent Employment Change
Home Health Aides	2,590	3,850	1,260	48.4
Interpreters and Translators	220	320	100	47.9
Personal Care Aides	5,160	7,390	2,230	43.3
Diagnostic Medical Sonographers	240	340	100	40.8
Physician Assistants	470	640	170	36.5
Substance Abuse and Behavioral Disorder Counselors	360	490	130	35.9
Physical Therapist Assistants	380	510	130	33.9
Veterinary Technologists and Technicians	590	780	190	33.2
Personal Financial Advisors	1,320	1,750	430	32.1
Medical Secretaries	2,420	3,170	750	31.2

Note: Projections cover New Hampshire; (1) Sorted by percent employment change and excludes occupations with numeric employment change less than 100
Source: www.projectionscentral.com, State Occupational Projections, 2012–2022 Long-Term Projections

Average Wages

Occupation	$/Hr.	Occupation	$/Hr.
Accountants and Auditors	35.81	Maids and Housekeeping Cleaners	9.88
Automotive Mechanics	21.59	Maintenance and Repair Workers	20.01
Bookkeepers	18.67	Marketing Managers	63.42
Carpenters	22.77	Nuclear Medicine Technologists	n/a
Cashiers	10.08	Nurses, Licensed Practical	23.25
Clerks, General Office	17.95	Nurses, Registered	31.78
Clerks, Receptionists/Information	12.41	Nursing Assistants	13.61
Clerks, Shipping/Receiving	15.91	Packers and Packagers, Hand	11.93
Computer Programmers	35.44	Physical Therapists	40.69
Computer Systems Analysts	43.24	Postal Service Mail Carriers	24.50
Computer User Support Specialists	29.17	Real Estate Brokers	n/a
Cooks, Restaurant	12.66	Retail Salespersons	12.77
Dentists	104.11	Sales Reps., Exc. Tech./Scientific	37.39
Electrical Engineers	49.86	Sales Reps., Tech./Scientific	49.17
Electricians	22.02	Secretaries, Exc. Legal/Med./Exec.	16.30
Financial Managers	60.17	Security Guards	14.44
First-Line Supervisors/Managers, Sales	23.82	Surgeons	n/a
Food Preparation Workers	10.09	Teacher Assistants*	14.77
General and Operations Managers	66.52	Teachers, Elementary School*	26.54
Hairdressers/Cosmetologists	16.29	Teachers, Secondary School*	27.76
Internists	119.89	Telemarketers	n/a
Janitors and Cleaners	15.42	Truck Drivers, Heavy/Tractor-Trailer	19.75
Landscaping/Groundskeeping Workers	12.86	Truck Drivers, Light/Delivery Svcs.	16.40
Lawyers	48.09	Waiters and Waitresses	10.39

Note: Wage data covers the New England City and Town Area Division—see Appendix B for areas included; (*) Hourly wages for elementary/secondary school teachers and teacher assistants were calculated by the editors from annual wage data based on a 40 hour work week; n/a not available.
Source: Bureau of Labor Statistics, Metro Area Occupational Employment and Wage Estimates, May 2015

TAXES

State Corporate Income Tax Rates

State	Tax Rate (%)	Income Brackets ($)	Num. of Brackets	Financial Institution Tax Rate (%)[a]	Federal Income Tax Ded.
New Hampshire	8.5 (q)	Flat rate	1	8.5 (q)	No

Note: Tax rates as of January 1, 2016; (a) Rates listed are the corporate income tax rate applied to financial institutions or excise taxes based on income. Some states have other taxes based upon the value of deposits or shares; (q) New Hampshire's 8.5% Business Profits Tax is imposed on both corporations and unincorporated associations with gross income over $50,000. In addition, New Hampshire levies a Business Enterprise Tax of 0.75% on the enterprise base (total compensation, interest and dividends paid) for businesses with gross income over $150,000 or base over $75,000. The Business Profits Tax is scheduled to decrease to 8.2% for tax years beginning on or after 2017.
Source: Federation of Tax Administrators, "State Corporate Income Tax Rates, 2016"

State Individual Income Tax Rates

State	Tax Rate (%)	Income Brackets ($)	Num. of Brackets	Personal Exempt. ($)[1] Single	Personal Exempt. ($)[1] Dependents	Fed. Inc. Tax Ded.
New Hampshire	State income tax of 5% on dividends and interest income only					

Note: Tax rates as of January 1, 2016; Local- and county-level taxes are not included; n/a not applicable; (1) Married joint filers generally receive double the single exemption
Source: Federation of Tax Administrators, "State Individual Income Tax Rates, 2016"

Various State and Local Tax Rates

State	State and Local Sales and Use (%)	State Sales and Use (%)	Gasoline[1] (¢/gal.)	Cigarette[2] ($/pack)	Spirits[3] ($/gal.)	Wine[4] ($/gal.)	Beer[5] ($/gal.)
New Hampshire	None	None	23.83	1.78	0 (g)	— (l)(m)	0.30

Note: All tax rates as of January 1, 2016; (1) The American Petroleum Institute has developed a methodology for determining the average tax rate on a gallon of fuel. Rates may include any of the following: excise taxes, environmental fees, storage tank fees, other fees or taxes, general sales tax, and local taxes. In states where gasoline is subject to the general sales tax, or where the fuel tax is based on the average sale price, the average rate determined by API is sensitive to changes in the price of gasoline. States that fully or partially apply general sales taxes to gasoline: CA, CO, GA, IL, IN, MI, NY; (2) The federal excise tax of $1.0066 per pack and local taxes are not included; (3) Rates are those applicable to off-premise sales of 40% alcohol by volume (a.b.v.) distilled spirits in 750ml containers. Local excise taxes are excluded; (4) Rates are those applicable to off-premise sales of 11% a.b.v. non-carbonated wine in 750ml containers; (5) Rates are those applicable to off-premise sales of 4.7% a.b.v. beer in 12 ounce containers; (g) Control states, where the government controls all sales. Products can be subject to ad valorem mark-up as well as excise taxes; (l) Different rates also applicable according to alcohol content, place of production, size of container, place purchased (on- or off-premise or on board airlines) or type of wine (carbonated, vermouth, etc.); (m) Control states, where the government controls all sales. Products can be subject to ad valorem mark-up as well as excise taxes.
Source: Tax Foundation, 2016 Facts & Figures: How Does Your State Compare?

State Business Tax Climate Index Rankings

State	Overall Rank	Corporate Tax Rank	Individual Income Tax Rank	Sales Tax Rank	Unemployment Insurance Tax Rank	Property Tax Rank
New Hampshire	7	48	9	2	44	43

Note: The index is a measure of how each state's tax laws affect economic performance. The lower the rank, the more favorable a state's tax system is for business. States without a given tax are given a ranking of 1. The scores/rankings for the District of Columbia do not affect other states. The 2016 index represents the tax climate as of July 1, 2015 (the beginning of Fiscal Year 2016).
Source: Tax Foundation, State Business Tax Climate Index 2016

TRANSPORTATION

Means of Transportation to Work

Area	Car/Truck/Van: Drove Alone	Car/Truck/Van: Car-pooled	Public Transportation: Bus	Public Transportation: Subway	Public Transportation: Railroad	Bicycle	Walked	Other Means	Worked at Home
City	84.4	6.3	0.6	0.1	0.0	0.3	1.2	0.6	6.5
MSA[1]	81.9	8.3	0.8	0.0	0.1	0.1	2.0	0.8	6.0
U.S.	76.4	9.6	2.6	1.8	0.6	0.6	2.8	1.3	4.4

Note: Figures are percentages and cover workers 16 years of age and older; (1) Figures cover the Manchester-Nashua, NH Metropolitan Statistical Area—see Appendix B for areas included
Source: U.S. Census Bureau, 2010-2014 American Community Survey 5-Year Estimates

Travel Time to Work

Area	Less Than 10 Minutes	10 to 19 Minutes	20 to 29 Minutes	30 to 44 Minutes	45 to 59 Minutes	60 to 89 Minutes	90 Minutes or More
City	9.4	27.1	31.2	14.0	7.1	8.1	3.1
MSA[1]	12.0	29.6	20.5	19.9	8.1	6.9	3.0
U.S.	13.3	29.6	21.0	20.2	7.7	5.7	2.6

Note: Figures are percentages and include workers 16 years old and over; (1) Figures cover the Manchester-Nashua, NH Metropolitan Statistical Area—see Appendix B for areas included
Source: U.S. Census Bureau, 2010-2014 American Community Survey 5-Year Estimates

Freeway Travel Time Index

Area	1985	1990	1995	2000	2005	2010	2014
Urban Area Rank[1,2]	n/a	n/a	n/a	n/a	n/a	n/a	n/a
Urban Area Index[1]	n/a	n/a	n/a	n/a	n/a	n/a	n/a
Average Index[3]	1.09	1.11	1.14	1.17	1.20	1.19	1.20

Note: Freeway Travel Time Index—the ratio of travel time in the peak period to the travel time at free-flow conditions. For example, a value of 1.30 indicates a 20-minute free-flow trip takes 26 minutes in the peak (20 minutes x 1.30 = 26 minutes); (1) Data for the Manchester-Nashua, NH urban area was not available; (2) Rank is based on 101 urban areas (#1 = highest travel time index); (3) Average of 101 urban areas
Source: Texas Transportation Institute, 2015 Urban Mobility Scorecard, August 2015

Freeway Commuter Stress Index

Area	1985	1990	1995	2000	2005	2010	2014
Urban Area Rank[1,2]	n/a	n/a	n/a	n/a	n/a	n/a	n/a
Urban Area Index[1]	n/a	n/a	n/a	n/a	n/a	n/a	n/a
Average Index[3]	1.13	1.16	1.19	1.22	1.25	1.24	1.25

Note: The Freeway Commuter Stress Index is the same as the Freeway Travel Time Index (see table above) except that it includes only the travel in the peak directions during the peak periods; the TTI includes travel in all directions during the peak period. Thus, the CSI is more indicative of the work trip experienced by each commuter on a daily basis. (1) Data for the Manchester-Nashua, NH urban area was not available; (2) Rank is based on 101 urban areas (#1 = highest stress index); (3) Average of 101 urban areas
Source: Texas Transportation Institute, 2015 Urban Mobility Scorecard, August 2015

Living Environment

COST OF LIVING

Cost of Living Index

Composite Index	Groceries	Housing	Utilities	Trans-portation	Health Care	Misc. Goods/ Services
118.3	111.0	123.2	137.3	104.5	116.3	116.2

Note: The Cost of Living Index measures regional differences in the cost of consumer goods and services, excluding taxes and non-consumer expenditures, for professional and managerial households in the top income quintile. It is based on more than 50,000 prices covering almost 60 different items for which prices are collected three times a year by chambers of commerce, economic development organizations or university applied economic centers in each participating urban area. The numbers shown should be read as a percentage above or below the national average of 100. For example, a value of 115.4 in the groceries column indicates that grocery prices are 15.4% higher than the national average. Small differences in the index numbers should not be interpreted as significant; Figures cover the Manchester NH urban area.
Source: The Council for Community and Economic Research, ACCRA Cost of Living Index, 2015

Grocery Prices

Area[1]	T-Bone Steak ($/pound)	Frying Chicken ($/pound)	Whole Milk ($/half gal.)	Eggs ($/dozen)	Orange Juice ($/64 oz.)	Coffee ($/11.5 oz.)
City[2]	11.15	1.45	2.81	2.79	3.30	4.97
Avg.	10.99	1.43	2.25	2.26	3.58	4.48
Min.	7.16	0.98	1.30	1.35	2.88	2.98
Max.	14.13	2.43	3.85	4.81	6.39	7.56

Note: (1) Values for the local area are compared with the average, minimum and maximum values for all 292 areas in the Cost of Living Index; (2) Figures cover the Manchester NH urban area; **T-Bone Steak** *(price per pound);* **Frying Chicken** *(price per pound, whole fryer);* **Whole Milk** *(half gallon carton);* **Eggs** *(price per dozen, Grade A, large);* **Orange Juice** *(64 oz. Tropicana or Florida Natural);* **Coffee** *(11.5 oz. can, vacuum-packed, Maxwell House, Hills Bros, or Folgers).*
Source: The Council for Community and Economic Research, ACCRA Cost of Living Index, 2015

Housing and Utility Costs

Area[1]	New Home Price ($)	Apartment Rent ($/month)	All Electric ($/month)	Part Electric ($/month)	Other Energy ($/month)	Telephone ($/month)
City[2]	362,649	1,318	-	114.46	128.88	36.25
Avg.	312,874	945	179.30	95.07	72.96	28.11
Min.	178,682	479	116.28	43.14	26.46	10.01
Max.	1,472,476	3,984	504.25	189.44	421.11	43.06

Note: (1) Values for the local area are compared with the average, minimum and maximum values for all 292 areas in the Cost of Living Index; (2) Figures cover the Manchester NH urban area; **New Home Price** *(2,400 sf living area, 8,000 sf lot, in urban area with full utilities);* **Apartment Rent** *(950 sf 2 bedroom/1.5 or 2 bath, unfurnished, excluding all utilities except water);* **All Electric** *(average monthly cost for an all-electric home);* **Part Electric** *(average monthly cost for a part-electric home);* **Other Energy** *(average monthly cost for natural gas, fuel oil, coal, wood, and any other forms of energy except electricity);* **Telephone** *(price includes basic monthly rate for a private residential line plus additional local usage charges incurred by a family of four).*
Source: The Council for Community and Economic Research, ACCRA Cost of Living Index, 2015

Health Care, Transportation, and Other Costs

Area[1]	Doctor ($/visit)	Dentist ($/visit)	Optometrist ($/visit)	Gasoline ($/gallon)	Beauty Salon ($/visit)	Men's Shirt ($)
City[2]	149.18	104.81	100.39	2.43	40.03	28.58
Avg.	105.15	89.02	99.78	2.38	35.30	28.10
Min.	66.87	56.09	48.53	1.95	18.91	13.38
Max.	182.34	150.36	228.33	4.09	67.91	63.80

Note: (1) Values for the local area are compared with the average, minimum and maximum values for all 292 areas in the Cost of Living Index; (2) Figures cover the Manchester NH urban area; **Doctor** *(general practitioners routine exam of an established patient);* **Dentist** *(adult teeth cleaning and periodic oral examination);* **Optometrist** *(full vision eye exam for established adult patient);* **Gasoline** *(one gallon regular unleaded, national brand, including all taxes, cash price at self-service pump if available);* **Beauty Salon** *(woman's shampoo, trim, and blow-dry);* **Men's Shirt** *(cotton/polyester dress shirt, pinpoint weave, long sleeves).*
Source: The Council for Community and Economic Research, ACCRA Cost of Living Index, 2015

HOUSING

House Price Index (HPI)

Area	National Ranking[2]	Quarterly Change (%)	One-Year Change (%)	Five-Year Change (%)
MSA[1]	130	0.00	4.70	5.10
U.S.[3]	–	1.45	5.76	22.85

Note: The HPI is a weighted repeat sales index. It measures average price changes in repeat sales or refinancings on the same properties. This information is obtained by reviewing repeat mortgage transactions on single-family properties whose mortgages have been purchased or securitized by Fannie Mae or Freddie Mac in January 1975; (1) Manchester-Nashua Metropolitan Statistical Area—see Appendix B for areas included; (2) Rankings are based on annual percentage change for all metro areas containing at least 15,000 transactions over the last 10 years and ranges from 1 to 266; (3) figures based on a weighted average of Census Division estimates using a seasonally adjusted, purchase-only index; all figures are for the period ending December 31, 2015

Source: Federal Housing Finance Agency, House Price Index, February 25, 2016

Median Single-Family Home Prices

Area	2013	2014	2015p	Percent Change 2014 to 2015
MSA[1]	229.2	234.8	253.2	7.8
U.S. Average	197.4	208.9	223.9	7.2

Note: Figures are median sales prices of existing single-family homes in thousands of dollars; (p) preliminary; n/a not available; (1) Manchester-Nashua, NH Metropolitan Statistical Area—see Appendix B for areas included

Source: National Association of Realtors, Median Sales Price of Existing Single-Family Homes for Metropolitan Areas, 4th Quarter 2015

Qualifying Income Based on Median Sales Price of Existing Single-Family Homes

Area	With 5% Down ($)	With 10% Down ($)	With 20% Down ($)
MSA[1]	55,652	52,723	46,865
U.S. Average	49,535	46,928	41,714

Note: Figures are preliminary; Qualifying income is based on a mortgage rate of 4.1%. Monthly principal and interest payment is limited to 25% of income; n/a not available; (1) Manchester-Nashua, NH Metropolitan Statistical Area—see Appendix B for areas included

Source: National Association of Realtors, Qualifying Income Based on Median Sales Price of Existing Single-Family Homes for Metropolitan Areas, 4th Quarter 2015

Median Apartment Condo-Coop Home Prices

Area	2013	2014	2015p	Percent Change 2014 to 2015
MSA[1]	155.6	156.6	164.7	5.2
U.S. Average	194.9	204.3	210.7	3.1

Note: Figures are median sales prices of existing apartment condo-coop homes in thousands of dollars; (p) preliminary; n/a not available; (1) Manchester-Nashua, NH Metropolitan Statistical Area—see Appendix B for areas included

Source: National Association of Realtors, Median Sales Price of Existing Apartment Condo-Coop Homes for Metropolitan Areas, 4th Quarter 2015

Gross Monthly Rent

Area	Under $200	$200 -299	$300 -499	$500 -749	$750 -999	$1,000 -1,499	$1,500 and up	Median ($)
City	1.1	0.0	5.4	4.7	1.0	63.2	24.6	1,324
MSA[1]	0.9	3.3	4.3	9.2	24.6	42.8	14.8	1,067
U.S.	1.5	3.2	7.4	21.0	24.1	26.9	15.9	920

Note: Figures are percentages except for Median; Gross rent is the contract rent plus the estimated average monthly cost of utilities (electricity, gas, and water and sewer) and fuels (oil, coal, kerosene, wood, etc.) if these are paid by the renter (or paid for the renter by someone else); (1) Figures cover the Manchester-Nashua, NH Metropolitan Statistical Area—see Appendix B for areas included

Source: U.S. Census Bureau, 2010-2014 American Community Survey 5-Year Estimates

Homeownership Rate

Area	2008 (%)	2009 (%)	2010 (%)	2011 (%)	2012 (%)	2013 (%)	2014 (%)	2015 (%)
MSA[1]	n/a	n/a	n/a	n/a	n/a	n/a	n/a	n/a
U.S.	67.8	67.4	66.9	66.1	65.4	65.1	64.5	63.7

Note: (1) Figures cover the Manchester-Nashua, NH Metropolitan Statistical Area—see Appendix B for areas included; n/a not available
Source: U.S. Census Bureau, Housing Vacancies and Homeownership Annual Statistics: 2015

Year Housing Structure Built

Area	2010 or Later	2000 -2009	1990 -1999	1980 -1989	1970 -1979	1960 -1969	1950 -1959	1940 -1949	Before 1940	Median Year
City	0.5	8.5	11.1	34.4	25.5	11.1	4.9	0.6	3.3	1981
MSA[1]	0.6	10.2	10.0	20.9	15.6	9.4	7.6	3.9	21.8	1975
U.S.	1.0	14.9	13.9	13.8	15.8	11.0	10.8	5.4	13.3	1976

Note: Figures are percentages except for Median Year; (1) Figures cover the Manchester-Nashua, NH Metropolitan Statistical Area—see Appendix B for areas included
Source: U.S. Census Bureau, 2010-2014 American Community Survey 5-Year Estimates

HEALTH

Health Risk Data

Category	MSA[1] (%)	U.S. (%)
Adults aged 18–64 who have any kind of health care coverage	84.8	79.6
Adults who reported being in good or excellent health	87.2	83.1
Adults who are current smokers	17.7	19.6
Adults who are heavy drinkers[2]	7.5	6.1
Adults who are binge drinkers[3]	16.1	16.9
Adults who are overweight (BMI 25.0 - 29.9)	37.2	35.8
Adults who are obese (BMI 30.0 - 99.8)	26.9	27.6
Adults who participated in any physical activities in the past month	78.9	77.1
Adults 50+ who have ever had a sigmoidoscopy or colonoscopy	79.3	67.3
Women aged 40+ who have had a mammogram within the past two years	78.2	74.0
Men aged 40+ who have had a PSA test within the past two years	42.4	45.2
Adults aged 65+ who have had flu shot within the past year	56.8	60.1
Adults who always wear a seatbelt	82.6	93.8

Note: Data as of 2012 unless otherwise noted; (1) Figures cover the Manchester-Nashua, NH Metropolitan Statistical Area—see Appendix B for areas included; (2) Heavy drinkers are classified as males having more than two drinks per day or females having more than one drink per day; (3) Binge drinkers are classified as males having five or more drinks on one occasion or females having four or more drinks on one occasion
Source: Centers for Disease Control and Prevention, Behaviorial Risk Factor Surveillance System, SMART: Selected Metropolitan/Micropolitan Area Risk Trends, 2012 (Note: the CDC has discontinued this dataset but will be releasing a replacement in mid-2016)

Chronic Health Indicators

Category	MSA[1] (%)	U.S. (%)
Adults who have ever been told they had a heart attack	4.7	4.5
Adults who have ever been told they had a stroke	2.3	2.9
Adults who have been told they currently have asthma	10.6	8.9
Adults who have ever been told they have arthritis	26.4	25.7
Adults who have ever been told they have diabetes[2]	8.7	9.7
Adults who have ever been told they had skin cancer	5.6	5.7
Adults who have ever been told they had any other types of cancer	5.8	6.5
Adults who have ever been told they have COPD	4.7	6.2
Adults who have ever been told they have kidney disease	2.3	2.5
Adults who have ever been told they have a form of depression	19.0	18.0

Note: Data as of 2012 unless otherwise noted; (1) Figures cover the Manchester-Nashua, NH Metropolitan Statistical Area—see Appendix B for areas included; (2) Figures do not include pregnancy-related, borderline, or pre-diabetes
Source: Centers for Disease Control and Prevention, Behaviorial Risk Factor Surveillance System, SMART: Selected Metropolitan/Micropolitan Area Risk Trends, 2012 (Note: the CDC has discontinued this dataset but will be releasing a replacement in mid-2016)

Mortality Rates for the Top 10 Causes of Death in the U.S.

ICD-10[a] Sub-Chapter	ICD-10[a] Code	Age-Adjusted Mortality Rate[1] per 100,000 population	
		County[2]	U.S.
Malignant neoplasms	C00-C97	154.4	163.6
Ischaemic heart diseases	I20-I25	86.3	102.2
Other forms of heart disease	I30-I51	49.6	50.1
Chronic lower respiratory diseases	J40-J47	43.2	41.4
Organic, including symptomatic, mental disorders	F01-F09	47.1	38.5
Cerebrovascular diseases	I60-I69	26.0	36.5
Other external causes of accidental injury	W00-X59	32.2	27.5
Other degenerative diseases of the nervous system	G30-G31	26.6	26.3
Diabetes mellitus	E10-E14	16.4	21.1
Hypertensive diseases	I10-I15	12.9	19.7

Note: (a) ICD-10 = International Classification of Diseases 10th Revision; (1) Mortality rates are a three year average covering 2012-2014; (2) Figures cover Hillsborough County.
Source: Centers for Disease Control and Prevention, National Center for Health Statistics. Underlying Cause of Death 1999-2014 on CDC WONDER Online Database, released 2015.

Mortality Rates for Selected Causes of Death

ICD-10[a] Sub-Chapter	ICD-10[a] Code	Age-Adjusted Mortality Rate[1] per 100,000 population	
		County[2]	U.S.
Assault	X85-Y09	Unreliable	5.1
Diseases of the liver	K70-K76	11.6	13.5
Human immunodeficiency virus (HIV) disease	B20-B24	Unreliable	2.1
Influenza and pneumonia	J09-J18	15.1	15.2
Intentional self-harm	X60-X84	16.2	12.7
Malnutrition	E40-E46	Unreliable	0.9
Obesity and other hyperalimentation	E65-E68	2.4	1.9
Renal failure	N17-N19	11.5	13.0
Transport accidents	V01-V99	8.3	11.6
Viral hepatitis	B15-B19	1.3	2.1

Note: (a) ICD-10 = International Classification of Diseases 10th Revision; (1) Mortality rates are a three year average covering 2012-2014; (2) Figures cover Hillsborough County; Data are Suppressed when the data meet the criteria for confidentiality constraints; Mortality rates are flagged as Unreliable when the rate would be calculated with a numerator of 20 or less.
Source: Centers for Disease Control and Prevention, National Center for Health Statistics. Underlying Cause of Death 1999-2014 on CDC WONDER Online Database, released 2015.

Health Insurance Coverage

Area	With Health Insurance	With Private Health Insurance	With Public Health Insurance	Without Health Insurance	Population Under Age 18 Without Health Insurance
City	94.1	87.1	18.2	5.9	2.3
MSA[1]	90.4	76.7	24.1	9.6	2.9
U.S.	85.8	65.8	31.1	14.2	7.1

Note: Figures are percentages that cover the civilian noninstitutionalized population; (1) Figures cover the Manchester-Nashua, NH Metropolitan Statistical Area—see Appendix B for areas included
Source: U.S. Census Bureau, 2010-2014 American Community Survey 5-Year Estimates

Number of Medical Professionals

Area	MDs[3]	DOs[3,4]	Dentists	Podiatrists	Chiropractors	Optometrists
County[1] (number)	952	88	310	19	103	68
County[1] (rate[2])	236.0	21.8	76.5	4.7	25.4	16.8
U.S. (rate[2])	272.5	20.9	64.7	5.8	25.9	15.2

Note: Data as of 2014 unless noted; (1) Data covers Hillsborough County; (2) Rate per 100,000 population; (3) Data as of 2013 and includes all active, non-federal physicians; (4) Doctor of Osteopathic Medicine
Source: U.S. Department of Health and Human Services, Health Resources and Services Administration, Bureau of Health Professions, Area Resource File (ARF) 2014-2015

EDUCATION

Public School District Statistics

District Name	Schls	Pupils	Pupil/ Teacher Ratio	Minority Pupils[1] (%)	Free Lunch Eligible[2] (%)	IEP[3] (%)
Merrimack School District	6	3,973	13.3	8.0	7.2	16.3

Note: Table includes school districts with 100 or more students; (1) Percentage of students that are not non-Hispanic white; (2) Percentage of students that are eligible for the free lunch program; (3) Percentage of students that have an Individualized Education Program.
Source: U.S. Department of Education, National Center for Education Statistics, Common Core of Data, Local Education Agency (School District) Universe Survey: School Year 2013-2014; U.S. Department of Education, National Center for Education Statistics, Common Core of Data, Public Elementary/Secondary School Universe Survey: School Year 2013-2014

Highest Level of Education

Area	Less than H.S.	H.S. Diploma	Some College, No Deg.	Associate Degree	Bachelor's Degree	Master's Degree	Prof. School Degree	Doctorate Degree
City	3.8	26.8	16.4	10.1	28.5	12.0	0.9	1.5
MSA[1]	9.1	27.5	18.4	9.5	22.7	10.0	1.5	1.3
U.S.	13.7	28.0	21.2	7.9	18.3	7.8	2.0	1.3

Note: Figures cover persons age 25 and over; (1) Figures cover the Manchester-Nashua, NH Metropolitan Statistical Area—see Appendix B for areas included
Source: U.S. Census Bureau, 2010-2014 American Community Survey 5-Year Estimates

Educational Attainment by Race

Area	High School Graduate or Higher (%)					Bachelor's Degree or Higher (%)				
	Total	White	Black	Asian	Hisp.[2]	Total	White	Black	Asian	Hisp.[2]
City	96.2	96.2	47.4	96.8	97.9	42.9	41.9	0.0	73.5	63.6
MSA[1]	90.9	91.6	81.5	85.2	70.3	35.5	35.2	24.8	57.0	17.5
U.S.	86.3	88.4	83.2	85.8	64.1	29.3	30.6	19.0	50.9	13.9

Note: Figures shown cover persons 25 years old and over; (1) Figures cover the Manchester-Nashua, NH Metropolitan Statistical Area—see Appendix B for areas included; (2) People of Hispanic origin can be of any race
Source: U.S. Census Bureau, 2010-2014 American Community Survey 5-Year Estimates

School Enrollment by Grade and Control

Area	Preschool (%)		Kindergarten (%)		Grades 1 - 4 (%)		Grades 5 - 8 (%)		Grades 9 - 12 (%)	
	Public	Private	Public	Private	Public	Private	Public	Private	Public	Private
City	47.1	52.9	83.7	16.3	94.5	5.5	87.8	12.2	90.4	9.6
MSA[1]	39.2	60.8	74.6	25.4	90.7	9.3	90.4	9.6	90.8	9.2
U.S.	57.4	42.6	87.8	12.2	89.8	10.2	89.9	10.1	90.6	9.4

Note: Figures shown cover persons 3 years old and over; (1) Figures cover the Manchester-Nashua, NH Metropolitan Statistical Area—see Appendix B for areas included
Source: U.S. Census Bureau, 2010-2014 American Community Survey 5-Year Estimates

Average Salaries of Public School Classroom Teachers

Area	2013-14		2014-15		Percent Change 2013-14 to 2014-15	Percent Change 2004-05 to 2014-15
	Dollars	Rank[1]	Dollars	Rank[1]		
New Hampshire	57,057	15	58,554	15	2.62	33.3
U.S. Average	56,610	–	57,379	–	1.36	20.8

Note: (1) State rank ranges from 1 to 51 where 1 indicates highest salary.
Source: National Education Association, Rankings & Estimates: Rankings of the States 2014 and Estimates of School Statistics 2015, March 2015

Higher Education

Four-Year Colleges			Two-Year Colleges			Medical Schools[1]	Law Schools[2]	Voc/ Tech[3]
Public	Private Non-profit	Private For-profit	Public	Private Non-profit	Private For-profit			
0	1	0	0	0	0	0	0	0

Note: Figures cover institutions located within the city limits and include main campuses only; (1) includes schools accredited by the Liaison Committee on Medical Education and the American Osteopathic Association's Commission on Osteopathic College Accreditation; (2) includes ABA-accredited schools, schools with provisional ABA accreditation, and state accredited schools; (3) includes all schools with programs that are less than 2 years.
Source: National Center for Education Statistics, Integrated Postsecondary Education System (IPEDS), 2014-15; Association of American Medical Colleges, Member List, March 21, 2016; American Osteopathic Association, Member List, March 21, 2016; Law School Admission Council, Official Guide to ABA-Approved Law Schools Online, March 21, 2016; Wikipedia, List of Medical Schools in the United States, March 21, 2016; Wikipedia, List of Law Schools in the United States, March 21, 2016

According to *U.S. News & World Report,* the Manchester-Nashua, NH metro area is home to one of the best liberal arts colleges in the U.S.: **St. Anselm College** (#112 tie). The indicators used to capture academic quality fall into a number of categories: assessment by administrators at peer institutions; retention of students; faculty resources; student selectivity; financial resources; alumni giving; high school counselor ratings of colleges; and graduation rate. *U.S. News & World Report, "America's Best Colleges 2016"*

PRESIDENTIAL ELECTION

2012 Presidential Election Results

Area	Obama (%)	Romney (%)	Other (%)
Hillsborough County	49.7	48.6	1.6
U.S.	51.0	47.2	1.8

Note: Results may not add to 100% due to rounding
Source: Dave Leip's Atlas of U.S. Presidential Elections

EMPLOYERS

Major Employers

Company Name	Industry
C & S Wholesale Grocers Inc	Grocery
Concord Hospital	Healthcare
Dartmouth-Hitchcock Keene	Healthcare
Dartmouth-Hitchcock Med Ctr	Healthcare
Elliot Hospital	Healthcare
Fidelity Investments	Financial services
Freudenberg-Nok	Healthcare
Hypertherm	Technology
J Jill	Retailer
Liberty Life Assurance Co	Insurance companies/services
Southern New Hampshire Health	Healthcare
St Joseph's Hospital	Healthcare
Sturm Ruger & Co. Inc	Firearms
Trustees of Dartmouth College	Education
UA Local 788 Marine Pipefitter	Union
United Physical Therapy	Healthcare
University of New Hampshire	Education
University System of NH	Education

Note: Companies shown are located within the Manchester-Nashua, NH Metropolitan Statistical Area.
Source: Hoovers.com; Wikipedia

PUBLIC SAFETY

Crime Rate

Area	All Crimes	Violent Crimes				Property Crimes		
		Murder	Rape[3]	Robbery	Aggrav. Assault	Burglary	Larceny -Theft	Motor Vehicle Theft
City	753.3	0.0	3.9	3.9	7.8	74.2	624.5	39.0
Metro[1]	2,342.1	1.7	39.2	78.0	148.1	343.0	1,651.2	80.9
U.S.	2,971.8	4.5	36.6	102.2	232.5	542.5	1,837.3	216.2

Note: Figures are crimes per 100,000 population; (1) Figures cover the Manchester-Nashua, NH Metropolitan Statistical Area—see Appendix B for areas included; (3) The city and U.S. figures shown were reported using the revised Uniform Crime Reporting (UCR) definition of rape. The suburban and metro area figures shown are an aggregate total of the data submitted using both the revised and legacy UCR definitions.
Source: FBI Uniform Crime Reports, 2014

Hate Crimes

Area	Number of Quarters Reported	Number of Incidents per Bias Motivation						
		Race	Religion	Sexual Orientation	Ethnicity	Disability	Gender	Gender Identity
City	4	0	0	0	0	0	0	0
U.S.	4	2,568	1,014	1,017	648	84	33	98

Source: Federal Bureau of Investigation, Hate Crime Statistics 2014

Identity Theft Consumer Complaints

Area	Complaints	Complaints per 100,000 Population	Rank[2]
MSA[1]	665	164.1	41
U.S.	490,220	152.4	-

Note: (1) Figures cover the Manchester-Nashua, NH Metropolitan Statistical Area—see Appendix B for areas included; (2) Rank ranges from 1 to 379 where 1 indicates greatest number of identity theft complaints per 100,000 population
Source: Federal Trade Commission, Consumer Sentinel Network Data Book for January–December 2015

Fraud and Other Consumer Complaints

Area	Complaints	Complaints per 100,000 Population	Rank[2]
MSA[1]	1,729	426.7	67
U.S.	2,593,159	806.0	-

Note: (1) Figures cover the Manchester-Nashua, NH Metropolitan Statistical Area—see Appendix B for areas included; (2) Rank ranges from 1 to 379 where 1 indicates greatest number of identity theft complaints per 100,000 population
Source: Federal Trade Commission, Consumer Sentinel Network Data Book for January–December 2015

RECREATION

Culture

Dance[1]	Theatre[1]	Instrumental Music[1]	Vocal Music[1]	Series and Festivals	Museums and Art Galleries[2]	Zoos and Aquariums[3]
0	0	0	0	0	0	0

Note: (1) Professional perfoming groups; (2) Based on organizations with SIC code 8412; (3) AZA-accredited
Source: The Grey House Performing Arts Directory, 2015-16; Association of Zoos & Aquariums, AZA Member Zoos & Aquariums, March 25, 2016; www.AccuLeads.com, March 29, 2016

Professional Sports Teams

Team Name	League	Year Established
No teams are located in the metro area		

Source: Wikipedia, Major Professional Sports Teams of the United States and Canada, March 24, 2016

CLIMATE

Average and Extreme Temperatures

Temperature	Jan	Feb	Mar	Apr	May	Jun	Jul	Aug	Sep	Oct	Nov	Dec	Yr.
Extreme High (°F)	68	66	85	95	97	98	102	101	98	90	80	68	102
Average High (°F)	31	34	43	57	69	77	83	80	72	61	48	35	57
Average Temp. (°F)	20	23	33	44	56	65	70	68	59	48	38	25	46
Average Low (°F)	9	11	22	32	42	51	57	55	46	35	28	15	34
Extreme Low (°F)	-33	-27	-16	8	21	30	35	29	22	10	-5	-22	-33

Note: Figures cover the years 1948-1990
Source: National Climatic Data Center, International Station Meteorological Climate Summary, 9/96

Average Precipitation/Snowfall/Humidity

Precip./Humidity	Jan	Feb	Mar	Apr	May	Jun	Jul	Aug	Sep	Oct	Nov	Dec	Yr.
Avg. Precip. (in.)	2.8	2.5	2.9	3.1	3.2	3.1	3.1	3.3	2.9	3.1	3.8	3.2	36.9
Avg. Snowfall (in.)	18	15	11	2	Tr	0	0	0	0	Tr	4	14	63
Avg. Rel. Hum. 7am (%)	76	76	76	75	75	80	82	87	89	86	83	79	80
Avg. Rel. Hum. 4pm (%)	59	55	52	46	47	52	51	53	55	53	61	63	54

Note: Figures cover the years 1948-1990; Tr = Trace amounts (<0.05 in. of rain; <0.5 in. of snow)
Source: National Climatic Data Center, International Station Meteorological Climate Summary, 9/96

Weather Conditions

Temperature			Daytime Sky			Precipitation		
5°F & below	32°F & below	90°F & above	Clear	Partly cloudy	Cloudy	0.01 inch or more precip.	0.1 inch or more snow/ice	Thunder-storms
32	171	12	87	131	147	125	32	19

Note: Figures are average number of days per year and cover the years 1948-1990
Source: National Climatic Data Center, International Station Meteorological Climate Summary, 9/96

HAZARDOUS WASTE

Superfund Sites

Merrimack has one hazardous waste site on the EPA's Superfund Final National Priorities List: **New Hampshire Plating Co.** There are a total of 1,323 Superfund sites on the list in the U.S. *U.S. Environmental Protection Agency, Final National Priorities List, March 18, 2016*

AIR & WATER QUALITY

Air Quality Trends: Ozone

	1990	1995	2000	2005	2010	2011	2012	2013	2014
MSA[1]	n/a	n/a	n/a	n/a	n/a	n/a	n/a	n/a	n/a

Note: (1) Data covers the Manchester-Nashua, NH Metropolitan Statistical Area—see Appendix B for areas included; n/a not available. The values shown are the composite ozone concentration averages among trend sites based on the highest fourth daily maximum 8-hour concentration in parts per million. These trends are based on sites having an adequate record of monitoring data during the trend period. Data from exceptional events are included.
Source: U.S. Environmental Protection Agency, Air Quality Monitoring Information, "Air Quality Trends by City, 1990-2014"

Air Quality Index

Area	Percent of Days when Air Quality was...[2]					AQI Statistics[2]	
	Good	Moderate	Unhealthy for Sensitive Groups	Unhealthy	Very Unhealthy	Maximum	Median
MSA[1]	91.0	8.8	0.3	0.0	0.0	109	36

Note: (1) Data covers the Manchester-Nashua, NH Metropolitan Statistical Area—see Appendix B for areas included; (2) Based on 365 days with AQI data in 2015. Air Quality Index (AQI) is an index for reporting daily air quality. EPA calculates the AQI for five major air pollutants regulated by the Clean Air Act: ground-level ozone, particle pollution (aka particulate matter), carbon monoxide, sulfur dioxide, and nitrogen dioxide. The AQI runs from 0 to 500. The higher the AQI value, the greater the level of air pollution and the greater the health concern. There are six AQI categories: "Good" AQI is between 0 and 50. Air quality is considered satisfactory; "Moderate" AQI is between 51 and 100. Air quality is acceptable; "Unhealthy for Sensitive Groups" When AQI values are between 101 and 150, members of sensitive groups may experience health effects; "Unhealthy" When AQI values are between 151 and 200 everyone may begin to experience health effects; "Very Unhealthy" AQI values between 201 and 300 trigger a health alert; "Hazardous" AQI values over 300 trigger warnings of emergency conditions (not shown).
Source: U.S. Environmental Protection Agency, Air Quality Index Report, 2015

Air Quality Index Pollutants

Area	Percent of Days when AQI Pollutant was...[2]					
	Carbon Monoxide	Nitrogen Dioxide	Ozone	Sulfur Dioxide	Particulate Matter 2.5	Particulate Matter 10
MSA[1]	0.0	0.0	78.4	0.0	21.6	0.0

Note: (1) Data covers the Manchester-Nashua, NH Metropolitan Statistical Area—see Appendix B for areas included; (2) Based on 365 days with AQI data in 2015. The Air Quality Index (AQI) is an index for reporting daily air quality. EPA calculates the AQI for five major air pollutants regulated by the Clean Air Act: ground-level ozone, particle pollution (also known as particulate matter), carbon monoxide, sulfur dioxide, and nitrogen dioxide. The AQI runs from 0 to 500. The higher the AQI value, the greater the level of air pollution and the greater the health concern.
Source: U.S. Environmental Protection Agency, Air Quality Index Report, 2015

Maximum Air Pollutant Concentrations: Particulate Matter, Ozone, CO and Lead

	Particulate Matter 10 (ug/m^3)	Particulate Matter 2.5 Wtd AM (ug/m^3)	Particulate Matter 2.5 24-Hr (ug/m^3)	Ozone (ppm)	Carbon Monoxide (ppm)	Lead (ug/m^3)
MSA[1] Level	n/a	6	13	0.07	0	n/a
NAAQS[2]	150	15	35	0.075	9	0.15
Met NAAQS[2]	n/a	Yes	Yes	Yes	Yes	n/a

Note: (1) Data covers the Manchester-Nashua, NH Metropolitan Statistical Area—see Appendix B for areas included; Data from exceptional events are included; (2) National Ambient Air Quality Standards; ppm = parts per million; ug/m^3 = micrograms per cubic meter; n/a not available.
Concentrations: Particulate Matter 10 (coarse particulate)—highest second maximum 24-hour concentration; Particulate Matter 2.5 Wtd AM (fine particulate)—highest weighted annual mean concentration; Particulate Matter 2.5 24-Hour (fine particulate)—highest 98th percentile 24-hour concentration; Ozone—highest fourth daily maximum 8-hour concentration; Carbon Monoxide—highest second maximum non-overlapping 8-hour concentration; Lead—maximum running 3-month average
Source: U.S. Environmental Protection Agency, Air Quality Monitoring Information, "Air Quality Statistics by City, 2014"

Maximum Air Pollutant Concentrations: Nitrogen Dioxide and Sulfur Dioxide

	Nitrogen Dioxide AM (ppb)	Nitrogen Dioxide 1-Hr (ppb)	Sulfur Dioxide AM (ppb)	Sulfur Dioxide 1-Hr (ppb)	Sulfur Dioxide 24-Hr (ppb)
MSA[1] Level	n/a	n/a	n/a	5	n/a
NAAQS[2]	53	100	30	75	140
Met NAAQS[2]	n/a	n/a	n/a	Yes	n/a

Note: (1) Data covers the Manchester-Nashua, NH Metropolitan Statistical Area—see Appendix B for areas included; Data from exceptional events are included; (2) National Ambient Air Quality Standards; ppm = parts per million; ug/m^3 = micrograms per cubic meter; n/a not available.
Concentrations: Nitrogen Dioxide AM—highest arithmetic mean concentration; Nitrogen Dioxide 1-Hr—highest 98th percentile 1-hour daily maximum concentration; Sulfur Dioxide AM—highest annual mean concentration; Sulfur Dioxide 1-Hr—highest 99th percentile 1-hour daily maximum concentration; Sulfur Dioxide 24-Hr—highest second maximum 24-hour concentration
Source: U.S. Environmental Protection Agency, Air Quality Monitoring Information, "Air Quality Statistics by City, 2014"

Drinking Water

Water System Name	Pop. Served	Primary Water Source Type	Violations[1]	
			Health Based	Monitoring/ Reporting
Merrimack Village District	25,000	Ground	0	0

Note: (1) Based on violation data from January 1, 2015 to December 31, 2015 (includes unresolved violations from earlier years)

Source: U.S. Environmental Protection Agency, Office of Ground Water and Drinking Water, Safe Drinking Water Information System (based on data extracted April 29, 2016)

Bernards, New Jersey

Background

Bernards is located in North-Central New Jersey, 25 miles west of Newark in Somerset County. It includes the communities of Basking Ridge, Liberty Corner and Lyons.

Bernards was formed in 1760 by a royal charter from King George II of England. The township was named for Sir Francis Bernard, who was the royal governor of New Jersey from 1758 until 1760 when he left to take a similar position in Massachusetts. At the time, the area was under the control of the Rev. Samuel Kennedy, fourth pastor of the Presbyterian Church in Basking Ridge. The territory was known as "The Ridge" and was the cultural center for the surrounding villages and hamlets.

In December 1776, the Township Continental Army General Charles Lee, second in command to George Washington, was captured by the British. Bernard's history is still evident today in many parts of the township.

Bernards architecture is eclectic, with many recognized historic sites. The Basking Ridge Presbyterian Church, an example of Greek Revival architecture was constructed in 1839 and its exterior has changed very little. The Coffee House, built in 1804 and a wonderful example of a New Jersey frame farmhouse, has been a residence, crossroads tavern, and community center for local farms in the early 19th century. Lyons Station, a one-story Tudor Revival-style structure, was designed and built by noted architect D.T. Mack in 1931.

Other places of interest include the Spooky Brook Golf Course, Day Camp Sunshine, Lord Stirling Stable, and Colonial Park.

Somerset County is one of the fastest growing counties in New Jersey. Mountain View Corporate Center, an 821,000 square foot campus, features six buildings ranging from 58,000 to 212,000 square feet.

Bernards has a seasonal climate with hot summers and cold winters. Median summer temperatures average 70 degrees, while winter averages can be as low as 20 degrees during of December and January. The city averages 4.5 inches of rainfall per month from April to October and 7 inches of snowfall per month from December to March.

Rankings

General Rankings

- New York* was identified as one of America's fastest-growing major metropolitan areas in terms of population growth by CNNMoney.com. The area ranked #1 out of 10. Criteria: population growth between July 2013 and July 2014. *CNNMoney, "10 Fastest-Growing Cities," May 27, 2015*

Business/Finance Rankings

- The personal finance site NerdWallet analyzed 183 American metropolitan areas with populations over 250,000 and more than 15,000 businesses to rank where entrepreneurs find the most success. Criteria included area economy, annual income, housing cost, unemployment rate, and the success rate of area businesses. New York* ranked #32. *www.nerdwallet.com, "Best Places to Start a Business," April 27, 2015*
- Based on the U.S. Department of Labor's Occupational Information Network Data Collection Program, the Brookings Institution defined job opportunities for STEM workers at various levels of educational attainment. The New York* metro area was one of the ten metro areas where workers in low-education-level STEM jobs earn the lowest relative wages. *www.brookings.edu, "The Hidden Stem Economy," June 10, 2013*
- Metro areas with the largest gap in income between rich and poor residents were identified by 24/7 Wall Street using the U.S. Census Bureau's 2013 American Community Survey. The New York* metro area placed #7 among metro areas with the widest wealth gap between rich and poor. *247wallst.com, "20 Cities with the Widest Gap between the Rich and Poor," July 8, 2015*
- Based on metro area social media reviews, the employment opinion group Glassdoor surveyed 50 of the largest U.S. metro areas and equally weighed cost of living, hiring opportunity, and job satisfaction to compose a list of "25 Best Cities for Jobs." The New York* metro area was ranked #21 in overall job satisfaction. *www.glassdoor.com, "Best Cities for Jobs," May 19, 2015*
- In a survey of economic confidence in the nation's 50 largest metropolitan areas conducted January–December 2014, the New York* metro area placed #23, according to Gallup's 2014 Economic Confidence Index. *Gallup, "San Jose and San Francisco Lead in Economic Confidence," March 19, 2015*
- The Brookings Institution ranked the 100 largest metro areas in the U.S. based on income inequality. New York* was ranked #2 (#1 = greatest ineqality). Criteria: the "95/20 ratio," a figure representing the income at which a household earns more than 95 percent of all other households, divided by the income at which a household earns more than only 20 percent of all other households. *Brookings Institution, "Income Inequality, 100 Largest U.S. Metro Areas, 2007-2014," January 14, 2016*
- Payscale.com ranked the 20 largest metro areas in terms of wage growth. The New York* metro area ranked #18. Criteria: private-sector wage growth between the 1st quarter of 2015 and the 1st quarter of 2016. *PayScale, "Wage Trends by Metro Area," 1st Quarter, 2016*
- The Newark* metro area appeared on the Milken Institute "2015 Best Performing Cities" list. Rank: #134 out of 200 large metro areas. Criteria: job growth; wage and salary growth; high-tech output growth. *Milken Institute, "Best-Performing Cities 2015," December 2015*
- *Forbes* ranked the 200 most populous metro areas to determine the nation's "Best Places for Business and Careers." The Newark* metro area was ranked #137. Criteria: costs (business and living); job growth (past and projected); income growth; educational attainment (college and high school); projected economic growth; cultural and recreational opportunities; net migration patterns; number of highly ranked colleges. *Forbes, "The Best Places for Business and Careers 2015," July 29, 2015*

Dating/Romance Rankings

- CreditDonkey, a financial education website, sought out the ten best U.S. cities for newlyweds, considering the number of married couples, divorce rate, average credit score, and average number of hours worked per week in metro areas with a million or more residents. The New York* metro area placed #5. *www.creditdonkey.com, "Study: Best Cities for Newlyweds," November 30, 2013*

Education Rankings

- Personal finance website *WalletHub* analyzed the 150 largest U.S. metropolitan statistical areas to determine where the most educated Americans are choosing to settle. Criteria: education quality and attainment gap; education levels; percentage of workers with degrees; public school rankings; quality and size of each metro area's universities. New York* was ranked #58 (#1 = most educated city). *www.WalletHub.com, "2015's Most and Least Educated Cities*

Environmental Rankings

- The New York* metro area came in at #155 for the relative comfort of its climate on Sperling's list of "chill cities," as measured by the Sperling Heat Index. All 361 metro areas are included. Criteria included daytime high temperatures, nighttime low temperatures, dew point, and relative humidity at the high temperatures. *www.bertsperling.com, "Sperling's Chill Cities," July 18, 2013*

- Sperling's BestPlaces assessed 379 metropolitan areas of the United States for the likelihood of dangerously extreme weather events or earthquakes. In general the Southeast and South-Central regions have the highest risk of weather extremes and earthquakes, while the Pacific Northwest enjoys the lowest risk. Of the least risky metropolitan areas, the Newark* metro area was ranked #208. *www.bestplaces.net, "Safest Places from Natural Disasters," April 2011*

- New York* was identified as one of America's dirtiest metro areas by *Forbes.* The area ranked #11 out of 20. Criteria: air quality; water quality; toxic releases; superfund sites. *Forbes, "America's 20 Dirtiest Cities," December 10, 2012*

- The U.S. Environmental Protection Agency (EPA) released a list of U.S. metropolitan areas with the most ENERGY STAR certified buildings in 2015. The New York* metro area was ranked #5 out of 25. *U.S. Environmental Protection Agency, "Top Cities With the Most ENERGY STAR Certified Buildings in 2016," March 30, 2016*

- New York* was highlighted as one of the 25 most ozone-polluted metro areas in the U.S. during 2011 through 2013. The area ranked #11. *American Lung Association, State of the Air 2015*

- New York* was highlighted as one of the 25 metro areas most polluted by year-round particle pollution (Annual PM 2.5) in the U.S. during 2011 through 2013. The area ranked #14. *American Lung Association, State of the Air 2015*

- New York* was highlighted as one of the 25 metro areas most polluted by short-term particle pollution (24-hour PM 2.5) in the U.S. during 2011 through 2013. The area ranked #15. *American Lung Association, State of the Air 2015*

Health/Fitness Rankings

- For each of the 50 most populous metro areas in the United States, the American College of Sports Medicine's American Fitness Index evaluated infrastructure, community assets, and policies that encourage healthy and fit lifestyles, including preventive health behaviors, levels of chronic disease conditions, health care access, and community resources and policies that support physical activity. The New York* metro area ranked #24 for "community fitness." *www.americanfitnessindex.org, "ACSM American Fitness Index Health and Community Fitness Status of the 50 Largest Metropolitan Areas," May 2015*

- *Business Insider* reported Trulia's analysis of the 100 largest U.S. metro areas to identify the nation's best cities for weight loss, based on healthful food options, access to outdoor activities, weight-loss centers, gyms, and opportunities to bike or walk to work. New York* ranked #6. *Businessinsider.com, "These Are the Best US Cities for Weight loss," January 17, 2013*
- The New York* metro area was identified as one of the worst cities for bed bugs in America by pest control company Orkin. The area ranked #4 out of 50 based on the number of bed bug treatments Orkin performed from January to December 2015. *Orkin, "Chicago Tops Bed Bug Cities List for Fourth Year in a Row," January 13, 2016*
- New York* was identified as a "2016 Spring Allergy Capital." The area ranked #31 out of 100. Three groups of factors were used to identify the most severe cities for people with allergies during the spring season: annual pollen levels; medicine utilization; access to board-certified allergists. *Asthma and Allergy Foundation of America, "Spring Allergy Capitals 2016"*
- New York* was identified as a "2015 Asthma Capital." The area ranked #35 out of the nation's 100 largest metropolitan areas. Criteria: estimated prevalence; self-reported prevalence; crude death rate for asthma; annual pollen score; annual air quality; public smoking laws; number of board-certified asthma specialists; school inhaler access laws; rescue medication use; controller medication use; ER visits for asthma; uninsured rate; poverty rate. *Asthma and Allergy Foundation of America, "Asthma Capitals 2015"*
- The New York* metro area ranked #113 out of 190 in The Gallup-Healthways Well-Being Index. Criteria: purpose; social well being; financial health; community and physical health. Results are based on telephone interviews with adults, aged 18 and older, living in metropolitan areas in the 50 U.S. states and the District of Columbia. *Gallup-Healthways, "State of American Well-Being," February 23, 2016*

Real Estate Rankings

- With data from RealtyTrac, Yahoo! Finance researchers listed the housing markets in which housing affordability is improving most, factoring in interest rates as well as median home prices. The New York* metro area was among the least affordable housing markets. *news.yahoo.com, "10 Cities Where Ordinary People Can No Longer Afford Homes," March 5, 2014*
- The Newark* metro area was identified as one of the 20 worst housing markets in the U.S. in 2015. The area ranked #10 out of 179 markets. Criteria: year-over-year change of median sales price of existing single-family homes between the 4th quarter of 2014 and the 4th quarter of 2015. *National Association of Realtors®, Median Sales Price of Existing Single-Family Homes for Metropolitan Areas, 4th Quarter 2015*
- The New York* metro area was identified as one of the 20 least affordable housing markets in the U.S. in 2015. The area ranked #9 out of 179 markets. Criteria: qualification for a mortgage loan on a typical home. *National Association of Realtors®, Affordability Index of Existing Single-Family Homes for Metropolitan Areas, 2015*
- Newark* was ranked #181 out of 225 metro areas in terms of housing affordability in 2015 by the National Association of Home Builders (#1 = most affordable). Criteria: the share of homes sold in that area affordable to a family earning the local median income, based on standard mortgage underwriting criteria. *National Association of Home Builders®, NAHB-Wells Fargo Housing Opportunity Index, 4th Quarter 2015*

Safety Rankings

- New York* was identified as one of the most disaster-proof places in the U.S. in terms of its vulnerability to natural and non-natural disasters. The city ranked #1 out of 5. Rankings are based on the U.S. Center for Disease Control's Cities Readiness Initiative (CRI), which assesses local emergency-management plans, protocols and capabilities for 72 Metropolitan Statistical Areas and four non-MSA large cities. *Forbes, "America's Most and Least Disaster-Proof Cities," December 12, 2011*

- The National Insurance Crime Bureau ranked 380 metro areas in the U.S. in terms of per capita rates of vehicle theft. The New York* metro area ranked #249 (#1 = highest rate). Criteria: number of vehicle theft offenses per 100,000 inhabitants in 2014. *National Insurance Crime Bureau, "Hot Spots 2014," June 24, 2015*

Seniors/Retirement Rankings

- From its Best Cities for Successful Aging indexes, the Milken Institute generated rankings for metropolitan areas, weighing data in eight categories—health care, wellness, living arrangements, transportation, financial characteristics, education and employment opportunities, community engagement, and overall livability. The New York* metro area was ranked #14 overall in the large metro area category. *Milken Institute, "Best Cities for Successful Aging, 2014"*

Sports/Recreation Rankings

- According to the personal finance website NerdWallet, the New York* metro area, at #4, is one of the nation's top dozen metro areas for sports fans. Criteria included the presence of all four major sports—MLB, NFL, NHL, and NBA, fan enthusiasm (as measured by game attendance), ticket affordability, and "sports culture," that is, number of sports bars. *www.nerdwallet.com, "Best Cities for Sports Fans," May 5, 2013*

Transportation Rankings

- New York* was identified as one of the most congested metro areas in the U.S. The area ranked #4 out of 10. Criteria: yearly delay per auto commuter in hours. *Texas A&M Transportation Institute, "2015 Urban Mobility Scorecard," August 2015*
- The New York* metro area appeared on *Forbes* list of places with the most extreme commutes. The metro area ranked #2 out of 10. Criteria: average travel time; percentage of mega commuters. Mega-commuters travel more than 90 minutes and 50 miles each way to work. *Forbes.com, "The Cities with the Most Extreme Commutes," March 5, 2013*

Miscellaneous Rankings

- The watchdog site Charity Navigator conducts an annual study of charities in the nation's major markets both to analyze statistical differences in their financial, accountability, and transparency practices and to track year-to-year variations in individual communities. The New York* metro area was ranked #17 among the 30 metro markets in the rating dimension of Overall Score. *www.charitynavigator.org, "Metro Market Study 2015," June 5, 2015*
- The Harris Poll's Happiness Index survey revealed that of the top ten U.S. markets, the New York* metro area residents ranked #6 in happiness. Criteria included strong assent to positive statements and strong disagreement with negative ones, and degree of agreement with a series of statements about respondents' personal relationships and general outlook. *www.harrisinteractive.com, "Dallas/Fort Worth Is "Happiest" City among America's Top Ten Markets," September 4, 2013*
- Energizer Personal Care, the makers of Edge® shave gel, in partnership with Sperling's BestPlaces, ranked 50 major metro areas in terms of everyday irritations. The New York* metro area ranked #2 the 50 metro area most iritating to guys. Criteria: high male-to-female ratio; poor sports team performance and high ticket prices; slow traffic; lack of job availability; unaffordable housing; extreme weather; lack of nightlife and fitness options. *Energizer Personal Care, "Most Irritatng Cities for Guys," August 26, 2013*
- Mars Chocolate North America, the makers of COMBOS®, in partnership with Sperling's BestPlaces, ranked 50 major metro areas in terms of their "manliness." The New York* metro area ranked #39. Criteria: number of professional sports teams; number of nearby NASCAR tracks and racing events; manly lifestyle; concentration of manly retail stores; manly occupations per capita; salty snack sales; "Board of Manliness" rankings. *Mars Chocolate North America, "America's Manliest Cities 2012"*

- The New York* metro area was selected as one of "America's Most Miserable Cities" by *Forbes.com.* The metro area ranked #10 out of 20. Criteria: violent crime; unemployment; foreclosures; income and property taxes; home prices; commute times; climate. *Forbes.com, "America's Most Miserable Cities" February 22, 2013*

- The National Alliance to End Homelessness ranked the 100 most populous metro areas with the highest rate of homelessness. The New York* metro area ranked #13. Criteria: number of homeless people per 10,000 population in 2011. *National Alliance to End Homelessness, The State of Homelessness in America 2012*

Bernards is located within the New York-Newark-Jersey City, NY-NJ-PA Metropolitan Statistical Area and the Newark, NJ-PA Metropolitan Division.

Business Environment

CITY FINANCES

City Government Finances

Component	2012 ($000)	2012 ($ per capita)
Total Revenues	31,546	1,183
Total Expenditures	29,990	1,125
Debt Outstanding	16,620	623
Cash and Securities[1]	37,928	1,423

Note: (1) Cash and security holdings of a government at the close of its fiscal year, including those of its dependent agencies, utilities, and liquor stores.
Source: U.S Census Bureau, State & Local Government Finances 2012

City Government Revenue by Source

Source	2012 ($000)	2012 ($ per capita)
General Revenue		
From Federal Government	0	0
From State Government	2,080	78
From Local Governments	822	30
Taxes		
Property	21,004	788
Sales and Gross Receipts	649	24
Personal Income	0	0
Corporate Income	0	0
Motor Vehicle License	0	0
Other Taxes	1,089	40
Current Charges	5,137	192
Liquor Store	0	0
Utility	0	0
Employee Retirement	0	0

Source: U.S Census Bureau, State & Local Government Finances 2012

City Government Expenditures by Function

Function	2012 ($000)	2012 ($ per capita)	2012 (%)
General Direct Expenditures			
Air Transportation	0	0	0.0
Corrections	0	0	0.0
Education	0	0	0.0
Employment Security Administration	0	0	0.0
Financial Administration	918	34	3.0
Fire Protection	90	3	0.3
General Public Buildings	286	10	0.9
Governmental Administration, Other	587	22	1.9
Health	756	28	2.5
Highways	2,434	91	8.1
Hospitals	0	0	0.0
Housing and Community Development	0	0	0.0
Interest on General Debt	792	29	2.6
Judicial and Legal	796	29	2.6
Libraries	2,259	84	7.5
Parking	0	0	0.0
Parks and Recreation	2,163	81	7.2
Police Protection	4,523	169	15.0
Public Welfare	0	0	0.0
Sewerage	4,512	169	15.0
Solid Waste Management	477	17	1.5
Veterans' Services	0	0	0.0
Liquor Store	0	0	0.0
Utility	0	0	0.0
Employee Retirement	0	0	0.0

Source: U.S Census Bureau, State & Local Government Finances 2012

DEMOGRAPHICS

Population Growth

Area	1990 Census	2000 Census	2010 Census	2014* Estimate	Population Growth (%) 1990-2014	Population Growth (%) 2010-2014
City	17,199	24,575	26,652	26,849	56.1	0.7
MSA[1]	16,845,992	18,323,002	18,897,109	19,865,045	17.9	5.1
U.S.	248,709,873	281,421,906	308,745,538	314,107,084	26.3	1.7

Note: (1) Figures cover the New York-Newark-Jersey City, NY-NJ-PA Metropolitan Statistical Area—see Appendix B for areas included; (*) 2010-2014 5-year estimated population
Source: U.S. Census Bureau, 1990 Census, Census 2000, Census 2010, 2010-2014 American Community Survey 5-Year Estimates

Household Size

Area	Persons in Household (%) One	Two	Three	Four	Five	Six	Seven or More	Average Household Size
City	27.9	25.2	17.9	19.3	6.5	2.4	0.4	2.70
MSA[1]	27.8	28.9	17.0	14.8	6.7	2.6	1.9	2.74
U.S.	27.5	33.5	15.8	13.1	6.0	2.3	1.4	2.64

Note: (1) Figures cover the New York-Newark-Jersey City, NY-NJ-PA Metropolitan Statistical Area—see Appendix B for areas included
Source: U.S. Census Bureau, 2010-2014 American Community Survey 5-Year Estimates

Race

Area	White Alone[2] (%)	Black Alone[2] (%)	Asian Alone[2] (%)	AIAN[3] Alone[2] (%)	NHOPI[4] Alone[2] (%)	Other Race Alone[2] (%)	Two or More Races (%)
City	81.1	2.0	13.9	0.0	0.0	0.1	2.8
MSA[1]	59.4	17.2	10.2	0.3	0.0	10.1	2.8
U.S.	73.8	12.6	5.0	0.8	0.2	4.7	2.9

Note: (1) Figures cover the New York-Newark-Jersey City, NY-NJ-PA Metropolitan Statistical Area—see Appendix B for areas included; (2) Alone is defined as not being in combination with one or more other races; (3) American Indian and Alaska Native; (4) Native Hawaiian and Other Pacific Islander
Source: U.S. Census Bureau, 2010-2014 American Community Survey 5-Year Estimates

Hispanic or Latino Origin

Area	Total (%)	Mexican (%)	Puerto Rican (%)	Cuban (%)	Other (%)
City	4.9	1.7	0.7	0.3	2.2
MSA[1]	23.3	3.0	6.4	0.7	13.1
U.S.	16.9	10.8	1.6	0.6	3.8

Note: Persons of Hispanic or Latino origin can be of any race; (1) Figures cover the New York-Newark-Jersey City, NY-NJ-PA Metropolitan Statistical Area—see Appendix B for areas included
Source: U.S. Census Bureau, 2010-2014 American Community Survey 5-Year Estimates

Ancestry

Area	German	Irish	English	American	Italian	Polish	French[2]	Scottish	Dutch
City	16.1	19.8	7.9	8.5	19.1	5.8	1.4	2.1	1.6
MSA[1]	7.2	10.6	3.1	4.4	13.7	4.2	1.1	0.7	0.7
U.S.	14.9	10.8	8.0	7.1	5.5	3.0	2.7	1.7	1.4

Note: Figures are the percentage of the total population reporting a particular ancestry. The nine most commonly reported ancestries in the U.S. are shown. Figures include multiple ancestries (e.g. if a person reported being Irish and Italian, they were included in both columns); (1) Figures cover the New York-Newark-Jersey City, NY-NJ-PA Metropolitan Statistical Area—see Appendix B for areas included; (2) Excludes Basque
Source: U.S. Census Bureau, 2010-2014 American Community Survey 5-Year Estimates

Foreign-Born Population

Area	Any Foreign Country	Asia	Mexico	Europe	Carribean	Central America[2]	South America	Africa	Canada
	Percent of Population Born in								
City	17.8	9.6	0.9	4.7	0.5	0.0	0.7	0.6	0.6
MSA[1]	28.5	8.0	1.7	4.6	6.5	1.9	4.3	1.2	0.2
U.S.	13.1	3.8	3.7	1.5	1.2	1.0	0.9	0.6	0.3

Note: (1) Figures cover the New York-Newark-Jersey City, NY-NJ-PA Metropolitan Statistical Area—see Appendix B for areas included; (2) Excludes Mexico.
Source: U.S. Census Bureau, 2010-2014 American Community Survey 5-Year Estimates

Marital Status

Area	Never Married	Now Married[2]	Separated	Widowed	Divorced
City	25.6	57.7	0.8	6.1	9.8
MSA[1]	37.7	45.8	2.5	6.0	7.9
U.S.	32.5	48.4	2.2	5.9	10.9

Note: Figures are percentages and cover the population 15 years of age and older; (1) Figures cover the New York-Newark-Jersey City, NY-NJ-PA Metropolitan Statistical Area—see Appendix B for areas included; (2) Excludes separated
Source: U.S. Census Bureau, 2010-2014 American Community Survey 5-Year Estimates

Disability Status

Area	All Ages	Under 18 Years Old	18 to 64 Years Old	65 Years and Over
City	6.5	2.1	3.6	30.2
MSA[1]	9.8	3.1	7.3	33.5
U.S.	12.3	4.1	10.2	36.3

Note: Figures show percent of the civilian noninstitutionalized population that reported having a disability. Disability status is determined from from six types of difficulty: vision, hearing, cognitive, ambulatory, self-care, and independent living. For children under 5 years old, hearing and vision difficulty are used to determine disability status. For children between the ages of 5 and 14, disability status is determined from hearing, vision, cognitive, ambulatory, and self-care difficulties. For people aged 15 years and older, they are considered to have a disability if they have difficulty with any one of the six difficulty types; (1) Figures cover the New York-Newark-Jersey City, NY-NJ-PA Metropolitan Statistical Area—see Appendix B for areas included.
Source: U.S. Census Bureau, 2010-2014 American Community Survey 5-Year Estimates

Age

Area	Under Age 5	Age 5–19	Age 20–34	Age 35–44	Age 45–54	Age 55–64	Age 65–74	Age 75–84	Age 85+	Median Age
	Percent of Population									
City	4.5	26.2	9.8	14.4	17.7	14.0	6.8	3.5	3.1	42.9
MSA[1]	6.2	18.8	21.2	13.6	14.6	12.0	7.3	4.2	2.0	37.8
U.S.	6.4	19.9	20.6	13.0	14.1	12.3	7.6	4.3	1.9	37.4

Note: (1) Figures cover the New York-Newark-Jersey City, NY-NJ-PA Metropolitan Statistical Area—see Appendix B for areas included
Source: U.S. Census Bureau, 2010-2014 American Community Survey 5-Year Estimates

Gender

Area	Males	Females	Males per 100 Females
City	12,515	14,334	87.3
MSA[1]	9,593,127	10,271,918	93.4
U.S.	154,515,159	159,591,925	96.8

Note: (1) Figures cover the New York-Newark-Jersey City, NY-NJ-PA Metropolitan Statistical Area—see Appendix B for areas included
Source: U.S. Census Bureau, 2010-2014 American Community Survey 5-Year Estimates

Religious Groups by Family

Area	Catholic	Baptist	Non-Den.	Methodist[2]	Lutheran	LDS[3]	Pente-costal	Presby-terian[4]	Muslim[5]	Judaism
MSA[1]	36.9	1.8	1.7	1.3	0.7	0.3	0.8	1.0	2.3	4.7
U.S.	19.1	9.3	4.0	4.0	2.3	2.0	1.9	1.6	0.8	0.7

Note: Figures are the number of adherents as a percentage of the total population; (1) Figures cover the New York-Northern New Jersey-Long Island, NY-NJ-PA Metropolitan Statistical Area—see Appendix B for areas included; (2) Methodist/Pietist; (3) Latter Day Saints; (4) Reformed; (5) Figures are estimates
Source: Association of Statisticians of American Religious Bodies, 2010 U.S. Religion Census: Religious Congregations & Membership Study

Religious Groups by Tradition

Area	Catholic	Evangelical Protestant	Mainline Protestant	Other Tradition	Black Protestant	Orthodox
MSA[1]	36.9	3.9	4.1	8.3	1.2	0.9
U.S.	19.1	16.2	7.3	4.3	1.6	0.3

Note: Figures are the number of adherents as a percentage of the total population; (1) Figures cover the New York-Northern New Jersey-Long Island, NY-NJ-PA Metropolitan Statistical Area—see Appendix B for areas included
Source: Association of Statisticians of American Religious Bodies, 2010 U.S. Religion Census: Religious Congregations & Membership Study

ECONOMY

Gross Metropolitan Product

Area	2013	2014	2015	2016	Rank[2]
MSA[1]	1,471.2	1,521.7	1,573.8	1,650.1	1

Note: Figures are in billions of dollars; (1) Figures cover the New York-Newark-Jersey City, NY-NJ-PA Metropolitan Statistical Area—see Appendix B for areas included; (2) Rank is based on 2016 data and ranges from 1 to 381
Source: The U.S. Conference of Mayors, U.S. Metro Economies: GMP and Employment 2014-2016, June 2015

Economic Growth

Area	2011-13 (%)	2014 (%)	2015 (%)	2016 (%)	Rank[2]
MSA[1]	1.6	1.8	2.0	2.8	116
U.S.	2.2	2.4	2.3	2.9	–

Note: Figures are real gross metropolitan product (GMP) growth rates and represent annual average percent change; (1) Figures cover the New York-Newark-Jersey City, NY-NJ-PA Metropolitan Statistical Area—see Appendix B for areas included; (2) Rank is based on 2016 data and ranges from 1 to 381
Source: The U.S. Conference of Mayors, U.S. Metro Economies: GMP and Employment 2014-2016, June 2015

Metropolitan Area Exports

Area	2009	2010	2011	2012	2013	2014	Rank[2]
MSA[1]	69,990.3	85,081.1	105,102.0	102,298.0	106,922.8	105,266.5	2

Note: Figures are in millions of dollars; (1) Figures cover the New York-Newark-Jersey City, NY-NJ-PA Metropolitan Statistical Area—see Appendix B for areas included; (2) Rank is based on 2014 data and ranges from 1 to 385
Source: U.S. Department of Commerce, International Trade Administration, Office of Trade & Industry Information, Manufacturing & Services, data extracted March 10, 2016

Building Permits

Area	Single-Family			Multi-Family			Total		
	2014	2015p	Pct. Chg.	2014	2015p	Pct. Chg.	2014	2015p	Pct. Chg.
City	12	11	-8.3	0	0	-	12	11	-8.3
MSA[1]	11,799	10,749	-8.9	36,185	75,646	109.1	47,984	86,395	80.0
U.S.	640,300	690,800	7.9	411,800	487,600	18.4	1,052,100	1,178,400	12.0

Note: (1) Figures cover the New York-Newark-Jersey City, NY-NJ-PA Metropolitan Statistical Area—see Appendix B for areas included; Figures represent new, privately-owned housing units authorized (unadjusted data); All permit data are based on estimates with imputation; (p) preliminary data.
Source: U.S. Census Bureau, Manufacturing, Mining, and Construction Statistics, Building Permits, 2014, 2015

Bankruptcy Filings

Area	Business Filings			Nonbusiness Filings		
	2014	2015	% Chg.	2014	2015	% Chg.
Somerset County	33	19	-42.4	522	512	-1.9
U.S.	26,983	24,735	-8.3	909,812	819,760	-9.9

Note: Business filings include Chapter 7, Chapter 11, Chapter 12, and Chapter 13; Nonbusiness filings include Chapter 7, Chapter 11, and Chapter 13
Source: Administrative Office of the U.S. Courts, Business and Nonbusiness Bankruptcy, County Cases Commenced by Chapter of the Bankruptcy Code, During the 12- Month Period Ending December 31, 2014 and Business and Nonbusiness Bankruptcy, County Cases Commenced by Chapter of the Bankruptcy Code, During the 12- Month Period Ending December 31, 2015

Housing Vacancy Rates

Area	Gross Vacancy Rate[2] (%)			Year-Round Vacancy Rate[3] (%)			Rental Vacancy Rate[4] (%)			Homeowner Vacancy Rate[5] (%)		
	2013	2014	2015	2013	2014	2015	2013	2014	2015	2013	2014	2015
MSA[1]	9.5	9.2	9.8	8.1	7.9	8.6	5.4	4.6	4.2	2.1	1.6	2.1
U.S.	13.6	13.4	12.9	10.7	10.4	10.0	8.3	7.6	7.1	2.0	1.9	1.8

Note: (1) Figures cover the New York-Newark-Jersey City, NY-NJ-PA Metropolitan Statistical Area—see Appendix B for areas included; (2) The percentage of the total housing inventory that is vacant; (3) The percentage of the housing inventory (excluding seasonal units) that is year-round vacant; (4) The percentage of rental inventory that is vacant for rent; (5) The percentage of homeowner inventory that is vacant for sale
Source: U.S. Census Bureau, Housing Vacancies and Homeownership Annual Statistics: 2015

INCOME

Income

Area	Per Capita ($)	Median Household ($)	Average Household ($)
City	67,750	126,667	185,757
MSA[1]	36,078	66,902	97,572
U.S.	28,555	53,482	74,596

Note: (1) Figures cover the New York-Newark-Jersey City, NY-NJ-PA Metropolitan Statistical Area—see Appendix B for areas included
Source: U.S. Census Bureau, 2010-2014 American Community Survey 5-Year Estimates

Household Income Distribution

Area	Percent of Households Earning							
	Under $15,000	$15,000 -24,999	$25,000 -34,999	$35,000 -49,999	$50,000 -74,999	$75,000 -99,000	$100,000 -149,999	$150,000 and up
City	3.9	3.2	2.7	6.1	11.6	10.9	18.6	43.1
MSA[1]	11.8	8.8	8.0	10.6	15.3	11.9	15.7	18.0
U.S.	12.5	10.7	10.2	13.5	17.8	12.2	13.0	10.0

Note: (1) Figures cover the New York-Newark-Jersey City, NY-NJ-PA Metropolitan Statistical Area—see Appendix B for areas included
Source: U.S. Census Bureau, 2010-2014 American Community Survey 5-Year Estimates

Poverty Rate

Area	All Ages	Under 18 Years Old	18 to 64 Years Old	65 Years and Over
City	3.7	3.7	3.1	6.7
MSA[1]	14.3	20.0	12.8	11.6
U.S.	15.6	21.9	14.6	9.4

Note: Figures are percentage of people whose income during the past 12 months was below the poverty level; (1) Figures cover the New York-Newark-Jersey City, NY-NJ-PA Metropolitan Statistical Area—see Appendix B for areas included
Source: U.S. Census Bureau, 2010-2014 American Community Survey 5-Year Estimates

EMPLOYMENT

Labor Force and Employment

Area	Civilian Labor Force			Workers Employed		
	Dec. 2014	Dec. 2015	% Chg.	Dec. 2014	Dec. 2015	% Chg.
City	12,845	13,047	1.5	12,378	12,703	2.6
MD[1]	1,263,429	1,278,694	1.2	1,193,847	1,224,747	2.5
U.S.	155,521,000	157,245,000	1.1	147,190,000	149,703,000	1.7

Note: Data is not seasonally adjusted and covers workers 16 years of age and older; (1) Figures cover the Newark, NJ-PA Metropolitan Division—see Appendix B for areas included
Source: Bureau of Labor Statistics, Local Area Unemployment Statistics

Unemployment Rate

Area	2015											
	Jan.	Feb.	Mar.	Apr.	May	Jun.	Jul.	Aug.	Sep.	Oct.	Nov.	Dec.
City	4.4	4.0	3.8	3.7	4.0	3.7	3.9	3.3	3.5	3.3	3.1	2.6
MD[1]	6.6	6.6	6.4	5.9	6.1	5.4	6.1	5.4	5.3	4.9	4.8	4.2
U.S.	6.1	5.8	5.6	5.1	5.3	5.5	5.6	5.2	4.9	4.8	4.8	4.8

Note: Data is not seasonally adjusted and covers workers 16 years of age and older; (1) Figures cover the Newark, NJ-PA Metropolitan Division—see Appendix B for areas included
Source: Bureau of Labor Statistics, Local Area Unemployment Statistics

Employment by Occupation

Occupation Classification	City (%)	MSA[1] (%)	U.S. (%)
Management, Business, Science, and Arts	67.5	40.3	36.4
Natural Resources, Construction, and Maintenance	3.7	7.0	9.0
Production, Transportation, and Material Moving	1.3	9.1	12.1
Sales and Office	20.0	24.2	24.4
Service	7.4	19.4	18.2

Note: Figures cover employed civilians 16 years of age and older; (1) Figures cover the New York-Newark-Jersey City, NY-NJ-PA Metropolitan Statistical Area—see Appendix B for areas included
Source: U.S. Census Bureau, 2010-2014 American Community Survey 5-Year Estimates

Employment by Industry

Sector	MD[1]		U.S.
	Number of Employees	Percent of Total	Percent of Total
Construction, Mining, and Logging	45,200	3.7	5.0
Education and Health Services	183,000	15.1	15.7
Financial Activities	81,200	6.7	5.7
Government	178,300	14.7	15.5
Information	23,000	1.9	1.9
Leisure and Hospitality	90,500	7.4	10.4
Manufacturing	76,300	6.3	8.6
Other Services	55,400	4.5	3.9
Professional and Business Services	224,100	18.5	13.9
Retail Trade	126,700	10.4	11.3
Transportation, Warehousing, and Utilities	62,500	5.1	3.9
Wholesale Trade	63,400	5.2	4.1

Note: Figures are non-farm employment as of December 2015. Figures are not seasonally adjusted and include workers 16 years of age and older; (1) Figures cover the Newark, NJ-PA Metropolitan Division—see Appendix B for areas included; n/a not available
Source: Bureau of Labor Statistics, Current Employment Statistics, Employment, Hours, and Earnings

Occupations with Greatest Projected Employment Growth: 2012 – 2022

Occupation[1]	2012 Employment	2022 Projected Employment	Numeric Employment Change	Percent Employment Change
Home Health Aides	31,140	46,280	15,140	48.6
Combined Food Preparation and Serving Workers, Including Fast Food	59,990	70,180	10,190	17.0
Retail Salespersons	125,690	134,870	9,180	7.3
Registered Nurses	79,840	88,880	9,040	11.3
Nursing Assistants	51,780	60,070	8,290	16.0
Laborers and Freight, Stock, and Material Movers, Hand	75,730	83,360	7,630	10.1
Software Developers, Applications	29,090	35,770	6,680	23.0
Receptionists and Information Clerks	51,160	57,830	6,670	13.0
Customer Service Representatives	63,450	69,530	6,080	9.6
Sales Representatives, Services, All Other	45,510	51,380	5,870	12.9

Note: Projections cover New Jersey; (1) Sorted by numeric employment change
Source: www.projectionscentral.com, State Occupational Projections, 2012–2022 Long-Term Projections

Fastest Growing Occupations: 2012 – 2022

Occupation[1]	2012 Employment	2022 Projected Employment	Numeric Employment Change	Percent Employment Change
Home Health Aides	31,140	46,280	15,140	48.6
Insulation Workers, Mechanical	370	540	170	48.2
Diagnostic Medical Sonographers	2,550	3,550	1,000	39.1
Occupational Therapy Assistants	370	500	130	37.5
Helpers—Electricians	1,310	1,800	490	37.5
Stonemasons	580	780	200	35.4
Physical Therapist Assistants	1,090	1,470	380	34.1
Skincare Specialists	1,050	1,400	350	33.2
Physician Assistants	1,450	1,920	470	32.8
Brickmasons and Blockmasons	2,150	2,830	680	31.7

Note: Projections cover New Jersey; (1) Sorted by percent employment change and excludes occupations with numeric employment change less than 100
Source: www.projectionscentral.com, State Occupational Projections, 2012–2022 Long-Term Projections

Average Wages

Occupation	$/Hr.	Occupation	$/Hr.
Accountants and Auditors	41.32	Maids and Housekeeping Cleaners	11.71
Automotive Mechanics	24.21	Maintenance and Repair Workers	20.80
Bookkeepers	21.35	Marketing Managers	81.89
Carpenters	31.15	Nuclear Medicine Technologists	44.57
Cashiers	10.30	Nurses, Licensed Practical	26.25
Clerks, General Office	16.08	Nurses, Registered	39.35
Clerks, Receptionists/Information	15.36	Nursing Assistants	13.68
Clerks, Shipping/Receiving	16.95	Packers and Packagers, Hand	10.53
Computer Programmers	44.01	Physical Therapists	44.49
Computer Systems Analysts	47.04	Postal Service Mail Carriers	24.73
Computer User Support Specialists	28.98	Real Estate Brokers	48.92
Cooks, Restaurant	13.86	Retail Salespersons	12.93
Dentists	77.83	Sales Reps., Exc. Tech./Scientific	37.17
Electrical Engineers	47.38	Sales Reps., Tech./Scientific	48.15
Electricians	35.49	Secretaries, Exc. Legal/Med./Exec.	19.97
Financial Managers	80.51	Security Guards	13.85
First-Line Supervisors/Managers, Sales	23.80	Surgeons	122.53
Food Preparation Workers	10.85	Teacher Assistants*	13.24
General and Operations Managers	81.78	Teachers, Elementary School*	33.13
Hairdressers/Cosmetologists	17.25	Teachers, Secondary School*	35.47
Internists	n/a	Telemarketers	14.24
Janitors and Cleaners	14.47	Truck Drivers, Heavy/Tractor-Trailer	22.90
Landscaping/Groundskeeping Workers	13.64	Truck Drivers, Light/Delivery Svcs.	16.49
Lawyers	75.62	Waiters and Waitresses	11.60

Note: Wage data covers the Newark-Union, NJ-PA Metropolitan Division—see Appendix B for areas included; (*) Hourly wages for elementary/secondary school teachers and teacher assistants were calculated by the editors from annual wage data based on a 40 hour work week; n/a not available.
Source: Bureau of Labor Statistics, Metro Area Occupational Employment and Wage Estimates, May 2015

TAXES

State Corporate Income Tax Rates

State	Tax Rate (%)	Income Brackets ($)	Num. of Brackets	Financial Institution Tax Rate (%)[a]	Federal Income Tax Ded.
New Jersey	9.0 (r)	Flat rate	1	9.0 (r)	No

Note: Tax rates as of January 1, 2016; (a) Rates listed are the corporate income tax rate applied to financial institutions or excise taxes based on income. Some states have other taxes based upon the value of deposits or shares; (r) In New Jersey small businesses with annual entire net income under $100,000 pay a tax rate of 7.5%; businesses with income under $50,000 pay 6.5%. The minimum Corporation Business Tax is based on New Jersey gross receipts. It ranges from $500 for a corporation with gross receipts less than $100,000, to $2,000 for a corporation with gross receipts of $1 million or more.
Source: Federation of Tax Administrators, "State Corporate Income Tax Rates, 2016"

State Individual Income Tax Rates

State	Tax Rate (%)	Income Brackets ($)	Num. of Brackets	Personal Exempt. ($)[1]		Fed. Inc. Tax Ded.
				Single	Dependents	
New Jersey	1.4 - 8.97	20,000 - 500,000 (n)	6	1,000	1,500	No

Note: Tax rates as of January 1, 2016; Local- and county-level taxes are not included; n/a not applicable; (1) Married joint filers generally receive double the single exemption; (n) The New Jersey rates reported are for single individuals. For married couples filing jointly, the tax rates also range from 1.4% to 8.97%, with 7 brackets and the same high and low income ranges.
Source: Federation of Tax Administrators, "State Individual Income Tax Rates, 2016"

Various State and Local Tax Rates

State	State and Local Sales and Use (%)	State Sales and Use (%)	Gasoline[1] (¢/gal.)	Cigarette[2] ($/pack)	Spirits[3] ($/gal.)	Wine[4] ($/gal.)	Beer[5] ($/gal.)
New Jersey	7.00	7.0 (e)	14.5	2.70	5.50	0.88	0.12

Note: All tax rates as of January 1, 2016; (1) The American Petroleum Institute has developed a methodology for determining the average tax rate on a gallon of fuel. Rates may include any of the following: excise taxes, environmental fees, storage tank fees, other fees or taxes, general sales tax, and local taxes. In states where gasoline is subject to the general sales tax, or where the fuel tax is based on the average sale price, the average rate determined by API is sensitive to changes in the price of gasoline. States that fully or partially apply general sales taxes to gasoline: CA, CO, GA, IL, IN, MI, NY; (2) The federal excise tax of $1.0066 per pack and local taxes are not included; (3) Rates are those applicable to off-premise sales of 40% alcohol by volume (a.b.v.) distilled spirits in 750ml containers. Local excise taxes are excluded; (4) Rates are those applicable to off-premise sales of 11% a.b.v. non-carbonated wine in 750ml containers; (5) Rates are those applicable to off-premise sales of 4.7% a.b.v. beer in 12 ounce containers; (e) Some counties in New Jersey are not subject to statewide sales tax rates and collect a local rate of 3.5%. Their average local score is represented as a negative.
Source: Tax Foundation, 2016 Facts & Figures: How Does Your State Compare?

State Business Tax Climate Index Rankings

State	Overall Rank	Corporate Tax Rank	Individual Income Tax Rank	Sales Tax Rank	Unemployment Insurance Tax Rank	Property Tax Rank
New Jersey	50	43	48	47	31	50

Note: The index is a measure of how each state's tax laws affect economic performance. The lower the rank, the more favorable a state's tax system is for business. States without a given tax are given a ranking of 1. The scores/rankings for the District of Columbia do not affect other states. The 2016 index represents the tax climate as of July 1, 2015 (the beginning of Fiscal Year 2016).
Source: Tax Foundation, State Business Tax Climate Index 2016

TRANSPORTATION

Means of Transportation to Work

Area	Car/Truck/Van		Public Transportation			Bicycle	Walked	Other Means	Worked at Home
	Drove Alone	Car-pooled	Bus	Subway	Railroad				
City	79.1	4.7	1.7	0.6	3.3	0.0	1.5	0.4	8.7
MSA[1]	50.6	6.8	8.0	18.5	3.6	0.6	6.0	1.9	4.1
U.S.	76.4	9.6	2.6	1.8	0.6	0.6	2.8	1.3	4.4

Note: Figures are percentages and cover workers 16 years of age and older; (1) Figures cover the New York-Newark-Jersey City, NY-NJ-PA Metropolitan Statistical Area—see Appendix B for areas included
Source: U.S. Census Bureau, 2010-2014 American Community Survey 5-Year Estimates

Travel Time to Work

Area	Less Than 10 Minutes	10 to 19 Minutes	20 to 29 Minutes	30 to 44 Minutes	45 to 59 Minutes	60 to 89 Minutes	90 Minutes or More
City	9.0	23.6	21.8	19.7	8.4	9.5	7.9
MSA[1]	7.8	19.9	16.6	23.6	12.1	13.9	6.2
U.S.	13.3	29.6	21.0	20.2	7.7	5.7	2.6

Note: Figures are percentages and include workers 16 years old and over; (1) Figures cover the New York-Newark-Jersey City, NY-NJ-PA Metropolitan Statistical Area—see Appendix B for areas included
Source: U.S. Census Bureau, 2010-2014 American Community Survey 5-Year Estimates

Freeway Travel Time Index

Area	1985	1990	1995	2000	2005	2010	2014
Urban Area Rank[1,2]	11	9	8	7	7	8	8
Urban Area Index[1]	1.16	1.20	1.24	1.29	1.33	1.33	1.34
Average Index[3]	1.09	1.11	1.14	1.17	1.20	1.19	1.20

Note: Freeway Travel Time Index—the ratio of travel time in the peak period to the travel time at free-flow conditions. For example, a value of 1.30 indicates a 20-minute free-flow trip takes 26 minutes in the peak (20 minutes x 1.30 = 26 minutes); (1) Covers the New York-Newark NY-NJ-CT urban area; (2) Rank is based on 101 urban areas (#1 = highest travel time index); (3) Average of 101 urban areas
Source: Texas Transportation Institute, 2015 Urban Mobility Scorecard, August 2015

Freeway Commuter Stress Index

Area	1985	1990	1995	2000	2005	2010	2014
Urban Area Rank[1,2]	19	19	13	12	11	11	12
Urban Area Index[1]	1.21	1.24	1.29	1.34	1.38	1.38	1.39
Average Index[3]	1.13	1.16	1.19	1.22	1.25	1.24	1.25

Note: The Freeway Commuter Stress Index is the same as the Freeway Travel Time Index (see table above) except that it includes only the travel in the peak directions during the peak periods; the TTI includes travel in all directions during the peak period. Thus, the CSI is more indicative of the work trip experienced by each commuter on a daily basis. (1) Covers the New York-Newark NY-NJ-CT urban area; (2) Rank is based on 101 urban areas (#1 = highest stress index); (3) Average of 101 urban areas

Source: Texas Transportation Institute, 2015 Urban Mobility Scorecard, August 2015

Living Environment

COST OF LIVING

Cost of Living Index

Composite Index	Groceries	Housing	Utilities	Trans- portation	Health Care	Misc. Goods/ Services
126.7	109.8	164.1	114.2	108.9	106.6	114.3

Note: The Cost of Living Index measures regional differences in the cost of consumer goods and services, excluding taxes and non-consumer expenditures, for professional and managerial households in the top income quintile. It is based on more than 50,000 prices covering almost 60 different items for which prices are collected three times a year by chambers of commerce, economic development organizations or university applied economic centers in each participating urban area. The numbers shown should be read as a percentage above or below the national average of 100. For example, a value of 115.4 in the groceries column indicates that grocery prices are 15.4% higher than the national average. Small differences in the index numbers should not be interpreted as significant; Figures cover the Newark-Elizabeth NJ urban area.
Source: The Council for Community and Economic Research, ACCRA Cost of Living Index, 2015

Grocery Prices

Area[1]	T-Bone Steak ($/pound)	Frying Chicken ($/pound)	Whole Milk ($/half gal.)	Eggs ($/dozen)	Orange Juice ($/64 oz.)	Coffee ($/11.5 oz.)
City[2]	11.86	1.83	2.42	2.41	3.59	4.25
Avg.	10.99	1.43	2.25	2.26	3.58	4.48
Min.	7.16	0.98	1.30	1.35	2.88	2.98
Max.	14.13	2.43	3.85	4.81	6.39	7.56

Note: (1) Values for the local area are compared with the average, minimum and maximum values for all 292 areas in the Cost of Living Index; (2) Figures cover the Newark-Elizabeth NJ urban area; **T-Bone Steak** *(price per pound);* **Frying Chicken** *(price per pound, whole fryer);* **Whole Milk** *(half gallon carton);* **Eggs** *(price per dozen, Grade A, large);* **Orange Juice** *(64 oz. Tropicana or Florida Natural);* **Coffee** *(11.5 oz. can, vacuum-packed, Maxwell House, Hills Bros, or Folgers).*
Source: The Council for Community and Economic Research, ACCRA Cost of Living Index, 2015

Housing and Utility Costs

Area[1]	New Home Price ($)	Apartment Rent ($/month)	All Electric ($/month)	Part Electric ($/month)	Other Energy ($/month)	Telephone ($/month)
City[2]	512,478	1,530	-	122.38	70.98	32.25
Avg.	312,874	945	179.30	95.07	72.96	28.11
Min.	178,682	479	116.28	43.14	26.46	10.01
Max.	1,472,476	3,984	504.25	189.44	421.11	43.06

Note: (1) Values for the local area are compared with the average, minimum and maximum values for all 292 areas in the Cost of Living Index; (2) Figures cover the Newark-Elizabeth NJ urban area; **New Home Price** *(2,400 sf living area, 8,000 sf lot, in urban area with full utilities);* **Apartment Rent** *(950 sf 2 bedroom/1.5 or 2 bath, unfurnished, excluding all utilities except water);* **All Electric** *(average monthly cost for an all-electric home);* **Part Electric** *(average monthly cost for a part-electric home);* **Other Energy** *(average monthly cost for natural gas, fuel oil, coal, wood, and any other forms of energy except electricity);* **Telephone** *(price includes basic monthly rate for a private residential line plus additional local usage charges incurred by a family of four).*
Source: The Council for Community and Economic Research, ACCRA Cost of Living Index, 2015

Health Care, Transportation, and Other Costs

Area[1]	Doctor ($/visit)	Dentist ($/visit)	Optometrist ($/visit)	Gasoline ($/gallon)	Beauty Salon ($/visit)	Men's Shirt ($)
City[2]	90.00	107.42	94.00	2.40	33.38	39.38
Avg.	105.15	89.02	99.78	2.38	35.30	28.10
Min.	66.87	56.09	48.53	1.95	18.91	13.38
Max.	182.34	150.36	228.33	4.09	67.91	63.80

Note: (1) Values for the local area are compared with the average, minimum and maximum values for all 292 areas in the Cost of Living Index; (2) Figures cover the Newark-Elizabeth NJ urban area; **Doctor** *(general practitioners routine exam of an established patient);* **Dentist** *(adult teeth cleaning and periodic oral examination);* **Optometrist** *(full vision eye exam for established adult patient);* **Gasoline** *(one gallon regular unleaded, national brand, including all taxes, cash price at self-service pump if available);* **Beauty Salon** *(woman's shampoo, trim, and blow-dry);* **Men's Shirt** *(cotton/polyester dress shirt, pinpoint weave, long sleeves).*
Source: The Council for Community and Economic Research, ACCRA Cost of Living Index, 2015

HOUSING

House Price Index (HPI)

Area	National Ranking[2]	Quarterly Change (%)	One-Year Change (%)	Five-Year Change (%)
MD[1]	235	-0.50	1.60	1.70
U.S.[3]	–	1.45	5.76	22.85

Note: The HPI is a weighted repeat sales index. It measures average price changes in repeat sales or refinancings on the same properties. This information is obtained by reviewing repeat mortgage transactions on single-family properties whose mortgages have been purchased or securitized by Fannie Mae or Freddie Mac in January 1975; (1) Newark Metropolitan Division—see Appendix B for areas included; (2) Rankings are based on annual percentage change for all metro areas containing at least 15,000 transactions over the last 10 years and ranges from 1 to 266; (3) figures based on a weighted average of Census Division estimates using a seasonally adjusted, purchase-only index; all figures are for the period ending December 31, 2015

Source: Federal Housing Finance Agency, House Price Index, February 25, 2016

Median Single-Family Home Prices

Area	2013	2014	2015p	Percent Change 2014 to 2015
MD[1]	381.3	381.5	376.9	-1.2
U.S. Average	197.4	208.9	223.9	7.2

Note: Figures are median sales prices of existing single-family homes in thousands of dollars; (p) preliminary; n/a not available; (1) Newark, NJ-PA Metropolitan Division—see Appendix B for areas included

Source: National Association of Realtors, Median Sales Price of Existing Single-Family Homes for Metropolitan Areas, 4th Quarter 2015

Qualifying Income Based on Median Sales Price of Existing Single-Family Homes

Area	With 5% Down ($)	With 10% Down ($)	With 20% Down ($)
MD[1]	77,384	73,311	65,165
U.S. Average	49,535	46,928	41,714

Note: Figures are preliminary; Qualifying income is based on a mortgage rate of 4.1%. Monthly principal and interest payment is limited to 25% of income; n/a not available; (1) Newark, NJ-PA Metropolitan Division—see Appendix B for areas included

Source: National Association of Realtors, Qualifying Income Based on Median Sales Price of Existing Single-Family Homes for Metropolitan Areas, 4th Quarter 2015

Median Apartment Condo-Coop Home Prices

Area	2013	2014	2015p	Percent Change 2014 to 2015
MD[1]	256.6	263.6	266.0	0.9
U.S. Average	194.9	204.3	210.7	3.1

Note: Figures are median sales prices of existing apartment condo-coop homes in thousands of dollars; (p) preliminary; n/a not available; (1) Newark, NJ-PA Metropolitan Division—see Appendix B for areas included

Source: National Association of Realtors, Median Sales Price of Existing Apartment Condo-Coop Homes for Metropolitan Areas, 4th Quarter 2015

Gross Monthly Rent

Area	Under $200	$200 -299	$300 -499	$500 -749	$750 -999	$1,000 -1,499	$1,500 and up	Median ($)
City	2.2	2.1	13.8	2.6	0.6	2.1	76.6	1,893
MSA[1]	1.1	3.9	4.8	7.3	13.5	36.1	33.3	1,246
U.S.	1.5	3.2	7.4	21.0	24.1	26.9	15.9	920

Note: Figures are percentages except for Median; Gross rent is the contract rent plus the estimated average monthly cost of utilities (electricity, gas, and water and sewer) and fuels (oil, coal, kerosene, wood, etc.) if these are paid by the renter (or paid for the renter by someone else); (1) Figures cover the New York-Newark-Jersey City, NY-NJ-PA Metropolitan Statistical Area—see Appendix B for areas included

Source: U.S. Census Bureau, 2010-2014 American Community Survey 5-Year Estimates

Homeownership Rate

Area	2008 (%)	2009 (%)	2010 (%)	2011 (%)	2012 (%)	2013 (%)	2014 (%)	2015 (%)
MSA[1]	52.6	51.7	51.6	50.9	51.5	50.6	50.7	49.9
U.S.	67.8	67.4	66.9	66.1	65.4	65.1	64.5	63.7

Note: (1) Figures cover the New York-Newark-Jersey City, NY-NJ-PA Metropolitan Statistical Area—see Appendix B for areas included
Source: U.S. Census Bureau, Housing Vacancies and Homeownership Annual Statistics: 2015

Year Housing Structure Built

Area	2010 or Later	2000 -2009	1990 -1999	1980 -1989	1970 -1979	1960 -1969	1950 -1959	1940 -1949	Before 1940	Median Year
City	0.1	11.9	27.5	25.9	8.9	12.6	5.0	2.5	5.7	1986
MSA[1]	0.6	7.4	6.0	7.8	10.0	13.9	16.5	9.5	28.4	1957
U.S.	1.0	14.9	13.9	13.8	15.8	11.0	10.8	5.4	13.3	1976

Note: Figures are percentages except for Median Year; (1) Figures cover the New York-Newark-Jersey City, NY-NJ-PA Metropolitan Statistical Area—see Appendix B for areas included
Source: U.S. Census Bureau, 2010-2014 American Community Survey 5-Year Estimates

HEALTH

Health Risk Data

Category	MD[1] (%)	U.S. (%)
Adults aged 18–64 who have any kind of health care coverage	80.5	79.6
Adults who reported being in good or excellent health	85.9	83.1
Adults who are current smokers	16.0	19.6
Adults who are heavy drinkers[2]	4.9	6.1
Adults who are binge drinkers[3]	17.4	16.9
Adults who are overweight (BMI 25.0 - 29.9)	36.8	35.8
Adults who are obese (BMI 30.0 - 99.8)	24.8	27.6
Adults who participated in any physical activities in the past month	75.1	77.1
Adults 50+ who have ever had a sigmoidoscopy or colonoscopy	65.7	67.3
Women aged 40+ who have had a mammogram within the past two years	77.6	74.0
Men aged 40+ who have had a PSA test within the past two years	45.2	45.2
Adults aged 65+ who have had flu shot within the past year	59.4	60.1
Adults who always wear a seatbelt	94.6	93.8

Note: Data as of 2012 unless otherwise noted; (1) Figures cover the Newark-Union, NJ-PA Metropolitan Division—see Appendix B for areas included; (2) Heavy drinkers are classified as males having more than two drinks per day or females having more than one drink per day; (3) Binge drinkers are classified as males having five or more drinks on one occasion or females having four or more drinks on one occasion
Source: Centers for Disease Control and Prevention, Behaviorial Risk Factor Surveillance System, SMART: Selected Metropolitan/Micropolitan Area Risk Trends, 2012 (Note: the CDC has discontinued this dataset but will be releasing a replacement in mid-2016)

Chronic Health Indicators

Category	MD[1] (%)	U.S. (%)
Adults who have ever been told they had a heart attack	3.6	4.5
Adults who have ever been told they had a stroke	2.3	2.9
Adults who have been told they currently have asthma	8.7	8.9
Adults who have ever been told they have arthritis	19.6	25.7
Adults who have ever been told they have diabetes[2]	8.5	9.7
Adults who have ever been told they had skin cancer	4.2	5.7
Adults who have ever been told they had any other types of cancer	5.3	6.5
Adults who have ever been told they have COPD	4.2	6.2
Adults who have ever been told they have kidney disease	2.1	2.5
Adults who have ever been told they have a form of depression	10.9	18.0

Note: Data as of 2012 unless otherwise noted; (1) Figures cover the Newark-Union, NJ-PA Metropolitan Division—see Appendix B for areas included; (2) Figures do not include pregnancy-related, borderline, or pre-diabetes
Source: Centers for Disease Control and Prevention, Behaviorial Risk Factor Surveillance System, SMART: Selected Metropolitan/Micropolitan Area Risk Trends, 2012 (Note: the CDC has discontinued this dataset but will be releasing a replacement in mid-2016)

Mortality Rates for the Top 10 Causes of Death in the U.S.

ICD-10[a] Sub-Chapter	ICD-10[a] Code	Age-Adjusted Mortality Rate[1] per 100,000 population	
		County[2]	U.S.
Malignant neoplasms	C00-C97	146.3	163.6
Ischaemic heart diseases	I20-I25	81.1	102.2
Other forms of heart disease	I30-I51	40.9	50.1
Chronic lower respiratory diseases	J40-J47	24.5	41.4
Organic, including symptomatic, mental disorders	F01-F09	34.9	38.5
Cerebrovascular diseases	I60-I69	30.6	36.5
Other external causes of accidental injury	W00-X59	19.5	27.5
Other degenerative diseases of the nervous system	G30-G31	16.6	26.3
Diabetes mellitus	E10-E14	17.7	21.1
Hypertensive diseases	I10-I15	16.4	19.7

Note: (a) ICD-10 = International Classification of Diseases 10th Revision; (1) Mortality rates are a three year average covering 2012-2014; (2) Figures cover Somerset County.
Source: Centers for Disease Control and Prevention, National Center for Health Statistics. Underlying Cause of Death 1999-2014 on CDC WONDER Online Database, released 2015.

Mortality Rates for Selected Causes of Death

ICD-10[a] Sub-Chapter	ICD-10[a] Code	Age-Adjusted Mortality Rate[1] per 100,000 population	
		County[2]	U.S.
Assault	X85-Y09	Unreliable	5.1
Diseases of the liver	K70-K76	7.6	13.5
Human immunodeficiency virus (HIV) disease	B20-B24	Suppressed	2.1
Influenza and pneumonia	J09-J18	12.4	15.2
Intentional self-harm	X60-X84	6.6	12.7
Malnutrition	E40-E46	Suppressed	0.9
Obesity and other hyperalimentation	E65-E68	Unreliable	1.9
Renal failure	N17-N19	10.2	13.0
Transport accidents	V01-V99	6.2	11.6
Viral hepatitis	B15-B19	Unreliable	2.1

Note: (a) ICD-10 = International Classification of Diseases 10th Revision; (1) Mortality rates are a three year average covering 2012-2014; (2) Figures cover Somerset County; Data are Suppressed when the data meet the criteria for confidentiality constraints; Mortality rates are flagged as Unreliable when the rate would be calculated with a numerator of 20 or less.
Source: Centers for Disease Control and Prevention, National Center for Health Statistics. Underlying Cause of Death 1999-2014 on CDC WONDER Online Database, released 2015.

Health Insurance Coverage

Area	With Health Insurance	With Private Health Insurance	With Public Health Insurance	Without Health Insurance	Population Under Age 18 Without Health Insurance
City	97.9	93.0	15.0	2.1	1.2
MSA[1]	87.7	65.3	31.8	12.3	4.4
U.S.	85.8	65.8	31.1	14.2	7.1

Note: Figures are percentages that cover the civilian noninstitutionalized population; (1) Figures cover the New York-Newark-Jersey City, NY-NJ-PA Metropolitan Statistical Area—see Appendix B for areas included
Source: U.S. Census Bureau, 2010-2014 American Community Survey 5-Year Estimates

Number of Medical Professionals

Area	MDs[3]	DOs[3,4]	Dentists	Podiatrists	Chiropractors	Optometrists
County[1] (number)	1,470	86	299	21	93	53
County[1] (rate[2])	443.7	26.0	89.9	6.3	28.0	15.9
U.S. (rate[2])	272.5	20.9	64.7	5.8	25.9	15.2

Note: Data as of 2014 unless noted; (1) Data covers Somerset County; (2) Rate per 100,000 population; (3) Data as of 2013 and includes all active, non-federal physicians; (4) Doctor of Osteopathic Medicine
Source: U.S. Department of Health and Human Services, Health Resources and Services Administration, Bureau of Health Professions, Area Resource File (ARF) 2014-2015

Best Hospitals

According to *U.S. News,* the Newark, NJ-PA metro area is home to two of the best hospitals in the U.S.: **Morristown Medical Center** (4 specialties); **Kessler Institute for Rehabilitation** (1 specialty). The hospitals listed were nationally ranked in at least one adult specialty. Only 137 hospitals nationwide were nationally ranked in one or more specialties. Fifteen hospitals in the U.S. made the Honor Roll with high scores in at least six specialties. *U.S. News Online, "America's Best Children's Hospitals 2015-16"*

EDUCATION

Public School District Statistics

District Name	Schls	Pupils	Pupil/ Teacher Ratio	Minority Pupils[1] (%)	Free Lunch Eligible[2] (%)	IEP[3] (%)
Bernards Township Public Schools	6	5,761	12.6	29.6	1.2	14.0

Note: Table includes school districts with 100 or more students; (1) Percentage of students that are not non-Hispanic white; (2) Percentage of students that are eligible for the free lunch program; (3) Percentage of students that have an Individualized Education Program.

Source: U.S. Department of Education, National Center for Education Statistics, Common Core of Data, Local Education Agency (School District) Universe Survey: School Year 2013-2014; U.S. Department of Education, National Center for Education Statistics, Common Core of Data, Public Elementary/Secondary School Universe Survey: School Year 2013-2014

Best High Schools

According to *U.S. News,* Bernards is home to one of the best high schools in the U.S.: **Bernards High School** (#478); Nearly 20,000 schools were ranked based on their performance on state assessments and how well they prepare students for college. Schools with the highest unrounded College Readiness Index values were numerically ranked from No. 1 to No. 500 and were the gold medal winners. *U.S. News & World Report, "Best High Schools 2015"*

Highest Level of Education

Area	Less than H.S.	H.S. Diploma	Some College, No Deg.	Associate Degree	Bachelor's Degree	Master's Degree	Prof. School Degree	Doctorate Degree
City	2.6	11.2	10.5	5.2	36.0	24.4	6.4	3.8
MSA[1]	14.9	25.9	15.7	6.6	21.7	10.9	3.0	1.4
U.S.	13.7	28.0	21.2	7.9	18.3	7.8	2.0	1.3

Note: Figures cover persons age 25 and over; (1) Figures cover the New York-Newark-Jersey City, NY-NJ-PA Metropolitan Statistical Area—see Appendix B for areas included

Source: U.S. Census Bureau, 2010-2014 American Community Survey 5-Year Estimates

Educational Attainment by Race

Area	High School Graduate or Higher (%)					Bachelor's Degree or Higher (%)				
	Total	White	Black	Asian	Hisp.[2]	Total	White	Black	Asian	Hisp.[2]
City	97.4	97.7	89.2	97.0	96.3	70.6	68.9	40.6	84.1	77.9
MSA[1]	85.1	89.6	83.0	82.5	67.7	37.0	41.9	22.5	52.7	16.7
U.S.	86.3	88.4	83.2	85.8	64.1	29.3	30.6	19.0	50.9	13.9

Note: Figures shown cover persons 25 years old and over; (1) Figures cover the New York-Newark-Jersey City, NY-NJ-PA Metropolitan Statistical Area—see Appendix B for areas included; (2) People of Hispanic origin can be of any race

Source: U.S. Census Bureau, 2010-2014 American Community Survey 5-Year Estimates

School Enrollment by Grade and Control

Area	Preschool (%)		Kindergarten (%)		Grades 1 - 4 (%)		Grades 5 - 8 (%)		Grades 9 - 12 (%)	
	Public	Private	Public	Private	Public	Private	Public	Private	Public	Private
City	39.0	61.0	88.9	11.1	89.3	10.7	92.8	7.2	85.3	14.7
MSA[1]	50.3	49.7	81.7	18.3	86.3	13.7	86.5	13.5	86.1	13.9
U.S.	57.4	42.6	87.8	12.2	89.8	10.2	89.9	10.1	90.6	9.4

Note: Figures shown cover persons 3 years old and over; (1) Figures cover the New York-Newark-Jersey City, NY-NJ-PA Metropolitan Statistical Area—see Appendix B for areas included

Source: U.S. Census Bureau, 2010-2014 American Community Survey 5-Year Estimates

Average Salaries of Public School Classroom Teachers

Area	2013-14 Dollars	2013-14 Rank[1]	2014-15 Dollars	2014-15 Rank[1]	Percent Change 2013-14 to 2014-15	Percent Change 2004-05 to 2014-15
New Jersey	68,238	6	69,038	6	1.17	22.2
U.S. Average	56,610	–	57,379	–	1.36	20.8

Note: (1) State rank ranges from 1 to 51 where 1 indicates highest salary.
Source: National Education Association, Rankings & Estimates: Rankings of the States 2014 and Estimates of School Statistics 2015, March 2015

Higher Education

Four-Year Colleges			Two-Year Colleges			Medical Schools[1]	Law Schools[2]	Voc/ Tech[3]
Public	Private Non-profit	Private For-profit	Public	Private Non-profit	Private For-profit			
0	0	0	0	0	0	0	0	0

Note: Figures cover institutions located within the city limits and include main campuses only; (1) includes schools accredited by the Liaison Committee on Medical Education and the American Osteopathic Association's Commission on Osteopathic College Accreditation; (2) includes ABA-accredited schools, schools with provisional ABA accreditation, and state accredited schools; (3) includes all schools with programs that are less than 2 years.
Source: National Center for Education Statistics, Integrated Postsecondary Education System (IPEDS), 2014-15; Association of American Medical Colleges, Member List, March 21, 2016; American Osteopathic Association, Member List, March 21, 2016; Law School Admission Council, Official Guide to ABA-Approved Law Schools Online, March 21, 2016; Wikipedia, List of Medical Schools in the United States, March 21, 2016; Wikipedia, List of Law Schools in the United States, March 21, 2016

According to *U.S. News & World Report,* the Newark, NJ-PA metro division is home to three of the best national universities in the U.S.: **Seton Hall University** (#123 tie); **New Jersey Institute of Technology** (#140 tie); **Rutgers, The State University of New Jersey–New Brunswick** (#140 tie). The indicators used to capture academic quality fall into a number of categories: assessment by administrators at peer institutions; retention of students; faculty resources; student selectivity; financial resources; alumni giving; high school counselor ratings of colleges; and graduation rate. *U.S. News & World Report, "America's Best Colleges 2016"*

According to *U.S. News & World Report,* the Newark, NJ-PA metro division is home to one of the best liberal arts colleges in the U.S.: **Drew University** (#112 tie). The indicators used to capture academic quality fall into a number of categories: assessment by administrators at peer institutions; retention of students; faculty resources; student selectivity; financial resources; alumni giving; high school counselor ratings of colleges; and graduation rate. *U.S. News & World Report, "America's Best Colleges 2016"*

According to *U.S. News & World Report,* the Newark, NJ-PA metro division is home to two of the top 100 law schools in the U.S.: **Seton Hall University, School of Law** (#65 tie); **Rutgers, The State University of New Jersey** (#92 tie). The rankings are based on a weighted average of 12 measures of quality: peer assessment score; assessment score by lawyers/judges; median LSAT scores; median undergrad GPA; acceptance rate; employment rates for graduates; placement success; bar passage rate; faculty resources; expenditures per student; student/faculty ratio; and library resources. *U.S. News & World Report, "America's Best Graduate Schools, Law, 2017"*

According to *U.S. News & World Report,* the Newark, NJ-PA metro division is home to one of the top 75 medical schools for research in the U.S.: **Rutgers New Jersey Medical School–Newark, New Jersey Medical School** (#73 tie). The rankings are based on a weighted average of 11 measures of quality: quality assessment; peer assessment score; assessment score by residency directors; research activity; total research activity; average research activity per faculty member; student selectivity; median MCAT total score; median undergraduate GPA; acceptance rate; and faculty resources. *U.S. News & World Report, "America's Best Graduate Schools, Medical, 2017"*

According to *U.S. News & World Report,* the Newark, NJ-PA metro division is home to one of the top 75 business schools in the U.S.: **The State University of New Jersey–Newark and New Brunswick, Rutgers Business School** (#53 tie). The rankings are based on a weighted average of the following nine measures: quality assessment; peer assessment; recruiter assessment; placement success; mean starting salary and bonus; student selectivity; mean GMAT and GRE scores; mean undergraduate GPA; and acceptance rate. *U.S. News & World Report, "America's Best Graduate Schools, Business, 2017"*

PRESIDENTIAL ELECTION

2012 Presidential Election Results

Area	Obama (%)	Romney (%)	Other (%)
Somerset County	52.0	46.8	1.2
U.S.	51.0	47.2	1.8

Note: Results may not add to 100% due to rounding
Source: Dave Leip's Atlas of U.S. Presidential Elections

EMPLOYERS

Major Employers

Company Name	Industry
American Express Company	Personal credit institutions
American International Group	Life insurance
Deloitte Consulting	Management consulting services
Hackensack University Medical Center	University
Merrill Lynch and Co	Security brokers & dealers
Mount Sinai Hospital	General medical & surgical hospitals
Mount Sinai School of Medicine	Medical training services
NewYork-Presbyterian Hospital	General medical & surgical hospitals
NYC Health and Hospitals Corp	Psychiatric hospitals
NYU School of Medicine	Offices & clinics of medical doctors
Paramount Comm Acq Corp	Investment holding companies, except banks
Patriarch Partners	Investment offices
Rutgers, The State Univ of NJ	Colleges & universities
Standard Americas	Agencies of foreign banks
The Long Island Rail Road Company	Local & suburban transit
U of Med and Dentistry of NJ	Colleges & universities
UMASS Memorial Health Care	Psychiatrist
United States Postal Service	U.s. postal service
Wellchoice	Health insurance carriers

Note: Companies shown are located within the New York-Newark-Jersey City, NY-NJ-PA Metropolitan Statistical Area.
Source: Hoovers.com; Wikipedia

PUBLIC SAFETY

Crime Rate

Area	All Crimes	Violent Crimes: Murder	Violent Crimes: Rape[3]	Violent Crimes: Robbery	Violent Crimes: Aggrav. Assault	Property Crimes: Burglary	Property Crimes: Larceny -Theft	Property Crimes: Motor Vehicle Theft
City	544.8	0.0	14.8	3.7	3.7	122.3	385.5	14.8
Metro[1]	1,910.7	5.8	10.9	175.5	123.9	330.2	1,032.3	232.1
U.S.	2,961.6	4.5	26.4	102.2	232.5	542.5	1,837.3	216.2

Note: Figures are crimes per 100,000 population; (1) Figures cover the Newark, NJ-PA Metropolitan Division—see Appendix B for areas included; (3) The city and U.S. figures shown were reported using the legacy Uniform Crime Reporting (UCR) definition of rape. The suburban and metro area figures shown are an aggregate total of the data submitted using both the revised and legacy UCR definitions.
Source: FBI Uniform Crime Reports, 2014

Hate Crimes

Area	Number of Quarters Reported	Race	Religion	Sexual Orientation	Ethnicity	Disability	Gender	Gender Identity
		Number of Incidents per Bias Motivation						
City	4	0	0	0	0	0	0	0
U.S.	4	2,568	1,014	1,017	648	84	33	98

Source: Federal Bureau of Investigation, Hate Crime Statistics 2014

Identity Theft Consumer Complaints

Area	Complaints	Complaints per 100,000 Population	Rank[2]
MSA[1]	27,397	136.4	77
U.S.	490,220	152.4	-

Note: (1) Figures cover the New York-Newark-Jersey City, NY-NJ-PA Metropolitan Statistical Area—see Appendix B for areas included; (2) Rank ranges from 1 to 379 where 1 indicates greatest number of identity theft complaints per 100,000 population
Source: Federal Trade Commission, Consumer Sentinel Network Data Book for January–December 2015

Fraud and Other Consumer Complaints

Area	Complaints	Complaints per 100,000 Population	Rank[2]
MSA[1]	74,212	369.3	172
U.S.	2,593,159	806.0	-

Note: (1) Figures cover the New York-Newark-Jersey City, NY-NJ-PA Metropolitan Statistical Area—see Appendix B for areas included; (2) Rank ranges from 1 to 379 where 1 indicates greatest number of identity theft complaints per 100,000 population
Source: Federal Trade Commission, Consumer Sentinel Network Data Book for January–December 2015

RECREATION

Culture

Dance[1]	Theatre[1]	Instrumental Music[1]	Vocal Music[1]	Series and Festivals	Museums and Art Galleries[2]	Zoos and Aquariums[3]
0	0	0	0	0	0	0

Note: (1) Professional perfoming groups; (2) Based on organizations with SIC code 8412; (3) AZA-accredited
Source: The Grey House Performing Arts Directory, 2015-16; Association of Zoos & Aquariums, AZA Member Zoos & Aquariums, March 25, 2016; www.AccuLeads.com, March 29, 2016

Professional Sports Teams

Team Name	League	Year Established
Brooklyn Nets	National Basketball Association (NBA)	1967
New Jersey Devils	National Hockey League (NHL)	1982
New York City FC	Major League Soccer (MLS)	2015
New York Giants	National Football League (NFL)	1925
New York Islanders	National Hockey League (NHL)	1972
New York Jets	National Football League (NFL)	1960
New York Knicks	National Basketball Association (NBA)	1946
New York Mets	Major League Baseball (MLB)	1962
New York Rangers	National Hockey League (NHL)	1926
New York Red Bulls	Major League Soccer (MLS)	1996
New York Yankees	Major League Baseball (MLB)	1903

Note: Includes teams located in the New York-Newark-Jersey City, NY-NJ-PA Metropolitan Statistical Area.
Source: Wikipedia, Major Professional Sports Teams of the United States and Canada, March 24, 2016

CLIMATE

Average and Extreme Temperatures

Temperature	Jan	Feb	Mar	Apr	May	Jun	Jul	Aug	Sep	Oct	Nov	Dec	Yr.
Extreme High (°F)	74	76	89	94	98	102	105	103	105	93	85	72	105
Average High (°F)	38	41	50	61	72	81	86	84	77	66	54	42	63
Average Temp. (°F)	32	33	42	52	63	72	77	76	68	57	47	36	55
Average Low (°F)	24	25	33	43	53	62	68	67	59	48	39	28	46
Extreme Low (°F)	-8	-7	6	16	33	41	52	45	35	25	15	-1	-8

Note: Figures cover the years 1935-1995
Source: National Climatic Data Center, International Station Meteorological Climate Summary, 9/96

Average Precipitation/Snowfall/Humidity

Precip./Humidity	Jan	Feb	Mar	Apr	May	Jun	Jul	Aug	Sep	Oct	Nov	Dec	Yr.
Avg. Precip. (in.)	3.4	3.0	4.0	3.7	3.9	3.3	4.2	4.1	3.6	3.0	3.8	3.4	43.5
Avg. Snowfall (in.)	8	8	5	1	Tr	0	0	0	0	Tr	1	5	27
Avg. Rel. Hum. 7am (%)	73	71	69	67	70	71	72	76	79	78	76	74	73
Avg. Rel. Hum. 4pm (%)	58	54	51	48	51	51	52	54	55	53	57	59	54

Note: Figures cover the years 1935-1995; Tr = Trace amounts (<0.05 in. of rain; <0.5 in. of snow)
Source: National Climatic Data Center, International Station Meteorological Climate Summary, 9/96

Weather Conditions

Temperature			Daytime Sky			Precipitation		
5°F & below	32°F & below	90°F & above	Clear	Partly cloudy	Cloudy	0.01 inch or more precip.	0.1 inch or more snow/ice	Thunder-storms
2	90	24	80	146	139	122	16	46

Note: Figures are average number of days per year and cover the years 1935-1995
Source: National Climatic Data Center, International Station Meteorological Climate Summary, 9/96

HAZARDOUS WASTE

Superfund Sites

Bernards has no sites on the EPA's Superfund Final National Priorities List. There are a total of 1,323 Superfund sites on the list in the U.S. *U.S. Environmental Protection Agency, Final National Priorities List, March 18, 2016*

AIR & WATER QUALITY

Air Quality Trends: Ozone

	1990	1995	2000	2005	2010	2011	2012	2013	2014
MSA[1]	0.101	0.107	0.091	0.092	0.082	0.082	0.080	0.072	0.069

Note: (1) Data covers the New York-Newark-Jersey City, NY-NJ-PA Metropolitan Statistical Area—see Appendix B for areas included. The values shown are the composite ozone concentration averages among trend sites based on the highest fourth daily maximum 8-hour concentration in parts per million. These trends are based on sites having an adequate record of monitoring data during the trend period. Data from exceptional events are included.
Source: U.S. Environmental Protection Agency, Air Quality Monitoring Information, "Air Quality Trends by City, 1990-2014"

Air Quality Index

Area	Percent of Days when Air Quality was...[2]					AQI Statistics[2]	
	Good	Moderate	Unhealthy for Sensitive Groups	Unhealthy	Very Unhealthy	Maximum	Median
MSA[1]	41.4	52.6	6.0	0.0	0.0	142	54

Note: (1) Data covers the New York-Newark-Jersey City, NY-NJ-PA Metropolitan Statistical Area—see Appendix B for areas included; (2) Based on 365 days with AQI data in 2015. Air Quality Index (AQI) is an index for reporting daily air quality. EPA calculates the AQI for five major air pollutants regulated by the Clean Air Act: ground-level ozone, particle pollution (aka particulate matter), carbon monoxide, sulfur dioxide, and nitrogen dioxide. The AQI runs from 0 to 500. The higher the AQI value, the greater the level of air pollution and the greater the health concern. There are six AQI categories: "Good" AQI is between 0 and 50. Air quality is considered satisfactory; "Moderate" AQI is between 51 and 100. Air quality is acceptable; "Unhealthy for Sensitive Groups" When AQI values are between 101 and 150, members of sensitive groups may experience health effects; "Unhealthy" When AQI values are between 151 and 200 everyone may begin to experience health effects; "Very Unhealthy" AQI values between 201 and 300 trigger a health alert; "Hazardous" AQI values over 300 trigger warnings of emergency conditions (not shown).
Source: U.S. Environmental Protection Agency, Air Quality Index Report, 2015

Air Quality Index Pollutants

Area	Percent of Days when AQI Pollutant was...[2]					
	Carbon Monoxide	Nitrogen Dioxide	Ozone	Sulfur Dioxide	Particulate Matter 2.5	Particulate Matter 10
MSA[1]	0.0	14.5	33.2	0.3	52.1	0.0

Note: (1) Data covers the New York-Newark-Jersey City, NY-NJ-PA Metropolitan Statistical Area—see Appendix B for areas included; (2) Based on 365 days with AQI data in 2015. The Air Quality Index (AQI) is an index for reporting daily air quality. EPA calculates the AQI for five major air pollutants regulated by the Clean Air Act: ground-level ozone, particle pollution (also known as particulate matter), carbon monoxide, sulfur dioxide, and nitrogen dioxide. The AQI runs from 0 to 500. The higher the AQI value, the greater the level of air pollution and the greater the health concern.
Source: U.S. Environmental Protection Agency, Air Quality Index Report, 2015

Maximum Air Pollutant Concentrations: Particulate Matter, Ozone, CO and Lead

	Particulate Matter 10 (ug/m^3)	Particulate Matter 2.5 Wtd AM (ug/m^3)	Particulate Matter 2.5 24-Hr (ug/m^3)	Ozone (ppm)	Carbon Monoxide (ppm)	Lead (ug/m^3)
MSA[1] Level	47	10.5	31	0.074	3	n/a
NAAQS[2]	150	15	35	0.075	9	0.15
Met NAAQS[2]	Yes	Yes	Yes	Yes	Yes	n/a

Note: (1) Data covers the New York-Newark-Jersey City, NY-NJ-PA Metropolitan Statistical Area—see Appendix B for areas included; Data from exceptional events are included; (2) National Ambient Air Quality Standards; ppm = parts per million; ug/m^3 = micrograms per cubic meter; n/a not available.
Concentrations: Particulate Matter 10 (coarse particulate)—highest second maximum 24-hour concentration; Particulate Matter 2.5 Wtd AM (fine particulate)—highest weighted annual mean concentration; Particulate Matter 2.5 24-Hour (fine particulate)—highest 98th percentile 24-hour concentration; Ozone—highest fourth daily maximum 8-hour concentration; Carbon Monoxide—highest second maximum non-overlapping 8-hour concentration; Lead—maximum running 3-month average
Source: U.S. Environmental Protection Agency, Air Quality Monitoring Information, "Air Quality Statistics by City, 2014"

Maximum Air Pollutant Concentrations: Nitrogen Dioxide and Sulfur Dioxide

	Nitrogen Dioxide AM (ppb)	Nitrogen Dioxide 1-Hr (ppb)	Sulfur Dioxide AM (ppb)	Sulfur Dioxide 1-Hr (ppb)	Sulfur Dioxide 24-Hr (ppb)
MSA[1] Level	22	70	n/a	15	n/a
NAAQS[2]	53	100	30	75	140
Met NAAQS[2]	Yes	Yes	n/a	Yes	n/a

Note: (1) Data covers the New York-Newark-Jersey City, NY-NJ-PA Metropolitan Statistical Area—see Appendix B for areas included; Data from exceptional events are included; (2) National Ambient Air Quality Standards; ppm = parts per million; ug/m^3 = micrograms per cubic meter; n/a not available.
Concentrations: Nitrogen Dioxide AM—highest arithmetic mean concentration; Nitrogen Dioxide 1-Hr—highest 98th percentile 1-hour daily maximum concentration; Sulfur Dioxide AM—highest annual mean concentration; Sulfur Dioxide 1-Hr—highest 99th percentile 1-hour daily maximum concentration; Sulfur Dioxide 24-Hr—highest second maximum 24-hour concentration
Source: U.S. Environmental Protection Agency, Air Quality Monitoring Information, "Air Quality Statistics by City, 2014"

Drinking Water

Water System Name	Pop. Served	Primary Water Source Type	Violations[1]	
			Health Based	Monitoring/ Reporting
NJ American Water Co.-Short Hills	217,230	Surface	0	2

Note: (1) Based on violation data from January 1, 2015 to December 31, 2015 (includes unresolved violations from earlier years)
Source: U.S. Environmental Protection Agency, Office of Ground Water and Drinking Water, Safe Drinking Water Information System (based on data extracted April 29, 2016)

Evesham, New Jersey

Background

Evensham is located in Burlington County, 13 miles southwest of Camden and 17 miles southwest of Philadelphia. The city borders Mount Laurel, Medford, and Camden County.

Present-day Evesham was settled by Quakers in 1672 and probably named for a town in England of the same name. The city was divided twice in its history, in 1847 and 1872, creating Medford and Mount Laurel, respectively. In 1955, the United States Army opened the PH-32 Nike Ajax facility in Evesham, one of 12 facilities intended to shield Philadelphia from an aerial assault during the Cold War. The facility was decommissioned in the mid-1960s and is currently used as a civil defense center. It is also the site of an upscale housing development.

The commercial center of Evesham is the historic Marlton Village, easily accessible from routes 70 and 73. This center offers businesses modern office space and upscale shopping, while still maintaining its old-time beauty.

Each fall, Evesham hosts the Olde Marlton Fall Festival, which features arts, crafts, food, and live entertainment in the city's historic downtown. Another major attraction in Evesham is the Indian Spring Country Club, with a 141-acre, 18-hole public golf course established in 1952.

A 14,000-square foot office building in the Evesham Corporate Center industrial park, is home to Lot Two, LLC, and the Elmwood Village Office Center along Route 70. More exciting to some than office space, however, is the state sponsored bikeway transportation system in the planning stages.

Evesham has a moderate climate with hot summers and cold winters. Median summer temperatures average 70 degrees, while winter averages are as low as 35 degrees during of December and January. The city averages 4.5 inches of rainfall per month from April to August and 6 inches of snowfall per month from December to March.

Rankings

Business/Finance Rankings

- The personal finance site NerdWallet analyzed 183 American metropolitan areas with populations over 250,000 and more than 15,000 businesses to rank where entrepreneurs find the most success. Criteria included area economy, annual income, housing cost, unemployment rate, and the success rate of area businesses. Camden* ranked #60. *www.nerdwallet.com, "Best Places to Start a Business," April 27, 2015*
- Based on metro area social media reviews, the employment opinion group Glassdoor surveyed 50 of the largest U.S. metro areas and equally weighed cost of living, hiring opportunity, and job satisfaction to compose a list of "25 Best Cities for Jobs." The Philadelphia* metro area was ranked #39 in overall job satisfaction. *www.glassdoor.com, "Best Cities for Jobs," May 19, 2015*
- In a survey of economic confidence in the nation's 50 largest metropolitan areas conducted January–December 2014, the Philadelphia* metro area placed #33, according to Gallup's 2014 Economic Confidence Index. *Gallup, "San Jose and San Francisco Lead in Economic Confidence," March 19, 2015*
- The Brookings Institution ranked the 100 largest metro areas in the U.S. based on income inequality. Philadelphia* was ranked #15 (#1 = greatest ineqality). Criteria: the "95/20 ratio," a figure representing the income at which a household earns more than 95 percent of all other households, divided by the income at which a household earns more than only 20 percent of all other households. *Brookings Institution, "Income Inequality, 100 Largest U.S. Metro Areas, 2007-2014," January 14, 2016*
- Payscale.com ranked the 20 largest metro areas in terms of wage growth. The Philadelphia* metro area ranked #15. Criteria: private-sector wage growth between the 1st quarter of 2015 and the 1st quarter of 2016. *PayScale, "Wage Trends by Metro Area," 1st Quarter, 2016*
- Philadelphia* was identified as one of America's most frugal metro areas by *Coupons.com.* The city ranked #14 out of 25. Criteria: online coupon usage. *Coupons.com, "Top 25 Most Frugal Cities of 2014," May 11, 2015*
- Philadelphia* was identified as one of America's most frugal metro areas by *Coupons.com.* The city ranked #12 out of 25. Criteria: Grocery IQ and coupons.com mobile app usage. *Coupons.com, "Top 25 Most On-the-Go Frugal Cities of 2013," April 10, 2014*
- The Camden* metro area appeared on the Milken Institute "2015 Best Performing Cities" list. Rank: #169 out of 200 large metro areas. Criteria: job growth; wage and salary growth; high-tech output growth. *Milken Institute, "Best-Performing Cities 2015," December 2015*
- *Forbes* ranked the 200 most populous metro areas to determine the nation's "Best Places for Business and Careers." The Camden* metro area was ranked #171. Criteria: costs (business and living); job growth (past and projected); income growth; educational attainment (college and high school); projected economic growth; cultural and recreational opportunities; net migration patterns; number of highly ranked colleges. *Forbes, "The Best Places for Business and Careers 2015," July 29, 2015*

Dating/Romance Rankings

- CreditDonkey, a financial education website, sought out the ten best U.S. cities for newlyweds, considering the number of married couples, divorce rate, average credit score, and average number of hours worked per week in metro areas with a million or more residents. The Philadelphia* metro area placed #6. *www.creditdonkey.com, "Study: Best Cities for Newlyweds," November 30, 2013*

Education Rankings

- Personal finance website *WalletHub* analyzed the 150 largest U.S. metropolitan statistical areas to determine where the most educated Americans are choosing to settle. Criteria: education quality and attainment gap; education levels; percentage of workers with degrees; public school rankings; quality and size of each metro area's universities. Philadelphia* was ranked #49 (#1 = most educated city). *www.WalletHub.com, "2015's Most and Least Educated Cities*

Environmental Rankings

- The Philadelphia* metro area came in at #196 for the relative comfort of its climate on Sperling's list of "chill cities," as measured by the Sperling Heat Index. All 361 metro areas are included. Criteria included daytime high temperatures, nighttime low temperatures, dew point, and relative humidity at the high temperatures. *www.bertsperling.com, "Sperling's Chill Cities," July 18, 2013*

- Sperling's BestPlaces assessed 379 metropolitan areas of the United States for the likelihood of dangerously extreme weather events or earthquakes. In general the Southeast and South-Central regions have the highest risk of weather extremes and earthquakes, while the Pacific Northwest enjoys the lowest risk. Of the least risky metropolitan areas, the Camden* metro area was ranked #331. *www.bestplaces.net, "Safest Places from Natural Disasters," April 2011*

- Philadelphia* was identified as one of America's dirtiest metro areas by *Forbes*. The area ranked #3 out of 20. Criteria: air quality; water quality; toxic releases; superfund sites. *Forbes, "America's 20 Dirtiest Cities," December 10, 2012*

- The U.S. Environmental Protection Agency (EPA) released a list of U.S. metropolitan areas with the most ENERGY STAR certified buildings in 2015. The Philadelphia* metro area was ranked #12 out of 25. *U.S. Environmental Protection Agency, "Top Cities With the Most ENERGY STAR Certified Buildings in 2016," March 30, 2016*

- Philadelphia* was highlighted as one of the 25 metro areas most polluted by year-round particle pollution (Annual PM 2.5) in the U.S. during 2011 through 2013. The area ranked #11. *American Lung Association, State of the Air 2015*

- Philadelphia* was highlighted as one of the 25 metro areas most polluted by short-term particle pollution (24-hour PM 2.5) in the U.S. during 2011 through 2013. The area ranked #22. *American Lung Association, State of the Air 2015*

Health/Fitness Rankings

- For each of the 50 most populous metro areas in the United States, the American College of Sports Medicine's American Fitness Index evaluated infrastructure, community assets, and policies that encourage healthy and fit lifestyles, including preventive health behaviors, levels of chronic disease conditions, health care access, and community resources and policies that support physical activity. The Philadelphia* metro area ranked #22 for "community fitness." *www.americanfitnessindex.org, "ACSM American Fitness Index Health and Community Fitness Status of the 50 Largest Metropolitan Areas," May 2015*

- *Business Insider* reported Trulia's analysis of the 100 largest U.S. metro areas to identify the nation's best cities for weight loss, based on healthful food options, access to outdoor activities, weight-loss centers, gyms, and opportunities to bike or walk to work. Philadelphia* ranked #8. *Businessinsider.com, "These Are the Best US Cities for Weight loss," January 17, 2013*

- The Philadelphia* metro area was identified as one of the worst cities for bed bugs in America by pest control company Orkin. The area ranked #6 out of 50 based on the number of bed bug treatments Orkin performed from January to December 2015. *Orkin, "Chicago Tops Bed Bug Cities List for Fourth Year in a Row," January 13, 2016*

- Philadelphia* was identified as a "2016 Spring Allergy Capital." The area ranked #21 out of 100. Three groups of factors were used to identify the most severe cities for people with allergies during the spring season: annual pollen levels; medicine utilization; access to board-certified allergists. *Asthma and Allergy Foundation of America, "Spring Allergy Capitals 2016"*

- Philadelphia* was identified as a "2015 Asthma Capital." The area ranked #3 out of the nation's 100 largest metropolitan areas. Criteria: estimated prevalence; self-reported prevalence; crude death rate for asthma; annual pollen score; annual air quality; public smoking laws; number of board-certified asthma specialists; school inhaler access laws; rescue medication use; controller medication use; ER visits for asthma; uninsured rate; poverty rate. *Asthma and Allergy Foundation of America, "Asthma Capitals 2015"*
- The Philadelphia* metro area ranked #131 out of 190 in The Gallup-Healthways Well-Being Index. Criteria: purpose; social well being; financial health; community and physical health. Results are based on telephone interviews with adults, aged 18 and older, living in metropolitan areas in the 50 U.S. states and the District of Columbia. *Gallup-Healthways, "State of American Well-Being," February 23, 2016*

Real Estate Rankings

- Camden* was ranked #70 out of 225 metro areas in terms of housing affordability in 2015 by the National Association of Home Builders (#1 = most affordable). Criteria: the share of homes sold in that area affordable to a family earning the local median income, based on standard mortgage underwriting criteria. *National Association of Home Builders®, NAHB-Wells Fargo Housing Opportunity Index, 4th Quarter 2015*
- The nation's largest metro areas were analyzed in terms of the percentage of households entering some stage of foreclosure in 2015. The Philadelphia* metro area ranked #19 out of 20 (#1 = highest foreclosure rate). *RealtyTrac, "2015 Year-End U.S. Foreclosure Market Report™," January 12, 2016*

Safety Rankings

- The National Insurance Crime Bureau ranked 380 metro areas in the U.S. in terms of per capita rates of vehicle theft. The Philadelphia* metro area ranked #158 (#1 = highest rate). Criteria: number of vehicle theft offenses per 100,000 inhabitants in 2014. *National Insurance Crime Bureau, "Hot Spots 2014," June 24, 2015*

Seniors/Retirement Rankings

- From its Best Cities for Successful Aging indexes, the Milken Institute generated rankings for metropolitan areas, weighing data in eight categories—health care, wellness, living arrangements, transportation, financial characteristics, education and employment opportunities, community engagement, and overall livability. The Philadelphia* metro area was ranked #57 overall in the large metro area category. *Milken Institute, "Best Cities for Successful Aging, 2014"*

Sports/Recreation Rankings

- According to the personal finance website NerdWallet, the Philadelphia* metro area, at #10, is one of the nation's top dozen metro areas for sports fans. Criteria included the presence of all four major sports—MLB, NFL, NHL, and NBA, fan enthusiasm (as measured by game attendance), ticket affordability, and "sports culture," that is, number of sports bars. *www.nerdwallet.com, "Best Cities for Sports Fans," May 5, 2013*

Transportation Rankings

- The Philadelphia* metro area appeared on *Forbes* list of places with the most extreme commutes. The metro area ranked #9 out of 10. Criteria: average travel time; percentage of mega commuters. Mega-commuters travel more than 90 minutes and 50 miles each way to work. *Forbes.com, "The Cities with the Most Extreme Commutes," March 5, 2013*

Miscellaneous Rankings

- The watchdog site Charity Navigator conducts an annual study of charities in the nation's major markets both to analyze statistical differences in their financial, accountability, and transparency practices and to track year-to-year variations in individual communities. The Philadelphia* metro area was ranked #26 among the 30 metro markets in the rating dimension of Overall Score. *www.charitynavigator.org, "Metro Market Study 2015," June 5, 2015*

- The Harris Poll's Happiness Index survey revealed that of the top ten U.S. markets, the Philadelphia* metro area residents ranked #3 in happiness. Criteria included strong assent to positive statements and strong disagreement with negative ones, and degree of agreement with a series of statements about respondents' personal relationships and general outlook. *www.harrisinteractive.com, "Dallas/Fort Worth Is "Happiest" City among America's Top Ten Markets," September 4, 2013*

- Energizer Personal Care, the makers of Edge® shave gel, in partnership with Sperling's BestPlaces, ranked 50 major metro areas in terms of everyday irritations. The Philadelphia* metro area ranked #4 the 50 metro area most iritating to guys. Criteria: high male-to-female ratio; poor sports team performance and high ticket prices; slow traffic; lack of job availability; unaffordable housing; extreme weather; lack of nightlife and fitness options. *Energizer Personal Care, "Most Irritatng Cities for Guys," August 26, 2013*

- Mars Chocolate North America, the makers of COMBOS®, in partnership with Sperling's BestPlaces, ranked 50 major metro areas in terms of their "manliness." The Philadelphia* metro area ranked #29. Criteria: number of professional sports teams; number of nearby NASCAR tracks and racing events; manly lifestyle; concentration of manly retail stores; manly occupations per capita; salty snack sales; "Board of Manliness" rankings. *Mars Chocolate North America, "America's Manliest Cities 2012"*

- The Camden* metro area was selected as one of "America's Most Miserable Cities" by *Forbes.com.* The metro area ranked #13 out of 20. Criteria: violent crime; unemployment; foreclosures; income and property taxes; home prices; commute times; climate. *Forbes.com, "America's Most Miserable Cities" February 22, 2013*

- The National Alliance to End Homelessness ranked the 100 most populous metro areas with the highest rate of homelessness. The Philadelphia* metro area ranked #27. Criteria: number of homeless people per 10,000 population in 2011. *National Alliance to End Homelessness, The State of Homelessness in America 2012*

Evesham is located within the Philadelphia-Camden-Wilmington, PA-NJ-DE-MD Metropolitan Statistical Area and the Camden, NJ Metropolitan Division.

Business Environment

CITY FINANCES

City Government Finances

Component	2012 ($000)	2012 ($ per capita)
Total Revenues	49,690	1,091
Total Expenditures	42,058	923
Debt Outstanding	86,658	1,902
Cash and Securities[1]	39,165	860

Note: (1) Cash and security holdings of a government at the close of its fiscal year, including those of its dependent agencies, utilities, and liquor stores.
Source: U.S Census Bureau, State & Local Government Finances 2012

City Government Revenue by Source

Source	2012 ($000)	2012 ($ per capita)
General Revenue		
From Federal Government	5	0
From State Government	3,565	78
From Local Governments	635	13
Taxes		
Property	22,961	504
Sales and Gross Receipts	545	11
Personal Income	0	0
Corporate Income	0	0
Motor Vehicle License	0	0
Other Taxes	730	16
Current Charges	12,342	271
Liquor Store	0	0
Utility	5,939	130
Employee Retirement	0	0

Source: U.S Census Bureau, State & Local Government Finances 2012

City Government Expenditures by Function

Function	2012 ($000)	2012 ($ per capita)	2012 (%)
General Direct Expenditures			
Air Transportation	0	0	0.0
Corrections	0	0	0.0
Education	0	0	0.0
Employment Security Administration	0	0	0.0
Financial Administration	971	21	2.3
Fire Protection	14	< 1	< 0.1
General Public Buildings	337	7	0.8
Governmental Administration, Other	828	18	1.9
Health	60	1	0.1
Highways	1,653	36	3.9
Hospitals	0	0	0.0
Housing and Community Development	65	1	0.1
Interest on General Debt	3,358	73	7.9
Judicial and Legal	521	11	1.2
Libraries	0	0	0.0
Parking	0	0	0.0
Parks and Recreation	1,736	38	4.1
Police Protection	7,575	166	18.0
Public Welfare	0	0	0.0
Sewerage	4,995	109	11.8
Solid Waste Management	2,715	59	6.4
Veterans' Services	0	0	0.0
Liquor Store	0	0	0.0
Utility	4,044	88	9.6
Employee Retirement	0	0	0.0

Source: U.S Census Bureau, State & Local Government Finances 2012

DEMOGRAPHICS

Population Growth

Area	1990 Census	2000 Census	2010 Census	2014* Estimate	Population Growth (%) 1990-2014	Population Growth (%) 2010-2014
City	35,309	42,275	45,538	45,669	29.3	0.3
MSA[1]	5,435,470	5,687,147	5,965,343	6,015,336	10.7	0.8
U.S.	248,709,873	281,421,906	308,745,538	314,107,084	26.3	1.7

Note: (1) Figures cover the Philadelphia-Camden-Wilmington, PA-NJ-DE-MD Metropolitan Statistical Area—see Appendix B for areas included; (*) 2010-2014 5-year estimated population
Source: U.S. Census Bureau, 1990 Census, Census 2000, Census 2010, 2010-2014 American Community Survey 5-Year Estimates

Household Size

Area	Persons in Household (%) One	Two	Three	Four	Five	Six	Seven or More	Average Household Size
City	24.0	31.4	18.9	16.8	7.1	1.2	0.4	2.64
MSA[1]	29.4	31.2	16.3	13.6	6.0	2.1	1.1	2.63
U.S.	27.5	33.5	15.8	13.1	6.0	2.3	1.4	2.64

Note: (1) Figures cover the Philadelphia-Camden-Wilmington, PA-NJ-DE-MD Metropolitan Statistical Area—see Appendix B for areas included
Source: U.S. Census Bureau, 2010-2014 American Community Survey 5-Year Estimates

Race

Area	White Alone[2] (%)	Black Alone[2] (%)	Asian Alone[2] (%)	AIAN[3] Alone[2] (%)	NHOPI[4] Alone[2] (%)	Other Race Alone[2] (%)	Two or More Races (%)
City	86.5	5.0	6.1	0.0	0.0	0.7	1.6
MSA[1]	68.1	20.9	5.3	0.2	0.0	3.1	2.3
U.S.	73.8	12.6	5.0	0.8	0.2	4.7	2.9

Note: (1) Figures cover the Philadelphia-Camden-Wilmington, PA-NJ-DE-MD Metropolitan Statistical Area—see Appendix B for areas included; (2) Alone is defined as not being in combination with one or more other races; (3) American Indian and Alaska Native; (4) Native Hawaiian and Other Pacific Islander
Source: U.S. Census Bureau, 2010-2014 American Community Survey 5-Year Estimates

Hispanic or Latino Origin

Area	Total (%)	Mexican (%)	Puerto Rican (%)	Cuban (%)	Other (%)
City	3.7	1.0	1.8	0.2	0.8
MSA[1]	8.3	1.7	4.3	0.2	2.1
U.S.	16.9	10.8	1.6	0.6	3.8

Note: Persons of Hispanic or Latino origin can be of any race; (1) Figures cover the Philadelphia-Camden-Wilmington, PA-NJ-DE-MD Metropolitan Statistical Area—see Appendix B for areas included
Source: U.S. Census Bureau, 2010-2014 American Community Survey 5-Year Estimates

Ancestry

Area	German	Irish	English	American	Italian	Polish	French[2]	Scottish	Dutch
City	19.7	27.2	8.7	3.5	24.4	7.8	2.0	1.8	1.1
MSA[1]	16.5	20.0	7.6	3.6	13.9	5.4	1.5	1.3	1.0
U.S.	14.9	10.8	8.0	7.1	5.5	3.0	2.7	1.7	1.4

Note: Figures are the percentage of the total population reporting a particular ancestry. The nine most commonly reported ancestries in the U.S. are shown. Figures include multiple ancestries (e.g. if a person reported being Irish and Italian, they were included in both columns); (1) Figures cover the Philadelphia-Camden-Wilmington, PA-NJ-DE-MD Metropolitan Statistical Area—see Appendix B for areas included; (2) Excludes Basque
Source: U.S. Census Bureau, 2010-2014 American Community Survey 5-Year Estimates

Foreign-Born Population

Area	Any Foreign Country	Asia	Mexico	Europe	Carribean	Central America[2]	South America	Africa	Canada
	Percent of Population Born in								
City	7.8	4.7	0.3	1.3	0.4	0.0	0.5	0.4	0.1
MSA[1]	9.9	4.0	0.9	1.9	1.1	0.4	0.6	0.8	0.1
U.S.	13.1	3.8	3.7	1.5	1.2	1.0	0.9	0.6	0.3

Note: (1) Figures cover the Philadelphia-Camden-Wilmington, PA-NJ-DE-MD Metropolitan Statistical Area—see Appendix B for areas included; (2) Excludes Mexico.
Source: U.S. Census Bureau, 2010-2014 American Community Survey 5-Year Estimates

Marital Status

Area	Never Married	Now Married[2]	Separated	Widowed	Divorced
City	28.7	54.9	1.2	5.9	9.3
MSA[1]	37.0	45.4	2.3	6.4	9.0
U.S.	32.5	48.4	2.2	5.9	10.9

Note: Figures are percentages and cover the population 15 years of age and older; (1) Figures cover the Philadelphia-Camden-Wilmington, PA-NJ-DE-MD Metropolitan Statistical Area—see Appendix B for areas included; (2) Excludes separated
Source: U.S. Census Bureau, 2010-2014 American Community Survey 5-Year Estimates

Disability Status

Area	All Ages	Under 18 Years Old	18 to 64 Years Old	65 Years and Over
City	7.9	3.1	4.5	31.4
MSA[1]	12.0	4.5	9.9	34.2
U.S.	12.3	4.1	10.2	36.3

Note: Figures show percent of the civilian noninstitutionalized population that reported having a disability. Disability status is determined from from six types of difficulty: vision, hearing, cognitive, ambulatory, self-care, and independent living. For children under 5 years old, hearing and vision difficulty are used to determine disability status. For children between the ages of 5 and 14, disability status is determined from hearing, vision, cognitive, ambulatory, and self-care difficulties. For people aged 15 years and older, they are considered to have a disability if they have difficulty with any one of the six difficulty types; (1) Figures cover the Philadelphia-Camden-Wilmington, PA-NJ-DE-MD Metropolitan Statistical Area—see Appendix B for areas included.
Source: U.S. Census Bureau, 2010-2014 American Community Survey 5-Year Estimates

Age

Area	Under Age 5	Age 5–19	Age 20–34	Age 35–44	Age 45–54	Age 55–64	Age 65–74	Age 75–84	Age 85+	Median Age
	Percent of Population									
City	5.0	19.5	18.0	13.7	16.7	13.0	7.2	4.5	2.3	40.7
MSA[1]	6.1	19.5	20.5	12.7	14.8	12.6	7.4	4.4	2.1	38.2
U.S.	6.4	19.9	20.6	13.0	14.1	12.3	7.6	4.3	1.9	37.4

Note: (1) Figures cover the Philadelphia-Camden-Wilmington, PA-NJ-DE-MD Metropolitan Statistical Area—see Appendix B for areas included
Source: U.S. Census Bureau, 2010-2014 American Community Survey 5-Year Estimates

Gender

Area	Males	Females	Males per 100 Females
City	22,333	23,336	95.7
MSA[1]	2,904,546	3,110,790	93.4
U.S.	154,515,159	159,591,925	96.8

Note: (1) Figures cover the Philadelphia-Camden-Wilmington, PA-NJ-DE-MD Metropolitan Statistical Area—see Appendix B for areas included
Source: U.S. Census Bureau, 2010-2014 American Community Survey 5-Year Estimates

Religious Groups by Family

Area	Catholic	Baptist	Non-Den.	Methodist[2]	Lutheran	LDS[3]	Pentecostal	Presbyterian[4]	Muslim[5]	Judaism
MSA[1]	33.4	3.9	2.8	2.9	1.8	0.3	0.8	2.1	1.2	1.3
U.S.	19.1	9.3	4.0	4.0	2.3	2.0	1.9	1.6	0.8	0.7

Note: Figures are the number of adherents as a percentage of the total population; (1) Figures cover the Philadelphia-Camden-Wilmington, PA-NJ-DE-MD Metropolitan Statistical Area—see Appendix B for areas included; (2) Methodist/Pietist; (3) Latter Day Saints; (4) Reformed; (5) Figures are estimates
Source: Association of Statisticians of American Religious Bodies, 2010 U.S. Religion Census: Religious Congregations & Membership Study

Religious Groups by Tradition

Area	Catholic	Evangelical Protestant	Mainline Protestant	Other Tradition	Black Protestant	Orthodox
MSA[1]	33.4	6.3	8.9	3.7	1.7	0.4
U.S.	19.1	16.2	7.3	4.3	1.6	0.3

Note: Figures are the number of adherents as a percentage of the total population; (1) Figures cover the Philadelphia-Camden-Wilmington, PA-NJ-DE-MD Metropolitan Statistical Area—see Appendix B for areas included
Source: Association of Statisticians of American Religious Bodies, 2010 U.S. Religion Census: Religious Congregations & Membership Study

ECONOMY

Gross Metropolitan Product

Area	2013	2014	2015	2016	Rank[2]
MSA[1]	383.4	393.8	406.6	425.5	8

Note: Figures are in billions of dollars; (1) Figures cover the Philadelphia-Camden-Wilmington, PA-NJ-DE-MD Metropolitan Statistical Area—see Appendix B for areas included; (2) Rank is based on 2016 data and ranges from 1 to 381
Source: The U.S. Conference of Mayors, U.S. Metro Economies: GMP and Employment 2014-2016, June 2015

Economic Growth

Area	2011-13 (%)	2014 (%)	2015 (%)	2016 (%)	Rank[2]
MSA[1]	0.7	1.0	1.7	2.6	159
U.S.	2.2	2.4	2.3	2.9	–

Note: Figures are real gross metropolitan product (GMP) growth rates and represent annual average percent change; (1) Figures cover the Philadelphia-Camden-Wilmington, PA-NJ-DE-MD Metropolitan Statistical Area—see Appendix B for areas included; (2) Rank is based on 2016 data and ranges from 1 to 381
Source: The U.S. Conference of Mayors, U.S. Metro Economies: GMP and Employment 2014-2016, June 2015

Metropolitan Area Exports

Area	2009	2010	2011	2012	2013	2014	Rank[2]
MSA[1]	19,067.4	22,710.0	26,155.7	22,991.5	24,929.2	26,321.2	11

Note: Figures are in millions of dollars; (1) Figures cover the Philadelphia-Camden-Wilmington, PA-NJ-DE-MD Metropolitan Statistical Area—see Appendix B for areas included; (2) Rank is based on 2014 data and ranges from 1 to 385
Source: U.S. Department of Commerce, International Trade Administration, Office of Trade & Industry Information, Manufacturing & Services, data extracted March 10, 2016

Building Permits

Area	Single-Family			Multi-Family			Total		
	2014	2015p	Pct. Chg.	2014	2015p	Pct. Chg.	2014	2015p	Pct. Chg.
City	1	5	400.0	5	0	-100.0	6	5	-16.7
MSA[1]	6,379	6,499	1.9	7,252	6,114	-15.7	13,631	12,613	-7.5
U.S.	640,300	690,800	7.9	411,800	487,600	18.4	1,052,100	1,178,400	12.0

Note: (1) Figures cover the Philadelphia-Camden-Wilmington, PA-NJ-DE-MD Metropolitan Statistical Area—see Appendix B for areas included; Figures represent new, privately-owned housing units authorized (unadjusted data); All permit data are based on estimates with imputation; (p) preliminary data.
Source: U.S. Census Bureau, Manufacturing, Mining, and Construction Statistics, Building Permits, 2014, 2015

Bankruptcy Filings

Area	Business Filings			Nonbusiness Filings		
	2014	2015	% Chg.	2014	2015	% Chg.
Burlington County	34	39	14.7	1,706	1,646	-3.5
U.S.	26,983	24,735	-8.3	909,812	819,760	-9.9

Note: Business filings include Chapter 7, Chapter 11, Chapter 12, and Chapter 13; Nonbusiness filings include Chapter 7, Chapter 11, and Chapter 13
Source: Administrative Office of the U.S. Courts, Business and Nonbusiness Bankruptcy, County Cases Commenced by Chapter of the Bankruptcy Code, During the 12- Month Period Ending December 31, 2014 and Business and Nonbusiness Bankruptcy, County Cases Commenced by Chapter of the Bankruptcy Code, During the 12- Month Period Ending December 31, 2015

Housing Vacancy Rates

Area	Gross Vacancy Rate[2] (%)			Year-Round Vacancy Rate[3] (%)			Rental Vacancy Rate[4] (%)			Homeowner Vacancy Rate[5] (%)		
	2013	2014	2015	2013	2014	2015	2013	2014	2015	2013	2014	2015
MSA[1]	10.4	10.2	10.7	10.2	10.0	10.2	11.6	9.7	7.6	1.6	2.0	2.4
U.S.	13.6	13.4	12.9	10.7	10.4	10.0	8.3	7.6	7.1	2.0	1.9	1.8

Note: (1) Figures cover the Philadelphia-Camden-Wilmington, PA-NJ-DE-MD Metropolitan Statistical Area—see Appendix B for areas included; (2) The percentage of the total housing inventory that is vacant; (3) The percentage of the housing inventory (excluding seasonal units) that is year-round vacant; (4) The percentage of rental inventory that is vacant for rent; (5) The percentage of homeowner inventory that is vacant for sale
Source: U.S. Census Bureau, Housing Vacancies and Homeownership Annual Statistics: 2015

INCOME

Income

Area	Per Capita ($)	Median Household ($)	Average Household ($)
City	42,757	93,732	111,778
MSA[1]	32,850	62,169	85,647
U.S.	28,555	53,482	74,596

Note: (1) Figures cover the Philadelphia-Camden-Wilmington, PA-NJ-DE-MD Metropolitan Statistical Area—see Appendix B for areas included
Source: U.S. Census Bureau, 2010-2014 American Community Survey 5-Year Estimates

Household Income Distribution

Area	Percent of Households Earning							
	Under $15,000	$15,000 -24,999	$25,000 -34,999	$35,000 -49,999	$50,000 -74,999	$75,000 -99,000	$100,000 -149,999	$150,000 and up
City	4.3	5.2	6.5	7.0	16.5	14.9	20.4	25.2
MSA[1]	11.7	8.9	8.8	11.9	16.6	12.4	15.6	14.1
U.S.	12.5	10.7	10.2	13.5	17.8	12.2	13.0	10.0

Note: (1) Figures cover the Philadelphia-Camden-Wilmington, PA-NJ-DE-MD Metropolitan Statistical Area—see Appendix B for areas included
Source: U.S. Census Bureau, 2010-2014 American Community Survey 5-Year Estimates

Poverty Rate

Area	All Ages	Under 18 Years Old	18 to 64 Years Old	65 Years and Over
City	4.2	5.3	3.5	5.1
MSA[1]	13.2	17.8	12.4	8.9
U.S.	15.6	21.9	14.6	9.4

Note: Figures are percentage of people whose income during the past 12 months was below the poverty level; (1) Figures cover the Philadelphia-Camden-Wilmington, PA-NJ-DE-MD Metropolitan Statistical Area—see Appendix B for areas included
Source: U.S. Census Bureau, 2010-2014 American Community Survey 5-Year Estimates

EMPLOYMENT

Labor Force and Employment

Area	Civilian Labor Force			Workers Employed		
	Dec. 2014	Dec. 2015	% Chg.	Dec. 2014	Dec. 2015	% Chg.
City	25,976	26,323	1.3	24,933	25,503	2.2
MD[1]	639,280	643,376	0.6	600,422	614,423	2.3
U.S.	155,521,000	157,245,000	1.1	147,190,000	149,703,000	1.7

Note: Data is not seasonally adjusted and covers workers 16 years of age and older; (1) Figures cover the Camden, NJ Metropolitan Division—see Appendix B for areas included
Source: Bureau of Labor Statistics, Local Area Unemployment Statistics

Unemployment Rate

Area	2015											
	Jan.	Feb.	Mar.	Apr.	May	Jun.	Jul.	Aug.	Sep.	Oct.	Nov.	Dec.
City	5.1	5.1	4.8	4.7	4.9	4.4	4.8	4.1	4.0	3.6	3.8	3.1
MD[1]	7.2	7.1	6.9	6.4	6.5	5.8	6.6	5.8	5.6	5.2	5.1	4.5
U.S.	6.1	5.8	5.6	5.1	5.3	5.5	5.6	5.2	4.9	4.8	4.8	4.8

Note: Data is not seasonally adjusted and covers workers 16 years of age and older; (1) Figures cover the Camden, NJ Metropolitan Division—see Appendix B for areas included
Source: Bureau of Labor Statistics, Local Area Unemployment Statistics

Employment by Occupation

Occupation Classification	City (%)	MSA[1] (%)	U.S. (%)
Management, Business, Science, and Arts	51.1	41.6	36.4
Natural Resources, Construction, and Maintenance	4.4	6.9	9.0
Production, Transportation, and Material Moving	5.5	9.6	12.1
Sales and Office	26.4	24.9	24.4
Service	12.6	17.0	18.2

Note: Figures cover employed civilians 16 years of age and older; (1) Figures cover the Philadelphia-Camden-Wilmington, PA-NJ-DE-MD Metropolitan Statistical Area—see Appendix B for areas included
Source: U.S. Census Bureau, 2010-2014 American Community Survey 5-Year Estimates

Employment by Industry

Sector	MD[1]		U.S.
	Number of Employees	Percent of Total	Percent of Total
Construction, Mining, and Logging	21,800	4.1	5.0
Education and Health Services	92,700	17.5	15.7
Financial Activities	29,000	5.4	5.7
Government	81,700	15.4	15.5
Information	7,000	1.3	1.9
Leisure and Hospitality	43,400	8.2	10.4
Manufacturing	36,700	6.9	8.6
Other Services	18,400	3.4	3.9
Professional and Business Services	79,300	14.9	13.9
Retail Trade	71,000	13.4	11.3
Transportation, Warehousing, and Utilities	19,100	3.6	3.9
Wholesale Trade	28,900	5.4	4.1

Note: Figures are non-farm employment as of December 2015. Figures are not seasonally adjusted and include workers 16 years of age and older; (1) Figures cover the Camden, NJ Metropolitan Division—see Appendix B for areas included; n/a not available
Source: Bureau of Labor Statistics, Current Employment Statistics, Employment, Hours, and Earnings

Occupations with Greatest Projected Employment Growth: 2012 – 2022

Occupation[1]	2012 Employment	2022 Projected Employment	Numeric Employment Change	Percent Employment Change
Home Health Aides	31,140	46,280	15,140	48.6
Combined Food Preparation and Serving Workers, Including Fast Food	59,990	70,180	10,190	17.0
Retail Salespersons	125,690	134,870	9,180	7.3
Registered Nurses	79,840	88,880	9,040	11.3
Nursing Assistants	51,780	60,070	8,290	16.0
Laborers and Freight, Stock, and Material Movers, Hand	75,730	83,360	7,630	10.1
Software Developers, Applications	29,090	35,770	6,680	23.0
Receptionists and Information Clerks	51,160	57,830	6,670	13.0
Customer Service Representatives	63,450	69,530	6,080	9.6
Sales Representatives, Services, All Other	45,510	51,380	5,870	12.9

Note: Projections cover New Jersey; (1) Sorted by numeric employment change
Source: www.projectionscentral.com, State Occupational Projections, 2012–2022 Long-Term Projections

Fastest Growing Occupations: 2012 – 2022

Occupation[1]	2012 Employment	2022 Projected Employment	Numeric Employment Change	Percent Employment Change
Home Health Aides	31,140	46,280	15,140	48.6
Insulation Workers, Mechanical	370	540	170	48.2
Diagnostic Medical Sonographers	2,550	3,550	1,000	39.1
Occupational Therapy Assistants	370	500	130	37.5
Helpers—Electricians	1,310	1,800	490	37.5
Stonemasons	580	780	200	35.4
Physical Therapist Assistants	1,090	1,470	380	34.1
Skincare Specialists	1,050	1,400	350	33.2
Physician Assistants	1,450	1,920	470	32.8
Brickmasons and Blockmasons	2,150	2,830	680	31.7

Note: Projections cover New Jersey; (1) Sorted by percent employment change and excludes occupations with numeric employment change less than 100
Source: www.projectionscentral.com, State Occupational Projections, 2012–2022 Long-Term Projections

Average Wages

Occupation	$/Hr.	Occupation	$/Hr.
Accountants and Auditors	41.77	Maids and Housekeeping Cleaners	11.20
Automotive Mechanics	22.72	Maintenance and Repair Workers	20.80
Bookkeepers	19.99	Marketing Managers	63.29
Carpenters	25.51	Nuclear Medicine Technologists	39.60
Cashiers	10.50	Nurses, Licensed Practical	24.36
Clerks, General Office	16.17	Nurses, Registered	37.36
Clerks, Receptionists/Information	13.97	Nursing Assistants	13.07
Clerks, Shipping/Receiving	17.64	Packers and Packagers, Hand	11.03
Computer Programmers	34.60	Physical Therapists	43.81
Computer Systems Analysts	41.00	Postal Service Mail Carriers	25.18
Computer User Support Specialists	23.33	Real Estate Brokers	n/a
Cooks, Restaurant	12.48	Retail Salespersons	13.13
Dentists	74.40	Sales Reps., Exc. Tech./Scientific	40.89
Electrical Engineers	50.77	Sales Reps., Tech./Scientific	67.99
Electricians	32.18	Secretaries, Exc. Legal/Med./Exec.	19.03
Financial Managers	72.92	Security Guards	14.31
First-Line Supervisors/Managers, Sales	21.72	Surgeons	n/a
Food Preparation Workers	10.18	Teacher Assistants*	12.58
General and Operations Managers	71.38	Teachers, Elementary School*	31.88
Hairdressers/Cosmetologists	15.75	Teachers, Secondary School*	34.29
Internists	101.41	Telemarketers	11.39
Janitors and Cleaners	14.33	Truck Drivers, Heavy/Tractor-Trailer	21.83
Landscaping/Groundskeeping Workers	11.89	Truck Drivers, Light/Delivery Svcs.	15.93
Lawyers	61.98	Waiters and Waitresses	10.37

Note: Wage data covers the Camden, NJ Metropolitan Division—see Appendix B for areas included; (*) Hourly wages for elementary/secondary school teachers and teacher assistants were calculated by the editors from annual wage data based on a 40 hour work week; n/a not available.
Source: Bureau of Labor Statistics, Metro Area Occupational Employment and Wage Estimates, May 2015

TAXES

State Corporate Income Tax Rates

State	Tax Rate (%)	Income Brackets ($)	Num. of Brackets	Financial Institution Tax Rate (%)[a]	Federal Income Tax Ded.
New Jersey	9.0 (r)	Flat rate	1	9.0 (r)	No

Note: Tax rates as of January 1, 2016; (a) Rates listed are the corporate income tax rate applied to financial institutions or excise taxes based on income. Some states have other taxes based upon the value of deposits or shares; (r) In New Jersey small businesses with annual entire net income under $100,000 pay a tax rate of 7.5%; businesses with income under $50,000 pay 6.5%. The minimum Corporation Business Tax is based on New Jersey gross receipts. It ranges from $500 for a corporation with gross receipts less than $100,000, to $2,000 for a corporation with gross receipts of $1 million or more.
Source: Federation of Tax Administrators, "State Corporate Income Tax Rates, 2016"

State Individual Income Tax Rates

State	Tax Rate (%)	Income Brackets ($)	Num. of Brackets	Personal Exempt. ($)[1] Single	Personal Exempt. ($)[1] Dependents	Fed. Inc. Tax Ded.
New Jersey	1.4 - 8.97	20,000 - 500,000 (n)	6	1,000	1,500	No

Note: Tax rates as of January 1, 2016; Local- and county-level taxes are not included; n/a not applicable; (1) Married joint filers generally receive double the single exemption; (n) The New Jersey rates reported are for single individuals. For married couples filing jointly, the tax rates also range from 1.4% to 8.97%, with 7 brackets and the same high and low income ranges.
Source: Federation of Tax Administrators, "State Individual Income Tax Rates, 2016"

Various State and Local Tax Rates

State	State and Local Sales and Use (%)	State Sales and Use (%)	Gasoline[1] (¢/gal.)	Cigarette[2] ($/pack)	Spirits[3] ($/gal.)	Wine[4] ($/gal.)	Beer[5] ($/gal.)
New Jersey	7.00	7.0 (e)	14.5	2.70	5.50	0.88	0.12

Note: All tax rates as of January 1, 2016; (1) The American Petroleum Institute has developed a methodology for determining the average tax rate on a gallon of fuel. Rates may include any of the following: excise taxes, environmental fees, storage tank fees, other fees or taxes, general sales tax, and local taxes. In states where gasoline is subject to the general sales tax, or where the fuel tax is based on the average sale price, the average rate determined by API is sensitive to changes in the price of gasoline. States that fully or partially apply general sales taxes to gasoline: CA, CO, GA, IL, IN, MI, NY; (2) The federal excise tax of $1.0066 per pack and local taxes are not included; (3) Rates are those applicable to off-premise sales of 40% alcohol by volume (a.b.v.) distilled spirits in 750ml containers. Local excise taxes are excluded; (4) Rates are those applicable to off-premise sales of 11% a.b.v. non-carbonated wine in 750ml containers; (5) Rates are those applicable to off-premise sales of 4.7% a.b.v. beer in 12 ounce containers; (e) Some counties in New Jersey are not subject to statewide sales tax rates and collect a local rate of 3.5%. Their average local score is represented as a negative.
Source: Tax Foundation, 2016 Facts & Figures: How Does Your State Compare?

State Business Tax Climate Index Rankings

State	Overall Rank	Corporate Tax Rank	Individual Income Tax Rank	Sales Tax Rank	Unemployment Insurance Tax Rank	Property Tax Rank
New Jersey	50	43	48	47	31	50

Note: The index is a measure of how each state's tax laws affect economic performance. The lower the rank, the more favorable a state's tax system is for business. States without a given tax are given a ranking of 1. The scores/rankings for the District of Columbia do not affect other states. The 2016 index represents the tax climate as of July 1, 2015 (the beginning of Fiscal Year 2016).
Source: Tax Foundation, State Business Tax Climate Index 2016

TRANSPORTATION

Means of Transportation to Work

Area	Car/Truck/Van		Public Transportation			Bicycle	Walked	Other Means	Worked at Home
	Drove Alone	Car-pooled	Bus	Subway	Railroad				
City	85.1	5.5	0.6	1.2	1.2	0.1	1.0	1.0	4.2
MSA[1]	73.4	7.8	5.5	1.6	2.3	0.6	3.7	0.9	4.0
U.S.	76.4	9.6	2.6	1.8	0.6	0.6	2.8	1.3	4.4

Note: Figures are percentages and cover workers 16 years of age and older; (1) Figures cover the Philadelphia-Camden-Wilmington, PA-NJ-DE-MD Metropolitan Statistical Area—see Appendix B for areas included
Source: U.S. Census Bureau, 2010-2014 American Community Survey 5-Year Estimates

Travel Time to Work

Area	Less Than 10 Minutes	10 to 19 Minutes	20 to 29 Minutes	30 to 44 Minutes	45 to 59 Minutes	60 to 89 Minutes	90 Minutes or More
City	8.9	28.4	20.7	19.1	10.5	9.2	3.1
MSA[1]	10.1	25.4	20.3	23.2	10.4	7.6	2.9
U.S.	13.3	29.6	21.0	20.2	7.7	5.7	2.6

Note: Figures are percentages and include workers 16 years old and over; (1) Figures cover the Philadelphia-Camden-Wilmington, PA-NJ-DE-MD Metropolitan Statistical Area—see Appendix B for areas included
Source: U.S. Census Bureau, 2010-2014 American Community Survey 5-Year Estimates

Freeway Travel Time Index

Area	1985	1990	1995	2000	2005	2010	2014
Urban Area Rank[1,2]	20	21	26	26	24	22	25
Urban Area Index[1]	1.12	1.15	1.18	1.21	1.25	1.24	1.24
Average Index[3]	1.09	1.11	1.14	1.17	1.20	1.19	1.20

Note: Freeway Travel Time Index—the ratio of travel time in the peak period to the travel time at free-flow conditions. For example, a value of 1.30 indicates a 20-minute free-flow trip takes 26 minutes in the peak (20 minutes x 1.30 = 26 minutes); (1) Covers the Philadelphia PA-NJ-DE-MD urban area; (2) Rank is based on 101 urban areas (#1 = highest travel time index); (3) Average of 101 urban areas
Source: Texas Transportation Institute, 2015 Urban Mobility Scorecard, August 2015

Freeway Commuter Stress Index

Area	1985	1990	1995	2000	2005	2010	2014
Urban Area Rank[1,2]	31	28	33	34	30	31	31
Urban Area Index[1]	1.15	1.19	1.22	1.25	1.29	1.28	1.28
Average Index[3]	1.13	1.16	1.19	1.22	1.25	1.24	1.25

Note: The Freeway Commuter Stress Index is the same as the Freeway Travel Time Index (see table above) except that it includes only the travel in the peak directions during the peak periods; the TTI includes travel in all directions during the peak period. Thus, the CSI is more indicative of the work trip experienced by each commuter on a daily basis. (1) Covers the Philadelphia PA-NJ-DE-MD urban area; (2) Rank is based on 101 urban areas (#1 = highest stress index); (3) Average of 101 urban areas

Source: Texas Transportation Institute, 2015 Urban Mobility Scorecard, August 2015

Living Environment

COST OF LIVING

Cost of Living Index

Composite Index	Groceries	Housing	Utilities	Trans-portation	Health Care	Misc. Goods/ Services
119.6	115.8	135.5	122.6	109.8	99.9	112.7

Note: The Cost of Living Index measures regional differences in the cost of consumer goods and services, excluding taxes and non-consumer expenditures, for professional and managerial households in the top income quintile. It is based on more than 50,000 prices covering almost 60 different items for which prices are collected three times a year by chambers of commerce, economic development organizations or university applied economic centers in each participating urban area. The numbers shown should be read as a percentage above or below the national average of 100. For example, a value of 115.4 in the groceries column indicates that grocery prices are 15.4% higher than the national average. Small differences in the index numbers should not be interpreted as significant; Figures cover the Philadelphia PA urban area.
Source: The Council for Community and Economic Research, ACCRA Cost of Living Index, 2015

Grocery Prices

Area[1]	T-Bone Steak ($/pound)	Frying Chicken ($/pound)	Whole Milk ($/half gal.)	Eggs ($/dozen)	Orange Juice ($/64 oz.)	Coffee ($/11.5 oz.)
City[2]	12.16	1.43	2.14	2.61	3.93	4.50
Avg.	10.99	1.43	2.25	2.26	3.58	4.48
Min.	7.16	0.98	1.30	1.35	2.88	2.98
Max.	14.13	2.43	3.85	4.81	6.39	7.56

Note: (1) Values for the local area are compared with the average, minimum and maximum values for all 292 areas in the Cost of Living Index; (2) Figures cover the Philadelphia PA urban area; **T-Bone Steak** *(price per pound);* **Frying Chicken** *(price per pound, whole fryer);* **Whole Milk** *(half gallon carton);* **Eggs** *(price per dozen, Grade A, large);* **Orange Juice** *(64 oz. Tropicana or Florida Natural);* **Coffee** *(11.5 oz. can, vacuum-packed, Maxwell House, Hills Bros, or Folgers).*
Source: The Council for Community and Economic Research, ACCRA Cost of Living Index, 2015

Housing and Utility Costs

Area[1]	New Home Price ($)	Apartment Rent ($/month)	All Electric ($/month)	Part Electric ($/month)	Other Energy ($/month)	Telephone ($/month)
City[2]	419,996	1,304	-	113.50	73.49	39.51
Avg.	312,874	945	179.30	95.07	72.96	28.11
Min.	178,682	479	116.28	43.14	26.46	10.01
Max.	1,472,476	3,984	504.25	189.44	421.11	43.06

Note: (1) Values for the local area are compared with the average, minimum and maximum values for all 292 areas in the Cost of Living Index; (2) Figures cover the Philadelphia PA urban area; **New Home Price** *(2,400 sf living area, 8,000 sf lot, in urban area with full utilities);* **Apartment Rent** *(950 sf 2 bedroom/1.5 or 2 bath, unfurnished, excluding all utilities except water);* **All Electric** *(average monthly cost for an all-electric home);* **Part Electric** *(average monthly cost for a part-electric home);* **Other Energy** *(average monthly cost for natural gas, fuel oil, coal, wood, and any other forms of energy except electricity);* **Telephone** *(price includes basic monthly rate for a private residential line plus additional local usage charges incurred by a family of four).*
Source: The Council for Community and Economic Research, ACCRA Cost of Living Index, 2015

Health Care, Transportation, and Other Costs

Area[1]	Doctor ($/visit)	Dentist ($/visit)	Optometrist ($/visit)	Gasoline ($/gallon)	Beauty Salon ($/visit)	Men's Shirt ($)
City[2]	119.17	95.44	104.35	2.53	51.48	40.96
Avg.	105.15	89.02	99.78	2.38	35.30	28.10
Min.	66.87	56.09	48.53	1.95	18.91	13.38
Max.	182.34	150.36	228.33	4.09	67.91	63.80

Note: (1) Values for the local area are compared with the average, minimum and maximum values for all 292 areas in the Cost of Living Index; (2) Figures cover the Philadelphia PA urban area; **Doctor** *(general practitioners routine exam of an established patient);* **Dentist** *(adult teeth cleaning and periodic oral examination);* **Optometrist** *(full vision eye exam for established adult patient);* **Gasoline** *(one gallon regular unleaded, national brand, including all taxes, cash price at self-service pump if available);* **Beauty Salon** *(woman's shampoo, trim, and blow-dry);* **Men's Shirt** *(cotton/polyester dress shirt, pinpoint weave, long sleeves).*
Source: The Council for Community and Economic Research, ACCRA Cost of Living Index, 2015

HOUSING

House Price Index (HPI)

Area	National Ranking[2]	Quarterly Change (%)	One-Year Change (%)	Five-Year Change (%)
MD[1]	174	1.30	3.50	-3.60
U.S.[3]	–	1.45	5.76	22.85

Note: The HPI is a weighted repeat sales index. It measures average price changes in repeat sales or refinancings on the same properties. This information is obtained by reviewing repeat mortgage transactions on single-family properties whose mortgages have been purchased or securitized by Fannie Mae or Freddie Mac in January 1975; (1) Camden Metropolitan Division—see Appendix B for areas included; (2) Rankings are based on annual percentage change for all metro areas containing at least 15,000 transactions over the last 10 years and ranges from 1 to 266; (3) figures based on a weighted average of Census Division estimates using a seasonally adjusted, purchase-only index; all figures are for the period ending December 31, 2015
Source: Federal Housing Finance Agency, House Price Index, February 25, 2016

Median Single-Family Home Prices

Area	2013	2014	2015p	Percent Change 2014 to 2015
MSA[1]	220.3	220.7	223.7	1.4
U.S. Average	197.4	208.9	223.9	7.2

Note: Figures are median sales prices of existing single-family homes in thousands of dollars; (p) preliminary; n/a not available; (1) Philadelphia-Camden-Wilmington, PA-NJ-DE-MD Metropolitan Statistical Area—see Appendix B for areas included
Source: National Association of Realtors, Median Sales Price of Existing Single-Family Homes for Metropolitan Areas, 4th Quarter 2015

Qualifying Income Based on Median Sales Price of Existing Single-Family Homes

Area	With 5% Down ($)	With 10% Down ($)	With 20% Down ($)
MSA[1]	47,533	45,032	40,028
U.S. Average	49,535	46,928	41,714

Note: Figures are preliminary; Qualifying income is based on a mortgage rate of 4.1%. Monthly principal and interest payment is limited to 25% of income; n/a not available; (1) Philadelphia-Camden-Wilmington, PA-NJ-DE-MD Metropolitan Statistical Area—see Appendix B for areas included
Source: National Association of Realtors, Qualifying Income Based on Median Sales Price of Existing Single-Family Homes for Metropolitan Areas, 4th Quarter 2015

Median Apartment Condo-Coop Home Prices

Area	2013	2014	2015p	Percent Change 2014 to 2015
MSA[1]	175.5	176.6	176.5	-0.1
U.S. Average	194.9	204.3	210.7	3.1

Note: Figures are median sales prices of existing apartment condo-coop homes in thousands of dollars; (p) preliminary; n/a not available; (1) Philadelphia-Camden-Wilmington, PA-NJ-DE-MD Metropolitan Statistical Area—see Appendix B for areas included
Source: National Association of Realtors, Median Sales Price of Existing Apartment Condo-Coop Homes for Metropolitan Areas, 4th Quarter 2015

Gross Monthly Rent

Area	Under $200	$200 -299	$300 -499	$500 -749	$750 -999	$1,000 -1,499	$1,500 and up	Median ($)
City	0.5	2.1	0.7	3.4	9.6	44.1	39.6	1,341
MSA[1]	1.6	3.1	4.7	13.0	26.5	34.6	16.5	1,011
U.S.	1.5	3.2	7.4	21.0	24.1	26.9	15.9	920

Note: Figures are percentages except for Median; Gross rent is the contract rent plus the estimated average monthly cost of utilities (electricity, gas, and water and sewer) and fuels (oil, coal, kerosene, wood, etc.) if these are paid by the renter (or paid for the renter by someone else); (1) Figures cover the Philadelphia-Camden-Wilmington, PA-NJ-DE-MD Metropolitan Statistical Area—see Appendix B for areas included
Source: U.S. Census Bureau, 2010-2014 American Community Survey 5-Year Estimates

Homeownership Rate

Area	2008 (%)	2009 (%)	2010 (%)	2011 (%)	2012 (%)	2013 (%)	2014 (%)	2015 (%)
MSA[1]	71.8	69.7	70.7	69.7	69.5	69.1	67.0	67.0
U.S.	67.8	67.4	66.9	66.1	65.4	65.1	64.5	63.7

Note: (1) Figures cover the Philadelphia-Camden-Wilmington, PA-NJ-DE-MD Metropolitan Statistical Area—see Appendix B for areas included
Source: U.S. Census Bureau, Housing Vacancies and Homeownership Annual Statistics: 2015

Year Housing Structure Built

Area	2010 or Later	2000 -2009	1990 -1999	1980 -1989	1970 -1979	1960 -1969	1950 -1959	1940 -1949	Before 1940	Median Year
City	0.5	11.1	19.2	30.3	20.9	11.7	4.9	0.4	1.0	1984
MSA[1]	0.6	8.4	9.2	10.1	12.4	12.3	16.0	9.1	21.9	1962
U.S.	1.0	14.9	13.9	13.8	15.8	11.0	10.8	5.4	13.3	1976

Note: Figures are percentages except for Median Year; (1) Figures cover the Philadelphia-Camden-Wilmington, PA-NJ-DE-MD Metropolitan Statistical Area—see Appendix B for areas included
Source: U.S. Census Bureau, 2010-2014 American Community Survey 5-Year Estimates

HEALTH

Health Risk Data

Category	MD[1] (%)	U.S. (%)
Adults aged 18–64 who have any kind of health care coverage	86.6	79.6
Adults who reported being in good or excellent health	82.5	83.1
Adults who are current smokers	19.1	19.6
Adults who are heavy drinkers[2]	5.4	6.1
Adults who are binge drinkers[3]	17.2	16.9
Adults who are overweight (BMI 25.0 - 29.9)	37.1	35.8
Adults who are obese (BMI 30.0 - 99.8)	29.1	27.6
Adults who participated in any physical activities in the past month	72.9	77.1
Adults 50+ who have ever had a sigmoidoscopy or colonoscopy	66.2	67.3
Women aged 40+ who have had a mammogram within the past two years	76.2	74.0
Men aged 40+ who have had a PSA test within the past two years	47.3	45.2
Adults aged 65+ who have had flu shot within the past year	65.5	60.1
Adults who always wear a seatbelt	93.1	93.8

Note: Data as of 2012 unless otherwise noted; (1) Figures cover the Camden, NJ Metropolitan Division—see Appendix B for areas included; (2) Heavy drinkers are classified as males having more than two drinks per day or females having more than one drink per day; (3) Binge drinkers are classified as males having five or more drinks on one occasion or females having four or more drinks on one occasion
Source: Centers for Disease Control and Prevention, Behaviorial Risk Factor Surveillance System, SMART: Selected Metropolitan/Micropolitan Area Risk Trends, 2012 (Note: the CDC has discontinued this dataset but will be releasing a replacement in mid-2016)

Chronic Health Indicators

Category	MD[1] (%)	U.S. (%)
Adults who have ever been told they had a heart attack	4.4	4.5
Adults who have ever been told they had a stroke	2.8	2.9
Adults who have been told they currently have asthma	10.5	8.9
Adults who have ever been told they have arthritis	25.2	25.7
Adults who have ever been told they have diabetes[2]	11.5	9.7
Adults who have ever been told they had skin cancer	4.5	5.7
Adults who have ever been told they had any other types of cancer	6.0	6.5
Adults who have ever been told they have COPD	6.5	6.2
Adults who have ever been told they have kidney disease	3.1	2.5
Adults who have ever been told they have a form of depression	16.9	18.0

Note: Data as of 2012 unless otherwise noted; (1) Figures cover the Camden, NJ Metropolitan Division—see Appendix B for areas included; (2) Figures do not include pregnancy-related, borderline, or pre-diabetes
Source: Centers for Disease Control and Prevention, Behaviorial Risk Factor Surveillance System, SMART: Selected Metropolitan/Micropolitan Area Risk Trends, 2012 (Note: the CDC has discontinued this dataset but will be releasing a replacement in mid-2016)

Mortality Rates for the Top 10 Causes of Death in the U.S.

ICD-10[a] Sub-Chapter	ICD-10[a] Code	Age-Adjusted Mortality Rate[1] per 100,000 population	
		County[2]	U.S.
Malignant neoplasms	C00-C97	167.6	163.6
Ischaemic heart diseases	I20-I25	90.0	102.2
Other forms of heart disease	I30-I51	56.6	50.1
Chronic lower respiratory diseases	J40-J47	33.3	41.4
Organic, including symptomatic, mental disorders	F01-F09	38.8	38.5
Cerebrovascular diseases	I60-I69	36.8	36.5
Other external causes of accidental injury	W00-X59	27.0	27.5
Other degenerative diseases of the nervous system	G30-G31	19.1	26.3
Diabetes mellitus	E10-E14	17.7	21.1
Hypertensive diseases	I10-I15	12.9	19.7

Note: (a) ICD-10 = International Classification of Diseases 10th Revision; (1) Mortality rates are a three year average covering 2012-2014; (2) Figures cover Burlington County.
Source: Centers for Disease Control and Prevention, National Center for Health Statistics. Underlying Cause of Death 1999-2014 on CDC WONDER Online Database, released 2015.

Mortality Rates for Selected Causes of Death

ICD-10[a] Sub-Chapter	ICD-10[a] Code	Age-Adjusted Mortality Rate[1] per 100,000 population	
		County[2]	U.S.
Assault	X85-Y09	2.5	5.1
Diseases of the liver	K70-K76	11.4	13.5
Human immunodeficiency virus (HIV) disease	B20-B24	Unreliable	2.1
Influenza and pneumonia	J09-J18	11.5	15.2
Intentional self-harm	X60-X84	9.6	12.7
Malnutrition	E40-E46	1.3	0.9
Obesity and other hyperalimentation	E65-E68	1.4	1.9
Renal failure	N17-N19	17.6	13.0
Transport accidents	V01-V99	8.2	11.6
Viral hepatitis	B15-B19	1.7	2.1

Note: (a) ICD-10 = International Classification of Diseases 10th Revision; (1) Mortality rates are a three year average covering 2012-2014; (2) Figures cover Burlington County; Data are Suppressed when the data meet the criteria for confidentiality constraints; Mortality rates are flagged as Unreliable when the rate would be calculated with a numerator of 20 or less.
Source: Centers for Disease Control and Prevention, National Center for Health Statistics. Underlying Cause of Death 1999-2014 on CDC WONDER Online Database, released 2015.

Health Insurance Coverage

Area	With Health Insurance	With Private Health Insurance	With Public Health Insurance	Without Health Insurance	Population Under Age 18 Without Health Insurance
City	94.9	86.3	20.3	5.1	4.1
MSA[1]	90.4	72.5	29.8	9.6	4.1
U.S.	85.8	65.8	31.1	14.2	7.1

Note: Figures are percentages that cover the civilian noninstitutionalized population; (1) Figures cover the Philadelphia-Camden-Wilmington, PA-NJ-DE-MD Metropolitan Statistical Area—see Appendix B for areas included
Source: U.S. Census Bureau, 2010-2014 American Community Survey 5-Year Estimates

Number of Medical Professionals

Area	MDs[3]	DOs[3,4]	Dentists	Podiatrists	Chiropractors	Optometrists
County[1] (number)	1,144	335	319	34	106	69
County[1] (rate[2])	254.1	74.4	70.9	7.6	23.6	15.3
U.S. (rate[2])	272.5	20.9	64.7	5.8	25.9	15.2

Note: Data as of 2014 unless noted; (1) Data covers Burlington County; (2) Rate per 100,000 population; (3) Data as of 2013 and includes all active, non-federal physicians; (4) Doctor of Osteopathic Medicine
Source: U.S. Department of Health and Human Services, Health Resources and Services Administration, Bureau of Health Professions, Area Resource File (ARF) 2014-2015

EDUCATION

Public School District Statistics

District Name	Schls	Pupils	Pupil/ Teacher Ratio	Minority Pupils[1] (%)	Free Lunch Eligible[2] (%)	IEP[3] (%)
Evesham Township School District	9	4,595	12.1	20.2	8.0	18.0
Lenape Regional High SD	4	6,976	11.6	16.1	6.9	16.3

Note: Table includes school districts with 100 or more students; (1) Percentage of students that are not non-Hispanic white; (2) Percentage of students that are eligible for the free lunch program; (3) Percentage of students that have an Individualized Education Program.
Source: U.S. Department of Education, National Center for Education Statistics, Common Core of Data, Local Education Agency (School District) Universe Survey: School Year 2013-2014; U.S. Department of Education, National Center for Education Statistics, Common Core of Data, Public Elementary/Secondary School Universe Survey: School Year 2013-2014

Highest Level of Education

Area	Less than H.S.	H.S. Diploma	Some College, No Deg.	Associate Degree	Bachelor's Degree	Master's Degree	Prof. School Degree	Doctorate Degree
City	4.9	22.4	18.1	7.4	29.8	12.1	3.3	1.9
MSA[1]	10.9	30.6	17.7	6.6	20.5	9.4	2.5	1.7
U.S.	13.7	28.0	21.2	7.9	18.3	7.8	2.0	1.3

Note: Figures cover persons age 25 and over; (1) Figures cover the Philadelphia-Camden-Wilmington, PA-NJ-DE-MD Metropolitan Statistical Area—see Appendix B for areas included
Source: U.S. Census Bureau, 2010-2014 American Community Survey 5-Year Estimates

Educational Attainment by Race

Area	High School Graduate or Higher (%)					Bachelor's Degree or Higher (%)				
	Total	White	Black	Asian	Hisp.[2]	Total	White	Black	Asian	Hisp.[2]
City	95.1	95.6	95.9	88.2	85.7	47.1	46.0	53.8	61.7	29.0
MSA[1]	89.1	91.8	84.4	82.5	66.8	34.2	37.9	18.0	54.0	15.2
U.S.	86.3	88.4	83.2	85.8	64.1	29.3	30.6	19.0	50.9	13.9

Note: Figures shown cover persons 25 years old and over; (1) Figures cover the Philadelphia-Camden-Wilmington, PA-NJ-DE-MD Metropolitan Statistical Area—see Appendix B for areas included; (2) People of Hispanic origin can be of any race
Source: U.S. Census Bureau, 2010-2014 American Community Survey 5-Year Estimates

School Enrollment by Grade and Control

Area	Preschool (%)		Kindergarten (%)		Grades 1 - 4 (%)		Grades 5 - 8 (%)		Grades 9 - 12 (%)	
	Public	Private	Public	Private	Public	Private	Public	Private	Public	Private
City	40.4	59.6	88.3	11.7	95.2	4.8	90.9	9.1	92.5	7.5
MSA[1]	43.6	56.4	80.0	20.0	84.8	15.2	83.4	16.6	83.8	16.2
U.S.	57.4	42.6	87.8	12.2	89.8	10.2	89.9	10.1	90.6	9.4

Note: Figures shown cover persons 3 years old and over; (1) Figures cover the Philadelphia-Camden-Wilmington, PA-NJ-DE-MD Metropolitan Statistical Area—see Appendix B for areas included
Source: U.S. Census Bureau, 2010-2014 American Community Survey 5-Year Estimates

Average Salaries of Public School Classroom Teachers

Area	2013-14		2014-15		Percent Change 2013-14 to 2014-15	Percent Change 2004-05 to 2014-15
	Dollars	Rank[1]	Dollars	Rank[1]		
New Jersey	68,238	6	69,038	6	1.17	22.2
U.S. Average	56,610	–	57,379	–	1.36	20.8

Note: (1) State rank ranges from 1 to 51 where 1 indicates highest salary.
Source: National Education Association, Rankings & Estimates: Rankings of the States 2014 and Estimates of School Statistics 2015, March 2015

Higher Education

Four-Year Colleges			Two-Year Colleges			Medical Schools[1]	Law Schools[2]	Voc/ Tech[3]
Public	Private Non-profit	Private For-profit	Public	Private Non-profit	Private For-profit			
0	0	0	0	0	0	0	0	0

Note: Figures cover institutions located within the city limits and include main campuses only; (1) includes schools accredited by the Liaison Committee on Medical Education and the American Osteopathic Association's Commission on Osteopathic College Accreditation; (2) includes ABA-accredited schools, schools with provisional ABA accreditation, and state accredited schools; (3) includes all schools with programs that are less than 2 years.

Source: National Center for Education Statistics, Integrated Postsecondary Education System (IPEDS), 2014-15; Association of American Medical Colleges, Member List, March 21, 2016; American Osteopathic Association, Member List, March 21, 2016; Law School Admission Council, Official Guide to ABA-Approved Law Schools Online, March 21, 2016; Wikipedia, List of Medical Schools in the United States, March 21, 2016; Wikipedia, List of Law Schools in the United States, March 21, 2016

PRESIDENTIAL ELECTION

2012 Presidential Election Results

Area	Obama (%)	Romney (%)	Other (%)
Burlington County	58.8	40.1	1.0
U.S.	51.0	47.2	1.8

Note: Results may not add to 100% due to rounding

Source: Dave Leip's Atlas of U.S. Presidential Elections

EMPLOYERS

Major Employers

Company Name	Industry
Abington Memorial Hospital	General medical & surgical hospitals
AstraZeneca Pharmaceuticals	Pharmaceutical preparations
City of Philadelphia	Police protection
Comcast Holdings Corporation	Cable & other pay television services
Cooper Health Care	Hospital management
E.I. du Pont de Nemours and Company	Agricultural chemicals
Einstein Community Health Associates	Offices & clinics of medical doctors
Glaxosmithkline	Commerical physical research
Lockheed Martin Corporation	Defense systems & equipment
Mercy Health System of SE Pennsylvania	General medical & surgical hospitals
On Time Staffing	Employment agencies
Richlieu Associates	Apartment building operators
Temple University	General medical & surgical hospitals
The University of Pennsylvania	Colleges & universities
The US Navy	Navy
The Vanguard Group	Management, investment, open-end
Thomas Jefferson University Hospital	General medical & surgical hospitals
Trustees of the University of Penn	General medical & surgical hospitals
Unisys Corporation	Computer integrated systems design
University of Delaware	Colleges & universities

Note: Companies shown are located within the Philadelphia-Camden-Wilmington, PA-NJ-DE-MD Metropolitan Statistical Area.

Source: Hoovers.com; Wikipedia

PUBLIC SAFETY

Crime Rate

Area	All Crimes	Violent Crimes				Property Crimes		
		Murder	Rape[3]	Robbery	Aggrav. Assault	Burglary	Larceny -Theft	Motor Vehicle Theft
City	1,194.6	0.0	15.3	24.1	35.1	177.5	922.8	19.7
Metro[1]	2,356.2	4.5	17.0	103.0	151.4	483.5	1,514.2	82.8
U.S.	2,961.6	4.5	26.4	102.2	232.5	542.5	1,837.3	216.2

Note: Figures are crimes per 100,000 population; (1) Figures cover the Camden, NJ Metropolitan Division—see Appendix B for areas included; (3) The city and U.S. figures shown were reported using the legacy Uniform Crime Reporting (UCR) definition of rape. The suburban and metro area figures shown are an aggregate total of the data submitted using both the revised and legacy UCR definitions.

Source: FBI Uniform Crime Reports, 2014

Hate Crimes

Area	Number of Quarters Reported	Number of Incidents per Bias Motivation: Race	Religion	Sexual Orientation	Ethnicity	Disability	Gender	Gender Identity
City	4	8	1	2	1	0	0	0
U.S.	4	2,568	1,014	1,017	648	84	33	98

Source: Federal Bureau of Investigation, Hate Crime Statistics 2014

Identity Theft Consumer Complaints

Area	Complaints	Complaints per 100,000 Population	Rank[2]
MSA[1]	9,168	151.5	51
U.S.	490,220	152.4	-

Note: (1) Figures cover the Philadelphia-Camden-Wilmington, PA-NJ-DE-MD Metropolitan Statistical Area—see Appendix B for areas included; (2) Rank ranges from 1 to 379 where 1 indicates greatest number of identity theft complaints per 100,000 population
Source: Federal Trade Commission, Consumer Sentinel Network Data Book for January–December 2015

Fraud and Other Consumer Complaints

Area	Complaints	Complaints per 100,000 Population	Rank[2]
MSA[1]	26,145	432.1	62
U.S.	2,593,159	806.0	-

Note: (1) Figures cover the Philadelphia-Camden-Wilmington, PA-NJ-DE-MD Metropolitan Statistical Area—see Appendix B for areas included; (2) Rank ranges from 1 to 379 where 1 indicates greatest number of identity theft complaints per 100,000 population
Source: Federal Trade Commission, Consumer Sentinel Network Data Book for January–December 2015

RECREATION

Culture

Dance[1]	Theatre[1]	Instrumental Music[1]	Vocal Music[1]	Series and Festivals	Museums and Art Galleries[2]	Zoos and Aquariums[3]
0	0	0	0	0	0	0

Note: (1) Professional perfoming groups; (2) Based on organizations with SIC code 8412; (3) AZA-accredited
Source: The Grey House Performing Arts Directory, 2015-16; Association of Zoos & Aquariums, AZA Member Zoos & Aquariums, March 25, 2016; www.AccuLeads.com, March 29, 2016

Professional Sports Teams

Team Name	League	Year Established
Philadelphia 76ers	National Basketball Association (NBA)	1963
Philadelphia Eagles	National Football League (NFL)	1933
Philadelphia Flyers	National Hockey League (NHL)	1967
Philadelphia Phillies	Major League Baseball (MLB)	1883
Philadelphia Union	Major League Soccer (MLS)	2010

Note: Includes teams located in the Philadelphia-Camden-Wilmington, PA-NJ-DE-MD Metropolitan Statistical Area.
Source: Wikipedia, Major Professional Sports Teams of the United States and Canada, March 24, 2016

CLIMATE

Average and Extreme Temperatures

Temperature	Jan	Feb	Mar	Apr	May	Jun	Jul	Aug	Sep	Oct	Nov	Dec	Yr.
Extreme High (°F)	74	74	85	94	96	100	104	101	100	89	84	72	104
Average High (°F)	39	42	51	63	73	82	86	85	78	67	55	43	64
Average Temp. (°F)	32	34	42	53	63	72	77	76	68	57	47	36	55
Average Low (°F)	24	26	33	43	53	62	67	66	59	47	38	28	45
Extreme Low (°F)	-7	-4	7	19	28	44	51	44	35	25	15	1	-7

Note: Figures cover the years 1948-1990
Source: National Climatic Data Center, International Station Meteorological Climate Summary, 9/96

Average Precipitation/Snowfall/Humidity

Precip./Humidity	Jan	Feb	Mar	Apr	May	Jun	Jul	Aug	Sep	Oct	Nov	Dec	Yr.
Avg. Precip. (in.)	3.2	2.8	3.7	3.5	3.7	3.6	4.1	4.0	3.3	2.7	3.4	3.3	41.4
Avg. Snowfall (in.)	7	7	4	Tr	Tr	0	0	0	0	Tr	1	4	22
Avg. Rel. Hum. 7am (%)	74	73	73	72	75	77	80	82	84	83	79	75	77
Avg. Rel. Hum. 4pm (%)	60	55	51	48	51	52	54	55	55	54	57	60	54

Note: Figures cover the years 1948-1990; Tr = Trace amounts (<0.05 in. of rain; <0.5 in. of snow)
Source: National Climatic Data Center, International Station Meteorological Climate Summary, 9/96

Weather Conditions

Temperature			Daytime Sky			Precipitation		
10°F & below	32°F & below	90°F & above	Clear	Partly cloudy	Cloudy	0.01 inch or more precip.	0.1 inch or more snow/ice	Thunder-storms
5	94	23	81	146	138	117	14	27

Note: Figures are average number of days per year and cover the years 1948-1990
Source: National Climatic Data Center, International Station Meteorological Climate Summary, 9/96

HAZARDOUS WASTE

Superfund Sites

Evesham has one hazardous waste site on the EPA's Superfund Final National Priorities List: **Ellis Property**. There are a total of 1,323 Superfund sites on the list in the U.S. *U.S. Environmental Protection Agency, Final National Priorities List, March 18, 2016*

AIR & WATER QUALITY

Air Quality Trends: Ozone

	1990	1995	2000	2005	2010	2011	2012	2013	2014
MSA[1]	0.102	0.109	0.099	0.091	0.083	0.084	0.084	0.069	0.071

Note: (1) Data covers the Philadelphia-Camden-Wilmington, PA-NJ-DE-MD Metropolitan Statistical Area—see Appendix B for areas included. The values shown are the composite ozone concentration averages among trend sites based on the highest fourth daily maximum 8-hour concentration in parts per million. These trends are based on sites having an adequate record of monitoring data during the trend period. Data from exceptional events are included.
Source: U.S. Environmental Protection Agency, Air Quality Monitoring Information, "Air Quality Trends by City, 1990-2014"

Air Quality Index

Area	Percent of Days when Air Quality was...[2]					AQI Statistics[2]	
	Good	Moderate	Unhealthy for Sensitive Groups	Unhealthy	Very Unhealthy	Maximum	Median
MSA[1]	37.3	57.8	4.7	0.3	0.0	161	55

Note: (1) Data covers the Philadelphia-Camden-Wilmington, PA-NJ-DE-MD Metropolitan Statistical Area—see Appendix B for areas included; (2) Based on 365 days with AQI data in 2015. Air Quality Index (AQI) is an index for reporting daily air quality. EPA calculates the AQI for five major air pollutants regulated by the Clean Air Act: ground-level ozone, particle pollution (aka particulate matter), carbon monoxide, sulfur dioxide, and nitrogen dioxide. The AQI runs from 0 to 500. The higher the AQI value, the greater the level of air pollution and the greater the health concern. There are six AQI categories: "Good" AQI is between 0 and 50. Air quality is considered satisfactory; "Moderate" AQI is between 51 and 100. Air quality is acceptable; "Unhealthy for Sensitive Groups" When AQI values are between 101 and 150, members of sensitive groups may experience health effects; "Unhealthy" When AQI values are between 151 and 200 everyone may begin to experience health effects; "Very Unhealthy" AQI values between 201 and 300 trigger a health alert; "Hazardous" AQI values over 300 trigger warnings of emergency conditions (not shown).
Source: U.S. Environmental Protection Agency, Air Quality Index Report, 2015

Air Quality Index Pollutants

Area	Percent of Days when AQI Pollutant was...[2]					
	Carbon Monoxide	Nitrogen Dioxide	Ozone	Sulfur Dioxide	Particulate Matter 2.5	Particulate Matter 10
MSA[1]	0.0	4.1	28.2	0.3	66.6	0.8

Note: (1) Data covers the Philadelphia-Camden-Wilmington, PA-NJ-DE-MD Metropolitan Statistical Area—see Appendix B for areas included; (2) Based on 365 days with AQI data in 2015. The Air Quality Index (AQI) is an index for reporting daily air quality. EPA calculates the AQI for five major air pollutants regulated by the Clean Air Act: ground-level ozone, particle pollution (also known as particulate matter), carbon monoxide, sulfur dioxide, and nitrogen dioxide. The AQI runs from 0 to 500. The higher the AQI value, the greater the level of air pollution and the greater the health concern.

Source: U.S. Environmental Protection Agency, Air Quality Index Report, 2015

Maximum Air Pollutant Concentrations: Particulate Matter, Ozone, CO and Lead

	Particulate Matter 10 (ug/m^3)	Particulate Matter 2.5 Wtd AM (ug/m^3)	Particulate Matter 2.5 24-Hr (ug/m^3)	Ozone (ppm)	Carbon Monoxide (ppm)	Lead (ug/m^3)
MSA[1] Level	60	12.6	32	0.074	1	0.01
NAAQS[2]	150	15	35	0.075	9	0.15
Met NAAQS[2]	Yes	Yes	Yes	Yes	Yes	Yes

Note: (1) Data covers the Philadelphia-Camden-Wilmington, PA-NJ-DE-MD Metropolitan Statistical Area—see Appendix B for areas included; Data from exceptional events are included; (2) National Ambient Air Quality Standards; ppm = parts per million; ug/m^3 = micrograms per cubic meter; n/a not available.

Concentrations: Particulate Matter 10 (coarse particulate)—highest second maximum 24-hour concentration; Particulate Matter 2.5 Wtd AM (fine particulate)—highest weighted annual mean concentration; Particulate Matter 2.5 24-Hour (fine particulate)—highest 98th percentile 24-hour concentration; Ozone—highest fourth daily maximum 8-hour concentration; Carbon Monoxide—highest second maximum non-overlapping 8-hour concentration; Lead—maximum running 3-month average

Source: U.S. Environmental Protection Agency, Air Quality Monitoring Information, "Air Quality Statistics by City, 2014"

Maximum Air Pollutant Concentrations: Nitrogen Dioxide and Sulfur Dioxide

	Nitrogen Dioxide AM (ppb)	Nitrogen Dioxide 1-Hr (ppb)	Sulfur Dioxide AM (ppb)	Sulfur Dioxide 1-Hr (ppb)	Sulfur Dioxide 24-Hr (ppb)
MSA[1] Level	18	59	n/a	14	n/a
NAAQS[2]	53	100	30	75	140
Met NAAQS[2]	Yes	Yes	n/a	Yes	n/a

Note: (1) Data covers the Philadelphia-Camden-Wilmington, PA-NJ-DE-MD Metropolitan Statistical Area—see Appendix B for areas included; Data from exceptional events are included; (2) National Ambient Air Quality Standards; ppm = parts per million; ug/m^3 = micrograms per cubic meter; n/a not available.

Concentrations: Nitrogen Dioxide AM—highest arithmetic mean concentration; Nitrogen Dioxide 1-Hr—highest 98th percentile 1-hour daily maximum concentration; Sulfur Dioxide AM—highest annual mean concentration; Sulfur Dioxide 1-Hr—highest 99th percentile 1-hour daily maximum concentration; Sulfur Dioxide 24-Hr—highest second maximum 24-hour concentration

Source: U.S. Environmental Protection Agency, Air Quality Monitoring Information, "Air Quality Statistics by City, 2014"

Drinking Water

Water System Name	Pop. Served	Primary Water Source Type	Violations[1]	
			Health Based	Monitoring/ Reporting
Evesham MUA	47,784	Ground	0	3

Note: (1) Based on violation data from January 1, 2015 to December 31, 2015 (includes unresolved violations from earlier years)

Source: U.S. Environmental Protection Agency, Office of Ground Water and Drinking Water, Safe Drinking Water Information System (based on data extracted April 29, 2016)

Marlboro, New Jersey

Background

Marlboro rests 43 miles south of New York City in Monmouth County and less than 18 miles west of the Jersey shore, making it accessible to both a bustling urban center and peaceful seaside recreational opportunities.

The Township was established in 1848, largely as a farming community. From its earliest settlements until fairly recently, Marlboro was a rural community composed of a number of small hamlets. Although each had small inns or taverns, the hub of activity centered around what is still referred to today as Marlboro Village. Historical research reveals that the name came from the discovery of marl on a farm just east of the village in 1768. Marl, composed of the remains of prehistoric fish, clams, etc., dates back to the period when New Jersey was part of the ocean bed. Farmers used the heavily demanded marl to improve the soil in the days before commercial fertilizers, and the export of marl to all parts of the country became one of Marlboro's first industries.

During the Revolutionary War, Marlboro was the scene of many skirmishes between British and American forces. When retreating from the Battle of Monmouth in 1778, the British troops passed through Marlboro on their way to ships at nearby Sandy Hook. They were attacked by American militiamen who mobilized along their route.

Today, Marlboro is a largely residential suburban community which, although surrounded by urban sprawl, continues to encourage reclamation of its remaining open spaces. The now 415-acre Big Brook Park, once part of the Marlboro State Hospital facility, was acquired by the county to help protect the Navesink Watershed. This protected open space is adjacent to Camp Arrowhead Reserves, and includes a piece of the Henry Hudson Trail along its westerly edge.

In 2004, Marlboro Township launched an education and government television station. Informational and educational programming, produced by Marlboro Township, can be seen in households throughout the municipality. The video messaging system features public information from the Township, the Board of Education, and local not-for-profit entities.

The school systems in Marlboro offer several innovative opportunities. The Marlboro Early Learning Center serves all pre-school handicapped, as well as all kindergarten children in the district. Students in grades one through five attend one of five elementary schools in the district. A district wide approach to curriculum development results in a common and equal teaching guide in all the schools. Each school, however, is unique in its implementation of the curricula.

Marlboro Middle School and the district's newest school, finished in 2003, Marlboro Memorial Middle School houses all students in the sixth through eighth grades. Seventh and eighth grade students are offered an Enrichment Opportunity Period, which enables them to select several electives throughout the year.

Rankings

General Rankings

- New York* was identified as one of America's fastest-growing major metropolitan areas in terms of population growth by CNNMoney.com. The area ranked #1 out of 10. Criteria: population growth between July 2013 and July 2014. *CNNMoney, "10 Fastest-Growing Cities," May 27, 2015*

Business/Finance Rankings

- The personal finance site NerdWallet analyzed 183 American metropolitan areas with populations over 250,000 and more than 15,000 businesses to rank where entrepreneurs find the most success. Criteria included area economy, annual income, housing cost, unemployment rate, and the success rate of area businesses. New York* ranked #32. *www.nerdwallet.com, "Best Places to Start a Business," April 27, 2015*
- Based on the U.S. Department of Labor's Occupational Information Network Data Collection Program, the Brookings Institution defined job opportunities for STEM workers at various levels of educational attainment. The New York* metro area was one of the ten metro areas where workers in low-education-level STEM jobs earn the lowest relative wages. *www.brookings.edu, "The Hidden Stem Economy," June 10, 2013*
- Metro areas with the largest gap in income between rich and poor residents were identified by 24/7 Wall Street using the U.S. Census Bureau's 2013 American Community Survey. The New York* metro area placed #7 among metro areas with the widest wealth gap between rich and poor. *247wallst.com, "20 Cities with the Widest Gap between the Rich and Poor," July 8, 2015*
- Based on metro area social media reviews, the employment opinion group Glassdoor surveyed 50 of the largest U.S. metro areas and equally weighed cost of living, hiring opportunity, and job satisfaction to compose a list of "25 Best Cities for Jobs." The New York* metro area was ranked #21 in overall job satisfaction. *www.glassdoor.com, "Best Cities for Jobs," May 19, 2015*
- In a survey of economic confidence in the nation's 50 largest metropolitan areas conducted January–December 2014, the New York* metro area placed #23, according to Gallup's 2014 Economic Confidence Index. *Gallup, "San Jose and San Francisco Lead in Economic Confidence," March 19, 2015*
- The Brookings Institution ranked the 100 largest metro areas in the U.S. based on income inequality. New York* was ranked #2 (#1 = greatest ineqality). Criteria: the "95/20 ratio," a figure representing the income at which a household earns more than 95 percent of all other households, divided by the income at which a household earns more than only 20 percent of all other households. *Brookings Institution, "Income Inequality, 100 Largest U.S. Metro Areas, 2007-2014," January 14, 2016*
- Payscale.com ranked the 20 largest metro areas in terms of wage growth. The New York* metro area ranked #18. Criteria: private-sector wage growth between the 1st quarter of 2015 and the 1st quarter of 2016. *PayScale, "Wage Trends by Metro Area," 1st Quarter, 2016*
- The New York* metro area appeared on the Milken Institute "2015 Best Performing Cities" list. Rank: #90 out of 200 large metro areas. Criteria: job growth; wage and salary growth; high-tech output growth. *Milken Institute, "Best-Performing Cities 2015," December 2015*
- *Forbes* ranked the 200 most populous metro areas to determine the nation's "Best Places for Business and Careers." The New York* metro area was ranked #111. Criteria: costs (business and living); job growth (past and projected); income growth; educational attainment (college and high school); projected economic growth; cultural and recreational opportunities; net migration patterns; number of highly ranked colleges. *Forbes, "The Best Places for Business and Careers 2015," July 29, 2015*

Dating/Romance Rankings

- CreditDonkey, a financial education website, sought out the ten best U.S. cities for newlyweds, considering the number of married couples, divorce rate, average credit score, and average number of hours worked per week in metro areas with a million or more residents. The New York* metro area placed #5. *www.creditdonkey.com, "Study: Best Cities for Newlyweds," November 30, 2013*

Education Rankings

- Personal finance website *WalletHub* analyzed the 150 largest U.S. metropolitan statistical areas to determine where the most educated Americans are choosing to settle. Criteria: education quality and attainment gap; education levels; percentage of workers with degrees; public school rankings; quality and size of each metro area's universities. New York* was ranked #58 (#1 = most educated city). *www.WalletHub.com, "2015's Most and Least Educated Cities*

Environmental Rankings

- The New York* metro area came in at #155 for the relative comfort of its climate on Sperling's list of "chill cities," as measured by the Sperling Heat Index. All 361 metro areas are included. Criteria included daytime high temperatures, nighttime low temperatures, dew point, and relative humidity at the high temperatures. *www.bertsperling.com, "Sperling's Chill Cities," July 18, 2013*

- Sperling's BestPlaces assessed 379 metropolitan areas of the United States for the likelihood of dangerously extreme weather events or earthquakes. In general the Southeast and South-Central regions have the highest risk of weather extremes and earthquakes, while the Pacific Northwest enjoys the lowest risk. Of the least risky metropolitan areas, the New York* metro area was ranked #207. *www.bestplaces.net, "Safest Places from Natural Disasters," April 2011*

- New York* was identified as one of America's dirtiest metro areas by *Forbes.* The area ranked #11 out of 20. Criteria: air quality; water quality; toxic releases; superfund sites. *Forbes, "America's 20 Dirtiest Cities," December 10, 2012*

- The U.S. Environmental Protection Agency (EPA) released a list of U.S. metropolitan areas with the most ENERGY STAR certified buildings in 2015. The New York* metro area was ranked #5 out of 25. *U.S. Environmental Protection Agency, "Top Cities With the Most ENERGY STAR Certified Buildings in 2016," March 30, 2016*

- New York* was highlighted as one of the 25 most ozone-polluted metro areas in the U.S. during 2011 through 2013. The area ranked #11. *American Lung Association, State of the Air 2015*

- New York* was highlighted as one of the 25 metro areas most polluted by year-round particle pollution (Annual PM 2.5) in the U.S. during 2011 through 2013. The area ranked #14. *American Lung Association, State of the Air 2015*

- New York* was highlighted as one of the 25 metro areas most polluted by short-term particle pollution (24-hour PM 2.5) in the U.S. during 2011 through 2013. The area ranked #15. *American Lung Association, State of the Air 2015*

Health/Fitness Rankings

- For each of the 50 most populous metro areas in the United States, the American College of Sports Medicine's American Fitness Index evaluated infrastructure, community assets, and policies that encourage healthy and fit lifestyles, including preventive health behaviors, levels of chronic disease conditions, health care access, and community resources and policies that support physical activity. The New York* metro area ranked #24 for "community fitness." *www.americanfitnessindex.org, "ACSM American Fitness Index Health and Community Fitness Status of the 50 Largest Metropolitan Areas," May 2015*

- *Business Insider* reported Trulia's analysis of the 100 largest U.S. metro areas to identify the nation's best cities for weight loss, based on healthful food options, access to outdoor activities, weight-loss centers, gyms, and opportunities to bike or walk to work. New York* ranked #6. *Businessinsider.com, "These Are the Best US Cities for Weight loss," January 17, 2013*
- The New York* metro area was identified as one of the worst cities for bed bugs in America by pest control company Orkin. The area ranked #4 out of 50 based on the number of bed bug treatments Orkin performed from January to December 2015. *Orkin, "Chicago Tops Bed Bug Cities List for Fourth Year in a Row," January 13, 2016*
- New York* was identified as a "2016 Spring Allergy Capital." The area ranked #31 out of 100. Three groups of factors were used to identify the most severe cities for people with allergies during the spring season: annual pollen levels; medicine utilization; access to board-certified allergists. *Asthma and Allergy Foundation of America, "Spring Allergy Capitals 2016"*
- New York* was identified as a "2015 Asthma Capital." The area ranked #35 out of the nation's 100 largest metropolitan areas. Criteria: estimated prevalence; self-reported prevalence; crude death rate for asthma; annual pollen score; annual air quality; public smoking laws; number of board-certified asthma specialists; school inhaler access laws; rescue medication use; controller medication use; ER visits for asthma; uninsured rate; poverty rate. *Asthma and Allergy Foundation of America, "Asthma Capitals 2015"*
- The New York* metro area ranked #113 out of 190 in The Gallup-Healthways Well-Being Index. Criteria: purpose; social well being; financial health; community and physical health. Results are based on telephone interviews with adults, aged 18 and older, living in metropolitan areas in the 50 U.S. states and the District of Columbia. *Gallup-Healthways, "State of American Well-Being," February 23, 2016*

Real Estate Rankings

- With data from RealtyTrac, Yahoo! Finance researchers listed the housing markets in which housing affordability is improving most, factoring in interest rates as well as median home prices. The New York* metro area was among the least affordable housing markets. *news.yahoo.com, "10 Cities Where Ordinary People Can No Longer Afford Homes," March 5, 2014*
- The New York* metro area was identified as one of the 20 least affordable housing markets in the U.S. in 2015. The area ranked #9 out of 179 markets. Criteria: qualification for a mortgage loan on a typical home. *National Association of Realtors®, Affordability Index of Existing Single-Family Homes for Metropolitan Areas, 2015*
- New York* was ranked #217 out of 225 metro areas in terms of housing affordability in 2015 by the National Association of Home Builders (#1 = most affordable). Criteria: the share of homes sold in that area affordable to a family earning the local median income, based on standard mortgage underwriting criteria. *National Association of Home Builders®, NAHB-Wells Fargo Housing Opportunity Index, 4th Quarter 2015*

Safety Rankings

- New York* was identified as one of the most disaster-proof places in the U.S. in terms of its vulnerability to natural and non-natural disasters. The city ranked #1 out of 5. Rankings are based on the U.S. Center for Disease Control's Cities Readiness Initiative (CRI), which assesses local emergency-management plans, protocols and capabilities for 72 Metropolitan Statistical Areas and four non-MSA large cities. *Forbes, "America's Most and Least Disaster-Proof Cities," December 12, 2011*
- The National Insurance Crime Bureau ranked 380 metro areas in the U.S. in terms of per capita rates of vehicle theft. The New York* metro area ranked #249 (#1 = highest rate). Criteria: number of vehicle theft offenses per 100,000 inhabitants in 2014. *National Insurance Crime Bureau, "Hot Spots 2014," June 24, 2015*

Seniors/Retirement Rankings

- From its Best Cities for Successful Aging indexes, the Milken Institute generated rankings for metropolitan areas, weighing data in eight categories—health care, wellness, living arrangements, transportation, financial characteristics, education and employment opportunities, community engagement, and overall livability. The New York* metro area was ranked #14 overall in the large metro area category. *Milken Institute, "Best Cities for Successful Aging, 2014"*

Sports/Recreation Rankings

- According to the personal finance website NerdWallet, the New York* metro area, at #4, is one of the nation's top dozen metro areas for sports fans. Criteria included the presence of all four major sports—MLB, NFL, NHL, and NBA, fan enthusiasm (as measured by game attendance), ticket affordability, and "sports culture," that is, number of sports bars. *www.nerdwallet.com, "Best Cities for Sports Fans," May 5, 2013*

Transportation Rankings

- New York* was identified as one of the most congested metro areas in the U.S. The area ranked #4 out of 10. Criteria: yearly delay per auto commuter in hours. *Texas A&M Transportation Institute, "2015 Urban Mobility Scorecard," August 2015*
- The New York* metro area appeared on *Forbes* list of places with the most extreme commutes. The metro area ranked #2 out of 10. Criteria: average travel time; percentage of mega commuters. Mega-commuters travel more than 90 minutes and 50 miles each way to work. *Forbes.com, "The Cities with the Most Extreme Commutes," March 5, 2013*

Miscellaneous Rankings

- The watchdog site Charity Navigator conducts an annual study of charities in the nation's major markets both to analyze statistical differences in their financial, accountability, and transparency practices and to track year-to-year variations in individual communities. The New York* metro area was ranked #17 among the 30 metro markets in the rating dimension of Overall Score. *www.charitynavigator.org, "Metro Market Study 2015," June 5, 2015*
- The Harris Poll's Happiness Index survey revealed that of the top ten U.S. markets, the New York* metro area residents ranked #6 in happiness. Criteria included strong assent to positive statements and strong disagreement with negative ones, and degree of agreement with a series of statements about respondents' personal relationships and general outlook. *www.harrisinteractive.com, "Dallas/Fort Worth Is "Happiest" City among America's Top Ten Markets," September 4, 2013*
- Energizer Personal Care, the makers of Edge® shave gel, in partnership with Sperling's BestPlaces, ranked 50 major metro areas in terms of everyday irritations. The New York* metro area ranked #2 the 50 metro area most iritating to guys. Criteria: high male-to-female ratio; poor sports team performance and high ticket prices; slow traffic; lack of job availability; unaffordable housing; extreme weather; lack of nightlife and fitness options. *Energizer Personal Care, "Most Irritatng Cities for Guys," August 26, 2013*
- Mars Chocolate North America, the makers of COMBOS®, in partnership with Sperling's BestPlaces, ranked 50 major metro areas in terms of their "manliness." The New York* metro area ranked #39. Criteria: number of professional sports teams; number of nearby NASCAR tracks and racing events; manly lifestyle; concentration of manly retail stores; manly occupations per capita; salty snack sales; "Board of Manliness" rankings. *Mars Chocolate North America, "America's Manliest Cities 2012"*
- The New York* metro area was selected as one of "America's Most Miserable Cities" by *Forbes.com.* The metro area ranked #10 out of 20. Criteria: violent crime; unemployment; foreclosures; income and property taxes; home prices; commute times; climate. *Forbes.com, "America's Most Miserable Cities" February 22, 2013*

- The National Alliance to End Homelessness ranked the 100 most populous metro areas with the highest rate of homelessness. The New York* metro area ranked #13. Criteria: number of homeless people per 10,000 population in 2011. *National Alliance to End Homelessness, The State of Homelessness in America 2012*

***Marlboro is located within the New York-Newark-Jersey City, NY-NJ-PA Metropolitan Statistical Area.**

Business Environment

CITY FINANCES

City Government Finances

Component	2012 ($000)	2012 ($ per capita)
Total Revenues	37,689	937
Total Expenditures	37,660	937
Debt Outstanding	45,953	1,143
Cash and Securities[1]	20,318	505

Note: (1) Cash and security holdings of a government at the close of its fiscal year, including those of its dependent agencies, utilities, and liquor stores.
Source: U.S Census Bureau, State & Local Government Finances 2012

City Government Revenue by Source

Source	2012 ($000)	2012 ($ per capita)
General Revenue		
From Federal Government	8	0
From State Government	2,636	65
From Local Governments	0	0
Taxes		
Property	23,861	593
Sales and Gross Receipts	160	3
Personal Income	0	0
Corporate Income	0	0
Motor Vehicle License	0	0
Other Taxes	672	16
Current Charges	900	22
Liquor Store	0	0
Utility	7,972	198
Employee Retirement	0	0

Source: U.S Census Bureau, State & Local Government Finances 2012

City Government Expenditures by Function

Function	2012 ($000)	2012 ($ per capita)	2012 (%)
General Direct Expenditures			
Air Transportation	0	0	0.0
Corrections	0	0	0.0
Education	0	0	0.0
Employment Security Administration	0	0	0.0
Financial Administration	1,100	27	2.9
Fire Protection	164	4	0.4
General Public Buildings	493	12	1.3
Governmental Administration, Other	938	23	2.4
Health	185	4	0.4
Highways	3,975	98	10.5
Hospitals	0	0	0.0
Housing and Community Development	4	< 1	< 0.1
Interest on General Debt	834	20	2.2
Judicial and Legal	374	9	0.9
Libraries	8	< 1	< 0.1
Parking	0	0	0.0
Parks and Recreation	1,663	41	4.4
Police Protection	9,076	225	24.1
Public Welfare	0	0	0.0
Sewerage	10	< 1	< 0.1
Solid Waste Management	210	5	0.5
Veterans' Services	0	0	0.0
Liquor Store	0	0	0.0
Utility	6,356	158	16.8
Employee Retirement	0	0	0.0

Source: U.S Census Bureau, State & Local Government Finances 2012

DEMOGRAPHICS

Population Growth

Area	1990 Census	2000 Census	2010 Census	2014* Estimate	Population Growth (%) 1990-2014	Population Growth (%) 2010-2014
City	27,974	36,398	40,191	40,370	44.3	0.4
MSA[1]	16,845,992	18,323,002	18,897,109	19,865,045	17.9	5.1
U.S.	248,709,873	281,421,906	308,745,538	314,107,084	26.3	1.7

Note: (1) Figures cover the New York-Newark-Jersey City, NY-NJ-PA Metropolitan Statistical Area—see Appendix B for areas included; (*) 2010-2014 5-year estimated population
Source: U.S. Census Bureau, 1990 Census, Census 2000, Census 2010, 2010-2014 American Community Survey 5-Year Estimates

Household Size

Area	Persons in Household (%)							Average Household Size
	One	Two	Three	Four	Five	Six	Seven or More	
City	13.2	29.2	18.1	25.5	9.5	2.9	1.2	3.11
MSA[1]	27.8	28.9	17.0	14.8	6.7	2.6	1.9	2.74
U.S.	27.5	33.5	15.8	13.1	6.0	2.3	1.4	2.64

Note: (1) Figures cover the New York-Newark-Jersey City, NY-NJ-PA Metropolitan Statistical Area—see Appendix B for areas included
Source: U.S. Census Bureau, 2010-2014 American Community Survey 5-Year Estimates

Race

Area	White Alone[2] (%)	Black Alone[2] (%)	Asian Alone[2] (%)	AIAN[3] Alone[2] (%)	NHOPI[4] Alone[2] (%)	Other Race Alone[2] (%)	Two or More Races (%)
City	79.2	1.6	17.0	0.1	0.0	0.4	1.7
MSA[1]	59.4	17.2	10.2	0.3	0.0	10.1	2.8
U.S.	73.8	12.6	5.0	0.8	0.2	4.7	2.9

Note: (1) Figures cover the New York-Newark-Jersey City, NY-NJ-PA Metropolitan Statistical Area—see Appendix B for areas included; (2) Alone is defined as not being in combination with one or more other races; (3) American Indian and Alaska Native; (4) Native Hawaiian and Other Pacific Islander
Source: U.S. Census Bureau, 2010-2014 American Community Survey 5-Year Estimates

Hispanic or Latino Origin

Area	Total (%)	Mexican (%)	Puerto Rican (%)	Cuban (%)	Other (%)
City	4.1	0.2	1.3	0.6	2.1
MSA[1]	23.3	3.0	6.4	0.7	13.1
U.S.	16.9	10.8	1.6	0.6	3.8

Note: Persons of Hispanic or Latino origin can be of any race; (1) Figures cover the New York-Newark-Jersey City, NY-NJ-PA Metropolitan Statistical Area—see Appendix B for areas included
Source: U.S. Census Bureau, 2010-2014 American Community Survey 5-Year Estimates

Ancestry

Area	German	Irish	English	American	Italian	Polish	French[2]	Scottish	Dutch
City	7.3	9.5	2.4	6.5	23.9	9.1	0.6	0.5	0.3
MSA[1]	7.2	10.6	3.1	4.4	13.7	4.2	1.1	0.7	0.7
U.S.	14.9	10.8	8.0	7.1	5.5	3.0	2.7	1.7	1.4

Note: Figures are the percentage of the total population reporting a particular ancestry. The nine most commonly reported ancestries in the U.S. are shown. Figures include multiple ancestries (e.g. if a person reported being Irish and Italian, they were included in both columns); (1) Figures cover the New York-Newark-Jersey City, NY-NJ-PA Metropolitan Statistical Area—see Appendix B for areas included; (2) Excludes Basque
Source: U.S. Census Bureau, 2010-2014 American Community Survey 5-Year Estimates

Foreign-Born Population

Area	Percent of Population Born in								
	Any Foreign Country	Asia	Mexico	Europe	Carribean	Central America[2]	South America	Africa	Canada
City	20.0	11.4	0.1	6.2	0.4	0.1	0.8	0.7	0.4
MSA[1]	28.5	8.0	1.7	4.6	6.5	1.9	4.3	1.2	0.2
U.S.	13.1	3.8	3.7	1.5	1.2	1.0	0.9	0.6	0.3

Note: (1) Figures cover the New York-Newark-Jersey City, NY-NJ-PA Metropolitan Statistical Area—see Appendix B for areas included; (2) Excludes Mexico.
Source: U.S. Census Bureau, 2010-2014 American Community Survey 5-Year Estimates

Marital Status

Area	Never Married	Now Married[2]	Separated	Widowed	Divorced
City	23.7	66.5	0.6	5.1	4.1
MSA[1]	37.7	45.8	2.5	6.0	7.9
U.S.	32.5	48.4	2.2	5.9	10.9

Note: Figures are percentages and cover the population 15 years of age and older; (1) Figures cover the New York-Newark-Jersey City, NY-NJ-PA Metropolitan Statistical Area—see Appendix B for areas included; (2) Excludes separated
Source: U.S. Census Bureau, 2010-2014 American Community Survey 5-Year Estimates

Disability Status

Area	All Ages	Under 18 Years Old	18 to 64 Years Old	65 Years and Over
City	6.5	2.4	4.1	26.6
MSA[1]	9.8	3.1	7.3	33.5
U.S.	12.3	4.1	10.2	36.3

Note: Figures show percent of the civilian noninstitutionalized population that reported having a disability. Disability status is determined from from six types of difficulty: vision, hearing, cognitive, ambulatory, self-care, and independent living. For children under 5 years old, hearing and vision difficulty are used to determine disability status. For children between the ages of 5 and 14, disability status is determined from hearing, vision, cognitive, ambulatory, and self-care difficulties. For people aged 15 years and older, they are considered to have a disability if they have difficulty with any one of the six difficulty types; (1) Figures cover the New York-Newark-Jersey City, NY-NJ-PA Metropolitan Statistical Area—see Appendix B for areas included.
Source: U.S. Census Bureau, 2010-2014 American Community Survey 5-Year Estimates

Age

Area	Percent of Population									Median Age
	Under Age 5	Age 5–19	Age 20–34	Age 35–44	Age 45–54	Age 55–64	Age 65–74	Age 75–84	Age 85+	
City	5.2	24.0	12.3	12.7	20.0	13.4	7.1	3.7	1.6	42.4
MSA[1]	6.2	18.8	21.2	13.6	14.6	12.0	7.3	4.2	2.0	37.8
U.S.	6.4	19.9	20.6	13.0	14.1	12.3	7.6	4.3	1.9	37.4

Note: (1) Figures cover the New York-Newark-Jersey City, NY-NJ-PA Metropolitan Statistical Area—see Appendix B for areas included
Source: U.S. Census Bureau, 2010-2014 American Community Survey 5-Year Estimates

Gender

Area	Males	Females	Males per 100 Females
City	19,532	20,838	93.7
MSA[1]	9,593,127	10,271,918	93.4
U.S.	154,515,159	159,591,925	96.8

Note: (1) Figures cover the New York-Newark-Jersey City, NY-NJ-PA Metropolitan Statistical Area—see Appendix B for areas included
Source: U.S. Census Bureau, 2010-2014 American Community Survey 5-Year Estimates

Religious Groups by Family

Area	Catholic	Baptist	Non-Den.	Methodist[2]	Lutheran	LDS[3]	Pente-costal	Presby-terian[4]	Muslim[5]	Judaism
MSA[1]	36.9	1.8	1.7	1.3	0.7	0.3	0.8	1.0	2.3	4.7
U.S.	19.1	9.3	4.0	4.0	2.3	2.0	1.9	1.6	0.8	0.7

Note: Figures are the number of adherents as a percentage of the total population; (1) Figures cover the New York-Northern New Jersey-Long Island, NY-NJ-PA Metropolitan Statistical Area—see Appendix B for areas included; (2) Methodist/Pietist; (3) Latter Day Saints; (4) Reformed; (5) Figures are estimates
Source: Association of Statisticians of American Religious Bodies, 2010 U.S. Religion Census: Religious Congregations & Membership Study

Religious Groups by Tradition

Area	Catholic	Evangelical Protestant	Mainline Protestant	Other Tradition	Black Protestant	Orthodox
MSA[1]	36.9	3.9	4.1	8.3	1.2	0.9
U.S.	19.1	16.2	7.3	4.3	1.6	0.3

Note: Figures are the number of adherents as a percentage of the total population; (1) Figures cover the New York-Northern New Jersey-Long Island, NY-NJ-PA Metropolitan Statistical Area—see Appendix B for areas included
Source: Association of Statisticians of American Religious Bodies, 2010 U.S. Religion Census: Religious Congregations & Membership Study

ECONOMY

Gross Metropolitan Product

Area	2013	2014	2015	2016	Rank[2]
MSA[1]	1,471.2	1,521.7	1,573.8	1,650.1	1

Note: Figures are in billions of dollars; (1) Figures cover the New York-Newark-Jersey City, NY-NJ-PA Metropolitan Statistical Area—see Appendix B for areas included; (2) Rank is based on 2016 data and ranges from 1 to 381
Source: The U.S. Conference of Mayors, U.S. Metro Economies: GMP and Employment 2014-2016, June 2015

Economic Growth

Area	2011-13 (%)	2014 (%)	2015 (%)	2016 (%)	Rank[2]
MSA[1]	1.6	1.8	2.0	2.8	116
U.S.	2.2	2.4	2.3	2.9	–

Note: Figures are real gross metropolitan product (GMP) growth rates and represent annual average percent change; (1) Figures cover the New York-Newark-Jersey City, NY-NJ-PA Metropolitan Statistical Area—see Appendix B for areas included; (2) Rank is based on 2016 data and ranges from 1 to 381
Source: The U.S. Conference of Mayors, U.S. Metro Economies: GMP and Employment 2014-2016, June 2015

Metropolitan Area Exports

Area	2009	2010	2011	2012	2013	2014	Rank[2]
MSA[1]	69,990.3	85,081.1	105,102.0	102,298.0	106,922.8	105,266.5	2

Note: Figures are in millions of dollars; (1) Figures cover the New York-Newark-Jersey City, NY-NJ-PA Metropolitan Statistical Area—see Appendix B for areas included; (2) Rank is based on 2014 data and ranges from 1 to 385
Source: U.S. Department of Commerce, International Trade Administration, Office of Trade & Industry Information, Manufacturing & Services, data extracted March 10, 2016

Building Permits

Area	Single-Family			Multi-Family			Total		
	2014	2015p	Pct. Chg.	2014	2015p	Pct. Chg.	2014	2015p	Pct. Chg.
City	6	7	16.7	5	30	500.0	11	37	236.4
MSA[1]	11,799	10,749	-8.9	36,185	75,646	109.1	47,984	86,395	80.0
U.S.	640,300	690,800	7.9	411,800	487,600	18.4	1,052,100	1,178,400	12.0

Note: (1) Figures cover the New York-Newark-Jersey City, NY-NJ-PA Metropolitan Statistical Area—see Appendix B for areas included; Figures represent new, privately-owned housing units authorized (unadjusted data); All permit data are based on estimates with imputation; (p) preliminary data.
Source: U.S. Census Bureau, Manufacturing, Mining, and Construction Statistics, Building Permits, 2014, 2015

Bankruptcy Filings

Area	Business Filings			Nonbusiness Filings		
	2014	2015	% Chg.	2014	2015	% Chg.
Monmouth County	66	48	-27.3	1,641	1,461	-11.0
U.S.	26,983	24,735	-8.3	909,812	819,760	-9.9

Note: Business filings include Chapter 7, Chapter 11, Chapter 12, and Chapter 13; Nonbusiness filings include Chapter 7, Chapter 11, and Chapter 13
Source: Administrative Office of the U.S. Courts, Business and Nonbusiness Bankruptcy, County Cases Commenced by Chapter of the Bankruptcy Code, During the 12- Month Period Ending December 31, 2014 and Business and Nonbusiness Bankruptcy, County Cases Commenced by Chapter of the Bankruptcy Code, During the 12- Month Period Ending December 31, 2015

Housing Vacancy Rates

Area	Gross Vacancy Rate[2] (%)			Year-Round Vacancy Rate[3] (%)			Rental Vacancy Rate[4] (%)			Homeowner Vacancy Rate[5] (%)		
	2013	2014	2015	2013	2014	2015	2013	2014	2015	2013	2014	2015
MSA[1]	9.5	9.2	9.8	8.1	7.9	8.6	5.4	4.6	4.2	2.1	1.6	2.1
U.S.	13.6	13.4	12.9	10.7	10.4	10.0	8.3	7.6	7.1	2.0	1.9	1.8

Note: (1) Figures cover the New York-Newark-Jersey City, NY-NJ-PA Metropolitan Statistical Area—see Appendix B for areas included; (2) The percentage of the total housing inventory that is vacant; (3) The percentage of the housing inventory (excluding seasonal units) that is year-round vacant; (4) The percentage of rental inventory that is vacant for rent; (5) The percentage of homeowner inventory that is vacant for sale
Source: U.S. Census Bureau, Housing Vacancies and Homeownership Annual Statistics: 2015

INCOME

Income

Area	Per Capita ($)	Median Household ($)	Average Household ($)
City	54,843	135,929	168,917
MSA[1]	36,078	66,902	97,572
U.S.	28,555	53,482	74,596

Note: (1) Figures cover the New York-Newark-Jersey City, NY-NJ-PA Metropolitan Statistical Area—see Appendix B for areas included
Source: U.S. Census Bureau, 2010-2014 American Community Survey 5-Year Estimates

Household Income Distribution

Area	Percent of Households Earning							
	Under $15,000	$15,000 -24,999	$25,000 -34,999	$35,000 -49,999	$50,000 -74,999	$75,000 -99,000	$100,000 -149,999	$150,000 and up
City	2.7	4.1	3.7	5.2	8.8	10.9	19.8	44.8
MSA[1]	11.8	8.8	8.0	10.6	15.3	11.9	15.7	18.0
U.S.	12.5	10.7	10.2	13.5	17.8	12.2	13.0	10.0

Note: (1) Figures cover the New York-Newark-Jersey City, NY-NJ-PA Metropolitan Statistical Area—see Appendix B for areas included
Source: U.S. Census Bureau, 2010-2014 American Community Survey 5-Year Estimates

Poverty Rate

Area	All Ages	Under 18 Years Old	18 to 64 Years Old	65 Years and Over
City	1.4	0.9	1.6	1.9
MSA[1]	14.3	20.0	12.8	11.6
U.S.	15.6	21.9	14.6	9.4

Note: Figures are percentage of people whose income during the past 12 months was below the poverty level; (1) Figures cover the New York-Newark-Jersey City, NY-NJ-PA Metropolitan Statistical Area—see Appendix B for areas included
Source: U.S. Census Bureau, 2010-2014 American Community Survey 5-Year Estimates

EMPLOYMENT

Labor Force and Employment

Area	Civilian Labor Force			Workers Employed		
	Dec. 2014	Dec. 2015	% Chg.	Dec. 2014	Dec. 2015	% Chg.
City	19,868	20,266	2.0	19,069	19,647	3.0
MD[1]	7,017,636	7,184,671	2.3	6,611,164	6,853,780	3.6
U.S.	155,521,000	157,245,000	1.1	147,190,000	149,703,000	1.7

Note: Data is not seasonally adjusted and covers workers 16 years of age and older; (1) Figures cover the New York-Jersey City-White Plains, NY-NJ Metropolitan Division—see Appendix B for areas included
Source: Bureau of Labor Statistics, Local Area Unemployment Statistics

Unemployment Rate

Area	2015											
	Jan.	Feb.	Mar.	Apr.	May	Jun.	Jul.	Aug.	Sep.	Oct.	Nov.	Dec.
City	4.9	4.5	4.3	4.3	4.8	4.1	4.8	4.2	4.0	3.9	3.6	3.1
MD[1]	6.7	6.8	6.2	5.8	5.8	5.4	5.7	5.2	4.9	4.7	4.8	4.6
U.S.	6.1	5.8	5.6	5.1	5.3	5.5	5.6	5.2	4.9	4.8	4.8	4.8

Note: Data is not seasonally adjusted and covers workers 16 years of age and older; (1) Figures cover the New York-Jersey City-White Plains, NY-NJ Metropolitan Division—see Appendix B for areas included
Source: Bureau of Labor Statistics, Local Area Unemployment Statistics

Employment by Occupation

Occupation Classification	City (%)	MSA[1] (%)	U.S. (%)
Management, Business, Science, and Arts	56.3	40.3	36.4
Natural Resources, Construction, and Maintenance	4.3	7.0	9.0
Production, Transportation, and Material Moving	4.6	9.1	12.1
Sales and Office	26.3	24.2	24.4
Service	8.5	19.4	18.2

Note: Figures cover employed civilians 16 years of age and older; (1) Figures cover the New York-Newark-Jersey City, NY-NJ-PA Metropolitan Statistical Area—see Appendix B for areas included
Source: U.S. Census Bureau, 2010-2014 American Community Survey 5-Year Estimates

Employment by Industry

Sector	MD[1]		U.S.
	Number of Employees	Percent of Total	Percent of Total
Construction, Mining, and Logging	256,300	3.7	5.0
Education and Health Services	1,350,800	19.7	15.7
Financial Activities	612,400	8.9	5.7
Government	917,500	13.3	15.5
Information	243,800	3.5	1.9
Leisure and Hospitality	638,900	9.3	10.4
Manufacturing	211,600	3.0	8.6
Other Services	296,100	4.3	3.9
Professional and Business Services	1,107,000	16.1	13.9
Retail Trade	686,300	10.0	11.3
Transportation, Warehousing, and Utilities	251,300	3.6	3.9
Wholesale Trade	284,100	4.1	4.1

Note: Figures are non-farm employment as of December 2015. Figures are not seasonally adjusted and include workers 16 years of age and older; (1) Figures cover the New York-Jersey City-White Plains, NY-NJ Metropolitan Division—see Appendix B for areas included; n/a not available
Source: Bureau of Labor Statistics, Current Employment Statistics, Employment, Hours, and Earnings

Occupations with Greatest Projected Employment Growth: 2012 – 2022

Occupation[1]	2012 Employment	2022 Projected Employment	Numeric Employment Change	Percent Employment Change
Home Health Aides	31,140	46,280	15,140	48.6
Combined Food Preparation and Serving Workers, Including Fast Food	59,990	70,180	10,190	17.0
Retail Salespersons	125,690	134,870	9,180	7.3
Registered Nurses	79,840	88,880	9,040	11.3
Nursing Assistants	51,780	60,070	8,290	16.0
Laborers and Freight, Stock, and Material Movers, Hand	75,730	83,360	7,630	10.1
Software Developers, Applications	29,090	35,770	6,680	23.0
Receptionists and Information Clerks	51,160	57,830	6,670	13.0
Customer Service Representatives	63,450	69,530	6,080	9.6
Sales Representatives, Services, All Other	45,510	51,380	5,870	12.9

Note: Projections cover New Jersey; (1) Sorted by numeric employment change
Source: www.projectionscentral.com, State Occupational Projections, 2012–2022 Long-Term Projections

Fastest Growing Occupations: 2012 – 2022

Occupation[1]	2012 Employment	2022 Projected Employment	Numeric Employment Change	Percent Employment Change
Home Health Aides	31,140	46,280	15,140	48.6
Insulation Workers, Mechanical	370	540	170	48.2
Diagnostic Medical Sonographers	2,550	3,550	1,000	39.1
Occupational Therapy Assistants	370	500	130	37.5
Helpers—Electricians	1,310	1,800	490	37.5
Stonemasons	580	780	200	35.4
Physical Therapist Assistants	1,090	1,470	380	34.1
Skincare Specialists	1,050	1,400	350	33.2
Physician Assistants	1,450	1,920	470	32.8
Brickmasons and Blockmasons	2,150	2,830	680	31.7

Note: Projections cover New Jersey; (1) Sorted by percent employment change and excludes occupations with numeric employment change less than 100
Source: www.projectionscentral.com, State Occupational Projections, 2012–2022 Long-Term Projections

Average Wages

Occupation	$/Hr.	Occupation	$/Hr.
Accountants and Auditors	46.43	Maids and Housekeeping Cleaners	16.84
Automotive Mechanics	20.21	Maintenance and Repair Workers	21.29
Bookkeepers	21.54	Marketing Managers	89.06
Carpenters	32.53	Nuclear Medicine Technologists	40.65
Cashiers	10.92	Nurses, Licensed Practical	25.33
Clerks, General Office	15.88	Nurses, Registered	41.54
Clerks, Receptionists/Information	15.02	Nursing Assistants	16.38
Clerks, Shipping/Receiving	16.94	Packers and Packagers, Hand	11.33
Computer Programmers	46.00	Physical Therapists	44.91
Computer Systems Analysts	50.45	Postal Service Mail Carriers	25.04
Computer User Support Specialists	28.75	Real Estate Brokers	50.12
Cooks, Restaurant	13.74	Retail Salespersons	12.99
Dentists	76.20	Sales Reps., Exc. Tech./Scientific	35.67
Electrical Engineers	48.32	Sales Reps., Tech./Scientific	51.39
Electricians	37.19	Secretaries, Exc. Legal/Med./Exec.	19.62
Financial Managers	90.86	Security Guards	15.32
First-Line Supervisors/Managers, Sales	24.90	Surgeons	113.38
Food Preparation Workers	11.50	Teacher Assistants*	13.73
General and Operations Managers	79.03	Teachers, Elementary School*	34.23
Hairdressers/Cosmetologists	17.87	Teachers, Secondary School*	39.55
Internists	97.62	Telemarketers	14.00
Janitors and Cleaners	15.87	Truck Drivers, Heavy/Tractor-Trailer	23.69
Landscaping/Groundskeeping Workers	15.52	Truck Drivers, Light/Delivery Svcs.	17.92
Lawyers	80.76	Waiters and Waitresses	14.08

Note: Wage data covers the Metropolitan Division—see Appendix B for areas included; (*) Hourly wages for elementary/secondary school teachers and teacher assistants were calculated by the editors from annual wage data based on a 40 hour work week; n/a not available.
Source: Bureau of Labor Statistics, Metro Area Occupational Employment and Wage Estimates, May 2015

TAXES

State Corporate Income Tax Rates

State	Tax Rate (%)	Income Brackets ($)	Num. of Brackets	Financial Institution Tax Rate (%)[a]	Federal Income Tax Ded.
New Jersey	9.0 (r)	Flat rate	1	9.0 (r)	No

Note: Tax rates as of January 1, 2016; (a) Rates listed are the corporate income tax rate applied to financial institutions or excise taxes based on income. Some states have other taxes based upon the value of deposits or shares; (r) In New Jersey small businesses with annual entire net income under $100,000 pay a tax rate of 7.5%; businesses with income under $50,000 pay 6.5%. The minimum Corporation Business Tax is based on New Jersey gross receipts. It ranges from $500 for a corporation with gross receipts less than $100,000, to $2,000 for a corporation with gross receipts of $1 million or more.
Source: Federation of Tax Administrators, "State Corporate Income Tax Rates, 2016"

State Individual Income Tax Rates

State	Tax Rate (%)	Income Brackets ($)	Num. of Brackets	Personal Exempt. ($)[1]		Fed. Inc. Tax Ded.
				Single	Dependents	
New Jersey	1.4 - 8.97	20,000 - 500,000 (n)	6	1,000	1,500	No

Note: Tax rates as of January 1, 2016; Local- and county-level taxes are not included; n/a not applicable; (1) Married joint filers generally receive double the single exemption; (n) The New Jersey rates reported are for single individuals. For married couples filing jointly, the tax rates also range from 1.4% to 8.97%, with 7 brackets and the same high and low income ranges.
Source: Federation of Tax Administrators, "State Individual Income Tax Rates, 2016"

Various State and Local Tax Rates

State	State and Local Sales and Use (%)	State Sales and Use (%)	Gasoline[1] (¢/gal.)	Cigarette[2] ($/pack)	Spirits[3] ($/gal.)	Wine[4] ($/gal.)	Beer[5] ($/gal.)
New Jersey	7.00	7.0 (e)	14.5	2.70	5.50	0.88	0.12

Note: All tax rates as of January 1, 2016; (1) The American Petroleum Institute has developed a methodology for determining the average tax rate on a gallon of fuel. Rates may include any of the following: excise taxes, environmental fees, storage tank fees, other fees or taxes, general sales tax, and local taxes. In states where gasoline is subject to the general sales tax, or where the fuel tax is based on the average sale price, the average rate determined by API is sensitive to changes in the price of gasoline. States that fully or partially apply general sales taxes to gasoline: CA, CO, GA, IL, IN, MI, NY; (2) The federal excise tax of $1.0066 per pack and local taxes are not included; (3) Rates are those applicable to off-premise sales of 40% alcohol by volume (a.b.v.) distilled spirits in 750ml containers. Local excise taxes are excluded; (4) Rates are those applicable to off-premise sales of 11% a.b.v. non-carbonated wine in 750ml containers; (5) Rates are those applicable to off-premise sales of 4.7% a.b.v. beer in 12 ounce containers; (e) Some counties in New Jersey are not subject to statewide sales tax rates and collect a local rate of 3.5%. Their average local score is represented as a negative.
Source: Tax Foundation, 2016 Facts & Figures: How Does Your State Compare?

State Business Tax Climate Index Rankings

State	Overall Rank	Corporate Tax Rank	Individual Income Tax Rank	Sales Tax Rank	Unemployment Insurance Tax Rank	Property Tax Rank
New Jersey	50	43	48	47	31	50

Note: The index is a measure of how each state's tax laws affect economic performance. The lower the rank, the more favorable a state's tax system is for business. States without a given tax are given a ranking of 1. The scores/rankings for the District of Columbia do not affect other states. The 2016 index represents the tax climate as of July 1, 2015 (the beginning of Fiscal Year 2016).
Source: Tax Foundation, State Business Tax Climate Index 2016

TRANSPORTATION

Means of Transportation to Work

Area	Car/Truck/Van		Public Transportation			Bicycle	Walked	Other Means	Worked at Home
	Drove Alone	Car-pooled	Bus	Subway	Railroad				
City	71.4	6.1	11.7	0.5	3.3	0.0	0.6	1.1	5.2
MSA[1]	50.6	6.8	8.0	18.5	3.6	0.6	6.0	1.9	4.1
U.S.	76.4	9.6	2.6	1.8	0.6	0.6	2.8	1.3	4.4

Note: Figures are percentages and cover workers 16 years of age and older; (1) Figures cover the New York-Newark-Jersey City, NY-NJ-PA Metropolitan Statistical Area—see Appendix B for areas included
Source: U.S. Census Bureau, 2010-2014 American Community Survey 5-Year Estimates

Travel Time to Work

Area	Less Than 10 Minutes	10 to 19 Minutes	20 to 29 Minutes	30 to 44 Minutes	45 to 59 Minutes	60 to 89 Minutes	90 Minutes or More
City	5.9	15.9	14.4	16.8	12.3	18.3	16.3
MSA[1]	7.8	19.9	16.6	23.6	12.1	13.9	6.2
U.S.	13.3	29.6	21.0	20.2	7.7	5.7	2.6

Note: Figures are percentages and include workers 16 years old and over; (1) Figures cover the New York-Newark-Jersey City, NY-NJ-PA Metropolitan Statistical Area—see Appendix B for areas included
Source: U.S. Census Bureau, 2010-2014 American Community Survey 5-Year Estimates

Freeway Travel Time Index

Area	1985	1990	1995	2000	2005	2010	2014
Urban Area Rank[1,2]	11	9	8	7	7	8	8
Urban Area Index[1]	1.16	1.20	1.24	1.29	1.33	1.33	1.34
Average Index[3]	1.09	1.11	1.14	1.17	1.20	1.19	1.20

Note: Freeway Travel Time Index—the ratio of travel time in the peak period to the travel time at free-flow conditions. For example, a value of 1.30 indicates a 20-minute free-flow trip takes 26 minutes in the peak (20 minutes x 1.30 = 26 minutes); (1) Covers the New York-Newark NY-NJ-CT urban area; (2) Rank is based on 101 urban areas (#1 = highest travel time index); (3) Average of 101 urban areas
Source: Texas Transportation Institute, 2015 Urban Mobility Scorecard, August 2015

Freeway Commuter Stress Index

Area	1985	1990	1995	2000	2005	2010	2014
Urban Area Rank[1,2]	19	19	13	12	11	11	12
Urban Area Index[1]	1.21	1.24	1.29	1.34	1.38	1.38	1.39
Average Index[3]	1.13	1.16	1.19	1.22	1.25	1.24	1.25

Note: The Freeway Commuter Stress Index is the same as the Freeway Travel Time Index (see table above) except that it includes only the travel in the peak directions during the peak periods; the TTI includes travel in all directions during the peak period. Thus, the CSI is more indicative of the work trip experienced by each commuter on a daily basis. (1) Covers the New York-Newark NY-NJ-CT urban area; (2) Rank is based on 101 urban areas (#1 = highest stress index); (3) Average of 101 urban areas
Source: Texas Transportation Institute, 2015 Urban Mobility Scorecard, August 2015

Living Environment

COST OF LIVING

Cost of Living Index

Composite Index	Groceries	Housing	Utilities	Transportation	Health Care	Misc. Goods/ Services
121.6	112.6	148.6	111.0	107.3	110.3	112.0

Note: The Cost of Living Index measures regional differences in the cost of consumer goods and services, excluding taxes and non-consumer expenditures, for professional and managerial households in the top income quintile. It is based on more than 50,000 prices covering almost 60 different items for which prices are collected three times a year by chambers of commerce, economic development organizations or university applied economic centers in each participating urban area. The numbers shown should be read as a percentage above or below the national average of 100. For example, a value of 115.4 in the groceries column indicates that grocery prices are 15.4% higher than the national average. Small differences in the index numbers should not be interpreted as significant; Figures cover the Middlesex-Monmouth NJ urban area.
Source: The Council for Community and Economic Research, ACCRA Cost of Living Index, 2015

Grocery Prices

Area[1]	T-Bone Steak ($/pound)	Frying Chicken ($/pound)	Whole Milk ($/half gal.)	Eggs ($/dozen)	Orange Juice ($/64 oz.)	Coffee ($/11.5 oz.)
City[2]	11.40	1.64	2.56	2.58	3.66	4.19
Avg.	10.99	1.43	2.25	2.26	3.58	4.48
Min.	7.16	0.98	1.30	1.35	2.88	2.98
Max.	14.13	2.43	3.85	4.81	6.39	7.56

Note: (1) Values for the local area are compared with the average, minimum and maximum values for all 292 areas in the Cost of Living Index; (2) Figures cover the Middlesex-Monmouth NJ urban area; **T-Bone Steak** *(price per pound);* **Frying Chicken** *(price per pound, whole fryer);* **Whole Milk** *(half gallon carton);* **Eggs** *(price per dozen, Grade A, large);* **Orange Juice** *(64 oz. Tropicana or Florida Natural);* **Coffee** *(11.5 oz. can, vacuum-packed, Maxwell House, Hills Bros, or Folgers).*
Source: The Council for Community and Economic Research, ACCRA Cost of Living Index, 2015

Housing and Utility Costs

Area[1]	New Home Price ($)	Apartment Rent ($/month)	All Electric ($/month)	Part Electric ($/month)	Other Energy ($/month)	Telephone ($/month)
City[2]	467,078	1,393		120.17	63.96	32.25
Avg.	312,874	945	179.30	95.07	72.96	28.11
Min.	178,682	479	116.28	43.14	26.46	10.01
Max.	1,472,476	3,984	504.25	189.44	421.11	43.06

Note: (1) Values for the local area are compared with the average, minimum and maximum values for all 292 areas in the Cost of Living Index; (2) Figures cover the Middlesex-Monmouth NJ urban area; **New Home Price** *(2,400 sf living area, 8,000 sf lot, in urban area with full utilities);* **Apartment Rent** *(950 sf 2 bedroom/1.5 or 2 bath, unfurnished, excluding all utilities except water);* **All Electric** *(average monthly cost for an all-electric home);* **Part Electric** *(average monthly cost for a part-electric home);* **Other Energy** *(average monthly cost for natural gas, fuel oil, coal, wood, and any other forms of energy except electricity);* **Telephone** *(price includes basic monthly rate for a private residential line plus additional local usage charges incurred by a family of four).*
Source: The Council for Community and Economic Research, ACCRA Cost of Living Index, 2015

Health Care, Transportation, and Other Costs

Area[1]	Doctor ($/visit)	Dentist ($/visit)	Optometrist ($/visit)	Gasoline ($/gallon)	Beauty Salon ($/visit)	Men's Shirt ($)
City[2]	86.08	115.37	101.58	2.38	33.58	37.72
Avg.	105.15	89.02	99.78	2.38	35.30	28.10
Min.	66.87	56.09	48.53	1.95	18.91	13.38
Max.	182.34	150.36	228.33	4.09	67.91	63.80

Note: (1) Values for the local area are compared with the average, minimum and maximum values for all 292 areas in the Cost of Living Index; (2) Figures cover the Middlesex-Monmouth NJ urban area; **Doctor** *(general practitioners routine exam of an established patient);* **Dentist** *(adult teeth cleaning and periodic oral examination);* **Optometrist** *(full vision eye exam for established adult patient);* **Gasoline** *(one gallon regular unleaded, national brand, including all taxes, cash price at self-service pump if available);* **Beauty Salon** *(woman's shampoo, trim, and blow-dry);* **Men's Shirt** *(cotton/polyester dress shirt, pinpoint weave, long sleeves).*
Source: The Council for Community and Economic Research, ACCRA Cost of Living Index, 2015

HOUSING

House Price Index (HPI)

Area	National Ranking[2]	Quarterly Change (%)	One-Year Change (%)	Five-Year Change (%)
MD[1]	157	0.30	4.00	4.80
U.S.[3]	–	1.45	5.76	22.85

Note: The HPI is a weighted repeat sales index. It measures average price changes in repeat sales or refinancings on the same properties. This information is obtained by reviewing repeat mortgage transactions on single-family properties whose mortgages have been purchased or securitized by Fannie Mae or Freddie Mac in January 1975; (1) New York-Jersey City-White Plains Metropolitan Division—see Appendix B for areas included; (2) Rankings are based on annual percentage change for all metro areas containing at least 15,000 transactions over the last 10 years and ranges from 1 to 266; (3) figures based on a weighted average of Census Division estimates using a seasonally adjusted, purchase-only index; all figures are for the period ending December 31, 2015

Source: Federal Housing Finance Agency, House Price Index, February 25, 2016

Median Single-Family Home Prices

Area	2013	2014	2015p	Percent Change 2014 to 2015
MD[1]	465.7	468.2	475.9	1.6
U.S. Average	197.4	208.9	223.9	7.2

Note: Figures are median sales prices of existing single-family homes in thousands of dollars; (p) preliminary; n/a not available; (1) New York-Jersey City-White Plains, NY-NJ Metropolitan Division—see Appendix B for areas included

Source: National Association of Realtors, Median Sales Price of Existing Single-Family Homes for Metropolitan Areas, 4th Quarter 2015

Qualifying Income Based on Median Sales Price of Existing Single-Family Homes

Area	With 5% Down ($)	With 10% Down ($)	With 20% Down ($)
MD[1]	103,341	97,902	87,024
U.S. Average	49,535	46,928	41,714

Note: Figures are preliminary; Qualifying income is based on a mortgage rate of 4.1%. Monthly principal and interest payment is limited to 25% of income; n/a not available; (1) New York-Jersey City-White Plains, NY-NJ Metropolitan Division—see Appendix B for areas included

Source: National Association of Realtors, Qualifying Income Based on Median Sales Price of Existing Single-Family Homes for Metropolitan Areas, 4th Quarter 2015

Median Apartment Condo-Coop Home Prices

Area	2013	2014	2015p	Percent Change 2014 to 2015
MD[1]	237.5	268.9	285.7	6.2
U.S. Average	194.9	204.3	210.7	3.1

Note: Figures are median sales prices of existing apartment condo-coop homes in thousands of dollars; (p) preliminary; n/a not available; (1) New York-Jersey City-White Plains, NY-NJ Metropolitan Division—see Appendix B for areas included

Source: National Association of Realtors, Median Sales Price of Existing Apartment Condo-Coop Homes for Metropolitan Areas, 4th Quarter 2015

Gross Monthly Rent

Area	Under $200	$200 -299	$300 -499	$500 -749	$750 -999	$1,000 -1,499	$1,500 and up	Median ($)
City	0.0	0.0	0.0	14.3	0.0	15.4	70.3	1,777
MSA[1]	1.1	3.9	4.8	7.3	13.5	36.1	33.3	1,246
U.S.	1.5	3.2	7.4	21.0	24.1	26.9	15.9	920

Note: Figures are percentages except for Median; Gross rent is the contract rent plus the estimated average monthly cost of utilities (electricity, gas, and water and sewer) and fuels (oil, coal, kerosene, wood, etc.) if these are paid by the renter (or paid for the renter by someone else); (1) Figures cover the New York-Newark-Jersey City, NY-NJ-PA Metropolitan Statistical Area—see Appendix B for areas included

Source: U.S. Census Bureau, 2010-2014 American Community Survey 5-Year Estimates

Homeownership Rate

Area	2008 (%)	2009 (%)	2010 (%)	2011 (%)	2012 (%)	2013 (%)	2014 (%)	2015 (%)
MSA[1]	52.6	51.7	51.6	50.9	51.5	50.6	50.7	49.9
U.S.	67.8	67.4	66.9	66.1	65.4	65.1	64.5	63.7

Note: (1) Figures cover the New York-Newark-Jersey City, NY-NJ-PA Metropolitan Statistical Area—see Appendix B for areas included
Source: U.S. Census Bureau, Housing Vacancies and Homeownership Annual Statistics: 2015

Year Housing Structure Built

Area	2010 or Later	2000 -2009	1990 -1999	1980 -1989	1970 -1979	1960 -1969	1950 -1959	1940 -1949	Before 1940	Median Year
City	1.0	14.9	27.3	26.2	13.5	11.1	2.8	1.2	2.0	1987
MSA[1]	0.6	7.4	6.0	7.8	10.0	13.9	16.5	9.5	28.4	1957
U.S.	1.0	14.9	13.9	13.8	15.8	11.0	10.8	5.4	13.3	1976

Note: Figures are percentages except for Median Year; (1) Figures cover the New York-Newark-Jersey City, NY-NJ-PA Metropolitan Statistical Area—see Appendix B for areas included
Source: U.S. Census Bureau, 2010-2014 American Community Survey 5-Year Estimates

HEALTH

Health Risk Data

Category	MD[1] (%)	U.S. (%)
Adults aged 18–64 who have any kind of health care coverage	78.3	79.6
Adults who reported being in good or excellent health	81.4	83.1
Adults who are current smokers	14.8	19.6
Adults who are heavy drinkers[2]	4.5	6.1
Adults who are binge drinkers[3]	16.9	16.9
Adults who are overweight (BMI 25.0 - 29.9)	36.8	35.8
Adults who are obese (BMI 30.0 - 99.8)	21.7	27.6
Adults who participated in any physical activities in the past month	74.2	77.1
Adults 50+ who have ever had a sigmoidoscopy or colonoscopy	70.5	67.3
Women aged 40+ who have had a mammogram within the past two years	78.5	74.0
Men aged 40+ who have had a PSA test within the past two years	47.8	45.2
Adults aged 65+ who have had flu shot within the past year	56.0	60.1
Adults who always wear a seatbelt	92.8	93.8

Note: Data as of 2012 unless otherwise noted; (1) Figures cover the New York-Jersey City-White Plains, NY-NJ Metropolitan Division—see Appendix B for areas included; (2) Heavy drinkers are classified as males having more than two drinks per day or females having more than one drink per day; (3) Binge drinkers are classified as males having five or more drinks on one occasion or females having four or more drinks on one occasion
Source: Centers for Disease Control and Prevention, Behaviorial Risk Factor Surveillance System, SMART: Selected Metropolitan/Micropolitan Area Risk Trends, 2012 (Note: the CDC has discontinued this dataset but will be releasing a replacement in mid-2016)

Chronic Health Indicators

Category	MD[1] (%)	U.S. (%)
Adults who have ever been told they had a heart attack	3.6	4.5
Adults who have ever been told they had a stroke	2.6	2.9
Adults who have been told they currently have asthma	8.0	8.9
Adults who have ever been told they have arthritis	22.2	25.7
Adults who have ever been told they have diabetes[2]	9.9	9.7
Adults who have ever been told they had skin cancer	3.3	5.7
Adults who have ever been told they had any other types of cancer	5.1	6.5
Adults who have ever been told they have COPD	5.3	6.2
Adults who have ever been told they have kidney disease	2.6	2.5
Adults who have ever been told they have a form of depression	13.3	18.0

Note: Data as of 2012 unless otherwise noted; (1) Figures cover the New York-Jersey City-White Plains, NY-NJ Metropolitan Division—see Appendix B for areas included; (2) Figures do not include pregnancy-related, borderline, or pre-diabetes
Source: Centers for Disease Control and Prevention, Behaviorial Risk Factor Surveillance System, SMART: Selected Metropolitan/Micropolitan Area Risk Trends, 2012 (Note: the CDC has discontinued this dataset but will be releasing a replacement in mid-2016)

Mortality Rates for the Top 10 Causes of Death in the U.S.

ICD-10[a] Sub-Chapter	ICD-10[a] Code	Age-Adjusted Mortality Rate[1] per 100,000 population	
		County[2]	U.S.
Malignant neoplasms	C00-C97	156.5	163.6
Ischaemic heart diseases	I20-I25	99.6	102.2
Other forms of heart disease	I30-I51	52.3	50.1
Chronic lower respiratory diseases	J40-J47	35.4	41.4
Organic, including symptomatic, mental disorders	F01-F09	39.1	38.5
Cerebrovascular diseases	I60-I69	33.2	36.5
Other external causes of accidental injury	W00-X59	24.6	27.5
Other degenerative diseases of the nervous system	G30-G31	20.0	26.3
Diabetes mellitus	E10-E14	17.2	21.1
Hypertensive diseases	I10-I15	11.6	19.7

Note: (a) ICD-10 = International Classification of Diseases 10th Revision; (1) Mortality rates are a three year average covering 2012-2014; (2) Figures cover Monmouth County.
Source: Centers for Disease Control and Prevention, National Center for Health Statistics. Underlying Cause of Death 1999-2014 on CDC WONDER Online Database, released 2015.

Mortality Rates for Selected Causes of Death

ICD-10[a] Sub-Chapter	ICD-10[a] Code	Age-Adjusted Mortality Rate[1] per 100,000 population	
		County[2]	U.S.
Assault	X85-Y09	1.9	5.1
Diseases of the liver	K70-K76	10.3	13.5
Human immunodeficiency virus (HIV) disease	B20-B24	1.5	2.1
Influenza and pneumonia	J09-J18	9.6	15.2
Intentional self-harm	X60-X84	8.1	12.7
Malnutrition	E40-E46	1.3	0.9
Obesity and other hyperalimentation	E65-E68	1.4	1.9
Renal failure	N17-N19	12.4	13.0
Transport accidents	V01-V99	6.0	11.6
Viral hepatitis	B15-B19	1.0	2.1

Note: (a) ICD-10 = International Classification of Diseases 10th Revision; (1) Mortality rates are a three year average covering 2012-2014; (2) Figures cover Monmouth County; Data are Suppressed when the data meet the criteria for confidentiality constraints; Mortality rates are flagged as Unreliable when the rate would be calculated with a numerator of 20 or less.
Source: Centers for Disease Control and Prevention, National Center for Health Statistics. Underlying Cause of Death 1999-2014 on CDC WONDER Online Database, released 2015.

Health Insurance Coverage

Area	With Health Insurance	With Private Health Insurance	With Public Health Insurance	Without Health Insurance	Population Under Age 18 Without Health Insurance
City	95.2	88.9	16.4	4.8	3.5
MSA[1]	87.7	65.3	31.8	12.3	4.4
U.S.	85.8	65.8	31.1	14.2	7.1

Note: Figures are percentages that cover the civilian noninstitutionalized population; (1) Figures cover the New York-Newark-Jersey City, NY-NJ-PA Metropolitan Statistical Area—see Appendix B for areas included
Source: U.S. Census Bureau, 2010-2014 American Community Survey 5-Year Estimates

Number of Medical Professionals

Area	MDs[3]	DOs[3,4]	Dentists	Podiatrists	Chiropractors	Optometrists
County[1] (number)	2,495	226	618	90	326	120
County[1] (rate[2])	396.3	35.9	98.2	14.3	51.8	19.1
U.S. (rate[2])	272.5	20.9	64.7	5.8	25.9	15.2

Note: Data as of 2014 unless noted; (1) Data covers Monmouth County; (2) Rate per 100,000 population; (3) Data as of 2013 and includes all active, non-federal physicians; (4) Doctor of Osteopathic Medicine
Source: U.S. Department of Health and Human Services, Health Resources and Services Administration, Bureau of Health Professions, Area Resource File (ARF) 2014-2015

Best Hospitals

According to *U.S. News,* the New York-Jersey City-White Plains, NY-NJ metro area is home to 11 of the best hospitals in the U.S.: **Hackensack University Medical Center** (5 specialties); **Robert Wood Johnson University Hospital** (1 specialty); **Hospital for Joint Diseases, NYU Langone Medical Center** (2 specialties); **Hospital for Special Surgery** (2 specialties); **Lenox Hill Hospital** (1 specialty); **Memorial Sloan Kettering Cancer Center** (4 specialties); **Mount Sinai Hospital** (9 specialties); **NYU Langone Medical Center** (Honor Roll/12 specialties); **New York Eye and Ear Infirmary** (2 specialties); **New York-Presbyterian University Hospital of Columbia and Cornell** (Honor Roll/15 specialties); **Rusk Rehabilitation at NYU Langone Medical Center** (1 specialty). The hospitals listed were nationally ranked in at least one adult specialty. Only 137 hospitals nationwide were nationally ranked in one or more specialties. Fifteen hospitals in the U.S. made the Honor Roll with high scores in at least six specialties. *U.S. News Online, "America's Best Children's Hospitals 2015-16"*

According to *U.S. News,* the New York-Jersey City-White Plains, NY-NJ metro area is home to seven of the best children's hospitals in the U.S.: **Joseph M. Sanzari Children's Hospital at Hackensack University Medical** (1 specialty); **Bristol-Myers Squibb Children's Hospital at RWJ Univ. Hosp.** (1 specialty); **Children's Hospital at Montefiore (Bronx)** (8 specialties); **Memorial Sloan-Kettering Cancer Center** (1 specialty); **Mount Sinai Kravis Children's Hospital** (7 specialties); **NY-Presbyterian Morgan Stanley-Komansky Children's Hospital** (10 specialties); **Maria Fareri Children's Hospital at Westchester Medical Center** (1 specialty). The hospitals listed were highly ranked in at least one pediatric specialty. Eighty-three children's hospitals in the U.S. were nationally ranked in at least one specialty. Twelve children's hospitals in the U.S. made the Honor Roll with high scores in at least three specialties. *U.S. News Online, "America's Best Children's Hospitals 2015-16"*

EDUCATION

Public School District Statistics

District Name	Schls	Pupils	Pupil/ Teacher Ratio	Minority Pupils[1] (%)	Free Lunch Eligible[2] (%)	IEP[3] (%)
Freehold Regional High SD	6	11,420	14.7	21.1	7.8	16.3
Marlboro Twp Board of Ed	8	5,245	12.2	30.8	2.9	14.9

Note: Table includes school districts with 100 or more students; (1) Percentage of students that are not non-Hispanic white; (2) Percentage of students that are eligible for the free lunch program; (3) Percentage of students that have an Individualized Education Program.
Source: U.S. Department of Education, National Center for Education Statistics, Common Core of Data, Local Education Agency (School District) Universe Survey: School Year 2013-2014; U.S. Department of Education, National Center for Education Statistics, Common Core of Data, Public Elementary/Secondary School Universe Survey: School Year 2013-2014

Highest Level of Education

Area	Less than H.S.	H.S. Diploma	Some College, No Deg.	Associate Degree	Bachelor's Degree	Master's Degree	Prof. School Degree	Doctorate Degree
City	3.7	17.9	12.6	6.7	34.8	16.8	4.9	2.6
MSA[1]	14.9	25.9	15.7	6.6	21.7	10.9	3.0	1.4
U.S.	13.7	28.0	21.2	7.9	18.3	7.8	2.0	1.3

Note: Figures cover persons age 25 and over; (1) Figures cover the New York-Newark-Jersey City, NY-NJ-PA Metropolitan Statistical Area—see Appendix B for areas included
Source: U.S. Census Bureau, 2010-2014 American Community Survey 5-Year Estimates

Educational Attainment by Race

Area	High School Graduate or Higher (%)					Bachelor's Degree or Higher (%)				
	Total	White	Black	Asian	Hisp.[2]	Total	White	Black	Asian	Hisp.[2]
City	96.3	96.5	93.1	96.4	91.4	59.1	54.3	50.5	83.2	30.4
MSA[1]	85.1	89.6	83.0	82.5	67.7	37.0	41.9	22.5	52.7	16.7
U.S.	86.3	88.4	83.2	85.8	64.1	29.3	30.6	19.0	50.9	13.9

Note: Figures shown cover persons 25 years old and over; (1) Figures cover the New York-Newark-Jersey City, NY-NJ-PA Metropolitan Statistical Area—see Appendix B for areas included; (2) People of Hispanic origin can be of any race
Source: U.S. Census Bureau, 2010-2014 American Community Survey 5-Year Estimates

School Enrollment by Grade and Control

Area	Preschool (%)		Kindergarten (%)		Grades 1 - 4 (%)		Grades 5 - 8 (%)		Grades 9 - 12 (%)	
	Public	Private	Public	Private	Public	Private	Public	Private	Public	Private
City	28.4	71.6	86.5	13.5	98.5	1.5	95.4	4.6	91.2	8.8
MSA[1]	50.3	49.7	81.7	18.3	86.3	13.7	86.5	13.5	86.1	13.9
U.S.	57.4	42.6	87.8	12.2	89.8	10.2	89.9	10.1	90.6	9.4

Note: Figures shown cover persons 3 years old and over; (1) Figures cover the New York-Newark-Jersey City, NY-NJ-PA Metropolitan Statistical Area—see Appendix B for areas included
Source: U.S. Census Bureau, 2010-2014 American Community Survey 5-Year Estimates

Average Salaries of Public School Classroom Teachers

Area	2013-14		2014-15		Percent Change 2013-14 to 2014-15	Percent Change 2004-05 to 2014-15
	Dollars	Rank[1]	Dollars	Rank[1]		
New Jersey	68,238	6	69,038	6	1.17	22.2
U.S. Average	56,610	–	57,379	–	1.36	20.8

Note: (1) State rank ranges from 1 to 51 where 1 indicates highest salary.
Source: National Education Association, Rankings & Estimates: Rankings of the States 2014 and Estimates of School Statistics 2015, March 2015

Higher Education

Four-Year Colleges			Two-Year Colleges			Medical Schools[1]	Law Schools[2]	Voc/ Tech[3]
Public	Private Non-profit	Private For-profit	Public	Private Non-profit	Private For-profit			
0	0	0	0	0	0	0	0	0

Note: Figures cover institutions located within the city limits and include main campuses only; (1) includes schools accredited by the Liaison Committee on Medical Education and the American Osteopathic Association's Commission on Osteopathic College Accreditation; (2) includes ABA-accredited schools, schools with provisional ABA accreditation, and state accredited schools; (3) includes all schools with programs that are less than 2 years.
Source: National Center for Education Statistics, Integrated Postsecondary Education System (IPEDS), 2014-15; Association of American Medical Colleges, Member List, March 21, 2016; American Osteopathic Association, Member List, March 21, 2016; Law School Admission Council, Official Guide to ABA-Approved Law Schools Online, March 21, 2016; Wikipedia, List of Medical Schools in the United States, March 21, 2016; Wikipedia, List of Law Schools in the United States, March 21, 2016

According to *U.S. News & World Report,* the New York-Jersey City-White Plains, NY-NJ metro division is home to nine of the best national universities in the U.S.: **Columbia University** (#4 tie); **New York University** (#32); **Yeshiva University** (#52 tie); **Fordham University** (#66 tie); **Rurgers, The State University of New Jersey–New Brunswick ,** (#72 tie); **Stevens Institute of Technology** (#75 tie); **New School** (#127 tie); **St. John's University** (#153 tie); **Pace University** (#180 tie). The indicators used to capture academic quality fall into a number of categories: assessment by administrators at peer institutions; retention of students; faculty resources; student selectivity; financial resources; alumni giving; high school counselor ratings of colleges; and graduation rate. *U.S. News & World Report, "America's Best Colleges 2016"*

According to *U.S. News & World Report,* the New York-Jersey City-White Plains, NY-NJ metro division is home to four of the best liberal arts colleges in the U.S.: **United States Military Academy** (#22); **Barnard College** (#29 tie); **Sarah Lawrence College** (#57 tie); **Purchase College–SUNY** (#171 tie). The indicators used to capture academic quality fall into a number of categories: assessment by administrators at peer institutions; retention of students; faculty resources; student selectivity; financial resources; alumni giving; high school counselor ratings of colleges; and graduation rate. *U.S. News & World Report, "America's Best Colleges 2016"*

According to *U.S. News & World Report,* the New York-Jersey City-White Plains, NY-NJ metro division is home to six of the top 100 law schools in the U.S.: **Columbia University, Law School** (#4 tie); **New York University, School of Law** (#6); **Fordham University, School of Law** (#37); **St. John's University, School of Law** (#74 tie); **Yeshiva University, Benjamin N. Cardozo School of Law** (#74 tie); **Brooklyn Law School** (#97 tie). The rankings are based on a weighted average of 12 measures of quality: peer assessment score; assessment score by lawyers/judges; median LSAT scores; median undergrad GPA; acceptance rate; employment rates for graduates; placement success; bar passage rate; faculty resources; expenditures per student; student/faculty ratio; and library resources. *U.S. News & World Report, "America's Best Graduate Schools, Law, 2017"*

According to *U.S. News & World Report,* the New York-Jersey City-White Plains, NY-NJ metro division is home to five of the top 75 medical schools for research in the U.S.: **Columbia University, College of Physicians and Surgeons** (#7); **New York University, School of Medicine** (#11 tie); **Cornell University, Weill Cornell Medical College** (#18 tie); **Icahn School of Medicine at Mount Sinai** (#21); **Yeshiva University, Albert Einstein College of Medicine** (#39). The rankings are based on a weighted average of 11 measures of quality: quality assessment; peer assessment score; assessment score by residency directors; research activity; total research activity; average research activity per faculty member; student selectivity; median MCAT total score; median undergraduate GPA; acceptance rate; and faculty resources. *U.S. News & World Report, "America's Best Graduate Schools, Medical, 2017"*

According to *U.S. News & World Report,* the New York-Jersey City-White Plains, NY-NJ metro division is home to two of the top 75 business schools in the U.S.: **Columbia University, Columbia Business School** (#10); **New York University, Leonard N. Stern School of Business** (#20). The rankings are based on a weighted average of the following nine measures: quality assessment; peer assessment; recruiter assessment; placement success; mean starting salary and bonus; student selectivity; mean GMAT and GRE scores; mean undergraduate GPA; and acceptance rate. *U.S. News & World Report, "America's Best Graduate Schools, Business, 2017"*

PRESIDENTIAL ELECTION

2012 Presidential Election Results

Area	Obama (%)	Romney (%)	Other (%)
Monmouth County	46.7	52.2	1.2
U.S.	51.0	47.2	1.8

Note: Results may not add to 100% due to rounding
Source: Dave Leip's Atlas of U.S. Presidential Elections

EMPLOYERS

Major Employers

Company Name	Industry
American Express Company	Personal credit institutions
American International Group	Life insurance
Deloitte Consulting	Management consulting services
Hackensack University Medical Center	University
Merrill Lynch and Co	Security brokers & dealers
Mount Sinai Hospital	General medical & surgical hospitals
Mount Sinai School of Medicine	Medical training services
NewYork-Presbyterian Hospital	General medical & surgical hospitals
NYC Health and Hospitals Corp	Psychiatric hospitals
NYU School of Medicine	Offices & clinics of medical doctors
Paramount Comm Acq Corp	Investment holding companies, except banks
Patriarch Partners	Investment offices
Rutgers, The State Univ of NJ	Colleges & universities
Standard Americas	Agencies of foreign banks
The Long Island Rail Road Company	Local & suburban transit
U of Med and Dentistry of NJ	Colleges & universities
UMASS Memorial Health Care	Psychiatrist
United States Postal Service	U.s. postal service
Wellchoice	Health insurance carriers

Note: Companies shown are located within the New York-Newark-Jersey City, NY-NJ-PA Metropolitan Statistical Area.
Source: Hoovers.com; Wikipedia

PUBLIC SAFETY

Crime Rate

Area	All Crimes	Violent Crimes: Murder	Violent Crimes: Rape[3]	Violent Crimes: Robbery	Violent Crimes: Aggrav. Assault	Property Crimes: Burglary	Property Crimes: Larceny -Theft	Property Crimes: Motor Vehicle Theft
City	681.5	0.0	2.5	0.0	27.3	104.1	532.8	14.9
Metro[1]	n/a	3.1	19.3	147.1	264.5	209.7	n/a	85.5
U.S.	2,961.6	4.5	26.4	102.2	232.5	542.5	1,837.3	216.2

Note: Figures are crimes per 100,000 population; (1) Figures cover the New York-Jersey City-White Plains, NY-NJ Metropolitan Division—see Appendix B for areas included; (3) The city and U.S. figures shown were reported using the legacy Uniform Crime Reporting (UCR) definition of rape. The suburban and metro area figures shown are an aggregate total of the data submitted using both the revised and legacy UCR definitions.
Source: FBI Uniform Crime Reports, 2014

Hate Crimes

Area	Number of Quarters Reported	Race	Religion	Sexual Orientation	Ethnicity	Disability	Gender	Gender Identity
City	4	0	2	1	0	0	0	0
U.S.	4	2,568	1,014	1,017	648	84	33	98

Number of Incidents per Bias Motivation (columns Race through Gender Identity)

Source: Federal Bureau of Investigation, Hate Crime Statistics 2014

Identity Theft Consumer Complaints

Area	Complaints	Complaints per 100,000 Population	Rank[2]
MSA[1]	27,397	136.4	77
U.S.	490,220	152.4	-

Note: (1) Figures cover the New York-Newark-Jersey City, NY-NJ-PA Metropolitan Statistical Area—see Appendix B for areas included; (2) Rank ranges from 1 to 379 where 1 indicates greatest number of identity theft complaints per 100,000 population
Source: Federal Trade Commission, Consumer Sentinel Network Data Book for January–December 2015

Fraud and Other Consumer Complaints

Area	Complaints	Complaints per 100,000 Population	Rank[2]
MSA[1]	74,212	369.3	172
U.S.	2,593,159	806.0	-

Note: (1) Figures cover the New York-Newark-Jersey City, NY-NJ-PA Metropolitan Statistical Area—see Appendix B for areas included; (2) Rank ranges from 1 to 379 where 1 indicates greatest number of identity theft complaints per 100,000 population
Source: Federal Trade Commission, Consumer Sentinel Network Data Book for January–December 2015

RECREATION

Culture

Dance[1]	Theatre[1]	Instrumental Music[1]	Vocal Music[1]	Series and Festivals	Museums and Art Galleries[2]	Zoos and Aquariums[3]
0	0	0	0	0	0	0

Note: (1) Professional perfoming groups; (2) Based on organizations with SIC code 8412; (3) AZA-accredited
Source: The Grey House Performing Arts Directory, 2015-16; Association of Zoos & Aquariums, AZA Member Zoos & Aquariums, March 25, 2016; www.AccuLeads.com, March 29, 2016

Professional Sports Teams

Team Name	League	Year Established
Brooklyn Nets	National Basketball Association (NBA)	1967
New Jersey Devils	National Hockey League (NHL)	1982
New York City FC	Major League Soccer (MLS)	2015
New York Giants	National Football League (NFL)	1925
New York Islanders	National Hockey League (NHL)	1972
New York Jets	National Football League (NFL)	1960
New York Knicks	National Basketball Association (NBA)	1946
New York Mets	Major League Baseball (MLB)	1962
New York Rangers	National Hockey League (NHL)	1926
New York Red Bulls	Major League Soccer (MLS)	1996
New York Yankees	Major League Baseball (MLB)	1903

Note: Includes teams located in the New York-Newark-Jersey City, NY-NJ-PA Metropolitan Statistical Area.
Source: Wikipedia, Major Professional Sports Teams of the United States and Canada, March 24, 2016

CLIMATE

Average and Extreme Temperatures

Temperature	Jan	Feb	Mar	Apr	May	Jun	Jul	Aug	Sep	Oct	Nov	Dec	Yr.
Extreme High (°F)	68	75	85	96	97	101	104	99	99	88	81	72	104
Average High (°F)	38	41	50	61	72	80	85	84	76	65	54	43	62
Average Temp. (°F)	32	34	43	53	63	72	77	76	68	58	48	37	55
Average Low (°F)	26	27	35	44	54	63	68	67	60	49	41	31	47
Extreme Low (°F)	-2	-2	8	21	36	46	53	50	40	29	17	-1	-2

Note: Figures cover the years 1962-1992
Source: National Climatic Data Center, International Station Meteorological Climate Summary, 9/96

Average Precipitation/Snowfall/Humidity

Precip./Humidity	Jan	Feb	Mar	Apr	May	Jun	Jul	Aug	Sep	Oct	Nov	Dec	Yr.
Avg. Precip. (in.)	3.5	3.1	4.0	3.9	4.5	3.8	4.5	4.1	4.1	3.3	4.5	3.8	47.0
Avg. Snowfall (in.)	7	8	4	Tr	Tr	0	0	0	0	Tr	Tr	3	23
Avg. Rel. Hum. 7am (%)	67	67	66	64	72	74	74	76	78	75	72	69	71
Avg. Rel. Hum. 4pm (%)	55	53	50	45	52	55	53	54	56	55	57	58	53

Note: Figures cover the years 1962-1992; Tr = Trace amounts (<0.05 in. of rain; <0.5 in. of snow)
Source: National Climatic Data Center, International Station Meteorological Climate Summary, 9/96

Weather Conditions

Temperature			Daytime Sky			Precipitation		
32°F & below	45°F & below	90°F & above	Clear	Partly cloudy	Cloudy	0.01 inch or more precip.	0.1 inch or more snow/ice	Thunder-storms
75	170	18	85	166	114	120	11	20

Note: Figures are average number of days per year and cover the years 1962-1992
Source: National Climatic Data Center, International Station Meteorological Climate Summary, 9/96

HAZARDOUS WASTE

Superfund Sites

Marlboro has one hazardous waste site on the EPA's Superfund Final National Priorities List: **Burnt Fly Bog**. There are a total of 1,323 Superfund sites on the list in the U.S. *U.S. Environmental Protection Agency, Final National Priorities List, March 18, 2016*

AIR & WATER QUALITY

Air Quality Trends: Ozone

	1990	1995	2000	2005	2010	2011	2012	2013	2014
MSA[1]	0.101	0.107	0.091	0.092	0.082	0.082	0.080	0.072	0.069

Note: (1) Data covers the New York-Newark-Jersey City, NY-NJ-PA Metropolitan Statistical Area—see Appendix B for areas included. The values shown are the composite ozone concentration averages among trend sites based on the highest fourth daily maximum 8-hour concentration in parts per million. These trends are based on sites having an adequate record of monitoring data during the trend period. Data from exceptional events are included.
Source: U.S. Environmental Protection Agency, Air Quality Monitoring Information, "Air Quality Trends by City, 1990-2014"

Air Quality Index

Area	Percent of Days when Air Quality was...[2]					AQI Statistics[2]	
	Good	Moderate	Unhealthy for Sensitive Groups	Unhealthy	Very Unhealthy	Maximum	Median
MSA[1]	41.4	52.6	6.0	0.0	0.0	142	54

Note: (1) Data covers the New York-Newark-Jersey City, NY-NJ-PA Metropolitan Statistical Area—see Appendix B for areas included; (2) Based on 365 days with AQI data in 2015. Air Quality Index (AQI) is an index for reporting daily air quality. EPA calculates the AQI for five major air pollutants regulated by the Clean Air Act: ground-level ozone, particle pollution (aka particulate matter), carbon monoxide, sulfur dioxide, and nitrogen dioxide. The AQI runs from 0 to 500. The higher the AQI value, the greater the level of air pollution and the greater the health concern. There are six AQI categories: "Good" AQI is between 0 and 50. Air quality is considered satisfactory; "Moderate" AQI is between 51 and 100. Air quality is acceptable; "Unhealthy for Sensitive Groups" When AQI values are between 101 and 150, members of sensitive groups may experience health effects; "Unhealthy" When AQI values are between 151 and 200 everyone may begin to experience health effects; "Very Unhealthy" AQI values between 201 and 300 trigger a health alert; "Hazardous" AQI values over 300 trigger warnings of emergency conditions (not shown).
Source: U.S. Environmental Protection Agency, Air Quality Index Report, 2015

Air Quality Index Pollutants

Area	Percent of Days when AQI Pollutant was...[2]					
	Carbon Monoxide	Nitrogen Dioxide	Ozone	Sulfur Dioxide	Particulate Matter 2.5	Particulate Matter 10
MSA[1]	0.0	14.5	33.2	0.3	52.1	0.0

Note: (1) Data covers the New York-Newark-Jersey City, NY-NJ-PA Metropolitan Statistical Area—see Appendix B for areas included; (2) Based on 365 days with AQI data in 2015. The Air Quality Index (AQI) is an index for reporting daily air quality. EPA calculates the AQI for five major air pollutants regulated by the Clean Air Act: ground-level ozone, particle pollution (also known as particulate matter), carbon monoxide, sulfur dioxide, and nitrogen dioxide. The AQI runs from 0 to 500. The higher the AQI value, the greater the level of air pollution and the greater the health concern.
Source: U.S. Environmental Protection Agency, Air Quality Index Report, 2015

Maximum Air Pollutant Concentrations: Particulate Matter, Ozone, CO and Lead

	Particulate Matter 10 (ug/m^3)	Particulate Matter 2.5 Wtd AM (ug/m^3)	Particulate Matter 2.5 24-Hr (ug/m^3)	Ozone (ppm)	Carbon Monoxide (ppm)	Lead (ug/m^3)
MSA[1] Level	47	10.5	31	0.074	3	n/a
NAAQS[2]	150	15	35	0.075	9	0.15
Met NAAQS[2]	Yes	Yes	Yes	Yes	Yes	n/a

Note: (1) Data covers the New York-Newark-Jersey City, NY-NJ-PA Metropolitan Statistical Area—see Appendix B for areas included; Data from exceptional events are included; (2) National Ambient Air Quality Standards; ppm = parts per million; ug/m^3 = micrograms per cubic meter; n/a not available.
Concentrations: Particulate Matter 10 (coarse particulate)—highest second maximum 24-hour concentration; Particulate Matter 2.5 Wtd AM (fine particulate)—highest weighted annual mean concentration; Particulate Matter 2.5 24-Hour (fine particulate)—highest 98th percentile 24-hour concentration; Ozone—highest fourth daily maximum 8-hour concentration; Carbon Monoxide—highest second maximum non-overlapping 8-hour concentration; Lead—maximum running 3-month average
Source: U.S. Environmental Protection Agency, Air Quality Monitoring Information, "Air Quality Statistics by City, 2014"

Maximum Air Pollutant Concentrations: Nitrogen Dioxide and Sulfur Dioxide

	Nitrogen Dioxide AM (ppb)	Nitrogen Dioxide 1-Hr (ppb)	Sulfur Dioxide AM (ppb)	Sulfur Dioxide 1-Hr (ppb)	Sulfur Dioxide 24-Hr (ppb)
MSA[1] Level	22	70	n/a	15	n/a
NAAQS[2]	53	100	30	75	140
Met NAAQS[2]	Yes	Yes	n/a	Yes	n/a

Note: (1) Data covers the New York-Newark-Jersey City, NY-NJ-PA Metropolitan Statistical Area—see Appendix B for areas included; Data from exceptional events are included; (2) National Ambient Air Quality Standards; ppm = parts per million; ug/m^3 = micrograms per cubic meter; n/a not available.
Concentrations: Nitrogen Dioxide AM—highest arithmetic mean concentration; Nitrogen Dioxide 1-Hr—highest 98th percentile 1-hour daily maximum concentration; Sulfur Dioxide AM—highest annual mean concentration; Sulfur Dioxide 1-Hr—highest 99th percentile 1-hour daily maximum concentration; Sulfur Dioxide 24-Hr—highest second maximum 24-hour concentration
Source: U.S. Environmental Protection Agency, Air Quality Monitoring Information, "Air Quality Statistics by City, 2014"

Drinking Water

Water System Name	Pop. Served	Primary Water Source Type	Violations[1]	
			Health Based	Monitoring/ Reporting
Marlboro Twp Water Utility Div	29,480	Purchased Surface	0	0

Note: (1) Based on violation data from January 1, 2015 to December 31, 2015 (includes unresolved violations from earlier years)
Source: U.S. Environmental Protection Agency, Office of Ground Water and Drinking Water, Safe Drinking Water Information System (based on data extracted April 29, 2016)

Princeton, New Jersey

Background

Princeton is located in Mercer County, in the heart of central New Jersey, covering about 18.1 square miles. The town's borough form of government was established in 2013 when the Borough of Princeton merged with Princeton Township. Princeton is situated equidistant from New York City and Philadelphia and is close to the many major roadways that serve both cities. US Highway Route 206 runs through the city and there is ready access to US Highway Route 1, the New Jersey Turnpike, the Garden State Parkway and Amtrak and New Jersey Transit which provide direct rail services to New York and Philadelphia.

Princeton is well known for being the home of Princeton University, the prestigious higher education institution that was founded in 1756. Princeton's long history with the university makes it primarily a college town. A substantial portion of the property of Princeton University lies within the borders of Princeton as does the property of the Institute for Advanced Study. Princeton is a hub for excellent public and private schools such as the Hun School, the Princeton Day School, and the Stuart Country Day School of the Sacred Heart. The area is also home to a variety of other well-known institutions such as the Dow Jones and Company, Siemens Corporate Research, and the Princeton Theological Seminary.

Despite a long history of being divided between two separate municipalities, Princeton's residents have strong community ties. The central borough, which was originally surrounded by the township, seceded in 1894 over a dispute regarding school taxes. The two municipalities would later form the Princeton Public Schools, with a few other combined public services before being officially reunited in 2013. Nassau Street is the main commercial street that runs through the town and most of the Princeton University campus. Before reunification, the borough and the township had similar populations.

While New Jersey's state capital is the city of Trenton, the governor's official residence has been in Princeton since 1945 when the Morven property was designated as the governor's mansion. An historic 18th century home at 55 Stockton Street, it served as the governor's mansion for nearly four decades from 1944 to 1981. Today, the governor's mansion is at Drumthwacket, at 354 Stockton Street, also in Princeton. It is one of three official governor's residences in the country that is not located in the state's capital city.

Princeton consistently ranks high on the list of most liveable cities, with a high quality of life and a vibrant community. The mixture of history, picturesque ivy covered walls and buildings, a bustling arts scene, and an array of fine and eclectic dining make it a desirable city to live and work in. It is also conveniently located to NYC and Philadelphia, and the endless offerings of these two major cities.

Historic Nassau Street is lined with bookshops, local stores, restaurants, and entertainment venues. Palmer Square is home to the historic Nassau Inn, and a variety of gift shops and outdoor dining options. Princeton University sits in the midst of the town, home to many of the country's leading scholars, scientists, and scribes. The gothic style Princeton University chapel is particularly exquisite in its architecture and mood. Princeton University also has its own art museum that houses renowned Chinese and classical art collections. There is also the famed McCarter Theater for theatrical performances and the Westminster Choir College for contemporary and classical vocal performances.

There are numerous recreation facilities in the area including a large pool complex, tennis and paddle tennis courts, athletic playing fields and various parks and playgrounds. Throughout the year, there are many different programs and activities on offer through the city's Recreation Department.

Princeton, like much of the northeastern United States, experiences a humid continental climate with cold winters and hot, humid summers. Highs in winter hover just above freezing and can drop well below zero, along with snowfall and precipitation. In summer, temperatures can reach into the 80s with a high percentage of humidity with balmy, warm evenings.

Rankings

Business/Finance Rankings

- The personal finance site NerdWallet analyzed 183 American metropolitan areas with populations over 250,000 and more than 15,000 businesses to rank where entrepreneurs find the most success. Criteria included area economy, annual income, housing cost, unemployment rate, and the success rate of area businesses. Trenton* ranked #27. *www.nerdwallet.com, "Best Places to Start a Business," April 27, 2015*
- The Trenton* metro area appeared on the Milken Institute "2015 Best Performing Cities" list. Rank: #87 out of 200 large metro areas. Criteria: job growth; wage and salary growth; high-tech output growth. *Milken Institute, "Best-Performing Cities 2015," December 2015*

Education Rankings

- The Trenton* metro area was selected as one of America's most innovative cities" by *The Business Insider*. The metro area was ranked #15 out of 20. Criteria: patents per capita. *The Business Insider, "The 20 Most Innovative Cities in the U.S.," February 1, 2013*
- Personal finance website *WalletHub* analyzed the 150 largest U.S. metropolitan statistical areas to determine where the most educated Americans are choosing to settle. Criteria: education quality and attainment gap; education levels; percentage of workers with degrees; public school rankings; quality and size of each metro area's universities. Trenton* was ranked #39 (#1 = most educated city). *www.WalletHub.com, "2015's Most and Least Educated Cities*

Environmental Rankings

- The Trenton* metro area came in at #189 for the relative comfort of its climate on Sperling's list of "chill cities," as measured by the Sperling Heat Index. All 361 metro areas are included. Criteria included daytime high temperatures, nighttime low temperatures, dew point, and relative humidity at the high temperatures. *www.bertsperling.com, "Sperling's Chill Cities," July 18, 2013*
- Sperling's BestPlaces assessed 379 metropolitan areas of the United States for the likelihood of dangerously extreme weather events or earthquakes. In general the Southeast and South-Central regions have the highest risk of weather extremes and earthquakes, while the Pacific Northwest enjoys the lowest risk. Of the least risky metropolitan areas, the Trenton* metro area was ranked #316. *www.bestplaces.net, "Safest Places from Natural Disasters," April 2011*

Health/Fitness Rankings

- The Gallup-Healthways Well-Being Index tracks Americans' optimism about their communities and satisfaction with the metro areas in which they live. At least 300 adult residents in each of 189 U.S. metropolitan areas were asked whether their metro was improving and the Trenton* metro area was one of the ten communities where residents were least optimistic. *www.gallup.com, "City Satisfaction Highest in Fort Collins-Loveland, Colo.," April 11, 2014*
- Gallup-Healthways Well-Being Index researchers asked at least 300 adult residents in each of 189 U.S. metropolitan areas how satisfied they were with the metro area in which they lived. The Trenton* metro area was one of the ten metros where residents were least likely to be satisfied. *www.gallup.com, "City Satisfaction Highest in Fort Collins-Loveland, Colo.," April 11, 2014*
- The Trenton* metro area ranked #147 out of 190 in The Gallup-Healthways Well-Being Index. Criteria: purpose; social well being; financial health; community and physical health. Results are based on telephone interviews with adults, aged 18 and older, living in metropolitan areas in the 50 U.S. states and the District of Columbia. *Gallup-Healthways, "State of American Well-Being," February 23, 2016*

Real Estate Rankings

- The Trenton* metro area was identified as one of the 20 worst housing markets in the U.S. in 2015. The area ranked #1 out of 179 markets. Criteria: year-over-year change of median sales price of existing single-family homes between the 4th quarter of 2014 and the 4th quarter of 2015. *National Association of Realtors®, Median Sales Price of Existing Single-Family Homes for Metropolitan Areas, 4th Quarter 2015*
- The nation's largest metro areas were analyzed in terms of the percentage of households entering some stage of foreclosure in 2015. The Trenton* metro area ranked #2 out of 20 (#1 = highest foreclosure rate). *RealtyTrac, "2015 Year-End U.S. Foreclosure Market Report™," January 12, 2016*

Safety Rankings

- The National Insurance Crime Bureau ranked 380 metro areas in the U.S. in terms of per capita rates of vehicle theft. The Trenton* metro area ranked #122 (#1 = highest rate). Criteria: number of vehicle theft offenses per 100,000 inhabitants in 2014. *National Insurance Crime Bureau, "Hot Spots 2014," June 24, 2015*

Seniors/Retirement Rankings

- From its Best Cities for Successful Aging indexes, the Milken Institute generated rankings for metropolitan areas, weighing data in eight categories—health care, wellness, living arrangements, transportation, financial characteristics, education and employment opportunities, community engagement, and overall livability. The Trenton* metro area was ranked #104 overall in the small metro area category. *Milken Institute, "Best Cities for Successful Aging, 2014"*

Transportation Rankings

- The Trenton* metro area appeared on *Forbes* list of places with the most extreme commutes. The metro area ranked #4 out of 10. Criteria: average travel time; percentage of mega commuters. Mega-commuters travel more than 90 minutes and 50 miles each way to work. *Forbes.com, "The Cities with the Most Extreme Commutes," March 5, 2013*

Princeton is located within the Trenton, NJ Metropolitan Statistical Area.

Business Environment

CITY FINANCES

City Government Finances

Component	2012 ($000)	2012 ($ per capita)
Total Revenues	29,657	2,409
Total Expenditures	28,899	2,348
Debt Outstanding	45,434	3,691
Cash and Securities[1]	18,452	1,499

Note: (1) Cash and security holdings of a government at the close of its fiscal year, including those of its dependent agencies, utilities, and liquor stores.
Source: U.S Census Bureau, State & Local Government Finances 2012

City Government Revenue by Source

Source	2012 ($000)	2012 ($ per capita)
General Revenue		
From Federal Government	1,105	89
From State Government	1,161	94
From Local Governments	1,598	129
Taxes		
Property	11,279	916
Sales and Gross Receipts	266	21
Personal Income	0	0
Corporate Income	0	0
Motor Vehicle License	0	0
Other Taxes	1,164	94
Current Charges	9,071	737
Liquor Store	0	0
Utility	0	0
Employee Retirement	0	0

Source: U.S Census Bureau, State & Local Government Finances 2012

City Government Expenditures by Function

Function	2012 ($000)	2012 ($ per capita)	2012 (%)
General Direct Expenditures			
Air Transportation	0	0	0.0
Corrections	0	0	0.0
Education	0	0	0.0
Employment Security Administration	0	0	0.0
Financial Administration	319	25	1.1
Fire Protection	830	67	2.8
General Public Buildings	530	43	1.8
Governmental Administration, Other	821	66	2.8
Health	536	43	1.8
Highways	760	61	2.6
Hospitals	0	0	0.0
Housing and Community Development	2,499	203	8.6
Interest on General Debt	1,783	144	6.1
Judicial and Legal	747	60	2.5
Libraries	1,283	104	4.4
Parking	1,370	111	4.7
Parks and Recreation	93	7	0.3
Police Protection	4,061	329	14.0
Public Welfare	70	5	0.2
Sewerage	1,660	134	5.7
Solid Waste Management	581	47	2.0
Veterans' Services	0	0	0.0
Liquor Store	0	0	0.0
Utility	0	0	0.0
Employee Retirement	0	0	0.0

Source: U.S Census Bureau, State & Local Government Finances 2012

DEMOGRAPHICS

Population Growth

Area	1990 Census	2000 Census	2010 Census	2014* Estimate	Population Growth (%) 1990-2014	Population Growth (%) 2010-2014
City	12,064	14,203	12,307	28,940	139.9	135.2
MSA[1]	325,804	350,761	366,513	369,526	13.4	0.8
U.S.	248,709,873	281,421,906	308,745,538	314,107,084	26.3	1.7

Note: (1) Figures cover the Trenton, NJ Metropolitan Statistical Area—see Appendix B for areas included; (*) 2010-2014 5-year estimated population
Source: U.S. Census Bureau, 1990 Census, Census 2000, Census 2010, 2010-2014 American Community Survey 5-Year Estimates

Household Size

Area	Persons in Household (%) One	Two	Three	Four	Five	Six	Seven or More	Average Household Size
City	26.4	37.3	16.1	14.4	4.6	0.8	0.1	2.48
MSA[1]	26.8	31.0	16.7	15.5	6.3	2.1	1.3	2.66
U.S.	27.5	33.5	15.8	13.1	6.0	2.3	1.4	2.64

Note: (1) Figures cover the Trenton, NJ Metropolitan Statistical Area—see Appendix B for areas included
Source: U.S. Census Bureau, 2010-2014 American Community Survey 5-Year Estimates

Race

Area	White Alone[2] (%)	Black Alone[2] (%)	Asian Alone[2] (%)	AIAN[3] Alone[2] (%)	NHOPI[4] Alone[2] (%)	Other Race Alone[2] (%)	Two or More Races (%)
City	73.8	6.3	15.5	0.3	0.0	1.4	2.6
MSA[1]	62.4	20.2	9.6	0.2	0.0	5.6	2.1
U.S.	73.8	12.6	5.0	0.8	0.2	4.7	2.9

Note: (1) Figures cover the Trenton, NJ Metropolitan Statistical Area—see Appendix B for areas included; (2) Alone is defined as not being in combination with one or more other races; (3) American Indian and Alaska Native; (4) Native Hawaiian and Other Pacific Islander
Source: U.S. Census Bureau, 2010-2014 American Community Survey 5-Year Estimates

Hispanic or Latino Origin

Area	Total (%)	Mexican (%)	Puerto Rican (%)	Cuban (%)	Other (%)
City	6.4	0.9	1.1	0.5	3.9
MSA[1]	15.9	1.8	4.8	0.3	9.0
U.S.	16.9	10.8	1.6	0.6	3.8

Note: Persons of Hispanic or Latino origin can be of any race; (1) Figures cover the Trenton, NJ Metropolitan Statistical Area—see Appendix B for areas included
Source: U.S. Census Bureau, 2010-2014 American Community Survey 5-Year Estimates

Ancestry

Area	German	Irish	English	American	Italian	Polish	French[2]	Scottish	Dutch
City	12.0	12.6	10.1	4.2	8.7	4.6	2.8	2.4	2.1
MSA[1]	10.3	12.2	6.0	2.8	13.7	7.0	1.5	1.3	0.9
U.S.	14.9	10.8	8.0	7.1	5.5	3.0	2.7	1.7	1.4

Note: Figures are the percentage of the total population reporting a particular ancestry. The nine most commonly reported ancestries in the U.S. are shown. Figures include multiple ancestries (e.g. if a person reported being Irish and Italian, they were included in both columns); (1) Figures cover the Trenton, NJ Metropolitan Statistical Area—see Appendix B for areas included; (2) Excludes Basque
Source: U.S. Census Bureau, 2010-2014 American Community Survey 5-Year Estimates

Foreign-Born Population

Area	Percent of Population Born in								
	Any Foreign Country	Asia	Mexico	Europe	Carribean	Central America[2]	South America	Africa	Canada
City	25.2	11.4	0.3	8.3	0.4	1.6	0.6	1.5	0.8
MSA[1]	21.2	6.8	1.0	3.8	2.6	3.3	1.9	1.4	0.3
U.S.	13.1	3.8	3.7	1.5	1.2	1.0	0.9	0.6	0.3

Note: (1) Figures cover the Trenton, NJ Metropolitan Statistical Area—see Appendix B for areas included; (2) Excludes Mexico.
Source: U.S. Census Bureau, 2010-2014 American Community Survey 5-Year Estimates

Marital Status

Area	Never Married	Now Married[2]	Separated	Widowed	Divorced
City	43.9	46.1	0.9	3.7	5.4
MSA[1]	36.5	47.4	2.1	5.8	8.3
U.S.	32.5	48.4	2.2	5.9	10.9

Note: Figures are percentages and cover the population 15 years of age and older; (1) Figures cover the Trenton, NJ Metropolitan Statistical Area—see Appendix B for areas included; (2) Excludes separated
Source: U.S. Census Bureau, 2010-2014 American Community Survey 5-Year Estimates

Disability Status

Area	All Ages	Under 18 Years Old	18 to 64 Years Old	65 Years and Over
City	6.2	2.3	4.0	22.0
MSA[1]	10.0	3.9	8.0	30.9
U.S.	12.3	4.1	10.2	36.3

Note: Figures show percent of the civilian noninstitutionalized population that reported having a disability. Disability status is determined from from six types of difficulty: vision, hearing, cognitive, ambulatory, self-care, and independent living. For children under 5 years old, hearing and vision difficulty are used to determine disability status. For children between the ages of 5 and 14, disability status is determined from hearing, vision, cognitive, ambulatory, and self-care difficulties. For people aged 15 years and older, they are considered to have a disability if they have difficulty with any one of the six difficulty types; (1) Figures cover the Trenton, NJ Metropolitan Statistical Area—see Appendix B for areas included.
Source: U.S. Census Bureau, 2010-2014 American Community Survey 5-Year Estimates

Age

Area	Percent of Population									Median Age
	Under Age 5	Age 5–19	Age 20–34	Age 35–44	Age 45–54	Age 55–64	Age 65–74	Age 75–84	Age 85+	
City	4.4	23.1	24.8	8.9	13.1	11.6	7.0	4.9	2.1	32.5
MSA[1]	5.9	19.8	20.4	13.6	15.0	12.2	7.0	4.2	2.0	38.3
U.S.	6.4	19.9	20.6	13.0	14.1	12.3	7.6	4.3	1.9	37.4

Note: (1) Figures cover the Trenton, NJ Metropolitan Statistical Area—see Appendix B for areas included
Source: U.S. Census Bureau, 2010-2014 American Community Survey 5-Year Estimates

Gender

Area	Males	Females	Males per 100 Females
City	14,379	14,561	98.8
MSA[1]	180,915	188,611	95.9
U.S.	154,515,159	159,591,925	96.8

Note: (1) Figures cover the Trenton, NJ Metropolitan Statistical Area—see Appendix B for areas included
Source: U.S. Census Bureau, 2010-2014 American Community Survey 5-Year Estimates

Religious Groups by Family

Area	Catholic	Baptist	Non-Den.	Methodist[2]	Lutheran	LDS[3]	Pente-costal	Presby-terian[4]	Muslim[5]	Judaism
MSA[1]	33.1	2.7	2.2	2.1	1.1	0.4	1.2	2.2	1.3	2.1
U.S.	19.1	9.3	4.0	4.0	2.3	2.0	1.9	1.6	0.8	0.7

Note: Figures are the number of adherents as a percentage of the total population; (1) Figures cover the Trenton-Ewing, NJ Metropolitan Statistical Area—see Appendix B for areas included; (2) Methodist/Pietist; (3) Latter Day Saints; (4) Reformed; (5) Figures are estimates
Source: Association of Statisticians of American Religious Bodies, 2010 U.S. Religion Census: Religious Congregations & Membership Study

Religious Groups by Tradition

Area	Catholic	Evangelical Protestant	Mainline Protestant	Other Tradition	Black Protestant	Orthodox
MSA[1]	33.1	4.7	8.0	4.6	1.4	0.5
U.S.	19.1	16.2	7.3	4.3	1.6	0.3

Note: Figures are the number of adherents as a percentage of the total population; (1) Figures cover the Trenton-Ewing, NJ Metropolitan Statistical Area—see Appendix B for areas included
Source: Association of Statisticians of American Religious Bodies, 2010 U.S. Religion Census: Religious Congregations & Membership Study

ECONOMY

Gross Metropolitan Product

Area	2013	2014	2015	2016	Rank[2]
MSA[1]	29.4	30.3	31.5	33.0	82

Note: Figures are in billions of dollars; (1) Figures cover the Trenton, NJ Metropolitan Statistical Area—see Appendix B for areas included; (2) Rank is based on 2016 data and ranges from 1 to 381
Source: The U.S. Conference of Mayors, U.S. Metro Economies: GMP and Employment 2014-2016, June 2015

Economic Growth

Area	2011-13 (%)	2014 (%)	2015 (%)	2016 (%)	Rank[2]
MSA[1]	3.4	1.4	2.4	2.7	135
U.S.	2.2	2.4	2.3	2.9	–

Note: Figures are real gross metropolitan product (GMP) growth rates and represent annual average percent change; (1) Figures cover the Trenton, NJ Metropolitan Statistical Area—see Appendix B for areas included; (2) Rank is based on 2016 data and ranges from 1 to 381
Source: The U.S. Conference of Mayors, U.S. Metro Economies: GMP and Employment 2014-2016, June 2015

Metropolitan Area Exports

Area	2009	2010	2011	2012	2013	2014	Rank[2]
MSA[1]	623.1	678.0	754.0	712.9	879.1	947.1	166

Note: Figures are in millions of dollars; (1) Figures cover the Trenton, NJ Metropolitan Statistical Area—see Appendix B for areas included; (2) Rank is based on 2014 data and ranges from 1 to 385
Source: U.S. Department of Commerce, International Trade Administration, Office of Trade & Industry Information, Manufacturing & Services, data extracted March 10, 2016

Building Permits

Area	Single-Family			Multi-Family			Total		
	2014	2015p	Pct. Chg.	2014	2015p	Pct. Chg.	2014	2015p	Pct. Chg.
City	20	39	95.0	0	340	-	20	379	1,795.0
MSA[1]	239	284	18.8	129	610	372.9	368	894	142.9
U.S.	640,300	690,800	7.9	411,800	487,600	18.4	1,052,100	1,178,400	12.0

Note: (1) Figures cover the Trenton, NJ Metropolitan Statistical Area—see Appendix B for areas included; Figures represent new, privately-owned housing units authorized (unadjusted data); All permit data are based on estimates with imputation; (p) preliminary data.
Source: U.S. Census Bureau, Manufacturing, Mining, and Construction Statistics, Building Permits, 2014, 2015

Bankruptcy Filings

Area	Business Filings 2014	Business Filings 2015	Business Filings % Chg.	Nonbusiness Filings 2014	Nonbusiness Filings 2015	Nonbusiness Filings % Chg.
Mercer County	50	26	-48.0	1,010	940	-6.9
U.S.	26,983	24,735	-8.3	909,812	819,760	-9.9

Note: Business filings include Chapter 7, Chapter 11, Chapter 12, and Chapter 13; Nonbusiness filings include Chapter 7, Chapter 11, and Chapter 13
Source: Administrative Office of the U.S. Courts, Business and Nonbusiness Bankruptcy, County Cases Commenced by Chapter of the Bankruptcy Code, During the 12- Month Period Ending December 31, 2014 and Business and Nonbusiness Bankruptcy, County Cases Commenced by Chapter of the Bankruptcy Code, During the 12- Month Period Ending December 31, 2015

Housing Vacancy Rates

Area	Gross Vacancy Rate[2] (%)			Year-Round Vacancy Rate[3] (%)			Rental Vacancy Rate[4] (%)			Homeowner Vacancy Rate[5] (%)		
	2013	2014	2015	2013	2014	2015	2013	2014	2015	2013	2014	2015
MSA[1]	n/a	n/a	n/a	n/a	n/a	n/a	n/a	n/a	n/a	n/a	n/a	n/a
U.S.	13.6	13.4	12.9	10.7	10.4	10.0	8.3	7.6	7.1	2.0	1.9	1.8

Note: (1) Figures cover the Trenton, NJ Metropolitan Statistical Area—see Appendix B for areas included; (2) The percentage of the total housing inventory that is vacant; (3) The percentage of the housing inventory (excluding seasonal units) that is year-round vacant; (4) The percentage of rental inventory that is vacant for rent; (5) The percentage of homeowner inventory that is vacant for sale; n/a not available
Source: U.S. Census Bureau, Housing Vacancies and Homeownership Annual Statistics: 2015

INCOME

Income

Area	Per Capita ($)	Median Household ($)	Average Household ($)
City	63,193	116,875	187,662
MSA[1]	38,076	74,118	104,437
U.S.	28,555	53,482	74,596

Note: (1) Figures cover the Trenton, NJ Metropolitan Statistical Area—see Appendix B for areas included
Source: U.S. Census Bureau, 2010-2014 American Community Survey 5-Year Estimates

Household Income Distribution

Area	Percent of Households Earning: Under $15,000	$15,000 -24,999	$25,000 -34,999	$35,000 -49,999	$50,000 -74,999	$75,000 -99,000	$100,000 -149,999	$150,000 and up
City	5.4	3.9	7.0	6.2	11.2	9.8	15.0	41.3
MSA[1]	9.8	7.6	7.2	10.0	15.9	12.5	16.7	20.4
U.S.	12.5	10.7	10.2	13.5	17.8	12.2	13.0	10.0

Note: (1) Figures cover the Trenton, NJ Metropolitan Statistical Area—see Appendix B for areas included
Source: U.S. Census Bureau, 2010-2014 American Community Survey 5-Year Estimates

Poverty Rate

Area	All Ages	Under 18 Years Old	18 to 64 Years Old	65 Years and Over
City	5.7	3.6	6.1	7.2
MSA[1]	11.7	16.9	10.6	7.6
U.S.	15.6	21.9	14.6	9.4

Note: Figures are percentage of people whose income during the past 12 months was below the poverty level; (1) Figures cover the Trenton, NJ Metropolitan Statistical Area—see Appendix B for areas included
Source: U.S. Census Bureau, 2010-2014 American Community Survey 5-Year Estimates

EMPLOYMENT

Labor Force and Employment

Area	Civilian Labor Force Dec. 2014	Civilian Labor Force Dec. 2015	Civilian Labor Force % Chg.	Workers Employed Dec. 2014	Workers Employed Dec. 2015	Workers Employed % Chg.
City	15,055	15,547	3.2	14,595	15,197	4.1
MSA[1]	195,102	200,573	2.8	185,497	193,151	4.1
U.S.	155,521,000	157,245,000	1.1	147,190,000	149,703,000	1.7

Note: Data is not seasonally adjusted and covers workers 16 years of age and older; (1) Figures cover the Trenton, NJ Metropolitan Statistical Area—see Appendix B for areas included
Source: Bureau of Labor Statistics, Local Area Unemployment Statistics

Unemployment Rate

Area	2015											
	Jan.	Feb.	Mar.	Apr.	May	Jun.	Jul.	Aug.	Sep.	Oct.	Nov.	Dec.
City	3.9	3.6	3.4	3.1	3.6	3.4	4.0	3.3	3.2	3.1	2.7	2.3
MSA[1]	6.0	5.8	5.6	5.3	5.5	4.9	5.7	5.0	4.8	4.4	4.2	3.7
U.S.	6.1	5.8	5.6	5.1	5.3	5.5	5.6	5.2	4.9	4.8	4.8	4.8

Note: Data is not seasonally adjusted and covers workers 16 years of age and older; (1) Figures cover the Trenton, NJ Metropolitan Statistical Area—see Appendix B for areas included
Source: Bureau of Labor Statistics, Local Area Unemployment Statistics

Employment by Occupation

Occupation Classification	City (%)	MSA[1] (%)	U.S. (%)
Management, Business, Science, and Arts	71.3	43.9	36.4
Natural Resources, Construction, and Maintenance	0.9	5.7	9.0
Production, Transportation, and Material Moving	2.0	9.2	12.1
Sales and Office	14.4	23.4	24.4
Service	11.4	17.8	18.2

Note: Figures cover employed civilians 16 years of age and older; (1) Figures cover the Trenton, NJ Metropolitan Statistical Area—see Appendix B for areas included
Source: U.S. Census Bureau, 2010-2014 American Community Survey 5-Year Estimates

Employment by Industry

Sector	MSA[1]		U.S.
	Number of Employees	Percent of Total	Percent of Total
Construction, Mining, and Logging	5,300	1.9	5.0
Education and Health Services	49,400	18.4	15.7
Financial Activities	19,500	7.2	5.7
Government	71,400	26.6	15.5
Information	5,600	2.0	1.9
Leisure and Hospitality	14,500	5.4	10.4
Manufacturing	7,900	2.9	8.6
Other Services	10,200	3.8	3.9
Professional and Business Services	45,500	17.0	13.9
Retail Trade	21,100	7.8	11.3
Transportation, Warehousing, and Utilities	10,000	3.7	3.9
Wholesale Trade	7,100	2.6	4.1

Note: Figures are non-farm employment as of December 2015. Figures are not seasonally adjusted and include workers 16 years of age and older; (1) Figures cover the Trenton, NJ Metropolitan Statistical Area—see Appendix B for areas included; n/a not available
Source: Bureau of Labor Statistics, Current Employment Statistics, Employment, Hours, and Earnings

Occupations with Greatest Projected Employment Growth: 2012 – 2022

Occupation[1]	2012 Employment	2022 Projected Employment	Numeric Employment Change	Percent Employment Change
Home Health Aides	31,140	46,280	15,140	48.6
Combined Food Preparation and Serving Workers, Including Fast Food	59,990	70,180	10,190	17.0
Retail Salespersons	125,690	134,870	9,180	7.3
Registered Nurses	79,840	88,880	9,040	11.3
Nursing Assistants	51,780	60,070	8,290	16.0
Laborers and Freight, Stock, and Material Movers, Hand	75,730	83,360	7,630	10.1
Software Developers, Applications	29,090	35,770	6,680	23.0
Receptionists and Information Clerks	51,160	57,830	6,670	13.0
Customer Service Representatives	63,450	69,530	6,080	9.6
Sales Representatives, Services, All Other	45,510	51,380	5,870	12.9

Note: Projections cover New Jersey; (1) Sorted by numeric employment change
Source: www.projectionscentral.com, State Occupational Projections, 2012–2022 Long-Term Projections

Fastest Growing Occupations: 2012 – 2022

Occupation[1]	2012 Employment	2022 Projected Employment	Numeric Employment Change	Percent Employment Change
Home Health Aides	31,140	46,280	15,140	48.6
Insulation Workers, Mechanical	370	540	170	48.2
Diagnostic Medical Sonographers	2,550	3,550	1,000	39.1
Occupational Therapy Assistants	370	500	130	37.5
Helpers—Electricians	1,310	1,800	490	37.5
Stonemasons	580	780	200	35.4
Physical Therapist Assistants	1,090	1,470	380	34.1
Skincare Specialists	1,050	1,400	350	33.2
Physician Assistants	1,450	1,920	470	32.8
Brickmasons and Blockmasons	2,150	2,830	680	31.7

Note: Projections cover New Jersey; (1) Sorted by percent employment change and excludes occupations with numeric employment change less than 100
Source: www.projectionscentral.com, State Occupational Projections, 2012–2022 Long-Term Projections

Average Wages

Occupation	$/Hr.	Occupation	$/Hr.
Accountants and Auditors	40.66	Maids and Housekeeping Cleaners	14.05
Automotive Mechanics	22.41	Maintenance and Repair Workers	22.36
Bookkeepers	22.33	Marketing Managers	72.75
Carpenters	28.59	Nuclear Medicine Technologists	43.36
Cashiers	10.54	Nurses, Licensed Practical	25.59
Clerks, General Office	19.11	Nurses, Registered	34.21
Clerks, Receptionists/Information	15.63	Nursing Assistants	13.25
Clerks, Shipping/Receiving	18.08	Packers and Packagers, Hand	11.08
Computer Programmers	44.28	Physical Therapists	42.42
Computer Systems Analysts	43.90	Postal Service Mail Carriers	25.12
Computer User Support Specialists	30.43	Real Estate Brokers	n/a
Cooks, Restaurant	12.77	Retail Salespersons	12.42
Dentists	74.92	Sales Reps., Exc. Tech./Scientific	36.67
Electrical Engineers	53.81	Sales Reps., Tech./Scientific	50.45
Electricians	31.56	Secretaries, Exc. Legal/Med./Exec.	22.11
Financial Managers	76.23	Security Guards	18.78
First-Line Supervisors/Managers, Sales	22.37	Surgeons	n/a
Food Preparation Workers	10.56	Teacher Assistants*	13.69
General and Operations Managers	78.08	Teachers, Elementary School*	32.27
Hairdressers/Cosmetologists	15.86	Teachers, Secondary School*	34.54
Internists	110.98	Telemarketers	12.29
Janitors and Cleaners	14.18	Truck Drivers, Heavy/Tractor-Trailer	19.43
Landscaping/Groundskeeping Workers	14.15	Truck Drivers, Light/Delivery Svcs.	17.16
Lawyers	61.95	Waiters and Waitresses	10.54

Note: Wage data covers the Trenton-Ewing, NJ Metropolitan Statistical Area—see Appendix B for areas included; (*) Hourly wages for elementary/secondary school teachers and teacher assistants were calculated by the editors from annual wage data based on a 40 hour work week; n/a not available.
Source: Bureau of Labor Statistics, Metro Area Occupational Employment and Wage Estimates, May 2015

TAXES

State Corporate Income Tax Rates

State	Tax Rate (%)	Income Brackets ($)	Num. of Brackets	Financial Institution Tax Rate (%)[a]	Federal Income Tax Ded.
New Jersey	9.0 (r)	Flat rate	1	9.0 (r)	No

Note: Tax rates as of January 1, 2016; (a) Rates listed are the corporate income tax rate applied to financial institutions or excise taxes based on income. Some states have other taxes based upon the value of deposits or shares; (r) In New Jersey small businesses with annual entire net income under $100,000 pay a tax rate of 7.5%; businesses with income under $50,000 pay 6.5%. The minimum Corporation Business Tax is based on New Jersey gross receipts. It ranges from $500 for a corporation with gross receipts less than $100,000, to $2,000 for a corporation with gross receipts of $1 million or more.
Source: Federation of Tax Administrators, "State Corporate Income Tax Rates, 2016"

State Individual Income Tax Rates

State	Tax Rate (%)	Income Brackets ($)	Num. of Brackets	Personal Exempt. ($)[1] Single	Personal Exempt. ($)[1] Dependents	Fed. Inc. Tax Ded.
New Jersey	1.4 - 8.97	20,000 - 500,000 (n)	6	1,000	1,500	No

Note: Tax rates as of January 1, 2016; Local- and county-level taxes are not included; n/a not applicable; (1) Married joint filers generally receive double the single exemption; (n) The New Jersey rates reported are for single individuals. For married couples filing jointly, the tax rates also range from 1.4% to 8.97%, with 7 brackets and the same high and low income ranges.
Source: Federation of Tax Administrators, "State Individual Income Tax Rates, 2016"

Various State and Local Tax Rates

State	State and Local Sales and Use (%)	State Sales and Use (%)	Gasoline[1] (¢/gal.)	Cigarette[2] ($/pack)	Spirits[3] ($/gal.)	Wine[4] ($/gal.)	Beer[5] ($/gal.)
New Jersey	7.00	7.0 (e)	14.5	2.70	5.50	0.88	0.12

Note: All tax rates as of January 1, 2016; (1) The American Petroleum Institute has developed a methodology for determining the average tax rate on a gallon of fuel. Rates may include any of the following: excise taxes, environmental fees, storage tank fees, other fees or taxes, general sales tax, and local taxes. In states where gasoline is subject to the general sales tax, or where the fuel tax is based on the average sale price, the average rate determined by API is sensitive to changes in the price of gasoline. States that fully or partially apply general sales taxes to gasoline: CA, CO, GA, IL, IN, MI, NY; (2) The federal excise tax of $1.0066 per pack and local taxes are not included; (3) Rates are those applicable to off-premise sales of 40% alcohol by volume (a.b.v.) distilled spirits in 750ml containers. Local excise taxes are excluded; (4) Rates are those applicable to off-premise sales of 11% a.b.v. non-carbonated wine in 750ml containers; (5) Rates are those applicable to off-premise sales of 4.7% a.b.v. beer in 12 ounce containers; (e) Some counties in New Jersey are not subject to statewide sales tax rates and collect a local rate of 3.5%. Their average local score is represented as a negative.
Source: Tax Foundation, 2016 Facts & Figures: How Does Your State Compare?

State Business Tax Climate Index Rankings

State	Overall Rank	Corporate Tax Rank	Individual Income Tax Rank	Sales Tax Rank	Unemployment Insurance Tax Rank	Property Tax Rank
New Jersey	50	43	48	47	31	50

Note: The index is a measure of how each state's tax laws affect economic performance. The lower the rank, the more favorable a state's tax system is for business. States without a given tax are given a ranking of 1. The scores/rankings for the District of Columbia do not affect other states. The 2016 index represents the tax climate as of July 1, 2015 (the beginning of Fiscal Year 2016).
Source: Tax Foundation, State Business Tax Climate Index 2016

TRANSPORTATION

Means of Transportation to Work

Area	Car/Truck/Van: Drove Alone	Car/Truck/Van: Car-pooled	Public Transportation: Bus	Public Transportation: Subway	Public Transportation: Railroad	Bicycle	Walked	Other Means	Worked at Home
City	49.2	4.4	2.7	0.8	6.6	5.1	18.0	0.7	12.5
MSA[1]	70.9	10.3	3.3	0.3	4.2	0.7	3.6	1.5	5.2
U.S.	76.4	9.6	2.6	1.8	0.6	0.6	2.8	1.3	4.4

Note: Figures are percentages and cover workers 16 years of age and older; (1) Figures cover the Trenton, NJ Metropolitan Statistical Area—see Appendix B for areas included
Source: U.S. Census Bureau, 2010-2014 American Community Survey 5-Year Estimates

Travel Time to Work

Area	Less Than 10 Minutes	10 to 19 Minutes	20 to 29 Minutes	30 to 44 Minutes	45 to 59 Minutes	60 to 89 Minutes	90 Minutes or More
City	23.7	34.3	12.4	9.0	5.5	6.4	8.6
MSA[1]	12.2	33.5	20.6	15.1	6.3	6.7	5.5
U.S.	13.3	29.6	21.0	20.2	7.7	5.7	2.6

Note: Figures are percentages and include workers 16 years old and over; (1) Figures cover the Trenton, NJ Metropolitan Statistical Area—see Appendix B for areas included
Source: U.S. Census Bureau, 2010-2014 American Community Survey 5-Year Estimates

Freeway Travel Time Index

Area	1985	1990	1995	2000	2005	2010	2014
Urban Area Rank[1,2]	n/a	n/a	n/a	n/a	n/a	n/a	n/a
Urban Area Index[1]	n/a	n/a	n/a	n/a	n/a	n/a	n/a
Average Index[3]	1.09	1.11	1.14	1.17	1.20	1.19	1.20

Note: Freeway Travel Time Index—the ratio of travel time in the peak period to the travel time at free-flow conditions. For example, a value of 1.30 indicates a 20-minute free-flow trip takes 26 minutes in the peak (20 minutes x 1.30 = 26 minutes); (1) Data for the Trenton, NJ urban area was not available; (2) Rank is based on 101 urban areas (#1 = highest travel time index); (3) Average of 101 urban areas
Source: Texas Transportation Institute, 2015 Urban Mobility Scorecard, August 2015

Freeway Commuter Stress Index

Area	1985	1990	1995	2000	2005	2010	2014
Urban Area Rank[1,2]	n/a	n/a	n/a	n/a	n/a	n/a	n/a
Urban Area Index[1]	n/a	n/a	n/a	n/a	n/a	n/a	n/a
Average Index[3]	1.13	1.16	1.19	1.22	1.25	1.24	1.25

Note: The Freeway Commuter Stress Index is the same as the Freeway Travel Time Index (see table above) except that it includes only the travel in the peak directions during the peak periods; the TTI includes travel in all directions during the peak period. Thus, the CSI is more indicative of the work trip experienced by each commuter on a daily basis. (1) Data for the Trenton, NJ urban area was not available; (2) Rank is based on 101 urban areas (#1 = highest stress index); (3) Average of 101 urban areas
Source: Texas Transportation Institute, 2015 Urban Mobility Scorecard, August 2015

Living Environment

COST OF LIVING

Cost of Living Index

Composite Index	Groceries	Housing	Utilities	Trans-portation	Health Care	Misc. Goods/ Services
n/a	n/a	n/a	n/a	n/a	n/a	n/a

Note: The Cost of Living Index measures regional differences in the cost of consumer goods and services, excluding taxes and non-consumer expenditures, for professional and managerial households in the top income quintile. It is based on more than 50,000 prices covering almost 60 different items for which prices are collected three times a year by chambers of commerce, economic development organizations or university applied economic centers in each participating urban area. The numbers shown should be read as a percentage above or below the national average of 100. For example, a value of 115.4 in the groceries column indicates that grocery prices are 15.4% higher than the national average. Small differences in the index numbers should not be interpreted as significant; n/a not available.

Source: The Council for Community and Economic Research, ACCRA Cost of Living Index, 2015

Grocery Prices

Area[1]	T-Bone Steak ($/pound)	Frying Chicken ($/pound)	Whole Milk ($/half gal.)	Eggs ($/dozen)	Orange Juice ($/64 oz.)	Coffee ($/11.5 oz.)
City[2]	n/a	n/a	n/a	n/a	n/a	n/a
Avg.	10.99	1.43	2.25	2.26	3.58	4.48
Min.	7.16	0.98	1.30	1.35	2.88	2.98
Max.	14.13	2.43	3.85	4.81	6.39	7.56

Note: (1) Values for the local area are compared with the average, minimum and maximum values for all 292 areas in the Cost of Living Index; (2) Figures cover the Princeton NJ urban area; n/a not available; **T-Bone Steak** *(price per pound);* **Frying Chicken** *(price per pound, whole fryer);* **Whole Milk** *(half gallon carton);* **Eggs** *(price per dozen, Grade A, large);* **Orange Juice** *(64 oz. Tropicana or Florida Natural);* **Coffee** *(11.5 oz. can, vacuum-packed, Maxwell House, Hills Bros, or Folgers).*

Source: The Council for Community and Economic Research, ACCRA Cost of Living Index, 2015

Housing and Utility Costs

Area[1]	New Home Price ($)	Apartment Rent ($/month)	All Electric ($/month)	Part Electric ($/month)	Other Energy ($/month)	Telephone ($/month)
City[2]	n/a	n/a	n/a	n/a	n/a	n/a
Avg.	312,874	945	179.30	95.07	72.96	28.11
Min.	178,682	479	116.28	43.14	26.46	10.01
Max.	1,472,476	3,984	504.25	189.44	421.11	43.06

Note: (1) Values for the local area are compared with the average, minimum and maximum values for all 292 areas in the Cost of Living Index; (2) Figures cover the Princeton NJ urban area; n/a not available; **New Home Price** *(2,400 sf living area, 8,000 sf lot, in urban area with full utilities);* **Apartment Rent** *(950 sf 2 bedroom/1.5 or 2 bath, unfurnished, excluding all utilities except water);* **All Electric** *(average monthly cost for an all-electric home);* **Part Electric** *(average monthly cost for a part-electric home);* **Other Energy** *(average monthly cost for natural gas, fuel oil, coal, wood, and any other forms of energy except electricity);* **Telephone** *(price includes basic monthly rate for a private residential line plus additional local usage charges incurred by a family of four).*

Source: The Council for Community and Economic Research, ACCRA Cost of Living Index, 2015

Health Care, Transportation, and Other Costs

Area[1]	Doctor ($/visit)	Dentist ($/visit)	Optometrist ($/visit)	Gasoline ($/gallon)	Beauty Salon ($/visit)	Men's Shirt ($)
City[2]	n/a	n/a	n/a	n/a	n/a	n/a
Avg.	105.15	89.02	99.78	2.38	35.30	28.10
Min.	66.87	56.09	48.53	1.95	18.91	13.38
Max.	182.34	150.36	228.33	4.09	67.91	63.80

Note: (1) Values for the local area are compared with the average, minimum and maximum values for all 292 areas in the Cost of Living Index; (2) Figures cover the Princeton NJ urban area; n/a not available; **Doctor** *(general practitioners routine exam of an established patient);* **Dentist** *(adult teeth cleaning and periodic oral examination);* **Optometrist** *(full vision eye exam for established adult patient);* **Gasoline** *(one gallon regular unleaded, national brand, including all taxes, cash price at self-service pump if available);* **Beauty Salon** *(woman's shampoo, trim, and blow-dry);* **Men's Shirt** *(cotton/polyester dress shirt, pinpoint weave, long sleeves).*

Source: The Council for Community and Economic Research, ACCRA Cost of Living Index, 2015

HOUSING

House Price Index (HPI)

Area	National Ranking[2]	Quarterly Change (%)	One-Year Change (%)	Five-Year Change (%)
MSA[1]	184	1.20	3.10	-2.00
U.S.[3]	–	1.45	5.76	22.85

Note: The HPI is a weighted repeat sales index. It measures average price changes in repeat sales or refinancings on the same properties. This information is obtained by reviewing repeat mortgage transactions on single-family properties whose mortgages have been purchased or securitized by Fannie Mae or Freddie Mac in January 1975; (1) Trenton Metropolitan Statistical Area—see Appendix B for areas included; (2) Rankings are based on annual percentage change for all metro areas containing at least 15,000 transactions over the last 10 years and ranges from 1 to 266; (3) figures based on a weighted average of Census Division estimates using a seasonally adjusted, purchase-only index; all figures are for the period ending December 31, 2015
Source: Federal Housing Finance Agency, House Price Index, February 25, 2016

Median Single-Family Home Prices

Area	2013	2014	2015p	Percent Change 2014 to 2015
MSA[1]	257.5	267.1	262.3	-1.8
U.S. Average	197.4	208.9	223.9	7.2

Note: Figures are median sales prices of existing single-family homes in thousands of dollars; (p) preliminary; n/a not available; (1) Trenton, NJ Metropolitan Statistical Area—see Appendix B for areas included
Source: National Association of Realtors, Median Sales Price of Existing Single-Family Homes for Metropolitan Areas, 4th Quarter 2015

Qualifying Income Based on Median Sales Price of Existing Single-Family Homes

Area	With 5% Down ($)	With 10% Down ($)	With 20% Down ($)
MSA[1]	50,781	48,108	42,763
U.S. Average	49,535	46,928	41,714

Note: Figures are preliminary; Qualifying income is based on a mortgage rate of 4.1%. Monthly principal and interest payment is limited to 25% of income; n/a not available; (1) Trenton, NJ Metropolitan Statistical Area—see Appendix B for areas included
Source: National Association of Realtors, Qualifying Income Based on Median Sales Price of Existing Single-Family Homes for Metropolitan Areas, 4th Quarter 2015

Median Apartment Condo-Coop Home Prices

Area	2013	2014	2015p	Percent Change 2014 to 2015
MSA[1]	190.8	186.8	198.3	6.2
U.S. Average	194.9	204.3	210.7	3.1

Note: Figures are median sales prices of existing apartment condo-coop homes in thousands of dollars; (p) preliminary; n/a not available; (1) Trenton, NJ Metropolitan Statistical Area—see Appendix B for areas included
Source: National Association of Realtors, Median Sales Price of Existing Apartment Condo-Coop Homes for Metropolitan Areas, 4th Quarter 2015

Gross Monthly Rent

Area	Under $200	$200 -299	$300 -499	$500 -749	$750 -999	$1,000 -1,499	$1,500 and up	Median ($)
City	2.1	1.8	5.0	6.3	13.0	26.6	45.1	1,344
MSA[1]	2.8	4.4	4.0	7.5	17.2	39.6	24.5	1,135
U.S.	1.5	3.2	7.4	21.0	24.1	26.9	15.9	920

Note: Figures are percentages except for Median; Gross rent is the contract rent plus the estimated average monthly cost of utilities (electricity, gas, and water and sewer) and fuels (oil, coal, kerosene, wood, etc.) if these are paid by the renter (or paid for the renter by someone else); (1) Figures cover the Trenton, NJ Metropolitan Statistical Area—see Appendix B for areas included
Source: U.S. Census Bureau, 2010-2014 American Community Survey 5-Year Estimates

Homeownership Rate

Area	2008 (%)	2009 (%)	2010 (%)	2011 (%)	2012 (%)	2013 (%)	2014 (%)	2015 (%)
MSA[1]	n/a	n/a	n/a	n/a	n/a	n/a	n/a	n/a
U.S.	67.8	67.4	66.9	66.1	65.4	65.1	64.5	63.7

Note: (1) Figures cover the Trenton, NJ Metropolitan Statistical Area—see Appendix B for areas included; n/a not available
Source: U.S. Census Bureau, Housing Vacancies and Homeownership Annual Statistics: 2015

Year Housing Structure Built

Area	2010 or Later	2000 -2009	1990 -1999	1980 -1989	1970 -1979	1960 -1969	1950 -1959	1940 -1949	Before 1940	Median Year
City	0.2	9.9	9.1	7.8	9.3	14.0	18.0	6.6	25.1	1960
MSA[1]	0.5	9.2	9.3	11.6	11.0	13.7	15.8	8.0	20.9	1964
U.S.	1.0	14.9	13.9	13.8	15.8	11.0	10.8	5.4	13.3	1976

Note: Figures are percentages except for Median Year; (1) Figures cover the Trenton, NJ Metropolitan Statistical Area—see Appendix B for areas included
Source: U.S. Census Bureau, 2010-2014 American Community Survey 5-Year Estimates

HEALTH

Health Risk Data

Category	MSA[1] (%)	U.S. (%)
Adults aged 18–64 who have any kind of health care coverage	85.2	79.6
Adults who reported being in good or excellent health	86.1	83.1
Adults who are current smokers	15.0	19.6
Adults who are heavy drinkers[2]	3.7	6.1
Adults who are binge drinkers[3]	15.7	16.9
Adults who are overweight (BMI 25.0 - 29.9)	38.8	35.8
Adults who are obese (BMI 30.0 - 99.8)	24.0	27.6
Adults who participated in any physical activities in the past month	78.1	77.1
Adults 50+ who have ever had a sigmoidoscopy or colonoscopy	64.0	67.3
Women aged 40+ who have had a mammogram within the past two years	75.0	74.0
Men aged 40+ who have had a PSA test within the past two years	43.8	45.2
Adults aged 65+ who have had flu shot within the past year	62.7	60.1
Adults who always wear a seatbelt	n/a	93.8

Note: Data as of 2012 unless otherwise noted; n/a not available; (1) Figures cover the Trenton-Ewing, NJ Metropolitan Statistical Area—see Appendix B for areas included; (2) Heavy drinkers are classified as males having more than two drinks per day or females having more than one drink per day; (3) Binge drinkers are classified as males having five or more drinks on one occasion or females having four or more drinks on one occasion
Source: Centers for Disease Control and Prevention, Behaviorial Risk Factor Surveillance System, SMART: Selected Metropolitan/Micropolitan Area Risk Trends, 2012 (Note: the CDC has discontinued this dataset but will be releasing a replacement in mid-2016)

Chronic Health Indicators

Category	MSA[1] (%)	U.S. (%)
Adults who have ever been told they had a heart attack	2.9	4.5
Adults who have ever been told they had a stroke	n/a	2.9
Adults who have been told they currently have asthma	7.4	8.9
Adults who have ever been told they have arthritis	23.1	25.7
Adults who have ever been told they have diabetes[2]	9.9	9.7
Adults who have ever been told they had skin cancer	5.6	5.7
Adults who have ever been told they had any other types of cancer	4.9	6.5
Adults who have ever been told they have COPD	6.5	6.2
Adults who have ever been told they have kidney disease	n/a	2.5
Adults who have ever been told they have a form of depression	16.2	18.0

Note: Data as of 2012 unless otherwise noted; n/a not available; (1) Figures cover the Trenton-Ewing, NJ Metropolitan Statistical Area—see Appendix B for areas included; (2) Figures do not include pregnancy-related, borderline, or pre-diabetes
Source: Centers for Disease Control and Prevention, Behaviorial Risk Factor Surveillance System, SMART: Selected Metropolitan/Micropolitan Area Risk Trends, 2012 (Note: the CDC has discontinued this dataset but will be releasing a replacement in mid-2016)

Mortality Rates for the Top 10 Causes of Death in the U.S.

ICD-10[a] Sub-Chapter	ICD-10[a] Code	Age-Adjusted Mortality Rate[1] per 100,000 population	
		County[2]	U.S.
Malignant neoplasms	C00-C97	155.1	163.6
Ischaemic heart diseases	I20-I25	92.2	102.2
Other forms of heart disease	I30-I51	57.3	50.1
Chronic lower respiratory diseases	J40-J47	27.4	41.4
Organic, including symptomatic, mental disorders	F01-F09	32.1	38.5
Cerebrovascular diseases	I60-I69	32.3	36.5
Other external causes of accidental injury	W00-X59	22.3	27.5
Other degenerative diseases of the nervous system	G30-G31	19.2	26.3
Diabetes mellitus	E10-E14	20.4	21.1
Hypertensive diseases	I10-I15	17.2	19.7

Note: (a) ICD-10 = International Classification of Diseases 10th Revision; (1) Mortality rates are a three year average covering 2012-2014; (2) Figures cover Mercer County.
Source: Centers for Disease Control and Prevention, National Center for Health Statistics. Underlying Cause of Death 1999-2014 on CDC WONDER Online Database, released 2015.

Mortality Rates for Selected Causes of Death

ICD-10[a] Sub-Chapter	ICD-10[a] Code	Age-Adjusted Mortality Rate[1] per 100,000 population	
		County[2]	U.S.
Assault	X85-Y09	8.7	5.1
Diseases of the liver	K70-K76	12.7	13.5
Human immunodeficiency virus (HIV) disease	B20-B24	3.8	2.1
Influenza and pneumonia	J09-J18	10.7	15.2
Intentional self-harm	X60-X84	6.3	12.7
Malnutrition	E40-E46	Unreliable	0.9
Obesity and other hyperalimentation	E65-E68	2.5	1.9
Renal failure	N17-N19	9.6	13.0
Transport accidents	V01-V99	7.8	11.6
Viral hepatitis	B15-B19	2.4	2.1

Note: (a) ICD-10 = International Classification of Diseases 10th Revision; (1) Mortality rates are a three year average covering 2012-2014; (2) Figures cover Mercer County; Data are Suppressed when the data meet the criteria for confidentiality constraints; Mortality rates are flagged as Unreliable when the rate would be calculated with a numerator of 20 or less.
Source: Centers for Disease Control and Prevention, National Center for Health Statistics. Underlying Cause of Death 1999-2014 on CDC WONDER Online Database, released 2015.

Health Insurance Coverage

Area	With Health Insurance	With Private Health Insurance	With Public Health Insurance	Without Health Insurance	Population Under Age 18 Without Health Insurance
City	95.2	90.5	14.9	4.8	0.8
MSA[1]	88.7	73.5	26.1	11.3	4.5
U.S.	85.8	65.8	31.1	14.2	7.1

Note: Figures are percentages that cover the civilian noninstitutionalized population; (1) Figures cover the Trenton, NJ Metropolitan Statistical Area—see Appendix B for areas included
Source: U.S. Census Bureau, 2010-2014 American Community Survey 5-Year Estimates

Number of Medical Professionals

Area	MDs[3]	DOs[3,4]	Dentists	Podiatrists	Chiropractors	Optometrists
County[1] (number)	1,449	94	287	31	95	64
County[1] (rate[2])	390.5	25.3	77.2	8.3	25.6	17.2
U.S. (rate[2])	272.5	20.9	64.7	5.8	25.9	15.2

Note: Data as of 2014 unless noted; (1) Data covers Mercer County; (2) Rate per 100,000 population; (3) Data as of 2013 and includes all active, non-federal physicians; (4) Doctor of Osteopathic Medicine
Source: U.S. Department of Health and Human Services, Health Resources and Services Administration, Bureau of Health Professions, Area Resource File (ARF) 2014-2015

EDUCATION

Public School District Statistics

District Name	Schls	Pupils	Pupil/ Teacher Ratio	Minority Pupils[1] (%)	Free Lunch Eligible[2] (%)	IEP[3] (%)
Princeton Charter School	1	343	10.8	46.1	2.0	7.6
Princeton Public Schools	6	3,416	11.1	40.1	10.0	16.0

Note: Table includes school districts with 100 or more students; (1) Percentage of students that are not non-Hispanic white; (2) Percentage of students that are eligible for the free lunch program; (3) Percentage of students that have an Individualized Education Program.
Source: U.S. Department of Education, National Center for Education Statistics, Common Core of Data, Local Education Agency (School District) Universe Survey: School Year 2013-2014; U.S. Department of Education, National Center for Education Statistics, Common Core of Data, Public Elementary/Secondary School Universe Survey: School Year 2013-2014

Best High Schools

According to *U.S. News,* Princeton is home to one of the best high schools in the U.S.: **Princeton High School** (#143); Nearly 20,000 schools were ranked based on their performance on state assessments and how well they prepare students for college. Schools with the highest unrounded College Readiness Index values were numerically ranked from No. 1 to No. 500 and were the gold medal winners. *U.S. News & World Report, "Best High Schools 2015"*

Highest Level of Education

Area	Less than H.S.	H.S. Diploma	Some College, No Deg.	Associate Degree	Bachelor's Degree	Master's Degree	Prof. School Degree	Doctorate Degree
City	3.8	6.5	6.9	1.9	26.1	29.1	8.7	17.0
MSA[1]	12.7	25.6	16.0	5.9	20.7	12.7	2.7	3.7
U.S.	13.7	28.0	21.2	7.9	18.3	7.8	2.0	1.3

Note: Figures cover persons age 25 and over; (1) Figures cover the Trenton, NJ Metropolitan Statistical Area—see Appendix B for areas included
Source: U.S. Census Bureau, 2010-2014 American Community Survey 5-Year Estimates

Educational Attainment by Race

Area	High School Graduate or Higher (%)					Bachelor's Degree or Higher (%)				
	Total	White	Black	Asian	Hisp.[2]	Total	White	Black	Asian	Hisp.[2]
City	96.2	96.5	91.7	97.9	77.0	80.9	83.2	43.2	91.6	44.0
MSA[1]	87.3	89.8	82.8	95.1	61.6	39.8	43.3	17.3	78.6	13.3
U.S.	86.3	88.4	83.2	85.8	64.1	29.3	30.6	19.0	50.9	13.9

Note: Figures shown cover persons 25 years old and over; (1) Figures cover the Trenton, NJ Metropolitan Statistical Area—see Appendix B for areas included; (2) People of Hispanic origin can be of any race
Source: U.S. Census Bureau, 2010-2014 American Community Survey 5-Year Estimates

School Enrollment by Grade and Control

Area	Preschool (%)		Kindergarten (%)		Grades 1 - 4 (%)		Grades 5 - 8 (%)		Grades 9 - 12 (%)	
	Public	Private	Public	Private	Public	Private	Public	Private	Public	Private
City	3.2	96.8	75.8	24.2	84.6	15.4	84.8	15.2	84.4	15.6
MSA[1]	45.3	54.7	88.7	11.3	90.4	9.6	89.8	10.2	88.9	11.1
U.S.	57.4	42.6	87.8	12.2	89.8	10.2	89.9	10.1	90.6	9.4

Note: Figures shown cover persons 3 years old and over; (1) Figures cover the Trenton, NJ Metropolitan Statistical Area—see Appendix B for areas included
Source: U.S. Census Bureau, 2010-2014 American Community Survey 5-Year Estimates

Average Salaries of Public School Classroom Teachers

Area	2013-14		2014-15		Percent Change 2013-14 to 2014-15	Percent Change 2004-05 to 2014-15
	Dollars	Rank[1]	Dollars	Rank[1]		
New Jersey	68,238	6	69,038	6	1.17	22.2
U.S. Average	56,610	–	57,379	–	1.36	20.8

Note: (1) State rank ranges from 1 to 51 where 1 indicates highest salary.
Source: National Education Association, Rankings & Estimates: Rankings of the States 2014 and Estimates of School Statistics 2015, March 2015

Higher Education

Four-Year Colleges			Two-Year Colleges			Medical Schools[1]	Law Schools[2]	Voc/ Tech[3]
Public	Private Non-profit	Private For-profit	Public	Private Non-profit	Private For-profit			
0	2	0	0	0	0	0	0	0

Note: Figures cover institutions located within the city limits and include main campuses only; (1) includes schools accredited by the Liaison Committee on Medical Education and the American Osteopathic Association's Commission on Osteopathic College Accreditation; (2) includes ABA-accredited schools, schools with provisional ABA accreditation, and state accredited schools; (3) includes all schools with programs that are less than 2 years.
Source: National Center for Education Statistics, Integrated Postsecondary Education System (IPEDS), 2014-15; Association of American Medical Colleges, Member List, March 21, 2016; American Osteopathic Association, Member List, March 21, 2016; Law School Admission Council, Official Guide to ABA-Approved Law Schools Online, March 21, 2016; Wikipedia, List of Medical Schools in the United States, March 21, 2016; Wikipedia, List of Law Schools in the United States, March 21, 2016

According to *U.S. News & World Report,* the Trenton, NJ metro area is home to one of the best national universities in the U.S.: **Princeton University** (#1). The indicators used to capture academic quality fall into a number of categories: assessment by administrators at peer institutions; retention of students; faculty resources; student selectivity; financial resources; alumni giving; high school counselor ratings of colleges; and graduation rate. *U.S. News & World Report, "America's Best Colleges 2016"*

PRESIDENTIAL ELECTION

2012 Presidential Election Results

Area	Obama (%)	Romney (%)	Other (%)
Mercer County	67.8	31.0	1.2
U.S.	51.0	47.2	1.8

Note: Results may not add to 100% due to rounding
Source: Dave Leip's Atlas of U.S. Presidential Elections

EMPLOYERS

Major Employers

Company Name	Industry
Bayada Nurses	Healthcare
Board of Education	Education
Capital Health Systems	Healthcare
Cenlar Capital Corp.	Mortgage loan servicing
College of NJ	Education
Congoleum Corp.	Manufacturing
Covance	Drug development
Horizon NJ Health	Healthcare
Hough Petroleum Corp.	Motor fuels and lubricants
New Jersey Ed. Assn.	Education
New Jersey Housing & Mortgage Finance Assn.	Financial services
New Jersey Re-Insurance Co.	Auto insurance
Novo Nordisk	Pharmaceuticals
Sandoz, Inc.	Pharmaceuticals
St Francis Medical Center	Healthcare
The Crest Group	Real estate
The Hibbert Company	Global fulfillment and distribution
The Times of Trenton Publishing Corp.	Publisher

Note: Companies shown are located within the Trenton, NJ Metropolitan Statistical Area.
Source: Hoovers.com; Wikipedia

PUBLIC SAFETY

Crime Rate

Area	All Crimes	Violent Crimes: Murder	Violent Crimes: Rape[3]	Violent Crimes: Robbery	Violent Crimes: Aggrav. Assault	Property Crimes: Burglary	Property Crimes: Larceny-Theft	Property Crimes: Motor Vehicle Theft
City	994.7	0.0	3.4	20.6	44.6	178.4	737.5	10.3
Metro[1]	2,163.3	8.6	11.3	150.2	177.1	475.5	1,172.2	168.5
U.S.	2,961.6	4.5	26.4	102.2	232.5	542.5	1,837.3	216.2

Note: Figures are crimes per 100,000 population; (1) Figures cover the Trenton, NJ Metropolitan Statistical Area—see Appendix B for areas included; (3) The city and U.S. figures shown were reported using the legacy Uniform Crime Reporting (UCR) definition of rape. The suburban and metro area figures shown are an aggregate total of the data submitted using both the revised and legacy UCR definitions.
Source: FBI Uniform Crime Reports, 2014

Hate Crimes

Area	Number of Quarters Reported	Race	Religion	Sexual Orientation	Ethnicity	Disability	Gender	Gender Identity
		Number of Incidents per Bias Motivation						
City	4	0	0	0	0	0	0	0
U.S.	4	2,568	1,014	1,017	648	84	33	98

Source: Federal Bureau of Investigation, Hate Crime Statistics 2014

Identity Theft Consumer Complaints

Area	Complaints	Complaints per 100,000 Population	Rank[2]
MSA[1]	519	139.7	69
U.S.	490,220	152.4	-

Note: (1) Figures cover the Trenton, NJ Metropolitan Statistical Area—see Appendix B for areas included; (2) Rank ranges from 1 to 379 where 1 indicates greatest number of identity theft complaints per 100,000 population
Source: Federal Trade Commission, Consumer Sentinel Network Data Book for January–December 2015

Fraud and Other Consumer Complaints

Area	Complaints	Complaints per 100,000 Population	Rank[2]
MSA[1]	1,701	457.8	41
U.S.	2,593,159	806.0	-

Note: (1) Figures cover the Trenton, NJ Metropolitan Statistical Area—see Appendix B for areas included; (2) Rank ranges from 1 to 379 where 1 indicates greatest number of identity theft complaints per 100,000 population
Source: Federal Trade Commission, Consumer Sentinel Network Data Book for January–December 2015

RECREATION

Culture

Dance[1]	Theatre[1]	Instrumental Music[1]	Vocal Music[1]	Series and Festivals	Museums and Art Galleries[2]	Zoos and Aquariums[3]
0	0	0	0	0	0	0

Note: (1) Professional perfoming groups; (2) Based on organizations with SIC code 8412; (3) AZA-accredited
Source: The Grey House Performing Arts Directory, 2015-16; Association of Zoos & Aquariums, AZA Member Zoos & Aquariums, March 25, 2016; www.AccuLeads.com, March 29, 2016

Professional Sports Teams

Team Name	League	Year Established
No teams are located in the metro area		

Source: Wikipedia, Major Professional Sports Teams of the United States and Canada, March 24, 2016

CLIMATE

Average and Extreme Temperatures

Temperature	Jan	Feb	Mar	Apr	May	Jun	Jul	Aug	Sep	Oct	Nov	Dec	Yr.
Extreme High (°F)	74	76	89	94	98	102	105	103	105	93	85	72	105
Average High (°F)	38	41	50	61	72	81	86	84	77	66	54	42	63
Average Temp. (°F)	32	33	42	52	63	72	77	76	68	57	47	36	55
Average Low (°F)	24	25	33	43	53	62	68	67	59	48	39	28	46
Extreme Low (°F)	-8	-7	6	16	33	41	52	45	35	25	15	-1	-8

Note: Figures cover the years 1935-1995
Source: National Climatic Data Center, International Station Meteorological Climate Summary, 9/96

Average Precipitation/Snowfall/Humidity

Precip./Humidity	Jan	Feb	Mar	Apr	May	Jun	Jul	Aug	Sep	Oct	Nov	Dec	Yr.
Avg. Precip. (in.)	3.4	3.0	4.0	3.7	3.9	3.3	4.2	4.1	3.6	3.0	3.8	3.4	43.5
Avg. Snowfall (in.)	8	8	5	1	Tr	0	0	0	0	Tr	1	5	27
Avg. Rel. Hum. 7am (%)	73	71	69	67	70	71	72	76	79	78	76	74	73
Avg. Rel. Hum. 4pm (%)	58	54	51	48	51	51	52	54	55	53	57	59	54

Note: Figures cover the years 1935-1995; Tr = Trace amounts (<0.05 in. of rain; <0.5 in. of snow)
Source: National Climatic Data Center, International Station Meteorological Climate Summary, 9/96

Weather Conditions

Temperature			Daytime Sky			Precipitation		
5°F & below	32°F & below	90°F & above	Clear	Partly cloudy	Cloudy	0.01 inch or more precip.	0.1 inch or more snow/ice	Thunder-storms
2	90	24	80	146	139	122	16	46

Note: Figures are average number of days per year and cover the years 1935-1995
Source: National Climatic Data Center, International Station Meteorological Climate Summary, 9/96

HAZARDOUS WASTE

Superfund Sites

Princeton has no sites on the EPA's Superfund Final National Priorities List. There are a total of 1,323 Superfund sites on the list in the U.S. *U.S. Environmental Protection Agency, Final National Priorities List, March 18, 2016*

AIR & WATER QUALITY

Air Quality Trends: Ozone

	1990	1995	2000	2005	2010	2011	2012	2013	2014
MSA[1]	0.105	0.107	0.099	0.089	0.086	0.079	0.080	0.070	0.071

Note: (1) Data covers the Trenton, NJ Metropolitan Statistical Area—see Appendix B for areas included. The values shown are the composite ozone concentration averages among trend sites based on the highest fourth daily maximum 8-hour concentration in parts per million. These trends are based on sites having an adequate record of monitoring data during the trend period. Data from exceptional events are included.
Source: U.S. Environmental Protection Agency, Air Quality Monitoring Information, "Air Quality Trends by City, 1990-2014"

Air Quality Index

Area	Percent of Days when Air Quality was...[2]					AQI Statistics[2]	
	Good	Moderate	Unhealthy for Sensitive Groups	Unhealthy	Very Unhealthy	Maximum	Median
MSA[1]	76.2	22.7	1.1	0.0	0.0	122	37

Note: (1) Data covers the Trenton, NJ Metropolitan Statistical Area—see Appendix B for areas included; (2) Based on 365 days with AQI data in 2015. Air Quality Index (AQI) is an index for reporting daily air quality. EPA calculates the AQI for five major air pollutants regulated by the Clean Air Act: ground-level ozone, particle pollution (aka particulate matter), carbon monoxide, sulfur dioxide, and nitrogen dioxide. The AQI runs from 0 to 500. The higher the AQI value, the greater the level of air pollution and the greater the health concern. There are six AQI categories: "Good" AQI is between 0 and 50. Air quality is considered satisfactory; "Moderate" AQI is between 51 and 100. Air quality is acceptable; "Unhealthy for Sensitive Groups" When AQI values are between 101 and 150, members of sensitive groups may experience health effects; "Unhealthy" When AQI values are between 151 and 200 everyone may begin to experience health effects; "Very Unhealthy" AQI values between 201 and 300 trigger a health alert; "Hazardous" AQI values over 300 trigger warnings of emergency conditions (not shown).
Source: U.S. Environmental Protection Agency, Air Quality Index Report, 2015

Air Quality Index Pollutants

Area	Percent of Days when AQI Pollutant was...[2]					
	Carbon Monoxide	Nitrogen Dioxide	Ozone	Sulfur Dioxide	Particulate Matter 2.5	Particulate Matter 10
MSA[1]	0.0	0.0	75.3	0.0	24.7	0.0

Note: (1) Data covers the Trenton, NJ Metropolitan Statistical Area—see Appendix B for areas included; (2) Based on 365 days with AQI data in 2015. The Air Quality Index (AQI) is an index for reporting daily air quality. EPA calculates the AQI for five major air pollutants regulated by the Clean Air Act: ground-level ozone, particle pollution (also known as particulate matter), carbon monoxide, sulfur dioxide, and nitrogen dioxide. The AQI runs from 0 to 500. The higher the AQI value, the greater the level of air pollution and the greater the health concern.
Source: U.S. Environmental Protection Agency, Air Quality Index Report, 2015

Maximum Air Pollutant Concentrations: Particulate Matter, Ozone, CO and Lead

	Particulate Matter 10 (ug/m^3)	Particulate Matter 2.5 Wtd AM (ug/m^3)	Particulate Matter 2.5 24-Hr (ug/m^3)	Ozone (ppm)	Carbon Monoxide (ppm)	Lead (ug/m^3)
MSA[1] Level	n/a	8.7	24	0.071	n/a	n/a
NAAQS[2]	150	15	35	0.075	9	0.15
Met NAAQS[2]	n/a	Yes	Yes	Yes	n/a	n/a

Note: (1) Data covers the Trenton, NJ Metropolitan Statistical Area—see Appendix B for areas included; Data from exceptional events are included; (2) National Ambient Air Quality Standards; ppm = parts per million; ug/m^3 = micrograms per cubic meter; n/a not available.
Concentrations: Particulate Matter 10 (coarse particulate)—highest second maximum 24-hour concentration; Particulate Matter 2.5 Wtd AM (fine particulate)—highest weighted annual mean concentration; Particulate Matter 2.5 24-Hour (fine particulate)—highest 98th percentile 24-hour concentration; Ozone—highest fourth daily maximum 8-hour concentration; Carbon Monoxide—highest second maximum non-overlapping 8-hour concentration; Lead—maximum running 3-month average
Source: U.S. Environmental Protection Agency, Air Quality Monitoring Information, "Air Quality Statistics by City, 2014"

Maximum Air Pollutant Concentrations: Nitrogen Dioxide and Sulfur Dioxide

	Nitrogen Dioxide AM (ppb)	Nitrogen Dioxide 1-Hr (ppb)	Sulfur Dioxide AM (ppb)	Sulfur Dioxide 1-Hr (ppb)	Sulfur Dioxide 24-Hr (ppb)
MSA[1] Level	n/a	n/a	n/a	n/a	n/a
NAAQS[2]	53	100	30	75	140
Met NAAQS[2]	n/a	n/a	n/a	n/a	n/a

Note: (1) Data covers the Trenton, NJ Metropolitan Statistical Area—see Appendix B for areas included; Data from exceptional events are included; (2) National Ambient Air Quality Standards; ppm = parts per million; ug/m^3 = micrograms per cubic meter; n/a not available.
Concentrations: Nitrogen Dioxide AM—highest arithmetic mean concentration; Nitrogen Dioxide 1-Hr—highest 98th percentile 1-hour daily maximum concentration; Sulfur Dioxide AM—highest annual mean concentration; Sulfur Dioxide 1-Hr—highest 99th percentile 1-hour daily maximum concentration; Sulfur Dioxide 24-Hr—highest second maximum 24-hour concentration
Source: U.S. Environmental Protection Agency, Air Quality Monitoring Information, "Air Quality Statistics by City, 2014"

Drinking Water

Water System Name	Pop. Served	Primary Water Source Type	Violations[1]	
			Health Based	Monitoring/ Reporting
Trenton Water Works	205,000	Surface	0	0

Note: (1) Based on violation data from January 1, 2015 to December 31, 2015 (includes unresolved violations from earlier years)
Source: U.S. Environmental Protection Agency, Office of Ground Water and Drinking Water, Safe Drinking Water Information System (based on data extracted April 29, 2016)

Ridgewood, New Jersey

Background

Ridgewood is an affluent small city in Bergen County, New Jersey located approximately 20 miles northwest of midtown Manhattan, and covers about five square miles. Its name was derived from the characteristics of the terrain and the wooded ridges that mark the area.

The village of Ridgewood was established in 1894, however the first recorded home built in Ridgewood dates back to 1700, two years after Johannes Van Emburgh purchased 250 acres of property in 1698. Throughout the 20th century Ridgewood acquired area from Franklin Township, Washington Township, and Ho-Ho-Kus, all of which neighbor Ridgewood. Today, the village council serves as Ridgewood's governing body and consists of five council members who are elected at large.

Ridgewood is officially a suburb of NYC, and Manhattan workers have an easy commute by car, train or bus. Ridgewood neighborhoods are intertwined around its many schools, local community hospital and religious centers. Academic excellence is the hallmark of the public school system in Ridgewood and it has a rich history of serving its disabled residents. In addition, the Ridgewood Community School offers an array of continuing education classes and trips designed for both adults and children. The Ridgewood Public Library is dedicated to the community and encourages life long learning and the enjoyment of books with programs and resources in a variety of formats. It is a well-equipped, busy hub with knowledgeable staff, and state of the art technology and facilities.

Residents of Ridgewood enjoy a strong sense of community due in part to the vast number of organizations and volunteers dedicated to its well being. Volunteers serve on local government advisory boards, in civic organizations, choral and musical groups, and social service associations. It is home to many corporate CEOs and managers, and offers a wide variety of services for all age groups. Quaint and quiet, Ridgewood is a great place to raise a family, while being close to the offerings of NYC.

The town offers a distinct, historic district with small mom and pop boutique stores alongside larger brand name establishments. The commercial district maintains the small town sentiment 'we care about you.' Ridgewood is a walking town and the downtown and commercial areas are easily accessible. The village is clean, safe, and beautiful, with tree lined streets and green spaces.

There are many park and open space facilities in Ridgewood. These facilities include a swimming pool, baseball fields, soccer fields, and a roller rink. There is also a band shell that offers free concerts and is the home of the local high school baseball team. There are sledding hills in winter as well as areas used for sleigh riding.

Ridgewood sees about 50 inches of rain per year and approximately 28 inches of snow. On average, there are 209 days of sunshine per year and the summer highs reach into the 80s, while the lows in winter drop into the teens and 20s. The climate is generally hot and humid in the summer months. Spring and fall are known for being the best seasons with extremely pleasant weather and colorful foliage.

Rankings

General Rankings

- New York* was identified as one of America's fastest-growing major metropolitan areas in terms of population growth by CNNMoney.com. The area ranked #1 out of 10. Criteria: population growth between July 2013 and July 2014. *CNNMoney, "10 Fastest-Growing Cities," May 27, 2015*

Business/Finance Rankings

- The personal finance site NerdWallet analyzed 183 American metropolitan areas with populations over 250,000 and more than 15,000 businesses to rank where entrepreneurs find the most success. Criteria included area economy, annual income, housing cost, unemployment rate, and the success rate of area businesses. New York* ranked #32. *www.nerdwallet.com, "Best Places to Start a Business," April 27, 2015*

- Based on the U.S. Department of Labor's Occupational Information Network Data Collection Program, the Brookings Institution defined job opportunities for STEM workers at various levels of educational attainment. The New York* metro area was one of the ten metro areas where workers in low-education-level STEM jobs earn the lowest relative wages. *www.brookings.edu, "The Hidden Stem Economy," June 10, 2013*

- Metro areas with the largest gap in income between rich and poor residents were identified by 24/7 Wall Street using the U.S. Census Bureau's 2013 American Community Survey. The New York* metro area placed #7 among metro areas with the widest wealth gap between rich and poor. *247wallst.com, "20 Cities with the Widest Gap between the Rich and Poor," July 8, 2015*

- Based on metro area social media reviews, the employment opinion group Glassdoor surveyed 50 of the largest U.S. metro areas and equally weighed cost of living, hiring opportunity, and job satisfaction to compose a list of "25 Best Cities for Jobs." The New York* metro area was ranked #21 in overall job satisfaction. *www.glassdoor.com, "Best Cities for Jobs," May 19, 2015*

- In a survey of economic confidence in the nation's 50 largest metropolitan areas conducted January–December 2014, the New York* metro area placed #23, according to Gallup's 2014 Economic Confidence Index. *Gallup, "San Jose and San Francisco Lead in Economic Confidence," March 19, 2015*

- The Brookings Institution ranked the 100 largest metro areas in the U.S. based on income inequality. New York* was ranked #2 (#1 = greatest ineqality). Criteria: the "95/20 ratio," a figure representing the income at which a household earns more than 95 percent of all other households, divided by the income at which a household earns more than only 20 percent of all other households. *Brookings Institution, "Income Inequality, 100 Largest U.S. Metro Areas, 2007-2014," January 14, 2016*

- Payscale.com ranked the 20 largest metro areas in terms of wage growth. The New York* metro area ranked #18. Criteria: private-sector wage growth between the 1st quarter of 2015 and the 1st quarter of 2016. *PayScale, "Wage Trends by Metro Area," 1st Quarter, 2016*

- The New York* metro area appeared on the Milken Institute "2015 Best Performing Cities" list. Rank: #90 out of 200 large metro areas. Criteria: job growth; wage and salary growth; high-tech output growth. *Milken Institute, "Best-Performing Cities 2015," December 2015*

- *Forbes* ranked the 200 most populous metro areas to determine the nation's "Best Places for Business and Careers." The New York* metro area was ranked #111. Criteria: costs (business and living); job growth (past and projected); income growth; educational attainment (college and high school); projected economic growth; cultural and recreational opportunities; net migration patterns; number of highly ranked colleges. *Forbes, "The Best Places for Business and Careers 2015," July 29, 2015*

Dating/Romance Rankings

- CreditDonkey, a financial education website, sought out the ten best U.S. cities for newlyweds, considering the number of married couples, divorce rate, average credit score, and average number of hours worked per week in metro areas with a million or more residents. The New York* metro area placed #5. *www.creditdonkey.com, "Study: Best Cities for Newlyweds," November 30, 2013*

Education Rankings

- Personal finance website *WalletHub* analyzed the 150 largest U.S. metropolitan statistical areas to determine where the most educated Americans are choosing to settle. Criteria: education quality and attainment gap; education levels; percentage of workers with degrees; public school rankings; quality and size of each metro area's universities. New York* was ranked #58 (#1 = most educated city). *www.WalletHub.com, "2015's Most and Least Educated Cities*

Environmental Rankings

- The New York* metro area came in at #155 for the relative comfort of its climate on Sperling's list of "chill cities," as measured by the Sperling Heat Index. All 361 metro areas are included. Criteria included daytime high temperatures, nighttime low temperatures, dew point, and relative humidity at the high temperatures. *www.bertsperling.com, "Sperling's Chill Cities," July 18, 2013*

- Sperling's BestPlaces assessed 379 metropolitan areas of the United States for the likelihood of dangerously extreme weather events or earthquakes. In general the Southeast and South-Central regions have the highest risk of weather extremes and earthquakes, while the Pacific Northwest enjoys the lowest risk. Of the least risky metropolitan areas, the New York* metro area was ranked #207. *www.bestplaces.net, "Safest Places from Natural Disasters," April 2011*

- New York* was identified as one of America's dirtiest metro areas by *Forbes*. The area ranked #11 out of 20. Criteria: air quality; water quality; toxic releases; superfund sites. *Forbes, "America's 20 Dirtiest Cities," December 10, 2012*

- The U.S. Environmental Protection Agency (EPA) released a list of U.S. metropolitan areas with the most ENERGY STAR certified buildings in 2015. The New York* metro area was ranked #5 out of 25. *U.S. Environmental Protection Agency, "Top Cities With the Most ENERGY STAR Certified Buildings in 2016," March 30, 2016*

- New York* was highlighted as one of the 25 most ozone-polluted metro areas in the U.S. during 2011 through 2013. The area ranked #11. *American Lung Association, State of the Air 2015*

- New York* was highlighted as one of the 25 metro areas most polluted by year-round particle pollution (Annual PM 2.5) in the U.S. during 2011 through 2013. The area ranked #14. *American Lung Association, State of the Air 2015*

- New York* was highlighted as one of the 25 metro areas most polluted by short-term particle pollution (24-hour PM 2.5) in the U.S. during 2011 through 2013. The area ranked #15. *American Lung Association, State of the Air 2015*

Health/Fitness Rankings

- For each of the 50 most populous metro areas in the United States, the American College of Sports Medicine's American Fitness Index evaluated infrastructure, community assets, and policies that encourage healthy and fit lifestyles, including preventive health behaviors, levels of chronic disease conditions, health care access, and community resources and policies that support physical activity. The New York* metro area ranked #24 for "community fitness." *www.americanfitnessindex.org, "ACSM American Fitness Index Health and Community Fitness Status of the 50 Largest Metropolitan Areas," May 2015*

- *Business Insider* reported Trulia's analysis of the 100 largest U.S. metro areas to identify the nation's best cities for weight loss, based on healthful food options, access to outdoor activities, weight-loss centers, gyms, and opportunities to bike or walk to work. New York* ranked #6. *Businessinsider.com, "These Are the Best US Cities for Weight loss," January 17, 2013*
- The New York* metro area was identified as one of the worst cities for bed bugs in America by pest control company Orkin. The area ranked #4 out of 50 based on the number of bed bug treatments Orkin performed from January to December 2015. *Orkin, "Chicago Tops Bed Bug Cities List for Fourth Year in a Row," January 13, 2016*
- New York* was identified as a "2016 Spring Allergy Capital." The area ranked #31 out of 100. Three groups of factors were used to identify the most severe cities for people with allergies during the spring season: annual pollen levels; medicine utilization; access to board-certified allergists. *Asthma and Allergy Foundation of America, "Spring Allergy Capitals 2016"*
- New York* was identified as a "2015 Asthma Capital." The area ranked #35 out of the nation's 100 largest metropolitan areas. Criteria: estimated prevalence; self-reported prevalence; crude death rate for asthma; annual pollen score; annual air quality; public smoking laws; number of board-certified asthma specialists; school inhaler access laws; rescue medication use; controller medication use; ER visits for asthma; uninsured rate; poverty rate. *Asthma and Allergy Foundation of America, "Asthma Capitals 2015"*
- The New York* metro area ranked #113 out of 190 in The Gallup-Healthways Well-Being Index. Criteria: purpose; social well being; financial health; community and physical health. Results are based on telephone interviews with adults, aged 18 and older, living in metropolitan areas in the 50 U.S. states and the District of Columbia. *Gallup-Healthways, "State of American Well-Being," February 23, 2016*

Real Estate Rankings

- With data from RealtyTrac, Yahoo! Finance researchers listed the housing markets in which housing affordability is improving most, factoring in interest rates as well as median home prices. The New York* metro area was among the least affordable housing markets. *news.yahoo.com, "10 Cities Where Ordinary People Can No Longer Afford Homes," March 5, 2014*
- The New York* metro area was identified as one of the 20 least affordable housing markets in the U.S. in 2015. The area ranked #9 out of 179 markets. Criteria: qualification for a mortgage loan on a typical home. *National Association of Realtors®, Affordability Index of Existing Single-Family Homes for Metropolitan Areas, 2015*
- New York* was ranked #217 out of 225 metro areas in terms of housing affordability in 2015 by the National Association of Home Builders (#1 = most affordable). Criteria: the share of homes sold in that area affordable to a family earning the local median income, based on standard mortgage underwriting criteria. *National Association of Home Builders®, NAHB-Wells Fargo Housing Opportunity Index, 4th Quarter 2015*

Safety Rankings

- New York* was identified as one of the most disaster-proof places in the U.S. in terms of its vulnerability to natural and non-natural disasters. The city ranked #1 out of 5. Rankings are based on the U.S. Center for Disease Control's Cities Readiness Initiative (CRI), which assesses local emergency-management plans, protocols and capabilities for 72 Metropolitan Statistical Areas and four non-MSA large cities. *Forbes, "America's Most and Least Disaster-Proof Cities," December 12, 2011*
- Ridgewood was identified as one of the safest cities in America by NeighborhoodScout. The city ranked #19 out of 100. Criteria: number of violent and property crimes per 1,000 residents. The editors only considered cities with 25,000 or more residents. *NeighborhoodScout, "Safest Cities in America 2016"*

- The National Insurance Crime Bureau ranked 380 metro areas in the U.S. in terms of per capita rates of vehicle theft. The New York* metro area ranked #249 (#1 = highest rate). Criteria: number of vehicle theft offenses per 100,000 inhabitants in 2014. *National Insurance Crime Bureau, "Hot Spots 2014," June 24, 2015*

Seniors/Retirement Rankings

- From its Best Cities for Successful Aging indexes, the Milken Institute generated rankings for metropolitan areas, weighing data in eight categories—health care, wellness, living arrangements, transportation, financial characteristics, education and employment opportunities, community engagement, and overall livability. The New York* metro area was ranked #14 overall in the large metro area category. *Milken Institute, "Best Cities for Successful Aging, 2014"*

Sports/Recreation Rankings

- According to the personal finance website NerdWallet, the New York* metro area, at #4, is one of the nation's top dozen metro areas for sports fans. Criteria included the presence of all four major sports—MLB, NFL, NHL, and NBA, fan enthusiasm (as measured by game attendance), ticket affordability, and "sports culture," that is, number of sports bars. *www.nerdwallet.com, "Best Cities for Sports Fans," May 5, 2013*

Transportation Rankings

- New York* was identified as one of the most congested metro areas in the U.S. The area ranked #4 out of 10. Criteria: yearly delay per auto commuter in hours. *Texas A&M Transportation Institute, "2015 Urban Mobility Scorecard," August 2015*
- The New York* metro area appeared on *Forbes* list of places with the most extreme commutes. The metro area ranked #2 out of 10. Criteria: average travel time; percentage of mega commuters. Mega-commuters travel more than 90 minutes and 50 miles each way to work. *Forbes.com, "The Cities with the Most Extreme Commutes," March 5, 2013*

Miscellaneous Rankings

- The watchdog site Charity Navigator conducts an annual study of charities in the nation's major markets both to analyze statistical differences in their financial, accountability, and transparency practices and to track year-to-year variations in individual communities. The New York* metro area was ranked #17 among the 30 metro markets in the rating dimension of Overall Score. *www.charitynavigator.org, "Metro Market Study 2015," June 5, 2015*
- The Harris Poll's Happiness Index survey revealed that of the top ten U.S. markets, the New York* metro area residents ranked #6 in happiness. Criteria included strong assent to positive statements and strong disagreement with negative ones, and degree of agreement with a series of statements about respondents' personal relationships and general outlook. *www.harrisinteractive.com, "Dallas/Fort Worth Is "Happiest" City among America's Top Ten Markets," September 4, 2013*
- Energizer Personal Care, the makers of Edge® shave gel, in partnership with Sperling's BestPlaces, ranked 50 major metro areas in terms of everyday irritations. The New York* metro area ranked #2 the 50 metro area most iritating to guys. Criteria: high male-to-female ratio; poor sports team performance and high ticket prices; slow traffic; lack of job availability; unaffordable housing; extreme weather; lack of nightlife and fitness options. *Energizer Personal Care, "Most Irritatng Cities for Guys," August 26, 2013*
- Mars Chocolate North America, the makers of COMBOS®, in partnership with Sperling's BestPlaces, ranked 50 major metro areas in terms of their "manliness." The New York* metro area ranked #39. Criteria: number of professional sports teams; number of nearby NASCAR tracks and racing events; manly lifestyle; concentration of manly retail stores; manly occupations per capita; salty snack sales; "Board of Manliness" rankings. *Mars Chocolate North America, "America's Manliest Cities 2012"*

- The New York* metro area was selected as one of "America's Most Miserable Cities" by *Forbes.com.* The metro area ranked #10 out of 20. Criteria: violent crime; unemployment; foreclosures; income and property taxes; home prices; commute times; climate. *Forbes.com, "America's Most Miserable Cities" February 22, 2013*

- The National Alliance to End Homelessness ranked the 100 most populous metro areas with the highest rate of homelessness. The New York* metro area ranked #13. Criteria: number of homeless people per 10,000 population in 2011. *National Alliance to End Homelessness, The State of Homelessness in America 2012*

Ridgewood is located within the New York-Newark-Jersey City, NY-NJ-PA Metropolitan Statistical Area.

Business Environment

CITY FINANCES

City Government Finances

Component	2012 ($000)	2012 ($ per capita)
Total Revenues	53,796	2,155
Total Expenditures	52,771	2,114
Debt Outstanding	55,202	2,211
Cash and Securities[1]	17,045	682

Note: (1) Cash and security holdings of a government at the close of its fiscal year, including those of its dependent agencies, utilities, and liquor stores.
Source: U.S Census Bureau, State & Local Government Finances 2012

City Government Revenue by Source

Source	2012 ($000)	2012 ($ per capita)
General Revenue		
From Federal Government	0	0
From State Government	2,342	93
From Local Governments	717	28
Taxes		
Property	33,410	1,338
Sales and Gross Receipts	575	23
Personal Income	0	0
Corporate Income	0	0
Motor Vehicle License	0	0
Other Taxes	1,294	51
Current Charges	2,613	104
Liquor Store	0	0
Utility	11,391	456
Employee Retirement	0	0

Source: U.S Census Bureau, State & Local Government Finances 2012

City Government Expenditures by Function

Function	2012 ($000)	2012 ($ per capita)	2012 (%)
General Direct Expenditures			
Air Transportation	0	0	0.0
Corrections	0	0	0.0
Education	0	0	0.0
Employment Security Administration	0	0	0.0
Financial Administration	569	22	1.0
Fire Protection	5,055	202	9.5
General Public Buildings	114	4	0.2
Governmental Administration, Other	623	24	1.1
Health	246	9	0.4
Highways	1,959	78	3.7
Hospitals	0	0	0.0
Housing and Community Development	0	0	0.0
Interest on General Debt	1,212	48	2.2
Judicial and Legal	389	15	0.7
Libraries	2,197	88	4.1
Parking	818	32	1.5
Parks and Recreation	1,691	67	3.2
Police Protection	6,005	240	11.3
Public Welfare	41	1	0.0
Sewerage	1,318	52	2.4
Solid Waste Management	2,543	101	4.8
Veterans' Services	0	0	0.0
Liquor Store	0	0	0.0
Utility	9,522	381	18.0
Employee Retirement	0	0	0.0

Source: U.S Census Bureau, State & Local Government Finances 2012

DEMOGRAPHICS

Population Growth

Area	1990 Census	2000 Census	2010 Census	2014* Estimate	Population Growth (%)	
					1990-2014	2010-2014
City	24,245	24,936	24,958	25,270	4.2	1.3
MSA[1]	16,845,992	18,323,002	18,897,109	19,865,045	17.9	5.1
U.S.	248,709,873	281,421,906	308,745,538	314,107,084	26.3	1.7

Note: (1) Figures cover the New York-Newark-Jersey City, NY-NJ-PA Metropolitan Statistical Area—see Appendix B for areas included; (*) 2010-2014 5-year estimated population
Source: U.S. Census Bureau, 1990 Census, Census 2000, Census 2010, 2010-2014 American Community Survey 5-Year Estimates

Household Size

Area	Persons in Household (%)							Average Household Size
	One	Two	Three	Four	Five	Six	Seven or More	
City	17.6	26.8	16.1	25.3	11.5	1.9	0.5	3.05
MSA[1]	27.8	28.9	17.0	14.8	6.7	2.6	1.9	2.74
U.S.	27.5	33.5	15.8	13.1	6.0	2.3	1.4	2.64

Note: (1) Figures cover the New York-Newark-Jersey City, NY-NJ-PA Metropolitan Statistical Area—see Appendix B for areas included
Source: U.S. Census Bureau, 2010-2014 American Community Survey 5-Year Estimates

Race

Area	White Alone[2] (%)	Black Alone[2] (%)	Asian Alone[2] (%)	AIAN[3] Alone[2] (%)	NHOPI[4] Alone[2] (%)	Other Race Alone[2] (%)	Two or More Races (%)
City	78.0	2.3	15.5	0.0	0.0	1.6	2.5
MSA[1]	59.4	17.2	10.2	0.3	0.0	10.1	2.8
U.S.	73.8	12.6	5.0	0.8	0.2	4.7	2.9

Note: (1) Figures cover the New York-Newark-Jersey City, NY-NJ-PA Metropolitan Statistical Area—see Appendix B for areas included; (2) Alone is defined as not being in combination with one or more other races; (3) American Indian and Alaska Native; (4) Native Hawaiian and Other Pacific Islander
Source: U.S. Census Bureau, 2010-2014 American Community Survey 5-Year Estimates

Hispanic or Latino Origin

Area	Total (%)	Mexican (%)	Puerto Rican (%)	Cuban (%)	Other (%)
City	7.1	1.2	0.8	0.5	4.6
MSA[1]	23.3	3.0	6.4	0.7	13.1
U.S.	16.9	10.8	1.6	0.6	3.8

Note: Persons of Hispanic or Latino origin can be of any race; (1) Figures cover the New York-Newark-Jersey City, NY-NJ-PA Metropolitan Statistical Area—see Appendix B for areas included
Source: U.S. Census Bureau, 2010-2014 American Community Survey 5-Year Estimates

Ancestry

Area	German	Irish	English	American	Italian	Polish	French[2]	Scottish	Dutch
City	11.9	20.0	8.6	4.3	17.5	5.2	1.8	1.9	2.3
MSA[1]	7.2	10.6	3.1	4.4	13.7	4.2	1.1	0.7	0.7
U.S.	14.9	10.8	8.0	7.1	5.5	3.0	2.7	1.7	1.4

Note: Figures are the percentage of the total population reporting a particular ancestry. The nine most commonly reported ancestries in the U.S. are shown. Figures include multiple ancestries (e.g. if a person reported being Irish and Italian, they were included in both columns); (1) Figures cover the New York-Newark-Jersey City, NY-NJ-PA Metropolitan Statistical Area—see Appendix B for areas included; (2) Excludes Basque
Source: U.S. Census Bureau, 2010-2014 American Community Survey 5-Year Estimates

Foreign-Born Population

Area	Any Foreign Country	Asia	Mexico	Europe	Carribean	Central America[2]	South America	Africa	Canada
	Percent of Population Born in								
City	21.3	11.8	0.0	4.5	1.5	1.0	0.9	0.8	0.6
MSA[1]	28.5	8.0	1.7	4.6	6.5	1.9	4.3	1.2	0.2
U.S.	13.1	3.8	3.7	1.5	1.2	1.0	0.9	0.6	0.3

Note: (1) Figures cover the New York-Newark-Jersey City, NY-NJ-PA Metropolitan Statistical Area—see Appendix B for areas included; (2) Excludes Mexico.
Source: U.S. Census Bureau, 2010-2014 American Community Survey 5-Year Estimates

Marital Status

Area	Never Married	Now Married[2]	Separated	Widowed	Divorced
City	24.3	63.4	0.7	4.8	6.8
MSA[1]	37.7	45.8	2.5	6.0	7.9
U.S.	32.5	48.4	2.2	5.9	10.9

Note: Figures are percentages and cover the population 15 years of age and older; (1) Figures cover the New York-Newark-Jersey City, NY-NJ-PA Metropolitan Statistical Area—see Appendix B for areas included; (2) Excludes separated
Source: U.S. Census Bureau, 2010-2014 American Community Survey 5-Year Estimates

Disability Status

Area	All Ages	Under 18 Years Old	18 to 64 Years Old	65 Years and Over
City	5.4	2.3	2.6	25.9
MSA[1]	9.8	3.1	7.3	33.5
U.S.	12.3	4.1	10.2	36.3

Note: Figures show percent of the civilian noninstitutionalized population that reported having a disability. Disability status is determined from from six types of difficulty: vision, hearing, cognitive, ambulatory, self-care, and independent living. For children under 5 years old, hearing and vision difficulty are used to determine disability status. For children between the ages of 5 and 14, disability status is determined from hearing, vision, cognitive, ambulatory, and self-care difficulties. For people aged 15 years and older, they are considered to have a disability if they have difficulty with any one of the six difficulty types; (1) Figures cover the New York-Newark-Jersey City, NY-NJ-PA Metropolitan Statistical Area—see Appendix B for areas included.
Source: U.S. Census Bureau, 2010-2014 American Community Survey 5-Year Estimates

Age

Area	Percent of Population									Median Age
	Under Age 5	Age 5–19	Age 20–34	Age 35–44	Age 45–54	Age 55–64	Age 65–74	Age 75–84	Age 85+	
City	5.0	27.6	10.1	13.9	18.5	12.3	6.6	3.6	2.4	41.4
MSA[1]	6.2	18.8	21.2	13.6	14.6	12.0	7.3	4.2	2.0	37.8
U.S.	6.4	19.9	20.6	13.0	14.1	12.3	7.6	4.3	1.9	37.4

Note: (1) Figures cover the New York-Newark-Jersey City, NY-NJ-PA Metropolitan Statistical Area—see Appendix B for areas included
Source: U.S. Census Bureau, 2010-2014 American Community Survey 5-Year Estimates

Gender

Area	Males	Females	Males per 100 Females
City	12,260	13,010	94.2
MSA[1]	9,593,127	10,271,918	93.4
U.S.	154,515,159	159,591,925	96.8

Note: (1) Figures cover the New York-Newark-Jersey City, NY-NJ-PA Metropolitan Statistical Area—see Appendix B for areas included
Source: U.S. Census Bureau, 2010-2014 American Community Survey 5-Year Estimates

Religious Groups by Family

Area	Catholic	Baptist	Non-Den.	Methodist[2]	Lutheran	LDS[3]	Pente-costal	Presby-terian[4]	Muslim[5]	Judaism
MSA[1]	36.9	1.8	1.7	1.3	0.7	0.3	0.8	1.0	2.3	4.7
U.S.	19.1	9.3	4.0	4.0	2.3	2.0	1.9	1.6	0.8	0.7

Note: Figures are the number of adherents as a percentage of the total population; (1) Figures cover the New York-Northern New Jersey-Long Island, NY-NJ-PA Metropolitan Statistical Area—see Appendix B for areas included; (2) Methodist/Pietist; (3) Latter Day Saints; (4) Reformed; (5) Figures are estimates
Source: Association of Statisticians of American Religious Bodies, 2010 U.S. Religion Census: Religious Congregations & Membership Study

Religious Groups by Tradition

Area	Catholic	Evangelical Protestant	Mainline Protestant	Other Tradition	Black Protestant	Orthodox
MSA[1]	36.9	3.9	4.1	8.3	1.2	0.9
U.S.	19.1	16.2	7.3	4.3	1.6	0.3

Note: Figures are the number of adherents as a percentage of the total population; (1) Figures cover the New York-Northern New Jersey-Long Island, NY-NJ-PA Metropolitan Statistical Area—see Appendix B for areas included
Source: Association of Statisticians of American Religious Bodies, 2010 U.S. Religion Census: Religious Congregations & Membership Study

ECONOMY

Gross Metropolitan Product

Area	2013	2014	2015	2016	Rank[2]
MSA[1]	1,471.2	1,521.7	1,573.8	1,650.1	1

Note: Figures are in billions of dollars; (1) Figures cover the New York-Newark-Jersey City, NY-NJ-PA Metropolitan Statistical Area—see Appendix B for areas included; (2) Rank is based on 2016 data and ranges from 1 to 381
Source: The U.S. Conference of Mayors, U.S. Metro Economies: GMP and Employment 2014-2016, June 2015

Economic Growth

Area	2011-13 (%)	2014 (%)	2015 (%)	2016 (%)	Rank[2]
MSA[1]	1.6	1.8	2.0	2.8	116
U.S.	2.2	2.4	2.3	2.9	–

Note: Figures are real gross metropolitan product (GMP) growth rates and represent annual average percent change; (1) Figures cover the New York-Newark-Jersey City, NY-NJ-PA Metropolitan Statistical Area—see Appendix B for areas included; (2) Rank is based on 2016 data and ranges from 1 to 381
Source: The U.S. Conference of Mayors, U.S. Metro Economies: GMP and Employment 2014-2016, June 2015

Metropolitan Area Exports

Area	2009	2010	2011	2012	2013	2014	Rank[2]
MSA[1]	69,990.3	85,081.1	105,102.0	102,298.0	106,922.8	105,266.5	2

Note: Figures are in millions of dollars; (1) Figures cover the New York-Newark-Jersey City, NY-NJ-PA Metropolitan Statistical Area—see Appendix B for areas included; (2) Rank is based on 2014 data and ranges from 1 to 385
Source: U.S. Department of Commerce, International Trade Administration, Office of Trade & Industry Information, Manufacturing & Services, data extracted March 10, 2016

Building Permits

Area	Single-Family			Multi-Family			Total		
	2014	2015p	Pct. Chg.	2014	2015p	Pct. Chg.	2014	2015p	Pct. Chg.
City	18	17	-5.6	2	4	100.0	20	21	5.0
MSA[1]	11,799	10,749	-8.9	36,185	75,646	109.1	47,984	86,395	80.0
U.S.	640,300	690,800	7.9	411,800	487,600	18.4	1,052,100	1,178,400	12.0

Note: (1) Figures cover the New York-Newark-Jersey City, NY-NJ-PA Metropolitan Statistical Area—see Appendix B for areas included; Figures represent new, privately-owned housing units authorized (unadjusted data); All permit data are based on estimates with imputation; (p) preliminary data.
Source: U.S. Census Bureau, Manufacturing, Mining, and Construction Statistics, Building Permits, 2014, 2015

Bankruptcy Filings

Area	Business Filings			Nonbusiness Filings		
	2014	2015	% Chg.	2014	2015	% Chg.
Bergen County	110	126	14.5	2,159	2,017	-6.6
U.S.	26,983	24,735	-8.3	909,812	819,760	-9.9

Note: Business filings include Chapter 7, Chapter 11, Chapter 12, and Chapter 13; Nonbusiness filings include Chapter 7, Chapter 11, and Chapter 13
Source: Administrative Office of the U.S. Courts, Business and Nonbusiness Bankruptcy, County Cases Commenced by Chapter of the Bankruptcy Code, During the 12- Month Period Ending December 31, 2014 and Business and Nonbusiness Bankruptcy, County Cases Commenced by Chapter of the Bankruptcy Code, During the 12- Month Period Ending December 31, 2015

Housing Vacancy Rates

Area	Gross Vacancy Rate[2] (%)			Year-Round Vacancy Rate[3] (%)			Rental Vacancy Rate[4] (%)			Homeowner Vacancy Rate[5] (%)		
	2013	2014	2015	2013	2014	2015	2013	2014	2015	2013	2014	2015
MSA[1]	9.5	9.2	9.8	8.1	7.9	8.6	5.4	4.6	4.2	2.1	1.6	2.1
U.S.	13.6	13.4	12.9	10.7	10.4	10.0	8.3	7.6	7.1	2.0	1.9	1.8

Note: (1) Figures cover the New York-Newark-Jersey City, NY-NJ-PA Metropolitan Statistical Area—see Appendix B for areas included; (2) The percentage of the total housing inventory that is vacant; (3) The percentage of the housing inventory (excluding seasonal units) that is year-round vacant; (4) The percentage of rental inventory that is vacant for rent; (5) The percentage of homeowner inventory that is vacant for sale
Source: U.S. Census Bureau, Housing Vacancies and Homeownership Annual Statistics: 2015

INCOME

Income

Area	Per Capita ($)	Median Household ($)	Average Household ($)
City	68,939	141,315	208,095
MSA[1]	36,078	66,902	97,572
U.S.	28,555	53,482	74,596

Note: (1) Figures cover the New York-Newark-Jersey City, NY-NJ-PA Metropolitan Statistical Area—see Appendix B for areas included
Source: U.S. Census Bureau, 2010-2014 American Community Survey 5-Year Estimates

Household Income Distribution

Area	Percent of Households Earning							
	Under $15,000	$15,000 -24,999	$25,000 -34,999	$35,000 -49,999	$50,000 -74,999	$75,000 -99,000	$100,000 -149,999	$150,000 and up
City	3.4	2.9	3.7	7.0	7.5	9.1	18.9	47.4
MSA[1]	11.8	8.8	8.0	10.6	15.3	11.9	15.7	18.0
U.S.	12.5	10.7	10.2	13.5	17.8	12.2	13.0	10.0

Note: (1) Figures cover the New York-Newark-Jersey City, NY-NJ-PA Metropolitan Statistical Area—see Appendix B for areas included
Source: U.S. Census Bureau, 2010-2014 American Community Survey 5-Year Estimates

Poverty Rate

Area	All Ages	Under 18 Years Old	18 to 64 Years Old	65 Years and Over
City	4.5	4.4	4.7	3.6
MSA[1]	14.3	20.0	12.8	11.6
U.S.	15.6	21.9	14.6	9.4

Note: Figures are percentage of people whose income during the past 12 months was below the poverty level; (1) Figures cover the New York-Newark-Jersey City, NY-NJ-PA Metropolitan Statistical Area—see Appendix B for areas included
Source: U.S. Census Bureau, 2010-2014 American Community Survey 5-Year Estimates

EMPLOYMENT

Labor Force and Employment

Area	Civilian Labor Force			Workers Employed		
	Dec. 2014	Dec. 2015	% Chg.	Dec. 2014	Dec. 2015	% Chg.
City	11,968	12,119	1.2	11,539	11,816	2.4
MD[1]	7,017,636	7,184,671	2.3	6,611,164	6,853,780	3.6
U.S.	155,521,000	157,245,000	1.1	147,190,000	149,703,000	1.7

Note: Data is not seasonally adjusted and covers workers 16 years of age and older; (1) Figures cover the New York-Jersey City-White Plains, NY-NJ Metropolitan Division—see Appendix B for areas included
Source: Bureau of Labor Statistics, Local Area Unemployment Statistics

Unemployment Rate

Area	2015											
	Jan.	Feb.	Mar.	Apr.	May	Jun.	Jul.	Aug.	Sep.	Oct.	Nov.	Dec.
City	4.3	4.0	4.1	3.8	4.1	3.7	3.9	3.5	3.5	3.3	3.1	2.5
MD[1]	6.7	6.8	6.2	5.8	5.8	5.4	5.7	5.2	4.9	4.7	4.8	4.6
U.S.	6.1	5.8	5.6	5.1	5.3	5.5	5.6	5.2	4.9	4.8	4.8	4.8

Note: Data is not seasonally adjusted and covers workers 16 years of age and older; (1) Figures cover the New York-Jersey City-White Plains, NY-NJ Metropolitan Division—see Appendix B for areas included
Source: Bureau of Labor Statistics, Local Area Unemployment Statistics

Employment by Occupation

Occupation Classification	City (%)	MSA[1] (%)	U.S. (%)
Management, Business, Science, and Arts	64.1	40.3	36.4
Natural Resources, Construction, and Maintenance	1.9	7.0	9.0
Production, Transportation, and Material Moving	3.8	9.1	12.1
Sales and Office	22.6	24.2	24.4
Service	7.6	19.4	18.2

Note: Figures cover employed civilians 16 years of age and older; (1) Figures cover the New York-Newark-Jersey City, NY-NJ-PA Metropolitan Statistical Area—see Appendix B for areas included
Source: U.S. Census Bureau, 2010-2014 American Community Survey 5-Year Estimates

Employment by Industry

Sector	MD[1]		U.S.
	Number of Employees	Percent of Total	Percent of Total
Construction, Mining, and Logging	256,300	3.7	5.0
Education and Health Services	1,350,800	19.7	15.7
Financial Activities	612,400	8.9	5.7
Government	917,500	13.3	15.5
Information	243,800	3.5	1.9
Leisure and Hospitality	638,900	9.3	10.4
Manufacturing	211,600	3.0	8.6
Other Services	296,100	4.3	3.9
Professional and Business Services	1,107,000	16.1	13.9
Retail Trade	686,300	10.0	11.3
Transportation, Warehousing, and Utilities	251,300	3.6	3.9
Wholesale Trade	284,100	4.1	4.1

Note: Figures are non-farm employment as of December 2015. Figures are not seasonally adjusted and include workers 16 years of age and older; (1) Figures cover the New York-Jersey City-White Plains, NY-NJ Metropolitan Division—see Appendix B for areas included; n/a not available
Source: Bureau of Labor Statistics, Current Employment Statistics, Employment, Hours, and Earnings

Occupations with Greatest Projected Employment Growth: 2012 – 2022

Occupation[1]	2012 Employment	2022 Projected Employment	Numeric Employment Change	Percent Employment Change
Home Health Aides	31,140	46,280	15,140	48.6
Combined Food Preparation and Serving Workers, Including Fast Food	59,990	70,180	10,190	17.0
Retail Salespersons	125,690	134,870	9,180	7.3
Registered Nurses	79,840	88,880	9,040	11.3
Nursing Assistants	51,780	60,070	8,290	16.0
Laborers and Freight, Stock, and Material Movers, Hand	75,730	83,360	7,630	10.1
Software Developers, Applications	29,090	35,770	6,680	23.0
Receptionists and Information Clerks	51,160	57,830	6,670	13.0
Customer Service Representatives	63,450	69,530	6,080	9.6
Sales Representatives, Services, All Other	45,510	51,380	5,870	12.9

Note: Projections cover New Jersey; (1) Sorted by numeric employment change
Source: www.projectionscentral.com, State Occupational Projections, 2012–2022 Long-Term Projections

Fastest Growing Occupations: 2012 – 2022

Occupation[1]	2012 Employment	2022 Projected Employment	Numeric Employment Change	Percent Employment Change
Home Health Aides	31,140	46,280	15,140	48.6
Insulation Workers, Mechanical	370	540	170	48.2
Diagnostic Medical Sonographers	2,550	3,550	1,000	39.1
Occupational Therapy Assistants	370	500	130	37.5
Helpers—Electricians	1,310	1,800	490	37.5
Stonemasons	580	780	200	35.4
Physical Therapist Assistants	1,090	1,470	380	34.1
Skincare Specialists	1,050	1,400	350	33.2
Physician Assistants	1,450	1,920	470	32.8
Brickmasons and Blockmasons	2,150	2,830	680	31.7

Note: Projections cover New Jersey; (1) Sorted by percent employment change and excludes occupations with numeric employment change less than 100
Source: www.projectionscentral.com, State Occupational Projections, 2012–2022 Long-Term Projections

Average Wages

Occupation	$/Hr.	Occupation	$/Hr.
Accountants and Auditors	46.43	Maids and Housekeeping Cleaners	16.84
Automotive Mechanics	20.21	Maintenance and Repair Workers	21.29
Bookkeepers	21.54	Marketing Managers	89.06
Carpenters	32.53	Nuclear Medicine Technologists	40.65
Cashiers	10.92	Nurses, Licensed Practical	25.33
Clerks, General Office	15.88	Nurses, Registered	41.54
Clerks, Receptionists/Information	15.02	Nursing Assistants	16.38
Clerks, Shipping/Receiving	16.94	Packers and Packagers, Hand	11.33
Computer Programmers	46.00	Physical Therapists	44.91
Computer Systems Analysts	50.45	Postal Service Mail Carriers	25.04
Computer User Support Specialists	28.75	Real Estate Brokers	50.12
Cooks, Restaurant	13.74	Retail Salespersons	12.99
Dentists	76.20	Sales Reps., Exc. Tech./Scientific	35.67
Electrical Engineers	48.32	Sales Reps., Tech./Scientific	51.39
Electricians	37.19	Secretaries, Exc. Legal/Med./Exec.	19.62
Financial Managers	90.86	Security Guards	15.32
First-Line Supervisors/Managers, Sales	24.90	Surgeons	113.38
Food Preparation Workers	11.50	Teacher Assistants*	13.73
General and Operations Managers	79.03	Teachers, Elementary School*	34.23
Hairdressers/Cosmetologists	17.87	Teachers, Secondary School*	39.55
Internists	97.62	Telemarketers	14.00
Janitors and Cleaners	15.87	Truck Drivers, Heavy/Tractor-Trailer	23.69
Landscaping/Groundskeeping Workers	15.52	Truck Drivers, Light/Delivery Svcs.	17.92
Lawyers	80.76	Waiters and Waitresses	14.08

Note: Wage data covers the Metropolitan Division—see Appendix B for areas included; (*) Hourly wages for elementary/secondary school teachers and teacher assistants were calculated by the editors from annual wage data based on a 40 hour work week; n/a not available.
Source: Bureau of Labor Statistics, Metro Area Occupational Employment and Wage Estimates, May 2015

TAXES

State Corporate Income Tax Rates

State	Tax Rate (%)	Income Brackets ($)	Num. of Brackets	Financial Institution Tax Rate (%)[a]	Federal Income Tax Ded.
New Jersey	9.0 (r)	Flat rate	1	9.0 (r)	No

Note: Tax rates as of January 1, 2016; (a) Rates listed are the corporate income tax rate applied to financial institutions or excise taxes based on income. Some states have other taxes based upon the value of deposits or shares; (r) In New Jersey small businesses with annual entire net income under $100,000 pay a tax rate of 7.5%; businesses with income under $50,000 pay 6.5%. The minimum Corporation Business Tax is based on New Jersey gross receipts. It ranges from $500 for a corporation with gross receipts less than $100,000, to $2,000 for a corporation with gross receipts of $1 million or more.
Source: Federation of Tax Administrators, "State Corporate Income Tax Rates, 2016"

State Individual Income Tax Rates

State	Tax Rate (%)	Income Brackets ($)	Num. of Brackets	Personal Exempt. ($)[1]		Fed. Inc. Tax Ded.
				Single	Dependents	
New Jersey	1.4 - 8.97	20,000 - 500,000 (n)	6	1,000	1,500	No

Note: Tax rates as of January 1, 2016; Local- and county-level taxes are not included; n/a not applicable; (1) Married joint filers generally receive double the single exemption; (n) The New Jersey rates reported are for single individuals. For married couples filing jointly, the tax rates also range from 1.4% to 8.97%, with 7 brackets and the same high and low income ranges.
Source: Federation of Tax Administrators, "State Individual Income Tax Rates, 2016"

Various State and Local Tax Rates

State	State and Local Sales and Use (%)	State Sales and Use (%)	Gasoline[1] (¢/gal.)	Cigarette[2] ($/pack)	Spirits[3] ($/gal.)	Wine[4] ($/gal.)	Beer[5] ($/gal.)
New Jersey	7.00	7.0 (e)	14.5	2.70	5.50	0.88	0.12

Note: All tax rates as of January 1, 2016; (1) The American Petroleum Institute has developed a methodology for determining the average tax rate on a gallon of fuel. Rates may include any of the following: excise taxes, environmental fees, storage tank fees, other fees or taxes, general sales tax, and local taxes. In states where gasoline is subject to the general sales tax, or where the fuel tax is based on the average sale price, the average rate determined by API is sensitive to changes in the price of gasoline. States that fully or partially apply general sales taxes to gasoline: CA, CO, GA, IL, IN, MI, NY; (2) The federal excise tax of $1.0066 per pack and local taxes are not included; (3) Rates are those applicable to off-premise sales of 40% alcohol by volume (a.b.v.) distilled spirits in 750ml containers. Local excise taxes are excluded; (4) Rates are those applicable to off-premise sales of 11% a.b.v. non-carbonated wine in 750ml containers; (5) Rates are those applicable to off-premise sales of 4.7% a.b.v. beer in 12 ounce containers; (e) Some counties in New Jersey are not subject to statewide sales tax rates and collect a local rate of 3.5%. Their average local score is represented as a negative.
Source: Tax Foundation, 2016 Facts & Figures: How Does Your State Compare?

State Business Tax Climate Index Rankings

State	Overall Rank	Corporate Tax Rank	Individual Income Tax Rank	Sales Tax Rank	Unemployment Insurance Tax Rank	Property Tax Rank
New Jersey	50	43	48	47	31	50

Note: The index is a measure of how each state's tax laws affect economic performance. The lower the rank, the more favorable a state's tax system is for business. States without a given tax are given a ranking of 1. The scores/rankings for the District of Columbia do not affect other states. The 2016 index represents the tax climate as of July 1, 2015 (the beginning of Fiscal Year 2016).
Source: Tax Foundation, State Business Tax Climate Index 2016

TRANSPORTATION

Means of Transportation to Work

Area	Car/Truck/Van		Public Transportation			Bicycle	Walked	Other Means	Worked at Home
	Drove Alone	Car-pooled	Bus	Subway	Railroad				
City	61.2	4.4	9.7	1.2	9.0	0.9	4.0	0.8	8.7
MSA[1]	50.6	6.8	8.0	18.5	3.6	0.6	6.0	1.9	4.1
U.S.	76.4	9.6	2.6	1.8	0.6	0.6	2.8	1.3	4.4

Note: Figures are percentages and cover workers 16 years of age and older; (1) Figures cover the New York-Newark-Jersey City, NY-NJ-PA Metropolitan Statistical Area—see Appendix B for areas included
Source: U.S. Census Bureau, 2010-2014 American Community Survey 5-Year Estimates

Travel Time to Work

Area	Less Than 10 Minutes	10 to 19 Minutes	20 to 29 Minutes	30 to 44 Minutes	45 to 59 Minutes	60 to 89 Minutes	90 Minutes or More
City	13.8	18.6	14.8	13.9	8.3	21.0	9.5
MSA[1]	7.8	19.9	16.6	23.6	12.1	13.9	6.2
U.S.	13.3	29.6	21.0	20.2	7.7	5.7	2.6

Note: Figures are percentages and include workers 16 years old and over; (1) Figures cover the New York-Newark-Jersey City, NY-NJ-PA Metropolitan Statistical Area—see Appendix B for areas included
Source: U.S. Census Bureau, 2010-2014 American Community Survey 5-Year Estimates

Freeway Travel Time Index

Area	1985	1990	1995	2000	2005	2010	2014
Urban Area Rank[1,2]	11	9	8	7	7	8	8
Urban Area Index[1]	1.16	1.20	1.24	1.29	1.33	1.33	1.34
Average Index[3]	1.09	1.11	1.14	1.17	1.20	1.19	1.20

Note: Freeway Travel Time Index—the ratio of travel time in the peak period to the travel time at free-flow conditions. For example, a value of 1.30 indicates a 20-minute free-flow trip takes 26 minutes in the peak (20 minutes x 1.30 = 26 minutes); (1) Covers the New York-Newark NY-NJ-CT urban area; (2) Rank is based on 101 urban areas (#1 = highest travel time index); (3) Average of 101 urban areas
Source: Texas Transportation Institute, 2015 Urban Mobility Scorecard, August 2015

Freeway Commuter Stress Index

Area	1985	1990	1995	2000	2005	2010	2014
Urban Area Rank[1,2]	19	19	13	12	11	11	12
Urban Area Index[1]	1.21	1.24	1.29	1.34	1.38	1.38	1.39
Average Index[3]	1.13	1.16	1.19	1.22	1.25	1.24	1.25

Note: The Freeway Commuter Stress Index is the same as the Freeway Travel Time Index (see table above) except that it includes only the travel in the peak directions during the peak periods; the TTI includes travel in all directions during the peak period. Thus, the CSI is more indicative of the work trip experienced by each commuter on a daily basis. (1) Covers the New York-Newark NY-NJ-CT urban area; (2) Rank is based on 101 urban areas (#1 = highest stress index); (3) Average of 101 urban areas

Source: Texas Transportation Institute, 2015 Urban Mobility Scorecard, August 2015

Living Environment

COST OF LIVING

Cost of Living Index

Composite Index	Groceries	Housing	Utilities	Trans- portation	Health Care	Misc. Goods/ Services
128.8	112.9	172.2	111.2	106.9	107.6	113.9

Note: The Cost of Living Index measures regional differences in the cost of consumer goods and services, excluding taxes and non-consumer expenditures, for professional and managerial households in the top income quintile. It is based on more than 50,000 prices covering almost 60 different items for which prices are collected three times a year by chambers of commerce, economic development organizations or university applied economic centers in each participating urban area. The numbers shown should be read as a percentage above or below the national average of 100. For example, a value of 115.4 in the groceries column indicates that grocery prices are 15.4% higher than the national average. Small differences in the index numbers should not be interpreted as significant; Figures cover the Bergen-Passaic NJ urban area.
Source: The Council for Community and Economic Research, ACCRA Cost of Living Index, 2015

Grocery Prices

Area[1]	T-Bone Steak ($/pound)	Frying Chicken ($/pound)	Whole Milk ($/half gal.)	Eggs ($/dozen)	Orange Juice ($/64 oz.)	Coffee ($/11.5 oz.)
City[2]	12.02	1.69	2.46	2.46	3.70	4.22
Avg.	10.99	1.43	2.25	2.26	3.58	4.48
Min.	7.16	0.98	1.30	1.35	2.88	2.98
Max.	14.13	2.43	3.85	4.81	6.39	7.56

Note: (1) Values for the local area are compared with the average, minimum and maximum values for all 292 areas in the Cost of Living Index; (2) Figures cover the Bergen-Passaic NJ urban area; **T-Bone Steak** *(price per pound);* **Frying Chicken** *(price per pound, whole fryer);* **Whole Milk** *(half gallon carton);* **Eggs** *(price per dozen, Grade A, large);* **Orange Juice** *(64 oz. Tropicana or Florida Natural);* **Coffee** *(11.5 oz. can, vacuum-packed, Maxwell House, Hills Bros, or Folgers).*
Source: The Council for Community and Economic Research, ACCRA Cost of Living Index, 2015

Housing and Utility Costs

Area[1]	New Home Price ($)	Apartment Rent ($/month)	All Electric ($/month)	Part Electric ($/month)	Other Energy ($/month)	Telephone ($/month)
City[2]	521,477	1,727	-	122.00	62.66	32.25
Avg.	312,874	945	179.30	95.07	72.96	28.11
Min.	178,682	479	116.28	43.14	26.46	10.01
Max.	1,472,476	3,984	504.25	189.44	421.11	43.06

Note: (1) Values for the local area are compared with the average, minimum and maximum values for all 292 areas in the Cost of Living Index; (2) Figures cover the Bergen-Passaic NJ urban area; **New Home Price** *(2,400 sf living area, 8,000 sf lot, in urban area with full utilities);* **Apartment Rent** *(950 sf 2 bedroom/1.5 or 2 bath, unfurnished, excluding all utilities except water);* **All Electric** *(average monthly cost for an all-electric home);* **Part Electric** *(average monthly cost for a part-electric home);* **Other Energy** *(average monthly cost for natural gas, fuel oil, coal, wood, and any other forms of energy except electricity);* **Telephone** *(price includes basic monthly rate for a private residential line plus additional local usage charges incurred by a family of four).*
Source: The Council for Community and Economic Research, ACCRA Cost of Living Index, 2015

Health Care, Transportation, and Other Costs

Area[1]	Doctor ($/visit)	Dentist ($/visit)	Optometrist ($/visit)	Gasoline ($/gallon)	Beauty Salon ($/visit)	Men's Shirt ($)
City[2]	99.07	98.83	113.17	2.35	38.27	40.11
Avg.	105.15	89.02	99.78	2.38	35.30	28.10
Min.	66.87	56.09	48.53	1.95	18.91	13.38
Max.	182.34	150.36	228.33	4.09	67.91	63.80

Note: (1) Values for the local area are compared with the average, minimum and maximum values for all 292 areas in the Cost of Living Index; (2) Figures cover the Bergen-Passaic NJ urban area; **Doctor** *(general practitioners routine exam of an established patient);* **Dentist** *(adult teeth cleaning and periodic oral examination);* **Optometrist** *(full vision eye exam for established adult patient);* **Gasoline** *(one gallon regular unleaded, national brand, including all taxes, cash price at self-service pump if available);* **Beauty Salon** *(woman's shampoo, trim, and blow-dry);* **Men's Shirt** *(cotton/polyester dress shirt, pinpoint weave, long sleeves).*
Source: The Council for Community and Economic Research, ACCRA Cost of Living Index, 2015

HOUSING

House Price Index (HPI)

Area	National Ranking[2]	Quarterly Change (%)	One-Year Change (%)	Five-Year Change (%)
MD[1]	157	0.30	4.00	4.80
U.S.[3]	–	1.45	5.76	22.85

Note: The HPI is a weighted repeat sales index. It measures average price changes in repeat sales or refinancings on the same properties. This information is obtained by reviewing repeat mortgage transactions on single-family properties whose mortgages have been purchased or securitized by Fannie Mae or Freddie Mac in January 1975; (1) New York-Jersey City-White Plains Metropolitan Division—see Appendix B for areas included; (2) Rankings are based on annual percentage change for all metro areas containing at least 15,000 transactions over the last 10 years and ranges from 1 to 266; (3) figures based on a weighted average of Census Division estimates using a seasonally adjusted, purchase-only index; all figures are for the period ending December 31, 2015

Source: Federal Housing Finance Agency, House Price Index, February 25, 2016

Median Single-Family Home Prices

Area	2013	2014	2015p	Percent Change 2014 to 2015
MD[1]	465.7	468.2	475.9	1.6
U.S. Average	197.4	208.9	223.9	7.2

Note: Figures are median sales prices of existing single-family homes in thousands of dollars; (p) preliminary; n/a not available; (1) New York-Jersey City-White Plains, NY-NJ Metropolitan Division—see Appendix B for areas included

Source: National Association of Realtors, Median Sales Price of Existing Single-Family Homes for Metropolitan Areas, 4th Quarter 2015

Qualifying Income Based on Median Sales Price of Existing Single-Family Homes

Area	With 5% Down ($)	With 10% Down ($)	With 20% Down ($)
MD[1]	103,341	97,902	87,024
U.S. Average	49,535	46,928	41,714

Note: Figures are preliminary; Qualifying income is based on a mortgage rate of 4.1%. Monthly principal and interest payment is limited to 25% of income; n/a not available; (1) New York-Jersey City-White Plains, NY-NJ Metropolitan Division—see Appendix B for areas included

Source: National Association of Realtors, Qualifying Income Based on Median Sales Price of Existing Single-Family Homes for Metropolitan Areas, 4th Quarter 2015

Median Apartment Condo-Coop Home Prices

Area	2013	2014	2015p	Percent Change 2014 to 2015
MD[1]	237.5	268.9	285.7	6.2
U.S. Average	194.9	204.3	210.7	3.1

Note: Figures are median sales prices of existing apartment condo-coop homes in thousands of dollars; (p) preliminary; n/a not available; (1) New York-Jersey City-White Plains, NY-NJ Metropolitan Division—see Appendix B for areas included

Source: National Association of Realtors, Median Sales Price of Existing Apartment Condo-Coop Homes for Metropolitan Areas, 4th Quarter 2015

Gross Monthly Rent

Area	Under $200	$200 -299	$300 -499	$500 -749	$750 -999	$1,000 -1,499	$1,500 and up	Median ($)
City	0.0	3.3	2.4	2.2	0.4	21.5	70.2	1,900
MSA[1]	1.1	3.9	4.8	7.3	13.5	36.1	33.3	1,246
U.S.	1.5	3.2	7.4	21.0	24.1	26.9	15.9	920

Note: Figures are percentages except for Median; Gross rent is the contract rent plus the estimated average monthly cost of utilities (electricity, gas, and water and sewer) and fuels (oil, coal, kerosene, wood, etc.) if these are paid by the renter (or paid for the renter by someone else); (1) Figures cover the New York-Newark-Jersey City, NY-NJ-PA Metropolitan Statistical Area—see Appendix B for areas included

Source: U.S. Census Bureau, 2010-2014 American Community Survey 5-Year Estimates

Homeownership Rate

Area	2008 (%)	2009 (%)	2010 (%)	2011 (%)	2012 (%)	2013 (%)	2014 (%)	2015 (%)
MSA[1]	52.6	51.7	51.6	50.9	51.5	50.6	50.7	49.9
U.S.	67.8	67.4	66.9	66.1	65.4	65.1	64.5	63.7

Note: (1) Figures cover the New York-Newark-Jersey City, NY-NJ-PA Metropolitan Statistical Area—see Appendix B for areas included
Source: U.S. Census Bureau, Housing Vacancies and Homeownership Annual Statistics: 2015

Year Housing Structure Built

Area	2010 or Later	2000 -2009	1990 -1999	1980 -1989	1970 -1979	1960 -1969	1950 -1959	1940 -1949	Before 1940	Median Year
City	0.1	2.2	1.8	3.9	3.3	9.8	25.6	11.3	42.1	1947
MSA[1]	0.6	7.4	6.0	7.8	10.0	13.9	16.5	9.5	28.4	1957
U.S.	1.0	14.9	13.9	13.8	15.8	11.0	10.8	5.4	13.3	1976

Note: Figures are percentages except for Median Year; (1) Figures cover the New York-Newark-Jersey City, NY-NJ-PA Metropolitan Statistical Area—see Appendix B for areas included
Source: U.S. Census Bureau, 2010-2014 American Community Survey 5-Year Estimates

HEALTH

Health Risk Data

Category	MD[1] (%)	U.S. (%)
Adults aged 18–64 who have any kind of health care coverage	78.3	79.6
Adults who reported being in good or excellent health	81.4	83.1
Adults who are current smokers	14.8	19.6
Adults who are heavy drinkers[2]	4.5	6.1
Adults who are binge drinkers[3]	16.9	16.9
Adults who are overweight (BMI 25.0 - 29.9)	36.8	35.8
Adults who are obese (BMI 30.0 - 99.8)	21.7	27.6
Adults who participated in any physical activities in the past month	74.2	77.1
Adults 50+ who have ever had a sigmoidoscopy or colonoscopy	70.5	67.3
Women aged 40+ who have had a mammogram within the past two years	78.5	74.0
Men aged 40+ who have had a PSA test within the past two years	47.8	45.2
Adults aged 65+ who have had flu shot within the past year	56.0	60.1
Adults who always wear a seatbelt	92.8	93.8

Note: Data as of 2012 unless otherwise noted; (1) Figures cover the New York-Jersey City-White Plains, NY-NJ Metropolitan Division—see Appendix B for areas included; (2) Heavy drinkers are classified as males having more than two drinks per day or females having more than one drink per day; (3) Binge drinkers are classified as males having five or more drinks on one occasion or females having four or more drinks on one occasion
Source: Centers for Disease Control and Prevention, Behaviorial Risk Factor Surveillance System, SMART: Selected Metropolitan/Micropolitan Area Risk Trends, 2012 (Note: the CDC has discontinued this dataset but will be releasing a replacement in mid-2016)

Chronic Health Indicators

Category	MD[1] (%)	U.S. (%)
Adults who have ever been told they had a heart attack	3.6	4.5
Adults who have ever been told they had a stroke	2.6	2.9
Adults who have been told they currently have asthma	8.0	8.9
Adults who have ever been told they have arthritis	22.2	25.7
Adults who have ever been told they have diabetes[2]	9.9	9.7
Adults who have ever been told they had skin cancer	3.3	5.7
Adults who have ever been told they had any other types of cancer	5.1	6.5
Adults who have ever been told they have COPD	5.3	6.2
Adults who have ever been told they have kidney disease	2.6	2.5
Adults who have ever been told they have a form of depression	13.3	18.0

Note: Data as of 2012 unless otherwise noted; (1) Figures cover the New York-Jersey City-White Plains, NY-NJ Metropolitan Division—see Appendix B for areas included; (2) Figures do not include pregnancy-related, borderline, or pre-diabetes
Source: Centers for Disease Control and Prevention, Behaviorial Risk Factor Surveillance System, SMART: Selected Metropolitan/Micropolitan Area Risk Trends, 2012 (Note: the CDC has discontinued this dataset but will be releasing a replacement in mid-2016)

Mortality Rates for the Top 10 Causes of Death in the U.S.

ICD-10[a] Sub-Chapter	ICD-10[a] Code	Age-Adjusted Mortality Rate[1] per 100,000 population	
		County[2]	U.S.
Malignant neoplasms	C00-C97	142.2	163.6
Ischaemic heart diseases	I20-I25	83.4	102.2
Other forms of heart disease	I30-I51	47.7	50.1
Chronic lower respiratory diseases	J40-J47	21.6	41.4
Organic, including symptomatic, mental disorders	F01-F09	29.4	38.5
Cerebrovascular diseases	I60-I69	27.2	36.5
Other external causes of accidental injury	W00-X59	18.9	27.5
Other degenerative diseases of the nervous system	G30-G31	15.9	26.3
Diabetes mellitus	E10-E14	14.0	21.1
Hypertensive diseases	I10-I15	13.6	19.7

Note: (a) ICD-10 = International Classification of Diseases 10th Revision; (1) Mortality rates are a three year average covering 2012-2014; (2) Figures cover Bergen County.
Source: Centers for Disease Control and Prevention, National Center for Health Statistics. Underlying Cause of Death 1999-2014 on CDC WONDER Online Database, released 2015.

Mortality Rates for Selected Causes of Death

ICD-10[a] Sub-Chapter	ICD-10[a] Code	Age-Adjusted Mortality Rate[1] per 100,000 population	
		County[2]	U.S.
Assault	X85-Y09	1.3	5.1
Diseases of the liver	K70-K76	7.0	13.5
Human immunodeficiency virus (HIV) disease	B20-B24	0.7	2.1
Influenza and pneumonia	J09-J18	10.9	15.2
Intentional self-harm	X60-X84	7.6	12.7
Malnutrition	E40-E46	Unreliable	0.9
Obesity and other hyperalimentation	E65-E68	1.0	1.9
Renal failure	N17-N19	11.9	13.0
Transport accidents	V01-V99	4.6	11.6
Viral hepatitis	B15-B19	1.5	2.1

Note: (a) ICD-10 = International Classification of Diseases 10th Revision; (1) Mortality rates are a three year average covering 2012-2014; (2) Figures cover Bergen County; Data are Suppressed when the data meet the criteria for confidentiality constraints; Mortality rates are flagged as Unreliable when the rate would be calculated with a numerator of 20 or less.
Source: Centers for Disease Control and Prevention, National Center for Health Statistics. Underlying Cause of Death 1999-2014 on CDC WONDER Online Database, released 2015.

Health Insurance Coverage

Area	With Health Insurance	With Private Health Insurance	With Public Health Insurance	Without Health Insurance	Population Under Age 18 Without Health Insurance
City	94.8	89.5	15.5	5.2	1.6
MSA[1]	87.7	65.3	31.8	12.3	4.4
U.S.	85.8	65.8	31.1	14.2	7.1

Note: Figures are percentages that cover the civilian noninstitutionalized population; (1) Figures cover the New York-Newark-Jersey City, NY-NJ-PA Metropolitan Statistical Area—see Appendix B for areas included
Source: U.S. Census Bureau, 2010-2014 American Community Survey 5-Year Estimates

Number of Medical Professionals

Area	MDs[3]	DOs[3,4]	Dentists	Podiatrists	Chiropractors	Optometrists
County[1] (number)	4,696	265	1,167	137	445	163
County[1] (rate[2])	506.3	28.6	125.0	14.7	47.7	17.5
U.S. (rate[2])	272.5	20.9	64.7	5.8	25.9	15.2

Note: Data as of 2014 unless noted; (1) Data covers Bergen County; (2) Rate per 100,000 population; (3) Data as of 2013 and includes all active, non-federal physicians; (4) Doctor of Osteopathic Medicine
Source: U.S. Department of Health and Human Services, Health Resources and Services Administration, Bureau of Health Professions, Area Resource File (ARF) 2014-2015

Best Hospitals

According to *U.S. News,* the New York-Jersey City-White Plains, NY-NJ metro area is home to 11 of the best hospitals in the U.S.: **Hackensack University Medical Center** (5 specialties); **Robert Wood Johnson University Hospital** (1 specialty); **Hospital for Joint Diseases, NYU Langone Medical Center** (2 specialties); **Hospital for Special Surgery** (2 specialties); **Lenox Hill Hospital** (1 specialty); **Memorial Sloan Kettering Cancer Center** (4 specialties); **Mount Sinai Hospital** (9 specialties); **NYU Langone Medical Center** (Honor Roll/12 specialties); **New York Eye and Ear Infirmary** (2 specialties); **New York-Presbyterian University Hospital of Columbia and Cornell** (Honor Roll/15 specialties); **Rusk Rehabilitation at NYU Langone Medical Center** (1 specialty). The hospitals listed were nationally ranked in at least one adult specialty. Only 137 hospitals nationwide were nationally ranked in one or more specialties. Fifteen hospitals in the U.S. made the Honor Roll with high scores in at least six specialties. *U.S. News Online, "America's Best Children's Hospitals 2015-16"*

According to *U.S. News,* the New York-Jersey City-White Plains, NY-NJ metro area is home to seven of the best children's hospitals in the U.S.: **Joseph M. Sanzari Children's Hospital at Hackensack University Medical** (1 specialty); **Bristol-Myers Squibb Children's Hospital at RWJ Univ. Hosp.** (1 specialty); **Children's Hospital at Montefiore (Bronx)** (8 specialties); **Memorial Sloan-Kettering Cancer Center** (1 specialty); **Mount Sinai Kravis Children's Hospital** (7 specialties); **NY-Presbyterian Morgan Stanley-Komansky Children's Hospital** (10 specialties); **Maria Fareri Children's Hospital at Westchester Medical Center** (1 specialty). The hospitals listed were highly ranked in at least one pediatric specialty. Eighty-three children's hospitals in the U.S. were nationally ranked in at least one specialty. Twelve children's hospitals in the U.S. made the Honor Roll with high scores in at least three specialties. *U.S. News Online, "America's Best Children's Hospitals 2015-16"*

EDUCATION

Public School District Statistics

District Name	Schls	Pupils	Pupil/ Teacher Ratio	Minority Pupils[1] (%)	Free Lunch Eligible[2] (%)	IEP[3] (%)
Ridgewood Public Schools	10	5,722	13.1	30.0	1.3	15.0

Note: Table includes school districts with 100 or more students; (1) Percentage of students that are not non-Hispanic white; (2) Percentage of students that are eligible for the free lunch program; (3) Percentage of students that have an Individualized Education Program.

Source: U.S. Department of Education, National Center for Education Statistics, Common Core of Data, Local Education Agency (School District) Universe Survey: School Year 2013-2014; U.S. Department of Education, National Center for Education Statistics, Common Core of Data, Public Elementary/Secondary School Universe Survey: School Year 2013-2014

Best High Schools

According to *U.S. News,* Ridgewood is home to one of the best high schools in the U.S.: **Ridgewood High School** (#307); Nearly 20,000 schools were ranked based on their performance on state assessments and how well they prepare students for college. Schools with the highest unrounded College Readiness Index values were numerically ranked from No. 1 to No. 500 and were the gold medal winners. *U.S. News & World Report, "Best High Schools 2015"*

Highest Level of Education

Area	Less than H.S.	H.S. Diploma	Some College, No Deg.	Associate Degree	Bachelor's Degree	Master's Degree	Prof. School Degree	Doctorate Degree
City	2.4	8.2	10.5	4.0	42.4	21.0	8.0	3.4
MSA[1]	14.9	25.9	15.7	6.6	21.7	10.9	3.0	1.4
U.S.	13.7	28.0	21.2	7.9	18.3	7.8	2.0	1.3

Note: Figures cover persons age 25 and over; (1) Figures cover the New York-Newark-Jersey City, NY-NJ-PA Metropolitan Statistical Area—see Appendix B for areas included

Source: U.S. Census Bureau, 2010-2014 American Community Survey 5-Year Estimates

Educational Attainment by Race

Area	High School Graduate or Higher (%)					Bachelor's Degree or Higher (%)				
	Total	White	Black	Asian	Hisp.[2]	Total	White	Black	Asian	Hisp.[2]
City	97.6	97.8	92.9	96.9	96.7	74.9	75.2	47.6	81.1	58.5
MSA[1]	85.1	89.6	83.0	82.5	67.7	37.0	41.9	22.5	52.7	16.7
U.S.	86.3	88.4	83.2	85.8	64.1	29.3	30.6	19.0	50.9	13.9

Note: Figures shown cover persons 25 years old and over; (1) Figures cover the New York-Newark-Jersey City, NY-NJ-PA Metropolitan Statistical Area—see Appendix B for areas included; (2) People of Hispanic origin can be of any race
Source: U.S. Census Bureau, 2010-2014 American Community Survey 5-Year Estimates

School Enrollment by Grade and Control

Area	Preschool (%)		Kindergarten (%)		Grades 1 - 4 (%)		Grades 5 - 8 (%)		Grades 9 - 12 (%)	
	Public	Private	Public	Private	Public	Private	Public	Private	Public	Private
City	13.3	86.7	90.1	9.9	96.8	3.2	93.4	6.6	84.0	16.0
MSA[1]	50.3	49.7	81.7	18.3	86.3	13.7	86.5	13.5	86.1	13.9
U.S.	57.4	42.6	87.8	12.2	89.8	10.2	89.9	10.1	90.6	9.4

Note: Figures shown cover persons 3 years old and over; (1) Figures cover the New York-Newark-Jersey City, NY-NJ-PA Metropolitan Statistical Area—see Appendix B for areas included
Source: U.S. Census Bureau, 2010-2014 American Community Survey 5-Year Estimates

Average Salaries of Public School Classroom Teachers

Area	2013-14		2014-15		Percent Change 2013-14 to 2014-15	Percent Change 2004-05 to 2014-15
	Dollars	Rank[1]	Dollars	Rank[1]		
New Jersey	68,238	6	69,038	6	1.17	22.2
U.S. Average	56,610	–	57,379	–	1.36	20.8

Note: (1) State rank ranges from 1 to 51 where 1 indicates highest salary.
Source: National Education Association, Rankings & Estimates: Rankings of the States 2014 and Estimates of School Statistics 2015, March 2015

Higher Education

Four-Year Colleges			Two-Year Colleges			Medical Schools[1]	Law Schools[2]	Voc/ Tech[3]
Public	Private Non-profit	Private For-profit	Public	Private Non-profit	Private For-profit			
0	0	0	0	0	0	0	0	0

Note: Figures cover institutions located within the city limits and include main campuses only; (1) includes schools accredited by the Liaison Committee on Medical Education and the American Osteopathic Association's Commission on Osteopathic College Accreditation; (2) includes ABA-accredited schools, schools with provisional ABA accreditation, and state accredited schools; (3) includes all schools with programs that are less than 2 years.
Source: National Center for Education Statistics, Integrated Postsecondary Education System (IPEDS), 2014-15; Association of American Medical Colleges, Member List, March 21, 2016; American Osteopathic Association, Member List, March 21, 2016; Law School Admission Council, Official Guide to ABA-Approved Law Schools Online, March 21, 2016; Wikipedia, List of Medical Schools in the United States, March 21, 2016; Wikipedia, List of Law Schools in the United States, March 21, 2016

According to *U.S. News & World Report,* the New York-Jersey City-White Plains, NY-NJ metro division is home to nine of the best national universities in the U.S.: **Columbia University** (#4 tie); **New York University** (#32); **Yeshiva University** (#52 tie); **Fordham University** (#66 tie); **Rurgers, The State University of New Jersey–New Brunswick ,** (#72 tie); **Stevens Institute of Technology** (#75 tie); **New School** (#127 tie); **St. John's University** (#153 tie); **Pace University** (#180 tie). The indicators used to capture academic quality fall into a number of categories: assessment by administrators at peer institutions; retention of students; faculty resources; student selectivity; financial resources; alumni giving; high school counselor ratings of colleges; and graduation rate. *U.S. News & World Report, "America's Best Colleges 2016"*

According to *U.S. News & World Report,* the New York-Jersey City-White Plains, NY-NJ metro division is home to four of the best liberal arts colleges in the U.S.: **United States Military Academy** (#22); **Barnard College** (#29 tie); **Sarah Lawrence College** (#57 tie); **Purchase College–SUNY** (#171 tie). The indicators used to capture academic quality fall into a number of categories: assessment by administrators at peer institutions; retention of students; faculty resources; student selectivity; financial resources; alumni giving; high school counselor ratings of colleges; and graduation rate. *U.S. News & World Report, "America's Best Colleges 2016"*

According to *U.S. News & World Report,* the New York-Jersey City-White Plains, NY-NJ metro division is home to six of the top 100 law schools in the U.S.: **Columbia University, Law School** (#4 tie); **New York University, School of Law** (#6); **Fordham University, School of Law** (#37); **St. John's University, School of Law** (#74 tie); **Yeshiva University, Benjamin N. Cardozo School of Law** (#74 tie); **Brooklyn Law School** (#97 tie). The rankings are based on a weighted average of 12 measures of quality: peer assessment score; assessment score by lawyers/judges; median LSAT scores; median undergrad GPA; acceptance rate; employment rates for graduates; placement success; bar passage rate; faculty resources; expenditures per student; student/faculty ratio; and library resources. *U.S. News & World Report, "America's Best Graduate Schools, Law, 2017"*

According to *U.S. News & World Report,* the New York-Jersey City-White Plains, NY-NJ metro division is home to five of the top 75 medical schools for research in the U.S.: **Columbia University, College of Physicians and Surgeons** (#7); **New York University, School of Medicine** (#11 tie); **Cornell University, Weill Cornell Medical College** (#18 tie); **Icahn School of Medicine at Mount Sinai** (#21); **Yeshiva University, Albert Einstein College of Medicine** (#39). The rankings are based on a weighted average of 11 measures of quality: quality assessment; peer assessment score; assessment score by residency directors; research activity; total research activity; average research activity per faculty member; student selectivity; median MCAT total score; median undergraduate GPA; acceptance rate; and faculty resources. *U.S. News & World Report, "America's Best Graduate Schools, Medical, 2017"*

According to *U.S. News & World Report,* the New York-Jersey City-White Plains, NY-NJ metro division is home to two of the top 75 business schools in the U.S.: **Columbia University, Columbia Business School** (#10); **New York University, Leonard N. Stern School of Business** (#20). The rankings are based on a weighted average of the following nine measures: quality assessment; peer assessment; recruiter assessment; placement success; mean starting salary and bonus; student selectivity; mean GMAT and GRE scores; mean undergraduate GPA; and acceptance rate. *U.S. News & World Report, "America's Best Graduate Schools, Business, 2017"*

PRESIDENTIAL ELECTION

2012 Presidential Election Results

Area	Obama (%)	Romney (%)	Other (%)
Bergen County	55.0	44.1	0.9
U.S.	51.0	47.2	1.8

Note: Results may not add to 100% due to rounding
Source: Dave Leip's Atlas of U.S. Presidential Elections

EMPLOYERS

Major Employers

Company Name	Industry
American Express Company	Personal credit institutions
American International Group	Life insurance
Deloitte Consulting	Management consulting services
Hackensack University Medical Center	University
Merrill Lynch and Co	Security brokers & dealers
Mount Sinai Hospital	General medical & surgical hospitals
Mount Sinai School of Medicine	Medical training services
NewYork-Presbyterian Hospital	General medical & surgical hospitals
NYC Health and Hospitals Corp	Psychiatric hospitals
NYU School of Medicine	Offices & clinics of medical doctors
Paramount Comm Acq Corp	Investment holding companies, except banks
Patriarch Partners	Investment offices
Rutgers, The State Univ of NJ	Colleges & universities
Standard Americas	Agencies of foreign banks
The Long Island Rail Road Company	Local & suburban transit
U of Med and Dentistry of NJ	Colleges & universities
UMASS Memorial Health Care	Psychiatrist
United States Postal Service	U.s. postal service
Wellchoice	Health insurance carriers

Note: Companies shown are located within the New York-Newark-Jersey City, NY-NJ-PA Metropolitan Statistical Area.
Source: Hoovers.com; Wikipedia

PUBLIC SAFETY

Crime Rate

Area	All Crimes	Violent Crimes				Property Crimes		
		Murder	Rape[3]	Robbery	Aggrav. Assault	Burglary	Larceny -Theft	Motor Vehicle Theft
City	718.2	0.0	0.0	7.8	15.7	172.7	510.2	11.8
Metro[1]	n/a	3.1	19.3	147.1	264.5	209.7	n/a	85.5
U.S.	2,961.6	4.5	26.4	102.2	232.5	542.5	1,837.3	216.2

Note: Figures are crimes per 100,000 population; (1) Figures cover the New York-Jersey City-White Plains, NY-NJ Metropolitan Division—see Appendix B for areas included; (3) The city and U.S. figures shown were reported using the legacy Uniform Crime Reporting (UCR) definition of rape. The suburban and metro area figures shown are an aggregate total of the data submitted using both the revised and legacy UCR definitions.
Source: FBI Uniform Crime Reports, 2014

Hate Crimes

Area	Number of Quarters Reported	Number of Incidents per Bias Motivation						
		Race	Religion	Sexual Orientation	Ethnicity	Disability	Gender	Gender Identity
City	4	0	1	0	1	0	0	0
U.S.	4	2,568	1,014	1,017	648	84	33	98

Source: Federal Bureau of Investigation, Hate Crime Statistics 2014

Identity Theft Consumer Complaints

Area	Complaints	Complaints per 100,000 Population	Rank[2]
MSA[1]	27,397	136.4	77
U.S.	490,220	152.4	-

Note: (1) Figures cover the New York-Newark-Jersey City, NY-NJ-PA Metropolitan Statistical Area—see Appendix B for areas included; (2) Rank ranges from 1 to 379 where 1 indicates greatest number of identity theft complaints per 100,000 population
Source: Federal Trade Commission, Consumer Sentinel Network Data Book for January–December 2015

Fraud and Other Consumer Complaints

Area	Complaints	Complaints per 100,000 Population	Rank[2]
MSA[1]	74,212	369.3	172
U.S.	2,593,159	806.0	-

Note: (1) Figures cover the New York-Newark-Jersey City, NY-NJ-PA Metropolitan Statistical Area—see Appendix B for areas included; (2) Rank ranges from 1 to 379 where 1 indicates greatest number of identity theft complaints per 100,000 population
Source: Federal Trade Commission, Consumer Sentinel Network Data Book for January–December 2015

RECREATION

Culture

Dance[1]	Theatre[1]	Instrumental Music[1]	Vocal Music[1]	Series and Festivals	Museums and Art Galleries[2]	Zoos and Aquariums[3]
0	0	0	0	0	0	0

Note: (1) Professional perfoming groups; (2) Based on organizations with SIC code 8412; (3) AZA-accredited
Source: The Grey House Performing Arts Directory, 2015-16; Association of Zoos & Aquariums, AZA Member Zoos & Aquariums, March 25, 2016; www.AccuLeads.com, March 29, 2016

Professional Sports Teams

Team Name	League	Year Established
Brooklyn Nets	National Basketball Association (NBA)	1967
New Jersey Devils	National Hockey League (NHL)	1982
New York City FC	Major League Soccer (MLS)	2015
New York Giants	National Football League (NFL)	1925
New York Islanders	National Hockey League (NHL)	1972
New York Jets	National Football League (NFL)	1960
New York Knicks	National Basketball Association (NBA)	1946
New York Mets	Major League Baseball (MLB)	1962
New York Rangers	National Hockey League (NHL)	1926
New York Red Bulls	Major League Soccer (MLS)	1996
New York Yankees	Major League Baseball (MLB)	1903

Note: Includes teams located in the New York-Newark-Jersey City, NY-NJ-PA Metropolitan Statistical Area.
Source: Wikipedia, Major Professional Sports Teams of the United States and Canada, March 24, 2016

CLIMATE

Average and Extreme Temperatures

Temperature	Jan	Feb	Mar	Apr	May	Jun	Jul	Aug	Sep	Oct	Nov	Dec	Yr.
Extreme High (°F)	68	75	85	96	97	101	104	99	99	88	81	72	104
Average High (°F)	38	41	50	61	72	80	85	84	76	65	54	43	62
Average Temp. (°F)	32	34	43	53	63	72	77	76	68	58	48	37	55
Average Low (°F)	26	27	35	44	54	63	68	67	60	49	41	31	47
Extreme Low (°F)	-2	-2	8	21	36	46	53	50	40	29	17	-1	-2

Note: Figures cover the years 1962-1992
Source: National Climatic Data Center, International Station Meteorological Climate Summary, 9/96

Average Precipitation/Snowfall/Humidity

Precip./Humidity	Jan	Feb	Mar	Apr	May	Jun	Jul	Aug	Sep	Oct	Nov	Dec	Yr.
Avg. Precip. (in.)	3.5	3.1	4.0	3.9	4.5	3.8	4.5	4.1	4.1	3.3	4.5	3.8	47.0
Avg. Snowfall (in.)	7	8	4	Tr	Tr	0	0	0	0	Tr	Tr	3	23
Avg. Rel. Hum. 7am (%)	67	67	66	64	72	74	74	76	78	75	72	69	71
Avg. Rel. Hum. 4pm (%)	55	53	50	45	52	55	53	54	56	55	57	58	53

Note: Figures cover the years 1962-1992; Tr = Trace amounts (<0.05 in. of rain; <0.5 in. of snow)
Source: National Climatic Data Center, International Station Meteorological Climate Summary, 9/96

Weather Conditions

Temperature			Daytime Sky			Precipitation		
32°F & below	45°F & below	90°F & above	Clear	Partly cloudy	Cloudy	0.01 inch or more precip.	0.1 inch or more snow/ice	Thunder-storms
75	170	18	85	166	114	120	11	20

Note: Figures are average number of days per year and cover the years 1962-1992
Source: National Climatic Data Center, International Station Meteorological Climate Summary, 9/96

HAZARDOUS WASTE

Superfund Sites

Ridgewood has no sites on the EPA's Superfund Final National Priorities List. There are a total of 1,323 Superfund sites on the list in the U.S. *U.S. Environmental Protection Agency, Final National Priorities List, March 18, 2016*

AIR & WATER QUALITY

Air Quality Trends: Ozone

	1990	1995	2000	2005	2010	2011	2012	2013	2014
MSA[1]	0.101	0.107	0.091	0.092	0.082	0.082	0.080	0.072	0.069

Note: (1) Data covers the New York-Newark-Jersey City, NY-NJ-PA Metropolitan Statistical Area—see Appendix B for areas included. The values shown are the composite ozone concentration averages among trend sites based on the highest fourth daily maximum 8-hour concentration in parts per million. These trends are based on sites having an adequate record of monitoring data during the trend period. Data from exceptional events are included.
Source: U.S. Environmental Protection Agency, Air Quality Monitoring Information, "Air Quality Trends by City, 1990-2014"

Air Quality Index

Area	Percent of Days when Air Quality was...[2]					AQI Statistics[2]	
	Good	Moderate	Unhealthy for Sensitive Groups	Unhealthy	Very Unhealthy	Maximum	Median
MSA[1]	41.4	52.6	6.0	0.0	0.0	142	54

Note: (1) Data covers the New York-Newark-Jersey City, NY-NJ-PA Metropolitan Statistical Area—see Appendix B for areas included; (2) Based on 365 days with AQI data in 2015. Air Quality Index (AQI) is an index for reporting daily air quality. EPA calculates the AQI for five major air pollutants regulated by the Clean Air Act: ground-level ozone, particle pollution (aka particulate matter), carbon monoxide, sulfur dioxide, and nitrogen dioxide. The AQI runs from 0 to 500. The higher the AQI value, the greater the level of air pollution and the greater the health concern. There are six AQI categories: "Good" AQI is between 0 and 50. Air quality is considered satisfactory; "Moderate" AQI is between 51 and 100. Air quality is acceptable; "Unhealthy for Sensitive Groups" When AQI values are between 101 and 150, members of sensitive groups may experience health effects; "Unhealthy" When AQI values are between 151 and 200 everyone may begin to experience health effects; "Very Unhealthy" AQI values between 201 and 300 trigger a health alert; "Hazardous" AQI values over 300 trigger warnings of emergency conditions (not shown).
Source: U.S. Environmental Protection Agency, Air Quality Index Report, 2015

Air Quality Index Pollutants

Area	Percent of Days when AQI Pollutant was...[2]					
	Carbon Monoxide	Nitrogen Dioxide	Ozone	Sulfur Dioxide	Particulate Matter 2.5	Particulate Matter 10
MSA[1]	0.0	14.5	33.2	0.3	52.1	0.0

Note: (1) Data covers the New York-Newark-Jersey City, NY-NJ-PA Metropolitan Statistical Area—see Appendix B for areas included; (2) Based on 365 days with AQI data in 2015. The Air Quality Index (AQI) is an index for reporting daily air quality. EPA calculates the AQI for five major air pollutants regulated by the Clean Air Act: ground-level ozone, particle pollution (also known as particulate matter), carbon monoxide, sulfur dioxide, and nitrogen dioxide. The AQI runs from 0 to 500. The higher the AQI value, the greater the level of air pollution and the greater the health concern.
Source: U.S. Environmental Protection Agency, Air Quality Index Report, 2015

Maximum Air Pollutant Concentrations: Particulate Matter, Ozone, CO and Lead

	Particulate Matter 10 (ug/m^3)	Particulate Matter 2.5 Wtd AM (ug/m^3)	Particulate Matter 2.5 24-Hr (ug/m^3)	Ozone (ppm)	Carbon Monoxide (ppm)	Lead (ug/m^3)
MSA[1] Level	47	10.5	31	0.074	3	n/a
NAAQS[2]	150	15	35	0.075	9	0.15
Met NAAQS[2]	Yes	Yes	Yes	Yes	Yes	n/a

Note: (1) Data covers the New York-Newark-Jersey City, NY-NJ-PA Metropolitan Statistical Area—see Appendix B for areas included; Data from exceptional events are included; (2) National Ambient Air Quality Standards; ppm = parts per million; ug/m^3 = micrograms per cubic meter; n/a not available.
Concentrations: Particulate Matter 10 (coarse particulate)—highest second maximum 24-hour concentration; Particulate Matter 2.5 Wtd AM (fine particulate)—highest weighted annual mean concentration; Particulate Matter 2.5 24-Hour (fine particulate)—highest 98th percentile 24-hour concentration; Ozone—highest fourth daily maximum 8-hour concentration; Carbon Monoxide—highest second maximum non-overlapping 8-hour concentration; Lead—maximum running 3-month average
Source: U.S. Environmental Protection Agency, Air Quality Monitoring Information, "Air Quality Statistics by City, 2014"

Maximum Air Pollutant Concentrations: Nitrogen Dioxide and Sulfur Dioxide

	Nitrogen Dioxide AM (ppb)	Nitrogen Dioxide 1-Hr (ppb)	Sulfur Dioxide AM (ppb)	Sulfur Dioxide 1-Hr (ppb)	Sulfur Dioxide 24-Hr (ppb)
MSA[1] Level	22	70	n/a	15	n/a
NAAQS[2]	53	100	30	75	140
Met NAAQS[2]	Yes	Yes	n/a	Yes	n/a

Note: (1) Data covers the New York-Newark-Jersey City, NY-NJ-PA Metropolitan Statistical Area—see Appendix B for areas included; Data from exceptional events are included; (2) National Ambient Air Quality Standards; ppm = parts per million; ug/m^3 = micrograms per cubic meter; n/a not available.
Concentrations: Nitrogen Dioxide AM—highest arithmetic mean concentration; Nitrogen Dioxide 1-Hr—highest 98th percentile 1-hour daily maximum concentration; Sulfur Dioxide AM—highest annual mean concentration; Sulfur Dioxide 1-Hr—highest 99th percentile 1-hour daily maximum concentration; Sulfur Dioxide 24-Hr—highest second maximum 24-hour concentration
Source: U.S. Environmental Protection Agency, Air Quality Monitoring Information, "Air Quality Statistics by City, 2014"

Drinking Water

Water System Name	Pop. Served	Primary Water Source Type	Violations[1]	
			Health Based	Monitoring/ Reporting
Ridgewood Water	61,700	Purchased Surface	0	0

Note: (1) Based on violation data from January 1, 2015 to December 31, 2015 (includes unresolved violations from earlier years)
Source: U.S. Environmental Protection Agency, Office of Ground Water and Drinking Water, Safe Drinking Water Information System (based on data extracted April 29, 2016)

South Brunswick, New Jersey

Background

South Brunswick is located in Middlesex County, 33 miles southwest of Newark and 46 miles from New York City.

South Brunswick was incorporated in 1798. In the 18th century, it was a rural agricultural region with small clustered settlements located on major transportation routes. Early settlers took advantage of fertile soils and favorable growing conditions. The 19th century brought increased commercial and residential growth, which coincided with new transportation routes. The Straight Turnpike, now Route 1, was built in 1804. In 1872, the state Legislature reduced the size of South Brunswick with the creation of Cranbury from the southern portion of South Brunswick. In 1919, the size of South Brunswick was further reduced with the formation of Plainsboro.

By 1980, South Brunswick's population approached 18,000; by 1990, it was over 25,000. Now it is a diverse community of over 43,000. Despite its rapid growth, much of South Brunswick's 42 square miles remain undeveloped with significant amounts of wetlands, woodlands and open space.

Manufacturing and wholesale trade make up most of the economic activity in South Brunswick. The township also benefits from its location along the Route 1 corridor between Princeton and New Brunswick, which is popular with high tech companies.

The South Brunswick School District is currently made up of nine school communities and continues to grow while maintaining its reputation as one of the finest public school systems in the state.

There are over 2,000 acres of municipal, county and state park land within South Brunswick. Recreational facilities include a Community Center and Senior Center. The township is also close to many art and music centers in nearby Princeton and New Brunswick.

South Brunswick has a seasonal climate with hot summers and cold winters. Median summer temperatures average 70 degrees, while winter averages can be as low as 20 degrees during the months of December and January. The city averages 4.5 inches of rainfall per month from April to October and 7.5 inches of snowfall per month from December to March.

Rankings

General Rankings

- New York* was identified as one of America's fastest-growing major metropolitan areas in terms of population growth by CNNMoney.com. The area ranked #1 out of 10. Criteria: population growth between July 2013 and July 2014. *CNNMoney, "10 Fastest-Growing Cities," May 27, 2015*

Business/Finance Rankings

- The personal finance site NerdWallet analyzed 183 American metropolitan areas with populations over 250,000 and more than 15,000 businesses to rank where entrepreneurs find the most success. Criteria included area economy, annual income, housing cost, unemployment rate, and the success rate of area businesses. New York* ranked #32. *www.nerdwallet.com, "Best Places to Start a Business," April 27, 2015*
- Based on the U.S. Department of Labor's Occupational Information Network Data Collection Program, the Brookings Institution defined job opportunities for STEM workers at various levels of educational attainment. The New York* metro area was one of the ten metro areas where workers in low-education-level STEM jobs earn the lowest relative wages. *www.brookings.edu, "The Hidden Stem Economy," June 10, 2013*
- Metro areas with the largest gap in income between rich and poor residents were identified by 24/7 Wall Street using the U.S. Census Bureau's 2013 American Community Survey. The New York* metro area placed #7 among metro areas with the widest wealth gap between rich and poor. *247wallst.com, "20 Cities with the Widest Gap between the Rich and Poor," July 8, 2015*
- Based on metro area social media reviews, the employment opinion group Glassdoor surveyed 50 of the largest U.S. metro areas and equally weighed cost of living, hiring opportunity, and job satisfaction to compose a list of "25 Best Cities for Jobs." The New York* metro area was ranked #21 in overall job satisfaction. *www.glassdoor.com, "Best Cities for Jobs," May 19, 2015*
- In a survey of economic confidence in the nation's 50 largest metropolitan areas conducted January–December 2014, the New York* metro area placed #23, according to Gallup's 2014 Economic Confidence Index. *Gallup, "San Jose and San Francisco Lead in Economic Confidence," March 19, 2015*
- The Brookings Institution ranked the 100 largest metro areas in the U.S. based on income inequality. New York* was ranked #2 (#1 = greatest ineqality). Criteria: the "95/20 ratio," a figure representing the income at which a household earns more than 95 percent of all other households, divided by the income at which a household earns more than only 20 percent of all other households. *Brookings Institution, "Income Inequality, 100 Largest U.S. Metro Areas, 2007-2014," January 14, 2016*
- Payscale.com ranked the 20 largest metro areas in terms of wage growth. The New York* metro area ranked #18. Criteria: private-sector wage growth between the 1st quarter of 2015 and the 1st quarter of 2016. *PayScale, "Wage Trends by Metro Area," 1st Quarter, 2016*
- The New York* metro area appeared on the Milken Institute "2015 Best Performing Cities" list. Rank: #90 out of 200 large metro areas. Criteria: job growth; wage and salary growth; high-tech output growth. *Milken Institute, "Best-Performing Cities 2015," December 2015*
- *Forbes* ranked the 200 most populous metro areas to determine the nation's "Best Places for Business and Careers." The New York* metro area was ranked #111. Criteria: costs (business and living); job growth (past and projected); income growth; educational attainment (college and high school); projected economic growth; cultural and recreational opportunities; net migration patterns; number of highly ranked colleges. *Forbes, "The Best Places for Business and Careers 2015," July 29, 2015*

Dating/Romance Rankings

- CreditDonkey, a financial education website, sought out the ten best U.S. cities for newlyweds, considering the number of married couples, divorce rate, average credit score, and average number of hours worked per week in metro areas with a million or more residents. The New York* metro area placed #5. *www.creditdonkey.com, "Study: Best Cities for Newlyweds," November 30, 2013*

Education Rankings

- Personal finance website *WalletHub* analyzed the 150 largest U.S. metropolitan statistical areas to determine where the most educated Americans are choosing to settle. Criteria: education quality and attainment gap; education levels; percentage of workers with degrees; public school rankings; quality and size of each metro area's universities. New York* was ranked #58 (#1 = most educated city). *www.WalletHub.com, "2015's Most and Least Educated Cities*

Environmental Rankings

- The New York* metro area came in at #155 for the relative comfort of its climate on Sperling's list of "chill cities," as measured by the Sperling Heat Index. All 361 metro areas are included. Criteria included daytime high temperatures, nighttime low temperatures, dew point, and relative humidity at the high temperatures. *www.bertsperling.com, "Sperling's Chill Cities," July 18, 2013*

- Sperling's BestPlaces assessed 379 metropolitan areas of the United States for the likelihood of dangerously extreme weather events or earthquakes. In general the Southeast and South-Central regions have the highest risk of weather extremes and earthquakes, while the Pacific Northwest enjoys the lowest risk. Of the least risky metropolitan areas, the New York* metro area was ranked #207. *www.bestplaces.net, "Safest Places from Natural Disasters," April 2011*

- New York* was identified as one of America's dirtiest metro areas by *Forbes*. The area ranked #11 out of 20. Criteria: air quality; water quality; toxic releases; superfund sites. *Forbes, "America's 20 Dirtiest Cities," December 10, 2012*

- The U.S. Environmental Protection Agency (EPA) released a list of U.S. metropolitan areas with the most ENERGY STAR certified buildings in 2015. The New York* metro area was ranked #5 out of 25. *U.S. Environmental Protection Agency, "Top Cities With the Most ENERGY STAR Certified Buildings in 2016," March 30, 2016*

- New York* was highlighted as one of the 25 most ozone-polluted metro areas in the U.S. during 2011 through 2013. The area ranked #11. *American Lung Association, State of the Air 2015*

- New York* was highlighted as one of the 25 metro areas most polluted by year-round particle pollution (Annual PM 2.5) in the U.S. during 2011 through 2013. The area ranked #14. *American Lung Association, State of the Air 2015*

- New York* was highlighted as one of the 25 metro areas most polluted by short-term particle pollution (24-hour PM 2.5) in the U.S. during 2011 through 2013. The area ranked #15. *American Lung Association, State of the Air 2015*

Health/Fitness Rankings

- For each of the 50 most populous metro areas in the United States, the American College of Sports Medicine's American Fitness Index evaluated infrastructure, community assets, and policies that encourage healthy and fit lifestyles, including preventive health behaviors, levels of chronic disease conditions, health care access, and community resources and policies that support physical activity. The New York* metro area ranked #24 for "community fitness." *www.americanfitnessindex.org, "ACSM American Fitness Index Health and Community Fitness Status of the 50 Largest Metropolitan Areas," May 2015*

- *Business Insider* reported Trulia's analysis of the 100 largest U.S. metro areas to identify the nation's best cities for weight loss, based on healthful food options, access to outdoor activities, weight-loss centers, gyms, and opportunities to bike or walk to work. New York* ranked #6. *Businessinsider.com, "These Are the Best US Cities for Weight loss," January 17, 2013*
- The New York* metro area was identified as one of the worst cities for bed bugs in America by pest control company Orkin. The area ranked #4 out of 50 based on the number of bed bug treatments Orkin performed from January to December 2015. *Orkin, "Chicago Tops Bed Bug Cities List for Fourth Year in a Row," January 13, 2016*
- New York* was identified as a "2016 Spring Allergy Capital." The area ranked #31 out of 100. Three groups of factors were used to identify the most severe cities for people with allergies during the spring season: annual pollen levels; medicine utilization; access to board-certified allergists. *Asthma and Allergy Foundation of America, "Spring Allergy Capitals 2016"*
- New York* was identified as a "2015 Asthma Capital." The area ranked #35 out of the nation's 100 largest metropolitan areas. Criteria: estimated prevalence; self-reported prevalence; crude death rate for asthma; annual pollen score; annual air quality; public smoking laws; number of board-certified asthma specialists; school inhaler access laws; rescue medication use; controller medication use; ER visits for asthma; uninsured rate; poverty rate. *Asthma and Allergy Foundation of America, "Asthma Capitals 2015"*
- The New York* metro area ranked #113 out of 190 in The Gallup-Healthways Well-Being Index. Criteria: purpose; social well being; financial health; community and physical health. Results are based on telephone interviews with adults, aged 18 and older, living in metropolitan areas in the 50 U.S. states and the District of Columbia. *Gallup-Healthways, "State of American Well-Being," February 23, 2016*

Real Estate Rankings

- With data from RealtyTrac, Yahoo! Finance researchers listed the housing markets in which housing affordability is improving most, factoring in interest rates as well as median home prices. The New York* metro area was among the least affordable housing markets. *news.yahoo.com, "10 Cities Where Ordinary People Can No Longer Afford Homes," March 5, 2014*
- The New York* metro area was identified as one of the 20 least affordable housing markets in the U.S. in 2015. The area ranked #9 out of 179 markets. Criteria: qualification for a mortgage loan on a typical home. *National Association of Realtors®, Affordability Index of Existing Single-Family Homes for Metropolitan Areas, 2015*
- New York* was ranked #217 out of 225 metro areas in terms of housing affordability in 2015 by the National Association of Home Builders (#1 = most affordable). Criteria: the share of homes sold in that area affordable to a family earning the local median income, based on standard mortgage underwriting criteria. *National Association of Home Builders®, NAHB-Wells Fargo Housing Opportunity Index, 4th Quarter 2015*

Safety Rankings

- New York* was identified as one of the most disaster-proof places in the U.S. in terms of its vulnerability to natural and non-natural disasters. The city ranked #1 out of 5. Rankings are based on the U.S. Center for Disease Control's Cities Readiness Initiative (CRI), which assesses local emergency-management plans, protocols and capabilities for 72 Metropolitan Statistical Areas and four non-MSA large cities. *Forbes, "America's Most and Least Disaster-Proof Cities," December 12, 2011*
- The National Insurance Crime Bureau ranked 380 metro areas in the U.S. in terms of per capita rates of vehicle theft. The New York* metro area ranked #249 (#1 = highest rate). Criteria: number of vehicle theft offenses per 100,000 inhabitants in 2014. *National Insurance Crime Bureau, "Hot Spots 2014," June 24, 2015*

Seniors/Retirement Rankings

- From its Best Cities for Successful Aging indexes, the Milken Institute generated rankings for metropolitan areas, weighing data in eight categories—health care, wellness, living arrangements, transportation, financial characteristics, education and employment opportunities, community engagement, and overall livability. The New York* metro area was ranked #14 overall in the large metro area category. *Milken Institute, "Best Cities for Successful Aging, 2014"*

Sports/Recreation Rankings

- According to the personal finance website NerdWallet, the New York* metro area, at #4, is one of the nation's top dozen metro areas for sports fans. Criteria included the presence of all four major sports—MLB, NFL, NHL, and NBA, fan enthusiasm (as measured by game attendance), ticket affordability, and "sports culture," that is, number of sports bars. *www.nerdwallet.com, "Best Cities for Sports Fans," May 5, 2013*

Transportation Rankings

- New York* was identified as one of the most congested metro areas in the U.S. The area ranked #4 out of 10. Criteria: yearly delay per auto commuter in hours. *Texas A&M Transportation Institute, "2015 Urban Mobility Scorecard," August 2015*
- The New York* metro area appeared on *Forbes* list of places with the most extreme commutes. The metro area ranked #2 out of 10. Criteria: average travel time; percentage of mega commuters. Mega-commuters travel more than 90 minutes and 50 miles each way to work. *Forbes.com, "The Cities with the Most Extreme Commutes," March 5, 2013*

Miscellaneous Rankings

- The watchdog site Charity Navigator conducts an annual study of charities in the nation's major markets both to analyze statistical differences in their financial, accountability, and transparency practices and to track year-to-year variations in individual communities. The New York* metro area was ranked #17 among the 30 metro markets in the rating dimension of Overall Score. *www.charitynavigator.org, "Metro Market Study 2015," June 5, 2015*
- The Harris Poll's Happiness Index survey revealed that of the top ten U.S. markets, the New York* metro area residents ranked #6 in happiness. Criteria included strong assent to positive statements and strong disagreement with negative ones, and degree of agreement with a series of statements about respondents' personal relationships and general outlook. *www.harrisinteractive.com, "Dallas/Fort Worth Is "Happiest" City among America's Top Ten Markets," September 4, 2013*
- Energizer Personal Care, the makers of Edge® shave gel, in partnership with Sperling's BestPlaces, ranked 50 major metro areas in terms of everyday irritations. The New York* metro area ranked #2 the 50 metro area most iritating to guys. Criteria: high male-to-female ratio; poor sports team performance and high ticket prices; slow traffic; lack of job availability; unaffordable housing; extreme weather; lack of nightlife and fitness options. *Energizer Personal Care, "Most Irritatng Cities for Guys," August 26, 2013*
- Mars Chocolate North America, the makers of COMBOS®, in partnership with Sperling's BestPlaces, ranked 50 major metro areas in terms of their "manliness." The New York* metro area ranked #39. Criteria: number of professional sports teams; number of nearby NASCAR tracks and racing events; manly lifestyle; concentration of manly retail stores; manly occupations per capita; salty snack sales; "Board of Manliness" rankings. *Mars Chocolate North America, "America's Manliest Cities 2012"*
- The New York* metro area was selected as one of "America's Most Miserable Cities" by *Forbes.com.* The metro area ranked #10 out of 20. Criteria: violent crime; unemployment; foreclosures; income and property taxes; home prices; commute times; climate. *Forbes.com, "America's Most Miserable Cities" February 22, 2013*

- The National Alliance to End Homelessness ranked the 100 most populous metro areas with the highest rate of homelessness. The New York* metro area ranked #13. Criteria: number of homeless people per 10,000 population in 2011. *National Alliance to End Homelessness, The State of Homelessness in America 2012*

South Brunswick is located within the New York-Newark-Jersey City, NY-NJ-PA Metropolitan Statistical Area.

Business Environment

CITY FINANCES

City Government Finances

Component	2012 ($000)	2012 ($ per capita)
Total Revenues	68,147	1,569
Total Expenditures	66,280	1,526
Debt Outstanding	95,414	2,197
Cash and Securities[1]	21,810	502

Note: (1) Cash and security holdings of a government at the close of its fiscal year, including those of its dependent agencies, utilities, and liquor stores.
Source: U.S Census Bureau, State & Local Government Finances 2012

City Government Revenue by Source

Source	2012 ($000)	2012 ($ per capita)
General Revenue		
From Federal Government	0	0
From State Government	6,325	145
From Local Governments	706	16
Taxes		
Property	32,482	748
Sales and Gross Receipts	1,034	23
Personal Income	0	0
Corporate Income	0	0
Motor Vehicle License	0	0
Other Taxes	1,608	37
Current Charges	16,007	368
Liquor Store	0	0
Utility	8,260	190
Employee Retirement	0	0

Source: U.S Census Bureau, State & Local Government Finances 2012

City Government Expenditures by Function

Function	2012 ($000)	2012 ($ per capita)	2012 (%)
General Direct Expenditures			
Air Transportation	0	0	0.0
Corrections	0	0	0.0
Education	0	0	0.0
Employment Security Administration	0	0	0.0
Financial Administration	1,671	38	2.5
Fire Protection	614	14	0.9
General Public Buildings	297	6	0.4
Governmental Administration, Other	930	21	1.4
Health	631	14	0.9
Highways	2,961	68	4.4
Hospitals	0	0	0.0
Housing and Community Development	0	0	0.0
Interest on General Debt	1,729	39	2.6
Judicial and Legal	638	14	0.9
Libraries	2,617	60	3.9
Parking	0	0	0.0
Parks and Recreation	5,006	115	7.5
Police Protection	9,333	214	14.0
Public Welfare	63	1	0.0
Sewerage	11,908	274	17.9
Solid Waste Management	2,634	60	3.9
Veterans' Services	0	0	0.0
Liquor Store	0	0	0.0
Utility	7,314	168	11.0
Employee Retirement	0	0	0.0

Source: U.S Census Bureau, State & Local Government Finances 2012

DEMOGRAPHICS

Population Growth

Area	1990 Census	2000 Census	2010 Census	2014* Estimate	Population Growth (%) 1990-2014	Population Growth (%) 2010-2014
City	25,792	37,734	43,417	44,355	72.0	2.2
MSA[1]	16,845,992	18,323,002	18,897,109	19,865,045	17.9	5.1
U.S.	248,709,873	281,421,906	308,745,538	314,107,084	26.3	1.7

Note: (1) Figures cover the New York-Newark-Jersey City, NY-NJ-PA Metropolitan Statistical Area—see Appendix B for areas included; (*) 2010-2014 5-year estimated population
Source: U.S. Census Bureau, 1990 Census, Census 2000, Census 2010, 2010-2014 American Community Survey 5-Year Estimates

Household Size

Area	Persons in Household (%)							Average Household Size
	One	Two	Three	Four	Five	Six	Seven or More	
City	18.4	28.2	19.7	22.4	7.9	2.4	0.7	2.91
MSA[1]	27.8	28.9	17.0	14.8	6.7	2.6	1.9	2.74
U.S.	27.5	33.5	15.8	13.1	6.0	2.3	1.4	2.64

Note: (1) Figures cover the New York-Newark-Jersey City, NY-NJ-PA Metropolitan Statistical Area—see Appendix B for areas included
Source: U.S. Census Bureau, 2010-2014 American Community Survey 5-Year Estimates

Race

Area	White Alone[2] (%)	Black Alone[2] (%)	Asian Alone[2] (%)	AIAN[3] Alone[2] (%)	NHOPI[4] Alone[2] (%)	Other Race Alone[2] (%)	Two or More Races (%)
City	49.8	7.5	39.8	0.3	0.0	1.0	1.7
MSA[1]	59.4	17.2	10.2	0.3	0.0	10.1	2.8
U.S.	73.8	12.6	5.0	0.8	0.2	4.7	2.9

Note: (1) Figures cover the New York-Newark-Jersey City, NY-NJ-PA Metropolitan Statistical Area—see Appendix B for areas included; (2) Alone is defined as not being in combination with one or more other races; (3) American Indian and Alaska Native; (4) Native Hawaiian and Other Pacific Islander
Source: U.S. Census Bureau, 2010-2014 American Community Survey 5-Year Estimates

Hispanic or Latino Origin

Area	Total (%)	Mexican (%)	Puerto Rican (%)	Cuban (%)	Other (%)
City	4.9	0.3	2.0	0.2	2.3
MSA[1]	23.3	3.0	6.4	0.7	13.1
U.S.	16.9	10.8	1.6	0.6	3.8

Note: Persons of Hispanic or Latino origin can be of any race; (1) Figures cover the New York-Newark-Jersey City, NY-NJ-PA Metropolitan Statistical Area—see Appendix B for areas included
Source: U.S. Census Bureau, 2010-2014 American Community Survey 5-Year Estimates

Ancestry

Area	German	Irish	English	American	Italian	Polish	French[2]	Scottish	Dutch
City	7.7	9.7	4.2	4.9	12.4	4.9	0.7	0.9	0.7
MSA[1]	7.2	10.6	3.1	4.4	13.7	4.2	1.1	0.7	0.7
U.S.	14.9	10.8	8.0	7.1	5.5	3.0	2.7	1.7	1.4

Note: Figures are the percentage of the total population reporting a particular ancestry. The nine most commonly reported ancestries in the U.S. are shown. Figures include multiple ancestries (e.g. if a person reported being Irish and Italian, they were included in both columns); (1) Figures cover the New York-Newark-Jersey City, NY-NJ-PA Metropolitan Statistical Area—see Appendix B for areas included; (2) Excludes Basque
Source: U.S. Census Bureau, 2010-2014 American Community Survey 5-Year Estimates

Foreign-Born Population

Area	Percent of Population Born in								
	Any Foreign Country	Asia	Mexico	Europe	Carribean	Central America[2]	South America	Africa	Canada
City	33.7	26.9	0.1	2.2	1.3	0.2	1.2	1.2	0.4
MSA[1]	28.5	8.0	1.7	4.6	6.5	1.9	4.3	1.2	0.2
U.S.	13.1	3.8	3.7	1.5	1.2	1.0	0.9	0.6	0.3

Note: (1) Figures cover the New York-Newark-Jersey City, NY-NJ-PA Metropolitan Statistical Area—see Appendix B for areas included; (2) Excludes Mexico.
Source: U.S. Census Bureau, 2010-2014 American Community Survey 5-Year Estimates

Marital Status

Area	Never Married	Now Married[2]	Separated	Widowed	Divorced
City	27.5	59.9	1.2	4.6	6.8
MSA[1]	37.7	45.8	2.5	6.0	7.9
U.S.	32.5	48.4	2.2	5.9	10.9

Note: Figures are percentages and cover the population 15 years of age and older; (1) Figures cover the New York-Newark-Jersey City, NY-NJ-PA Metropolitan Statistical Area—see Appendix B for areas included; (2) Excludes separated
Source: U.S. Census Bureau, 2010-2014 American Community Survey 5-Year Estimates

Disability Status

Area	All Ages	Under 18 Years Old	18 to 64 Years Old	65 Years and Over
City	7.3	2.8	5.5	28.3
MSA[1]	9.8	3.1	7.3	33.5
U.S.	12.3	4.1	10.2	36.3

Note: Figures show percent of the civilian noninstitutionalized population that reported having a disability. Disability status is determined from from six types of difficulty: vision, hearing, cognitive, ambulatory, self-care, and independent living. For children under 5 years old, hearing and vision difficulty are used to determine disability status. For children between the ages of 5 and 14, disability status is determined from hearing, vision, cognitive, ambulatory, and self-care difficulties. For people aged 15 years and older, they are considered to have a disability if they have difficulty with any one of the six difficulty types; (1) Figures cover the New York-Newark-Jersey City, NY-NJ-PA Metropolitan Statistical Area—see Appendix B for areas included.
Source: U.S. Census Bureau, 2010-2014 American Community Survey 5-Year Estimates

Age

Area	Percent of Population									Median Age
	Under Age 5	Age 5–19	Age 20–34	Age 35–44	Age 45–54	Age 55–64	Age 65–74	Age 75–84	Age 85+	
City	4.4	23.4	14.9	16.4	18.1	11.5	6.2	3.3	1.6	39.6
MSA[1]	6.2	18.8	21.2	13.6	14.6	12.0	7.3	4.2	2.0	37.8
U.S.	6.4	19.9	20.6	13.0	14.1	12.3	7.6	4.3	1.9	37.4

Note: (1) Figures cover the New York-Newark-Jersey City, NY-NJ-PA Metropolitan Statistical Area—see Appendix B for areas included
Source: U.S. Census Bureau, 2010-2014 American Community Survey 5-Year Estimates

Gender

Area	Males	Females	Males per 100 Females
City	21,736	22,619	96.1
MSA[1]	9,593,127	10,271,918	93.4
U.S.	154,515,159	159,591,925	96.8

Note: (1) Figures cover the New York-Newark-Jersey City, NY-NJ-PA Metropolitan Statistical Area—see Appendix B for areas included
Source: U.S. Census Bureau, 2010-2014 American Community Survey 5-Year Estimates

Religious Groups by Family

Area	Catholic	Baptist	Non-Den.	Methodist[2]	Lutheran	LDS[3]	Pente-costal	Presby-terian[4]	Muslim[5]	Judaism
MSA[1]	36.9	1.8	1.7	1.3	0.7	0.3	0.8	1.0	2.3	4.7
U.S.	19.1	9.3	4.0	4.0	2.3	2.0	1.9	1.6	0.8	0.7

Note: Figures are the number of adherents as a percentage of the total population; (1) Figures cover the New York-Northern New Jersey-Long Island, NY-NJ-PA Metropolitan Statistical Area—see Appendix B for areas included; (2) Methodist/Pietist; (3) Latter Day Saints; (4) Reformed; (5) Figures are estimates
Source: Association of Statisticians of American Religious Bodies, 2010 U.S. Religion Census: Religious Congregations & Membership Study

Religious Groups by Tradition

Area	Catholic	Evangelical Protestant	Mainline Protestant	Other Tradition	Black Protestant	Orthodox
MSA[1]	36.9	3.9	4.1	8.3	1.2	0.9
U.S.	19.1	16.2	7.3	4.3	1.6	0.3

Note: Figures are the number of adherents as a percentage of the total population; (1) Figures cover the New York-Northern New Jersey-Long Island, NY-NJ-PA Metropolitan Statistical Area—see Appendix B for areas included
Source: Association of Statisticians of American Religious Bodies, 2010 U.S. Religion Census: Religious Congregations & Membership Study

ECONOMY

Gross Metropolitan Product

Area	2013	2014	2015	2016	Rank[2]
MSA[1]	1,471.2	1,521.7	1,573.8	1,650.1	1

Note: Figures are in billions of dollars; (1) Figures cover the New York-Newark-Jersey City, NY-NJ-PA Metropolitan Statistical Area—see Appendix B for areas included; (2) Rank is based on 2016 data and ranges from 1 to 381
Source: The U.S. Conference of Mayors, U.S. Metro Economies: GMP and Employment 2014-2016, June 2015

Economic Growth

Area	2011-13 (%)	2014 (%)	2015 (%)	2016 (%)	Rank[2]
MSA[1]	1.6	1.8	2.0	2.8	116
U.S.	2.2	2.4	2.3	2.9	–

Note: Figures are real gross metropolitan product (GMP) growth rates and represent annual average percent change; (1) Figures cover the New York-Newark-Jersey City, NY-NJ-PA Metropolitan Statistical Area—see Appendix B for areas included; (2) Rank is based on 2016 data and ranges from 1 to 381
Source: The U.S. Conference of Mayors, U.S. Metro Economies: GMP and Employment 2014-2016, June 2015

Metropolitan Area Exports

Area	2009	2010	2011	2012	2013	2014	Rank[2]
MSA[1]	69,990.3	85,081.1	105,102.0	102,298.0	106,922.8	105,266.5	2

Note: Figures are in millions of dollars; (1) Figures cover the New York-Newark-Jersey City, NY-NJ-PA Metropolitan Statistical Area—see Appendix B for areas included; (2) Rank is based on 2014 data and ranges from 1 to 385
Source: U.S. Department of Commerce, International Trade Administration, Office of Trade & Industry Information, Manufacturing & Services, data extracted March 10, 2016

Building Permits

Area	Single-Family			Multi-Family			Total		
	2014	2015p	Pct. Chg.	2014	2015p	Pct. Chg.	2014	2015p	Pct. Chg.
City	65	172	164.6	0	0	-	65	172	164.6
MSA[1]	11,799	10,749	-8.9	36,185	75,646	109.1	47,984	86,395	80.0
U.S.	640,300	690,800	7.9	411,800	487,600	18.4	1,052,100	1,178,400	12.0

Note: (1) Figures cover the New York-Newark-Jersey City, NY-NJ-PA Metropolitan Statistical Area—see Appendix B for areas included; Figures represent new, privately-owned housing units authorized (unadjusted data); All permit data are based on estimates with imputation; (p) preliminary data.
Source: U.S. Census Bureau, Manufacturing, Mining, and Construction Statistics, Building Permits, 2014, 2015

Bankruptcy Filings

Area	Business Filings 2014	Business Filings 2015	Business Filings % Chg.	Nonbusiness Filings 2014	Nonbusiness Filings 2015	Nonbusiness Filings % Chg.
Middlesex County	66	48	-27.3	2,000	1,749	-12.6
U.S.	26,983	24,735	-8.3	909,812	819,760	-9.9

Note: Business filings include Chapter 7, Chapter 11, Chapter 12, and Chapter 13; Nonbusiness filings include Chapter 7, Chapter 11, and Chapter 13

Source: Administrative Office of the U.S. Courts, Business and Nonbusiness Bankruptcy, County Cases Commenced by Chapter of the Bankruptcy Code, During the 12- Month Period Ending December 31, 2014 and Business and Nonbusiness Bankruptcy, County Cases Commenced by Chapter of the Bankruptcy Code, During the 12- Month Period Ending December 31, 2015

Housing Vacancy Rates

Area	Gross Vacancy Rate[2] (%)			Year-Round Vacancy Rate[3] (%)			Rental Vacancy Rate[4] (%)			Homeowner Vacancy Rate[5] (%)		
	2013	2014	2015	2013	2014	2015	2013	2014	2015	2013	2014	2015
MSA[1]	9.5	9.2	9.8	8.1	7.9	8.6	5.4	4.6	4.2	2.1	1.6	2.1
U.S.	13.6	13.4	12.9	10.7	10.4	10.0	8.3	7.6	7.1	2.0	1.9	1.8

Note: (1) Figures cover the New York-Newark-Jersey City, NY-NJ-PA Metropolitan Statistical Area—see Appendix B for areas included; (2) The percentage of the total housing inventory that is vacant; (3) The percentage of the housing inventory (excluding seasonal units) that is year-round vacant; (4) The percentage of rental inventory that is vacant for rent; (5) The percentage of homeowner inventory that is vacant for sale

Source: U.S. Census Bureau, Housing Vacancies and Homeownership Annual Statistics: 2015

INCOME

Income

Area	Per Capita ($)	Median Household ($)	Average Household ($)
City	45,645	110,167	130,803
MSA[1]	36,078	66,902	97,572
U.S.	28,555	53,482	74,596

Note: (1) Figures cover the New York-Newark-Jersey City, NY-NJ-PA Metropolitan Statistical Area—see Appendix B for areas included

Source: U.S. Census Bureau, 2010-2014 American Community Survey 5-Year Estimates

Household Income Distribution

Area	Percent of Households Earning: Under $15,000	$15,000 -24,999	$25,000 -34,999	$35,000 -49,999	$50,000 -74,999	$75,000 -99,000	$100,000 -149,999	$150,000 and up
City	3.0	4.4	3.5	6.1	14.2	11.9	25.7	31.1
MSA[1]	11.8	8.8	8.0	10.6	15.3	11.9	15.7	18.0
U.S.	12.5	10.7	10.2	13.5	17.8	12.2	13.0	10.0

Note: (1) Figures cover the New York-Newark-Jersey City, NY-NJ-PA Metropolitan Statistical Area—see Appendix B for areas included

Source: U.S. Census Bureau, 2010-2014 American Community Survey 5-Year Estimates

Poverty Rate

Area	All Ages	Under 18 Years Old	18 to 64 Years Old	65 Years and Over
City	2.8	3.6	2.7	2.0
MSA[1]	14.3	20.0	12.8	11.6
U.S.	15.6	21.9	14.6	9.4

Note: Figures are percentage of people whose income during the past 12 months was below the poverty level; (1) Figures cover the New York-Newark-Jersey City, NY-NJ-PA Metropolitan Statistical Area—see Appendix B for areas included

Source: U.S. Census Bureau, 2010-2014 American Community Survey 5-Year Estimates

EMPLOYMENT

Labor Force and Employment

Area	Civilian Labor Force			Workers Employed		
	Dec. 2014	Dec. 2015	% Chg.	Dec. 2014	Dec. 2015	% Chg.
City	24,194	24,713	2.1	23,176	23,941	3.3
MD[1]	7,017,636	7,184,671	2.3	6,611,164	6,853,780	3.6
U.S.	155,521,000	157,245,000	1.1	147,190,000	149,703,000	1.7

Note: Data is not seasonally adjusted and covers workers 16 years of age and older; (1) Figures cover the New York-Jersey City-White Plains, NY-NJ Metropolitan Division—see Appendix B for areas included
Source: Bureau of Labor Statistics, Local Area Unemployment Statistics

Unemployment Rate

Area	2015											
	Jan.	Feb.	Mar.	Apr.	May	Jun.	Jul.	Aug.	Sep.	Oct.	Nov.	Dec.
City	4.8	4.7	4.7	4.5	4.8	4.1	4.8	4.2	4.1	3.6	3.6	3.1
MD[1]	6.7	6.8	6.2	5.8	5.8	5.4	5.7	5.2	4.9	4.7	4.8	4.6
U.S.	6.1	5.8	5.6	5.1	5.3	5.5	5.6	5.2	4.9	4.8	4.8	4.8

Note: Data is not seasonally adjusted and covers workers 16 years of age and older; (1) Figures cover the New York-Jersey City-White Plains, NY-NJ Metropolitan Division—see Appendix B for areas included
Source: Bureau of Labor Statistics, Local Area Unemployment Statistics

Employment by Occupation

Occupation Classification	City (%)	MSA[1] (%)	U.S. (%)
Management, Business, Science, and Arts	57.7	40.3	36.4
Natural Resources, Construction, and Maintenance	4.2	7.0	9.0
Production, Transportation, and Material Moving	6.0	9.1	12.1
Sales and Office	22.0	24.2	24.4
Service	10.0	19.4	18.2

Note: Figures cover employed civilians 16 years of age and older; (1) Figures cover the New York-Newark-Jersey City, NY-NJ-PA Metropolitan Statistical Area—see Appendix B for areas included
Source: U.S. Census Bureau, 2010-2014 American Community Survey 5-Year Estimates

Employment by Industry

Sector	MD[1]		U.S.
	Number of Employees	Percent of Total	Percent of Total
Construction, Mining, and Logging	256,300	3.7	5.0
Education and Health Services	1,350,800	19.7	15.7
Financial Activities	612,400	8.9	5.7
Government	917,500	13.3	15.5
Information	243,800	3.5	1.9
Leisure and Hospitality	638,900	9.3	10.4
Manufacturing	211,600	3.0	8.6
Other Services	296,100	4.3	3.9
Professional and Business Services	1,107,000	16.1	13.9
Retail Trade	686,300	10.0	11.3
Transportation, Warehousing, and Utilities	251,300	3.6	3.9
Wholesale Trade	284,100	4.1	4.1

Note: Figures are non-farm employment as of December 2015. Figures are not seasonally adjusted and include workers 16 years of age and older; (1) Figures cover the New York-Jersey City-White Plains, NY-NJ Metropolitan Division—see Appendix B for areas included; n/a not available
Source: Bureau of Labor Statistics, Current Employment Statistics, Employment, Hours, and Earnings

Occupations with Greatest Projected Employment Growth: 2012 – 2022

Occupation[1]	2012 Employment	2022 Projected Employment	Numeric Employment Change	Percent Employment Change
Home Health Aides	31,140	46,280	15,140	48.6
Combined Food Preparation and Serving Workers, Including Fast Food	59,990	70,180	10,190	17.0
Retail Salespersons	125,690	134,870	9,180	7.3
Registered Nurses	79,840	88,880	9,040	11.3
Nursing Assistants	51,780	60,070	8,290	16.0
Laborers and Freight, Stock, and Material Movers, Hand	75,730	83,360	7,630	10.1
Software Developers, Applications	29,090	35,770	6,680	23.0
Receptionists and Information Clerks	51,160	57,830	6,670	13.0
Customer Service Representatives	63,450	69,530	6,080	9.6
Sales Representatives, Services, All Other	45,510	51,380	5,870	12.9

Note: Projections cover New Jersey; (1) Sorted by numeric employment change
Source: www.projectionscentral.com, State Occupational Projections, 2012–2022 Long-Term Projections

Fastest Growing Occupations: 2012 – 2022

Occupation[1]	2012 Employment	2022 Projected Employment	Numeric Employment Change	Percent Employment Change
Home Health Aides	31,140	46,280	15,140	48.6
Insulation Workers, Mechanical	370	540	170	48.2
Diagnostic Medical Sonographers	2,550	3,550	1,000	39.1
Occupational Therapy Assistants	370	500	130	37.5
Helpers—Electricians	1,310	1,800	490	37.5
Stonemasons	580	780	200	35.4
Physical Therapist Assistants	1,090	1,470	380	34.1
Skincare Specialists	1,050	1,400	350	33.2
Physician Assistants	1,450	1,920	470	32.8
Brickmasons and Blockmasons	2,150	2,830	680	31.7

Note: Projections cover New Jersey; (1) Sorted by percent employment change and excludes occupations with numeric employment change less than 100
Source: www.projectionscentral.com, State Occupational Projections, 2012–2022 Long-Term Projections

Average Wages

Occupation	$/Hr.	Occupation	$/Hr.
Accountants and Auditors	46.43	Maids and Housekeeping Cleaners	16.84
Automotive Mechanics	20.21	Maintenance and Repair Workers	21.29
Bookkeepers	21.54	Marketing Managers	89.06
Carpenters	32.53	Nuclear Medicine Technologists	40.65
Cashiers	10.92	Nurses, Licensed Practical	25.33
Clerks, General Office	15.88	Nurses, Registered	41.54
Clerks, Receptionists/Information	15.02	Nursing Assistants	16.38
Clerks, Shipping/Receiving	16.94	Packers and Packagers, Hand	11.33
Computer Programmers	46.00	Physical Therapists	44.91
Computer Systems Analysts	50.45	Postal Service Mail Carriers	25.04
Computer User Support Specialists	28.75	Real Estate Brokers	50.12
Cooks, Restaurant	13.74	Retail Salespersons	12.99
Dentists	76.20	Sales Reps., Exc. Tech./Scientific	35.67
Electrical Engineers	48.32	Sales Reps., Tech./Scientific	51.39
Electricians	37.19	Secretaries, Exc. Legal/Med./Exec.	19.62
Financial Managers	90.86	Security Guards	15.32
First-Line Supervisors/Managers, Sales	24.90	Surgeons	113.38
Food Preparation Workers	11.50	Teacher Assistants*	13.73
General and Operations Managers	79.03	Teachers, Elementary School*	34.23
Hairdressers/Cosmetologists	17.87	Teachers, Secondary School*	39.55
Internists	97.62	Telemarketers	14.00
Janitors and Cleaners	15.87	Truck Drivers, Heavy/Tractor-Trailer	23.69
Landscaping/Groundskeeping Workers	15.52	Truck Drivers, Light/Delivery Svcs.	17.92
Lawyers	80.76	Waiters and Waitresses	14.08

Note: Wage data covers the Metropolitan Division—see Appendix B for areas included; (*) Hourly wages for elementary/secondary school teachers and teacher assistants were calculated by the editors from annual wage data based on a 40 hour work week; n/a not available.
Source: Bureau of Labor Statistics, Metro Area Occupational Employment and Wage Estimates, May 2015

TAXES

State Corporate Income Tax Rates

State	Tax Rate (%)	Income Brackets ($)	Num. of Brackets	Financial Institution Tax Rate (%)[a]	Federal Income Tax Ded.
New Jersey	9.0 (r)	Flat rate	1	9.0 (r)	No

Note: Tax rates as of January 1, 2016; (a) Rates listed are the corporate income tax rate applied to financial institutions or excise taxes based on income. Some states have other taxes based upon the value of deposits or shares; (r) In New Jersey small businesses with annual entire net income under $100,000 pay a tax rate of 7.5%; businesses with income under $50,000 pay 6.5%. The minimum Corporation Business Tax is based on New Jersey gross receipts. It ranges from $500 for a corporation with gross receipts less than $100,000, to $2,000 for a corporation with gross receipts of $1 million or more.
Source: Federation of Tax Administrators, "State Corporate Income Tax Rates, 2016"

State Individual Income Tax Rates

State	Tax Rate (%)	Income Brackets ($)	Num. of Brackets	Personal Exempt. ($)[1]		Fed. Inc. Tax Ded.
				Single	Dependents	
New Jersey	1.4 - 8.97	20,000 - 500,000 (n)	6	1,000	1,500	No

Note: Tax rates as of January 1, 2016; Local- and county-level taxes are not included; n/a not applicable; (1) Married joint filers generally receive double the single exemption; (n) The New Jersey rates reported are for single individuals. For married couples filing jointly, the tax rates also range from 1.4% to 8.97%, with 7 brackets and the same high and low income ranges.
Source: Federation of Tax Administrators, "State Individual Income Tax Rates, 2016"

Various State and Local Tax Rates

State	State and Local Sales and Use (%)	State Sales and Use (%)	Gasoline[1] (¢/gal.)	Cigarette[2] ($/pack)	Spirits[3] ($/gal.)	Wine[4] ($/gal.)	Beer[5] ($/gal.)
New Jersey	7.00	7.0 (e)	14.5	2.70	5.50	0.88	0.12

Note: All tax rates as of January 1, 2016; (1) The American Petroleum Institute has developed a methodology for determining the average tax rate on a gallon of fuel. Rates may include any of the following: excise taxes, environmental fees, storage tank fees, other fees or taxes, general sales tax, and local taxes. In states where gasoline is subject to the general sales tax, or where the fuel tax is based on the average sale price, the average rate determined by API is sensitive to changes in the price of gasoline. States that fully or partially apply general sales taxes to gasoline: CA, CO, GA, IL, IN, MI, NY; (2) The federal excise tax of $1.0066 per pack and local taxes are not included; (3) Rates are those applicable to off-premise sales of 40% alcohol by volume (a.b.v.) distilled spirits in 750ml containers. Local excise taxes are excluded; (4) Rates are those applicable to off-premise sales of 11% a.b.v. non-carbonated wine in 750ml containers; (5) Rates are those applicable to off-premise sales of 4.7% a.b.v. beer in 12 ounce containers; (e) Some counties in New Jersey are not subject to statewide sales tax rates and collect a local rate of 3.5%. Their average local score is represented as a negative.
Source: Tax Foundation, 2016 Facts & Figures: How Does Your State Compare?

State Business Tax Climate Index Rankings

State	Overall Rank	Corporate Tax Rank	Individual Income Tax Rank	Sales Tax Rank	Unemployment Insurance Tax Rank	Property Tax Rank
New Jersey	50	43	48	47	31	50

Note: The index is a measure of how each state's tax laws affect economic performance. The lower the rank, the more favorable a state's tax system is for business. States without a given tax are given a ranking of 1. The scores/rankings for the District of Columbia do not affect other states. The 2016 index represents the tax climate as of July 1, 2015 (the beginning of Fiscal Year 2016).
Source: Tax Foundation, State Business Tax Climate Index 2016

TRANSPORTATION

Means of Transportation to Work

Area	Car/Truck/Van		Public Transportation			Bicycle	Walked	Other Means	Worked at Home
	Drove Alone	Car-pooled	Bus	Subway	Railroad				
City	79.4	7.6	5.1	0.2	3.1	0.1	0.6	0.7	3.4
MSA[1]	50.6	6.8	8.0	18.5	3.6	0.6	6.0	1.9	4.1
U.S.	76.4	9.6	2.6	1.8	0.6	0.6	2.8	1.3	4.4

Note: Figures are percentages and cover workers 16 years of age and older; (1) Figures cover the New York-Newark-Jersey City, NY-NJ-PA Metropolitan Statistical Area—see Appendix B for areas included
Source: U.S. Census Bureau, 2010-2014 American Community Survey 5-Year Estimates

Travel Time to Work

Area	Less Than 10 Minutes	10 to 19 Minutes	20 to 29 Minutes	30 to 44 Minutes	45 to 59 Minutes	60 to 89 Minutes	90 Minutes or More
City	6.1	21.8	19.2	23.5	10.1	10.2	9.1
MSA[1]	7.8	19.9	16.6	23.6	12.1	13.9	6.2
U.S.	13.3	29.6	21.0	20.2	7.7	5.7	2.6

Note: Figures are percentages and include workers 16 years old and over; (1) Figures cover the New York-Newark-Jersey City, NY-NJ-PA Metropolitan Statistical Area—see Appendix B for areas included
Source: U.S. Census Bureau, 2010-2014 American Community Survey 5-Year Estimates

Freeway Travel Time Index

Area	1985	1990	1995	2000	2005	2010	2014
Urban Area Rank[1,2]	11	9	8	7	7	8	8
Urban Area Index[1]	1.16	1.20	1.24	1.29	1.33	1.33	1.34
Average Index[3]	1.09	1.11	1.14	1.17	1.20	1.19	1.20

Note: Freeway Travel Time Index—the ratio of travel time in the peak period to the travel time at free-flow conditions. For example, a value of 1.30 indicates a 20-minute free-flow trip takes 26 minutes in the peak (20 minutes x 1.30 = 26 minutes); (1) Covers the New York-Newark NY-NJ-CT urban area; (2) Rank is based on 101 urban areas (#1 = highest travel time index); (3) Average of 101 urban areas
Source: Texas Transportation Institute, 2015 Urban Mobility Scorecard, August 2015

Freeway Commuter Stress Index

Area	1985	1990	1995	2000	2005	2010	2014
Urban Area Rank[1,2]	19	19	13	12	11	11	12
Urban Area Index[1]	1.21	1.24	1.29	1.34	1.38	1.38	1.39
Average Index[3]	1.13	1.16	1.19	1.22	1.25	1.24	1.25

Note: The Freeway Commuter Stress Index is the same as the Freeway Travel Time Index (see table above) except that it includes only the travel in the peak directions during the peak periods; the TTI includes travel in all directions during the peak period. Thus, the CSI is more indicative of the work trip experienced by each commuter on a daily basis. (1) Covers the New York-Newark NY-NJ-CT urban area; (2) Rank is based on 101 urban areas (#1 = highest stress index); (3) Average of 101 urban areas
Source: Texas Transportation Institute, 2015 Urban Mobility Scorecard, August 2015

Living Environment

COST OF LIVING

Cost of Living Index

Composite Index	Groceries	Housing	Utilities	Trans-portation	Health Care	Misc. Goods/ Services
121.6	112.6	148.6	111.0	107.3	110.3	112.0

Note: The Cost of Living Index measures regional differences in the cost of consumer goods and services, excluding taxes and non-consumer expenditures, for professional and managerial households in the top income quintile. It is based on more than 50,000 prices covering almost 60 different items for which prices are collected three times a year by chambers of commerce, economic development organizations or university applied economic centers in each participating urban area. The numbers shown should be read as a percentage above or below the national average of 100. For example, a value of 115.4 in the groceries column indicates that grocery prices are 15.4% higher than the national average. Small differences in the index numbers should not be interpreted as significant; Figures cover the Middlesex-Monmouth NJ urban area.
Source: The Council for Community and Economic Research, ACCRA Cost of Living Index, 2015

Grocery Prices

Area[1]	T-Bone Steak ($/pound)	Frying Chicken ($/pound)	Whole Milk ($/half gal.)	Eggs ($/dozen)	Orange Juice ($/64 oz.)	Coffee ($/11.5 oz.)
City[2]	11.40	1.64	2.56	2.58	3.66	4.19
Avg.	10.99	1.43	2.25	2.26	3.58	4.48
Min.	7.16	0.98	1.30	1.35	2.88	2.98
Max.	14.13	2.43	3.85	4.81	6.39	7.56

Note: (1) Values for the local area are compared with the average, minimum and maximum values for all 292 areas in the Cost of Living Index; (2) Figures cover the Middlesex-Monmouth NJ urban area; **T-Bone Steak** *(price per pound);* **Frying Chicken** *(price per pound, whole fryer);* **Whole Milk** *(half gallon carton);* **Eggs** *(price per dozen, Grade A, large);* **Orange Juice** *(64 oz. Tropicana or Florida Natural);* **Coffee** *(11.5 oz. can, vacuum-packed, Maxwell House, Hills Bros, or Folgers).*
Source: The Council for Community and Economic Research, ACCRA Cost of Living Index, 2015

Housing and Utility Costs

Area[1]	New Home Price ($)	Apartment Rent ($/month)	All Electric ($/month)	Part Electric ($/month)	Other Energy ($/month)	Telephone ($/month)
City[2]	467,078	1,393		120.17	63.96	32.25
Avg.	312,874	945	179.30	95.07	72.96	28.11
Min.	178,682	479	116.28	43.14	26.46	10.01
Max.	1,472,476	3,984	504.25	189.44	421.11	43.06

Note: (1) Values for the local area are compared with the average, minimum and maximum values for all 292 areas in the Cost of Living Index; (2) Figures cover the Middlesex-Monmouth NJ urban area; **New Home Price** *(2,400 sf living area, 8,000 sf lot, in urban area with full utilities);* **Apartment Rent** *(950 sf 2 bedroom/1.5 or 2 bath, unfurnished, excluding all utilities except water);* **All Electric** *(average monthly cost for an all-electric home);* **Part Electric** *(average monthly cost for a part-electric home);* **Other Energy** *(average monthly cost for natural gas, fuel oil, coal, wood, and any other forms of energy except electricity);* **Telephone** *(price includes basic monthly rate for a private residential line plus additional local usage charges incurred by a family of four).*
Source: The Council for Community and Economic Research, ACCRA Cost of Living Index, 2015

Health Care, Transportation, and Other Costs

Area[1]	Doctor ($/visit)	Dentist ($/visit)	Optometrist ($/visit)	Gasoline ($/gallon)	Beauty Salon ($/visit)	Men's Shirt ($)
City[2]	86.08	115.37	101.58	2.38	33.58	37.72
Avg.	105.15	89.02	99.78	2.38	35.30	28.10
Min.	66.87	56.09	48.53	1.95	18.91	13.38
Max.	182.34	150.36	228.33	4.09	67.91	63.80

Note: (1) Values for the local area are compared with the average, minimum and maximum values for all 292 areas in the Cost of Living Index; (2) Figures cover the Middlesex-Monmouth NJ urban area; **Doctor** *(general practitioners routine exam of an established patient);* **Dentist** *(adult teeth cleaning and periodic oral examination);* **Optometrist** *(full vision eye exam for established adult patient);* **Gasoline** *(one gallon regular unleaded, national brand, including all taxes, cash price at self-service pump if available);* **Beauty Salon** *(woman's shampoo, trim, and blow-dry);* **Men's Shirt** *(cotton/polyester dress shirt, pinpoint weave, long sleeves).*
Source: The Council for Community and Economic Research, ACCRA Cost of Living Index, 2015

HOUSING

House Price Index (HPI)

Area	National Ranking[2]	Quarterly Change (%)	One-Year Change (%)	Five-Year Change (%)
MD[1]	157	0.30	4.00	4.80
U.S.[3]	–	1.45	5.76	22.85

Note: The HPI is a weighted repeat sales index. It measures average price changes in repeat sales or refinancings on the same properties. This information is obtained by reviewing repeat mortgage transactions on single-family properties whose mortgages have been purchased or securitized by Fannie Mae or Freddie Mac in January 1975; (1) New York-Jersey City-White Plains Metropolitan Division—see Appendix B for areas included; (2) Rankings are based on annual percentage change for all metro areas containing at least 15,000 transactions over the last 10 years and ranges from 1 to 266; (3) figures based on a weighted average of Census Division estimates using a seasonally adjusted, purchase-only index; all figures are for the period ending December 31, 2015

Source: Federal Housing Finance Agency, House Price Index, February 25, 2016

Median Single-Family Home Prices

Area	2013	2014	2015p	Percent Change 2014 to 2015
MD[1]	465.7	468.2	475.9	1.6
U.S. Average	197.4	208.9	223.9	7.2

Note: Figures are median sales prices of existing single-family homes in thousands of dollars; (p) preliminary; n/a not available; (1) New York-Jersey City-White Plains, NY-NJ Metropolitan Division—see Appendix B for areas included

Source: National Association of Realtors, Median Sales Price of Existing Single-Family Homes for Metropolitan Areas, 4th Quarter 2015

Qualifying Income Based on Median Sales Price of Existing Single-Family Homes

Area	With 5% Down ($)	With 10% Down ($)	With 20% Down ($)
MD[1]	103,341	97,902	87,024
U.S. Average	49,535	46,928	41,714

Note: Figures are preliminary; Qualifying income is based on a mortgage rate of 4.1%. Monthly principal and interest payment is limited to 25% of income; n/a not available; (1) New York-Jersey City-White Plains, NY-NJ Metropolitan Division—see Appendix B for areas included

Source: National Association of Realtors, Qualifying Income Based on Median Sales Price of Existing Single-Family Homes for Metropolitan Areas, 4th Quarter 2015

Median Apartment Condo-Coop Home Prices

Area	2013	2014	2015p	Percent Change 2014 to 2015
MD[1]	237.5	268.9	285.7	6.2
U.S. Average	194.9	204.3	210.7	3.1

Note: Figures are median sales prices of existing apartment condo-coop homes in thousands of dollars; (p) preliminary; n/a not available; (1) New York-Jersey City-White Plains, NY-NJ Metropolitan Division—see Appendix B for areas included

Source: National Association of Realtors, Median Sales Price of Existing Apartment Condo-Coop Homes for Metropolitan Areas, 4th Quarter 2015

Gross Monthly Rent

Area	Under $200	$200 -299	$300 -499	$500 -749	$750 -999	$1,000 -1,499	$1,500 and up	Median ($)
City	0.6	1.5	3.0	1.3	5.7	47.2	40.7	1,412
MSA[1]	1.1	3.9	4.8	7.3	13.5	36.1	33.3	1,246
U.S.	1.5	3.2	7.4	21.0	24.1	26.9	15.9	920

Note: Figures are percentages except for Median; Gross rent is the contract rent plus the estimated average monthly cost of utilities (electricity, gas, and water and sewer) and fuels (oil, coal, kerosene, wood, etc.) if these are paid by the renter (or paid for the renter by someone else); (1) Figures cover the New York-Newark-Jersey City, NY-NJ-PA Metropolitan Statistical Area—see Appendix B for areas included

Source: U.S. Census Bureau, 2010-2014 American Community Survey 5-Year Estimates

Homeownership Rate

Area	2008 (%)	2009 (%)	2010 (%)	2011 (%)	2012 (%)	2013 (%)	2014 (%)	2015 (%)
MSA[1]	52.6	51.7	51.6	50.9	51.5	50.6	50.7	49.9
U.S.	67.8	67.4	66.9	66.1	65.4	65.1	64.5	63.7

Note: (1) Figures cover the New York-Newark-Jersey City, NY-NJ-PA Metropolitan Statistical Area—see Appendix B for areas included
Source: U.S. Census Bureau, Housing Vacancies and Homeownership Annual Statistics: 2015

Year Housing Structure Built

Area	2010 or Later	2000 -2009	1990 -1999	1980 -1989	1970 -1979	1960 -1969	1950 -1959	1940 -1949	Before 1940	Median Year
City	0.9	10.3	26.5	28.8	13.1	8.7	7.8	1.0	3.0	1986
MSA[1]	0.6	7.4	6.0	7.8	10.0	13.9	16.5	9.5	28.4	1957
U.S.	1.0	14.9	13.9	13.8	15.8	11.0	10.8	5.4	13.3	1976

Note: Figures are percentages except for Median Year; (1) Figures cover the New York-Newark-Jersey City, NY-NJ-PA Metropolitan Statistical Area—see Appendix B for areas included
Source: U.S. Census Bureau, 2010-2014 American Community Survey 5-Year Estimates

HEALTH

Health Risk Data

Category	MD[1] (%)	U.S. (%)
Adults aged 18–64 who have any kind of health care coverage	78.3	79.6
Adults who reported being in good or excellent health	81.4	83.1
Adults who are current smokers	14.8	19.6
Adults who are heavy drinkers[2]	4.5	6.1
Adults who are binge drinkers[3]	16.9	16.9
Adults who are overweight (BMI 25.0 - 29.9)	36.8	35.8
Adults who are obese (BMI 30.0 - 99.8)	21.7	27.6
Adults who participated in any physical activities in the past month	74.2	77.1
Adults 50+ who have ever had a sigmoidoscopy or colonoscopy	70.5	67.3
Women aged 40+ who have had a mammogram within the past two years	78.5	74.0
Men aged 40+ who have had a PSA test within the past two years	47.8	45.2
Adults aged 65+ who have had flu shot within the past year	56.0	60.1
Adults who always wear a seatbelt	92.8	93.8

Note: Data as of 2012 unless otherwise noted; (1) Figures cover the New York-Jersey City-White Plains, NY-NJ Metropolitan Division—see Appendix B for areas included; (2) Heavy drinkers are classified as males having more than two drinks per day or females having more than one drink per day; (3) Binge drinkers are classified as males having five or more drinks on one occasion or females having four or more drinks on one occasion
Source: Centers for Disease Control and Prevention, Behaviorial Risk Factor Surveillance System, SMART: Selected Metropolitan/Micropolitan Area Risk Trends, 2012 (Note: the CDC has discontinued this dataset but will be releasing a replacement in mid-2016)

Chronic Health Indicators

Category	MD[1] (%)	U.S. (%)
Adults who have ever been told they had a heart attack	3.6	4.5
Adults who have ever been told they had a stroke	2.6	2.9
Adults who have been told they currently have asthma	8.0	8.9
Adults who have ever been told they have arthritis	22.2	25.7
Adults who have ever been told they have diabetes[2]	9.9	9.7
Adults who have ever been told they had skin cancer	3.3	5.7
Adults who have ever been told they had any other types of cancer	5.1	6.5
Adults who have ever been told they have COPD	5.3	6.2
Adults who have ever been told they have kidney disease	2.6	2.5
Adults who have ever been told they have a form of depression	13.3	18.0

Note: Data as of 2012 unless otherwise noted; (1) Figures cover the New York-Jersey City-White Plains, NY-NJ Metropolitan Division—see Appendix B for areas included; (2) Figures do not include pregnancy-related, borderline, or pre-diabetes
Source: Centers for Disease Control and Prevention, Behaviorial Risk Factor Surveillance System, SMART: Selected Metropolitan/Micropolitan Area Risk Trends, 2012 (Note: the CDC has discontinued this dataset but will be releasing a replacement in mid-2016)

Mortality Rates for the Top 10 Causes of Death in the U.S.

ICD-10[a] Sub-Chapter	ICD-10[a] Code	Age-Adjusted Mortality Rate[1] per 100,000 population	
		County[2]	U.S.
Malignant neoplasms	C00-C97	150.7	163.6
Ischaemic heart diseases	I20-I25	101.6	102.2
Other forms of heart disease	I30-I51	47.1	50.1
Chronic lower respiratory diseases	J40-J47	25.4	41.4
Organic, including symptomatic, mental disorders	F01-F09	28.8	38.5
Cerebrovascular diseases	I60-I69	28.2	36.5
Other external causes of accidental injury	W00-X59	22.0	27.5
Other degenerative diseases of the nervous system	G30-G31	14.7	26.3
Diabetes mellitus	E10-E14	17.6	21.1
Hypertensive diseases	I10-I15	14.4	19.7

Note: (a) ICD-10 = International Classification of Diseases 10th Revision; (1) Mortality rates are a three year average covering 2012-2014; (2) Figures cover Middlesex County.
Source: Centers for Disease Control and Prevention, National Center for Health Statistics. Underlying Cause of Death 1999-2014 on CDC WONDER Online Database, released 2015.

Mortality Rates for Selected Causes of Death

ICD-10[a] Sub-Chapter	ICD-10[a] Code	Age-Adjusted Mortality Rate[1] per 100,000 population	
		County[2]	U.S.
Assault	X85-Y09	1.6	5.1
Diseases of the liver	K70-K76	8.7	13.5
Human immunodeficiency virus (HIV) disease	B20-B24	1.1	2.1
Influenza and pneumonia	J09-J18	10.6	15.2
Intentional self-harm	X60-X84	6.2	12.7
Malnutrition	E40-E46	Unreliable	0.9
Obesity and other hyperalimentation	E65-E68	2.0	1.9
Renal failure	N17-N19	12.0	13.0
Transport accidents	V01-V99	6.3	11.6
Viral hepatitis	B15-B19	1.4	2.1

Note: (a) ICD-10 = International Classification of Diseases 10th Revision; (1) Mortality rates are a three year average covering 2012-2014; (2) Figures cover Middlesex County; Data are Suppressed when the data meet the criteria for confidentiality constraints; Mortality rates are flagged as Unreliable when the rate would be calculated with a numerator of 20 or less.
Source: Centers for Disease Control and Prevention, National Center for Health Statistics. Underlying Cause of Death 1999-2014 on CDC WONDER Online Database, released 2015.

Health Insurance Coverage

Area	With Health Insurance	With Private Health Insurance	With Public Health Insurance	Without Health Insurance	Population Under Age 18 Without Health Insurance
City	92.9	85.1	15.1	7.1	4.6
MSA[1]	87.7	65.3	31.8	12.3	4.4
U.S.	85.8	65.8	31.1	14.2	7.1

Note: Figures are percentages that cover the civilian noninstitutionalized population; (1) Figures cover the New York-Newark-Jersey City, NY-NJ-PA Metropolitan Statistical Area—see Appendix B for areas included
Source: U.S. Census Bureau, 2010-2014 American Community Survey 5-Year Estimates

Number of Medical Professionals

Area	MDs[3]	DOs[3,4]	Dentists	Podiatrists	Chiropractors	Optometrists
County[1] (number)	2,968	153	689	85	194	138
County[1] (rate[2])	357.2	18.4	82.4	10.2	23.2	16.5
U.S. (rate[2])	272.5	20.9	64.7	5.8	25.9	15.2

Note: Data as of 2014 unless noted; (1) Data covers Middlesex County; (2) Rate per 100,000 population; (3) Data as of 2013 and includes all active, non-federal physicians; (4) Doctor of Osteopathic Medicine
Source: U.S. Department of Health and Human Services, Health Resources and Services Administration, Bureau of Health Professions, Area Resource File (ARF) 2014-2015

Best Hospitals

According to *U.S. News,* the New York-Jersey City-White Plains, NY-NJ metro area is home to 11 of the best hospitals in the U.S.: **Hackensack University Medical Center** (5 specialties); **Robert Wood Johnson University Hospital** (1 specialty); **Hospital for Joint Diseases, NYU Langone Medical Center** (2 specialties); **Hospital for Special Surgery** (2 specialties); **Lenox Hill Hospital** (1 specialty); **Memorial Sloan Kettering Cancer Center** (4 specialties); **Mount Sinai Hospital** (9 specialties); **NYU Langone Medical Center** (Honor Roll/12 specialties); **New York Eye and Ear Infirmary** (2 specialties); **New York-Presbyterian University Hospital of Columbia and Cornell** (Honor Roll/15 specialties); **Rusk Rehabilitation at NYU Langone Medical Center** (1 specialty). The hospitals listed were nationally ranked in at least one adult specialty. Only 137 hospitals nationwide were nationally ranked in one or more specialties. Fifteen hospitals in the U.S. made the Honor Roll with high scores in at least six specialties. *U.S. News Online, "America's Best Children's Hospitals 2015-16"*

According to *U.S. News,* the New York-Jersey City-White Plains, NY-NJ metro area is home to seven of the best children's hospitals in the U.S.: **Joseph M. Sanzari Children's Hospital at Hackensack University Medical** (1 specialty); **Bristol-Myers Squibb Children's Hospital at RWJ Univ. Hosp.** (1 specialty); **Children's Hospital at Montefiore (Bronx)** (8 specialties); **Memorial Sloan-Kettering Cancer Center** (1 specialty); **Mount Sinai Kravis Children's Hospital** (7 specialties); **NY-Presbyterian Morgan Stanley-Komansky Children's Hospital** (10 specialties); **Maria Fareri Children's Hospital at Westchester Medical Center** (1 specialty). The hospitals listed were highly ranked in at least one pediatric specialty. Eighty-three children's hospitals in the U.S. were nationally ranked in at least one specialty. Twelve children's hospitals in the U.S. made the Honor Roll with high scores in at least three specialties. *U.S. News Online, "America's Best Children's Hospitals 2015-16"*

EDUCATION

Public School District Statistics

District Name	Schls	Pupils	Pupil/ Teacher Ratio	Minority Pupils[1] (%)	Free Lunch Eligible[2] (%)	IEP[3] (%)
South Brunswick School District	10	8,804	13.5	68.0	8.8	12.4

Note: Table includes school districts with 100 or more students; (1) Percentage of students that are not non-Hispanic white; (2) Percentage of students that are eligible for the free lunch program; (3) Percentage of students that have an Individualized Education Program.

Source: U.S. Department of Education, National Center for Education Statistics, Common Core of Data, Local Education Agency (School District) Universe Survey: School Year 2013-2014; U.S. Department of Education, National Center for Education Statistics, Common Core of Data, Public Elementary/Secondary School Universe Survey: School Year 2013-2014

Highest Level of Education

Area	Less than H.S.	H.S. Diploma	Some College, No Deg.	Associate Degree	Bachelor's Degree	Master's Degree	Prof. School Degree	Doctorate Degree
City	5.7	16.3	11.2	7.2	35.1	17.9	3.2	3.3
MSA[1]	14.9	25.9	15.7	6.6	21.7	10.9	3.0	1.4
U.S.	13.7	28.0	21.2	7.9	18.3	7.8	2.0	1.3

Note: Figures cover persons age 25 and over; (1) Figures cover the New York-Newark-Jersey City, NY-NJ-PA Metropolitan Statistical Area—see Appendix B for areas included

Source: U.S. Census Bureau, 2010-2014 American Community Survey 5-Year Estimates

Educational Attainment by Race

Area	High School Graduate or Higher (%)					Bachelor's Degree or Higher (%)				
	Total	White	Black	Asian	Hisp.[2]	Total	White	Black	Asian	Hisp.[2]
City	94.3	94.9	91.9	94.7	92.1	59.5	47.4	50.1	80.3	38.9
MSA[1]	85.1	89.6	83.0	82.5	67.7	37.0	41.9	22.5	52.7	16.7
U.S.	86.3	88.4	83.2	85.8	64.1	29.3	30.6	19.0	50.9	13.9

Note: Figures shown cover persons 25 years old and over; (1) Figures cover the New York-Newark-Jersey City, NY-NJ-PA Metropolitan Statistical Area—see Appendix B for areas included; (2) People of Hispanic origin can be of any race

Source: U.S. Census Bureau, 2010-2014 American Community Survey 5-Year Estimates

School Enrollment by Grade and Control

Area	Preschool (%)		Kindergarten (%)		Grades 1 - 4 (%)		Grades 5 - 8 (%)		Grades 9 - 12 (%)	
	Public	Private	Public	Private	Public	Private	Public	Private	Public	Private
City	27.0	73.0	82.8	17.2	95.7	4.3	97.2	2.8	93.6	6.4
MSA[1]	50.3	49.7	81.7	18.3	86.3	13.7	86.5	13.5	86.1	13.9
U.S.	57.4	42.6	87.8	12.2	89.8	10.2	89.9	10.1	90.6	9.4

Note: Figures shown cover persons 3 years old and over; (1) Figures cover the New York-Newark-Jersey City, NY-NJ-PA Metropolitan Statistical Area—see Appendix B for areas included
Source: U.S. Census Bureau, 2010-2014 American Community Survey 5-Year Estimates

Average Salaries of Public School Classroom Teachers

Area	2013-14		2014-15		Percent Change 2013-14 to 2014-15	Percent Change 2004-05 to 2014-15
	Dollars	Rank[1]	Dollars	Rank[1]		
New Jersey	68,238	6	69,038	6	1.17	22.2
U.S. Average	56,610	–	57,379	–	1.36	20.8

Note: (1) State rank ranges from 1 to 51 where 1 indicates highest salary.
Source: National Education Association, Rankings & Estimates: Rankings of the States 2014 and Estimates of School Statistics 2015, March 2015

Higher Education

Four-Year Colleges			Two-Year Colleges			Medical Schools[1]	Law Schools[2]	Voc/ Tech[3]
Public	Private Non-profit	Private For-profit	Public	Private Non-profit	Private For-profit			
0	0	0	0	0	0	0	0	0

Note: Figures cover institutions located within the city limits and include main campuses only; (1) includes schools accredited by the Liaison Committee on Medical Education and the American Osteopathic Association's Commission on Osteopathic College Accreditation; (2) includes ABA-accredited schools, schools with provisional ABA accreditation, and state accredited schools; (3) includes all schools with programs that are less than 2 years.
Source: National Center for Education Statistics, Integrated Postsecondary Education System (IPEDS), 2014-15; Association of American Medical Colleges, Member List, March 21, 2016; American Osteopathic Association, Member List, March 21, 2016; Law School Admission Council, Official Guide to ABA-Approved Law Schools Online, March 21, 2016; Wikipedia, List of Medical Schools in the United States, March 21, 2016; Wikipedia, List of Law Schools in the United States, March 21, 2016

According to *U.S. News & World Report,* the New York-Jersey City-White Plains, NY-NJ metro division is home to nine of the best national universities in the U.S.: **Columbia University** (#4 tie); **New York University** (#32); **Yeshiva University** (#52 tie); **Fordham University** (#66 tie); **Rurgers, The State University of New Jersey–New Brunswick ,** (#72 tie); **Stevens Institute of Technology** (#75 tie); **New School** (#127 tie); **St. John's University** (#153 tie); **Pace University** (#180 tie). The indicators used to capture academic quality fall into a number of categories: assessment by administrators at peer institutions; retention of students; faculty resources; student selectivity; financial resources; alumni giving; high school counselor ratings of colleges; and graduation rate. *U.S. News & World Report, "America's Best Colleges 2016"*

According to *U.S. News & World Report,* the New York-Jersey City-White Plains, NY-NJ metro division is home to four of the best liberal arts colleges in the U.S.: **United States Military Academy** (#22); **Barnard College** (#29 tie); **Sarah Lawrence College** (#57 tie); **Purchase College–SUNY** (#171 tie). The indicators used to capture academic quality fall into a number of categories: assessment by administrators at peer institutions; retention of students; faculty resources; student selectivity; financial resources; alumni giving; high school counselor ratings of colleges; and graduation rate. *U.S. News & World Report, "America's Best Colleges 2016"*

According to *U.S. News & World Report,* the New York-Jersey City-White Plains, NY-NJ metro division is home to six of the top 100 law schools in the U.S.: **Columbia University, Law School** (#4 tie); **New York University, School of Law** (#6); **Fordham University, School of Law** (#37); **St. John's University, School of Law** (#74 tie); **Yeshiva University, Benjamin N. Cardozo School of Law** (#74 tie); **Brooklyn Law School** (#97 tie). The rankings are based on a weighted average of 12 measures of quality: peer assessment score; assessment score by lawyers/judges; median LSAT scores; median undergrad GPA; acceptance rate; employment rates for graduates; placement success; bar passage rate; faculty resources; expenditures per student; student/faculty ratio; and library resources. *U.S. News & World Report, "America's Best Graduate Schools, Law, 2017"*

According to *U.S. News & World Report,* the New York-Jersey City-White Plains, NY-NJ metro division is home to five of the top 75 medical schools for research in the U.S.: **Columbia University, College of Physicians and Surgeons** (#7); **New York University, School of Medicine** (#11 tie); **Cornell University, Weill Cornell Medical College** (#18 tie); **Icahn School of Medicine at Mount Sinai** (#21); **Yeshiva University, Albert Einstein College of Medicine** (#39). The rankings are based on a weighted average of 11 measures of quality: quality assessment; peer assessment score; assessment score by residency directors; research activity; total research activity; average research activity per faculty member; student selectivity; median MCAT total score; median undergraduate GPA; acceptance rate; and faculty resources. *U.S. News & World Report, "America's Best Graduate Schools, Medical, 2017"*

According to *U.S. News & World Report,* the New York-Jersey City-White Plains, NY-NJ metro division is home to two of the top 75 business schools in the U.S.: **Columbia University, Columbia Business School** (#10); **New York University, Leonard N. Stern School of Business** (#20). The rankings are based on a weighted average of the following nine measures: quality assessment; peer assessment; recruiter assessment; placement success; mean starting salary and bonus; student selectivity; mean GMAT and GRE scores; mean undergraduate GPA; and acceptance rate. *U.S. News & World Report, "America's Best Graduate Schools, Business, 2017"*

PRESIDENTIAL ELECTION

2012 Presidential Election Results

Area	Obama (%)	Romney (%)	Other (%)
Middlesex County	62.9	36.0	1.1
U.S.	51.0	47.2	1.8

Note: Results may not add to 100% due to rounding
Source: Dave Leip's Atlas of U.S. Presidential Elections

EMPLOYERS

Major Employers

Company Name	Industry
American Express Company	Personal credit institutions
American International Group	Life insurance
Deloitte Consulting	Management consulting services
Hackensack University Medical Center	University
Merrill Lynch and Co	Security brokers & dealers
Mount Sinai Hospital	General medical & surgical hospitals
Mount Sinai School of Medicine	Medical training services
NewYork-Presbyterian Hospital	General medical & surgical hospitals
NYC Health and Hospitals Corp	Psychiatric hospitals
NYU School of Medicine	Offices & clinics of medical doctors
Paramount Comm Acq Corp	Investment holding companies, except banks
Patriarch Partners	Investment offices
Rutgers, The State Univ of NJ	Colleges & universities
Standard Americas	Agencies of foreign banks
The Long Island Rail Road Company	Local & suburban transit
U of Med and Dentistry of NJ	Colleges & universities
UMASS Memorial Health Care	Psychiatrist
United States Postal Service	U.s. postal service
Wellchoice	Health insurance carriers

Note: Companies shown are located within the New York-Newark-Jersey City, NY-NJ-PA Metropolitan Statistical Area.
Source: Hoovers.com; Wikipedia

PUBLIC SAFETY

Crime Rate

Area	All Crimes	Violent Crimes				Property Crimes		
		Murder	Rape[3]	Robbery	Aggrav. Assault	Burglary	Larceny -Theft	Motor Vehicle Theft
City	880.3	0.0	6.7	6.7	8.9	252.8	572.1	33.3
Metro[1]	n/a	3.1	19.3	147.1	264.5	209.7	n/a	85.5
U.S.	2,961.6	4.5	26.4	102.2	232.5	542.5	1,837.3	216.2

Note: Figures are crimes per 100,000 population; (1) Figures cover the New York-Jersey City-White Plains, NY-NJ Metropolitan Division—see Appendix B for areas included; (3) The city and U.S. figures shown were reported using the legacy Uniform Crime Reporting (UCR) definition of rape. The suburban and metro area figures shown are an aggregate total of the data submitted using both the revised and legacy UCR definitions.
Source: FBI Uniform Crime Reports, 2014

Hate Crimes

Area	Number of Quarters Reported	Number of Incidents per Bias Motivation						
		Race	Religion	Sexual Orientation	Ethnicity	Disability	Gender	Gender Identity
City	4	0	2	1	4	0	0	0
U.S.	4	2,568	1,014	1,017	648	84	33	98

Source: Federal Bureau of Investigation, Hate Crime Statistics 2014

Identity Theft Consumer Complaints

Area	Complaints	Complaints per 100,000 Population	Rank[2]
MSA[1]	27,397	136.4	77
U.S.	490,220	152.4	-

Note: (1) Figures cover the New York-Newark-Jersey City, NY-NJ-PA Metropolitan Statistical Area—see Appendix B for areas included; (2) Rank ranges from 1 to 379 where 1 indicates greatest number of identity theft complaints per 100,000 population
Source: Federal Trade Commission, Consumer Sentinel Network Data Book for January–December 2015

Fraud and Other Consumer Complaints

Area	Complaints	Complaints per 100,000 Population	Rank[2]
MSA[1]	74,212	369.3	172
U.S.	2,593,159	806.0	-

Note: (1) Figures cover the New York-Newark-Jersey City, NY-NJ-PA Metropolitan Statistical Area—see Appendix B for areas included; (2) Rank ranges from 1 to 379 where 1 indicates greatest number of identity theft complaints per 100,000 population
Source: Federal Trade Commission, Consumer Sentinel Network Data Book for January–December 2015

RECREATION

Culture

Dance[1]	Theatre[1]	Instrumental Music[1]	Vocal Music[1]	Series and Festivals	Museums and Art Galleries[2]	Zoos and Aquariums[3]
0	0	0	0	0	0	0

Note: (1) Professional perfoming groups; (2) Based on organizations with SIC code 8412; (3) AZA-accredited
Source: The Grey House Performing Arts Directory, 2015-16; Association of Zoos & Aquariums, AZA Member Zoos & Aquariums, March 25, 2016; www.AccuLeads.com, March 29, 2016

Professional Sports Teams

Team Name	League	Year Established
Brooklyn Nets	National Basketball Association (NBA)	1967
New Jersey Devils	National Hockey League (NHL)	1982
New York City FC	Major League Soccer (MLS)	2015
New York Giants	National Football League (NFL)	1925
New York Islanders	National Hockey League (NHL)	1972
New York Jets	National Football League (NFL)	1960
New York Knicks	National Basketball Association (NBA)	1946
New York Mets	Major League Baseball (MLB)	1962
New York Rangers	National Hockey League (NHL)	1926
New York Red Bulls	Major League Soccer (MLS)	1996
New York Yankees	Major League Baseball (MLB)	1903

Note: Includes teams located in the New York-Newark-Jersey City, NY-NJ-PA Metropolitan Statistical Area.
Source: Wikipedia, Major Professional Sports Teams of the United States and Canada, March 24, 2016

CLIMATE

Average and Extreme Temperatures

Temperature	Jan	Feb	Mar	Apr	May	Jun	Jul	Aug	Sep	Oct	Nov	Dec	Yr.
Extreme High (°F)	68	75	85	96	97	101	104	99	99	88	81	72	104
Average High (°F)	38	41	50	61	72	80	85	84	76	65	54	43	62
Average Temp. (°F)	32	34	43	53	63	72	77	76	68	58	48	37	55
Average Low (°F)	26	27	35	44	54	63	68	67	60	49	41	31	47
Extreme Low (°F)	-2	-2	8	21	36	46	53	50	40	29	17	-1	-2

Note: Figures cover the years 1962-1992
Source: National Climatic Data Center, International Station Meteorological Climate Summary, 9/96

Average Precipitation/Snowfall/Humidity

Precip./Humidity	Jan	Feb	Mar	Apr	May	Jun	Jul	Aug	Sep	Oct	Nov	Dec	Yr.
Avg. Precip. (in.)	3.5	3.1	4.0	3.9	4.5	3.8	4.5	4.1	4.1	3.3	4.5	3.8	47.0
Avg. Snowfall (in.)	7	8	4	Tr	Tr	0	0	0	0	Tr	Tr	3	23
Avg. Rel. Hum. 7am (%)	67	67	66	64	72	74	74	76	78	75	72	69	71
Avg. Rel. Hum. 4pm (%)	55	53	50	45	52	55	53	54	56	55	57	58	53

Note: Figures cover the years 1962-1992; Tr = Trace amounts (<0.05 in. of rain; <0.5 in. of snow)
Source: National Climatic Data Center, International Station Meteorological Climate Summary, 9/96

Weather Conditions

Temperature			Daytime Sky			Precipitation		
32°F & below	45°F & below	90°F & above	Clear	Partly cloudy	Cloudy	0.01 inch or more precip.	0.1 inch or more snow/ice	Thunder-storms
75	170	18	85	166	114	120	11	20

Note: Figures are average number of days per year and cover the years 1962-1992
Source: National Climatic Data Center, International Station Meteorological Climate Summary, 9/96

HAZARDOUS WASTE

Superfund Sites

South Brunswick has no sites on the EPA's Superfund Final National Priorities List. There are a total of 1,323 Superfund sites on the list in the U.S. *U.S. Environmental Protection Agency, Final National Priorities List, March 18, 2016*

AIR & WATER QUALITY

Air Quality Trends: Ozone

	1990	1995	2000	2005	2010	2011	2012	2013	2014
MSA[1]	0.101	0.107	0.091	0.092	0.082	0.082	0.080	0.072	0.069

Note: (1) Data covers the New York-Newark-Jersey City, NY-NJ-PA Metropolitan Statistical Area—see Appendix B for areas included. The values shown are the composite ozone concentration averages among trend sites based on the highest fourth daily maximum 8-hour concentration in parts per million. These trends are based on sites having an adequate record of monitoring data during the trend period. Data from exceptional events are included.
Source: U.S. Environmental Protection Agency, Air Quality Monitoring Information, "Air Quality Trends by City, 1990-2014"

Air Quality Index

Area	Percent of Days when Air Quality was...[2]					AQI Statistics[2]	
	Good	Moderate	Unhealthy for Sensitive Groups	Unhealthy	Very Unhealthy	Maximum	Median
MSA[1]	41.4	52.6	6.0	0.0	0.0	142	54

Note: (1) Data covers the New York-Newark-Jersey City, NY-NJ-PA Metropolitan Statistical Area—see Appendix B for areas included; (2) Based on 365 days with AQI data in 2015. Air Quality Index (AQI) is an index for reporting daily air quality. EPA calculates the AQI for five major air pollutants regulated by the Clean Air Act: ground-level ozone, particle pollution (aka particulate matter), carbon monoxide, sulfur dioxide, and nitrogen dioxide. The AQI runs from 0 to 500. The higher the AQI value, the greater the level of air pollution and the greater the health concern. There are six AQI categories: "Good" AQI is between 0 and 50. Air quality is considered satisfactory; "Moderate" AQI is between 51 and 100. Air quality is acceptable; "Unhealthy for Sensitive Groups" When AQI values are between 101 and 150, members of sensitive groups may experience health effects; "Unhealthy" When AQI values are between 151 and 200 everyone may begin to experience health effects; "Very Unhealthy" AQI values between 201 and 300 trigger a health alert; "Hazardous" AQI values over 300 trigger warnings of emergency conditions (not shown).
Source: U.S. Environmental Protection Agency, Air Quality Index Report, 2015

Air Quality Index Pollutants

Area	Percent of Days when AQI Pollutant was...[2]					
	Carbon Monoxide	Nitrogen Dioxide	Ozone	Sulfur Dioxide	Particulate Matter 2.5	Particulate Matter 10
MSA[1]	0.0	14.5	33.2	0.3	52.1	0.0

Note: (1) Data covers the New York-Newark-Jersey City, NY-NJ-PA Metropolitan Statistical Area—see Appendix B for areas included; (2) Based on 365 days with AQI data in 2015. The Air Quality Index (AQI) is an index for reporting daily air quality. EPA calculates the AQI for five major air pollutants regulated by the Clean Air Act: ground-level ozone, particle pollution (also known as particulate matter), carbon monoxide, sulfur dioxide, and nitrogen dioxide. The AQI runs from 0 to 500. The higher the AQI value, the greater the level of air pollution and the greater the health concern.
Source: U.S. Environmental Protection Agency, Air Quality Index Report, 2015

Maximum Air Pollutant Concentrations: Particulate Matter, Ozone, CO and Lead

	Particulate Matter 10 (ug/m^3)	Particulate Matter 2.5 Wtd AM (ug/m^3)	Particulate Matter 2.5 24-Hr (ug/m^3)	Ozone (ppm)	Carbon Monoxide (ppm)	Lead (ug/m^3)
MSA[1] Level	47	10.5	31	0.074	3	n/a
NAAQS[2]	150	15	35	0.075	9	0.15
Met NAAQS[2]	Yes	Yes	Yes	Yes	Yes	n/a

Note: (1) Data covers the New York-Newark-Jersey City, NY-NJ-PA Metropolitan Statistical Area—see Appendix B for areas included; Data from exceptional events are included; (2) National Ambient Air Quality Standards; ppm = parts per million; ug/m^3 = micrograms per cubic meter; n/a not available.
Concentrations: Particulate Matter 10 (coarse particulate)—highest second maximum 24-hour concentration; Particulate Matter 2.5 Wtd AM (fine particulate)—highest weighted annual mean concentration; Particulate Matter 2.5 24-Hour (fine particulate)—highest 98th percentile 24-hour concentration; Ozone—highest fourth daily maximum 8-hour concentration; Carbon Monoxide—highest second maximum non-overlapping 8-hour concentration; Lead—maximum running 3-month average
Source: U.S. Environmental Protection Agency, Air Quality Monitoring Information, "Air Quality Statistics by City, 2014"

Maximum Air Pollutant Concentrations: Nitrogen Dioxide and Sulfur Dioxide

	Nitrogen Dioxide AM (ppb)	Nitrogen Dioxide 1-Hr (ppb)	Sulfur Dioxide AM (ppb)	Sulfur Dioxide 1-Hr (ppb)	Sulfur Dioxide 24-Hr (ppb)
MSA[1] Level	22	70	n/a	15	n/a
NAAQS[2]	53	100	30	75	140
Met NAAQS[2]	Yes	Yes	n/a	Yes	n/a

Note: (1) Data covers the New York-Newark-Jersey City, NY-NJ-PA Metropolitan Statistical Area—see Appendix B for areas included; Data from exceptional events are included; (2) National Ambient Air Quality Standards; ppm = parts per million; ug/m^3 = micrograms per cubic meter; n/a not available.
Concentrations: Nitrogen Dioxide AM—highest arithmetic mean concentration; Nitrogen Dioxide 1-Hr—highest 98th percentile 1-hour daily maximum concentration; Sulfur Dioxide AM—highest annual mean concentration; Sulfur Dioxide 1-Hr—highest 99th percentile 1-hour daily maximum concentration; Sulfur Dioxide 24-Hr—highest second maximum 24-hour concentration
Source: U.S. Environmental Protection Agency, Air Quality Monitoring Information, "Air Quality Statistics by City, 2014"

Drinking Water

Water System Name	Pop. Served	Primary Water Source Type	Violations[1]	
			Health Based	Monitoring/ Reporting
South Brunswick Twp WDI	45,450	Purchased Surface	0	0

Note: (1) Based on violation data from January 1, 2015 to December 31, 2015 (includes unresolved violations from earlier years)
Source: U.S. Environmental Protection Agency, Office of Ground Water and Drinking Water, Safe Drinking Water Information System (based on data extracted April 29, 2016)

West Windsor, New Jersey

Background

West Windsor is centrally located on the eastern border of Mercer County. Princeton lies to the north, East Windsor and Plainsboro to the east, Hamilton and Lawrence to the west, and Robbinsville to the south.

The area was originally inhabited by the Lenni Lenape ("true people") Indians, also known as the Delaware Indians. Captain Thomas Yong of England discovered what is now known as West Windsor, during his exploration of the Delaware Bay area in 1634. In 1682, after many Europeans settled in this area, William Penn signed a treaty with the Lenni Lenape Indians to purchase the land and established West Windsor. In 1737, William Penn's heirs sold the property to the Dutch farming families of Schenk and Covenhoven. In 1751 it became the Town of Windsor. Finally, in 1797 it was officially incorporated.

West Windsor is an area rich in history and culture, with part of the prestigious Princeton University campus located within West Windsor's borders. On October 30, 1938, however, a radio broadcast of H.G. Wells' War of The Worlds, put West Windsor in a different national spotlight. Performed as a Halloween special aired over the CBS Radio network, narrator Orson Welles began telling the story of an alien spacecraft that landed on a farm near Grovers Mill, located in West Windsor. Terrified listeners, thinking that news of an impending Martian attack was real, began fleeing their homes to seek shelter. Today, a monument at Grovers Mill commemorates the broadcast and is a popular tourist stop.

For the more conservative history buff, The Schenk House (circa 1750) shows what life was like in early-day West Windsor. Max Zaitz gifted it to West Windsor Historical Society in 1995, with a mission to preserve and document the farming past of West Windsor. It has housed the Historical Society of West Windsor since its founding in 1983.

The McCarter Theatre Center for the Performing Arts is West Windsor's theatrical gem, built for the Princeton University Triangle Club. Since opening night, on February 21, 1930, it has served as an endless avenue of fine productions with appearances of many well-known companies and actors. "Our Town" had its world premiere there and such actors as Katharine Hepburn and James Stewart have performed at the McCarter in the 1930s. More recently, its diverse program has included such artists as Bill Cosby, James Taylor, Billy Joel, Carol Burnett, Bob Dylan, Bette Midler, George Winston and many more.

Another popular attraction is the "Dinky" which is a one-car train shuttle that runs between Princeton Junction and Princeton stations. It is listed in the history books as the shortest and most expensive per-mile, regularly scheduled train passenger route in the United States, traveling 2.7 miles each way.

Since 1993, West Windsor's government is made up of an elected Mayor and five City Council members. Some of the many educational institutions that serve West Windsor are Princeton University, Mercer Community College, Westminster Choir College of Rider University, Princeton Theological Seminary, as well as many high ranking high schools and elementary schools.

Rankings

Business/Finance Rankings

- The personal finance site NerdWallet analyzed 183 American metropolitan areas with populations over 250,000 and more than 15,000 businesses to rank where entrepreneurs find the most success. Criteria included area economy, annual income, housing cost, unemployment rate, and the success rate of area businesses. Trenton* ranked #27. *www.nerdwallet.com, "Best Places to Start a Business," April 27, 2015*
- The Trenton* metro area appeared on the Milken Institute "2015 Best Performing Cities" list. Rank: #87 out of 200 large metro areas. Criteria: job growth; wage and salary growth; high-tech output growth. *Milken Institute, "Best-Performing Cities 2015," December 2015*

Education Rankings

- The Trenton* metro area was selected as one of America's most innovative cities" by *The Business Insider*. The metro area was ranked #15 out of 20. Criteria: patents per capita. *The Business Insider, "The 20 Most Innovative Cities in the U.S.," February 1, 2013*
- Personal finance website *WalletHub* analyzed the 150 largest U.S. metropolitan statistical areas to determine where the most educated Americans are choosing to settle. Criteria: education quality and attainment gap; education levels; percentage of workers with degrees; public school rankings; quality and size of each metro area's universities. Trenton* was ranked #39 (#1 = most educated city). *www.WalletHub.com, "2015's Most and Least Educated Cities*

Environmental Rankings

- The Trenton* metro area came in at #189 for the relative comfort of its climate on Sperling's list of "chill cities," as measured by the Sperling Heat Index. All 361 metro areas are included. Criteria included daytime high temperatures, nighttime low temperatures, dew point, and relative humidity at the high temperatures. *www.bertsperling.com, "Sperling's Chill Cities," July 18, 2013*
- Sperling's BestPlaces assessed 379 metropolitan areas of the United States for the likelihood of dangerously extreme weather events or earthquakes. In general the Southeast and South-Central regions have the highest risk of weather extremes and earthquakes, while the Pacific Northwest enjoys the lowest risk. Of the least risky metropolitan areas, the Trenton* metro area was ranked #316. *www.bestplaces.net, "Safest Places from Natural Disasters," April 2011*

Health/Fitness Rankings

- The Gallup-Healthways Well-Being Index tracks Americans' optimism about their communities and satisfaction with the metro areas in which they live. At least 300 adult residents in each of 189 U.S. metropolitan areas were asked whether their metro was improving and the Trenton* metro area was one of the ten communities where residents were least optimistic. *www.gallup.com, "City Satisfaction Highest in Fort Collins-Loveland, Colo.," April 11, 2014*
- Gallup-Healthways Well-Being Index researchers asked at least 300 adult residents in each of 189 U.S. metropolitan areas how satisfied they were with the metro area in which they lived. The Trenton* metro area was one of the ten metros where residents were least likely to be satisfied. *www.gallup.com, "City Satisfaction Highest in Fort Collins-Loveland, Colo.," April 11, 2014*
- The Trenton* metro area ranked #147 out of 190 in The Gallup-Healthways Well-Being Index. Criteria: purpose; social well being; financial health; community and physical health. Results are based on telephone interviews with adults, aged 18 and older, living in metropolitan areas in the 50 U.S. states and the District of Columbia. *Gallup-Healthways, "State of American Well-Being," February 23, 2016*

Real Estate Rankings

- The Trenton* metro area was identified as one of the 20 worst housing markets in the U.S. in 2015. The area ranked #1 out of 179 markets. Criteria: year-over-year change of median sales price of existing single-family homes between the 4th quarter of 2014 and the 4th quarter of 2015. *National Association of Realtors®, Median Sales Price of Existing Single-Family Homes for Metropolitan Areas, 4th Quarter 2015*
- The nation's largest metro areas were analyzed in terms of the percentage of households entering some stage of foreclosure in 2015. The Trenton* metro area ranked #2 out of 20 (#1 = highest foreclosure rate). *RealtyTrac, "2015 Year-End U.S. Foreclosure Market Report™," January 12, 2016*

Safety Rankings

- The National Insurance Crime Bureau ranked 380 metro areas in the U.S. in terms of per capita rates of vehicle theft. The Trenton* metro area ranked #122 (#1 = highest rate). Criteria: number of vehicle theft offenses per 100,000 inhabitants in 2014. *National Insurance Crime Bureau, "Hot Spots 2014," June 24, 2015*

Seniors/Retirement Rankings

- From its Best Cities for Successful Aging indexes, the Milken Institute generated rankings for metropolitan areas, weighing data in eight categories—health care, wellness, living arrangements, transportation, financial characteristics, education and employment opportunities, community engagement, and overall livability. The Trenton* metro area was ranked #104 overall in the small metro area category. *Milken Institute, "Best Cities for Successful Aging, 2014"*

Transportation Rankings

- The Trenton* metro area appeared on *Forbes* list of places with the most extreme commutes. The metro area ranked #4 out of 10. Criteria: average travel time; percentage of mega commuters. Mega-commuters travel more than 90 minutes and 50 miles each way to work. *Forbes.com, "The Cities with the Most Extreme Commutes," March 5, 2013*

West Windsor is located within the Trenton, NJ Metropolitan Statistical Area.

Business Environment

CITY FINANCES

City Government Finances

Component	2012 ($000)	2012 ($ per capita)
Total Revenues	41,396	1,523
Total Expenditures	38,291	1,409
Debt Outstanding	45,158	1,662
Cash and Securities[1]	57,032	2,099

Note: (1) Cash and security holdings of a government at the close of its fiscal year, including those of its dependent agencies, utilities, and liquor stores.
Source: U.S Census Bureau, State & Local Government Finances 2012

City Government Revenue by Source

Source	2012 ($000)	2012 ($ per capita)
General Revenue		
From Federal Government	0	0
From State Government	2,329	85
From Local Governments	98	3
Taxes		
Property	25,102	924
Sales and Gross Receipts	802	29
Personal Income	0	0
Corporate Income	0	0
Motor Vehicle License	0	0
Other Taxes	2,482	91
Current Charges	4,746	174
Liquor Store	0	0
Utility	0	0
Employee Retirement	0	0

Source: U.S Census Bureau, State & Local Government Finances 2012

City Government Expenditures by Function

Function	2012 ($000)	2012 ($ per capita)	2012 (%)
General Direct Expenditures			
Air Transportation	0	0	0.0
Corrections	0	0	0.0
Education	0	0	0.0
Employment Security Administration	0	0	0.0
Financial Administration	844	31	2.2
Fire Protection	1,050	38	2.7
General Public Buildings	283	10	0.7
Governmental Administration, Other	985	36	2.5
Health	335	12	0.8
Highways	1,752	64	4.5
Hospitals	0	0	0.0
Housing and Community Development	0	0	0.0
Interest on General Debt	1,415	52	3.6
Judicial and Legal	643	23	1.6
Libraries	0	0	0.0
Parking	598	22	1.5
Parks and Recreation	462	17	1.2
Police Protection	5,928	218	15.4
Public Welfare	0	0	0.0
Sewerage	439	16	1.1
Solid Waste Management	2,233	82	5.8
Veterans' Services	0	0	0.0
Liquor Store	0	0	0.0
Utility	0	0	0.0
Employee Retirement	0	0	0.0

Source: U.S Census Bureau, State & Local Government Finances 2012

DEMOGRAPHICS

Population Growth

Area	1990 Census	2000 Census	2010 Census	2014* Estimate	Population Growth (%) 1990-2014	Population Growth (%) 2010-2014
City	16,021	21,907	27,165	28,108	75.4	3.5
MSA[1]	325,804	350,761	366,513	369,526	13.4	0.8
U.S.	248,709,873	281,421,906	308,745,538	314,107,084	26.3	1.7

Note: (1) Figures cover the Trenton, NJ Metropolitan Statistical Area—see Appendix B for areas included; (*) 2010-2014 5-year estimated population
Source: U.S. Census Bureau, 1990 Census, Census 2000, Census 2010, 2010-2014 American Community Survey 5-Year Estimates

Household Size

Area	Persons in Household (%) One	Two	Three	Four	Five	Six	Seven or More	Average Household Size
City	16.1	31.1	19.4	23.5	7.1	2.1	0.4	2.89
MSA[1]	26.8	31.0	16.7	15.5	6.3	2.1	1.3	2.66
U.S.	27.5	33.5	15.8	13.1	6.0	2.3	1.4	2.64

Note: (1) Figures cover the Trenton, NJ Metropolitan Statistical Area—see Appendix B for areas included
Source: U.S. Census Bureau, 2010-2014 American Community Survey 5-Year Estimates

Race

Area	White Alone[2] (%)	Black Alone[2] (%)	Asian Alone[2] (%)	AIAN[3] Alone[2] (%)	NHOPI[4] Alone[2] (%)	Other Race Alone[2] (%)	Two or More Races (%)
City	50.6	2.4	41.8	0.0	0.0	2.7	2.5
MSA[1]	62.4	20.2	9.6	0.2	0.0	5.6	2.1
U.S.	73.8	12.6	5.0	0.8	0.2	4.7	2.9

Note: (1) Figures cover the Trenton, NJ Metropolitan Statistical Area—see Appendix B for areas included; (2) Alone is defined as not being in combination with one or more other races; (3) American Indian and Alaska Native; (4) Native Hawaiian and Other Pacific Islander
Source: U.S. Census Bureau, 2010-2014 American Community Survey 5-Year Estimates

Hispanic or Latino Origin

Area	Total (%)	Mexican (%)	Puerto Rican (%)	Cuban (%)	Other (%)
City	6.0	0.9	1.2	0.0	3.9
MSA[1]	15.9	1.8	4.8	0.3	9.0
U.S.	16.9	10.8	1.6	0.6	3.8

Note: Persons of Hispanic or Latino origin can be of any race; (1) Figures cover the Trenton, NJ Metropolitan Statistical Area—see Appendix B for areas included
Source: U.S. Census Bureau, 2010-2014 American Community Survey 5-Year Estimates

Ancestry

Area	German	Irish	English	American	Italian	Polish	French[2]	Scottish	Dutch
City	7.1	8.8	5.4	2.4	9.6	4.2	2.4	1.8	0.2
MSA[1]	10.3	12.2	6.0	2.8	13.7	7.0	1.5	1.3	0.9
U.S.	14.9	10.8	8.0	7.1	5.5	3.0	2.7	1.7	1.4

Note: Figures are the percentage of the total population reporting a particular ancestry. The nine most commonly reported ancestries in the U.S. are shown. Figures include multiple ancestries (e.g. if a person reported being Irish and Italian, they were included in both columns); (1) Figures cover the Trenton, NJ Metropolitan Statistical Area—see Appendix B for areas included; (2) Excludes Basque
Source: U.S. Census Bureau, 2010-2014 American Community Survey 5-Year Estimates

Foreign-Born Population

Area	Percent of Population Born in: Any Foreign Country	Asia	Mexico	Europe	Carribean	Central America[2]	South America	Africa	Canada
City	38.2	28.4	0.5	5.5	0.7	0.1	1.5	0.7	0.6
MSA[1]	21.2	6.8	1.0	3.8	2.6	3.3	1.9	1.4	0.3
U.S.	13.1	3.8	3.7	1.5	1.2	1.0	0.9	0.6	0.3

Note: (1) Figures cover the Trenton, NJ Metropolitan Statistical Area—see Appendix B for areas included; (2) Excludes Mexico.
Source: U.S. Census Bureau, 2010-2014 American Community Survey 5-Year Estimates

Marital Status

Area	Never Married	Now Married[2]	Separated	Widowed	Divorced
City	21.8	69.3	0.5	4.0	4.4
MSA[1]	36.5	47.4	2.1	5.8	8.3
U.S.	32.5	48.4	2.2	5.9	10.9

Note: Figures are percentages and cover the population 15 years of age and older; (1) Figures cover the Trenton, NJ Metropolitan Statistical Area—see Appendix B for areas included; (2) Excludes separated
Source: U.S. Census Bureau, 2010-2014 American Community Survey 5-Year Estimates

Disability Status

Area	All Ages	Under 18 Years Old	18 to 64 Years Old	65 Years and Over
City	4.9	3.9	2.8	18.7
MSA[1]	10.0	3.9	8.0	30.9
U.S.	12.3	4.1	10.2	36.3

Note: Figures show percent of the civilian noninstitutionalized population that reported having a disability. Disability status is determined from from six types of difficulty: vision, hearing, cognitive, ambulatory, self-care, and independent living. For children under 5 years old, hearing and vision difficulty are used to determine disability status. For children between the ages of 5 and 14, disability status is determined from hearing, vision, cognitive, ambulatory, and self-care difficulties. For people aged 15 years and older, they are considered to have a disability if they have difficulty with any one of the six difficulty types; (1) Figures cover the Trenton, NJ Metropolitan Statistical Area—see Appendix B for areas included.
Source: U.S. Census Bureau, 2010-2014 American Community Survey 5-Year Estimates

Age

Area	Percent of Population: Under Age 5	Age 5–19	Age 20–34	Age 35–44	Age 45–54	Age 55–64	Age 65–74	Age 75–84	Age 85+	Median Age
City	5.8	23.6	12.8	16.7	17.3	12.2	6.4	3.6	1.5	40.5
MSA[1]	5.9	19.8	20.4	13.6	15.0	12.2	7.0	4.2	2.0	38.3
U.S.	6.4	19.9	20.6	13.0	14.1	12.3	7.6	4.3	1.9	37.4

Note: (1) Figures cover the Trenton, NJ Metropolitan Statistical Area—see Appendix B for areas included
Source: U.S. Census Bureau, 2010-2014 American Community Survey 5-Year Estimates

Gender

Area	Males	Females	Males per 100 Females
City	13,623	14,485	94.0
MSA[1]	180,915	188,611	95.9
U.S.	154,515,159	159,591,925	96.8

Note: (1) Figures cover the Trenton, NJ Metropolitan Statistical Area—see Appendix B for areas included
Source: U.S. Census Bureau, 2010-2014 American Community Survey 5-Year Estimates

Religious Groups by Family

Area	Catholic	Baptist	Non-Den.	Methodist[2]	Lutheran	LDS[3]	Pente-costal	Presby-terian[4]	Muslim[5]	Judaism
MSA[1]	33.1	2.7	2.2	2.1	1.1	0.4	1.2	2.2	1.3	2.1
U.S.	19.1	9.3	4.0	4.0	2.3	2.0	1.9	1.6	0.8	0.7

Note: Figures are the number of adherents as a percentage of the total population; (1) Figures cover the Trenton-Ewing, NJ Metropolitan Statistical Area—see Appendix B for areas included; (2) Methodist/Pietist; (3) Latter Day Saints; (4) Reformed; (5) Figures are estimates
Source: Association of Statisticians of American Religious Bodies, 2010 U.S. Religion Census: Religious Congregations & Membership Study

Religious Groups by Tradition

Area	Catholic	Evangelical Protestant	Mainline Protestant	Other Tradition	Black Protestant	Orthodox
MSA[1]	33.1	4.7	8.0	4.6	1.4	0.5
U.S.	19.1	16.2	7.3	4.3	1.6	0.3

Note: Figures are the number of adherents as a percentage of the total population; (1) Figures cover the Trenton-Ewing, NJ Metropolitan Statistical Area—see Appendix B for areas included
Source: Association of Statisticians of American Religious Bodies, 2010 U.S. Religion Census: Religious Congregations & Membership Study

ECONOMY

Gross Metropolitan Product

Area	2013	2014	2015	2016	Rank[2]
MSA[1]	29.4	30.3	31.5	33.0	82

Note: Figures are in billions of dollars; (1) Figures cover the Trenton, NJ Metropolitan Statistical Area—see Appendix B for areas included; (2) Rank is based on 2016 data and ranges from 1 to 381
Source: The U.S. Conference of Mayors, U.S. Metro Economies: GMP and Employment 2014-2016, June 2015

Economic Growth

Area	2011-13 (%)	2014 (%)	2015 (%)	2016 (%)	Rank[2]
MSA[1]	3.4	1.4	2.4	2.7	135
U.S.	2.2	2.4	2.3	2.9	–

Note: Figures are real gross metropolitan product (GMP) growth rates and represent annual average percent change; (1) Figures cover the Trenton, NJ Metropolitan Statistical Area—see Appendix B for areas included; (2) Rank is based on 2016 data and ranges from 1 to 381
Source: The U.S. Conference of Mayors, U.S. Metro Economies: GMP and Employment 2014-2016, June 2015

Metropolitan Area Exports

Area	2009	2010	2011	2012	2013	2014	Rank[2]
MSA[1]	623.1	678.0	754.0	712.9	879.1	947.1	166

Note: Figures are in millions of dollars; (1) Figures cover the Trenton, NJ Metropolitan Statistical Area—see Appendix B for areas included; (2) Rank is based on 2014 data and ranges from 1 to 385
Source: U.S. Department of Commerce, International Trade Administration, Office of Trade & Industry Information, Manufacturing & Services, data extracted March 10, 2016

Building Permits

Area	Single-Family			Multi-Family			Total		
	2014	2015p	Pct. Chg.	2014	2015p	Pct. Chg.	2014	2015p	Pct. Chg.
City	3	6	100.0	73	94	28.8	76	100	31.6
MSA[1]	239	284	18.8	129	610	372.9	368	894	142.9
U.S.	640,300	690,800	7.9	411,800	487,600	18.4	1,052,100	1,178,400	12.0

Note: (1) Figures cover the Trenton, NJ Metropolitan Statistical Area—see Appendix B for areas included; Figures represent new, privately-owned housing units authorized (unadjusted data); All permit data are based on estimates with imputation; (p) preliminary data.
Source: U.S. Census Bureau, Manufacturing, Mining, and Construction Statistics, Building Permits, 2014, 2015

Bankruptcy Filings

Area	Business Filings 2014	Business Filings 2015	Business Filings % Chg.	Nonbusiness Filings 2014	Nonbusiness Filings 2015	Nonbusiness Filings % Chg.
Mercer County	50	26	-48.0	1,010	940	-6.9
U.S.	26,983	24,735	-8.3	909,812	819,760	-9.9

Note: Business filings include Chapter 7, Chapter 11, Chapter 12, and Chapter 13; Nonbusiness filings include Chapter 7, Chapter 11, and Chapter 13
Source: Administrative Office of the U.S. Courts, Business and Nonbusiness Bankruptcy, County Cases Commenced by Chapter of the Bankruptcy Code, During the 12- Month Period Ending December 31, 2014 and Business and Nonbusiness Bankruptcy, County Cases Commenced by Chapter of the Bankruptcy Code, During the 12- Month Period Ending December 31, 2015

Housing Vacancy Rates

Area	Gross Vacancy Rate[2] (%)			Year-Round Vacancy Rate[3] (%)			Rental Vacancy Rate[4] (%)			Homeowner Vacancy Rate[5] (%)		
	2013	2014	2015	2013	2014	2015	2013	2014	2015	2013	2014	2015
MSA[1]	n/a	n/a	n/a	n/a	n/a	n/a	n/a	n/a	n/a	n/a	n/a	n/a
U.S.	13.6	13.4	12.9	10.7	10.4	10.0	8.3	7.6	7.1	2.0	1.9	1.8

Note: (1) Figures cover the Trenton, NJ Metropolitan Statistical Area—see Appendix B for areas included; (2) The percentage of the total housing inventory that is vacant; (3) The percentage of the housing inventory (excluding seasonal units) that is year-round vacant; (4) The percentage of rental inventory that is vacant for rent; (5) The percentage of homeowner inventory that is vacant for sale; n/a not available
Source: U.S. Census Bureau, Housing Vacancies and Homeownership Annual Statistics: 2015

INCOME

Income

Area	Per Capita ($)	Median Household ($)	Average Household ($)
City	66,221	161,716	191,715
MSA[1]	38,076	74,118	104,437
U.S.	28,555	53,482	74,596

Note: (1) Figures cover the Trenton, NJ Metropolitan Statistical Area—see Appendix B for areas included
Source: U.S. Census Bureau, 2010-2014 American Community Survey 5-Year Estimates

Household Income Distribution

Area	Percent of Households Earning							
	Under $15,000	$15,000 -24,999	$25,000 -34,999	$35,000 -49,999	$50,000 -74,999	$75,000 -99,000	$100,000 -149,999	$150,000 and up
City	3.9	4.4	2.9	5.5	7.7	7.6	15.3	52.6
MSA[1]	9.8	7.6	7.2	10.0	15.9	12.5	16.7	20.4
U.S.	12.5	10.7	10.2	13.5	17.8	12.2	13.0	10.0

Note: (1) Figures cover the Trenton, NJ Metropolitan Statistical Area—see Appendix B for areas included
Source: U.S. Census Bureau, 2010-2014 American Community Survey 5-Year Estimates

Poverty Rate

Area	All Ages	Under 18 Years Old	18 to 64 Years Old	65 Years and Over
City	4.6	5.2	4.1	5.3
MSA[1]	11.7	16.9	10.6	7.6
U.S.	15.6	21.9	14.6	9.4

Note: Figures are percentage of people whose income during the past 12 months was below the poverty level; (1) Figures cover the Trenton, NJ Metropolitan Statistical Area—see Appendix B for areas included
Source: U.S. Census Bureau, 2010-2014 American Community Survey 5-Year Estimates

EMPLOYMENT

Labor Force and Employment

Area	Civilian Labor Force Dec. 2014	Civilian Labor Force Dec. 2015	Civilian Labor Force % Chg.	Workers Employed Dec. 2014	Workers Employed Dec. 2015	Workers Employed % Chg.
City	14,504	14,984	3.3	14,059	14,640	4.1
MSA[1]	195,102	200,573	2.8	185,497	193,151	4.1
U.S.	155,521,000	157,245,000	1.1	147,190,000	149,703,000	1.7

Note: Data is not seasonally adjusted and covers workers 16 years of age and older; (1) Figures cover the Trenton, NJ Metropolitan Statistical Area—see Appendix B for areas included
Source: Bureau of Labor Statistics, Local Area Unemployment Statistics

Unemployment Rate

Area	2015											
	Jan.	Feb.	Mar.	Apr.	May	Jun.	Jul.	Aug.	Sep.	Oct.	Nov.	Dec.
City	3.7	3.4	3.3	3.3	3.6	3.3	3.8	3.1	3.3	3.1	3.0	2.3
MSA[1]	6.0	5.8	5.6	5.3	5.5	4.9	5.7	5.0	4.8	4.4	4.2	3.7
U.S.	6.1	5.8	5.6	5.1	5.3	5.5	5.6	5.2	4.9	4.8	4.8	4.8

Note: Data is not seasonally adjusted and covers workers 16 years of age and older; (1) Figures cover the Trenton, NJ Metropolitan Statistical Area—see Appendix B for areas included
Source: Bureau of Labor Statistics, Local Area Unemployment Statistics

Employment by Occupation

Occupation Classification	City (%)	MSA[1] (%)	U.S. (%)
Management, Business, Science, and Arts	74.8	43.9	36.4
Natural Resources, Construction, and Maintenance	1.7	5.7	9.0
Production, Transportation, and Material Moving	1.8	9.2	12.1
Sales and Office	16.3	23.4	24.4
Service	5.5	17.8	18.2

Note: Figures cover employed civilians 16 years of age and older; (1) Figures cover the Trenton, NJ Metropolitan Statistical Area—see Appendix B for areas included
Source: U.S. Census Bureau, 2010-2014 American Community Survey 5-Year Estimates

Employment by Industry

Sector	MSA[1]		U.S.
	Number of Employees	Percent of Total	Percent of Total
Construction, Mining, and Logging	5,300	1.9	5.0
Education and Health Services	49,400	18.4	15.7
Financial Activities	19,500	7.2	5.7
Government	71,400	26.6	15.5
Information	5,600	2.0	1.9
Leisure and Hospitality	14,500	5.4	10.4
Manufacturing	7,900	2.9	8.6
Other Services	10,200	3.8	3.9
Professional and Business Services	45,500	17.0	13.9
Retail Trade	21,100	7.8	11.3
Transportation, Warehousing, and Utilities	10,000	3.7	3.9
Wholesale Trade	7,100	2.6	4.1

Note: Figures are non-farm employment as of December 2015. Figures are not seasonally adjusted and include workers 16 years of age and older; (1) Figures cover the Trenton, NJ Metropolitan Statistical Area—see Appendix B for areas included; n/a not available
Source: Bureau of Labor Statistics, Current Employment Statistics, Employment, Hours, and Earnings

Occupations with Greatest Projected Employment Growth: 2012 – 2022

Occupation[1]	2012 Employment	2022 Projected Employment	Numeric Employment Change	Percent Employment Change
Home Health Aides	31,140	46,280	15,140	48.6
Combined Food Preparation and Serving Workers, Including Fast Food	59,990	70,180	10,190	17.0
Retail Salespersons	125,690	134,870	9,180	7.3
Registered Nurses	79,840	88,880	9,040	11.3
Nursing Assistants	51,780	60,070	8,290	16.0
Laborers and Freight, Stock, and Material Movers, Hand	75,730	83,360	7,630	10.1
Software Developers, Applications	29,090	35,770	6,680	23.0
Receptionists and Information Clerks	51,160	57,830	6,670	13.0
Customer Service Representatives	63,450	69,530	6,080	9.6
Sales Representatives, Services, All Other	45,510	51,380	5,870	12.9

Note: Projections cover New Jersey; (1) Sorted by numeric employment change
Source: www.projectionscentral.com, State Occupational Projections, 2012–2022 Long-Term Projections

Fastest Growing Occupations: 2012 – 2022

Occupation[1]	2012 Employment	2022 Projected Employment	Numeric Employment Change	Percent Employment Change
Home Health Aides	31,140	46,280	15,140	48.6
Insulation Workers, Mechanical	370	540	170	48.2
Diagnostic Medical Sonographers	2,550	3,550	1,000	39.1
Occupational Therapy Assistants	370	500	130	37.5
Helpers—Electricians	1,310	1,800	490	37.5
Stonemasons	580	780	200	35.4
Physical Therapist Assistants	1,090	1,470	380	34.1
Skincare Specialists	1,050	1,400	350	33.2
Physician Assistants	1,450	1,920	470	32.8
Brickmasons and Blockmasons	2,150	2,830	680	31.7

Note: Projections cover New Jersey; (1) Sorted by percent employment change and excludes occupations with numeric employment change less than 100
Source: www.projectionscentral.com, State Occupational Projections, 2012–2022 Long-Term Projections

Average Wages

Occupation	$/Hr.	Occupation	$/Hr.
Accountants and Auditors	40.66	Maids and Housekeeping Cleaners	14.05
Automotive Mechanics	22.41	Maintenance and Repair Workers	22.36
Bookkeepers	22.33	Marketing Managers	72.75
Carpenters	28.59	Nuclear Medicine Technologists	43.36
Cashiers	10.54	Nurses, Licensed Practical	25.59
Clerks, General Office	19.11	Nurses, Registered	34.21
Clerks, Receptionists/Information	15.63	Nursing Assistants	13.25
Clerks, Shipping/Receiving	18.08	Packers and Packagers, Hand	11.08
Computer Programmers	44.28	Physical Therapists	42.42
Computer Systems Analysts	43.90	Postal Service Mail Carriers	25.12
Computer User Support Specialists	30.43	Real Estate Brokers	n/a
Cooks, Restaurant	12.77	Retail Salespersons	12.42
Dentists	74.92	Sales Reps., Exc. Tech./Scientific	36.67
Electrical Engineers	53.81	Sales Reps., Tech./Scientific	50.45
Electricians	31.56	Secretaries, Exc. Legal/Med./Exec.	22.11
Financial Managers	76.23	Security Guards	18.78
First-Line Supervisors/Managers, Sales	22.37	Surgeons	n/a
Food Preparation Workers	10.56	Teacher Assistants*	13.69
General and Operations Managers	78.08	Teachers, Elementary School*	32.27
Hairdressers/Cosmetologists	15.86	Teachers, Secondary School*	34.54
Internists	110.98	Telemarketers	12.29
Janitors and Cleaners	14.18	Truck Drivers, Heavy/Tractor-Trailer	19.43
Landscaping/Groundskeeping Workers	14.15	Truck Drivers, Light/Delivery Svcs.	17.16
Lawyers	61.95	Waiters and Waitresses	10.54

Note: Wage data covers the Trenton-Ewing, NJ Metropolitan Statistical Area—see Appendix B for areas included; (*) Hourly wages for elementary/secondary school teachers and teacher assistants were calculated by the editors from annual wage data based on a 40 hour work week; n/a not available.
Source: Bureau of Labor Statistics, Metro Area Occupational Employment and Wage Estimates, May 2015

TAXES

State Corporate Income Tax Rates

State	Tax Rate (%)	Income Brackets ($)	Num. of Brackets	Financial Institution Tax Rate (%)[a]	Federal Income Tax Ded.
New Jersey	9.0 (r)	Flat rate	1	9.0 (r)	No

Note: Tax rates as of January 1, 2016; (a) Rates listed are the corporate income tax rate applied to financial institutions or excise taxes based on income. Some states have other taxes based upon the value of deposits or shares; (r) In New Jersey small businesses with annual entire net income under $100,000 pay a tax rate of 7.5%; businesses with income under $50,000 pay 6.5%. The minimum Corporation Business Tax is based on New Jersey gross receipts. It ranges from $500 for a corporation with gross receipts less than $100,000, to $2,000 for a corporation with gross receipts of $1 million or more.
Source: Federation of Tax Administrators, "State Corporate Income Tax Rates, 2016"

State Individual Income Tax Rates

State	Tax Rate (%)	Income Brackets ($)	Num. of Brackets	Personal Exempt. ($)[1]		Fed. Inc. Tax Ded.
				Single	Dependents	
New Jersey	1.4 - 8.97	20,000 - 500,000 (n)	6	1,000	1,500	No

Note: Tax rates as of January 1, 2016; Local- and county-level taxes are not included; n/a not applicable; (1) Married joint filers generally receive double the single exemption; (n) The New Jersey rates reported are for single individuals. For married couples filing jointly, the tax rates also range from 1.4% to 8.97%, with 7 brackets and the same high and low income ranges.
Source: Federation of Tax Administrators, "State Individual Income Tax Rates, 2016"

Various State and Local Tax Rates

State	State and Local Sales and Use (%)	State Sales and Use (%)	Gasoline[1] (¢/gal.)	Cigarette[2] ($/pack)	Spirits[3] ($/gal.)	Wine[4] ($/gal.)	Beer[5] ($/gal.)
New Jersey	7.00	7.0 (e)	14.5	2.70	5.50	0.88	0.12

Note: All tax rates as of January 1, 2016; (1) The American Petroleum Institute has developed a methodology for determining the average tax rate on a gallon of fuel. Rates may include any of the following: excise taxes, environmental fees, storage tank fees, other fees or taxes, general sales tax, and local taxes. In states where gasoline is subject to the general sales tax, or where the fuel tax is based on the average sale price, the average rate determined by API is sensitive to changes in the price of gasoline. States that fully or partially apply general sales taxes to gasoline: CA, CO, GA, IL, IN, MI, NY; (2) The federal excise tax of $1.0066 per pack and local taxes are not included; (3) Rates are those applicable to off-premise sales of 40% alcohol by volume (a.b.v.) distilled spirits in 750ml containers. Local excise taxes are excluded; (4) Rates are those applicable to off-premise sales of 11% a.b.v. non-carbonated wine in 750ml containers; (5) Rates are those applicable to off-premise sales of 4.7% a.b.v. beer in 12 ounce containers; (e) Some counties in New Jersey are not subject to statewide sales tax rates and collect a local rate of 3.5%. Their average local score is represented as a negative.
Source: Tax Foundation, 2016 Facts & Figures: How Does Your State Compare?

State Business Tax Climate Index Rankings

State	Overall Rank	Corporate Tax Rank	Individual Income Tax Rank	Sales Tax Rank	Unemployment Insurance Tax Rank	Property Tax Rank
New Jersey	50	43	48	47	31	50

Note: The index is a measure of how each state's tax laws affect economic performance. The lower the rank, the more favorable a state's tax system is for business. States without a given tax are given a ranking of 1. The scores/rankings for the District of Columbia do not affect other states. The 2016 index represents the tax climate as of July 1, 2015 (the beginning of Fiscal Year 2016).
Source: Tax Foundation, State Business Tax Climate Index 2016

TRANSPORTATION

Means of Transportation to Work

Area	Car/Truck/Van		Public Transportation			Bicycle	Walked	Other Means	Worked at Home
	Drove Alone	Car-pooled	Bus	Subway	Railroad				
City	61.6	6.2	1.2	1.1	19.8	0.6	0.3	0.9	8.3
MSA[1]	70.9	10.3	3.3	0.3	4.2	0.7	3.6	1.5	5.2
U.S.	76.4	9.6	2.6	1.8	0.6	0.6	2.8	1.3	4.4

Note: Figures are percentages and cover workers 16 years of age and older; (1) Figures cover the Trenton, NJ Metropolitan Statistical Area—see Appendix B for areas included
Source: U.S. Census Bureau, 2010-2014 American Community Survey 5-Year Estimates

Travel Time to Work

Area	Less Than 10 Minutes	10 to 19 Minutes	20 to 29 Minutes	30 to 44 Minutes	45 to 59 Minutes	60 to 89 Minutes	90 Minutes or More
City	7.1	23.7	16.1	12.3	6.6	16.7	17.5
MSA[1]	12.2	33.5	20.6	15.1	6.3	6.7	5.5
U.S.	13.3	29.6	21.0	20.2	7.7	5.7	2.6

Note: Figures are percentages and include workers 16 years old and over; (1) Figures cover the Trenton, NJ Metropolitan Statistical Area—see Appendix B for areas included
Source: U.S. Census Bureau, 2010-2014 American Community Survey 5-Year Estimates

Freeway Travel Time Index

Area	1985	1990	1995	2000	2005	2010	2014
Urban Area Rank[1,2]	n/a	n/a	n/a	n/a	n/a	n/a	n/a
Urban Area Index[1]	n/a	n/a	n/a	n/a	n/a	n/a	n/a
Average Index[3]	1.09	1.11	1.14	1.17	1.20	1.19	1.20

Note: Freeway Travel Time Index—the ratio of travel time in the peak period to the travel time at free-flow conditions. For example, a value of 1.30 indicates a 20-minute free-flow trip takes 26 minutes in the peak (20 minutes x 1.30 = 26 minutes); (1) Data for the Trenton, NJ urban area was not available; (2) Rank is based on 101 urban areas (#1 = highest travel time index); (3) Average of 101 urban areas
Source: Texas Transportation Institute, 2015 Urban Mobility Scorecard, August 2015

Freeway Commuter Stress Index

Area	1985	1990	1995	2000	2005	2010	2014
Urban Area Rank[1,2]	n/a	n/a	n/a	n/a	n/a	n/a	n/a
Urban Area Index[1]	n/a	n/a	n/a	n/a	n/a	n/a	n/a
Average Index[3]	1.13	1.16	1.19	1.22	1.25	1.24	1.25

Note: The Freeway Commuter Stress Index is the same as the Freeway Travel Time Index (see table above) except that it includes only the travel in the peak directions during the peak periods; the TTI includes travel in all directions during the peak period. Thus, the CSI is more indicative of the work trip experienced by each commuter on a daily basis. (1) Data for the Trenton, NJ urban area was not available; (2) Rank is based on 101 urban areas (#1 = highest stress index); (3) Average of 101 urban areas
Source: Texas Transportation Institute, 2015 Urban Mobility Scorecard, August 2015

Living Environment

COST OF LIVING

Cost of Living Index

Composite Index	Groceries	Housing	Utilities	Trans-portation	Health Care	Misc. Goods/ Services
121.6	112.6	148.6	111.0	107.3	110.3	112.0

Note: The Cost of Living Index measures regional differences in the cost of consumer goods and services, excluding taxes and non-consumer expenditures, for professional and managerial households in the top income quintile. It is based on more than 50,000 prices covering almost 60 different items for which prices are collected three times a year by chambers of commerce, economic development organizations or university applied economic centers in each participating urban area. The numbers shown should be read as a percentage above or below the national average of 100. For example, a value of 115.4 in the groceries column indicates that grocery prices are 15.4% higher than the national average. Small differences in the index numbers should not be interpreted as significant; Figures cover the Middlesex-Monmouth NJ urban area.
Source: The Council for Community and Economic Research, ACCRA Cost of Living Index, 2015

Grocery Prices

Area[1]	T-Bone Steak ($/pound)	Frying Chicken ($/pound)	Whole Milk ($/half gal.)	Eggs ($/dozen)	Orange Juice ($/64 oz.)	Coffee ($/11.5 oz.)
City[2]	11.40	1.64	2.56	2.58	3.66	4.19
Avg.	10.99	1.43	2.25	2.26	3.58	4.48
Min.	7.16	0.98	1.30	1.35	2.88	2.98
Max.	14.13	2.43	3.85	4.81	6.39	7.56

Note: (1) Values for the local area are compared with the average, minimum and maximum values for all 292 areas in the Cost of Living Index; (2) Figures cover the Middlesex-Monmouth NJ urban area; **T-Bone Steak** *(price per pound);* **Frying Chicken** *(price per pound, whole fryer);* **Whole Milk** *(half gallon carton);* **Eggs** *(price per dozen, Grade A, large);* **Orange Juice** *(64 oz. Tropicana or Florida Natural);* **Coffee** *(11.5 oz. can, vacuum-packed, Maxwell House, Hills Bros, or Folgers).*
Source: The Council for Community and Economic Research, ACCRA Cost of Living Index, 2015

Housing and Utility Costs

Area[1]	New Home Price ($)	Apartment Rent ($/month)	All Electric ($/month)	Part Electric ($/month)	Other Energy ($/month)	Telephone ($/month)
City[2]	467,078	1,393	-	120.17	63.96	32.25
Avg.	312,874	945	179.30	95.07	72.96	28.11
Min.	178,682	479	116.28	43.14	26.46	10.01
Max.	1,472,476	3,984	504.25	189.44	421.11	43.06

Note: (1) Values for the local area are compared with the average, minimum and maximum values for all 292 areas in the Cost of Living Index; (2) Figures cover the Middlesex-Monmouth NJ urban area; **New Home Price** *(2,400 sf living area, 8,000 sf lot, in urban area with full utilities);* **Apartment Rent** *(950 sf 2 bedroom/1.5 or 2 bath, unfurnished, excluding all utilities except water);* **All Electric** *(average monthly cost for an all-electric home);* **Part Electric** *(average monthly cost for a part-electric home);* **Other Energy** *(average monthly cost for natural gas, fuel oil, coal, wood, and any other forms of energy except electricity);* **Telephone** *(price includes basic monthly rate for a private residential line plus additional local usage charges incurred by a family of four).*
Source: The Council for Community and Economic Research, ACCRA Cost of Living Index, 2015

Health Care, Transportation, and Other Costs

Area[1]	Doctor ($/visit)	Dentist ($/visit)	Optometrist ($/visit)	Gasoline ($/gallon)	Beauty Salon ($/visit)	Men's Shirt ($)
City[2]	86.08	115.37	101.58	2.38	33.58	37.72
Avg.	105.15	89.02	99.78	2.38	35.30	28.10
Min.	66.87	56.09	48.53	1.95	18.91	13.38
Max.	182.34	150.36	228.33	4.09	67.91	63.80

Note: (1) Values for the local area are compared with the average, minimum and maximum values for all 292 areas in the Cost of Living Index; (2) Figures cover the Middlesex-Monmouth NJ urban area; **Doctor** *(general practitioners routine exam of an established patient);* **Dentist** *(adult teeth cleaning and periodic oral examination);* **Optometrist** *(full vision eye exam for established adult patient);* **Gasoline** *(one gallon regular unleaded, national brand, including all taxes, cash price at self-service pump if available);* **Beauty Salon** *(woman's shampoo, trim, and blow-dry);* **Men's Shirt** *(cotton/polyester dress shirt, pinpoint weave, long sleeves).*
Source: The Council for Community and Economic Research, ACCRA Cost of Living Index, 2015

HOUSING

House Price Index (HPI)

Area	National Ranking[2]	Quarterly Change (%)	One-Year Change (%)	Five-Year Change (%)
MSA[1]	184	1.20	3.10	-2.00
U.S.[3]	–	1.45	5.76	22.85

Note: The HPI is a weighted repeat sales index. It measures average price changes in repeat sales or refinancings on the same properties. This information is obtained by reviewing repeat mortgage transactions on single-family properties whose mortgages have been purchased or securitized by Fannie Mae or Freddie Mac in January 1975; (1) Trenton Metropolitan Statistical Area—see Appendix B for areas included; (2) Rankings are based on annual percentage change for all metro areas containing at least 15,000 transactions over the last 10 years and ranges from 1 to 266; (3) figures based on a weighted average of Census Division estimates using a seasonally adjusted, purchase-only index; all figures are for the period ending December 31, 2015

Source: Federal Housing Finance Agency, House Price Index, February 25, 2016

Median Single-Family Home Prices

Area	2013	2014	2015p	Percent Change 2014 to 2015
MSA[1]	257.5	267.1	262.3	-1.8
U.S. Average	197.4	208.9	223.9	7.2

Note: Figures are median sales prices of existing single-family homes in thousands of dollars; (p) preliminary; n/a not available; (1) Trenton, NJ Metropolitan Statistical Area—see Appendix B for areas included

Source: National Association of Realtors, Median Sales Price of Existing Single-Family Homes for Metropolitan Areas, 4th Quarter 2015

Qualifying Income Based on Median Sales Price of Existing Single-Family Homes

Area	With 5% Down ($)	With 10% Down ($)	With 20% Down ($)
MSA[1]	50,781	48,108	42,763
U.S. Average	49,535	46,928	41,714

Note: Figures are preliminary; Qualifying income is based on a mortgage rate of 4.1%. Monthly principal and interest payment is limited to 25% of income; n/a not available; (1) Trenton, NJ Metropolitan Statistical Area—see Appendix B for areas included

Source: National Association of Realtors, Qualifying Income Based on Median Sales Price of Existing Single-Family Homes for Metropolitan Areas, 4th Quarter 2015

Median Apartment Condo-Coop Home Prices

Area	2013	2014	2015p	Percent Change 2014 to 2015
MSA[1]	190.8	186.8	198.3	6.2
U.S. Average	194.9	204.3	210.7	3.1

Note: Figures are median sales prices of existing apartment condo-coop homes in thousands of dollars; (p) preliminary; n/a not available; (1) Trenton, NJ Metropolitan Statistical Area—see Appendix B for areas included

Source: National Association of Realtors, Median Sales Price of Existing Apartment Condo-Coop Homes for Metropolitan Areas, 4th Quarter 2015

Gross Monthly Rent

Area	Under $200	$200 -299	$300 -499	$500 -749	$750 -999	$1,000 -1,499	$1,500 and up	Median ($)
City	1.3	2.0	1.5	5.6	7.0	18.2	64.3	1,748
MSA[1]	2.8	4.4	4.0	7.5	17.2	39.6	24.5	1,135
U.S.	1.5	3.2	7.4	21.0	24.1	26.9	15.9	920

Note: Figures are percentages except for Median; Gross rent is the contract rent plus the estimated average monthly cost of utilities (electricity, gas, and water and sewer) and fuels (oil, coal, kerosene, wood, etc.) if these are paid by the renter (or paid for the renter by someone else); (1) Figures cover the Trenton, NJ Metropolitan Statistical Area—see Appendix B for areas included

Source: U.S. Census Bureau, 2010-2014 American Community Survey 5-Year Estimates

Homeownership Rate

Area	2008 (%)	2009 (%)	2010 (%)	2011 (%)	2012 (%)	2013 (%)	2014 (%)	2015 (%)
MSA[1]	n/a	n/a	n/a	n/a	n/a	n/a	n/a	n/a
U.S.	67.8	67.4	66.9	66.1	65.4	65.1	64.5	63.7

Note: (1) Figures cover the Trenton, NJ Metropolitan Statistical Area—see Appendix B for areas included; n/a not available

Source: U.S. Census Bureau, Housing Vacancies and Homeownership Annual Statistics: 2015

Year Housing Structure Built

Area	2010 or Later	2000 -2009	1990 -1999	1980 -1989	1970 -1979	1960 -1969	1950 -1959	1940 -1949	Before 1940	Median Year
City	2.8	21.5	22.5	29.3	8.6	5.5	4.5	1.7	3.5	1989
MSA[1]	0.5	9.2	9.3	11.6	11.0	13.7	15.8	8.0	20.9	1964
U.S.	1.0	14.9	13.9	13.8	15.8	11.0	10.8	5.4	13.3	1976

Note: Figures are percentages except for Median Year; (1) Figures cover the Trenton, NJ Metropolitan Statistical Area—see Appendix B for areas included

Source: U.S. Census Bureau, 2010-2014 American Community Survey 5-Year Estimates

HEALTH

Health Risk Data

Category	MSA[1] (%)	U.S. (%)
Adults aged 18–64 who have any kind of health care coverage	85.2	79.6
Adults who reported being in good or excellent health	86.1	83.1
Adults who are current smokers	15.0	19.6
Adults who are heavy drinkers[2]	3.7	6.1
Adults who are binge drinkers[3]	15.7	16.9
Adults who are overweight (BMI 25.0 - 29.9)	38.8	35.8
Adults who are obese (BMI 30.0 - 99.8)	24.0	27.6
Adults who participated in any physical activities in the past month	78.1	77.1
Adults 50+ who have ever had a sigmoidoscopy or colonoscopy	64.0	67.3
Women aged 40+ who have had a mammogram within the past two years	75.0	74.0
Men aged 40+ who have had a PSA test within the past two years	43.8	45.2
Adults aged 65+ who have had flu shot within the past year	62.7	60.1
Adults who always wear a seatbelt	n/a	93.8

Note: Data as of 2012 unless otherwise noted; n/a not available; (1) Figures cover the Trenton-Ewing, NJ Metropolitan Statistical Area—see Appendix B for areas included; (2) Heavy drinkers are classified as males having more than two drinks per day or females having more than one drink per day; (3) Binge drinkers are classified as males having five or more drinks on one occasion or females having four or more drinks on one occasion

Source: Centers for Disease Control and Prevention, Behaviorial Risk Factor Surveillance System, SMART: Selected Metropolitan/Micropolitan Area Risk Trends, 2012 (Note: the CDC has discontinued this dataset but will be releasing a replacement in mid-2016)

Chronic Health Indicators

Category	MSA[1] (%)	U.S. (%)
Adults who have ever been told they had a heart attack	2.9	4.5
Adults who have ever been told they had a stroke	n/a	2.9
Adults who have been told they currently have asthma	7.4	8.9
Adults who have ever been told they have arthritis	23.1	25.7
Adults who have ever been told they have diabetes[2]	9.9	9.7
Adults who have ever been told they had skin cancer	5.6	5.7
Adults who have ever been told they had any other types of cancer	4.9	6.5
Adults who have ever been told they have COPD	6.5	6.2
Adults who have ever been told they have kidney disease	n/a	2.5
Adults who have ever been told they have a form of depression	16.2	18.0

Note: Data as of 2012 unless otherwise noted; n/a not available; (1) Figures cover the Trenton-Ewing, NJ Metropolitan Statistical Area—see Appendix B for areas included; (2) Figures do not include pregnancy-related, borderline, or pre-diabetes

Source: Centers for Disease Control and Prevention, Behaviorial Risk Factor Surveillance System, SMART: Selected Metropolitan/Micropolitan Area Risk Trends, 2012 (Note: the CDC has discontinued this dataset but will be releasing a replacement in mid-2016)

Mortality Rates for the Top 10 Causes of Death in the U.S.

ICD-10[a] Sub-Chapter	ICD-10[a] Code	Age-Adjusted Mortality Rate[1] per 100,000 population	
		County[2]	U.S.
Malignant neoplasms	C00-C97	155.1	163.6
Ischaemic heart diseases	I20-I25	92.2	102.2
Other forms of heart disease	I30-I51	57.3	50.1
Chronic lower respiratory diseases	J40-J47	27.4	41.4
Organic, including symptomatic, mental disorders	F01-F09	32.1	38.5
Cerebrovascular diseases	I60-I69	32.3	36.5
Other external causes of accidental injury	W00-X59	22.3	27.5
Other degenerative diseases of the nervous system	G30-G31	19.2	26.3
Diabetes mellitus	E10-E14	20.4	21.1
Hypertensive diseases	I10-I15	17.2	19.7

Note: (a) ICD-10 = International Classification of Diseases 10th Revision; (1) Mortality rates are a three year average covering 2012-2014; (2) Figures cover Mercer County.
Source: Centers for Disease Control and Prevention, National Center for Health Statistics. Underlying Cause of Death 1999-2014 on CDC WONDER Online Database, released 2015.

Mortality Rates for Selected Causes of Death

ICD-10[a] Sub-Chapter	ICD-10[a] Code	Age-Adjusted Mortality Rate[1] per 100,000 population	
		County[2]	U.S.
Assault	X85-Y09	8.7	5.1
Diseases of the liver	K70-K76	12.7	13.5
Human immunodeficiency virus (HIV) disease	B20-B24	3.8	2.1
Influenza and pneumonia	J09-J18	10.7	15.2
Intentional self-harm	X60-X84	6.3	12.7
Malnutrition	E40-E46	Unreliable	0.9
Obesity and other hyperalimentation	E65-E68	2.5	1.9
Renal failure	N17-N19	9.6	13.0
Transport accidents	V01-V99	7.8	11.6
Viral hepatitis	B15-B19	2.4	2.1

Note: (a) ICD-10 = International Classification of Diseases 10th Revision; (1) Mortality rates are a three year average covering 2012-2014; (2) Figures cover Mercer County; Data are Suppressed when the data meet the criteria for confidentiality constraints; Mortality rates are flagged as Unreliable when the rate would be calculated with a numerator of 20 or less.
Source: Centers for Disease Control and Prevention, National Center for Health Statistics. Underlying Cause of Death 1999-2014 on CDC WONDER Online Database, released 2015.

Health Insurance Coverage

Area	With Health Insurance	With Private Health Insurance	With Public Health Insurance	Without Health Insurance	Population Under Age 18 Without Health Insurance
City	95.7	90.1	13.6	4.3	2.7
MSA[1]	88.7	73.5	26.1	11.3	4.5
U.S.	85.8	65.8	31.1	14.2	7.1

Note: Figures are percentages that cover the civilian noninstitutionalized population; (1) Figures cover the Trenton, NJ Metropolitan Statistical Area—see Appendix B for areas included
Source: U.S. Census Bureau, 2010-2014 American Community Survey 5-Year Estimates

Number of Medical Professionals

Area	MDs[3]	DOs[3,4]	Dentists	Podiatrists	Chiropractors	Optometrists
County[1] (number)	1,449	94	287	31	95	64
County[1] (rate[2])	390.5	25.3	77.2	8.3	25.6	17.2
U.S. (rate[2])	272.5	20.9	64.7	5.8	25.9	15.2

Note: Data as of 2014 unless noted; (1) Data covers Mercer County; (2) Rate per 100,000 population; (3) Data as of 2013 and includes all active, non-federal physicians; (4) Doctor of Osteopathic Medicine
Source: U.S. Department of Health and Human Services, Health Resources and Services Administration, Bureau of Health Professions, Area Resource File (ARF) 2014-2015

EDUCATION

Public School District Statistics

District Name	Schls	Pupils	Pupil/ Teacher Ratio	Minority Pupils[1] (%)	Free Lunch Eligible[2] (%)	IEP[3] (%)
West Windsor-Plainsboro Reg SD	10	9,724	13.1	71.0	3.7	10.1

Note: Table includes school districts with 100 or more students; (1) Percentage of students that are not non-Hispanic white; (2) Percentage of students that are eligible for the free lunch program; (3) Percentage of students that have an Individualized Education Program.
Source: U.S. Department of Education, National Center for Education Statistics, Common Core of Data, Local Education Agency (School District) Universe Survey: School Year 2013-2014; U.S. Department of Education, National Center for Education Statistics, Common Core of Data, Public Elementary/Secondary School Universe Survey: School Year 2013-2014

Best High Schools

According to *U.S. News,* West Windsor is home to one of the best high schools in the U.S.: **West Windsor-?Plainsboro High School South** (#237); Nearly 20,000 schools were ranked based on their performance on state assessments and how well they prepare students for college. Schools with the highest unrounded College Readiness Index values were numerically ranked from No. 1 to No. 500 and were the gold medal winners. *U.S. News & World Report, "Best High Schools 2015"*

Highest Level of Education

Area	Less than H.S.	H.S. Diploma	Some College, No Deg.	Associate Degree	Bachelor's Degree	Master's Degree	Prof. School Degree	Doctorate Degree
City	2.9	6.6	8.1	2.6	32.4	28.8	8.2	10.4
MSA[1]	12.7	25.6	16.0	5.9	20.7	12.7	2.7	3.7
U.S.	13.7	28.0	21.2	7.9	18.3	7.8	2.0	1.3

Note: Figures cover persons age 25 and over; (1) Figures cover the Trenton, NJ Metropolitan Statistical Area—see Appendix B for areas included
Source: U.S. Census Bureau, 2010-2014 American Community Survey 5-Year Estimates

Educational Attainment by Race

Area	High School Graduate or Higher (%)					Bachelor's Degree or Higher (%)				
	Total	White	Black	Asian	Hisp.[2]	Total	White	Black	Asian	Hisp.[2]
City	97.1	96.8	97.4	97.3	93.3	79.8	75.3	51.5	88.7	51.3
MSA[1]	87.3	89.8	82.8	95.1	61.6	39.8	43.3	17.3	78.6	13.3
U.S.	86.3	88.4	83.2	85.8	64.1	29.3	30.6	19.0	50.9	13.9

Note: Figures shown cover persons 25 years old and over; (1) Figures cover the Trenton, NJ Metropolitan Statistical Area—see Appendix B for areas included; (2) People of Hispanic origin can be of any race
Source: U.S. Census Bureau, 2010-2014 American Community Survey 5-Year Estimates

School Enrollment by Grade and Control

Area	Preschool (%)		Kindergarten (%)		Grades 1 - 4 (%)		Grades 5 - 8 (%)		Grades 9 - 12 (%)	
	Public	Private	Public	Private	Public	Private	Public	Private	Public	Private
City	25.0	75.0	92.5	7.5	90.9	9.1	95.5	4.5	92.5	7.5
MSA[1]	45.3	54.7	88.7	11.3	90.4	9.6	89.8	10.2	88.9	11.1
U.S.	57.4	42.6	87.8	12.2	89.8	10.2	89.9	10.1	90.6	9.4

Note: Figures shown cover persons 3 years old and over; (1) Figures cover the Trenton, NJ Metropolitan Statistical Area—see Appendix B for areas included
Source: U.S. Census Bureau, 2010-2014 American Community Survey 5-Year Estimates

Average Salaries of Public School Classroom Teachers

Area	2013-14		2014-15		Percent Change 2013-14 to 2014-15	Percent Change 2004-05 to 2014-15
	Dollars	Rank[1]	Dollars	Rank[1]		
New Jersey	68,238	6	69,038	6	1.17	22.2
U.S. Average	56,610	–	57,379	–	1.36	20.8

Note: (1) State rank ranges from 1 to 51 where 1 indicates highest salary.
Source: National Education Association, Rankings & Estimates: Rankings of the States 2014 and Estimates of School Statistics 2015, March 2015

Higher Education

Four-Year Colleges			Two-Year Colleges			Medical Schools[1]	Law Schools[2]	Voc/ Tech[3]
Public	Private Non-profit	Private For-profit	Public	Private Non-profit	Private For-profit			
0	0	0	1	0	0	0	0	0

Note: Figures cover institutions located within the city limits and include main campuses only; (1) includes schools accredited by the Liaison Committee on Medical Education and the American Osteopathic Association's Commission on Osteopathic College Accreditation; (2) includes ABA-accredited schools, schools with provisional ABA accreditation, and state accredited schools; (3) includes all schools with programs that are less than 2 years.
Source: National Center for Education Statistics, Integrated Postsecondary Education System (IPEDS), 2014-15; Association of American Medical Colleges, Member List, March 21, 2016; American Osteopathic Association, Member List, March 21, 2016; Law School Admission Council, Official Guide to ABA-Approved Law Schools Online, March 21, 2016; Wikipedia, List of Medical Schools in the United States, March 21, 2016; Wikipedia, List of Law Schools in the United States, March 21, 2016

According to *U.S. News & World Report,* the Trenton, NJ metro area is home to one of the best national universities in the U.S.: **Princeton University** (#1). The indicators used to capture academic quality fall into a number of categories: assessment by administrators at peer institutions; retention of students; faculty resources; student selectivity; financial resources; alumni giving; high school counselor ratings of colleges; and graduation rate. *U.S. News & World Report, "America's Best Colleges 2016"*

PRESIDENTIAL ELECTION

2012 Presidential Election Results

Area	Obama (%)	Romney (%)	Other (%)
Mercer County	67.8	31.0	1.2
U.S.	51.0	47.2	1.8

Note: Results may not add to 100% due to rounding
Source: Dave Leip's Atlas of U.S. Presidential Elections

EMPLOYERS

Major Employers

Company Name	Industry
Bayada Nurses	Healthcare
Board of Education	Education
Capital Health Systems	Healthcare
Cenlar Capital Corp.	Mortgage loan servicing
College of NJ	Education
Congoleum Corp.	Manufacturing
Covance	Drug development
Horizon NJ Health	Healthcare
Hough Petroleum Corp.	Motor fuels and lubricants
New Jersey Ed. Assn.	Education
New Jersey Housing & Mortgage Finance Assn.	Financial services
New Jersey Re-Insurance Co.	Auto insurance
Novo Nordisk	Pharmaceuticals
Sandoz, Inc.	Pharmaceuticals
St Francis Medical Center	Healthcare
The Crest Group	Real estate
The Hibbert Company	Global fulfillment and distribution
The Times of Trenton Publishing Corp.	Publisher

Note: Companies shown are located within the Trenton, NJ Metropolitan Statistical Area.
Source: Hoovers.com; Wikipedia

PUBLIC SAFETY

Crime Rate

Area	All Crimes	Violent Crimes				Property Crimes		
		Murder	Rape[3]	Robbery	Aggrav. Assault	Burglary	Larceny -Theft	Motor Vehicle Theft
City	1,338.1	0.0	7.0	17.4	17.4	160.3	1,111.6	24.4
Metro[1]	2,163.3	8.6	11.3	150.2	177.1	475.5	1,172.2	168.5
U.S.	2,961.6	4.5	26.4	102.2	232.5	542.5	1,837.3	216.2

Note: Figures are crimes per 100,000 population; (1) Figures cover the Trenton, NJ Metropolitan Statistical Area—see Appendix B for areas included; (3) The city and U.S. figures shown were reported using the legacy Uniform Crime Reporting (UCR) definition of rape. The suburban and metro area figures shown are an aggregate total of the data submitted using both the revised and legacy UCR definitions.
Source: FBI Uniform Crime Reports, 2014

Hate Crimes

Area	Number of Quarters Reported	Number of Incidents per Bias Motivation						
		Race	Religion	Sexual Orientation	Ethnicity	Disability	Gender	Gender Identity
City	4	0	0	0	0	0	0	0
U.S.	4	2,568	1,014	1,017	648	84	33	98

Source: Federal Bureau of Investigation, Hate Crime Statistics 2014

Identity Theft Consumer Complaints

Area	Complaints	Complaints per 100,000 Population	Rank[2]
MSA[1]	519	139.7	69
U.S.	490,220	152.4	-

Note: (1) Figures cover the Trenton, NJ Metropolitan Statistical Area—see Appendix B for areas included; (2) Rank ranges from 1 to 379 where 1 indicates greatest number of identity theft complaints per 100,000 population
Source: Federal Trade Commission, Consumer Sentinel Network Data Book for January–December 2015

Fraud and Other Consumer Complaints

Area	Complaints	Complaints per 100,000 Population	Rank[2]
MSA[1]	1,701	457.8	41
U.S.	2,593,159	806.0	-

Note: (1) Figures cover the Trenton, NJ Metropolitan Statistical Area—see Appendix B for areas included; (2) Rank ranges from 1 to 379 where 1 indicates greatest number of identity theft complaints per 100,000 population
Source: Federal Trade Commission, Consumer Sentinel Network Data Book for January–December 2015

RECREATION

Culture

Dance[1]	Theatre[1]	Instrumental Music[1]	Vocal Music[1]	Series and Festivals	Museums and Art Galleries[2]	Zoos and Aquariums[3]
0	0	0	0	0	0	0

Note: (1) Professional perfoming groups; (2) Based on organizations with SIC code 8412; (3) AZA-accredited
Source: The Grey House Performing Arts Directory, 2015-16; Association of Zoos & Aquariums, AZA Member Zoos & Aquariums, March 25, 2016; www.AccuLeads.com, March 29, 2016

Professional Sports Teams

Team Name	League	Year Established
No teams are located in the metro area		

Source: Wikipedia, Major Professional Sports Teams of the United States and Canada, March 24, 2016

CLIMATE

Average and Extreme Temperatures

Temperature	Jan	Feb	Mar	Apr	May	Jun	Jul	Aug	Sep	Oct	Nov	Dec	Yr.
Extreme High (°F)	74	76	89	94	98	102	105	103	105	93	85	72	105
Average High (°F)	38	41	50	61	72	81	86	84	77	66	54	42	63
Average Temp. (°F)	32	33	42	52	63	72	77	76	68	57	47	36	55
Average Low (°F)	24	25	33	43	53	62	68	67	59	48	39	28	46
Extreme Low (°F)	-8	-7	6	16	33	41	52	45	35	25	15	-1	-8

Note: Figures cover the years 1935-1995
Source: National Climatic Data Center, International Station Meteorological Climate Summary, 9/96

Average Precipitation/Snowfall/Humidity

Precip./Humidity	Jan	Feb	Mar	Apr	May	Jun	Jul	Aug	Sep	Oct	Nov	Dec	Yr.
Avg. Precip. (in.)	3.4	3.0	4.0	3.7	3.9	3.3	4.2	4.1	3.6	3.0	3.8	3.4	43.5
Avg. Snowfall (in.)	8	8	5	1	Tr	0	0	0	0	Tr	1	5	27
Avg. Rel. Hum. 7am (%)	73	71	69	67	70	71	72	76	79	78	76	74	73
Avg. Rel. Hum. 4pm (%)	58	54	51	48	51	51	52	54	55	53	57	59	54

Note: Figures cover the years 1935-1995; Tr = Trace amounts (<0.05 in. of rain; <0.5 in. of snow)
Source: National Climatic Data Center, International Station Meteorological Climate Summary, 9/96

Weather Conditions

Temperature			Daytime Sky			Precipitation		
5°F & below	32°F & below	90°F & above	Clear	Partly cloudy	Cloudy	0.01 inch or more precip.	0.1 inch or more snow/ice	Thunderstorms
2	90	24	80	146	139	122	16	46

Note: Figures are average number of days per year and cover the years 1935-1995
Source: National Climatic Data Center, International Station Meteorological Climate Summary, 9/96

HAZARDOUS WASTE

Superfund Sites

West Windsor has no sites on the EPA's Superfund Final National Priorities List. There are a total of 1,323 Superfund sites on the list in the U.S. *U.S. Environmental Protection Agency, Final National Priorities List, March 18, 2016*

AIR & WATER QUALITY

Air Quality Trends: Ozone

	1990	1995	2000	2005	2010	2011	2012	2013	2014
MSA[1]	0.105	0.107	0.099	0.089	0.086	0.079	0.080	0.070	0.071

Note: (1) Data covers the Trenton, NJ Metropolitan Statistical Area—see Appendix B for areas included. The values shown are the composite ozone concentration averages among trend sites based on the highest fourth daily maximum 8-hour concentration in parts per million. These trends are based on sites having an adequate record of monitoring data during the trend period. Data from exceptional events are included.
Source: U.S. Environmental Protection Agency, Air Quality Monitoring Information, "Air Quality Trends by City, 1990-2014"

Air Quality Index

Area	Percent of Days when Air Quality was...[2]					AQI Statistics[2]	
	Good	Moderate	Unhealthy for Sensitive Groups	Unhealthy	Very Unhealthy	Maximum	Median
MSA[1]	76.2	22.7	1.1	0.0	0.0	122	37

Note: (1) Data covers the Trenton, NJ Metropolitan Statistical Area—see Appendix B for areas included; (2) Based on 365 days with AQI data in 2015. Air Quality Index (AQI) is an index for reporting daily air quality. EPA calculates the AQI for five major air pollutants regulated by the Clean Air Act: ground-level ozone, particle pollution (aka particulate matter), carbon monoxide, sulfur dioxide, and nitrogen dioxide. The AQI runs from 0 to 500. The higher the AQI value, the greater the level of air pollution and the greater the health concern. There are six AQI categories: "Good" AQI is between 0 and 50. Air quality is considered satisfactory; "Moderate" AQI is between 51 and 100. Air quality is acceptable; "Unhealthy for Sensitive Groups" When AQI values are between 101 and 150, members of sensitive groups may experience health effects; "Unhealthy" When AQI values are between 151 and 200 everyone may begin to experience health effects; "Very Unhealthy" AQI values between 201 and 300 trigger a health alert; "Hazardous" AQI values over 300 trigger warnings of emergency conditions (not shown).
Source: U.S. Environmental Protection Agency, Air Quality Index Report, 2015

Air Quality Index Pollutants

Area	Percent of Days when AQI Pollutant was...[2]					
	Carbon Monoxide	Nitrogen Dioxide	Ozone	Sulfur Dioxide	Particulate Matter 2.5	Particulate Matter 10
MSA[1]	0.0	0.0	75.3	0.0	24.7	0.0

Note: (1) Data covers the Trenton, NJ Metropolitan Statistical Area—see Appendix B for areas included; (2) Based on 365 days with AQI data in 2015. The Air Quality Index (AQI) is an index for reporting daily air quality. EPA calculates the AQI for five major air pollutants regulated by the Clean Air Act: ground-level ozone, particle pollution (also known as particulate matter), carbon monoxide, sulfur dioxide, and nitrogen dioxide. The AQI runs from 0 to 500. The higher the AQI value, the greater the level of air pollution and the greater the health concern.
Source: U.S. Environmental Protection Agency, Air Quality Index Report, 2015

Maximum Air Pollutant Concentrations: Particulate Matter, Ozone, CO and Lead

	Particulate Matter 10 (ug/m³)	Particulate Matter 2.5 Wtd AM (ug/m³)	Particulate Matter 2.5 24-Hr (ug/m³)	Ozone (ppm)	Carbon Monoxide (ppm)	Lead (ug/m³)
MSA[1] Level	n/a	8.7	24	0.071	n/a	n/a
NAAQS[2]	150	15	35	0.075	9	0.15
Met NAAQS[2]	n/a	Yes	Yes	Yes	n/a	n/a

Note: (1) Data covers the Trenton, NJ Metropolitan Statistical Area—see Appendix B for areas included; Data from exceptional events are included; (2) National Ambient Air Quality Standards; ppm = parts per million; ug/m³ = micrograms per cubic meter; n/a not available.
Concentrations: Particulate Matter 10 (coarse particulate)—highest second maximum 24-hour concentration; Particulate Matter 2.5 Wtd AM (fine particulate)—highest weighted annual mean concentration; Particulate Matter 2.5 24-Hour (fine particulate)—highest 98th percentile 24-hour concentration; Ozone—highest fourth daily maximum 8-hour concentration; Carbon Monoxide—highest second maximum non-overlapping 8-hour concentration; Lead—maximum running 3-month average
Source: U.S. Environmental Protection Agency, Air Quality Monitoring Information, "Air Quality Statistics by City, 2014"

Maximum Air Pollutant Concentrations: Nitrogen Dioxide and Sulfur Dioxide

	Nitrogen Dioxide AM (ppb)	Nitrogen Dioxide 1-Hr (ppb)	Sulfur Dioxide AM (ppb)	Sulfur Dioxide 1-Hr (ppb)	Sulfur Dioxide 24-Hr (ppb)
MSA[1] Level	n/a	n/a	n/a	n/a	n/a
NAAQS[2]	53	100	30	75	140
Met NAAQS[2]	n/a	n/a	n/a	n/a	n/a

Note: (1) Data covers the Trenton, NJ Metropolitan Statistical Area—see Appendix B for areas included; Data from exceptional events are included; (2) National Ambient Air Quality Standards; ppm = parts per million; ug/m³ = micrograms per cubic meter; n/a not available.
Concentrations: Nitrogen Dioxide AM—highest arithmetic mean concentration; Nitrogen Dioxide 1-Hr—highest 98th percentile 1-hour daily maximum concentration; Sulfur Dioxide AM—highest annual mean concentration; Sulfur Dioxide 1-Hr—highest 99th percentile 1-hour daily maximum concentration; Sulfur Dioxide 24-Hr—highest second maximum 24-hour concentration
Source: U.S. Environmental Protection Agency, Air Quality Monitoring Information, "Air Quality Statistics by City, 2014"

Drinking Water

Water System Name	Pop. Served	Primary Water Source Type	Violations[1]	
			Health Based	Monitoring/ Reporting
NJ American Water Co.	n/a	n/a	n/a	n/a

Note: (1) Based on violation data from January 1, 2015 to December 31, 2015 (includes unresolved violations from earlier years); n/a not available
Source: U.S. Environmental Protection Agency, Office of Ground Water and Drinking Water, Safe Drinking Water Information System (based on data extracted April 29, 2016)

Appendix A: Comparative Statistics

Population Growth: City

Area	1990 Census	2000 Census	2010 Census	2014* Estimate	Population Growth (%) 1990-2014	Population Growth (%) 2010-2014
Aliso Viejo, CA	8,963	40,166	47,823	49,437	451.6	3.4
Allen, TX	19,208	43,554	84,246	89,845	367.7	6.6
Alpharetta, GA	15,338	34,854	57,551	60,903	297.1	5.8
Ankeny, IA	19,065	27,117	45,582	49,488	159.6	8.6
Apex, NC	7,092	20,212	37,476	40,631	472.9	8.4
Ballwin, MO	29,423	31,283	30,404	30,478	3.6	0.2
Beavercreek, OH	33,946	37,984	45,193	45,738	34.7	1.2
Bella Vista, AR	9,091	16,582	26,461	27,273	200.0	3.1
Bernards, NJ	17,199	24,575	26,652	26,849	56.1	0.7
Bethlehem, NY	27,552	31,304	33,656	34,163	24.0	1.5
Bloomfield, MI	42,137	43,021	41,070	41,571	-1.3	1.2
Bowie, MD	39,831	50,269	54,727	56,335	41.4	2.9
Bozeman, MT	23,499	27,509	37,280	39,123	66.5	4.9
Brentwood, TN	17,287	23,445	37,060	39,059	125.9	5.4
Broomfield, CO	24,789	38,272	55,889	59,027	138.1	5.6
Carmel, IN	27,705	37,733	79,191	83,474	201.3	5.4
Cedar Park, TX	9,798	26,049	48,937	58,088	492.9	18.7
Cheshire, CT	25,684	28,543	29,261	29,272	14.0	0.0
Chesterfield, MO	41,843	46,802	47,484	47,651	13.9	0.4
Collierville, TN	15,439	31,872	43,965	46,780	203.0	6.4
Coppell, TX	16,881	35,958	38,659	40,021	137.1	3.5
Cornelius, NC	5,815	11,969	24,866	26,246	351.3	5.5
Cranberry, PA	14,764	23,625	28,098	29,023	96.6	3.3
Cupertino, CA	44,842	50,546	58,302	59,787	33.3	2.5
Danville, CA	32,328	41,715	42,039	42,891	32.7	2.0
Draper, UT	7,250	25,220	42,274	44,656	515.9	5.6
Dublin, OH	17,231	31,392	41,751	42,378	145.9	1.5
Eastchester, NY	30,867	31,318	32,363	32,737	6.1	1.2
Eden Prairie, MN	39,311	54,901	60,797	62,096	58.0	2.1
Edmond, OK	52,239	68,315	81,405	85,084	62.9	4.5
Evesham, NJ	35,309	42,275	45,538	45,669	29.3	0.3
Fishers, IN	12,437	37,835	76,794	81,060	551.8	5.6
Flower Mound, TX	15,788	50,702	64,669	67,630	328.4	4.6
Folsom, CA	29,701	51,884	72,203	73,334	146.9	1.6
Foster City, CA	28,176	28,803	30,567	31,809	12.9	4.1
Franklin, TN	22,236	41,842	62,487	66,596	199.5	6.6
Friendswood, TX	23,020	29,037	35,805	37,001	60.7	3.3
Germantown, TN	33,414	37,348	38,844	39,207	17.3	0.9
Glastonbury, CT	27,901	31,876	34,427	34,661	24.2	0.7
Grand Blanc, MI	25,180	29,827	37,508	37,019	47.0	-1.3
Guilderland, NY	28,877	32,688	35,303	35,511	23.0	0.6
Hampden, PA	20,384	24,135	28,044	28,291	38.8	0.9
Holly Springs, NC	2,351	9,192	24,661	27,339	1,062.9	10.9
Huntersville, NC	9,131	24,960	46,773	49,279	439.7	5.4
Independence, KY	10,645	14,982	24,757	25,638	140.8	3.6
Johns Creek, GA	n/a	n/a	76,728	80,979	n/a	5.5
Keller, TX	13,683	27,345	39,627	41,913	206.3	5.8
Kirkland, WA	39,914	45,054	48,787	83,320	108.7	70.8
Lafayette, CO	15,609	23,197	24,453	25,812	65.4	5.6
Lake Oswego, OR	32,216	35,278	36,619	37,310	15.8	1.9
League City, TX	30,247	45,444	83,560	88,979	194.2	6.5
Leawood, KS	19,683	27,656	31,867	32,842	66.9	3.1
Lee's Summit, MO	46,585	70,700	91,364	92,813	99.2	1.6
Leesburg, VA	16,240	28,311	42,616	46,211	184.6	8.4
Lehi, UT	9,766	19,028	47,407	51,982	432.3	9.7
Lenexa, KS	34,268	40,238	48,190	49,573	44.7	2.9
Lexington, MA	28,974	30,355	31,394	32,306	11.5	2.9
Los Altos, CA	26,400	27,693	28,976	29,762	12.7	2.7
Lower Makefield, PA	25,083	32,681	32,559	32,622	30.1	0.2
Madison, AL	16,813	29,329	42,938	44,866	166.9	4.5
Mamaroneck, NY	27,706	28,967	29,156	29,501	6.5	1.2
Manheim, PA	28,823	33,697	38,133	38,770	34.5	1.7
Manlius, NY	30,656	31,872	32,370	32,391	5.7	0.1
Maple Grove, MN	38,868	50,365	61,567	64,364	65.6	4.5
Marion, IA	21,274	26,294	34,768	35,809	68.3	3.0
Marlboro, NJ	27,974	36,398	40,191	40,370	44.3	0.4
Mason, OH	12,046	22,016	30,712	31,289	159.7	1.9
McCandless, PA	28,781	29,022	28,457	28,788	0.0	1.2

Table continued on next page.

Area	1990 Census	2000 Census	2010 Census	2014* Estimate	Population Growth (%) 1990-2014	2010-2014
Menomonee Falls, WI	26,840	32,647	35,626	35,828	33.5	0.6
Meridian, ID	12,266	34,919	75,092	81,025	560.6	7.9
Merrimack, NH	22,156	25,119	25,494	25,563	15.4	0.3
Mount Lebanon, PA	33,655	33,017	33,137	33,085	-1.7	-0.2
Mount Pleasant, SC	33,294	47,609	67,843	72,379	117.4	6.7
Needham, MA	27,557	28,911	28,886	29,540	7.2	2.3
Newtown, CT	20,779	25,031	27,560	27,960	34.6	1.5
Northbrook, IL	33,020	33,435	33,170	33,396	1.1	0.7
Northville, MI	17,300	21,036	28,497	28,682	65.8	0.6
Novi, MI	33,103	47,386	55,224	56,887	71.8	3.0
O'Fallon, IL	17,169	21,910	28,281	29,100	69.5	2.9
O'Fallon, MO	21,851	46,169	79,329	81,978	275.2	3.3
Orchard Park, NY	24,632	27,637	29,054	29,351	19.2	1.0
Oviedo, FL	11,588	26,316	33,342	35,602	207.2	6.8
Parker, CO	5,562	23,558	45,297	47,515	754.3	4.9
Parkland, FL	4,201	13,835	23,962	25,895	516.4	8.1
Peachtree City, GA	18,908	31,580	34,364	34,701	83.5	1.0
Pflugerville, TX	5,830	16,335	46,936	52,138	794.3	11.1
Plainfield, IL	6,409	13,038	39,581	40,641	534.1	2.7
Princeton, NJ	12,064	14,203	12,307	28,940	139.9	135.2
Queen Creek, AZ	2,860	4,316	26,361	28,529	897.5	8.2
Rancho Palos Verdes, CA	42,293	41,145	41,643	42,282	0.0	1.5
Redmond, WA	36,936	45,256	54,144	56,704	53.5	4.7
Richland, WA	33,058	38,708	48,058	51,116	54.6	6.4
Ridgefield, CT	20,919	23,643	24,638	25,025	19.6	1.6
Ridgewood, NJ	24,245	24,936	24,958	25,270	4.2	1.3
Rio Rancho, NM	32,674	51,765	87,521	90,627	177.4	3.5
Sahuarita, AZ	1,752	3,242	25,259	26,441	1,409.2	4.7
Sammamish, WA	23,254	34,104	45,780	49,077	111.0	7.2
San Ramon, CA	35,463	44,722	72,148	73,826	108.2	2.3
Saratoga, CA	28,177	29,843	29,926	30,627	8.7	2.3
Schertz, TX	10,628	18,694	31,465	35,093	230.2	11.5
Shrewsbury, MA	24,146	31,640	35,608	36,114	49.6	1.4
South Brunswick, NJ	25,792	37,734	43,417	44,355	72.0	2.2
South Jordan, UT	12,183	29,437	50,418	56,528	364.0	12.1
South Kingstown, RI	24,631	27,921	30,639	30,546	24.0	-0.3
South Windsor, CT	22,090	24,412	25,709	25,795	16.8	0.3
Southlake, TX	7,155	21,519	26,575	27,755	287.9	4.4
Spring Hill, TN	2,362	7,715	29,036	31,467	1,232.2	8.4
Stow, OH	27,702	32,139	34,837	34,741	25.4	-0.3
Sugar Land, TX	44,150	63,328	78,817	82,420	86.7	4.6
Sun Prairie, WI	15,836	20,369	29,364	30,601	93.2	4.2
Syracuse, UT	4,977	9,398	24,331	25,374	409.8	4.3
Tredyffrin, PA	28,021	29,062	29,332	29,455	5.1	0.4
Upper Arlington, OH	34,171	33,686	33,771	34,191	0.1	1.2
Upper Dublin, PA	24,028	25,878	25,569	26,042	8.4	1.8
Vestavia Hills, AL	22,183	24,476	34,033	34,061	53.5	0.1
Webster, NY	31,639	37,926	42,641	43,402	37.2	1.8
Wellesley, MA	26,615	26,613	27,982	28,858	8.4	3.1
West Fargo, ND	12,276	14,940	25,830	28,371	131.1	9.8
West Linn, OR	17,500	22,261	25,109	25,710	46.9	2.4
West Windsor, NJ	16,021	21,907	27,165	28,108	75.4	3.5
Westlake, OH	27,018	31,719	32,729	32,513	20.3	-0.7
Weston, FL	10,099	49,286	65,333	67,567	569.0	3.4
Westport, CT	24,410	25,749	26,391	27,055	10.8	2.5
Wilmette, IL	26,685	27,651	27,087	27,345	2.5	1.0
Woodbury, MN	20,075	46,463	61,961	64,544	221.5	4.2
Yorba Linda, CA	52,827	58,918	64,234	66,335	25.6	3.3
U.S.	248,709,873	281,421,906	308,745,538	314,107,084	26.3	1.7

Note: (*) 2010-2014 5-year estimated population
Source: U.S. Census Bureau, Census 2010, 2000, 1990, 2010-2014 American Community Survey 5-Year Estimates

Population Growth: Metro Area

Area	1990 Census	2000 Census	2010 Census	2014* Estimate	Population Growth (%) 1990-2014	2010-2014
Aliso Viejo, CA	11,273,720	12,365,627	12,828,837	13,060,534	15.8	1.8
Allen, TX	3,989,294	5,161,544	6,371,773	6,703,020	68.0	5.2
Alpharetta, GA	3,069,411	4,247,981	5,268,860	5,455,053	77.7	3.5
Ankeny, IA	416,346	481,394	569,633	590,741	41.9	3.7
Apex, NC	541,081	797,071	1,130,490	1,189,579	119.9	5.2
Ballwin, MO	2,580,897	2,698,687	2,812,896	2,797,737	8.4	-0.5
Beavercreek, OH	843,857	848,153	841,502	801,259	-5.0	-4.8
Bella Vista, AR	239,474	347,045	463,204	483,396	101.9	4.4
Bernards, NJ	16,845,992	18,323,002	18,897,109	19,865,045	17.9	5.1
Bethlehem, NY	809,443	825,875	870,716	875,567	8.2	0.6
Bloomfield, MI	4,248,699	4,452,557	4,296,250	4,292,647	1.0	-0.1
Bowie, MD	4,122,914	4,796,183	5,582,170	5,863,608	42.2	5.0
Bozeman, MT	50,491	67,831	89,513	93,108	84.4	4.0
Brentwood, TN	1,048,218	1,311,789	1,589,934	1,730,515	65.1	8.8
Broomfield, CO	1,666,935	2,179,296	2,543,482	2,651,392	59.1	4.2
Carmel, IN	1,294,217	1,525,104	1,756,241	1,931,182	49.2	10.0
Cedar Park, TX	846,217	1,249,763	1,716,289	1,835,016	116.8	6.9
Cheshire, CT	804,219	824,008	862,477	863,148	7.3	0.1
Chesterfield, MO	2,580,897	2,698,687	2,812,896	2,797,737	8.4	-0.5
Collierville, TN	1,067,263	1,205,204	1,316,100	1,337,014	25.3	1.6
Coppell, TX	3,989,294	5,161,544	6,371,773	6,703,020	68.0	5.2
Cornelius, NC	1,024,331	1,330,448	1,758,038	2,298,915	124.4	30.8
Cranberry, PA	2,468,289	2,431,087	2,356,285	2,358,793	-4.4	0.1
Cupertino, CA	1,534,280	1,735,819	1,836,911	1,898,457	23.7	3.4
Danville, CA	3,686,592	4,123,740	4,335,391	4,466,251	21.1	3.0
Draper, UT	768,075	968,858	1,124,197	1,123,643	46.3	0.0
Dublin, OH	1,405,176	1,612,694	1,836,536	1,948,188	38.6	6.1
Eastchester, NY	16,845,992	18,323,002	18,897,109	19,865,045	17.9	5.1
Eden Prairie, MN	2,538,834	2,968,806	3,279,833	3,424,786	34.9	4.4
Edmond, OK	971,042	1,095,421	1,252,987	1,297,998	33.7	3.6
Evesham, NJ	5,435,470	5,687,147	5,965,343	6,015,336	10.7	0.8
Fishers, IN	1,294,217	1,525,104	1,756,241	1,931,182	49.2	10.0
Flower Mound, TX	3,989,294	5,161,544	6,371,773	6,703,020	68.0	5.2
Folsom, CA	1,481,126	1,796,857	2,149,127	2,197,422	48.4	2.2
Foster City, CA	3,686,592	4,123,740	4,335,391	4,466,251	21.1	3.0
Franklin, TN	1,048,218	1,311,789	1,589,934	1,730,515	65.1	8.8
Friendswood, TX	3,767,335	4,715,407	5,946,800	6,204,141	64.7	4.3
Germantown, TN	1,067,263	1,205,204	1,316,100	1,337,014	25.3	1.6
Glastonbury, CT	1,123,706	1,148,618	1,212,381	1,215,159	8.1	0.2
Grand Blanc, MI	430,459	436,141	425,790	418,654	-2.7	-1.7
Guilderland, NY	809,443	825,875	870,716	875,567	8.2	0.6
Hampden, PA	474,242	509,074	549,475	555,154	17.1	1.0
Holly Springs, NC	541,081	797,071	1,130,490	1,189,579	119.9	5.2
Huntersville, NC	1,024,331	1,330,448	1,758,038	2,298,915	124.4	30.8
Independence, KY	1,844,917	2,009,632	2,130,151	2,131,793	15.5	0.1
Johns Creek, GA	3,069,411	4,247,981	5,268,860	5,455,053	77.7	3.5
Keller, TX	3,989,294	5,161,544	6,371,773	6,703,020	68.0	5.2
Kirkland, WA	2,559,164	3,043,878	3,439,809	3,557,037	39.0	3.4
Lafayette, CO	208,898	269,758	294,567	305,166	46.1	3.6
Lake Oswego, OR	1,523,741	1,927,881	2,226,009	2,288,796	50.2	2.8
League City, TX	3,767,335	4,715,407	5,946,800	6,204,141	64.7	4.3
Leawood, KS	1,636,528	1,836,038	2,035,334	2,040,869	24.7	0.3
Lee's Summit, MO	1,636,528	1,836,038	2,035,334	2,040,869	24.7	0.3
Leesburg, VA	4,122,914	4,796,183	5,582,170	5,863,608	42.2	5.0
Lehi, UT	269,407	376,774	526,810	550,774	104.4	4.5
Lenexa, KS	1,636,528	1,836,038	2,035,334	2,040,869	24.7	0.3
Lexington, MA	4,133,895	4,391,344	4,552,402	4,650,876	12.5	2.2
Los Altos, CA	1,534,280	1,735,819	1,836,911	1,898,457	23.7	3.4
Lower Makefield, PA	5,435,470	5,687,147	5,965,343	6,015,336	10.7	0.8
Madison, AL	293,047	342,376	417,593	430,396	46.9	3.1
Mamaroneck, NY	16,845,992	18,323,002	18,897,109	19,865,045	17.9	5.1
Manheim, PA	422,822	470,658	519,445	526,839	24.6	1.4
Manlius, NY	659,864	650,154	662,577	662,236	0.4	-0.1
Maple Grove, MN	2,538,834	2,968,806	3,279,833	3,424,786	34.9	4.4
Marion, IA	210,640	237,230	257,940	261,429	24.1	1.4
Marlboro, NJ	16,845,992	18,323,002	18,897,109	19,865,045	17.9	5.1
Mason, OH	1,844,917	2,009,632	2,130,151	2,131,793	15.5	0.1
McCandless, PA	2,468,289	2,431,087	2,356,285	2,358,793	-4.4	0.1

Table continued on next page.

Area	1990 Census	2000 Census	2010 Census	2014* Estimate	Population Growth (%) 1990-2014	2010-2014
Menomonee Falls, WI	1,432,149	1,500,741	1,555,908	1,565,368	9.3	0.6
Meridian, ID	319,596	464,840	616,561	639,616	100.1	3.7
Merrimack, NH	336,073	380,841	400,721	402,776	19.8	0.5
Mount Lebanon, PA	2,468,289	2,431,087	2,356,285	2,358,793	-4.4	0.1
Mount Pleasant, SC	506,875	549,033	664,607	697,281	37.6	4.9
Needham, MA	4,133,895	4,391,344	4,552,402	4,650,876	12.5	2.2
Newtown, CT	827,645	882,567	916,829	934,215	12.9	1.9
Northbrook, IL	8,182,076	9,098,316	9,461,105	9,516,448	16.3	0.6
Northville, MI	4,248,699	4,452,557	4,296,250	4,292,647	1.0	-0.1
Novi, MI	4,248,699	4,452,557	4,296,250	4,292,647	1.0	-0.1
O'Fallon, IL	2,580,897	2,698,687	2,812,896	2,797,737	8.4	-0.5
O'Fallon, MO	2,580,897	2,698,687	2,812,896	2,797,737	8.4	-0.5
Orchard Park, NY	1,189,288	1,170,111	1,135,509	1,135,667	-4.5	0.0
Oviedo, FL	1,224,852	1,644,561	2,134,411	2,226,835	81.8	4.3
Parker, CO	1,666,935	2,179,296	2,543,482	2,651,392	59.1	4.2
Parkland, FL	4,056,100	5,007,564	5,564,635	5,775,204	42.4	3.8
Peachtree City, GA	3,069,411	4,247,981	5,268,860	5,455,053	77.7	3.5
Pflugerville, TX	846,217	1,249,763	1,716,289	1,835,016	116.8	6.9
Plainfield, IL	8,182,076	9,098,316	9,461,105	9,516,448	16.3	0.6
Princeton, NJ	325,804	350,761	366,513	369,526	13.4	0.8
Queen Creek, AZ	2,238,480	3,251,876	4,192,887	4,337,542	93.8	3.5
Rancho Palos Verdes, CA	11,273,720	12,365,627	12,828,837	13,060,534	15.8	1.8
Redmond, WA	2,559,164	3,043,878	3,439,809	3,557,037	39.0	3.4
Richland, WA	150,033	191,822	253,340	266,561	77.7	5.2
Ridgefield, CT	827,645	882,567	916,829	934,215	12.9	1.9
Ridgewood, NJ	16,845,992	18,323,002	18,897,109	19,865,045	17.9	5.1
Rio Rancho, NM	599,416	729,649	887,077	899,137	50.0	1.4
Sahuarita, AZ	666,880	843,746	980,263	993,144	48.9	1.3
Sammamish, WA	2,559,164	3,043,878	3,439,809	3,557,037	39.0	3.4
San Ramon, CA	3,686,592	4,123,740	4,335,391	4,466,251	21.1	3.0
Saratoga, CA	1,534,280	1,735,819	1,836,911	1,898,457	23.7	3.4
Schertz, TX	1,407,745	1,711,703	2,142,508	2,239,222	59.1	4.5
Shrewsbury, MA	709,728	750,963	798,552	924,722	30.3	15.8
South Brunswick, NJ	16,845,992	18,323,002	18,897,109	19,865,045	17.9	5.1
South Jordan, UT	768,075	968,858	1,124,197	1,123,643	46.3	0.0
South Kingstown, RI	1,509,789	1,582,997	1,600,852	1,604,317	6.3	0.2
South Windsor, CT	1,123,706	1,148,618	1,212,381	1,215,159	8.1	0.2
Southlake, TX	3,989,294	5,161,544	6,371,773	6,703,020	68.0	5.2
Spring Hill, TN	1,048,218	1,311,789	1,589,934	1,730,515	65.1	8.8
Stow, OH	657,575	694,960	703,200	703,017	6.9	0.0
Sugar Land, TX	3,767,335	4,715,407	5,946,800	6,204,141	64.7	4.3
Sun Prairie, WI	432,323	501,774	568,593	620,368	43.5	9.1
Syracuse, UT	351,799	442,656	547,184	614,521	74.7	12.3
Tredyffrin, PA	5,435,470	5,687,147	5,965,343	6,015,336	10.7	0.8
Upper Arlington, OH	1,405,176	1,612,694	1,836,536	1,948,188	38.6	6.1
Upper Dublin, PA	5,435,470	5,687,147	5,965,343	6,015,336	10.7	0.8
Vestavia Hills, AL	956,894	1,052,238	1,128,047	1,135,534	18.7	0.7
Webster, NY	1,002,410	1,037,831	1,054,323	1,082,578	8.0	2.7
Wellesley, MA	4,133,895	4,391,344	4,552,402	4,650,876	12.5	2.2
West Fargo, ND	153,296	174,367	208,777	218,290	42.4	4.6
West Linn, OR	1,523,741	1,927,881	2,226,009	2,288,796	50.2	2.8
West Windsor, NJ	325,804	350,761	366,513	369,526	13.4	0.8
Westlake, OH	2,102,219	2,148,143	2,077,240	2,067,490	-1.7	-0.5
Weston, FL	4,056,100	5,007,564	5,564,635	5,775,204	42.4	3.8
Westport, CT	827,645	882,567	916,829	934,215	12.9	1.9
Wilmette, IL	8,182,076	9,098,316	9,461,105	9,516,448	16.3	0.6
Woodbury, MN	2,538,834	2,968,806	3,279,833	3,424,786	34.9	4.4
Yorba Linda, CA	11,273,720	12,365,627	12,828,837	13,060,534	15.8	1.8
U.S.	248,709,873	281,421,906	308,745,538	314,107,084	26.3	1.7

Note: (*) 2010-2014 5-year estimated population; Figures cover the Metropolitan Statistical Area (MSA)—see Appendix B for areas included

Source: U.S. Census Bureau, Census 2010, 2000, 1990, 2010-2014 American Community Survey 5-Year Estimates

Household Size: City

City	Persons in Household (%) One	Two	Three	Four	Five	Six	Seven or More	Average Household Size
Aliso Viejo, CA	24.8	30.4	19.6	17.4	4.7	1.8	1.0	2.60
Allen, TX	14.9	28.3	21.2	21.4	9.7	2.9	1.2	3.05
Alpharetta, GA	25.5	28.2	16.5	20.7	6.3	2.3	0.2	2.72
Ankeny, IA	23.5	35.5	17.0	16.0	5.0	2.0	0.6	2.53
Apex, NC	19.2	26.8	20.8	19.8	9.9	2.6	0.6	2.91
Ballwin, MO	18.4	37.4	19.3	17.8	5.5	0.9	0.4	2.76
Beavercreek, OH	26.4	36.2	17.0	11.6	5.9	2.0	0.6	2.51
Bella Vista, AR	19.5	55.1	8.9	9.3	3.6	1.9	1.3	2.33
Bernards, NJ	27.9	25.2	17.9	19.3	6.5	2.4	0.4	2.70
Bethlehem, NY	26.6	34.4	16.5	14.9	5.2	1.6	0.4	2.56
Bloomfield, MI	23.6	40.5	12.7	13.7	6.1	2.8	0.2	2.52
Bowie, MD	23.4	31.0	18.0	15.1	7.7	3.5	0.9	2.82
Bozeman, MT	33.0	38.1	14.9	9.7	3.5	0.3	0.3	2.21
Brentwood, TN	9.2	32.6	21.2	22.7	10.0	2.4	1.6	3.04
Broomfield, CO	25.8	32.1	15.8	16.4	7.3	1.5	0.8	2.58
Carmel, IN	20.2	35.8	16.1	17.3	7.7	1.6	0.9	2.72
Cedar Park, TX	20.4	30.9	15.8	21.9	6.5	2.7	1.4	3.02
Cheshire, CT	23.0	32.6	17.7	17.8	6.2	2.0	0.4	2.72
Chesterfield, MO	25.2	38.6	15.8	14.0	4.6	1.1	0.3	2.50
Collierville, TN	14.3	30.2	22.2	22.3	8.7	1.4	0.5	3.04
Coppell, TX	18.6	28.6	22.2	21.7	6.4	2.0	0.2	2.80
Cornelius, NC	27.0	37.1	19.5	9.5	4.7	1.5	0.4	2.46
Cranberry, PA	20.4	30.3	19.1	20.7	6.9	1.8	0.6	2.72
Cupertino, CA	19.6	24.2	22.2	25.5	6.2	1.2	0.8	2.90
Danville, CA	20.7	34.1	14.7	20.8	7.0	1.9	0.5	2.74
Draper, UT	11.8	32.4	13.0	20.1	12.2	5.3	5.0	3.42
Dublin, OH	18.6	32.4	16.1	22.8	7.8	1.6	0.3	2.82
Eastchester, NY	29.8	30.6	15.6	13.8	7.4	1.9	0.5	2.54
Eden Prairie, MN	24.3	33.8	17.6	15.2	5.8	2.5	0.4	2.54
Edmond, OK	23.3	37.0	17.2	13.9	5.7	2.0	0.6	2.64
Evesham, NJ	24.0	31.4	18.9	16.8	7.1	1.2	0.4	2.64
Fishers, IN	21.0	28.5	18.3	19.1	9.0	3.0	0.7	2.92
Flower Mound, TX	12.3	27.7	22.1	26.0	9.4	2.0	0.2	3.11
Folsom, CA	24.6	30.6	18.7	18.2	5.7	1.6	0.3	2.63
Foster City, CA	23.9	35.4	17.2	16.8	4.4	1.6	0.4	2.63
Franklin, TN	27.3	31.6	13.9	17.5	6.5	1.9	0.9	2.54
Friendswood, TX	20.5	32.4	18.1	18.4	6.7	2.2	1.3	2.83
Germantown, TN	19.0	41.6	15.5	15.4	6.1	1.0	1.0	2.79
Glastonbury, CT	23.0	35.2	16.5	16.2	6.3	1.7	0.7	2.61
Grand Blanc, MI	26.7	35.0	14.2	12.6	8.7	1.9	0.5	2.56
Guilderland, NY	31.3	37.7	15.0	10.8	3.3	1.4	0.1	2.34
Hampden, PA	28.1	37.8	13.4	12.7	5.1	2.1	0.4	2.37
Holly Springs, NC	16.0	27.4	18.5	24.1	11.3	2.0	0.3	3.01
Huntersville, NC	23.1	30.9	19.9	17.9	6.1	1.4	0.3	2.79
Independence, KY	15.7	29.7	22.3	17.6	10.2	2.5	1.7	3.04
Johns Creek, GA	16.9	26.8	20.5	24.3	8.0	1.9	1.1	3.10
Keller, TX	15.5	32.7	19.8	19.9	9.7	1.3	0.8	2.97
Kirkland, WA	29.8	35.6	15.1	13.8	4.1	0.7	0.5	2.39
Lafayette, CO	29.0	33.4	16.1	15.2	4.0	1.4	0.6	2.45
Lake Oswego, OR	30.4	36.1	14.8	12.8	4.3	1.2	0.1	2.29
League City, TX	21.0	30.6	19.9	17.4	7.4	2.8	0.6	2.71
Leawood, KS	19.5	39.5	13.2	17.4	7.4	1.6	1.2	2.61
Lee's Summit, MO	21.9	33.7	17.5	16.7	7.1	1.6	1.1	2.75
Leesburg, VA	18.7	28.5	18.9	18.4	9.1	3.6	2.5	3.08
Lehi, UT	9.3	21.3	14.5	18.5	18.8	11.7	5.6	4.00
Lenexa, KS	25.7	37.4	15.2	13.5	5.4	2.0	0.5	2.49
Lexington, MA	20.6	32.2	16.8	19.5	8.6	1.4	0.6	2.74
Los Altos, CA	20.3	34.4	16.4	20.8	6.6	1.2	0.1	2.70
Lower Makefield, PA	19.0	36.6	17.6	17.0	6.7	2.7	0.1	2.72
Madison, AL	23.4	33.2	17.9	16.8	6.0	1.9	0.4	2.75
Mamaroneck, NY	27.5	27.9	14.2	20.0	8.0	1.9	0.1	2.64
Manheim, PA	26.1	35.6	16.9	14.1	5.3	1.0	0.7	2.46
Manlius, NY	27.3	37.7	14.8	12.3	5.2	1.5	0.7	2.43
Maple Grove, MN	20.6	36.0	17.4	17.3	6.6	1.3	0.6	2.68
Marion, IA	28.6	34.3	15.8	13.0	5.7	1.5	0.7	2.46
Marlboro, NJ	13.2	29.2	18.1	25.5	9.5	2.9	1.2	3.11
Mason, OH	21.9	31.8	14.9	21.8	7.4	1.7	0.2	2.81

Table continued on next page.

City	Persons in Household (%) One	Two	Three	Four	Five	Six	Seven or More	Average Household Size
McCandless, PA	28.1	35.7	14.8	15.9	4.1	0.8	0.2	2.40
Menomonee Falls, WI	28.0	36.0	14.5	14.7	4.2	1.2	1.0	2.45
Meridian, ID	19.2	35.4	13.6	17.4	8.1	4.3	1.6	2.93
Merrimack, NH	19.1	41.7	14.0	16.0	6.5	1.3	1.0	2.65
Mount Lebanon, PA	33.1	32.3	14.8	11.8	6.0	1.3	0.3	2.34
Mount Pleasant, SC	27.1	35.8	16.4	14.4	4.4	1.3	0.2	2.52
Needham, MA	22.5	30.0	16.6	20.9	7.9	1.8	0.1	2.72
Newtown, CT	19.9	31.4	19.4	17.0	8.6	2.8	0.6	2.84
Northbrook, IL	21.6	35.3	16.4	16.9	7.4	2.1	0.0	2.68
Northville, MI	28.7	30.3	16.6	15.8	5.5	2.9	0.0	2.57
Novi, MI	31.8	29.0	15.0	16.2	5.9	1.3	0.5	2.43
O'Fallon, IL	25.0	30.0	18.0	15.9	7.1	2.2	1.4	2.73
O'Fallon, MO	20.6	29.5	17.8	19.8	8.4	2.6	0.8	2.78
Orchard Park, NY	27.1	32.7	15.6	17.0	5.0	2.0	0.2	2.51
Oviedo, FL	14.0	30.2	20.3	24.4	6.3	3.5	0.9	3.38
Parker, CO	19.2	27.3	18.8	23.0	8.1	1.5	1.8	2.88
Parkland, FL	9.0	26.9	25.4	27.0	8.3	2.6	0.4	3.25
Peachtree City, GA	21.9	34.9	16.4	15.2	7.6	2.0	1.6	2.83
Pflugerville, TX	19.2	30.7	17.9	21.8	6.4	2.4	1.3	2.86
Plainfield, IL	12.3	25.2	16.5	26.1	12.6	5.3	1.7	3.38
Princeton, NJ	26.4	37.3	16.1	14.4	4.6	0.8	0.1	2.48
Queen Creek, AZ	13.6	26.6	16.7	20.8	11.2	7.7	3.1	3.36
Rancho Palos Verdes, CA	20.8	39.6	16.3	15.3	5.7	1.6	0.4	2.68
Redmond, WA	30.7	31.5	18.0	14.6	2.9	1.5	0.5	2.38
Richland, WA	28.6	37.4	14.3	10.7	4.7	3.0	0.9	2.51
Ridgefield, CT	18.1	32.9	16.1	22.9	8.2	0.9	0.5	2.83
Ridgewood, NJ	17.6	26.8	16.1	25.3	11.5	1.9	0.5	3.05
Rio Rancho, NM	23.1	34.3	15.6	15.8	6.9	3.2	0.7	2.80
Sahuarita, AZ	16.9	37.0	15.6	17.0	8.5	3.0	1.6	2.88
Sammamish, WA	9.3	28.8	22.0	27.5	9.5	1.7	0.8	3.11
San Ramon, CA	18.6	26.0	19.0	27.3	5.6	2.6	0.6	2.91
Saratoga, CA	14.2	35.2	18.8	24.6	5.1	1.4	0.3	2.82
Schertz, TX	19.6	33.6	19.8	16.0	7.6	1.7	1.3	2.84
Shrewsbury, MA	23.0	29.4	17.3	21.7	6.5	1.0	0.9	2.75
South Brunswick, NJ	18.4	28.2	19.7	22.4	7.9	2.4	0.7	2.91
South Jordan, UT	11.7	29.1	15.1	16.8	12.4	8.6	6.0	3.63
South Kingstown, RI	28.1	37.7	14.0	13.1	5.5	0.8	0.3	2.40
South Windsor, CT	22.8	32.6	17.9	16.6	7.3	1.3	1.3	2.67
Southlake, TX	10.8	29.7	19.1	26.3	11.8	1.3	0.7	3.13
Spring Hill, TN	17.9	28.3	17.5	21.4	9.7	4.3	0.5	3.08
Stow, OH	28.4	34.3	15.8	14.1	5.3	1.5	0.1	2.49
Sugar Land, TX	14.9	31.9	20.9	18.8	8.5	2.4	2.2	3.00
Sun Prairie, WI	24.5	36.0	17.1	13.2	6.1	1.7	1.1	2.60
Syracuse, UT	7.8	26.5	13.2	18.6	18.2	10.7	4.7	3.89
Tredyffrin, PA	31.0	31.1	14.0	15.5	5.6	2.3	0.1	2.44
Upper Arlington, OH	25.2	36.9	14.3	15.2	5.7	1.6	0.7	2.59
Upper Dublin, PA	20.1	33.3	21.5	14.6	7.4	2.5	0.3	2.70
Vestavia Hills, AL	29.7	32.8	14.4	15.1	6.4	1.0	0.3	2.45
Webster, NY	25.9	37.4	14.2	13.7	6.4	1.2	0.9	2.52
Wellesley, MA	20.4	31.3	14.5	19.7	11.0	2.7	0.2	2.82
West Fargo, ND	25.9	34.2	16.3	14.1	7.2	1.5	0.5	2.43
West Linn, OR	21.6	36.5	17.4	16.7	6.4	0.6	0.4	2.57
West Windsor, NJ	16.1	31.1	19.4	23.5	7.1	2.1	0.4	2.89
Westlake, OH	34.8	34.6	10.4	11.3	6.1	1.8	0.8	2.33
Weston, FL	12.8	29.0	19.6	27.3	8.8	1.9	0.2	3.22
Westport, CT	18.9	32.9	17.7	19.5	9.1	1.0	0.5	2.81
Wilmette, IL	20.5	31.6	15.6	20.2	8.2	2.8	0.8	2.87
Woodbury, MN	20.5	33.9	16.7	18.7	6.8	1.9	1.2	2.73
Yorba Linda, CA	13.5	31.8	20.0	21.6	8.5	3.5	0.7	2.99
U.S.	27.5	33.5	15.8	13.1	6.0	2.3	1.4	2.64

U.S. Census Bureau, 2010-2014 American Community Survey 5-Year Estimates

Household Size: Metro Area

Metro Area	Persons in Household (%)							Average Household Size
	One	Two	Three	Four	Five	Six	Seven or More	
Aliso Viejo, CA	24.5	28.0	16.6	15.4	8.3	3.8	3.1	3.03
Allen, TX	25.1	30.7	16.6	15.1	7.4	2.9	1.8	2.79
Alpharetta, GA	26.5	31.3	16.8	14.7	6.5	2.4	1.4	2.77
Ankeny, IA	26.7	34.3	15.8	13.6	6.2	2.1	1.0	2.52
Apex, NC	25.8	32.6	17.2	15.1	5.9	2.1	1.0	2.64
Ballwin, MO	29.2	33.8	15.7	12.8	5.5	1.7	0.8	2.48
Beavercreek, OH	32.3	34.1	14.8	11.2	4.8	1.6	0.8	2.36
Bella Vista, AR	24.4	34.4	15.7	14.0	6.8	2.7	1.8	2.66
Bernards, NJ	27.8	28.9	17.0	14.8	6.7	2.6	1.9	2.74
Bethlehem, NY	31.6	35.5	15.0	11.4	4.3	1.4	0.6	2.42
Bloomfield, MI	29.9	31.9	15.6	13.2	5.7	2.2	1.2	2.56
Bowie, MD	27.1	30.6	16.7	14.7	6.5	2.6	1.5	2.73
Bozeman, MT	27.0	38.8	15.9	12.2	4.2	1.1	0.5	2.38
Brentwood, TN	27.6	33.9	16.2	13.3	5.7	1.9	1.1	2.59
Broomfield, CO	29.1	33.2	15.2	13.0	5.6	2.2	1.3	2.55
Carmel, IN	28.4	33.4	15.8	13.1	6.0	2.0	1.0	2.57
Cedar Park, TX	27.6	32.9	15.8	13.8	6.0	2.1	1.4	2.66
Cheshire, CT	30.2	32.0	16.5	13.2	5.4	1.7	0.8	2.55
Chesterfield, MO	29.2	33.8	15.7	12.8	5.5	1.7	0.8	2.48
Collierville, TN	28.0	32.2	16.7	13.3	5.8	2.2	1.5	2.68
Coppell, TX	25.1	30.7	16.6	15.1	7.4	2.9	1.8	2.79
Cornelius, NC	26.5	33.6	17.1	13.6	6.0	1.9	1.0	2.64
Cranberry, PA	32.3	35.3	14.9	11.4	4.1	1.2	0.5	2.32
Cupertino, CA	21.3	29.2	18.6	17.6	7.6	2.8	2.5	2.95
Danville, CA	28.1	31.4	16.2	14.0	5.8	2.3	1.7	2.67
Draper, UT	22.6	29.3	15.9	14.4	8.9	4.8	3.6	3.03
Dublin, OH	28.9	33.1	15.7	13.3	5.7	1.9	1.0	2.54
Eastchester, NY	27.8	28.9	17.0	14.8	6.7	2.6	1.9	2.74
Eden Prairie, MN	27.8	33.7	15.0	14.0	5.9	2.0	1.3	2.54
Edmond, OK	28.1	34.0	15.8	12.8	5.8	2.1	1.1	2.58
Evesham, NJ	29.4	31.2	16.3	13.6	6.0	2.1	1.1	2.63
Fishers, IN	28.4	33.4	15.8	13.1	6.0	2.0	1.0	2.57
Flower Mound, TX	25.1	30.7	16.6	15.1	7.4	2.9	1.8	2.79
Folsom, CA	25.8	32.7	15.7	14.1	6.7	2.7	2.0	2.72
Foster City, CA	28.1	31.4	16.2	14.0	5.8	2.3	1.7	2.67
Franklin, TN	27.6	33.9	16.2	13.3	5.7	1.9	1.1	2.59
Friendswood, TX	24.4	29.7	16.9	15.4	8.1	3.2	2.1	2.90
Germantown, TN	28.0	32.2	16.7	13.3	5.8	2.2	1.5	2.68
Glastonbury, CT	28.2	33.6	16.0	14.2	5.5	1.6	0.6	2.48
Grand Blanc, MI	29.7	33.9	15.9	11.9	5.6	1.8	0.8	2.49
Guilderland, NY	31.6	35.5	15.0	11.4	4.3	1.4	0.6	2.42
Hampden, PA	29.6	35.3	15.4	12.1	4.6	1.7	1.0	2.40
Holly Springs, NC	25.8	32.6	17.2	15.1	5.9	2.1	1.0	2.64
Huntersville, NC	26.5	33.6	17.1	13.6	6.0	1.9	1.0	2.64
Independence, KY	28.2	33.9	15.6	13.2	5.8	2.0	1.0	2.55
Johns Creek, GA	26.5	31.3	16.8	14.7	6.5	2.4	1.4	2.77
Keller, TX	25.1	30.7	16.6	15.1	7.4	2.9	1.8	2.79
Kirkland, WA	28.9	33.4	15.8	13.4	5.1	1.9	1.1	2.53
Lafayette, CO	27.8	36.4	15.5	13.2	4.7	1.4	0.6	2.43
Lake Oswego, OR	27.4	34.6	15.6	13.1	5.6	2.0	1.4	2.56
League City, TX	24.4	29.7	16.9	15.4	8.1	3.2	2.1	2.90
Leawood, KS	28.8	33.6	15.3	13.0	5.8	2.0	1.1	2.54
Lee's Summit, MO	28.8	33.6	15.3	13.0	5.8	2.0	1.1	2.54
Leesburg, VA	27.1	30.6	16.7	14.7	6.5	2.6	1.5	2.73
Lehi, UT	12.3	26.3	15.9	17.0	12.5	9.2	6.4	3.62
Lenexa, KS	28.8	33.6	15.3	13.0	5.8	2.0	1.1	2.54
Lexington, MA	28.3	32.3	16.4	14.5	5.7	1.7	0.8	2.54
Los Altos, CA	21.3	29.2	18.6	17.6	7.6	2.8	2.5	2.95
Lower Makefield, PA	29.4	31.2	16.3	13.6	6.0	2.1	1.1	2.63
Madison, AL	29.5	34.3	16.1	12.8	4.8	1.4	0.7	2.50
Mamaroneck, NY	27.8	28.9	17.0	14.8	6.7	2.6	1.9	2.74
Manheim, PA	24.0	36.6	15.5	13.2	5.8	2.3	2.2	2.64
Manlius, NY	30.1	33.8	15.8	12.1	5.1	1.7	1.0	2.47
Maple Grove, MN	27.8	33.7	15.0	14.0	5.9	2.0	1.3	2.54
Marion, IA	28.4	36.3	14.4	13.0	4.8	1.9	0.9	2.42
Marlboro, NJ	27.8	28.9	17.0	14.8	6.7	2.6	1.9	2.74
Mason, OH	28.2	33.9	15.6	13.2	5.8	2.0	1.0	2.55

Table continued on next page.

Metro Area	Persons in Household (%) One	Two	Three	Four	Five	Six	Seven or More	Average Household Size
McCandless, PA	32.3	35.3	14.9	11.4	4.1	1.2	0.5	2.32
Menomonee Falls, WI	30.8	33.3	14.9	12.6	5.2	1.8	1.0	2.47
Meridian, ID	24.4	34.7	14.7	14.5	6.7	2.8	1.8	2.71
Merrimack, NH	24.5	36.0	16.3	14.8	5.7	1.5	0.9	2.56
Mount Lebanon, PA	32.3	35.3	14.9	11.4	4.1	1.2	0.5	2.32
Mount Pleasant, SC	28.2	34.9	16.6	12.8	4.8	1.6	0.8	2.57
Needham, MA	28.3	32.3	16.4	14.5	5.7	1.7	0.8	2.54
Newtown, CT	25.4	30.3	16.9	16.6	7.2	2.2	1.0	2.74
Northbrook, IL	28.1	29.9	15.8	14.3	7.0	2.7	1.8	2.72
Northville, MI	29.9	31.9	15.6	13.2	5.7	2.2	1.2	2.56
Novi, MI	29.9	31.9	15.6	13.2	5.7	2.2	1.2	2.56
O'Fallon, IL	29.2	33.8	15.7	12.8	5.5	1.7	0.8	2.48
O'Fallon, MO	29.2	33.8	15.7	12.8	5.5	1.7	0.8	2.48
Orchard Park, NY	32.8	33.6	14.9	11.6	4.6	1.5	0.7	2.35
Oviedo, FL	26.0	35.0	16.7	13.2	5.8	2.0	1.0	2.80
Parker, CO	29.1	33.2	15.2	13.0	5.6	2.2	1.3	2.55
Parkland, FL	28.7	31.9	16.6	13.3	5.8	2.1	1.3	2.80
Peachtree City, GA	26.5	31.3	16.8	14.7	6.5	2.4	1.4	2.77
Pflugerville, TX	27.6	32.9	15.8	13.8	6.0	2.1	1.4	2.66
Plainfield, IL	28.1	29.9	15.8	14.3	7.0	2.7	1.8	2.72
Princeton, NJ	26.8	31.0	16.7	15.5	6.3	2.1	1.3	2.66
Queen Creek, AZ	26.6	34.5	14.4	12.7	6.5	3.0	2.0	2.75
Rancho Palos Verdes, CA	24.5	28.0	16.6	15.4	8.3	3.8	3.1	3.03
Redmond, WA	28.9	33.4	15.8	13.4	5.1	1.9	1.1	2.53
Richland, WA	23.8	32.1	15.1	14.3	8.0	4.2	2.2	2.89
Ridgefield, CT	25.4	30.3	16.9	16.6	7.2	2.2	1.0	2.74
Ridgewood, NJ	27.8	28.9	17.0	14.8	6.7	2.6	1.9	2.74
Rio Rancho, NM	29.4	33.5	15.4	12.3	5.7	2.1	1.2	2.57
Sahuarita, AZ	30.8	35.2	14.0	10.4	5.6	2.4	1.3	2.50
Sammamish, WA	28.9	33.4	15.8	13.4	5.1	1.9	1.1	2.53
San Ramon, CA	28.1	31.4	16.2	14.0	5.8	2.3	1.7	2.67
Saratoga, CA	21.3	29.2	18.6	17.6	7.6	2.8	2.5	2.95
Schertz, TX	25.2	31.0	16.8	14.2	7.4	3.0	2.1	2.85
Shrewsbury, MA	26.5	32.6	16.9	15.1	6.0	1.8	0.7	2.59
South Brunswick, NJ	27.8	28.9	17.0	14.8	6.7	2.6	1.9	2.74
South Jordan, UT	22.6	29.3	15.9	14.4	8.9	4.8	3.6	3.03
South Kingstown, RI	29.4	32.7	16.7	13.4	5.2	1.5	0.7	2.49
South Windsor, CT	28.2	33.6	16.0	14.2	5.5	1.6	0.6	2.48
Southlake, TX	25.1	30.7	16.6	15.1	7.4	2.9	1.8	2.79
Spring Hill, TN	27.6	33.9	16.2	13.3	5.7	1.9	1.1	2.59
Stow, OH	30.3	34.9	15.1	12.2	4.8	1.7	0.8	2.44
Sugar Land, TX	24.4	29.7	16.9	15.4	8.1	3.2	2.1	2.90
Sun Prairie, WI	29.9	36.5	14.5	12.2	4.4	1.5	0.6	2.36
Syracuse, UT	17.9	30.7	15.5	15.5	10.7	5.9	3.4	3.11
Tredyffrin, PA	29.4	31.2	16.3	13.6	6.0	2.1	1.1	2.63
Upper Arlington, OH	28.9	33.1	15.7	13.3	5.7	1.9	1.0	2.54
Upper Dublin, PA	29.4	31.2	16.3	13.6	6.0	2.1	1.1	2.63
Vestavia Hills, AL	28.3	34.4	16.8	12.8	5.0	1.6	0.8	2.55
Webster, NY	30.1	35.2	15.1	12.0	4.8	1.6	0.8	2.42
Wellesley, MA	28.3	32.3	16.4	14.5	5.7	1.7	0.8	2.54
West Fargo, ND	32.1	34.3	14.9	11.5	5.0	1.4	0.4	2.34
West Linn, OR	27.4	34.6	15.6	13.1	5.6	2.0	1.4	2.56
West Windsor, NJ	26.8	31.0	16.7	15.5	6.3	2.1	1.3	2.66
Westlake, OH	32.8	33.0	14.8	11.5	5.0	1.7	0.9	2.39
Weston, FL	28.7	31.9	16.6	13.3	5.8	2.1	1.3	2.80
Westport, CT	25.4	30.3	16.9	16.6	7.2	2.2	1.0	2.74
Wilmette, IL	28.1	29.9	15.8	14.3	7.0	2.7	1.8	2.72
Woodbury, MN	27.8	33.7	15.0	14.0	5.9	2.0	1.3	2.54
Yorba Linda, CA	24.5	28.0	16.6	15.4	8.3	3.8	3.1	3.03
U.S.	27.5	33.5	15.8	13.1	6.0	2.3	1.4	2.64

Note: Figures cover the Metropolitan Statistical Area (MSA)—see Appendix B for areas included
Source: U.S. Census Bureau, 2010-2014 American Community Survey 5-Year Estimates

Race: City

City	White Alone[1] (%)	Black Alone[1] (%)	Asian Alone[1] (%)	AIAN[2] Alone[1] (%)	NHOPI[3] Alone[1] (%)	Other Race Alone[1] (%)	Two or More Races (%)
Aliso Viejo, CA	70.0	2.7	15.5	0.3	0.0	5.5	6.0
Allen, TX	72.8	8.0	13.4	0.7	0.1	1.5	3.4
Alpharetta, GA	68.9	10.7	15.1	0.1	0.2	1.1	3.9
Ankeny, IA	93.7	0.9	2.3	0.0	0.0	0.6	2.5
Apex, NC	80.0	8.5	6.7	0.2	0.0	1.8	2.7
Ballwin, MO	88.8	2.3	5.7	0.1	0.0	0.3	2.9
Beavercreek, OH	88.9	2.8	5.3	0.2	0.0	0.5	2.4
Bella Vista, AR	95.9	0.7	1.1	0.7	0.2	0.1	1.4
Bernards, NJ	81.1	2.0	13.9	0.0	0.0	0.1	2.8
Bethlehem, NY	90.2	2.5	4.5	0.0	0.0	0.9	1.9
Bloomfield, MI	80.7	7.6	8.5	0.2	0.2	0.3	2.5
Bowie, MD	42.2	47.6	4.0	0.3	0.0	1.9	4.0
Bozeman, MT	92.7	0.5	2.2	1.6	0.0	0.3	2.7
Brentwood, TN	87.4	4.1	5.5	0.2	0.0	0.2	2.7
Broomfield, CO	86.9	1.0	6.0	0.4	0.0	2.2	3.5
Carmel, IN	84.1	2.7	9.7	0.1	0.0	1.0	2.4
Cedar Park, TX	81.7	5.7	7.9	0.3	0.0	1.3	3.1
Cheshire, CT	82.1	4.7	7.7	0.1	0.0	2.8	2.6
Chesterfield, MO	84.7	3.6	9.3	0.1	0.0	0.8	1.5
Collierville, TN	77.9	13.4	6.4	0.4	0.0	0.4	1.5
Coppell, TX	70.8	5.2	19.4	0.3	0.0	1.9	2.3
Cornelius, NC	90.1	4.9	2.8	0.1	0.0	0.7	1.4
Cranberry, PA	94.6	1.1	2.3	0.0	0.0	0.2	1.7
Cupertino, CA	30.8	0.6	65.0	0.2	0.3	0.6	2.5
Danville, CA	83.4	1.1	11.5	0.2	0.1	0.4	3.4
Draper, UT	90.9	0.8	2.5	0.6	0.3	2.6	2.2
Dublin, OH	79.3	2.1	15.8	0.0	0.0	0.6	2.2
Eastchester, NY	84.8	4.9	6.4	0.0	0.0	1.3	2.5
Eden Prairie, MN	79.8	5.5	10.6	0.3	0.1	0.9	2.8
Edmond, OK	81.7	6.0	3.6	2.2	0.3	1.3	5.0
Evesham, NJ	86.5	5.0	6.1	0.0	0.0	0.7	1.6
Fishers, IN	86.7	4.6	5.4	0.1	0.0	0.5	2.8
Flower Mound, TX	83.3	3.8	9.3	0.6	0.1	0.7	2.3
Folsom, CA	70.4	5.8	14.1	0.5	0.6	4.1	4.4
Foster City, CA	45.4	1.9	45.9	0.2	0.2	1.0	5.5
Franklin, TN	86.8	5.6	4.7	0.0	0.0	1.4	1.6
Friendswood, TX	88.6	3.0	4.8	0.3	0.0	1.1	2.3
Germantown, TN	87.4	5.0	6.2	0.1	0.0	0.3	1.1
Glastonbury, CT	85.4	2.4	9.6	0.0	0.0	1.3	1.4
Grand Blanc, MI	81.1	11.6	4.2	0.0	0.1	0.4	2.6
Guilderland, NY	87.3	3.4	7.0	0.1	0.1	1.1	1.0
Hampden, PA	88.5	1.5	8.0	0.0	0.2	0.2	1.6
Holly Springs, NC	78.7	13.9	3.9	0.0	0.0	1.0	2.6
Huntersville, NC	84.6	9.3	1.8	0.4	0.1	1.1	2.7
Independence, KY	95.2	1.6	0.9	0.0	0.2	0.4	1.7
Johns Creek, GA	62.6	10.9	22.5	0.2	0.0	0.9	2.8
Keller, TX	88.8	2.3	4.0	0.2	0.0	2.0	2.7
Kirkland, WA	78.5	1.4	13.0	0.4	0.0	1.6	5.1
Lafayette, CO	86.4	0.5	5.4	0.5	0.1	3.3	3.8
Lake Oswego, OR	88.3	0.6	6.7	0.1	0.1	1.3	2.9
League City, TX	81.0	7.6	5.7	0.2	0.0	2.6	3.0
Leawood, KS	92.5	1.4	3.6	0.3	0.0	0.3	1.8
Lee's Summit, MO	84.2	8.8	2.3	0.1	0.4	1.5	2.7
Leesburg, VA	74.3	8.0	9.0	0.0	0.2	5.7	2.8
Lehi, UT	93.8	0.2	1.3	0.5	0.7	2.1	1.4
Lenexa, KS	86.5	5.7	3.9	0.2	0.1	0.9	2.8
Lexington, MA	73.3	1.1	21.9	0.2	0.0	0.3	3.1
Los Altos, CA	69.6	0.6	24.0	0.1	0.0	0.6	5.0
Lower Makefield, PA	88.8	2.1	6.9	0.0	0.0	1.0	1.1
Madison, AL	75.1	14.7	5.6	0.8	0.2	0.7	2.8
Mamaroneck, NY	81.4	3.7	5.0	0.1	0.0	6.5	3.5
Manheim, PA	88.4	2.9	3.9	0.3	0.0	2.4	1.9
Manlius, NY	91.5	3.0	3.7	0.3	0.0	0.1	1.4
Maple Grove, MN	87.0	3.8	6.6	0.1	0.0	0.3	2.2
Marion, IA	93.6	1.9	2.0	0.2	0.0	0.7	1.6
Marlboro, NJ	79.2	1.6	17.0	0.1	0.0	0.4	1.7

Table continued on next page.

City	White Alone[1] (%)	Black Alone[1] (%)	Asian Alone[1] (%)	AIAN[2] Alone[1] (%)	NHOPI[3] Alone[1] (%)	Other Race Alone[1] (%)	Two or More Races (%)
Mason, OH	82.7	4.5	10.3	0.0	0.0	0.8	1.7
McCandless, PA	90.8	1.9	6.4	0.1	0.0	0.2	0.7
Menomonee Falls, WI	90.8	2.5	4.7	0.1	0.0	0.7	1.3
Meridian, ID	94.0	0.8	2.0	0.0	0.1	0.8	2.3
Merrimack, NH	95.8	0.1	2.0	0.1	0.0	0.8	1.3
Mount Lebanon, PA	92.7	1.1	3.9	0.1	0.0	0.3	1.8
Mount Pleasant, SC	92.1	4.4	1.8	0.1	0.1	0.1	1.5
Needham, MA	88.4	2.1	6.7	0.0	0.0	0.2	2.5
Newtown, CT	91.8	1.2	2.1	0.0	0.0	3.2	1.8
Northbrook, IL	84.9	0.7	11.7	0.0	0.0	0.7	2.0
Northville, MI	79.9	3.0	14.7	0.1	0.1	0.2	1.9
Novi, MI	71.7	7.4	17.6	0.1	0.0	0.8	2.4
O'Fallon, IL	78.1	14.7	2.5	0.1	0.0	0.8	3.8
O'Fallon, MO	90.0	4.3	3.5	0.1	0.0	0.3	1.7
Orchard Park, NY	97.4	0.9	0.7	0.1	0.0	0.2	0.8
Oviedo, FL	82.5	8.5	5.4	0.3	0.1	1.2	2.0
Parker, CO	90.8	1.3	2.6	0.2	0.1	0.9	4.0
Parkland, FL	83.9	6.8	6.3	0.2	0.0	1.3	1.6
Peachtree City, GA	83.2	8.5	4.7	0.3	0.1	1.2	2.1
Pflugerville, TX	70.2	15.5	8.7	0.4	0.0	2.3	2.8
Plainfield, IL	80.2	6.0	8.4	0.0	0.0	2.8	2.6
Princeton, NJ	73.8	6.3	15.5	0.3	0.0	1.4	2.6
Queen Creek, AZ	86.9	2.8	1.2	1.5	0.1	6.2	1.3
Rancho Palos Verdes, CA	61.9	2.6	28.0	0.2	0.2	1.7	5.4
Redmond, WA	62.9	1.6	29.3	0.2	0.3	1.9	3.9
Richland, WA	84.3	1.6	5.4	1.1	0.1	3.3	4.3
Ridgefield, CT	95.1	0.7	2.0	0.1	0.0	0.9	1.2
Ridgewood, NJ	78.0	2.3	15.5	0.0	0.0	1.6	2.5
Rio Rancho, NM	81.6	3.7	1.7	2.3	0.1	6.4	4.3
Sahuarita, AZ	84.9	3.7	4.2	0.5	0.1	2.9	3.7
Sammamish, WA	73.7	0.8	20.7	0.2	0.2	0.7	3.8
San Ramon, CA	49.3	2.3	40.5	0.3	0.4	1.8	5.5
Saratoga, CA	50.5	0.4	45.1	0.2	0.0	0.4	3.3
Schertz, TX	79.3	9.5	3.1	0.4	0.0	3.7	4.0
Shrewsbury, MA	77.1	2.8	16.4	0.1	0.0	1.0	2.6
South Brunswick, NJ	49.8	7.5	39.8	0.3	0.0	1.0	1.7
South Jordan, UT	92.2	0.4	2.1	0.1	0.9	1.3	3.0
South Kingstown, RI	90.2	2.6	2.3	2.0	0.0	1.3	1.6
South Windsor, CT	81.2	5.1	10.3	0.3	0.2	1.4	1.6
Southlake, TX	87.5	3.1	6.8	0.2	0.0	0.6	1.8
Spring Hill, TN	90.9	4.8	1.0	0.6	0.0	1.7	0.9
Stow, OH	93.6	2.3	1.8	0.2	0.0	0.2	2.0
Sugar Land, TX	51.6	7.2	36.6	0.3	0.0	1.7	2.5
Sun Prairie, WI	86.9	5.4	3.7	0.1	0.0	1.2	2.7
Syracuse, UT	93.5	1.3	1.3	0.1	0.0	1.2	2.7
Tredyffrin, PA	83.7	1.8	12.2	0.1	0.0	0.2	2.1
Upper Arlington, OH	91.9	1.2	4.4	0.2	0.0	0.3	1.9
Upper Dublin, PA	85.0	6.0	7.4	0.0	0.0	0.1	1.5
Vestavia Hills, AL	90.0	3.3	5.2	0.2	0.0	0.7	0.6
Webster, NY	92.7	1.7	3.3	0.0	0.0	0.3	1.9
Wellesley, MA	83.5	2.0	10.8	0.1	0.0	1.2	2.4
West Fargo, ND	90.9	3.8	1.8	0.9	0.1	0.3	2.3
West Linn, OR	89.5	0.6	5.0	0.3	0.1	1.1	3.4
West Windsor, NJ	50.6	2.4	41.8	0.0	0.0	2.7	2.5
Westlake, OH	89.8	2.1	5.5	0.0	0.0	0.4	2.0
Weston, FL	85.4	4.4	4.3	0.4	0.0	3.1	2.4
Westport, CT	90.0	0.8	6.0	0.1	0.0	0.8	2.2
Wilmette, IL	84.2	1.1	12.7	0.2	0.0	0.4	1.3
Woodbury, MN	81.2	5.5	8.9	0.2	0.1	0.7	3.2
Yorba Linda, CA	75.2	1.0	17.0	0.3	0.1	1.5	4.8
U.S.	73.8	12.6	5.0	0.8	0.2	4.7	2.9

Note: (1) Alone is defined as not being in combination with one or more other races; (2) American Indian and Alaska Native; (3) Native Hawaiian and Other Pacific Islander

Source: U.S. Census Bureau, 2010-2014 American Community Survey 5-Year Estimates

Race: Metro Area

Metro Area	White Alone[1] (%)	Black Alone[1] (%)	Asian Alone[1] (%)	AIAN[2] Alone[1] (%)	NHOPI[3] Alone[1] (%)	Other Race Alone[1] (%)	Two or More Races (%)
Aliso Viejo, CA	55.7	6.8	15.1	0.5	0.3	17.9	3.8
Allen, TX	69.5	15.0	5.7	0.4	0.1	6.5	2.7
Alpharetta, GA	56.1	32.9	5.2	0.3	0.0	3.4	2.2
Ankeny, IA	87.6	4.8	3.3	0.2	0.1	1.6	2.3
Apex, NC	69.5	20.2	4.8	0.3	0.0	2.9	2.3
Ballwin, MO	76.5	18.3	2.2	0.2	0.0	0.6	2.1
Beavercreek, OH	79.0	15.6	2.1	0.2	0.0	0.6	2.5
Bella Vista, AR	84.1	2.2	2.7	1.3	1.1	5.8	2.7
Bernards, NJ	59.4	17.2	10.2	0.3	0.0	10.1	2.8
Bethlehem, NY	84.5	7.7	3.6	0.2	0.0	1.3	2.8
Bloomfield, MI	70.2	22.5	3.6	0.3	0.0	1.1	2.3
Bowie, MD	55.9	25.4	9.5	0.3	0.1	5.1	3.7
Bozeman, MT	95.2	0.3	1.1	1.0	0.1	0.3	2.1
Brentwood, TN	77.8	15.3	2.3	0.3	0.0	2.3	2.0
Broomfield, CO	81.5	5.5	3.8	0.8	0.1	4.8	3.5
Carmel, IN	77.9	14.6	2.3	0.2	0.0	2.6	2.3
Cedar Park, TX	78.3	7.3	5.0	0.5	0.1	5.9	2.9
Cheshire, CT	75.2	12.7	3.7	0.2	0.0	5.6	2.5
Chesterfield, MO	76.5	18.3	2.2	0.2	0.0	0.6	2.1
Collierville, TN	48.0	46.0	1.9	0.2	0.1	2.1	1.7
Coppell, TX	69.5	15.0	5.7	0.4	0.1	6.5	2.7
Cornelius, NC	69.2	22.0	3.0	0.4	0.0	3.1	2.2
Cranberry, PA	87.5	8.2	2.0	0.1	0.0	0.3	1.9
Cupertino, CA	50.3	2.6	32.2	0.5	0.4	9.4	4.5
Danville, CA	54.0	8.0	24.0	0.5	0.7	7.5	5.4
Draper, UT	83.9	1.6	3.4	0.8	1.5	6.1	2.6
Dublin, OH	78.0	14.5	3.3	0.2	0.0	1.2	2.9
Eastchester, NY	59.4	17.2	10.2	0.3	0.0	10.1	2.8
Eden Prairie, MN	81.2	7.4	5.9	0.6	0.0	1.8	3.0
Edmond, OK	74.2	10.1	3.0	3.6	0.1	2.7	6.3
Evesham, NJ	68.1	20.9	5.3	0.2	0.0	3.1	2.3
Fishers, IN	77.9	14.6	2.3	0.2	0.0	2.6	2.3
Flower Mound, TX	69.5	15.0	5.7	0.4	0.1	6.5	2.7
Folsom, CA	66.6	7.2	12.4	0.8	0.8	6.4	5.9
Foster City, CA	54.0	8.0	24.0	0.5	0.7	7.5	5.4
Franklin, TN	77.8	15.3	2.3	0.3	0.0	2.3	2.0
Friendswood, TX	65.6	17.2	6.9	0.4	0.1	7.6	2.1
Germantown, TN	48.0	46.0	1.9	0.2	0.1	2.1	1.7
Glastonbury, CT	77.2	10.8	4.3	0.2	0.0	4.5	3.0
Grand Blanc, MI	74.7	20.4	1.0	0.5	0.0	0.5	2.9
Guilderland, NY	84.5	7.7	3.6	0.2	0.0	1.3	2.8
Hampden, PA	82.1	10.2	3.0	0.1	0.0	1.8	2.7
Holly Springs, NC	69.5	20.2	4.8	0.3	0.0	2.9	2.3
Huntersville, NC	69.2	22.0	3.0	0.4	0.0	3.1	2.2
Independence, KY	82.8	12.2	2.1	0.2	0.0	0.8	1.9
Johns Creek, GA	56.1	32.9	5.2	0.3	0.0	3.4	2.2
Keller, TX	69.5	15.0	5.7	0.4	0.1	6.5	2.7
Kirkland, WA	72.5	5.6	11.9	0.9	0.8	2.5	5.7
Lafayette, CO	87.7	0.9	4.2	0.5	0.1	3.7	3.0
Lake Oswego, OR	82.0	2.8	6.0	0.8	0.5	3.8	4.1
League City, TX	65.6	17.2	6.9	0.4	0.1	7.6	2.1
Leawood, KS	79.1	12.5	2.5	0.4	0.1	2.4	2.9
Lee's Summit, MO	79.1	12.5	2.5	0.4	0.1	2.4	2.9
Leesburg, VA	55.9	25.4	9.5	0.3	0.1	5.1	3.7
Lehi, UT	91.7	0.6	1.4	0.5	0.8	2.5	2.5
Lenexa, KS	79.1	12.5	2.5	0.4	0.1	2.4	2.9
Lexington, MA	78.1	7.7	7.0	0.2	0.0	4.1	3.0
Los Altos, CA	50.3	2.6	32.2	0.5	0.4	9.4	4.5
Lower Makefield, PA	68.1	20.9	5.3	0.2	0.0	3.1	2.3
Madison, AL	71.5	21.7	2.2	0.6	0.1	1.1	2.7
Mamaroneck, NY	59.4	17.2	10.2	0.3	0.0	10.1	2.8
Manheim, PA	88.9	3.9	2.0	0.2	0.0	3.1	1.9
Manlius, NY	85.0	8.2	2.7	0.6	0.0	1.0	2.6
Maple Grove, MN	81.2	7.4	5.9	0.6	0.0	1.8	3.0
Marion, IA	91.2	3.8	1.6	0.3	0.0	0.9	2.1
Marlboro, NJ	59.4	17.2	10.2	0.3	0.0	10.1	2.8

Table continued on next page.

Metro Area	White Alone[1] (%)	Black Alone[1] (%)	Asian Alone[1] (%)	AIAN[2] Alone[1] (%)	NHOPI[3] Alone[1] (%)	Other Race Alone[1] (%)	Two or More Races (%)
Mason, OH	82.8	12.2	2.1	0.2	0.0	0.8	1.9
McCandless, PA	87.5	8.2	2.0	0.1	0.0	0.3	1.9
Menomonee Falls, WI	74.5	16.5	3.1	0.4	0.0	2.8	2.6
Meridian, ID	91.5	0.8	2.0	0.7	0.2	2.0	2.7
Merrimack, NH	90.8	2.2	3.5	0.1	0.0	1.1	2.2
Mount Lebanon, PA	87.5	8.2	2.0	0.1	0.0	0.3	1.9
Mount Pleasant, SC	67.2	27.1	1.7	0.3	0.1	1.2	2.4
Needham, MA	78.1	7.7	7.0	0.2	0.0	4.1	3.0
Newtown, CT	74.3	11.1	4.9	0.2	0.0	7.1	2.4
Northbrook, IL	66.6	17.0	6.0	0.2	0.0	7.9	2.2
Northville, MI	70.2	22.5	3.6	0.3	0.0	1.1	2.3
Novi, MI	70.2	22.5	3.6	0.3	0.0	1.1	2.3
O'Fallon, IL	76.5	18.3	2.2	0.2	0.0	0.6	2.1
O'Fallon, MO	76.5	18.3	2.2	0.2	0.0	0.6	2.1
Orchard Park, NY	80.9	12.1	2.6	0.6	0.1	1.7	2.2
Oviedo, FL	71.9	16.2	4.1	0.3	0.1	4.5	3.0
Parker, CO	81.5	5.5	3.8	0.8	0.1	4.8	3.5
Parkland, FL	71.6	21.3	2.4	0.2	0.0	2.6	1.9
Peachtree City, GA	56.1	32.9	5.2	0.3	0.0	3.4	2.2
Pflugerville, TX	78.3	7.3	5.0	0.5	0.1	5.9	2.9
Plainfield, IL	66.6	17.0	6.0	0.2	0.0	7.9	2.2
Princeton, NJ	62.4	20.2	9.6	0.2	0.0	5.6	2.1
Queen Creek, AZ	80.0	5.1	3.5	2.2	0.2	5.9	3.0
Rancho Palos Verdes, CA	55.7	6.8	15.1	0.5	0.3	17.9	3.8
Redmond, WA	72.5	5.6	11.9	0.9	0.8	2.5	5.7
Richland, WA	75.9	1.7	2.5	0.7	0.1	15.9	3.2
Ridgefield, CT	74.3	11.1	4.9	0.2	0.0	7.1	2.4
Ridgewood, NJ	59.4	17.2	10.2	0.3	0.0	10.1	2.8
Rio Rancho, NM	71.8	2.7	2.0	5.5	0.1	14.1	3.8
Sahuarita, AZ	78.8	3.6	2.7	3.2	0.1	8.2	3.5
Sammamish, WA	72.5	5.6	11.9	0.9	0.8	2.5	5.7
San Ramon, CA	54.0	8.0	24.0	0.5	0.7	7.5	5.4
Saratoga, CA	50.3	2.6	32.2	0.5	0.4	9.4	4.5
Schertz, TX	79.0	6.5	2.2	0.6	0.1	8.5	3.0
Shrewsbury, MA	86.2	4.1	3.9	0.2	0.0	2.8	2.7
South Brunswick, NJ	59.4	17.2	10.2	0.3	0.0	10.1	2.8
South Jordan, UT	83.9	1.6	3.4	0.8	1.5	6.1	2.6
South Kingstown, RI	83.6	5.4	2.7	0.4	0.0	5.1	2.7
South Windsor, CT	77.2	10.8	4.3	0.2	0.0	4.5	3.0
Southlake, TX	69.5	15.0	5.7	0.4	0.1	6.5	2.7
Spring Hill, TN	77.8	15.3	2.3	0.3	0.0	2.3	2.0
Stow, OH	82.9	11.9	2.2	0.2	0.0	0.4	2.4
Sugar Land, TX	65.6	17.2	6.9	0.4	0.1	7.6	2.1
Sun Prairie, WI	87.1	4.3	4.3	0.2	0.0	1.5	2.4
Syracuse, UT	89.4	1.1	1.5	0.6	0.4	4.2	2.7
Tredyffrin, PA	68.1	20.9	5.3	0.2	0.0	3.1	2.3
Upper Arlington, OH	78.0	14.5	3.3	0.2	0.0	1.2	2.9
Upper Dublin, PA	68.1	20.9	5.3	0.2	0.0	3.1	2.3
Vestavia Hills, AL	66.8	28.5	1.3	0.3	0.0	2.0	1.1
Webster, NY	81.4	11.4	2.7	0.3	0.0	1.8	2.3
Wellesley, MA	78.1	7.7	7.0	0.2	0.0	4.1	3.0
West Fargo, ND	91.1	2.5	2.1	1.2	0.0	0.6	2.4
West Linn, OR	82.0	2.8	6.0	0.8	0.5	3.8	4.1
West Windsor, NJ	62.4	20.2	9.6	0.2	0.0	5.6	2.1
Westlake, OH	74.4	20.0	2.1	0.2	0.0	1.0	2.3
Weston, FL	71.6	21.3	2.4	0.2	0.0	2.6	1.9
Westport, CT	74.3	11.1	4.9	0.2	0.0	7.1	2.4
Wilmette, IL	66.6	17.0	6.0	0.2	0.0	7.9	2.2
Woodbury, MN	81.2	7.4	5.9	0.6	0.0	1.8	3.0
Yorba Linda, CA	55.7	6.8	15.1	0.5	0.3	17.9	3.8
U.S.	73.8	12.6	5.0	0.8	0.2	4.7	2.9

Note: (1) Figures cover the Metropolitan Statistical Area (MSA)—see Appendix B for areas included; (1) Alone is defined as not being in combination with one or more other races; (2) American Indian and Alaska Native; (3) Native Hawaiian & Other Pacific Islander
Source: U.S. Census Bureau, 2010-2014 American Community Survey 5-Year Estimates

Hispanic Origin: City

City	Hispanic or Latino (%)	Mexican (%)	Puerto Rican (%)	Cuban (%)	Other Hispanic or Latino (%)
Aliso Viejo, CA	16.5	11.7	0.3	0.1	4.3
Allen, TX	10.8	7.4	1.2	0.4	1.8
Alpharetta, GA	8.2	3.4	0.8	0.3	3.6
Ankeny, IA	2.0	1.5	0.0	0.0	0.5
Apex, NC	7.6	2.9	2.1	0.2	2.4
Ballwin, MO	1.8	0.6	0.2	0.1	0.9
Beavercreek, OH	3.0	1.6	0.8	0.1	0.5
Bella Vista, AR	3.9	3.3	0.1	0.0	0.5
Bernards, NJ	4.9	1.7	0.7	0.3	2.2
Bethlehem, NY	2.6	0.1	1.1	0.0	1.4
Bloomfield, MI	1.2	0.7	0.1	0.1	0.4
Bowie, MD	6.7	0.9	1.0	0.6	4.3
Bozeman, MT	3.0	1.9	0.1	0.1	0.9
Brentwood, TN	2.6	1.1	0.1	0.4	0.9
Broomfield, CO	11.6	8.8	0.2	0.3	2.4
Carmel, IN	3.5	2.0	0.1	0.2	1.3
Cedar Park, TX	16.0	12.5	0.6	0.6	2.3
Cheshire, CT	6.8	0.9	4.2	0.1	1.6
Chesterfield, MO	3.5	1.7	0.5	0.3	1.0
Collierville, TN	2.9	2.1	0.1	0.1	0.6
Coppell, TX	11.3	8.3	0.4	0.2	2.4
Cornelius, NC	7.2	3.3	2.0	0.4	1.5
Cranberry, PA	1.0	0.5	0.3	0.0	0.2
Cupertino, CA	4.7	3.0	0.3	0.0	1.4
Danville, CA	5.8	3.5	0.1	0.1	2.0
Draper, UT	7.6	4.9	0.1	0.0	2.7
Dublin, OH	4.5	2.2	0.9	0.2	1.2
Eastchester, NY	7.3	1.1	2.9	0.1	3.3
Eden Prairie, MN	3.1	1.8	0.2	0.0	1.1
Edmond, OK	5.0	3.4	0.2	0.3	1.0
Evesham, NJ	3.7	1.0	1.8	0.2	0.8
Fishers, IN	3.3	1.8	0.1	0.0	1.3
Flower Mound, TX	8.5	5.9	0.4	0.2	1.9
Folsom, CA	11.8	8.9	0.4	0.1	2.4
Foster City, CA	5.5	3.5	0.3	0.0	1.7
Franklin, TN	6.7	4.2	0.3	0.8	1.3
Friendswood, TX	14.9	10.8	0.7	0.5	2.8
Germantown, TN	3.0	0.8	0.6	0.2	1.3
Glastonbury, CT	3.9	0.6	1.3	0.2	1.8
Grand Blanc, MI	2.2	1.6	0.1	0.2	0.2
Guilderland, NY	3.4	0.3	1.5	0.0	1.6
Hampden, PA	2.3	0.9	1.0	0.0	0.4
Holly Springs, NC	3.8	0.7	1.7	0.4	0.9
Huntersville, NC	5.1	2.7	0.8	0.3	1.3
Independence, KY	2.1	0.5	0.1	0.0	1.5
Johns Creek, GA	5.5	2.2	0.6	0.6	2.2
Keller, TX	7.2	4.7	0.6	0.1	1.8
Kirkland, WA	6.4	4.2	0.2	0.0	2.1
Lafayette, CO	14.7	11.1	0.1	0.1	3.4
Lake Oswego, OR	4.0	2.8	0.1	0.1	1.0
League City, TX	18.9	11.6	1.5	0.4	5.4
Leawood, KS	1.9	0.8	0.1	0.4	0.6
Lee's Summit, MO	3.9	2.8	0.4	0.1	0.7
Leesburg, VA	19.1	1.9	1.5	0.3	15.4
Lehi, UT	7.8	5.3	0.2	0.0	2.3
Lenexa, KS	8.0	5.4	0.0	0.2	2.3
Lexington, MA	1.8	0.5	0.0	0.1	1.3
Los Altos, CA	3.6	1.6	0.1	0.0	2.0
Lower Makefield, PA	1.6	0.3	0.5	0.2	0.5
Madison, AL	4.5	2.2	1.4	0.1	0.9
Mamaroneck, NY	12.0	2.3	2.3	0.3	7.0
Manheim, PA	8.4	0.6	4.7	0.6	2.5
Manlius, NY	1.3	0.2	0.4	0.0	0.6
Maple Grove, MN	2.1	0.9	0.1	0.1	1.1
Marion, IA	1.5	0.7	0.1	0.1	0.7
Marlboro, NJ	4.1	0.2	1.3	0.6	2.1
Mason, OH	4.6	2.1	0.2	0.6	1.7

Table continued on next page.

City	Hispanic or Latino (%)	Mexican (%)	Puerto Rican (%)	Cuban (%)	Other Hispanic or Latino (%)
McCandless, PA	1.2	0.5	0.2	0.0	0.5
Menomonee Falls, WI	2.4	1.1	0.3	0.0	1.0
Meridian, ID	7.1	5.8	0.3	0.0	0.9
Merrimack, NH	2.6	0.7	0.7	0.3	1.0
Mount Lebanon, PA	2.2	0.9	0.6	0.1	0.7
Mount Pleasant, SC	2.8	1.1	0.3	0.0	1.5
Needham, MA	2.5	0.3	0.7	0.3	1.3
Newtown, CT	8.1	0.8	1.6	0.4	5.3
Northbrook, IL	2.7	0.8	0.3	0.6	1.1
Northville, MI	4.2	2.9	0.1	0.0	1.2
Novi, MI	2.8	1.9	0.2	0.0	0.7
O'Fallon, IL	3.1	1.8	0.9	0.1	0.3
O'Fallon, MO	2.0	1.4	0.2	0.0	0.4
Orchard Park, NY	1.9	0.2	0.5	0.0	1.1
Oviedo, FL	19.5	1.3	7.9	2.4	7.9
Parker, CO	7.6	5.4	0.4	0.0	1.8
Parkland, FL	19.3	1.8	1.8	3.5	12.2
Peachtree City, GA	7.9	4.4	0.8	0.6	2.0
Pflugerville, TX	27.4	22.1	1.1	0.9	3.3
Plainfield, IL	10.5	7.6	1.1	0.3	1.4
Princeton, NJ	6.4	0.9	1.1	0.5	3.9
Queen Creek, AZ	17.7	11.0	1.4	0.2	5.1
Rancho Palos Verdes, CA	7.8	5.1	0.3	0.3	2.1
Redmond, WA	9.3	6.8	0.6	0.0	1.8
Richland, WA	9.0	7.4	0.5	0.0	1.1
Ridgefield, CT	5.2	0.5	0.8	0.8	3.2
Ridgewood, NJ	7.1	1.2	0.8	0.5	4.6
Rio Rancho, NM	38.9	18.6	0.5	0.1	19.7
Sahuarita, AZ	30.2	26.3	0.7	0.1	3.1
Sammamish, WA	4.1	1.8	0.1	0.1	2.0
San Ramon, CA	8.6	5.1	0.4	0.1	3.1
Saratoga, CA	3.3	1.9	0.3	0.1	1.0
Schertz, TX	26.6	22.3	1.8	0.0	2.5
Shrewsbury, MA	3.5	0.3	1.6	0.0	1.6
South Brunswick, NJ	4.9	0.3	2.0	0.2	2.3
South Jordan, UT	5.1	3.0	0.5	0.0	1.5
South Kingstown, RI	3.9	0.3	1.2	0.2	2.2
South Windsor, CT	5.6	0.6	1.9	1.0	2.1
Southlake, TX	6.0	2.9	0.6	0.0	2.4
Spring Hill, TN	7.5	5.6	0.8	0.1	1.1
Stow, OH	1.2	0.5	0.2	0.0	0.5
Sugar Land, TX	11.1	7.7	0.5	0.3	2.6
Sun Prairie, WI	3.6	2.1	0.1	0.0	1.3
Syracuse, UT	6.4	3.6	0.0	0.1	2.7
Tredyffrin, PA	1.7	0.5	0.3	0.1	0.8
Upper Arlington, OH	2.8	1.1	0.7	0.2	0.7
Upper Dublin, PA	2.1	1.0	0.3	0.0	0.7
Vestavia Hills, AL	1.4	0.6	0.1	0.0	0.7
Webster, NY	2.6	0.4	1.4	0.2	0.6
Wellesley, MA	4.9	0.9	0.9	0.5	2.6
West Fargo, ND	1.0	0.9	0.0	0.0	0.0
West Linn, OR	4.6	3.8	0.7	0.0	0.1
West Windsor, NJ	6.0	0.9	1.2	0.0	3.9
Westlake, OH	3.4	0.9	1.3	0.2	0.9
Weston, FL	47.8	1.7	3.4	3.8	38.9
Westport, CT	4.6	0.8	1.1	0.4	2.3
Wilmette, IL	4.6	1.8	0.6	0.7	1.6
Woodbury, MN	4.6	3.1	0.1	0.0	1.4
Yorba Linda, CA	17.0	12.9	0.2	0.6	3.2
U.S.	16.9	10.8	1.6	0.6	3.8

Note: Persons of Hispanic or Latino origin can be of any race
Source: U.S. Census Bureau, 2010-2014 American Community Survey 5-Year Estimates

Hispanic Origin: Metro Area

Metro Area	Hispanic or Latino (%)	Mexican (%)	Puerto Rican (%)	Cuban (%)	Other Hispanic or Latino (%)
Aliso Viejo, CA	44.8	35.0	0.5	0.4	8.9
Allen, TX	27.8	23.6	0.6	0.2	3.4
Alpharetta, GA	10.4	5.9	0.9	0.4	3.2
Ankeny, IA	6.9	5.3	0.2	0.1	1.3
Apex, NC	10.3	6.0	1.0	0.3	3.0
Ballwin, MO	2.7	1.8	0.2	0.1	0.6
Beavercreek, OH	2.3	1.3	0.4	0.1	0.5
Bella Vista, AR	15.3	11.5	0.3	0.1	3.4
Bernards, NJ	23.3	3.0	6.4	0.7	13.1
Bethlehem, NY	4.5	0.7	2.3	0.2	1.4
Bloomfield, MI	4.1	2.9	0.5	0.1	0.6
Bowie, MD	14.5	2.2	1.0	0.3	11.0
Bozeman, MT	2.9	2.1	0.1	0.1	0.7
Brentwood, TN	6.7	4.3	0.4	0.2	1.7
Broomfield, CO	22.7	18.0	0.5	0.1	4.0
Carmel, IN	6.2	4.5	0.3	0.1	1.3
Cedar Park, TX	31.7	26.7	0.6	0.4	4.0
Cheshire, CT	16.0	1.9	9.8	0.3	4.0
Chesterfield, MO	2.7	1.8	0.2	0.1	0.6
Collierville, TN	5.1	3.7	0.3	0.1	1.0
Coppell, TX	27.8	23.6	0.6	0.2	3.4
Cornelius, NC	9.4	4.6	0.9	0.3	3.7
Cranberry, PA	1.4	0.5	0.4	0.1	0.5
Cupertino, CA	27.7	23.5	0.4	0.1	3.6
Danville, CA	21.8	14.8	0.6	0.2	6.2
Draper, UT	17.2	13.0	0.3	0.1	3.8
Dublin, OH	3.7	2.1	0.5	0.1	1.0
Eastchester, NY	23.3	3.0	6.4	0.7	13.1
Eden Prairie, MN	5.5	3.7	0.3	0.1	1.4
Edmond, OK	11.9	9.9	0.3	0.1	1.7
Evesham, NJ	8.3	1.7	4.3	0.2	2.1
Fishers, IN	6.2	4.5	0.3	0.1	1.3
Flower Mound, TX	27.8	23.6	0.6	0.2	3.4
Folsom, CA	20.6	17.0	0.7	0.1	2.8
Foster City, CA	21.8	14.8	0.6	0.2	6.2
Franklin, TN	6.7	4.3	0.4	0.2	1.7
Friendswood, TX	35.9	27.7	0.6	0.4	7.3
Germantown, TN	5.1	3.7	0.3	0.1	1.0
Glastonbury, CT	13.3	0.9	9.0	0.3	3.0
Grand Blanc, MI	3.1	2.5	0.2	0.1	0.3
Guilderland, NY	4.5	0.7	2.3	0.2	1.4
Hampden, PA	5.2	0.9	2.7	0.2	1.4
Holly Springs, NC	10.3	6.0	1.0	0.3	3.0
Huntersville, NC	9.4	4.6	0.9	0.3	3.7
Independence, KY	2.8	1.4	0.3	0.1	1.0
Johns Creek, GA	10.4	5.9	0.9	0.4	3.2
Keller, TX	27.8	23.6	0.6	0.2	3.4
Kirkland, WA	9.3	6.7	0.6	0.1	1.9
Lafayette, CO	13.6	10.5	0.3	0.2	2.6
Lake Oswego, OR	11.2	9.1	0.3	0.2	1.6
League City, TX	35.9	27.7	0.6	0.4	7.3
Leawood, KS	8.5	6.5	0.3	0.2	1.5
Lee's Summit, MO	8.5	6.5	0.3	0.2	1.5
Leesburg, VA	14.5	2.2	1.0	0.3	11.0
Lehi, UT	10.9	7.3	0.2	0.1	3.3
Lenexa, KS	8.5	6.5	0.3	0.2	1.5
Lexington, MA	9.7	0.6	2.7	0.2	6.2
Los Altos, CA	27.7	23.5	0.4	0.1	3.6
Lower Makefield, PA	8.3	1.7	4.3	0.2	2.1
Madison, AL	4.9	3.3	0.6	0.1	0.8
Mamaroneck, NY	23.3	3.0	6.4	0.7	13.1
Manheim, PA	9.3	0.9	6.2	0.4	1.7
Manlius, NY	3.7	0.5	1.8	0.3	1.1
Maple Grove, MN	5.5	3.7	0.3	0.1	1.4
Marion, IA	2.5	1.9	0.1	0.0	0.5
Marlboro, NJ	23.3	3.0	6.4	0.7	13.1
Mason, OH	2.8	1.4	0.3	0.1	1.0

Table continued on next page.

Metro Area	Hispanic or Latino (%)	Mexican (%)	Puerto Rican (%)	Cuban (%)	Other Hispanic or Latino (%)
McCandless, PA	1.4	0.5	0.4	0.1	0.5
Menomonee Falls, WI	9.9	6.6	2.3	0.1	0.9
Meridian, ID	12.9	11.1	0.3	0.1	1.4
Merrimack, NH	5.6	1.7	1.7	0.1	2.1
Mount Lebanon, PA	1.4	0.5	0.4	0.1	0.5
Mount Pleasant, SC	5.3	3.0	0.8	0.2	1.4
Needham, MA	9.7	0.6	2.7	0.2	6.2
Newtown, CT	17.9	2.1	5.9	0.4	9.4
Northbrook, IL	21.2	16.8	2.1	0.2	2.0
Northville, MI	4.1	2.9	0.5	0.1	0.6
Novi, MI	4.1	2.9	0.5	0.1	0.6
O'Fallon, IL	2.7	1.8	0.2	0.1	0.6
O'Fallon, MO	2.7	1.8	0.2	0.1	0.6
Orchard Park, NY	4.4	0.5	3.0	0.1	0.9
Oviedo, FL	26.7	3.1	13.5	2.0	8.1
Parker, CO	22.7	18.0	0.5	0.1	4.0
Parkland, FL	42.4	2.4	3.9	18.2	17.9
Peachtree City, GA	10.4	5.9	0.9	0.4	3.2
Pflugerville, TX	31.7	26.7	0.6	0.4	4.0
Plainfield, IL	21.2	16.8	2.1	0.2	2.0
Princeton, NJ	15.9	1.8	4.8	0.3	9.0
Queen Creek, AZ	29.8	26.8	0.6	0.2	2.3
Rancho Palos Verdes, CA	44.8	35.0	0.5	0.4	8.9
Redmond, WA	9.3	6.7	0.6	0.1	1.9
Richland, WA	29.6	27.3	0.4	0.1	1.8
Ridgefield, CT	17.9	2.1	5.9	0.4	9.4
Ridgewood, NJ	23.3	3.0	6.4	0.7	13.1
Rio Rancho, NM	47.4	26.1	0.4	0.4	20.5
Sahuarita, AZ	35.4	32.1	0.6	0.2	2.5
Sammamish, WA	9.3	6.7	0.6	0.1	1.9
San Ramon, CA	21.8	14.8	0.6	0.2	6.2
Saratoga, CA	27.7	23.5	0.4	0.1	3.6
Schertz, TX	54.4	48.7	1.0	0.2	4.4
Shrewsbury, MA	10.0	0.7	5.8	0.1	3.4
South Brunswick, NJ	23.3	3.0	6.4	0.7	13.1
South Jordan, UT	17.2	13.0	0.3	0.1	3.8
South Kingstown, RI	10.9	0.8	3.7	0.1	6.3
South Windsor, CT	13.3	0.9	9.0	0.3	3.0
Southlake, TX	27.8	23.6	0.6	0.2	3.4
Spring Hill, TN	6.7	4.3	0.4	0.2	1.7
Stow, OH	1.7	0.8	0.5	0.0	0.4
Sugar Land, TX	35.9	27.7	0.6	0.4	7.3
Sun Prairie, WI	5.4	3.9	0.4	0.1	1.0
Syracuse, UT	11.9	8.8	0.2	0.1	2.8
Tredyffrin, PA	8.3	1.7	4.3	0.2	2.1
Upper Arlington, OH	3.7	2.1	0.5	0.1	1.0
Upper Dublin, PA	8.3	1.7	4.3	0.2	2.1
Vestavia Hills, AL	4.3	3.3	0.2	0.1	0.7
Webster, NY	6.5	0.7	4.3	0.3	1.2
Wellesley, MA	9.7	0.6	2.7	0.2	6.2
West Fargo, ND	2.7	2.0	0.1	0.1	0.6
West Linn, OR	11.2	9.1	0.3	0.2	1.6
West Windsor, NJ	15.9	1.8	4.8	0.3	9.0
Westlake, OH	5.0	1.3	2.9	0.1	0.8
Weston, FL	42.4	2.4	3.9	18.2	17.9
Westport, CT	17.9	2.1	5.9	0.4	9.4
Wilmette, IL	21.2	16.8	2.1	0.2	2.0
Woodbury, MN	5.5	3.7	0.3	0.1	1.4
Yorba Linda, CA	44.8	35.0	0.5	0.4	8.9
U.S.	16.9	10.8	1.6	0.6	3.8

Note: Persons of Hispanic or Latino origin can be of any race; Figures cover the Metropolitan Statistical Area (MSA)—see Appendix B for areas included
Source: U.S. Census Bureau, 2010-2014 American Community Survey 5-Year Estimates

Age: City

City	Percent of Population							
	Under Age 5	Age 5–19	Age 20–34	Age 35–44	Age 45–54	Age 55–64	Age 65–74	Age 75–84
Aliso Viejo, CA	8.5	19.8	19.8	18.4	17.7	8.7	5.1	1.0
Allen, TX	7.5	25.6	16.0	19.0	16.6	8.9	4.0	1.8
Alpharetta, GA	7.8	24.0	16.2	16.4	16.4	10.9	4.3	2.4
Ankeny, IA	8.4	20.5	26.1	14.6	11.5	9.6	5.4	2.8
Apex, NC	7.9	26.9	13.9	20.5	16.7	8.3	3.9	1.4
Ballwin, MO	5.0	20.4	15.7	13.2	14.5	15.0	9.7	5.1
Beavercreek, OH	4.7	17.6	21.0	12.3	14.0	14.7	9.2	4.5
Bella Vista, AR	5.9	13.7	12.1	11.7	11.8	11.8	17.7	10.2
Bernards, NJ	4.5	26.2	9.8	14.4	17.7	14.0	6.8	3.5
Bethlehem, NY	5.9	20.4	13.9	13.1	15.9	15.5	7.5	5.2
Bloomfield, MI	4.6	19.4	11.1	10.6	15.5	16.6	12.7	6.3
Bowie, MD	6.7	19.6	18.1	14.5	17.4	12.0	6.5	3.5
Bozeman, MT	5.1	17.6	40.9	12.3	8.3	7.7	4.0	2.2
Brentwood, TN	5.6	27.4	9.0	15.1	18.2	13.3	7.5	2.7
Broomfield, CO	6.3	20.7	19.8	15.9	14.7	11.5	6.5	2.9
Carmel, IN	6.3	24.4	13.2	15.2	16.6	12.6	7.0	3.0
Cedar Park, TX	7.8	23.8	19.0	18.6	13.7	9.1	4.9	2.1
Cheshire, CT	3.4	21.9	14.9	12.8	18.0	14.5	7.8	4.3
Chesterfield, MO	4.7	19.0	13.2	10.5	16.9	13.7	11.7	6.9
Collierville, TN	5.5	25.3	14.2	14.3	17.9	12.9	6.0	2.9
Coppell, TX	5.4	25.5	13.9	16.1	20.6	12.3	4.0	1.6
Cornelius, NC	6.3	20.3	19.5	16.6	14.6	11.5	7.2	3.0
Cranberry, PA	6.6	23.8	13.9	16.9	17.5	11.8	5.4	2.6
Cupertino, CA	5.9	22.9	12.1	17.9	17.7	10.4	6.7	4.1
Danville, CA	5.5	23.9	8.5	12.4	18.2	15.7	8.1	5.0
Draper, UT	9.4	26.1	20.4	16.3	12.7	9.2	3.7	1.7
Dublin, OH	6.7	25.1	12.3	15.9	17.7	13.2	5.8	2.1
Eastchester, NY	4.8	21.3	14.1	13.7	17.4	11.5	8.6	5.9
Eden Prairie, MN	6.7	21.2	18.3	13.7	17.7	13.2	5.6	2.4
Edmond, OK	6.4	22.3	20.7	12.2	14.3	12.0	7.0	3.6
Evesham, NJ	5.0	19.5	18.0	13.7	16.7	13.0	7.2	4.5
Fishers, IN	8.2	26.3	17.8	18.2	15.2	7.8	3.9	2.0
Flower Mound, TX	5.5	27.3	11.9	17.4	20.7	10.8	4.3	1.6
Folsom, CA	6.2	19.4	18.7	17.0	16.5	11.5	5.8	3.3
Foster City, CA	6.3	16.7	17.3	17.2	13.7	12.6	9.4	4.9
Franklin, TN	6.4	22.0	17.6	16.7	14.7	11.9	5.5	3.9
Friendswood, TX	4.4	24.4	14.1	12.6	17.9	12.7	8.7	3.6
Germantown, TN	5.5	20.6	10.9	12.3	15.7	17.8	10.4	5.3
Glastonbury, CT	5.5	21.8	10.3	14.1	18.2	14.8	8.6	4.3
Grand Blanc, MI	6.0	22.4	18.7	14.4	13.6	11.5	7.8	3.6
Guilderland, NY	3.7	20.4	19.6	11.2	15.1	15.3	7.5	5.1
Hampden, PA	4.8	19.5	13.9	14.2	14.6	16.6	9.5	4.7
Holly Springs, NC	10.1	24.9	17.1	19.6	13.4	8.0	5.2	1.3
Huntersville, NC	7.4	21.6	19.0	18.2	17.1	8.8	5.3	1.5
Independence, KY	10.6	23.5	20.2	16.1	12.2	10.2	4.8	1.7
Johns Creek, GA	6.3	26.1	12.5	16.3	18.7	12.1	5.2	2.0
Keller, TX	5.1	26.2	12.7	15.3	18.6	11.7	6.5	3.1
Kirkland, WA	6.7	15.9	23.3	14.9	14.8	13.0	6.9	3.0
Lafayette, CO	6.6	18.7	19.3	16.6	15.1	14.2	5.5	3.3
Lake Oswego, OR	4.3	19.7	11.6	13.5	16.2	17.1	10.1	4.3
League City, TX	7.4	22.2	20.3	15.7	15.5	10.6	5.1	2.4
Leawood, KS	5.3	24.0	7.5	14.2	16.5	16.1	9.2	4.8
Lee's Summit, MO	7.2	22.8	17.0	13.7	15.3	11.8	6.4	3.6
Leesburg, VA	8.2	22.5	21.6	16.2	15.5	9.2	4.0	1.8
Lehi, UT	13.9	31.8	22.5	14.2	7.0	5.6	3.0	1.5
Lenexa, KS	6.9	19.4	21.3	13.7	12.6	14.8	6.1	2.9
Lexington, MA	5.3	23.6	8.0	12.5	17.6	14.7	9.0	6.0
Los Altos, CA	5.4	21.6	7.4	13.6	16.7	14.7	10.1	6.4
Lower Makefield, PA	4.7	22.3	11.3	13.1	18.4	15.8	9.3	3.5
Madison, AL	5.8	23.2	18.6	13.5	18.4	11.4	6.2	1.9
Mamaroneck, NY	6.4	21.0	14.4	13.3	16.5	12.4	7.7	5.8
Manheim, PA	5.7	19.4	13.8	12.5	14.7	12.6	9.9	7.0
Manlius, NY	5.0	19.5	13.2	12.1	16.9	15.2	9.5	5.9
Maple Grove, MN	6.8	21.6	16.8	15.9	16.2	14.1	5.8	2.0
Marion, IA	5.9	21.7	20.1	14.1	14.3	10.5	7.4	4.4
Marlboro, NJ	5.2	24.0	12.3	12.7	20.0	13.4	7.1	3.7
Mason, OH	5.4	27.8	12.2	14.3	17.9	10.4	6.4	4.0

Table continued on next page.

City	Percent of Population							
	Under Age 5	Age 5–19	Age 20–34	Age 35–44	Age 45–54	Age 55–64	Age 65–74	Age 75–84
McCandless, PA	6.1	16.8	17.3	11.0	15.2	15.2	9.5	5.3
Menomonee Falls, WI	5.3	18.7	15.5	12.1	15.7	13.7	9.0	6.4
Meridian, ID	7.9	25.6	18.1	15.3	13.5	9.7	6.1	2.7
Merrimack, NH	5.4	18.8	15.2	13.9	19.5	15.0	7.0	3.5
Mount Lebanon, PA	5.1	19.8	14.0	12.4	15.8	13.5	9.1	6.1
Mount Pleasant, SC	5.8	19.3	19.3	15.3	14.7	12.2	7.5	4.4
Needham, MA	7.0	22.4	10.2	13.5	15.5	14.1	8.2	4.5
Newtown, CT	4.2	24.3	10.9	13.1	20.2	12.8	7.5	5.3
Northbrook, IL	4.6	21.2	8.3	12.4	15.8	14.2	11.6	7.9
Northville, MI	4.6	21.0	13.1	14.0	17.9	12.3	8.9	5.3
Novi, MI	5.6	20.8	17.1	15.1	16.1	12.1	5.9	4.3
O'Fallon, IL	6.9	23.8	17.9	16.9	14.2	10.7	5.8	3.2
O'Fallon, MO	7.3	24.2	18.3	16.1	14.7	9.4	5.2	3.2
Orchard Park, NY	4.4	20.5	12.8	11.5	17.8	14.9	9.3	6.3
Oviedo, FL	6.1	24.7	20.8	14.7	16.0	10.5	3.9	2.0
Parker, CO	7.5	26.7	17.1	19.6	15.5	8.2	3.8	1.2
Parkland, FL	7.1	27.0	12.7	16.2	16.6	12.5	5.5	1.2
Peachtree City, GA	4.3	24.7	13.4	12.4	17.1	14.8	8.4	3.1
Pflugerville, TX	7.2	24.3	16.1	17.9	15.4	12.2	4.7	1.5
Plainfield, IL	7.0	29.5	14.4	19.6	15.8	7.8	3.9	1.5
Princeton, NJ	4.4	23.1	24.8	8.9	13.1	11.6	7.0	4.9
Queen Creek, AZ	10.4	30.7	15.4	17.6	11.6	7.7	4.6	1.6
Rancho Palos Verdes, CA	3.5	19.8	9.2	10.3	18.1	13.9	12.0	9.5
Redmond, WA	8.1	15.0	27.9	18.3	11.2	9.9	4.7	3.1
Richland, WA	7.2	20.1	19.3	12.1	14.3	12.4	8.7	4.1
Ridgefield, CT	4.6	27.4	7.8	12.9	19.2	14.5	6.8	5.1
Ridgewood, NJ	5.0	27.6	10.1	13.9	18.5	12.3	6.6	3.6
Rio Rancho, NM	6.6	23.3	18.2	14.1	14.2	11.5	7.3	3.2
Sahuarita, AZ	9.6	22.8	17.5	14.1	9.6	9.6	10.2	5.5
Sammamish, WA	7.2	27.8	10.5	19.3	18.1	10.3	4.8	1.4
San Ramon, CA	6.4	25.4	13.7	19.5	17.2	9.3	5.3	2.3
Saratoga, CA	2.9	21.9	8.1	11.8	19.9	15.5	9.9	6.2
Schertz, TX	7.2	21.9	19.5	12.5	15.1	12.0	7.3	3.6
Shrewsbury, MA	5.6	22.9	15.0	14.7	16.9	11.2	7.5	4.1
South Brunswick, NJ	4.4	23.4	14.9	16.4	18.1	11.5	6.2	3.3
South Jordan, UT	9.5	26.5	20.9	13.5	11.9	10.0	4.9	2.1
South Kingstown, RI	3.2	27.6	17.8	8.3	13.1	14.0	8.1	5.2
South Windsor, CT	5.4	20.8	14.2	12.9	17.6	13.6	8.2	5.2
Southlake, TX	4.6	30.6	6.5	14.2	23.1	13.5	4.1	1.9
Spring Hill, TN	9.5	25.6	19.5	19.4	13.4	6.7	4.8	0.8
Stow, OH	5.2	19.1	19.7	12.3	14.6	14.0	8.4	5.0
Sugar Land, TX	5.5	21.0	16.0	12.8	17.3	15.7	7.2	3.2
Sun Prairie, WI	8.1	21.4	22.1	14.8	13.2	10.9	5.8	2.6
Syracuse, UT	9.9	34.3	15.2	17.0	11.0	6.8	3.9	1.7
Tredyffrin, PA	5.3	20.1	14.6	12.7	17.0	14.5	8.1	5.7
Upper Arlington, OH	6.4	21.1	13.6	13.2	15.3	13.8	8.3	5.2
Upper Dublin, PA	4.9	21.6	11.6	12.3	17.6	15.2	9.3	4.5
Vestavia Hills, AL	5.6	21.2	15.7	13.8	14.8	13.0	7.2	5.3
Webster, NY	6.0	19.3	14.6	13.3	16.0	13.8	9.4	4.7
Wellesley, MA	5.1	30.2	13.3	11.3	15.4	10.9	7.0	4.5
West Fargo, ND	8.0	20.7	24.3	14.7	13.4	10.0	5.9	2.3
West Linn, OR	3.5	21.6	13.0	14.1	17.1	16.5	8.9	3.7
West Windsor, NJ	5.8	23.6	12.8	16.7	17.3	12.2	6.4	3.6
Westlake, OH	4.3	19.2	12.7	13.4	15.3	15.2	10.0	5.8
Weston, FL	4.6	28.4	11.8	16.0	19.5	11.0	4.8	2.7
Westport, CT	4.9	25.9	6.9	11.7	19.6	14.8	9.1	5.2
Wilmette, IL	5.4	25.3	8.1	12.9	16.4	14.2	9.5	5.1
Woodbury, MN	7.1	23.0	18.0	15.3	16.1	10.9	5.7	2.7
Yorba Linda, CA	6.1	20.4	16.2	12.2	17.6	14.0	8.2	3.6
U.S.	6.4	19.9	20.6	13.0	14.1	12.3	7.6	4.3

Source: U.S. Census Bureau, 2010-2014 American Community Survey 5-Year Estimates

Age: Metro Area

Metro Area	Percent of Population							
	Under Age 5	Age 5–19	Age 20–34	Age 35–44	Age 45–54	Age 55–64	Age 65–74	Age 75–84
Aliso Viejo, CA	6.4	20.0	22.6	14.2	14.0	11.0	6.4	3.6
Allen, TX	7.4	22.4	21.5	14.7	14.0	10.4	5.7	2.8
Alpharetta, GA	6.9	21.7	20.7	15.2	14.6	10.9	6.1	2.8
Ankeny, IA	7.3	20.9	21.3	13.7	13.7	11.4	6.4	3.5
Apex, NC	6.8	21.5	20.8	15.7	14.6	10.6	5.9	2.8
Ballwin, MO	6.1	19.7	19.9	12.5	14.8	12.9	7.6	4.5
Beavercreek, OH	6.0	19.3	19.8	11.8	14.1	13.3	8.4	5.1
Bella Vista, AR	7.4	22.2	22.6	13.4	12.5	10.2	6.7	3.5
Bernards, NJ	6.2	18.8	21.2	13.6	14.6	12.0	7.3	4.2
Bethlehem, NY	5.3	19.0	20.2	12.3	15.1	13.5	7.9	4.5
Bloomfield, MI	5.9	20.1	18.3	13.1	15.3	13.3	7.6	4.3
Bowie, MD	6.7	19.4	22.0	14.7	14.9	11.6	6.3	3.0
Bozeman, MT	6.1	18.5	28.5	12.6	12.3	11.6	6.0	2.9
Brentwood, TN	6.7	19.9	21.8	14.0	14.2	11.8	6.8	3.4
Broomfield, CO	6.7	19.8	21.9	14.7	14.1	11.9	6.4	3.1
Carmel, IN	7.0	21.1	20.5	13.7	14.3	11.6	6.6	3.6
Cedar Park, TX	7.0	20.5	25.1	15.4	13.0	10.2	5.3	2.5
Cheshire, CT	5.4	19.4	19.9	12.6	15.1	12.9	7.8	4.5
Chesterfield, MO	6.1	19.7	19.9	12.5	14.8	12.9	7.6	4.5
Collierville, TN	7.1	21.7	20.8	13.3	13.9	12.0	6.6	3.4
Coppell, TX	7.4	22.4	21.5	14.7	14.0	10.4	5.7	2.8
Cornelius, NC	6.7	20.9	19.9	14.9	14.5	11.4	6.9	3.4
Cranberry, PA	5.1	17.2	18.7	11.8	15.0	14.5	8.9	5.9
Cupertino, CA	6.7	19.4	21.4	15.2	14.6	10.9	6.4	3.6
Danville, CA	5.8	17.3	21.6	14.8	14.7	12.5	7.3	4.0
Draper, UT	8.4	23.2	24.2	13.7	11.6	9.7	5.2	2.7
Dublin, OH	6.8	20.4	22.1	13.8	14.0	11.6	6.5	3.4
Eastchester, NY	6.2	18.8	21.2	13.6	14.6	12.0	7.3	4.2
Eden Prairie, MN	6.7	20.3	21.0	13.4	15.0	12.1	6.4	3.5
Edmond, OK	7.2	20.4	22.7	12.6	13.1	11.6	6.9	3.8
Evesham, NJ	6.1	19.5	20.5	12.7	14.8	12.6	7.4	4.4
Fishers, IN	7.0	21.1	20.5	13.7	14.3	11.6	6.6	3.6
Flower Mound, TX	7.4	22.4	21.5	14.7	14.0	10.4	5.7	2.8
Folsom, CA	6.4	20.5	21.2	12.9	14.0	12.0	7.2	4.0
Foster City, CA	5.8	17.3	21.6	14.8	14.7	12.5	7.3	4.0
Franklin, TN	6.7	19.9	21.8	14.0	14.2	11.8	6.8	3.4
Friendswood, TX	7.7	22.4	22.0	14.3	13.6	10.8	5.6	2.6
Germantown, TN	7.1	21.7	20.8	13.3	13.9	12.0	6.6	3.4
Glastonbury, CT	5.2	19.5	19.0	12.5	15.6	13.2	7.9	4.6
Grand Blanc, MI	6.2	20.7	18.1	12.5	14.7	13.2	8.0	4.8
Guilderland, NY	5.3	19.0	20.2	12.3	15.1	13.5	7.9	4.5
Hampden, PA	5.8	18.7	19.2	12.5	14.7	13.7	8.2	4.8
Holly Springs, NC	6.8	21.5	20.8	15.7	14.6	10.6	5.9	2.8
Huntersville, NC	6.7	20.9	19.9	14.9	14.5	11.4	6.9	3.4
Independence, KY	6.6	20.6	19.8	12.8	14.7	12.6	7.1	4.0
Johns Creek, GA	6.9	21.7	20.7	15.2	14.6	10.9	6.1	2.8
Keller, TX	7.4	22.4	21.5	14.7	14.0	10.4	5.7	2.8
Kirkland, WA	6.4	18.4	22.4	14.5	14.6	12.2	6.6	3.3
Lafayette, CO	5.3	19.9	23.8	13.4	14.1	12.5	6.5	3.1
Lake Oswego, OR	6.2	19.1	21.2	14.6	13.9	12.7	7.1	3.4
League City, TX	7.7	22.4	22.0	14.3	13.6	10.8	5.6	2.6
Leawood, KS	6.9	20.7	20.0	13.3	14.3	12.2	7.0	3.8
Lee's Summit, MO	6.9	20.7	20.0	13.3	14.3	12.2	7.0	3.8
Leesburg, VA	6.7	19.4	22.0	14.7	14.9	11.6	6.3	3.0
Lehi, UT	10.6	28.6	27.5	11.6	8.3	6.4	3.9	2.2
Lenexa, KS	6.9	20.7	20.0	13.3	14.3	12.2	7.0	3.8
Lexington, MA	5.5	18.6	21.4	13.2	15.1	12.5	7.3	4.3
Los Altos, CA	6.7	19.4	21.4	15.2	14.6	10.9	6.4	3.6
Lower Makefield, PA	6.1	19.5	20.5	12.7	14.8	12.6	7.4	4.4
Madison, AL	6.1	19.9	20.4	13.0	15.7	12.1	7.4	4.0
Mamaroneck, NY	6.2	18.8	21.2	13.6	14.6	12.0	7.3	4.2
Manheim, PA	6.7	20.7	18.9	11.8	13.9	12.4	8.0	5.1
Manlius, NY	5.7	20.3	19.8	11.7	15.1	13.1	7.6	4.6
Maple Grove, MN	6.7	20.3	21.0	13.4	15.0	12.1	6.4	3.5
Marion, IA	6.3	20.4	19.8	12.9	14.2	12.3	7.5	4.7
Marlboro, NJ	6.2	18.8	21.2	13.6	14.6	12.0	7.3	4.2
Mason, OH	6.6	20.6	19.8	12.8	14.7	12.6	7.1	4.0

Table continued on next page.

Metro Area	Percent of Population							
	Under Age 5	Age 5–19	Age 20–34	Age 35–44	Age 45–54	Age 55–64	Age 65–74	Age 75–84
McCandless, PA	5.1	17.2	18.7	11.8	15.0	14.5	8.9	5.9
Menomonee Falls, WI	6.5	20.4	20.5	12.5	14.5	12.5	6.8	4.3
Meridian, ID	7.1	22.6	20.4	13.6	13.1	11.3	7.0	3.4
Merrimack, NH	5.7	19.4	18.7	13.5	16.7	13.2	7.2	3.9
Mount Lebanon, PA	5.1	17.2	18.7	11.8	15.0	14.5	8.9	5.9
Mount Pleasant, SC	6.6	18.9	23.2	12.9	13.7	12.2	7.6	3.4
Needham, MA	5.5	18.6	21.4	13.2	15.1	12.5	7.3	4.3
Newtown, CT	5.9	21.0	17.4	13.5	16.1	12.3	7.3	4.4
Northbrook, IL	6.5	20.7	21.1	13.7	14.2	11.8	6.7	3.7
Northville, MI	5.9	20.1	18.3	13.1	15.3	13.3	7.6	4.3
Novi, MI	5.9	20.1	18.3	13.1	15.3	13.3	7.6	4.3
O'Fallon, IL	6.1	19.7	19.9	12.5	14.8	12.9	7.6	4.5
O'Fallon, MO	6.1	19.7	19.9	12.5	14.8	12.9	7.6	4.5
Orchard Park, NY	5.3	18.6	19.8	11.6	14.9	13.6	8.2	5.4
Oviedo, FL	6.0	19.7	22.2	13.7	14.1	11.4	7.4	4.0
Parker, CO	6.7	19.8	21.9	14.7	14.1	11.9	6.4	3.1
Parkland, FL	5.7	17.8	19.6	13.7	14.9	11.9	8.4	5.5
Peachtree City, GA	6.9	21.7	20.7	15.2	14.6	10.9	6.1	2.8
Pflugerville, TX	7.0	20.5	25.1	15.4	13.0	10.2	5.3	2.5
Plainfield, IL	6.5	20.7	21.1	13.7	14.2	11.8	6.7	3.7
Princeton, NJ	5.9	19.8	20.4	13.6	15.0	12.2	7.0	4.2
Queen Creek, AZ	7.0	21.4	21.1	13.5	12.9	10.9	7.6	4.1
Rancho Palos Verdes, CA	6.4	20.0	22.6	14.2	14.0	11.0	6.4	3.6
Redmond, WA	6.4	18.4	22.4	14.5	14.6	12.2	6.6	3.3
Richland, WA	8.3	23.4	20.9	12.5	12.7	11.3	6.4	3.2
Ridgefield, CT	5.9	21.0	17.4	13.5	16.1	12.3	7.3	4.4
Ridgewood, NJ	6.2	18.8	21.2	13.6	14.6	12.0	7.3	4.2
Rio Rancho, NM	6.5	20.1	21.1	12.6	13.8	12.7	7.7	4.0
Sahuarita, AZ	6.1	19.5	21.0	11.6	12.6	12.7	9.2	5.3
Sammamish, WA	6.4	18.4	22.4	14.5	14.6	12.2	6.6	3.3
San Ramon, CA	5.8	17.3	21.6	14.8	14.7	12.5	7.3	4.0
Saratoga, CA	6.7	19.4	21.4	15.2	14.6	10.9	6.4	3.6
Schertz, TX	7.1	22.2	21.8	13.2	13.2	11.0	6.6	3.5
Shrewsbury, MA	5.6	20.0	18.8	13.2	16.0	12.9	7.2	4.0
South Brunswick, NJ	6.2	18.8	21.2	13.6	14.6	12.0	7.3	4.2
South Jordan, UT	8.4	23.2	24.2	13.7	11.6	9.7	5.2	2.7
South Kingstown, RI	5.3	18.9	19.9	12.7	15.2	13.0	7.8	4.6
South Windsor, CT	5.2	19.5	19.0	12.5	15.6	13.2	7.9	4.6
Southlake, TX	7.4	22.4	21.5	14.7	14.0	10.4	5.7	2.8
Spring Hill, TN	6.7	19.9	21.8	14.0	14.2	11.8	6.8	3.4
Stow, OH	5.5	19.3	19.6	12.1	14.8	13.7	8.0	4.7
Sugar Land, TX	7.7	22.4	22.0	14.3	13.6	10.8	5.6	2.6
Sun Prairie, WI	6.0	18.8	24.1	13.0	13.9	12.3	6.6	3.6
Syracuse, UT	9.1	25.6	22.0	12.8	11.3	9.4	5.4	3.1
Tredyffrin, PA	6.1	19.5	20.5	12.7	14.8	12.6	7.4	4.4
Upper Arlington, OH	6.8	20.4	22.1	13.8	14.0	11.6	6.5	3.4
Upper Dublin, PA	6.1	19.5	20.5	12.7	14.8	12.6	7.4	4.4
Vestavia Hills, AL	6.5	19.6	20.1	13.2	14.1	12.8	7.8	4.3
Webster, NY	5.5	19.7	19.7	11.8	15.0	13.3	8.1	4.6
Wellesley, MA	5.5	18.6	21.4	13.2	15.1	12.5	7.3	4.3
West Fargo, ND	6.9	19.6	28.2	11.9	12.0	10.6	5.5	3.6
West Linn, OR	6.2	19.1	21.2	14.6	13.9	12.7	7.1	3.4
West Windsor, NJ	5.9	19.8	20.4	13.6	15.0	12.2	7.0	4.2
Westlake, OH	5.7	19.4	17.9	12.3	15.0	13.8	8.3	5.1
Weston, FL	5.7	17.8	19.6	13.7	14.9	11.9	8.4	5.5
Westport, CT	5.9	21.0	17.4	13.5	16.1	12.3	7.3	4.4
Wilmette, IL	6.5	20.7	21.1	13.7	14.2	11.8	6.7	3.7
Woodbury, MN	6.7	20.3	21.0	13.4	15.0	12.1	6.4	3.5
Yorba Linda, CA	6.4	20.0	22.6	14.2	14.0	11.0	6.4	3.6
U.S.	6.4	19.9	20.6	13.0	14.1	12.3	7.6	4.3

Note: Figures cover the Metropolitan Statistical Area (MSA)—see Appendix B for areas included
Source: U.S. Census Bureau, 2010-2014 American Community Survey 5-Year Estimates

Religious Groups by Family

Area[1]	Catholic	Baptist	Non-Den.	Methodist[2]	Lutheran	LDS[3]	Pente-costal	Presby-terian[4]	Muslim[5]	Judaism
Aliso Viejo, CA	33.8	2.7	3.6	1.0	0.6	1.7	1.7	0.9	0.7	0.9
Allen, TX	13.3	18.7	7.7	5.2	0.7	1.1	2.1	0.9	2.4	0.3
Alpharetta, GA	7.4	17.4	6.8	7.8	0.5	0.7	2.6	1.8	0.7	0.5
Ankeny, IA	13.6	4.7	3.3	6.9	8.2	0.9	2.3	2.9	0.3	0.3
Apex, NC	9.1	12.1	5.9	6.7	0.9	0.8	2.2	2.2	0.9	0.3
Ballwin, MO	19.8	10.0	3.8	3.4	4.1	0.6	1.2	3.0	0.4	0.7
Beavercreek, OH	12.4	9.6	4.2	4.4	2.0	0.8	1.4	2.1	0.2	0.3
Bella Vista, AR	9.1	22.9	5.7	4.8	0.8	1.7	2.2	0.9	0.1	<0.1
Bernards, NJ	36.9	1.8	1.7	1.3	0.7	0.3	0.8	1.0	2.3	4.7
Bethlehem, NY	26.8	1.2	2.2	2.9	1.5	0.3	0.5	2.1	1.2	1.0
Bloomfield, MI	21.3	4.5	4.9	2.1	3.1	0.3	1.2	1.3	1.8	0.8
Bowie, MD	14.5	7.3	4.8	4.5	1.2	1.1	1.0	1.3	2.3	1.1
Bozeman, MT	7.1	2.0	3.9	2.8	3.6	4.0	1.6	3.2	0.3	0.3
Brentwood, TN	4.1	25.2	5.8	6.1	0.3	0.7	2.1	2.1	0.3	0.1
Broomfield, CO	16.0	2.9	4.6	1.7	2.1	2.4	1.2	1.5	0.5	0.6
Carmel, IN	10.5	10.2	7.1	4.9	1.6	0.7	1.6	1.6	0.2	0.3
Cedar Park, TX	16.0	10.3	4.5	3.6	1.9	1.1	0.8	1.0	1.2	0.2
Cheshire, CT	35.3	1.4	1.9	1.5	0.6	0.3	1.0	2.2	0.5	1.2
Chesterfield, MO	19.8	10.0	3.8	3.4	4.1	0.6	1.2	3.0	0.4	0.7
Collierville, TN	5.2	30.8	5.4	6.2	0.3	0.6	4.7	2.4	0.3	0.6
Coppell, TX	13.3	18.7	7.7	5.2	0.7	1.1	2.1	0.9	2.4	0.3
Cornelius, NC	5.9	17.2	6.7	8.6	1.3	0.7	3.2	4.5	0.2	0.3
Cranberry, PA	32.8	2.3	2.8	5.6	3.3	0.3	1.1	4.6	0.3	0.7
Cupertino, CA	26.0	1.3	4.2	1.0	0.5	1.4	1.1	0.7	1.0	0.6
Danville, CA	20.7	2.5	2.4	1.9	0.5	1.5	1.2	1.1	1.2	0.8
Draper, UT	8.9	0.8	0.5	0.5	0.5	58.9	0.6	0.3	0.4	0.1
Dublin, OH	11.7	5.3	3.5	4.7	2.4	0.7	1.9	2.0	0.8	0.5
Eastchester, NY	36.9	1.8	1.7	1.3	0.7	0.3	0.8	1.0	2.3	4.7
Eden Prairie, MN	21.7	2.4	2.9	2.7	14.4	0.6	1.7	1.8	0.4	0.7
Edmond, OK	6.3	25.3	7.0	10.6	0.7	1.2	3.1	0.9	0.2	0.1
Evesham, NJ	33.4	3.9	2.8	2.9	1.8	0.3	0.8	2.1	1.2	1.3
Fishers, IN	10.5	10.2	7.1	4.9	1.6	0.7	1.6	1.6	0.2	0.3
Flower Mound, TX	13.3	18.7	7.7	5.2	0.7	1.1	2.1	0.9	2.4	0.3
Folsom, CA	16.1	3.1	4.0	1.7	0.7	3.3	2.0	0.8	0.8	0.2
Foster City, CA	20.7	2.5	2.4	1.9	0.5	1.5	1.2	1.1	1.2	0.8
Franklin, TN	4.1	25.2	5.8	6.1	0.3	0.7	2.1	2.1	0.3	0.1
Friendswood, TX	17.0	16.0	7.2	4.8	1.0	1.1	1.5	0.8	2.6	0.3
Germantown, TN	5.2	30.8	5.4	6.2	0.3	0.6	4.7	2.4	0.3	0.6
Glastonbury, CT	30.3	1.9	2.1	1.9	1.3	0.3	0.9	3.6	0.2	1.2
Grand Blanc, MI	10.7	6.9	3.4	3.0	3.2	0.5	2.9	1.4	2.5	0.1
Guilderland, NY	26.8	1.2	2.2	2.9	1.5	0.3	0.5	2.1	1.2	1.0
Hampden, PA	14.1	1.6	3.2	9.8	5.5	0.6	2.0	5.1	0.8	0.7
Holly Springs, NC	9.1	12.1	5.9	6.7	0.9	0.8	2.2	2.2	0.9	0.3
Huntersville, NC	5.9	17.2	6.7	8.6	1.3	0.7	3.2	4.5	0.2	0.3
Independence, KY	19.0	9.5	3.6	3.8	1.1	0.5	2.2	1.5	0.2	0.5
Johns Creek, GA	7.4	17.4	6.8	7.8	0.5	0.7	2.6	1.8	0.7	0.5
Keller, TX	13.3	18.7	7.7	5.2	0.7	1.1	2.1	0.9	2.4	0.3
Kirkland, WA	12.3	2.1	5.0	1.2	2.0	3.3	2.8	1.4	0.4	0.4
Lafayette, CO	20.1	2.3	4.7	1.7	3.0	2.9	0.4	2.0	0.1	0.7
Lake Oswego, OR	10.5	2.3	4.5	1.0	1.6	3.7	2.0	0.9	0.1	0.3
League City, TX	17.0	16.0	7.2	4.8	1.0	1.1	1.5	0.8	2.6	0.3
Leawood, KS	12.6	13.1	5.2	5.8	2.2	2.4	2.6	1.6	0.3	0.4
Lee's Summit, MO	12.6	13.1	5.2	5.8	2.2	2.4	2.6	1.6	0.3	0.4
Leesburg, VA	14.5	7.3	4.8	4.5	1.2	1.1	1.0	1.3	2.3	1.1
Lehi, UT	1.3	<0.1	<0.1	0.1	<0.1	88.5	0.1	<0.1	<0.1	<0.1
Lenexa, KS	12.6	13.1	5.2	5.8	2.2	2.4	2.6	1.6	0.3	0.4
Lexington, MA	44.3	1.1	1.0	0.9	0.3	0.4	0.6	1.6	0.4	1.4
Los Altos, CA	26.0	1.3	4.2	1.0	0.5	1.4	1.1	0.7	1.0	0.6
Lower Makefield, PA	33.4	3.9	2.8	2.9	1.8	0.3	0.8	2.1	1.2	1.3
Madison, AL	3.9	27.6	3.1	7.5	0.7	1.1	1.2	1.7	0.2	0.1
Mamaroneck, NY	36.9	1.8	1.7	1.3	0.7	0.3	0.8	1.0	2.3	4.7
Manheim, PA	9.8	0.8	8.2	6.9	4.3	0.3	1.0	4.1	0.1	0.3
Manlius, NY	30.1	2.1	1.9	4.8	1.3	0.4	1.1	1.3	0.9	0.6
Maple Grove, MN	21.7	2.4	2.9	2.7	14.4	0.6	1.7	1.8	0.4	0.7
Marion, IA	18.8	2.3	3.0	7.3	11.3	0.8	1.8	3.2	0.5	0.1
Marlboro, NJ	36.9	1.8	1.7	1.3	0.7	0.3	0.8	1.0	2.3	4.7
Mason, OH	19.0	9.5	3.6	3.8	1.1	0.5	2.2	1.5	0.2	0.5
McCandless, PA	32.8	2.3	2.8	5.6	3.3	0.3	1.1	4.6	0.3	0.7

Table continued on next page.

Area[1]	Catholic	Baptist	Non-Den.	Methodist[2]	Lutheran	LDS[3]	Pente-costal	Presby-terian[4]	Muslim[5]	Judaism
Menomonee Falls, WI	24.6	3.1	3.8	1.5	10.7	0.4	1.9	1.5	0.5	0.5
Meridian, ID	8.0	2.9	4.1	2.1	1.1	15.8	2.3	0.6	0.1	0.1
Merrimack, NH	31.1	1.3	2.3	1.1	0.5	0.6	0.4	2.0	0.3	0.5
Mount Lebanon, PA	32.8	2.3	2.8	5.6	3.3	0.3	1.1	4.6	0.3	0.7
Mount Pleasant, SC	6.1	12.4	7.0	10.0	1.1	0.9	2.0	2.3	0.1	0.3
Needham, MA	44.3	1.1	1.0	0.9	0.3	0.4	0.6	1.6	0.4	1.4
Newtown, CT	44.1	1.9	2.3	2.0	0.8	0.5	1.1	3.0	0.5	1.9
Northbrook, IL	34.2	3.2	4.4	1.9	3.0	0.3	1.2	1.9	3.2	0.8
Northville, MI	21.3	4.5	4.9	2.1	3.1	0.3	1.2	1.3	1.8	0.8
Novi, MI	21.3	4.5	4.9	2.1	3.1	0.3	1.2	1.3	1.8	0.8
O'Fallon, IL	19.8	10.0	3.8	3.4	4.1	0.6	1.2	3.0	0.4	0.7
O'Fallon, MO	19.8	10.0	3.8	3.4	4.1	0.6	1.2	3.0	0.4	0.7
Orchard Park, NY	35.6	2.7	2.0	2.3	3.3	0.3	1.0	1.9	1.6	0.7
Oviedo, FL	13.2	6.9	5.6	2.9	0.9	0.9	3.2	1.3	1.3	0.2
Parker, CO	16.0	2.9	4.6	1.7	2.1	2.4	1.2	1.5	0.5	0.6
Parkland, FL	18.5	5.3	4.1	1.2	0.4	0.5	1.7	0.6	0.9	1.5
Peachtree City, GA	7.4	17.4	6.8	7.8	0.5	0.7	2.6	1.8	0.7	0.5
Pflugerville, TX	16.0	10.3	4.5	3.6	1.9	1.1	0.8	1.0	1.2	0.2
Plainfield, IL	34.2	3.2	4.4	1.9	3.0	0.3	1.2	1.9	3.2	0.8
Princeton, NJ	33.1	2.7	2.2	2.1	1.1	0.4	1.2	2.2	1.3	2.1
Queen Creek, AZ	13.3	3.4	5.1	1.0	1.6	6.1	2.9	0.6	0.1	0.3
Rancho Palos Verdes, CA	33.8	2.7	3.6	1.0	0.6	1.7	1.7	0.9	0.7	0.9
Redmond, WA	12.3	2.1	5.0	1.2	2.0	3.3	2.8	1.4	0.4	0.4
Richland, WA	13.4	2.5	4.9	2.0	2.0	8.5	2.2	0.9	0.3	<0.1
Ridgefield, CT	44.1	1.9	2.3	2.0	0.8	0.5	1.1	3.0	0.5	1.9
Ridgewood, NJ	36.9	1.8	1.7	1.3	0.7	0.3	0.8	1.0	2.3	4.7
Rio Rancho, NM	27.1	3.7	4.2	1.4	0.9	2.3	1.4	1.0	0.2	0.2
Sahuarita, AZ	20.7	3.3	3.7	1.3	1.5	2.9	1.5	1.0	<0.1	0.5
Sammamish, WA	12.3	2.1	5.0	1.2	2.0	3.3	2.8	1.4	0.4	0.4
San Ramon, CA	20.7	2.5	2.4	1.9	0.5	1.5	1.2	1.1	1.2	0.8
Saratoga, CA	26.0	1.3	4.2	1.0	0.5	1.4	1.1	0.7	1.0	0.6
Schertz, TX	28.4	8.5	6.0	3.0	1.6	1.4	1.3	0.7	0.9	0.2
Shrewsbury, MA	38.4	1.1	1.7	0.9	0.9	0.3	1.0	2.0	<0.1	0.5
South Brunswick, NJ	36.9	1.8	1.7	1.3	0.7	0.3	0.8	1.0	2.3	4.7
South Jordan, UT	8.9	0.8	0.5	0.5	0.5	58.9	0.6	0.3	0.4	0.1
South Kingstown, RI	47.0	1.4	1.2	0.8	0.5	0.3	0.5	1.0	0.1	0.7
South Windsor, CT	30.3	1.9	2.1	1.9	1.3	0.3	0.9	3.6	0.2	1.2
Southlake, TX	13.3	18.7	7.7	5.2	0.7	1.1	2.1	0.9	2.4	0.3
Spring Hill, TN	4.1	25.2	5.8	6.1	0.3	0.7	2.1	2.1	0.3	0.1
Stow, OH	19.4	2.8	6.8	3.8	1.7	0.4	1.0	2.2	0.3	0.3
Sugar Land, TX	17.0	16.0	7.2	4.8	1.0	1.1	1.5	0.8	2.6	0.3
Sun Prairie, WI	21.8	1.1	1.5	3.6	12.7	0.5	0.3	2.1	0.4	0.4
Syracuse, UT	5.7	0.9	0.9	0.2	0.4	68.7	1.2	0.1	<0.1	<0.1
Tredyffrin, PA	33.4	3.9	2.8	2.9	1.8	0.3	0.8	2.1	1.2	1.3
Upper Arlington, OH	11.7	5.3	3.5	4.7	2.4	0.7	1.9	2.0	0.8	0.5
Upper Dublin, PA	33.4	3.9	2.8	2.9	1.8	0.3	0.8	2.1	1.2	1.3
Vestavia Hills, AL	5.7	39.0	7.0	7.8	0.3	0.6	4.8	2.1	0.3	0.3
Webster, NY	24.0	2.7	4.0	3.2	1.8	0.6	0.6	2.3	0.8	0.9
Wellesley, MA	44.3	1.1	1.0	0.9	0.3	0.4	0.6	1.6	0.4	1.4
West Fargo, ND	17.4	0.4	0.4	3.3	32.5	0.6	1.5	1.8	0.1	<0.1
West Linn, OR	10.5	2.3	4.5	1.0	1.6	3.7	2.0	0.9	0.1	0.3
West Windsor, NJ	33.1	2.7	2.2	2.1	1.1	0.4	1.2	2.2	1.3	2.1
Westlake, OH	28.8	4.3	3.3	2.8	2.5	0.3	1.1	2.0	0.1	1.4
Weston, FL	18.5	5.3	4.1	1.2	0.4	0.5	1.7	0.6	0.9	1.5
Westport, CT	44.1	1.9	2.3	2.0	0.8	0.5	1.1	3.0	0.5	1.9
Wilmette, IL	34.2	3.2	4.4	1.9	3.0	0.3	1.2	1.9	3.2	0.8
Woodbury, MN	21.7	2.4	2.9	2.7	14.4	0.6	1.7	1.8	0.4	0.7
Yorba Linda, CA	33.8	2.7	3.6	1.0	0.6	1.7	1.7	0.9	0.7	0.9
U.S.	19.1	9.3	4.0	4.0	2.3	2.0	1.9	1.6	0.8	0.7

Note: Figures are the number of adherents as a percentage of the total population; (1) Figures cover the Metropolitan Statistical Area—see Appendix B for areas included; (2) Methodist/Pietist; (3) Latter Day Saints; (4) Reformed; (5) Figures are estimates

Source: Association of Statisticians of American Religious Bodies, 2010 U.S. Religion Census: Religious Congregations & Membership Study

Religious Groups by Tradition

Area	Catholic	Evangelical Protestant	Mainline Protestant	Other Tradition	Black Protestant	Orthodox
Aliso Viejo, CA	33.8	9.0	2.3	4.6	0.8	0.6
Allen, TX	13.3	28.3	6.9	4.7	1.7	0.1
Alpharetta, GA	7.4	26.0	9.8	2.9	3.1	0.2
Ankeny, IA	13.6	12.3	16.8	1.8	0.9	0.1
Apex, NC	9.1	19.9	10.1	3.2	1.7	0.2
Ballwin, MO	19.8	17.4	7.3	2.3	2.1	0.2
Beavercreek, OH	12.4	16.0	9.5	2.5	2.7	0.5
Bella Vista, AR	9.1	32.6	7.0	2.1	0.1	<0.1
Bernards, NJ	36.9	3.9	4.1	8.3	1.2	0.9
Bethlehem, NY	26.8	4.5	7.3	3.1	0.5	0.3
Bloomfield, MI	21.3	10.6	4.7	3.5	3.3	0.9
Bowie, MD	14.5	12.4	8.7	5.9	2.3	0.6
Bozeman, MT	7.1	13.5	6.5	4.9	0.1	<0.1
Brentwood, TN	4.1	32.9	8.0	1.7	3.3	0.4
Broomfield, CO	16.0	11.0	4.5	4.6	0.3	0.3
Carmel, IN	10.5	18.2	9.6	1.6	1.8	0.2
Cedar Park, TX	16.0	16.1	6.3	3.9	1.3	0.1
Cheshire, CT	35.3	3.8	6.1	2.3	0.7	0.4
Chesterfield, MO	19.8	17.4	7.3	2.3	2.1	0.2
Collierville, TN	5.2	29.4	8.3	2.1	13.4	<0.1
Coppell, TX	13.3	28.3	6.9	4.7	1.7	0.1
Cornelius, NC	5.9	27.5	13.3	1.6	2.7	0.4
Cranberry, PA	32.8	7.3	13.8	2.0	0.8	0.6
Cupertino, CA	26.0	8.2	2.4	6.8	0.1	0.4
Danville, CA	20.7	6.1	3.8	5.2	1.0	0.6
Draper, UT	8.9	2.6	1.2	60.0	0.1	0.4
Dublin, OH	11.7	11.8	9.5	3.1	1.1	0.2
Eastchester, NY	36.9	3.9	4.1	8.3	1.2	0.9
Eden Prairie, MN	21.7	12.8	14.5	2.2	0.4	0.2
Edmond, OK	6.3	39.0	9.8	2.7	1.9	0.1
Evesham, NJ	33.4	6.3	8.9	3.7	1.7	0.4
Fishers, IN	10.5	18.2	9.6	1.6	1.8	0.2
Flower Mound, TX	13.3	28.3	6.9	4.7	1.7	0.1
Folsom, CA	16.1	11.3	2.2	5.8	0.5	0.3
Foster City, CA	20.7	6.1	3.8	5.2	1.0	0.6
Franklin, TN	4.1	32.9	8.0	1.7	3.3	0.4
Friendswood, TX	17.0	24.9	6.6	4.9	1.3	0.2
Germantown, TN	5.2	29.4	8.3	2.1	13.4	<0.1
Glastonbury, CT	30.3	4.8	8.2	2.6	0.7	0.3
Grand Blanc, MI	10.7	14.0	5.3	4.1	4.8	0.3
Guilderland, NY	26.8	4.5	7.3	3.1	0.5	0.3
Hampden, PA	14.1	11.4	17.7	4.0	1.2	0.3
Holly Springs, NC	9.1	19.9	10.1	3.2	1.7	0.2
Huntersville, NC	5.9	27.5	13.3	1.6	2.7	0.4
Independence, KY	19.0	15.5	7.1	1.5	1.1	0.1
Johns Creek, GA	7.4	26.0	9.8	2.9	3.1	0.2
Keller, TX	13.3	28.3	6.9	4.7	1.7	0.1
Kirkland, WA	12.3	11.9	4.6	5.9	0.3	0.4
Lafayette, CO	20.1	9.7	6.4	4.8	<0.1	0.2
Lake Oswego, OR	10.5	11.6	3.6	5.2	0.1	0.3
League City, TX	17.0	24.9	6.6	4.9	1.3	0.2
Leawood, KS	12.6	20.5	9.9	3.6	2.6	0.1
Lee's Summit, MO	12.6	20.5	9.9	3.6	2.6	0.1
Leesburg, VA	14.5	12.4	8.7	5.9	2.3	0.6
Lehi, UT	1.3	0.4	<0.1	88.8	<0.1	<0.1
Lenexa, KS	12.6	20.5	9.9	3.6	2.6	0.1
Lexington, MA	44.3	3.2	4.5	3.4	0.1	1.0
Los Altos, CA	26.0	8.2	2.4	6.8	0.1	0.4
Lower Makefield, PA	33.4	6.3	8.9	3.7	1.7	0.4
Madison, AL	3.9	33.3	9.6	1.8	1.8	<0.1
Mamaroneck, NY	36.9	3.9	4.1	8.3	1.2	0.9
Manheim, PA	9.8	23.6	13.7	1.0	0.4	0.3
Manlius, NY	30.1	5.0	9.1	2.9	0.8	0.6
Maple Grove, MN	21.7	12.8	14.5	2.2	0.4	0.2
Marion, IA	18.8	13.7	17.5	1.9	0.1	0.2
Marlboro, NJ	36.9	3.9	4.1	8.3	1.2	0.9
Mason, OH	19.0	15.5	7.1	1.5	1.1	0.1
McCandless, PA	32.8	7.3	13.8	2.0	0.8	0.6

Table continued on next page.

Area	Catholic	Evangelical Protestant	Mainline Protestant	Other Tradition	Black Protestant	Orthodox
Menomonee Falls, WI	24.6	14.6	7.1	2.3	2.4	0.6
Meridian, ID	8.0	12.9	4.3	16.7	<0.1	<0.1
Merrimack, NH	31.1	5.1	4.4	1.8	<0.1	0.7
Mount Lebanon, PA	32.8	7.3	13.8	2.0	0.8	0.6
Mount Pleasant, SC	6.1	19.6	11.1	1.8	7.3	0.1
Needham, MA	44.3	3.2	4.5	3.4	0.1	1.0
Newtown, CT	44.1	5.1	9.0	3.5	0.4	1.0
Northbrook, IL	34.2	9.7	5.1	5.0	2.0	0.9
Northville, MI	21.3	10.6	4.7	3.5	3.3	0.9
Novi, MI	21.3	10.6	4.7	3.5	3.3	0.9
O'Fallon, IL	19.8	17.4	7.3	2.3	2.1	0.2
O'Fallon, MO	19.8	17.4	7.3	2.3	2.1	0.2
Orchard Park, NY	35.6	5.8	7.1	3.2	2.2	0.4
Oviedo, FL	13.2	17.8	4.7	3.2	1.2	0.3
Parker, CO	16.0	11.0	4.5	4.6	0.3	0.3
Parkland, FL	18.5	11.4	2.4	3.5	1.7	0.2
Peachtree City, GA	7.4	26.0	9.8	2.9	3.1	0.2
Pflugerville, TX	16.0	16.1	6.3	3.9	1.3	0.1
Plainfield, IL	34.2	9.7	5.1	5.0	2.0	0.9
Princeton, NJ	33.1	4.7	8.0	4.6	1.4	0.5
Queen Creek, AZ	13.3	13.2	2.6	7.8	0.1	0.3
Rancho Palos Verdes, CA	33.8	9.0	2.3	4.6	0.8	0.6
Redmond, WA	12.3	11.9	4.6	5.9	0.3	0.4
Richland, WA	13.4	12.5	4.5	9.3	<0.1	<0.1
Ridgefield, CT	44.1	5.1	9.0	3.5	0.4	1.0
Ridgewood, NJ	36.9	3.9	4.1	8.3	1.2	0.9
Rio Rancho, NM	27.1	11.2	3.2	3.9	0.2	0.1
Sahuarita, AZ	20.7	10.0	3.7	4.5	0.4	0.2
Sammamish, WA	12.3	11.9	4.6	5.9	0.3	0.4
San Ramon, CA	20.7	6.1	3.8	5.2	1.0	0.6
Saratoga, CA	26.0	8.2	2.4	6.8	0.1	0.4
Schertz, TX	28.4	16.9	5.0	3.1	0.4	<0.1
Shrewsbury, MA	38.4	4.6	5.4	2.3	<0.1	0.9
South Brunswick, NJ	36.9	3.9	4.1	8.3	1.2	0.9
South Jordan, UT	8.9	2.6	1.2	60.0	0.1	0.4
South Kingstown, RI	47.0	2.8	4.7	1.6	<0.1	0.5
South Windsor, CT	30.3	4.8	8.2	2.6	0.7	0.3
Southlake, TX	13.3	28.3	6.9	4.7	1.7	0.1
Spring Hill, TN	4.1	32.9	8.0	1.7	3.3	0.4
Stow, OH	19.4	11.9	8.2	1.2	0.9	0.6
Sugar Land, TX	17.0	24.9	6.6	4.9	1.3	0.2
Sun Prairie, WI	21.8	7.2	15.3	2.2	0.1	<0.1
Syracuse, UT	5.7	3.4	0.7	69.3	0.1	<0.1
Tredyffrin, PA	33.4	6.3	8.9	3.7	1.7	0.4
Upper Arlington, OH	11.7	11.8	9.5	3.1	1.1	0.2
Upper Dublin, PA	33.4	6.3	8.9	3.7	1.7	0.4
Vestavia Hills, AL	5.7	45.2	8.3	1.4	10.1	0.1
Webster, NY	24.0	7.3	8.5	2.9	0.9	0.2
Wellesley, MA	44.3	3.2	4.5	3.4	0.1	1.0
West Fargo, ND	17.4	10.7	30.8	0.8	<0.1	<0.1
West Linn, OR	10.5	11.6	3.6	5.2	0.1	0.3
West Windsor, NJ	33.1	4.7	8.0	4.6	1.4	0.5
Westlake, OH	28.8	9.0	7.5	2.6	2.1	0.8
Weston, FL	18.5	11.4	2.4	3.5	1.7	0.2
Westport, CT	44.1	5.1	9.0	3.5	0.4	1.0
Wilmette, IL	34.2	9.7	5.1	5.0	2.0	0.9
Woodbury, MN	21.7	12.8	14.5	2.2	0.4	0.2
Yorba Linda, CA	33.8	9.0	2.3	4.6	0.8	0.6
U.S.	19.1	16.2	7.3	4.3	1.6	0.3

Note: Figures are the number of adherents as a percentage of the total population; (1) Figures cover the Metropolitan Statistical Area—see Appendix B for areas included; Source: Association of Statisticians of American Religious Bodies, 2010 U.S. Religion Census: Religious Congregations & Membership Study

Ancestry: City

City	German	Irish	English	American	Italian	Polish	French[1]	Scottish	Dutch
Aliso Viejo, CA	12.9	11.7	9.5	3.5	6.8	2.4	3.3	1.8	1.2
Allen, TX	15.6	10.0	9.3	6.9	3.9	2.2	2.3	2.1	1.4
Alpharetta, GA	11.4	11.3	8.5	5.9	4.6	1.8	1.9	2.2	0.8
Ankeny, IA	38.3	14.2	11.5	4.8	3.1	1.5	2.4	1.3	4.4
Apex, NC	19.1	15.4	14.4	7.0	8.8	4.4	1.8	3.1	1.9
Ballwin, MO	33.8	20.3	11.4	6.6	6.9	4.3	3.5	2.3	1.5
Beavercreek, OH	24.1	12.9	11.0	13.7	4.2	3.4	2.5	2.1	1.6
Bella Vista, AR	18.8	10.3	13.1	9.2	3.3	1.3	2.6	3.4	1.8
Bernards, NJ	16.1	19.8	7.9	8.5	19.1	5.8	1.4	2.1	1.6
Bethlehem, NY	18.4	28.6	13.4	5.6	15.5	6.1	5.0	1.9	4.5
Bloomfield, MI	17.2	13.2	10.3	5.6	6.6	8.8	3.5	3.0	1.7
Bowie, MD	9.9	9.4	6.0	3.7	4.2	2.3	1.2	1.8	0.6
Bozeman, MT	26.3	14.9	13.2	4.0	5.7	3.2	4.0	3.7	3.1
Brentwood, TN	19.3	13.0	16.6	10.5	4.0	2.7	2.5	3.7	1.3
Broomfield, CO	23.4	13.4	13.4	7.1	6.3	3.9	3.0	2.7	2.1
Carmel, IN	25.9	13.2	11.1	7.7	3.9	3.4	2.3	2.6	2.4
Cedar Park, TX	17.9	11.6	9.3	6.7	3.1	2.4	3.2	2.2	1.8
Cheshire, CT	11.0	22.6	8.9	2.7	26.3	8.8	3.7	1.6	0.3
Chesterfield, MO	28.9	14.9	11.1	6.9	4.5	3.5	3.5	1.9	1.3
Collierville, TN	15.1	12.9	11.6	10.5	4.9	2.1	2.4	2.0	1.8
Coppell, TX	15.6	8.9	13.5	6.5	4.0	1.2	3.3	1.9	1.0
Cornelius, NC	21.0	11.8	11.2	7.3	9.2	3.2	4.3	3.7	1.3
Cranberry, PA	37.4	22.8	8.8	3.9	18.7	9.3	2.6	2.0	0.9
Cupertino, CA	5.4	3.7	4.0	2.2	2.8	0.7	1.2	1.2	0.5
Danville, CA	18.1	14.1	12.7	6.0	10.5	2.4	3.6	2.1	1.6
Draper, UT	14.0	7.8	28.5	4.9	3.3	2.0	1.5	4.5	3.6
Dublin, OH	28.8	15.6	10.9	6.4	7.7	4.3	3.8	2.0	1.7
Eastchester, NY	9.2	17.9	5.0	6.1	35.9	3.0	1.3	1.1	0.6
Eden Prairie, MN	32.1	11.4	7.1	2.7	3.1	3.6	2.7	1.7	1.8
Edmond, OK	17.5	11.7	10.0	8.3	2.5	1.5	2.7	2.5	1.8
Evesham, NJ	19.7	27.2	8.7	3.5	24.4	7.8	2.0	1.8	1.1
Fishers, IN	26.4	14.5	10.3	8.4	3.6	4.0	4.4	2.7	1.7
Flower Mound, TX	20.4	14.4	13.8	7.0	5.3	2.9	4.3	3.0	1.7
Folsom, CA	15.9	11.1	9.6	4.4	7.3	2.2	2.8	2.1	1.3
Foster City, CA	7.7	5.7	5.2	2.6	4.0	1.5	1.6	0.9	0.3
Franklin, TN	16.1	15.4	15.2	9.1	5.3	1.8	2.8	3.5	1.3
Friendswood, TX	16.0	13.5	12.1	9.1	4.1	1.6	3.2	2.4	1.4
Germantown, TN	13.2	12.0	17.5	11.2	4.6	1.9	3.7	4.1	1.2
Glastonbury, CT	12.6	21.1	12.9	5.3	19.4	10.0	6.2	2.4	0.8
Grand Blanc, MI	18.4	10.5	10.7	7.3	3.9	7.3	3.6	2.8	2.0
Guilderland, NY	18.7	23.9	12.3	4.8	18.9	6.1	5.4	1.9	3.7
Hampden, PA	32.7	17.9	9.2	4.6	8.9	4.7	2.4	2.1	2.0
Holly Springs, NC	17.0	16.4	11.6	7.5	10.6	6.0	1.9	3.0	1.7
Huntersville, NC	21.1	16.5	12.7	6.4	8.7	4.1	3.6	3.0	1.5
Independence, KY	39.6	18.7	9.4	10.0	2.8	2.1	2.1	2.0	1.1
Johns Creek, GA	10.4	9.1	9.0	5.6	4.6	2.5	2.4	1.8	1.0
Keller, TX	20.3	14.2	13.9	8.1	5.5	2.4	3.8	3.6	1.3
Kirkland, WA	17.7	11.8	12.8	3.7	4.1	2.3	3.9	3.3	2.6
Lafayette, CO	23.1	15.6	14.5	7.0	5.3	4.2	3.4	4.2	2.7
Lake Oswego, OR	20.9	13.6	14.8	5.6	5.5	3.4	3.4	5.1	2.5
League City, TX	17.2	13.8	8.9	5.9	5.9	2.2	4.5	2.1	1.0
Leawood, KS	33.0	18.6	16.3	6.5	6.9	2.7	3.3	3.2	1.6
Lee's Summit, MO	24.9	12.8	12.8	6.8	4.3	1.7	2.7	2.2	1.5
Leesburg, VA	14.0	9.9	11.3	4.4	6.3	3.1	3.5	2.6	1.5
Lehi, UT	12.1	6.5	29.5	5.9	2.4	0.6	1.8	6.1	1.9
Lenexa, KS	29.8	15.1	12.9	5.2	3.0	2.4	3.1	2.0	1.4
Lexington, MA	7.3	15.5	11.1	4.2	12.3	3.2	2.2	2.5	0.9
Los Altos, CA	15.4	10.9	13.7	3.0	6.9	2.6	2.6	2.9	2.0
Lower Makefield, PA	19.3	23.3	10.9	5.6	16.6	8.9	2.5	2.3	0.9
Madison, AL	13.2	9.8	11.9	11.6	2.7	1.8	1.8	2.2	1.2
Mamaroneck, NY	9.1	14.8	5.8	10.1	15.0	4.5	4.7	2.1	0.5
Manheim, PA	35.3	15.0	12.2	6.6	8.2	3.8	1.7	2.0	1.0
Manlius, NY	20.9	25.8	14.3	5.6	17.0	5.7	4.6	2.1	2.6
Maple Grove, MN	32.3	12.2	5.4	4.0	2.8	5.1	5.4	1.5	1.6
Marion, IA	39.4	16.9	11.1	5.7	2.9	2.0	2.4	2.3	2.7
Marlboro, NJ	7.3	9.5	2.4	6.5	23.9	9.1	0.6	0.5	0.3
Mason, OH	29.5	12.2	10.3	6.6	6.2	3.0	2.4	2.1	1.4
McCandless, PA	34.0	19.2	7.9	4.2	18.5	10.0	2.5	2.1	0.6
Menomonee Falls, WI	51.5	11.1	6.4	3.4	5.0	10.9	3.3	1.6	2.2

Table continued on next page.

City	German	Irish	English	American	Italian	Polish	French[1]	Scottish	Dutch
Meridian, ID	15.9	8.0	15.3	6.2	3.3	1.8	2.0	2.5	1.9
Merrimack, NH	8.0	22.6	16.2	3.5	10.9	4.3	16.9	3.7	1.0
Mount Lebanon, PA	25.9	22.1	10.5	3.9	19.5	7.6	1.8	2.3	0.9
Mount Pleasant, SC	18.2	17.0	14.4	9.9	6.5	2.7	3.8	4.5	1.5
Needham, MA	8.6	25.0	11.7	5.4	12.3	5.1	1.9	2.4	0.7
Newtown, CT	17.0	20.9	11.9	5.3	24.6	6.8	3.7	2.8	1.3
Northbrook, IL	17.1	11.4	5.4	6.9	6.0	10.0	1.6	1.4	0.5
Northville, MI	19.0	10.2	10.9	5.5	8.3	13.1	3.5	2.8	1.5
Novi, MI	18.2	11.9	8.9	4.7	8.0	9.8	3.1	2.2	1.3
O'Fallon, IL	28.4	14.2	11.8	5.2	3.1	5.0	3.8	2.2	2.0
O'Fallon, MO	39.3	18.0	9.2	6.7	7.2	4.2	4.8	1.5	1.4
Orchard Park, NY	30.5	22.1	8.9	3.5	18.8	21.6	3.1	2.3	1.2
Oviedo, FL	14.4	11.2	8.8	7.9	8.2	3.7	2.9	2.2	2.0
Parker, CO	27.6	17.0	13.4	6.0	6.7	3.1	3.5	3.7	1.6
Parkland, FL	7.6	11.5	6.0	8.7	14.2	7.0	2.6	0.5	0.3
Peachtree City, GA	17.0	14.3	13.2	9.6	6.1	2.3	2.5	2.7	2.5
Pflugerville, TX	14.9	8.9	6.8	4.0	1.7	1.8	2.4	1.1	1.5
Plainfield, IL	20.4	20.6	6.3	4.0	13.0	12.4	1.6	1.3	1.7
Princeton, NJ	12.0	12.6	10.1	4.2	8.7	4.6	2.8	2.4	2.1
Queen Creek, AZ	17.9	11.8	11.9	4.8	5.0	1.9	4.1	3.5	2.8
Rancho Palos Verdes, CA	10.9	8.1	10.3	5.0	6.5	2.3	2.2	1.9	1.2
Redmond, WA	12.1	7.5	8.6	3.3	3.0	1.8	2.3	2.6	1.2
Richland, WA	22.7	12.7	15.0	9.0	3.9	1.8	3.0	2.6	2.0
Ridgefield, CT	17.7	24.4	13.7	5.5	23.6	5.7	3.0	3.0	0.9
Ridgewood, NJ	11.9	20.0	8.6	4.3	17.5	5.2	1.8	1.9	2.3
Rio Rancho, NM	14.8	9.8	9.4	5.5	4.2	2.9	2.6	2.4	1.3
Sahuarita, AZ	12.3	13.7	9.9	2.9	5.4	3.4	1.8	1.3	1.8
Sammamish, WA	15.9	10.4	11.7	4.4	4.4	2.6	2.4	3.3	1.9
San Ramon, CA	8.7	8.2	6.9	3.7	6.7	1.2	1.9	1.5	0.7
Saratoga, CA	8.5	7.6	8.3	1.7	5.7	1.5	1.4	1.8	0.9
Schertz, TX	19.3	11.5	11.2	5.5	2.7	2.7	4.0	1.6	1.8
Shrewsbury, MA	5.7	21.5	8.9	4.4	17.1	5.3	10.3	1.8	0.2
South Brunswick, NJ	7.7	9.7	4.2	4.9	12.4	4.9	0.7	0.9	0.7
South Jordan, UT	13.2	5.8	30.4	6.4	4.4	1.0	1.8	5.0	3.1
South Kingstown, RI	9.1	22.5	15.8	2.8	17.9	5.2	8.3	3.1	0.6
South Windsor, CT	9.1	18.4	13.1	2.0	16.1	9.2	6.7	2.7	0.8
Southlake, TX	20.9	15.3	14.5	8.1	7.2	3.0	3.8	2.5	1.7
Spring Hill, TN	16.9	16.2	15.4	10.7	3.9	2.3	4.7	3.6	1.5
Stow, OH	26.0	15.1	11.9	8.5	8.8	5.9	2.4	2.9	1.2
Sugar Land, TX	8.6	5.8	5.7	4.5	2.6	1.1	2.0	1.4	0.6
Sun Prairie, WI	44.1	14.2	7.7	3.8	3.7	6.9	2.0	0.9	3.7
Syracuse, UT	9.9	6.8	27.6	9.6	2.0	1.3	1.7	5.4	2.8
Tredyffrin, PA	20.5	22.4	13.9	4.2	13.9	5.2	2.9	3.0	1.4
Upper Arlington, OH	32.8	20.0	16.6	5.8	9.7	3.8	2.1	2.7	1.0
Upper Dublin, PA	20.4	22.6	8.9	5.1	14.8	8.3	1.3	1.9	0.9
Vestavia Hills, AL	9.7	11.6	17.9	14.6	5.2	1.1	3.8	4.7	1.0
Webster, NY	23.2	18.0	11.8	4.6	27.4	6.1	2.6	2.1	3.9
Wellesley, MA	10.6	22.4	13.9	4.4	12.9	3.9	2.5	2.7	1.7
West Fargo, ND	44.1	4.8	3.6	2.3	1.9	2.5	3.0	1.2	1.3
West Linn, OR	22.6	11.2	14.1	3.8	5.9	2.5	4.0	3.9	2.4
West Windsor, NJ	7.1	8.8	5.4	2.4	9.6	4.2	2.4	1.8	0.2
Westlake, OH	27.4	22.0	11.7	4.4	8.7	6.5	1.7	2.3	0.5
Weston, FL	7.3	6.2	3.3	5.9	7.9	3.8	1.6	0.8	0.4
Westport, CT	11.7	16.7	11.5	7.1	17.7	7.7	3.1	3.1	1.7
Wilmette, IL	23.4	16.3	10.4	5.3	7.1	8.0	2.9	1.9	1.3
Woodbury, MN	33.5	13.0	7.8	2.3	5.0	4.9	4.0	1.9	1.1
Yorba Linda, CA	15.6	10.8	11.1	5.7	6.1	2.6	3.2	1.8	2.4
U.S.	14.9	10.8	8.0	7.1	5.5	3.0	2.7	1.7	1.4

Note: Figures are the percentage of the total population reporting a particular ancestry. The nine most commonly reported ancestries in the U.S. are shown. Figures include multiple ancestries (e.g. if a person reported being Irish and Italian, they were included in both columns); (1) Excludes Basque

Source: U.S. Census Bureau, 2010-2014 American Community Survey 5-Year Estimates

Ancestry: Metro Area

Metro Area	German	Irish	English	American	Italian	Polish	French[1]	Scottish	Dutch
Aliso Viejo, CA	6.0	4.8	4.4	3.2	3.0	1.3	1.4	1.0	0.7
Allen, TX	10.3	8.1	7.6	6.6	2.2	1.1	2.0	1.7	1.0
Alpharetta, GA	7.4	7.5	7.5	9.8	2.6	1.3	1.5	1.8	0.8
Ankeny, IA	29.4	13.7	9.4	5.4	3.2	1.4	2.3	1.7	3.9
Apex, NC	11.1	10.0	11.0	11.3	4.7	2.2	1.9	2.7	1.0
Ballwin, MO	29.3	13.8	8.1	7.3	4.8	2.6	3.6	1.5	1.3
Beavercreek, OH	24.5	12.7	9.0	9.8	3.6	2.1	2.4	1.9	1.5
Bella Vista, AR	13.0	10.3	9.0	8.5	2.0	1.1	2.2	2.0	1.4
Bernards, NJ	7.2	10.6	3.1	4.4	13.7	4.2	1.1	0.7	0.7
Bethlehem, NY	16.2	23.0	10.0	5.2	17.2	6.8	7.0	2.0	3.7
Bloomfield, MI	16.5	10.2	7.3	5.4	6.4	10.6	3.8	2.2	1.3
Bowie, MD	10.7	9.3	7.6	4.7	4.4	2.3	1.7	1.8	0.8
Bozeman, MT	28.5	15.4	13.5	4.6	5.2	2.7	4.2	3.4	4.5
Brentwood, TN	10.7	11.2	10.3	13.7	2.7	1.2	2.2	2.3	1.1
Broomfield, CO	19.4	11.6	10.0	5.0	5.2	2.6	2.7	2.4	1.6
Carmel, IN	20.6	11.7	9.3	9.5	2.7	1.9	2.1	2.0	1.6
Cedar Park, TX	14.3	8.7	8.6	4.7	2.9	1.6	2.8	2.2	1.0
Cheshire, CT	8.4	15.9	6.9	2.8	22.8	7.2	3.8	1.4	0.6
Chesterfield, MO	29.3	13.8	8.1	7.3	4.8	2.6	3.6	1.5	1.3
Collierville, TN	6.6	7.5	6.6	7.6	2.2	0.7	1.4	1.5	0.7
Coppell, TX	10.3	8.1	7.6	6.6	2.2	1.1	2.0	1.7	1.0
Cornelius, NC	12.4	9.4	8.4	10.0	3.7	1.7	1.7	2.3	1.1
Cranberry, PA	28.6	18.8	8.3	4.5	16.4	9.0	1.8	1.9	1.3
Cupertino, CA	7.2	5.5	5.2	2.0	4.5	1.2	1.6	1.2	0.8
Danville, CA	8.5	7.9	6.3	2.6	5.3	1.5	2.0	1.6	0.9
Draper, UT	11.4	6.0	21.9	5.1	3.0	1.0	1.9	4.0	2.4
Dublin, OH	25.2	14.2	9.3	7.7	5.5	2.4	2.2	2.1	1.6
Eastchester, NY	7.2	10.6	3.1	4.4	13.7	4.2	1.1	0.7	0.7
Eden Prairie, MN	32.4	11.8	6.0	3.3	2.8	4.6	3.7	1.4	1.6
Edmond, OK	14.3	11.0	8.2	8.7	1.8	1.0	2.1	1.9	1.6
Evesham, NJ	16.5	20.0	7.6	3.6	13.9	5.4	1.5	1.3	1.0
Fishers, IN	20.6	11.7	9.3	9.5	2.7	1.9	2.1	2.0	1.6
Flower Mound, TX	10.3	8.1	7.6	6.6	2.2	1.1	2.0	1.7	1.0
Folsom, CA	13.0	9.6	8.7	3.5	5.4	1.4	2.6	2.0	1.3
Foster City, CA	8.5	7.9	6.3	2.6	5.3	1.5	2.0	1.6	0.9
Franklin, TN	10.7	11.2	10.3	13.7	2.7	1.2	2.2	2.3	1.1
Friendswood, TX	8.7	6.0	5.5	4.8	2.1	1.3	2.3	1.2	0.7
Germantown, TN	6.6	7.5	6.6	7.6	2.2	0.7	1.4	1.5	0.7
Glastonbury, CT	9.2	16.0	9.4	4.0	16.8	10.2	7.2	1.8	0.7
Grand Blanc, MI	16.7	10.3	9.3	6.8	2.8	5.5	4.3	2.2	1.9
Guilderland, NY	16.2	23.0	10.0	5.2	17.2	6.8	7.0	2.0	3.7
Hampden, PA	32.1	13.2	7.0	6.0	7.4	3.6	1.9	1.6	1.9
Holly Springs, NC	11.1	10.0	11.0	11.3	4.7	2.2	1.9	2.7	1.0
Huntersville, NC	12.4	9.4	8.4	10.0	3.7	1.7	1.7	2.3	1.1
Independence, KY	29.7	14.3	8.8	10.4	4.2	1.5	2.0	1.7	1.2
Johns Creek, GA	7.4	7.5	7.5	9.8	2.6	1.3	1.5	1.8	0.8
Keller, TX	10.3	8.1	7.6	6.6	2.2	1.1	2.0	1.7	1.0
Kirkland, WA	16.8	10.7	10.4	4.2	3.7	2.0	3.2	2.8	1.8
Lafayette, CO	22.0	13.5	13.2	4.9	5.9	3.7	3.7	3.7	2.1
Lake Oswego, OR	19.7	11.6	11.2	5.1	4.0	1.9	3.2	3.1	2.2
League City, TX	8.7	6.0	5.5	4.8	2.1	1.3	2.3	1.2	0.7
Leawood, KS	23.2	13.3	10.2	8.1	3.5	1.7	2.6	2.0	1.6
Lee's Summit, MO	23.2	13.3	10.2	8.1	3.5	1.7	2.6	2.0	1.6
Leesburg, VA	10.7	9.3	7.6	4.7	4.4	2.3	1.7	1.8	0.8
Lehi, UT	11.5	5.2	28.6	5.4	2.4	0.7	2.0	5.5	1.9
Lenexa, KS	23.2	13.3	10.2	8.1	3.5	1.7	2.6	2.0	1.6
Lexington, MA	6.3	23.4	10.5	4.5	14.6	3.7	5.6	2.5	0.6
Los Altos, CA	7.2	5.5	5.2	2.0	4.5	1.2	1.6	1.2	0.8
Lower Makefield, PA	16.5	20.0	7.6	3.6	13.9	5.4	1.5	1.3	1.0
Madison, AL	9.9	9.2	9.9	13.9	2.2	1.0	1.8	2.0	0.9
Mamaroneck, NY	7.2	10.6	3.1	4.4	13.7	4.2	1.1	0.7	0.7
Manheim, PA	36.5	10.7	7.8	8.0	5.8	2.8	1.7	1.5	1.5
Manlius, NY	17.9	21.3	11.9	7.5	16.3	6.2	5.1	1.9	2.2
Maple Grove, MN	32.4	11.8	6.0	3.3	2.8	4.6	3.7	1.4	1.6
Marion, IA	40.5	16.3	9.2	5.9	1.8	1.4	2.6	1.7	2.5
Marlboro, NJ	7.2	10.6	3.1	4.4	13.7	4.2	1.1	0.7	0.7
Mason, OH	29.7	14.3	8.8	10.4	4.2	1.5	2.0	1.7	1.2
McCandless, PA	28.6	18.8	8.3	4.5	16.4	9.0	1.8	1.9	1.3
Menomonee Falls, WI	35.8	10.2	4.6	2.6	4.5	11.7	2.7	1.0	1.3

Table continued on next page.

Metro Area	German	Irish	English	American	Italian	Polish	French[1]	Scottish	Dutch
Meridian, ID	16.8	8.9	14.4	9.8	3.1	1.5	2.3	3.0	1.9
Merrimack, NH	8.1	21.2	13.8	4.2	10.1	4.7	15.5	3.3	0.9
Mount Lebanon, PA	28.6	18.8	8.3	4.5	16.4	9.0	1.8	1.9	1.3
Mount Pleasant, SC	11.5	10.4	8.8	13.0	3.6	1.8	2.6	2.4	1.0
Needham, MA	6.3	23.4	10.5	4.5	14.6	3.7	5.6	2.5	0.6
Newtown, CT	9.2	14.8	8.0	4.4	17.6	5.4	2.5	1.8	0.8
Northbrook, IL	15.5	11.6	4.4	2.9	7.0	9.4	1.5	1.0	1.3
Northville, MI	16.5	10.2	7.3	5.4	6.4	10.6	3.8	2.2	1.3
Novi, MI	16.5	10.2	7.3	5.4	6.4	10.6	3.8	2.2	1.3
O'Fallon, IL	29.3	13.8	8.1	7.3	4.8	2.6	3.6	1.5	1.3
O'Fallon, MO	29.3	13.8	8.1	7.3	4.8	2.6	3.6	1.5	1.3
Orchard Park, NY	25.4	17.2	7.7	3.8	16.9	16.9	2.5	1.7	1.0
Oviedo, FL	10.3	8.6	7.1	8.0	5.3	2.1	2.2	1.5	0.9
Parker, CO	19.4	11.6	10.0	5.0	5.2	2.6	2.7	2.4	1.6
Parkland, FL	5.3	5.1	3.3	5.8	5.4	2.2	1.4	0.7	0.5
Peachtree City, GA	7.4	7.5	7.5	9.8	2.6	1.3	1.5	1.8	0.8
Pflugerville, TX	14.3	8.7	8.6	4.7	2.9	1.6	2.8	2.2	1.0
Plainfield, IL	15.5	11.6	4.4	2.9	7.0	9.4	1.5	1.0	1.3
Princeton, NJ	10.3	12.2	6.0	2.8	13.7	7.0	1.5	1.3	0.9
Queen Creek, AZ	14.5	9.3	8.3	5.8	4.6	2.6	2.4	1.7	1.4
Rancho Palos Verdes, CA	6.0	4.8	4.4	3.2	3.0	1.3	1.4	1.0	0.7
Redmond, WA	16.8	10.7	10.4	4.2	3.7	2.0	3.2	2.8	1.8
Richland, WA	18.2	9.5	10.2	8.6	2.4	1.4	2.8	2.2	1.7
Ridgefield, CT	9.2	14.8	8.0	4.4	17.6	5.4	2.5	1.8	0.8
Ridgewood, NJ	7.2	10.6	3.1	4.4	13.7	4.2	1.1	0.7	0.7
Rio Rancho, NM	10.7	7.4	6.7	4.4	3.2	1.5	2.0	1.7	1.0
Sahuarita, AZ	14.5	10.2	8.8	3.5	4.6	2.4	2.8	1.9	1.5
Sammamish, WA	16.8	10.7	10.4	4.2	3.7	2.0	3.2	2.8	1.8
San Ramon, CA	8.5	7.9	6.3	2.6	5.3	1.5	2.0	1.6	0.9
Saratoga, CA	7.2	5.5	5.2	2.0	4.5	1.2	1.6	1.2	0.8
Schertz, TX	11.9	6.1	5.4	4.0	2.0	1.6	1.9	1.2	0.7
Shrewsbury, MA	6.6	20.3	10.6	4.1	13.3	6.5	14.4	2.2	0.8
South Brunswick, NJ	7.2	10.6	3.1	4.4	13.7	4.2	1.1	0.7	0.7
South Jordan, UT	11.4	6.0	21.9	5.1	3.0	1.0	1.9	4.0	2.4
South Kingstown, RI	5.1	18.7	11.2	3.3	15.4	4.1	11.1	1.9	0.5
South Windsor, CT	9.2	16.0	9.4	4.0	16.8	10.2	7.2	1.8	0.7
Southlake, TX	10.3	8.1	7.6	6.6	2.2	1.1	2.0	1.7	1.0
Spring Hill, TN	10.7	11.2	10.3	13.7	2.7	1.2	2.2	2.3	1.1
Stow, OH	23.8	14.9	9.4	6.9	9.4	5.1	2.0	2.1	1.5
Sugar Land, TX	8.7	6.0	5.5	4.8	2.1	1.3	2.3	1.2	0.7
Sun Prairie, WI	40.2	13.9	8.9	3.3	3.5	5.0	2.8	1.5	2.2
Syracuse, UT	11.7	5.9	26.1	8.2	2.7	0.7	1.9	4.6	2.8
Tredyffrin, PA	16.5	20.0	7.6	3.6	13.9	5.4	1.5	1.3	1.0
Upper Arlington, OH	25.2	14.2	9.3	7.7	5.5	2.4	2.2	2.1	1.6
Upper Dublin, PA	16.5	20.0	7.6	3.6	13.9	5.4	1.5	1.3	1.0
Vestavia Hills, AL	6.9	9.3	9.3	15.3	2.3	0.7	1.6	2.2	0.9
Webster, NY	21.4	16.5	12.7	5.0	16.6	4.9	3.1	2.1	3.7
Wellesley, MA	6.3	23.4	10.5	4.5	14.6	3.7	5.6	2.5	0.6
West Fargo, ND	39.9	8.1	4.3	2.0	1.3	2.8	3.6	1.2	1.2
West Linn, OR	19.7	11.6	11.2	5.1	4.0	1.9	3.2	3.1	2.2
West Windsor, NJ	10.3	12.2	6.0	2.8	13.7	7.0	1.5	1.3	0.9
Westlake, OH	20.1	14.3	7.5	4.0	10.0	8.0	1.6	1.7	1.0
Weston, FL	5.3	5.1	3.3	5.8	5.4	2.2	1.4	0.7	0.5
Westport, CT	9.2	14.8	8.0	4.4	17.6	5.4	2.5	1.8	0.8
Wilmette, IL	15.5	11.6	4.4	2.9	7.0	9.4	1.5	1.0	1.3
Woodbury, MN	32.4	11.8	6.0	3.3	2.8	4.6	3.7	1.4	1.6
Yorba Linda, CA	6.0	4.8	4.4	3.2	3.0	1.3	1.4	1.0	0.7
U.S.	14.9	10.8	8.0	7.1	5.5	3.0	2.7	1.7	1.4

Note: Figures are the percentage of the total population reporting a particular ancestry. The nine most commonly reported ancestries in the U.S. are shown. Figures include multiple ancestries (e.g. if a person reported being Irish and Italian, they were included in both columns); Figures cover the Metropolitan Statistical Area—see Appendix B for areas included; (1) Excludes Basque
Source: U.S. Census Bureau, 2010-2014 American Community Survey 5-Year Estimates

Foreign-Born Population: City

City	Percent of Population Born in: Any Foreign Country	Asia	Mexico	Europe	Carribean	Central America[1]	South America	Africa	Canada
Aliso Viejo, CA	22.5	14.3	3.0	1.8	0.3	0.4	1.5	0.7	0.5
Allen, TX	17.1	9.9	2.1	1.6	0.3	0.3	0.6	1.9	0.3
Alpharetta, GA	22.0	11.8	2.1	3.5	0.8	0.4	1.8	1.0	0.5
Ankeny, IA	3.4	1.2	0.0	1.5	0.0	0.3	0.0	0.3	0.1
Apex, NC	10.1	4.7	1.6	1.2	0.1	0.4	0.6	0.9	0.6
Ballwin, MO	7.3	4.5	0.1	2.1	0.0	0.2	0.1	0.1	0.1
Beavercreek, OH	7.5	5.1	0.5	1.2	0.1	0.0	0.1	0.3	0.1
Bella Vista, AR	3.6	0.8	0.6	1.7	0.1	0.1	0.0	0.2	0.2
Bernards, NJ	17.8	9.6	0.9	4.7	0.5	0.0	0.7	0.6	0.6
Bethlehem, NY	6.7	3.7	0.0	1.7	0.2	0.0	0.1	0.7	0.2
Bloomfield, MI	15.2	9.2	0.3	3.1	0.2	0.1	0.2	0.7	1.3
Bowie, MD	13.0	3.4	0.2	1.1	1.9	1.8	0.6	3.8	0.2
Bozeman, MT	4.3	2.2	0.3	0.7	0.0	0.1	0.2	0.2	0.4
Brentwood, TN	8.0	5.1	0.2	1.0	0.3	0.1	0.3	0.5	0.6
Broomfield, CO	9.2	3.9	2.0	1.9	0.1	0.3	0.2	0.2	0.6
Carmel, IN	11.9	7.3	0.7	1.8	0.2	0.2	0.4	0.7	0.5
Cedar Park, TX	11.8	5.2	2.8	1.0	0.8	0.3	0.6	0.9	0.2
Cheshire, CT	10.2	5.2	0.4	3.2	0.1	0.1	0.5	0.3	0.5
Chesterfield, MO	11.3	7.1	0.5	2.1	0.2	0.1	0.6	0.2	0.3
Collierville, TN	6.4	4.3	0.5	0.7	0.1	0.0	0.3	0.2	0.3
Coppell, TX	20.8	13.7	3.0	1.0	0.1	0.2	1.5	1.1	0.2
Cornelius, NC	7.7	1.6	1.5	2.7	0.3	0.5	0.2	0.4	0.4
Cranberry, PA	3.3	1.5	0.1	0.9	0.1	0.0	0.1	0.0	0.5
Cupertino, CA	50.3	43.6	0.6	3.8	0.1	0.1	0.5	0.6	0.8
Danville, CA	12.6	7.3	0.3	3.1	0.1	0.2	0.3	0.5	0.6
Draper, UT	6.9	1.8	1.2	1.5	0.0	0.4	1.1	0.3	0.6
Dublin, OH	16.1	12.2	0.3	2.0	0.2	0.0	0.2	0.6	0.5
Eastchester, NY	16.8	5.4	0.5	7.6	0.4	0.2	1.2	0.7	0.4
Eden Prairie, MN	13.9	8.4	0.8	1.6	0.1	0.2	0.7	1.7	0.3
Edmond, OK	6.6	3.5	1.0	0.6	0.1	0.2	0.4	0.6	0.2
Evesham, NJ	7.8	4.7	0.3	1.3	0.4	0.0	0.5	0.4	0.1
Fishers, IN	7.9	4.9	0.6	0.8	0.2	0.2	0.6	0.4	0.1
Flower Mound, TX	11.4	6.2	1.6	1.3	0.3	0.1	0.6	0.5	0.8
Folsom, CA	15.3	10.3	1.0	2.0	0.1	0.5	0.2	0.2	0.7
Foster City, CA	43.1	33.8	0.5	5.5	0.1	0.4	0.9	1.0	0.6
Franklin, TN	9.5	4.0	2.5	0.9	0.5	0.2	0.6	0.3	0.2
Friendswood, TX	8.7	3.5	1.3	1.3	0.4	0.5	0.9	0.5	0.4
Germantown, TN	7.1	4.2	0.2	1.2	0.1	0.1	0.5	0.4	0.2
Glastonbury, CT	12.4	5.4	0.2	3.6	0.2	0.2	1.1	0.9	0.7
Grand Blanc, MI	6.4	4.3	0.1	0.8	0.1	0.0	0.5	0.3	0.4
Guilderland, NY	9.4	6.4	0.0	1.2	0.3	0.4	0.2	0.5	0.4
Hampden, PA	10.3	6.3	0.2	1.6	0.0	0.1	0.2	1.2	0.3
Holly Springs, NC	6.9	2.9	0.0	1.0	0.7	0.2	0.5	1.2	0.4
Huntersville, NC	5.9	1.8	1.5	1.2	0.3	0.2	0.4	0.1	0.3
Independence, KY	2.2	0.9	0.1	0.2	0.1	0.3	0.4	0.1	0.2
Johns Creek, GA	25.4	17.4	1.0	3.1	0.5	0.2	1.3	0.8	0.5
Keller, TX	6.7	2.8	0.6	1.4	0.0	0.7	0.5	0.4	0.2
Kirkland, WA	20.0	10.1	1.5	5.1	0.0	0.2	0.7	0.7	1.3
Lafayette, CO	10.8	3.2	2.7	2.3	0.0	1.4	0.7	0.1	0.4
Lake Oswego, OR	11.3	5.5	1.0	2.6	0.2	0.0	0.2	0.5	1.0
League City, TX	9.4	3.7	1.5	1.0	0.2	1.4	0.6	0.5	0.4
Leawood, KS	5.2	2.6	0.1	1.5	0.2	0.0	0.4	0.3	0.2
Lee's Summit, MO	3.8	1.8	0.3	0.6	0.1	0.2	0.2	0.2	0.2
Leesburg, VA	22.5	8.2	1.0	1.8	0.2	7.7	1.9	1.3	0.3
Lehi, UT	4.2	0.9	1.5	0.3	0.1	0.2	0.9	0.0	0.3
Lenexa, KS	8.8	3.4	1.8	0.7	0.1	0.9	0.7	1.0	0.2
Lexington, MA	24.4	16.4	0.1	5.5	0.1	0.1	0.5	0.7	0.8
Los Altos, CA	23.3	14.4	0.2	5.8	0.0	0.3	0.5	0.4	1.4
Lower Makefield, PA	8.3	4.7	0.0	2.6	0.2	0.0	0.1	0.5	0.2
Madison, AL	7.8	4.4	0.5	1.6	0.0	0.1	0.4	0.4	0.3
Mamaroneck, NY	19.9	4.4	1.3	7.0	0.7	1.6	3.2	0.7	0.8
Manheim, PA	7.7	2.8	0.2	1.7	0.9	0.4	0.6	0.6	0.6
Manlius, NY	6.2	3.0	0.0	1.9	0.1	0.0	0.4	0.2	0.5
Maple Grove, MN	9.1	5.0	0.2	2.2	0.1	0.0	0.5	0.6	0.3
Marion, IA	3.9	1.7	0.3	0.4	0.3	0.3	0.1	0.4	0.4
Marlboro, NJ	20.0	11.4	0.1	6.2	0.4	0.1	0.8	0.7	0.4

Table continued on next page.

City	Percent of Population Born in								
	Any Foreign Country	Asia	Mexico	Europe	Carribean	Central America[1]	South America	Africa	Canada
Mason, OH	11.2	7.3	0.2	1.6	0.1	0.1	1.1	0.4	0.1
McCandless, PA	7.5	4.7	0.1	1.8	0.1	0.0	0.3	0.4	0.2
Menomonee Falls, WI	5.4	3.2	0.3	1.5	0.0	0.1	0.1	0.0	0.1
Meridian, ID	4.9	1.1	0.9	1.6	0.1	0.0	0.4	0.3	0.4
Merrimack, NH	4.7	1.7	0.0	1.6	0.1	0.0	0.5	0.0	0.8
Mount Lebanon, PA	9.1	4.1	0.1	3.4	0.3	0.0	0.3	0.6	0.1
Mount Pleasant, SC	4.6	1.1	0.4	1.6	0.4	0.1	0.3	0.1	0.5
Needham, MA	12.7	5.3	0.3	4.8	0.3	0.2	0.6	0.4	0.8
Newtown, CT	8.2	1.9	0.3	3.4	0.5	0.6	1.0	0.2	0.3
Northbrook, IL	19.1	10.3	0.4	6.7	0.4	0.2	0.5	0.4	0.1
Northville, MI	16.2	11.2	0.4	3.2	0.0	0.1	0.5	0.1	0.8
Novi, MI	18.8	13.5	0.8	2.7	0.1	0.2	0.2	0.2	0.9
O'Fallon, IL	3.9	2.2	0.1	0.9	0.2	0.1	0.0	0.1	0.2
O'Fallon, MO	3.7	2.5	0.2	0.6	0.0	0.0	0.1	0.2	0.1
Orchard Park, NY	3.6	0.6	0.0	1.9	0.0	0.1	0.2	0.0	0.7
Oviedo, FL	11.8	2.6	0.2	1.7	2.7	0.7	2.6	0.9	0.5
Parker, CO	5.0	1.9	0.9	1.1	0.1	0.4	0.1	0.1	0.4
Parkland, FL	22.6	5.3	0.5	3.9	5.2	0.5	5.6	0.1	1.4
Peachtree City, GA	11.6	3.9	2.8	2.0	0.8	0.2	0.9	0.6	0.4
Pflugerville, TX	15.3	6.0	4.5	0.9	0.7	0.7	0.6	1.7	0.1
Plainfield, IL	11.5	6.7	2.0	1.8	0.0	0.2	0.4	0.3	0.1
Princeton, NJ	25.2	11.4	0.3	8.3	0.4	1.6	0.6	1.5	0.8
Queen Creek, AZ	4.0	0.9	1.4	0.8	0.1	0.0	0.1	0.1	0.5
Rancho Palos Verdes, CA	26.5	18.6	0.8	4.4	0.0	0.4	0.5	0.7	0.8
Redmond, WA	37.3	23.6	3.5	5.8	0.0	0.5	1.1	1.0	1.7
Richland, WA	8.1	3.8	0.9	1.8	0.2	0.0	0.1	0.6	0.6
Ridgefield, CT	9.4	1.3	0.1	5.0	0.5	0.2	1.1	0.5	0.6
Ridgewood, NJ	21.3	11.8	0.0	4.5	1.5	1.0	0.9	0.8	0.6
Rio Rancho, NM	5.9	1.2	3.0	0.7	0.1	0.2	0.3	0.0	0.2
Sahuarita, AZ	10.0	1.9	4.7	1.1	0.2	0.2	1.1	0.1	0.6
Sammamish, WA	24.7	14.4	0.5	5.1	0.1	0.1	0.7	0.8	2.7
San Ramon, CA	32.1	25.3	0.8	2.8	0.2	0.2	1.1	0.5	0.8
Saratoga, CA	37.9	30.9	0.4	4.5	0.1	0.1	0.5	0.5	0.5
Schertz, TX	7.4	2.3	2.5	1.2	0.2	0.8	0.1	0.0	0.2
Shrewsbury, MA	21.2	12.5	0.0	3.7	0.4	0.4	2.0	1.5	0.5
South Brunswick, NJ	33.7	26.9	0.1	2.2	1.3	0.2	1.2	1.2	0.4
South Jordan, UT	4.5	1.5	0.9	1.2	0.0	0.0	0.3	0.0	0.3
South Kingstown, RI	5.5	1.8	0.0	1.8	0.6	0.4	0.5	0.4	0.0
South Windsor, CT	13.9	6.5	0.0	2.9	1.2	0.2	1.4	0.8	1.0
Southlake, TX	9.4	3.6	1.1	2.6	0.1	0.1	0.6	0.4	0.6
Spring Hill, TN	4.3	0.9	1.3	0.5	0.0	0.6	0.4	0.3	0.0
Stow, OH	4.2	1.9	0.2	1.3	0.0	0.2	0.1	0.2	0.3
Sugar Land, TX	34.0	25.8	1.8	1.6	0.3	0.6	1.3	1.8	0.6
Sun Prairie, WI	4.3	2.0	0.5	0.5	0.0	0.2	0.4	0.3	0.3
Syracuse, UT	2.0	0.4	0.1	0.5	0.0	0.2	0.7	0.0	0.1
Tredyffrin, PA	13.5	8.7	0.1	3.0	0.2	0.1	0.8	0.4	0.2
Upper Arlington, OH	7.6	3.8	0.3	2.2	0.1	0.1	0.2	0.5	0.4
Upper Dublin, PA	9.3	6.5	0.3	1.6	0.1	0.1	0.4	0.2	0.1
Vestavia Hills, AL	6.4	4.0	0.5	1.2	0.0	0.1	0.0	0.3	0.2
Webster, NY	9.4	3.4	0.2	4.2	0.3	0.2	0.3	0.1	0.6
Wellesley, MA	14.0	7.4	0.1	3.5	0.3	0.1	0.9	0.6	0.8
West Fargo, ND	5.1	1.5	0.0	0.4	0.0	0.0	0.0	2.9	0.2
West Linn, OR	9.1	4.0	2.0	1.4	0.0	0.1	0.1	0.7	0.4
West Windsor, NJ	38.2	28.4	0.5	5.5	0.7	0.1	1.5	0.7	0.6
Westlake, OH	9.4	5.3	0.1	2.6	0.2	0.0	0.6	0.3	0.2
Weston, FL	39.9	3.0	0.9	2.9	4.4	1.3	26.4	0.2	0.8
Westport, CT	12.4	5.1	0.4	4.1	0.2	0.3	0.7	0.4	1.0
Wilmette, IL	17.7	10.2	0.5	5.3	0.3	0.1	0.7	0.2	0.3
Woodbury, MN	10.5	5.9	0.7	0.9	0.1	0.1	0.5	1.7	0.5
Yorba Linda, CA	18.0	11.7	2.1	1.6	0.2	0.4	0.6	0.5	0.8
U.S.	13.1	3.8	3.7	1.5	1.2	1.0	0.9	0.6	0.3

Note: (1) Excludes Mexico

Source: U.S. Census Bureau, 2010-2014 American Community Survey 5-Year Estimates

Foreign-Born Population: Metro Area

Metro Area	Percent of Population Born in								
	Any Foreign Country	Asia	Mexico	Europe	Carribean	Central America[1]	South America	Africa	Canada
Aliso Viejo, CA	33.8	12.3	13.3	1.7	0.3	4.3	0.9	0.5	0.3
Allen, TX	17.5	4.4	9.0	0.8	0.2	1.3	0.5	1.0	0.2
Alpharetta, GA	13.3	4.0	3.1	1.2	1.4	1.1	0.9	1.3	0.2
Ankeny, IA	7.5	2.6	1.8	1.3	0.0	0.5	0.2	0.9	0.1
Apex, NC	11.7	3.9	3.2	1.1	0.6	1.0	0.6	1.1	0.3
Ballwin, MO	4.5	1.9	0.6	1.2	0.1	0.1	0.1	0.3	0.1
Beavercreek, OH	3.7	1.9	0.3	0.6	0.1	0.1	0.1	0.4	0.1
Bella Vista, AR	10.9	1.9	5.4	0.5	0.1	1.7	0.3	0.1	0.1
Bernards, NJ	28.5	8.0	1.7	4.6	6.5	1.9	4.3	1.2	0.2
Bethlehem, NY	6.9	2.8	0.2	1.7	0.6	0.1	0.8	0.4	0.3
Bloomfield, MI	8.9	4.6	0.8	2.2	0.1	0.1	0.1	0.3	0.6
Bowie, MD	21.9	7.8	0.9	1.9	1.0	4.6	2.3	3.0	0.2
Bozeman, MT	2.9	1.1	0.4	0.8	0.0	0.1	0.1	0.1	0.3
Brentwood, TN	7.4	2.2	2.1	0.6	0.2	0.8	0.3	0.9	0.2
Broomfield, CO	12.2	2.9	5.5	1.5	0.1	0.5	0.4	0.9	0.3
Carmel, IN	6.2	2.0	2.0	0.6	0.2	0.4	0.2	0.7	0.1
Cedar Park, TX	14.7	3.8	7.2	1.0	0.3	1.1	0.5	0.5	0.3
Cheshire, CT	11.7	3.1	1.0	3.3	1.3	0.5	1.6	0.7	0.3
Chesterfield, MO	4.5	1.9	0.6	1.2	0.1	0.1	0.1	0.3	0.1
Collierville, TN	5.0	1.6	1.7	0.4	0.1	0.5	0.2	0.5	0.1
Coppell, TX	17.5	4.4	9.0	0.8	0.2	1.3	0.5	1.0	0.2
Cornelius, NC	9.2	2.2	2.4	1.1	0.5	1.3	0.8	0.6	0.2
Cranberry, PA	3.4	1.6	0.1	1.0	0.1	0.1	0.2	0.2	0.1
Cupertino, CA	36.9	22.9	8.1	2.9	0.1	1.0	0.7	0.5	0.5
Danville, CA	29.9	16.3	5.6	2.9	0.2	2.5	0.9	0.6	0.4
Draper, UT	11.9	2.7	5.0	1.3	0.1	0.6	1.0	0.5	0.3
Dublin, OH	7.0	2.8	0.9	0.8	0.2	0.2	0.2	1.6	0.1
Eastchester, NY	28.5	8.0	1.7	4.6	6.5	1.9	4.3	1.2	0.2
Eden Prairie, MN	9.7	3.9	1.4	1.1	0.1	0.3	0.5	2.1	0.2
Edmond, OK	8.1	2.4	3.8	0.4	0.1	0.6	0.2	0.4	0.1
Evesham, NJ	9.9	4.0	0.9	1.9	1.1	0.4	0.6	0.8	0.1
Fishers, IN	6.2	2.0	2.0	0.6	0.2	0.4	0.2	0.7	0.1
Flower Mound, TX	17.5	4.4	9.0	0.8	0.2	1.3	0.5	1.0	0.2
Folsom, CA	17.7	7.9	4.8	2.7	0.1	0.6	0.3	0.4	0.3
Foster City, CA	29.9	16.3	5.6	2.9	0.2	2.5	0.9	0.6	0.4
Franklin, TN	7.4	2.2	2.1	0.6	0.2	0.8	0.3	0.9	0.2
Friendswood, TX	22.5	5.4	9.8	1.0	0.5	3.4	1.0	1.0	0.2
Germantown, TN	5.0	1.6	1.7	0.4	0.1	0.5	0.2	0.5	0.1
Glastonbury, CT	12.8	3.3	0.4	3.9	2.2	0.4	1.4	0.6	0.6
Grand Blanc, MI	2.3	1.2	0.1	0.5	0.0	0.0	0.1	0.1	0.2
Guilderland, NY	6.9	2.8	0.2	1.7	0.6	0.1	0.8	0.4	0.3
Hampden, PA	5.6	2.6	0.2	1.0	0.5	0.2	0.3	0.6	0.2
Holly Springs, NC	11.7	3.9	3.2	1.1	0.6	1.0	0.6	1.1	0.3
Huntersville, NC	9.2	2.2	2.4	1.1	0.5	1.3	0.8	0.6	0.2
Independence, KY	4.2	1.8	0.5	0.7	0.1	0.3	0.2	0.5	0.1
Johns Creek, GA	13.3	4.0	3.1	1.2	1.4	1.1	0.9	1.3	0.2
Keller, TX	17.5	4.4	9.0	0.8	0.2	1.3	0.5	1.0	0.2
Kirkland, WA	17.1	8.5	2.5	2.8	0.1	0.5	0.4	1.2	0.7
Lafayette, CO	10.6	3.2	3.6	2.3	0.1	0.3	0.4	0.2	0.4
Lake Oswego, OR	12.5	4.5	3.7	2.4	0.1	0.4	0.3	0.5	0.5
League City, TX	22.5	5.4	9.8	1.0	0.5	3.4	1.0	1.0	0.2
Leawood, KS	6.4	2.0	2.2	0.6	0.2	0.4	0.2	0.6	0.1
Lee's Summit, MO	6.4	2.0	2.2	0.6	0.2	0.4	0.2	0.6	0.1
Leesburg, VA	21.9	7.8	0.9	1.9	1.0	4.6	2.3	3.0	0.2
Lehi, UT	7.1	1.0	2.8	0.6	0.1	0.5	1.3	0.1	0.4
Lenexa, KS	6.4	2.0	2.2	0.6	0.2	0.4	0.2	0.6	0.1
Lexington, MA	17.1	5.4	0.2	3.2	3.0	1.4	1.8	1.4	0.5
Los Altos, CA	36.9	22.9	8.1	2.9	0.1	1.0	0.7	0.5	0.5
Lower Makefield, PA	9.9	4.0	0.9	1.9	1.1	0.4	0.6	0.8	0.1
Madison, AL	5.2	1.8	1.4	0.8	0.3	0.3	0.2	0.4	0.1
Mamaroneck, NY	28.5	8.0	1.7	4.6	6.5	1.9	4.3	1.2	0.2
Manheim, PA	4.6	1.5	0.3	0.9	0.7	0.2	0.4	0.5	0.1
Manlius, NY	5.7	2.2	0.1	1.6	0.6	0.1	0.3	0.5	0.3
Maple Grove, MN	9.7	3.9	1.4	1.1	0.1	0.3	0.5	2.1	0.2
Marion, IA	2.9	1.3	0.4	0.4	0.1	0.1	0.1	0.3	0.2
Marlboro, NJ	28.5	8.0	1.7	4.6	6.5	1.9	4.3	1.2	0.2

Table continued on next page.

Metro Area	Percent of Population Born in: Any Foreign Country	Asia	Mexico	Europe	Carribean	Central America[1]	South America	Africa	Canada
Mason, OH	4.2	1.8	0.5	0.7	0.1	0.3	0.2	0.5	0.1
McCandless, PA	3.4	1.6	0.1	1.0	0.1	0.1	0.2	0.2	0.1
Menomonee Falls, WI	6.9	2.2	2.4	1.4	0.1	0.2	0.2	0.3	0.1
Meridian, ID	6.7	1.5	3.1	1.1	0.0	0.2	0.2	0.3	0.3
Merrimack, NH	8.7	2.9	0.6	1.7	0.7	0.3	0.8	0.6	1.0
Mount Lebanon, PA	3.4	1.6	0.1	1.0	0.1	0.1	0.2	0.2	0.1
Mount Pleasant, SC	5.1	1.3	1.4	1.0	0.3	0.5	0.3	0.2	0.2
Needham, MA	17.1	5.4	0.2	3.2	3.0	1.4	1.8	1.4	0.5
Newtown, CT	20.5	3.9	1.2	4.7	3.2	2.2	4.3	0.6	0.4
Northbrook, IL	17.6	4.8	7.0	3.8	0.3	0.5	0.6	0.5	0.2
Northville, MI	8.9	4.6	0.8	2.2	0.1	0.1	0.1	0.3	0.6
Novi, MI	8.9	4.6	0.8	2.2	0.1	0.1	0.1	0.3	0.6
O'Fallon, IL	4.5	1.9	0.6	1.2	0.1	0.1	0.1	0.3	0.1
O'Fallon, MO	4.5	1.9	0.6	1.2	0.1	0.1	0.1	0.3	0.1
Orchard Park, NY	6.0	2.4	0.1	1.6	0.4	0.1	0.3	0.5	0.6
Oviedo, FL	16.3	2.8	1.3	1.6	4.9	1.0	3.8	0.5	0.3
Parker, CO	12.2	2.9	5.5	1.5	0.1	0.5	0.4	0.9	0.3
Parkland, FL	38.7	2.0	1.1	2.3	20.4	4.2	7.8	0.4	0.6
Peachtree City, GA	13.3	4.0	3.1	1.2	1.4	1.1	0.9	1.3	0.2
Pflugerville, TX	14.7	3.8	7.2	1.0	0.3	1.1	0.5	0.5	0.3
Plainfield, IL	17.6	4.8	7.0	3.8	0.3	0.5	0.6	0.5	0.2
Princeton, NJ	21.2	6.8	1.0	3.8	2.6	3.3	1.9	1.4	0.3
Queen Creek, AZ	14.4	2.9	7.9	1.4	0.2	0.5	0.3	0.4	0.7
Rancho Palos Verdes, CA	33.8	12.3	13.3	1.7	0.3	4.3	0.9	0.5	0.3
Redmond, WA	17.1	8.5	2.5	2.8	0.1	0.5	0.4	1.2	0.7
Richland, WA	14.5	1.8	10.0	1.1	0.1	0.5	0.2	0.4	0.3
Ridgefield, CT	20.5	3.9	1.2	4.7	3.2	2.2	4.3	0.6	0.4
Ridgewood, NJ	28.5	8.0	1.7	4.6	6.5	1.9	4.3	1.2	0.2
Rio Rancho, NM	9.8	1.7	6.2	0.8	0.3	0.2	0.3	0.1	0.2
Sahuarita, AZ	12.8	2.2	7.7	1.2	0.1	0.3	0.3	0.4	0.4
Sammamish, WA	17.1	8.5	2.5	2.8	0.1	0.5	0.4	1.2	0.7
San Ramon, CA	29.9	16.3	5.6	2.9	0.2	2.5	0.9	0.6	0.4
Saratoga, CA	36.9	22.9	8.1	2.9	0.1	1.0	0.7	0.5	0.5
Schertz, TX	11.9	1.8	7.8	0.7	0.2	0.6	0.3	0.3	0.1
Shrewsbury, MA	10.7	3.3	0.3	2.2	1.0	0.5	1.5	1.4	0.6
South Brunswick, NJ	28.5	8.0	1.7	4.6	6.5	1.9	4.3	1.2	0.2
South Jordan, UT	11.9	2.7	5.0	1.3	0.1	0.6	1.0	0.5	0.3
South Kingstown, RI	12.7	2.1	0.3	4.4	1.9	1.5	1.0	1.4	0.2
South Windsor, CT	12.8	3.3	0.4	3.9	2.2	0.4	1.4	0.6	0.6
Southlake, TX	17.5	4.4	9.0	0.8	0.2	1.3	0.5	1.0	0.2
Spring Hill, TN	7.4	2.2	2.1	0.6	0.2	0.8	0.3	0.9	0.2
Stow, OH	4.2	2.1	0.2	1.2	0.0	0.1	0.1	0.2	0.2
Sugar Land, TX	22.5	5.4	9.8	1.0	0.5	3.4	1.0	1.0	0.2
Sun Prairie, WI	6.8	3.1	1.7	1.0	0.0	0.2	0.4	0.3	0.2
Syracuse, UT	5.5	1.0	2.6	0.6	0.0	0.4	0.6	0.1	0.2
Tredyffrin, PA	9.9	4.0	0.9	1.9	1.1	0.4	0.6	0.8	0.1
Upper Arlington, OH	7.0	2.8	0.9	0.8	0.2	0.2	0.2	1.6	0.1
Upper Dublin, PA	9.9	4.0	0.9	1.9	1.1	0.4	0.6	0.8	0.1
Vestavia Hills, AL	3.9	1.1	1.8	0.3	0.1	0.3	0.1	0.2	0.1
Webster, NY	6.6	2.3	0.2	2.0	0.9	0.2	0.3	0.4	0.4
Wellesley, MA	17.1	5.4	0.2	3.2	3.0	1.4	1.8	1.4	0.5
West Fargo, ND	5.2	2.3	0.1	0.9	0.0	0.1	0.1	1.4	0.3
West Linn, OR	12.5	4.5	3.7	2.4	0.1	0.4	0.3	0.5	0.5
West Windsor, NJ	21.2	6.8	1.0	3.8	2.6	3.3	1.9	1.4	0.3
Westlake, OH	5.7	2.0	0.3	2.4	0.2	0.2	0.2	0.3	0.2
Weston, FL	38.7	2.0	1.1	2.3	20.4	4.2	7.8	0.4	0.6
Westport, CT	20.5	3.9	1.2	4.7	3.2	2.2	4.3	0.6	0.4
Wilmette, IL	17.6	4.8	7.0	3.8	0.3	0.5	0.6	0.5	0.2
Woodbury, MN	9.7	3.9	1.4	1.1	0.1	0.3	0.5	2.1	0.2
Yorba Linda, CA	33.8	12.3	13.3	1.7	0.3	4.3	0.9	0.5	0.3
U.S.	13.1	3.8	3.7	1.5	1.2	1.0	0.9	0.6	0.3

Note: Figures cover the Metropolitan Statistical Area—see Appendix B for areas included; (1) Excludes Mexico
Source: U.S. Census Bureau, 2010-2014 American Community Survey 5-Year Estimates

Marital Status: City

City	Never Married	Now Married[1]	Separated	Widowed	Divorced
Aliso Viejo, CA	29.7	55.9	1.2	3.0	10.2
Allen, TX	24.8	62.3	1.0	2.6	9.4
Alpharetta, GA	26.0	60.3	0.6	4.1	9.0
Ankeny, IA	25.5	60.3	1.2	3.8	9.2
Apex, NC	26.7	60.5	1.2	2.7	8.8
Ballwin, MO	23.5	62.4	0.8	5.0	8.3
Beavercreek, OH	27.4	58.3	1.2	5.3	7.8
Bella Vista, AR	13.5	72.0	0.3	6.4	7.7
Bernards, NJ	25.6	57.7	0.8	6.1	9.8
Bethlehem, NY	27.2	57.5	1.2	6.6	7.5
Bloomfield, MI	21.8	63.6	0.4	6.4	7.9
Bowie, MD	33.3	48.4	1.8	6.5	10.0
Bozeman, MT	53.3	35.0	1.0	3.3	7.4
Brentwood, TN	20.2	70.8	0.6	3.0	5.4
Broomfield, CO	26.2	58.2	1.1	4.6	9.9
Carmel, IN	22.6	66.3	0.6	3.6	6.9
Cedar Park, TX	26.9	57.2	1.4	3.7	10.7
Cheshire, CT	30.2	54.6	0.6	6.1	8.4
Chesterfield, MO	21.1	61.7	0.8	6.7	9.8
Collierville, TN	24.4	63.8	1.0	3.9	6.9
Coppell, TX	24.3	64.5	0.9	2.8	7.5
Cornelius, NC	26.7	54.3	1.6	4.0	13.3
Cranberry, PA	21.6	66.7	1.4	4.2	6.2
Cupertino, CA	22.7	65.4	0.7	5.9	5.4
Danville, CA	19.6	64.4	0.6	6.1	9.3
Draper, UT	25.3	60.7	1.5	2.3	10.3
Dublin, OH	21.7	67.1	0.6	3.3	7.3
Eastchester, NY	29.2	54.9	1.3	6.7	7.9
Eden Prairie, MN	26.5	60.3	1.4	3.3	8.5
Edmond, OK	28.0	56.5	0.9	5.2	9.4
Evesham, NJ	28.7	54.9	1.2	5.9	9.3
Fishers, IN	24.5	62.4	1.1	2.3	9.7
Flower Mound, TX	22.9	65.6	1.0	2.7	7.8
Folsom, CA	29.1	53.8	1.6	4.2	11.3
Foster City, CA	23.9	61.3	1.3	5.9	7.5
Franklin, TN	23.2	61.3	0.7	5.1	9.7
Friendswood, TX	22.8	60.2	1.0	5.2	10.7
Germantown, TN	20.2	65.8	0.4	5.5	8.1
Glastonbury, CT	25.6	57.0	1.0	5.8	10.6
Grand Blanc, MI	26.3	55.6	2.0	5.6	10.5
Guilderland, NY	34.4	49.7	1.7	5.6	8.6
Hampden, PA	21.9	62.0	1.0	7.0	8.1
Holly Springs, NC	19.6	66.4	2.1	3.1	8.8
Huntersville, NC	23.9	62.8	1.3	3.8	8.2
Independence, KY	23.9	57.8	2.0	3.6	12.7
Johns Creek, GA	23.3	64.6	1.3	3.4	7.4
Keller, TX	21.3	66.0	1.1	3.6	8.0
Kirkland, WA	28.3	55.1	1.0	3.6	12.0
Lafayette, CO	29.7	51.9	1.2	4.0	13.3
Lake Oswego, OR	21.5	59.6	1.5	5.5	12.0
League City, TX	24.6	59.9	1.2	3.3	11.0
Leawood, KS	18.3	69.7	0.2	5.0	6.7
Lee's Summit, MO	24.2	59.2	1.2	4.9	10.5
Leesburg, VA	28.6	57.3	2.3	3.6	8.2
Lehi, UT	22.1	70.1	0.9	1.7	5.3
Lenexa, KS	28.6	55.5	1.3	4.3	10.3
Lexington, MA	23.3	63.7	0.3	6.4	6.2
Los Altos, CA	18.7	68.0	0.6	6.8	5.9
Lower Makefield, PA	24.7	62.3	1.3	3.9	8.0
Madison, AL	27.6	58.3	1.0	4.0	9.1
Mamaroneck, NY	26.1	59.8	1.5	6.0	6.6
Manheim, PA	24.0	59.5	2.4	7.6	6.5
Manlius, NY	23.5	58.9	1.3	6.5	9.8
Maple Grove, MN	23.0	63.4	0.9	3.1	9.5
Marion, IA	24.7	54.1	1.5	4.8	14.8
Marlboro, NJ	23.7	66.5	0.6	5.1	4.1
Mason, OH	23.0	61.1	1.2	5.2	9.5
McCandless, PA	27.3	57.9	0.7	6.9	7.2
Menomonee Falls, WI	22.3	59.6	0.5	8.8	8.8

Table continued on next page.

City	Never Married	Now Married[1]	Separated	Widowed	Divorced
Meridian, ID	22.8	62.5	0.9	3.9	9.9
Merrimack, NH	25.6	60.7	1.0	3.6	9.2
Mount Lebanon, PA	25.2	56.7	1.9	7.7	8.6
Mount Pleasant, SC	25.9	56.2	2.4	5.3	10.1
Needham, MA	23.0	62.6	0.9	7.1	6.4
Newtown, CT	25.4	60.3	0.4	5.0	8.9
Northbrook, IL	19.2	65.4	0.9	7.4	7.1
Northville, MI	24.0	61.6	0.5	5.6	8.3
Novi, MI	26.6	57.0	1.1	5.9	9.3
O'Fallon, IL	28.8	54.4	2.0	4.8	10.1
O'Fallon, MO	25.6	59.3	1.3	4.2	9.5
Orchard Park, NY	25.0	57.8	1.0	7.9	8.2
Oviedo, FL	34.4	53.8	1.3	2.9	7.6
Parker, CO	22.9	64.6	0.9	1.8	9.9
Parkland, FL	26.4	62.1	1.6	3.2	6.6
Peachtree City, GA	24.1	61.5	1.1	4.5	8.8
Pflugerville, TX	25.9	55.8	2.8	3.0	12.5
Plainfield, IL	26.3	61.9	0.8	3.0	8.0
Princeton, NJ	43.9	46.1	0.9	3.7	5.4
Queen Creek, AZ	21.4	65.5	1.1	2.8	9.3
Rancho Palos Verdes, CA	20.6	63.3	1.2	7.4	7.5
Redmond, WA	27.1	58.6	1.2	3.3	9.7
Richland, WA	26.4	54.3	1.4	5.4	12.5
Ridgefield, CT	19.8	66.9	0.6	5.0	7.7
Ridgewood, NJ	24.3	63.4	0.7	4.8	6.8
Rio Rancho, NM	28.4	52.1	1.2	5.2	13.1
Sahuarita, AZ	18.8	64.7	1.6	4.3	10.7
Sammamish, WA	19.7	72.9	0.4	1.9	5.1
San Ramon, CA	23.7	65.3	1.1	3.4	6.4
Saratoga, CA	18.6	70.1	0.8	6.2	4.3
Schertz, TX	24.0	59.4	1.6	4.6	10.3
Shrewsbury, MA	27.7	58.7	0.8	5.1	7.7
South Brunswick, NJ	27.5	59.9	1.2	4.6	6.8
South Jordan, UT	24.8	64.7	0.8	2.6	7.1
South Kingstown, RI	41.2	44.9	0.3	6.2	7.3
South Windsor, CT	22.7	59.8	0.4	6.1	11.0
Southlake, TX	19.0	71.9	0.7	2.6	5.8
Spring Hill, TN	20.3	65.7	1.0	2.7	10.3
Stow, OH	26.6	55.3	1.0	6.3	10.8
Sugar Land, TX	24.0	64.4	1.1	4.3	6.2
Sun Prairie, WI	29.8	53.1	2.0	3.9	11.2
Syracuse, UT	23.6	67.1	0.6	1.9	6.9
Tredyffrin, PA	25.3	59.0	1.7	5.3	8.7
Upper Arlington, OH	23.7	62.7	0.9	4.8	7.9
Upper Dublin, PA	24.8	62.6	1.2	6.4	5.1
Vestavia Hills, AL	20.9	61.3	0.7	6.8	10.3
Webster, NY	23.7	59.2	1.6	7.0	8.6
Wellesley, MA	35.1	54.6	0.9	4.1	5.2
West Fargo, ND	27.7	57.5	0.7	3.3	10.8
West Linn, OR	23.8	61.8	0.9	3.6	9.9
West Windsor, NJ	21.8	69.3	0.5	4.0	4.4
Westlake, OH	24.0	56.7	0.7	7.8	10.8
Weston, FL	25.6	60.4	1.0	3.2	9.7
Westport, CT	22.5	62.3	0.9	4.9	9.4
Wilmette, IL	21.9	64.3	0.9	5.6	7.2
Woodbury, MN	25.3	62.0	0.9	3.2	8.5
Yorba Linda, CA	25.7	62.0	0.8	5.1	6.4
U.S.	32.5	48.4	2.2	5.9	10.9

Note: Figures are percentages and cover the population 15 years of age and older; (1) Excludes separated
Source: U.S. Census Bureau, 2010-2014 American Community Survey 5-Year Estimates

Marital Status: Metro Area

Metro Area	Never Married	Now Married[1]	Separated	Widowed	Divorced
Aliso Viejo, CA	39.6	44.3	2.5	5.0	8.6
Allen, TX	31.3	50.7	2.5	4.5	11.1
Alpharetta, GA	34.1	47.8	2.3	4.7	11.1
Ankeny, IA	28.6	53.7	1.5	5.0	11.2
Apex, NC	31.5	51.9	2.7	4.5	9.4
Ballwin, MO	31.8	48.9	1.8	6.3	11.2
Beavercreek, OH	31.4	46.7	2.0	6.8	13.0
Bella Vista, AR	27.7	54.8	1.5	5.1	10.9
Bernards, NJ	37.7	45.8	2.5	6.0	7.9
Bethlehem, NY	35.8	46.3	2.1	6.4	9.4
Bloomfield, MI	33.9	46.6	1.6	6.5	11.4
Bowie, MD	36.0	48.5	2.2	4.4	8.8
Bozeman, MT	36.4	50.1	1.1	3.4	8.9
Brentwood, TN	30.8	49.9	2.0	5.3	12.0
Broomfield, CO	31.7	50.2	1.7	4.2	12.2
Carmel, IN	31.2	49.0	1.8	5.3	12.8
Cedar Park, TX	35.8	47.6	2.0	3.6	11.0
Cheshire, CT	36.3	45.1	1.4	6.3	10.8
Chesterfield, MO	31.8	48.9	1.8	6.3	11.2
Collierville, TN	36.5	42.6	3.4	6.0	11.6
Coppell, TX	31.3	50.7	2.5	4.5	11.1
Cornelius, NC	31.4	49.9	2.9	5.5	10.3
Cranberry, PA	31.5	48.8	2.0	8.0	9.7
Cupertino, CA	32.5	53.2	1.7	4.5	8.2
Danville, CA	35.9	47.7	1.9	5.2	9.4
Draper, UT	30.9	52.7	1.9	4.0	10.5
Dublin, OH	33.4	48.0	1.9	5.1	11.7
Eastchester, NY	37.7	45.8	2.5	6.0	7.9
Eden Prairie, MN	32.9	51.5	1.3	4.4	10.0
Edmond, OK	29.7	49.8	2.2	5.7	12.6
Evesham, NJ	37.0	45.4	2.3	6.4	9.0
Fishers, IN	31.2	49.0	1.8	5.3	12.8
Flower Mound, TX	31.3	50.7	2.5	4.5	11.1
Folsom, CA	33.1	47.7	2.3	5.4	11.5
Foster City, CA	35.9	47.7	1.9	5.2	9.4
Franklin, TN	30.8	49.9	2.0	5.3	12.0
Friendswood, TX	32.7	50.0	2.8	4.5	10.0
Germantown, TN	36.5	42.6	3.4	6.0	11.6
Glastonbury, CT	34.1	47.5	1.5	5.9	11.1
Grand Blanc, MI	33.0	44.8	2.0	6.6	13.5
Guilderland, NY	35.8	46.3	2.1	6.4	9.4
Hampden, PA	31.0	50.3	2.1	6.6	9.9
Holly Springs, NC	31.5	51.9	2.7	4.5	9.4
Huntersville, NC	31.4	49.9	2.9	5.5	10.3
Independence, KY	31.3	49.5	1.8	5.8	11.5
Johns Creek, GA	34.1	47.8	2.3	4.7	11.1
Keller, TX	31.3	50.7	2.5	4.5	11.1
Kirkland, WA	32.2	50.1	1.6	4.4	11.7
Lafayette, CO	37.1	47.7	1.1	3.5	10.6
Lake Oswego, OR	31.3	49.7	1.8	4.8	12.5
League City, TX	32.7	50.0	2.8	4.5	10.0
Leawood, KS	29.7	50.8	1.8	5.5	12.2
Lee's Summit, MO	29.7	50.8	1.8	5.5	12.2
Leesburg, VA	36.0	48.5	2.2	4.4	8.8
Lehi, UT	31.7	58.7	1.1	2.6	6.0
Lenexa, KS	29.7	50.8	1.8	5.5	12.2
Lexington, MA	36.4	47.4	1.8	5.4	8.9
Los Altos, CA	32.5	53.2	1.7	4.5	8.2
Lower Makefield, PA	37.0	45.4	2.3	6.4	9.0
Madison, AL	29.2	51.1	1.8	5.8	12.0
Mamaroneck, NY	37.7	45.8	2.5	6.0	7.9
Manheim, PA	28.8	55.6	1.8	6.0	7.8
Manlius, NY	35.4	45.6	2.5	6.1	10.5
Maple Grove, MN	32.9	51.5	1.3	4.4	10.0
Marion, IA	28.4	52.8	1.5	5.7	11.5
Marlboro, NJ	37.7	45.8	2.5	6.0	7.9
Mason, OH	31.3	49.5	1.8	5.8	11.5
McCandless, PA	31.5	48.8	2.0	8.0	9.7
Menomonee Falls, WI	35.8	46.9	1.3	5.8	10.2

Table continued on next page.

Metro Area	Never Married	Now Married[1]	Separated	Widowed	Divorced
Meridian, ID	27.3	54.5	1.3	4.7	12.1
Merrimack, NH	29.9	52.1	1.4	5.1	11.5
Mount Lebanon, PA	31.5	48.8	2.0	8.0	9.7
Mount Pleasant, SC	33.3	46.7	3.1	5.7	11.2
Needham, MA	36.4	47.4	1.8	5.4	8.9
Newtown, CT	32.3	51.2	1.4	5.8	9.4
Northbrook, IL	36.2	47.2	1.8	5.6	9.1
Northville, MI	33.9	46.6	1.6	6.5	11.4
Novi, MI	33.9	46.6	1.6	6.5	11.4
O'Fallon, IL	31.8	48.9	1.8	6.3	11.2
O'Fallon, MO	31.8	48.9	1.8	6.3	11.2
Orchard Park, NY	35.3	45.0	1.9	7.3	10.5
Oviedo, FL	34.5	45.9	2.6	5.4	11.7
Parker, CO	31.7	50.2	1.7	4.2	12.2
Parkland, FL	34.1	43.2	3.0	6.9	12.8
Peachtree City, GA	34.1	47.8	2.3	4.7	11.1
Pflugerville, TX	35.8	47.6	2.0	3.6	11.0
Plainfield, IL	36.2	47.2	1.8	5.6	9.1
Princeton, NJ	36.5	47.4	2.1	5.8	8.3
Queen Creek, AZ	33.1	47.9	1.8	5.1	12.2
Rancho Palos Verdes, CA	39.6	44.3	2.5	5.0	8.6
Redmond, WA	32.2	50.1	1.6	4.4	11.7
Richland, WA	29.0	53.2	2.0	4.7	11.1
Ridgefield, CT	32.3	51.2	1.4	5.8	9.4
Ridgewood, NJ	37.7	45.8	2.5	6.0	7.9
Rio Rancho, NM	33.7	45.7	1.7	5.4	13.5
Sahuarita, AZ	33.4	45.4	2.1	6.1	13.1
Sammamish, WA	32.2	50.1	1.6	4.4	11.7
San Ramon, CA	35.9	47.7	1.9	5.2	9.4
Saratoga, CA	32.5	53.2	1.7	4.5	8.2
Schertz, TX	32.3	48.1	2.7	5.4	11.5
Shrewsbury, MA	33.0	48.8	1.7	5.8	10.6
South Brunswick, NJ	37.7	45.8	2.5	6.0	7.9
South Jordan, UT	30.9	52.7	1.9	4.0	10.5
South Kingstown, RI	35.1	45.3	1.9	6.6	11.1
South Windsor, CT	34.1	47.5	1.5	5.9	11.1
Southlake, TX	31.3	50.7	2.5	4.5	11.1
Spring Hill, TN	30.8	49.9	2.0	5.3	12.0
Stow, OH	32.9	47.5	1.5	6.3	11.8
Sugar Land, TX	32.7	50.0	2.8	4.5	10.0
Sun Prairie, WI	35.0	49.7	1.1	4.2	10.0
Syracuse, UT	25.3	59.6	1.6	3.6	9.7
Tredyffrin, PA	37.0	45.4	2.3	6.4	9.0
Upper Arlington, OH	33.4	48.0	1.9	5.1	11.7
Upper Dublin, PA	37.0	45.4	2.3	6.4	9.0
Vestavia Hills, AL	29.3	48.7	2.4	6.9	12.7
Webster, NY	35.0	46.3	2.3	6.3	10.1
Wellesley, MA	36.4	47.4	1.8	5.4	8.9
West Fargo, ND	38.1	47.6	0.8	4.4	9.0
West Linn, OR	31.3	49.7	1.8	4.8	12.5
West Windsor, NJ	36.5	47.4	2.1	5.8	8.3
Westlake, OH	33.7	45.6	1.8	7.0	11.9
Weston, FL	34.1	43.2	3.0	6.9	12.8
Westport, CT	32.3	51.2	1.4	5.8	9.4
Wilmette, IL	36.2	47.2	1.8	5.6	9.1
Woodbury, MN	32.9	51.5	1.3	4.4	10.0
Yorba Linda, CA	39.6	44.3	2.5	5.0	8.6
U.S.	32.5	48.4	2.2	5.9	10.9

Note: Figures are percentages and cover the population 15 years of age and older; Figures cover the Metropolitan Statistical Area—see Appendix B for areas included; (1) Excludes separated
Source: U.S. Census Bureau, 2010-2014 American Community Survey 5-Year Estimates

Disability Status: City

City	All Ages	Under 18 Years Old	18 to 64 Years Old	65 Years and Over
Aliso Viejo, CA	5.1	2.6	3.6	29.7
Allen, TX	6.1	2.1	5.3	33.3
Alpharetta, GA	6.0	1.6	3.6	39.6
Ankeny, IA	6.9	1.9	5.4	33.6
Apex, NC	5.0	2.8	4.8	17.8
Ballwin, MO	8.0	0.8	6.2	27.3
Beavercreek, OH	10.5	4.3	8.2	28.5
Bella Vista, AR	13.6	1.4	7.3	29.1
Bernards, NJ	6.5	2.1	3.6	30.2
Bethlehem, NY	9.6	5.0	6.8	28.3
Bloomfield, MI	9.1	3.2	5.3	24.4
Bowie, MD	8.2	2.2	6.5	29.7
Bozeman, MT	7.5	2.4	5.3	40.6
Brentwood, TN	5.9	1.9	4.6	23.3
Broomfield, CO	8.2	2.9	5.5	36.2
Carmel, IN	6.3	2.6	4.0	28.4
Cedar Park, TX	8.8	3.9	7.7	39.3
Cheshire, CT	8.5	2.7	5.7	28.4
Chesterfield, MO	8.5	4.4	4.4	25.5
Collierville, TN	7.6	4.1	5.1	32.6
Coppell, TX	4.7	1.2	3.6	30.7
Cornelius, NC	8.0	2.5	6.2	29.8
Cranberry, PA	6.6	3.1	4.2	34.3
Cupertino, CA	6.1	1.2	3.6	29.6
Danville, CA	7.1	2.4	3.1	27.8
Draper, UT	5.6	2.8	5.4	25.5
Dublin, OH	5.4	2.3	3.5	29.1
Eastchester, NY	7.7	2.0	3.8	29.0
Eden Prairie, MN	6.3	4.7	4.2	26.7
Edmond, OK	9.0	3.3	6.5	34.1
Evesham, NJ	7.9	3.1	4.5	31.4
Fishers, IN	5.4	4.6	3.7	26.8
Flower Mound, TX	5.4	1.3	5.6	25.0
Folsom, CA	7.5	2.4	4.7	36.8
Foster City, CA	5.2	1.0	2.6	21.1
Franklin, TN	7.5	2.1	5.5	33.7
Friendswood, TX	8.4	2.6	6.0	31.4
Germantown, TN	7.9	1.1	4.3	29.7
Glastonbury, CT	7.3	2.8	4.7	25.7
Grand Blanc, MI	9.6	3.4	7.3	32.5
Guilderland, NY	8.1	3.4	5.9	25.1
Hampden, PA	8.8	1.9	4.7	33.7
Holly Springs, NC	5.1	4.2	4.5	15.3
Huntersville, NC	6.7	2.1	5.9	32.1
Independence, KY	11.0	4.9	11.8	33.3
Johns Creek, GA	4.7	4.0	3.3	18.3
Keller, TX	7.2	3.4	5.3	31.8
Kirkland, WA	8.1	3.2	5.8	32.7
Lafayette, CO	9.6	2.4	8.4	32.1
Lake Oswego, OR	8.1	4.2	3.3	29.0
League City, TX	8.6	3.1	7.3	36.0
Leawood, KS	6.6	1.4	3.1	25.0
Lee's Summit, MO	8.6	2.6	6.5	34.9
Leesburg, VA	6.3	2.6	4.5	42.9
Lehi, UT	5.5	2.6	5.2	34.7
Lenexa, KS	8.0	3.9	6.2	28.5
Lexington, MA	6.7	1.8	3.4	24.7
Los Altos, CA	5.5	0.6	2.8	19.6
Lower Makefield, PA	4.9	2.0	3.3	17.1
Madison, AL	7.9	1.8	6.7	36.0
Mamaroneck, NY	7.8	1.8	5.1	28.8
Manheim, PA	9.9	3.7	5.4	29.8
Manlius, NY	9.2	4.5	6.0	25.8
Maple Grove, MN	5.2	1.3	4.2	24.1
Marion, IA	7.5	2.9	6.6	20.8
Marlboro, NJ	6.5	2.4	4.1	26.6
Mason, OH	7.5	2.2	4.9	33.1
McCandless, PA	9.5	4.4	5.0	31.9

Table continued on next page.

City	All Ages	Under 18 Years Old	18 to 64 Years Old	65 Years and Over
Menomonee Falls, WI	10.4	1.6	6.2	34.1
Meridian, ID	7.6	2.8	6.6	28.4
Merrimack, NH	8.1	3.9	6.0	26.9
Mount Lebanon, PA	9.5	3.8	5.9	28.2
Mount Pleasant, SC	7.7	2.1	5.2	29.7
Needham, MA	7.6	2.2	4.4	28.1
Newtown, CT	8.5	3.2	4.9	33.3
Northbrook, IL	7.9	2.2	4.6	21.9
Northville, MI	8.6	2.1	5.0	29.9
Novi, MI	7.3	2.1	5.0	28.4
O'Fallon, IL	9.0	3.0	6.9	36.8
O'Fallon, MO	8.2	4.6	5.5	37.9
Orchard Park, NY	8.4	1.8	4.6	30.3
Oviedo, FL	7.5	2.5	6.6	35.5
Parker, CO	6.1	4.7	4.8	27.2
Parkland, FL	5.7	2.2	3.6	32.9
Peachtree City, GA	6.4	3.2	4.5	21.1
Pflugerville, TX	8.6	4.4	8.2	28.7
Plainfield, IL	4.4	1.6	3.7	31.7
Princeton, NJ	6.2	2.3	4.0	22.0
Queen Creek, AZ	6.3	2.1	6.8	27.5
Rancho Palos Verdes, CA	9.6	2.4	4.4	27.7
Redmond, WA	7.4	2.7	4.7	40.9
Richland, WA	11.8	5.9	8.9	33.5
Ridgefield, CT	6.0	2.3	3.4	25.5
Ridgewood, NJ	5.4	2.3	2.6	25.9
Rio Rancho, NM	12.2	3.1	11.2	38.1
Sahuarita, AZ	7.9	4.3	6.7	18.6
Sammamish, WA	4.7	2.7	3.7	24.3
San Ramon, CA	4.6	1.8	2.9	30.8
Saratoga, CA	6.8	1.6	2.7	25.4
Schertz, TX	14.2	4.6	13.7	39.7
Shrewsbury, MA	8.4	3.1	5.3	32.7
South Brunswick, NJ	7.3	2.8	5.5	28.3
South Jordan, UT	7.2	1.3	7.0	34.3
South Kingstown, RI	9.9	4.0	7.3	27.3
South Windsor, CT	9.8	5.2	5.6	33.8
Southlake, TX	5.7	1.5	4.2	32.0
Spring Hill, TN	4.8	3.4	4.1	20.9
Stow, OH	9.5	2.7	8.0	25.6
Sugar Land, TX	5.9	2.6	3.7	23.9
Sun Prairie, WI	10.1	4.5	9.6	31.0
Syracuse, UT	6.0	1.9	6.1	35.7
Tredyffrin, PA	7.0	1.4	4.0	27.2
Upper Arlington, OH	8.3	5.8	4.2	28.2
Upper Dublin, PA	7.4	2.5	4.9	23.6
Vestavia Hills, AL	8.2	1.9	4.5	32.6
Webster, NY	9.5	1.9	6.9	29.5
Wellesley, MA	6.6	1.7	4.7	25.6
West Fargo, ND	8.9	2.0	7.5	37.0
West Linn, OR	8.2	4.2	5.6	27.3
West Windsor, NJ	4.9	3.9	2.8	18.7
Westlake, OH	9.8	3.4	6.4	29.7
Weston, FL	4.2	0.8	3.7	19.7
Westport, CT	6.4	3.1	3.7	21.3
Wilmette, IL	7.5	1.5	4.6	26.9
Woodbury, MN	5.5	2.5	3.8	26.2
Yorba Linda, CA	7.4	1.9	4.2	31.6
U.S.	12.3	4.1	10.2	36.3

Note: Figures show percent of the civilian noninstitutionalized population that reported having a disability. Disability status is determined from from six types of difficulty: vision, hearing, cognitive, ambulatory, self-care, and independent living. For children under 5 years old, hearing and vision difficulty are used to determine disability status. For children between the ages of 5 and 14, disability status is determined from hearing, vision, cognitive, ambulatory, and self-care difficulties. For people aged 15 years and older, they are considered to have a disability if they have difficulty with any one of the six difficulty types.
Source: U.S. Census Bureau, 2010-2014 American Community Survey 5-Year Estimates

Disability Status: Metro Area

Metro Area	All Ages	Under 18 Years Old	18 to 64 Years Old	65 Years and Over
Aliso Viejo, CA	9.2	2.8	6.8	36.1
Allen, TX	9.5	3.4	8.2	35.6
Alpharetta, GA	9.8	3.3	8.5	35.2
Ankeny, IA	10.2	3.2	9.2	31.8
Apex, NC	8.8	3.4	7.3	33.2
Ballwin, MO	12.1	4.3	10.0	35.2
Beavercreek, OH	14.3	5.1	12.3	35.9
Bella Vista, AR	10.8	3.5	9.2	36.5
Bernards, NJ	9.8	3.1	7.3	33.5
Bethlehem, NY	11.8	4.5	9.4	33.3
Bloomfield, MI	13.9	4.8	12.2	37.4
Bowie, MD	8.0	2.8	6.2	30.3
Bozeman, MT	7.8	2.7	5.9	31.1
Brentwood, TN	11.6	3.7	10.2	36.5
Broomfield, CO	9.2	3.0	7.6	33.0
Carmel, IN	12.0	4.6	10.6	36.3
Cedar Park, TX	9.3	3.8	8.1	33.9
Cheshire, CT	11.3	3.8	8.7	33.7
Chesterfield, MO	12.1	4.3	10.0	35.2
Collierville, TN	12.9	4.3	11.7	39.9
Coppell, TX	9.5	3.4	8.2	35.6
Cornelius, NC	11.1	3.7	9.6	35.7
Cranberry, PA	13.9	5.0	10.9	35.0
Cupertino, CA	7.7	2.2	5.2	33.5
Danville, CA	9.5	2.7	6.9	33.3
Draper, UT	9.0	3.2	8.0	34.7
Dublin, OH	11.8	4.8	10.3	35.9
Eastchester, NY	9.8	3.1	7.3	33.5
Eden Prairie, MN	9.2	3.6	7.6	30.8
Edmond, OK	13.4	4.3	11.8	40.7
Evesham, NJ	12.0	4.5	9.9	34.2
Fishers, IN	12.0	4.6	10.6	36.3
Flower Mound, TX	9.5	3.4	8.2	35.6
Folsom, CA	12.2	4.2	10.2	37.3
Foster City, CA	9.5	2.7	6.9	33.3
Franklin, TN	11.6	3.7	10.2	36.5
Friendswood, TX	9.6	3.5	8.2	37.0
Germantown, TN	12.9	4.3	11.7	39.9
Glastonbury, CT	11.2	4.1	8.5	33.4
Grand Blanc, MI	16.1	5.9	15.0	38.0
Guilderland, NY	11.8	4.5	9.4	33.3
Hampden, PA	12.1	4.6	9.5	33.9
Holly Springs, NC	8.8	3.4	7.3	33.2
Huntersville, NC	11.1	3.7	9.6	35.7
Independence, KY	12.1	4.2	10.6	35.3
Johns Creek, GA	9.8	3.3	8.5	35.2
Keller, TX	9.5	3.4	8.2	35.6
Kirkland, WA	10.7	3.5	8.9	35.8
Lafayette, CO	8.1	2.7	6.6	27.9
Lake Oswego, OR	12.0	4.1	10.2	36.4
League City, TX	9.6	3.5	8.2	37.0
Leawood, KS	11.6	3.7	10.2	35.5
Lee's Summit, MO	11.6	3.7	10.2	35.5
Leesburg, VA	8.0	2.8	6.2	30.3
Lehi, UT	7.3	2.9	6.6	34.6
Lenexa, KS	11.6	3.7	10.2	35.5
Lexington, MA	10.3	3.8	7.9	33.0
Los Altos, CA	7.7	2.2	5.2	33.5
Lower Makefield, PA	12.0	4.5	9.9	34.2
Madison, AL	12.6	3.8	10.6	38.5
Mamaroneck, NY	9.8	3.1	7.3	33.5
Manheim, PA	11.1	4.4	8.8	31.6
Manlius, NY	12.0	4.7	10.1	32.1
Maple Grove, MN	9.2	3.6	7.6	30.8
Marion, IA	10.3	4.1	8.4	29.8
Marlboro, NJ	9.8	3.1	7.3	33.5
Mason, OH	12.1	4.2	10.6	35.3
McCandless, PA	13.9	5.0	10.9	35.0

Table continued on next page.

Metro Area	All Ages	Under 18 Years Old	18 to 64 Years Old	65 Years and Over
Menomonee Falls, WI	11.6	4.7	9.7	33.9
Meridian, ID	11.3	4.2	9.7	35.7
Merrimack, NH	10.7	4.7	8.8	32.2
Mount Lebanon, PA	13.9	5.0	10.9	35.0
Mount Pleasant, SC	11.4	3.7	9.5	35.5
Needham, MA	10.3	3.8	7.9	33.0
Newtown, CT	8.8	3.1	6.4	30.2
Northbrook, IL	9.7	3.1	7.6	35.0
Northville, MI	13.9	4.8	12.2	37.4
Novi, MI	13.9	4.8	12.2	37.4
O'Fallon, IL	12.1	4.3	10.0	35.2
O'Fallon, MO	12.1	4.3	10.0	35.2
Orchard Park, NY	13.0	4.7	10.8	33.3
Oviedo, FL	11.3	4.3	9.0	34.7
Parker, CO	9.2	3.0	7.6	33.0
Parkland, FL	11.0	3.1	7.5	34.5
Peachtree City, GA	9.8	3.3	8.5	35.2
Pflugerville, TX	9.3	3.8	8.1	33.9
Plainfield, IL	9.7	3.1	7.6	35.0
Princeton, NJ	10.0	3.9	8.0	30.9
Queen Creek, AZ	10.4	3.3	8.6	32.6
Rancho Palos Verdes, CA	9.2	2.8	6.8	36.1
Redmond, WA	10.7	3.5	8.9	35.8
Richland, WA	10.8	3.6	9.8	35.8
Ridgefield, CT	8.8	3.1	6.4	30.2
Ridgewood, NJ	9.8	3.1	7.3	33.5
Rio Rancho, NM	13.2	3.7	11.5	38.3
Sahuarita, AZ	13.7	4.2	11.6	34.5
Sammamish, WA	10.7	3.5	8.9	35.8
San Ramon, CA	9.5	2.7	6.9	33.3
Saratoga, CA	7.7	2.2	5.2	33.5
Schertz, TX	13.3	5.1	11.7	41.6
Shrewsbury, MA	11.6	4.7	9.4	34.5
South Brunswick, NJ	9.8	3.1	7.3	33.5
South Jordan, UT	9.0	3.2	8.0	34.7
South Kingstown, RI	13.2	4.7	10.9	35.6
South Windsor, CT	11.2	4.1	8.5	33.4
Southlake, TX	9.5	3.4	8.2	35.6
Spring Hill, TN	11.6	3.7	10.2	36.5
Stow, OH	12.4	4.3	10.2	33.8
Sugar Land, TX	9.6	3.5	8.2	37.0
Sun Prairie, WI	9.4	3.7	7.7	30.4
Syracuse, UT	9.8	3.2	9.2	35.5
Tredyffrin, PA	12.0	4.5	9.9	34.2
Upper Arlington, OH	11.8	4.8	10.3	35.9
Upper Dublin, PA	12.0	4.5	9.9	34.2
Vestavia Hills, AL	15.0	4.4	13.6	40.3
Webster, NY	12.4	4.8	10.5	32.5
Wellesley, MA	10.3	3.8	7.9	33.0
West Fargo, ND	9.3	2.5	7.7	34.7
West Linn, OR	12.0	4.1	10.2	36.4
West Windsor, NJ	10.0	3.9	8.0	30.9
Westlake, OH	13.3	4.9	11.0	35.0
Weston, FL	11.0	3.1	7.5	34.5
Westport, CT	8.8	3.1	6.4	30.2
Wilmette, IL	9.7	3.1	7.6	35.0
Woodbury, MN	9.2	3.6	7.6	30.8
Yorba Linda, CA	9.2	2.8	6.8	36.1
U.S.	12.3	4.1	10.2	36.3

Note: Figures show percent of the civilian noninstitutionalized population that reported having a disability. Disability status is determined from from six types of difficulty: vision, hearing, cognitive, ambulatory, self-care, and independent living. For children under 5 years old, hearing and vision difficulty are used to determine disability status. For children between the ages of 5 and 14, disability status is determined from hearing, vision, cognitive, ambulatory, and self-care difficulties. For people aged 15 years and older, they are considered to have a disability if they have difficulty with any one of the six difficulty types; Figures cover the Metropolitan Statistical Area—see Appendix B for areas included

Source: U.S. Census Bureau, 2010-2014 American Community Survey 5-Year Estimates

Male/Female Ratio: City

City	Males	Females	Males per 100 Females
Aliso Viejo, CA	23,511	25,926	90.7
Allen, TX	43,207	46,638	92.6
Alpharetta, GA	30,377	30,526	99.5
Ankeny, IA	25,101	24,387	102.9
Apex, NC	19,687	20,944	94.0
Ballwin, MO	14,436	16,042	90.0
Beavercreek, OH	23,063	22,675	101.7
Bella Vista, AR	13,147	14,126	93.1
Bernards, NJ	12,515	14,334	87.3
Bethlehem, NY	16,642	17,521	95.0
Bloomfield, MI	19,702	21,869	90.1
Bowie, MD	27,119	29,216	92.8
Bozeman, MT	20,408	18,715	109.0
Brentwood, TN	19,492	19,567	99.6
Broomfield, CO	29,245	29,782	98.2
Carmel, IN	40,238	43,236	93.1
Cedar Park, TX	28,166	29,922	94.1
Cheshire, CT	15,170	14,102	107.6
Chesterfield, MO	22,225	25,426	87.4
Collierville, TN	22,169	24,611	90.1
Coppell, TX	19,880	20,141	98.7
Cornelius, NC	12,651	13,595	93.1
Cranberry, PA	14,388	14,635	98.3
Cupertino, CA	29,342	30,445	96.4
Danville, CA	20,200	22,691	89.0
Draper, UT	23,960	20,696	115.8
Dublin, OH	20,407	21,971	92.9
Eastchester, NY	15,560	17,177	90.6
Eden Prairie, MN	31,185	30,911	100.9
Edmond, OK	41,832	43,252	96.7
Evesham, NJ	22,333	23,336	95.7
Fishers, IN	39,351	41,709	94.3
Flower Mound, TX	33,012	34,618	95.4
Folsom, CA	39,652	33,682	117.7
Foster City, CA	15,441	16,368	94.3
Franklin, TN	31,834	34,762	91.6
Friendswood, TX	18,629	18,372	101.4
Germantown, TN	19,413	19,794	98.1
Glastonbury, CT	16,872	17,789	94.8
Grand Blanc, MI	18,169	18,850	96.4
Guilderland, NY	17,280	18,231	94.8
Hampden, PA	13,284	15,007	88.5
Holly Springs, NC	13,579	13,760	98.7
Huntersville, NC	24,607	24,672	99.7
Independence, KY	12,407	13,231	93.8
Johns Creek, GA	39,833	41,146	96.8
Keller, TX	21,045	20,868	100.8
Kirkland, WA	40,649	42,671	95.3
Lafayette, CO	12,617	13,195	95.6
Lake Oswego, OR	17,553	19,757	88.8
League City, TX	44,833	44,146	101.6
Leawood, KS	16,377	16,465	99.5
Lee's Summit, MO	44,641	48,172	92.7
Leesburg, VA	22,730	23,481	96.8
Lehi, UT	26,349	25,633	102.8
Lenexa, KS	24,055	25,518	94.3
Lexington, MA	15,634	16,672	93.8
Los Altos, CA	14,391	15,371	93.6
Lower Makefield, PA	16,155	16,467	98.1
Madison, AL	22,341	22,525	99.2
Mamaroneck, NY	14,110	15,391	91.7
Manheim, PA	18,536	20,234	91.6
Manlius, NY	14,928	17,463	85.5
Maple Grove, MN	31,044	33,320	93.2
Marion, IA	17,767	18,042	98.5
Marlboro, NJ	19,532	20,838	93.7
Mason, OH	15,042	16,247	92.6
McCandless, PA	13,915	14,873	93.6

Table continued on next page.

City	Males	Females	Males per 100 Females
Menomonee Falls, WI	16,996	18,832	90.3
Meridian, ID	39,142	41,883	93.5
Merrimack, NH	12,416	13,147	94.4
Mount Lebanon, PA	15,746	17,339	90.8
Mount Pleasant, SC	34,755	37,624	92.4
Needham, MA	14,295	15,245	93.8
Newtown, CT	13,986	13,974	100.1
Northbrook, IL	16,172	17,224	93.9
Northville, MI	13,674	15,008	91.1
Novi, MI	27,809	29,078	95.6
O'Fallon, IL	14,082	15,018	93.8
O'Fallon, MO	40,556	41,422	97.9
Orchard Park, NY	13,843	15,508	89.3
Oviedo, FL	17,361	18,241	95.2
Parker, CO	23,872	23,643	101.0
Parkland, FL	12,629	13,266	95.2
Peachtree City, GA	16,715	17,986	92.9
Pflugerville, TX	24,509	27,629	88.7
Plainfield, IL	20,007	20,634	97.0
Princeton, NJ	14,379	14,561	98.8
Queen Creek, AZ	14,090	14,439	97.6
Rancho Palos Verdes, CA	20,139	22,143	90.9
Redmond, WA	29,244	27,460	106.5
Richland, WA	25,632	25,484	100.6
Ridgefield, CT	12,250	12,775	95.9
Ridgewood, NJ	12,260	13,010	94.2
Rio Rancho, NM	44,171	46,456	95.1
Sahuarita, AZ	13,086	13,355	98.0
Sammamish, WA	24,438	24,639	99.2
San Ramon, CA	36,512	37,314	97.9
Saratoga, CA	15,022	15,605	96.3
Schertz, TX	16,885	18,208	92.7
Shrewsbury, MA	17,729	18,385	96.4
South Brunswick, NJ	21,736	22,619	96.1
South Jordan, UT	28,443	28,085	101.3
South Kingstown, RI	14,417	16,129	89.4
South Windsor, CT	12,991	12,804	101.5
Southlake, TX	14,068	13,687	102.8
Spring Hill, TN	15,506	15,961	97.1
Stow, OH	16,488	18,253	90.3
Sugar Land, TX	40,973	41,447	98.9
Sun Prairie, WI	14,475	16,126	89.8
Syracuse, UT	13,328	12,046	110.6
Tredyffrin, PA	13,875	15,580	89.1
Upper Arlington, OH	16,322	17,869	91.3
Upper Dublin, PA	12,433	13,609	91.4
Vestavia Hills, AL	16,440	17,621	93.3
Webster, NY	20,926	22,476	93.1
Wellesley, MA	12,563	16,295	77.1
West Fargo, ND	14,864	13,507	110.0
West Linn, OR	12,558	13,152	95.5
West Windsor, NJ	13,623	14,485	94.0
Westlake, OH	15,407	17,106	90.1
Weston, FL	33,506	34,061	98.4
Westport, CT	12,964	14,091	92.0
Wilmette, IL	13,584	13,761	98.7
Woodbury, MN	30,863	33,681	91.6
Yorba Linda, CA	33,344	32,991	101.1
U.S.	154,515,159	159,591,925	96.8

Source: U.S. Census Bureau, 2010-2014 American Community Survey 5-Year Estimates

Male/Female Ratio: Metro Area

Metro Area	Males	Females	Males per 100 Females
Aliso Viejo, CA	6,438,759	6,621,775	97.2
Allen, TX	3,300,766	3,402,254	97.0
Alpharetta, GA	2,649,723	2,805,330	94.5
Ankeny, IA	290,553	300,188	96.8
Apex, NC	580,492	609,087	95.3
Ballwin, MO	1,354,888	1,442,849	93.9
Beavercreek, OH	387,853	413,406	93.8
Bella Vista, AR	240,613	242,783	99.1
Bernards, NJ	9,593,127	10,271,918	93.4
Bethlehem, NY	427,575	447,992	95.4
Bloomfield, MI	2,081,346	2,211,301	94.1
Bowie, MD	2,859,981	3,003,627	95.2
Bozeman, MT	47,971	45,137	106.3
Brentwood, TN	843,981	886,534	95.2
Broomfield, CO	1,319,273	1,332,119	99.0
Carmel, IN	943,352	987,830	95.5
Cedar Park, TX	918,393	916,623	100.2
Cheshire, CT	416,027	447,121	93.0
Chesterfield, MO	1,354,888	1,442,849	93.9
Collierville, TN	641,599	695,415	92.3
Coppell, TX	3,300,766	3,402,254	97.0
Cornelius, NC	1,117,511	1,181,404	94.6
Cranberry, PA	1,143,001	1,215,792	94.0
Cupertino, CA	953,276	945,181	100.9
Danville, CA	2,202,384	2,263,867	97.3
Draper, UT	564,616	559,027	101.0
Dublin, OH	957,480	990,708	96.6
Eastchester, NY	9,593,127	10,271,918	93.4
Eden Prairie, MN	1,692,444	1,732,342	97.7
Edmond, OK	639,781	658,217	97.2
Evesham, NJ	2,904,546	3,110,790	93.4
Fishers, IN	943,352	987,830	95.5
Flower Mound, TX	3,300,766	3,402,254	97.0
Folsom, CA	1,076,441	1,120,981	96.0
Foster City, CA	2,202,384	2,263,867	97.3
Franklin, TN	843,981	886,534	95.2
Friendswood, TX	3,083,945	3,120,196	98.8
Germantown, TN	641,599	695,415	92.3
Glastonbury, CT	592,094	623,065	95.0
Grand Blanc, MI	201,815	216,839	93.1
Guilderland, NY	427,575	447,992	95.4
Hampden, PA	271,491	283,663	95.7
Holly Springs, NC	580,492	609,087	95.3
Huntersville, NC	1,117,511	1,181,404	94.6
Independence, KY	1,042,464	1,089,329	95.7
Johns Creek, GA	2,649,723	2,805,330	94.5
Keller, TX	3,300,766	3,402,254	97.0
Kirkland, WA	1,773,931	1,783,106	99.5
Lafayette, CO	153,300	151,866	100.9
Lake Oswego, OR	1,130,354	1,158,442	97.6
League City, TX	3,083,945	3,120,196	98.8
Leawood, KS	1,000,049	1,040,820	96.1
Lee's Summit, MO	1,000,049	1,040,820	96.1
Leesburg, VA	2,859,981	3,003,627	95.2
Lehi, UT	276,831	273,943	101.1
Lenexa, KS	1,000,049	1,040,820	96.1
Lexington, MA	2,254,371	2,396,505	94.1
Los Altos, CA	953,276	945,181	100.9
Lower Makefield, PA	2,904,546	3,110,790	93.4
Madison, AL	212,007	218,389	97.1
Mamaroneck, NY	9,593,127	10,271,918	93.4
Manheim, PA	257,612	269,227	95.7
Manlius, NY	322,275	339,961	94.8
Maple Grove, MN	1,692,444	1,732,342	97.7
Marion, IA	129,625	131,804	98.3
Marlboro, NJ	9,593,127	10,271,918	93.4
Mason, OH	1,042,464	1,089,329	95.7
McCandless, PA	1,143,001	1,215,792	94.0

Table continued on next page.

Metro Area	Males	Females	Males per 100 Females
Menomonee Falls, WI	761,325	804,043	94.7
Meridian, ID	319,467	320,149	99.8
Merrimack, NH	199,502	203,274	98.1
Mount Lebanon, PA	1,143,001	1,215,792	94.0
Mount Pleasant, SC	340,925	356,356	95.7
Needham, MA	2,254,371	2,396,505	94.1
Newtown, CT	454,762	479,453	94.9
Northbrook, IL	4,650,729	4,865,719	95.6
Northville, MI	2,081,346	2,211,301	94.1
Novi, MI	2,081,346	2,211,301	94.1
O'Fallon, IL	1,354,888	1,442,849	93.9
O'Fallon, MO	1,354,888	1,442,849	93.9
Orchard Park, NY	549,332	586,335	93.7
Oviedo, FL	1,088,823	1,138,012	95.7
Parker, CO	1,319,273	1,332,119	99.0
Parkland, FL	2,800,775	2,974,429	94.2
Peachtree City, GA	2,649,723	2,805,330	94.5
Pflugerville, TX	918,393	916,623	100.2
Plainfield, IL	4,650,729	4,865,719	95.6
Princeton, NJ	180,915	188,611	95.9
Queen Creek, AZ	2,153,952	2,183,590	98.6
Rancho Palos Verdes, CA	6,438,759	6,621,775	97.2
Redmond, WA	1,773,931	1,783,106	99.5
Richland, WA	135,373	131,188	103.2
Ridgefield, CT	454,762	479,453	94.9
Ridgewood, NJ	9,593,127	10,271,918	93.4
Rio Rancho, NM	442,039	457,098	96.7
Sahuarita, AZ	488,310	504,834	96.7
Sammamish, WA	1,773,931	1,783,106	99.5
San Ramon, CA	2,202,384	2,263,867	97.3
Saratoga, CA	953,276	945,181	100.9
Schertz, TX	1,101,982	1,137,240	96.9
Shrewsbury, MA	456,142	468,580	97.3
South Brunswick, NJ	9,593,127	10,271,918	93.4
South Jordan, UT	564,616	559,027	101.0
South Kingstown, RI	776,584	827,733	93.8
South Windsor, CT	592,094	623,065	95.0
Southlake, TX	3,300,766	3,402,254	97.0
Spring Hill, TN	843,981	886,534	95.2
Stow, OH	340,894	362,123	94.1
Sugar Land, TX	3,083,945	3,120,196	98.8
Sun Prairie, WI	308,134	312,234	98.7
Syracuse, UT	308,872	305,649	101.1
Tredyffrin, PA	2,904,546	3,110,790	93.4
Upper Arlington, OH	957,480	990,708	96.6
Upper Dublin, PA	2,904,546	3,110,790	93.4
Vestavia Hills, AL	546,799	588,735	92.9
Webster, NY	526,377	556,201	94.6
Wellesley, MA	2,254,371	2,396,505	94.1
West Fargo, ND	109,607	108,683	100.9
West Linn, OR	1,130,354	1,158,442	97.6
West Windsor, NJ	180,915	188,611	95.9
Westlake, OH	995,456	1,072,034	92.9
Weston, FL	2,800,775	2,974,429	94.2
Westport, CT	454,762	479,453	94.9
Wilmette, IL	4,650,729	4,865,719	95.6
Woodbury, MN	1,692,444	1,732,342	97.7
Yorba Linda, CA	6,438,759	6,621,775	97.2
U.S.	154,515,159	159,591,925	96.8

Note: Figures cover the Metropolitan Statistical Area (MSA)—see Appendix B for areas included
Source: U.S. Census Bureau, 2010-2014 American Community Survey 5-Year Estimates

Gross Metropolitan Product

MSA[1]	2013	2014	2015	2016	Rank[2]
Aliso Viejo, CA	826.8	859.7	887.9	930.8	2
Allen, TX	447.6	470.0	486.7	518.5	6
Alpharetta, GA	307.2	321.1	335.5	354.0	10
Ankeny, IA	42.7	44.0	45.6	47.9	63
Apex, NC	66.9	70.7	74.3	78.9	44
Ballwin, MO	146.0	150.2	154.6	161.1	22
Beavercreek, OH	37.5	38.4	39.6	41.2	70
Bella Vista, AR	23.8	25.3	26.3	27.9	93
Bernards, NJ	1,471.2	1,521.7	1,573.8	1,650.1	1
Bethlehem, NY	46.5	47.8	49.3	51.3	59
Bloomfield, MI	224.7	231.1	239.2	248.9	14
Bowie, MD	463.9	477.0	495.8	523.2	5
Bozeman, MT	n/a	n/a	n/a	n/a	n/a
Brentwood, TN	100.8	105.4	110.2	115.6	34
Broomfield, CO	178.9	188.8	194.9	205.3	18
Carmel, IN	126.5	132.3	138.0	144.6	25
Cedar Park, TX	103.9	110.2	114.7	122.3	33
Cheshire, CT	44.2	45.7	47.2	49.2	60
Chesterfield, MO	146.0	150.2	154.6	161.1	22
Collierville, TN	67.9	69.5	71.6	74.8	47
Coppell, TX	447.6	470.0	486.7	518.5	6
Cornelius, NC	139.0	146.4	153.6	162.2	21
Cranberry, PA	131.3	135.3	139.5	145.7	24
Cupertino, CA	196.8	210.1	220.3	233.3	16
Danville, CA	388.2	408.6	426.9	451.0	7
Draper, UT	76.2	79.0	82.4	86.8	42
Dublin, OH	114.3	118.3	122.8	129.1	31
Eastchester, NY	1,471.2	1,521.7	1,573.8	1,650.1	1
Eden Prairie, MN	227.8	236.7	246.4	258.6	13
Edmond, OK	72.0	74.3	75.4	78.6	45
Evesham, NJ	383.4	393.8	406.6	425.5	8
Fishers, IN	126.5	132.3	138.0	144.6	25
Flower Mound, TX	447.6	470.0	486.7	518.5	6
Folsom, CA	108.2	113.4	117.8	124.1	32
Foster City, CA	388.2	408.6	426.9	451.0	7
Franklin, TN	100.8	105.4	110.2	115.6	34
Friendswood, TX	517.4	542.5	535.1	562.6	4
Germantown, TN	67.9	69.5	71.6	74.8	47
Glastonbury, CT	86.6	89.9	93.0	96.5	40
Grand Blanc, MI	12.6	12.8	13.3	13.8	169
Guilderland, NY	46.5	47.8	49.3	51.3	59
Hampden, PA	31.8	32.8	33.9	35.4	77
Holly Springs, NC	66.9	70.7	74.3	78.9	44
Huntersville, NC	139.0	146.4	153.6	162.2	21
Independence, KY	119.1	122.9	127.3	133.2	28
Johns Creek, GA	307.2	321.1	335.5	354.0	10
Keller, TX	447.6	470.0	486.7	518.5	6
Kirkland, WA	285.0	296.9	309.1	324.3	12
Lafayette, CO	21.3	22.2	22.7	23.8	108
Lake Oswego, OR	163.7	171.6	180.3	191.0	19
League City, TX	517.4	542.5	535.1	562.6	4
Leawood, KS	117.3	121.8	126.4	132.3	29
Lee's Summit, MO	117.3	121.8	126.4	132.3	29
Leesburg, VA	463.9	477.0	495.8	523.2	5
Lehi, UT	19.1	20.4	21.7	23.1	112
Lenexa, KS	117.3	121.8	126.4	132.3	29
Lexington, MA	370.8	384.4	398.4	418.3	9
Los Altos, CA	196.8	210.1	220.3	233.3	16
Lower Makefield, PA	383.4	393.8	406.6	425.5	8
Madison, AL	22.9	23.6	24.5	25.7	102
Mamaroneck, NY	1,471.2	1,521.7	1,573.8	1,650.1	1
Manheim, PA	23.2	24.1	24.9	25.9	101
Manlius, NY	30.1	30.6	31.3	32.5	84
Maple Grove, MN	227.8	236.7	246.4	258.6	13
Marion, IA	17.2	17.7	18.2	19.0	128
Marlboro, NJ	1,471.2	1,521.7	1,573.8	1,650.1	1
Mason, OH	119.1	122.9	127.3	133.2	28
McCandless, PA	131.3	135.3	139.5	145.7	24
Menomonee Falls, WI	94.4	97.2	100.5	105.0	38

Table continued on next page.

MSA[1]	2013	2014	2015	2016	Rank[2]
Meridian, ID	28.5	29.8	31.2	32.8	83
Merrimack, NH	23.6	24.2	25.1	26.4	99
Mount Lebanon, PA	131.3	135.3	139.5	145.7	24
Mount Pleasant, SC	32.7	34.2	35.8	37.8	76
Needham, MA	370.8	384.4	398.4	418.3	9
Newtown, CT	93.5	96.7	100.5	105.1	37
Northbrook, IL	590.2	611.0	630.3	658.6	3
Northville, MI	224.7	231.1	239.2	248.9	14
Novi, MI	224.7	231.1	239.2	248.9	14
O'Fallon, IL	146.0	150.2	154.6	161.1	22
O'Fallon, MO	146.0	150.2	154.6	161.1	22
Orchard Park, NY	51.6	52.9	54.5	56.7	56
Oviedo, FL	110.4	116.5	122.9	130.4	30
Parker, CO	178.9	188.8	194.9	205.3	18
Parkland, FL	281.1	295.0	309.2	325.7	11
Peachtree City, GA	307.2	321.1	335.5	354.0	10
Pflugerville, TX	103.9	110.2	114.7	122.3	33
Plainfield, IL	590.2	611.0	630.3	658.6	3
Princeton, NJ	29.4	30.3	31.5	33.0	82
Queen Creek, AZ	209.5	219.0	228.4	241.4	15
Rancho Palos Verdes, CA	826.8	859.7	887.9	930.8	2
Redmond, WA	285.0	296.9	309.1	324.3	12
Richland, WA	11.5	11.9	12.3	12.9	175
Ridgefield, CT	93.5	96.7	100.5	105.1	37
Ridgewood, NJ	1,471.2	1,521.7	1,573.8	1,650.1	1
Rio Rancho, NM	42.0	44.2	45.4	47.4	64
Sahuarita, AZ	35.4	36.3	37.5	39.4	74
Sammamish, WA	285.0	296.9	309.1	324.3	12
San Ramon, CA	388.2	408.6	426.9	451.0	7
Saratoga, CA	196.8	210.1	220.3	233.3	16
Schertz, TX	96.0	100.5	103.9	109.9	35
Shrewsbury, MA	37.1	38.5	39.7	41.4	69
South Brunswick, NJ	1,471.2	1,521.7	1,573.8	1,650.1	1
South Jordan, UT	76.2	79.0	82.4	86.8	42
South Kingstown, RI	73.3	75.9	78.4	81.7	43
South Windsor, CT	86.6	89.9	93.0	96.5	40
Southlake, TX	447.6	470.0	486.7	518.5	6
Spring Hill, TN	100.8	105.4	110.2	115.6	34
Stow, OH	31.5	32.1	32.8	34.2	79
Sugar Land, TX	517.4	542.5	535.1	562.6	4
Sun Prairie, WI	42.9	44.6	46.6	49.1	61
Syracuse, UT	24.1	25.2	26.3	27.6	95
Tredyffrin, PA	383.4	393.8	406.6	425.5	8
Upper Arlington, OH	114.3	118.3	122.8	129.1	31
Upper Dublin, PA	383.4	393.8	406.6	425.5	8
Vestavia Hills, AL	59.7	61.3	63.7	66.3	50
Webster, NY	52.5	53.8	55.2	57.4	55
Wellesley, MA	370.8	384.4	398.4	418.3	9
West Fargo, ND	14.5	15.6	16.4	17.3	142
West Linn, OR	163.7	171.6	180.3	191.0	19
West Windsor, NJ	29.4	30.3	31.5	33.0	82
Westlake, OH	122.9	125.9	129.4	134.6	27
Weston, FL	281.1	295.0	309.2	325.7	11
Westport, CT	93.5	96.7	100.5	105.1	37
Wilmette, IL	590.2	611.0	630.3	658.6	3
Woodbury, MN	227.8	236.7	246.4	258.6	13
Yorba Linda, CA	826.8	859.7	887.9	930.8	2

Note: Figures are in billions of dollars; (1) Metropolitan Statistical Area—see Appendix B for areas included; (2) Rank is based on 2015 data and ranges from 1 to 381.
Source: The U.S. Conference of Mayors, U.S. Metro Economies: GMP and Employment 2014-2016, June 2015

Economic Growth

Area	2011-13 (%)	2014 (%)	2015 (%)	2016 (%)	Rank[2]
Aliso Viejo, CA	1.5	2.6	2.0	3.0	83
Allen, TX	3.9	4.3	4.6	4.1	9
Alpharetta, GA	1.8	2.8	3.1	3.5	33
Ankeny, IA	3.7	1.2	2.4	3.0	83
Apex, NC	3.1	4.0	3.6	4.3	6
Ballwin, MO	0.9	1.2	1.5	2.2	236
Beavercreek, OH	0.5	0.7	1.7	2.0	283
Bella Vista, AR	3.7	4.8	3.2	4.2	7
Bernards, NJ	1.6	1.8	2.0	2.8	116
Bethlehem, NY	1.3	1.1	1.4	2.2	236
Bloomfield, MI	1.7	1.2	2.1	2.2	236
Bowie, MD	-0.1	1.0	2.4	3.4	38
Bozeman, MT	n/a	n/a	n/a	n/a	n/a
Brentwood, TN	3.9	2.6	3.0	2.9	99
Broomfield, CO	3.9	4.7	2.9	3.2	61
Carmel, IN	3.0	3.3	2.8	2.9	99
Cedar Park, TX	4.2	4.2	4.5	4.4	5
Cheshire, CT	1.3	1.7	1.9	2.1	262
Chesterfield, MO	0.9	1.2	1.5	2.2	236
Collierville, TN	1.0	0.8	1.7	2.6	159
Coppell, TX	3.9	4.3	4.6	4.1	9
Cornelius, NC	4.2	3.6	3.4	3.6	31
Cranberry, PA	2.1	1.5	1.6	2.4	201
Cupertino, CA	3.8	3.4	3.7	4.1	9
Danville, CA	4.2	3.8	3.2	3.7	27
Draper, UT	4.3	2.1	2.8	3.3	49
Dublin, OH	4.1	1.8	2.3	3.2	61
Eastchester, NY	1.6	1.8	2.0	2.8	116
Eden Prairie, MN	2.0	2.4	2.7	3.0	83
Edmond, OK	4.0	2.9	1.6	1.9	303
Evesham, NJ	0.7	1.0	1.7	2.6	159
Fishers, IN	3.0	3.3	2.8	2.9	99
Flower Mound, TX	3.9	4.3	4.6	4.1	9
Folsom, CA	2.6	3.1	2.6	3.3	49
Foster City, CA	4.2	3.8	3.2	3.7	27
Franklin, TN	3.9	2.6	3.0	2.9	99
Friendswood, TX	7.1	4.7	0.2	2.8	116
Germantown, TN	1.0	0.8	1.7	2.6	159
Glastonbury, CT	0.8	2.0	2.0	1.9	303
Grand Blanc, MI	0.6	0.4	2.1	1.9	303
Guilderland, NY	1.3	1.1	1.4	2.2	236
Hampden, PA	1.3	1.3	2.0	2.2	236
Holly Springs, NC	3.1	4.0	3.6	4.3	6
Huntersville, NC	4.2	3.6	3.4	3.6	31
Independence, KY	2.8	1.6	2.2	2.7	135
Johns Creek, GA	1.8	2.8	3.1	3.5	33
Keller, TX	3.9	4.3	4.6	4.1	9
Kirkland, WA	3.6	2.6	2.7	3.1	69
Lafayette, CO	3.4	2.5	1.5	2.5	178
Lake Oswego, OR	3.7	3.1	3.3	3.8	20
League City, TX	7.1	4.7	0.2	2.8	116
Leawood, KS	1.5	2.2	2.4	2.7	135
Lee's Summit, MO	1.5	2.2	2.4	2.7	135
Leesburg, VA	-0.1	1.0	2.4	3.4	38
Lehi, UT	6.9	5.2	4.7	4.0	14
Lenexa, KS	1.5	2.2	2.4	2.7	135
Lexington, MA	2.0	1.9	2.1	3.0	83
Los Altos, CA	3.8	3.4	3.7	4.1	9
Lower Makefield, PA	0.7	1.0	1.7	2.6	159
Madison, AL	0.7	1.3	2.2	3.0	83
Mamaroneck, NY	1.6	1.8	2.0	2.8	116
Manheim, PA	1.3	2.4	1.9	2.1	262
Manlius, NY	0.4	-0.4	0.9	1.9	303
Maple Grove, MN	2.0	2.4	2.7	3.0	83
Marion, IA	1.3	1.1	1.4	2.7	135
Marlboro, NJ	1.6	1.8	2.0	2.8	116
Mason, OH	2.8	1.6	2.2	2.7	135
McCandless, PA	2.1	1.5	1.6	2.4	201
Menomonee Falls, WI	0.3	1.2	1.9	2.5	178

Table continued on next page.

Area	2011-13 (%)	2014 (%)	2015 (%)	2016 (%)	Rank[2]
Meridian, ID	3.0	2.5	2.9	3.0	83
Merrimack, NH	0.3	0.8	2.3	3.0	83
Mount Lebanon, PA	2.1	1.5	1.6	2.4	201
Mount Pleasant, SC	1.8	3.0	3.3	3.4	38
Needham, MA	2.0	1.9	2.1	3.0	83
Newtown, CT	1.3	1.7	2.6	2.6	159
Northbrook, IL	1.6	1.9	1.7	2.6	159
Northville, MI	1.7	1.2	2.1	2.2	236
Novi, MI	1.7	1.2	2.1	2.2	236
O'Fallon, IL	0.9	1.2	1.5	2.2	236
O'Fallon, MO	0.9	1.2	1.5	2.2	236
Orchard Park, NY	0.6	1.0	1.5	2.1	262
Oviedo, FL	2.1	3.6	4.0	4.1	9
Parker, CO	3.9	4.7	2.9	3.2	61
Parkland, FL	2.8	3.2	3.3	3.4	38
Peachtree City, GA	1.8	2.8	3.1	3.5	33
Pflugerville, TX	4.2	4.2	4.5	4.4	5
Plainfield, IL	1.6	1.9	1.7	2.6	159
Princeton, NJ	3.4	1.4	2.4	2.7	135
Queen Creek, AZ	2.4	2.8	2.8	3.7	27
Rancho Palos Verdes, CA	1.5	2.6	2.0	3.0	83
Redmond, WA	3.6	2.6	2.7	3.1	69
Richland, WA	-2.1	1.8	2.0	3.1	69
Ridgefield, CT	1.3	1.7	2.6	2.6	159
Ridgewood, NJ	1.6	1.8	2.0	2.8	116
Rio Rancho, NM	0.7	3.6	2.5	2.3	218
Sahuarita, AZ	1.4	0.9	1.7	2.8	116
Sammamish, WA	3.6	2.6	2.7	3.1	69
San Ramon, CA	4.2	3.8	3.2	3.7	27
Saratoga, CA	3.8	3.4	3.7	4.1	9
Schertz, TX	3.3	3.7	4.0	3.4	38
Shrewsbury, MA	1.6	2.0	1.8	2.2	236
South Brunswick, NJ	1.6	1.8	2.0	2.8	116
South Jordan, UT	4.3	2.1	2.8	3.3	49
South Kingstown, RI	1.4	1.7	1.7	2.2	236
South Windsor, CT	0.8	2.0	2.0	1.9	303
Southlake, TX	3.9	4.3	4.6	4.1	9
Spring Hill, TN	3.9	2.6	3.0	2.9	99
Stow, OH	1.5	-0.1	1.0	2.1	262
Sugar Land, TX	7.1	4.7	0.2	2.8	116
Sun Prairie, WI	2.5	2.3	3.0	3.3	49
Syracuse, UT	4.2	3.1	2.7	3.3	49
Tredyffrin, PA	0.7	1.0	1.7	2.6	159
Upper Arlington, OH	4.1	1.8	2.3	3.2	61
Upper Dublin, PA	0.7	1.0	1.7	2.6	159
Vestavia Hills, AL	1.9	1.0	2.3	2.2	236
Webster, NY	1.0	1.3	1.2	2.1	262
Wellesley, MA	2.0	1.9	2.1	3.0	83
West Fargo, ND	4.8	6.9	4.0	2.9	99
West Linn, OR	3.7	3.1	3.3	3.8	20
West Windsor, NJ	3.4	1.4	2.4	2.7	135
Westlake, OH	1.7	0.9	1.4	2.1	262
Weston, FL	2.8	3.2	3.3	3.4	38
Westport, CT	1.3	1.7	2.6	2.6	159
Wilmette, IL	1.6	1.9	1.7	2.6	159
Woodbury, MN	2.0	2.4	2.7	3.0	83
Yorba Linda, CA	1.5	2.6	2.0	3.0	83
U.S.	2.2	2.4	2.3	2.9	–

Note: Figures are real gross metropolitan product (GMP) growth rates and represent annual average percent change; (1) Metropolitan Statistical Area—see Appendix B for areas included; (2) Rank is based on 2016 data and ranges from 1 to 381
Source: The U.S. Conference of Mayors, U.S. Metro Economies: GMP and Employment 2014-2016, June 2015

Metropolitan Area Exports

Area	2009	2010	2011	2012	2013	2014	Rank[2]
Aliso Viejo, CA	51,528.4	62,167.6	72,688.9	75,007.5	76,305.7	75,471.2	3
Allen, TX	19,881.8	22,500.4	26,648.7	27,820.9	27,596.0	28,669.4	9
Alpharetta, GA	13,405.9	15,009.7	17,229.1	18,169.1	18,827.9	19,870.3	18
Ankeny, IA	782.3	767.9	970.1	1,183.2	1,279.4	1,361.8	131
Apex, NC	1,799.5	1,912.4	2,254.4	2,308.1	2,280.6	2,713.1	87
Ballwin, MO	9,026.7	11,239.5	12,307.6	14,642.3	12,393.6	10,359.8	31
Beavercreek, OH	3,771.0	2,509.8	2,749.2	2,790.4	2,740.1	3,026.1	80
Bella Vista, AR	811.4	678.0	568.2	667.6	699.1	786.9	181
Bernards, NJ	69,990.3	85,081.2	105,102.0	102,298.0	106,922.8	105,266.6	2
Bethlehem, NY	3,205.1	3,362.9	3,525.1	3,420.1	3,946.1	4,547.0	63
Bloomfield, MI	28,405.2	43,964.7	49,422.8	55,387.3	53,906.5	50,279.3	5
Bowie, MD	9,226.1	11,082.9	10,237.9	14,609.7	16,225.0	13,053.6	23
Bozeman, MT	n/a	n/a	n/a	n/a	n/a	n/a	n/a
Brentwood, TN	4,406.6	5,748.5	5,878.7	6,402.1	8,702.8	9,620.9	33
Broomfield, CO	4,309.8	4,990.9	3,771.3	3,355.8	3,618.4	4,958.6	59
Carmel, IN	8,030.9	9,446.7	9,560.7	10,436.0	9,747.5	9,539.4	34
Cedar Park, TX	5,963.7	8,867.8	8,626.3	8,976.6	8,870.8	9,400.0	35
Cheshire, CT	1,594.7	1,778.8	1,856.7	1,965.3	1,903.9	1,834.5	110
Chesterfield, MO	9,026.7	11,239.5	12,307.6	14,642.3	12,393.6	10,359.8	31
Collierville, TN	8,442.9	11,069.1	11,978.6	11,360.1	11,276.4	11,002.0	28
Coppell, TX	19,881.8	22,500.4	26,648.7	27,820.9	27,596.0	28,669.4	9
Cornelius, NC	4,133.4	5,424.6	6,253.3	6,322.6	10,684.1	12,885.3	24
Cranberry, PA	8,343.0	12,160.7	15,165.5	14,134.7	10,444.4	10,015.8	32
Cupertino, CA	21,405.8	26,333.0	26,712.1	26,687.7	23,413.1	21,128.8	16
Danville, CA	16,040.3	21,355.4	23,573.8	23,031.7	25,305.3	26,863.7	10
Draper, UT	7,783.5	10,719.2	15,579.2	15,990.0	11,867.2	8,361.5	39
Dublin, OH	2,872.7	3,554.4	4,327.5	5,488.6	5,731.4	6,245.6	48
Eastchester, NY	69,990.3	85,081.2	105,102.0	102,298.0	106,922.8	105,266.6	2
Eden Prairie, MN	20,096.7	23,192.8	26,189.1	25,155.7	23,747.5	21,198.2	15
Edmond, OK	987.6	1,196.1	1,592.8	1,574.6	1,581.7	1,622.0	117
Evesham, NJ	19,067.4	22,710.0	26,155.8	22,991.6	24,929.2	26,321.3	11
Fishers, IN	8,030.9	9,446.7	9,560.7	10,436.0	9,747.5	9,539.4	34
Flower Mound, TX	19,881.8	22,500.4	26,648.7	27,820.9	27,596.0	28,669.4	9
Folsom, CA	3,502.0	4,070.5	4,686.0	5,194.6	5,777.1	7,143.9	43
Foster City, CA	16,040.3	21,355.4	23,573.8	23,031.7	25,305.3	26,863.7	10
Franklin, TN	4,406.6	5,748.5	5,878.7	6,402.1	8,702.8	9,620.9	33
Friendswood, TX	65,820.9	80,569.7	104,457.3	110,297.8	114,962.6	118,966.0	1
Germantown, TN	8,442.9	11,069.1	11,978.6	11,360.1	11,276.4	11,002.0	28
Glastonbury, CT	7,542.1	7,894.2	9,321.6	9,680.4	10,152.2	10,463.9	30
Grand Blanc, MI	354.1	367.1	367.6	399.2	474.6	561.3	209
Guilderland, NY	3,205.1	3,362.9	3,525.1	3,420.1	3,946.1	4,547.0	63
Hampden, PA	1,805.3	2,077.9	2,595.7	2,894.4	3,030.4	3,052.8	78
Holly Springs, NC	1,799.5	1,912.4	2,254.4	2,308.1	2,280.6	2,713.1	87
Huntersville, NC	4,133.4	5,424.6	6,253.3	6,322.6	10,684.1	12,885.3	24
Independence, KY	15,488.7	17,598.5	18,744.2	19,966.8	20,976.4	22,280.7	14
Johns Creek, GA	13,405.9	15,009.7	17,229.1	18,169.1	18,827.9	19,870.3	18
Keller, TX	19,881.8	22,500.4	26,648.7	27,820.9	27,596.0	28,669.4	9
Kirkland, WA	36,942.3	35,409.6	41,117.5	50,301.7	56,686.4	61,938.4	4
Lafayette, CO	727.2	1,058.7	946.7	1,128.0	1,046.0	1,016.1	159
Lake Oswego, OR	15,482.4	18,544.9	20,875.7	20,337.7	17,606.8	18,667.2	20
League City, TX	65,820.9	80,569.7	104,457.3	110,297.8	114,962.6	118,966.0	1
Leawood, KS	5,888.9	7,374.1	7,958.9	7,880.8	8,012.1	8,262.9	40
Lee's Summit, MO	5,888.9	7,374.1	7,958.9	7,880.8	8,012.1	8,262.9	40
Leesburg, VA	9,226.1	11,082.9	10,237.9	14,609.7	16,225.0	13,053.6	23
Lehi, UT	1,772.8	2,024.6	2,056.4	2,058.1	2,789.2	2,533.4	89
Lenexa, KS	5,888.9	7,374.1	7,958.9	7,880.8	8,012.1	8,262.9	40
Lexington, MA	18,972.6	21,804.5	22,292.8	21,234.8	22,212.8	23,378.5	13
Los Altos, CA	21,405.8	26,333.0	26,712.1	26,687.7	23,413.1	21,128.8	16
Lower Makefield, PA	19,067.4	22,710.0	26,155.8	22,991.6	24,929.2	26,321.3	11
Madison, AL	1,136.5	986.8	1,293.3	1,491.5	1,518.7	1,440.4	127
Mamaroneck, NY	69,990.3	85,081.2	105,102.0	102,298.0	106,922.8	105,266.6	2
Manheim, PA	786.1	983.8	1,076.4	1,084.2	1,062.4	974.3	164
Manlius, NY	1,314.6	1,759.1	2,054.1	1,915.5	1,753.3	1,922.5	105
Maple Grove, MN	20,096.7	23,192.8	26,189.1	25,155.7	23,747.5	21,198.2	15
Marion, IA	734.8	749.5	880.8	889.1	930.2	879.0	172
Marlboro, NJ	69,990.3	85,081.2	105,102.0	102,298.0	106,922.8	105,266.6	2
Mason, OH	15,488.7	17,598.5	18,744.2	19,966.8	20,976.4	22,280.7	14
McCandless, PA	8,343.0	12,160.7	15,165.5	14,134.7	10,444.4	10,015.8	32
Menomonee Falls, WI	6,505.4	7,654.5	8,826.3	9,175.6	8,874.6	8,696.0	38

Table continued on next page.

Area	2009	2010	2011	2012	2013	2014	Rank[2]
Meridian, ID	2,849.7	3,647.7	4,131.5	4,088.2	3,657.9	3,143.4	75
Merrimack, NH	1,743.0	2,612.1	2,494.1	1,634.9	1,445.8	1,575.4	119
Mount Lebanon, PA	8,343.0	12,160.7	15,165.5	14,134.7	10,444.4	10,015.8	32
Mount Pleasant, SC	1,455.7	2,120.0	2,299.4	2,429.8	3,464.3	5,866.7	49
Needham, MA	18,972.6	21,804.5	22,292.8	21,234.8	22,212.8	23,378.5	13
Newtown, CT	8,450.9	9,339.6	11,250.4	10,332.6	11,055.2	12,103.0	26
Northbrook, IL	28,196.6	33,672.0	39,522.4	40,568.0	44,910.6	47,340.1	6
Northville, MI	28,405.2	43,964.7	49,422.8	55,387.3	53,906.5	50,279.3	5
Novi, MI	28,405.2	43,964.7	49,422.8	55,387.3	53,906.5	50,279.3	5
O'Fallon, IL	9,026.7	11,239.5	12,307.6	14,642.3	12,393.6	10,359.8	31
O'Fallon, MO	9,026.7	11,239.5	12,307.6	14,642.3	12,393.6	10,359.8	31
Orchard Park, NY	3,561.8	3,792.1	4,179.7	4,305.1	4,376.6	4,798.7	60
Oviedo, FL	2,947.1	3,453.6	3,230.0	3,850.6	3,227.7	3,134.8	76
Parker, CO	4,309.8	4,990.9	3,771.3	3,355.8	3,618.4	4,958.6	59
Parkland, FL	31,175.0	35,866.9	43,129.9	47,858.7	41,771.5	37,969.5	7
Peachtree City, GA	13,405.9	15,009.7	17,229.1	18,169.1	18,827.9	19,870.3	18
Pflugerville, TX	5,963.7	8,867.8	8,626.3	8,976.6	8,870.8	9,400.0	35
Plainfield, IL	28,196.6	33,672.0	39,522.4	40,568.0	44,910.6	47,340.1	6
Princeton, NJ	623.1	678.0	754.1	713.0	879.2	947.1	166
Queen Creek, AZ	7,947.5	9,342.7	10,914.4	10,834.3	11,473.5	12,764.4	25
Rancho Palos Verdes, CA	51,528.4	62,167.6	72,688.9	75,007.5	76,305.7	75,471.2	3
Redmond, WA	36,942.3	35,409.6	41,117.5	50,301.7	56,686.4	61,938.4	4
Richland, WA	704.2	728.4	1,002.5	882.5	739.5	798.4	179
Ridgefield, CT	8,450.9	9,339.6	11,250.4	10,332.6	11,055.2	12,103.0	26
Ridgewood, NJ	69,990.3	85,081.2	105,102.0	102,298.0	106,922.8	105,266.6	2
Rio Rancho, NM	357.6	519.9	951.9	1,790.6	1,389.6	1,564.0	121
Sahuarita, AZ	1,978.0	2,099.3	2,310.0	2,508.3	2,589.9	2,277.4	95
Sammamish, WA	36,942.3	35,409.6	41,117.5	50,301.7	56,686.4	61,938.4	4
San Ramon, CA	16,040.3	21,355.4	23,573.8	23,031.7	25,305.3	26,863.7	10
Saratoga, CA	21,405.8	26,333.0	26,712.1	26,687.7	23,413.1	21,128.8	16
Schertz, TX	4,390.0	6,416.2	10,506.5	14,010.2	19,287.6	25,781.8	12
Shrewsbury, MA	2,035.9	2,355.7	2,397.0	2,966.2	3,393.6	3,126.6	77
South Brunswick, NJ	69,990.3	85,081.2	105,102.0	102,298.0	106,922.8	105,266.6	2
South Jordan, UT	7,783.5	10,719.2	15,579.2	15,990.0	11,867.2	8,361.5	39
South Kingstown, RI	5,392.0	5,791.9	7,139.1	5,830.8	6,609.0	6,595.1	44
South Windsor, CT	7,542.1	7,894.2	9,321.6	9,680.4	10,152.2	10,463.9	30
Southlake, TX	19,881.8	22,500.4	26,648.7	27,820.9	27,596.0	28,669.4	9
Spring Hill, TN	4,406.6	5,748.5	5,878.7	6,402.1	8,702.8	9,620.9	33
Stow, OH	2,957.7	3,144.8	3,889.0	3,821.5	3,544.5	3,393.7	71
Sugar Land, TX	65,820.9	80,569.7	104,457.3	110,297.8	114,962.6	118,966.0	1
Sun Prairie, WI	1,571.6	1,906.5	1,958.1	2,168.7	2,292.1	2,369.5	94
Syracuse, UT	626.2	831.3	896.5	855.5	1,310.0	1,363.6	130
Tredyffrin, PA	19,067.4	22,710.0	26,155.8	22,991.6	24,929.2	26,321.3	11
Upper Arlington, OH	2,872.7	3,554.4	4,327.5	5,488.6	5,731.4	6,245.6	48
Upper Dublin, PA	19,067.4	22,710.0	26,155.8	22,991.6	24,929.2	26,321.3	11
Vestavia Hills, AL	1,449.9	1,687.8	2,383.3	1,939.2	1,865.3	1,803.5	111
Webster, NY	4,874.0	5,116.4	5,492.9	5,329.8	5,092.0	5,150.2	56
Wellesley, MA	18,972.6	21,804.5	22,292.8	21,234.8	22,212.8	23,378.5	13
West Fargo, ND	465.9	548.6	730.8	785.9	817.9	782.8	183
West Linn, OR	15,482.4	18,544.9	20,875.7	20,337.7	17,606.8	18,667.2	20
West Windsor, NJ	623.1	678.0	754.1	713.0	879.2	947.1	166
Westlake, OH	8,012.6	10,260.9	11,276.1	11,063.7	11,137.9	10,706.5	29
Weston, FL	31,175.0	35,866.9	43,129.9	47,858.7	41,771.5	37,969.5	7
Westport, CT	8,450.9	9,339.6	11,250.4	10,332.6	11,055.2	12,103.0	26
Wilmette, IL	28,196.6	33,672.0	39,522.4	40,568.0	44,910.6	47,340.1	6
Woodbury, MN	20,096.7	23,192.8	26,189.1	25,155.7	23,747.5	21,198.2	15
Yorba Linda, CA	51,528.4	62,167.6	72,688.9	75,007.5	76,305.7	75,471.2	3

Note: Figures are in millions of dollars; (1) Metropolitan Statistical Area—see Appendix B for areas included; (2) Rank is based on 2014 data and ranges from 1 to 385; n/a not available
Source: U.S. Department of Commerce, International Trade Administration, Office of Trade & Industry Information, Manufacturing & Services, data extracted March 10, 2016

Building Permits: City

City	Single-Family			Multi-Family			Total		
	2014	2015	Pct. Chg.	2014	2015	Pct. Chg.	2014	2015	Pct. Chg.
Aliso Viejo, CA	0	0	-	0	637	-	0	637	-
Allen, TX	503	466	-7.4	830	330	-60.2	1,333	796	-40.3
Alpharetta, GA	288	277	-3.8	0	235	-	288	512	77.8
Ankeny, IA	974	890	-8.6	206	171	-17.0	1,180	1,061	-10.1
Apex, NC	578	683	18.2	0	0	-	578	683	18.2
Ballwin, MO	37	17	-54.1	0	0	-	37	17	-54.1
Beavercreek, OH	n/a	n/a	n/a	n/a	n/a	n/a	n/a	n/a	n/a
Bella Vista, AR	51	68	33.3	0	0	-	51	68	33.3
Bernards, NJ	12	11	-8.3	0	0	-	12	11	-8.3
Bethlehem, NY	58	58	0.0	41	248	504.9	99	306	209.1
Bloomfield, MI	61	64	4.9	0	0	-	61	64	4.9
Bowie, MD	n/a	n/a	n/a	n/a	n/a	n/a	n/a	n/a	n/a
Bozeman, MT	295	287	-2.7	376	493	31.1	671	780	16.2
Brentwood, TN	251	240	-4.4	0	0	-	251	240	-4.4
Broomfield, CO	439	403	-8.2	381	44	-88.5	820	447	-45.5
Carmel, IN	352	275	-21.9	714	1,368	91.6	1,066	1,643	54.1
Cedar Park, TX	596	439	-26.3	43	470	993.0	639	909	42.3
Cheshire, CT	41	41	0.0	0	0	-	41	41	0.0
Chesterfield, MO	n/a	n/a	n/a	n/a	n/a	n/a	n/a	n/a	n/a
Collierville, TN	142	160	12.7	0	120	-	142	280	97.2
Coppell, TX	118	203	72.0	0	0	-	118	203	72.0
Cornelius, NC	n/a	n/a	n/a	n/a	n/a	n/a	n/a	n/a	n/a
Cranberry, PA	110	103	-6.4	60	120	100.0	170	223	31.2
Cupertino, CA	41	52	26.8	2	127	6,250.0	43	179	316.3
Danville, CA	29	63	117.2	16	2	-87.5	45	65	44.4
Draper, UT	172	220	27.9	47	38	-19.1	219	258	17.8
Dublin, OH	202	118	-41.6	0	2	-	202	120	-40.6
Eastchester, NY	3	7	133.3	0	0	-	3	7	133.3
Eden Prairie, MN	61	73	19.7	0	0	-	61	73	19.7
Edmond, OK	561	530	-5.5	24	14	-41.7	585	544	-7.0
Evesham, NJ	1	5	400.0	5	0	-100.0	6	5	-16.7
Fishers, IN	564	498	-11.7	548	375	-31.6	1,112	873	-21.5
Flower Mound, TX	355	460	29.6	0	341	-	355	801	125.6
Folsom, CA	300	244	-18.7	0	0	-	300	244	-18.7
Foster City, CA	0	26	-	232	320	37.9	232	346	49.1
Franklin, TN	477	702	47.2	324	162	-50.0	801	864	7.9
Friendswood, TX	189	152	-19.6	0	0	-	189	152	-19.6
Germantown, TN	n/a	n/a	n/a	n/a	n/a	n/a	n/a	n/a	n/a
Glastonbury, CT	25	39	56.0	0	2	-	25	41	64.0
Grand Blanc, MI	111	118	6.3	0	0	-	111	118	6.3
Guilderland, NY	101	70	-30.7	0	0	-	101	70	-30.7
Hampden, PA	93	84	-9.7	35	0	-100.0	128	84	-34.4
Holly Springs, NC	406	657	61.8	0	0	-	406	657	61.8
Huntersville, NC	n/a	n/a	n/a	n/a	n/a	n/a	n/a	n/a	n/a
Independence, KY	107	108	0.9	24	0	-100.0	131	108	-17.6
Johns Creek, GA	125	292	133.6	0	0	-	125	292	133.6
Keller, TX	339	218	-35.7	187	0	-100.0	526	218	-58.6
Kirkland, WA	241	320	32.8	430	200	-53.5	671	520	-22.5
Lafayette, CO	104	123	18.3	105	133	26.7	209	256	22.5
Lake Oswego, OR	77	89	15.6	28	6	-78.6	105	95	-9.5
League City, TX	990	1,135	14.6	368	75	-79.6	1,358	1,210	-10.9
Leawood, KS	73	62	-15.1	8	0	-100.0	81	62	-23.5
Lee's Summit, MO	321	313	-2.5	250	209	-16.4	571	522	-8.6
Leesburg, VA	n/a	n/a	n/a	n/a	n/a	n/a	n/a	n/a	n/a
Lehi, UT	453	533	17.7	266	180	-32.3	719	713	-0.8
Lenexa, KS	193	249	29.0	446	40	-91.0	639	289	-54.8
Lexington, MA	99	87	-12.1	0	0	-	99	87	-12.1
Los Altos, CA	35	42	20.0	182	4	-97.8	217	46	-78.8
Lower Makefield, PA	46	62	34.8	0	3	-	46	65	41.3
Madison, AL	338	466	37.9	0	0	-	338	466	37.9
Mamaroneck, NY	3	7	133.3	0	0	-	3	7	133.3
Manheim, PA	97	110	13.4	0	0	-	97	110	13.4
Manlius, NY	42	49	16.7	0	0	-	42	49	16.7
Maple Grove, MN	306	192	-37.3	196	205	4.6	502	397	-20.9
Marion, IA	146	180	23.3	75	261	248.0	221	441	99.5
Marlboro, NJ	6	7	16.7	5	30	500.0	11	37	236.4
Mason, OH	142	132	-7.0	281	5	-98.2	423	137	-67.6

Table continued on next page.

City	Single-Family 2014	Single-Family 2015	Single-Family Pct. Chg.	Multi-Family 2014	Multi-Family 2015	Multi-Family Pct. Chg.	Total 2014	Total 2015	Total Pct. Chg.
McCandless, PA	28	32	14.3	0	16	-	28	48	71.4
Menomonee Falls, WI	47	90	91.5	56	224	300.0	103	314	204.9
Meridian, ID	764	1,056	38.2	496	414	-16.5	1,260	1,470	16.7
Merrimack, NH	23	25	8.7	0	0	-	23	25	8.7
Mount Lebanon, PA	5	5	0.0	0	0	-	5	5	0.0
Mount Pleasant, SC	739	940	27.2	593	401	-32.4	1,332	1,341	0.7
Needham, MA	106	95	-10.4	0	0	-	106	95	-10.4
Newtown, CT	19	29	52.6	0	0	-	19	29	52.6
Northbrook, IL	46	38	-17.4	0	0	-	46	38	-17.4
Northville, MI	57	43	-24.6	0	0	-	57	43	-24.6
Novi, MI	198	173	-12.6	5	116	2,220.0	203	289	42.4
O'Fallon, IL	126	120	-4.8	0	0	-	126	120	-4.8
O'Fallon, MO	344	378	9.9	98	172	75.5	442	550	24.4
Orchard Park, NY	70	67	-4.3	2	10	400.0	72	77	6.9
Oviedo, FL	42	172	309.5	0	0	-	42	172	309.5
Parker, CO	348	325	-6.6	306	403	31.7	654	728	11.3
Parkland, FL	547	430	-21.4	9	0	-100.0	556	430	-22.7
Peachtree City, GA	39	36	-7.7	0	0	-	39	36	-7.7
Pflugerville, TX	597	427	-28.5	276	424	53.6	873	851	-2.5
Plainfield, IL	163	139	-14.7	0	12	-	163	151	-7.4
Princeton, NJ	20	39	95.0	0	340	-	20	379	1,795.0
Queen Creek, AZ	693	987	42.4	0	0	-	693	987	42.4
Rancho Palos Verdes, CA	8	28	250.0	0	0	-	8	28	250.0
Redmond, WA	216	200	-7.4	264	696	163.6	480	896	86.7
Richland, WA	231	274	18.6	112	117	4.5	343	391	14.0
Ridgefield, CT	22	16	-27.3	20	10	-50.0	42	26	-38.1
Ridgewood, NJ	18	17	-5.6	2	4	100.0	20	21	5.0
Rio Rancho, NM	741	711	-4.0	79	64	-19.0	820	775	-5.5
Sahuarita, AZ	183	271	48.1	0	0	-	183	271	48.1
Sammamish, WA	278	192	-30.9	0	0	-	278	192	-30.9
San Ramon, CA	0	7	-	48	53	10.4	48	60	25.0
Saratoga, CA	19	14	-26.3	0	0	-	19	14	-26.3
Schertz, TX	299	575	92.3	0	0	-	299	575	92.3
Shrewsbury, MA	57	4	-93.0	0	0	-	57	4	-93.0
South Brunswick, NJ	65	172	164.6	0	0	-	65	172	164.6
South Jordan, UT	806	751	-6.8	324	14	-95.7	1,130	765	-32.3
South Kingstown, RI	48	24	-50.0	0	0	-	48	24	-50.0
South Windsor, CT	25	43	72.0	0	0	-	25	43	72.0
Southlake, TX	202	224	10.9	0	0	-	202	224	10.9
Spring Hill, TN	571	537	-6.0	4	0	-100.0	575	537	-6.6
Stow, OH	41	41	0.0	0	0	-	41	41	0.0
Sugar Land, TX	175	143	-18.3	254	0	-100.0	429	143	-66.7
Sun Prairie, WI	114	160	40.4	152	10	-93.4	266	170	-36.1
Syracuse, UT	150	240	60.0	28	12	-57.1	178	252	41.6
Tredyffrin, PA	17	9	-47.1	0	0	-	17	9	-47.1
Upper Arlington, OH	23	14	-39.1	0	0	-	23	14	-39.1
Upper Dublin, PA	15	13	-13.3	0	0	-	15	13	-13.3
Vestavia Hills, AL	109	88	-19.3	0	272	-	109	360	230.3
Webster, NY	65	64	-1.5	109	236	116.5	174	300	72.4
Wellesley, MA	66	95	43.9	0	0	-	66	95	43.9
West Fargo, ND	541	476	-12.0	441	138	-68.7	982	614	-37.5
West Linn, OR	38	51	34.2	0	0	-	38	51	34.2
West Windsor, NJ	3	6	100.0	73	94	28.8	76	100	31.6
Westlake, OH	57	28	-50.9	0	0	-	57	28	-50.9
Weston, FL	4	2	-50.0	0	0	-	4	2	-50.0
Westport, CT	109	79	-27.5	54	12	-77.8	163	91	-44.2
Wilmette, IL	44	48	9.1	0	0	-	44	48	9.1
Woodbury, MN	297	257	-13.5	45	160	255.6	342	417	21.9
Yorba Linda, CA	94	206	119.1	0	69	-	94	275	192.6
U.S.	640,300	690,800	7.9	411,800	487,600	18.4	1,052,100	1,178,400	12.0

Note: Figures represent new, privately-owned housing units authorized (unadjusted data); All permit data are based on estimates with imputation

Source: U.S. Census Bureau, Manufacturing, Mining, and Construction Statistics, Building Permits, 2014, 2015

Building Permits: Metro Area

Metro Area	Single-Family			Multi-Family			Total		
	2014	2015	Pct. Chg.	2014	2015	Pct. Chg.	2014	2015	Pct. Chg.
Aliso Viejo, CA	8,300	8,458	1.9	18,650	25,211	35.2	26,950	33,669	24.9
Allen, TX	22,550	28,363	25.8	18,868	28,038	48.6	41,418	56,401	36.2
Alpharetta, GA	16,984	19,885	17.1	9,699	10,126	4.4	26,683	30,011	12.5
Ankeny, IA	2,952	3,495	18.4	1,484	1,949	31.3	4,436	5,444	22.7
Apex, NC	7,680	8,681	13.0	3,967	3,293	-17.0	11,647	11,974	2.8
Ballwin, MO	4,538	5,008	10.4	2,454	2,290	-6.7	6,992	7,298	4.4
Beavercreek, OH	743	770	3.6	36	113	213.9	779	883	13.4
Bella Vista, AR	2,388	2,816	17.9	965	976	1.1	3,353	3,792	13.1
Bernards, NJ	11,799	10,749	-8.9	36,185	75,646	109.1	47,984	86,395	80.0
Bethlehem, NY	1,203	1,186	-1.4	1,028	2,520	145.1	2,231	3,706	66.1
Bloomfield, MI	4,830	5,197	7.6	1,465	2,020	37.9	6,295	7,217	14.6
Bowie, MD	12,411	12,418	0.1	12,393	10,376	-16.3	24,804	22,794	-8.1
Bozeman, MT	701	872	24.4	490	624	27.3	1,191	1,496	25.6
Brentwood, TN	9,075	10,813	19.2	5,869	6,997	19.2	14,944	17,810	19.2
Broomfield, CO	8,064	9,288	15.2	7,703	8,569	11.2	15,767	17,857	13.3
Carmel, IN	4,965	5,054	1.8	3,041	3,647	19.9	8,006	8,701	8.7
Cedar Park, TX	11,515	11,574	0.5	8,434	10,545	25.0	19,949	22,119	10.9
Cheshire, CT	484	238	-50.8	656	614	-6.4	1,140	852	-25.3
Chesterfield, MO	4,538	5,008	10.4	2,454	2,290	-6.7	6,992	7,298	4.4
Collierville, TN	2,539	2,581	1.7	615	1,378	124.1	3,154	3,959	25.5
Coppell, TX	22,550	28,363	25.8	18,868	28,038	48.6	41,418	56,401	36.2
Cornelius, NC	11,306	11,742	3.9	7,231	7,048	-2.5	18,537	18,790	1.4
Cranberry, PA	3,082	1,032	-66.5	1,108	1,397	26.1	4,190	2,429	-42.0
Cupertino, CA	1,861	1,954	5.0	8,176	4,364	-46.6	10,037	6,318	-37.1
Danville, CA	3,716	4,595	23.7	6,285	8,171	30.0	10,001	12,766	27.6
Draper, UT	3,159	3,722	17.8	2,159	2,828	31.0	5,318	6,550	23.2
Dublin, OH	3,497	3,421	-2.2	3,547	4,027	13.5	7,044	7,448	5.7
Eastchester, NY	11,799	10,749	-8.9	36,185	75,646	109.1	47,984	86,395	80.0
Eden Prairie, MN	6,689	6,786	1.5	4,736	4,927	4.0	11,425	11,713	2.5
Edmond, OK	5,959	5,539	-7.0	1,911	486	-74.6	7,870	6,025	-23.4
Evesham, NJ	6,379	6,499	1.9	7,252	6,114	-15.7	13,631	12,613	-7.5
Fishers, IN	4,965	5,054	1.8	3,041	3,647	19.9	8,006	8,701	8.7
Flower Mound, TX	22,550	28,363	25.8	18,868	28,038	48.6	41,418	56,401	36.2
Folsom, CA	3,694	5,174	40.1	465	1,009	117.0	4,159	6,183	48.7
Foster City, CA	3,716	4,595	23.7	6,285	8,171	30.0	10,001	12,766	27.6
Franklin, TN	9,075	10,813	19.2	5,869	6,997	19.2	14,944	17,810	19.2
Friendswood, TX	38,315	36,662	-4.3	25,426	20,201	-20.5	63,741	56,863	-10.8
Germantown, TN	2,539	2,581	1.7	615	1,378	124.1	3,154	3,959	25.5
Glastonbury, CT	754	792	5.0	639	866	35.5	1,393	1,658	19.0
Grand Blanc, MI	271	103	-62.0	72	24	-66.7	343	127	-63.0
Guilderland, NY	1,203	1,186	-1.4	1,028	2,520	145.1	2,231	3,706	66.1
Hampden, PA	1,201	1,142	-4.9	401	522	30.2	1,602	1,664	3.9
Holly Springs, NC	7,680	8,681	13.0	3,967	3,293	-17.0	11,647	11,974	2.8
Huntersville, NC	11,306	11,742	3.9	7,231	7,048	-2.5	18,537	18,790	1.4
Independence, KY	3,218	3,481	8.2	1,988	1,182	-40.5	5,206	4,663	-10.4
Johns Creek, GA	16,984	19,885	17.1	9,699	10,126	4.4	26,683	30,011	12.5
Keller, TX	22,550	28,363	25.8	18,868	28,038	48.6	41,418	56,401	36.2
Kirkland, WA	8,665	8,587	-0.9	13,288	16,380	23.3	21,953	24,967	13.7
Lafayette, CO	560	683	22.0	811	481	-40.7	1,371	1,164	-15.1
Lake Oswego, OR	5,462	7,128	30.5	6,894	6,701	-2.8	12,356	13,829	11.9
League City, TX	38,315	36,662	-4.3	25,426	20,201	-20.5	63,741	56,863	-10.8
Leawood, KS	4,170	4,507	8.1	4,031	4,488	11.3	8,201	8,995	9.7
Lee's Summit, MO	4,170	4,507	8.1	4,031	4,488	11.3	8,201	8,995	9.7
Leesburg, VA	12,411	12,418	0.1	12,393	10,376	-16.3	24,804	22,794	-8.1
Lehi, UT	2,679	3,101	15.8	2,616	1,435	-45.1	5,295	4,536	-14.3
Lenexa, KS	4,170	4,507	8.1	4,031	4,488	11.3	8,201	8,995	9.7
Lexington, MA	4,991	4,779	-4.2	7,033	10,469	48.9	12,024	15,248	26.8
Los Altos, CA	1,861	1,954	5.0	8,176	4,364	-46.6	10,037	6,318	-37.1
Lower Makefield, PA	6,379	6,499	1.9	7,252	6,114	-15.7	13,631	12,613	-7.5
Madison, AL	1,784	2,116	18.6	1,033	486	-53.0	2,817	2,602	-7.6
Mamaroneck, NY	11,799	10,749	-8.9	36,185	75,646	109.1	47,984	86,395	80.0
Manheim, PA	970	65	-93.3	139	20	-85.6	1,109	85	-92.3
Manlius, NY	652	340	-47.9	511	354	-30.7	1,163	694	-40.3
Maple Grove, MN	6,689	6,786	1.5	4,736	4,927	4.0	11,425	11,713	2.5
Marion, IA	644	489	-24.1	237	332	40.1	881	821	-6.8
Marlboro, NJ	11,799	10,749	-8.9	36,185	75,646	109.1	47,984	86,395	80.0
Mason, OH	3,218	3,481	8.2	1,988	1,182	-40.5	5,206	4,663	-10.4

Table continued on next page.

Metro Area	Single-Family			Multi-Family			Total		
	2014	2015	Pct. Chg.	2014	2015	Pct. Chg.	2014	2015	Pct. Chg.
McCandless, PA	3,082	1,032	-66.5	1,108	1,397	26.1	4,190	2,429	-42.0
Menomonee Falls, WI	1,257	1,341	6.7	1,098	1,577	43.6	2,355	2,918	23.9
Meridian, ID	3,481	4,293	23.3	1,702	1,204	-29.3	5,183	5,497	6.1
Merrimack, NH	464	353	-23.9	504	322	-36.1	968	675	-30.3
Mount Lebanon, PA	3,082	1,032	-66.5	1,108	1,397	26.1	4,190	2,429	-42.0
Mount Pleasant, SC	4,144	4,520	9.1	2,011	1,691	-15.9	6,155	6,211	0.9
Needham, MA	4,991	4,779	-4.2	7,033	10,469	48.9	12,024	15,248	26.8
Newtown, CT	987	781	-20.9	902	1,802	99.8	1,889	2,583	36.7
Northbrook, IL	7,723	7,577	-1.9	7,956	8,160	2.6	15,679	15,737	0.4
Northville, MI	4,830	5,197	7.6	1,465	2,020	37.9	6,295	7,217	14.6
Novi, MI	4,830	5,197	7.6	1,465	2,020	37.9	6,295	7,217	14.6
O'Fallon, IL	4,538	5,008	10.4	2,454	2,290	-6.7	6,992	7,298	4.4
O'Fallon, MO	4,538	5,008	10.4	2,454	2,290	-6.7	6,992	7,298	4.4
Orchard Park, NY	1,057	999	-5.5	821	685	-16.6	1,878	1,684	-10.3
Oviedo, FL	9,806	12,328	25.7	6,309	7,873	24.8	16,115	20,201	25.4
Parker, CO	8,064	9,288	15.2	7,703	8,569	11.2	15,767	17,857	13.3
Parkland, FL	5,791	7,102	22.6	9,468	15,994	68.9	15,259	23,096	51.4
Peachtree City, GA	16,984	19,885	17.1	9,699	10,126	4.4	26,683	30,011	12.5
Pflugerville, TX	11,515	11,574	0.5	8,434	10,545	25.0	19,949	22,119	10.9
Plainfield, IL	7,723	7,577	-1.9	7,956	8,160	2.6	15,679	15,737	0.4
Princeton, NJ	239	284	18.8	129	610	372.9	368	894	142.9
Queen Creek, AZ	11,557	16,940	46.6	8,784	6,006	-31.6	20,341	22,946	12.8
Rancho Palos Verdes, CA	8,300	8,458	1.9	18,650	25,211	35.2	26,950	33,669	24.9
Redmond, WA	8,665	8,587	-0.9	13,288	16,380	23.3	21,953	24,967	13.7
Richland, WA	1,078	1,245	15.5	186	289	55.4	1,264	1,534	21.4
Ridgefield, CT	987	781	-20.9	902	1,802	99.8	1,889	2,583	36.7
Ridgewood, NJ	11,799	10,749	-8.9	36,185	75,646	109.1	47,984	86,395	80.0
Rio Rancho, NM	2,128	2,019	-5.1	415	283	-31.8	2,543	2,302	-9.5
Sahuarita, AZ	2,296	2,477	7.9	954	1,055	10.6	3,250	3,532	8.7
Sammamish, WA	8,665	8,587	-0.9	13,288	16,380	23.3	21,953	24,967	13.7
San Ramon, CA	3,716	4,595	23.7	6,285	8,171	30.0	10,001	12,766	27.6
Saratoga, CA	1,861	1,954	5.0	8,176	4,364	-46.6	10,037	6,318	-37.1
Schertz, TX	6,220	6,446	3.6	4,112	2,055	-50.0	10,332	8,501	-17.7
Shrewsbury, MA	1,274	149	-88.3	110	24	-78.2	1,384	173	-87.5
South Brunswick, NJ	11,799	10,749	-8.9	36,185	75,646	109.1	47,984	86,395	80.0
South Jordan, UT	3,159	3,722	17.8	2,159	2,828	31.0	5,318	6,550	23.2
South Kingstown, RI	1,441	1,477	2.5	334	320	-4.2	1,775	1,797	1.2
South Windsor, CT	754	792	5.0	639	866	35.5	1,393	1,658	19.0
Southlake, TX	22,550	28,363	25.8	18,868	28,038	48.6	41,418	56,401	36.2
Spring Hill, TN	9,075	10,813	19.2	5,869	6,997	19.2	14,944	17,810	19.2
Stow, OH	684	438	-36.0	79	175	121.5	763	613	-19.7
Sugar Land, TX	38,315	36,662	-4.3	25,426	20,201	-20.5	63,741	56,863	-10.8
Sun Prairie, WI	1,243	1,401	12.7	2,562	2,103	-17.9	3,805	3,504	-7.9
Syracuse, UT	1,990	2,108	5.9	688	765	11.2	2,678	2,873	7.3
Tredyffrin, PA	6,379	6,499	1.9	7,252	6,114	-15.7	13,631	12,613	-7.5
Upper Arlington, OH	3,497	3,421	-2.2	3,547	4,027	13.5	7,044	7,448	5.7
Upper Dublin, PA	6,379	6,499	1.9	7,252	6,114	-15.7	13,631	12,613	-7.5
Vestavia Hills, AL	2,318	2,468	6.5	1,046	1,190	13.8	3,364	3,658	8.7
Webster, NY	1,269	1,333	5.0	522	1,272	143.7	1,791	2,605	45.4
Wellesley, MA	4,991	4,779	-4.2	7,033	10,469	48.9	12,024	15,248	26.8
West Fargo, ND	1,242	1,344	8.2	2,524	1,354	-46.4	3,766	2,698	-28.4
West Linn, OR	5,462	7,128	30.5	6,894	6,701	-2.8	12,356	13,829	11.9
West Windsor, NJ	239	284	18.8	129	610	372.9	368	894	142.9
Westlake, OH	2,256	2,505	11.0	644	413	-35.9	2,900	2,918	0.6
Weston, FL	5,791	7,102	22.6	9,468	15,994	68.9	15,259	23,096	51.4
Westport, CT	987	781	-20.9	902	1,802	99.8	1,889	2,583	36.7
Wilmette, IL	7,723	7,577	-1.9	7,956	8,160	2.6	15,679	15,737	0.4
Woodbury, MN	6,689	6,786	1.5	4,736	4,927	4.0	11,425	11,713	2.5
Yorba Linda, CA	8,300	8,458	1.9	18,650	25,211	35.2	26,950	33,669	24.9
U.S.	640,300	690,800	7.9	411,800	487,600	18.4	1,052,100	1,178,400	12.0

Note: Figures cover the Metropolitan Statistical Area—see Appendix B for areas included; Figures represent new, privately-owned housing units authorized (unadjusted data); All permit data are based on estimates with imputation
Source: U.S. Census Bureau, Manufacturing, Mining, and Construction Statistics, Building Permits, 2014, 2015

Housing Vacancy Rates

Metro Area[1]	Gross Vacancy Rate[2] (%)			Year-Round Vacancy Rate[3] (%)			Rental Vacancy Rate[4] (%)			Homeowner Vacancy Rate[5] (%)		
	2013	2014	2015	2013	2014	2015	2013	2014	2015	2013	2014	2015
Aliso Viejo, CA	6.2	5.8	5.4	5.7	5.5	5.0	4.2	4.6	3.3	1.2	0.8	0.8
Allen, TX	9.0	9.2	8.0	8.8	9.0	7.8	8.2	9.8	8.3	1.9	1.5	1.4
Alpharetta, GA	12.4	11.0	11.0	11.8	10.3	10.7	10.2	8.8	8.2	2.1	2.5	2.2
Ankeny, IA	n/a	n/a	n/a	n/a	n/a	n/a	n/a	n/a	n/a	n/a	n/a	n/a
Apex, NC	7.3	6.4	6.8	7.2	6.4	6.7	6.9	5.3	6.6	1.8	0.6	1.7
Ballwin, MO	15.1	12.3	10.7	14.9	12.0	10.3	13.2	10.3	9.7	3.5	2.4	3.1
Beavercreek, OH	12.9	10.1	11.4	12.8	10.1	11.4	11.6	8.9	9.4	3.2	0.4	2.3
Bella Vista, AR	n/a	n/a	n/a	n/a	n/a	n/a	n/a	n/a	n/a	n/a	n/a	n/a
Bernards, NJ	9.5	9.2	9.8	8.1	7.9	8.6	5.4	4.6	4.2	2.1	1.6	2.1
Bethlehem, NY	9.4	10.8	13.2	7.6	7.4	8.9	8.4	4.2	6.5	2.2	1.4	1.8
Bloomfield, MI	11.6	11.1	9.7	11.4	10.7	9.5	12.1	9.5	6.8	1.7	1.2	1.1
Bowie, MD	8.3	7.8	7.7	8.2	7.5	7.4	7.2	6.7	5.7	1.3	1.4	0.9
Bozeman, MT	n/a	n/a	n/a	n/a	n/a	n/a	n/a	n/a	n/a	n/a	n/a	n/a
Brentwood, TN	6.6	7.0	8.3	6.4	6.7	8.2	5.3	4.0	4.9	0.9	2.4	3.1
Broomfield, CO	6.3	6.1	7.4	5.5	5.1	5.6	5.3	3.3	4.8	1.2	0.8	0.7
Carmel, IN	9.2	8.8	7.4	8.7	8.7	7.4	10.9	10.9	8.4	1.5	2.2	1.0
Cedar Park, TX	12.5	12.4	9.2	11.9	11.6	8.5	12.1	10.9	6.0	1.1	0.8	1.3
Cheshire, CT	9.9	7.4	8.7	9.5	7.1	8.6	7.8	4.8	5.8	2.6	1.2	2.1
Chesterfield, MO	15.1	12.3	10.7	14.9	12.0	10.3	13.2	10.3	9.7	3.5	2.4	3.1
Collierville, TN	12.9	14.1	11.2	12.7	14.1	11.0	13.4	15.1	10.7	1.8	2.0	1.4
Coppell, TX	9.0	9.2	8.0	8.8	9.0	7.8	8.2	9.8	8.3	1.9	1.5	1.4
Cornelius, NC	9.3	7.9	8.2	8.7	7.8	7.8	6.4	6.0	6.4	3.5	1.7	1.8
Cranberry, PA	12.7	12.2	13.5	12.5	11.7	13.2	7.8	6.1	7.1	1.7	1.2	1.5
Cupertino, CA	5.0	4.7	5.7	4.9	4.5	5.6	3.0	2.9	3.5	0.6	0.6	0.9
Danville, CA	6.5	5.9	5.7	6.4	5.9	5.7	3.9	3.2	3.6	1.1	0.4	0.7
Draper, UT	7.4	7.8	5.2	6.8	7.6	5.1	6.7	9.8	5.8	1.5	1.8	1.3
Dublin, OH	9.8	10.2	9.6	9.8	9.9	9.2	6.3	7.0	6.5	1.1	1.7	1.5
Eastchester, NY	9.5	9.2	9.8	8.1	7.9	8.6	5.4	4.6	4.2	2.1	1.6	2.1
Eden Prairie, MN	5.7	5.7	6.4	5.1	5.3	6.0	5.4	4.4	4.9	0.9	1.4	0.8
Edmond, OK	13.0	13.4	11.9	12.6	12.9	11.1	8.7	10.1	7.6	2.0	1.7	2.0
Evesham, NJ	10.4	10.2	10.7	10.2	10.0	10.2	11.6	9.7	7.6	1.6	2.0	2.4
Fishers, IN	9.2	8.8	7.4	8.7	8.7	7.4	10.9	10.9	8.4	1.5	2.2	1.0
Flower Mound, TX	9.0	9.2	8.0	8.8	9.0	7.8	8.2	9.8	8.3	1.9	1.5	1.4
Folsom, CA	9.7	10.2	8.8	8.4	7.6	6.0	7.0	6.5	5.3	1.2	1.0	1.4
Foster City, CA	6.5	5.9	5.7	6.4	5.9	5.7	3.9	3.2	3.6	1.1	0.4	0.7
Franklin, TN	6.6	7.0	8.3	6.4	6.7	8.2	5.3	4.0	4.9	0.9	2.4	3.1
Friendswood, TX	9.6	8.9	9.2	9.0	8.4	8.7	10.0	8.6	9.6	2.3	1.3	1.5
Germantown, TN	12.9	14.1	11.2	12.7	14.1	11.0	13.4	15.1	10.7	1.8	2.0	1.4
Glastonbury, CT	9.9	8.2	10.5	9.2	7.5	9.7	9.0	6.0	6.1	1.0	1.3	1.5
Grand Blanc, MI	n/a	n/a	n/a	n/a	n/a	n/a	n/a	n/a	n/a	n/a	n/a	n/a
Guilderland, NY	9.4	10.8	13.2	7.6	7.4	8.9	8.4	4.2	6.5	2.2	1.4	1.8
Hampden, PA	n/a	n/a	n/a	n/a	n/a	n/a	n/a	n/a	n/a	n/a	n/a	n/a
Holly Springs, NC	7.3	6.4	6.8	7.2	6.4	6.7	6.9	5.3	6.6	1.8	0.6	1.7
Huntersville, NC	9.3	7.9	8.2	8.7	7.8	7.8	6.4	6.0	6.4	3.5	1.7	1.8
Independence, KY	11.2	10.1	10.5	10.0	9.3	10.0	8.9	7.9	10.1	2.6	2.2	2.2
Johns Creek, GA	12.4	11.0	11.0	11.8	10.3	10.7	10.2	8.8	8.2	2.1	2.5	2.2
Keller, TX	9.0	9.2	8.0	8.8	9.0	7.8	8.2	9.8	8.3	1.9	1.5	1.4
Kirkland, WA	6.9	6.9	5.6	6.6	6.7	5.4	4.3	4.4	3.8	1.7	1.2	1.1
Lafayette, CO	n/a	n/a	n/a	n/a	n/a	n/a	n/a	n/a	n/a	n/a	n/a	n/a
Lake Oswego, OR	6.5	6.3	6.0	6.1	6.2	5.5	3.1	3.6	3.4	1.2	1.3	1.0
League City, TX	9.6	8.9	9.2	9.0	8.4	8.7	10.0	8.6	9.6	2.3	1.3	1.5
Leawood, KS	10.8	9.0	7.3	10.4	8.6	7.1	10.1	9.5	7.9	2.0	1.5	1.3
Lee's Summit, MO	10.8	9.0	7.3	10.4	8.6	7.1	10.1	9.5	7.9	2.0	1.5	1.3
Leesburg, VA	8.3	7.8	7.7	8.2	7.5	7.4	7.2	6.7	5.7	1.3	1.4	0.9
Lehi, UT	n/a	n/a	n/a	n/a	n/a	n/a	n/a	n/a	n/a	n/a	n/a	n/a
Lenexa, KS	10.8	9.0	7.3	10.4	8.6	7.1	10.1	9.5	7.9	2.0	1.5	1.3
Lexington, MA	7.8	9.2	9.9	6.2	6.4	6.3	6.8	4.9	3.3	1.1	0.8	1.1
Los Altos, CA	5.0	4.7	5.7	4.9	4.5	5.6	3.0	2.9	3.5	0.6	0.6	0.9
Lower Makefield, PA	10.4	10.2	10.7	10.2	10.0	10.2	11.6	9.7	7.6	1.6	2.0	2.4
Madison, AL	n/a	n/a	n/a	n/a	n/a	n/a	n/a	n/a	n/a	n/a	n/a	n/a
Mamaroneck, NY	9.5	9.2	9.8	8.1	7.9	8.6	5.4	4.6	4.2	2.1	1.6	2.1
Manheim, PA	n/a	n/a	n/a	n/a	n/a	n/a	n/a	n/a	n/a	n/a	n/a	n/a
Manlius, NY	16.0	13.7	11.1	13.3	12.1	10.4	10.5	8.1	9.2	0.4	2.7	2.3
Maple Grove, MN	5.7	5.7	6.4	5.1	5.3	6.0	5.4	4.4	4.9	0.9	1.4	0.8
Marion, IA	n/a	n/a	n/a	n/a	n/a	n/a	n/a	n/a	n/a	n/a	n/a	n/a
Marlboro, NJ	9.5	9.2	9.8	8.1	7.9	8.6	5.4	4.6	4.2	2.1	1.6	2.1
Mason, OH	11.2	10.1	10.5	10.0	9.3	10.0	8.9	7.9	10.1	2.6	2.2	2.2

Table continued on next page.

Metro Area[1]	Gross Vacancy Rate[2] (%)			Year-Round Vacancy Rate[3] (%)			Rental Vacancy Rate[4] (%)			Homeowner Vacancy Rate[5] (%)		
	2013	2014	2015	2013	2014	2015	2013	2014	2015	2013	2014	2015
McCandless, PA	12.7	12.2	13.5	12.5	11.7	13.2	7.8	6.1	7.1	1.7	1.2	1.5
Menomonee Falls, WI	12.1	9.5	8.0	9.8	7.8	7.3	9.0	4.5	4.5	1.2	1.5	0.8
Meridian, ID	n/a	n/a	n/a	n/a	n/a	n/a	n/a	n/a	n/a	n/a	n/a	n/a
Merrimack, NH	n/a	n/a	n/a	n/a	n/a	n/a	n/a	n/a	n/a	n/a	n/a	n/a
Mount Lebanon, PA	12.7	12.2	13.5	12.5	11.7	13.2	7.8	6.1	7.1	1.7	1.2	1.5
Mount Pleasant, SC	-1.0	-1.0	14.3	-1.0	-1.0	12.4	-1.0	-1.0	8.7	-1.0	-1.0	2.2
Needham, MA	7.8	9.2	9.9	6.2	6.4	6.3	6.8	4.9	3.3	1.1	0.8	1.1
Newtown, CT	10.2	10.8	11.3	9.4	9.2	10.1	5.1	5.6	7.1	2.6	1.6	1.8
Northbrook, IL	10.5	10.3	9.7	10.3	10.2	9.4	10.9	9.1	7.4	2.8	2.6	2.3
Northville, MI	11.6	11.1	9.7	11.4	10.7	9.5	12.1	9.5	6.8	1.7	1.2	1.1
Novi, MI	11.6	11.1	9.7	11.4	10.7	9.5	12.1	9.5	6.8	1.7	1.2	1.1
O'Fallon, IL	15.1	12.3	10.7	14.9	12.0	10.3	13.2	10.3	9.7	3.5	2.4	3.1
O'Fallon, MO	15.1	12.3	10.7	14.9	12.0	10.3	13.2	10.3	9.7	3.5	2.4	3.1
Orchard Park, NY	9.6	10.3	12.3	9.0	10.0	11.8	10.4	8.0	11.9	1.0	2.1	2.5
Oviedo, FL	20.5	18.8	14.3	15.5	15.2	11.3	14.7	14.6	8.0	2.8	3.1	4.1
Parker, CO	6.3	6.1	7.4	5.5	5.1	5.6	5.3	3.3	4.8	1.2	0.8	0.7
Parkland, FL	20.2	19.6	16.9	10.3	10.4	8.5	6.7	7.0	6.4	1.7	1.8	1.4
Peachtree City, GA	12.4	11.0	11.0	11.8	10.3	10.7	10.2	8.8	8.2	2.1	2.5	2.2
Pflugerville, TX	12.5	12.4	9.2	11.9	11.6	8.5	12.1	10.9	6.0	1.1	0.8	1.3
Plainfield, IL	10.5	10.3	9.7	10.3	10.2	9.4	10.9	9.1	7.4	2.8	2.6	2.3
Princeton, NJ	n/a	n/a	n/a	n/a	n/a	n/a	n/a	n/a	n/a	n/a	n/a	n/a
Queen Creek, AZ	18.4	17.5	15.3	11.5	11.3	9.5	9.7	9.7	6.3	2.4	2.9	2.0
Rancho Palos Verdes, CA	6.2	5.8	5.4	5.7	5.5	5.0	4.2	4.6	3.3	1.2	0.8	0.8
Redmond, WA	6.9	6.9	5.6	6.6	6.7	5.4	4.3	4.4	3.8	1.7	1.2	1.1
Richland, WA	n/a	n/a	n/a	n/a	n/a	n/a	n/a	n/a	n/a	n/a	n/a	n/a
Ridgefield, CT	10.2	10.8	11.3	9.4	9.2	10.1	5.1	5.6	7.1	2.6	1.6	1.8
Ridgewood, NJ	9.5	9.2	9.8	8.1	7.9	8.6	5.4	4.6	4.2	2.1	1.6	2.1
Rio Rancho, NM	8.4	8.6	9.3	7.7	7.3	8.3	7.8	7.5	7.2	2.4	1.9	2.7
Sahuarita, AZ	14.5	10.0	11.8	12.5	8.4	9.8	13.9	9.0	10.1	1.9	2.1	1.7
Sammamish, WA	6.9	6.9	5.6	6.6	6.7	5.4	4.3	4.4	3.8	1.7	1.2	1.1
San Ramon, CA	6.5	5.9	5.7	6.4	5.9	5.7	3.9	3.2	3.6	1.1	0.4	0.7
Saratoga, CA	5.0	4.7	5.7	4.9	4.5	5.6	3.0	2.9	3.5	0.6	0.6	0.9
Schertz, TX	9.0	8.6	9.0	8.3	8.2	7.8	9.1	7.3	9.6	1.4	1.2	0.8
Shrewsbury, MA	10.8	11.0	10.1	8.6	6.8	7.8	6.4	4.5	2.9	3.1	1.9	1.9
South Brunswick, NJ	9.5	9.2	9.8	8.1	7.9	8.6	5.4	4.6	4.2	2.1	1.6	2.1
South Jordan, UT	7.4	7.8	5.2	6.8	7.6	5.1	6.7	9.8	5.8	1.5	1.8	1.3
South Kingstown, RI	12.3	13.2	11.0	8.9	9.9	7.8	6.6	6.8	3.3	2.3	1.6	1.7
South Windsor, CT	9.9	8.2	10.5	9.2	7.5	9.7	9.0	6.0	6.1	1.0	1.3	1.5
Southlake, TX	9.0	9.2	8.0	8.8	9.0	7.8	8.2	9.8	8.3	1.9	1.5	1.4
Spring Hill, TN	6.6	7.0	8.3	6.4	6.7	8.2	5.3	4.0	4.9	0.9	2.4	3.1
Stow, OH	11.6	9.6	11.6	11.3	9.5	11.6	7.8	6.3	11.8	2.4	0.8	0.5
Sugar Land, TX	9.6	8.9	9.2	9.0	8.4	8.7	10.0	8.6	9.6	2.3	1.3	1.5
Sun Prairie, WI	n/a	n/a	n/a	n/a	n/a	n/a	n/a	n/a	n/a	n/a	n/a	n/a
Syracuse, UT	n/a	n/a	n/a	n/a	n/a	n/a	n/a	n/a	n/a	n/a	n/a	n/a
Tredyffrin, PA	10.4	10.2	10.7	10.2	10.0	10.2	11.6	9.7	7.6	1.6	2.0	2.4
Upper Arlington, OH	9.8	10.2	9.6	9.8	9.9	9.2	6.3	7.0	6.5	1.1	1.7	1.5
Upper Dublin, PA	10.4	10.2	10.7	10.2	10.0	10.2	11.6	9.7	7.6	1.6	2.0	2.4
Vestavia Hills, AL	14.2	14.3	16.0	13.2	13.8	15.6	9.9	13.0	17.7	1.8	2.7	2.2
Webster, NY	9.6	9.1	8.0	7.2	6.3	6.2	6.1	6.6	6.5	0.2	1.1	0.8
Wellesley, MA	7.8	9.2	9.9	6.2	6.4	6.3	6.8	4.9	3.3	1.1	0.8	1.1
West Fargo, ND	n/a	n/a	n/a	n/a	n/a	n/a	n/a	n/a	n/a	n/a	n/a	n/a
West Linn, OR	6.5	6.3	6.0	6.1	6.2	5.5	3.1	3.6	3.4	1.2	1.3	1.0
West Windsor, NJ	n/a	n/a	n/a	n/a	n/a	n/a	n/a	n/a	n/a	n/a	n/a	n/a
Westlake, OH	9.9	9.2	11.0	9.9	9.2	10.9	9.2	7.0	7.4	1.9	1.5	1.4
Weston, FL	20.2	19.6	16.9	10.3	10.4	8.5	6.7	7.0	6.4	1.7	1.8	1.4
Westport, CT	10.2	10.8	11.3	9.4	9.2	10.1	5.1	5.6	7.1	2.6	1.6	1.8
Wilmette, IL	10.5	10.3	9.7	10.3	10.2	9.4	10.9	9.1	7.4	2.8	2.6	2.3
Woodbury, MN	5.7	5.7	6.4	5.1	5.3	6.0	5.4	4.4	4.9	0.9	1.4	0.8
Yorba Linda, CA	6.2	5.8	5.4	5.7	5.5	5.0	4.2	4.6	3.3	1.2	0.8	0.8
U.S.	13.6	13.4	12.9	10.7	10.4	10.0	8.3	7.6	7.1	2.0	1.9	1.8

Note: (1) Metropolitan Statistical Area—see Appendix B for areas included; (2) The percentage of the total housing inventory that is vacant; (3) The percentage of the housing inventory (excluding seasonal units) that is year-round vacant; (4) The percentage of rental inventory that is vacant for rent; (5) The percentage of homeowner inventory that is vacant for sale; n/a not available
Source: U.S. Census Bureau, Housing Vacancies and Homeownership Annual Statistics: 2015

Bankruptcy Filings

City	Area Covered	Business Filings			Nonbusiness Filings		
		2014	2015	% Chg.	2014	2015	% Chg.
Aliso Viejo, CA	Orange County	397	424	6.8	7,279	5,898	-19.0
Allen, TX	Collin County	146	144	-1.4	1,514	1,362	-10.0
Alpharetta, GA	Fulton County	161	138	-14.3	5,080	4,863	-4.3
Ankeny, IA	Polk County	39	24	-38.5	978	822	-16.0
Apex, NC	Wake County	110	85	-22.7	1,823	1,612	-11.6
Ballwin, MO	Saint Louis County	43	68	58.1	4,418	3,924	-11.2
Beavercreek, OH	Greene County	8	12	50.0	381	369	-3.1
Bella Vista, AR	Benton County	29	33	13.8	656	576	-12.2
Bernards, NJ	Somerset County	33	19	-42.4	522	512	-1.9
Bethlehem, NY	Albany County	18	21	16.7	650	576	-11.4
Bloomfield, MI	Oakland County	162	163	0.6	4,091	3,721	-9.0
Bowie, MD	Prince George's County	58	74	27.6	4,443	4,032	-9.3
Bozeman, MT	Gallatin County	8	6	-25.0	145	123	-15.2
Brentwood, TN	Williamson County	39	24	-38.5	350	310	-11.4
Broomfield, CO	Broomfield County	3	5	66.7	153	131	-14.4
Carmel, IN	Hamilton County	52	54	3.8	889	766	-13.8
Cedar Park, TX	Williamson County	60	49	-18.3	516	481	-6.8
Cheshire, CT	New Haven County	64	46	-28.1	1,998	1,813	-9.3
Chesterfield, MO	Saint Louis County	43	68	58.1	4,418	3,924	-11.2
Collierville, TN	Shelby County	106	61	-42.5	12,422	11,817	-4.9
Coppell, TX	Dallas County	379	238	-37.2	4,779	4,105	-14.1
Cornelius, NC	Mecklenburg County	63	58	-7.9	1,326	1,254	-5.4
Cranberry, PA	Butler County	10	9	-10.0	226	282	24.8
Cupertino, CA	Santa Clara County	147	124	-15.6	3,173	2,413	-24.0
Danville, CA	Contra Costa County	104	93	-10.6	2,467	1,850	-25.0
Draper, UT	Salt Lake County	114	94	-17.5	5,837	5,242	-10.2
Dublin, OH	Franklin County	82	63	-23.2	4,806	4,651	-3.2
Eastchester, NY	Westchester County	164	110	-32.9	1,213	1,240	2.2
Eden Prairie, MN	Hennepin County	110	99	-10.0	2,625	2,330	-11.2
Edmond, OK	Oklahoma County	57	69	21.1	2,365	2,197	-7.1
Evesham, NJ	Burlington County	34	39	14.7	1,706	1,646	-3.5
Fishers, IN	Hamilton County	52	54	3.8	889	766	-13.8
Flower Mound, TX	Denton County	82	78	-4.9	1,200	1,002	-16.5
Folsom, CA	Sacramento County	128	111	-13.3	5,064	4,145	-18.1
Foster City, CA	San Mateo County	73	60	-17.8	998	826	-17.2
Franklin, TN	Williamson County	39	24	-38.5	350	310	-11.4
Friendswood, TX	Galveston County	30	40	33.3	368	362	-1.6
Germantown, TN	Shelby County	106	61	-42.5	12,422	11,817	-4.9
Glastonbury, CT	Hartford County	79	74	-6.3	1,563	1,403	-10.2
Grand Blanc, MI	Genesee County	24	26	8.3	2,490	2,362	-5.1
Guilderland, NY	Albany County	18	21	16.7	650	576	-11.4
Hampden, PA	Cumberland County	25	19	-24.0	414	370	-10.6
Holly Springs, NC	Wake County	110	85	-22.7	1,823	1,612	-11.6
Huntersville, NC	Mecklenburg County	63	58	-7.9	1,326	1,254	-5.4
Independence, KY	Kenton County	13	10	-23.1	719	660	-8.2
Johns Creek, GA	Fulton County	161	138	-14.3	5,080	4,863	-4.3
Keller, TX	Tarrant County	177	250	41.2	4,302	4,110	-4.5
Kirkland, WA	King County	185	136	-26.5	4,752	3,924	-17.4
Lafayette, CO	Boulder County	33	26	-21.2	544	441	-18.9
Lake Oswego, OR	Clackamas County	42	24	-42.9	1,235	1,017	-17.7
League City, TX	Galveston County	30	40	33.3	368	362	-1.6
Leawood, KS	Johnson County	80	75	-6.3	1,369	1,121	-18.1
Lee's Summit, MO	Jackson County	45	45	0.0	2,916	2,533	-13.1
Leesburg, VA	Loudoun County	42	49	16.7	569	548	-3.7
Lehi, UT	Utah County	43	40	-7.0	2,003	1,715	-14.4
Lenexa, KS	Johnson County	80	75	-6.3	1,369	1,121	-18.1
Lexington, MA	Middlesex County	96	111	15.6	1,591	1,330	-16.4
Los Altos, CA	Santa Clara County	147	124	-15.6	3,173	2,413	-24.0
Lower Makefield, PA	Bucks County	57	43	-24.6	1,214	1,121	-7.7
Madison, AL	Madison County	35	25	-28.6	1,334	1,316	-1.3
Mamaroneck, NY	Westchester County	164	110	-32.9	1,213	1,240	2.2
Manheim, PA	Lancaster County	16	21	31.3	684	584	-14.6
Manlius, NY	Onondaga County	30	24	-20.0	1,067	1,005	-5.8
Maple Grove, MN	Hennepin County	110	99	-10.0	2,625	2,330	-11.2
Marion, IA	Linn County	5	8	60.0	347	315	-9.2
Marlboro, NJ	Monmouth County	66	48	-27.3	1,641	1,461	-11.0
Mason, OH	Warren County	14	18	28.6	600	593	-1.2
McCandless, PA	Allegheny County	88	111	26.1	2,209	2,288	3.6

Table continued on next page.

City	Area Covered	Business Filings 2014	Business Filings 2015	Business Filings % Chg.	Nonbusiness Filings 2014	Nonbusiness Filings 2015	Nonbusiness Filings % Chg.
Menomonee Falls, WI	Waukesha County	44	25	-43.2	1,030	940	-8.7
Meridian, ID	Ada County	47	47	0.0	1,177	969	-17.7
Merrimack, NH	Hillsborough County	78	32	-59.0	750	570	-24.0
Mount Lebanon, PA	Allegheny County	88	111	26.1	2,209	2,288	3.6
Mount Pleasant, SC	Charleston County	29	18	-37.9	448	389	-13.2
Needham, MA	Norfolk County	42	45	7.1	778	699	-10.2
Newtown, CT	Fairfield County	91	83	-8.8	1,506	1,393	-7.5
Northbrook, IL	Cook County	569	511	-10.2	33,968	33,318	-1.9
Northville, MI	Wayne County	109	107	-1.8	9,516	9,339	-1.9
Novi, MI	Oakland County	162	163	0.6	4,091	3,721	-9.0
O'Fallon, IL	Saint Clair County	19	18	-5.3	1,141	1,139	-0.2
O'Fallon, MO	Saint Charles County	28	16	-42.9	1,311	1,242	-5.3
Orchard Park, NY	Erie County	81	88	8.6	1,965	1,860	-5.3
Oviedo, FL	Seminole County	80	71	-11.3	1,530	1,320	-13.7
Parker, CO	Douglas County	45	45	0.0	797	670	-15.9
Parkland, FL	Broward County	241	202	-16.2	7,870	6,714	-14.7
Peachtree City, GA	Fayette County	13	10	-23.1	401	398	-0.7
Pflugerville, TX	Travis County	112	105	-6.3	838	741	-11.6
Plainfield, IL	Will County	93	62	-33.3	3,522	2,987	-15.2
Princeton, NJ	Mercer County	50	26	-48.0	1,010	940	-6.9
Queen Creek, AZ	Maricopa County	545	496	-9.0	13,283	11,293	-15.0
Rancho Palos Verdes, CA	Los Angeles County	1,212	1,235	1.9	29,341	23,618	-19.5
Redmond, WA	King County	185	136	-26.5	4,752	3,924	-17.4
Richland, WA	Benton County	5	19	280.0	466	442	-5.2
Ridgefield, CT	Fairfield County	91	83	-8.8	1,506	1,393	-7.5
Ridgewood, NJ	Bergen County	110	126	14.5	2,159	2,017	-6.6
Rio Rancho, NM	Sandoval County	11	13	18.2	309	280	-9.4
Sahuarita, AZ	Pima County	75	71	-5.3	2,460	2,214	-10.0
Sammamish, WA	King County	185	136	-26.5	4,752	3,924	-17.4
San Ramon, CA	Contra Costa County	104	93	-10.6	2,467	1,850	-25.0
Saratoga, CA	Santa Clara County	147	124	-15.6	3,173	2,413	-24.0
Schertz, TX	Guadalupe County	5	2	-60.0	130	136	4.6
Shrewsbury, MA	Worcester County	52	44	-15.4	1,561	1,380	-11.6
South Brunswick, NJ	Middlesex County	66	48	-27.3	2,000	1,749	-12.6
South Jordan, UT	Salt Lake County	114	94	-17.5	5,837	5,242	-10.2
South Kingstown, RI	Washington County	11	17	54.5	220	196	-10.9
South Windsor, CT	Hartford County	79	74	-6.3	1,563	1,403	-10.2
Southlake, TX	Tarrant County	177	250	41.2	4,302	4,110	-4.5
Spring Hill, TN	Williamson County	39	24	-38.5	350	310	-11.4
Stow, OH	Summit County	30	27	-10.0	2,376	2,232	-6.1
Sugar Land, TX	Fort Bend County	48	61	27.1	838	775	-7.5
Sun Prairie, WI	Dane County	40	29	-27.5	991	847	-14.5
Syracuse, UT	Davis County	18	17	-5.6	1,469	1,302	-11.4
Tredyffrin, PA	Chester County	46	27	-41.3	670	600	-10.4
Upper Arlington, OH	Franklin County	82	63	-23.2	4,806	4,651	-3.2
Upper Dublin, PA	Montgomery County	82	64	-22.0	1,196	1,197	0.1
Vestavia Hills, AL	Jefferson County	55	54	-1.8	4,020	4,336	7.9
Webster, NY	Monroe County	45	38	-15.6	1,030	905	-12.1
Wellesley, MA	Norfolk County	42	45	7.1	778	699	-10.2
West Fargo, ND	Cass County	9	3	-66.7	257	165	-35.8
West Linn, OR	Clackamas County	42	24	-42.9	1,235	1,017	-17.7
West Windsor, NJ	Mercer County	50	26	-48.0	1,010	940	-6.9
Westlake, OH	Cuyahoga County	88	93	5.7	6,065	5,648	-6.9
Weston, FL	Broward County	241	202	-16.2	7,870	6,714	-14.7
Westport, CT	Fairfield County	91	83	-8.8	1,506	1,393	-7.5
Wilmette, IL	Cook County	569	511	-10.2	33,968	33,318	-1.9
Woodbury, MN	Washington County	32	30	-6.3	639	572	-10.5
Yorba Linda, CA	Orange County	397	424	6.8	7,279	5,898	-19.0
U.S.	U.S.	26,983	24,735	-8.3	909,812	819,760	-9.9

Note: Business filings include Chapter 7, Chapter 11, Chapter 12, and Chapter 13; Nonbusiness filings include Chapter 7, Chapter 11, and Chapter 13

Source: Administrative Office of the U.S. Courts, Business and Nonbusiness Bankruptcy, County Cases Commenced by Chapter of the Bankruptcy Code, During the 12- Month Period Ending December 31, 2014 and Business and Nonbusiness Bankruptcy, County Cases Commenced by Chapter of the Bankruptcy Code, During the 12- Month Period Ending December 31, 2015

Income: City

City	Per Capita ($)	Median Household ($)	Average Household ($)
Aliso Viejo, CA	44,986	102,325	119,475
Allen, TX	40,741	102,120	123,007
Alpharetta, GA	42,644	87,837	115,032
Ankeny, IA	33,555	75,069	84,761
Apex, NC	35,852	89,392	103,680
Ballwin, MO	40,300	82,685	105,277
Beavercreek, OH	39,325	79,243	95,917
Bella Vista, AR	31,734	62,500	74,892
Bernards, NJ	67,750	126,667	185,757
Bethlehem, NY	44,297	92,188	113,018
Bloomfield, MI	63,030	108,235	158,104
Bowie, MD	42,544	106,396	119,456
Bozeman, MT	26,350	46,422	62,333
Brentwood, TN	58,745	138,395	181,595
Broomfield, CO	38,706	80,430	99,462
Carmel, IN	52,207	107,916	141,596
Cedar Park, TX	33,632	79,323	96,203
Cheshire, CT	43,583	107,716	125,801
Chesterfield, MO	52,010	94,263	127,077
Collierville, TN	41,346	106,783	124,236
Coppell, TX	49,098	111,325	135,828
Cornelius, NC	46,223	81,059	111,332
Cranberry, PA	43,110	100,020	117,275
Cupertino, CA	55,867	134,872	159,497
Danville, CA	65,783	140,616	178,684
Draper, UT	34,083	94,852	120,088
Dublin, OH	54,045	117,860	150,700
Eastchester, NY	65,243	104,891	164,891
Eden Prairie, MN	50,435	95,697	129,002
Edmond, OK	38,298	71,825	100,864
Evesham, NJ	42,757	93,732	111,778
Fishers, IN	38,600	91,646	110,153
Flower Mound, TX	45,981	121,549	139,559
Folsom, CA	38,472	100,163	110,870
Foster City, CA	55,318	114,651	142,467
Franklin, TN	40,447	81,432	102,973
Friendswood, TX	42,963	95,120	119,925
Germantown, TN	52,763	110,169	140,261
Glastonbury, CT	55,678	108,157	145,318
Grand Blanc, MI	30,476	58,392	77,817
Guilderland, NY	41,921	79,074	101,378
Hampden, PA	43,812	80,573	103,822
Holly Springs, NC	34,257	91,755	102,567
Huntersville, NC	39,446	85,258	104,900
Independence, KY	24,821	65,776	73,401
Johns Creek, GA	43,998	108,114	132,303
Keller, TX	45,415	114,266	132,628
Kirkland, WA	48,902	90,611	115,173
Lafayette, CO	39,288	71,038	95,616
Lake Oswego, OR	57,359	84,244	132,173
League City, TX	37,953	90,972	105,172
Leawood, KS	76,304	133,702	201,273
Lee's Summit, MO	34,153	78,186	92,467
Leesburg, VA	39,533	101,719	117,864
Lehi, UT	22,510	74,200	86,003
Lenexa, KS	38,390	75,400	94,694
Lexington, MA	69,064	137,456	189,916
Los Altos, CA	84,705	157,500	227,294
Lower Makefield, PA	56,319	126,492	152,640
Madison, AL	42,284	92,965	112,609
Mamaroneck, NY	71,721	116,969	191,034
Manheim, PA	37,520	67,796	93,959
Manlius, NY	41,252	75,609	100,174
Maple Grove, MN	43,833	92,267	114,692
Marion, IA	31,037	62,532	75,025
Marlboro, NJ	54,843	135,929	168,917
Mason, OH	37,459	83,466	104,860
McCandless, PA	41,258	81,257	100,943
Menomonee Falls, WI	36,386	73,936	88,453

Table continued on next page.

City	Per Capita ($)	Median Household ($)	Average Household ($)
Meridian, ID	26,738	63,225	75,177
Merrimack, NH	39,833	91,429	104,710
Mount Lebanon, PA	49,275	80,914	115,754
Mount Pleasant, SC	42,485	76,202	103,123
Needham, MA	62,497	129,154	173,737
Newtown, CT	48,740	108,667	139,282
Northbrook, IL	58,154	115,085	154,913
Northville, MI	54,794	101,949	139,451
Novi, MI	44,800	80,299	109,602
O'Fallon, IL	36,234	79,795	98,266
O'Fallon, MO	31,809	78,634	88,857
Orchard Park, NY	44,024	81,326	110,581
Oviedo, FL	28,457	82,259	94,851
Parker, CO	36,763	98,170	106,038
Parkland, FL	49,671	126,905	161,017
Peachtree City, GA	38,599	86,352	104,908
Pflugerville, TX	30,514	74,196	86,565
Plainfield, IL	36,007	111,536	119,533
Princeton, NJ	63,193	116,875	187,662
Queen Creek, AZ	30,547	83,809	102,621
Rancho Palos Verdes, CA	57,201	120,697	149,400
Redmond, WA	50,787	99,586	120,434
Richland, WA	36,298	69,372	89,543
Ridgefield, CT	75,716	147,936	212,297
Ridgewood, NJ	68,939	141,315	208,095
Rio Rancho, NM	27,400	59,243	74,099
Sahuarita, AZ	26,856	65,183	76,183
Sammamish, WA	56,662	144,775	174,961
San Ramon, CA	51,569	129,062	149,528
Saratoga, CA	77,667	167,917	219,907
Schertz, TX	30,578	72,463	84,890
Shrewsbury, MA	41,521	97,365	113,750
South Brunswick, NJ	45,645	110,167	130,803
South Jordan, UT	29,964	91,228	105,016
South Kingstown, RI	33,669	72,021	95,139
South Windsor, CT	44,569	94,217	117,942
Southlake, TX	74,380	170,742	232,034
Spring Hill, TN	28,763	76,840	84,968
Stow, OH	32,098	64,073	77,987
Sugar Land, TX	45,611	105,400	138,698
Sun Prairie, WI	30,905	66,956	77,991
Syracuse, UT	26,687	86,158	98,162
Tredyffrin, PA	60,231	112,472	146,396
Upper Arlington, OH	53,970	100,736	136,783
Upper Dublin, PA	53,381	106,869	144,242
Vestavia Hills, AL	51,102	81,352	126,102
Webster, NY	33,760	67,201	84,003
Wellesley, MA	71,733	159,615	237,462
West Fargo, ND	32,129	69,104	81,282
West Linn, OR	41,622	83,933	106,954
West Windsor, NJ	66,221	161,716	191,715
Westlake, OH	46,435	76,250	109,566
Weston, FL	40,452	91,613	124,595
Westport, CT	90,945	151,771	255,021
Wilmette, IL	67,116	126,471	188,450
Woodbury, MN	44,047	98,974	119,421
Yorba Linda, CA	47,852	115,994	144,599
U.S.	28,555	53,482	74,596

Source: U.S. Census Bureau, 2010-2014 American Community Survey 5-Year Estimates

Income: Metro Area

Metro Area	Per Capita ($)	Median Household ($)	Average Household ($)
Aliso Viejo, CA	29,506	60,337	86,928
Allen, TX	29,766	59,175	81,743
Alpharetta, GA	28,880	56,618	78,422
Ankeny, IA	31,342	61,640	79,073
Apex, NC	31,468	62,794	83,004
Ballwin, MO	30,024	54,959	74,420
Beavercreek, OH	26,345	47,162	62,881
Bella Vista, AR	25,291	48,627	67,424
Bernards, NJ	36,078	66,902	97,572
Bethlehem, NY	32,069	61,841	78,155
Bloomfield, MI	28,182	52,305	71,184
Bowie, MD	43,884	91,756	117,989
Bozeman, MT	29,468	54,298	71,625
Brentwood, TN	28,521	52,805	72,921
Broomfield, CO	34,173	64,206	86,081
Carmel, IN	27,778	52,434	71,052
Cedar Park, TX	32,035	61,900	84,202
Cheshire, CT	32,794	61,646	83,146
Chesterfield, MO	30,024	54,959	74,420
Collierville, TN	25,191	47,647	66,395
Coppell, TX	29,766	59,175	81,743
Cornelius, NC	28,403	52,591	73,846
Cranberry, PA	30,272	51,883	70,519
Cupertino, CA	42,176	92,960	123,393
Danville, CA	42,540	80,008	112,073
Draper, UT	26,516	61,529	78,463
Dublin, OH	29,145	55,115	74,004
Eastchester, NY	36,078	66,902	97,572
Eden Prairie, MN	34,593	68,019	88,061
Edmond, OK	26,994	50,967	69,147
Evesham, NJ	32,850	62,169	85,647
Fishers, IN	27,778	52,434	71,052
Flower Mound, TX	29,766	59,175	81,743
Folsom, CA	29,252	59,439	78,856
Foster City, CA	42,540	80,008	112,073
Franklin, TN	28,521	52,805	72,921
Friendswood, TX	29,594	58,689	83,923
Germantown, TN	25,191	47,647	66,395
Glastonbury, CT	35,991	68,959	90,995
Grand Blanc, MI	22,536	41,879	55,656
Guilderland, NY	32,069	61,841	78,155
Hampden, PA	30,404	57,461	74,177
Holly Springs, NC	31,468	62,794	83,004
Huntersville, NC	28,403	52,591	73,846
Independence, KY	29,008	55,204	73,857
Johns Creek, GA	28,880	56,618	78,422
Keller, TX	29,766	59,175	81,743
Kirkland, WA	36,061	68,969	90,467
Lafayette, CO	38,524	69,407	94,871
Lake Oswego, OR	30,560	58,832	77,479
League City, TX	29,594	58,689	83,923
Leawood, KS	30,101	57,056	75,695
Lee's Summit, MO	30,101	57,056	75,695
Leesburg, VA	43,884	91,756	117,989
Lehi, UT	20,927	60,647	75,227
Lenexa, KS	30,101	57,056	75,695
Lexington, MA	39,572	74,494	101,462
Los Altos, CA	42,176	92,960	123,393
Lower Makefield, PA	32,850	62,169	85,647
Madison, AL	30,960	55,881	77,454
Mamaroneck, NY	36,078	66,902	97,572
Manheim, PA	26,892	57,120	71,532
Manlius, NY	27,741	53,191	69,201
Maple Grove, MN	34,593	68,019	88,061
Marion, IA	30,337	59,000	73,992
Marlboro, NJ	36,078	66,902	97,572
Mason, OH	29,008	55,204	73,857
McCandless, PA	30,272	51,883	70,519
Menomonee Falls, WI	29,733	53,628	73,078

Table continued on next page.

Metro Area	Per Capita ($)	Median Household ($)	Average Household ($)
Meridian, ID	24,715	50,776	66,347
Merrimack, NH	34,767	70,906	89,012
Mount Lebanon, PA	30,272	51,883	70,519
Mount Pleasant, SC	28,033	52,517	70,756
Needham, MA	39,572	74,494	101,462
Newtown, CT	49,688	83,163	135,743
Northbrook, IL	31,488	61,497	84,504
Northville, MI	28,182	52,305	71,184
Novi, MI	28,182	52,305	71,184
O'Fallon, IL	30,024	54,959	74,420
O'Fallon, MO	30,024	54,959	74,420
Orchard Park, NY	28,171	50,726	66,507
Oviedo, FL	24,876	48,559	66,823
Parker, CO	34,173	64,206	86,081
Parkland, FL	27,240	48,435	72,352
Peachtree City, GA	28,880	56,618	78,422
Pflugerville, TX	32,035	61,900	84,202
Plainfield, IL	31,488	61,497	84,504
Princeton, NJ	38,076	74,118	104,437
Queen Creek, AZ	26,893	53,310	72,307
Rancho Palos Verdes, CA	29,506	60,337	86,928
Redmond, WA	36,061	68,969	90,467
Richland, WA	26,182	59,476	74,453
Ridgefield, CT	49,688	83,163	135,743
Ridgewood, NJ	36,078	66,902	97,572
Rio Rancho, NM	26,144	48,875	65,948
Sahuarita, AZ	25,524	46,233	63,627
Sammamish, WA	36,061	68,969	90,467
San Ramon, CA	42,540	80,008	112,073
Saratoga, CA	42,176	92,960	123,393
Schertz, TX	25,298	52,786	70,400
Shrewsbury, MA	31,558	64,629	82,290
South Brunswick, NJ	36,078	66,902	97,572
South Jordan, UT	26,516	61,529	78,463
South Kingstown, RI	30,218	56,267	75,674
South Windsor, CT	35,991	68,959	90,995
Southlake, TX	29,766	59,175	81,743
Spring Hill, TN	28,521	52,805	72,921
Stow, OH	27,823	50,776	67,560
Sugar Land, TX	29,594	58,689	83,923
Sun Prairie, WI	32,778	61,227	78,465
Syracuse, UT	24,890	63,393	76,587
Tredyffrin, PA	32,850	62,169	85,647
Upper Arlington, OH	29,145	55,115	74,004
Upper Dublin, PA	32,850	62,169	85,647
Vestavia Hills, AL	26,706	48,438	67,422
Webster, NY	28,320	52,717	69,429
Wellesley, MA	39,572	74,494	101,462
West Fargo, ND	29,754	53,634	71,169
West Linn, OR	30,560	58,832	77,479
West Windsor, NJ	38,076	74,118	104,437
Westlake, OH	28,499	49,551	68,050
Weston, FL	27,240	48,435	72,352
Westport, CT	49,688	83,163	135,743
Wilmette, IL	31,488	61,497	84,504
Woodbury, MN	34,593	68,019	88,061
Yorba Linda, CA	29,506	60,337	86,928
U.S.	28,555	53,482	74,596

Note: Figures cover the Metropolitan Statistical Area (MSA)—see Appendix B for areas included
Source: U.S. Census Bureau, 2010-2014 American Community Survey 5-Year Estimates

Household Income Distribution: City

City	Percent of Households Earning							
	Under $15,000	$15,000 -24,999	$25,000 -34,999	$35,000 -49,999	$50,000 -74,999	$75,000 -99,000	$100,000 -149,999	$150,000 and up
Aliso Viejo, CA	4.2	3.2	3.6	7.3	14.2	16.1	23.5	27.9
Allen, TX	3.7	3.3	5.0	8.8	14.3	13.1	23.5	28.3
Alpharetta, GA	5.8	5.6	4.9	8.3	17.5	14.8	19.1	23.9
Ankeny, IA	5.4	5.3	7.4	11.5	20.2	17.6	21.6	10.8
Apex, NC	4.5	3.6	5.6	10.4	16.1	14.9	24.7	20.3
Ballwin, MO	3.8	6.5	8.6	10.9	16.8	14.1	20.2	19.2
Beavercreek, OH	4.3	5.9	6.7	11.7	18.5	15.5	20.0	17.4
Bella Vista, AR	5.2	7.7	9.4	15.4	23.0	15.1	16.3	8.0
Bernards, NJ	3.9	3.2	2.7	6.1	11.6	10.9	18.6	43.1
Bethlehem, NY	3.8	5.0	4.5	9.6	17.5	14.7	22.5	22.5
Bloomfield, MI	5.0	4.4	5.7	7.7	12.2	10.3	18.5	36.1
Bowie, MD	2.9	2.9	4.4	7.5	13.1	14.5	28.2	26.5
Bozeman, MT	14.6	13.5	11.0	13.8	19.3	13.3	8.9	5.5
Brentwood, TN	2.3	2.0	4.1	5.5	9.2	10.7	20.2	46.1
Broomfield, CO	6.8	6.3	7.1	9.3	16.9	15.0	21.0	17.7
Carmel, IN	4.3	4.1	5.1	7.1	12.8	12.0	23.9	30.7
Cedar Park, TX	4.9	6.0	6.0	11.2	18.9	15.8	20.6	16.5
Cheshire, CT	3.2	4.6	4.3	7.3	12.7	13.4	24.0	30.4
Chesterfield, MO	4.7	6.7	5.8	9.0	14.4	12.5	17.9	29.0
Collierville, TN	1.9	4.6	4.2	9.4	12.2	14.0	23.7	29.9
Coppell, TX	3.5	3.3	4.5	7.6	13.8	10.8	24.0	32.4
Cornelius, NC	4.9	6.0	7.0	13.2	14.6	13.4	20.1	20.8
Cranberry, PA	2.7	3.9	4.7	8.1	16.5	14.1	24.3	25.7
Cupertino, CA	5.1	4.5	2.8	5.5	9.3	8.2	18.8	45.7
Danville, CA	3.6	2.8	2.9	5.1	11.4	8.7	19.9	45.7
Draper, UT	3.5	4.7	3.4	8.5	18.9	14.5	24.8	21.7
Dublin, OH	2.7	1.9	2.9	4.3	13.8	14.0	23.9	36.4
Eastchester, NY	4.9	4.9	4.9	8.9	14.8	9.9	16.7	35.0
Eden Prairie, MN	5.0	4.2	5.5	7.6	16.6	13.2	20.0	28.0
Edmond, OK	9.4	7.3	7.1	10.7	17.2	13.1	17.3	17.9
Evesham, NJ	4.3	5.2	6.5	7.0	16.5	14.9	20.4	25.2
Fishers, IN	2.5	3.9	5.4	9.8	17.6	16.3	23.1	21.3
Flower Mound, TX	1.8	2.8	2.7	5.2	12.0	13.3	27.1	35.0
Folsom, CA	5.1	4.0	5.7	7.6	13.3	14.2	25.4	24.7
Foster City, CA	4.0	3.6	3.2	5.2	11.8	13.3	21.9	36.9
Franklin, TN	6.3	7.0	7.8	10.7	14.4	12.6	19.9	21.2
Friendswood, TX	5.9	3.3	5.3	8.5	15.3	13.1	20.1	28.3
Germantown, TN	3.4	3.4	5.1	6.8	15.3	10.3	24.5	31.3
Glastonbury, CT	5.0	4.5	2.9	7.1	13.9	12.7	20.4	33.4
Grand Blanc, MI	8.4	7.1	12.2	15.3	16.3	15.8	14.1	10.8
Guilderland, NY	5.3	5.2	7.5	11.9	17.8	13.5	20.7	18.2
Hampden, PA	3.6	6.7	8.3	9.8	16.5	16.1	20.4	18.5
Holly Springs, NC	4.8	2.7	5.5	7.7	14.5	21.2	26.8	16.8
Huntersville, NC	6.6	4.9	4.4	9.9	17.3	13.4	21.9	21.6
Independence, KY	6.6	6.5	6.5	13.1	25.5	18.5	18.3	5.1
Johns Creek, GA	4.2	4.2	3.9	7.0	15.2	11.9	21.0	32.6
Keller, TX	5.2	4.0	5.6	5.7	11.2	11.2	22.9	34.2
Kirkland, WA	5.8	4.8	5.8	11.4	14.5	12.1	22.4	23.2
Lafayette, CO	6.7	7.8	5.7	14.9	17.4	13.7	16.5	17.2
Lake Oswego, OR	6.7	7.0	7.8	8.3	14.4	13.7	14.5	27.7
League City, TX	3.5	5.2	4.7	9.7	16.2	16.8	22.4	21.4
Leawood, KS	4.1	3.9	4.9	6.4	9.2	7.9	18.0	45.6
Lee's Summit, MO	6.2	6.7	6.4	10.8	18.0	15.3	21.5	15.3
Leesburg, VA	2.1	4.6	4.2	10.6	14.6	13.1	22.2	28.7
Lehi, UT	4.4	4.8	6.4	10.4	24.6	19.8	21.1	8.6
Lenexa, KS	5.0	7.4	7.3	12.2	17.8	14.6	20.0	15.7
Lexington, MA	5.4	3.8	4.4	5.5	7.1	9.0	18.1	46.6
Los Altos, CA	4.0	3.4	3.5	6.4	7.9	7.8	15.0	51.9
Lower Makefield, PA	3.5	2.6	3.5	5.6	10.0	12.2	23.3	39.4
Madison, AL	3.7	5.6	7.6	10.5	16.1	10.0	23.0	23.5
Mamaroneck, NY	6.4	4.5	5.6	6.0	12.5	8.5	15.0	41.4
Manheim, PA	6.2	7.3	7.8	15.1	17.6	13.5	16.1	16.5
Manlius, NY	6.6	6.9	6.8	11.4	18.0	12.1	19.1	19.2
Maple Grove, MN	4.3	4.2	5.1	7.8	17.1	15.0	24.0	22.6
Marion, IA	7.5	10.2	9.1	13.3	19.1	16.4	16.0	8.3
Marlboro, NJ	2.7	4.1	3.7	5.2	8.8	10.9	19.8	44.8
Mason, OH	4.4	4.8	7.7	9.2	18.0	14.8	19.0	22.0

Table continued on next page.

City	Percent of Households Earning							
	Under $15,000	$15,000 -24,999	$25,000 -34,999	$35,000 -49,999	$50,000 -74,999	$75,000 -99,000	$100,000 -149,999	$150,000 and up
McCandless, PA	6.0	7.9	7.0	10.3	16.0	13.1	21.9	17.9
Menomonee Falls, WI	5.8	8.7	8.6	11.4	16.2	16.6	18.6	14.2
Meridian, ID	6.3	7.2	9.5	14.3	24.9	15.3	13.6	8.8
Merrimack, NH	3.4	3.8	4.4	8.8	17.2	17.6	25.2	19.5
Mount Lebanon, PA	7.7	8.0	7.7	9.1	15.1	11.3	19.5	21.4
Mount Pleasant, SC	6.1	6.8	6.7	10.6	19.2	12.5	17.7	20.4
Needham, MA	6.3	2.7	2.5	5.8	10.2	11.7	17.1	43.8
Newtown, CT	4.2	4.9	5.8	7.4	9.2	15.0	18.3	35.2
Northbrook, IL	4.5	6.4	6.3	7.2	10.0	9.1	18.8	37.7
Northville, MI	4.9	6.7	5.7	7.6	13.4	11.3	17.2	33.2
Novi, MI	6.0	5.5	7.2	10.8	17.7	11.9	17.6	23.3
O'Fallon, IL	7.0	8.8	6.0	8.4	17.1	11.4	23.4	17.9
O'Fallon, MO	4.4	6.1	6.9	11.7	18.2	17.2	22.3	13.2
Orchard Park, NY	3.3	7.0	8.7	10.8	17.0	13.2	21.6	18.4
Oviedo, FL	5.1	4.0	5.6	11.8	19.0	15.4	22.3	16.8
Parker, CO	4.4	3.6	4.8	8.3	15.7	14.3	27.9	20.9
Parkland, FL	3.2	3.7	3.6	6.0	10.7	12.5	19.4	41.1
Peachtree City, GA	6.0	4.4	5.6	9.8	17.2	14.4	20.8	21.8
Pflugerville, TX	7.3	6.2	4.9	9.6	22.3	16.1	20.5	13.1
Plainfield, IL	2.6	3.1	1.6	7.4	15.9	13.2	27.1	29.1
Princeton, NJ	5.4	3.9	7.0	6.2	11.2	9.8	15.0	41.3
Queen Creek, AZ	4.9	3.9	7.6	9.8	16.3	15.9	23.9	17.7
Rancho Palos Verdes, CA	4.2	4.4	4.6	5.9	13.3	9.6	18.4	39.7
Redmond, WA	6.7	4.2	4.8	7.6	14.7	12.4	21.9	27.8
Richland, WA	8.4	8.5	7.4	12.4	16.1	14.1	18.4	14.8
Ridgefield, CT	4.9	4.0	2.9	5.7	9.0	9.2	14.7	49.4
Ridgewood, NJ	3.4	2.9	3.7	7.0	7.5	9.1	18.9	47.4
Rio Rancho, NM	8.2	8.7	8.8	16.3	21.1	13.4	14.0	9.6
Sahuarita, AZ	3.2	6.2	5.2	14.4	30.1	18.8	14.8	7.3
Sammamish, WA	3.1	1.8	2.2	3.1	7.8	9.4	24.9	47.9
San Ramon, CA	2.3	3.0	4.1	5.8	9.3	10.8	22.5	42.3
Saratoga, CA	3.9	3.2	3.2	4.3	6.8	8.2	13.8	56.8
Schertz, TX	6.4	5.4	5.2	13.0	22.2	14.2	22.1	11.5
Shrewsbury, MA	5.0	4.6	5.8	9.6	12.5	14.2	22.8	25.7
South Brunswick, NJ	3.0	4.4	3.5	6.1	14.2	11.9	25.7	31.1
South Jordan, UT	2.7	2.8	4.1	8.0	19.1	18.7	25.1	19.5
South Kingstown, RI	7.2	7.6	8.5	13.3	15.3	13.0	17.2	18.0
South Windsor, CT	4.0	6.0	4.4	8.3	15.3	14.1	22.8	25.0
Southlake, TX	4.8	2.3	3.6	3.3	6.7	6.4	16.4	56.6
Spring Hill, TN	2.2	5.9	7.2	10.0	22.7	21.4	20.8	9.9
Stow, OH	6.2	7.9	8.0	15.5	20.4	14.8	16.7	10.5
Sugar Land, TX	4.4	3.2	5.4	7.5	13.2	13.0	20.7	32.8
Sun Prairie, WI	6.4	6.4	9.2	13.7	21.0	16.4	16.9	9.9
Syracuse, UT	2.0	2.2	5.3	9.6	20.3	22.2	27.3	11.0
Tredyffrin, PA	4.3	4.9	4.5	6.5	11.6	12.4	20.3	35.5
Upper Arlington, OH	4.5	4.8	5.7	7.9	15.5	11.1	20.6	29.8
Upper Dublin, PA	3.9	4.2	4.2	6.9	12.5	14.4	21.2	32.7
Vestavia Hills, AL	5.6	7.5	8.8	10.5	14.6	10.0	17.3	25.7
Webster, NY	6.8	7.5	10.0	11.2	19.8	15.3	17.7	11.8
Wellesley, MA	3.2	5.8	2.4	3.6	8.6	8.7	14.0	53.9
West Fargo, ND	5.8	7.7	9.4	12.0	21.6	17.1	16.5	9.8
West Linn, OR	6.1	5.0	6.6	10.3	17.2	14.2	18.7	21.9
West Windsor, NJ	3.9	4.4	2.9	5.5	7.7	7.6	15.3	52.6
Westlake, OH	6.2	5.3	7.6	10.9	19.2	13.1	18.5	19.2
Weston, FL	6.1	4.8	6.0	8.7	15.0	12.8	18.8	27.8
Westport, CT	4.9	3.2	3.9	3.9	9.7	10.5	13.4	50.3
Wilmette, IL	4.1	3.4	4.3	6.7	11.6	10.4	16.5	42.9
Woodbury, MN	2.9	5.0	3.9	8.0	16.5	14.3	23.6	25.7
Yorba Linda, CA	3.2	4.2	3.3	7.4	12.3	11.4	22.6	35.7
U.S.	12.5	10.7	10.2	13.5	17.8	12.2	13.0	10.0

Source: U.S. Census Bureau, 2010-2014 American Community Survey 5-Year Estimates

Household Income Distribution: Metro Area

Metro Area	Percent of Households Earning							
	Under $15,000	$15,000 -24,999	$25,000 -34,999	$35,000 -49,999	$50,000 -74,999	$75,000 -99,000	$100,000 -149,999	$150,000 and up
Aliso Viejo, CA	11.3	9.8	9.1	12.2	16.6	12.1	14.5	14.4
Allen, TX	10.0	9.3	9.9	13.3	18.2	12.4	14.8	12.2
Alpharetta, GA	11.2	9.5	9.9	13.7	18.3	12.4	13.7	11.3
Ankeny, IA	9.0	8.5	9.4	13.3	19.7	14.3	15.6	10.2
Apex, NC	9.0	8.3	9.4	13.4	17.8	13.2	15.9	12.9
Ballwin, MO	11.7	10.2	10.0	13.6	18.3	12.8	13.7	9.6
Beavercreek, OH	14.4	12.1	11.6	14.4	17.9	11.8	11.2	6.6
Bella Vista, AR	13.0	11.2	11.5	15.4	18.4	10.6	11.8	8.0
Bernards, NJ	11.8	8.8	8.0	10.6	15.3	11.9	15.7	18.0
Bethlehem, NY	10.3	9.0	8.8	12.4	18.7	13.8	16.6	10.4
Bloomfield, MI	13.7	10.8	10.1	13.4	17.5	12.2	13.1	9.2
Bowie, MD	6.3	5.0	5.4	8.9	15.3	13.1	20.1	25.9
Bozeman, MT	11.1	10.2	10.9	14.0	19.9	13.9	12.3	7.8
Brentwood, TN	11.3	10.5	10.4	15.0	19.0	12.5	12.3	8.9
Broomfield, CO	9.4	8.2	8.9	12.6	18.0	13.5	16.0	13.4
Carmel, IN	11.7	10.5	10.7	14.6	18.6	12.6	12.9	8.3
Cedar Park, TX	10.1	8.6	8.8	13.2	18.1	13.0	15.3	12.8
Cheshire, CT	11.7	9.4	8.6	11.8	16.6	12.7	15.6	13.7
Chesterfield, MO	11.7	10.2	10.0	13.6	18.3	12.8	13.7	9.6
Collierville, TN	14.9	12.1	11.1	13.8	17.7	11.2	11.7	7.6
Coppell, TX	10.0	9.3	9.9	13.3	18.2	12.4	14.8	12.2
Cornelius, NC	12.1	10.5	10.5	14.5	18.3	12.2	12.3	9.6
Cranberry, PA	12.7	11.5	10.8	13.3	18.3	12.4	12.6	8.4
Cupertino, CA	6.9	6.1	6.1	8.8	13.4	11.8	18.6	28.2
Danville, CA	9.2	7.2	6.7	9.6	14.8	11.8	17.5	23.3
Draper, UT	8.7	8.7	9.0	13.2	21.0	14.9	14.9	9.6
Dublin, OH	11.9	9.9	9.9	13.8	18.4	12.7	13.7	9.6
Eastchester, NY	11.8	8.8	8.0	10.6	15.3	11.9	15.7	18.0
Eden Prairie, MN	8.6	7.8	8.1	12.0	18.2	14.5	17.5	13.4
Edmond, OK	12.4	10.9	11.3	14.4	18.9	12.1	12.2	7.8
Evesham, NJ	11.7	8.9	8.8	11.9	16.6	12.4	15.6	14.1
Fishers, IN	11.7	10.5	10.7	14.6	18.6	12.6	12.9	8.3
Flower Mound, TX	10.0	9.3	9.9	13.3	18.2	12.4	14.8	12.2
Folsom, CA	11.2	9.4	9.3	12.9	17.6	12.7	15.1	11.9
Foster City, CA	9.2	7.2	6.7	9.6	14.8	11.8	17.5	23.3
Franklin, TN	11.3	10.5	10.4	15.0	19.0	12.5	12.3	8.9
Friendswood, TX	10.7	9.9	9.8	12.8	17.2	12.0	14.1	13.5
Germantown, TN	14.9	12.1	11.1	13.8	17.7	11.2	11.7	7.6
Glastonbury, CT	9.6	8.6	7.8	10.8	16.8	13.5	17.3	15.6
Grand Blanc, MI	17.0	12.8	12.5	15.3	18.2	10.6	9.2	4.5
Guilderland, NY	10.3	9.0	8.8	12.4	18.7	13.8	16.6	10.4
Hampden, PA	9.3	9.4	9.9	14.3	20.1	14.0	14.2	8.6
Holly Springs, NC	9.0	8.3	9.4	13.4	17.8	13.2	15.9	12.9
Huntersville, NC	12.1	10.5	10.5	14.5	18.3	12.2	12.3	9.6
Independence, KY	12.5	10.2	9.7	13.2	18.5	12.6	13.5	9.8
Johns Creek, GA	11.2	9.5	9.9	13.7	18.3	12.4	13.7	11.3
Keller, TX	10.0	9.3	9.9	13.3	18.2	12.4	14.8	12.2
Kirkland, WA	8.9	7.4	7.9	12.0	17.7	13.6	17.4	15.0
Lafayette, CO	10.2	8.3	8.0	11.3	15.5	12.0	16.7	18.0
Lake Oswego, OR	10.5	9.1	9.4	13.5	18.7	13.7	14.8	10.1
League City, TX	10.7	9.9	9.8	12.8	17.2	12.0	14.1	13.5
Leawood, KS	10.9	9.5	9.9	13.7	18.6	13.4	14.4	9.6
Lee's Summit, MO	10.9	9.5	9.9	13.7	18.6	13.4	14.4	9.6
Leesburg, VA	6.3	5.0	5.4	8.9	15.3	13.1	20.1	25.9
Lehi, UT	8.5	8.7	8.9	14.1	21.6	15.3	14.8	8.0
Lenexa, KS	10.9	9.5	9.9	13.7	18.6	13.4	14.4	9.6
Lexington, MA	10.2	7.7	7.1	9.9	15.4	12.7	17.7	19.3
Los Altos, CA	6.9	6.1	6.1	8.8	13.4	11.8	18.6	28.2
Lower Makefield, PA	11.7	8.9	8.8	11.9	16.6	12.4	15.6	14.1
Madison, AL	12.2	9.6	10.2	13.2	16.5	11.8	15.3	11.1
Mamaroneck, NY	11.8	8.8	8.0	10.6	15.3	11.9	15.7	18.0
Manheim, PA	9.0	9.6	10.4	14.5	21.0	14.3	13.6	7.7
Manlius, NY	13.1	10.4	10.2	13.6	18.7	12.8	13.3	7.9
Maple Grove, MN	8.6	7.8	8.1	12.0	18.2	14.5	17.5	13.4
Marion, IA	9.3	9.5	9.7	13.3	20.1	15.2	14.8	8.2
Marlboro, NJ	11.8	8.8	8.0	10.6	15.3	11.9	15.7	18.0
Mason, OH	12.5	10.2	9.7	13.2	18.5	12.6	13.5	9.8

Table continued on next page.

Metro Area	Percent of Households Earning							
	Under $15,000	$15,000 -24,999	$25,000 -34,999	$35,000 -49,999	$50,000 -74,999	$75,000 -99,000	$100,000 -149,999	$150,000 and up
McCandless, PA	12.7	11.5	10.8	13.3	18.3	12.4	12.6	8.4
Menomonee Falls, WI	12.3	11.1	10.3	13.2	17.6	12.7	13.7	9.1
Meridian, ID	11.6	10.8	11.4	15.3	20.3	12.5	11.1	6.9
Merrimack, NH	7.5	8.0	8.0	11.2	17.9	14.4	18.8	14.4
Mount Lebanon, PA	12.7	11.5	10.8	13.3	18.3	12.4	12.6	8.4
Mount Pleasant, SC	12.8	10.4	10.3	14.0	18.9	12.5	12.6	8.4
Needham, MA	10.2	7.7	7.1	9.9	15.4	12.7	17.7	19.3
Newtown, CT	8.3	7.1	6.9	9.4	13.9	11.6	16.0	26.7
Northbrook, IL	11.1	9.3	8.9	12.2	17.4	13.0	15.1	13.1
Northville, MI	13.7	10.8	10.1	13.4	17.5	12.2	13.1	9.2
Novi, MI	13.7	10.8	10.1	13.4	17.5	12.2	13.1	9.2
O'Fallon, IL	11.7	10.2	10.0	13.6	18.3	12.8	13.7	9.6
O'Fallon, MO	11.7	10.2	10.0	13.6	18.3	12.8	13.7	9.6
Orchard Park, NY	13.8	11.6	10.6	13.4	18.4	12.3	12.8	7.1
Oviedo, FL	12.0	11.7	12.1	15.5	19.1	11.2	11.0	7.3
Parker, CO	9.4	8.2	8.9	12.6	18.0	13.5	16.0	13.4
Parkland, FL	14.3	11.9	10.9	14.1	16.9	10.9	11.4	9.5
Peachtree City, GA	11.2	9.5	9.9	13.7	18.3	12.4	13.7	11.3
Pflugerville, TX	10.1	8.6	8.8	13.2	18.1	13.0	15.3	12.8
Plainfield, IL	11.1	9.3	8.9	12.2	17.4	13.0	15.1	13.1
Princeton, NJ	9.8	7.6	7.2	10.0	15.9	12.5	16.7	20.4
Queen Creek, AZ	11.4	10.3	10.6	14.6	18.7	12.4	13.2	8.9
Rancho Palos Verdes, CA	11.3	9.8	9.1	12.2	16.6	12.1	14.5	14.4
Redmond, WA	8.9	7.4	7.9	12.0	17.7	13.6	17.4	15.0
Richland, WA	10.1	10.2	8.6	13.4	19.2	14.4	15.0	9.1
Ridgefield, CT	8.3	7.1	6.9	9.4	13.9	11.6	16.0	26.7
Ridgewood, NJ	11.8	8.8	8.0	10.6	15.3	11.9	15.7	18.0
Rio Rancho, NM	14.2	11.8	11.0	13.9	17.7	11.8	11.9	7.7
Sahuarita, AZ	14.8	12.1	11.7	14.8	17.7	11.3	11.0	6.6
Sammamish, WA	8.9	7.4	7.9	12.0	17.7	13.6	17.4	15.0
San Ramon, CA	9.2	7.2	6.7	9.6	14.8	11.8	17.5	23.3
Saratoga, CA	6.9	6.1	6.1	8.8	13.4	11.8	18.6	28.2
Schertz, TX	12.4	10.4	10.5	14.0	18.7	12.4	13.0	8.5
Shrewsbury, MA	10.7	9.3	8.5	11.3	16.8	13.7	16.8	12.9
South Brunswick, NJ	11.8	8.8	8.0	10.6	15.3	11.9	15.7	18.0
South Jordan, UT	8.7	8.7	9.0	13.2	21.0	14.9	14.9	9.6
South Kingstown, RI	13.5	10.2	9.2	12.2	16.9	12.7	14.6	10.7
South Windsor, CT	9.6	8.6	7.8	10.8	16.8	13.5	17.3	15.6
Southlake, TX	10.0	9.3	9.9	13.3	18.2	12.4	14.8	12.2
Spring Hill, TN	11.3	10.5	10.4	15.0	19.0	12.5	12.3	8.9
Stow, OH	13.4	10.9	10.6	14.4	18.9	12.3	11.9	7.6
Sugar Land, TX	10.7	9.9	9.8	12.8	17.2	12.0	14.1	13.5
Sun Prairie, WI	9.8	8.4	9.6	13.2	18.9	14.3	15.7	10.2
Syracuse, UT	7.6	7.4	8.8	13.8	22.2	16.0	16.0	8.3
Tredyffrin, PA	11.7	8.9	8.8	11.9	16.6	12.4	15.6	14.1
Upper Arlington, OH	11.9	9.9	9.9	13.8	18.4	12.7	13.7	9.6
Upper Dublin, PA	11.7	8.9	8.8	11.9	16.6	12.4	15.6	14.1
Vestavia Hills, AL	14.4	11.8	11.1	13.9	17.6	11.6	11.7	7.9
Webster, NY	12.1	10.9	10.8	13.8	18.5	13.0	13.2	7.7
Wellesley, MA	10.2	7.7	7.1	9.9	15.4	12.7	17.7	19.3
West Fargo, ND	11.0	10.3	11.6	14.1	19.3	13.1	12.7	7.9
West Linn, OR	10.5	9.1	9.4	13.5	18.7	13.7	14.8	10.1
West Windsor, NJ	9.8	7.6	7.2	10.0	15.9	12.5	16.7	20.4
Westlake, OH	14.5	11.4	10.6	13.8	17.8	11.9	12.1	7.9
Weston, FL	14.3	11.9	10.9	14.1	16.9	10.9	11.4	9.5
Westport, CT	8.3	7.1	6.9	9.4	13.9	11.6	16.0	26.7
Wilmette, IL	11.1	9.3	8.9	12.2	17.4	13.0	15.1	13.1
Woodbury, MN	8.6	7.8	8.1	12.0	18.2	14.5	17.5	13.4
Yorba Linda, CA	11.3	9.8	9.1	12.2	16.6	12.1	14.5	14.4
U.S.	12.5	10.7	10.2	13.5	17.8	12.2	13.0	10.0

Note: Figures cover the Metropolitan Statistical Area (MSA)—see Appendix B for areas included
Source: Source: U.S. Census Bureau, 2010-2014 American Community Survey 5-Year Estimates

Poverty Rate: City

City	All Ages	Under 18 Years Old	18 to 64 Years Old	65 Years and Over
Aliso Viejo, CA	5.2	5.6	4.7	8.8
Allen, TX	5.9	7.5	5.4	2.7
Alpharetta, GA	5.1	6.6	4.3	6.3
Ankeny, IA	6.5	6.3	7.2	2.1
Apex, NC	2.9	2.8	3.0	3.0
Ballwin, MO	3.5	2.3	4.4	2.0
Beavercreek, OH	5.3	3.8	6.0	4.2
Bella Vista, AR	4.3	2.5	5.9	2.9
Bernards, NJ	3.7	3.7	3.1	6.7
Bethlehem, NY	3.9	2.6	4.0	5.8
Bloomfield, MI	6.0	6.0	6.0	6.1
Bowie, MD	3.3	2.8	3.6	3.1
Bozeman, MT	21.0	10.8	24.9	6.0
Brentwood, TN	2.9	3.1	2.8	2.5
Broomfield, CO	6.3	6.9	6.3	5.4
Carmel, IN	3.6	4.1	3.7	2.3
Cedar Park, TX	6.0	7.4	5.6	4.4
Cheshire, CT	2.1	1.0	2.0	4.4
Chesterfield, MO	4.8	5.9	5.0	3.3
Collierville, TN	3.8	5.6	3.3	2.1
Coppell, TX	4.2	5.2	4.0	2.7
Cornelius, NC	7.1	7.9	7.7	2.4
Cranberry, PA	2.2	2.6	1.9	3.6
Cupertino, CA	4.1	2.2	4.2	7.2
Danville, CA	4.2	4.4	3.6	5.9
Draper, UT	5.1	6.1	4.9	1.2
Dublin, OH	2.7	3.6	1.9	4.9
Eastchester, NY	3.6	3.7	3.7	3.3
Eden Prairie, MN	5.2	6.7	4.5	5.7
Edmond, OK	10.4	10.1	11.3	6.0
Evesham, NJ	4.2	5.3	3.5	5.1
Fishers, IN	3.3	3.4	3.3	2.4
Flower Mound, TX	3.1	3.6	2.9	3.2
Folsom, CA	4.4	3.1	4.3	8.1
Foster City, CA	3.9	3.8	3.5	5.7
Franklin, TN	7.3	10.7	6.1	5.6
Friendswood, TX	5.2	5.7	4.9	5.7
Germantown, TN	4.1	5.2	4.0	2.8
Glastonbury, CT	3.7	2.7	3.7	5.4
Grand Blanc, MI	10.4	11.5	11.4	3.9
Guilderland, NY	5.9	6.1	6.3	4.0
Hampden, PA	3.0	4.2	2.8	2.1
Holly Springs, NC	2.2	0.5	2.9	4.7
Huntersville, NC	5.7	5.9	5.7	5.0
Independence, KY	9.4	15.2	7.0	3.9
Johns Creek, GA	4.6	4.5	4.4	6.3
Keller, TX	4.2	5.0	3.9	4.0
Kirkland, WA	6.4	5.4	6.8	5.5
Lafayette, CO	9.2	15.8	7.6	5.1
Lake Oswego, OR	7.6	10.2	7.3	5.3
League City, TX	4.9	6.3	4.6	2.3
Leawood, KS	3.3	2.9	3.2	4.5
Lee's Summit, MO	6.6	9.6	5.7	3.9
Leesburg, VA	5.2	5.8	4.8	6.1
Lehi, UT	6.5	7.8	5.7	2.1
Lenexa, KS	7.6	10.6	6.9	5.2
Lexington, MA	4.4	3.4	4.4	5.5
Los Altos, CA	2.7	1.4	2.8	3.8
Lower Makefield, PA	2.5	2.1	2.9	1.6
Madison, AL	6.6	9.1	5.9	4.3
Mamaroneck, NY	7.0	6.1	7.9	5.4
Manheim, PA	5.3	8.2	5.4	1.9
Manlius, NY	5.3	5.8	5.3	5.0
Maple Grove, MN	5.1	8.4	3.5	6.9
Marion, IA	6.3	6.4	6.4	5.2
Marlboro, NJ	1.4	0.9	1.6	1.9
Mason, OH	3.2	2.0	3.0	7.0
McCandless, PA	5.0	3.4	4.5	8.4

Table continued on next page.

City	All Ages	Under 18 Years Old	18 to 64 Years Old	65 Years and Over
Menomonee Falls, WI	4.2	4.1	3.1	7.7
Meridian, ID	8.6	9.6	8.3	6.9
Merrimack, NH	3.8	4.9	3.3	4.7
Mount Lebanon, PA	5.6	6.4	5.2	5.6
Mount Pleasant, SC	8.0	8.8	8.3	5.4
Needham, MA	3.2	2.5	2.4	6.7
Newtown, CT	5.2	5.3	5.5	3.6
Northbrook, IL	3.7	3.7	3.4	4.4
Northville, MI	3.1	1.9	3.1	4.8
Novi, MI	6.4	8.5	6.1	4.3
O'Fallon, IL	7.9	9.7	7.6	4.9
O'Fallon, MO	4.9	5.5	4.5	5.4
Orchard Park, NY	2.4	2.6	2.6	1.3
Oviedo, FL	6.5	6.0	6.7	6.8
Parker, CO	4.2	4.9	3.5	7.9
Parkland, FL	4.3	5.4	3.4	6.5
Peachtree City, GA	7.7	11.1	6.8	5.1
Pflugerville, TX	10.4	15.2	8.8	4.5
Plainfield, IL	4.2	6.2	3.1	4.5
Princeton, NJ	5.7	3.6	6.1	7.2
Queen Creek, AZ	8.6	11.6	6.7	5.8
Rancho Palos Verdes, CA	4.4	4.8	4.3	4.1
Redmond, WA	7.6	7.9	7.1	10.2
Richland, WA	9.7	14.3	8.8	6.2
Ridgefield, CT	3.1	2.8	2.9	4.8
Ridgewood, NJ	4.5	4.4	4.7	3.6
Rio Rancho, NM	11.3	13.7	11.0	8.0
Sahuarita, AZ	6.3	10.3	5.0	2.7
Sammamish, WA	2.9	3.5	2.2	6.2
San Ramon, CA	3.6	3.5	3.6	4.3
Saratoga, CA	3.6	4.3	3.2	3.7
Schertz, TX	7.3	11.6	6.5	2.2
Shrewsbury, MA	5.0	4.7	4.7	6.9
South Brunswick, NJ	2.8	3.6	2.7	2.0
South Jordan, UT	4.1	3.5	4.7	2.8
South Kingstown, RI	8.7	8.1	10.5	3.6
South Windsor, CT	4.0	4.6	3.3	5.7
Southlake, TX	3.2	2.4	3.2	6.5
Spring Hill, TN	4.1	5.8	3.2	4.5
Stow, OH	6.3	7.1	6.2	5.4
Sugar Land, TX	5.1	5.7	5.1	3.8
Sun Prairie, WI	9.0	13.6	7.4	6.6
Syracuse, UT	2.4	3.3	2.0	0.7
Tredyffrin, PA	4.2	5.1	4.1	3.5
Upper Arlington, OH	4.8	6.6	4.6	2.8
Upper Dublin, PA	2.9	4.3	1.9	4.3
Vestavia Hills, AL	4.6	3.8	5.6	2.3
Webster, NY	6.9	9.5	6.6	4.3
Wellesley, MA	3.5	3.2	3.8	2.8
West Fargo, ND	8.7	12.7	6.9	10.1
West Linn, OR	5.5	6.0	5.7	3.8
West Windsor, NJ	4.6	5.2	4.1	5.3
Westlake, OH	4.7	4.9	4.1	6.4
Weston, FL	7.8	8.1	7.4	9.5
Westport, CT	4.3	3.3	4.8	4.1
Wilmette, IL	3.0	2.2	2.7	5.6
Woodbury, MN	3.5	3.1	3.4	5.0
Yorba Linda, CA	3.0	3.2	2.8	4.0
U.S.	15.6	21.9	14.6	9.4

Note: Figures are percentage of people whose income during the past 12 months was below the poverty level;
Source: U.S. Census Bureau, 2010-2014 American Community Survey 5-Year Estimates

Poverty Rate: Metro Area

Metro Area	All Ages	Under 18 Years Old	18 to 64 Years Old	65 Years and Over
Aliso Viejo, CA	17.1	24.0	15.4	12.2
Allen, TX	14.8	21.4	12.9	8.7
Alpharetta, GA	15.7	22.2	14.0	9.6
Ankeny, IA	11.2	15.2	10.4	6.6
Apex, NC	12.3	16.5	11.3	7.1
Ballwin, MO	13.2	18.9	12.3	7.5
Beavercreek, OH	16.9	25.8	15.9	8.0
Bella Vista, AR	16.4	21.6	15.7	8.2
Bernards, NJ	14.3	20.0	12.8	11.6
Bethlehem, NY	11.5	16.3	11.0	6.9
Bloomfield, MI	16.9	24.6	15.7	9.1
Bowie, MD	8.4	10.8	7.8	6.8
Bozeman, MT	13.9	11.3	16.2	4.6
Brentwood, TN	14.4	20.7	13.1	8.2
Broomfield, CO	12.0	16.6	11.1	7.5
Carmel, IN	14.6	20.8	13.5	7.0
Cedar Park, TX	14.9	19.3	14.4	7.0
Cheshire, CT	12.7	18.4	11.8	7.9
Chesterfield, MO	13.2	18.9	12.3	7.5
Collierville, TN	19.4	29.0	16.9	10.8
Coppell, TX	14.8	21.4	12.9	8.7
Cornelius, NC	15.3	21.2	14.1	9.0
Cranberry, PA	12.3	17.3	11.9	8.0
Cupertino, CA	10.0	11.9	9.5	8.7
Danville, CA	11.3	13.5	11.1	9.0
Draper, UT	12.7	16.6	11.8	6.7
Dublin, OH	15.1	20.8	14.2	7.4
Eastchester, NY	14.3	20.0	12.8	11.6
Eden Prairie, MN	10.6	13.9	9.9	7.1
Edmond, OK	15.7	21.9	14.8	7.6
Evesham, NJ	13.2	17.8	12.4	8.9
Fishers, IN	14.6	20.8	13.5	7.0
Flower Mound, TX	14.8	21.4	12.9	8.7
Folsom, CA	16.1	21.3	15.6	8.6
Foster City, CA	11.3	13.5	11.1	9.0
Franklin, TN	14.4	20.7	13.1	8.2
Friendswood, TX	16.3	23.7	13.9	10.3
Germantown, TN	19.4	29.0	16.9	10.8
Glastonbury, CT	10.7	14.3	10.3	7.4
Grand Blanc, MI	21.2	32.1	20.3	7.2
Guilderland, NY	11.5	16.3	11.0	6.9
Hampden, PA	11.2	16.3	10.7	5.6
Holly Springs, NC	12.3	16.5	11.3	7.1
Huntersville, NC	15.3	21.2	14.1	9.0
Independence, KY	14.1	19.9	13.2	7.7
Johns Creek, GA	15.7	22.2	14.0	9.6
Keller, TX	14.8	21.4	12.9	8.7
Kirkland, WA	11.7	15.2	11.0	8.4
Lafayette, CO	14.6	14.6	16.0	5.9
Lake Oswego, OR	13.9	18.1	13.5	8.0
League City, TX	16.3	23.7	13.9	10.3
Leawood, KS	12.6	18.0	11.6	6.8
Lee's Summit, MO	12.6	18.0	11.6	6.8
Leesburg, VA	8.4	10.8	7.8	6.8
Lehi, UT	13.8	12.5	15.6	5.2
Lenexa, KS	12.6	18.0	11.6	6.8
Lexington, MA	10.4	12.8	9.9	8.8
Los Altos, CA	10.0	11.9	9.5	8.7
Lower Makefield, PA	13.2	17.8	12.4	8.9
Madison, AL	13.5	18.9	12.6	8.2
Mamaroneck, NY	14.3	20.0	12.8	11.6
Manheim, PA	10.6	15.1	9.7	6.8
Manlius, NY	15.4	22.4	14.6	7.9
Maple Grove, MN	10.6	13.9	9.9	7.1
Marion, IA	9.5	11.2	9.7	5.8
Marlboro, NJ	14.3	20.0	12.8	11.6
Mason, OH	14.1	19.9	13.2	7.7
McCandless, PA	12.3	17.3	11.9	8.0

Table continued on next page.

Metro Area	All Ages	Under 18 Years Old	18 to 64 Years Old	65 Years and Over
Menomonee Falls, WI	15.5	23.4	14.0	8.0
Meridian, ID	15.6	20.1	14.9	8.4
Merrimack, NH	8.6	11.9	8.0	5.9
Mount Lebanon, PA	12.3	17.3	11.9	8.0
Mount Pleasant, SC	15.8	22.6	14.7	8.8
Needham, MA	10.4	12.8	9.9	8.8
Newtown, CT	9.1	11.4	8.7	6.7
Northbrook, IL	14.1	20.3	12.6	9.2
Northville, MI	16.9	24.6	15.7	9.1
Novi, MI	16.9	24.6	15.7	9.1
O'Fallon, IL	13.2	18.9	12.3	7.5
O'Fallon, MO	13.2	18.9	12.3	7.5
Orchard Park, NY	14.5	21.8	13.6	8.5
Oviedo, FL	16.2	23.0	15.1	9.6
Parker, CO	12.0	16.6	11.1	7.5
Parkland, FL	17.3	23.7	15.7	15.0
Peachtree City, GA	15.7	22.2	14.0	9.6
Pflugerville, TX	14.9	19.3	14.4	7.0
Plainfield, IL	14.1	20.3	12.6	9.2
Princeton, NJ	11.7	16.9	10.6	7.6
Queen Creek, AZ	17.1	24.5	16.0	8.0
Rancho Palos Verdes, CA	17.1	24.0	15.4	12.2
Redmond, WA	11.7	15.2	11.0	8.4
Richland, WA	15.6	23.7	13.0	7.9
Ridgefield, CT	9.1	11.4	8.7	6.7
Ridgewood, NJ	14.3	20.0	12.8	11.6
Rio Rancho, NM	18.7	26.2	17.6	10.6
Sahuarita, AZ	19.0	26.7	19.2	8.3
Sammamish, WA	11.7	15.2	11.0	8.4
San Ramon, CA	11.3	13.5	11.1	9.0
Saratoga, CA	10.0	11.9	9.5	8.7
Schertz, TX	16.6	23.7	14.6	10.6
Shrewsbury, MA	11.5	15.5	10.8	8.3
South Brunswick, NJ	14.3	20.0	12.8	11.6
South Jordan, UT	12.7	16.6	11.8	6.7
South Kingstown, RI	13.7	19.1	12.7	9.9
South Windsor, CT	10.7	14.3	10.3	7.4
Southlake, TX	14.8	21.4	12.9	8.7
Spring Hill, TN	14.4	20.7	13.1	8.2
Stow, OH	15.0	21.3	14.6	7.3
Sugar Land, TX	16.3	23.7	13.9	10.3
Sun Prairie, WI	12.6	14.3	13.2	5.6
Syracuse, UT	9.9	12.1	9.4	6.2
Tredyffrin, PA	13.2	17.8	12.4	8.9
Upper Arlington, OH	15.1	20.8	14.2	7.4
Upper Dublin, PA	13.2	17.8	12.4	8.9
Vestavia Hills, AL	16.9	24.9	15.4	9.6
Webster, NY	14.6	21.6	13.9	7.0
Wellesley, MA	10.4	12.8	9.9	8.8
West Fargo, ND	12.7	13.0	13.6	6.9
West Linn, OR	13.9	18.1	13.5	8.0
West Windsor, NJ	11.7	16.9	10.6	7.6
Westlake, OH	15.5	23.2	14.3	9.1
Weston, FL	17.3	23.7	15.7	15.0
Westport, CT	9.1	11.4	8.7	6.7
Wilmette, IL	14.1	20.3	12.6	9.2
Woodbury, MN	10.6	13.9	9.9	7.1
Yorba Linda, CA	17.1	24.0	15.4	12.2
U.S.	15.6	21.9	14.6	9.4

Note: Figures are percentage of people whose income during the past 12 months was below the poverty level; Figures cover the Metropolitan Statistical Area—see Appendix B for areas included
Source: U.S. Census Bureau, 2010-2014 American Community Survey 5-Year Estimates

Employment by Industry

Metro Area[1]	(A)	(B)	(C)	(D)	(E)	(F)	(G)	(H)	(I)	(J)	(K)	(L)	(M)	(N)
Aliso Viejo, CA[2]	6.1	6.0	12.8	7.5	10.2	1.6	13.2	9.9	<0.1	3.0	18.4	10.0	1.7	5.1
Allen, TX[2]	5.2	n/a	11.8	9.1	11.5	2.7	10.0	6.7	n/a	3.3	18.7	10.2	3.7	6.6
Alpharetta, GA	4.2	4.2	12.2	6.1	12.3	3.3	10.4	6.1	<0.1	3.7	18.5	11.3	5.4	6.0
Ankeny, IA	4.9	n/a	13.6	15.9	12.3	1.8	8.3	5.7	n/a	3.9	13.5	11.7	3.0	5.0
Apex, NC	5.7	n/a	11.9	4.9	16.0	3.3	11.1	5.6	n/a	4.0	19.2	11.8	2.1	3.9
Ballwin, MO	4.6	n/a	17.9	6.3	12.0	2.0	10.5	8.3	n/a	3.5	15.3	10.7	3.7	4.6
Beavercreek, OH	3.1	n/a	18.7	4.6	16.4	2.1	9.9	10.5	n/a	3.5	13.1	10.7	3.5	3.4
Bella Vista, AR	4.1	n/a	10.8	2.8	14.1	0.8	10.0	10.9	n/a	2.9	20.0	11.3	6.9	4.9
Bernards, NJ[2]	3.7	n/a	15.1	6.7	14.7	1.9	7.4	6.3	n/a	4.5	18.5	10.4	5.1	5.2
Bethlehem, NY	4.1	n/a	20.2	5.6	22.1	1.8	8.2	5.5	n/a	3.9	11.4	10.7	2.9	3.0
Bloomfield, MI[2]	3.6	n/a	14.4	6.1	8.0	1.6	9.3	12.2	n/a	3.9	21.9	11.7	2.0	4.6
Bowie, MD[2]	4.5	n/a	12.6	4.4	22.5	2.3	9.8	1.3	n/a	6.3	23.0	8.7	2.2	1.9
Bozeman, MT	n/a	n/a	n/a	n/a	n/a	n/a	n/a	n/a	n/a	n/a	n/a	n/a	n/a	n/a
Brentwood, TN	4.3	n/a	15.4	6.4	12.4	2.2	10.5	8.6	n/a	4.0	16.3	10.4	4.6	4.4
Broomfield, CO	6.7	n/a	12.5	7.4	13.7	3.2	10.8	4.9	n/a	3.8	18.0	9.8	3.7	4.9
Carmel, IN	4.4	4.3	14.4	6.0	12.7	1.5	10.0	8.6	<0.1	4.2	15.9	10.8	6.5	4.4
Cedar Park, TX	6.0	n/a	11.5	5.5	17.6	2.7	11.9	5.7	n/a	4.1	16.9	10.6	1.7	5.2
Cheshire, CT[3]	3.7	n/a	28.2	4.4	12.7	1.2	8.2	8.4	n/a	3.7	10.7	10.9	3.4	3.9
Chesterfield, MO	4.6	n/a	17.9	6.3	12.0	2.0	10.5	8.3	n/a	3.5	15.3	10.7	3.7	4.6
Collierville, TN	3.4	n/a	14.3	4.3	12.5	0.9	10.1	7.0	n/a	3.7	16.0	10.5	11.2	5.6
Coppell, TX[2]	5.2	n/a	11.8	9.1	11.5	2.7	10.0	6.7	n/a	3.3	18.7	10.2	3.7	6.6
Cornelius, NC	5.0	n/a	10.1	7.6	13.5	2.3	10.9	9.2	n/a	3.3	16.7	11.4	4.4	5.0
Cranberry, PA	5.4	4.5	20.7	5.9	10.1	1.5	9.9	7.3	0.9	4.4	15.2	11.2	4.1	3.8
Cupertino, CA	4.1	4.1	15.1	3.3	8.8	7.2	9.0	15.1	<0.1	2.6	20.9	8.6	1.6	3.4
Danville, CA[2]	5.9	5.8	16.2	4.3	15.2	2.0	9.6	7.9	<0.1	3.4	16.4	10.8	3.6	4.3
Draper, UT	5.3	n/a	11.4	8.0	15.3	2.6	8.4	7.9	n/a	2.9	17.1	11.0	4.9	4.5
Dublin, OH	3.4	n/a	14.4	7.6	16.2	1.5	9.6	6.7	n/a	3.9	16.9	10.1	5.2	4.0
Eastchester, NY[2]	3.7	n/a	19.7	8.9	13.3	3.5	9.3	3.0	n/a	4.3	16.1	10.0	3.6	4.1
Eden Prairie, MN	3.6	n/a	16.5	7.6	13.0	2.0	8.9	10.0	n/a	4.1	15.6	9.7	3.5	5.0
Edmond, OK	7.5	4.7	14.3	5.2	20.5	1.2	10.7	5.8	2.8	3.8	12.6	10.9	3.2	3.7
Evesham, NJ[2]	4.1	n/a	17.5	5.4	15.4	1.3	8.2	6.9	n/a	3.4	14.9	13.4	3.6	5.4
Fishers, IN	4.4	4.3	14.4	6.0	12.7	1.5	10.0	8.6	<0.1	4.2	15.9	10.8	6.5	4.4
Flower Mound, TX[2]	5.2	n/a	11.8	9.1	11.5	2.7	10.0	6.7	n/a	3.3	18.7	10.2	3.7	6.6
Folsom, CA	5.6	5.6	15.3	5.5	25.0	1.5	10.1	3.9	<0.1	3.2	12.9	11.0	2.7	2.7
Foster City, CA[2]	3.9	3.9	12.3	6.9	11.7	5.6	12.6	3.2	<0.1	3.7	25.2	8.0	3.9	2.5
Franklin, TN	4.3	n/a	15.4	6.4	12.4	2.2	10.5	8.6	n/a	4.0	16.3	10.4	4.6	4.4
Friendswood, TX	10.5	7.4	12.4	5.0	12.9	1.0	10.2	7.9	3.1	3.5	15.5	10.3	4.7	5.7
Germantown, TN	3.4	n/a	14.3	4.3	12.5	0.9	10.1	7.0	n/a	3.7	16.0	10.5	11.2	5.6
Glastonbury, CT[3]	3.3	n/a	18.4	9.9	15.8	2.0	8.2	9.6	n/a	3.7	12.7	9.9	2.9	3.0
Grand Blanc, MI	3.2	n/a	20.3	4.4	13.7	2.9	10.6	8.5	n/a	3.9	10.9	14.5	2.7	3.9
Guilderland, NY	4.1	n/a	20.2	5.6	22.1	1.8	8.2	5.5	n/a	3.9	11.4	10.7	2.9	3.0
Hampden, PA	3.1	n/a	16.2	6.5	17.5	1.3	8.9	6.2	n/a	4.2	14.1	9.9	8.2	3.6
Holly Springs, NC	5.7	n/a	11.9	4.9	16.0	3.3	11.1	5.6	n/a	4.0	19.2	11.8	2.1	3.9
Huntersville, NC	5.0	n/a	10.1	7.6	13.5	2.3	10.9	9.2	n/a	3.3	16.7	11.4	4.4	5.0
Independence, KY	4.0	n/a	15.4	6.4	12.2	1.2	10.0	10.7	n/a	3.6	15.8	10.5	4.0	5.7
Johns Creek, GA	4.2	4.2	12.2	6.1	12.3	3.3	10.4	6.1	<0.1	3.7	18.5	11.3	5.4	6.0
Keller, TX[2]	7.0	n/a	12.8	5.5	13.4	1.1	11.2	9.3	n/a	3.6	11.1	11.7	7.8	4.9
Kirkland, WA[2]	5.3	5.3	12.7	5.1	13.2	6.0	9.5	10.4	<0.1	3.4	15.1	10.9	3.4	4.4
Lafayette, CO	3.0	n/a	13.1	4.0	20.3	4.3	10.7	9.6	n/a	3.2	17.9	9.4	0.9	3.1
Lake Oswego, OR	4.9	4.8	14.6	5.9	13.5	2.2	10.0	10.8	0.1	3.5	15.3	10.5	3.4	4.9
League City, TX	10.5	7.4	12.4	5.0	12.9	1.0	10.2	7.9	3.1	3.5	15.5	10.3	4.7	5.7
Leawood, KS	4.3	n/a	14.2	7.1	14.0	1.8	9.5	7.2	n/a	3.9	17.4	10.7	4.6	4.8
Lee's Summit, MO	4.3	n/a	14.2	7.1	14.0	1.8	9.5	7.2	n/a	3.9	17.4	10.7	4.6	4.8
Leesburg, VA[2]	4.5	n/a	12.6	4.4	22.5	2.3	9.8	1.3	n/a	6.3	23.0	8.7	2.2	1.9
Lehi, UT	8.4	n/a	21.8	3.2	13.1	4.9	8.0	7.9	n/a	2.1	12.7	13.0	1.4	3.0
Lenexa, KS	4.3	n/a	14.2	7.1	14.0	1.8	9.5	7.2	n/a	3.9	17.4	10.7	4.6	4.8
Lexington, MA[4]	3.6	n/a	22.7	8.5	11.0	3.1	9.4	4.5	n/a	3.8	19.0	8.2	2.4	3.2
Los Altos, CA	4.1	4.1	15.1	3.3	8.8	7.2	9.0	15.1	<0.1	2.6	20.9	8.6	1.6	3.4
Lower Makefield, PA[2]	4.8	n/a	17.3	7.5	8.0	2.0	7.9	8.6	n/a	4.4	18.9	11.9	2.8	5.4
Madison, AL	3.7	n/a	9.0	2.8	21.8	1.1	8.7	10.5	n/a	3.1	23.6	11.3	1.3	2.6
Mamaroneck, NY[2]	3.7	n/a	19.7	8.9	13.3	3.5	9.3	3.0	n/a	4.3	16.1	10.0	3.6	4.1
Manheim, PA	6.3	n/a	17.8	3.5	8.1	1.2	9.2	14.6	n/a	5.6	9.2	12.9	4.6	6.5
Manlius, NY	3.5	n/a	20.1	4.7	17.9	1.3	9.7	7.7	n/a	3.8	9.8	12.0	4.3	4.6
Maple Grove, MN	3.6	n/a	16.5	7.6	13.0	2.0	8.9	10.0	n/a	4.1	15.6	9.7	3.5	5.0
Marion, IA	5.4	n/a	14.1	7.5	11.4	2.9	8.1	14.1	n/a	3.7	9.2	10.8	8.2	3.9
Marlboro, NJ[2]	3.7	n/a	19.7	8.9	13.3	3.5	9.3	3.0	n/a	4.3	16.1	10.0	3.6	4.1
Mason, OH	4.0	n/a	15.4	6.4	12.2	1.2	10.0	10.7	n/a	3.6	15.8	10.5	4.0	5.7
McCandless, PA	5.4	4.5	20.7	5.9	10.1	1.5	9.9	7.3	0.9	4.4	15.2	11.2	4.1	3.8
Menomonee Falls, WI	3.4	3.4	19.2	5.9	10.3	1.6	8.2	14.1	<0.1	5.3	14.5	9.3	3.2	4.6

Table continued on next page.

Metro Area[1]	(A)	(B)	(C)	(D)	(E)	(F)	(G)	(H)	(I)	(J)	(K)	(L)	(M)	(N)
Meridian, ID	6.2	n/a	15.1	5.6	15.6	1.5	9.5	8.6	n/a	3.5	13.9	12.1	3.3	4.6
Merrimack, NH[4]	3.8	n/a	14.2	6.0	10.5	1.4	8.5	15.3	n/a	4.2	11.9	17.0	2.4	4.2
Mount Lebanon, PA	5.4	4.5	20.7	5.9	10.1	1.5	9.9	7.3	0.9	4.4	15.2	11.2	4.1	3.8
Mount Pleasant, SC	5.2	n/a	11.6	4.2	19.3	1.6	12.7	7.7	n/a	4.0	14.5	12.2	4.1	2.4
Needham, MA[4]	3.6	n/a	22.7	8.5	11.0	3.1	9.4	4.5	n/a	3.8	19.0	8.2	2.4	3.2
Newtown, CT[3]	n/a	n/a	n/a	n/a	12.6	n/a	9.1	n/a	n/a	n/a	11.8	17.3	n/a	n/a
Northbrook, IL[2]	3.3	3.3	15.7	6.8	11.6	1.9	9.7	7.6	<0.1	4.3	18.3	10.0	5.1	5.2
Northville, MI[2]	2.5	n/a	18.0	4.6	11.5	1.0	9.9	12.1	n/a	3.9	16.8	9.5	5.5	4.0
Novi, MI[2]	3.6	n/a	14.4	6.1	8.0	1.6	9.3	12.2	n/a	3.9	21.9	11.7	2.0	4.6
O'Fallon, MO	4.6	n/a	17.9	6.3	12.0	2.0	10.5	8.3	n/a	3.5	15.3	10.7	3.7	4.6
O'Fallon, IL	4.6	n/a	17.9	6.3	12.0	2.0	10.5	8.3	n/a	3.5	15.3	10.7	3.7	4.6
Orchard Park, NY	3.6	n/a	17.3	6.1	16.2	1.3	10.0	9.2	n/a	4.2	12.4	11.8	3.3	3.9
Oviedo, FL	5.3	5.3	12.2	6.0	10.2	1.9	20.5	3.6	<0.1	3.5	16.9	12.6	3.1	3.6
Parker, CO	6.7	n/a	12.5	7.4	13.7	3.2	10.8	4.9	n/a	3.8	18.0	9.8	3.7	4.9
Parkland, FL[2]	n/a	5.3	12.7	7.1	12.5	2.3	11.3	3.4	n/a	4.6	17.6	13.7	3.2	5.9
Peachtree City, GA	4.2	4.2	12.2	6.1	12.3	3.3	10.4	6.1	<0.1	3.7	18.5	11.3	5.4	6.0
Pflugerville, TX	6.0	n/a	11.5	5.5	17.6	2.7	11.9	5.7	n/a	4.1	16.9	10.6	1.7	5.2
Plainfield, IL[2]	3.3	3.3	15.7	6.8	11.6	1.9	9.7	7.6	<0.1	4.3	18.3	10.0	5.1	5.2
Princeton, NJ	1.9	n/a	18.4	7.2	26.6	2.0	5.4	2.9	n/a	3.8	17.0	7.8	3.7	2.6
Queen Creek, AZ	5.2	5.1	14.7	8.6	12.0	1.9	10.6	6.1	0.1	3.3	17.2	12.4	3.6	3.9
Rancho Palos Verdes, CA[2]	3.0	2.9	17.5	4.9	13.2	4.7	11.3	8.1	<0.1	3.4	14.0	10.1	4.0	5.2
Redmond, WA[2]	5.3	5.3	12.7	5.1	13.2	6.0	9.5	10.4	<0.1	3.4	15.1	10.9	3.4	4.4
Richland, WA	6.0	n/a	13.8	3.7	17.8	0.7	9.7	6.7	n/a	3.1	19.8	12.4	2.8	3.0
Ridgefield, CT[3]	3.0	n/a	17.3	9.8	11.0	2.9	10.1	7.5	n/a	4.2	15.8	12.0	2.5	3.3
Ridgewood, NJ[2]	3.7	n/a	19.7	8.9	13.3	3.5	9.3	3.0	n/a	4.3	16.1	10.0	3.6	4.1
Rio Rancho, NM	5.2	n/a	16.4	4.6	21.5	2.1	10.5	4.2	n/a	3.0	14.9	11.5	2.6	3.0
Sahuarita, AZ	4.3	3.7	17.1	4.9	21.1	1.2	11.4	6.0	0.5	3.3	13.7	11.7	2.8	2.0
Sammamish, WA[2]	5.3	5.3	12.7	5.1	13.2	6.0	9.5	10.4	<0.1	3.4	15.1	10.9	3.4	4.4
San Ramon, CA[2]	5.9	5.8	16.2	4.3	15.2	2.0	9.6	7.9	<0.1	3.4	16.4	10.8	3.6	4.3
Saratoga, CA	4.1	4.1	15.1	3.3	8.8	7.2	9.0	15.1	<0.1	2.6	20.9	8.6	1.6	3.4
Schertz, TX	5.8	5.1	15.3	8.4	17.1	2.1	12.1	4.7	0.7	3.7	12.5	11.5	2.6	3.5
Shrewsbury, MA[3]	3.6	n/a	23.7	5.4	15.6	1.2	8.1	9.8	n/a	3.7	9.2	10.8	4.5	3.6
South Brunswick, NJ[2]	3.7	n/a	19.7	8.9	13.3	3.5	9.3	3.0	n/a	4.3	16.1	10.0	3.6	4.1
South Jordan, UT	5.3	n/a	11.4	8.0	15.3	2.6	8.4	7.9	n/a	2.9	17.1	11.0	4.9	4.5
South Kingstown, RI[3]	4.0	3.9	21.5	6.1	12.3	1.7	10.9	9.0	<0.1	4.7	12.0	11.4	2.6	3.4
South Windsor, CT[3]	3.3	n/a	18.4	9.9	15.8	2.0	8.2	9.6	n/a	3.7	12.7	9.9	2.9	3.0
Southlake, TX[2]	7.0	n/a	12.8	5.5	13.4	1.1	11.2	9.3	n/a	3.6	11.1	11.7	7.8	4.9
Spring Hill, TN	4.3	n/a	15.4	6.4	12.4	2.2	10.5	8.6	n/a	4.0	16.3	10.4	4.6	4.4
Stow, OH	3.5	n/a	16.1	4.0	14.1	1.2	9.9	11.6	n/a	4.2	15.0	11.4	3.0	5.4
Sugar Land, TX	10.5	7.4	12.4	5.0	12.9	1.0	10.2	7.9	3.1	3.5	15.5	10.3	4.7	5.7
Sun Prairie, WI	3.9	n/a	11.7	5.9	22.4	4.2	8.6	8.5	n/a	5.0	12.5	10.7	2.4	3.7
Syracuse, UT	7.1	n/a	12.6	4.0	20.5	0.8	9.0	13.0	n/a	2.6	11.6	12.1	3.4	2.8
Tredyffrin, PA[2]	4.8	n/a	17.3	7.5	8.0	2.0	7.9	8.6	n/a	4.4	18.9	11.9	2.8	5.4
Upper Arlington, OH	3.4	n/a	14.4	7.6	16.2	1.5	9.6	6.7	n/a	3.9	16.9	10.1	5.2	4.0
Upper Dublin, PA[2]	4.8	n/a	17.3	7.5	8.0	2.0	7.9	8.6	n/a	4.4	18.9	11.9	2.8	5.4
Vestavia Hills, AL	5.5	5.0	13.6	8.1	15.8	1.5	9.2	7.1	0.5	4.5	12.4	11.8	4.4	5.5
Webster, NY	3.6	3.5	23.7	3.9	15.3	1.7	8.2	11.1	0.1	4.0	12.4	10.5	2.0	3.2
Wellesley, MA[4]	3.6	n/a	22.7	8.5	11.0	3.1	9.4	4.5	n/a	3.8	19.0	8.2	2.4	3.2
West Fargo, ND	6.2	n/a	15.8	7.6	13.1	2.1	10.1	7.0	n/a	3.6	11.7	12.0	3.8	6.4
West Linn, OR	4.9	4.8	14.6	5.9	13.5	2.2	10.0	10.8	0.1	3.5	15.3	10.5	3.4	4.9
West Windsor, NJ	1.9	n/a	18.4	7.2	26.6	2.0	5.4	2.9	n/a	3.8	17.0	7.8	3.7	2.6
Westlake, OH	3.2	n/a	19.2	6.1	12.9	1.3	9.6	11.7	n/a	3.8	14.0	9.9	2.9	4.9
Weston, FL[2]	n/a	5.3	12.7	7.1	12.5	2.3	11.3	3.4	n/a	4.6	17.6	13.7	3.2	5.9
Westport, CT[3]	3.0	n/a	17.3	9.8	11.0	2.9	10.1	7.5	n/a	4.2	15.8	12.0	2.5	3.3
Wilmette, IL[2]	3.3	3.3	15.7	6.8	11.6	1.9	9.7	7.6	<0.1	4.3	18.3	10.0	5.1	5.2
Woodbury, MN	3.6	n/a	16.5	7.6	13.0	2.0	8.9	10.0	n/a	4.1	15.6	9.7	3.5	5.0
Yorba Linda, CA[2]	6.1	6.0	12.8	7.5	10.2	1.6	13.2	9.9	<0.1	3.0	18.4	10.0	1.7	5.1
U.S.	5.0	4.5	15.7	5.7	15.5	1.9	10.4	8.6	0.5	3.9	13.9	11.3	3.9	4.1

Note: All figures are percentages covering non-farm employment as of December 2015 and are not seasonally adjusted; (1) Figures cover the Metropolitan Statistical Area (MSA) except where noted. See Appendix B for areas included; (2) Metropolitan Division; (3) New England City and Town Area; (4) New England City and Town Area Division; (A) Construction, Mining, and Logging (some areas report Construction separate from Mining and Logging); (B) Construction; (C) Education and Health Services; (D) Financial Activities; (E) Government; (F) Information; (G) Leisure and Hospitality; (H) Manufacturing; (I) Mining and Logging; (J) Other Services; (K) Professional and Business Services; (L) Retail Trade; (M) Transportation and Utilities; (N) Wholesale Trade; n/a not available

Source: Bureau of Labor Statistics, Current Employment Statistics, Employment, Hours, and Earnings

Labor Force, Employment and Job Growth: City

City	Civilian Labor Force			Workers Employed		
	Dec. 2014	Dec. 2015	% Chg.	Dec. 2014	Dec. 2015	% Chg.
Aliso Viejo, CA	29,342	29,700	1.2	28,271	28,758	1.7
Allen, TX	51,019	51,243	0.4	49,323	49,767	0.9
Alpharetta, GA	33,497	33,937	1.3	32,027	32,607	1.8
Ankeny, IA	30,371	30,657	0.9	29,610	30,033	1.4
Apex, NC	22,297	23,205	4.0	21,594	22,342	3.4
Ballwin, MO	16,910	17,328	2.4	16,326	16,874	3.3
Beavercreek, OH	22,580	22,689	0.4	21,735	21,879	0.6
Bella Vista, AR	11,292	11,713	3.7	10,759	11,255	4.6
Bernards, NJ	12,845	13,047	1.5	12,378	12,703	2.6
Bethlehem, NY	17,486	18,002	2.9	16,909	17,463	3.2
Bloomfield, MI	20,210	20,384	0.8	19,486	19,791	1.5
Bowie, MD	32,304	33,027	2.2	30,955	31,836	2.8
Bozeman, MT	24,691	25,656	3.9	23,975	25,027	4.3
Brentwood, TN	19,140	20,051	4.7	18,348	19,320	5.3
Broomfield, CO	33,660	33,572	-0.2	32,481	32,624	0.4
Carmel, IN	45,598	46,885	2.8	43,824	45,476	3.7
Cedar Park, TX	33,502	33,725	0.6	32,462	32,816	1.0
Cheshire, CT	15,340	15,261	-0.5	14,758	14,755	0.0
Chesterfield, MO	24,675	25,312	2.5	23,847	24,648	3.3
Collierville, TN	22,949	23,680	3.1	21,876	22,666	3.6
Coppell, TX	23,148	23,252	0.4	22,338	22,536	0.8
Cornelius, NC	15,302	16,118	5.3	14,835	15,560	4.8
Cranberry, PA	16,281	16,639	2.2	15,807	16,195	2.4
Cupertino, CA	29,487	30,359	2.9	28,453	29,448	3.5
Danville, CA	20,466	20,625	0.7	19,609	19,885	1.4
Draper, UT	21,089	21,368	1.3	20,490	20,818	1.6
Dublin, OH	23,809	24,011	0.8	23,156	23,313	0.6
Eastchester, NY	15,480	16,035	3.5	14,842	15,491	4.3
Eden Prairie, MN	35,211	35,891	1.9	34,359	35,055	2.0
Edmond, OK	45,069	46,985	4.2	43,947	45,868	4.3
Evesham, NJ	25,976	26,323	1.3	24,933	25,503	2.2
Fishers, IN	45,650	47,050	3.0	43,975	45,633	3.7
Flower Mound, TX	38,359	38,552	0.5	37,134	37,475	0.9
Folsom, CA	34,539	34,894	1.0	33,102	33,636	1.6
Foster City, CA	18,702	19,135	2.3	18,100	18,597	2.7
Franklin, TN	36,792	38,545	4.7	35,307	37,177	5.3
Friendswood, TX	19,927	19,664	-1.3	19,248	18,927	-1.6
Germantown, TN	18,887	19,432	2.8	18,007	18,658	3.6
Glastonbury, CT	18,712	18,686	-0.1	18,016	18,047	0.1
Grand Blanc, MI	18,456	18,524	0.3	17,784	17,990	1.1
Guilderland, NY	19,164	19,697	2.7	18,482	19,087	3.2
Hampden, PA	15,792	16,412	3.9	15,388	16,006	4.0
Holly Springs, NC	14,278	14,892	4.3	13,869	14,350	3.4
Huntersville, NC	28,361	29,878	5.3	27,478	28,821	4.8
Independence, KY	13,223	13,150	-0.5	12,750	12,637	-0.8
Johns Creek, GA	42,889	43,443	1.2	40,992	41,735	1.8
Keller, TX	22,546	22,357	-0.8	21,817	21,682	-0.6
Kirkland, WA	49,834	50,190	0.7	48,046	48,316	0.5
Lafayette, CO	15,655	15,472	-1.1	15,154	15,051	-0.6
Lake Oswego, OR	19,647	20,155	2.5	18,787	19,412	3.3
League City, TX	52,581	51,764	-1.5	50,831	49,981	-1.6
Leawood, KS	16,713	16,835	0.7	16,238	16,405	1.0
Lee's Summit, MO	53,279	54,137	1.6	51,244	52,566	2.5
Leesburg, VA	25,932	26,160	0.8	25,014	25,358	1.3
Lehi, UT	22,842	23,307	2.0	22,198	22,723	2.3
Lenexa, KS	29,595	29,797	0.6	28,605	28,898	1.0
Lexington, MA	15,648	15,544	-0.6	15,149	15,034	-0.7
Los Altos, CA	14,333	14,772	3.0	13,929	14,416	3.5
Lower Makefield, PA	16,818	17,209	2.3	16,332	16,792	2.8
Madison, AL	22,885	23,243	1.5	22,019	22,180	0.7
Mamaroneck, NY	14,080	14,661	4.1	13,559	14,152	4.3
Manheim, PA	19,080	19,756	3.5	18,482	19,170	3.7
Manlius, NY	16,519	16,983	2.8	15,849	16,428	3.6
Maple Grove, MN	37,785	38,498	1.8	36,822	37,567	2.0
Marion, IA	19,548	19,424	-0.6	18,807	18,820	0.0
Marlboro, NJ	19,868	20,266	2.0	19,069	19,647	3.0
Mason, OH	15,852	16,000	0.9	15,321	15,402	0.5
McCandless, PA	15,706	16,055	2.2	15,207	15,610	2.6

Table continued on next page.

City	Civilian Labor Force			Workers Employed		
	Dec. 2014	Dec. 2015	% Chg.	Dec. 2014	Dec. 2015	% Chg.
Menomonee Falls, WI	19,777	19,741	-0.1	19,057	19,071	0.0
Meridian, ID	40,426	41,368	2.3	38,738	40,065	3.4
Merrimack, NH	15,723	15,551	-1.0	15,167	15,102	-0.4
Mount Lebanon, PA	16,692	17,086	2.3	16,213	16,642	2.6
Mount Pleasant, SC	40,218	41,329	2.7	38,550	39,919	3.5
Needham, MA	15,071	14,915	-1.0	14,594	14,462	-0.9
Newtown, CT	14,345	14,222	-0.8	13,758	13,666	-0.6
Northbrook, IL	16,194	16,224	0.1	15,595	15,552	-0.2
Northville, MI	14,456	14,493	0.2	14,135	14,226	0.6
Novi, MI	30,485	30,755	0.8	29,427	29,888	1.5
O'Fallon, MO	46,014	47,250	2.6	44,461	46,000	3.4
O'Fallon, IL	13,489	13,869	2.8	12,750	13,110	2.8
Orchard Park, NY	15,040	15,499	3.0	14,368	14,888	3.6
Oviedo, FL	20,148	20,407	1.2	19,303	19,623	1.6
Parker, CO	27,813	27,674	-0.5	26,828	26,918	0.3
Parkland, FL	14,282	14,396	0.8	13,783	13,939	1.1
Peachtree City, GA	17,667	17,893	1.2	16,841	17,144	1.8
Pflugerville, TX	30,258	30,492	0.7	29,386	29,683	1.0
Plainfield, IL	21,815	21,774	-0.1	20,730	20,708	-0.1
Princeton, NJ	15,055	15,547	3.2	14,595	15,197	4.1
Queen Creek, AZ	14,540	14,806	1.8	13,918	14,253	2.4
Rancho Palos Verdes, CA	19,221	19,135	-0.4	18,522	18,600	0.4
Redmond, WA	33,399	33,675	0.8	32,134	32,314	0.5
Richland, WA	25,517	25,745	0.8	23,915	24,319	1.6
Ridgefield, CT	11,806	11,825	0.1	11,344	11,418	0.6
Ridgewood, NJ	11,968	12,119	1.2	11,539	11,816	2.4
Rio Rancho, NM	41,741	41,702	0.0	39,510	39,358	-0.3
Sahuarita, AZ	11,359	11,522	1.4	10,817	11,018	1.8
Sammamish, WA	25,593	25,793	0.7	24,609	24,747	0.5
San Ramon, CA	39,376	39,722	0.8	37,986	38,521	1.4
Saratoga, CA	14,789	15,236	3.0	14,333	14,834	3.5
Schertz, TX	17,211	17,302	0.5	16,667	16,801	0.8
Shrewsbury, MA	19,750	19,658	-0.4	19,018	18,959	-0.3
South Brunswick, NJ	24,194	24,713	2.1	23,176	23,941	3.3
South Jordan, UT	29,710	30,120	1.3	28,870	29,322	1.5
South Kingstown, RI	16,347	16,580	1.4	15,453	15,896	2.8
South Windsor, CT	13,921	13,918	0.0	13,318	13,375	0.4
Southlake, TX	13,564	13,427	-1.0	13,066	12,992	-0.5
Spring Hill, TN	16,557	17,469	5.5	15,896	16,745	5.3
Stow, OH	18,537	18,635	0.5	17,747	17,889	0.8
Sugar Land, TX	45,579	44,959	-1.3	44,190	43,466	-1.6
Sun Prairie, WI	18,700	18,807	0.5	18,097	18,275	0.9
Syracuse, UT	12,328	12,443	0.9	12,001	12,150	1.2
Tredyffrin, PA	15,784	16,019	1.4	15,337	15,662	2.1
Upper Arlington, OH	18,126	18,284	0.8	17,587	17,710	0.7
Upper Dublin, PA	13,756	14,096	2.4	13,338	13,723	2.8
Vestavia Hills, AL	17,197	17,330	0.7	16,702	16,758	0.3
Webster, NY	21,630	22,292	3.0	20,728	21,449	3.4
Wellesley, MA	13,115	13,056	-0.4	12,678	12,626	-0.4
West Fargo, ND	18,081	18,102	0.1	17,605	17,720	0.6
West Linn, OR	13,982	14,284	2.1	13,337	13,780	3.3
West Windsor, NJ	14,504	14,984	3.3	14,059	14,640	4.1
Westlake, OH	17,018	16,805	-1.2	16,369	16,284	-0.5
Weston, FL	35,751	36,071	0.9	34,307	34,695	1.1
Westport, CT	12,374	12,337	-0.3	11,863	11,898	0.3
Wilmette, IL	12,827	12,827	0.0	12,332	12,298	-0.2
Woodbury, MN	36,651	37,451	2.1	35,824	36,560	2.0
Yorba Linda, CA	34,522	34,923	1.1	33,111	33,681	1.7
U.S.	155,521,000	157,245,000	1.1	147,190,000	149,703,000	1.7

Note: Data is not seasonally adjusted and covers workers 16 years of age and older
Source: Bureau of Labor Statistics, Local Area Unemployment Statistics

Labor Force, Employment and Job Growth: Metro Area

Metro Area[1]	Civilian Labor Force			Workers Employed		
	Dec. 2014	Dec. 2015	% Chg.	Dec. 2014	Dec. 2015	% Chg.
Aliso Viejo, CA[2]	1,584,967	1,602,110	1.0	1,511,008	1,537,037	1.7
Allen, TX[2]	2,392,061	2,403,448	0.4	2,296,944	2,317,383	0.8
Alpharetta, GA	2,815,375	2,835,654	0.7	2,647,261	2,695,404	1.8
Ankeny, IA	340,970	342,746	0.5	326,880	331,881	1.5
Apex, NC	629,675	653,397	3.7	604,111	624,803	3.4
Ballwin, MO	1,448,218	1,479,973	2.1	1,372,069	1,416,204	3.2
Beavercreek, OH	380,778	382,981	0.5	363,107	365,680	0.7
Bella Vista, AR	241,432	250,333	3.6	231,793	242,314	4.5
Bernards, NJ[2]	1,263,429	1,278,694	1.2	1,193,847	1,224,747	2.5
Bethlehem, NY	439,631	451,970	2.8	420,126	434,012	3.3
Bloomfield, MI[2]	1,245,341	1,252,111	0.5	1,173,548	1,191,493	1.5
Bowie, MD[2]	2,576,993	2,610,615	1.3	2,459,715	2,507,911	1.9
Bozeman, MT	56,832	59,093	3.9	54,968	57,381	4.3
Brentwood, TN	896,903	939,376	4.7	854,219	900,228	5.3
Broomfield, CO	1,497,400	1,488,871	-0.5	1,437,876	1,442,519	0.3
Carmel, IN	996,479	1,020,083	2.3	942,497	978,074	3.7
Cedar Park, TX	1,052,087	1,059,421	0.7	1,016,673	1,027,086	1.0
Cheshire, CT[3]	323,360	322,103	-0.3	305,248	306,200	0.3
Chesterfield, MO	1,448,218	1,479,973	2.1	1,372,069	1,416,204	3.2
Collierville, TN	602,176	621,661	3.2	559,876	583,671	4.2
Coppell, TX[2]	2,392,061	2,403,448	0.4	2,296,944	2,317,383	0.8
Cornelius, NC	1,184,609	1,239,605	4.6	1,125,541	1,179,140	4.7
Cranberry, PA	1,195,363	1,222,689	2.2	1,141,244	1,170,651	2.5
Cupertino, CA	1,039,234	1,068,398	2.8	992,810	1,027,507	3.4
Danville, CA[2]	1,361,975	1,371,421	0.6	1,292,276	1,310,864	1.4
Draper, UT	609,378	617,220	1.2	590,573	599,822	1.5
Dublin, OH	1,034,102	1,041,176	0.6	994,183	1,000,710	0.6
Eastchester, NY[2]	7,017,636	7,184,671	2.3	6,611,164	6,853,780	3.6
Eden Prairie, MN	1,905,506	1,942,269	1.9	1,843,783	1,881,640	2.0
Edmond, OK	646,136	674,376	4.3	624,543	652,097	4.4
Evesham, NJ[2]	639,280	643,376	0.6	600,422	614,423	2.3
Fishers, IN	996,479	1,020,083	2.3	942,497	978,074	3.7
Flower Mound, TX[2]	2,392,061	2,403,448	0.4	2,296,944	2,317,383	0.8
Folsom, CA	1,046,596	1,054,618	0.7	980,489	996,693	1.6
Foster City, CA[2]	977,381	999,542	2.2	942,144	967,640	2.7
Franklin, TN	896,903	939,376	4.7	854,219	900,228	5.3
Friendswood, TX	3,280,203	3,246,266	-1.0	3,148,828	3,096,889	-1.6
Germantown, TN	602,176	621,661	3.2	559,876	583,671	4.2
Glastonbury, CT[3]	616,412	614,187	-0.3	581,558	583,499	0.3
Grand Blanc, MI	184,709	184,534	0.0	174,034	176,047	1.1
Guilderland, NY	439,631	451,970	2.8	420,126	434,012	3.3
Hampden, PA	285,455	295,159	3.4	274,548	285,719	4.0
Holly Springs, NC	629,675	653,397	3.7	604,111	624,803	3.4
Huntersville, NC	1,184,609	1,239,605	4.6	1,125,541	1,179,140	4.7
Independence, KY	1,069,102	1,071,770	0.2	1,022,870	1,026,072	0.3
Johns Creek, GA	2,815,375	2,835,654	0.7	2,647,261	2,695,404	1.8
Keller, TX[2]	1,198,013	1,188,246	-0.8	1,150,482	1,143,078	-0.6
Kirkland, WA[2]	1,557,418	1,579,774	1.4	1,492,562	1,505,578	0.8
Lafayette, CO	177,034	174,620	-1.3	171,184	170,017	-0.6
Lake Oswego, OR	1,212,803	1,239,291	2.1	1,142,161	1,181,273	3.4
League City, TX	3,280,203	3,246,266	-1.0	3,148,828	3,096,889	-1.6
Leawood, KS	1,107,078	1,118,856	1.0	1,055,730	1,076,324	1.9
Lee's Summit, MO	1,107,078	1,118,856	1.0	1,055,730	1,076,324	1.9
Leesburg, VA[2]	2,576,993	2,610,615	1.3	2,459,715	2,507,911	1.9
Lehi, UT	265,249	271,083	2.2	258,088	264,188	2.3
Lenexa, KS	1,107,078	1,118,856	1.0	1,055,730	1,076,324	1.9
Lexington, MA[4]	2,627,900	2,607,376	-0.7	2,512,440	2,500,406	-0.4
Los Altos, CA	1,039,234	1,068,398	2.8	992,810	1,027,507	3.4
Lower Makefield, PA[2]	1,033,653	1,055,610	2.1	996,185	1,022,725	2.6
Madison, AL	206,534	208,299	0.8	196,222	197,695	0.7
Mamaroneck, NY[2]	7,017,636	7,184,671	2.3	6,611,164	6,853,780	3.6
Manheim, PA	267,649	275,998	3.1	258,069	267,678	3.7
Manlius, NY	307,613	316,488	2.8	290,543	301,211	3.6
Maple Grove, MN	1,905,506	1,942,269	1.9	1,843,783	1,881,640	2.0
Marion, IA	144,082	143,099	-0.6	137,538	137,950	0.3
Marlboro, NJ[2]	7,017,636	7,184,671	2.3	6,611,164	6,853,780	3.6
Mason, OH	1,069,102	1,071,770	0.2	1,022,870	1,026,072	0.3
McCandless, PA	1,195,363	1,222,689	2.2	1,141,244	1,170,651	2.5

Table continued on next page.

Metro Area[1]	Civilian Labor Force			Workers Employed		
	Dec. 2014	Dec. 2015	% Chg.	Dec. 2014	Dec. 2015	% Chg.
Menomonee Falls, WI	823,371	819,599	-0.4	782,000	783,077	0.1
Meridian, ID	313,572	323,203	3.0	300,918	311,157	3.4
Merrimack, NH[4]	2,627,900	2,607,376	-0.7	2,512,440	2,500,406	-0.4
Mount Lebanon, PA	1,195,363	1,222,689	2.2	1,141,244	1,170,651	2.5
Mount Pleasant, SC	348,192	357,044	2.5	329,245	340,926	3.5
Needham, MA[4]	2,627,900	2,607,376	-0.7	2,512,440	2,500,406	-0.4
Newtown, CT[3]	106,905	105,885	-0.9	102,297	101,609	-0.6
Northbrook, IL[2]	3,743,002	3,771,441	0.7	3,525,255	3,562,874	1.0
Northville, MI[2]	758,003	752,875	-0.6	700,376	704,860	0.6
Novi, MI[2]	1,245,341	1,252,111	0.5	1,173,548	1,191,493	1.5
O'Fallon, MO	1,448,218	1,479,973	2.1	1,372,069	1,416,204	3.2
O'Fallon, IL	1,448,218	1,479,973	2.1	1,372,069	1,416,204	3.2
Orchard Park, NY	541,740	557,071	2.8	511,083	529,580	3.6
Oviedo, FL	1,211,468	1,222,042	0.8	1,149,268	1,169,073	1.7
Parker, CO	1,497,400	1,488,871	-0.5	1,437,876	1,442,519	0.3
Parkland, FL[2]	995,560	999,633	0.4	945,682	956,378	1.1
Peachtree City, GA	2,815,375	2,835,654	0.7	2,647,261	2,695,404	1.8
Pflugerville, TX	1,052,087	1,059,421	0.7	1,016,673	1,027,086	1.0
Plainfield, IL[2]	3,743,002	3,771,441	0.7	3,525,255	3,562,874	1.0
Princeton, NJ	195,102	200,573	2.8	185,497	193,151	4.1
Queen Creek, AZ	2,140,674	2,175,140	1.6	2,023,418	2,072,215	2.4
Rancho Palos Verdes, CA[2]	5,030,364	4,991,657	-0.7	4,662,182	4,707,516	0.9
Redmond, WA[2]	1,557,418	1,579,774	1.4	1,492,562	1,505,578	0.8
Richland, WA	127,305	127,581	0.2	115,587	117,644	1.7
Ridgefield, CT[3]	462,757	463,036	0.0	437,814	440,819	0.6
Ridgewood, NJ[2]	7,017,636	7,184,671	2.3	6,611,164	6,853,780	3.6
Rio Rancho, NM	414,520	413,685	-0.2	391,974	390,197	-0.4
Sahuarita, AZ	465,594	470,703	1.1	438,925	447,052	1.8
Sammamish, WA[2]	1,557,418	1,579,774	1.4	1,492,562	1,505,578	0.8
San Ramon, CA[2]	1,361,975	1,371,421	0.6	1,292,276	1,310,864	1.4
Saratoga, CA	1,039,234	1,068,398	2.8	992,810	1,027,507	3.4
Schertz, TX	1,096,505	1,103,232	0.6	1,056,403	1,064,694	0.7
Shrewsbury, MA[3]	348,073	345,834	-0.6	329,698	329,149	-0.1
South Brunswick, NJ[2]	7,017,636	7,184,671	2.3	6,611,164	6,853,780	3.6
South Jordan, UT	609,378	617,220	1.2	590,573	599,822	1.5
South Kingstown, RI[3]	675,936	681,101	0.7	634,087	647,538	2.1
South Windsor, CT[3]	616,412	614,187	-0.3	581,558	583,499	0.3
Southlake, TX[2]	1,198,013	1,188,246	-0.8	1,150,482	1,143,078	-0.6
Spring Hill, TN	896,903	939,376	4.7	854,219	900,228	5.3
Stow, OH	357,895	360,364	0.6	340,430	343,115	0.7
Sugar Land, TX	3,280,203	3,246,266	-1.0	3,148,828	3,096,889	-1.6
Sun Prairie, WI	376,562	379,938	0.9	364,184	368,342	1.1
Syracuse, UT	300,508	303,649	1.0	290,572	294,090	1.2
Tredyffrin, PA[2]	1,033,653	1,055,610	2.1	996,185	1,022,725	2.6
Upper Arlington, OH	1,034,102	1,041,176	0.6	994,183	1,000,710	0.6
Upper Dublin, PA[2]	1,033,653	1,055,610	2.1	996,185	1,022,725	2.6
Vestavia Hills, AL	530,623	535,298	0.8	504,964	506,858	0.3
Webster, NY	516,206	530,419	2.7	488,916	506,134	3.5
Wellesley, MA[4]	2,627,900	2,607,376	-0.7	2,512,440	2,500,406	-0.4
West Fargo, ND	131,007	131,990	0.7	127,473	128,859	1.0
West Linn, OR	1,212,803	1,239,291	2.1	1,142,161	1,181,273	3.4
West Windsor, NJ	195,102	200,573	2.8	185,497	193,151	4.1
Westlake, OH	1,018,479	1,007,659	-1.0	967,544	967,796	0.0
Weston, FL[2]	995,560	999,633	0.4	945,682	956,378	1.1
Westport, CT[3]	462,757	463,036	0.0	437,814	440,819	0.6
Wilmette, IL[2]	3,743,002	3,771,441	0.7	3,525,255	3,562,874	1.0
Woodbury, MN	1,905,506	1,942,269	1.9	1,843,783	1,881,640	2.0
Yorba Linda, CA[2]	1,584,967	1,602,110	1.0	1,511,008	1,537,037	1.7
U.S.	155,521,000	157,245,000	1.1	147,190,000	149,703,000	1.7

Note: Data is not seasonally adjusted and covers workers 16 years of age and older; (1) Figures cover the Metropolitan Statistical Area (MSA) except where noted. See Appendix B for areas included; (2) Metropolitan Division; (3) New England City and Town Area; (4) New England City and Town Area Division
Source: Bureau of Labor Statistics, Local Area Unemployment Statistics

Unemployment Rate: City

City	2015 Jan.	Feb.	Mar.	Apr.	May	Jun.	Jul.	Aug.	Sep.	Oct.	Nov.	Dec.
Aliso Viejo, CA	3.9	3.6	3.4	3.2	3.3	3.4	3.7	3.5	3.1	3.4	3.3	3.2
Allen, TX	3.7	3.5	3.2	3.0	3.2	3.3	3.4	3.1	3.2	3.3	3.2	2.9
Alpharetta, GA	4.5	4.5	4.5	4.4	4.7	4.8	4.8	4.5	4.4	4.1	3.8	3.9
Ankeny, IA	2.7	2.5	2.2	2.2	2.3	2.6	2.4	2.2	2.3	2.1	2.0	2.0
Apex, NC	3.7	3.5	3.5	3.2	3.9	4.0	4.1	4.0	3.4	3.7	3.6	3.7
Ballwin, MO	3.9	4.0	4.2	4.1	4.1	4.0	4.0	3.4	3.3	3.1	2.8	2.6
Beavercreek, OH	4.8	4.1	4.2	3.7	4.0	4.1	3.8	3.4	3.5	3.3	3.6	3.6
Bella Vista, AR	5.4	5.0	4.7	4.6	4.6	4.6	5.2	4.2	4.2	4.0	3.8	3.9
Bernards, NJ	4.4	4.0	3.8	3.7	4.0	3.7	3.9	3.3	3.5	3.3	3.1	2.6
Bethlehem, NY	4.1	3.9	3.5	3.5	3.6	3.6	3.8	3.4	3.5	3.1	3.0	3.0
Bloomfield, MI	4.1	3.5	3.4	2.8	3.8	3.7	4.0	3.5	3.2	3.5	2.9	2.9
Bowie, MD	4.6	4.2	4.1	3.9	4.4	4.6	4.4	4.2	4.4	4.4	4.1	3.6
Bozeman, MT	3.3	2.9	3.0	2.6	2.3	2.6	2.5	2.4	2.2	2.5	2.6	2.5
Brentwood, TN	4.8	4.4	3.9	3.8	4.3	4.9	4.8	4.3	4.2	3.9	3.8	3.6
Broomfield, CO	4.0	4.0	3.9	3.8	3.8	3.9	3.5	3.3	2.9	2.9	3.0	2.8
Carmel, IN	4.3	3.8	3.7	2.9	3.3	3.5	3.4	3.0	2.9	3.0	3.2	3.0
Cedar Park, TX	3.4	3.0	2.9	2.7	2.8	3.1	3.0	3.0	2.9	3.1	2.9	2.7
Cheshire, CT	4.5	4.5	4.3	3.8	3.8	3.7	3.8	3.7	3.4	3.3	3.2	3.3
Chesterfield, MO	3.9	4.0	4.1	3.9	4.3	4.1	4.0	3.4	3.2	3.0	2.8	2.6
Collierville, TN	5.6	5.1	4.7	4.5	4.8	5.2	5.1	4.7	4.9	4.6	4.5	4.3
Coppell, TX	4.0	3.7	3.4	3.3	3.4	3.4	3.6	3.4	3.4	3.6	3.4	3.1
Cornelius, NC	3.7	3.4	3.5	3.2	3.8	3.9	4.2	4.2	3.9	4.0	4.0	3.5
Cranberry, PA	3.7	3.3	3.2	3.0	3.6	3.7	3.9	3.7	3.4	3.2	3.0	2.7
Cupertino, CA	3.8	3.5	3.3	3.1	3.2	3.2	3.4	3.2	2.9	3.1	3.1	3.0
Danville, CA	4.5	4.2	4.0	3.7	3.8	3.9	4.1	3.9	3.5	3.7	3.6	3.6
Draper, UT	3.3	3.4	3.3	2.9	3.2	3.5	3.6	3.6	3.1	3.1	2.8	2.6
Dublin, OH	3.6	3.1	3.1	2.8	3.1	3.2	3.2	2.7	2.9	2.8	3.0	2.9
Eastchester, NY	4.5	4.2	3.8	4.0	4.2	4.2	4.5	4.2	4.6	4.2	3.8	3.4
Eden Prairie, MN	3.1	2.9	3.1	2.8	3.0	3.1	3.2	2.9	2.7	2.6	2.2	2.3
Edmond, OK	2.8	2.8	2.5	2.6	3.1	3.5	3.0	3.0	2.7	2.6	2.5	2.4
Evesham, NJ	5.1	5.1	4.8	4.7	4.9	4.4	4.8	4.1	4.0	3.6	3.8	3.1
Fishers, IN	4.1	3.7	3.7	2.9	3.3	3.4	3.4	3.1	2.8	3.0	3.2	3.0
Flower Mound, TX	3.7	3.4	3.3	3.1	3.1	3.3	3.4	3.2	3.1	3.1	3.1	2.8
Folsom, CA	4.4	4.1	3.9	3.7	3.7	3.8	4.0	3.8	3.4	3.7	3.6	3.6
Foster City, CA	3.5	3.2	3.1	2.9	3.0	3.0	3.2	3.0	2.7	2.9	2.9	2.8
Franklin, TN	4.6	4.1	3.7	3.5	3.8	4.2	4.3	3.8	3.9	3.6	3.6	3.5
Friendswood, TX	3.8	3.6	3.5	3.2	3.4	3.8	3.9	3.8	3.7	3.9	4.0	3.7
Germantown, TN	5.3	4.9	4.5	4.5	4.8	5.0	4.8	4.3	4.5	4.1	4.2	4.0
Glastonbury, CT	4.4	4.4	4.1	3.7	3.7	3.8	3.8	3.7	3.5	3.4	3.2	3.4
Grand Blanc, MI	4.5	3.9	4.0	3.4	4.0	4.0	4.3	3.4	3.1	3.1	3.0	2.9
Guilderland, NY	4.4	4.1	3.6	3.7	3.8	3.9	4.0	3.4	3.8	3.5	3.5	3.1
Hampden, PA	3.5	3.1	3.2	2.8	3.2	3.4	3.6	3.3	3.0	2.8	2.6	2.5
Holly Springs, NC	3.6	3.5	3.5	3.1	3.7	4.0	4.2	4.1	3.7	3.9	3.9	3.6
Huntersville, NC	3.8	3.7	3.5	3.3	3.8	4.1	4.2	4.1	3.7	3.8	3.8	3.5
Independence, KY	4.4	4.2	4.1	3.8	4.2	4.0	4.0	3.4	3.5	3.2	3.6	3.9
Johns Creek, GA	4.7	4.6	4.5	4.3	4.6	4.9	4.9	4.6	4.5	4.3	3.9	3.9
Keller, TX	3.7	3.5	3.4	2.9	3.1	3.4	3.6	3.3	3.3	3.5	3.4	3.0
Kirkland, WA	4.1	4.1	3.5	2.6	3.1	3.3	3.4	2.9	3.2	3.4	3.8	3.7
Lafayette, CO	3.7	3.9	3.5	3.5	3.3	3.4	3.2	3.1	2.7	2.8	2.8	2.7
Lake Oswego, OR	4.6	4.3	4.2	3.9	4.1	4.6	4.8	4.6	4.4	4.3	3.9	3.7
League City, TX	3.7	3.6	3.6	3.3	3.5	3.6	3.7	3.6	3.6	3.7	3.7	3.4
Leawood, KS	3.1	3.0	3.1	3.3	3.4	3.4	3.6	3.2	2.7	2.6	2.5	2.6
Lee's Summit, MO	4.5	4.8	4.6	4.3	4.4	4.2	4.3	4.0	3.6	3.5	3.1	2.9
Leesburg, VA	3.8	3.8	3.7	3.5	3.9	3.9	3.5	3.3	3.2	3.3	3.0	3.1
Lehi, UT	3.4	3.4	3.3	2.9	3.1	3.4	3.6	3.5	3.0	2.9	2.8	2.5
Lenexa, KS	3.9	3.7	3.6	3.6	3.7	3.8	4.1	3.8	3.2	3.4	3.0	3.0
Lexington, MA	3.5	3.3	3.2	2.9	3.4	4.0	3.7	3.2	3.4	3.4	3.4	3.3
Los Altos, CA	3.0	2.8	2.6	2.5	2.6	2.6	2.7	2.6	2.3	2.5	2.5	2.4
Lower Makefield, PA	3.7	3.5	3.5	3.4	3.9	4.0	4.0	3.6	3.1	3.0	2.9	2.4
Madison, AL	4.8	4.4	4.5	4.1	4.7	5.2	5.1	5.1	4.5	4.4	4.4	4.6
Mamaroneck, NY	4.5	4.5	4.0	3.6	3.9	3.7	4.0	3.7	3.7	3.6	3.5	3.5
Manheim, PA	4.2	3.7	3.7	3.2	4.1	4.4	4.4	4.2	3.9	3.6	3.4	3.0
Manlius, NY	4.8	4.6	4.1	4.0	4.0	4.0	4.1	3.7	3.6	3.4	3.3	3.3
Maple Grove, MN	3.1	3.1	3.3	3.0	3.0	3.3	3.2	3.0	2.8	2.6	2.4	2.4
Marion, IA	4.1	3.8	3.6	3.0	3.0	3.0	2.9	2.8	2.9	2.7	2.9	3.1
Marlboro, NJ	4.9	4.5	4.3	4.3	4.8	4.1	4.8	4.2	4.0	3.9	3.6	3.1
Mason, OH	4.2	3.6	3.5	3.1	3.5	3.9	3.9	3.3	3.5	3.4	3.8	3.7
McCandless, PA	4.1	4.0	3.8	3.1	3.5	3.7	4.4	4.0	3.5	3.2	3.3	2.8

Table continued on next page.

City	2015											
	Jan.	Feb.	Mar.	Apr.	May	Jun.	Jul.	Aug.	Sep.	Oct.	Nov.	Dec.
Menomonee Falls, WI	4.1	4.2	4.0	3.4	4.0	4.1	3.6	3.1	3.3	3.3	3.5	3.4
Meridian, ID	4.8	4.6	4.9	4.5	3.7	4.0	4.4	4.3	3.8	3.1	3.3	3.1
Merrimack, NH	4.1	4.2	3.8	3.5	3.5	3.6	3.7	3.5	3.1	3.2	3.1	2.9
Mount Lebanon, PA	3.7	3.5	3.5	3.1	3.7	3.6	3.9	3.7	3.5	3.1	3.0	2.6
Mount Pleasant, SC	4.5	4.5	4.1	4.0	4.3	4.3	3.9	3.8	3.9	3.8	3.3	3.4
Needham, MA	3.5	3.3	3.1	2.7	3.1	3.5	3.4	3.1	3.2	3.2	3.2	3.0
Newtown, CT	4.9	5.1	4.7	4.5	4.2	4.1	4.4	4.4	3.8	3.7	3.7	3.9
Northbrook, IL	4.4	4.8	4.6	4.3	4.4	4.6	4.5	4.3	3.7	3.8	4.1	4.1
Northville, MI	2.5	2.1	2.0	1.7	2.3	2.3	2.4	2.2	2.0	2.3	1.8	1.8
Novi, MI	3.9	3.4	3.3	2.7	3.7	3.6	3.9	3.4	3.1	3.4	2.8	2.8
O'Fallon, MO	4.0	4.1	4.1	3.9	3.9	3.9	3.8	3.4	3.1	2.9	2.7	2.6
O'Fallon, IL	6.2	5.6	5.5	4.5	4.7	5.2	5.4	5.1	5.1	5.4	6.2	5.5
Orchard Park, NY	5.0	5.0	4.6	4.3	4.2	3.9	4.1	3.7	4.1	3.8	3.8	3.9
Oviedo, FL	4.7	4.4	4.3	3.9	4.2	4.1	4.1	4.0	3.9	3.8	3.7	3.8
Parker, CO	3.8	3.9	3.6	3.6	3.6	3.9	3.5	3.3	3.0	2.9	2.9	2.7
Parkland, FL	4.1	3.8	3.7	3.6	4.0	3.9	3.9	3.9	4.0	3.6	3.3	3.2
Peachtree City, GA	5.1	5.0	4.7	4.5	5.1	5.3	5.4	4.8	4.6	4.5	3.9	4.2
Pflugerville, TX	3.1	2.9	2.7	2.5	2.7	3.0	3.1	2.9	2.8	2.9	2.9	2.7
Plainfield, IL	6.2	5.8	5.6	5.2	5.4	5.9	5.8	5.3	4.5	4.6	4.7	4.9
Princeton, NJ	3.9	3.6	3.4	3.1	3.6	3.4	4.0	3.3	3.2	3.1	2.7	2.3
Queen Creek, AZ	4.4	3.9	3.8	3.7	3.6	4.4	4.5	4.6	4.6	4.2	3.9	3.7
Rancho Palos Verdes, CA	4.0	3.7	3.5	3.4	3.6	3.6	3.6	3.4	3.0	2.8	2.7	2.8
Redmond, WA	4.3	4.3	3.5	2.9	3.3	3.4	3.4	3.0	3.3	3.7	4.0	4.0
Richland, WA	7.1	7.0	5.8	5.5	5.9	5.5	5.9	5.6	5.1	5.1	5.0	5.5
Ridgefield, CT	4.7	4.7	4.3	3.9	3.9	3.9	3.8	3.6	3.5	3.4	3.3	3.4
Ridgewood, NJ	4.3	4.0	4.1	3.8	4.1	3.7	3.9	3.5	3.5	3.3	3.1	2.5
Rio Rancho, NM	5.8	5.9	5.6	5.3	5.6	6.8	6.8	6.4	6.4	6.2	5.8	5.6
Sahuarita, AZ	5.4	5.3	4.5	4.5	4.3	5.4	5.7	5.8	5.2	4.7	4.5	4.4
Sammamish, WA	4.4	4.4	3.6	2.9	3.3	3.5	3.6	3.2	3.4	3.7	4.1	4.1
San Ramon, CA	3.8	3.5	3.3	3.1	3.2	3.3	3.5	3.3	2.9	3.1	3.1	3.0
Saratoga, CA	3.3	3.1	2.9	2.7	2.8	2.8	3.0	2.8	2.6	2.8	2.7	2.6
Schertz, TX	3.6	3.3	3.1	2.8	3.0	3.3	3.4	3.1	3.2	3.3	3.2	2.9
Shrewsbury, MA	4.1	4.0	3.7	3.2	3.4	3.9	3.8	3.5	3.5	3.6	3.6	3.6
South Brunswick, NJ	4.8	4.7	4.7	4.5	4.8	4.1	4.8	4.2	4.1	3.6	3.6	3.1
South Jordan, UT	3.2	3.6	3.5	3.2	3.2	3.6	3.7	3.6	3.0	3.0	2.7	2.6
South Kingstown, RI	6.9	6.5	6.5	4.8	5.4	5.6	5.6	5.1	4.2	3.7	4.3	4.1
South Windsor, CT	5.2	5.2	4.9	4.5	4.4	4.2	4.5	4.3	3.9	3.8	3.7	3.9
Southlake, TX	4.0	3.6	3.5	3.2	3.3	3.6	3.7	3.5	3.5	3.6	3.5	3.2
Spring Hill, TN	4.6	4.3	3.8	3.8	4.4	4.8	4.9	4.4	4.4	4.4	4.5	4.1
Stow, OH	5.4	4.7	4.6	3.8	4.1	4.5	4.3	3.8	3.7	3.8	4.2	4.0
Sugar Land, TX	3.5	3.3	3.3	3.1	3.3	3.6	3.7	3.5	3.6	3.7	3.6	3.3
Sun Prairie, WI	3.7	3.7	3.7	2.9	3.5	3.5	3.0	2.7	2.7	2.7	2.8	2.8
Syracuse, UT	3.0	3.1	2.9	2.7	2.7	3.1	3.4	3.3	3.0	2.7	2.3	2.4
Tredyffrin, PA	3.5	3.2	3.1	2.9	3.4	3.5	3.7	3.4	3.2	2.9	2.7	2.2
Upper Arlington, OH	3.8	3.3	3.2	2.8	3.2	3.4	3.3	2.8	3.0	2.9	3.2	3.1
Upper Dublin, PA	3.7	3.4	3.4	3.3	4.0	3.8	4.3	4.0	3.7	3.4	3.0	2.6
Vestavia Hills, AL	3.9	3.7	3.6	3.4	4.0	4.0	4.2	4.2	3.6	3.5	3.2	3.3
Webster, NY	4.9	4.9	4.5	4.4	4.4	4.2	4.4	4.1	4.3	3.8	3.8	3.8
Wellesley, MA	3.7	3.2	3.1	3.0	3.4	4.2	3.9	3.3	3.4	3.4	3.6	3.3
West Fargo, ND	3.3	3.2	3.2	2.4	2.1	2.4	1.9	2.0	1.8	1.7	1.7	2.1
West Linn, OR	4.8	4.4	4.4	4.0	4.1	4.6	4.8	4.5	4.5	4.1	3.6	3.5
West Windsor, NJ	3.7	3.4	3.3	3.3	3.6	3.3	3.8	3.1	3.3	3.1	3.0	2.3
Westlake, OH	4.5	4.8	4.2	4.0	4.9	5.2	4.5	3.9	4.1	3.5	3.1	3.1
Weston, FL	4.5	4.3	4.3	4.0	4.4	4.5	4.2	4.2	4.1	3.8	3.7	3.8
Westport, CT	4.8	4.7	4.5	4.1	4.2	4.1	4.1	3.9	3.7	3.7	3.6	3.6
Wilmette, IL	4.6	4.7	4.4	4.2	4.6	4.6	4.4	3.9	3.5	3.8	4.2	4.1
Woodbury, MN	2.9	2.7	2.7	2.6	2.8	3.0	3.0	2.7	2.6	2.5	2.3	2.4
Yorba Linda, CA	4.4	4.0	3.8	3.6	3.7	3.8	4.1	3.9	3.5	3.8	3.7	3.6
U.S.	6.1	5.8	5.6	5.1	5.3	5.5	5.6	5.2	4.9	4.8	4.8	4.8

Note: Data is not seasonally adjusted and covers workers 16 years of age and older; All figures are percentages
Source: Bureau of Labor Statistics, Local Area Unemployment Statistics

Unemployment Rate: Metro Area

Metro Area[1]	2015											
	Jan.	Feb.	Mar.	Apr.	May	Jun.	Jul.	Aug.	Sep.	Oct.	Nov.	Dec.
Aliso Viejo, CA[2]	5.0	4.6	4.4	4.1	4.2	4.3	4.7	4.5	4.0	4.3	4.2	4.1
Allen, TX[2]	4.4	4.1	4.0	3.6	3.7	4.0	4.0	3.8	3.8	3.9	3.9	3.6
Alpharetta, GA	6.2	6.1	5.9	5.6	5.9	6.0	6.1	5.6	5.5	5.4	4.9	4.9
Ankeny, IA	4.6	4.4	4.0	3.5	3.3	3.4	3.2	3.1	3.1	3.0	2.9	3.2
Apex, NC	4.7	4.5	4.5	4.3	4.9	5.1	5.2	5.1	4.5	4.7	4.6	4.4
Ballwin, MO	6.0	6.0	5.9	5.3	5.5	5.6	5.7	5.1	4.6	4.6	4.6	4.3
Beavercreek, OH	6.0	5.3	5.2	4.5	4.7	4.9	4.9	4.2	4.2	4.2	4.5	4.5
Bella Vista, AR	4.7	4.4	4.2	4.0	4.3	4.2	4.3	3.6	3.5	3.4	3.1	3.2
Bernards, NJ[2]	6.6	6.6	6.4	5.9	6.1	5.4	6.1	5.4	5.3	4.9	4.8	4.2
Bethlehem, NY	5.4	5.1	4.6	4.4	4.4	4.5	4.8	4.3	4.4	4.1	4.0	4.0
Bloomfield, MI[2]	6.7	5.7	5.5	4.5	5.9	5.9	6.3	5.5	5.0	5.5	4.6	4.8
Bowie, MD[2]	5.0	5.0	4.8	4.4	4.7	4.9	4.7	4.4	4.3	4.3	4.2	3.9
Bozeman, MT	3.6	3.3	3.3	2.9	2.8	2.8	2.5	2.3	2.3	3.0	3.4	2.9
Brentwood, TN	5.6	5.0	4.6	4.2	4.6	5.1	5.1	4.6	4.7	4.3	4.3	4.2
Broomfield, CO	4.5	4.5	4.3	4.1	4.1	4.3	3.8	3.6	3.2	3.1	3.2	3.1
Carmel, IN	6.2	5.7	5.5	4.3	4.5	4.5	4.4	4.2	3.8	4.0	4.2	4.1
Cedar Park, TX	3.7	3.4	3.3	3.0	3.1	3.3	3.5	3.2	3.3	3.3	3.3	3.1
Cheshire, CT[3]	6.7	6.8	6.4	5.8	5.6	5.5	5.8	5.6	5.1	4.9	4.9	4.9
Chesterfield, MO	6.0	6.0	5.9	5.3	5.5	5.6	5.7	5.1	4.6	4.6	4.6	4.3
Collierville, TN	7.9	7.0	6.5	5.9	6.6	7.0	7.0	6.4	6.4	6.1	6.1	6.1
Coppell, TX[2]	4.4	4.1	4.0	3.6	3.7	4.0	4.0	3.8	3.8	3.9	3.9	3.6
Cornelius, NC	5.7	5.5	5.3	5.1	5.6	5.8	5.9	5.7	5.2	5.2	5.1	4.9
Cranberry, PA	5.9	5.7	5.5	4.6	5.2	5.5	5.8	5.5	4.9	4.6	4.5	4.3
Cupertino, CA	4.8	4.4	4.2	3.9	4.0	4.0	4.3	4.1	3.7	4.0	3.9	3.8
Danville, CA[2]	5.5	5.1	4.8	4.5	4.7	4.7	5.1	4.8	4.3	4.6	4.5	4.4
Draper, UT	3.6	3.7	3.5	3.1	3.3	3.6	3.7	3.6	3.1	3.1	2.9	2.8
Dublin, OH	5.0	4.5	4.4	3.8	4.0	4.2	4.2	3.6	3.7	3.6	3.9	3.9
Eastchester, NY[2]	6.7	6.8	6.2	5.8	5.8	5.4	5.7	5.2	4.9	4.7	4.8	4.6
Eden Prairie, MN	4.1	4.0	4.1	3.5	3.5	3.8	3.7	3.4	3.1	2.9	2.8	3.1
Edmond, OK	3.7	3.6	3.3	3.4	3.8	4.3	3.9	3.9	3.6	3.6	3.6	3.3
Evesham, NJ[2]	7.2	7.1	6.9	6.4	6.5	5.8	6.6	5.8	5.6	5.2	5.1	4.5
Fishers, IN	6.2	5.7	5.5	4.3	4.5	4.5	4.4	4.2	3.8	4.0	4.2	4.1
Flower Mound, TX[2]	4.4	4.1	4.0	3.6	3.7	4.0	4.0	3.8	3.8	3.9	3.9	3.6
Folsom, CA	6.7	6.3	5.9	5.5	5.6	5.6	6.0	5.7	5.1	5.5	5.5	5.5
Foster City, CA[2]	4.0	3.7	3.5	3.3	3.4	3.4	3.7	3.4	3.1	3.3	3.2	3.2
Franklin, TN	5.6	5.0	4.6	4.2	4.6	5.1	5.1	4.6	4.7	4.3	4.3	4.2
Friendswood, TX	4.5	4.3	4.2	4.0	4.2	4.5	4.7	4.6	4.6	4.8	4.9	4.6
Germantown, TN	7.9	7.0	6.5	5.9	6.6	7.0	7.0	6.4	6.4	6.1	6.1	6.1
Glastonbury, CT[3]	6.8	6.8	6.5	5.8	5.5	5.4	5.7	5.6	5.0	4.8	4.8	5.0
Grand Blanc, MI	7.1	6.2	6.3	5.4	6.4	6.3	6.8	5.4	5.0	5.0	4.8	4.6
Guilderland, NY	5.4	5.1	4.6	4.4	4.4	4.5	4.8	4.3	4.4	4.1	4.0	4.0
Hampden, PA	4.8	4.6	4.5	3.9	4.5	4.7	4.9	4.5	4.0	3.8	3.5	3.2
Holly Springs, NC	4.7	4.5	4.5	4.3	4.9	5.1	5.2	5.1	4.5	4.7	4.6	4.4
Huntersville, NC	5.7	5.5	5.3	5.1	5.6	5.8	5.9	5.7	5.2	5.2	5.1	4.9
Independence, KY	5.5	4.9	4.8	4.1	4.3	4.6	4.6	3.9	3.9	3.8	4.2	4.3
Johns Creek, GA	6.2	6.1	5.9	5.6	5.9	6.0	6.1	5.6	5.5	5.4	4.9	4.9
Keller, TX[2]	4.4	4.1	4.1	3.8	3.9	4.1	4.3	4.1	4.1	4.2	4.1	3.8
Kirkland, WA[2]	4.6	4.5	4.4	3.8	4.1	4.6	4.7	4.6	4.7	4.7	5.1	4.7
Lafayette, CO	3.7	3.9	3.6	3.5	3.5	3.8	3.3	3.2	2.6	2.7	2.8	2.6
Lake Oswego, OR	6.1	5.7	5.3	4.9	5.0	5.4	5.9	5.5	5.2	5.0	4.8	4.7
League City, TX	4.5	4.3	4.2	4.0	4.2	4.5	4.7	4.6	4.6	4.8	4.9	4.6
Leawood, KS	5.9	5.9	5.3	5.1	5.3	5.3	5.5	5.2	4.4	4.2	3.9	3.8
Lee's Summit, MO	5.9	5.9	5.3	5.1	5.3	5.3	5.5	5.2	4.4	4.2	3.9	3.8
Leesburg, VA[2]	5.0	5.0	4.8	4.4	4.7	4.9	4.7	4.4	4.3	4.3	4.2	3.9
Lehi, UT	3.3	3.5	3.2	2.9	3.1	3.6	3.7	3.6	3.0	3.0	2.7	2.5
Lenexa, KS	5.9	5.9	5.3	5.1	5.3	5.3	5.5	5.2	4.4	4.2	3.9	3.8
Lexington, MA[4]	4.9	4.8	4.4	3.8	4.0	4.5	4.5	4.1	4.1	4.1	4.1	4.1
Los Altos, CA	4.8	4.4	4.2	3.9	4.0	4.0	4.3	4.1	3.7	4.0	3.9	3.8
Lower Makefield, PA[2]	4.7	4.5	4.3	3.8	4.4	4.5	4.8	4.5	3.9	3.7	3.5	3.1
Madison, AL	5.6	5.2	5.3	4.8	5.5	6.1	6.1	5.9	5.3	5.0	5.0	5.1
Mamaroneck, NY[2]	6.7	6.8	6.2	5.8	5.8	5.4	5.7	5.2	4.9	4.7	4.8	4.6
Manheim, PA	4.7	4.5	4.2	3.6	4.2	4.5	4.7	4.4	3.7	3.5	3.4	3.0
Manlius, NY	6.6	6.3	5.7	5.4	5.4	5.4	5.6	5.0	5.1	4.7	4.8	4.8
Maple Grove, MN	4.1	4.0	4.1	3.5	3.5	3.8	3.7	3.4	3.1	2.9	2.8	3.1
Marion, IA	5.1	4.8	4.4	3.7	3.5	3.7	3.6	3.6	3.5	3.3	3.3	3.6
Marlboro, NJ[2]	6.7	6.8	6.2	5.8	5.8	5.4	5.7	5.2	4.9	4.7	4.8	4.6
Mason, OH	5.5	4.9	4.8	4.1	4.3	4.6	4.6	3.9	3.9	3.8	4.2	4.3
McCandless, PA	5.9	5.7	5.5	4.6	5.2	5.5	5.8	5.5	4.9	4.6	4.5	4.3

Table continued on next page.

Metro Area[1]	2015 Jan.	Feb.	Mar.	Apr.	May	Jun.	Jul.	Aug.	Sep.	Oct.	Nov.	Dec.
Menomonee Falls, WI	5.6	5.6	5.6	4.7	5.2	5.5	5.2	4.5	4.2	4.2	4.4	4.5
Meridian, ID	4.4	4.2	4.1	3.8	3.4	3.6	3.7	3.8	3.5	3.4	3.7	3.7
Merrimack, NH[4]	4.9	4.8	4.4	3.8	4.0	4.5	4.5	4.1	4.1	4.1	4.1	4.1
Mount Lebanon, PA	5.9	5.7	5.5	4.6	5.2	5.5	5.8	5.5	4.9	4.6	4.5	4.3
Mount Pleasant, SC	5.9	5.8	5.3	5.2	5.7	5.8	5.5	5.3	5.1	5.0	4.5	4.5
Needham, MA[4]	4.9	4.8	4.4	3.8	4.0	4.5	4.5	4.1	4.1	4.1	4.1	4.1
Newtown, CT[3]	5.4	5.6	5.3	4.7	4.4	4.3	4.6	4.5	4.0	3.9	3.8	4.0
Northbrook, IL[2]	6.9	6.5	6.0	5.7	5.9	6.1	6.2	5.6	5.1	5.3	5.4	5.5
Northville, MI[2]	8.5	7.3	6.9	5.9	7.7	7.7	8.2	7.5	6.7	7.7	6.2	6.4
Novi, MI[2]	6.7	5.7	5.5	4.5	5.9	5.9	6.3	5.5	5.0	5.5	4.6	4.8
O'Fallon, MO	6.0	6.0	5.9	5.3	5.5	5.6	5.7	5.1	4.6	4.6	4.6	4.3
O'Fallon, IL	6.0	6.0	5.9	5.3	5.5	5.6	5.7	5.1	4.6	4.6	4.6	4.3
Orchard Park, NY	6.7	6.4	5.9	5.5	5.3	5.3	5.8	5.2	5.3	4.8	4.9	4.9
Oviedo, FL	5.6	5.4	5.2	4.9	5.2	5.1	5.3	5.1	4.9	4.7	4.5	4.3
Parker, CO	4.5	4.5	4.3	4.1	4.1	4.3	3.8	3.6	3.2	3.1	3.2	3.1
Parkland, FL[2]	5.5	5.3	5.2	4.9	5.2	5.1	5.3	5.2	4.9	4.7	4.5	4.3
Peachtree City, GA	6.2	6.1	5.9	5.6	5.9	6.0	6.1	5.6	5.5	5.4	4.9	4.9
Pflugerville, TX	3.7	3.4	3.3	3.0	3.1	3.3	3.5	3.2	3.3	3.3	3.3	3.1
Plainfield, IL[2]	6.9	6.5	6.0	5.7	5.9	6.1	6.2	5.6	5.1	5.3	5.4	5.5
Princeton, NJ	6.0	5.8	5.6	5.3	5.5	4.9	5.7	5.0	4.8	4.4	4.2	3.7
Queen Creek, AZ	5.8	5.4	4.8	4.8	4.6	5.4	5.7	5.8	5.5	5.2	5.0	4.7
Rancho Palos Verdes, CA[2]	7.9	7.4	7.1	6.8	6.8	6.9	7.2	6.7	6.2	6.0	5.8	5.7
Redmond, WA[2]	4.6	4.5	4.4	3.8	4.1	4.6	4.7	4.6	4.7	4.7	5.1	4.7
Richland, WA	9.9	9.2	7.5	6.5	6.7	6.0	6.5	6.0	5.4	5.7	6.5	7.8
Ridgefield, CT[3]	6.4	6.7	6.3	5.6	5.4	5.2	5.4	5.3	4.9	4.7	4.7	4.8
Ridgewood, NJ[2]	6.7	6.8	6.2	5.8	5.8	5.4	5.7	5.2	4.9	4.7	4.8	4.6
Rio Rancho, NM	5.9	6.0	5.6	5.4	5.6	6.8	6.7	6.5	6.4	6.3	6.0	5.7
Sahuarita, AZ	5.9	5.6	4.9	5.1	4.9	5.9	6.2	6.1	5.7	5.5	5.3	5.0
Sammamish, WA[2]	4.6	4.5	4.4	3.8	4.1	4.6	4.7	4.6	4.7	4.7	5.1	4.7
San Ramon, CA[2]	5.5	5.1	4.8	4.5	4.7	4.7	5.1	4.8	4.3	4.6	4.5	4.4
Saratoga, CA	4.8	4.4	4.2	3.9	4.0	4.0	4.3	4.1	3.7	4.0	3.9	3.8
Schertz, TX	4.1	3.8	3.7	3.4	3.5	3.8	3.9	3.7	3.7	3.8	3.8	3.5
Shrewsbury, MA[3]	5.9	5.8	5.4	4.6	4.7	5.2	5.3	4.9	4.8	4.7	4.7	4.8
South Brunswick, NJ[2]	6.7	6.8	6.2	5.8	5.8	5.4	5.7	5.2	4.9	4.7	4.8	4.6
South Jordan, UT	3.6	3.7	3.5	3.1	3.3	3.6	3.7	3.6	3.1	3.1	2.9	2.8
South Kingstown, RI[3]	7.3	7.0	6.8	5.5	5.6	5.6	5.8	5.6	4.8	4.8	5.0	4.9
South Windsor, CT[3]	6.8	6.8	6.5	5.8	5.5	5.4	5.7	5.6	5.0	4.8	4.8	5.0
Southlake, TX[2]	4.4	4.1	4.1	3.8	3.9	4.1	4.3	4.1	4.1	4.2	4.1	3.8
Spring Hill, TN	5.6	5.0	4.6	4.2	4.6	5.1	5.1	4.6	4.7	4.3	4.3	4.2
Stow, OH	6.4	5.7	5.5	4.6	4.7	5.0	4.9	4.2	4.2	4.2	4.6	4.8
Sugar Land, TX	4.5	4.3	4.2	4.0	4.2	4.5	4.7	4.6	4.6	4.8	4.9	4.6
Sun Prairie, WI	3.8	3.9	3.9	3.1	3.6	3.7	3.3	2.8	2.8	2.7	3.0	3.1
Syracuse, UT	3.8	3.9	3.7	3.2	3.4	3.8	4.0	3.9	3.5	3.4	3.1	3.1
Tredyffrin, PA[2]	4.7	4.5	4.3	3.8	4.4	4.5	4.8	4.5	3.9	3.7	3.5	3.1
Upper Arlington, OH	5.0	4.5	4.4	3.8	4.0	4.2	4.2	3.6	3.7	3.6	3.9	3.9
Upper Dublin, PA[2]	4.7	4.5	4.3	3.8	4.4	4.5	4.8	4.5	3.9	3.7	3.5	3.1
Vestavia Hills, AL	5.5	5.1	5.1	4.8	5.5	5.9	6.0	5.9	5.4	5.1	5.2	5.3
Webster, NY	6.2	6.0	5.5	5.2	5.1	5.1	5.4	4.8	4.9	4.5	4.6	4.6
Wellesley, MA[4]	4.9	4.8	4.4	3.8	4.0	4.5	4.5	4.1	4.1	4.1	4.1	4.1
West Fargo, ND	3.6	3.4	3.3	2.6	2.5	2.7	2.4	2.2	2.1	1.8	1.9	2.4
West Linn, OR	6.1	5.7	5.3	4.9	5.0	5.4	5.9	5.5	5.2	5.0	4.8	4.7
West Windsor, NJ	6.0	5.8	5.6	5.3	5.5	4.9	5.7	5.0	4.8	4.4	4.2	3.7
Westlake, OH	5.8	6.1	5.3	4.8	5.3	5.4	5.1	4.3	4.2	3.8	3.9	4.0
Weston, FL[2]	5.5	5.3	5.2	4.9	5.2	5.1	5.3	5.2	4.9	4.7	4.5	4.3
Westport, CT[3]	6.4	6.7	6.3	5.6	5.4	5.2	5.4	5.3	4.9	4.7	4.7	4.8
Wilmette, IL[2]	6.9	6.5	6.0	5.7	5.9	6.1	6.2	5.6	5.1	5.3	5.4	5.5
Woodbury, MN	4.1	4.0	4.1	3.5	3.5	3.8	3.7	3.4	3.1	2.9	2.8	3.1
Yorba Linda, CA[2]	5.0	4.6	4.4	4.1	4.2	4.3	4.7	4.5	4.0	4.3	4.2	4.1
U.S.	6.1	5.8	5.6	5.1	5.3	5.5	5.6	5.2	4.9	4.8	4.8	4.8

Note: Data is not seasonally adjusted and covers workers 16 years of age and older; All figures are percentages; (1) Figures cover the Metropolitan Statistical Area (MSA) except where noted. See Appendix B for areas included; (2) Metropolitan Division; (3) New England City and Town Area; (4) New England City and Town Area Division

Source: Bureau of Labor Statistics, Local Area Unemployment Statistics

Average Hourly Wages: Occupations A – C

Metro Area[1]	Accountants/ Auditors	Automotive Mechanics	Book-keepers	Carpenters	Cashiers	Clerks, Gen. Office	Clerks, Recep./Info.
Aliso Viejo, CA[2]	37.26	25.15	21.75	24.95	11.29	16.51	14.99
Allen, TX[2]	38.66	21.09	19.97	16.53	9.60	16.57	13.29
Alpharetta, GA	38.06	19.15	19.46	19.77	9.38	14.20	14.19
Ankeny, IA	32.25	21.01	18.02	21.46	9.89	16.54	13.93
Apex, NC	33.11	20.12	18.63	17.07	9.29	14.30	13.44
Ballwin, MO	37.50	20.95	19.10	26.82	10.22	15.53	12.44
Beavercreek, OH	35.20	17.57	18.09	20.74	9.71	15.12	12.05
Bella Vista, AR	29.64	17.26	16.88	16.73	9.04	12.24	11.98
Bernards, NJ[2]	41.32	24.21	21.35	31.15	10.30	16.08	15.36
Bethlehem, NY	35.85	20.00	19.63	21.30	10.28	15.46	14.89
Bloomfield, MI[2]	38.84	20.93	18.98	23.50	10.66	15.98	13.16
Bowie, MD[2]	43.03	23.59	21.96	22.16	10.63	18.51	15.29
Bozeman, MT	n/a	n/a	n/a	n/a	n/a	n/a	n/a
Brentwood, TN	32.68	21.81	18.70	19.27	9.80	15.79	13.93
Broomfield, CO	36.90	20.68	19.30	21.18	10.49	18.98	15.39
Carmel, IN	32.87	22.25	18.90	21.12	9.33	14.92	13.67
Cedar Park, TX	33.89	19.44	19.90	17.86	10.42	16.44	13.33
Cheshire, CT[3]	34.56	21.35	22.03	24.84	10.84	17.81	15.59
Chesterfield, MO	37.50	20.95	19.10	26.82	10.22	15.53	12.44
Collierville, TN	31.64	19.05	18.09	18.35	9.21	14.95	12.58
Coppell, TX[2]	38.66	21.09	19.97	16.53	9.60	16.57	13.29
Cornelius, NC	37.36	21.38	18.38	16.97	9.47	14.42	13.64
Cranberry, PA	33.01	17.91	17.45	23.70	9.22	15.01	12.68
Cupertino, CA	48.36	25.59	23.98	29.24	12.25	19.84	17.28
Danville, CA[2]	41.65	25.00	22.97	30.64	12.48	18.66	16.89
Draper, UT	34.49	19.26	17.93	18.38	9.90	14.32	12.97
Dublin, OH	34.62	19.42	19.10	21.40	9.71	15.60	12.71
Eastchester, NY[2]	46.43	20.21	21.54	32.53	10.92	15.88	15.02
Eden Prairie, MN	34.30	20.89	19.75	26.22	10.43	16.68	14.44
Edmond, OK	31.23	19.76	17.48	18.16	9.40	13.77	12.39
Evesham, NJ[2]	41.77	22.72	19.99	25.51	10.50	16.17	13.97
Fishers, IN	32.87	22.25	18.90	21.12	9.33	14.92	13.67
Flower Mound, TX[2]	38.66	21.09	19.97	16.53	9.60	16.57	13.29
Folsom, CA	33.75	21.38	20.18	23.10	11.90	17.08	15.07
Foster City, CA[2]	43.70	27.46	24.88	32.84	13.41	20.58	17.81
Franklin, TN	32.68	21.81	18.70	19.27	9.80	15.79	13.93
Friendswood, TX	41.91	21.26	20.37	18.17	9.85	17.80	13.28
Germantown, TN	31.64	19.05	18.09	18.35	9.21	14.95	12.58
Glastonbury, CT[3]	36.17	19.62	20.84	24.27	10.82	17.91	16.53
Grand Blanc, MI	32.50	18.20	17.31	23.74	10.04	15.33	13.41
Guilderland, NY	35.85	20.00	19.63	21.30	10.28	15.46	14.89
Hampden, PA	33.43	17.31	17.68	23.15	9.43	15.99	13.29
Holly Springs, NC	33.11	20.12	18.63	17.07	9.29	14.30	13.44
Huntersville, NC	37.36	21.38	18.38	16.97	9.47	14.42	13.64
Independence, KY	33.20	17.61	17.59	20.71	9.72	15.30	12.80
Johns Creek, GA	38.06	19.15	19.46	19.77	9.38	14.20	14.19
Keller, TX[2]	36.70	20.37	18.67	16.58	9.86	16.27	12.56
Kirkland, WA[2]	37.75	22.12	20.99	26.81	13.58	17.44	16.06
Lafayette, CO	37.93	24.16	19.87	19.50	12.26	19.84	14.19
Lake Oswego, OR	32.30	21.20	19.51	23.15	12.01	16.79	14.29
League City, TX	41.91	21.26	20.37	18.17	9.85	17.80	13.28
Leawood, KS	33.45	18.68	18.37	24.09	9.86	15.39	14.08
Lee's Summit, MO	33.45	18.68	18.37	24.09	9.86	15.39	14.08
Leesburg, VA[2]	43.03	23.59	21.96	22.16	10.63	18.51	15.29
Lehi, UT	33.17	18.05	17.12	17.69	9.58	12.44	12.07
Lenexa, KS	33.45	18.68	18.37	24.09	9.86	15.39	14.08
Lexington, MA[4]	41.34	23.83	22.55	31.66	11.36	18.73	16.16
Los Altos, CA	48.36	25.59	23.98	29.24	12.25	19.84	17.28
Lower Makefield, PA[2]	36.82	20.64	19.72	26.76	10.12	16.09	13.17
Madison, AL	36.90	17.29	17.75	16.16	9.31	12.28	12.10
Mamaroneck, NY[2]	46.43	20.21	21.54	32.53	10.92	15.88	15.02
Manheim, PA	32.65	19.23	17.12	18.45	9.57	14.90	13.27
Manlius, NY	34.40	17.38	18.60	20.84	9.92	14.29	13.56
Maple Grove, MN	34.30	20.89	19.75	26.22	10.43	16.68	14.44
Marion, IA	30.76	18.00	17.27	19.92	9.25	16.58	13.95
Marlboro, NJ[2]	46.43	20.21	21.54	32.53	10.92	15.88	15.02
Mason, OH	33.20	17.61	17.59	20.71	9.72	15.30	12.80
McCandless, PA	33.01	17.91	17.45	23.70	9.22	15.01	12.68

Table continued on next page.

Metro Area[1]	Accountants/ Auditors	Automotive Mechanics	Book-keepers	Carpenters	Cashiers	Clerks, Gen. Office	Clerks, Recep./Info.
Menomonee Falls, WI	34.24	19.83	18.32	25.19	9.88	16.39	13.65
Meridian, ID	32.15	19.11	17.16	16.82	9.83	14.14	12.82
Merrimack, NH[4]	35.81	21.59	18.67	22.77	10.08	17.95	12.41
Mount Lebanon, PA	33.01	17.91	17.45	23.70	9.22	15.01	12.68
Mount Pleasant, SC	29.32	19.93	17.05	20.00	9.08	12.95	13.71
Needham, MA[4]	41.34	23.83	22.55	31.66	11.36	18.73	16.16
Newtown, CT[3]	35.04	22.49	21.16	27.70	11.64	16.36	16.17
Northbrook, IL[2]	35.11	22.85	19.63	31.04	10.38	16.40	14.47
Northville, MI[2]	34.91	19.00	19.34	25.46	10.71	16.30	13.67
Novi, MI[2]	38.84	20.93	18.98	23.50	10.66	15.98	13.16
O'Fallon, MO	37.50	20.95	19.10	26.82	10.22	15.53	12.44
O'Fallon, IL	37.50	20.95	19.10	26.82	10.22	15.53	12.44
Orchard Park, NY	34.74	16.40	18.27	22.00	10.04	13.98	14.11
Oviedo, FL	31.71	18.53	17.20	17.84	9.69	13.93	12.90
Parker, CO	36.90	20.68	19.30	21.18	10.49	18.98	15.39
Parkland, FL[2]	34.83	20.65	17.61	18.54	9.91	13.55	13.11
Peachtree City, GA	38.06	19.15	19.46	19.77	9.38	14.20	14.19
Pflugerville, TX	33.89	19.44	19.90	17.86	10.42	16.44	13.33
Plainfield, IL[2]	35.11	22.85	19.63	31.04	10.38	16.40	14.47
Princeton, NJ	40.66	22.41	22.33	28.59	10.54	19.11	15.63
Queen Creek, AZ	33.16	19.59	18.26	19.55	10.31	16.85	13.39
Rancho Palos Verdes, CA[2]	37.94	19.33	21.13	25.74	10.92	15.88	14.57
Redmond, WA[2]	37.75	22.12	20.99	26.81	13.58	17.44	16.06
Richland, WA	32.99	21.74	19.20	18.47	11.49	15.99	13.71
Ridgefield, CT[3]	41.89	22.23	22.17	25.29	11.58	18.19	16.69
Ridgewood, NJ[2]	46.43	20.21	21.54	32.53	10.92	15.88	15.02
Rio Rancho, NM	32.26	19.30	17.16	17.41	10.04	12.59	12.81
Sahuarita, AZ	27.57	19.17	17.28	17.47	10.76	16.20	12.69
Sammamish, WA[2]	37.75	22.12	20.99	26.81	13.58	17.44	16.06
San Ramon, CA[2]	41.65	25.00	22.97	30.64	12.48	18.66	16.89
Saratoga, CA	48.36	25.59	23.98	29.24	12.25	19.84	17.28
Schertz, TX	34.57	20.32	17.91	18.32	9.84	16.17	11.99
Shrewsbury, MA[3]	35.33	20.49	19.45	23.98	10.81	15.94	15.05
South Brunswick, NJ[2]	46.43	20.21	21.54	32.53	10.92	15.88	15.02
South Jordan, UT	34.49	19.26	17.93	18.38	9.90	14.32	12.97
South Kingstown, RI[3]	38.05	19.67	19.03	22.70	10.76	16.47	14.63
South Windsor, CT[3]	36.17	19.62	20.84	24.27	10.82	17.91	16.53
Southlake, TX[2]	36.70	20.37	18.67	16.58	9.86	16.27	12.56
Spring Hill, TN	32.68	21.81	18.70	19.27	9.80	15.79	13.93
Stow, OH	33.14	17.48	17.11	25.27	9.86	14.28	12.02
Sugar Land, TX	41.91	21.26	20.37	18.17	9.85	17.80	13.28
Sun Prairie, WI	32.66	19.04	18.56	28.54	9.74	16.51	13.43
Syracuse, UT	34.42	22.97	17.29	17.57	9.73	14.04	11.65
Tredyffrin, PA[2]	36.82	20.64	19.72	26.76	10.12	16.09	13.17
Upper Arlington, OH	34.62	19.42	19.10	21.40	9.71	15.60	12.71
Upper Dublin, PA[2]	36.82	20.64	19.72	26.76	10.12	16.09	13.17
Vestavia Hills, AL	33.02	21.05	18.89	17.70	8.93	12.18	12.82
Webster, NY	33.79	18.75	18.43	20.32	9.88	14.76	13.41
Wellesley, MA[4]	41.34	23.83	22.55	31.66	11.36	18.73	16.16
West Fargo, ND	27.50	19.72	18.20	19.42	9.78	13.24	12.59
West Linn, OR	32.30	21.20	19.51	23.15	12.01	16.79	14.29
West Windsor, NJ	40.66	22.41	22.33	28.59	10.54	19.11	15.63
Westlake, OH	34.77	18.70	18.43	24.98	10.56	15.06	12.37
Weston, FL[2]	34.83	20.65	17.61	18.54	9.91	13.55	13.11
Westport, CT[3]	41.89	22.23	22.17	25.29	11.58	18.19	16.69
Wilmette, IL[2]	35.11	22.85	19.63	31.04	10.38	16.40	14.47
Woodbury, MN	34.30	20.89	19.75	26.22	10.43	16.68	14.44
Yorba Linda, CA[2]	37.26	25.15	21.75	24.95	11.29	16.51	14.99

Notes: (1) Figures cover the Metropolitan Statistical Area (MSA) except where noted. See Appendix B for areas included; (2) Metropolitan Division; (3) New England City and Town Area; (4) New England City and Town Area Division; n/a not available
Source: Bureau of Labor Statistics, May 2015 Metro Area Occupational Employment and Wage Estimates

Average Hourly Wages: Occupations C – E

Metro Area	Clerks, Ship./Rec.	Computer Programmers	Computer Systems Analysts	Comp. User Support Specialists	Cooks, Restaurant	Dentists	Electrical Engineers
Aliso Viejo, CA[2]	15.87	39.49	45.84	28.56	12.43	84.50	53.89
Allen, TX[2]	13.93	43.02	45.75	24.91	12.47	94.23	46.31
Alpharetta, GA	14.09	40.72	42.17	25.87	11.38	83.66	43.06
Ankeny, IA	17.24	35.63	40.00	22.49	10.63	85.33	35.79
Apex, NC	14.92	38.69	43.33	26.93	10.91	99.46	49.25
Ballwin, MO	16.25	40.55	44.34	25.26	11.65	83.85	48.11
Beavercreek, OH	15.23	32.62	42.80	22.15	10.63	91.36	42.25
Bella Vista, AR	14.41	n/a	32.59	18.99	11.43	99.55	38.34
Bernards, NJ[2]	16.95	44.01	47.04	28.98	13.86	77.83	47.38
Bethlehem, NY	17.06	36.64	36.96	22.98	12.62	93.42	50.25
Bloomfield, MI[2]	16.11	35.12	41.45	25.16	11.58	77.55	41.86
Bowie, MD[2]	17.38	47.38	49.66	29.48	12.68	77.21	55.22
Bozeman, MT	n/a	n/a	n/a	n/a	n/a	n/a	n/a
Brentwood, TN	14.55	37.17	35.57	23.61	11.05	87.93	37.16
Broomfield, CO	16.40	43.27	46.67	28.45	11.65	88.30	46.01
Carmel, IN	14.60	34.28	37.67	25.88	11.08	57.12	39.11
Cedar Park, TX	15.26	43.51	40.50	24.54	11.05	79.37	55.18
Cheshire, CT[3]	15.39	36.35	43.82	25.53	12.74	81.31	41.30
Chesterfield, MO	16.25	40.55	44.34	25.26	11.65	83.85	48.11
Collierville, TN	14.32	34.05	35.03	24.17	10.71	65.93	36.66
Coppell, TX[2]	13.93	43.02	45.75	24.91	12.47	94.23	46.31
Cornelius, NC	15.32	41.84	45.32	25.43	10.80	106.94	51.71
Cranberry, PA	15.82	33.79	39.05	25.33	11.08	55.05	42.98
Cupertino, CA	17.59	45.16	55.19	37.61	13.19	91.18	64.71
Danville, CA[2]	17.62	45.15	45.26	30.35	11.82	94.70	53.69
Draper, UT	14.77	36.95	35.35	23.59	12.34	73.82	44.91
Dublin, OH	13.83	35.33	39.92	23.12	11.74	95.76	38.89
Eastchester, NY[2]	16.94	46.00	50.45	28.75	13.74	76.20	48.32
Eden Prairie, MN	16.89	38.85	43.76	26.27	12.47	90.82	44.95
Edmond, OK	15.95	34.15	35.30	20.96	11.58	76.51	41.84
Evesham, NJ[2]	17.64	34.60	41.00	23.33	12.48	74.40	50.77
Fishers, IN	14.60	34.28	37.67	25.88	11.08	57.12	39.11
Flower Mound, TX[2]	13.93	43.02	45.75	24.91	12.47	94.23	46.31
Folsom, CA	15.45	39.27	39.06	27.42	12.24	78.99	44.34
Foster City, CA[2]	19.15	51.96	55.39	35.68	14.96	93.40	55.57
Franklin, TN	14.55	37.17	35.57	23.61	11.05	87.93	37.16
Friendswood, TX	15.07	42.67	49.39	27.58	10.96	75.83	51.64
Germantown, TN	14.32	34.05	35.03	24.17	10.71	65.93	36.66
Glastonbury, CT[3]	16.88	36.77	44.04	28.45	12.22	91.66	44.18
Grand Blanc, MI	14.27	n/a	39.90	24.04	10.85	92.88	n/a
Guilderland, NY	17.06	36.64	36.96	22.98	12.62	93.42	50.25
Hampden, PA	15.51	37.33	37.49	24.32	10.99	82.57	41.60
Holly Springs, NC	14.92	38.69	43.33	26.93	10.91	99.46	49.25
Huntersville, NC	15.32	41.84	45.32	25.43	10.80	106.94	51.71
Independence, KY	16.31	32.03	43.40	24.77	11.41	81.77	37.40
Johns Creek, GA	14.09	40.72	42.17	25.87	11.38	83.66	43.06
Keller, TX[2]	14.67	37.60	43.50	23.57	11.18	79.09	48.43
Kirkland, WA[2]	18.12	59.37	47.95	29.93	13.58	94.95	51.87
Lafayette, CO	16.38	46.98	41.57	27.14	12.68	92.45	47.98
Lake Oswego, OR	16.25	38.95	42.92	24.96	12.18	82.52	44.70
League City, TX	15.07	42.67	49.39	27.58	10.96	75.83	51.64
Leawood, KS	15.42	36.37	40.43	24.12	10.81	78.43	44.86
Lee's Summit, MO	15.42	36.37	40.43	24.12	10.81	78.43	44.86
Leesburg, VA[2]	17.38	47.38	49.66	29.48	12.68	77.21	55.22
Lehi, UT	13.31	38.13	38.09	18.65	12.24	74.10	41.43
Lenexa, KS	15.42	36.37	40.43	24.12	10.81	78.43	44.86
Lexington, MA[4]	17.83	48.37	44.94	31.22	14.10	82.28	52.77
Los Altos, CA	17.59	45.16	55.19	37.61	13.19	91.18	64.71
Lower Makefield, PA[2]	16.16	42.35	44.65	27.85	12.44	87.79	46.24
Madison, AL	14.44	47.04	40.71	24.24	10.52	87.51	47.71
Mamaroneck, NY[2]	16.94	46.00	50.45	28.75	13.74	76.20	48.32
Manheim, PA	16.31	31.91	36.26	21.55	11.24	75.58	43.76
Manlius, NY	15.53	33.92	37.01	26.95	12.09	98.69	44.71
Maple Grove, MN	16.89	38.85	43.76	26.27	12.47	90.82	44.95
Marion, IA	16.70	32.35	36.78	20.74	10.31	105.89	41.67
Marlboro, NJ[2]	16.94	46.00	50.45	28.75	13.74	76.20	48.32
Mason, OH	16.31	32.03	43.40	24.77	11.41	81.77	37.40

Table continued on next page.

Metro Area	Clerks, Ship./Rec.	Computer Program-mers	Computer Systems Analysts	Comp. User Support Specialists	Cooks, Restaurant	Dentists	Electrical Engineers
McCandless, PA	15.82	33.79	39.05	25.33	11.08	55.05	42.98
Menomonee Falls, WI	17.17	32.25	43.93	25.29	11.47	101.09	41.20
Meridian, ID	13.94	32.04	38.55	20.80	10.27	107.79	41.19
Merrimack, NH[4]	15.91	35.44	43.24	29.17	12.66	104.11	49.86
Mount Lebanon, PA	15.82	33.79	39.05	25.33	11.08	55.05	42.98
Mount Pleasant, SC	15.46	36.08	37.09	24.12	11.40	101.35	38.46
Needham, MA[4]	17.83	48.37	44.94	31.22	14.10	82.28	52.77
Newtown, CT[3]	15.19	40.11	44.53	23.12	13.09	76.85	37.34
Northbrook, IL[2]	16.37	37.27	42.42	26.66	11.75	61.93	45.45
Northville, MI[2]	17.91	38.39	45.88	21.55	12.17	72.86	45.78
Novi, MI[2]	16.11	35.12	41.45	25.16	11.58	77.55	41.86
O'Fallon, MO	16.25	40.55	44.34	25.26	11.65	83.85	48.11
O'Fallon, IL	16.25	40.55	44.34	25.26	11.65	83.85	48.11
Orchard Park, NY	15.67	33.36	35.27	20.87	12.52	98.60	39.36
Oviedo, FL	14.15	35.08	39.31	20.76	12.15	77.38	42.40
Parker, CO	16.40	43.27	46.67	28.45	11.65	88.30	46.01
Parkland, FL[2]	14.54	33.95	38.15	22.18	12.85	59.61	43.18
Peachtree City, GA	14.09	40.72	42.17	25.87	11.38	83.66	43.06
Pflugerville, TX	15.26	43.51	40.50	24.54	11.05	79.37	55.18
Plainfield, IL[2]	16.37	37.27	42.42	26.66	11.75	61.93	45.45
Princeton, NJ	18.08	44.28	43.90	30.43	12.77	74.92	53.81
Queen Creek, AZ	15.95	39.92	43.97	24.43	11.50	75.56	50.79
Rancho Palos Verdes, CA[2]	14.82	45.98	45.58	27.56	12.17	83.24	50.86
Redmond, WA[2]	18.12	59.37	47.95	29.93	13.58	94.95	51.87
Richland, WA	14.74	n/a	43.46	25.37	12.32	84.44	52.00
Ridgefield, CT[3]	17.32	41.64	45.62	27.07	15.17	93.45	44.69
Ridgewood, NJ[2]	16.94	46.00	50.45	28.75	13.74	76.20	48.32
Rio Rancho, NM	14.04	50.99	35.79	21.36	10.80	77.11	44.75
Sahuarita, AZ	14.82	36.77	37.61	23.31	10.91	70.15	37.40
Sammamish, WA[2]	18.12	59.37	47.95	29.93	13.58	94.95	51.87
San Ramon, CA[2]	17.62	45.15	45.26	30.35	11.82	94.70	53.69
Saratoga, CA	17.59	45.16	55.19	37.61	13.19	91.18	64.71
Schertz, TX	13.89	45.44	45.03	23.72	10.59	78.54	45.79
Shrewsbury, MA[3]	17.44	38.53	43.64	26.51	12.80	106.87	46.38
South Brunswick, NJ[2]	16.94	46.00	50.45	28.75	13.74	76.20	48.32
South Jordan, UT	14.77	36.95	35.35	23.59	12.34	73.82	44.91
South Kingstown, RI[3]	15.91	37.25	39.68	24.00	12.22	79.84	47.60
South Windsor, CT[3]	16.88	36.77	44.04	28.45	12.22	91.66	44.18
Southlake, TX[2]	14.67	37.60	43.50	23.57	11.18	79.09	48.43
Spring Hill, TN	14.55	37.17	35.57	23.61	11.05	87.93	37.16
Stow, OH	15.40	32.12	41.17	21.83	10.37	89.47	34.31
Sugar Land, TX	15.07	42.67	49.39	27.58	10.96	75.83	51.64
Sun Prairie, WI	15.66	38.00	35.16	23.01	11.19	95.28	42.26
Syracuse, UT	14.56	32.14	34.32	21.30	11.29	42.32	45.25
Tredyffrin, PA[2]	16.16	42.35	44.65	27.85	12.44	87.79	46.24
Upper Arlington, OH	13.83	35.33	39.92	23.12	11.74	95.76	38.89
Upper Dublin, PA[2]	16.16	42.35	44.65	27.85	12.44	87.79	46.24
Vestavia Hills, AL	14.60	37.71	35.89	23.32	10.50	68.83	45.00
Webster, NY	15.32	30.78	39.30	23.83	11.59	104.50	44.12
Wellesley, MA[4]	17.83	48.37	44.94	31.22	14.10	82.28	52.77
West Fargo, ND	15.34	25.11	n/a	21.60	12.57	101.62	41.80
West Linn, OR	16.25	38.95	42.92	24.96	12.18	82.52	44.70
West Windsor, NJ	18.08	44.28	43.90	30.43	12.77	74.92	53.81
Westlake, OH	15.60	33.46	39.07	22.06	10.86	88.96	36.49
Weston, FL[2]	14.54	33.95	38.15	22.18	12.85	59.61	43.18
Westport, CT[3]	17.32	41.64	45.62	27.07	15.17	93.45	44.69
Wilmette, IL[2]	16.37	37.27	42.42	26.66	11.75	61.93	45.45
Woodbury, MN	16.89	38.85	43.76	26.27	12.47	90.82	44.95
Yorba Linda, CA[2]	15.87	39.49	45.84	28.56	12.43	84.50	53.89

Notes: (1) Figures cover the Metropolitan Statistical Area (MSA) except where noted. See Appendix B for areas included; (2) Metropolitan Division; (3) New England City and Town Area; (4) New England City and Town Area Division; n/a not available
Source: Bureau of Labor Statistics, May 2015 Metro Area Occupational Employment and Wage Estimates

Average Hourly Wages: Occupations E – I

Metro Area	Electricians	Financial Managers	First-Line Supervisors/ Mgrs., Sales	Food Preparation Workers	General/ Operations Managers	Hairdressers/ Cosmetologists	Internists
Aliso Viejo, CA[2]	25.64	68.25	21.08	11.02	66.05	14.23	129.18
Allen, TX[2]	21.15	72.30	22.54	9.99	69.69	12.15	72.19
Alpharetta, GA	22.23	68.91	19.56	9.93	60.10	13.42	129.01
Ankeny, IA	27.48	59.93	19.84	9.77	52.60	16.42	97.55
Apex, NC	18.95	60.83	21.26	9.98	65.42	13.57	121.22
Ballwin, MO	30.18	63.93	21.20	10.12	53.15	12.87	127.15
Beavercreek, OH	21.46	52.43	18.33	10.61	55.52	10.71	102.23
Bella Vista, AR	18.47	68.74	16.62	9.03	47.63	11.88	n/a
Bernards, NJ[2]	35.49	80.51	23.80	10.85	81.78	17.25	n/a
Bethlehem, NY	29.11	61.18	22.39	10.73	55.68	16.92	112.72
Bloomfield, MI[2]	31.88	60.90	22.50	11.79	57.93	13.62	90.64
Bowie, MD[2]	26.93	74.37	22.57	11.70	70.62	17.08	71.81
Bozeman, MT	n/a	n/a	n/a	n/a	n/a	n/a	n/a
Brentwood, TN	23.15	52.67	19.88	9.83	54.46	14.41	78.03
Broomfield, CO	23.14	77.09	22.01	10.50	66.33	13.40	72.69
Carmel, IN	27.05	54.70	19.41	9.58	55.69	13.07	125.04
Cedar Park, TX	22.59	66.68	21.89	11.33	57.71	15.75	118.26
Cheshire, CT[3]	28.51	60.98	22.43	13.00	66.12	15.82	107.57
Chesterfield, MO	30.18	63.93	21.20	10.12	53.15	12.87	127.15
Collierville, TN	23.78	52.87	20.61	9.24	52.68	15.31	132.08
Coppell, TX[2]	21.15	72.30	22.54	9.99	69.69	12.15	72.19
Cornelius, NC	20.33	73.51	21.77	10.08	64.08	14.53	119.44
Cranberry, PA	26.49	68.98	21.38	10.36	59.56	11.69	104.14
Cupertino, CA	36.59	82.91	24.43	11.88	76.18	12.87	112.31
Danville, CA[2]	37.97	72.46	23.00	11.41	66.83	14.25	102.30
Draper, UT	24.71	57.31	19.33	9.56	46.90	11.94	102.22
Dublin, OH	21.62	63.86	18.95	10.59	54.97	11.81	124.26
Eastchester, NY[2]	37.19	90.86	24.90	11.50	79.03	17.87	97.62
Eden Prairie, MN	30.25	68.00	20.97	12.51	55.19	13.88	119.37
Edmond, OK	21.55	49.38	18.55	9.81	49.12	11.51	82.11
Evesham, NJ[2]	32.18	72.92	21.72	10.18	71.38	15.75	101.41
Fishers, IN	27.05	54.70	19.41	9.58	55.69	13.07	125.04
Flower Mound, TX[2]	21.15	72.30	22.54	9.99	69.69	12.15	72.19
Folsom, CA	33.30	59.81	20.20	11.03	53.98	13.24	100.33
Foster City, CA[2]	44.77	89.78	24.32	12.28	74.80	16.55	90.30
Franklin, TN	23.15	52.67	19.88	9.83	54.46	14.41	78.03
Friendswood, TX	23.23	75.80	22.64	10.49	70.02	13.24	76.11
Germantown, TN	23.78	52.87	20.61	9.24	52.68	15.31	132.08
Glastonbury, CT[3]	25.35	68.35	23.15	11.17	61.27	14.53	83.89
Grand Blanc, MI	29.93	52.11	18.47	12.02	47.48	12.05	46.45
Guilderland, NY	29.11	61.18	22.39	10.73	55.68	16.92	112.72
Hampden, PA	25.17	57.83	22.52	10.22	57.39	13.76	n/a
Holly Springs, NC	18.95	60.83	21.26	9.98	65.42	13.57	121.22
Huntersville, NC	20.33	73.51	21.77	10.08	64.08	14.53	119.44
Independence, KY	23.11	60.83	18.86	10.86	54.76	12.00	69.49
Johns Creek, GA	22.23	68.91	19.56	9.93	60.10	13.42	129.01
Keller, TX[2]	21.26	59.46	24.27	10.52	59.54	13.01	82.45
Kirkland, WA[2]	34.06	63.43	22.63	13.06	64.86	19.81	100.32
Lafayette, CO	23.59	69.87	25.94	10.75	64.82	17.65	103.76
Lake Oswego, OR	34.05	56.19	20.38	11.65	53.66	14.27	101.27
League City, TX	23.23	75.80	22.64	10.49	70.02	13.24	76.11
Leawood, KS	28.55	62.77	19.02	10.13	53.31	13.36	92.96
Lee's Summit, MO	28.55	62.77	19.02	10.13	53.31	13.36	92.96
Leesburg, VA[2]	26.93	74.37	22.57	11.70	70.62	17.08	71.81
Lehi, UT	22.95	53.20	17.64	9.77	40.09	11.75	n/a
Lenexa, KS	28.55	62.77	19.02	10.13	53.31	13.36	92.96
Lexington, MA[4]	33.33	68.75	22.66	12.90	71.11	17.84	112.54
Los Altos, CA	36.59	82.91	24.43	11.88	76.18	12.87	112.31
Lower Makefield, PA[2]	32.08	75.65	24.01	11.37	66.61	14.62	84.76
Madison, AL	18.98	63.42	19.82	8.94	64.69	14.75	n/a
Mamaroneck, NY[2]	37.19	90.86	24.90	11.50	79.03	17.87	97.62
Manheim, PA	22.17	56.94	23.59	10.37	50.82	11.90	n/a
Manlius, NY	26.70	59.97	20.60	11.18	53.59	12.83	102.96
Maple Grove, MN	30.25	68.00	20.97	12.51	55.19	13.88	119.37
Marion, IA	28.69	55.29	17.28	9.88	45.25	9.64	n/a
Marlboro, NJ[2]	37.19	90.86	24.90	11.50	79.03	17.87	97.62
Mason, OH	23.11	60.83	18.86	10.86	54.76	12.00	69.49

Table continued on next page.

Metro Area	Electricians	Financial Managers	First-Line Supervisors/ Mgrs., Sales	Food Preparation Workers	General/ Operations Managers	Hairdressers/ Cosmetologists	Internists
McCandless, PA	26.49	68.98	21.38	10.36	59.56	11.69	104.14
Menomonee Falls, WI	30.28	62.59	19.22	9.90	62.49	13.43	102.20
Meridian, ID	22.18	46.56	18.65	9.72	38.80	13.23	n/a
Merrimack, NH[4]	22.02	60.17	23.82	10.09	66.52	16.29	119.89
Mount Lebanon, PA	26.49	68.98	21.38	10.36	59.56	11.69	104.14
Mount Pleasant, SC	22.55	53.83	19.85	10.98	47.30	15.51	94.77
Needham, MA[4]	33.33	68.75	22.66	12.90	71.11	17.84	112.54
Newtown, CT[3]	25.37	60.73	21.83	11.89	67.21	15.58	n/a
Northbrook, IL[2]	35.46	63.54	22.18	10.44	58.83	13.34	83.00
Northville, MI[2]	31.99	58.52	18.59	12.30	57.48	13.85	75.38
Novi, MI[2]	31.88	60.90	22.50	11.79	57.93	13.62	90.64
O'Fallon, MO	30.18	63.93	21.20	10.12	53.15	12.87	127.15
O'Fallon, IL	30.18	63.93	21.20	10.12	53.15	12.87	127.15
Orchard Park, NY	28.15	59.01	19.81	10.83	51.65	10.90	n/a
Oviedo, FL	18.74	62.20	20.70	10.71	58.06	12.42	97.37
Parker, CO	23.14	77.09	22.01	10.50	66.33	13.40	72.69
Parkland, FL[2]	19.45	66.68	23.10	10.52	66.56	12.01	66.56
Peachtree City, GA	22.23	68.91	19.56	9.93	60.10	13.42	129.01
Pflugerville, TX	22.59	66.68	21.89	11.33	57.71	15.75	118.26
Plainfield, IL[2]	35.46	63.54	22.18	10.44	58.83	13.34	83.00
Princeton, NJ	31.56	76.23	22.37	10.56	78.08	15.86	110.98
Queen Creek, AZ	23.49	59.68	20.03	10.42	51.00	12.18	84.97
Rancho Palos Verdes, CA[2]	29.84	72.17	20.71	11.08	62.25	13.93	82.36
Redmond, WA[2]	34.06	63.43	22.63	13.06	64.86	19.81	100.32
Richland, WA	33.20	49.69	19.69	12.40	53.24	13.78	n/a
Ridgefield, CT[3]	30.15	75.74	23.59	14.89	81.02	14.75	100.52
Ridgewood, NJ[2]	37.19	90.86	24.90	11.50	79.03	17.87	97.62
Rio Rancho, NM	21.27	49.63	19.99	10.13	48.59	13.36	103.89
Sahuarita, AZ	22.24	45.92	19.70	10.62	38.38	11.55	n/a
Sammamish, WA[2]	34.06	63.43	22.63	13.06	64.86	19.81	100.32
San Ramon, CA[2]	37.97	72.46	23.00	11.41	66.83	14.25	102.30
Saratoga, CA	36.59	82.91	24.43	11.88	76.18	12.87	112.31
Schertz, TX	21.58	74.58	22.64	10.33	56.28	11.63	102.17
Shrewsbury, MA[3]	33.90	52.49	21.18	11.07	57.60	16.75	n/a
South Brunswick, NJ[2]	37.19	90.86	24.90	11.50	79.03	17.87	97.62
South Jordan, UT	24.71	57.31	19.33	9.56	46.90	11.94	102.22
South Kingstown, RI[3]	25.53	64.39	22.98	11.29	62.82	13.95	94.75
South Windsor, CT[3]	25.35	68.35	23.15	11.17	61.27	14.53	83.89
Southlake, TX[2]	21.26	59.46	24.27	10.52	59.54	13.01	82.45
Spring Hill, TN	23.15	52.67	19.88	9.83	54.46	14.41	78.03
Stow, OH	24.59	55.92	20.08	11.45	53.40	11.43	74.82
Sugar Land, TX	23.23	75.80	22.64	10.49	70.02	13.24	76.11
Sun Prairie, WI	27.83	58.87	18.18	10.03	55.94	13.87	119.94
Syracuse, UT	23.02	46.90	18.86	9.98	34.84	11.68	n/a
Tredyffrin, PA[2]	32.08	75.65	24.01	11.37	66.61	14.62	84.76
Upper Arlington, OH	21.62	63.86	18.95	10.59	54.97	11.81	124.26
Upper Dublin, PA[2]	32.08	75.65	24.01	11.37	66.61	14.62	84.76
Vestavia Hills, AL	22.93	65.09	21.83	9.46	63.70	11.48	120.46
Webster, NY	30.11	63.06	21.80	10.37	58.76	12.59	n/a
Wellesley, MA[4]	33.33	68.75	22.66	12.90	71.11	17.84	112.54
West Fargo, ND	26.80	54.51	20.21	12.48	50.06	14.19	n/a
West Linn, OR	34.05	56.19	20.38	11.65	53.66	14.27	101.27
West Windsor, NJ	31.56	76.23	22.37	10.56	78.08	15.86	110.98
Westlake, OH	28.52	58.15	19.54	10.87	54.68	13.97	77.03
Weston, FL[2]	19.45	66.68	23.10	10.52	66.56	12.01	66.56
Westport, CT[3]	30.15	75.74	23.59	14.89	81.02	14.75	100.52
Wilmette, IL[2]	35.46	63.54	22.18	10.44	58.83	13.34	83.00
Woodbury, MN	30.25	68.00	20.97	12.51	55.19	13.88	119.37
Yorba Linda, CA[2]	25.64	68.25	21.08	11.02	66.05	14.23	129.18

Notes: (1) Figures cover the Metropolitan Statistical Area (MSA) except where noted. See Appendix B for areas included; (2) Metropolitan Division; (3) New England City and Town Area; (4) New England City and Town Area Division; n/a not available
Source: Bureau of Labor Statistics, May 2015 Metro Area Occupational Employment and Wage Estimates

Average Hourly Wages: Occupations J – N

Metro Area	Janitors/ Cleaners	Landscapers	Lawyers	Maids/ House- keepers	Main- tenance Repairers	Marketing Managers	Nuclear Medicine Techs
Aliso Viejo, CA[2]	12.80	12.75	76.75	11.34	19.96	65.03	52.24
Allen, TX[2]	10.15	12.52	73.09	9.56	17.84	70.82	37.60
Alpharetta, GA	11.57	12.98	66.05	9.32	18.24	64.91	35.79
Ankeny, IA	11.85	14.18	58.64	10.24	18.66	57.84	33.84
Apex, NC	10.33	12.09	60.11	9.69	18.93	67.65	32.80
Ballwin, MO	11.59	13.20	55.39	10.36	19.01	66.57	33.83
Beavercreek, OH	12.05	13.30	59.25	10.00	18.48	58.23	32.26
Bella Vista, AR	10.93	11.85	63.97	8.92	16.10	70.65	n/a
Bernards, NJ[2]	14.47	13.64	75.62	11.71	20.80	81.89	44.57
Bethlehem, NY	13.02	14.32	51.56	10.69	20.07	76.15	39.82
Bloomfield, MI[2]	12.22	13.36	57.37	11.00	17.36	58.43	33.31
Bowie, MD[2]	13.08	13.95	80.09	12.55	21.71	75.26	39.84
Bozeman, MT	n/a	n/a	n/a	n/a	n/a	n/a	n/a
Brentwood, TN	11.28	12.56	60.22	9.94	18.53	47.48	31.17
Broomfield, CO	12.11	13.95	68.61	10.39	19.00	70.66	36.55
Carmel, IN	11.89	12.22	59.31	9.80	18.60	53.84	34.81
Cedar Park, TX	11.16	12.82	66.76	9.76	17.11	73.67	34.83
Cheshire, CT[3]	15.58	17.64	60.45	11.36	22.16	61.13	37.84
Chesterfield, MO	11.59	13.20	55.39	10.36	19.01	66.57	33.83
Collierville, TN	10.69	12.16	61.29	9.44	18.15	44.53	34.58
Coppell, TX[2]	10.15	12.52	73.09	9.56	17.84	70.82	37.60
Cornelius, NC	10.76	12.21	66.87	9.18	19.20	65.66	32.52
Cranberry, PA	12.84	13.02	67.07	10.44	18.79	69.88	28.76
Cupertino, CA	13.50	15.50	98.08	15.18	23.36	94.90	57.52
Danville, CA[2]	15.37	15.75	75.13	15.77	21.70	79.92	55.63
Draper, UT	10.02	12.66	58.35	10.41	18.97	59.22	34.64
Dublin, OH	12.74	12.57	53.27	10.21	19.08	65.49	33.00
Eastchester, NY[2]	15.87	15.52	80.76	16.84	21.29	89.06	40.65
Eden Prairie, MN	13.40	14.32	64.64	11.42	21.64	66.76	37.32
Edmond, OK	10.90	11.41	51.21	9.45	16.70	45.33	33.20
Evesham, NJ[2]	14.33	11.89	61.98	11.20	20.80	63.29	39.60
Fishers, IN	11.89	12.22	59.31	9.80	18.60	53.84	34.81
Flower Mound, TX[2]	10.15	12.52	73.09	9.56	17.84	70.82	37.60
Folsom, CA	13.63	13.99	64.01	12.55	20.05	57.90	56.48
Foster City, CA[2]	14.30	19.61	85.63	17.69	27.89	89.58	55.14
Franklin, TN	11.28	12.56	60.22	9.94	18.53	47.48	31.17
Friendswood, TX	10.54	11.76	77.69	9.46	18.45	78.07	35.74
Germantown, TN	10.69	12.16	61.29	9.44	18.15	44.53	34.58
Glastonbury, CT[3]	15.34	14.82	65.46	12.62	20.71	64.39	39.03
Grand Blanc, MI	12.45	12.40	45.59	11.19	15.35	51.67	30.03
Guilderland, NY	13.02	14.32	51.56	10.69	20.07	76.15	39.82
Hampden, PA	11.85	13.49	63.09	9.50	18.80	64.00	34.90
Holly Springs, NC	10.33	12.09	60.11	9.69	18.93	67.65	32.80
Huntersville, NC	10.76	12.21	66.87	9.18	19.20	65.66	32.52
Independence, KY	11.88	12.16	58.49	10.49	19.40	61.36	32.60
Johns Creek, GA	11.57	12.98	66.05	9.32	18.24	64.91	35.79
Keller, TX[2]	10.63	12.61	54.80	10.07	17.49	60.31	34.75
Kirkland, WA[2]	15.07	16.94	65.19	12.32	21.61	69.13	42.98
Lafayette, CO	13.35	14.44	58.47	11.06	19.16	73.56	n/a
Lake Oswego, OR	13.29	15.14	60.08	12.25	20.66	57.98	40.97
League City, TX	10.54	11.76	77.69	9.46	18.45	78.07	35.74
Leawood, KS	12.82	12.89	57.35	10.01	17.76	61.85	32.84
Lee's Summit, MO	12.82	12.89	57.35	10.01	17.76	61.85	32.84
Leesburg, VA[2]	13.08	13.95	80.09	12.55	21.71	75.26	39.84
Lehi, UT	10.00	11.86	49.87	9.38	17.31	54.32	n/a
Lenexa, KS	12.82	12.89	57.35	10.01	17.76	61.85	32.84
Lexington, MA[4]	16.71	16.71	78.96	14.49	22.61	68.56	36.73
Los Altos, CA	13.50	15.50	98.08	15.18	23.36	94.90	57.52
Lower Makefield, PA[2]	14.65	14.39	62.53	11.62	19.96	79.14	35.59
Madison, AL	10.55	10.16	66.06	8.46	19.72	65.00	n/a
Mamaroneck, NY[2]	15.87	15.52	80.76	16.84	21.29	89.06	40.65
Manheim, PA	13.22	14.47	53.63	10.51	19.68	66.95	n/a
Manlius, NY	13.10	13.58	50.44	10.29	18.42	67.17	37.50
Maple Grove, MN	13.40	14.32	64.64	11.42	21.64	66.76	37.32
Marion, IA	14.53	13.78	50.42	10.08	21.72	59.45	n/a
Marlboro, NJ[2]	15.87	15.52	80.76	16.84	21.29	89.06	40.65
Mason, OH	11.88	12.16	58.49	10.49	19.40	61.36	32.60

Table continued on next page.

Metro Area	Janitors/ Cleaners	Landscapers	Lawyers	Maids/ House-keepers	Main-tenance Repairers	Marketing Managers	Nuclear Medicine Techs
McCandless, PA	12.84	13.02	67.07	10.44	18.79	69.88	28.76
Menomonee Falls, WI	11.91	12.80	51.49	10.55	18.99	56.31	35.67
Meridian, ID	11.41	12.94	49.52	10.53	15.47	60.19	n/a
Merrimack, NH[4]	15.42	12.86	48.09	9.88	20.01	63.42	n/a
Mount Lebanon, PA	12.84	13.02	67.07	10.44	18.79	69.88	28.76
Mount Pleasant, SC	10.39	11.89	40.49	9.89	18.13	48.09	33.66
Needham, MA[4]	16.71	16.71	78.96	14.49	22.61	68.56	36.73
Newtown, CT[3]	15.02	15.97	68.53	11.71	23.48	53.44	n/a
Northbrook, IL[2]	14.23	14.34	62.12	12.44	21.36	58.77	35.61
Northville, MI[2]	12.80	13.17	52.07	11.87	18.83	71.40	30.26
Novi, MI[2]	12.22	13.36	57.37	11.00	17.36	58.43	33.31
O'Fallon, MO	11.59	13.20	55.39	10.36	19.01	66.57	33.83
O'Fallon, IL	11.59	13.20	55.39	10.36	19.01	66.57	33.83
Orchard Park, NY	12.87	13.23	47.48	11.38	18.75	69.36	34.17
Oviedo, FL	10.82	11.76	78.47	10.27	16.23	53.58	35.01
Parker, CO	12.11	13.95	68.61	10.39	19.00	70.66	36.55
Parkland, FL[2]	10.35	12.70	n/a	10.28	16.53	58.89	35.89
Peachtree City, GA	11.57	12.98	66.05	9.32	18.24	64.91	35.79
Pflugerville, TX	11.16	12.82	66.76	9.76	17.11	73.67	34.83
Plainfield, IL[2]	14.23	14.34	62.12	12.44	21.36	58.77	35.61
Princeton, NJ	14.18	14.15	61.95	14.05	22.36	72.75	43.36
Queen Creek, AZ	11.49	11.74	63.45	10.33	17.82	57.96	37.87
Rancho Palos Verdes, CA[2]	13.89	14.45	83.22	12.64	21.34	70.61	48.58
Redmond, WA[2]	15.07	16.94	65.19	12.32	21.61	69.13	42.98
Richland, WA	13.72	14.34	45.01	11.41	22.34	61.14	n/a
Ridgefield, CT[3]	15.35	17.04	87.43	12.27	23.42	80.11	46.76
Ridgewood, NJ[2]	15.87	15.52	80.76	16.84	21.29	89.06	40.65
Rio Rancho, NM	10.88	11.59	42.98	9.16	16.82	39.71	35.71
Sahuarita, AZ	11.20	12.00	51.38	9.62	16.65	52.73	n/a
Sammamish, WA[2]	15.07	16.94	65.19	12.32	21.61	69.13	42.98
San Ramon, CA[2]	15.37	15.75	75.13	15.77	21.70	79.92	55.63
Saratoga, CA	13.50	15.50	98.08	15.18	23.36	94.90	57.52
Schertz, TX	10.69	12.62	58.39	9.69	15.86	68.65	33.06
Shrewsbury, MA[3]	15.29	15.39	50.62	11.86	20.44	59.80	n/a
South Brunswick, NJ[2]	15.87	15.52	80.76	16.84	21.29	89.06	40.65
South Jordan, UT	10.02	12.66	58.35	10.41	18.97	59.22	34.64
South Kingstown, RI[3]	13.55	14.43	61.40	12.45	20.45	63.64	41.16
South Windsor, CT[3]	15.34	14.82	65.46	12.62	20.71	64.39	39.03
Southlake, TX[2]	10.63	12.61	54.80	10.07	17.49	60.31	34.75
Spring Hill, TN	11.28	12.56	60.22	9.94	18.53	47.48	31.17
Stow, OH	14.65	12.98	49.57	10.94	18.75	58.29	32.75
Sugar Land, TX	10.54	11.76	77.69	9.46	18.45	78.07	35.74
Sun Prairie, WI	11.50	13.62	51.37	10.34	19.28	54.07	n/a
Syracuse, UT	11.43	11.59	43.86	9.67	18.01	47.78	n/a
Tredyffrin, PA[2]	14.65	14.39	62.53	11.62	19.96	79.14	35.59
Upper Arlington, OH	12.74	12.57	53.27	10.21	19.08	65.49	33.00
Upper Dublin, PA[2]	14.65	14.39	62.53	11.62	19.96	79.14	35.59
Vestavia Hills, AL	10.41	12.59	58.47	8.79	18.76	71.08	31.26
Webster, NY	11.98	13.81	49.71	10.89	19.15	56.80	33.94
Wellesley, MA[4]	16.71	16.71	78.96	14.49	22.61	68.56	36.73
West Fargo, ND	12.86	12.80	50.58	10.16	18.77	49.57	n/a
West Linn, OR	13.29	15.14	60.08	12.25	20.66	57.98	40.97
West Windsor, NJ	14.18	14.15	61.95	14.05	22.36	72.75	43.36
Westlake, OH	12.64	13.10	55.05	10.62	18.99	60.52	33.71
Weston, FL[2]	10.35	12.70	n/a	10.28	16.53	58.89	35.89
Westport, CT[3]	15.35	17.04	87.43	12.27	23.42	80.11	46.76
Wilmette, IL[2]	14.23	14.34	62.12	12.44	21.36	58.77	35.61
Woodbury, MN	13.40	14.32	64.64	11.42	21.64	66.76	37.32
Yorba Linda, CA[2]	12.80	12.75	76.75	11.34	19.96	65.03	52.24

Notes: (1) Figures cover the Metropolitan Statistical Area (MSA) except where noted. See Appendix B for areas included; (2) Metropolitan Division; (3) New England City and Town Area; (4) New England City and Town Area Division; n/a not available

Source: Bureau of Labor Statistics, May 2015 Metro Area Occupational Employment and Wage Estimates

Average Hourly Wages: Occupations N – R

Metro Area	Nurses, Licensed Practical	Nurses, Registered	Nursing Assistants	Packers/ Packagers	Physical Therapists	Postal Mail Carriers	R.E. Brokers
Aliso Viejo, CA[2]	24.65	42.74	13.85	11.64	45.41	25.84	n/a
Allen, TX[2]	22.70	34.89	12.27	10.71	49.69	25.03	64.35
Alpharetta, GA	19.58	31.73	11.41	10.96	39.70	24.82	51.40
Ankeny, IA	20.06	27.44	13.34	10.34	38.76	24.61	n/a
Apex, NC	20.84	29.41	11.51	10.92	36.66	25.11	29.24
Ballwin, MO	20.33	29.20	12.03	11.44	37.83	24.38	15.47
Beavercreek, OH	20.70	29.55	12.79	9.72	43.43	24.63	n/a
Bella Vista, AR	19.66	27.00	10.53	11.62	35.20	24.41	n/a
Bernards, NJ[2]	26.25	39.35	13.68	10.53	44.49	24.73	48.92
Bethlehem, NY	19.92	29.85	13.21	14.41	34.21	24.56	n/a
Bloomfield, MI[2]	23.80	37.09	13.69	13.40	44.15	25.14	30.04
Bowie, MD[2]	23.74	37.41	13.90	11.06	41.93	24.56	45.36
Bozeman, MT	n/a	n/a	n/a	n/a	n/a	n/a	n/a
Brentwood, TN	19.18	28.49	10.99	11.15	40.76	25.00	25.28
Broomfield, CO	24.11	34.48	15.10	11.42	36.71	24.73	33.01
Carmel, IN	19.97	29.83	12.31	11.36	40.48	24.57	20.52
Cedar Park, TX	22.24	32.27	12.37	11.42	44.13	24.78	46.87
Cheshire, CT[3]	27.02	38.49	16.09	12.84	40.66	25.81	29.11
Chesterfield, MO	20.33	29.20	12.03	11.44	37.83	24.38	15.47
Collierville, TN	19.95	29.68	11.65	10.33	42.77	24.66	23.80
Coppell, TX[2]	22.70	34.89	12.27	10.71	49.69	25.03	64.35
Cornelius, NC	20.03	29.22	11.20	11.66	39.89	24.61	33.59
Cranberry, PA	20.26	30.34	13.68	11.37	39.01	24.20	62.40
Cupertino, CA	28.36	58.47	15.92	12.48	47.60	26.04	n/a
Danville, CA[2]	28.78	60.05	16.42	11.99	47.88	26.11	44.42
Draper, UT	22.79	30.47	12.16	10.81	35.87	25.18	n/a
Dublin, OH	19.97	31.13	12.05	11.61	36.67	23.97	53.78
Eastchester, NY[2]	25.33	41.54	16.38	11.33	44.91	25.04	50.12
Eden Prairie, MN	21.42	37.00	14.83	12.13	36.96	24.43	n/a
Edmond, OK	19.19	29.21	11.51	11.94	39.38	24.20	14.26
Evesham, NJ[2]	24.36	37.36	13.07	11.03	43.81	25.18	n/a
Fishers, IN	19.97	29.83	12.31	11.36	40.48	24.57	20.52
Flower Mound, TX[2]	22.70	34.89	12.27	10.71	49.69	25.03	64.35
Folsom, CA	28.21	54.33	17.78	13.37	47.23	25.32	69.32
Foster City, CA[2]	29.72	64.26	19.09	13.19	51.47	26.23	41.41
Franklin, TN	19.18	28.49	10.99	11.15	40.76	25.00	25.28
Friendswood, TX	23.96	36.92	12.21	11.10	43.13	24.68	51.39
Germantown, TN	19.95	29.68	11.65	10.33	42.77	24.66	23.80
Glastonbury, CT[3]	27.04	36.53	14.90	14.20	39.83	24.89	48.04
Grand Blanc, MI	21.95	31.88	12.70	13.23	39.55	24.88	n/a
Guilderland, NY	19.92	29.85	13.21	14.41	34.21	24.56	n/a
Hampden, PA	22.07	32.43	13.86	11.18	42.77	24.61	n/a
Holly Springs, NC	20.84	29.41	11.51	10.92	36.66	25.11	29.24
Huntersville, NC	20.03	29.22	11.20	11.66	39.89	24.61	33.59
Independence, KY	20.65	30.76	12.47	10.97	41.41	24.88	73.93
Johns Creek, GA	19.58	31.73	11.41	10.96	39.70	24.82	51.40
Keller, TX[2]	22.96	35.38	11.86	11.96	41.14	24.91	27.74
Kirkland, WA[2]	25.93	39.54	15.43	13.38	42.87	25.00	41.23
Lafayette, CO	22.45	36.29	13.80	11.48	34.27	24.85	33.53
Lake Oswego, OR	24.42	40.95	14.36	12.61	40.28	24.58	35.58
League City, TX	23.96	36.92	12.21	11.10	43.13	24.68	51.39
Leawood, KS	19.56	30.45	12.30	11.13	37.13	24.23	n/a
Lee's Summit, MO	19.56	30.45	12.30	11.13	37.13	24.23	n/a
Leesburg, VA[2]	23.74	37.41	13.90	11.06	41.93	24.56	45.36
Lehi, UT	19.03	28.39	11.40	10.40	39.82	24.80	n/a
Lenexa, KS	19.56	30.45	12.30	11.13	37.13	24.23	n/a
Lexington, MA[4]	26.51	46.05	14.83	12.24	40.26	25.82	59.92
Los Altos, CA	28.36	58.47	15.92	12.48	47.60	26.04	n/a
Lower Makefield, PA[2]	24.53	34.49	14.24	12.00	41.20	24.93	40.89
Madison, AL	17.52	27.61	11.63	11.61	46.15	24.72	34.44
Mamaroneck, NY[2]	25.33	41.54	16.38	11.33	44.91	25.04	50.12
Manheim, PA	20.14	29.23	13.26	12.32	41.25	24.41	n/a
Manlius, NY	18.53	29.16	13.27	12.62	35.69	24.12	40.56
Maple Grove, MN	21.42	37.00	14.83	12.13	36.96	24.43	n/a
Marion, IA	19.32	25.92	12.06	9.55	35.19	24.78	n/a
Marlboro, NJ[2]	25.33	41.54	16.38	11.33	44.91	25.04	50.12
Mason, OH	20.65	30.76	12.47	10.97	41.41	24.88	73.93

Table continued on next page.

Metro Area	Nurses, Licensed Practical	Nurses, Registered	Nursing Assistants	Packers/ Packagers	Physical Therapists	Postal Mail Carriers	R.E. Brokers
McCandless, PA	20.26	30.34	13.68	11.37	39.01	24.20	62.40
Menomonee Falls, WI	22.18	32.85	13.15	12.36	35.94	24.41	63.87
Meridian, ID	19.34	30.00	11.69	13.87	34.91	24.26	24.24
Merrimack, NH[4]	23.25	31.78	13.61	11.93	40.69	24.50	n/a
Mount Lebanon, PA	20.26	30.34	13.68	11.37	39.01	24.20	62.40
Mount Pleasant, SC	19.97	32.84	12.82	11.02	37.55	24.29	30.24
Needham, MA[4]	26.51	46.05	14.83	12.24	40.26	25.82	59.92
Newtown, CT[3]	25.51	38.93	15.27	13.74	45.79	25.07	n/a
Northbrook, IL[2]	24.67	35.96	12.89	12.25	41.57	25.13	38.44
Northville, MI[2]	23.40	32.23	13.44	11.94	40.69	25.31	36.14
Novi, MI[2]	23.80	37.09	13.69	13.40	44.15	25.14	30.04
O'Fallon, MO	20.33	29.20	12.03	11.44	37.83	24.38	15.47
O'Fallon, IL	20.33	29.20	12.03	11.44	37.83	24.38	15.47
Orchard Park, NY	19.78	33.55	14.06	11.36	35.56	24.53	n/a
Oviedo, FL	19.35	29.62	11.85	10.45	41.89	24.89	59.59
Parker, CO	24.11	34.48	15.10	11.42	36.71	24.73	33.01
Parkland, FL[2]	21.07	33.22	12.03	10.17	41.56	25.26	34.73
Peachtree City, GA	19.58	31.73	11.41	10.96	39.70	24.82	51.40
Pflugerville, TX	22.24	32.27	12.37	11.42	44.13	24.78	46.87
Plainfield, IL[2]	24.67	35.96	12.89	12.25	41.57	25.13	38.44
Princeton, NJ	25.59	34.21	13.25	11.08	42.42	25.12	n/a
Queen Creek, AZ	24.62	35.34	14.21	11.28	40.14	24.88	32.71
Rancho Palos Verdes, CA[2]	23.86	46.61	14.67	10.74	44.29	25.56	39.75
Redmond, WA[2]	25.93	39.54	15.43	13.38	42.87	25.00	41.23
Richland, WA	23.66	30.68	13.30	12.36	42.09	25.55	n/a
Ridgefield, CT[3]	27.02	37.63	15.94	11.75	44.15	25.24	n/a
Ridgewood, NJ[2]	25.33	41.54	16.38	11.33	44.91	25.04	50.12
Rio Rancho, NM	23.03	32.57	13.49	10.12	40.31	24.90	n/a
Sahuarita, AZ	23.18	32.28	13.11	10.47	42.61	25.44	35.70
Sammamish, WA[2]	25.93	39.54	15.43	13.38	42.87	25.00	41.23
San Ramon, CA[2]	28.78	60.05	16.42	11.99	47.88	26.11	44.42
Saratoga, CA	28.36	58.47	15.92	12.48	47.60	26.04	n/a
Schertz, TX	20.92	31.88	12.02	11.39	44.93	24.61	29.65
Shrewsbury, MA[3]	25.97	43.25	14.81	12.16	38.08	24.03	n/a
South Brunswick, NJ[2]	25.33	41.54	16.38	11.33	44.91	25.04	50.12
South Jordan, UT	22.79	30.47	12.16	10.81	35.87	25.18	n/a
South Kingstown, RI[3]	25.44	36.83	13.91	11.15	38.96	24.65	34.30
South Windsor, CT[3]	27.04	36.53	14.90	14.20	39.83	24.89	48.04
Southlake, TX[2]	22.96	35.38	11.86	11.96	41.14	24.91	27.74
Spring Hill, TN	19.18	28.49	10.99	11.15	40.76	25.00	25.28
Stow, OH	19.05	30.95	11.97	14.23	40.89	24.30	n/a
Sugar Land, TX	23.96	36.92	12.21	11.10	43.13	24.68	51.39
Sun Prairie, WI	22.04	36.24	14.44	16.01	36.90	24.14	n/a
Syracuse, UT	20.73	28.09	10.94	10.58	45.18	24.70	23.20
Tredyffrin, PA[2]	24.53	34.49	14.24	12.00	41.20	24.93	40.89
Upper Arlington, OH	19.97	31.13	12.05	11.61	36.67	23.97	53.78
Upper Dublin, PA[2]	24.53	34.49	14.24	12.00	41.20	24.93	40.89
Vestavia Hills, AL	18.41	28.38	10.74	10.02	40.96	24.56	n/a
Webster, NY	19.25	29.62	13.11	12.00	37.60	24.19	n/a
Wellesley, MA[4]	26.51	46.05	14.83	12.24	40.26	25.82	59.92
West Fargo, ND	18.90	28.40	13.55	11.27	34.98	23.98	n/a
West Linn, OR	24.42	40.95	14.36	12.61	40.28	24.58	35.58
West Windsor, NJ	25.59	34.21	13.25	11.08	42.42	25.12	n/a
Westlake, OH	21.04	31.55	12.33	11.55	40.18	24.82	n/a
Weston, FL[2]	21.07	33.22	12.03	10.17	41.56	25.26	34.73
Westport, CT[3]	27.02	37.63	15.94	11.75	44.15	25.24	n/a
Wilmette, IL[2]	24.67	35.96	12.89	12.25	41.57	25.13	38.44
Woodbury, MN	21.42	37.00	14.83	12.13	36.96	24.43	n/a
Yorba Linda, CA[2]	24.65	42.74	13.85	11.64	45.41	25.84	n/a

Notes: (1) Figures cover the Metropolitan Statistical Area (MSA) except where noted. See Appendix B for areas included; (2) Metropolitan Division; (3) New England City and Town Area; (4) New England City and Town Area Division; n/a not available
Source: Bureau of Labor Statistics, May 2015 Metro Area Occupational Employment and Wage Estimates

Average Hourly Wages: Occupations R – T

Metro Area	Retail Salespersons	Sales Reps., Except Tech./Scien.	Sales Reps., Tech./Scien.	Secretaries, Exc. Leg./Med./Exec.	Security Guards	Surgeons	Teacher Assistants
Aliso Viejo, CA[2]	13.50	30.76	41.69	18.85	12.56	87.38	16.42
Allen, TX[2]	13.72	38.76	38.45	17.16	13.24	120.03	11.50
Alpharetta, GA	11.85	32.41	39.40	17.34	12.62	128.18	10.47
Ankeny, IA	13.58	34.68	33.82	17.33	14.01	111.55	11.04
Apex, NC	12.05	31.22	50.21	16.86	12.75	n/a	11.10
Ballwin, MO	13.21	32.93	35.44	16.37	13.13	n/a	12.99
Beavercreek, OH	11.36	28.01	33.83	16.30	13.47	119.89	13.87
Bella Vista, AR	11.36	36.32	44.72	15.83	13.34	n/a	9.51
Bernards, NJ[2]	12.93	37.17	48.15	19.97	13.85	122.53	13.24
Bethlehem, NY	13.03	34.58	46.74	18.43	15.78	127.78	12.93
Bloomfield, MI[2]	12.66	32.88	43.24	16.88	12.90	121.74	13.01
Bowie, MD[2]	12.25	37.76	54.87	20.99	18.56	99.71	15.41
Bozeman, MT	n/a	n/a	n/a	n/a	n/a	n/a	n/a
Brentwood, TN	12.79	30.04	34.59	15.59	13.63	113.16	11.65
Broomfield, CO	13.11	34.35	54.54	18.54	13.79	121.51	13.73
Carmel, IN	12.16	32.46	47.36	17.08	12.36	n/a	11.56
Cedar Park, TX	13.43	31.88	37.05	16.12	14.84	101.40	11.47
Cheshire, CT[3]	12.48	31.05	46.95	20.12	15.36	102.31	14.40
Chesterfield, MO	13.21	32.93	35.44	16.37	13.13	n/a	12.99
Collierville, TN	13.08	30.03	38.00	15.91	10.50	127.78	11.98
Coppell, TX[2]	13.72	38.76	38.45	17.16	13.24	120.03	11.50
Cornelius, NC	12.56	37.19	42.39	16.74	12.37	123.15	11.39
Cranberry, PA	12.65	31.91	43.31	16.24	11.24	117.58	11.51
Cupertino, CA	14.30	35.36	56.30	22.03	15.74	125.24	15.16
Danville, CA[2]	14.35	33.64	48.56	20.82	14.78	118.49	15.50
Draper, UT	12.53	34.52	48.47	16.23	14.03	n/a	11.18
Dublin, OH	11.97	32.72	41.85	16.68	12.44	117.66	13.40
Eastchester, NY[2]	12.99	35.67	51.39	19.62	15.32	113.38	13.73
Eden Prairie, MN	12.38	37.53	58.26	19.51	16.78	129.05	15.40
Edmond, OK	12.98	29.00	33.15	15.34	14.35	107.54	8.87
Evesham, NJ[2]	13.13	40.89	67.99	19.03	14.31	n/a	12.58
Fishers, IN	12.16	32.46	47.36	17.08	12.36	n/a	11.56
Flower Mound, TX[2]	13.72	38.76	38.45	17.16	13.24	120.03	11.50
Folsom, CA	13.42	32.76	42.49	18.02	13.09	123.73	15.20
Foster City, CA[2]	15.57	31.16	53.91	22.36	16.41	92.50	17.85
Franklin, TN	12.79	30.04	34.59	15.59	13.63	113.16	11.65
Friendswood, TX	12.62	36.83	47.56	17.28	13.23	106.63	10.55
Germantown, TN	13.08	30.03	38.00	15.91	10.50	127.78	11.98
Glastonbury, CT[3]	13.26	36.73	46.11	20.92	14.25	108.58	13.61
Grand Blanc, MI	11.27	24.51	70.77	15.44	10.70	n/a	12.55
Guilderland, NY	13.03	34.58	46.74	18.43	15.78	127.78	12.93
Hampden, PA	12.90	29.69	33.61	17.07	13.54	83.51	11.02
Holly Springs, NC	12.05	31.22	50.21	16.86	12.75	n/a	11.10
Huntersville, NC	12.56	37.19	42.39	16.74	12.37	123.15	11.39
Independence, KY	12.41	35.53	40.93	16.83	12.87	84.18	13.25
Johns Creek, GA	11.85	32.41	39.40	17.34	12.62	128.18	10.47
Keller, TX[2]	13.34	32.63	36.37	15.05	14.26	n/a	9.44
Kirkland, WA[2]	14.69	35.49	43.24	20.26	16.99	108.64	16.41
Lafayette, CO	15.79	38.60	37.25	17.92	13.67	132.34	15.71
Lake Oswego, OR	13.40	33.08	40.16	18.08	15.19	n/a	14.68
League City, TX	12.62	36.83	47.56	17.28	13.23	106.63	10.55
Leawood, KS	11.65	32.40	44.34	16.32	13.51	123.07	11.75
Lee's Summit, MO	11.65	32.40	44.34	16.32	13.51	123.07	11.75
Leesburg, VA[2]	12.25	37.76	54.87	20.99	18.56	99.71	15.41
Lehi, UT	12.39	33.29	36.32	14.03	13.25	107.92	11.54
Lenexa, KS	11.65	32.40	44.34	16.32	13.51	123.07	11.75
Lexington, MA[4]	13.15	40.34	50.17	22.35	14.81	106.45	15.07
Los Altos, CA	14.30	35.36	56.30	22.03	15.74	125.24	15.16
Lower Makefield, PA[2]	13.45	35.34	51.26	17.80	13.24	132.08	13.31
Madison, AL	11.85	28.38	43.33	17.35	12.52	n/a	9.22
Mamaroneck, NY[2]	12.99	35.67	51.39	19.62	15.32	113.38	13.73
Manheim, PA	13.02	32.78	34.73	15.88	12.75	n/a	12.60
Manlius, NY	12.47	33.59	35.86	16.75	17.10	129.11	12.98
Maple Grove, MN	12.38	37.53	58.26	19.51	16.78	129.05	15.40
Marion, IA	11.59	31.01	39.26	14.45	n/a	n/a	13.25
Marlboro, NJ[2]	12.99	35.67	51.39	19.62	15.32	113.38	13.73
Mason, OH	12.41	35.53	40.93	16.83	12.87	84.18	13.25

Table continued on next page.

Metro Area	Retail Salespersons	Sales Reps., Except Tech./Scien.	Sales Reps., Tech./Scien.	Secretaries, Exc. Leg./ Med./Exec.	Security Guards	Surgeons	Teacher Assistants
McCandless, PA	12.65	31.91	43.31	16.24	11.24	117.58	11.51
Menomonee Falls, WI	12.08	35.50	41.74	18.95	12.85	94.06	13.63
Meridian, ID	13.07	31.08	33.56	14.78	12.78	n/a	11.76
Merrimack, NH[4]	12.77	37.39	49.17	16.30	14.44	n/a	14.77
Mount Lebanon, PA	12.65	31.91	43.31	16.24	11.24	117.58	11.51
Mount Pleasant, SC	11.28	28.39	38.22	16.08	14.28	n/a	10.63
Needham, MA[4]	13.15	40.34	50.17	22.35	14.81	106.45	15.07
Newtown, CT[3]	13.06	42.41	48.57	18.54	15.69	104.90	15.61
Northbrook, IL[2]	13.08	35.53	36.28	18.19	14.91	122.87	14.05
Northville, MI[2]	12.62	33.87	41.29	16.79	13.11	92.00	13.22
Novi, MI[2]	12.66	32.88	43.24	16.88	12.90	121.74	13.01
O'Fallon, MO	13.21	32.93	35.44	16.37	13.13	n/a	12.99
O'Fallon, IL	13.21	32.93	35.44	16.37	13.13	n/a	12.99
Orchard Park, NY	12.02	30.51	39.69	16.75	11.79	n/a	11.49
Oviedo, FL	11.88	28.91	37.43	15.84	10.90	116.31	11.54
Parker, CO	13.11	34.35	54.54	18.54	13.79	121.51	13.73
Parkland, FL[2]	12.70	27.99	45.70	16.02	11.00	108.95	11.20
Peachtree City, GA	11.85	32.41	39.40	17.34	12.62	128.18	10.47
Pflugerville, TX	13.43	31.88	37.05	16.12	14.84	101.40	11.47
Plainfield, IL[2]	13.08	35.53	36.28	18.19	14.91	122.87	14.05
Princeton, NJ	12.42	36.67	50.45	22.11	18.78	n/a	13.69
Queen Creek, AZ	12.07	29.63	41.79	17.04	13.85	127.07	12.06
Rancho Palos Verdes, CA[2]	13.66	29.08	41.19	19.31	12.83	124.06	14.90
Redmond, WA[2]	14.69	35.49	43.24	20.26	16.99	108.64	16.41
Richland, WA	13.99	25.93	30.95	18.60	18.77	n/a	13.93
Ridgefield, CT[3]	15.11	36.05	48.83	20.92	14.12	128.44	16.24
Ridgewood, NJ[2]	12.99	35.67	51.39	19.62	15.32	113.38	13.73
Rio Rancho, NM	12.55	25.79	29.94	15.50	12.74	n/a	10.52
Sahuarita, AZ	11.93	23.79	37.14	15.75	11.50	126.79	11.74
Sammamish, WA[2]	14.69	35.49	43.24	20.26	16.99	108.64	16.41
San Ramon, CA[2]	14.35	33.64	48.56	20.82	14.78	118.49	15.50
Saratoga, CA	14.30	35.36	56.30	22.03	15.74	125.24	15.16
Schertz, TX	13.32	33.05	39.01	15.61	12.35	117.11	11.01
Shrewsbury, MA[3]	12.27	36.85	42.11	19.80	14.18	n/a	15.05
South Brunswick, NJ[2]	12.99	35.67	51.39	19.62	15.32	113.38	13.73
South Jordan, UT	12.53	34.52	48.47	16.23	14.03	n/a	11.18
South Kingstown, RI[3]	14.03	31.65	38.16	18.76	13.70	123.50	15.54
South Windsor, CT[3]	13.26	36.73	46.11	20.92	14.25	108.58	13.61
Southlake, TX[2]	13.34	32.63	36.37	15.05	14.26	n/a	9.44
Spring Hill, TN	12.79	30.04	34.59	15.59	13.63	113.16	11.65
Stow, OH	12.82	29.79	37.10	16.75	16.44	120.99	13.57
Sugar Land, TX	12.62	36.83	47.56	17.28	13.23	106.63	10.55
Sun Prairie, WI	12.33	29.81	36.40	18.06	12.17	n/a	13.05
Syracuse, UT	12.68	30.52	40.77	14.63	15.75	125.98	13.72
Tredyffrin, PA[2]	13.45	35.34	51.26	17.80	13.24	132.08	13.31
Upper Arlington, OH	11.97	32.72	41.85	16.68	12.44	117.66	13.40
Upper Dublin, PA[2]	13.45	35.34	51.26	17.80	13.24	132.08	13.31
Vestavia Hills, AL	12.92	33.37	42.34	17.26	10.69	98.93	10.53
Webster, NY	13.11	31.11	43.30	17.16	14.88	128.11	12.46
Wellesley, MA[4]	13.15	40.34	50.17	22.35	14.81	106.45	15.07
West Fargo, ND	13.65	32.15	38.06	16.94	11.75	n/a	14.47
West Linn, OR	13.40	33.08	40.16	18.08	15.19	n/a	14.68
West Windsor, NJ	12.42	36.67	50.45	22.11	18.78	n/a	13.69
Westlake, OH	13.18	33.12	38.36	16.69	13.75	n/a	13.62
Weston, FL[2]	12.70	27.99	45.70	16.02	11.00	108.95	11.20
Westport, CT[3]	15.11	36.05	48.83	20.92	14.12	128.44	16.24
Wilmette, IL[2]	13.08	35.53	36.28	18.19	14.91	122.87	14.05
Woodbury, MN	12.38	37.53	58.26	19.51	16.78	129.05	15.40
Yorba Linda, CA[2]	13.50	30.76	41.69	18.85	12.56	87.38	16.42

Notes: (1) Figures cover the Metropolitan Statistical Area (MSA) except where noted. See Appendix B for areas included; (2) Metropolitan Division; (3) New England City and Town Area; (4) New England City and Town Area Division; n/a not available
Source: Bureau of Labor Statistics, May 2015 Metro Area Occupational Employment and Wage Estimates

Average Hourly Wages: Occupations T – Z

Metro Area	Teachers, Elementary School	Teachers, Secondary School	Tele-marketers	Truck Driv., Heavy/ Trac. Trail.	Truck Drivers, Light	Waiters/ Waitresses
Aliso Viejo, CA[2]	36.66	38.38	13.81	20.45	18.28	13.53
Allen, TX[2]	26.09	26.60	15.35	20.54	16.36	11.51
Alpharetta, GA	26.05	27.22	14.98	19.95	17.48	9.22
Ankeny, IA	26.25	27.57	13.73	21.84	16.44	9.18
Apex, NC	22.47	22.86	17.78	20.73	15.64	10.40
Ballwin, MO	27.63	27.07	12.35	20.70	17.44	9.46
Beavercreek, OH	28.56	30.52	12.50	18.53	15.27	9.79
Bella Vista, AR	23.95	27.23	11.11	21.07	14.34	9.07
Bernards, NJ[2]	33.13	35.47	14.24	22.90	16.49	11.60
Bethlehem, NY	29.27	30.95	15.14	20.63	16.76	12.71
Bloomfield, MI[2]	32.81	30.56	14.67	20.22	15.80	10.50
Bowie, MD[2]	33.75	35.25	12.83	20.66	18.42	12.66
Bozeman, MT	n/a	n/a	n/a	n/a	n/a	n/a
Brentwood, TN	25.00	24.34	12.79	20.00	17.31	9.16
Broomfield, CO	25.45	27.26	14.15	23.01	17.39	10.53
Carmel, IN	24.21	26.14	13.23	21.79	16.94	10.14
Cedar Park, TX	25.32	25.29	12.23	18.73	16.51	10.57
Cheshire, CT[3]	35.38	36.67	22.18	22.13	17.77	10.95
Chesterfield, MO	27.63	27.07	12.35	20.70	17.44	9.46
Collierville, TN	24.62	25.44	12.44	20.48	16.76	8.79
Coppell, TX[2]	26.09	26.60	15.35	20.54	16.36	11.51
Cornelius, NC	21.35	22.34	13.05	19.97	15.39	9.98
Cranberry, PA	28.52	30.61	10.57	20.56	15.84	9.97
Cupertino, CA	36.39	36.28	17.42	20.79	18.60	13.01
Danville, CA[2]	35.79	35.54	15.39	22.83	19.08	13.20
Draper, UT	27.75	28.12	12.10	19.34	15.70	11.94
Dublin, OH	29.20	30.86	11.84	21.92	17.28	10.50
Eastchester, NY[2]	34.23	39.55	14.00	23.69	17.92	14.08
Eden Prairie, MN	30.58	32.31	14.42	21.24	18.30	10.29
Edmond, OK	19.09	19.62	10.16	19.73	18.76	10.79
Evesham, NJ[2]	31.88	34.29	11.39	21.83	15.93	10.37
Fishers, IN	24.21	26.14	13.23	21.79	16.94	10.14
Flower Mound, TX[2]	26.09	26.60	15.35	20.54	16.36	11.51
Folsom, CA	33.21	33.73	13.27	20.21	18.39	13.30
Foster City, CA[2]	33.40	36.46	17.46	24.39	19.99	15.41
Franklin, TN	25.00	24.34	12.79	20.00	17.31	9.16
Friendswood, TX	27.66	27.65	12.77	19.67	15.55	10.59
Germantown, TN	24.62	25.44	12.44	20.48	16.76	8.79
Glastonbury, CT[3]	35.68	34.92	13.44	22.32	17.04	11.02
Grand Blanc, MI	29.67	29.24	11.43	18.64	14.84	10.18
Guilderland, NY	29.27	30.95	15.14	20.63	16.76	12.71
Hampden, PA	28.19	27.25	13.19	22.35	17.04	9.50
Holly Springs, NC	22.47	22.86	17.78	20.73	15.64	10.40
Huntersville, NC	21.35	22.34	13.05	19.97	15.39	9.98
Independence, KY	27.50	28.06	13.26	20.87	16.51	9.50
Johns Creek, GA	26.05	27.22	14.98	19.95	17.48	9.22
Keller, TX[2]	26.00	26.80	11.41	20.35	15.84	9.49
Kirkland, WA[2]	29.39	31.11	14.10	22.24	18.43	15.73
Lafayette, CO	28.17	28.00	12.13	21.11	16.65	12.73
Lake Oswego, OR	29.00	29.09	13.35	20.35	17.01	11.88
League City, TX	27.66	27.65	12.77	19.67	15.55	10.59
Leawood, KS	23.84	22.74	14.09	21.09	17.22	9.56
Lee's Summit, MO	23.84	22.74	14.09	21.09	17.22	9.56
Leesburg, VA[2]	33.75	35.25	12.83	20.66	18.42	12.66
Lehi, UT	26.24	30.94	11.23	22.65	14.05	10.39
Lenexa, KS	23.84	22.74	14.09	21.09	17.22	9.56
Lexington, MA[4]	35.84	36.26	16.27	24.97	17.56	13.95
Los Altos, CA	36.39	36.28	17.42	20.79	18.60	13.01
Lower Makefield, PA[2]	34.75	34.36	14.45	22.60	15.97	10.32
Madison, AL	24.73	24.42	n/a	18.61	14.34	10.14
Mamaroneck, NY[2]	34.23	39.55	14.00	23.69	17.92	14.08
Manheim, PA	29.33	29.59	n/a	20.04	13.85	10.51
Manlius, NY	30.65	34.49	13.53	22.47	14.76	10.89
Maple Grove, MN	30.58	32.31	14.42	21.24	18.30	10.29
Marion, IA	25.40	25.06	10.08	19.66	16.43	9.44
Marlboro, NJ[2]	34.23	39.55	14.00	23.69	17.92	14.08
Mason, OH	27.50	28.06	13.26	20.87	16.51	9.50

Table continued on next page.

Metro Area	Teachers, Elementary School	Teachers, Secondary School	Tele-marketers	Truck Driv., Heavy/ Trac. Trail.	Truck Drivers, Light	Waiters/ Waitresses
McCandless, PA	28.52	30.61	10.57	20.56	15.84	9.97
Menomonee Falls, WI	28.25	29.84	13.54	20.16	16.33	9.10
Meridian, ID	23.23	21.61	11.63	18.12	14.77	9.49
Merrimack, NH[4]	26.54	27.76	n/a	19.75	16.40	10.39
Mount Lebanon, PA	28.52	30.61	10.57	20.56	15.84	9.97
Mount Pleasant, SC	23.24	24.33	11.51	20.34	14.32	10.61
Needham, MA[4]	35.84	36.26	16.27	24.97	17.56	13.95
Newtown, CT[3]	36.23	35.93	n/a	20.87	17.39	10.86
Northbrook, IL[2]	30.77	36.04	12.71	23.64	17.54	10.57
Northville, MI[2]	29.44	30.57	12.87	21.95	18.58	10.39
Novi, MI[2]	32.81	30.56	14.67	20.22	15.80	10.50
O'Fallon, MO	27.63	27.07	12.35	20.70	17.44	9.46
O'Fallon, IL	27.63	27.07	12.35	20.70	17.44	9.46
Orchard Park, NY	29.31	31.08	12.16	21.28	16.19	11.34
Oviedo, FL	22.91	22.61	11.25	19.41	15.62	12.80
Parker, CO	25.45	27.26	14.15	23.01	17.39	10.53
Parkland, FL[2]	23.89	26.25	12.89	19.25	17.31	11.80
Peachtree City, GA	26.05	27.22	14.98	19.95	17.48	9.22
Pflugerville, TX	25.32	25.29	12.23	18.73	16.51	10.57
Plainfield, IL[2]	30.77	36.04	12.71	23.64	17.54	10.57
Princeton, NJ	32.27	34.54	12.29	19.43	17.16	10.54
Queen Creek, AZ	20.48	23.77	13.83	20.26	16.21	10.61
Rancho Palos Verdes, CA[2]	35.30	36.88	13.48	20.54	17.16	13.26
Redmond, WA[2]	29.39	31.11	14.10	22.24	18.43	15.73
Richland, WA	26.18	28.22	11.58	23.04	16.79	12.61
Ridgefield, CT[3]	38.04	39.42	18.73	23.76	17.38	11.87
Ridgewood, NJ[2]	34.23	39.55	14.00	23.69	17.92	14.08
Rio Rancho, NM	26.58	24.43	11.51	20.47	15.60	10.14
Sahuarita, AZ	18.46	18.98	9.95	18.53	16.26	10.54
Sammamish, WA[2]	29.39	31.11	14.10	22.24	18.43	15.73
San Ramon, CA[2]	35.79	35.54	15.39	22.83	19.08	13.20
Saratoga, CA	36.39	36.28	17.42	20.79	18.60	13.01
Schertz, TX	25.54	25.84	11.76	20.93	14.16	11.05
Shrewsbury, MA[3]	33.07	33.97	16.06	24.12	17.67	12.38
South Brunswick, NJ[2]	34.23	39.55	14.00	23.69	17.92	14.08
South Jordan, UT	27.75	28.12	12.10	19.34	15.70	11.94
South Kingstown, RI[3]	33.30	32.25	13.67	20.65	17.27	10.52
South Windsor, CT[3]	35.68	34.92	13.44	22.32	17.04	11.02
Southlake, TX[2]	26.00	26.80	11.41	20.35	15.84	9.49
Spring Hill, TN	25.00	24.34	12.79	20.00	17.31	9.16
Stow, OH	29.49	30.19	12.79	21.32	14.59	9.44
Sugar Land, TX	27.66	27.65	12.77	19.67	15.55	10.59
Sun Prairie, WI	25.16	25.91	14.50	22.23	17.05	12.48
Syracuse, UT	24.91	26.66	10.54	21.69	13.98	10.81
Tredyffrin, PA[2]	34.75	34.36	14.45	22.60	15.97	10.32
Upper Arlington, OH	29.20	30.86	11.84	21.92	17.28	10.50
Upper Dublin, PA[2]	34.75	34.36	14.45	22.60	15.97	10.32
Vestavia Hills, AL	24.73	24.58	13.15	21.98	14.63	9.61
Webster, NY	28.76	28.32	11.75	20.11	15.02	11.53
Wellesley, MA[4]	35.84	36.26	16.27	24.97	17.56	13.95
West Fargo, ND	23.39	22.62	10.26	21.38	16.25	9.77
West Linn, OR	29.00	29.09	13.35	20.35	17.01	11.88
West Windsor, NJ	32.27	34.54	12.29	19.43	17.16	10.54
Westlake, OH	28.92	28.93	13.70	21.42	16.10	10.20
Weston, FL[2]	23.89	26.25	12.89	19.25	17.31	11.80
Westport, CT[3]	38.04	39.42	18.73	23.76	17.38	11.87
Wilmette, IL[2]	30.77	36.04	12.71	23.64	17.54	10.57
Woodbury, MN	30.58	32.31	14.42	21.24	18.30	10.29
Yorba Linda, CA[2]	36.66	38.38	13.81	20.45	18.28	13.53

Notes: (1) Figures cover the Metropolitan Statistical Area (MSA) except where noted. See Appendix B for areas included; (2) Metropolitan Division; (3) New England City and Town Area; (4) New England City and Town Area Division; Hourly wages for elementary and secondary school teachers were calculated by the editors from annual wage data assuming a 40 hour work week; n/a not available
Source: Bureau of Labor Statistics, May 2015 Metro Area Occupational Employment and Wage Estimates

Means of Transportation to Work: City

City	Car/Truck/Van		Public Transportation			Bicycle	Walked	Other Means	Worked at Home
	Drove Alone	Car-pooled	Bus	Subway	Railroad				
Aliso Viejo, CA	78.8	9.3	0.8	0.0	0.1	0.2	1.6	0.5	8.6
Allen, TX	81.4	7.6	0.1	0.4	0.9	0.0	0.8	1.1	7.6
Alpharetta, GA	78.9	5.1	0.7	0.6	0.1	0.0	2.4	1.0	11.3
Ankeny, IA	87.5	6.6	0.6	0.0	0.0	0.4	0.7	0.7	3.5
Apex, NC	80.4	9.3	0.4	0.0	0.0	0.2	1.0	1.1	7.6
Ballwin, MO	86.2	4.2	0.2	0.1	0.0	0.0	1.8	0.4	7.2
Beavercreek, OH	86.8	5.7	0.1	0.0	0.0	0.3	1.9	0.6	4.6
Bella Vista, AR	83.6	9.1	0.4	0.0	0.0	0.0	1.0	0.5	5.5
Bernards, NJ	79.1	4.7	1.7	0.6	3.3	0.0	1.5	0.4	8.7
Bethlehem, NY	84.1	6.4	1.2	0.0	0.2	0.5	1.3	1.2	5.2
Bloomfield, MI	86.1	5.5	0.4	0.0	0.0	0.1	0.5	0.7	6.7
Bowie, MD	73.1	10.6	1.6	7.4	0.7	0.1	1.9	0.7	3.9
Bozeman, MT	71.3	6.6	1.0	0.2	0.0	5.5	9.5	0.7	5.1
Brentwood, TN	82.7	6.2	0.3	0.0	0.0	0.1	0.8	1.2	8.8
Broomfield, CO	78.3	7.0	4.2	0.0	0.0	0.3	1.0	1.4	7.9
Carmel, IN	83.5	7.4	0.2	0.1	0.0	0.4	0.8	0.6	7.1
Cedar Park, TX	82.5	7.0	0.4	0.0	0.3	0.3	0.9	0.5	7.9
Cheshire, CT	80.5	7.6	1.1	0.1	0.2	0.0	4.1	0.6	5.9
Chesterfield, MO	86.6	5.3	0.3	0.0	0.0	0.1	0.7	0.7	6.3
Collierville, TN	90.0	4.1	0.0	0.0	0.0	0.0	0.4	0.5	5.0
Coppell, TX	83.1	5.9	0.4	0.2	0.0	0.1	0.4	1.1	8.8
Cornelius, NC	77.2	7.9	3.1	0.0	0.0	0.1	0.8	1.0	10.0
Cranberry, PA	83.7	7.2	1.3	0.0	0.0	0.0	1.1	0.6	6.1
Cupertino, CA	79.6	9.5	1.3	0.2	0.5	0.7	1.4	1.0	5.7
Danville, CA	76.4	6.7	0.4	4.6	0.9	0.3	1.0	0.9	8.8
Draper, UT	80.1	7.2	1.1	0.3	0.7	0.1	0.9	1.7	7.9
Dublin, OH	85.6	5.6	0.3	0.0	0.0	0.2	0.5	0.8	7.1
Eastchester, NY	60.0	3.9	1.3	1.3	23.8	0.0	4.8	0.3	4.5
Eden Prairie, MN	81.6	6.6	2.9	0.0	0.0	0.2	1.4	0.9	6.4
Edmond, OK	85.0	7.0	0.4	0.0	0.0	0.1	1.6	0.9	5.0
Evesham, NJ	85.1	5.5	0.6	1.2	1.2	0.1	1.0	1.0	4.2
Fishers, IN	84.6	7.6	0.1	0.0	0.0	0.2	0.4	0.8	6.2
Flower Mound, TX	82.1	5.5	0.2	0.1	0.2	0.0	1.1	1.0	9.9
Folsom, CA	79.1	9.3	0.6	0.7	0.8	0.7	1.2	1.5	6.1
Foster City, CA	74.2	11.9	1.1	1.2	2.2	0.9	1.4	1.2	6.0
Franklin, TN	80.2	9.1	0.6	0.0	0.0	0.1	1.0	1.0	8.0
Friendswood, TX	84.6	7.1	1.4	0.0	0.0	0.2	0.5	0.9	5.3
Germantown, TN	90.0	3.5	0.0	0.0	0.0	0.0	0.7	0.8	5.0
Glastonbury, CT	84.0	5.6	0.6	0.0	0.1	0.1	2.3	1.1	6.3
Grand Blanc, MI	89.3	6.3	0.1	0.0	0.0	0.1	0.4	0.3	3.6
Guilderland, NY	84.4	6.3	1.3	0.1	0.0	0.2	2.7	1.4	3.7
Hampden, PA	89.3	5.1	0.2	0.0	0.0	0.2	0.2	0.3	4.5
Holly Springs, NC	81.3	7.1	0.2	0.0	0.0	0.0	0.5	1.6	9.3
Huntersville, NC	81.5	7.7	1.4	0.1	0.0	0.2	0.6	1.2	7.3
Independence, KY	84.8	11.1	0.8	0.0	0.0	0.1	0.3	0.2	2.6
Johns Creek, GA	77.4	8.2	0.1	0.4	0.1	0.1	1.2	0.9	11.5
Keller, TX	85.3	4.8	0.1	0.0	0.1	0.1	0.4	1.2	8.1
Kirkland, WA	72.5	8.4	7.8	0.0	0.0	0.5	2.1	1.2	7.6
Lafayette, CO	75.4	7.3	3.4	0.0	0.0	1.0	1.5	1.3	10.0
Lake Oswego, OR	73.9	6.4	4.3	0.1	0.1	0.3	1.6	0.9	12.4
League City, TX	85.9	7.5	1.4	0.0	0.0	0.2	0.2	1.2	3.7
Leawood, KS	86.8	3.5	0.1	0.0	0.0	0.1	0.4	0.9	8.2
Lee's Summit, MO	86.4	6.2	0.3	0.1	0.0	0.0	0.4	0.9	5.8
Leesburg, VA	76.2	10.1	4.2	0.2	0.2	0.4	2.5	1.0	5.2
Lehi, UT	76.8	10.2	1.2	0.3	0.6	0.2	0.8	1.2	8.7
Lenexa, KS	86.6	6.5	0.3	0.0	0.0	0.2	0.8	0.4	5.2
Lexington, MA	74.3	6.6	2.3	4.3	0.6	1.3	1.2	0.8	8.6
Los Altos, CA	78.2	5.2	0.5	0.3	1.3	3.1	2.9	0.3	8.3
Lower Makefield, PA	78.1	6.2	0.2	0.2	6.1	0.0	0.8	0.2	8.1
Madison, AL	90.7	6.1	0.1	0.0	0.0	0.3	0.1	0.7	2.0
Mamaroneck, NY	46.8	4.5	1.7	1.6	31.5	0.5	3.8	1.9	7.7
Manheim, PA	83.9	7.3	0.8	0.1	0.8	0.4	1.9	1.1	3.8
Manlius, NY	86.9	6.1	0.2	0.1	0.0	0.2	1.3	0.8	4.3
Maple Grove, MN	83.9	6.2	3.9	0.0	0.0	0.1	0.5	0.5	4.9
Marion, IA	85.8	8.1	0.9	0.0	0.0	0.3	1.1	0.8	3.0
Marlboro, NJ	71.4	6.1	11.7	0.5	3.3	0.0	0.6	1.1	5.2
Mason, OH	89.6	4.6	0.5	0.0	0.0	0.0	0.4	0.3	4.6

Table continued on next page.

City	Car/Truck/Van: Drove Alone	Car/Truck/Van: Car-pooled	Public Transportation: Bus	Public Transportation: Subway	Public Transportation: Railroad	Bicycle	Walked	Other Means	Worked at Home
McCandless, PA	79.8	11.0	2.2	0.0	0.1	0.1	1.2	0.8	4.8
Menomonee Falls, WI	86.8	8.0	0.2	0.1	0.1	0.1	1.1	0.5	3.1
Meridian, ID	82.3	8.8	0.2	0.0	0.0	0.4	0.7	0.6	7.2
Merrimack, NH	84.4	6.3	0.6	0.1	0.0	0.3	1.2	0.6	6.5
Mount Lebanon, PA	72.3	7.5	5.2	2.0	0.0	0.2	3.1	3.3	6.4
Mount Pleasant, SC	83.1	4.9	0.2	0.0	0.0	1.0	1.4	0.5	9.0
Needham, MA	72.5	6.6	0.4	1.3	8.5	0.4	1.9	0.8	7.7
Newtown, CT	82.7	6.0	0.2	0.1	1.5	0.0	1.2	0.5	7.9
Northbrook, IL	69.5	6.6	0.4	0.6	10.4	0.2	2.1	0.7	9.5
Northville, MI	90.0	4.4	0.3	0.0	0.0	0.2	0.6	0.2	4.3
Novi, MI	89.2	6.0	0.3	0.1	0.0	0.2	0.4	0.5	3.4
O'Fallon, IL	85.9	7.3	0.6	0.7	0.1	0.0	1.3	1.0	3.2
O'Fallon, MO	87.6	5.9	0.0	0.1	0.0	0.1	0.7	0.8	4.9
Orchard Park, NY	90.5	3.9	0.6	0.0	0.0	0.0	1.2	0.5	3.4
Oviedo, FL	84.9	7.0	0.2	0.0	0.0	0.3	0.8	1.0	5.6
Parker, CO	80.6	8.1	1.1	0.5	0.5	0.2	0.4	1.3	7.4
Parkland, FL	82.1	5.7	0.1	0.0	0.2	0.0	1.0	1.4	9.5
Peachtree City, GA	78.1	9.1	0.6	0.3	0.1	0.2	0.4	3.1	8.1
Pflugerville, TX	81.0	10.9	0.6	0.0	0.0	0.1	0.7	1.7	4.9
Plainfield, IL	84.1	6.6	0.8	0.0	1.8	0.0	0.9	1.3	4.5
Princeton, NJ	49.2	4.4	2.7	0.8	6.6	5.1	18.0	0.7	12.5
Queen Creek, AZ	79.1	7.6	0.1	0.1	0.0	0.1	0.7	2.4	10.0
Rancho Palos Verdes, CA	79.6	8.7	1.2	0.2	0.0	0.3	0.4	0.8	8.9
Redmond, WA	71.2	10.1	7.1	0.1	0.0	1.0	4.0	0.9	5.6
Richland, WA	80.6	10.4	1.3	0.0	0.0	0.8	2.2	0.6	4.0
Ridgefield, CT	78.4	4.2	0.4	0.7	3.7	0.5	1.6	0.2	10.3
Ridgewood, NJ	61.2	4.4	9.7	1.2	9.0	0.9	4.0	0.8	8.7
Rio Rancho, NM	84.8	7.8	0.6	0.0	0.7	0.2	0.4	1.4	4.1
Sahuarita, AZ	79.0	12.9	0.0	0.0	0.0	0.1	0.8	2.8	4.3
Sammamish, WA	72.5	10.0	5.2	0.0	0.0	0.3	1.3	0.7	10.1
San Ramon, CA	75.8	7.5	0.7	4.2	0.6	0.3	1.8	1.2	8.1
Saratoga, CA	81.5	7.4	0.3	0.1	0.5	0.4	0.4	0.2	9.2
Schertz, TX	84.8	9.1	0.5	0.0	0.0	0.0	0.7	0.9	4.0
Shrewsbury, MA	82.4	9.0	0.2	0.1	1.3	0.2	1.8	0.5	4.5
South Brunswick, NJ	79.4	7.6	5.1	0.2	3.1	0.1	0.6	0.7	3.4
South Jordan, UT	79.0	7.9	1.0	0.7	1.1	0.2	0.9	1.4	7.8
South Kingstown, RI	78.9	5.6	1.5	0.0	1.0	0.6	7.1	0.7	4.7
South Windsor, CT	85.0	7.6	1.3	0.0	0.1	0.1	0.1	0.6	5.1
Southlake, TX	81.3	3.8	0.1	0.0	0.0	0.0	0.8	2.0	12.0
Spring Hill, TN	80.2	9.0	0.2	0.0	0.0	0.1	2.0	0.3	8.2
Stow, OH	90.6	4.7	0.7	0.0	0.0	0.0	0.9	0.3	2.8
Sugar Land, TX	79.4	10.5	2.3	0.0	0.0	0.2	0.7	0.8	6.2
Sun Prairie, WI	83.5	8.2	0.3	0.0	0.0	0.3	1.3	1.5	5.0
Syracuse, UT	82.7	8.2	0.3	0.0	1.0	0.3	0.6	1.2	5.6
Tredyffrin, PA	75.5	4.9	0.3	0.5	7.7	0.0	2.5	0.6	8.0
Upper Arlington, OH	83.8	4.7	1.1	0.0	0.0	0.9	1.5	0.9	7.1
Upper Dublin, PA	80.4	4.9	0.3	0.8	5.1	0.6	1.0	1.0	5.7
Vestavia Hills, AL	88.5	4.9	0.1	0.0	0.0	0.2	1.7	0.5	4.0
Webster, NY	87.7	5.8	0.4	0.0	0.0	0.1	1.3	0.9	3.9
Wellesley, MA	61.0	5.4	0.8	1.8	6.5	0.6	13.1	1.2	9.6
West Fargo, ND	86.0	8.0	0.6	0.0	0.0	0.2	1.1	0.9	3.2
West Linn, OR	79.1	6.2	1.6	0.0	0.0	0.6	1.4	0.7	10.4
West Windsor, NJ	61.6	6.2	1.2	1.1	19.8	0.6	0.3	0.9	8.3
Westlake, OH	84.2	7.1	1.6	0.1	0.0	0.1	1.0	0.5	5.3
Weston, FL	80.5	7.7	0.1	0.1	0.1	0.0	1.3	1.1	9.2
Westport, CT	61.1	2.7	0.1	0.9	18.3	0.0	2.0	0.5	14.4
Wilmette, IL	57.9	6.4	1.8	2.4	17.4	0.2	2.1	0.2	11.5
Woodbury, MN	82.9	7.7	3.4	0.0	0.0	0.2	0.7	0.2	4.9
Yorba Linda, CA	81.7	8.3	0.6	0.0	0.5	0.3	0.7	1.1	6.7
U.S.	76.4	9.6	2.6	1.8	0.6	0.6	2.8	1.3	4.4

Note: Figures are percentages and cover workers 16 years of age and older
Source: U.S. Census Bureau, 2010-2014 American Community Survey 5-Year Estimates

Means of Transportation to Work: Metro Area

Metro Area	Car/Truck/Van		Public Transportation			Bicycle	Walked	Other Means	Worked at Home
	Drove Alone	Car-pooled	Bus	Subway	Railroad				
Aliso Viejo, CA	73.9	10.3	5.3	0.4	0.2	0.9	2.6	1.3	5.1
Allen, TX	80.9	10.1	1.0	0.2	0.3	0.2	1.2	1.5	4.7
Alpharetta, GA	77.9	10.4	2.2	0.7	0.1	0.2	1.4	1.4	5.8
Ankeny, IA	83.3	9.0	0.9	0.0	0.0	0.2	1.6	0.7	4.2
Apex, NC	80.7	9.3	1.0	0.0	0.0	0.2	1.3	1.2	6.4
Ballwin, MO	83.0	7.7	2.1	0.4	0.1	0.3	1.8	0.9	3.9
Beavercreek, OH	83.3	8.1	1.6	0.0	0.0	0.3	2.5	0.9	3.3
Bella Vista, AR	80.2	11.4	0.5	0.0	0.0	0.3	2.2	1.0	4.4
Bernards, NJ	50.6	6.8	8.0	18.5	3.6	0.6	6.0	1.9	4.1
Bethlehem, NY	80.5	7.7	3.0	0.1	0.1	0.2	3.7	1.0	3.7
Bloomfield, MI	84.1	8.7	1.6	0.0	0.0	0.2	1.3	0.8	3.2
Bowie, MD	66.0	10.1	5.5	7.9	0.7	0.7	3.2	1.0	4.9
Bozeman, MT	73.1	8.6	0.8	0.1	0.0	3.0	6.0	1.2	7.2
Brentwood, TN	82.1	9.8	1.0	0.0	0.1	0.2	1.3	0.9	4.6
Broomfield, CO	76.0	9.1	3.6	0.5	0.2	0.9	2.1	1.1	6.4
Carmel, IN	83.8	8.7	1.0	0.0	0.0	0.3	1.6	0.9	3.7
Cedar Park, TX	76.0	10.5	2.3	0.0	0.1	0.8	1.8	1.5	6.9
Cheshire, CT	79.3	8.1	3.0	0.1	1.0	0.5	3.6	0.8	3.6
Chesterfield, MO	83.0	7.7	2.1	0.4	0.1	0.3	1.8	0.9	3.9
Collierville, TN	83.8	10.0	1.1	0.0	0.0	0.1	1.2	1.0	2.7
Coppell, TX	80.9	10.1	1.0	0.2	0.3	0.2	1.2	1.5	4.7
Cornelius, NC	80.5	9.9	1.5	0.1	0.1	0.2	1.4	1.1	5.1
Cranberry, PA	77.5	8.8	4.8	0.2	0.0	0.3	3.4	1.2	3.8
Cupertino, CA	76.5	10.5	2.2	0.2	1.1	1.8	1.9	1.4	4.6
Danville, CA	60.6	10.1	7.6	6.1	1.0	1.9	4.4	2.3	6.1
Draper, UT	75.7	12.2	2.4	0.3	0.4	0.8	2.1	1.5	4.6
Dublin, OH	82.7	7.9	1.6	0.0	0.0	0.4	2.2	0.8	4.3
Eastchester, NY	50.6	6.8	8.0	18.5	3.6	0.6	6.0	1.9	4.1
Eden Prairie, MN	78.2	8.4	4.3	0.1	0.1	0.9	2.3	0.9	4.9
Edmond, OK	83.0	10.3	0.4	0.0	0.0	0.3	1.6	1.0	3.3
Evesham, NJ	73.4	7.8	5.5	1.6	2.3	0.6	3.7	0.9	4.0
Fishers, IN	83.8	8.7	1.0	0.0	0.0	0.3	1.6	0.9	3.7
Flower Mound, TX	80.9	10.1	1.0	0.2	0.3	0.2	1.2	1.5	4.7
Folsom, CA	75.5	11.2	1.9	0.3	0.3	1.9	2.1	1.3	5.6
Foster City, CA	60.6	10.1	7.6	6.1	1.0	1.9	4.4	2.3	6.1
Franklin, TN	82.1	9.8	1.0	0.0	0.1	0.2	1.3	0.9	4.6
Friendswood, TX	79.9	11.1	2.3	0.0	0.0	0.3	1.3	1.6	3.4
Germantown, TN	83.8	10.0	1.1	0.0	0.0	0.1	1.2	1.0	2.7
Glastonbury, CT	81.4	7.9	3.0	0.0	0.1	0.2	2.7	1.0	3.7
Grand Blanc, MI	85.1	8.9	1.2	0.0	0.0	0.1	1.2	0.6	2.9
Guilderland, NY	80.5	7.7	3.0	0.1	0.1	0.2	3.7	1.0	3.7
Hampden, PA	81.4	9.1	1.4	0.1	0.0	0.3	3.5	0.7	3.5
Holly Springs, NC	80.7	9.3	1.0	0.0	0.0	0.2	1.3	1.2	6.4
Huntersville, NC	80.5	9.9	1.5	0.1	0.1	0.2	1.4	1.1	5.1
Independence, KY	83.2	8.1	2.0	0.0	0.0	0.2	2.1	0.7	3.8
Johns Creek, GA	77.9	10.4	2.2	0.7	0.1	0.2	1.4	1.4	5.8
Keller, TX	80.9	10.1	1.0	0.2	0.3	0.2	1.2	1.5	4.7
Kirkland, WA	69.8	10.2	8.1	0.2	0.4	1.1	3.6	1.2	5.5
Lafayette, CO	64.9	8.4	5.3	0.0	0.0	4.2	4.9	1.4	10.8
Lake Oswego, OR	70.8	9.8	4.7	0.6	0.2	2.3	3.5	1.7	6.5
League City, TX	79.9	11.1	2.3	0.0	0.0	0.3	1.3	1.6	3.4
Leawood, KS	83.3	8.9	1.1	0.0	0.0	0.2	1.3	1.0	4.3
Lee's Summit, MO	83.3	8.9	1.1	0.0	0.0	0.2	1.3	1.0	4.3
Leesburg, VA	66.0	10.1	5.5	7.9	0.7	0.7	3.2	1.0	4.9
Lehi, UT	73.1	12.8	1.2	0.1	0.3	1.2	4.1	1.1	6.0
Lenexa, KS	83.3	8.9	1.1	0.0	0.0	0.2	1.3	1.0	4.3
Lexington, MA	68.5	7.4	4.1	5.8	2.0	0.9	5.3	1.4	4.6
Los Altos, CA	76.5	10.5	2.2	0.2	1.1	1.8	1.9	1.4	4.6
Lower Makefield, PA	73.4	7.8	5.5	1.6	2.3	0.6	3.7	0.9	4.0
Madison, AL	86.7	7.6	0.3	0.0	0.0	0.1	1.0	1.2	2.9
Mamaroneck, NY	50.6	6.8	8.0	18.5	3.6	0.6	6.0	1.9	4.1
Manheim, PA	79.3	9.2	1.0	0.0	0.2	0.7	3.5	1.3	4.8
Manlius, NY	80.1	8.3	2.2	0.0	0.0	0.4	4.6	0.9	3.5
Maple Grove, MN	78.2	8.4	4.3	0.1	0.1	0.9	2.3	0.9	4.9
Marion, IA	82.4	8.9	0.8	0.0	0.0	0.4	2.5	1.0	3.9
Marlboro, NJ	50.6	6.8	8.0	18.5	3.6	0.6	6.0	1.9	4.1
Mason, OH	83.2	8.1	2.0	0.0	0.0	0.2	2.1	0.7	3.8

Table continued on next page.

Metro Area	Car/Truck/Van Drove Alone	Car/Truck/Van Car-pooled	Public Transportation Bus	Public Transportation Subway	Public Transportation Railroad	Bicycle	Walked	Other Means	Worked at Home
McCandless, PA	77.5	8.8	4.8	0.2	0.0	0.3	3.4	1.2	3.8
Menomonee Falls, WI	80.2	8.6	3.6	0.0	0.0	0.5	2.8	0.8	3.5
Meridian, ID	79.2	8.6	0.4	0.0	0.0	1.4	2.0	1.6	7.0
Merrimack, NH	81.9	8.3	0.8	0.0	0.1	0.1	2.0	0.8	6.0
Mount Lebanon, PA	77.5	8.8	4.8	0.2	0.0	0.3	3.4	1.2	3.8
Mount Pleasant, SC	80.7	8.8	1.4	0.0	0.0	0.9	2.8	1.0	4.3
Needham, MA	68.5	7.4	4.1	5.8	2.0	0.9	5.3	1.4	4.6
Newtown, CT	72.8	8.4	2.7	0.3	6.3	0.3	2.7	0.9	5.5
Northbrook, IL	70.9	8.4	4.6	3.6	3.2	0.6	3.2	1.1	4.3
Northville, MI	84.1	8.7	1.6	0.0	0.0	0.2	1.3	0.8	3.2
Novi, MI	84.1	8.7	1.6	0.0	0.0	0.2	1.3	0.8	3.2
O'Fallon, IL	83.0	7.7	2.1	0.4	0.1	0.3	1.8	0.9	3.9
O'Fallon, MO	83.0	7.7	2.1	0.4	0.1	0.3	1.8	0.9	3.9
Orchard Park, NY	82.2	7.8	3.0	0.2	0.0	0.4	2.9	1.0	2.4
Oviedo, FL	80.9	9.5	1.9	0.0	0.0	0.5	1.1	1.4	4.7
Parker, CO	76.0	9.1	3.6	0.5	0.2	0.9	2.1	1.1	6.4
Parkland, FL	78.2	9.5	3.4	0.2	0.2	0.6	1.8	1.4	4.7
Peachtree City, GA	77.9	10.4	2.2	0.7	0.1	0.2	1.4	1.4	5.8
Pflugerville, TX	76.0	10.5	2.3	0.0	0.1	0.8	1.8	1.5	6.9
Plainfield, IL	70.9	8.4	4.6	3.6	3.2	0.6	3.2	1.1	4.3
Princeton, NJ	70.9	10.3	3.3	0.3	4.2	0.7	3.6	1.5	5.2
Queen Creek, AZ	76.6	11.3	2.0	0.0	0.0	0.8	1.5	1.8	5.9
Rancho Palos Verdes, CA	73.9	10.3	5.3	0.4	0.2	0.9	2.6	1.3	5.1
Redmond, WA	69.8	10.2	8.1	0.2	0.4	1.1	3.6	1.2	5.5
Richland, WA	80.1	12.1	1.1	0.0	0.0	0.3	2.0	0.8	3.6
Ridgefield, CT	72.8	8.4	2.7	0.3	6.3	0.3	2.7	0.9	5.5
Ridgewood, NJ	50.6	6.8	8.0	18.5	3.6	0.6	6.0	1.9	4.1
Rio Rancho, NM	80.0	9.5	1.4	0.0	0.3	1.0	1.9	1.4	4.4
Sahuarita, AZ	76.5	9.9	2.6	0.0	0.0	1.8	2.4	2.1	4.7
Sammamish, WA	69.8	10.2	8.1	0.2	0.4	1.1	3.6	1.2	5.5
San Ramon, CA	60.6	10.1	7.6	6.1	1.0	1.9	4.4	2.3	6.1
Saratoga, CA	76.5	10.5	2.2	0.2	1.1	1.8	1.9	1.4	4.6
Schertz, TX	79.3	11.2	2.2	0.0	0.0	0.2	1.8	1.1	4.1
Shrewsbury, MA	82.0	8.9	0.7	0.1	0.6	0.1	2.8	0.8	4.0
South Brunswick, NJ	50.6	6.8	8.0	18.5	3.6	0.6	6.0	1.9	4.1
South Jordan, UT	75.7	12.2	2.4	0.3	0.4	0.8	2.1	1.5	4.6
South Kingstown, RI	80.9	8.5	1.7	0.1	0.8	0.4	3.2	1.0	3.3
South Windsor, CT	81.4	7.9	3.0	0.0	0.1	0.2	2.7	1.0	3.7
Southlake, TX	80.9	10.1	1.0	0.2	0.3	0.2	1.2	1.5	4.7
Spring Hill, TN	82.1	9.8	1.0	0.0	0.1	0.2	1.3	0.9	4.6
Stow, OH	86.3	6.7	1.5	0.0	0.0	0.1	1.7	0.5	3.2
Sugar Land, TX	79.9	11.1	2.3	0.0	0.0	0.3	1.3	1.6	3.4
Sun Prairie, WI	73.9	8.7	4.2	0.0	0.0	2.5	5.2	0.8	4.5
Syracuse, UT	79.4	11.2	1.5	0.1	0.5	0.4	1.4	1.2	4.3
Tredyffrin, PA	73.4	7.8	5.5	1.6	2.3	0.6	3.7	0.9	4.0
Upper Arlington, OH	82.7	7.9	1.6	0.0	0.0	0.4	2.2	0.8	4.3
Upper Dublin, PA	73.4	7.8	5.5	1.6	2.3	0.6	3.7	0.9	4.0
Vestavia Hills, AL	85.2	9.3	0.6	0.0	0.0	0.1	1.0	0.7	2.9
Webster, NY	81.8	7.7	2.1	0.0	0.0	0.5	3.6	0.8	3.6
Wellesley, MA	68.5	7.4	4.1	5.8	2.0	0.9	5.3	1.4	4.6
West Fargo, ND	82.0	7.8	1.1	0.0	0.0	0.6	3.7	1.0	3.6
West Linn, OR	70.8	9.8	4.7	0.6	0.2	2.3	3.5	1.7	6.5
West Windsor, NJ	70.9	10.3	3.3	0.3	4.2	0.7	3.6	1.5	5.2
Westlake, OH	82.5	7.3	2.9	0.2	0.1	0.4	2.2	0.9	3.6
Weston, FL	78.2	9.5	3.4	0.2	0.2	0.6	1.8	1.4	4.7
Westport, CT	72.8	8.4	2.7	0.3	6.3	0.3	2.7	0.9	5.5
Wilmette, IL	70.9	8.4	4.6	3.6	3.2	0.6	3.2	1.1	4.3
Woodbury, MN	78.2	8.4	4.3	0.1	0.1	0.9	2.3	0.9	4.9
Yorba Linda, CA	73.9	10.3	5.3	0.4	0.2	0.9	2.6	1.3	5.1
U.S.	76.4	9.6	2.6	1.8	0.6	0.6	2.8	1.3	4.4

Note: Figures are percentages and cover workers 16 years of age and older; (1) Figures cover the Metropolitan Statistical Area—see Appendix B for areas included

Source: U.S. Census Bureau, 2010-2014 American Community Survey 5-Year Estimates

Travel Time to Work: City

City	Less Than 10 Minutes	10 to 19 Minutes	20 to 29 Minutes	30 to 44 Minutes	45 to 59 Minutes	60 to 89 Minutes	90 Minutes or More
Aliso Viejo, CA	11.2	25.5	24.9	25.2	5.5	5.3	2.5
Allen, TX	10.8	24.8	23.7	22.3	11.1	6.1	1.2
Alpharetta, GA	11.3	34.2	17.7	17.0	10.7	6.8	2.2
Ankeny, IA	16.9	27.4	32.4	19.8	1.3	1.0	1.3
Apex, NC	10.6	28.5	29.1	22.8	5.3	2.2	1.5
Ballwin, MO	9.6	24.3	25.7	30.1	8.3	1.1	0.8
Beavercreek, OH	12.0	47.2	27.2	8.3	2.0	2.1	1.1
Bella Vista, AR	8.3	19.5	33.4	27.2	7.8	2.2	1.7
Bernards, NJ	9.0	23.6	21.8	19.7	8.4	9.5	7.9
Bethlehem, NY	10.7	36.4	32.6	14.6	3.3	1.4	1.1
Bloomfield, MI	9.2	31.0	23.9	25.0	6.7	3.3	0.9
Bowie, MD	7.0	14.5	16.4	26.5	15.5	16.3	3.9
Bozeman, MT	33.6	47.6	10.1	4.6	1.2	1.9	1.0
Brentwood, TN	7.5	31.1	27.4	25.4	6.2	1.2	1.3
Broomfield, CO	10.2	24.9	21.0	28.1	8.9	5.1	1.7
Carmel, IN	11.6	29.0	19.9	27.3	8.8	2.5	1.1
Cedar Park, TX	9.4	22.1	24.7	27.5	10.9	4.9	0.5
Cheshire, CT	16.8	21.3	21.2	27.6	8.5	2.8	1.8
Chesterfield, MO	10.6	31.1	27.4	24.5	4.9	0.7	0.9
Collierville, TN	12.3	24.1	23.0	31.0	7.2	1.3	1.2
Coppell, TX	10.3	26.7	26.6	25.1	7.1	2.5	1.7
Cornelius, NC	13.8	22.2	17.1	27.2	13.0	4.5	2.3
Cranberry, PA	11.6	25.7	14.2	28.0	15.0	3.4	2.2
Cupertino, CA	7.6	21.4	32.0	28.1	6.4	3.6	0.9
Danville, CA	11.9	25.2	17.4	18.2	11.4	13.5	2.4
Draper, UT	11.8	24.8	31.1	22.7	5.7	1.5	2.4
Dublin, OH	15.6	25.4	28.3	22.7	4.2	2.3	1.5
Eastchester, NY	13.1	21.5	15.3	20.3	10.4	16.8	2.5
Eden Prairie, MN	11.2	36.2	25.2	19.0	5.3	2.1	1.1
Edmond, OK	14.9	30.0	29.0	20.1	3.5	1.0	1.5
Evesham, NJ	8.9	28.4	20.7	19.1	10.5	9.2	3.1
Fishers, IN	8.5	22.3	22.8	31.8	9.4	3.0	2.2
Flower Mound, TX	9.8	20.1	21.6	28.9	13.4	4.3	1.9
Folsom, CA	15.4	30.9	19.4	21.8	6.1	3.8	2.5
Foster City, CA	8.4	28.7	20.0	23.6	10.8	7.4	1.1
Franklin, TN	12.9	31.6	21.0	23.4	8.0	1.7	1.4
Friendswood, TX	8.5	22.9	19.2	22.4	13.6	11.3	2.1
Germantown, TN	13.0	34.7	29.2	19.0	2.5	0.9	0.7
Glastonbury, CT	12.9	30.8	25.4	21.1	5.0	2.8	1.9
Grand Blanc, MI	13.9	33.4	20.0	13.0	7.9	10.1	1.7
Guilderland, NY	10.1	36.6	29.9	18.1	3.1	1.2	0.9
Hampden, PA	10.3	43.4	28.6	11.7	3.3	1.3	1.2
Holly Springs, NC	7.5	18.2	24.8	33.8	10.5	4.1	1.2
Huntersville, NC	7.2	27.1	24.4	30.2	6.9	2.4	1.7
Independence, KY	7.3	27.2	30.4	20.7	8.1	4.5	1.7
Johns Creek, GA	7.8	23.2	18.9	23.6	14.3	9.2	3.1
Keller, TX	7.4	18.9	17.7	32.7	15.4	6.1	1.8
Kirkland, WA	9.6	29.0	25.0	23.4	7.6	4.3	1.1
Lafayette, CO	10.0	25.8	31.6	20.1	6.4	4.5	1.6
Lake Oswego, OR	12.0	28.2	29.4	21.9	5.1	2.0	1.4
League City, TX	7.7	26.2	19.2	23.1	12.1	9.7	2.0
Leawood, KS	12.7	38.1	26.7	18.0	2.7	0.5	1.3
Lee's Summit, MO	14.2	24.3	21.5	28.8	8.8	1.6	0.7
Leesburg, VA	13.7	23.6	15.9	21.4	9.6	10.6	5.3
Lehi, UT	13.9	27.7	24.5	24.2	5.8	2.5	1.4
Lenexa, KS	13.0	38.4	27.1	17.7	1.9	0.9	0.9
Lexington, MA	8.8	20.3	18.9	26.7	15.1	8.4	1.8
Los Altos, CA	9.6	32.8	30.8	18.6	2.8	3.7	1.6
Lower Makefield, PA	7.9	25.4	19.1	19.6	9.9	11.8	6.3
Madison, AL	10.5	42.0	31.6	13.2	1.2	1.0	0.4
Mamaroneck, NY	10.2	14.6	11.6	23.5	15.8	21.1	3.1
Manheim, PA	13.5	38.3	23.2	14.4	4.9	3.8	1.8
Manlius, NY	13.2	33.6	34.9	12.6	2.3	2.1	1.2
Maple Grove, MN	8.4	23.8	26.4	29.5	7.8	3.7	0.5
Marion, IA	16.5	37.5	29.5	9.7	3.8	2.2	0.7
Marlboro, NJ	5.9	15.9	14.4	16.8	12.3	18.3	16.3
Mason, OH	10.9	25.7	28.3	23.4	8.0	3.1	0.7
McCandless, PA	8.9	26.6	23.4	28.6	7.1	4.6	0.8

Table continued on next page.

City	Less Than 10 Minutes	10 to 19 Minutes	20 to 29 Minutes	30 to 44 Minutes	45 to 59 Minutes	60 to 89 Minutes	90 Minutes or More
Menomonee Falls, WI	14.6	31.9	27.8	18.9	3.3	1.7	1.7
Meridian, ID	8.6	32.0	32.7	21.4	2.3	1.6	1.4
Merrimack, NH	9.4	27.1	31.2	14.0	7.1	8.1	3.1
Mount Lebanon, PA	12.4	22.2	20.3	29.2	10.3	4.1	1.6
Mount Pleasant, SC	11.7	32.8	27.8	21.4	4.0	1.1	1.3
Needham, MA	9.2	23.7	17.6	25.4	15.4	6.9	1.8
Newtown, CT	10.1	20.7	18.9	24.6	12.2	9.6	3.8
Northbrook, IL	13.7	24.8	17.4	19.7	11.5	11.5	1.5
Northville, MI	7.5	22.8	21.2	33.5	9.3	4.2	1.4
Novi, MI	10.0	24.8	21.7	27.3	11.4	4.1	0.6
O'Fallon, IL	14.6	30.5	22.1	21.2	8.0	2.1	1.4
O'Fallon, MO	9.9	25.3	21.5	28.7	10.5	3.0	1.2
Orchard Park, NY	12.5	29.5	29.5	22.1	3.6	1.1	1.8
Oviedo, FL	6.4	21.4	21.5	31.1	13.8	3.6	2.1
Parker, CO	9.7	24.5	22.8	25.7	9.6	4.6	3.0
Parkland, FL	7.3	22.8	22.3	30.3	11.0	4.6	1.6
Peachtree City, GA	14.3	26.4	10.7	24.5	14.5	8.0	1.5
Pflugerville, TX	9.4	26.0	26.5	24.4	7.3	4.0	2.4
Plainfield, IL	5.7	19.1	17.4	19.9	17.7	14.3	6.0
Princeton, NJ	23.7	34.3	12.4	9.0	5.5	6.4	8.6
Queen Creek, AZ	9.0	12.7	23.5	28.7	16.3	7.7	2.1
Rancho Palos Verdes, CA	4.7	17.9	23.4	30.5	11.2	9.7	2.5
Redmond, WA	13.9	38.1	20.7	17.6	6.2	2.8	0.6
Richland, WA	20.8	39.2	20.1	10.0	5.8	2.7	1.3
Ridgefield, CT	13.1	18.9	15.4	25.2	13.3	6.8	7.2
Ridgewood, NJ	13.8	18.6	14.8	13.9	8.3	21.0	9.5
Rio Rancho, NM	9.6	23.7	15.3	27.6	15.6	5.4	2.8
Sahuarita, AZ	9.7	20.6	22.0	30.9	12.2	3.1	1.5
Sammamish, WA	6.9	15.4	25.8	34.7	11.2	4.4	1.6
San Ramon, CA	9.6	25.5	12.8	18.2	14.7	15.3	4.0
Saratoga, CA	3.6	21.2	28.5	33.3	7.2	4.6	1.6
Schertz, TX	10.0	27.2	23.0	25.4	8.8	4.8	0.8
Shrewsbury, MA	8.1	31.0	21.0	16.9	10.2	9.9	3.0
South Brunswick, NJ	6.1	21.8	19.2	23.5	10.1	10.2	9.1
South Jordan, UT	10.5	26.2	27.5	26.3	5.5	3.3	0.8
South Kingstown, RI	17.1	30.9	14.7	21.3	9.5	4.1	2.4
South Windsor, CT	12.4	28.4	32.8	18.9	4.7	1.7	1.0
Southlake, TX	11.8	20.3	20.7	28.7	12.6	4.2	1.7
Spring Hill, TN	9.6	12.0	16.5	36.9	17.6	6.2	1.3
Stow, OH	12.5	30.6	24.9	20.0	6.9	3.6	1.5
Sugar Land, TX	7.7	20.7	19.3	31.5	13.7	5.6	1.5
Sun Prairie, WI	17.4	32.2	22.6	21.1	3.5	1.8	1.2
Syracuse, UT	11.4	30.5	19.2	21.4	11.1	4.4	2.0
Tredyffrin, PA	14.9	30.4	18.8	16.6	7.6	9.3	2.5
Upper Arlington, OH	12.4	40.6	29.9	13.1	2.0	1.0	1.0
Upper Dublin, PA	12.3	25.9	18.2	23.8	11.6	6.0	2.1
Vestavia Hills, AL	9.6	41.9	30.4	13.7	2.0	1.5	1.0
Webster, NY	14.6	28.8	33.2	18.9	2.3	1.0	1.2
Wellesley, MA	15.6	22.1	15.6	25.1	13.2	7.1	1.4
West Fargo, ND	20.7	49.3	18.1	7.0	1.5	2.5	0.8
West Linn, OR	8.7	26.1	27.2	28.5	5.5	3.0	1.0
West Windsor, NJ	7.1	23.7	16.1	12.3	6.6	16.7	17.5
Westlake, OH	11.8	27.6	25.3	24.4	7.1	2.4	1.4
Weston, FL	9.4	23.0	18.5	25.0	14.5	7.6	2.0
Westport, CT	11.0	25.6	13.6	17.1	5.6	12.4	14.6
Wilmette, IL	10.0	19.2	12.8	23.8	17.1	13.4	3.7
Woodbury, MN	10.8	26.6	26.4	23.0	8.9	3.4	0.9
Yorba Linda, CA	8.1	20.2	18.6	30.7	10.3	7.9	4.1
U.S.	13.3	29.6	21.0	20.2	7.7	5.7	2.6

Note: Figures are percentages and include workers 16 years old and over
Source: U.S. Census Bureau, 2010-2014 American Community Survey 5-Year Estimates

Travel Time to Work: Metro Area

Metro Area	Less Than 10 Minutes	10 to 19 Minutes	20 to 29 Minutes	30 to 44 Minutes	45 to 59 Minutes	60 to 89 Minutes	90 Minutes or More
Aliso Viejo, CA	8.1	26.1	20.5	24.9	9.2	8.2	3.0
Allen, TX	9.8	26.5	21.2	24.8	9.9	5.8	1.8
Alpharetta, GA	7.8	23.4	20.4	24.7	11.9	8.8	3.0
Ankeny, IA	15.6	36.5	27.4	14.6	3.1	1.6	1.1
Apex, NC	10.2	28.9	25.9	22.8	7.0	3.5	1.7
Ballwin, MO	11.2	28.2	24.0	23.2	8.0	3.9	1.5
Beavercreek, OH	15.2	35.9	25.7	15.5	3.7	2.6	1.4
Bella Vista, AR	16.3	35.8	23.0	16.4	5.1	1.9	1.3
Bernards, NJ	7.8	19.9	16.6	23.6	12.1	13.9	6.2
Bethlehem, NY	13.0	33.0	24.3	20.5	5.5	2.4	1.3
Bloomfield, MI	10.0	26.9	23.1	24.2	9.0	5.0	1.8
Bowie, MD	6.3	19.2	18.0	25.8	13.7	12.6	4.4
Bozeman, MT	24.7	43.8	18.1	8.2	1.7	1.9	1.6
Brentwood, TN	9.7	27.4	22.8	23.5	9.7	5.1	1.7
Broomfield, CO	8.9	26.0	23.6	25.5	8.9	5.1	1.9
Carmel, IN	12.0	27.7	24.5	23.6	7.4	3.5	1.4
Cedar Park, TX	10.7	28.9	22.4	22.5	8.5	5.0	1.9
Cheshire, CT	12.5	32.3	23.0	19.7	6.0	4.1	2.3
Chesterfield, MO	11.2	28.2	24.0	23.2	8.0	3.9	1.5
Collierville, TN	10.7	28.9	25.7	23.7	7.1	2.7	1.2
Coppell, TX	9.8	26.5	21.2	24.8	9.9	5.8	1.8
Cornelius, NC	10.6	28.9	23.0	23.2	8.2	4.1	1.9
Cranberry, PA	12.5	27.6	21.3	21.8	9.1	5.8	2.0
Cupertino, CA	8.4	29.2	25.7	22.3	7.4	5.3	1.9
Danville, CA	7.8	24.9	19.1	24.1	11.1	10.0	3.0
Draper, UT	10.9	33.3	26.8	20.0	5.1	2.6	1.3
Dublin, OH	11.8	30.3	27.0	21.0	5.6	2.9	1.4
Eastchester, NY	7.8	19.9	16.6	23.6	12.1	13.9	6.2
Eden Prairie, MN	10.9	28.1	24.8	23.0	7.8	4.1	1.3
Edmond, OK	14.0	33.1	25.3	19.2	4.7	2.2	1.5
Evesham, NJ	10.1	25.4	20.3	23.2	10.4	7.6	2.9
Fishers, IN	12.0	27.7	24.5	23.6	7.4	3.5	1.4
Flower Mound, TX	9.8	26.5	21.2	24.8	9.9	5.8	1.8
Folsom, CA	11.8	29.7	22.6	21.7	7.0	4.0	3.1
Foster City, CA	7.8	24.9	19.1	24.1	11.1	10.0	3.0
Franklin, TN	9.7	27.4	22.8	23.5	9.7	5.1	1.7
Friendswood, TX	8.5	24.8	20.6	25.5	10.7	7.7	2.1
Germantown, TN	10.7	28.9	25.7	23.7	7.1	2.7	1.2
Glastonbury, CT	13.2	31.3	24.1	20.7	6.0	3.1	1.5
Grand Blanc, MI	13.2	32.8	22.5	14.0	7.8	7.2	2.5
Guilderland, NY	13.0	33.0	24.3	20.5	5.5	2.4	1.3
Hampden, PA	14.7	34.7	23.8	16.5	5.9	2.7	1.8
Holly Springs, NC	10.2	28.9	25.9	22.8	7.0	3.5	1.7
Huntersville, NC	10.6	28.9	23.0	23.2	8.2	4.1	1.9
Independence, KY	11.2	29.1	25.3	22.8	7.0	3.3	1.4
Johns Creek, GA	7.8	23.4	20.4	24.7	11.9	8.8	3.0
Keller, TX	9.8	26.5	21.2	24.8	9.9	5.8	1.8
Kirkland, WA	9.0	25.1	22.0	24.9	9.8	6.8	2.5
Lafayette, CO	15.7	35.2	21.4	16.2	6.1	3.8	1.5
Lake Oswego, OR	11.3	28.9	23.4	22.1	7.9	4.6	1.8
League City, TX	8.5	24.8	20.6	25.5	10.7	7.7	2.1
Leawood, KS	13.1	31.4	25.3	20.7	5.9	2.3	1.2
Lee's Summit, MO	13.1	31.4	25.3	20.7	5.9	2.3	1.2
Leesburg, VA	6.3	19.2	18.0	25.8	13.7	12.6	4.4
Lehi, UT	19.2	35.5	20.0	14.3	5.8	3.5	1.7
Lenexa, KS	13.1	31.4	25.3	20.7	5.9	2.3	1.2
Lexington, MA	10.2	23.8	18.8	23.9	11.2	9.3	2.9
Los Altos, CA	8.4	29.2	25.7	22.3	7.4	5.3	1.9
Lower Makefield, PA	10.1	25.4	20.3	23.2	10.4	7.6	2.9
Madison, AL	11.1	34.0	28.2	19.4	4.4	1.7	1.1
Mamaroneck, NY	7.8	19.9	16.6	23.6	12.1	13.9	6.2
Manheim, PA	15.7	33.6	22.8	17.0	5.1	3.6	2.1
Manlius, NY	16.0	35.7	25.4	15.3	4.1	2.2	1.4
Maple Grove, MN	10.9	28.1	24.8	23.0	7.8	4.1	1.3
Marion, IA	19.3	38.8	21.0	13.6	4.1	2.1	1.2
Marlboro, NJ	7.8	19.9	16.6	23.6	12.1	13.9	6.2
Mason, OH	11.2	29.1	25.3	22.8	7.0	3.3	1.4
McCandless, PA	12.5	27.6	21.3	21.8	9.1	5.8	2.0

Table continued on next page.

Metro Area	Less Than 10 Minutes	10 to 19 Minutes	20 to 29 Minutes	30 to 44 Minutes	45 to 59 Minutes	60 to 89 Minutes	90 Minutes or More
Menomonee Falls, WI	12.4	31.6	26.0	20.4	5.5	2.6	1.5
Meridian, ID	14.0	34.0	25.6	19.0	4.1	2.1	1.2
Merrimack, NH	12.0	29.6	20.5	19.9	8.1	6.9	3.0
Mount Lebanon, PA	12.5	27.6	21.3	21.8	9.1	5.8	2.0
Mount Pleasant, SC	10.5	29.2	25.2	22.4	7.6	3.4	1.6
Needham, MA	10.2	23.8	18.8	23.9	11.2	9.3	2.9
Newtown, CT	11.8	31.4	18.6	17.2	7.1	8.6	5.3
Northbrook, IL	9.0	22.4	18.7	24.7	11.8	10.1	3.2
Northville, MI	10.0	26.9	23.1	24.2	9.0	5.0	1.8
Novi, MI	10.0	26.9	23.1	24.2	9.0	5.0	1.8
O'Fallon, IL	11.2	28.2	24.0	23.2	8.0	3.9	1.5
O'Fallon, MO	11.2	28.2	24.0	23.2	8.0	3.9	1.5
Orchard Park, NY	14.8	34.3	26.2	17.9	3.8	1.8	1.2
Oviedo, FL	7.4	27.0	23.6	25.9	9.6	4.5	2.0
Parker, CO	8.9	26.0	23.6	25.5	8.9	5.1	1.9
Parkland, FL	7.5	25.0	23.3	27.0	9.0	6.1	2.0
Peachtree City, GA	7.8	23.4	20.4	24.7	11.9	8.8	3.0
Pflugerville, TX	10.7	28.9	22.4	22.5	8.5	5.0	1.9
Plainfield, IL	9.0	22.4	18.7	24.7	11.8	10.1	3.2
Princeton, NJ	12.2	33.5	20.6	15.1	6.3	6.7	5.5
Queen Creek, AZ	10.0	27.2	23.4	24.8	8.6	4.5	1.5
Rancho Palos Verdes, CA	8.1	26.1	20.5	24.9	9.2	8.2	3.0
Redmond, WA	9.0	25.1	22.0	24.9	9.8	6.8	2.5
Richland, WA	15.6	37.8	22.6	13.1	5.8	3.6	1.4
Ridgefield, CT	11.8	31.4	18.6	17.2	7.1	8.6	5.3
Ridgewood, NJ	7.8	19.9	16.6	23.6	12.1	13.9	6.2
Rio Rancho, NM	11.2	32.9	25.4	19.9	5.8	3.1	1.8
Sahuarita, AZ	10.9	30.0	24.6	23.1	6.9	2.9	1.7
Sammamish, WA	9.0	25.1	22.0	24.9	9.8	6.8	2.5
San Ramon, CA	7.8	24.9	19.1	24.1	11.1	10.0	3.0
Saratoga, CA	8.4	29.2	25.7	22.3	7.4	5.3	1.9
Schertz, TX	10.6	29.3	24.8	22.3	7.2	3.9	1.9
Shrewsbury, MA	12.5	27.7	19.2	20.1	9.5	8.1	2.8
South Brunswick, NJ	7.8	19.9	16.6	23.6	12.1	13.9	6.2
South Jordan, UT	10.9	33.3	26.8	20.0	5.1	2.6	1.3
South Kingstown, RI	13.4	32.1	21.5	18.2	6.8	5.4	2.6
South Windsor, CT	13.2	31.3	24.1	20.7	6.0	3.1	1.5
Southlake, TX	9.8	26.5	21.2	24.8	9.9	5.8	1.8
Spring Hill, TN	9.7	27.4	22.8	23.5	9.7	5.1	1.7
Stow, OH	13.3	33.0	23.7	18.8	6.7	3.2	1.3
Sugar Land, TX	8.5	24.8	20.6	25.5	10.7	7.7	2.1
Sun Prairie, WI	16.3	33.2	24.3	17.5	4.9	2.5	1.3
Syracuse, UT	16.8	32.9	22.9	16.4	5.9	3.5	1.6
Tredyffrin, PA	10.1	25.4	20.3	23.2	10.4	7.6	2.9
Upper Arlington, OH	11.8	30.3	27.0	21.0	5.6	2.9	1.4
Upper Dublin, PA	10.1	25.4	20.3	23.2	10.4	7.6	2.9
Vestavia Hills, AL	9.6	27.6	23.3	24.0	8.9	4.7	1.7
Webster, NY	16.0	34.5	25.9	16.0	4.1	2.4	1.2
Wellesley, MA	10.2	23.8	18.8	23.9	11.2	9.3	2.9
West Fargo, ND	21.4	49.4	16.9	7.3	1.9	1.7	1.2
West Linn, OR	11.3	28.9	23.4	22.1	7.9	4.6	1.8
West Windsor, NJ	12.2	33.5	20.6	15.1	6.3	6.7	5.5
Westlake, OH	11.2	28.4	25.1	23.6	7.1	3.2	1.5
Weston, FL	7.5	25.0	23.3	27.0	9.0	6.1	2.0
Westport, CT	11.8	31.4	18.6	17.2	7.1	8.6	5.3
Wilmette, IL	9.0	22.4	18.7	24.7	11.8	10.1	3.2
Woodbury, MN	10.9	28.1	24.8	23.0	7.8	4.1	1.3
Yorba Linda, CA	8.1	26.1	20.5	24.9	9.2	8.2	3.0
U.S.	13.3	29.6	21.0	20.2	7.7	5.7	2.6

Note: Figures are percentages and include workers 16 years old and over; Figures cover the Metropolitan Statistical Area—see Appendix B for areas included
Source: U.S. Census Bureau, 2010-2014 American Community Survey 5-Year Estimates

2012 Presidential Election Results

City	Area Covered	Obama	Romney	Other
Aliso Viejo, CA	Orange County	45.4	52.4	2.2
Allen, TX	Collin County	33.5	65.1	1.5
Alpharetta, GA	Fulton County	64.3	34.5	1.2
Ankeny, IA	Polk County	56.1	42.0	1.9
Apex, NC	Wake County	54.9	43.5	1.6
Ballwin, MO	St. Louis County	56.2	42.5	1.3
Beavercreek, OH	Greene County	38.3	60.0	1.7
Bella Vista, AR	Benton County	28.6	68.9	2.5
Bernards, NJ	Somerset County	52.0	46.8	1.2
Bethlehem, NY	Albany County	64.4	33.5	2.1
Bloomfield, MI	Oakland County	53.4	45.4	1.2
Bowie, MD	Prince George's County	89.6	9.3	1.0
Bozeman, MT	Gallatin County	45.9	50.9	3.3
Brentwood, TN	Williamson County	26.1	72.6	1.3
Broomfield, CO	Broomfield County	51.8	45.8	2.4
Carmel, IN	Hamilton County	32.0	66.3	1.7
Cedar Park, TX	Williamson County	37.9	59.5	2.6
Cheshire, CT	New Haven County	60.6	38.3	1.1
Chesterfield, MO	St. Louis County	56.2	42.5	1.3
Collierville, TN	Shelby County	62.6	36.6	0.8
Coppell, TX	Dallas County	57.1	41.7	1.2
Cornelius, NC	Mecklenburg County	60.7	38.2	1.1
Cranberry, PA	Butler County	31.9	66.8	1.3
Cupertino, CA	Santa Clara County	69.9	27.6	2.5
Danville, CA	Contra Costa County	65.8	31.9	2.3
Draper, UT	Salt Lake County	38.8	58.2	3.0
Dublin, OH	Franklin County	60.1	38.4	1.5
Eastchester, NY	Westchester County	60.4	38.2	1.4
Eden Prairie, MN	Hennepin County	62.3	35.3	2.4
Edmond, OK	Oklahoma County	41.7	58.3	0.0
Evesham, NJ	Burlington County	58.8	40.1	1.0
Fishers, IN	Hamilton County	32.0	66.3	1.7
Flower Mound, TX	Denton County	33.3	65.0	1.7
Folsom, CA	Sacramento County	57.5	40.0	2.5
Foster City, CA	San Mateo County	72.1	25.7	2.2
Franklin, TN	Williamson County	26.1	72.6	1.3
Friendswood, TX	Galveston County	35.8	62.8	1.4
Germantown, TN	Shelby County	62.6	36.6	0.8
Glastonbury, CT	Hartford County	62.4	36.5	1.1
Grand Blanc, MI	Genesee County	63.3	35.2	1.5
Guilderland, NY	Albany County	64.4	33.5	2.1
Hampden, PA	Cumberland County	40.0	58.5	1.5
Holly Springs, NC	Wake County	54.9	43.5	1.6
Huntersville, NC	Mecklenburg County	60.7	38.2	1.1
Independence, KY	Kenton County	36.8	61.2	2.0
Johns Creek, GA	Fulton County	64.3	34.5	1.2
Keller, TX	Tarrant County	41.4	57.1	1.4
Kirkland, WA	King County	68.8	28.8	2.3
Lafayette, CO	Boulder County	69.7	27.9	2.4
Lake Oswego, OR	Clackamas County	50.7	47.1	2.2
League City, TX	Galveston County	35.8	62.8	1.4
Leawood, KS	Johnson County	40.1	58.0	1.9
Lee's Summit, MO	Jackson County	58.7	39.7	1.6
Leesburg, VA	Loudoun County	51.5	47.1	1.4
Lehi, UT	Utah County	9.8	88.3	2.0
Lenexa, KS	Johnson County	40.1	58.0	1.9
Lexington, MA	Middlesex County	62.6	35.7	1.8
Los Altos, CA	Santa Clara County	69.9	27.6	2.5
Lower Makefield, PA	Bucks County	50.0	48.8	1.2
Madison, AL	Madison County	40.0	58.6	1.4
Mamaroneck, NY	Westchester County	60.4	38.2	1.4
Manheim, PA	Lancaster County	39.7	58.9	1.5
Manlius, NY	Onondaga County	59.7	38.6	1.8
Maple Grove, MN	Hennepin County	62.3	35.3	2.4
Marion, IA	Linn County	57.9	40.2	1.9
Marlboro, NJ	Monmouth County	46.7	52.2	1.2
Mason, OH	Warren County	29.5	69.1	1.4
McCandless, PA	Allegheny County	56.6	42.2	1.2
Menomonee Falls, WI	Waukesha County	32.2	67.0	0.8

Table continued on next page.

City	Area Covered	Obama	Romney	Other
Meridian, ID	Ada County	42.7	54.0	3.2
Merrimack, NH	Hillsborough County	49.7	48.6	1.6
Mount Lebanon, PA	Allegheny County	56.6	42.2	1.2
Mount Pleasant, SC	Charleston County	50.4	48.0	1.6
Needham, MA	Norfolk County	57.4	41.3	1.3
Newtown, CT	Fairfield County	55.3	43.8	0.9
Northbrook, IL	Cook County	74.0	24.6	1.3
Northville, MI	Wayne County	72.8	26.1	1.0
Novi, MI	Oakland County	53.4	45.4	1.2
O'Fallon, IL	St. Clair County	56.4	41.9	1.7
O'Fallon, MO	St. Charles County	38.7	59.7	1.7
Orchard Park, NY	Erie County	56.9	41.3	1.8
Oviedo, FL	Seminole County	46.2	52.7	1.1
Parker, CO	Douglas County	36.0	62.6	1.4
Parkland, FL	Broward County	67.2	32.3	0.5
Peachtree City, GA	Fayette County	33.7	65.0	1.2
Pflugerville, TX	Travis County	60.1	36.2	3.6
Plainfield, IL	Will County	51.1	47.4	1.5
Princeton, NJ	Mercer County	67.8	31.0	1.2
Queen Creek, AZ	Maricopa County	43.1	54.9	2.0
Rancho Palos Verdes, CA	Los Angeles County	68.6	29.1	2.3
Redmond, WA	King County	68.8	28.8	2.3
Richland, WA	Benton County	35.3	62.3	2.4
Ridgefield, CT	Fairfield County	55.3	43.8	0.9
Ridgewood, NJ	Bergen County	55.0	44.1	0.9
Rio Rancho, NM	Sandoval County	50.3	45.2	4.5
Sahuarita, AZ	Pima County	52.1	46.1	1.8
Sammamish, WA	King County	68.8	28.8	2.3
San Ramon, CA	Contra Costa County	65.8	31.9	2.3
Saratoga, CA	Santa Clara County	69.9	27.6	2.5
Schertz, TX	Guadalupe County	31.8	66.9	1.3
Shrewsbury, MA	Worcester County	53.7	44.5	1.8
South Brunswick, NJ	Middlesex County	62.9	36.0	1.1
South Jordan, UT	Salt Lake County	38.8	58.2	3.0
South Kingstown, RI	Washington County	57.1	40.4	2.6
South Windsor, CT	Hartford County	62.4	36.5	1.1
Southlake, TX	Tarrant County	41.4	57.1	1.4
Spring Hill, TN	Williamson County	26.1	72.6	1.3
Stow, OH	Summit County	56.7	41.9	1.4
Sugar Land, TX	Fort Bend County	46.1	52.9	1.0
Sun Prairie, WI	Dane County	71.1	27.6	1.3
Syracuse, UT	Davis County	18.1	80.0	1.9
Tredyffrin, PA	Chester County	49.2	49.6	1.1
Upper Arlington, OH	Franklin County	60.1	38.4	1.5
Upper Dublin, PA	Montgomery County	56.5	42.4	1.1
Vestavia Hills, AL	Jefferson County	52.6	46.6	0.8
Webster, NY	Monroe County	57.8	40.4	1.8
Wellesley, MA	Norfolk County	57.4	41.3	1.3
West Fargo, ND	Cass County	47.0	49.9	3.1
West Linn, OR	Clackamas County	50.7	47.1	2.2
West Windsor, NJ	Mercer County	67.8	31.0	1.2
Westlake, OH	Cuyahoga County	68.8	30.2	1.0
Weston, FL	Broward County	67.2	32.3	0.5
Westport, CT	Fairfield County	55.3	43.8	0.9
Wilmette, IL	Cook County	74.0	24.6	1.3
Woodbury, MN	Washington County	49.4	48.6	2.0
Yorba Linda, CA	Orange County	45.4	52.4	2.2
U.S.	U.S.	51.0	47.2	1.8

Note: Results are percentages and may not add to 100% due to rounding
Source: Dave Leip's Atlas of U.S. Presidential Elections

House Price Index (HPI)

Metro Area[1]	National Ranking[3]	Quarterly Change (%)	One-Year Change (%)	Five-Year Change (%)
Aliso Viejo, CA[2]	88	1.00	6.10	29.10
Allen, TX[2]	19	1.10	10.90	30.70
Alpharetta, GA	49	0.70	7.90	16.00
Ankeny, IA	148	0.20	4.30	9.70
Apex, NC	116	0.20	5.00	10.80
Ballwin, MO	164	0.50	3.80	4.00
Beavercreek, OH	162	0.70	3.90	0.80
Bella Vista, AR	145	1.60	4.30	13.10
Bernards, NJ[2]	235	-0.50	1.60	1.70
Bethlehem, NY	222	1.00	2.10	0.80
Bloomfield, MI[2]	107	-0.20	5.30	33.30
Bowie, MD[2]	180	0.30	3.20	17.20
Bozeman, MT	n/a	n/a	n/a	n/a
Brentwood, TN	46	1.40	8.20	22.40
Broomfield, CO	8	1.50	13.50	41.30
Carmel, IN	129	0.30	4.70	9.30
Cedar Park, TX	20	0.60	10.50	41.10
Cheshire, CT	252	-0.70	1.00	-5.30
Chesterfield, MO	164	0.50	3.80	4.00
Collierville, TN	178	0.50	3.30	5.30
Coppell, TX[2]	19	1.10	10.90	30.70
Cornelius, NC	84	1.50	6.10	12.10
Cranberry, PA	144	-0.10	4.40	13.60
Cupertino, CA	15	1.20	11.30	51.20
Danville, CA[2]	13	1.20	11.70	47.60
Draper, UT	89	1.30	6.10	21.80
Dublin, OH	81	0.30	6.20	11.90
Eastchester, NY[2]	157	0.30	4.00	4.80
Eden Prairie, MN	112	0.20	5.20	13.00
Edmond, OK	105	1.90	5.40	14.90
Evesham, NJ[2]	174	1.30	3.50	-3.60
Fishers, IN	129	0.30	4.70	9.30
Flower Mound, TX[2]	19	1.10	10.90	30.70
Folsom, CA	57	0.90	7.50	36.60
Foster City, CA[2]	4	2.90	14.10	54.90
Franklin, TN	46	1.40	8.20	22.40
Friendswood, TX	59	0.70	7.40	32.70
Germantown, TN	178	0.50	3.30	5.30
Glastonbury, CT	258	-0.10	0.50	-4.00
Grand Blanc, MI	135	0.80	4.60	19.10
Guilderland, NY	222	1.00	2.10	0.80
Hampden, PA	202	0.60	2.50	0.70
Holly Springs, NC	116	0.20	5.00	10.80
Huntersville, NC	84	1.50	6.10	12.10
Independence, KY	165	-0.10	3.80	4.30
Johns Creek, GA	49	0.70	7.90	16.00
Keller, TX[2]	25	1.30	10.20	23.60
Kirkland, WA[2]	18	1.60	10.90	28.40
Lafayette, CO	7	2.30	13.50	35.70
Lake Oswego, OR	10	1.90	12.40	30.70
League City, TX	59	0.70	7.40	32.70
Leawood, KS	79	1.80	6.40	8.50
Lee's Summit, MO	79	1.80	6.40	8.50
Leesburg, VA[2]	180	0.30	3.20	17.20
Lehi, UT	67	1.70	6.80	23.10
Lenexa, KS	79	1.80	6.40	8.50
Lexington, MA[2]	100	0.50	5.50	16.70
Los Altos, CA	15	1.20	11.30	51.20
Lower Makefield, PA[2]	195	0.80	2.70	3.70
Madison, AL	209	0.80	2.40	0.00
Mamaroneck, NY[2]	157	0.30	4.00	4.80
Manheim, PA	170	1.10	3.80	2.80
Manlius, NY	259	0.40	0.40	2.80
Maple Grove, MN	112	0.20	5.20	13.00
Marion, IA	234	0.40	1.60	4.30
Marlboro, NJ[2]	157	0.30	4.00	4.80
Mason, OH	165	-0.10	3.80	4.30
McCandless, PA	144	-0.10	4.40	13.60

Table continued on next page.

Metro Area[1]	National Ranking[3]	Quarterly Change (%)	One-Year Change (%)	Five-Year Change (%)
Menomonee Falls, WI	175	0.30	3.50	2.60
Meridian, ID	26	2.60	10.10	33.40
Merrimack, NH	130	0.00	4.70	5.10
Mount Lebanon, PA	144	-0.10	4.40	13.60
Mount Pleasant, SC	28	0.60	10.10	20.20
Needham, MA[2]	109	1.10	5.20	14.80
Newtown, CT	242	-1.00	1.30	-0.70
Northbrook, IL[2]	146	0.80	4.30	4.70
Northville, MI[2]	75	1.30	6.50	28.40
Novi, MI[2]	107	-0.20	5.30	33.30
O'Fallon, IL	164	0.50	3.80	4.00
O'Fallon, MO	164	0.50	3.80	4.00
Orchard Park, NY	173	-0.10	3.50	12.20
Oviedo, FL	33	1.60	9.50	25.20
Parker, CO	8	1.50	13.50	41.30
Parkland, FL[2]	41	1.60	8.60	36.30
Peachtree City, GA	49	0.70	7.90	16.00
Pflugerville, TX	20	0.60	10.50	41.10
Plainfield, IL[2]	146	0.80	4.30	4.70
Princeton, NJ	184	1.20	3.10	-2.00
Queen Creek, AZ	55	0.80	7.70	43.60
Rancho Palos Verdes, CA[2]	61	1.30	7.20	31.30
Redmond, WA[2]	18	1.60	10.90	28.40
Richland, WA	124	-0.60	4.80	10.50
Ridgefield, CT	242	-1.00	1.30	-0.70
Ridgewood, NJ[2]	157	0.30	4.00	4.80
Rio Rancho, NM	233	-0.30	1.60	-0.60
Sahuarita, AZ	156	2.40	4.00	6.70
Sammamish, WA[2]	18	1.60	10.90	28.40
San Ramon, CA[2]	13	1.20	11.70	47.60
Saratoga, CA	15	1.20	11.30	51.20
Schertz, TX	69	-0.70	6.70	18.80
Shrewsbury, MA	160	0.80	3.90	4.90
South Brunswick, NJ[2]	157	0.30	4.00	4.80
South Jordan, UT	89	1.30	6.10	21.80
South Kingstown, RI	139	0.30	4.50	3.40
South Windsor, CT	258	-0.10	0.50	-4.00
Southlake, TX[2]	25	1.30	10.20	23.60
Spring Hill, TN	46	1.40	8.20	22.40
Stow, OH	121	3.40	4.90	4.80
Sugar Land, TX	59	0.70	7.40	32.70
Sun Prairie, WI	143	0.80	4.40	7.40
Syracuse, UT	63	1.20	7.00	13.90
Tredyffrin, PA[2]	195	0.80	2.70	3.70
Upper Arlington, OH	81	0.30	6.20	11.90
Upper Dublin, PA[2]	195	0.80	2.70	3.70
Vestavia Hills, AL	176	-0.10	3.40	5.50
Webster, NY	182	-0.30	3.20	4.90
Wellesley, MA[2]	109	1.10	5.20	14.80
West Fargo, ND	62	0.10	7.20	25.60
West Linn, OR	10	1.90	12.40	30.70
West Windsor, NJ	184	1.20	3.10	-2.00
Westlake, OH	183	-0.90	3.10	3.10
Weston, FL[2]	41	1.60	8.60	36.30
Westport, CT	242	-1.00	1.30	-0.70
Wilmette, IL[2]	146	0.80	4.30	4.70
Woodbury, MN	112	0.20	5.20	13.00
Yorba Linda, CA[2]	88	1.00	6.10	29.10
U.S.[4]	–	1.45	5.76	22.85

Note: The HPI is a weighted repeat sales index. It measures average price changes in repeat sales or refinancings on the same properties. This information is obtained by reviewing repeat mortgage transactions on single-family properties whose mortgages have been purchased or securitized by Fannie Mae or Freddie Mac in January 1975; (1) figures cover the Metropolitan Statistical Area (MSA) unless noted otherwise—see Appendix B for areas included; (2) Metropolitan Division—see Appendix B for areas included; (3) Rankings are based on annual percentage change, for all MSAs containing at least 15,000 transactions over the last 10 years and ranges from 1 to 266; (4) figures based on a weighted division average; all figures are for the period ended December 31, 2015; n/a not available; n/r not ranked

Source: Federal Housing Finance Agency, House Price Index, February 25, 2016

Homeownership Rate

Metro Area	2008	2009	2010	2011	2012	2013	2014	2015
Aliso Viejo, CA	52.1	50.4	49.7	50.1	49.9	48.7	49.0	49.1
Allen, TX	60.9	61.6	63.8	62.6	61.8	59.9	57.7	57.8
Alpharetta, GA	67.5	67.7	67.2	65.8	62.1	61.6	61.6	61.7
Ankeny, IA	n/a	n/a	n/a	n/a	n/a	n/a	n/a	n/a
Apex, NC	70.7	65.7	65.9	66.7	67.7	65.5	65.5	67.4
Ballwin, MO	72.2	72.5	72.2	71.1	72.0	72.7	71.1	68.7
Beavercreek, OH	67.4	67.9	67.4	68.4	67.1	64.4	65.0	60.8
Bella Vista, AR	n/a	n/a	n/a	n/a	n/a	n/a	n/a	n/a
Bernards, NJ	52.6	51.7	51.6	50.9	51.5	50.6	50.7	49.9
Bethlehem, NY	69.5	71.1	72.8	72.4	70.6	67.9	67.5	65.9
Bloomfield, MI	75.5	73.9	73.6	73.5	73.4	71.7	71.2	74.0
Bowie, MD	68.1	67.2	67.3	67.6	66.9	66.0	65.0	64.6
Bozeman, MT	n/a	n/a	n/a	n/a	n/a	n/a	n/a	n/a
Brentwood, TN	71.3	71.8	70.4	69.6	64.9	63.9	67.1	67.4
Broomfield, CO	66.9	65.3	65.7	63.0	61.8	61.0	61.9	61.6
Carmel, IN	75.0	71.0	68.8	68.3	67.1	67.5	66.9	64.6
Cedar Park, TX	65.5	64.0	65.8	58.4	60.1	59.6	61.1	57.5
Cheshire, CT	65.5	64.1	65.6	66.3	62.2	62.0	62.4	64.6
Chesterfield, MO	72.2	72.5	72.2	71.1	72.0	72.7	71.1	68.7
Collierville, TN	63.9	61.5	61.9	60.1	60.5	56.2	57.2	59.6
Coppell, TX	60.9	61.6	63.8	62.6	61.8	59.9	57.7	57.8
Cornelius, NC	65.4	66.1	66.1	63.6	58.3	58.9	58.1	62.3
Cranberry, PA	73.2	71.7	70.4	70.3	67.9	68.3	69.1	71.0
Cupertino, CA	54.6	57.2	58.9	60.4	58.6	56.4	56.4	50.7
Danville, CA	56.4	57.3	58.0	56.1	53.2	55.2	54.6	56.3
Draper, UT	72.0	68.8	65.5	66.4	66.9	66.8	68.2	69.1
Dublin, OH	61.2	61.5	62.2	59.7	60.7	60.5	60.0	59.0
Eastchester, NY	52.6	51.7	51.6	50.9	51.5	50.6	50.7	49.9
Eden Prairie, MN	69.9	70.9	71.2	69.1	70.8	71.7	69.7	67.9
Edmond, OK	69.5	69.0	70.0	69.6	67.3	67.6	65.7	61.4
Evesham, NJ	71.8	69.7	70.7	69.7	69.5	69.1	67.0	67.0
Fishers, IN	75.0	71.0	68.8	68.3	67.1	67.5	66.9	64.6
Flower Mound, TX	60.9	61.6	63.8	62.6	61.8	59.9	57.7	57.8
Folsom, CA	61.1	64.3	61.1	57.2	58.6	60.4	60.1	60.8
Foster City, CA	56.4	57.3	58.0	56.1	53.2	55.2	54.6	56.3
Franklin, TN	71.3	71.8	70.4	69.6	64.9	63.9	67.1	67.4
Friendswood, TX	64.8	63.6	61.4	61.3	62.1	60.5	60.4	60.3
Germantown, TN	63.9	61.5	61.9	60.1	60.5	56.2	57.2	59.6
Glastonbury, CT	70.5	72.1	71.3	71.4	70.8	69.8	68.5	66.1
Grand Blanc, MI	n/a	n/a	n/a	n/a	n/a	n/a	n/a	n/a
Guilderland, NY	69.5	71.1	72.8	72.4	70.6	67.9	67.5	65.9
Hampden, PA	n/a	n/a	n/a	n/a	n/a	n/a	n/a	n/a
Holly Springs, NC	70.7	65.7	65.9	66.7	67.7	65.5	65.5	67.4
Huntersville, NC	65.4	66.1	66.1	63.6	58.3	58.9	58.1	62.3
Independence, KY	64.7	62.4	62.8	65.2	63.4	63.3	65.5	65.9
Johns Creek, GA	67.5	67.7	67.2	65.8	62.1	61.6	61.6	61.7
Keller, TX	60.9	61.6	63.8	62.6	61.8	59.9	57.7	57.8
Kirkland, WA	61.3	61.2	60.9	60.7	60.4	61.0	61.3	59.5
Lafayette, CO	n/a	n/a	n/a	n/a	n/a	n/a	n/a	n/a
Lake Oswego, OR	62.6	64.0	63.7	63.7	63.9	60.9	59.8	58.9
League City, TX	64.8	63.6	61.4	61.3	62.1	60.5	60.4	60.3
Leawood, KS	70.2	69.5	68.8	68.5	65.1	65.6	66.1	65.0
Lee's Summit, MO	70.2	69.5	68.8	68.5	65.1	65.6	66.1	65.0
Leesburg, VA	68.1	67.2	67.3	67.6	66.9	66.0	65.0	64.6
Lehi, UT	n/a	n/a	n/a	n/a	n/a	n/a	n/a	n/a
Lenexa, KS	70.2	69.5	68.8	68.5	65.1	65.6	66.1	65.0
Lexington, MA	66.2	65.5	66.0	65.5	66.0	66.3	62.8	59.3
Los Altos, CA	54.6	57.2	58.9	60.4	58.6	56.4	56.4	50.7
Lower Makefield, PA	71.8	69.7	70.7	69.7	69.5	69.1	67.0	67.0
Madison, AL	n/a	n/a	n/a	n/a	n/a	n/a	n/a	n/a
Mamaroneck, NY	52.6	51.7	51.6	50.9	51.5	50.6	50.7	49.9
Manheim, PA	n/a	n/a	n/a	n/a	n/a	n/a	n/a	n/a
Manlius, NY	62.4	61.3	61.1	61.5	57.0	58.9	60.4	62.8
Maple Grove, MN	69.9	70.9	71.2	69.1	70.8	71.7	69.7	67.9
Marion, IA	n/a	n/a	n/a	n/a	n/a	n/a	n/a	n/a
Marlboro, NJ	52.6	51.7	51.6	50.9	51.5	50.6	50.7	49.9
Mason, OH	64.7	62.4	62.8	65.2	63.4	63.3	65.5	65.9
McCandless, PA	73.2	71.7	70.4	70.3	67.9	68.3	69.1	71.0
Menomonee Falls, WI	60.9	61.6	62.4	62.3	61.9	60.0	55.9	57.0

Table continued on next page.

Metro Area	2008	2009	2010	2011	2012	2013	2014	2015
Meridian, ID	n/a	n/a	n/a	n/a	n/a	n/a	n/a	n/a
Merrimack, NH	n/a	n/a	n/a	n/a	n/a	n/a	n/a	n/a
Mount Lebanon, PA	73.2	71.7	70.4	70.3	67.9	68.3	69.1	71.0
Mount Pleasant, SC	-1.0	-1.0	-1.0	-1.0	-1.0	-1.0	-1.0	65.8
Needham, MA	66.2	65.5	66.0	65.5	66.0	66.3	62.8	59.3
Newtown, CT	72.6	70.3	71.3	71.6	70.6	70.7	67.7	66.6
Northbrook, IL	68.4	69.2	68.2	67.7	67.1	68.2	66.3	64.3
Northville, MI	75.5	73.9	73.6	73.5	73.4	71.7	71.2	74.0
Novi, MI	75.5	73.9	73.6	73.5	73.4	71.7	71.2	74.0
O'Fallon, IL	72.2	72.5	72.2	71.1	72.0	72.7	71.1	68.7
O'Fallon, MO	72.2	72.5	72.2	71.1	72.0	72.7	71.1	68.7
Orchard Park, NY	63.9	60.3	64.5	67.6	63.5	65.5	64.1	63.9
Oviedo, FL	70.5	72.4	70.8	68.6	68.0	65.5	62.3	58.4
Parker, CO	66.9	65.3	65.7	63.0	61.8	61.0	61.9	61.6
Parkland, FL	66.0	67.1	63.8	64.2	61.8	60.1	58.8	58.6
Peachtree City, GA	67.5	67.7	67.2	65.8	62.1	61.6	61.6	61.7
Pflugerville, TX	65.5	64.0	65.8	58.4	60.1	59.6	61.1	57.5
Plainfield, IL	68.4	69.2	68.2	67.7	67.1	68.2	66.3	64.3
Princeton, NJ	n/a	n/a	n/a	n/a	n/a	n/a	n/a	n/a
Queen Creek, AZ	70.2	69.8	66.5	63.3	63.1	62.2	61.9	61.0
Rancho Palos Verdes, CA	52.1	50.4	49.7	50.1	49.9	48.7	49.0	49.1
Redmond, WA	61.3	61.2	60.9	60.7	60.4	61.0	61.3	59.5
Richland, WA	n/a	n/a	n/a	n/a	n/a	n/a	n/a	n/a
Ridgefield, CT	72.6	70.3	71.3	71.6	70.6	70.7	67.7	66.6
Ridgewood, NJ	52.6	51.7	51.6	50.9	51.5	50.6	50.7	49.9
Rio Rancho, NM	68.2	65.7	65.5	67.1	62.8	65.9	64.4	64.3
Sahuarita, AZ	63.5	65.5	64.3	67.2	64.9	66.1	66.7	61.4
Sammamish, WA	61.3	61.2	60.9	60.7	60.4	61.0	61.3	59.5
San Ramon, CA	56.4	57.3	58.0	56.1	53.2	55.2	54.6	56.3
Saratoga, CA	54.6	57.2	58.9	60.4	58.6	56.4	56.4	50.7
Schertz, TX	66.1	69.8	70.1	66.5	67.5	70.1	70.2	66.0
Shrewsbury, MA	68.5	64.4	64.1	65.8	61.9	63.3	62.5	64.2
South Brunswick, NJ	52.6	51.7	51.6	50.9	51.5	50.6	50.7	49.9
South Jordan, UT	72.0	68.8	65.5	66.4	66.9	66.8	68.2	69.1
South Kingstown, RI	63.9	61.7	61.0	61.3	61.7	60.1	61.6	60.0
South Windsor, CT	70.5	72.1	71.3	71.4	70.8	69.8	68.5	66.1
Southlake, TX	60.9	61.6	63.8	62.6	61.8	59.9	57.7	57.8
Spring Hill, TN	71.3	71.8	70.4	69.6	64.9	63.9	67.1	67.4
Stow, OH	77.3	77.1	76.9	70.9	70.0	66.0	69.0	74.0
Sugar Land, TX	64.8	63.6	61.4	61.3	62.1	60.5	60.4	60.3
Sun Prairie, WI	n/a	n/a	n/a	n/a	n/a	n/a	n/a	n/a
Syracuse, UT	n/a	n/a	n/a	n/a	n/a	n/a	n/a	n/a
Tredyffrin, PA	71.8	69.7	70.7	69.7	69.5	69.1	67.0	67.0
Upper Arlington, OH	61.2	61.5	62.2	59.7	60.7	60.5	60.0	59.0
Upper Dublin, PA	71.8	69.7	70.7	69.7	69.5	69.1	67.0	67.0
Vestavia Hills, AL	73.3	75.1	76.2	76.1	73.2	72.1	71.9	71.3
Webster, NY	75.0	74.7	71.4	68.3	68.2	69.3	68.0	64.9
Wellesley, MA	66.2	65.5	66.0	65.5	66.0	66.3	62.8	59.3
West Fargo, ND	n/a	n/a	n/a	n/a	n/a	n/a	n/a	n/a
West Linn, OR	62.6	64.0	63.7	63.7	63.9	60.9	59.8	58.9
West Windsor, NJ	n/a	n/a	n/a	n/a	n/a	n/a	n/a	n/a
Westlake, OH	73.1	70.9	70.7	69.8	64.2	65.8	69.2	68.4
Weston, FL	66.0	67.1	63.8	64.2	61.8	60.1	58.8	58.6
Westport, CT	72.6	70.3	71.3	71.6	70.6	70.7	67.7	66.6
Wilmette, IL	68.4	69.2	68.2	67.7	67.1	68.2	66.3	64.3
Woodbury, MN	69.9	70.9	71.2	69.1	70.8	71.7	69.7	67.9
Yorba Linda, CA	52.1	50.4	49.7	50.1	49.9	48.7	49.0	49.1
U.S.	67.8	67.4	66.9	66.1	65.4	65.1	64.5	63.7

Note: Figures are percentages and cover the Metropolitan Statistical Area—see Appendix B for areas included
Source: U.S. Census Bureau, Housing Vacancies and Homeownership Annual Statistics: 2015

Year Housing Structure Built: City

City	2010 or Later	2000 -2009	1990 -1999	1980 -1989	1970 -1979	1960 -1969	1950 -1959	1940 -1949	Before 1940	Median Year
Aliso Viejo, CA	1.8	13.3	56.1	22.1	4.7	0.7	0.3	0.3	0.6	1994
Allen, TX	4.5	43.3	28.5	13.9	6.7	1.4	1.2	0.2	0.3	1999
Alpharetta, GA	0.7	20.5	48.7	20.9	6.6	1.4	0.5	0.2	0.5	1994
Ankeny, IA	5.8	37.1	19.1	8.7	13.5	8.8	3.6	1.4	2.0	1996
Apex, NC	3.9	38.8	42.4	8.0	3.3	0.8	0.5	0.8	1.4	1998
Ballwin, MO	0.1	5.0	15.7	12.2	29.4	25.6	9.8	1.1	1.1	1974
Beavercreek, OH	1.2	22.9	15.5	9.2	19.4	13.8	12.6	2.8	2.6	1979
Bella Vista, AR	0.3	27.9	25.9	25.4	15.5	3.2	0.5	0.6	0.8	1992
Bernards, NJ	0.1	11.9	27.5	25.9	8.9	12.6	5.0	2.5	5.7	1986
Bethlehem, NY	0.6	11.2	15.0	14.7	12.0	10.0	11.3	7.3	17.9	1973
Bloomfield, MI	0.3	4.0	8.9	11.9	19.3	27.1	23.3	2.4	2.8	1968
Bowie, MD	0.2	9.9	26.0	16.3	8.5	35.2	2.1	1.0	0.8	1981
Bozeman, MT	3.4	30.7	15.3	9.4	14.4	8.1	5.2	3.1	10.5	1989
Brentwood, TN	1.4	28.5	20.0	22.0	18.2	8.6	0.4	0.4	0.6	1990
Broomfield, CO	2.7	34.0	23.0	11.0	17.7	5.3	5.5	0.1	0.7	1994
Carmel, IN	3.2	29.0	26.4	14.7	15.6	6.8	2.8	0.7	0.9	1993
Cedar Park, TX	7.1	46.7	27.7	12.6	3.5	1.4	0.4	0.5	0.1	2001
Cheshire, CT	0.3	8.9	11.7	16.1	15.1	17.4	15.7	6.1	8.6	1971
Chesterfield, MO	0.7	9.3	18.1	24.4	33.2	11.9	1.7	0.2	0.5	1981
Collierville, TN	0.7	30.5	40.1	15.5	8.0	1.8	1.5	0.5	1.3	1995
Coppell, TX	1.0	14.3	42.2	34.5	4.9	1.1	1.1	0.5	0.4	1992
Cornelius, NC	1.5	37.5	32.8	16.9	6.6	2.6	0.6	0.3	1.1	1997
Cranberry, PA	3.4	20.5	29.8	20.2	15.1	4.3	4.4	0.5	1.7	1991
Cupertino, CA	0.5	7.7	12.2	11.2	22.0	27.5	15.4	2.7	0.8	1972
Danville, CA	1.1	5.0	23.2	15.3	31.1	14.8	7.8	1.3	0.6	1978
Draper, UT	1.2	47.4	39.7	2.3	3.4	1.3	1.5	0.9	2.2	2000
Dublin, OH	2.0	25.0	29.2	31.8	7.8	1.6	1.4	0.2	1.0	1992
Eastchester, NY	0.0	3.1	2.3	3.8	7.4	10.8	18.9	11.4	42.3	1947
Eden Prairie, MN	0.4	16.0	24.7	35.4	15.9	3.7	2.5	0.3	1.1	1987
Edmond, OK	3.1	22.2	20.2	21.4	19.2	7.5	3.2	1.6	1.7	1988
Evesham, NJ	0.5	11.1	19.2	30.3	20.9	11.7	4.9	0.4	1.0	1984
Fishers, IN	3.5	40.9	35.8	14.0	2.8	1.6	0.8	0.3	0.3	1998
Flower Mound, TX	1.7	24.1	51.3	16.0	4.4	1.6	0.5	0.2	0.2	1995
Folsom, CA	0.9	32.4	29.9	20.1	8.2	2.6	3.2	0.9	1.9	1994
Foster City, CA	0.0	3.6	6.8	18.7	48.1	19.5	2.0	0.4	0.8	1976
Franklin, TN	3.9	27.7	35.1	15.1	8.5	3.8	2.5	1.2	2.1	1995
Friendswood, TX	2.6	25.5	17.3	16.1	28.2	9.0	1.0	0.1	0.2	1987
Germantown, TN	0.6	12.1	15.0	27.2	37.2	5.4	0.8	0.6	1.1	1982
Glastonbury, CT	0.4	6.5	15.0	17.6	17.6	12.5	15.1	3.7	11.5	1974
Grand Blanc, MI	0.5	24.0	16.4	11.6	16.4	15.0	10.2	3.1	2.8	1982
Guilderland, NY	0.9	8.8	16.7	15.6	17.1	13.5	12.1	6.7	8.6	1975
Hampden, PA	2.3	17.7	20.7	12.0	19.8	15.5	8.2	1.3	2.5	1982
Holly Springs, NC	3.5	55.3	31.3	4.4	1.8	0.9	0.9	0.7	1.2	2002
Huntersville, NC	2.6	44.1	35.0	9.8	3.1	3.1	0.9	0.8	0.6	1999
Independence, KY	4.2	38.4	18.0	6.0	18.0	9.0	3.3	1.1	2.1	1996
Johns Creek, GA	1.1	20.3	49.4	25.5	2.2	0.5	0.3	0.1	0.4	1994
Keller, TX	2.9	33.0	30.5	20.1	9.3	2.3	0.6	0.3	0.9	1995
Kirkland, WA	0.9	12.8	16.0	22.0	24.7	15.8	3.6	1.6	2.7	1981
Lafayette, CO	2.7	13.5	35.0	22.2	15.6	3.5	2.6	1.3	3.7	1990
Lake Oswego, OR	1.4	10.5	17.1	21.5	24.1	9.4	7.2	4.4	4.3	1980
League City, TX	3.8	46.5	19.5	15.5	9.3	3.0	1.6	0.4	0.5	2000
Leawood, KS	0.2	18.8	21.4	22.7	10.4	7.9	14.9	2.3	1.4	1986
Lee's Summit, MO	0.9	24.9	26.8	18.8	14.9	6.9	3.8	0.8	2.2	1991
Leesburg, VA	1.8	26.8	27.4	19.9	12.6	5.5	3.2	0.2	2.7	1992
Lehi, UT	4.5	55.6	17.8	4.9	6.2	2.0	2.7	2.1	4.1	2002
Lenexa, KS	1.0	20.0	16.5	25.5	26.2	5.8	3.2	0.8	1.0	1985
Lexington, MA	1.3	12.0	4.4	7.3	7.1	14.3	21.8	8.3	23.4	1958
Los Altos, CA	1.0	7.0	4.9	5.2	10.9	19.7	39.8	7.4	4.0	1960
Lower Makefield, PA	0.3	5.2	25.3	23.4	13.9	11.6	13.1	3.2	3.9	1982
Madison, AL	3.1	32.4	29.9	22.3	6.2	4.2	0.9	0.4	0.6	1995
Mamaroneck, NY	0.4	2.8	2.9	4.4	5.3	10.7	15.9	8.5	49.2	1941
Manheim, PA	2.8	13.7	15.3	13.2	14.2	12.7	14.4	3.7	10.0	1976
Manlius, NY	0.9	7.4	9.4	15.8	15.9	14.4	16.4	6.0	13.9	1969
Maple Grove, MN	2.0	23.8	22.3	24.2	20.0	3.7	1.9	0.9	1.2	1989
Marion, IA	1.9	24.5	22.0	8.6	12.8	11.5	9.1	1.8	7.8	1988
Marlboro, NJ	1.0	14.9	27.3	26.2	13.5	11.1	2.8	1.2	2.0	1987
Mason, OH	0.3	27.0	35.6	11.7	11.1	1.5	8.7	0.9	3.2	1994
McCandless, PA	1.1	4.1	8.6	16.4	26.1	19.2	17.2	3.0	4.4	1972

Table continued on next page.

City	2010 or Later	2000 -2009	1990 -1999	1980 -1989	1970 -1979	1960 -1969	1950 -1959	1940 -1949	Before 1940	Median Year
Menomonee Falls, WI	1.8	12.7	22.1	7.9	8.7	20.4	19.1	3.1	4.3	1974
Meridian, ID	4.6	47.6	31.1	6.1	6.8	1.3	0.6	0.8	1.2	2000
Merrimack, NH	0.5	8.5	11.1	34.4	25.5	11.1	4.9	0.6	3.3	1981
Mount Lebanon, PA	0.1	3.5	3.3	5.8	6.6	9.3	22.8	16.0	32.6	1951
Mount Pleasant, SC	2.0	33.2	24.2	17.6	11.7	6.1	3.5	0.8	0.8	1994
Needham, MA	1.7	10.5	4.2	8.6	7.6	11.3	20.6	9.5	26.1	1957
Newtown, CT	0.6	13.1	16.1	11.5	14.8	15.2	12.0	4.7	12.0	1974
Northbrook, IL	0.2	9.2	8.3	11.1	25.0	23.9	13.2	5.1	4.0	1972
Northville, MI	1.5	26.6	19.6	20.2	19.6	6.1	3.4	0.8	2.2	1989
Novi, MI	1.3	22.0	25.4	19.8	20.6	4.7	3.9	0.3	2.0	1989
O'Fallon, IL	2.4	26.0	26.7	14.4	9.6	7.8	7.0	1.9	4.2	1992
O'Fallon, MO	2.4	42.4	34.1	10.1	4.0	3.6	1.5	0.6	1.3	1998
Orchard Park, NY	0.3	11.8	12.5	9.6	19.4	11.5	18.4	5.9	10.6	1972
Oviedo, FL	2.2	24.3	42.8	22.3	5.0	1.3	0.7	1.1	0.4	1994
Parker, CO	1.4	42.4	37.0	15.5	1.9	0.6	0.4	0.4	0.5	1998
Parkland, FL	3.4	40.0	37.1	17.1	1.4	0.6	0.4	0.0	0.0	1998
Peachtree City, GA	1.4	16.3	36.4	30.1	12.7	2.3	0.3	0.0	0.4	1991
Pflugerville, TX	2.1	44.6	31.6	16.2	3.1	0.9	1.0	0.1	0.3	1999
Plainfield, IL	1.4	65.7	20.2	2.9	3.7	2.1	1.8	0.4	1.9	2003
Princeton, NJ	0.2	9.9	9.1	7.8	9.3	14.0	18.0	6.6	25.1	1960
Queen Creek, AZ	3.5	82.9	6.4	3.7	1.6	0.5	0.9	0.4	0.2	2004
Rancho Palos Verdes, CA	0.3	2.6	2.4	5.9	25.0	40.8	20.5	1.1	1.4	1967
Redmond, WA	2.3	20.7	22.3	19.1	22.2	11.1	1.4	0.3	0.4	1988
Richland, WA	2.7	22.0	13.0	5.9	19.0	8.2	7.5	20.6	1.2	1977
Ridgefield, CT	0.9	7.4	11.2	14.2	16.9	24.2	11.4	2.5	11.4	1970
Ridgewood, NJ	0.1	2.2	1.8	3.9	3.3	9.8	25.6	11.3	42.1	1947
Rio Rancho, NM	1.8	38.8	20.0	24.2	11.7	2.3	0.8	0.1	0.3	1995
Sahuarita, AZ	4.4	75.9	10.9	1.9	3.1	2.2	0.6	0.7	0.4	2004
Sammamish, WA	2.6	28.7	25.2	25.8	11.6	3.0	1.1	0.7	1.1	1993
San Ramon, CA	2.5	33.1	16.5	21.4	17.3	8.0	0.6	0.3	0.4	1991
Saratoga, CA	0.8	5.8	4.3	7.1	22.9	27.1	24.5	3.8	3.7	1967
Schertz, TX	8.0	34.2	24.2	13.1	11.4	4.2	3.1	0.9	1.0	1997
Shrewsbury, MA	0.7	11.8	17.4	11.3	14.2	7.7	15.0	7.0	14.9	1974
South Brunswick, NJ	0.9	10.3	26.5	28.8	13.1	8.7	7.8	1.0	3.0	1986
South Jordan, UT	7.0	45.7	29.6	7.0	6.7	2.4	0.4	0.6	0.9	2001
South Kingstown, RI	0.8	11.6	15.0	14.7	15.9	7.2	9.9	4.7	20.2	1975
South Windsor, CT	1.0	8.3	12.0	26.3	13.4	13.5	15.9	2.5	7.1	1978
Southlake, TX	1.5	25.6	49.5	15.9	4.2	1.7	1.0	0.6	0.0	1995
Spring Hill, TN	4.7	70.1	19.0	2.4	2.0	1.2	0.3	0.0	0.4	2004
Stow, OH	0.0	13.1	18.3	17.5	20.0	13.1	11.7	2.8	3.5	1979
Sugar Land, TX	3.3	20.0	24.6	33.6	14.8	2.2	0.7	0.1	0.7	1989
Sun Prairie, WI	0.7	33.8	20.3	8.0	14.9	10.9	4.9	2.2	4.3	1992
Syracuse, UT	2.9	58.9	17.5	6.0	8.6	2.7	1.8	0.6	1.1	2002
Tredyffrin, PA	0.1	2.2	8.4	20.9	15.6	18.7	18.9	4.5	10.7	1968
Upper Arlington, OH	0.1	2.5	1.3	5.0	11.8	21.0	35.8	11.2	11.2	1958
Upper Dublin, PA	0.6	5.2	13.3	14.9	18.8	20.7	13.6	4.6	8.2	1972
Vestavia Hills, AL	0.2	14.7	15.1	15.5	20.3	20.1	11.3	2.3	0.4	1978
Webster, NY	0.6	17.4	19.1	12.1	16.0	10.5	13.9	3.2	7.3	1979
Wellesley, MA	1.9	7.0	3.8	5.2	7.2	8.4	17.4	12.8	36.3	1951
West Fargo, ND	4.5	39.5	16.0	7.9	19.5	5.8	4.2	1.0	1.6	1996
West Linn, OR	0.9	15.8	26.9	16.6	20.7	7.5	5.7	1.3	4.7	1986
West Windsor, NJ	2.8	21.5	22.5	29.3	8.6	5.5	4.5	1.7	3.5	1989
Westlake, OH	0.1	9.7	21.2	22.3	19.1	7.1	14.5	3.5	2.5	1981
Weston, FL	0.0	22.9	52.5	17.4	6.1	0.6	0.5	0.1	0.0	1995
Westport, CT	2.8	8.2	4.9	10.6	11.0	15.3	22.6	5.8	18.7	1962
Wilmette, IL	0.2	6.9	3.9	2.2	6.5	13.5	25.7	8.6	32.7	1953
Woodbury, MN	2.6	28.5	39.2	15.7	8.1	3.7	1.5	0.2	0.6	1995
Yorba Linda, CA	1.6	14.4	12.7	31.8	22.8	12.4	3.1	0.3	1.1	1983
U.S.	1.0	14.9	13.9	13.8	15.8	11.0	10.8	5.4	13.3	1976

Note: Figures are percentages except for Median Year
Source: U.S. Census Bureau, 2010-2014 American Community Survey 5-Year Estimates

Year Housing Structure Built: Metro Area

Metro Area	2010 or Later	2000 -2009	1990 -1999	1980 -1989	1970 -1979	1960 -1969	1950 -1959	1940 -1949	Before 1940	Median Year
Aliso Viejo, CA	0.5	6.8	7.5	12.6	16.5	16.0	19.0	8.9	12.2	1966
Allen, TX	1.9	23.3	16.5	19.5	15.3	9.5	7.7	3.1	3.1	1986
Alpharetta, GA	0.9	26.9	22.5	18.1	13.1	8.1	5.0	2.1	3.2	1990
Ankeny, IA	2.3	18.9	14.4	9.4	14.1	9.0	10.1	4.7	17.1	1976
Apex, NC	2.2	30.1	25.2	16.7	10.4	6.4	4.3	1.8	2.9	1993
Ballwin, MO	0.8	12.2	12.4	11.3	13.5	12.8	13.8	6.5	16.7	1970
Beavercreek, OH	0.4	8.4	9.2	8.3	16.6	17.3	16.6	7.2	16.1	1966
Bella Vista, AR	1.5	26.5	24.8	16.3	13.5	6.9	4.0	2.4	4.0	1991
Bernards, NJ	0.6	7.4	6.0	7.8	10.0	13.9	16.5	9.5	28.4	1957
Bethlehem, NY	0.8	9.0	9.8	10.9	12.3	9.5	10.7	6.2	30.8	1962
Bloomfield, MI	0.3	8.8	11.1	9.0	14.4	12.7	19.8	10.6	13.3	1965
Bowie, MD	1.2	15.7	14.4	16.5	15.0	12.9	10.0	5.6	8.7	1979
Bozeman, MT	2.0	30.0	19.5	11.8	15.9	6.0	3.8	2.3	8.7	1991
Brentwood, TN	1.8	21.7	19.0	15.8	15.2	10.4	7.6	3.3	5.3	1985
Broomfield, CO	1.1	18.4	15.5	15.0	19.3	10.4	10.0	3.1	7.1	1980
Carmel, IN	1.4	17.3	16.5	10.6	13.3	11.8	11.0	5.0	13.1	1977
Cedar Park, TX	2.8	30.5	19.4	19.0	14.1	5.5	4.1	2.1	2.6	1991
Cheshire, CT	0.5	5.6	7.4	12.7	12.9	12.5	15.0	7.0	26.4	1961
Chesterfield, MO	0.8	12.2	12.4	11.3	13.5	12.8	13.8	6.5	16.7	1970
Collierville, TN	1.0	17.2	17.0	13.7	16.9	11.5	11.6	5.3	5.8	1979
Coppell, TX	1.9	23.3	16.5	19.5	15.3	9.5	7.7	3.1	3.1	1986
Cornelius, NC	1.5	26.0	20.7	15.0	12.6	9.1	7.1	3.5	4.6	1989
Cranberry, PA	0.6	6.7	7.6	7.5	12.1	11.1	17.0	9.5	28.0	1957
Cupertino, CA	0.7	9.8	10.6	12.7	22.6	18.9	15.4	4.2	5.2	1973
Danville, CA	0.6	8.3	8.0	10.8	15.4	13.4	14.4	8.6	20.5	1965
Draper, UT	1.7	17.1	16.3	13.4	20.0	9.0	9.7	4.2	8.7	1979
Dublin, OH	1.1	15.4	16.9	12.2	14.5	11.9	10.8	4.4	12.9	1977
Eastchester, NY	0.6	7.4	6.0	7.8	10.0	13.9	16.5	9.5	28.4	1957
Eden Prairie, MN	0.8	15.2	14.6	14.8	15.4	10.0	10.1	4.1	15.0	1977
Edmond, OK	2.1	16.2	11.3	15.9	18.3	13.3	10.5	5.5	7.0	1978
Evesham, NJ	0.6	8.4	9.2	10.1	12.4	12.3	16.0	9.1	21.9	1962
Fishers, IN	1.4	17.3	16.5	10.6	13.3	11.8	11.0	5.0	13.1	1977
Flower Mound, TX	1.9	23.3	16.5	19.5	15.3	9.5	7.7	3.1	3.1	1986
Folsom, CA	0.7	18.5	14.3	16.7	19.4	11.2	10.7	4.0	4.6	1980
Foster City, CA	0.6	8.3	8.0	10.8	15.4	13.4	14.4	8.6	20.5	1965
Franklin, TN	1.8	21.7	19.0	15.8	15.2	10.4	7.6	3.3	5.3	1985
Friendswood, TX	2.5	24.9	14.6	16.3	19.6	9.5	6.9	2.9	2.8	1985
Germantown, TN	1.0	17.2	17.0	13.7	16.9	11.5	11.6	5.3	5.8	1979
Glastonbury, CT	0.3	7.2	7.7	13.8	13.4	14.1	16.8	7.6	19.0	1965
Grand Blanc, MI	0.1	10.4	11.3	7.5	16.1	16.0	18.8	8.0	11.9	1967
Guilderland, NY	0.8	9.0	9.8	10.9	12.3	9.5	10.7	6.2	30.8	1962
Hampden, PA	1.0	10.3	12.0	12.1	15.0	10.8	12.8	5.6	20.4	1970
Holly Springs, NC	2.2	30.1	25.2	16.7	10.4	6.4	4.3	1.8	2.9	1993
Huntersville, NC	1.5	26.0	20.7	15.0	12.6	9.1	7.1	3.5	4.6	1989
Independence, KY	0.9	12.6	14.7	10.7	13.3	11.2	12.7	5.4	18.5	1972
Johns Creek, GA	0.9	26.9	22.5	18.1	13.1	8.1	5.0	2.1	3.2	1990
Keller, TX	1.9	23.3	16.5	19.5	15.3	9.5	7.7	3.1	3.1	1986
Kirkland, WA	1.5	16.8	16.0	15.4	15.4	11.5	7.9	4.7	10.8	1980
Lafayette, CO	1.1	13.7	20.2	16.3	22.0	12.0	5.5	1.7	7.5	1981
Lake Oswego, OR	1.0	16.1	18.9	11.7	18.0	9.2	7.5	4.9	12.7	1979
League City, TX	2.5	24.9	14.6	16.3	19.6	9.5	6.9	2.9	2.8	1985
Leawood, KS	0.7	15.0	14.3	12.6	15.9	12.5	12.2	4.9	11.9	1975
Lee's Summit, MO	0.7	15.0	14.3	12.6	15.9	12.5	12.2	4.9	11.9	1975
Leesburg, VA	1.2	15.7	14.4	16.5	15.0	12.9	10.0	5.6	8.7	1979
Lehi, UT	2.0	30.5	21.1	9.5	15.7	5.5	5.9	3.9	5.9	1992
Lenexa, KS	0.7	15.0	14.3	12.6	15.9	12.5	12.2	4.9	11.9	1975
Lexington, MA	0.7	8.0	7.2	10.7	11.0	10.5	11.1	5.6	35.1	1958
Los Altos, CA	0.7	9.8	10.6	12.7	22.6	18.9	15.4	4.2	5.2	1973
Lower Makefield, PA	0.6	8.4	9.2	10.1	12.4	12.3	16.0	9.1	21.9	1962
Madison, AL	2.4	21.9	19.7	16.2	12.6	14.3	7.4	2.3	3.2	1986
Mamaroneck, NY	0.6	7.4	6.0	7.8	10.0	13.9	16.5	9.5	28.4	1957
Manheim, PA	1.4	11.3	14.3	14.4	12.7	8.7	9.9	4.2	23.1	1973
Manlius, NY	0.6	6.8	8.7	11.5	12.9	11.7	14.6	6.5	26.6	1962
Maple Grove, MN	0.8	15.2	14.6	14.8	15.4	10.0	10.1	4.1	15.0	1977
Marion, IA	1.3	16.0	15.4	6.7	14.2	12.2	11.0	4.5	18.7	1973
Marlboro, NJ	0.6	7.4	6.0	7.8	10.0	13.9	16.5	9.5	28.4	1957
Mason, OH	0.9	12.6	14.7	10.7	13.3	11.2	12.7	5.4	18.5	1972
McCandless, PA	0.6	6.7	7.6	7.5	12.1	11.1	17.0	9.5	28.0	1957

Table continued on next page.

Metro Area	2010 or Later	2000 -2009	1990 -1999	1980 -1989	1970 -1979	1960 -1969	1950 -1959	1940 -1949	Before 1940	Median Year
Menomonee Falls, WI	0.5	8.5	10.8	7.8	13.3	11.2	17.2	7.5	23.2	1962
Meridian, ID	1.5	27.9	22.5	10.5	17.7	5.3	5.2	3.7	5.7	1991
Merrimack, NH	0.6	10.2	10.0	20.9	15.6	9.4	7.6	3.9	21.8	1975
Mount Lebanon, PA	0.6	6.7	7.6	7.5	12.1	11.1	17.0	9.5	28.0	1957
Mount Pleasant, SC	1.9	26.3	16.3	17.5	15.6	9.4	5.8	2.8	4.5	1987
Needham, MA	0.7	8.0	7.2	10.7	11.0	10.5	11.1	5.6	35.1	1958
Newtown, CT	0.8	6.9	6.8	11.4	13.6	14.5	17.1	7.6	21.4	1963
Northbrook, IL	0.4	12.0	10.8	8.8	14.0	11.9	13.6	6.1	22.4	1967
Northville, MI	0.3	8.8	11.1	9.0	14.4	12.7	19.8	10.6	13.3	1965
Novi, MI	0.3	8.8	11.1	9.0	14.4	12.7	19.8	10.6	13.3	1965
O'Fallon, IL	0.8	12.2	12.4	11.3	13.5	12.8	13.8	6.5	16.7	1970
O'Fallon, MO	0.8	12.2	12.4	11.3	13.5	12.8	13.8	6.5	16.7	1970
Orchard Park, NY	0.5	5.2	7.0	6.5	10.4	10.9	17.8	9.1	32.6	1955
Oviedo, FL	1.1	27.1	21.2	21.6	13.8	6.4	5.8	1.4	1.6	1990
Parker, CO	1.1	18.4	15.5	15.0	19.3	10.4	10.0	3.1	7.1	1980
Parkland, FL	0.5	14.1	14.8	19.9	22.0	12.8	10.4	3.2	2.2	1980
Peachtree City, GA	0.9	26.9	22.5	18.1	13.1	8.1	5.0	2.1	3.2	1990
Pflugerville, TX	2.8	30.5	19.4	19.0	14.1	5.5	4.1	2.1	2.6	1991
Plainfield, IL	0.4	12.0	10.8	8.8	14.0	11.9	13.6	6.1	22.4	1967
Princeton, NJ	0.5	9.2	9.3	11.6	11.0	13.7	15.8	8.0	20.9	1964
Queen Creek, AZ	1.0	28.0	20.9	18.3	16.8	7.0	5.5	1.4	1.0	1990
Rancho Palos Verdes, CA	0.5	6.8	7.5	12.6	16.5	16.0	19.0	8.9	12.2	1966
Redmond, WA	1.5	16.8	16.0	15.4	15.4	11.5	7.9	4.7	10.8	1980
Richland, WA	2.4	22.6	14.7	7.6	23.2	9.0	9.5	7.8	3.3	1979
Ridgefield, CT	0.8	6.9	6.8	11.4	13.6	14.5	17.1	7.6	21.4	1963
Ridgewood, NJ	0.6	7.4	6.0	7.8	10.0	13.9	16.5	9.5	28.4	1957
Rio Rancho, NM	0.7	19.3	18.2	16.8	18.1	9.6	10.0	3.8	3.5	1983
Sahuarita, AZ	0.9	19.7	17.9	17.5	20.7	9.2	8.6	3.1	2.4	1983
Sammamish, WA	1.5	16.8	16.0	15.4	15.4	11.5	7.9	4.7	10.8	1980
San Ramon, CA	0.6	8.3	8.0	10.8	15.4	13.4	14.4	8.6	20.5	1965
Saratoga, CA	0.7	9.8	10.6	12.7	22.6	18.9	15.4	4.2	5.2	1973
Schertz, TX	2.4	23.8	14.9	16.2	15.7	9.4	8.2	4.4	5.0	1985
Shrewsbury, MA	0.6	9.1	9.1	12.6	11.7	8.5	10.5	5.8	32.1	1962
South Brunswick, NJ	0.6	7.4	6.0	7.8	10.0	13.9	16.5	9.5	28.4	1957
South Jordan, UT	1.7	17.1	16.3	13.4	20.0	9.0	9.7	4.2	8.7	1979
South Kingstown, RI	0.4	6.7	7.9	10.4	12.3	10.3	11.8	6.6	33.6	1958
South Windsor, CT	0.3	7.2	7.7	13.8	13.4	14.1	16.8	7.6	19.0	1965
Southlake, TX	1.9	23.3	16.5	19.5	15.3	9.5	7.7	3.1	3.1	1986
Spring Hill, TN	1.8	21.7	19.0	15.8	15.2	10.4	7.6	3.3	5.3	1985
Stow, OH	0.4	9.6	12.2	8.7	14.0	13.0	16.4	6.9	18.9	1966
Sugar Land, TX	2.5	24.9	14.6	16.3	19.6	9.5	6.9	2.9	2.8	1985
Sun Prairie, WI	1.1	17.9	15.9	11.0	16.5	9.9	8.8	3.7	15.2	1978
Syracuse, UT	2.0	23.0	17.6	12.8	16.2	8.7	9.0	4.1	6.6	1984
Tredyffrin, PA	0.6	8.4	9.2	10.1	12.4	12.3	16.0	9.1	21.9	1962
Upper Arlington, OH	1.1	15.4	16.9	12.2	14.5	11.9	10.8	4.4	12.9	1977
Upper Dublin, PA	0.6	8.4	9.2	10.1	12.4	12.3	16.0	9.1	21.9	1962
Vestavia Hills, AL	1.1	16.6	17.1	13.7	16.6	11.6	10.9	5.3	7.0	1979
Webster, NY	0.6	7.4	9.4	10.8	13.4	12.5	11.3	5.8	28.8	1963
Wellesley, MA	0.7	8.0	7.2	10.7	11.0	10.5	11.1	5.6	35.1	1958
West Fargo, ND	2.4	20.0	17.2	11.4	18.1	8.3	9.0	2.8	10.8	1981
West Linn, OR	1.0	16.1	18.9	11.7	18.0	9.2	7.5	4.9	12.7	1979
West Windsor, NJ	0.5	9.2	9.3	11.6	11.0	13.7	15.8	8.0	20.9	1964
Westlake, OH	0.5	7.4	8.5	6.7	12.6	13.1	18.7	8.5	24.2	1959
Weston, FL	0.5	14.1	14.8	19.9	22.0	12.8	10.4	3.2	2.2	1980
Westport, CT	0.8	6.9	6.8	11.4	13.6	14.5	17.1	7.6	21.4	1963
Wilmette, IL	0.4	12.0	10.8	8.8	14.0	11.9	13.6	6.1	22.4	1967
Woodbury, MN	0.8	15.2	14.6	14.8	15.4	10.0	10.1	4.1	15.0	1977
Yorba Linda, CA	0.5	6.8	7.5	12.6	16.5	16.0	19.0	8.9	12.2	1966
U.S.	1.0	14.9	13.9	13.8	15.8	11.0	10.8	5.4	13.3	1976

Note: Figures are percentages except for Median Year; Figures cover the Metropolitan Statistical Area—see Appendix B for areas included
Source: U.S. Census Bureau, 2010-2014 American Community Survey 5-Year Estimates

Highest Level of Education: City

City	Less than H.S.	H.S. Diploma	Some College, No Deg.	Associate Degree	Bachelors Degree	Masters Degree	Profess. School Degree	Doctorate Degree
Aliso Viejo, CA	4.6	11.3	18.0	9.2	38.8	13.2	2.9	1.9
Allen, TX	4.2	13.2	22.2	7.8	34.2	14.7	2.0	1.8
Alpharetta, GA	3.2	10.8	16.8	6.8	39.4	17.8	3.1	2.1
Ankeny, IA	2.5	17.4	20.2	14.7	32.7	9.6	1.6	1.3
Apex, NC	2.9	8.6	17.6	9.9	40.7	15.8	2.4	2.0
Ballwin, MO	3.0	15.8	21.4	6.1	33.9	14.7	3.5	1.5
Beavercreek, OH	3.5	18.9	18.4	9.1	24.5	19.2	2.9	3.4
Bella Vista, AR	5.5	26.3	24.2	9.5	22.1	10.2	1.3	1.0
Bernards, NJ	2.6	11.2	10.5	5.2	36.0	24.4	6.4	3.8
Bethlehem, NY	2.8	16.0	13.4	11.1	23.0	22.3	7.9	3.5
Bloomfield, MI	2.8	9.5	13.2	5.1	34.8	20.7	11.1	2.9
Bowie, MD	4.7	18.5	23.0	5.8	27.5	15.6	2.3	2.6
Bozeman, MT	2.5	11.8	24.6	6.6	35.6	12.4	2.1	4.3
Brentwood, TN	2.3	10.4	14.3	5.1	42.6	16.2	5.7	3.4
Broomfield, CO	5.2	15.2	22.1	8.0	31.9	13.6	2.0	2.0
Carmel, IN	1.9	10.2	14.4	4.7	38.6	18.9	6.8	4.6
Cedar Park, TX	4.7	17.0	26.2	7.9	30.3	10.5	2.0	1.4
Cheshire, CT	5.6	22.5	13.8	6.3	26.1	17.0	5.0	3.6
Chesterfield, MO	2.3	11.6	16.7	5.4	35.2	19.2	6.4	3.2
Collierville, TN	3.4	16.4	20.8	6.7	33.8	14.6	2.8	1.5
Coppell, TX	3.5	11.0	16.4	5.9	38.5	18.5	4.3	1.9
Cornelius, NC	5.4	16.6	18.1	7.8	34.2	12.8	2.8	2.4
Cranberry, PA	2.4	19.3	14.0	6.4	37.4	15.9	2.7	1.9
Cupertino, CA	3.5	6.2	10.2	4.5	33.1	31.2	4.1	7.3
Danville, CA	2.3	9.0	17.0	7.5	41.0	16.6	3.8	2.8
Draper, UT	3.7	18.3	28.7	9.4	24.7	10.2	3.5	1.4
Dublin, OH	1.7	7.4	12.0	5.3	43.7	20.3	5.4	4.2
Eastchester, NY	6.0	16.7	13.8	5.4	29.8	19.5	6.5	2.3
Eden Prairie, MN	2.7	10.6	17.3	8.7	39.1	15.6	3.5	2.4
Edmond, OK	4.1	15.8	23.1	5.1	31.6	13.5	4.2	2.6
Evesham, NJ	4.9	22.4	18.1	7.4	29.8	12.1	3.3	1.9
Fishers, IN	2.3	11.7	18.1	6.8	40.4	14.8	3.9	2.1
Flower Mound, TX	2.7	11.7	20.5	7.6	40.3	14.0	2.2	1.0
Folsom, CA	8.0	17.2	19.9	9.2	28.5	12.3	3.1	1.9
Foster City, CA	4.1	10.2	16.2	6.5	33.4	20.1	4.4	5.1
Franklin, TN	5.7	13.8	18.1	6.2	36.3	14.4	3.4	1.9
Friendswood, TX	4.8	15.8	21.7	9.4	33.3	10.8	2.1	2.0
Germantown, TN	1.9	10.0	18.1	5.0	38.4	16.9	7.0	2.8
Glastonbury, CT	3.8	14.9	12.9	7.2	28.9	21.9	7.6	2.8
Grand Blanc, MI	5.0	23.7	24.2	12.1	20.5	10.4	2.8	1.3
Guilderland, NY	3.5	20.6	14.3	10.8	24.7	18.2	3.8	4.1
Hampden, PA	5.1	23.1	14.9	8.1	29.2	14.4	3.7	1.7
Holly Springs, NC	3.6	14.2	16.0	11.4	36.4	14.5	1.8	2.1
Huntersville, NC	5.0	14.6	18.8	7.8	38.2	11.0	2.5	2.1
Independence, KY	10.0	30.9	22.1	7.9	20.1	6.3	2.2	0.5
Johns Creek, GA	4.1	10.1	15.3	6.6	39.1	19.0	3.1	2.6
Keller, TX	3.1	12.4	21.8	5.8	38.6	13.6	2.8	1.9
Kirkland, WA	3.5	12.2	20.1	8.6	35.9	15.2	2.7	1.6
Lafayette, CO	5.3	14.9	16.7	7.4	33.7	16.3	2.2	3.4
Lake Oswego, OR	2.2	9.9	17.4	5.4	37.5	16.9	7.7	3.0
League City, TX	5.4	20.0	22.7	10.8	27.7	9.0	2.7	1.8
Leawood, KS	0.8	6.5	14.4	4.0	41.7	18.1	11.6	3.0
Lee's Summit, MO	3.6	21.2	23.6	9.0	27.6	11.0	2.4	1.6
Leesburg, VA	11.4	16.7	15.9	6.6	31.1	14.8	1.7	1.8
Lehi, UT	3.9	17.1	27.5	12.5	29.5	7.0	1.5	1.0
Lenexa, KS	4.0	13.8	20.9	6.9	34.2	14.4	3.8	2.0
Lexington, MA	3.2	8.6	7.3	4.2	27.0	28.7	8.0	13.1
Los Altos, CA	1.3	4.9	10.1	4.8	32.2	30.9	8.1	7.8
Lower Makefield, PA	2.1	14.1	11.8	5.4	33.7	22.2	6.7	4.1
Madison, AL	4.3	13.3	20.4	6.8	33.1	17.5	2.0	2.5
Mamaroneck, NY	6.4	12.0	10.3	3.3	34.0	21.8	9.1	3.1
Manheim, PA	8.7	28.0	14.5	6.3	24.4	12.7	3.8	1.6
Manlius, NY	3.0	18.9	15.0	10.9	25.3	17.6	5.5	3.8
Maple Grove, MN	2.7	17.3	20.2	10.4	33.8	12.2	2.2	1.2
Marion, IA	4.3	25.9	22.4	13.8	23.9	7.6	1.7	0.5
Marlboro, NJ	3.7	17.9	12.6	6.7	34.8	16.8	4.9	2.6
Mason, OH	3.6	20.0	15.2	6.7	31.2	17.4	3.4	2.4

Table continued on next page.

City	Less than H.S.	H.S. Diploma	Some College, No Deg.	Associate Degree	Bachelors Degree	Masters Degree	Profess. School Degree	Doctorate Degree
McCandless, PA	2.9	19.4	15.0	7.9	31.4	16.8	3.4	3.2
Menomonee Falls, WI	5.4	26.3	17.9	9.7	27.5	10.6	1.7	1.0
Meridian, ID	5.1	23.9	28.7	8.9	24.3	6.3	1.8	0.8
Merrimack, NH	3.8	26.8	16.4	10.1	28.5	12.0	0.9	1.5
Mount Lebanon, PA	2.4	15.9	12.2	5.7	33.0	18.8	7.4	4.6
Mount Pleasant, SC	2.4	12.8	19.1	7.3	37.8	13.9	4.3	2.4
Needham, MA	2.1	9.9	8.8	5.1	32.4	26.4	10.0	5.3
Newtown, CT	5.5	18.1	15.3	6.7	29.8	18.6	4.2	1.8
Northbrook, IL	3.1	10.0	13.9	4.2	37.5	17.9	10.1	3.3
Northville, MI	3.1	13.3	15.6	7.5	29.4	22.9	5.6	2.6
Novi, MI	5.1	14.7	17.4	6.8	31.2	18.9	3.8	1.9
O'Fallon, IL	3.8	16.3	20.8	10.3	27.6	17.9	1.8	1.4
O'Fallon, MO	5.6	24.9	23.7	8.3	24.9	10.8	0.9	0.8
Orchard Park, NY	3.7	22.8	15.0	13.2	24.7	14.7	4.5	1.4
Oviedo, FL	5.2	18.6	21.3	12.3	28.1	11.1	1.8	1.6
Parker, CO	2.4	14.1	22.5	9.3	37.0	11.2	2.1	1.3
Parkland, FL	2.8	11.6	16.3	7.5	38.1	14.8	5.8	3.1
Peachtree City, GA	5.2	14.5	18.8	8.0	35.0	13.7	2.8	2.0
Pflugerville, TX	6.7	20.6	25.7	10.7	24.8	9.4	0.5	1.5
Plainfield, IL	4.1	17.2	19.1	10.8	30.1	16.2	1.4	1.1
Princeton, NJ	3.8	6.5	6.9	1.9	26.1	29.1	8.7	17.0
Queen Creek, AZ	4.0	16.2	29.4	12.7	25.7	8.6	2.0	1.4
Rancho Palos Verdes, CA	2.5	9.4	16.1	7.2	33.7	17.7	8.5	4.9
Redmond, WA	4.5	9.2	16.3	7.6	34.9	22.6	1.6	3.3
Richland, WA	4.5	18.2	22.1	11.4	25.2	12.2	2.0	4.3
Ridgefield, CT	1.8	9.4	12.0	4.3	38.0	25.0	6.9	2.7
Ridgewood, NJ	2.4	8.2	10.5	4.0	42.4	21.0	8.0	3.4
Rio Rancho, NM	6.3	25.8	28.2	11.0	18.1	7.9	1.4	1.3
Sahuarita, AZ	4.9	20.0	29.7	10.2	23.4	9.6	0.9	1.2
Sammamish, WA	1.6	6.3	12.7	6.8	44.4	21.0	3.3	3.9
San Ramon, CA	2.5	8.7	15.7	8.1	39.5	18.4	3.9	3.2
Saratoga, CA	1.8	5.1	10.4	5.1	35.7	30.1	6.4	5.4
Schertz, TX	7.2	25.0	25.4	11.0	19.3	10.3	1.3	0.5
Shrewsbury, MA	5.2	18.4	12.8	8.4	28.2	18.5	4.1	4.3
South Brunswick, NJ	5.7	16.3	11.2	7.2	35.1	17.9	3.2	3.3
South Jordan, UT	3.6	17.0	29.2	11.4	25.3	10.7	1.4	1.4
South Kingstown, RI	6.2	18.8	16.9	5.3	29.7	14.4	3.4	5.3
South Windsor, CT	5.7	21.3	14.1	8.1	28.1	16.7	4.4	1.7
Southlake, TX	1.5	8.2	16.4	5.4	43.5	17.6	5.6	1.9
Spring Hill, TN	3.7	21.9	23.0	8.5	31.2	10.4	0.5	0.7
Stow, OH	6.3	24.4	19.7	9.2	26.6	10.1	2.2	1.6
Sugar Land, TX	7.3	12.4	20.3	5.8	32.1	15.5	2.9	3.7
Sun Prairie, WI	4.8	20.2	20.4	12.1	28.7	11.0	2.1	0.7
Syracuse, UT	1.8	21.0	28.1	12.5	25.6	8.9	1.2	0.9
Tredyffrin, PA	2.3	8.3	9.3	4.0	41.5	23.6	6.5	4.6
Upper Arlington, OH	1.5	8.9	11.5	3.9	39.6	17.6	10.2	6.8
Upper Dublin, PA	3.3	15.5	12.1	4.8	34.5	18.5	7.5	3.8
Vestavia Hills, AL	2.2	10.0	16.3	4.4	37.3	17.4	8.1	4.4
Webster, NY	5.2	22.7	16.3	13.4	23.3	15.3	1.7	2.1
Wellesley, MA	1.9	6.7	5.6	3.6	33.6	29.5	11.2	7.9
West Fargo, ND	5.4	19.7	22.9	16.3	26.3	6.7	0.9	1.7
West Linn, OR	1.8	12.8	24.1	7.3	33.9	13.5	4.6	2.1
West Windsor, NJ	2.9	6.6	8.1	2.6	32.4	28.8	8.2	10.4
Westlake, OH	4.5	17.1	17.9	6.9	33.0	13.5	5.1	2.0
Weston, FL	3.0	13.0	17.3	8.8	33.5	16.3	6.0	2.1
Westport, CT	2.0	11.6	8.1	2.6	38.0	26.6	8.1	3.0
Wilmette, IL	1.2	5.7	8.9	3.0	35.1	25.6	14.3	6.2
Woodbury, MN	2.7	14.2	16.9	9.0	36.1	14.8	3.2	3.0
Yorba Linda, CA	4.5	12.7	23.8	9.6	30.8	13.0	3.8	1.8
U.S.	13.7	28.0	21.2	7.9	18.3	7.8	2.0	1.3

Note: Figures cover persons age 25 and over
Source: U.S. Census Bureau, 2010-2014 American Community Survey 5-Year Estimates

Highest Level of Education: Metro Area

Metro Area	Less than H.S.	H.S. Diploma	Some College, No Deg.	Associate Degree	Bachelors Degree	Masters Degree	Profess. School Degree	Doctorate Degree
Aliso Viejo, CA	21.5	19.9	19.9	7.1	20.7	7.2	2.4	1.3
Allen, TX	15.9	22.9	22.6	6.6	21.4	8.0	1.7	1.0
Alpharetta, GA	12.1	24.7	20.9	7.1	22.7	9.0	2.2	1.3
Ankeny, IA	7.4	26.4	20.9	10.1	24.8	7.2	2.1	1.1
Apex, NC	9.8	19.5	19.3	8.9	27.8	10.7	2.1	1.9
Ballwin, MO	9.7	27.2	23.2	8.3	19.3	8.9	2.0	1.3
Beavercreek, OH	10.6	29.9	23.7	9.3	15.4	8.4	1.5	1.1
Bella Vista, AR	15.8	30.3	20.8	5.2	17.7	7.2	1.7	1.3
Bernards, NJ	14.9	25.9	15.7	6.6	21.7	10.9	3.0	1.4
Bethlehem, NY	8.0	28.1	17.7	11.7	18.9	11.5	2.2	1.8
Bloomfield, MI	11.5	27.7	23.8	8.4	17.3	8.5	1.9	0.9
Bowie, MD	9.8	19.1	17.2	5.6	25.1	16.0	4.3	3.0
Bozeman, MT	3.6	19.6	24.1	6.0	31.2	9.8	2.4	3.2
Brentwood, TN	12.4	28.9	20.7	6.6	20.6	7.3	2.0	1.5
Broomfield, CO	10.2	20.8	21.7	7.5	25.6	10.4	2.4	1.4
Carmel, IN	11.3	29.6	20.7	7.7	20.1	7.6	2.0	1.1
Cedar Park, TX	11.7	19.3	21.6	6.4	26.8	10.1	2.3	1.8
Cheshire, CT	11.1	30.5	17.9	7.1	18.0	10.4	2.8	2.1
Chesterfield, MO	9.7	27.2	23.2	8.3	19.3	8.9	2.0	1.3
Collierville, TN	14.0	29.1	24.0	6.8	17.0	6.6	1.7	1.0
Coppell, TX	15.9	22.9	22.6	6.6	21.4	8.0	1.7	1.0
Cornelius, NC	13.1	25.1	22.0	8.4	21.6	7.5	1.5	0.8
Cranberry, PA	7.7	35.4	16.6	9.4	19.0	8.5	2.0	1.4
Cupertino, CA	13.5	15.7	17.2	7.1	25.7	14.9	2.7	3.3
Danville, CA	12.1	17.0	19.0	6.9	27.1	11.8	3.6	2.5
Draper, UT	10.7	23.3	26.4	8.7	20.0	7.4	2.0	1.5
Dublin, OH	9.9	29.0	20.5	7.2	21.4	8.4	2.0	1.5
Eastchester, NY	14.9	25.9	15.7	6.6	21.7	10.9	3.0	1.4
Eden Prairie, MN	6.9	22.8	21.4	9.9	25.9	9.2	2.4	1.4
Edmond, OK	12.2	27.4	25.1	6.9	18.7	6.8	1.8	1.2
Evesham, NJ	10.9	30.6	17.7	6.6	20.5	9.4	2.5	1.7
Fishers, IN	11.3	29.6	20.7	7.7	20.1	7.6	2.0	1.1
Flower Mound, TX	15.9	22.9	22.6	6.6	21.4	8.0	1.7	1.0
Folsom, CA	12.0	21.5	26.2	9.7	19.9	6.9	2.4	1.4
Foster City, CA	12.1	17.0	19.0	6.9	27.1	11.8	3.6	2.5
Franklin, TN	12.4	28.9	20.7	6.6	20.6	7.3	2.0	1.5
Friendswood, TX	18.5	23.5	21.8	6.2	19.5	7.2	1.9	1.4
Germantown, TN	14.0	29.1	24.0	6.8	17.0	6.6	1.7	1.0
Glastonbury, CT	10.2	27.5	17.9	8.1	20.4	11.6	2.8	1.5
Grand Blanc, MI	11.0	33.1	27.1	9.7	12.0	5.5	1.1	0.6
Guilderland, NY	8.0	28.1	17.7	11.7	18.9	11.5	2.2	1.8
Hampden, PA	10.2	36.0	16.7	8.0	17.9	7.9	2.3	1.1
Holly Springs, NC	9.8	19.5	19.3	8.9	27.8	10.7	2.1	1.9
Huntersville, NC	13.1	25.1	22.0	8.4	21.6	7.5	1.5	0.8
Independence, KY	10.7	30.9	20.0	8.0	19.3	8.2	1.8	1.2
Johns Creek, GA	12.1	24.7	20.9	7.1	22.7	9.0	2.2	1.3
Keller, TX	15.9	22.9	22.6	6.6	21.4	8.0	1.7	1.0
Kirkland, WA	8.4	20.9	23.1	9.2	24.5	9.9	2.4	1.7
Lafayette, CO	6.0	12.8	17.2	5.7	31.5	17.8	3.4	5.5
Lake Oswego, OR	9.3	21.9	25.4	8.5	22.1	8.9	2.4	1.5
League City, TX	18.5	23.5	21.8	6.2	19.5	7.2	1.9	1.4
Leawood, KS	9.2	26.5	23.4	7.4	21.5	8.9	2.2	1.1
Lee's Summit, MO	9.2	26.5	23.4	7.4	21.5	8.9	2.2	1.1
Leesburg, VA	9.8	19.1	17.2	5.6	25.1	16.0	4.3	3.0
Lehi, UT	6.5	17.3	28.7	10.9	25.4	7.8	1.5	1.8
Lenexa, KS	9.2	26.5	23.4	7.4	21.5	8.9	2.2	1.1
Lexington, MA	9.2	24.0	15.5	7.2	24.5	13.5	3.2	2.8
Los Altos, CA	13.5	15.7	17.2	7.1	25.7	14.9	2.7	3.3
Lower Makefield, PA	10.9	30.6	17.7	6.6	20.5	9.4	2.5	1.7
Madison, AL	11.5	23.3	22.0	7.8	22.3	10.3	1.5	1.4
Mamaroneck, NY	14.9	25.9	15.7	6.6	21.7	10.9	3.0	1.4
Manheim, PA	15.7	38.6	14.7	6.3	16.1	6.2	1.4	0.9
Manlius, NY	10.6	29.9	17.8	11.8	16.7	9.8	1.9	1.4
Maple Grove, MN	6.9	22.8	21.4	9.9	25.9	9.2	2.4	1.4
Marion, IA	6.3	29.4	23.3	11.9	20.4	6.6	1.5	0.8
Marlboro, NJ	14.9	25.9	15.7	6.6	21.7	10.9	3.0	1.4
Mason, OH	10.7	30.9	20.0	8.0	19.3	8.2	1.8	1.2

Table continued on next page.

Metro Area	Less than H.S.	H.S. Diploma	Some College, No Deg.	Associate Degree	Bachelors Degree	Masters Degree	Profess. School Degree	Doctorate Degree
McCandless, PA	7.7	35.4	16.6	9.4	19.0	8.5	2.0	1.4
Menomonee Falls, WI	10.1	27.3	21.4	8.3	21.7	8.1	2.0	1.1
Meridian, ID	9.9	25.1	26.8	8.4	20.2	6.7	1.8	1.1
Merrimack, NH	9.1	27.5	18.4	9.5	22.7	10.0	1.5	1.3
Mount Lebanon, PA	7.7	35.4	16.6	9.4	19.0	8.5	2.0	1.4
Mount Pleasant, SC	11.2	25.6	22.4	8.7	20.6	8.1	2.1	1.3
Needham, MA	9.2	24.0	15.5	7.2	24.5	13.5	3.2	2.8
Newtown, CT	10.8	22.5	15.4	5.8	25.5	14.7	3.8	1.5
Northbrook, IL	13.1	24.8	20.2	6.9	21.5	9.8	2.5	1.3
Northville, MI	11.5	27.7	23.8	8.4	17.3	8.5	1.9	0.9
Novi, MI	11.5	27.7	23.8	8.4	17.3	8.5	1.9	0.9
O'Fallon, IL	9.7	27.2	23.2	8.3	19.3	8.9	2.0	1.3
O'Fallon, MO	9.7	27.2	23.2	8.3	19.3	8.9	2.0	1.3
Orchard Park, NY	9.8	29.8	19.0	11.8	16.5	10.0	1.9	1.3
Oviedo, FL	12.2	28.2	21.2	10.0	19.0	6.8	1.7	0.9
Parker, CO	10.2	20.8	21.7	7.5	25.6	10.4	2.4	1.4
Parkland, FL	15.9	27.7	18.5	8.8	18.5	6.8	2.6	1.2
Peachtree City, GA	12.1	24.7	20.9	7.1	22.7	9.0	2.2	1.3
Pflugerville, TX	11.7	19.3	21.6	6.4	26.8	10.1	2.3	1.8
Plainfield, IL	13.1	24.8	20.2	6.9	21.5	9.8	2.5	1.3
Princeton, NJ	12.7	25.6	16.0	5.9	20.7	12.7	2.7	3.7
Queen Creek, AZ	13.6	23.9	25.3	8.5	18.6	7.5	1.8	1.1
Rancho Palos Verdes, CA	21.5	19.9	19.9	7.1	20.7	7.2	2.4	1.3
Redmond, WA	8.4	20.9	23.1	9.2	24.5	9.9	2.4	1.7
Richland, WA	16.2	24.8	23.7	10.0	16.1	6.4	1.2	1.5
Ridgefield, CT	10.8	22.5	15.4	5.8	25.5	14.7	3.8	1.5
Ridgewood, NJ	14.9	25.9	15.7	6.6	21.7	10.9	3.0	1.4
Rio Rancho, NM	12.5	24.8	24.7	7.9	17.0	9.1	2.0	2.1
Sahuarita, AZ	12.5	22.8	26.2	8.4	17.6	8.5	2.0	1.9
Sammamish, WA	8.4	20.9	23.1	9.2	24.5	9.9	2.4	1.7
San Ramon, CA	12.1	17.0	19.0	6.9	27.1	11.8	3.6	2.5
Saratoga, CA	13.5	15.7	17.2	7.1	25.7	14.9	2.7	3.3
Schertz, TX	16.4	25.8	23.9	7.5	17.1	6.7	1.6	1.0
Shrewsbury, MA	10.6	29.6	18.1	9.0	20.2	9.3	1.7	1.5
South Brunswick, NJ	14.9	25.9	15.7	6.6	21.7	10.9	3.0	1.4
South Jordan, UT	10.7	23.3	26.4	8.7	20.0	7.4	2.0	1.5
South Kingstown, RI	15.7	28.4	18.1	8.4	18.0	8.2	1.8	1.3
South Windsor, CT	10.2	27.5	17.9	8.1	20.4	11.6	2.8	1.5
Southlake, TX	15.9	22.9	22.6	6.6	21.4	8.0	1.7	1.0
Spring Hill, TN	12.4	28.9	20.7	6.6	20.6	7.3	2.0	1.5
Stow, OH	9.2	33.7	20.3	7.8	18.7	7.4	1.7	1.3
Sugar Land, TX	18.5	23.5	21.8	6.2	19.5	7.2	1.9	1.4
Sun Prairie, WI	5.7	22.8	19.3	9.8	25.5	11.0	2.9	2.9
Syracuse, UT	7.4	25.2	28.4	10.1	20.1	6.8	1.3	0.8
Tredyffrin, PA	10.9	30.6	17.7	6.6	20.5	9.4	2.5	1.7
Upper Arlington, OH	9.9	29.0	20.5	7.2	21.4	8.4	2.0	1.5
Upper Dublin, PA	10.9	30.6	17.7	6.6	20.5	9.4	2.5	1.7
Vestavia Hills, AL	13.8	28.1	22.8	7.6	17.4	6.9	2.3	1.2
Webster, NY	10.3	27.7	17.6	11.9	18.2	10.9	1.9	1.5
Wellesley, MA	9.2	24.0	15.5	7.2	24.5	13.5	3.2	2.8
West Fargo, ND	5.4	22.6	23.0	13.5	24.8	7.1	1.8	1.8
West Linn, OR	9.3	21.9	25.4	8.5	22.1	8.9	2.4	1.5
West Windsor, NJ	12.7	25.6	16.0	5.9	20.7	12.7	2.7	3.7
Westlake, OH	11.0	30.2	22.2	7.8	17.7	7.8	2.2	1.2
Weston, FL	15.9	27.7	18.5	8.8	18.5	6.8	2.6	1.2
Westport, CT	10.8	22.5	15.4	5.8	25.5	14.7	3.8	1.5
Wilmette, IL	13.1	24.8	20.2	6.9	21.5	9.8	2.5	1.3
Woodbury, MN	6.9	22.8	21.4	9.9	25.9	9.2	2.4	1.4
Yorba Linda, CA	21.5	19.9	19.9	7.1	20.7	7.2	2.4	1.3
U.S.	13.7	28.0	21.2	7.9	18.3	7.8	2.0	1.3

Note: Figures cover persons age 25 and over; Figures cover the Metropolitan Statistical Area—see Appendix B for areas included
Source: U.S. Census Bureau, 2010-2014 American Community Survey 5-Year Estimates

School Enrollment by Grade and Control: City

City	Preschool (%)		Kindergarten (%)		Grades 1 - 4 (%)		Grades 5 - 8 (%)		Grades 9 - 12 (%)	
	Public	Private	Public	Private	Public	Private	Public	Private	Public	Private
Aliso Viejo, CA	30.3	69.7	75.2	24.8	84.2	15.8	86.2	13.8	90.4	9.6
Allen, TX	25.2	74.8	90.0	10.0	91.1	8.9	93.3	6.7	97.1	2.9
Alpharetta, GA	39.6	60.4	82.2	17.8	94.1	5.9	89.4	10.6	89.8	10.2
Ankeny, IA	48.8	51.2	93.8	6.2	92.3	7.7	97.4	2.6	96.2	3.8
Apex, NC	22.8	77.2	92.1	7.9	89.7	10.3	90.0	10.0	96.1	3.9
Ballwin, MO	43.5	56.5	72.0	28.0	78.3	21.7	77.6	22.4	78.2	21.8
Beavercreek, OH	39.4	60.6	73.2	26.8	84.2	15.8	90.6	9.4	86.8	13.2
Bella Vista, AR	20.7	79.3	92.5	7.5	78.4	21.6	83.1	16.9	90.9	9.1
Bernards, NJ	39.0	61.0	88.9	11.1	89.3	10.7	92.8	7.2	85.3	14.7
Bethlehem, NY	20.0	80.0	80.7	19.3	91.0	9.0	92.1	7.9	84.5	15.5
Bloomfield, MI	32.6	67.4	65.1	34.9	80.0	20.0	71.8	28.2	75.3	24.7
Bowie, MD	28.9	71.1	79.2	20.8	74.4	25.6	73.3	26.7	72.9	27.1
Bozeman, MT	33.0	67.0	88.0	12.0	92.9	7.1	85.9	14.1	88.9	11.1
Brentwood, TN	22.4	77.6	80.4	19.6	86.9	13.1	82.7	17.3	81.5	18.5
Broomfield, CO	35.3	64.7	82.7	17.3	89.8	10.2	92.0	8.0	95.1	4.9
Carmel, IN	28.5	71.5	80.7	19.3	83.8	16.2	90.0	10.0	83.4	16.6
Cedar Park, TX	33.0	67.0	84.3	15.7	97.3	2.7	92.4	7.6	95.5	4.5
Cheshire, CT	40.7	59.3	89.7	10.3	95.3	4.7	88.6	11.4	89.3	10.7
Chesterfield, MO	38.8	61.2	64.6	35.4	83.2	16.8	81.5	18.5	76.2	23.8
Collierville, TN	24.1	75.9	82.2	17.8	80.3	19.7	79.0	21.0	80.3	19.7
Coppell, TX	33.9	66.1	82.5	17.5	90.2	9.8	87.9	12.1	90.8	9.2
Cornelius, NC	11.9	88.1	67.8	32.2	90.7	9.3	89.7	10.3	94.3	5.7
Cranberry, PA	30.0	70.0	79.6	20.4	84.0	16.0	83.5	16.5	89.1	10.9
Cupertino, CA	16.8	83.2	83.0	17.0	93.2	6.8	92.4	7.6	91.3	8.7
Danville, CA	21.5	78.5	80.5	19.5	83.8	16.2	83.7	16.3	92.6	7.4
Draper, UT	46.1	53.9	78.9	21.1	86.0	14.0	85.3	14.7	85.3	14.7
Dublin, OH	29.0	71.0	86.2	13.8	84.6	15.4	86.7	13.3	88.8	11.2
Eastchester, NY	24.4	75.6	92.5	7.5	94.6	5.4	88.2	11.8	86.1	13.9
Eden Prairie, MN	52.4	47.6	86.1	13.9	84.4	15.6	81.6	18.4	88.8	11.2
Edmond, OK	55.3	44.7	78.4	21.6	85.4	14.6	85.6	14.4	87.3	12.7
Evesham, NJ	40.4	59.6	88.3	11.7	95.2	4.8	90.9	9.1	92.5	7.5
Fishers, IN	38.8	61.2	78.2	21.8	88.5	11.5	92.6	7.4	86.6	13.4
Flower Mound, TX	21.5	78.5	78.3	21.7	88.3	11.7	94.7	5.3	91.7	8.3
Folsom, CA	42.4	57.6	69.3	30.7	88.8	11.2	89.4	10.6	90.5	9.5
Foster City, CA	9.8	90.2	87.6	12.4	81.6	18.4	83.1	16.9	81.4	18.6
Franklin, TN	32.1	67.9	79.3	20.7	85.4	14.6	83.2	16.8	84.2	15.8
Friendswood, TX	32.5	67.5	92.3	7.7	94.7	5.3	93.8	6.2	94.6	5.4
Germantown, TN	9.5	90.5	71.8	28.2	70.0	30.0	62.7	37.3	55.8	44.2
Glastonbury, CT	31.5	68.5	90.8	9.2	98.7	1.3	89.8	10.2	93.4	6.6
Grand Blanc, MI	82.0	18.0	83.4	16.6	92.5	7.5	88.6	11.4	95.2	4.8
Guilderland, NY	23.0	77.0	95.7	4.3	95.0	5.0	97.3	2.7	93.7	6.3
Hampden, PA	23.1	76.9	87.8	12.2	92.1	7.9	91.7	8.3	93.2	6.8
Holly Springs, NC	10.3	89.7	83.6	16.4	87.6	12.4	90.9	9.1	89.3	10.7
Huntersville, NC	31.9	68.1	81.7	18.3	80.7	19.3	82.0	18.0	81.2	18.8
Independence, KY	42.2	57.8	89.1	10.9	87.3	12.7	81.5	18.5	89.0	11.0
Johns Creek, GA	38.0	62.0	87.8	12.2	91.2	8.8	92.5	7.5	91.5	8.5
Keller, TX	28.3	71.7	83.8	16.2	83.0	17.0	80.9	19.1	82.2	17.8
Kirkland, WA	20.4	79.6	78.6	21.4	79.0	21.0	88.1	11.9	88.8	11.2
Lafayette, CO	41.5	58.5	94.9	5.1	91.0	9.0	94.0	6.0	97.2	2.8
Lake Oswego, OR	26.7	73.3	84.9	15.1	83.0	17.0	86.5	13.5	90.4	9.6
League City, TX	45.1	54.9	86.6	13.4	92.3	7.7	94.2	5.8	95.9	4.1
Leawood, KS	35.4	64.6	61.4	38.6	67.3	32.7	63.8	36.2	66.5	33.5
Lee's Summit, MO	35.2	64.8	87.8	12.2	90.3	9.7	94.4	5.6	91.3	8.7
Leesburg, VA	30.7	69.3	92.3	7.7	94.8	5.2	93.1	6.9	95.2	4.8
Lehi, UT	36.2	63.8	95.8	4.2	95.5	4.5	94.0	6.0	97.1	2.9
Lenexa, KS	32.1	67.9	80.1	19.9	82.1	17.9	75.6	24.4	78.5	21.5
Lexington, MA	19.8	80.2	90.6	9.4	93.6	6.4	87.7	12.3	86.7	13.3
Los Altos, CA	23.6	76.4	82.6	17.4	83.1	16.9	76.1	23.9	72.2	27.8
Lower Makefield, PA	17.1	82.9	73.0	27.0	86.0	14.0	86.6	13.4	70.1	29.9
Madison, AL	62.7	37.3	72.4	27.6	91.0	9.0	91.7	8.3	89.9	10.1
Mamaroneck, NY	23.3	76.7	96.2	3.8	84.1	15.9	87.0	13.0	78.2	21.8
Manheim, PA	31.2	68.8	86.4	13.6	85.3	14.7	89.9	10.1	86.0	14.0
Manlius, NY	52.0	48.0	77.7	22.3	91.2	8.8	94.0	6.0	85.6	14.4
Maple Grove, MN	50.7	49.3	86.7	13.3	81.9	18.1	91.4	8.6	91.6	8.4
Marion, IA	56.0	44.0	83.8	16.2	85.3	14.7	90.7	9.3	94.8	5.2
Marlboro, NJ	28.4	71.6	86.5	13.5	98.5	1.5	95.4	4.6	91.2	8.8
Mason, OH	57.1	42.9	78.8	21.2	83.2	16.8	89.7	10.3	87.7	12.3
McCandless, PA	47.0	53.0	79.7	20.3	87.2	12.8	82.6	17.4	90.6	9.4

Table continued on next page.

City	Preschool (%)		Kindergarten (%)		Grades 1 - 4 (%)		Grades 5 - 8 (%)		Grades 9 - 12 (%)	
	Public	Private	Public	Private	Public	Private	Public	Private	Public	Private
Menomonee Falls, WI	35.6	64.4	73.9	26.1	72.8	27.2	72.1	27.9	84.4	15.6
Meridian, ID	38.5	61.5	95.5	4.5	92.5	7.5	95.0	5.0	96.7	3.3
Merrimack, NH	47.1	52.9	83.7	16.3	94.5	5.5	87.8	12.2	90.4	9.6
Mount Lebanon, PA	35.4	64.6	90.5	9.5	98.0	2.0	93.0	7.0	94.5	5.5
Mount Pleasant, SC	33.0	67.0	68.0	32.0	81.8	18.2	80.3	19.7	85.6	14.4
Needham, MA	20.0	80.0	100.0	0.0	82.3	17.7	79.4	20.6	79.7	20.3
Newtown, CT	36.0	64.0	81.1	18.9	93.8	6.2	87.1	12.9	88.3	11.7
Northbrook, IL	29.2	70.8	78.3	21.7	85.7	14.3	90.6	9.4	94.9	5.1
Northville, MI	29.2	70.8	80.3	19.7	80.8	19.2	90.7	9.3	81.5	18.5
Novi, MI	54.1	45.9	88.8	11.2	89.6	10.4	92.6	7.4	87.9	12.1
O'Fallon, IL	69.3	30.7	83.0	17.0	91.0	9.0	88.2	11.8	97.5	2.5
O'Fallon, MO	35.2	64.8	89.4	10.6	83.2	16.8	88.1	11.9	85.5	14.5
Orchard Park, NY	47.7	52.3	77.5	22.5	88.0	12.0	83.0	17.0	83.6	16.4
Oviedo, FL	51.6	48.4	64.8	35.2	87.2	12.8	84.2	15.8	91.6	8.4
Parker, CO	50.7	49.3	92.5	7.5	91.8	8.2	93.1	6.9	93.8	6.2
Parkland, FL	10.0	90.0	86.2	13.8	88.4	11.6	85.9	14.1	77.1	22.9
Peachtree City, GA	43.4	56.6	94.5	5.5	89.5	10.5	84.2	15.8	90.4	9.6
Pflugerville, TX	51.1	48.9	84.5	15.5	84.7	15.3	94.3	5.7	96.0	4.0
Plainfield, IL	57.8	42.2	86.4	13.6	90.9	9.1	89.2	10.8	96.6	3.4
Princeton, NJ	3.2	96.8	75.8	24.2	84.6	15.4	84.8	15.2	84.4	15.6
Queen Creek, AZ	38.0	62.0	97.4	2.6	90.8	9.2	89.9	10.1	82.8	17.2
Rancho Palos Verdes, CA	23.9	76.1	81.4	18.6	87.8	12.2	90.7	9.3	93.8	6.2
Redmond, WA	22.5	77.5	79.2	20.8	88.0	12.0	80.2	19.8	90.3	9.7
Richland, WA	45.9	54.1	87.7	12.3	85.1	14.9	88.8	11.2	93.8	6.2
Ridgefield, CT	10.7	89.3	84.2	15.8	94.4	5.6	94.8	5.2	92.0	8.0
Ridgewood, NJ	13.3	86.7	90.1	9.9	96.8	3.2	93.4	6.6	84.0	16.0
Rio Rancho, NM	70.3	29.7	87.0	13.0	90.3	9.7	91.5	8.5	95.1	4.9
Sahuarita, AZ	77.8	22.2	90.1	9.9	97.9	2.1	95.7	4.3	90.3	9.7
Sammamish, WA	27.7	72.3	61.0	39.0	90.5	9.5	89.4	10.6	87.9	12.1
San Ramon, CA	22.2	77.8	77.1	22.9	91.8	8.2	96.9	3.1	95.6	4.4
Saratoga, CA	27.5	72.5	85.2	14.8	85.6	14.4	87.5	12.5	80.5	19.5
Schertz, TX	48.7	51.3	92.5	7.5	84.8	15.2	95.2	4.8	92.7	7.3
Shrewsbury, MA	52.7	47.3	82.8	17.2	88.6	11.4	87.5	12.5	87.7	12.3
South Brunswick, NJ	27.0	73.0	82.8	17.2	95.7	4.3	97.2	2.8	93.6	6.4
South Jordan, UT	47.3	52.7	92.3	7.7	92.6	7.4	95.7	4.3	95.4	4.6
South Kingstown, RI	42.0	58.0	92.0	8.0	92.3	7.7	97.7	2.3	77.4	22.6
South Windsor, CT	64.1	35.9	92.8	7.2	92.1	7.9	96.7	3.3	84.5	15.5
Southlake, TX	24.6	75.4	81.1	18.9	86.4	13.6	90.1	9.9	89.7	10.3
Spring Hill, TN	57.2	42.8	87.4	12.6	95.9	4.1	89.2	10.8	83.2	16.8
Stow, OH	27.5	72.5	71.0	29.0	85.2	14.8	87.6	12.4	88.7	11.3
Sugar Land, TX	27.9	72.1	79.3	20.7	83.4	16.6	91.5	8.5	92.6	7.4
Sun Prairie, WI	48.0	52.0	86.8	13.2	94.2	5.8	91.3	8.7	95.9	4.1
Syracuse, UT	59.0	41.0	99.4	0.6	98.5	1.5	98.1	1.9	97.6	2.4
Tredyffrin, PA	8.1	91.9	73.3	26.7	90.2	9.8	88.0	12.0	84.4	15.6
Upper Arlington, OH	43.5	56.5	93.1	6.9	92.2	7.8	87.2	12.8	87.9	12.1
Upper Dublin, PA	10.5	89.5	79.4	20.6	81.3	18.7	83.8	16.2	82.6	17.4
Vestavia Hills, AL	25.8	74.2	80.5	19.5	89.0	11.0	91.2	8.8	94.2	5.8
Webster, NY	47.6	52.4	88.4	11.6	91.2	8.8	90.0	10.0	87.4	12.6
Wellesley, MA	23.3	76.7	66.4	33.6	82.6	17.4	79.4	20.6	82.4	17.6
West Fargo, ND	65.8	34.2	100.0	0.0	99.6	0.4	95.7	4.3	93.1	6.9
West Linn, OR	30.9	69.1	84.0	16.0	91.9	8.1	91.4	8.6	90.3	9.7
West Windsor, NJ	25.0	75.0	92.5	7.5	90.9	9.1	95.5	4.5	92.5	7.5
Westlake, OH	39.0	61.0	72.7	27.3	81.1	18.9	80.7	19.3	81.8	18.2
Weston, FL	34.1	65.9	79.4	20.6	79.3	20.7	88.6	11.4	84.7	15.3
Westport, CT	28.4	71.6	89.5	10.5	94.8	5.2	82.5	17.5	87.3	12.7
Wilmette, IL	20.5	79.5	83.7	16.3	80.8	19.2	83.6	16.4	89.0	11.0
Woodbury, MN	32.8	67.2	83.3	16.7	89.4	10.6	86.4	13.6	89.3	10.7
Yorba Linda, CA	28.9	71.1	83.7	16.3	77.7	22.3	80.5	19.5	85.3	14.7
U.S.	57.4	42.6	87.8	12.2	89.8	10.2	89.9	10.1	90.6	9.4

Note: Figures shown cover persons 3 years old and over
Source: U.S. Census Bureau, 2010-2014 American Community Survey 5-Year Estimates

School Enrollment by Grade and Control: Metro Area

Metro Area	Preschool (%)		Kindergarten (%)		Grades 1 - 4 (%)		Grades 5 - 8 (%)		Grades 9 - 12 (%)	
	Public	Private	Public	Private	Public	Private	Public	Private	Public	Private
Aliso Viejo, CA	58.3	41.7	88.2	11.8	90.3	9.7	90.6	9.4	91.8	8.2
Allen, TX	55.8	44.2	89.3	10.7	92.2	7.8	92.0	8.0	92.4	7.6
Alpharetta, GA	54.2	45.8	87.7	12.3	90.2	9.8	89.5	10.5	90.3	9.7
Ankeny, IA	61.2	38.8	89.4	10.6	90.4	9.6	90.8	9.2	91.0	9.0
Apex, NC	36.0	64.0	87.4	12.6	89.4	10.6	89.2	10.8	90.5	9.5
Ballwin, MO	53.9	46.1	81.1	18.9	83.2	16.8	83.4	16.6	85.5	14.5
Beavercreek, OH	62.7	37.3	86.4	13.6	86.9	13.1	88.9	11.1	88.5	11.5
Bella Vista, AR	63.0	37.0	91.4	8.6	92.3	7.7	92.3	7.7	93.3	6.7
Bernards, NJ	50.3	49.7	81.7	18.3	86.3	13.7	86.5	13.5	86.1	13.9
Bethlehem, NY	45.3	54.7	87.5	12.5	92.2	7.8	91.8	8.2	92.3	7.7
Bloomfield, MI	65.2	34.8	88.2	11.8	89.7	10.3	90.5	9.5	91.4	8.6
Bowie, MD	41.1	58.9	84.5	15.5	88.0	12.0	87.6	12.4	88.8	11.2
Bozeman, MT	33.1	66.9	84.9	15.1	84.8	15.2	88.6	11.4	87.0	13.0
Brentwood, TN	49.4	50.6	88.5	11.5	88.6	11.4	85.7	14.3	85.3	14.7
Broomfield, CO	57.0	43.0	90.1	9.9	92.2	7.8	91.9	8.1	92.5	7.5
Carmel, IN	46.7	53.3	84.7	15.3	88.9	11.1	89.9	10.1	89.2	10.8
Cedar Park, TX	49.0	51.0	89.7	10.3	92.3	7.7	92.3	7.7	93.3	6.7
Cheshire, CT	59.1	40.9	87.5	12.5	91.4	8.6	90.8	9.2	89.3	10.7
Chesterfield, MO	53.9	46.1	81.1	18.9	83.2	16.8	83.4	16.6	85.5	14.5
Collierville, TN	61.5	38.5	85.5	14.5	86.1	13.9	85.3	14.7	85.3	14.7
Coppell, TX	55.8	44.2	89.3	10.7	92.2	7.8	92.0	8.0	92.4	7.6
Cornelius, NC	47.7	52.3	90.5	9.5	91.3	8.7	90.2	9.8	90.7	9.3
Cranberry, PA	47.7	52.3	85.0	15.0	88.5	11.5	88.2	11.8	89.8	10.2
Cupertino, CA	34.4	65.6	81.9	18.1	87.1	12.9	87.7	12.3	89.1	10.9
Danville, CA	40.4	59.6	83.6	16.4	85.3	14.7	85.6	14.4	88.0	12.0
Draper, UT	50.3	49.7	91.0	9.0	92.8	7.2	93.3	6.7	93.4	6.6
Dublin, OH	49.2	50.8	87.5	12.5	89.2	10.8	88.6	11.4	89.6	10.4
Eastchester, NY	50.3	49.7	81.7	18.3	86.3	13.7	86.5	13.5	86.1	13.9
Eden Prairie, MN	55.6	44.4	86.8	13.2	87.9	12.1	88.6	11.4	90.9	9.1
Edmond, OK	71.2	28.8	89.8	10.2	91.1	8.9	90.9	9.1	91.8	8.2
Evesham, NJ	43.6	56.4	80.0	20.0	84.8	15.2	83.4	16.6	83.8	16.2
Fishers, IN	46.7	53.3	84.7	15.3	88.9	11.1	89.9	10.1	89.2	10.8
Flower Mound, TX	55.8	44.2	89.3	10.7	92.2	7.8	92.0	8.0	92.4	7.6
Folsom, CA	53.1	46.9	88.8	11.2	91.8	8.2	92.2	7.8	91.7	8.3
Foster City, CA	40.4	59.6	83.6	16.4	85.3	14.7	85.6	14.4	88.0	12.0
Franklin, TN	49.4	50.6	88.5	11.5	88.6	11.4	85.7	14.3	85.3	14.7
Friendswood, TX	58.9	41.1	90.6	9.4	93.3	6.7	93.9	6.1	93.6	6.4
Germantown, TN	61.5	38.5	85.5	14.5	86.1	13.9	85.3	14.7	85.3	14.7
Glastonbury, CT	55.7	44.3	90.0	10.0	93.2	6.8	93.3	6.7	91.6	8.4
Grand Blanc, MI	80.2	19.8	92.3	7.7	92.8	7.2	92.2	7.8	93.9	6.1
Guilderland, NY	45.3	54.7	87.5	12.5	92.2	7.8	91.8	8.2	92.3	7.7
Hampden, PA	44.2	55.8	79.9	20.1	87.1	12.9	88.9	11.1	89.2	10.8
Holly Springs, NC	36.0	64.0	87.4	12.6	89.4	10.6	89.2	10.8	90.5	9.5
Huntersville, NC	47.7	52.3	90.5	9.5	91.3	8.7	90.2	9.8	90.7	9.3
Independence, KY	51.6	48.4	83.1	16.9	83.6	16.4	82.7	17.3	83.3	16.7
Johns Creek, GA	54.2	45.8	87.7	12.3	90.2	9.8	89.5	10.5	90.3	9.7
Keller, TX	55.8	44.2	89.3	10.7	92.2	7.8	92.0	8.0	92.4	7.6
Kirkland, WA	41.1	58.9	84.0	16.0	89.0	11.0	89.0	11.0	90.9	9.1
Lafayette, CO	41.9	58.1	91.9	8.1	90.1	9.9	90.7	9.3	94.7	5.3
Lake Oswego, OR	38.7	61.3	84.4	15.6	89.3	10.7	91.0	9.0	91.9	8.1
League City, TX	58.9	41.1	90.6	9.4	93.3	6.7	93.9	6.1	93.6	6.4
Leawood, KS	51.5	48.5	86.7	13.3	88.7	11.3	88.6	11.4	89.7	10.3
Lee's Summit, MO	51.5	48.5	86.7	13.3	88.7	11.3	88.6	11.4	89.7	10.3
Leesburg, VA	41.1	58.9	84.5	15.5	88.0	12.0	87.6	12.4	88.8	11.2
Lehi, UT	43.4	56.6	92.6	7.4	95.1	4.9	94.6	5.4	95.2	4.8
Lenexa, KS	51.5	48.5	86.7	13.3	88.7	11.3	88.6	11.4	89.7	10.3
Lexington, MA	42.8	57.2	86.5	13.5	90.9	9.1	89.4	10.6	86.9	13.1
Los Altos, CA	34.4	65.6	81.9	18.1	87.1	12.9	87.7	12.3	89.1	10.9
Lower Makefield, PA	43.6	56.4	80.0	20.0	84.8	15.2	83.4	16.6	83.8	16.2
Madison, AL	45.3	54.7	83.7	16.3	86.6	13.4	87.3	12.7	87.3	12.7
Mamaroneck, NY	50.3	49.7	81.7	18.3	86.3	13.7	86.5	13.5	86.1	13.9
Manheim, PA	43.6	56.4	82.1	17.9	76.8	23.2	77.1	22.9	85.7	14.3
Manlius, NY	63.5	36.5	90.1	9.9	93.3	6.7	93.2	6.8	92.9	7.1
Maple Grove, MN	55.6	44.4	86.8	13.2	87.9	12.1	88.6	11.4	90.9	9.1
Marion, IA	61.9	38.1	86.3	13.7	86.0	14.0	88.9	11.1	91.5	8.5
Marlboro, NJ	50.3	49.7	81.7	18.3	86.3	13.7	86.5	13.5	86.1	13.9
Mason, OH	51.6	48.4	83.1	16.9	83.6	16.4	82.7	17.3	83.3	16.7
McCandless, PA	47.7	52.3	85.0	15.0	88.5	11.5	88.2	11.8	89.8	10.2

Table continued on next page.

Metro Area	Preschool (%)		Kindergarten (%)		Grades 1 - 4 (%)		Grades 5 - 8 (%)		Grades 9 - 12 (%)	
	Public	Private	Public	Private	Public	Private	Public	Private	Public	Private
Menomonee Falls, WI	53.4	46.6	76.6	23.4	81.1	18.9	80.3	19.7	86.3	13.7
Meridian, ID	43.6	56.4	91.8	8.2	92.9	7.1	94.3	5.7	93.1	6.9
Merrimack, NH	39.2	60.8	74.6	25.4	90.7	9.3	90.4	9.6	90.8	9.2
Mount Lebanon, PA	47.7	52.3	85.0	15.0	88.5	11.5	88.2	11.8	89.8	10.2
Mount Pleasant, SC	46.3	53.7	83.7	16.3	89.3	10.7	89.0	11.0	89.0	11.0
Needham, MA	42.8	57.2	86.5	13.5	90.9	9.1	89.4	10.6	86.9	13.1
Newtown, CT	38.5	61.5	83.3	16.7	86.9	13.1	85.5	14.5	86.2	13.8
Northbrook, IL	57.4	42.6	85.1	14.9	88.3	11.7	89.1	10.9	90.6	9.4
Northville, MI	65.2	34.8	88.2	11.8	89.7	10.3	90.5	9.5	91.4	8.6
Novi, MI	65.2	34.8	88.2	11.8	89.7	10.3	90.5	9.5	91.4	8.6
O'Fallon, IL	53.9	46.1	81.1	18.9	83.2	16.8	83.4	16.6	85.5	14.5
O'Fallon, MO	53.9	46.1	81.1	18.9	83.2	16.8	83.4	16.6	85.5	14.5
Orchard Park, NY	66.3	33.7	86.5	13.5	89.8	10.2	89.2	10.8	89.9	10.1
Oviedo, FL	50.3	49.7	84.9	15.1	88.8	11.2	88.8	11.2	90.6	9.4
Parker, CO	57.0	43.0	90.1	9.9	92.2	7.8	91.9	8.1	92.5	7.5
Parkland, FL	47.6	52.4	82.9	17.1	86.8	13.2	87.5	12.5	87.8	12.2
Peachtree City, GA	54.2	45.8	87.7	12.3	90.2	9.8	89.5	10.5	90.3	9.7
Pflugerville, TX	49.0	51.0	89.7	10.3	92.3	7.7	92.3	7.7	93.3	6.7
Plainfield, IL	57.4	42.6	85.1	14.9	88.3	11.7	89.1	10.9	90.6	9.4
Princeton, NJ	45.3	54.7	88.7	11.3	90.4	9.6	89.8	10.2	88.9	11.1
Queen Creek, AZ	58.0	42.0	92.0	8.0	92.8	7.2	94.4	5.6	94.0	6.0
Rancho Palos Verdes, CA	58.3	41.7	88.2	11.8	90.3	9.7	90.6	9.4	91.8	8.2
Redmond, WA	41.1	58.9	84.0	16.0	89.0	11.0	89.0	11.0	90.9	9.1
Richland, WA	55.6	44.4	89.8	10.2	92.1	7.9	94.0	6.0	96.7	3.3
Ridgefield, CT	38.5	61.5	83.3	16.7	86.9	13.1	85.5	14.5	86.2	13.8
Ridgewood, NJ	50.3	49.7	81.7	18.3	86.3	13.7	86.5	13.5	86.1	13.9
Rio Rancho, NM	61.4	38.6	88.2	11.8	89.8	10.2	89.4	10.6	90.1	9.9
Sahuarita, AZ	57.6	42.4	87.1	12.9	91.7	8.3	92.5	7.5	92.5	7.5
Sammamish, WA	41.1	58.9	84.0	16.0	89.0	11.0	89.0	11.0	90.9	9.1
San Ramon, CA	40.4	59.6	83.6	16.4	85.3	14.7	85.6	14.4	88.0	12.0
Saratoga, CA	34.4	65.6	81.9	18.1	87.1	12.9	87.7	12.3	89.1	10.9
Schertz, TX	64.1	35.9	89.9	10.1	92.4	7.6	92.1	7.9	93.4	6.6
Shrewsbury, MA	58.2	41.8	90.2	9.8	92.2	7.8	91.7	8.3	90.8	9.2
South Brunswick, NJ	50.3	49.7	81.7	18.3	86.3	13.7	86.5	13.5	86.1	13.9
South Jordan, UT	50.3	49.7	91.0	9.0	92.8	7.2	93.3	6.7	93.4	6.6
South Kingstown, RI	51.0	49.0	85.9	14.1	89.3	10.7	90.2	9.8	87.1	12.9
South Windsor, CT	55.7	44.3	90.0	10.0	93.2	6.8	93.3	6.7	91.6	8.4
Southlake, TX	55.8	44.2	89.3	10.7	92.2	7.8	92.0	8.0	92.4	7.6
Spring Hill, TN	49.4	50.6	88.5	11.5	88.6	11.4	85.7	14.3	85.3	14.7
Stow, OH	55.1	44.9	82.0	18.0	87.0	13.0	87.4	12.6	89.9	10.1
Sugar Land, TX	58.9	41.1	90.6	9.4	93.3	6.7	93.9	6.1	93.6	6.4
Sun Prairie, WI	53.3	46.7	89.5	10.5	90.3	9.7	90.2	9.8	95.0	5.0
Syracuse, UT	55.0	45.0	94.5	5.5	97.0	3.0	96.9	3.1	97.2	2.8
Tredyffrin, PA	43.6	56.4	80.0	20.0	84.8	15.2	83.4	16.6	83.8	16.2
Upper Arlington, OH	49.2	50.8	87.5	12.5	89.2	10.8	88.6	11.4	89.6	10.4
Upper Dublin, PA	43.6	56.4	80.0	20.0	84.8	15.2	83.4	16.6	83.8	16.2
Vestavia Hills, AL	40.7	59.3	81.7	18.3	90.5	9.5	90.4	9.6	89.9	10.1
Webster, NY	57.2	42.8	90.4	9.6	90.5	9.5	91.1	8.9	91.2	8.8
Wellesley, MA	42.8	57.2	86.5	13.5	90.9	9.1	89.4	10.6	86.9	13.1
West Fargo, ND	58.6	41.4	90.7	9.3	90.1	9.9	91.5	8.5	89.3	10.7
West Linn, OR	38.7	61.3	84.4	15.6	89.3	10.7	91.0	9.0	91.9	8.1
West Windsor, NJ	45.3	54.7	88.7	11.3	90.4	9.6	89.8	10.2	88.9	11.1
Westlake, OH	53.7	46.3	80.8	19.2	81.3	18.7	81.5	18.5	84.3	15.7
Weston, FL	47.6	52.4	82.9	17.1	86.8	13.2	87.5	12.5	87.8	12.2
Westport, CT	38.5	61.5	83.3	16.7	86.9	13.1	85.5	14.5	86.2	13.8
Wilmette, IL	57.4	42.6	85.1	14.9	88.3	11.7	89.1	10.9	90.6	9.4
Woodbury, MN	55.6	44.4	86.8	13.2	87.9	12.1	88.6	11.4	90.9	9.1
Yorba Linda, CA	58.3	41.7	88.2	11.8	90.3	9.7	90.6	9.4	91.8	8.2
U.S.	57.4	42.6	87.8	12.2	89.8	10.2	89.9	10.1	90.6	9.4

Note: Figures shown cover persons 3 years old and over; Figures cover the Metropolitan Statistical Area—see Appendix B for areas included;
Source: U.S. Census Bureau, 2010-2014 American Community Survey 5-Year Estimates

Educational Attainment by Race: City

City	High School Graduate or Higher (%)					Bachelor's Degree or Higher (%)				
	Total	White	Black	Asian	Hisp.[1]	Total	White	Black	Asian	Hisp.[1]
Aliso Viejo, CA	95.4	97.0	96.8	96.7	80.6	56.9	57.0	64.4	67.7	28.8
Allen, TX	95.8	96.3	98.6	93.8	79.9	52.6	52.2	42.8	69.1	35.2
Alpharetta, GA	96.8	97.0	96.1	98.0	80.6	62.4	62.3	39.6	81.7	45.2
Ankeny, IA	97.5	97.6	99.5	97.7	89.5	45.2	45.4	28.8	46.4	41.1
Apex, NC	97.1	97.2	96.5	95.5	79.0	60.9	61.0	37.8	86.2	36.9
Ballwin, MO	97.0	97.2	100.0	91.7	100.0	53.6	52.6	28.5	80.7	28.8
Beavercreek, OH	96.5	96.6	96.9	93.6	96.5	50.0	48.6	66.4	67.5	55.1
Bella Vista, AR	94.5	94.7	65.8	91.9	55.8	34.5	34.7	16.8	45.5	15.1
Bernards, NJ	97.4	97.7	89.2	97.0	96.3	70.6	68.9	40.6	84.1	77.9
Bethlehem, NY	97.2	97.4	88.5	97.1	99.3	56.7	56.5	29.6	80.3	48.5
Bloomfield, MI	97.2	97.8	96.1	92.9	97.6	69.4	70.4	43.5	80.8	75.6
Bowie, MD	95.3	94.5	97.1	91.6	80.8	48.0	45.9	50.0	68.9	24.9
Bozeman, MT	97.5	97.5	100.0	100.0	94.1	54.4	55.1	74.1	61.3	33.5
Brentwood, TN	97.7	97.8	97.8	96.5	87.5	67.9	67.9	55.1	81.4	45.8
Broomfield, CO	94.8	95.9	94.8	89.0	79.4	49.5	50.2	38.4	57.2	20.3
Carmel, IN	98.1	98.6	98.8	94.8	89.7	68.8	68.4	61.6	77.8	52.5
Cedar Park, TX	95.3	95.2	96.7	95.0	84.9	44.1	42.7	33.7	67.2	29.9
Cheshire, CT	94.4	96.4	79.5	89.8	84.6	51.7	53.2	8.8	75.4	24.6
Chesterfield, MO	97.7	98.1	91.4	97.1	93.3	64.0	64.1	34.4	76.4	48.7
Collierville, TN	96.6	97.8	89.5	95.3	92.6	52.7	52.1	46.4	72.9	43.8
Coppell, TX	96.5	96.6	99.9	95.3	86.1	63.2	62.1	53.4	72.0	51.0
Cornelius, NC	94.6	95.2	93.6	74.3	74.7	52.2	52.7	47.0	52.6	31.2
Cranberry, PA	97.6	97.8	100.0	82.8	100.0	57.9	57.8	57.6	59.5	62.8
Cupertino, CA	96.5	95.9	97.9	97.3	85.7	75.6	60.2	30.9	85.5	41.0
Danville, CA	97.7	98.2	97.5	94.9	91.7	64.2	63.9	39.2	70.4	53.4
Draper, UT	96.3	96.9	79.7	97.6	85.8	39.8	40.6	0.0	71.9	15.4
Dublin, OH	98.3	98.8	99.5	96.7	89.1	73.7	72.3	44.6	85.9	71.6
Eastchester, NY	94.0	94.1	89.4	99.4	84.8	58.1	58.7	35.8	71.3	42.1
Eden Prairie, MN	97.3	98.8	83.0	92.6	82.2	60.7	60.9	28.9	76.5	45.4
Edmond, OK	95.9	96.4	94.7	94.2	78.6	51.9	52.7	38.2	74.8	33.5
Evesham, NJ	95.1	95.6	95.9	88.2	85.7	47.1	46.0	53.8	61.7	29.0
Fishers, IN	97.7	98.3	93.5	94.1	78.5	61.1	61.1	48.2	74.8	35.7
Flower Mound, TX	97.3	98.0	97.9	96.0	88.8	57.6	56.0	54.3	82.5	45.8
Folsom, CA	92.0	95.2	68.3	94.8	80.0	45.7	45.8	9.1	73.5	31.7
Foster City, CA	95.9	96.4	90.8	96.1	95.2	63.0	58.8	40.0	70.7	30.8
Franklin, TN	94.3	95.4	81.0	98.9	58.5	56.1	58.3	19.2	69.5	19.2
Friendswood, TX	95.2	95.7	95.6	88.8	88.4	48.3	47.5	50.1	65.9	41.5
Germantown, TN	98.1	98.2	97.3	96.6	92.9	65.1	64.2	61.1	82.4	57.4
Glastonbury, CT	96.2	97.0	89.8	89.3	90.3	61.2	61.5	43.4	64.5	57.4
Grand Blanc, MI	95.0	95.1	94.7	96.2	88.9	35.0	34.4	28.7	64.7	30.9
Guilderland, NY	96.5	96.6	90.7	97.0	83.5	50.8	48.2	35.9	83.9	49.1
Hampden, PA	94.9	95.4	89.7	89.2	90.4	48.9	47.9	36.4	63.6	28.2
Holly Springs, NC	96.4	98.5	86.1	97.5	89.9	54.9	56.3	43.6	75.2	25.5
Huntersville, NC	95.0	95.3	94.8	94.4	56.1	53.7	53.5	49.6	81.8	24.2
Independence, KY	90.0	90.1	88.1	100.0	88.0	29.1	29.0	43.3	36.4	5.9
Johns Creek, GA	95.9	97.3	96.5	92.0	84.3	63.8	63.5	47.2	72.8	37.0
Keller, TX	96.9	97.8	93.9	97.4	79.0	56.8	56.7	53.4	83.1	34.4
Kirkland, WA	96.5	97.4	98.5	93.7	76.8	55.6	54.7	48.6	65.9	33.9
Lafayette, CO	94.7	95.8	100.0	90.2	75.6	55.6	57.7	61.5	54.5	23.5
Lake Oswego, OR	97.8	98.4	100.0	100.0	72.9	65.2	66.4	50.0	60.1	42.4
League City, TX	94.6	95.2	97.1	90.5	83.3	41.2	41.0	36.1	55.5	28.7
Leawood, KS	99.2	99.3	96.7	98.6	100.0	74.3	74.4	60.8	91.8	82.9
Lee's Summit, MO	96.4	96.7	94.7	96.2	80.1	42.6	43.8	34.5	40.2	36.3
Leesburg, VA	88.6	91.0	87.5	86.8	59.2	49.4	53.2	31.4	54.3	14.6
Lehi, UT	96.1	96.0	100.0	96.9	81.5	39.1	38.9	0.0	65.2	19.7
Lenexa, KS	96.0	96.4	96.4	94.3	74.6	54.3	54.7	43.1	69.6	21.1
Lexington, MA	96.8	97.3	76.3	97.4	95.8	76.7	76.2	37.5	82.2	87.8
Los Altos, CA	98.7	98.9	100.0	98.5	94.2	79.0	77.4	64.7	83.8	48.6
Lower Makefield, PA	97.9	98.1	87.9	97.2	100.0	66.6	65.3	43.2	86.3	64.5
Madison, AL	95.7	96.9	96.6	85.1	83.8	55.2	58.3	40.9	60.1	51.5
Mamaroneck, NY	93.6	95.2	96.8	87.9	79.1	68.1	72.1	50.9	76.4	28.3
Manheim, PA	91.3	93.4	95.7	67.9	72.8	42.5	43.8	36.9	35.0	14.3
Manlius, NY	97.0	97.5	90.6	87.4	98.8	52.1	51.4	64.0	68.3	39.9
Maple Grove, MN	97.3	98.0	84.3	93.2	87.7	49.4	48.6	42.1	61.9	42.4
Marion, IA	95.7	96.2	89.4	87.9	78.1	33.7	33.6	17.0	61.9	32.4
Marlboro, NJ	96.3	96.5	93.1	96.4	91.4	59.1	54.3	50.5	83.2	30.4
Mason, OH	96.4	96.5	91.2	97.6	89.4	54.5	51.8	49.0	79.7	49.3
McCandless, PA	97.1	97.0	90.4	100.0	100.0	54.8	52.9	62.4	84.9	57.6

Table continued on next page.

City	High School Graduate or Higher (%)					Bachelor's Degree or Higher (%)				
	Total	White	Black	Asian	Hisp.[1]	Total	White	Black	Asian	Hisp.[1]
Menomonee Falls, WI	94.6	94.7	95.2	92.8	93.5	40.8	39.3	45.2	76.6	25.3
Meridian, ID	94.9	95.5	80.4	87.5	81.1	33.3	33.0	33.9	59.1	16.1
Merrimack, NH	96.2	96.2	47.4	96.8	97.9	42.9	41.9	0.0	73.5	63.6
Mount Lebanon, PA	97.6	97.9	86.1	93.3	99.7	63.8	63.6	12.0	84.2	64.9
Mount Pleasant, SC	97.6	98.7	84.3	75.2	99.9	58.4	60.5	19.6	43.9	57.5
Needham, MA	97.9	98.3	91.8	96.7	94.0	74.1	74.9	26.5	79.1	65.5
Newtown, CT	94.5	95.6	78.8	78.9	89.5	54.4	55.5	26.7	63.9	41.0
Northbrook, IL	96.9	97.2	89.8	98.9	84.4	68.9	69.1	1.6	74.4	58.8
Northville, MI	96.9	98.0	90.3	93.2	95.9	60.5	58.3	53.8	77.1	51.8
Novi, MI	94.9	95.0	93.0	96.2	85.0	55.9	52.2	35.4	81.7	38.9
O'Fallon, IL	96.2	96.7	93.2	91.2	95.9	48.8	49.7	40.8	54.9	42.8
O'Fallon, MO	94.4	94.4	96.9	95.4	83.4	37.5	35.9	42.3	74.6	29.4
Orchard Park, NY	96.3	96.3	91.1	96.7	100.0	45.3	45.2	43.3	67.5	63.3
Oviedo, FL	94.8	95.7	90.1	88.4	91.0	42.6	43.9	33.6	46.8	33.1
Parker, CO	97.6	97.9	77.5	98.0	90.7	51.6	52.2	34.5	62.9	33.4
Parkland, FL	97.2	98.0	97.3	88.5	96.7	61.8	61.1	71.6	65.7	50.3
Peachtree City, GA	94.8	95.4	95.0	93.1	70.2	53.5	53.9	49.2	69.1	33.8
Pflugerville, TX	93.3	94.2	95.8	80.5	85.2	36.2	36.9	34.6	44.5	23.5
Plainfield, IL	95.9	97.3	94.7	87.8	84.2	48.8	49.5	52.8	58.4	27.4
Princeton, NJ	96.2	96.5	91.7	97.9	77.0	80.9	83.2	43.2	91.6	44.0
Queen Creek, AZ	96.0	97.0	90.2	96.1	90.1	37.7	38.5	38.8	66.1	24.3
Rancho Palos Verdes, CA	97.5	98.0	99.1	97.2	93.2	64.8	62.9	49.6	74.4	41.6
Redmond, WA	95.5	95.7	99.8	97.0	72.9	62.4	53.9	50.5	84.0	28.4
Richland, WA	95.5	96.4	91.7	88.8	88.5	43.7	44.1	19.0	63.0	19.5
Ridgefield, CT	98.2	98.2	94.0	100.0	92.7	72.6	72.1	66.4	94.5	66.3
Ridgewood, NJ	97.6	97.8	92.9	96.9	96.7	74.9	75.2	47.6	81.1	58.5
Rio Rancho, NM	93.7	93.8	97.2	91.8	89.2	28.6	28.2	45.3	53.8	20.8
Sahuarita, AZ	95.1	95.4	97.8	96.7	90.8	35.2	36.6	43.8	15.1	23.1
Sammamish, WA	98.4	98.8	91.4	97.5	94.9	72.5	69.6	70.1	83.7	71.6
San Ramon, CA	97.5	98.0	99.3	97.7	93.3	65.0	56.4	62.4	78.6	39.8
Saratoga, CA	98.2	98.4	91.1	98.1	82.5	77.6	70.5	23.6	88.1	30.3
Schertz, TX	92.8	93.1	97.3	72.8	88.8	31.4	30.4	43.2	41.6	19.5
Shrewsbury, MA	94.8	95.4	97.9	93.0	80.9	55.2	51.6	53.1	76.3	33.2
South Brunswick, NJ	94.3	94.9	91.9	94.7	92.1	59.5	47.4	50.1	80.3	38.9
South Jordan, UT	96.4	97.0	68.8	94.2	84.9	38.7	38.5	6.3	62.7	28.6
South Kingstown, RI	93.8	94.2	85.0	100.0	100.0	52.8	53.4	45.7	85.4	77.9
South Windsor, CT	94.3	95.0	88.2	92.0	90.8	50.9	49.6	46.0	69.7	36.0
Southlake, TX	98.5	98.9	94.0	97.2	94.6	68.5	67.1	64.8	87.9	54.6
Spring Hill, TN	96.3	96.4	99.5	81.1	81.9	42.8	43.1	51.2	44.7	12.4
Stow, OH	93.7	94.3	84.9	76.4	95.8	40.5	40.1	46.0	56.1	58.3
Sugar Land, TX	92.7	95.1	95.5	89.8	81.3	54.2	49.9	54.7	62.1	36.0
Sun Prairie, WI	95.2	95.7	93.4	92.4	61.6	42.5	43.3	24.1	61.2	20.3
Syracuse, UT	98.2	98.5	100.0	91.1	90.2	36.6	37.4	30.9	19.4	18.6
Tredyffrin, PA	97.7	98.5	86.3	93.9	88.4	76.2	75.1	56.9	86.2	67.5
Upper Arlington, OH	98.5	98.9	75.3	98.7	91.1	74.2	73.9	46.7	90.1	63.1
Upper Dublin, PA	96.7	97.4	90.2	94.2	81.2	64.3	65.6	31.7	72.4	48.6
Vestavia Hills, AL	97.8	98.1	89.0	99.3	90.9	67.1	67.5	40.1	85.9	40.8
Webster, NY	94.8	95.5	87.5	84.2	86.5	42.3	41.7	46.4	64.3	35.4
Wellesley, MA	98.1	98.5	94.3	97.2	95.9	82.2	83.0	39.0	80.8	70.2
West Fargo, ND	94.6	96.1	57.5	68.1	67.8	35.7	36.5	32.0	19.0	28.7
West Linn, OR	98.2	98.9	67.8	98.2	87.3	54.1	54.7	34.5	58.7	19.9
West Windsor, NJ	97.1	96.8	97.4	97.3	93.3	79.8	75.3	51.5	88.7	51.3
Westlake, OH	95.5	96.0	72.0	99.1	87.8	53.6	52.3	41.3	79.0	51.7
Weston, FL	97.0	97.0	97.3	94.9	96.7	57.9	57.9	64.3	64.3	54.4
Westport, CT	98.0	98.4	85.6	93.0	100.0	75.7	76.7	25.3	72.6	64.0
Wilmette, IL	98.8	99.1	97.0	97.8	100.0	81.1	81.9	56.2	79.6	81.1
Woodbury, MN	97.3	97.9	90.2	97.2	87.1	57.2	55.9	44.1	77.2	33.2
Yorba Linda, CA	95.5	95.8	100.0	94.6	89.3	49.4	44.9	45.1	71.0	36.7
U.S.	86.3	88.4	83.2	85.8	64.1	29.3	30.6	19.0	50.9	13.9

Note: Figures shown cover persons 25 years old and over; (1) People of Hispanic origin can be of any race
Source: U.S. Census Bureau, 2010-2014 American Community Survey 5-Year Estimates

Educational Attainment by Race: Metro Area

Metro Area	High School Graduate or Higher (%)					Bachelor's Degree or Higher (%)				
	Total	White	Black	Asian	Hisp.[1]	Total	White	Black	Asian	Hisp.[1]
Aliso Viejo, CA	78.5	81.1	88.5	87.2	57.4	31.7	33.6	23.9	50.0	11.1
Allen, TX	84.1	85.5	88.7	87.3	55.7	32.0	33.6	23.7	56.3	11.3
Alpharetta, GA	87.9	89.3	88.5	86.4	61.4	35.3	39.0	27.1	53.3	16.5
Ankeny, IA	92.6	94.1	84.4	80.1	59.7	35.1	36.2	18.2	44.4	13.7
Apex, NC	90.2	92.3	87.0	90.2	55.8	42.5	45.9	27.5	67.5	15.9
Ballwin, MO	90.3	91.9	83.5	88.2	76.8	31.5	33.6	17.3	62.8	24.9
Beavercreek, OH	89.4	90.2	85.5	87.7	76.3	26.5	27.3	18.3	56.2	26.2
Bella Vista, AR	84.2	86.4	88.0	89.0	42.4	27.9	28.3	28.3	60.6	9.4
Bernards, NJ	85.1	89.6	83.0	82.5	67.7	37.0	41.9	22.5	52.7	16.7
Bethlehem, NY	92.0	93.0	85.1	86.9	78.7	34.4	34.9	18.1	60.1	26.6
Bloomfield, MI	88.5	90.2	83.9	88.7	68.6	28.6	30.4	17.1	63.9	17.3
Bowie, MD	90.2	92.9	89.9	90.5	65.8	48.3	55.8	31.3	62.7	23.6
Bozeman, MT	96.4	96.5	92.6	100.0	86.6	46.7	47.1	47.2	62.5	29.5
Brentwood, TN	87.6	89.0	85.0	83.3	59.2	31.3	32.6	24.1	48.9	12.9
Broomfield, CO	89.8	91.5	89.6	85.0	65.9	39.8	42.1	24.3	46.9	13.3
Carmel, IN	88.7	90.4	84.6	86.1	57.7	30.8	32.7	17.6	58.4	13.6
Cedar Park, TX	88.3	89.8	89.2	91.9	67.7	41.0	42.9	24.5	65.7	18.9
Cheshire, CT	88.9	90.6	84.8	89.6	71.7	33.4	35.4	19.6	65.2	14.0
Chesterfield, MO	90.3	91.9	83.5	88.2	76.8	31.5	33.6	17.3	62.8	24.9
Collierville, TN	86.0	91.0	81.7	85.3	56.7	26.3	33.6	16.9	52.0	12.3
Coppell, TX	84.1	85.5	88.7	87.3	55.7	32.0	33.6	23.7	56.3	11.3
Cornelius, NC	86.9	88.6	85.4	84.6	59.5	31.4	33.9	22.4	52.5	15.1
Cranberry, PA	92.3	92.7	87.7	89.5	84.4	30.9	31.2	16.9	71.3	33.5
Cupertino, CA	86.5	88.4	91.8	89.2	65.6	46.5	44.1	31.5	61.2	14.3
Danville, CA	87.9	91.3	89.5	85.3	68.2	44.9	49.6	23.9	50.5	18.4
Draper, UT	89.3	91.9	82.5	83.2	63.0	30.8	32.1	19.8	46.4	11.7
Dublin, OH	90.1	91.2	85.5	89.8	68.7	33.3	34.5	19.6	66.3	21.0
Eastchester, NY	85.1	89.6	83.0	82.5	67.7	37.0	41.9	22.5	52.7	16.7
Eden Prairie, MN	93.1	95.3	81.8	79.8	65.7	39.0	40.7	20.2	44.0	17.6
Edmond, OK	87.8	89.2	88.8	80.9	56.2	28.5	30.0	19.9	43.4	10.5
Evesham, NJ	89.1	91.8	84.4	82.5	66.8	34.2	37.9	18.0	54.0	15.2
Fishers, IN	88.7	90.4	84.6	86.1	57.7	30.8	32.7	17.6	58.4	13.6
Flower Mound, TX	84.1	85.5	88.7	87.3	55.7	32.0	33.6	23.7	56.3	11.3
Folsom, CA	88.0	90.9	88.1	81.8	70.0	30.7	32.1	20.2	39.8	14.6
Foster City, CA	87.9	91.3	89.5	85.3	68.2	44.9	49.6	23.9	50.5	18.4
Franklin, TN	87.6	89.0	85.0	83.3	59.2	31.3	32.6	24.1	48.9	12.9
Friendswood, TX	81.5	82.1	88.3	85.9	58.3	30.0	31.0	24.3	54.3	12.1
Germantown, TN	86.0	91.0	81.7	85.3	56.7	26.3	33.6	16.9	52.0	12.3
Glastonbury, CT	89.8	91.9	83.7	88.4	69.2	36.3	38.4	19.3	64.1	14.9
Grand Blanc, MI	89.0	90.0	85.3	91.8	84.8	19.2	20.3	12.7	54.2	16.4
Guilderland, NY	92.0	93.0	85.1	86.9	78.7	34.4	34.9	18.1	60.1	26.6
Hampden, PA	89.8	91.0	85.7	81.5	72.0	29.2	30.4	13.5	50.9	15.4
Holly Springs, NC	90.2	92.3	87.0	90.2	55.8	42.5	45.9	27.5	67.5	15.9
Huntersville, NC	86.9	88.6	85.4	84.6	59.5	31.4	33.9	22.4	52.5	15.1
Independence, KY	89.3	90.2	83.8	90.9	70.7	30.5	31.6	16.5	65.7	23.7
Johns Creek, GA	87.9	89.3	88.5	86.4	61.4	35.3	39.0	27.1	53.3	16.5
Keller, TX	84.1	85.5	88.7	87.3	55.7	32.0	33.6	23.7	56.3	11.3
Kirkland, WA	91.6	93.7	87.6	85.9	70.5	38.4	39.4	20.5	48.6	19.3
Lafayette, CO	94.0	95.6	85.7	91.6	64.2	58.2	60.1	38.7	65.1	21.2
Lake Oswego, OR	90.7	92.6	86.4	84.7	62.3	34.9	35.7	22.9	44.6	15.2
League City, TX	81.5	82.1	88.3	85.9	58.3	30.0	31.0	24.3	54.3	12.1
Leawood, KS	90.8	92.5	86.1	84.1	65.5	33.6	36.1	17.9	52.6	15.2
Lee's Summit, MO	90.8	92.5	86.1	84.1	65.5	33.6	36.1	17.9	52.6	15.2
Leesburg, VA	90.2	92.9	89.9	90.5	65.8	48.3	55.8	31.3	62.7	23.6
Lehi, UT	93.5	94.3	87.5	92.8	70.9	36.5	36.8	35.2	57.7	18.1
Lenexa, KS	90.8	92.5	86.1	84.1	65.5	33.6	36.1	17.9	52.6	15.2
Lexington, MA	90.8	93.5	82.3	84.2	69.1	44.0	46.2	23.8	58.2	19.7
Los Altos, CA	86.5	88.4	91.8	89.2	65.6	46.5	44.1	31.5	61.2	14.3
Lower Makefield, PA	89.1	91.8	84.4	82.5	66.8	34.2	37.9	18.0	54.0	15.2
Madison, AL	88.5	89.5	86.2	86.8	62.5	35.4	37.6	26.2	53.1	23.2
Mamaroneck, NY	85.1	89.6	83.0	82.5	67.7	37.0	41.9	22.5	52.7	16.7
Manheim, PA	84.3	85.2	82.9	71.7	69.9	24.7	25.5	14.6	31.5	7.9
Manlius, NY	89.4	91.0	76.7	74.5	74.0	29.9	30.7	15.4	50.6	23.6
Maple Grove, MN	93.1	95.3	81.8	79.8	65.7	39.0	40.7	20.2	44.0	17.6
Marion, IA	93.7	94.3	82.8	92.2	72.4	29.2	29.1	16.7	58.3	20.3
Marlboro, NJ	85.1	89.6	83.0	82.5	67.7	37.0	41.9	22.5	52.7	16.7
Mason, OH	89.3	90.2	83.8	90.9	70.7	30.5	31.6	16.5	65.7	23.7
McCandless, PA	92.3	92.7	87.7	89.5	84.4	30.9	31.2	16.9	71.3	33.5

Table continued on next page.

Metro Area	High School Graduate or Higher (%)					Bachelor's Degree or Higher (%)				
	Total	White	Black	Asian	Hisp.[1]	Total	White	Black	Asian	Hisp.[1]
Menomonee Falls, WI	89.9	92.8	80.0	82.9	64.8	32.9	36.6	12.4	51.1	12.1
Meridian, ID	90.1	91.0	80.5	84.4	62.1	29.8	30.1	18.7	48.0	11.4
Merrimack, NH	90.9	91.6	81.5	85.2	70.3	35.5	35.2	24.8	57.0	17.5
Mount Lebanon, PA	92.3	92.7	87.7	89.5	84.4	30.9	31.2	16.9	71.3	33.5
Mount Pleasant, SC	88.8	92.2	81.1	84.1	68.1	32.1	38.7	15.0	38.7	19.1
Needham, MA	90.8	93.5	82.3	84.2	69.1	44.0	46.2	23.8	58.2	19.7
Newtown, CT	89.2	92.2	84.2	89.6	68.7	45.4	50.4	19.7	66.7	18.1
Northbrook, IL	86.9	89.9	85.1	90.5	62.5	35.1	38.5	20.3	62.8	12.8
Northville, MI	88.5	90.2	83.9	88.7	68.6	28.6	30.4	17.1	63.9	17.3
Novi, MI	88.5	90.2	83.9	88.7	68.6	28.6	30.4	17.1	63.9	17.3
O'Fallon, IL	90.3	91.9	83.5	88.2	76.8	31.5	33.6	17.3	62.8	24.9
O'Fallon, MO	90.3	91.9	83.5	88.2	76.8	31.5	33.6	17.3	62.8	24.9
Orchard Park, NY	90.2	92.0	81.7	77.2	73.2	29.6	31.2	14.8	55.1	19.7
Oviedo, FL	87.8	89.7	82.8	85.6	80.4	28.4	29.8	19.5	47.4	19.5
Parker, CO	89.8	91.5	89.6	85.0	65.9	39.8	42.1	24.3	46.9	13.3
Parkland, FL	84.1	85.7	78.8	86.7	77.4	29.1	31.7	17.4	47.8	24.0
Peachtree City, GA	87.9	89.3	88.5	86.4	61.4	35.3	39.0	27.1	53.3	16.5
Pflugerville, TX	88.3	89.8	89.2	91.9	67.7	41.0	42.9	24.5	65.7	18.9
Plainfield, IL	86.9	89.9	85.1	90.5	62.5	35.1	38.5	20.3	62.8	12.8
Princeton, NJ	87.3	89.8	82.8	95.1	61.6	39.8	43.3	17.3	78.6	13.3
Queen Creek, AZ	86.4	87.9	88.8	87.5	63.4	28.8	29.7	22.7	53.0	10.6
Rancho Palos Verdes, CA	78.5	81.1	88.5	87.2	57.4	31.7	33.6	23.9	50.0	11.1
Redmond, WA	91.6	93.7	87.6	85.9	70.5	38.4	39.4	20.5	48.6	19.3
Richland, WA	83.8	89.5	90.1	80.6	49.4	25.2	27.6	21.4	52.1	6.7
Ridgefield, CT	89.2	92.2	84.2	89.6	68.7	45.4	50.4	19.7	66.7	18.1
Ridgewood, NJ	85.1	89.6	83.0	82.5	67.7	37.0	41.9	22.5	52.7	16.7
Rio Rancho, NM	87.5	89.8	91.6	86.7	77.7	30.1	33.6	29.8	46.5	16.6
Sahuarita, AZ	87.5	89.5	88.8	86.9	72.5	30.1	32.1	22.5	46.5	13.6
Sammamish, WA	91.6	93.7	87.6	85.9	70.5	38.4	39.4	20.5	48.6	19.3
San Ramon, CA	87.9	91.3	89.5	85.3	68.2	44.9	49.6	23.9	50.5	18.4
Saratoga, CA	86.5	88.4	91.8	89.2	65.6	46.5	44.1	31.5	61.2	14.3
Schertz, TX	83.6	84.7	90.1	85.0	73.4	26.4	27.4	25.3	50.2	14.8
Shrewsbury, MA	89.4	90.7	87.0	82.8	67.7	32.7	33.1	23.3	53.4	14.7
South Brunswick, NJ	85.1	89.6	83.0	82.5	67.7	37.0	41.9	22.5	52.7	16.7
South Jordan, UT	89.3	91.9	82.5	83.2	63.0	30.8	32.1	19.8	46.4	11.7
South Kingstown, RI	84.3	86.1	77.8	78.5	62.6	29.4	30.7	19.0	43.1	12.0
South Windsor, CT	89.8	91.9	83.7	88.4	69.2	36.3	38.4	19.3	64.1	14.9
Southlake, TX	84.1	85.5	88.7	87.3	55.7	32.0	33.6	23.7	56.3	11.3
Spring Hill, TN	87.6	89.0	85.0	83.3	59.2	31.3	32.6	24.1	48.9	12.9
Stow, OH	90.8	91.9	85.5	78.2	77.8	29.0	30.1	16.2	51.6	29.5
Sugar Land, TX	81.5	82.1	88.3	85.9	58.3	30.0	31.0	24.3	54.3	12.1
Sun Prairie, WI	94.3	95.3	87.7	88.7	69.3	42.5	42.8	21.7	66.1	22.8
Syracuse, UT	92.6	94.0	94.0	88.7	68.0	29.0	30.1	22.8	31.2	12.4
Tredyffrin, PA	89.1	91.8	84.4	82.5	66.8	34.2	37.9	18.0	54.0	15.2
Upper Arlington, OH	90.1	91.2	85.5	89.8	68.7	33.3	34.5	19.6	66.3	21.0
Upper Dublin, PA	89.1	91.8	84.4	82.5	66.8	34.2	37.9	18.0	54.0	15.2
Vestavia Hills, AL	86.2	87.8	84.2	91.1	56.7	27.8	31.1	18.6	59.8	12.6
Webster, NY	89.7	91.8	77.0	82.3	67.7	32.4	34.5	13.3	52.2	15.6
Wellesley, MA	90.8	93.5	82.3	84.2	69.1	44.0	46.2	23.8	58.2	19.7
West Fargo, ND	94.6	95.4	81.3	84.9	80.9	35.5	35.9	29.0	53.6	14.0
West Linn, OR	90.7	92.6	86.4	84.7	62.3	34.9	35.7	22.9	44.6	15.2
West Windsor, NJ	87.3	89.8	82.8	95.1	61.6	39.8	43.3	17.3	78.6	13.3
Westlake, OH	89.0	91.1	81.5	88.6	72.2	28.9	31.7	13.9	65.9	14.8
Weston, FL	84.1	85.7	78.8	86.7	77.4	29.1	31.7	17.4	47.8	24.0
Westport, CT	89.2	92.2	84.2	89.6	68.7	45.4	50.4	19.7	66.7	18.1
Wilmette, IL	86.9	89.9	85.1	90.5	62.5	35.1	38.5	20.3	62.8	12.8
Woodbury, MN	93.1	95.3	81.8	79.8	65.7	39.0	40.7	20.2	44.0	17.6
Yorba Linda, CA	78.5	81.1	88.5	87.2	57.4	31.7	33.6	23.9	50.0	11.1
U.S.	86.3	88.4	83.2	85.8	64.1	29.3	30.6	19.0	50.9	13.9

Note: Figures shown cover persons 25 years old and over; Figures cover the Metropolitan Statistical Area—see Appendix B for areas included; (1) People of Hispanic origin can be of any race
Source: U.S. Census Bureau, 2010-2014 American Community Survey 5-Year Estimates

Cost of Living Index

Urban Area	Composite	Groceries	Housing	Utilities	Transp.	Health	Misc.
Aliso Viejo, CA[1]	148.8	107.6	244.7	113.9	135.0	107.6	104.8
Allen, TX[2]	100.9	101.1	91.0	101.6	122.3	99.1	101.9
Alpharetta, GA[3]	99.9	103.7	97.8	93.6	104.8	101.4	100.4
Ankeny, IA[4]	89.8	92.0	83.7	89.8	95.1	96.6	91.4
Apex, NC[5]	90.5	102.3	72.6	98.0	89.5	99.6	97.8
Ballwin, MO[6]	92.5	104.6	72.3	116.6	98.5	99.8	94.3
Beavercreek, OH[7]	92.8	96.5	75.6	96.2	100.3	88.6	102.9
Bella Vista, AR[8]	88.3	91.5	76.1	103.6	93.8	90.9	90.3
Bernards, NJ[9]	126.7	109.8	164.1	114.2	108.9	106.6	114.3
Bethlehem, NY[10]	112.8	109.9	123.2	90.6	107.1	99.5	115.7
Bloomfield, MI[11]	95.4	88.8	91.1	104.5	104.8	96.4	95.5
Bowie, MD[12]	129.5	108.6	201.6	101.8	109.2	88.5	97.5
Bozeman, MT	102.8	103.8	113.3	85.5	97.7	104.8	100.2
Brentwood, TN[13]	95.3	95.7	82.4	97.6	97.9	86.6	105.7
Broomfield, CO[14]	109.7	99.2	130.7	94.6	98.2	107.8	104.9
Carmel, IN[15]	91.2	92.9	82.4	90.9	91.8	99.3	96.8
Cedar Park, TX[16]	96.0	84.2	90.7	101.6	97.5	103.5	102.1
Cheshire, CT[17]	124.3	131.5	142.7	101.2	107.2	113.8	120.1
Chesterfield, MO[18]	92.5	104.6	72.3	116.6	98.5	99.8	94.3
Collierville, TN[19]	84.5	89.4	68.2	94.9	88.2	88.2	91.5
Coppell, TX[20]	100.9	101.1	91.0	101.6	122.3	99.1	101.9
Cornelius, NC[21]	96.5	101.6	82.3	105.5	96.5	102.9	102.9
Cranberry, PA[22]	98.7	99.6	96.2	101.2	113.2	96.4	95.0
Cupertino, CA	n/a	n/a	n/a	n/a	n/a	n/a	n/a
Danville, CA[23]	147.2	128.5	228.0	106.6	124.5	114.4	110.5
Draper, UT[24]	96.4	96.1	93.9	83.8	110.8	92.2	98.4
Dublin, OH[25]	90.5	92.9	78.1	99.3	91.0	95.9	96.5
Eastchester, NY[26]	173.5	133.9	291.6	133.1	125.8	114.3	125.4
Eden Prairie, MN[27]	108.3	108.0	112.3	93.1	111.9	105.5	108.8
Edmond, OK	96.2	88.8	94.5	102.8	96.2	95.1	98.6
Evesham, NJ[28]	119.6	115.8	135.5	122.6	109.8	99.9	112.7
Fishers, IN[29]	91.2	92.9	82.4	90.9	91.8	99.3	96.8
Flower Mound, TX[30]	100.9	101.1	91.0	101.6	122.3	99.1	101.9
Folsom, CA[31]	115.2	118.6	138.4	77.3	118.1	98.7	107.2
Foster City, CA[32]	176.7	127.9	320.6	108.3	131.7	118.1	118.2
Franklin, TN[33]	95.3	95.7	82.4	97.6	97.9	86.6	105.7
Friendswood, TX[34]	91.3	82.1	90.1	101.5	90.7	100.4	91.7
Germantown, TN[35]	84.5	89.4	68.2	94.9	88.2	88.2	91.5
Glastonbury, CT[36]	124.5	129.7	133.0	129.4	110.4	118.2	119.2
Grand Blanc, MI	n/a	n/a	n/a	n/a	n/a	n/a	n/a
Guilderland, NY[37]	112.8	109.9	123.2	90.6	107.1	99.5	115.7
Hampden, PA[38]	98.9	97.2	90.1	115.7	89.1	91.3	106.1
Holly Springs, NC[39]	90.5	102.3	72.6	98.0	89.5	99.6	97.8
Huntersville, NC[40]	96.5	101.6	82.3	105.5	96.5	102.9	102.9
Independence, KY[41]	87.6	89.1	72.4	93.8	101.9	101.4	91.3
Johns Creek, GA[42]	99.9	103.7	97.8	93.6	104.8	101.4	100.4
Keller, TX[43]	102.8	91.6	99.7	95.2	100.8	101.7	113.1
Kirkland, WA[44]	140.5	124.6	184.6	107.8	120.9	120.6	128.8
Lafayette, CO	n/a	n/a	n/a	n/a	n/a	n/a	n/a
Lake Oswego, OR[45]	129.6	115.5	167.5	83.5	118.8	110.6	123.7
League City, TX[46]	91.3	82.1	90.1	101.5	90.7	100.4	91.7
Leawood, KS[47]	94.2	91.1	91.7	90.5	93.4	95.4	98.8
Lee's Summit, MO[48]	94.2	91.1	91.7	90.5	93.4	95.4	98.8
Leesburg, VA[49]	147.1	111.9	246.8	96.3	114.0	94.2	110.3
Lehi, UT	n/a	n/a	n/a	n/a	n/a	n/a	n/a
Lenexa, KS[50]	n/a	n/a	n/a	n/a	n/a	n/a	n/a
Lexington, MA[51]	136.8	111.7	192.6	102.8	109.0	123.3	121.3
Los Altos, CA	n/a	n/a	n/a	n/a	n/a	n/a	n/a
Lower Makefield, PA[52]	119.6	115.8	135.5	122.6	109.8	99.9	112.7
Madison, AL[53]	91.3	93.6	73.3	101.2	95.4	94.9	100.8
Mamaroneck, NY[54]	173.5	133.9	291.6	133.1	125.8	114.3	125.4
Manheim, PA	n/a	n/a	n/a	n/a	n/a	n/a	n/a
Manlius, NY	n/a	n/a	n/a	n/a	n/a	n/a	n/a
Maple Grove, MN[55]	108.3	108.0	112.3	93.1	111.9	105.5	108.8
Marion, IA[56]	94.7	95.6	85.2	105.9	95.1	100.6	97.9
Marlboro, NJ[57]	121.6	112.6	148.6	111.0	107.3	110.3	112.0
Mason, OH[58]	91.0	89.2	78.8	102.6	99.2	97.7	94.7
McCandless, PA[59]	98.7	99.6	96.2	101.2	113.2	96.4	95.0
Menomonee Falls, WI[60]	100.4	101.3	99.7	108.2	97.7	117.4	96.7

Table continued on next page.

Urban Area	Composite	Groceries	Housing	Utilities	Transp.	Health	Misc.
Meridian, ID[61]	90.9	84.5	80.1	85.2	105.3	105.5	97.5
Merrimack, NH[62]	118.3	111.0	123.2	137.3	104.5	116.3	116.2
Mount Lebanon, PA[63]	98.7	99.6	96.2	101.2	113.2	96.4	95.0
Mount Pleasant, SC[64]	101.0	106.6	96.5	115.5	91.4	106.4	100.6
Needham, MA[65]	144.5	105.0	194.5	151.8	109.8	130.4	129.1
Newtown, CT[66]	147.1	130.8	209.8	132.1	106.3	114.5	123.0
Northbrook, IL[67]	116.3	116.7	136.2	104.2	114.3	99.1	105.9
Northville, MI[68]	95.4	88.8	91.1	104.5	104.8	96.4	95.5
Novi, MI[69]	95.4	88.8	91.1	104.5	104.8	96.4	95.5
O'Fallon, IL[71]	92.5	104.6	72.3	116.6	98.5	99.8	94.3
O'Fallon, MO[70]	92.5	104.6	72.3	116.6	98.5	99.8	94.3
Orchard Park, NY[72]	95.4	91.6	101.8	98.3	102.0	86.3	89.6
Oviedo, FL[73]	98.3	104.8	95.7	95.9	102.0	95.0	97.8
Parker, CO[74]	109.7	99.2	130.7	94.6	98.2	107.8	104.9
Parkland, FL[75]	114.3	103.1	145.4	96.0	111.2	99.3	101.0
Peachtree City, GA[76]	99.9	103.7	97.8	93.6	104.8	101.4	100.4
Pflugerville, TX[77]	91.0	84.8	89.5	95.8	89.4	102.7	92.4
Plainfield, IL[78]	101.0	104.5	103.4	99.9	106.9	105.5	95.2
Princeton, NJ	n/a	n/a	n/a	n/a	n/a	n/a	n/a
Queen Creek, AZ[79]	95.9	98.5	95.1	96.7	99.8	97.2	93.9
Rancho Palos Verdes, CA[80]	140.4	106.3	214.1	115.7	132.4	109.3	106.0
Redmond, WA[81]	140.5	124.6	184.6	107.8	120.9	120.6	128.8
Richland, WA[82]	95.0	93.4	97.2	88.9	108.3	105.2	89.9
Ridgefield, CT[83]	147.1	130.8	209.8	132.1	106.3	114.5	123.0
Ridgewood, NJ[84]	128.8	112.9	172.2	111.2	106.9	107.6	113.9
Rio Rancho, NM[85]	96.0	94.2	96.9	92.0	101.6	97.3	95.0
Sahuarita, AZ[86]	92.9	96.7	83.5	91.5	96.7	103.6	97.0
Sammamish, WA[87]	140.5	124.6	184.6	107.8	120.9	120.6	128.8
San Ramon, CA[88]	147.2	128.5	228.0	106.6	124.5	114.4	110.5
Saratoga, CA	n/a	n/a	n/a	n/a	n/a	n/a	n/a
Schertz, TX[89]	87.3	83.5	74.1	87.2	83.9	94.4	100.2
Shrewsbury, MA	n/a	n/a	n/a	n/a	n/a	n/a	n/a
South Brunswick, NJ[90]	121.6	112.6	148.6	111.0	107.3	110.3	112.0
South Jordan, UT[91]	96.4	96.1	93.9	83.8	110.8	92.2	98.4
South Kingstown, RI[92]	123.4	118.6	136.5	125.8	105.8	114.8	120.6
South Windsor, CT[93]	124.5	129.7	133.0	129.4	110.4	118.2	119.2
Southlake, TX[94]	102.8	91.6	99.7	95.2	100.8	101.7	113.1
Spring Hill, TN[95]	95.3	95.7	82.4	97.6	97.9	86.6	105.7
Stow, OH[96]	101.3	117.0	110.3	93.7	104.6	90.4	90.0
Sugar Land, TX[97]	98.2	85.6	105.6	97.2	90.8	91.4	100.8
Sun Prairie, WI[98]	104.6	102.8	111.6	92.2	105.5	121.7	100.6
Syracuse, UT	n/a	n/a	n/a	n/a	n/a	n/a	n/a
Tredyffrin, PA[99]	119.6	115.8	135.5	122.6	109.8	99.9	112.7
Upper Arlington, OH[100]	90.5	92.9	78.1	99.3	91.0	95.9	96.5
Upper Dublin, PA[101]	119.6	115.8	135.5	122.6	109.8	99.9	112.7
Vestavia Hills, AL[102]	91.7	101.4	80.6	97.5	90.5	84.2	96.9
Webster, NY[103]	99.3	97.7	94.0	89.3	112.2	98.2	103.3
Wellesley, MA[104]	136.8	111.7	192.6	102.8	109.0	123.3	121.3
West Fargo, ND[105]	99.2	109.7	92.7	98.4	98.3	115.0	99.0
West Linn, OR[106]	129.6	115.5	167.5	83.5	118.8	110.6	123.7
West Windsor, NJ[107]	121.6	112.6	148.6	111.0	107.3	110.3	112.0
Westlake, OH[108]	101.2	108.8	93.7	100.3	99.2	108.7	104.6
Weston, FL[109]	114.3	103.1	145.4	96.0	111.2	99.3	101.0
Westport, CT[110]	147.1	130.8	209.8	132.1	106.3	114.5	123.0
Wilmette, IL[111]	116.3	116.7	136.2	104.2	114.3	99.1	105.9
Woodbury, MN[112]	108.3	108.0	112.3	93.1	111.9	105.5	108.8
Yorba Linda, CA[113]	148.8	107.6	244.7	113.9	135.0	107.6	104.8
U.S.	100.0	100.0	100.0	100.0	100.0	100.0	100.0

Note: The Cost of Living Index measures regional differences in the cost of consumer goods and services, excluding taxes and non-consumer expenditures, for professional and managerial households in the top income quintile. It is based on more than 50,000 prices covering almost 60 different items for which prices are collected three times a year by chambers of commerce, economic development organizations or university applied economic centers in each participating urban area. The numbers shown should be read as a percentage above or below the national average of 100. For example, a value of 115.4 in the groceries column indicates that grocery prices are 15.4% higher than the national average. Small differences in the index numbers should not be interpreted as significant. In cases where data is not available for the city, data for the metro area or for a neighboring city has been provided and noted as follows: (1) Orange County CA; (2) Plano TX; (3) Atlanta GA; (4) Des Moines IA; (5) Raleigh NC; (6) St. Louis MO-IL; (7) Dayton OH; (8) Fayetteville AR; (9) Newark-Elizabeth NJ; (10) Albany NY; (11) Detroit MI; (12) Bethesda-Gaithersburg-Frederick MD; (13) Nashville-Franklin TN; (14) Denver CO; (15) Indianapolis IN; (16) Austin TX; (17) New Haven CT; (18) St. Louis MO-IL; (19) Memphis TN; (20) Plano TX; (21) Charlotte NC; (22) Pittsburgh PA; (23) Oakland CA; (24) Salt Lake City UT; (25) Columbus OH; (26) Brooklyn NY; (27) Minneapolis MN; (28) Philadelphia PA; (29) Indianapolis IN; (30) Plano TX; (31) Sacramento CA; (32) San Francisco CA; (33) Nashville-Franklin TN; (34) Brazoria County TX; (35) Memphis TN; (36) Hartford CT; (37) Albany NY; (38) Harrisburg PA; (39) Raleigh NC; (40) Charlotte NC; (41) Covington KY; (42) Atlanta GA; (43) Fort Worth TX; (44) Seattle WA; (45) Portland OR; (46) Brazoria County TX; (47) Kansas City MO-KS; (48) Kansas City MO-KS; (49) Washington-Arlington-Alexandria DC-VA; (50) Kansas City MO-KS; (51) Framingham-Natick MA; (52) Philadelphia PA; (53) Huntsville AL; (54) Brooklyn NY; (55) Minneapolis MN; (56) Cedar Rapids IA; (57) Middlesex-Monmouth NJ; (58) Cincinnati OH; (59) Pittsburgh PA; (60) Milwaukee-Waukesha WI; (61) Boise ID; (62) Manchester NH; (63) Pittsburgh PA; (64) Charleston-N Charleston SC; (65) Boston MA; (66) Stamford CT; (67) Chicago IL; (68) Detroit MI; (69) Detroit MI; (71) St. Louis MO-IL; (70) St. Louis MO-IL; (72) Buffalo NY; (73) Orlando FL; (74) Denver CO; (75) Fort Lauderdale FL; (76) Atlanta GA; (77) Round Rock TX; (78) Joliet-Will County IL; (79) Phoenix AZ; (80) Los Angeles-Long Beach CA; (81) Seattle WA; (82) Kennewick-Richland-Pasco WA; (83) Stamford CT; (84) Bergen-Passaic NJ; (85) Albuquerque NM; (86) Tucson AZ; (87) Seattle WA; (88) Oakland CA; (89) San Antonio TX; (90) Middlesex-Monmouth NJ; (91) Salt Lake City UT; (92) Providence RI; (93) Hartford CT; (94) Fort Worth TX; (95) Nashville-Franklin TN; (96) Akron OH; (97) Houston TX; (98) Madison WI; (99) Philadelphia PA; (100) Columbus OH; (101) Philadelphia PA; (102) Birmingham AL; (103) Rochester NY; (104) Framingham-Natick MA; (105) Fargo-Moorhead ND-MN; (106) Portland OR; (107) Middlesex-Monmouth NJ; (108) Cleveland OH; (109) Fort Lauderdale FL; (110) Stamford CT; (111) Chicago IL; (112) Minneapolis MN; (113) Orange County CA

Source: The Council for Community and Economic Research (formerly ACCRA), Cost of Living Index, 2015

Grocery Prices

Urban Area	T-Bone Steak ($/pound)	Frying Chicken ($/pound)	Whole Milk ($/half gal.)	Eggs ($/dozen)	Orange Juice ($/64 oz.)	Coffee ($/11.5 oz.)
Aliso Viejo, CA[1]	11.16	1.48	2.43	3.59	3.52	5.35
Allen, TX[2]	10.11	2.04	2.16	2.16	4.02	4.49
Alpharetta, GA[3]	12.83	1.42	2.30	2.07	3.75	4.58
Ankeny, IA[4]	9.63	1.57	1.85	2.13	3.18	4.24
Apex, NC[5]	11.61	1.45	2.38	2.10	3.53	4.57
Ballwin, MO[6]	11.55	2.02	2.46	2.48	3.61	4.56
Beavercreek, OH[7]	10.65	1.59	2.21	2.21	3.36	4.26
Bella Vista, AR[8]	10.76	1.03	2.22	2.17	3.51	3.98
Bernards, NJ[9]	11.86	1.83	2.42	2.41	3.59	4.25
Bethlehem, NY[10]	10.16	1.66	2.40	2.65	3.43	4.40
Bloomfield, MI[11]	10.81	1.20	1.85	1.98	3.00	4.06
Bowie, MD[12]	11.56	1.66	2.44	2.17	3.53	4.34
Bozeman, MT	9.08	1.48	2.13	1.95	3.35	5.26
Brentwood, TN[13]	11.50	1.17	1.87	2.14	3.35	4.06
Broomfield, CO[14]	10.92	1.50	1.99	2.44	4.05	5.49
Carmel, IN[15]	10.31	1.17	1.90	2.07	3.54	4.18
Cedar Park, TX[16]	10.15	1.10	1.83	2.11	3.11	4.06
Cheshire, CT[17]	11.71	1.53	3.39	3.10	3.56	3.71
Chesterfield, MO[18]	11.55	2.02	2.46	2.48	3.61	4.56
Collierville, TN[19]	10.88	1.09	1.90	1.99	3.41	4.41
Coppell, TX[20]	10.11	2.04	2.16	2.16	4.02	4.49
Cornelius, NC[21]	11.68	1.44	2.34	2.03	3.48	4.15
Cranberry, PA[22]	11.46	1.75	1.98	1.91	3.75	4.66
Cupertino, CA	n/a	n/a	n/a	n/a	n/a	n/a
Danville, CA[23]	11.54	2.28	2.75	3.66	4.75	5.98
Draper, UT[24]	9.97	1.43	1.82	1.95	3.77	4.45
Dublin, OH[25]	12.50	1.17	1.87	1.82	3.33	5.25
Eastchester, NY[26]	12.62	2.28	2.45	2.47	4.21	5.58
Eden Prairie, MN[27]	14.13	1.90	2.26	1.92	3.78	4.64
Edmond, OK	10.92	1.25	2.41	2.19	3.14	3.55
Evesham, NJ[28]	12.16	1.43	2.14	2.61	3.93	4.50
Fishers, IN[29]	10.31	1.17	1.90	2.07	3.54	4.18
Flower Mound, TX[30]	10.11	2.04	2.16	2.16	4.02	4.49
Folsom, CA[31]	11.32	1.96	2.75	3.31	3.48	6.83
Foster City, CA[32]	11.33	1.96	2.77	3.55	4.55	5.99
Franklin, TN[33]	11.50	1.17	1.87	2.14	3.35	4.06
Friendswood, TX[34]	9.66	1.11	1.83	2.16	3.20	4.23
Germantown, TN[35]	10.88	1.09	1.90	1.99	3.41	4.41
Glastonbury, CT[36]	11.62	1.64	2.99	2.51	3.83	3.85
Grand Blanc, MI	n/a	n/a	n/a	n/a	n/a	n/a
Guilderland, NY[37]	10.16	1.66	2.40	2.65	3.43	4.40
Hampden, PA[38]	11.49	1.67	1.99	2.33	3.07	3.74
Holly Springs, NC[39]	11.61	1.45	2.38	2.10	3.53	4.57
Huntersville, NC[40]	11.68	1.44	2.34	2.03	3.48	4.15
Independence, KY[41]	10.69	1.28	2.07	2.03	3.35	3.76
Johns Creek, GA[42]	12.83	1.42	2.30	2.07	3.75	4.58
Keller, TX[43]	10.12	1.44	2.14	2.20	3.65	3.99
Kirkland, WA[44]	12.02	1.86	2.22	2.38	4.11	5.76
Lafayette, CO	n/a	n/a	n/a	n/a	n/a	n/a
Lake Oswego, OR[45]	9.89	1.97	2.17	2.49	3.59	5.75
League City, TX[46]	9.66	1.11	1.83	2.16	3.20	4.23
Leawood, KS[47]	10.00	1.19	2.17	2.15	3.06	4.46
Lee's Summit, MO[48]	10.00	1.19	2.17	2.15	3.06	4.46
Leesburg, VA[49]	12.08	1.63	2.47	2.41	3.55	4.83
Lehi, UT	n/a	n/a	n/a	n/a	n/a	n/a
Lenexa, KS[50]	n/a	n/a	n/a	n/a	n/a	n/a
Lexington, MA[51]	11.86	1.66	2.61	2.81	3.46	4.04
Los Altos, CA	n/a	n/a	n/a	n/a	n/a	n/a
Lower Makefield, PA[52]	12.16	1.43	2.14	2.61	3.93	4.50
Madison, AL[53]	11.50	1.21	2.07	2.10	3.30	4.19
Mamaroneck, NY[54]	12.62	2.28	2.45	2.47	4.21	5.58
Manheim, PA	n/a	n/a	n/a	n/a	n/a	n/a
Manlius, NY	n/a	n/a	n/a	n/a	n/a	n/a
Maple Grove, MN[55]	14.13	1.90	2.26	1.92	3.78	4.64
Marion, IA[56]	9.22	1.79	2.28	2.16	3.58	4.00
Marlboro, NJ[57]	11.40	1.64	2.56	2.58	3.66	4.19
Mason, OH[58]	11.08	1.05	1.30	2.08	3.42	4.27
McCandless, PA[59]	11.46	1.75	1.98	1.91	3.75	4.66
Menomonee Falls, WI[60]	12.29	1.78	2.07	2.70	4.02	4.22
Meridian, ID[61]	9.95	1.05	1.76	1.86	3.51	4.68

Table continued on next page.

Urban Area	T-Bone Steak ($/pound)	Frying Chicken ($/pound)	Whole Milk ($/half gal.)	Eggs ($/dozen)	Orange Juice ($/64 oz.)	Coffee ($/11.5 oz.)
Merrimack, NH[62]	11.15	1.45	2.81	2.79	3.30	4.97
Mount Lebanon, PA[63]	11.46	1.75	1.98	1.91	3.75	4.66
Mount Pleasant, SC[64]	11.26	1.65	2.31	2.42	3.68	4.67
Needham, MA[65]	10.99	1.78	2.21	2.39	3.63	4.46
Newtown, CT[66]	12.44	1.35	2.89	3.05	4.21	5.49
Northbrook, IL[67]	11.95	1.43	2.39	2.82	4.05	4.92
Northville, MI[68]	10.81	1.20	1.85	1.98	3.00	4.06
Novi, MI[69]	10.81	1.20	1.85	1.98	3.00	4.06
O'Fallon, IL[71]	11.55	2.02	2.46	2.48	3.61	4.56
O'Fallon, MO[70]	11.55	2.02	2.46	2.48	3.61	4.56
Orchard Park, NY[72]	13.05	1.31	1.89	2.20	2.96	3.93
Oviedo, FL[73]	11.81	1.52	2.59	2.53	3.38	3.81
Parker, CO[74]	10.92	1.50	1.99	2.44	4.05	5.49
Parkland, FL[75]	12.46	1.41	2.75	2.44	3.59	2.98
Peachtree City, GA[76]	12.83	1.42	2.30	2.07	3.75	4.58
Pflugerville, TX[77]	10.16	1.04	2.54	2.18	3.08	4.02
Plainfield, IL[78]	10.28	1.45	2.45	1.97	3.60	6.03
Princeton, NJ	n/a	n/a	n/a	n/a	n/a	n/a
Queen Creek, AZ[79]	11.14	1.83	1.73	2.12	3.69	4.68
Rancho Palos Verdes, CA[80]	11.05	1.56	2.35	3.38	3.54	5.27
Redmond, WA[81]	12.02	1.86	2.22	2.38	4.11	5.76
Richland, WA[82]	10.53	1.32	2.26	2.08	3.36	4.95
Ridgefield, CT[83]	12.44	1.35	2.89	3.05	4.21	5.49
Ridgewood, NJ[84]	12.02	1.69	2.46	2.46	3.70	4.22
Rio Rancho, NM[85]	9.98	1.61	1.74	2.12	3.14	4.87
Sahuarita, AZ[86]	11.20	1.31	1.68	2.12	3.28	4.88
Sammamish, WA[87]	12.02	1.86	2.22	2.38	4.11	5.76
San Ramon, CA[88]	11.54	2.28	2.75	3.66	4.75	5.98
Saratoga, CA	n/a	n/a	n/a	n/a	n/a	n/a
Schertz, TX[89]	8.68	1.23	2.09	2.12	2.88	3.79
Shrewsbury, MA	n/a	n/a	n/a	n/a	n/a	n/a
South Brunswick, NJ[90]	11.40	1.64	2.56	2.58	3.66	4.19
South Jordan, UT[91]	9.97	1.43	1.82	1.95	3.77	4.45
South Kingstown, RI[92]	11.97	1.59	3.22	3.12	3.75	5.02
South Windsor, CT[93]	11.62	1.64	2.99	2.51	3.83	3.85
Southlake, TX[94]	10.12	1.44	2.14	2.20	3.65	3.99
Spring Hill, TN[95]	11.50	1.17	1.87	2.14	3.35	4.06
Stow, OH[96]	10.20	1.98	2.74	1.87	3.92	5.42
Sugar Land, TX[97]	9.52	1.17	1.76	2.14	3.23	4.34
Sun Prairie, WI[98]	10.58	2.05	2.22	1.94	3.64	4.92
Syracuse, UT	n/a	n/a	n/a	n/a	n/a	n/a
Tredyffrin, PA[99]	12.16	1.43	2.14	2.61	3.93	4.50
Upper Arlington, OH[100]	12.50	1.17	1.87	1.82	3.33	5.25
Upper Dublin, PA[101]	12.16	1.43	2.14	2.61	3.93	4.50
Vestavia Hills, AL[102]	10.25	1.32	2.45	2.44	4.14	4.19
Webster, NY[103]	13.66	1.57	2.14	2.34	3.47	4.11
Wellesley, MA[104]	11.86	1.66	2.61	2.81	3.46	4.04
West Fargo, ND[105]	10.55	1.51	3.13	2.73	4.29	4.81
West Linn, OR[106]	9.89	1.97	2.17	2.49	3.59	5.75
West Windsor, NJ[107]	11.40	1.64	2.56	2.58	3.66	4.19
Westlake, OH[108]	13.34	1.73	2.56	2.16	3.81	4.87
Weston, FL[109]	12.46	1.41	2.75	2.44	3.59	2.98
Westport, CT[110]	12.44	1.35	2.89	3.05	4.21	5.49
Wilmette, IL[111]	11.95	1.43	2.39	2.82	4.05	4.92
Woodbury, MN[112]	14.13	1.90	2.26	1.92	3.78	4.64
Yorba Linda, CA[113]	11.16	1.48	2.43	3.59	3.52	5.35
Average*	10.99	1.43	2.25	2.26	3.58	4.48
Minimum*	7.16	0.98	1.30	1.35	2.88	2.98
Maximum*	14.13	2.43	3.85	4.81	6.39	7.56

Note: T-Bone Steak (price per pound); Frying Chicken (price per pound, whole fryer); Whole Milk (half gallon carton); Eggs (price per dozen, Grade A, large); Orange Juice (64 oz. Tropicana or Florida Natural); Coffee (11.5 oz. can, vacuum-packed, Maxwell House, Hills Bros, or Folgers); (*) Values for the local area are compared with the average, minimum, and maximum values for all 308 areas in the Cost of Living Index report; n/a not available; In cases where data is not available for the city, data for the metro area or for a neighboring city has been provided and noted as follows: (1) Orange County CA; (2) Plano TX; (3) Atlanta GA; (4) Des Moines IA; (5) Raleigh NC; (6) St. Louis MO-IL; (7) Dayton OH; (8) Fayetteville AR; (9) Newark-Elizabeth NJ; (10) Albany NY; (11) Detroit MI; (12) Bethesda-Gaithersburg-Frederick MD; (13) Nashville-Franklin TN; (14) Denver CO; (15) Indianapolis IN; (16) Austin TX; (17) New Haven CT; (18) St. Louis MO-IL; (19) Memphis TN; (20) Plano TX; (21) Charlotte NC; (22) Pittsburgh PA; (23) Oakland CA; (24) Salt Lake City UT; (25) Columbus OH; (26) Brooklyn NY; (27) Minneapolis MN; (28) Philadelphia PA; (29) Indianapolis IN; (30) Plano TX; (31) Sacramento CA; (32) San Francisco CA; (33) Nashville-Franklin TN; (34) Brazoria County TX; (35) Memphis TN; (36) Hartford CT; (37) Albany NY; (38) Harrisburg PA; (39) Raleigh NC; (40) Charlotte NC; (41) Covington KY; (42) Atlanta GA; (43) Fort Worth TX; (44) Seattle WA; (45) Portland OR; (46) Brazoria County TX; (47) Kansas City MO-KS; (48) Kansas City MO-KS; (49) Washington-Arlington-Alexandria DC-VA; (50) Kansas City MO-KS; (51) Framingham-Natick MA; (52) Philadelphia PA; (53) Huntsville AL; (54) Brooklyn NY; (55) Minneapolis MN; (56) Cedar Rapids IA; (57) Middlesex-Monmouth NJ; (58) Cincinnati OH; (59) Pittsburgh PA; (60) Milwaukee-Waukesha WI; (61) Boise ID; (62) Manchester NH; (63) Pittsburgh PA; (64) Charleston-N Charleston SC; (65) Boston MA; (66) Stamford CT; (67) Chicago IL; (68) Detroit MI; (69) Detroit MI; (71) St. Louis MO-IL; (70) St. Louis MO-IL; (72) Buffalo NY; (73) Orlando FL; (74) Denver CO; (75) Fort Lauderdale FL; (76) Atlanta GA; (77) Round Rock TX; (78) Joliet-Will County IL; (79) Phoenix AZ; (80) Los Angeles-Long Beach CA; (81) Seattle WA; (82) Kennewick-Richland-Pasco WA; (83) Stamford CT; (84) Bergen-Passaic NJ; (85) Albuquerque NM; (86) Tucson AZ; (87) Seattle WA; (88) Oakland CA; (89) San Antonio TX; (90) Middlesex-Monmouth NJ; (91) Salt Lake City UT; (92) Providence RI; (93) Hartford CT; (94) Fort Worth TX; (95) Nashville-Franklin TN; (96) Akron OH; (97) Houston TX; (98) Madison WI; (99) Philadelphia PA; (100) Columbus OH; (101) Philadelphia PA; (102) Birmingham AL; (103) Rochester NY; (104) Framingham-Natick MA; (105) Fargo-Moorhead ND-MN; (106) Portland OR; (107) Middlesex-Monmouth NJ; (108) Cleveland OH; (109) Fort Lauderdale FL; (110) Stamford CT; (111) Chicago IL; (112) Minneapolis MN; (113) Orange County CA

Source: The Council for Community and Economic Research (formerly ACCRA), Cost of Living Index, 2015

Housing and Utility Costs

Urban Area	New Home Price ($)	Apartment Rent ($/month)	All Electric ($/month)	Part Electric ($/month)	Other Energy ($/month)	Telephone ($/month)
Aliso Viejo, CA[1]	809,108	1,998	-	129.72	57.14	33.57
Allen, TX[2]	265,095	1,005	-	122.11	55.60	27.38
Alpharetta, GA[3]	289,012	1,050	-	88.79	57.58	29.30
Ankeny, IA[4]	288,831	651	-	75.11	60.31	29.30
Apex, NC[5]	221,534	717	-	92.53	55.26	31.99
Ballwin, MO[6]	207,522	832	-	95.19	70.93	40.32
Beavercreek, OH[7]	229,972	756	-	70.85	59.10	34.95
Bella Vista, AR[8]	250,223	642	-	79.71	78.12	33.40
Bernards, NJ[9]	512,478	1,530	-	122.38	70.98	32.25
Bethlehem, NY[10]	397,061	1,123	-	89.88	71.82	23.65
Bloomfield, MI[11]	269,215	955	-	108.88	66.14	30.00
Bowie, MD[12]	652,136	1,732	-	106.79	73.56	26.86
Bozeman, MT	363,664	995	-	80.72	88.31	18.46
Brentwood, TN[13]	237,572	913	-	101.02	77.31	24.50
Broomfield, CO[14]	398,144	1,306	-	92.34	59.91	28.60
Carmel, IN[15]	236,995	950	-	78.56	75.38	25.68
Cedar Park, TX[16]	255,904	1,073	-	114.72	43.11	32.03
Cheshire, CT[17]	438,228	1,355	-	109.68	81.09	24.00
Chesterfield, MO[18]	207,522	832	-	95.19	70.93	40.32
Collierville, TN[19]	203,013	694	-	89.14	54.91	30.75
Coppell, TX[20]	265,095	1,005	-	122.11	55.60	27.38
Cornelius, NC[21]	244,547	880	170.61	-	-	31.67
Cranberry, PA[22]	279,873	1,068	-	100.25	100.22	21.74
Cupertino, CA	n/a	n/a	n/a	n/a	n/a	n/a
Danville, CA[23]	747,967	1,912	-	129.66	75.31	24.33
Draper, UT[24]	295,695	894	-	74.45	73.10	22.33
Dublin, OH[25]	231,820	835	-	94.43	73.91	27.99
Eastchester, NY[26]	963,047	2,337	-	116.78	139.53	30.33
Eden Prairie, MN[27]	345,759	1,098	-	93.62	69.52	24.99
Edmond, OK	296,318	921	-	82.21	74.11	33.24
Evesham, NJ[28]	419,996	1,304	-	113.50	73.49	39.51
Fishers, IN[29]	236,995	950	-	78.56	75.38	25.68
Flower Mound, TX[30]	265,095	1,005	-	122.11	55.60	27.38
Folsom, CA[31]	398,011	1,575	-	99.01	37.79	20.43
Foster City, CA[32]	978,744	3,230	-	135.14	75.78	24.12
Franklin, TN[33]	237,572	913	-	101.02	77.31	24.50
Friendswood, TX[34]	263,601	998	-	104.32	63.25	29.66
Germantown, TN[35]	203,013	694	-	89.14	54.91	30.75
Glastonbury, CT[36]	429,480	1,123	-	148.46	119.90	24.95
Grand Blanc, MI	n/a	n/a	n/a	n/a	n/a	n/a
Guilderland, NY[37]	397,061	1,123	-	89.88	71.82	23.65
Hampden, PA[38]	276,979	875	203.34	-	-	30.91
Holly Springs, NC[39]	221,534	717	-	92.53	55.26	31.99
Huntersville, NC[40]	244,547	880	170.61	-	-	31.67
Independence, KY[41]	224,020	725	-	64.47	79.49	30.01
Johns Creek, GA[42]	289,012	1,050	-	88.79	57.58	29.30
Keller, TX[43]	247,911	1,429	-	122.03	52.89	23.67
Kirkland, WA[44]	548,187	1,980	178.75	-	-	31.32
Lafayette, CO	n/a	n/a	n/a	n/a	n/a	n/a
Lake Oswego, OR[45]	439,773	2,211	-	74.74	76.31	21.34
League City, TX[46]	263,601	998	-	104.32	63.25	29.66
Leawood, KS[47]	291,595	835	-	85.41	77.39	23.34
Lee's Summit, MO[48]	291,595	835	-	85.41	77.39	23.34
Leesburg, VA[49]	801,674	2,092	-	81.62	80.95	27.32
Lehi, UT	n/a	n/a	n/a	n/a	n/a	n/a
Lenexa, KS[50]	n/a	n/a	n/a	n/a	n/a	n/a
Lexington, MA[51]	592,300	1,888	-	57.91	106.18	31.39
Los Altos, CA	n/a	n/a	n/a	n/a	n/a	n/a
Lower Makefield, PA[52]	419,996	1,304	-	113.50	73.49	39.51
Madison, AL[53]	219,464	778	153.20	-	-	32.84
Mamaroneck, NY[54]	963,047	2,337	-	116.78	139.53	30.33
Manheim, PA	n/a	n/a	n/a	n/a	n/a	n/a
Manlius, NY	n/a	n/a	n/a	n/a	n/a	n/a
Maple Grove, MN[55]	345,759	1,098	-	93.62	69.52	24.99
Marion, IA[56]	267,450	776	-	125.54	57.75	29.00
Marlboro, NJ[57]	467,078	1,393	-	120.17	63.96	32.25
Mason, OH[58]	232,736	857	-	108.97	81.78	24.99
McCandless, PA[59]	279,873	1,068	-	100.25	100.22	21.74
Menomonee Falls, WI[60]	322,327	877	-	99.46	70.33	33.76
Meridian, ID[61]	258,125	700	-	70.21	70.23	24.99

Table continued on next page.

Urban Area	New Home Price ($)	Apartment Rent ($/month)	All Electric ($/month)	Part Electric ($/month)	Other Energy ($/month)	Telephone ($/month)
Merrimack, NH[62]	362,649	1,318	-	114.46	128.88	36.25
Mount Lebanon, PA[63]	279,873	1,068	-	100.25	100.22	21.74
Mount Pleasant, SC[64]	272,824	1,147	211.29	-	-	28.92
Needham, MA[65]	553,220	2,262	-	151.70	140.48	34.64
Newtown, CT[66]	626,189	2,199	-	147.95	111.00	29.01
Northbrook, IL[67]	431,884	1,236	-	97.38	76.61	30.05
Northville, MI[68]	269,215	955	-	108.88	66.14	30.00
Novi, MI[69]	269,215	955	-	108.88	66.14	30.00
O'Fallon, IL[71]	207,522	832	-	95.19	70.93	40.32
O'Fallon, MO[70]	207,522	832	-	95.19	70.93	40.32
Orchard Park, NY[72]	345,149	789	-	87.45	81.33	27.21
Oviedo, FL[73]	287,272	958	178.39	-	-	23.31
Parker, CO[74]	398,144	1,306	-	92.34	59.91	28.60
Parkland, FL[75]	443,005	1,483	161.87	-	-	27.31
Peachtree City, GA[76]	289,012	1,050	-	88.79	57.58	29.30
Pflugerville, TX[77]	254,738	1,044	-	121.69	52.80	24.15
Plainfield, IL[78]	295,329	1,196	-	98.64	78.21	26.41
Princeton, NJ	n/a	n/a	n/a	n/a	n/a	n/a
Queen Creek, AZ[79]	292,558	880	194.92	-	-	19.99
Rancho Palos Verdes, CA[80]	617,169	2,420	-	134.81	57.31	33.57
Redmond, WA[81]	548,187	1,980	178.75	-	-	31.32
Richland, WA[82]	319,328	793	135.02	-	-	28.75
Ridgefield, CT[83]	626,189	2,199	-	147.95	111.00	29.01
Ridgewood, NJ[84]	521,477	1,727	-	122.00	62.66	32.25
Rio Rancho, NM[85]	296,671	948	-	120.52	51.03	22.26
Sahuarita, AZ[86]	253,513	839	-	103.26	63.52	23.09
Sammamish, WA[87]	548,187	1,980	178.75	-	-	31.32
San Ramon, CA[88]	747,967	1,912	-	129.66	75.31	24.33
Saratoga, CA	n/a	n/a	n/a	n/a	n/a	n/a
Schertz, TX[89]	208,293	848	-	96.27	37.03	28.01
Shrewsbury, MA	n/a	n/a	n/a	n/a	n/a	n/a
South Brunswick, NJ[90]	467,078	1,393	-	120.17	63.96	32.25
South Jordan, UT[91]	295,695	894	-	74.45	73.10	22.33
South Kingstown, RI[92]	399,678	1,473	-	112.75	97.49	36.19
South Windsor, CT[93]	429,480	1,123	-	148.46	119.90	24.95
Southlake, TX[94]	247,911	1,429	-	122.03	52.89	23.67
Spring Hill, TN[95]	237,572	913	-	101.02	77.31	24.50
Stow, OH[96]	377,533	767	-	54.45	96.52	28.30
Sugar Land, TX[97]	288,271	1,328	-	115.19	42.89	29.01
Sun Prairie, WI[98]	362,264	958	-	106.11	75.77	19.99
Syracuse, UT	n/a	n/a	n/a	n/a	n/a	n/a
Tredyffrin, PA[99]	419,996	1,304	-	113.50	73.49	39.51
Upper Arlington, OH[100]	231,820	835	-	94.43	73.91	27.99
Upper Dublin, PA[101]	419,996	1,304	-	113.50	73.49	39.51
Vestavia Hills, AL[102]	243,880	833	-	103.98	74.91	24.33
Webster, NY[103]	275,153	1,023	-	44.32	95.44	27.95
Wellesley, MA[104]	592,300	1,888	-	57.91	106.18	31.39
West Fargo, ND[105]	289,825	897	-	75.18	83.93	29.55
West Linn, OR[106]	439,773	2,211	-	74.74	76.31	21.34
West Windsor, NJ[107]	467,078	1,393	-	120.17	63.96	32.25
Westlake, OH[108]	276,479	983	-	69.04	90.29	30.79
Weston, FL[109]	443,005	1,483	161.87	-	-	27.31
Westport, CT[110]	626,189	2,199	-	147.95	111.00	29.01
Wilmette, IL[111]	431,884	1,236	-	97.38	76.61	30.05
Woodbury, MN[112]	345,759	1,098	-	93.62	69.52	24.99
Yorba Linda, CA[113]	809,108	1,998	-	129.72	57.14	33.57
Average*	312,874	945	179.30	95.07	72.96	28.11
Minimum*	178,682	479	116.28	43.14	26.46	10.01
Maximum*	1,472,476	3,984	504.25	189.44	421.11	43.06

Note: New Home Price (2,400 sf living area, 8,000 sf lot, in urban area with full utilities); Apartment Rent (950 sf 2 bedroom/1.5 or 2 bath, unfurnished, excluding all utilities except water); All Electric (average monthly cost for an all-electric home); Part Electric (average monthly cost for a part-electric home); Other Energy (average monthly cost for natural gas, fuel oil, coal, wood, and any other forms of energy except electricity); Telephone (price includes basic monthly rate for a private residential line plus additional local usage charges incurred by a family of four); (*) Values for the local area are compared with the average, minimum, and maximum values for all 308 areas in the Cost of Living Index report; n/a not available; In cases where data is not available for the city, data for the metro area or for a neighboring city has been provided and noted as follows: (1) Orange County CA; (2) Plano TX; (3) Atlanta GA; (4) Des Moines IA; (5) Raleigh NC; (6) St. Louis MO-IL; (7) Dayton OH; (8) Fayetteville AR; (9) Newark-Elizabeth NJ; (10) Albany NY; (11) Detroit MI; (12) Bethesda-Gaithersburg-Frederick MD; (13) Nashville-Franklin TN; (14) Denver CO; (15) Indianapolis IN; (16) Austin TX; (17) New Haven CT; (18) St. Louis MO-IL; (19) Memphis TN; (20) Plano TX; (21) Charlotte NC; (22) Pittsburgh PA; (23) Oakland CA; (24) Salt Lake City UT; (25) Columbus OH; (26) Brooklyn NY; (27) Minneapolis MN; (28) Philadelphia PA; (29) Indianapolis IN; (30) Plano TX; (31) Sacramento CA; (32) San Francisco CA; (33) Nashville-Franklin TN; (34) Brazoria County TX; (35) Memphis TN; (36) Hartford CT; (37) Albany NY; (38) Harrisburg PA; (39) Raleigh NC; (40) Charlotte NC; (41) Covington KY; (42) Atlanta GA; (43) Fort Worth TX; (44) Seattle WA; (45) Portland OR; (46) Brazoria County TX; (47) Kansas City MO-KS; (48) Kansas City MO-KS; (49) Washington-Arlington-Alexandria DC-VA; (50) Kansas City MO-KS; (51) Framingham-Natick MA; (52) Philadelphia PA; (53) Huntsville AL; (54) Brooklyn NY; (55) Minneapolis MN; (56) Cedar Rapids IA; (57) Middlesex-Monmouth NJ; (58) Cincinnati OH; (59) Pittsburgh PA; (60) Milwaukee-Waukesha WI; (61) Boise ID; (62) Manchester NH; (63) Pittsburgh PA; (64) Charleston-N Charleston SC; (65) Boston MA; (66) Stamford CT; (67) Chicago IL; (68) Detroit MI; (69) Detroit MI; (71) St. Louis MO-IL; (70) St. Louis MO-IL; (72) Buffalo NY; (73) Orlando FL; (74) Denver CO; (75) Fort Lauderdale FL; (76) Atlanta GA; (77) Round Rock TX; (78) Joliet-Will County IL; (79) Phoenix AZ; (80) Los Angeles-Long Beach CA; (81) Seattle WA; (82) Kennewick-Richland-Pasco WA; (83) Stamford CT; (84) Bergen-Passaic NJ; (85) Albuquerque NM; (86) Tucson AZ; (87) Seattle WA; (88) Oakland CA; (89) San Antonio TX; (90) Middlesex-Monmouth NJ; (91) Salt Lake City UT; (92) Providence RI; (93) Hartford CT; (94) Fort Worth TX; (95) Nashville-Franklin TN; (96) Akron OH; (97) Houston TX; (98) Madison WI; (99) Philadelphia PA; (100) Columbus OH; (101) Philadelphia PA; (102) Birmingham AL; (103) Rochester NY; (104) Framingham-Natick MA; (105) Fargo-Moorhead ND-MN; (106) Portland OR; (107) Middlesex-Monmouth NJ; (108) Cleveland OH; (109) Fort Lauderdale FL; (110) Stamford CT; (111) Chicago IL; (112) Minneapolis MN; (113) Orange County CA

Source: The Council for Community and Economic Research (formerly ACCRA), Cost of Living Index, 2015

Health Care, Transportation, and Other Costs

Urban Area	Doctor ($/visit)	Dentist ($/visit)	Optometrist ($/visit)	Gasoline ($/gallon)	Beauty Salon ($/visit)	Men's Shirt ($)
Aliso Viejo, CA[1]	96.52	104.00	101.81	3.38	59.39	26.79
Allen, TX[2]	110.27	85.39	102.34	2.99	36.49	25.90
Alpharetta, GA[3]	95.50	102.54	89.05	2.46	45.03	24.26
Ankeny, IA[4]	122.87	76.90	95.35	2.20	27.14	18.18
Apex, NC[5]	95.90	100.93	100.47	2.22	40.52	23.52
Ballwin, MO[6]	94.95	91.43	83.95	2.31	35.77	23.78
Beavercreek, OH[7]	78.17	79.67	92.73	2.38	51.02	31.90
Bella Vista, AR[8]	91.43	78.47	93.33	2.14	32.26	16.03
Bernards, NJ[9]	90.00	107.42	94.00	2.40	33.38	39.38
Bethlehem, NY[10]	103.13	92.42	88.87	2.61	42.00	42.52
Bloomfield, MI[11]	100.13	86.47	79.43	2.44	47.83	21.95
Bowie, MD[12]	70.27	81.75	72.39	2.58	47.00	32.38
Bozeman, MT	132.50	81.41	99.01	2.42	35.60	19.66
Brentwood, TN[13]	80.64	79.53	76.03	2.23	34.13	26.96
Broomfield, CO[14]	125.38	97.33	101.85	2.29	35.84	29.52
Carmel, IN[15]	95.01	90.00	87.83	2.28	28.73	37.94
Cedar Park, TX[16]	103.05	93.88	124.00	2.22	48.22	26.75
Cheshire, CT[17]	126.59	111.48	117.01	2.52	52.93	29.98
Chesterfield, MO[18]	94.95	91.43	83.95	2.31	35.77	23.78
Collierville, TN[19]	86.77	81.25	68.33	2.13	26.88	23.75
Coppell, TX[20]	110.27	85.39	102.34	2.99	36.49	25.90
Cornelius, NC[21]	99.40	97.23	118.48	2.39	36.82	33.83
Cranberry, PA[22]	92.67	84.22	87.11	2.68	40.30	25.12
Cupertino, CA	n/a	n/a	n/a	n/a	n/a	n/a
Danville, CA[23]	123.63	113.02	116.21	3.13	55.17	35.17
Draper, UT[24]	96.03	77.91	93.12	2.54	36.55	26.36
Dublin, OH[25]	104.66	96.39	57.71	2.21	32.93	23.65
Eastchester, NY[26]	114.33	115.09	97.67	2.75	64.44	25.75
Eden Prairie, MN[27]	133.87	84.35	82.36	2.62	33.40	30.95
Edmond, OK	96.33	81.63	110.46	2.02	33.82	28.83
Evesham, NJ[28]	119.17	95.44	104.35	2.53	51.48	40.96
Fishers, IN[29]	95.01	90.00	87.83	2.28	28.73	37.94
Flower Mound, TX[30]	110.27	85.39	102.34	2.99	36.49	25.90
Folsom, CA[31]	92.46	87.18	109.14	2.97	42.32	31.24
Foster City, CA[32]	125.52	119.23	121.18	3.24	61.93	37.26
Franklin, TN[33]	80.64	79.53	76.03	2.23	34.13	26.96
Friendswood, TX[34]	101.09	91.48	100.73	2.20	28.27	35.72
Germantown, TN[35]	86.77	81.25	68.33	2.13	26.88	23.75
Glastonbury, CT[36]	123.77	122.94	116.73	2.57	47.06	26.88
Grand Blanc, MI	n/a	n/a	n/a	n/a	n/a	n/a
Guilderland, NY[37]	103.13	92.42	88.87	2.61	42.00	42.52
Hampden, PA[38]	89.59	83.97	51.43	2.12	27.70	28.15
Holly Springs, NC[39]	95.90	100.93	100.47	2.22	40.52	23.52
Huntersville, NC[40]	99.40	97.23	118.48	2.39	36.82	33.83
Independence, KY[41]	92.47	101.64	101.00	2.40	31.88	21.32
Johns Creek, GA[42]	95.50	102.54	89.05	2.46	45.03	24.26
Keller, TX[43]	108.96	95.72	87.06	2.36	57.07	44.34
Kirkland, WA[44]	114.72	125.99	139.39	2.87	52.26	32.17
Lafayette, CO	n/a	n/a	n/a	n/a	n/a	n/a
Lake Oswego, OR[45]	133.08	99.07	124.06	2.89	50.33	33.26
League City, TX[46]	101.09	91.48	100.73	2.20	28.27	35.72
Leawood, KS[47]	93.36	87.39	94.68	2.16	31.21	28.60
Lee's Summit, MO[48]	93.36	87.39	94.68	2.16	31.21	28.60
Leesburg, VA[49]	88.18	88.13	72.50	2.72	58.04	32.37
Lehi, UT	n/a	n/a	n/a	n/a	n/a	n/a
Lenexa, KS[50]	n/a	n/a	n/a	n/a	n/a	n/a
Lexington, MA[51]	163.83	108.44	119.59	2.47	48.68	45.26
Los Altos, CA	n/a	n/a	n/a	n/a	n/a	n/a
Lower Makefield, PA[52]	119.17	95.44	104.35	2.53	51.48	40.96
Madison, AL[53]	78.61	91.92	111.44	2.21	33.47	31.00
Mamaroneck, NY[54]	114.33	115.09	97.67	2.75	64.44	25.75
Manheim, PA	n/a	n/a	n/a	n/a	n/a	n/a
Manlius, NY	n/a	n/a	n/a	n/a	n/a	n/a
Maple Grove, MN[55]	133.87	84.35	82.36	2.62	33.40	30.95
Marion, IA[56]	131.25	73.83	126.22	2.25	35.73	22.57
Marlboro, NJ[57]	86.08	115.37	101.58	2.38	33.58	37.72
Mason, OH[58]	96.44	87.39	89.32	2.37	31.50	20.98
McCandless, PA[59]	92.67	84.22	87.11	2.68	40.30	25.12
Menomonee Falls, WI[60]	182.34	91.28	52.76	2.43	31.59	26.07
Meridian, ID[61]	128.96	87.20	117.98	2.47	30.63	25.65

Table continued on next page.

Urban Area	Doctor ($/visit)	Dentist ($/visit)	Optometrist ($/visit)	Gasoline ($/gallon)	Beauty Salon ($/visit)	Men's Shirt ($)
Merrimack, NH[62]	149.18	104.81	100.39	2.43	40.03	28.58
Mount Lebanon, PA[63]	92.67	84.22	87.11	2.68	40.30	25.12
Mount Pleasant, SC[64]	106.73	103.50	104.64	2.23	41.10	33.92
Needham, MA[65]	165.53	120.84	109.50	2.42	51.60	31.55
Newtown, CT[66]	123.75	110.00	111.67	2.47	64.17	27.43
Northbrook, IL[67]	99.17	99.44	95.00	2.70	45.00	25.27
Northville, MI[68]	100.13	86.47	79.43	2.44	47.83	21.95
Novi, MI[69]	100.13	86.47	79.43	2.44	47.83	21.95
O'Fallon, IL[71]	94.95	91.43	83.95	2.31	35.77	23.78
O'Fallon, MO[70]	94.95	91.43	83.95	2.31	35.77	23.78
Orchard Park, NY[72]	82.12	76.49	57.69	2.67	26.74	20.24
Oviedo, FL[73]	85.45	88.74	64.24	2.41	40.70	22.40
Parker, CO[74]	125.38	97.33	101.85	2.29	35.84	29.52
Parkland, FL[75]	85.67	89.45	90.43	2.49	52.58	25.80
Peachtree City, GA[76]	95.50	102.54	89.05	2.46	45.03	24.26
Pflugerville, TX[77]	109.00	93.33	100.51	2.10	38.89	18.66
Plainfield, IL[78]	131.40	84.25	109.32	2.50	36.01	22.71
Princeton, NJ	n/a	n/a	n/a	n/a	n/a	n/a
Queen Creek, AZ[79]	97.83	98.67	84.67	2.49	28.33	23.10
Rancho Palos Verdes, CA[80]	98.29	105.22	121.62	3.39	59.95	25.91
Redmond, WA[81]	114.72	125.99	139.39	2.87	52.26	32.17
Richland, WA[82]	117.67	108.47	103.40	2.53	34.53	19.92
Ridgefield, CT[83]	123.75	110.00	111.67	2.47	64.17	27.43
Ridgewood, NJ[84]	99.07	98.83	113.17	2.35	38.27	40.11
Rio Rancho, NM[85]	90.15	94.77	98.91	2.35	41.03	29.12
Sahuarita, AZ[86]	121.93	89.60	91.60	2.23	43.60	34.05
Sammamish, WA[87]	114.72	125.99	139.39	2.87	52.26	32.17
San Ramon, CA[88]	123.63	113.02	116.21	3.13	55.17	35.17
Saratoga, CA	n/a	n/a	n/a	n/a	n/a	n/a
Schertz, TX[89]	98.06	82.29	91.22	2.06	37.50	29.25
Shrewsbury, MA	n/a	n/a	n/a	n/a	n/a	n/a
South Brunswick, NJ[90]	86.08	115.37	101.58	2.38	33.58	37.72
South Jordan, UT[91]	96.03	77.91	93.12	2.54	36.55	26.36
South Kingstown, RI[92]	149.00	98.00	125.00	2.51	41.67	31.67
South Windsor, CT[93]	123.77	122.94	116.73	2.57	47.06	26.88
Southlake, TX[94]	108.96	95.72	87.06	2.36	57.07	44.34
Spring Hill, TN[95]	80.64	79.53	76.03	2.23	34.13	26.96
Stow, OH[96]	85.13	73.53	76.20	2.34	32.80	22.84
Sugar Land, TX[97]	82.63	85.82	92.74	2.24	49.96	36.38
Sun Prairie, WI[98]	173.00	99.11	64.11	2.35	40.78	29.61
Syracuse, UT	n/a	n/a	n/a	n/a	n/a	n/a
Tredyffrin, PA[99]	119.17	95.44	104.35	2.53	51.48	40.96
Upper Arlington, OH[100]	104.66	96.39	57.71	2.21	32.93	23.65
Upper Dublin, PA[101]	119.17	95.44	104.35	2.53	51.48	40.96
Vestavia Hills, AL[102]	90.61	66.78	109.22	2.18	30.89	36.41
Webster, NY[103]	94.40	90.45	112.93	2.70	37.27	25.76
Wellesley, MA[104]	163.83	108.44	119.59	2.47	48.68	45.26
West Fargo, ND[105]	149.75	93.57	77.88	2.27	27.80	22.77
West Linn, OR[106]	133.08	99.07	124.06	2.89	50.33	33.26
West Windsor, NJ[107]	86.08	115.37	101.58	2.38	33.58	37.72
Westlake, OH[108]	114.21	101.78	81.99	2.27	39.76	32.53
Weston, FL[109]	85.67	89.45	90.43	2.49	52.58	25.80
Westport, CT[110]	123.75	110.00	111.67	2.47	64.17	27.43
Wilmette, IL[111]	99.17	99.44	95.00	2.70	45.00	25.27
Woodbury, MN[112]	133.87	84.35	82.36	2.62	33.40	30.95
Yorba Linda, CA[113]	96.52	104.00	101.81	3.38	59.39	26.79
Average*	105.15	89.02	99.78	2.38	35.30	28.10
Minimum*	66.87	56.09	48.53	1.95	18.91	13.38
Maximum*	182.34	150.36	228.33	4.09	67.91	63.80

Note: Doctor (general practitioners routine exam of an established patient); Dentist (adult teeth cleaning and periodic oral examination); Optometrist (full vision eye exam for established adult patient); Gasoline (one gallon regular unleaded, national brand, including all taxes, cash price at self-service pump if available); Beauty Salon (woman's shampoo, trim, and blow-dry); Men's Shirt (cotton/polyester dress shirt, pinpoint weave, long sleeves); (*) Values for the local area are compared with the average, minimum, and maximum values for all 308 areas in the Cost of Living Index report; n/a not available; In cases where data is not available for the city, data for the metro area or for a neighboring city has been provided and noted as follows: (1) Orange County CA; (2) Plano TX; (3) Atlanta GA; (4) Des Moines IA; (5) Raleigh NC; (6) St. Louis MO-IL; (7) Dayton OH; (8) Fayetteville AR; (9) Newark-Elizabeth NJ; (10) Albany NY; (11) Detroit MI; (12) Bethesda-Gaithersburg-Frederick MD; (13) Nashville-Franklin TN; (14) Denver CO; (15) Indianapolis IN; (16) Austin TX; (17) New Haven CT; (18) St. Louis MO-IL; (19) Memphis TN; (20) Plano TX; (21) Charlotte NC; (22) Pittsburgh PA; (23) Oakland CA; (24) Salt Lake City UT; (25) Columbus OH; (26) Brooklyn NY; (27) Minneapolis MN; (28) Philadelphia PA; (29) Indianapolis IN; (30) Plano TX; (31) Sacramento CA; (32) San Francisco CA; (33) Nashville-Franklin TN; (34) Brazoria County TX; (35) Memphis TN; (36) Hartford CT; (37) Albany NY; (38) Harrisburg PA; (39) Raleigh NC; (40) Charlotte NC; (41) Covington KY; (42) Atlanta GA; (43) Fort Worth TX; (44) Seattle WA; (45) Portland OR; (46) Brazoria County TX; (47) Kansas City MO-KS; (48) Kansas City MO-KS; (49) Washington-Arlington-Alexandria DC-VA; (50) Kansas City MO-KS; (51) Framingham-Natick MA; (52) Philadelphia PA; (53) Huntsville AL; (54) Brooklyn NY; (55) Minneapolis MN; (56) Cedar Rapids IA; (57) Middlesex-Monmouth NJ; (58) Cincinnati OH; (59) Pittsburgh PA; (60) Milwaukee-Waukesha WI; (61) Boise ID; (62) Manchester NH; (63) Pittsburgh PA; (64) Charleston-N Charleston SC; (65) Boston MA; (66) Stamford CT; (67) Chicago IL; (68) Detroit MI; (69) Detroit MI; (71) St. Louis MO-IL; (70) St. Louis MO-IL; (72) Buffalo NY; (73) Orlando FL; (74) Denver CO; (75) Fort Lauderdale FL; (76) Atlanta GA; (77) Round Rock TX; (78) Joliet-Will County IL; (79) Phoenix AZ; (80) Los Angeles-Long Beach CA; (81) Seattle WA; (82) Kennewick-Richland-Pasco WA; (83) Stamford CT; (84) Bergen-Passaic NJ; (85) Albuquerque NM; (86) Tucson AZ; (87) Seattle WA; (88) Oakland CA; (89) San Antonio TX; (90) Middlesex-Monmouth NJ; (91) Salt Lake City UT; (92) Providence RI; (93) Hartford CT; (94) Fort Worth TX; (95) Nashville-Franklin TN; (96) Akron OH; (97) Houston TX; (98) Madison WI; (99) Philadelphia PA; (100) Columbus OH; (101) Philadelphia PA; (102) Birmingham AL; (103) Rochester NY; (104) Framingham-Natick MA; (105) Fargo-Moorhead ND-MN; (106) Portland OR; (107) Middlesex-Monmouth NJ; (108) Cleveland OH; (109) Fort Lauderdale FL; (110) Stamford CT; (111) Chicago IL; (112) Minneapolis MN; (113) Orange County CA

Source: The Council for Community and Economic Research (formerly ACCRA), Cost of Living Index, 2015

Number of Medical Professionals

City	Area Covered	MDs[1]	DOs[1,2]	Dentists	Podiatrists	Chiropractors	Optometrists
Aliso Viejo, CA	Orange County	309.2	19.1	103.8	5.7	44.6	23.9
Allen, TX	Collin County	251.8	17.6	62.9	4.0	31.7	15.9
Alpharetta, GA	Fulton County	488.4	9.9	67.1	4.1	48.4	14.0
Ankeny, IA	Polk County	212.5	107.3	65.2	9.8	46.3	22.6
Apex, NC	Wake County	273.3	8.7	66.7	3.0	24.4	15.6
Ballwin, MO	St. Louis County	503.2	27.0	83.1	9.3	50.8	26.2
Beavercreek, OH	Greene County	285.1	64.2	81.2	6.1	21.4	25.0
Bella Vista, AR	Benton County	128.1	13.5	44.2	2.9	31.4	13.2
Bernards, NJ	Somerset County	443.7	26.0	89.9	6.3	28.0	15.9
Bethlehem, NY	Albany County	535.4	31.6	86.6	7.8	17.2	14.9
Bloomfield, MI	Oakland County	541.0	104.9	101.9	17.5	30.9	17.9
Bowie, MD	Prince George's County	167.0	4.4	59.6	6.1	9.2	8.6
Bozeman, MT	Gallatin County	223.9	10.6	70.9	3.1	54.5	16.4
Brentwood, TN	Williamson County	585.5	16.6	77.0	3.9	40.9	21.4
Broomfield, CO	Broomfield County	189.0	28.2	95.0	3.2	56.3	27.4
Carmel, IN	Hamilton County	565.3	23.2	73.0	3.3	34.7	21.8
Cedar Park, TX	Williamson County	168.9	18.0	53.1	4.5	27.8	16.1
Cheshire, CT	New Haven County	548.9	11.1	73.6	9.6	24.7	15.8
Chesterfield, MO	St. Louis County	503.2	27.0	83.1	9.3	50.8	26.2
Collierville, TN	Shelby County	379.3	6.6	66.8	3.4	11.3	28.0
Coppell, TX	Dallas County	311.3	19.9	76.5	3.9	32.8	12.1
Cornelius, NC	Mecklenburg County	310.0	10.3	65.5	3.2	31.2	13.3
Cranberry, PA	Butler County	133.2	32.9	65.6	6.5	54.9	23.7
Cupertino, CA	Santa Clara County	392.9	8.2	107.0	5.9	39.0	24.3
Danville, CA	Contra Costa County	281.4	10.3	81.0	4.4	29.7	17.1
Draper, UT	Salt Lake County	351.1	12.2	73.3	5.5	26.1	12.6
Dublin, OH	Franklin County	410.9	62.2	83.7	6.7	23.2	25.3
Eastchester, NY	Westchester County	641.7	17.5	105.3	14.1	26.8	15.6
Eden Prairie, MN	Hennepin County	481.9	16.4	89.5	3.5	66.5	18.2
Edmond, OK	Oklahoma County	392.9	41.9	95.1	5.0	25.3	18.1
Evesham, NJ	Burlington County	254.1	74.4	70.9	7.6	23.6	15.3
Fishers, IN	Hamilton County	565.3	23.2	73.0	3.3	34.7	21.8
Flower Mound, TX	Denton County	171.0	18.4	51.9	3.2	36.0	17.1
Folsom, CA	Sacramento County	293.3	12.8	72.8	4.4	22.0	16.7
Foster City, CA	San Mateo County	432.0	6.3	98.2	5.8	32.3	21.2
Franklin, TN	Williamson County	585.5	16.6	77.0	3.9	40.9	21.4
Friendswood, TX	Galveston County	453.7	16.6	39.5	4.1	28.0	16.9
Germantown, TN	Shelby County	379.3	6.6	66.8	3.4	11.3	28.0
Glastonbury, CT	Hartford County	419.2	22.5	100.1	6.2	21.5	18.0
Grand Blanc, MI	Genesee County	222.1	62.6	67.3	7.5	24.2	17.2
Guilderland, NY	Albany County	535.4	31.6	86.6	7.8	17.2	14.9
Hampden, PA	Cumberland County	242.9	46.4	68.1	7.0	23.4	20.1
Holly Springs, NC	Wake County	273.3	8.7	66.7	3.0	24.4	15.6
Huntersville, NC	Mecklenburg County	310.0	10.3	65.5	3.2	31.2	13.3
Independence, KY	Kenton County	264.4	14.1	47.0	5.5	19.5	12.8
Johns Creek, GA	Fulton County	488.4	9.9	67.1	4.1	48.4	14.0
Keller, TX	Tarrant County	174.6	38.9	54.6	4.0	23.6	14.0
Kirkland, WA	King County	466.0	13.5	102.2	6.4	44.0	20.3
Lafayette, CO	Boulder County	358.6	23.2	94.1	4.8	69.6	23.9
Lake Oswego, OR	Clackamas County	247.6	24.5	75.7	3.0	35.7	12.9
League City, TX	Galveston County	453.7	16.6	39.5	4.1	28.0	16.9
Leawood, KS	Johnson County	479.6	44.6	78.2	3.5	58.7	24.4
Lee's Summit, MO	Jackson County	289.7	55.0	79.6	6.0	39.4	18.2
Leesburg, VA	Loudoun County	186.3	9.4	60.6	3.0	20.9	16.3
Lehi, UT	Utah County	120.5	14.9	63.6	3.7	24.2	9.6
Lenexa, KS	Johnson County	479.6	44.6	78.2	3.5	58.7	24.4
Lexington, MA	Middlesex County	520.2	9.4	90.7	7.2	21.7	17.6
Los Altos, CA	Santa Clara County	392.9	8.2	107.0	5.9	39.0	24.3
Lower Makefield, PA	Bucks County	236.6	63.9	78.8	9.1	45.3	22.2
Madison, AL	Madison County	270.8	10.9	55.4	3.7	22.3	18.3
Mamaroneck, NY	Westchester County	641.7	17.5	105.3	14.1	26.8	15.6
Manheim, PA	Lancaster County	172.8	39.6	51.2	5.6	24.8	14.1
Manlius, NY	Onondaga County	489.5	16.2	72.4	9.8	26.7	15.6
Maple Grove, MN	Hennepin County	481.9	16.4	89.5	3.5	66.5	18.2
Marion, IA	Linn County	190.2	19.0	69.3	7.8	55.1	15.6
Marlboro, NJ	Monmouth County	396.3	35.9	98.2	14.3	51.8	19.1
Mason, OH	Warren County	242.7	29.6	35.2	3.2	23.5	13.5
McCandless, PA	Allegheny County	610.6	34.7	90.2	10.6	41.0	18.3
Menomonee Falls, WI	Waukesha County	463.3	26.9	86.3	5.6	43.8	21.0

Table continued on next page.

City	Area Covered	MDs[1]	DOs[1,2]	Dentists	Podiatrists	Chiropractors	Optometrists
Meridian, ID	Ada County	286.9	23.8	80.2	3.5	51.8	17.6
Merrimack, NH	Hillsborough County	236.0	21.8	76.5	4.7	25.4	16.8
Mount Lebanon, PA	Allegheny County	610.6	34.7	90.2	10.6	41.0	18.3
Mount Pleasant, SC	Charleston County	778.5	25.2	101.3	5.0	42.8	19.9
Needham, MA	Norfolk County	671.7	10.6	114.1	6.9	25.0	19.8
Newtown, CT	Fairfield County	376.8	14.1	90.2	9.0	34.2	12.1
Northbrook, IL	Cook County	413.7	21.5	82.7	11.5	25.8	18.3
Northville, MI	Wayne County	290.8	35.1	61.8	8.9	17.1	9.2
Novi, MI	Oakland County	541.0	104.9	101.9	17.5	30.9	17.9
O'Fallon, IL	St. Clair County	159.9	16.1	68.9	5.6	44.0	18.1
O'Fallon, MO	St. Charles County	100.6	18.2	53.5	5.0	56.1	16.3
Orchard Park, NY	Erie County	371.7	21.5	79.1	8.2	36.1	14.3
Oviedo, FL	Seminole County	186.4	20.4	56.3	6.6	29.6	19.0
Parker, CO	Douglas County	197.8	32.0	62.0	4.1	33.7	19.7
Parkland, FL	Broward County	241.4	35.5	69.5	10.6	33.7	20.9
Peachtree City, GA	Fayette County	299.0	9.2	92.1	14.6	46.5	18.2
Pflugerville, TX	Travis County	300.4	17.9	66.7	4.7	31.0	15.2
Plainfield, IL	Will County	125.1	20.8	51.2	5.8	30.6	12.4
Princeton, NJ	Mercer County	390.5	25.3	77.2	8.3	25.6	17.2
Queen Creek, AZ	Maricopa County	236.4	32.4	63.7	5.9	33.8	13.8
Rancho Palos Verdes, CA	Los Angeles County	283.7	11.3	79.6	5.8	27.4	15.8
Redmond, WA	King County	466.0	13.5	102.2	6.4	44.0	20.3
Richland, WA	Benton County	201.1	27.1	67.6	5.4	37.5	27.3
Ridgefield, CT	Fairfield County	376.8	14.1	90.2	9.0	34.2	12.1
Ridgewood, NJ	Bergen County	506.3	28.6	125.0	14.7	47.7	17.5
Rio Rancho, NM	Sandoval County	135.6	8.8	40.7	1.5	8.7	8.7
Sahuarita, AZ	Pima County	351.4	23.0	57.6	5.1	19.0	14.4
Sammamish, WA	King County	466.0	13.5	102.2	6.4	44.0	20.3
San Ramon, CA	Contra Costa County	281.4	10.3	81.0	4.4	29.7	17.1
Saratoga, CA	Santa Clara County	392.9	8.2	107.0	5.9	39.0	24.3
Schertz, TX	Guadalupe County	70.5	10.5	29.2	1.4	12.2	9.5
Shrewsbury, MA	Worcester County	356.9	18.5	66.6	6.3	20.4	17.2
South Brunswick, NJ	Middlesex County	357.2	18.4	82.4	10.2	23.2	16.5
South Jordan, UT	Salt Lake County	351.1	12.2	73.3	5.5	26.1	12.6
South Kingstown, RI	Washington County	226.8	29.2	52.1	6.3	21.3	18.9
South Windsor, CT	Hartford County	419.2	22.5	100.1	6.2	21.5	18.0
Southlake, TX	Tarrant County	174.6	38.9	54.6	4.0	23.6	14.0
Spring Hill, TN	Williamson County	585.5	16.6	77.0	3.9	40.9	21.4
Stow, OH	Summit County	319.5	77.0	58.3	10.7	19.9	17.3
Sugar Land, TX	Fort Bend County	237.0	14.8	47.1	3.4	11.8	15.2
Sun Prairie, WI	Dane County	576.8	17.3	67.0	5.2	40.9	19.8
Syracuse, UT	Davis County	137.9	15.8	62.8	3.9	26.4	10.6
Tredyffrin, PA	Chester County	246.5	42.8	63.2	8.2	25.4	18.1
Upper Arlington, OH	Franklin County	410.9	62.2	83.7	6.7	23.2	25.3
Upper Dublin, PA	Montgomery County	593.4	82.2	101.6	12.6	39.2	22.9
Vestavia Hills, AL	Jefferson County	575.9	13.2	81.7	4.5	14.2	28.9
Webster, NY	Monroe County	470.4	15.7	75.5	6.1	25.7	17.2
Wellesley, MA	Norfolk County	671.7	10.6	114.1	6.9	25.0	19.8
West Fargo, ND	Cass County	407.5	9.8	72.5	3.0	59.9	28.7
West Linn, OR	Clackamas County	247.6	24.5	75.7	3.0	35.7	12.9
West Windsor, NJ	Mercer County	390.5	25.3	77.2	8.3	25.6	17.2
Westlake, OH	Cuyahoga County	677.5	49.1	97.3	16.4	16.6	16.1
Weston, FL	Broward County	241.4	35.5	69.5	10.6	33.7	20.9
Westport, CT	Fairfield County	376.8	14.1	90.2	9.0	34.2	12.1
Wilmette, IL	Cook County	413.7	21.5	82.7	11.5	25.8	18.3
Woodbury, MN	Washington County	273.2	11.4	67.4	2.8	61.8	21.7
Yorba Linda, CA	Orange County	309.2	19.1	103.8	5.7	44.6	23.9
U.S.	U.S.	272.5	20.9	64.7	5.8	25.9	15.2

Note: All figures are rates per 100,000 population; Data as of 2014 unless noted; (1) Data as of 2013; (2) Doctor of Osteopathic Medicine; Source: U.S. Department of Health and Human Services, Health Resources and Services Administration, Bureau of Health Professions, Area Resource File (ARF) 2014-2015

Health Insurance Coverage: City

City	With Health Insurance	With Private Health Insurance	With Public Health Insurance	Without Health Insurance	Population Under Age 18 Without Health Insurance
Aliso Viejo, CA	90.8	84.1	11.4	9.2	3.8
Allen, TX	88.4	81.5	12.3	11.6	8.6
Alpharetta, GA	91.6	84.7	12.3	8.4	4.6
Ankeny, IA	96.3	88.7	17.5	3.7	2.1
Apex, NC	92.6	87.9	10.3	7.4	3.2
Ballwin, MO	92.7	85.0	20.3	7.3	5.1
Beavercreek, OH	94.4	85.7	22.2	5.6	4.1
Bella Vista, AR	93.9	81.5	37.5	6.1	2.7
Bernards, NJ	97.9	93.0	15.0	2.1	1.2
Bethlehem, NY	96.8	88.7	22.0	3.2	1.9
Bloomfield, MI	96.1	88.9	26.0	3.9	2.4
Bowie, MD	92.7	85.4	18.8	7.3	2.5
Bozeman, MT	90.2	82.1	15.1	9.8	4.1
Brentwood, TN	96.6	91.3	13.9	3.4	1.5
Broomfield, CO	92.0	81.9	18.8	8.0	4.9
Carmel, IN	95.2	90.1	14.1	4.8	3.0
Cedar Park, TX	89.2	81.5	14.8	10.8	6.7
Cheshire, CT	94.3	86.7	18.7	5.7	2.0
Chesterfield, MO	95.5	88.8	22.4	4.5	3.1
Collierville, TN	95.4	90.1	14.8	4.6	3.0
Coppell, TX	90.5	86.5	8.2	9.5	6.6
Cornelius, NC	88.4	81.3	14.9	11.6	8.6
Cranberry, PA	95.4	90.3	14.6	4.6	3.7
Cupertino, CA	96.6	88.4	16.1	3.4	0.9
Danville, CA	97.4	92.7	18.2	2.6	0.9
Draper, UT	92.8	88.1	11.0	7.2	4.6
Dublin, OH	97.5	93.6	11.0	2.5	1.2
Eastchester, NY	96.3	87.4	20.8	3.7	0.3
Eden Prairie, MN	94.0	85.5	16.7	6.0	3.2
Edmond, OK	90.4	81.1	20.1	9.6	5.7
Evesham, NJ	94.9	86.3	20.3	5.1	4.1
Fishers, IN	94.1	89.7	9.3	5.9	2.7
Flower Mound, TX	93.3	89.5	8.9	6.7	4.9
Folsom, CA	94.3	86.7	17.1	5.7	1.9
Foster City, CA	96.1	87.3	19.0	3.9	1.7
Franklin, TN	91.8	85.3	15.8	8.2	5.5
Friendswood, TX	91.9	84.7	17.9	8.1	3.9
Germantown, TN	95.5	88.4	21.2	4.5	1.3
Glastonbury, CT	95.5	86.4	21.4	4.5	1.8
Grand Blanc, MI	93.2	78.8	27.8	6.8	1.6
Guilderland, NY	96.6	88.3	21.7	3.4	0.3
Hampden, PA	96.4	87.8	23.1	3.6	1.5
Holly Springs, NC	94.4	88.3	14.2	5.6	3.0
Huntersville, NC	89.9	84.5	12.1	10.1	5.3
Independence, KY	92.1	79.3	20.9	7.9	5.6
Johns Creek, GA	89.7	84.5	11.2	10.3	5.1
Keller, TX	93.2	88.2	13.6	6.8	3.4
Kirkland, WA	91.4	83.0	17.2	8.6	4.4
Lafayette, CO	89.3	75.7	20.9	10.7	4.4
Lake Oswego, OR	93.4	85.4	21.3	6.6	3.9
League City, TX	90.0	83.7	13.6	10.0	5.0
Leawood, KS	97.8	92.2	18.0	2.2	1.6
Lee's Summit, MO	93.8	84.9	18.6	6.2	3.3
Leesburg, VA	88.4	81.8	11.9	11.6	6.1
Lehi, UT	91.6	84.9	12.3	8.4	5.5
Lenexa, KS	90.8	82.6	18.2	9.2	4.9
Lexington, MA	98.5	90.6	21.4	1.5	0.3
Los Altos, CA	97.8	90.7	20.8	2.2	1.2
Lower Makefield, PA	97.7	92.7	17.1	2.3	1.1
Madison, AL	92.7	85.9	17.7	7.3	3.3
Mamaroneck, NY	94.4	83.6	21.5	5.6	2.6
Manheim, PA	94.9	83.8	28.8	5.1	2.1
Manlius, NY	95.4	84.7	27.0	4.6	2.4
Maple Grove, MN	96.1	88.4	16.0	3.9	3.0
Marion, IA	92.9	78.8	26.6	7.1	1.6
Marlboro, NJ	95.2	88.9	16.4	4.8	3.5
Mason, OH	95.5	89.8	15.1	4.5	1.7

Table continued on next page.

City	With Health Insurance	With Private Health Insurance	With Public Health Insurance	Without Health Insurance	Population Under Age 18 Without Health Insurance
McCandless, PA	96.3	89.1	21.6	3.7	1.4
Menomonee Falls, WI	96.7	86.4	25.8	3.3	0.7
Meridian, ID	88.2	78.3	18.9	11.8	8.5
Merrimack, NH	94.1	87.1	18.2	5.9	2.3
Mount Lebanon, PA	95.4	86.9	26.5	4.6	3.3
Mount Pleasant, SC	91.5	84.8	17.3	8.5	6.3
Needham, MA	98.7	92.1	20.6	1.3	0.3
Newtown, CT	96.3	85.9	20.6	3.7	0.9
Northbrook, IL	96.4	87.2	25.1	3.6	1.2
Northville, MI	95.0	89.9	20.9	5.0	2.4
Novi, MI	93.3	85.4	19.9	6.7	1.9
O'Fallon, IL	94.6	81.8	24.2	5.4	2.9
O'Fallon, MO	93.2	86.1	15.5	6.8	4.8
Orchard Park, NY	97.6	90.8	22.7	2.4	0.5
Oviedo, FL	90.2	79.0	18.2	9.8	2.3
Parker, CO	94.5	89.5	11.2	5.5	2.7
Parkland, FL	95.0	87.3	12.6	5.0	1.2
Peachtree City, GA	91.3	83.5	19.5	8.7	5.6
Pflugerville, TX	87.3	75.9	19.2	12.7	7.8
Plainfield, IL	92.8	84.7	13.0	7.2	4.7
Princeton, NJ	95.2	90.5	14.9	4.8	0.8
Queen Creek, AZ	95.4	86.0	16.0	4.6	3.5
Rancho Palos Verdes, CA	95.2	86.3	27.1	4.8	2.8
Redmond, WA	92.3	85.1	14.3	7.7	2.3
Richland, WA	90.9	77.1	28.2	9.1	4.4
Ridgefield, CT	96.0	88.4	17.2	4.0	5.2
Ridgewood, NJ	94.8	89.5	15.5	5.2	1.6
Rio Rancho, NM	90.0	70.4	30.8	10.0	5.1
Sahuarita, AZ	93.3	78.3	29.2	6.7	5.2
Sammamish, WA	97.4	94.4	8.7	2.6	1.7
San Ramon, CA	95.1	90.2	11.1	4.9	2.5
Saratoga, CA	97.4	90.9	20.6	2.6	1.4
Schertz, TX	87.8	78.5	23.7	12.2	10.4
Shrewsbury, MA	97.5	87.2	22.3	2.5	2.1
South Brunswick, NJ	92.9	85.1	15.1	7.1	4.6
South Jordan, UT	91.0	84.0	13.7	9.0	7.5
South Kingstown, RI	93.7	84.9	23.0	6.3	2.2
South Windsor, CT	97.9	88.1	21.5	2.1	0.9
Southlake, TX	96.8	93.5	9.4	3.2	2.1
Spring Hill, TN	94.3	87.1	12.7	5.7	2.6
Stow, OH	95.0	85.0	21.3	5.0	2.0
Sugar Land, TX	87.6	79.0	15.6	12.4	8.8
Sun Prairie, WI	94.8	81.1	26.0	5.2	2.3
Syracuse, UT	95.1	89.5	12.3	4.9	1.4
Tredyffrin, PA	97.2	91.9	19.2	2.8	1.0
Upper Arlington, OH	96.0	89.1	19.9	4.0	2.3
Upper Dublin, PA	95.8	88.3	21.4	4.2	2.4
Vestavia Hills, AL	97.0	90.4	19.5	3.0	1.0
Webster, NY	96.2	84.5	26.8	3.8	2.1
Wellesley, MA	98.5	92.9	17.2	1.5	1.4
West Fargo, ND	92.6	84.9	19.4	7.4	5.9
West Linn, OR	92.2	83.9	20.5	7.8	6.4
West Windsor, NJ	95.7	90.1	13.6	4.3	2.7
Westlake, OH	95.4	86.1	23.7	4.6	3.7
Weston, FL	87.8	79.1	13.6	12.2	10.2
Westport, CT	96.0	89.9	18.7	4.0	2.4
Wilmette, IL	95.9	89.5	18.8	4.1	4.0
Woodbury, MN	96.0	90.4	14.4	4.0	3.0
Yorba Linda, CA	93.9	84.7	17.6	6.1	3.8
U.S.	85.8	65.8	31.1	14.2	7.1

Note: Figures are percentages that cover the civilian noninstitutionalized population
Source: U.S. Census Bureau, 2010-2014 American Community Survey 5-Year Estimates

Health Insurance Coverage: Metro Area

Metro Area	With Health Insurance	With Private Health Insurance	With Public Health Insurance	Without Health Insurance	Population Under Age 18 Without Health Insurance
Aliso Viejo, CA	80.3	56.7	29.9	19.7	8.2
Allen, TX	78.9	61.8	24.1	21.1	12.5
Alpharetta, GA	81.9	65.5	24.4	18.1	9.1
Ankeny, IA	92.6	76.7	27.4	7.4	3.1
Apex, NC	86.5	72.7	22.4	13.5	7.2
Ballwin, MO	89.6	72.6	28.0	10.4	4.4
Beavercreek, OH	89.3	68.5	33.7	10.7	4.6
Bella Vista, AR	83.9	64.9	28.3	16.1	7.3
Bernards, NJ	87.7	65.3	31.8	12.3	4.4
Bethlehem, NY	93.3	77.0	30.0	6.7	3.0
Bloomfield, MI	88.5	68.7	33.3	11.5	3.9
Bowie, MD	88.8	77.1	21.4	11.2	5.0
Bozeman, MT	87.5	76.9	18.6	12.5	8.2
Brentwood, TN	86.8	68.9	27.2	13.2	5.7
Broomfield, CO	86.2	70.1	24.7	13.8	8.3
Carmel, IN	86.7	69.0	27.9	13.3	6.9
Cedar Park, TX	82.4	68.5	21.9	17.6	10.0
Cheshire, CT	91.7	69.9	33.0	8.3	3.1
Chesterfield, MO	89.6	72.6	28.0	10.4	4.4
Collierville, TN	85.0	62.4	32.3	15.0	6.2
Coppell, TX	78.9	61.8	24.1	21.1	12.5
Cornelius, NC	84.5	66.7	27.4	15.5	6.8
Cranberry, PA	92.5	76.1	32.3	7.5	2.7
Cupertino, CA	89.3	73.0	24.2	10.7	3.9
Danville, CA	89.2	72.5	26.5	10.8	4.7
Draper, UT	84.4	72.1	20.1	15.6	11.4
Dublin, OH	89.0	71.2	27.4	11.0	4.8
Eastchester, NY	87.7	65.3	31.8	12.3	4.4
Eden Prairie, MN	92.2	77.7	25.1	7.8	4.9
Edmond, OK	83.5	65.5	28.9	16.5	8.2
Evesham, NJ	90.4	72.5	29.8	9.6	4.1
Fishers, IN	86.7	69.0	27.9	13.3	6.9
Flower Mound, TX	78.9	61.8	24.1	21.1	12.5
Folsom, CA	87.4	67.2	31.5	12.6	5.4
Foster City, CA	89.2	72.5	26.5	10.8	4.7
Franklin, TN	86.8	68.9	27.2	13.2	5.7
Friendswood, TX	77.1	58.2	25.3	22.9	13.2
Germantown, TN	85.0	62.4	32.3	15.0	6.2
Glastonbury, CT	92.8	73.8	30.7	7.2	2.7
Grand Blanc, MI	90.5	63.2	43.1	9.5	3.0
Guilderland, NY	93.3	77.0	30.0	6.7	3.0
Hampden, PA	91.0	76.6	28.7	9.0	6.0
Holly Springs, NC	86.5	72.7	22.4	13.5	7.2
Huntersville, NC	84.5	66.7	27.4	15.5	6.8
Independence, KY	89.8	72.5	27.7	10.2	4.7
Johns Creek, GA	81.9	65.5	24.4	18.1	9.1
Keller, TX	78.9	61.8	24.1	21.1	12.5
Kirkland, WA	88.3	73.5	24.8	11.7	4.9
Lafayette, CO	89.7	78.3	20.0	10.3	6.3
Lake Oswego, OR	86.9	70.1	27.6	13.1	5.4
League City, TX	77.1	58.2	25.3	22.9	13.2
Leawood, KS	87.5	73.2	25.1	12.5	6.5
Lee's Summit, MO	87.5	73.2	25.1	12.5	6.5
Leesburg, VA	88.8	77.1	21.4	11.2	5.0
Lehi, UT	87.3	77.5	17.0	12.7	9.1
Lenexa, KS	87.5	73.2	25.1	12.5	6.5
Lexington, MA	95.7	77.0	30.0	4.3	1.7
Los Altos, CA	89.3	73.0	24.2	10.7	3.9
Lower Makefield, PA	90.4	72.5	29.8	9.6	4.1
Madison, AL	87.6	73.8	26.7	12.4	3.6
Mamaroneck, NY	87.7	65.3	31.8	12.3	4.4
Manheim, PA	86.8	71.1	28.5	13.2	14.7
Manlius, NY	92.3	72.2	34.0	7.7	3.8
Maple Grove, MN	92.2	77.7	25.1	7.8	4.9
Marion, IA	93.3	78.5	27.9	6.7	2.8
Marlboro, NJ	87.7	65.3	31.8	12.3	4.4
Mason, OH	89.8	72.5	27.7	10.2	4.7

Table continued on next page.

Metro Area	With Health Insurance	With Private Health Insurance	With Public Health Insurance	Without Health Insurance	Population Under Age 18 Without Health Insurance
McCandless, PA	92.5	76.1	32.3	7.5	2.7
Menomonee Falls, WI	90.9	69.5	32.3	9.1	3.4
Meridian, ID	85.0	68.9	26.9	15.0	8.0
Merrimack, NH	90.4	76.7	24.1	9.6	2.9
Mount Lebanon, PA	92.5	76.1	32.3	7.5	2.7
Mount Pleasant, SC	84.5	67.6	28.4	15.5	8.0
Needham, MA	95.7	77.0	30.0	4.3	1.7
Newtown, CT	88.7	72.4	26.4	11.3	5.1
Northbrook, IL	86.5	66.8	28.7	13.5	4.1
Northville, MI	88.5	68.7	33.3	11.5	3.9
Novi, MI	88.5	68.7	33.3	11.5	3.9
O'Fallon, IL	89.6	72.6	28.0	10.4	4.4
O'Fallon, MO	89.6	72.6	28.0	10.4	4.4
Orchard Park, NY	93.5	72.6	35.6	6.5	2.9
Oviedo, FL	79.9	60.5	28.5	20.1	11.9
Parker, CO	86.2	70.1	24.7	13.8	8.3
Parkland, FL	75.9	52.4	30.9	24.1	12.8
Peachtree City, GA	81.9	65.5	24.4	18.1	9.1
Pflugerville, TX	82.4	68.5	21.9	17.6	10.0
Plainfield, IL	86.5	66.8	28.7	13.5	4.1
Princeton, NJ	88.7	73.5	26.1	11.3	4.5
Queen Creek, AZ	83.7	62.3	31.4	16.3	11.4
Rancho Palos Verdes, CA	80.3	56.7	29.9	19.7	8.2
Redmond, WA	88.3	73.5	24.8	11.7	4.9
Richland, WA	84.1	62.7	32.5	15.9	6.4
Ridgefield, CT	88.7	72.4	26.4	11.3	5.1
Ridgewood, NJ	87.7	65.3	31.8	12.3	4.4
Rio Rancho, NM	84.6	59.3	36.3	15.4	6.6
Sahuarita, AZ	85.5	60.8	37.4	14.5	10.7
Sammamish, WA	88.3	73.5	24.8	11.7	4.9
San Ramon, CA	89.2	72.5	26.5	10.8	4.7
Saratoga, CA	89.3	73.0	24.2	10.7	3.9
Schertz, TX	81.4	62.0	30.1	18.6	9.8
Shrewsbury, MA	95.9	74.7	33.1	4.1	1.5
South Brunswick, NJ	87.7	65.3	31.8	12.3	4.4
South Jordan, UT	84.4	72.1	20.1	15.6	11.4
South Kingstown, RI	91.7	70.3	33.9	8.3	3.3
South Windsor, CT	92.8	73.8	30.7	7.2	2.7
Southlake, TX	78.9	61.8	24.1	21.1	12.5
Spring Hill, TN	86.8	68.9	27.2	13.2	5.7
Stow, OH	89.9	71.6	30.3	10.1	4.4
Sugar Land, TX	77.1	58.2	25.3	22.9	13.2
Sun Prairie, WI	93.2	81.1	23.7	6.8	3.3
Syracuse, UT	88.6	77.9	20.2	11.4	7.1
Tredyffrin, PA	90.4	72.5	29.8	9.6	4.1
Upper Arlington, OH	89.0	71.2	27.4	11.0	4.8
Upper Dublin, PA	90.4	72.5	29.8	9.6	4.1
Vestavia Hills, AL	87.9	68.4	31.3	12.1	4.5
Webster, NY	92.6	73.5	33.0	7.4	4.6
Wellesley, MA	95.7	77.0	30.0	4.3	1.7
West Fargo, ND	91.7	80.8	22.2	8.3	5.3
West Linn, OR	86.9	70.1	27.6	13.1	5.4
West Windsor, NJ	88.7	73.5	26.1	11.3	4.5
Westlake, OH	89.9	69.6	32.8	10.1	4.5
Weston, FL	75.9	52.4	30.9	24.1	12.8
Westport, CT	88.7	72.4	26.4	11.3	5.1
Wilmette, IL	86.5	66.8	28.7	13.5	4.1
Woodbury, MN	92.2	77.7	25.1	7.8	4.9
Yorba Linda, CA	80.3	56.7	29.9	19.7	8.2
U.S.	85.8	65.8	31.1	14.2	7.1

Note: Figures are percentages that cover the civilian noninstitutionalized population; Figures cover the Metropolitan Statistical Area (MSA)—see Appendix B for areas included

Source: U.S. Census Bureau, 2010-2014 American Community Survey 5-Year Estimates

Crime Rate: City

City	All Crimes	Violent Crimes: Murder	Violent Crimes: Forcible Rape	Violent Crimes: Robbery	Violent Crimes: Aggrav. Assault	Property Crimes: Burglary	Property Crimes: Larceny -Theft	Property Crimes: Motor Vehicle Theft
Aliso Viejo, CA	607.8	2.0	*9.9	9.9	47.4	88.8	416.4	33.5
Allen, TX	1,279.2	0.0	*24.5	20.2	33.0	160.8	974.6	66.0
Alpharetta, GA	2,035.4	0.0	4.7	33.1	22.1	236.3	1,685.6	53.6
Ankeny, IA	1,393.6	0.0	*20.7	0.0	88.5	203.4	1,007.6	73.4
Apex, NC	1,128.7	0.0	6.9	23.0	34.6	251.1	799.3	13.8
Ballwin, MO	714.4	0.0	*16.4	6.6	3.3	59.0	602.9	26.2
Beavercreek, OH	2,249.4	0.0	*13.1	24.0	15.3	211.6	1,952.7	32.7
Bella Vista, AR	738.0	0.0	*43.0	0.0	96.7	111.1	480.1	7.2
Bernards, NJ	544.8	0.0	14.8	3.7	3.7	122.3	385.5	14.8
Bethlehem, NY	1,408.2	0.0	*20.2	17.3	60.6	167.4	1,111.0	31.7
Bloomfield, MI	824.0	2.4	*7.1	16.6	14.2	159.1	588.9	35.6
Bowie, MD	1,610.5	1.7	1.7	54.2	75.2	236.1	1,124.4	117.2
Bozeman, MT	2,934.0	0.0	*76.5	7.4	98.7	175.2	2,433.1	143.1
Brentwood, TN	917.6	2.5	*9.8	12.3	22.1	174.2	682.1	14.7
Broomfield, CO	1,758.0	0.0	*24.7	8.2	18.1	187.8	1,459.8	59.3
Carmel, IN	945.7	1.1	*2.3	6.9	3.4	82.2	786.9	62.8
Cedar Park, TX	1,620.6	1.6	*55.0	11.0	37.7	221.4	1,234.3	59.7
Cheshire, CT	844.8	3.4	*0.0	6.9	10.3	137.4	587.2	99.6
Chesterfield, MO	1,598.0	0.0	*8.4	10.5	52.3	87.8	1,416.0	23.0
Collierville, TN	1,781.9	0.0	*20.9	18.8	113.1	152.9	1,423.9	52.3
Coppell, TX	1,271.3	0.0	*17.2	19.6	19.6	193.9	979.2	41.7
Cornelius, NC	1,529.4	0.0	7.3	29.2	84.0	193.5	1,190.0	25.6
Cranberry, PA	1,384.3	0.0	*0.0	10.1	10.1	93.9	1,243.5	26.8
Cupertino, CA	1,760.1	0.0	*6.6	31.4	28.1	434.3	1,182.2	77.6
Danville, CA	1,043.8	0.0	6.9	2.3	29.8	247.2	673.0	84.7
Draper, UT	2,435.3	0.0	*34.8	17.4	67.3	321.5	1,842.2	152.1
Dublin, OH	1,091.4	0.0	*0.0	15.9	2.3	151.7	894.4	27.2
Eastchester, NY	731.3	0.0	0.0	10.0	20.0	125.2	561.0	15.0
Eden Prairie, MN	1,381.8	0.0	*17.5	6.3	11.1	155.5	1,166.0	25.4
Edmond, OK	1,831.8	1.1	*13.6	15.8	61.1	330.4	1,328.3	81.5
Evesham, NJ	1,194.6	0.0	15.3	24.1	35.1	177.5	922.8	19.7
Fishers, IN	972.0	2.3	*2.3	5.8	10.5	58.4	848.2	44.4
Flower Mound, TX	971.7	2.9	*10.1	11.5	24.4	120.7	770.4	31.6
Folsom, CA	1,887.4	1.4	10.9	31.4	64.1	332.7	1,358.3	88.6
Foster City, CA	1,157.3	0.0	9.1	6.1	27.4	246.7	755.3	112.7
Franklin, TN	1,545.0	0.0	*27.0	7.1	106.4	146.1	1,231.5	27.0
Friendswood, TX	920.8	0.0	*28.9	5.3	21.0	184.2	644.5	36.8
Germantown, TN	1,190.0	0.0	*0.0	15.2	63.3	159.5	944.4	7.6
Glastonbury, CT	880.9	0.0	*2.9	14.3	11.5	229.6	602.6	20.1
Grand Blanc, MI	1,742.6	2.7	*57.4	10.9	90.1	314.1	1,226.3	41.0
Guilderland, NY	2,043.7	11.8	*14.7	11.8	35.3	182.6	1,772.8	14.7
Hampden, PA	982.9	0.0	*17.3	38.1	10.4	72.7	830.7	13.8
Holly Springs, NC	959.2	3.3	0.0	23.3	40.0	156.5	719.4	16.7
Huntersville, NC	2,069.1	1.9	13.6	29.2	68.1	290.0	1,613.7	52.6
Independence, KY	817.2	3.8	*22.7	11.3	11.3	177.8	559.9	30.3
Johns Creek, GA	738.2	0.0	3.6	9.5	20.2	109.2	581.6	14.2
Keller, TX	910.5	2.3	*16.0	0.0	36.6	132.7	697.8	25.2
Kirkland, WA	2,461.6	1.2	*34.0	17.6	45.7	317.5	1,830.1	215.6
Lafayette, CO	1,840.8	3.7	*40.2	21.9	29.2	233.7	1,409.8	102.3
Lake Oswego, OR	1,414.0	0.0	10.6	10.6	29.1	269.6	975.3	118.9
League City, TX	2,053.0	3.2	*32.3	28.0	42.0	341.6	1,531.4	74.4
Leawood, KS	1,295.6	0.0	*6.0	3.0	60.1	216.4	971.0	39.1
Lee's Summit, MO	2,007.6	2.1	*20.3	20.3	44.9	261.8	1,547.1	111.1
Leesburg, VA	1,602.8	4.1	*26.6	22.5	65.4	110.4	1,341.2	32.7
Lehi, UT	1,335.6	0.0	33.9	8.9	25.0	256.8	939.7	71.3
Lenexa, KS	1,696.3	3.9	*15.7	11.8	78.6	165.1	1,240.3	180.8
Lexington, MA	696.0	0.0	*0.0	9.1	21.2	102.9	547.7	15.1
Los Altos, CA	1,087.4	0.0	6.6	9.9	6.6	390.0	637.9	36.4
Lower Makefield, PA	945.2	0.0	*9.1	0.0	30.5	192.1	695.1	18.3
Madison, AL	2,353.5	4.3	*23.7	43.1	251.9	325.1	1,612.8	92.6
Mamaroneck, NY	994.4	0.0	0.0	5.2	98.4	145.0	730.2	15.5
Manheim, PA	1,780.1	2.6	*5.1	23.0	12.8	255.4	1,448.1	33.2
Manlius, NY	1,590.9	0.0	*4.1	16.3	40.7	240.1	1,265.4	24.4
Maple Grove, MN	1,814.5	3.0	*4.5	13.6	13.6	179.3	1,562.8	37.7
Marion, IA	1,576.2	0.0	*30.2	21.9	82.2	309.8	1,085.5	46.6
Marlboro, NJ	681.5	0.0	2.5	0.0	27.3	104.1	532.8	14.9

Table continued on next page.

City	All Crimes	Violent Crimes				Property Crimes		
		Murder	Forcible Rape	Robbery	Aggrav. Assault	Burglary	Larceny -Theft	Motor Vehicle Theft
Mason, OH	1,241.4	0.0	*22.3	3.2	9.5	101.9	1,069.5	35.0
McCandless, PA	1,040.4	6.9	*0.0	3.4	27.6	103.3	885.4	13.8
Menomonee Falls, WI	1,252.9	0.0	0.0	16.7	5.6	127.8	1,069.5	33.3
Meridian, ID	1,465.0	2.3	*22.2	1.2	54.8	220.5	1,130.3	33.8
Merrimack, NH	753.3	0.0	*3.9	3.9	7.8	74.2	624.5	39.0
Mount Lebanon, PA	714.0	0.0	*3.0	6.1	18.2	84.7	593.0	9.1
Mount Pleasant, SC	1,942.6	2.6	*11.7	24.8	142.1	182.5	1,483.7	95.2
Needham, MA	663.6	0.0	*0.0	0.0	13.3	106.7	523.5	20.0
Newtown, CT	647.9	0.0	*17.7	3.5	17.7	230.1	357.6	21.2
Northbrook, IL	1,077.2	0.0	*11.9	5.9	3.0	127.6	919.9	8.9
Northville, MI	1,312.5	0.0	*20.8	6.9	52.1	131.9	1,024.3	76.4
Novi, MI	1,534.4	1.7	*22.2	11.9	44.3	90.4	1,295.7	68.2
O'Fallon, IL	1,616.8	0.0	*41.0	10.3	88.9	232.4	1,203.2	41.0
O'Fallon, MO	1,363.3	0.0	*10.8	10.8	50.3	120.9	1,141.8	28.7
Orchard Park, NY	1,372.6	3.4	*3.4	13.6	23.7	240.6	1,043.8	44.1
Oviedo, FL	1,379.9	2.7	*8.0	10.7	128.1	331.0	859.4	40.0
Parker, CO	1,363.6	0.0	*24.3	8.1	97.1	161.9	1,023.7	48.6
Parkland, FL	662.6	3.7	*0.0	7.4	14.7	114.1	500.7	22.1
Peachtree City, GA	1,294.7	0.0	2.9	14.3	11.4	77.2	1,068.9	120.0
Pflugerville, TX	1,657.0	0.0	*32.7	16.3	61.7	210.5	1,277.7	58.1
Plainfield, IL	836.6	0.0	*14.2	21.3	37.9	87.7	647.0	28.4
Princeton, NJ	994.7	0.0	3.4	20.6	44.6	178.4	737.5	10.3
Queen Creek, AZ	n/a	n/a	n/a	n/a	n/a	n/a	n/a	n/a
Rancho Palos Verdes, CA	1,163.1	0.0	11.7	18.8	25.8	424.4	614.4	68.0
Redmond, WA	3,044.0	1.7	*12.0	13.7	24.0	413.3	2,438.6	140.6
Richland, WA	2,430.5	0.0	*20.6	24.3	123.5	316.2	1,854.2	91.7
Ridgefield, CT	261.0	0.0	*0.0	0.0	4.0	11.9	241.2	4.0
Ridgewood, NJ	718.2	0.0	0.0	7.8	15.7	172.7	510.2	11.8
Rio Rancho, NM	2,139.5	1.1	10.8	30.1	146.3	440.0	1,390.8	120.5
Sahuarita, AZ	1,477.6	0.0	*7.4	11.0	14.7	187.5	1,198.2	58.8
Sammamish, WA	772.3	2.0	5.9	2.0	5.9	256.8	454.8	45.1
San Ramon, CA	1,027.3	0.0	*4.0	14.7	12.0	278.5	616.9	101.3
Saratoga, CA	986.4	0.0	*35.3	6.4	19.3	437.0	449.8	38.6
Schertz, TX	1,945.3	2.7	*35.2	32.5	105.5	284.1	1,393.4	92.0
Shrewsbury, MA	576.8	0.0	*2.7	2.7	0.0	142.2	415.6	13.7
South Brunswick, NJ	880.3	0.0	6.7	6.7	8.9	252.8	572.1	33.3
South Jordan, UT	2,301.9	0.0	*19.5	30.8	27.6	245.1	1,860.4	118.5
South Kingstown, RI	956.8	0.0	*16.3	3.3	26.0	237.6	647.7	26.0
South Windsor, CT	1,391.2	0.0	*19.3	11.6	3.9	231.9	1,066.6	58.0
Southlake, TX	1,470.0	0.0	*0.0	3.5	20.9	195.5	1,229.1	20.9
Spring Hill, TN	1,123.3	0.0	*9.0	17.9	83.7	140.4	848.5	23.9
Stow, OH	1,976.7	2.9	37.4	14.4	14.4	227.3	1,654.4	25.9
Sugar Land, TX	1,762.4	1.2	*7.1	42.3	65.8	258.7	1,330.9	56.4
Sun Prairie, WI	2,468.0	0.0	19.2	16.0	67.2	188.9	2,151.1	25.6
Syracuse, UT	1,034.3	7.7	*15.3	3.8	23.0	99.6	869.6	15.3
Tredyffrin, PA	815.7	0.0	*6.8	6.8	23.7	169.2	585.6	23.7
Upper Arlington, OH	1,173.4	0.0	*0.0	11.6	0.0	251.4	901.7	8.7
Upper Dublin, PA	809.6	0.0	*3.8	26.6	15.2	98.8	649.9	15.2
Vestavia Hills, AL	1,405.5	0.0	*0.0	17.6	47.0	217.6	1,061.5	61.7
Webster, NY	1,182.5	2.3	*13.6	15.8	29.4	151.5	945.1	24.9
Wellesley, MA	652.8	0.0	*3.4	13.6	30.6	132.6	459.0	13.6
West Fargo, ND	1,934.1	0.0	*19.4	9.7	151.8	413.3	1,181.8	158.2
West Linn, OR	992.3	0.0	11.4	0.0	19.1	64.9	870.2	26.7
West Windsor, NJ	1,338.1	0.0	7.0	17.4	17.4	160.3	1,111.6	24.4
Westlake, OH	1,234.0	0.0	0.0	6.2	30.8	163.5	968.7	64.8
Weston, FL	614.8	1.4	*17.4	8.7	37.6	89.7	432.5	27.5
Westport, CT	1,278.7	0.0	*0.0	14.5	14.5	185.3	1,038.9	25.4
Wilmette, IL	1,319.9	0.0	*10.9	7.3	18.2	207.8	1,057.4	18.2
Woodbury, MN	1,823.0	0.0	*13.5	10.5	30.1	220.9	1,487.8	60.1
Yorba Linda, CA	1,103.4	1.5	*19.2	10.3	35.4	205.3	747.4	84.2
U.S.	2,971.8	4.5	36.6	102.2	232.5	542.5	1,837.3	216.2

Note: Figures are crimes per 100,000 population in 2014 except where noted; n/a not available; (1) 2013 data; (*) Figures shown were reported using the revised Uniform Crime Reporting (UCR) definition of rape. The U.S. figure for rape is 26.4 using the legacy definition.
Source: FBI Uniform Crime Reports, 2013, 2014

Crime Rate: Suburbs

Suburbs[1]	All Crimes	Violent Crimes: Murder	Violent Crimes: Forcible Rape	Violent Crimes: Robbery	Violent Crimes: Aggrav. Assault	Property Crimes: Burglary	Property Crimes: Larceny -Theft	Property Crimes: Motor Vehicle Theft
Aliso Viejo, CA	1,954.5	1.9	20.8	62.6	115.0	296.5	1,255.4	202.2
Allen, TX	n/a	n/a	n/a	n/a	n/a	n/a	n/a	n/a
Alpharetta, GA	3,648.0	6.2	20.5	155.4	220.2	731.6	2,176.0	338.2
Ankeny, IA	2,951.4	2.0	33.3	53.9	247.5	504.7	1,889.2	220.8
Apex, NC	n/a	n/a	n/a	n/a	n/a	n/a	n/a	n/a
Ballwin, MO	2,902.8	8.9	36.0	104.4	284.8	474.9	1,777.8	215.9
Beavercreek, OH	n/a	4.5	50.0	115.4	114.0	865.4	n/a	170.3
Bella Vista, AR	n/a	n/a	n/a	n/a	n/a	n/a	n/a	n/a
Bernards, NJ	1,925.6	5.8	10.8	177.3	125.2	332.4	1,039.4	234.5
Bethlehem, NY	2,534.2	3.8	28.8	75.5	166.7	389.3	1,791.1	78.9
Bloomfield, MI	1,699.8	1.5	37.1	39.9	138.2	251.9	1,099.4	131.9
Bowie, MD	2,610.3	4.3	26.7	141.0	182.6	265.4	1,772.0	218.2
Bozeman, MT	n/a	n/a	n/a	n/a	n/a	n/a	n/a	n/a
Brentwood, TN	3,230.8	4.0	47.6	111.3	461.2	518.0	1,962.5	126.2
Broomfield, CO	n/a	2.8	55.5	76.6	202.6	n/a	1,901.3	297.7
Carmel, IN	4,026.6	8.2	40.4	218.9	408.3	816.1	2,180.0	354.8
Cedar Park, TX	3,222.4	2.4	48.8	59.2	186.9	500.2	2,260.6	164.4
Cheshire, CT	3,073.5	3.1	22.6	140.5	171.9	416.5	2,035.5	283.4
Chesterfield, MO	2,901.2	9.0	36.2	105.0	285.8	477.0	1,771.1	217.1
Collierville, TN	5,292.5	13.3	52.0	279.6	721.0	1,165.8	2,765.1	295.8
Coppell, TX	n/a	n/a	n/a	n/a	n/a	n/a	n/a	n/a
Cornelius, NC	3,234.0	4.6	22.5	100.2	268.1	606.0	2,091.1	141.6
Cranberry, PA	2,116.1	5.5	15.6	85.0	184.5	350.1	1,402.6	72.7
Cupertino, CA	2,520.1	2.3	25.8	82.0	145.6	470.9	1,274.9	518.6
Danville, CA	3,870.0	5.6	24.6	243.0	250.4	624.0	2,003.5	718.9
Draper, UT	4,921.8	2.3	61.2	92.8	201.1	596.9	3,483.3	484.1
Dublin, OH	3,445.1	4.9	55.1	129.9	111.3	730.8	2,218.8	194.3
Eastchester, NY	n/a	3.1	19.3	147.3	264.9	209.8	n/a	85.6
Eden Prairie, MN	2,783.5	1.9	34.0	95.9	134.1	406.8	1,929.6	181.2
Edmond, OK	3,954.8	5.4	52.5	111.7	320.4	822.4	2,263.2	379.3
Evesham, NJ	2,400.0	4.6	17.1	105.9	155.7	495.0	1,536.5	85.1
Fishers, IN	4,022.2	8.1	40.4	218.7	407.6	816.4	2,175.8	355.3
Flower Mound, TX	n/a	n/a	n/a	n/a	n/a	n/a	n/a	n/a
Folsom, CA	2,919.3	4.1	24.9	118.8	273.1	559.7	1,586.9	351.8
Foster City, CA	4,322.3	3.6	36.5	237.5	253.4	529.2	2,766.6	495.6
Franklin, TN	3,245.1	4.1	47.6	113.3	465.3	525.1	1,962.1	127.6
Friendswood, TX	3,792.4	5.9	33.3	233.6	297.7	691.6	2,141.4	389.0
Germantown, TN	5,288.2	13.2	52.4	278.1	718.6	1,159.2	2,771.1	295.6
Glastonbury, CT	2,540.9	3.9	25.0	96.8	134.4	395.2	1,702.3	183.3
Grand Blanc, MI	3,545.7	8.2	71.1	127.4	493.1	935.1	1,765.8	144.9
Guilderland, NY	2,507.8	3.3	29.0	75.7	167.6	388.5	1,764.1	79.6
Hampden, PA	2,204.2	4.1	37.1	84.4	121.6	340.0	1,554.5	62.4
Holly Springs, NC	n/a	n/a	n/a	n/a	n/a	n/a	n/a	n/a
Huntersville, NC	3,239.7	4.6	22.5	101.0	270.4	608.1	2,091.0	142.2
Independence, KY	3,255.2	4.6	36.9	113.9	114.7	643.4	2,208.0	133.9
Johns Creek, GA	3,673.9	6.2	20.6	156.2	220.9	735.4	2,194.7	339.8
Keller, TX	n/a	n/a	n/a	n/a	n/a	n/a	n/a	n/a
Kirkland, WA	4,628.5	2.4	29.8	109.8	160.6	798.4	2,944.1	583.4
Lafayette, CO	n/a	1.7	67.4	26.0	149.7	363.6	n/a	142.4
Lake Oswego, OR	3,185.6	2.0	33.6	69.7	156.8	432.8	2,191.2	299.4
League City, TX	3,800.7	5.9	33.2	235.2	299.8	693.7	2,141.3	391.5
Leawood, KS	3,535.4	6.7	55.2	115.0	311.9	634.6	2,007.7	404.2
Lee's Summit, MO	3,570.1	6.8	56.0	117.6	320.3	645.3	2,012.1	412.0
Leesburg, VA	2,608.7	4.3	26.4	141.2	182.6	266.7	1,768.6	218.9
Lehi, UT	n/a	n/a	n/a	n/a	n/a	n/a	n/a	n/a
Lenexa, KS	3,544.8	6.6	55.4	115.8	313.6	639.6	2,010.0	403.8
Lexington, MA	n/a	n/a	n/a	n/a	n/a	n/a	n/a	n/a
Los Altos, CA	2,518.8	2.3	25.5	81.5	144.1	471.1	1,282.0	512.3
Lower Makefield, PA	1,656.8	1.4	12.1	41.4	72.7	218.4	1,250.8	60.0
Madison, AL	3,804.9	5.3	43.9	115.6	331.2	737.3	2,329.9	241.8
Mamaroneck, NY	n/a	3.1	19.3	147.3	264.8	209.8	n/a	85.6
Manheim, PA	1,738.8	2.4	40.2	53.0	79.2	273.4	1,244.4	46.3
Manlius, NY	2,601.7	3.6	40.0	82.3	161.9	466.5	1,758.3	89.2
Maple Grove, MN	2,776.5	1.8	34.3	95.9	134.1	406.6	1,922.6	181.1
Marion, IA	2,833.4	4.4	27.3	59.8	129.7	553.4	1,902.0	156.9
Marlboro, NJ	n/a	3.1	19.3	147.5	265.2	210.0	n/a	85.7

Table continued on next page.

Suburbs[1]	All Crimes	Violent Crimes				Property Crimes		
		Murder	Forcible Rape	Robbery	Aggrav. Assault	Burglary	Larceny -Theft	Motor Vehicle Theft
Mason, OH	3,254.7	4.6	36.9	114.2	114.9	645.6	2,204.3	134.1
McCandless, PA	2,120.1	5.4	15.6	85.1	184.2	349.9	1,407.0	72.8
Menomonee Falls, WI	3,701.7	6.4	34.0	256.6	351.3	546.0	2,018.4	489.0
Meridian, ID	2,079.8	1.6	48.0	15.8	184.9	357.5	1,372.8	99.4
Merrimack, NH	2,449.4	1.8	41.6	83.0	157.5	361.2	1,720.4	83.8
Mount Lebanon, PA	2,126.6	5.5	15.6	85.2	184.6	350.6	1,412.0	73.0
Mount Pleasant, SC	3,446.7	8.6	34.4	85.6	289.2	549.4	2,229.6	249.8
Needham, MA	n/a	n/a	n/a	n/a	n/a	n/a	n/a	n/a
Newtown, CT	1,888.6	2.0	20.0	103.0	126.0	306.3	1,171.0	160.2
Northbrook, IL	2,627.5	7.0	29.9	168.7	223.2	366.3	1,644.7	187.7
Northville, MI	4,283.7	19.3	57.3	252.9	667.4	788.6	1,740.5	757.7
Novi, MI	1,688.8	1.5	36.9	40.1	138.3	254.2	1,086.1	131.7
O'Fallon, IL	2,892.3	8.9	35.7	104.4	283.8	472.9	1,771.0	215.6
O'Fallon, MO	2,925.5	9.1	36.5	106.2	288.9	481.1	1,784.2	219.5
Orchard Park, NY	3,171.5	6.4	31.6	159.5	248.4	534.9	2,048.9	141.9
Oviedo, FL	4,752.4	6.8	63.4	156.7	467.3	986.6	2,820.8	250.7
Parker, CO	n/a	2.8	55.4	76.3	200.4	n/a	1,907.5	296.9
Parkland, FL	3,563.2	4.1	33.9	143.4	243.0	644.9	2,284.7	209.2
Peachtree City, GA	3,644.4	6.1	20.5	154.9	219.2	730.0	2,177.4	336.3
Pflugerville, TX	3,214.0	2.4	49.4	58.8	185.5	499.2	2,254.7	163.9
Plainfield, IL	2,630.7	7.0	29.9	168.8	223.3	366.8	1,647.1	187.8
Princeton, NJ	2,262.8	9.3	12.0	161.2	188.3	500.8	1,209.2	181.9
Queen Creek, AZ	n/a	n/a	n/a	n/a	n/a	n/a	n/a	n/a
Rancho Palos Verdes, CA	2,576.9	5.2	22.0	160.6	235.9	437.0	1,353.5	362.7
Redmond, WA	4,595.2	2.4	30.3	109.0	160.0	791.7	2,920.5	581.3
Richland, WA	2,415.2	6.3	34.5	35.0	138.1	482.1	1,563.0	156.1
Ridgefield, CT	1,895.4	2.0	20.5	102.8	126.1	312.2	1,171.6	160.2
Ridgewood, NJ	n/a	3.1	19.3	147.3	265.0	209.7	n/a	85.6
Rio Rancho, NM	5,340.0	5.2	59.1	187.3	552.0	991.0	3,035.4	510.0
Sahuarita, AZ	n/a	n/a	n/a	n/a	n/a	n/a	n/a	n/a
Sammamish, WA	4,632.7	2.4	30.4	109.0	159.9	793.6	2,955.6	581.9
San Ramon, CA	3,904.0	5.6	24.8	245.6	253.5	627.6	2,020.9	725.9
Saratoga, CA	2,521.0	2.3	25.0	81.6	144.0	470.3	1,285.3	512.5
Schertz, TX	4,645.3	5.8	59.8	88.0	255.0	736.7	3,133.5	366.6
Shrewsbury, MA	2,371.8	1.0	26.1	77.2	335.2	452.2	1,379.9	100.3
South Brunswick, NJ	n/a	3.1	19.3	147.5	265.3	209.5	n/a	85.6
South Jordan, UT	4,964.7	2.4	62.5	93.1	205.3	605.1	3,505.6	490.7
South Kingstown, RI	2,491.5	2.0	38.1	70.6	223.8	461.5	1,537.2	158.4
South Windsor, CT	2,512.7	3.9	24.3	96.1	133.5	393.6	1,680.4	180.8
Southlake, TX	n/a	n/a	n/a	n/a	n/a	n/a	n/a	n/a
Spring Hill, TN	3,217.2	4.0	47.5	110.8	458.2	517.2	1,954.0	125.6
Stow, OH	n/a	4.9	44.6	82.7	153.4	684.4	n/a	129.9
Sugar Land, TX	3,802.4	5.9	33.6	234.7	299.2	694.3	2,143.3	391.4
Sun Prairie, WI	2,234.9	2.2	23.9	50.5	137.4	304.5	1,648.6	67.8
Syracuse, UT	2,291.1	1.5	51.4	26.0	80.6	308.6	1,680.8	142.3
Tredyffrin, PA	1,657.5	1.4	12.2	41.2	72.7	218.7	1,251.6	59.9
Upper Arlington, OH	3,432.1	4.9	54.8	129.4	110.8	726.2	2,212.2	193.8
Upper Dublin, PA	1,656.2	1.3	12.2	40.9	72.7	219.6	1,249.6	59.9
Vestavia Hills, AL	n/a	8.0	44.8	165.5	373.8	944.6	n/a	261.6
Webster, NY	2,562.7	3.0	42.7	87.7	134.0	431.8	1,759.6	104.0
Wellesley, MA	n/a	n/a	n/a	n/a	n/a	n/a	n/a	n/a
West Fargo, ND	2,505.1	2.5	56.9	46.2	157.4	391.0	1,703.3	147.8
West Linn, OR	3,181.5	2.0	33.5	69.5	156.3	434.3	2,186.3	299.5
West Windsor, NJ	2,232.4	9.3	11.7	161.3	190.4	501.9	1,177.3	180.5
Westlake, OH	n/a	n/a	n/a	n/a	n/a	n/a	n/a	n/a
Weston, FL	3,632.4	4.2	34.0	146.6	247.4	658.2	2,328.7	213.3
Westport, CT	1,868.3	2.0	20.6	102.6	126.0	307.7	1,149.5	159.9
Wilmette, IL	2,625.3	6.9	29.9	168.5	223.0	365.8	1,643.6	187.5
Woodbury, MN	2,776.4	1.9	34.1	96.0	133.8	405.8	1,924.1	180.7
Yorba Linda, CA	1,951.1	1.9	20.6	62.9	115.7	295.1	1,252.8	202.1
U.S.	2,971.8	4.5	36.6	102.2	232.5	542.5	1,837.3	216.2

Note: Figures are crimes per 100,000 population in 2014 except where noted; n/a not available; (1) All areas within the metro area that are located outside the city limits; (2) 2013 data; (3) The suburban area figures for rape are an aggregate total of the data submitted using both the revised and legacy Uniform Crime Reporting (UCR) definitions. The U.S. figure for rape is 26.4 using the legacy definition.
Source: FBI Uniform Crime Reports, 2013, 2014

Crime Rate: Metro Area

Metro Area[1]	All Crimes	Violent Crimes				Property Crimes		
		Murder	Forcible Rape	Robbery	Aggrav. Assault	Burglary	Larceny -Theft	Motor Vehicle Theft
Aliso Viejo, CA[2]	1,932.9	1.9	20.6	61.7	114.0	293.2	1,241.9	199.5
Allen, TX[2]	n/a	n/a	n/a	n/a	n/a	n/a	n/a	n/a
Alpharetta, GA	3,629.7	6.1	20.4	154.0	217.9	725.9	2,170.4	334.9
Ankeny, IA	2,815.4	1.8	32.2	49.2	233.6	478.4	1,812.2	208.0
Apex, NC	n/a	n/a	n/a	n/a	n/a	n/a	n/a	n/a
Ballwin, MO	2,879.0	8.8	35.8	103.4	281.8	470.4	1,765.0	213.8
Beavercreek, OH	n/a	4.2	47.9	110.2	108.4	828.1	n/a	162.5
Bella Vista, AR	n/a	n/a	n/a	n/a	n/a	n/a	n/a	n/a
Bernards, NJ[2]	1,910.7	5.8	10.9	175.5	123.9	330.2	1,032.3	232.1
Bethlehem, NY	2,489.9	3.6	28.5	73.2	162.5	380.6	1,764.4	77.1
Bloomfield, MI[2]	1,685.3	1.5	36.6	39.5	136.1	250.4	1,090.9	130.3
Bowie, MD[2]	2,598.3	4.3	26.4	139.9	181.4	265.1	1,764.2	217.0
Bozeman, MT	n/a	n/a	n/a	n/a	n/a	n/a	n/a	n/a
Brentwood, TN	3,177.9	3.9	46.8	109.1	451.1	510.1	1,933.3	123.7
Broomfield, CO	n/a	2.8	54.9	75.0	198.5	n/a	1,891.6	292.5
Carmel, IN	3,889.8	7.9	38.7	209.4	390.3	783.5	2,118.1	341.8
Cedar Park, TX	3,169.8	2.4	49.0	57.6	182.0	491.0	2,226.9	160.9
Cheshire, CT	2,993.1	3.1	21.8	135.7	166.1	406.5	1,983.3	276.8
Chesterfield, MO	2,879.0	8.8	35.8	103.4	281.8	470.4	1,765.0	213.8
Collierville, TN	5,168.1	12.8	50.9	270.4	699.4	1,129.9	2,717.5	287.1
Coppell, TX[2]	n/a	n/a	n/a	n/a	n/a	n/a	n/a	n/a
Cornelius, NC	3,214.3	4.5	22.3	99.4	266.0	601.2	2,080.7	140.2
Cranberry, PA	2,106.8	5.4	15.4	84.1	182.3	346.9	1,400.5	72.1
Cupertino, CA	2,496.5	2.3	25.2	80.4	142.0	469.8	1,272.0	504.9
Danville, CA[2]	3,824.5	5.5	24.3	239.2	246.8	618.0	1,982.1	708.7
Draper, UT	4,822.9	2.2	60.2	89.8	195.8	585.9	3,418.0	470.9
Dublin, OH	3,392.8	4.8	53.9	127.3	108.9	718.0	2,189.3	190.6
Eastchester, NY[2]	n/a	3.1	19.3	147.1	264.5	209.7	n/a	85.5
Eden Prairie, MN	2,758.2	1.8	33.7	94.3	131.9	402.3	1,915.8	178.4
Edmond, OK	3,814.4	5.2	49.9	105.4	303.2	789.8	2,201.4	359.6
Evesham, NJ[2]	2,356.2	4.5	17.0	103.0	151.4	483.5	1,514.2	82.8
Fishers, IN	3,889.8	7.9	38.7	209.4	390.3	783.5	2,118.1	341.8
Flower Mound, TX[2]	n/a	n/a	n/a	n/a	n/a	n/a	n/a	n/a
Folsom, CA	2,885.5	4.0	24.5	115.9	266.3	552.3	1,579.4	343.2
Foster City, CA[2]	4,257.7	3.5	35.9	232.8	248.8	523.4	2,725.5	487.8
Franklin, TN	3,177.9	3.9	46.8	109.1	451.1	510.1	1,933.3	123.7
Friendswood, TX	3,775.5	5.8	33.2	232.2	296.1	688.6	2,132.6	387.0
Germantown, TN	5,168.1	12.8	50.9	270.4	699.4	1,129.9	2,717.5	287.1
Glastonbury, CT	2,484.4	3.8	24.2	94.0	130.2	389.5	1,664.9	177.7
Grand Blanc, MI	3,386.0	7.7	69.9	117.1	457.5	880.1	1,718.0	135.7
Guilderland, NY	2,489.9	3.6	28.5	73.2	162.5	380.6	1,764.4	77.1
Hampden, PA	2,141.1	3.9	36.1	82.0	115.8	326.2	1,517.1	59.9
Holly Springs, NC	n/a	n/a	n/a	n/a	n/a	n/a	n/a	n/a
Huntersville, NC	3,214.3	4.5	22.3	99.4	266.0	601.2	2,080.7	140.2
Independence, KY	3,225.2	4.6	36.7	112.6	113.4	637.6	2,187.7	132.6
Johns Creek, GA	3,629.7	6.1	20.4	154.0	217.9	725.9	2,170.4	334.9
Keller, TX[2]	n/a	n/a	n/a	n/a	n/a	n/a	n/a	n/a
Kirkland, WA[2]	4,563.4	2.4	29.9	107.0	157.2	783.9	2,910.6	572.3
Lafayette, CO	n/a	1.9	65.0	25.7	139.2	352.3	n/a	138.9
Lake Oswego, OR	3,157.0	2.0	33.2	68.8	154.8	430.2	2,171.6	296.5
League City, TX	3,775.5	5.8	33.2	232.2	296.1	688.6	2,132.6	387.0
Leawood, KS	3,499.3	6.6	54.4	113.2	307.9	627.9	1,991.0	398.3
Lee's Summit, MO	3,499.3	6.6	54.4	113.2	307.9	627.9	1,991.0	398.3
Leesburg, VA[2]	2,598.3	4.3	26.4	139.9	181.4	265.1	1,764.2	217.0
Lehi, UT	n/a	n/a	n/a	n/a	n/a	n/a	n/a	n/a
Lenexa, KS	3,499.3	6.6	54.4	113.2	307.9	627.9	1,991.0	398.3
Lexington, MA[2]	n/a	n/a	n/a	n/a	n/a	n/a	n/a	n/a
Los Altos, CA	2,496.5	2.3	25.2	80.4	142.0	469.8	1,272.0	504.9
Lower Makefield, PA[2]	1,644.8	1.3	12.1	40.7	72.0	218.0	1,241.5	59.3
Madison, AL	3,651.8	5.2	41.8	107.9	322.8	693.8	2,254.2	226.0
Mamaroneck, NY[2]	n/a	3.1	19.3	147.1	264.5	209.7	n/a	85.5
Manheim, PA	1,741.9	2.4	37.6	50.8	74.3	272.1	1,259.4	45.3
Manlius, NY	2,564.2	3.5	38.6	79.8	157.4	458.1	1,740.0	86.8
Maple Grove, MN	2,758.2	1.8	33.7	94.3	131.9	402.3	1,915.8	178.4
Marion, IA	2,659.7	3.8	27.7	54.5	123.1	519.7	1,789.2	141.7
Marlboro, NJ[2]	n/a	3.1	19.3	147.1	264.5	209.7	n/a	85.5

Table continued on next page.

Metro Area[1]	All Crimes	Violent Crimes: Murder	Violent Crimes: Forcible Rape	Violent Crimes: Robbery	Violent Crimes: Aggrav. Assault	Property Crimes: Burglary	Property Crimes: Larceny-Theft	Property Crimes: Motor Vehicle Theft
Mason, OH	3,225.2	4.6	36.7	112.6	113.4	637.6	2,187.7	132.6
McCandless, PA	2,106.8	5.4	15.4	84.1	182.3	346.9	1,400.5	72.1
Menomonee Falls, WI	3,645.7	6.3	33.2	251.1	343.4	536.5	1,996.7	478.6
Meridian, ID	2,000.4	1.7	44.6	13.9	168.1	339.8	1,341.5	90.9
Merrimack, NH	2,342.1	1.7	39.2	78.0	148.1	343.0	1,651.2	80.9
Mount Lebanon, PA	2,106.8	5.4	15.4	84.1	182.3	346.9	1,400.5	72.1
Mount Pleasant, SC	3,288.0	8.0	32.0	79.2	273.7	510.7	2,150.9	233.5
Needham, MA[2]	n/a	n/a	n/a	n/a	n/a	n/a	n/a	n/a
Newtown, CT	1,850.8	1.9	20.0	100.0	122.7	304.0	1,146.2	155.9
Northbrook, IL[2]	2,620.4	6.9	29.9	167.9	222.2	365.2	1,641.4	186.9
Northville, MI[2]	4,235.3	19.0	56.7	248.9	657.4	777.9	1,728.8	746.6
Novi, MI[2]	1,685.3	1.5	36.6	39.5	136.1	250.4	1,090.9	130.3
O'Fallon, IL	2,879.0	8.8	35.8	103.4	281.8	470.4	1,765.0	213.8
O'Fallon, MO	2,879.0	8.8	35.8	103.4	281.8	470.4	1,765.0	213.8
Orchard Park, NY	3,124.7	6.3	30.9	155.7	242.5	527.2	2,022.8	139.3
Oviedo, FL	4,697.9	6.8	62.5	154.4	461.8	976.0	2,789.2	247.3
Parker, CO	n/a	2.8	54.9	75.0	198.5	n/a	1,891.6	292.5
Parkland, FL[2]	3,521.2	4.1	33.4	141.5	239.7	637.2	2,258.8	206.5
Peachtree City, GA	3,629.7	6.1	20.4	154.0	217.9	725.9	2,170.4	334.9
Pflugerville, TX	3,169.8	2.4	49.0	57.6	182.0	491.0	2,226.9	160.9
Plainfield, IL[2]	2,620.4	6.9	29.9	167.9	222.2	365.2	1,641.4	186.9
Princeton, NJ	2,163.3	8.6	11.3	150.2	177.1	475.5	1,172.2	168.5
Queen Creek, AZ[3]	n/a	4.8	29.5	115.3	242.8	731.0	2,219.4	n/a
Rancho Palos Verdes, CA[2]	2,570.9	5.2	22.0	160.0	235.0	436.9	1,350.4	361.5
Redmond, WA[2]	4,563.4	2.4	29.9	107.0	157.2	783.9	2,910.6	572.3
Richland, WA	2,418.2	5.1	31.8	32.9	135.3	450.1	1,619.3	143.6
Ridgefield, CT	1,850.8	1.9	20.0	100.0	122.7	304.0	1,146.2	155.9
Ridgewood, NJ[2]	n/a	3.1	19.3	147.1	264.5	209.7	n/a	85.5
Rio Rancho, NM	5,010.8	4.8	54.1	171.1	510.3	934.3	2,866.3	469.9
Sahuarita, AZ	n/a	n/a	n/a	n/a	n/a	n/a	n/a	n/a
Sammamish, WA[2]	4,563.4	2.4	29.9	107.0	157.2	783.9	2,910.6	572.3
San Ramon, CA[2]	3,824.5	5.5	24.3	239.2	246.8	618.0	1,982.1	708.7
Saratoga, CA	2,496.5	2.3	25.2	80.4	142.0	469.8	1,272.0	504.9
Schertz, TX	4,602.4	5.8	59.4	87.1	252.6	729.5	3,105.8	362.2
Shrewsbury, MA	2,295.2	0.9	25.1	74.1	320.9	438.9	1,338.7	96.6
South Brunswick, NJ[2]	n/a	3.1	19.3	147.1	264.5	209.7	n/a	85.5
South Jordan, UT	4,822.9	2.2	60.2	89.8	195.8	585.9	3,418.0	470.9
South Kingstown, RI	2,462.2	1.9	37.7	69.3	220.0	457.3	1,520.2	155.9
South Windsor, CT	2,484.4	3.8	24.2	94.0	130.2	389.5	1,664.9	177.7
Southlake, TX[2]	n/a	n/a	n/a	n/a	n/a	n/a	n/a	n/a
Spring Hill, TN	3,177.9	3.9	46.8	109.1	451.1	510.1	1,933.3	123.7
Stow, OH	n/a	4.8	44.3	79.4	146.6	661.9	n/a	124.8
Sugar Land, TX	3,775.5	5.8	33.2	232.2	296.1	688.6	2,132.6	387.0
Sun Prairie, WI	2,246.4	2.1	23.7	48.8	134.0	298.8	1,673.4	65.7
Syracuse, UT	2,239.0	1.7	49.9	25.1	78.2	299.9	1,647.1	137.0
Tredyffrin, PA[2]	1,644.8	1.3	12.1	40.7	72.0	218.0	1,241.5	59.3
Upper Arlington, OH	3,392.8	4.8	53.9	127.3	108.9	718.0	2,189.3	190.6
Upper Dublin, PA[2]	1,644.8	1.3	12.1	40.7	72.0	218.0	1,241.5	59.3
Vestavia Hills, AL	n/a	7.8	43.4	161.1	364.1	923.0	n/a	255.6
Webster, NY	2,506.5	2.9	41.5	84.7	129.8	420.3	1,726.4	100.8
Wellesley, MA[2]	n/a	n/a	n/a	n/a	n/a	n/a	n/a	n/a
West Fargo, ND	2,427.5	2.2	51.8	41.2	156.7	394.1	1,632.4	149.2
West Linn, OR	3,157.0	2.0	33.2	68.8	154.8	430.2	2,171.6	296.5
West Windsor, NJ	2,163.3	8.6	11.3	150.2	177.1	475.5	1,172.2	168.5
Westlake, OH	n/a	n/a	n/a	n/a	n/a	n/a	n/a	n/a
Weston, FL[2]	3,521.2	4.1	33.4	141.5	239.7	637.2	2,258.8	206.5
Westport, CT	1,850.8	1.9	20.0	100.0	122.7	304.0	1,146.2	155.9
Wilmette, IL[2]	2,620.4	6.9	29.9	167.9	222.2	365.2	1,641.4	186.9
Woodbury, MN	2,758.2	1.8	33.7	94.3	131.9	402.3	1,915.8	178.4
Yorba Linda, CA[2]	1,932.9	1.9	20.6	61.7	114.0	293.2	1,241.9	199.5
U.S.	2,971.8	4.5	36.6	102.2	232.5	542.5	1,837.3	216.2

Note: Figures are crimes per 100,000 population in 2014 except where noted; n/a not available; (1) Figures cover the Metropolitan Statistical Area except where noted; (2) Metropolitan Division (MD); (3) 2013 data; (4) The metro area figures for rape are an aggregate total of the data submitted using both the revised and legacy Uniform Crime Reporting (UCR) definitions. The U.S. figure for rape is 26.4 using the legacy definition.

Source: FBI Uniform Crime Reports, 2013, 2014

Temperature & Precipitation: Yearly Averages and Extremes

City	Extreme Low (°F)	Average Low (°F)	Average Temp. (°F)	Average High (°F)	Extreme High (°F)	Average Precip. (in.)	Average Snow (in.)
Aliso Viejo, CA	25	53	64	75	112	11.9	Trace
Allen, TX	-2	56	67	77	112	33.9	3
Alpharetta, GA	-8	52	62	72	105	49.8	2
Ankeny, IA	-24	40	50	60	108	31.8	33
Apex, NC	-9	48	60	71	105	42.0	8
Ballwin, MO	-18	46	56	66	115	36.8	20
Beavercreek, OH	-25	42	52	62	102	37.4	29
Bella Vista, AR	-10	49	61	73	111	41.8	6
Bernards, NJ	-8	46	55	63	105	43.5	27
Bethlehem, NY	-28	37	48	58	100	35.8	63
Bloomfield, MI	-21	39	49	58	104	32.4	41
Bowie, MD	-5	49	58	67	104	39.5	18
Bozeman, MT	-32	36	47	59	105	14.6	59
Brentwood, TN	-17	49	60	70	107	47.4	11
Broomfield, CO	-25	37	51	64	103	15.5	63
Carmel, IN	-23	42	53	62	104	40.2	25
Cedar Park, TX	-2	58	69	79	109	31.1	1
Cheshire, CT	-7	44	52	60	103	41.4	25
Chesterfield, MO	-18	46	56	66	115	36.8	20
Collierville, TN	0	52	65	77	107	54.8	1
Coppell, TX	-2	56	67	77	112	33.9	3
Cornelius, NC	-5	50	61	71	104	42.8	6
Cranberry, PA	-18	41	51	60	103	37.1	43
Cupertino, CA	21	50	59	68	105	13.5	Trace
Danville, CA	27	52	59	66	106	17.6	Trace
Draper, UT	-22	40	52	64	107	15.6	63
Dublin, OH	-19	42	52	62	104	37.9	28
Eastchester, NY	-2	47	55	62	104	47.0	23
Eden Prairie, MN	-34	35	45	54	105	27.1	52
Edmond, OK	-8	49	60	71	110	32.8	10
Evesham, NJ	-7	45	55	64	104	41.4	22
Fishers, IN	-23	42	53	62	104	40.2	25
Flower Mound, TX	-2	56	67	77	112	33.9	3
Folsom, CA	18	48	61	73	115	17.3	Trace
Foster City, CA	24	49	57	65	106	19.3	Trace
Franklin, TN	-17	49	60	70	107	47.4	11
Friendswood, TX	7	58	69	79	107	46.9	Trace
Germantown, TN	0	52	65	77	107	54.8	1
Glastonbury, CT	-26	40	50	60	102	44.2	46
Grand Blanc, MI	-25	38	47	57	101	30.5	47
Guilderland, NY	-28	37	48	58	100	35.8	63
Hampden, PA	-9	44	53	62	107	39.0	35
Holly Springs, NC	-9	48	60	71	105	42.0	8
Huntersville, NC	-5	50	61	71	104	42.8	6
Independence, KY	-25	44	54	64	103	40.9	23
Johns Creek, GA	-8	52	62	72	105	49.8	2
Keller, TX	-1	55	66	76	113	32.3	3
Kirkland, WA	0	44	52	59	99	38.4	13
Lafayette, CO	-25	37	51	64	103	15.5	63
Lake Oswego, OR	-3	45	54	62	107	37.5	7
League City, TX	7	58	69	79	107	46.9	Trace
Leawood, KS	-23	44	54	64	109	38.1	21
Lee's Summit, MO	-23	44	54	64	109	38.1	21
Leesburg, VA	-5	49	58	67	104	39.5	18
Lehi, UT	-22	40	52	64	107	15.6	63
Lenexa, KS	-23	44	54	64	109	38.1	21
Lexington, MA	-12	44	52	59	102	42.9	41
Los Altos, CA	21	50	59	68	105	13.5	Trace
Lower Makefield, PA	-7	45	55	64	104	41.4	22
Madison, AL	-11	50	61	71	104	56.8	4
Mamaroneck, NY	-2	47	55	62	104	47.0	23
Manheim, PA	-9	44	53	62	107	39.0	35
Manlius, NY	-26	38	48	57	98	38.5	107
Maple Grove, MN	-34	35	45	54	105	27.1	52
Marion, IA	-34	36	47	57	105	34.4	33
Marlboro, NJ	-2	47	55	62	104	47.0	23
Mason, OH	-25	44	54	64	103	40.9	23
McCandless, PA	-18	41	51	60	103	37.1	43

Table continued on next page.

City	Extreme Low (°F)	Average Low (°F)	Average Temp. (°F)	Average High (°F)	Extreme High (°F)	Average Precip. (in.)	Average Snow (in.)
Menomonee Falls, WI	-26	38	47	55	103	32.0	49
Meridian, ID	-25	39	51	63	111	11.8	22
Merrimack, NH	-33	34	46	57	102	36.9	63
Mount Lebanon, PA	-18	41	51	60	103	37.1	43
Mount Pleasant, SC	6	55	66	76	104	52.1	1
Needham, MA	-12	44	52	59	102	42.9	41
Newtown, CT	-16	39	n/a	60	100	48.8	38.6
Northbrook, IL	-27	40	49	59	104	35.4	39
Northville, MI	-21	39	49	58	104	32.4	41
Novi, MI	-21	39	49	58	104	32.4	41
O'Fallon, MO	-18	46	56	66	115	36.8	20
O'Fallon, IL	-18	46	56	66	115	36.8	20
Orchard Park, NY	-20	40	48	56	99	38.1	90
Oviedo, FL	19	62	72	82	100	47.7	Trace
Parker, CO	-25	37	51	64	103	15.5	63
Parkland, FL	30	69	76	83	98	57.1	0
Peachtree City, GA	-8	52	62	72	105	49.8	2
Pflugerville, TX	-2	58	69	79	109	31.1	1
Plainfield, IL	-27	40	49	59	104	35.4	39
Princeton, NJ	-8	46	55	63	105	43.5	27
Queen Creek, AZ	17	59	72	86	122	7.3	Trace
Rancho Palos Verdes, CA	27	55	63	70	110	11.3	Trace
Redmond, WA	0	44	52	59	99	38.4	13
Richland, WA	-25	36	50	63	110	8.2	24
Ridgefield, CT	-7	44	52	60	103	41.4	25
Ridgewood, NJ	-2	47	55	62	104	47.0	23
Rio Rancho, NM	-17	43	57	70	105	8.5	11
Sahuarita, AZ	16	55	69	82	117	11.6	2
Sammamish, WA	0	44	52	59	99	38.4	13
San Ramon, CA	27	52	59	66	106	17.6	Trace
Saratoga, CA	21	50	59	68	105	13.5	Trace
Schertz, TX	0	58	69	80	108	29.6	1
Shrewsbury, MA	-13	38	47	56	99	47.6	62
South Brunswick, NJ	-2	47	55	62	104	47.0	23
South Jordan, UT	-22	40	52	64	107	15.6	63
South Kingstown, RI	-13	42	51	60	104	45.3	35
South Windsor, CT	-26	40	50	60	102	44.2	46
Southlake, TX	-1	55	66	76	113	32.3	3
Spring Hill, TN	-17	49	60	70	107	47.4	11
Stow, OH	-24	40	50	59	101	36.7	47
Sugar Land, TX	7	58	69	79	107	46.9	Trace
Sun Prairie, WI	-37	35	46	57	104	31.1	42
Syracuse, UT	-22	40	52	64	107	15.6	63
Tredyffrin, PA	-7	45	55	64	104	41.4	22
Upper Arlington, OH	-19	42	52	62	104	37.9	28
Upper Dublin, PA	-7	45	55	64	104	41.4	22
Vestavia Hills, AL	-6	51	63	74	106	53.5	2
Webster, NY	-19	39	48	57	100	31.8	92
Wellesley, MA	-12	44	52	59	102	42.9	41
West Fargo, ND	-36	31	41	52	106	19.6	40
West Linn, OR	-3	45	54	62	107	37.5	7
West Windsor, NJ	-8	46	55	63	105	43.5	27
Westlake, OH	-19	41	50	59	104	37.1	55
Weston, FL	30	69	76	83	98	57.1	0
Westport, CT	-7	44	52	60	103	41.4	25
Wilmette, IL	-27	40	49	59	104	35.4	39
Woodbury, MN	-34	35	45	54	105	27.1	52
Yorba Linda, CA	25	53	64	75	112	11.9	Trace

Source: National Climatic Data Center, International Station Meteorological Climate Summary, 9/96

Weather Conditions

City	Temperature			Daytime Sky			Precipitation		
	10°F & below	32°F & below	90°F & above	Clear	Partly cloudy	Cloudy	0.01 inch or more precip.	1.0 inch or more snow/ice	Thunder-storms
Aliso Viejo, CA	0	2	18	95	192	78	41	0	4
Allen, TX	1	34	102	108	160	97	78	2	49
Alpharetta, GA	1	49	38	98	147	120	116	3	48
Ankeny, IA	n/a	137	26	99	129	137	106	25	46
Apex, NC	n/a	n/a	39	98	143	124	110	3	42
Ballwin, MO	13	100	43	97	138	130	109	14	46
Beavercreek, OH	18	117	17	80	121	164	133	28	40
Bella Vista, AR	3	76	76	117	121	127	98	5	59
Bernards, NJ	n/a	90	24	80	146	139	122	16	46
Bethlehem, NY	n/a	147	11	58	149	158	133	36	24
Bloomfield, MI	n/a	136	12	74	134	157	135	38	32
Bowie, MD	2	71	34	84	144	137	112	9	30
Bozeman, MT	n/a	149	29	75	163	127	97	41	27
Brentwood, TN	5	76	51	98	135	132	119	8	54
Broomfield, CO	24	155	33	99	177	89	90	38	39
Carmel, IN	19	119	19	83	128	154	127	24	43
Cedar Park, TX	< 1	20	111	105	148	112	83	1	41
Cheshire, CT	n/a	n/a	7	80	146	139	118	17	22
Chesterfield, MO	13	100	43	97	138	130	109	14	46
Collierville, TN	1	53	86	101	152	112	104	2	59
Coppell, TX	1	34	102	108	160	97	78	2	49
Cornelius, NC	1	65	44	98	142	125	113	3	41
Cranberry, PA	n/a	121	8	62	137	166	154	42	35
Cupertino, CA	0	5	5	106	180	79	57	< 1	6
Danville, CA	0	< 1	3	99	168	98	59	0	6
Draper, UT	n/a	128	56	94	152	119	92	38	38
Dublin, OH	n/a	118	19	72	137	156	136	29	40
Eastchester, NY	n/a	n/a	18	85	166	114	120	11	20
Eden Prairie, MN	n/a	156	16	93	125	147	113	41	37
Edmond, OK	5	79	70	124	131	110	80	8	50
Evesham, NJ	5	94	23	81	146	138	117	14	27
Fishers, IN	19	119	19	83	128	154	127	24	43
Flower Mound, TX	1	34	102	108	160	97	78	2	49
Folsom, CA	0	21	73	175	111	79	58	< 1	2
Foster City, CA	0	6	4	136	130	99	63	< 1	5
Franklin, TN	5	76	51	98	135	132	119	8	54
Friendswood, TX	n/a	n/a	96	83	168	114	101	1	62
Germantown, TN	1	53	86	101	152	112	104	2	59
Glastonbury, CT	n/a	134	18	69	151	145	126	26	20
Grand Blanc, MI	n/a	143	8	74	122	169	133	47	33
Guilderland, NY	n/a	147	11	58	149	158	133	36	24
Hampden, PA	n/a	106	22	83	134	148	124	20	31
Holly Springs, NC	n/a	n/a	39	98	143	124	110	3	42
Huntersville, NC	1	65	44	98	142	125	113	3	41
Independence, KY	14	107	23	80	126	159	127	25	39
Johns Creek, GA	1	49	38	98	147	120	116	3	48
Keller, TX	1	40	100	123	136	106	79	3	47
Kirkland, WA	n/a	38	3	57	121	187	157	8	8
Lafayette, CO	24	155	33	99	177	89	90	38	39
Lake Oswego, OR	n/a	37	11	67	116	182	152	4	7
League City, TX	n/a	n/a	96	83	168	114	101	1	62
Leawood, KS	22	110	39	112	134	119	103	17	51
Lee's Summit, MO	22	110	39	112	134	119	103	17	51
Leesburg, VA	2	71	34	84	144	137	112	9	30
Lehi, UT	n/a	128	56	94	152	119	92	38	38
Lenexa, KS	22	110	39	112	134	119	103	17	51
Lexington, MA	n/a	97	12	88	127	150	253	48	18
Los Altos, CA	0	5	5	106	180	79	57	< 1	6
Lower Makefield, PA	5	94	23	81	146	138	117	14	27
Madison, AL	2	66	49	70	118	177	116	2	54
Mamaroneck, NY	n/a	n/a	18	85	166	114	120	11	20
Manheim, PA	n/a	106	22	83	134	148	124	20	31
Manlius, NY	n/a	136	9	56	135	174	170	67	27
Maple Grove, MN	n/a	156	16	93	125	147	113	41	37
Marion, IA	n/a	156	16	89	132	144	109	28	42
Marlboro, NJ	n/a	n/a	18	85	166	114	120	11	20

Table continued on next page.

City	Temperature			Daytime Sky			Precipitation		
	10°F & below	32°F & below	90°F & above	Clear	Partly cloudy	Cloudy	0.01 inch or more precip.	1.0 inch or more snow/ice	Thunder-storms
Mason, OH	14	107	23	80	126	159	127	25	39
McCandless, PA	n/a	121	8	62	137	166	154	42	35
Menomonee Falls, WI	n/a	141	10	90	118	157	126	38	35
Meridian, ID	n/a	124	45	106	133	126	91	22	14
Merrimack, NH	n/a	171	12	87	131	147	125	32	19
Mount Lebanon, PA	n/a	121	8	62	137	166	154	42	35
Mount Pleasant, SC	< 1	33	53	89	162	114	114	1	59
Needham, MA	n/a	97	12	88	127	150	253	48	18
Newtown, CT	n/a	132	9	n/a	n/a	n/a	n/a	n/a	21
Northbrook, IL	n/a	132	17	83	136	146	125	31	38
Northville, MI	n/a	136	12	74	134	157	135	38	32
Novi, MI	n/a	136	12	74	134	157	135	38	32
O'Fallon, MO	13	100	43	97	138	130	109	14	46
O'Fallon, IL	13	100	43	97	138	130	109	14	46
Orchard Park, NY	n/a	131	4	47	144	174	169	65	30
Oviedo, FL	n/a	n/a	90	76	208	81	115	0	80
Parker, CO	24	155	33	99	177	89	90	38	39
Parkland, FL	n/a	n/a	55	48	263	54	128	0	74
Peachtree City, GA	1	49	38	98	147	120	116	3	48
Pflugerville, TX	< 1	20	111	105	148	112	83	1	41
Plainfield, IL	n/a	132	17	83	136	146	125	31	38
Princeton, NJ	n/a	90	24	80	146	139	122	16	46
Queen Creek, AZ	0	10	167	186	125	54	37	< 1	23
Rancho Palos Verdes, CA	0	< 1	5	131	125	109	34	0	1
Redmond, WA	n/a	38	3	57	121	187	157	8	8
Richland, WA	n/a	149	32	102	133	130	70	18	6
Ridgefield, CT	n/a	n/a	7	80	146	139	118	17	22
Ridgewood, NJ	n/a	n/a	18	85	166	114	120	11	20
Rio Rancho, NM	4	114	65	140	161	64	60	9	38
Sahuarita, AZ	0	18	140	177	119	69	54	2	42
Sammamish, WA	n/a	38	3	57	121	187	157	8	8
San Ramon, CA	0	< 1	3	99	168	98	59	0	6
Saratoga, CA	0	5	5	106	180	79	57	< 1	6
Schertz, TX	n/a	n/a	112	97	153	115	81	1	36
Shrewsbury, MA	n/a	141	4	81	144	140	131	32	23
South Brunswick, NJ	n/a	n/a	18	85	166	114	120	11	20
South Jordan, UT	n/a	128	56	94	152	119	92	38	38
South Kingstown, RI	n/a	117	9	85	134	146	123	21	21
South Windsor, CT	n/a	134	18	69	151	145	126	26	20
Southlake, TX	1	40	100	123	136	106	79	3	47
Spring Hill, TN	5	76	51	98	135	132	119	8	54
Stow, OH	n/a	129	8	67	134	164	153	48	38
Sugar Land, TX	n/a	n/a	96	83	168	114	101	1	62
Sun Prairie, WI	n/a	161	14	88	119	158	118	38	40
Syracuse, UT	n/a	128	56	94	152	119	92	38	38
Tredyffrin, PA	5	94	23	81	146	138	117	14	27
Upper Arlington, OH	n/a	118	19	72	137	156	136	29	40
Upper Dublin, PA	5	94	23	81	146	138	117	14	27
Vestavia Hills, AL	1	57	59	91	161	113	119	1	57
Webster, NY	n/a	135	11	58	137	170	157	65	27
Wellesley, MA	n/a	97	12	88	127	150	253	48	18
West Fargo, ND	n/a	180	15	81	145	139	100	38	31
West Linn, OR	n/a	37	11	67	116	182	152	4	7
West Windsor, NJ	n/a	90	24	80	146	139	122	16	46
Westlake, OH	n/a	123	12	63	127	175	157	48	34
Weston, FL	n/a	n/a	55	48	263	54	128	0	74
Westport, CT	n/a	n/a	7	80	146	139	118	17	22
Wilmette, IL	n/a	132	17	83	136	146	125	31	38
Woodbury, MN	n/a	156	16	93	125	147	113	41	37
Yorba Linda, CA	0	2	18	95	192	78	41	0	4

Note: Figures are average number of days per year

Source: National Climatic Data Center, International Station Meteorological Climate Summary, 9/96

Air Quality Index

MSA[1] (Days[2])	Percent of Days when Air Quality was... Good	Moderate	Unhealthy for Sensitive Groups	Unhealthy	Very Unhealthy	AQI Statistics Maximum	Median
Aliso Viejo, CA (365)	19.7	57.8	19.5	3.0	0.0	182	67
Allen, TX (365)	59.7	32.3	7.9	0.0	0.0	147	47
Alpharetta, GA (365)	40.0	57.8	2.2	0.0	0.0	147	55
Ankeny, IA (365)	83.3	16.7	0.0	0.0	0.0	98	36
Apex, NC (365)	71.2	28.2	0.5	0.0	0.0	105	44
Ballwin, MO (365)	38.6	59.2	1.6	0.5	0.0	154	55
Beavercreek, OH (365)	66.8	32.6	0.5	0.0	0.0	119	43
Bella Vista, AR (365)	93.2	6.8	0.0	0.0	0.0	74	34
Bernards, NJ (365)	41.4	52.6	6.0	0.0	0.0	142	54
Bethlehem, NY (365)	84.4	15.3	0.3	0.0	0.0	107	36
Bloomfield, MI (365)	41.1	55.6	3.0	0.3	0.0	165	54
Bowie, MD (365)	47.9	50.7	1.4	0.0	0.0	132	51
Bozeman, MT (365)	87.4	11.8	0.5	0.3	0.0	174	22
Brentwood, TN (365)	64.9	35.1	0.0	0.0	0.0	97	44
Broomfield, CO (365)	35.9	59.5	4.7	0.0	0.0	146	54
Carmel, IN (365)	46.8	52.3	0.5	0.3	0.0	157	52
Cedar Park, TX (365)	70.1	29.0	0.8	0.0	0.0	124	42
Cheshire, CT (365)	64.1	32.6	3.3	0.0	0.0	145	43
Chesterfield, MO (365)	38.6	59.2	1.6	0.5	0.0	154	55
Collierville, TN (365)	71.2	28.2	0.5	0.0	0.0	109	42
Coppell, TX (365)	59.7	32.3	7.9	0.0	0.0	147	47
Cornelius, NC (365)	59.2	40.3	0.5	0.0	0.0	109	47
Cranberry, PA (365)	35.1	58.4	6.0	0.5	0.0	175	57
Cupertino, CA (365)	67.1	31.0	1.9	0.0	0.0	135	44
Danville, CA (365)	57.3	39.7	3.0	0.0	0.0	124	47
Draper, UT (365)	67.9	27.4	4.1	0.5	0.0	153	44
Dublin, OH (365)	67.9	32.1	0.0	0.0	0.0	97	43
Eastchester, NY (365)	41.4	52.6	6.0	0.0	0.0	142	54
Eden Prairie, MN (365)	54.5	44.1	1.4	0.0	0.0	137	48
Edmond, OK (365)	72.9	27.1	0.0	0.0	0.0	100	42
Evesham, NJ (365)	37.3	57.8	4.7	0.3	0.0	161	55
Fishers, IN (365)	46.8	52.3	0.5	0.3	0.0	157	52
Flower Mound, TX (365)	59.7	32.3	7.9	0.0	0.0	147	47
Folsom, CA (365)	37.8	55.3	6.3	0.5	0.0	179	56
Foster City, CA (365)	57.3	39.7	3.0	0.0	0.0	124	47
Franklin, TN (365)	64.9	35.1	0.0	0.0	0.0	97	44
Friendswood, TX (365)	44.1	47.1	7.4	1.4	0.0	182	53
Germantown, TN (365)	71.2	28.2	0.5	0.0	0.0	109	42
Glastonbury, CT (365)	62.7	35.3	1.9	0.0	0.0	122	43
Grand Blanc, MI (357)	77.9	21.8	0.3	0.0	0.0	131	38
Guilderland, NY (365)	84.4	15.3	0.3	0.0	0.0	107	36
Hampden, PA (365)	45.2	53.7	1.1	0.0	0.0	124	52
Holly Springs, NC (365)	71.2	28.2	0.5	0.0	0.0	105	44
Huntersville, NC (365)	59.2	40.3	0.5	0.0	0.0	109	47
Independence, KY (365)	46.6	51.5	1.9	0.0	0.0	127	51
Johns Creek, GA (365)	40.0	57.8	2.2	0.0	0.0	147	55
Keller, TX (365)	59.7	32.3	7.9	0.0	0.0	147	47
Kirkland, WA (335)	54.6	40.6	3.9	0.9	0.0	162	48
Lafayette, CO (365)	85.8	13.4	0.8	0.0	0.0	109	40
Lake Oswego, OR (334)	73.7	24.9	0.6	0.9	0.0	171	37.5
League City, TX (365)	44.1	47.1	7.4	1.4	0.0	182	53
Leawood, KS (365)	44.9	44.7	10.4	0.0	0.0	134	53
Lee's Summit, MO (365)	44.9	44.7	10.4	0.0	0.0	134	53
Leesburg, VA (365)	47.9	50.7	1.4	0.0	0.0	132	51
Lehi, UT (365)	71.2	27.4	1.4	0.0	0.0	120	43
Lenexa, KS (365)	44.9	44.7	10.4	0.0	0.0	134	53
Lexington, MA (365)	61.6	37.8	0.3	0.0	0.3	615	46
Los Altos, CA (365)	67.1	31.0	1.9	0.0	0.0	135	44
Lower Makefield, PA (365)	37.3	57.8	4.7	0.3	0.0	161	55
Madison, AL (334)	90.4	9.6	0.0	0.0	0.0	71	34.5
Mamaroneck, NY (365)	41.4	52.6	6.0	0.0	0.0	142	54
Manheim, PA (365)	53.7	44.1	2.2	0.0	0.0	140	49
Manlius, NY (365)	86.0	14.0	0.0	0.0	0.0	100	33
Maple Grove, MN (365)	54.5	44.1	1.4	0.0	0.0	137	48
Marion, IA (365)	75.1	24.7	0.3	0.0	0.0	112	41
Marlboro, NJ (365)	41.4	52.6	6.0	0.0	0.0	142	54
Mason, OH (365)	46.6	51.5	1.9	0.0	0.0	127	51

Table continued on next page.

MSA[1] (Days[2])	Percent of Days when Air Quality was...					AQI Statistics	
	Good	Moderate	Unhealthy for Sensitive Groups	Unhealthy	Very Unhealthy	Maximum	Median
McCandless, PA (365)	35.1	58.4	6.0	0.5	0.0	175	57
Menomonee Falls, WI (340)	70.6	28.8	0.6	0.0	0.0	104	42
Meridian, ID (303)	80.5	15.8	3.0	0.7	0.0	155	40
Merrimack, NH (365)	91.0	8.8	0.3	0.0	0.0	109	36
Mount Lebanon, PA (365)	35.1	58.4	6.0	0.5	0.0	175	57
Mount Pleasant, SC (365)	87.9	11.8	0.3	0.0	0.0	114	36
Needham, MA (365)	61.6	37.8	0.3	0.0	0.3	615	46
Newtown, CT (365)	61.9	33.4	4.4	0.3	0.0	151	44
Northbrook, IL (365)	33.2	64.4	1.9	0.5	0.0	183	55
Northville, MI (365)	41.1	55.6	3.0	0.3	0.0	165	54
Novi, MI (365)	41.1	55.6	3.0	0.3	0.0	165	54
O'Fallon, IL (365)	38.6	59.2	1.6	0.5	0.0	154	55
O'Fallon, MO (365)	38.6	59.2	1.6	0.5	0.0	154	55
Orchard Park, NY (365)	66.8	32.9	0.3	0.0	0.0	101	43
Oviedo, FL (365)	87.7	12.3	0.0	0.0	0.0	87	37
Parker, CO (365)	35.9	59.5	4.7	0.0	0.0	146	54
Parkland, FL (365)	71.2	28.8	0.0	0.0	0.0	95	42
Peachtree City, GA (365)	40.0	57.8	2.2	0.0	0.0	147	55
Pflugerville, TX (365)	70.1	29.0	0.8	0.0	0.0	124	42
Plainfield, IL (365)	33.2	64.4	1.9	0.5	0.0	183	55
Princeton, NJ (365)	76.2	22.7	1.1	0.0	0.0	122	37
Queen Creek, AZ (365)	18.6	71.2	6.6	0.8	2.7	881	66
Rancho Palos Verdes, CA (365)	19.7	57.8	19.5	3.0	0.0	182	67
Redmond, WA (335)	54.6	40.6	3.9	0.9	0.0	162	48
Richland, WA (331)	81.3	16.0	2.1	0.3	0.3	485	31
Ridgefield, CT (365)	61.9	33.4	4.4	0.3	0.0	151	44
Ridgewood, NJ (365)	41.4	52.6	6.0	0.0	0.0	142	54
Rio Rancho, NM (365)	76.4	23.3	0.3	0.0	0.0	117	44
Sahuarita, AZ (365)	78.6	21.4	0.0	0.0	0.0	95	43
Sammamish, WA (335)	54.6	40.6	3.9	0.9	0.0	162	48
San Ramon, CA (365)	57.3	39.7	3.0	0.0	0.0	124	47
Saratoga, CA (365)	67.1	31.0	1.9	0.0	0.0	135	44
Schertz, TX (365)	63.6	34.0	2.5	0.0	0.0	132	44
Shrewsbury, MA (365)	85.8	14.0	0.3	0.0	0.0	109	36
South Brunswick, NJ (365)	41.4	52.6	6.0	0.0	0.0	142	54
South Jordan, UT (365)	67.9	27.4	4.1	0.5	0.0	153	44
South Kingstown, RI (365)	65.2	33.4	1.1	0.3	0.0	170	44
South Windsor, CT (365)	62.7	35.3	1.9	0.0	0.0	122	43
Southlake, TX (365)	59.7	32.3	7.9	0.0	0.0	147	47
Spring Hill, TN (365)	64.9	35.1	0.0	0.0	0.0	97	44
Stow, OH (365)	48.5	51.2	0.3	0.0	0.0	135	52
Sugar Land, TX (365)	44.1	47.1	7.4	1.4	0.0	182	53
Sun Prairie, WI (339)	82.3	17.4	0.3	0.0	0.0	106	38
Syracuse, UT (365)	70.4	26.6	2.7	0.3	0.0	189	44
Tredyffrin, PA (365)	37.3	57.8	4.7	0.3	0.0	161	55
Upper Arlington, OH (365)	67.9	32.1	0.0	0.0	0.0	97	43
Upper Dublin, PA (365)	37.3	57.8	4.7	0.3	0.0	161	55
Vestavia Hills, AL (365)	57.3	41.6	0.8	0.0	0.3	356	48
Webster, NY (365)	81.1	18.9	0.0	0.0	0.0	78	36
Wellesley, MA (365)	61.6	37.8	0.3	0.0	0.3	615	46
West Fargo, ND (365)	86.0	13.2	0.8	0.0	0.0	140	36
West Linn, OR (334)	73.7	24.9	0.6	0.9	0.0	171	37.5
West Windsor, NJ (365)	76.2	22.7	1.1	0.0	0.0	122	37
Westlake, OH (365)	39.7	56.7	3.3	0.3	0.0	156	55
Weston, FL (365)	71.2	28.8	0.0	0.0	0.0	95	42
Westport, CT (365)	61.9	33.4	4.4	0.3	0.0	151	44
Wilmette, IL (365)	33.2	64.4	1.9	0.5	0.0	183	55
Woodbury, MN (365)	54.5	44.1	1.4	0.0	0.0	137	48
Yorba Linda, CA (365)	19.7	57.8	19.5	3.0	0.0	182	67

Note: The Air Quality Index (AQI) is an index for reporting daily air quality. EPA calculates the AQI for five major air pollutants regulated by the Clean Air Act: ground-level ozone, particle pollution (also known as particulate matter), carbon monoxide, sulfur dioxide, and nitrogen dioxide. The AQI runs from 0 to 500. The higher the AQI value, the greater the level of air pollution and the greater the health concern. There are six AQI categories: "Good" The AQI is between 0 and 50. Air quality is considered satisfactory; "Moderate" The AQI is between 51 and 100. Air quality is acceptable; "Unhealthy for Sensitive Groups" When AQI values are between 101 and 150, members of sensitive groups may experience health effects; "Unhealthy" When AQI values are between 151 and 200 everyone may begin to experience health effects; "Very Unhealthy" AQI values between 201 and 300 trigger a health alert; "Hazardous" AQI values over 300 trigger health warnings of emergency conditions; Data covers the entire county unless noted otherwise; (1) Data covers the Metropolitan Statistical Area—see Appendix B for areas included; (2) Number of days with AQI data in 2015

Source: U.S. Environmental Protection Agency, Air Quality Index Report, 2015

Air Quality Index Pollutants

MSA[1] (Days[2])	Percent of Days when AQI Pollutant was... Carbon Monoxide	Nitrogen Dioxide	Ozone	Sulfur Dioxide	Particulate Matter 2.5	Particulate Matter 10
Aliso Viejo, CA (365)	0.0	1.9	49.0	0.0	48.5	0.5
Allen, TX (365)	0.0	4.7	52.6	0.0	42.7	0.0
Alpharetta, GA (365)	0.0	1.6	24.7	0.0	73.2	0.5
Ankeny, IA (365)	0.0	3.0	33.2	0.0	63.0	0.8
Apex, NC (365)	0.0	0.8	38.9	0.0	60.3	0.0
Ballwin, MO (365)	0.0	2.2	18.6	0.8	75.1	3.3
Beavercreek, OH (365)	0.0	0.0	42.5	0.5	57.0	0.0
Bella Vista, AR (365)	0.0	0.0	86.0	0.0	14.0	0.0
Bernards, NJ (365)	0.0	14.5	33.2	0.3	52.1	0.0
Bethlehem, NY (365)	0.0	0.0	58.9	0.0	41.1	0.0
Bloomfield, MI (365)	0.0	2.5	15.6	14.2	58.9	8.8
Bowie, MD (365)	0.0	7.4	30.4	0.0	62.2	0.0
Bozeman, MT (365)	1.6	9.6	0.0	0.0	88.8	0.0
Brentwood, TN (365)	0.0	11.2	22.2	0.0	66.6	0.0
Broomfield, CO (365)	0.0	28.2	49.6	0.0	20.0	2.2
Carmel, IN (365)	0.0	1.6	24.7	9.0	63.8	0.8
Cedar Park, TX (365)	0.0	8.8	43.8	0.0	47.4	0.0
Cheshire, CT (365)	0.0	3.8	44.9	0.0	51.2	0.0
Chesterfield, MO (365)	0.0	2.2	18.6	0.8	75.1	3.3
Collierville, TN (365)	0.0	3.8	37.0	0.0	59.2	0.0
Coppell, TX (365)	0.0	4.7	52.6	0.0	42.7	0.0
Cornelius, NC (365)	0.0	1.4	44.7	0.0	54.0	0.0
Cranberry, PA (365)	0.0	0.0	16.4	7.4	76.2	0.0
Cupertino, CA (365)	0.0	2.5	51.0	0.0	46.3	0.3
Danville, CA (365)	0.0	6.3	33.4	0.0	60.3	0.0
Draper, UT (365)	0.0	13.2	62.2	0.3	21.6	2.7
Dublin, OH (365)	0.0	9.6	32.6	0.0	57.5	0.3
Eastchester, NY (365)	0.0	14.5	33.2	0.3	52.1	0.0
Eden Prairie, MN (365)	0.0	1.9	18.6	0.0	51.0	28.5
Edmond, OK (365)	0.0	11.8	49.0	0.0	37.3	1.9
Evesham, NJ (365)	0.0	4.1	28.2	0.3	66.6	0.8
Fishers, IN (365)	0.0	1.6	24.7	9.0	63.8	0.8
Flower Mound, TX (365)	0.0	4.7	52.6	0.0	42.7	0.0
Folsom, CA (365)	0.0	0.0	51.5	0.0	48.5	0.0
Foster City, CA (365)	0.0	6.3	33.4	0.0	60.3	0.0
Franklin, TN (365)	0.0	11.2	22.2	0.0	66.6	0.0
Friendswood, TX (365)	0.0	6.3	34.8	0.8	54.2	3.8
Germantown, TN (365)	0.0	3.8	37.0	0.0	59.2	0.0
Glastonbury, CT (365)	0.0	9.0	34.5	0.0	56.4	0.0
Grand Blanc, MI (357)	0.0	0.0	31.4	0.0	68.6	0.0
Guilderland, NY (365)	0.0	0.0	58.9	0.0	41.1	0.0
Hampden, PA (365)	0.0	0.0	15.3	0.0	84.7	0.0
Holly Springs, NC (365)	0.0	0.8	38.9	0.0	60.3	0.0
Huntersville, NC (365)	0.0	1.4	44.7	0.0	54.0	0.0
Independence, KY (365)	0.0	10.4	23.0	5.5	59.7	1.4
Johns Creek, GA (365)	0.0	1.6	24.7	0.0	73.2	0.5
Keller, TX (365)	0.0	4.7	52.6	0.0	42.7	0.0
Kirkland, WA (335)	0.3	15.5	25.7	0.0	58.5	0.0
Lafayette, CO (365)	0.0	0.0	90.7	0.0	8.5	0.8
Lake Oswego, OR (334)	0.0	1.2	43.1	0.0	55.7	0.0
League City, TX (365)	0.0	6.3	34.8	0.8	54.2	3.8
Leawood, KS (365)	0.0	3.8	19.5	20.3	46.8	9.6
Lee's Summit, MO (365)	0.0	3.8	19.5	20.3	46.8	9.6
Leesburg, VA (365)	0.0	7.4	30.4	0.0	62.2	0.0
Lehi, UT (365)	0.0	17.0	59.5	0.0	21.6	1.9
Lenexa, KS (365)	0.0	3.8	19.5	20.3	46.8	9.6
Lexington, MA (365)	0.0	3.3	27.9	0.0	68.5	0.3
Los Altos, CA (365)	0.0	2.5	51.0	0.0	46.3	0.3
Lower Makefield, PA (365)	0.0	4.1	28.2	0.3	66.6	0.8
Madison, AL (334)	0.0	0.0	61.4	0.0	22.2	16.5
Mamaroneck, NY (365)	0.0	14.5	33.2	0.3	52.1	0.0
Manheim, PA (365)	0.0	0.8	33.4	0.0	65.8	0.0
Manlius, NY (365)	0.0	0.0	71.5	0.0	28.5	0.0
Maple Grove, MN (365)	0.0	1.9	18.6	0.0	51.0	28.5
Marion, IA (365)	0.0	0.0	28.2	5.2	65.8	0.8
Marlboro, NJ (365)	0.0	14.5	33.2	0.3	52.1	0.0
Mason, OH (365)	0.0	10.4	23.0	5.5	59.7	1.4

Table continued on next page.

MSA[1] (Days[2])	Percent of Days when AQI Pollutant was...					
	Carbon Monoxide	Nitrogen Dioxide	Ozone	Sulfur Dioxide	Particulate Matter 2.5	Particulate Matter 10
McCandless, PA (365)	0.0	0.0	16.4	7.4	76.2	0.0
Menomonee Falls, WI (340)	0.3	3.8	43.2	0.0	50.9	1.8
Meridian, ID (303)	0.3	6.9	47.9	0.0	34.3	10.6
Merrimack, NH (365)	0.0	0.0	78.4	0.0	21.6	0.0
Mount Lebanon, PA (365)	0.0	0.0	16.4	7.4	76.2	0.0
Mount Pleasant, SC (365)	0.0	0.3	39.7	0.0	59.7	0.3
Needham, MA (365)	0.0	3.3	27.9	0.0	68.5	0.3
Newtown, CT (365)	0.5	0.0	34.8	0.0	64.7	0.0
Northbrook, IL (365)	0.0	6.8	9.9	2.5	73.2	7.7
Northville, MI (365)	0.0	2.5	15.6	14.2	58.9	8.8
Novi, MI (365)	0.0	2.5	15.6	14.2	58.9	8.8
O'Fallon, IL (365)	0.0	2.2	18.6	0.8	75.1	3.3
O'Fallon, MO (365)	0.0	2.2	18.6	0.8	75.1	3.3
Orchard Park, NY (365)	0.0	6.8	32.1	0.0	61.1	0.0
Oviedo, FL (365)	0.0	0.0	54.2	0.0	45.5	0.3
Parker, CO (365)	0.0	28.2	49.6	0.0	20.0	2.2
Parkland, FL (365)	0.0	1.1	18.1	0.3	67.1	13.4
Peachtree City, GA (365)	0.0	1.6	24.7	0.0	73.2	0.5
Pflugerville, TX (365)	0.0	8.8	43.8	0.0	47.4	0.0
Plainfield, IL (365)	0.0	6.8	9.9	2.5	73.2	7.7
Princeton, NJ (365)	0.0	0.0	75.3	0.0	24.7	0.0
Queen Creek, AZ (365)	0.0	3.8	31.0	0.0	24.7	40.5
Rancho Palos Verdes, CA (365)	0.0	1.9	49.0	0.0	48.5	0.5
Redmond, WA (335)	0.3	15.5	25.7	0.0	58.5	0.0
Richland, WA (331)	0.0	0.0	21.5	0.0	68.0	10.6
Ridgefield, CT (365)	0.5	0.0	34.8	0.0	64.7	0.0
Ridgewood, NJ (365)	0.0	14.5	33.2	0.3	52.1	0.0
Rio Rancho, NM (365)	0.0	0.0	79.2	0.0	9.3	11.5
Sahuarita, AZ (365)	0.0	2.5	65.8	0.0	5.5	26.3
Sammamish, WA (335)	0.3	15.5	25.7	0.0	58.5	0.0
San Ramon, CA (365)	0.0	6.3	33.4	0.0	60.3	0.0
Saratoga, CA (365)	0.0	2.5	51.0	0.0	46.3	0.3
Schertz, TX (365)	0.0	6.0	38.1	0.0	55.9	0.0
Shrewsbury, MA (365)	0.0	8.2	70.4	0.0	21.4	0.0
South Brunswick, NJ (365)	0.0	14.5	33.2	0.3	52.1	0.0
South Jordan, UT (365)	0.0	13.2	62.2	0.3	21.6	2.7
South Kingstown, RI (365)	0.0	14.2	32.6	0.0	53.2	0.0
South Windsor, CT (365)	0.0	9.0	34.5	0.0	56.4	0.0
Southlake, TX (365)	0.0	4.7	52.6	0.0	42.7	0.0
Spring Hill, TN (365)	0.0	11.2	22.2	0.0	66.6	0.0
Stow, OH (365)	0.3	0.0	9.6	0.5	89.6	0.0
Sugar Land, TX (365)	0.0	6.3	34.8	0.8	54.2	3.8
Sun Prairie, WI (339)	0.0	0.0	51.6	2.1	44.8	1.5
Syracuse, UT (365)	0.0	4.1	65.8	0.0	27.7	2.5
Tredyffrin, PA (365)	0.0	4.1	28.2	0.3	66.6	0.8
Upper Arlington, OH (365)	0.0	9.6	32.6	0.0	57.5	0.3
Upper Dublin, PA (365)	0.0	4.1	28.2	0.3	66.6	0.8
Vestavia Hills, AL (365)	0.0	2.7	16.7	1.6	77.8	1.1
Webster, NY (365)	0.0	3.6	47.1	0.3	49.0	0.0
Wellesley, MA (365)	0.0	3.3	27.9	0.0	68.5	0.3
West Fargo, ND (365)	0.0	0.3	38.4	0.0	53.2	8.2
West Linn, OR (334)	0.0	1.2	43.1	0.0	55.7	0.0
West Windsor, NJ (365)	0.0	0.0	75.3	0.0	24.7	0.0
Westlake, OH (365)	0.3	2.5	15.3	17.0	57.0	7.9
Weston, FL (365)	0.0	1.1	18.1	0.3	67.1	13.4
Westport, CT (365)	0.5	0.0	34.8	0.0	64.7	0.0
Wilmette, IL (365)	0.0	6.8	9.9	2.5	73.2	7.7
Woodbury, MN (365)	0.0	1.9	18.6	0.0	51.0	28.5
Yorba Linda, CA (365)	0.0	1.9	49.0	0.0	48.5	0.5

Note: The Air Quality Index (AQI) is an index for reporting daily air quality. EPA calculates the AQI for five major air pollutants regulated by the Clean Air Act: ground-level ozone, particle pollution (also known as particulate matter), carbon monoxide, sulfur dioxide, and nitrogen dioxide. The AQI runs from 0 to 500. The higher the AQI value, the greater the level of air pollution and the greater the health concern; (1) Data covers the Metropolitan Statistical Area—see Appendix B for areas included; (2) Number of days with AQI data in 2015
Source: U.S. Environmental Protection Agency, Air Quality Index Report, 2015

Air Quality Trends: Ozone

MSA[1]	1990	1995	2000	2005	2010	2011	2012	2013	2014
Aliso Viejo, CA	0.123	0.106	0.087	0.080	0.073	0.075	0.076	0.072	0.080
Allen, TX	0.095	0.105	0.096	0.097	0.080	0.090	0.080	0.081	0.076
Alpharetta, GA	0.104	0.103	0.101	0.087	0.076	0.078	0.079	0.066	0.072
Ankeny, IA	n/a	n/a	n/a	n/a	n/a	n/a	n/a	n/a	n/a
Apex, NC	0.093	0.081	0.087	0.082	0.071	0.074	0.071	0.061	0.063
Ballwin, MO	0.085	0.092	0.082	0.087	0.075	0.078	0.085	0.069	0.068
Beavercreek, OH	0.074	0.087	0.074	0.080	0.071	0.074	0.077	0.067	0.065
Bella Vista, AR	n/a	n/a	n/a	n/a	n/a	n/a	n/a	n/a	n/a
Bernards, NJ	0.101	0.107	0.091	0.092	0.082	0.082	0.080	0.072	0.069
Bethlehem, NY	0.086	0.079	0.070	0.082	0.072	0.066	0.071	0.063	0.061
Bloomfield, MI	0.083	0.088	0.076	0.083	0.074	0.079	0.081	0.068	0.069
Bowie, MD	0.087	0.093	0.081	0.081	0.078	0.079	0.077	0.069	0.068
Bozeman, MT	n/a	n/a	n/a	n/a	n/a	n/a	n/a	n/a	n/a
Brentwood, TN	0.089	0.086	0.085	0.078	0.073	0.071	0.078	0.068	0.069
Broomfield, CO	0.074	0.069	0.069	0.073	0.070	0.076	0.078	0.078	0.072
Carmel, IN	0.086	0.095	0.082	0.080	0.069	0.072	0.074	0.062	0.063
Cedar Park, TX	0.088	0.089	0.088	0.082	0.074	0.075	0.074	0.069	0.062
Cheshire, CT	0.121	0.117	0.087	0.092	0.079	0.092	0.087	0.087	0.087
Chesterfield, MO	0.085	0.092	0.082	0.087	0.075	0.078	0.085	0.069	0.068
Collierville, TN	0.088	0.095	0.092	0.086	0.076	0.078	0.080	0.066	0.067
Coppell, TX	0.095	0.105	0.096	0.097	0.080	0.090	0.080	0.081	0.076
Cornelius, NC	0.098	0.094	0.094	0.088	0.080	0.083	0.079	0.064	0.066
Cranberry, PA	0.080	0.098	0.082	0.084	0.076	0.073	0.080	0.068	0.067
Cupertino, CA	0.079	0.085	0.070	0.065	0.073	0.065	0.064	0.064	0.069
Danville, CA	0.058	0.074	0.057	0.055	0.061	0.060	0.057	0.056	0.065
Draper, UT	n/a	n/a	n/a	n/a	n/a	n/a	n/a	n/a	n/a
Dublin, OH	0.090	0.091	0.085	0.084	0.073	0.075	0.077	0.065	0.067
Eastchester, NY	0.101	0.107	0.091	0.092	0.082	0.082	0.080	0.072	0.069
Eden Prairie, MN	0.068	0.084	0.065	0.074	0.066	0.064	0.073	0.066	0.063
Edmond, OK	0.078	0.086	0.082	0.077	0.071	0.082	0.080	0.071	0.069
Evesham, NJ	0.102	0.109	0.099	0.091	0.083	0.084	0.084	0.069	0.071
Fishers, IN	0.086	0.095	0.082	0.080	0.069	0.072	0.074	0.062	0.063
Flower Mound, TX	0.095	0.105	0.096	0.097	0.080	0.090	0.080	0.081	0.076
Folsom, CA	0.088	0.093	0.087	0.087	0.074	0.074	0.079	0.070	0.073
Foster City, CA	0.058	0.074	0.057	0.055	0.061	0.060	0.057	0.056	0.065
Franklin, TN	0.089	0.086	0.085	0.078	0.073	0.071	0.078	0.068	0.069
Friendswood, TX	0.119	0.114	0.102	0.087	0.079	0.081	0.080	0.075	0.064
Germantown, TN	0.088	0.095	0.092	0.086	0.076	0.078	0.080	0.066	0.067
Glastonbury, CT	0.103	0.097	0.082	0.094	0.079	0.073	0.080	0.080	0.078
Grand Blanc, MI	0.076	0.081	0.073	0.080	0.068	0.073	0.084	0.066	0.068
Guilderland, NY	0.086	0.079	0.070	0.082	0.072	0.066	0.071	0.063	0.061
Hampden, PA	0.091	0.086	0.080	0.084	0.075	0.071	0.072	0.066	0.063
Holly Springs, NC	0.093	0.081	0.087	0.082	0.071	0.074	0.071	0.061	0.063
Huntersville, NC	0.098	0.094	0.094	0.088	0.080	0.083	0.079	0.064	0.066
Independence, KY	0.092	0.090	0.082	0.086	0.076	0.079	0.082	0.065	0.069
Johns Creek, GA	0.104	0.103	0.101	0.087	0.076	0.078	0.079	0.066	0.072
Keller, TX	0.095	0.105	0.096	0.097	0.080	0.090	0.080	0.081	0.076
Kirkland, WA	0.082	0.062	0.056	0.053	0.053	0.054	0.059	0.048	0.052
Lafayette, CO	n/a	n/a	n/a	n/a	n/a	n/a	n/a	n/a	n/a
Lake Oswego, OR	0.081	0.065	0.059	0.059	0.056	0.056	0.059	0.053	0.057
League City, TX	0.119	0.114	0.102	0.087	0.079	0.081	0.080	0.075	0.064
Leawood, KS	0.075	0.098	0.088	0.084	0.072	0.080	0.085	0.067	0.066
Lee's Summit, MO	0.075	0.098	0.088	0.084	0.072	0.080	0.085	0.067	0.066
Leesburg, VA	0.087	0.093	0.081	0.081	0.078	0.079	0.077	0.069	0.068
Lehi, UT	0.070	0.068	0.083	0.078	0.070	0.065	0.077	0.077	0.068
Lenexa, KS	0.075	0.098	0.088	0.084	0.072	0.080	0.085	0.067	0.066
Lexington, MA	n/a	n/a	n/a	n/a	n/a	n/a	n/a	n/a	n/a
Los Altos, CA	0.079	0.085	0.070	0.065	0.073	0.065	0.064	0.064	0.069
Lower Makefield, PA	0.102	0.109	0.099	0.091	0.083	0.084	0.084	0.069	0.071
Madison, AL	0.079	0.080	0.088	0.075	0.071	0.072	0.076	0.064	0.064
Mamaroneck, NY	0.101	0.107	0.091	0.092	0.082	0.082	0.080	0.072	0.069
Manheim, PA	0.087	0.102	0.090	0.085	0.082	0.078	0.081	0.066	0.066
Manlius, NY	0.089	0.090	0.074	0.077	0.073	0.069	0.074	0.065	0.063
Maple Grove, MN	0.068	0.084	0.065	0.074	0.066	0.064	0.073	0.066	0.063
Marion, IA	n/a	n/a	n/a	n/a	n/a	n/a	n/a	n/a	n/a
Marlboro, NJ	0.101	0.107	0.091	0.092	0.082	0.082	0.080	0.072	0.069
Mason, OH	0.092	0.090	0.082	0.086	0.076	0.079	0.082	0.065	0.069
McCandless, PA	0.080	0.098	0.082	0.084	0.076	0.073	0.080	0.068	0.067
Menomonee Falls, WI	0.095	0.106	0.082	0.092	0.079	0.074	0.092	0.069	0.072

Table continued on next page.

MSA[1]	1990	1995	2000	2005	2010	2011	2012	2013	2014
Meridian, ID	n/a	n/a	n/a	n/a	n/a	n/a	n/a	n/a	n/a
Merrimack, NH	n/a	n/a	n/a	n/a	n/a	n/a	n/a	n/a	n/a
Mount Lebanon, PA	0.080	0.098	0.082	0.084	0.076	0.073	0.080	0.068	0.067
Mount Pleasant, SC	0.068	0.071	0.078	0.073	0.067	0.066	0.063	0.059	0.060
Needham, MA	n/a	n/a	n/a	n/a	n/a	n/a	n/a	n/a	n/a
Newtown, CT	0.106	0.103	0.088	0.094	0.081	0.084	0.087	0.083	0.075
Northbrook, IL	0.074	0.093	0.072	0.084	0.070	0.072	0.082	0.066	0.067
Northville, MI	0.083	0.088	0.076	0.083	0.074	0.079	0.081	0.068	0.069
Novi, MI	0.083	0.088	0.076	0.083	0.074	0.079	0.081	0.068	0.069
O'Fallon, IL	0.085	0.092	0.082	0.087	0.075	0.078	0.085	0.069	0.068
O'Fallon, MO	0.085	0.092	0.082	0.087	0.075	0.078	0.085	0.069	0.068
Orchard Park, NY	0.089	0.088	0.083	0.090	0.072	0.071	0.081	0.068	0.062
Oviedo, FL	0.081	0.075	0.080	0.083	0.069	0.075	0.071	0.063	0.062
Parker, CO	0.074	0.069	0.069	0.073	0.070	0.076	0.078	0.078	0.072
Parkland, FL	0.068	0.072	0.075	0.065	0.064	0.060	0.062	0.061	0.062
Peachtree City, GA	0.104	0.103	0.101	0.087	0.076	0.078	0.079	0.066	0.072
Pflugerville, TX	0.088	0.089	0.088	0.082	0.074	0.075	0.074	0.069	0.062
Plainfield, IL	0.074	0.093	0.072	0.084	0.070	0.072	0.082	0.066	0.067
Princeton, NJ	0.105	0.107	0.099	0.089	0.086	0.079	0.080	0.070	0.071
Queen Creek, AZ	0.080	0.087	0.082	0.077	0.076	0.077	0.080	0.076	0.075
Rancho Palos Verdes, CA	0.123	0.106	0.087	0.080	0.073	0.075	0.076	0.072	0.080
Redmond, WA	0.082	0.062	0.056	0.053	0.053	0.054	0.059	0.048	0.052
Richland, WA	n/a	n/a	n/a	n/a	n/a	n/a	n/a	n/a	n/a
Ridgefield, CT	0.106	0.103	0.088	0.094	0.081	0.084	0.087	0.083	0.075
Ridgewood, NJ	0.101	0.107	0.091	0.092	0.082	0.082	0.080	0.072	0.069
Rio Rancho, NM	0.071	0.070	0.073	0.074	0.066	0.070	0.070	0.067	0.064
Sahuarita, AZ	0.073	0.078	0.074	0.075	0.068	0.072	0.069	0.069	0.065
Sammamish, WA	0.082	0.062	0.056	0.053	0.053	0.054	0.059	0.048	0.052
San Ramon, CA	0.058	0.074	0.057	0.055	0.061	0.060	0.057	0.056	0.065
Saratoga, CA	0.079	0.085	0.070	0.065	0.073	0.065	0.064	0.064	0.069
Schertz, TX	0.090	0.095	0.078	0.084	0.072	0.079	0.081	0.076	0.069
Shrewsbury, MA	0.097	0.096	0.076	0.085	0.070	0.065	0.070	0.067	0.065
South Brunswick, NJ	0.101	0.107	0.091	0.092	0.082	0.082	0.080	0.072	0.069
South Jordan, UT	n/a	n/a	n/a	n/a	n/a	n/a	n/a	n/a	n/a
South Kingstown, RI	0.106	0.107	0.087	0.090	0.072	0.078	0.072	0.073	0.067
South Windsor, CT	0.103	0.097	0.082	0.094	0.079	0.073	0.080	0.080	0.078
Southlake, TX	0.095	0.105	0.096	0.097	0.080	0.090	0.080	0.081	0.076
Spring Hill, TN	0.089	0.086	0.085	0.078	0.073	0.071	0.078	0.068	0.069
Stow, OH	0.090	0.092	0.085	0.091	0.074	0.073	0.072	0.059	0.060
Sugar Land, TX	0.119	0.114	0.102	0.087	0.079	0.081	0.080	0.075	0.064
Sun Prairie, WI	0.077	0.084	0.072	0.079	0.062	0.068	0.074	0.067	0.068
Syracuse, UT	n/a	n/a	n/a	n/a	n/a	n/a	n/a	n/a	n/a
Tredyffrin, PA	0.102	0.109	0.099	0.091	0.083	0.084	0.084	0.069	0.071
Upper Arlington, OH	0.090	0.091	0.085	0.084	0.073	0.075	0.077	0.065	0.067
Upper Dublin, PA	0.102	0.109	0.099	0.091	0.083	0.084	0.084	0.069	0.071
Vestavia Hills, AL	0.093	0.096	0.091	0.082	0.075	0.078	0.077	0.066	0.066
Webster, NY	0.087	0.096	0.070	0.065	0.071	0.058	0.072	0.066	0.064
Wellesley, MA	n/a	n/a	n/a	n/a	n/a	n/a	n/a	n/a	n/a
West Fargo, ND	n/a	n/a	n/a	n/a	n/a	n/a	n/a	n/a	n/a
West Linn, OR	0.081	0.065	0.059	0.059	0.056	0.056	0.059	0.053	0.057
West Windsor, NJ	0.105	0.107	0.099	0.089	0.086	0.079	0.080	0.070	0.071
Westlake, OH	0.085	0.092	0.076	0.083	0.077	0.080	0.087	0.068	0.069
Weston, FL	0.068	0.072	0.075	0.065	0.064	0.060	0.062	0.061	0.062
Westport, CT	0.106	0.103	0.088	0.094	0.081	0.084	0.087	0.083	0.075
Wilmette, IL	0.074	0.093	0.072	0.084	0.070	0.072	0.082	0.066	0.067
Woodbury, MN	0.068	0.084	0.065	0.074	0.066	0.064	0.073	0.066	0.063
Yorba Linda, CA	0.123	0.106	0.087	0.080	0.073	0.075	0.076	0.072	0.080

Note: (1) Data covers the Metropolitan Statistical Area—see Appendix B for areas included; n/a not available. The values shown are the composite ozone concentration averages among trend sites based on the highest fourth daily maximum 8-hour concentration in parts per million. These trends are based on sites having an adequate record of monitoring data during the trend period. Data from exceptional events are included.

Source: U.S. Environmental Protection Agency, Air Quality Monitoring Information, "Air Quality Trends by City, 1990-2014"

Maximum Air Pollutant Concentrations: Particulate Matter, Ozone, CO and Lead

Metro Aea	PM 10 (ug/m³)	PM 2.5 Wtd AM (ug/m³)	PM 2.5 24-Hr (ug/m³)	Ozone (ppm)	Carbon Monoxide (ppm)	Lead (ug/m³)
Aliso Viejo, CA	95	12.6	35	0.097	4	0.07
Allen, TX	80	10.7	23	0.079	1	0.04
Alpharetta, GA	61	11.2	22	0.079	2	0
Ankeny, IA	43	8.6	21	0.061	1	n/a
Apex, NC	34	11.1	22	0.063	1	n/a
Ballwin, MO	159	11.4	29	0.072	1	0.36
Beavercreek, OH	35	9.8	25	0.069	1	0.01
Bella Vista, AR	n/a	8.7	21	0.064	n/a	n/a
Bernards, NJ	47	10.5	31	0.074	3	n/a
Bethlehem, NY	n/a	7.2	19	0.061	1	n/a
Bloomfield, MI	150	11.7	27	0.073	2	0.03
Bowie, MD	43	9.3	21	0.071	2	0
Bozeman, MT	n/a	n/a	n/a	n/a	1	n/a
Brentwood, TN	37	10.5	22	0.071	1	n/a
Broomfield, CO	97	10	29	0.077	2	0.03
Carmel, IN	58	12.8	31	0.066	3	0.02
Cedar Park, TX	78	10	22	0.063	0	n/a
Cheshire, CT	34	8.7	26	0.072	1	n/a
Chesterfield, MO	159	11.4	29	0.072	1	0.36
Collierville, TN	47	9.6	25	0.067	1	0
Coppell, TX	80	10.7	23	0.079	1	0.04
Cornelius, NC	39	9.2	20	0.068	1	n/a
Cranberry, PA	63	13.4	32	0.071	2	0.2
Cupertino, CA	52	8.4	27	0.073	2	0.13
Danville, CA	37	10.8	26	0.076	3	n/a
Draper, UT	87	7.5	48	0.072	2	0.1
Dublin, OH	46	10.3	24	0.07	1	n/a
Eastchester, NY	47	10.5	31	0.074	3	n/a
Eden Prairie, MN	76	9.9	28	0.064	2	0.12
Edmond, OK	85	9.4	22	0.07	1	n/a
Evesham, NJ	60	12.6	32	0.074	1	0.01
Fishers, IN	58	12.8	31	0.066	3	0.02
Flower Mound, TX	80	10.7	23	0.079	1	0.04
Folsom, CA	83	8.8	28	0.083	2	n/a
Foster City, CA	37	10.8	26	0.076	3	n/a
Franklin, TN	37	10.5	22	0.071	1	n/a
Friendswood, TX	110	11	24	0.072	2	0
Germantown, TN	47	9.6	25	0.067	1	0
Glastonbury, CT	25	8.1	22	0.08	1	n/a
Grand Blanc, MI	n/a	8.9	24	0.068	n/a	n/a
Guilderland, NY	n/a	7.2	19	0.061	1	n/a
Hampden, PA	39	9.8	27	0.063	n/a	n/a
Holly Springs, NC	34	11.1	22	0.063	1	n/a
Huntersville, NC	39	9.2	20	0.068	1	n/a
Independence, KY	75	12.9	28	0.073	1	0.01
Johns Creek, GA	61	11.2	22	0.079	2	0
Keller, TX	80	10.7	23	0.079	1	0.04
Kirkland, WA	23	7.9	30	0.067	2	n/a
Lafayette, CO	55	7.5	26	0.07	n/a	n/a
Lake Oswego, OR	30	7	23	0.062	1	n/a
League City, TX	110	11	24	0.072	2	0
Leawood, KS	90	9.5	22	0.068	1	0.01
Lee's Summit, MO	90	9.5	22	0.068	1	0.01
Leesburg, VA	43	9.3	21	0.071	2	0
Lehi, UT	69	7.3	29	0.076	2	n/a
Lenexa, KS	90	9.5	22	0.068	1	0.01
Lexington, MA	66	10.1	19	0.07	1	n/a
Los Altos, CA	52	8.4	27	0.073	2	0.13
Lower Makefield, PA	60	12.6	32	0.074	1	0.01
Madison, AL	62	9	21	0.064	n/a	n/a
Mamaroneck, NY	47	10.5	31	0.074	3	n/a
Manheim, PA	37	15.9	40	0.066	n/a	0.23
Manlius, NY	n/a	6.5	16	0.063	n/a	n/a
Maple Grove, MN	76	9.9	28	0.064	2	0.12
Marion, IA	52	9.7	24	0.061	1	n/a
Marlboro, NJ	47	10.5	31	0.074	3	n/a
Mason, OH	75	12.9	28	0.073	1	0.01

Table continued on next page.

Metro Aea	PM 10 (ug/m³)	PM 2.5 Wtd AM (ug/m³)	PM 2.5 24-Hr (ug/m³)	Ozone (ppm)	Carbon Monoxide (ppm)	Lead (ug/m³)
McCandless, PA	63	13.4	32	0.071	2	0.2
Menomonee Falls, WI	53	10.5	30	0.074	1	n/a
Meridian, ID	61	n/a	n/a	0.065	2	n/a
Merrimack, NH	n/a	6	13	0.07	0	n/a
Mount Lebanon, PA	63	13.4	32	0.071	2	0.2
Mount Pleasant, SC	30	8.8	18	0.06	n/a	n/a
Needham, MA	66	10.1	19	0.07	1	n/a
Newtown, CT	35	9.9	25	0.081	1	n/a
Northbrook, IL	93	11.7	27	0.076	2	0.15
Northville, MI	150	11.7	27	0.073	2	0.03
Novi, MI	150	11.7	27	0.073	2	0.03
O'Fallon, IL	159	11.4	29	0.072	1	0.36
O'Fallon, MO	159	11.4	29	0.072	1	0.36
Orchard Park, NY	n/a	n/a	n/a	0.063	1	n/a
Oviedo, FL	43	6.4	14	0.067	2	n/a
Parker, CO	97	10	29	0.077	2	0.03
Parkland, FL	61	6.3	15	0.068	2	n/a
Peachtree City, GA	61	11.2	22	0.079	2	0
Pflugerville, TX	78	10	22	0.063	0	n/a
Plainfield, IL	93	11.7	27	0.076	2	0.15
Princeton, NJ	n/a	8.7	24	0.071	n/a	n/a
Queen Creek, AZ	985	10.9	37	0.08	3	0.05
Rancho Palos Verdes, CA	95	12.6	35	0.097	4	0.07
Redmond, WA	23	7.9	30	0.067	2	n/a
Richland, WA	130	n/a	n/a	n/a	n/a	n/a
Ridgefield, CT	35	9.9	25	0.081	1	n/a
Ridgewood, NJ	47	10.5	31	0.074	3	n/a
Rio Rancho, NM	155	7.4	20	0.064	1	0
Sahuarita, AZ	143	6.3	17	0.069	1	0
Sammamish, WA	23	7.9	30	0.067	2	n/a
San Ramon, CA	37	10.8	26	0.076	3	n/a
Saratoga, CA	52	8.4	27	0.073	2	0.13
Schertz, TX	71	8.9	20	0.072	n/a	n/a
Shrewsbury, MA	67	7.1	18	0.065	1	n/a
South Brunswick, NJ	47	10.5	31	0.074	3	n/a
South Jordan, UT	87	7.5	48	0.072	2	0.1
South Kingstown, RI	58	7.2	17	0.067	2	n/a
South Windsor, CT	25	8.1	22	0.08	1	n/a
Southlake, TX	80	10.7	23	0.079	1	0.04
Spring Hill, TN	37	10.5	22	0.071	1	n/a
Stow, OH	n/a	10.8	23	0.061	1	n/a
Sugar Land, TX	110	11	24	0.072	2	0
Sun Prairie, WI	41	9.3	25	0.069	n/a	n/a
Syracuse, UT	81	7.6	44	0.074	2	n/a
Tredyffrin, PA	60	12.6	32	0.074	1	0.01
Upper Arlington, OH	46	10.3	24	0.07	1	n/a
Upper Dublin, PA	60	12.6	32	0.074	1	0.01
Vestavia Hills, AL	98	11.8	26	0.065	2	n/a
Webster, NY	n/a	7.3	17	0.064	1	n/a
Wellesley, MA	66	10.1	19	0.07	1	n/a
West Fargo, ND	72	5.5	17	0.059	0	n/a
West Linn, OR	30	7	23	0.062	1	n/a
West Windsor, NJ	n/a	8.7	24	0.071	n/a	n/a
Westlake, OH	93	12.5	27	0.075	4	0.03
Weston, FL	61	6.3	15	0.068	2	n/a
Westport, CT	35	9.9	25	0.081	1	n/a
Wilmette, IL	93	11.7	27	0.076	2	0.15
Woodbury, MN	76	9.9	28	0.064	2	0.12
Yorba Linda, CA	95	12.6	35	0.097	4	0.07
NAAQS[1]	150	15	35	0.075	9	0.15

Note: Data from exceptional events are included; Data covers the Metropolitan Statistical Area—see Appendix B for areas included; (1) National Ambient Air Quality Standards; ppm = parts per million; ug/m³ = micrograms per cubic meter; n/a not available
Concentrations: Particulate Matter 10 (coarse particulate)—highest second maximum 24-hour concentration; Particulate Matter 2.5 Wtd AM (fine particulate)—highest weighted annual mean concentration; Particulate Matter 2.5 24-Hour (fine particulate)—highest 98th percentile 24-hour concentration; Ozone—highest fourth daily maximum 8-hour concentration; Carbon Monoxide—highest second maximum non-overlapping 8-hour concentration; Lead—maximum running 3-month average
Source: U.S. Environmental Protection Agency, Air Quality Monitoring Information, "Air Quality Statistics by City, 2014"

Maximum Air Pollutant Concentrations: Nitrogen Dioxide and Sulfur Dioxide

Metro Area	Nitrogen Dioxide AM (ppb)	Nitrogen Dioxide 1-Hr (ppb)	Sulfur Dioxide AM (ppb)	Sulfur Dioxide 1-Hr (ppb)	Sulfur Dioxide 24-Hr (ppb)
Aliso Viejo, CA	27	69	n/a	9	n/a
Allen, TX	10	48	n/a	17	n/a
Alpharetta, GA	11	53	n/a	6	n/a
Ankeny, IA	9	35	n/a	1	n/a
Apex, NC	10	39	n/a	6	n/a
Ballwin, MO	14	60	n/a	41	n/a
Beavercreek, OH	n/a	n/a	n/a	26	n/a
Bella Vista, AR	n/a	n/a	n/a	n/a	n/a
Bernards, NJ	22	70	n/a	15	n/a
Bethlehem, NY	n/a	n/a	n/a	8	n/a
Bloomfield, MI	16	52	n/a	72	n/a
Bowie, MD	11	47	n/a	16	n/a
Bozeman, MT	2	28	n/a	n/a	n/a
Brentwood, TN	10	n/a	n/a	13	n/a
Broomfield, CO	25	77	n/a	18	n/a
Carmel, IN	17	46	n/a	106	n/a
Cedar Park, TX	5	31	n/a	5	n/a
Cheshire, CT	13	50	n/a	17	n/a
Chesterfield, MO	14	60	n/a	41	n/a
Collierville, TN	8	42	n/a	11	n/a
Coppell, TX	10	48	n/a	17	n/a
Cornelius, NC	9	41	n/a	6	n/a
Cranberry, PA	10	44	n/a	105	n/a
Cupertino, CA	13	55	n/a	2	n/a
Danville, CA	17	58	n/a	16	n/a
Draper, UT	14	48	n/a	6	n/a
Dublin, OH	12	51	n/a	17	n/a
Eastchester, NY	22	70	n/a	15	n/a
Eden Prairie, MN	16	50	n/a	12	n/a
Edmond, OK	7	46	n/a	3	n/a
Evesham, NJ	18	59	n/a	14	n/a
Fishers, IN	17	46	n/a	106	n/a
Flower Mound, TX	10	48	n/a	17	n/a
Folsom, CA	11	55	n/a	5	n/a
Foster City, CA	17	58	n/a	16	n/a
Franklin, TN	10	n/a	n/a	13	n/a
Friendswood, TX	13	52	n/a	25	n/a
Germantown, TN	8	42	n/a	11	n/a
Glastonbury, CT	14	51	n/a	7	n/a
Grand Blanc, MI	n/a	n/a	n/a	n/a	n/a
Guilderland, NY	n/a	n/a	n/a	8	n/a
Hampden, PA	n/a	n/a	n/a	n/a	n/a
Holly Springs, NC	10	39	n/a	6	n/a
Huntersville, NC	9	41	n/a	6	n/a
Independence, KY	23	59	n/a	71	n/a
Johns Creek, GA	11	53	n/a	6	n/a
Keller, TX	10	48	n/a	17	n/a
Kirkland, WA	12	47	n/a	n/a	n/a
Lafayette, CO	n/a	n/a	n/a	n/a	n/a
Lake Oswego, OR	8	35	n/a	3	n/a
League City, TX	13	52	n/a	25	n/a
Leawood, KS	13	53	n/a	125	n/a
Lee's Summit, MO	13	53	n/a	125	n/a
Leesburg, VA	11	47	n/a	16	n/a
Lehi, UT	17	62	n/a	n/a	n/a
Lenexa, KS	13	53	n/a	125	n/a
Lexington, MA	17	53	n/a	32	n/a
Los Altos, CA	13	55	n/a	2	n/a
Lower Makefield, PA	18	59	n/a	14	n/a
Madison, AL	n/a	n/a	n/a	n/a	n/a
Mamaroneck, NY	22	70	n/a	15	n/a
Manheim, PA	9	42	n/a	12	n/a
Manlius, NY	n/a	n/a	n/a	5	n/a
Maple Grove, MN	16	50	n/a	12	n/a
Marion, IA	n/a	n/a	n/a	113	n/a
Marlboro, NJ	22	70	n/a	15	n/a
Mason, OH	23	59	n/a	71	n/a

Table continued on next page.

Metro Area	Nitrogen Dioxide AM (ppb)	Nitrogen Dioxide 1-Hr (ppb)	Sulfur Dioxide AM (ppb)	Sulfur Dioxide 1-Hr (ppb)	Sulfur Dioxide 24-Hr (ppb)
McCandless, PA	10	44	n/a	105	n/a
Menomonee Falls, WI	16	53	n/a	27	n/a
Meridian, ID	n/a	n/a	n/a	5	n/a
Merrimack, NH	n/a	n/a	n/a	5	n/a
Mount Lebanon, PA	10	44	n/a	105	n/a
Mount Pleasant, SC	7	36	n/a	11	n/a
Needham, MA	17	53	n/a	32	n/a
Newtown, CT	9	48	n/a	8	n/a
Northbrook, IL	21	67	n/a	53	n/a
Northville, MI	16	52	n/a	72	n/a
Novi, MI	16	52	n/a	72	n/a
O'Fallon, IL	14	60	n/a	41	n/a
O'Fallon, MO	14	60	n/a	41	n/a
Orchard Park, NY	9	n/a	n/a	8	n/a
Oviedo, FL	5	36	n/a	7	n/a
Parker, CO	25	77	n/a	18	n/a
Parkland, FL	9	50	n/a	5	n/a
Peachtree City, GA	11	53	n/a	6	n/a
Pflugerville, TX	5	31	n/a	5	n/a
Plainfield, IL	21	67	n/a	53	n/a
Princeton, NJ	n/a	n/a	n/a	n/a	n/a
Queen Creek, AZ	25	64	n/a	8	n/a
Rancho Palos Verdes, CA	27	69	n/a	9	n/a
Redmond, WA	12	47	n/a	n/a	n/a
Richland, WA	n/a	n/a	n/a	n/a	n/a
Ridgefield, CT	9	48	n/a	8	n/a
Ridgewood, NJ	22	70	n/a	15	n/a
Rio Rancho, NM	12	42	n/a	6	n/a
Sahuarita, AZ	11	43	n/a	6	n/a
Sammamish, WA	12	47	n/a	n/a	n/a
San Ramon, CA	17	58	n/a	16	n/a
Saratoga, CA	13	55	n/a	2	n/a
Schertz, TX	11	46	n/a	18	n/a
Shrewsbury, MA	13	49	n/a	9	n/a
South Brunswick, NJ	22	70	n/a	15	n/a
South Jordan, UT	14	48	n/a	6	n/a
South Kingstown, RI	10	44	n/a	13	n/a
South Windsor, CT	14	51	n/a	7	n/a
Southlake, TX	10	48	n/a	17	n/a
Spring Hill, TN	10	n/a	n/a	13	n/a
Stow, OH	n/a	n/a	n/a	21	n/a
Sugar Land, TX	13	52	n/a	25	n/a
Sun Prairie, WI	n/a	n/a	n/a	10	n/a
Syracuse, UT	14	n/a	n/a	n/a	n/a
Tredyffrin, PA	18	59	n/a	14	n/a
Upper Arlington, OH	12	51	n/a	17	n/a
Upper Dublin, PA	18	59	n/a	14	n/a
Vestavia Hills, AL	14	51	n/a	41	n/a
Webster, NY	n/a	n/a	n/a	21	n/a
Wellesley, MA	17	53	n/a	32	n/a
West Fargo, ND	4	34	n/a	3	n/a
West Linn, OR	8	35	n/a	3	n/a
West Windsor, NJ	n/a	n/a	n/a	n/a	n/a
Westlake, OH	12	48	n/a	80	n/a
Weston, FL	9	50	n/a	5	n/a
Westport, CT	9	48	n/a	8	n/a
Wilmette, IL	21	67	n/a	53	n/a
Woodbury, MN	16	50	n/a	12	n/a
Yorba Linda, CA	27	69	n/a	9	n/a
NAAQS[1]	53	100	30	75	140

Note: Data from exceptional events are included; Data covers the Metropolitan Statistical Area—see Appendix B for areas included; (1) National Ambient Air Quality Standards; ppb = parts per billion; n/a not available

Concentrations: Nitrogen Dioxide AM—highest arithmetic mean concentration; Nitrogen Dioxide 1-Hr—highest 98th percentile 1-hour daily maximum concentration; Sulfur Dioxide AM—highest annual mean concentration; Sulfur Dioxide 1-Hr—highest 99th percentile 1-hour daily maximum concentration; Sulfur Dioxide 24-Hr—highest second maximum 24-hour concentration

Source: U.S. Environmental Protection Agency, Air Quality Monitoring Information, "Air Quality Statistics by City, 2014"

Appendix B: Metropolitan Area Definitions

Metropolitan Statistical Areas (MSA), Metropolitan Divisions (MD), New England City and Town Areas (NECTA), and New England City and Town Area Divisions (NECTAD)

Note: *In February 2013, the Office of Management and Budget (OMB) announced changes to metropolitan area definitions. Both current and historical definitions are shown below. If the change only affected the name of the metro area, the counties included were not repeated.*

Akron, OH MSA
Portage and Summit Counties

Albuquerque, NM MSA
Bernalillo, Sandoval, Torrance, and Valencia Counties

Aliso Viejo, CA
See Los Angeles, CA (Anaheim-Santa Ana-Irvine, CA MD)

Allen, TX
See Dallas, TX (Dallas-Plano-Irving, TX MD)

Alpharetta, GA
See Atlanta-Sandy Springs-Roswell, GA MSA

Ankeny, IA
See Des Moines-West Des Moines, IA MSA

Apex, NC
See Raleigh, NC MSA

Atlanta-Sandy Springs-Roswell, GA MSA
Barrow, Bartow, Butts, Carroll, Cherokee, Clayton, Cobb, Coweta, Dawson, DeKalb, Douglas, Fayette, Forsyth, Fulton, Gwinnett, Haralson, Heard, Henry, Jasper, Lamar, Meriwether, Morgan, Newton, Paulding, Pickens, Pike, Rockdale, Spalding, and Walton Counties
Previous name: Atlanta-Sandy Springs-Marietta, GA MSA
Barrow, Bartow, Butts, Carroll, Cherokee, Clayton, Cobb, Coweta, Dawson, DeKalb, Douglas, Fayette, Forsyth, Fulton, Gwinnett, Haralson, Heard, Henry, Jasper, Lamar, Meriwether, Newton, Paulding, Pickens, Pike, Rockdale, Spalding, and Walton Counties

Austin-Round Rock, TX MSA
Previous name: Austin-Round Rock-San Marcos, TX MSA
Bastrop, Caldwell, Hays, Travis, and Williamson Counties

Ballwin, MO
See St. Louis, MO-IL MSA

Beavercreek, OH
See Dayton, OH MSA

Bella Vista, AR
See Fayetteville-Springdale-Rogers, AR-MO MSA

Bernards, NJ
See New York, NY (Newark, NJ-PA MD)

Bethlehem, NY
See Albany-Schenectady-Troy, NY MSA

Birmingham-Hoover, AL MSA
Bibb, Blount, Chilton, Jefferson, St. Clair, Shelby, and Walker Counties

Bloomfield, MI
See Detroit, MI (Warren-Troy-Farmington Hills, MI MD)

Boise City, ID MSA
Previous name: Boise City-Nampa, ID MSA
Ada, Boise, Canyon, Gem, and Owyhee Counties

Boston, MA

Boston-Cambridge-Newton, MA-NH MSA
Previous name: Boston-Cambridge-Quincy, MA-NH MSA
Essex, Middlesex, Norfolk, Plymouth, and Suffolk Counties, MA; Rockingham and Strafford Counties, NH

Boston, MA MD
Previous name: Boston-Quincy, MA MD
Norfolk, Plymouth, and Suffolk Counties

Cambridge-Newton-Framingham, MA MD
Essex and Middlesex Counties

Boston-Cambridge-Nashua, MA-NH NECTA
Includes 157 cities and towns in Massachusetts and 34 cities and towns in New Hampshire
Previous name: Boston-Cambridge-Quincy, MA-NH NECTA
Includes 155 cities and towns in Massachusetts and 38 cities and towns in New Hampshire

Boston-Cambridge-Newton, MA NECTA Division
Includes 92 cities and towns in Massachusetts
Previous name: Boston-Cambridge-Quincy, MA NECTA Division
Includes 97 cities and towns in Massachusetts

Boulder, CO MSA
Boulder County

Bowie, MD
See Washington, DC (Washington-Arlington-Alexandria, DC-VA-MD-WV MD)

Bozeman, MT MSA
Gallatin County

Brentwood, TN
See Nashville-Davidson—Murfreesboro—Franklin, TN MSA

Bridgeport, CT

Bridgeport-Stamford-Norwalk, CT MSA
Fairfield County

Bridgeport-Stamford-Norwalk, CT NECTA
Includes 24 cities and towns in Connecticut

Broomfield, CO
See Denver-Aurora-Lakewood, CO MSA

Buffalo-Cheektowaga-Niagara Falls, NY MSA
Previous name: Buffalo-Niagara Falls, NY MSA
Erie and Niagara Counties

Carmel, IN
See Indianapolis-Carmel-Anderson, IN MSA

Cedar Park, TX
See Austin-Round Rock, TX MSA

Cedar Rapids, IA MSA
Benton, Jones, and Linn Counties

Charleston-North Charleston, SC MSA
Previous name: Charleston-North Charleston-Summerville, SC MSA
Berkeley, Charleston, and Dorchester Counties

Charlotte-Concord-Gastonia, NC-SC MSA
Cabarrus, Gaston, Iredell, Lincoln, Mecklenburg, Rowan, and Union Counties, NC; Chester, Lancaster, and York Counties, SC
Previous name: Charlotte-Gastonia-Rock Hill, NC-SC MSA
Anson, Cabarrus, Gaston, Mecklenburg, and Union Counties, NC; York County, SC

Cheshire, CT
See New Haven-Milford, CT MSA

Chesterfield, MO
See St. Louis, MO-IL MSA

Chicago, IL

Chicago-Naperville-Elgin, IL-IN-WI MSA
Previous name: Chicago-Joliet-Naperville, IL-IN-WI MSA
Cook, DeKalb, DuPage, Grundy, Kane, Kendall, Lake, McHenry, and Will Counties, IL; Jasper, Lake, Newton, and Porter Counties, IN; Kenosha County, WI

Chicago-Naperville-Arlington Heights, IL MD
Cook, DuPage, Grundy, Kendall, McHenry, and Will Counties
Previous name: Chicago-Joliet-Naperville, IL MD
Cook, DeKalb, DuPage, Grundy, Kane, Kendall, McHenry, and Will Counties

Lake County-Kenosha County, IL-WI MD
Lake County, IL; Kenosha County, WI

Chino Hills, CA
See Riverside-San Bernardino-Ontario, CA MSA

Cincinnati, OH-KY-IN MSA
Previous name: Cincinnati-Middletown, OH-KY-IN MSA
Dearborn, Ohio, and Union Counties, OH; Boone, Bracken, Campbell, Gallatin, Grant, Kenton, and Pendleton County, KY; Brown, Butler, Clermont, Hamilton, and Warren Counties, IN

Cleveland-Elyria, OH MSA
Previous name: Cleveland-Elyria-Mentor, OH MSA
Cuyahoga, Geauga, Lake, Lorain, and Medina Counties

Collierville, TN
See Memphis, TN-MS-AR MSA

Columbus, OH MSA
Delaware, Fairfield, Franklin, Licking, Madison, Morrow, Pickaway, and Union Counties

Coppell, TX
See Dallas, TX (Dallas-Plano-Irving, TX MD)

Cornelius, NC
See Charlotte-Concord-Gastonia, NC-SC MSA

Cranberry, PA
See Pittsburgh, PA MSA

Cupertino, CA
See San Jose-Sunnyvale-Santa Clara, CA MSA

Dallas, TX

Dallas-Fort Worth-Arlington, TX MSA
Collin, Dallas, Denton, Ellis, Hunt, Johnson, Kaufman, Parker, Rockwall, Tarrant, and Wise Counties

Dallas-Plano-Irving, TX MD
Collin, Dallas, Denton, Ellis, Hunt, Kaufman, and Rockwall Counties

Danville, CA
See San Francisco, CA (Oakland-Hayward-Berkeley, CA MD)

Dayton, OH MSA
Greene, Miami, and Montgomery Counties
Previous name: Dayton, OH MSA
Greene, Miami, Montgomery, and Preble Counties

Denver-Aurora-Lakewood, CO MSA
Previous name: Denver-Aurora-Broomfield, CO MSA
Adams, Arapahoe, Broomfield, Clear Creek, Denver, Douglas, Elbert, Gilpin, Jefferson, and Park Counties

Des Moines-West Des Moines, IA MSA
Dallas, Guthrie, Madison, Polk, and Warren Counties

Detroit, MI

Detroit-Warren-Dearborn, MI MSA
Previous name: Detroit-Warren-Livonia, MI MSA
Lapeer, Livingston, Macomb, Oakland, St. Clair, and Wayne Counties

Detroit-Dearborn-Livonia, MI MD
Previous name: Detroit-Livonia-Dearborn, MI MD
Wayne County

Warren-Troy-Farmington Hills, MI MD
Lapeer, Livingston, Macomb, Oakland, and St. Clair Counties

Draper, UT
See Salt Lake City, UT MSA

Dublin, OH
See Columbus, OH MSA

Eastchester, NY
See New York, NY (New York-Jersey City-White Plains, NY-NJ MD)

Eden Prairie, MN
See Minneapolis-St. Paul-Bloomington, MN-WI, MSA

Edmond, OK
See Oklahoma City, OK MSA

Evesham, NJ
See Philadelphia, PA (Camden, NJ MD)

Fargo, ND-MN MSA
Cass County, ND; Clay County, MN

Fayetteville-Springdale-Rogers, AR-MO MSA
Benton, Madison, and Washington Counties, AR; McDonald County, MO

Fishers, IN
See Indianapolis-Carmel-Anderson, IN MSA

Flint, MI MSA
Genesee County

Flower Mound, TX
See Dallas, TX (Dallas-Plano-Irving, TX MD)

Folsom, CA
See Sacramento—Roseville—Arden-Arcade, CA MSA

Fort Worth, TX

Dallas-Fort Worth-Arlington, TX MSA
Collin, Dallas, Denton, Ellis, Hunt, Johnson, Kaufman, Parker, Rockwall, Tarrant, and Wise Counties

Fort Worth-Arlington, TX MD
Hood, Johnson, Parker, Somervell, Tarrant, and Wise Counties

Foster City, CA
See San Francisco, CA (San Francisco-Redwood City-South San Francisco, CA MD)

Franklin, TN
See Nashville-Davidson—Murfreesboro—Franklin, TN MSA

Friendswood, TX
See Houston-The Woodlands-Sugar Land, TX MSA

Germantown, TN
See Memphis, TN-MS-AR MSA

Glastonbury, CT
See Hartford-West Hartford-East Hartford, CT MSA

Grand Blanc, MI
See Flint, MI MSA

Guilderland, NY
See Albany-Schenectady-Troy, NY MSA

Hampden, PA
See Harrisburg-Carlisle, PA MSA

Harrisburg-Carlisle, PA MSA
Cumberland, Dauphin, and Perry Counties

Hartford, CT

Hartford-West Hartford-East Hartford, CT MSA
Hartford, Middlesex, and Tolland Counties

Hartford-West Hartford-East Hartford, CT NECTA
Includes 54 cities and towns in Connecticut
Previous name: Hartford-West Hartford-East Hartford, CT NECTA
Includes 52 cities and towns in Connecticut

Holly Springs, NC
See Raleigh, NC MSA

Houston-The Woodlands-Sugar Land-Baytown, TX MSA
Austin, Brazoria, Chambers, Fort Bend, Galveston, Harris, Liberty, Montgomery, and Waller Counties
Previous name: Houston-Sugar Land-Baytown, TX MSA
Austin, Brazoria, Chambers, Fort Bend, Galveston, Harris, Liberty, Montgomery, San Jacinto, and Waller Counties

Huntersville, NC
See Charlotte-Concord-Gastonia, NC-SC MSA

Huntsville, AL MSA
Limestone and Madison Counties

Independence, KY
See Cincinnati, OH-KY-IN MSA

Indianapolis-Carmel, IN MSA
Boone, Brown, Hamilton, Hancock, Hendricks, Johnson, Marion, Morgan, Putnam, and Shelby Counties

Johns Creek, GA
See Atlanta-Sandy Springs-Roswell, GA MSA

Kansas City, MO-KS MSA
Franklin, Johnson, Leavenworth, Linn, Miami, and Wyandotte Counties, KS; Bates, Caldwell, Cass, Clay, Clinton, Jackson, Lafayette, Platte, and Ray Counties, MO

Keller, TX
See Fort Worth, TX (Fort Worth-Arlington, TX MD)

Kennewick-Richland, WA MSA
Previous name: Kennewick-Pasco-Richland, WA MSA
Benton and Franklin Counties

Kirkland, WA
See Seattle, WA (Seattle-Bellevue-Everett, WA MD)

Lafayette, CO
See Boulder, CO MSA

Lake Oswego, OR
See Portland-Vancouver-Hillsboro, OR-WA MSA

Lancaster, PA
Lancaster County

League City, TX
See Houston-The Woodlands-Sugar Land, TX MSA

Leawood, KS
See Kansas City, MO-KS MSA

Lee's Summit, MO
See Kansas City, MO-KS MSA

Leesburg, VA
See Washington, DC (Washington-Arlington-Alexandria, DC-VA-MD-WV MD)

Lehi, UT
See Provo-Orem, UT MSA

Lenexa, KS
See Kansas City, MO-KS MSA

Lexington, MA
See Boston, MA (Cambridge-Newton-Framingham, MA MD)

Los Altos, CA
See San Jose-Sunnyvale-Santa Clara, CA MSA

Los Angeles, CA

Los Angeles-Long Beach-Anaheim, CA MSA
Previous name: Los Angeles-Long Beach-Santa Ana, CA MSA
Los Angeles and Orange Counties

Los Angeles-Long Beach-Glendale, CA MD
Los Angeles County

Anaheim-Santa Ana-Irvine, CA MD
Previous name: Santa Ana-Anaheim-Irvine, CA MD
Orange County

Lower Makefield, PA
See Philadelphia, PA (Montgomery County-Bucks County-Chester County, PA MD)

Madison, AL
See Huntsville, AL MSA

Madison, WI MSA
Columbia, Dane, and Iowa Counties

Mamaroneck, NY
See New York, NY (New York-Jersey City-White Plains, NY-NJ MD)

Manchester, NH

Manchester-Nashua, NH MSA
Hillsborough County

Manchester, NH NECTA
Includes 11 cities and towns in New Hampshire
Previous name: Manchester, NH NECTA
Includes 9 cities and towns in New Hampshire

Manheim, PA
See Lancaster, PA MSA

Manlius, NY
See Syracuse, NY MSA

Maple Grove, MN
See Minneapolis-St. Paul-Bloomington, MN-WI MSA

Marion, IA
See Cedar Rapids, IA MSA

Marlboro, NJ
See New York, NY (New York-Jersey City-White Plains, NY-NJ MD)

Mason, OH
See Cincinnati, OH-KY-IN MSA

McCandless, PA
See Pittsburgh, PA MSA

Memphis, TN-MS-AR MSA
Crittenden County, AR; Benton, DeSoto, Marshall, Tate, and Tunica Counties, MS; Fayette, Shelby, and Tipton Counties, TN
Previous name: Memphis, TN-MS-AR MSA
Crittenden County, AR; DeSoto, Marshall, Tate, and Tunica Counties, MS; Fayette, Shelby, and Tipton Counties, TN

Menomonee Falls, WI
See Milwaukee-Waukesha-West Allis, WI MSA

Meridian, ID
See Boise City, ID MSA

Merrimack, NH
See Manchester-Nashua, NH MSA

Miami, FL

Miami-Fort Lauderdale-West Palm Beach, FL MSA
Previous name: Miami-Fort Lauderdale-Pompano Beach, FL MSA
Broward, Miami-Dade, and Palm Beach Counties

Fort Lauderdale-Pompano Beach-Deerfield Beach, FL MD
Broward County

Miami-Miami Beach-Kendall, FL MD
Miami-Dade County

Milwaukee-Waukesha-West Allis, WI MSA
Milwaukee, Ozaukee, Washington, and Waukesha Counties

Minneapolis-St. Paul-Bloomington, MN-WI MSA
Anoka, Carver, Chisago, Dakota, Hennepin, Isanti, Le Sueur, Mille Lacs, Ramsey, Scott, Sherburne, Sibley, Washington, and Wright Counties, MN; Pierce and St. Croix Counties, WI

Mount Lebanon, PA
See Pittsburgh, PA MSA

Mount Pleasant, SC
See Charleston-North Charleston, SC MSA

Nashville-Davidson-Murfreesboro-Franklin, TN MSA
Cannon, Cheatham, Davidson, Dickson, Hickman, Macon, Robertson, Rutherford, Smith, Sumner, Trousdale, Williamson, and Wilson Counties

Needham, MA
See Boston, MA (Boston, MA MD)

New Haven, CT
New Haven-Milford, CT MSA
New Haven County
New Haven, CT NECTA
Includes 23 cities and towns in Connecticut
Previous name: New Haven, CT NECTA
Includes 22 cities and towns in Connecticut

New York, NY
New York-Newark-Jersey City, NY-NJ-PA MSA
Bergen, Essex, Hudson, Hunterdon, Middlesex, Monmouth, Morris, Ocean, Passaic, Somerset, Sussex, and Union Counties, NJ; Bronx, Dutchess, Kings, Nassau, New York, Orange, Putnam, Queens, Richmond, Rockland, Suffolk, and Westchester Counties, NY; Pike County, PA
Previous name: New York-Northern New Jersey-Long Island, NY-NJ-PA MSA
Bergen, Essex, Hudson, Hunterdon, Middlesex, Monmouth, Morris, Ocean, Passaic, Somerset, Sussex, and Union Counties, NJ; Bronx, Kings, Nassau, New York, Putnam, Queens, Richmond, Rockland, Suffolk, and Westchester Counties, NY; Pike County, PA
Nassau-Suffolk, NY MD
Nassau and Suffolk Counties
New York-Jersey City-White Plains, NY-NJ MD
Bergen, Hudson, Middlesex, Monmouth, Ocean, and Passaic Counties, NJ; Bronx, Kings, New York, Putnam, Queens, Richmond, Rockland, and Westchester Counties, NY
Previous name: New York-Wayne-White Plains, NY-NJ MD
Bergen, Hudson, and Passaic Counties, NJ; Bronx, Kings, New York, Putnam, Queens, Richmond, Rockland, and Westchester Counties, NY

Newark, NJ-PA MD
Essex, Hunterdon, Morris, Somerset, Sussex, and Union Counties, NJ; Pike County, PA
Previous name: Newark-Union, NJ-PA MD
Essex, Hunterdon, Morris, Sussex, and Union Counties, NJ; Pike County, PA

Newtown, CT
See Bridgeport, CT

Northbrook, IL
See Chicago, IL (Chicago-Naperville-Arlington Heights, IL MD)

Northville, MI
See Detroit, MI (Detroit-Dearborn-Livonia, MI MD)

Novi, MI
See Detroit, MI (Warren-Troy-Farmington Hills, MI MD)

O'Fallon, IL
See St. Louis, MO-IL MSA

O'Fallon, MO
See St. Louis, MO-IL MSA

Ogden-Clearfield, UT MSA
Box Elder, Davis, Morgan, and Weber Counties
Previous name: Ogden-Clearfield, UT MSA
Davis, Morgan, and Weber Counties

Oklahoma City, OK MSA
Canadian, Cleveland, Grady, Lincoln, Logan, McClain, and Oklahoma Counties

Orchard Park, NY
See Buffalo-Cheektowaga-Niagara Falls, NY MSA

Orlando-Kissimmee-Sanford, FL MSA
Lake, Orange, Osceola, and Seminole Counties

Oviedo, FL
See Orlando-Kissimmee-Sanford, FL MSA

Parker, CO
See Denver-Aurora-Lakewood, CO MSA

Parkland, FL
See Miami, FL (Fort Lauderdale-Pompano Beach-Deerfield Beach, FL MD)

Peachtree City, GA
See Atlanta-Sandy Springs-Roswell, GA MSA

Pflugerville, TX
See Austin-Round Rock, TX MSA

Philadelphia, PA
Philadelphia-Camden-Wilmington, PA-NJ-DE-MD MSA
New Castle County, DE; Cecil County, MD; Burlington, Camden, Gloucester, and Salem Counties, NJ; Bucks, Chester, Delaware, Montgomery, and Philadelphia Counties, PA
Camden, NJ MD
Burlington, Camden, and Gloucester Counties
Montgomery County-Bucks County-Chester County, PA MD
Bucks, Chester, and Montgomery Counties
Philadelphia, PA MD
Delaware and Philadelphia Counties
Previous name: Philadelphia, PA MD
Bucks, Chester, Delaware, Montgomery, and Philadelphia Counties

Pittsburgh, PA MSA
Allegheny, Armstrong, Beaver, Butler, Fayette, Washington, and Westmoreland Counties

Plainfield, IL
See Chicago, IL (Chicago-Naperville-Arlington Heights, IL MD)

Portland-Vancouver-Hillsboro, OR-WA MSA
Clackamas, Columbia, Multnomah, Washington, and Yamhill Counties, OR; Clark and Skamania Counties, WA

Princeton, NJ
See Trenton, NJ MSA

Providence, RI
Providence-New Bedford-Fall River, RI-MA MSA
Previous name: Providence-New Bedford-Fall River, RI-MA MSA
Bristol County, MA; Bristol, Kent, Newport, Providence, and Washington Counties, RI
Providence-Warwick, RI-MA NECTA
Includes 12 cities and towns in Massachusetts and 36 cities and towns in Rhode Island
Previous name: Providence-Fall River-Warwick, RI-MA NECTA
Includes 12 cities and towns in Massachusetts and 37 cities and towns in Rhode Island

Provo-Orem, UT MSA
Juab and Utah Counties

Queen Creek, AZ
See Phoenix-Mesa-Scottsdale, AZ MSA

Raleigh, NC MSA
Previous name: Raleigh-Cary, NC MSA
Franklin, Johnston, and Wake Counties

Rancho Palos Verdes, CA
See Los Angeles, CA (Los Angeles-Long Beach-Glendale, CA MD)

Redmond, WA
See Seattle, WA (Seattle-Bellevue-Everett, WA MD)

Richland, WA
See Kennewick-Richland, WA MSA

Ridgefield, CT
See Bridgeport-Stamford-Norwalk, CT MSA

Ridgewood, NJ
See New York, NY (New York-Jersey City-White Plains, NY-NJ MD)

Rio Rancho, NM
See Albuquerque, NM MSA

Rochester, NY MSA
Livingston, Monroe, Ontario, Orleans, Wayne, and Yates Counties
Previous name: Rochester, NY MSA
Livingston, Monroe, Ontario, Orleans, and Wayne Counties

Sacramento—Roseville—Arden-Arcade, CA MSA
El Dorado, Placer, Sacramento, and Yolo Counties
Previous name: Sacramento—Arden-Arcade — Roseville, CA MSA
El Dorado, Placer, Sacramento, and Yolo Counties

Sahuarita, AZ
See Tucson, AZ MSA

Saint Louis, MO-IL MSA
Bond, Calhoun, Clinton, Jersey, Macoupin, Madison, Monroe, Saint Clair Counties, IL; Franklin, Jefferson, Lincoln, Saint Charles, Saint Louis, and Warren Counties, MO; Saint Louis city, MO
Previous name: Saint Louis, MO-IL MSA
Bond, Calhoun, Clinton, Jersey, Macoupin, Madison, Monroe, Saint Clair Counties, IL; Franklin, Jefferson, Lincoln, Saint Charles, Saint Louis, Warren, and Washington Counties, MO; Saint Louis city, MO

Salt Lake City, UT MSA
Salt Lake and Tooele Counties

Sammamish, WA
See Seattle, WA (Seattle-Bellevue-Everett, WA MD)

San Antonio-New Braunfels, TX MSA
Atascosa, Bandera, Bexar, Comal, Guadalupe, Kendall, Medina, and Wilson Counties

San Francisco, CA

San Francisco-Oakland-Hayward, CA MSA
Previous name: San Francisco-Oakland-Fremont, CA MSA
Alameda, Contra Costa, Marin, San Francisco, and San Mateo Counties

Oakland-Hayward-Berkeley, CA MD
Previous name: Oakland-Fremont-Hayward, CA MD
Alameda and Contra Costa Counties

San Francisco-Redwood City-South San Francisco, CA MD
San Francisco and San Mateo Counties
Previous name: San Francisco-San Mateo-Redwood City, CA MD
Marin, San Francisco, and San Mateo Counties

San Jose-Sunnyvale-Santa Clara, CA MSA
San Benito and Santa Clara Counties

San Ramon, CA
See San Francisco, CA (Oakland-Hayward-Berkeley, CA MD)

Saratoga, CA
See San Jose-Sunnyvale-Santa Clara, CA MSA

Schertz, TX
See San Antonio-New Braunfels, TX MSA

Seattle, WA

Seattle-Tacoma-Bellevue, WA MSA
King, Pierce, and Snohomish Counties

Seattle-Bellevue-Everett, WA MD
King and Snohomish Counties

Shrewsbury, MA
See Worcester, MA-CT MSA

South Brunswick, NJ
See New York, NY (New York-Jersey City-White Plains, NY-NJ MD)

South Jordan, UT
See Salt Lake City, UT MSA

South Kingstown, RI
See Providence-Warwick, RI-MA MSA

South Windsor, CT
See Hartford-West Hartford-East Hartford, CT MSA

Southlake, TX
See Fort Worth, TX (Fort Worth-Arlington, TX MD)

Spring Hill, TN
See Nashville-Davidson—Murfreesboro—Franklin, TN MSA

Stow, OH
See Akron, OH MSA

Sugar Land, TX
See Houston-The Woodlands-Sugar Land, TX MSA

Sun Prairie, WI
See Madison, WI MSA

Syracuse, NY MSA
Madison, Onondaga, and Oswego Counties

Syracuse, UT
See Ogden-Clearfield, UT MSA

Tredyffrin, PA
See Philadelphia, PA (Montgomery County-Bucks County-Chester County, PA MD)

Trenton, NJ MSA
Previous name: Trenton-Ewing, NJ MSA
Mercer County

Tucson, AZ MSA
Pima County

Upper Arlington, OH
See Columbus, OH MSA

Upper Dublin, PA
See Philadelphia, PA (Montgomery County-Bucks County-Chester County, PA MD)

Vestavia Hills, AL
See Birmingham-Hoover, AL MSA

Washington, DC

Washington-Arlington-Alexandria, DC-VA-MD-WV MSA
District of Columbia; Calvert, Charles, Frederick, Montgomery, and Prince George's Counties, MD; Alexandria, Fairfax, Falls Church, Fredericksburg, Manassas Park, and Manassas cities, VA; Arlington, Clarke, Culpepper, Fairfax, Fauquier, Loudoun, Prince William, Rappahannock, Spotsylvania, Stafford, and Warren Counties, VA; Jefferson County, WV
Previous name: Washington-Arlington-Alexandria, DC-VA-MD-WV MSA
District of Columbia; Calvert, Charles, Frederick, Montgomery, and Prince George's Counties, MD; Alexandria, Fairfax, Falls Church, Fredericksburg, Manassas Park, and Manassas cities, VA; Arlington, Clarke, Fairfax, Fauquier, Loudoun, Prince William, Spotsylvania, Stafford, and Warren Counties, VA; Jefferson County, WV

Washington-Arlington-Alexandria, DC-VA-MD-WV MD
District of Columbia; Calvert, Charles, and Prince George's Counties, MD; Alexandria, Fairfax, Falls Church, Fredericksburg, Manassas Park, and Manassas cities, VA; Arlington, Clarke, Culpepper, Fairfax, Fauquier, Loudoun, Prince William, Rappahannock, Spotsylvania, Stafford, and Warren Counties, VA; Jefferson County, WV
Previous name: Washington-Arlington-Alexandria, DC-VA-MD-WV MD
District of Columbia; Calvert, Charles, and Prince George's Counties, MD; Alexandria, Fairfax, Falls Church, Fredericksburg, Manassas Park, and Manassas cities, VA; Arlington, Clarke, Fairfax, Fauquier, Loudoun, Prince William, Spotsylvania, Stafford, and Warren Counties, VA; Jefferson County, WV

Webster, NY
See Rochester, NY MSA

Wellesley, MA
See Boston, MA (Boston, MA MD)

West Fargo, ND
See Fargo, ND-MN MSA

West Linn, OR
See Portland-Vancouver-Hillsboro, OR-WA MSA

West Windsor, NJ
See Trenton, NJ MSA

Westlake, OH
See Cleveland-Elyria, OH MSA

Weston, FL
See Miami, FL (Fort Lauderdale-Pompano Beach-Deerfield Beach, FL MD)

Westport, CT
See Bridgeport-Stamford-Norwalk, CT MSA

Wilmette, IL
See Chicago, IL (Chicago-Naperville-Arlington Heights, IL MD)

Woodbury, MN
See Minneapolis-St. Paul-Bloomington, MN-WI MSA

Worcester, MA

Worcester, MA-CT MSA
Windham County, CT; Worcester County, MA
Previous name: Worcester, MA MSA
Worcester County

Worcester, MA-CT NECTA
Includes 40 cities and towns in Massachusetts and 8 cities and towns in Connecticut
Previous name: Worcester, MA-CT NECTA
Includes 37 cities and towns in Massachusetts and 3 cities and towns in Connecticut

Yorba Linda, CA
See Los Angeles, CA (Anaheim-Santa Ana-Irvine, CA MD)

Appendix C: Government Type and Primary County

This appendix includes the government structure of each place included in this book. It also includes the county or county equivalent in which each place is located. If a place spans more that one county, the county in which the majority of the population resides is shown.

Aliso Viejo, CA
Government Type: City
County: Orange

Allen, TX
Government Type: City
County: Collin

Alpharetta, GA
Government Type: City
County: Fulton

Ankeny, IA
Government Type: City
County: Polk

Apex, NC
Government Type: Town
County: Wake

Ballwin, MO
Government Type: City
County: Saint Louis

Beavercreek, OH
Government Type: City
County: Greene

Bella Vista, AR
Government Type: Town
County: Benton

Bernards, NJ
Government Type: Township
County: Somerset

Bethlehem, NY
Government Type: Town
County: Albany

Bloomfield, MI
Government Type: Charter Township
County: Oakland

Bowie, MD
Government Type: City
County: Prince George's

Bozeman, MT
Government Type: City
County: Gallatin

Brentwood, TN
Government Type: City
County: Williamson

Broomfield, CO
Government Type: City
County: Broomfield

Carmel, IN
Government Type: City
County: Hamilton

Cedar Park, TX
Government Type: City
County: Williamson

Cheshire, CT
Government Type: Town
County: New Haven

Chesterfield, MO
Government Type: City
County: Saint Louis

Collierville, TN
Government Type: Town
County: Shelby

Coppell, TX
Government Type: City
County: Dallas

Cornelius, NC
Government Type: Town
County: Mecklenburg

Cranberry, PA
Government Type: Township
County: Butler

Cupertino, CA
Government Type: City
County: Santa Clara

Danville, CA
Government Type: Town
County: Contra Costa

Draper, UT
Government Type: City
County: Salt Lake

Dublin, OH
Government Type: City
County: Franklin

Eastchester, NY
Government Type: Town
County: Westchester

Eden Prairie, MN
Government Type: City
County: Hennepin

Edmond, OK
Government Type: City
County: Oklahoma

Evesham, NJ
Government Type: Township
County: Burlington

Fishers, IN
Government Type: Town
County: Hamilton

Flower Mound, TX
Government Type: Town
County: Denton

Folsom, CA
Government Type: City
County: Sacramento

Foster City, CA
Government Type: City
County: San Mateo

Franklin, TN
Government Type: City
County: Williamson

Friendswood, TX
Government Type: City
County: Galveston

Germantown, TN
Government Type: City
County: Shelby

Glastonbury, CT
Government Type: Town
County: Hartford

Grand Blanc, MI
Government Type: Charter Township
County: Genesee

Guilderland, NY
Government Type: Town
County: Albany

Hampden, PA
Government Type: Township
County: Cumberland

Holly Springs, NC
Government Type: Town
County: Wake

Huntersville, NC
Government Type: Town
County: Mecklenburg

Independence, KY
Government Type: City
County: Kenton

Johns Creek, GA
Government Type: City
County: Fulton

Keller, TX
Government Type: City
County: Tarrant

Kirkland, WA
Government Type: City
County: King

Lafayette, CO
Government Type: City
County: Boulder

Lake Oswego, OR
Government Type: City
County: Clackamas

League City, TX
Government Type: City
County: Galveston

Leawood, KS
Government Type: City
County: Johnson

Lee's Summit, MO
Government Type: City
County: Jackson

Leesburg, VA
Government Type: Town
County: Loudoun

Lehi, UT
Government Type: City
County: Utah

Lenexa, KS
Government Type: City
County: Johnson

Lexington, MA
Government Type: Town
County: Middlesex

Los Altos, CA
Government Type: City
County: Santa Clara

Lower Makefield, PA
Government Type: Township
County: Bucks

Madison, AL
Government Type: City
County: Madison

Mamaroneck, NY
Government Type: Town
County: Westchester

Manheim, PA
Government Type: Township
County: Lancaster

Manlius, NY
Government Type: Town
County: Onondaga

Maple Grove, MN
Government Type: City
County: Hennepin

Marion, IA
Government Type: City
County: Linn

Marlboro, NJ
Government Type: Township
County: Monmouth

Mason, OH
Government Type: City
County: Warren

McCandless, PA
Government Type: Township
County: Allegheny

Menomonee Falls, WI
Government Type: Village
County: Waukesha

Meridian, ID
Government Type: City
County: Ada

Merrimack, NH
Government Type: Town
County: Hillsborough

Mount Lebanon, PA
Government Type: Township
County: Allegheny

Mount Pleasant, SC
Government Type: Town
County: Charleston

Needham, MA
Government Type: Town
County: Norfolk

Newtown, CT
Government Type: Town
County: Fairfield

Northbrook, IL
Government Type: Village
County: Cook

Northville, MI
Government Type: Township
County: Wayne

Novi, MI
Government Type: City
County: Oakland

O'Fallon, IL
Government Type: City
County: Saint Clair

O'Fallon, MO
Government Type: City
County: Saint Charles

Orchard Park, NY
Government Type: Town
County: Erie

Oviedo, FL
Government Type: City
County: Seminole

Parker, CO
Government Type: Town
County: Douglas

Parkland, FL
Government Type: City
County: Broward

Peachtree City, GA
Government Type: City
County: Fayette

Pflugerville, TX
Government Type: City
County: Travis

Plainfield, IL
Government Type: Village
County: Will

Princeton, NJ
Government Type: Borough
County: Mercer

Queen Creek, AZ
Government Type: Town
County: Maricopa

Rancho Palos Verdes, CA
Government Type: City
County: Los Angeles

Redmond, WA
Government Type: City
County: King

Richland, WA
Government Type: City
County: Benton

Ridgefield, CT
Government Type: Town
County: Fairfield

Ridgewood, NJ
Government Type: Village
County: Bergen

Rio Rancho, NM
Government Type: City
County: Sandoval

Sahuarita, AZ
Government Type: Town
County: Pima

Sammamish, WA
Government Type: City
County: King

San Ramon, CA
Government Type: City
County: Contra Costa

Saratoga, CA
Government Type: City
County: Santa Clara

Schertz, TX
Government Type: City
County: Guadalupe

Shrewsbury, MA
Government Type: Town
County: Worcester

South Brunswick, NJ
Government Type: Township
County: Middlesex

South Jordan, UT
Government Type: City
County: Salt Lake

South Kingstown, RI
Government Type: Town
County: Washington

South Windsor, CT
Government Type: Town
County: Hartford

Southlake, TX
Government Type: City
County: Tarrant

Spring Hill, TN
Government Type: City
County: Williamson

Stow, OH
Government Type: City
County: Summit

Sugar Land, TX
Government Type: City
County: Fort Bend

Sun Prairie, WI
Government Type: City
County: Dane

Syracuse, UT
Government Type: City
County: Davis

Tredyffrin, PA
Government Type: Township
County: Chester

Upper Arlington, OH
Government Type: City
County: Franklin

Upper Dublin, PA
Government Type: Township
County: Montgomery

Vestavia Hills, AL
Government Type: City
County: Jefferson

Webster, NY
Government Type: Town
County: Monroe

Wellesley, MA
Government Type: Town
County: Norfolk

West Fargo, ND
Government Type: City
County: Cass

West Linn, OR
Government Type: City
County: Clackamas

West Windsor, NJ
Government Type: Township
County: Mercer

Westlake, OH
Government Type: City
County: Cuyahoga

Weston, FL
Government Type: City
County: Broward

Westport, CT
Government Type: Town
County: Fairfield

Wilmette, IL
Government Type: Village
County: Cook

Woodbury, MN
Government Type: City
County: Washington

Yorba Linda, CA
Government Type: City
County: Orange

Appendix D: Chambers of Commerce

Aliso Viejo, CA
Alisa Viejo Chamber of Commerce
12 Journey
Suite 100
Alisa Viejo, CA 92656-5335
Phone: 949- 243-7042
http://alisoviejochamber.com

Allen, TX
Allen Chamber of Commerce
210 West McDermott Drive
Allen, TX 75013
Phone: 972-727-5585
Fax: 972-727-9000
http://www.allenfairviewchamber.com

Alpharetta, GA
Greater North Fulton Chamber of Commerce
11605 Haynes Bridge Road
Suite 100
Alpharetta, GA 30009
Phone: 866-840-5770
Fax: 770-594-1059
http://www.gnfcc.com

Ankeny, IA
Ankeny Area Chamber of Commerce
210 South Ankeny Blvd.
PO Box 488
Ankeny, IA 50023
Phone: 515-964-0685
Fax: 515-964-0487
http://www.ankeny.org

Apex, NC
Apex Chamber of Commerce
220 North Salem Street
Apex, NC 27502
Phone: 919-362-6456
Fax: 919-362-9050
http://www.apexchamber.com/

Ballwin, MO
West St. Louis County Chamber of Commerce
15965 Manchester Road
Suite 102
Ellisville, MO 63011
Phone: 636-230-9900
Fax: 636-230-9912
http://www.westcountychamber.com

Beavercreek, OH
Beavercreek Chamber of Commerce
3210 Beaver-Vu Drive
Beavercreek, OH 45434
Phone: 937-426-2202
Fax: 937-426-2204
http://www.beavercreekchamber.org

Bella Vista, AR
Bentonville/Bella Vista Chamber of Commerce
200 East Central Avenue
Bentonville, AR 72712
Phone: 479-273-2841
Fax: 429-273-2180
http://bbvchamber.com

Bernards, NJ
Bernards Township Regional Chamber of Commerce
PO Box 11
Basking Ridge, NJ 07920
Phone: 908-766-6755
http://bernardstwpregionalchamber.org

Bethlehem, NY
Bethlehem Chamber of Commerce
318 Delaware Avenue
Suite 11
Delmar, NY 12054
Phone: 518-439-0512
Fax: 518-475-0910
http://www.bethlehemchamber.com

Bloomfield, MI
Birmingham Bloomfield Chamber
725 S. Adams Road
Suite 130
Birmingham, MI 48009
Phone: 248-644-1700
Fax: 248-644-0286
http://www.bbcc.com

Bowie, MD
Greater Bowie Chamber of Commerce
2614 Kenhill Drive
Suite 117
Bowie, MD 20715
Phone: 301-262-0920
Fax: 304-262-0921
http://www.bowiechamber.org

Bozeman, MT
Bozeman Chamber of Commerce
2000 Commerce Way
Bozeman, MT 59715
Phone: 406-586-5421
Fax: 406-586-8286
http://bozemanchamber.com

Brentwood, TN
Wliamson, Inc.
5005 Meridian Boulevard
Franklin, TN 37067
Phone: 615-771-1912
http://www.williamsonchamber.com

Broomfield, CO
Broomfield Chamber of Commerce
2095 W. 6th Avenue
Broomfield, CO 80020
Phone: 303-466-1775
Fax: 303-466-4481
http://accessbroomfield.chambermaster.com

Carmel, IN
OneZone - Carmel and Fishers Chambers of Commerce
10305 Allisonville Road
Suite B
Fishers, IN 46038
Phone: 317-436-4653
http://www.onezonecommerce.com

Cedar Park, TX
Cedar Park Chamber of Commerce
1460 E. Whitestone Blvd.
Suite 180
Cedar Park, TX 78630
Phone: 512-260-7800
Fax: 512-260-9269
http://www.cedarparkchamber.org

Cheshire, CT
Cheshire Chamber of Commerce
195 South Main Street
Cheshire, CT 06410
Phone: 203-272-2345
Fax: 203-271-3044
http://www.cheshirechamber.org

Chesterfield, MO
Chesterfield Chamber of Commerce
101 Chesterfield Business Parkway
Chesterfield, MO 63005
Phone: 636-532-3399
http://www.chesterfieldmochamber.com

Collierville, TN
Collierville Chamber of Commerce
485 Halle Park Drive
Collierville, TN 38017
Phone: 901-853-1949
Fax: 901-853-2399
http://www.colliervillechamber.com

Coppell, TX
Coppell Chamber of Commerce
708 Main St
Coppell, TX 75019
Phone: 972-393-2829
Fax: 972-393-0659
http://coppellchamber.org

Cornelius, NC
Lake Norman Chamber of Commerce
19900 W. Catawba Ave
Cornelius, NC 28031
Phone: 704-892-1922
Fax: 704-892-5313
https://www.lakenormanchamber.org

Cranberry, PA
Pittsburgh North Regional Chamber - Cranberry Twp Satellite Office
2525 Rochester Road
Suite 200
Cranberry Twp, PA 16066
Phone: 724-934-9700
http://www.pghnorthchamber.com

Cupertino, CA
Cupertino Chamber of Commerce
20455 Silverado Avenue
Cupertino, CA 95014
Phone: 408-252-7054
Fax: 408-252-0638
http://cupertino-chamber.org

Danville, CA
Danville Area Chamber of Commerce
117-E Town & Country Dr.
Danville, CA 94526
Phone: 925-837-4400
http://www.danvilleareachamber.com

Draper, UT
Draper Area Chamber of Commerce
1160 East Pioneer Road
Draper, UT 84020
Phone: 801-553-0928
Fax: 801-816-0478
http://draperchamber.com

Dublin, OH
Dublin Chamber of Commerce
129 South High Street
Dublin, OH 43017
Phone: 614-889-2001
Fax: 614-889-2888
http://www.dublinchamber.org

Eastchester, NY
Eastchester Tuckahoe Chamber of Commerce
65 Main Street
Suite 202
Tuckahoe, NY 10707
Phone: 914-779-7344
http://www.etcoc.com

Eden Prairie, MN
Eden Prairie Chamber of Commerce
11455 Viking Drive
Suite 270
Eden Prairie, MN 55344
Phone: 952-944-2830
Fax: 952-944-0229
http://epchamber.org

Edmond, OK
Edmond Area Chamber of Commerce
825 East 2nd Street
Suite 100
Edmond, OK 73003
Phone: 405-341-2808
Fax: 405-340-5512
http://www.edmondchamber.com

Evesham, NJ
Burlington County Regional Chamber of Commerce
520 Fellowship Road
Suite E502
Mount Laurel, NJ 08054
Phone: 856-439-2520
Fax: 856-439-2523
http://www.bcrcc.com

Fishers, IN
OneZone - Carmel and Fishers Chambers of Commerce
10305 Allisonville Road
Suite B
Fishers, IN 46038
Phone: 317-436-4653
http://www.onezonecommerce.com

Flower Mound, TX
Flower Mound Chamber of Commerce
700 Parker Square
Suite 100
Flower Mound, TX 75028
Phone: 972-539-0500
Fax: 972-539-4307
http://www.flowermoundchamber.com

Folsom, CA
Folsom Chamber of Commerce
200 Wool Street
Folsom, CA 95630
Phone: 916-985-2698
http://www.folsomchamber.com

Foster City, CA
Foster City Chamber of Commerce
1031 E. Hillsdale Blvd
Suite F
Foster City, CA 94404
Phone: 650-573-7600
Fax: 650-573-5201
http://fostercitychamber.com

Franklin, TN
Williamson, Inc.
5005 Meridian Boulevard
Suite 150
Franklin, TN 37067
Phone: 615-771-1912
http://www.williamsonchamber.com

Friendswood, TX
Friendswood Chamber of Commerce
1100 South Friendswood Drive
Friendswood, TX 77546
Phone: 281-482-3329
Fax: 281-482-3911
http://www.friendswoodchamber.com

Germantown, TN
Germantown Area Chamber of Commerce
2195 Germantown Road South
Germantown, TN 38138
Phone: 901-755-1200
Fax: 901-755-9168
http://www.germantownchamber.com

Glastonbury, CT
CT River Valley Chamber of Commerce
2400 Main Street
Suite 2
Glastonbury, CT 06033
Phone: 860-659-3587
Fax: 860-659-0102
http://www.crvchamber.org

Grand Blanc, MI
Grand Blanc Chamber of Commerce
512 E. Grand Blanc Rd.
Grand Blanc, MI 48439
Phone: 810-695-4222
http://grandblancchamber.com

Guilderland, NY
Guilderland Chamber of Commerce
2050 Western Avenue
Suite 201
Guilderland, NY 12084
Phone: 518-456-6611
Fax: 518-456-6690
http://www.guilderlandchamber.com

Hampden, PA
West Shore Chamber of Commerce
4211 Trindle Road
Camp Hill, PA 17011
Phone: 717-761-0702
Fax: 717-761-4315
https://www.wschamber.org

Holly Springs, NC
Holly Springs Chamber of Commerce
344 Raleigh Street
Suite 100
Holly Springs, NC 27540
Phone: 919-567-1796
Fax: 919-567-1380
http://www.hollyspringschamber.org

Huntersville, NC
Lake Norman Chamber of Commerce
19900 W. Catawba Ave
Cornelius, NC 28031
Phone: 704-892-1922
Fax: 704-892-5313
https://www.lakenormanchamber.org

Independence, KY
Northern Kentucky Chamber of Commerce
300 Buttermilk Pike
Suite 330
Fort Mitchell, KY 17416
Phone: 859-578-8800
Fax: 859-578-8802
http://www.nkychamber.com

Johns Creek, GA
Johns Creek Chamber of Commerce
10475 Medlock Bridge Rd
Suite 122
Johns Creek, GA 30097
Phone: 770-495-0545
Fax: 770-495-4646
http://www.johnscreekchamber.com

Keller, TX
Greater Keller Chamber of Commerce
420 Johnson Road
Keller, TX 76248
Phone: 817-431-2169
Fax: 817-431-3789
http://www.kellerchamber.com

Kirkland, WA
Greater Kirkland Chamber of Commerce
440 Central Way
Kirkland, WA 98033
Phone: 425-822-7066
Fax: 425-827-4878
http://kirklandchamber.org

Lafayette, CO
Lafayette Chamber
1290 S. Public Road
Lafayette, CO 80026
Phone: 303-666-9555
Fax: 303-666-4392
http://www.lafayettecolorado.com

Lake Oswego, OR
Lake Oswego Chamber of Commerce
459 3rd Street
Lake Oswego, OR 97034
Phone: 503-636-3634
Fax: 503-636-7427
http://www.lake-oswego.com

League City, TX
League City Regional Chamber of Commerce
217 E Main Street
League City, TX 77573
Phone: 281-338-7339
Fax: 281-554-8103
www.leaguecitychamber.com

Leawood, KS
Leawood Chamber of Commerce
13451 Briar
Suite 201
Leawood, KS 66209
Phone: 913-498-1514
Fax: 913-491-0134
http://www.leawoodchamber.org

Lee's Summit, MO
Lee's Summit Chamber of Commerce
220 SE Main Street
Lee's Summit, MO 64063-2332
Phone: 816-524-2424
Fax: 816-524-5246
http://www.lschamber.com

Leesburg, VA
Loudoun County Chamber of Commerce
19301 Winmeade Drive
Suite 210
Lansdowne, VA 20176
Phone: 703-777-2176
Fax: 703-777-1392
http://www.loudounchamber.org

Lehi, UT
Lehi Area Chamber of Commerce
235 East State St.
Lehi, UT 84043
Phone: 801-901-6664
http://lehiareachamber.com

Lenexa, KS
Lenexa Chamber of Commerce
11180 Lackman Rd.
Lenexa, KS 66219
Phone: 913-888-1414
http://www.lenexa.org

Lexington, MA
Lexington Chamber of Commerce
1875 Massachusetts Avenue
Lexington, MA 02420
Phone: 781-862-2480
Fax: 781-862-1450
http://www.lexingtonchamber.org

Los Altos, CA
Los Altos Chamber of Commerce
321 University Avenue
Los Altos, CA 94022
Phone: 650-948-1455
Fax: 650-948-6238
http://losaltoschamber.org

Lower Makefield, PA
Central Bucks Chamber of Commerce
252 West Swamp Road
Suite 23
Doylestown, PA 18901
Phone: 215-348-3913
Fax: 215-348-7154
http://centralbuckschamber.com

Madison, AL
Madison Chamber of Commerce
130 Park Square Lane
Madison, AL 35758
Phone: 256-325-8317
Fax: 256-461-0840
http://www.madisonalchamber.com

Mamaroneck, NY
Mamaroneck Chamber of Commerce
430 Center Avenue
Mamaroneck, NY 10543
Phone: 914-698-4400
http://www.mamaroneckchamberofcommerce.org

Manheim, PA
Manheim Area Chamber of Commerce
15 East High Street
Manheim, PA 17545
Phone: 717-665-6330
http://manheimchamber.com

Manlius, NY
Greater Manlius Chamber of Commerce
425 East Genessee Street
Fayetteville, NY 13066
Phone: 315-637-4760
Fax: 315-637-4762
http://www.manliuschamber.com

Maple Grove, MN
North Hennepin Area Chamber of Commerce
229 1st Avenue Northeast
Osseo, MN 55369
Phone: 763-424-6744
Fax: 763-424-6927
http://www.nhachamber.com

Marion, IA
Cedar Rapids Metro Economic Alliance
501 First St. SE
Cedar Rapids, IA 52401
Phone: 319-398-5317
Fax: 319-398-5228
http://www.cedarrapids.org

Marlboro, NJ
Greater Monmouth Chamber of Commerce
10 East Main Street
Suite 1A
Freehold, NJ 07728
Phone: 732-462-3030
Fax: 732-462-2123
http://www.greatermonmouthchamber.com

Mason, OH
Mason Deerfield Chamber
316 W. Main Street
Mason, OH 45040
Phone: 513-336-0125
Fax: 513-398-6371
http://business.madechamber.org

McCandless, PA
Pittsburgh North Regional Chamber
5000 Brooktree Road
Suite 100
Wexford, PA 15090
Phone: 724-934-9700
Fax: 724-934-9710
http://www.pghnorthchamber.com

Menomonee Falls, WI
Menomonee Falls Chamber of Commerce
N88 W16621 Appleton Avenue
Menomonee Falls, WI 53051
Phone: 262-251-2430
Fax: 262-251-0969
http://www.fallschamber.com

Meridian, ID
Meridan Chamber of Commerce
215 East Franklin Road
Meridian, ID 83642
Phone: 208-888-2817
Fax: 208-888-2682
http://www.meridianchamber.org

Merrimack, NH
Merrimack Chamber of Commerce
246 Daniel Webster Highway
Merrimack, NH 03054
Phone: 603-424-3669
Fax: 603-429-4325
http://www.merrimackchamber.org

Mount Lebanon, PA
South Hills Chamber of Commerce
61 McMurray Road
Suite 105
Pittsburgh, PA 15241
Phone: 412-306-8090
Fax: 412-221-4205
https://www.shchamber.org

Mount Pleasant, SC
Charleston Metro Chamber of Commerce
4500 Leeds Avenue
Suite 100
North Charleston, SC 29405
Phone: 843-577-2510
http://www.charlestonchamber.net

Needham, MA
Newton-Needham Regional Chamber
281 Neddham Street
Newton, MA 02464
Phone: 617-244-5300
Fax: 617-244-5302
http://www.nnchamber.com

Newtown, CT
Chamber of Commerce of Newtown, Inc
45 Main Street
Newtown, CT 06470
Phone: 203-426-2695
http://www.newtown-ct.com

Northbrook, IL
Northbrook Chamber of Commerce
2002 Walters Avenue
Northbrook, IL 60062
Phone: 847-498-5555
http://northbrookchamber.org

Northville, MI
Northville Chamber of Commerce
195 S. Main Street
Northville, MI 48167
Phone: 248-349-7640
Fax: 248-349-8730
http://www.northville.org

Novi, MI
Novi Chamber of Commerce
41875 W 11 Mile Road
Suite 201
Novi, MI 48375
Phone: 248-349-3743
Fax: 248-349-9719
http://www.novichamber.com

O'Fallon, IL
O'Fallon Shiloh Chamber of Commerce
116 E. First Street
O'Fallon, IN 62269
Phone: 618-632-3377
Fax: 618- 632-8162
http://ofallonchamber.com

O'Fallon, MO
O'Fallon Chamber of Commerce & Industries
2145 Bryan Valley Commercial Dr
O'Fallon, MO 63366
Phone: 636-240-1818
Fax: 888-349-1897
http://www.ofallonchamber.org

Orchard Park, NY
The Orchard Park Chamber of Commerce
4211 North Buffalo Street
Orchard Park, NY 14127
Phone: 716-662-3366
Fax: 716-662-5946
http://orchardparkchamber.org

Oviedo, FL
Oviedo Winter Springs Regional Chamber of Commerce
376 North Central Ave
Oviedo, FL 32765
Phone: 407-365-6500
Fax: 407- 650-2712
http://www.oviedowintersprings.org

Parker, CO
Parker Area Chamber of Commerce
19590 E Mainstreet
Suite 100
Parker, CO 80138
Phone: 303-841-4268
Fax: 303-841-8061
http://www.parkerchamber.com

Parkland, FL
Parkland Chamber of Commerce
10561 Trails End
Parkland, FL
Phone: 954-937-0232
http://www.parklandchamber.org

Peachtree City, GA
Fayette Chamber of Commerce
600 West Lanier Avenue
Suite 205
Fayetteville, GA 30214
Phone: 770-461-9983
Fax: 770-461-9622
http://fayettechamber.org

Pflugerville, TX
Pflugerville Chamber of Commerce
101 S. Third St.
Pflugerville, TX 78660
Phone: 512-251-7799
Fax: 512-251-7802
http://www.pfchamber.com

Plainfield, IL
Plainfield Area Chamber of Commerce
24109 W. Lockport Street
Plainfield, IL 60544
Phone: 815-436-4431
Fax: 815-436-0520
http://www.plainfieldchamber.com

Princeton, NJ
Princeton Regional Chamber of Commerce
182 Nassau St.
Suite 301
Princeton, NJ 08542
Phone: 609-924-1776
Fax: 609-924-5776
http://www.princetonchamber.org

Queen Creek, AZ
Queen Creek Chamber of Commerce
22246 South Ellsworth Rd
Queen Creek, AZ 85142
Phone: 480-888-1709
Fax: 480-289-4801
http://www.queencreekchamber.com

Rancho Palos Verdes, CA
Palos Verdes Peninsula Chamber of Commerce
707 Silver Spur Road
Suite 100
Rolling Hills Estates, CA 90274
Phone: 310-377-8111
https://www.palosverdeschamber.com

Redmond, WA
OneRedmond
8383 158th Ave NE
Suite 225
Redmond, WA 98052
Phone: 425-885-4014
Fax: 425-882-0996
http://www.oneredmond.org

Richland, WA
Tri-City Regional Chamber of Commerce
7130 W Grandridge Blvd
Suite C
Kennewick, WA 99336
Phone: 509-736-0510
Fax: 509-783-1733
http://www.tricityregionalchamber.com

Ridgefield, CT
Ridgefield Chamber of Commerce
9 Bailey Avenue
Ridgefield, CT 06877
Phone: 203-438-5992
http://destinationridgefield.com

Ridgewood, NJ
Ridgewood Chamber of Commerce
27 Chestnut Street
Suite 1B
Ridgewood, NJ 07450
Phone: 201-445-2600
http://www.ridgewoodchamber.com

Rio Rancho, NM
Rio Rancho Regional Chamber of Commerce
4001 Southern Blvd SE
Suite B
Rio Rancho, NM 87124
Phone: 505-892-1533
Fax: 505-892-6157
http://rrrcc.org

Sahuarita, AZ
Green Valley/Sahuarita Chamber of Commerce
275 West Continental Rd
Suite 123
Green Valley, AZ 85622
Phone: 520-625-7575
Fax: 520-648-6154
http://greenvalleysahuarita.com

Sammamish, WA
Sammamish Chamber of Commerce
704 228th Avenue Northeast
Suite 123
Sammamish, WA 98074
Phone: 425-681-4910
Fax: 425-484-6266
http://sammamishchamber.org

San Ramon, CA
San Ramon Chamber of Commerce
2410 Camino Ramon
Suite 125
San Ramon, CA 94583
Phone: 925-242-0600
Fax: 925-242-0603
www.sanramon.org

Saratoga, CA
Saratoga Chamber of Commerce
14460 Big Basin Way
Saratoga, CA 95070
Phone: 408-867-0753
http://www.saratogachamber.org

Schertz, TX
Schertz Chamber of Commerce
1730 Schertz Parkway
Schertz, TX 78154
Phone: 210-619-1950
Fax: 210-619-1959
http://www.thechamber.info

Shrewsbury, MA
Corridor Nine Area Chamber of Commerce
30 Lyman Street
Westborough, MA 01581
Phone: 508-836-4444
Fax: 508-836-2652
http://www.corridornine.org

South Brunswick, NJ
Middlesex County Regional Chamber of Commerce
109 Church Street
New Brunswick, NJ 08901
Phone: 732-745-8090
https://www.mcrcc.org

South Jordan, UT
South Jordan Chamber of Commerce
11565 S District Main Drive
Suite 600
South Jordan, UT 84095
Phone: 801-253-5200
Fax: 801-253-5201
http://www.southjordanchamber.com

South Kingstown, RI
Southern Rhode Island Chamber of Commerce
230 Old Tower Hill Road
Wakefield, RI 02879
Phone: 401-783-2801
Fax: 401-789-3120
http://www.srichamber.com

South Windsor, CT
South Windsor Chamber of Commerce
22 Morgan Farms Drive
South Windsor, CT 06880
Phone: 860-644-9442
Fax: 860-648-1911
http://www.southwindsorchamber.com

Southlake, TX
Southlake Chamber of Commerce
1501 Corporate Circle
Suite 100
Southlake, TX 76092
Phone: 817-481-8200
Fax: 817-749-8202
http://southlakechamber.chambermaster.com

Spring Hill, TN
Spring Hill Chamber of Commerce
5000 Northfield Lane
Suite 100
Spring Hill, TN 37174
Phone: 931-486-0625
http://springhillchamber.com

Stow, OH
Stow-Munroe Falls Chamber of Commerce
4301 Darrow Road
Suite 2450
Stow, OH 44224
Phone: 330-688-1579
Fax: 330-688-6234
http://smfcc.chambermaster.com

Sugar Land, TX
Fort Bend Chamber of Commerce
445 Commerce Green Blvd
Sugar Land, TX 77478
Phone: 281-491-0800
Fax: 281-491-0112
http://www.fortbendchamber.com

Sun Prairie, WI
Sun Prairie Chamber Of Commerce
109 East Main Street
Sun Prairie, WI 53590
Phone: 608-837-4547
Fax: 608-837-8765
http://www.sunprairiechamber.com

Syracuse, UT
Syracuse Chamber of Commerce
PO Box 160595
Clearfield, UT 84016
Phone: 801-645-0247
http://syracuseutahchamber.com

Tredyffrin, PA
The Main Line Chamber of Commerce
175 Strafford Avenue
Suite 130
Wayne, PA 19087
Phone: 610-687-6232
Fax: 610-687-8085
http://www.mlcc.org

Upper Arlington, OH
Upper Arlington Area Chamber of Commerce
1250 Old Henderson Rd
Suite B
Columbus, OH 43220
Phone: 614-481-5710
Fax: 614-481-5711
http://www.uachamber.org

Upper Dublin, PA
Eastern Montgomery County Chamber of Commerce
436 Old York Rd
Jenkintown, PA 19046
Phone: 215-887-5122
http://www.emccc.org

Vestavia Hills, AL
Vestavia Hills Chamber of Commerce
1975 Merryvale Road
Vestavia Hills, AL 35216
Phone: 205-823-5011
Fax: 205-823-8974
http://vestaviahills.org

Webster, NY
Webster Chamber of Commerce
1110 Crosspointe Lane
Suite C
Webster, NY 14580
Phone: 585-265-3960
Fax: 585-265-3702
http://www.websterchamber.com

Wellesley, MA
Wellesley Chamber of Commerce
One Hollis Street
Suite 232
Wellesley, MA 02482-4671
Phone: 781-235-2446
Fax: 781-235-7326
http://wellesleychamber.org

West Fargo, ND
West Fargo Chamber of Commerce
202 First Avenue North
Moorhead, ND 56560
Phone: 218-223-1100
Fax: 218-233-1200
http://www.fmwfchamber.com

West Linn, OR
West Linn Chamber of Commerce
21420 Willamette Drive
West Linn, OR 97068
Phone: 503-655-6744
http://westlinnchamber.com

West Windsor, NJ
MIDJersey Chamber of Commerce
423 Riverview Plaza
Trenton, NJ 08611
Phone: 609-689-9960
Fax: 609-586-9989
http://midjerseychamber.org

Westlake, OH
West Shore Chamber of Commerce
PO Box 45297
Westlake, OH 44145
Phone: 440-835-8787
Fax: 440-835-8798
http://www.westshorechamber.org

Weston, FL
Weston Area Chamber of Commerce
1290 Weston Road
Weston, FL 33326
Phone: 954-389-0600

Westport, CT
Westport-Westin Chamber of Commerce
41 Riverside Avenue
Westport, CT 06880
Phone: 203-227-9234
Fax: 203-454-4019
http://www.westportwestonchamber.com

Wilmette, IL
The Wilmette/Kenilworth Chamber of Commerce
351 Linden Avenue
Wilmette, IL 60091
Phone: 847-251-3800
Fax: 847-251-6321
http://www.wilmettechamber.org

Woodbury, MN
Woodbury Area Chamber of Commerce
700 Commerce Drive
Suite 245
Woodbury, MN 55125
Phone: 651-578-0722
Fax: 651-578-7276
http://www.woodburychamber.org

Yorba Linda, CA
Yorba Linda Chamber of Commerce
17670 Yorba Linda Boulevard
Yorba Linda, CA 92886
Phone: 714-993-9537
http://www.yorbalindachamber.org

Appendix E: State Departments of Labor

Alabama
Alabama Department of Labor
P.O. Box 303500
Montgomery, AL 36130-3500
Phone: (334) 242-3072
http://www.labor.alabama.gov

Alaska
Dept of Labor and Workforce Devel.
P.O. Box 11149
Juneau, AK 99822-2249
Phone: (907) 465-2700
http://www.labor.state.ak.us

Arizona
Industrial Commission or Arizona
800 West Washington Street
Phoenix, AZ 85007
Phone: (602) 542-4515
http://www.ica.state.az.us

Arkansas
Department of Labor
10421 West Markham
Little Rock, AR 72205
Phone: (501) 682-4500
http://www.labor.ar.gov

California
Labor and Workforce Development
445 Golden Gate Ave., 10th Floor
San Francisco, CA 94102
Phone: (916) 263-1811
http://www.labor.ca.gov

Colorado
Dept of Labor and Employment
633 17th St., 2nd Floor
Denver, CO 80202-3660
Phone: (888) 390-7936
http://www.colorado.gov/CDLE

Connecticut
Department of Labor
200 Folly Brook Blvd.
Wethersfield, CT 06109-1114
Phone: (860) 263-6000
http://www.ctdol.state.ct.us

Delaware
Department of Labor
4425 N. Market St., 4th Floor
Wilmington, DE 19802
Phone: (302) 451-3423
http://dol.delaware.gov

District of Columbia
Department of Employment Services
614 New York Ave., NE, Suite 300
Washington, DC 20002
Phone: (202) 671-1900
http://does.dc.gov

Florida
Florida Department of Economic Opportunity
The Caldwell Building
107 East Madison St. Suite 100
Tallahassee, FL 32399-4120
Phone: (800) 342-3450
http://www.floridajobs.org

Georgia
Department of Labor
Sussex Place, Room 600
148 Andrew Young Intl Blvd., NE
Atlanta, GA 30303
Phone: (404) 656-3011
http://dol.georgia.gov

Hawaii
Dept of Labor & Industrial Relations
830 Punchbowl Street
Honolulu, HI 96813
Phone: (808) 586-8842
http://labor.hawaii.gov

Idaho
Department of Labor
317 W. Main St.
Boise, ID 83735-0001
Phone: (208) 332-3579
http://www.labor.idaho.gov

Illinois
Department of Labor
160 N. LaSalle Street, 13th Floor
Suite C-1300
Chicago, IL 60601
Phone: (312) 793-2800
http://www.illinois.gov/idol

Indiana
Indiana Department of Labor
402 West Washington Street, Room W195
Indianapolis, IN 46204
Phone: (317) 232-2655
http://www.in.gov/dol

Iowa
Iowa Workforce Development
1000 East Grand Avenue
Des Moines, IA 50319-0209
Phone: (515) 242-5870
http://www.iowadivisionoflabor.gov

Kansas
Department of Labor
401 S.W. Topeka Blvd.
Topeka, KS 66603-3182
Phone: (785) 296-5000
http://www.dol.ks.gov

Kentucky
Department of Labor
1047 U.S. Hwy 127 South, Suite 4
Frankfort, KY 40601-4381
Phone: (502) 564-3070
http://www.labor.ky.gov

Louisiana
Louisiana Workforce Commission
1001 N. 23rd Street
Baton Rouge, LA 70804-9094
Phone: (225) 342-3111
http://www.laworks.net

Maine
Department of Labor
45 Commerce Street
Augusta, ME 04330
Phone: (207) 623-7900
http://www.state.me.us/labor

Maryland
Department of Labor, Licensing & Regulation
500 N. Calvert Street
Suite 401
Baltimore, MD 21202
Phone: (410) 767-2357
http://www.dllr.state.md.us

Massachusetts
Dept of Labor & Workforce Development
One Ashburton Place
Room 2112
Boston, MA 02108
Phone: (617) 626-7100
http://www.mass.gov/lwd

Michigan
Dept of Labor & Economic Growth
P.O. Box 30004
Lansing, MI 48909
Phone: (517) 335-0400
http://www.michigan.gov/cis

Minnesota
Dept of Labor and Industry
443 Lafayette Road North
Saint Paul, MN 55155
Phone: (651) 284-5070
http://www.doli.state.mn.us

Mississippi
Dept of Employment Security
P.O. Box 1699
Jackson, MS 39215-1699
Phone: (601) 321-6000
http://www.mdes.ms.gov

Missouri
Labor and Industrial Relations
P.O. Box 599
3315 W. Truman Boulevard
Jefferson City, MO 65102-0599
Phone: (573) 751-7500
http://labor.mo.gov

Montana
Dept of Labor and Industry
P.O. Box 1728
Helena, MT 59624-1728
Phone: (406) 444-9091
http://www.dli.mt.gov

Nebraska
Department of Labor
550 S 16th Street
Lincoln, NE 68508
Phone: (402) 471-9000
https://dol.nebraska.gov

Nevada
Dept of Business and Industry
555 E. Washington Ave.
Suite 4100
Las Vegas, NV 89101-1050
Phone: (702) 486-2650
http://www.laborcommissioner.com

New Hampshire
Department of Labor
State Office Park South
95 Pleasant Street
Concord, NH 03301
Phone: (603) 271-3176
https://www.nh.gov/labor

New Jersey
Department of Labor & Workforce Development
John Fitch Plaza, 13th Floor
Suite D
Trenton, NJ 08625-0110
Phone: (609) 777-3200
http://lwd.dol.state.nj.us/labor

New Mexico
Department of Workforce Solutions
401 Broadway, NE
Albuquerque, NM 87103-1928
Phone: (505) 841-8450
http://www.dws.state.nm.us

New York
Department of Labor
State Office Bldg. # 12
W.A. Harriman Campus
Albany, NY 12240
Phone: (518) 457-5519
http://www.labor.ny.gov

North Carolina
Department of Labor
4 West Edenton Street
Raleigh, NC 27601-1092
Phone: (919) 733-7166
http://www.nclabor.com

North Dakota
North Dakota Department of Labor and Human Rights
State Capitol Building
600 East Boulevard, Dept 406
Bismark, ND 58505-0340
Phone: (701) 328-2660
http://www.nd.gov/labor

Ohio
Department of Commerce
77 South High Street, 22nd Floor
Columbus, OH 43215
Phone: (614) 644-2239
http://www.com.state.oh.us

Oklahoma
Department of Labor
4001 N. Lincoln Blvd.
Oklahoma City, OK 73105-5212
Phone: (405) 528-1500
https://www.ok.gov/odol

Oregon
Bureau of Labor and Industries
800 NE Oregon St., #32
Portland, OR 97232
Phone: (971) 673-0761
http://www.oregon.gov/boli

Pennsylvania
Dept of Labor and Industry
1700 Labor and Industry Bldg
7th and Forster Streets
Harrisburg, PA 17120
Phone: (717) 787-5279
http://www.dli.pa.gov

Rhode Island
Department of Labor and Training
1511 Pontiac Avenue
Cranston, RI 02920
Phone: (401) 462-8000
http://www.dlt.state.ri.us

South Carolina
Dept of Labor, Licensing & Regulations
P.O. Box 11329
Columbia, SC 29211-1329
Phone: (803) 896-4300
http://www.llr.state.sc.us

South Dakota
Department of Labor & Regulation
700 Governors Drive
Pierre, SD 57501-2291
Phone: (605) 773-3682
http://dlr.sd.gov

Tennessee
Dept of Labor & Workforce Development
Andrew Johnson Tower
710 James Robertson Pkwy
Nashville, TN 37243-0655
Phone: (615) 741-6642
http://www.tn.gov/workforce

Texas
Texas Workforce Commission
101 East 15th St.
Austin, TX 78778
Phone: (512) 475-2670
http://www.twc.state.tx.us

Utah
Utah Labor Commission
160 East 300 South, 3rd Floor
Salt Lake City, UT 84114-6600
Phone: (801) 530-6800
http://laborcommission.utah.gov

Vermont
Department of Labor
5 Green Mountain Drive
P.O. Box 488
Montpelier, VT 05601-0488
Phone: (802) 828-4000
http://labor.vermont.gov

Virginia
Dept of Labor and Industry
Powers-Taylor Building
13 S. 13th Street
Richmond, VA 23219
Phone: (804) 371-2327
http://www.doli.virginia.gov

Washington
Dept of Labor and Industries
P.O. Box 44001
Olympia, WA 98504-4001
Phone: (360) 902-4200
http://www.lni.wa.gov

West Virginia
Division of Labor
749 B Bulding 6
Capitol Complex
Charleston, WV 25305
Phone: (304) 558-7890
http://www.wvlabor.com

Wisconsin
Dept of Workforce Development
201 E. Washington Ave., #A400
P.O. Box 7946
Madison, WI 53707-7946
Phone: (608) 266-6861
http://dwd.wisconsin.gov

Wyoming
Department of Workforce Services
1510 East Pershing Blvd.
Cheyenne, WY 82002
Phone: (307) 777-7261
http://www.wyomingworkforce.org

Source: *U.S. Department of Labor; Original research*

2016 Title List

Visit www.GreyHouse.com for Product Information, Table of Contents, and Sample Pages.

General Reference

An African Biographical Dictionary
America's College Museums
American Environmental Leaders: From Colonial Times to the Present
Encyclopedia of African-American Writing
Encyclopedia of Constitutional Amendments
Encyclopedia of Gun Control & Gun Rights
An Encyclopedia of Human Rights in the United States
Encyclopedia of Invasions & Conquests
Encyclopedia of Prisoners of War & Internment
Encyclopedia of Religion & Law in America
Encyclopedia of Rural America
Encyclopedia of the Continental Congress
Encyclopedia of the United States Cabinet, 1789-2010
Encyclopedia of War Journalism
Encyclopedia of Warrior Peoples & Fighting Groups
The Environmental Debate: A Documentary History
The Evolution Wars: A Guide to the Debates
From Suffrage to the Senate: America's Political Women
Global Terror & Political Risk Assessment
Nations of the World
Political Corruption in America
Privacy Rights in the Digital Era
The Religious Right: A Reference Handbook
Speakers of the House of Representatives, 1789-2009
This is Who We Were: 1880-1900
This is Who We Were: A Companion to the 1940 Census
This is Who We Were: In the 1910s
This is Who We Were: In the 1920s
This is Who We Were: In the 1940s
This is Who We Were: In the 1950s
This is Who We Were: In the 1960s
This is Who We Were: In the 1970s
U.S. Land & Natural Resource Policy
The Value of a Dollar 1600-1865: Colonial Era to the Civil War
The Value of a Dollar: 1860-2014
Working Americans 1770-1869 Vol. IX: Revolutionary War to the Civil War
Working Americans 1880-1999 Vol. I: The Working Class
Working Americans 1880-1999 Vol. II: The Middle Class
Working Americans 1880-1999 Vol. III: The Upper Class
Working Americans 1880-1999 Vol. IV: Their Children
Working Americans 1880-2015 Vol. V: Americans At War
Working Americans 1880-2005 Vol. VI: Women at Work
Working Americans 1880-2006 Vol. VII: Social Movements
Working Americans 1880-2007 Vol. VIII: Immigrants
Working Americans 1880-2009 Vol. X: Sports & Recreation
Working Americans 1880-2010 Vol. XI: Inventors & Entrepreneurs
Working Americans 1880-2011 Vol. XII: Our History through Music
Working Americans 1880-2012 Vol. XIII: Education & Educators
World Cultural Leaders of the 20th & 21st Centuries

Education Information

Charter School Movement
Comparative Guide to American Elementary & Secondary Schools
Complete Learning Disabilities Directory
Educators Resource Directory
Special Education: A Reference Book for Policy and Curriculum Development

Health Information

Comparative Guide to American Hospitals
Complete Directory for Pediatric Disorders
Complete Directory for People with Chronic Illness
Complete Directory for People with Disabilities
Complete Mental Health Directory
Diabetes in America: Analysis of an Epidemic
Directory of Drug & Alcohol Residential Rehab Facilities
Directory of Health Care Group Purchasing Organizations
Directory of Hospital Personnel
HMO/PPO Directory
Medical Device Register
Older Americans Information Directory

Business Information

Complete Television, Radio & Cable Industry Directory
Directory of Business Information Resources
Directory of Mail Order Catalogs
Directory of Venture Capital & Private Equity Firms
Environmental Resource Handbook
Food & Beverage Market Place
Grey House Homeland Security Directory
Grey House Performing Arts Directory
Grey House Safety & Security Directory
Grey House Transportation Security Directory
Hudson's Washington News Media Contacts Directory
New York State Directory
Rauch Market Research Guides
Sports Market Place Directory

Statistics & Demographics

American Tally
America's Top-Rated Cities
America's Top-Rated Smaller Cities
America's Top-Rated Small Towns & Cities
Ancestry & Ethnicity in America
The Asian Databook
Comparative Guide to American Suburbs
The Hispanic Databook
Profiles of America
"Profiles of" Series - State Handbooks
Weather America

Financial Ratings Series

TheStreet Ratings' Guide to Bond & Money Market Mutual Funds
TheStreet Ratings' Guide to Common Stocks
TheStreet Ratings' Guide to Exchange-Traded Funds
TheStreet Ratings' Guide to Stock Mutual Funds
TheStreet Ratings' Ultimate Guided Tour of Stock Investing
Weiss Ratings' Consumer Guides
Weiss Ratings' Guide to Banks
Weiss Ratings' Guide to Credit Unions
Weiss Ratings' Guide to Health Insurers
Weiss Ratings' Guide to Life & Annuity Insurers
Weiss Ratings' Guide to Property & Casualty Insurers

Bowker's Books In Print® Titles

American Book Publishing Record® Annual
American Book Publishing Record® Monthly
Books In Print®
Books In Print® Supplement
Books Out Loud™
Bowker's Complete Video Directory™
Children's Books In Print®
El-Hi Textbooks & Serials In Print®
Forthcoming Books®
Large Print Books & Serials™
Law Books & Serials In Print™
Medical & Health Care Books In Print™
Publishers, Distributors & Wholesalers of the US™
Subject Guide to Books In Print®
Subject Guide to Children's Books In Print®

Canadian General Reference

Associations Canada
Canadian Almanac & Directory
Canadian Environmental Resource Guide
Canadian Parliamentary Guide
Canadian Venture Capital & Private Equity Firms
Financial Post Directory of Directors
Financial Services Canada
Governments Canada
Health Guide Canada
The History of Canada
Libraries Canada
Major Canadian Cities

SALEM PRESS

SALEM PRESS

2016 Title List

Visit **www.SalemPress.com** for Product Information, Table of Contents, and Sample Pages.

Science, Careers & Mathematics

Ancient Creatures
Applied Science
Applied Science: Engineering & Mathematics
Applied Science: Science & Medicine
Applied Science: Technology
Biomes and Ecosystems
Careers in Building Construction
Careers in Business
Careers in Chemistry
Careers in Communications & Media
Careers in Environment & Conservation
Careers in Healthcare
Careers in Hospitality & Tourism
Careers in Human Services
Careers in Law, Criminal Justice & Emergency Services
Careers in Manufacturing
Careers in Physics
Careers in Sales, Insurance & Real Estate
Careers in Science & Engineering
Careers in Technology Services & Repair
Computer Technology Innovators
Contemporary Biographies in Business
Contemporary Biographies in Chemistry
Contemporary Biographies in Communications & Media
Contemporary Biographies in Environment & Conservation
Contemporary Biographies in Healthcare
Contemporary Biographies in Hospitality & Tourism
Contemporary Biographies in Law & Criminal Justice
Contemporary Biographies in Physics
Earth Science
Earth Science: Earth Materials & Resources
Earth Science: Earth's Surface and History
Earth Science: Physics & Chemistry of the Earth
Earth Science: Weather, Water & Atmosphere
Encyclopedia of Energy
Encyclopedia of Environmental Issues
Encyclopedia of Environmental Issues: Atmosphere and Air Pollution
Encyclopedia of Environmental Issues: Ecology and Ecosystems
Encyclopedia of Environmental Issues: Energy and Energy Use
Encyclopedia of Environmental Issues: Policy and Activism
Encyclopedia of Environmental Issues: Preservation/Wilderness Issues
Encyclopedia of Environmental Issues: Water and Water Pollution
Encyclopedia of Global Resources
Encyclopedia of Global Warming
Encyclopedia of Mathematics & Society
Encyclopedia of Mathematics & Society: Engineering, Tech, Medicine
Encyclopedia of Mathematics & Society: Great Mathematicians
Encyclopedia of Mathematics & Society: Math & Social Sciences
Encyclopedia of Mathematics & Society: Math Development/Concepts
Encyclopedia of Mathematics & Society: Math in Culture & Society
Encyclopedia of Mathematics & Society: Space, Science, Environment
Encyclopedia of the Ancient World
Forensic Science
Geography Basics
Internet Innovators
Inventions and Inventors
Magill's Encyclopedia of Science: Animal Life
Magill's Encyclopedia of Science: Plant life
Notable Natural Disasters
Principles of Astronomy
Principles of Chemistry
Principles of Physics
Science and Scientists
Solar System
Solar System: Great Astronomers
Solar System: Study of the Universe
Solar System: The Inner Planets
Solar System: The Moon and Other Small Bodies
Solar System: The Outer Planets
Solar System: The Sun and Other Stars
World Geography

Literature

American Ethnic Writers
Classics of Science Fiction & Fantasy Literature
Critical Insights: Authors
Critical Insights: Film
Critical Insights: Literary Collection Bundles
Critical Insights: Themes
Critical Insights: Works
Critical Survey of Drama
Critical Survey of Graphic Novels: Heroes & Super Heroes
Critical Survey of Graphic Novels: History, Theme & Technique
Critical Survey of Graphic Novels: Independents/Underground Classics
Critical Survey of Graphic Novels: Manga
Critical Survey of Long Fiction
Critical Survey of Mystery & Detective Fiction
Critical Survey of Mythology and Folklore: Heroes and Heroines
Critical Survey of Mythology and Folklore: Love, Sexuality & Desire
Critical Survey of Mythology and Folklore: World Mythology
Critical Survey of Poetry
Critical Survey of Poetry: American Poets
Critical Survey of Poetry: British, Irish & Commonwealth Poets
Critical Survey of Poetry: Cumulative Index
Critical Survey of Poetry: European Poets
Critical Survey of Poetry: Topical Essays
Critical Survey of Poetry: World Poets
Critical Survey of Shakespeare's Plays
Critical Survey of Shakespeare's Sonnets
Critical Survey of Short Fiction
Critical Survey of Short Fiction: American Writers
Critical Survey of Short Fiction: British, Irish, Commonwealth Writers
Critical Survey of Short Fiction: Cumulative Index
Critical Survey of Short Fiction: European Writers
Critical Survey of Short Fiction: Topical Essays
Critical Survey of Short Fiction: World Writers
Critical Survey of Young Adult Literature
Cyclopedia of Literary Characters
Cyclopedia of Literary Places
Holocaust Literature
Introduction to Literary Context: American Poetry of the 20th Century
Introduction to Literary Context: American Post-Modernist Novels
Introduction to Literary Context: American Short Fiction
Introduction to Literary Context: English Literature
Introduction to Literary Context: Plays
Introduction to Literary Context: World Literature
Magill's Literary Annual 2015
Magill's Survey of American Literature
Magill's Survey of World Literature
Masterplots
Masterplots II: African American Literature
Masterplots II: American Fiction Series
Masterplots II: British & Commonwealth Fiction Series
Masterplots II: Christian Literature
Masterplots II: Drama Series
Masterplots II: Juvenile & Young Adult Literature, Supplement
Masterplots II: Nonfiction Series
Masterplots II: Poetry Series
Masterplots II: Short Story Series
Masterplots II: Women's Literature Series
Notable African American Writers
Notable American Novelists
Notable Playwrights
Notable Poets
Recommended Reading: 600 Classics Reviewed
Short Story Writers

Grey House Publishing | Salem Press | H.W. Wilson | 4919 Route, 22 PO Box 56, Amenia NY 12501-0056

 SALEM PRESS

2016 Title List

Visit **www.SalemPress.com** for Product Information, Table of Contents, and Sample Pages.

History and Social Science

The 2000s in America
50 States
African American History
Agriculture in History
American First Ladies
American Heroes
American Indian Culture
American Indian History
American Indian Tribes
American Presidents
American Villains
America's Historic Sites
Ancient Greece
The Bill of Rights
The Civil Rights Movement
The Cold War
Countries, Peoples & Cultures
Countries, Peoples & Cultures: Central & South America
Countries, Peoples & Cultures: Central, South & Southeast Asia
Countries, Peoples & Cultures: East & South Africa
Countries, Peoples & Cultures: East Asia & the Pacific
Countries, Peoples & Cultures: Eastern Europe
Countries, Peoples & Cultures: Middle East & North Africa
Countries, Peoples & Cultures: North America & the Caribbean
Countries, Peoples & Cultures: West & Central Africa
Countries, Peoples & Cultures: Western Europe
Defining Documents: American Revolution
Defining Documents: Civil Rights
Defining Documents: Civil War
Defining Documents: Emergence of Modern America
Defining Documents: Exploration & Colonial America
Defining Documents: Manifest Destiny
Defining Documents: Postwar 1940s
Defining Documents: Reconstruction
Defining Documents: 1920s
Defining Documents: 1930s
Defining Documents: 1950s
Defining Documents: 1960s
Defining Documents: 1970s
Defining Documents: American West
Defining Documents: Ancient World
Defining Documents: Middle Ages
Defining Documents: Vietnam War
Defining Documents: World War I
Defining Documents: World War II
The Eighties in America
Encyclopedia of American Immigration
Encyclopedia of Flight
Encyclopedia of the Ancient World
Fashion Innovators
The Fifties in America
The Forties in America
Great Athletes
Great Athletes: Baseball
Great Athletes: Basketball
Great Athletes: Boxing & Soccer
Great Athletes: Cumulative Index
Great Athletes: Football
Great Athletes: Golf & Tennis
Great Athletes: Olympics
Great Athletes: Racing & Individual Sports
Great Events from History: 17th Century
Great Events from History: 18th Century
Great Events from History: 19th Century
Great Events from History: 20th Century (1901-1940)
Great Events from History: 20th Century (1941-1970)
Great Events from History: 20th Century (1971-2000)
Great Events from History: Ancient World
Great Events from History: Cumulative Indexes
Great Events from History: Gay, Lesbian, Bisexual, Transgender Events
Great Events from History: Middle Ages
Great Events from History: Modern Scandals
Great Events from History: Renaissance & Early Modern Era
Great Lives from History: 17th Century
Great Lives from History: 18th Century
Great Lives from History: 19th Century
Great Lives from History: 20th Century
Great Lives from History: African Americans
Great Lives from History: American Women
Great Lives from History: Ancient World
Great Lives from History: Asian & Pacific Islander Americans
Great Lives from History: Cumulative Indexes
Great Lives from History: Incredibly Wealthy
Great Lives from History: Inventors & Inventions
Great Lives from History: Jewish Americans
Great Lives from History: Latinos
Great Lives from History: Middle Ages
Great Lives from History: Notorious Lives
Great Lives from History: Renaissance & Early Modern Era
Great Lives from History: Scientists & Science
Historical Encyclopedia of American Business
Issues in U.S. Immigration
Magill's Guide to Military History
Milestone Documents in African American History
Milestone Documents in American History
Milestone Documents in World History
Milestone Documents of American Leaders
Milestone Documents of World Religions
Music Innovators
Musicians & Composers 20th Century
The Nineties in America
The Seventies in America
The Sixties in America
Survey of American Industry and Careers
The Thirties in America
The Twenties in America
United States at War
U.S.A. in Space
U.S. Court Cases
U.S. Government Leaders
U.S. Laws, Acts, and Treaties
U.S. Legal System
U.S. Supreme Court
Weapons and Warfare
World Conflicts: Asia and the Middle East
World Political Yearbook

Health

Addictions & Substance Abuse
Adolescent Health & Wellness
Cancer
Complementary & Alternative Medicine
Genetics & Inherited Conditions
Health Issues
Infectious Diseases & Conditions
Magill's Medical Guide
Psychology & Behavioral Health
Psychology Basics

HW WILSON

HW WILSON

2016 Title List

Visit www.HWWilsonInPrint.com for Product Information, Table of Contents and Sample Pages

Current Biography
Current Biography Cumulative Index 1946-2013
Current Biography Monthly Magazine
Current Biography Yearbook: 2003
Current Biography Yearbook: 2004
Current Biography Yearbook: 2005
Current Biography Yearbook: 2006
Current Biography Yearbook: 2007
Current Biography Yearbook: 2008
Current Biography Yearbook: 2009
Current Biography Yearbook: 2010
Current Biography Yearbook: 2011
Current Biography Yearbook: 2012
Current Biography Yearbook: 2013
Current Biography Yearbook: 2014
Current Biography Yearbook: 2015

Core Collections
Children's Core Collection
Fiction Core Collection
Graphic Novels Core Collection
Middle & Junior High School Core
Public Library Core Collection: Nonfiction
Senior High Core Collection
Young Adult Fiction Core Collection

The Reference Shelf
Aging in America
American Military Presence Overseas
The Arab Spring
The Brain
The Business of Food
Campaign Trends & Election Law
Conspiracy Theories
The Digital Age
Dinosaurs
Embracing New Paradigms in Education
Faith & Science
Families: Traditional and New Structures
The Future of U.S. Economic Relations: Mexico, Cuba, and Venezuela
Global Climate Change
Graphic Novels and Comic Books
Immigration
Immigration in the U.S.
Internet Safety
Marijuana Reform
The News and its Future
The Paranormal
Politics of the Ocean
Racial Tension in a "Postracial" Age
Reality Television
Representative American Speeches: 2008-2009
Representative American Speeches: 2009-2010
Representative American Speeches: 2010-2011
Representative American Speeches: 2011-2012
Representative American Speeches: 2012-2013
Representative American Speeches: 2013-2014
Representative American Speeches: 2014-2015
Representative American Speeches: 2015-2016
Rethinking Work
Revisiting Gender
Robotics
Russia
Social Networking
Social Services for the Poor
Space Exploration & Development
Sports in America
The Supreme Court
The Transformation of American Cities
U.S. Infrastructure
U.S. National Debate Topic: Surveillance
U.S. National Debate Topic: The Ocean
U.S. National Debate Topic: Transportation Infrastructure
Whistleblowers

Readers' Guide
Abridged Readers' Guide to Periodical Literature
Readers' Guide to Periodical Literature

Indexes
Index to Legal Periodicals & Books
Short Story Index
Book Review Digest

Sears List
Sears List of Subject Headings
Sears: Lista de Encabezamientos de Materia

Facts About Series
Facts About American Immigration
Facts About China
Facts About the 20th Century
Facts About the Presidents
Facts About the World's Languages

Nobel Prize Winners
Nobel Prize Winners: 1901-1986
Nobel Prize Winners: 1987-1991
Nobel Prize Winners: 1992-1996
Nobel Prize Winners: 1997-2001

World Authors
World Authors: 1995-2000
World Authors: 2000-2005

Famous First Facts
Famous First Facts
Famous First Facts About American Politics
Famous First Facts About Sports
Famous First Facts About the Environment
Famous First Facts: International Edition

American Book of Days
The American Book of Days
The International Book of Days

Junior Authors & Illustrators
Eleventh Book of Junior Authors & Illustrations

Monographs
The Barnhart Dictionary of Etymology
Celebrate the World
Guide to the Ancient World
Indexing from A to Z
The Poetry Break
Radical Change: Books for Youth in a Digital Age

Wilson Chronology
Wilson Chronology of Asia and the Pacific
Wilson Chronology of Human Rights
Wilson Chronology of Ideas
Wilson Chronology of the Arts
Wilson Chronology of the World's Religions
Wilson Chronology of Women's Achievements